MW01202229

JOEL WHITBURN PRESENTS

TOP POP ALBUMS

SEVENTH EDITION

Billboard.

55-Year History Of Every Album & CD
That Made THE BILLBOARD 200 Albums Chart!

For Anyone
With A Heart For
The Charts!

Produced by
Joel Whitburn
TPA #7

1. Complete Chart Data
2. Covering 1955-2009
3. Over 30,000 Albums & CDs
4. Over 6,500 Artists
5. Top Album & Artist Rankings
6. Top Artist Achievements & Bios

Chart Data Compiled From *Billboard*'s Pop Albums Charts, 1955-2009,
and Bubbling Under The Top Pop Albums Charts, 1970-1985.

ISBN 0-89820-183-7
ISBN 978-0-89820-183-3

Record Research Inc.
P.O. Box 200
Menomonee Falls, Wisconsin 53052-0200 U.S.A.

Phone: (262) 251-5408
Fax: (262) 251-9452
E-Mail: books@recordresearch.com
Website: www.recordresearch.com

CONTENTS

AUTHOR'S NOTE

Behind my desk in Menomonee Falls, I have a custom-built display case which houses the current Top 10 best-selling albums in the country. This week alone it contains a wide array of musical genres, including R&B/Hip-Hop (Drake), Rock (Tom Petty & The Heartbreakers), Pop (Justin Bieber), Adult Contemporary (Sarah McLachlan), Adult Alternative (Jack Johnson) and Country (Lady Antebellum); there's also popular movie (*Twilight: Eclipse)* and TV *(Glee: Journey To Regionals)* soundtracks. It's this weekly diversity that makes *The Billboard 200* such a delight. It truly is the pulse of the American record-buying public.

This seventh edition of *Top Pop Albums* covers a whopping 55 years — the entire history of the rock era. To help make this edition even more complete, we've added hundreds of non-charting albums by key artists, especially from the 1955-64 era. These often colorful and highly collectable albums were crowded out of the charts by the soundtracks and original cast albums that dominated those particular years. You'll also find major artists arranged by sub-category; this makes it much easier to sort out the regular studio releases from all the compilations, live albums, etc. I hope you'll enjoy the rich history and diversity in the pages ahead.

JOEL WHITBURN

About the Author:

From an eager record-collecting teenager in the 1950s to a world-renowned musicologist in the 21st century, Joel Whitburn's passion for music and the Billboard charts is ongoing. Joel turned his chart-watching hobby into a business in 1970 with the publication of his first book. Over the past 40 years, Joel's company, Record Research, has published over 200 reference books, which chronicle over a century of American music. These, as well as Joel's books published by Billboard Books, are required reading for virtually anyone with a serious interest in music. He has also collaborated with Rhino Records on a series of over 150 CD compilations of America's top charted hits. Joel's own comprehensive charted music collection is the backbone of his research.

Ever the hobbyist, Joel participates in a wide variety of water, winter and motor sports, but the active, six-and-a-half footer ranks basketball and softball as his top sports. The Wisconsinite and his wife Fran, a native of Honduras, enjoy spending time in southern Florida and central Wisconsin.

Special thanks...

...to my Record Research staff: Paul Haney, Jeanne Olynick, Brent Olynick, Kim Bloxdorf and Jessica Olynick.

WHAT'S NEW IN THIS EDITION?

This seventh edition of *Top Pop Albums* (formerly titled *Billboard Albums*) marks the debut of the following new features:

BUBBLING UNDER

All albums that charted on *Billboard's* "Bubbling Under The Top Pop Albums" are now integrated in the main "Billboard 200" listings (see page 10 for a complete history of the "Bubbling Under" chart).

NON-CHARTED ALBUMS

Hundreds of non-charted albums by major artists are now listed directly after the main charted albums. Most (but not all) of these highly collectable albums charted between 1955-64. These listings give a more complete picture of an artist's discography.

SUBCATEGORIES FOR MAJOR ARTISTS

Many artists now have their albums divided in subcategories. This makes it easier to differentiate regular studio albums from greatest hits compilations, live albums, soundtracks, etc.

EXPLANATION OF ARTIST AND ALBUM AWARDS

GRAMMY AWARDS

The National Academy of Recording Arts & Sciences introduced the Grammy Awards in 1958. Each year thousands of music industry professionals vote for winners in several different music genres. The actual awards show is televised each February. You'll find the award(s) won directly underneath each honored album. You'll find the Best New Artist and other Grammy artist award information directly beneath the artist bio.

GRAMMY HALL OF FAME

The Recording Academy's Trustees established the Grammy Hall of Fame Award in 1973 to honor recordings of lasting qualitative or historical significance that are at least 25 years old. A special committee of eminent and knowledgeable music professionals selects inductees annually each January. The honored titles have the designation [**Grammy: Hall of Fame**] directly beneath the album title.

ROCK & ROLL HALL OF FAME

The Rock and Roll Hall of Fame Foundation was created in 1983 (the actual museum opened in Cleveland in 1995). Each year since 1986, a selection committee has designated nominees, which are then voted on by a group of approximately 1,000 music industry professionals. The winners are announced at the end of each year and the induction ceremonies are held the following spring, The Induction Year for each individual is shown directly beneath the artist bio [**R&R Hall of Fame**].

ROLLING STONE 500

In 2003, *Rolling Stone* magazine polled approximately 300 music industry professionals to vote for their favorite albums of all time. The results were later published and the albums that ranked are noted [**RS500**] directly beneath the album title.

COUNTRY MUSIC ASSOCIATION AWARDS

Country music industry professionals in Nashville founded the Country Music Association [**CMA**] in 1958. In 1961, the CMA created the Country Music Hall of Fame [**C&W Hall of Fame**]. The Induction Year for each individual is shown directly beneath the artist bio.

In November 1967, the CMA held its first awards show; one year later the event was televised for the first time and has been every year since. Nominees and winners are determined by a vote of Country music industry professionals. Artist awards are found directly beneath the bio. Album awards are found directly beneath the album title.

GRAND OLE OPRY

The *Grand Ole Opry* radio show was first broadcast on Nashville's WSM radio station on Saturday night, November 28, 1925. The show was picked up by NBC radio in October 1939 and was heard throughout the nation. The show has also been televised on various network and cable outlets over the years. Periodically, the current members vote to induct a new member. The induction year [**OPRY**] is shown directly beneath the artist bio.

NATIONAL RECORDING REGISTRY

In 2000, the U.S. Congress passed a bill to establish the National Recording Registry in the Library of Congress to maintain and preserve sound recordings that are culturally, historically or aesthetically significant. Each April, new inductees are announced. These recordings are noted [**NRR**] directly beneath the album title.

Billboard magazine began publishing a Top 5 Popular Albums chart in 1945. This chart was published on a sporatic basis until the week of March 24, 1956, when the chart first appeared weekly on a consistant basis. Today, *Billboard's* Popular Albums chart numbers 200 positions and is known as *The Billboard 200*. Throughout its long history, this chart has been home to America's most popular long-play recordings (from vinyl albums to compact discs to digital downloads) representing hundreds of musical genres.

Every album that hit the Popular Albums charts from January 1, 1955 through December 26, 2009, appears in this book. The research cutoff date for albums that were on the December 26, 2009 chart is May 29, 2010; weeks charted and peak positions are current through that chart.

To make this book a complete digest of all of *Billboard's* Popular Albums charts of the rock era, we also consulted two Popular Albums charts not outlined in the *Synopsis Of Billboard's Pop Albums Charts* (page 10). The "Most Played by Jockeys" chart, published from July 14, 1956, to December 8, 1958, was a top 15 chart. The "Pop Albums Coming Up Strong" chart, published from July 14, 1956 through August 26, 1957, served the purpose of a "Bubbling Under The Top LPs" chart. We checked the "Most Played by Jockeys" and "Pop Albums Coming Up Strong" charts <u>only</u> for albums, which made these charts but did not make the *Billboard* Popular Albums charts. To the 47 albums that <u>only charted</u> on the "Most Played by Jockeys" chart, we added 10 points (or positions) to their peak position. To the 39 albums that <u>only charted</u> on the "Coming Up Strong" charts, we added 15 points (or positions) to their peak position.

From 1959 to 1963, *Billboard* ran concurrent Mono and Stereo charts. For the characteristics and method of researching those charts, see the *Synopsis Of Billboard's Pop Albums Charts*.

Prior to 1963, *Billboard* charted all best-selling Christmas albums on the Popular Albums charts. From 1963 through 1973, *Billboard* did not chart Christmas albums on their Popular Albums charts, but issued special "Christmas Albums" charts for three to four weeks during each holiday season. *Billboard* discontinued the Christmas chart from 1974 through 1982 and returned to charting best-selling Chrismas albums on their regular albums charts. *Billboard* again published "Christmas Albums" charts from 1983-85; however, they also charted the best-selling Christmas albums on their Popular Albums charts. They did not publish a "Christmas Albums" chart in 1986, but have annually since 1987. Albums that only made the "Christmas Albums" chart are indicated with a superscript "**X**" following their peak position in the peak column. For albums that made the Popular Albums charts and the "Christmas Albums" charts, their peak positions on the latter chart appears in title trivia.

From 1976 through 1991, *Billboard* did not publish an issue on the final week of the year. The last published chart of the year was considered "frozen" and all chart positions of that final issue remained the same for the unpublished week. This frozen chart data is included in our tabulations. Since 1992, *Billboard* has <u>compiled</u> a Popular Albums chart for the last week of the year, even though an issue is <u>not published</u>. This chart is only available through *Billboard's* computerized information network (BIN) or by mail. Our tabulations include this unpublished chart data.

Also included is our research of *Billboard's* Midline, later known as Catalog, Albums charts. The biweekly "Midline LPs" chart first appeared in *Billboard* on July 24, 1982. The 50-position chart was cut back to 40 positions on October 24, 1982, was renamed "Top Midline Albums," and appeared in *Billboard* every three weeks, until its final chart on October 22, 1988. The Midline chart generally included albums that were $2.00-$3.00 less than the albums on the "Top 200 Albums" chart. On May 25, 1991, *Billboard* introduced the weekly, 50-position "Top Pop Catalog Albums" chart. The Catalog chart was a continuation of the Midline chart as it included several albums that had earlier appeared on the latter chart. According to *Billboard*, "Catalog albums are two-year-old titles that have fallen below #100 on "*The Billboard 200*" or reissues of older albums." The Catalog Albums chart still runs today. For albums that hit the Midline/Catalog chart but not the "*The Billboard 200*" chart, we show a superscript "**C**" following the peak position in the peak column. For all titles that hit the Midline/Catalog charts and "*The Billboard 200*," we show its peak position from the Midline/Catalog charts on the line to the right of the title. As of December 5, 2009, Billboard began allowing Catalog albums to make "*The Billboard 200*" regardless of age. The catalog information to the right of each title only includes information from when the title **was not** included on the main "Top 200 Albums" chart.

Billboard's compilation of the Popular Albums charts has always been based on album sales. For over 30 years, *Billboard* tallied the Popular Albums charts from rankings of best-selling albums as reported by a representative sampling of stores nationwide. On May 25, 1991, *Billboard* ushered in a new era in sales charts compilation. *Billboard* now bases the Popular Albums chart on actual units sold data as collected by point-of-sale scanning machines which read the album's UPC bar code. The music research firm Nielsen SoundScan Inc. provides *Billboard* with the actual sales of all albums from a continually revised representative sampling of stores.

MONO VS. STEREO NUMBERS

During the 1960s, *Billboard* frequently showed both mono and stereo numbers for an album on the album charts. The only numbering system that had major differences was the Columbia label. We have shown both the mono and stereo numbers for those albums on Columbia in the main artist listings. For the labels listed below we generally show stereo numbers only in the main artist listings. For your information, here is a list of other mono/stereo variations used on the charts (variations are shown in bold — label numbers are examples only):

RECORD COMPANY	MONO	STEREO
Coral, Decca & Brunswick	57487	**7**57487
Dolton & Sunset	**2**049	**8**049
Epic	2**4**022	2**6**022
Hi	**1**2002	**3**2002
Kapp	**1**368	**3**368
Liberty	**3**522	**7**522
London	**3**338 or 5943	338 or **2**5943
Mercury	**2**0837	**6**0837
Philips	**200**223	**600**223
United Artists	**3**536	**6**536
Viva	6010	**3**6010

SYNOPSIS OF BILLBOARD'S POP ALBUMS CHARTS

DATE	POSITIONS	CHART TITLE
1/8/55	15	**BEST SELLING POPULAR ALBUMS** (a biweekly chart featuring a 15-position "LP's" chart and a 15-position "EP's" chart – "EP's" chart discontinued after 11/26/1955)
3/24/56	10-15-20-30	**BEST SELLING POPULAR ALBUMS** (published weekly with size varying from a top 10 to a top 30)
6/2/56	15	**BEST SELLING POP ALBUMS**
9/2/57	25	**BEST SELLING POP LPs**
5/25/59	50	**BEST SELLING MONOPHONIC LPs**
5/25/59	30	**BEST SELLING STEREOPHONIC LPs** (separate Stereo and Mono charts published through 8/10/1963)
1/4/60	40	**MONO ACTION CHARTS** (mono albums charted 39 weeks or less)
1/4/60	30	**STEREO ACTION CHARTS** (stereo albums charted 19 weeks or less; changed to 29 weeks or less on 5/30/1960)
1/4/60	25	**ESSENTIAL INVENTORY – MONO** (mono albums charted 40 weeks or more)
1/4/60	20	**ESSENTIAL INVENTORY – STEREO** (stereo albums charted 20 weeks or more; changed to 30 weeks or more on 5/30/1960)
1/9/61	25	**ACTION ALBUMS – MONOPHONIC** (mono albums charted nine weeks or less)
1/9/61	15	**ACTION ALBUMS – STEREOPHONIC** (stereo albums charted nine weeks or less)
1/9/61	—	Approximately 200 albums listed by category (no positions) and shown as essential inventory
4/3/61	150	**TOP LP's – MONAURAL**
4/3/61	50	**TOP LP's – STEREO**
8/17/63	150	**TOP LP's** (one chart)
4/1/67	175	**TOP LP's**
5/13/67	200	**TOP LP's**
11/25/67	200	**TOP LP's** (three pages)
2/15/69	200	**TOP LP's** (two pages with A-Z artist listing)
2/19/72	200	**TOP LP's & TAPES**
10/20/84	200	**TOP 200 ALBUMS**
1/5/85	200	**TOP POP ALBUMS**
9/7/91	200	**THE BILLBOARD 200 TOP ALBUMS**
3/14/92	200	**THE BILLBOARD 200**

An album appearing on both the Mono and Stereo charts in the same week is tabulated as one weekly appearance. The album's highest position is determined by the chart (Mono or Stereo) on which the album reached its highest position.

The Essential Inventory charts list albums which have already been charted for months on the Mono and Stereo charts; therefore, we researched the Essential Inventory charts for weeks charted only and did not count peak positions reached on this chart.

Synopsis of *Billboard's* **Bubbling Under The Top Pop Albums** chart:

DATE	POSITIONS	CHART TITLE
12/26/70	4-35	**BUBBLING UNDER THE TOP LP's**
7/13/74	10	**BUBBLING UNDER THE TOP LP's**
10/20/84	10	**BUBBLING UNDER THE 200 ALBUMS**
2/9/85	10	**BUBBLING UNDER THE TOP POP ALBUMS**
8/24/85	final chart	**BUBBLING UNDER THE TOP POP ALBUMS**

Synopsis of *Billboard's* **Midline/Catalog Albums** and **Christmas Albums** charts:

DATE	POSITIONS	CHART TITLE
7/24/82	50	**MIDLINE LPs** (a biweekly chart)
10/24/82	40	**TOP MIDLINE ALBUMS** (a triweekly chart – discontinued after 10/22/1988)
5/25/91	50	**TOP POP CATALOG ALBUMS** (a weekly chart)

DATE	POSITIONS	CHART TITLE
1963-73	5-117	**CHRISTMAS LP's**
1983-85	10	**CHRISTMAS ALBUMS**
1987-93	30	**TOP CHRISTMAS ALBUMS**
1994-01	40	**TOP HOLIDAY ALBUMS**
2002-09	50	**TOP HOLIDAY ALBUMS**

The Artist Section lists by artist name, alphabetically, every album that charted on *Billboard* magazine's Pop Albums charts from January 1, 1955 through December 25, 2009. (See page ??? for a chart synopsis.) Each artist's charted hits are listed in chronological order and are sequentially numbered.

EXPLANATION OF COLUMNAR HEADINGS

DEBUT: Date album first charted

PEAK: Highest charted position (highlighted in bold type)

WKS: Total weeks charted

RIAA: RIAA-certified gold or platinum album

Catalog: Peak position/Weeks charted on the Catalog chart

Label & Number: Original label and number of album when first charted

EXPLANATION OF SYMBOLS AND NUMBERS

2^1 — Superscript number to the right of the #1, #2 or #3 peak position is the total weeks the album held that position

$+$ — Beside debut date indicates that album peaked in a year other than when it first charted

$\uparrow$ — Beside the peak position and/or weeks charted indicates that the album was still on the charts as of the May 29, 2010 research cutoff date

25^C — Superscript C following the peak position in the "PEAK" column indicates album only charted on the Catalog Albums chart and <u>not</u> on the Pop Albums chart. The preceding peak position is from the Catalog chart.

15^X — Superscript X following the peak position in the "PEAK" column indicates album only charted on the Christmas Albums chart and <u>not</u> on the Pop Albums chart. The preceding peak position is from the Christmas chart.

    For an album that charted on the Christmas <u>and</u> the Popular Albums charts, its Christmas chart's peak position and year of debut appears in title trivia.

Cat: — Indicates that an album which hit the Pop Albums chart <u>also</u> hit the Catalog chart. The "Cat:" appears on the line to the right of an album title and is followed by its Catalog chart's peak position and weeks charted.

[ ] — Number in brackets after a label number indicates the number of records or CDs in a multi-disc set.

● — RIAA-certified gold album (500,000 units sold)

▲ — RIAA-certified platinum album (1,000,000 units sold)

    The Recording Industry Association of America (RIAA) began certifying gold albums in 1958, platinum albums in 1976 and multi-platinum albums in 1984. Some record labels have never requested RIAA certification for albums which would otherwise have qualified for these awards.

    A superscript number to the right of the platinum triangle indicates album was awarded multi-platinum status (ex.: ▲^{3} indicates an album was certified triple platinum).

UNDERLINED & SHADED TITLES

For any artist with 10 or more charted hits, the artist's highest charting title is underlined for easy indentification. The biggest hit is mostly a reflection of chart performance; however, there are exceptions. When a particular album has numerous awards, RIAA certifications and/or is considered an artist's signature album, this takes precedence over strict chart performance. In some cases, more than one album will fit this criteria; therefore, more than one album may be underlined.

All Top 10 albums are shaded with a light gray background.

LETTER(S) IN BRACKETS AFTER TITLES (Sym column)

C - Comedy

E - Earlier Recordings/Releases

EP - 7" Extended Play or Mini Album (10" or 12" EP, lower-priced CD)

F - Foreign Language

G - Greatest Hits

I - Instrumental Recording

K - Compilation

L - Live Recording

N - Novelty

OC - Original Cast

R - Reissue or re-release **with a new label number** of a previously charted album or Christmas re-release of album with or without the same label number

S - Movie Soundtrack

T - Talk/Spoken Word Recording

TV - Television Program Soundtrack

X - Christmas (If an album also charted on *Billboard's* special Christmas charts, a title note lists the highest position reached and year it made the Christmas albums chart). For example a note may read:

Christmas charts: 5/'67, 10/'68

(indicating that an album peaked at position five on the Christmas chart in 1967 and position 10 in 1968.)

ARTIST & TITLE NOTES

Pertinent biographical information is shown below <u>every</u> artist name. Directly under some album titles are notes indicating guest artists, the location of live recordings, the names of famous producers, etc. Duets and other important name variations are shown in bold capital letters. We highlighted in bold type the names of artists mentioned in the artist and title notes of other charted pop album artists if they have their own album listing elsewhere in this book. All movie and TV titles, and other major works, appear in italics.

ALBUMS BY ARTIST

Lists, alphabetically by artist name, every album that charted on *Billboard's* Pop Albums chart from January 1, 1955 through December 26, 2009.

A

AALIYAH
Born Aaliyah Haughton on 1/16/1979 in Brooklyn, New York; raised in Detroit, Michigan. Died in a plane crash (in Abaco, Bahamas) on 8/25/2001 (age 22). Female R&B singer/actress. Acted in the movies *Romeo Must Die* and *Queen Of The Damned*. Married **R. Kelly** on 7/31/1994 (marriage later annulled).

6/11/94	18	37	▲²	1 Age Ain't Nothing But A Number	Cat:#15/3	Blackground 41533
9/14/96+	18	67	▲²	2 One In A Million	Cat:❶³/22	Blackground 92715
8/4/01	❶¹	68	▲²	3 Aaliyah		Blackground 10082
12/28/02	3¹	26	▲	4 I Care 4 U	[K]	Blackground 060082

ABBA   All-Time: #259
Pop group formed in Stockholm, Sweden: Anni-Frid (**Frida**) Lyngstad (vocals; born on 11/15/1945) and **Agnetha Faltskog** (vocals; born on 4/5/1950), Bjorn Ulvaeus (guitar; born on 4/25/1945) and Benny Andersson (keyboards; born on 12/16/1946). ABBA is an acronym of members' first initials. Benny and Bjorn first recorded together in 1966. Bjorn and Agnetha were married from 1971-79. Benny and Frida were married from 1978-81. Disbanded in 1982. Bjorn and Benny co-wrote the musical *Chess* with Sir Tim Rice. The Broadway musical/movie *Mamma Mia!* features the music of Abba.

AWARD: R&R Hall of Fame: 2010

8/17/74	145	8		1 Waterloo		Atlantic 18101
11/15/75	174	3		2 Abba		Atlantic 18146
1/22/77	20	50	●	3 Arrival		Atlantic 18207
2/18/78	14	41	▲	4 The Album		Atlantic 19164
7/7/79	19	27	●	5 Voulez-Vous		Atlantic 16000
12/13/80+	17	38	●	6 Super Trouper		Atlantic 16023
1/9/82	29	17		7 The Visitors		Atlantic 19332
				GREATEST HITS & COMPILATIONS:		
9/18/76	48	61	▲	8 Greatest Hits		Atlantic 18189
12/22/79+	46	14	●	9 Greatest Hits, Vol. 2		Atlantic 16009
12/18/82+	62	18		10 The Singles (The First Ten Years)		Atlantic 80036 [2]
4/28/84	208	2		11 I Love Abba		Atlantic 80142
10/9/93	63	126↑	▲⁶	12 Gold - Greatest Hits	Cat:❶¹²/409	Polydor 517007
11/24/01	186	1		13 The Definitive Collection	Cat:#43/2	Polydor 549974 [2]
				RS500: #180		
12/14/02+	9ᶜ	18	●	14 The Best Of Abba: 20th Century Masters: The Millennium Collection		Polydor 543948
8/2/08	11ᶜ	10		15 Number Ones		Polydor 008021

ABBOTT, Gregory
Born on 4/2/1954 in Harlem, New York. R&B singer/songwriter. Married to **Freda Payne** from 1976-79.

11/1/86+	22	36	●	1 Shake You Down		Columbia 40437
6/4/88	132	9		2 I'll Prove It To You		Columbia 44087

ABC
Electro-pop/dance band from Sheffield, Yorkshire, England: Martin Fry (vocals; born on 3/9/1958), Mark White (guitar; born on 4/1/1961), Stephen Singleton (sax), Mark Lickley (bass) and David Palmer (drums). After their second album the latter three left, leaving duo of Fry and White.

9/25/82+	24	39	●	1 The Lexicon Of Love		Mercury 4059
12/17/83+	69	14		2 Beauty Stab		Mercury 814661
10/5/85	30	41		3 How To Be A...Zillionaire!		Mercury 824904
8/22/87	48	25		4 Alphabet City		Mercury 832391

ABDUL, Paula
Born on 6/19/1962 in San Fernando, California. Female pop-dance singer/choreographer. While still a teen, was the choreographer and member of the NBA's Los Angeles Lakers cheerleaders. Choreographed **Janet Jackson**'s *Control* videos and **Tracey Ullman**'s TV show. Married to actor Emilio Estevez from 1992-93. One of the judges on TV's *American Idol* from 2002-09.

7/23/88+	❶¹⁰	175	▲⁷	1 Forever Your Girl		Virgin 90943
5/26/90	7	35	▲	2 Shut Up And Dance (The Dance Mixes)	[K]	Virgin 91362
6/1/91	❶²	70	▲³	3 Spellbound		Captive 91611
7/1/95	18	18	●	4 Head Over Heels		Captive 40525

ABK
Born James Lowery on 6/26/1975 in Detroit, Michigan. Native American hardcore rapper. Performs with white face paint. Affiliated with **Insane Clown Posse**. ABK: Any Body Killa.

4/26/03	98	1		1 Hatchet Warrior		Psychopathic 4012
8/14/04	152	1		2 Dirty History		Psychopathic 4026

ABN
Male rap duo from Houston, Texas: Frazier "**Trae**" Thompson and Joseph "**Z-Ro**" McVey. ABN: Assholes By Nature.

8/2/08	62	3		1 It Is What It Is		J Prince 511943

ABOVE THE LAW
Rap group from Pamona, California: Gregory Hutchinson, Kevin Gulley, Anthony Stewart and Arthur Goodman. Hutchinson is the nephew of **Willie Hutch**. Goodman left in early 1994. Members of **The West Coast Rap All-Stars**.

4/14/90	75	16		1 Livin' Like Hustlers		Ruthless 46041
8/3/91	120	4		2 Vocally Pimpin'	[EP]	Ruthless 47934
2/20/93	37	7		3 Black Mafia Life		Ruthless 24477
7/30/94	113	13		4 Uncle Sam's Curse		Ruthless 5524

(columns: DEBUT | PEAK | WKS | RIAA | Album Title | Catalog | Label & Number)

ABOVE THE LAW — cont'd

| 11/9/96 | 80 | 2 | | 5 Time Will Reveal | | Tommy Boy 1154 |
| 3/14/98 | 142 | 2 | | 6 Legends | | Tommy Boy 1233 |

ABRAMS, Colonel
Born Colonel Abrams in Detroit, Michigan; raised in New York City. R&B singer/songwriter.

| 4/19/86 | 75 | 11 | | 1 Colonel Abrams | | MCA 5682 |

ACACIA STRAIN, The
Deathcore band from Chicopee, Massachusetts: Vincent Bennett (vocals), Daniel Laskiewicz (guitar), Jack Strong (bass) and Kevin Boutot (drums).

| 9/6/08 | 107 | 1 | | 1 Continent | | Prosthetic 10061 |

ACADEMY IS..., The
Alternative-rock band from Barrington, Illinois: William Beckett (vocals), Michael Carden (guitar), Thomas Conrad (guitar), Adam Siska (bass) and Andy Mrotek (drums). Conrad left in late 2006.

2/11/06	185	1		1 Almost Here		Fueled By Ramen 071
4/21/07	32	7		2 Santi		Decaydance 94667
9/6/08	17	3		3 Fast Times At Barrington High		Decaydance 512263

ACCEPT
Heavy metal band from Germany: Udo Dirkschneider (vocals), Wolf Hoffmann (guitar) Hermann Frank (guitar), Peter Baltes (bass) and Stefan Kaufmann (drums). Jorg Fischer replaced Frank in 1985. In 1987, Dirkschneider and Fischer left; replaced by Colorado-born David Reece and Jim Stacey.

2/4/84	74	26	●	1 Balls To The Wall		Portrait 39241
3/30/85	94	14		2 Metal Heart		Portrait 39974
5/17/86	114	9		3 Russian Roulette		Portrait 40354
6/24/89	139	9		4 Eat The Heat		Epic 44368

ACCEPTANCE
Alternative-rock band from Seattle, Washington: Jason Vena (vocals), Christain McAlhaney (guitar), Kaylan Cloyd (guitar), Ryan Zwiefelhofer (bass) and Nick Radovanovic (drums).

| 5/14/05 | 122 | 1 | | 1 Phantoms | | Columbia 89016 |

AC/DC   1980s: #4 / All-Time: #60
Hard-rock band formed in Sydney, Australia: Ronald "Bon" Scott (vocals; born on 7/9/1946; died of asphyxiation on 2/19/1980, age 33), brothers Angus Young (guitar; born on 3/31/1955) and Malcolm Young (guitar; born on 1/6/1953), Mark Evans (bass; born on 3/2/1956) and Phil Rudd (drums; born on 5/19/1954). Cliff Williams (born on 12/14/1949) replaced Evans in 1977. Brian Johnson (vocals; born on 10/5/1947) replaced Scott after his death. Simon Wright (born on 6/19/1963) replaced Rudd in 1985. Wright joined **Dio** in 1989; replaced by Chris Slade (born on 10/30/1946) of **The Firm**. Rudd returned to replace Slade in 1995. Angus and Malcolm are the younger brothers of George Young of **The Easybeats**. Group made a cameo concert appearance in the 1997 movie *Private Parts*.
AWARD: R&R Hall of Fame: 2003

8/13/77	154	11	▲²	1 Let There Be Rock	Cat:#9/23	Atco 151
6/24/78	133	17	▲	2 Powerage		Atlantic 19180
8/25/79	17	83	▲⁷	3 Highway To Hell	Cat:#4/41	Atlantic 19244
				RS500 #199		
8/23/80	4	137↑	▲²²	4 Back In Black	Cat:❶⁷/868	Atlantic 16018
				RS500 #73		
				first album with new vocalist Brian Johnson		
12/12/81	❶³	30	▲⁴	5 For Those About To Rock We Salute You	Cat:#13/4	Atlantic 11111
9/10/83	15	23	▲	6 Flick Of The Switch		Atlantic 80100
7/20/85	32	30	▲	7 Fly On The Wall		Atlantic 81263
3/5/88	12	24	▲	8 Blow Up Your Video		Atlantic 81828
10/6/90	2¹	77	▲⁵	9 The Razors Edge	Cat:#30/3	Atco 91413
10/14/95	4	30	▲²	10 Ballbreaker		EastWest 61780
3/18/00	7	28	▲	11 Stiff Upper Lip		EastWest 62494
11/8/08	❶²	35	▲²	12 Black Ice		Columbia 33829
				EARLY ALBUMS:		
4/18/81	3⁶	55	▲⁶	13 Dirty Deeds Done Dirt Cheap	Cat:#5/11	Atlantic 16033
7/18/81+	146	19	▲³	14 High Voltage	Cat:#3/16	Atco 142
				above 2 albums recorded in 1976 (Bon Scott on vocals)		
11/17/84	76	14	▲	15 '74 Jailbreak	[EP]	Atlantic 80178
				Australian releases from 1975-76 (Bon Scott on vocals)		
				GREATEST HITS & COMPILATIONS:		
12/6/97	90	5	▲	16 Bonfire		EastWest 62119 [5]
				box set tribute to former lead singer Bon Scott; contains recordings from 1976-80		
11/28/09	39	2		17 Backtracks		Columbia 54099 [2]
				LIVE ALBUMS:		
12/23/78+	113	14	▲	18 If You Want Blood You've Got It	Cat:#23/2	Atlantic 19212
				recorded during the group's 1978 *Powerage* world tour		
11/14/92	34	14	▲²	19 Live (Special Collector's Edition)	Cat:#19/4	Atco 92212 [2]
				recorded during the group's 1991 *The Razors Edge* world tour		
11/14/92	15	48	▲³	20 Live	Cat:#6/183	Atco 92215
				14 tracks from album #19 above		

				AC/DC — cont'd		
				REISSUE:		
12/8/07	73	3		21 **Sight & Sound Collection**		Columbia 17326 [2]
				re-issue of *Back In Black* and *Dirty Deeds Done Dirt Cheap* albums		
				SOUNDTRACK:		
6/21/86	33	42	▲⁵	22 **Who Made Who**	Cat:#14/44	Atlantic 81650
				soundtrack from the movie *Maximum Overdrive*		

ACE
Pop-rock band formed in London, England: **Paul Carrack** (vocals, keyboards), Phil Harris (guitar), Alan King (guitar), Terry Comer (bass) and Fran Byrne (drums). Harris replaced by Jon Woodhead by 1976. Disbanded in 1977. Carrack later joined **Squeeze** and **Mike + The Mechanics**.

3/15/75	11	22		1 **Five-A-Side (An Ace Album)**		Anchor 2001
12/27/75+	153	6		2 **Time For Another**		Anchor 2013
2/12/77	170	2		3 **No Strings**		Anchor 2020

ACE HOOD
Born Antoine McColister on 5/11/1988 in Deerfield Beach, Florida. Male rapper.

12/6/08	36	3		1 **Gutta**		We The Best 011773
7/18/09	23	5		2 **Ruthless**		We The Best 013066

ACE OF BASE
Pop-dance group from Gothenburg, Sweden: vocalists/sisters Jenny Berggren and Linn Berggren with keyboardists Jonas "Joker" Berggren (their brother) and Ulf "Buddha" Ekberg.

12/11/93+	❶²	102	▲⁹	1 **The Sign**		Arista 18740
12/2/95+	29	29	▲	2 **The Bridge**		Arista 18806
8/1/98	101	10		3 **Cruel Summer**		Arista 19021

ACE SPECTRUM
R&B vocal group from Harlem, New York: Ed Zant, Aubrey Johnson, Elliot Isaac and Rudy Gay.

7/13/74	209	1		1 **Inner Spectrum**		Atlantic 7299
8/23/75	138	7		2 **Low Rent Rendezvous**		Atlantic 18143

ACKLES, David
Born on 2/20/1937 in Rock Island, Illinois; raised in Pasadena, California. Died of cancer on 3/2/1999 (age 62). Pop singer/songwriter/actor. Played "Tuck Worden" in the *Rusty* movie series from 1947-49.

8/12/72	167	10		1 **American Gothic**		Elektra 75032

ACKLIN, Barbara
Born on 2/28/1943 in Oakland, California; raised in Chicago, Illinois. Died of pneumonia on 11/27/1998 (age 55). R&B singer/songwriter.

10/5/68	146	5		1 **Love Makes A Woman**		Brunswick 754137

ADAM & THE ANTS — see **ANT, Adam**

ADAMS, Andy — see **EGG CREAM**

ADAMS, Bryan   All-Time: #314
Born on 11/5/1959 in Kingston, Ontario, Canada (to British parents). Rock singer/songwriter/guitarist. Lead singer of Sweeney Todd from 1976-77. Teamed with Jim Vallance in 1978 in successful songwriting partnership. Cameo appearance as a gas station attendant in the movie *Pink Cadillac*.

1/30/82	118	13		1 **You Want It, You Got It**	Cat:#39/4	A&M 4864
2/19/83	8	89	▲	2 **Cuts Like A Knife**		A&M 4919
11/24/84+	❶²	83	▲⁵	3 **Reckless**	Cat:#4/11	A&M 5013
4/18/87	7	33	▲	4 **Into The Fire**		A&M 3907
10/12/91	6	75	▲⁴	5 **Waking Up The Neighbours**		A&M 5367
11/27/93+	6	66	▲⁵	6 **So Far So Good**	Cat:#38/13 [G]	A&M 540157
6/22/96	31	50	▲	7 **18 Til I Die**		A&M 540551
12/27/97+	88	14		8 **MTV Unplugged**	[L]	A&M 540831
				recorded on 9/26/1997 at the Hammerstein Ballroom in New York City		
11/14/98	103	2		9 **On A Day Like Today**		A&M 541014
5/28/05	134	1		10 **Room Service**		Bad Man 004571
11/5/05	65	4		11 **Anthology**	[G]	A&M 005613 [2]
5/31/08	80	4		12 **11**		Badman 4259

ADAMS, Jay Boy
Born in Fort Worth, Texas; raised in Colorado City, Texas. Country-rock singer/guitarist.

10/1/77	210	1		1 **Jay Boy Adams**		Atlantic 18221

ADAMS, Oleta
Born on 5/4/1962 in Seattle, Washington; raised in Yakima, Washington. Female R&B singer/pianist.

9/1/90+	20	44	●	1 **Circle Of One**		Fontana 846346
8/21/93	67	13		2 **Evolution**		Fontana 514965
11/25/95	194	1		3 **Moving On**		Fontana 528684

ADAMS, Ryan

Born David Ryan Adams on 11/5/1974 in Jacksonville, North Carolina. Adult Alternative singer/songwriter/guitarist. One-half of **Whiskeytown** duo. The Cardinals: J.P. Bowersock (guitar), Cindy Cashdollar (steel guitar), Catherine Popper (bass) and Brad Pemberton (drums).

10/13/01	59	9		1 Gold		Lost Highway 170235 [2]
10/12/02	28	5		2 Demolition	[K]	Lost Highway 170333
				collection of previously recorded demos		
11/22/03	33	4		3 Rock N Roll		Lost Highway 001376
11/22/03	78	1		4 Love Is Hell Pt. 1	[EP]	Lost Highway 001548
12/27/03	171	1		5 Love Is Hell Pt. 2	[EP]	Lost Highway 001549
5/21/05	26	6		6 Cold Roses		Lost Highway 004343 [2]
10/15/05	33	3		7 Jacksonville City Nights		Lost Highway 004707
				RYAN ADAMS & THE CARDINALS (above 2)		
1/7/06	144	3		8 29		Lost Highway 005872
7/14/07	7	11		9 Easy Tiger		Lost Highway 008760
11/10/07	40	3		10 Follow The Lights	[EP]	Lost Highway 010177
11/15/08	11	4		11 Cardinology		Lost Highway 012195
				RYAN ADAMS & THE CARDINALS (above 2)		

ADAMS, Yolanda

Born on 8/27/1962 in Houston, Texas. Black female gospel singer.

10/9/99+	24	54	▲	1 Mountain High...Valley Low		Elektra 62439
				Grammy: Contemporary Soul Gospel Album		
12/2/00	86	9		2 Christmas With Yolanda Adams	[X]	Elektra 62567
				Christmas chart: 4/'00		
4/7/01	63	11		3 The Experience	[L]	Elektra 62629
				Grammy: Contemporary Soul Gospel Album		
				recorded at Constitution Hall in Washington DC		
12/22/01+	42	36	●	4 Believe		Elektra 62690
9/17/05	23	22		5 Day By Day		Elektra 83789
5/26/07	60	2		6 The Best Of Me		Elektra 156604
12/15/07	179	2		7 What A Wonderful Time	[X]	Columbia 09432
				Christmas chart: 16/'07		

ADC BAND

Funk band from Detroit, Michigan: Audrey Matthews (vocals), Michael Judkins (vocals, keyboards), Pervis Johnson (guitar), Kublah Khan (congas), Mark Patterson (bass) and Artwell Matthews (drums). ADC: Aid for Dependant Children.

12/16/78+	139	9		1 Long Stroke		Cotillion 5210

ADDEO, Leo, & His Orchestra

Born on 10/14/1914 in Brooklyn, New York. Died in May 1979 (age 64). Orchestra leader/arranger. His orchestra featured guitarists Al Caiola and Billy Mure (of **The Palm Beach Band Boys**).

1/9/61	143	13		1 Hawaii In Hi-Fi	[I]	RCA Camden 510

ADDERLEY, "Cannonball", Quintet

Born Julian Adderley on 9/15/1928 in Tampa, Florida. Died of a stroke on 8/8/1975 (age 46). Jazz/R&B saxophonist. Nickname derived from "cannibal" due to his love of eating. His quintet consisted of brother Nat Adderley (coronet; born on 11/25/1931; died of diabetes on 1/2/2000, age 68), Joe Zawinul (keyboards), Walter Booker (bass) and Roy McCurdy (drums). Zawinul left in 1971 to form **Weather Report**; replaced by **George Duke**.

5/5/62	30	21		1 Nancy Wilson/Cannonball Adderley		Capitol 1657
3/30/63	11	25		2 Jazz Workshop Revisited	[I-L]	Riverside 444
				CANNONBALL ADDERLEY Sextet		
				recorded in San Francisco, California		
2/25/67	13	27		3 Mercy, Mercy, Mercy!	[I-L]	Capitol 2663
				Grammy: Jazz Album		
				despite liner notes claiming this album was recorded at the Club De Lisa in Chicago, it was actually recorded at the Capitol studios in Los Angeles in front of an invited live audience		
6/10/67	148	12		4 Why Am I Treated So Bad!	[I-L]	Capitol 2617
12/9/67	186	2		5 74 Miles Away - Walk Tall	[I-L]	Capitol 2822
				recorded in Hollywood, California		
3/14/70	136	22		6 Country Preacher	[I-L]	Capitol 404
				recorded in Chicago, Illinois; introduction by Rev. Jesse Jackson		
9/26/70	194	2		7 Experience In E, Tensity, Dialogues	[I]	Capitol 484
3/6/71	169	2		8 The Price You Got To Pay To Be Free	[L]	Capitol 636 [2]
2/26/72	167	3		9 The Black Messiah	[L]	Capitol 846 [2]
				recorded at the Troubadour Club in West Hollywood, California		
7/1/72	74	20		10 Soul Zodiac		Capitol 11025 [2]
				"CANNONBALL" ADDERLEY (above 2)		
				featuring the Nat Adderley Sextet; narration by Rick Holmes		
9/29/73	179	5		11 Inside Straight	[I-L]	Fantasy 9435
9/20/75	121	8		12 Phenix	[I-K]	Fantasy 79004 [2]
				"CANNONBALL" ADDERLEY		

~ ~ ~ ~ ~ ~ ~ ~ ~ ~ **NON-CHARTED ALBUM** ~ ~ ~ ~ ~ ~ ~ ~ ~ ~
1959 **The Cannonball Adderley Quintet In San Francisco**
Grammy: Hall of Fame

ADDISON, Shari

Born on 7/7/1964 in Chicago, Illinois. Female gospel singer.

1/31/09	176	1		1 Shari Addison		BET 33091

Billboard			R I A A	ARTIST		
DEBUT	PEAK	WKS		Album Title	Catalog	Label & Number

ADDISON ROAD
Christian rock band from Dallas, Texas: husband-and-wife Ryan Simmons (guitar) and Jenny Simmons (vocals), with Ryan Gregg (guitar), Travis Lawrence (bass) and Jeff Sutton (drums).

4/5/08	182	1		1 Addison Road		Ino 20849

ADDRISI BROTHERS, The
Pop singing/songwriting duo from Boston, Massachusetts: brothers Dick Addrisi (born on 7/4/1941) and Don Addrisi (born on 12/14/1938; died of cancer on 11/11/1984, age 45). Discovered by **Lenny Bruce** in 1956 while performing music for the family trapeze act (The Flying Addrisis); family then moved to Los Angeles, California.

4/8/72	137	3		1 We've Got To Get It On Again		Columbia 31296
7/2/77	118	14		2 Addrisi Brothers		Buddah 5694

ADE, King Sunny, & His African Beats
Born Sunday Adeniyi on 9/1/1946 in Oshogbo, Nigeria. Black singer/songwriter/guitarist. Best known for his JuJu style (hybrid of western pop and native African music).

4/9/83	111	29		1 JuJu Music .... [F]		Mango 9712
8/20/83	91	10		2 Synchro System .... [F]		Mango 9737

ADELE
Born Adele Adkins on 5/5/1988 in Tottenham, North London, England. Female pop singer/songwriter/guitarist.
AWARD: Grammy: Best New Artist 2008

6/28/08+	10	63	●	1 19	Cat:#18/11	XL 30624
2/21/09	105	1		2 iTunes Live From Soho .... [EP-L]		XL digital

ADEMA
Hard-rock band from Bakersfield, California: Mark Chavez (vocals), Mike Ransom (guitar), Tim Fluckey (guitar), Dave DeRoo (bass) and Kris Kohls (drums). Chavez is the half-brother of Jonathan Davis (of **Korn**). Ransom left in 2004. Luke Caraccioli replaced Chavez in late 2004. Bobby Reeves replaced Caraccioli in late 2005.

9/8/01	27	36	●	1 Adema		Arista 14696
9/6/03	43	4		2 Unstable		Arista 53914
4/23/05	152	2		3 Planets		Earache 292

ADKINS, Trace
All-Time: #374
Born Tracy Adkins on 1/13/1962 in Springhill, Louisiana; raised in Sarepta, Louisiana. Male country singer/songwriter/guitarist. Sang with the New Commitment gospel group while in high school. Played football for Louisiana Tech. Appeared as a contestant on TV's *The Celebrity Apprentice* in 2008.
AWARD: OPRY: 2003

10/19/96+	53	56	▲	1 Dreamin' Out Loud		Capitol 37222
11/8/97	50	21	●	2 Big Time		Capitol 55856
11/20/99	82	3		3 More...		Capitol 96618
10/27/01	59	20	●	4 Chrome		Capitol 30618
7/26/03	9	24	▲	5 Greatest Hits Collection, Volume I	[G]	Capitol 81512
12/20/03	31	55	▲	6 Comin' On Strong		Capitol 40517
4/9/05	11	78	▲²	7 Songs About Me		Capitol 64512
9/2/06	3¹	52	●	8 Dangerous Man		Capitol 56731
12/22/07	22	64	●	9 American Man: Greatest Hits Volume II .... Cat:#45/1	[G]	Capitol 76927
12/13/08	32	18		10 X: Ten		Capitol 20281

ADRENALIN
Rock band from Detroit, Michigan: Marc Gilbert (vocals), brothers Mike Romeo (guitar) and Jim Romeo (sax), brothers Mark Pastoria (keyboards) and Brian Pastoria (drums), Mike "Flash" Haggerty (guitar) and Bruce Schafer (bass).

8/11/84	203	8		1 American Heart		Rocshire 9517

ADVENTURES, The
Pop band from Belfast, Ireland: Terry Sharpe (male vocals), husband-and-wife Patrick Gribben (guitar) and Eileen Gribben (female vocals), Gerard "Spud" Murphy (guitar), Tony Ayre (bass) and Paul Crowder (drums).

4/16/88	144	9		1 The Sea Of Love		Elektra 60772

AEROSMITH
1980s: #11 / All-Time: #39
Hard-rock band formed in Boston, Massachusetts: Steven Tyler (vocals; born on 3/26/1948), Joe Perry (guitar; born on 9/10/1950), Brad Whitford (guitar; born on 2/23/1952), Tom Hamilton (bass; born on 12/31/1951) and Joey Kramer (drums; born on 6/21/1950). Perry left for own **Joe Perry Project** in 1979; replaced by Jimmy Crespo (of **The Flame**). Whitford left in 1981; replaced by Rick Dufay. Original band reunited in April 1984. Tyler is the father of actress/model Liv Tyler. Group appeared in the movies *Sgt. Pepper's Lonely Hearts Club Band* and *Wayne's World 2*. Also see **Whitford/St. Holmes**.
AWARD: R&R Hall of Fame: 2001

10/13/73+	21	59	▲²	1 Aerosmith		Columbia 32005
4/6/74+	74	86	▲³	2 Get Your Wings		Columbia 32847
4/26/75	11	128	▲⁸	3 Toys In The Attic .... Cat:#9/197		Columbia 33479
				RS500 #228		
5/29/76	3³	53	▲⁴	4 Rocks		Columbia 34165
				RS500 #176		
12/24/77+	11	20	▲²	5 Draw The Line		Columbia 34856
12/1/79+	14	19	▲	6 Night In The Ruts		Columbia 36050
9/25/82	32	19	●	7 Rock In A Hard Place		Columbia 38061

DEBUT	PEAK	WKS	RIAA	Album Title	Catalog	Label & Number
				AEROSMITH — cont'd		
11/30/85	36	28	●	8 Done With Mirrors		Geffen 24091
9/19/87	11	67	▲⁵	9 Permanent Vacation	Cat:#36/33	Geffen 24162
9/30/89	5	110	▲⁷	10 Pump	Cat:#37/12	Geffen 24254
5/8/93	❶¹	92	▲⁷	11 Get A Grip		Geffen 24455
4/5/97	❶¹	77	▲²	12 Nine Lives		Columbia 67547
3/24/01	2¹	27	▲	13 Just Push Play		Columbia 62088
4/17/04	5	15	●	14 Honkin' On Bobo		Columbia 87025
				GREATEST HITS & COMPILATIONS:		
11/29/80	53	40	▲¹¹	15 Aerosmith's Greatest Hits	Cat:❶⁸³/677	Columbia 36865
12/10/88+	133	11	●	16 Gems		Columbia 44487
12/7/91+	45	9	▲	17 Pandora's Box		Columbia 46209 [3]
				recordings from 1972-82		
11/19/94	6	48	▲⁴	18 Big Ones	Cat:#9/125	Geffen 24716
12/8/01	191	1	●	19 Young Lust: The Aerosmith Anthology		Geffen 493119 [2]
7/20/02	4	32	▲²	20 O, Yeah! Ultimate Aerosmith Hits	Cat:#36/6	Columbia 86700 [2]
11/4/06	33	10		21 Devil's Got A New Disguise: The Very Best Of Aerosmith	Cat:#16/33	Geffen 00867
7/19/08	45ᶜ	1		22 The Best Of Aerosmith: 20th Century Masters: The Millenium Collection		Geffen 001101
				LIVE ALBUMS:		
11/11/78+	13	22	▲	23 Live! Bootleg		Columbia 35564 [2]
4/26/86	84	12	▲	24 Classics Live!		Columbia 40329
11/7/98	12	20	▲	25 A Little South Of Sanity		Geffen 25221 [2]
11/12/05	24	5		26 Rockin' The Joint		Columbia 97800
				recorded on 1/11/2002 at the Hard Rock Hotel in Las Vegas, Nevada		

AESOP ROCK
Born Ian Bavitz on 6/5/1976 in Northport, Long Island, New York. Male alternative rapper.

DEBUT	PEAK	WKS	RIAA	Album Title	Catalog	Label & Number
10/11/03	112	1		1 Bazooka Tooth		Definitive Jux 68
3/12/05	190	1		2 Fast Cars, Danger, Fire And Knives .... [EP]		Definitive Jux 106
9/15/07	50	4		3 None Shall Pass		Definitive Jux 144
12/5/09	131	1		4 Felt 3: A Tribute To Rosie Perez		Rhymesayers 0116
				SLUG & MURS WITH AESOP ROCK		

AFGHAN WHIGS, The
Alternative-rock band from Cincinnati, Ohio: Greg Dulli (vocals), Rick McCollum (guitar), John Curley (bass) and Paul Buchignani (drums). Michael Horrigan replaced Buchignani in 1997. Dulli also formed **The Gutter Twins**.

DEBUT	PEAK	WKS	RIAA	Album Title	Catalog	Label & Number
3/30/96	79	2		1 Black Love		Elektra 61896
11/14/98	176	1		2 1965		Columbia 69450

AFI
Hardcore punk-rock band formed in Ukiah, California: Davey "Havok" Marchand (vocals), Jade Puget (guitar), Hunter Burgan (bass) and Adam Carson (drums). AFI: A Fire Inside. Marchand and Puget also recorded as **Blaqk Audio**.

DEBUT	PEAK	WKS	RIAA	Album Title	Catalog	Label & Number
10/14/00	174	1		1 The Art Of Drowning		Nitro 15835
3/29/03	5	51	▲	2 Sing The Sorrow	Cat:#46/1	DreamWorks 450380
11/20/04	88	1		3 AFI .... [E]		Nitro 15859
				recordings from 1996-2000		
6/24/06	❶¹	38	●	4 Decemberunderground		Tiny Evil 006854
12/1/07	133	1		5 I Heard A Voice: Live From Long Beach Arena .... [L]		Tiny Evil 010268
10/17/09	12	7		6 Crash Love		DGC 013380

AFRIQUE
R&B-jazz studio band formed in Los Angeles, California: **David T. Walker** and Arthur Wright (guitars), Charles Kynard (organ), Joe Kelso, Paul Jeffery and Steve Kravitz (horns), King Errisson, **Paul Humphrey**, Wallace Snow, Charles Taggart and Chino Valdes (percussion), Chuck Rainey (bass) and Ray Pound (drums). Same group also recorded as The Chubukos.

DEBUT	PEAK	WKS	RIAA	Album Title	Catalog	Label & Number
6/16/73	152	8		1 Soul Makossa .... [I]		Mainstream 394

AFRO CELT SOUND SYSTEM
Band combines traditional West African and Irish music: N'Faly Kouyate and Iarla O'Lionaird (vocals), Simon Emmerson, James McNally, Martin Russell, Johnny Kalsi, Emer Mayock, Demba Barry, Moussa Sissokho and Mass.

DEBUT	PEAK	WKS	RIAA	Album Title	Catalog	Label & Number
7/7/01	176	4		1 Volume 3: Further In Time		Real World 10184

AFRO-CUBAN BAND
Disco studio group based in New York and produced by Michael Zager. Previously known as Love Childs Afro Cuban Blues Band.

DEBUT	PEAK	WKS	RIAA	Album Title	Catalog	Label & Number
9/16/78	204	4		1 Rhythm Of Life		Arista 4188

AFROMAN
Born Joseph Foreman on 7/28/1974 in Los Angeles, California; later based in Hattiesburg, Mississippi. Novelty rapper/songwriter.

DEBUT	PEAK	WKS	RIAA	Album Title	Catalog	Label & Number
9/15/01	10	19	●	1 The Good Times		Universal 014979

AFTERS, The
Christian pop-rock band from Mesquite, Texas: Josh Havens (vocals, guitar), Matt Fuqua (guitar), Brad Wigg (bass) and Marc Dodd (drums).

DEBUT	PEAK	WKS	RIAA	Album Title	Catalog	Label & Number
3/15/08	41	3		1 Never Going Back To OK		Ino 09358

AFTER 7
R&B vocal trio from Indianapolis, Indiana: Keith Mitchell with brothers Melvin Edmonds and **Kevon Edmonds**. Keith is the cousin of Antonio "L.A." Reid. Kevon and Melvin are the brothers of **Babyface**.

10/14/89+	35	72	▲	1 After 7		Virgin 91061
9/12/92	76	36	●	2 Takin' My Time		Virgin 86349
8/5/95	40	17	●	3 Reflections		Virgin 40547
3/29/97	97	8		4 The Very Best Of After 7	[G]	Virgin 42756

AFTER THE FIRE
Rock band formed in London, England: Andy Piercy (vocals, bass), John Russell (guitar), **Peter Banks** (keyboards) and Pete King (drums). Banks was a member of **Yes** and **Flash**.

3/12/83	25	20		1 ATF		Epic 38282

AFU-RA
Born Aaron Phillip in Brooklyn, New York. Male rapper.

11/11/00	183	1		1 Body Of The Life Force		D&D 8210
6/15/02	184	2		2 Life Force Radio		D&D 8356

AGAINST ME!
Punk-rock band from Gainesville, Florida: **Tom Gabel** (vocals, guitar), James Bowman (guitar), Andrew Seward (bass) and Warren Oakes (drums).

9/24/05	114	1		1 Searching For A Former Clarity		Fat Wreck Chords 684
7/28/07	57	2		2 New Wave		Sire 101304

AGNEW, Todd
Born on 3/15/1971 in Dallas, Texas; raised in Memphis, Tennessee. Contemporary Christian singer/songwriter.

9/3/05	86	2		1 Reflection Of Something		Ardent 72526
7/8/06	❶3C	5		2 Grace Like Rain		Ardent 72530
				first released in 2003		
8/4/07	100	2		3 Better Questions		Ardent 72547

AGUILAR, Pepe
Born on 8/7/1968 in San Antonio, Texas; raised in Zacatecas, Mexico. Latin singer. Son of Latin recording legends Antonio Aguilar and Flor Silvestre.

4/12/03	118	4		1 Y Tenerte Otra Vez	[F]	Univision 310119
10/22/05	198	1		2 Dos Idolos	[F]	Fonovisa 310540
				MARCO ANTONIO SOLIS & PEPE AGUILAR		

AGUILERA, Christina
Born on 12/18/1980 in Staten Island, New York (Irish mother; Ecuadorian father); raised in Wexford, Pennsylvania. Pop-dance singer/songwriter. Regular on TV's *The Mickey Mouse Club* (1992-93).
AWARD: Grammy: Best New Artist 1999

9/11/99	❶1	97	▲8	1 Christina Aguilera		RCA 67690
9/30/00	27	18	●	2 Mi Reflejo	[F]	RCA 69323
11/11/00	28	12	▲	3 My Kind Of Christmas	[X]	RCA 69343
				Christmas chart: 1/'00		
9/8/01	71	4		4 Just Be Free	[E-K]	Platinum 2844
				her first recordings from 1995		
11/16/02	21	79	▲4	5 Stripped	Cat:#14/9	RCA 68037
9/2/06	❶1	46	▲	6 Back To Basics		RCA 82639 [2]
11/29/08	9	23		7 Keeps Gettin' Better: A Decade Of Hits	[G]	RCA 30261

A-HA
Pop trio from Oslo, Norway: Morten Harket (vocals), Pal Waaktaar (guitar) and Magne "Mags" Furuholmen (keyboards).

7/20/85	15	47	▲	1 Hunting High And Low		Warner 25300
11/1/86	74	20		2 Scoundrel Days		Warner 25501
6/4/88	148	6		3 Stay On These Roads		Warner 25733

AHN, Priscilla
Born Priscilla Hartranft in 1984 in Fort Stewart, Georgia; raised in Pennsylvania. Folk singer/songwriter/guitarist.

7/26/08	147	1		1 A Good Day		Blue Note 95283
1/17/09	188	1		2 Live Session	[EP-L]	Blue Note digital

AIDEN
Punk-rock band from Seattle, Washington: Wil Francis (vocals), Jake Wambold (guitar), Angel Ibarra (guitar), Nick Wiggins (bass) and Jake Davison (drums).

10/22/05	196	1		1 Nightmare Anatomy		Victory 259
9/8/07	54	3		2 Conviction		Victory 349
5/30/09	95	1		3 Knives		Victory 504

AIKEN, Clay
Born Clayton Grissom (Aiken is his mother's maiden name) on 11/30/1978 in Raleigh, North Carolina. Male singer. Finished in second place on the 2003 season of TV's *American Idol*.

11/1/03	❶2	35	▲2	1 Measure Of A Man		RCA 54638
12/4/04	4	7	▲	2 Merry Christmas With Love	Cat:#8/16 [X]	RCA 62622
				Christmas charts: 1/'04, 8/'05, 18/'06		
10/7/06	21	14	●	3 A Thousand Different Ways		RCA 78846

AIKEN, Clay — cont'd

5/24/08	4	5		4 On My Way Here		S Records 28089
4/18/09	173	1		5 Playlist: The Very Best Of Clay Aiken .... [G]		RCA 47028

AIKIN, Crystal
Born in Tacoma, Washington. Gospel singer.

1/31/09	127	1		1 Crystal Aikin		BET 29754

AIR
Electronic duo from Versailles, France: Nicolas Godin and Jean-Benoit Dunckel.

3/18/00	161	1		1 The Virgin Suicides .... [I-S]		Astralwerks 48848
6/16/01	88	3		2 10,000Hz Legend		Astralwerks 10332
2/14/04	61	6		3 Talkie Walkie		Astralwerks 96632
3/24/07	40	3		4 Pocket Symphony		Aircheology 83761
10/24/09	100	1		5 Love 2		Astralwerks 66396

AIRBORNE TOXIC EVENT, The
Rock band formed in Los Angeles, California: Mikel Jollett (vocals), Steven Chen (guitar), Anna Bulbrook (keyboards), Noah Harmon (bass) and Daren Taylor (drums).

8/23/08+	108	28		1 The Airborne Toxic Event		Majordomo 10975

AIRBOURNE
Rock band from Warrnambool, Victoria, Australia: brothers Joel O'Keeffe (vocals, guitar) and Ryan O'Keeffe (drums), with David Roads (guitar) and Justin Street (bass).

2/16/08	106	2		1 Runnin' Wild		Roadrunner 617963

AIR FORCE — see BAKER, Ginger

AIR SUPPLY
Pop vocal duo formed in Australia: Russell Hitchcock (born on 6/15/1949 in Melbourne, Australia) and Graham Russell (born on 6/1/1950 in Nottingham, England). Their regular backing band included David Moyse and Rex Goh (guitars), Frank Esler-Smith (keyboards), David Green (bass) and Ralph Cooper (drums).

5/17/80	22	104	▲²	1 Lost In Love		Arista 4268
6/13/81	10	60	▲	2 The One That You Love		Arista 9551
6/19/82	25	38	▲	3 Now And Forever		Arista 9587
8/20/83	7	51	▲⁵	4 Greatest Hits .... [G]		Arista 8024
6/29/85	26	21	●	5 Air Supply		Arista 8283
9/6/86	84	9		6 Hearts In Motion		Arista 8426
12/19/87+	10ˣ	3		7 The Christmas Album .... [X]		Arista 8528
				Christmas charts: 17/'87, 10/'88		
6/21/03	186	1		8 Ultimate Air Supply .... [G]		Arista 52204

AIRTO
Born Airto Moreira on 8/5/1941 in Itaiopolis, Brazil. Male jazz percussionist/singer. Married to jazz vocalist **Flora Purim**.

3/23/74	114	9		1 In Concert .... [I]		CTI 6041
				DEODATO / AIRTO		
11/29/75	207	1		2 Identity		Arista 4068

AIRWAVES
Pop trio from Wales: Ray Martinez (vocals, guitar), John David (bass) and Dave Charles (drums).

5/13/78	204	3		1 New Day		A&M 4689

AKENS, Jewel
Born on 9/12/1940 in Houston, Texas. Male R&B singer/producer.

~ ~ ~ ~ ~ ~ ~ ~ ~ ~ **NON-CHARTED ALBUM** ~ ~ ~ ~ ~ ~ ~ ~ ~ ~ ~
1965 **The Birds And The Bees**

AKINS, Rhett
Born Thomas Rhett Akins on 10/13/1969 in Valdosta, Georgia. Country singer/songwriter/guitarist.

6/22/96	102	10		1 Somebody New		Decca 11424

AKINYELE
Born Akinyele Adams in 1970 in Queens, New York. Male hardcore rapper.

8/31/96	127	4		1 Put It In Your Mouth (a.k.a. Fella) .... [EP]		Stress 11142

AKKERMAN, Jan
Born on 12/24/1946 in Amsterdam, Holland. Progressive-rock guitarist. Former member of **Focus**.

10/13/73	192	4		1 Profile .... [I]		Sire 7407
3/2/74	195	2		2 Tabernakel .... [I]		Atco 7032
4/8/78	198	2		3 Jan Akkerman .... [I]		Atlantic 19159

AKON
Born Aliaune Thiam on 4/16/1973 in St. Louis, Missouri; raised in Dakar, Senegal, and Jersey City, New Jersey. Male R&B singer/songwriter/producer.

7/17/04+	18	72	▲	1 Trouble		SRC 000860
12/2/06	2⁴	68	▲³	2 Konvicted		SRC 007968
12/20/08	7	38		3 Freedom		Konvict 012334

Billboard			R I A A	ARTIST		
DEBUT	PEAK	WKS		Album Title	Catalog	Label & Number

AKWID
Latin rap duo from Los Angeles, California: Sergio "Wikid" Gomez and Francisco "AK" Gomez.

7/3/04	132	5		1 KOMP 104.9: Radio Compa .... [F]	Aries 31020
7/9/05	192	1		2 Kickin' It...Juntos! .... [F-K]	Univision 310478
				AKWID & JAE-P	
9/17/05	157	2		3 Los Aguacates De Jiquilpan... [F]	Univision 310381
3/29/08	196	1		4 La Novela... [F]	Univision 311070

ALABAMA
1980s: #9 / 1990s: #27 / All-Time: #65

Country band formed in Fort Payne, Alabama: **Randy Owen** (vocals, guitar; born on 12/13/1949), Jeff Cook (keyboards, fiddle; born on 8/27/1949), Teddy Gentry (bass; born on 1/22/1952) and Mark Herndon (drums; born on 5/11/1955). Randy, Jeff and Teddy are cousins.

AWARDS: C&W Hall of Fame: 2005 ★ CMA: Vocal Group 1981, 1982 & 1983 / Instrumental Group 1981 & 1982 / Entertainer 1982, 1983 & 1984

7/19/80	71	21	▲²	1 My Home's In Alabama	RCA Victor 3644
3/28/81	16	161	▲⁴	2 Feels So Right	RCA Victor 3930
3/13/82	14	114	▲⁵	3 Mountain Music	RCA Victor 4229
				Grammy: Country Vocal Group	
3/26/83	10	70	▲⁴	4 The Closer You Get...	RCA Victor 4663
				Grammy: Country Vocal Group ★ CMA: Album of the Year	
2/11/84	21	62	▲⁴	5 Roll On .... Cat:#33/4	RCA Victor 4939
2/23/85	28	40	▲²	6 40 Hour Week	RCA Victor 5339
10/25/86	42	30	▲	7 The Touch	RCA Victor 5649
10/17/87	55	28	▲	8 Just Us	RCA Victor 6495
2/18/89	62	21	▲	9 Southern Star	RCA 8587
6/16/90	57	41	▲	10 Pass It On Down	RCA 2108
8/29/92	46	51	▲	11 American Pride	RCA 66044
10/30/93	76	38	▲	12 Cheap Seats	RCA 66296
9/2/95	100	21	▲	13 In Pictures	RCA 66525
4/26/97	55	26	●	14 Dancin' On The Boulevard	RCA 67426
7/3/99	51	10	●	15 Twentieth Century	RCA 67793
2/3/01	37	8		16 When It All Goes South	RCA 69337
				CHRISTMAS ALBUMS:	
11/23/85	75	9	▲²	17 Christmas .... Cat:#25/12	RCA Victor 7014
				Christmas charts: 1/'85, 16/'87, 8/'88, 18/'89, 20/'90, 15/'91, 30/'92, 28/'93	
11/30/96	117	6		18 Christmas Volume II..	RCA 66927
				Christmas charts: 12/'96, 25/'03, 29/'04	
				GREATEST HITS & COMPILATIONS:	
3/1/86	24	38	▲⁵	19 Greatest Hits..	RCA Victor 7170
10/26/91	72	31	▲	20 Greatest Hits II	RCA 61040
10/15/94+	56	49	▲²	21 Greatest Hits - Vol. III	RCA 66410
9/12/98	13	33	▲⁵	22 For The Record - 41 Number One Hits	RCA 67633 [2]
2/22/03	15	11		23 In The Mood: The Love Songs	RCA 67052 [2]
10/30/04	52	4		24 Ultimate Alabama: 20 #1 Hits	RCA 64196
2/18/06	120	1		25 Livin' Lovin' Rockin' Rollin': The 25th Anniversary Collection..........	RCA 71918 [3]
				LIVE ALBUMS:	
6/25/88	76	19	▲	26 Alabama Live	RCA 6825
10/25/03	64	5		27 The American Farewell Tour	RCA 54371
				RELIGIOUS ALBUMS:	
11/11/06	15	7		28 Songs Of Inspiration	RCA 00532
4/14/07	33	1		29 Songs Of Inspiration II	RCA 06065

ALABAMA STATE TROUPERS, The
Concert revue featuring vocalists **Don Nix** and Jeanie Greene with legendary 1920s blues singer/guitarist Walter "Furry" Lewis (died on 9/14/1981, age 88). Backed by the Mt. Zion Band and the Mt. Zion Choir.

| 2/26/72 | 218 | 2 | | 1 Road Show .... [L] | Elektra 75022 [2] |
| | | | | recorded on 10/15/1971 in Long Beach, California, and on 10/17/1971 in Pasadena, California | |

ALACRANES MUSICAL
Tejano family band from Durango, Mexico: Oscar Urbina, Joel Urbina, Eduardo Urbina, Oscar Urbina Jr., Guillermo Ibarra, Rene Urbina, Adam Cervantes and Chris Urbina. Group name is Spanish for "Musical Scorpions."

6/11/05	151	2		1 100% Originales .... [F-K]	Univision 310384
7/8/06	126	2		2 A Paso Firme .... [F]	Univision 310839
6/9/07	47	8		3 Ahora Y Siempre.. [F]	Univision 311054
9/13/08	26	8		4 Tu Inspiration .... [F]	Fonovisa 311305
3/7/09	141	1		5 Live: En Vivo Desde Mexico .... [F-L]	Fonovisa 353810

ALARM, The
Rock band from Rhyl, Wales: Mike Peters (vocals), Dave Sharp (guitar), Eddie MacDonald (bass) and Nigel Twist (drums).

7/30/83+	126	37		1 The Alarm .... [EP]		I.R.S. 70504
3/10/84	50	22		2 Declaration		I.R.S. 70608
11/9/85+	39	36		3 Strength		I.R.S. 5666
11/7/87	77	30		4 Eye Of The Hurricane		I.R.S. 42061
10/29/88	167	5		5 Electric Folklore Live .... [L]		I.R.S. 39108
				recorded on 4/26/1988 in Boston, Massachusetts		
10/14/89	75	23		6 Change.		I.R.S. 82018
12/15/90	177	3		7 Standards .... [G]		I.R.S. 13056
5/18/91	161	1		8 Raw		I.R.S. 13087

ALBERT, Morris
Born Mauricio Alberto Kaisermann on 9/7/1951 in Sao Paulo, Brazil. Adult Contemporary singer/songwriter.

9/6/75	37	31		1 Feelings		RCA Victor 1018
6/12/76	135	7		2 Morris Albert		RCA Victor 1496
6/18/77	201	6		3 Love And Life		RCA Victor 2070

ALBRIGHT, Gerald
Born on 8/30/1957 in Los Angeles, California. R&B session saxophonist.

2/27/88	181	5		1 Just Between Us .... [I]		Atlantic 81813
3/12/94	151	10		2 Smooth .... [I]		Atlantic 82552
10/17/98	169	3		3 Pleasures Of The Night		Verve Forecast 557613
				WILL DOWNING & GERALD ALBRIGHT		

AL B. SURE!
Born Albert Brown on 6/4/1969 in Boston, Massachusetts; raised in Mt. Vernon, New York. R&B singer/songwriter.

5/14/88	20	54	▲²	1 In Effect Mode		Warner 25662
11/3/90	20	19	●	2 Private Times...And The Whole 9!		Warner 26005
10/10/92	41	11		3 Sexy Versus		Warner 26973
7/11/09	85	3		4 Honey I'm Home		Hidden Beach 00092

ALCATRAZZ
Hard-rock band: Graham Bonnet (vocals), **Yngwie J. Malmsteen** (guitar), Jimmy Waldo (keyboards), Gary Shea (bass) and Jan Uvena (drums). Shea and Waldo were with **New England**. Bonnet was also with **Rainbow**, **Michael Schenker Group** and **Impellitteri**. By 1985, **Steve Vai** had replaced Malmsteen. Group named after the notorious maximum-security prison near San Francisco, California.

1/7/84	128	18		1 No Parole From Rock 'N' Roll		Rocshire 22016
6/9/84	133	10		2 Live Sentence .... [L]		Rocshire 22020
				recorded on 1/28/1984 in Tokyo, Japan		
4/20/85	145	16		3 Disturbing The Peace		Capitol 12385

ALCHEMIST, The
Born Alan Maman on 10/14/1975 in Beverly Hills, California. White hip-hop singer/songwriter/producer.

10/9/04	101	2		1 1st Infantry		Koch 9548
7/25/09	63	2		2 Chemical Warfare		ALC 4220

ALDA RESERVE
Rock band from England: Brad Ellis (vocals, keyboards), Mark Suall (guitar), Tony Shanahan (bass) and Matthew "Chips" Patuto (drums).

11/24/79	210	4		1 Love Goes On		Sire 6079

ALDEAN, Jason
Born Jason Aldine Williams on 2/28/1977 in Macon, Georgia. Country singer/guitarist.

8/13/05	37	104	▲	1 Jason Aldean .... **Cat:**#25/9		Broken Bow 76572
6/16/07	4	47	●	2 Relentless .... **Cat:**#35/7		Broken Bow 7047
4/25/09	4	58↑	▲	3 Wide Open		Broken Bow 7637

ALDRICH, Ronnie, And His Two Pianos
Born on 2/15/1916 in Erith, Kent, England. Died of cancer on 9/30/1993 (age 77). Pianist/arranger. Musical director of the *Benny Hill* TV variety series.

10/23/61+	20	33		1 Melody And Percussion For Two Pianos .... [I]		London Phase 4 44007
10/6/62	36	4		2 Ronnie Aldrich And His Two Pianos .... [I]		London Phase 4 44018
5/22/71	169	6		3 Love Story .... [I]		London Phase 4 22 [2]

ALESANA
Rock band from Raleigh, North Carolina: Dennis Lee (vocals), Patrick Thompson (guitar), Shawn Milke (guitar), Shane Crump (bass) and Jeremy Bryan (drums).

6/21/08	96	2		1 Where Myth Fades To Legend		Fearless 30110

ALESSI
Identical twin brothers Billy and Bobby Alessi. Born on 7/12/1953 in West Hempstead, New York.

2/4/78	210	1		1 All For A Reason		A&M 4657

ALEXIS Y FIDO
Reggaeton duo from Puerto Rico: Raul "Alexis" Ortiz and Joel "Fido" Martinez.

12/3/05	164	1		1 The Pitbulls .... [F]		Sony 95913

ALEXISONFIRE
Alternative-rock band from St. Catharines, Ontario, Canada: George Pettit (vocals), Dallas Green (vocals, guitar), Wade MacNeil (guitar, vocals), Chris Steele (bass) and Jordan "Ratbeard" Hastings (drums).

DEBUT	PEAK	WKS		Album Title	Catalog	Label & Number
9/9/06	189	1		1 Crisis		Distort 438
7/11/09	81	1		2 Old Crows / Young Cardinals		Vagrant 540

ALI
Born Ali Jones on 7/13/1971 in St. Louis, Missouri. Male rapper. Member of **St. Lunatics**.

5/18/02	24	6		1 Heavy Starch		Fo' Reel 017104
9/1/07	174	1		2 Kinfolk		Derrty 007160
				ALI & GIPP		

ALI, Tatyana
Born on 1/24/1979 in North Bellmore, Long Island, New York; raised in Los Angeles, California. R&B singer/actress. Played "Ashley Banks" on TV's *The Fresh Prince Of Bel-Air*.

9/12/98	106	11		1 Kiss The Sky		MJJ Music 68656

ALIADOS DE LA SIERRA
Latin band from Mexico. Group name is Spanish for "Allies Of The Sierra."

11/24/07	136	1		1 Con Los Ojos Cerrados [F]		Disa 730028
3/28/09	133	1		2 Solo Por Ti [F]		Disa 730157

ALIAS
Rock band formed in Los Angeles, California: former **Sheriff** members Freddy Curci (vocals) and Steve DeMarchi (guitar), with former **Heart** members Roger Fisher (guitar), Steve Fossen (bass) and Mike Derosier (drums).

10/6/90+	114	28		1 Alias		EMI 93908

ALICE DEEJAY
Techno-dance act from Amsterdam, Netherlands. Formed by producers Eelke Kalberg, Sebastiaan Molijn and DJ Jurgen. Fronted by female singer Judy with Gaby and Jane.

4/15/00	76	26		1 Who Needs Guitars Anyway?		Republic 157672

ALICE IN CHAINS
1990s: #30 / All-Time: #335

Male hard-rock band formed in Seattle, Washington: Layne Staley (vocals; born on 8/22/1967; died of a drug overdose on 4/5/2002, age 34), **Jerry Cantrell** (guitar; born on 3/18/1966), Mike Starr (bass; born on 4/4/1966) and Sean Kinney (drums; born on 5/27/1966). Starr replaced by Mike Inez (former bassist for **Ozzy Osbourne**; born on 5/14/1966) by 1994. In 1995, Inez recorded with **Slash's Snakepit** and Staley recorded with **Mad Season**. Scott Olson (guitar) joined in 1996.

4/27/91	42	59	▲²	1 Facelift	Cat:#23/65	Columbia 46075
10/17/92	6	102	▲⁴	2 Dirt	Cat:#28/29	Columbia 52475
2/12/94	❶¹	59	▲²	3 Jar Of Flies [EP]		Columbia 57628
4/15/95	29ᶜ	7		4 Sap [EP]		Columbia 67059
11/25/95	❶¹	46	▲²	5 Alice In Chains		Columbia 67248
8/17/96	3¹	33	▲	6 MTV Unplugged [L]		Columbia 67703
				recorded on 4/10/1996 at the Majestic Theater in New York City		
7/17/99	20	17	▲	7 Nothing Safe [K]		Columbia 63649
11/13/99	123	1		8 Music Bank [K]		Columbia 69580 [4]
12/23/00	142	2		9 Live [L]		Columbia 85274
				recorded from 1991-93		
9/15/01	112	4	●	10 Greatest Hits [G]	Cat:#50/1	Columbia 85922
9/23/06	139	1		11 The Essential Alice In Chains [G]		Legacy 92090 [2]
10/17/09	5	32	●	12 Black Gives Way To Blue		Virgin 67159

ALIEN ANT FARM
Alternative-rock band from Riverside, California: Dryden Mitchell (vocals), Terry Corso (guitar), Tye Zamora (bass) and Mike Cosgrove (drums).

3/24/01	11	64	▲	1 ANThology		New Noize 450293
9/6/03	42	4		2 truANT		El Tonal 000568
8/5/06	114	1		3 Up In The Attic		El Tonal 006823

ALISHA
Born Alisha Itkin on 4/16/1968 in Brooklyn, New York. White female dance singer.

6/23/90	166	4		1 Bounce Back		MCA 6378

ALIVE 'N KICKIN'
Pop-rock band from Brooklyn, New York: Pepe Cardona (male vocals), Sandy Toder (female vocals), John Parisio (guitar), Bruce Sudano (organ), Thomas Wilson (bass) and Vito Albano (drums). Sudano married **Donna Summer** on 7/16/1980 and was a member of **Brooklyn Dreams**.

10/17/70	129	3		1 Alive 'N Kickin'		Roulette 42052
				produced by **Tommy James**		

ALKAHOLIKS, Tha
Rap trio from Los Angeles, California: James Robinson ("J-Ro"), Rico Smith ("Tash") and Eric Brooks ("E-Swift"). Changed name to **Tha Liks** in 2001.

9/11/93	124	6		1 21 & Over		Loud 66280
3/18/95	50	3		2 Coast II Coast		Loud 66446
9/13/97	57	5		3 Likwidation		Loud 67435
7/28/01	47	4		4 X.O. Experience		Loud 85782
				THA LIKS		

ALKALINE TRIO
Punk-rock trio from Chicago, Illinois: Matt Skiba (vocals, guitar), Daniel Andriano (bass) and Mike Felumlee (drums). Derek Grant replaced Felumlee in 2002.

DEBUT	PEAK	WKS			Catalog	Label & Number
4/21/01	199	1		1 From Here To Infirmary		Vagrant 353
5/31/03	20	12		2 Good Mourning		Vagrant 381
6/11/05	25	7		3 Crimson		Vagrant 409
2/17/07	64	2		4 Remains		Vagrant 441
7/19/08	13	5		5 Agony & Irony		Epic 17247

ALL-AMERICAN REJECTS, The
Rock band from Stillwater, Oklahoma: Tyson Ritter (vocals, bass), Nick Wheeler (guitar), Mike Kennerty (guitar) and Chris Gaylor (drums).

2/22/03	25	41	▲	1 The All-American Rejects		Doghouse 450407
7/30/05	6	97	▲2	2 Move Along		Doghouse 004791
1/3/09	15	38	●	3 When The World Comes Down		Doghouse 012297

ALLAN, Davie, And The Arrows
Born in 1945 in Los Angeles, California. Session guitarist. The Arrows consisted of Jared Hendler (keyboards), Drew Bennett (bass) and Larry Brown (drums).

10/15/66+	17	71		1 The Wild Angels	[S]	Tower 5043
4/22/67	94	18		2 The Wild Angels, Vol. II	[I-S]	Tower 5056
8/19/67	165	2		3 Devil's Angels	[I-S]	Tower 5074

ALLAN, Gary
Born Gary Allan Herzberg on 12/5/1967 in Montebello, California; raised in La Mirada, California. Country singer/guitarist.

11/9/96+	136	16		1 Used Heart For Sale		Decca 11482
6/6/98	132	6		2 It Would Be You		Decca 70012
11/13/99	84	47	▲	3 Smoke Rings In The Dark	Cat:#40/4	MCA Nashville 70101
10/20/01	39	42	▲	4 Alright Guy		MCA Nashville 70201
10/18/03	17	45	▲	5 See If I Care		MCA Nashville 000111
10/29/05	3[1]	43	●	6 Tough All Over		MCA Nashville 003711
3/24/07	5	27	●	7 Greatest Hits	Cat:#42/2 [G]	MCA Nashville 008196
11/10/07	3[1]	43	●	8 Living Hard		MCA Nashville 008962

ALLEN, Dayton
Born Dayton Allen Bolke on 9/24/1919 in Brooklyn, New York. Died of a stroke on 11/11/2004 (age 85). Comedian on **Steve Allen**'s TV show. Voice of *Deputy Dawg* TV cartoon and "Phineas T. Bluster" of TV's *Howdy Doody*.

12/19/60	35	1		1 Why Not!	[C]	Grand Award 424

ALLEN, Deborah
Born Deborah Lynn Thurmond on 9/30/1953 in Memphis, Tennessee. Country singer/songwriter.

12/3/83+	67	20		1 Cheat The Night	[EP]	RCA Victor 8514

ALLEN, Donna
Born in Key West, Florida; raised in Tampa. R&B/dance singer. Former cheerleader for the NFL's Tampa Bay Buccaneers.

4/4/87	133	13		1 Perfect Timing		21 Records 90548

ALLEN, Kris
Born on 6/21/1985 in Jacksonville, Arkansas; raised in Conway, Arkansas. Male singer. Winner on the 2009 season of TV's *American Idol*.

6/6/09	50	2		1 Season 8 Favorites Performances	[L]	19 Records digital
12/5/09	11	18		2 Kris Allen		19 Records 54802

ALLEN, Lily
Born on 5/2/1985 in Hammersmith, London, England. Pop-rock singer/songwriter.

2/17/07	20	36	●	1 Alright, Still...	Cat:#16/1	Capitol 75466
2/28/09	5	21		2 It's Not Me, It's You		Capitol 67233

ALLEN, Peter
Born Peter Allen Woolnough on 2/10/1944 in Tenterfield, New South Wales, Australia. Died of AIDS on 6/18/1992 (age 48). Cabaret-style performer/songwriter/author. Married to **Liza Minnelli** from 1967-74. Co-writer of "Arthur's Theme" and "I Honestly Love You."

12/10/77	209	1		1 It's Time For Peter Allen	[L]	A&M 3706 [2]
				recorded at Avery Fischer Hall and The Bottom Line in New York City and The Roxy in Los Angeles		
4/21/79	171	3		2 I Could Have Been A Sailor		A&M 4739
11/29/80+	123	20		3 Bi-Coastal		A&M 4825
3/12/83	170	6		4 Not The Boy Next Door		Arista 9613

ALLEN, Steve
Born on 12/26/1921 in Manhattan, New York; raised in Chicago, Illinois. Died of heart failure on 10/30/2000 (age 78). Comedian/actor/songwriter/author. In 1954, became the first host of TV's *The Tonight Show*. Played **Benny Goodman** in the 1956 movie *The Benny Goodman Story*. Hosted own variety and talk shows (1956-80). Married actress Jayne Meadows on 7/31/1954.

5/14/55	7	5		1 Music For Tonight	[I]	Coral 57004
3/16/63	65	11		2 Funny Fone-Calls	[C]	Dot 3472
4/27/63	41	22		3 Gravy Waltz And 11 Current Hits!	[I]	Dot 3515

Billboard			R I A A	ARTIST		
DEBUT	PEAK	WKS		Album Title	Catalog	Label & Number

ALLEN, Woody
Born Allen Konigsberg on 12/1/1935 in Brooklyn, New York. Prolific movie director/actor/comedian/writer. Married to actress Louise Lasser from 1966-69. Had a longtime relationship with actress Mia Farrow (never married; highly publicized breakup in 1992). Married Farrow's adopted daughter, Soon-Yi Previn, on 12/22/1997.

8/15/64	63	11		1 Woody Allen .... [C]		Colpix 518
				no track titles listed on this album		

ALL-4-ONE
Male interracial vocal group from Los Angeles, California: Jamie Jones (born on 11/6/1974), Delious Kennedy (born on 12/21/1970), Alfred Nevarez (born on 5/17/1973) and Tony Borowiak (born on 10/12/1972).

4/30/94	7	72	▲⁴	1 All-4-One		Blitzz 82588
6/24/95	27	35	▲	2 And The Music Speaks		Blitzz 82746
12/2/95	91	7		3 An All-4-One Christmas .... [X]		Blitzz 82846
				Christmas charts: 13/'95, 30/'96		

ALLFRUMTHA I
Male rap duo from Inglewood, California: Ryan Garner and Marcus Moore.

5/23/98	168	1		1 AllFrumTha I		Priority 50588

ALLMAN, Gregg
Born on 12/8/1947 in Nashville, Tennessee; raised in Daytona Beach, Florida. Southern-rock singer/organist. Brother of **Duane Allman**; member of **The Allman Brothers Band**. Married six times, including **Cher** from 1975-79 (their son, Elijah Blue, fronts the group **Deadsy**). Played "Gaines" in the 1991 movie *Rush*. His band included brothers Dan Toler (guitar) and David Toler (drums), Tim Heding (keyboards), Chaz Trippy (percussion) and Bruce Waibel (bass; committed suicide on 9/2/2003, age 45).

11/24/73+	13	39	●	1 Laid Back		Capricorn 0116
11/16/74	50	12		2 The Gregg Allman Tour .... [L]		Capricorn 0141 [2]
				recorded at Carnegie Hall and the Capitol Theater in New Jersey		

THE GREGG ALLMAN BAND:
6/11/77	42	12		3 Playin' Up A Storm		Capricorn 0181
3/7/87	30	28	●	4 I'm No Angel		Epic 40531
8/6/88	117	11		5 Just Before The Bullets Fly		Epic 44033

ALLMAN BROTHERS BAND, The   1970s: #42 / All-Time: #123
Southern-rock band formed in Macon, Georgia. Original lineup: brothers **Gregg Allman** (vocals, organ) and **Duane Allman** (lead guitar), **Dickey Betts** (guitar; vocals), Berry Oakley (bass), Butch Trucks (drums) and Jai Johnny Johanson (drums). Gregg and Duane first recorded together as the **Allman Joys** and Hour Glass. Duane Allman died in a motorcycle crash on 10/29/1971 (age 24). Berry Oakley died in a motorcycle crash on 11/11/1972 (age 24); replaced by Lamar Williams (died on 1/21/1983, age 36). Chuck Leavell (keyboards) added in 1972. Group split up in 1976. Leavell, Williams and Johanson formed the fusion-rock band **Sea Level**. Allman, Betts and Trucks reunited in late 1978 with Dan Toler (guitar) and David Goldflies (bass). By early 1980, Dan's brother David Toler (drums) had joined. Group once again split up in 1982. Allman, Betts, Trucks and Johanson reunited in 1989 with **Warren Haynes** (guitar), Allen Woody (bass) and Johnny Neel (keyboards). Neel left in 1991; replaced by Mark Quinones. Haynes and Woody formed **Gov't Mule**. Woody died of a heart attack on 8/26/2000 (age 44). By 2003, **Derek Trucks** (guitar; nephew of Butch Trucks) had replaced Betts and Otiel Burbridge (bass) had joined.
AWARD: R&R Hall of Fame: 1995

1/24/70	188	5		1 The Allman Brothers Band .... Cat:#50/4		Atco 308
10/24/70	38	22		2 Idlewild South		Atco 342
8/25/73	❶⁵	56	▲	3 Brothers And Sisters		Capricorn 0111
9/13/75	5	14	●	4 Win, Lose Or Draw		Capricorn 0156
3/17/79	9	24	●	5 Enlightened Rogues		Capricorn 0218
8/23/80	27	13		6 Reach For The Sky		Arista 9535
8/22/81	44	12		7 Brothers Of The Road		Arista 9564
7/21/90	53	16		8 Seven Turns		Epic 46144
7/20/91	85	17		9 Shades Of Two Worlds		Epic 47877
5/21/94	45	21	●	10 Where It All Begins		Epic 64232
4/5/03	37	7		11 Hittin' The Note		Peach 84599

EARLY ALBUMS:
5/13/72	129	8		12 Duane & Gregg Allman		Bold 301
				recorded in 1968		
11/3/73	171	8		13 Early Allman		Dial 6005
				ALLMAN JOYS		
				recorded in 1966		

GREATEST HITS & COMPILATIONS:
12/9/72+	28	26	●	14 An Anthology		Capricorn 0108 [2]
8/31/74	49	16		15 An Anthology, Vol. II		Capricorn 0139 [2]
				DUANE ALLMAN (above 2)		
12/13/75+	43	14		16 The Road Goes On Forever, A Collection Of Their Greatest Recordings		Capricorn 0164 [2]
11/21/81	189	3	●	17 The Best Of The Allman Brothers Band		Polydor 6339
7/15/89	103	11	●	18 Dreams		Polydor 839417 [6]

LIVE ALBUMS:
7/24/71	13	47	▲	19 At Fillmore East .... Cat:#23/8		Capricorn 802 [2]
				Grammy: Hall of Fame ★ RS500 #49 ★ NRR		
				recorded on 3/12/1971 in New York City		
3/18/72	4	48	▲	20 Eat A Peach Cat:#21/21		Capricorn 0102 [2]
12/4/76	75	10		21 Wipe The Windows-Check The Oil-Dollar Gas		Capricorn 0177 [2]
6/27/92	80	8		22 An Evening With The Allman Brothers Band		Epic 48998
5/27/95	88	4		23 2nd Set - An Evening With The Allman Brothers Band		Epic 66795
4/10/04	190	1		24 One Way Out: Live At The Beacon Theatre		Sanctuary 84682 [2]

ALLMAN BROTHERS BAND, The — cont'd
REISSUE:

3/10/73	25	55	● 25 Beginnings..		Atco 805 [2]

reissue of albums #1 and #2 above

ALL SAINTS
Female interracial vocal group formed in London, England: sisters Natalie Appleton and Nicky Appleton (from Canada), with Shaznay Lewis and Melanie Blatt (from England). Natalie Appleton married Liam Howlett (of **Prodigy**) on 6/6/2002.

3/28/98	40	49	▲ 1 All Saints..	London 828997

ALL SHALL PERISH
Deathcore band from Oakland, California: Hernan "Eddie" Hermida (vocals), Jason Richardson (guitar), Beniko Orum (guitar), Mike Tiner (bass) and Matt Kuykendall (drums).

10/4/08	126	1	1 Awaken The Dreamers..	Nuclear Blast 2170

ALL THAT REMAINS
Heavy metal band from Springfield, Massachusetts: Philip Labonte (vocals), Mike Martin (guitar), Oli Herbert (guitar), Jeanne Sagan (bass) and Jason Costa (drums).

7/29/06	75	3	1 The Fall Of Ideals..	Prosthetic 82956
10/4/08	16	21	2 Overcome..	Prosthetic 82999

ALL TIME LOW
Pop-punk band from Baltimore, Maryland: Alex Gaskarth (vocals, guitar), Jack Barakat (guitar), Zack Merrick (bass) and Rian Dawson (drums).

10/13/07	62	4	1 So Wrong, It's Right..	Hopeless 693
7/25/09	4	13	2 Nothing Personal	Hopeless 710

ALLURE
Female R&B vocal group from Long Island, New York: Alia Davis, Akissa Mendez, Lalisha McLean and Linnie Belcher.

5/24/97	108	27	● 1 Allure..	Crave 67848

ALMEIDA, Laurindo, and The Bossa Nova All Stars
Born on 9/2/1917 in Sao Paulo, Brazil. Died of cancer on 7/26/1995 (age 77). Male guitarist/bandleader. Member of **Stan Kenton**'s orchestra until 1950. Helped popularize the bossa nova style. Worked on the scores of many movies.

12/8/62+	9	27	1 Viva Bossa Nova!	[I]	Capitol 1759

ALMOND, Marc
Born Peter Mark Sinclair Almond on 7/9/1957 in Southport, Lancashire, England. Male singer/songwriter/multi-instrumentalist. Half of the **Soft Cell** duo.

1/28/89	144	11	1 The Stars We Are..	Capitol 91042

ALMOST, The
Alternative-rock band formed in Clearwater, Florida: Aaron Gillespie (vocals), Jay Vilardi (guitar), Alex Aponte (bass) and Kenny Bozich (drums). Gillespie is also the drummer for **Underoath**.

4/21/07	39	20	1 Southern Weather..		Tooth & Nail 52481
10/10/09	31[X]	1	2 No Gift To Bring..	[X-EP]	Tooth & Nail 42971
11/21/09	67	2	3 Monster Monster..		Tooth & Nail 08630

ALONSO, Tite Curet
Born on 2/26/1926 in Guayama, Puerto Rico. Died of a heart attack on 8/5/2003 (age 77). Latin singer/songwriter.

2/7/09	199	1	1 A Man And His Songs: Alma De Poeta............................	[F-K]	Fania 130425 [2]

ALPERT, Herb, & The Tijuana Brass   1960s: #17 / All-Time: #42
Born on 3/31/1935 in Los Angeles, California. Trumpeter/songwriter/producer. Played trumpet since age eight. Recorded as Dore Alpert in 1962. Formed highly successful Tijuana Brass group. Co-founder (with Jerry Moss) of both A&M record label in 1962 and Almos Sounds label in 1994. Married singer Lani Hall (of **Sergio Medes & Brasil '66**) on 12/15/1974.
AWARDS: Grammy: Trustees 1997 ★ R&R Hall of Fame: 2006 (Lifetime Achievement/Non-Performer)

12/29/62+	10	157	● 1 The Lonely Bull..	[I]	A&M 101
1/15/66	17	56	● 2 Herb Alpert's Tijuana Brass, Volume 2............................	[I]	A&M 103
			released in 1963		
1/16/65+	6	163	● 3 South Of The Border..	[I]	A&M 108
5/15/65	❶[8]	185	● 4 Whipped Cream & Other Delights............................	[I]	A&M 110
10/16/65+	❶[6]	164	● 5 Going Places..	[I]	A&M 112
5/14/66	❶[9]	129	● 6 What Now My Love..	[I]	A&M 4114
12/10/66	2[6]	85	● 7 S.R.O..	[I]	A&M 4119
6/3/67	❶[1]	53	● 8 Sounds Like..	[I]	A&M 4124
12/23/67+	4	49	● 9 Herb Alpert's Ninth..	[I]	A&M 4134
5/11/68	❶[2]	54	● 10 The Beat Of The Brass..	[I]	A&M 4146
12/7/68	❶[2X]	10	● 11 Christmas Album..	[X-I]	A&M 4166
			Christmas charts: 1/'68, 6/'69, 17/'70		
7/5/69	28	26	● 12 Warm..	[I]	A&M 4190

Billboard			R I A A	ARTIST		
DEBUT	PEAK	WKS		Album Title	Catalog	Label & Number

ALPERT, Herb, & The Tijuana Brass — cont'd

DEBUT	PEAK	WKS				
11/22/69+	30	20		13 **The Brass Are Comin'** .... [I]		A&M 4228
3/21/70	43	32	●	14 **Greatest Hits** .... [G-I]		A&M 4245
7/24/71	111	10		15 **Summertime** .... [I]		A&M 4314
6/17/72	135	9		16 **Solid Brass** .... [I-K]		A&M 4341
12/8/73	196	4		17 **Foursider** .... [I-K]		A&M 3521 [2]
6/1/74	66	11		18 **You Smile-The Song Begins** .... [I]		A&M 3620
4/26/75	88	10		19 **Coney Island** .... [I]		A&M 4521
2/11/78	65	19		20 **Herb Alpert/Hugh Masekela** .... [I]		Horizon 728

HERB ALPERT:

DEBUT	PEAK	WKS				
10/13/79	6	39	▲	21 **Rise** .... [I]		A&M 4790
7/26/80	28	12		22 **Beyond** .... [I]		A&M 3717
8/16/80	206	1		23 **Greatest Hits Vol. 2** .... [G]		A&M 4627
8/22/81	61	10		24 **Magic Man** .... [I]		A&M 3728
5/29/82	100	26		25 **Fandango** .... [I]		A&M 3731
9/24/83	120	8		26 **Blow Your Own Horn** .... [I]		A&M 4949
8/25/84	75	10		27 **Bullish** .... [I]		A&M 5022

HERB ALPERT/TIJUANA BRASS

DEBUT	PEAK	WKS				
8/24/85	151	10		28 **Wild Romance** .... [I]		A&M 5082
4/25/87	18	31	●	29 **Keep Your Eye On Me** .... [I]		A&M 5125

ALPHAVILLE
Male pop trio from Berlin, Germany: Marian Gold (vocals), Frank Mertens (keyboards) and Bernhard Lloyd (drums). Ricky Echolette replaced Mertens by 1986.

DEBUT	PEAK	WKS				
12/22/84+	180	15		1 **Forever Young**		Atlantic 80186
8/30/86	174	6		2 **Afternoons In Utopia**		Atlantic 81667

ALTER BRIDGE
Rock band from Tallahassee, Florida: Myles Kennedy (vocals), Mark Tremonti (guitar), Brian Marshall (bass) and Scott Phillips (drums). The latter three were members of **Creed**.

DEBUT	PEAK	WKS				
8/28/04	5	14	●	1 **One Day Remains**		Wind-Up 13097
10/27/07	13	14		2 **Blackbird**		Universal 009955

ALVIN, Dave
Born on 11/11/1955 in Downey, California. Rock singer/songwriter/guitarist. Former member of **The Blasters**, **X** and **The Knitters**.

DEBUT	PEAK	WKS				
9/26/87	116	13		1 **Romeo's Escape**		Epic 40921

ALY & AJ
Teen pop vocal/songwriting duo from Torrance, California: sisters Alyson "Aly" Michalka (born on 3/25/1989) and Amanda Joy "AJ" Michalka (born on 4/10/1991). Both are also actresses and appeared in several TV shows.

DEBUT	PEAK	WKS				
9/3/05	36	65	●	1 **Into The Rush**		Hollywood 162505
11/25/06	78	7		2 **Acoustic Hearts Of Winter** .... [X]		Hollywood 162639
				Christmas charts: 14/'06, 28/'07		
7/28/07	15	18		3 **Insomniatic**		Hollywood 162642

AMANT
Disco studio group assembled by producer Ray Martinez.

DEBUT	PEAK	WKS				
3/31/79	203	4		1 **Amant**		Marlin 2227

AMAZING BLONDEL
Medieval-styled trio from Scunthorpe, England: John David Gladwin (lute, oboe), Terry Wincott (pipe organ, flute) and Edward Baird (guitar, percussion). Named for Richard the Lionhearted's legendary favorite minstrel.

DEBUT	PEAK	WKS				
2/17/73	210	3		1 **England**		Island 9327

AMAZING RHYTHM ACES, The
Country-rock band from Knoxville, Tennessee: Russell Smith (vocals, guitar), Barry "Byrd" Burton (guitar), Billy Earhart III (keyboards), James Hooker (piano), Jeff "Stick" Davis (bass) and Butch McDade (drums). Burton left in 1977; replaced by Duncan Cameron (joined **Sawyer Brown** in 1991). McDade died of cancer on 11/29/1998 (age 52).

DEBUT	PEAK	WKS				
10/18/75	120	8		1 **Stacked Deck**		ABC 913
6/5/76	157	7		2 **Too Stuffed To Jump**		ABC 940
4/16/77	114	11		3 **Toucan Do It Too**		ABC 1005
4/15/78	116	9		4 **Burning The Ballroom Down**		ABC 1063
2/17/79	144	7		5 **The Amazing Rhythm Aces**		ABC 1123
10/4/80	175	3		6 **How The Hell Do You Spell Rythum?**		Warner 3476

AMAZING SPIDER-MAN, The — see VARIOUS ARTIST COMPILATIONS

AMB
White male rap duo from Denver, Colorado: brothers James "Otis" and Michael "Bonez Dubb" Garcia. AMB: Axe Murder Boyz.

DEBUT	PEAK	WKS				
5/6/06	199	1		1 **Blood In, Blood Out**		Psychopathic 4057

AMBER PACIFIC
Pop-punk band from Seattle, Washington: Matt Young (vocals), Will Nutter (guitar), Greg Strong (bass) and Dango (drums).

DEBUT	PEAK	WKS				
6/9/07	64	2		1 **Truth In Sincerity**		Hopeless 692

AMBOY DUKES, The
Hard-rock band from Detroit, Michigan: John Drake (vocals), **Ted Nugent** (lead guitar), Steve Farmer (guitar), Rick Lorber (keyboards), Bill White (bass) and Dave Palmer (drums). Several personnel changes with Nugent the only constant until his solo career started in 1975.

2/10/68	183	4		1 The Amboy Dukes..		Mainstream 6104
6/15/68	74	23		2 Journey To The Center Of The Mind		Mainstream 6112
3/21/70	191	2		3 Marriage On The Rocks/Rock Bottom....................................		Polydor 4012
3/6/71	129	5		4 Survival Of The Fittest/Live .... [L]		Polydor 4035

TED NUGENT AND THE AMBOY DUKES
recorded on 7/31/1970 at the Eastowne Theater in Detroit, Michigan

AMBROSIA
Pop band formed in Los Angeles, California: David Pack (vocals, guitar), Joe Puerta (vocals, bass), Christopher North (keyboards; no longer an "official" member after 1977, although still played on the albums) and Burleigh Drummond (drums). Puerta later joined **Bruce Hornsby & The Range**.

5/3/75	22	33		1 Ambrosia		20th Century 434
9/18/76	79	17		2 Somewhere I've Never Travelled		20th Century 510
8/12/78	19	29		3 Life Beyond L.A.		Warner 3135
4/19/80	25	33		4 One Eighty		Warner 3368
5/29/82	115	7		5 Road Island		Warner 3638

AMECHE, Don, & Frances Langford
Ameche was born on 5/31/1908 in Kenosha, Wisconsin; died of cancer on 12/6/1993 (age 85). Langford was born on 4/4/1913 in Lakeland, Florida; died of heart failure on 7/11/2005 (age 92). Both began their movie careers in 1935. Their ongoing skit as the quarreling "John & Blanche Bickerson" began as a radio comedy in 1946.

4/7/62	76	12		1 The Bickersons .... [C]		Columbia 1692
11/3/62	109	6		2 The Bickersons Fight Back .... [C]		Columbia 1883

AMERICA
All-Time: #228
Soft-rock trio formed in London, England (all children of U.S. military personnel): Lee "Dewey" Bunnell (vocals, guitar; born on 1/19/1952), Dan Peek (vocals, guitar; born on 11/1/1950) and Gerry Beckley (vocals, keyboards; born on 9/12/1952). Peek left to pursue Christian music career in 1976.

AWARD: Grammy: Best New Artist 1972

2/19/72	❶⁵	40	▲	1 America		Warner 2576
12/2/72+	9	32	▲	2 Homecoming		Warner 2655
11/17/73	28	18		3 Hat Trick		Warner 2728
7/13/74	3¹	53	●	4 Holiday		Warner 2808
4/5/75	4	44	●	5 Hearts		Warner 2852
11/22/75	3⁶	63	▲⁴	6 History/America's Greatest Hits Cat:#41/1 [G]		Warner 2894
5/1/76	11	22	●	7 Hideaway		Warner 2932
3/12/77	21	14		8 Harbor		Warner 3017
12/17/77+	129	7		9 America/Live .... [L]		Warner 3136

recorded at the Greek Theatre in Los Angeles, California

7/7/79	110	6		10 Silent Letter		Capitol 11950
9/6/80	142	6		11 Alibi		Capitol 12098
8/28/82	41	28		12 View From The Ground...		Capitol 12209
7/2/83	81	14		13 Your Move...		Capitol 12277
11/10/84	185	3		14 Perspective		Capitol 12370
10/6/01	152	5		15 The Complete Greatest Hits .... [G]		Warner Archives 74375
2/3/07	52	2		16 Here & Now		Burgundy 85749 [2]

AMERICAN ANGEL
Hard-rock band from New Jersey: Rocco Furriero (vocals), Petey DeGeorge (guitar), Danny Monchek (guitar), Steve Evetts (bass) and Eric Nilla (drums).

3/24/90	164	9		1 American Angel		Grudge 4518

AMERICAN BREED, The
Interracial pop-rock band from Chicago, Illinois: Gary Loizzo (vocals, guitar), Al Ciner (guitar), Chuck Colbert (bass) and Lee Graziano (drums). Later members Kevin Murphy (keyboards) and Andre Fischer (drums) went on to form **Rufus**.

2/24/68	99	10		1 Bend Me, Shape Me		Acta 38003

AMERICAN DREAM, The
Rock band from Philadelphia, Pennsylvania: Nicky Indelicato (vocals), Nick Jameson (guitar), Don Lee Van Winkle (guitar), Don Ferris (bass) and Mickey Brook (drums). Jameson went on to produce several albums as a member of **Foghat**.

2/28/70	194	2		1 The American Dream		Ampex 10101

produced by **Todd Rundgren**

AMERICAN FLYER
Soft-rock band formed in New York: Craig Fuller (**Pure Prairie League**), Eric Kaz (**Blues Magoos**), Steve Katz (**Blood, Sweat & Tears**) and Doug Yule (**The Velvet Underground**).

9/4/76	87	10		1 American Flyer		United Artists 650
7/2/77	171	5		2 Spirit Of A Woman		United Artists 720

AMERICAN HEAD CHARGE
Heavy metal band from Minneapolis, Minnesota: Martin Cock (vocals), Wayne Kile (guitar), David Rogers (guitar), Aaron Zilch (keyboards), Justin Fouler (keyboards), Chad Hanks (bass) and Christopher Emery (drums).

9/15/01	118	1		1 The War Of Art...		American 586327

Billboard			R I A A	ARTIST		
DEBUT	PEAK	WKS		Album Title	Catalog	Label & Number

AMERICAN HI-FI
Male rock band from Boston, Massachusetts: Stacy Jones (vocals), Jaime Arentzen (guitar), Drew Parsons (bass) and Brian Nolan (drums). Jones was drummer with **Letters To Cleo**.

3/17/01	81	25		1 American Hi-Fi..		Island 542871
3/15/03	80	2		2 The Art Of Losing..		Island 063657
4/30/05	129	1		3 Hearts On Parade...		Maverick 48991

AMERICAN STANDARD BAND
Pop-rock band from New York: Kevin Falvey (vocals, keyboards), Cliff Goodwin (guitar), Deric Dyer (sax), Howard Hersh (bass) and John Riley (drums).

4/28/79	201	3		1 American Standard Band		Island 9540

AMERIE
Born Amerie Rogers on 1/12/1980 in Fitchburg, Massachusetts (Korean mother; African-American father); raised in several different areas as miltary father traveled frequently, eventually settled in Washington DC. Female R&B singer.

8/17/02	9	29	●	1 All I Have		Rise 85959
5/14/05	5	16	●	2 Touch		Columbia 90763
11/21/09	46	3		3 In Love & War		Def Jam 013225

AMES, Ed
Born Edmond Urick on 7/9/1927 in Malden, Massachusetts (to Ukrainian parents). Adult Contemporary singer/actor. Member of **The Ames Brothers**. Appeared in several TV shows; best known as "Mingo" on the *Daniel Boone* TV series (1964-68). Known as "The Boston Baritone."

11/5/66	90	7		1 More I Cannot Wish You..		RCA Victor 3636
3/4/67	4	81	●	2 My Cup Runneth Over		RCA Victor 3774
7/8/67	77	38		3 Time, Time		RCA Victor 3834
12/9/67	11[X]	8		4 Christmas With Ed Ames... [X]		RCA Victor 3838
				Christmas charts: 11/'67, 12/'68		
12/16/67+	24	25		5 When The Snow Is On The Roses		RCA Victor 3913
2/24/68	13	50	●	6 Who Will Answer? And Other Songs Of Our Time		RCA Victor 3961
8/10/68	135	14		7 Apologize		RCA Victor 4028
12/21/68	186	6		8 The Hits Of Broadway And Hollywood...................................		RCA Victor 4079
3/8/69	114	14		9 A Time For Living, A Time For Hope		RCA Victor 4128
7/5/69	157	6		10 The Windmills Of Your Mind		RCA Victor 4172
10/18/69	119	16		11 The Best Of Ed Ames .... [G]		RCA Victor 4184
1/3/70	172	6		12 Love Of The Common People		RCA Victor 4249
7/11/70	194	2		13 Sing Away The World		RCA Victor 4381
2/20/71	199	1		14 The Songs Of Bacharach And David....................................		RCA Victor 4453

AMES, Nancy
Born Nancy Alfaro in 1937 in Washington DC. Singer/actress. Her grandfather was president of Panama. Cast as the "TW3 Girl" on TV's satirical revue *That Was The Week That Was*.

9/26/64	133	4		1 This Is The Girl That Is .... [F]		Liberty 7369
10/29/66	133	8		2 Latin Pulse .... [F]		Epic 26189

AMES BROTHERS, The
Pop vocal group from Malden, Massachusetts: brothers **Ed Ames**, Gene Ames, Vic Ames and Joe Ames. One of the most popular vocal groups of the 1950s. Vic died in a car crash on 1/23/1978 (age 52). Gene died on 4/26/1997 (age 74). Joe died on 12/22/2007 (age 86). Also see *Merry Christmas* (Christmas Albums section).

12/2/57	16	4		1 There'll Always Be A Christmas................................... [X]		RCA Victor 1541

AMG
Born Jason Lewis on 9/29/1970 in Brooklyn, New York. Male hardcore rapper.

12/21/91+	63	32	●	1 Bitch Betta Have My Money		Select 21642
6/24/95	100	3		2 Ballin' Outta Control		Select 21654

AMICI FOREVER
Operatic vocal group formed in England: males Geoff Sewell, David Habbin and Nick Garrett, with females Jo Appleby and Tsakane Valentine.

1/31/04	74	7		1 The Opera Band .... [F]		Victor 52739
7/9/05	198	2		2 Defined .... [F]		RCA Victor 68883

AMIL
Born Amil Whitehead on 9/19/1978 in Brooklyn, New York. Female rapper.

10/7/00	45	6		1 A.M.I.L. (All Money Is Legal)		Roc-A-Fella 63936

AMMONS, Gene
Born Eugene Ammons on 4/14/1925 in Chicago, Illinois. Died of cancer on 8/6/1974 (age 49). Jazz/R&B tenor saxophonist. Nicknamed "Jug." Son of boogie-woogie pianist Albert Ammons.

12/22/62+	53	17		1 Bad! Bossa Nova .... [I]		Prestige 7257
6/6/70	174	2		2 The Boss Is Back!.. [I]		Prestige 7739

AMON AMARTH
Death metal band formed in Tumba, Sweden: Johan Hegg (vocals), Johan Soderberg (guitar), Olavi Mikkonen (guitar), Ted Lundstrom (bass) and Fredrik Andersson (drums).

10/18/08	50	4		1 Twilight Of The Thunder God..		Metal Blade 14693

				ARTIST / Album Title	Catalog	Label & Number

AMOS, Tori All-Time: #268
Born Myra Ellen Amos on 8/22/1963 in Newton, North Carolina; raised in Baltimore, Maryland. Alternative pop-rock singer/songwriter/pianist.

DEBUT	PEAK	WKS	RIAA	# Title	Catalog	Label & Number
4/4/92	54	38	▲²	1 Little Earthquakes	Cat:#24/22	Atlantic 82358
2/19/94	12	35	▲²	2 Under The Pink		Atlantic 82567
2/10/96	2¹	29	▲	3 Boys For Pele		Atlantic 82862
9/7/96	94	3		4 Hey Jupiter [EP-L]		Atlantic 82955
5/23/98	5	20	▲	5 From The Choirgirl Hotel		Atlantic 83095
10/9/99	12	11	▲	6 To Venus And Back [L]		Atlantic 83230 [2]
				Disc 1: new studio recordings; Disc 2: live recordings		
10/6/01	4	9		7 Strange Little Girls		Atlantic 83486
11/16/02	7	22	●	8 Scarlet's Walk		Epic 86412
12/6/03	40	9		9 A Tori Amos Collection: Tales Of A Librarian [G]		Atlantic 83658
3/12/05	5	10		10 The Beekeeper		Epic 92800
5/19/07	5	6		11 American Doll Posse		Epic 86140
6/6/09	9	9		12 Abnormally Attracted To Sin		Universal 012873
11/28/09	66	2		13 Midwinter Graces [X]		Universal 013629
				Christmas chart: 9/09		

ANA
Born Ana Rodriguez on 2/22/1972 in Cuba; raised in Orlando, Florida. Female dance singer.

6/23/90	191	2		1 Body Language		Parc 45355

ANASTACIA
Born Anastacia Newkirk on 9/17/1973 in Brooklyn, New York; raised in Chicago, Illinois. Female pop-dance singer.

4/14/01	168	4		1 Not That Kind		Daylight 69948
7/6/02	27	13		2 Freak Of Nature		Daylight 86010

ANASTASIO, Trey
Born Ernest Giuseppe Anastasio III on 9/30/1964 in Princeton, New Jersey. Rock singer/songwriter/guitarist. Leader of band **Phish**. Member of **Oysterhead**.

5/18/02	45	5		1 Trey Anastasio		Elektra 62749
5/17/03	102	1		2 Plasma [L]		Elektra 62867 [2]
11/19/05	64	2		3 Shine		Columbia 96428
10/21/06	102	1		4 Bar 17		Rubber Jungle 01
8/11/07	167	1		5 The Horseshoe Curve		Rubber Jungle 04

ANBERLIN
Alternative-rock band from Winter Haven, Florida: Stephen Christian (vocals), Joseph Milligan (guitar), Nathan Strayer (guitar), Deon Rexroat (bass) and Nathan Young (drums).

2/19/05	144	1		1 Never Take Friendship Personal		Tooth & Nail 66607
3/10/07	19	6		2 Cities		Tooth & Nail 73673
10/18/08	13	7		3 New Surrender		Universal 011710

ANDA, Geza
Born on 11/19/1921 in Budapest, Hungary. Died on 6/13/1976 (age 54). Classical pianist.

6/29/68	115	17		1 Mozart: Piano Concertos Nos. 17 & 21 [I]		DG 138783

ANDERSEN, Eric
Born on 2/14/1943 in Pittsburgh, Pennsylvania. Folk singer/songwriter.

7/15/72	169	11		1 Blue River		Columbia 31062
4/19/75	113	9		2 Be True To You		Arista 4033
6/12/76	208	4		3 Sweet Surprise		Arista 4075

ANDERSON, Bill
Born James William Anderson III on 11/1/1937 in Columbia, South Carolina. Country singer/songwriter/actor. Known as "Whispering Bill."
AWARDS: C&W Hall of Fame: 2001 ★ OPRY: 1961

7/6/63	36	17		1 Still		Decca 74427

ANDERSON, Carl
Born on 2/27/1945 in Lynchburg, Virginia. Died of leukemia on 2/23/2004 (age 58). R&B singer/actor. Played "Judas" in the original Broadway cast and movie version of the rock opera *Jesus Christ Superstar*.

8/23/86	87	12		1 Carl Anderson		Epic 40410

ANDERSON, Ernestine
Born on 11/11/1928 in Houston, Texas. Jazz singer.

10/20/58	15	6		1 Hot Cargo!		Mercury 20354

ANDERSON, Ian
Born on 8/10/1947 in Dunfermline, Fife, Scotland; raised in Blackpool, Lancashire, England. Rock singer/songwriter/fluitist. Leader of **Jethro Tull**.

1/21/84	202	4		1 Walk Into Light		Chrysalis 41443

ANDERSON, John
Born on 12/13/1954 in Orlando, Florida; raised in Apopka, Florida. Country singer/songwriter/guitarist.
AWARD: CMA: Horizon 1983

4/9/83	58	12	●	1 Wild & Blue		Warner 23721
10/29/83	163	5		2 All The People Are Talkin'		Warner 23912
10/6/84	202	3	●	3 Greatest Hits	[G]	Warner 25169
2/29/92	35	75	▲²	4 Seminole Wind		BNA 61029
7/10/93	75	20	●	5 Solid Ground		BNA 66232
8/16/97	138	4		6 Takin' The Country Back		Mercury 536004
6/2/07	170	1		7 Easy Money		Raybaw 44438

ANDERSON, John W. — see KASANDRA

ANDERSON, Jon
Born on 10/25/1944 in Accrington, Lancashire, England. Rock singer/songwriter. Lead singer of **Yes**; one-half of **Jon & Vangelis** duo.

7/24/76	47	13		1 Olias Of Sunhillow		Atlantic 18180
12/6/80+	143	11		2 Song Of Seven		Atlantic 16021
7/3/82	176	5		3 Animation		Atlantic 19355
12/28/85+	166	5		4 3 Ships	[X]	Elektra 60469

ANDERSON, Keith
Born on 1/12/1968 in Miami, Oklahoma. Country singer/songwriter/guitarist.

5/21/05	71	27	●	1 Three Chord Country And American Rock & Roll		Arista Nashville 66294
8/23/08	12	8		2 C'mon!		Columbia 10333

ANDERSON, Laurie
Born on 6/5/1947 in Glen Ellyn, Illinois. Avant-garde performance artist.

2/6/82	203	3		1 O Superman	[EP]	Warner 49888
5/29/82	124	12		2 Big Science		Warner 3674
3/17/84	60	19		3 Mister Heartbreak		Warner 25077
1/26/85	192	5		4 United States Live	[L]	Warner 25192 [5]
				recorded in February 1983 at the Brooklyn Academy of Music		
4/26/86	145	12		5 Home Of The Brave	[S]	Warner 25400
11/18/89	171	12		6 Strange Angels		Warner 25900
11/12/94	195	1		7 Bright Red		Warner 45534

ANDERSON, Lynn
Born on 9/26/1947 in Grand Forks, North Dakota; raised in Sacramento, California. Country singer/songwriter/guitarist/actress. Daughter of country singer/songwriter Liz Anderson. Married to singer/songwriter Glenn Sutton from 1968-77
AWARD: CMA: Female Vocalist 1971

4/12/69	197	2		1 With Love, From Lynn		Chart 1013
5/3/69	180	3		2 The Best Of Lynn Anderson	[G]	Chart 1009
1/9/71	19	33	▲	3 Rose Garden		Columbia 30411
7/24/71	99	14		4 You're My Man		Columbia 30793
10/30/71	174	4		5 The World Of Lynn Anderson	[K]	Columbia 30902 [2]
12/4/71	132	5		6 How Can I Unlove You		Columbia 30925
12/18/71	13ˣ	1		7 The Christmas Album	[X]	Columbia 30957
4/8/72	114	9		8 Cry		Columbia 31316
9/9/72	160	7		9 Listen To A Country Song		Columbia 31647
11/11/72	129	14	●	10 Lynn Anderson's Greatest Hits	[G]	Columbia 31641
3/17/73	201	3		11 Keep Me In Mind		Columbia 32078
8/11/73	179	3		12 Top Of The World		Columbia 32429

ANDERSON, Michael
Born in Grand Rapids, Michigan. Rock singer/songwriter.

8/13/88	194	2		1 Sound Alarm		A&M 5203

ANDERSON, Sunshine
Born on 10/26/1973 in Charlotte, North Carolina. Female R&B singer.

5/5/01	5	17	●	1 Your Woman		Soulife 93011
2/10/07	86	4		2 Sunshine At Midnight		Music World 010

ANDERSON, BRUFORD, WAKEMAN, HOWE — see YES

ANDREWS, Jessica
Born on 12/29/1983 in Huntingdon, Tennessee. Country singer/songwriter.

3/17/01	22	31	●	1 Who I Am		DreamWorks 450248
5/3/03	34	8		2 Now		DreamWorks 450356

ANDREWS, Julie
Born Julia Wells on 10/1/1935 in Walton-on-Thames, Surrey, England. Actress/singer. Appeared in several movies and Broadway shows. Married movie director Blake Edwards on 11/12/1969. Named Dame by Queen Elizabeth on 12/31/1999.

9/1/62	85	9	1 Julie And Carol At Carnegie Hall .... [L]	Columbia 2240 / 5840

JULIE ANDREWS & CAROL BURNETT
recorded on 6/11/1962

12/2/67	9ˣ	6	2 A Christmas Treasure [X]	RCA Victor 3829

JULIE ANDREWS WITH ANDRE PREVIN
Christmas charts: 9/'67, 52/'68

ANDREWS SISTERS
Female vocal trio from Minneapolis, Minnesota: sisters Patty Andrews (born on 2/26/1918), Maxene Andrews (born on 1/13/1916; died on 10/21/1995, age 79) and LaVerne Andrews (born on 7/6/1911; died on 5/8/1967, age 55). The most popular female vocal group of the 1940s.

10/6/73	126	9	1 The Best Of The Andrews Sisters .... [G]	MCA 4024 [2]
10/13/73	167	7	2 Boogie Woogie Bugle Girls.. [K]	Paramount 6075
7/13/74	137	3	3 Over Here! .... [OC]	Columbia 32961
7/20/74	198	1	4 In The Mood .... [K]	Paramount 1023 [2]

ANDREW W.K.
Born Andrew Wilkes Krier on 5/9/1979 in Los Angeles, California; raised in Detroit, Michigan. Hard-rock singer/songwriter.

4/13/02	84	8	1 I Get Wet	Island 586588
9/27/03	61	1	2 The Wolf	Island 001051

ANDY ANDY
Born Andy Villalona in the Dominican Republic. Latin singer.

7/9/05	157	9	1 Ironia .... [F]	WEPA 1060

...AND YOU WILL KNOW US BY THE TRAIL OF DEAD
Punk-rock band from Austin, Texas: Jason Reece (vocals, guitar), Conrad Keely (vocals, drums), Kevin Allen (guitar) and Neil Busch (bass).

2/12/05	81	1	1 Worlds Apart..	Interscope 003290
12/2/06	188	1	2 So Divided	Interscope 007821
3/7/09	169	1	3 The Century Of Self	Richter Scale 35013

ANGEL
Hard-rock band from Washington DC: Frank DiMino (vocals), Punky Meadows (guitar), Gregg Giuffria (keyboards), Mickey Jones (bass) and Barry Brandt (drums). Felix Robinson replaced Jones by 1978. Giuffria later formed **Giuffria** and **House Of Lords**. Jones died on 9/5/2009.

12/20/75+	156	6	1 Angel	Casablanca 7021
6/19/76	155	10	2 Helluva Band	Casablanca 7028
3/5/77	76	12	3 On Earth As It Is In Heaven	Casablanca 7043
2/4/78	55	13	4 White Hot	Casablanca 7085
3/3/79	159	5	5 Sinful	Casablanca 7127
2/23/80	149	4	6 Live Without A Net .... [L]	Casablanca 7203 [2]

ANGEL, Ashley Parker
Born Ashley Ward Parker (stepfather's last name is Angel) on 8/1/1981 in Redding, California. Male pop singer/songwriter. Former member of **O-Town**.

6/3/06	5	8	1 Soundtrack To Your Life	Blackground 006740

ANGEL CITY
Hard-rock band from Sydney, Australia: Bernard "Doc" Neeson (vocals; born in Belfast, Ireland), brothers Rick Brewster and John Brewster (guitars), Jim Hilbun (bass) and Brent Eccles (drums).

5/10/80	152	7	1 Face To Face	Epic 36344
11/8/80	133	6	2 Darkroom	Epic 36543
3/20/82	174	5	3 Night Attack	Epic 37702
2/9/85	201	8	4 Two Minute Warning	MCA 5509

ANGELS, The
Female vocal trio from Orange, New Jersey: Peggy Santiglia (lead singer; born on 5/4/1944), with sisters Barbara Allbut (born on 9/24/1940) and Phyllis "Jiggs" Allbut (born on 9/24/1942).

9/28/63	33	14	1 My Boyfriend's Back	Smash 67039

~ ~ ~ ~ ~ ~ ~ ~ ~ ~ **NON-CHARTED ALBUM** ~ ~ ~ ~ ~ ~ ~ ~ ~ ~
1962 ...And The Angels Sing

ANGELS AND AIRWAVES
Alternative-rock band from San Diego, California: Tom DeLonge (vocals, guitar), David Kennedy (guitar), Ryan Sinn (bass) and Atom Willard (drums). DeLong is also a member of **Blink-182**. DeLong and Kennedy are also members of **Box Car Racer**. Sinn is also a member of **The Distillers**. Willard was a member of **The Offspring** from 2004-06.

6/10/06	4	20	● 1 We Don't Need To Whisper	Suretone 006759
11/24/07	9	13	2 I-Empire	Suretone 010101

ANIMAL COLLECTIVE
Experimental-rock band from Baltimore, Maryland: David Portner (vocals), Josh Dibb (guitar), Brian Weitz (keyboards) and Noah Lennox (drums).

9/29/07	72	2	1 Strawberry Jam	Domino 156
2/7/09	13	13	2 Merriweather Post Pavilion	Domino 219

Billboard			R I A A	ARTIST		
DEBUT	PEAK	WKS		Album Title	Catalog	Label & Number

ANIMAL LOGIC
All-star rock trio: Deborah Holland (vocals), **Stanley Clarke** (bass) and **Stewart Copeland** (drums).

12/9/89+	106	21		1 Animal Logic..		I.R.S. 82020

ANIMALS, The   All-Time: #297
Rock band from Newcastle, England: **Eric Burdon** (vocals; born on 5/11/1941), Hilton Valentine (guitar; born on 5/21/1943), **Alan Price** (keyboards; born on 4/19/1942), Bryan "Chas" Chandler (bass; born on 12/18/1938; died of a heart attack on 7/17/1996, age 57) and John Steel (drums; born on 2/4/1941). Price left in May 1965; replaced by Dave Rowberry (died of heart failure on 6/6/2003, age 62). Chandler pursued a management career and discovered **Jimi Hendrix** in 1966. Steel left in 1966; replaced by Barry Jenkins. Group disbanded in July 1968. After a period with **War**, Burdon and the other originals reunited in 1976 and again in 1983.
         AWARD: R&R Hall of Fame: 1994

9/5/64	7	27		1 The Animals		MGM 4264
3/20/65	99	9		2 The Animals On Tour..		MGM 4281
9/18/65	57	25		3 Animal Tracks...		MGM 4305
2/12/66	6	113	●	4 The Best Of The Animals [G]		MGM 4324
8/20/66	20	30		5 Animalization...		MGM 4384
12/3/66+	33	22		6 Animalism...		MGM 4414
				ERIC BURDON & THE ANIMALS:		
3/25/67	121	13		7 Eric Is Here		MGM 4433
6/10/67	71	24		8 The Best Of Eric Burdon And The Animals, Vol. II .... [G]		MGM 4454
9/23/67	42	20		9 Winds Of Change		MGM 4484
4/6/68	79	29		10 The Twain Shall Meet		MGM 4537
8/24/68	152	8		11 Every One Of Us		MGM 4553
1/11/69	123	10		12 Love Is		MGM 4591 [2]
3/15/69	153	6		13 The Greatest Hits Of Eric Burdon And The Animals .... Cat:#40/6 [G]		MGM 4602
				THE ANIMALS:		
8/25/73	188	2		14 Best Of The Animals .... [G]		Abkco 4226
8/27/77	70	11		15 Before We Were So Rudely Interrupted		United Artists 790
9/10/83	66	10		16 Ark		I.R.S. 70037
9/15/84	193	4		17 Rip It To Shreds - The Animals Greatest Hits Live! .... [L]		I.R.S. 70043
				recorded on 12/31/1983 at Wembley Arena in London		
2/7/09	45^C	1		18 The Best Of The Animals .... [G]		ABKCO 714324

ANIMALYMICS — see GOULDMAN, Graham

ANIMOTION
Techno-pop band formed in Los Angeles, California: Astrid Plane (female vocals), Bill Wadhams (male vocals, keyboards), Don Kirkpatrick (guitar), Charles Ottavio (bass) and Frency O'Brien (drums). Plane and Wadhams left by 1988; replaced by Cynthia Rhodes and Paul Engemann. Rhodes was an actress (in movies *Staying Alive* and *Dirty Dancing*). Engemann was formerly with **Device**. Rhodes married **Richard Marx** on 1/8/1989. Plane and Ottavio married on 10/13/1990.

2/23/85	28	30		1 Animotion		Mercury 822580
3/15/86	71	14		2 Strange Behavior		Casablanca 826691
3/25/89	110	17		3 Animotion		Polydor 837314

ANJULIE
Born Anjulie Persaud in Oakville, Ontario, Canada. Female singer/songwriter.

8/22/09	108	3		1 Anjulie		Monster 30498

ANKA, Paul   All-Time: #273
Born on 7/30/1941 in Ottawa, Ontario, Canada. Pop singer/songwriter. Wrote "She's A Lady" for **Tom Jones** and the English lyrics to "My Way" for **Frank Sinatra**. Also wrote theme for TV's *The Tonight Show*. Own TV variety show in 1973. Cameo appearances in the 1962 movie *The Longest Day* and the 1992 movie *Captain Ron*.

7/4/60	4	140		1 Paul Anka Sings His Big 15 [G]		ABC-Paramount 323
12/5/60+	23	27		2 Anka At The Copa.. [L]		ABC-Paramount 353
				recorded on 7/6/1960 at the Copacabana in New York City		
9/25/61	72	12		3 Paul Anka Sings His Big 15, Vol. 2 .... [G]		ABC-Paramount 390
4/14/62	61	12		4 Young, Alive And In Love!		RCA Victor 2502
9/15/62	137	2		5 Let's Sit This One Out		RCA Victor 2575
7/6/63	65	33		6 Paul Anka's 21 Golden Hits.. [G]		RCA Victor 2691
				newly recorded versions of his ABC-Paramount hits		
3/15/69	101	11		7 Goodnight My Love		RCA Victor 4142
12/27/69+	194	2		8 Life Goes On		RCA Victor 4250
1/15/72	188	4		9 Paul Anka		Buddah 5093
6/3/72	192	4		10 Jubilation		Buddah 5114
8/31/74	9	28	●	11 Anka		United Artists 314
12/14/74+	125	9		12 Paul Anka Gold... [G]		Sire 3704 [2]
				original ABC-Paramount recordings		
4/5/75	36	29		13 Feelings		United Artists 367
12/13/75+	22	25	●	14 Times Of Your Life .... [K]		United Artists 569
				9 of 10 cuts from previous 2 United Artists albums		
10/23/76+	85	15		15 The Painter		United Artists 653
6/18/77	195	3		16 The Music Man		United Artists 746
11/25/78	179	7		17 Listen To Your Heart		RCA Victor 2892
5/9/81	171	6		18 Both Sides Of Love		RCA Victor 3926
8/13/83	156	8		19 Walk A Fine Line		Columbia 38442

Billboard			R I A A	ARTIST		
DEBUT	PEAK	WKS		Album Title	Catalog	Label & Number

ANKA, Paul — cont'd

| 6/25/05 | 120 | 2 | | 20 Rock Swings .... | | Verve 004751 |
| 9/22/07 | 139 | 2 | | 21 Classic Songs, My Way .... | | Decca 008707 |

~ ~ ~ ~ ~ ~ ~ ~ ~ **NON-CHARTED ALBUMS** ~ ~ ~ ~ ~ ~ ~ ~ ~

1958 **Paul Anka**
1959 **My Heart Sings**
1960 **Swings For Young Lovers**
1960 **It's Christmas Everywhere**
1962 **Paul Anka Sings His Big Big Big 15, Vol. 3**
1962 **Diana**

ANNETTE
Born Annette Funicello on 10/22/1942 in Utica, New York. Became a Mouseketeer in 1955. Acted in several teen movies in the early 1960s. Co-starred with **Frankie Avalon** in the 1987 movie *Back To The Beach*. Diagnosed with multiple sclerosis in 1987.

3/21/60	21	21		1 Annette Sings Anka		Buena Vista 3302
9/26/60	38	3		2 Hawaiiannette		Buena Vista 3303
10/19/63	39	13		3 Annette's Beach Party .... [S]		Buena Vista 3316

half of the songs are from the movie *Beach Party* starring Annette and **Frankie Avalon**

~ ~ ~ ~ ~ ~ ~ ~ ~ **NON-CHARTED ALBUMS** ~ ~ ~ ~ ~ ~ ~ ~ ~

1959 **Annette**
1960 **Italiannette**
1961 **Dance Annette**
1962 **The Story Of My Teens**
1963 **Muscle Beach Party**
1964 **Annette On Campus**
1964 **Annette At Bikini Beach**
1964 **Annette's Pajama Party**
1964 **Annette Sings Golden Surfin' Hits**

ANN-MARGRET
Born Ann-Margret Olsson on 4/28/1941 in Valsjobyn, Jamtland, Sweden; raised in Wilmette, Illinois. Actress/dancer/singer. Acted in several movies.

2/29/64	83	9		1 Beauty And The Beard		RCA Victor 2690
				AL HIRT & ANN-MARGRET		
11/14/64	141	4		2 David Merrick Presents Hits From His Broadway Hits		RCA Victor 2947
				JOHN GARY & ANN-MARGRET		

ANOINTED
Gospel trio from Columbus, Ohio: Steve Crawford and his sister Da'dra Crawford, with Denise Walls.

| 5/8/99 | 159 | 2 | | 1 Anointed .... | | Myrrh 69616 |

ANOTHER BAD CREATION
R&B vocal group from Atlanta, Georgia: Chris Sellers, Dave Shelton, Romell Chapman, with brothers Marliss Pugh and Demetrius Pugh.

| 3/9/91 | 7 | 52 | ▲ | 1 Coolin' At The Playground Ya' Know! | | Motown 6318 |

ANT, Adam
Born Stuart Goddard on 11/3/1954 in Marylebone, London, England. New-wave singer/songwriter. Formed romantic-punk group **Adam And The Ants** in 1976. Three original Ants left to join **Bow Wow Wow** and Ant headed new lineup in 1980: Marco Pirroni (guitar), Terry Miall (percussion), Kevin Mooney (bass) and Chris Hughes (drums). Ant went solo in 1982. Acted in several movies and TV shows.

2/28/81	44	35	●	1 Kings Of The Wild Frontier		Epic 37033
12/12/81+	94	21		2 Prince Charming		Epic 37615
				ADAM AND THE ANTS (above 2)		
12/11/82+	16	36	●	3 Friend Or Foe		Epic 38370
12/10/83	65	26		4 Strip		Epic 39108
10/19/85	131	7		5 Vive Le Rock		Epic 40159
3/3/90	57	20		6 Manners & Physique		MCA 6315
3/25/95	143	9		7 Wonderful		Capitol 30335

ANTHONY, Marc
Born Marco Antonio Muniz on 9/16/1968 in the Bronx, New York. Latin singer/actor. Starred in **Paul Simon**'s Broadway musical *The Capeman*. Married **Jennifer Lopez** on 6/5/2004.

11/22/97	74	9	●	1 Contra La Corriente .... [F]		RMM 82156
				Grammy: Tropical Latin Album		
10/16/99	8	83	▲³	2 Marc Anthony	Cat:#18/18	Columbia 69726
12/4/99+	151	18	●	3 Desde Un Principio / From The Beginning .... [F]		Sony Discos 83580
12/8/01	57	12	●	4 Libre .... [F]		Sony Discos 84617
6/8/02	3¹	20	●	5 Mended		Columbia 85300
6/26/04	26	9		6 Amar Sin Mentiras .... [F]		Sony Discos 95194
8/14/04	122	3		7 Valio La Pena .... [F]		Sony Discos 95310
7/29/06	101	9		8 Sigo Siendo Yo: Grandes Exitos .... [F]		Sony 81251
8/11/07	31	11		9 El Cantante .... [F-S]		Sony 11824

ANTHONY, Ray   **1950s: #23**
Born Raymond Antonini on 1/20/1922 in Bentleyville, Pennsylvania; raised in Cleveland, Ohio. Big band leader/trumpeter. Own TV series in the 1950s. Appeared in the movie *Daddy Long Legs*. Married to actress Mamie Van Doren from 1955-61.

3/19/55	10	3		1 Golden Horn .... [I]		Capitol 563
				LP: T-563 (#10); EP: ECF-563 (#11)		
6/23/56	15	1		2 Dream Dancing .... [I]		Capitol 723
10/28/57	11	21		3 Young Ideas .... [I]		Capitol 866
5/19/58	12	10		4 The Dream Girl .... [I]		Capitol 969
7/21/62	14	19		5 Worried Mind .... [I]		Capitol 1752

Billboard			R I A A	ARTIST		
DEBUT	PEAK	WKS		Album Title	Catalog	Label & Number

ANTHRAX
Heavy metal band formed in Queens, New York: Joey Belladonna (vocals; born on 10/30/1960), Scott Ian (guitar; born on 12/31/1963), Dan Spitz (guitar; born on 1/28/1963), Frank Bello (bass; born on 7/9/1965) and Charlie Benante (drums; born on 11/27/1962). Belladonna left in early 1992; replaced by John Bush (of **Armored Saint**; born on 8/24/1963). Spitz left in 1994. Group appeared on TV's *Married...With Children* in 1992.

12/21/85+	113	18		1 Spreading The Disease..		Island 90480
4/11/87	62	36	●	2 Among The Living..		Island 90584
12/19/87+	53	40	▲	3 I'm The Man.. [EP-L]		Island 90685
				recorded on 7/11/1987 in Dallas, Texas		
10/8/88	30	36	●	4 State Of Euphoria...		Island 91004
9/8/90	24	31	●	5 Persistence Of Time..		Island 846480
7/13/91	27	25	●	6 Attack Of The Killer B's................................... [K]		Island 848804
				unreleased material and B-sides recorded from 1988-91		
6/12/93	7	17	●	7 Sound Of White Noise		Elektra 61430
11/11/95	47	3		8 Stomp 442..		Elektra 61856
8/8/98	118	2		9 Volume 8 - The Threat Is Real!...............................		Ignition 4034
5/24/03	122	1		10 We've Come For You All..		Sanctuary 84609

ANTI-FLAG
Punk-rock band from Pittsburgh, Pennsylvania: Justin Sane (vocals, guitar), Chris Head (guitar), Chris "#2" Barker (bass) and Pat Thetic (drums).

11/8/03	91	1		1 The Terror State..		Fat Wreck Chords 643
4/8/06	100	2		2 For Blood And Empire		RCA 76836
4/19/08	118	1		3 Bright Lights Of America..		RCA 25142
6/27/09	122	1		4 The People Or The Gun		SideOneDummy 1385

ANTONY & THE JOHNSONS
Born Antony Hegarty in 1971 in Chichester, West Sussex, England; raised in San Francisco, California. Singer/songwriter/performance artist.

10/25/08	179	1		1 Another World .... [EP]		Secretly Canadian 193
2/7/09	65	3		2 The Crying Light..		Secretly Canadian 194

ANVIL
Heavy metal band from Toronto, Ontario, Canada: Steve "Lips" Kudlow (vocals, guitar), Dave Allison (guitar), Ian Dickson (bass) and Robb Reiner (drums). Band was featured in the critically acclaimed 2008 documentary movie *Anvil! The Story Of Anvil*.

7/18/87	191	2		1 Strength Of Steel...		Enigma 73267

AORTA
Rock band from Chicago, Illinois: Jim Donlinger (vocals, guitar), Jim Nyeholt (keyboards), Bobby Jones (bass) and Billy Herman (drums).

4/12/69	167	8		1 Aorta..		Columbia 9785

APACHE
Born Anthony Teaks in Jersey City, New Jersey. Died on 1/22/2010. Male rapper.

2/27/93	69	6		1 Apache Ain't Shit..		Tommy Boy 1068

APEX THEORY, The
Alternative-rock band from Los Angeles, California: Andy Khachaturian (vocals), Art Karamian (guitar), David Hakopyan (bass) and Sammy J. Watson (drums).

4/20/02	157	1		1 Topsy-Turvy..		DreamWorks 450292

APHEX TWIN
Born Richard James on 8/18/1971 in Truro, Cornwall, England. Techno artist.

11/10/01	154	1		1 Drukqs..		Warp 31174 [2]

APOCALYPTICA
Heavy metal band from Helsinki, Finland: Eicca Toppinen, Paavo Lotjonen, Pertta Kivilaasko and Mikko Siren. All are classically trained cellists.

5/3/08	59	39		1 Worlds Collide...		20-20 Ent. 21580

APOLLONIA 6
Born Patricia Apollonia Kotero on 8/2/1959 in Santa Monica, California. R&B-dance singer/actress. Acted in the movie *Purple Rain* and on TV's *Falcon Crest*. The other members of **Apollonia 6** were Susan Moonsie and Brenda Bennett (also members of **Vanity 6**).

10/27/84	62	17		1 Apollonia 6...		Warner 25108

APOLLO 100
Studio group from England: Tom Parker, Clem Cattini, Vic Flick, Jim Lawless and Brian Odgers.

2/19/72	47	16		1 Joy.. [I]		Mega 1010

APPALOOSA
Folk-rock band from Boston, Massachusetts: John Parker Compton (vocals, guitar), Robin Batteau (violin), Gene Rosor (cello) and David Reiser (bass).

8/16/69	178	4		1 Appaloosa...		Columbia 9819

APPICE, Carmine
Born on 12/15/1946 in Staten Island, New York. Rock singer/drummer. Member of **Vanilla Fudge**, **Cactus**, **KGB** and **Blue Murder**.

4/7/73	12	27	●	1 Jeff Beck, Tim Bogert, Carmine Appice..........................		Epic 32140

APPLE, Fiona
Born Fiona Apple Maggart on 9/13/1977 in Manhattan, New York. Adult Alternative singer/songwriter/pianist. Daughter of singer Diane McAfee and actor Brandon Maggart.

9/28/96+	15	91	▲³	1 Tidal..		Clean Slate 67439
11/27/99	13	20	●	2 When The Pawn....		Clean Slate 69195

entire album title: When The Pawn Hits The Conflicts He Thinks Like A King What He Knows Throws The Blows When He Goes To The Fight And He'll Win The Whole Thing 'Fore He Enters The Ring There's No Body To Batter When Your Mind Is Your Might So When You Go Solo, You Hold Your Own Hand And Remember That Depth Is The Greatest Of Heights And If You Know Where You Stand, Then You Know Where To Land And If You Fall It Won't Matter, Cuz You'll Know That You're Right

10/22/05	7	21	●	3 Extraordinary Machine		Clean Slate 86683

APRIL WINE
Rock band formed in Halifax, Nova Scotia, Canada: Myles Goodwyn (vocals, guitar), Brian Greenway (guitar), Gary Moffet (guitar), Steve Lang (bass) and Jerry Mercer (drums). Lang, Moffet and Mercer replaced by Daniel Barbe (keyboards), Jean Pellerin (bass) and Marty Simon (drums) in 1985.

10/28/72	205	2		1 April Wine		Big Tree 2012
4/21/79	114	11		2 First Glance		Capitol 11852
11/10/79	64	40	●	3 Harder...Faster		Capitol 12013
1/31/81	26	34	▲	4 The Nature Of The Beast		Capitol 12125
7/10/82	37	20		5 Power Play		Capitol 12218
3/17/84	62	12		6 Animal Grace		Capitol 12311
10/5/85	174	4		7 Walking Through Fire		Capitol 12433

AQUA
Pop-dance group from Denmark: Lene Grawford Nystrom, Rene Dif, Claus Norreen and Soren Rasted.

9/27/97	7	50	▲³	1 Aquarium		MCA 11705
4/8/00	82	6		2 Aquarius		MCA 157305

AQUABATS, The
Ska-rock band from Huntington Beach, California: Christian Jacobs (vocals), Courtney Pollack (guitar), James Briggs, Adam Diebert and Boyd Terry (horns), Charles Grey (keyboards), Chad Larson (bass) and Travis Barker (drums). Barker later joined Blink-182 and Transplants.

11/15/97	172	1		1 The Fury Of The Aquabats!		Goldenvoice 43512

AQUALUNG
Born Matthew Hales on 1/17/1972 in London, England. White male singer/songwriter/guitarist.

9/3/05+	108	9		1 Strange And Beautiful		Red Ink 23888
3/31/07	88	1		2 Aqualung Presents Memory Man		Columbia 80723

AQUARIAN DREAM
Disco band from Philadelphia, Pennsylvania: Patricia Shannon and Connie Harvey (vocals), Pete Bartee (guitar), Claude Bartee (horns), Winston Daley (keyboards), David Worthy (percussion), Ernie Adams (bass) and Jim Morrison (drums).

10/9/76	154	6		1 Norman Connors Presents Aquarian Dream		Buddah 5672

AQUARIANS
Instrumental studio group: Vladimir Vassilieff (piano; died on 9/5/1986, age 52), Joe Pass (guitar; died on 5/23/1994, age 65), Joe Roccisano (flute; died on 11/9/1997, age 58), Stan Gilbert (bass) and Carl Lott (drums).

11/1/69	192	2		1 Jungle Grass .... [I]		United Artists 73053

ARABIAN PRINCE
Born Michael Lezan in Compton, California. Male rapper. Former member of Bobby Jimmy & The Critters.

12/16/89	193	3		1 Brother Arab		Orpheus 175614

ARBORS, The
Pop vocal group formed in Ann Arbor, Michigan, by two pairs of brothers: Edward Farran and Fred Farran, and Scott Herrick and Tom Herrick. Edward Farran died of kidney failure on 1/2/2003 (age 64).

2/11/67	144	2		1 A Symphony For Susan		Date 3003

ARCADE
Hard-rock band formed in Los Angeles, California: Stephen Pearcy (vocals; of Ratt), Frank Wilsex (guitar; of Sea Hags), Donny Syracuse (guitar), Michael Andrews (bass) and Fred Coury (drums; of Cinderella).

4/24/93	133	2		1 Arcade		Epic 53012

ARCADE FIRE
Alternative-rock band from Montreal, Quebec, Canada: husband-and-wife Win Butler and Regine Chassagne, William Butler (Win's brother), Richard Parry and Tim Kingsbury. All members play several different instruments.

1/22/05	131	8		1 Funeral .... Cat:#45/1		Merge 225
3/24/07	2¹	17		2 Neon Bible		Merge 285

ARCADIA
Pop-rock trio from England: Duran Duran's Simon LeBon (vocals), Nick Rhodes (keyboards) and Roger Taylor (drums).

12/21/85+	23	17	▲	1 So Red The Rose		Capitol 12428

ARC ANGELS
Rock band formed in Austin, Texas: Charlie Sexton (vocals, guitar), Doyle Bramhall II (guitar), Tommy Shannon (bass) and Chris Layton (drums). Shannon, Layton and Bramhall's father were members of Stevie Ray Vaughan's band. ARC: Austin Rehearsal Complex.

5/16/92	127	22		1 Arc Angels		DGC 24465

Billboard DEBUT	PEAK	WKS	R I A A	ARTIST Album Title	Catalog	Label & Number

ARCH ENEMY
Death metal band from Halmstad, Sweden: Angela Grossow (vocals), brothers Michael Amott (guitar) and Christopher Amott (guitar), Sharlee D'Angelo (bass) and Daniel Erlandsson (drums).

8/13/05	87	2		1 Doomsday Machine		Century Media 8283
10/13/07	84	2		2 Rise Of The Tyrant		Century Media 8400

ARCHER, Tasmin
Born on 8/3/1963 in Bradford, Yorkshire, England (of Jamaican parentage). Black female singer.

4/24/93	115	10		1 Great Expectations		SBK 80134

ARCHIES, The
Studio group created by Don Kirshner and Jeff Barry. Based on the Saturday morning cartoon TV series: Archie Andrews (vocals, guitar), Veronica Lodge (organ), Betty Cooper (tambourine), Reggie Mantle (bass) and Forsythe "Jughead" Jones (drums). Actual vocalists include prolific session singers Ron Dante, Toni Wine and Donna Marie.

11/2/68+	88	21		1 The Archies..		Calendar 101
9/6/69	66	36		2 Everything's Archie		Calendar 103
1/3/70	125	10		3 Jingle Jangle		Kirshner 105
9/12/70	137	6		4 Sunshine		Kirshner 107
11/28/70	114	12		5 The Archies Greatest Hits	[G]	Kirshner 109
4/24/71	207	1		6 This Is Love		Kirshner 110

ARCHULETA, David
Born on 12/28/1990 in Miami, Florida; raised in Murray, Utah. Pop singer. Finished in second place on the 2008 season of TV's *American Idol.*

11/29/08	2[1]	29	●	1 David Archuleta		19 Records 34752
10/31/09	30	11		2 Christmas From The Heart	[X]	19 Records 57494
				Christmas chart: 2/'09		

ARCTIC MONKEYS
Alternative-rock band from Sheffield, Yorkshire, England: Alex Turner (vocals, guitar), Jamie Cook (guitar), Andy Nicholson (bass) and Matt Helders (drums). Nick O'Malley replaced Nicholson in May 2006. Turner also formed **The Last Shadow Puppets.**

3/11/06	24	19		1 Whatever People Say I Am, That's What I'm Not		Domino 086
5/12/07	7	7		2 Favourite Worst Nightmare		Domino 136
9/12/09	15	6		3 Humbug..		Domino 237

ARDEN, Jann
Born Jann Arden Richards on 3/27/1962 in Calgary, Alberta, Canada. Adult Alternative-pop singer/songwriter.

3/30/96	76	32	●	1 Living Under June..		A&M 540336

AREA CODE 615
Country session band formed in Nashville, Tennessee: Wayne Moss (guitar), Mac Gayden (guitar), **Charlie McCoy** (harmonica), Weldon Myrick (steel guitar), Bobby Thompson (banjo), Buddy Spicher (fiddle), David Briggs (piano), Norman Putnam (bass) and Ken Buttrey (drums). All were prolific studio musicians.

10/18/69	191	4		1 Area Code 615...	[I]	Polydor 4002

ARENA, Tina
Born Philopina Arena on 11/1/1967 in Melbourne, Australia. Alternative pop singer.

5/18/96	101	8		1 Don't Ask..		Epic 67533

ARENA BRASS
Studio group conducted by Robert Mersey.

1/5/63	130	5		1 The Lonely Bull	[I]	Epic 26039

ARGENT
Rock band formed in Hertfordshire, England: Rod Argent (vocals, keyboards; born on 6/14/1945), **Russ Ballard** (guitar), Jim Rodford (bass) and Robert Henrit (drums). Argent was leader of **The Zombies.** Henrit later joined **Charlie.** Rodford and Henrit later joined **The Kinks.**

7/1/72	23	23		1 All Together Now		Epic 31556
4/7/73	90	11		2 In Deep		Epic 32195
5/4/74	149	6		3 Nexus		Epic 32573
1/11/75	151	4		4 Encore-Live In Concert	[L]	Epic 33079 [2]
3/29/75	171	3		5 Circus		Epic 33422

ARJONA, Ricardo
Born on 1/19/1964 in Antigua, Guatemala. Latin singer/songwriter/guitarist.

9/16/00	136	3		1 Galeria Caribe	[F]	Sony Discos 84014
12/24/05	126	2		2 Adentro	[F]	Sony 67549
9/8/07	59	6		3 Quien Dijo Ayer	[F-K]	Sony 11335 [2]
12/6/08	55	3		4 5to Piso	[F]	Warner Latina 516669

ARMADA ORCHESTRA, The
Studio group featuring members of **The London Symphony Orchestra.**

1/17/76	196	2		1 The Armada Orchestra	[I]	Scepter 5123

ARMAGEDDON
Rock band formed in England: Keith Relf (vocals), Martin Pugh (guitar), Louis Cennamo (bass) and Bobby Caldwell (drums). Relf was a member of **The Yardbirds**; died from electrocution on 5/14/1976 (age 33). Caldwell (not to be confused with the same-named solo artist) was with **Johnny Winter**'s band.

6/7/75	151	6		1 Armageddon		A&M 4513

Billboard			R I A A	ARTIST		
DEBUT	PEAK	WKS		Album Title	Catalog	Label & Number

ARMANDO'S, Don, Second Avenue Rhumba Band
Born Don Armando Bonilla on 8/9/1946 in East Harlem, New York. Died on 11/16/2002 (age 56). Latin disco percussionist. Member of **Dr. Buzzard's Original Savannah Band**. Featured lead vocalist Fonda Rae.

| 2/2/80 | 208 | 1 | | 1 Don Armando's Second Avenue Rhumba Band .... | | ZE 33005 |

ARMATRADING, Joan
Born on 12/9/1950 in Basseterre, St. Kitts, West Indies; raised in Birmingham, England. Black female eclectic-rock singer/songwriter/guitarist.

10/9/76+	67	27		1 Joan Armatrading		A&M 4588
10/22/77	52	21		2 Show Some Emotion		A&M 4663
11/11/78	125	12		3 To The Limit		A&M 4732
12/8/79+	136	18		4 How Cruel .... [EP]		A&M 3302
6/7/80	28	23		5 Me Myself I		A&M 4809
10/17/81+	88	32		6 Walk Under Ladders		A&M 4876
4/30/83	32	22		7 The Key		A&M 4912
1/21/84	113	10		8 Track Record .... [G]		A&M 4987
3/30/85	73	19		9 Secret Secrets		A&M 5040
7/5/86	68	16		10 Sleight Of Hand		A&M 5130
8/20/88	100	13		11 The Shouting Stage		A&M 5211
6/30/90	161	10		12 Heart And Flowers		A&M 5298

ARMORED SAINT
Heavy metal band from Los Angeles, California: John Bush (vocals), Dave Prichard (guitar), Phil Sandoval (guitar), Joey Vera (bass) and Gonzo (drums). Sandoval left in 1986. Prichard died of leukemia on 2/27/1990 (age 26). Bush joined **Anthrax** in 1992.

12/22/84+	138	16		1 March Of The Saint		Chrysalis 41476
12/7/85+	108	19		2 Delirious Nomad		Chrysalis 41516
9/26/87	114	12		3 Raising Fear		Chrysalis 41601

ARMOR FOR SLEEP
Alternative-rock band from New Jersey: Ben Jorgensen (vocals), PJ Decicco (guitar), Anthony Dilonno (bass) and Nash Breen (drums).

| 3/12/05 | 101 | 3 | | 1 What To Do When You Are Dead .... | | Equal Vision 104 |
| 11/17/07 | 93 | 2 | | 2 Smile For Them .... | | Sire 132348 |

ARMSTRONG, Louis
Born Daniel Louis Armstrong on 8/4/1901 in New Orleans, Louisiana. Died of heart failure on 7/6/1971 (age 69). Legendary singer/trumpet player. Nicknamed "Satchmo." Numerous appearances on radio, TV and in movies.
AWARDS: Grammy: Lifetime Achievement 1972 ★ R&R Hall of Fame: 1990 (Early Influence)

10/1/55	10	1		1 Satch Plays Fats		Columbia 708
				LOUIS ARMSTRONG and His All-Stars		
				a tribute to Fats Waller		
12/15/56	12	2		2 Ella And Louis		Verve 4003
				ELLA FITZGERALD and LOUIS ARMSTRONG		
5/16/64	❶⁶	74	●	3 Hello, Dolly!		Kapp 3364
12/19/98	21ˣ	3		4 It's Christmas Time .... Cat:#13/5 [X]		LaserLight 15152
				BING CROSBY • FRANK SINATRA • LOUIS ARMSTRONG		
7/15/00	192	1		5 The Millennium Collection: The Best Of Louis Armstrong .... [G]		MCA 11940
1/27/01	142	5		6 Ken Burns Jazz - The Definitive Louis Armstrong .... [K-TV]		Legacy 61440
				songs from the Ken Burns PBS-TV special *Jazz*		

~ ~ ~ ~ ~ ~ ~ ~ ~ ~ **NON-CHARTED ALBUM** ~ ~ ~ ~ ~ ~ ~ ~ ~ ~ ~
1957 Porgy And Bess *[w/ Ella Fitzgerald]*
Grammy: Hall of Fame

ARMSTRONG, Tim
Born on 11/25/1966 in Berkeley, California. Hard-rock singer/songwriter/guitarist. Member of **Rancid** and the **Transplants**. Married to Brody Dalle of **The Distillers** from 1997-2003.

| 6/9/07 | 59 | 3 | | 1 A Poet's Life.. | | Hellcat 80491 |

ARMY OF ANYONE
Rock band formed in Los Angeles, California: Richard Patrick (vocals), brothers Dean DeLeo (guitar) and Robert DeLeo (bass), with Ray Luzier (drums). Patrick was lead singer of **Filter**. The DeLeo brothers were members of **Stone Temple Pilots** and **Talk Show**.

| 12/2/06 | 56 | 1 | | 1 Army Of Anyone.. | | Firm 60010 |

ARNOLD, Eddy   **All-Time: #290**
Born Richard Edward Arnold on 5/15/1918 in Henderson, Tennessee. Died on 5/8/2008 (age 89). Legendary country singer/songwriter/guitarist. Once known as "The Tennessee Plowboy."
AWARDS: Grammy: Lifetime Achievement 2005 ★ C&W Hall of Fame: 1966 ★ CMA: Entertainer 1967 ★ OPRY: 1943

10/26/63	131	5		1 Cattle Call		RCA Victor 2578
10/16/65+	7	58	●	2 My World		RCA Victor 3466
3/26/66	26	28		3 I Want To Go With You		RCA Victor 3507
7/30/66	46	22		4 The Last Word In Lonesome		RCA Victor 3622
12/24/66+	27ˣ	8		5 Christmas with Eddy Arnold .... [X]		RCA Victor 2554
				first released in 1962; Christmas charts: 64/66, 27/67, 39/68		
12/24/66+	36	30		6 Somebody Like Me...		RCA Victor 3715
3/18/67	57	24		7 Lonely Again..		RCA Victor 3753

Billboard			R I A A	ARTIST		
DEBUT	PEAK	WKS		Album Title	Catalog	Label & Number
				ARNOLD, Eddy — cont'd		
5/6/67	34	57	●	8 The Best Of Eddy Arnold .... [G]		RCA Victor 3565
10/7/67	34	36		9 Turn The World Around		RCA Victor 3869
2/24/68	122	21		10 The Everlovin' World Of Eddy Arnold		RCA Victor 3931
6/15/68	56	32		11 The Romantic World Of Eddy Arnold		RCA Victor 4009
11/9/68	70	13		12 Walkin' In Love Land		RCA Victor 4089
3/8/69	77	13		13 Songs Of The Young World		RCA Victor 4110
7/5/69	167	5		14 The Glory Of Love		RCA Victor 4179
11/1/69	116	8		15 The Warmth Of Eddy		RCA Victor 4231
5/2/70	191	3		16 Love & Guitars		RCA Victor 4304
5/30/70	146	2		17 The Best Of Eddy Arnold, Volume II .... [G]		RCA Victor 4320
3/13/71	141	4		18 Portrait Of My Woman		RCA Victor 4471
				ARPEGGIO		
				Black disco studio group assembled by producer Simon Soussan.		
2/10/79	75	16		1 Let The Music Play		Polydor 6180
				ARRESTED DEVELOPMENT		
				Hip-hop group from Atlanta, Georgia: Todd "Speech" Thomas, **Dionne Farris**, Aerle Taree, Tim Barnwell, Montsho Eshe, Rasa Don and Baba Oje.		
				AWARD: Grammy: Best New Artist 1992		
4/18/92+	7	76	▲4	1 3 Years, 5 Months & 2 Days In The Life Of ...		Chrysalis 21929
				title refers to the length of time between group's formation and the signing of its recording contract		
4/10/93	60	12	●	2 Unplugged .... [L]		Chrysalis 21994
				recorded on 1/6/1993		
7/2/94	55	8		3 Zingalamaduni		Chrysalis 29274
				title is Swahili for "Beehive of Culture"		
				ARRINGTON, Steve		
				Born on 3/5/1956 in Dayton, Ohio. R&B singer/drummer. Former member of **Slave**.		
3/12/83	101	17		1 Steve Arrington's Hall Of Fame: I		Atlantic 80049
2/25/84	141	9		2 Positive Power		Atlantic 80127
				STEVE ARRINGTON'S Hall Of Fame (above 2)		
5/18/85	185	5		3 Dancin' In The Key Of Life		Atlantic 81245
				ARROWS, The — see ALLAN, Davie		
				ARROYO, Bronson		
				Born on 2/24/1977 in Key West, Florida. Professional baseball pitcher (with the Boston Red Sox in 2005 and the Cinicinnati Reds in 2006). Album below features his cover versions of recent hits.		
7/30/05	123	2		1 Covering The Bases		Bronson Arroyo 69000
				ARTFUL DODGER		
				Rock band from Fairfax, Virginia: Billy Paliselli (vocals), Gary Herrewig (guitar), Gary Cox (guitar), Steve Cooper (bass) and Steve Brigida (drums). Cox left by 1980.		
9/11/76	208	2		1 Honor Among Thieves		Columbia 34273
8/30/80	209	1		2 Rave On		Ariola America 1503
				ARTIFACTS		
				Black rap duo from Newark, New Jersey: Raheem "El The Sensei" Brown and William "Tame One" Williams.		
11/12/94	137	1		1 Between A Rock And A Hard Place		Big Beat 92397
5/3/97	134	1		2 That's Them		Big Beat 92753
				ART IN AMERICA		
				Pop-rock trio from Detroit, Michigan: brothers Chris Flynn (vocals, guitar) and Dan Flynn (drums), with sister Shishonee Flynn (vocals, harp).		
3/26/83	176	3		1 Art In America		Pavillion 38517
				ARTISTS AGAINST AIDS		
				All-star group organized to benefit worldwide AIDS research. Featured performers include **Christina Aguilera**, **Backstreet Boys**, **Destiny's Child**, **Eve**, **Nelly Furtado**, **Ja Rule**, **Lil' Kim**, **Jennifer Lopez**, ***NSYNC** and **Britney Spears**.		
11/17/01	18	7		1 What's Going On .... [EP]		Play-Tone 86199
				ARTISTS UNITED AGAINST APARTHEID		
				Benefit group of 49 superstar artists formed to protest the South African apartheid government; proceeds went to political prisoners in South Africa. Organized by **Little Steven** and Arthur Baker. Featuring **Pat Benatar**, Bono (**U2**), **Jackson Browne**, **Jimmy Cliff**, **Bob Dylan**, **Peter Gabriel**, **Bonnie Raitt**, **Lou Reed**, **Bruce Springsteen** and many others.		
11/23/85	31	18		1 Sun City		Manhattan 53019
				ART OF NOISE, The		
				Techno-pop trio from England: Anne Dudley (keyboards), J.J. Jeczalik (keyboards, programmer) and Gary Langan (engineer).		
7/14/84	85	13		1 (Who's Afraid Of?) The Art Of Noise!		Island 90179
5/3/86	53	30		2 In Visible Silence		Chrysalis 41528
10/17/87	134	9		3 In-No-Sense? Nonsense!		Chrysalis 41570
12/17/88+	83	14		4 The Best Of The Art Of Noise .... [G]		China 837367

A's, The
Pop-rock band from Philadelphia, Pennsylvania: Richard Bush (vocals), Rick DiFonzo (guitar), Rocco Notte (keyboards), Terry Bortman (bass) and Mike Snyder (drums).

9/29/79	201	3		1 The A's		Arista 4238
7/11/81	146	7		2 A Woman's Got The Power		Arista 9554

AS CITIES BURN
Hard-rock band from Mandeville, Louisiana: Cody Bonnette (vocals), Chris Lott (guitar), Colin Kimble (bass) and Aaron Lunsford (drums).

9/1/07	135	1		1 Come Now Sleep		Tooth & Nail 82908
5/9/09	109	1		2 Hell Or High Water		Tooth & Nail 23491

ASH, Daniel
Born on 7/31/1957 in Northampton, England. Alternative-rock singer/songwriter/guitarist. Former member of **Bauhaus** and **Love And Rockets**.

3/9/91	109	10		1 Coming Down		Beggars Banquet 3014

ASHANTI
Born Ashanti Douglas on 10/13/1980 in Glen Cove, Long Island, New York. R&B singer/songwriter/actress. Played "Kyra" in the 2005 movie *Coach Carter*. Member of **The Inc.**

4/20/02	❶³	55	▲³	1 Ashanti		Murder Inc. 586830
				Grammy: Contemporary R&B Album		
6/7/03	142	6		2 Ashanti: The 7 Series .... [EP-K]		Murder Inc. 000494
				contains seven songs from album #1 above		
7/19/03	❶²	30	▲	3 Chapter II		Murder Inc. 000143
12/6/03	160	5		4 Ashanti's Christmas .... [X]		The Inc. 001612
				Christmas chart: 13/03		
1/1/05	7	20	▲	5 Concrete Rose		The Inc. 003409
12/24/05	59	5		6 Collectables By Ashanti .... [K]		The Inc. 005924
6/21/08	6	17		7 The Declaration		The Inc. 011318

ASHCROFT, Richard
Born on 9/11/1971 in Wigan, Lancashire, England. Alternative-rock singer/songwriter. Former lead singer of **The Verve**.

7/15/00	127	1		1 Alone With Everybody		Virgin 49494

ASHES DIVIDE
Born William Howerdel on 5/18/1970 in West Milford, New Jersey. Eclectic-rock singer/songwriter/musician. One-half of **A Perfect Circle**.

4/26/08	36	3		1 Keep Telling Myself It's Alright		Island 010770

ASHFORD & SIMPSON
All-Time: #468

Husband-and-wife vocal/songwriting duo: Nickolas Ashford (born on 5/4/1942 in Fairfield, South Carolina) and Valerie Simpson (born on 8/26/1946 in Brooklyn, New York). Joined staff at Motown and wrote and produced for many of the label's top stars. They married on 11/30/1974. Valerie's brother, Ray Simpson, was the lead singer of **Village People**.

11/10/73+	156	13		1 Gimme Something Real		Warner 2739
7/20/74	195	4		2 I Wanna Be Selfish		Warner 2789
5/8/76	189	4		3 Come As You Are		Warner 2858
2/5/77	180	3		4 So So Satisfied		Warner 2992
10/15/77	52	46	●	5 Send It		Warner 3088
9/9/78	20	28	●	6 Is It Still Good To Ya		Warner 3219
9/1/79	23	23	●	7 Stay Free		Warner 3357
8/23/80	38	12		8 A Musical Affair		Warner 3458
10/17/81	125	6		9 Performance .... [L]		Warner 3524 [2]
5/29/82	45	20		10 Street Opera		Capitol 12207
9/17/83	84	12		11 High-Rise		Capitol 12282
11/10/84+	29	36		12 Solid		Capitol 12366
9/6/86	74	18		13 Real Love		Capitol 12469
3/18/89	135	8		14 Love Or Physical		Capitol 46946

ASHTON, Susan
Born Susan Hill on 7/17/1967 in Irving, Texas. Contemporary Christian singer/songwriter.

10/26/96	163	1		1 A Distant Call		Sparrow 51458

ASHTON, GARDNER & DYKE
Pop trio from England: Tony Ashton (vocals, keyboards; born on 3/1/1946; died of cancer on 5/28/2001, age 55), Kim Gardner (bass; born on 1/27/1948; died of cancer on 10/24/2001, age 53) and Roy Dyke (drums; born on 2/13/1946).

8/7/71	185	6		1 Resurrection Shuffle		Capitol 563

ASIA
Rock supergroup from England: John Wetton (vocals, bass; **King Crimson**, **Uriah Heep**, **U.K.**), Steve Howe (guitar; **Yes**), Geoff Downes (keyboards; Yes, **The Buggles**) and Carl Palmer (drums; **Emerson, Lake & Palmer**, **Atomic Rooster**). Howe replaced by Mandy Meyer (**Krokus**) in 1985. Meyer replaced by Pat Thrall (**Automatic Man**) in 1990.

4/3/82	❶⁹	64	▲⁴	1 Asia		Geffen 2008
8/27/83	6	25	▲	2 Alpha		Geffen 4008
12/7/85	67	17		3 Astra		Geffen 24072
9/1/90	114	10	●	4 Then & Now .... [G]		Geffen 24298

Billboard DEBUT	PEAK	WKS	R I A A	ARTIST Album Title	Catalog	Label & Number
				ASIA — cont'd		
9/30/06	183	1		5 The Definitive Collection	[G]	Geffen 007432
5/3/08	73	1		6 Phoenix		Frontiers 12869
				AS I LAY DYING		
				Heavy metal band from San Diego, California: Tim Lambesis (vocals), Phil Sgrosso (guitar), Nick Hipa (guitar), Clint Norris (bass) and Jordan Mancino (drums). Lambesis also records solo as **Austrian Death Machine**.		
7/2/05	35	9		1 Shadows Are Security		Metal Blade 14522
6/3/06	129	2		2 A Long March: The First Recordings	[K]	Metal Blade 14572
9/8/07	8	8		3 An Ocean Between Us		Metal Blade 14632
				ASKING ALEXANDRIA		
				Hard-rock band from York, North Yorkshire, England: Danny Worsnop (vocals), Cameron Liddell (guitar), Ben Bruce (guitar), Sam Bettley (bass) and James Cassells (drums).		
10/3/09	170	1		1 Stand Up And Scream		Sumerian 022
				ASLEEP AT THE WHEEL		
				Western swing band from Paw Paw, West Virginia: Ray Benson (male vocals, guitar), Chris O'Connell (female vocals, guitar), Reuben "Lucky Oceans" Gosfield (steel guitar), Danny Levin (fiddle, mandolin), and Jim "Floyd Domino" Haber (piano). Numerous personnel changes with Benson the only constant.		
9/20/75	136	8		1 Texas Gold		Capitol 11441
9/18/76	179	3		2 Wheelin' And Dealin'		Capitol 11546
4/16/77	162	4		3 The Wheel		Capitol 11620
8/19/78	209	2		4 Collision Course		Capitol 11726
9/6/80	191	2		5 Framed		MCA 5131
11/20/93	159	7		6 Tribute To The Music Of Bob Wills And The Texas Playboys		Liberty 81470
2/21/09	90	7		7 Willie & The Wheel		Bismeaux 1287
				WILLIE NELSON & ASLEEP AT THE WHEEL		
				ASSJACK		
				Hard-rock trio formed in Nashville, Tennessee: **Hank Williams III** (vocals, guitar), Gary Lindsey (vocals) and Zach Shedd (bass).		
8/22/09	92	2		1 AssJack		Sidewalk 79150
				ASSOCIATION, The All-Time: #499		
				Pop band formed in Los Angeles, California: Gary Alexander (guitar; born on 9/25/1943), Russ Giguere (guitar; born on 10/18/1943), Jim Yester (guitar; born on 11/24/1939), Terry Kirkman (keyboards; born on 12/12/1939), Brian Cole (bass; born on 9/8/1942; died of a heroin overdose on 8/2/1972, age 29) and Ted Bluechel (drums; born on 12/2/1942). All shared vocals. Larry Ramos (guitar; born on 4/19/1942) joined in 1967. Richard Thompson replaced Giguere in 1970.		
8/20/66	5	59	●	1 And Then...Along Comes The Association		Valiant 5002
1/7/67	34	15		2 Renaissance		Valiant 5004
7/22/67	8	68	●	3 Insight Out		Warner 1696
5/4/68	23	26		4 Birthday		Warner 1733
12/28/68+	4	75	▲²	5 Greatest Hits	[G]	Warner 1767
5/10/69	99	18		6 Goodbye, Columbus	[S]	Warner 1786
10/4/69	32	17		7 The Association		Warner 1800
7/18/70	79	12		8 The Association "Live"	[L]	Warner 1868 [2]
8/14/71	158	4		9 Stop Your Motor		Warner 1927
5/20/72	194	5		10 Waterbeds In Trinidad!		Columbia 31348
				AS TALL AS LIONS		
				Alternative-rock band from Long Island, New York: Dan Nigro (vocals), Saen Fitzgerald (guitar), Julio Tavarez (bass) and Cliff Sarcona (drums).		
9/5/09	88	1		1 You Can't Take It It With You		Triple Crown 03096
				ASTLEY, Jon		
				Born in Manchester, England. Rock singer/songwriter/producer. His sister, Karen Astley, was married to **Pete Townshend** from 1968-2000.		
8/1/87	135	10		1 Everyone Loves The Pilot (Except The Crew)		Atlantic 81740
				ASTLEY, Rick		
				Born on 2/6/1966 in Newton-le-Willows, Lancashire, England. Pop singer/guitarist.		
1/23/88	10	60	▲²	1 Whenever You Need Somebody		RCA 6822
1/28/89	19	23	●	2 Hold Me In Your Arms		RCA 8589
3/30/91	31	18		3 Free		RCA 3004
10/16/93	185	1		4 Body & Soul		RCA 66295
				ASTRONAUTS, The		
				Surf-rock band from Boulder, Colorado: guitarists Bob Demmon, Dennis Lindsey, Rich Fifield and Storm Patterson, with drummer Jim Gallagher. Fifield and Patterson share vocals.		
8/3/63	61	14		1 Surfin' With The Astronauts		RCA Victor 2760
2/8/64	100	9		2 Everything Is A-OK!	[L]	RCA Victor 2782
3/28/64	123	5		3 Competition Coupe		RCA Victor 2858
				ASWAD		
				Reggae trio from London, England: Brinsley Forde (vocals, guitar), Tony Robinson (keyboards) and Angus Gaye (drums). Aswad means "black" in Arabic.		
8/13/88	173	7		1 Distant Thunder		Mango 9810

43

Billboard			R I A A	ARTIST Album Title	Catalog	Label & Number
DEBUT	PEAK	WKS				

ATARIS, The
Rock band formed in Anderson, Indiana; later based in Santa Barbara, California: Kris Roe (vocals, guitar), John Collura (guitar), Mike Davenport (bass) and Chris Knapp (drums).

3/22/03	24	36	●	1 **So Long, Astoria**	Columbia 86184
3/10/07	85	1		2 **Welcome The Night**	Isola 84791

ATC
Pop vocal group: males Joe Murray (from New Zealand) and Livio Salvi (from Italy), and females Sarah Egglestone (from Australia) and Tracey Packham (from England). ATC: A Touch of Class.

2/24/01	73	11		1 **Planet Pop**	Republic 013572

A*TEENS
Teen vocal group from Stockholm, Sweden: Dhani Lennevald, Sara Lumholdt, Amit Paul and Marie Serenholt. Began as an **Abba** tribute group.

6/3/00	71	41	●	1 **The ABBA Generation**	Stockholm 159007
3/17/01	50	28	●	2 **Teen Spirit**	Stockholm 013666
7/6/02	45	7		3 **Pop 'Til You Drop!**	Stockholm 018435

ATKINS, Chet   All-Time: #303
Born on 6/20/1924 in Luttrell, Tennessee. Died of cancer on 6/30/2001 (age 77). Legendary country guitarist. Moved to Nashville in 1950 and became prolific studio musician/producer. RCA's A&R manager in Nashville from 1960-68; RCA Vice President from 1968-82. Also see **Nashville String Band**.
AWARDS: Grammy: Lifetime Achievement 1993 ★ R&R Hall of Fame: 2002 (Sideman) ★ C&W Hall of Fame: 1973 ★ CMA: Musician 1967, 1968, 1969, 1981, 1982, 1983, 1984, 1985 & 1988 ★ Billboard Century: 1997 ★ OPRY: 1950

6/16/58	21	4		1 **Chet Atkins At Home** .... [I]	RCA Victor 1544
2/22/60	16	12		2 **Teensville** .... [I]	RCA Victor 2161
2/13/61	7	24		3 **Chet Atkins' Workshop** .... [I]	RCA Victor 2232
7/10/61	119	10		4 **The Most Popular Guitar** .... [I]	RCA Victor 2346
3/17/62	31	24		5 **Down Home** .... [I]	RCA Victor 2450
10/13/62	33	9		6 **Caribbean Guitar** .... [I]	RCA Victor 2549
3/23/63	135	5		7 **Our Man In Nashville** .... [I]	RCA Victor 2616
9/21/63	93	6		8 **Teen Scene** .... [I]	RCA Victor 2719
12/14/63+	12ˣ	16		9 **Christmas with Chet Atkins** .... [X]	RCA Victor 2423
				first released in 1961; Christmas charts: 16/'63, 22/'64, 28/'66, 43/'67, 32/'68, 12/'69	
2/29/64	64	8		10 **Guitar Country** .... [I]	RCA Victor 2783
4/9/66	112	13		11 **Chet Atkins Picks On The Beatles** .... [I]	RCA Victor 3531
6/18/66	62	23		12 **The "Pops" Goes Country** .... [I]	RCA Victor 2870
				CHET ATKINS/BOSTON POPS/ARTHUR FIEDLER	
12/17/66+	140	4		13 **From Nashville With Love** .... [I]	RCA Victor 3647
5/6/67	148	9		14 **It's A Guitar World** .... [I]	RCA Victor 3728
1/20/68	189	2		15 **Class Guitar** .... [I]	RCA Victor 3885
3/30/68	184	3		16 **Solo Flights** .... [I]	RCA Victor 3922
10/11/69	160	4		17 **Chet Picks On The Pops** .... [I]	RCA Victor 3104
				CHET ATKINS/BOSTON POPS/ARTHUR FIEDLER	
12/13/69+	150	7		18 **Solid Gold '69** .... [I]	RCA Victor 4244
4/25/70	139	5		19 **Yesterdroovin'** .... [I]	RCA Victor 4331
5/29/76	172	5		20 **Chester & Lester** .... [I]	RCA Victor 1167
				CHET ATKINS & LES PAUL *Grammy: Country Instrumental Album*	
4/27/85	145	13		21 **Stay Tuned** .... [I]	Columbia 39591
11/3/90	127	25		22 **Neck And Neck** .... [I]	Columbia 45307
				CHET ATKINS & MARK KNOPFLER	

ATKINS, Rodney
Born on 3/28/1969 in Knoxville, Tennessee. Country singer/songwriter/guitarist.

8/5/06	3¹	107	▲	1 **If You're Going Through Hell** Cat:#50/1	Curb 78945
4/18/09	15	8		2 **It's America**	Curb 79132

ATLANTA
Country band from Atlanta, Georgia: Brad Griffis and Bill Davidson (vocals), Tony Ingram (vocals, fiddle), Alan David (guitar), Allen Collay and Bill Packard (keyboards), Jeff Baker (harmonica), Dick Stevens (bass) and John Holder (drums).

5/26/84	140	7		1 **Pictures**	MCA 5463

ATLANTA DISCO BAND, The
Disco studio group assembled by producer Dave Crawford. Includes several members of **MFSB**.

1/17/76	172	9		1 **Bad Luck** .... [I]	Ariola America 50004

ATLANTA RHYTHM SECTION
Soft-rock band formed in Doraville, Georgia: Ronnie Hammond (vocals; born on 11/10/1950), Barry Bailey (guitar; born on 6/12/1948), J.R. Cobb (guitar; born on 2/5/1944), Dean Daughtry (keyboards; born on 9/8/1946), Paul Goddard (bass; born on 6/23/1945) and Robert Nix (drums; born on 3/1/1947). Daughtry and Nix were with **Roy Orbison**'s band, **The Candymen**. Cobb, Daughtry and band manager/producer Buddy Buie were with the **Classics IV**. Nix left in late 1978; replaced by Roy Yeager (born on 2/4/1946).

4/15/72	210	2		1 **Atlanta Rhythm Section**	Decca 75265
9/14/74	74	12		2 **Third Annual Pipe Dream**	Polydor 6027
9/6/75	113	9		3 **Dog Days**	Polydor 6041
6/5/76	146	15		4 **Red Tape**	Polydor 6060
1/15/77	11	39	●	5 **A Rock And Roll Alternative**	Polydor 6080

DEBUT	PEAK	WKS	R I A A	ARTIST / Album Title	Catalog	Label & Number
				ATLANTA RHYTHM SECTION — cont'd		
4/9/77	154	4		6 **Atlanta Rhythm Section**... [E]		MCA 4114 [2]
				recordings from 1972-73		
4/1/78	7	40	▲	7 Champagne Jam		Polydor 6134
6/23/79	26	21	●	8 **Underdog**		Polydor 6200
11/10/79	51	12		9 **Are You Ready!** .... [L]		Polydor 6236 [2]
8/16/80	65	11		10 **The Boys From Doraville**		Polydor 6285
9/19/81	70	16		11 **Quinella**		Columbia 37550
				ATLANTIC STARR		
				Urban contemporary band from White Plains, New York: brothers Wayne Lewis (vocals, keyboards), Jonathan Lewis (trumpet) and David Lewis (vocals, guitar), with **Sharon Bryant** (vocals), Cliff Archer (bass) and Porter Carroll (drums). Barbara Weathers replaced Bryant in 1984. Porscha Martin replaced Weathers in 1989. Rachel Oliver replaced Martin in 1991. Aisha Tanner replaced Oliver in 1993.		
8/26/78	67	13		1 **Atlantic Starr**...		A&M 4711
6/2/79	142	7		2 **Straight To The Point**		A&M 4764
3/14/81	47	30		3 **Radiant**		A&M 4833
3/27/82	18	29		4 **Brilliance**		A&M 4883
11/19/83+	91	28		5 **Yours Forever**		A&M 4948
5/25/85+	17	68	●	6 **As The Band Turns**		A&M 5019
4/25/87	18	31	▲	7 **All In The Name Of Love**		Warner 25560
5/20/89	125	6		8 **We're Movin' Up**		Warner 25849
2/8/92	134	14		9 **Love Crazy**		Reprise 26545
				ATLAS SOUND		
				Born Bradford Cox in 1982 in Athens, Georgia. Experimental-rock singer/songwriter.		
11/7/09	182	1		1 **Logos**		Kranky 138
				ATMOSPHERE		
				Hip-hop trio from Minneapolis, Minnesota: Sean "Slug" Daley (rapper), Anthony "Ant" Davis (producer) and Mr. Dibbs (DJ).		
6/29/02	139	1		1 **God Loves Ugly**		Fat Beats 35001
10/11/03	83	2		2 **Seven's Travels**		Rhymesayers 86690
1/22/05	165	2		3 **Headshots: Se7en** .... [E-K]		Rhymesayers 53
				contains early recordings from 1997-99		
10/22/05	66	3		4 **You Can't Imagine How Much Fun We're Having**..........		Rhymesayers 69
5/10/08	5	10		5 When Life Gives You Lemons, You Paint That Shit Gold		Rhymesayers 0096
				ATOMIC ROOSTER		
				Progressive-rock band from England co-founded by Vincent Crane (keyboards) and Carl Palmer (drums; **Emerson, Lake & Palmer, Asia**); both were with **The Crazy World of Arthur Brown**. Palmer left before first album below. Crane headed fluctuating lineup including vocalist Chris Farlowe on third album (earlier of **Colosseum**). Crane committed suicide on 2/14/1989 (age 44).		
7/3/71	90	15		1 **Death Walks Behind You**.......................................		Elektra 74094
12/11/71+	167	9		2 **In Hearing Of Atomic Rooster**		Elektra 74109
10/7/72	149	8		3 **Made In England**...		Elektra 75039
				ATREYU		
				Hard-rock band from Anaheim, California: Alex Varkatzas (vocals), Dan Jacobs (guitar), Travis Miguel (guitar), Marc McKnight (bass) and Brandon Saller (drums).		
7/17/04	32	7		1 **The Curse**..		Victory 218
4/15/06	9	11		2 A Death-Grip On Yesterday		Victory 267
2/10/07	103	3		3 **The Best Of Atreyu** .... [G]		Victory 345
9/15/07	8	27		4 Lead Sails Paper Anchor		Hollywood 000386
11/14/09	18	3		5 **Congregation Of The Damned**		Hollywood 034940
				ATTACK ATTACK!		
				Rock band from Westerville, Ohio: Caleb Shomo (vocals), Andrew Whiting (guitar), Johnny Franck (guitar), John Holgado (bass) and Andrew Wetzel (drums).		
11/29/08	193	1		1 **Someday Came Suddenly**		Rise 073
				AT THE DRIVE-IN		
				Alternative-rock band from El Paso, Texas: Cedric Bixler (vocals), Omar Rodriguez (guitar), Jim Ward (guitar), Paul Hinojos (bass) and Tony Hajjar (drums). Ward, Hinojos and Hajjar are also members of **Sparta**.		
9/30/00+	116	14		1 **Relationship Of Command**		Grand Royal 49999
6/11/05	95	3		2 **This Station Is Non-Operational** .... [K]		Fearless 30074
				ATTITUDES		
				Band of top session musicians: **David Foster** (keyboards), Danny Kortchmar (guitar), Paul Stallworth (bass) and Jim Keltner (drums).		
3/20/76	206	1		1 **Attitudes**...		Dark Horse 22008
				AUDIENCE		
				Soft-rock band from London, England: Howard Werth (vocals, guitar), Patrick Neubergh (sax), Nick Judd (keyboards), Trevor Williams (bass) and Tony Connor (drums).		
9/11/71	204	1		1 **The House On The Hill**		Elektra 74100
6/24/72	175	5		2 **Lunch**		Elektra 75026

Billboard			R I A A	ARTIST Album Title	Catalog	Label & Number
DEBUT	PEAK	WKS				

AUDIO ADRENALINE
Christian pop-rock band from Grayson, Kentucky: Mark Stuart (vocals), Barry Blair (guitar), Bob Herdman (keyboards), Will McGinniss (bass) and Ben Cissel (drums). Tyler Burkum replaced Blair in early 1997.

3/9/96	77	11	●	1 Bloom		ForeFront 25144
12/6/97	99	5		2 Some Kind Of Zombie.................		ForeFront 25182
10/2/99	76	7		3 Underdog		ForeFront 25225
4/7/01	186	2		4 Hit Parade .... [G]		ForeFront 25273
12/8/01	169	2		5 Lift....................		ForeFront 25299
3/15/03	116	3		6 Worldwide		ForeFront 40877
				Grammy: Rock Gospel Album		
9/17/05	122	2		7 Until My Heart Caves In		ForeFront 63758
				Grammy: Rock Gospel Album		
8/19/06	103	2		8 Adios: The Greatest Hits .... [G]		ForeFront 55086

AUDIOSLAVE
Hard-rock band of former **Rage Against The Machine** members Tom Morello (guitar), Tim Commerford (bass) and Brad Wilk (drums), with **Chris Cornell** (vocals; **Soundgarden**).

12/7/02	7	100	▲³	1 Audioslave	Cat:#3/47	Interscope 86968
6/11/05	❶¹	39	▲	2 Out Of Exile		Epic 004603
9/23/06	2¹	20	●	3 Revelations		Interscope 97728

AUDIO TWO
Rap duo from Brooklyn, New York: brothers Kirk Robinson and Gene Robinson.

6/25/88	185	4		1 What More Can I Say?		First Priority 90907

AUDIOVENT
Alternative-rock band from Calabasas, California: Jason Boyd (vocals), Ben Einziger (guitar), Paul Fried (bass) and Jamin Wilcox (drums).

6/22/02	156	6		1 Dirty Sexy Knights In Paris		Atlantic 83544

AUDITION, The
Pop-rock band from Chicago, Illinois: Danny Stevens (vocals), Seth Johnson (guitar), Timmy Klepek (bass) and Ryan O'Connor (drums).

2/9/08	157	1		1 Champion....................		Victory 339

AUER, Barbara Ann
Born in Los Angeles, California. Aerobic dance instructor.

6/20/81	145	15		1 Aerobic Dancing...................		Gateway 7610

AUERBACH, Dan
Born on 5/14/1979 in Akron, Ohio. Rock singer/songwriter/guitarist. Member of **The Black Keys**.

2/28/09	101	5		1 Keep It Hid		Nonesuch 517241

AUF DER MAUR
Born Melissa Auf Der Maur on 3/17/1972 in Montreal, Quebec, Canada. Rock singer/bassist. Former member of **Hole**.

6/19/04	187	1		1 Auf Der Maur................		Capitol 82537

AUGER, Brian
Born on 7/18/1939 in London, England. Jazz-rock keyboardist. The Trinity consisted of Julie Driscoll (vocals), Gary Boyle (guitar), Dave Ambrose (bass) and Clive Thacker (drums). Disbanded in mid-1970. Everchanging personnel of Oblivion Express included future **Average White Band** members Robbie McIntosh and Steve Ferrone, and Alex Ligertwood, later of **Santana**.

JULIE DRISCOLL/BRIAN AUGER & THE TRINITY:

5/10/69	194	2		1 Jools & Brian		Capitol 136
6/14/69	41	16		2 Streetnoise		Atco 701 [2]

BRIAN AUGER & THE TRINITY:

8/1/70	184	3		3 Befour....................		RCA Victor 4372

BRIAN AUGER'S OBLIVION EXPRESS:

4/17/71	209	3		4 Brian Auger's Oblivion Express		RCA Victor 4462
11/13/71	211	2		5 A Better Land........................		RCA Victor 4540
6/3/72	170	7		6 Second Wind		RCA Victor 4703
8/4/73	64	31		7 Closer To It!		RCA Victor 0140
4/6/74	45	20		8 Straight Ahead......................		RCA Victor 0454
12/7/74+	51	13		9 Live Oblivion, Vol. 1 .... [L]		RCA Victor 0645
				recorded at the Whiskey-A-Go-Go in Hollywood, California		
10/11/75	115	8		10 Reinforcements		RCA Victor 1210
3/13/76	169	4		11 Live Oblivion, Vol. 2 .... [L]		RCA Victor 1230 [2]
				recorded at the Whiskey-A-Go-Go in Hollywood, California		
2/19/77	127	5		12 Happiness Heartaches..............		Warner 2981
4/23/77	151	3		13 The Best Of Brian Auger .... [G]		RCA Victor 2249

AUGUSTANA
Alternative-rock band formed in Los Angeles, California: Dan Layus (vocals, guitar), Josiah Rosen (guitar), Jared Palomar (keyboards, bass) and Justin South (drums).

1/13/07	96	18		1 All The Stars And Boulevards........		Epic 93433
5/17/08	21	6		2 Can't Love, Can't Hurt................		Epic 03064

AUGUST BURNS RED
Hard-rock band from Lancaster, Pennsylvania: Jake Luhrs (vocals), J.B. Brubaker (guitar), Brent Rambler (guitar), Dustin Davidson (bass) and Matt Greiner (drums).

DEBUT	PEAK	WKS				
7/7/07	81	2		1 The Messengers		Solid State 89352
8/1/09	24	6		2 Constellations .... **[L]**		Solid State 64385

AURACLE
Jazz-pop band formed in New York: **Rick Braun** (sax), Stephen Kujala (woodwinds), Steven Rehbein (percussion), John Serry (keyboards), Bill Staebell (bass) and Ron Wagner (drums).

7/22/78	201	5		1 Glider .... **[I]**		Chrysalis 1172

AURRA
Funk band from Dayton, Ohio: Starleana Young (female vocals), Curt Jones (male vocals), Steve Washington (trumpet), Tom Lockett (sax) and Phillip Fields (keyboards). Young, Washington and Lockett were members of **Slave**. Young and Jones later formed the duo **Deja**.

6/13/81	103	13		1 Send Your Love		Salsoul 8538
2/27/82	38	15		2 A Little Love..		Salsoul 8551
3/26/83	208	1		3 Live And Let Live		Salsoul 8559

AUSTIN, Patti
Born on 8/10/1948 in Harlem, New York. R&B/jazz-styled singer/actress. Debuted at Harlem's Apollo Theatre at age four. Signed to a record contract with RCA at age five. By the late 1960s, was a prolific session and commercial jingle singer. Played "Millie" in the 1988 movie *Tucker: The Man and His Dream*.

12/3/77+	116	13		1 Havana Candy		CTI 5006
7/19/80	208	2		2 Body Language		CTI 36503
10/3/81+	36	44		3 Every Home Should Have One..		Qwest 3591
3/31/84	87	18		4 Patti Austin		Qwest 23974
11/9/85	182	4		5 Gettin' Away With Murder		Qwest 25276
4/14/90	93	17		6 Love Is Gonna Getcha		GRP 9603

AUSTIN, Sherrie
Born Sherrie Krenn on 8/28/1970 in Sydney, Australia; raised in Townsville, Australia. Country singer/songwriter/actress. Played "Pippa McKenna" on TV's *The Facts of Life* (1987-88). Former member of pop duo Colourhaus (under her real last name).

8/28/99	150	3		1 Love In The Real World		Arista 18881
8/30/03	144	1		2 Streets Of Heaven		Broken Bow 75872

AUSTRIAN DEATH MACHINE
Born Timothy Lambesis on 11/21/1980 in San Diego, California. Hard-rock singer/songwriter. Lead singer of **As I Lay Dying**.

8/9/08	179	1		1 Total Brutal		Metal Blade 14683
10/17/09	105	1		2 Double Brutal..		Metal Blade 14769 [2]

AUTOGRAPH
Hard-rock band from Los Angeles, California: Steve Plunkett (vocals, guitar), Steve Lynch (guitar), Steven Isham (keyboards), Randy Rand (bass) and Keni Richards (drums). Isham died of cancer on 12/9/2008 (age 56).

1/5/85	29	29	●	1 Sign In Please		RCA Victor 8040
11/16/85	92	15		2 That's The Stuff		RCA Victor 7009
4/11/87	108	15		3 Loud And Clear		RCA Victor 5796

AUTOMATIC MAN
Rock band formed in San Francisco, California: Todd "Bayete" Cochran (vocals, keyboards), Pat Thrall (guitar; of **Asia**), Donni Harvey (bass) and **Michael Shrieve** (drums, of **Santana**). After first album, Shrieve and Harvey left; replaced by Glenn Symmonds and Jerome Rinson.

10/2/76	120	7		1 Automatic Man		Island 9397
10/8/77	109	8		2 Visitors		Island 9429

AUTOPILOT OFF
Alternative-rock band formed in Monroe, New York: Chris Johnson (vocals, guitar), Chris Hughes (guitar), Rob Kucharek (bass) and Phil Robinson (drums).

5/1/04	119	1		1 Make A Sound		Island 001899

AVALON
Christian vocal group: Jody McBrayer and Michael Passons (male vocals), Nikki Hassman and Janna Potter (female vocals). Cherie Paliotta replaced Hassman after first album.

2/20/99	153	1	●	1 A Maze Of Grace		Sparrow 51639
4/10/99	81	13	●	2 In A Different Light..		Sparrow 51687
11/18/00	115	8		3 Joy – A Christmas Collection .... Cat:#9/1 **[X]**		Sparrow 51733
				Christmas chart: 13/'02		
6/9/01	37	11		4 Oxygen		Sparrow 51796
4/12/03	112	12		5 The Very Best Of Avalon: Testify To Love .... **[G]**		Sparrow 42949
3/13/04	104	8		6 The Creed		Sparrow 84901
2/11/06	160	1		7 Stand		Sparrow 74733

Billboard			R I A A	**ARTIST**		
DEBUT	**PEAK**	**WKS**		Album Title	Catalog	Label & Number

AVALON, Frankie
Born Francis Avallone on 9/18/1939 in Philadelphia, Pennsylvania. Teen idol managed by Bob Marcucci. Worked in bands in 1953 in Atlantic City, New Jersey. Performed on radio and TV with Paul Whiteman, mid-1950s. Singer/trumpet player with Rocco & His Saints in 1956, which included **Bobby Rydell**. Appeared in several movies, many of which co-starred **Annette**.

DEBUT	PEAK	WKS				
12/28/59+	9	14		1 Swingin' On A Rainbow		Chancellor 5004
10/23/61+	59	20		2 A Whole Lotta Frankie [G]		Chancellor 5018

~ ~ ~ ~ ~ ~ ~ ~ ~ ~ **NON-CHARTED ALBUMS** ~ ~ ~ ~ ~ ~ ~ ~ ~ ~ ~ ~

1958 **Frankie Avalon**	1961 **...And Now About Mr. Avalon**
1959 **The Young Frankie Avalon**	1962 **Italiano**
1960 **Fabian/Avalon (The Hit Makers)**	1962 **You're Mine**
1960 **Summer Scene**	1962 **Frankie Avalon's Christmas Album**
1960 **Young And In Love**	

AVANT
Born Myron Avant on 4/26/1976 in Cleveland, Ohio. Male R&B singer/songwriter. Played "Dexter" in the 2004 movie *Barbershop 2: Back In Business*.

5/27/00	45	44	●	1 My Thoughts	Magic Johnson 112069
4/13/02	6	30	●	2 Ecstasy	Magic Johnson 112809
12/27/03	18	26	●	3 Private Room	Magic Johnson 001567
5/13/06	4	20		4 Director	Magic Johnson 005875
12/27/08	26	11		5 Avant	Capitol 07582

AVENGED SEVENFOLD
Hard-rock band from Huntington Beach, California: Matt "M. Shadows" Sanders (vocals), Brian "Synyster Gates" Haner (guitar), Zach "Zacky Vengeance" Baker (guitar), John "Johnny Christ" Seward (bass) and Jimmy "The Rev" Sullivan (drums).

6/25/05	30	61	●	1 City Of Evil	Hopeless 48613
11/17/07	4	73	●	2 Avenged Sevenfold **Cat:#38/3**	Hopeless 303804
10/4/08	24	5		3 Live In The LBC & Diamonds In The Rough [L]	Hopeless 466684

AVENTURA
Latin group from the Bronx, New York: Anthony Santos, Lenny Santos, Max Santos and Henry Santos Jeter (none are related).

5/14/05	133	2		1 God's Project [F]	Premium Latin 94082
1/6/07	124	38		2 K.O.B.: Live [F-L]	Premium Latin 20560 [2]
12/1/07	97	18		3 Kings Of Bachata: Sold Out At Madison Square Garden [F-L]	Sony Discos 605 [2]
6/27/09	5	45		4 The Last [F]	Premium Latin 20800

AVERAGE WHITE BAND (AWB)   All-Time: #474
White funk band formed in Glasgow, Scotland: Alan Gorrie (vocals, bass; born on 7/19/1946), Onnie McIntyre (guitar, vocals; born on 9/25/1945), Hamish Stuart (guitar, vocals; born on 10/8/1949), Malcolm Duncan (sax; born on 8/25/1945), Roger Ball (sax, keyboards; born on 6/4/1944) and Robbie McIntosh (drums; born on 5/6/1950; died of a drug overdose on 9/23/1974, age 24). Gorrie and McIntyre were members of **Forever More**. McIntosh and Ferrone were members of **Brian Auger's Oblivion Express**. Steve Ferrone (born on 4/25/1950) joined after McIntosh's death. Stuart later joined **Paul McCartney**'s touring band.

10/13/73	216	3		1 Show Your Hand	MCA 345
4/5/75	39	13		2 Put It Where You Want It [R]	MCA 475
				reissue of #1 above	
9/21/74+	❶¹	43	●	3 AWB	Atlantic 7308
6/28/75	4	24	●	4 Cut The Cake	Atlantic 18140
7/17/76	9	32	▲	5 Soul Searching	Atlantic 18179
1/22/77	28	18	●	6 Person To Person [L]	Atlantic 1002 [2]
7/23/77	33	21		7 Benny And Us	Atlantic 19105
				AVERAGE WHITE BAND & BEN E. KING	
4/1/78	28	17	●	8 Warmer Communications	Atlantic 19162
4/7/79	32	15		9 Feel No Fret	Atlantic 19207
9/20/80	182	2		10 Volume VIII [G]	Atlantic 19266
5/31/80	116	12		11 Shine	Arista 9523
8/7/82	202	2		12 Cupid's In Fashion	Arista 9594

AVETT BROTHERS, The
Folk-rock trio from Concord, North Carolina: brothers Seth Avett (vocals, guitar) and Scott Avett (vocals, banjo), with Bob Crawford (bass).

6/2/07	134	2		1 Emotionalism	Ramseur 2716
8/9/08	82	3		2 The Second Gleam [EP]	Ramseur 2724
10/17/09	16	14		3 I And Love And You	American 35099

AVI, Zee
Born Izyan Alirahman in 1986 in Miri, Sarawak, Malaysia. Female singer/songwriter/guitarist.

6/6/09	130	1		1 Zee Avi	Monotone 012731

AXE
Rock band from Gainesville, Florida: Bobby Barth (vocals, guitar), Michael Osborne (guitar). Edgar Riley (keyboards), Wayne Haner (bass) and Ted Mueller (drums). Disbanded in 1984. Group made the Adult Contemporary chart in 1976 as Babyface. Osborne died in a car crash on 7/21/1984 (age 34).

6/26/82	81	20		1 Offering	Atco 148
9/10/83	156	6		2 Nemesis	Atco 90099

Billboard			R I A A	ARTIST		
DEBUT	PEAK	WKS		Album Title	Catalog	Label & Number

AXTON, Hoyt
Born on 3/25/1938 in Duncan, Oklahoma. Died of a heart attack on 10/26/1999 (age 61). Country singer/songwriter/actor. Son of songwriter Mae Axton ("Heartbreak Hotel"). Acted in the movies *The Black Stallion* and *Gremlins*.

7/10/71	215	1		1 Joy To The World		Capitol 788
4/12/75	188	2		2 Southbound		A&M 4510
4/10/76	171	4		3 Fearless		A&M 4571

AYALA, Ramon, Y Banda Noches
Born on 8/13/1943 in Donna, Texas. Latin singer/bassist.

6/16/07	40^C	3		1 Arriba El Norte, Arriba El Sur	[F]	Freddie 1837

AYERS, Roy
Born on 9/10/1940 in Los Angeles, California. R&B-jazz vibraphone player/keyboardist/vocalist. With **Herbie Mann** from 1966-70. In 1970, formed **Ubiquity** whose guest players included drummer **Billy Cobham**, guitarist **George Benson**, trombonist Wayne Henderson (**The Crusaders**) and vocalist **Dee Dee Bridgewater**.

ROY AYERS UBIQUITY:

10/5/74	156	4		1 Change Up The Groove		Polydor 6032
2/21/76	90	18		2 Mystic Voyage		Polydor 6057
8/14/76	51	17		3 Everybody Loves The Sunshine		Polydor 6070
10/23/76	206	1		4 Daddy Bug & Friends	[I]	Atlantic 1692
1/15/77	74	12		5 Vibrations		Polydor 6091
7/2/77	72	25		6 Lifeline		Polydor 6108

ROY AYERS:

3/11/78	33	13		7 Let's Do It		Polydor 6126
8/19/78	48	15		8 You Send Me..		Polydor 6159
5/26/79	67	15		9 Fever...		Polydor 6204
12/15/79+	82	18		10 No Stranger To Love		Polydor 6246
7/5/80	205	2		11 Prime Time		Polydor 6276

ROY AYERS & WAYNE HENDERSON

11/1/80	157	3		12 Love Fantasy		Polydor 6301
8/15/81	197	2		13 Africa, Center Of The World		Polydor 6327
3/20/82	160	7		14 Feeling Good		Polydor 6348
1/12/85	201	6		15 In The Dark	[I]	Columbia 39422

AZ
Born Anthony Cruz in Brooklyn, New York. Male rapper. Member of **The Firm**. Acted in the movies *Belly* and *Envy*.

10/28/95	15	6		1 Doe Or Die..		EMI 32631
4/25/98	22	6		2 Pieces Of A Man		Noo Trybe 56715
6/30/01	23	7		3 9 Lives		Motown 013786
6/29/02	29	9		4 AZiatic		Motown 018074
9/24/05	73	2		5 A*W*O*L		Quiet Money 29
4/19/08	141	2		6 Undeniable..		New Era 5027

AZTECA
Latin jazz-rock ensemble led by brothers Pete Escovedo (vocals) and Thomas **Coke Escovedo** (percussion). Pete is the father of **Sheila E**. Coke died on 7/13/1986 (age 45).

1/13/73	151	9		1 Azteca..		Columbia 31776
10/27/73	209	5		2 Pyramid Of The Moon		Columbia 32451

AZTEC CAMERA
Pop-rock band formed by singer/songwriter Roddy Frame (born on 1/29/1964 in East Kilbride, Scotland). Numerous personnel changes with Frame the only constant.

9/10/83	129	10		1 High Land, Hard Rain....................................		Sire 23899
10/13/84	175	6		2 Knife		Sire 25183
				produced by **Mark Knopfler**		
4/13/85	181	3		3 Aztec Camera	[EP-L]	Sire 25285
				recorded on 10/16/1984 at the Dominion Theatre in London		
12/19/87	193	3		4 Love		Sire 25646

AZTEC TWO-STEP
Pop-rock duo from Boston, Massachusetts: guitarists/vocalists Rex Fowler and Neal Shulman.

11/15/75	209	3		1 Second Step		RCA Victor 1161
12/25/76+	181	4		2 Two's Company		RCA Victor 1497
2/18/78	210	1		3 Adjoining Suites...		RCA Victor 2453

AZ YET
R&B vocal group from Philadelphia, Pennsylvania: Dion Allen, Darryl Anthony, Marc Nelson, Shawn Rivera and Kenny Terry.

11/16/96	60	41	▲	1 Az Yet		LaFace 26034

B

BABE RUTH
Rock band from Hatfield, Hertfordshire, England: Janita "Jenny" Haan (vocals), Alan Shacklock (guitar), Dave Punshon (piano), Dave Hewitt (bass) and Dick Powell (drums). In 1974, Steve Gurl replaced Punshon and Ed Spevock replaced Powell. In mid-1975, Bernie Marsden replaced Shacklock. Group named after the baseball great.

8/11/73	178	6	1 First Base		Harvest 11151
2/22/75	75	7	2 Babe Ruth		Harvest 11367
10/25/75	169	6	3 Stealin' Home..		Harvest 11451

BABY — see BIRDMAN

BABY BASH
Born Ronald Bryant on 10/18/1975 in Vallejo, California; raised in Houston, Texas. Latin male rapper.

10/11/03	48	26	● 1 Tha Smokin' Nephew		Universal 001258
4/2/05	11	11	2 Super Saucy		Universal 004101
11/17/07	30	6	3 Cyclone		Arista 05784

BABY BOY DA PRINCE
Born Lawrence Cennett in 1986 in New Orleans, Louisiana. Male rapper.

4/7/07	26	12	1 Across The Water...		Extreme 007608

BABY EINSTEIN MUSIC BOX ORCHESTRA, The
Studio group assembled by producer Bill Weisbach. Musicians include Weisbach, Clive Smith, Dan Willis, Tom Nazziola and Laura Koepke.

1/29/05+	169	16	● 1 Baby Einstein: Lullaby Classics............................ Cat:#13/89 [I]		Buena Vista 861085
1/10/09	94	2	2 Baby Einstein: Baby's Holiday Symphony .... [X-I]		Buena Vista 002606
			Christmas chart: 8/'08		

BABYFACE
Born Kenneth Edmonds on 4/10/1959 in Indianapolis, Indiana. R&B singer/songwriter/multi-instrumentalist. Formerly with **Manchild** and **The Deele**. Brother of Melvin Edmonds and **Kevon Edmonds** of After 7. Formed prolific songwriting partnership with Mark "L.A. Reid" Rooney; they co-founded LaFace Records in 1989.

AWARD: Grammys: Producer of the Year 1992, 1995, 1996 & 1997

8/5/89+	14	61	▲³ 1 Tender Lover		Solar 45288
9/4/93	16	83	▲³ 2 For The Cool In You		Epic 53558
11/16/96	6	46	▲² 3 The Day		Epic 67293
12/13/97	106	13	● 4 MTV Unplugged NYC 1997 .... [L]		Epic 68779
12/12/98	101	5	5 Christmas with Babyface .... Cat:#43/1 [X]		Epic 69617
			Christmas charts: 11/'98, 33/'99		
12/2/00	75	7	6 A Collection Of His Greatest Hits .... [G]		Epic 85132
9/29/01	25	11	7 Face2Face...		Arista 14667
8/13/05	10	10	8 Grown & Sexy		Arista 70568
10/6/07	48	4	9 Playlist...		Mercury 009495
			KENNY "BABYFACE" EDMONDS		

BABY HUEY
Born James Ramey on 1/1/1944 in Richmond, Indiana. Died of natural causes on 10/28/1970 (age 26). R&B singer.

5/8/71	214	2	1 The Baby Huey Story/The Living Legend		Curtom 8007

BABYLON A.D.
Hard-rock band from San Francisco, California: Derek Davis (vocals), Danny De La Rosa (guitar), Ron Freschi (guitar), Robb Reid (bass) and James Pacheco (drums).

12/2/89+	88	28	1 Babylon A.D.		Arista 8580

BABYS, The
Pop-rock band from England: **John Waite** (vocals), Walt Stocker (guitar), Mike Corby (keyboards) and Tony Brock (drums). In 1978, Jonathan Cain replaced Corby and Ricky Phillips (bass) joined. Cain later joined **Journey**. Waite later formed **Bad English** with Phillips and Cain.

3/5/77	133	13	1 The Babys		Chrysalis 1129
10/8/77	34	26	2 Broken Heart...		Chrysalis 1150
1/27/79	22	25	3 Head First...		Chrysalis 1195
1/19/80	42	22	4 Union Jacks		Chrysalis 1267
11/15/80	71	15	5 On The Edge		Chrysalis 1305
11/7/81	138	7	6 Anthology .... [G]		Chrysalis 1351

BACH, Sebastian
Born Sebastian Bierk on 4/13/1968 in Freeport, Bahamas; raised in Peterborough, Ontario, Canada. Former lead singer of **Skid Row**.

12/8/07	191	1	1 Angel Down		MRV 10013

BACHARACH, Burt
Born on 5/12/1928 in Kansas City, Missouri. Conductor/arranger/composer. Formed prolific songwriting team with lyricist Hal David. Married to actress Angie Dickinson from 1965-80. Married to songwriter **Carole Bayer Sager** from 1982-91. Composed songs for several movies.

AWARD: Grammys: Trustees 1997 / Lifetime Achievement 2008

10/28/67+	96	65	● 1 Reach Out		A&M 4131
6/28/69	51	87	● 2 Make It Easy On Yourself		A&M 4188

Billboard			R I A A	ARTIST		
DEBUT	**PEAK**	**WKS**		**Album Title**	**Catalog**	**Label & Number**

BACHARACH, Burt — cont'd

6/19/71	18	24	●	3 Burt Bacharach		A&M 3501
1/5/74	181	6		4 Living Together		A&M 3527
12/14/74	173	5		5 Burt Bacharach's Greatest Hits	[G]	A&M 3661
10/17/98	78	6		6 Painted From Memory		Mercury 538002
				ELVIS COSTELLO WITH BURT BACHARACH		
11/29/03	73	2		7 Here I Am: Isley Meets Bacharach		DreamWorks 001005
				RONALD ISLEY / BURT BACHARACH		
11/15/08	72	1		8 Live At The Sydney Opera House	[L]	Verve 012193
				BURT BACHARACH with The Sydney Symphony Orchestra		

BACHELORS, The
Pop vocal trio from Dublin, Ireland: brothers Declan Cluskey (born on 12/12/1942) and Conleth Cluskey (born on 3/18/1941), with John Stokes (born on 8/13/1940).

6/20/64	70	16	1 Presenting: The Bachelors		London 353
11/7/64	142	3	2 Back Again		London 393
4/3/65	136	4	3 No Arms Can Ever Hold You		London 418
9/4/65	89	6	4 Marie		London 435

BACHMAN, Tal
Born on 8/13/1968 in Winnipeg, Manitoba, Canada. Male rock singer/songwriter/guitarist. Son of Randy Bachman (of **Bachman-Turner Overdrive**).

8/7/99	124	10	1 Tal Bachman		Columbia 67956

BACHMAN-TURNER OVERDRIVE   **All-Time: #492**
Hard-rock band from Vancouver, British Columbia, Canada: brothers Randy Bachman (vocals, guitar; born on 9/27/1943) and Robbie Bachman (drums; born on 2/18/1953), with C. Fred Turner (vocals, bass; born on 10/16/1943) and Blair Thornton (guitar; born on 7/23/1950). Originally known as Brave Belt. Randy was a member of **The Guess Who**. Randy left in 1977 to form **Ironhorse**. Randy and Turner formed **Union** in 1981. Randy and Tim regrouped with C.F. Turner in 1984. Randy is the father of **Tal Bachman**.

8/18/73+	70	68	●	1 Bachman-Turner Overdrive		Mercury 673
1/19/74	4	75	●	2 Bachman-Turner Overdrive II		Mercury 696
8/31/74	❶¹	50	●	3 Not Fragile		Mercury 1004
3/8/75	180	3		4 Bachman-Turner-Bachman As Brave Belt	[E]	Reprise 2210
				first released in 1972 as *Brave Belt II* on Reprise 2057		
5/31/75	5	22	●	5 Four Wheel Drive		Mercury 1027
1/3/76	23	21	●	6 Head On		Mercury 1067
8/14/76	19	15	▲	7 Best Of B.T.O. (So Far) .... Cat.#29/8	[G]	Mercury 1101
3/19/77	70	9		8 Freeways		Mercury 3700
3/18/78	130	4		9 Street Action		Mercury 3713
4/7/79	165	4		10 Rock N' Roll Nights		Mercury 3748
				BTO (above 2)		
9/29/84	191	2		11 Bachman Turner Overdrive		Compleat 1010

BACKBONE
Born Jamahr Williams in Atlanta, Georgia. Male rapper. Member of **Dungeon Family**.

7/7/01	128	3	1 Concrete Law		Universal 014117
			BACKBONE AKA MR. FAT FACE 100 Featuring Slic Patna		

BACKSTREET BOYS   **All-Time: #377**
"Boy band" formed in Orlando, Florida: Nick Carter (born on 1/28/1980 in Jamestown, New York), Howie Dorough (born on 8/22/1973 in Orlando, Florida), Brian Littrell (born on 2/20/1975 in Lexington, Kentucky), A.J. McLean (born on 1/9/1978 in West Palm Beach, Florida) and Kevin Richardson (born on 10/3/1971 in Lexington, Kentucky). Richardson left in 2006. Carter is the older brother **Aaron Carter**.

8/30/97+	4	133	▲¹⁴	1 Backstreet Boys .... Cat.#2⁴/41		Jive 41589
6/5/99	❶¹⁰	93	▲¹³	2 Millennium .... Cat.#23/7		Jive 41672
12/9/00	❶²	42	▲⁸	3 Black & Blue		Jive 41743
11/17/01	4	24	▲	4 The Hits - Chapter One	[G]	Jive 41779
7/2/05	3¹	16	▲	5 Never Gone		Jive 69611
11/17/07	7	5		6 Unbreakable		Jive 16967
10/24/09	9	5		7 This Is Us		Jive 56504

BACK STREET CRAWLER
Rock band from England: Terry Wilson-Slesser (vocals), **Paul Kossoff** (guitar; **Free**), Mike Montgomery (keyboards), Terry Wilson (bass) and Tony Brunagel (drums). After first album, John Bundrick replaced Montgomery. Kossoff died of heart failure on 3/19/1976 (age 25; after completion of second album). Geoff Whitehorn replaced Kossoff and group shortened name to **Crawler**.

11/15/75	111	10	1 The Band Plays On		Atco 125
8/14/76	140	5	2 2nd Street		Atco 138
9/10/77	85	13	3 Crawler		Epic 34900
10/14/78	210	1	4 Snake, Rattle & Roll		Epic 35482
			CRAWLER (above 2)		

BAD AZZ
Born Jamarr Stamps in 1975 in Los Angeles, California. Male rapper.

10/17/98	182	1	1 Word On Tha Streets		Priority 50741
8/4/01	59	8	2 Personal Business		Doggy Style 50076

BAD BOY'S DA BAND
Rap group assembled and produced by **P. Diddy** for the reality TV series *Making The Band 2:* Dylan John, Sara Stokes, Lloyd "Ness" Mathis, Frederick Watson, Lynese "Babs" Wiley and Rodney "Young City" Hill.

10/18/03	2¹	9	●	1 **Too Hot For T.V.**	Bad Boy 001118

BAD BRAINS
Highly influential punk-rock band formed in Washington DC: Paul "H.R." Hudson (vocals), Gary "Dr. Know" Miller (guitar), Darryl Jenifer (bass) and Earl Hudson (drums).

7/14/07	100	1		1 **Build A Nation**	Megaforce 1048

BAD COMPANY   All-Time: #296
Rock band from England: **Paul Rodgers** (vocals; born on 12/17/1949), Mick Ralphs (guitar; born on 3/31/1948), Raymond "Boz" Burrell (bass; born on 8/1/1946; died on 9/21/2006, age 60) and Simon Kirke (drums; born on 7/28/1949). Rodgers and Kirke from **Free**; Ralphs from **Mott The Hoople**; and Burrell from **King Crimson**. Rodgers, who left group in late 1982, was a member of **The Firm** (1984-86) and **The Law** (in 1991). Vocalist Brian Howe joined in 1986. Burrell left in 1987. Dave "Bucket" Colwell (guitar) and Rick Wills (of **Foreigner**; bass) joined in late 1992. Howe left in early 1995; replaced by Robert Hart. Band named after a 1972 Jeff Bridges movie.

7/27/74	❶¹	64	▲5	1 **Bad Company**	Swan Song 8410
4/19/75	3¹	33	▲3	2 **Straight Shooter** Cat:#12/23	Swan Song 8413
2/14/76	5	28	▲	3 **Run With The Pack**	Swan Song 8415
3/26/77	15	24	●	4 **Burnin' Sky**	Swan Song 8500
3/31/79	3²	37	▲2	5 **Desolation Angels**	Swan Song 8506
9/4/82	26	18		6 **Rough Diamonds**	Swan Song 90001
1/18/86	137	14	▲2	7 **10 From 6** Cat:#11/71 [G]	Atlantic 81625
10/25/86	106	9		8 **Fame And Fortune**	Atlantic 81684
9/17/88	58	40	●	9 **Dangerous Age**	Atlantic 81884
6/30/90	35	75	▲	10 **Holy Water**	Atco 91371
10/10/92	40	20	●	11 **Here Comes Trouble**	Atco 91759
6/24/95	159	3		12 **Company Of Strangers**	EastWest 61808
4/10/99	189	1		13 **The 'Original' Bad Co. Anthology** .... [K]	Elektra 62349 [2]

BAD ENGLISH
Pop-rock band formed in Los Angeles, California: **John Waite** (vocals), **Neal Schon** (guitar), **Jonathan Cain** (keyboards), Ricky Phillips (bass) and Deen Castronovo (drums). Waite, Phillips and Cain were members of **The Babys**. Cain and Schon were members of **Journey**.

7/15/89	21	52	▲	1 **Bad English**	Epic 45083
9/14/91	72	8		2 **Backlash**	Epic 46935

BADFINGER
Rock band from Swansea, Wales: Pete Ham (guitar; born on 4/27/1947; committed suicide on 4/23/1975, age 27), Joey Molland (guitar; born on 6/21/1948), Tom Evans (bass; born on 6/5/1947; committed suicide on 11/23/1983, age 36) and Mike Gibbins (drums; born on 3/12/1949). All but Gibbins shared vocals. Group disbanded after Ham's death; Molland and Evans reunited in 1979 with new lineup.

3/28/70	55	17		1 **Magic Christian Music**	Apple 3364
11/28/70	28	15		2 **No Dice**	Apple 3367
12/25/71+	31	32		3 **Straight Up** .... Cat:#23/1	Apple 3387
12/15/73+	122	8		4 **Ass**	Apple 3411
3/9/74	161	5		5 **Badfinger**	Warner 2762
11/9/74	148	6		6 **Wish You Were Here**	Warner 2827
3/24/79	125	8		7 **Airwaves**	Elektra 175
3/28/81	155	6		8 **Say No More**	Radio 16030

BADGER
Rock band from England: Tony Kaye (keyboards; **Yes**, **Badfinger**), Brian Parrish (guitar), Dave Foster (bass) and Roy Dyke (drums).

8/11/73	167	8		1 **One Live Badger** .... [L]	Atco 7022
				recorded on 12/15/1972 at the Rainbow Theatre	

BADLANDS
Hard-rock band from England: Ray Gillen (vocals), Jake E. Lee (guitar), Greg Chaisson (bass) and Eric Singer (drums; **Black Sabbath**). Singer replaced by Jeff Martin in 1990. Gillen died of cancer on 12/1/1993 (age 33).

6/10/89	57	26		1 **Badlands**	Atlantic 81966
6/29/91	140	3		2 **Voodoo Highway**	Atlantic 82251

BADLY DRAWN BOY
Born Damon Gough on 10/2/1970 in Bolton, Lancashire, England. Adult Alternative singer/songwriter/guitarist/pianist.

6/8/02	180	2		1 **About A Boy** .... [S]	Artist Direct 01019
11/23/02	135	1		2 **Have You Fed The Fish?**	Artist Direct 01066

BAD RELIGION
Punk-rock band from Woodland Hills, California: Greg Graffin (vocals), Brett Gurewitz (guitar), Greg Hetson (guitar), Jay Bentley (bass) and Bobby Schayer (drums). Brian Baker replaced Gurewitz in 1995. Gurewitz owns the Epitaph record label.

9/24/94	87	7	●	1 **Stranger Than Fiction**	Atlantic 82658
3/16/96	56	5		2 **The Gray Race**	Atlantic 82870
				co-produced by **Ric Ocasek**	
5/23/98	78	2		3 **No Substance**	Atlantic 83094
5/27/00	88	2		4 **The New America**	Atlantic 83303
2/9/02	49	5		5 **The Process Of Belief**	Epitaph 86635

Billboard DEBUT	PEAK	WKS	R I A A	ARTIST Album Title	Catalog	Label & Number

BAD RELIGION — cont'd

6/26/04	40	5		6 The Empire Strikes First		Epitaph 86694
7/28/07	35	5		7 New Maps Of Hell		Epitaph 86863

BADU, Erykah
Born Erica Wright on 2/26/1971 in Dallas, Texas. R&B singer/songwriter/actress. Played "Rose Rose" in the 1999 movie *The Cider House Rules*.

3/1/97	2¹	58	▲³	1 Baduizm		Kedar 53027
				Grammy: R&B Album		
12/6/97	4	30	▲²	2 Live [L]		Kedar 53109
				recorded on 10/1/1997 at Sony Studios in New York City		
12/9/00	11	25	▲	3 Mama's Gun		Motown 153259
10/4/03	3¹	11	●	4 World Wide Underground		Motown 000739
3/15/08	2¹	15		5 New Amerykah, Part One: 4th World War		Universal Motown 010800

BAERWALD, David
Born on 7/11/1960 in Oxford, Ohio. Pop-rock singer/songwriter. Half of the **David & David** duo.

7/7/90	149	19		1 Bedtime Stories		A&M 5289

BAEZ, Joan   1960s: #42 / All-Time: #95
Born on 1/9/1941 in Staten Island, New York (British mother; Mexican father); raised in Palo Alto, California. Folk singer/songwriter/guitarist. Became a political activist while attending Boston University in the late 1950s. Made her professional debut in July 1959 at the first Newport Folk Festival. Orientation changed from traditional to popular folk songs in the early 1960s. Influential in fostering career of **Bob Dylan**.
AWARD: Grammy: Lifetime Achievement 2007

3/3/62	15	140	●	1 Joan Baez		Vanguard 2077
				first released in 1960		
11/27/61+	13	125	●	2 Joan Baez, Vol. 2		Vanguard 2097
11/21/64	12	66		3 Joan Baez/5		Vanguard 79160
10/23/65	10	27		4 Farewell, Angelina		Vanguard 79200
12/3/66	6ˣ	13		5 Noel [X]		Vanguard 79230
				Christmas charts: 6/'66, 10/'67, 11/'71, 11/'72, 12/'73		
9/2/67	38	20		6 Joan		Vanguard 79240
8/10/68	84	25		7 Baptism		Vanguard 79275
1/25/69	30	20	●	8 Any Day Now		Vanguard 79306 [2]
				songs of **Bob Dylan**		
6/7/69	36	14		9 David's Album		Vanguard 79308
				dedicated to her husband, David Harris, imprisoned for draft resistance		
3/21/70	80	14		10 One Day At A Time		Vanguard 79310
9/18/71	11	23	●	11 Blessed Are		Vanguard 6570 [2]
1/1/72	164	5		12 Carry It On [S]		Vanguard 79313
5/27/72	48	24		13 Come From The Shadows		A&M 4339
5/19/73	138	9		14 Where Are You Now, My Son?		A&M 4390
5/17/75	11	46	●	15 Diamonds & Rust		A&M 4527
11/6/76	62	17		16 Gulf Winds		A&M 4603
6/25/77	54	14		17 Blowin' Away		Portrait 34697
8/4/79	113	7		18 Honest Lullaby		Portrait 35766
9/27/08	128	1		19 Day After Tomorrow		Bobolink 83002

GREATEST HITS & COMPILATIONS:

11/23/63	45	18		20 The Best Of Joan Baez		Squire 33001
11/21/70	73	11		21 The First 10 Years		Vanguard 6560 [2]
12/16/72+	188	7		22 The Joan Baez Ballad Book		Vanguard 41/42 [2]
7/7/73	163	8		23 Hits/Greatest & Others		Vanguard 79332
4/3/76	205	6		24 The Joan Baez Lovesong Album		Vanguard 79/80 [2]
12/17/77+	121	8		25 The Best Of Joan C. Baez		A&M 4668

LIVE ALBUMS:

10/27/62	10	114	●	26 Joan Baez In Concert		Vanguard 2122
12/7/63+	7	36		27 Joan Baez In Concert, Part 2		Vanguard 2123
2/7/76	34	17		28 From Every Stage		A&M 3704 [2]

BAHAMADIA
Born Antonia Reed in 1976 in Philadelphia, Pennsylvania. Female rapper.

4/20/96	126	5		1 Kollage		Chrysalis 35484

BAHA MEN
Dance-junkanoo band from the Bahamas led by Isaiah Taylor, with Rick Carey and Omerit Hield (vocals), Marvin Prosper (rapper), Herschel Small and Patrick Carey (guitars), Tony Flowers (percussion), Jeff Cher (keyboards) and Colyn Grant (drums).

8/26/00	5	46	▲³	1 Who Let The Dogs Out		S-Curve 751052
4/13/02	57	12		2 Move It Like This		S-Curve 37980

BAILEY, Philip
Born on 5/8/1951 in Denver, Colorado. R&B singer/songwriter. Falsetto vocalist of **Earth, Wind & Fire**.

9/10/83	71	14	1 Continuation		Columbia 38725
11/10/84+	22	35	2 Chinese Wall		Columbia 39542
5/24/86	84	11	3 Inside Out..		Columbia 40209

BAILEY, Razzy
Born Erastus Bailey on 2/14/1939 in Hugley, Alabama; raised in Lafayette, Alabama. Country singer/songwriter/guitarist.

6/20/81	183	2	1 Makin' Friends		RCA Victor 4026
2/27/82	176	4	2 Feelin' Right		RCA Victor 4228

BAILEY RAE, Corinne
Born on 2/26/1979 in Leeds, West Yorkshire, England. Black female singer/songwriter.

7/8/06+	4	72	▲ 1 Corinne Bailey Rae		Capitol 66361

BAINBRIDGE, Merril
Born on 6/2/1968 in Melbourne, Australia. Female singer/songwriter.

10/26/96	101	20	1 The Garden		Universal 53019

BAIO, Scott
Born on 9/22/1961 in Brooklyn, New York. Singer/actor. Played "Chaci Arcola" on TV's *Happy Days*.

9/4/82	181	4	1 Scott Baio		RCA Victor 8025

BAJA MARIMBA BAND
Instrumental band led by marimbist Julius Wechter (born on 5/10/1935 in Chicago, Illinois; died of cancer on 2/1/1999, age 63). Band featured various studio musicians with Wechter the only constant. Wechter also played with **Herb Alpert** and **Martin Denny**.

4/25/64	88	12	1 Baja Marimba Band .... [I]		A&M 104
4/24/65	123	3	2 Baja Marimba Band Rides Again.. [I]		A&M 109
1/8/66	102	16	3 For Animals Only .... [I]		A&M 113
11/19/66+	54	43	4 Watch Out! [I]		A&M 4118
5/27/67	77	44	5 Heads Up! .... [I]		A&M 4123

JULIUS WECHTER AND THE BAJA MARIMBA BAND:

1/20/68	168	9	6 Fowl Play .... [I]		A&M 4136
8/31/68	171	8	7 Do You Know The Way To San Jose? .... [I]		A&M 4150
3/8/69	117	10	8 Those Were The Days .... [I]		A&M 4167
10/18/69	176	3	9 Fresh Air .... [I]		A&M 4200
4/4/70	180	6	10 Greatest Hits .... [G-I]		A&M 4248

BAKER, Anita   **All-Time: #496**
Born on 1/26/1958 in Toledo, Ohio; raised in Detroit, Michigan. R&B/jazz-styled singer. Began singing in her church choir in 1970. Member of Chapter 8 from 1976-80. Worked as a receptionist in a law firm in 1981. Signed to the Beverly Glen record label in 1982. Signed to Elektra in 1985.

10/29/83	139	11	1 The Songstress		Beverly Glen 10002
4/19/86+	11	157	▲5 2 Rapture		Elektra 60444
			Grammy: Female R&B Vocal		
11/5/88	❶4	42	▲3 3 Giving You The Best That I Got		Elektra 60827
			Grammy: Female R&B Vocal		
7/21/90	5	40	▲ 4 Compositions		Elektra 60922
			Grammy: Female R&B Vocal		
10/1/94	3²	38	▲2 5 Rhythm Of Love		Elektra 61555
7/6/02	118	16	● 6 The Best Of Anita Baker .... [G]		Atlantic 78209
9/25/04	4	20	● 7 My Everything		Blue Note 77102
12/10/05	120	5	8 Christmas Fantasy .... [X]		Blue Note 32173
			Christmas chart: 17/'05		

BAKER, Chet
Born Chesney Baker on 12/23/1929 in Yale, Oklahoma. Died on 5/13/1988 (age 58). White jazz trumpet player/singer. Movie biography *Let's Get Lost* was released in 1989. Featured player with the studio created **Mariachi Brass**.

2/26/66	120	4	1 A Taste Of Tequila .... [I]		World Pacific 21839
			MARIACHI BRASS Featuring Chet Baker		

~ ~ ~ ~ ~ ~ ~ ~ ~ ~ **NON-CHARTED ALBUM** ~ ~ ~ ~ ~ ~ ~ ~ ~ ~ ~

1956 **Chet Baker Sings**
Grammy: Hall of Fame

BAKER, George, Selection
Born Johannes Bouwens on 12/8/1944 in the Netherlands. His Selection consisted of Jan Hop, Jacobus Greuter, George The and Jan Visser. Female singer Lydia Bont joined in 1975.

7/4/70	107	6	1 Little Green Bag		Colossus 1002
1/31/76	153	7	2 Paloma Blanca...		Warner 2905

BAKER, Ginger
Born Peter Baker on 8/19/1939 in Lewisham, London, England. Rock drummer/singer. Member of **Cream**, **Blind Faith** and **Baker Gurvitz Army**. Ten-member Air Force featured **Steve Winwood** (vocals), Denny Laine (guitar; **Moody Blues**, **Wings**) and Rick Grech (bass; **Family**, **Traffic**, Blind Faith).

5/23/70	33	15	1 Ginger Baker's Air Force .... [L]		Atco 703 [2]
			recorded at the Royal Albert Hall in London, England		
1/9/71	211	2	2 Ginger Baker's Air Force 2		Atco 343

BAKER, Ginger — cont'd

9/2/72	205	4	3 Live! .... [L]	Signpost 8401

FELA RANSOME-KUTI AND THE AFRICA '70 WITH GINGER BAKER

9/23/72	201	5	4 Stratavarious .... [I]	Atco 7013
11/4/72	205	5	5 At His Best .... [K]	Polydor 3504 [2]

includes recordings with Blind Faith and **Cream**

BAKER, LaVern

Born Delores Williams on 11/11/1929 in Chicago, Illinois. Died of heart failure on 3/10/1997 (age 67). Recorded as "Little Miss Share Cropper" and "Bea Baker." One of the most popular female R&B singers of the early rock era.

AWARD: R&R Hall of Fame: 1991

~ ~ ~ ~ ~ ~ ~ ~ ~ **NON-CHARTED ALBUMS** ~ ~ ~ ~ ~ ~ ~ ~ ~ ~ ~

1956 **LaVern**
1957 **LaVern Baker**
1962 **See See Rider**
1963 **The Best Of LaVern Baker**

BAKER GURVITZ ARMY

Rock trio from England: **Ginger Baker** (drums) with brothers Paul Gurvitz (bass) and Adrian Gurvitz (guitar). All shared vocals.

2/15/75	140	7	1 The Baker Gurvitz Army	Janus 7015
11/15/75	165	5	2 Elysian Encounter	Atco 123

BALAAM & THE ANGEL

Gothic-rock trio formed in Cannock, Staffordshire, England: brothers Mark Morris (vocals), Jim Morris (guitar) and Des Morris (drums). All three were born in Scotland. Band named after a 1836 Gustav Jaeger painting.

4/30/88	174	3	1 Live Free Or Die...	Virgin 90869

BALANCE

Pop-rock trio from the Bronx, New York: Peppy Castro (vocals; **Blues Magoos**), Bob Kulick (guitar; brother of Bruce Kulick of **Kiss**) and Doug Katsaros (keyboards).

8/29/81	133	12	1 Balance	Portrait 37357

BALDHEAD SLICK & DA CLICK — see GURU

BALDRY, Long John

Born on 1/12/1941 in Haddon, Derbyshire, England. Died of a chest infection on 7/21/2005 (age 64). Blues-rock singer. Formed Steampacket with **Rod Stewart** and Bluesology with **Elton John**. Nicknamed "Long John" because of his 6'7" height.

7/3/71	83	18	1 It Ain't Easy...	Warner 1921
5/6/72	180	6	2 Everything Stops For Tea...	Warner 2614

above 2 produced by **Rod Stewart** and **Elton John**

BALIN, Marty

Born Martyn Buchwald on 1/30/1942 in Cincinnati, Ohio. Pop-rock singer/songwriter. Member of **Jefferson Airplane/Starship** and **KBC Band**.

6/6/81	35	23	1 Balin	EMI America 17054
3/12/83	156	6	2 Lucky	EMI America 17088

BALL, David

Born on 7/9/1953 in Rock Hill, South Carolina. Country singer/songwriter/guitarist.

7/2/94	53	55	▲ 1 Thinkin' Problem	Warner 45562
10/20/01	120	15	2 Amigo	Dualtone 01109

BALL, Kenny, and His Jazzmen

Born on 5/22/1931 in Ilford, Essex, England. Trumpet player. His Jazzmen consisted of Diz Disley (banjo), Johnny Bennett (trombone), Dave Jones (clarinet), Colin Bates (piano), Vic Pitts (bass) and Ron Bowden (drums).

3/17/62	13	32	1 Midnight In Moscow .... [I]	Kapp 1276

BALLARD, Hank, And The Midnighters

Born on 11/18/1927 in Detroit, Michigan. Died of cancer on 3/2/2003 (age 75). R&B singer. The Midnighters consisted of Henry Booth, Charles Sutton, Lawson Smith and Sonny Woods.

AWARD: R&R Hall of Fame: 1990

~ ~ ~ ~ ~ ~ ~ ~ ~ **NON-CHARTED ALBUMS** ~ ~ ~ ~ ~ ~ ~ ~ ~ ~ ~

1958 **Their Greatest Juke Box Hits**
1959 **Singin' And Swingin' The Twist**
1959 **The One And Only Hank Ballard And His Midnighters**
1963 **Hank Ballard's Biggest Hits**

BALLARD, Russ

Born on 10/31/1945 in Waltham Cross, Hertfordshire, England. Pop-rock singer/songwriter/producer. Guitarist of **Argent** from 1969-74.

8/16/80	187	2	1 Barnet Dogs	Epic 36186
6/9/84	147	13	2 Russ Ballard	EMI America 17108
8/3/85	166	4	3 The Fire Still Burns	EMI America 17162

BALLAS HOUGH BAND

Pop-rock band formed in London, England, by Mark Ballas (born on 5/24/1986 in Houston, Texas) and Derek Hough (born on 5/17/1985 in Salt Lake City, Utah). Both were professional dancers on TV's *Dancing With The Stars*. Their band: Emily Grace (keyboards), Sam Marder (bass) and Harry Sullivan (drums).

3/28/09	98	1	1 BHB	Hollywood 002959

					Catalog	Label & Number

BALLINGER, Lon
Born in Toronto, Ontario, Canada. Male DJ/dance producer.

5/12/01	167	2		1 Webster Hall Tranzworld 4 .... [I]		Webster Hall NYC 22

BALLIN' JACK
Interracial jazz-rock band from San Francisco, California: Jim Walters (vocals, trumpet), Glenn Thomas (guitar), Jim Coile (sax), Tim McFarland (trombone), Luther Rabb (bass) and Ronnie Hammond (drums). Rabb and Hammond joined **War** in 1979. Rabb died on 1/21/2006 (age 63).

1/2/71	180	8		1 Ballin' Jack		Columbia 30344

BALTIMORA
Born Jimmy McShane on 5/23/1957 in Londonderry, Northern Ireland. Died of AIDS on 3/28/1995 (age 37). Pop singer.

1/18/86	49	17		1 Living In The Background		Manhattan 53026

BALTIMORE AND OHIO MARCHING BAND, The
Studio group assembled by producers Joey Day and Alan Dischel.

1/20/68	177	3		1 Lapland .... [I]		Jubilee 8008

BANANARAMA
Female vocal trio formed in London, England: Sarah Dallin (born on 12/17/1961), Keren Woodward (born on 4/2/1961) and Siobhan Fahey (born on 9/10/1957). Group name is a combination of the children's TV show *The Banana Splits* and the **Roxy Music** song "Pyjamarama." Fahey married David A. Stewart (of **Eurythmics**) on 8/1/1987; later formed the duo **Shakespear's Sister**.

4/16/83	63	19		1 Deep Sea Skiving		London 810102
6/2/84	30	36		2 Bananarama		London 820036
8/16/86	15	28	●	3 True Confessions		London 828013
9/26/87	44	26		4 Wow!		London 828061
12/3/88	151	9		5 Greatest Hits Collection .... [G]		London 828127

BAND, The   1970s: #47 / All-Time: #234
Rock band formed in Woodstock, New York: **Robbie Robertson** (guitar, vocals; born on 7/5/1943), **Levon Helm** (drums, vocals; born on 5/26/1942), Richard Manuel (piano; born on 4/3/1943; committed suicide on 3/4/1986, age 42), Garth Hudson (organ; born on 8/2/1937) and **Rick Danko** (bass; born on 12/9/1943; died on 12/10/1999, age 56). All hailed from Canada (except Helm from Arkansas). Group's "farewell concert" on Thanksgiving Day in 1976 was documented in the Martin Scorsese movie *The Last Waltz*. Helm, Danko and Hudson reunited in 1993 with Jim Weider (guitar), Richard Bell (piano) and Randy Ciarlante (drums).
AWARDS: Grammy: Lifetime Achievement 2008 ★ R&R Hall of Fame: 1994

8/10/68	30	40	●	1 Music From Big Pink		Capitol 2955
				Grammy: Hall of Fame ★ RS500 #34		
10/18/69+	9	49	▲	2 The Band		Capitol 132
				Grammy: Hall of Fame ★ RS500 #45		
9/5/70	5	22	●	3 Stage Fright		Capitol 425
10/16/71	21	14		4 Cahoots		Capitol 651
9/9/72	6	28	●	5 Rock Of Ages [L]		Capitol 11045 [2]
				recorded on 12/31/1971 at the Academy of Music in New York City		
11/17/73+	28	20		6 Moondog Matinee		Capitol 11214
2/9/74	❶⁴	21	●	7 Planet Waves		Asylum 1003
7/13/74	3²	19	▲	8 Before The Flood [L]		Asylum 201 [2]
7/26/75	7	14	●	9 The Basement Tapes [E]		Columbia 33682 [2]
				BOB DYLAN & THE BAND (above 3)		
				RS500 #291		
12/13/75+	26	19		10 Northern Lights-Southern Cross		Capitol 11440
9/4/76	51	14	●	11 The Best Of The Band .... [G]		Capitol 11553
3/26/77	64	10		12 Islands		Capitol 11602
4/29/78	16	20		13 The Last Waltz .... Cat:#16/1 [L-S]		Warner 3146 [3]
				recorded on 11/25/1976 at Winterland in San Francisco, California		
11/20/93	166	1		14 Jericho		Pyramid 71564
5/2/09	13ᶜ	1		15 Greatest Hits .... [G]		Capitol 24941

BANDA EL RECODO
Group of various Mexican musicians assembled by producer Don Cruz.

4/7/01	188	2	●	1 Contigo Por Siempre... .... [F]		Fonovisa 6102
8/17/02	150	2		2 No Me Se Rajar .... [F]		Fonovisa 86228

BAND OF HORSES
Alternative-rock trio formed in Seattle, Washington; later based in Charleston, South Carolina: Ben Bridwell (vocals, guitar), Rob Hampon (bass) and Creighton Barrett (drums).

10/27/07	35	4		1 Cease To Begin		Sub Pop 745

BAND OF THE BLACK WATCH, The
Military unit from Canada. Led by pipe major Bruce Bolton.

3/20/76	164	4		1 Scotch On The Rocks .... [I]		Private Stock 2007

BANDY, Moe
Born Marion Bandy on 2/12/1944 in Meridian, Mississippi; raised in San Antonio, Texas. Country singer/guitarist.
AWARD: CMA: Vocal Duo (w/ Joe Stampley) 1980

4/11/81	170	4		1 Hey Joe! / Hey Moe!		Columbia 37003
7/21/84	205	3		2 The Good Ol' Boys - Alive And Well		Columbia 39426
				MOE BANDY & JOE STAMPLEY (above 2)		

BANG
Rock trio from Florida: Frank Ferrara (vocals, bass), Frank Gilcken (guitar) and Tony D'Lorio (drums).

| 4/8/72 | 164 | 10 | | 1 **Bang** .... | | Capitol 11015 |

B ANGIE B
Born Angela Boyd in 1968 in Morton, Mississippi. R&B singer.

| 5/4/91 | 133 | 6 | | 1 **B Angie B** .... | | Bust It 95236 |

BANGLES
Female pop-rock band formed in Los Angeles, California: **Susanna Hoffs** (vocals, guitar; born on 1/17/1959), sisters Vicki Peterson (guitar; born on 1/11/1958) and Debbi Peterson (drums; born on 8/22/1961) and Michael Steele (bass; born on 6/2/1955). Originally named The Bangs. Steele was previously in **The Runaways**. Vicki Peterson married John Cowsill (of **The Cowsills**) on 10/25/2003.

8/4/84	80	30		1 **All Over The Place**..		Columbia 39220
2/1/86+	**2**²	82	▲³	2 **Different Light**		Columbia 40039
11/5/88+	15	42	▲	3 **Everything**		Columbia 44056
5/26/90	97	9	▲	4 **Greatest Hits**.. [G]		Columbia 46125

BANGOR FLYING CIRCUS
Pop trio from Chicago, Illinois: David Wolinski (vocals, guitar), Alan DeCarlo (keyboards, bass) and Michael Tegza (drums). Wolinski and DeCarlo went on to form **Madura**. Wolinski later joined **Rufus**.

| 12/27/69 | 190 | 2 | | 1 **Bangor Flying Circus**... | | Dunhill/ABC 50069 |

BANG TANGO
Hard-rock band from Los Angeles, California: Joe LeSte (vocals), Mark Knight (guitar), Kyle Stevens (guitar), Kyle Kyle (bass) and Tigg Ketler (drums).

| 7/1/89 | 58 | 39 | | 1 **Psycho Cafe** .... | | Mechanic 6300 |
| 6/15/91 | 113 | 3 | | 2 **Dancin' On Coals**... | | Mechanic 10196 |

BANHART, Devendra
Born on 5/30/1981 in Houston, Texas. Eclectic male singer/songwriter.

| 10/13/07 | 115 | 1 | | 1 **Smokey Rolls Down Thunder Canyon** .... | | XL 283 |
| 11/14/09 | 139 | 1 | | 2 **What Will We Be** .... | | Warner 520960 |

BANJO BARONS
Banjo band conducted by Teo Macero (died on 2/19/2008, age 83).

| 4/21/73 | 207 | 2 | | 1 **Dueling Banjos**.. [I] | | Harmony 32214 |

BANKS, Ant
Born Anthony Banks in Oakland, California. Male rapper/producer. Also see **T.W.D.Y.**

4/10/93	123	7		1 **Sittin' On Somethin' Phat**		Jive 41496
7/2/94	80	5		2 **The Big Badass**		Jive 41534
7/26/97	20	10		3 **Big Thangs**		Priority 50698

BANKS, Lloyd
Born Christopher Lloyd on 4/30/1982 in New Carrollton, Maryland; raised in Jamaica, Queens, New York. Male rapper. Member of **G-Unit**.

| 7/17/04 | ❶² | 36 | ▲ | 1 **The Hunger For More** | | G-Unit 002826 |
| 10/28/06 | 3¹ | 8 | | 2 **Rotten Apple** | | G-Unit 007023 |

BANKS, Peter
Born on 4/8/1947 in England. Rock singer/keyboardist. Former member of **Yes** and **Flash**; later joned **After The Fire**.

| 9/8/73 | 152 | 8 | | 1 **Two Sides Of Peter Banks**.. | | Sovereign 11217 |

BANKS, Tony
Born on 3/27/1951 in East Heathly, Sussex, England. Rock singer/songwriter/keyboardist. Member of **Genesis**.

| 12/15/79+ | 171 | 5 | | 1 **A Curious Feeling** .... | | Charisma 2207 |
| 7/2/83 | 202 | 3 | | 2 **The Fugitive** .... | | Atlantic 80071 |

BANNER, David
Born Lavell Crump on 4/11/1973 in Jackson, Mississippi. Male rapper.

6/7/03	9	22		1 **Mississippi: The Album**		SRC 000312
1/10/04	69	14		2 **MTA2: Baptized In Dirty Water**		SRC 001720
10/8/05	6	8		3 **Certified**		SRC 004975
8/2/08	8	14		4 **The Greatest Story Ever Told**		SRC 009956

BANTON, Buju
Born Mark Myrie on 7/15/1973 in Kingston, Jamaica. Dancehall reggae singer. The name Buju Banton is taken from the Jamaican word for breadfruit.

8/21/93	159	7		1 **Voice Of Jamaica**		Mercury 518013
8/5/95	148	2		2 **'Til Shiloh**		Loose Cannon 524119
9/9/00	128	2		3 **Unchained Spirit**		Anti 86580
3/29/03	198	1		4 **Friends For Life**		VP 83634

BARBARA, Ana
Born Altagracia Motta on 1/10/1973 in Rio Verde, Mexico. Latin singer.

| 4/16/05 | 154 | 3 | | 1 **Confesiones** .... [F] | | Fonovisa 351791 |
| | | | | **ANA BARBARA & JENNIFER PENA** | | |

BARBER, Frank, Orch.
Born in England. Composer/conductor/arranger.

6/5/82	94	16	1 Hooked On Big Bands	[I]	Victory 702

BARBIERI, Gato
Born Leandro Barbieri on 11/28/1934 in Rosario, Argentina. Tenor saxophonist.

5/5/73	166	7		1 Last Tango In Paris	[I-S]	United Artists 045
				Grammy: Instrumental Album		
11/24/73	203	8		2 Chapter One: Latin America	[I]	Impulse 9248
10/26/74	160	3		3 Chapter Three - Viva Emiliano Zapata	[I]	Impulse! 9279
10/2/76+	75	32	●	4 Caliente!	[I]	A&M 4597
10/29/77	66	20		5 Ruby, Ruby	[I]	A&M 4655
7/29/78	96	7		6 Tropico	[I]	A&M 4710
8/11/79	116	9		7 Euphoria	[I]	A&M 4774

BARBOUR, Keith
Born on 1/21/1941 in Brooklyn, New York. Pop singer/songwriter. Formerly with **The New Christy Minstrels**. Married to actress Deidre Hall from 1972-78.

11/1/69	163	4	1 Echo Park		Epic 26485

BARCLAY JAMES HARVEST
Art-rock band from Oldham, England: John Lees (vocals, guitar), Stewart Wolstenholme (keyboards), Les Holroyd (bass) and Mel Pritchard (drums). Pritchard died on 1/27/2004 (age 56).

2/19/77	174	3	1 Octoberon		MCA 2234

BARDENS, Pete
Born on 6/19/1945 in London, England. Died of cancer on 1/22/2002 (age 56). Rock keyboardist. Former member of **Them**, **Camel** and **Keats**.

10/17/87	148	5	1 Seen One Earth	[I]	Cinema 12555

BARDEUX
Female dance duo from Los Angeles, California: Stacy Smith and Lisa "Jaz" Teaney. Melanie Taylor replaced Jaz in 1989.

4/30/88	104	12	1 Bold As Love		Enigma 73312
10/14/89	133	7	2 Shangri-La		Enigma 73522

BARE, Bobby
Born on 4/7/1935 in Ironton, Ohio. Country singer/songwriter/guitarist. Played "Pvt. Cranshaw" in the 1964 movie *A Distant Trumpet*. Hosted own TV series in the mid-1980s.
AWARD: OPRY: 1965

10/26/63	119	3	1 "Detroit City" And Other Hits		RCA Victor 2776
2/1/64	133	5	2 500 Miles Away From Home		RCA Victor 2835
8/21/76	205	6	3 The Winner And Other Losers		RCA Victor 1786
6/27/81	204	2	4 As Is		Columbia 37157

BAREILLES, Sara
Born on 12/7/1979 in Eureka, California. Adult Alternative-pop singer/songwriter/pianist.

7/21/07+	7	53	●	1 Little Voice	Epic 94821

BARENAKED LADIES — All-Time: #450
Alternative-rock band from Toronto, Ontario, Canada: Steven Page (vocals, guitar; born on 6/22/1970), Ed Robertson (vocals, guitar; born on 10/25/1970), brothers Andrew Creeggan (keyboards; born on 7/4/1971) and Jim Creeggan (bass; born on 2/12/1970) and Tyler Stewart (drums; born on 9/21/1967). Kevin Hearn (born on 7/3/1969) replaced Andrew Creeggan in 1996.

7/25/98	36^C	13	●	1 Gordon	[E]	Reprise 26956
				released in 1992		
9/3/94	175	1		2 Maybe You Should Drive		Reprise 45709
4/6/96	111	2	●	3 Born On A Pirate Ship		Reprise 46128
7/5/97+	86	56	▲	4 Rock Spectacle	Cat:#16/19 [L]	Reprise 46393
7/25/98	3^1	63	▲4	5 Stunt		Reprise 46963
9/30/00	5	27	▲	6 Maroon		Reprise 47814
12/1/01	38	15	●	7 Disc One: All Their Greatest Hits (1991-2001)	[G]	Reprise 48075
11/8/03	10	10		8 Everything To Everyone		Reprise 48209
11/27/04	64	7		9 Barenaked For The Holidays	Cat:#26/5 [X]	Desperation 40015
				Christmas charts: 5/'04, 24/'05, 44/'06, 36/'07		
9/30/06	17	6		10 Barenaked Ladies Are Me		Desperation 44351
2/24/07	102	2		11 Barenaked Ladies Are Men		Desperation 43247
5/24/08	61	8		12 Snacktime!		Desperation 533699

BAR-KAYS — All-Time: #421
Funk band from Memphis, Tennessee: Jimmy King (guitar), Ronnie Caldwell (organ), Phalon Jones (sax), Ben Cauley (trumpet), James Alexander (bass) and Carl Cunningham (drums). The plane crash that killed **Otis Redding** (on 12/10/1967 in Madison, Wisconsin) also claimed the lives of all the Bar-Kays except Alexander (not on the plane) and Cauley (survived the crash). Alexander re-formed the group with Larry Dodson (vocals), Barry Wilkins (guitar), Harvey Henderson (sax), Winston Stewart (organ) and Willie Hall (drums).

2/27/71	90	12	1 Black Rock		Volt 6011
2/24/73	212	5	2 Do You See What I See?		Volt 8001
11/13/76+	69	22	3 Too Hot To Stop		Mercury 1099
12/10/77+	47	23	● 4 Flying High On Your Love		Mercury 1181
11/11/78+	72	15	5 Money Talks		Stax 4106

			R I A A	ARTIST		
DEBUT	**PEAK**	**WKS**		**Album Title**	**Catalog**	**Label & Number**

				ARTIST / Album Title	Catalog	Label & Number
				BAR-KAYS — cont'd		
12/23/78+	86	17		6 Light Of Life		Mercury 3732
11/10/79	35	24	●	7 Injoy		Mercury 3781
12/13/80+	57	16		8 As One		Mercury 3844
11/14/81+	55	29	●	9 Nightcruising		Mercury 4028
11/20/82	51	29		10 Propositions		Mercury 4065
4/21/84	52	22		11 Dangerous		Mercury 818478
9/21/85	115	9		12 Banging The Wall		Mercury 824727
11/7/87	110	14		13 Contagious		Mercury 830305

BARLOWGIRL
Christian rock trio from Elgin, Illinois: sisters Rebecca Barlow (guitar), Alyssa Barlow (vocals, keyboards, bass) and Lauren Barlow (vocals, drums).

10/15/05	85	7		1 Another Journal Entry		Fervent 86446
7/7/07	13[C]	5		2 Barlowgirl		Fervent 30046
8/11/07	40	7		3 How Can We Be Silent		Fervent 887197
12/13/08	180	1		4 Home For Christmas .... [X]		Fervent 997685
				Christmas charts: 2/'08, 22/'09		
9/26/09	85	5		5 Love & War		Fervent 887861

BARNES, Dave
Born on 6/20/1978 in South Carolina; raised in Kosciusko, Mississippi. Singer/songwriter/guitarist.

4/19/08	94	2		1 Me & You & The World		Razor & Tie 82976
2/21/09	158	1		2 You, The Night And Candlelight .... [EP]		Razor & Tie 80972

BARNES, Jimmy
Born on 4/28/1956 in Glasgow, Scotland; raised in Australia. Rock singer/songwriter. Lead singer of **Cold Chisel**.

3/8/86	109	16		1 Jimmy Barnes		Geffen 24089
6/11/88	104	15		2 Freight Train Heart		Geffen 24146

BARONESS
Hard-rock band from Savannah, Georgia: John Baizley (vocals, guitar), Peter Adams (guitar), Summer Welch (bass) and Allen Blickle (drums).

10/31/09	117	1		1 Blue Record		Relapse 7053

BARRABAS
Disco band from Spain: Jo Tejada (vocals), Ricky Morales (guitar), Juan Vidal (keyboards), Ernesto Duarte Duarte (percussion), Miguel Morales (bass) and Daniel Louis (drums).

8/23/75	149	7		1 Heart Of The City		Atco 118

BARRERE, Paul
Born on 7/3/1948 in Burbank, California. Rock singer/songwriter/guitarist. Former member of **Little Feat**.

3/5/83	204	5		1 On My Own Two Feet		Mirage 90070

BARRETT, Syd
Born Roger Barrett on 1/6/1946 in Cambridge, England. Died on 7/9/2006 (age 60). Rock singer/guitarist. Member of **Pink Floyd** from 1965-68.

8/17/74	163	4		1 The Madcap Laughs/Barrett		Harvest 11314 [2]

BARRY, Claudja
Born in 1952 in Jamaica; raised in Toronto, Ontario, Canada. Disco singer/actress.

2/25/78	131	10		1 Claudja		Salsoul 5525
6/2/79	101	10		2 Boogie Woogie Dancin' Shoes		Chrysalis 1232

BARRY, Len
Born Leonard Borisoff on 6/12/1942 in Philadelphia, Pennsylvania. Lead singer of **The Dovells** from 1957-63.

11/20/65	90	13		1 1-2-3		Decca 74720

BARRY And The TAMERLANES
Pop vocal trio from Los Angeles, California: songwriters Barry DeVorzon, Terry Smith and Bodie Chandler. DeVorzon founded the Valiant label and began his ongoing prolific songwriting career in the mid-1950s.

~ ~ ~ ~ ~ ~ ~ ~ ~ ~ **NON-CHARTED ALBUM** ~ ~ ~ ~ ~ ~ ~ ~ ~ ~
1963 **I Wonder What She's Doing Tonight**

BARTOLI, Cecilia
Born on 6/4/1966 in Rome, Italy. Opera singer.

11/14/09	189	1		1 Sacrificium		Decca 013412

BARTON, Lou Ann
Born on 2/17/1954 in Fort Worth, Texas. Female blues singer.

4/24/82	133	9		1 Old Enough		Asylum 60032
				produced by **Glenn Frey**		

BASEMENT JAXX
Electro-dance/rock production duo from England: Simon Ratcliffe and Felix Buxton.

7/14/01	149	3		1 Rooty		Astralwerks 10423
11/8/03	172	1		2 Kish Kash		XL 93878
10/10/09	173	1		3 Scars		XL 2175

BASIA
Born Basia Trzetrzelewska on 9/30/1959 in Jaworzno, Poland. Female pop singer.

2/20/88	36	77	▲	1 Time And Tide		Epic 40767
3/3/90	20	38	▲	2 London Warsaw New York		Epic 45472
5/21/94	27	18	●	3 The Sweetest Illusion		Epic 64255

BASIC BLACK
R&B band from Los Angeles, California: Darryl Adams (vocals), Walter Scott and Lloyd Turner (keyboards) and Kelvin Bradshaw (drums).

11/17/90	178	1		1 Basic Black		Motown 6307

BASIE, Count   All-Time: #473
Born William Basie on 8/21/1904 in Red Bank, New Jersey. Died of cancer on 4/26/1984 (age 79). Legendary jazz, big-band leader/pianist/organist. Appeared in many movies.
AWARD: Grammys: Trustees 1981 / Lifetime Achievement 2002

2/2/63	5	42		1 Sinatra-Basie		Reprise 1008
				FRANK SINATRA & COUNT BASIE		
7/20/63	19	27		2 This Time By Basie! Hits Of The 50's And 60's	[I]	Reprise 6070
				Grammy: Dance Band		
9/7/63	123	5		3 Li'l Ol' Groovemaker...Basie!	[I]	Verve 8549
10/19/63	69	20		4 Ella And Basie!		Verve 4061
				ELLA FITZGERALD & COUNT BASIE		
				Grammy: Hall of Fame		
2/22/64	150	1		5 More Hits Of The 50's And 60's	[I]	Verve 8563
8/22/64	13	31		6 It Might As Well Be Swing		Reprise 1012
				FRANK SINATRA & COUNT BASIE		
3/27/65	141	4		7 Our Shining Hour		Verve 8605
				SAMMY DAVIS, JR. & COUNT BASIE		
3/26/66	107	13		8 Arthur Prysock/Count Basie		Verve 8646
12/10/66	143	2		9 Broadway Basie's...Way	[I]	Command 905
4/6/68	145	6		10 The Board Of Directors		Dot 25838
				COUNT BASIE & THE MILLS BROTHERS		
6/1/68	195	3		11 Manufacturers Of Soul		Brunswick 754134
				JACKIE WILSON & COUNT BASIE		
10/21/06	23	11		12 Ray Sings Basie Swings	[L]	Hear 30026
				RAY CHARLES & THE COUNT BASIE ORCHESTRA		
11/15/08	28	9		13 A Swingin' Christmas	[X]	RPM 32250
				TONY BENNETT Featuring The Count Basie Big Band		
				Christmas chart: 6/'08		

BASIL, Toni
Born Antonia Basilotta on 9/22/1943 in Philadelphia, Pennsylvania. Choreographer/actress. Worked on TV shows *Shindig* and *Hullabaloo*. Choreographed the movie *American Grafitti*. Appeared in the movie *Easy Rider*.

10/23/82	22	30	●	1 Word Of Mouth		Chrysalis 1410
2/4/84	206	2		2 Toni Basil		Chrysalis 41449

BASS, Fontella
Born on 7/3/1940 in St. Louis, Missouri. R&B singer/pianist.

2/26/66	93	8		1 The New Look		Checker 2997

BASS BOY
Born James McCauley in Sarasota, Florida. Mixer/scratcher of bass-heavy samples. Also see **Bass Outlaws**.

6/6/92	160	12		1 I Got The Bass	[I]	Newtown 2209

BASSEY, Shirley
Born on 1/8/1937 in Cardiff, Wales (African father). R&B singer. Began professional career at age 16 as a member of the touring show *Memories Of Al Jolson*. Became a popular club attraction in America in 1961. Named Dame by Queen Elizabeth on 12/31/1999.

4/24/65	85	9		1 Shirley Bassey Belts The Best!		United Artists 6419
10/17/70	105	13		2 Shirley Bassey Is Really "Something"		United Artists 6765
6/12/71	123	24		3 Something Else		United Artists 6797
3/18/72	94	13		4 I Capricorn		United Artists 5565
11/25/72	171	8		5 And I Love You So		United Artists 5643
5/26/73	60	19		6 Never, Never, Never		United Artists 055
9/22/73	136	8		7 Live At Carnegie Hall	[L]	United Artists 111 [2]
				recorded on 5/11/1973		
9/21/74	142	6		8 Nobody Does It Like Me		United Artists 214
11/29/75	186	3		9 Good, Bad But Beautiful		United Artists 542
10/9/76	149	8		10 Love, Life And Feelings		United Artists 605
1/22/77	205	5		11 Shirley Bassey's Greatest Hits	[G]	United Artists 715 [2]
7/23/77	204	5		12 You Take My Heart Away		United Artists 751

BASS OUTLAWS
Hardcore bass duo from Florida: **Bass Boy** and **Techmaster P.E.B.**

1/30/93	165	8		1 Illegal Bass	[I]	Newtown 2210

BATDORF & RODNEY
Pop duo formed in Los Angeles, California: John Batdorf and Mark Rodney. Batdorf formed the group **Silver** in 1976.

3/11/72	214	1	1 Off The Shelf	Atlantic 8298
10/28/72	185	7	2 Batdorf & Rodney	Asylum 5056
7/12/75	140	10	3 Life Is You	Arista 4041

BATES, Jeff
Born on 9/19/1963 in Bunker Hill, Mississippi. Country singer/songwriter/guitarist.

6/7/03	117	13	1 Rainbow Man	Cat:#11/4	RCA 67071
4/29/06	62	3	2 Leave The Light On		RCA 78801

BAT FOR LASHES
Born Natasha Khan on 10/25/1979 in London, England. Female alternative-rock singer/songwriter/guitarist.

4/25/09	141	2	1 Two Suns	Echo Label 93020

BATON ROUGE
Hard-rock band from New Orleans, Louisiana: Kelly Keeling (vocals, guitar), Lance Bulen (guitar), David Cremin (keyboards), Scott Bender (bass) and Corky McClellan (drums).

6/2/90	160	12	1 Shake Your Soul	Atlantic 82073

BATTISTELLI, Francesca
Born on 5/18/1985 in Manhattan, New York. Christian singer/songwriter.

3/14/09	91	35	1 My Paper Heart	Fervent 887378

BATTLE, Kathleen, & Jessye Norman
Duo of opera stars. Battle was born on 8/13/1948 in Portsmouth, Ohio. Norman was born on 9/15/1945 in Augusta, Georgia.

5/4/91	186	2	1 Spirituals In Concert	[L]	Deutsche G. 429790
			recorded on 3/18/1990 at Carnegie Hall		

BAUHAUS
Goth-rock band from Northampton, England: **Peter Murphy** (vocals, keyboards), **Daniel Ash** (guitar), David Jay (bass) and Kevin Haskins (drums). Disbanded in 1983. Murphy went solo. The latter three formed **Love & Rockets**.

8/12/89	169	6	1 Swing The Heartache - The BBC Sessions	[E]	Beggars Banquet 9804 [2]
			recorded from 1980-83		
3/22/08	105	1	2 Go Away White		Bauhaus 001

BAXTER, Les, & His Orchestra
Born on 3/14/1922 in Mexia, Texas. Died of a heart attack on 1/15/1996 (age 73). Orchestra leader/arranger. **1950s: #45**

6/11/55	14	4	1 Blue Mirage	[EP]	Capitol 599
1/28/56	6	1	2 Tamboo!	[I]	Capitol 655
3/16/57	21	2	3 Skins!	[I]	Capitol 774

BAY CITY ROLLERS
Pop-rock band from Edinburgh, Scotland: Les McKeown (vocals; born on 11/12/1955), brothers Alan Longmuir (guitar; born on 6/20/1948) and Derek Longmuir (drums; born on 5/19/1951), Eric Faulkner (guitar; born on 10/21/1955) and Stuart "Woody" Wood (bass; born on 2/25/1957). Alan Longmuir left in mid-1976; returned in 1978. Ian Mitchell (guitar) joined briefly in 1976.

9/27/75+	20	35	●	1 Bay City Rollers		Arista 4049
3/20/76	31	16	●	2 Rock N' Roll Love Letter		Arista 4071
9/18/76	26	25	●	3 Dedication		Arista 4093
7/23/77	23	11	●	4 It's A Game		Arista 7004
12/3/77+	77	11	●	5 Greatest Hits	[G]	Arista 4158
10/14/78	129	4		6 Strangers In The Wind		Arista 4194

BAYSIDE
Punk-rock band from Long Island, New York: Anthony Raneri (vocals), Jack O'Shea (guitar), Nick Ghanbarian (bass) and John "Beatz" Holohan (drums).

9/10/05	153	1	1 Bayside		Victory 258
3/18/06	200	1	2 Acoustic	[L]	Victory 293
2/24/07	75	3	3 The Walking Wounded		Victory 336
10/18/08	54	2	4 Shudder		Victory 457

BAZAN, David
Born in January 1976 in Seattle, Washington. Alternative-rock singer/songwriter.

9/19/09	116	1	1 Curse Your Branches	Barusk 083

B.B.&Q. BAND — see BROOKLYN, BRONX & QUEENS BAND

BBMAK
Male pop trio from Liverpool, England: Mark Barry, Christian Burns and Steve McNally.

6/3/00	38	44	●	1 Sooner Or Later	Hollywood 62260
9/14/02	25	5		2 Into Your Head	Hollywood 62320

BEACH BOYS, The
1960s: #19 / 1970s: #39 / All-Time: #12

Surf-rock band from Hawthorne, California: brothers **Brian Wilson** (keyboards, bass; born on 6/20/1942), **Carl Wilson** (guitar; born on 12/21/1946; died of cancer on 2/6/1998, age 51) and **Dennis Wilson** (drums; born on 12/4/1944; drowned on 12/28/1983, age 39); their cousin Mike Love (lead vocals, saxophone; born on 3/15/1941) and Al Jardine (guitar; born on 9/3/1942). Jardine replaced by David Marks from March 1962 to March 1963. Brian quit touring with group in December 1964; replaced briefly by **Glen Campbell** until Bruce Johnston (born on 6/27/1944) joined permanently in April 1965. Brian continued to write for and produce group; returned to stage in 1983. Daryl Dragon (**Captain & Tennille**) was a keyboardist in their stage band. Carnie and Wendy Wilson, daughters of Brian Wilson, were members of **Wilson Phillips**.

AWARDS: Grammy: Lifetime Achievement 2001 ★ R&R Hall of Fame: 1988

DEBUT	PEAK	WKS			Title	Catalog	Label & Number
11/24/62+	32	37		1	Surfin' Safari		Capitol 1808
5/4/63	2²	78	●	2	Surfin' U.S.A.		Capitol 1890
10/12/63	7	56	●	3	Surfer Girl		Capitol 1981
11/9/63+	4	46	▲	4	Little Deuce Coupe		Capitol 1998
4/11/64	13	38	●	5	Shut Down, Volume 2		Capitol 2027
8/1/64	4	49	●	6	All Summer Long		Capitol 2110
3/27/65	4	50	●	7	The Beach Boys Today!		Capitol 2269
					RS500 #270		
7/24/65	2¹	33	●	8	Summer Days (And Summer Nights!!)		Capitol 2354
11/27/65+	6	24		9	Beach Boys' Party!		Capitol 2398
5/28/66	10	39	▲	10	Pet Sounds		Capitol 2458
					Grammy: Hall of Fame ★ RS500 #2 ★ NRR		
9/30/67	41	21		11	Smiley Smile		Brother 9001
12/30/67+	24	15		12	Wild Honey		Capitol 2859
7/6/68	126	10		13	Friends		Capitol 2895
3/1/69	68	11		14	20/20		Capitol 133
9/26/70	151	4		15	Sunflower		Brother 6382
					RS500 #380		
9/11/71	29	17		16	Surf's Up		Brother 6453
1/27/73	36	30		17	Holland		Brother 2118
7/17/76	8	27	●	18	15 Big Ones		Brother 2251
4/30/77	53	7		19	Love You		Brother 2258
10/21/78	151	4		20	M.I.U. Album		Brother 2268
					MIU: Maharishi International University		
4/7/79	100	13		21	L.A. (Light Album)		Caribou 35752
4/12/80	75	6		22	Keepin' The Summer Alive		Caribou 36283
6/29/85	52	14		23	The Beach Boys		Caribou 39946
9/7/96	101	8		24	Stars And Stripes Vol. 1		River North 1205
					CHRISTMAS ALBUMS:		
12/5/64	6ˣ	13	●	25	The Beach Boys' Christmas Album		Capitol 2164
					Christmas charts: 6/'64, 7/'65, 26/'66, 72/'67, 14/'68		
11/25/00+	20ˣ	3		26	The Beach Boys Ultimate Christmas	Cat:#26/2	Capitol 95734
					GREATEST HITS & COMPILATIONS:		
7/23/66	8	78	▲²	27	Best Of The Beach Boys		Capitol 2545
8/12/67	50	22	▲²	28	Best Of The Beach Boys, Vol. 2		Capitol 2706
9/7/68	153	6		29	Best Of The Beach Boys, Vol. 3		Capitol 2945
7/20/74	❶¹	156	▲³	30	Endless Summer		Capitol 11307 [2]
5/3/75	8	43	●	31	Spirit Of America		Capitol 11384 [2]
7/19/75	25	23		32	Good Vibrations-Best Of The Beach Boys		Brother 2223
12/26/81+	156	8		33	Ten Years Of Harmony (1970-1980)		Caribou 37445 [2]
7/3/82	180	6		34	Sunshine Dream		Capitol 12220 [2]
7/26/86	96	12	▲²	35	Made In U.S.A.		Capitol 12396 [2]
9/16/89	46	22	▲	36	Still Cruisin'		Capitol 92639
4/20/96	198	1	▲²	37	20 Good Vibrations - The Greatest Hits	Cat:#22/18	Capitol 29418
3/18/00	95	11		38	The Greatest Hits - Volume 1: 20 Good Vibrations	Cat:#7/64	Capitol 21860
3/18/00	192	1		39	The Greatest Hits - Volume 2: 20 More Good Vibrations		Capitol 20238
3/18/00	26ᶜ	1		40	The Best Of The Beach Boys		EMI-Capitol 19707
7/20/02	159	1		41	The Beach Boys Classics Selected By Brian Wilson		Capitol 40087
6/28/03	16	104	▲²	42	The Very Best Of The Beach Boys: Sounds Of Summer	Cat:❶⁵/142	Capitol 82710
6/9/07	40	7		43	The Warmth Of The Sun		Capitol 44964
					LIVE ALBUMS:		
11/7/64	❶⁴	62	●	44	Beach Boys Concert		Capitol 2198
					recorded on 8/1/1964 at the Civic Auditorium in Sacramento, California		
12/8/73+	25	24	●	45	The Beach Boys In Concert		Brother 6484 [2]
12/11/76+	75	10		46	Beach Boys '69 (The Beach Boys Live In London)		Capitol 11584
					REISSUES:		
8/16/69	136	6		47	Close-Up		Capitol 253 [2]
6/3/72	50	20		48	Pet Sounds/Carl And The Passions - So Tough		Brother 2083 [2]
8/3/74	50	11		49	Wild Honey & 20/20		Brother 2166 [2]
11/9/74	125	6		50	Friends & Smiley Smile		Brother 2167 [2]
6/16/90	162	5		51	Pet Sounds	Cat:#8/6	Capitol 48421

Billboard			R I A A	ARTIST		
DEBUT	PEAK	WKS		Album Title	Catalog	Label & Number

BEACH HOUSE
Electro-pop duo formed in Baltimore, Maryland: Victoria Legrand and Alex Scally.

| 3/15/08 | 195 | 1 | | 1 Devotion .... | | Carpark 42 |

BEACON STREET UNION
Rock band from Boston, Massachusetts: John Lincoln Wright (vocals), Paul Tartachny (guitar), Robert Rhodes (keyboards), Wayne Ulaky (bass) and Richard Weisberg (drums).

| 3/9/68 | 75 | 16 | | 1 The Eyes Of The Beacon Street Union.. | | MGM 4517 |
| 9/14/68 | 173 | 10 | | 2 The Clown Died In Marvin Gardens .... | | MGM 4568 |

BEAR, Edward — see EDWARD

BEARS, The
Pop-rock band formed in Los Angeles, California: **Adrian Belew** (vocals), Rob Fetters (guitar), Bob Nyswonger (bass) and Chris Arduser (drums).

| 4/30/88 | 159 | 5 | | 1 Rise And Shine .... | | I.R.S. 42139 |

BEAST
Rock band from Denver, Colorado: David Raines (vocals), Robert Yeazel (guitar), Gerry Fike (organ), Michael Kerns (flute), Dominick Todero (trumpet), Ken Passarelli (bass) and Larry Ferris (drums).

| 9/13/69 | 195 | 2 | | 1 Beast .... | | Cotillion 9012 |

BEASTIE BOYS   1990s: #40 / All-Time: #172
White rap-punk trio from Brooklyn, New York: Adam "King Ad-Rock" Horovitz (born on 10/31/1966), Adam "MCA" Yauch (born on 8/15/1967) and Michael "Mike D" Diamond (born on 11/20/1965). Horovitz was married to actress Ione Skye (daughter of **Donovan**) from 1991-99. Group ran own Grand Royal record label from 1993-2001.

11/29/86+	❶⁷	68	▲⁹	1 Licensed To Ill Cat:❶²⁶/437	Def Jam 40238
				RS500 #217	
8/12/89	14	15	▲²	2 Paul's Boutique.. Cat:#6/29	Capitol 91743
				RS500 #156	
5/9/92	10	35	▲²	3 Check Your Head Cat:#11/16	Capitol 98938
2/26/94	46	7		4 Some Old Bullshit .... [K]	Grand Royal 89843
6/18/94	❶¹	62	▲³	5 Ill Communication Cat:#21/11	Grand Royal 28599
6/10/95	50	8		6 Root Down.. [EP-L]	Grand Royal 33603
4/20/96	45	7		7 The In Sound From Way Out! .... [I]	Grand Royal 33590
8/1/98	❶³	48	▲³	8 Hello Nasty	Grand Royal 37716
				Grammy: Alternative Album	
12/11/99	19	17		9 Beastie Boys Anthology: The Sounds Of Science .... [K]	Grand Royal 22940 [2]
7/3/04	❶¹	19	▲	10 To The 5 Boroughs	Capitol 84571
11/26/05	42	11		11 Solid Gold Hits .... [G]	Brooklyn Dust 44049
7/14/07	15	9		12 The Mix-Up .... [I]	Brooklyn Dust 94085
				Grammy: Pop Instrumental Album	

BEAT FARMERS, The
Alternative-rock band from Los Angeles, California: Joey Harris (vocals, guitar), Jerry Raney (guitar), Rollie Love (bass) and Country Dick Montana (drums). Montana died of a heart attack on 11/8/1995 (age 40).

6/8/85	186	3		1 Tales Of The New West...	Rhino 853
7/12/86	135	9		2 Van Go..	MCA/Curb 5759
9/5/87	131	8		3 The Pursuit Of Happiness	MCA/Curb 5993

BEATLES, The   1960s: #1 / 1970s: #43 / 2000s: #21 / All-Time: #3
The world's #1 rock band was formed in Liverpool, England, in the late 1950s. Known in early forms as The Quarrymen, Johnny & the Moondogs, The Rainbows, and the Silver Beatles. Named The Beatles in 1960. Originally consisted of **John Lennon** (vocals, rhythm guitar; born on 10/9/1940; shot to death on 12/8/1980, age 40), **Paul McCartney** (vocals, bass; born on 6/18/1942), **George Harrison** (lead guitar; born on 2/24/1943; died of lung cancer on 11/29/2001, age 58) and **Ringo Starr** (drums; born on 7/7/1940). Early member Stuart Sutcliffe (bass; born on 6/23/1940; died of a brain hemorrhage on 4/10/1962, age 21) left in April 1961. Original drummer Pete Best (drums; born on 11/24/1941) was fired in August 1962. Group managed by Brian Epstein (born on 9/19/1934; died of a sleeping-pill overdose on 8/27/1967, age 32) and produced by **George Martin**. First U.S. tour in February 1964. Group starred in the movies *A Hard Day's Night* (1964), *Help* (1965), *Magical Mystery Tour* (1967) and *Let It Be* (1970); contributed soundtrack to the animated movie *Yellow Submarine* (1968). Started own Apple label in 1968. McCartney publicly announced group's dissolution on 4/10/1970. Also see **Various Artists Compilations: Come Together - America Salutes The Beatles.**
AWARDS: Grammys: Best New Artist 1964 / Trustees 1972 ★ R&R Hall of Fame: 1988

2/1/64	❶¹¹	71	▲⁵	1 Meet The Beatles!	Capitol 2047
				Grammy: Hall of Fame ★ RS500 #59	
2/8/64	2⁹	49		2 Introducing...The Beatles	Vee-Jay 1062
				first pressings included "Love Me Do" and "P.S. I Love You;" replaced with "Please Please Me" and "Ask Me Why"	
4/25/64	❶⁵	55	▲²	3 The Beatles' Second Album	Capitol 2080
8/8/64	2⁹	41	▲²	4 Something New	Capitol 2108
				includes 5 songs from the soundtrack album *A Hard Day's Night*	
1/2/65	❶⁹	71	▲³	5 Beatles '65	Capitol 2228

BEATLES, The — cont'd

DEBUT	PEAK	WKS	RIAA	#	Album Title	Catalog	Label & Number
6/26/65	**❶**[6]	41	▲	6 Beatles VI		Capitol 2358
12/25/65+	**❶**[6]	63	▲[6]	7 Rubber Soul	Cat:#4/44	Capitol 2442
				Grammy: Hall of Fame ★ RS500 #5		
				producer George Martin said this was the first rock album to be thought of as a work of art		
9/3/66	**❶**[6]	80	▲[5]	8 Revolver	Cat:#5/43	Capitol 2576
				Grammy: Hall of Fame ★ RS500 #3		
				producer George Martin stated that The Beatles started developing their best songwriting skills for this album		
6/24/67	**❶**[15]	184	▲[11]	9 Sgt. Pepper's Lonely Hearts Club Band	Cat:**❶**[1]/229	Capitol 2653
				Grammys: Album of the Year / Pop Album / Hall of Fame ★ RS500 #1 ★ NRR		
12/14/68	**❶**[9]	168	▲[19]	10 The Beatles [White Album]	Cat:#2[2]/112	Apple 101 [2]
				Grammy: Hall of Fame ★ RS500 #10		
				John Lennon stated that "every track is an individual track - there isn't any Beatle music on it"		
10/18/69	**❶**[11]	148	▲[12]	11 Abbey Road	Cat:**❶**[2]/221	Apple 383
				Grammy: Hall of Fame ★ RS500 #14		
				the last album recorded by The Beatles and now regarded by many as one of their best albums		
5/30/70	**❶**[4]	60	▲[4]	12 Let It Be	Cat:#8/12 **[S]**	Apple 34001
				Grammy: Soundtrack Album ★ RS500 #86		
				originally recorded in January 1969 for an unreleased album *Get Back*; re-produced by Phil Spector		

EARLY ALBUMS:

DEBUT	PEAK	WKS	RIAA	#	Album Title	Catalog	Label & Number
2/15/64	68	14		13 The Beatles With Tony Sheridan And Their Guests		MGM 4215
				recorded in 1961 in Hamburg, Germany, with Tony Sheridan (lead singer) and Pete Best (drums); other cuts are by American studio musicians The Titans		
4/4/64	104	6		14 Jolly What! The Beatles & Frank Ifield .... **[K]**		Vee-Jay 1085
				4 tracks are by The Beatles and 8 by Frank Ifield		
10/10/64	142	3		15 The Beatles vs. The Four Seasons .... **[R]**		Vee-Jay 30 [2]
				12 tracks by The Beatles and The Four Seasons; The Beatles tracks are the same as the second pressing of #2 above		
5/16/70	117	7		16 The Beatles Featuring Tony Sheridan - In The Beginning (Circa 1960)........		Polydor 4504
				recorded in Hamburg, Germany, as 'Tony Sheridan and the Beat Brothers,' and 'The Beatles with Tony Sheridan'		
12/24/94	3[1]	24	▲[4]	17 Live At The BBC	**[L]**	Apple 31796 [2]
				56 songs as performed for Britain's BBC radio broadcasts between March 1962 and June 1965		

GREATEST HITS & COMPILATIONS:

DEBUT	PEAK	WKS	RIAA	#	Album Title	Catalog	Label & Number
7/9/66	**❶**[5]	31	▲[2]	18 "Yesterday"...And Today		Capitol 2553
				originally released with the infamous "Butcher Cover" and quickly recalled and replaced with the "Trunk Cover"		
3/21/70	2[4]	33	▲[3]	19 Hey Jude		Apple 385
4/14/73	3[2]	164	▲[15]	20 The Beatles/1962-1966	Cat:#2[2]/63	Apple 3403 [2]
4/14/73	**❶**[1]	169	▲[16]	21 The Beatles/1967-1970	Cat:**❶**[4]/88	Apple 3404 [2]
6/26/76	2[2]	30	▲	22 Rock 'N' Roll Music		Capitol 11537 [2]
7/24/82	11[C]	71	▲	23 Rock 'N' Roll Music, Volume 1	**[R]**	Capitol 16020
7/24/82	7[C]	95	▲	24 Rock 'N' Roll Music, Volume 2	**[R]**	Capitol 16021
11/12/77	24	31	▲[3]	25 Love Songs		Capitol 11711 [2]
4/12/80	21	15	●	26 Rarities		Capitol 12060
4/10/82	19	12	●	27 Reel Music		Capitol 12199
11/13/82+	50	28	▲[2]	28 20 Greatest Hits		Capitol 12245
4/2/88	149	6	▲	29 Past Masters - Volume One .... Cat:#39/1		Capitol 90043
4/2/88	121	7	▲	30 Past Masters - Volume Two .... Cat:#30/2		Capitol 90044
12/9/95	**❶**[3]	29	▲[8]	31 Anthology 1		Apple 34445 [2]
4/6/96	**❶**[1]	37	▲[4]	32 Anthology 2		Apple 34448 [2]
11/16/96	**❶**[1]	16	▲[3]	33 Anthology 3		Apple 46332 [2]
12/2/00	**❶**[8]	111	▲[11]	34 1	Cat:**❶**[9]/357	Apple 29325
				The Beatles' combined 27 #1 hits from the U.S. and U.K. charts		
12/9/06	4	76	▲[2]	35 Love	Cat:#21/50	Apple 79808

LIVE ALBUMS:

DEBUT	PEAK	WKS	RIAA	#	Album Title	Catalog	Label & Number
5/21/77	2[2]	17	▲	36 The Beatles At The Hollywood Bowl	**[E]**	Capitol 11638
				recorded at the 1964 and 1965 concerts in Los Angeles, California		
7/2/77	111	7		37 The Beatles Live! At The Star-Club In Hamburg, Germany; 1962........ **[E]**		Lingasong 7001 [2]

REISSUES:

DEBUT	PEAK	WKS	RIAA	#	Album Title	Catalog	Label & Number
10/31/64	63	11		38 Songs, Pictures And Stories Of The Fabulous Beatles........		Vee-Jay 1092
				reissue of #2 above (second pressing; also see #15 above)		
4/24/65	43	35	▲	39 The Early Beatles .... **[E]**		Capitol 2309
				reissue by Capitol of the Vee-Jay recordings (all on the first or second pressings of #2 above)		
11/14/92+	12[C]	8	▲	40 Please Please Me		Capitol 46435
				U.S. issue of The Beatles first British album		
12/6/03	5	14	▲	41 Let It Be...Naked		Apple 95713
				reissue of #12 above, minus Phil Spector's orchestral overdubs		
12/4/04	35	6	▲	42 The Capitol Albums Vol. 1		Apple 66878 [4]
				box set of albums #1, 3, 4 & 5 above; each presented in both stereo and mono mixes		
4/29/06	46	2	●	43 The Capitol Albums Vol. 2		Apple 57716 [4]
				box set of albums #6, 7, 39 & 49; each presented in both stereo and mono mixes		
9/26/09	13[C]	6		44 With The Beatles		Apple 82420
				U.S. issue of The Beatles second British album		
9/26/09	14[C]	6		45 Beatles For Sale		Apple 82414
				U.S. issue of The Beatles fourth British album		
9/26/09	15	13	▲[3]	46 The Beatles In Stereo		Apple 99449 [16]
				box set of albums #7, 8, 9, 10, 11, 12, 29, 30, 40, 44, 45, 48, 49, 50 & 51		

Billboard DEBUT	PEAK	WKS	R I A A	ARTIST Album Title	Catalog	Label & Number

BEATLES, The — cont'd

9/26/09	40	4	▲	47 **The Beatles In Mono**		Apple 99451 [13]
				box set of albums #7, 8, 9, 10, 40, 44, 45, 48, 49 & 50, with new *Mono Masters* disc		

SOUNDTRACKS:

7/18/64	❶ 14	52	▲4	48 **A Hard Day's Night** .... Cat:#11/10		United Artists 6366
				Grammy: Hall of Fame ★ RS500 #388		
				includes instrumentals produced by musical director George Martin		
8/28/65	❶ 9	44	▲3	49 **Help!** .... Cat:#7/16		Capitol 2386
				RS500 #332		
				includes 5 instrumentals produced by musical director Ken Thorne		
12/23/67+	❶ 8	91	▲6	50 **Magical Mystery Tour** .... Cat:#10/30		Capitol 2835
				6 tracks are from the television movie		
2/8/69	2 2	25	▲	51 **Yellow Submarine** .... Cat:#17/5		Apple 153
				6 tracks are vocals from the animated movie; plus 6 re-recorded instrumental selections		
10/2/99	15	15	●	52 **Yellow Submarine Songtrack** .... [R]		Apple 21481
				remixes of the original 6 vocals from #51 above, plus 9 more new remixed songs		

SPECIALTY ALBUMS:

6/6/64	20	13		53 **The American Tour With Ed Rudy** .... [T]		RadioPulsebeat 2
				American radio reporter Ed Rudy interviews The Beatles and their fans		
12/12/64+	7	17	●	54 **The Beatles' Story** .... [T]		Capitol 2222 [2]
				50-minute documentary featuring interviews and portions of several of the Beatles' recordings		

BEATNUTS, The

Latin hip-hop trio from Queens, New York: Jerry "JuJu" Tineo, "Psycho" Les Fernandez and Bert "Fashion" Smalls (left after first album; later changed name to Al Tariq).

7/9/94	182	2		1 **The Beatnuts**		Relativity 1179
7/12/97	154	1		2 **Stone Crazy**		Relativity 1508
9/18/99	35	8		3 **A Musical Massacre**		Violator 1722
4/7/01	51	7		4 **Take It Or Squeeze It**		Loud 1906
9/18/04	196	1		5 **Milk Me**		Penalty 7001

BEATS INTERNATIONAL

Dance band from England: Lester Noel (male vocals), Lindy Layton (female vocals), Andy Boucher (keyboards), Norman Cook (bass) and Luke Creswell (drums). Cook was a member of **The Housemartins** and later recorded as **Fatboy Slim**.

5/19/90	162	6		1 **Let Them Eat Bingo**		Elektra 60921

BEAU, Toby — see TOBY

BEAU BRUMMELS, The

Rock band from San Francisco, California: Sal Valentino (vocals), Ron Elliott (guitar), Ron Meagher (bass) and John Petersen (drums). Petersen later joined **Harpers Bizarre**.

5/8/65	24	21		1 **Introducing The Beau Brummels**		Autumn 103
				produced by Sly Stone		
9/30/67	197	2		2 **Triangle**		Warner 1692
7/5/75	180	3		3 **The Beau Brummels**		Warner 2842

BEAUVOIR, Jean

Born in Chicago, Illinois (of Haitian parents); raised in Brooklyn, New York. Male rock singer/bassist. Member of the **Plasmatics** and **Little Steven and the Disciples Of Soul**.

6/28/86	93	15		1 **Drums Along The Mohawk**		Columbia 40403

BEAVIS & BUTT-HEAD — see TELEVISION SOUNDTRACKS

BE-BOP DELUXE

Rock band from Wakefield, Yorkshire, England: Bill Nelson (vocals), Andy Clark (keyboards), Charles Tumahai (bass) and Simon Fox (drums). Tumahai died of a heart attack on 12/21/1995 (age 46).

9/27/75	203	6		1 **Futurama**		Harvest 11432
2/7/76	96	17		2 **Sunburst Finish**		Harvest 11478
10/16/76	88	8		3 **Modern Music**		Harvest 11575
8/20/77	65	15		4 **Live! In The Air Age** .... [L]		Harvest 11666 [2]
3/11/78	95	9		5 **Drastic Plastic**		Harvest 11750
2/17/79	202	6		6 **The Best Of And The Rest Of Be Bop Deluxe** .... [K]		Harvest 11870 [2]

BECK   **All-Time: #493**

Born Beck David Campbell (later changed his last name to his mother's maiden name of Hansen) on 7/8/1970 in Los Angeles, California. Alternative-rock singer/songwriter/guitarist. Married actress Marissa Ribisi on 4/3/2004.

3/19/94	13	24	▲	1 **Mellow Gold**		DGC 24634
7/6/96	16	88	▲2	2 **Odelay** .... Cat:#16/1		DGC 24823
				Grammy: Alternative Album ★ RS500 #305		
11/21/98	13	14	●	3 **Mutations**		DGC 25309
				Grammy: Alternative Album		
12/11/99	34	18	●	4 **Midnite Vultures**		DGC 490485
10/12/02	8	26	●	5 **Sea Change**		DGC 493393
				RS500 #440		
4/16/05	2 1	26	●	6 **Guero**		Interscope 003481
12/31/05	191	1		7 **Guerolito** .... [K]		Interscope 005972
				contains new mixes and versions of songs from #6 above		

			R I A A	ARTIST		
DEBUT	**PEAK**	**WKS**		**Album Title**	**Catalog**	**Label & Number**

BECK — cont'd

| 10/21/06 | 7 | 23 | | 8 The Information | | Interscope 007576 |
| 7/26/08 | 4 | 15 | | 9 Modern Guilt | | DGC 011507 |

BECK, Jeff   **All-Time: #224**

Born on 6/24/1944 in Wallington, Surrey, England. Prolific rock guitarist. With **The Yardbirds** from 1965-66. Lineup of **Jeff Beck Group** from 1968-69: Beck, **Rod Stewart** (vocals), **Ronnie Wood** (bass), **Nicky Hopkins** (keyboards) and Tony Newman (drums); group's lineup from 1970-72: Beck, Bob Tench (vocals), Clive Chaman (bass), Max Middleton (piano) and Cozy Powell (drums; **Emerson, Lake & Powell; Black Sabbath**). Member of **The Honeydrippers**.

    AWARD: R&R Hall of Fame: 2009

8/24/68	15	33	●	1 Truth		Epic 26413
7/12/69	15	21	●	2 Beck-Ola		Epic 26478
11/6/71	46	16		3 Rough And Ready		Epic 30973
5/13/72	19	26	●	4 Jeff Beck Group		Epic 31331
4/7/73	12	27	●	5 Jeff Beck, Tim Bogert, Carmine Appice		Epic 32140
				JEFF BECK GROUP (above 3)		
4/12/75	4	25	▲	6 Blow By Blow Cat:#12/209 [I]		Epic 33409
6/26/76	16	25	▲	7 Wired Cat:#21/96 [I]		Epic 33849
4/2/77	23	15	●	8 Jeff Beck With The Jan Hammer Group Live [I-L]		Epic 34433
				recorded at Scorpio Sound Studios in London, England		
7/12/80	21	20		9 There And Back [I]		Epic 35684
7/20/85	39	18		10 Flash		Epic 39483
10/21/89	49	18		11 Jeff Beck's Guitar Shop [I]		Epic 44313
				JEFF BECK WITH TERRY BOZZIO & TONY HYMAS		
				Grammy: Rock Instrumental Album		
7/17/93	171	1		12 Crazy Legs		Epic 53562
				JEFF BECK and The Big Town Playboys		
				tribute to Gene Vincent		
4/3/99	99	5		13 Who Else! [I]		Epic 67987
2/24/01	110	2		14 You Had It Coming [I]		Epic 61625
8/23/03	122	1		15 Jeff [I]		Epic 86941

BECK, Joe

Born on 7/29/1945 in Philadelphia, Pennsylvania. Died on 7/22/2008 (age 62). Jazz-funk guitarist.

| 6/28/75 | 140 | 5 | | 1 Beck [I] | | Kudu 21 |

BECKETT

Born Alston Beckett Cyrus on 8/1/1949 in Layou, West Indies. Disco singer/songwriter.

| 8/20/77 | 210 | 1 | | 1 Disco Calypso | | Casablanca 7059 |

BEDINGFIELD, Daniel

Born on 12/3/1979 in Auckland, New Zealand; raised in Lewisham, London, England. Pop singer/songwriter. Brother of **Natasha Bedingfield**.

| 9/14/02 | 41 | 35 | ● | 1 Gotta Get Thru This | | Island 065113 |

BEDINGFIELD, Natasha

Born on 11/26/1981 in London, England. Pop singer/songwriter. Sister of **Daniel Bedingfield**.

| 8/20/05 | 26 | 47 | ● | 1 Unwritten | | Epic 93988 |
| 2/9/08 | 3[1] | 61 | ● | 2 Pocketful Of Sunshine | | Phonogenic 11748 |

BEDLAM

Hard-rock band formed in England: Francesco Aiello (vocals), brothers Dave Ball (guitar) and Dennis Ball (bass), and Cozy Powell (drums; **Whitesnake; Emerson, Lake & Powell; Black Sabbath**). Powell died in a car crash on 4/5/1998 (age 50).

| 9/29/73 | 207 | 3 | | 1 Bedlam | | Chrysalis 1048 |

BEE GEES   **1970s: #10 / All-Time: #30**

Pop-disco trio of brothers from Manchester, England: **Barry Gibb** (born on 9/1/1946) and twins Maurice Gibb and **Robin Gibb** (born on 12/22/1949). Moved to Australia in 1958, performed as the Gibbs, later as BG's, finally the Bee Gees. Returned to England in February 1967, with guitarist Vince Melouney and drummer Colin Peterson. Melouney left in December 1968; Robin left for solo career in 1969. When Peterson left in August 1969, Barry and Maurice went solo. After eight months, the brothers reunited. Maurice was married to **Lulu** from 1969-73. Composed soundtracks for *Saturday Night Fever* and *Staying Alive*. Acted in the movie *Sgt. Pepper's Lonely Hearts Club Band*. Youngest brother, **Andy Gibb**, was a successful solo singer (died on 3/10/1988). Maurice died of heart failure on 1/12/2003 (age 53).

    AWARDS: Grammy: Legend 2003 ★ R&R Hall of Fame: 1997

8/26/67	7	52		1 Bee Gees' 1st		Atco 223
2/10/68	12	22		2 Horizontal		Atco 233
8/31/68	17	27		3 Idea		Atco 253
2/22/69	20	25		4 Odessa		Atco 702 [2]
5/9/70	94	8		5 Cucumber Castle		Atco 327
1/30/71	32	14		6 2 Years On		Atco 353
9/25/71	34	14		7 Trafalgar		Atco 7003
11/4/72	35	14		8 To Whom It May Concern		Atco 7012
2/3/73	69	13		9 Life In A Tin Can		RSO 870
6/15/74	178	5		10 Mr. Natural		RSO 4800
6/21/75+	14	75	●	11 Main Course		RSO 4807

			R I A A	ARTIST Album Title	Catalog	Label & Number
DEBUT	**PEAK**	**WKS**				

BEE GEES — cont'd

DEBUT	PEAK	WKS				Label & Number
10/2/76	**8**	63	▲	12 **Children Of The World**		RSO 3003
2/17/79	**❶**[6]	55	▲	13 **Spirits Having Flown**		RSO 3041
11/21/81	41	12		14 **Living Eyes**		RSO 3098
10/17/87	96	9		15 **E-S-P**		Warner 25541
8/19/89	68	13		16 **One**		Warner 25887
11/20/93	153	3		17 **Size Isn't Everything**		Polydor 521055
5/24/97	11	21	▲	18 **Still Waters**		Polydor 537302
5/12/01	16	8		19 **This Is Where I Came In**		Universal 549626

EARLY ALBUMS:

DEBUT	PEAK	WKS				Label & Number
12/7/68+	99	12		20 **Rare Precious & Beautiful**		Atco 264
				early Australian recordings (1963-1966)		
3/28/70	100	8		21 **Rare Precious & Beautiful, Volume 2**		Atco 321
				more Australian recordings (1963-1966)		

GREATEST HITS & COMPILATIONS:

DEBUT	PEAK	WKS				Label & Number
7/26/69	**9**	49	●	22 **Best Of Bee Gees**	Cat:#37/1	Atco 292
8/4/73	98	16		23 **Best Of Bee Gees, Vol. 2**		RSO 875
11/13/76+	50	33	●	24 **Bee Gees Gold, Volume One**		RSO 3006
11/17/79+	**❶**[1]	32	▲[2]	25 **Bee Gees Greatest**	Cat:**❶**[2]/76	RSO 4200 [2]
12/8/01	49	40	▲	26 **Their Greatest Hits - The Record**	Cat:#13/6	Universal 589400 [2]
11/27/04	23	60	●	27 **Number Ones**	Cat:#13/10	Polydor 003777
12/24/05	166	3		28 **Love Songs**		Polydor 005561
11/21/09	116	3		29 **The Ultimate Bee Gees**		Reprise 521352 [2]

LIVE ALBUMS:

DEBUT	PEAK	WKS				Label & Number
6/4/77	**8**	90	▲	30 **Here At Last...Bee Gees...Live**		RSO 3901 [2]
				recorded on 12/20/1976 at the Los Angeles Forum		
11/21/98+	72	42	▲	31 **One Night Only**	Cat:**❶**[2]/52	Polydor 559220
				recorded on 11/14/1997 at the MGM Grand in Las Vegas, Nevada		

SOUNDTRACKS:

DEBUT	PEAK	WKS				Label & Number
11/26/77+	**❶**[24]	120	▲[15]	32 **Saturday Night Fever**	Cat:#6/28	RSO 4001 [2]
				Grammys: Album of the Year / Group Pop Vocal / Hall of Fame ★ RS500 #131		
7/16/83	6	27	▲	33 **Staying Alive**		RSO 813269

BEELOW
Born Bruce Moore in Baton Rouge, Louisiana. Male rapper.

DEBUT	PEAK	WKS				Label & Number
3/18/00	146	2		1 **Ballaholic**		Ballin 417105

BEENIE MAN
Born Moses Davis on 8/22/1973 in Kingston, Jamaica. Reggae singer/rapper.

DEBUT	PEAK	WKS				Label & Number
3/21/98	151	12		1 **Many Moods Of Moses**		VP 1513
7/29/00	68	20		2 **Art And Life**		Shocking Vibes 49093
				Grammy: Reggae Album		
9/7/02	18	9		3 **Tropical Storm**		Shocking Vibes 13134
7/31/04	51	10		4 **Back To Basics**		Shocking Vibes 95173
9/16/06	65	4		5 **Undisputed**		Shocking Vibes 11742

BEGA, Lou
Born David Lubega on 4/13/1975 in Munich, Germany (Sicilian mother/Ugandan father). Latin pop-dance singer/songwriter.

DEBUT	PEAK	WKS				Label & Number
9/11/99	**3**[1]	47	▲[3]	1 **A Little Bit Of Mambo**		RCA 67887

BEHEMOTH
Death metal band from Gdansk, Poland: Adam Darski (vocals, guitar), Patryk Sztybor (guitar), Tomasz Wroblewski (bass) and Zbigniew Prominski (drums).

DEBUT	PEAK	WKS				Label & Number
8/4/07	149	1		1 **The Apostasy**		Century Media 18374
8/29/09	55	3		2 **Evangelion**		Metal Blade 14745

BEIRUT
Born Zachary Condon on 2/13/1986 in Santa Fe, New Mexico. Folk singer/songwriter.

DEBUT	PEAK	WKS				Label & Number
10/27/07	118	2		1 **The Flying Club Cup**		Ba Da Bing! 55
3/7/09	87	3		2 **March Of The Zapotec** And Realpeople Holland		Pompeii 001 [2]

BELAFONTE, Harry   1950s: #4 / 1960s: #45 / All-Time: #72
Born on 3/1/1927 in Harlem, New York. Calypso singer/actor. Rode the crest of the calypso craze to worldwide stardom. Starred in several movies. Involved in several humanatarian causes; became UNICEF goodwill ambassador in 1987. Father of actress Shari Belafonte.
          AWARD: Grammy: Lifetime Achievement 2000

DEBUT	PEAK	WKS				Label & Number
1/28/56	**3**[1]	4		1 **"Mark Twain" And Other Folk Favorites**		RCA Victor 1022
2/25/56	**❶**[6]	61	●	2 **Belafonte**		RCA Victor 1150

Billboard			R I A A	ARTIST		
DEBUT	PEAK	WKS		Album Title	Catalog	Label & Number

BELAFONTE, Harry — cont'd

6/16/56	❶³¹	99	●	3 Calypso		RCA Victor 1248
3/30/57	2²	20		4 An Evening With Belafonte		RCA Victor 1402
9/16/57	3²	16		5 Belafonte Sings Of The Caribbean		RCA Victor 1505
10/20/58	16	15		6 Belafonte Sings The Blues		RCA Victor 1006
5/25/59	18	11		7 Love Is A Gentle Thing		RCA Victor 1927
6/22/59	13	22		8 Porgy & Bess		RCA Victor 1507
				LENA HORNE & HARRY BELAFONTE		
11/9/59+	3¹	168	●	9 Belafonte At Carnegie Hall [L]		RCA Victor 6006 [2]
				Grammy: Hall of Fame		
				recorded on 4/20/1959		
12/26/60+	3¹	39	●	10 Belafonte Returns To Carnegie Hall [L]		RCA Victor 6007 [2]
				recorded on 5/2/1960		
3/21/60	34	1		11 My Lord What A Mornin'		RCA Victor 2022
8/28/61	3¹	67	●	12 Jump Up Calypso		RCA Victor 2388
5/12/62	8	24		13 The Midnight Special		RCA Victor 2449
				Bob Dylan (harmonica on title track - his first appearance on record)		
10/20/62	25	22		14 The Many Moods Of Belafonte		RCA Victor 2574
12/22/62	125	2		15 To Wish You A Merry Christmas [X]		RCA Victor 2626
				first released in 1958 on RCA 1887; Christmas charts: 34/'64, 58/'66, 47/'67		
6/22/63	30	26		16 Streets I Have Walked		RCA Victor 2695
4/18/64	17	20		17 Belafonte At The Greek Theatre [L]		RCA Victor 6009 [2]
				recorded on 8/23/1963		
10/17/64	103	7		18 Ballads, Blues And Boasters		RCA Victor 2953
7/10/65	85	11		19 An Evening With Belafonte/Makeba		RCA Victor 3420
				HARRY BELAFONTE & MIRIAM MAKEBA		
				Grammy: Folk Album		
4/9/66	124	8		20 An Evening With Belafonte/Mouskouri		RCA Victor 3415
				HARRY BELAFONTE & NANA MOUSKOURI		
7/16/66	82	10		21 In My Quiet Room		RCA Victor 3571
4/29/67	172	2		22 Calypso In Brass		RCA Victor 3658
7/29/67	199	3		23 Belafonte On Campus		RCA Victor 3779
1/10/70	192	3		24 Homeward Bound		RCA Victor 4255

BELEW, Adrian
Born Robert Steven Belew on 12/23/1949 in Covington, Kentucky. Rock singer/songwriter/guitarist. Member of **King Crimson** from 1981-84 and **The Bears** from 1985-88.

7/24/82	82	9		1 Lone Rhino		Island 9751
10/1/83	146	7		2 Twang Bar King		Island 90108
7/22/89	114	11		3 Mr. Music Head		Atlantic 81959
6/2/90	118	11		4 Young Lions		Atlantic 82099

BELL, Archie, & The Drells
Born on 9/1/1944 in Henderson, Texas. R&B singer. The Drells consisted of James Wise, Lee Bell and Willie Parnell.

5/25/68	142	8		1 Tighten Up		Atlantic 8181
8/16/69	163	3		2 There's Gonna Be A Showdown		Atlantic 8226
1/10/76	95	20		3 Dance Your Troubles Away		TSOP 33844

BELL, Drake
Born Jared Drake Bell on 6/27/1986 in Orange County, California. Pop singer/songwriter/actor. Appeared in several movies and TV shows. Best-known as "Drake Parker" on TV's *Drake & Josh.*

12/23/06	81	5		1 It's Only Time		Universal Motown 008086

BELL, Joshua
Born on 12/9/1967 in Bloomington, Indiana. Classical violinist.

1/31/04	176	2		1 Romance Of The Violin [I]		Sony Classical 87894
9/20/08	134	2		2 Vivaldi: The Four Seasons [I]		Sony Classical 10132
				JOSHUA BELL with Academy Of St. Martin In The Fields		
10/17/09	118	4		3 At Home With Friends [I]		Sony Classical 52716

BELL, Maggie
Born on 1/12/1945 in Glasgow, Scotland. Rock singer. Member of Stone The Crows.

4/20/74	122	13		1 Queen Of The Night		Atlantic 7293
4/5/75	130	8		2 Suicide Sal		Swan Song 8412

BELL, Vincent
Born Vincent Gambella on 7/28/1935 in Brooklyn, New York. Prolific studio guitarist.

6/20/70	75	8		1 Airport Love Theme [I]		Decca 75212

BELL, William
Born William Yarborough on 7/16/1939 in Memphis, Tennessee. R&B singer/songwriter.

5/1/71	209	2		1 Wow...		Stax 2037
4/2/77	63	12		2 Coming Back For More		Mercury 1146

BELLAMY BROTHERS
Country duo from Darby, Florida: brothers Howard Bellamy (born on 2/2/1946) and David Bellamy (born on 9/16/1950). One of the top country acts of the 1980s.

5/15/76	69	12	● 1 Bellamy Brothers		Warner/Curb 2941

BELL & JAMES
R&B duo formed in Portland, Oregon: Leroy Bell and Casey James. Began as songwriting team for Bell's uncle, producer Thom Bell.

2/3/79	31	19	1 Bell & James		A&M 4728
11/3/79	125	4	2 Only Make Believe		A&M 4784

BELL BIV DeVOE
R&B vocal trio from Boston, Massachusetts: Ricky Bell (born on 9/18/1967), Michael Bivins (born on 8/10/1968) and Ronnie DeVoe (born on 11/17/1967). All were members of **New Edition**.

4/7/90	5	77	▲⁴ 1 Poison		MCA 6387
9/14/91	18	27	● 2 WBBD - Bootcity! The Remix Album .... [K]		MCA 10345
7/10/93	19	18	● 3 Hootie Mack		MCA 10682

BELLE, Regina
Born on 7/15/1963 in Englewood, New Jersey. Female R&B singer.

7/11/87	85	15	1 All By Myself		Columbia 40537
9/16/89	63	44	● 2 Stay With Me		Columbia 44367
3/6/93	63	23	● 3 Passion		Columbia 48826
9/23/95	115	9	4 Reachin' Back		Columbia 66813
5/31/08	119	2	5 Love Forever Shines		Pendulum 300208

BELLE AND SEBASTIAN
Alternative-pop band from Glasgow, Scotland: Stuart Murdoch (male vocals), Isobel Campbell (female vocals), Stevie Jackson (guitar), Chris Geddes (keyboards), Stuart David (bass) and Richard Colburn (drums). Group name taken from a French children's TV series. Also see **God Help The Girl**.

7/31/99	39ᶜ	1	1 Tigermilk		Jeepster 361
6/24/00	80	3	2 Fold Your Hands Child, You Walk Like A Peasant ...		Jeepster 429
6/22/02	150	1	3 Storytelling .... [S]		Jeepster 512
10/25/03	84	2	4 Dear Catastrophe Waitress		Rough Trade 83216
2/25/06	65	6	5 The Life Pursuit		Matador 687
12/6/08	141	1	6 The BBC Sessions		Matador 845

BELLE STARS, The
Female band from England: Jennie McKeown (vocals), Sarah-Jane Owen (guitar), Stella Barker (guitar), Miranda Joyce (sax), Clare Hirts (sax), Lesley Shone (bass) and Judy Parsons (drums).

5/28/83	191	2	1 The Belle Stars		Warner 23866

BELLS, The
Pop band from Montreal, Quebec, Canada: Jacki Ralph (female vocals), Cliff Edwards (male vocals), Charles Clarke (guitar), Dennis Will (keyboards), Michael Waye (bass) and Douglas Gravelle (drums).

5/1/71	90	14	1 Fly, Little White Dove, Fly		Polydor 4510

BELLUS, Tony
Born Anthony Bellusci on 4/17/1936 in Chicago, Illinois. Pop singer/accordionist. First recorded for Shi-Fi in 1958.

~ ~ ~ ~ ~ ~ ~ ~ ~ ~ **NON-CHARTED ALBUM** ~ ~ ~ ~ ~ ~ ~ ~ ~ ~
1959 **Robbin' The Cradle**

BELLY
Alternative-rock band from Newport, Rhode Island: Tanya Donelly (vocals, guitar) with brothers Thomas Gorman (guitar) and Chris Gorman (drums). Gail Greenwood (bass) joined by mid-1993. Donelly was a member of Throwing Muses and **The Breeders**.

2/20/93	59	28	● 1 Star		Sire 45187
3/4/95	57	6	2 King		Sire 45833

BELMONTS, The
Doo-wop trio from the Bronx, New York: Angelo D'Aleo, Fred Milano and Carlo Mastrangelo. Sang with **Dion** from 1957-60. Frank Lyndon replaced Mastrangelo in May 1962.

10/27/62	113	7	1 The Belmonts' Carnival Of Hits .... [G]		Sabina 5001

BELOVED, The
Pop-rock duo from England: Jon Marsh (vocals, keyboards) and Steve Waddington (guitars).

4/14/90	154	9	1 Happiness		Atlantic 82047

BELTRAN, Graciela
Born on 12/29/1975 in Sinaloa, Mexico. Female Latin singer.

4/22/95	147	4	1 Las Reinas Del Pueblo .... [F]		EMI Latin 32639
			SELENA & GRACIELA BELTRAN		
2/11/06	168	1	2 Rancherisimas Con Banda .... [F]		Univision 310383

BELUSHI - AYKROYD
Duo of actors/singers/comedians. Jim Belushi was born on 6/15/1954 in Chicago, Illinois. Dan Aykroyd was born on 7/1/1952 in Ottawa, Ontario, Canada. Aykroyd and Jim's older brother John (died of a drug overdose on 3/5/1982, age 33) were the original **Blues Brothers**.

6/21/03	166	2	1 Have Love Will Travel		Have Love 480200

BELVIN, Jesse
Born on 12/15/1933 in Texarkana, Texas; raised in Los Angeles, California. Died in a car crash on 2/6/1960 (age 26).
R&B singer/songwriter.
~ ~ ~ ~ ~ ~ ~ ~ ~ ~ **NON-CHARTED ALBUM** ~ ~ ~ ~ ~ ~ ~ ~ ~ ~ ~
1959 **Just Jesse Belvin**

BENATAR, Pat   **1980s: #16 / All-Time: #239**
Born Patricia Andrzejewski on 1/10/1953 in Brooklyn, New York; raised in Lindenhurst, Long Island, New York. Rock singer/
songwriter. Married to Dennis Benatar from 1971-79; married her producer/guitarist Neil Giraldo on 2/20/1982. Played "Jeanette
Florescu" in the 1980 movie *Union City*.

DEBUT	PEAK	WKS	RIAA	#	Album Title	Catalog	Label & Number
10/20/79+	12	122	▲	1	In The Heat Of The Night		Chrysalis 1236
8/23/80+	2⁵	93	▲⁴	2	Crimes Of Passion		Chrysalis 1275
					Grammy: Female Rock Vocal		
7/25/81	❶¹	54	▲²	3	Precious Time		Chrysalis 1346
11/20/82+	4	46	▲	4	Get Nervous		Chrysalis 1396
10/15/83	13	34	▲	5	Live From Earth	[L]	Chrysalis 41444
11/24/84	14	22	▲	6	Tropico		Chrysalis 41471
12/14/85	26	20	●	7	Seven The Hard Way		Chrysalis 41507
7/23/88	28	29	●	8	Wide Awake In Dreamland		Chrysalis 41628
11/25/89	67	20	▲	9	Best Shots	[G]	Chrysalis 21715
4/27/91	37	22		10	True Love		Chrysalis 21805
6/19/93	85	9		11	Gravity's Rainbow		Chrysalis 21982
6/21/97	171	1		12	Innamorata		CMC Int'l. 86216
8/30/03	187	1		13	Go		Bel Chiasso 79743
6/25/05	47	15	●	14	Greatest Hits	[G]	Capitol 78858

BENEDICTINE MONKS OF SANTO DOMINGO DE SILOS, The
Group of 36 monks who live in an eighth-century monastery in north-central Spain. They sing 1,000-year-old Gregorian chants
in Latin.

DEBUT	PEAK	WKS	RIAA	#	Album Title	Catalog	Label & Number
4/2/94	3¹	53	▲²	1	Chant	[F]	Angel 55138
11/26/94	78	7		2	Chant Noel (Chants For The Holiday Season)	[X-F]	Angel 55206
					Christmas chart: 9/'94		
12/23/95+	172	3		3	Chant II	[E-F-L]	Angel 55504
					recorded on 11/21/1972 at Teatro Real in Madrid, Spain		

BENET, Eric
Born Eric Benet Jordan on 10/15/1970 in Milwaukee, Wisconsin. R&B singer/songwriter. Married to actress Halle Berry from
2001-05.

DEBUT	PEAK	WKS	RIAA	#	Album Title	Catalog	Label & Number
4/26/97	174	5		1	True To Myself		Warner 46270
5/15/99	25	49	●	2	A Day In The Life		Warner 47072
7/9/05	133	1		3	Hurricane		Reprise 47970
9/27/08	11	13		4	Love & Life		Friday 511399

BENNETT, Boyd
Born on 12/7/1924 in Muscle Shoals, Alabama; raised in Nashville, Tennessee. Died of lung failure on 6/2/2002 (age 77).
White rockabilly singer/songwriter/drummer.
~ ~ ~ ~ ~ ~ ~ ~ ~ ~ **NON-CHARTED ALBUM** ~ ~ ~ ~ ~ ~ ~ ~ ~ ~ ~
1955 **Boyd Bennett**

BENNETT, Paris
Born on 8/21/1988 in Rockford, Illinois; later based in Fayetteville, Georgia. Female R&B singer. Finalist on the fifth season of
TV's *American Idol* in 2006.

DEBUT	PEAK	WKS	RIAA	#	Album Title	Catalog	Label & Number
5/26/07	133	1		1	Princess P		306 Records 2760

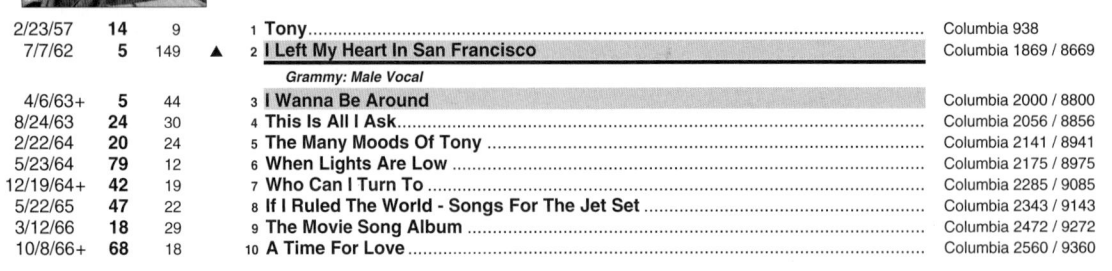

BENNETT, Tony   **1960s: #43 / All-Time: #70**
Born Anthony Benedetto on 8/3/1926 in Queens, New York. Legendary pop/jazz-styled singer. Breakthrough with **Bob Hope**
in 1949 who suggested that he change his then-stage name, Joe Bari, to Tony Bennett. Recorded mostly pop until early 1960s,
when he switched to a more Adult Contemporary style. By the 1990s, had become one of the most honored jazz vocalists and
appealed to a whole new generation of fans. Played "Hymie Kelly" in the 1966 movie *The Oscar*.
AWARDS: Grammy: Lifetime Achievement 2001 ★ Billboard Century: 2006

DEBUT	PEAK	WKS	RIAA	#	Album Title	Catalog	Label & Number
2/23/57	14	9		1	Tony		Columbia 938
7/7/62	5	149	▲	2	I Left My Heart In San Francisco		Columbia 1869 / 8669
					Grammy: Male Vocal		
4/6/63+	5	44		3	I Wanna Be Around		Columbia 2000 / 8800
8/24/63	24	30		4	This Is All I Ask		Columbia 2056 / 8856
2/22/64	20	24		5	The Many Moods Of Tony		Columbia 2141 / 8941
5/23/64	79	12		6	When Lights Are Low		Columbia 2175 / 8975
12/19/64+	42	19		7	Who Can I Turn To		Columbia 2285 / 9085
5/22/65	47	22		8	If I Ruled The World - Songs For The Jet Set		Columbia 2343 / 9143
3/12/66	18	29		9	The Movie Song Album		Columbia 2472 / 9272
10/8/66+	68	18		10	A Time For Love		Columbia 2560 / 9360

DEBUT	PEAK	WKS	R I A A	ARTIST / Album Title	Catalog	Label & Number

BENNETT, Tony — cont'd

DEBUT	PEAK	WKS		#	Album Title	Label & Number
5/13/67	178	6		11	Tony Makes It Happen!	Columbia 2653 / 9453
1/13/68	164	7		12	For Once In My Life	Columbia 9573
9/6/69	137	5		13	I've Gotta Be Me	Columbia 9882
2/28/70	144	11		14	Tony Sings The Great Hits Of Today!	Columbia 9980
11/14/70	193	2		15	Tony Bennett's "Something"	Columbia 30280
3/6/71	67	13		16	Love Story	Columbia 30558
2/19/72	182	4		17	Summer Of '42	Columbia 31219
7/1/72	167	14		18	With Love	Columbia 31460
12/9/72	196	6		19	The Good Things In Life	MGM/Verve 5088
6/21/86	160	8		20	The Art Of Excellence	Columbia 40344
10/3/92	102	26	●	21	Perfectly Frank	Columbia 52965
					Grammy: Traditional Pop Album tribute to **Frank Sinatra**	
10/23/93+	128	16	●	22	Steppin' Out	Columbia 57424
					Grammy: Traditional Pop Album	
11/11/95	96	9		23	Here's To The Ladies	Columbia 67349
					Grammy: Traditional Pop Album	
2/22/97	101	5		24	On Holiday - A Tribute To Billie Holiday	Columbia 67774
					Grammy: Traditional Pop Album	
10/16/99	161	3		25	Bennett Sings Ellington Hot & Cool	RPM 63668
					Grammy: Traditional Pop Album	
11/24/01	50	10		26	Playin' With My Friends: Bennett Sings The Blues	RPM 85833
					Grammy: Traditional Pop Album	
11/23/02	41	18	●	27	A Wonderful World	RPM 86734
					TONY BENNETT & K.D. LANG *Grammy: Traditional Pop Album*	
11/27/04	65	5		28	The Art Of Romance	RPM 92820
					Grammy: Traditional Pop Album	
10/14/06	3[1]	44	▲	29	Duets: An American Classic	RPM 80979
10/13/07	16	6		30	Tony Bennett Sings The Ultimate American Songbook Vol. 1	RPM 15320

CHRISTMAS ALBUMS:

DEBUT	PEAK	WKS		#	Album Title	Label & Number
12/14/68	10[X]	15		31	Snowfall/The Tony Bennett Christmas Album **Cat:#17/14**	Columbia 9739
					Christmas charts: 10/'68, 22/'94, 31/'95, 49/'02, 42/'07	
12/1/01	102	6		32	Our Favorite Things [L]	Sony Classical 89468
					TONY BENNETT / CHARLOTTE CHURCH / PLACIDO DOMINGO / VANESSA WILLIAMS recorded on 12/21/2000 at the Konzerthaus in Vienna, Austria; Christmas chart: 10/'01	
11/15/08	28	9		33	A Swingin' Christmas	RPM 32250
					TONY BENNETT Featuring The Count Basie Big Band Christmas chart: 6/'08	

GREATEST HITS & COMPILATIONS:

DEBUT	PEAK	WKS		#	Album Title	Label & Number
8/21/65	20	42	●	34	Tony's Greatest Hits, Volume III	Columbia 2373 / 9173
5/10/69	174	8		35	Tony Bennett's Greatest Hits, Volume IV	Columbia 9814
10/21/72	175	7	●	36	Tony Bennett's All-Time Greatest Hits	Columbia 31494 [2]
8/10/02	125	4		37	The Essential Tony Bennett	RPM 86634 [2]
1/24/09	27[C]	1		38	The Ultimate Tony Bennett	Legacy 63570

LIVE ALBUMS:

DEBUT	PEAK	WKS		#	Album Title	Label & Number
10/13/62	37	19		39	Tony Bennett At Carnegie Hall	Columbia 23 [2]
					recorded on 6/9/1962	
11/20/71	195	2		40	Get Happy with the London Philharmonic Orchestra	Columbia 30953
					recorded on 1/31/1971	
7/16/94+	48	27	▲	41	MTV Unplugged	Columbia 66214
					Grammys: Album of the Year / Traditional Pop Album recorded on 4/12/1994	

BENNO, Marc
Born on 7/1/1947 in Dallas, Texas. Rock guitarist/songwriter/singer. Formed partnership, **Asylum Choir**, with **Leon Russell** in 1968. Songwriter for **Rita Coolidge** and session work for **The Doors**.

DEBUT	PEAK	WKS		#	Album Title	Label & Number
4/8/72	201	8		1	Look Inside The Asylum Choir [E]	Smash 67107
12/4/71+	70	20		2	Asylum Choir II [E]	Shelter 8910
					LEON RUSSELL & MARC BENNO (above 2) above 2 recorded in 1968-69	
9/23/72	171	8		3	Ambush	A&M 4364

BENOIT, David
Born on 1/1/1953 in Bakersfield, California. Jazz pianist.

DEBUT	PEAK	WKS		#	Album Title	Label & Number
6/4/88	129	14		1	Every Step Of The Way [I]	GRP 1047
5/13/89	101	14		2	Urban Daydreams [I]	GRP 9587
11/11/89	187	3		3	Waiting For Spring [I]	GRP 9595
10/27/90	161	4		4	Inner Motion [I]	GRP 9621
3/12/94	118	7		5	The Benoit/Freeman Project [I]	GRP 9739
					DAVID BENOIT & RUSS FREEMAN	

BENSON, Brendan
Born on 11/14/1970 in Royal Oak, Michigan. Rock singer/songwriter/guitarist. Member of **The Raconteurs**.

DEBUT	PEAK	WKS		#	Album Title	Label & Number
9/5/09	110	1		1	My Old, Familiar Friend	ATO 0079

BENSON, George
All-Time: #141

Born on 3/22/1943 in Pittsburgh, Pennsylvania. R&B/jazz-styled singer/songwriter/guitarist. Played guitar from age eight. Session player for **Brother Jack McDuff** and **Jimmy Smith**. House musician at CTI Records from 1968-73. Heavily influenced by **Wes Montgomery**. Member of group **Fuse One**.

8/23/69	145	3		1	Tell It Like It Is .... [I]		A&M 3020
7/24/76	125	8		2	The Other Side Of Abbey Road .... [I]		A&M 3028
					recorded in 1969		
12/28/74+	78	19		3	Bad Benson .... [I]		CTI 6045
6/26/76	51	16		4	Good King Bad .... [I]		CTI 6062
10/30/76	100	8		5	Benson & Farrell .... [I]		CTI 6069
					GEORGE BENSON & JOE FARRELL		
1/29/77	122	8		6	George Benson In Concert-Carnegie Hall .... [I-L]		CTI 6072
					recorded on 1/11/1975		
12/25/76	206	2		7	Blue Benson .... [I]		CTI 6084
4/17/76	❶²	78	▲³	8	Breezin' .... [I]		Warner 2919
					Grammys: Pop Instrumental Album / Hall of Fame		
2/12/77	9	35	▲	9	In Flight		Warner 2983
2/11/78	5	38	▲	10	Weekend In L.A. .... [L]		Warner 3139 [2]
					recorded on 10/1/1977 at the Roxy		
3/17/79	7	26	●	11	Livin' Inside Your Love		Warner 3277 [2]
8/9/80	3²	38	▲	12	Give Me The Night		Warner 3453
					Grammy: Male R&B Vocal		
11/21/81+	14	26	●	13	The George Benson Collection .... [G]		Warner 3577 [2]
6/18/83	27	35	●	14	In Your Eyes		Warner 23744
1/26/85	45	32	●	15	20/20		Warner 25178
9/20/86	77	24		16	While The City Sleeps...		Warner 25475
7/11/87	59	31	●	17	Collaboration .... [I]		Warner 25580
					GEORGE BENSON & EARL KLUGH		
9/24/88	76	10		18	Twice The Love		Warner 25705
8/5/89	140	6		19	Tenderly		Warner 25907
8/17/96	150	10		20	That's Right .... [I]		GRP 9823
6/10/00	125	3		21	Absolute Benson .... [I]		GRP 543586
7/26/03	138	1		22	The Greatest Hits Of All .... [G]		Rhino 78284
6/26/04	195	1		23	Irreplaceable		GRP 000599
11/11/06	58	7		24	Givin' It Up		Monster 2316
					GEORGE BENSON & AL JARREAU		
9/12/09	96	3		25	Songs And Stories		Monster 30364

BENTLEY, Dierks

Born on 11/20/1975 in Phoenix, Arizona; raised in Lawrenceville, New Jersey. Country singer/songwriter/guitarist.
AWARDS: CMA: Horizon 2005 ★ OPRY: 2005

9/6/03	26	76	▲	1	Dierks Bentley		Capitol 39814
5/28/05	6	80	▲	2	Modern Day Drifter		Capitol 66475
11/4/06	5	52	●	3	Long Trip Alone		Capitol 67320
5/24/08	9	21		4	Greatest Hits: Every Mile A Memory	[G]		Capitol 09070
2/21/09	3¹	34		5	Feel That Fire		Capitol 02158

BENTON, Barbi

Born Barbara Klein on 1/28/1950 in New York; raised in Sacramento, California. Country singer/actress/model.

9/18/76	208	1		1	Something New		Playboy 411

BENTON, Brook

Born Benjamin Franklin Peay on 9/19/1931 in Lugoff, South Carolina. Died of spinal meningitis on 4/9/1988 (age 56). R&B singer/songwriter. Member of The Camden Jubilee Singers. To New York in 1948, joined Bill Langford's Langfordaires. Member of the Jerusalem Stars in 1951. First recorded under own name for Okeh in 1955.

6/5/61	82	20		1	Golden Hits .... [G]		Mercury 60607
9/25/61	70	13		2	The Boll Weevil Song And 11 Other Great Hits.........		Mercury 60641
2/17/62	77	7		3	If You Believe...		Mercury 60619
10/27/62	40	15		4	Singing The Blues - Lie To Me		Mercury 60740
4/13/63	82	6		5	Golden Hits, Volume 2 .... [G]		Mercury 60774
10/28/67	156	4		6	Laura (What's He Got That I Ain't Got)		Reprise 6268
7/19/69	189	2		7	Do Your Own Thing		Cotillion 9002
2/21/70	27	23		8	Brook Benton Today		Cotillion 9018
8/22/70	199	2		9	Home Style		Cotillion 9028

~ ~ ~ ~ ~ ~ ~ ~ **NON-CHARTED ALBUMS** ~ ~ ~ ~ ~ ~ ~ ~ ~ ~ ~
1959 **It's Just A Matter Of Time**   1960 **I Love You In So Many Ways**
1959 **Endlessly**   1960 **The Two Of Us** [w/ Dinah Washington]

Billboard DEBUT	PEAK	WKS	R I A A	ARTIST / Album Title	Catalog	Label & Number

BENZINO
Born Raymond Scott on 10/24/1964 in Boston, Massachusetts. Male rapper/producer. Former member of **Made Men**.

11/17/01	84	3		1 The Benzino Project	Motown 014981
2/1/03	65	3		2 Redemption	Surrender 62827
3/12/05	117	1		3 Arch Nemesis	Zno 10

BERG, Gertrude
Born Tilly Edelstein on 10/3/1898 in Harlem, New York. Died of heart failure on 9/14/1966 (age 67). Radio, TV and Broadway actress. Played "Molly Goldberg" on radio and TV's *The Goldbergs*.

7/17/65	131	12		1 How To Be A Jewish Mother .... [C]	Amy 8007

BERGEN, Polly
Born Nellie Burgin on 7/14/1930 in Knoxville, Tennessee. Singer/actress. Appeared in several movies and TV shows.

6/10/57	10	5		1 Bergen Sings Morgan	Columbia 994
				tribute to Helen Morgan	
11/4/57	20	1		2 The Party's Over	Columbia 1031

BERING STRAIT
Country band from Obninsk, Russia: Natasha Borzilova (vocals, guitar), Ilya Toshinsky (guitar), Lydia Salnikova (keyboards), Alexander "Sasha" Ostrovsky (dobro), Sergei "Spooky" Olkhovsky (bass) and Alexander Arzamastsev (drums).

3/15/03	98	4		1 Bering Strait..	Universal South 170218

BERKNER, Laurie, Band
Born in March 1969 in France; raised in Princeton, New Jersey. Singer/songwriter/guitarist specializing in children's songs.

8/23/08	130	2		1 Rocketship Run	Two Tomatoes 23406

BERLIN
Electro-pop band from Los Angeles, California: Terri Nunn (vocals), Rick Olsen (guitar), Matt Reid and David Diamond (keyboards), John Crawford (bass) and Rob Brill (drums). Pared down to a trio in 1985 with Nunn, Crawford and Brill.

2/19/83	30	34	▲	1 Pleasure Victim	Geffen 2036
3/31/84	28	30	●	2 Love Life	Geffen 4025
11/8/86	61	20		3 Count Three And Pray	Geffen 24121

BERMAN, Shelley   **1950s: #31**
Born Sheldon Berman on 2/3/1925 in Chicago, Illinois. Stand-up comedian/actor. Appeared in several TV shows and movies.

4/27/59	2⁵	134		1 Inside Shelley Berman .... [C]	Verve 15003
				Grammy: Comedy Album	
11/30/59	6	77		2 Outside Shelley Berman .... [C]	Verve 15007
7/25/60	4	52		3 The Edge Of Shelley Berman .... [C]	Verve 15013
11/6/61+	25	19		4 A Personal Appearance .... [C]	Verve 15027
				no track titles listed for above 4 albums	
9/26/64	88	8		5 The Sex Life Of The Primate (And Other Bits Of Gossip) ...... [C]	Verve 15043
				with Jerry Stiller, Anne Meara and Lovelady Powell	

BERNARDI, Herschel
Born on 10/20/1923 in Brooklyn, New York. Died on 5/9/1986 (age 62). Actor/singer. Played "Tevye" in Broadway's *Fiddler On The Roof*.

11/12/66+	138	5		1 Fiddler On The Roof	Columbia 6610

BERNSTEIN, Leonard
Born on 8/25/1918 in Lawrence, Massachusetts. Died of a heart attack on 10/14/1990 (age 72). Conductor/pianist/composer. Conductor of numerous major orchestras worldwide, including the New York Philharmonic and the Vienna Philharmonic. Composed music for several movies and Broadway shows.
AWARD: Grammy: Lifetime Achievement 1985

12/12/60+	13	15		1 Bernstein Plays Brubeck Plays Bernstein .... [I]	Columbia 1466 / 8257
				side 1: **New York Philharmonic** with the **Dave Brubeck Quartet** conducted by Leonard Bernstein; side 2: **Dave Brubeck Quartet**	
12/21/63+	8ˣ	12	●	2 The Joy Of Christmas [X]	Columbia 5899 / 6499
				LEONARD BERNSTEIN/NEW YORK PHILHARMONIC/THE MORMON TABERNACLE CHOIR	
				Christmas charts: 12/'63, 32/'64, 8/'65, 62/'66, 106/'67, 28/'68, 20/'70	
12/25/71+	53	20		3 Mass (From The Liturgy Of The Roman Mass)	Columbia 31008 [2]
				created for the opening of the **John F. Kennedy** *Center for the Performing Arts*	
5/25/85	70	20		4 West Side Story	DG 415253 [2]
				studio production featuring opera stars **Kiri Te Kanawa**, **José Carreras**, Tatiana Troyanos, Kurt Ollmann and Marilyn Horne	

BERRY, Chuck
Born on 10/18/1926 in St. Louis, Missouri. Black rock and roll singer/songwriter/guitarist. Acclaimed as one of rock and roll's most influential artists. Performed in several movies including own documentary/concert tribute *Hail! Hail! Rock 'N' Roll*.
AWARDS: Grammy: Lifetime Achievement 1984 ★ R&R Hall of Fame: 1986

8/24/63	29	17		1 Chuck Berry On Stage	Chess 1480
				not a live album; audience dubbed in; although "Surfin' USA" is listed on the cover, it does not appear on the album	
6/6/64	34	21		2 Chuck Berry's Greatest Hits .... [G]	Chess 1485
12/12/64+	124	7		3 St. Louis To Liverpool	Chess 1488
5/20/67+	72	20		4 Chuck Berry's Golden Decade...................................... [G]	Chess 1514 [2]
6/10/72	8	47	●	5 The London Chuck Berry Sessions [L]	Chess 60020
				side 1: studio; side 2: recorded live at the Lanchester Arts Festival in Coventry, England (with **Average White Band** backing)	
11/4/72	185	7		6 St. Louie To Frisco To Memphis .... [L]	Mercury 6501 [2]
				record 1: live at the Fillmore with the **Steve Miller Band**	
2/24/73	110	8		7 Chuck Berry's Golden Decade, Vol. 2 .... [G]	Chess 60023 [2]
9/8/73	175	6		8 Chuck Berry/Bio	Chess 50043

Billboard			R I A A	ARTIST		
DEBUT	PEAK	WKS		Album Title	Catalog	Label & Number

~ ~ ~ ~ ~ ~ **NON-CHARTED ALBUMS by CHUCK BERRY** ~ ~ ~ ~ ~ ~ ~

1957 After School Session	1962 Chuck Berry Twist
1958 One Dozen Berrys	1965 Chuck Berry In London
1959 Chuck Berry Is On Top	1965 Fresh Berry's
1960 Rockin' At The Hops	1984 The Great Twenty-Eight
1961 New Juke Box Hits	*RS500 #21*

BERRY, John
Born on 9/14/1959 in Aiken, South Carolina; raised in Atlanta, Georgia. Country singer/songwriter/guitarist.

4/16/94	85	43	▲	1 John Berry		Liberty 80472
3/25/95	69	39	●	2 Standing On The Edge		Patriot 28495
12/2/95	110	6		3 O Holy Night .... Cat:#36/3	[X]	Capitol 32663
				Christmas chart: 18/'95		
10/5/96	83	13	●	4 Faces		Capitol 35464

BETA BAND, The
Electronic band from Edinburgh, Scotland: Stephen Mason (vocals), John MacLean (DJ/sampler), Richard Greentree (bass) and Robin Jones (drums).

8/4/01	200	1		1 Hot Shots II		Astralwerks 10446

BETH, Karen
Born in 1948 in Brooklyn, New York. Folk-rock singer/songwriter/keyboardist.

9/6/69	171	6		1 The Joys Of Life		Decca 75148
1/9/71	201	1		2 Harvest		Decca 75247

BETO Y SUS CANARIOS
Latin band from Mexico: Edilberto Mendoza, Pedro Diaz, Eduardo Cervantes, Gabino Palaces, Crescencio Mendoza, Miguel Navarrese, Jose Rivers, Cuauhtemoc Gonzalez, Luis Roman, Artemio Garcia, Courteous Norberto and Epigmenio Gaytan. Group name is Spanish for "Beto And Its Canaries."

8/6/05	62	5		1 Ardientes	[F]	Disa 726828

BETTER THAN EZRA
Rock trio from New Orleans, Louisiana: Kevin Griffin (vocals, guitar), Tom Drummond (bass) and Cary Bonnecaze (drums). Travis McNabb replaced Bonnecaze by 1996.

4/22/95	35	42	▲	1 Deluxe		Elektra 61784
8/31/96	64	19		2 Friction, Baby		Elektra 61944
9/12/98	129	1		3 How Does Your Garden Grow?		Elektra 62247
8/25/01	110	3		4 Closer		Beyond 578137
6/18/05	84	3		5 Before The Robots		Song 51617
5/30/09	62	1		6 Paper Empire		Ezra Dry Goods 01

BETTS, Dickey
Born on 12/12/1943 in Sarasota, Florida. Southern-rock singer/guitarist. Member of **The Allman Brothers Band**. In the late 1970s, formed Great Southern: Dan Toler (guitar), Ken Tibbets (bass), Tom Broome (keyboards) and Jerry Thompson and Doni Sharbono (drums). By 1978, Tibbets, Broome and Thompson left; Dave Goldflies (bass), Michael Workman (keyboards) and David Toler (drums; brother of Dan) joined. The Toler brothers later joined **The Gregg Allman Band**. **The Dickey Betts Band** included: Warren Haynes (guitar), Johnny Neel (piano), Marty Privette (bass) and Matt Abts (drums). Haynes and Neel were also with The Allman Brothers Band. Haynes later formed **Gov't Mule**. Betts was fired from the Allman Brothers Band in 2000.

8/31/74	19	16		1 Highway Call		Capricorn 0123
				RICHARD BETTS		
4/30/77	31	12		2 Dickey Betts & Great Southern		Arista 4123
4/29/78	157	5		3 Atlanta's Burning Down		Arista 4168
11/12/88	187	4		4 Pattern Disruptive		Epic 44289
				THE DICKEY BETTS BAND		

BETWEEN THE BURIED AND ME
Heavy metal band from Raleigh, North Carolina: Tommy Rogers (vocals, keyboards), Paul Waggoner (guitar), Dusty Waring (guitar), Dan Briggs (bass) and Blake Richardson (drums).

9/24/05	121	1		1 Alaska		Victory 262
7/1/06	151	1		2 The Anatomy Of		Victory 297
10/6/07	57	2		3 Colors		Victory 351
11/1/08	100	1		4 Colors: Live	[L]	Victory 439
11/14/09	36	2		5 The Great Misdirect		Victory 533

BETWEEN THE TREES
Pop-punk trio from Orlando, Florida: Ryan Kirkland (vocals), with brothers Jeremy Butler (bass) and Josh Butler (drums).

8/29/09	138	1		1 Spain		Bonded 005

BEYONCE
Born Beyonce Knowles on 9/4/1981 in Houston, Texas. R&B singer/songwriter/actress. Member of **Destiny's Child**. Sister of **Solange**. Acted in several movies. Married **Jay-Z** on 4/4/2008.
AWARD: Billboard Woman of the Year: 2009

7/12/03	❶¹	100	▲⁴	1 Dangerously In Love .... Cat:#7/18		Columbia 86386
				Grammy: Contemporary R&B Album		
5/15/04	17	8		2 Live At Wembley	[L]	Columbia 58626
9/23/06	❶¹	74	▲³	3 B'Day		Columbia 90920
9/15/07	105	3		4 Irremplazable	[EP-F]	Music World 12804
				contains Spanish versions of some of her hits		

BEYONCE — cont'd

12/6/08	❶[1]	78↑	▲[2]	5 I Am...Sasha Fierce		Music World 19492
				Grammy: Contemporary R&B Album		
7/4/09	35	13		6 Above And Beyonce: Video Collection & Dance Mixes .... [EP]		Music World 75394

B-52's, The
All-Time: #425

New-wave dance band formed in Athens, Georgia: Fred Schneider (vocals, keyboards; born on 7/1/1951), Kate Pierson (vocals, organ; born on 4/27/1948), Cindy Wilson (guitar, vocals; born on 2/28/1957) and her brother Ricky Wilson (guitar; born on 3/19/1953; died of AIDS on 10/12/1985, age 32) and Keith Strickland (drums; born on 10/26/1953). After Ricky Wilson's death, Strickland moved to guitar. Cindy Wilson left in 1991; replaced on tour by **Julee Cruise**. Appeared as The B.C. 52's in the 1994 movie *The Flintstones*. B-52 is slang for the bouffant hairstyle worn by Kate and Cindy.

8/11/79+	59	74	▲	1 The B-52's		Warner 3355
				RS500 #152		
9/20/80	18	27	●	2 Wild Planet		Warner 3471
8/8/81	55	11		3 Party Mix! .... [EP-K]		Warner 3596
				6-cut party remix of Wild Planet album		
2/20/82	35	18		4 Mesopotamia .... Cat:#31/8 [EP]		Warner 3641
5/21/83	29	26	●	5 Whammy!		Warner 23819
10/4/86	85	15		6 Bouncing Off The Satellites		Warner 25504
7/22/89+	4	65	▲[4]	7 Cosmic Thing		Reprise 25854
2/23/91	184	3		8 Party Mix!/Mesopotamia .... [R]		Reprise 26401
				albums #3 and 4 above released together on 1 CD; Mesopotamia remixed in summer of 1990		
7/11/92	16	15	●	9 Good Stuff		Reprise 26943
6/13/98	93	11		10 Time Capsule - Songs For A Future Generation .... [G]		Reprise 46920
4/12/08	11	7		11 Funplex		Astralwerks 28730

B5

Male teen R&B vocal group from Atlanta, Georgia: brothers Dustin, Kelly, Patrick, Carnell and Bryan Breeding. Group name is short for Breeding Five.

8/6/05	19	9		1 B5		Bad Boy 83812
9/29/07	27	3		2 Don't Talk, Just Listen		Bad Boy 116156

B.G.

Born Christopher Dorsey on 9/3/1980 in New Orleans, Louisiana. Male rapper. B.G.: Baby Gangsta. Member of **Cash Money Millionaires** and **Hot Boys**.

11/15/97	184	1		1 It's All On U Vol. 2		Cash Money 9616
5/8/99	9	42	●	2 Chopper City In The Ghetto		Cash Money 53265
12/9/00	21	15	●	3 Checkmate		Cash Money 860909
3/15/02	21	12		4 Livin' Legend		Koch 8465
8/14/04	22	9		5 Life After Cash Money		Koch 5708
6/11/05	21	7		6 The Heart Of Tha Streetz Vol. 1		Choppa City 5819
4/8/06	6	8		7 The Heart Of Tha Streetz Vol. 2 (I Am What I Am)		Choppa City 5849
8/26/06	191	1		8 Play It How It Go: Collection .... [G]		CT Media 101
3/17/07	21	3		9 We Got This		Choppa City 5700
10/4/08	117	2		10 Life In The Concrete Jungle		Choppa City 513058
12/26/09	77	2		11 Too Hood 2 Be Hollywood		Choppa City 2073

B.G. KNOCC OUT & DRESTA

Male rap duo from Los Angeles, California: Arlandis "B.G. Knocc Out" Hinton and Andre "Dresta" Wicker. Hinton served several years in prison for attempted murder.

9/2/95	128	5		1 Real Brothas		OutBurst 527899

BICE, Bo

Born Harold Bice on 11/1/1975 in Huntsville, Alabama. Male singer. Finished in second place on the 2005 season of TV's *American Idol*.

12/31/05	4	20	●	1 The Real Thing		RCA 71196
11/17/07	150	1		2 See The Light		Sugarmoney 40929

BICKERSONS, The — see AMECHE, Don

BIDDU ORCHESTRA

Born Biddu Appaiah in 1944 in Bangalore, India; later based in England. Male dance songwriter/producer/arranger.

2/21/76	170	3		1 Biddu Orchestra .... [I]		Epic 33903

BIEBER, Justin

Born on 3/1/1994 in Stratford, Ontario, Canada. Teen idol singer.

12/5/09+	5	26↑	▲	1 My World .... [EP]		SchoolBoy 013719

BIG & RICH

Country duo formed in Nashville, Tennessee: **Big Kenny** Alphin and **John Rich** (former member of **Lonestar**).

5/22/04	6	99	▲[2]	1 Horse Of A Different Color .... Cat:#38/4		Warner 48520
11/13/04	90	8		2 Big & Rich's Super Galactic Fan Pak .... [EP]		Warner 48904
12/3/05	7	39	▲	3 Comin' To Your City		Warner 49470
6/23/07	6	28	●	4 Between Raising Hell And Amazing Grace		Warner 43255
10/17/09	148	2		5 Greatest Hits .... [G]		Warner 519706

Billboard			R I A A	ARTIST		
DEBUT	PEAK	WKS		Album Title	Catalog	Label & Number

BIG AUDIO DYNAMITE
Alternative-rock band formed in England: Mick Jones (vocals, guitar; **The Clash**), Don Letts and Dan Donovan (keyboards), Leo Williams (bass) and Greg Roberts (drums). Disbanded in 1989. Jones formed **Big Audio Dynamite II** in 1990 with Nick Hawkins (guitar; **Sigue Sigue Sputnik**), Gary Stonadge (bass) and Chris Kavanagh (drums). By 1994, group simply known as Big Audio. Hawkins died of a heart attack on 10/10/2005 (age 40).

11/23/85+	103	35		1 This Is Big Audio Dynamite..		Columbia 40220
11/1/86	119	23		2 No. 10, Upping St.		Columbia 40445
8/13/88	102	12		3 Tighten Up Vol. '88		Columbia 44074
9/23/89	85	13		4 Megatop Phoenix		Columbia 45212
8/24/91	76	37	●	5 The Globe..		Columbia 46147
				BIG AUDIO DYNAMITE II		

BIG BAD VOODOO DADDY
Eclectic-jazz band from Ventura, California: Scotty Morris (vocals, guitar), Joshua Levy (piano), Jeff Harvis, Karl Hunter, Glen Marhevka and Andy Rowley (horns), Dirk Shumaker (bass) and Kurt Sodergen (drums). Harvis left after first album. Group appeared as the band in the 1996 movie *Swingers*.

3/14/98	47	56	▲	1 Big Bad Voodoo Daddy		Coolsville 93338
11/6/99	93	3		2 This Beautiful Life		Coolsville 90387
7/26/03	195	1		3 Save My Soul		Big Bad 79742

BIG BOPPER
Born Jiles Perry Richardson on 10/24/1930 in Sabine Pass, Texas. DJ at KTRM in Beaumont, Texas. Wrote "Running Bear" for **Johnny Preston**. Died with **Buddy Holly** and **Ritchie Valens** in the 2/3/1959 plane crash (age 28).

~ ~ ~ ~ ~ ~ ~ ~ ~ ~ ~ **NON-CHARTED ALBUM** ~ ~ ~ ~ ~ ~ ~ ~ ~ ~ ~ ~

1959 Chantilly Lace

BIG BROTHER & THE HOLDING COMPANY
Rock band formed in San Francisco, California: **Janis Joplin** (vocals), Sam Andrew (guitar), James Gurley (guitar), Peter Albin (bass) and David Getz (drums). Joplin died of a heroin overdose on 10/4/1970 (age 27). Gurley died of a heart attack on 12/20/2009 (age 69).

9/2/67	60	30		1 Big Brother & The Holding Company.......................................		Mainstream 6099
8/31/68	❶[8]	66	▲[2]	2 Cheap Thrills		Columbia 9700
				RS500 #338		
11/28/70	134	6		3 Be A Brother		Columbia 30222
5/15/71	185	4		4 Big Brother & The Holding Company....................................... [R]		Columbia 30631
9/4/71	157	3		5 How Hard It Is		Columbia 30738

BIG BUB
Born Frederick Lee Drakeford in Englewood, New Jersey. Black singer/rapper. Former member of **Today**.

11/8/97	104	3		1 Timeless		Kedar 53074

BIG COUNTRY
Pop-rock band from Dunfermline, Scotland: Stuart Adamson (vocals, guitar), Bruce Watson (guitar), Tony Butler (bass) and Mark Brzezicki (drums). Adamson committed suicide on 12/16/2001 (age 43).

9/24/83	18	42	●	1 The Crossing		Mercury 812870
5/5/84	65	12		2 Wonderland .... [EP]		Mercury 818835
11/24/84	70	17		3 Steeltown		Mercury 822831
7/19/86	59	17		4 The Seer		Mercury 826844
10/29/88	160	6		5 Peace In Our Time		Reprise 25787

BIG DADDY WEAVE
Christian pop band from Nashville, Tennessee: brothers Mike Weaver (vocals, guitar) and Jay Weaver (bass), Jeremy Redmon (guitar), Joe Shirk (sax) and Jeff Jones (drums).

10/18/03	177	1		1 Fields Of Grace		Fervent 30040
10/10/09	5[X]	5		2 Christ Is Come .... [X]		Fervent 887875

BIGDUMBFACE
Rock band formed in Jacksonville, Florida: Wes Borland (vocals, guitar), Kyle Weeks (guitar), Chris Gibbs (bass) and Greg Isabel (drums). Borland is also a member of **Limp Bizkit**.

3/24/01	194	1		1 Duke Lion Fights The Terror!!..		Flip 490893

BIG ED
Born Edward Knight in 1971 in Richmond, California. Died of cancer in August 2001 (age 30). Male rapper.

9/19/98	16	6		1 The Assassin		No Limit 50729

BIG GIPP
Born Cameron Gipp on 4/28/1973 in Atlanta, Georgia. Male rapper. Member of **Goodie Mob**.

8/30/03	161	2		1 Mutant Mindframe		Koch 8481
9/1/07	174	1		2 Kinfolk		Derrty 007160
				ALI & GIPP		

BIG HEAD TODD AND THE MONSTERS
Rock trio from Boulder, Colorado: Todd Park Mohr (guitar, keyboards), Rob Squires (bass) and Brian Nevin (drums). All share vocals.

3/13/93+	117	64	▲	1 Sister Sweetly		Giant 24486
10/15/94	30	8		2 Strategem..		Giant 24580
3/1/97	54	10		3 Beautiful World		Revolution 24661
4/13/02	166	1		4 Riviera		Warner 48266

Billboard			R I A A	ARTIST		
DEBUT	PEAK	WKS		Album Title	Catalog	Label & Number

BIG KENNY
Born William Kenneth Alphin on 11/1/1963 in Culpepper, Virginia. Country singer/songwriter/guitarist. One-half of **Big & Rich**.

11/28/09	197	1		1 The Quiet Times Of A Rock And Roll Farm Boy		Love Everybody 521815

BIG KUNTRY KING
Born Sean Merrett in Atlanta, Georgia. Male rapper.

10/18/08	98	1		1 My Turn To Eat		Grand Hustle 514113

BIG L
Born Lamont Coleman on 5/30/1974 in Harlem, New York. Shot to death on 2/15/1999 (age 24). Male rapper. Member of **D.I.T.C.**

4/15/95	149	2		1 Lifestylez Ov Da Poor & Dangerous		Columbia 53795
8/19/00	13	9	●	2 The Big Picture		Rawkus 26136

BIG MIKE
Born Michael Barnett on 9/27/1971 in New Orleans, Louisiana. Male rapper. Member of **The Geto Boys**.

7/16/94	40	20	●	1 Somethin' Serious		Rap-A-Lot 53907
4/26/97	16	11		2 Still Serious		Rap-A-Lot 44099
6/12/99	63	3		3 Hard To Hit		Rap-A-Lot 50104

BIG MOE
Born Kenneth Moore on 6/27/1974 in Houston, Texas. Died of a heart attack on 10/14/2007 (age 33). Male rapper.

8/5/00	176	2		1 City Of Syrup		Wreckshop 4441
5/11/02	29	7		2 Purple World		Wreckshop 50244

BIG MOUNTAIN
Multi-cultural reggae band from San Diego, California: Joaquin "Quino" McWhinney (vocals, rhythm guitar), Jerome Cruz (guitar), Manfred Reinke (keyboards), Gregory Blakney (percussion), Lance Rhodes (drums) and Lynn Copeland (bass).

8/6/94	174	5		1 Unity		Giant 24563

BIG PIG
Rock band from Australia: male singers Nick Disbray, Tony Antoniades, Tim Rosewarne and Oleh Witer, with female singer Sherine, and drummers Adrian Scaglione and Neil Baker.

3/26/88	93	17		1 Bonk		A&M 5185

BIG PINK, The
Electro-rock duo from London, England: Robbie Furze and Milo Cordell.

10/10/09	138	1		1 A Brief History Of Love		4AD 2916

BIG PUN
Born Christopher Rios on 11/9/1971 in the Bronx, New York. Died of a heart attack on 2/7/2000 (age 28). Male rapper. Name is short for Big Punisher.

5/16/98	5	28	▲	1 Capital Punishment		Loud 67512
4/22/00	3[1]	23	●	2 Yeeeah Baby		Loud 63843
4/21/01	7	9		3 Endangered Species		Loud 1963

BIG STAR
Pop-rock band from Memphis, Tennessee: Alex Chilton (vocals; **Box Tops**), Chris Bell (guitar; left after *#1 Record*), Andy Hummel (bass) and Jody Stephens (drums). Chilton died of heart failure on 3/17/2010 (age 59).

~ ~ ~ ~ ~ ~ ~ ~ ~ ~ **NON-CHARTED ALBUMS** ~ ~ ~ ~ ~ ~ ~ ~ ~ ~

1972 **#1 Record**
     RS500 #438
1974 **Radio City**
     RS500 #403
1978 **Big Star's 3rd: Sister Lovers**
     RS500 #456

BIG TRAY DEEE
Born Tracy Davis on 4/27/1966 in Long Beach, California. Male rapper. Member of **Tha Eastsidaz**.

9/7/02	95	3		1 The General's List		Empire 39040

BIG TYMERS
Rap duo from New Orleans, Louisiana: Byron "**Mannie Fresh**" Thomas and Bryan "**Birdman**" Williams. Members of **Cash Money Millionaires**.

3/14/98	168	1		1 How You Luv That?		Cash Money 9617
10/10/98	105	2		2 How You Luv That? Vol. 2		Cash Money 53170
6/3/00	3[1]	29	▲	3 I Got That Work		Cash Money 157673
5/18/02	❶[1]	29	▲	4 Hood Rich		Cash Money 860997
12/27/03	21	16	●	5 Big Money Heavyweight		Cash Money 000815

BILAL
Born Bilal Oliver on 8/21/1979 in Philadelphia, Pennsylvania. Male R&B singer.

8/18/01	31	11		1 1st Born Second		Moyo 493009

BILK, Mr. Acker
Born Bernard Stanley Bilk on 1/28/1929 in Pensford, Somerset, England. Clarinet player.

5/5/62	3[6]	29	●	1 Stranger On The Shore	[I]	Atco 129
9/1/62	48	9		2 Above The Stars & Other Romantic Fancies	[I]	Atco 144

Billboard DEBUT	PEAK	WKS	R I A A	ARTIST / Album Title	Catalog	Label & Number
				BILLION DOLLAR BABIES		
				Backing band for **Alice Cooper**: Michael Bruce (vocals), Mike Marconi (guitar), Bob Dolin (keyboards), Dennis Dunaway (bass) and Neal Smith (drums). Group named after Cooper's 1973 album.		
6/11/77	198	2		1 Battle Axe		Polydor 6100
				BILLY & THE BEATERS — see VERA, Billy		
				BILLY SATELLITE		
				Rock band from Oakland, California: Monty Byrom (vocals), Danny Chauncey (guitar), Ira Walker (bass) and Tom Falletti (drums). Chauncey later joined **38 Special**.		
9/1/84	139	6		1 Billy Satellite		Capitol 12340
				BILLY TALENT		
				Punk-rock band from Streetsville, Ontario, Canada: Ben Kowalewicz (vocals), Ian D'Sa (guitar), Jon Gallant (bass) and Aaron Solowoniuk (drums).		
10/4/03	194	1		1 Billy Talent		Atlantic 83614
7/15/06	134	1		2 Billy Talent II		Atlantic 83941
10/10/09	107	1		3 Billy Talent III		Roadrunner 617817
				BINGHAM, Ryan, & The Dead Horses		
				Born George Ryan Bingham on 3/31/1981 in Hobbs, New Mexico. Folk-rock singer/songwriter. The Dead Horses: Cory Schaub (guitar), Elijah Ford (bass) and Matt Smith (drums).		
6/20/09	65	1		1 Roadhouse Sun		Lost Highway 012739
				BIOHAZARD		
				Hard-rock band from Brooklyn, New York: Bobby Hambel (vocals), Billy Graziadei (guitar), Evan Seinfeld (bass) and Danny Schuler (drums). Hambel left in 1995, Graziadei and Seinfeld took over vocals. Rob Echeverria (guitar) joined in 1998.		
6/11/94	48	8		1 State Of The World Address		Warner 45595
7/13/96	170	1		2 Mata Leão		Warner 46208
6/26/99	187	1		3 New World Disorder		King 546032
				BIONIC BOOGIE		
				Disco studio group assembled by producer Gregg Diamond.		
1/28/78	88	16		1 Bionic Boogie		Polydor 6123
				BIRCH, Diane		
				Born on 1/24/1983 in Michigan. Singer/songwriter/pianist.		
6/20/09	87	4		1 Bible Belt		S-Curve 51101
				BIRD, Andrew		
				Born on 7/11/1973 in Chicago, Illinois. Folk-rock singer/songwriter/multi-instrumentalist.		
4/7/07	76	3		1 Armchair Apocrypha .... Cat:#39/1		Fat Possum 1058
2/7/09	12	14		2 Noble Beast		Fat Possum 1124
				BIRD AND THE BEE, The		
				Electro-pop duo from Los Angeles, California: Inara George and Greg Kurstin.		
2/14/09	78	1		1 Ray Guns Are Not Just The Future		Blue Note 34556
				BIRDMAN		
				Born Bryan Williams on 2/15/1969 in New Orleans, Louisiana. Male rapper/songwriter. Founder and CEO of Cash Money record label. Member of **Big Tymers** and **Cash Money Millionaires**. Previously nicknamed **Baby**.		
12/14/02	24	20	●	1 Birdman .... BABY (AKA DA #1 STUNNA)		Cash Money 060076
7/9/05	9	7		2 Fast Money		Cash Money 004220
11/18/06	3[1]	37	●	3 Like Father, Like Son .... Cat:#45/1 BIRDMAN & LIL WAYNE		Cash Money 007563
12/29/07	18	17		4 5 Star Stunna		Cash Money 010351
4/19/08	198	1		5 Happy Fathers Day.. LIL WAYNE & BIRDMAN		BCD 63170
12/12/09	33	18		6 Priceless		Cash Money 013090
				BIRDSONG, Edwin		
				Born in 1950 in Los Angeles, California. Funk singer/keyboardist.		
8/28/71	218	1		1 What It Is		Polydor 4071
				BIRKIN, Jane, & Serge Gainsbourg		
				Actress Birkin was born on 12/14/1946 in London, England. Singer/songwriter Lucien "Serge" Gainsbourg was born on 4/2/1928 in Paris, France. Died of heart failure on 3/2/1991 (age 62). Couple were married from 1968-80; parents of **Charlotte Gainsbourg**.		
3/7/70	196	2		1 Je T'Aime (Beautiful Love) .... [F]		Fontana 67610
				BIRTHA		
				Female rock band from Glendale, California: Shele Pinizzotto (guitar), Sherry Hagler (keyboards), Rosemary Butler (bass) and Liver Favela (drums). All shared vocals.		
9/30/72	209	4		1 Birtha		Dunhill 50127

Billboard			R I A A	ARTIST	Catalog	Label & Number
DEBUT	PEAK	WKS		Album Title		
				BISBAL, David		
				Born on 6/5/1979 in Almeria, Spain. Latin pop singer.		
10/21/06	150	2		1 **Premonicion**	[F]	Vale 007713
11/7/09	119	2		2 **Sin Mirar Atras**	[F]	Vale 013491
				BISHOP, Elvin		
				Born on 10/21/1942 in Glendale, California; raised in Tulsa, Oklahoma. White blues-rock guitarist. Member of **Paul Butterfield**'s band from 1965-68.		
1/2/71	202	1		1 **Feel It!**		Fillmore 30239
				THE ELVIN BISHOP GROUP		
12/2/72	206	3		2 **Rock My Soul**		Epic 31563
				THE ELVIN BISHOP BAND		
7/27/74	100	17		3 **Let It Flow**		Capricorn 0134
5/10/75	46	17		4 **Juke Joint Jump**		Capricorn 0151
1/24/76	18	34		5 **Struttin' My Stuff**		Capricorn 0165
11/20/76	70	12		6 **Hometown Boy Makes Good!**		Capricorn 0176
8/27/77	38	12		7 **Live! Raisin' Hell**	[L]	Capricorn 0185 [2]
12/16/78	201	9		8 **Hog Heaven**		Capricorn 0215
				BISHOP, Stephen		
				Born on 11/14/1951 in San Diego, California. Pop-rock singer/songwriter. Wrote several movie themes. Cameo as the "Charming Guy With Guitar" in the 1978 movie *National Lampoon's Animal House*.		
1/8/77	34	32		1 **Careless**		ABC 954
9/16/78	35	19	●	2 **Bish**		ABC 1082
				BIZARRE		
				Born Rufus Johnson on 7/5/1976 in Detroit, Michigan. Male rapper. Member of **D12**.		
7/16/05	48	3		1 **Hannicap Circus**		Red Head 87535
				BIZ MARKIE		
				Born Marcel Hall on 4/8/1964 in Harlem, New York. Male rapper.		
3/19/88	90	18		1 **Goin' Off**		Cold Chillin' 25675
10/28/89	66	30	●	2 **The Biz Never Sleeps**		Cold Chillin' 26003
				THE DIABOLICAL BIZ MARKIE		
9/14/91	113	2		3 **I Need A Haircut**		Cold Chillin' 26648
				BIZZY BONE		
				Born Bryon McCane on 9/12/1976 in Columbus, Ohio. Male rapper. Member of **Bone Thugs-N-Harmony**.		
10/24/98	3[1]	19	●	1 **Heaven'z Movie**		Mo Thugs 1670
4/7/01	44	7		2 **The Gift**		AMC 71150
11/6/04	152	1		3 **Alpha And Omega**		7th Sign 970036
10/15/05	183	1		4 **Speaking In Tongues**		845 Records 105
3/18/06	168	1		5 **Thugs Revenge**		PMC 900094
5/10/08	148	1		6 **A Song For You**		After Platinum 7935
				BJOERLING, Jussi		
				Born on 2/5/1911 in Stora Tuna, Sweden. Died on 9/9/1960 (age 49). Male opera tenor.		
4/17/61	142	1		1 **The Beloved Bjoerling, Volume One**	[E]	Capitol 7239
				recordings from 1936-48		
				BJORK		
				Born Bjork Gudmundsdottir on 11/21/1965 in Reykjavik, Iceland. Female singer/actress. Lead singer of **The Sugarcubes**. Played "Selma Jezkova" in the 2000 movie *Dancer In The Dark*.		
7/31/93	61	31	▲	1 **Debut**		Elektra 61468
7/1/95	32	20	▲	2 **Post**		Elektra 61740
				RS500 #373		
2/1/97	66	5		3 **Telegram**	[K]	Elektra 61897
				contains remixes of songs from #2 above		
10/11/97	28	9	●	4 **Homogenic**		Elektra 62061
10/7/00	41	7		5 **Selmasongs**		Elektra 62533
9/15/01	19	10		6 **Vespertine**		Elektra 62653
11/23/02	115	2		7 **Greatest Hits**	[G]	Elektra 62787
9/18/04	14	7		8 **Medulla**		Elektra 62984
5/26/07	9	5		9 **Volta**		Elektra 135868
7/18/09	118	1		10 **Voltaic**	[L]	Nonesuch 519646
				BLACK('S), Bill, Combo		
				Born on 9/17/1926 in Memphis, Tennessee. Died of a brain tumor on 10/21/1965 (age 39). White bass guitarist. Session work in Memphis; backed **Elvis Presley** (with Scotty Moore, guitar; D.J. Fontana, drums) on most of his early records. Formed own band in 1959. Labeled as "The Untouchable Sound." Larry Rogers and Bob Tucker led group after Black's death; recorded well into the 1970s.		
				AWARD: R&R Hall of Fame: 2009 (Sideman)		
11/14/60	23	28		1 **Solid And Raunchy**	[I]	Hi 12003
1/20/62	35	19		2 **Let's Twist Her**	[I]	Hi 12006
				originally released in 1961 as *Bill Black's Record Hop*		
7/11/64	143	4		3 **Plays Tunes By Chuck Berry**	[I]	Hi 32017
11/28/64	139	3		4 **Bill Black's Combo Goes Big Band**	[I]	Hi 32020

Billboard			R I A A	ARTIST		
DEBUT	PEAK	WKS		Album Title	Catalog	Label & Number

BLACK('S), Bill, Combo — cont'd

| 8/19/67 | 195 | 2 | | 5 Bill Black's Greatest Hits .... [G-I] | Hi 32012 |
| 9/13/69 | 168 | 4 | | 6 Solid And Raunchy The 3rd .... [I] | Hi 32052 |

~ ~ ~ ~ ~ ~ ~ ~ ~ ~ **NON-CHARTED ALBUMS** ~ ~ ~ ~ ~ ~ ~ ~ ~ ~ ~ ~

1960 **Smokie**   1961 **That Wonderful Feeling**
1960 **Saxy Jazz**

BLACK, Clint   **1990s: #24 / All-Time: #339**

Born on 2/4/1962 in Long Branch, New Jersey; raised in Katy, Texas. Country singer/songwriter/guitarist. Began singing professionally in 1981 at the Benton Springs Club in Houston. Married actress Lisa Hartman on 10/20/1991.
AWARDS: CMA: Horizon 1989 / Male Vocalist 1990 ★ OPRY: 1991

6/10/89+	31	143	▲³	1 Killin' Time	RCA 9668
11/24/90	18	80	▲³	2 Put Yourself In My Shoes	RCA 2372
8/1/92	8	41	▲	3 The Hard Way	RCA 66003
7/31/93	14	52	▲	4 No Time To Kill	RCA 66239
10/22/94	37	33	▲	5 One Emotion	RCA 66419
11/11/95	138	7		6 Looking For Christmas .... [X]	RCA 66593
				Christmas chart: 20/'95	
10/12/96	12	40	▲	7 The Greatest Hits .... [G]	RCA 66671
8/16/97	43	43	●	8 Nothin' But The Taillights	RCA 67515
10/16/99	75	23	●	9 D'lectrified	RCA 67823
12/8/01	97	7		10 Greatest Hits II .... [G]	RCA 67005
3/20/04	27	7		11 Spend My Time	Equity 3001

BLACK, Frank

Born Charles Thompson on 4/6/1965 in Long Beach, California. Alternative-rock singer/guitarist. Former leader of the **Pixies**.

3/27/93	117	5		1 Frank Black	4 A D 61467
6/11/94	131	2		2 Teenager Of The Year	4 A D 61618
2/17/96	127	1		3 The Cult Of Ray	American 43070

BLACK, Lewis

Born on 8/30/1948 in Washington DC; raised in Silver Spring, Maryland. Stand-up comedian. Regular on TV's *The Daily Show*.

| 5/13/06 | 144 | 4 | | 1 The Carnegie Hall Performance .... [C] | Comedy Central 0041 [2] |
| 8/23/08 | 64 | 3 | | 2 Anticipation .... [C] | Comedy Central 0069 |

BLACK, Stanley, and His Orchestra

Born on 6/14/1913 in London, England. Died of heart failure on 11/26/2002 (age 89). Pianist/arranger/composer. Wrote many movie scores.

2/10/62	30	8		1 Exotic Percussion .... [I]	London Phase 4 44004
8/18/62	33	10		2 Spain .... [I]	London Phase 4 44016
8/10/63	50	4		3 Film Spectacular .... [I]	London Phase 4 44025
6/12/65	148	3		4 Music Of A People .... [I]	London Phase 4 44060

BLACKALICIOUS

Rap duo from Sacramento, California: Xavier "Chief Xcel" Mosley and Tim "The Gift of Gab" Parker.

| 5/18/02 | 49 | 9 | | 1 Blazing Arrow .... | MCA 112806 |
| 10/15/05 | 102 | 1 | | 2 The Craft .... | Quannum 86745 |

BLACK BOX

Male Italian dance trio of producer Daniele Davoli and musicians Mirko Limoni and Valerio Semplici. **Martha Wash** is the uncredited lead vocalist.

| 8/11/90 | 56 | 61 | ● | 1 Dreamland .... | RCA 2221 |

BLACKBYRDS, The

R&B band from Washington DC. Core members: **Donald Byrd** (trumpet), Joe Hall (vocals, bass), Kevin Toney (vocals, keyboards) and Keith Killgo (vocals, drums).

6/22/74	96	23		1 The Blackbyrds	Fantasy 9444
12/7/74+	30	39		2 Flying Start	Fantasy 9472
7/5/75	150	6		3 Cornbread, Earl And Me .... [S]	Fantasy 9483
11/22/75+	16	40	●	4 City Life	Fantasy 9490
11/27/76+	34	24	●	5 Unfinished Business	Fantasy 9518
10/8/77	43	30	●	6 Action	Fantasy 9535
1/6/79	159	7		7 Night Grooves .... [G]	Fantasy 9570
1/17/81	133	11		8 Better Days	Fantasy 9602

BLACK CROWES, The   **All-Time: #341**

Rock and roll band from Atlanta, Georgia: brothers **Chris Robinson** (vocals; born on 12/20/1966) and Rich Robinson (guitar; born on 5/24/1969, with Jeff Cease (guitar), Johnny Colt (bass) and Steve Gorman (drums). Marc Ford replaced Cease in late 1991. Eddie Harsch (keyboards) joined in late 1992. Ford left in August 1997. Audley Freed replaced Colt in 1998. Colt joined Train in late 2003. Chris Robinson was married to actress Kate Hudson (daughter of Goldie Hawn) from 2000-07.

3/24/90+	4	165	▲⁵	1 Shake Your Money Maker Cat:#32/15	Def American 24278
5/30/92	❶¹	51	▲²	2 The Southern Harmony And Musical Companion	Def American 26916
11/19/94	11	18	●	3 Amorica	American 43000
8/10/96	15	14		4 Three Snakes And One Charm	American 43082
1/30/99	26	10		5 By Your Side	American 69361

Billboard DEBUT	PEAK	WKS	R I A A	ARTIST Album Title	Catalog	Label & Number
				BLACK CROWES, The — cont'd		
7/8/00	143	4		6 A Tribute To A Work In Progress...Greatest Hits 1990-1999 .... [G]		American 63666
7/22/00	64	9	●	7 Live At The Greek .... [L]		TVT 2140 [2]
				JIMMY PAGE & THE BLACK CROWES		
5/26/01	20	6		8 Lions...		V2 27091
9/7/02	137	1		9 Live .... [L]		V2 27134 [2]
10/14/06	128	1		10 The Lost Crows: The Tall Sessions/The Band Sessions .... [K]		American 74771 [2]
				recordings from 1993 (Tall Sessions) and 1997 (Band Sessions)		
3/22/08	5	9		11 Warpaint		Silver Arrow 01
9/19/09	12	6		12 Before The Frost...Until The Freeze .... [L]		Silver Arrow 02
				BLACK DAHLIA MURDER, The		
				Hard-rock band from Detroit, Michigan: Trevor Strnad (vocals), John Kempainen (guitar), Brian Eschbach (guitar), David Lock (bass) and Zach Gibson (drums). Group named after the infamous unsolved murder of actress Elizabeth Short in January 1947.		
7/30/05	118	1		1 Miasma		Metal Blade 14536
10/6/07	72	2		2 Nocturnal		Metal Blade 14642
10/3/09	43	3		3 Deflorate...		Metal Blade 14753
				BLACK EYED PEAS		
				Multiracial hip-hop group from Los Angeles, California: Will Adams (**will.i.am**), Allan Pineda (apl.de.ap), Jaime Gomez (Taboo) and Stacy Ferguson (**Fergie**). Ferguson was a member of **Wild Orchid**.		
7/18/98	129	9		1 Behind The Front		Interscope 90152
10/14/00	67	5		2 Bridging The Gap		Interscope 490661
7/12/03+	14	106	▲²	3 Elephunk .... Cat:#4/23		A&M 000699
6/25/05	2¹	73	▲³	4 Monkey Business		A&M 004341
6/27/09	❶²	49↑	▲²	5 The E.N.D.		Interscope 012887
				Grammy: Pop Vocal Album		
				BLACK FLAG		
				Hardcore punk band from Los Angeles, California: Henry Rollins (vocals; **Rollins Band**), Greg Ginn (guitar), Dez Cadena (guitar), Charles Dukowski (bass) and Roberto "Robo" Valverde (drums).		
				~ ~ ~ ~ ~ ~ ~ ~ ~ ~ **NON-CHARTED ALBUM** ~ ~ ~ ~ ~ ~ ~ ~ ~ ~ ~		
				1981 **Damaged**		
				RS500 #340		
				BLACKFOOT		
				Southern-rock band from Jacksonville, Florida: Rickey Medlocke (vocals, guitar), Charlie Hargrett (guitar), Greg Walker (bass) and Jakson Spires (drums). Medlocke and Walker were original members of **Lynyrd Skynyrd** (Medlocke rejoined group in 1995). Hargrett left in 1983. **Ken Hensley** (keyboards; **Uriah Heep**) joined in early 1984. Spires died of a brain hemorrhage on 3/16/2005 (age 53).		
5/12/79	42	41	▲	1 Strikes		Atco 112
6/21/80	50	20		2 Tomcattin'		Atco 101
7/25/81	48	12		3 Marauder		Atco 107
6/11/83	82	13		4 Siogo		Atco 90080
10/27/84	176	5		5 Vertical Smiles..		Atco 90218
				BLACK 47		
				Rock band formed in the Bronx, New York: Larry Kirwan (vocals, guitar), Geoffrey Blythe (sax), Chris Byrne (pipes), Fred Parcells (trombone), David Conrad (bass) and Thomas Hamlin (drums). All are originally from Ireland. Group name stands for the blackest year of the Irish potato famine (1847).		
4/10/93	176	1		1 Fire Of Freedom		SBK 80686
				co-produced by Ric Ocasek		
				BLACKHAWK		
				Country vocal trio formed in Nashville, Tennessee: **Henry Paul**, **Van Stephenson** and Dave Robbins. Stephenson died of cancer on 4/8/2001 (age 47).		
2/19/94	98	83	▲²	1 BlackHawk		Arista 18708
9/30/95	22	32	●	2 Strong Enough		Arista 18792
8/16/97	79	9		3 Love & Gravity		Arista 18837
10/17/98	192	2		4 The Sky's The Limit..		Arista Nashville 18872
6/3/00	152	3		5 Greatest Hits.. [G]		Arista Nashville 18907
				BLACK HEAT		
				Funk band from New York: Bradley Owens (guitar), Johnell Grey (keyboards), Namon "Chip" Jones (bass), Esco Cromer (drums), Raymond Green (percussion), Ray Thompson (sax, flute) and Rodney Edwards (trumpet). All shared vocals.		
4/6/74	201	9		1 No Time To Burn		Atlantic 7294
				BLACK IVORY		
				R&B vocal trio from Brooklyn, New York: Leroy Burgess, Stuart Bascombe and Russell Patterson.		
4/22/72	158	9		1 Don't Turn Around		Today 1005
1/20/73	188	9		2 Baby, Won't You Change Your Mind		Today 1008
				BLACKJACK		
				Rock band formed in New York: Michael Bolotin (vocals), Bruce Kulick (guitar), Jimmy Haslip (bass) and Sandy Gennaro (drums). Haslip joined the **Yellowjackets**. Bolotin began solo career in 1983 as **Michael Bolton**. Kulick joined **Kiss** in 1985.		
7/21/79	127	7		1 Blackjack...		Polydor 6215

BLACK KEYS, The
Rock duo from Akron, Ohio: **Dan Auerbach** (vocals, guitar) and Patrick Carney (drums).

9/25/04	143	1	1 Rubber Factory		Fat Possum 80379
5/20/06	199	1	2 Chulahoma [EP]		Fat Possum 1032
9/30/06	95	2	3 Magic Potion		Nonesuch 79967
4/19/08	14	11	4 Attack & Release		Nonesuch 292476
12/12/09	110	2	5 BlakRoc		BlakRoc 33032

BLACK KIDS
Alternative-pop band from Jacksonville, Florida: brothers Reggie Youngblood (vocals, guitar) and Ali Youngblood (keyboards), Dawn Watley (keyboards), Owen Holmes (bass) and Kevin Snow (drums).

8/9/08	127	3	1 Partie Traumatic		Almostgold 31783

BLACK LABEL SOCIETY
Hard-rock band from Jersey City, New Jersey: Zakk Wylde (vocals, guitar, bass) and Craig Nunenmacher (drums). Wylde was lead guitarist for **Ozzy Osbourne** and his own band, **Pride & Glory**.

3/23/02	149	1	1 1919*Eternal		Spitfire 15176
5/10/03	50	7	2 The Blessed Hellride		Spitfire 15091
5/8/04	40	5	3 Hangover Music Vol. VI		Spitfire 15081
3/26/05	15	8	4 Mafia		Artemis 51610
9/30/06	21	4	5 Shot To Hell		Roadrunner 618048
5/9/09	111	2	6 Skullage		Armoury 25030

BLACK LIGHT BURNS
Hard-rock band formed in Los Angeles, California: Wes Borland (vocals, bass), Danny Lohner (guitar), John Freese (keyboards) and Josh Eustis (drums). Borland was a member of **Limp Bizkit**.

6/23/07	133	1	1 Cruel Melody		I Am: Wolfpack 40079

BLACK MIKE
Born in Queens, New York. Male rapper.

11/29/08+	190	2	1 That's Me [EP]		Grind Power 931

BLACK MOON
Rap trio from Brooklyn, New York: Kenyatta "**Buckshot** Shorty" Blake (lead vocals), 5 Ft. Excellerator and Edward "DJ Evil Dee" Dewgarde.

4/3/99	35	5	1 War Zone		Duck Down 50039

BLACKMORE, Ritchie — see RAINBOW

BLACK MOUNTAIN
Hard-rock band from Vancouver, British Columbia, Canada: Stephen McBean (male vocals, guitar), Amber Webber (female vocals), Jeremy Schmidt (keyboards), Matt Camirand (bass) and Joshua Wells (drums).

2/9/08	101	2	1 In The Future		Jagjaguwar 090

BLACK 'N BLUE
Hard-rock band from Portland, Oregon: Jaime St. James (vocals), Tom Thayer (guitar), Jeff Warner (guitar), Patrick Young (bass) and Pete Holmes (drums).

9/15/84	116	11	1 Black 'N Blue		Geffen 24041
10/25/86	110	20	2 Nasty Nasty		Geffen 24111
4/23/88	133	9	3 In Heat		Geffen 24180

BLACK OAK ARKANSAS
Southern-rock band from Black Oak, Arkansas: Jim "Dandy" Mangrum (vocals), Ricky Reynolds, Jimmy Henderson and Stan Knight (guitars), Pat Daugherty (bass) and Wayne Evans (drums).

8/28/71	127	12	● 1 Black Oak Arkansas		Atco 354
2/12/72	103	10	2 Keep The Faith		Atco 381
7/8/72	93	19	3 If An Angel Came To See You, Would You Make Her Feel At Home?		Atco 7008
3/17/73	90	16	4 Raunch 'N' Roll/Live [L]		Atco 7019
11/24/73+	52	22	● 5 High On The Hog		Atco 7035
7/27/74	56	12	6 Street Party		Atco 101
5/31/75	145	8	7 Ain't Life Grand		Atco 111
10/18/75+	99	17	8 X-Rated		MCA 2155
2/28/76	194	2	9 Live! Mutha [L]		Atco 128
			recorded on 5/11/1975 at the Long Beach Auditorium in California		
6/12/76	173	7	10 Balls Of Fire		MCA 2199

BLACK PEARL
Rock band formed in San Francisco, California: Bernie "B.B." Fieldings (vocals), Bruce Benson (guitar), Jeff Morris (guitar), Jerry Causi (bass) and Tom Molcahy (drums). Benson, Morris and Causi were members of The Barbarians.

5/3/69	130	5	1 Black Pearl		Atlantic 8220
10/17/70	189	2	2 Black Pearl-Live! [L]		Prophesy 1001
			recorded in October 1968 at the Fillmore West		

BLACK REBEL MOTORCYCLE CLUB
Eclectic-rock trio from San Francisco, California: Peter Hayes (vocals, guitar), Robert Turner (bass) and Nick Jago (drums).

9/20/03	47	4	1 Take Them On, On Your Own		Virgin 80095
9/10/05	90	3	2 Howl		RCA 71601
5/19/07	46	4	3 Baby 81		Abstract Dragon 03802

			R I A A	ARTIST		
DEBUT	**PEAK**	**WKS**		**Album Title**	**Catalog**	**Label & Number**

BLACK ROB
Born Robert Ross in 1970 in Harlem, New York. Male rapper.

3/25/00	**3**[1]	19	▲	1 Life Story		Bad Boy 73026
11/5/05	**40**	3		2 The Black Rob Report..		Bad Boy 83840

BLACK SABBATH   **All-Time: #137**

Heavy-metal rock band from Birmingham, England: **Ozzy Osbourne** (vocals; born on 12/3/1948), Tony **Iommi** (guitar; born on 2/19/1948), Terry "Geezer" Butler (bass; born on 7/17/1949) and William Ward (drums; born on 5/5/1948). Osbourne left in 1979; replaced by Ronnie James **Dio** (**Rainbow**). Ward left for a year in 1981; replaced by Vinnie Appice (younger brother of **Carmine Appice**). In 1983, Ian **Gillan** (**Deep Purple**) replaced Dio who, with Appice, formed Dio. Fluctuating lineup since 1986. Iommi was the only original member in lineups that included vocalists Glenn Hughes (1986; ex-bassist of Deep Purple) and Tony Martin (since 1987); bassists Dave Spitz (1986-87), Bob Daisley (1987), Laurence Cottle (1989) and Neil Murray (since 1990); drummers Eric Singer (1986-87), Bev Bevan (1987; **Move**, **ELO**) and Cozy Powell (since 1989; **Jeff Beck Group**, **Emerson, Lake & Powell**), and keyboardist Geoff Nicholls (1983-89). Singer later joined **Kiss**. In 1991, reunion of Iommi, Butler, Appice and Dio. Lineup in 1994: Iommi, Butler, Martin, Nichols and Bobby Rondinelli (drums). Powell died in a car crash on 4/5/1998 (age 50). Original lineup reunited in 1997. Dio died of stomach cancer on 5/16/2010 (age 67). Also see **Heaven & Hell**. Also see **Various Artists Compilations**: *Nativity In Black: A Tribute To Black Sabbath*.
        AWARD: R&R Hall of Fame: 2006

8/29/70	**23**	65	▲	1 Black Sabbath .... **Cat:**#29/29		Warner 1871
				RS500 #241		
2/20/71	**12**	70	▲[4]	2 Paranoid		Warner 1887
				RS500 #130		
9/4/71	**8**	43	▲[2]	3 Master Of Reality **Cat:**#6/19		Warner 2562
				RS500 #298		
10/21/72	**13**	31	▲	4 Black Sabbath, Vol. 4 .... **Cat:**#42/2		Warner 2602
1/26/74	**11**	32	▲	5 Sabbath Bloody Sabbath .... **Cat:**#34/19		Warner 2695
8/23/75	**28**	14	●	6 Sabotage		Warner 2822
10/30/76	**51**	12	●	7 Technical Ecstasy		Warner 2969
10/28/78	**69**	14	●	8 Never Say Die!		Warner 3186
6/14/80	**28**	24	▲	9 Heaven And Hell		Warner 3372
11/28/81	**29**	18	●	10 Mob Rules		Warner 3605
10/22/83	**39**	16		11 Born Again		Warner 23978
2/15/86	**78**	11		12 Seventh Star		Warner 25337
				BLACK SABBATH Featuring Tony Iommi		
12/26/87+	**168**	6		13 The Eternal Idol		Warner 25548
5/13/89	**115**	8		14 Headless Cross		I.R.S. 82002
7/18/92	**44**	8		15 Dehumanizer		Reprise 26965
2/26/94	**122**	2		16 Cross Purposes		I.R.S. 13222
				GREATEST HITS & COMPILATIONS:		
2/28/76	**48**	10	▲[2]	17 We Sold Our Soul For Rock 'N' Roll		Warner 2923 [2]
4/1/06	**96**	10		18 Greatest Hits 1970-78...		Warner 73365
4/21/07	**54**	9		19 The Dio Years		Warner 116668
				LIVE ALBUMS:		
2/5/83	**37**	12		20 Live Evil..		Warner 23742 [2]
11/7/98	**11**	18	▲	21 Reunion		Epic 69115 [2]
				recorded on 12/5/1997 in Birmingham, England		
9/7/02	**114**	1		22 Past Lives		Divine 84561 [2]
				contains recordings made at various locations and dates during the 1970s		

BLACK SHEEP
Rap duo from the Bronx, New York: Andres "Dres" Titus and William "Mista Lawnge" McLean.

11/9/91+	**30**	41	●	1 A Wolf In Sheep's Clothing		Mercury 848368
12/24/94	**107**	3		2 Non-Fiction		Mercury 522685

BLACK STAR
Rap duo formed in New York: **Mos Def** and **Talib Kweli**.

10/17/98	**53**	5		1 Black Star		Rawkus 1158

BLACK STONE CHERRY
Southern-rock band from Edmonton, Kentucky: Chris Robertson (vocals, guitar), Ben Wells (guitar), Jon Lawhon (bass) and John Fred Young (drums). Young is the son of Richard Young and the nephew of Fred Young, both of **The Kentucky Headhunters**.

8/5/06	**90**	3		1 Black Stone Cherry		In De Goot 618086
9/6/08	**28**	4		2 Folklore And Superstition		In De Goot 617940

BLACKstreet
R&B/hip-hop group formed in New York: Teddy Riley, Chauncey Hannibal, Levi Little and **Dave Hollister**. Riley was a member of **Guy**. Hollister and Little left in late 1995; replaced by Eric Williams and Mark Middleton.

7/9/94	**52**	51	▲	1 Blackstreet...		Interscope 92351
9/28/96	**3**[1]	60	▲[4]	2 Another Level		Interscope 90071
4/10/99	**9**	12	●	3 Finally		Lil' Man 90274
3/29/03	**14**	5		4 Level II		DreamWorks 450392

BLACK TIDE
Hard-rock band from Miami, Florida: Gabriel Garcia (vocals, guitar), Alex Nunez (guitar), Zachary Sandler (bass) and Steven Spence (drums).

4/5/08	**73**	4		1 Light From Above		Interscope 010565

BLACK UHURU
Reggae vocal trio from Jamaica: Don Carlos, Duckie Simpson and Garth Dennis. Carlos and Dennis left in 1977, Michael Rose and female vocalist Puma Jones joined. Rose and Jones left in 1985, Delroy Reid and Janet Reid were added. Carlos, Simpson and Dennis reunited in 1987. Uhuru means freedom in Swahili.

| 7/24/82 | 146 | 7 | | 1 Chill Out .... | | Island 9752 |
| 3/10/90 | 121 | 11 | | 2 Now .... | | Mesa 79021 |

BLADES, Ruben
Born on 7/16/1948 in Panama City, Panama. Latin singer/actor. Appeared in several movies.

| 5/7/88 | 156 | 6 | | 1 Nothing But The Truth .... | | Elektra 60754 |

BLAKEY, Art
Born on 10/11/1919 in Pittsburgh, Pennsylvania. Died of cancer on 10/16/1990 (age 71). Black jazz drummer. Played in **Billy Eckstine**'s band from 1944-47.
> AWARD: Grammy: Lifetime Achievement 2005

~ ~ ~ ~ ~ ~ ~ ~ ~ **NON-CHARTED ALBUMS** ~ ~ ~ ~ ~ ~ ~ ~ ~ ~ ~

1956 **A Night At Birdland, Volume 1**   1958 **Art Blakey And The Jazz Messengers: Moanin'**
Grammy: Hall of Fame   *Grammy: Hall of Fame*
1956 **A Night At Birdland, Volume 2**
Grammy: Hall of Fame

BLAKROC — see BLACK KEYS

BLANCHARD, Jack, & Misty Morgan
Husband-and-wife country duo. Both born in Buffalo, New York. Jack (born on 5/8/1942) plays saxophone and keyboards. Misty (born on 5/23/1945) plays keyboards. Met and married while working in Florida in 1963.

| 7/4/70 | 185 | 5 | | 1 Birds Of A Feather .... | | Wayside 001 |

BLANCMANGE
Techno-rock duo from England: Neil Arthur (vocals, guitar) and Stephen Luscombe (keyboards).

| 3/26/83 | 206 | 4 | | 1 Happy Families .... | | Island 90053 |
| 9/29/84 | 204 | 3 | | 2 Mange Tout .... | | Sire 25172 |

BLAND, Bobby
Born on 1/27/1930 in Rosemark, Tennessee. Blues singer/guitarist. Nicknamed "Blue." In the late 1940s, sang in gospel group The Miniatures in Memphis, Tennessee. Member of legendary blues band the Beale Streeters in 1949. Driver and valet for **B.B. King** in the early 1950s.
> AWARDS: Grammy: Lifetime Achievement 1997 ★ R&R Hall of Fame: 1992

9/1/62	53	7		1 Here's The Man!!!		Duke 75
7/13/63	11	26		2 Call On Me/That's The Way Love Is		Duke 77
8/1/64	119	8		3 Ain't Nothing You Can Do		Duke 78
11/3/73+	136	19		4 His California Album		Dunhill/ABC 50163
				BOBBY BLUE BLAND		
8/3/74	172	7		5 Dreamer		Dunhill/ABC 50169
10/26/74+	43	20	●	6 Together For The First Time...Live .... [L]		Dunhill/ABC 50190 [2]
				B.B. KING & BOBBY BLAND		
9/13/75	154	5		7 Get On Down With Bobby Bland		ABC 895
7/17/76	73	14		8 Together Again...Live .... [L]		ABC/Impulse 9317
				BOBBY BLAND & B.B. KING		
5/14/77	185	4		9 Reflections In Blue		ABC 1018
7/1/78	185	3		10 Come Fly With Me		ABC 1075
10/27/79	187	2		11 I Feel Good, I Feel Fine		MCA 3157
9/19/81	207	2		12 Try Me, I'm Real		MCA 5233
7/17/82	201	8		13 Here We Go Again		MCA 5297

~ ~ ~ ~ ~ ~ ~ ~ ~ **NON-CHARTED ALBUMS** ~ ~ ~ ~ ~ ~ ~ ~ ~ ~ ~

1961 **Two Steps From The Blues**   1966 **The Soul Of The Man**
RS500 #215   1967 **The Best Of Bobby Bland**

BLANK, Amanda
Born Amanda Mallory in Philadelphia, Pennsylvania. Female rapper.

| 8/22/09 | 109 | 1 | | 1 I Love You .... | | Downtown 70089 |

BLAQK AUDIO
Electronic-rock duo from San Francisco, California: Davey "Havok" Marchand (vocals) and Jade Puget (instruments). Both are also members of **AFI**.

| 9/1/07 | 18 | 5 | | 1 Cexcells .... | | Tiny Evil 009512 |

BLAQUE
Female R&B vocal trio from Atlanta, Georgia: Shamari Fears, Natina Reed and Brandi Williams.

| 6/19/99+ | 53 | 54 | ▲ | 1 Blaque .... | | Track Masters 68987 |

BLASTERS, The
Rock band formed in Los Angeles, California: brothers Phil Alvin (vocals, guitar) and **Dave Alvin** (guitar), Gene Taylor (piano), John Bazz (bass), and Bill Bateman (drums).

1/9/82	36	30		1 The Blasters		Slash 3680
10/30/82	117	8		2 Over There-Live At The Venue, London .... [EP-L]		Slash 23735
				recorded on 5/22/1982		

Billboard			R I A A	ARTIST		
DEBUT	PEAK	WKS		Album Title	Catalog	Label & Number
				BLASTERS, The — cont'd		
5/14/83	95	8		3 Non Fiction		Slash 23818
3/23/85	86	19		4 Hard Line		Slash 25093

BLAZE YA DEAD HOMIE
Born Christopher Rouleau on 7/1/1975 in Mt. Clemens, Michigan. White male rapper.

| 11/6/04 | 167 | 1 | | 1 Colton Grundy .... | | Psychopathic 40432 |
| 9/8/07 | 100 | 1 | | 2 Clockwork Gray .... | | Psychopathic 4300 |

BLAZE

BLED, The
Hard-rock band from Tucson, Arizona: James Munoz (vocals), Ross Ott (guitar), Jeremy Talley (guitar), Darren Simoes (bass) and Mike Pedicone (drums).

| 9/10/05 | 87 | 1 | | 1 Found In The Flood .... | | Vagrant 413 |

BLEEDING THROUGH
Hard-rock band from Anaheim, California: Brandon Schieppati (vocals), Scott Danough (guitar), Brian Leppke (guitar), Marta Peterson (keyboards), Ryan Wombacher (bass) and Derek Youngsma (drums).

| 1/28/06 | 48 | 3 | | 1 The Truth .... | | Trustkill 72 |
| 10/18/08 | 104 | 1 | | 2 Declaration .... | | Trustkill 116 |

B-LEGIT
Born Brandt Jones in 1970 in Vallejo, California. Male rapper. Member of **The Click**. Cousin of **E-40**.

12/14/96	55	10		1 The Hemp Museum		Sick Wid' It 41593
9/30/00	64	6		2 Hempin' Ain't Easy		Koch 8167
10/12/02	111	3		3 Hard 2 B-Legit		Koch 8322

BLESSID UNION OF SOULS
Interracial pop-rock band from Cincinnati, Ohio: Eliot Sloan (vocals, piano), Jeff Pence (guitar), Charly Roth (keyboards), Tony Clark (bass) and Eddie Hedges (drums). Group name taken from a line in the TV series *M*A*S*H*.

4/22/95	78	29	●	1 Home		EMI 31836
6/7/97	127	10		2 Blessid Union Of Souls		EMI 56716
6/5/99	143	15		3 Walking Off The Buzz		Push 27047
3/17/01	178	1		4 The Singles .... [G]		V2 27086

| | | | | **BLESSING, Adam — see DAMNATION OF** | | |

BLESSTHEFALL
Heavy metal band from Phoenix, Arizona: Beau Bokan (vocals), Eric Lambert (guitar), Mike Frisby (guitar), Jared Warth (bass) and Matt Traynor (drums).

| 10/24/09 | 56 | 2 | | 1 Witness .... | | Fearless 30131 |

BLEU, Corbin
Born Corbin Bleu Reivers on 2/21/1989 in Brooklyn, New York (Jamaican father; American mother). Male singer/dancer/actor. Played "Chad Danforth" in the popular TV movie series *High School Musical*.

| 5/19/07 | 36 | 14 | | 1 Another Side .... | | Walt Disney 000343 |

BLIGE, Mary J. 2000s: #43 / All-Time: #189
Born Mary Jane Blige on 1/11/1971 in the Bronx, New York; spent first few years in Savannah, Georgia; mainly raised in Yonkers, New York. R&B singer/songwriter. Began singing in her church choir as a child. Signed to Uptown/MCA by rapper **Heavy D**. Played "Mrs. Butler" in the 2001 movie *Prison Song*.

8/15/92	6	58	▲³	1 What's The 411?		Uptown 10681
12/25/93+	118	14	●	2 What's The 411? Remix .... [K]		Uptown 10942
12/17/94+	7	46	▲³	3 My Life		Uptown 11156
				RS500 #279		
5/10/97	❶¹	57	▲³	4 Share My World		MCA 11606
8/15/98	21	12	●	5 The Tour .... [L]		MCA 11848
9/4/99	2¹	57	▲²	6 Mary		MCA 11929
9/15/01	2¹	24	▲²	7 No More Drama		MCA 112616
2/23/02	14	33		8 No More Drama .... [R]		MCA 112808
				contains some different cuts and new mixes of songs from #7 above		
8/31/02	76	4		9 Dance For Me .... [K]		MCA 112959
				contains new remixes from #7 above		
9/13/03	❶¹	25	▲	10 Love & Life		Geffen 000956
1/7/06	❶²	72	▲³	11 The Breakthrough		Geffen 005722
12/30/06	9	21		12 Reflections (A Retrospective) [G]		Matriarch 008112
12/8/07	95	1		13 Mary J. Blige & Friends .... Cat:❶²/4 [EP]		Matriarch 71315
1/5/08	❶¹	36		14 Growing Pains		Matriarch 010313
				Grammy: Contemporary R&B Album		

BLIND BOYS OF ALABAMA, The

Legendary Southern gospel group from Talladega, Alabama: Bobby Butler, Jimmy Carter, Clarence Fountain, Ricke McKinnie, Tracie Pierce, George Scott and Joe Williams. Scott died on 3/9/2005 (age 75).

AWARD: Grammy: Lifetime Achievement 2009

DEBUT	PEAK	WKS		ALBUM	CATALOG	LABEL
12/20/03+	164	3		1 Go Tell It On The Mountain .... [X]		Real World 90600
				Grammy: Traditional Soul Gospel Album		
				Christmas chart: 20/'03		
10/9/04	81	6		2 There Will Be A Light		Virgin 71206
				BEN HARPER AND THE BLIND BOYS OF ALABAMA		

BLIND FAITH

Rock supergroup from England: **Eric Clapton** (The Yardbirds, **Cream**), **Steve Winwood** (**Spencer Davis Group**, **Traffic**), **Ginger Baker** (Cream) and **Rick Grech** (**Family**, Traffic). Formed and disbanded in 1969.

8/16/69	❶²	37	▲	1 Blind Faith		Atco 304
				original cover depicted a prepubescent nude girl; quickly withdrawn and replaced by a photo of the band		
2/26/77	126	8		2 Blind Faith .... [R]		RSO 3016
				re-issued with the original, controversial cover		

BLIND MELON

Male rock band formed in Los Angeles, California: Shannon Hoon (vocals), Rogers Stevens (guitar) Christopher Thorn (guitar), Brad Smith (bass) and Glen Graham (drums). Hoon died of a drug overdose on 10/21/1995 (age 28).

7/24/93	3¹	44	▲⁴	1 Blind Melon		Capitol 96585
9/2/95	28	9		2 Soup		Capitol 28732
11/30/96	161	1		3 Nico .... [K]		Capitol 37451
				recordings from 1991-95		
5/10/08	133	1		4 For My Friends		Wishbone 101028

BLIND PILOT

Pop duo from Portland, Oregon: Israel Nebeker and Ryan Dobrowski.

7/26/08	149	1		1 3 Rounds And A Sound		Expunged 0007

BLINDSIDE

Rock band from Stockholm, Sweden: Christian Lindskog (vocals), Simon Grenehed (guitar), Tomas Naslund (bass) and Marcus Dahlstrom (drums).

9/7/02	83	9		1 Silence		Elektra 62765
3/13/04	39	4		2 About A Burning Fire		Elektra 62918
8/20/05	89	1		3 The Great Depression		Wasa 00436

BLINK-182

Punk-rock trio from San Diego, California: Tom DeLonge (vocals, guitar), Mark Hoppus (vocals, bass) and Scott Raynor (drums). Travis Barker (formerly of **The Aquabats**) replaced Raynor in late 1998. DeLonge and Barker also formed **Box Car Racer**. Barker is also a member of the **Transplants**.

7/5/97+	67	48	▲	1 Dude Ranch .... Cat:#27/7		MCA 11624
6/19/99	9	86	▲⁵	2 Enema Of The State Cat:#6/19		MCA 11950
11/25/00	8	17	●	3 The Mark, Tom, And Travis Show (The Enema Strikes Back!) [L]		MCA 112379
6/30/01	❶¹	58	▲²	4 Take Off Your Pants And Jacket		MCA 112627
12/6/03	3¹	47	▲	5 Blink-182		Geffen 001336
11/19/05	6	20		6 Greatest Hits [G]		Geffen 005607

BLITZEN TRAPPER

Folk-rock band from Portland, Oregon: Eric Earley (vocals, guitar), Erik Menteer (guitar), Marty Marquis (guitar), Drew Laughery (keyboards), Michael Van Pelt (bass) and Brian Koch (drums).

1/24/09	189	1		1 Furr		Sub Pop 755

BLOC PARTY

Alternative-rock band from London, England: Kele Okereke (vocals, guitar), Russell Lissack (guitar), Gordon Moakes (bass) and Matt Tong (drums).

4/9/05	114	16		1 Silent Alarm		Vice 93815
2/24/07	12	7		2 A Weekend In The City		Vice 94598
11/15/08	18	3		3 Intimacy.............		Atlantic 512336

BLODWYN PIG

Blues-rock band from England: Mick Abrahams (vocals, guitar; **Jethro Tull**), Jack Lancaster (sax), Andy Pyle (bass) and Ron Berg (drums).

12/13/69+	149	5		1 Ahead Rings Out		A&M 4210
6/27/70	96	5		2 Getting To This		A&M 4243

BLONDE REDHEAD

Alternative-rock trio formed in New York: Japanese female Kazu Makino (vocals), with Italian brothers Amedeo Pace (guitar) and Simone Pace (drums).

4/10/04	180	1		1 Misery Is A Butterfly		4AD 2409
4/28/07	63	2		2 23		4AD 2717

BLONDIE

New-wave rock band formed in New York: **Debbie Harry** (vocals; born on 7/1/1945), Chris Stein (guitar; born on 1/5/1950), Frank Infante (guitar; born in 1952), **Jimmy Destri** (keyboards; born on 4/13/1954), Nigel Harrison (bass; born on 4/18/1951) and Clem Burke (drums; born on 11/24/1955). Harry had been in the folk-rock band **The Wind In The Willows**. Group disbanded in 1982. Harrison and Burke joined **Chequered Past**. Harrison was also a member of **Silverhead** and **Nite City**. Harry, Stein, Destri and Burke reunited in 1999.

> AWARD: R&R Hall of Fame: 2006

DEBUT	PEAK	WKS	RIAA	#	Album Title	Catalog	Label & Number
2/25/78	**72**	17		1	Plastic Letters		Chrysalis 1166
9/23/78+	**6**	103	▲	2	Parallel Lines		Chrysalis 1192
					RS500 #140		
10/20/79	**17**	51	▲	3	Eat To The Beat		Chrysalis 1225
12/13/80+	**7**	34	▲	4	Autoamerican		Chrysalis 1290
10/31/81	**30**	23	▲²	5	The Best Of Blondie	Cat:#13/25 **[G]**	Chrysalis 1337
6/19/82	**33**	12		6	The Hunter		Chrysalis 1384
3/13/99	**18**	15		7	No Exit		Beyond 78003
4/24/04	**160**	1		8	The Curse Of Blondie		Sanctuary 84666

BLOOD BROTHERS, The

Punk-rock band from Seattle, Washington: Jordan Billie (vocals, guitar), Johnny Whitney (vocals, keyboards), Cody Votolato (guitar), Morgan Henderson (bass) and Mark Gajadhar (drums).

DEBUT	PEAK	WKS		#	Album Title		Label & Number
10/30/04	**157**	1		1	Crimes		V2 27214
10/28/06	**92**	1		2	Young Machetes		Radar 27338

BLOODHOUND GANG

Electro-rock band from Trappe, Pennsylvania: James "Jimmy Pop Ali" Franks (vocals), Matt "Lupus Thunder" Stigliano (guitar), Q-Ball (DJ), Evil Jared Hasselhoff (bass) and Spanky G (drums). Willie The New Guy replaced Spanky G in 1999.

DEBUT	PEAK	WKS		#	Album Title		Label & Number
1/18/97	**57**	26	●	1	One Fierce Beer Coaster		Geffen 25124
3/18/00	**14**	29	▲	2	Hooray For Boobies		Republic 490455
10/15/05	**24**	6		3	Hefty Fine		Republic 005284

BLOOD RAW

Born Bruce Falson on 1/2/1981 in Panama City, Florida. Male rapper. Member of **U.S.D.A.**

DEBUT	PEAK	WKS		#	Album Title		Label & Number
7/5/08	**29**	3		1	My Life: The True Testimony		CTE 011143

BLOODROCK

Hard-rock band from Fort Worth, Texas: Jim Rutledge (vocals), Lee Pickens (guitar), Nick Taylor (guitar), Stevie Hill (keyboards), Eddie Grundy (bass) and Rick Cobb (drums). Rutledge left in 1972, replaced by Warren Ham.

DEBUT	PEAK	WKS		#	Album Title		Label & Number
4/25/70	**160**	5		1	Bloodrock		Capitol 435
11/7/70+	**21**	37	●	2	Bloodrock 2		Capitol 491
4/10/71	**27**	23		3	Bloodrock 3		Capitol 765
11/6/71	**88**	7		4	Bloodrock U.S.A.		Capitol 645
6/3/72	**67**	22		5	Bloodrock Live	**[L]**	Capitol 11038 [2]
					recorded at the Chicago Ampitheater		
9/30/72	**104**	14		6	Bloodrock Passage		Capitol 11109

BLOODS & CRIPS

Rap group formed by producer Ron Phillips in Los Angeles, California. Made up of members of two notorious rival street gangs. Features a revolving lineup of rappers.

DEBUT	PEAK	WKS		#	Album Title		Label & Number
3/27/93	**86**	19		1	Bangin On Wax		Dangerous 19138
10/8/94	**139**	4		2	Bangin On Wax 2		Dangerous 6715

BLOODSTONE

R&B vocal group from Kansas City, Missouri: Charles Love, Willis Draffen, Charles McCormick and Harry Williams. Group starred in the 1975 movie *Train Ride To Hollywood*. Draffen died on 2/8/2002 (age 56).

DEBUT	PEAK	WKS		#	Album Title		Label & Number
4/14/73	**30**	36		1	Natural High		London 620
1/5/74	**110**	22		2	Unreal		London 634
8/10/74	**141**	8		3	I Need Time		London 647
2/22/75	**147**	6		4	Riddle Of The Sphinx		London 645
7/17/82	**95**	11		5	We Go A Long Way Back		T-Neck 38115

BLOOD, SWEAT & TEARS   All-Time: #382

Pop-jazz band formed by **Al Kooper** (Royal Teens, **Blues Project**) in New York. Nucleus consisted of Kooper (keyboards), Steve Katz (guitar; Blues Project), Jim Fielder (bass) and Bobby Colomby (drums). Kooper replaced by lead singer **David Clayton-Thomas** by 1969. Clayton-Thomas replaced by Jerry Fisher in 1972. Katz left in 1973. Clayton-Thomas rejoined in 1974.

DEBUT	PEAK	WKS		#	Album Title		Label & Number
4/13/68	**47**	55	●	1	Child Is Father To The Man		Columbia 9619
					Grammy: Hall of Fame ★ RS500 #264		
2/1/69	**❶**⁷	109	▲⁴	2	Blood, Sweat & Tears		Columbia 9720
					Grammys: Album of the Year / Hall of Fame		
7/18/70	**❶**²	41	●	3	Blood, Sweat & Tears 3		Columbia 30090
7/10/71	**10**	23	●	4	B, S & T; 4		Columbia 30590
3/11/72	**19**	27	▲²	5	Blood, Sweat & Tears Greatest Hits	**[G]**	Columbia 31170
11/4/72	**32**	17		6	New Blood		Columbia 31780
8/25/73	**72**	12		7	No Sweat		Columbia 32180
9/7/74	**149**	6		8	Mirror Image		Columbia 32929
5/31/75	**47**	13		9	New City		Columbia 33484
7/31/76	**165**	3		10	More Than Ever		Columbia 34233
12/3/77	**205**	4		11	Brand New Day		ABC 1015

BLOOM, Bobby
Born in 1945 in Brooklyn, New York. Died from an accidental shooting on 2/28/1974 (age 28). Pop singer/songwriter. Much session work in the 1960s.

| 11/28/70 | 126 | 3 | | 1 The Bobby Bloom Album .... | | L&R 1035 |

BLOOMFIELD, Mike
Born on 7/28/1944 in Chicago, Illinois. Died of a drug overdose on 2/15/1981 (age 36). Blues-rock singer/guitarist. With The **Paul Butterfield** Blues Band and **Electric Flag**. Later joined **KGB**.

8/31/68	12	37	●	1 Super Session		Columbia 9701
				MIKE BLOOMFIELD / AL KOOPER / STEVE STILLS		
2/8/69	18	20		2 The Live Adventures Of Mike Bloomfield And Al Kooper .... [L]		Columbia 6 [2]
				MIKE BLOOMFIELD & AL KOOPER		
				recorded on 9/27/1968 at the Fillmore in San Francisco, California		
10/11/69	127	5		3 It's Not Killing Me		Columbia 9883
				MICHAEL BLOOMFIELD		
6/16/73	105	12		4 Triumvirate...		Columbia 32172
				MIKE BLOOMFIELD / JOHN PAUL HAMMOND / DR. JOHN		

BLOW, Kurtis
Born Kurtis Walker on 8/9/1959 in Harlem, New York. Highly influential rapper. Appeared in the 1985 movie *Krush Groove*.

10/18/80	71	10		1 Kurtis Blow		Mercury 3854
7/18/81	137	5		2 Deuce		Mercury 4020
10/9/82	167	5		3 Tough .... [EP]		Mercury 505
9/17/83+	203	3		4 Party Time?		Mercury 812757
10/13/84+	83	37		5 Ego Trip		Mercury 822420
11/2/85	153	15		6 America		Mercury 826141
12/13/86	196	2		7 Kingdom Blow		Mercury 830215

BLOWFLY
Born Clarence Reid on 2/14/1945 in Cochran, Georgia. X-rated singer/songwriter/producer.

| 5/24/80 | 82 | 20 | | 1 Blowfly's Party [X-Rated] .... | | Weird World 2034 |

BLOW MONKEYS, The
Pop-rock band from England: "Dr. Robert" Howard (vocals, guitar), Neville Henry (sax), Mick Anker (bass) and Tony Kiley (drums).

| 6/21/86 | 35 | 18 | | 1 Animal Magic .... | | RCA Victor 8065 |
| 4/25/87 | 134 | 8 | | 2 She Was Only A Grocer's Daughter .... | | RCA Victor 6246 |

BLUE CHEER
Hard-rock trio formed in Boston, Massachusetts; later based in San Francisco, California: Dickie Peterson (vocals, bass), Leigh Stephens (guitar) and Paul Whaley (drums). Considered to be the first "heavy metal" band. Peterson died on 10/12/2009 (age 61).

3/9/68	11	27		1 Vincebus Eruptum		Philips 264
9/28/68	90	16		2 Outsideinside		Philips 278
5/3/69	84	14		3 New! Improved! Blue Cheer		Philips 305
11/7/70	188	5		4 The Original Human Being		Philips 347

BLUE COLLAR COMEDY TOUR
All-star "redneck" comedy collective: **Jeff Foxworthy**, **Bill Engvall**, **Larry The Cable Guy** and **Ron White**. The first three also starred in the TV sketch comedy series *Blue Collar TV*.

1/24/04	104	32	●	1 Blue Collar Comedy Tour: The Movie .... Cat:#22/1 [C-S]		Warner 48424
12/11/04	50	13		2 Blue Collar Comedy Tour Rides Again .... [C-TV]		Warner 48930
6/24/06	19	9		3 Blue Collar Comedy Tour: One For The Road......................... [C-TV]		Jack 44252 [2]

BLUE MAGIC
R&B vocal group from Philadelphia, Pennsylvania: Theodore Mills (lead), brothers Vernon Sawyer and Wendell Sawyer, Keith Beaton and Richard Pratt.

3/16/74	45	34		1 Blue Magic		Atco 7038
12/28/74+	71	13		2 The Magic Of The Blue		Atco 103
10/4/75	50	12		3 Thirteen Blue Magic Lane		Atco 120
9/25/76	170	5		4 Mystic Dragons		Atco 140

BLUE MAN GROUP
Experimental musical theatre trio: Matt Goldman, Phil Stanton and Chris Wink. Perform with various inventive percussion instruments while dressed in blue-painted skin, skullcaps and black clothing.

| 5/19/01 | 175 | 1 | ● | 1 Audio... [I] | | Blue Man Group 48613 |
| 5/10/03 | 60 | 6 | | 2 The Complex .... | | Blue Man Group 83631 |

BLUE MERCEDES
Pop-dance duo from London, England: David Titlow (vocals) and Duncan Millar (keyboards).

| 5/14/88 | 165 | 5 | | 1 Rich And Famous .... | | MCA 42143 |

BLUE MERLE
Alternative-rock band from Nashville, Tennessee: Luke Reynolds (vocals, guitar), Beau Stapleton (mandolin), Jason Oettel (bass) and William Ellis (drums).

| 3/5/05 | 199 | 1 | | 1 Burning In The Sun .... | | Island 002961 |

BLUE MURDER
All-star rock trio: John Sykes (guitar, vocals; **Thin Lizzy**, **Whitesnake**), Tony Franklin (bass; **The Firm**) and **Carmine Appice** (drums; **Vanilla Fudge**, **Cactus**, and **KGB**).

| 5/13/89 | 69 | 21 | | 1 Blue Murder .... | | Geffen 24212 |

BLUE NILE, The
Melodic-pop trio from Glasgow, Scotland: Paul Buchanan (vocals, guitar), Robert Bell (bass) and Paul Moore (keyboards).

2/24/90	108	14		1 Hats		A&M 5284

BLUE OCTOBER
Rock band from Houston, Texas: brothers Justin Furstenfeld (vocals, guitar) and Jeremy Furstenfeld (drums), with C.B. Hudson (guitar), Ryan Delahoussaye (keyboards) and Matt Noveskey (bass).

4/22/06	29	62	▲	1 Foiled...	Universal Motown 006262
10/13/07	106	2		2 Foiled For The Last Time..	Brando 009890 [2]
4/11/09	13	16		3 Approaching Normal	Brando 012721

BLUE OYSTER CULT   All-Time: #337
Hard-rock band from Long Island, New York: Eric Bloom (vocals; born on 21/1/1944), Donald "Buck Dharma" Roeser (guitar; born on 11/12/1947), Allen Lanier (keyboards; born on 6/25/1946), and brothers Joe Bouchard (bass; born on 11/9/1948) and Albert Bouchard (born on 5/24/1947). Rick Downey replaced Albert Bouchard in 1982. Downey left in 1984. Tommy Zvoncheck (keyboards) and Jimmy Wilcox (drums) joined in 1985. Original lineup reunited in 1988. Bloom is a cousin of DJ Howard Stern.

5/20/72	172	8		1 Blue Oyster Cult		Columbia 31063
3/17/73	122	13		2 Tyranny And Mutation		Columbia 32017
4/27/74	53	14	●	3 Secret Treaties		Columbia 32858
3/15/75	22	13		4 On Your Feet Or On Your Knees .... [L]		Columbia 33371 [2]
				recorded at the Academy of Music in New York City		
6/19/76	29	35	▲	5 Agents Of Fortune	Cat:#17/12	Columbia 34164
11/12/77	43	14	●	6 Spectres		Columbia 35019
9/30/78	44	12	▲	7 Some Enchanted Evening .... Cat:#27/35 [L]		Columbia 35563
7/7/79	44	17		8 Mirrors		Columbia 36009
7/12/80	34	16		9 Cultosaurus Erectus		Columbia 36550
7/11/81	24	31	●	10 Fire Of Unknown Origin		Columbia 37389
5/15/82	29	19		11 Extraterrestrial Live .... [L]		Columbia 37946 [2]
11/26/83+	93	16		12 The Revolution By Night		Columbia 38947
2/22/86	63	14		13 Club Ninja		Columbia 39979
8/20/88	122	8		14 Imaginos		Columbia 40618

BLUE RIDGE RANGERS — see FOGERTY, John

BLUES BROTHERS
Duo of comedians John Belushi (as "Jake Blues") and Dan Aykroyd (as "Elwood Blues"). Originally created for TV's *Saturday Night Live*. Starred in their own 1980 movie. Belushi was born on 1/24/1949 in Wheaton, Illinois. Died of a drug overdose on 3/5/1982 (age 33). Aykroyd was born on 7/1/1952 in Ottawa, Ontario, Canada. Backing band included Paul Shaffer, **Steve Cropper** and Donald "Duck" Dunn. Actor John Goodman replaced Belushi for the *Blues Brothers 2000* movie. Also see **Belushi - Aykroyd**.

12/23/78+	❶¹	29	▲²	1 Briefcase Full Of Blues [L]	Atlantic 19217
				recorded at the Universal Ampitheater in Los Angeles	
6/28/80	13	19	▲	2 The Blues Brothers .... [S]	Atlantic 16017
12/27/80+	49	12		3 Made In America .... [L]	Atlantic 16025
				recorded at the Universal Ampitheater in Los Angeles	
1/9/82	143	3		4 Best Of The Blues Brothers .... [G]	Atlantic 19331
2/21/98	12	10	●	5 Blues Brothers 2000 .... [S]	Universal 53116

BLUES IMAGE
Rock band from Tampa, Florida: Mike Pinera (vocals, guitar; **Iron Butterfly**), Frank Konte (keyboards), Joe Lala (percussion), Malcolm Jones (bass) and Manuel Bertematti (drums).

8/16/69	112	9		1 Blues Image	Atco 300
4/25/70	147	13		2 Open	Atco 317
2/27/71	204	3		3 Red White & Blues Image	Atco 348

BLUES MAGOOS
Psychedelic-rock band from the Bronx, New York: Emil "Peppy Castro" Thielhelm (vocals, guitar), Mike Esposito (guitar), Ralph Scala (keyboards), Ronnie Gilbert (bass) and Geoff Daking (drums). Castro later became lead singer of **Balance**.

12/3/66+	21	32		1 Psychedelic Lollipop	Mercury 61096
4/22/67	74	16		2 Electric Comic Book	Mercury 61104

BLUES PROJECT, The
Blues-rock band formed in New York: Danny Kalb (vocals, guitar), Steve Katz (guitar), **Al Kooper** (organ), Andy Kulberg (bass) and Roy Blumenfeld (drums). Kooper and Katz went on to form **Blood, Sweat & Tears**. Kulberg died of cancer on 1/28/2002 (age 57).

5/21/66	77	21		1 Live At The Cafe Au Go Go.. [L]	Verve Folkways 3000
				recorded on 11/25/1965 in New York City	
12/17/66+	52	36		2 Projections	Verve Folkways 3008
10/7/67	71	11		3 The Blues Project Live At Town Hall .... [L]	Verve Forecast 3025
8/9/69	199	2		4 Best Of The Blues Project... [G]	Verve Forecast 3077
11/10/73	219	2		5 Reunion In Central Park .... [L]	MCA 8003 [2]
				THE ORIGINAL BLUES PROJECT	
				recorded on 6/24/1973	

BLUE STEEL
Rock band from Texas: Leonard Arnold (vocals, guitar), Richard Bowden and Howard Burke (guitars), Marc Durham (bass), and Mickey McGee and Michael Huey (drums). Bowden later formed country-novelty duo with Sandy Pinkard.

10/6/79	203	2		1 No More Lonely Nights	Infinity 9018

Billboard			R I A A	ARTIST		
DEBUT	PEAK	WKS		Album Title	Catalog	Label & Number

BLUES TRAVELER
Blues-rock band formed in Princeton, New Jersey: John Popper (vocals, harmonica), Chan Kinchla (guitar), Bobby Sheehan (bass) and Brendan Hill (drums). Sheehan died of a drug overdose on 8/20/1999 (age 31); replaced by Chan's brother, Tad Kinchla. Ben Wilson (keyboards) joined in 2000.

3/2/91	136	12	●	1 Blues Traveler .... Cat:#41/3		A&M 5308
9/21/91	125	5	●	2 Travelers & Thieves		A&M 5373
4/24/93	72	13	●	3 Save His Soul		A&M 540080
10/1/94+	8	96	▲⁶	4 Four		A&M 540265
7/20/96	46	11	▲	5 Live From The Fall .... [L]		A&M 540515 [2]
7/19/97	11	24	▲	6 Straight On Till Morning		A&M 540750
5/26/01	91	6		7 Bridge		A&M 490895
8/23/03	147	1		8 Truth Be Told		Sanctuary 84620

BLUE SWEDE
Pop band from Stockholm, Sweden: Bjorn Skifs (vocals), Michael Areklew (guitar), Anders Berglund (keyboards), Hinke Ekestubbe (sax), Thomas Berglund (trumpet), Bosse Liljedahl (bass) and Jan Guldback (drums).

4/6/74	80	17		1 Hooked On A Feeling		EMI 11286

BLUETREE
Rock band from Belfast, Northern Ireland: Aaron Boyd (vocals, guitar), Pete Kernoghan (DJ), Conor McCrory (guitar) and Pete Nickell (bass).

3/14/09	103	6		1 God Of This City		Lucid 1228063

BLUNT, James
Born James Blount on 2/22/1974 in Tidworth, Wiltshire, England. Male singer/songwriter/guitarist/pianist.

10/22/05+	2²	78	▲²	1 Back To Bedlam .... Cat:#32/2		Custard 97250
10/6/07	7	25	●	2 All The Lost Souls		Custard 286396

BLUR
Pop-rock band from London, England: Damon Albarn (vocals), Graham Coxon (guitar), Alex James (bass) and Dave Rowntree (drums). Albarn later co-founded Gorillaz and The Good, The Bad & The Queen.

10/14/95	150	1		1 The Great Escape		Food 40855
3/29/97	61	37	●	2 Blur		Food 42876
4/10/99	80	5		3 13		Food 99129
12/9/00	186	1		4 Blur: The Best Of .... Cat:#30/1 [G-L]		Food 50457 [2]
				disc 2: recorded on 12/12/1999 at Wembley Arena		
5/24/03	56	3		5 Think Tank		Parlophone 84242

BoA
Born Kwon Boa on 11/5/1986 in Guri, South Korea. Female singer/songwriter.

4/4/09	127	1		1 BoA		SM USA 01

BOB & EARL
R&B vocal duo from Los Angeles, California: Bob Relf (born on 1/10/1937; died on 11/20/2007, age 70) and Earl Nelson (born on 9/8/1928; died on 7/12/2008, age 79). Nelson also recorded as Jackie Lee.

~ ~ ~ ~ ~ ~ ~ ~ ~ ~ **NON-CHARTED ALBUM** ~ ~ ~ ~ ~ ~ ~ ~ ~ ~ ~
1964 **Harlem Shuffle Starring Bob & Earl**

BOB & TOM
DJ morning team of Bob Kevoian and Tom Griswold of radio station WFBQ in Indianapolis, Indiana (also nationally syndicated).

9/27/97	164	2		1 Fun House .... [C]		Big Mouth 97

BOB B. SOXX And The Blue Jeans
Vocal trio formed by producer Phil Spector: Bobby Sheen (The Alley Cats) with Darlene Love and Fanita James (both formerly with The Blossoms). Love and James later replaced by Gloria Jones (also with The Blossoms) and Carolyn Willis. Sheen died of pneumonia on 11/23/2000 (age 58).

~ ~ ~ ~ ~ ~ ~ ~ ~ ~ **NON-CHARTED ALBUM** ~ ~ ~ ~ ~ ~ ~ ~ ~ ~ ~
1963 **Zip-A-Dee Doo Dah**

BOBBY & THE MIDNITES
Rock band formed in San Francisco, California: Bob Weir (vocals, guitar), Brent Mydland (keyboards), Bobby Cochran (guitar), Matthew Kelly (harmonica), Alphonso Johnson (bass) and Billy Cobham (drums). Weir and Mydland were both members of the Grateful Dead. Mydland died of a drug overdose on 7/26/1990 (age 37).

11/21/81	158	7		1 Bobby & The Midnites		Arista 9568
8/25/84	166	4		2 Where The Beat Meets The Street		Columbia 39276

BOBBY JIMMY & THE CRITTERS
Comedic rap group from Los Angeles, California: Russ Parr ("Bobby Jimmy"), Arabian Prince, Buckwheat and Bo.

11/29/86	200	1		1 Roaches: The Beginning .... [N]		Macola 0933

BOBO, Willie
Born William Correa on 2/28/1934 in Harlem, New York. Died on 9/15/1983 (age 49). Latin-jazz percussionist. Joined the bands of Tito Puente (1954-57), Cal Tjader (1958-61) and Mongo Santamaria (1961-62).

2/26/66	137	8		1 Spanish Grease .... [I]		Verve 8631

Billboard DEBUT	PEAK	WKS	R I A A	ARTIST Album Title	Catalog	Label & Number

BOCELLI, Andrea
2000s: #10 / All-Time: #154

Born on 9/22/1958 in Lajatico, Tuscany, Italy. Male operatic tenor. Visually impared since birth, lost eyesight completely at age 12. Studied law at the University of Pisa and worked briefly as a lawyer before his singing career.

DEBUT	PEAK	WKS	RIAA	#	Album Title	Catalog	Label & Number
12/20/97+	35	91	▲²	1	Romanza	Cat:❶²/110 [F]	Philips 539207
3/28/98	153	21	●	2	Viaggio Italiano	Cat:#19/1 [F]	Philips 533123
4/25/98	59	69	▲	3	Aria: The Opera Album	Cat:#29/4 [F]	Philips 462033
4/17/99	4	72	▲²	4	Sogno	[F]	Polydor 547222
5/8/99	163	2		5	Sueno	[F]	Polydor 547224
11/27/99+	22	30	▲	6	Sacred Arias	[F]	Philips 462600
9/30/00	23	23	●	7	Verdi	[F]	Philips 464600
11/3/01	11	39	▲	8	Cieli Di Toscana	[F]	Philips 589341
11/23/02	12	20	▲	9	Sentimento	[F]	Philips 470400
11/27/04	16	22	▲	10	Andrea	[F]	Philips 003513
2/18/06	3¹	59	▲	11	Amore	[F]	Sugar 006069
3/18/06	110	12		12	Amor	[F]	Sugar 006144
					Spanish version of #11 above		
11/25/06	11	19		13	Under The Desert Sky	[F]	Sugar 007831
11/17/07	9	27		14	The Best Of Andrea Bocelli: Vivere	Cat:#43/3 [F-G]	Sugar 009988
11/24/07	193	3		15	Lo Mejor De Andrea Bocelli: Vivere	[F-G]	Sugar 653534
2/16/08	22	20		16	Vivere: Live In Tuscany	[F-L]	Sugar 010665
11/22/08	8	22		17	Incanto	[F]	Sugar 012161
11/21/09	2⁵	10	▲²	18	My Christmas	[X]	Sugar 013437
					Christmas chart: 1/09		
12/19/09	180	2		19	Mi Navidad	[X-F]	Sugar 653936
					Spanish version of #18 above; Christmas chart: 18/09		

BoDEANS
Rock and roll band from Waukesha, Wisconsin: Kurt Neumann and Sam Llanas (vocals, guitars), Bob Griffin (bass) and Guy Hoffman (drums). In 1989, Hoffman left; Michael Ramos (keyboards) and Danny Gayol (drums) joined. In 1995, Gayol was replaced by Nick Kitsos.

DEBUT	PEAK	WKS	RIAA	#	Album Title	Catalog	Label & Number
6/7/86	115	19		1	Love & Hope & Sex & Dreams		Slash 25403
10/10/87	86	20		2	Outside Looking In		Slash 25629
7/22/89	94	13		3	Home		Slash 25876
4/20/91	105	5		4	Black And White		Slash 26487
10/30/93	127	3		5	Go Slow Down		Slash 45455
8/26/95	161	1		6	Joe Dirt Car	[L]	Slash 45945 [2]
11/23/96	132	2		7	Blend		Slash 46216
7/10/04	194	1		8	Resolution		Zoe 431046
3/22/08	194	1		9	Still		He & He 40391

BODY COUNT
Speed-metal band formed in Los Angeles, California: Tracy "**Ice-T**" Morrow (vocals), Ernie C (guitar), Dennis "D-Roc" Miles (guitar; died of cancer on 8/17/2004, age 45), Lloyd "Mooseman" Roberts (bass; shot to death on 2/1/2001, age 42) and Victor "Beatmaster V" Wilson (drums; died of leukemia on 4/30/1996, age 37).

DEBUT	PEAK	WKS	RIAA	#	Album Title	Catalog	Label & Number
4/18/92	26	20	●	1	Body Count		Sire 26878
9/24/94	74	3		2	Born Dead		Virgin 39802

BOFILL, Angela
Born on 5/2/1954 in the Bronx, New York (Cuban father; Puerto Rican mother); raised in Harlem, New York. Jazz-styled singer/songwriter. Trained in opera at the Manhattan School of Music. Father was lead singer for Cuban bandleader Machito.

DEBUT	PEAK	WKS	RIAA	#	Album Title	Catalog	Label & Number
2/17/79	47	26		1	Angie		GRP 5000
11/3/79+	34	33		2	Angel of the Night		GRP 5501
11/21/81	61	22		3	Something About You		Arista 9576
2/12/83	40	32		4	Too Tough		Arista 9616
11/26/83+	81	21		5	Teaser		Arista 8198

BOGERT, Tim
Born on 8/27/1944 in Richfield, New Jersey. Hard-rock bassist. Member of **Vanilla Fudge** and **Cactus**.

DEBUT	PEAK	WKS	RIAA	#	Album Title	Catalog	Label & Number
4/7/73	12	27	●	1	Jeff Beck, Tim Bogert, Carmine Appice		Epic 32140

BOGGUSS, Suzy
Born on 12/30/1956 in Aledo, Illinois. Country singer/songwriter/guitarist.
AWARD: CMA: Horizon 1992

DEBUT	PEAK	WKS	RIAA	#	Album Title	Catalog	Label & Number
2/1/92	83	53	▲	1	Aces		Capitol 95847
10/31/92	116	23	●	2	Voices In The Wind		Liberty 98585
10/9/93	121	18	●	3	Something Up My Sleeve		Liberty 89261
4/2/94	190	1	●	4	Greatest Hits	[G]	Liberty 28457

Billboard			R I A A	ARTIST Album Title	Catalog	Label & Number
DEBUT	PEAK	WKS				

BOHANNON, Hamilton
Born on 3/7/1942 in Newnan, Georgia. R&B session drummer. Worked for **Stevie Wonder** from 1965-67.

8/27/77	203	4		1 Phase II		Mercury 1159
8/12/78	58	19		2 Summertime Groove		Mercury 3728
8/4/79	202	3		3 Too Hot To Hold		Mercury 3778

BOHN, Rudi, and His Band
Born in Germany. Polka bandleader.

| 10/16/61 | 38 | 9 | | 1 Percussive Oompah | [I] | London Phase 4 44009 |

BOLAND, Jason, & The Stragglers
Born in Harrah, Oklahoma. Country singer/songwriter/guitarist. Formed backing band The Stragglers in Stillwater, Oklahoma: Roger Ray (guitar), Noah Jeffries (banjo), Grant Tracy (bass) and Brad Rice (drums).

| 9/13/08 | 160 | 1 | | 1 Comal County Blue | | Apex 001 |

BOLIN, Tommy
Born on 8/1/1951 in Sioux City, Iowa. Died of a drug overdose on 12/4/1976 (age 25). Rock singer/guitarist. Member of **The James Gang**, **Deep Purple** and **Zephyr**.

| 12/20/75+ | 96 | 14 | | 1 Teaser | | Nemperor 436 |
| 10/2/76 | 98 | 8 | ● | 2 Private Eyes | | Columbia 34329 |

BOLTON, Michael   1990s: #15 / All-Time: #192
Born Michael Bolotin on 2/26/1954 in New Haven, Connecticut. Adult Contemporary singer/songwriter. First recorded for Epic in 1968. Lead singer of **Blackjack** in the late 1970s. Began recording as Michael Bolton in 1983.

8/9/75	209	3		1 Michael Bolotin		RCA Victor 0992
5/7/83	89	13	●	2 Michael Bolton		Columbia 38537
10/10/87+	46	41	▲²	3 The Hunger	Cat:#8/37	Columbia 40473
7/22/89+	3³	202	▲⁶	4 Soul Provider	Cat:#32/14	Columbia 45012
5/11/91	❶¹	149	▲⁸	5 Time, Love & Tenderness		Columbia 46771
10/17/92	❶¹	47	▲⁴	6 Timeless (The Classics)		Columbia 52783
12/4/93	3²	45	▲³	7 The One Thing		Columbia 53567
10/7/95	5	42	▲³	8 Greatest Hits 1985-1995	[G]	Columbia 67300
10/19/96	11	15	▲	9 This Is The Time – The Christmas Album	Cat:#6/9 [X]	Columbia 67621
				Christmas charts: 2/'96, 7/'97, 26/'98		
11/22/97	39	17	●	10 All That Matters		Columbia 68510
12/20/97	192	2		11 Merry Christmas From Vienna	[X-L]	Sony Classical 62970
				PLÁCIDO DOMINGO / YING HUANG / MICHAEL BOLTON		
				recorded on 12/16/1996 at the Austria Center in Vienna		
2/14/98	112	8		12 My Secret Passion - The Arias	[F]	Sony Classical 63077
5/11/02	36	6		13 Only A Woman Like You		Jive 41780
9/20/03	76	5		14 Vintage		PMG 73973
10/1/05	128	1		15 Til The End Of Forever	[L]	Montaigne 70005
6/10/06	51	12		16 Bolton Swings Sinatra: The Second Time Around		PMG 30038

BOLTZ, Ray
Born in 1953 in Muncie, Indiana. Contemporary Christian singer/songwriter.

9/9/95	194	1	●	1 The Concert Of A Lifetime	[L]	Word 641601
10/26/96	173	1		2 No Greater Sacrifice		Word 67867
11/29/97	169	5		3 A Christmas Album	[X]	Word 68512
				Christmas chart: 15/'97		

BOMSHEL
Female duo formed in Nashville, Tennessee: Buffy Lawson (from Lexington, Kentucky) and Kristy Osmonson (from Sandpoint, Idaho). Kelley Shepard (from Detroit, Michigan) replaced Lawson in December 2007.

| 11/7/09 | 87 | 2 | | 1 Fight Like A Girl | | Curb 78946 |

BONAMASSA, Joe
Born on 5/8/1977 in Utica, New York. Blues-rock guitarist.

9/8/07	184	1		1 Sloe Gin		J&R Adventures 60283
9/6/08	136	1		2 Live: From Nowhere In Particular	[L]	J&R Adventures 65328
3/14/09	103	3		3 The Ballad Of John Henry		J&R Adventures 91646

BONAMY, James
Born on 4/29/1972 in Winter Park, Florida; raised in Daytona Beach, Florida. Country singer.

| 8/3/96 | 112 | 13 | | 1 What I Live To Do | | Epic 67069 |

BOND
Female classical-folk group from England: Eos Chater and Haylie Ecker (violins), Tania Davis (viola) and Gay-Yee Westerhoff (cello).

4/21/01	108	8		1 Born .... [I]		MBO 467091
11/2/02	61	6		2 Shine .... [I]		Decca 470500
7/3/04	76	6		3 Classified .... [I]		Decca 002332

BOND, Angelo
Born in Detroit, Michigan. Male R&B singer/songwriter.

8/2/75	179	2		1 Bondage		ABC 889

BOND, Graham
Born on 10/28/1937 in Romford, Sussex, England. Committed suicide on 5/8/1974 (age 36). Alto saxophonist/organist. Joined Alexis Korner's Blues Inc. in 1962. Formed the Graham Bond Organization in 1963. Joined **Ginger Baker**'s Air Force.

1/30/71	210	1		1 Holy Magick		Mercury 61327

BOND, Johnny
Born Cyrus Bond on 6/1/1915 in Enville, Oklahoma. Died of a heart attack on 6/12/1978 (age 63). Country singer/songwriter/ actor. Appeared in several movies.
   AWARD: C&W Hall of Fame: 1999

5/29/65	142	3		1 Ten Little Bottles .... [N]		Starday 333

BONDS, Gary (U.S.)
Born Gary Anderson on 6/6/1939 in Jacksonville, Florida; raised in Norfolk, Virginia. Black rock and roll singer/songwriter.

8/7/61	6	28		1 Dance 'Til Quarter To Three		Legrand 3001
				U.S. BONDS		
5/2/81	27	20		2 Dedication		EMI America 17051
6/26/82	52	17		3 On The Line		EMI America 17068
				above 2 produced by **Bruce Springsteen** and "**Little Steven**" Van Zant		

~ ~ ~ ~ ~ ~ ~ ~ ~ ~ **NON-CHARTED ALBUMS** ~ ~ ~ ~ ~ ~ ~ ~ ~ ~ ~
1962 Twist Up Calypso   1962 The Greatest Hits Of Gary (U.S.) Bonds

BONE BROTHERS
Rap duo from Cleveland, Ohio: Steven "**Layzie Bone**" Howse and Byron "**Bizzy Bone**" McCane. Both were members of **Bone Thugs-N-Harmony**.

3/12/05	60	3		1 Bone Brothers		Mo Thugs 5719
5/26/07	122	2		2 Bone Brothers 2		Real Talk 35

BONE CRUSHER
Born Wayne Hardnett on 8/23/1971 in Atlanta, Georgia. Male rapper.

5/17/03	11	19		1 AttenCHUN!		Break-Em-Off 50995

BONE THUGS-N-HARMONY   All-Time: #269
Male rap group from Cleveland, Ohio: Anthony Henderson ("**Krayzie Bone**"), Steven Howse ("**Layzie Bone**"), Bryon McCane ("**Bizzy Bone**"), Charles Scruggs ("**Wish Bone**") and Stanley Howse ("**Flesh-N-Bone**"; left in 1996). Previously known as **Bone Enterprise**. Also see **Bone Brothers**.

7/30/94	12	96	▲²	1 Creepin On Ah Come Up .... [EP]		Ruthless 5526
7/22/95	188	2		2 Faces Of Death .... [E]		Stoney Burke 70020
				BONE ENTERPRISE recordings from 1993		
8/12/95	❶²	104	▲⁴	3 E. 1999 Eternal	Cat:#12/19	Ruthless 5539
8/16/97	❶¹	32	▲⁴	4 The Art Of War		Ruthless 6340 [2]
12/12/98	32	28	▲	5 The Collection Volume One .... [G]		Ruthless 69715
3/18/00	2¹	28	▲	6 BTNHRESURRECTION		Ruthless 63581
12/2/00	41	11		7 The Collection Volume Two .... [K]		Ruthless 85172
11/16/02	12	16		8 Thug World Order		Ruthless 86594
12/4/04+	95	69	▲	9 Greatest Hits	Cat:#29/13 [G]	Ruthless 25423 [2]
10/7/06	25	4		10 Thug Stories		Mo Thugs 5864
5/26/07	2¹	20	●	11 Strength & Loyalty		Mo Thugs 820902
12/1/07	73	2		12 T.H.U.G.S.		Ruthless 8808

BONEY JAMES
Born James Oppenheim on 9/1/1961 in Lowell, Massachusetts; raised in New Rochelle, New York. Male saxophonist.

6/14/97	112	11	●	1 Sweet Thing .... [I]		Warner 46548
3/13/99	91	18	●	2 Body Language .... [I]		Warner 47283
6/17/00	78	15		3 Shake It Up .... [I]		Warner 47557
				BONEY JAMES / RICK BRAUN		
11/10/01	82	5		4 Ride .... [I]		Warner 48004
8/21/04	66	5		5 Pure .... [I]		Warner 48786
10/14/06	44	5		6 Shine .... [I]		Concord 30049
2/21/09	77	4		7 Send One Your Love		Concord 30815

BONEY M
Vocal group created in Germany by producer/composer Frank Farian. Consisted of Marcia Barrett, Maizie Williams, Liz Mitchell and Bobby Farrell. All were from the West Indies. Farian created the Far Corporation in 1986 and **Milli Vanilli** in 1988.

12/17/77	206	3		1 Love For Sale		Atlantic 19145
9/2/78	134	10		2 Nightflight To Venus		Sire 6062

BONFIGLIO
Born Robert Bonfiglio in 1946 in Iowa; raised in New York. Classical harmonica player.

10/21/95	21 C	1	1 Through The Raindrops .... [I]	High Harmony 1000

released in 1992

BONGOS, The
Pop-rock band from Hoboken, New Jersey: Richard Barone (vocals), James Mastro (guitar), Rob Norris (bass) and Frank Giannini (drums).

3/16/85	209	1	1 Beat Hotel	RCA Victor 8043

BONHAM
Hard-rock band formed in England: Jason Bonham (drums; born on 7/15/1966; son of **Led Zeppelin**'s John Bonham), Daniel MacMaster (vocals), Ian Hatton (guitar) and John Smithson (keyboards, bass).

10/7/89	38	29	●	1 The Disregard Of Timekeeping	WTG 45009

BONHAM, Tracy
Born on 3/16/1967 in Eugene, Oregon. Adult Alternative singer/songwriter/guitarist.

4/27/96	54	25	●	1 The Burdens Of Being Upright	Island 524187

BON IVER
Born Justin Vernon on 4/30/1981 in Eau Claire, Wisconsin. Folk-rock singer/songwriter/guitarist. Vernon also formed **Volcano Choir**.

3/8/08+	64	15		1 For Emma, Forever Ago	Jagjaguwar 115
2/7/09	16	6		2 Blood Bank .... [EP]	Jagjaguwar 134

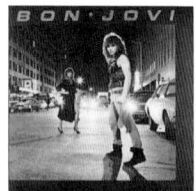

BON JOVI
2000s: #37 / All-Time: #85

Rock band from Sayreville, New Jersey: **Jon Bon Jovi** (vocals; born on 3/2/1962), **Richie Sambora** (guitar; born on 7/11/1959), Dave Bryan (keyboards; born on 2/7/1962), Alec John Such (bass; born on 11/14/1956) and Tico Torres (drums; born on 10/7/1953). Jon acted in the movies *Moonlight and Valentino, The Leading Man, No Looking Back, U-571* and *Pay It Forward*. Sambora was married to actress Heather Locklear from 1994-2007.

2/25/84	43	86	▲2	1 Bon Jovi	Mercury 814982
5/18/85	37	104	▲	2 7800° Fahrenheit	Mercury 824509
9/13/86	❶8	95↑	▲12	3 Slippery When Wet Cat:#3/141	Mercury 830264
10/8/88	❶4	76	▲7	4 New Jersey	Mercury 836345
8/25/90	3 3	41	▲2	5 Blaze Of Glory/Young Guns II [S]	Mercury 846473
				JON BON JOVI	
				songs from and songs inspired by the movie Young Guns II starring Emilio Estevez and Kiefer Sutherland	
11/21/92	5	46	▲2	6 Keep The Faith	Mercury 514045
11/5/94	8	56	▲4	7 Cross Road Cat:❶1/253 [G]	Mercury 526013
7/15/95	9	20	▲	8 These Days	Mercury 528181
7/5/97	31	9		9 Destination Anywhere	Mercury 534903
				JON BON JOVI	
7/1/00	9	51	▲2	10 Crush	Island 542474
6/9/01	20	14		11 One Wild Night: Live 1985 - 2001 .... [L]	Island 548684
10/26/02	2 1	29	●	12 Bounce	Island 063055
11/22/03	14	12		13 This Left Feels Right	Island 001540
				contains new acoustic versions of several previous hits	
12/4/04	53	5	●	14 100,000,000 Bon Jovi Fans Can't Be Wrong .... [K]	Island 003543 [4]
				box set of unreleased songs spanning their entire career; contains a 60-page booklet	
10/8/05	2 1	59	▲	15 Have A Nice Day	Island 005371
7/7/07	❶1	45	▲	16 Lost Highway	Island 008902
11/28/09	❶1	25↑	●	17 The Circle	Island 013685

BONNIE "PRINCE" BILLY
Born Will Oldham on 12/24/1970 in Louisville, Kentucky. Adult Alternative singer/songwriter/guitarist/actor. Appeared in several movies.

10/7/06	194	1	1 The Letting Go	Drag City 420
4/4/09	114	2	2 Beware	Domino 666

BONOFF, Karla
Born on 12/27/1951 in Los Angeles, California. Pop singer/songwriter/pianist.

10/1/77	52	40	●	1 Karla Bonoff	Columbia 34672
9/29/79	31	26		2 Restless Nights	Columbia 35799
4/3/82	49	35		3 Wild Heart Of The Young	Columbia 37444

BONUS, Jack
Born in San Francisco, California. Blues-rock singer/guitarist/saxophonist.

6/17/72	203	3	1 Jack Bonus	Grunt 1005

Billboard			R I A A	ARTIST		
DEBUT	PEAK	WKS		Album Title	Catalog	Label & Number

BONZO DOG BAND
Satirical rock band formed in London, England: Vivian Stanshall (vocals), Neil Innes (guitar), Roger Spear (horns), Rodney Slater (horns), Sam Spoons (percussion), Dennis Cowan (bass) and Larry Smith (drums). Stanshall died in a house fire on 3/5/1995 (age 51).

6/10/72	199	2		1 Let's Make Up And Be Friendly		United Artists 5584

BOO & GOTTI
Male rap duo from Chicago, Illinois: James "Boo" Griffin and Mwata "Gotti" Mitchell.

9/13/03	195	1		1 Perfect Timing		Cash Money 000542

BOOGIE BOYS, The
Rap trio from New York: William "Boogie Knight" Stroman, Joe "Romeo J.D." Malloy and Rudy "Lil' Rahiem" Sheriff.

8/31/85	53	17		1 City Life		Capitol 12409
8/9/86	124	9		2 Survival Of The Freshest		Capitol 12488
3/19/88	117	11		3 Romeo Knight		Capitol 46917

BOOGIE DOWN PRODUCTIONS
Rap group from the Bronx, New York. Founded by Lawrence Parker ("**KRS-ONE**") and Scott Sterling (shot to death on 8/25/1987, age 24). Group includes a revolving lineup of rappers.

4/30/88	75	23	●	1 By All Means Necessary		Jive 1097
7/22/89	36	17		2 Ghetto Music: The Blueprint Of Hip Hop		Jive 1187
8/25/90	32	16	●	3 Edutainment		Jive 1358
4/6/91	115	7		4 Live Hardcore Worldwide	[L]	Jive 1425
3/14/92	42	9		5 Sex And Violence		Jive 41470

~ ~ ~ ~ ~ ~ ~ ~ ~ ~ **NON-CHARTED ALBUM** ~ ~ ~ ~ ~ ~ ~ ~ ~ ~
1987 **Criminal Minded**
RS500 #444

BOOKER, Chuckii
Born on 12/19/1962 in Los Angeles, California. R&B singer/songwriter/multi-instrumentalist.

7/22/89	116	10		1 Chuckii		Atlantic 81947

BOOKER T. & THE MG'S
Instrumental band from Memphis, Tennessee: Booker T. Jones (keyboards; born on 11/12/1944), **Steve Cropper** (guitar; born on 10/21/1941), Donald "Duck" Dunn (bass; born on 11/24/1941) and Al Jackson, Jr. (drums; born on 11/27/1935; shot to death on 10/1/1975, age 39). MG stands for Memphis Group. Cropper and Dunn had been in the **Mar-Keys**. Cropper and Dunn later joined the **Blues Brothers** band. Jones married and recorded with Priscilla Coolidge (sister of **Rita Coolidge**).
AWARDS: Grammy: Lifetime Achievement 2007 ★ R&R Hall of Fame: 1992

11/10/62+	33	17		1 Green Onions	[I]	Stax 701
12/17/66+	13[X]	10		2 Booker T. & The MG's In The Christmas Spirit	[X-I]	Stax 713
				Christmas charts: 31/'66, 13/'67, 54/'68, 14/'69		
6/24/67	35	29		3 Hip Hug-Her	[I]	Stax 717
8/26/67	98	4		4 Back To Back	[I-L]	Stax 720
				THE MAR-KEYS / BOOKER T. & THE MG's		
5/18/68	176	4		5 Doin' Our Thing	[I]	Stax 724
10/19/68	127	9		6 Soul Limbo	[I]	Stax 2001
11/23/68	167	11		7 The Best Of Booker T. & The MG's	[G-I]	Atlantic 8202
2/8/69	98	27		8 Uptight	[S]	Stax 2006
6/14/69	53	18		9 The Booker T. Set	[I]	Stax 2009
5/2/70	107	15		10 McLemore Avenue	[I]	Stax 2027
11/14/70	132	8		11 Booker T. & The M.G.'s Greatest Hits	[G-I]	Stax 2033
2/13/71	43	38		12 Melting Pot	[I]	Stax 2035
8/14/71	106	6		13 Booker T. & Priscilla		A&M 3504 [2]
7/22/72	190	4		14 Home Grown		A&M 4351
				BOOKER T. & PRISCILLA (above 2)		
4/2/77	209	3		15 Universal Language	[I]	Asylum 1093
5/9/09	135	2		16 Potato Hole	[I]	Anti 86948
				BOOKER T.		
				Grammy: Pop Instrumental Album		

~ ~ ~ ~ ~ ~ ~ ~ ~ ~ **NON-CHARTED ALBUMS** ~ ~ ~ ~ ~ ~ ~ ~ ~ ~
1964 **Soul Dressing**   1966 **And Now! Booker T. & The MG's**

BOOK OF LOVE
Electro-dance/pop band from New York: Susan Ottaviano (vocals), Ted Ottaviano and Lauren Roselli (keyboards), and Jade Lee (percussion). The Ottavianos are not related.

7/23/88	156	10		1 Lullaby		Sire 25700
2/23/91	174	4		2 Candy Carol		Sire 26389

BOOM, Taka
Born Yvonne Stevens on 10/8/1954 in Chicago, Illinois. R&B singer. Sister of **Chaka Khan**.

6/9/79	171	4		1 Taka Boom		Ariola 50041

BOOMKAT
Pop-rock duo from Tucson, Arizona: brother-and sister Kellin Manning and Taryn Manning. Taryn acted in such movies as *Crossroads* and *8 Mile*.

4/26/03	88	2		1 Boomkatalog.One		DreamWorks 450386

BOOMTOWN RATS, The

Rock band formed in Dublin, Ireland: **Bob Geldof** (vocals), Gerry Cott (guitar), Garry Roberts (guitar), John "Johnnie Fingers" Moylett (keyboards), Pete Briquette (bass) and Simon Crowe (drums). Cott left in 1980. Geldof organized Band Aid in 1984.

DEBUT	PEAK	WKS				Label & Number
3/3/79	112	13		1 A Tonic For The Troops		Columbia 35750
12/1/79+	103	16		2 The Fine Art Of Surfacing		Columbia 36248
2/21/81	116	8		3 Mondo Bongo		Columbia 37062
9/25/82	201	5		4 V Deep		Columbia 38195
5/25/85	188	4		5 In The Long Grass		Columbia 39335

BOONDOX

Born David Hutto in Covington, Georgia. Male rapper.

5/31/08	113	1		1 Krimson Creek		Psychopathic 4400

BOONE, Daniel

Born Peter Lee Stirling on 7/31/1942 in Birmingham, England. Pop singer/songwriter.

10/7/72	142	9		1 Beautiful Sunday		Mercury 649

BOONE, Debby

Born on 9/22/1956 in Hackensack, New Jersey. Daughter of **Pat Boone**. Married Gabriel Ferrer (son of **Rosemary Clooney** and actor Jose Ferrer) on 9/1/1979.

AWARD: Grammy: Best New Artist 1977

10/29/77	6	37	▲	1 You Light Up My Life		Warner/Curb 3118
8/12/78	147	5		2 Midstream		Warner/Curb 3130

BOONE, Pat   1950s: #8 / All-Time: #214

Born Charles Eugene Boone on 6/1/1934 in Jacksonville, Florida; raised in Nashville, Tennessee. Direct descendant of Daniel Boone. Married country singer Red Foley's daughter, Shirley, on 11/7/1953. Father of **Debby Boone**. Hosted own TV show, *The Pat Boone-Chevy Showroom*, 1957-60. Appeared in several movies. Wrote several books. Recording artist Nick Todd is his younger brother.

10/7/57	20	2		1 Pat Boone		Dot 3012
				released in 1956		
10/27/56	14	4		2 Howdy!		Dot 3030
6/24/57	13	7		3 A Closer Walk With Thee	[EP]	Dot 1056
9/2/57	5	5		4 Four By Pat	[EP]	Dot 1057
7/8/57	19	3		5 "Pat"		Dot 3050
10/21/57	3²	36	●	6 Pat's Great Hits	[G]	Dot 3071
12/23/57+	12	13		7 April Love	[S]	Dot 9000
12/23/57	21	4		8 Hymns We Love		Dot 3068
7/28/58	2¹	32		9 Star Dust		Dot 3118
11/24/58	13	2		10 Yes Indeed!		Dot 3121
7/13/59	17	11		11 Tenderly		Dot 3180
5/23/60	26	3		12 Moonglow		Dot 3270
7/17/61	29	30		13 Moody River		Dot 3384
1/6/62	39	2		14 White Christmas	[X]	Dot 3222
				first released in 1959; Christmas chart: 50/'66		
12/29/62	116	1		15 White Christmas	[X-R]	Dot 3222
9/15/62	66	13		16 Pat Boone's Golden Hits	[G]	Dot 3455
2/15/97	125	2		17 In A Metal Mood: No More Mr. Nice Guy		Hip-O 40025

~ ~ ~ ~ ~ ~ ~ ~ ~ ~   **NON-CHARTED ALBUMS**   ~ ~ ~ ~ ~ ~ ~ ~ ~ ~ ~ ~

1959 **Pat Boone Sings**   1961 **Great! Great! Great!**
1960 **Pat's Great Hits, Volume 2**   1963 **Pat Boone Sings Guess Who?**
1960 **This And That**

BOOT CAMP CLIK

Collective of rap acts: BDI, **Cocoa Brovaz**, **Heltah Skeltah**, **Originoo Gunn Clappaz**, The Reps, B.T.J's, Swan & Boogie Brown, F.L.O.W. and Illa Noyz.

6/7/97	15	9		1 For The People		Priority 50646

BOOTLEG

Born Ira Dorsey in Flint, Michigan. Male rapper. Member of group **The Dayton Family**.

4/17/99	91	5		1 Death Before Dishonesty		Relativity 1726
7/28/01	174	2		2 Hated By Many Loved By Few		Overcore 2330

BOOTSY'S RUBBER BAND

Born William Collins on 10/26/1951 in Cincinnati, Ohio. R&B singer/songwriter/bassist. Member of **James Brown**'s band from 1969-71. Joined Funkadelic/Parliament in 1972.

5/1/76	59	27		1 Stretchin' Out In Bootsy's Rubber Band		Warner 2920
2/5/77	16	23	●	2 Ahh...The Name Is Bootsy, Baby!		Warner 2972
2/25/78	16	24	●	3 Bootsy? Player Of The Year		Warner 3093
7/21/79	52	9		4 This Boot Is Made For Fonk-n-		Warner 3295
12/6/80	70	9		5 Ultra Wave		Warner 3433
				BOOTSY		
5/29/82	120	8		6 The One Giveth, The Count Taketh Away		Warner 3667
				WILLIAM "BOOTSY" COLLINS		

Billboard DEBUT	PEAK	WKS	R I A A	ARTIST / Album Title	Catalog	Label & Number
				BOO-YAA T.R.I.B.E.		
				Rap group from Los Angeles, California: Samoan brothers Ted Devoux, Donald Devoux, David Devoux, Danny Devoux, Paul Devoux and Roscoe Devoux.		
4/28/90	117	15		1 New Funky Nation		4th & B'way 4017
				BORDEN, Lizzy — see LIZZY		
				BORN JAMERICANS		
				Dancehall reggae duo: Horace Payne and Norman Howell.		
6/25/94	188	1		1 Kids From Foreign		Delicious Vinyl 92349
				BORN OF OSIRIS		
				Heavy metal band from Palatine, Illinois: Ronnie Canizaro (vocals), Lee McKinney (guitar), Jason Richardson (guitar), Joe Buras (keyboards), David Darocha (bass) and Cameron Losch (drums).		
7/25/09	73	2		1 A Higher Place		Sumerian 202
				BOSE		
4/7/07	160	1		Born Miguel Borlani on 4/3/1956 in Aries, Panama. Latin singer/songwriter. B.O.S.E.: Bass Overdrive System Experts.		
				1 Papito .... [F]		Warner Latina 699903
				BOSS		
				Female hardcore rap duo based in Los Angeles, California: Lichelle "Boss" Laws and Irene "Dee" Moore.		
6/12/93	22	18		1 Born Gangstaz		DJ West 52903
				BOSTON		
				Rock band from Boston, Massachusetts: Brad Delp (vocals), Tom Scholz (guitar, keyboards), Barry Goudreau (guitar), Fran Sheehan (bass) and Sib Hashian (drums). Goudreau formed **Orion The Hunter** in 1982. By 1986, reduced to a duo of Scholz and Delp. Delp and Goudreau formed **RTZ**. Lineup in 1994: Scholz, Fran Cosmo (vocals), Tommy Funderburk (vocals), Gary Pihl (guitar), David Sikes (bass) and Doug Huffman (drums). Lineup in 2002: Scholz, Delp, Cosmo, Pihl, Anthony Cosmo (guitar; Fran's son), Kimberley Dahme (bass) and Jeff Neal (drums). Scholz is an avid inventor with several patented inventions. Delp committed suicide on 3/9/2007 (age 55).		
9/25/76	3⁶	132	▲¹⁷	1 Boston Cat:#37/29		Epic 34188
9/2/78	❶²	45	▲⁷	2 Don't Look Back Cat:#20/21		Epic 35050
10/18/86	❶⁴	50	▲⁴	3 Third Stage		MCA 6188
6/25/94	7	16	▲	4 Walk On		MCA 10973
6/21/97	47	16	▲²	5 Greatest Hits .... Cat:#12/40 [G]		Epic 67622
11/23/02	42	3		6 Corporate America		Artemis 751142
				BOSTON POPS ORCHESTRA **All-Time: #305**		
				Founded in 1885 by Henry Lee Higginson, conductor of the Boston Symphony Orchestra. Arthur Fiedler (born on 12/17/1894 in Boston, Massachusetts; died on 7/10/1979, age 84) joined the orchestra in 1915 as a violist; began his reign as its conductor in 1930 and remained until his death. National public TV program *Evening at Pops* began in 1969. **John Williams** succeeded Fiedler in 1980. Keith Lockhart (former Cincinnati Pops conductor) succeeded Williams in 1995.		
				BOSTON POPS/ARTHUR FIEDLER:		
2/2/59	9	16		1 Offenbach: Gaite Parisienne; Khachaturian: Gayne Ballet Suite [I]		RCA Victor 2267
7/14/62	29	14		2 Pops Roundup .... [I]		RCA Victor 2595
3/9/63	36	6		3 Our Man In Boston .... [I]		RCA Victor 2599
4/6/63	5	23		4 "Jalousie" And Other Favorites In The Latin Flavor [I]		RCA Victor 2661
6/22/63	29	14		5 Star Dust .... [I]		RCA Victor 2670
10/19/63	116	4		6 Concert In The Park .... [I]		RCA Victor 2677
9/26/64	18	31		7 "Pops" Goes The Trumpet .... [I]		RCA Victor 2729
				AL HIRT/BOSTON POPS/ARTHUR FIEDLER		
11/21/64+	53	14		8 Peter And The Commissar .... [C]		RCA Victor 2773
				ALLAN SHERMAN/BOSTON POPS/ARTHUR FIEDLER		
10/23/65	86	16		9 Nero Goes "Pops" .... [I]		RCA Victor 2821
				PETER NERO/ARTHUR FIEDLER/BOSTON POPS		
12/25/65	58ˣ	1		10 Pops Christmas Party .... [X-I]		RCA Victor 2329
5/14/66	145	3		11 The Duke At Tanglewood .... [I-L]		RCA Victor 2857
				DUKE ELLINGTON/BOSTON POPS/ARTHUR FIEDLER		
6/18/66	62	23		12 The "Pops" Goes Country .... [I]		RCA Victor 2870
				CHET ATKINS/BOSTON POPS/ARTHUR FIEDLER		
10/26/68	157	7		13 Up Up And Away .... [I]		RCA Victor 3041
4/5/69	192	2		14 Glenn Miller's Biggest Hits .... [I]		RCA Victor 3064
10/11/69	160	4		15 Chet Picks On The Pops .... [I]		RCA Victor 3104
				CHET ATKINS/BOSTON POPS/ARTHUR FIEDLER		
12/19/70	9ˣ	2		16 A Christmas Festival [X-I]		Polydor 24-5004
1/9/71	190	2		17 Fabulous Broadway .... [I]		Polydor 5003
7/3/71	219	1		18 Encore (Fiedler's Greatest Hits) .... [G-I]		Polydor 5005
				BOSTON POPS/ARTHUR FIEDLER		
12/4/71	174	5		19 Arthur Fiedler "Superstar" .... [I]		Polydor 5008
2/26/72	196	3		20 The Music Of Paul Simon .... [I]		Polydor 5018
9/8/79	147	6		21 Saturday Night Fiedler .... [I]		Midsong Int'l. 011
12/20/80+	181	6		22 Pops In Space .... [I]		Philips 9500 921
5/17/86	155	8		23 Swing, Swing, Swing .... [I]		Philips 412626
				BOSTON POPS/JOHN WILLIAMS (above 2)		
7/20/96	62	7		24 Summon The Heroes .... [I]		Sony Classical 62592
				BOSTON POPS		
				official centennial Olympic theme for the 1996 Summer Olympics in Atlanta, Georgia		

Billboard DEBUT	PEAK	WKS	R I A A	ARTIST / Album Title	Catalog	Label & Number
				BOSTON SYMPHONY ORCHESTRA		
				Orchestra founded in 1880. Conductors have included **Charles Munch**, **Erich Leinsdorf** and Seiji Ozawa.		
5/11/63	17	8		1 **Ravel: Bolero/Pavan For A Dead Princess/La Valse** .... [I]		RCA Victor 2664
				Charles Munch, conductor		
5/18/63	41	4		2 **Mahler: Symphony No. 1** .... [I]		RCA Victor 2642
				Erich Leinsdorf, conductor		
3/28/64	82	12		3 **Mozart: Requiem Mass**		RCA Victor 7030 [2]
				a Requiem Mass conducted by **Erich Leinsdorf** in memory of President **John F. Kennedy** - celebrated by Richard Cardinal Cushing, the Archbishop of Boston, on 1/19/1964 at Boston's Cathedral of the Holy Cross		
				BOTTI, Chris		
				Born on 10/12/1962 in Portland, Oregon. Contemporary pop-jazz trumpet player.		
10/16/04	37	32	●	1 **When I Fall In Love** .... [I]		Columbia 92872
11/5/05	18	24		2 **To Love Again: The Duets**		Columbia 94823
12/2/06	124	5		3 **December** .... Cat:#38/1 [X-I]		Columbia 75381
				Christmas charts: 36/'06, 23/'07, 26/'08, 34/'09		
10/13/07	27	26		4 **Italia** .... [I]		Columbia 07606
4/18/09	13	14		5 **Chris Botti: In Boston** .... [I-L]		Columbia 38735
				BOUNCING SOULS, The		
				Punk-rock band from New Brunswick, New Jersey: Greg Attonito (vocals), Pete Steinkopf (guitar), Bryan Kienlen (bass) and Michael McDermott (drums).		
9/13/03	168	1		1 **Anchors Aweigh**		Epitaph 86669
6/24/06	141	1		2 **The Gold Record**		Epitaph 86808
				BOUNTY KILLER		
				Born Rodney Pryce on 6/26/1972 in Riverton City, Jamaica. Reggae singer.		
10/5/96	145	4		1 **My Xperience**		TVT 1461
				BOURGEOIS TAGG		
				Rock band from Los Angeles, California: Brent Bourgeois (vocals, keyboards), Larry Tagg (vocals, bass), Lyle Workman (guitar), Scott Moon (keyboards) and Michael Urbano (drums). Urbano later joined **Smash Mouth**.		
5/31/86	139	7		1 **Bourgeois Tagg**		Island 90496
10/24/87	84	21		2 **YoYo**		Island 90638
				BOWEN, Jimmy		
				Born on 11/30/1937 in Santa Rita, New Mexico. Rock and roll singer/producer.		
				~ ~ ~ ~ ~ ~ ~ ~ ~ ~ **NON-CHARTED ALBUMS** ~ ~ ~ ~ ~ ~ ~ ~ ~ ~ ~		
				1957 **Jimmy Bowen** 1959 **Buddy Knox & Jimmy Bowen**		
				BOWEN, Wade		
				Born in Waco, Texas. Country singer/songwriter.		
10/18/08	176	1		1 **If We Ever Make It Home**		Sustain 001181

				BOWIE, David **1970s: #7 / 1980s: #33 / All-Time: #26**		
				Born David Jones on 1/8/1947 in Brixton, London, England. Pop-rock singer/actor. Adopted new personas (Ziggy Stardust, Alladin Sane, Thin White Duke) to accompany several of his musical phases. Married to Angie Barnett from 1970-80. Acted in several movies. Starred in *The Elephant Man* on Broadway. Formed **Tin Machine** in 1988. Married Somalian actress/supermodel Iman on 4/24/1992. Also see **Spiders From Mars**.		
				AWARDS: Grammy: Lifetime Achievement 2006 ★ R&R Hall of Fame: 1996		
4/15/72+	93	16		1 **Hunky Dory** .... Cat:#39/16		RCA Victor 4623
				RS500 #107		
6/17/72+	75	72	●	2 **The Rise And Fall Of Ziggy Stardust And The Spiders From Mars**.... Cat:❶[46]/277		RCA Victor 4702
				Grammy: Hall of Fame ★ RS500 #35		
				also see #36 & #37 below		
5/12/73	17	22	●	3 **Aladdin Sane** .... Cat:#41/20		RCA Victor 4852
				RS500 #277		
11/10/73	23	21		4 **Bowie Pin Ups** .... Cat:#32/16		RCA Victor 0291
6/15/74	5	25	●	5 **Diamond Dogs** Cat:#9/48		RCA Victor 0576
				original cover features Bowie as a dog with his genitals visible — controversial and quickly withdrawn		
3/22/75	9	51	●	6 **Young Americans**		RCA Victor 0998
2/7/76	3[2]	32	●	7 **Station To Station**		RCA Victor 1327
				RS500 #323		
1/29/77	11	19		8 **Low**		RCA Victor 2030
				RS500 #249		
11/12/77	35	19		9 **"Heroes"** .... Cat:#18/60		RCA Victor 2522
6/16/79	20	15		10 **Lodger**		RCA Victor 3254
10/4/80	12	27		11 **Scary Monsters**		RCA Victor 3647
4/30/83	4	68	▲	12 **Let's Dance**		EMI America 17093
10/20/84	11	24	▲	13 **Tonight**		EMI America 17138
5/23/87	34	26	●	14 **Never Let Me Down**		EMI America 17267
4/24/93	39	8		15 **Black Tie White Noise**		Savage 50212
10/14/95	21	6		16 **Outside - The Nathan Adler Diaries: A Hyper Cycle**		Virgin 40711

Billboard			R I A A	ARTIST Album Title	Catalog	Label & Number
DEBUT	PEAK	WKS				

BOWIE, David — cont'd

3/1/97	39	6		17 Earthling		Virgin 42627
10/23/99	47	4		18 'Hours...		Virgin 48157
6/29/02	14	9		19 Heathen		Columbia 86630
10/4/03	29	4		20 Reality		Iso 90576

EARLY ALBUMS:

11/18/72+	16	36		21 Space Oddity .... first released in 1968 as *Man Of Words, Man Of Music* on Mercury 61246		RCA Victor 4813
11/18/72+	105	23		22 The Man Who Sold The World .... first released in 1970 on Mercury 61325		RCA Victor 4816
3/17/73	144	9		23 Images 1966-1967 .... first recordings in London on Pye and Decca labels		London 628/9 [2]
10/14/00	181	1		24 Bowie At The Beeb .... recorded from 1968-72 for the BBC		Virgin 28958 [3]

GREATEST HITS & COMPILATIONS:

6/19/76	10	39	▲	25 **Changesonebowie** RS500 #425		RCA Victor 1732
12/12/81+	68	18		26 Changestwobowie		RCA Victor 4202
8/27/83	99	9		27 Golden Years		RCA Victor 4792
4/21/84	147	6		28 Fame And Fashion (David Bowie's All Time Greatest Hits)		RCA Victor 4919
10/14/89	97	16	●	29 Sound + Vision .... recordings from 1969-80		Rykodisc 0120 [6]
4/7/90	39	27	▲	30 Changesbowie		Rykodisc 20171
11/9/02	70	18	●	31 Best Of Bowie .... single disc version of #32 below	Cat:#36/10	Virgin 41929
11/9/02	108	1		32 Best Of Bowie		Virgin 41930 [2]

LIVE ALBUMS:

10/26/74	8	21	●	33 **David Live** recorded on 7/12/1974 at the Tower Theatre in Philadelphia, Pennsylvania		RCA Victor 0771 [2]
10/21/78	44	13		34 Stage .... recorded on 4/28/1978 at the Spectrum in Philadelphia, Pennsylvania		RCA Victor 2913 [2]
8/9/08	41ᶜ	1		35 Live Santa Monica '72		EMI 83221

REISSUES:

7/7/90	93	9		36 The Rise And Fall Of Ziggy Stardust And The Spiders From Mars .... reissue of #2 above with five additional tracks		Rykodisc 10134
8/3/02	17ᶜ	1		37 The Rise And Fall Of Ziggy Stardust And The Spiders From Mars (30th Anniversary Edition) .... reissue of #2 above with 12 additional tracks		Virgin 39826 [2]

SOUNDTRACKS:

4/3/82	135	7		38 Christiane F.		RCA Victor 4239
6/26/82	204	2 .		39 Bertolt Brecht's Baal .... songs from BBC-TV production (aired 3/2/1982) of play by Bertolt Brecht, composer famous for "Mack The Knife"; Bowie starred as Baal	[TV]	RCA Victor 4346
11/12/83	89	15		40 Ziggy Stardust/The Motion Picture .... recorded on 7/3/1973 at the Hammersmith Odeon in London, England		RCA Victor 4862 [2]
7/19/86	68	8		41 Labyrinth		EMI America 17206

SPECIALTY ALBUM:

5/6/78	136	8		42 David Bowie Narrates Prokofiev's "Peter And The Wolf" .... **DAVID BOWIE/EUGENE ORMANDY & THE PHILADELPHIA ORCHESTRA** side 1: above title; side 2: Britten: Young Person's Guide to the Orchestra - both sides feature The Philadelphia Orch.		RCA Victor 2743

BOWLING FOR SOUP
Punk-rock band from Wichita Falls, Texas: Jaret Reddick (vocals, guitar), Chris Burney (guitar), Erik Chandler (bass) and Gary Wiseman (drums).

3/15/03	129	15		1 Drunk Enough To Dance		Ffroe 41819
10/2/04	37	50	●	2 A Hangover You Don't Deserve		Silvertone 62294
11/25/06	88	2		3 The Great Burrito Extortion Case		Ffroe 00198
10/31/09	104	1		4 Sorry For Partyin'		Jive 56156

BOW WOW
Born Shad Moss on 3/9/1987 in Columbus, Ohio. Teen male rapper/actor. Starred in the movies *Like Mike* and *Roll Bounce*; also acted in the movies *All About The Benjamins* and *Johnson Family Vacation*. First recorded as **Lil Bow Wow**.

10/14/00	8	52	▲²	1 Beware Of Dog		So So Def 69981
1/5/02	11	31	▲	2 Doggy Bag		So So Def 86130
				LIL BOW WOW (above 2)		
9/6/03	3¹	25	●	3 Unleashed		Columbia 87103
7/30/05	3¹	35	▲	4 Wanted		Columbia 93505
1/6/07	6	24	●	5 The Price Of Fame		Columbia 87932
12/29/07	11	13	●	6 Face Off		T.U.G. 11492
				BOW WOW & OMARION		
4/18/09	16	5		7 New Jack City II		Columbia 12471

BOW WOW WOW
New-wave band assembled in London by Malcolm McLaren (former **Sex Pistols** manager): Annabella Lwin (vocals; born Myant Myant Aye in Burma), Matthew Ashman (guitar), Leroy Gorman (bass) and Dave Barbarossa (drums). The latter three were members of **Adam And The Ants** until 1980. Barbarossa later joined **Republica**. Ashman died of diabetes on 11/21/1995 (age 35).

11/21/81	192	2		1 See Jungle! See Jungle! Go Join Your Gang Yeah! City All Over, Go Ape Crazy		RCA Victor 4147
5/15/82	67	22		2 The Last Of The Mohicans .... **[EP]**		RCA Victor 4314
9/18/82	123	9		3 I Want Candy		RCA Victor 4375
3/26/83	82	13		4 When The Going Gets Tough, The Tough Get Going		RCA Victor 4570

BOX CAR RACER
Punk-rock band from San Diego, California: Tom DeLonge (vocals, guitar), David Kennedy (guitar), Anthony Celestino (bass) and Travis Barker (drums). DeLonge and Barker are also members of **Blink-182**.

6/8/02	12	17		1 Box Car Racer		MCA 112894

BOXER REBELLION, The
Alternative-rock band formed in London, England: Nathan Nicholson (vocals), Todd Howe (guitar), Adam Harrison (bass) and Piers Hewitt (drums).

1/31/09	82	1		1 Union		Boxer Rebellion digital

BOX OF FROGS
Rock band from England: John Fiddler (vocals), Chris Dreja (guitar), Paul Samwell-Smith (bass) and Jim McCarty (drums). The latter three were members of **The Yardbirds**. McCarty also with **Renaissance** and **Illusion**.

7/7/84	45	20		1 Box Of Frogs		Epic 39327
6/14/86	177	3		2 Strange Land		Epic 39923

BOX TOPS, The
Pop-rock band from Memphis, Tennessee: Alex Chilton (vocals), Gary Talley (guitar), John Evans (organ), Bill Cunningham (bass) and Danny Smythe (drums). Evans and Smythe left in late 1967; replaced by Rick Allen and Tom Boggs. Disbanded in 1970. Chilton later formed the power-pop band **Big Star**. Cunningham is the brother of B.B. Cunningham of **The Hombres**. Boggs died of cancer on 5/5/2008 (age 63). Chilton died of heart failure on 3/17/2010 (age 59).

11/18/67+	87	15		1 The Letter / Neon Rainbow		Bell 6011
4/27/68	59	19		2 Cry Like A Baby		Bell 6017
12/7/68+	45	26		3 The Box Tops Super Hits .... **[G]**		Bell 6025
9/6/69	77	11		4 Dimensions..		Bell 6032

BOYCE, Tommy, & Bobby Hart
Songwriting/singing/production duo. Boyce was born on 9/29/1939 in Charlottesville, Virginia. Died of a self-inflicted gunshot wound on 11/23/1994 (age 55). Hart was born on 2/18/1939 in Phoenix, Arizona.

9/9/67	200	1		1 Test Patterns		A&M 4126
4/20/68	109	5		2 I Wonder What She's Doing Tonite?		A&M 4143

BOYD, Neal E.
Born on 11/18/1975 in Sikeston, Missouri. Black opera singer. Winner on the third season of TV's *America's Got Talent* in 2008.

7/11/09	195	1		1 My American Dream		Decca 012897

BOYER, Charles
Born on 8/28/1899 in Figeac, France. Committed suicide on 8/26/1978 (age 78). Prolific actor.

1/8/66	148	2		1 Where Does Love Go .... **[T]**		Valiant 5001

BOY GEORGE
Born George O'Dowd on 6/14/1961 in Eltham, Kent, England. Former lead singer of **Culture Club**.

8/1/87	145	5		1 Sold		Virgin 90617
3/25/89	126	11		2 High Hat		Virgin 91022
11/20/93	169	3		3 At Worst...The Best Of Boy George And Culture Club .... **[G]**		SBK 39014

BOY HOWDY
Country band formed in Los Angeles, California: brothers Cary Parks and Larry Parks (guitars), with Jeffrey Steele (vocals, bass) and Hugh Wright (drums).

1/29/94	103	14		1 She'd Give Anything .... **[EP]**		Curb 77656

BOYLAN, Terence
Born in 1948 in Buffalo, New York. Singer/songwriter/guitarist. Brother of record producer John Boylan.

11/5/77	181	3		1 Terence Boylan		Asylum 1091

BOYLE, Susan
Born on 4/1/1961 in Blackburn, Scotland. Female singer. Finished in second place on the 2009 season of TV's *Britain's Got Talent*.

12/12/09	❶⁶	25↑	▲⁴	1 I Dreamed A Dream		Syco 59829

BOY MEETS GIRL
Songwriting/recording duo from Seattle: Shannon Rubicam and George Merrill. Married from 1988-2000.

5/4/85	76	11		1 Boy Meets Girl		A&M 5046
10/22/88+	50	26		2 Reel Life		RCA 8414

BOYS, The
R&B vocal group from Northridge, California: brothers Khiry Samad, Hakeem Samad, Tajh Samad and Bilal Samad.

11/26/88+	33	36	▲	1 Messages From The Boys		Motown 6260
10/27/90	108	7	●	2 The Boys		Motown 6302
5/30/92	191	1		3 The Saga Continues...		Motown 6336

BOYS CLUB
Vocal duo from Minneapolis, Minnesota: Gene Hunt and Joe Pasquale. Hunt (real name: Eugene Wolfgramm) was a member of **The Jets**.

DEBUT	PEAK	WKS			
11/26/88+	93	16		1 Boys Club	MCA 42242

BOYS DON'T CRY
Pop-rock band from England: Nick Richards (vocals), Nico Ramsden (guitar), Brian Chatton (keyboards), Mark Smith (bass) and Jeff Seopardi (drums).

6/21/86	55	19		1 Boys Don't Cry	Profile 1219

BOYSETSFIRE
Punk-rock band from Delaware: Nathan Gray (vocals), Chad Istvan (guitar), Josh Latshaw (guitar), Rob Avery (bass) and Matt Krupanski (drums).

9/28/02	185	1		1 Live For Today .... [EP-L]	Wind-Up 18007
4/19/03	141	1		2 Tomorrow Come Today	Wind-Up 13071

BOYS LIKE GIRLS
Alternative-rock band from Andover, Massachusetts: Martin Johnson (vocals, guitar), Paul DiGiovanni (guitar), Bryan Donahue (bass) and John Keefe (drums).

4/21/07	55	64	●	1 Boys Like Girls	Columbia 05572
9/26/09	8	20		2 Love Drunk	Columbia 49192

BOYS NIGHT OUT
Alternative-rock band from Burlington, Ontario, Canada: Connor Lavat-Fraser (male vocals), Kara Dupuy (female vocals, keyboards), Jeff Davis (guitar), Shawn Butchart (guitar), Dave Costa (bass) and Brian Southall (drums).

8/13/05	194	1		1 Trainwreck	Ferret 055

BOYZ N DA HOOD
Male rap group formed in Atlanta, Georgia: Jay **"Young Jeezy"** Jenkins, Jacoby **"Jody Breeze"** White, Miguel **"Big Gee"** Scott and Lee **"Big Duke"** Dixon.

7/9/05	5	14		1 Boyz N Da Hood	Bad Boy 83810
10/20/07	51	3		2 Back Up N Da Chevy	Block 135996

BOYZONE
Male vocal group from Dublin, Ireland: Mikey Graham, Keith Duffy, Shane Lynch, Ronan Keating and Stephen Gately. Gately died on 10/9/2009 (age 33).

9/18/99	167	4		1 Where We Belong..............................	Ravenous 559171

BOYZ II MEN   1990s: #35 / All-Time: #275
R&B vocal group from Philadelphia, Pennsylvania: Wanya Morris (born on 7/29/1974), Michael McCary (born on 12/16/1972), **Shawn Stockman** (born on 9/26/1973) and **Nathan Morris** (born on 6/18/1972). Discovered by Michael Bivins (**New Edition, Bell Biv DeVoe**). Group appeared in the 1992 TV mini-series *The Jacksons: An American Dream*.

6/1/91	3¹	133	▲⁹	1 Cooleyhighharmony Cat:❶⁷/75	Motown 6320
				Grammy: R&B Vocal Group	
10/23/93	19	15	▲²	2 Christmas Interpretations .... Cat:#3/30 [X]	Motown 6365
				Christmas charts: 2/'93, 5/'94, 6/'95, 13/'96, 21/'97	
1/8/94	154	6		3 Cooleyhighharmony .... Cat:#27/2 [R]	Motown 0231
				expanded edition of their first album, includes 7 extra tracks	
9/17/94	❶⁵	99	▲¹²	4 II Cat:#46/2	Motown 0323
				Grammy: R&B Album	
11/25/95	17	19	▲	5 The Remix Collection.................................... [K]	Motown 0584
10/11/97	❶¹	50	▲²	6 Evolution	Motown 0819
9/30/00	4	23	●	7 Nathan/Michael/Shawn/Wanya	Universal 159281
12/1/01	89	15	●	8 Legacy: The Greatest Hits Collection .... Cat:#12/10 [G]	Universal 016083
8/10/02+	10	11		9 Full Circle	Arista 14741
9/11/04	52	4		10 Throwback	Koch 5735
1/17/04	23ˣ	1		11 The Best Of Boyz II Men The Christmas Collection 20th Century Masters .... [X]	Motown 000611
2/3/07	38ᶜ	3		12 The Best Of Boyz II Men The Millennium Collection 20th Century Masters .... [G]	Motown 001098
12/1/07	27	17		13 Motown: A Journey Through Hitsville USA	Decca 009444
12/12/09	114	2		14 Love	Decca 013393

BRADY, Wayne
Born on 6/2/1972 in Orlando, Florida. Black actor/comedian/singer. Appeared in several movies and TV shows. Hosted own TV talk show.

10/4/08	157	2		1 A Long Time Coming	Peak 23066

BRADY BUNCH, The
Vocal group consisting of the child actors of TV's *The Brady Bunch*. Barry Williams (Greg), Chris Knight (Peter), Mike Lookinland (Bobby), Maureen McCormick (Marsha), Eve Plumb (Jan) and Susan Olsen (Cindy).

12/25/71	6ˣ	1		1 Merry Christmas From The Brady Bunch [X]	Paramount 5026
5/13/72	108	19		2 Meet The Brady Bunch	Paramount 6032
1/20/73	210	4		3 The Kids From The Brady Bunch	Paramount 6037
7/28/73	218	5		4 Phonographic Album	Paramount 6058

BRAGG, Billy
Born Steven William Bragg on 12/20/1957 in Barking, Essex, England. Rock singer/songwriter.

11/5/88	198	1	1 Workers Playtime		Elektra 60824
7/11/98	90	7	2 Mermaid Avenue		Elektra 62204
6/17/00	88	4	3 Mermaid Avenue Vol. II		Elektra 62522

BILLY BRAGG & WILCO (above 2)

BRAINS, The
New-wave rock band from Atlanta, Georgia: Tom Gray (vocals), Rick Price (guitar), Bryan Smithwick (bass) and Charles Wolff (drums).

4/11/81	208	1	1 Electronic Eden		Mercury 4012

BRAINSTORM
Disco group from Detroit, Michigan: Belita Woods, Charles Overton, Jeryl Bright, Larry Sims, Gerald Kent, Trenita Womack, Lamont Johnson, Willie Wooten and Renell Gonsalves.

3/26/77	145	16	1 Stormin'		Tabu 2048
5/19/79	204	3	2 Funky Entertainment		Tabu 35749

BRAMLETT, Bonnie
Born Bonnie O'Farrell on 11/8/1944 in Acton, Illinois. Folk-rock singer/actress. Half of **Delaney & Bonnie**. Married to Delaney Bramlett from 1967-72. Their daughter Bekka briefly joined **Fleetwood Mac**. Played "Bonnie Watkins" on TV's *Roseanne*.

6/30/73	222	2	1 Sweet..		Columbia 31786
2/22/75	168	5	2 It's Time		Capricorn 0148

BRAM TCHAIKOVSKY
Rock trio from Lincolnshire, England: Peter Bramall (vocals, guitar), Micky Broadbent (bass) and Keith Boyce (drums).

6/30/79	36	18	1 Strange Man, Changed Man		Polydor 6211
5/17/80	108	10	2 Pressure		Polydor 6273
5/23/81	158	8	3 Funland		Arista 4292

BRANCH, Michelle
Born on 7/2/1983 in Phoenix, Arizona; raised in Flagstaff and Sedona, Arizona. Adult Alternative pop-rock singer/songwriter/guitarist.

9/1/01+	28	86	▲	1 The Spirit Room		Maverick 47985
7/12/03	2¹	33	▲	2 Hotel Paper		Maverick 48426

BRAND NEW
Punk-pop band from Merrick, New York: Jesse Lacey (vocals), Vincent Accardi (guitar), Garrett Tierney (bass) and Brian Lane (drums).

7/5/03	63	26	●	1 Deja Entendu		Triple Crown 82896
12/9/06	31	9		2 The Devil And God Are Raging Inside Me		Interscope 008034
10/10/09	6	6		3 Daisy		Interscope 013357

BRAND NEW HEAVIES, The
Funk band from London, England: N'dea Davenport (vocals), Simon Bartholomew (guitar), Andrew Levy (bass) and Jan Kincaid (drums). Davenport left in 1996; replaced by Siedah Garrett.

8/22/92	139	3	1 Heavy Rhyme Experience: Vol. 1		Delicious Vinyl 92178
4/9/94	95	9	2 Brother Sister		Delicious Vinyl 92319
5/31/97	118	5	3 Shelter		Delicious Vinyl 5019

BRAND NUBIAN
Rap trio from New Rochelle, New York: Maxwell Dixon ("**Grand Puba**"), Derek Murphy ("**Sadat X**") and Lorenzo DeChalus ("**Lord Jamar**"). Dixon left in 1992, replaced by Terence Perry ("**Sincere Allah**"). Dixon returned in 1998.

2/23/91	130	28	1 One For All		Elektra 60946
2/20/93	12	10	2 In God We Trust		Elektra 61381
11/19/94	54	3	3 Everything Is Everything		Elektra 61682
10/17/98	59	5	4 Foundation..		Arista 19024

BRANDOS, The
Rock band from New York: Dave Kincaid (vocals), Ed Rupprecht (guitar), Ernie Mendillo (bass) and Larry Mason (drums).

9/26/87	108	19	1 Honor Among Thieves..		Relativity 8192

BRANDT, Paul
Born on 7/21/1972 in Calgary, Alberta, Canada. Country singer/songwriter/guitarist.

6/29/96	102	30	●	1 Calm Before The Storm		Reprise 46180

BRAND X
Jazz-fusion band from England: Phil Collins (drums; **Genesis**), John Goodsall (guitar), Robin Lumley (keyboards), Percy Jones (bass) and Morris Pert (percussion).

11/13/76	191	3	1 Unorthodox Behaviour .... [I]		Passport 98019
5/21/77	125	8	2 Moroccan Roll .... [I]		Passport 98022
12/17/77	204	4	3 Livestock .... [I]		Passport 9824
11/3/79	165	6	4 Product .... [I]		Passport 9840
7/19/80	204	4	5 Do They Hurt? .... [I]		Passport 9845

BRANDY
Born Brandy Norwood on 2/11/1979 in McComb, Mississippi; raised in Los Angeles, California. R&B singer/actress. Played "Danesha Turrell" on TV's *Thea* in 1993 and starred as "Moesha Mitchell" on the 1996 TV series *Moesha*. Starred in the 1997 TV production of *Cinderella*. Played "Karla Wilson" in the 1998 movie *I Still Know What You Did Last Summer*. Sister of **Ray J**. One of the judges on the 2006 TV show *America's Got Talent*.

DEBUT	PEAK	WKS	RIAA	#	Album Title	Catalog	Label & Number
10/15/94+	20	89	▲⁴	1	Brandy		Atlantic 82610
6/27/98	2¹	72	▲⁴	2	Never S-a-y Never		Atlantic 83039
3/23/02	2¹	30	▲	3	Full Moon		Atlantic 83493
7/17/04	3¹	13	●	4	Afrodisiac		Atlantic 83633
4/23/05	27	5		5	The Best Of Brandy	[G]	Atlantic 74647
12/27/08	15	13		6	Human		Knockout 27271

BRANIGAN, Laura
Born on 7/3/1957 in Brewster, New York. Died of a brain aneurysm on 8/26/2004 (age 47). Singer/actress. Played "Monica" in the 1985 movie *Delta Pi*.

DEBUT	PEAK	WKS	RIAA	#	Album Title	Catalog	Label & Number
9/25/82	34	36	●	1	Branigan		Atlantic 19289
4/9/83	29	37	●	2	Branigan 2		Atlantic 80052
4/28/84	23	45	▲	3	Self Control		Atlantic 80147
8/10/85	71	15		4	Hold Me		Atlantic 81265
8/1/87	87	28		5	Touch		Atlantic 81747
4/28/90	133	6		6	Laura Branigan		Atlantic 82086

BRANNEN, John
Born on 3/19/1952 in Savannah, Georgia; raised in Charleston, South Carolina. Country-rock singer.

DEBUT	PEAK	WKS	RIAA	#	Album Title	Catalog	Label & Number
3/12/88	156	14		1	Mystery Street		Apache 71650

BRASS CONSTRUCTION
Disco band from Brooklyn, New York: Randy Muller (vocals, keyboards), Joe Wong (guitar), Wayne Parris, Morris Price, Jesse Ward and Mickey Grudge (horn section), Sandy Billups (congas), Wade Williamston (bass) and Larry Payton (drums). Muller later formed **Skyy**.

DEBUT	PEAK	WKS	RIAA	#	Album Title	Catalog	Label & Number
2/7/76	10	35	▲	1	Brass Construction		United Artists 545
11/20/76	26	22	●	2	Brass Construction II		United Artists 677
11/19/77	66	14	●	3	Brass Construction III		United Artists 775
11/18/78	174	4		4	Brass Construction IV		United Artists 916
12/15/79+	89	20		5	Brass Construction 5		United Artists 977
9/20/80	121	5		6	Brass Construction 6		United Artists 1060
5/22/82	114	8		7	Attitudes		Liberty 51121
6/11/83	176	6		8	Conversations		Capitol 12268

BRASS RING, The
Studio group assembled by producer/arranger/saxophonist Phil Bodner (born on 6/13/1917; died on 2/24/2008, age 90).

DEBUT	PEAK	WKS	RIAA	#	Album Title	Catalog	Label & Number
6/25/66	109	8		1	Love Theme From The Flight Of The Phoenix	[I]	Dunhill 50008
4/15/67	157	3		2	Sunday Night At The Movies	[I]	Dunhill 50015
6/24/67	193	2		3	The Dis-Advantages Of You	[I]	Dunhill 50017

BRATZ
Studio group based on the popular line of pre-teen dolls: Sasha, Cloe, Jade, Yasmin and Roxxi.

DEBUT	PEAK	WKS	RIAA	#	Album Title	Catalog	Label & Number
8/13/05	79	20		1	Rock Angelz		Hip-O 004902
4/29/06	106	1		2	Genie Magic		Hip-O 006521
10/7/06	184	1		3	Forever Diamondz		Hip-O 007315
3/10/07	166	1		4	Fashion Pixiez		Hip-O 008519

BRAUN, Bob
Born Robert Brown on 4/20/1929 in Ludlow, Kentucky. Died of Parkinson's disease on 1/15/2001 (age 71). Pop singer.

DEBUT	PEAK	WKS	RIAA	#	Album Title	Catalog	Label & Number
10/27/62	99	6		1	Till Death Do Us Part		Decca 74339

BRAUN, Rick
Born on 7/6/1960 in Allentown, Pennsylvania. Jazz saxophonist. Member of **Auracle**.

DEBUT	PEAK	WKS	RIAA	#	Album Title	Catalog	Label & Number
6/17/00	78	15		1	Shake It Up	[I]	Warner 47557
					BONEY JAMES / RICK BRUAN		
3/17/01	182	1		2	Kisses In The Rain	[I]	Warner 47994

BRAVE BELT — see BACHMAN-TURNER OVERDRIVE

BRAVEHEARTS
Male rap duo from Queens, New York: Jabari "Jungle" Jones and Mike "Wiz" Epps.

DEBUT	PEAK	WKS	RIAA	#	Album Title	Catalog	Label & Number
1/10/04	75	7		1	Bravehearted		Ill Will 86712

BRAVERY, The
Alternative-rock band from New York: Sam Endicott (vocals, guitar), Michael Zakarin (guitar), John Conway (keyboards), Mike Hindirt (bass) and Anthony Burulcich (drums).

DEBUT	PEAK	WKS	RIAA	#	Album Title	Catalog	Label & Number
4/16/05	18	24		1	The Bravery		Island 004163
6/9/07	24	7		2	The Sun And The Moon		Island 008283
12/19/09	135	1		3	Stir The Blood		Island 013602

BRAXTON, Toni
Born on 10/7/1967 in Severn, Maryland. Female R&B singer/actress. Recorded in 1990 with her younger sisters as **The Braxtons**. Sister of **Tamar** Braxton. Married Keri Lewis (of **Mint Condition**) on 4/21/2001. Played "Juanita Slocumb" in the 2001 movie *Kingdom Come*.

AWARD: Grammy: Best New Artist 1993

DEBUT	PEAK	WKS	RIAA		Album Title	Catalog	Label & Number
7/31/93+	❶²	96	▲⁸	1	Toni Braxton	Cat:#46/1	LaFace 26007
7/6/96	2¹	92	▲⁸	2	Secrets		LaFace 26020
5/13/00	2¹	47	▲²	3	The Heat		LaFace 26069
11/10/01	119	7	●	4	Snowflakes	Cat:#36/1 [X]	Arista 14723
					Christmas charts: 9/'01, 5/'02		
12/7/02	13	14	●	5	More Than A Woman		Arista 14749
11/22/03	119	2		6	Ultimate Toni Braxton	[G]	Arista 51699
10/15/05	4	15	●	7	Libra		Blackground 005441

BRAXTONS, The
Vocal trio of sisters from Severn, Maryland: **Tamar**, Trina and Towanda Braxton. Began as a quintet, with Traci and **Toni** Braxton. Toni went solo in 1992; Traci went solo in 1995.

DEBUT	PEAK	WKS			Album Title		Label & Number
8/31/96	113	6		1	So Many Ways		Atlantic 82875

BRAZEROS MUSICAL DE DURANGO
Latin band formed in Chicago, Illinois: Eduardo Navar, Filiberto Valdez, Jorge Moral, Jose Ayala, Juan Loredo, Raymundo Nunez and Alex Salgado.

DEBUT	PEAK	WKS			Album Title		Label & Number
10/30/04	199	1		1	El Grupo Joven De La Musica Duranguense	[F]	Disa 726904
9/6/06	186	1		2	Rosas Rojas	[F]	Disa 720908
7/21/07	164	1		3	Volvio El Dolor	[F]	Disa 721081

BREAD
All-Time: #483

Soft-rock band formed in Los Angeles, California: **David Gates** (vocals, guitar, keyboards; born on 12/11/1940), James Griffin (guitar; born on 8/10/1943; died of cancer on 1/11/2005, age 61), Robb Royer (guitar) and Jim Gordon (drums). Mike Botts (born on 12/8/1944; died of cancer on 12/9/2005, age 61) replaced Gordon after first album. Larry Knechtel (born on 8/4/1940; died on 8/20/2009, age 69) replaced Royer in 1971. Disbanded in 1973, reunited briefly in 1976.

DEBUT	PEAK	WKS			Album Title		Label & Number
10/18/69	127	9		1	Bread		Elektra 74044
8/8/70	12	32	●	2	On The Waters		Elektra 74076
3/27/71	21	25	●	3	Manna		Elektra 74086
2/5/72	3¹	56	●	4	Baby I'm-A Want You		Elektra 75015
11/18/72	18	29	●	5	Guitar Man		Elektra 75047
1/15/77	26	16	●	6	Lost Without Your Love		Elektra 1094
					GREATEST HITS & COMPILATIONS:		
3/31/73	2¹	119	▲⁵	7	The Best Of Bread		Elektra 75056
6/1/74	32	18	●	8	The Best Of Bread, Volume Two		Elektra 1005
8/11/01	163	1		9	The Best Of Bread		Elektra 74311
7/28/07	32ᶜ	7		10	Anthology Of Bread		Elektra 60414

BREAKFAST CLUB
Pop-dance band from Manhattan, New York: brothers Dan Gilroy (vocals) and Eddie Gilroy (guitar), Gary Burke (bass) and Stephen Bray (drums). **Madonna** was the group's drummer for a short time in 1979.

DEBUT	PEAK	WKS			Album Title		Label & Number
3/28/87	43	30		1	Breakfast Club		MCA 5821

BREAKING BENJAMIN
Hard-rock band from Wilkes-Barre, Pennsylvania: Ben Burnley (vocals, guitar), Aaron Fink (guitar), Mark Klepaski (bass) and Jeremy Hummel (drums). Chad Szeliga replaced Hummel in late 2005.

DEBUT	PEAK	WKS			Album Title		Label & Number
9/14/02	136	2		1	Saturate		Hollywood 62356
7/17/04	20	59	▲	2	We Are Not Alone		Hollywood 162428
8/26/06	2¹	78	▲	3	Phobia		Hollywood 162607
10/17/09	4	33↑	●	4	Dear Agony		Hollywood 002398

BREAKS, The
Pop-rock band from Memphis, Tennessee: Susanne Jerome Taylor (vocals), Pat Taylor (guitar), Tom Ward (keyboards), Rob Caudill (bass) and Russ Caudill (drums).

DEBUT	PEAK	WKS			Album Title		Label & Number
9/17/83	203	5		1	The Breaks		RCA Victor 4675

BREAKWATER
Disco band from Philadelphia, Pennsylvania: Gene Robinson (vocals), Lincoln Gilmore (guitar), Kae Williams (keyboards), John Braddock (percussion), Vince Garnell and Greg Scott (horns), Steve Green (bass) and James Jones (drums).

DEBUT	PEAK	WKS			Album Title		Label & Number
4/21/79	173	5		1	Breakwater		Arista 4208
6/7/80	141	5		2	Splashdown		Arista 4264

B REAL
Born Louis Freese on 6/2/1970 in Los Angeles, California. Male rapper. Member of **Cypress Hill**.

DEBUT	PEAK	WKS			Album Title		Label & Number
3/14/09	148	1		1	Smoke N Mirrors		Duck Down 2090

BREATHE
Pop band from London, England: David Glasper (vocals), Marcus Lillington (guitar), Michael Delahunty (bass) and Ian Spice (drums). Delahunty left in 1988.

DEBUT	PEAK	WKS			Album Title		Label & Number
6/4/88	34	51	●	1	All That Jazz		A&M 5163
9/22/90	116	20		2	Peace Of Mind		A&M 5320

Billboard			R I A A	ARTIST	Catalog	Label & Number
DEBUT	PEAK	WKS		Album Title		

BREATHE CAROLINA
Electronica duo from Denver, Colorado: David Schmitt and Kyle Even.

10/4/08	186	1		1 It's Classy Not Classic		Rise 069
9/5/09	43	2		2 Hello Fascination		Fearless 30127

BRECKER BROTHERS, The
White jazz-funk duo from Philadelphia, Pennsylvania: brothers Randy Brecker (trumpet; born on 11/27/1945) and Michael Brecker (reeds; born on 3/29/1949; died on 1/13/2007, age 57). Both were prolific sessionmen. The brothers began recording together in their group, **Dreams**; also with **Spyro Gyra**.

6/7/75	102	13		1 The Brecker Brothers	[I]	Arista 4037
2/28/76	82	16		2 Back To Back	[I]	Arista 4061
5/7/77	135	6		3 Don't Stop The Music	[I]	Arista 4122
11/4/78	207	1		4 Heavy Metal Be-Bop	[I]	Arista 4185
6/28/80	204	1		5 Detente	[I]	Arista 4272
6/20/81	176	3		6 Straphangin'	[I]	Arista 9550

BREEDERS, The
Rock band from Dayton, Ohio: twin sisters/guitarists/vocalists Kim Deal and Kelley Deal, bassist Josephine Wiggs (native of Bedfordshire, England) and drummer Jim MacPherson. Kim was a member of the **Pixies**. Tanya Donelly (Throwing Muses, **Belly**) was an early member.

9/18/93+	33	36	▲	1 Last Splash		4AD 61508
6/8/02	130	2		2 Title TK		4AD 62766
4/26/08	98	2		3 Mountain Battles		4AD 2803

BREMERS, Beverly
Born on 3/10/1950 in Chicago, Illinois. Pop singer/actress.

9/16/72	124	8		1 I'll Make You Music		Scepter 5102

BRENDA & THE TABULATIONS
R&B vocal group from Philadelphia, Pennsylvania: Brenda Payton, Jerry Jones, Eddie Jackson and Maurice Coates. Payton died on 6/14/1992 (age 46).

7/1/67	191	4		1 Dry Your Eyes		Dionn 2000

BRENNAN, Walter
Born on 7/25/1894 in Swampscott, Massachusetts. Died of emphysema on 9/21/1974 (age 80). Famous character actor. Appeared in several movies and TV shows.

6/23/62	54	10		1 Old Rivers		Liberty 3233

BRENT, Teddy
Born in Detroit, Michigan. Funk singer/songwriter.

4/12/08	147	6		1 Fashionable		Kass 21347

BREWER, Teresa
Born Theresa Breuer on 5/7/1931 in Toledo, Ohio. Died on 10/17/2007 (age 76). Pop singer.

3/19/55	10	3		1 Especially For You...	[EP]	Coral 81115
11/10/73	220	2		2 Music, Music, Music		Flying Dutchman 12013

BREWER & SHIPLEY
Folk-rock duo formed in Los Angeles, California: Mike Brewer (born in 1944 in Oklahoma City, Oklahoma) and Tom Shipley (born in 1942 in Mineral Ridge, Ohio).

3/6/71	34	26		1 Tarkio		Kama Sutra 2024
12/25/71+	164	8		2 Shake Off The Demon		Kama Sutra 2039
1/27/73	174	7		3 Rural Space		Kama Sutra 2058
5/11/74	185	5		4 ST-11261		Capitol 11261
				album title refers to the label prefix and number		
8/2/75	202	1		5 Welcome To Riddle Bridge		Capitol 11402

BREWSTER, Lincoln
Born on 7/30/1971 in Fairbanks, Alaska; raised in Homer, Alaska. Christian rock singer/songwriter/guitarist.

10/11/08	56	4		1 Today Is The Day		Integrity 33578

B RICH
Born Brian Rich in Baltimore, Maryland. Male rapper.

7/6/02	100	4		1 80 Dimes		Atlantic 83555

BRICK
Disco-jazz band from Atlanta, Georgia: Jimmy Brown (sax), Reggie Hargis (guitar), Don Nevins (keyboards), Ray Ransom (bass) and Eddie Irons (drums). All share vocals.

11/13/76+	19	24		1 Good High		Bang 408
9/10/77	15	32		2 Brick		Bang 409
5/19/79	100	8		3 Stoneheart		Bang 35969
7/12/80	179	5		4 Waiting On You		Bang 36262
9/5/81	89	10		5 Summer Heat		Bang 37471

BRICKELL, Edie
Born on 3/10/1966 in Oak Cliff, Texas. Adult Alternative singer/songwriter. New Bohemians: Kenny Withrow (guitar), Brad Houser (bass) and John Bush (drums). Joining the band by 1990 were Wes Burt-Martin (guitar) and Matt Chamberlain (drums). Brickell married **Paul Simon** on 5/30/1992.

DEBUT	PEAK	WKS			Catalog	Label & Number
9/24/88+	4	54	▲²	1 Shooting Rubberbands At The Stars		Geffen 24192
11/17/90	32	18		2 Ghost Of A Dog		Geffen 24304
				EDIE BRICKELL & NEW BOHEMIANS (above 2)		
9/3/94	68	10		3 Picture Perfect Morning		Geffen 24715
11/1/03	188	1		4 Volcano		Universal 000963

BRICKMAN, Jim   All-Time: #358
Born on 11/20/1961 in Cleveland, Ohio. New Age pianist/songwriter. Classically-trained at the Cleveland Institute of Music. Began career writing commercial jingles. Also see **Various Artists Compilations: Jim Brickman's Visions Of Love**.

DEBUT	PEAK	WKS			Catalog	Label & Number
2/17/96	187	4	●	1 By Heart: Piano Solos	[I]	Windham Hill 11164
2/15/97	30	29	●	2 Picture This	[I]	Windham Hill 11211
2/13/99	42	16	●	3 Destiny	[I]	Windham Hill 11396
9/9/00	75	12		4 My Romance...An Evening With Jim Brickman	[I-L]	Windham Hill 11557
				recorded on 3/27/2000 at the Capitol Theatre in Salt Lake City, Utah		
10/13/01	54	12		5 Simple Things	[I]	Windham Hill 11589
8/24/02	73	8		6 Love Songs & Lullabies	[I]	Windham Hill 11647
5/22/04	134	3		7 Greatest Hits	[G]	Windham Hill 60616
5/7/05	88	3		8 Grace	[I]	Windham Hill 67979
10/22/05	142	1		9 The Disney Songbook		Walt Disney 861380
10/21/06	105	1		10 Escape	[I]	SLG 17615
10/11/08	199	1		11 Unspoken	[I]	SLG 17745
10/17/09	89	1		12 Beautiful World	[I]	Somerset 49268
				CHRISTMAS ALBUMS:		
11/1/97	48	11	●	13 The Gift	Cat:#16/8 [I]	Windham Hill 11242
				Christmas charts: 3/'97, 17/'98, 26/'99, 25/'05		
11/15/03	87	8		14 Peace		Windham Hill 52896
				Christmas charts: 7/'03, 50/'05		
10/20/07	96	6		15 Homecoming	[I]	SLG 17659
				Christmas charts: 1/'07, 41/'08		
1/12/08	9ˣ	2		16 Christmas Romance	Cat:#10/2 [I]	Compass 39871
11/29/08	82	1		17 The Hymns & Carols Of Christmas		Brickhouse Direct 06304
				Christmas chart: 22/'08		
11/28/09+	85	2		18 Joy		Compass 49026
				Christmas chart: 6/'09		

BRIDES OF DESTRUCTION
Hard-rock band formed in Los Angeles, California: London LeGrand (vocals), Tracii Guns (guitar; **L.A. Guns**), Nikki Sixx (bass; **Motley Crue**) and Scot Coogan (drums).

DEBUT	PEAK	WKS			Catalog	Label & Number
3/27/04	92	1		1 Here Come The Brides		Sanctuary 84674

BRIDES OF FUNKENSTEIN, The
Female R&B-funk vocal duo: Dawn Silva and Lynn Mabry. Members of the **Parliament/Funkadelic** aggregation. Trio in 1980 of Silva, Sheila Horn and Jeanette McGruder.

DEBUT	PEAK	WKS			Catalog	Label & Number
11/4/78	70	13		1 Funk Or Walk		Atlantic 19201
2/16/80	93	7		2 Never Buy Texas From A Cowboy		Atlantic 19261

BRIDGES, Alicia
Born on 7/15/1953 in Lawndale, North Carolina. Disco singer/songwriter.

DEBUT	PEAK	WKS			Catalog	Label & Number
9/30/78+	33	32		1 Alicia Bridges		Polydor 6158

BRIDGEWATER, Dee Dee
Born on 5/27/1950 in Memphis, Tennessee; raised in Flint, Michigan. Jazz singer/actress.

DEBUT	PEAK	WKS			Catalog	Label & Number
5/6/78	170	7		1 Just Family		Elektra 119
5/26/79	182	4		2 Bad For Me		Elektra 188

BRIGHTER SIDE OF DARKNESS
R&B vocal group from Chicago: Darryl Lamont, Ralph Eskridge, Randolph Murph and Larry Washington.

DEBUT	PEAK	WKS			Catalog	Label & Number
4/14/73	202	4		1 Love Jones		20th Century 405

BRIGHT EYES
Born Connor Oberst on 2/15/1980 in Omaha, Nebraska. Adult Alternative singer/songwriter/guitarist. Member of **Monsters Of Folk**.

DEBUT	PEAK	WKS			Catalog	Label & Number
8/31/02	161	1		1 Lifted or The Story Is In The Soil, Keep Your Ear To The Ground		Saddle Creek 0046
2/12/05	10	17		2 I'm Wide Awake, It's Morning		Saddle Creek 0072
2/12/05	15	10		3 Digital Ash In A Digital Urn		Saddle Creek 0073
11/11/06	107	1		4 Noise Floor (Rarities: 1998-2005)	[K]	Saddle Creek 99
3/24/07	57	2		5 Four Winds	[EP]	Saddle Creek 101
4/28/07	4	10		6 Cassadaga		Saddle Creek 103
8/23/08	15	6		7 Conor Oberst		Merge 340
5/23/09	40	4		8 Outer South		Merge 349
				CONOR OBERST & THE MYSTIC VALLEY BAND		

BRIGHTMAN, Sarah
Born on 8/14/1960 in Berkhamstead, Hertfordshire, England. Singer/actress. Starred on Broadway's *The Phantom Of The Opera*. Married to **Andrew Lloyd Webber** from 1984-90.

DEBUT	PEAK	WKS			Album Title	Catalog	Label & Number
2/28/98	71	27	▲	1	Time To Say Goodbye	Cat:#35/6	Angel 56511
5/8/99	65	24		2	Eden		Angel 56769
9/16/00	17	31	●	3	La Luna		Angel 56968
6/28/03	29	16		4	Harem		Angel 37180
2/16/08	13	11		5	Symphony		Manhattan 46078
11/22/08	38	8		6	A Winter Symphony	[X]	Manhattan 34123
					Christmas charts: 6/'08, 42/'09		

GREATEST HITS & COMPILATIONS:

6/26/99	110	17	●	7	The Andrew Lloyd Webber Collection		Really Useful 539330
12/8/01+	66	18	●	8	Classics		Angel 33257
5/11/02	124	4		9	Encore		Really Useful 589050
10/21/06	100	5		10	Diva: The Singles Collection		Nemo Studios 73671

LIVE ALBUMS:

10/16/04	126	3		11	The Harem World Tour: Live From Las Vegas		Nemo Studio 57801
3/28/09	191	1		12	Symphony: Live In Vienna		Manhattan 21681

BRILEY, Martin
Born on 8/17/1949 in London, England. Rock singer/songwriter/guitarist.

5/7/83	55	22	1	One Night With A Stranger		Mercury 810332
2/9/85	85	10	2	Dangerous Moments		Mercury 822423

BRING ME THE HORIZON
Heavy metal band from Sheffield, Yorkshire, England: Oliver Sykes (vocals), Lee Malia (guitar), Curtis Ward (guitar), Matt Kean (bass) and Matt Nicholls (drums).

12/6/08	107	2	1	Suicide Season		Visible Noise 87006

BRINKLEY, David — HUNTLEY, Chet

BRISTOL, Johnny
Born on 2/3/1939 in Morganton, North Carolina. Died of a heart attack on 3/21/2004 (age 65). R&B singer/songwriter/producer.

8/31/74	82	17	1	Hang On In There Baby		MGM 4959
12/11/76+	154	11	2	Bristol's Creme		Atlantic 18197

BRITISH LIONS
Rock band from Birmingham, England: John Fiddler (vocals), Ray Major (guitar), Morgan Fisher (keyboards), Pete "Overend" Watts (bass) and Dale "Buffin" Griffin (drums). Fisher, Watts and Griffin were members of **Mott The Hoople**.

4/29/78	83	15	1	British Lions		RSO 3032

BRITNY FOX
Hard-rock band from Philadelphia, Pennsylvania: "Dizzy" Dean Davidson (vocals), Michael Kelly Smith (guitar), Billy Childs (bass) and Johnny Dee (drums).

7/23/88	39	37	●	1	Britny Fox		Columbia 44140
11/25/89	79	23		2	Boys In Heat		Columbia 45300

BRITTEN, Benjamin
Born on 11/22/1913 in Lowestoft, Norfolk, England. Died on 12/4/1976 (age 63). Composer/conductor.

9/7/63	68	8	1	Britten: War Requiem		London 4255 [2]
				Grammys: Classical Choral Album / Hall of Fame		

BROADWAY SYMPHONY ORCHESTRA
Studio group assembled by producer Luther Henderson.

7/3/82	207	1	1	Turned-On Broadway	[I]	RCA Victor 4327

BROCK, Chad
Born on 7/31/1963 in Ocala, Florida. Country singer/songwriter/guitarist.

5/20/00	125	2	1	Yes!		Warner 47659

BRODSKY QUARTET, The — see COSTELLO, Elvis

BRODY, Dean
Born in Jaffray, British Columbia, Canada. Country singer/songwriter/guitarist.

5/16/09	187	1	1	Dean Brody		Broken Bow 71372

BROKENCYDE
Crunkcore band from Albuquerque, New Mexico: Se7en, Mikl, Phat J and Antz.

7/4/09	86	2	1	I'm Not A Fan But The Kids Like It		Breaksilence 123

BROKEN SOCIAL SCENE
Alternative-rock band from Toronto, Ontario, Canada. Formed by **Kevin Drew** and Brendan Canning and featuring a revolving lineup of local singers and musicians.

10/22/05	105	2	1	Broken Social Scene		Arts & Crafts 014

BROMBERG, David
Born on 9/19/1945 in Philadelphia, Pennsylvania. Folk singer/songwriter/guitarist.

3/25/72	194	2		1 David Bromberg		Columbia 31104
2/23/74	167	5		2 Wanted Dead Or Alive..		Columbia 32717
7/12/75	173	3		3 Midnight On The Water..		Columbia 33397
10/9/76	104	11		4 How Late'll Ya Play 'Til? .... **[L]**		Fantasy 79007 [2]
				record 1: studio; record 2: recorded on 6/18/1976 at the Great American Music Hall in San Francisco, California		
11/19/77	132	9		5 Reckless Abandon		Fantasy 9540
6/17/78	130	9		6 Bandit In A Bathing Suit		Fantasy 9555
2/24/79	152	4		7 My Own House		Fantasy 9572

BRONCO
Latin group from Apodaca, Mexico: Ramiro Delgado, Aurelio Esparza, Jose Esparza, Javier Villarreal and Jose Villarreal.

4/19/03	153	2		1 30 Inolvidables .... **[F-G]**		Fonovisa 350787
8/9/03	97	5		2 Siempre Arriba .... **[F]**		Fonovisa 350927
2/21/04	127	5		3 Cronica De Dos Grandes .... **[F]**		Fonovisa 351279
				BRONCO / LOS BUKIS		
8/21/04	142	3		4 Sin Riendas .... **[F]**		Fonovisa 351485
2/12/05	120	4		5 Recuerdos Con Amor... **[F]**		Fonovisa 351606
				BRONCO / LOS BUKIS		
9/10/05	175	1		6 Por Ti .... **[F]**		Fonovisa 351927
1/28/06	166	3		7 Los Inicios De Nuestra Historia................................... **[F-K]**		Fonovisa 352231
				BRONCO / LOS BUKIS		

BRONSKI BEAT
Techno-pop trio from England: **Jimmy Somerville** (vocals), Steve Bronski and Larry Steinbachek (synthesizers). Somerville formed the **Communards**.

1/19/85	36	25		1 The Age Of Consent		MCA 5538
8/2/86	147	6		2 Truthdare Doubledare...		MCA 5751

BROOD, Herman
Born on 11/5/1946 in Zwolle, Netherlands. Committed suicide on 7/11/2001 (age 54). Leader of Dutch rock band Wild Romance.

5/26/79	122	19		1 Herman Brood & His Wild Romance		Ariola 50059
6/28/80	207	2		2 Go Nutz		Ariola America 1500

BROOKE, Jonatha
Born on 1/23/1964 in Illinois; raised in Boston, Massachusetts. Female folk-pop singer/songwriter/guitarist.

3/3/01	192	1		1 Steady Pull...		Bad Dog 60801

BROOKLYN BRIDGE
Pop band from Long Island, New York: Johnny Maestro (lead vocals), Fred Ferrara, Les Cauchi and Mike Gregorie (backing vocals), Richie Macioce (guitar), Tom Sullivan and Joe Ruvio (saxophones), Shelly Davis (trumpet), Carolyn Wood (organ), Jimmy Rosica (bass) and Artie Catanzarita (drums). Maestro was lead singer of The Crests. Maestro died of cancer on 3/24/2010 (age 70).

3/29/69	54	30		1 Brooklyn Bridge		Buddah 5034
10/11/69	145	8		2 The Second Brooklyn Bridge		Buddah 5042

BROOKLYN, BRONX & QUEENS BAND, The
R&B band from New York: Lucious Floyd (vocals), Abdul Walli Mohammed (guitar), Kevin Nance (keyboards), PeeWee Ford (bass) and Dwayne Perdue (drums).

8/29/81	109	9		1 The Brooklyn, Bronx & Queens Band		Capitol 12155

BROOKLYN DREAMS
Disco trio from Brooklyn, New York: Joe "Bean" Esposito (vocals, guitar), Bruce Sudano (keyboards; **Alive And Kicking**) and Eddie Hokenson (drums). Sudano married **Donna Summer** on 7/16/1980.

3/24/79	151	7		1 Sleepless Nights		Casablanca 7135

BROOKLYN TABERNACLE CHOIR, The
Church choir founded in 1972 by Pastor Jim Cymbala in Brooklyn, New York. Comprised of 240 members.

5/6/00	59	3		1 God Is Working - Live... **[L]**		Word 63805
11/17/01	25ˣ	3		2 Light Of The World .... **[X]**		Word/Epic 85911
				Christmas chart: 25/'01		
12/6/03	137	2		3 Live...This Is Your House .... **[L]**		Word-Curb 82502 [2]
2/16/08	80	2		4 I'll Say Yes .... **[L]**		Integrity 21732

BROOKS, Albert
Born Albert Einstein on 7/22/1947 in Los Angeles. Comedian/director/actor. Son of radio comedian Harry "Parkyarkarkus" Parke. Acted in several movies. Brother of comedian daredevil Bob "Super Dave Osborne" Einstein.

1/19/74	211	3		1 Comedy Minus One .... **[C]**		ABC 800
7/26/75	205	3		2 A Star Is Bought .... **[C]**		Asylum 1035

BROOKS, Donnie
Born John Abohosh on 2/6/1936 in Dallas, Texas; raised in Ventura, California. Died of heart failure on 2/23/2007 (age 71). Pop singer.

~ ~ ~ ~ ~ ~ ~ ~ ~ ~   ***NON-CHARTED ALBUM***   ~ ~ ~ ~ ~ ~ ~ ~ ~ ~ ~

1961 The Happiest...Donnie Brooks

BROOKS, Garth
1990s: #1 / All-Time: #57

Born Troyal Garth Brooks on 2/7/1962 in Luba, Oklahoma; raised in Yukon, Oklahoma. Country singer/songwriter/guitarist. Attended Oklahoma State University on a track scholarship. Played local clubs and worked as a bouncer. Also recorded as alter-ego Chris Gaines. Married **Trisha Yearwood** on 12/10/2005. The #1 country artist of the 1990s.
AWARDS: CMA: Horizon 1990 / Entertainer 1991, 1992, 1997 & 1998 ★ OPRY: 1990

						Catalog	Label & Number
5/12/90+	13	224	▲10	1	Garth Brooks	Cat:#48/1	Capitol 90897
9/22/90+	3[2]	224	▲17	2	No Fences	Cat:#17/15	Capitol 93866
					CMA: Album of the Year		
9/28/91	❶18	132	▲14	3	Ropin' The Wind		Capitol 96330
					Grammy: Male Country Vocal ★ CMA: Album of the Year		
10/10/92	❶7	64	▲9	4	The Chase		Liberty 98743
9/18/93	❶5	76	▲8	5	In Pieces		Liberty 80857
12/9/95	2[2]	66	▲7	6	Fresh Horses		Capitol 32080
12/13/97	❶5	58	▲10	7	Sevens		Capitol 56599
5/23/98	❶2	34		8	The Limited Series [K-R]		Capitol 94572 [6]
					package of albums #1-6 above with one additional track on each; includes a 61-page booklet		
12/5/98	❶5	56	▲21	9	Double Live [L]		Capitol 97424 [2]
10/16/99	2[1]	18	▲2	10	Garth Brooks In...The Life Of Chris Gaines		Capitol 20051
12/1/01	❶1	28	▲5	11	Scarecrow		Capitol 31330
					CHRISTMAS ALBUMS:		
9/12/92	2[1]	24	▲3	12	Beyond The Season	Cat:#3/42	Liberty 98742
					Christmas charts: 1/'92, 11/'93, 16/'94, 17/'95, 25/'96, 37/'97, 10/'98		
12/11/99	7	7	▲	13	Garth Brooks & The Magic Of Christmas	Cat:#6/8	Capitol 23550
					Christmas charts: 1/'99, 10/'00		
12/1/01	99	6		14	Garth Brooks & The Magic Of Christmas: Songs From Call Me Claus [R]		Capitol 35624
					Christmas chart: 11/'01; reissue of #13 above with 4 additional cuts from the TV special *Call Me Claus*		
					GREATEST HITS & COMPILATIONS:		
12/31/94+	❶8	110	▲10	15	The Hits	Cat:❶12/102	Liberty 29689
11/24/07	3[1]	84↑	▲5	16	The Ultimate Hits	Cat:#17/32	Pearl 213 [2]

BROOKS, Mel — see REINER, Carl

BROOKS, Meredith
Born on 6/12/1958 in Oregon City, Oregon. Female rock singer/guitarist. Former member of **The Graces**.

5/24/97	22	47	▲	1	Blurring The Edges		Capitol 36919

BROOKS & DUNN
1990s: #18 / All-Time: #151

Duo of Kix Brooks (born on 5/12/1955 in Shreveport, Louisiana) and Ronnie Dunn (born on 6/1/1953 in Coleman, Texas). Brooks had written several hits and Dunn had won a national talent competition before teaming up. The most successful country duo of all-time.
AWARD: CMA: Vocal Duo 1992, 1993, 1994, 1995, 1996, 1997, 1998, 1999, 2001, 2002, 2003, 2004, 2005 & 2006 / Entertainer 1996

9/7/91+	10	153	▲6	1	Brand New Man		Arista 18658
3/13/93	9	99	▲5	2	Hard Workin' Man		Arista 18716
10/15/94	15	59	▲3	3	Waitin' On Sundown		Arista 18765
5/4/96	5	70	▲2	4	Borderline		Arista 18810
10/4/97	4	86	▲4	5	The Greatest Hits Collection	Cat:#21/141 [G]	Arista Nashville 18852
6/20/98	11	40	▲2	6	If You See Her		Arista Nashville 18865
10/9/99	31	14	●	7	Tight Rope		Arista Nashville 18895
5/5/01	4	70	▲	8	Steers & Stripes		Arista Nashville 67003
11/23/02	81	8		9	It Won't Be Christmas Without You [X]		Arista Nashville 67053
					Christmas charts: 11/'02, 38/'04		
8/2/03	4	53	▲	10	Red Dirt Road		Arista Nashville 67070
11/6/04	7	34	▲	11	The Greatest Hits Collection II [G]		Arista Nashville 63271
9/17/05	3[1]	94	▲	12	Hillbilly Deluxe		Arista Nashville 69946
10/20/07	13	20		13	Cowboy Town	Cat:#29/2	Arista Nashville 11163
9/26/09	5	33↑		14	#1s...And Then Some [G]		Arista Nashville 49922 [2]

BROOM, Bobby
Born on 1/18/1961 in New York. Jazz guitarist.

8/15/81	203	7		1	Clean Sweep [I]		Arista/GRP 5504

Billboard			R I A A	ARTIST		
DEBUT	PEAK	WKS		Album Title	Catalog	Label & Number

BROS
Pop trio from Camberley, England: twin brothers Matt Goss (vocals) and Luke Goss (drums), with Craig Logan (bass). Group's name rhymes with "cross."

7/23/88	171	5		1 Push		Epic 44285

BROTHA LYNCH HUNG
Born Kevin Mann on 1/10/1972 in Sacramento, California. Hardcore rapper.

3/18/95	162	2		1 Season Of Da Siccness - The Resurrection		Black Market 53967
10/18/97	28	5		2 Loaded		Black Market 50648
7/15/00	86	6		3 EBK4		Black Market 4321
9/15/01	79	5		4 Blocc Movement...		JCOR 860950
				BROTHA LYNCH HUNG & C-BO		
6/28/03	132	2		5 Lynch By Inch: Suicide Note		Siccmade 70132 [2]

BROTHER ALI
Born Ali Newman in 1977 in Madison, Wisconsin; raised in Michigan and Minnesota. White male rapper.

4/28/07	69	1		1 The Undisputed Truth		Rhymesayers 0080
3/28/09	119	1		2 The Truth Is Here .... [EP]		Rhymesayers 0104
10/10/09	56	2		3 Us		Rhymesayers 0113

BROTHER CANE
Rock band from Birmingham, Alabama: Damon Johnson (vocals, guitar), Roman Glick (guitar), David Anderson (bass) and Scott Collier (drums). Johnson later joined **Whiskey Falls**.

8/12/95	184	7		1 Seeds...		Virgin 40564

BROTHERHOOD OF MAN, The
Studio group from England featuring Tony Burrows (lead singer of Edison Lighthouse, First Class, **The Pipkins** and **White Plains**).

8/8/70	168	8		1 United We Stand...		Deram 18046

BROTHERS FOUR, The
Folk-pop group formed in Seattle, Washington: Dick Foley, Bob Flick, John Paine and Mike Kirkland.

4/18/60	11	19		1 The Brothers Four		Columbia 1402 / 8197
2/13/61	4	35		2 B.M.O.C. (Best Music On/Off Campus)		Columbia 1578 / 8378
12/18/61	71	14		3 The Brothers Four Song Book		Columbia 1697 / 8497
10/6/62	102	4		4 The Brothers Four: In Person .... [L]		Columbia 1828 / 8628
5/4/63	81	12		5 Cross-Country Concert .... [L]		Columbia 1946 / 8746
10/12/63	56	20		6 The Big Folk Hits		Columbia 2033 / 8833
10/31/64	134	4		7 More Big Folk Hits...		Columbia 2213 / 9013
5/1/65	118	5		8 The Honey Wind Blows		Columbia 2305 / 9105
11/13/65+	76	15		9 Try To Remember...		Columbia 2379 / 9179
7/30/66	97	7		10 A Beatles' Songbook (The Brothers Four Sing Lennon/McCartney)		Columbia 2502 / 9302

BROTHERS JOHNSON, The
R&B duo from Los Angeles, California: brothers George Johnson (guitar; born on 5/17/1953) and Louis Johnson (bass; born on 4/13/1955). Discovered by **Quincy Jones** while playing with **Billy Preston**'s band. Duo split up in 1984. Louis was also a member of **Passage**.

3/6/76	9	49	▲	1 Look Out For #1		A&M 4567
5/21/77	13	31	▲	2 Right On Time...		A&M 4644
8/12/78	7	24	▲	3 Blam!!		A&M 4714
3/8/80	5	30	▲	4 Light Up The Night		A&M 3716
7/18/81	48	13		5 Winners		A&M 3724
1/22/83	138	5		6 Blast! (The Latest And The Greatest) .... [G]		A&M 4927
8/4/84	91	11		7 Out Of Control		A&M 4965

BROUSSARD, Marc
Born on 1/14/1982 in Carencro, Louisiana. Adult Contemporary singer/songwriter.

7/14/07	96	3		1 S.O.S.: Save Our Soul		Vanguard 79826
10/4/08	136	1		2 Keep Coming Back		Atlantic 512257

BROWN, Arthur [The Crazy World Of]
Born Arthur Wilton on 6/24/1942 in Whitby, Yorkshire, England. White theatrical rock singer. His band consisted of Sean Nicholas (guitar), Vince Crane (organ; **Atomic Rooster**) and Carl Palmer (drums; Atomic Rooster, **Emerson, Lake & Palmer**, **Asia**). Crane committed suicide on 2/14/1989 (age 44).

9/7/68	7	24		1 The Crazy World Of Arthur Brown		Track 8198

BROWN, Bobby
Born on 2/5/1969 in Roxbury, Massachusetts. R&B singer/songwriter. Former member of **New Edition**. Appeared in the movies *Ghostbusters II, Panther* and *A Thin Line Between Love & Hate*. Established own Bosstown recording studio and label in Atlanta in 1991. Married to **Whitney Houston** from 1992-2007. Arrested several times for various incidents during the 1990s.

12/13/86+	88	17		1 King Of Stage		MCA 5827
7/23/88+	❶⁶	97	▲⁷	2 Don't Be Cruel		MCA 42185
12/2/89+	9	33	▲	3 Dance!...Ya Know It! .... [K]		MCA 6342
9/12/92	2¹	43	▲²	4 Bobby		MCA 10417
11/22/97	61	3		5 Forever		MCA 11691

Billboard			R I A	ARTIST
DEBUT	**PEAK**	**WKS**	A	**Album Title**

						Catalog	Label & Number

BROWN, Buster
Born Wayman Glasco on 8/15/1911 in Cordele, Georgia. Died on 1/31/1976 (age 64). R&B singer/harmonica player.

~ ~ ~ ~ ~ ~ ~ ~ ~ ~ **NON-CHARTED ALBUM** ~ ~ ~ ~ ~ ~ ~ ~ ~ ~ ~
1960 **The New King Of The Blues**

BROWN, Charles
Born on 9/13/1922 in Texas City, Texas. Died of heart failure on 1/21/1999 (age 76). R&B singer/pianist.
AWARD: R&R Hall of Fame: 1999 (Early Influence)

12/12/64+	17ˣ	10		1 Charles Brown Sings Christmas Songs.. [X]	King 775

first released in 1961; Christmas charts: 22/'64, 29/'66, 19/'67, 36/'68, 17/'70

BROWN, Chris
Born on 5/5/1989 in Tappahannock, Washington. Male teen R&B singer. Arrested for a domestic abuse incident against girlfriend **Rihanna** in 2009.

12/17/05	2¹	71	▲²	1 Chris Brown	Cat:#50/1	Jive 82876
11/24/07	4	65	▲	2 Exclusive		Jive 12049
12/26/09	7	13		3 Graffiti		Jive 61434

BROWN, Chuck
Born in 1936 in Washington DC. Funk singer/guitarist. The Soul Searchers: John Buchanan and Curtis Johnson (keyboards), Don Tillery (trumpet), Leroy Fleming (sax), Gregory Gerran (congas), Jerry Wilder (bass) and Ricky Wellman (drums).

3/10/73	210	3		1 We The People..	Sussex 7020

THE SOUL SEARCHERS

2/17/79	31	14	●	2 Bustin' Loose..	Source 3076

CHUCK BROWN & THE SOUL SEARCHERS

6/2/01	193	1		3 Your Game... Live At The 9:30 Club, Washington, D.C. .... [L]	Raw Venture 9
5/12/07	37	4		4 We're About The Business..	Full Circle 15

BROWN, Clint
Born in Orlando, Florida. Christian singer/songwriter.

2/23/08	197	1		1 Fall Like Rain..	Tribe 2008

BROWN, Danny Joe
Born on 8/24/1951 in Jacksonville, Florida. Died of diabetes complications on 3/10/2005 (age 53). Hard-rock singer. Member of **Molly Hatchet**. Brown's band included: Bobby Ingram, Steve Wheeler and Kenny McVay (guitars), John Galvin (keyboards), Buzzy Meekins (bass) and Jimmy Glenn (drums).

7/4/81	120	7		1 Danny Joe Brown And The Danny Joe Brown Band	Epic 37385

BROWN, Dennis
Born on 2/1/1957 in Kingston, Jamaica. Died of a collapsed lung on 7/1/1999 (age 42). Reggae singer/songwriter.

5/2/81	208	2		1 Foul Play..	A&M 4850

BROWN, Foxy
Born Inga Marchand on 9/6/1979 in Brooklyn, New York. Female rapper. Took her name from the action movie character played by actress Pam Grier. Member of **The Firm**.

12/7/96	7	43	▲	1 Ill Na Na	Violator 533684
2/13/99	❶¹	20	▲	2 Chyna Doll	Violator 558933
8/4/01	5	13	●	3 Broken Silence	Def Jam 548834
5/31/08	83	2		4 Brooklyn's Don Diva	Black Roses 5030

BROWN, Horace
Born in Charlotte, North Carolina. R&B singer.

7/6/96	145	2		1 Horace Brown..	Motown 530625

BROWN, James   **1960s: #24 / 1970s: #21 / All-Time: #27**
Born on 5/3/1933 in Barnwell, South Carolina; raised in Augusta, Georgia. Died of heart failure on 12/25/2006 (age 73). Acclaimed as one of the most influential "soul" artists of all-time. Various nicknames include "The Godfather of Soul" and "The Hardest Working Man In Show Business." On 12/15/1988, received a six-year prison sentence after leading police on an interstate car chase; released from prison on 2/27/1991.
AWARDS: Grammy: Lifetime Achievement 1992 ★ R&R Hall of Fame: 1986

9/28/63	73	17		1 Prisoner Of Love	King 851
9/11/65+	26	27		2 Papa's Got A Brand New Bag	King 938
1/22/66	36	17		3 I Got You (I Feel Good)	King 946
9/10/66	90	9		4 It's A Man's Man's Man's World	King 985
4/8/67	88	14		5 Raw Soul	King 1016
9/16/67	35	17		6 Cold Sweat..	King 1020
3/23/68	17	14		7 I Can't Stand Myself (When You Touch Me)...............................	King 1030
5/18/68	135	14		8 I Got The Feelin'	King 1031
4/12/69	53	22		9 Say It Loud-I'm Black And I'm Proud	King 1047
5/31/69	99	14		10 Gettin' Down To It..	King 1051
9/6/69	26	24		11 It's A Mother..	King 1063
5/16/70	125	10		12 Soul On Top	King 1100

				BROWN, James — cont'd		
7/4/70	121	6		13 It's A New Day So Let A Man Come In		King 1095
9/4/71	22	18		14 Hot Pants		Polydor 4054
7/8/72	60	21		15 There It Is		Polydor 5028
12/9/72+	68	17		16 Get On The Good Foot		Polydor 3004 [2]
1/5/74	34	36	●	17 The Payback		Polydor 3007 [2]
7/27/74	35	19		18 Hell		Polydor 9001 [2]
1/25/75	56	10		19 Reality		Polydor 6039
5/24/75	103	8		20 Sex Machine Today		Polydor 6042
10/4/75	193	2		21 Everybody's Doin' The Hustle & Dead On The Double Bump		Polydor 6054
8/14/76	147	8		22 Get Up Offa That Thing		Polydor 6071
1/15/77	126	10		23 Bodyheat		Polydor 6093
5/6/78	121	22		24 Jam/1980's		Polydor 6140
8/11/79	152	6		25 The Original Disco Man		Polydor 6212
10/18/86	156	6		26 Gravity		Scotti Brothers 40380
6/18/88	96	14		27 I'm Real		Scotti Brothers 44241
				CHRISTMAS ALBUMS:		
12/3/66+	13^X	11		28 James Brown Sings Christmas Songs		King 1010
				Christmas charts: 15/'66, 13/'67, 15/'68		
12/13/69	10^X	3		29 **A Soulful Christmas**		King 1040
				first released in 1968		
				GREATEST HITS & COMPILATIONS:		
6/17/72	83	16		30 James Brown Soul Classics		Polydor 5401
10/6/73	202	3		31 Soul Classics Vol. II		Polydor 5402
1/13/07	6^c	8	▲	32 20 All-Time Greatest Hits		Polydor 511326
				RS500 #414		
4/12/08	170	2		33 Soul Brother No. 1		Starbucks 009440
				INSTRUMENTAL ALBUMS:		
4/10/65	124	10		34 Grits & Soul		Smash 67057
11/20/65+	42	19		35 James Brown Plays James Brown - Today & Yesterday		Smash 67072
4/16/66	101	11		36 James Brown Plays New Breed		Smash 67080
12/3/66	135	3		37 Handful Of Soul		Smash 67084
7/15/67	164	5		38 James Brown Plays The Real Thing		Smash 67093
8/24/68	150	5		39 James Brown Plays Nothing But Soul		King 1034
8/23/69	40	22		40 James Brown Plays & Directs The Popcorn		King 1055
2/14/70	43	12		41 Ain't It Funky		King 1092
5/1/71	137	4		42 Sho Is Funky Down Here		King 1110
				LIVE ALBUMS:		
6/29/63	2^2	66		43 **Live At The Apollo**		King 826
				Grammy: Hall of Fame ★ RS500 #24 ★ NRR		
				recorded on 10/24/1962 at the Apollo Theater in Harlem, New York		
2/29/64	10	22		44 **Pure Dynamite! Live At The Royal**		King 883
				recorded at The Royal Theater in Baltimore		
5/9/64	61	18		45 Showtime		Smash 67054
6/10/67	41	17		46 Live At The Garden		King 1018
9/7/68	32	39		47 Live At The Apollo, Volume II		King 1022 [2]
				recorded at the Apollo Theater in New York City		
9/12/70	29	31		48 Sex Machine		King 1115 [2]
1/30/71	61	15		49 Super Bad		King 1127
12/25/71+	39	21		50 Revolution Of The Mind - Live At The Apollo, Volume III		Polydor 3003 [2]
8/16/80	170	5		51 James Brown...Live/Hot On The One		Polydor 6290 [2]
				recorded in Tokyo, Japan		
11/22/80	163	3		52 Live And Lowdown At The Apollo, Vol. 1 [R]		Solid Smoke 8006
				reissue of #43 above		
				SOUNDTRACKS:		
3/3/73	31	21		53 Black Caesar		Polydor 6014
7/28/73	92	11		54 Slaughter's Big Rip-Off		Polydor 6015

~ ~ ~ ~ ~ ~ ~ ~ ~ **NON-CHARTED ALBUMS** ~ ~ ~ ~ ~ ~ ~ ~ ~ ~ ~

1958 Please Please Please	1986 In The Jungle Groove
1959 Try Me!	*RS500 #330*
1960 Think!	1991 Star Time ●
1961 The Amazing James Brown And The Famous Flames	*RS500 #79*

BROWN, Jim Ed
Born on 4/1/1934 in Sparkman, Arkansas. Country singer. Leader of **The Browns**.
AWARDS: CMA: Vocal Duo (w/ Helen Cornelius) 1977 ★ OPRY: 1963

2/6/71	81	9		1 Morning		RCA Victor 4461

BROWN, Jocelyn
Born on 11/25/1950 in Kinston, North Carolina. Female R&B singer.

11/24/84	208	1		1 Somebody Else's Guy		Vinyl Dreams 1

BROWN, Julie
Born on 8/31/1958 in Van Nuys, California. Comedic singer/actress. Appeared in several movies and TV shows. Not to be confused with former MTV VJ "Downtown" Julie Brown.

2/2/85	168	7	1 Goddess In Progress .... [EP-N]	Rhino 610

BROWN, Les, And His Orchestra
Born on 3/14/1912 in Reinerton, Pennsylvania. Died of cancer on 1/4/2001 (age 88). Big band leader/clarinetist.

2/19/55	15	1	1 Concert At The Palladium .... [I-L]	Coral CX-1 [2]
			recorded in September 1953 at the Hollywood Palladium	

BROWN, Maxine
Born on 8/18/1939 in Kingstree, South Carolina. R&B singer.

11/29/69	195	2	1 We'll Cry Together..	Commonwealth U. 6001

~ ~ ~ ~ ~ ~ ~ ~ ~ **NON-CHARTED ALBUMS** ~ ~ ~ ~ ~ ~ ~ ~ ~ ~
1963 **The Fabulous Sound Of Maxine Brown**   1965 **Saying Something** *[w/ Chuck Jackson]*

BROWN, Norman
Born on 12/18/1970 in Shreveport, Louisiana; raised in Kansas City, Missouri; later based in Los Angeles, California. Jazz guitarist/singer.

6/4/94	140	13	●	1 After The Storm... [I]	MoJazz 0301
7/6/96	162	3		2 Better Days Ahead .... [I]	MoJazz 530545
7/20/02	198	1		3 Just Chillin' .... [I]	Warner 47995
				Grammy: Pop Instrumental Album	
10/9/04	160	1		4 West Coast Coolin'	Warner 48713
5/12/07	107	1		5 Stay With Me	Peak 30218

BROWN, Odell, & The Organ-Izers
Born in 1938 in Louisville, Kentucky. Jazz organist. The Organ-Izers: Artee "Duke" Payne, Tommy Purvis and Curtis Prince.

9/9/67	173	4	1 Mellow Yellow .... [I]	Cadet 788

BROWN, Peter
Born on 7/11/1953 in Blue Island, Illinois; later based in Miami, Florida. Disco singer/songwriter/keyboardist.

1/14/78	11	44	1 A Fantasy Love Affair	Drive 104
1/26/80	206	4	2 Stargazer	Drive 108

BROWN, Ruth
Born Ruth Weston on 1/12/1928 in Portsmouth, Virginia. Died on 11/17/2006 (age 78). R&B pioneer. Acted in several movies and TV shows.
AWARD: R&R Hall of Fame: 1993

~ ~ ~ ~ ~ ~ ~ ~ ~ **NON-CHARTED ALBUMS** ~ ~ ~ ~ ~ ~ ~ ~ ~ ~ ~
1957 **Ruth Brown**   1959 **Miss Rhythm**

BROWN, Shannon
Born on 7/23/1973 in Spirit Lake, Iowa. Female country singer/songwriter.

3/18/06	163	1	1 Corn Fed	Warner 49323

BROWN, Shirley
Born on 1/6/1947 in West Memphis, Arkansas; raised in St. Louis, Missouri. R&B singer.

1/25/75	98	11	1 Woman To Woman	Truth 4206

BROWN, Sleepy
Born Patrick Brown on 6/29/1973 in Savannah, Georgia. R&B singer/songwriter.

10/21/06	53	3	1 Mr. Brown	Purple Ribbon 35582

BROWN, Zac, Band
Born in Dahlonega, Georgia. Country singer/songwriter/guitarist. His band: Jimmy DeMartini (fiddle), Coy Bowles (keyboards), John Hopkins (bass) and Chris Fryar (drums).
AWARD: Grammy: Best New Artist 2009

12/6/08+	9	78↑	▲² 1 The Foundation	Roar 516931
9/26/09	115	5	2 The Foundation .... [R]	Cracker Barrel 521278
			reissue of #1 above, with 3 live tracks replacing 3 studio tracks	
8/22/09	95	1	3 Live From Bonnaroo .... [EP-L]	Roar digital

BROWNE, Duncan
Born on 3/25/1947 in England. Died of cancer on 5/28/1993 (age 46). Folk-rock singer/songwriter.

5/19/79	174	5	1 The Wild Places..	Sire 6065

DEBUT	PEAK	WKS	R I A A	ARTIST / Album Title	Catalog	Label & Number

BROWNE, Jackson
All-Time: #174

Born Clyde Jackson Browne on 10/9/1948 in Heidelberg, Germany (U.S. Army base); raised in Los Angeles, California. Pop-rock singer/songwriter/guitarist/pianist. Worked with the **Eagles** and **Warren Zevon**. His wife, Phyllis Majors, committed suicide on 3/25/1976. Longtime relationship with actress Daryl Hannah (never married). A prominent activist against nuclear power.

AWARD: R&R Hall of Fame: 2004

DEBUT	PEAK	WKS			Catalog	Label & Number
3/18/72	53	23	▲	1 Jackson Browne		Asylum 5051
				album also known as *Saturate Before Using*		
11/10/73	43	38	▲	2 For Everyman		Asylum 5067
				RS500 #457		
10/12/74	14	29	▲	3 Late For The Sky		Asylum 1017
				RS500 #372		
11/20/76	5	35	▲3	4 The Pretender		Asylum 1079
				RS500 #391		
1/7/78	3²	65	▲7	5 Running On Empty		Asylum 113
7/19/80	❶¹	38	▲2	6 Hold Out		Asylum 511
8/20/83	8	33	▲	7 Lawyers In Love		Asylum 60268
3/22/86	23	31	●	8 Lives In The Balance		Asylum 60457
6/24/89	45	16		9 World In Motion		Elektra 60830
11/13/93	40	21	●	10 I'm Alive		Elektra 61524
3/2/96	36	9		11 Looking East		Elektra 61867
10/11/97	47	13	▲	12 The Next Voice You Hear - The Best Of Jackson Browne [G]		Elektra 62111
10/12/02	36	6		13 The Naked Ride Home		Elektra 62793
4/3/04	46	10	●	14 The Very Best Of Jackson Browne [G]		Elektra 78091 [2]
10/29/05	55	5		15 Solo Acoustic Vol. 1 [L]		Inside 5251
3/22/08	24	5		16 Solo Acoustic Vol. 2 [L]		Inside 8021
10/11/08	20	6		17 Time The Conqueror		Inside 80923

BROWNE, Tom
Born in 1954 in Jamaica, Queens, New York. Jazz-funk trumpeter. Member of **Fuse One**.

8/11/79	147	6		1 Browne Sugar [I]		GRP 5003
7/26/80	18	26	●	2 Love Approach [I]		GRP 5008
2/21/81	37	19		3 Magic		GRP 5503
12/12/81+	97	14		4 Yours Truly		GRP 5507
12/3/83+	147	12		5 Rockin' Radio [I]		Arista 8107

BROWNS, The
Country vocal trio from Sparkman, Arkansas: siblings **Jim Ed Brown**, Maxine Brown and Bonnie Brown.

AWARD: OPRY: 1963

~ ~ ~ ~ ~ ~ ~ ~ ~ ~ **NON-CHARTED ALBUMS** ~ ~ ~ ~ ~ ~ ~ ~ ~ ~

1959 Sweet Sounds By The Browns Featuring The Three Bells   1960 The Browns Sing Their Hits

BROWNSTONE
Female R&B vocal trio form Los Angeles, California: Monica Doby, Nichole Gilbert and Charmayne Maxwell. Doby left group for health reasons in June 1995; replaced by Kina Cosper.

1/28/95	29	37	▲	1 From The Bottom Up		MJJ Music 57827
7/12/97	51	11		2 Still Climbing		MJJ Music 67524

BROWNSVILLE STATION
Rock trio from Ann Arbor, Michigan: Michael Lutz (vocals, bass), Michael "Cub" Koda (guitar), and Henry Weck (drums). Koda died of kidney failure on 7/1/2000 (age 51).

10/7/72	191	5		1 A Night On The Town		Big Tree 2010
9/15/73+	98	19		2 Yeah!		Big Tree 2102
6/15/74	170	8		3 School Punks		Big Tree 89500
6/4/77	204	2		4 Brownsville Station		Private Stock 2026

BRUBECK, Dave, Quartet
1950s: #16 / All-Time: #211

Born David Warren on 12/6/1920 in Concord, California. Leader of jazz quartet consisting of Brubeck (piano), **Paul Desmond** (alto sax), Eugene Wright (bass) and Joe Morello (drums). One of America's all-time most popular jazz groups on college campuses. Desmond died on 5/30/1977 (age 52).

AWARD: Grammy: Lifetime Achievement 1996

2/5/55	8	3		1 Dave Brubeck At Storyville: 1954 [I-L]		Columbia 590
				recorded at the Storyville nightclub in Boston		
3/19/55	5	11		2 Brubeck Time [I]		Columbia 622
				LP: Columbia CL-622 (#5); EP: Columbia B-473 (#10)		
11/12/55	7	2		3 Jazz: Red Hot And Cool [I-L]		Columbia 699
				recorded at the Basin Street nightclub in New York City; LP: Columbia CL-699 (#7); EP: Columbia B-699 (#8)		
7/8/57	18	1		4 Jazz Impressions Of The U.S.A. [I]		Columbia 984
9/30/57	24	1		5 Jazz Goes To Junior College [I-L]		Columbia 1034
				sequel to Brubeck's 1954 album *Jazz Goes To College* (#8)		

Billboard			R I A A	ARTIST		
DEBUT	PEAK	WKS		Album Title	Catalog	Label & Number

BRUBECK, Dave, Quartet — cont'd

11/28/60+	2¹	164	▲	6 Time Out Featuring "Take Five"	Cat:#42/2 [I]	Columbia 1397 / 8192
				Grammy: Hall of Fame ★ NRR		
12/12/60+	13	15		7 Bernstein Plays Brubeck Plays Bernstein .... [I]		Columbia 1466 / 8257
				side 1: **New York Philharmonic** with the Dave Brubeck Quartet conducted by **Leonard Bernstein**; side 2: Dave Brubeck Quartet		
12/25/61+	8	46		8 Time Further Out	[I]	Columbia 1690 / 8490
6/16/62	24	21		9 Countdown - Time In Outer Space	[I]	Columbia 1775 / 8575
3/16/63	14	15		10 Bossa Nova U.S.A.	[I]	Columbia 8798
7/27/63	37	4		11 The Dave Brubeck Quartet At Carnegie Hall	[I-L]	Columbia 826 [2]
12/21/63	137	3		12 Brandenburg Gate: Revisited	[I]	Columbia 1963 / 8763
4/18/64	81	9		13 Time Changes	[I]	Columbia 2127 / 8927
2/27/65	142	4		14 Jazz Impressions Of New York	[I]	Columbia 2275 / 9075
10/9/65	122	3		15 Angel Eyes	[I]	Columbia 2348 / 9148
3/26/66	133	5		16 My Favorite Things	[I]	Columbia 2437 / 9237
7/30/66	104	4	●	17 Dave Brubeck's Greatest Hits	[G-I]	Columbia 2484 / 9284
11/9/74	206	2		18 Brother, The Great Spirit Made Us All	[I]	Atlantic 1660
				DAVE BRUBECK: TWO GENERATIONS OF BRUBECK		
1/10/76	167	5		19 1975: The Duets	[I]	Horizon 703
				DAVE BRUBECK & PAUL DESMOND		

BRUCE, Jack
Born John Asher on 5/14/1943 in Glasgow, Scotland. Bass player of **Cream**. Started career with Alexis Korner's Blues Inc. (C.C.S.). Prior to Cream was with the Graham Bond Organization, **John Mayall**'s Bluesbreakers and **Manfred Mann**. Also see **West, Bruce & Laing**.

10/25/69	55	11	1 Songs For A Tailor	Atco 306
8/14/71	202	4	2 Harmony Row	Atco 365
11/11/72	204	5	3 At His Best .... [K]	Polydor 3505 [2]
12/7/74	160	3	4 Out Of The Storm	RSO 4805
5/7/77	153	5	5 How's Tricks	RSO 3021
			JACK BRUCE BAND	
12/13/80	182	2	6 I've Always Wanted To Do This	Epic 36827
			JACK BRUCE & FRIENDS	
3/21/81	37	16	7 B.L.T.	Chrysalis 1324
			JACK BRUCE / BILL LORDAN / ROBIN TROWER	
1/30/82	109	6	8 Truce	Chrysalis 1352
			JACK BRUCE & ROBIN TROWER	

BRUCE, Lenny
Born Leonard Schneider on 10/13/1925 in Mineola, Long Island, New York. Died of a heroin overdose on 8/3/1966 (age 40). Satirical comedian. Dustin Hoffman portrayed Bruce in the 1974 autobiographical movie. Also see **Movie Soundtracks**: *Lenny*.

3/15/75	178	2	1 Lenny Bruce/Carnegie Hall .... [C]	United Artists 9800 [3]
			recorded on 2/4/1961	
3/29/75	206	4	2 The Law, Language And Lenny Bruce .... [C]	Warner 9101
			no track titles listed on this album	
4/5/75	191	2	3 The Real Lenny Bruce .... [C-E]	Fantasy 79003 [2]
			recorded 1958-1959	

BRUFORD, Bill
Born on 5/17/1949 in Sevenoaks, Kent, England. Rock drummer. Member of **Yes**, **King Crimson** and **U.K.**

7/7/79	123	5	1 One Of A Kind .... [I]	Polydor 6205
3/29/80	191	2	2 Gradually Going Tornado	Polydor 6261

BRUNI, Carla
Born on 12/23/1967 in Turin, Italy. Female singer/songwriter. Married French President Nicolas Sarkozy on 2/2/2008.

8/23/08	195	1	1 Comme Si De Rien N'Etait .... [F]	Teorema 70045

BRUTHA
Family R&B vocal group from Los Angeles, California: brothers Anthony Harrell, Jacob Harrell, Grady Harrell and Jared Overton.

1/10/09	81	7	1 Brutha	Goodfellas 012390

BRYAN, Luke
Born Thomas Luther Bryan on 7/17/1976 in Leesburg, Georgia. Country singer/songwriter/guitarist.

9/1/07	24	8	1 I'll Stay Me	Capitol 63251
10/24/09	6	32↑	2 Doin' My Thing	Capitol 65833

BRYANT, Anita
Born on 3/25/1940 in Barnsdall, Oklahoma. Adult Contemporary singer.

9/15/62	145	2	1 In A Velvet Mood	Columbia 1885 / 8685
1/21/67	146	4	2 Mine Eyes Have Seen The Glory	Columbia 2573 / 9373
12/2/67	25ˣ	5	3 Christmas With Anita Bryant/Do You Hear What I Hear? .... [X]	Columbia 2720 / 9520

BRYANT, Ray
Born Raphael Bryant on 12/24/1931 in Philadelphia, Pennsylvania. Jazz pianist.

6/25/66	111	12	1 Gotta Travel On .... [I]	Cadet 767
5/13/67	193	3	2 Slow Freight .... [I]	Cadet 781

BRYANT, Sharon
Born on 8/14/1956 in Westchester County, New York. R&B singer. Member of **Atlantic Starr** from 1976-84.

DEBUT	PEAK	WKS		Album Title	Catalog	Label & Number
9/9/89	139	13		1 Here I Am		Wing 837313

BRYSON, Peabo   1980s: #46 / All-Time: #342
Born Robert Peabo Bryson on 4/13/1951 in Greenville, South Carolina. R&B singer. Began career with Al Freeman & The Upsetters in 1965; with Mose Dillard & The Tex-Town Display from 1968-73. Married Juanita Leonard, former wife of boxer Sugar Ray Leonard, in 1992.

DEBUT	PEAK	WKS		Album Title	Catalog	Label & Number
3/11/78	49	29	●	1 Reaching For The Sky		Capitol 11729
12/9/78+	35	26	●	2 Crosswinds		Capitol 11875
12/15/79+	44	19		3 We're The Best Of Friends		Capitol 12019
				NATALIE COLE & PEABO BRYSON		
5/3/80	79	16		4 Paradise		Capitol 12063
12/20/80+	52	19		5 Live & More [L]		Atlantic 7004 [2]
				ROBERTA FLACK & PEABO BRYSON		
				recorded at the Holiday Star Theater in Merrillville, Indiana		
2/28/81	82	11		6 Turn The Hands Of Time		Capitol 12138
11/28/81+	40	24		7 I Am Love		Capitol 12179
12/4/82+	55	21		8 Don't Play With Fire		Capitol 12241
8/13/83	25	42	●	9 Born To Love		Capitol 12284
				PEABO BRYSON & ROBERTA FLACK		
6/16/84	44	26		10 Straight From The Heart		Elektra 60362
7/14/84	168	10		11 The Peabo Bryson Collection [G]		Capitol 12348
7/6/85	102	13		12 Take No Prisoners		Elektra 60427
2/13/88	157	6		13 Positive		Elektra 60753
7/13/91	88	19	●	14 Can You Stop The Rain		Columbia 46823
1/14/06	10ˣ	2		15 Christmas With You [X]		Time Life 19161
				Christmas chart: 10/'05		

BT
Born Brian Transeau on 10/4/1970 in Washington DC. Electronic keyboardist/producer.

DEBUT	PEAK	WKS		Album Title	Catalog	Label & Number
8/26/00	166	2		1 Movement In Still Life		Nettwerk 30154
8/23/03	138	1		2 Emotional Technology		Nettwerk 30344

B.T. EXPRESS
R&B-disco band from Brooklyn, New York. Core members: Barbara Joyce (female vocals), brothers Louis Risbrook (male vocals, bass) and Bill Risbrook (sax), Richard Thompson (guitar), Carlos Ward (flute) and Dennis Rowe (congas). Keyboardist Michael Jones, who was with the group from 1976-79, later recorded solo as techno-funk musician **Kashif**.

DEBUT	PEAK	WKS		Album Title	Catalog	Label & Number
11/23/74+	5	31	●	1 Do It ('Til You're Satisfied)		Roadshow 5117
8/2/75	19	19		2 Non-Stop		Roadshow 41001
5/29/76	43	12		3 Energy To Burn		Columbia 34178
5/28/77	111	5		4 Function At The Junction		Columbia 34702
2/25/78	67	11		5 Shout!		Columbia 35078
5/31/80	164	4		6 B.T. Express 1980		Columbia 36333

B2K
Male R&B vocal group from Los Angeles, California: Jarell "J-Boog" Houston (born on 8/11/1985), Mario "Raz-B" Thornton (born on 6/13/1985), Dreux "Lil Fizz" Frederic (born on 11/26/1985) and Omari "**Omarion**" Grandberry (born on 11/12/1984). Houston is the cousin of **Marques Houston**. Group starred in the 2004 movie *You Got Served*.

DEBUT	PEAK	WKS		Album Title	Catalog	Label & Number
3/30/02	2¹	33	●	1 B2K		Epic 85457
8/10/02	129	4		2 B2K: The Remixes - Vol. 1 [K]		Epic 86643
12/14/02	132	4		3 Santa Hooked Me Up [X]		Epic 85856
				Christmas chart: 19/'02		
12/28/02	10	35	▲	4 Pandemonium!		Epic 86995
7/19/03	192	1		5 B2K: The Remixes - Vol. 2 [K]		Epic 86885
1/10/04	34	12	●	6 You Got Served [S]		Epic 90744

BUBBLE PUPPY, The
Psychedelic-rock band from Houston, Texas: Rod Prince (vocals), Todd Potter (guitar), Roy Cox (bass) and David Fore (drums).

DEBUT	PEAK	WKS		Album Title	Catalog	Label & Number
5/17/69	176	6		1 A Gathering Of Promises		Int'l. Artists 10

BUBLE, Michael   2000s: #14 / All-Time: #291
Born on 9/9/1975 in Burnaby, British Columbia, Canada. Adult Contemporary singer.

DEBUT	PEAK	WKS		Album Title	Catalog	Label & Number
3/1/03	47	63↑	▲	1 Michael Buble — Cat:●⁵/209		143 Records 48376
12/20/03	56	3		2 Let It Snow! — Cat:#2¹/23 [X-EP]		143 Records 48599
				Christmas charts: 9/'03, 48/'06, 4/'07, 10/'08, 8/'09		
4/17/04	55	5		3 Come Fly With Me		143 Records 48683
2/26/05	7	130↑	▲³	4 It's Time — Cat:●⁸/139		143 Records 48946
12/10/05	82	11		5 Caught In The Act [L]		143 Records 49444
5/19/07	●¹	106↑	▲	6 Call Me Irresponsible — Cat:#6/35		143 Records 100313
				Grammy: Traditional Pop Vocal Album		
5/17/08	35	2		7 A Taste Of Buble [EP]		143 Records 462716
7/4/09	14	9		8 Michael Buble Meets Madison Square Garden [L]		143 Records 517750
				Grammy: Traditional Pop Album		
10/24/09	●²	32↑	▲	9 Crazy Love		143 Records 520733
12/5/09	32	6		10 Let It Snow! [X-EP-R]		143 Records 48599

Billboard			R I A A	ARTIST		
DEBUT	PEAK	WKS		Album Title	Catalog	Label & Number

BUCHANAN, Roy
Born on 9/23/1939 in Ozark, Arkansas; raised in Pixley, California. Committed suicide on 8/14/1988 (age 48). Prolific rock/blues guitarist.

9/9/72	107	12		1 Roy Buchanan		Polydor 5033
3/10/73	86	13		2 Second Album [I]		Polydor 5046
2/23/74	152	10		3 That's What I Am Here For		Polydor 6020
12/28/74+	160	6		4 In The Beginning		Polydor 6035
5/15/76	148	7		5 A Street Called Straight		Atlantic 18170
6/18/77	105	8		6 Loading Zone [I]		Atlantic 18219
5/20/78	119	7		7 You're Not Alone [I]		Atlantic 19170
1/24/81	193	2		8 My Babe		Waterhouse 12
8/3/85	161	13		9 When A Guitar Plays The Blues		Alligator 4741
6/28/86	153	8		10 Dancing On The Edge		Alligator 4747

BUCKCHERRY
Hard-rock band from Los Angeles, California: Joshua Todd (vocals), Keith Nelson (guitar), Yugomir "Yogi" Lonich (guitar), Jon Brightman (bass) and Devon Glenn (drums). Disbanded in 2002. Todd and Nelson re-formed the band in 2005 with Steve Dacanay (guitar), Jimmy Ashhurst (bass) and Xavier Muriel (drums).

4/24/99	74	30	●	1 Buckcherry		DreamWorks 450044
4/14/01	64	5		2 Time Bomb		DreamWorks 450287
4/29/06+	39	126	▲	3 15 Cat:#12/8		Eleven Seven 001
10/4/08	8	19		4 Black Butterfly		Eleven Seven 511262
10/17/09	172	1		5 Live & Loud 2009 [L]		Eleven Seven 730

BUCKINGHAM, Lindsey
Born on 10/3/1949 in Palo Alto, California. Rock singer/songwriter/guitarist. Formed **Buckingham Nicks** duo with then-girlfriend, Stevie Nicks. Both joined **Fleetwood Mac** in 1975.

11/7/81	32	24		1 Law And Order		Asylum 561
1/29/83+	28 C	22		2 Buckingham Nicks		Polydor 5058
				first released in 1973		
9/1/84	45	16		3 Go Insane		Elektra 60363
7/4/92	128	9		4 Out Of The Cradle		Reprise 26182
10/21/06	80	2		5 Under The Skin		Reprise 44359
4/12/08	186	1		6 Live At The Bass Performance Hall [L]		Reprise 359804
10/4/08	48	2		7 Gift Of Screws		Reprise 512970

BUCKINGHAMS, The
Rock band from Chicago, Illinois: Dennis Tufano (vocals; born on 9/11/1946), Carl Giammarese (guitar; born on 8/21/1947), Dennis Miccoli (keyboards), Nick Fortuna (bass; born on 5/1/1946) and Jon Paulos (drums; born on 3/31/1947; died of a drug overdose on 3/26/1980, age 32). Martin Grebb (born on 9/2/1946) replaced Miccoli in 1967. Grebb formed **The Fabulous Rhinestones**. Also see **Tufano & Giammarese**.

3/25/67	109	8		1 Kind Of A Drag		U.S.A. 107
6/10/67	58	23		2 Time & Charges		Columbia 9469
2/10/68	53	16		3 Portraits		Columbia 9598
9/21/68	161	5		4 In One Ear And Gone Tomorrow		Columbia 9703
5/24/69	73	12		5 The Buckinghams' Greatest Hits [G]		Columbia 9812

BUCKLEY, Jeff
Born on 11/17/1966 in Anaheim, California. Drowned on 5/29/1997 (age 30). Adult Alternative singer/songwriter/guitarist. Son of **Tim Buckley**.

5/20/95	149	7	●	1 Grace Cat:#10/2		Columbia 57528
				RS500 #303		
6/13/98	64	3		2 Sketches For My Sweetheart The Drunk		Columbia 67228 [2]
5/27/00	133	1		3 Mystery White Boy - Live '95-'96 [L]		Columbia 69592
6/20/09	125	1		4 Grace Around The World [K-L]		Columbia 51706

BUCKLEY, Tim
Born on 2/14/1947 in Washington DC. Died of a drug overdose on 6/29/1975 (age 28). Folk singer/songwriter. Father of **Jeff Buckley**.

11/4/67	171	5		1 Goodbye And Hello		Elektra 74018
4/19/69	81	12		2 Happy Sad		Elektra 74045
2/7/70	192	2		3 Blue Afternoon		Straight 1060
10/27/73	201	5		4 Sefronia		DiscReet 2157
10/19/74	208	2		5 Look At The Fool		DiscReet 2301

BUCKNER & GARCIA
Novelty duo from Atlanta, Georgia: Jerry Buckner (keyboards) and Gary Garcia (vocals).

| 3/13/82 | 24 | 16 | ● | 1 Pac-Man Fever [N] | | Columbia 37941 |

BUCK-O-NINE
Ska-rock band from San Diego, California: Jon Pebsworth (vocals), Jonas Kleiner (guitar), Anthony Curry (trumpet), Dan Albert (trombone), Craig Yarnold (sax), Scott Kennerly (bass) and Steve Bauer (drums).

| 9/6/97 | 190 | 1 | | 1 Twenty-Eight Teeth | | TVT 5760 |

BUCKSHOT
Born Kenyatta Blake in Brooklyn, New York. Male rapper. Member of **Black Moon**.

| 10/3/09 | 62 | 2 | | 1 Survival Skills | | Duck Down 2120 |
| | | | | KRS-ONE & BUCKSHOT | | |

BUCKWHEAT
Pop band from Los Angeles, California: Debbie Campbell (vocals), Michael Smotherman (vocals, keyboards), Randy James (guitar), Mark Durham (bass) and Timmy Harrison (drums). Campbell died on 2/28/2004 (age 53).

4/1/72	179	6		1 Movin' On		London 609

BUCKWHEAT ZYDECO
Born Stanley Dural on 11/14/1947 in Lafayette, Louisiana. Singer/songwriter/accordianist.

11/14/87	172	5		1 On A Night Like This..		Island 90622
9/17/88	104	7		2 Taking It Home		Island 90968
7/7/90	140	11		3 Where There's Smoke There's Fire..		Island 842925

BUD AND TRAVIS
Folk duo from San Francisco, California: Oliver "Bud" Dashiell (born on 9/28/1929; died of a brain tumor on 6/2/1989, age 59) and Travis Edmonson (born on 9/23/1932; died on 5/9/2009, age 76).

11/9/63	126	4		1 Bud & Travis...In Concert.. [L]		Liberty 11001 [2]
				recorded on 3/24/1960 at the Civic Auditorium in Santa Monica, California		
3/28/64	129	6		2 Perspective On Bud & Travis		Liberty 7341

BUDDEN, Joe
Born on 8/31/1980 in Harlem, New York; raised in Jersey City, New Jersey. Male rapper. Member of **Slaughterhouse**.

6/28/03	8	16		1 Joe Budden		Def Jam 000505
11/15/08	184	1		2 Halfway House..		Amalgam digital
3/14/09	42	2		3 Padded Room		Amalgam 08002

BUDDZ, Collie
Born Colin Harper on 8/21/1981 in New Orleans, Louisiana; raised in Bermuda. Male rapper.

7/21/07	68	3		1 Collie Buddz		Columbia 78322

BUENA VISTA SOCIAL CLUB
Group of Cuban musicians assembled by American guitarist **Ry Cooder**: Company Segundo (vocals), **Ibrahim Ferrer** (vocals), Eliades Ochoa (guitar) and Ruben Gonzalez (piano). Segundo died of kidney failure on 7/13/2003 (age 95). Gonzalez died on 12/8/2003 (age 84). Ferrer died on 8/6/2005 (age 78).

3/14/98+	80	19	▲	1 Buena Vista Social Club .... Cat:❶³/57 [F]		World Circuit 79478
				Grammy: Tropical Latin Album ★ RS500 #260		
11/1/08	200	1		2 At Carnegie Hall .... [L]		World Circuit 514415

BUFFALO SPRINGFIELD, The
All-star rock band formed in Los Angeles, California: **Stephen Stills** (vocals, guitar), **Neil Young** and **Richie Furay** (guitars), Bruce Palmer (bass) and Dewey Martin (drums). **Jim Messina** replaced Palmer after second album. Disbanded in 1968. Stills and Young with **Crosby, Stills, Nash & Young**. Furay and Messina formed **Poco**. Palmer died of a heart attack on 10/4/2004 (age 58). Martin died on 1/31/2009 (age 68).
AWARD: R&R Hall of Fame: 1997

3/25/67	80	16		1 Buffalo Springfield		Atco 200
11/18/67+	44	14		2 Buffalo Springfield Again		Atco 226
				RS500 #188		
8/17/68	42	19		3 Last Time Around..		Atco 256
3/1/69	42	24	▲	4 Retrospective/The Best Of Buffalo Springfield............................. Cat:#33/6 [G]		Atco 283
12/8/73	104	13		5 Buffalo Springfield .... [K]		Atco 806 [2]
8/4/01	194	1		6 Box Set... [K]		Atco 74324 [4]
				contains all of the group's recorded output, including several demos; contains an 81 page booklet		

BUFFALO TOM
Rock trio from Boston, Massachusetts: Bill Janovitz (vocals, guitar), Chris Colbourn (bass) and Tom Maginnis (drums).

10/9/93	185	1		1 Big Red Letter Day		Beggars Banquet 92292
7/29/95	160	1		2 Sleepy Eyed		EastWest 61782

BUFFETT, Jimmy   1980s: #18 / 1990s: #26 / 2000s: 45 / All-Time: #23
Born on 12/25/1946 in Pascagoula, Mississippi; raised in Mobile, Alabama. Singer/songwriter/guitarist. Has BS degree in journalism from the University of Southern Mississippi. After working in New Orleans, moved to Nashville in 1969. Nashville correspondent for *Billboard* magazine, 1969-70. Settled in Key West in 1971. Author of several books. Appeared in the 1978 movie *FM*. Faithful fans known as "Parrotheads."

7/28/73	205	2		1 A White Sport Coat And A Pink Crustacean..		Dunhill/ABC 50150
3/2/74	176	13		2 Living And Dying In 3/4 Time .... Cat:#21/56		Dunhill/ABC 50132
2/8/75	25	27		3 A1A		Dunhill/ABC 50183
2/14/76	65	14		4 Havana Daydreamin'		ABC 914
2/12/77	12	42	▲	5 Changes In Latitudes, Changes In Attitudes.................................... Cat:#10/218		ABC 990
4/8/78	10	29	▲	6 Son Of A Son Of A Sailor	Cat:#30/48		ABC 1046
9/15/79	14	28	●	7 Volcano		MCA 5102
2/21/81	30	18		8 Coconut Telegraph		MCA 5169
1/23/82	31	15		9 Somewhere Over China		MCA 5285
10/8/83	59	24		10 One Particular Harbour		MCA 5447
9/29/84	87	14		11 Riddles In The Sand		MCA 5512

DEBUT	PEAK	WKS	R I A A	ARTIST / Album Title	Catalog	Label & Number
				BUFFETT, Jimmy — cont'd		
7/6/85	53	20		12 Last Mango In Paris		MCA 5600
6/28/86	66	16		13 Floridays		MCA 5730
7/9/88	46	14		14 Hot Water		MCA 42093
7/15/89	57	13		15 Off To See The Lizard		MCA 6314
6/12/93	169	2		16 Before The Beach .... [E]		Margaritaville 10823
6/11/94	5	19	▲	17 Fruitcakes		Margaritaville 11043
8/19/95	6	17	●	18 Barometer Soup		Margaritaville 11247
6/22/96	4	18	▲	19 Banana Wind		Margaritaville 11451
10/26/96	27	14	▲	20 Christmas Island .... Cat:#12/18 [X]		Margaritaville/MCA 11489
				Christmas charts: 4/'96, 17/'97, 25/'99, 48/'02, 32/'03, 40/'04, 24/'06		
5/16/98	15	11	●	21 Don't Stop The Carnival		Margaritaville 524485
6/5/99	8	17	●	22 Beach House On The Moon		Margaritaville 524660
4/6/02	5	16		23 Far Side Of The World		Mailboat 2005
7/31/04	❶¹	39	▲	24 License To Chill .... Cat:#40/2		Mailboat 62270
10/28/06	4	13	●	25 Take The Weather With You		Mailboat 00332
12/26/09	17	12		26 Buffet Hotel		Mailboat 2121
				GREATEST HITS & COMPILATIONS:		
11/16/85	100	24	▲⁷	27 Songs You Know By Heart - Jimmy Buffett's Greatest Hit(s) Cat:❶⁵/533		MCA 5633
6/6/92	68	19	▲⁴	28 Boats Beaches Bars & Ballads		Margaritaville 10613 [4]
5/3/03	9	46	▲²	29 Meet Me In Margaritaville: The Ultimate Collection	Cat:#25/18	Mailboat 067781 [2]
				LIVE ALBUMS:		
11/11/78	72	18	●	30 You Had To Be There		ABC 1008 [2]
11/17/90	68	15	●	31 Feeding Frenzy .... Cat:#32/4		MCA 10022
11/27/99	37	13	●	32 Buffett Live: Tuesdays, Thursdays, Saturdays .... Cat:#29/2		Mailboat 2000
4/9/05	66	8		33 Live In Hawaii		Mailboat 2109 [2]
12/3/05	41	6		34 Live At Fenway Park		Mailboat 2115 [2]
4/21/07	11	11		35 Live At Texas Stadium		MCA Nashville 005894
				ALAN JACKSON / GEORGE STRAIT / JIMMY BUFFETT		
11/24/07	54	6		36 Jimmy Buffett Live In Anguilla		Mailboat 2111 [2]

BUGGLES, The
New-wave duo from England: Geoff Downes and Trevor Horn. Both joined the group **Yes** in 1980. Downes joined **Asia** in 1981. Horn became a prolific producer.

DEBUT	PEAK	WKS				
3/27/82	161	5		1 Adventures In Modern Recording		Carrere 37926

BUGNON, Alex
Born on 10/10/1958 in Montreux, Switzerland. Jazz keyboardist. Nephew of **Donald Byrd**.

4/1/89	127	11		1 Love Season		Orpheus 75602
5/26/90	131	7		2 Head Over Heels .... [I]		Orpheus 75615

BUILDING 429
Christian rock band from Raleigh, North Carolina: Jason Roy (vocals, guitar), Jesse Garcia (keyboards), Scotty Beshears (bass) and Michael Anderson (drums).

4/1/06	81	2		1 Rise		Word/Curb/W. 886405
5/19/07	140	1		2 Iris To Iris		Word-Curb 887093
11/8/08+	119	5		3 Building 429		Ino 34325

BUILT TO SPILL
Rock trio from Boise, Idaho: **Doug Martsch** (vocals, guitar), Brett Nelson (bass) and Andy Capps (drums).

3/13/99	120	1		1 Keep It Like A Secret		Warner 46952
7/28/01	94	2		2 Ancient Melodies Of The Future		Warner 47954
4/29/06	63	3		3 You In Reverse		Warner 49363
10/24/09	50	3		4 There Is No Enemy		Warner 514116

BULGARIAN STATE FEMALE VOCAL CHOIR
Twenty-six-member female choir, conducted by Dora Hriztova. Established in 1951 in Bulgaria by Philip Koutev, choir's vocal sound is a combination of Bulgarian folk and Western classical music.

12/17/88+	165	10		1 Le Mystere Des Voix Bulgares .... [F-K]		Nonesuch 79165

BULLDOG
Rock band formed in New York: Billy Hocher (vocals, bass), Eric Thorngren (guitar), Gene Cornish (guitar), John Turi (keyboards) and Dino Danelli (drums). Cornish and Danelli were members of **The Rascals**. Thorngren later became a prolific record mixer. Also see **Fotomaker**.

11/18/72+	176	11		1 Bulldog		Decca 75370

BULLENS, Cindy
Born on 11/30/1957 in West Newbury, Massachusetts. Pop-rock singer/guitarist.

3/24/79	202	2		1 Desire Wire		United Artists 933
12/15/79+	203	5		2 Steal The Night		Casablanca 7185

BULLETBOYS
Hard-rock band from Los Angeles, California: Marq Torien (vocals), Mick Sweda (guitar), Lonnie Vencent (bass) and Jimmy D'Anda (drums).

10/29/88+	34	47	●	1 BulletBoys		Warner 25782
3/30/91	69	8		2 Freakshow		Warner 26168

BULLET FOR MY VALENTINE
Hard-rock band from Bridgend, South Wales: Matthew Tuck (vocals, guitar), Michael Paget (guitar), Jason James (bass) and Michael Thomas (drums).

3/4/06	128	28	●	1 The Poison	Cat:#36/5	Trustkill 74
2/16/08	4	17		2 Scream Aim Fire		Jive 21393

BUN-B
Born Bernard Freeman on 3/19/1973 in Port Arthur, Texas. Male rapper. Member of **UGK**.

11/5/05	6	24	●	1 Trill		Rap-A-Lot 4 Life 68539
6/7/08	2[1]	16		2 II Trill		J Prince 445884

BURNHAM, Bo
Born Robert Burnham on 8/21/1990 in Hamilton, Massachusetts. Comedic singer/songwriter/pianist.

7/5/08	123	1	1 Bo Fo Sho	[EP-N]	Comedy Central digital
3/28/09	105	4	2 Bo Burnham	[L-N]	Comedy Central 0078

BUONO, Victor
Born Charles Victor Buono on 2/3/1938 in San Diego, California. Died of a heart attack on 1/1/1982 (age 43). Prolific character actor.

9/18/71	66	17	1 Heavy!	[C]	Dore 325

BUOYS, The
Rock band from Wilkes-Barre, Pennsylvania: Bill Kelly (vocals), Carl Siracuse (guitar), Fran Brozena (keyboards), Jerry Hludzik (bass) and Chris Hanlon (drums). **Rupert Holmes** was their composer/arranger.

8/14/71	202	3	1 The Buoys		Scepter 24001

BURDON, Eric, And War
Born on 5/11/1941 in Walker, Newcastle, England. Rock singer. Leader of **The Animals**. Starred in the 1982 movie *Comeback* and made a cameo appearance in the 1991 movie *The Doors*.

5/16/70	18	27	1 Eric Burdon Declares "War"		MGM 4663
12/26/70+	82	9	2 The Black-Man's Burdon		MGM 4710 [2]
			ERIC BURDON AND WAR (above 2)		
12/21/74+	51	16	3 Sun Secrets		Capitol 11359
8/9/75	171	5	4 Stop		Capitol 11426
			THE ERIC BURDON BAND (above 2)		
12/25/76+	140	5	5 Love Is All Around		ABC 988
			WAR FEATURING ERIC BURDON		
			recorded 1969-70		

BURGER, Anthony
Born on 6/5/1961 in Franklin, Tennessee. Died of a heart attack while performing a concert on 2/22/2006 (age 44). Gospel pianist.

5/6/06	65	4	1 The Best Of Anthony Burger From The Homecoming Series	[I-K-L]	Gaither 42657

BURKE, Solomon
Born on 3/21/1940 in Philadelphia, Pennsylvania. R&B singer. Preached and broadcast from own church, "Solomon's Temple," in Philadelphia from 1945-55 as the "Wonder Boy Preacher." Church was founded for him by his grandmother. First recorded for Apollo in 1954. Left music to attend mortuary school; returned in 1960.
AWARD: R&R Hall of Fame: 2001

7/31/65	141	3	1 The Best Of Solomon Burke	[G]	Atlantic 8109
7/5/69	140	4	2 Proud Mary		Bell 6033
8/10/02	138	2	3 Don't Give Up On Me		Fat Possum 80358

~ ~ ~ ~ ~ ~ ~ ~ ~ **NON-CHARTED ALBUMS** ~ ~ ~ ~ ~ ~ ~ ~ ~ ~ ~
1962 **Solomon Burke's Greatest Hits**   1964 **Rock 'N Soul**
1963 **If You Need Me**

BURNETT, Carol
Born on 4/26/1933 in San Antonio, Texas. Comedic actress. Star of own variety TV show from 1967-78.

9/1/62	85	9	1 Julie And Carol At Carnegie Hall	[L]	Columbia 2240 / 5840
			JULIE ANDREWS & CAROL BURNETT		
			recorded on 6/11/1962		
1/29/72	199	2	2 Carol Burnett Featuring If I Could Write A Song		Columbia 31048

BURNETT, T-Bone
Born John Burnett on 1/14/1948 in St. Louis, Missouri; raised in Fort Worth, Texas. Rock singer/songwriter/guitarist/producer. Married to **Sam Phillips** from 1989-2004.

10/23/82	208	1	1 Trap Door		Warner 23691
10/1/83	188	5	2 Proof Through The Night		Warner 23921

BURNETTE, Billy
Born on 5/8/1953 in Memphis, Tennessee. Son of **Dorsey Burnette**, nephew of **Johnny Burnette** and cousin of **Rocky Burnette**. Member of **Fleetwood Mac** from 1987-1993.

11/8/80	208	2	1 Billy Burnette		Columbia 36792

BURNETTE, Dorsey
Born on 12/28/1932 in Memphis, Tennessee. Died of a heart attack on 8/19/1979 (age 46). Older brother of **Johnny Burnette** and father of **Billy Burnette**. Recorded with brother Johnny in the Rock & Roll Trio from 1956-57 and as The Texans in 1961.

~ ~ ~ ~ ~ ~ ~ ~ ~ ~ **NON-CHARTED ALBUM** ~ ~ ~ ~ ~ ~ ~ ~ ~ ~ ~
1960 **Tall Oak Tree**

Billboard			R I A A	ARTIST		
DEBUT	PEAK	WKS		Album Title	Catalog	Label & Number

BURNETTE, Johnny
Born on 3/25/1934 in Memphis, Tennessee. Died in a boating accident on Clear Lake in California on 8/14/1964 (age 30). Johnny, older brother **Dorsey Burnette**, and Paul Burlison were rockabilly pioneers when they formed the Johnny Burnette Rock & Roll Trio. They released seven records on the Coral label, 1956-57. Recorded with brother Dorsey as The Texans in 1961. Father of **Rocky Burnette**.

~ ~ ~ ~ ~ ~ ~ ~ ~ ~ **NON-CHARTED ALBUMS** ~ ~ ~ ~ ~ ~ ~ ~ ~ ~ ~
1956 **Johnny Burnette And The Rock'n Roll Trio**	1962 **Johnny Burnette's Hits And Other Favorites**
1960 **Dreamin'**	1962 **Roses Are Red**
1961 **Johnny Burnette**	1964 **The Johnny Burnette Story**
1961 **Johnny Burnette Sings**	

BURNETTE, Rocky
Born Jonathan Burnette on 6/12/1953 in Memphis, Tennessee. Pop-rock singer/songwriter/guitarist. Son of **Johnny Burnette**, nephew of **Dorsey Burnette** and cousin of **Billy Burnette**.

6/21/80	53	14		1 **The Son Of Rock And Roll**		EMI America 17033

BURN HALO
Hard-rock band from Anaheim, California: James Hart (vocals), Joey Cunha (guitar), Allen Wheeler (guitar), Aaron Baylor (bass) and Tim Russell (drums). Hart was also the lead singer of **Eighteen Visions**.

4/18/09	129	1		1 **Burn Halo**		Rawkhead 10001

BURNING SENSATIONS
Rock band from Los Angeles, California: Tim McGovern (vocals, guitar), Morley Bartnof (keyboards), Jeff Hollie (sax), Michael Temple (percussion), Rob Hasick (bass) and Barry Wisdom (drums).

7/30/83	175	4		1 **Burning Sensations** .... **[EP]**		Capitol 15009

BURNS & SCHREIBER
Comedy duo of TV writers/actors/producers Jack Burns (born on 11/15/1933 in Boston, Massachusetts) and Avery Schreiber (born on 4/9/1935 in Chicago, Illinois). Both appeared in several movies and TV shows.

12/1/73	215	1		1 **Pure B.S.!** .... **[C]**		Little David 1006

BURNS, George
Born Nathan Birnbaum on 1/20/1896 in Brooklyn, New York. Died on 3/9/1996 (age 100). Popular radio, movie and TV comedian. Starred in several movies including *The Sunshine Boys* and *Oh God*.

2/9/80	93	10		1 **I Wish I Was Eighteen Again**		Mercury 5025

BURRELL, Kenny
Born on 7/31/1931 in Detroit, Michigan. Jazz guitarist.

11/30/63	108	4		1 **Blue Bash!** .... **[I]**		Verve 8553
				KENNY BURRELL & JIMMY SMITH		
12/17/66+	15^X	8		2 **Have Yourself A Soulful Little Christmas** .... **[X-I]**		Cadet 779
				Christmas charts: 43/'66, 21/'67, 15/'68		
12/17/66	146	2		3 **The Tender Gender** .... **[I]**		Cadet 772
8/31/68	191	2		4 **Blues-The Common Ground** .... **[I]**		Verve 8746

BURRELL, Kim
Born on 8/26/1972 in Houston, Texas. Gospel singer.

3/24/01	138	3		1 **Live In Concert** .... **[L]**		Tommy Boy 1450

BURTNICK, Glen
Born on 4/8/1955 in New Brunswick, New Jersey. Pop-rock singer/guitarist. Member of **Styx** from 1990-2004.

10/24/87	147	6		1 **Heroes & Zeros**		A&M 5166

BURTON, Jenny
Born on 11/18/1957 in Brooklyn, New York. Disco singer.

3/24/84	181	4		1 **In Black And White**		Atlantic 80122

BURY YOUR DEAD
Metalcore band from Worcester, Massachusetts: Mat Bruso (vocals), Brendan MacDonald (guitar), Eric Ellis (guitar), Aaron Patrick (bass) and Mark Castillo (drums).

7/29/06	129	1		1 **Beauty And The Breakdown**		Victory 300
4/5/08	176	1		2 **Bury Your Dead**		Victory 409
6/13/09	142	1		3 **It's Nothing Personal**		Victory 512

BUS BOYS, The
Black rock and roll band from Los Angeles, California: Gus Lounderman (vocals), brothers Brian (keyboards) and Kevin (bass) O'Neal, Victor Johnson (guitar), Michael Jones (keyboards) and Steve Felix (drums). Group appeared in the movie *48 HRS*.

11/29/80+	85	15		1 **Minimum Wage Rock & Roll**		Arista 4280
8/21/82	139	7		2 **American Worker**		Arista 9569

BUSH
Rock band from London, England: Gavin Rossdale (vocals, guitar; born on 10/30/1967), Nigel Pulsford (guitar; born on 4/11/1963), Dave Parsons (bass; born on 7/2/1965) and Robin Goodridge (drums; born on 9/10/1966). Rossdale married **Gwen Stefani** (lead singer of **No Doubt**) on 9/14/2002. Also see **Institute**.

1/28/95+	4	109	▲^{6}	1 **Sixteen Stone**	Cat:#3/42	Trauma 92531
12/7/96	❶^2	45	▲^{3}	2 **Razorblade Suitcase**		Trauma 90091
11/29/97	36	15	●	3 **Deconstructed** .... **[K]**		Trauma 90161
				contains remixes of previous recordings		

BUSH — cont'd

11/13/99	11	30	▲	4 The Science Of Things		Trauma 490483
11/10/01	22	6		5 Golden State		Atlantic 83488

BUSH, Kate
Born on 7/30/1958 in Bexleyheath, Kent, England. Eclectic singer/songwriter.

11/13/82	157	11		1 The Dreaming		EMI America 17084
7/9/83	148	6		2 Kate Bush [EP]		EMI America 19004
2/18/84	201	7		3 Lionheart		EMI America 17008
10/26/85	30	27		4 Hounds Of Love		EMI America 17171
12/20/86+	76	27		5 The Whole Story [G]		EMI America 17242
11/4/89	43	26	●	6 The Sensual World		Columbia 44164
11/20/93	28	14		7 The Red Shoes		Columbia 53737
11/26/05	48	2		8 Aerial		Columbia 97772 [2]

BUSHKIN, Joe
Born on 11/7/1916 in Manhattan, New York. Died on 11/3/2004 (age 87). Pianist/composer.

5/26/56	14	1		1 Midnight Rhapsody [I]		Capitol 711

BUSHWICK BILL
Born Richard Shaw on 12/8/1966 in Kingston, Jamaica. Member of **The Geto Boys**. Lost his right eye in a shooting on 5/10/1991.

10/17/92	32	9		1 Little Big Man		Rap-A-Lot 57189
7/29/95	43	7		2 Phantom Of The Rapra		Rap-A-Lot 40512

BUSTA RHYMES   All-Time: #485
Born Trevor Smith on 5/20/1972 in Brooklyn, New York. Male rapper/songwriter/actor. Member of **Leaders Of The New School** and **Flipmode Squad**. Played "Freddie Harris" in the 2002 movie *Halloween Resurrection*.

4/13/96	6	21	▲	1 The Coming		Elektra 61742
10/4/97	3[1]	44	▲	2 When Disaster Strikes...		Elektra 62064
1/2/99	12	32	▲	3 E.L.E.: Extinction Level Event * The Final World Front		Flipmode 62211
7/8/00	4	14	▲	4 Anarchy		Flipmode 62517
12/15/01	7	32	▲	5 Genesis		J Records 20009
12/14/02	43	34	●	6 It Ain't Safe No More...		J Records 20043
7/1/06	❶[1]	16	●	7 The Big Bang		Aftermath 006748
6/6/09	5	11		8 Back On My B.S.		Universal Motown 012387

BUTCHER, Jon, Axis
Born Jon Toombs in Boston, Massachusetts. Black rock singer/guitarist. The Axis included Chris Martin (bass) and Derek Blevins (drums). Martin left in early 1985. Thom Gimbel (keyboards) and Jimmy Johnson (bass) joined in 1985. Butcher went solo in early 1987.

3/26/83	91	13		1 Jon Butcher Axis		Polydor 810059
3/31/84	160	6		2 Stare At The Sun		Polydor 817493
10/12/85	66	17		3 Along The Axis		Capitol 12425
4/4/87	77	27		4 Wishes		Capitol 12542
2/18/89	121	8		5 Pictures From The Front		Capitol 90238
				JON BUTCHER (above 2)		

BUTLER, Carl
Born on 6/2/1927 in Knoxville, Tennessee. Died on 9/4/1992 (age 65). Country singer.
AWARD: OPRY: 1962

4/27/63	104	9		1 Don't Let Me Cross Over		Columbia 2002

BUTLER, Jerry
Born on 12/8/1939 in Sunflower, Mississippi; raised in Chicago, Illinois. R&B singer. Older brother of Billy Butler. Sang in the Northern Jubilee Gospel Singers, with **Curtis Mayfield**. Later with the Quails. In 1957, Butler and Mayfield joined the Roosters with Sam Gooden and brothers Arthur Brooks and Richard Brooks. Changed name to **The Impressions** in 1957. Left for solo career in autumn of 1958. Also worked as a Cook County Commissioner in Illinois. Dubbed "The Ice Man." Host of the popular PBS-TV "Doo Wop" specials.

10/3/64	102	11		1 Delicious Together		Vee-Jay 1099
				BETTY EVERETT & JERRY BUTLER		
1/20/68	154	7		2 Mr. Dream Merchant		Mercury 61146
3/16/68	178	2		3 Jerry Butler's Golden Hits Live [L]		Mercury 61151
				recorded in September 1967 at Morgan State College in Baltimore, Maryland		
7/27/68	195	2		4 The Soul Goes On		Mercury 61171
1/4/69	29	47		5 The Ice Man Cometh		Mercury 61198
10/4/69	41	23		6 Ice On Ice		Mercury 61234
6/27/70	167	5		7 The Best Of Jerry Butler [G]		Mercury 61281
7/11/70	172	4		8 You & Me		Mercury 61269
2/6/71	186	4		9 Jerry Butler Sings Assorted Sounds		Mercury 61320
3/27/71	143	5		10 Gene & Jerry - One & One		Mercury 61330
				GENE CHANDLER & JERRY BUTLER		
10/2/71+	123	22		11 The Sagittarius Movement		Mercury 61347
6/17/72	92	24		12 The Spice Of Life		Mercury 7502 [2]
11/4/72	212	2		13 Melinda [S]		Pride 0006
7/14/73	201	11		14 The Love We Have, The Love We Had		Mercury 660
				JERRY BUTLER & BRENDA LEE EAGER		

Billboard DEBUT	PEAK	WKS	R I A A	ARTIST Album Title	Catalog	Label & Number
				BUTLER, Jerry — cont'd		
2/5/77	199	2		15 **The Vintage Years** .... [G]		Sire 3717 [2]
3/12/77	146	11		16 **Suite For The Single Girl**		Motown 878
6/18/77	53	12		17 **Thelma & Jerry**		Motown 887
				THELMA HOUSTON & JERRY BUTLER		
1/13/79	160	4		18 **Nothing Says I Love You Like I Love You**..........................		Philadelphia Int'l. 35510
				~ ~ ~ ~ ~ ~ ~ ~ ~ **NON-CHARTED ALBUMS** ~ ~ ~ ~ ~ ~ ~ ~ ~ ~		
				1959 **Moon River** (1962) ... 1959 **Jerry Butler, Esq.**		
				1960 **He Will Break Your Heart** — 1962 **The Best Of Jerry Butler** [Vee Jay label]		
				1961 **Aware Of Love** — 1965 **More Of The Best Of Jerry Butler**		
				BUTLER, John, Trio		
				Born on 4/1/1975 in Torrance, California. Eclectic-rock singer/songwriter. Formed trio in Fremantle, Australia, with Bryon Luiters and Nicky Bomba.		
4/14/07	110	1		1 **Grand National**		Jarrah 101649
				BUTLER, Jonathan		
				Born on 10/1/1961 in Capetown, South Africa; later based in London, England. R&B singer/songwriter/guitarist.		
5/24/86	101	16		1 **Introducing Jonathan Butler**		Jive 8408
5/30/87	50	33	●	2 **Jonathan Butler**		Jive 1032 [2]
11/5/88	113	22		3 **More Than Friends**		Jive 1136
10/14/06	146	3		4 **Gospel Goes Classical, Vol. 1** .... [L]		Maranatha! 1894
				JUANITA BYNUM & JONATHAN BUTLER		
				BUTTERFIELD, Billy		
				Born Charles William Butterfield on 1/14/1917 in Middleton, Ohio. Died on 3/18/1988 (age 71). Legendary trumpeter.		
11/23/59+	8	36		1 **Conniff Meets Butterfield** [I]		Columbia 1346 / 8155
9/14/63	85	13		2 **Just Kiddin' Around**.. [I]		Columbia 2022 / 8822
				RAY CONNIFF & BILLY BUTTERFIELD (above 2)		
				BUTTERFIELD, Paul		
				Born on 12/17/1942 in Chicago, Illinois. Died of heart failure on 5/4/1987 (age 44). White blues singer/harmonica player. Formed interracial blues band in Chicago in 1965. His University of Chicago classmate **Elvin Bishop** was guitarist with group through 1968. **Mike Bloomfield** was the slide guitarist from 1965-66. Various members including saxophonist **David Sanborn** worked on and off with Butterfield from 1967-72.		
12/4/65+	123	9		1 **The Paul Butterfield Blues Band**		Elektra 7294
				RS500 #476		
				THE BUTTERFIELD BLUES BAND:		
10/8/66+	65	29		2 **East-West**		Elektra 7315
				Grammy: Hall of Fame		
1/13/68	52	16		3 **The Resurrection Of Pigboy Crabshaw**		Elektra 74015
				Pigboy Crabshaw is **Elvin Bishop**'s nickname		
8/24/68	79	17		4 **In My Own Dream**		Elektra 74025
11/1/69	102	10		5 **Keep On Moving**		Elektra 74053
1/16/71	72	12		6 **The Butterfield Blues Band/Live** .... [L]		Elektra 2001 [2]
				recorded at The Troubador in Los Angeles, California		
9/4/71	124	6		7 **Sometimes I Just Feel Like Smilin'**		Elektra 75013
5/20/72	136	6		8 **Golden Butter/The Best Of The Paul Butterfield Blues Band** .... [G]		Elektra 2005 [2]
				PAUL BUTTERFIELD'S BETTER DAYS:		
2/3/73	145	13		9 **Better Days**		Bearsville 2119
11/3/73	156	8		10 **It All Comes Back**		Bearsville 2170
				BUTTHOLE SURFERS		
				Punk-rock band from San Antonio, Texas: Gibby Haynes (vocals), Paul Leary (guitar), Jeff Pinkus (bass) and King Coffey (drums).		
4/10/93	154	12		1 **Independent Worm Saloon**		Capitol 98798
6/1/96	31	24	●	2 **Electriclarryland**		Capitol 29842
9/15/01	130	2		3 **Weird Revolution**		Surfdog 162269
				BUZZCOCKS		
				Punk-rock band from Manchester, England: **Pete Shelley** (vocals, guitar), Steve Diggle (guitar), Steve Garvey (bass) and John Maher (drums).		
2/23/80	163	6		1 **A Different Kind Of Tension**		I.R.S. 009
				~ ~ ~ ~ ~ ~ ~ ~ ~ ~ **NON-CHARTED ALBUM** ~ ~ ~ ~ ~ ~ ~ ~ ~ ~		
				1979 **Singles Going Steady**		
				RS500 #358		
				B*WITCHED		
				Female vocal group from Dublin, Ireland: twin sisters Edele Lynch and Keavy Lynch, with Sinead O'Carroll and Lindsay Armaou.		
4/3/99	12	29	▲	1 **B*Witched**		Epic 69751
11/13/99	91	10	●	2 **Awake And Breathe**		Epic 63985
				BY ALL MEANS		
				R&B trio from Los Angeles, California: Lynn Roderick (female vocals), James Varner (male vocals, piano) and Billy Sheppard (guitar).		
1/20/90	160	11		1 **Beyond A Dream**		Island 91319

Billboard DEBUT	PEAK	WKS	R I A A	ARTIST / Album Title	Catalog	Label & Number

BYNUM, Juanita
Born on 1/16/1959 in Chicago, Illinois. Gospel singer/speaker/author. Wrote several books and is a popular religious teacher/speaker.

2/4/06	40	27	●	1 A Piece Of My Passion		Flow 9301
10/14/06	146	3		2 Gospel Goes Classical, Vol. 1	[L]	Maranatha! 1894
				JUANITA BYNUM & JONATHAN BUTLER		
1/27/07	44ˣ	1		3 Christmas At Home With Juanita Bynum	[X]	Flow 9309
11/29/08	137	3		4 Pour My Love On You		Flow 9338 [2]

BYRD, Charlie
Born on 9/16/1925 in Chuckatuck, Virginia. Died of cancer on 11/30/1999 (age 74). Jazz and classical guitar virtuoso.

9/15/62+	❶¹	70		1 Jazz Samba	[I]	Verve 8432
				STAN GETZ & CHARLIE BYRD		
				Grammy: Hall of Fame		
3/23/63	128	5		2 Bossa Nova Pelos Passaros	[I]	Riverside 9436
12/9/67	40ˣ	4		3 Christmas Carols For Solo Guitar	[X-I]	Columbia 2555 / 9355
6/28/69	197	4		4 Aquarius	[I]	Columbia 9841
9/6/69	129	4		5 Let Go	[I-L]	Columbia 9869
				THE CHARLIE BYRD QUARTET		
				recorded on 2/28/1969 at the Century Plaza Hotel in Los Angeles, California		

BYRD, Donald
Born on 12/9/1932 in Detroit, Michigan. R&B-jazz trumpeter/flugelhorn player. Founded **The Blackbyrds** in 1974 while teaching jazz at Howard University in Washington DC.

7/11/64	110	8		1 A New Perspective	[I]	Blue Note 84124
4/28/73	36	34		2 Black Byrd		Blue Note 047
3/30/74	33	28		3 Street Lady	[I]	Blue Note 140
3/29/75	42	19		4 Stepping Into Tomorrow	[I]	Blue Note 368
11/15/75+	49	29		5 Places And Spaces		Blue Note 549
12/18/76+	167	4		6 Donald Byrd's Best	[G]	Blue Note 700
2/12/77	60	14		7 Caricatures		Blue Note 633
11/18/78	191	4		8 Thank You...For F.U.M.L. (Funking Up My Life)		Elektra 144
11/24/79	204	1		9 Donald Byrd And 125th Street, N.Y.C.		Elektra 247
10/3/81	93	10		10 Love Byrd		Elektra 531

BYRD, Tracy
Born on 12/17/1966 in Beaumont, Texas; raised in Vidor, Texas. Male country singer/songwriter/guitarist.

5/15/93	115	6	●	1 Tracy Byrd		MCA 10649
6/25/94+	30	78	▲²	2 No Ordinary Man		MCA 10991
8/5/95	44	31	●	3 Love Lessons		MCA 11242
11/9/96+	106	22	●	4 Big Love		MCA 11485
5/30/98	58	8		5 I'm From The Country		MCA Nashville 70016
3/13/99	70	10	●	6 Keepers / Greatest Hits	[G]	MCA Nashville 70048
11/20/99	174	1		7 It's About Time		RCA 67881
8/11/01	119	3		8 Ten Rounds		RCA 67009
7/19/03	33	7		9 The Truth About Men		RCA 67073
2/26/05	61	2		10 Greatest Hits	[G]	BNA 64861
11/18/06	165	1		11 Different Things		Blind Mule 101

BYRDS, The   All-Time: #263
Folk-rock band formed in Los Angeles, California: **Roger McGuinn** (guitar), **David Crosby** (guitar), **Gene Clark** (tambourine, guitar), **Chris Hillman** (bass) and Mike Clarke (drums). All shared vocals. McGuinn had been with the **Chad Mitchell Trio**. Gene Clark had been with the **New Christy Minstrels**; left in 1966. Crosby left in late 1967 to form **Crosby, Stills & Nash**. Re-formed in 1968 with McGuinn, Hillman, Kevin Kelly (drums) and **Gram Parsons** (guitar). Hillman and Parsons left that same year to form the **Flying Burrito Brothers**. McGuinn again re-formed with Clarence White (guitar), John York (bass) and Gene Parsons (drums). Reunions with original members in 1973 and 1979. Gram Parsons died of a heroin overdose on 9/19/1973 (age 26). **McGuinn, Clark & Hillman** later recorded as a trio. In 1986, Hillman formed popular country group **The Desert Rose Band**. McGuinn, Crosby and Hillman reunited on stage on 2/24/1990 for a **Roy Orbison** tribute. Gene Clark died on 5/24/1991 (age 46). Mike Clarke, also with the Flying Burrito Brothers and **Firefall**, died of liver failure on 12/19/1993 (age 49).

AWARD: R&R Hall of Fame: 1991

6/26/65	6	38		1 Mr. Tambourine Man		Columbia 2372 / 9172
				RS500 #232		
1/1/66	17	40		2 Turn! Turn! Turn!		Columbia 2454 / 9254
8/27/66	24	28		3 Fifth Dimension		Columbia 2549 / 9349
3/18/67	24	24		4 Younger Than Yesterday		Columbia 2642 / 9442
				RS500 #124		
9/2/67	6	29	▲	5 The Byrds' Greatest Hits	[G]	Columbia 2716 / 9516
				RS500 #178		
2/3/68	47	19		6 The Notorious Byrd Brothers		Columbia 2775 / 9575
				RS500 #171		
8/31/68	77	10		7 Sweetheart Of The Rodeo		Columbia 9670
				Grammy: Hall of Fame ★ RS500 #117		
3/15/69	153	7		8 Dr. Byrds & Mr. Hyde		Columbia 9755
9/6/69	84	12		9 Preflyte	[E]	Together 1001
				recorded in 1964; also see #16 below		
12/13/69+	36	17		10 Ballad Of Easy Rider		Columbia 9942

			R I A	ARTIST		
DEBUT	PEAK	WKS		Album Title	Catalog	Label & Number

BYRDS, The — cont'd

10/17/70	40	21		11 **The Byrds (Untitled)**.. [L]		Columbia 30127 [2]
				record 1: live; record 2: studio		
7/24/71	46	10		12 **Byrdmaniax**...		Columbia 30640
12/25/71+	152	7		13 **Farther Along**...		Columbia 31050
12/16/72+	114	13		14 **The Best Of The Byrds (Greatest Hits, Volume II)**.................... [G]		Columbia 31795
3/24/73	20	17		15 **Byrds**..		Asylum 5058
				reunion of original 5 Byrds		
9/8/73	183	3		16 **Preflyte**.. [E-R]		Columbia 32183
				new cover features a futuristic drawing of the band		
11/10/90	151	4		17 **The Byrds**.. [K]		Columbia 46773 [4]

BYRNE, David
Born on 5/14/1952 in Dumbarton, Scotland; raised in Baltimore, Maryland. Lead singer of the **Talking Heads**. Composed scores for several movies and plays. Formed own Luaka Bop record label.

3/21/81	44	13		1 **My Life In The Bush Of Ghosts**.. [I]		Sire 6093
				BRIAN ENO & DAVID BYRNE		
12/19/81+	104	12		2 **The Catherine Wheel**... [OC]		Sire 3645
6/1/85	141	6		3 **Music For The Knee Plays**...		ECM 25022
10/21/89	71	18		4 **Rei Momo**..		Luaka Bop 25990
3/21/92	125	6		5 **Uh-Oh**...		Luaka Bop 26799
6/11/94	139	6		6 **David Byrne**...		Luaka Bop 45558
7/5/97	155	1		7 **Feelings**...		Luaka Bop 46605
5/26/01	120	4		8 **Look Into The Eyeball**...		Luaka Bop 50924
4/3/04	178	1		9 **Grown Backwards**...		Nonesuch 79826
1/17/09	174	2		10 **Everything That Happens Will Happen Today**............................		Opal 002
				DAVID BYRNE & BRIAN ENO		

BYRNES, Edward
Born Edward Breitenberger on 7/30/1933 in Brooklyn, New York. Played "Kookie" on TV's *77 Sunset Strip*.

~ ~ ~ ~ ~ ~ ~ ~ ~ ~ **NON-CHARTED ALBUM** ~ ~ ~ ~ ~ ~ ~ ~ ~ ~ ~
1959 **Kookie Star Of "77 Sunset Strip"**

BYRON, D.L.
Born David Byron in Brooklyn, New York. Singer/songwriter/guitarist.

| 2/16/80 | 133 | 10 | | 1 **This Day And Age** .... | | Arista 4258 |

B'ZZ, The
Rock band from Chicago, Illinois: Tom Holland (vocals), Michael Tafoya (guitar), Anatole Halinkovitch (keyboards), David Angel (bass) and Stephan Riley (drums).

| 3/12/83 | 210 | 1 | | 1 **Get Up** .... | | Epic 38230 |

C

CAB, The
Pop-rock band from Las Vegas, Nevada: Alex DeLeon (vocals), Ian Crawford (guitar), Alex Marshall (keyboards), Cash Colligan (bass) and Alex Johnson (drums).

| 5/17/08 | 108 | 1 | | 1 **Whisper War** .... | | Decaydance 442364 |

CABRERA, Ryan
Born on 7/18/1982 in Dallas, Texas. Pop singer/songwriter.

9/4/04	8	36	●	1 **Take It All Away**		E.V.L.A. 83702
10/8/05	24	7		2 **You Stand Watching**		E.V.L.A. 83823
5/31/08	177	1		3 **The Moon Under Water**		Papa Joe 90097

CACTUS
Rock band formed in New York: Russell "Rusty Day" Davidson (vocals), Jim McCarty (guitar), **Tim Bogert** (bass) and **Carmine Appice** (drums). McCarty was with **Mitch Ryder & The Detroit Wheels**. Bogert and Appice were with **Vanilla Fudge**. Day and McCarty left in 1972, replaced by Peter French (vocals), Werner Fritzschings (guitar) and Duane Hitchings (keyboards). Hitchings formed New Cactus Band in 1972 with Mike Pinera (vocals, guitar; **Iron Butterfly, Blues Image, Ramatam**), Roland Robinson (bass) and Jerry Norris (drums). Day was shot to death on 6/3/1982 (age 36). Hitchings and Appice later joined **Rod Stewart**'s band.

7/25/70	54	18		1 **Cactus**..		Atco 340
3/20/71	88	13		2 **One Way...Or Another**..		Atco 356
11/27/71	155	10		3 **Restrictions**...		Atco 377
10/28/72	162	5		4 **'Ot 'N' Sweaty**.. [L]		Atco 7011
5/12/73	183	6		5 **Son Of Cactus**..		Atco 7017
				NEW CACTUS BAND		

CACTUS WORLD NEWS
Rock band from Dublin, Ireland: Eoin McEvoy (vocals), Frank Kearns (guitar), Fergal MacAindris (bass) and Wayne Sheehy (drums).

| 8/9/86 | 179 | 5 | | 1 **Urban Beaches** .... | | MCA 5747 |

Billboard			R I A A	ARTIST Album Title	Catalog	Label & Number
DEBUT	PEAK	WKS				

CADETS, The / JACKS, The
R&B vocal group from Los Angeles, California: Aaron Collins, Ted Taylor, William "Dub" Jones (bass man for **The Coasters**; died on 1/16/2000, age 71), Willie Davis and Lloyd McCraw. Recorded as both **The Jacks** on RPM with Davis as lead and The Cadets on Modern with Collins or Jones as lead.

~ ~ ~ ~ ~ ~ ~ ~ ~ ~ **NON-CHARTED ALBUMS** ~ ~ ~ ~ ~ ~ ~ ~ ~ ~ ~ ~
1957 **Jumpin' With The Jacks**   1957 **Rockin' N' Reelin' With The Cadets**

CADILLAC DON & J-MONEY
Male hip-hop duo from Crawford, Mississippi: Donald "Cadillac Don" Sharp and Tiyon "J-Money" Rogers.

11/25/06	156	1	1 **Look At Me**	35*35 68794

CADILLACS, The
R&B vocal group from Harlem, New York: Earl "Speedoo" Carroll (lead vocals), LaVern Drake, Earl Wade, Charles Brooks and Robert Phillips. By 1958, Drake and Brooks replaced by J.R. Bailey and Bobby Spencer. Varying personnel. Carroll joined **The Coasters** in 1961. Bailey died in January 1980 (age 45).

~ ~ ~ ~ ~ ~ ~ ~ ~ **NON-CHARTED ALBUMS** ~ ~ ~ ~ ~ ~ ~ ~ ~ ~ ~
1957 **The Fabulous Cadillacs**   1962 **Twisting With The Cadillacs**
1959 **The Crazy Cadillacs**

CAEDMON'S CALL
Christian folk-rock band from Houston, Texas: Danielle Glenn (female vocals), Cliff Young (male vocals, guitar), **Derek Webb** (guitar), Garett Buell (percussion), Aric Nitzberg (bass) and Todd Bragg (drums). Randy Holsapple (keyboards) joined in 1998. Josh Moore replaced Holsapple and Jeff Miller replaced Nitzberg in early 2000. Band named after a seventh-century folk tale about a herdsman's God-given singing voice.

4/12/97	110	2	1 **Caedmon's Call**	Warner Alliance 46463
5/1/99	61	9	2 **40 Acres**	Essential 10486
10/28/00	58	2	3 **Long Line Of Leavers**	Essential 10559
10/13/01	72	4	4 **In The Company Of Angels - A Call To Worship**	Essential 10621
2/22/03	66	4	5 **Back Home**	Essential 10694
10/30/04	175	1	6 **Share The Well**	Essential 10739
9/15/07	54	1	7 **Overdressed**	Ino 09355

CAFE JACQUES
Pop-rock trio formed in England: Chris Thomson (vocals), Mike Ogletree (guitar) and Peter Veitch (keyboards).

4/1/78	210	1	1 **Round The Back**	Columbia 35294

CAFFERTY, John, And The Beaver Brown Band
Rock band from Narragansett, Rhode Island: John Cafferty (vocals, guitar), Gary Gramolini (guitar), Robert Cotoia (keyboards), Michael Antunes (sax), Pat Lupo (bass) and Ken Silva (drums). Wrote and recorded the music for the soundtrack *Eddie And The Cruisers*. Cotoia died on 9/3/2004 (age 51).

10/15/83+	9	62	▲³	1 **Eddie And The Cruisers** [S]	Scotti Brothers 38929
6/8/85	40	32		2 **Tough All Over**	Scotti Brothers 39405
8/26/89	121	6		3 **Eddie And The Cruisers II** [S]	Scotti Brothers 45297

CAGE
Born Christian Palko in 1970 on a U.S. military base in West Germany; raised in Brooklyn, New York. Male rapper. Member of **Smut Peddlers**.

8/24/02	193	1	1 **Movies For The Blind**	Eastern Conference 102
7/25/09	133	1	2 **Depart From Me**	Definitive Jux 179

CAGE, Byron
Born on 12/15/1962 in Grand Rapids, Michigan; later based in Fort Washington, Maryland. Gospel singer.

12/17/05	188	1	1 **An Invitation To Worship**	GospoCentric 71281
10/6/07	118	1	2 **Live At The Apollo: The Proclamation** [L]	GospoCentric 11114
11/14/09	102	2	3 **Faithful To Believe**	GospoCentric 43343

CAGE THE ELEPHANT
Punk-rock band from Bowling Green, Kentucky: brothers Matt Schultz (vocals) and Brad Schultz (guitar), with Lincoln Parish (guitar), Dan Tichenor (bass) and Jared Champion (drums).

5/2/09	67	53↑	1 **Cage The Elephant**	DSP 49658

CAGLE, Chris
Born Christian Cagle on 11/10/1968 in DeRidder, Louisiana; raised in Baytown, Texas. Male country singer/songwriter/guitarist.

7/7/01+	164	24	●	1 **Play It Loud**	Capitol 34170
4/19/03	15	36	●	2 **Chris Cagle**	Capitol 40516
10/22/05	24	20		3 **Anywhere But Here**	Capitol 77380
3/8/08	8	9		4 **My Life's Been A Country Song**	Capitol 88106

CAILLAT, Colbie
Born on 5/28/1985 in Newbury Park, California; raised in Malibu, California. Adult Alternative-pop singer/songwriter/guitarist. Daughter of record producer Ken Caillat.

8/4/07	5	79	▲²	1 **Coco** Cat:#18/19	Universal Rep. 009219
11/29/08	176	1		2 **Coco: Summer Sessions** [EP]	Universal Rep. digital
				contains live and acoustic versions of some songs from #1 above	
9/12/09	❶¹	38↑	●	3 **Breakthrough**	Universal Rep. 013194

126

CAIN, Tane
Born Tane McClure on 6/8/1958 in Pacific Palasades, California. Female singer/songwriter. Daughter of actor Doug McClure. Formerly married to Jonathan Cain (of **The Babys**, **Journey**, **Bad English**). First name pronounced: tawnee.

9/11/82	121	10	1 Tane Cain		RCA Victor 4381

CAKE
Rock band from Sacramento, California: John McCrea (vocals, guitar), Greg Brown (guitar), Vince DiFiore (trumpet), Victor Damiani (bass) and Todd Roper (drums). Gabe Nelson replaced Damiani in 1997. Xan McCurdy replaced Brown in 1998. Roper left in 2002.

10/5/96+	36	51	▲	1 Fashion Nugget .... **Cat:#48/1**	Capricorn 532867
10/24/98	33	36	▲	2 Prolonging The Magic	Capricorn 538092
8/11/01	13	14	●	3 Comfort Eagle	Columbia 62132
10/23/04	17	7		4 Pressure Chief	Columbia 92629

CALDERA
Jazz band formed in New York: Jorge Strunz (guitar), Eduardo Del Barrio (piano), Steve Tavaglione (flute), Mike Azevedo (congas), Hector Andrade (percussion), Dean Cortez (bass) and Carlos Vega (drums). Also see **Strunz & Farah**.

10/1/77	159	4	1 Sky Islands .... **[I]**	Capitol 11658

CALDERON, Tego
Born on 2/1/1972 in Santurce, Puerto Rico. Male Latin reggae rapper.

9/16/06	43	4	1 The Underdog / El Subestimado .... **[F]**	Jiggiri 94122
9/15/07	136	2	2 El Abayarde Contra-Ataca .... **[F]**	Warner Latina 285692

CALDWELL, Bobby
Born on 8/15/1951 in Manhattan, New York; raised in Miami, Florida. White singer/songwriter/multi-instrumentalist.

11/18/78+	21	31	1 Bobby Caldwell	Clouds 8804
3/29/80	113	15	2 Cat In The Hat	Clouds 8810
4/17/82	133	13	3 Carry On	Polydor 6347

CALE, J.J.
Born John Weldon Cale on 12/5/1938 in Oklahoma City, Oklahoma. Rock singer/songwriter/guitarist.

1/22/72	51	32	1 Naturally	Shelter 8098
12/30/72+	92	11	2 Really	Shelter 8912
6/15/74	128	11	3 Okie	Shelter 2107
9/25/76	84	18	4 Troubadour	Shelter 52002
9/8/79	136	9	5 5	Shelter 3163
2/28/81	110	7	6 Shades	MCA 5158
4/3/82	149	8	7 Grasshopper	Mercury 4038
3/17/90	131	10	8 Travel-Log	Silvertone 1306
11/25/06	23	20	●	9 The Road To Escondido	Duck 44418
				J.J. CALE & ERIC CLAPTON	
3/14/09	113	2	10 Roll On	Rounder 613258

CALE, John
Born on 3/9/1940 in Crynant, West Glamorgan, Wales. Eclectic-rock singer/songwriter/producer. Member of the **Velvet Underground**.

9/6/75	203	4	1 Slow Dazzle	Island 9317
2/9/80	201	3	2 Sabotage/Live .... **[L]**	I.R.S. 004
			recorded at the CBGB club in New York City in June 1979	
4/11/81	154	5	3 Honi Soit (o nee swa)	A&M 4849
5/12/90	103	8	4 Songs For Drella	Sire 26140
			LOU REED & JOHN CALE	
			fictitious account of the life of Andy Warhol	

CALEXICO
Experimental-rock band from Tuscon, Arizona. Formed by Joey Burns and John Convertino and featuring a revolving lineup of various singers and musicians.

10/1/05	135	1	1 In The Reins .... **[EP]**	Overcoat 28
			CALEXICO / IRON & WINE	
4/29/06	156	2	2 Garden Ruin	Quarterstick 97
9/27/08	98	2	3 Carried To Dust	Quarterstick 108

CALHOUN, Slimm
Born Brian Loving in College Park, Georgia. Male rapper.

4/28/01	78	5	1 The Skinny	Aquemini 62520

CALHOUNS
Male rap trio from Atlanta, Georgia: Freddy "**Cool Breeze**" Calhoun, Paul "Pauly Calhoun" Whiteside and Sedric "Lucky Calhoun" Barnett.

9/7/02	168	1	1 Made In The Dirdy South	Empire 39046

CALIFORNIA RAISINS, The
Studio group assembled by producer Ross Vannelli (brother of **Gino Vannelli**). Features R&B singer/drummer **Buddy Miles** and singer Alfie Silas. Based on the Claymation characters of a California Raisin Growers TV commercial.

12/5/87+	60	36	▲	1 The California Raisins Sing The Hit Songs	Priority 9706
10/8/88	140	15		2 Sweet, Delicious, & Marvelous	Priority 9755
12/24/88	27^X	3		3 Christmas With The California Raisins .... **[X]**	Priority 7923

Billboard			R I A A	ARTIST		
DEBUT	PEAK	WKS		Album Title	Catalog	Label & Number

CALL, The
Rock band from San Francisco, California: Michael Been (vocals, guitar), Tom Ferrier (guitar), Greg Freeman (bass) and Scott Musick (drums). Jim Goodwin (keyboards) replaced Freeman in 1984.

3/26/83	84	15		1 Modern Romans		Mercury 810307
6/16/84	204	3		2 Scene Beyond Dreams		Mercury 422818
3/8/86	82	30		3 Reconciled		Elektra 60440
7/4/87	123	13		4 Into The Woods		Elektra 60739
7/1/89	64	22		5 Let The Day Begin		MCA 6303

CALLAS, Maria
Born Maria Kalogeropoulos on 12/2/1923 in Queens, New York. Died of heart failure on 9/16/1977 (age 53). Renowned operatic soprano.

2/27/65	87	8		1 Bizet: Carmen		Angel 3650 [3]

CALLE 13
Male reggae rap duo from Puerto Rico: Rene "Residente" Perez and Eduardo "Visitante" Cabra.

7/29/06	189	4		1 Calle 13	[F]	White Lion 96875
5/12/07	52	4		2 Residente O Visitante	[F]	Sony 03170
11/8/08	89	2		3 Los De Atras Vienen Conmigo	[F]	Sony 36801
				Grammy: Latin Urban Album		

CALLING, The
Rock band from Los Angeles, California: Alex Band (vocals), Aaron Kamin (guitar), Sean Woolstenhulme (guitar), Billy Mohler (bass) and Nate Wood (drums).

11/17/01+	36	38	●	1 Camino Palmero		RCA 67585
6/26/04	54	3		2 Two		RCA 56612

CALLOWAY
R&B duo from Cincinnati, Ohio: brothers Reggie Calloway and Vincent Calloway. Both were members of **Midnight Star**.

3/31/90	80	14		1 All The Way		Solar 75310

CALLY
Born Cally Gage in England. Female techno-house DJ.

4/4/09	172	1		1 Simple Instrumentals	[I]	Simple digital
				no track titles listed on this album		

CAMBRIDGE, Godfrey
Born on 2/26/1933 in Harlem, New York. Died of a heart attack on 11/29/1976 (age 43). Black actor/comedian. Starred in the 1970 movie *Watermelon Man*.

7/11/64	42	13		1 Ready Or Not...Here's Godfrey Cambridge	[C]	Epic 13101
4/3/65	142	9		2 Them Cotton Pickin' Days Is Over	[C]	Epic 13102

CAMEL
Rock band from Surrey, England: **Pete Bardens** (keyboards; **Them**), Andy Latimer (vocals, guitar), Doug Ferguson (bass) and Andy Ward (drums).

11/30/74	149	13		1 Mirage		Janus 7009
7/19/75	162	5		2 The Snow Goose	[I]	Janus 7016
5/22/76	118	13		3 Moonmadness		Janus 7024
11/12/77	136	5		4 Rain Dances		Janus 7035
2/10/79	134	10		5 Breathless		Arista 4206
1/12/80	208	1		6 I Can See Your House From Here		Arista 4254

CAMEO   **1980s: #44 / All-Time: #298**
R&B-funk band founded by Larry Blackmon (producer, vocals, drums) as The New York City Players. Varying members also included Gregory Johnson, Tomi Jenkins, brothers Nathan Leftenant and Arnett Leftenant, Wayne Cooper, Gary Dow, Eric Durham, Anthony Lockett, Charlie Singleton, Jeryl Bright, Thomas Campbell, Stephen Moore, Aaron Mills and Kevin Kendricks. In mid-'80s, Blackmon relocated group to Atlanta and formed own label, Atlanta Artists. By 1986, group pared to trio of Blackmon, Jenkins and Nathan Leftenant (left by 1992 and Singleton returned).

8/20/77	116	15		1 Cardiac Arrest		Chocolate City 2003
2/18/78	58	23		2 We All Know Who We Are		Chocolate City 2004
11/4/78	83	15		3 Ugly Ego		Chocolate City 2006
7/28/79	46	21	●	4 Secret Omen		Chocolate City 2008
5/24/80	25	26	●	5 Cameosis		Chocolate City 2011
12/6/80+	44	17	●	6 Feel Me		Chocolate City 2016
6/20/81	44	13		7 Knights Of The Sound Table		Chocolate City 2019
4/10/82	23	24	●	8 Alligator Woman		Chocolate City 2021
5/7/83	53	12		9 Style		Atlanta Artists 811072
3/17/84	27	24	●	10 She's Strange		Atlanta Artists 814984
7/13/85	58	27	●	11 Single Life		Atlanta Artists 824546
9/27/86	8	54	▲	12 Word Up!		Atlanta Artists 830265
11/12/88	56	19		13 Machismo		Atlanta Artists 836002
7/14/90	84	8		14 Real Men...Wear Black		Atlanta Artists 846297

CAMERA OBSCURA
Alternative-rock band from Glasgow, Scotland: Tracyanne Campbell (vocals, guitar), Kenny McKeeve (guitar), Carey Lander (keyboards), Gavin Dunbar (bass) and Lee Thomson (drums).

5/9/09	87	4		1 My Maudlin Career		4AD 2907

Billboard			R I A A	ARTIST		
DEBUT	PEAK	WKS		Album Title	Catalog	Label & Number

CAMERON, Rafael
Born in 1951 in Georgetown, Guyana. Disco singer.

| 8/2/80 | 67 | 18 | | 1 Cameron | | Salsoul 8535 |
| 7/18/81 | 101 | 12 | | 2 Cameron's In Love | | Salsoul 8542 |

CAMILA
Latin soft-rock trio from Mexico: Mario Domm, Samo and Pablo Hurtado.

| 8/4/07 | 76 | 36 | | 1 Todo Cambio [F] | | Sony 78272 |

CAMOUFLAGE
Dance trio from Germany: Marcus Meyn (vocals), Heiko Maile (keyboards) and Oliver Kreyssig (backing vocals; left in 1990).

| 1/14/89 | 100 | 14 | | 1 Voices & Images | | Atlantic 81886 |

CAMP, Jeremy
Born on 1/12/1978 in Lafayette, Indiana. Contemporary Christian singer/songwriter/guitarist.

2/28/04	102	20	●	1 Carried Me: The Worship Project		BEC 39613
11/13/04+	2³ᶜ	6	●	2 Stay		BEC 40456
				first released in 2002		
12/4/04	45	32	●	3 Restored		BEC 98615
11/26/05	111	7		4 Live-Unplugged: Franklin, TN [L]		BEC 77661
11/18/06	29	16	●	5 Beyond Measure		BEC 63723
12/13/08	38	27		6 Speaking Louder Than Before		BEC 26780

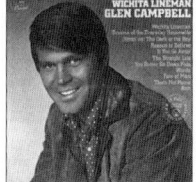

CAMPBELL, Glen
All-Time: #99

Born on 4/22/1936 in Delight, Arkansas. Country-pop singer/songwriter/guitarist. Became prolific studio musician; with **The Champs** in 1960, **The Hondells** in 1964, **The Beach Boys** in 1965 and Sagittarius in 1967. Own TV show *The Glen Campbell Goodtime Hour*, 1968-72. Acted in the movies *True Grit*, *Norwood* and *Strange Homecoming*; voice in the animated movie *Rock-A-Doodle*. Also see **The Folkswingers**.

AWARDS: C&W Hall of Fame: 2005 ★ CMA: Male Vocalist 1968 / Entertainer 1968

12/2/67+	5	75	▲	1 Gentle On My Mind		Capitol 2809
12/30/67+	15	80	▲	2 By The Time I Get To Phoenix		Capitol 2851
				Grammy: Album of the Year		
4/6/68	26	51	●	3 Hey, Little One		Capitol 2878
6/22/68	24	33		4 A New Place In The Sun		Capitol 2907
10/12/68	11	47	●	5 Bobbie Gentry & Glen Campbell		Capitol 2928
11/16/68	❶⁵	46	▲²	6 Wichita Lineman		Capitol 103
12/7/68	❶²ˣ	10	●	7 That Christmas Feeling [X]		Capitol 2978
				Christmas charts: 1/'68, 4/'69, 23/'70, 14/'71		
4/12/69	2¹	42	▲	8 Galveston		Capitol 210
9/20/69	13	29	●	9 Glen Campbell - "Live" [L]		Capitol 268 [2]
				recorded at the Garden States Art Center in Holmdel, New Jersey		
2/7/70	12	28	●	10 Try A Little Kindness		Capitol 389
5/23/70	38	19		11 Oh Happy Day		Capitol 443
6/27/70	90	13		12 Norwood [S]		Capitol 475
10/3/70	27	21		13 The Glen Campbell Goodtime Album		Capitol 493
4/17/71	39	27	▲	14 Glen Campbell's Greatest Hits [G]		Capitol 752
8/7/71	87	9		15 The Last Time I Saw Her		Capitol 733
12/11/71+	128	8		16 Anne Murray / Glen Campbell		Capitol 869
11/25/72+	148	13		17 Glen Travis Campbell		Capitol 11117
6/9/73	154	6		18 I Knew Jesus (Before He Was A Star)		Capitol 11185
1/19/74	205	1		19 I Remember Hank Williams		Capitol 11253
11/16/74	166	5		20 Reunion (The Songs Of Jimmy Webb)		Capitol 11336
8/9/75	17	30	●	21 Rhinestone Cowboy		Capitol 11430
5/1/76	63	9		22 Bloodline		Capitol 11516
11/27/76	116	6		23 The Best Of Glen Campbell [G]		Capitol 11577
3/19/77	22	22	●	24 Southern Nights		Capitol 11601
1/7/78	171	5		25 Live At The Royal Festival Hall [L]		Capitol 11707 [2]
12/16/78	164	5		26 Basic		Capitol 11722
2/28/81	178	3		27 It's The World Gone Crazy		Capitol 12124
2/15/03	89	1		28 All The Best [G]		Capitol 41816
9/6/08	155	1		29 Meet Glen Campbell		Capitol 34132

CAMPBELL, Jo Ann
Born on 7/20/1938 in Jacksonville, Florida. Female singer/actress.

~ ~ ~ ~ ~ ~ ~ ~ ~ ~ **NON-CHARTED ALBUMS** ~ ~ ~ ~ ~ ~ ~ ~ ~ ~ ~ ~

1962 **Twistin' And Listenin'**   1962 **All The Hits By Jo Ann Campbell**

Billboard DEBUT	PEAK	WKS	R I A A	ARTIST Album Title	Catalog	Label & Number
				CAMPBELL, Tevin		
				Born on 11/12/1976 in Waxahachie, Texas. Male R&B singer. Appeared in the 1990 movie *Graffiti Bridge*.		
12/7/91+	38	44	▲	1 T.E.V.I.N.		Qwest 26291
11/13/93	18	49	▲²	2 I'm Ready		Qwest 45388
7/13/96	46	8		3 Back To The World		Qwest 46003
3/13/99	88	4		4 Tevin Campbell		Qwest 47008
				CAMPER VAN BEETHOVEN		
				Rock band from Santa Cruz, California: David Lowery (vocals, guitar), Greg Lisher (guitar), Morgan Fichter (violin), Victor Krummenacher (bass) and Chris Pedersen (drums). Lowery later formed **Cracker**.		
6/18/88	124	17		1 Our Beloved Revolutionary Sweetheart		Virgin 90918
10/7/89	141	13		2 Key Lime Pie		Virgin 91289
				CAMP LO		
				Male rap duo from the Bronx, New York: Salahadeen Wallace and Saladine Wilds.		
3/1/97	27	9		1 Uptown Saturday Night		Profile 1470
				CAM'RON		
				Born Cameron Giles on 2/4/1976 in Harlem, New York. Male rapper/songwriter. Brother of **Freekey Zekey**. Member of **The Diplomats**.		
8/8/98	6	10	●	1 Confessions Of Fire		Untertainment 68976
10/7/00	14	9		2 S.D.E.		Untertainment 69873
6/1/02	2¹	28	▲	3 Come Home With Me		Roc-A-Fella 586876
12/25/04	20	14	●	4 Purple Haze		Roc-A-Fella 002728
6/3/06	2¹	10		5 Killa Season		Diplomatic Man 68589
5/30/09	3¹	8		6 Crime Pays		Diplomatic Man 518073
				CANADIAN BRASS		
				Brass band formed in Canada: Chuck Daellenbach, Gene Watts, Jeff Nelsen, Chris Coletti and Brandon Ridenour.		
10/10/09	8ˣ	3		1 Christmas Tradition [X-I]		Opening Day 7345
				C & C MUSIC FACTORY		
				Dance group led by producers/songwriters Robert Clivilles (percussion; born on 8/30/1964) and David Cole (keyboards; born on 6/3/1962; died of spinal meningitis on 1/24/1995, age 32). Featured vocalists include Freedom Williams, Deborah Cooper and **Martha Wash**.		
1/12/91	2⁷	85	▲⁵	1 Gonna Make You Sweat		Columbia 47093
2/29/92	87	9		2 Greatest Remixes Vol. I [K] **CLIVILLES + COLE**		Columbia 48840
8/27/94	106	9		3 Anything Goes!		Columbia 66160
				CANDLEBOX		
				Rock band from Seattle, Washington: Kevin Martin (vocals), Peter Klett (guitar), Bardi Martin (bass) and Scott Mercado (drums). Dave Krusen replaced Mercado in 1997.		
10/9/93+	7	104	▲⁴	1 Candlebox		Maverick 45313
10/21/95	11	17	●	2 Lucy		Maverick 45962
8/8/98	65	9		3 Happy Pills		Maverick 46975
8/9/08	32	3		4 Into The Sun		Silent Majority 51140
				CANDLEMASS		
				Hard-rock band from Sweden: Messiah Marcolin (vocals), Lars Johansson (guitar), Mats Bjorkman (guitar), Leif Edling (bass) and Jan Lindh (drums).		
1/21/89	174	6		1 Ancient Dreams		Metal Blade 73340
				CANDYMAN		
				Born John Shaffer on 6/25/1968 in Los Angeles, California. Male rapper.		
10/27/90+	40	36	●	1 Ain't No Shame In My Game		Epic 46947
				CANDYMEN, The		
				Former backing band for **Roy Orbison**: Rodney Justo (vocals), John Adkins (guitar), Dean Daughtry (piano), Billy Gilmore (bass) and Bob Nix (drums). Daughter joined the **Classics IV**. Justo, Daughtry and Nix later joined the **Atlanta Rhythm Section**. Adkins died in June 1989 (age 47).		
11/11/67	195	4		1 The Candymen		ABC 616
				CANIBUS		
				Born Germaine Williams on 12/9/1974 in Jamaica; raised in New Jersey. Male rapper.		
9/26/98	2¹	7	●	1 Can-I-Bus		Universal 53136
8/5/00	23	7		2 2000 B.C. (Before Can-I-Bus)		Universal 159054
8/9/03	194	1		3 Rip The Jacker		Babygrande 5

Billboard			R I A A	ARTIST		
DEBUT	PEAK	WKS		Album Title	Catalog	Label & Number

CANNED HEAT
Blues-rock band from Los Angeles, California: Bob "The Bear" Hite (vocals, harmonica), Alan "Blind Owl" Wilson (guitar, harmonica, vocals), Henry Vestine (guitar), Larry Taylor (bass) and Frank Cook (drums). Cook replaced by Fito DeLa Parra in 1968. Vestine replaced by **Harvey Mandel** in 1969. Wilson died of a drug overdose on 9/3/1970 (age 27). Hite died of a drug-related heart attack on 4/6/1981 (age 36). Vestine died of heart failure on 10/20/1997 (age 52).

DEBUT	PEAK	WKS		Album Title	Catalog	Label & Number
8/12/67	76	23		1 Canned Heat		Liberty 7526
2/24/68	16	52		2 Boogie With Canned Heat		Liberty 7541
12/7/68+	18	17		3 Living The Blues	[L]	Liberty 27200 [2]
				record 2: recorded live at the Kaleidoscope in Hollywood; also see #10 below		
10/30/71	182	2		4 Living The Blues	[L-R]	United Artists 9955 [2]
				new cover features a drawing of an open mouth		
8/9/69	37	15		5 Hallelujah		Liberty 7618
12/6/69+	86	19		6 Canned Heat Cook Book (The Best Of Canned Heat)	[G]	Liberty 11000
1/17/70	173	5		7 Vintage-Canned Heat	[E]	Janus 3009
9/12/70	59	19		8 Future Blues		Liberty 11002
2/27/71	73	16		9 Hooker 'N Heat		Liberty 35002 [2]
				CANNED HEAT & JOHN LEE HOOKER		
7/17/71	133	9		10 Canned Heat Concert (Recorded Live In Europe)	[L]	United Artists 5509
3/4/72	87	12		11 Historical Figures And Ancient Heads		United Artists 5557
4/21/73	209	4		12 The New Age		United Artists 049
2/2/74	217	5		13 One More River To Cross		Atlantic 7289

CANNIBAL AND THE HEADHUNTERS
Latino vocal group from Los Angeles, California: Frankie "Cannibal" Garcia, brothers Robert Jaramillo and Joe Jaramillo, and Richard Lopez. Garcia died on 1/21/1996 (age 49). Joe Jaramillo died on 5/24/2000 (age 51).

DEBUT	PEAK	WKS		Album Title	Catalog	Label & Number
5/8/65	141	4		1 Land Of 1000 Dances		Rampart 3302

CANNIBAL CORPSE
Death-metal band from Buffalo, New York: George Fisher (vocals), Jack Owen (guitar), Rob Barrett (guitar), Alex Webster (bass) and Paul Mazurkiewicz (drums).

DEBUT	PEAK	WKS		Album Title	Catalog	Label & Number
6/8/96	151	1		1 Vile		Metal Blade 14204
4/8/06	170	1		2 Kill		Metal Blade 14560
2/21/09	66	2		3 Evisceration Plague		Metal Blade 14718

CANNON, Ace
Born Hubert Cannon on 5/5/1934 in Grenada, Mississippi. Male saxophonist.

DEBUT	PEAK	WKS		Album Title	Catalog	Label & Number
5/19/62	44	17		1 "Tuff"-Sax	[I]	Hi 32007
12/18/65	23[X]	5		2 Christmas Cheers From Ace Cannon	[X]	Hi 32022
				Christmas charts: 23/'65, 64/'67		

CANNON, Freddy
Born Frederick Picariello on 12/4/1939 in Lynn, Massachusetts. Pop singer. Nickname "Boom Boom" came from big bass drum-sound on his records.

DEBUT	PEAK	WKS		Album Title	Catalog	Label & Number
9/1/62	101	5		1 Freddy Cannon At Palisades Park		Swan 507

~ ~ ~ ~ ~ ~ ~ ~ ~ ~ **NON-CHARTED ALBUMS** ~ ~ ~ ~ ~ ~ ~ ~ ~ ~ ~

1960 **The Explosive! Freddy Cannon**
1960 **Freddy Cannon Sings Happy Shades Of Blue**
1961 **Freddy Cannon's Solid Gold Hits!**
1963 **Freddie Cannon "Steps Out"**
1964 **Freddie Cannon** ["Abigail Beecher"]
1965 **Action!**
1966 **Freddy Cannon's Greatest Hits**

CANNON, Nick
Born on 10/8/1980 in San Diego, California. R&B singer/actor. Regular on TV's *All That* (1998-2001). Starred in the 2002 movie *Drumline*. Married **Mariah Carey** on 4/30/2008.

DEBUT	PEAK	WKS		Album Title	Catalog	Label & Number
12/27/03	83	10		1 Nick Cannon		Nick 48500

CANO, Eddie
Born on 6/6/1927 in Los Angeles, California. Died on 1/30/1988 (age 60). Latin-jazz pianist/bandleader.

DEBUT	PEAK	WKS		Album Title	Catalog	Label & Number
9/1/62	31	12		1 Eddie Cano At P.J.'s	[I]	Reprise 6030

CANTRELL, Blu
Born Tiffany Cobb on 10/1/1976 in Providence, Rhode Island. Female R&B singer.

DEBUT	PEAK	WKS		Album Title	Catalog	Label & Number
8/18/01	8	15	●	1 So Blu		Arista 14703
7/12/03	37	7		2 Bittersweet		Arista 52728

CANTRELL, Jerry
Born on 3/18/1966 in Tacoma, Washington. Rock singer/songwriter/guitarist. Member of **Alice In Chains**.

DEBUT	PEAK	WKS		Album Title	Catalog	Label & Number
4/25/98	28	14		1 Boggy Depot		Columbia 68147
7/6/02	33	5		2 Degradation Trip		Roadrunner 618451

CANTRELL, Lana
Born on 8/7/1943 in Sydney, Australia. Female singer/actress.

DEBUT	PEAK	WKS		Album Title	Catalog	Label & Number
11/16/68	166	2		1 Lana!		RCA Victor 4026

Billboard		R I A	ARTIST		
DEBUT	PEAK	WKS	Album Title	Catalog	Label & Number

CAPALDI, Jim
Born on 8/24/1944 in Evesham, Worcestershire, England. Died of cancer on 1/28/2005 (age 60). Rock singer/drummer. Member of **Traffic**.

3/4/72	82	11	1 Oh How We Danced		Island 9314
9/7/74	191	3	2 Whale Meat Again		Island 9254
2/14/76	193	4	3 Short Cut Draw Blood		Island 9336
5/21/83	91	12	4 Fierce Heart		Atlantic 80059
12/17/88+	183	8	5 Some Come Running		Island 91024

CAPITOLS, The
R&B trio from Detroit, Michigan: Sam George (vocals, drums), Donald Storball (guitar) and Richard McDougall (keyboards). George was fatally stabbed on 3/17/1982 (age 39).

7/23/66	95	12	1 Dance The Cool Jerk		Atco 190

CAPONE-N-NOREAGA
Rap duo from Queens, New York: Kiam "Capone" Holley and Victor "**Noreaga**" Santiago. Capone is a member of **QB Finest**.

7/5/97	21	10	1 The War Report		Penalty 3041
12/9/00	31	14	2 The Reunion		Tommy Boy 3110
4/4/09	136	1	3 Channel 10		SMC 284

CAPPADONNA
Born Darryl Hill on 9/18/1969 in Staten Island, New York. Male rapper.

4/11/98	3[1]	10	● 1 The Pillage		Razor Sharp 67947
4/21/01	51	4	2 The Yin And The Yang		Razor Sharp 69821

CAPTAIN & TENNILLE
Pop duo: Daryl "The Captain" Dragon (born on 8/27/1942 in Los Angeles, California) and his wife, Toni Tennille (born on 5/8/1943 in Montgomery, Alabama). Dragon is the son of noted conductor **Carmen Dragon**. Keyboardist with **The Beach Boys**; nicknamed "The Captain" by Mike Love. Married on 2/14/1974; duo had own TV show on ABC from 1976-77.

6/14/75	2[1]	104	● 1 Love Will Keep Us Together		A&M 3405
3/20/76	9	61	▲ 2 Song Of Joy		A&M 4570
4/23/77	18	15	● 3 Come In From The Rain		A&M 4700
12/10/77+	55	12	● 4 Captain & Tennille's Greatest Hits .... [G]		A&M 4667
7/22/78	131	30	5 Dream		A&M 4707
11/17/79+	23	24	● 6 Make Your Move		Casablanca 7188

CAPTAIN BEEFHEART
Born Don Van Vliet on 1/15/1941 in Glendale, California. Multi-octave rock singer. Collaborations with high school friend **Frank Zappa**. Backed by various personnel. Beefheart retired from music in 1986 to become a professional painter.

1/30/71	203	1	1 Lick My Decals Off, Baby		Straight 6420
2/19/72	131	9	2 The Spotlight Kid		Reprise 2050
12/23/72+	191	7	3 Clear Spot		Reprise 2115
4/27/74	192	4	4 Unconditionally Guaranteed		Mercury 709
			CAPTAIN BEEFHEART & THE MAGIC BAND (above 2)		
11/1/75	66	8	5 Bongo Fury .... [L]		DiscReet 2234
			FRANK ZAPPA/CAPTAIN BEEFHEART/THE MOTHERS		
			recorded on 5/20/1975 in Austin, Texas		
10/25/80	203	2	6 Doc At The Radar Station		Virgin 13148

~ ~ ~ ~ ~ ~ ~ ~ ~ ~ **NON-CHARTED ALBUM** ~ ~ ~ ~ ~ ~ ~ ~ ~ ~ ~

1969 **Trout Mask Replica**
RS500 #58

CAPTAIN BEYOND
Rock band formed in Los Angeles, California: Rod Evans (vocals; **Deep Purple**), Larry Rheinhart (guitar), Lee Dorman (bass; **Iron Butterfly**) and Bobby Caldwell (drums; **Armageddon**). Various personnel after first album. Evans left after second album; replaced by Willy Daffern.

8/19/72	134	12	1 Captain Beyond		Capricorn 0105
9/1/73	90	10	2 Sufficiently Breathless		Capricorn 0115
6/11/77	181	2	3 Dawn Explosion		Warner 3047

CAPTAIN SKY
Born Daryl Cameron on 7/10/1957 in Chicago, Illinois. R&B singer/songwriter/producer.

1/27/79	157	12	1 The Adventures Of Captain Sky		AVI 6042
10/25/80	210	1	2 Concerned Party #1		TEC 1202

CAPUANO, Carla
Born in Westfield, New Jersey. Aerobic dance instructor.

3/13/82	152	8	1 Aerobic Dance Hits, Volume One		Casablanca 7263

CARA, Irene
Born Irene Escalera on 3/18/1959 in the Bronx, New York. Dance singer/actress/pianist. Appeared in several movies and TV shows.

1/30/82	76	17	1 Anyone Can See		Network 60003
12/10/83+	77	37	2 What A Feelin'		Geffen 4021

Billboard			R I A A	ARTIST		
DEBUT	PEAK	WKS		Album Title	Catalog	Label & Number

CARAVAN
Rock band from Canterbury, England: Pye Hastings (vocals, guitar), Dave Sinclair (piano), Geoff Richardson (viola), Mike Wedgwood (bass) and Richard Coughlan (drums).

10/26/74	207	1		1 Caravan & The New Symphonia .... **[L]**		London 650
				recorded on 10/28/1973 at Theatre Royal, Drury Lane; The New Symphonia is a 39-piece orchestra		
8/23/75	124	10		2 Cunning Stunts		BTM 5000

CARAVELLES, The
Female pop vocal duo from England: Andrea Simpson (born on 9/12/1946) and Lois Wilkinson (born on 4/3/1944).

| 2/15/64 | 127 | 4 | | 1 You Don't Have To Be A Baby To Cry .... | | Smash 67044 |

CARBON LEAF
Pop-rock band from Richmond, Virginia: Barry Privett (vocals), Terry Clark (guitar), Carter Gravatt (keyboards), Jordan Medas (bass) and Scott Milstead (drums).

| 9/30/06 | 170 | 1 | | 1 Love, Loss, Hope, Repeat | | Vanguard 79799 |
| 6/6/09 | 136 | 1 | | 2 Nothing Rhymes With Woman .... | | Vanguard 79852 |

CARDIGANS, The
Pop-rock band from Jonkoping, Sweden: Nina Persson (vocals), Peter Svensson (guitar), Lars-Olof Johansson (keyboards), Magnus Sveningsson (bass) and Bengt Lagersburg (drums).

| 1/4/97 | 35 | 27 | ▲ | 1 First Band On The Moon .... | | Stockholm 533117 |
| 11/21/98 | 151 | 1 | | 2 Gran Turismo .... | | Stockholm 559081 |

CAREY, Mariah   1990s: #2 / 2000s: #40 / All-Time: #77
Born on 3/27/1970 in Greenlawn, Long Island, New York. Singer/songwriter/producer. Daughter of former opera singer Patricia Carey. Mariah sang backup for **Brenda K. Starr**. Married to Tommy Mottola, president of Sony Music Entertainment, from 1993-98. Starred in the 2001 movie *Glitter*. Married **Nick Cannon** on 4/30/2008.
      AWARD: Grammy: Best New Artist 1990

6/30/90+	❶[11]	113	▲[9]	1 Mariah Carey	Cat:#30/26	Columbia 45202
10/5/91	4	54	▲[4]	2 Emotions		Columbia 47980
6/20/92	3[5]	57	▲[3]	3 MTV Unplugged EP	**[EP-L]**	Columbia 52758
				recorded on 3/16/1992		
9/18/93	❶[8]	128	▲[10]	4 Music Box		Columbia 53205
10/21/95	❶[6]	81	▲[9]	5 Daydream	Cat:#45/1	Columbia 66700
10/4/97	❶[1]	55	▲[5]	6 Butterfly		Columbia 67835
11/20/99	2[2]	35	▲[3]	7 Rainbow		Columbia 63800
9/29/01	7	12	▲	8 Glitter	**[S]**	Virgin 10797
12/21/02	3[1]	22	▲	9 Charmbracelet		Island 063467
4/30/05	❶[2]	74	▲[6]	10 The Emancipation Of Mimi	Cat:#15/2	Island 003943
				Grammy: Contemporary R&B Album		
5/3/08	❶[2]	27	▲	11 E=MC2		Island 010272
10/17/09	3[1]	27	●	12 Memoirs Of An Imperfect Angel		Island 013226
				CHRISTMAS ALBUMS:		
11/19/94	3[1]	13	▲[5]	13 Merry Christmas	Cat:❶[2]/98	Columbia 64222
				Christmas charts: 1/'94, 3/'95, 3/'96, 7/'97, 7/'98, 14/'99, 19/'00, 20/'01, 19/'02, 17/'03, 18/'04, 11/'05, 18/'06, 27/'07, 24/'08, 39/'09		
12/19/09	133	3		14 Merry Christmas .... **[R]**		Columbia 64222
				GREATEST HITS & COMPILATIONS:		
12/5/98	4	62	▲[5]	15 #1's	Cat:#13/3	Columbia 69670
12/22/01	52	11	▲	16 Greatest Hits .... Cat:#5/3		Columbia 85960 [2]
11/1/03	26	5		17 The Remixes		Columbia 87154 [2]
2/7/09	10	9		18 The Ballads		Columbia 41303

CAREY, Tony
Born on 10/16/1952 in Watsonville, California. Rock singer/songwriter/keyboardist. Former member of **Rainbow** and **Planet P**.

| 4/2/83 | 167 | 9 | | 1 Tony Carey [I Won't Be Home Tonight] .... | | Rocshire 0001 |
| 3/31/84 | 60 | 24 | | 2 Some Tough City .... | | MCA 5464 |

CARGILL, Henson
Born on 2/5/1941 in Oklahoma City, Oklahoma. Died on 3/24/2007 (age 66). Country singer/guitarist.

| 3/23/68 | 179 | 2 | | 1 Skip A Rope .... | | Monument 18094 |

CARIBOU
Born Daniel Snaith in 1978 in London, Ontario, Canada. Electronic singer/songwriter/musician.

| 9/8/07 | 193 | 1 | | 1 Andorra .... | | Merge 308 |

CARLILE, Brandi
Born on 6/1/1981 in Ravensdale, Washington. White female singer/songwriter/guitarist.

| 4/21/07 | 41 | 25 | | 1 The Story .... | | Columbia 00802 |
| 10/24/09 | 26 | 6 | | 2 Give Up The Ghost .... | | Columbia 24740 |

Billboard			R I A A	ARTIST		
DEBUT	PEAK	WKS		Album Title	Catalog	Label & Number

CARLIN, George
Born on 5/12/1937 in Manhattan, New York. Died of heart failure on 6/22/2008 (age 71). Stand-up comedian/actor. Appeared in several movies. Starred in own TV series.

2/19/72	13	35	●	1 FM & AM .... [C]		Little David 7214
				Grammy: Comedy Album		
10/14/72	22	35	●	2 Class Clown .... Cat:#42/1 [C]		Little David 1004
				Grammy: Hall of Fame		
11/10/73	35	21	●	3 Occupation: Foole... [C]		Little David 1005
12/7/74+	19	17	●	4 Toledo Window Box .... [C]		Little David 3003
11/8/75+	34	15		5 An Evening With Wally Londo Featuring Bill Slaszo .... [C]		Little David 1008
5/21/77	90	9		6 On The Road .... [C]		Little David 1075
1/6/79	112	8		7 Indecent Exposure (Some Of The Best Of George Carlin) .... [C-K]		Little David 1076
12/19/81+	145	13		8 A Place For My Stuff! .... [C]		Atlantic 19326
8/4/84	136	11		9 Carlin On Campus .... [C]		Eardrum 1001

CARLISLE, Belinda
Born on 8/17/1958 in Hollywood, California. Lead singer of the **Go-Go's**. Married Morgan Mason (son of actor James Mason) on 4/12/1986.

6/7/86	13	34	●	1 Belinda		I.R.S. 5741
10/24/87+	13	51	▲	2 Heaven On Earth		MCA 42080
10/21/89	37	25	●	3 Runaway Horses		MCA 6339

CARLISLE, Bob
Born on 9/29/1956 in Santa Ana, California. Contemporary Christian singer/songwriter/guitarist.

5/10/97	❶²	39	▲²	1 Butterfly Kisses (Shades Of Grace)	Cat:#14/1	Jive 41613
10/17/98	191	2		2 Stories From The Heart		Benson 2312

CARLOS, Walter
Born on 11/14/1939 in Pawtucket, Rhode Island. Classical musician who performs on the Moog Synthesizer. Had a sex change and known as Wendy Carlos by 1982.

1/18/69	10	56	●	1 Switched-On Bach .... [I]		Columbia 7194
				Grammys: Classical Album / Hall of Fame ★ NRR		
1/3/70	199	2		2 The Well-Tempered Synthesizer .... [I]		Columbia 7286
7/8/72	146	9		3 Walter Carlos' Clockwork Orange .... [I]		Columbia 31480
7/8/72	168	7		4 Sonic Seasonings .... [I]		Columbia 31234 [2]
12/13/75	201	4		5 By Request .... [I]		Columbia 32088

CARLTON, Carl
Born on 10/22/1952 in Detroit, Michigan. R&B singer/songwriter.

1/18/75	132	7		1 Everlasting Love		ABC 857
8/8/81	34	19		2 Carl Carlton		20th Century 628
10/23/82	133	7		3 The Bad C.C.		RCA Victor 4425

CARLTON, Larry
Born on 3/2/1948 in Torrance, California. Top session guitarist. Joined **Fourplay** in 1997.

8/26/78	174	10		1 Larry Carlton .... [I]		Warner 3221
9/6/80	138	8		2 Strikes Twice .... [I]		Warner 3380
1/30/82	99	16		3 Sleepwalk .... [I]		Warner 3635
6/18/83	126	11		4 Friends .... [I]		Warner 23834
6/28/86	141	11		5 Alone/But Never Alone .... [I]		MCA 5689
8/1/87	180	6		6 Discovery .... [I]		MCA 42003
6/10/89	126	8		7 On Solid Ground .... [I]		MCA 6237
6/30/90	156	5		8 Collection .... [I-K]		GRP 9611

CARLTON, Vanessa
Born on 8/16/1980 in Milford, Pennsylvania. Adult Contemporary singer/songwriter/pianist.

5/18/02	5	51	▲	1 Be Not Nobody		A&M 493307
11/27/04	33	7		2 Harmonium		A&M 003480
10/27/07	44	3		3 Heroes & Thieves		The Inc. 009991

CARMAN
Born Carman Licciardello on 1/19/1956 in Trenton, New Jersey. Male Christian singer.

11/18/95	45	8	●	1 R.I.O.T. (Righteous Invasion Of Truth)		Sparrow 1422
4/19/97	102	12	●	2 I Surrender All - 30 Classic Hymns..		Sparrow 51565
2/14/98	94	8		3 Mission 3:16		Sparrow 51640
4/10/99	179	4		4 Passion For Praise Volume One		Sparrow 51704
11/11/00	53	7	●	5 Heart Of A Champion: A Collection Of 30 Hits .... [K]		Sparrow 51766 [2]

CARMEN, Eric
Born on 8/11/1949 in Cleveland, Ohio. Pop-rock singer/songwriter/pianist. Lead singer of the **Raspberries** from 1970-74.

11/15/75+	21	51	●	1 Eric Carmen		Arista 4057
9/10/77	45	13		2 Boats Against The Current...		Arista 4124
10/28/78	137	12		3 Change Of Heart		Arista 4184
6/28/80	160	5		4 Tonight You're Mine		Arista 9513
2/9/85	128	10		5 Eric Carmen		Geffen 24042
6/11/88	59	20		6 The Best Of Eric Carmen .... [G]		Arista 8547

CARN, Jean
Born Sarah Jean Perkins on 3/15/1947 in Columbus, Georgia; raised in Atlanta, Georgia. Female R&B session singer.

DEBUT	PEAK	WKS			Catalog	Label & Number
2/19/77	122	10		1 Jean Carn		Philadelphia Int'l. 34394
8/15/81	176	3		2 Sweet And Wonderful		TSOP 36775
7/17/82	210	1		3 Trust Me		Motown 6010
9/6/86	162	6		4 Closer Than Close		Omni 90492
				JEAN CARNE		

CARNES, Kim
Born on 7/20/1945 in Los Angeles, California. Pop singer/songwriter/pianist. Member of **The New Christy Minstrels** with husband/co-writer Dave Ellingson.

3/31/79	206	3		1 St. Vincent's Court		EMI America 17004
7/5/80	57	17		2 Romance Dance		EMI America 17030
5/2/81	❶⁴	52	▲	3 Mistaken Identity		EMI America 17052
9/25/82	49	22		4 Voyeur		EMI America 17078
11/19/83	97	16		5 Cafe Racers		EMI America 17106
6/29/85	48	14		6 Barking At Airplanes		EMI America 17159
6/14/86	116	7		7 Light House		EMI America 17198

CARNIVAL, The
Band of musicians that formerly worked with **Sergio Mendes**: Janis Hansen (vocals), Jose Soares (percussion), Bob Matthews (bass) and Joao Palma (drums).

12/6/69	191	2		1 The Carnival		World Pacific 21894

CAROLINA LIAR
Rock band formed in Los Angeles, California: Chad Wolf (vocals; born in South Carolina), with Swedish natives Jim Gandara (guitar), Rick Goransson (guitar), Johan Carlsson (keyboards), Erik Haager (bass) and Max Grahn (drums).

5/2/09	140	11		1 Coming To Terms		Atlantic 474364

CARPENTER, Mary Chapin
Born on 2/21/1958 in Princeton, New Jersey. Country singer/songwriter/guitarist.

AWARD: CMA: Female Vocalist 1992 & 1993

12/9/89+	183	10	●	1 State Of The Heart		Columbia 44228
11/3/90+	70	52	▲	2 Shooting Straight In The Dark		Columbia 46077
7/18/92	31	134	▲⁵	3 Come On Come On		Columbia 48881
10/22/94	10	40	▲²	4 Stones In The Road		Columbia 64327
				Grammy: Country Album		
11/9/96	20	19	●	5 A Place In The World		Columbia 67501
6/12/99	43	17	●	6 Party Doll And Other Favorites [K]		Columbia 68751
6/16/01	52	10		7 Time*Sex*Love*		Columbia 85176
5/15/04	50	5		8 Between Here And Gone		Columbia 86619
3/24/07	59	5		9 The Calling		Zoe 431111
12/20/08	155	2		10 Come Darkness, Come Light: Twelve Songs Of Christmas [X]		Zoe 431123
				Christmas chart: 7/'08		

CARPENTERS   **All-Time: #217**
Brother-sister duo originally from New Haven, Connecticut: Richard Carpenter (born on 10/15/1946) and Karen Carpenter (born 3/2/1950; died of heart failure due to anorexia nervosa on 2/4/1983, age 32). Moved to Downey, California, in 1963. Richard played piano from age nine. Karen played drums in group with Richard and bass player Wes Jacobs in 1965. The trio recorded for RCA in 1966. After a period with the band Spectrum, the Carpenters recorded as a duo for A&M in 1969. Also see **Various Artists Compilations: If I Were A Carpenter.**

AWARD: Grammy: Best New Artist 1970

3/6/71	150	16		1 Ticket To Ride		A&M 4205
				first released in 1969 as *Offering*		
9/19/70	2¹	87	▲²	2 Close To You		A&M 4271
				RS500 #175		
6/5/71	2²	59	▲⁴	3 Carpenters		A&M 3502
				Grammy: Pop Vocal Duo		
				also known among fans as *The Tan Album*		
7/8/72	4	41	▲³	4 A Song For You		A&M 3511
6/2/73	2¹	41	▲²	5 Now & Then		A&M 3519
6/28/75	13	18	▲	6 Horizon		A&M 4530
7/10/76	33	16	●	7 A Kind Of Hush		A&M 4581
10/22/77	49	18		8 Passage		A&M 4703
7/4/81	52	15		9 Made In America		A&M 3723
11/19/83+	46	19	●	10 Voice Of The Heart		A&M 4954
				CHRISTMAS ALBUMS:		
12/9/78+	145	7	▲	11 Christmas Portrait		A&M 4726
				also released on A&M 3210; Christmas charts: 5/'83, 2/'84, 7/'85, 7/'87, 7/'88, 8/'89		
1/5/85	190	1	●	12 An Old-Fashioned Christmas	Cat:#46/1	A&M 3270
				Christmas charts: 29/'87, 29/'88, 25/'90		
12/22/90+	159	3		13 Christmas Portrait – The Special Edition	Cat:#5/70 [R]	A&M 5173
				expanded edition of #10 above with new sequencing plus some substituted songs; Christmas charts: 8/'90, 5/'91, 10/'92, 18/'93, 20/'94, 21/'95, 24/'96, 19/'97, 40/'98, 36/'00, 32/'01, 34/'02, 47/'05, 41/'06, 41/'07, 43/'08, 41/'09		
12/5/09	152	4		14 Christmas Portrait – The Special Edition [R]		A&M 5173

CARPENTERS — cont'd
GREATEST HITS & COMPILATIONS:

12/1/73+	**❶**[1]	49	▲[7] 15 The Singles 1969-1973	Cat:#48/1	A&M 3601
5/25/85	144	8	▲[2] 16 Yesterday Once More		A&M 6601 [2]
4/18/98	106	25	● 17 Love Songs		A&M 540838
2/28/04	101	10	18 Carpenters Gold: 35th Anniversary Edition		A&M 001777 [2]

CARR, Cathy
Born Angela Catherine Cordovano on 6/28/1936 in the Bronx, New York. Died on 11/22/1988 (age 52). Pop singer.

~ ~ ~ ~ ~ ~ ~ ~ ~ ~ **NON-CHARTED ALBUM** ~ ~ ~ ~ ~ ~ ~ ~ ~ ~
1956 Ivory Tower

CARR, Kurt, & The Kurt Carr Singers
Born in Hartford, Connecticut. Gospel singer/songwriter/producer.

4/13/02	46[C]	1	● 1 Awesome Wonder .... [L]		Gospo Centric 70016
4/9/05	109	6	2 One Church .... [L]		Gospo Centric 70058
			KURT CARR PROJECT		
11/15/08	62	3	3 Just The Beginning		KCG 29753 [2]

CARR, Vikki
Born Florencia Martinez Cardona on 7/19/1941 in El Paso, Texas. Adult Contemporary singer. Regular on **Ray Anthony**'s TV show.

7/18/64	114	4	1 Discovery!		Liberty 7354
10/21/67+	12	47	2 It Must Be Him		Liberty 7533
3/23/68	63	16	3 Vikki!		Liberty 7548
3/29/69	29	34	4 For Once In My Life .... [L]		Liberty 7604
			recorded at the Persian Room in New York City		
5/9/70	111	8	5 Nashville by Carr		Liberty 11001
7/10/71	60	14	6 Vikki Carr's Love Story		Columbia 30662
1/8/72	118	4	7 Superstar		Columbia 31040
6/24/72	146	12	8 The First Time Ever (I Saw Your Face)		Columbia 31453
9/9/72	106	25	9 En Espanol .... [F]		Columbia 31470
6/23/73	142	7	10 Ms. America		Columbia 32251
11/24/73	172	7	11 Live At The Greek Theatre .... [L]		Columbia 32656 [2]
9/28/74	155	5	12 One Hell Of A Woman		Columbia 32860
3/1/75	203	3	13 Hoy (Today) .... [F]		Columbia 33340

CARRACK, Paul
Born on 4/22/1951 in Sheffield, Yorkshire, England. Pop-rock singer/guitarist/keyboardist. Lead singer of **Ace**, **Squeeze** and **Mike + The Mechanics**.

9/11/82	78	14	1 Suburban Voodoo		Epic 38161
11/21/87+	67	31	2 One Good Reason		Chrysalis 41578
11/11/89	120	18	3 Groove Approved		Chrysalis 21709

CARRADINE, Keith
Born on 8/8/1949 in San Mateo, California. Singer/guitarist/actor. Son of actor John Carradine. Half-brother of actor David Carradine. Acted in several movies.

6/26/76	61	17	1 I'm Easy		Asylum 1066

CARRERAS, Jose
Born on 12/5/1946 in Barcelona, Spain. Operatic tenor. Member of **The Three Tenors**.

12/18/93	154	3	1 Christmas In Vienna .... [X-L]		Sony Classical 53358
			PLACIDO DOMINGO / DIANA ROSS / JOSE CARRERAS		
			recorded on 12/23/1992 at the Rathaus in Vienna, Austria		
12/21/96	196	2	2 A Celebration Of Christmas .... [X-L]		Elektra 62000
			JOSE CARRERAS / NATALIE COLE / PLACIDO DOMINGO		
			recorded on 12/23/1995 at the Austria Center in Vienna		

CARRINGTON, Rodney
Born on 10/19/1968 in Longview, Texas. Country comedian. Starred in the TV sitcom *Rodney*.

9/2/00	153	3	● 1 Morning Wood .... [C]		Capitol 24827
3/1/03	82	7	2 Nut Sack .... [C]		Capitol 36579
3/13/04	112	4	● 3 Greatest Hits .... [C-K]		Capitol 94164 [2]
4/21/07	68	6	4 King Of The Mountains .... [C]		Capitol 63998
7/4/09	76	3	5 El Nino Loco .... [N]		Capitol 06288

CARRINGTON, Terri Lyne
Born on 8/4/1965 in Medford, Massachusetts. Female jazz drummer. Member of the house band on TV's *The Arsenio Hall Show* until June 1989.

4/29/89	169	7	1 Real Life Story .... [I]		Forecast 837697

CARROLL, David, And His Orchestra
Born Rodell Schreier on 10/15/1913 in Chicago, Illinois. Died on 3/22/2008 (age 94). Arranger/conductor.

6/1/59	21	6	1 Let's Dance		Mercury 60001
1/11/60	6	30	2 Let's Dance Again		Mercury 60152

Billboard			R I A A	ARTIST Album Title	Catalog	Label & Number
DEBUT	**PEAK**	**WKS**				
				CARROLL, Jason Michael Born on 6/13/1978 in Houston, Texas; raised in Franklinton, North Carolina. Country singer/songwriter.		
2/24/07	8	38		1 Waitin' In The Country		Arista Nashville 01487
5/16/09	28	6		2 Growing Up Is Getting Old		Arista Nashville 26910
				CARROLL, Jim, Band Born on 8/1/1950 in Brooklyn, New York. Died of a heart attack on 9/11/2009 (age 59). Poet/rock singer. His band included Brian Linsley and Terrell Winn (guitars), Steve Linsley (bass) and Wayne Woods (drums). The 1995 movie *The Basketball Diaries* was based on Carroll's autobiographical book.		
11/15/80+	73	23		1 Catholic Boy		Atco 132
5/22/82	156	7		2 Dry Dreams		Atco 145
3/10/84	207	2		3 I Write Your Name		Atlantic 80123
				CARS, The **All-Time: #440** Rock and roll band from Boston, Massachusetts: **Ric Ocasek** (vocals, guitar; born on 3/23/1949), **Benjamin Orr** (bass, vocals; born on 8/9/1947; died on 10/3/2000, age 53), **Elliot Easton** (guitar; born on 12/18/1953), Greg Hawkes (keyboards; born on 3/15/1950) and David Robinson (drums; born on 1/2/1953). Robinson was a member of **The Modern Lovers**.		
7/1/78+	18	139	▲6	1 The Cars... **Cat:#24/25** RS500 #282		Elektra 135
6/30/79	3⁴	62	▲4	2 Candy-O		Elektra 507
9/6/80	5	28	▲	3 Panorama		Elektra 514
11/28/81	9	41	▲2	4 Shake It Up		Elektra 567
4/7/84	3¹	69	▲4	5 Heartbeat City		Elektra 60296
11/23/85	12	39	▲6	6 The Cars Greatest Hits .... **Cat:#39/1** **[G]**		Elektra 60464
9/12/87	26	23	●	7 Door To Door		Elektra 60747
3/9/02	144	1		8 Complete Greatest Hits .... **[G]**		Elektra 78288
6/24/06	193	1		9 It's Alive!.. **[L]**		Eleven Seven 051
				THE NEW CARS		
4/11/09	49ᶜ	1		10 Rhino HiFive: The Cars .... **[EP-K]**		Elektra digital
				CARSON, Jeff Born Jeff Herndon on 12/16/1964 in Tulsa, Oklahoma; raised in Gravette, Arkansas. Country singer/songwriter/guitarist.		
8/12/95	152	7		1 Jeff Carson		MCG/Curb 77744
				CARTEL Rock band from Atlanta, Georgia: Will Pugh (vocals), Joe Pepper (guitar), Nic Hudson (guitar), Jeff Lett (bass) and Kevin Sanders (drums).		
7/1/06	140	14		1 Chroma..		Epic 83850
9/8/07	20	5		2 Cartel		Militia Group 09835
11/7/09	59	2		3 Cycles		Wind-Up 13161
				CARTER, Aaron Born on 12/7/1987 in Tampa, Florida. White teen rapper. Younger brother of **Nick Carter** of the **Backstreet Boys**. Was a contestant on the 2009 TV show *Dancing With The Stars*.		
10/14/00+	4	67	▲3	1 Aaron's Party (Come Get It)		Jive 41708
8/25/01	7	33	▲	2 Oh Aaron		Jive 41768
9/21/02	18	17		3 Another Earthquake		Jive 41818
				CARTER, Betty Born Lillie Mae Jones on 5/16/1930 in Flint, Michigan. Died of cancer on 9/26/1998 (age 68). Acclaimed jazz singer. With Lionel Hampton's band from 1948-51.		
9/4/61	52	15		1 Ray Charles & Betty Carter		ABC-Paramount 385
				CARTER, Carlene Born Rebecca Carlene Smith on 9/26/1955 in Madison, Tennessee. Country singer/songwriter/guitarist. Daughter of country singers **June Carter** and Carl Smith. Married to **Nick Lowe** from 1979-90.		
10/20/79	204	4		1 Two Sides To Every Woman		Warner 3375
10/4/80	139	6		2 Musical Shapes		Warner 3465
8/28/93	196	1		3 Little Love Letters		Giant 24499
				CARTER, Clarence Born on 1/14/1936 in Montgomery, Alabama. R&B singer/guitarist. Blind since age one. Married for a time to **Candi Staton**.		
12/7/68	200	2		1 This Is Clarence Carter		Atlantic 8192
4/5/69	169	4		2 The Dynamic Clarence Carter		Atlantic 8199
8/16/69	138	3		3 Testifyin'...		Atlantic 8238
9/26/70	44	12		4 Patches		Atlantic 8267
5/22/71	103	10		5 The Best Of Clarence Carter .... **[G]**		Atlantic 8282
2/28/81	189	3		6 Let's Burn..		Venture 1005
				CARTER, Deana Born on 1/4/1966 in Nashville, Tennessee. Country singer/songwriter.		
9/28/96+	10	86	▲5	1 Did I Shave My Legs For This?		Capitol 37514
11/7/98	57	12	●	2 Everything's Gonna Be Alright		Capitol 21142
4/5/03	58	3		3 I'm Just A Girl		Arista Nashville 67054
3/26/05	150	1		4 The Story Of My Life		Vanguard 79765

CARTER, June
Born Valerie June Carter on 6/23/1929 in Maces Springs, Virginia. Died of heart failure on 5/15/2003 (age 73). Country singer/songwriter. Member of The Carter Family. Married to **Carl Smith** from 1952-56; their daughter is **Carlene Carter**. Worked with **Elvis Presley**, then joined the **Johnny Cash** road show in 1961. Married Cash on 3/1/1968. Reese Witherspoon won the Best Actress Oscar for her portrayal of Carter in the 2005 movie *Walk The Line*.

AWARD: CMA: Vocal Group (w/ Johnny Cash) 1969

| 10/7/67 | 194 | 3 | | 1 Carryin' On With Johnny Cash & June Carter | | Columbia 2728 / 9528 |
| 3/18/06 | 126 | 4 | | 2 16 Biggest Hits ..... [G] | | Legacy 77087 |

JOHNNY CASH & JUNE CARTER (above 2)

CARTER, Mel
Born on 4/22/1939 in Cincinnati, Ohio. Black Adult Contemporary singer/actor. Appeared in several TV shows in the 1970s.

| 9/18/65 | 62 | 12 | | 1 Hold Me, Thrill Me, Kiss Me | | Imperial 12289 |
| 10/1/66 | 81 | 11 | | 2 Easy Listening | | Imperial 12319 |

~ ~ ~ ~ ~ ~ ~ ~ ~ ~ **NON-CHARTED ALBUM** ~ ~ ~ ~ ~ ~ ~ ~ ~ ~ ~
1963 **When A Boy Falls In Love**

CARTER, Nick
Born on 1/28/1980 in Jamestown, New York; raised in Tampa, Florida. Member of the **Backstreet Boys**. Older brother of **Aaron Carter**.

| 11/16/02 | 17 | 9 | ● | 1 Now Or Never | | Jive 41828 |

CARTER, Regina
Born on 8/6/1966 in Detroit, Michigan. Black female classical violinist.

| 5/31/03 | 189 | 1 | | 1 Paganini: After A Dream ..... [I] | | Verve 065554 |

CARTER, Ron
Born on 5/4/1937 in Ferndale, Michigan. Jazz bassist. Also see **V.S.O.P.**

3/12/77	193	1		1 Pastels ..... [I]		Milestone 9073
10/21/78	178	3		2 A Song For You ..... [I]		Milestone 9086
7/7/79	202	6		3 Parade ..... [I]		Milestone 9088

CARTER, Valerie
Born in 1954 in Brooklyn, New York. White session singer.

| 4/2/77 | 182 | 5 | | 1 Just A Stone's Throw Away | | Columbia 34155 |

CARTWRIGHT, Lionel
Born on 2/10/1960 in Gallipolis, Ohio; raised in West Virginia. Country singer/actor.

| 10/5/91 | 170 | 2 | | 1 Chasin' The Sun | | MCA 10307 |

CASABLANCAS, Julian
Born on 8/23/1978 in Manhattan, New York. Rock singer/songwriter. Lead singer of **The Strokes**.

| 11/21/09 | 35 | 2 | | 1 Phrazes For The Young | | Cult 48421 |

CASA DE LEONES
Reggaeton group from Puerto Rico: Miguel DeJesus, Jaime Borges, Hector Padilla, Randy Ortiz and Joel Munoz.

| 7/7/07 | 126 | 2 | | 1 Los Leones ..... [F] | | Warner Latina 232444 |

CASCADA
Dance trio formed in Germany: fronted by female vocalist Natalie Horler (born on 9/23/1981 in Bonn, Germany), with male musicians/producers Yann "Yanou" Peifer and Manuel "DJ Manian" Reuter. Group name is Spanish for "waterfall."

3/11/06	67	16		1 Everytime We Touch		Robbins 75064
3/22/08	70	3		2 Perfect Day		Robbins 75079
9/5/09	155	1		3 Evacuate The Dancefloor		Robbins 75084

CASCADES, The
Pop band from San Diego, California: John Gummoe (vocals, guitar), Eddie Snyder (piano), David Wilson (sax), David Stevens (bass) and David Zabo (drums). Wilson died of cancer on 11/14/2000 (age 63).

| 4/20/63 | 111 | 10 | | 1 Rhythm Of The Rain | | Valiant 405 |

CASE
Born Casey Woodard on 1/10/1973 in Harlem, New York. Male R&B singer/songwriter.

8/31/96	42	6		1 Case		Def Jam 533134
5/8/99	33	28	●	2 Personal Conversation		Def Jam 538871
5/12/01	5	17	●	3 Open Letter		Def Soul 548626
4/11/09	111	2		4 The Rose Experience		Indigo Blue 10191

CASE, Neko
Born on 9/8/1970 in Alexandria, Virginia; raised in Tacoma, Washington. Female singer/songwriter/guitarist. Lead singer of **The New Pornographers**.

| 3/25/06 | 54 | 7 | | 1 Fox Confessor Brings The Flood | | Anti 86777 |
| 3/21/09 | 3[1] | 13 | | 2 Middle Cyclone | | Anti 86973 |

CASEY, Marty, & Lovehammers
Born on 9/26/1973 in Hickory Hills, Illinois. Pop-rock singer/songwriter/guitarist. Finished in second place on the TV reality series *Rock Star: INXS*. Lovehammers: brothers Dino (bass) and Bobby (drums) Kourelis, with Billy Sawilchik (guitar).

| 2/11/06 | 67 | 2 | | 1 Marty Casey & Lovehammers | | Burnett 76873 |

CASH, Johnny   1960s: #40 / All-Time: #45

Born J.R. Cash on 2/26/1932 in Kingsland, Arkansas (later adopted the name John Ray). Died of diabetes on 9/12/2003 (age 71). Country singer/songwriter/guitarist. Formed trio with Luther Perkins (guitar) and Marshall Grant (bass) in 1955. Hosted own TV show for ABC from 1969-71. Worked with **June Carter** from 1961; married her in March 1968. Father of **Rosanne Cash**. Joaquin Phoenix portrayed Cash in the 2005 movie *Walk The Line*. Also see **Highwaymen** and **Various Artists Compilations:** *Kindred Spirits: A Tribute To Johnny Cash*.

AWARDS: Grammys: Legend 1991 / Lifetime Achievement 1999 ★ R&R Hall of Fame: 1992 ★ C&W Hall of Fame: 1980 ★ CMA: Vocal Group (w/ June Carter) 1969 / Male Vocalist 1969 / Entertainer 1969 ★ RIAA: American Music Legend ★ OPRY: 1956

DEBUT	PEAK	WKS			Album Title	Catalog	Label & Number
12/8/58	19	11		1	The Fabulous Johnny Cash		Columbia 1253 / 8122
3/16/63	80	15		2	Blood, Sweat & Tears		Columbia 1930 / 8730
7/25/64	53	17	●	3	I Walk The Line		Columbia 2190 / 8990
					includes a new recording of "I Walk The Line" and 6 other "Sun" recordings		
11/7/64	47	13		4	Bitter Tears (Ballads Of The American Indian)		Columbia 2248 / 9048
3/20/65	49	13		5	Orange Blossom Special		Columbia 2309 / 9109
7/9/66	88	9		6	Everybody Loves A Nut	[N]	Columbia 2492 / 9292
10/7/67	194	3		7	Carryin' On With Johnny Cash & June Carter		Columbia 2728 / 9528
					JOHNNY CASH & JUNE CARTER		
2/14/70	6	30	●	8	Hello, I'm Johnny Cash		Columbia 9943
6/26/71	56	12		9	Man In Black		Columbia 30550
4/29/72	112	9		10	A Thing Called Love		Columbia 31332
9/16/72	176	7		11	Johnny Cash: America (A 200-Year Salute In Story And Song)		Columbia 31645
2/24/73	188	4		12	Any Old Wind That Blows		Columbia 32091
7/17/76	185	2		13	One Piece At A Time		Columbia 34193
7/4/81	201	4		14	The Baron		Columbia 37179
6/21/86	87	12		15	Class Of '55 (Memphis Rock & Roll Homecoming)	Cat:#13/2	America Smash 830002
					CARL PERKINS / JERRY LEE LEWIS / ROY ORBISON / JOHNNY CASH		
5/14/94	110	9		16	American Recordings		American 45520
					Grammy: Contemporary Folk Album ★ RS500 #364		
11/23/96	170	2		17	Unchained		American 43097
					Grammy: Country Album		
11/4/00	88	4		18	American III: Solitary Man		American 69691
11/23/02+	22	62	▲	19	American IV: The Man Comes Around	Cat:#24/14	American 063339
					CMA: Album of the Year		
7/22/06	❶¹	17	●	20	American V: A Hundred Highways		American 002769
					CHRISTMAS ALBUMS:		
12/13/69	7ˣ	5		21	The Christmas Spirit		Columbia 2117 / 8917
					first released in 1963; Christmas charts: 7/'69, 14/'70		
1/15/05	34ˣ	1		22	Christmas With Johnny Cash	[K]	Legacy 90701
1/13/07	39ˣ	1		23	Country Christmas	[K]	LaserLight 32833
					GREATEST HITS & COMPILATIONS:		
7/27/63	26	68	●	24	Ring Of Fire (The Best Of Johnny Cash)		Columbia 2053 / 8853
					not a "best of" album, but a selection of songs from previous Columbia albums		
7/22/67+	82	71	▲²	25	Johnny Cash's Greatest Hits, Volume 1		Columbia 2678 / 9478
9/27/69	95	13		26	Original Golden Hits, Volume I		Sun 100
9/27/69	98	8		27	Original Golden Hits, Volume II		Sun 101
10/11/69	186	2		28	Johnny Cash		Harmony 11342
11/29/69	164	6		29	Get Rhythm		Sun 105
12/27/69	197	2		30	Story Songs Of The Trains And Rivers		Sun 104
5/16/70	186	3		31	The Singing Story Teller		Sun 115
					all Sun albums were recorded from 1955-58		
6/6/70	54	34	●	32	The World Of Johnny Cash		Columbia 29 [2]
10/23/71	94	8	▲	33	The Johnny Cash Collection (His Greatest Hits, Volume II)		Columbia 30887
5/8/99	185	1	▲²	34	16 Biggest Hits	Cat:❶²⁶/203	Columbia 69739
9/27/03+	5ᶜ	36	▲	35	Super Hits		Columbia 66773
9/27/03	102	10	▲	36	The Essential Johnny Cash	Cat:#3/37	Legacy 86290 [2]
12/17/05	173	4	●	37	The Legend		Legacy 92802 [4]
11/12/05+	5	78	▲²	38	The Legend Of Johnny Cash		Legacy 005288
12/9/06	144	5		39	The Legend Of Johnny Cash: Vol. II		Legacy 008056
3/18/06	126	4		40	16 Biggest Hits		Legacy 77087
					JOHNNY CASH & JUNE CARTER		
6/10/06	108	3		41	Personal File		Legacy 94265 [2]
2/24/07	109	3		42	JC: Johnny Cash		Madacy 52550 [2]
					LIVE ALBUMS:		
6/15/68	13	122	▲³	43	Johnny Cash At Folsom Prison	Cat:#2¹/67	Columbia 9639
					CMA: Album of the Year ★ RS500: #88 ★ NRR		
7/5/69	❶⁴	70	▲³	44	Johnny Cash At San Quentin	Cat:#26/2	Columbia 9827
					Grammy: Hall of Fame ★ CMA: Album of the Year		
12/27/69+	181	4		45	Showtime	[K]	Sun 106
					live effects dubbed in		
11/14/70	44	18	●	46	The Johnny Cash Show		Columbia 30100
					recorded at the *Grand Ole Opry* with **The Statler Brothers** and The Carter Family		

Billboard DEBUT	PEAK	WKS	R I A A	ARTIST / Album Title	Catalog	Label & Number

CASH, Johnny — cont'd

5/22/82	205	3		47 The Survivors		Columbia 37961
				JOHNNY CASH / JERRY LEE LEWIS / CARL PERKINS		
				recorded on 4/23/1981 at the Sporthalle Boeblingen in Stuttgart, West Germany		
6/27/98	150	2		48 VH1 Storytellers		American 69416
				JOHNNY CASH & WILLIE NELSON		

RELIGIOUS ALBUMS:

2/15/69	54	20		49 The Holy Land		Columbia 9726
5/12/73	205	4		50 The Gospel Road .... [S]		Columbia 32253 [2]
				narration and songs by Cash with Kris Kristofferson, Rita Coolidge, Larry Gatlin and The Statler Brothers		
4/24/04	194	1		51 My Mother's Hymn Book		American 002362
3/24/07	184	1		52 Cash: Ultimate Gospel .... [K]		Columbia 00739

SOUNDTRACKS:

12/12/70	176	6		53 I Walk The Line		Columbia 30397
2/6/71	209	1		54 Little Fauss And Big Halsy		Columbia 30385
				includes one song by Carl Perkins		

~ ~ ~ ~ ~ ~ ~ ~ ~ ~   *NON-CHARTED ALBUMS*   ~ ~ ~ ~ ~ ~ ~ ~ ~ ~ ~

1956 **Johnny Cash With His Hot And Blue Guitar**	1960 **Now, There Was A Song!**
1958 **The Songs That Made Him Famous**	1960 **Ride This Train**
1959 **Hymns By Johnny Cash**	1962 **The Sound Of Johnny Cash**
1959 **Songs Of Our Soil**	

CASH, Ray
Born Wardell Raymond Cheeks in 1980 in Cleveland, Ohio. Hardcore rapper.

7/15/06	41	4		1 Cash On Delivery		Ghet-O-Vision 92685

CASH, Rosanne
Born on 5/24/1955 in Memphis, Tennessee. Country singer/songwriter. Daughter of **Johnny Cash**. Married to **Rodney Crowell** from 1979-92. Married producer John Leventhal in 1995. Released short-story collection *Bodies of Water* in 1996.

3/28/81	26	32	●	1 **Seven Year Ache**		Columbia 36965
7/10/82	76	12		2 Somewhere In The Stars		Columbia 37570
6/22/85	101	21		3 Rhythm & Romance		Columbia 39463
8/15/87+	138	20	●	4 King's Record Shop		Columbia 40777
4/1/89	152	7	●	5 Hits 1979-1989 .... [G]		Columbia 45054
11/17/90	175	4		6 Interiors		Columbia 46079
3/27/93	160	2		7 The Wheel		Columbia 52729
4/12/03	130	3		8 Rules Of Travel		Capitol 37757
2/11/06	78	8		9 Black Cadillac		Capitol 48738
10/24/09	22	16		10 The List		Manhattan 96576

CASHFLOW
Funk-rap band from Atlanta, Georgia: Kary Hubbert (vocals), James Duffie and Regis Ferguson (keyboards) and Gaylord Parsons (drums).

5/3/86	144	11		1 Ca$hflow		Atlanta Artists 826028

CASHIS
Born Ramone Johnson on 4/9/1978 in Chicago, Illinois; raised in Irvine, California. Male rapper.

6/9/07	106	2		1 The County Hounds EP .... [EP]		Shady 008810

CASHMAN & WEST
Duo of pop record producers/songwriters/singers Dennis "Terry Cashman" Minogue (born on 7/5/1941) and Thomas "Tommy West" Picardo. (born on 8/17/1942). Produced all of **Jim Croce**'s recordings.

10/14/72	168	8		1 A Song Or Two		Dunhill/ABC 50126
8/11/73	192	2		2 Moondog Serenade		Dunhill/ABC 50141
11/23/74	202	2		3 Lifesong		ABC/Dunhill 50179

CASH MONEY MILLIONAIRES
Rap collective of Cash Money artists: **B.G.**, **Big Tymers**, **Juvenile**, **Lil' Wayne** and **Turk**.

9/30/00	13	24	●	1 Baller Blockin		Cash Money 153291

CASINOS, The
Pop vocal group from Cincinnati, Ohio: Gene Hughes (lead), Pete Bolton, Bob Armstrong, Tom Mathews, Ray White, Mickey Denton, Glen Hughes, Joe Patterson and Bill Hawkins. Gene Hughes died in a car crash on 2/3/2004 (age 67).

5/13/67	187	4		1 Then You Can Tell Me Goodbye		Fraternity 1019

CASSIDY
Born Barry Reese on 7/7/1982 in Philadelphia, Pennsylvania. Male rapper.

4/3/04	2[1]	15	●	1 Split Personality		Full Surface 57018
7/16/05	5	9		2 I'm A Hustla		Full Surface 68073
11/24/07	10	5		3 B.A.R.S. The Barry Adrian Reese Story		Full Surface 18699

DEBUT	PEAK	WKS	R I A A	ARTIST / Album Title	Catalog	Label & Number

CASSIDY, David
Born on 4/12/1950 in Manhattan, New York. Son of actor Jack Cassidy and actress Evelyn Ward. Played "Keith Partridge," the lead singer of TV's **The Partridge Family**. Married to actress Kay Lenz from 1977-83. Co-starred with his half-brother **Shaun Cassidy** on Broadway's *Blood Brothers* in 1993.

DEBUT	PEAK	WKS	RIAA			Label & Number
2/12/72	15	23	●	1 Cherish		Bell 6070
11/11/72	41	17		2 Rock Me Baby		Bell 1109
11/3/90	136	11		3 David Cassidy		Enigma 73554
5/18/02	147	1		4 Then And Now	[G]	Decca 017454

CASSIDY, Eva
Born on 2/2/1963 in Oxon Hill, Maryland. Died of cancer on 11/2/1996 (age 33). Adult Alternative singer/songwriter/guitarist.

DEBUT	PEAK	WKS	RIAA			Label & Number
4/7/01	❶⁹ᶜ	46	▲	1 Songbird *released in 1998*		Blix Street 10045
6/9/01	2¹ᶜ	7		2 Live At Blues Alley *recorded on 1/2/1996 in Washington DC*	[L]	Blix Street 10046
7/21/01	161	1		3 Time After Time		Blix Street 10073
9/7/02	32	11		4 Imagine		Blix Street 10075
8/30/03	112	5		5 American Tune		Blix Street 10079
9/13/08	136	4		6 Somewhere		Blix Street 10090

CASSIDY, Shaun
Born on 9/27/1958 in Los Angeles, California. Son of actor Jack Cassidy and actress Shirley Jones of TV's **The Partridge Family**. Played "Joe Hardy" on TV's *The Hardy Boys*. Co-starred with his half-brother **David Cassidy** on Broadway's *Blood Brothers* in 1993. Cast member of the TV soap *General Hospital* in 1987. Married to model Ann Pennington from 1979-91.

DEBUT	PEAK	WKS	RIAA			Label & Number
6/25/77	3²	57	▲	1 Shaun Cassidy		Warner/Curb 3067
11/26/77+	6	37	▲	2 Born Late		Warner/Curb 3126
8/19/78	33	13	▲	3 Under Wraps		Warner/Curb 3222

CASSIE
Born Casandra Ventura on 8/26/1986 in New London, Connecticut. Female R&B singer/songwriter/former fashion model.

DEBUT	PEAK	WKS	RIAA			Label & Number
8/26/06	4	13		1 Cassie		Bad Boy 83981

CASTELLS, The
Pop vocal group from Santa Rosa, California: Bob Ussery, Tom Hicks, Joe Kelly and Chuck Girard (later with **The Hondells**).

~ ~ ~ ~ ~ ~ ~ ~ ~ ~ **NON-CHARTED ALBUM** ~ ~ ~ ~ ~ ~ ~ ~ ~ ~ ~

1962 **So This Is Love**

CASTING CROWNS
Christian pop band from Daytona Beach, Florida: Mark Hall (vocals), Hector Cervantes (guitar), Juan Devevo (guitar), Megan Garrett (keyboards), Melodee Devevo (violin), Chris Huffman (bass) and Andy Williams (drums).

DEBUT	PEAK	WKS	RIAA			Label & Number
10/18/03+	59	90	▲	1 Casting Crowns	Cat:#7/48	Beach Street 10723
9/17/05	9	75	▲	2 Lifesong *Grammy: Pop Gospel Album*	Cat:#34/4	Beach Street 10770
9/15/07	2¹	76	●	3 The Altar And The Door	Cat:#26/12	Beach Street 10117
9/6/08	114	4		4 The Altar And The Door: Live	[L]	Beach Street 10131
10/25/08	24	13	●	5 Peace On Earth *Christmas charts: 2/'08, 2/'09*	Cat:❶/4 [X]	Beach Street 10129
12/5/09	4	26↑	●	6 Until The Whole World Hears		Beach Street 10135
12/5/09	15	6		7 Peace On Earth	[X-R]	Beach Street 10129

CASTOR, Jimmy, Bunch
Born on 6/22/1943 in the Bronx, New York. R&B singer/saxophonist/composer/arranger. Formed the Jimmy Castor Bunch in 1972, with Harry Jensen (guitar), Gerry Thomas (keyboards), Lenny Fridie (congas), Doug Gibson (bass) and Bobby Manigault (drums).

DEBUT	PEAK	WKS	RIAA			Label & Number
4/22/72	27	23		1 It's Just Begun		RCA Victor 4640
9/23/72	192	4		2 Phase Two		RCA Victor 4783
3/1/75	74	17		3 Butt Of Course		Atlantic 18124
9/25/76	132	9		4 E-Man Groovin'		Atlantic 18186

CASTRO, Christian
Born on 12/8/1974 in Mexico City, Mexico. Latin singer/actor. Son of Mexican movie star Veronica Castro.

DEBUT	PEAK	WKS	RIAA			Label & Number
7/14/07	114	9		1 El Indomable	[F]	Universal Latino 009199

CASUAL
Born Jonathan Owens in Oakland, California. Male rapper.

DEBUT	PEAK	WKS	RIAA			Label & Number
2/19/94	108	2		1 Fear Itself		Jive 41520

CASUALTIES, The
Punk-rock band from Jersey City, New Jersey: Jorge Herrera (vocals), Jake Kolatis (guitar), Rick Lopez (bass) and Meggers Anderson (drums).

DEBUT	PEAK	WKS	RIAA			Label & Number
9/9/06	200	1		1 Under Attack		Side One Dummy 1300

CATE BROS.
Pop-rock duo of twins Ernie Cate (vocals, piano) and Earl Cate (guitar). Born on 12/26/1942 in Fayetteville, Arkansas.

DEBUT	PEAK	WKS	RIAA			Label & Number
2/7/76	158	9		1 Cate Bros.		Asylum 1050
10/30/76	182	2		2 In One Eye And Out The Other		Asylum 1080

CATHEDRALS, The
Gospel group formed in Akron, Ohio: Glen Payne, George Younce, Scott Fowler and **Ernie Haase**. Younce and Haase are also member of **Old Friends Quartet**. Payne died of cancer on 10/15/1999 (age 72).

12/11/99	93	4	1 **A Farewell Celebration** .... [L]	Spring House 42223

CATHERINE WHEEL
Rock band from England: Rob Dickinson (vocals), Brian Futter (guitar), Dave Hawes (bass) and Neil Sims (drums). Dickinson is the cousin of **Bruce Dickinson** (of **Iron Maiden**).

6/24/95	163	1	1 **Happy Days**..	Mercury 526850
9/13/97	178	1	2 **Adam And Eve**	Mercury 534864

CATHY JEAN and THE ROOMMATES
Born Cathy Jean Giordano on 9/8/1945 in Brooklyn, New York. The Roommates were a vocal quartet from Queens, New York: Steve Susskind (lead), Jack Sailson and Felix Alvarez (tenors) and Bob Minsky (bass).

~ ~ ~ ~ ~ ~ ~ ~ ~ ~ **NON-CHARTED ALBUM** ~ ~ ~ ~ ~ ~ ~ ~ ~ ~ ~
1961 **At The Hop!**

CAT MOTHER and The All Night News Boys
Rock band from Brooklyn, New York: Larry Packer (guitar), Bob Smith (piano), Charley Chin (banjo), Roy Michaels (bass) and Michael Equine (drums). All share vocals.

7/5/69	55	15	1 **The Street Giveth...And The Street Taketh Away** .... produced by **Jimi Hendrix**	Polydor 4001
5/27/72	212	2	2 **Cat Mother**	Polydor 5017

CAT POWER
Born Charlyn Marshall on 1/21/1972 in Atlanta, Georgia. Female Adult Alternative singer/songwriter/pianist.

3/8/03	105	4	1 **You Are Free**	Matador 427
2/11/06	34	6	2 **The Greatest**	Matador 626
2/9/08	12	7	3 **Jukebox**...	Matador 754

CAUSE & EFFECT
Pop duo based in Northern California: Sean Rowley (keyboards) and Robert Rowe (vocals, guitar). Rowley died of asthma-related cardiac arrest on 11/12/1992 (age 23).

4/4/92	141	11	1 **Another Minute**	SRC 11019

CAVALERA CONSPIRACY
Heavy metal band formed in Los Angeles, California: brothers Max Cavalera (vocals, guitar) and Igor Cavalera (drums), with Marc Rizzo (guitar) and Joe Duplantier (bass). The Cavalera brothers were founders of **Sepultura**. Duplantier is also the lead singer of **Gojira**.

4/12/08	72	2	1 **Inflikted**	Roadrunner 179552

CAVALIERE, Felix
Born on 11/29/1942 in Pelham, New York. "Blue-eyed" soul singer/songwriter/keyboardist. Member of **The Rascals**.

4/19/80	203	5	1 **Castles In The Air**	Epic 35990

CAVE, Nick, & The Bad Seeds
Born on 9/22/1957 in Warracknabeal, Victoria, Australia. Rock singer/pianist. The Bad Seeds: Mick Harvey and Blixa Bargeld (guitars), Conway Savage (organ), Warren Ellis (violin), Martyn Casey (bass) and Thomas Wylder (drums). Band also recorded as **Grinderman**.

3/22/97	155	1	1 **The Boatman's Call**	Reprise 46530
4/28/01	180	1	2 **No More Shall We Part**	Reprise 48039
3/1/03	182	1	3 **Nocturama**	Mute 86668
11/13/04	126	1	4 **Abattoir Blues / The Lyre Of Orpheus**	Anti 86729 [2]
4/28/07	150	1	5 **Grinderman**	Mute 86861
4/26/08	64	3	6 **Dig, Lazarus Dig!!!**	Anti 86943

CAVE IN
Rock band from Boston, Massachusetts: Stephen Brodsky (vocals, guitar), Adam McGrath (guitar), Caleb Scofield (bass) and John-Robert Conners (drums).

4/5/03	169	1	1 **Antenna**	RCA 68131

CAVO
Hard-rock band from St. Louis, Missouri: Casey Walker (vocals), Chris Hobbs (guitar), Brian Smith (bass) and Chad LaRoy (drums).

8/29/09	47	7	1 **Bright Nights Dark Days**	Reprise 517657

C-BO
Born Shawn Thomas in 1973 in Sacramento, California. Male rapper.

6/24/95	99	9	1 **Tales From The Crypt**	AWOL 7197
3/1/97	65	6	2 **One Life 2 Live**	AWOL 7201
3/14/98	41	6	3 **Til My Casket Drops**	AWOL 45496
3/27/99	81	2	4 **The Final Chapter**	AWOL 47206
8/12/00	91	6	5 **Enemy Of The State**	West Coast Mafia 2829
9/15/01	79	5	6 **Blocc Movement**	JCOR 860950
			BROTHA LYNCH HUNG & C-BO	
8/10/02	136	2	7 **West Coast Mafia**	West Coast Mafia 2002
8/9/03	199	1	8 **The Mobfather**	West Coast Mafia 2010

C.C.S.
Jazz-rock collective from England. Put together by the core trio of Alexis Korner (born on 4/19/1928; died of lung cancer on 1/1/1984, age 55) and Peter Thorup (born on 12/14/1948; died on 8/3/2007, age 58), with arranger John Cameron. C.C.S.: Collective Consciousness Society.

4/3/71	197	2		1 Whole Lotta Love		RAK 30559

CEDARMONT KIDS SINGERS
Cedarmont Kids Christian series of recordings for children, featuring a chorus of 14 little girls.

11/25/95+	30^X	7		1 Christmas Carols	Cat:#48/1 [X]	Benson 4054
				Christmas charts: 33/'95, 30/'06, 50/'07, 39/'08		
12/2/95	29^X	7		2 Christmas Favorites	Cat:#42/1 [X]	Benson 4058
				Christmas charts: 29/'95, 34/'07, 33/'08, 33/'09		
4/15/00	25^C	16	▲	3 Toddler Tunes: 25 Classic Songs For Toddlers		Benson 4056
				released in 1995		
4/29/06	185	1		4 Easter Favorites		Cedarmont Kids 80335

CEE-LO
Born Thomas Callaway on 5/30/1974 in Atlanta, Georgia. Male rapper. Member of **Goodie Mob**.

5/11/02	11	13		1 Cee-Lo Green And His Perfect Imperfections		Arista 14682
3/20/04	13	8		2 Cee-Lo Green...Is The Soul Machine		Arista 52111

CELI BEE & THE BUZZY BUNCH
Disco group from Puerto Rico. Led by female singer Celinas Soto.

7/23/77	169	5		1 Celi Bee & The Buzzy Bunch		APA 77001

CELLA DWELLAS
Rap duo from Brooklyn, New York: Ug and Phantasm.

4/13/96	160	1		1 Realms 'N Reality		Loud 66521

CELLY CELL
Born Michael McCarver in Vallejo, California. Male rapper.

5/18/96	26	17		1 Killa Kali		Sick Wid' It 41577
8/15/98	53	6		2 The G Filez		Sick Wid' It 41622

CELTIC THUNDER
Celtic music band formed in Northern Ireland: Paul Byrom, George Donaldson, Keith harkin, Ryan Kelly and Damian McGinty.

4/5/08	48	14		1 Celtic Thunder		Celtic Thunder 001
10/4/08	61	14		2 Act Two	[L]	Celtic Thunder 011606
8/1/09	55	6		3 Take Me Home		Celtic Thunder 013087

CELTIC WOMAN
Female group that performs traditional Celtic music: Chloe Agnew, Lisa Kelly, Orla Fallon, Meav NiMhaolchatha and Mairead Nesbitt.

4/2/05+	53	87	▲	1 Celtic Woman	Cat:#3/13	Manhattan 60233
11/11/06	35	10	●	2 A Christmas Celebration	Cat:#3/20 [X]	Manhattan 70124
				Christmas charts: 7/'06, 5/'07, 16/'08, 14/'09		
12/5/09	65	6		3 A Christmas Celebration	[X-R]	Manhattan 70124
2/17/07	4	41	●	4 A New Journey		Manhattan 75110
11/15/08	75	12		5 The Greatest Journey: Essential Collection	[G]	Manhattan 34124
12/6/08	89	5		6 A Celtic Family Christmas	[X-EP]	Manhattan 35623
				CELTIC WOMAN Featuring The High Kings		
				Christmas charts: 20/'08, 29/'09		

CENA, John & Tha Trademarc
Born on 4/23/1977 in West Newbury, Massachusetts. White rapper/professional wrestler.

5/28/05	15	17		1 You Can't See Me		Columbia 92498

CENTRAL LINE
R&B-dance band from London, England: Linton Beckles (vocals, drums), Henry Defoe (guitar), Lipson Francis (keyboards) and Camelle Hinds (bass).

1/9/82	145	9		1 Central Line		Mercury 4033

CERRONE
Born Jean-Marc Cerrone on 5/24/1952 in St. Michel, France. Composer/producer/drummer. A pioneer of the Euro-disco sound. Also see **Kongas**.

2/26/77	153	10		1 Love In C Minor		Cotillion 9913
8/6/77	162	5		2 Cerrone's Paradise		Cotillion 9917
1/21/78	129	8		3 Cerrone 3 - Supernature		Cotillion 5202
11/18/78+	118	13		4 Cerrone IV - The Golden Touch		Cotillion 5208

CETERA, Peter
Born on 9/13/1944 in Chicago, Illinois. Lead singer/bassist of **Chicago** from 1967-85.

1/23/82	143	10		1 Peter Cetera		Full Moon 3624
7/12/86	23	43	▲	2 Solitude/Solitaire		Full Moon 25474
8/20/88	58	17		3 One More Story		Full Moon 25704
8/8/92	163	9		4 World Falling Down		Warner 26894
6/7/97	134	13		5 You're The Inspiration - A Collection	[G]	River North 61250

CEU
Born Maria Ceu Whitaker on 4/17/1980 in Sao Paulo, Brazil. Female singer/songwriter.

4/21/07	57	7	1 Ceu .... [F]	Urban Jungle 361129

CHACKSFIELD, Frank, And His Orch.
Born on 5/9/1914 in Battle, Sussex, England. Died on 6/9/1995 (age 81). Pianist/bandleader.

1/9/61	36	14	1 Ebb Tide	Richmond 30078
11/28/64	120	9	2 The New Ebb Tide	London Phase 4 44053

CHAD & JEREMY
Soft-rock duo from London, England: Chad Stuart (born on 12/10/1941) and Jeremy Clyde (born on 3/22/1941).

9/26/64+	22	39	1 Yesterday's Gone	World Artists 2002
3/27/65	69	14	2 Chad & Jeremy Sing For You	World Artists 2005
6/26/65	37	18	3 Before And After	Columbia 9174
11/6/65	77	11	4 I Don't Want To Lose You Baby	Columbia 9198
4/23/66	49	23	5 The Best Of Chad & Jeremy .... [G]	Capitol 2470
8/20/66	144	4	6 More Chad & Jeremy .... [K]	Capitol 2546
9/24/66	61	14	7 Distant Shores	Columbia 9364
11/11/67	186	5	8 Of Cabbages And Kings	Columbia 9471

CHAIRMEN OF THE BOARD
R&B vocal group from Detroit, Michigan: General Norman Johnson, Danny Woods, Harrison Kennedy and Eddie Curtis.

5/2/70	133	10	1 Give Me Just A Little More Time	Invictus 7300
11/28/70+	117	16	2 In Session	Invictus 7304
5/6/72	178	3	3 Bittersweet	Invictus 9801

CHAKACHAS, The
Studio group from Belgium. Featuring saxophonist Victor Ingeveld.

4/8/72	117	11	1 Jungle Fever .... [F]	Polydor 5504

CHAKIRIS, George
Born on 9/16/1934 in Norwood, Ohio. Actor/singer. Best-known for playing "Bernardo" in the movie *West Side Story*.

9/1/62	28	16	1 George Chakiris	Capitol 1750
2/2/63	45	17	2 Memories Are Made Of These	Capitol 1813

CHAM
Born Damian Beckett on 2/24/1977 in Kingston, Jamaica. Male reggae singer/songwriter.

9/2/06	53	4	1 Ghetto Story	Madhouse 83975

CHAMBERLAIN, Richard
Born George Richard Chamberlain on 3/31/1935 in Beverly Hills, California. Leading movie, theater and TV actor. Played lead role in TV's *Dr. Kildare* from 1961-66.

2/2/63	5	36	1 Richard Chamberlain Sings	MGM 4088

CHAMBERS, Kasey
Born on 6/4/1976 in Mount Gambier, South Australia. Female country singer/songwriter/guitarist.

3/2/02	104	4	1 Barricades & Brickwalls	Warner 48028

CHAMBERS BROTHERS, The
Black psychedlic-rock band from Lee County, Mississippi: brothers George Chambers (bass), Willie Chambers (guitar), Lester Chambers (harmonica) and Joe Chambers (guitar), with Brian Keenan (drums). All shared vocals. Keenan died of a heart attack on 10/5/1985 (age 42).

2/17/68	4	58	●	1 The Time Has Come	Columbia 9522
10/12/68	16	21		2 A New Time-A New Day	Columbia 9671
12/27/69+	58	33		3 Love, Peace And Happiness .... [L]	Columbia 20 [2]
				record 2: live at Bill Graham's Fillmore East	
12/5/70	193	2		4 The Chambers Brothers Greatest Hits .... [E]	Vault 135 [2]
				reissue of 1965-1966 recordings	
2/27/71	145	7		5 New Generation	Columbia 30032
12/4/71+	166	7		6 The Chambers Brothers' Greatest Hits .... [G]	Columbia 30871

CHAMILLIONAIRE
Born Hakeem Seriki on 11/28/1979 in Houston, Texas. Male rapper/songwriter.

12/10/05	10	46	▲	1 The Sound Of Revenge	Universal 005423
10/6/07	8	8		2 Ultimate Victory	Chamillitary 00812

CHAMPAIGN
R&B band from Champaign, Illinois: Pauli Carman and Rena Jones (vocals), Leon Reeder (guitar), Michael Day and Dana Walden (keyboards), Michael Reed (bass) and Rocky Maffit (drums).

3/21/81	53	20	1 How 'Bout Us	Columbia 37008
4/2/83	64	24	2 Modern Heart	Columbia 38284
11/10/84	184	3	3 Woman In Flames	Columbia 39365

CHAMPLIN, Bill
Born on 5/21/1947 in Oakland, California. Singer/songwriter/guitarist. Founder of **Sons Of Champlin**. Joined **Chicago** in 1982.

2/6/82	178	4	1 Runaway	Elektra 563

CHAMPS, The

Rock and roll instrumental band from Los Angeles, California. Fluctuating lineup featured Jim Seals, Dash Crofts (**Seals & Crofts**) and **Glen Campbell**.

~ ~ ~ ~ ~ ~ ~ ~ ~ ~ **NON-CHARTED ALBUMS** ~ ~ ~ ~ ~ ~ ~ ~ ~ ~ ~

1958 **Go Champs Go!**   1962 **Great Dance Hits Featuring Limbo Rock**
1959 **Everybody's Rockin' With The Champs**

CHANDLER, Gene

Born Eugene Dixon on 7/6/1940 in Chicago, Illinois. R&B singer/producer. Joined The Dukays vocal group in 1957. Own label, Mr. Chand, 1969-73.

3/31/62	69	8	1 **The Duke Of Earl**		Vee-Jay 1040
1/8/66	124	3	2 **Gene Chandler - Live On Stage In '65** .... [L]		Constellation 1425
			recorded at the Regal Theater in Chicago, Illinois		
10/31/70	178	9	3 **The Gene Chandler Situation**		Mercury 61304
3/27/71	143	5	4 **Gene & Jerry - One & One**		Mercury 61330
			GENE CHANDLER & JERRY BUTLER		
11/25/78+	47	20	5 **Get Down**		Chi-Sound 578
8/25/79	153	3	6 **When You're #1**		20th Century 598
6/7/80	87	18	7 **Gene Chandler '80**		20th Century 605

~ ~ ~ ~ ~ ~ ~ ~ ~ ~ **NON-CHARTED ALBUMS** ~ ~ ~ ~ ~ ~ ~ ~ ~ ~ ~

1964 **The Greatest Hits Of Gene Chandler**   1964 **Just Be True**

CHANGE

European-American dance group formed in Italy by producers Jacques Fred Petrus and Mauro Malavasi.

5/10/80	29	25	● 1 **The Glow Of Love**		RFC 3438
4/18/81	46	22	2 **Miracles**		Atlantic 19301
5/15/82	66	9	3 **Sharing Your Love**		Atlantic 19342
4/2/83	161	7	4 **This Is Your Time**		Atlantic 80053
4/28/84	102	15	5 **Change of Heart**		Atlantic 80151
4/20/85	208	2	6 **Turn On Your Radio**		Atlantic 81243

CHANGE OF PACE, A

Hard-rock band from Peoria, Arizona: Torry Jasper (vocals), Adam Rodgers (guitar), Dan Parker (guitar), Johnny Abdullah (bass) and Jonathan Kelly (drums).

9/2/06	156	1	1 **Prepare The Masses**		Immortal 60026

CHANGING FACES

Female R&B vocal duo from Brooklyn, New York: Charisse Rose and Cassandra Lucas.

9/10/94	25	25	● 1 **Changing Faces**		Big Beat 92369
6/28/97	21	15	● 2 **All Day, All Night**		Big Beat 92720
10/28/00	46	6	3 **Visit Me**		Atlantic 83401

CHANNEL, Bruce

Born on 11/28/1940 in Jacksonville, Texas. Pop singer.

5/19/62	114	5	1 **Hey! Baby (and 11 Other Songs About Your Baby)**		Smash 67008

CHANNEL LIVE

Rap duo from New Jersey: Hokiem Green and Vincent Morgan.

4/8/95	58	5	1 **Station Identification**		Capitol 28968

CHANSON

R&B duo formed in Los Angeles, California: James Jamerson Jr. (born in Detroit, Michigan) and David Williams (born in Newport News, Virginia). Jamerson is the son of the prominent Motown session bassist.

10/14/78+	41	21	1 **Chanson**		Ariola 50039

CHANTAY'S

Teen surf-rock band from Santa Ana, California: Bob Spickard (lead guitar), Brian Carman (rhythm guitar), Rob Marshall (piano), Warren Waters (bass) and Bob Welsh (drums).

5/18/63	26	18	1 **Pipeline** .... [I]		Dot 25516

CHANTELS, The

Female R&B vocal group from the Bronx, New York: Arlene Smith, Sonia Goring, Rene Minus, Jackie Landry and Lois Harris. Landry died of cancer on 12/23/1997 (age 56).

~ ~ ~ ~ ~ ~ ~ ~ ~ ~ **NON-CHARTED ALBUMS** ~ ~ ~ ~ ~ ~ ~ ~ ~ ~ ~

1958 **We Are The Chantels**   1961 **The Chantels On Tour (Look In My Eyes)**

CHANTICLEER

Classical vocal ensemble formed in 1978 in San Francisco, California. Group varies from eight to twelve members.

11/3/07	50^X	1	1 **Let It Snow** .... [X]		Rhino 284988

CHAO, Manu

Born Jose Manuel Chao on 6/21/1961 in Paris, France (Spanish parents). Eclectic singer/songwriter/guitarist.

9/22/07	71	3	1 **La Radiolina** .... [F]		Because 68496

CHAPIN, Harry
Born on 12/7/1942 in Greenwich Village, New York. Died in a car crash on 7/16/1981 (age 38). Folk-rock singer/songwriter.

DEBUT	PEAK	WKS			Label & Number
3/18/72	60	27	●	1 Heads & Tales..	Elektra 75023
10/28/72	160	8		2 Sniper and Other Love Songs...................................	Elektra 75042
12/29/73+	61	23		3 Short Stories...	Elektra 75065
9/7/74	4	33	●	4 Verities & Balderdash..	Elektra 1012
10/4/75	53	8		5 Portrait Gallery...	Elektra 1041
5/1/76	48	19	▲²	6 Greatest Stories-Live.. [L]	Elektra 2009 [2]
10/30/76	87	6		7 On The Road To Kingdom Come................................	Elektra 1082
9/17/77	58	10		8 Dance Band On The Titanic......................................	Elektra 301 [2]
7/1/78	133	8		9 Living Room Suite...	Elektra 142
10/27/79	163	3		10 Legends Of The Lost And Found - New Greatest Stories Live .... [L]	Elektra 703 [2]
11/1/80	58	15		11 Sequel..	Boardwalk 36872

CHAPMAN, Gary
Born on 8/19/1957 in Waurika, Oklahoma; raised in DeLeon, Texas. Contemporary Christian singer/songwriter. Married to **Amy Grant** from 1982-99. Hosted TNN's *Prime Time Country* from 1996-99.

DEBUT	PEAK	WKS			Label & Number
3/16/96	192	1		1 Shelter...	Reunion 16200

CHAPMAN, Steven Curtis   All-Time: #459
Born on 11/21/1962 in Paducah, Kentucky. Contemporary Christian singer/songwriter.

DEBUT	PEAK	WKS			Label & Number
11/18/95	61	9	●	1 The Music Of Christmas .... Cat:#39/3 [X]	Sparrow 51489
				Christmas charts: 7/95, 39/96, 39/98	
12/9/95	195	1	▲	2 Heaven In The Real World...................................	Sparrow 51408
				released in July 1994	
9/21/96	20	36	●	3 Signs Of Life...	Sparrow 51554
11/8/97	85	16	●	4 Greatest Hits... [G]	Sparrow 51630
7/3/99	31	34	▲	5 Speechless..	Sparrow 51695
				Grammy: Pop Gospel Album	
10/13/01	14	30	●	6 Declaration..	Sparrow 51770
2/15/03	12	12	●	7 All About Love.. Cat:❶¹/3	Sparrow 41762
10/9/04	22	14		8 All Things New...	Sparrow 76897
12/3/05	90	5		9 All I Really Want For Christmas................ Cat:❶²/10 [X]	Sparrow 11231
				Christmas charts: 6/05, 2/06, 24/07, 17/08	
11/10/07	47	26		10 This Moment... Cat:#44/3	Sparrow 86393
11/21/09	27	8		11 Beauty Will Rise...	Sparrow 26516

CHAPMAN, Tracy
Born on 3/30/1964 in Cleveland, Ohio. Folk-R&B singer/songwriter/guitarist.
AWARD: Grammy: Best New Artist 1988

DEBUT	PEAK	WKS			Label & Number
4/30/88	❶¹	61	▲⁶	1 Tracy Chapman.. Cat:#5/65	Elektra 60774
				Grammy: Contemporary Folk Album ★ RS500 #261	
10/21/89	9	26	▲	2 Crossroads..	Elektra 60888
5/16/92	53	11	●	3 Matters Of The Heart..	Elektra 61215
12/2/95+	4	95	▲⁵	4 New Beginning..	Elektra 61850
3/4/00	33	22	●	5 Telling Stories...	Elektra 62478
11/2/02	25	9		6 Let It Rain..	Elektra 62803
10/1/05	49	8		7 Where You Live..	Elektra 83803
11/29/08	57	2		8 Our Bright Future..	Elektra 514061

CHARIOT, The
Christian hard-rock band from Douglasville, Georgia: Josh Scogin (vocals), Bryan Taylor (guitar), Stephen Harrison (guitar), Jon Kindler (bass) and Dave Kennedy (drums).

DEBUT	PEAK	WKS			Label & Number
4/21/07	169	1		1 The Fiancee	Solid State 49015
5/23/09	112	1		2 Wars And Rumors Of Wars	Solid State 43862

CHARLATANS UK, The
Rock band from Northwich, England: Tim Burgess (vocals), Jon Baker (guitar), Rob Collins (organ), Martin Blunt (bass) and Jon Brookes (drums). Mark Collins (guitar) replaced Baker in 1993. Simply known as The Charlatans by 1994. Rob Collins died in a car crash on 7/23/1996 (age 32).

DEBUT	PEAK	WKS			Label & Number
11/10/90+	73	27		1 Some Friendly	Beggars Banquet 2411
5/2/92	173	2		2 Between 10th & 11th..	Beggars Banquet 61108

CHARLENE
Born Charlene D'Angelo on 6/1/1950 in Hollywood, California. Pop-R&B singer.

DEBUT	PEAK	WKS			Label & Number
4/10/82	36	20		1 I've Never Been To Me	Motown 6009
11/27/82	162	7		2 Used To Be	Motown 6027

Billboard			R I A A	ARTIST		
DEBUT	PEAK	WKS		Album Title	Catalog	Label & Number

CHARLES, Ray
1960s: #5 / All-Time: #16

Born Ray Charles Robinson on 9/23/1930 in Albany, Georgia; raised in Greenville, Florida. Died of liver disease on 6/10/2004 (age 73). Legendary R&B singer/pianist. Partially blind at age five, completely blind at seven (glaucoma). Studied classical piano and clarinet at State School for Deaf and Blind Children, St. Augustine, Florida, 1937-45. With local Florida bands; moved to Seattle in 1948. Formed the McSon Trio (also known as the Maxim Trio and the Maxine Trio) with Gossady McGhee (guitar) and Milton Garred (bass). First recordings were very much in the King Cole Trio style. Formed own band in 1954. The 1950s female vocal group, The Cookies, became his backing group, The Raeletts. Popular performer, with many TV and movie appearances. Jamie Foxx portrayed Charles in the 2004 movie *Ray*.

AWARDS: Grammy: Lifetime Achievement 1987 ★ R&R Hall of Fame: 1986

DEBUT	PEAK	WKS	RIAA	#	Album Title	Catalog	Label & Number
2/15/60	17	82		1	The Genius Of Ray Charles		Atlantic 1312
					Grammys: Male Vocal / Hall of Fame ★ RS500 #263		
10/10/60	9	50		2	The Genius Hits The Road		ABC-Paramount 335
3/6/61	11	31		3	Dedicated To You		ABC-Paramount 355
3/27/61	4	48		4	Genius + Soul = Jazz		Impulse! 2
9/4/61	52	15		5	Ray Charles & Betty Carter		ABC-Paramount 385
4/21/62	❶¹⁴	101	●	6	Modern Sounds In Country And Western Music		ABC-Paramount 410
					Grammy: Hall of Fame ★ RS500 #104		
11/3/62	2²	67	●	7	Modern Sounds In Country And Western Music (Volume Two)		ABC-Paramount 435
8/31/63	2²	36		8	Ingredients In A Recipe For Soul		ABC-Paramount 465
3/21/64	9	23		9	Sweet & Sour Tears		ABC-Paramount 480
8/29/64	36	16		10	Have A Smile With Me		ABC-Paramount 495
9/11/65	116	7		11	Country & Western Meets Rhythm & Blues		ABC-Paramount 520
3/12/66	15	36		12	Crying Time		ABC-Paramount 544
9/17/66	52	17		13	Ray's Moods		ABC 550
7/8/67	76	34		14	Ray Charles Invites You To Listen		ABC/TRC 595
4/13/68	51	24		15	A Portrait Of Ray		ABC/TRC 625
4/5/69	167	11		16	I'm All Yours-Baby!		ABC/TRC 675
7/26/69	172	3		17	Doing His Thing		ABC/TRC 695
8/22/70	192	4		18	Love Country Style		ABC/TRC 707
5/29/71	52	16		19	Volcanic Action Of My Soul		ABC/TRC 726
4/29/72	52	22		20	A Message From The People		ABC/TRC 755
11/25/72+	186	8		21	Through The Eyes Of Love		ABC/TRC 765
3/9/74	206	4		22	Come Live With Me		Crossover 9000
6/28/75	175	3		23	Renaissance		Crossover 9005
12/4/76	138	11		24	Porgy & Bess		RCA Victor 1831 [2]
					RAY CHARLES & CLEO LAINE		
11/12/77	78	20		25	True To Life		Atlantic 19142
1/5/80	204	1		26	Ain't It So		Atlantic 19251
10/18/80	203	1		27	Brother Ray Is At It Again!		Atlantic 19281
2/23/85	75	20		28	Friendship		Columbia 39415
5/15/93	145	8		29	My World		Warner 26735
9/18/04+	❶¹	56	▲³	30	Genius Loves Company		Concord 2248
					Grammy: Album of the Year / Pop Vocal		
12/18/04	121	2		31	Ray Charles Celebrates A Gospel Christmas With The Voices Of Jubilation! . [X]		Urban Works 50827
					Christmas charts: 9/'04, 50/'05		
10/8/05	36	7		32	Genius & Friends		Atlantic 73185
					GREATEST HITS & COMPILATIONS:		
8/28/61+	20	73		33	What'd I Say		Atlantic 8029
11/13/61+	73	12		34	The Genius Sings The Blues		Atlantic 8052
12/18/61+	11	52		35	Do The Twist!		Atlantic 8054
8/11/62	14	38		36	The Ray Charles Story		Atlantic 900 [2]
8/18/62	5	47	●	37	Ray Charles' Greatest Hits		ABC-Paramount 415
3/25/67	77	62	●	38	A Man And His Soul		ABC 590 [2]
11/20/71	152	10		39	A 25th Anniversary In Show Business Salute To Ray Charles		ABC 731 [2]
					record 1: Atlantic hits; record 2: ABC hits		
6/26/04	❶¹²ᶜ	78	●	40	The Very Best Of Ray Charles		Rhino 79822
					released in 2000		
6/26/04	3¹ᶜ	24	●	41	Anthology		Rhino 75759
					released in 1988		
4/25/09	35	6		42	Genius: The Ultimate Ray Charles Collection		Concord 31293
					INSTRUMENTAL ALBUMS:		
8/28/61	49	17		43	The Genius After Hours		Atlantic 1369
7/11/70	155	2		44	My Kind Of Jazz		Tangerine 1512
					LIVE ALBUMS:		
7/18/60	13	37		45	Ray Charles In Person		Atlantic 8039
					Grammy: Hall of Fame		
					recorded on 5/28/1959 at Herndon Stadium in Atlanta, Georgia		
2/20/65	80	18		46	Ray Charles Live In Concert		ABC-Paramount 500
					recorded at on 9/20/1964 the Shrine Auditorium in Los Angeles, California		
5/5/73	216	4		47	Genius Live In Concert .... [R]		Bluesway 6053
					reissue of #46 above		
5/19/73	182	5		48	Ray Charles Live .... [R]		Atlantic 503 [2]
					record 1: recorded on 7/5/1958 at the Newport Jazz Festival; record 2: reissue of #45 above		

CHARLES, Ray — cont'd

10/21/06	23	11		49 Ray Sings Basie Swings		Hear 30026

RAY CHARLES & THE COUNT BASIE ORCHESTRA
vocals taken from a 1973 Ray Charles concert in Europe; current Count Basie band recorded new instrumentation to create the album

SOUNDTRACKS:

11/6/04	9	39	▲	50 Ray		Atlantic 76540

Grammy: Soundtrack Album

2/19/05	46	8		51 More Music From Ray		Atlantic 78703

~ ~ ~ ~ ~ ~ ~ ~ ~ **NON-CHARTED ALBUMS** ~ ~ ~ ~ ~ ~ ~ ~ ~ ~ ~
1957 **Rock & Roll**	1991 **The Birth Of Soul: The Complete Atlantic Rhythm**
1957 **The Great Ray Charles**	**& Blues Recordings, 1952-1959**
1958 **Yes Indeed!**	*RS500 #53*

CHARLES, Ray, Singers
Born Charles Raymond Offenberg on 9/13/1918 in Chicago, Illinois. Arranger/conductor for many TV shows.

4/4/64	11	33	1 Something Special For Young Lovers		Command 866
9/5/64	45	22	2 Al-Di-La And Other Extra-Special Songs For Young Lovers		Command 870
12/5/64+	88	20	3 Songs For Lonesome Lovers		Command 874
8/21/65	125	6	4 Songs For Latin Lovers		Command 886

CHARLES, Sonny
Born Charles Hemphill on 9/4/1940 in Fort Wayne, Indiana. R&B singer. Leader of **The Checkmates, Ltd.**

12/25/82+	136	7	1 The Sun Still Shines		Highrise 102

CHARLES & EDDIE
R&B vocal duo: Charles Pettigrew (from Philadelphia) and Eddie Chacon (from Oakland). Pettigrew died of cancer on 4/6/2001 (age 37).

10/31/92	153	5	1 Duophonic		Capitol 97150

CHARLESTON CITY ALL-STARS
Group of studio musicians conducted by **Enoch Light**.

7/8/57+	16	14	1 The Roaring 20's, Volume 2	[I]	Grand Award 340
9/2/57	17	2	2 The Roaring 20's, Volume 3	[I]	Grand Award 353

CHARLIE
Rock band from England: Terry Thomas (guitar), Julian Colbeck (guitar), John Anderson (bass) and Steve Gadd (drums). Varying membership also included Bob Henrit (drums; **Argent**; joined by 1983) and Terry Slesser (vocals; joined in 1980). Henrit joined **The Kinks** in 1984.

6/4/77	111	15	1 No Second Chance		Janus 7032
4/15/78	75	14	2 Lines		Janus 7036
9/1/79	60	10	3 Fight Dirty		Arista 4239
10/17/81	201	6	4 Good Morning America		RCA Victor 4137
7/23/83	145	9	5 Charlie		Mirage 90098

CHARMS, The
Black doo-wop group from Cincinnati, Ohio: Otis Williams, Richard Parker, Donald Peak, Joe Penn and Rolland Bradley. Group first recorded for Rockin' label in 1953. Otis, not to be confused with the same-named member of The Temptations, later recorded country music.

~ ~ ~ ~ ~ ~ ~ ~ ~ **NON-CHARTED ALBUMS** ~ ~ ~ ~ ~ ~ ~ ~ ~ ~ ~
1957 **Sing Their All Time Hits**	1959 **This Is Otis Williams And His Charms**

CHARO & The Salsoul Orchestra
Born Maria Rosario Martinez on 3/13/1941 in Murcia, Spain. Singer/actress/guitarist. Known as "The Cuchi-Cuchi Girl." Married to bandleader Xavier Cugat from 1966-78.

11/26/77+	100	15	1 Cuchi-Cuchi		Salsoul 5519

CHASE
Jazz-rock band organized by trumpeter Bill Chase (born on 10/20/1934 in Boston, Massachusetts; formerly with **Woody Herman** and **Stan Kenton**). Varying lineup. Chase (age 39) along with bandmates John Emma, Wallace Yohn and Walter Clark were killed in a plane crash on 8/9/1974 near Jackson, Minnesota.

5/8/71	22	26	1 Chase		Epic 30472
4/8/72	71	12	2 Ennea		Epic 31097
4/27/74	155	10	3 Pure Music		Epic 32572

CHASE, Chevy
Born Cornelius Crane Chase on 10/8/1943 in Manhattan, New York. Comedian/actor/keyboardist. An original cast member of TV's *Saturday Night Live*, 1975-76. Went on to star in several movies. Hosted own late night TV talk show in 1993.

9/13/80	201	5	1 Chevy Chase	[N]	Arista 9519

CHASEZ, JC
Born Joshua Chasez on 8/8/1976 in Washington DC. Pop singer/songwriter. Member of *NSYNC.

3/13/04	17	4	1 Schizophrenic		Jive 53724

Billboard DEBUT	PEAK	WKS	R I A A	ARTIST Album Title	Catalog	Label & Number

CHAYANNE
Born Elmer Figueroa on 6/29/1968 in Puerto Rico. Latin singer/actor.

7/13/02	199	1		1 Grandes Exitos .... [F-G]		Sony Discos 84667
9/13/03	87	5		2 Sincero .... [F]		Sony Discos 70627
4/16/05	182	3		3 Desde Siempre.. [F]		Sony Discos 95678
10/15/05	62	5		4 Cautivo .... [F]		Sony Discos 95886
4/28/07	42	5		5 Mi Tempo .... [F]		Sony 06119

CHEAP TRICK   All-Time: #206
Rock band from Rockford, Illinois: Robin Zander (vocals; born on 1/23/1953), Rick Nielsen (guitar; born on 12/22/1946), Tom Petersson (bass; born on 5/9/1950) and Brad "Bun E. Carlos" Carlson (drums; born on 6/12/1951). Petersson replaced by Jon Brant in 1980; returned in 1988, replacing Brant. Carlos also joined **Tinted Windows**.

4/9/77	207	1		1 Cheap Trick..		Epic 34400
9/24/77	73	12	▲	2 In Color..		Epic 34884
				RS500 #448		
6/10/78	48	22	▲	3 Heaven Tonight		Epic 35312
2/24/79	4	53	▲³	4 Cheap Trick At Budokan Cat:#34/56 [L]		Epic 35795
				RS500 #430		
				recorded on 4/28/1978 in Japan		
10/6/79	6	25	▲	5 Dream Police		Epic 35773
7/5/80	39	12		6 Found All The Parts .... [EP]		Epic 36453
11/15/80	24	15	●	7 All Shook Up		Epic 36498
5/29/82	39	27	●	8 One On One		Epic 38021
9/10/83	61	11		9 Next Position Please		Epic 38794
8/17/85	35	18		10 Standing On The Edge		Epic 39592
10/18/86	115	9		11 The Doctor		Epic 40405
5/7/88	16	47	▲	12 Lap Of Luxury		Epic 40922
8/4/90	48	17		13 Busted		Epic 46013
10/19/91	174	3	▲	14 The Greatest Hits .... [G]		Epic 48681
4/9/94	123	2		15 Woke Up With A Monster		Warner 45425
5/17/97	99	2		16 Cheap Trick		Red Ant 002
8/9/03	128	1		17 Special One..		Cheap Trick 36333
6/24/06	101	2		18 Rockford		Cheap Trick 36788
8/8/09	78	1		19 The Latest		Cheap Trick 2009
9/12/09	83	1		20 Sgt. Pepper Live .... [L]		Cheap Trick 37000

CHECKER, Chubby   1960s: #34 / All-Time: #186
Born Ernest Evans on 10/3/1941 in Andrews, South Carolina; raised in Philadelphia, Pennsylvania. Did impersonations of famous singers. First recorded for Parkway in 1959. Dick Clark's then-wife Bobbie suggested that Evans change his name to Chubby Checker due to his resemblance to a teenage **Fats Domino**. Cover version of Hank Ballard's "The Twist" started worldwide dance craze. On 4/12/1964, married Miss World 1962, Dutch-born Catharina Lodders ("Loddy Lo" written for her). In the movies *Don't Knock The Twist* and *Twist Around The Clock*.

10/31/60+	3¹	86		1 Twist With Chubby Checker		Parkway 7001
5/29/61	110	16		2 It's Pony Time		Parkway 7003
9/25/61+	11	47		3 Let's Twist Again		Parkway 7004
12/4/61+	8	38		4 For Twisters Only		Parkway 7002
12/11/61+	2⁶	67		5 Your Twist Party [K]		Parkway 7007
12/18/61+	7	30		6 Bobby Rydell/Chubby Checker		Cameo 1013
3/31/62	17	27		7 For Teen Twisters Only		Parkway 7009
4/28/62	54	11		8 Twistin' Round The World		Parkway 7008
6/9/62	29	20		9 Don't Knock The Twist .... [S]		Parkway 7011
10/27/62	23	24		10 All The Hits (For Your Dancin' Party)		Parkway 7014
11/17/62	117	4		11 Down To Earth		Cameo 1029
				CHUBBY CHECKER & DEE DEE SHARP		
12/15/62+	11	24		12 Limbo Party		Parkway 7020
12/29/62+	27	23		13 Chubby Checker's Biggest Hits................................ [G]		Parkway 7022
3/30/63	87	17		14 Let's Limbo Some More		Parkway 7027
8/10/63	90	4		15 Beach Party		Parkway 7030
10/12/63	104	4		16 Chubby Checker In Person...................................... [L]		Parkway 7026
				labeled as *Twist It Up*; recorded at the Under 21 Club in Somers Point, New Jersey		
12/23/72+	152	10		17 Chubby Checker's Greatest Hits .... [G]		Abkco 4219 [2]
3/6/82	186	2		18 The Change Has Come		MCA 5291

~ ~ ~ ~ ~ ~ ~ ~ ~ **NON-CHARTED ALBUMS** ~ ~ ~ ~ ~ ~ ~ ~ ~ ~

1963 **Golden Hits** *[w/ Bobby Rydell]*   1965 **The Chubby Checker Discotheque**
1964 **Chubby Checker With Sy Oliver And His Orchestra** 1966 **18 Golden Hits**
1964 **Chubby's Folk Album** *["Loddy Lo"]*

Billboard			R I A A	ARTIST		
DEBUT	PEAK	WKS		Album Title	Catalog	Label & Number

CHECKMATES, LTD., The
R&B group from Fort Wayne, Indiana: **Sonny Charles** and Bobby Stevens (vocals), Harvey Trees (guitar), Bill Van Buskirk (bass) and Marvin Smith (drums). Smith died of a heart attack on 12/15/2007 (age 68).

| 10/18/69 | 178 | 4 | | 1 **Love Is All We Have To Give** .... | | A&M 4183 |

CHEECH & CHONG
Duo of comedians Richard "Cheech" Marin (born on 7/13/1946 in Watts, California) and Thomas Chong (born on 5/24/1938, Edmonton, Alberta, Canada). Starred in several movies. Chong, the father of actress Rae Dawn Chong, was the guitarist of **Bobby Taylor & The Vancouvers**. Cheech was a cast member of TV's *Golden Palace* and *Nash Bridges*.

9/25/71+	28	64	●	1 **Cheech And Chong** .... [C]	Ode 77010
7/1/72	2¹	111	●	2 **Big Bambu**	[C]	Ode 77014
9/8/73	2¹	69	●	3 **Los Cochinos**	[C]	Ode 77019
				Grammy: Comedy Album	
10/19/74	5	25	●	4 **Cheech & Chong's Wedding Album**	[C]	Ode 77025
6/26/76	25	13		5 **Sleeping Beauty** .... [C]	Ode 77040
12/2/78+	162	7		6 **Up In Smoke** .... [C-S]	Warner 3249
7/19/80	173	3		7 **Let's Make A New Dope Deal** .... [C]	Warner 3391
10/24/81	201	4		8 **Cheech & Chong's Greatest Hit** .... [C-G]	Warner 3614
10/12/85	71	11		9 **Get Out Of My Room** .... [C]	MCA 5640

CHEETAH GIRLS, The
Female pop vocal trio: Adrienne Bailon, Kiely Williams and Sabrina Bryan. The trio starred in the same-named Disney channel TV movies with **Raven-Symon**. Bailon and Williams were members of **3LW**.

| 10/13/07 | 44 | 9 | | 1 **TCG** .... | Hollywood 000305 |
| 9/6/08 | 13 | 19 | | 2 **One World** .... [S] | Walt Disney 002046 |

CHEMICAL BROTHERS, The
Techno-dance DJ duo from England: Tom Rowlands (born on 6/9/1970) and Ed Simons (born on 1/11/1971).

4/26/97	14	25	●	1 **Dig Your Own Hole** .... [I]	Astralwerks 6180
10/10/98	95	4		2 **Brother's Gonna Work It Out** .... [I]	Astralwerks 6243
7/10/99	32	14		3 **Surrender** .... [I]	Freestyle Dust 47610
2/16/02	32	7		4 **Come With Us** .... [I]	Freestyle Dust 11682
10/18/03	123	1		5 **Singles 93 - 03** .... [G-I]	Freestyle Dust 92714 [2]
2/12/05	59	3		6 **Push The Button** .... [I]	Freestyle Dust 63282
				Grammy: Electronic Dance Album	
8/4/07	65	2		7 **We Are The Night** .... [I]	Freestyle Dust 94158
				Grammy: Electronic/Dance Album	

CHENOWETH, Kristin
Born on 7/24/1968 in Broken Arrow, Oklahoma. Actress/singer. Acted in several TV shows and movies.

| 11/1/08 | 77 | 8 | | 1 **A Lovely Way To Spend Christmas** .... [X] | Sony Classical 34256 |
| | | | | Christmas charts: 7/'08, 28/'09 | |

CHEQUERED PAST
Hard-rock band formed in Los Angeles, California: Michael Des Barres (vocals; **Silverhead**; **Detective**), Tony Sales (guitar), **Steve Jones** (guitar), Nigel Harrison (bass) and Clem Burke (drums). Sales was a member of **Utopia** and later **Tin Machine**. Jones was a founding member of the **Sex Pistols**. Harrison and Burke were members of **Blondie**.

| 9/15/84 | 151 | 6 | | 1 **Chequered Past** .... | EMI America 17123 |

CHER   **All-Time: #116**
Born Cherilyn Sarkasian on 5/20/1946 in El Centro, California. Adopted by stepfather at age 15 and last name changed to La Piere. Worked as backup singer for Phil Spector. Recorded as "Bonnie Jo Mason" and "Cherilyn" in 1964. Recorded with Sonny Bono as "Caesar & Cleo" in 1963, then as **Sonny & Cher** from 1965-73. Married to Bono from 1963-75. Married to **Gregg Allman** from 1975-79. Own TV series with Bono from 1971-74, 1976-77. Member of the group Black Rose in 1980. Acclaimed movie actress (won the 1987 Best Actress Oscar for *Moonstruck*).

9/18/65	16	24		1 **All I Really Want To Do**	Imperial 12292
4/23/66	26	19		2 **The Sonny Side Of Cher**	Imperial 12301
10/1/66	59	16		3 **Cher**	Imperial 12320
11/18/67+	47	14		4 **With Love - Cher**	Imperial 12358
8/16/69	160	3		5 **3614 Jackson Highway**	Atco 298
9/25/71	16	45	●	6 **Gypsys, Tramps & Thieves**	Kapp 3649
7/29/72	43	22		7 **Foxy Lady**	Kapp 5514
4/14/73	140	8		8 **Bittersweet White Light**	MCA 2101
9/22/73	28	25	●	9 **Half-Breed**	MCA 2104
6/1/74	69	14		10 **Dark Lady**	MCA 2113
5/10/75	153	7		11 **Stars**	Warner 2850
2/24/79	25	21	●	12 **Take Me Home**	Casablanca 7133
12/5/87+	32	41	▲	13 **Cher**	Geffen 24164
7/22/89	10	53	▲³	14 **Heart Of Stone**	Geffen 24239
7/6/91	48	34	●	15 **Love Hurts**	Geffen 24369
7/13/96	64	10		16 **It's A Man's World**	Reprise 46179

CHER — cont'd

DEBUT	PEAK	WKS	RIAA	#	Album Title	Catalog	Label & Number
11/28/98+	4	76	▲⁴	17	Believe	Cat:#49/2	Warner 47121
3/16/02	9	21	●	18	Living Proof		Warner 47619
9/13/03	40	6		19	Live: The Farewell Tour	[L]	Warner 73953

GREATEST HITS & COMPILATIONS:

DEBUT	PEAK	WKS	RIAA	#	Album Title	Catalog	Label & Number
11/30/68	195	3		20	Cher's Golden Greats		Imperial 12406
1/8/72	92	10		21	Cher Superpak		United Artists 88 [2]
10/7/72	95	9		22	Cher Superpak, Vol. II		United Artists 94 [2]
					Superpaks: Imperial recordings		
11/16/74	152	7		23	Greatest Hits		MCA 2127
3/27/99	57	23	●	24	If I Could Turn Back Time - Cher's Greatest Hits	Cat:#12/1	Geffen 24509
4/19/03	4	51	▲²	25	The Very Best Of Cher	Cat:#50/1	Warner 73852
9/13/03	83	5		26	The Very Best Of Cher: Special Edition		Warner 73956 [2]
					deluxe package of albums #19 & 25 above		

CHERISH
Female R&B vocal group from Atlanta, Georgia: sisters Farrah, Neosha, Fallon and Felisha King (Fallon and Felisha are twins).

DEBUT	PEAK	WKS	RIAA	#	Album Title	Catalog	Label & Number
9/2/06	4	25	●	1	Unappreciated		Sho'Nuff 54077
5/31/08	40	5		2	The Truth		Sho'Nuff 00806

CHERISH THE LADIES
Female Irish-American folk band formed in New York: Joanie Madden, Kathleen Boyle, Michelle Burke, Mary Coogan, Roisin Dillon and Mirella Murray.

DEBUT	PEAK	WKS	RIAA	#	Album Title	Catalog	Label & Number
10/18/08	50ˣ	1		1	On Christmas Night	[X]	Rounder 617061

CHERRELLE
Born Cheryl Norton on 10/13/1958 in Los Angeles, California. R&B singer. Cousin of singer **Pebbles**.

DEBUT	PEAK	WKS	RIAA	#	Album Title	Catalog	Label & Number
9/8/84	144	8		1	Fragile		Tabu 39144
2/1/86	36	30		2	High Priority		Tabu 40094
11/19/88	106	15		3	Affair		Tabu 44148

CHERRY, Ava
Born in Chicago, Illinois. Dance-R&B singer.

DEBUT	PEAK	WKS	RIAA	#	Album Title	Catalog	Label & Number
3/15/80	206	2		1	Ripe!!!		RSO 3072

CHERRY, Don
Born on 1/11/1924 in Wichita Falls, Texas. Pop singer. Not to be confused with the jazz trumpeter/father of Eagle-Eye and Neneh Cherry.

DEBUT	PEAK	WKS	RIAA	#	Album Title	Catalog	Label & Number
9/22/56	15	7		1	Swingin' For Two		Columbia 893

CHERRY, Eagle-Eye
Born on 5/7/1969 in Stockholm, Sweden; raised in Brooklyn, New York. Son of jazz trumpeter Don Cherry. Half-brother of **Neneh Cherry**.

DEBUT	PEAK	WKS	RIAA	#	Album Title	Catalog	Label & Number
8/22/98	45	39	▲	1	Desireless		Work 69434

CHERRY, Neneh
Born on 3/10/1964 in Stockholm, Sweden; raised in Brooklyn, New York. Female R&B singer. Stepdaughter of jazz trumpeter Don Cherry. Half-sister of **Eagle-Eye Cherry**.

DEBUT	PEAK	WKS	RIAA	#	Album Title	Catalog	Label & Number
6/24/89	40	35		1	Raw Like Sushi		Virgin 91252

CHERRY POPPIN' DADDIES
Retro-swing band from Eugene, Oregon: Steve Perry (vocals, guitar), Jason Moss (guitar), Dana Heitman, Sean Flannery and Ian Early (horns), Darren Cassidy (bass) and Tim Donahue (drums).

DEBUT	PEAK	WKS	RIAA	#	Album Title	Catalog	Label & Number
2/28/98	17	53	▲²	1	Zoot Suit Riot		Mojo 53081

CHESNEY, Kenny
2000s: #5 / All-Time: #148

Born on 3/26/1968 in Knoxville, Tennessee; raised in Luttrell, Tennessee. Country singer/songwriter/guitarist. Married actress Renee Zellweger on 5/9/2005; marriage annulled on 9/16/2005.
AWARD: CMA: Entertainer 2004, 2006, 2007 & 2008

DEBUT	PEAK	WKS	RIAA	#	Album Title	Catalog	Label & Number
9/28/96+	78	30	▲	1	Me And You		BNA 66908
8/2/97	95	34	▲	2	I Will Stand		BNA 67498
3/20/99	51	82	▲²	3	Everywhere We Go		BNA 67655
10/14/00	13	104	▲⁴	4	Greatest Hits	Cat:#3/190 [G]	BNA 67976
5/11/02	❶¹	104	▲⁴	5	No Shoes, No Shirt, No Problems	Cat:#2¹/32	BNA 67038
10/25/03	42	12	●	6	All I Want For Christmas Is A Real Good Tan	Cat:#14/16 [X]	BNA 51808
					Christmas charts: 3/'03, 18/'04, 27/'05, 34/'06, 49/'07, 46/'08, 41/'09		
2/21/04	❶¹	94	▲⁴	7	When The Sun Goes Down	Cat:#46/1	BNA 58801
					CMA: Album of the Year		
8/14/04	3¹ᶜ	2		8	In My Wildest Dreams	[E]	BNA 62661
					released in 1994		
2/12/05	❶¹	27	▲	9	Be As You Are: Songs From An Old Blue Chair		BNA 61530

Billboard			R I A A	ARTIST		
DEBUT	PEAK	WKS		Album Title	Catalog	Label & Number
				CHESNEY, Kenny — cont'd		
11/26/05	**❶**¹	98	▲³	10 The Road And The Radio		BNA 72960
10/7/06	4	17	●	11 LIVE: Live Those Songs Again	[L]	BNA 86578
9/29/07	3¹	61	▲	12 Just Who I Am: Poets & Pirates		BNA 11457
11/1/08	**❶**¹	38		13 Lucky Old Sun		Blue Chair 36726
6/6/09	3¹	51↑		14 Greatest Hits II	[G]	BNA 49530
				CHESNUTT, Cody		
				Born in Atlanta, Georgia. Male R&B singer/songwriter.		
4/5/03	128	1		1 The Headphone Masterpiece		Ready Set Go! 001 [2]
				CHESNUTT, Mark		
				Born on 9/6/1963 in Beaumont, Texas. Country singer/songwriter/guitarist.		
				AWARD: CMA: Horizon 1993		
10/27/90	132	38	▲	1 Too Cold At Home		MCA 10032
4/18/92	68	57	▲	2 Longnecks & Short Stories		MCA 10530
7/10/93	43	48	▲	3 Almost Goodbye		MCA 10851
10/1/94	98	17	●	4 What A Way To Live..		Decca 11094
10/21/95	116	4		5 Wings		Decca 11261
12/7/96+	130	14	▲	6 Greatest Hits	[G]	Decca 11529
10/11/97	165	4		7 Thank God For Believers		Decca 70006
2/27/99	65	7		8 I Don't Want To Miss A Thing................................		Decca 70035
6/8/02	184	1		9 Mark Chesnutt		Columbia 86540
10/9/04	170	1		10 Savin' The Honky Tonk		Vivaton! 01
				CHESTER FRENCH		
				Alternative-pop duo formed in Cambridge, Massachusetts: David "D.A." Wallach and Max Drummey.		
5/9/09	77	1		1 Love The Future		Star Trak 012582
				CHEVELLE		
				Rock trio from Chicago, Illinois: brothers Pete Loeffler (vocals, guitar), Joe Loeffler (bass) and Sam Loeffler (drums).		
10/26/02	14	49	▲	1 Wonder What's Next.............................. **Cat:**#39/3		Epic 86157
10/9/04	8	38	●	2 This Type Of Thinking (Could Do Us In)		Epic 86908
4/21/07	12	12		3 Vena Sera...		Epic 02698
9/19/09	6	13		4 Sci-Fi Crimes		Epic 41325
				CHI-ALI		
				Born Chi-Ali Griffith on 5/27/1976 in the Bronx, New York. Male rapper. Acted in the HBO-TV movie *Strapped*. In 2002, sentenced to 12-14 years in prison for manslaughter.		
4/18/92	189	2		1 The Fabulous Chi-Ali		Violator 1082
				CHIC		
				Disco band formed in New York: **Norma Jean** Wright and Luci Martin (vocals), **Nile Rodgers** (guitar), Bernard Edwards (bass) and Tony Thompson (drums). Rodgers joined **The Honeydrippers** in 1984. Thompson joined **The Power Station** in 1985 and Edwards became their producer. Edwards died of pneumonia on 4/18/1996 (age 43). Thompson died of cancer on 11/12/2003 (age 48).		
12/17/77+	27	40	●	1 Chic		Atlantic 19153
12/2/78	4	48	▲	2 C'est Chic		Atlantic 19209
8/25/79	5	17	▲	3 Risque		Atlantic 16003
12/22/79+	88	9		4 Les Plus Grands Succes De Chic - Chic's Greatest Hits	[G]	Atlantic 16011
7/26/80	30	15		5 Real People..		Atlantic 16016
12/19/81+	124	9		6 Take It Off..		Atlantic 19323
12/4/82	173	6		7 Tongue In Chic		Atlantic 80031
				CHICAGO 1970s: #6 / All-Time: #25		
				Jazz-oriented rock band from Chicago, Illinois: **Peter Cetera** (vocals, bass; born on 9/13/1944), Robert Lamm (vocals, keyboards; born on 10/13/1944), Terry Kath (vocals, guitar; born on 1/31/1946; died of an accidental self-inflicted gunshot on 1/23/1978, age 31), James Pankow (trombone; born on 8/20/1947), Lee Loughnane (trumpet; born on 10/21/1946), Walt Parazaider (reeds; born on 3/14/1945) and Danny Seraphine (drums; born on 8/28/1948). Originally called The Big Thing, later Chicago Transit Authority. To Los Angeles in 1968. Brazilian percussionest Laudir DeOliveira was a member from 1973-80. Donnie Dacus (guitar) was a member from 1978-80 (played "Woof" in the movie version of *Hair*). Chris Pinnick (guitar) was a member from 1980-84. **Bill Champlin** (vocals, keyboards) joined in 1982. Cetera left in 1985; replaced by Jason Scheff. Dawayne Bailey (guitar) was a member from 1986-94. Seraphine left in 1989; replaced by Tris Imboden. Bruce Gaitsch (guitar) was a brief member in 1995; replaced by Keith Howland.		
5/17/69	17	171	▲²	1 Chicago Transit Authority		Columbia 8 [2]
2/14/70	4	134	●	2 Chicago II		Columbia 24 [2]
1/30/71	2²	63	▲	3 Chicago III		Columbia 30110 [2]
11/13/71+	3¹	46	▲	4 Chicago At Carnegie Hall	[L]	Columbia 30865 [4]
				recorded in April 1971		
7/29/72	**❶**⁹	51	▲²	5 Chicago V		Columbia 31102
7/14/73	**❶**⁵	73	▲²	6 Chicago VI		Columbia 32400
3/30/74	**❶**¹	69	▲	7 Chicago VII		Columbia 32810 [2]
4/12/75	**❶**²	29	▲	8 Chicago VIII		Columbia 33100

Billboard DEBUT	PEAK	WKS	R I A A	ARTIST / Album Title	Catalog	Label & Number
				CHICAGO — cont'd		
7/4/76	3[1]	44	▲[2]	9 Chicago X		Columbia 34200
10/1/77	6	20	▲	10 Chicago XI		Columbia 34860
10/21/78	12	29	▲	11 Hot Streets		Columbia 35512
9/1/79	21	10	●	12 Chicago 13		Columbia 36105
8/9/80	71	9		13 Chicago XIV		Columbia 36517
6/26/82	9	38	▲	14 Chicago 16		Full Moon 23689
6/2/84+	4	72	▲[6]	15 Chicago 17		Warner 25060
10/18/86+	35	45	●	16 Chicago 18		Warner 25509
7/9/88+	37	42	▲	17 19		Reprise 25714
2/16/91	66	11		18 Twenty 1		Reprise 26391
6/10/95	90	7		19 Night & Day		Giant 24615
4/8/06	41	2		20 Chicago XXX		Rhino 73362
7/5/08	122	2		21 Chicago XXXII: Stone Of Sisyphus		Rhino 491580
				CHRISTMAS ALBUMS:		
11/28/98	47	7	●	22 Chicago 25	Cat:#9/7	Chicago 3035
				Christmas charts: 4/'98, 18/'99		
12/6/03	102	4		23 Chicago Christmas What's It Gonna Be, Santa?		Rhino 73892
				Christmas charts: 14/'03, 46/'04		
				GREATEST HITS & COMPILATIONS:		
11/29/75	❶[5]	72	▲[5]	24 Chicago IX - Chicago's Greatest Hits	Cat:#9/110	Columbia 33900
12/12/81	171	5		25 Chicago - Greatest Hits, Volume II		Columbia 37682
12/9/89+	37	25	▲[5]	26 Greatest Hits 1982-1989	Cat:#20/203	Reprise 26080
5/10/97	55	27	●	27 The Heart Of Chicago 1967-1997		Reprise 46554
5/30/98	154	2		28 The Heart Of Chicago 1967-1998 Volume II		Reprise 46911
7/20/02	38	25	▲[2]	29 The Very Best Of: Only The Beginning		Rhino 76170 [2]
2/12/05	57	4		30 Love Songs		Rhino 78451
10/20/07	100	7	●	31 The Best Of Chicago: 40th Anniversary Edition	Cat:#33/1	Rhino 309116 [2]
				CHICKENFOOT		
				Hard-rock supergroup: Sammy Hagar (vocals), Joe Satriani (guitar), Michael Anthony (bass) and Chad Smith (drums). Hagar and Anthony were members of Van Halen. Smith is also a member of Red Hot Chili Peppers.		
6/20/09	4	32	●	1 Chickenfoot		Redline 20091
				CHIEFTAINS, The		
				Traditional folk band from Ireland: Kevin Conneff (vocals), Paddy Moloney (pipes, whistles), Martin Fay and Sean Keane (fiddles), Derek Bell (harpsichord) and Matt Molloy (flute). Bell died on 10/15/2002 (age 66).		
2/28/76	187	4		1 The Chieftains 5 [I]		Island 9334
7/23/88	102	13		2 Irish Heartbeat		Mercury 834496
				VAN MORRISON & THE CHIEFTAINS		
12/14/91+	107	5	●	3 The Bells Of Dublin Cat:#49/2 [X]		RCA Victor 60824
				Christmas charts: 14/'91, 25/'92		
3/14/92	120	4		4 An Irish Evening-Live At The Grand Opera House, Belfast [L]		RCA Victor 60916
				Grammy: Traditional Folk Album		
				recorded on 7/31/1991		
2/11/95	22	19	●	5 The Long Black Veil		RCA Victor 62702
3/30/96	193	1		6 Film Cuts [I]		RCA Victor 68438
3/13/99	56	13		7 Tears Of Stone		RCA Victor 68968
3/18/00	96	4		8 Water From The Well		RCA Victor 63637
3/23/02	77	4		9 The Wide World Over: A 40 Year Celebration [K]		RCA Victor 63917
10/5/02	91	6		10 Down The Old Plank Road: The Nashville Sessions		RCA Victor 63971
9/27/03	180	2		11 Further Down The Old Plank Road		Victor 52897
				CHIFFONS, The		
				Female R&B vocal group from the Bronx, New York: Judy Craig, Barbara Lee Jones, Patricia Bennett and Sylvia Peterson. Jones died of a heart attack on 5/15/1992 (age 44).		
5/18/63	97	11		1 He's So Fine		Laurie 2018
8/20/66	149	3		2 Sweet Talkin' Guy		Laurie 2036
				~ ~ ~ ~ ~ ~ ~ ~ ~ ~ **NON-CHARTED ALBUM** ~ ~ ~ ~ ~ ~ ~ ~ ~ ~		
				1963 One Fine Day		
				CHILD, Desmond, And Rouge		
				Born John Charles Barrett on 10/28/1953 in Miami, Florida. Prolific producer/songwriter. Formed vocal group Rouge with Diane Grasselli, Myriam Valle and Maria Vidal.		
3/24/79	157	6		1 Desmond Child And Rouge		Capitol 11908
				CHILD, Jane		
				Born on 2/15/1969 in Scarborough, Ontario, Canada. Singer/songwriter/keyboardist.		
3/3/90	49	22		1 Jane Child		Warner 25858

Billboard			R I A A	ARTIST		
DEBUT	PEAK	WKS		Album Title	Catalog	Label & Number
				CHILDREN OF BODOM		
				Heavy metal band from Espoo, Finland: Alexi Laiho (vocals, guitar), Roope Latuala (guitar), Janne Warman (keyboards), Henkka Blacksmith (bass) and Jaska Raatikainen (drums).		
11/12/05	195	1		1 **Are You Dead Yet?**		Spinefarm 001
5/3/08	22	4		2 **Blooddrunk**		Spinefarm 310
10/10/09	81	1		3 **Skeletons In The Closet**		Spinefarm 1764
				CHILDS, Toni		
				Born on 7/20/1960 in Orange, California. Female rock singer.		
6/25/88	63	45	●	1 **Union**		A&M 5175
7/13/91	115	13		2 **House Of Hope**		A&M 5358
				CHI-LITES, The		
				R&B vocal group from Chicago, Illinois: Eugene Record, Robert Lester, Marshall Thompson and Creadel Jones. Jones died on 8/25/1994 (age 53). Record died of cancer on 7/22/2005 (age 64). Lester died on 1/22/2010 (age 67).		
9/13/69	180	3		1 **Give It Away**		Brunswick 754152
8/21/71	12	32		2 **(For God's Sake) Give More Power To The People**		Brunswick 754170
4/29/72	5	36		3 **A Lonely Man**		Brunswick 754179
10/21/72	55	24		4 **The Chi-Lites Greatest Hits**	[G]	Brunswick 754184
3/24/73	50	13		5 **A Letter To Myself**		Brunswick 754188
9/15/73	89	14		6 **Chi-Lites**		Brunswick 754197
7/13/74	181	5		7 **Toby**		Brunswick 754200
11/29/80	179	6		8 **Heavenly Body**		Chi-Sound 619
4/10/82	162	7		9 **Me And You**		Chi-Sound 635
6/4/83	98	12		10 **Bottom's Up**		Larc 8103
				CHILLDRIN OF DA GHETTO		
				Male rap trio from Chicago, Illinois: Goldiiz, Bad Seed and P-Child.		
11/6/99	158	1		1 **Chilldrin Of Da Ghetto**		Hoo Bangin' 50020
				CHILLIWACK		
				Rock band from Vancouver, British Columbia, Canada: Bill Henderson (vocals, guitar), Brian MacLeod (guitar), Ab Bryant (bass) and Rick Taylor (drums). Bryant and MacLeod later joined **Headpins**. Bryant was also with **Prism**. MacLeod died of brain cancer on 4/25/1992 (age 41).		
2/26/72	210	2		1 **Chilliwack**		A&M 3509 [2]
11/1/75	210	1		2 **Rockerbox**		Sire 7511
3/26/77	142	13		3 **Dreams, Dreams, Dreams**		Mushroom 5006
8/12/78	191	4		4 **Lights From The Valley**		Mushroom 5011
10/3/81	78	30		5 **Wanna Be A Star**		Millennium 7759
11/27/82	112	10		6 **Opus X**		Millennium 7766
				CHIMAIRA		
				Heavy metal band from Cleveland, Ohio: Mark Hunter (vocals), Rob Arnold (guitar), Matt DeVries (guitar), Chris Spicuzza (electronics), Jim LaMarca (bass) and Andols Herrick (drums).		
5/31/03	117	1		1 **The Impossibility Of Reason**		Roadrunner 618397
8/27/05	74	2		2 **Chimaira**		Roadrunner 618262
3/24/07	42	3		3 **Resurrection**		Ferret 078
5/9/09	30	4		4 **The Infection**		Ferret 121
				CHIMES, The		
				Dance trio from Scotland: Pauline Henry (vocals), Mike Peden (bass) and James Locke (drums).		
6/2/90	162	6		1 **The Chimes**		Columbia 46008
				CHINA CRISIS		
				Rock band from Liverpool, England: Garry Daly (vocals, keyboards), Eddie Lundon (guitar), Gary Johnson (bass) and Kevin Wilkinson (drums).		
3/24/84	202	4		1 **Working With Fire And Steel**		Warner 25062
6/1/85	171	4		2 **Flaunt The Imperfection**		Warner 25296
3/7/87	114	12		3 **What Price Paradise**		A&M 5148
				CHINGO BLING		
				Born Pedro Herrera in Houston, Texas. Latin rapper.		
9/1/07	123	2		1 **They Can't Deport Us All**		Big Chile 123452
				CHINGY		
				Born Howard Bailey on 3/9/1980 in St. Louis, Missouri. Male rapper.		
8/2/03	2[1]	56	▲[2]	1 **Jackpot**		DTP 82976
11/27/04	10	16	▲	2 **Powerballin'**		Capitol 97686
10/7/06	9	14	●	3 **Hoodstar**		Slot-A-Lot 12135
1/5/08	84	5		4 **Hate It Or Love It**		DTP 010227
				CHIODOS		
				Alternative-rock band from Davison, Michigan: Craig Owens (vocals), Pat McManaman (guitar), Jason Hale (guitar), Bradley Bell (keyboards), Matt Goddard (bass) and Derrick Frost (drums).		
11/4/06	164	1		1 **All's Well That Ends Well**		Equal Vision 136
9/22/07	5	7		2 **Bone Palace Ballet**		Equal Vision 141

Billboard			R I A A	ARTIST		
DEBUT	PEAK	WKS		Album Title	Catalog	Label & Number

CHIPMUNKS, The
All-Time: #258

Characters created by Ross Bagdasarian ("David Seville") who named Alvin, Simon and Theodore after Liberty executives Alvin Bennett, Simon Waronker and Theodore Keep. The Chipmunks starred in own prime-time animated TV show in the early 1960s and a Saturday morning cartoon series in the mid-1980s. Bagdasarian died on 1/16/1972 (age 52). His son, Ross Jr., resurrected the act in 1980. Act revived popularity in 2007 with movie *Alvin And The Chipmunks*.

DAVID SEVILLE AND THE CHIPMUNKS:

11/30/59+	4	41		1 Let's All Sing With The Chipmunks [N]		Liberty 3132
				Grammy: Children's Album		
6/20/60	31	5		2 Sing Again With The Chipmunks [N]		Liberty 3159

THE CHIPMUNKS WITH DAVID SEVILLE:

12/22/62	84	2	▲	3 Christmas With The Chipmunks [X-N]	Cat:#44/4	Liberty 7256
				Christmas charts: 33/'65, 36/'66, 33/'67, 23/'87, 21/'88		
12/7/63	9ˣ	13		4 Christmas With The Chipmunks, Vol. 2 [X-N]		Liberty 7334
				Christmas charts: 9/'63, 18/'64, 18/'67, 31/'68		
9/5/64	14	23		5 The Chipmunks Sing The Beatles Hits [N]		Liberty 7388

THE CHIPMUNKS:

8/9/80	34	26	●	6 Chipmunk Punk [N]		Excelsior 6008
6/6/81	56	35	●	7 Urban Chipmunk [N]	Cat:#25/4	RCA 4027
11/21/81+	72	9	●	8 A Chipmunk Christmas [X-N]		RCA 4041
				Christmas charts: 10/'83, 8/'84		
6/5/82	109	6		9 Chipmunk Rock [N]		RCA 4304

ALVIN & THE CHIPMUNKS:

10/24/92+	21	28	▲	10 Chipmunks In Low Places [N]		Epic 53006
12/17/94	147	3		11 A Very Merry Chipmunk [X-N]		Chipmunk/Epic 64434
				Christmas chart: 33/'94		
11/20/04+	38ˣ	5		12 Merry Christmas From The Chipmunks [X-N]		Capitol 90302
				Christmas charts: 45/'04, 38/'05		
11/18/06	38ˣ	5		13 Christmas With The Chipmunks [X-N]		Madacy 6449
				Christmas charts: 38/'06, 49/'07		
11/25/06+	12ˣ	17		14 Christmas With The Chipmunks [X-N]	Cat:#7/11	Capitol 65136
				Christmas charts: 43/'06, 12/'07		
11/10/07+	37ˣ	4		15 Christmas With The Chipmunks [X-N]	Cat:#42/2	Madacy 53003 [2]
12/22/07+	5	58	▲	16 Alvin And The Chipmunks [N-S]		Fox 82986
11/22/08	78	14		17 Undeniable [N]		Chipmunk 83009
12/5/09	64	7		18 Christmas With The Chipmunks [X-N]	Cat:#4/11	Capitol 36588
				Christmas charts: 13/'08, 14/'09		
12/19/09+	6	24↑	●	19 Alvin And The Chipmunks: The Squeakquel [N-S]		Fox 522421

!!! (CHK CHK CHK)

Punk-disco band from Sacramento, California: Nic Offer (vocals), Mario Andreoni (guitar), Tyler Pope (guitar), Dan Gorman (trumpet), Allan Wilson (sax), Jason Racine (percussion), Justin Van Der Volgen (bass) and John Pugh (drums).

3/24/07	195	1		1 Myth Takes	Warp 154

CHOCOLATE MILK

R&B band from New Orleans, Louisiana: Frank Richard (vocals), Amadee Castanell (saxophone), Joe Foxx (trumpet), Robert Dabon (keyboards), Mario Tio (guitar) and Dwight Richards (drums).

10/25/75	191	3		1 Action Speaks Louder Than Words	RCA Victor 1188
10/9/76	202	6		2 Comin'	RCA Victor 1830
6/24/78	171	5		3 We're All In This Together	RCA Victor 2331
4/14/79	161	6		4 Milky Way	RCA Victor 3081
12/12/81+	162	10		5 Blue Jeans	RCA Victor 3896

CHOIR OF THE VIENNA HOFBURGKAPELLE

Austrian choir. Conducted by Josef Schabasser.

7/30/94	185	1		1 Mystical Chants [F]	Special Music 5118

CHOPPA

Born Darwin Turner in New Orleans, Louisiana. Male rapper.

3/22/03	54	8		1 Straight From The N.O.	New No Limit 075007

CHRISTIAN

Born Cristian Castro on 12/8/1974 in Mexico City, Mexico. Latin singer.

6/23/01	193	1		1 Azul [F]	Ariola 85324
10/18/03	167	1		2 Amar Es [F]	Ariola 55195

CHRISTIANS, The

Rock trio from Liverpool, England: brothers Garry Christian (vocals) and Russell Christian (sax), with multi-instrumentalist Henry Priestman.

3/12/88	158	8		1 The Christians	Island 90852

CHRISTIE

Pop-rock trio from England: Jeff Christie (vocals, bass), Vic Elmes (guitar) and Mike Blakely (drums). Blakely's brother, Alan, was a member of **The Tremeloes**.

12/12/70+	115	10		1 Yellow River	Epic 30403

CHRISTIE, Lou
Born Lugee Sacco on 2/19/1943 in Glenwillard, Pennsylvania. Pop singer/songwriter.

DEBUT	PEAK	WKS		ARTIST / Album Title	Catalog	Label & Number
8/24/63	124	6		1 Lou Christie		Roulette 25208
3/5/66	103	14		2 Lightnin' Strikes		MGM 4360

~ ~ ~ ~ ~ ~ ~ ~ ~ ~ **NON-CHARTED ALBUMS** ~ ~ ~ ~ ~ ~ ~ ~ ~ ~
1966 **Lou Christie Strikes Again** [Roulette label]   1966 **Lou Christie Strikes Again** [Colpix label]

CHRISTION
R&B vocal duo from Oakland, California: Kenny Ski and Allen Anthony.

| 11/22/97 | 146 | 2 | | 1 Ghetto Cyrano .... | | Roc-A-Fella 536281 |

CHRISTOPHER, Gavin
Born on 3/5/1956 in Chicago, Illinois. Male R&B singer/songwriter/producer.

| 7/5/86 | 74 | 15 | | 1 One Step Closer .... | | Manhattan 53024 |

CHRISTY, June
Born Shirley Luster on 11/20/1925 in Springfield, Illinois. Died of kidney failure on 6/21/1990 (age 64). Jazz singer. Achieved national fame with the **Stan Kenton** band. Orchestra conducted by Pete Rugolo.

| 9/29/56 | 14 | 4 | | 1 The Misty Miss Christy .... | | Capitol 725 |
| 7/22/57 | 16 | 4 | | 2 June - Fair and Warmer! .... | | Capitol 833 |

CHUBB ROCK
Born Richard Simpson on 5/28/1968 in Jamaica; raised in Brooklyn, New York. Male rapper.

3/23/91	73	10		1 Treat 'Em Right.......................		Select 9063
6/8/91	71	21		2 The One		Select 21640
9/19/92	127	3		3 I Gotta Get Mine Yo! - Book Of Rhymes.......................		Select 61299

CHUCK D
Born Carlton Ridenhour on 8/1/1960 in Roosevelt, Long Island, New York. Male rapper. Leader of **Public Enemy**.

| 11/9/96 | 190 | 1 | | 1 Autobiography Of Mistachuck .... | | Mercury 532944 |

CHUMBAWAMBA
Post-punk rock band from Leeds, England: Alice Nutter, Lou Watts, Danbert Nubacon, Paul Greco, Jude Abbott, Dunstan Bruce, Neil Ferguson and Harry Hamer.

| 10/11/97+ | 3² | 43 | ▲³ | 1 Tubthumper | | Republic 53099 |

CHUNKY A
Chunkston Arthur Hall is actually comedian Arsenio Hall. Born on 2/12/1957 in Cleveland, Ohio. Hosted own late night talk show (1989-1994) and starred in own sitcom (1997). Acted in several movies.

| 12/16/89+ | 71 | 13 | | 1 Large And In Charge .... [N] | | MCA 6354 |

CHURCH, The
Alternative pop-rock band from Canberra, Australia: Steve Kilbey (vocals, bass), Peter Koppes (guitar), Marty Willson-Piper (guitar) and Richard Ploog (drums). Ploog left in 1991, replaced by Jay Dee Daugherty.

6/21/86	146	11		1 Heyday		Warner 25370
3/12/88	41	36	●	2 Starfish.......................		Arista 8521
3/31/90	66	20		3 Gold Afternoon Fix		Arista 8579
3/28/92	176	2		4 Priest = Aura		Arista 18683

CHURCH, Charlotte
Born on 2/21/1986 in Llandaff, Cardiff, Wales. Teenage classical singer.

4/3/99	28	77	▲²	1 Voice Of An Angel .... Cat:#38/2		Sony Classical 60957
12/4/99+	40	28	▲	2 Charlotte Church.......................		Sony Classical 64356
11/4/00	7	12	▲	3 Dream A Dream Cat:❶¹/17 [X]		Sony Classical 89463
				Christmas charts: 1/00, 5/01, 11/02, 24/03		
10/27/01	15	20	●	4 Enchantment		Columbia 89710
12/1/01	102	6		5 Our Favorite Things .... [X-L]		Sony Classical 89468
				TONY BENNETT / CHARLOTTE CHURCH / PLACIDO DOMINGO / VANESSA WILLIAMS recorded on 12/21/2000 at the Konzerthaus in Vienna, Austria; Christmas chart: 10/01		
12/14/02	76	10		6 Prelude: The Best Of Charlotte Church .... [G]		Columbia 86990

CHURCH, Eric
Born on 5/3/1977 in Granite Falls, North Carolina. Country singer/songwriter.

| 8/5/06 | 29 | 20 | | 1 Sinners Like Me .... | | Capitol 60745 |
| 4/11/09 | 17 | 33 | | 2 Carolina....................... | | Capitol 20810 |

CIARA
Born Ciara Harris on 10/25/1985 in Austin, Texas; raised in Atlanta, Georgia. Female R&B singer.

10/16/04	3¹	71	▲³	1 Goodies		LaFace 62819
12/23/06	❶¹	37	▲	2 Ciara: The Evolution		LaFace 03336
5/23/09	3¹	10		3 Fantasy Ride		LaFace 31390

CIBO MATTO
Rock band formed in New York: **Sean Lennon** (son of **John Lennon**; bass), Miho Hatori (vocals, guitar), Yuka Honda (keyboards) and Timo Ellis (drums).

| 6/26/99 | 171 | 1 | | 1 Stereo * Type A....................... | | Warner 47345 |

CINCOTTI, Peter
Born on 7/11/1983 in Manhattan, New York. Jazz singer/pianist. Played Dick "**King Richard**" Behrke in the 2004 movie *Beyond The Sea*.

3/29/03	118	6		1 Peter Cincotti		Concord 2159
10/2/04	128	2		2 On The Moon		Concord 2221

CINDERELLA
Hard-rock band from Philadelphia, Pennsylvania: Tom Keifer (vocals, guitar), Jeff LaBar (guitar), Eric Brittingham (bass) and Fred Coury (drums; left in 1992 and formed **Arcade**).

7/19/86+	3²	70	▲³	1 Night Songs		Mercury 830076
7/23/88	10	66	▲³	2 Long Cold Winter		Mercury 834612
12/8/90	19	32	▲	3 Heartbreak Station		Mercury 848018
11/26/94	178	1		4 Still Climbing		Mercury 522947

CINEMATIC SUNRISE
Rock band from Detroit, Michigan: Craig Owens (vocals), Bryan Beeler (guitar), Mick Martin (guitar), Brad Bell (piano), Marcus VanKirk (bass) and Dave Shapiro (drums).

5/31/08	196	1		1 A Coloring Storybook And Long Playing Record		Equal Vision 147

CIRCA SURVIVE
Punk-rock band from Philadelphia, Pennsylvania: **Anthony Green** (vocals), Colin Frangicetto (guitar), Brendan Ekstrom (guitar), Nick Beard (bass) and Steve Clifford (drums).

5/7/05	183	1		1 Juturna		Equal Vision 103
6/16/07	24	5		2 On Letting Go		Equal Vision 139

CIRCUS OF POWER
Hard-rock band formed in New York: Alex Mitchell (vocals), Ricky Mahler (guitar), Gary Sunshine (bass) and Ryan Maher (drums).

11/12/88	185	2		1 Circus Of Power		RCA 8464

CISSEL, Chuck
Born in Tulsa, Oklahoma. R&B singer/actor. Acted in several Broadway shows.

2/23/80	204	4		1 Just For You		Arista 4257

CISTERCIAN MONKS OF STIFT HEILIGENKREUZ, The
Traditional chants recorded by a group of monks from the Heiligenkreuz Abbey near Baden, Austria.

7/19/08	183	1		1 Chant: Music For The Soul .... **[F]**		Decca 011489

CITIZEN COPE
Born Clarence Greenwood in Memphis, Tennessee; later based in Brooklyn, New York. Eclectic singer/songwriter/musician.

9/30/06	69	2		1 Every Waking Moment		RCA 86993

CITY BOY
Pop-rock band from Birmingham, England: Lol Mason (vocals), Mike Slamer (guitar), Max Thomas (keyboards), Steve Broughton (percussion), Chris Dunn (bass) and Roger Kent (drums). In 1978, Roy Ward replaced Kent.

8/28/76	177	3		1 City Boy		Mercury 1098
2/12/77	170	4		2 Dinner At The Ritz		Mercury 1121
10/8/77	207	2		3 Young Men Gone West		Mercury 1182
9/16/78	115	9		4 Book Early		Mercury 3737

CITY HIGH
Hip-hop trio from Willingboro, New Jersey: Claudette Ortiz, Robby Pardio and Ryan Toby.

6/9/01	34	40	●	1 City High		Booga Base. 490890

CITY OF REFUGE SANCTUARY CHOIR, The
Gospel choir based in Gardena, California. Directed by Bishop Noel Jones.

7/14/07	172	1		1 Welcome To The City		Tyscot 4159

C.J. & CO.
Disco group from Detroit, Michigan: Cornelius Brown, Curtis Durden, Joni Tolbert, Connie Durden and Charles Clark.

7/9/77	60	23		1 Devil's Gun		Westbound 6100
9/2/78	204	1		2 Deadeye Dick		Westbound 6104

CKY
Punk-rock band from West Chester, Pennsylvania: Deron Miller (vocals, guitar), Chad Ginsburg (guitar), Vern Zaborowski (bass) and Jess Margera (drums). Margera is the brother of Bam Margera of MTV's *Jackass* and *Viva La Bam*. CKY: Camp Kill Yourself.

10/12/02	99	3		1 Infiltrate-Destroy-Rebuild		Island 063100
7/16/05	35	6		2 An Answer Can Be Found		Island 004837
6/6/09	46	2		3 Carver City		Roadrunner 618005

CLANCY BROTHERS & TOMMY MAKEM
Folk band from Ireland: brothers Tom Clancy, Liam Clancy and Pat Clancy with Tommy Makem. Tom acted off-Broadway and in TV through the 1980s. Tom died of cancer on 11/7/1990 (age 67). Pat died of cancer on 11/11/1998 (age 76). Tommy died of lung cancer on 8/1/2007 (age 74). Liam died on 12/4/2009 (age 74).

11/16/63	60	12		1 In Person At Carnegie Hall .... **[L]**		Columbia 1950
				recorded on 11/3/1962		
5/2/64	91	6		2 The First Hurrah!		Columbia 2165

Billboard			R I A A	ARTIST		
DEBUT	**PEAK**	**WKS**		Album Title	Catalog	Label & Number

CLANNAD
Folk-pop band from Ireland: Maire Brennan (vocals) with brothers Pol and Ciaran Brennan, and twin uncles Noel and Padraig Duggan. Pol left by 1993. Group name is Gaelic for family. Singer **Enya**, the sister of the Brennans, was a member from 1980-82.

3/22/86	131	12		1 Macalla	RCA Victor 8063
3/5/88	183	5		2 Sirius	RCA 6846
3/20/93	46	24	●	3 Anam	Atlantic 82409
7/3/93	110	11	●	4 Banba	Atlantic 82503
3/23/96	195	1		5 Lore	Atlantic 82753

CLANTON, Jimmy
Born on 9/2/1940 in Baton Rouge, Louisiana. Rock and roll teen idol. Brother of Ike Clanton. Toured with Dick Clark's Caravan Of Stars. Starred in the 1958 movie *Go, Johnny, Go!*. DJ in Lancaster, Pennsylvania, from 1972-76.

~ ~ ~ ~ ~ ~ ~ ~ ~ ~ **NON-CHARTED ALBUMS** ~ ~ ~ ~ ~ ~ ~ ~ ~ ~ ~

1958 **Just A Dream**	1961 **Teenage Millionaire** *[soundtrack]*
1960 **Jimmy's Happy/Jimmy's Blue**	1962 **Venus In Blue Jeans**
1960 **My Best To You**	1964 **The Best Of Jimmy Clanton**

CLAPTON, Eric   1970s: #22 / 1980s: #32 / 1990s: #9 / All-Time: #11
Born on 3/30/1945 in Ripley, Surrey, England. Prolific rock-blues singer/songwriter/guitarist. With The Roosters in 1963, **The Yardbirds**, 1963-65, and **John Mayall**'s Bluesbreakers, 1965-66. Formed **Cream** with **Jack Bruce** and **Ginger Baker** in 1966. Formed **Blind Faith** in 1968; worked with **John Lennon**'s Plastic Ono Band, and **Delaney & Bonnie**. Formed **Derek and The Dominos** in 1970. After two years of reclusion (1971-72), Clapton performed his comeback concert at London's Rainbow Theatre in January 1973. Began actively recording and touring again in 1974. Clapton's four-year-old son, Conor, died on 3/20/1991 in a 53-floor fall in New York City. Nicknamed "Slowhand" in 1964 while with The Yardbirds.
AWARD: R&R Hall of Fame: 2000

7/25/70	13	30		1 Eric Clapton		Atco 329
11/21/70	16	65	●	2 Layla		Atco 704 [2]
				DEREK AND THE DOMINOS		
				Grammy: Hall of Fame ★ RS500 #115		
7/20/74	❶⁴	25	●	3 461 Ocean Boulevard		RSO 4801
				RS500 #409		
				address where recorded in Miami, Florida		
4/12/75	21	14		4 There's One In Every Crowd		RSO 4806
10/16/76	15	21		5 No Reason To Cry		RSO 3004
11/26/77+	2⁵	74	▲³	6 Slowhand	Cat:#48/1	RSO 3030
				RS500 #325		
12/2/78+	8	37	▲	7 Backless		RSO 3039
3/21/81	7	21	●	8 Another Ticket		RSO 3095
2/19/83	16	19		9 Money And Cigarettes		Duck 23773
4/6/85	34	28	▲	10 Behind The Sun		Duck 25166
12/27/86+	37	34	●	11 August		Duck 25476
11/25/89+	16	51	▲²	12 Journeyman		Duck 26074
2/1/92	24	31	●	13 Rush	[I-S]	Reprise 26794
3/28/98	4	29	▲	14 Pilgrim		Duck 46577
7/1/00	3¹	43	▲²	15 Riding With The King		Reprise 47612
				B.B. KING & ERIC CLAPTON		
				Grammy: Traditional Blues Album		
3/31/01	5	16	●	16 Reptile		Duck 47966
4/17/04	6	18	●	17 Me And Mr. Johnson		Duck 48423
				all songs written by blues legend Robert Johnson		
9/17/05	13	14	●	18 Back Home		Duck 49395
11/25/06	23	20	●	19 The Road To Escondido		Duck 44418
				J.J. CALE & ERIC CLAPTON		

GREATEST HITS & COMPILATIONS:

4/15/72	6	42	●	20 History Of Eric Clapton		Atco 803 [2]
10/14/72	87	17		21 Eric Clapton At His Best		Polydor 3503 [2]
2/17/73	67	11		22 Clapton		Polydor 5526
5/22/82	101	14	▲⁷	23 Time Pieces/The Best Of Eric Clapton	Cat:❶³⁷/327	RSO 3099
5/7/88	34	26	▲³	24 Crossroads		Polydor 835261 [6]
3/25/95	80	30	▲²	25 The Cream Of Clapton	Cat:#15/103	Chronicles 527116
8/14/99	52	9	●	26 Blues		Polydor 547178 [2]
10/30/99	20	28	▲	27 Clapton Chronicles - The Best Of Eric Clapton		Duck 47553
5/7/05	143	5		28 The Best Of Eric Clapton: 20th Century Masters The Millennium Collection	Cat:#20/14	Chronicles 002759
10/27/07	14	19	●	29 Complete Clapton		Duck 294332 [2]

LIVE ALBUMS:

1/27/73	20	21	●	30 Derek & The Dominos In Concert		RSO 8800 [2]
				DEREK & THE DOMINOS		
				recorded at the Fillmore East in New York City		
9/22/73	18	14		31 Eric Clapton's Rainbow Concert		RSO 877
				recorded at the Rainbow Theatre in London		
9/6/75	20	13		32 E.C. Was Here		RSO 4809

Billboard		R I A A	ARTIST		
DEBUT	PEAK	WKS	Album Title	Catalog	Label & Number

CLAPTON, Eric — cont'd

DEBUT	PEAK	WKS				Label & Number
5/3/80	2⁶	31	●	33 **Just One Night**		RSO 4202 [2]
				recorded December 1979 at the Budokan concert hall in Japan		
10/26/91	38	19	●	34 **24 Nights**		Duck 26420 [2]
				recorded at the Royal Albert Hall in London, England		
9/12/92+	❶³	137	▲¹⁰	35 **Unplugged**	Cat:#25/28	Duck 45024
				Grammys: Album of the Year / Male Rock Vocal		
				recorded on 3/12/1992		
10/1/94	❶¹	41	▲³	36 **From The Cradle**		Duck 45735
				Grammy: Traditional Blues Album		
4/20/96	137	1		37 **Crossroads 2 (Live In The Seventies)**		Chronicles 529305 [4]
11/23/02	43	9		38 **One More Car, One More Rider**		Duck 48374 [2]
12/25/04	172	2		39 **Sessions For Robert J**		Duck 48926
6/6/09	14	11		40 **Live From Madison Square Garden**		Wincraft 517584 [2]
				ERIC CLAPTON & STEVE WINWOOD		
				REISSUES:		
8/10/74	107	10		41 **Layla**		Polydor 3501 [2]
2/19/77	183	2		42 **Layla**		RSO 3801 [2]
10/6/90	157	5		43 **The Layla Sessions - 20th Anniversary Edition**		Polydor 847083 [3]
				DEREK AND THE DOMINOS (above 3)		
3/5/77	194	2		44 **Eric Clapton**		RSO 3008

CLAP YOUR HANDS SAY YEAH
Alternative-rock band formed in Brooklyn, New York: Alec Ounsworth (vocals, guitar), Robbie Guertin (guitar), twin brothers Lee Sargent (guitar) and Tyler Sargent (bass), and Sean Greenhalgh (drums).

DEBUT	PEAK	WKS			Label & Number
2/17/07	47	2	1 **Some Loud Thunder**		Clap Your Hands 68611

CLARK, Claudine
Born on 4/26/1941 in Macon, Georgia; raised in Philadelphia, Pennsylvania. R&B singer/songwriter.

~ ~ ~ ~ ~ ~ ~ ~ ~ ~ ~ **NON-CHARTED ALBUM** ~ ~ ~ ~ ~ ~ ~ ~ ~ ~ ~
1962 **Party Lights**

CLARK, Dave, Five　　　　　　　　　　　　　　　　　　　　　　　**All-Time: #320**
Born on 12/15/1939 in Tottenham, London, England. Pop-rock drummer. His group consisted of Mike Smith (vocals, keyboards), Lenny Davidson (guitar), Denny Payton (sax) and Rick Huxley (bass). Group starred in the 1965 movie *Having A Wild Weekend*. Clark co-wrote and produced the 1986 London stage musical *Time*. Payton died on 12/17/2006 (age 63). Smith died on 2/28/2008 (age 64).
AWARD: R&R Hall of Fame: 2008

DEBUT	PEAK	WKS				Label & Number
4/11/64	3¹	32	●	1 **Glad All Over**		Epic 26093
6/20/64	5	22		2 **The Dave Clark Five Return!**		Epic 26104
8/29/64	11	28		3 **American Tour**		Epic 26117
1/2/65	6	21		4 **Coast To Coast**		Epic 26128
4/3/65	24	23		5 **Weekend In London**		Epic 26139
8/14/65	15	21		6 **Having A Wild Weekend**	[S]	Epic 26162
12/11/65+	32	16		7 **I Like It Like That**		Epic 26178
2/26/66	9	62	●	8 **The Dave Clark Five's Greatest Hits**	[G]	Epic 26185
6/25/66	77	11		9 **Try Too Hard**		Epic 26198
10/1/66	127	6		10 **Satisfied With You**		Epic 26212
12/10/66+	103	7		11 **The Dave Clark Five/More Greatest Hits**	[G]	Epic 26221
3/25/67	119	7		12 **5 By 5**		Epic 26236
8/12/67	149	3		13 **You Got What It Takes**		Epic 26312
8/21/93	127	1		14 **The History Of The Dave Clark Five**	[K]	Hollywood 61482 [2]

CLARK, Dee
Born Delecta Clark on 11/7/1938 in Blytheville, Arkansas; raised in Chicago, Illinois. Died of a heart attack on 12/7/1990 (age 52). Male R&B singer.

~ ~ ~ ~ ~ ~ ~ ~ ~ ~ **NON-CHARTED ALBUMS** ~ ~ ~ ~ ~ ~ ~ ~ ~ ~
1959 **Dee Clark**　　　　　　　　　　　　　1961 **Hold On...It's Dee Clark**
1960 **How About That**　　　　　　　　　1964 **The Best Of Dee Clark**
1960 **You're Looking Good**

CLARK, Dick — see VARIOUS ARTISTS COMPILATIONS: "Dick Clark..."

CLARK, Gene
Born Harold Eugene Clark on 11/17/1941 in Tipton, Missouri. Died on 5/24/1991 (age 49). Rock singer/guitarist. Member of **The Byrds** and **McGuinn, Clark & Hillman**.

DEBUT	PEAK	WKS			Label & Number
11/2/74	144	5	1 **No Other**		Asylum 1016

CLARK, Mike E.
Born in Detroit, Michigan; raised in Roseville, Michigan. DJ/record producer.

DEBUT	PEAK	WKS			Label & Number
7/11/09	125	1	1 **Murder Mix Volume 1**		Psychopathic 4608

CLARK, Petula
Born on 11/15/1932 in Epsom, Surrey, England. Pop singer/actress. Hosted own radio and TV shows in England. Starred in several movies including *Finian's Rainbow* and *Goodbye Mr. Chips*.

All-Time: #412

DEBUT	PEAK	WKS			Label & Number
2/13/65	21	36		1 Downtown	Warner 1590
5/29/65	42	17		2 I Know A Place	Warner 1598
10/23/65	129	9		3 The World's Greatest International Hits!	Warner 1608
4/9/66	68	12		4 My Love	Warner 1630
9/3/66	43	16		5 I Couldn't Live Without Your Love	Warner 1645
2/18/67	49	27		6 Color My World/Who Am I	Warner 1673
9/2/67	27	27		7 These Are My Songs	Warner 1698
2/17/68	93	23		8 The Other Man's Grass Is Always Greener	Warner 1719
9/7/68	51	21		9 Petula	Warner 1743
12/28/68+	57	17		10 Petula Clark's Greatest Hits, Vol. 1 [G]	Warner 1765
5/17/69	37	11		11 Portrait Of Petula	Warner 1789
12/27/69+	176	7		12 Just Pet	Warner 1823
8/8/70	198	2		13 Memphis	Warner 1862
4/10/71	178	3		14 Warm And Tender	Warner 1885

CLARK, Roy
Born on 4/15/1933 in Meherrin, Virginia. Country singer/songwriter/guitarist/banjo player. Co-hosted TV's *Hee-Haw*.
AWARDS: C&W Hall of Fame: 2009 ★ CMA: Comedian 1970 / Entertainer 1973 / Instrumental Group (w/ Buck Trent) 1975 & 1976 / Musician 1977, 1978 & 1980 ★ OPRY: 1987

DEBUT	PEAK	WKS			Label & Number
7/5/69	50	20		1 Yesterday, When I Was Young	Dot 25953
1/3/70	129	9		2 The Everlovin' Soul Of Roy Clark	Dot 25972
8/29/70	176	6		3 I Never Picked Cotton	Dot 25980
4/3/71	178	8		4 The Best Of Roy Clark [G]	Dot 25986
8/14/71	197	2		5 The Incredible Roy Clark	Dot 25990
7/29/72	112	12		6 Roy Clark Country!	Dot 25997
12/16/72	207	3		7 Roy Clark Live! [L]	Dot 26005
				recorded at the Landmark Hotel in Las Vegas	
5/5/73	172	6		8 Roy Clark / Superpicker [I]	Dot 26008
2/9/74	204	5		9 Roy Clark's Family Album	Dot 26018
4/13/74	186	3		10 Roy Clark / The Entertainer	ABC/Dot 2001

CLARK, Terri
Born Terri Sauson (Clark is her stepfather's last name) on 8/5/1968 in Montreal, Quebec, Canada; raised in Medicine Hat, Alberta, Canada. Female country singer/songwriter/guitarist.
AWARD: OPRY: 2004

DEBUT	PEAK	WKS			Label & Number
9/23/95+	79	47	▲	1 Terri Clark	Mercury 526991
11/23/96	58	25	▲	2 Just The Same	Mercury 532879
6/6/98	70	16	▲	3 How I Feel	Mercury 558211
10/7/00	85	3		4 Fearless	Mercury 170157
2/1/03	27	8		5 Pain To Kill	Mercury 170325
8/14/04	14	34	●	6 Greatest Hits 1994-2004 [G]	Mercury 001906
11/19/05	26	5		7 Life Goes On	Mercury 002579

CLARK-COLE, Dorinda
Born on 10/19/1957 in Detroit, Michigan. Gospel singer. Member of **The Clark Sisters**. Sister of **Karen Clark-Sheard**. Aunt of **Kierra KiKi Sheard**.

DEBUT	PEAK	WKS			Label & Number
9/17/05	159	1		1 Live From Houston-The Rose Of Gospel [L]	GospoCentric 70611
5/3/08	104	1		2 Take It Back	Gospo Centric 10027

CLARKE, Stanley
Born on 6/30/1951 in Philadelphia, Pennsylvania. R&B-jazz bassist/violinist/cellist. With **Chick Corea** in **Return To Forever** in 1973. Much session work, solo debut in 1974. Member of **Fuse One**, **Animal Logic** and **S.M.V.**

DEBUT	PEAK	WKS			Label & Number
1/18/75	59	16		1 Stanley Clarke [I]	Nemperor 431
11/1/75	34	19		2 Journey To Love [I]	Nemperor 433
9/25/76	34	22		3 School Days [I]	Nemperor 439
4/29/78	57	19		4 Modern Man [I]	Nemperor 35303
7/21/79	62	14		5 I Wanna Play For You [I-L]	Nemperor 35680 [2]
6/28/80	95	11		6 Rocks, Pebbles And Sand	Epic 36506
5/9/81	33	23		7 The Clarke/Duke Project	Epic 36918
				STANLEY CLARKE/GEORGE DUKE	
8/21/82	114	8		8 Let Me Know You	Epic 38086
11/26/83+	146	10		9 The Clarke/Duke Project II	Epic 38934
				STANLEY CLARKE/GEORGE DUKE	
4/28/84	149	13		10 Time Exposure	Epic 38688
7/27/85	203	4		11 Find Out!	Epic 40040
				THE STANLEY CLARKE BAND	

CLARKS, The
Rock band from Pittsburgh, Pennsylvania: Scott Blasey (vocals, guitar), Rob James (guitar), Greg Joseph (bass) and Dave Minarik (drums).

DEBUT	PEAK	WKS			Label & Number
6/29/02	143	1		1 Another Happy Ending	Razor & Tie 82884
6/26/04	196	1		2 Fast Moving Cars	Razor & Tie 82918
6/27/09	136	1		3 Restless Days	High Wire 019

Billboard DEBUT	PEAK	WKS	R I A A	ARTIST / Album Title	Catalog	Label & Number

CLARK-SHEARD, Karen
Born on 11/15/1960 in Detroit, Michigan. Gospel singer. Member of **The Clark Sisters**. Sister of **Dorinda Clark-Cole**. Mother of **Kierra KiKi Sheard**.

DEBUT	PEAK	WKS				
8/17/02	82	6		1 2nd Chance		Elektra 62767
11/22/03	188	1		2 The Heavens Are Telling		Elektra 62894
2/11/06	124	2		3 It's Not Over		Word-Curb 86379

CLARK SISTERS, The
Family gospel group from Detroit, Michigan: **Karen Clark-Sheard**, Jackie Clark, **Dorinda Clark-Cole**, Niecy Clark and Elbernita Clark.

4/28/07	56	5		1 Live...One Last Time	[L]	EMI Gospel 81094
				Grammy: Traditional Gospel Album		
10/24/09	18ˣ	1		2 The Clark Sisters' Family Christmas	[X]	Karew 94724

CLARKSON, Kelly
Born on 4/24/1982 in Burleson, Texas. Female pop singer. Winner of TV's first *American Idol* talent series.

5/3/03	❶¹	50	▲²	1 Thankful	Cat:#12/55	RCA 68159
12/18/04	3¹	104	▲⁶	2 Breakaway	Cat:❶¹/58	RCA 64491
				Grammy: Pop Vocal Album		
7/14/07	2¹	18	▲	3 My December		RCA 06900
3/28/09	❶²	47		4 All I Ever Wanted		S Records 32715

CLASH, The
Punk-rock band formed in London, England: John "**Joe Strummer**" Mellor (vocals; born on 8/21/1952; died of a heart attack on 12/22/2002, age 50), Mick Jones (guitar; born on 6/26/1955), Paul Simonon (bass; born on 12/15/1955) and Nicky "Topper" Headon (drums; born on 5/30/1955). Political activists who wrote songs protesting racism and oppression. Headon left in May 1983; replaced by Peter Howard. Jones (not to be confused with Mick Jones of Foreigner) left band in 1984 to form **Big Audio Dynamite**. Strummer disbanded The Clash in early 1986, and appeared in the 1987 movie *Straight To Hell*. Simonon formed **Havana 3 A.M.** in 1990; later joined **The Good, The Bad & The Queen**.
AWARD: R&R Hall of Fame: 2003

2/24/79	128	10		1 Give 'Em Enough Rope		Epic 35543
9/8/79	126	6	●	2 The Clash		Epic 36060
				RS500 #77		
2/9/80	27	33	▲	3 London Calling	Cat:#5/2	Epic 36328 [2]
				RS500 #8		
11/22/80	74	16		4 Black Market Clash		Epic 36846
2/7/81	24	20	●	5 Sandinista!		Epic 37037 [3]
				RS500 #404		
6/12/82+	7	61	▲²	6 Combat Rock		Epic 37689
12/7/85+	88	12		7 Cut The Crap		Epic 40017
5/28/88	142	8	▲	8 The Story Of The Clash, Volume I	[G]	Epic 44035 [2]
11/13/99	193	1		9 From Here To Eternity Live	[L]	Epic 65747
				recorded from 1978-82		
3/29/03	99	2		10 The Essential Clash	[G]	Epic 89056 [2]
10/25/08	93	2		11 Live At Shea Stadium	[L]	Epic 34880

CLASSIC CRIME, The
Alternative-rock band from Seattle, Washington: Matt MacDonald (vocals), Robert Negrin (guitar), Justin DuQue (guitar), Alan Clark (bass) and Paul Erickson (drums).

8/9/08	123	1		1 The Silver Cord		Tooth & Nail 06165

CLASSICS IV
Soft-rock band from Jacksonville, Florida: Dennis Yost (vocals), J.R. Cobb (guitar), Wally Eaton (guitar), Joe Wilson (bass; replaced by Dean Daughtry) and Kim Venable (drums). Cobb, Daughtry and producer Buddy Buie joined the **Atlanta Rhythm Section** in 1974. Yost died of respiratory failure on 12/7/2008 (age 65).

3/9/68	140	7		1 Spooky		Imperial 12371
2/1/69	196	3		2 Mamas And Papas/Soul Train		Imperial 12407
4/26/69	45	20		3 Traces		Imperial 12429
12/6/69+	50	20		4 Dennis Yost & The Classics IV/Golden Greats-Volume I	[G]	Imperial 16000

CLAY, Andrew Dice
Born Andrew Silverstein on 9/29/1957 in Brooklyn, New York. Stand-up comedian/actor. Appeared in several movies and TV shows.

4/29/89	94	47		1 Dice	[C]	Def American 24214
4/21/90	39	24		2 The Day The Laughter Died	[C]	Def American 24287 [2]
5/4/91	81	12		3 Dice Rules	[C]	Def American 26555
5/2/92	144	4		4 40 Too Long	[C]	Def American 26854

CLAY, Cassius
Born on 1/18/1942 in Louisville, Kentucky. Former world heavyweight boxing champ. Changed name to Muhammad Ali in 1966. Also see **Soundtracks**: *The Greatest*.

10/12/63	61	20		1 I Am The Greatest!	[C]	Columbia 2093 / 8893

CLAY, Tom
Born Thomas Clague on 8/20/1929 in Binghamton, New York. Died of cancer on 11/22/1995 (age 66). Was a DJ at KGBS in Los Angeles when he created this recording.

8/28/71	92	5		1 What The World Needs Now Is Love		MoWest 103

Billboard			R I A A	ARTIST		
DEBUT	PEAK	WKS		Album Title	Catalog	Label & Number

CLAYDERMAN, Richard
Born Phillipe Pages on 12/28/1953 in Paris, France. Romantic pianist. Known as "The Prince Of Romance."

11/24/84	160	9		1 Amour .... [I]		Columbia 39603

CLAYPOOL, Les
Born on 9/29/1963 in Richmond, California. Alternative-rock singer/bassist. Member of **Primus** and **Oysterhead**.

9/14/96	182	1		1 Highball With The Devil		Interscope 90085
				LES CLAYPOOL & THE HOLY MACKEREL		
10/12/02	145	1		2 Purple Onion		Prawn Song 0005
				THE LES CLAYPOOL FROG BRIGADE		
10/9/04	118	1		3 The Big Eyeball In The Sky		Prawn Song 0006
				COLONEL CLAYPOOL'S BUCKET OF BERNIE BRAINS		
6/17/06	115	1		4 Of Whales And Woe		Prawn Song 0011
4/4/09	110	1		5 Of Fungi And Foe		Prawn Song 0014

CLAYTON, Merry
Born Mary Clayton on 12/25/1948 in New Orleans, Louisiana; later based in Los Angeles, California. R&B session singer. Played "Audrey James" in the 1987 movie *Maid To Order*.

11/20/71+	180	11		1 Merry Clayton		Ode 77012
9/6/75	146	8		2 Keep Your Eye On The Sparrow		Ode 77030

CLAYTON-THOMAS, David
Born David Thomsett on 9/13/1941 in Kingston, Surrey, England; raised in Willowdale, Ontario, Canada. Lead singer of **Blood, Sweat & Tears**.

9/27/69	159	8		1 David Clayton-Thomas!		Decca 75146
4/15/72	184	3		2 David Clayton-Thomas		Columbia 31000
10/28/72	202	2		3 Tequila Sunrise		Columbia 31700

CLEAR LIGHT
Folk-rock band from Los Angeles, California: Cliff DeYoung (vocals), Bob Seal (guitar), Ralph Schuckett (organ), Michael Ney (percussion), Douglas Lubahn (bass) and Dallas Taylor (drums). DeYoung later pursued a solo music and acting career. Taylor later became a prominent session drummer.

11/25/67+	126	13		1 Clear Light		Elektra 74011

CLEFTONES, The
Black doo-wop group from Queens, New York: Herbie Cox (lead), Charlie James (first tenor), Berman Patterson (second tenor), William McClain (baritone) and Warren Corbin (bass). Originally called the Silvertones.

~ ~ ~ ~ ~ ~ ~ ~ ~ ~ **NON-CHARTED ALBUMS** ~ ~ ~ ~ ~ ~ ~ ~ ~ ~
1961 **Heart And Soul**   1961 **For Sentimental Reasons**

CLEGG, Johnny, & Savuka
Born on 7/13/1953 in Rochdale, Lancashire, England; raised in South Africa. Singer/guitarist/dancer. Former member of **Juluka**. Savuka: Steve Mavuso (keyboards), Keith Hutchinson (sax), Solly Letwaba (bass) and Dudu Zulu and Derek De Beer (drums).

9/10/88	155	7		1 Shadow Man		Capitol 90411
5/12/90	123	13		2 Cruel, Crazy, Beautiful World		Capitol 93446

CLEMONS, Clarence
Born on 1/11/1942 in Norfolk, Virginia. R&B saxophonist. Member of **Bruce Springsteen**'s E Street Band. Known as the "Big Man."

11/5/83	174	5		1 Rescue		Columbia 38933
11/23/85+	62	18		2 Hero		Columbia 40010

CLEOPATRA
Black teen vocal trio from Manchester, England: sisters Cleopatra Higgins, Zainam Higgins and Yonah Higgins.

7/25/98	109	14		1 Comin' Atcha!		Maverick 46926

CLEVELAND, James
Born on 12/23/1932 in Chicago, Illinois. Died of heart failure on 2/9/1991 (age 58). Legendary gospel choir leader.

12/13/69	12X	1		1 Merry Christmas .... [X]		Savoy 14195

~ ~ ~ ~ ~ ~ ~ ~ ~ ~ **NON-CHARTED ALBUM** ~ ~ ~ ~ ~ ~ ~ ~ ~ ~
1962 **Peace Be Still**
Grammy: Hall of Fame

CLEVELAND ORCHESTRA
Conducted by Michael Tilson Thomas.

3/29/75	152	4		1 Carl Orff: Carmina Burana..		Columbia 33172
				Grammy: Choral Album		

CLIBURN, Van
Born Harvey Lavan Cliburn on 7/12/1934 in Shreveport, Louisiana. Classical pianist.
AWARD: Grammy: Lifetime Achievement 2004

8/4/58	❶⁷	125	▲	1 Tchaikovsky: Piano Concerto No. 1 [I]		RCA Victor 2252
				Grammys: Classical Album / Hall of Fame		
7/13/59+	10	60		2 Rachmaninoff: Piano Concerto No. 3 [I-L]		RCA Victor 2355
				Grammy: Classical Album recorded on 5/19/1958 at Carnegie Hall		
1/9/61	134	13		3 Schumann: Piano Concerto in A Minor .... [I]		RCA Victor 2455
2/3/62	71	29	●	4 My Favorite Chopin .... [I]		RCA Victor 2576
3/10/62	25	13		5 Brahms: Piano Concerto No. 2 .... [I]		RCA Victor 2581

DEBUT	PEAK	WKS	R I A A	ARTIST Album Title	Catalog	Label & Number
				CLICK, The All-star rap group: **E-40**, **B-Legit The Savage**, **Suga T** and **D-Shot**.		
11/25/95	21	21	●	1 Game Related		Sick Wid' It 41562
10/13/01	99	4		2 Money And Muscle		Sick Wid' It 41716
				CLICK FIVE, The Punk-rock band from Boston, Massachusetts: Eric Dill (vocal, guitar), Joe Guese (guitar), Ben Romans (keyboards), Ethan Mentzer (bass) and Joey Zehr (drums).		
9/3/05	15	20		1 Greetings From Imrie House		Lava 93826
7/14/07	136	1		2 Modern Minds And Pastimes		Lava 168508
				CLIFF, Jimmy Born James Chambers on 4/1/1948 in St. James, Jamaica. Reggae singer/composer. Starred in the movies *The Harder They Come* (1975) and *Club Paradise* (1986). **AWARD: R&R Hall of Fame: 2010**		
9/22/73	214	3		1 Unlimited		Reprise 2147
3/22/75	140	8		2 The Harder They Come .... [S] *Grammy: Hall of Fame ★ RS500 #119*		Mango 9202
11/1/75	195	2		3 Follow My Mind		Reprise 2218
1/20/79	209	1		4 Give Thankx		Warner 3240
12/6/80	201	8		5 I Am The Living		MCA 5153
11/28/81	207	2		6 Give The People What They Want		MCA 5217
8/14/82	186	2		7 Special		Columbia 38099
12/3/83	207	1		8 The Power And The Glory		Columbia 38986
7/26/86	122	6		9 Club Paradise .... [S]		Columbia 40404
				CLIFFORD, Buzz Born Reese Francis Clifford III on 10/8/1942 in Berwyn, Illinois. Teen pop-novelty singer. ~ ~ ~ ~ ~ ~ ~ ~ ~ ~ ~ **NON-CHARTED ALBUM** ~ ~ ~ ~ ~ ~ ~ ~ ~ ~ ~ 1961 **Baby Sittin' With Buzz Clifford**		
				CLIFFORD, Linda Born on 6/14/1948 in Brooklyn, New York. R&B-disco singer.		
5/20/78	22	22		1 If My Friends Could See Me Now		Curtom 5021
4/7/79	26	17		2 Let Me Be Your Woman		RSO 3902 [2]
12/1/79	117	9		3 Here's My Love		RSO 3067
7/19/80	180	4		4 The Right Combination .... **LINDA CLIFFORD & CURTIS MAYFIELD**		RSO 3084
10/4/80	160	6		5 I'm Yours		RSO 3087
				CLIFFORD, Mike Born on 11/6/1943 in Los Angeles, California. White pop singer/actor. In the 1970s Broadway production of *Grease*. ~ ~ ~ ~ ~ ~ ~ ~ ~ ~ ~ **NON-CHARTED ALBUM** ~ ~ ~ ~ ~ ~ ~ ~ ~ ~ ~ 1965 **For The Love Of Mike!** *["Close To Cathy"]*		
				CLIMAX Pop band from Los Angeles, California: Sonny Geraci (vocals), Walter Nims (guitar), Virgil Weber (keyboards), Steve York (bass) and Robert Neilson (drums). Geraci was a member of **The Outsiders**.		
6/24/72	177	7		1 Climax		Rocky Road 3506
				CLIMAX Latin trio from Mexico: Osskar Atilano, Mr. Grillo and Nelly Bedolla. Also known as Grupo Climax.		
8/28/04	79	15		1 Za Za Za .... [F]		Balboa 539
				CLIMAX BLUES BAND Blues-rock band formed in Stafford, Staffordshire, England: Colin Cooper (vocals, sax), Peter Haycock (guitar, vocals), Derek Holt (bass) and John Cuffley (drums). Cooper died of cancer on 7/3/2008 (age 68).		
11/28/70	197	1		1 The Climax Chicago Blues Band Plays On............		Sire 97023
6/26/71	204	8		2 Climax Blues Band...		Sire 4901
2/19/72	211	5		3 Tightly Knit		Sire 5903
2/17/73	150	10		4 Rich Man		Sire 7402
12/1/73+	107	30		5 FM/Live .... [L] recorded at the Academy of Music in New York City; concert broadcast over WNEW-FM in New York City		Sire 7411 [2]
6/15/74	37	29		6 Sense Of Direction		Sire 7501
9/13/75	69	11		7 Stamp Album		Sire 7507
10/23/76+	27	44		8 Gold Plated		Sire 7523
4/29/78	71	11		9 Shine On		Sire 6056
6/16/79	170	6		10 Real To Reel...		Sire 3334
4/25/81	75	16		11 Flying The Flag..		Warner 3493
				CLIMIE FISHER Pop-rock duo formed in London, England: Simon Climie (vocals; born on 4/7/1960) and Rob Fisher (keyboards; born on 11/5/1959; died following surgery on 8/25/1999, age 39). Fisher was also a member of **Naked Eyes**.		
5/28/88	120	16		1 Everything...		Capitol 48338

Billboard			R I A A	ARTIST		
DEBUT	PEAK	WKS		Album Title	Catalog	Label & Number

CLINE, Patsy
Born Virginia Patterson Hensley on 9/8/1932 in Gore, Virginia. Killed in a plane crash on 3/5/1963 (age 30) near Camden, Tennessee. Legendary country singer. Jessica Lange portrayed Cline in the 1985 biographical movie *Sweet Dreams*. Also see **Various Artists Compilations:** *Remembering Patsy Cline*.

AWARDS: Grammy: Lifetime Achievement 1995 ★ C&W Hall of Fame: 1973 ★ OPRY: 1961

DEBUT	PEAK	WKS				
3/31/62+	73	21		1 Patsy Cline Showcase		Decca 4202
11/16/85	29	18	●	2 Sweet Dreams - The Life And Times Of Patsy Cline .... [S]		MCA 6149
				GREATEST HITS & COMPILATIONS:		
8/31/63	74	12	▲	3 The Patsy Cline Story		Decca 7176 [2]
3/7/87+	5^C	376	▲10	4 Patsy Cline's Greatest Hits		MCA 12
				first released in 1967 on Decca 74854		
11/30/91+	24^C	5		5 20 Golden Hits		DeLuxe 7887
				first released in 1989		
1/4/92	166	1	▲	6 The Patsy Cline Collection		MCA 10421 [4]
6/8/96	31^C	2		7 The Legendary Patsy Cline		Pair 1236
1/29/00+	20^C	14	▲	8 Heartaches		MCA 20265
9/20/08	41^C	1		9 The Definitive Collection		MCA Nashville 001791

~ ~ ~ ~ ~ ~ ~ ~ ~ ~ **NON-CHARTED ALBUMS** ~ ~ ~ ~ ~ ~ ~ ~ ~ ~ ~
1957 **Patsy Cline**   2000 **The Ultimate Collection**
1962 **Sentimentally Yours**   *RS500 #234*
1964 **A Portrait Of Patsy Cline**

CLINTON, George
Born on 7/22/1941 in Kannapolis, North Carolina. Highly prolific and influential funk music singer/songwriter/producer. Formed the seminal groups **Parliament** and **Funkadelic**. Those groups spawned several influential musicians and spawned several offshoot groups including **Bootsy's Rubber Band**, **The Brides Of Funkenstein** and the **P-Funk All Stars**.

DEBUT	PEAK	WKS				
12/18/82+	40	33		1 Computer Games		Capitol 12246
1/7/84	102	18		2 You Shouldn't-Nuf Bit Fish...		Capitol 12308
8/10/85	163	6		3 Some Of My Best Jokes Are Friends		Capitol 12417
5/24/86	81	12		4 R&B Skeletons In The Closet		Capitol 12481
9/2/89	192	4		5 The Cinderella Theory		Paisley Park 25994
10/30/93	145	3		6 Hey Man...Smell My Finger		Paisley Park 25518
6/29/96	121	4		7 The Awesome Power Of A Fully-Operational Mothership...............		550 Music 67144
				GEORGE CLINTON & THE P-FUNK ALLSTARS		
11/16/96	138	4		8 Greatest Funkin' Hits .... [K]		Capitol 33911

CLIPSE
Male rap duo from Virginia Beach, Virginia: brothers Gene "Malice" Thornton and Terrence "Pusha T" Thornton. Also see **Re-Up Gang**.

DEBUT	PEAK	WKS				
9/7/02	4	31	●	1 Lord Willin'		Star Trak 14735
12/16/06	14	8		2 Hell Hath No Fury		Re-Up Gang 52119
12/26/09	46	5		3 Til The Casket Drops		Columbia 21099

CLIQUE, The
Pop-rock band from Beaumont, Texas: Randy Shaw (vocals), Sid Templeton (guitar), David Dunham (sax), Tommy Pena (bass) and Jerry "Function" Cope (drums).

DEBUT	PEAK	WKS				
1/17/70	177	3		1 The Clique..		White Whale 7126

CLIVILLES & COLE — see C & C MUSIC FACTORY

CLOONEY, Rosemary
Born on 5/23/1928 in Maysville, Kentucky. Died of cancer on 6/29/2002 (age 74). One of the most popular female singers of the early 1950s. Married to actor Jose Ferrer from 1953-61; their son Gabriel married **Debby Boone**. Her nephew, George Clooney, is a popular TV and movie actor.

AWARD: Grammy: Lifetime Achievement 2002

DEBUT	PEAK	WKS				
7/22/57	14	7		1 Ring Around Rosie..		Columbia 1006
				ROSEMARY CLOONEY AND THE HI-LO'S		
12/21/96	186	1		2 White Christmas .... [X]		Concord Jazz 4719

CLOVER
Country-rock band from San Francisco, California: Alex Call (vocals, guitar), **Huey Lewis** (vocals, harmonica), John McFee (guitar), Sean Hopper (keyboards), John Ciambotti (bass) and Tony Braunagel (drums). Lewis and Hopper later formed The News. McFee later joined **The Doobie Brothers**. Ciamobotti died on 3/24/2010 (age 67).

DEBUT	PEAK	WKS				
2/25/78	207	5		1 Love On The Wire..		Mercury 3708

CLOVERS, The
R&B vocal group from Washington DC: John "Buddy" Bailey (died on 2/3/1994, age 63), Matthew McQuater (died on 12/19/2000, age 73), Harold Lucas (died on 1/6/1994, age 61), Harold Winley and Billy Mitchell (died on 11/5/2002, age 71), with Bill Harris (guitar; died on 12/10/1988, age 63).

~ ~ ~ ~ ~ ~ ~ ~ ~ ~ **NON-CHARTED ALBUMS** ~ ~ ~ ~ ~ ~ ~ ~ ~ ~ ~
1956 **The Clovers**   1959 **Love Potion Number 9**
1958 **The Clovers In Clover**   1959 **The Clovers Dance Party**

CLUB NOUVEAU
R&B group from Sacramento, California: Jay King (producer/owner of King Jay Records; founded the **Timex Social Club**), Valerie Watson, Samuelle Prater, Denzil Foster and Thomas McElroy. Foster and McElroy formed a prolific production duo and also recorded as FMob.

12/20/86+	6	44	▲	1 Life, Love & Pain		Warner 25531
6/18/88	98	6		2 Listen To The Message		Warner 25687

CLUTCH
Rock band from Germantown, Maryland: Neil Fallon (vocals), Tim Sult (guitar), Dan Maines (bass) and Jean Paul Gaster (drums).

5/2/98	104	1	1 The Elephant Riders	Columbia 69113
3/31/01	135	1	2 Pure Rock Fury	Atlantic 83433
4/17/04	147	1	3 Blast Tyrant	DRT 00410
7/9/05	94	2	4 Robot Hive / Exodus	DRT 00433
4/14/07	52	3	5 From Beale Street To Oblivion	Issachar 00449
8/1/09	38	4	6 Strange Cousins From The West	Weathermaker 009

CLYNE, Roger, And The Peacemakers
Born on 1/13/1968 in Tucson, Arizona. Rock singer/songwriter.

4/7/07	185	1	1 No More Beautiful World	Emma Java 928814

C-MURDER
Born Corey Miller on 3/9/1971 in New Orleans, Louisiana. Male rapper. Brother of **Master P** and **Silkk The Shocker**. Member of **Tru**. Convicted of murder and sentanced to life in prison on 10/1/2003.

4/4/98	3[1]	27	▲	1 Life Or Death	No Limit 50723
3/27/99	2[1]	11	●	2 Bossalinie	No Limit 50035
9/23/00	9	11		3 Trapped In Crime	Tru 50083
11/10/01	45	3		4 C-P-3.com	Tru 50178
5/18/02	67	5		5 Tru Dawgs	Tru 9993
4/9/05	41	6		6 The Truest $#!@ I Ever Said	Tru 9900
7/19/08	130	1		7 Screamin' 4 Vengeance	Tru 427324

C NOTE
Male pop vocal group from Orlando, Florida: Jose Martinez, Raul Molina, David Perez and Andrew Rogers.

6/12/99	163	1	1 Different Kind Of Love	Epic 69537

COAL CHAMBER
Heavy metal band from Los Angeles, California: Brad Fafara (vocals), Miquel Rascon (guitar), Rayna Rose (bass) and Mike Cox (drums). Fafara is the nephew of actor Stanley Fafara (played "Whitey Whitney" on TV's *Leave It To Beaver).* Fafara later formed **Devildriver**.

9/25/99	22	8	●	1 Chamber Music	Roadrunner 8659
5/25/02	34	6		2 Dark Days	Roadrunner 618484

COASTERS, The
R&B vocal group from Los Angeles, California: Carl Gardner, Leon Hughes, Billy Guy and Bobby Nunn, with Adolph Jacobs (guitar). Gardner and Nunn had been in **The Robins**. Cornelius Gunter (brother of Shirley Gunter) joined in 1957; left in 1961. Will "Dub" Jones (of **The Cadets**) replaced Nunn in late 1958 and is heard on "Charlie Brown" and "Along Came Jones." Earl "Speedoo" Carroll (of **The Cadillacs**) joined group in 1961. Bobby Nunn died of a heart attack on 11/5/1986 (age 61). Gunter was shot to death on 2/26/1990 (age 51). Jones died of diabetes on 1/16/2000 (age 71). Guy died of a heart attack on 11/5/2002 (age 66).
    AWARD: R&R Hall of Fame: 1987

~ ~ ~ ~ ~ ~ ~ ~ ~ **NON-CHARTED ALBUMS** ~ ~ ~ ~ ~ ~ ~ ~ ~ ~
    1958 **The Coasters**   1960 **One By One**
    1959 **The Coasters' Greatest Hits**   1962 **Coast Along With The Coasters**

COATES, Odia
Born on 11/13/1941 in Vicksburg, Mississippi; raised in Los Angeles, California. Died of cancer on 5/19/1991 (age 49). Female R&B singer. Member of the **Edwin Hawkins Singers**.

7/26/75	202	9	1 Odia Coates	United Artists 228

COBHAM, Billy
Born on 5/16/1944 in Panama; raised in Harlem, New York. Jazz-rock drummer. Formerly with **Miles Davis** and **John McLaughlin**.

11/17/73+	26	43	1 Spectrum	[I]	Atlantic 7268
5/4/74	23	21	2 Crosswinds	[I]	Atlantic 7300
12/21/74+	36	13	3 Total Eclipse	[I]	Atlantic 18121
6/28/75	74	8	4 Shabazz (Recorded Live In Europe)	[I-L]	Atlantic 18139
			recorded on 7/13/1974 at the Rainbow Theatre in London, England		
11/15/75	79	7	5 A Funky Thide Of Sings	[I]	Atlantic 18149
4/10/76	128	8	6 Life & Times	[I]	Atlantic 18166
10/23/76	99	9	7 "Live"-On Tour In Europe	[L]	Atlantic 18194
			THE BILLY COBHAM & GEORGE DUKE BAND		
6/3/78	172	4	8 Inner Conflicts	[I]	Atlantic 19174
10/14/78	166	6	9 Simplicity Of Expression-Depth Of Thought		Columbia 35457

Billboard		R I A	ARTIST		
DEBUT	PEAK	WKS	Album Title	Catalog	Label & Number

COBRA STARSHIP
Rock band formed in New Jersey: Gabe Saporta (vocals), Alex Suarez (guitar), Victoria Asher (keyboards), Ryland Blackinton (bass) and Nate Navarro (drums). Saporta was the singer/bassist for the band **Midtown**.

10/28/06	125	1	1 While The City Sleeps, We Rule The Streets		Decaydance 089
11/10/07	80	3	2 Viva La Cobra!		Decaydance 344636
8/29/09	4	8	3 Hot Mess		Decaydance 517002

COCHRAN, Anita
Born on 2/6/1967 in Pontiac, Michigan. Country singer/songwriter/guitarist.

2/28/98	173	4	1 Back To You		Warner 46395

COCHRAN, Eddie
Born Edward Ray Cochrane on 10/3/1938 in Albert Lea, Minnesota. Killed in a car crash on 4/17/1960 (age 21) in Chippenham, Wiltshire, England; accident also injured **Gene Vincent**. Influential rock and roll singer/guitarist.
AWARD: R&R Hall of Fame: 1987

~ ~ ~ ~ ~ ~ ~ ~ ~ ~ **NON-CHARTED ALBUMS** ~ ~ ~ ~ ~ ~ ~ ~ ~ ~ ~
1957 **Singin' To My Baby**   1962 **Never To Be Forgotten**
1960 **12 Of His Biggest Hits**

COCHRAN, Tammy
Born on 1/30/1972 in Austinburg, Ohio. Country singer/songwriter.

11/2/02	95	2	1 Life Happened		Epic 86052

COCHRAN, Wayne
Born in 1939 in Thomaston, Georgia. Flamboyant rock and roll singer.

3/30/68	167	4	1 Wayne Cochran!		Chess 1519

COCHRANE, Tom / RED RIDER
Born on 5/13/1953 in Lynn Lake, Manitoba, Canada. Rock singer/songwriter/guitarist. Red Rider: Ken Greer (guitar), Peter Boynton (keyboards), Jeff Jones (bass) and Rob Baker (drums). Steve Sexton replaced Boynton in 1982; left in early 1984.

RED RIDER:

4/26/80	146	5	1 Don't Fight It		Capitol 12028
9/12/81	65	24	2 As Far As Siam		Capitol 12145
2/5/83	66	16	3 Neruda...		Capitol 12226
			dedicated to exiled Chilean poet Pablo Neruda		
6/23/84	137	8	4 Breaking Curfew..		Capitol 12317

TOM COCHRANE AND RED RIDER:

8/2/86	112	12	5 Tom Cochrane And Red Rider		Capitol 12484
11/12/88	144	13	6 Victory Day		RCA 8532

TOM COCHRANE:

5/9/92	46	29	● 7 Mad Mad World...		Capitol 97723

COCKBURN, Bruce
Born on 5/27/1945 in Ottawa, Canada. Pop-rock singer/songwriter. Name pronounced: coe-burn.

2/23/80	45	24	1 Dancing In The Dragon's Jaws		Millennium 7747
10/18/80	81	9	2 Humans		Millennium 7752
5/23/81	174	5	3 Bruce Cockburn/Resume		Millennium 7757
1/23/82	208	2	4 Inner City Front		Millennium 7761
8/25/84+	74	31	5 Stealing Fire		Gold Mountain 80012
7/26/86	143	8	6 World Of Wonders...		MCA 5772
2/25/89	182	7	7 Big Circumstance..		Gold Castle 71320
3/19/94	176	2	8 Dart To The Heart		Columbia 53831
2/22/97	178	1	9 The Charity Of Night		Rykodisc 10366

COCKER, Jarvis
Born on 9/19/1963 in Sheffield, Yorkshire, England. Pop-rock singer/songwriter. Former lead singer of **Pulp**. No relation to Joe Cocker.

6/6/09	155	1	1 Further Complications...		Rough Trade 540

COCKER, Joe   **All-Time: #205**
Born John Robert Cocker on 5/20/1944 in Sheffield, Yorkshire, England. Pop-rock singer. Assembled the **Grease Band** in the mid-1960s. Successful tour with 43-piece revue, Mad Dogs & Englishmen, in 1970. Notable spastic stage antics were based on **Ray Charles**'s movements at the piano.

5/31/69	35	37	● 1 With A Little Help From My Friends		A&M 4182
11/22/69+	11	53	● 2 Joe Cocker!		A&M 4224
9/5/70	2¹	53	● 3 Mad Dogs & Englishmen [L-S]		A&M 6002 [2]
			recorded on 3/27/1970 at the Fillmore East in New York City		
12/2/72+	30	21	4 Joe Cocker...		A&M 4368
8/24/74	11	36	5 I Can Stand A Little Rain		A&M 3633
8/30/75	42	10	6 Jamaica Say You Will		A&M 4529
5/15/76	70	10	7 Stingray..		A&M 4574
12/10/77	114	8	8 Joe Cocker's Greatest Hits .... [G]		A&M 4670
9/16/78	76	13	9 Luxury You Can Afford		Asylum 145
7/10/82	105	23	10 Sheffield Steel		Island 9750
5/19/84	133	9	11 Civilized Man		Capitol 12335

Billboard			R I A A	ARTIST		
DEBUT	PEAK	WKS		Album Title	Catalog	Label & Number

COCKER, Joe — cont'd

4/12/86	50	18		12 Cocker		Capitol 12394
11/14/87+	89	27		13 Unchain My Heart		Capitol 48285
9/16/89+	52	30		14 One Night Of Sin		Capitol 92861
6/23/90	95	14		15 Joe Cocker Live [L]		Capitol 93416
				recorded on 10/15/1989 in Lowell, Massachusetts		
8/1/92	111	10		16 Night Calls		Capitol 97801
1/31/04	122	5		17 Ultimate Collection [G]		A&M 001572
2/19/05	61	3		18 Heart & Soul		New Door 003823
9/15/07	167	1		19 Classic Cocker [G]		Capitol 02356

COCK ROBIN
Pop band from Los Angeles, California: Peter Kingsbery (vocals, bass), Anna LaCazio (vocals, keyboards), Clive Wright (guitars) and Louis Molino (drums).

7/13/85	61	19		1 Cock Robin		Columbia 39582
9/5/87	166	3		2 After Here Through Midland		Columbia 40375

COCOA BROVAZ
Rap duo from Brooklyn, New York: Tek and Steele. Formerly known as **Smif-N-Wessun**. Members of **Boot Camp Clik**.

1/28/95	59	8		1 Dah Shinin'		Wreck 2005
				SMIF-N-WESSUN		
4/18/98	21	7		2 The Rude Awakening		Duck Down 50699

COCTEAU TWINS
Pop trio from Grangemouth, Scotland: Elizabeth Fraser (vocals), Robin Guthrie (guitar) and Simon Raymonde (bass). Guthrie and Fraser also recorded in 1984 as This Mortal Coil. Group name taken from a **Simple Minds** song.

10/15/88	109	18		1 Blue Bell Knoll		Capitol 90892
10/6/90	99	19		2 Heaven or Las Vegas		Capitol 93669
11/20/93	78	3		3 Four-Calendar Cafe		Capitol 99375
6/1/96	99	2		4 Milk & Kisses		Capitol 37049

CODE BLUE
Rock trio formed in England: Dean Chamberlain (guitar), Gary Tibbs (bass) and Randall Marsh (drums). All shared vocals.

10/4/80	202	2		1 Code Blue		Warner 3461
				album and cover packaged in a large blue plastic bag		

COE, David Allan
Born on 9/6/1939 in Akron, Ohio. Country singer. Billed as "The Mysterious Rhinestone Cowboy" until 1978. In the movie *Take This Job And Shove It* (also wrote the title tune for **Johnny Paycheck**).

4/17/76	202	4		1 Longhaired Redneck		Columbia 33916
6/18/83	39^C	10	▲	2 Greatest Hits [G]		Columbia 35627
7/9/83	179	5		3 Castles In The Sand		Columbia 38535

COFFEY, Dennis, And The Detroit Guitar Band
Born in 1940 in Detroit, Michigan. White session guitarist for Motown.

11/13/71+	36	25		1 Evolution [I]		Sussex 7004
3/25/72	90	14		2 Goin' For Myself [I]		Sussex 7010
1/20/73	189	6		3 Electric Coffey [I]		Sussex 7021
1/17/76	147	7		4 Finger Lickin Good [I]		Westbound 212

COFFEY, Kellie
Born on 4/22/1971 in Moore, Oklahoma. Female country singer/songwriter.

5/25/02	54	14		1 When You Lie Next To Me		BNA 67040

COHEED AND CAMBRIA
Hard-rock band from Nyack, New York: Claudio Sanchez (vocals, guitar), Travis Stever (guitar), Mic Todd (bass) and Josh Eppard (drums). Sanchez also recorded as **The Prize Fighter Inferno**.

10/25/03	52	23	●	1 In Keeping Secrets Of Silent Earth: 3		Equal Vision 87
10/8/05	7	18	●	2 Good Apollo I'm Burning Star IV / Volume One: From Fear Through The Eyes Of Madness		Equal Vision 97683
10/8/05	44^C	1		3 The Second Stage Turbine Blade		Equal Vision 114
				released in 2002		
11/10/07	6	9		4 No World For Tomorrow		Columbia 16454

COHEN, Leonard
Born on 9/21/1934 in Montreal, Quebec, Canada. Singer/songwriter/poet/novelist. His numerous works include novels *The Favorite Game* and *Beautiful Losers*, six volumes of poetry, several documentaries, and songs recorded by **Judy Collins**, **Tim Hardin** and **Jennifer Warnes**. Also see Various Artists Compilations: *Tower Of Song - The Songs Of Leonard Cohen*.
AWARDS: Grammy: Lifetime Achievement 2010 ★ R&R Hall of Fame: 2008

3/2/68	83	14	●	1 Songs Of Leonard Cohen		Columbia 9533
4/12/69	63	17		2 Songs From A Room		Columbia 9767
5/1/71	145	11		3 Songs Of Love And Hate		Columbia 30103
5/26/73	156	5		4 Leonard Cohen: Live Songs [L]		Columbia 31724
10/27/01	143	3		5 Ten New Songs		Columbia 85953
11/13/04	131	1		6 Dear Heather		Columbia 92891
4/18/09	76	8		7 Live In London [L]		Columbia 40502 [2]

COHEN, Myron
Born on 7/1/1902 in Grodno, Poland; raised in Brooklyn, New York. Died of a heart attack on 3/10/1986 (age 83). Stand-up comedian.

4/2/66	102	13		1 Everybody Gotta Be Someplace .... [C]		RCA Victor 3534

COHN, Marc
Born on 7/5/1959 in Cleveland, Ohio. Pop-rock singer/songwriter/pianist. Married ABC-TV news anchor Elizabeth Vargas on 7/20/2002. Shot in the head during an attempted car jacking on 8/7/2005 (fully recovered).
AWARD: Grammy: Best New Artist 1991

4/27/91+	38	63	▲	1 Marc Cohn...		Atlantic 82178
6/12/93	63	15		2 The Rainy Season		Atlantic 82491
4/4/98	114	6		3 Burning The Daze...		Atlantic 82909

COKO
Born Cheryl Gamble on 6/13/1974 in the Bronx, New York. Female R&B singer. Member of **SWV**.

8/28/99	68	6		1 Hot Coko		RCA 67766

COLD
Hard-rock band from Jacksonville, Florida: Ronald "Scooter" Ward (vocals, guitar), Stephen "Kelly" Hayes (guitar), Terry Balsamo (guitar), Jeremy Marshall (bass) and Sam McCandless (drums).

9/30/00+	98	27		1 13 Ways To Bleed On Stage...		Geffen 490726
5/31/03	3[1]	21	●	2 Year Of The Spider		Flip 000006
9/17/05	26	5		3 A Different Kind Of Pain		Flip 94107

COLD BLOOD
Rock band from San Francisco, California. Core members: Lydia Pense (vocals), Michael Sasaki (guitar), Raul Matute (piano), Rod Ellicott (bass), Max Haskett (trumpet) and Danny Hull (sax). Haskett later joined **Rubicon**.

12/27/69+	23	29		1 Cold Blood		San Francisco 200
1/23/71	60	13		2 Sisyphus		San Francisco 205
4/22/72	133	11		3 First Taste Of Sin		Reprise 2074
4/28/73	97	14		4 Thriller!...		Reprise 2130
8/10/74	126	8		5 Lydia		Warner 2806
3/13/76	179	4		6 Lydia Pense & Cold Blood		ABC 917

COLD CHISEL
Rock band from Adelaide, Australia: **Jimmy Barnes** (vocals), Ian Moss (guitar), Don Walker (keyboards), Phil Small (bass) and Steven Prestwich (drums).

6/13/81	171	6		1 East...		Elektra 336

COLDPLAY   2000s: #36 / All-Time: #436
Alternative-rock band formed in London, England: Chris Martin (vocals; born on 3/2/1977), Jon Buckland (guitar; born on 9/11/1977), Guy Berryman (bass; born on 4/12/1978) and Will Champion (drums; born on 7/31/1978). Martin married actress Gwyneth Paltrow on 12/5/2003.

12/30/00+	51	76	▲[2]	1 Parachutes... Cat:❶[1]/131		Nettwerk 30162
				Grammy: Alternative Album		
9/14/02	5	104	▲[4]	2 A Rush Of Blood To The Head .... Cat:❶[8]/112		Capitol 40504
				Grammy: Alternative Album ★ RS500 #473		
11/22/03	13	17	●	3 Coldplay Live 2003 .... [L]		Capitol 99014
6/25/05	❶[3]	64	▲[3]	4 X&Y .... Cat:❶[1]/8		Capitol 74786
7/5/08	❶[2]	75	▲[2]	5 Viva La Vida Or Death And All His Friends .... Cat:#41/6		Capitol 16886
				Grammy: Rock Album		
12/13/08	15	8		6 Prospekt's March .... [EP]		Capitol 65787

COLD WAR KIDS
Rock band from Fullerton, California: Nathan Willett (vocals, piano), Jonnie Russell (guitar), Matt Maust (bass) and Matt Aveiro (drums).

5/12/07	173	5		1 Robbers & Cowards		Downtown 70009
10/11/08	21	4		2 Loyalty To Loyalty..		Downtown 70042

COLE, Cozy
Born William Cole on 10/17/1909 in East Orange, New Jersey. Died of cancer on 1/31/1981 (age 71). Lead drummer for many swing bands.

~ ~ ~ ~ ~ ~ ~ ~ ~ ~   *NON-CHARTED ALBUM*   ~ ~ ~ ~ ~ ~ ~ ~ ~ ~
1958 **Cozy Cole Hits!** *["Topsy"]*

COLE, Jude
Born on 6/18/1960 in Carbon Cliff, Illinois; raised in East Moline, Illinois. Male pop-rock singer/guitarist. Member of **The Records** from 1979-81.

5/5/90	138	12		1 A View From 3rd Street...		Reprise 26164
10/17/92	177	3		2 Start The Car...		Reprise 26898

COLE, Keyshia
Born on 10/15/1983 in Oakland, California. Female R&B singer/songwriter. Starred in own BET reality series *The Way It Is*.

7/9/05	6	64	▲	1 The Way It Is		A&M 003554
10/13/07	2[1]	57	▲	2 Just Like You		Confidential 009475
1/3/09	2[1]	40	●	3 A Different Me		Imani 012395

Billboard			R I A A	ARTIST		
DEBUT	PEAK	WKS		Album Title	Catalog	Label & Number

COLE, Lloyd, And The Commotions
Born on 1/31/1961 in Buxton, England; raised in Glasgow, Scotland. Rock singer/songwriter/guitarist. The Commotions: Neil Clark (guitar), Blair Cowan (keyboards), Lawrence Donegan (bass) and Steven Irvine (drums).

3/30/85	201	8		1 Rattlesnakes		Geffen 24064

COLE, Nat "King"　　　　　　　　　1950s: #6 / 1960s: #33 / All-Time: #44
Born Nathaniel Adams Coles on 3/17/1919 in Montgomery, Alabama; raised in Chicago, Illinois. Died of cancer on 2/15/1965 (age 45). R&B-jazz singer/songwriter/pianist. Father of **Natalie Cole**. Formed The King Cole Trio in 1939. Long series of top-selling records led to his solo career in 1950. Appeared in several movies. Hosted own TV variety series from 1956-57.
AWARDS: Grammy: Lifetime Achievement 1990 ★ R&R Hall of Fame: 2000 (Early Influence)

11/27/54+	5	20		1 Nat 'King' Cole Sings　　　　　　　　　　　　　　　　　[EP]		Capitol 9120
7/9/55	9	8		2 Moods In Song　　　　　　　　　　　　　　　　　　　　[EP]		Capitol 633
4/28/56	16	2		3 Ballads Of The Day		Capitol 680
3/9/57	13	2		4 After Midnight..		Capitol 782
				with the King Cole Trio		
4/6/57	❶⁸	94	▲	5 Love Is The Thing		Capitol 824
9/23/57	18	3		6 This Is Nat "King" Cole		Capitol 870
12/16/57+	18	6		7 Just One Of Those Things		Capitol 903
5/5/58	18	3		8 St. Louis Blues .... [S]		Capitol 993
				Cole portrayed W.C. Handy in the movie about Handy's life		
9/22/58	12	5		9 Cole Espanol .... [F]		Capitol 1031
12/1/58	17	2		10 The Very Thought Of You		Capitol 1084
6/22/59	45	5		11 To Whom It May Concern		Capitol 1190
4/18/60	33	2		12 Tell Me All About Yourself		Capitol 1331
10/24/60	4	23		13 Wild Is Love		Capitol 1392
5/15/61	79	17		14 The Touch Of Your Lips		Capitol 1574
5/5/62	27	16		15 Nat King Cole Sings/George Shearing Plays		Capitol 1675
				NAT KING COLE & GEORGE SHEARING		
9/22/62	3⁴	162	▲	16 Ramblin' Rose		Capitol 1793
12/29/62+	24	36		17 Dear Lonely Hearts		Capitol 1838
5/25/63	68	6		18 Where Did Everyone Go?		Capitol 1859
7/6/63	14	36		19 Those Lazy-Hazy-Crazy Days Of Summer		Capitol 1932
8/1/64	18	45		20 I Don't Want To Be Hurt Anymore		Capitol 2118
9/26/64	74	23		21 My Fair Lady		Capitol 2117
2/6/65	4	38		22 L-O-V-E		Capitol 2195
3/20/65	30	39	▲	23 Unforgettable .... Cat:#39/7 [E]		Capitol 357
				first released as a 10" album in 1952		
7/3/65	77	9		24 Songs From "Cat Ballou" And Other Motion Pictures .... [K]		Capitol 2340
2/19/66	74	11		25 Nat King Cole At The Sands .... [L]		Capitol 2434
8/23/69	197	3		26 Close-Up .... [R]		Capitol 252 [2]
				reissue of Ballads Of The Day and Nat King Cole's Top Pops albums		
				CHRISTMAS ALBUMS:		
12/5/92	8ˣ	43		27 It's Christmas Time　　　　　　　　　　　Cat:#6/41		LaserLight 15152
				BING CROSBY • FRANK SINATRA • NAT KING COLE		
				Christmas charts: 8/'92, 17/'93, 12/'94, 13/'95, 8/'96, 22/'97		
11/20/99+	9ˣ	30		28 Christmas Favorites Featuring The Christmas Song　Cat:#7/26		EMI-Capitol 57729
				an EMI-Capitol Music Special Markets release of 10 selections from #18 above; Christmas charts: 30/'99, 9/'00, 31/'01, 28/'02, 42/'03		
12/6/08+	44	7		29 NBC Sounds Of The Season: The Nat King Cole Holiday Collection .... [EP]		NBC 36054
				Christmas chart: 4/'08		
12/19/09	164	2	▲⁶	30 The Christmas Song .... Cat:#4/86		Capitol 31227
				Christmas charts: 6/'63, 12/'64, 8/'65, 8/'66, 3/'67, 5/'68, 1/'69, 4/'70, 3/'71, 1/'72, 5/'73, 5/'83, 5/'85, 6/'87, 6/'88, 8/'89, 6/'90, 4/'91, 8/'92, 12/'93, 12/'94, 11/'95, 10/'96, 13/'97, 20/'98, 28/'99, 26/'00, 25/'01, 27/'02, 27/'03, 25/'04, 28/'05, 37/'06, 26/'07, 36/'08, 42/'09		
				GREATEST HITS & COMPILATIONS:		
9/4/65	60	14		31 Looking Back...		Capitol 2361
11/26/66	145	3		32 The Great Songs!		Capitol 2558
9/14/68	187	5	▲	33 The Best Of Nat King Cole................................ Cat:#48/2		Capitol 2944
7/13/91	86	28	●	34 Collectors Series .... Cat:#12/1		Capitol 93590
2/12/05	41	6		35 The World Of Nat King Cole		Capitol 74712
5/20/06	131	2		36 The Very Best Of Nat King Cole..		Capitol 59324

Billboard			R I A A	ARTIST		
DEBUT	PEAK	WKS		Album Title	Catalog	Label & Number

COLE, Natalie
All-Time: #134

Born on 2/6/1950 in Los Angeles, California. R&B singer. Daughter of **Nat "King" Cole**. Professional debut at age 11. Marriages include Marvin Yancy (her producer) and Andre Fischer (former drummer of **Rufus**). Hosted own syndicated variety TV show *Big Break* in 1990. Made acting debut in 1993 TV series *I'll Fly Away*. Starred in the 1995 movie *Lily In Winter*.

AWARD: Grammy: Best New Artist 1975

8/30/75	18	56	●	1 Inseparable		Capitol 11429
5/29/76	13	30	●	2 Natalie		Capitol 11517
3/5/77	8	28	▲	3 Unpredictable		Capitol 11600
12/10/77+	16	39	▲	4 Thankful		Capitol 11708
7/15/78	31	16	●	5 Natalie...Live!	[L]	Capitol 11709 [2]
4/7/79	52	15	●	6 I Love You So		Capitol 11928
12/15/79+	44	19		7 We're The Best Of Friends		Capitol 12019
				NATALIE COLE & PEABO BRYSON		
6/14/80	77	22		8 Don't Look Back		Capitol 12079
9/26/81	132	4		9 Happy Love		Capitol 12165
9/17/83	182	3		10 I'm Ready		Epic 38280
6/29/85	140	9		11 Dangerous		Modern 90270
8/8/87+	42	58		12 Everlasting		Manhattan 53051
5/27/89	59	23		13 Good To Be Back		EMI 48902
6/29/91	❶⁵	110	▲⁷	14 Unforgettable With Love	Cat:#36/1	Elektra 61049
				Grammys: Album & Traditional Pop Vocal		
7/3/93	26	19	●	15 Take A Look		Elektra 61496
				Grammy: Jazz Vocal		
11/26/94	36	8	●	16 Holly & Ivy	Cat:#25/6 [X]	Elektra 61704
				Christmas charts: 6/'94, 25/'95		
10/12/96	20	21	▲	17 Stardust		Elektra 61946
12/21/96	196	2		18 A Celebration Of Christmas	[X-L]	Elektra 62000
				JOSE CARRERAS / NATALIE COLE / PLACIDO DOMINGO		
				recorded on 12/23/1995 at the Austria Center in Vienna		
7/10/99	163	3		19 Snowfall On The Sahara		Elektra 62401
12/18/99+	157	4		20 The Magic Of Christmas	[X]	Elektra 62433
				NATALIE COLE with the London Symphony Orchestra		
				Christmas chart: 21/'99		
12/23/00	154	2		21 Greatest Hits Volume I	[G]	Elektra 62582
10/5/02	32	9		22 Ask A Woman Who Knows		Verve 589774
10/14/06	97	2		23 Leavin'		Verve 006223
9/27/08	19	9		24 Still Unforgettable		DMI 512320
				Grammy: Traditional Pop Vocal Album		

COLE, Paula

Born on 4/5/1968 in Rockport, Masschusetts. Adult Alternative singer/songwriter.

AWARD: Grammy: Best New Artist 1997

2/22/97+	20	77	▲²	1 This Fire		Imago 46424
10/16/99	97	4		2 Amen		Imago 47490
				PAULA COLE BAND		
6/30/07	163	1		3 Courage		Decca 008292

COLEMAN, Durell

Born in 1958 in Roanoke, Virginia. Male R&B singer.

9/28/85	155	7		1 Durell Coleman		Island 90293

COLEMAN, Ornette

Born on 3/19/1930 in Fort Worth, Texas. Black jazz alto saxophonist.

5/16/09	24ᶜ	1		1 The Shape Of Jazz To Come	[I]	Atlantic 1317
				RS500 #246		

COLLECTIVE SOUL

Rock band from Stockbridge, Georgia: brothers Ed Roland (vocals; born on 8/3/1963) and Dean Roland (guitar; born on 10/10/1971), with Ross Childress (guitar; born on 9/8/1971), Will Turpin (bass; born on 2/8/1971) and Shane Evans (drums; born on 4/26/1971).

4/30/94	15	40	▲²	1 Hints Allegations And Things Left Unsaid		Atlantic 82596
4/1/95	23	76	▲³	2 Collective Soul		Atlantic 82745
3/29/97	16	26	▲	3 Disciplined Breakdown		Atlantic 82984
2/27/99	21	35	▲	4 Dosage		Atlantic 83162
10/28/00	22	15	●	5 Blender		Atlantic 83400
10/6/01	50	8		6 7even Year Itch: Greatest Hits 1994-2001	[G]	Atlantic 83510
12/4/04	66	2		7 Youth		El 60001
6/11/05	129	1		8 From The Ground Up	[EP]	El 90502
2/25/06	183	1		9 Home	[L]	El 90601
9/12/09	24	4		10 Collective Soul		El 617876

Billboard			R I A A	ARTIST
DEBUT	PEAK	WKS		Album Title	Catalog	Label & Number

COLLEGE BOYZ, The
Black male rap group from Los Angeles, California: Rom, Squeak, The Q and DJ B-Selector.

5/2/92	118	11		1 Radio Fusion Radio		Virgin 91658

COLLIE, Mark
Born on 1/18/1956 in Waynesboro, Tennessee. Country singer/songwriter/guitarist.

1/30/93	156	8		1 Mark Collie		MCA 10658

COLLINS, Albert
Born on 10/1/1932 in Leona, Texas. Died of cancer on 11/24/1993 (age 61). Blues singer/guitarist. Cousin of Lightnin' Hopkins. Nicknamed "The Master of the Telecaster" and "The Iceman."

2/12/72	196	2		1 There's Gotta Be A Change		Tumbleweed 103
2/15/86	124	18		2 Showdown!		Alligator 4743

ALBERT COLLINS / ROBERT CRAY / JOHNNY COPELAND
Grammy: Blues Album

COLLINS, "Bootsy" — see BOOTSY

COLLINS, Edwyn
Born on 8/23/1959 in Edinburgh, Scotland. Pop-rock singer/songwriter.

10/28/95	183	4		1 Gorgeous George		Bar None 058

COLLINS, Judy   **All-Time: #241**
Born on 5/1/1939 in Seattle, Washington. Contemporary folk singer/songwriter. Moved to Los Angeles, then to Denver at age nine, where her father, Chuck Collins, was a radio personality. **Stephen Stills** wrote "Suite: Judy Blue Eyes" for her. Appeared in the New York Shakespeare Festival's production of *Peer Gynt*. Nominated for a 1974 Academy Award for co-directing *Antonia: A Portrait of the Woman*, a documentary about Judy's former classical mentor and a pioneer female orchestra conductor, Dr. Antonia Brico.

3/28/64	126	10		1 Judy Collins #3		Elektra 7243
10/2/65	69	13		2 Judy Collins' Fifth Album		Elektra 7300
1/7/67	46	34	●	3 In My Life		Elektra 7320
1/6/68	5	75	●	4 Wildflowers		Elektra 74012
12/21/68+	29	33	●	5 Who Knows Where The Time Goes		Elektra 74033
9/20/69	29	29		6 Recollections	[K]	Elektra 74055
				recordings from 1963-65		
12/5/70+	17	35	●	7 Whales & Nightingales		Elektra 75010
12/4/71+	64	13		8 Living		Elektra 75014
5/27/72	37	24	▲	9 Colors Of The Day/The Best Of Judy Collins	[G]	Elektra 75030
2/10/73	27	20		10 True Stories And Other Dreams		Elektra 75053
4/12/75	17	34	▲	11 Judith		Elektra 1032
9/11/76	25	20		12 Bread & Roses		Elektra 1076
8/6/77	42	27		13 So Early In The Spring, The First 15 Years	[K]	Elektra 6002 [2]
3/17/79	54	16		14 Hard Times For Lovers		Elektra 171
5/3/80	142	6		15 Running For My Life		Elektra 253
3/13/82	190	5		16 Times Of Our Lives		Elektra 60001

COLLINS, Phil   **1990s: #47 / All-Time: #182**
Born on 1/30/1951 in Chiswick, London, England. Pop singer/songwriter/drummer. Stage actor as a young child; played the "Artful Dodger" in the London production of *Oliver*. With group Flaming Youth in 1969. Joined **Genesis** in 1970; became lead singer in 1975. Also with jazz-rock group **Brand X**. Starred in the 1988 movie *Buster*. Left Genesis in April 1996.

3/14/81	7	164	▲4	1 Face Value	Cat:#4/112	Atlantic 16029
11/27/82+	8	141	▲3	2 Hello, I Must Be Going!	Cat:#14/28	Atlantic 80035
3/9/85	●7	123	▲12	3 No Jacket Required	Cat:#13/15	Atlantic 81240
				Grammys: Album & Male Pop Vocal		
12/2/89+	●3	90	▲4	4 ...But Seriously		Atlantic 82050
11/24/90+	11	97	▲4	5 Serious Hits...Live!	[L]	Atlantic 82157
11/27/93	13	30	▲	6 Both Sides		Atlantic 82550
11/9/96	23	20	●	7 Dance Into The Light		Atlantic 82949
10/24/98	18	102	▲3	8 ...Hits	Cat:#10/134 [G]	Atlantic 83139
11/30/02	30	16		9 Testify		Atlantic 83563
10/16/04	51	6	●	10 Love Songs: A Compilation...Old And New	[K]	Face Value 78058 [2]

COLLINS, Tyler
Born on 9/1/1966 in Harlem, New York; raised in Detroit, Michigan. Female R&B singer.

5/26/90	85	22		1 Girls Nite Out		RCA 9642

COLON, Willie
Born on 4/28/1950 in the Bronx, New York. Latin trombonist/bandleader.

10/20/07	49X	1		1 Asalto Navideno	[X-F]	Fania 130076
				Hector LaVoe (vocals)		

Billboard			R I A A	ARTIST Album Title	Catalog	Label & Number
DEBUT	PEAK	WKS				

COLOR ME BADD
Vocal group from Oklahoma City, Oklahoma: Bryan Abrams (born on 11/16/1969), Sam Watters (born on 7/23/1970), Mark Calderon (born on 9/27/1970) and Kevin Thornton (born on 6/17/1969). Formed while in high school in Oklahoma City.

DEBUT	PEAK	WKS	RIAA	#	Album Title	Label & Number
8/10/91	3²	77	▲³	1	C.M.B.	Giant 24429
1/16/93	189	1		2	Young, Gifted And Badd - The Remixes .... [K]	Giant 24480
12/4/93	56	17	●	3	Time And Chance..	Giant 24524
6/1/96	113	4		4	Now & Forever	Giant 24622

COLOSSEUM
Jazz-rock band from England: Chris Farlowe (vocals; **Atomic Rooster**), Dave Clempson (guitar), Mark Clarke (bass), Dave Greenslade (organ), Dick Heckstall-Smith (sax) and Jon Hiseman (drums). Hiseman and Heckstall-Smith were with **John Mayall**'s Bluesbreakers.

| 11/20/71 | 192 | 3 | | 1 | Colosseum Live .... [L] | Warner 1942 [2] |

COLTER, Jessi
Born Mirriam Johnson on 5/25/1943 in Phoenix, Arizona. Country singer/songwriter/pianist. Married to **Duane Eddy** from 1961-68. Married **Waylon Jennings** in October 1969. Mother of **Shooter Jennings**.

5/3/75	50	27		1	I'm Jessi Colter	Capitol 11363
2/7/76	109	8		2	Jessi	Capitol 11477
8/7/76	79	8		3	Diamond In The Rough	Capitol 11543
3/21/81	43	19	●	4	Leather And Lace	RCA Victor 3931
					WAYLON & JESSI	

COLTON, Graham
Born on 11/6/1981 in Oklahoma City, Oklahoma. Pop singer/songwriter.

| 11/17/07 | 153 | 1 | | 1 | Here Right Now .... | Universal 009810 |

COLTRANE, Alice
Born Alice MacLeod on 8/27/1937 in Detroit, Michigan. Died of respiratory failure on 1/12/2007 (age 69). Jazz keyboardist. Married to **John Coltrane** from 1964-67 (his death).

11/13/71	190	2		1	Universal Consciousness .... [I]	Impulse! 9210
10/12/74	79	8		2	Illuminations.. [I]	Columbia 32900
					TURIYA ALICE COLTRANE / DEVADIP CARLOS SANTANA	

COLTRANE, Chi
Born on 11/16/1948 in Racine, Wisconsin. Female rock singer/pianist. First name pronounced: shy.

| 9/23/72 | 148 | 10 | | 1 | Chi Coltrane .... | Columbia 31275 |

COLTRANE, John
Born on 9/23/1926 in Hamlet, North Carolina. Died of liver cancer on 7/17/1967 (age 40). Legendary jazz tenor saxophonist. With Dizzy Gillespie in the early 1950s, **Miles Davis** in 1955, **Thelonious Monk** in 1957, then solo. Married to **Alice Coltrane** from 1964-67 (his death).

AWARD: Grammy: Lifetime Achievement 1992

11/18/67	194	3		1	Expression .... [I]	Impulse! 9120
11/13/71	186	3		2	Sun Ship .... [I]	Impulse! 9211
2/17/01	21ᶜ	2	●	3	A Love Supreme .... [I]	Impulse! 050155
					Grammy: Hall of Fame ★ RS500 #47	
10/15/05	107	14		4	At Carnegie Hall.. [L]	Thelonious 35173
					THELONIOUS MONK QUARTET WITH JOHN COLTRANE recorded on 11/29/1957	
6/28/08	107	7		5	A Man Called Trane .... [K]	Starbucks 8288
10/18/08	41ᶜ	1		6	Thelonious Monk With John Coltrane .... [I]	Original Jazz Cl. 86039
					Grammy: Hall of Fame	
1/17/09	31ᶜ	1		7	My Favorite Things .... [I]	Atlantic 1361
					Grammy: Hall of Fame	
3/28/09	33ᶜ	1		8	Blue Train .... [I]	Blue Note 1577
					Grammy: Hall of Fame	

~ ~ ~ ~ ~ ~ ~ ~ **NON-CHARTED ALBUMS** ~ ~ ~ ~ ~ ~ ~ ~ ~ ~
| 1960 **Giant Steps** | 1962 **Ballads** |
| *RS500 #102* | *Grammy: Jazz Album* |

COLVIN, Shawn
Born Shanna Colvin on 1/10/1956 in Vermillion, South Dakota. Female contemporary folk singer/songwriter/guitarist.

12/16/89+	111	24		1	Steady On	Columbia 45209
					Grammy: Contemporary Folk Album	
11/14/92	142	14		2	Fat City	Columbia 47122
9/10/94	48	11		3	Cover Girl...	Columbia 57875
10/19/96	39	52	▲	4	A Few Small Repairs	Columbia 67119
12/19/98	181	2		5	Holiday Songs And Lullabies .... [X]	Columbia 69550
					Christmas chart: 18/'98	
4/14/01	101	7		6	Whole New You	Columbia 69889
9/30/06	109	3		7	These Four Walls	Nonesuch 79937

COMEBACK KID
Punk-rock band from Winnipeg, Manitoba, Canada: Andrew Neufeld (vocals), Jeremy Hiebert (guitar), Casey Hjelmberg (guitar), Matt Keil (bass) and Kyle Profeta (drums).

| 3/10/07 | 129 | 1 | | 1 | Broadcasting... .... | Victory 323 |

COMMAND ALL-STARS — see LIGHT, Enoch

COMMANDER CODY And His Lost Planet Airmen
Born George Frayne on 7/19/1944 in Boise, Idaho; raised in Brooklyn, New York. Rock singer/keyboardist. His Lost Planet Airmen consisted of John Tichy, Don Bolton and Bill Kirchen (guitars), Andy Stein (fiddle, sax), Bruce Barlow (bass) and Lance Dickerson (drums). Dickerson died on 11/10/2003 (age 55).

11/27/71+	82	33	1 Lost In The Ozone		Paramount 6017
9/9/72	94	13	2 Hot Licks, Cold Steel & Truckers Favorites		Paramount 6031
6/16/73	104	9	3 Country Casanova		Paramount 6054
2/16/74	105	14	4 Live From Deep In The Heart Of Texas...............................	[L]	Paramount 1017
			recorded November 1973 in Austin, Texas		
3/1/75	58	10	5 Commander Cody & His Lost Planet Airmen		Warner 2847
10/11/75	168	6	6 Tales From The Ozone		Warner 2883
7/31/76	170	3	7 We've Got A Live One Here!	[L]	Warner 2939 [2]
9/3/77	163	5	8 Rock 'N Roll Again		Arista 4125
			COMMANDER CODY BAND		

COMMISSIONED
Contemporary gospel group from Detroit, Michigan: **Marvin Sapp**, **Fred Hammond**, Marcus Colo, Keith Staten, Mitchell Jones, Michael Williams and Karl Reid.

5/11/02	100	2	1 The Commissioned Reunion "Live"	[L]	Verity 43190 [2]

COMMITMENTS, The
Band of Irish actors/musicians who starred in the movie of the same name: Robert Arkin, Michael Aherne, Angeline Ball, Maria Doyle, Dave Finnegan, Bronagh Gallagher, Glen Hansard, Dick Massey, Kenneth McCluskey, Johnny Murphy and Andrew Strong. All did their own performing.

9/14/91	8	76	▲² 1 The Commitments	[S]	MCA 10286
4/4/92	118	12	2 The Commitments - Vol. 2	[S]	MCA 10506

COMMODORES
All-Time: #190

R&B band formed in Tuskegee, Alabama: **Lionel Richie** (vocals, sax; born on 6/20/1949), William King (trumpet; born on 1/29/1949), Thomas McClary (guitar; born on 10/6/1950), Milan Williams (keyboards; born on 3/28/1948; died of cancer on 7/9/2006, age 58), Ronald LaPread (bass; born on 9/4/1950) and Walter "Clyde" Orange (drums; born on 12/9/1946). First recorded for Motown in 1972. Group appeared in the 1978 movie *Thank God It's Friday*. Richie left group in 1982.

8/24/74	138	9	1 Machine Gun..		Motown 798
3/22/75	26	33	2 Caught In The Act		Motown 820
11/8/75	29	32	3 Movin' On		Motown 848
7/10/76	12	39	4 Hot On The Tracks		Motown 867
4/2/77	3³	53	5 Commodores		Motown 884
11/12/77	3²	28	6 Commodores Live!	[L]	Motown 894 [2]
5/27/78	3⁸	33	▲ 7 Natural High		Motown 902
11/25/78+	23	20	8 Commodores' Greatest Hits..	[G]	Motown 912
8/18/79	3²	41	9 Midnight Magic		Motown 926
6/28/80	7	33	▲ 10 Heroes		Motown 939
7/11/81	13	40	▲ 11 In The Pocket		Motown 955
12/4/82+	37	24	12 All The Great Hits	[G]	Motown 6028
6/11/83	141	7	13 Commodores Anthology	[G]	Motown 6044 [2]
10/1/83	103	11	14 Commodores 13		Motown 6054
2/16/85	12	37	● 15 Nightshift		Motown 6124
11/22/86	101	15	16 United		Polydor 831194

COMMON
Born Lonnie Lynn on 3/13/1972 in Chicago, Illinois. Male rapper/songwriter. First recorded as **Common Sense**.

10/22/94	179	2	1 Resurrection		Relativity 1208
			COMMON SENSE		
10/18/97	62	5	2 One Day It'll All Make Sense		Relativity 1535
4/15/00	16	31	● 3 Like Water For Chocolate		MCA 111970
12/28/02	47	13	4 Electric Circus		MCA 113114
6/11/05	2¹	27	● 5 Be		G.O.O.D. 004670
8/18/07	❶¹	23	● 6 Finding Forever		G.O.O.D. 009382
12/27/08	12	13	7 Universal Mind Control		G.O.O.D. 011986

COMMUNARDS
Dance duo: **Jimmy Somerville** (vocals; born on 6/22/1961 in Glasgow, Scotland) and Richard Coles (keyboards; born on 6/23/1962 in Northampton, England). Somerville was also lead singer of **Bronski Beat**.

12/20/86+	90	16	1 Communards		MCA 5794
2/6/88	93	9	2 Red		MCA 42106

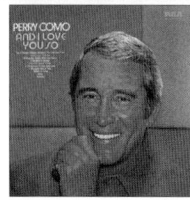

COMO, Perry   1950s: #14 / All-Time: #145

Born Pierino Como on 5/18/1912 in Canonsburg, Pennsylvania. Died on 5/12/2001 (age 88). Owned barbershop in hometown. With Freddy Carlone band in 1933; with Ted Weems from 1936-42. Appeared in several movies. Hosted own TV shows from 1948-63. One of the most popular singers of the 20th century.

AWARD: Grammy: Lifetime Achievement 2002

DEBUT	PEAK	WKS			Catalog	Label & Number
10/15/55	7	10		1 **So Smooth**		RCA Victor 1085
				LP: RCA Victor LPM-1085 (#7); EP: RCA Victor EPB-1085 (#10)		
9/2/57	8	10		2 **We Get Letters**		RCA Victor 1463
12/16/57	11	9		3 **Dream Along With Me**		RCA Camden 403
6/23/58	18	2		4 **Saturday Night With Mr. C.**		RCA Victor 1004
9/1/58	24	2		5 **Como's Golden Records**	[G]	RCA Victor 1007
1/5/59	16	7		6 **When You Come To The End Of The Day**		RCA Victor 1885
11/2/59	17	12		7 **Como Swings**		RCA Victor 2010
9/25/61	50	13		8 **Sing To Me, Mr. C.**		RCA Victor 2390
9/29/62	32	21		9 **By Request**		RCA Victor 2567
12/8/62	90	6		10 **The Best Of Irving Berlin's Songs From "Mr. President"**		RCA Victor 2630
9/21/63	59	18		11 **The Songs I Love**		RCA Victor 2708
5/29/65	47	17		12 **The Scene Changes**		RCA Victor 3396
6/11/66	86	9		13 **Lightly Latin**		RCA Victor 3552
10/22/66	81	16		14 **Perry Como In Italy**		RCA Victor 3608
6/21/69	93	11		15 **Seattle**		RCA Victor 4183
1/16/71	22	27		16 **It's Impossible**		RCA Victor 4473
6/26/71	101	9		17 **I Think Of You**		RCA Victor 4539
5/26/73	34	19	●	18 **And I Love You So**		RCA Victor 0100
8/17/74	138	10		19 **Perry**		RCA Victor 0585
12/20/75+	142	9		20 **Just Out Of Reach**		RCA Victor 0863
				CHRISTMAS ALBUMS:		
12/16/57	8	5		21 **Perry Como Sings Merry Christmas Music**		RCA Victor 1243
12/15/58	9	4		22 **Perry Como Sings Merry Christmas Music**	[R]	RCA Victor 1243
1/4/60	22	1	●	23 **Season's Greetings From Perry Como**		RCA Victor 2066
				Christmas charts: 5/'63, 34/'64, 15/'65, 11/'66, 22/'67, 17/'68		
12/31/60	27	1		24 **Season's Greetings From Perry Como**	[R]	RCA Victor 2066
1/6/62	33	3		25 **Season's Greetings From Perry Como**	[R]	RCA Victor 2066
12/15/62	74	3		26 **Season's Greetings From Perry Como**	[R]	RCA Victor 2066
12/21/63+	15 [X]	15		27 **Perry Como Sings Merry Christmas Music**		RCA Camden 660
				reissue of album first charted in 1946 on RCA Victor 161 and in 1957 on RCA Victor 1243; Christmas charts: 17/'63, 15/'64, 55/'65, 63/'66, 16/'67, 16/'68		
12/5/70	5 [X]	5	●	28 **The Perry Como Christmas Album**		RCA Victor 4016
				first released in 1968; Christmas charts: 5/'70, 18/'73		
11/15/03	50 [X]	1		29 **Christmas With Perry Como**		BMG 44553

COMPANY B

Female dance trio from Miami, Florida: Lori Ledesma, Lezlee Livrano and Susan Johnson.

7/18/87	143	6	1 **Company B**	Atlantic 81763

COMPANY OF THIEVES

Alternative-rock band from Chicago, Illinois: Genevieve Schatz (vocals), Marc Walloch (guitar), Mike Miamone (keyboards), Bob Buckstaff (bass) and Mike Ortiz (drums).

1/24/09	162	1	1 **Ordinary Riches**	Wind-Up digital

COMPANY OF WOLVES

Hard-rock band from New Jersey: Kyf Brewer (vocals), Steve Conte (guitar), John Conte (bass) and Frankie Larocka (drums).

3/17/90	166	6	1 **Company Of Wolves**	Mercury 842184

COMPTON'S MOST WANTED

Rap trio from Los Angeles, California: Aaron **"MC Eiht"** Tyler, Terry "DJ Slip" Allen and Michael "DJ Mike T" Bryant.

7/7/90	133	7		1 **It's A Compton Thang**	Orpheus 75627
8/3/91	92	9		2 **Straight Checkn 'Em**	Orpheus 47926
10/17/92	66	9		3 **Music To Driveby**	Orpheus 52984
8/6/94	5	14	●	4 **We Come Strapped**	Epic Street 57696
4/27/96	16	8		5 **Death Threatz**	Epic Street 67139
				MC EIHT Featuring CMW (above 2)	

COMRADS, The

Rap duo from Los Angeles, California: K-Mac and Gangsta.

7/26/97	113	2	1 **The Comrads**	Street Life 75507
7/22/00	153	2	2 **Wake Up & Ball**	Hoo-Bangin' 50001

CONCENTRATION CAMP II

Gathering of solo rappers: **Young Bleed**, C-Loc, Lay Lo, Lucky Knuckles and Boo The Boss Playa.

5/30/98	84	2	1 **Da Holocaust**	Priority 53536

CONCRETE BLONDE
Rock trio formed in Los Angeles, California: Johnette Napolitano (vocals, bass), James Andrew Mankey (guitar) and Harry Rushakoff (drums). Paul Thompson replaced Rushakoff in early 1990; Rushakoff returned in late 1991, replacing Thompson. Group originally known as Dream 6, renamed by Michael Stipe of **R.E.M.**

DEBUT	PEAK	WKS		Album Title		Label & Number
2/21/87	96	16		1 Concrete Blonde		I.R.S. 5835
5/13/89	148	18		2 Free		I.R.S. 82001
6/9/90	49	44	●	3 Bloodletting		I.R.S. 82037
3/28/92	73	15		4 Walking In London		I.R.S. 13137
11/6/93	67	5		5 Mexican Moon		Capitol 81129

CONDON, Mark
Born in Lancaster, Ohio. Christian choral director.

9/9/00	106	3		1 Marvelous Things		Hosanna! 17802

CONEY HATCH
Rock band from Toronto, Ontario, Canada: Carl Dixon (vocals), Steve Shelski (guitar), Andy Curran (bass) and Dave Ketchum (drums).

9/17/83	186	2		1 Outa Hand		Mercury 812869

CONFEDERATE RAILROAD
Country-rock band from Marietta, Georgia: Danny Shirley (vocals), Michael Lamb (guitar), Gates Nichols (steel guitar), Chris McDaniel (keyboards), Wayne Secrest (bass) and Mark DuFresne (drums). Jimmy Dormire replaced Lamb in 1995.

9/19/92+	53	80	▲²	1 Confederate Railroad		Atlantic 82335
4/9/94	52	22	▲	2 Notorious		Atlantic 82505
7/8/95	152	5		3 When And Where		Atlantic 82774

CON FUNK SHUN
Funk band from Vallejo, California: **Michael Cooper** (vocals, guitar), Danny Thomas (keyboards), Karl Fuller, Paul Harrell and Felton Pilate (horns), Cedric Martin (bass) and Louis McCall (drums).

10/15/77	51	28	●	1 Secrets		Mercury 1180
7/1/78	32	19	●	2 Loveshine		Mercury 3725
6/2/79	46	22	●	3 Candy		Mercury 3754
4/12/80	30	20	●	4 Spirit Of Love		Mercury 3806
12/13/80+	51	19		5 Touch		Mercury 4002
12/12/81+	82	13		6 Con Funk Shun 7		Mercury 4030
12/4/82	115	29		7 To The Max		Mercury 4067
12/3/83+	105	21		8 Fever		Mercury 814447
5/18/85	62	26		9 Electric Lady		Mercury 824345
7/19/86	121	11		10 Burnin' Love		Mercury 826963

CONJUNTO ATARDECER
Latin band from Durango, Mexico: Mario Madrigal, Heraclio Cepeda, Daniel Rubio, Roberto Villa, Emmanuel Ruacho, Oscar Navarro and Alexis Soto.

11/18/06	190	1		1 El Decimo...Y Siguen Los No. 1 Del Pasito Duranguense	[F]	Universal Latino 007889
9/5/09	103	3		2 Contigo Para Siempre	[F]	Disa 721307

CONJUNTO PRIMAVERA
Latin norteno band from Ojinaga, Chihuahua, Mexico: Tony Melendez (vocals), Rolando Perez (guitar), Felix Contreras (keyboards), Juan Dominguez (sax), Oscar Ochoa (bass) and Adan Huerta (drums). Group name is Spanish for "Joint Spring."

2/12/00	153	4	●	1 Morir De Amor	[F]	Fonovisa 9926
4/14/01	139	5	●	2 Ansia De Amar	[F]	Fonovisa 6104
9/7/02	117	5	●	3 Perdoname Mi Amor	[F]	Fonovisa 86237
4/19/03	159	3		4 Nuestra Historia	[F-K]	Fonovisa 50786
9/6/03	124	4		5 Decide Tu	[F]	Fonovisa 350875
5/8/04	107	5		6 Dejando Huella	[F]	Fonovisa 351248
2/19/05	58	5		7 Hoy Como Ayer	[F]	Fonovisa 351613
7/23/05	158	2		8 Dejando Huella II	[F]	Fonovisa 351902
3/18/06	82	4		9 Algo De Mi	[F]	Fonovisa 352250
9/16/06	174	2		10 Para Ti...Nuestra Historia	[F-K]	Fonovisa 352602 [2]
2/17/07	89	3		11 El Amor Que Nunca Fue	[F]	Fonovisa 352971
2/23/08	87	3		12 Que Ganas De Volver	[F]	Fonovisa 353487
2/14/09	103	3		13 Mentir Por Amor	[F]	Fonovisa 353833

CONLEE, John
Born on 8/11/1946 in Versailles, Kentucky. Country singer./songwriter/guitarist.
AWARD: OPRY: 1981

6/11/83	166	6	●	1 John Conlee's Greatest Hits	[G]	MCA 5405

CONLEY, Arthur
Born on 1/4/1946 in Atlanta, Georgia. Died of cancer on 11/17/2003 (age 57). R&B singer.

5/13/67	93	13		1 Sweet Soul Music		Atco 215
8/19/67	193	2		2 Shake, Rattle & Roll		Atco 220
7/6/68	185	2		3 Soul Directions		Atco 243

CONLEY, Earl Thomas
Born on 10/17/1941 in West Portsmouth, Ohio. Country singer/songwriter/guitarist.

11/24/84	210	1		1 Treadin' Water		RCA Victor 5175

Billboard			R I A A	ARTIST		
DEBUT	PEAK	WKS		Album Title	Catalog	Label & Number

CONNELLS, The
Rock band from Raleigh, North Carolina: brothers Mike Connell (guitar) and David Connell (bass) with Doug MacMillan (vocals), Peele Wimberley (drums) and George Huntley (guitar). Steve Potak (keyboards) joined by 1993.

5/6/89	163	10		1 Fun & Games		TVT 2550
11/10/90+	168	18		2 One Simple Word		TVT 2580
10/16/93	199	1		3 Ring		TVT 2590

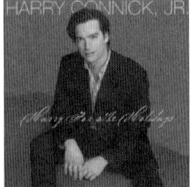

CONNICK, Harry Jr.   **1990s: #22 / All-Time: #150**
Born on 9/11/1967 in New Orleans, Louisiana. Jazz-pop singer/pianist/actor. Father served as New Orleans District Attorney from 1974-2003; mother was a Louisiana Supreme Court Justice. Acted in several movies. Married model/actress Jill Goodacre on 4/16/1994.

5/25/91+	133	44	▲	1 20 .... *recorded in 1987*		Columbia 44369
8/19/89	42	122	▲²	2 When Harry Met Sally... **[S]** *Grammy: Jazz Vocal*		Columbia 45319
7/21/90+	22	96	▲²	3 We Are In Love .... **Cat:#46/1** *Grammy: Jazz Vocal*		Columbia 46146
7/21/90	94	11		4 Lofty's Roach Souffle .... **[I]** HARRY CONNICK, JR. TRIO *trio includes Benjamin Wolfe (bass) and Shannon Powell (drums)*		Columbia 46223
10/12/91+	17	51	▲²	5 Blue Light, Red Light		Columbia 48685
12/12/92+	19	18	▲	6 25		Columbia 53172
7/30/94	16	33	▲	7 She		Columbia 64376
7/20/96	38	12	●	8 Star Turtle		Columbia 67575
11/29/97	53	15	●	9 To See You		Columbia 68787
6/19/99	36	13	●	10 Come By Me		Columbia 69618
11/10/01	88	4		11 Songs I Heard *Grammy: Traditional Pop Vocal*		Columbia 86077
11/10/01	94	4		12 30 .... *recorded in 1997*		Columbia 69794
2/21/04	5	23	▲	13 Only You		Columbia 90551
5/27/06	97	2		14 Harry On Broadway, Act I/The Pajama Game .... **[OC]**		Columbia 82883
2/17/07	11	8		15 Oh, My Nola		Columbia 88851
10/10/09	8	21↑		16 Your Songs		Columbia 47228
				CHRISTMAS ALBUMS:		
11/13/93+	13	10	▲³	17 When My Heart Finds Christmas .... **Cat:❶¹/81** *Christmas charts: 1/'93, 3/'94, 4/'95, 7/'96, 8/'97, 23/'98, 20/'99, 22/'00, 22/'01, 12/'02, 13/'03, 23/'04, 35/'05, 39/'09*		Columbia 57550
11/15/03	12	9	▲	18 Harry For The Holidays .... **Cat:#3/18** *Christmas charts: 1/'03, 6/'04, 17/'05, 40/'06*		Columbia 90550
11/22/08	20	8		19 What A Night! A Christmas Album .... **Cat:#44/1** *Christmas charts: 5/'08, 14/'09*		Columbia 37020
12/5/09	106	5		20 What A Night! A Christmas Album .... **[R]**		Columbia 37020

CONNIFF, Ray, and His Orchestra & Chorus   **1950s: #19 / 1960s: #4 / All-Time: #18**
Born on 11/6/1916 in Attleboro, Massachusetts. Died of a stroke on 10/12/2002 (age 85). Legendary arranger/conductor. Played trombone with Bunny Berigan, Bob Crosby, **Harry James**, Vaughn Monroe and Artie Shaw bands. Conniff's non-instrumental albums feature the Ray Conniff Singers.

3/23/57	11	16		1 'S Wonderful! .... **[I]**		Columbia 925
12/23/57+	10	37	●	2 'S Marvelous **[I]**		Columbia 1074
6/23/58+	9	52		3 'S Awful Nice **[I]**		Columbia 1137 / 8001
9/29/58	9	50	●	4 Concert In Rhythm **[I]**		Columbia 1163 / 8022
5/25/59+	10	20		5 Broadway In Rhythm **[I]**		Columbia 1252 / 8064
6/29/59	29	8		6 Hollywood In Rhythm .... **[I]**		Columbia 1310 / 8117
11/23/59+	8	36		7 Conniff Meets Butterfield **[I]** RAY CONNIFF & BILLY BUTTERFIELD		Columbia 1346 / 8155
2/15/60	8	54		8 It's The Talk Of The Town		Columbia 1334 / 8143
3/7/60	13	33		9 Concert In Rhythm - Volume II .... **[I]**		Columbia 1415 / 8212
8/15/60+	6	28		10 Young At Heart		Columbia 1489 / 8281
10/10/60	4	58		11 Say It With Music (A Touch Of Latin) **[I]**		Columbia 1490 / 8282
2/13/61	4	34	●	12 Memories Are Made Of This **[I]**		Columbia 1574 / 8374
9/11/61	14	34		13 Somebody Loves Me		Columbia 1642 / 8442
2/17/62	5	34	●	14 So Much In Love		Columbia 1720 / 8520

Billboard DEBUT	PEAK	WKS	R I A A	ARTIST Album Title	Catalog	Label & Number
				CONNIFF, Ray, and His Orchestra & Chorus — cont'd		
5/5/62	6	25		15 'S Continental [I]		Columbia 1776 / 8576
10/6/62	28	16		16 Rhapsody In Rhythm .... [I]		Columbia 1878 / 8678
3/9/63	20	15		17 The Happy Beat... [I]		Columbia 1949 / 8749
9/14/63	85	13		18 Just Kiddin' Around... [I]		Columbia 2022 / 8822
				RAY CONNIFF & BILLY BUTTERFIELD		
2/15/64	73	17		19 You Make Me Feel So Young .... [I]		Columbia 2118 / 8918
5/30/64	50	19		20 Speak To Me Of Love		Columbia 2150 / 8950
10/3/64	23	27		21 Invisible Tears		Columbia 2264 / 9064
4/3/65	141	5		22 Friendly Persuasion .... [I]		Columbia 2210 / 9010
6/5/65	34	19		23 Music From Mary Poppins, The Sound Of Music, My Fair Lady, & Other Great Movie Themes		Columbia 2366 / 9166
9/18/65	54	16		24 Love Affair		Columbia 2352 / 9152
4/2/66	80	9		25 Happiness Is		Columbia 2461 / 9261
7/16/66	3[4]	90	▲	26 Somewhere My Love		Columbia 2519 / 9319
3/18/67	78	10		27 Ray Conniff's World Of Hits .... [I]		Columbia 2500 / 9300
5/13/67	180	2		28 En Espanol! .... [F]		Columbia 2608 / 9408
6/3/67	30	46		29 This Is My Song		Columbia 2676 / 9476
10/28/67+	39	15		30 Hawaiian Album		Columbia 2747 / 9547
2/17/68	25	41	●	31 It Must Be Him		Columbia 2795 / 9595
6/1/68	22	39	●	32 Honey		Columbia 9661
10/26/68+	70	22		33 Turn Around Look At Me		Columbia 9712
3/8/69	101	14		34 I Love How You Love Me		Columbia 9777
7/12/69	158	5	●	35 Ray Conniff's Greatest Hits .... [G]		Columbia 9839
12/20/69+	103	21		36 Jean		Columbia 9920
4/25/70	47	28		37 Bridge Over Troubled Water		Columbia 1022
9/26/70	177	5		38 Concert In Stereo/Live At The Sahara/Tahoe........................ [L]		Columbia 30122 [2]
12/26/70+	120	13		39 We've Only Just Begun		Columbia 30410
3/27/71	98	15		40 Love Story..		Columbia 30498
9/11/71	185	5		41 Great Contemporary Instrumental Hits .... [I]		Columbia 30755
2/12/72	138	11		42 I'd Like To Teach The World To Sing		Columbia 31220
6/3/72	114	14		43 Love Theme From "The Godfather"		Columbia 31473
10/7/72	180	10		44 Alone Again (Naturally)		Columbia 31629
2/10/73	165	10		45 I Can See Clearly Now		Columbia 32090
7/7/73	176	5		46 You Are The Sunshine Of My Life		Columbia 32376
10/13/73	194	4		47 Harmony		Columbia 32553
3/29/75	204	6		48 Laughter In The Rain		Columbia 33332
				CHRISTMAS ALBUMS:		
12/28/59+	14	2	▲	49 Christmas With Conniff .... Christmas charts: 39/'65, 35/'67, 11/'68, 7/'69		Columbia 1390 / 8185
12/31/60	15	1		50 Christmas With Conniff .... [R]		Columbia 1390 / 8185
12/18/61+	16	6		51 Christmas With Conniff .... [R]		Columbia 1390 / 8185
12/8/62	32	4	▲	52 We Wish You A Merry Christmas .... Christmas charts: 7/'63, 10/'64, 13/'65, 20/'66, 12/'67, 18/'68, 5/'72		Columbia 1892 / 8692
12/25/65+	15[X]	5		53 Here We Come A-Caroling .... Christmas charts: 17/'65, 15/'66		Columbia 2406 / 9206
12/12/70+	10[X]	3		54 Two All-TIme Great Albums In One Great Package [R] reissue of #27 & 53 above		Columbia GP 3 [2]
				CONNOR, Sarah Born on 6/13/1980 in Delmenhorst, Germany. White R&B singer.		
3/27/04	106	2		1 Sarah Connor		Epic 91110
				CONNORS, Norman Born on 3/1/1948 in Philadelphia, Pennsylvania. Jazz drummer with Archie Shepp, **John Coltrane**, **Pharoah Sanders** and others. Own group on Buddah in 1972. Featured vocalists are **Michael Henderson**, **Jean Carn** and **Phyllis Hyman**. Formed disco group **Aquarian Dream**.		
10/11/75	150	5		1 Saturday Night Special		Buddah 5643
7/24/76	39	24	●	2 You Are My Starship		Buddah 5655
4/9/77	94	16		3 Romantic Journey		Buddah 5682
5/27/78	68	17		4 This Is Your Life		Arista 4177
1/13/79	175	5		5 The Best Of Norman Connors & Friends .... [G]		Buddah 5716
7/21/79	137	7		6 Invitation		Arista 4216
9/27/80	145	6		7 Take It To The Limit		Arista 9534
12/5/81	197	2		8 Mr. C		Arista 9575
				CONSCIOUS DAUGHTERS, The Black female hardcore rap duo from Oakland, California: Carla Green and Karryl Smith.		
2/26/94	126	9		1 Ear To The Street		Scarface 53877
				CONSEQUENCE Born Dexter Mills on 6/14/1977 in Queens, New York. Male rapper. Cousin of **Q-Tip**.		
3/24/07	113	2		1 Don't Quit Your Day Job		G.O.O.D. 94805

Billboard			R I A A	ARTIST		
DEBUT	PEAK	WKS		Album Title	Catalog	Label & Number

CONSTANTINE
Born Constantine Maroulis on 9/17/1975 in Brooklyn, New York. Hard-rock singer. Finalist on the fourth season of TV's *American Idol* in 2005. Leader of **Pray For The Soul Of Betty**.

| 8/25/07 | 75 | 2 | | 1 Constantine .... | | 6th Place 1078 |

CONTOURS, The
R&B vocal group from Detroit, Michigan: Billy Gordon, Billy Hoggs, Joe Billingslea, Sylvester Potts and Hubert Johnson, with Huey Davis (guitar). Johnson committed suicide on 7/11/1981 (age 40). Davis died on 2/23/2002 (age 63).

~ ~ ~ ~ ~ ~ ~ ~ ~ ~ ~ **NON-CHARTED ALBUM** ~ ~ ~ ~ ~ ~ ~ ~ ~ ~ ~
1962 **Do You Love Me**

CONTRABAND
Hard-rock band formed in Los Angeles, California: Richard Black (vocals), Tracii Guns (guitar; **L.A. Guns**), Michael Schenker (guitar), Share Pedersen (bass; **Vixen**) and Bobby Blotzer (drums; **Ratt**).

| 6/29/91 | 187 | 1 | | 1 Contraband .... | | Impact 10247 |

CONTROL
Latin group from Mexico. Led by Sergio Alcocer.

| 9/6/03 | 196 | 1 | | 1 La Historia .... [F-K] | | EMI Latin 90878 |

CONTROLLERS, The
R&B vocal group from Fairfield, Alabama: brothers Reginald McArthur and Larry McArthur, with Lenard Brown and Ricky Lewis.

| 12/17/77+ | 146 | 6 | | 1 In Control .... | | Juana 200,001 |

CONVERGE
Hard-rock band from Boston, Massachusetts: Jacob Bannon (vocals), Kurt Ballou (guitar), Nate Newton (bass) and Ben Koller (drums).

10/9/04	171	1		1 You Fail Me		Epitaph 86715
11/11/06	151	1		2 No Heroes		Epitaph 86827
11/7/09	74	2		3 Axe To Fall		Epitaph 87035

CONWAY, Julie
Born in Brooklyn, New York. Aerobics instructor.

| 1/9/61 | 73 | 17 | | 1 Good Housekeeping's Plan For Reducing Off-The-Record .... | | Harmony 7143 |
| | | | | music by The Bob Price Quartet; the first aerobics album | | |

CONWELL, Tommy, And The Young Rumblers
Born in Philadelphia, Pennsylvania. Rock singer/guitarist. The Young Rumblers: Chris Day (guitar), Rob Miller (keyboards; **Hooters**), Paul Slivka (bass) and Jim Hannum (drums).

| 9/3/88 | 103 | 28 | | 1 Rumble .... | | Columbia 44186 |

COO COO CAL
Born Calvin Bellamy on 4/30/1970 in Milwaukee, Wisconsin. Male rapper.

| 10/6/01 | 45 | 7 | | 1 Disturbed .... | | Tommy Boy 1466 |

COODER, Ry
Born Ryland Cooder on 3/15/1947 in Los Angeles, California. Blues-rock singer/guitarist. Scored several movies. Member of **Little Village**.

2/13/71	216	1		1 Ry Cooder		Reprise 6402
2/12/72	113	8		2 Into The Purple Valley		Reprise 2052
6/8/74	167	6		3 Paradise And Lunch		Reprise 2179
10/23/76	177	5		4 Chicken Skin Music		Reprise 2254
9/10/77	158	5		5 Show Time .... [L]		Warner 3059
				recorded on 12/14/1976 at the Great American Music Hall in San Francisco		
8/11/79	62	15		6 Bop Till You Drop		Warner 3358
7/12/80	206	3		7 The Long Riders .... [I-S]		Warner 3448
1/24/81	43	16		8 Borderline		Warner 3489
6/12/82	105	7		9 The Slide Area		Warner 3651
3/9/85	210	1		10 Paris, Texas .... [I-S]		Warner 25270
5/10/86	85	9		11 Crossroads .... [S]		Warner 25399
11/28/87	177	12		12 Get Rhythm		Warner 25639
2/15/03	52	8		13 Mambo Sinuendo .... [I]		Perro Verde 79691
				RY COODER & MANUEL GALBAN		
				Grammy: Pop Instrumental Album		
7/2/05	149	2		14 Chavez Ravine		Perro Verde 79877
3/24/07	168	1		15 My Name Is Buddy: Another Record By Ry Cooder		Perdo Verde 79961

COOK, Barbara
Born on 10/25/1927 in Atlanta, Georgia. Singer/actress. Appeared in Broadway's *Plain and Fancy*, *Candide*, *The Music Man* and *She Loves Me*.

| 7/4/81 | 209 | 3 | | 1 It's Better With A Band .... [L] | | MMG 104 |
| | | | | recorded on 9/14/1980 at Carnegie Hall in New York City | | |

COOK, Dane
Born on 3/18/1972 in Boston, Massachusetts. Stand-up comedian/actor. Appeared in several movies.

9/3/05+	❶⁹ᶜ	102	●	1 Harmful If Swallowed [C]		Comedy Central 0017
				released in 2003		
8/13/05	4	84	▲²	2 Retaliation	Cat:#38/5 [C]	Comedy Central 0034 [2]
12/1/07	11	23	●	3 Rough Around The Edges: Live From Madison Square Garden .... [C]		Comedy Central 0051
6/6/09	4	18		4 Isolated Incident [C]		Comedy Central 0085

COOK, David
Born on 12/20/1982 in Houston, Texas; raised in Blue Springs, Missouri. Pop-rock singer. Winner on the 2008 season of TV's *American Idol*.

12/6/08	3¹	44	▲	1 David Cook		19 Records 33463

COOK, Kristy Lee
Born on 1/18/1984 in Seattle, Washington. Country singer. Finalist on the 2008 season of TV's *American Idol*.

10/4/08	49	2		1 Why Wait		19 Records 33393

COOKE, Sam   All-Time: #470
Born on 1/22/1931 in Clarksdale, Mississippi; raised in Chicago, Illinois. Died from a gunshot wound on 12/11/1964 (age 33) in Los Angeles, California; shot by a female motel manager under mysterious circumstances. Son of a Baptist minister. Lead singer of the Soul Stirrers from 1950-56. Uncle of **R.B. Greaves**. Revered as the definitive soul singer.
AWARDS: Grammy: Lifetime Achievement 1999 ★ R&R Hall of Fame: 1986

3/10/58	16	2		1 Sam Cooke		Keen 2001
6/30/62	72	8		2 Twistin' The Night Away		RCA Victor 2555
3/23/63	94	9		3 Mr. Soul		RCA Victor 2673
9/14/63	62	19		4 Night Beat		RCA Victor 2709
4/4/64	34	19		5 Ain't That Good News		RCA Victor 2899
2/13/65	44	23		6 Shake...		RCA Victor 3367
10/30/65	120	7		7 Try A Little Love		RCA Victor 3435
				GREATEST HITS & COMPILATIONS:		
10/20/62	22	35		8 The Best Of Sam Cooke	Cat:#39/4	RCA Victor 2625
7/24/65	128	8		9 The Best Of Sam Cooke, Volume 2		RCA Victor 3373
4/5/86	175	8		10 The Man And His Music		RCA Victor 7127 [2]
3/4/06	22ᶜ	4		11 Portrait Of A Legend 1951-1964		Abkco 792642
				RS500 #106		
				LIVE ALBUMS:		
10/31/64+	29	55		12 Sam Cooke At The Copa		RCA Victor 2970
6/22/85	134	8		13 Live At The Harlem Square Club, 1963		RCA Victor 5181
				RS500 #443		
				recorded on 1/12/1963 in Miami, Florida		

~ ~ ~ ~ ~ ~ ~ ~ ~ ~   **NON-CHARTED ALBUMS**   ~ ~ ~ ~ ~ ~ ~ ~ ~ ~ ~

1958 **Encore**   1960 **I Thank God**
1959 **Tribute To The Lady**   1960 **The Wonderful World Of Sam Cooke**

COOKIES, The
Female R&B vocal trio from Brooklyn, New York: Earl-Jean McCrea, Dorothy Jones and Margaret Ross.

~ ~ ~ ~ ~ ~ ~ ~ ~ ~   **NON-CHARTED ALBUM**   ~ ~ ~ ~ ~ ~ ~ ~ ~ ~ ~

1964 **The Dimension Dolls (volume 1)**
[w/ Little Eva & Carole King]

COOL BREEZE
Born Freddy Calhoun in Atlanta, Georgia. Male rapper. Member of **Calhouns** and **Dungeon Family**.

4/10/99	38	6		1 East Points Greatest Hit		Organized Noize 90159

COOLIDGE, Rita   All-Time: #431
Born on 5/1/1944 in Nashville, Tennessee. Pop-rock singer. Did backup work for **Delaney & Bonnie**, **Leon Russell**, **Joe Cocker** and **Eric Clapton**. With **Kris Kristofferson** from 1971, married to him from 1973-80. Known as "The Delta Lady," for whom Leon Russell wrote the song of the same name. In the 1983 movie *Club Med*.

4/3/71	105	10		1 Rita Coolidge		A&M 4291
12/18/71+	135	8		2 Nice Feelin'		A&M 3130
11/11/72+	46	24		3 The Lady's Not For Sale		A&M 4370
9/22/73	26	33	●	4 Full Moon		A&M 4403
				KRIS KRISTOFFERSON & RITA COOLIDGE		
5/25/74	55	15		5 Fall Into Spring		A&M 3627
12/21/74+	103	12		6 Breakaway		Monument 33278
				KRIS KRISTOFFERSON & RITA COOLIDGE		
12/6/75+	85	10		7 It's Only Love		A&M 4531
4/2/77	6	54	▲	8 Anytime...Anywhere		A&M 4616
6/17/78	32	22	●	9 Love Me Again		A&M 4699
2/3/79	106	9		10 Natural Act		A&M 4690
				KRIS KRISTOFFERSON & RITA COOLIDGE		
9/22/79	95	16		11 Satisfied		A&M 4781
2/14/81	107	8		12 Rita Coolidge/Greatest Hits .... [G]		A&M 4836
9/12/81	160	4		13 Heartbreak Radio		A&M 3727

COOLIO
Born Artis Ivey on 8/1/1963 in Los Angeles, California. Male rapper.

8/6/94	8	30	▲	1 It Takes A Thief	Tommy Boy 1083
11/25/95+	9	62	▲²	2 Gangsta's Paradise	Tommy Boy 1141
9/13/97	39	9	●	3 My Soul	Tommy Boy 1180

COOL KIDS, The
Alternative hip-hop duo formed in Chicago, Illinois: Antoine "Mikey" Reed and Evan "Chuck" Ingersoll.

6/7/08	152	1		1 The Bake Sale	C.A.K.E. 001

COOPER, Alice
All-Time: #149

Born Vincent Furnier on 2/4/1948 in Detroit, Michigan; raised in Phoenix, Arizona. Formed hard-rock band, Alice Cooper: Furnier (vocals), Glen Buxton (guitar), Michael Bruce (keyboards), Dennis Dunaway (bass) and Neal Smith (drums). Furnier went on to assume the Alice Cooper name for himself. Band split in 1974. Cooper went solo and became known for his bizarre stage antics. Appeared in the movies *Prince Of Darkness* and *Wayne's World*, among others. Hosts own nightly syndicated radio show. Also see **Billion Dollar Babies**.

6/28/69	193	6		1 Pretties For You		Straight 1051
3/20/71	35	38	▲	2 Love It To Death		Warner 1883
				RS500 #460		
12/4/71+	21	54	▲	3 Killer		Warner 2567
7/1/72	2³	32	▲	4 School's Out		Warner 2623
3/17/73	❶¹	50	▲	5 Billion Dollar Babies		Warner 2685
12/8/73+	10	21	●	6 Muscle Of Love		Warner 2748
8/31/74	8	23	▲	7 Alice Cooper's Greatest Hits	[G]	Warner 2803
3/22/75	5	37	▲	8 Welcome To My Nightmare		Atlantic 18130
7/17/76	27	32	●	9 Alice Cooper Goes To Hell		Warner 2896
5/28/77	42	16		10 Lace And Whiskey		Warner 3027
12/17/77+	131	6		11 The Alice Cooper Show	[L]	Warner 3138
12/16/78+	60	11		12 From The Inside		Warner 3263
5/24/80	44	17		13 Flush The Fashion		Warner 3436
9/19/81	125	5		14 Special Forces		Warner 3581
10/18/86	59	21		15 Constrictor		MCA 5761
10/24/87	73	15		16 Raise Your Fist And Yell		MCA 42091
8/12/89	20	43	▲	17 Trash		Epic 45137
7/20/91	47	13		18 Hey Stoopid		Epic 46786
7/30/94	68	3		19 The Last Temptation		Epic 52771
6/24/00	193	1		20 Brutal Planet		Spitfire 5038
10/27/01	197	1		21 Dragontown		Eagle Rock 15200
10/18/03	184	1		22 The Eyes Of Alice Cooper		Eagle 20028
8/20/05	169	1		23 Dirty Diamonds		New West 6078
8/16/08	53	3		24 Along Came A Spider		Steamhammer 9060

COOPER, Michael
Born on 11/15/1952 in Vallejo, California. R&B singer/songwriter/guitarist. Leader of **Con Funk Shun**.

1/16/88	98	25	1 Love Is Such A Funny Game		Warner 25653

COOPER, Pat
Born Pasquale Caputo on 7/31/1929 in Brooklyn, New York. Stand-up comedian/actor. Appeared in several movies.

5/28/66	82	42	1 Our Hero...Pat Cooper	[C]	United Artists 6446
12/17/66+	84	14	2 Spaghetti Sauce & Other Delights	[C]	United Artists 6548
3/22/69	193	2	3 More Saucy Stories From...Pat Cooper	[C]	United Artists 6690

COOPER BROTHERS
Pop-rock band from Ottawa, Ontario, Canada: brothers Richard Cooper (guitar) and Brian Cooper (bass), Terry King (guitar), Darryl Alguire (guitar), Charles Robinson (flute), Al Serwa (keyboards) and Glenn Bell (drums). All but Serwa share vocals.

7/21/79	204	2	1 Pitfalls Of The Ballroom		Capricorn 0226

COPE, Julian
Born on 10/21/1957 in Deri, South Wales; raised in Tamworth, England. Pop-rock singer/songwriter/bassist. Leader of the **Teardrop Explodes**.

2/21/87	109	6	1 Julian Cope	[EP]	Island 90560
4/4/87	105	12	2 Saint Julian		Island 90571
12/10/88+	155	13	3 My Nation Underground		Island 91025

COPELAND
Alternative-rock band from Florida: Aaron Marsh (vocals, guitar), Bryan Laurenson (guitar), James Likeness (bass) and Jon Bucklew (drums).

4/9/05	115	1	1 In Motion		The Militia Group 030
11/18/06	90	1	2 Eat, Sleep, Repeat		The Militia Group 049
11/1/08	48	1	3 You Are My Sunshine		Tooth & Nail 13502

COPELAND, Johnny
Born on 3/27/1937 in Haynesville, Louisiana; later based in Houston, Texas. Died of heart failure on 7/4/1997 (age 60). Blues guitarist. Known as "The Texas Twister."

2/15/86	124	18	1 Showdown!		Alligator 4743

ALBERT COLLINS / ROBERT CRAY / JOHNNY COPELAND
Grammy: Blues Album

COPELAND, Stewart
Born on 7/16/1952 in South Norfolk, Virginia; partially raised in Egypt and Lebanon (father was in CIA; mother was an archaeologist). Rock drummer. Member of **The Police** and **Oysterhead**. Prior to The Police, worked as **Joan Armatrading**'s road manager. Founded **Animal Logic** in 1989. His brother, Miles Copeland, founded the IRS record label.

12/17/83+	157	5	1 Rumble Fish .... **[I-S]**		A&M 4983
9/7/85	148	8	2 The Rhythmatist		A&M 5084

COPPERHEAD
Rock band formed in San Francisco, California: Gary Philippet (vocals, guitar), John Cipollina (guitar; **Quicksilver Messenger Service**), Jim McPherson (keyboards), Hutch Hutchinson (bass) and David Weber (drums). Cipollina died on 5/29/1989 (age 45).

6/23/73	208	5	1 Copperhead		Columbia 32250

CORAL, The
Pop-rock band from Holylake, Wirral, England: James Skelly (vocals, guitar), Lee Southall (guitar), Bill Ryder-Jones (trumpet), Nick Power (organ), Paul Duffy (bass) and Ian Skelly (drums).

3/22/03	189	1	1 The Coral		Deltasonic 87192

COREA, Chick
Born Anthony Corea on 6/12/1941 in Chelsea, Massachusetts. Jazz-rock pianist. Worked with **Stan Getz**, Blue Mitchell, **Sarah Vaughan** and Gary Burton before joining the **Miles Davis** band in 1968. Formed group **Return To Forever** in 1973.

3/6/76	42	15	1 The Leprechaun .... **[I]**		Polydor 6062
			Grammy: Jazz Album		
1/15/77	55	12	2 My Spanish Heart .... **[I]**		Polydor 9003 [2]
3/11/78	61	14	3 The Mad Hatter .... **[I]**		Polydor 6130
8/19/78	86	10	4 Friends .... **[I]**		Polydor 6160
			Grammy: Jazz Album		
3/31/79	100	8	5 An Evening With Herbie Hancock & Chick Corea .... **[I-L]**		Columbia 35663 [2]
11/24/79	175	2	6 An Evening With Chick Corea & Herbie Hancock .... **[I-L]**		Polydor 6238 [2]
5/10/80	170	3	7 Tap Step .... **[I]**		Warner 3425
8/1/81	179	4	8 Three Quartets .... **[I]**		Warner 3552
10/16/82	207	2	9 Touchstone .... **[I]**		Warner 23699

COREY
Born Corey Hodges on 11/13/1988 in Atlanta, Georgia. Teen R&B singer.

4/6/02	73	5	1 I'm Just Corey		Noontime 016713

CORGAN, Billy
Born on 3/17/1967 in Chicago, Illinois. Alternative-rock singer/songwriter/guitarist. Leader of **Smashing Pumpkins** and **Zwan**.

7/9/05	31	3	1 TheFutureEmbrace		Martha's Music 48712

CORMEGA
Born Cory McKay in Queens, New York. Male rapper. Member of **QB Finest**.

8/11/01	111	8	1 The Realness		Legal Hustle 9203
7/13/02	95	2	2 The True Meaning		Legal Hustle 9214
6/12/04	174	1	3 Legal Hustle		Legal Hustle 5727

CORNELIUS BROTHERS & SISTER ROSE
Family R&B trio from Dania, Florida: Edward Cornelius, Carter Cornelius and Rose Cornelius. Carter died of a heart attack on 11/7/1991 (age 43).

7/29/72	29	25	1 Cornelius Brothers & Sister Rose		United Artists 5568

CORNELL, Chris
Born on 7/20/1964 in Seattle, Washington. Hard-rock singer/songwriter/guitarist. Lead singer of **Soundgarden** and **Audioslave**.

10/9/99	18	8	1 Euphoria Morning		A&M 490412
6/23/07	17	6	2 Carry On		Suretone 008742
3/28/09	10	4	3 Scream		Mosley 012018

CORNERSHOP
Rock band formed in London, England: Tjinder Singh (vocals), Ben Ayers (guitar), Anthony Saffrey (sitar), Peter Bengry (percussion) and Nick Simms (drums).

1/24/98	144	5	1 When I Was Born For The 7th Time		Luaka Bop 46576

CORONA
Dance duo: Italian producer Francesco Bontempi and Brazilian singer Olga DeSouza.

6/17/95	154	7	1 The Rhythm Of The Night		EastWest 61817

CORPORATION, The
Rock band from Milwaukee, Wisconsin: Danny Peil (vocals), Gerry Smith (guitar), John Kondos (keyboards), Pat McCarthy (horns), Ken Berdoll (bass) and Nick Kondos (drums).

3/1/69	197	4	1 The Corporation		Capitol 175

CORROSION OF CONFORMITY

Hard-rock band from Raleigh, North Carolina: Pepper Keenan (vocals, guitar), Woody Weatherman (guitar), Mike Dean (bass) and Reed Mullin (drums). Keenan was also a member of **Down**.

10/15/94+	155	15	1 Deliverance	Columbia 66208
11/2/96	104	2	2 Wiseblood	Columbia 67583
4/23/05	108	1	3 In The Arms Of God	Sanctuary 84739

CORRS, The

Sibling pop band from Ireland: Andrea Corr (vocals), Jim Corr (guitar), Sharon Corr (violin) and Caroline Corr (drums).

1/20/96	131	4	● 1 Forgiven, Not Forgotten	143 Records 92612
3/27/99	72	17	● 2 Talk On Corners - Special Edition	143 Records 83164
9/30/00	21	44	▲ 3 In Blue	143 Records 83352
3/30/02	52	24	4 VH-1 Presents The Corrs: Live In Dublin ... [L] recorded on 1/25/2002 at Ardmore Studios	Lava 83533
6/26/04	51	4	5 Borrowed Heaven	Atlantic 83670

CORTEZ, Dave "Baby"

Born David Cortez Clowney on 8/13/1938 in Detroit, Michigan. R&B keyboardist/composer.

9/29/62	107	3	1 Rinky Dink ... [I]	Chess 1473

~ ~ ~ ~ ~ ~ ~ ~ ~ **NON-CHARTED ALBUMS** ~ ~ ~ ~ ~ ~ ~ ~ ~ ~

1959 **The Happy Organ** *[RCA Victor label]*   1960 **Dave "Baby" Cortez** *[Clock label]*

CORYELL, Larry

Born on 4/2/1943 in Galveston, Texas. Jazz/rock guitarist. Founder of **Eleventh House**.

5/31/69	196	3	1 Lady Coryell	Vanguard 6509
11/25/72	212	2	2 Offering ... [I]	Vanguard 79319
6/2/73	206	6	3 The Real Great Escape	Vanguard 79329
2/12/77	209	1	4 The Lion and the Ram ... [I]	Arista 4108
8/27/77	205	3	5 Back Together Again **LARRY CORYELL & ALPHONSE MOUZON**	Atlantic 18220

COSBY, Bill
1960s: #36 / All-Time: #127

Born on 7/12/1937 in Philadelphia, Pennsylvania. Stand-up comedian/actor. Played "Alexander Scott" on TV's *I Spy*. Hosted and did voices for the animated series *Fat Albert*. Star of the highly-rated NBC-TV series *The Cosby Show*. Also starred in several other TV shows and movies.

6/27/64+	21	128	▲ 1 Bill Cosby Is A Very Funny Fellow, Right! ... [C]	Warner 1518
11/21/64+	32	140	▲ 2 I Started Out As A Child ... [C] *Grammy: Comedy Album*	Warner 1567
8/28/65+	19	152	▲ 3 Why Is There Air? ... [C] *Grammy: Comedy Album*	Warner 1606
5/28/66	7	106	▲ 4 Wonderfulness ... [C] *Grammy: Comedy Album*	Warner 1634
5/13/67	2[1]	73	▲ 5 Revenge ... [C] *Grammy: Comedy Album*	Warner 1691
9/2/67	18	26	6 Bill Cosby Sings/Silver Throat ... [N]	Warner 1709
2/24/68	74	11	7 Bill Cosby Sings/Hooray For The Salvation Army Band! ... [N]	Warner 1728
4/6/68	7	46	● 8 To Russell, My Brother, Whom I Slept With ... [C] *Grammy: Comedy Album*	Warner 1734
10/26/68+	16	25	● 9 200 M.P.H. ... [C]	Warner 1757
2/8/69	37	19	10 It's True! It's True! ... [C]	Warner 1770
7/12/69	62	16	11 8:15 12:15 ... [C] title: times of shows at Harrah's Lake Tahoe; no track titles listed on album	Tetragrammaton 5100 [2]
9/6/69	51	25	▲ 12 The Best Of Bill Cosby ... [C-K]	Warner 1798
10/18/69+	70	24	13 Bill Cosby ... [C] *Grammy: Comedy Album*	Uni 73066
3/14/70	80	16	14 More Of The Best Of Bill Cosby ... [C-K]	Warner 1836
9/12/70	165	6	15 "Live" Madison Square Garden Center ... [C]	Uni 73082
3/6/71	72	8	16 When I Was A Kid ... [C]	Uni 73100
12/11/71+	181	7	17 For Adults Only ... [C]	Uni 73112
9/30/72	191	4	18 Inside The Mind Of Bill Cosby ... [C]	Uni 73139
6/16/73	187	4	19 Fat Albert ... [C]	MCA 333
6/5/76	100	12	20 Bill Cosby Is Not Himself These Days (Rat Own, Rat Own, Rat Own) ... [N]	Capitol 11530
3/11/78	201	4	21 Bill's Best Friend ... [C]	Capitol 11731
12/18/82+	64	14	22 Bill Cosby "Himself" ... [C-S]	Motown 6026
6/21/86	26	15	● 23 Those Of You With Or Without Children, You'll Understand ... [C] *Grammy: Comedy Album*	Geffen 24104

COSCULLUELA
Born Jose Cosculluela on 10/15/1980 in Humacao, Puerto Rico. Reggaeton singer/songwriter.

12/19/09	185	1		1 **El Principe** .... [F]		Reggaeton 653935

COSTA, Matt
Born on 6/16/1982 in Huntington Beach, California. Alternative-pop singer/songwriter/guitarist.

2/9/08	59	3		1 **Unfamiliar Faces**		Brushfire 009867

COSTA, Nikka
Born on 6/4/1972 in Los Angeles, California. Female singer/songwriter. Daughter of prolific producer/arranger Don Costa.

6/9/01	120	9		1 **Everybody Got Their Something**		Cheeba Sound 10096
6/11/05	157	1		2 **Can'tneverdidnothin'**		Virgin 80429
11/1/08	157	1		3 **Pebble To A Pearl**		Stax 30942

COSTANDINOS, Alec R.
Born Alexandre Kouyoumdjiam in 1944 in Cairo, Egypt; later based in France. Disco producer. Assembled group **Love And Kisses**.

3/25/78	92	17		1 **Romeo & Juliet**		Casablanca 7086

Shakespeare play set to a disco beat; side 1: Acts I & II; side 2: Acts III & IV

COSTELLO, Elvis   1980s: #24 / All-Time: #86
Born Declan McManus on 8/25/1954 in Paddington, London, England; raised in Liverpool, England. Eclectic pop-rock singer/songwriter/guitarist. Changed name to Elvis Costello in 1976 (Costello is his mother's maiden name). In 1977, formed backing band The Attractions: Steve "Nieve" Nason (keyboards), Bruce Thomas (bass; **Southerland Brothers & Quiver**) and Peter Thomas (drums). Married to Cait O'Riordan, former bassist with **The Pogues**, from 1986-2002. Appeared in the 1987 movie *Straight To Hell*. Married **Diana Krall** on 12/6/2003.
    AWARD: R&R Hall of Fame: 2003

12/3/77+	32	36	▲	1 **My Aim Is True** .... Cat:#40/1		Columbia 35037
				RS500 #168		
4/15/78	30	17	●	2 **This Year's Model** .... Cat:#6/174		Columbia 35331
				RS500 #98		
1/27/79	10	25	●	3 **Armed Forces** Cat:#31/56		Columbia 35709
				RS500 #482		

ELVIS COSTELLO & THE ATTRACTIONS:

3/22/80	11	15		4 **Get Happy!!** .... Cat:#16/42		Columbia 36347
10/11/80	28	14		5 **Taking Liberties** .... [K]		Columbia 36839
2/14/81	28	15		6 **Trust**		Columbia 37051
11/14/81	50	13		7 **Almost Blue**		Columbia 37562
7/24/82	30	24		8 **Imperial Bedroom**		Columbia 38157
				RS500 #166		
8/13/83	24	24		9 **Punch The Clock**		Columbia 38897
7/7/84	35	21		10 **Goodbye Cruel World**		Columbia 39429
11/30/85+	116	16	▲	11 **The Best Of Elvis Costello & The Attractions** .... [G]		Columbia 40101
3/22/86	39	18		12 **King Of America**		Columbia 40173
10/11/86	84	11		13 **Blood & Chocolate**		Columbia 40518

ELVIS COSTELLO:

2/25/89	32	25	●	14 **Spike**		Warner 25848
6/1/91	55	7		15 **Mighty Like A Rose**		Warner 26575
2/6/93	125	8		16 **The Juliet Letters**		Warner 45180

ELVIS COSTELLO AND THE BRODSKY QUARTET

3/26/94	34	10		17 **Brutal Youth**		Warner 45535
5/27/95	102	3		18 **Kojak Variety**		Warner 45903
6/1/96	53	5		19 **All This Useless Beauty**		Warner 46198

ELVIS COSTELLO & THE ATTRACTIONS

10/17/98	78	6		20 **Painted From Memory**		Mercury 538002

ELVIS COSTELLO WITH BURT BACHARACH

5/11/02	20	9		21 **When I Was Cruel**		Island 586775
10/19/02	180	1		22 **Cruel Smile** .... [K]		Island 063388

ELVIS COSTELLO & THE IMPOSTERS
    contains previously unreleased studio and live recordings

10/11/03	57	3		23 **North**		Deutsche Gr. 000999
10/9/04	40	4		24 **The Delivery Man**		Lost Highway 002593

ELVIS COSTELLO & THE IMPOSTERS

3/18/06	188	1		25 **My Flame Burns Blue** .... [L]		DG 005994

ELVIS COSTELLO with The Metropole Orkest

6/24/06	103	3		26 **The River In Reverse**		Verve Forecast 006660

ELVIS COSTELLO & ALLEN TOUSSAINT

5/19/07	110	1		27 **The Best Of Elvis Costello: The First Ten Years** .... [K]		Hip-O 008640
5/24/08	59	3		28 **Momofuku**		Lost Highway 011109

ELVIS COSTELLO & THE IMPOSTERS

6/20/09	13	6		29 **Secret, Profane & Sugarcane**		Hear 31280

Billboard			R I A A	ARTIST		
DEBUT	PEAK	WKS		Album Title	Catalog	Label & Number

COTTER, Brad
Born on 9/29/1973 in Opelika, Alabama; raised in Auburn, Alabama. Country singer/songwriter. Winner of TV's second *Nashville Star* talent series in 2004.

| 7/24/04 | 27 | 6 | | 1 Patient Man .... | | Epic 92559 |

COTTON, Gene
Born on 6/30/1944 in Columbus, Ohio. Singer/songwriter/guitarist.

| 4/8/78 | 202 | 9 | | 1 Save The Dancer .... | | Ariola America 50031 |

COTTON, James, Band
Born on 7/1/1935 in Tunica, Mississippi. Blues singer/harmonica player. His band: Luther Tucker (guitar), Albert Gianquinto (keyboards), Bob Anderson (bass) and Francis Clay (drums).

| 12/16/67 | 194 | 2 | | 1 The James Cotton Blues Band .... | | Verve Forecast 3023 |
| 1/18/75 | 146 | 9 | | 2 100% Cotton .... | | Buddah 5620 |

COTTON, Josie
Born Kathleen Josey on 5/15/1951 in Dallas, Texas. Pop-rock singer/actress. Appeared in the 1983 movie *Valley Girl*.

| 8/7/82 | 147 | 12 | | 1 Convertible Music .... | | Elektra 60140 |

COTTRELL, Travis
Born in Boone, North Carolina. Christian singer/songwriter.

| 10/25/08 | 11ˣ | 4 | | 1 Ring The Bells .... [X] | | Indelible 70034 |
| | | | | Christmas charts: 11/'08, 37/'09 | | |

COUCHOIS
Rock band from Los Angeles, California: brothers Chris Couchois (vocals), Pat Couchois (guitar) and Mike Couchois (drums), with Howard Messer (bass) and Chas Carlson (keyboards). Also see **Ratchell**.

| 4/21/79 | 170 | 4 | | 1 Couchois .... | | Warner 3289 |

COUGAR, John — see MELLENCAMP

COULSON, DEAN, McGUINNESS, FLINT — see McGUINNES FLINT

COULTER, Phil
Born on 2/1/1942 in Londonderry, Northern Ireland. Prolific arranger/producer.

| 4/5/97 | 186 | 1 | | 1 Legends .... [I] | | RCA Victor 68776 |
| | | | | **JAMES GALWAY & PHIL COULTER** | | |

COUNTDOWN SINGERS, The
Group of various studio singers and musicians from Canada.

2/25/95	145	2		1 A Time For Romance - Unchained Melodies		Madacy 0338
9/16/95	51	5		2 Love Songs From The Movies		Madacy 4902
9/7/96	93	16		3 Macarena Tropical Disco		Madacy 0346
				THE COUNTDOWN DANCE MASTERS		
1/1/00	194	1		4 Mambo #5		Madacy 0353
6/23/07	145	2		5 Forever 80s		Madacy 52381 [3]
6/16/01	162	1		6 100 Songs For Kids		Madacy 00831 [4]
4/25/09	❶¹ᶜ	2		7 150 Fun Songs For Kids		Madacy Kids 50804 [3]
				THE COUNTDOWN KIDS (above 2)		

COUNT FIVE
Psychedelic garage-rock band from San Jose, California: Kenn Ellner (vocals), John Michalski (guitar), Sean Byrne (guitar), Roy Chaney (bass) and Craig Atkinson (drums). Atkinson died on 10/13/1998 (age 50). Byrne died on 12/17/2008 (age 61).

| 12/3/66 | 122 | 6 | | 1 Psychotic Reaction .... | | Double Shot 1001 |

COUNTING CROWS   **All-Time: #405**
Rock band from San Francisco, California: Adam Duritz (vocals; born on 8/1/1964), David Bryson (guitar), Charlie Gillingham (piano), Matt Malley (bass) and Steve Bowman (drums). Ben Mize replaced Bowman in 1994. Dan Vickrey (guitar) joined in 1996.

1/1/94	4	93	▲⁷	1 August And Everything After	Cat:#19/39	DGC 24528
11/2/96	❶¹	50	▲²	2 Recovering The Satellites		DGC 24975
8/1/98	19	9	▲	3 Across A Wire - Live In New York .... [L]		DGC 25222 [2]
				Disc 1: recorded on 8/12/1997 at Chelsea Studios; Disc 2: recorded on 11/6/1997 at Hammerstein Ballroom		
11/20/99	8	23	▲	4 This Desert Life		DGC 490415
7/27/02	5	34	●	5 Hard Candy		Geffen 493356
12/13/03	32	31	●	6 Films About Ghosts: The Best Of... .... [G]		Geffen 001676
7/8/06	52	3		7 New Amsterdam: Live At Heineken Music Hall February 4-6, 2003 .... [L]		Geffen 006969
4/12/08	3¹	16		8 Saturday Nights & Sunday Mornings		DGC 010212
8/9/08	66	1		9 iTunes: Live From Soho .... [L]		DGC digital

COUNTRY JOE AND THE FISH
Born Joseph McDonald on 1/1/1942 in El Monte, California. Highly political rock singer/guitarist. The Fish: Barry Melton (guitar), David Cohen (guitar), Bruce Barthol (bass) and Chicken Hirsch (drums).

6/10/67	39	38		1 Electric Music For The Mind And Body		Vanguard 79244
12/23/67+	67	28		2 I-Feel-Like-I'm-Fixin'-To-Die		Vanguard 79266
7/13/68	23	16		3 Together		Vanguard 79277
6/21/69	48	11		4 Here We Are Again		Vanguard 79299
1/3/70	74	9		5 Country Joe & The Fish/Greatest Hits .... [G]		Vanguard 6545
5/2/70	111	9		6 C.J. Fish		Vanguard 6555

COUNTRY JOE McDONALD:

6/12/71	205	5		7 Hold On It's Coming..		Vanguard 79314
8/7/71	185	4		8 War, War, War		Vanguard 79315
10/30/71	197	2		9 The Life And Times Of Country Joe & The Fish From Haight-Ashbury		
				To Woodstock .... [K]		Vanguard 27/28 [2]
2/19/72	179	4		10 Incredible! Live! .... [L]		Vanguard 79316
				recorded at the Bitter End in New York City		
11/1/75+	124	14		11 Paradise With An Ocean View		Fantasy 9495
9/11/76	202	3		12 Love Is A Fire		Fantasy 9511

COUNTS, The
Funk band from Detroit, Michigan: Mose Davis (vocals, organ), Leroy Emmanuel (guitar), Demetrus Cates (sax), Jim White (sax), Raoul Keith Mangrum (percussion) and Andrew Gibson (drums).

7/1/72	193	2		1 What's Up Front That-Counts		Westbound 2011

COURSE OF NATURE
Rock trio from Enterprise, Alabama: Mark Wilkerson (vocals, guitar), John Mildrum (bass) and Rickey Shelton (drums).

3/16/02	166	5		1 Superkala		Lava 83526

COURTNEY, David
Born in 1949 in Brighton, Sussex, England. Pop singer/songwriter/drummer. Formed a songwriting partnership with **Leo Sayer** in the mid-1970s.

2/21/76	194	4		1 David Courtney's First Day		United Artists 553

COVAY, Don
Born on 3/24/1938 in Orangeburg, South Carolina. R&B singer/songwriter.

8/18/73	204	4		1 Super Dude I		Mercury 653

~ ~ ~ ~ ~ ~ ~ ~ ~ ~ **NON-CHARTED ALBUM** ~ ~ ~ ~ ~ ~ ~ ~ ~ ~
1964 **Mercy!** *[w/ The Goodtimers]*

COVEN
Pop band from Chicago, Illinois: Jinx Dawson (female vocals), Oz (male vocals), Christopher Nelson (guitar), John Hobbs (keyboards) and Steve Ross (drums).

2/19/72	201	2		1 Coven		MGM 4801

COVERDALE·PAGE
Hard-rock duo from England: David Coverdale (vocalist of **Deep Purple** and **Whitesnake**) and **Jimmy Page** (guitarist of **The Yardbirds**, **Led Zeppelin** and **The Firm**).

4/3/93	5	24	▲	1 Coverdale·Page		Geffen 24487

COVER GIRLS, The
Female dance trio from the Bronx, New York: Louise Sabater, Caroline Jackson and Sunshine Wright (replaced by Margo Urban in 1989).

8/15/87+	64	61		1 Show Me..		Fever 4
10/7/89+	108	19		2 We Can't Go Wrong......................................		Capitol 91041

COVINGTON, Bucky
Born William Covington on 11/8/1977 in Rockingham, North Carolina. Country singer. Finalist on the 2006 season of TV's *American Idol*.

5/5/07	4	22		1 Bucky Covington		Lyric Street 002930

COWARD, Noel
Born on 12/16/1899 in Teddington, Middlesex, England. Died of a heart attack on 3/26/1973 (age 73). Enormously popular and enduring actor/playwright/personality in England. Knighted by Queen Elizabeth II in 1970.

1/28/56	14	1		1 Noel Coward At Las Vegas .... [L]		Columbia 5063
				recorded at the Desert Inn		

COWBOY
Pop-rock band formed in Alabama: Scott Boyer (vocals), Tommy Talton (guitar) and Pete Kowalke (guitars), Bill Pilmore (keyboards), George Clark (bass) and Tomm Wynn (drums). Lineup in 1977: Boyer, Talton, Chip Condon (keyboards), Arch Pearson (bass) and Chip Miller (drums).

1/2/71	210	1		1 Reach For The Sky.......................................		Atco 351
12/10/77+	204	3		2 Cowboy		Capricorn 0194

COWBOY JUNKIES
Alternative-rock band from Toronto, Ontario, Canada: siblings Margo Timmins (vocals), Michael Timmins (guitar) and Peter Timmins (drums), with Alan Anton (bass).

1/28/89	26	29	▲	1 The Trinity Session		RCA 8568
3/31/90	47	16		2 The Caution Horses.....................................		RCA 2058
2/29/92	76	15		3 Black Eyed Man..		RCA 61049
12/11/93+	114	14		4 Pale Sun, Crescent Moon		RCA 66344
3/16/96	55	21		5 Lay It Down...		Geffen 24952
7/18/98	98	5		6 Miles From Our Home...................................		Geffen 25201
6/2/01	107	2		7 Open...		Latent 431020
6/26/04	127	2		8 One Soul Now		Zoe 431036

Billboard			R I A A	ARTIST		
DEBUT	PEAK	WKS		Album Title	Catalog	Label & Number

COWBOY MOUTH
Rock band from New Orleans, Louisiana: John Thomas Griffith (vocals), Paul Sanchez (guitar), Rob Savoy (bass) and Fred LeBlanc (drums).

6/28/97	192	1		1 Are You With Me?		MCA 11447

COWBOY TROY
Born Troy Coleman on 12/19/1971 in Victoria, Texas. Black country singer/songwriter/rapper. Calls his style of music "hick-hop."

6/4/05	15	15		1 Loco Motive		Raybaw 49316
6/23/07	153	1		2 Black In The Saddle		Raybaw 43233

COWSILLS, The
Family pop group from Newport, Rhode Island: brothers Bill, Bob, Paul, Barry and John, with their younger sister Susan and mother Barbara Cowsill. Bob, Paul, John and Susan reunited for touring in 1990. Susan married Peter Holsapple of **The dB's** on 4/18/1993. Group was the inspiration for TV's **The Partridge Family**. John married Vicki Peterson (of the **Bangles**) on 10/25/2003. Barbara died of emphysema on 1/31/1985 (age 56). Barry went missing during Hurricane Katrina on 9/1/2005; his body was found on 12/28/2005 (age 51). Bill died of emphysema on 2/18/2006 (age 58).

11/4/67+	31	17		1 The Cowsills		MGM 4498
3/9/68	89	14		2 We Can Fly		MGM 4534
9/7/68	105	12		3 Captain Sad And His Ship Of Fools		MGM 4554
1/18/69	127	9		4 The Best Of The Cowsills	[G]	MGM 4597
5/10/69	16	24		5 The Cowsills In Concert	[L]	MGM 4619
5/8/71	200	1		6 On My Side		London 587

COX, Deborah
Born on 7/13/1974 in Toronto, Ontario, Canada. R&B singer/songwriter.

10/28/95	102	16	▲	1 Deborah Cox		Arista 18781
10/17/98	72	46	●	2 One Wish		Arista 19022
11/23/02	38	8		3 The Morning After		J Records 20014
7/7/07	175	1		4 Destination Moon		Decca 008332
11/29/08	106	2		5 The Promise		Deco 5209

COX, Mick, Band
Rock band formed in England: Mick Cox (guitar), Tony O'Malley (vocals), Mick Weaver (keyboards), Chris Stewart (bass) and Andrew Steele (drums).

6/30/73	207	5		1 The Mick Cox Band		Capitol 11175

COYOTE SISTERS, The
White female vocal trio: Marty Gwinn, Leah Kunkel (sister of Mama Cass of **The Mamas & The Papas**) and Renee Armand.

9/8/84	201	6		1 The Coyote Sisters		Morocco 6063

COZIER, Jimmy
Born on 10/15/1977 in Brooklyn, New York. R&B singer/songwriter.

8/11/01	63	7		1 Jimmy Cozier		J Records 20004

CRABB, Jason
Born in Beaver Dam, Kentucky. White Southern Gospel singer/songwriter. Member of **The Crabb Family**.

7/18/09	62	3		1 Jason Crabb		Gaither 21143
				Grammy: Gospel Bluegrass Album		

CRABB FAMILY, The
White Southern Gospel group of siblings from Beaver Dam, Kentucky: **Jason Crabb**, twins Adam and Aaron Crabb, Kelly Bowling and Terah Penhollow.

4/15/06	195	1		1 Blur The Lines		Clear Cool 71477

CRABBY APPLETON
Pop-rock band from Los Angeles, California: Michael Fennelly (vocals, guitar), Casey Foutz (keyboards), Flaco Falcon (percussion), Hank Harvey (bass) and Phil Jones (drums).

6/27/70	175	6		1 Crabby Appleton		Elektra 74067

CRACKER
Rock trio from Redlands, California: David Lowery (vocals; **Camper Van Beethoven**), John Hickman (guitar) and Dave Faragher (bass). Faragher left in 1995. Bob Rupe (bass) and Charlie Quintana (drums) joined in 1996. Frank Furnaro replaced Quintana in 1997. Kenny Margolis (keyboards) joined in early 1998.

9/11/93+	59	45	●	1 Kerosene Hat		Virgin 39012
4/20/96	63	6		2 The Golden Age		Virgin 41498
9/12/98	182	1		3 Gentleman's Blues		Virgin 46263
5/23/09	189	1		4 Sunrise In The Land Of Milk And Honey		429 Records 17770

CRACK THE SKY
Rock band from Steubenville, Ohio: **John Palumbo** (vocals), Jim Griffiths (guitar), Rick Witkowski (guitar), Joe Macre (bass) and Joey D'Amico (drums). In 1977, Gary Lee Chappell replaced Palumbo. Group split in 1979. Palumbo, Witkowski and D'Amico reunited in 1989 with Vince DePaul (keyboards).

1/24/76	161	6		1 Crack The Sky		Lifesong 6000
10/30/76	142	5		2 Animal Notes		Lifesong 6005
3/11/78	124	8		3 Safety In Numbers		Lifesong 6015
6/24/89	186	5		4 From The Greenhouse		Grudge 4500
4/7/90	164	10		5 Dog City		Grudge 4520

Billboard			R I A A	ARTIST		
DEBUT	PEAK	WKS		Album Title	Catalog	Label & Number

CRADDOCK, Billy "Crash"
Born on 6/13/1939 in Greensboro, North Carolina. Country-rock singer/songwriter/guitarist.

8/24/74	142	5		1 Rub It In		ABC 817

CRADLE OF FILTH
Heavy metal band from England: Dani Davey (vocals), Paul Allender (guitar), Martin Powell (keyboards), Dave Pubis (bass) and Adrian Erlandsson (drums).

4/12/03	140	1		1 Damnation And A Day		Red Ink 71423
10/16/04	89	2		2 Nymphetamine		Roadrunner 618282
11/4/06	66	2		3 Thornography		Roadrunner 618113
11/15/08	48	2		4 Godspeed On The Devil's Thunder		Roadrunner 617923 [2]

CRAMER, Floyd
Born on 10/27/1933 in Campti, Louisiana; raised in Huttig, Arkansas. Died of cancer on 12/31/1997 (age 64). Legendary country session pianist.
AWARDS: R&R Hall of Fame: 2003 (Sideman) ★ C&W Hall of Fame: 2003

8/14/61	70	16		1 On The Rebound .... [I]		RCA Victor 2359
5/26/62	113	6		2 Floyd Cramer Gets Organ-ized .... [I]		RCA Victor 2488
10/13/62	130	2		3 I Remember Hank Williams .... [I]		RCA Victor 2544
10/23/65+	107	13		4 Class Of '65 .... [I]		RCA Victor 3405
9/17/66	123	7		5 Class Of '66 .... [I]		RCA Victor 3650
5/6/67	166	6		6 Here's What's Happening! .... [I]		RCA Victor 3746
12/2/67	26ˣ	5		7 We Wish You a Merry Christmas .... [X-I]		RCA Victor 3828
4/25/70	183	3		8 The Big Ones, Volume II .... [I]		RCA Victor 4312
5/24/80	170	5		9 Dallas .... [I-TV]		RCA Victor 3613

CRANBERRIES, The
Pop-rock band from Limerick, Ireland: Dolores O'Riordan (vocals; born on 9/6/1971), brothers Noel Hogan (guitar; born on 12/25/1971) and Mike Hogan (bass; born on 4/29/1973), and Fergal Lawler (drums; born on 3/4/1971).

7/17/93	18	130	▲5	1 Everybody Else Is Doing It, So Why Can't We? .... Cat:#23/14		Island 514156
10/22/94+	6	90	▲7	2 No Need To Argue		Island 524050
5/18/96	4	51	▲2	3 To The Faithful Departed		Island 524234
5/15/99	13	10	●	4 Bury The Hatchet		Island 524611
11/10/01	46	4		5 Wake Up And Smell The Coffee		MCA 112739

CRANE, Les
Born Lesley Stein on 12/3/1933 in Long Beach, New York; later based in San Francisco, California. Died on 7/13/2008 (age 74). Hosted TV talk show *ABC's Nightlife* in 1964. Married to actress Tina Louise from 1966-70.

12/4/71+	32	11		1 Desiderata .... [T]		Warner 2570

CRANSTON, Lamont — see LAMONT

CRASH TEST DUMMIES
Pop-rock band from Winnipeg, Manitoba, Canada: brothers Brad Roberts (vocals) and Dan Roberts (bass), with Ellen Reid (keyboards), Benjamin Darvill (harmonica) and Mitch Dorge (drums).

1/29/94	9	42	▲2	1 God Shuffled His Feet	Cat:#29/7	Arista 16531
10/19/96	78	5		2 A Worm's Life		Arista 39779

CRAWFORD, Hank
Born on 12/21/1934 in Memphis, Tennessee. Died on 1/29/2009 (age 74). Jazz alto saxophonist. With Ray Charles's band from 1958-63.

8/8/64	143	2		1 True Blue .... [I]		Atlantic 1423
2/16/74	202	6		2 Wildflower .... [I]		Kudu 15
10/26/74	201	4		3 Don't You Worry 'Bout A Thing .... [I]		Kudu 19
4/17/76	159	7		4 I Hear A Symphony .... [I]		Kudu 26
1/29/77	167	3		5 Hank Crawford's Back .... [I]		Kudu 33

CRAWFORD, Johnny
Born on 3/26/1946 in Los Angeles, California. Teen pop singer/actor. One of the original Mouseketeers. Played "Mark McCain" on TV's *The Rifleman*.

9/1/62	40	10		1 A Young Man's Fancy		Del-Fi 1223
5/25/63	126	5		2 His Greatest Hits .... [G]		Del-Fi 1229

~ ~ ~ ~ ~ ~ ~ ~ ~ ~ **NON-CHARTED ALBUM** ~ ~ ~ ~ ~ ~ ~ ~ ~ ~ ~
1961 The Captivating Johnny Crawford

CRAWFORD, Michael
Born Michael Dumble-Smith on 1/19/1942 in Salisbury, Wiltshire, England. Actor/singer. Starred in several Broadway shows.

7/30/88	192	2		1 Songs From The Stage And Screen		Columbia 44321
11/30/91+	54	31	▲	2 Michael Crawford Performs Andrew Lloyd Webber		Atlantic 82347
11/4/00	28ᶜ	1		3 With Love		Atlantic 82403
				first released in 1989		
10/16/93	39	21	●	4 A Touch Of Music In The Night		Atlantic 82531
3/21/98	57	13	●	5 On Eagle's Wings		Atlantic 83076
12/4/99	98	6		6 A Christmas Album .... [X]		Atlantic 83222
				Christmas chart: 11/'99		

Billboard			R I A A	ARTIST		
DEBUT	PEAK	WKS		Album Title	Catalog	Label & Number

CRAWFORD, Randy
Born Veronica Crawford on 2/18/1952 in Macon, Georgia; raised in Cincinnati, Ohio. Female R&B singer.

DEBUT	PEAK	WKS				Label & Number
5/31/80	180	7		1 Now We May Begin		Warner 3421
5/23/81	71	19		2 Secret Combination		Warner 3541
6/26/82	148	10		3 Windsong		Warner 23687
11/5/83	164	5		4 Nightline		Warner 23976
7/26/86	178	4		5 Abstract Emotions		Warner 25423
11/18/89	159	13		6 Rich And Poor		Warner 26002

CRAWLER — see BACK STREET CRAWLER

CRAY, Robert, Band
Born on 8/1/1953 in Columbus, Georgia. Blues-rock singer/guitarist. Played bass with fictional band Otis Day & The Knights in the 1978 movie *Animal House*. Band formed in 1974 as backing tour group for **Albert Collins**. Lineup from 1986-89: Richard Cousins (bass), Peter Boe (keyboards) and David Olson (drums). Lineup in 1990: Cousins, Tim Kaihatsu (guitar), Jim Pugh (keyboards) and Kevin Hayes (drums). Karl Sevareid (bass) joined in 1992. Cousins and Kaihatsu left in 1996.

DEBUT	PEAK	WKS				Label & Number
2/15/86	124	18		1 Showdown!		Alligator 4743
				ALBERT COLLINS / ROBERT CRAY / JOHNNY COPELAND		
				Grammy: Blues Album		
3/7/87	143	11		2 Bad Influence .... [E]		Hightone 8001
				released in 1983		
4/5/86	141	21		3 False Accusations		Hightone 8005
12/20/86+	13	49	▲²	4 Strong Persuader		Mercury 830568
				Grammy: Contemporary Blues Album		
8/27/88	32	32	●	5 Don't Be Afraid Of The Dark		Mercury 834923
				Grammy: Contemporary Blues Album		
10/6/90	51	32	●	6 Midnight Stroll		Mercury 846652
				THE ROBERT CRAY BAND FEATURING THE MEMPHIS HORNS		
9/26/92	103	7		7 I Was Warned		Mercury 512721
10/23/93	143	3		8 Shame + A Sin		Mercury 518237
5/27/95	127	6		9 Some Rainy Morning		Mercury 526867
5/24/97	184	3		10 Sweet Potato Pie		Mercury 534483
5/15/99	181	2		11 Take Your Shoes Off		Rykodisc 10479
				Grammy: Contemporary Blues Album		
1/31/09	46ᶜ	1		12 Heavy Picks: The Robert Cray Collection .... [G]		Mercury 546557

CRAZY FROG
Novelty production based on a computer animation character created by Erik Wernquist. First made popular as a ringtone.

DEBUT	PEAK	WKS				Label & Number
9/10/05	19	12		1 Crazy Hits .... [N]		Next Plateau 005360
9/9/06	40	7		2 More Crazy Hits .... [N]		Next Plateau 007149

CRAZY HORSE
Backing band for **Neil Young**. Lineup in 1971: Danny Whitten (vocals, guitar), Jack Nitzsche (piano), Billy Talbot (bass) and Ralph Molina (drums). Lineup in 1972: Talbot, Molina, George Whitsell (vocals, guitar), Greg Leroy (guitar), John Blanton (piano). Whitten died of a heroin overdose on 11/18/1972 (age 29). Also see **Neil Young**.

DEBUT	PEAK	WKS				Label & Number
3/27/71	84	11		1 Crazy Horse		Reprise 6438
2/5/72	170	6		2 Loose		Reprise 2059

CRAZY OTTO   **1950s: #30**
Born Fritz Schulz-Reichel on 7/4/1912 in Meiningen, Germany. Died on 2/14/1990 (age 77). Honky-tonk pianist.

DEBUT	PEAK	WKS				Label & Number
4/16/55	❶¹	10		1 Crazy Otto .... [I]		Decca 8113
4/16/55	2¹	11		2 Crazy Otto (Part 1) .... [EP-I]		Decca 2201
4/30/55	3¹	10		3 Crazy Otto (Part 2) .... [EP-I]		Decca 2202

CRAZY TOWN
White rock-rap band from Los Angeles, California: Seth "Shifty Shellshock" Binzer and Bret "Epic" Mazur (vocals), Adam "DJ AM" Goldstein (DJ), Craig Tyler and Anthony Valli (guitars), Doug Miller (bass) and James Bradley (drums). Goldstein died of a drug overdose on 8/28/2009 (age 36).

DEBUT	PEAK	WKS				Label & Number
12/9/00+	9	34	▲	1 The Gift Of Game		Columbia 63654
11/30/02	120	1		2 Darkhorse		Columbia 85647

CREACH, Papa John
Born on 5/28/1917 in Beaver Hills, Pennsylvania. Died on 2/22/1994 (age 76). Black rock fiddler. Worked with **Jefferson Airplane/Starship** and **Hot Tuna**.

DEBUT	PEAK	WKS				Label & Number
1/1/72	94	14		1 Papa John Creach		Grunt 1003

CREAM   **All-Time: #353**
All-star rock trio from England: **Eric Clapton** (guitar), **Jack Bruce** (bass) and **Ginger Baker** (drums). Baker and Bruce had been in Alexis Korner's Blues Inc. (**C.C.S.**) and the **Graham Bond** Organization. Clapton and Bruce were in **John Mayall's** Bluesbreakers. After Cream disbanded, Clapton and Baker formed **Blind Faith**.
AWARDS: Grammy: Lifetime Achievement 2006 ★ R&R Hall of Fame: 1993

DEBUT	PEAK	WKS				Label & Number
5/13/67+	39	92	●	1 Fresh Cream		Atco 206
				RS500 #101		
12/9/67+	4	77	▲	2 Disraeli Gears		Atco 232
				Grammy: Hall of Fame ★ RS500 #112		
7/13/68	❶⁴	46	●	3 Wheels Of Fire		Atco 700 [2]
				RS500 #203		

Billboard			R I A A	ARTIST		
DEBUT	PEAK	WKS		Album Title	Catalog	Label & Number

CREAM — cont'd

2/15/69	2²	26	●	4 Goodbye		Atco 7001

GREATEST HITS & COMPILATIONS:

7/19/69	3¹	44	●	5 Best Of Cream		Atco 291
10/28/72	135	10		6 Heavy Cream		Polydor 3502 [2]
6/25/83	205	1	▲	7 Strange Brew - The Very Best Of Cream	Cat:#20/45	RSO 811639
5/27/95	49ᶜ	1	●	8 The Very Best Of Cream		Polydor 3752

LIVE ALBUMS:

5/2/70	15	21		9 Live Cream		Atco 328
4/1/72	27	16		10 Live Cream - Volume II		Atco 7005
10/22/05	59	4		11 Royal Albert Hall: London May 2-3-5-6 2005		Reprise 49416 [2]

REISSUES:

2/19/77	165	6		12 Disraeli Gears		RSO 3010
2/19/77	197	4		13 Wheels Of Fire		RSO 3802 [2]

CREATIVE SOURCE
R&B vocal group from Los Angeles, California: Don Wyatt, Celeste Rhodes, Steve Flanagan, Barbara Berryman and Barbara Lewis.

1/19/74	152	10		1 Creative Source		Sussex 8027

CREATURES, The
Duo from England: Siouxsie Sioux (vocals) and her husband, Peter "Budgie" Clark (percussion). Both are members of **Siouxsie And The Banshees**.

3/3/90	197	2		1 Boomerang		Geffen 24275

CREED   All-Time: #372
Rock band formed in Tallahassee, Florida: Scott Stapp (vocals; born on 8/8/1973), Mark Tremonti (guitar; born on 4/18/1974), Brian Marshall (bass; born on 4/24/1974) and Scott Phillips (drums; born on 2/22/1973). Marshall left in late 2000. Group disbanded in June 2004. Tremonti, Marshall and Phillips formed **Alter Bridge**.

10/18/97+	22	112	▲⁶	1 My Own Prison	Cat:❶⁵⁴/157	Wind-Up 13049
10/16/99	❶²	104	▲¹¹	2 Human Clay	Cat:❶¹³/82	Wind-Up 13053
12/8/01	❶⁸	74	▲⁶	3 Weathered		Wind-Up 13075
12/11/04	15	86	▲²	4 Greatest Hits	Cat:#4/141 **[G]**	Wind-Up 13103
11/14/09	2¹	19		5 Full Circle		Wind-Up 13187

CREEDENCE CLEARWATER REVIVAL   All-Time: #103
Rock band formed in El Cerrito, California: **John Fogerty** (vocals, guitar; born on 5/28/1945), brother **Tom Fogerty** (guitar; born on 11/9/1941; died of respiratory failure on 9/6/1990, age 48), Stu Cook (keyboards, bass; born on 4/25/1945) and Doug "Cosmo" Clifford (drums; born on 4/24/1945). First recorded as the Blue Velvets for the Orchestra label in 1959. Recorded as the Golliwogs for Fantasy in 1964. Renamed Creedence Clearwater Revival in 1967. Tom Fogerty left for a solo career in 1971 and group disbanded in October 1972. Cook and Clifford joined the **Don Harrison Band**; both later formed Creedence Clearwater Revisited.
AWARD: R&R Hall of Fame: 1993

7/20/68	52	73	▲	1 Creedence Clearwater Revival		Fantasy 8382
2/8/69	7	88	▲²	2 Bayou Country		Fantasy 8387
9/13/69	❶⁴	88	▲³	3 Green River	Cat:#24/80	Fantasy 8393
				RS500 #95		
12/13/69+	3⁶	60	▲²	4 Willy And The Poorboys	Cat:#22/80	Fantasy 8397
				RS500 #392		
7/25/70	❶⁹	69	▲⁴	5 Cosmo's Factory	Cat:#11/105	Fantasy 8402
				RS500 #265		
12/26/70+	5	42	▲	6 Pendulum		Fantasy 8410
4/29/72	12	24	●	7 Mardi Gras		Fantasy 9404

GREATEST HITS & COMPILATIONS:

12/2/72+	15	37	▲²	8 Creedence Gold		Fantasy 9418
7/21/73	61	18	●	9 More Creedence Gold		Fantasy 9430
3/6/76+	99	51↑	▲⁸	10 Chronicle (The 20 Greatest Hits)	Cat:❶¹/678	Fantasy CCR-2 [2]
10/30/82	202	7		11 Chooglin'		Fantasy 9621
11/19/05	13	19	●	12 The Long Road Home: The Ultimate John Fogerty-Creedence Collection	Cat:#8/1	Fantasy 9686
8/22/09	25	4		13 Opus Collection		Concord 1512

LIVE ALBUMS:

11/24/73	143	10		14 Live In Europe		Fantasy CCR-1 [2]
				recorded in September 1971		
12/20/80+	62	20	▲	15 The Concert	Cat:#32/12	Fantasy 4501
				originally titled The Royal Albert Hall Concert, the album was actually recorded at the Oakland Coliseum in 1970		

CRENSHAW, Marshall
Born on 11/11/1953 in Detroit, Michigan. Rockabilly singer/guitarist. Played **John Lennon** in the road show of *Beatlemania* in 1976. Appeared in the 1986 movie *Peggy Sue Got Married* and portrayed **Buddy Holly** in the 1987 movie *La Bamba*.

5/29/82	50	27		1 Marshall Crenshaw	Warner 3673
6/18/83	52	14		2 Field Day	Warner 23873
10/12/85	110	18		3 Downtown	Warner 25319

CRESPO, Elvis
Born on 7/30/1971 in Brooklyn, New York. Latin singer/songwriter.

5/23/98+	106	43	▲	1 Suavemente	[F]	Sony Discos 82634
5/22/99	49	10	●	2 Pintame	[F]	Sony Discos 82917
				Grammy: Merengue Album		
2/12/00	155	1		3 The Remixes..	[F-K]	Sony Discos 83622
5/22/04	171	1		4 Saborealo	[F]	Ole 197112

CRESTS, The
Interracial doo-wop group from Brooklyn, New York: Johnny Maestro, Harold Torres, Talmadge Gough, J.T. Carter and Patricia Van Dross (older sister of **Luther Vandross**). Maestro later formed **Brooklyn Bridge**. Maestro died of cancer on 3/24/2010 (age 70).

~ ~ ~ ~ ~ ~ ~ ~ ~ ~ **NON-CHARTED ALBUMS** ~ ~ ~ ~ ~ ~ ~ ~ ~ ~ ~
1960 **The Crests Sing All Biggies**   1961 **The Best Of The Crests/16 Fabulous Hits**

CRETONES, The
Rock band from Los Angeles, California: Mark Goldenberg (vocals, guitar), Steve Leonard (keyboards), Peter Bernstein (bass) and Steve Beers (drums).

3/29/80	125	10		1 Thin Red Line	Planet 5

CREW-CUTS, The
Pop vocal group from Toronto, Ontario, Canada: brothers John Perkins (lead) and Ray Perkins (bass), Pat Barrett (tenor), and Rudi Maugeri (baritone; died of cancer on 5/7/2004, age 73).

~ ~ ~ ~ ~ ~ ~ ~ ~ ~ **NON-CHARTED ALBUM** ~ ~ ~ ~ ~ ~ ~ ~ ~ ~ ~
1956 **Rock And Roll Bash**

CREWE, Bob, Generation
Born on 11/12/1937 in Newark, New Jersey. Prolific songwriter/arranger/producer.

2/25/67	100	11		1 Music To Watch Girls By	[I]	DynoVoice 9003

CRICKETS, The — see HOLLY, Buddy / VEE, Bobby

CRIME BOSS
Born Thurston Slaughter in Houston, Texas. Male rapper.

3/11/95	113	11		1 All In The Game	Suave 0003
4/26/97	25	5		2 Conflicts & Confusion	Suave House 1566

CRIME MOB
Rap group from Cedar Grove, Tennessee: Princess, Diamond, Lil Jay, Killa C, Jock and Cyco Black.

8/21/04	90	14		1 Crime Mob...	Crunk 48803
4/7/07	31	7		2 Hated On Mostly	Crunk 44298

CRISS, Gary
Born in Brazil. Disco singer.

9/9/78	201	3		1 Rio De Janeiro	Salsoul 8504

CRISS, Peter
Born Peter Crisscoula on 12/20/1945 in Brooklyn, New York. Rock singer/songwriter/drummer. Member of **Kiss** (1973-81, 1996).

10/14/78	43	20	▲	1 Peter Criss	Casablanca 7122

CRITTERS, The
Pop band from Plainfield, New Jersey: Don Ciccone (vocals, guitar), Jimmy Ryan (guitar), Chris Darway (organ), Kenny Gorka (bass) and Jack Decker (drums). Ciccone later joined **The 4 Seasons**.

9/24/66	147	2		1 Younger Girl	Kapp 3485

CROCE, Jim
Born on 1/10/1943 in Philadelphia, Pennsylvania. Killed in a plane crash on 9/20/1973 (age 30) in Natchitoches, Louisiana. Singer/songwriter/guitarist. Recorded with wife Ingrid for Capitol in 1968. Lead guitarist on his hits, Maury Muehleisen, was killed in the same crash.

7/1/72+	❶⁵	93	●	1 You Don't Mess Around With Jim		ABC 756
2/17/73	7	84	●	2 Life And Times		ABC 769
12/15/73+	2²	53	●	3 I Got A Name		ABC 797
10/5/74	2²	46	▲	4 Photographs & Memories/His Greatest Hits	Cat:#16/19 [G]	ABC 835
11/1/75+	87	18		5 The Faces I've Been	[E-K]	Lifesong 900 [2]
				recordings from 1961-71		
2/26/77	170	3		6 Time In A Bottle/Jim Croce's Greatest Love Songs..	[K]	Lifesong 6007

CROCKER, Frankie — see HEART AND SOUL ORCHESTRA

CROOKED X
Hard-rock band from Coweta, Oklahoma: Forrest French (vocals, guitar), Jesse Cooper (guitar), Josh McDowell (bass) and Boomer Simpson (drums).

2/14/09	176	1	1 Crooked X		MPM 50020

CROPPER, Steve
Born on 10/21/1941 in Willow Springs, Missouri. Prolific session guitarist. Member of **Booker T. & The MG's**, **The Mar-Keys** and **The Blues Brothers** band.

7/12/69	171	5	1 Jammed Together .... [I]		Stax 2020
			ALBERT KING / STEVE CROPPER / POP STAPLES		
2/21/81	210	2	2 Playin' My Thang		MCA 5171

CROSBY, Bing   1950s: #34
Born Harry Lillis Crosby on 5/3/1903 in Tacoma, Washington. Died of a heart attack on 10/14/1977 (age 74). One of the most popular entertainers of the 20th century. Charted over 300 hit singles from 1931-54. Starred in several movies (won Academy Award for *Going My Way* in 1944). Married to actress Dixie Lee from 1930 until her death in 1952; their son Gary Crosby began recording in 1950. Married to actress Kathryn Grant from 1957 until his death; their daughter Mary Crosby became an actress. Bing's youngest brother, Bob Crosby, was a popular swing-era bandleader.
    AWARD: Grammy: Lifetime Achievement 1962

3/31/58	13	2	1 Shillelaghs And Shamrocks		Decca 8207
5/30/64	116	7	2 America, I Hear You Singing		Reprise 2020
			FRANK SINATRA / BING CROSBY / FRED WARING		
3/29/69	162	8	3 Hey Jude/Hey Bing!		Amos 7001
12/10/77+	98	9	4 Bing Crosby's Greatest Hits .... [G]		MCA 3031
			CHRISTMAS ALBUMS:		
12/22/56	21	1	5 A Christmas Sing With Bing Around The World		Decca DL 8419
12/2/57	❶¹	7	● 6 Merry Christmas	Cat:#8/25	Decca 8128
			first released in 1945 on Decca 403; #1 for six consecutive seasons from 1945-50 (38 weeks at #1); Christmas charts: 4/'63, 2/'64, 3/'65, 5/'66, 8/'67, 6/'68, 3/'69, 6/'70, 4/'71, 2/'72, 8/'73, 3/'83, 21/'87, 13/'88, 15/'89, 15/'90, 10/'91, 12/'92, 11/'95, 14/'96, 33/'98		
12/15/58+	2¹	4	7 Merry Christmas .... [R]		Decca 8128
12/28/59+	17	2	8 Merry Christmas .... [R]		Decca 8128
12/19/60	9	3	9 Merry Christmas .... [R]		Decca 8128
12/18/61+	22	7	10 Merry Christmas .... [R]		Decca 8128
12/22/62	46	2	11 Merry Christmas .... [R]		Decca 8128
12/22/62	50	2	12 I Wish You A Merry Christmas		Warner 1484
			Christmas chart: 40/'65		
12/12/64	9ˣ	3	13 12 Songs Of Christmas		Reprise 2022
			BING CROSBY / FRANK SINATRA / FRED WARING And The Pennsylvanians		
12/5/92	8ˣ	43	14 It's Christmas Time	Cat:#6/41	LaserLight 15152
			BING CROSBY • FRANK SINATRA • NAT KING COLE		
			Christmas charts: 8/'92, 17/'93, 12/'94, 13/'95, 8/'96, 22/'97, 22/'98		
12/19/98	21ˣ	3	15 It's Christmas Time .... Cat:#13/5		LaserLight 15152
			BING CROSBY • FRANK SINATRA • LOUIS ARMSTRONG		
			above 2 are the same album, with Louis Armstrong tracks substituted for Nat King Cole		
12/4/93+	26ˣ	24	▲⁴ 16 White Christmas .... Cat:#24/19		LaserLight 15444
			Christmas charts: 30/'93, 33/'94, 26/'95, 36/'96, 32/'97, 44/'02		
1/13/07	28ˣ	1	17 White Christmas		LaserLight 32830
1/13/07	49ˣ	1	18 Christmas With Bing Crosby		Lifestyles 160001
12/19/09	159	1	19 Christmas Classics		Capitol 63928
			Christmas chart: 49/'09		
12/19/09	166	2	20 White Christmas .... Cat:#3/60		MCA 731143
			Christmas charts: 23/'99, 23/'00, 19/'01, 17/'02, 8/'03, 11/'04, 21/'05, 22/'06, 43/'07, 31/'08, 43/'09		

CROSBY, David
Born on 8/14/1941 in Los Angeles, California. Folk-rock singer/songwriter/guitarist. Member of **The Byrds** from 1964-68 and later **Crosby, Stills & Nash**. Son of cinematographer Floyd Crosby (*High Noon*). Frequent troubles with the law due to drug charges. Movie cameos in *Backdraft*, *Hook* and *Thunderheart*; appeared on TV's *Roseanne*. Underwent a successful liver transplant on 11/19/1994. In early 2000, it was announced that he was the biological father (via artificial insemination) of two children for the couple of **Melissa Etheridge** and Julie Cypher.

3/20/71	12	18	● 1 If I Could Only Remember My Name		Atlantic 7203
2/18/89	104	10	2 Oh Yes I Can		A&M 5232
6/5/93	133	8	3 Thousand Roads		Atlantic 82484
			DAVID CROSBY/GRAHAM NASH:		
4/22/72	4	26	● 4 Graham Nash/David Crosby		Atlantic 7220
10/11/75	6	31	● 5 Wind On The Water		ABC 902
7/24/76	26	15	● 6 Whistling Down The Wire		ABC 956
11/19/77	52	8	7 Crosby/Nash - Live .... [L]		ABC 1042
10/28/78	150	4	8 The Best Of Crosby/Nash .... [G]		ABC 1102
8/28/04	142	1	9 Crosby & Nash		Sanctuary 84683 [2]

CROSBY, STILLS & NASH [& YOUNG]　　　　　　　All-Time: #180

Folk-rock trio formed in Laurel Canyon, California: **David Crosby** (guitar; born on 8/14/1941), **Stephen Stills** (guitar, keyboards, bass; born on 1/3/1945) and **Graham Nash** (guitar; born on 2/2/1942). Crosby had been in **The Byrds**, Stills had been in **The Buffalo Springfield**, and Nash was with **The Hollies**. **Neil Young** (guitar; born on 11/12/1945), formerly with Buffalo Springfield, joined group in 1970; left in 1974. Reunion in 1988. Crosby, Stills, Nash & Young reunited for a tour and album in 2000.

AWARDS: Grammy: Best New Artist 1969 ★ R&R Hall of Fame: 1997

CROSBY, STILLS & NASH:

DEBUT	PEAK	WKS	RIAA	#	Album Title	Catalog	Label & Number
6/28/69	6	107	▲⁴	1	Crosby, Stills & Nash	Cat:#39/1	Atlantic 8229
					Grammy: Hall of Fame ★ RS500 #259		
7/9/77	2⁴	33	▲⁴	2	CSN	Cat:#21/21	Atlantic 19104
7/17/82	8	41	▲	3	Daylight Again		Atlantic 19360
7/2/83	43	12		4	Allies	[L]	Atlantic 80075
7/14/90	57	11		5	Live It Up		Atlantic 82107
9/3/94	98	2		6	After The Storm		Atlantic 82654
1/10/81	122	5		7	Replay	[K]	Atlantic 16026
1/4/92	109	2	▲	8	CSN	[K]	Atlantic 82319 [4]
4/2/05	24	8		9	Greatest Hits	[G]	Atlantic 76537
6/20/09	104	1		10	Demos	[K]	Atlantic 519624
					CROSBY, STILLS, NASH & YOUNG:		
4/4/70	❶¹	97	▲⁷	11	Deja Vu	Cat:#27/4	Atlantic 7200
					RS500 #148		
4/24/71	❶¹	42	▲⁴	12	4 Way Street	Cat:#29/5 [L]	Atlantic 902 [2]
9/7/74	❶¹	27	▲⁶	13	So Far	Cat:❶⁵/111 [G]	Atlantic 18100
12/3/88+	16	22	▲	14	American Dream		Atlantic 81888
11/13/99	26	9		15	Looking Forward		Reprise 47436
8/9/08	153	1		16	Deja Vu: Live	[L-S]	Reprise 512606

CROSS, Christopher

Born Christopher Geppert on 5/3/1951 in San Antonio, Texas. Pop-rock singer/songwriter/guitarist.

AWARD: Grammy: Best New Artist 1980

DEBUT	PEAK	WKS	RIAA	#	Album Title	Label & Number
2/16/80	6	116	▲⁵	1	Christopher Cross	Warner 3383
					Grammy: Album of the Year	
2/19/83	11	31	●	2	Another Page	Warner 23757
11/30/85	127	6	.	3	Every Turn Of The World	Warner 25341

CROSS, David

Born on 4/4/1964 in Atlanta, Georgia. Stand-up comedian/actor. Appeared in several movies and TV shows.

DEBUT	PEAK	WKS	#	Album Title	Label & Number
5/22/04	194	1	1	It's Not Funny	[C] Sub Pop 635

CROSS CANADIAN RAGWEED

Country band from Stillwater, Oklahoma: Cody Canada (vocals, guitar), Grady Cross (guitar), Jeremy Plato (bass) and Randy Ragsdale (drums).

DEBUT	PEAK	WKS	#	Album Title	Label & Number
3/27/04	51	2	1	Soul Gravy	Universal South 001887
10/22/05	37	3	2	Garage	Universal South 003818
11/18/06	120	2	3	Back To Tulsa: Live And Loud At Cain's Ballroom	[L] Universal South 007018 [2]
10/20/07	30	3	4	Mission California	Universal South 008889
9/19/09	33	3	5	Happiness And All The Other Things	Universal South 013231

CROSS COUNTRY

Pop trio: Jay Siegel (vocals), with brothers Mitch Margo (guitar) and Phil Margo (percussion). All were members of **The Tokens**.

DEBUT	PEAK	WKS	#	Album Title	Label & Number
10/13/73	198	2	1	Cross Country	Atco 7024

CROSSE, Clay

Born Walter Clayton Crossnoe on 2/11/1967 in Memphis, Tennessee. Christian singer/songwriter.

DEBUT	PEAK	WKS	#	Album Title	Label & Number
7/19/97	141	5	1	Stained Glass	Reunion 10005

CROSSFADE

Rock band from Columbia, South Carolina: Tony Byroads (vocals), Ed Sloan (guitar), Mitch James (bass) and Brian Geiger (drums).

DEBUT	PEAK	WKS	RIAA	#	Album Title	Label & Number
7/31/04+	41	70	▲	1	Crossfade	Columbia 87148
9/16/06	30	5		2	Falling Away	Columbia 84238

CROSS MOVEMENT, The

Christian hip-hop group from New Jersey: William Branch, Virgil Byrd, Brady Goodwin and John Wells.

DEBUT	PEAK	WKS	#	Album Title	Label & Number
5/10/03	134	1	1	Holy Culture	BEC 82654

CROUCH, Andrae

Born on 7/1/1942 in Los Angeles, California. Leading gospel choir leader/songwriter.

DEBUT	PEAK	WKS	#	Album Title	Label & Number
10/17/81	208	1	1	Don't Give Up	Warner 3513
				Grammy: Contemporary Soul Gospel Album	

Billboard			R I A A	ARTIST		
DEBUT	PEAK	WKS		Album Title	Catalog	Label & Number

CROW
Rock-blues band from Minneapolis, Minnesota: Dave Waggoner (vocals), Dick Weigand (guitar), Kink Middlemist (organ), Larry Weigand (bass) and Denny Craswell (drums). Craswell was a member of The Castaways.

9/13/69+	69	24		1 Crow Music		Amaret 5002
6/6/70	181	4		2 Crow By Crow		Amaret 5006
2/27/71	207	6		3 Mosaic		Amaret 5009

CROW, Sheryl   **All-Time: #366**
Born on 2/11/1962 in Kennett, Missouri. Adult Alternative rock singer/songwriter/guitarist. After attending the University of Missouri, worked as a grade school music teacher, until moving to Los Angeles in 1986. Worked as backing singer for **Michael Jackson**, **Don Henley**, **George Harrison** and others. Crow's compositions covered by **Eric Clapton** and **Wynonna Judd**.
AWARD: Grammy: Best New Artist 1994

3/19/94+	3[1]	100	▲[7]	1 Tuesday Night Music Club Cat:#44/5		A&M 540126
10/12/96	6	63	▲[3]	2 Sheryl Crow		A&M 540587
				Grammy: Rock Album		
10/17/98	5	53	▲	3 The Globe Sessions		A&M 540959
				Grammy: Rock Album		
12/25/99	107	11		4 Sheryl Crow And Friends: Live From Central Park .... [L]		A&M 490574
5/4/02	2[1]	61	▲	5 C'mon, C'mon		A&M 493260
11/22/03+	2[2]	80	▲[3]	6 The Very Best Of Sheryl Crow Cat:#5/48 [G]		A&M 001521
10/15/05	2[1]	42	▲	7 Wildflower		A&M 005229
2/23/08	2[1]	23		8 Detours		A&M 010599

CROWBAR — see KING BISCUIT BOY

CROWDED HOUSE
Pop-rock band formed in Melbourne, Australia: Neil Finn (vocals, guitar, piano), Nick Seymour (bass) and Paul Hester (drums). Finn and Hester were members of **Split Enz**. Neil's brother, **Tim Finn** (also of Split Enz), joined band in 1991; left in 1993, replaced by Mark Hart. Hester left band in April 1994. Group disbanded in June 1996. Hester committed suicide on 3/26/2005 (age 46). Also see **The Finn Brothers**.

8/30/86+	12	58	▲	1 Crowded House		Capitol 12485
7/23/88	40	19		2 Temple Of Low Men		Capitol 48763
7/20/91	83	17		3 Woodface		Capitol 93559
1/29/94	73	7		4 Together Alone		Capitol 27048
7/28/07	46	3		5 Time On Earth		ATO 21580

CROWDER, David, Band
Christian rock band from Waco, Texas: David Crowder (vocals, guitar), Jason Solley (guitar), Jack Parker (keyboards), Mike Hogan (violin), Mike Dodson (bass) and Jeremy Bush (drums).

10/4/03	84	1		1 Illuminate		Sixsteps 90230
10/15/05	39	8		2 A Collision		Sixsteps 11229
7/15/06	118	1		3 B Collision		Sixsteps 48093
10/13/07	22	9		4 Remedy		Sixsteps 92684
9/6/08	88	1		5 Remedy: Club Tour Edition .... [L]		Sixsteps 07134
10/10/09	11	13		6 Church Music		Sixsteps 26515

CROWELL, Rodney
Born on 8/7/1950 in Houston, Texas. Country singer/songwriter/guitarist. Married to **Rosanne Cash** from 1979-92. Member of **The Notorious Cherry Bombs**.

4/26/80	155	10		1 But What Will The Neighbors Think		Warner 3407
10/3/81	105	8		2 Rodney Crowell		Warner 3587
8/23/86	177	5		3 Street Language		Columbia 40116
10/6/90	180	2		4 Keys To The Highway		Columbia 45242
6/6/92	155	9		5 Life Is Messy		Columbia 47985

CROWFOOT
Rock trio from Milwaukee, Wisconsin: Sam McCue (guitar), Russell Dashiell (bass) and Don Francisco (drums). All shared vocals.

10/23/71	211	1		1 Find The Sun		ABC 745

CROWN HEIGHTS AFFAIR
Disco band from New York: Phil Thomas (vocals), William Anderson (guitar), Howard Young (keyboards), Bert Reid, James Baynard and Ray Reid (horns), Muki Wilson (bass) and Ray Rock (drums). Bert Reid died of cancer on 12/12/2004.

10/4/75	121	17		1 Dreaming A Dream		De-Lite 2017
2/19/77	207	1		2 Do It Your Way		De-Lite 2022
9/9/78	205	3		3 Dream World		De-Lite 9506
5/12/79	207	3		4 Dance Lady Dance		De-Lite 9512
3/29/80	148	12		5 Sure Shot		De-Lite 9517

CRU
Rap trio from Brooklyn, New York: Chadio, Yogi and Mighty Ha.

9/13/97	102	3		1 Da Dirty 30		Violator 537607

CRUCIAL CONFLICT
Hip-hop group from Chicago, Illinois: Corey Johnson, Marrico King, Ralph Leverston and Wondosas Martin.

7/20/96	12	18	●	1 The Final Tic		Pallas 53006
11/21/98	38	4		2 Good Side Bad Side		Pallas 53163

CRUISE, Julee
Born on 12/1/1956 in Creston, Iowa. Eclectic-pop singer/actress.

| 6/2/90 | 74 | 20 | 1 Floating Into The Night | Warner 25859 |

CRUNCHY BLACK
Born Darnell Carlton in 1977 in Memphis, Tennessee. Male rapper. Former member of **Three 6 Mafia**.

| 10/7/06 | 163 | 1 | 1 On My Own | Hypnotize Minds 3616 |

CRUSADERS, The   All-Time: #254
Instrumental jazz-oriented band from Houston, Texas: **Joe Sample** (keyboards), **Wilton Felder** (reeds), Nesbert "**Stix**"**Hooper** (drums) and **Wayne Henderson** (trombone). First known as **The Jazz Crusaders**. Henderson left in 1975. **Larry Carlton** was a frequent guitarist from 1972-77. Hooper left in 1983. Sample and Felder reunited with a new lineup in 1991.

1/4/69	184	2	1 Powerhouse	[I]	Pacific Jazz 20136
10/17/70+	90	16	2 Old Socks, New Shoes...New Socks, Old Shoes	[I]	Chisa 804
			THE JAZZ CRUSADERS (above 2)		
6/26/71	168	4	3 Pass The Plate	[I]	Chisa 807
3/4/72	96	29	4 Crusaders 1	[I]	Blue Thumb 6001 [2]
3/10/73	45	29	5 The 2nd Crusade	[I]	Blue Thumb 7000 [2]
10/13/73	203	8	6 At Their Best	[I-K]	Motown 796
11/24/73	173	14	7 Unsung Heroes	[I]	Blue Thumb 6007
4/13/74	73	20	8 Scratch	[I-L]	Blue Thumb 6010
10/26/74	31	23	● 9 Southern Comfort	[I]	Blue Thumb 9002 [2]
8/23/75	26	17	10 Chain Reaction	[I]	Blue Thumb 6022
5/22/76	38	18	11 Those Southern Knights	[I]	Blue Thumb 6024
12/18/76+	122	10	12 The Best Of The Crusaders	[G-I]	Blue Thumb 6027 [2]
6/18/77	41	15	13 Free As The Wind	[I]	Blue Thumb 6029
7/15/78	34	18	● 14 Images	[I]	Blue Thumb 6030
6/9/79	18	39	● 15 Street Life	[I]	MCA 3094
7/12/80	29	16	16 Rhapsody And Blues	[I]	MCA 5124
10/10/81	59	16	17 Standing Tall	[I]	MCA 5254
7/17/82	144	7	18 Royal Jam	[I-L]	MCA 8017 [2]
			recorded September 1981 at the Royal Festival Hall in London, England		
4/21/84	79	22	19 Ghetto Blaster	[I]	MCA 5429
5/11/91	174	2	20 Healing The Wounds	[I]	GRP 9638

CRUZ, Celia
Born on 10/21/1924 in Havana, Cuba. Died of brain cancer on 7/16/2003 (age 78). Known as "The Queen of Salsa Music."

8/2/03	106	7	1 Hits Mix	[F-K]	Sony Discos 87607
8/16/03	40	7	● 2 Regalo Del Alma	[F]	Sony Discos 70620
8/16/03	95	7	3 Exitos Eternos	[F-K]	Universal Latino 000756

CRUZADOS
Rock band from Los Angeles, California: Tito Larriva (vocals), Steven Hufsteter (guitar), Tony Marsico (bass) and Chalo Quintana (drums). Marshall Rohner (guitar) replaced Hufsteter in early 1987. Rohner left in 1989 to join **TSOL**.

| 11/2/85 | 76 | 18 | 1 Cruzados | Arista 8383 |
| 8/1/87 | 106 | 21 | 2 After Dark | Arista 8439 |

CRYAN' SHAMES, The
Rock and roll band from Hinsdale, Illinois: Tom Doody (vocals), Jim Fairs (guitar), Jerry Stone (guitar), Jim Pilster (tambourine), Dave Purple (bass) and Dennis Conroy (drums).

5/13/67	192	4	1 Sugar & Spice	Columbia 9389
1/13/68	156	5	2 A Scratch In The Sky	Columbia 9586
2/15/69	184	9	3 Synthesis	Columbia 9719

CRYSTAL, Billy
Born on 3/14/1947 in Long Beach, Long Island, New York. Actor/comedian. Starred in several movies and TV shows.

| 9/21/85 | 65 | 13 | 1 Mahvelous! | [C] | A&M 5096 |

CRYSTAL GRASS
Disco studio group assembled by producer Lee Hallyday.

| 7/26/75 | 204 | 2 | 1 Crystal World | Polydor 6516 |

CRYSTAL METHOD, The
Electronic-dance duo from Los Angeles, California: Ken Jordan and Scott Kirkland.

9/13/97	92	43	▲ 1 Vegas	[I]	Outpost 30003
8/18/01	32	10	2 Tweekend	[I]	Geffen 493063
8/10/02	160	1	3 Community Service		Ultra 1125
1/31/04	36	5	4 Legion Of Boom		V2 27176
5/30/09	38	2	5 Divided By Night		Tiny E 009

CRYSTALS, The
Rock and roll "girl group" from Brooklyn, New York: Barbara Alston, Dee Dee Kenniebrew, Mary Thomas, Patricia Wright and Myrna Gerrard. La La Brooks replaced Gerrard in 1962. Thomas left in 1962. Wright was replaced by Frances Collins in 1964.

| 3/16/63 | 131 | 2 | 1 He's A Rebel | Philles 4001 |

~ ~ ~ ~ ~ ~ ~ ~ ~ ~ **NON-CHARTED ALBUMS** ~ ~ ~ ~ ~ ~ ~ ~ ~ ~
1962 **The Crystals Twist Uptown**   1963 **The Crystals Sing The Greatest Hits, Volume 1**

Billboard DEBUT	PEAK	WKS	R I A A	ARTIST Album Title	Catalog	Label & Number
				CSS Dance-rock band from Sao Paulo, Brazil: Adriano Cintra, Luisa "Lovefoxxx" Matsushita, Luiza Sa, Ana Rezende and Carolina Parra. CSS: Cansei Ser Sexy.		
8/9/08	189	1		1 Donkey		Sub Pop 770
				CUBA, Joe, Sextet Born Gilberto Calderon on 4/22/1931 in Manhattan, New York. Died on 2/15/2009 (age 77). Latin conga player. Other members of his sextet: Jose "Cheo" Feliciano (vocals, not to be confused with the solo star), Tommy Berrios (vibes), Nick Jimenez (piano), Jules Cordero (bass) and Jimmy Sabater (drums).		
9/17/66	119	3		1 We Must Be Doing Something Right! .... [F]		Tico 1133
1/7/67	131	6		2 Wanted Dead Or Alive (Bang! Bang! Push, Push, Push) .... [F]		Tico 1146
				CUBAN LINK Born Felix Delgado on 12/18/1974 in Cuba; raised in Brooklyn, New York. Male rapper.		
9/3/05	188	1		1 Chain Reaction		M.O.B. 1301
				CUFF LINKS, The Group is actually the overdubbed voice of Ron Dante (of **The Archies**).		
12/6/69+	138	11		1 Tracy..		Decca 75160
				CULBERTSON, Brian Born on 1/12/1973 in Decatur, Illinois. Smooth jazz singer/pianist.		
7/12/03	197	1		1 Come On Up		Warner 48300
8/13/05	161	1		2 It's On Tonight		GRP 004535
5/17/08	99	1		3 Bringing Back The Funk...		GRP 010927
				CULLUM, Jamie Born on 8/20/1979 in Essex, England. Male jazz-pop singer/songwriter/pianist.		
5/29/04	83	20		1 Twentysomething..		Verve Forecast 002273
10/29/05	49	4		2 Catching Tales..		Verve Forecast 005478
				CULT, The Hard-rock band formed in England: Ian Astbury (vocals; born on 5/14/1962), Billy Duffy (guitar; born on 5/12/1961), Jamie Stewart (bass) and Les Warner (drums). Numerous personnel changes with Astbury and Duffy the only constants.		
12/28/85+	87	34	●	1 Love..		Sire 25359
4/25/87	38	32	▲	2 Electric		Sire 25555
4/29/89	10	33	▲	3 Sonic Temple		Sire 25871
10/12/91	25	12		4 Ceremony		Sire 26673
10/29/94	69	4		5 The Cult...		Sire 45673
6/23/01	37	8		6 Beyond Good And Evil		Lava 83440
10/20/07	70	2		7 Born Into This		New Wilderness 617971
				CULTURE CLUB Pop band formed in London, England: George "**Boy George**" O'Dowd (vocals), Roy Hay (guitar, keyboards), Michael Craig (bass) and Jon Moss (drums). Designer Sue Clowes originated distinctive costuming for the group. Boy George went solo in 1987. **AWARD: Grammy: Best New Artist 1983**		
1/8/83	14	88	▲	1 Kissing To Be Clever		Epic 38398
11/5/83+	2[6]	59	▲[4]	2 Colour By Numbers		Epic 39107
11/24/84	26	20	▲	3 Waking Up With The House On Fire		Virgin 39881
4/26/86	32	17		4 From Luxury To Heartache		Virgin 40345
11/20/93	169	3		5 At Worst...The Best Of Boy George And Culture Club............... [G]		SBK 39014
8/29/98	148	2		6 VH1 Storytellers / Greatest Moments .... [G-L]		Virgin 46191 [2]
				Disc 1: recorded live; Disc 2: greatest hits		
				CUMMINGS, Burton Born on 12/31/1947 in Winnipeg, Manitoba, Canada. Pop-rock singer/songwriter/pianist. Lead singer of **The Guess Who**.		
11/6/76+	30	20		1 Burton Cummings..		Portrait 34261
7/9/77	51	6		2 My Own Way To Rock		Portrait 34698
8/26/78	203	2		3 Dream Of A Child		Portrait 35481
				CUOMO, Rivers Born on 6/13/1970 in Manhattan, New York; raised in Pomfret, Connecticut. Alternative-pop singer/songwriter/guitarist. Leader of **Weezer**.		
1/5/08	163	1		1 Alone: The Home Recordings Of Rivers Cuomo		DGC 010417
12/13/08	175	1		2 Alone II: The Home Recordings Of Rivers Cuomo		DGC 012341
				CUPID Born Bryson Bernard on 10/10/1982 in Lafayette, Louisiana. Male rapper/songwriter.		
9/29/07	58	2		1 Time For A Change		Asylum 242364
				CURB, Mike, Congregation Born on 12/24/1944 in Savannah, Georgia. Pop music mogul and politician. President of MGM Records from 1969-73. Elected lieutenant governor of California in 1978. Formed own company, Sidewalk Records, in 1964; became Curb Records in 1974.		
7/4/70	105	5		1 Come Together		CoBurt 1002
11/21/70	185	2		2 Sweet Gingerbread Man		CoBurt 1003
3/13/71	117	8		3 Burning Bridges And Other Great Motion Picture Themes		MGM 4761
7/10/71	205	6		4 Put Your Hand In The Hand...		MGM 4788

Billboard
DEBUT | PEAK | WKS
R I A A
ARTIST
Album Title
Catalog
Label & Number

DEBUT	PEAK	WKS	RIAA	ARTIST / Album Title	Catalog	Label & Number
				CURB, Mike, Congregation — cont'd		
2/19/72	206	4		5 Softly Whispering I Love You		MGM 4821
7/1/72	208	1		6 The World Of Steve & Eydie		MGM 4803
				STEVE LAWRENCE & EYDIE GORME with The Mike Curb Congregation		

CURE, The All-Time: #216

Techno-rock band from England: Robert Smith (vocals, guitar), Porl Thompson (guitar), Laurence "Lol" Tolhurst (keyboards), Simon Gallup (bass) and Boris Williams (drums). Numerous personnel changes with Smith the only constant.

DEBUT	PEAK	WKS	RIAA	ARTIST / Album Title	Catalog	Label & Number
8/13/83	179	8		1 The Walk [EP]		Sire 23928
6/23/84	180	4		2 The Top		Sire 25086
10/5/85	59	49	●	3 The Head On The Door		Elektra 60435
6/20/87	35	52	▲	4 Kiss Me, Kiss Me, Kiss Me		Elektra 60737 [2]
5/20/89	12	55	▲²	5 Disintegration		Elektra 60855
				RS500 #326		
5/9/92	2¹	26	▲	6 Wish		Fiction 61309
5/25/96	12	14	●	7 Wild Mood Swings		Fiction 61744
3/4/00	16	8		8 Bloodflowers		Fiction 62236
7/17/04	7	11		9 The Cure		I Am 002870
11/15/08	16	4		10 4:13 Dream		Suretone 010913
				GREATEST HITS & COMPILATIONS:		
2/25/84	181	5		11 Japanese Whispers		Sire 25076
6/14/86	48	57	▲²	12 Standing On A Beach - The Singles		Elektra 60477
11/17/90	14	41	▲	13 Mixed Up		Elektra 60978
11/15/97	32	13	●	14 Galore - The Singles 1987-1997		Fiction 62117
12/1/01	58	3		15 Greatest Hits	Cat:#44/1	Fiction 62726
2/14/04	106	1		16 Join The Dots: B-Side & Rarities 1978-2001		Fiction 78043 [4]
				LIVE ALBUMS:		
10/9/93	42	6		17 Show		Fiction 61551
11/13/93	118	2		18 Paris		Fiction 61552
				~ ~ ~ ~ ~ ~ ~ ~ ~ ~ **NON-CHARTED ALBUM** ~ ~ ~ ~ ~ ~ ~ ~ ~ ~ ~		
				1980 **Boys Don't Cry**		
				RS500 #442		

CURIOSITY KILLED THE CAT

Pop-rock band formed in London, England: Ben Volpeliere-Pierrot (vocals), Julian Brookhouse (guitar), Nick Thorpe (bass) and Miguel Drummond (drums).

DEBUT	PEAK	WKS	RIAA	ARTIST / Album Title	Catalog	Label & Number
8/22/87	55	29		1 Keep Your Distance		Mercury 832025

CURRINGTON, Billy

Born on 11/19/1973 in Savannah, Georgia; raised in Rincon, Georgia. Country singer/songwriter/pianist.

DEBUT	PEAK	WKS	RIAA	ARTIST / Album Title	Catalog	Label & Number
10/18/03	107	2		1 Billy Currington		Mercury 000164
11/5/05	11	71	▲	2 Doin' Somethin' Right		Mercury 003712
11/1/08	13	63	●	3 Little Bit Of Everything	Cat:#26/2	Mercury 009550

CURRY, Tim

Born on 4/19/1946 in Grappenhall, Cheshire, England. Actor/singer. Starred in several movies.

DEBUT	PEAK	WKS	RIAA	ARTIST / Album Title	Catalog	Label & Number
9/8/79	53	24		1 Fearless		A&M 4773
8/29/81	112	8		2 Simplicity		A&M 4830

CURSIVE

Alternative-rock band from Omaha, Nebraska: Tim Kasher (vocals, guitar), Ted Stevens (guitar), Matt Maginn (bass) and Clint Schnase (drums). Kasher also formed **The Good Life**.

DEBUT	PEAK	WKS	RIAA	ARTIST / Album Title	Catalog	Label & Number
9/9/06	96	1		1 Happy Hollow		Saddle Creek 94
3/28/09	104	2		2 Mama, I'm Swollen		Saddle Creek 132

CUSTOM

Born Duane Lavold in Calgary, Alberta, Canada. Adult Alternative singer/songwriter.

DEBUT	PEAK	WKS	RIAA	ARTIST / Album Title	Catalog	Label & Number
4/6/02	124	3		1 Fast		Artist Direct 01016

CUT COPY

Electro-pop band from Melbourne, Australia: Dan Whitford (vocals, keyboards), Tim Hoey (guitar), Bennett Foddy (bass) and Mitchell Scott (drums).

DEBUT	PEAK	WKS	RIAA	ARTIST / Album Title	Catalog	Label & Number
5/3/08	167	1		1 In Ghost Colours		Modular 050

CUTE IS WHAT WE AIM FOR

Punk-pop band from Buffalo, New York: Shaant Hacikyan (vocals), Jeff Czum (guitar), Jack Marin (bass) and Tom Falcone (drums).

DEBUT	PEAK	WKS	RIAA	ARTIST / Album Title	Catalog	Label & Number
7/8/06	75	3		1 The Same Old Blood Rush With A New Touch		Fueled By Ramen 087
7/12/08	21	6		2 Rotation		Fueled By Ramen 511251

CUTLASS, Frankie

Born Francis Parker in Puerto Rico. Hip-hop producer.

DEBUT	PEAK	WKS	RIAA	ARTIST / Album Title	Catalog	Label & Number
3/1/97	129	6		1 Politics & Bullsh*t		Relativity 1548

Billboard			R I A A	ARTIST		
DEBUT	PEAK	WKS		Album Title	Catalog	Label & Number

CUTTING CREW
Pop-rock band formed in England: Nick Van Eede (vocals), Kevin MacMichael (guitar), Colin Farley (bass) and Martin Beedle (drums). MacMichael died of cancer on 12/31/2002 (age 51).

3/21/87	16	45	●	1 Broadcast		Virgin 90573
6/3/89	150	6		2 The Scattering		Virgin 91239

CYMANDE
Afro-rock band from the West Indies: Ray King (vocals), Pat Patterson (guitar), Peter Serreo (sax), Mike Rose (flute), Pablo Gonsales (congas), Joe Dee (percussion), Derek Gibbs (sax) and Sam Kelly (drums).

1/13/73	85	17		1 Cymande		Janus 3044
6/30/73	180	4		2 Second Time Round		Janus 3054

CYMARRON
Male pop vocal trio from Memphis, Tennessee: Richard Mainegra, Rick Yancey and Sherrill Parks.

10/2/71	187	3		1 Rings		Entrance 30962

CYMBAL, Johnny
Born on 2/3/1945 in Ochtree, Scotland. Died of a heart attack on 3/16/1993 (age 48). Pop singer/songwriter/producer. Also recorded as Derek.

~ ~ ~ ~ ~ ~ ~ ~ ~ ~ **NON-CHARTED ALBUM** ~ ~ ~ ~ ~ ~ ~ ~ ~ ~ ~
1963 **Mr. Bass Man**

CYMONE, Andre
Born Andre Simon Anderson in Minneapolis, Minnesota. R&B singer/songwriter/producer. Former bass player of **Prince**'s band, The Revolution. Went solo in 1981. Much production work for **Jody Watley**.

10/15/83	185	4		1 Survivin' In The 80's		Columbia 38902
9/21/85	121	8		2 A.C.		Columbia 40037

CYPRESS HILL   All-Time: #451
Latin rap trio from Los Angeles, California: Senen "Sen Dog" Reyes, Louis "B-Real" Freeze and Lawrence "DJ Muggs" Muggerud. Reyes is the brother of **Mellow Man Ace**. Group appeared in the 1993 movie *The Meteor Man*. Freeze was also a member of **The Psycho Realm**.

1/4/92	31	89	▲²	1 Cypress Hill		Ruffhouse 47889
8/7/93	❶²	56	▲³	2 Black Sunday		Ruffhouse 53931
11/18/95	3¹	34	▲	3 Cypress Hill III (Temples Of Boom)		Ruffhouse 66991
8/31/96	21	12	●	4 Unreleased & Revamped	[E-EP]	Ruffhouse 67780
10/24/98	11	16	●	5 IV		Ruffhouse 69037
5/13/00	5	26	▲	6 Skull & Bones		Columbia 69990 [2]
12/30/00+	119	6		7 Live At The Fillmore	[L]	Columbia 85184
				recorded on 8/16/2000 in San Francisco, California		
12/22/01	64	8		8 Stoned Raiders		Columbia 85740
4/10/04	21	9		9 Till Death Do Us Part		Columbia 90781

CYRKLE, The
Pop band formed in Easton, Pennsylvania: Don Dannemann (vocals, guitar), Mike Losekamp (keyboards), Tom Dawes (bass) and Marty Fried (drums). Dawes died of a stroke on 10/13/2007 (age 64).

8/6/66	47	15		1 Red Rubber Ball		Columbia 2544 / 9344
4/1/67	164	2		2 Neon		Columbia 2632 / 9432

CYRUS, Billy Ray   All-Time: #446
Born on 8/25/1961 in Flatwoods, Kentucky. Country singer/actor. Played "Dr. Clint Cassidy" on the PAX-TV series *Doc* (2001-04). Father of TV's *Hannah Montana* star **Miley Cyrus** (plays her manager "Robbie Stewart" on the show).

6/6/92	❶¹⁷	97	▲⁹	1 Some Gave All		Mercury 510635
7/10/93	3¹	43	▲	2 It Won't Be The Last		Mercury 514758
11/26/94	73	12	●	3 Storm In The Heartland		Mercury 526081
9/7/96	125	4		4 Trail Of Tears		Mercury 532829
11/4/00	102	2		5 Southern Rain		Monument 62105
11/15/03	131	1		6 The Other Side		Word-Curb 886274
8/5/06	113	2		7 Wanna Be Your Joe		New Door 006997
8/11/07	20	29		8 Home At Last		Walt Disney 000707
4/25/09	41	4		9 Back To Tennessee		Walt Disney 002344

CYRUS, Miley   2000s: #18 / All-Time: #324
Born Destiny Hope Cyrus on 11/23/1992 in Franklin, Tennessee. Teen singer/actress. Daughter of **Billy Ray Cyrus**. Star of the Disney TV series *Hannah Montana*. Legally changed her name to Miley Ray Cyrus in January 2008.

HANNAH MONTANA:

11/11/06	❶²	78	▲³	1 Hannah Montana	Cat:#26/15 [TV]	Walt Disney 861620
7/14/07	❶¹	65	▲³	2 Hannah Montana 2 / Meet Miley Cyrus	Cat:#41/1 [S]	Walt Disney 000465 [2]
2/16/08	7	14		3 Hannah Montana 2: Non-Stop Dance Party		Walt Disney 001106
9/6/08	103	5		4 Hannah Montana: Hits Remixed		Walt Disney 002169
4/11/09	❶¹	55	▲	5 Hannah Montana: The Movie	[S]	Walt Disney 003101
7/25/09	2¹	27		6 Hannah Montana 3		Walt Disney 002970

Billboard DEBUT	PEAK	WKS	R I A A	ARTIST Album Title	Catalog	Label & Number
				MILEY CYRUS:		
3/29/08	3[1]	34		7 Best Of Both Worlds Concert	[L]	Hollywood 001250
8/9/08	❶[1]	48	▲	8 Breakout		Hollywood 002129
9/12/09	2[2]	38↑	▲	9 The Time Of Our Lives	[EP]	Hollywood 004719

D

DA BACKWUDZ
Male rap duo from Decatur, Georgia: Marcus "Big Marc" Thomas and James "Sho Nuff" Redding.

5/6/06	94	3		1 Wood Work		Major Way 006364

DA BEATMINERZ
Rap production group from Brooklyn, New York: Mr. Walt, Rich Blak, Evil Dee, Baby Paul and Chocolate Ty.

8/18/01	143	4		1 Brace 4 Impak		Rawkus 26168

DA BRAT
Born Shawntae Harris on 4/14/1974 in Chicago, Illinois. Female rapper/songwriter/actress. Discovered by her producer/ songwriter **Jermaine Dupri** at a **Kris Kross** concert. Played "Louise" in the 2001 **Mariah Carey** movie *Glitter*.

7/16/94	11	46	▲	1 Funkdafied		So So Def 66164
11/16/96	20	17	●	2 Anuthatantrum		So So Def 67813
4/29/00	5	24	▲	3 Unrestricted		So So Def 69772
8/2/03	17	6		4 Limelite, Luv & Niteclubz		So So Def 51586

D.A.D.
Hard-rock band from Copenhagen, Denmark: brothers Jesper Binzer (vocals) and Jacob Binzer (guitar), Stig Pedersen (bass) and Peter Jensen (drums). D.A.D. is abbreviation for Disneyland After Dark.

9/30/89	116	11		1 No Fuel Left For The Pilgrims		Warner 25999

dada
Rock trio from Los Angeles, California: Joie Calio (vocals, bass), Michael Gurley (guitar) and Phil Leavitt (drums).

1/16/93	111	10		1 Puzzle		I.R.S. 13141
10/8/94	178	1		2 American Highway Flower		I.R.S. 27986

DADDY DEWDROP
Born Richard Monda in 1940 in Cleveland, Ohio. Pop singer. Songwriter for the TV cartoon series *Sabrina & The Groovy Ghoulies*.

6/26/71	211	3		1 Daddy Dewdrop	[N]	Sunflower 5006

DADDY YANKEE
Born Raymond Ayala on 2/3/1977 in Rio Piedras, Puerto Rico. Reggae singer.

7/31/04+	26	54	▲	1 Barrio Fino	[F]	VI 450639
4/2/05	104	2		2 Ahora Le Toca Al Cangri	[F-L]	El Cartel 450710
4/16/05	158	1		3 Los Homerun-es	Cat:#20/3 [E-F]	Machete 450582
12/31/05	24	38	●	4 Barrio Fino: En Directo	[F-L]	El Cartel 005792
6/23/07	9	13		5 El Cartel: The Big Boss	[F]	El Cartel 008937
8/30/08	13	16		6 Talento De Barrio	[S]	El Cartel 080020

DAEMYON, Jerald
Born in Detroit, Michigan. Classically trained violinist.

2/10/96	195	2		1 Thinking About You	[I]	GRP 9829

DAFT PUNK
Electronica-dance duo from Paris, France: Thomas Bangalter and Guy-Manuel de Homem-Christo.

7/26/97	150	18	●	1 Homework		Soma 42609
3/31/01	44	17		2 Discovery		Virgin 49606
4/2/05	98	1		3 Human After All		Virgin 63562
12/22/07	169	3		4 Alive 2007	[L]	Virgin 09841
				Grammy: Electronic/Dance Album		
2/28/09	35[C]	1		5 Musique Vol. I: 1993-2005	[K]	Virgin 58405

DA HEADBUSSAZ
Male rap trio from Memphis, Tennessee: DJ Paul Beauregard, Jordan "**Juicy J**" Houston and **Fiend**. DJ Paul and Juicy J are also members of **Three 6 Mafia**, **Prophet Posse** and **Tear Da Club Up Thugs**.

11/2/02	98	4		1 Dat's How It Happen To'm		Hypnotize Minds 3602

DA HOOD
Rap group assembled by **Mack 10**: Skoop, DV, Mr. K-Mac, Cousteau and Techniec.

8/10/02	40	7		1 Mack 10 Presents Da Hood		Hoo-Bangin' 9996

DA'KRASH
Funk band from St. Louis, Missouri: Robert Jordan (vocals), Brian Tate, Edgar Hinton, Dee Dee James and Gabriel Acevedo.

4/16/88	184	3		1 Da'Krash		Capitol 48355

Billboard DEBUT	PEAK	WKS	R I A A	ARTIST / Album Title	Catalog	Label & Number

DALE, Dick, and The Del-Tones
Born Richard Monsour on 5/4/1937 in Boston, Massachusetts. Influential surf-rock guitarist.

1/26/63	59	17		1 Surfers' Choice .... **[E]**		Deltone 1886
				first released in 1962 on Deltone 1001		
12/14/63+	106	11		2 Checkered Flag		Capitol 2002

~ ~ ~ ~ ~ ~ ~ ~ ~ **NON-CHARTED ALBUMS** ~ ~ ~ ~ ~ ~ ~ ~ ~ ~
1963 **King Of The Surf Guitar**   1964 **Summer Surf**
1964 **Mr. Eliminator**

DALE & GRACE
Pop vocal duo: Dale Houston (born on 4/23/1940 in Seminary, Mississippi; died of heart failure on 9/27/2007, age 67) and Grace Broussard (born in 1939 in Prairieville, Louisiana).

2/1/64	100	7		1 I'm Leaving It Up To You		Montel 100

DA LENCH MOB
Rap trio from Los Angeles, California: Terry Gray, DeSean Cooper and Jerome Washington. Cooper left in 1993, replaced by Maulkie.

10/10/92	24	21	●	1 Guerillas In Tha Mist		Street Know. 92206
11/19/94	81	2		2 Planet Of Da Apes		Street Know. 53939

DALTON, Kathy
Born in Memphis, Tennessee. Pop-country singer.

11/16/74	190	3		1 Boogie Bands & One Night Stands		DiscReet 2208

DALTREY, Roger
Born on 3/1/1944 in Hammersmith, London, England. Lead singer of **The Who**. Starred in the movies *Tommy*, *Lisztomania*, *The Legacy* and *McVicar*.

5/26/73	45	20		1 Daltrey		Track 328
8/9/75	28	23		2 Ride A Rock Horse		MCA 2147
7/9/77	46	19		3 One Of The Boys		MCA 2271
8/16/80	22	15		4 McVicar .... **[S]**		Polydor 6284
3/27/82	185	5		5 Best Bits .... **[G]**		MCA 5301
3/17/84	102	9		6 Parting Should Be Painless		Atlantic 80128
10/12/85	42	26		7 Under A Raging Moon		Atlantic 81269

DAMAGEPLAN
Hard-rock band formed in Texas: Pat Lachman (vocals), "Dimebag" Darrell Abbott (guitar), Bob "Zilla" Kakaha (bass) and Vinnie Paul Abbott (drums). Brothers Darrell and Vinnie were members of **Pantera**. Darrell was shot to death on stage on 12/8/2004 (age 38).

2/28/04	38	6		1 New Found Power		Elektra 62939

DAMIAN, Michael
Born Michael Damian Weir on 4/26/1962 in San Diego, California. Pop singer/actor. Played "Danny Romalotti" on the TV soap opera *The Young & The Restless*.

6/17/89	61	26		1 Where Do We Go From Here		Cypress 0130

DAMITA JO
Born Damita Jo DuBlanc on 8/5/1930 in Austin, Texas. Died on 12/25/1998 (age 68). Female singer. Regular on **Redd Foxx**'s TV variety series in 1977.

3/27/65	121	4		1 This Is Damita Jo		Epic 26131
5/6/67	169	2		2 If You Go Away		Epic 26244

~ ~ ~ ~ ~ ~ ~ ~ ~ ~ **NON-CHARTED ALBUMS** ~ ~ ~ ~ ~ ~ ~ ~ ~ ~
1961 **The Big 15** *[w/ Steve Gibson & the Red Caps]*   1961 **I'll Save The Last Dance For You**

DAMNATION OF ADAM BLESSING, The
Rock band from Cleveland, Ohio: Adam Blessing (vocals), Bob Kalamasz (guitar), Jim Quinn (guitar), Ray Benick (bass) and Bill Schwark (drums).

3/28/70	181	2		1 The Damnation Of Adam Blessing		United Artists 6738

DAMN YANKEES
All-star rock band: **Ted Nugent** (guitar, vocals), **Tommy Shaw** (guitar, vocals), Jack Blades (bass, vocals) and Michael Cartellone (drums). Nugent was with the **Amboy Dukes**. Shaw was with **Styx**. Blades was with **Night Ranger**. Shaw and Blades also recorded as a duo in 1995.

3/31/90+	13	78	▲²	1 Damn Yankees		Warner 26159
8/29/92	22	28	●	2 Don't Tread		Warner 45025

DAMON('S), Liz, Orient Express
Damon is the leader of the three-woman, six-man vocal/instrumental group from Hawaii.

3/6/71	190	2		1 Liz Damon's Orient Express		White Whale 5003

DAMONE
Pop-rock band from Waltham, Massachusetts: Noelle Leblanc (vocals, guitar), Mike Woods (guitar), Mike Vazquez (bass) and Dustin Hengst (drums).

6/10/06	168	1		1 Out Here All Night		Island 006483

Billboard DEBUT	PEAK	WKS	R I A A	ARTIST / Album Title	Catalog	Label & Number
				DAMONE, Vic Born Vito Farinola on 6/12/1928 in Brooklyn, New York. Adult Contemporary singer. Appeared in the movies *Kismet*, *Meet Me In Las Vegas* and *Hell To Eternity*. Hosted own TV series (1956-57). Married to actress Diahann Carroll from 1987-96.		
10/13/56	14	8		1 That Towering Feeling!		Columbia 900
3/3/62	64	17		2 Linger Awhile with Vic Damone		Capitol 1646
10/13/62	57	10		3 The Lively Ones		Capitol 1748
7/10/65	86	10		4 You Were Only Fooling		Warner 1602
				DA MUZICIANZ Hip-hop trio from Atlanta, Georgia: brothers Deongelo "D-Roc" Holmes (of **Ying Yang Twins**), Brandon "Mr. Ball" Sams and Courtney "Birthday Boy" Holmes.		
6/10/06	137	2		1 Da Muzicianz		Collipark 2800
				DAN, Leo Born Leopoldo Dante Tevez on 3/22/1942 in Argentina. Latin singer.		
2/10/07	194	2		1 La Historia	[F-K]	Sony 02936
				DANA, Bill — see JIMENEZ, Jose		
				DANA, Vic Born on 8/26/1942 in Buffalo, New York; raised in Los Angeles, California. Adult Contemporary singer.		
11/16/63+	111	9		1 More		Dolton 8026
5/16/64	116	5		2 Shangri-La		Dolton 8028
4/10/65	13	21		3 Red Roses For A Blue Lady		Dolton 8034
12/30/67	114^X	1		4 Little Altar Boy And Other Christmas Songs	[X]	Dolton 8049
				DANA DANE Born Dana McLeese in Brooklyn, New York. Male rapper.		
9/12/87	46	32	●	1 Dana Dane With Fame		Profile 1233
11/10/90	150	4		2 Dana Dane 4-Ever		Profile 1298
				DANCE GAVIN DANCE Hard-rock band from Sacramento, California: Kurt Travis (vocals), Will Swan (guitar), Tim Feerick (bass) and Matt Mingus (drums).		
9/6/08	172	1		1 Dance Gavin Dance		Rise 068
6/27/09	143	1		2 Happiness		Rise 80
				DANDY WARHOLS, The Rock band from Portland, Oregon: Courtney Taylor (vocals), Peter Holmstrom (guitar), Zia McCabe (bass) and Brent DeBoer (drums).		
8/19/00	182	1		1 Thirteen Tales From Urban Bohemia		Capitol 57787
9/6/03	118	2		2 Welcome To The Monkey House		Capitol 84368
10/1/05	89	1		3 Odditorium Or Warlords Of Mars		Capitol 74590
9/6/08	128	1		4 ...Earth To The Dandy Warhols...		Beat The World 001
				D'ANGELO Born Michael D'Angelo Archer on 2/11/1974 in Richmond, Virginia. R&B singer/songwriter.		
7/22/95+	22	65	▲	1 Brown Sugar		EMI 32629
2/12/00	❶²	33	▲	2 Voodoo *Grammy: R&B Album ★ RS500 #488*		Virgin 48499
				DANGER DANGER Hard-rock band from Queens, New York: Ted Poley (vocals), Andy Timmons (guitar), Kasey Smith (keyboards), Bruno Ravel (bass) and Steve West (drums).		
8/19/89	88	42		1 Danger Danger		CBS Associated 44342
10/19/91	123	5		2 Screw It!		Epic 46977
				DANGER DOOM Electronic-rap duo formed in New York: Brian "Danger Mouse" Burton and Daniel "**MF Doom**" Dumile.		
10/29/05	41	4		1 The Mouse And The Mask		Epitaph 86775
				DANGERFIELD, Rodney Born Jacob Cohen on 11/22/1921 in Babylon, Long Island, New York. Died of heart failure on 10/5/2004 (age 82). Stand-up comedian/actor. Starred in several movies.		
8/2/80	48	19		1 No Respect *Grammy: Comedy Album*	[C]	Casablanca 7229
11/12/83	36	20		2 Rappin' Rodney	[C]	RCA Victor 4869
				DANGEROUS TOYS Hard-rock band from Austin, Texas: Jason McMaster (vocals), Scott Dalhover (guitar), Danny Aaron (guitar), Mike Watson (bass) and Mark Geary (drums).		
6/17/89	65	36	●	1 Dangerous Toys		Columbia 45031
6/22/91	67	9		2 Hellacious Acres		Columbia 46754
				DANGER RADIO Rock band from Edmonds, Washington: Andrew DeTorres (vocals), Elan Wright (guitar), Andy Brookins (guitar), Spencer Phillips (keyboards), Robbie Cochrane (bass) and Nico Hartikainen (drums).		
7/26/08	198	1		1 Used And Abused		Photo Finish 510959

Billboard

DEBUT	PEAK	WKS	R I A A	ARTIST Album Title	Catalog	Label & Number

DANIELS, Charlie, Band   **All-Time: #389**

Born on 10/28/1936 in Wilmington, North Carolina. Country-rock singer/songwriter/fiddle player. His band consisted of Tom Crain (guitar), Joe "Taz" DiGregorio (keyboards), Charles Hayward (bass), James W. Marshall (drums) and Fred Edwards (drums). Marshall and Edwards left in 1986; replaced by Jack Gavin. Group appeared in the movie *Urban Cowboy*.

AWARDS: CMA: Instrumental Group 1979 & 1980 / Musician 1979 ★ OPRY: 2008

DEBUT	PEAK	WKS	R I A A	#	Album Title	Catalog	Label & Number
7/28/73	164	9		1	Honey In The Rock		Kama Sutra 2071
12/28/74+	38	34	▲	2	Fire On The Mountain		Kama Sutra 2603
10/4/75	57	12		3	Nightrider		Kama Sutra 2607
5/15/76	35	18	●	4	Saddle Tramp		Epic 34150
12/4/76	83	10		5	High Lonesome		Epic 34377
11/12/77	105	11	●	6	Midnight Wind		Epic 34970
5/12/79	5	43	▲³	7	Million Mile Reflections		Epic 35751
8/9/80	11	33	▲	8	Full Moon		Epic 36571
4/3/82	26	19	●	9	Windows		Epic 37694
7/23/83	84	12	▲⁴	10	A Decade Of Hits	Cat:#25/69 [G]	Epic 38795
11/12/88	181	2		11	Homesick Heroes		Epic 44324
11/25/89+	82	25	▲	12	Simple Man		Epic 45316
5/25/91	139	3		13	Renegade		Epic 46835
9/20/97+	26ᶜ	5	▲²	14	Super Hits	[G]	Epic 64182

DANITY KANE

Female R&B vocal group assembled by **Diddy** for the reality TV series *Making The Band 3*: Shannon Bex, Aundrea Fimbres, Aubrey O'Day, Dawn Richard and Wanita Woodgette.

DEBUT	PEAK	WKS	R I A A	#	Album Title	Catalog	Label & Number
9/9/06	❶¹	23	▲	1	Danity Kane		Bad Boy 83989
4/5/08	❶¹	21	●	2	Welcome To The Dollhouse		Bad Boy 444604

DANKO, Rick

Born on 12/29/1942 in Simcoe, Ontario, Canada. Died on 12/10/1999 (age 56). Rock singer/bassist. Member of **The Band**.

DEBUT	PEAK	WKS	R I A A	#	Album Title	Catalog	Label & Number
12/24/77+	119	8		1	Rick Danko		Arista 4141

DANNY WILSON

Pop trio from Dundee, Scotland: brothers Gary Clark (vocals, guitar) and Kit Clark (keyboards, drums), with Ged Grimes (bass). Group named after the 1952 **Frank Sinatra** movie *Meet Danny Wilson*.

DEBUT	PEAK	WKS	R I A A	#	Album Title	Catalog	Label & Number
7/18/87	79	16		1	Meet Danny Wilson		Virgin 90596

DANTE AND THE EVERGREENS

Born Donald Drowty on 9/8/1941 in Los Angeles, California. Pop singer. The Evergreens: Bill Young, Tony Moon and Frank Rosenthal.

~ ~ ~ ~ ~ ~ ~ ~ ~ ~ **NON-CHARTED ALBUM** ~ ~ ~ ~ ~ ~ ~ ~ ~ ~ ~

1961 **Dante & The Evergreens**

DANZIG

Born Glenn Anzalone on 6/23/1955 in Lodi, New Jersey. Hard-rock singer/songwriter. His band: John Christ (guitar), Eerie Von (bass) and Chuck Biscuits (drums). Joey Castillo replaced Biscuits in 1994. John Lazie replaced Von in 1996.

DEBUT	PEAK	WKS	R I A A	#	Album Title	Catalog	Label & Number
10/8/88	125	9	●	1	Danzig	Cat:#3/20	Def American 24208
7/14/90	74	13		2	Danzig II - Lucifuge		Def American 24281
8/1/92	24	7		3	Danzig III - How The Gods Kill		Def American 26914
6/12/93+	54	20		4	Thrall - Demonsweatlive	[EP-L]	Def American 45286
					side 1 titled "Thrall"; side 2 titled "Demonsweatlive" (recorded live on 10/31/1992 at Irvine Meadows, California)		
10/22/94	29	8		5	Danzig 4		American 45647
11/16/96	41	3		6	Danzig 5 - Blackacidevil		Hollywood 62084
11/20/99	149	1		7	6:66 - Satans Child		Evilive 61005
6/22/02	158	1		8	777: I Luciferi		Evilive 15204
9/18/04	183	1		9	Circle Of Snakes		Evillive 82496
7/28/07	164	1		10	The Lost Tracks Of Danzig	[K]	Evilive 99 [2]

D'ARBY, Terence Trent

Born on 3/15/1962 in Manhattan, New York; later based in London, England. R&B singer/songwriter/producer. Last name originally spelled Darby. Was a member of the U.S. boxing team.

DEBUT	PEAK	WKS	R I A A	#	Album Title	Catalog	Label & Number
10/24/87+	4	60	▲²	1	Introducing The Hardline According To Terence Trent D'Arby		Columbia 40964
					Grammy: Male R&B Vocal		
11/25/89	61	15		2	Terence Trent D'Arby's Neither Fish Nor Flesh		Columbia 45351
5/29/93	119	7		3	Terence Trent D'Arby's Symphony Or Damn		Columbia 53616
5/27/95	178	1		4	Terence Trent D'Arby's Vibrator		Work 67070

DAREYES DE LA SIERRA

Traditional Mexican band from Navojoa, Sonora, Mexico. Led by Jose Darrey Castro.

DEBUT	PEAK	WKS	R I A A	#	Album Title	Catalog	Label & Number
8/30/08	117	5		1	Con Banda	[F]	Disa 721149

DARIN, Bobby
All-Time: #329

Born Walden Robert Cassotto on 5/14/1936 in the Bronx, New York. Died of heart failure on 12/20/1973 (age 37). Pop singer/pianist/songwriter/entertainer. Married to actress Sandra Dee from 1960-67. Acted in several movies. **Kevin Spacey** portrayed Darin in the 2004 movie *Beyond The Sea*.

AWARDS: Grammy: Best New Artist 1959 / Lifetime Achievement 2010 ★ R&R Hall of Fame: 1990

10/5/59+	7	52	1 That's All		Atco 104
3/7/60	6	50	2 This Is Darin		Atco 115
10/17/60	9	38	3 Darin At The Copa [L]		Atco 122
5/22/61	18	42	4 The Bobby Darin Story [G]		Atco 131
9/11/61	92	10	5 Love Swings		Atco 134
1/27/62	48	31	6 Twist With Bobby Darin		Atco 138
5/12/62	96	11	7 Bobby Darin Sings Ray Charles		Atco 140
10/6/62	45	10	8 Things & Other Things		Atco 146
11/17/62	100	6	9 Oh! Look At Me Now		Capitol 1791
3/16/63	43	15	10 You're The Reason I'm Living		Capitol 1866
8/24/63	98	5	11 18 Yellow Roses		Capitol 1942
12/26/64+	107	8	12 From Hello Dolly To Goodbye Charlie		Capitol 2194
7/10/65	132	4	13 Venice Blue		Capitol 2322
2/11/67	142	5	14 If I Were A Carpenter		Atlantic 8135
4/6/74	204	6	15 Darin 1936-1973		Motown 813

~ ~ ~ ~ ~ ~ ~ ~ ~ **NON-CHARTED ALBUMS** ~ ~ ~ ~ ~ ~ ~ ~ ~
1958 **Bobby Darin**   1960 **It's You...Or No One**
1960 **Bobby Darin For Teenagers Only**   1960 **The 25th Day Of December With Bobby Darin**

DARK ANGEL
Hard-rock band from Los Angeles, California: Ron Rinehart (vocals), Jim Durkin (guitar), Eric Meyer (guitar), Mike Gonzalez (bass) and Gene Hoglan (drums).

4/1/89	159	6	1 Leave Scars		Combat 8264

DARKEST HOUR
Hard-rock band from Washington DC: John Henry (vocals), Mike Schleibaum (guitar), Kris Norris (guitar), Paul Burnette (bass) and Ryan Parrish (drums).

7/16/05	138	1	1 Undoing Ruin		Victory 244
7/28/07	110	2	2 Deliver Us		Victory 347
7/11/09	104	1	3 Eternal Return		Victory 495

DARK LOTUS
Rap collaboration between **Insane Clown Posse** and **Twiztid**.

8/4/01	158	1	1 Tales From The Lotus Pod		Psychopathic 2700
			no track titles listed on this album		
4/24/04	71	1	2 Black Rain		Psychopathic 4024
5/3/08	45	2	3 The Opaque Brotherhood		Psychopathic 4603

DARKNESS, The
Rock band from London, England: brothers Justin Hawkins (vocals) and Dan Hawkins (guitar), with Frankie Poullain (bass) and Ed Graham (drums). Richie Edwards replaced Poullain in early 2005.

1/3/04	36	28	● 1 Permission To Land		Atlantic 60817
12/17/05	58	2	2 One Way Ticket To Hell...And Back		Atlantic 62838

DARK NEW DAY
Hard-rock band formed in Orlando, Florida: brothers Clint Lowery (guitar; **Sevendust**) and Corey Lowery (bass; **Stereomud**), Brett Hestla (vocals), Troy McLawhorn (guitar) and Will Hunt (drums).

7/2/05	103	2	1 Twelve Year Silence		Warner 49318

DARLING CRUEL
Rock band from Los Angeles, California: Greg Darling (vocals), Danni Bardot (guitar), Janis Massey (sax, flute), Orlando Sims (bass) and Erik Gloege (drums).

9/9/89	160	8	1 Passion Crimes		Mika 837920

DARRELL, Johnny
Born on 7/23/1940 in Hopewell, Alabama. Died of diabetes on 10/7/1997 (age 57). Country singer/guitarist.

9/6/69	172	3	1 Why You Been Gone So Long		United Artists 6707

DARREN, James
Born James Ercolani on 6/8/1936 in Philadelphia, Pennsylvania. Pop singer/actor. Starred in several movies. Regular on TV's *The Time Tunnel* from 1966-67 and *T.J. Hooker* from 1983-86.

9/25/61	132	3	1 Gidget Goes Hawaiian (James Darren Sings The Movies)		Colpix 418
5/11/63	48	18	2 Teen-Age Triangle [G]		Colpix 444
			JAMES DARREN / SHELLEY FABARES / PAUL PETERSEN		
6/3/67	187	3	3 James Darren/All		Warner 1688

~ ~ ~ ~ ~ ~ ~ ~ ~ ~ **NON-CHARTED ALBUMS** ~ ~ ~ ~ ~ ~ ~ ~ ~ ~
1959 **Album No. 1**   1964 **More Teenage Triangle**
[w/ Shelley Fabares & Paul Petersen]

			R I A A	ARTIST Album Title	Catalog	Label & Number

DARTELLS, The
Rock and roll band from Oxnard, California: Doug Phillips (vocals, bass), Dick Burns (guitar), Randy Ray (organ), Corky Wilkie and Rich Peil (saxophones), and Gary Peeler (drums). Phillips died on 5/5/1995 (age 50). Burns died on 11/5/2007 (age 64).

| 7/6/63 | 95 | 5 | | 1 **Hot Pastrami!** | | Dot 25522 |

DAS EFX
Hip-hop duo from Brooklyn, New York: Andre "Dray" Weston (born on 9/9/1970) and Willie "Skoob" Hines (born on 11/27/1970). DAS is an acronym for Dray And Skoob (which is "books" spelled backward).

4/25/92	16	42	▲	1 **Dead Serious**		EastWest 91827
12/4/93	20	12		2 **Straight Up Sewaside**		EastWest 92265
10/14/95	22	6		3 **Hold It Down**		EastWest 61829
4/11/98	48	3		4 **Generation EFX**		EastWest 62063

DASH, Sarah
Born on 8/18/1943 in Trenton, New Jersey. R&B singer. Member of **LaBelle**.

| 1/20/79 | 182 | 7 | | 1 **Sarah Dash** | | Kirshner 35477 |

DASHBOARD CONFESSIONAL
Rock band from Boca Raton, Florida: Christopher Carrabba (vocals, guitar), John Lefler (guitar), Scott Shoenbeck (bass) and Mike Marsh (drums).

4/6/02	108	27	●	1 **The Places You Have Come To Fear The Most**		Vagrant 0354
1/4/03	111	6		2 **MTV Unplugged V 2.0** [L]		Vagrant 0378
8/30/03	2¹	35	●	3 **A Mark • A Mission • A Brand • A Scar**		Vagrant 0385
7/15/06	2¹	22	●	4 **Dusk And Summer**		Vagrant 006061
10/20/07	18	6		5 **The Shade Of Poison Trees**		Vagrant 477
11/28/09	19	3		6 **Alter The Ending**		Vagrant 013475

DA' T.R.U.T.H.
Born Emanuel Lambert on 12/15/1976 in Philadelphia, Pennsylvania. Christian rapper.

| 8/8/09 | 110 | 1 | | 1 **The Big Picture** | | Cross Movement 30036 |

DAUGHTRY
Rock band formed in North Carolina: Chris Daughtry (born on 12/26/1979 in Roanoke Rapids, North Carolina; finalist on the 2006 season of TV's *American Idol*), Josh Steeley (guitar), Jeremy Brady (guitar), Josh Paul (bass) and Joey Barnes (drums).

| 12/9/06+ | ❶² | 164 | ▲⁴ | 1 **Daughtry** Cat:#27/12 | | RCA 88860 |
| 8/1/09 | ❶¹ | 44↑ | ● | 2 **Leave This Town** | | 19 Records 53744 |

DAVE & SUGAR
Country singer Dave Rowland with female duo of Vicki Hackeman and Jackie Frantz. Sue Powell replaced Frantz in 1977. Melissa Dean replaced Hackemen in 1979. Jamie Jaye replaced Powell in 1980.

| 9/17/77 | 157 | 4 | | 1 **That's The Way Love Should Be** | | RCA Victor 2477 |
| 3/7/81 | 179 | 4 | | 2 **Greatest Hits** [G] | | RCA Victor 3915 |

DAVE DEE, DOZY, BEAKY, MICK AND TICH
Pop band from Wiltshire, England: "Dave Dee" Harmon (vocals), Trevor "Dozy" Davies (guitar), John "Beaky" Dymond (guitar), Michael "Mick" Wilson (bass) and Ian "Tich" Amey (drums). Harmon died of cancer on 1/9/2009 (age 65).

| 8/5/67 | 155 | 3 | | 1 **Greatest Hits** [G] | | Fontana 67567 |

DAVID, Craig
Born on 5/5/1981 in Southampton, England. R&B singer/songwriter.

| 8/4/01 | 11 | 62 | ▲ | 1 **Born To Do It** | | Wildstar 88081 |
| 12/7/02 | 32 | 14 | ● | 2 **Slicker Than Your Average** | | Wildstar 80027 |

DAVID & DAVID
Pop-rock duo from Los Angeles, California: **David Baerwald** and David Ricketts.

| 8/16/86 | 39 | 38 | ● | 1 **Boomtown** | | A&M 5134 |

DAVIDSON, Dianne
Born in Denver, Colorado. Folk singer/songwriter/guitarist.

| 4/29/72 | 212 | 2 | | 1 **Back Woods Woman** | | Janus 3043 |

DAVIDSON, John
Born on 12/13/1941 in Pittsburgh, Pennsylvania. Singer/actor. Hosted own TV talk show from 1980-82. Co-hosted TV's *That's Incredible* and a version of *Hollywood Squares*.

10/8/66	19	24		1 **The Time Of My Life!**		Columbia 9380
4/8/67	125	8		2 **My Best To You**		Columbia 9448
12/2/67	79	12		3 **A Kind Of Hush**		Columbia 9534
6/29/68	151	10		4 **Goin' Places**		Columbia 9654
5/17/69	153	7		5 **John Davidson**		Columbia 9795
11/22/69	165	5		6 **My Cherie Amour**		Columbia 9859

DAVIES, Dave
Born on 2/3/1947 in Muswell Hill, London, England. Rock singer/guitarist. Younger brother of **Ray Davies**. Member of **The Kinks**.

7/26/80	42	14		1 **AFL1-3603**		RCA Victor 3603
				title refers to label number bar code		
7/18/81	152	8		2 **Glamour**		RCA Victor 4036
9/3/83	202	3		3 **Chosen People**		Warner 23917

DEBUT	PEAK	WKS			Catalog	Label & Number
				DAVIES, Ray Born on 6/21/1944 in Muswell Hill, London, England. Rock singer/songwriter/guitarist. Older brother of **Dave Davies**. Leader of **The Kinks**.		
3/11/06	122	1		1 Other People's Lives		V2 27285
3/8/08	140	1		2 Working Man's Cafe		Ammal 6136
				DAVINA Born Davina Bussey on 12/31/1966 in Detroit, Michigan. Female R&B singer.		
4/25/98	180	2		1 Best Of Both Worlds		Loud 67536
				DAVIS, Alana Born on 5/6/1974 in Manhattan, New York. Adult Alternative singer/songwriter.		
1/31/98	157	7		1 Blame It On Me		Elektra 62112
				DAVIS, Betty Born Betty Mabry on 7/26/1945 in Durham, North Carolina. Funk singer/songwriter. Married to **Miles Davis** from 1968-69.		
9/22/73	202	6		1 Betty Davis		Just Sunshine 5
11/22/75	202	5		2 Nasty Girl		Island 9329
				DAVIS, Chip Born Louis Davis on 11/15/1947 in Sylvania, Ohio. New Age songwriter/producer/musician. Founder of **Mannheim Steamroller**.		
11/23/96	168	1		1 Holiday Musik [I-X] Christmas chart: 6/'96		American Gram. 296
11/21/98	9ˣ	1		2 Chip Davis Presents Renaissance Holiday [I-X]		American Gram. 298
				DAVIS, Danny, & The Nashville Brass Born George Nowlan on 4/29/1925 in Dorchester, Massachusetts. Died of a heart attack on 6/12/2008 (age 83). Country trumpet player/bandleader. Played and sang in swing bands including Gene Krupa, Bob Crosby, Freddy Martin, Blue Barron, and **Sammy Kaye**. Formed The Nashville Brass in 1968. AWARD: CMA: Instrumental Group 1969, 1970, 1971, 1972, 1973 & 1974		
2/15/69	78	24		1 The Nashville Sound [I]		RCA Victor 4059
7/12/69	143	6		2 More Nashville Sounds [I] Grammy: Country Instrumental Album		RCA Victor 4176
12/27/69+	141	20		3 Movin' On [I]		RCA Victor 4232
5/30/70	102	12		4 You Ain't Heard Nothin' Yet [I]		RCA Victor 4334
10/31/70	140	12		5 Down Homers [I]		RCA Victor 4424
12/12/70	11ˣ	3		6 Christmas With Danny Davis And The Nashville Brass [X-I]		RCA Victor 4377
4/3/71	161	3		7 Somethin' Else [I]		RCA Victor 4476
9/18/71	184	4		8 Super Country [I]		RCA Victor 4571
2/12/72	202	6		9 Nashville Brass Turns To Gold [I]		RCA Victor 4627
11/25/72	193	5		10 Turn On Some Happy! [I]		RCA Victor 4803
3/15/80	150	5		11 Danny Davis & Willie Nelson With The Nashville Brass new instrumental backing for earlier recordings by Nelson		RCA Victor 3549
				DAVIS, Jimmy, & Junction Born in Memphis, Tennessee. Rock singer/guitarist. His band Junction: Tommy Burroughs (guitar), John Scott (piano) and Chuck Reynolds (drums).		
10/31/87	122	8		1 Kick The Wall		MCA 42015
				DAVIS, Linda Born on 11/26/1962 in Dodson, Texas. Country singer. Mother of Hillary Scott (of **Lady Antebellum**).		
5/14/94	124	3		1 Shoot For The Moon		Arista 18749
2/17/96	164	4		2 Some Things Are Meant To Be		Arista 18804
				DAVIS, Mac Born Scott Davis on 1/21/1942 in Lubbock, Texas. Country-pop singer/songwriter/guitarist. Worked as a regional rep for Vee-Jay and Liberty Records. Acted in several movies. Host of own musical variety TV series from 1974-76.		
10/19/74	182	4		1 Song Painter released in 1970		Columbia 9969
12/25/71+	160	17		2 I Believe In Music		Columbia 30926
9/16/72	11	44	▲	3 Baby Don't Get Hooked On Me		Columbia 31770
4/21/73	120	13		4 Mac Davis		Columbia 32206
5/4/74	13	45	▲	5 Stop And Smell The Roses		Columbia 32582
2/8/75	21	14	●	6 All The Love In The World		Columbia 32927
7/5/75	64	10		7 Burnin' Thing		Columbia 33551
4/10/76	156	9		8 Forever Lovers		Columbia 34105
6/10/78	207	6		9 Fantasy		Columbia 35284
5/24/80	69	15	●	10 It's Hard To Be Humble		Casablanca 7207
10/18/80	67	9		11 Texas In My Rear View Mirror		Casablanca 7239
1/16/82	174	3		12 Midnight Crazy		Casablanca 7257
				DAVIS, Martha Born on 1/15/1951 in Berkeley, California. Lead singer of **The Motels**.		
11/14/87	127	13		1 Policy		Capitol 48054

DAVIS, Miles
All-Time: #232

Born on 5/26/1926 in Alton, Illinois. Died of a stroke and pneumonia on 9/28/1991 (age 65). Innovative jazz trumpeter who influenced the jazz fusion movement. Began career in 1944 with **Billy Eckstine**'s orchestra. With Six Brown Cats group in 1944. With Charlie Parker and Coleman Hawkins. Recorded with Parker on Savoy and Dial from 1945-46. Formed own quintet in 1955. Band members included **Herbie Hancock** and **Wayne Shorter**. Married to **Betty Davis** from 1968-69. Married to actress Cicely Tyson from 1981-88.

AWARDS: Grammy: Lifetime Achievement 1990 ★ R&R Hall of Fame: 2006

DEBUT	PEAK	WKS				
3/24/62	116	10		1 Someone My Prince Will Come	[I]	Columbia 1656 / 8456
9/14/63	62	15		2 Seven Steps To Heaven	[I]	Columbia 2051 / 8851
4/11/64	93	9		3 Quiet Nights	[I]	Columbia 2106 / 8906
9/6/69	134	6		4 In A Silent Way	[I]	Columbia 9875
				Grammy: Hall of Fame		
5/16/70	35	29	▲	5 Bitches Brew	[I]	Columbia 26 [2]
				Grammys: Jazz Album / Hall of Fame ★ RS500 #94		
4/24/71	159	8		6 A Tribute To Jack Johnson	[I-S]	Columbia 30455
				movie is a biography of the world heavyweight boxing champ (1908-1915)		
12/25/71+	125	13		7 Live-Evil	[I]	Columbia 30954 [2]
11/18/72	156	11		8 On The Corner	[I]	Columbia 31906
6/8/74	179	5		9 Big Fun	[I]	Columbia 32866 [2]
1/4/75	141	8		10 Get Up With It	[I]	Columbia 33236 [2]
				tribute to Duke Ellington		
7/25/81	53	18		11 The Man With The Horn	[I]	Columbia 36790
5/21/83	136	7		12 Star People	[I]	Columbia 38657
6/30/84	169	11		13 Decoy	[I]	Columbia 38991
6/1/85	111	12		14 You're Under Arrest	[I]	Columbia 40023
10/25/86	141	10		15 Tutu	[I]	Warner 25490
				Grammy: Jazz Album		
6/17/89	177	5		16 Amandla	[I]	Warner 25873
7/25/92	190	4		17 Doo-Bop	[I]	Warner 26938
				Grammy: R&B Instrumental Album		
				EARLY ALBUMS:		
6/14/97+	2¹ᶜ	167	▲⁵	18 Kind Of Blue	[I]	Columbia 40579
				Grammy: Hall of Fame ★ RS500 #12 ★ NRR		
				first released in 1959 on Columbia 1355/8163		
2/17/01	36ᶜ	1	●	19 Sketches Of Spain	[I]	Columbia 65142
				Grammys: Jazz Album / Hall of Fame ★ RS500 #356		
				first released in 1960 on Columbia 1480/8271		
11/29/08	44ᶜ	1		20 Birth Of The Cool	[I]	Blue Note 30117
				his first recordings from 1949-50; first released in 1956 on Capitol 762		
				GREATEST HITS & COMPILATIONS:		
10/13/73	189	3		21 Basic Miles - The Classic Performances Of Miles Davis	[I]	Columbia 32025
5/7/77	190	2		22 Water Babies	[I]	Columbia 34396
4/11/81	179	2		23 Directions	[I]	Columbia 36472 [2]
				LIVE ALBUMS:		
10/2/61	68	19		24 Miles Davis In Person	[I]	Columbia 1669 [2]
				recorded at The Blackhawk in San Francisco, California		
10/6/62	59	7		25 Miles Davis At Carnegie Hall	[I]	Columbia 1812 / 8612
				recorded on 5/19/1961		
9/26/64	116	10		26 Miles Davis In Europe	[I]	Columbia 2183 / 8983
				recorded at the Antibes International Jazz Festival in France		
4/24/65	138	9		27 My Funny Valentine	[I]	Columbia 2306 / 9106
				recorded on 2/12/1964 at the Philharmonic Hall in New York City		
12/12/70+	123	12		28 Miles Davis At Fillmore	[I]	Columbia 30038 [2]
				recorded at the Fillmore East in New York City		
5/5/73	152	8		29 In Concert	[I]	Columbia 32092 [2]
				recorded at the Philharmonic Hall in New York City		
3/13/76	168	5		30 Agharta	[I]	Columbia 33967 [2]
				recorded on 2/1/1975 at the Osaka Festival Hall in Japan		
5/29/82	159	7		31 We Want Miles	[I]	Columbia 38005 [2]
				Grammy: Jazz Album		

~ ~ ~ ~ ~ ~ ~ ~ ~ **NON-CHARTED ALBUMS** ~ ~ ~ ~ ~ ~ ~ ~ ~ ~ ~

1957 **Miles Ahead**　　　　　　　　　　　　　　1958 **Porgy And Bess**
　　Grammy: Hall of Fame　　　　　　　　　　　　*Grammy: Hall of Fame*
1958 **Milestones**
　　Grammy: Hall of Fame

DAVIS, Paul

Born on 4/21/1948 in Meridian, Mississippi. Died of a heart attack on 4/21/2008 (age 60). Pop-country singer/songwriter/producer.

DEBUT	PEAK	WKS				
1/11/75	148	6		1 Ride 'Em Cowboy		Bang 401
1/21/78	82	18		2 Singer Of Songs - Teller Of Tales		Bang 410
4/26/80	173	4		3 Paul Davis		Bang 36094
12/19/81+	52	29		4 Cool Night		Arista 9578

DAVIS, Sammy Jr.   All-Time: #416

Born on 12/8/1925 in Harlem, New York. Died of cancer on 5/16/1990 (age 64). One of America's all-time great entertainers. With father and uncle in dance act the Will Mastin Trio from the early 1940s. First recorded for Capitol in 1950. Lost his left eye and had his nose smashed in an auto accident near San Bernardino, California, on 11/19/1954; returned to performing in January 1955. Frequent appearances on TV, Broadway and in movies. Member of **The Rat Pack**.

AWARD: Grammy: Lifetime Achievement 2001

5/14/55	❶³	14		1 **Starring Sammy Davis, Jr.**		Decca 8118
				LP: Decca DL-8118 (#1³); EP: Decca ED-2214 (#1¹)		
10/15/55	5	5		2 **Just For Lovers**		Decca 8170
				LP: Decca DL-8170 (#5); EP: Decca ED-2285 (#11)		
10/20/62	14	22		3 What Kind Of Fool Am I And Other Show-Stoppers		Reprise 6051
3/16/63	96	6		4 Sammy Davis Jr. At The Cocoanut Grove .... [L]		Reprise 6063 [2]
5/25/63	73	15		5 As Long As She Needs Me		Reprise 6082
3/14/64	139	3		6 Sammy Davis Jr. Salutes The Stars Of The London Palladium		Reprise 6095
4/4/64	26	18		7 The Shelter Of Your Arms		Reprise 6114
3/27/65	141	4		8 Our Shining Hour		Verve 8605
				SAMMY DAVIS, JR. & COUNT BASIE		
9/4/65	104	4		9 Sammy's Back On Broadway		Reprise 6169
1/11/69	24	25		10 I've Gotta Be Me		Reprise 6324
4/29/72	11	26		11 Sammy Davis Jr. Now		MGM 4832
10/14/72	128	15		12 Portrait Of Sammy Davis, Jr.		MGM 4852

DAVIS, Skeeter

Born Mary Penick on 12/30/1931 in Dry Ridge, Kentucky. Died of cancer on 9/19/2004 (age 72). Country singer. Married to DJ/TV host Ralph Emery (1960-64) and **NRBQ** bassist Joey Spampinato (1983-96).

AWARD: OPRY: 1959

4/13/63	61	15		1 The End Of The World		RCA Victor 2699

DAVIS, Spencer, Group

Born on 7/17/1939 in Swansea, South Wales. Singer/rhythm guitarist. Formed his R&B-styled rock band in Birmingham, England, in 1963. Featured **Steve Winwood** (vocals, guitar, keyboards), his brother Muff Winwood (bass) and Pete York (drums). Steve Winwood left in 1967 to form **Traffic**.

3/25/67	54	25		1 Gimme Some Lovin'		United Artists 6578
7/15/67	83	9		2 I'm A Man		United Artists 6589
3/30/68	195	3		3 Spencer Davis' Greatest Hits .... [G]		United Artists 6641
9/22/73	206	4		4 Gluggo		Vertigo 1015

DAVIS, Tyrone

Born on 5/4/1938 in Greenville, Mississippi; raised in Saginaw, Michigan. Died of a stroke on 2/9/2005 (age 66). R&B singer. His younger sister, Jean Davis, was a member of **Facts Of Life**.

3/29/69	146	6		1 Can I Change My Mind		Dakar 9005
7/11/70	90	11		2 Turn Back The Hands Of Time		Dakar 9027
7/1/72	182	6		3 I Had It All The Time		Dakar 76901
8/11/73	174	6		4 Without You In My Life		Dakar 76904
10/2/76	89	9		5 Love And Touch		Columbia 34268
4/7/79	115	12		6 In The Mood With Tyrone Davis		Columbia 35723
1/8/83	137	6		7 Tyrone Davis		Highrise 103

DAVIS, Wild Bill — see HODGES, Johnny

DAWN

Pop vocal trio formed in New York: Tony Orlando (from Manhattan, New York), Telma Hopkins (from Louisville, Kentucky) and Joyce Vincent (from Detroit, Michigan). Orlando was manager for April-Blackwood Music at the time of trio's first hit. Own TV show from 1974-76. Hopkins later acted on TV's *Bosom Buddies*, *Gimme A Break* and *Family Matters*.

12/19/70+	35	23		1 Candida		Bell 6052
				also see #6 below		
				DAWN FEATURING TONY ORLANDO:		
12/18/71	178	2		2 Dawn Featuring Tony Orlando		Bell 6069
				also see #7 below		
3/24/73	30	34	●	3 Tuneweaving		Bell 1112
10/20/73+	43	58	●	4 Dawn's New Ragtime Follies		Bell 1130
				TONY ORLANDO & DAWN:		
12/7/74+	16	17		5 Prime Time		Bell 1317
1/18/75	170	4		6 Candida & Knock Three Times .... [R]		Bell 1320
				reissue of album #1 above		
1/11/75	165	5		7 Tony Orlando & Dawn II .... [R]		Bell 1322
				reissue of album #2 above		
4/26/75	20	17		8 He Don't Love You (Like I Love You)		Elektra 1034
6/28/75	16	32	●	9 Greatest Hits .... [G]		Arista 4045
11/1/75	93	6		10 Skybird		Arista 4059
3/20/76	94	6		11 To Be With You		Elektra 1049

DAY, Bobby
Born Robert Byrd on 7/1/1930 in Ft. Worth, Texas. Died of cancer on 7/15/1990 (age 60). R&B singer/songwriter. Formed the Hollywood Flames in 1950. One-half of the duo **Bob & Earl** from 1957-60.

~ ~ ~ ~ ~ ~ ~ ~ ~ ~ ~ ~ **NON-CHARTED ALBUM** ~ ~ ~ ~ ~ ~ ~ ~ ~ ~ ~

1959 Rockin' With Robin

DAY, Doris
1950s: #20

Born Doris Kappelhoff on 4/3/1922 in Cincinnati, Ohio. Singer/actress. Lead singer with Les Brown's big band. Starred in several movies. Star of own TV series from 1968-73.

AWARD: Grammy: Lifetime Achievement 2008

2/5/55	11	3	1 Young At Heart .... [S]	Columbia 6339
			EP: Columbia B-455 (#11); LP: Columbia CL-6339 (#15)	
6/25/55	❶⁹	15	2 Love Me Or Leave Me .... [S]	Columbia 710
			EP: Columbia EPB-540 (#1⁹); LP: Columbia CL-710 (#1⁹)	
2/9/57	11	6	3 Day By Day	Columbia 942
5/30/60	26	7	4 Listen To Day	Columbia DD1
10/2/61	97	8	5 I Have Dreamed	Columbia 1660 / 8460
3/14/64	102	8	6 Love Him!	Columbia 2131 / 8931
12/30/67	92ˣ	1	7 The Doris Day Christmas Album .... [X]	Columbia 2226 / 9026
			first released in 1964	

DAY, Howie
Born on 1/15/1981 in Bangor, Maine. Pop-rock singer/songwriter.

5/17/03	135	1	1 The Madrigals .... [EP]	Epic 89083
10/25/03	46	41	● 2 Stop All The World Now	Epic 86807
9/26/09	82	1	3 Sound The Alarm	Epic 93801

DAY, Morris
Born on 12/13/1957 in Springfield, Illinois; raised in Minneapolis, Minnesota. Lead singer of **The Time**. Acted in several movies.

10/19/85	37	31	1 Color Of Success	Warner 25320
3/12/88	41	15	2 Daydreaming	Warner 25651
7/10/04	197	1	3 It's About Time .... [L]	Hollywood 162435

DAYE, Cory
Born on 4/25/1952 in the Bronx, New York. Female singer. Member of **Dr. Buzzard's Original Savannah Band**.

10/13/79	171	5	1 Cory And Me	New York Int'l. 3408

DAYNE, Taylor
Born Leslie Wunderman on 3/7/1962 in Baldwin, Long Island, New York. White female dance/pop singer.

1/30/88	21	69	▲² 1 Tell It To My Heart .... **Cat**:#42/2	Arista 8529
11/18/89+	25	55	▲² 2 Can't Fight Fate	Arista 8581
7/31/93	51	22	● 3 Soul Dancing	Arista 18705
2/23/08	179	1	4 Satisfied	Intention 200203

DA YOUNGSTA'S
Hip-hop trio from Philadelphia, Pennsylvania: brothers Taji Goodman and Qur'an Goodman, with Tarik Dawson.

5/8/93	126	5	1 The Aftermath	EastWest 92245

DAYS OF THE NEW
Rock band from Louisville, Kentucky: Travis Meeks (vocals), Todd Whitener (guitar), Jesse Vest (bass) and Matt Taul (drums). Whitener, Vest and Taul left in 1999 to form **Tantric**; Meeks continued group name as a solo project.

9/13/97	54	56	▲ 1 Days Of The New	Outpost 30004
9/18/99	40	10	2 Days Of The New	Outpost 30037
10/13/01	91	2	3 Days Of The New	Outpost 490767

DAYTON FAMILY, The
Rap group from Flint, Michigan: brothers Eric Dorsey and Ira ("**Bootleg**") Dorsey, with Matt Hinkle and Raheen Peterson.

10/19/96	45	7	1 F.B.I.	Relativity 1544
6/8/02	107	5	2 Welcome To The Dope House	In The Paint 8313

DAY TO REMEMBER, A
Heavy metal band from Ocala, Florida: Jeremy McKinnon (vocals), Tom Denney (guitar), Neil Westfall (guitar), Joshua Woodard (bass) and Alex Shelnutt (drums).

2/21/09	21	21	1 Homesick	Victory 448

DAY26
R&B vocal group assembled by **P.Diddy** for the reality TV series *Making The Band 4*: Brian Andrews, Robert Curry, Michael McCluney, Qwanell Mosley and Willie Taylor.

4/12/08	❶¹	14	1 DAY26	Bad Boy 444540
5/2/09	2¹	9	2 Forever In A Day	Bad Boy 517897

DAZZ BAND
Funk-dance band from Cleveland, Ohio: Skip Martin (vocals), Eric Fearman (guitar), Bobby Harris (sax), Pierre DeMudd (trumpet), Kevin Frederick (keyboards), and brothers Michael Wiley (bass) and Isaac Wiley (drums). First known as **Kinsman Dazz**.

12/9/78+	203	4	1 Kinsman Dazz	20th Century 574
6/27/81	154	11	2 Let The Music Play	Motown 957
4/3/82	14	34	● 3 Keep It Live	Motown 6004

Billboard			R I A A	ARTIST		
DEBUT	PEAK	WKS		Album Title	Catalog	Label & Number

DAZZ BAND — cont'd

2/12/83	59	16		4 On The One		Motown 6031
12/17/83+	73	33		5 Joystick		Motown 6084
10/20/84	83	29		6 Jukebox		Motown 6117
8/17/85	98	12		7 Hot Spot		Motown 6149
8/30/86	100	11		8 Wild And Free		Geffen 24110

D-BLOCK
Collective of various rappers on the D-Block record label.

6/27/09	39	3		1 No Security		D-Block 5091

dB's, The
Pop-rock band from Chapel Hill, North Carolina: Peter Holsapple (vocals, keyboards), Jeff Beninato (guitar), Gene Holder (bass) and Will Rigby (drums). Holsapple married Susan Cowsill of **The Cowsills** on 4/18/1993.

11/28/87	171	8		1 The Sound Of Music		I.R.S. 42055

DC TALK
Contemporary rock/hip-hop Christian trio from Washington DC: Toby "**TobyMac**" McKeehan (born on 10/22/1964), Michael Tait (born on 5/18/1966) and Kevin Smith (born on 8/17/1967).

12/9/95	16	79	▲²	1 Jesus Freak		ForeFront 25140
				Grammy: Rock Gospel Album		
9/13/97	109	11	●	2 Welcome To The Freak Show [L]		ForeFront 25184
				Grammy: Rock Gospel Album		
10/10/98	4	38	▲	3 Supernatural		ForeFront 46525
12/9/00	81	14	●	4 Intermission: The Greatest Hits [G]		ForeFront 25274
5/12/01	142	3		5 Solo [EP]		ForeFront 25296
				Grammy: Rock Gospel Album		

DEACON, Dan
Born on 8/28/1981 in West Babylon, New York; raised in Baltimore, Maryland. Electronic musician.

4/11/09	199	1		1 Bromst [I]		Carpark 48

DEAD BOYS
Punk-rock band from Cleveland, Ohio: Stiv Bators (vocals), Gene Connor (guitar), Jimmy Zero (guitar), Jeff Magnum (bass) and Johnny Blitz (drums). Bators later formed **Lords Of The New Church**. Bators died on 6/4/1990 (age 40) after being hit by a car in Paris, France.

10/22/77	189	4		1 Young, Loud And Snotty		Sire 6038
7/22/78	206	2		2 We Have Come For Your Children		Sire 6054

DEAD BY SUNRISE
Hard-rock band formed in Los Angeles, California: Chester Bennington (vocals), Ryan Shuck (guitar), Amir Derakh (guitar), Brandon Belsky (bass) and Elias Andra (drums). Bennington is also lead singer of **Linkin Park**. Shuck and Derakh are also members of **Orgy**.

10/31/09	29	3		1 Out Of Ashes		Warner 520658

DEAD CAN DANCE
Alternative-pop duo formed in Australia: Lisa Gerard (vocals) and Brendan Perry (guitar).

10/2/93	122	11		1 Into The Labyrinth		4 A D 45384
11/12/94	131	3		2 Toward The Within		4 A D 45769
7/13/96	75	8		3 Spiritchaser		4 A D 46230

DEAD KENNEDYS
Punk-rock band formed in San Francisco, California: Eric "Jello Biafra" Boucher (vocals), Raymond "East Bay Ray" Pepperell (guitar), Jeff "Klaus Fluoride" Lyall (bass) and Darren "D.H. Pelligro" Henley (drums).

2/21/81	204	2		1 Fresh Fruit For Rotting Vegetables		I.R.S. 70014

DEAD MILKMEN, The
Punk-rock band from Philadelphia, Pennsylvania: Rodney "Anonymous" Linderman (vocals), Joe "Joe Jack Talcum" Genaro (guitar), David "Dave Blood" Schulthise (bass) and Dean "Clean" Sabatino (drums). Schulthise committed suicide on 3/10/2004 (age 47).

8/1/87	163	7		1 Bucky Fellini		Enigma 73260
12/24/88+	101	23		2 Beelzebubba		Enigma 73351
6/2/90	164	7		3 Metaphysical Graffiti		Enigma 73564

DEAD ON
Hard-rock band from Long Island, New York: Mike Raptis (vocals), Michael Caronia (guitar), Tony Frazzitta (guitar), John Linder (bass) and Mike Caputo (drums).

2/10/90	159	6		1 Dead On		SBK 93249

DEAD OR ALIVE
Dance band from Liverpool, England: Pete Burns (vocals), Tim Lever (keyboards), Mike Percy (bass) and Steve Coy (drums).

7/13/85	31	20	●	1 Youthquake		Epic 40119
12/27/86+	52	25		2 Mad, Bad, And Dangerous To Know		Epic 40572
7/30/88	195	2		3 Rip It Up [K]		Epic 44255
7/22/89	106	9		4 Nude		Epic 45224

Billboard			R A A	ARTIST		
DEBUT	PEAK	WKS		Album Title	Catalog	Label & Number

DEAD PREZ
Male rap duo from Brooklyn, New York: Clayton Gavin and Lavon Alford.

4/1/00	73	10	1 Lets Get Free		Loud 1867
11/8/03	144	1	2 Turn Off The Radio The Mixtape Vol. 2: Get Free Or Die Tryin'		Boss Up 9228
4/17/04	60	4	3 RBG: Revolutionary But Gangsta		Columbia 89050

DEADSY
Rock band from Los Angeles, California: P. Exeter Blue I (vocals, guitar), Carlton Megalodon (guitar), Dr. Nner (keyboards), Creature (bass) and Alec Pure (drums). P. Exeter Blue I is actually Elijah Blue, the son of **Cher** and **Gregg Allman**.

6/1/02	100	3	1 Commencement		Elementree 450301
9/9/06	176	1	2 Phantasmagore		Elementree 60027

DEAD WEATHER, The
Rock band formed in Nashville, Tennessee: Alison Mosshart (female vocals), Jack White (male vocals, drums), Dean Fertita (guitar) and Jack Lawrence (bass). White is a member of **The White Stripes**. Mosshart is a member of **The Kills**. Both White and Lawrence are members of **The Raconteurs**.

8/1/09	6	10	1 Horehound		Third Man 519785

DEAL, Bill, & The Rhondels
Brassy-rock band from Virginia Beach, Virginia: Bill Deal (vocals, organ), Bob Fisher (guitar), Mike Kerwin, Jeff Pollard, Ronny Rosenbaum and Ken Dawson (horn section), Don Queinsenburry (bass) and Ammon Tharp (drums). Deal died of a heart attack on 12/10/2003 (age 59).

4/11/70	185	2	1 The Best Of Bill Deal & The Rhondels .... [G]		Heritage 35006

DEAN, Billy
Born on 4/2/1962 in Quincy, Florida. Country singer/songwriter/guitarist.

5/25/91	99	26	● 1 Young Man		Capitol 94302
7/4/92	88	37	● 2 Billy Dean		Capitol 96728
2/13/93	83	16	● 3 Fire In The Dark		Liberty 98947
4/2/94	148	11	● 4 Greatest Hits .... [G]		Liberty 28357
4/20/96	143	5	5 It's What I Do		Capitol 30525
4/16/05	50	3	6 Let Them Be Little		Curb 78662

DEAN, Jimmy
Born on 8/10/1928 in Plainview, Texas. Died on 6/13/2010 (age 81). Country singer/pianist/guitarist. Hosted own CBS-TV series (1957-58); ABC-TV series (1963-66). Business interests include a restaurant chain and a line of pork sausage. Married country singer Donna Meade on 10/27/1991.

12/4/61+	23	28	1 Big Bad John And Other Fabulous Songs And Tales		Columbia 1735 / 8535
11/3/62	144	2	2 Portrait Of Jimmy Dean		Columbia 1894 / 8694
12/11/65	13ˣ	8	3 Jimmy Dean's Christmas Card .... [X]		Columbia 2404 / 9204
			Christmas charts: 13/'65, 37/'66, 80/'67		

DEAN, Paul
Born on 2/19/1946 in Calgary, Alberta, Canada. Rock singer/guitarist. Member of **Loverboy**.

2/25/89	195	2	1 Hard Core		Columbia 44462

DeANDA, Paula
Born on 11/3/1989 in San Angelo, Texas. Teen pop singer/songwriter.

9/16/06	54	19	1 Paula DeAnda		Arista 83611

DEAR HUNTER, The
Rock band formed in Boston, Massachusetts: brothers Casey Crescenzo (vocals) and Nick Crescenzo (drums), Erick Serna (guitar), Andy Wildrick (keyboards) and Nate Patterson (bass).

7/11/09	182	1	1 Act III: Life And Death		Triple Crown 03091

DEATH ANGEL
Hard-rock band from San Francisco, California: Mark Osegueda (vocals), Rob Cavestany (guitar), brothers Gus Pepa (guitar) and Dennis Pepa (bass), and Andy Galeon (drums). All members are related.

8/6/88	143	11	1 Frolic Through The Park		Enigma 73332

DEATH CAB FOR CUTIE
Pop-rock band from Bellingham, Washington: Benjamin Gibbard (vocals, guitar), Chris Walla (keyboards), Nick Harmer (bass) and Jason McGerr (drums). Gibbard also formed **The Postal Service**.

10/25/03	97	2	● 1 Transatlanticism .... Cat:#47/2		Barsuk 32
9/17/05	4	50	▲ 2 Plans		Barsuk 83834
5/31/08	❶¹	32	● 3 Narrow Stairs		Barsuk 452796
10/4/08	135	1	4 iTunes: Live From Las Vegas Exclusively At The Palms .... [EP-L]		Barsuk digital
4/18/09	42	8	5 The Open Door .... [EP]		Barsuk 518246

DEAUVILLE, Ronnie
Born on 8/28/1925 in Miami, Florida. Died on 12/24/1990 (age 65). Male singer with **Ray Anthony**'s band from 1950-51.

12/9/57	13	2	1 Smoke Dreams		Era 20002

DeBARGE

R&B family band from Grand Rapids, Michigan: **El DeBarge** (keyboards) with brothers Mark (trumpet, saxophone), James (keyboards), Randy (bass) and sister **Bunny DeBarge** (vocals). Their brothers Bobby and Tommy were in **Switch**; brother **Chico DeBarge** also recorded. James was briefly married to **Janet Jackson** in 1984.

9/11/82+	24	48	●	1 All This Love		Gordy 6012
10/22/83+	36	40	●	2 In A Special Way		Gordy 6061
3/23/85	19	48	●	3 Rhythm Of The Night		Gordy 6123

DeBARGE, Bunny

Born on 3/15/1955 in Grand Rapids, Michigan. Female singer. Member of **DeBarge**.

3/14/87	172	5		1 In Love		Motown 6217

DeBARGE, Chico

Born Jonathan DeBarge on 6/23/1966 in Grand Rapids, Michigan. Male singer. DeBarge sibling, but not a member of the group **DeBarge**. Served six years in prison in the early 1990s for conpiracy to sell drugs.

11/15/86+	90	30		1 Chico DeBarge		Motown 6214
12/6/97	86	38	●	2 Long Time No See		Kedar 53088
11/13/99	41	7		3 The Game		Motown 153263
8/1/09	93	2		4 Addiction		Reality 00004

DeBARGE, El

Born Eldra DeBarge on 6/4/1961 in Grand Rapids, Michigan. Male singer/songwriter. Lead singer of **DeBarge**.

6/21/86	24	23	●	1 El DeBarge		Gordy 6181
6/18/94	137	7		2 Heart, Mind & Soul		Reprise 45375

DeBARGE, Kristinia

Born on 3/8/1990 in Pasadena, California. Female R&B singer. Daughter of James DeBarge (of family group **DeBarge**).

8/15/09	23	6		1 Exposed		Soda Pop 013094

DeBURGH, Chris

Born Christopher Davison on 10/15/1948 in Buenos Aires, Argentina (of Irish parentage). Adult Contemporary singer/songwriter. DeBurgh was his mother's maiden name.

4/9/83	43	22		1 The Getaway		A&M 4929
6/30/84	69	19		2 Man On The Line		A&M 5002
9/20/86+	25	32	●	3 Into The Light		A&M 5121

DeCARO, Nick

Born on 6/23/1938 in the Bronx, New York. Died on 3/4/1992 (age 53). Prolific record producer/arranger/conductor.

4/19/69	165	5		1 Happy Heart [I]		A&M 4176

DECEMBERADIO

Christian rock band from Christiansburg, Virginia: Josh Reedy (vocals, bass), Brian Bunn (guitar), Eric Miker (guitar) and Boone Daughdrill (drums).

9/13/08	116	1		1 Satisfied		Slanted 1140

DECEMBERISTS, The

Alternative-pop band from Portland, Oregon: Colin Meloy (vocals, guitar), Chris Funk (guitar), Jenny Conlee (keyboards), Jesse Emerson (bass) and Rachel Blumberg (drums).

4/9/05	128	2		1 Picaresque		Kill Rock Stars 60425
10/21/06	35	17		2 The Crane Wife		Capitol 35984
4/4/09	14	13		3 The Hazards Of Love		Capitol 14710

DECO

Funk duo from Akron, Ohio: Phillip Ingram and Zane Giles. Ingram, the brother of **James Ingram**, was also a member of **Switch**.

3/23/85	209	2		1 Fast Forward [S]		Qwest 25263

DECYFER DOWN

Christian hard-rock band from Morehead City, North Carolina: T.J. Harris (vocals), Brandon Mills (guitar), Chris Clonts (bass) and Josh Oliver (drums).

5/23/09	66	4		1 Crash		Ino 09359

DEE, Dave — see DAVE DEE

DEE, Joey, & the Starliters

Born Joseph DiNicola on 6/11/1940 in Passaic, New Jersey. Rock and roll singer. Appeared in the movies *Hey, Let's Twist* and *Two Tickets To Paris*.

12/11/61+	2[6]	40		1 Doin' The Twist At The Peppermint Lounge [L]		Roulette 25166
2/17/62	18	23		2 Hey, Let's Twist! [S]		Roulette 25168
6/30/62	97	7		3 Back At The Peppermint Lounge-Twistin' [L]		Roulette 25173

~ ~ ~ ~ ~ ~ ~ ~ ~ ~ **NON-CHARTED ALBUMS** ~ ~ ~ ~ ~ ~ ~ ~ ~ ~ ~ ~

1962 **All The World Is Twistin'!**   1963 **Joey Dee**

DEE, Kiki

Born Pauline Matthews on 3/6/1947 in Bradford, Yorkshire, England. Female pop-rock singer.

6/15/74	202	3		1 Loving & Free		Rocket 395
11/16/74	28	18		2 I've Got The Music In Me		Rocket 458
				THE KIKI DEE BAND		
5/14/77	159	5		3 Kiki Dee		Rocket 2257

Billboard	R I A A	ARTIST		
DEBUT	PEAK	WKS	Album Title	Catalog	Label & Number

DEE, Lenny
Born Leonard DeStoppelaire on 1/5/1923 in Chicago, Illinois. Male organist.

7/9/55	11	3	1 **Dee-lightful!** .... [I]	Decca 8114
6/8/68	196	3	2 **Gentle On My Mind** .... [I]	Decca 74994
3/8/69	199	2	3 **Turn Around, Look At Me** .... [I]	Decca 75073
1/3/70	189	3	4 **Spinning Wheel** .... [I]	Decca 75152

DEEE-LITE
Dance trio formed in New York: Super DJ Dmitry Brill (from Kirovograd, Soviet Union), Jungle DJ Towa "Towa" Tei (from Tokyo, Japan) and vocalist Lady Miss Kier (Kier Kirby from Youngstown, Ohio). Group's name inspired by the tune "It's De-lovely" from the 1936 Cole Porter musical *Red, Hot & Blue*. Brill and Kier are married. Tei left by 1994, replaced by Ani.

9/15/90	20	41	● 1 **World Clique**	Elektra 60957
7/11/92	67	8	2 **Infinity Within**	Elektra 61313
8/20/94	127	4	3 **Dewdrops In The Garden**	Elektra 61526

DEELE, The
R&B band from Cincinnati, Ohio: Darnell "Dee" Bristol and Carlos "Satin" Greene (lead vocals), Stanley Burke (guitar), Kenny "**Babyface**" Edmonds (keyboards; **Manchild**), Kevin Roberson (bass) and Antonio "L.A." Reid (drums). Edmonds and Reid later formed LaFace Records. Reid then became president of Arista Records.

2/4/84	78	19	1 **Street Beat**	Solar 60285
7/6/85	155	8	2 **Material Thangz**	Solar 60410
2/27/88	54	25	● 3 **Eyes Of A Stranger**	Solar 72555

DEEP BLUE SOMETHING
Pop-rock band from Dallas, Texas: brothers Todd Pipes (vocals, bass) and Toby Pipes (guitar), Kirk Tatom (guitar) and John Kirtland (drums).

9/9/95+	46	35	● 1 **Home**	RainMaker 92608

DEEP FOREST
Experimental keyboard duo from France: Michel Sanchez and Eric Mouquet.

8/21/93+	59	25	● 1 **Deep Forest** .... [F]	550 Music 57840
7/8/95	62	12	2 **Boheme** .... [F]	550 Music 67115
3/7/98	127	5	3 **Comparsa** .... [F]	550 Music 68726

DEEP PURPLE   **All-Time: #191**
Hard-rock band from England: Rod Evans (vocals), **Ritchie Blackmore** (guitar), Jon Lord (keyboards), Nicky Simper (bass) and Ian Paice (drums). Evans and Simper left in 1969; replaced by Ian Gillan (vocals) and **Roger Glover** (bass). Evans formed **Captain Beyond**. Gillan and Glover left in late 1973; replaced by **David Coverdale** (vocals) and Glenn Hughes (bass). Blackmore left in early 1975 to form **Rainbow** (which Glover later joined); replaced by American **Tommy Bolin** (ex-**James Gang** guitarist; died on 12/4/1976). Band split in July 1976. Coverdale formed **Whitesnake**. Blackmore, Lord, Paice, Gillan and Glover reunited in 1984. Hughes joined **Black Sabbath** as vocalist in 1986. Gillan (who was with Black Sabbath for 1983 *Born Again* album) left in 1989 to form Garth Rockett & The Moonshiners; replaced by **Joe Lynn Turner** (ex-Rainbow), then returned in 1992 to take Turner's place.

9/7/68	24	23	1 **Shades Of Deep Purple**	Tetragrammaton 102
1/11/69	54	14	2 **The Book Of Taliesyn**	Tetragrammaton 107
7/12/69	162	6	3 **Deep Purple**	Tetragrammaton 119
9/12/70	143	21	● 4 **Deep Purple In Rock**	Warner 1877
8/21/71	32	18	● 5 **Fireball**	Warner 2564
4/15/72+	7	118	▲² 6 **Machine Head**	Warner 2607
1/20/73	15	49	● 7 **Who Do We Think We Are!**	Warner 2678
3/2/74	9	30	● 8 **Burn**	Warner 2766
12/7/74	20	15	● 9 **Stormbringer**	Warner 2832
12/6/75+	43	14	10 **Come Taste The Band**	Warner 2895
12/1/84+	17	32	▲ 11 **Perfect Strangers**	Mercury 824003
1/31/87	34	22	12 **The House Of Blue Light**	Mercury 831318
11/10/90	87	19	13 **Slaves And Masters**	RCA 2421
8/21/93	192	1	14 **The Battle Rages On...**	Giant 24517
			GREATEST HITS & COMPILATIONS:	
10/21/72	57	20	15 **(Purple Passages)**	Warner 2644 [2]
10/21/78	201	6	16 **When We Rock, We Rock And When We Roll, We Roll**	Warner 3223
11/1/80	148	4	▲ 17 **Deepest Purple/The Very Best Of Deep Purple**	Warner 3486
			LIVE ALBUMS:	
5/16/70	149	8	18 **Deep Purple/The Royal Philharmonic Ork. "Concerto For Group And Orchestra"**. recorded at the Royal Albert Hall	Warner 1860
4/21/73	6	52	▲ 19 **Made In Japan** recorded on 8/17/1972 in Tokyo, Japan	Warner 2701 [2]
11/27/76	148	6	20 **Made In Europe**	Warner 2995
7/17/82	206	1	21 **Deep Purple In Concert** .... recorded in 1970 and 1972	Portrait 38050 [2]
7/23/88	105	9	22 **Nobody's Perfect**	Mercury 835897 [2]

Billboard			R I A A	ARTIST		
DEBUT	PEAK	WKS		Album Title	Catalog	Label & Number

DEERHOOF
Experimental-rock band from San Francisco, California: Satomi Matsuzaki (vocals, bass), John Dietrich (guitar), Ed Rodriguez (guitar) and Greg Saunier (drums).

2/10/07	152	1		1 Friend Opportunity	Kill Rock Stars 472
10/25/08	150	1		2 Offend Maggie	Kill Rock Stars 485

DEERHUNTER
Alternative-rock band from Atlanta, Georgia: Bradford Cox (vocals), Lockett Pundt (guitar), Josh Fauver (bass) and Moses Archuleta (drums).

11/15/08	123	2		1 Microcastle	Kranky 127

DEES, Rick, And His Cast Of Idiots
Born Rigdon Dees on 3/14/1950 in Jacksonville, Florida. One of America's top radio DJs.

3/5/77	157	5		1 The Original Disco Duck................................... [N]	RSO 3017

DEES, Stephen
Born in Philadelphia, Pennsylvania. Pop-rock singer/songwriter/bassist.

5/21/77	207	2		1 Hip Shot	RCA Victor 2186

DEFAULT
Rock band from Vancouver, British Columbia, Canada: Dallas Smith (vocals), Jeremy Hora (guitar), David Benedict (bass) and Daniel Craig (drums).

11/17/01+	51	47	▲	1 The Fallout	TVT 2310
12/13/03	105	3		2 Elocation	TVT 6000
10/29/05	90	2		3 One Thing Remains	TVT 6060

DEF LEPPARD   1980s: #45 / 1990s: #32 / All-Time: #119
Hard-rock band from Sheffield, Yorkshire, England: Joe Elliott (vocals; born on 8/1/1959), Steve Clark (guitar; born on 4/23/1960; died of alcohol-related respiratory failure on 1/8/1991, age 30), Pete Willis (guitar; born on 2/16/1960), Rick Savage (bass; born on 12/2/1960) and Rick Allen (drums; born on 11/1/1963). Phil Collen (born on 12/8/1957) replaced Willis in late 1982. Allen lost his left arm in a car crash on 12/31/1984. Guitarist Vivian Campbell (born on 8/25/1962; formerly of **Whitesnake** and **Dio**) joined in April 1992.

5/3/80	51	51	▲	1 On Through The Night	Mercury 3828
8/8/81	38	106	▲²	2 High 'n' Dry	Mercury 4021
				also see #4 below	
2/5/83	2²	116	▲¹⁰	3 Pyromania Cat:#24/11	Mercury 810308
				RS500 #384	
6/2/84	72	18		4 High 'n' Dry .... [R]	Mercury 818836
				added remixed version of "Bringin' On The Heartbreak" plus "Me & My Wine" (previously unavailable)	
8/22/87+	❶⁶	133	▲¹²	5 Hysteria Cat:#2¹/129	Mercury 830675
				RS500 #472	
4/18/92	❶⁵	65	▲³	6 Adrenalize	Mercury 512185
10/23/93	9	26	▲	7 Retro Active .... [K]	Mercury 518305
				compilation of previously unreleased songs and alternate versions	
11/18/95	15	66	▲⁴	8 Vault: Greatest Hits 1980-1995 .... Cat:❶⁶/433 [G]	Mercury 528815
6/1/96	14	12	●	9 Slang	Mercury 532486
6/26/99	11	16	●	10 Euphoria..	Mercury 546212
8/17/02	11	8		11 X	Island 063121
6/4/05	10	30	▲	12 Rock Of Ages: The Definitive Collection .... [G]	Island 004647 [2]
6/10/06	16	11		13 Yeah!	Bludgeon Riffola 005340
5/17/08	5	8		14 Songs From The Sparkle Lounge	Bludgeon Riffola 011004

DeFRANCO FAMILY Featuring Tony DeFranco
Family vocal group from Port Colborne, Ontario, Canada: Tony, Merlina, Nino, Marisa and Benny DeFranco.

10/13/73	109	16		1 Heartbeat, It's A Lovebeat	20th Century 422
6/29/74	163	7		2 Save The Last Dance For Me	20th Century 441

DEF SQUAD
All-star rap trio: **Keith Murray**, **Redman** and **Erick Sermon**.

7/18/98	2¹	11		1 El Nino	Def Jam 558343

DEFTONES
Alternative-rock band from Sacramento, California: Chino Moreno (vocals), Stephen Carpenter (guitar), Chi Cheng (bass) and Abe Cunningham (drums). Moreno also formed **Team Sleep**.

11/11/00	46ᶜ	1	▲	1 Adrenaline.. [E]	Maverick 46054
				released in 1995	
11/15/97	29	17	●	2 Around The Fur	Maverick 46810
7/8/00	3¹	38	▲	3 White Pony	Maverick 47667
6/7/03	2¹	13	●	4 Deftones	Maverick 48350
10/22/05	43	3		5 B-Sides & Rarities .... [K]	Maverick 76460
11/18/06	10	8		6 Saturday Night Wrist	Maverick 43239

Billboard			R I A A	ARTIST Album Title	Catalog	Label & Number
DEBUT	PEAK	WKS				

DeGARMO, Diana
Born on 6/16/1987 in Snellville, Georgia. Female vocalist. Finished in second place on the 2004 season of TV's *American Idol*.

| 12/25/04 | 52 | 4 | | 1 Blue Skies .... | | RCA 64490 |

DEGRAW, Gavin
Born on 2/4/1977 in South Fallsburg, New York. Pop-rock singer/songwriter.

8/9/03+	103	12	▲	1 Chariot		J Records 20058
8/14/04	56	59	▲	2 Chariot-Stripped		J Records 63461 [2]
				contains acoustic versions of songs from #1 above		
5/24/08	7	14		3 Gavin DeGraw		J Records 06291
11/29/08	167	1		4 iTunes: Live From Soho .... [L]		J Records digital
4/18/09	19	3		5 Free		J Records 47478

DEJA
Male-female R&B duo from Dayton, Ohio: Curt Jones and Starleana Young. Both were members of **Slave** and **Aurra**.

| 12/5/87+ | 186 | 6 | | 1 Serious .... | | Virgin 90601 |

DEKKER, Desmond, & The Aces
Born Desmond Dacris on 7/16/1941 in Kingston, Jamaica. Died of a heart attack on 5/25/2006 (age 64). Reggae singer.

| 9/6/69 | 153 | 3 | | 1 Israelites.. | | Uni 73059 |

DE LA HOYA, Oscar
Born on 2/4/1973 in Montebello, California. Professional boxer.

| 10/28/00 | 121 | 5 | | 1 Oscar De La Hoya .... [F] | | EMI Latin 21967 |

DEL AMITRI
Pop-rock band from Glasgow, Scotland: Justin Currie (vocals, bass), David Cummings (guitar), Iain Harvie (guitar) and Brian McDermott (drums).

4/7/90	95	19		1 Waking Hours		A&M 5287
9/26/92	178	3		2 Change Everything		A&M 5385
8/26/95	170	8		3 Twisted		A&M 540311
7/12/97	160	1		4 Some Other Sucker's Parade		A&M 540705

DELANEY & BONNIE & FRIENDS
Folk-rock duo: Delaney Bramlett (born on 7/1/1939 in Pontotoc County, Mississippi; died on 12/27/2008, age 69) and wife Bonnie Bramlett (born on 11/8/1944 in Alton, Illinois). Married fom 1967-72. Backing artists (Friends) included, at various times, **Leon Russell**, **Rita Coolidge**, **Dave Mason**, **Eric Clapton**, **Duane Allman** (**Allman Brothers Band**) and many others. Friends **Bobby Whitlock**, Carl Radle and Jim Gordon later became Eric Clapton's Dominos. Their daughter Bekka was the lead singer of **Mick Fleetwood**'s Zoo, then joined **Fleetwood Mac** briefly in 1993. Also see **Eric Clapton**.

7/26/69	175	3		1 Accept No Substitute - The Original Delaney & Bonnie & Friends		Elektra 74039
4/18/70	29	17		2 Delaney & Bonnie & Friends On Tour with Eric Clapton .... [L]		Atco 326
10/10/70	58	10		3 To Bonnie From Delaney		Atco 341
4/3/71	65	23		4 Motel Shot		Atco 358
4/15/72	133	6		5 D&B Together		Columbia 31377

DE LA SOUL
Alternative-rap trio from Amityville, Long Island, New York: Kelvin "Posdnous" Mercer, David "Trugoy the Dove" Jolicoeur and Vincent "Pasemaster Mase" Mason.

4/1/89	24	29	▲	1 3 Feet High And Rising		Tommy Boy 1019
				RS500 #346		
6/1/91	26	17	●	2 De La Soul Is Dead..		Tommy Boy 1029
10/9/93	40	7		3 Buhloone Mindstate		Tommy Boy 1063
7/20/96	13	9		4 Stakes Is High		Tommy Boy 1149
8/26/00	9	12		5 Art Official Intelligence: Mosaic Thump		Tommy Boy 1361
12/22/01	136	1		6 AOI: Bionix		Tommy Boy 1362
10/23/04	87	5		7 The Grind Date		AOI 87526

DELBERT & GLEN — see McCLINTON, Delbert

DELEGATION
Disco trio formed in England: Ricky Bailey and Ray Patterson (from Jamaica), with Bruce Dunbar (from Texas).

| 2/17/79 | 84 | 16 | | 1 The Promise Of Love .... | | Shadybrook 010 |

DELFONICS, The
R&B vocal group from Philadelphia, Pennsylvania: brothers William Hart and Wilbert Hart, Ritchie Daniels and Randy Cain. Daniels left for the service in 1968, group continued as a trio. Cain was replaced by **Major Harris** in 1971. Harris went solo in 1974. Cain died on 4/9/2009 (age 63).

6/8/68	100	6		1 La La Means I Love You		Philly Groove 1150
3/8/69	155	6		2 Sound Of Sexy Soul..		Philly Groove 1151
11/29/69+	111	19		3 The Delfonics Super Hits .... [G]		Philly Groove 1152
8/15/70	61	18		4 The Delfonics		Philly Groove 1153
6/24/72	123	11		5 Tell Me This Is A Dream		Philly Groove 1154
4/6/74	205	4		6 Alive & Kicking		Philly Groove 1501

DEL FUEGOS, The

Rock band from Boston, Massachusetts: brothers Dan Zanes (vocals, guitar) and Warren Zanes (guitar), Tom Lloyd (bass) and Woody Giessmann (drums). Warren Zanes and Giessmann left in 1988; replaced by Adam Roth and Joe Donnelly.

DEBUT	PEAK	WKS				
10/26/85	132	34		1 Boston, Mass.		Slash 25339
4/18/87	167	6		2 Stand Up		Slash 25540
10/28/89	139	22		3 Smoking In The Fields		RCA 9860

DELILAH

Born in Philadelphia, Pennsylvania. Female R&B-disco singer.

2/24/79	209	1		1 Dancing In The Fire		ABC 1131

DELINQUENT HABITS

Latino hip-hop trio from Los Angeles, California: Kemo (David Thomas) and Ives (Ivan Martin) with DJ/producer O.G. Style (Alejandro Martinez).

6/22/96	74	8		1 Delinquent Habits		Loud 66929

DELIRIOUS?

Christian rock band from Littlehampton, West Sussex, England: Martin Smith (vocals), Stuart Garrard (guitar), Tim Jupp (keyboards), Jon Thatcher (bass) and Stewart Smith (drums).

6/26/99	137	1		1 Mezzamorphis		Sparrow 51677
10/28/00	177	1		2 Glo		Sparrow 51739

DEL-LORDS, The

Rock band formed in New York: Scott Kempner (vocals, guitar), Eric Ambel (guitar), Manny Caiati (bass) and Frank Funaro (drums). Kempner was a member of the **Dictators**.

2/2/85	203	4		1 Frontier Days		EMI America 17133

DELLS, The

R&B vocal group from Harvey, Illinois: Johnny Carter (lead; born on 6/2/1934; died of lung cancer on 8/21/2009, age 75), Marvin Junior (baritone lead; born on 1/31/1936), Verne Allison (tenor; born on 6/22/1936), Mickey McGill (baritone; born on 2/17/1937) and Chuck Barksdale (bass; born on 6/11/1935).

AWARD: R&R Hall of Fame: 2004

5/25/68	29	29		1 There Is		Cadet 804
3/8/69	146	10		2 The Dells Musical Menu/Always Together		Cadet 822
6/14/69	102	22		3 The Dells Greatest Hits	[G]	Cadet 824
8/23/69	54	24		4 Love Is Blue		Cadet 829
3/14/70	126	12		5 Like It Is, Like It Was		Cadet 837
8/28/71	81	16		6 Freedom Means		Cadet 50004
6/24/72	162	5		7 The Dells Sing Dionne Warwicke's Greatest Hits		Cadet 50017
6/23/73	99	9		8 Give Your Baby A Standing Ovation		Cadet 50037
11/3/73	202	6		9 The Dells		Cadet 50046
5/4/74	156	6		10 The Dells vs. The Dramatics		Cadet 60027
9/21/74	114	8		11 The Mighty Mighty Dells		Cadet 60030
3/1/75	210	1		12 The Dells Greatest Hits Volume 2	[G]	Cadet 60036
9/20/75	207	1		13 We Got To Get Our Thing Together		Cadet 60044
6/25/77	208	1		14 They Said It Couldn't Be Done, But We Did It		Mercury 1145
2/18/78	204	3		15 Love Connection		Mercury 3711
9/23/78	169	3		16 New Beginnings		ABC 1100
3/3/79	203	4		17 Face To Face		ABC 1113
8/30/80	137	12		18 I Touched A Dream		20th Century 618

~ ~ ~ ~ ~ ~ ~ ~ ~ ~ **NON-CHARTED ALBUM** ~ ~ ~ ~ ~ ~ ~ ~ ~ ~
1959 **Oh, What A Nite**

DELL-VIKINGS, The

Interracial doo-wop group formed in Pittsburgh, Pennsylvania: Clarence Quick, Kripp Johnson, Norman Wright, Dave Lerchey and William Blakely. Quick died of a heart attack on 5/5/1983 (age 46). Johnson died on 6/22/1990 (age 57).

~ ~ ~ ~ ~ ~ ~ ~ ~ ~ **NON-CHARTED ALBUMS** ~ ~ ~ ~ ~ ~ ~ ~ ~ ~
1957 **Come Go With The Del Vikings**   1958 **Swinging, Singing Record Session**
1957 **They Sing...They Swing**

DeLORY, Al

Born on 1/31/1930 in Los Angeles, California. Prolific producer/arranger/conductor. Sang in the pop trio The Balladeers.

3/13/71	220	2		1 Love Story	[I]	Capitol 677

DEL THA FUNKY HOMOSAPIEN

Born Teren Jones on 8/12/1972 in Oakland, California. Male rapper. Cousin of **Ice Cube**. Member of **Deltron 3030**.

12/11/93	125	1		1 No Need For Alarm		Elektra 61529
4/29/00	118	1		2 Both Sides Of The Brain		Hiero Imperium 230103
3/29/08	122	1		3 Eleventh Hour		Definitive Jux 156

DELTRON 3030

Hip-hop trio: **Del Tha Funkee Homosapien**, Dan Nakamura and Kid Koala. Nakamura later formed **Gorillaz**, **Handsome Boy Modeling School** and **Head Automatica**.

11/4/00	194	1		1 Deltron 3030		75 Ark 75033

DeLUCA, Rocco, & The Burden
Born on 12/27/1975 in Torrance, California. Alternative-rock singer/songwriter/guitarist.

2/3/07	177	1		1 I Trust You To Kill Me		Ironworks 165
3/28/09	123	1		2 Mercy		Ironworks 012672

DeLUNA, Kat
Born Kathleen DeLuna on 11/17/1987 in the Bronx, New York. R&B-dance singer/songwriter.

8/25/07	58	4		1 9 Lives		Epic 04023

DEMENSIONS, The
White pop vocal group from the Bronx, New York: Lenny Dell, Marisa Martelli, Howard Margolin and Charlie Peterson.

~ ~ ~ ~ ~ ~ ~ ~ ~ ~ **NON-CHARTED ALBUM** ~ ~ ~ ~ ~ ~ ~ ~ ~ ~

1963 **My Foolish Heart**

DEM FRANCHIZE BOYZ
Hip-hop group from Atlanta, Georgia: Maurice "Parlac" Gleaton, Bernard "Jizzal Man" Leverette, Jamal "Pimpin" Willingham and Gerald "Buddie" Tiller.

10/2/04	106	4		1 Dem Franchize Boyz		Tight 2 Def 003274
2/25/06	5	27	●	2 On Top Of Our Game		So So Def 53423
10/18/08	118	1		3 Our World, Our Way		Koch 4585

DEMIAN, Max — see MAX DEMIAN

DEMON HUNTER
Christian hard-rock band from California: brothers Ryan Clark (vocals) and Donald Clark (guitar), Kris McCaddon (guitar), Jon Dunn (bass) and Jesse Sprinkle (drums).

11/12/05	136	1		1 The Triptych		Solid State 31606
11/24/07	85	1		2 Storm The Gates Of Hell		Solid State 95605

DENNEN, Brett
Born on 10/28/1979 in Oakdale, Claifornia. Folk-pop singer/songwriter/guitarist.

11/8/08	41	2		1 Hope For The Hopeless		Downtown 1425

DENNEY, Kevin
Born on 1/27/1976 in Monticello, Kentucky. Country singer/songwriter/guitarist.

5/11/02	119	2		1 Kevin Denney		Lyric Street 65020

DENNIS, Cathy
Born on 3/25/1969 in Norwich, Norfolk, England. White dance/pop singer/songwriter.

12/15/90+	67	40		1 Move To This		Polydor 847267

DENNIS, Cheri
Born on 8/7/1979 in Cleveland, Ohio; later based in New York. Female R&B singer.

3/15/08	74	2		1 In And Out Of Love		Bad Boy 83952

DENNY, Martin (The Exotic Sounds of)   1950s: #41
Born on 4/10/1911 in Manhattan, New York. Died on 3/2/2005 (age 93). Composer/arranger/pianist. Originated "The Exotic Sounds of Martin Denny" in Hawaii, featuring Julius Wechter (of **Baja Marimba Band**) on vibes and marimba.

5/4/59	❶⁵	63		1 Exotica	[I]	Liberty 7034
8/31/59+	8	71		2 Quiet Village	[I]	Liberty 7122
11/23/59	50	1		3 Exotica-Vol. III	[I]	Liberty 7116
9/29/62	6	27		4 A Taste Of Honey	[I]	Liberty 7237
1/16/65	123	7		5 Hawaii Tattoo	[I]	Liberty 7394

DENNY, Sandy
Born Alexandra Denny on 1/6/1941 in Wimbledon, London, England. Died of a brain hemorrhage on 4/21/1978 (age 37). Lead singer of **Fairport Convention**.

1/6/73	204	4		1 Sandy		A&M 4371
7/20/74	197	2		2 Like An Old Fashioned Waltz		Island 9340

DENVER, John   1970s: #15 / All-Time: #75
Born Henry John Deutschendorf on 12/31/1943 in Roswell, New Mexico. Died on 10/12/1997 (age 53) at the controls of a light plane that crashed off the California coast. Country-pop singer/songwriter/guitarist. With the **Chad Mitchell Trio** from 1964-68. Wrote "Leaving On A Jet Plane." Starred in the 1977 movie *Oh, God.*

AWARD: CMA: Entertainer 1975

10/25/69	148	3		1 Rhymes & Reasons		RCA Victor 4207
5/2/70	197	2		2 Take Me To Tomorrow		RCA Victor 4278
4/17/71	15	80	▲	3 Poems, Prayers & Promises		RCA Victor 4499
12/4/71+	75	16	●	4 Aerie		RCA Victor 4607
9/16/72+	4	53	▲²	5 Rocky Mountain High		RCA Victor 4731
6/16/73	16	35	●	6 Farewell Andromeda		RCA Victor 0101

DENVER, John — cont'd

6/29/74	❶¹	96	▲³	7 Back Home Again		RCA Victor 0548
10/4/75	❶²	45	▲²	8 Windsong		RCA Victor 1183
9/4/76	7	30	▲	9 Spirit		RCA Victor 1694
12/3/77+	45	25	▲	10 I Want To Live		RCA Victor 2521
1/27/79	25	15	●	11 John Denver		RCA Victor 3075
3/1/80	39	17		12 Autograph		RCA Victor 3449
7/4/81	32	30	●	13 Some Days Are Diamonds		RCA Victor 4055
3/20/82	39	33		14 Seasons Of The Heart		RCA Victor 4256
6/25/83	202	1		15 Rocky Mountain Holiday		RCA Victor 4721

JOHN DENVER & THE MUPPETS

10/15/83	61	15		16 It's About Time		RCA Victor 4683
7/6/85	90	19		17 Dreamland Express		RCA Victor 5458
11/10/90	185	6		18 The Flower That Shattered The Stone		Windstar 53334
11/1/97	165	1		19 All Aboard!		Sony Wonder 63412

CHRISTMAS ALBUMS:

11/8/75	14	11	▲²	20 Rocky Mountain Christmas		RCA Victor 1201
				Christmas charts: 39/'98, 17/'05		
12/20/75+	138	6		21 John Denver Gift Pak	[R]	RCA Victor 1263 [2]
				consists of albums #8 & 20 in a special Christmas sleeve		
12/18/76+	115	5		22 Rocky Mountain Christmas	[R]	RCA Victor 1201
11/10/79+	26	12	▲	23 A Christmas Together	Cat:#13/10 [N]	RCA Victor 3451
				JOHN DENVER & THE MUPPETS		
				Christmas charts: 10/'83, 25/'96, 17/'97, 26/'98, 37/'01		
12/22/90	28ˣ	5		24 Christmas Like A Lullaby		Windstar 53335

GREATEST HITS & COMPILATIONS:

12/8/73+	❶³	175	▲⁹	25 John Denver's Greatest Hits	Cat:#5/11	RCA Victor 0374
3/5/77	6	18	▲²	26 John Denver's Greatest Hits, Volume 2	Cat:#13/3	RCA Victor 2195
11/24/84	203	8	●	27 Greatest Hits Volume 3		RCA Victor 5313
11/1/97	22ᶜ	1	▲	28 The Rocky Mountain Collection		RCA 66837 [2]
12/13/97	130	8		29 A Celebration Of Life (1943-1997) - The Last Recordings		River North 1360
5/20/00	9ᶜ	14		30 The Best Of John Denver		Madacy 4750
10/23/04	52	6		31 Definitive All-Time Greatest Hits		RCA 60764

LIVE ALBUMS:

3/8/75	2²	50	▲³	32 An Evening With John Denver		RCA Victor 0764 [2]
				recorded at the Universal Amiptheater in Los Angeles, California		
7/1/95	104	4	●	33 The Wildlife Concert		Legacy 64655 [2]
				recorded on 2/23/1995 at the Sony Music Studios in New York City		
11/1/97	52	10		34 The Best Of John Denver Live		Legacy 65183
				recorded on 2/23/1995 at Sony Studios in New York City		

DEODATO

Born Eumir Deodato on 6/21/1942 in Rio de Janeiro, Brazil. Keyboardist/producer/arranger.

1/20/73	3¹	26	1 Prelude	[I]	CTI 6021
8/11/73	19	35	2 Deodato 2	[I]	CTI 6029
8/18/73	213	2	3 Donato/Deodato	[I]	Muse 5017
3/23/74	114	9	4 In Concert	[I]	CTI 6041

DEODATO / AIRTO

5/4/74	63	16	5 Whirlwinds	[I]	MCA 410
11/16/74	102	9	6 Artistry	[I]	MCA 457
9/6/75	110	9	7 First Cuckoo	[I]	MCA 491
10/9/76	86	11	8 Very Together	[I]	MCA 2219
4/29/78	98	17	9 Love Island	[I]	Warner 3132
8/18/79	202	5	10 Knights Of Fantasy	[I]	Warner 3321
9/27/80	186	3	11 Night Cruiser	[I]	Warner 3467

DEPARTMENT OF EAGLES

Experimental-rock duo formed in Brooklyn, New York: Daniel Rossen (of **Grizzly Bear**) and Fred Nicolaus.

10/25/08	166	1	1 In Ear Park		4AD 2818

DEPECHE MODE   All-Time: #226

All-synthesized electro-pop band formed in Basildon, Essex, England: singer Dave Gahan (born on 5/9/1962) and synthesizer players **Martin L. Gore** (born on 7/23/1961), Vince Clarke (born on 7/3/1960) and Andy Fletcher (born on 7/9/1960). Clarke left in 1982 (formed **Yaz**, then **Erasure**), replaced by Alan Wilder (born on 6/1/1959; left in 1995). Group name is French for fast fashion.

12/26/81+	192	9		1 Speak & Spell		Sire 23642
12/4/82	177	8		2 A Broken Frame		Sire 23751
10/8/83	201	5		3 Construction Time Again		Sire 23900
7/28/84+	71	30	●	4 People Are People		Sire 25124
1/19/85	51	42	▲	5 Some Great Reward		Sire 25194
4/26/86	90	26	●	6 Black Celebration		Sire 25429
10/24/87	35	59	▲	7 Music For The Masses	Cat:#31/2	Sire 25614
4/7/90	7	74	▲³	8 Violator		Sire 26081
				RS500 #342		

Billboard DEBUT	PEAK	WKS	R I A A	ARTIST Album Title	Catalog	Label & Number
				DEPECHE MODE — cont'd		
4/10/93	❶¹	29	▲	9 **Songs Of Faith And Devotion**		Sire 45243
5/3/97	5	19	●	10 **Ultra**		Mute 46522
6/2/01	8	14	●	11 **Exciter**		Mute 47960
11/5/05	7	16		12 **Playing The Angel**		Sire 49348
5/9/09	3¹	10		13 **Sounds Of The Universe**		Mute 96769
				GREATEST HITS & COMPILATIONS:		
12/7/85+	113	18	▲	14 **Catching Up With Depeche Mode**		Sire 25346
2/6/99	114	3		15 **The Singles 81-85**		Mute 47298
10/24/98	38	10	▲	16 **The Singles 86-98**		Mute 47110 [2]
12/2/06	148	1		17 **The Best Of Depeche Mode: Volume 1**		Sire 44256
				LIVE ALBUMS:		
4/1/89	45	19	●	18 **101** .... [S]		Sire 25853 [2]
				recorded on 6/18/1988 at the Rose Bowl in Pasadena, California		
12/25/93	193	1		19 **Songs Of Faith And Devotion/Live...**		Sire 45505
				recorded in Copenhagen, Milan and New Orleans		

DEREK AND THE DOMINOS — see CLAPTON, Eric

DERRINGER, Rick
Born Richard Zehringer on 8/5/1947 in Celina, Ohio. Rock singer/guitarist. Member of **The McCoys** and the **Edgar Winter Group**. Producer for "**Weird Al**" Yankovic.

12/1/73+	25	31		1 **All American Boy**		Blue Sky 32481
4/26/75	141	8		2 **Spring Fever**		Blue Sky 33423
7/31/76	154	9		3 **Derringer**		Blue Sky 34181
2/19/77	169	3		4 **Sweet Evil**		Blue Sky 34470
7/16/77	123	10		5 **Derringer Live** .... [L]		Blue Sky 34848
11/3/79	203	1		6 **Guitars And Women**		Blue Sky 36092
10/25/80	205	1		7 **Face To Face**		Blue Sky 36551

DeSARIO, Teri
Born in Miami, Florida. Female dance-pop singer/songwriter.

| 1/19/80 | 80 | 13 | | 1 **Moonlight Madness**.......................... | | Casablanca 7178 |

DESCENDENTS
Punk-rock band from Los Angeles, California: Milo Aukerman (vocals), Stephen Egerton (guitar), Karl Alvarez (bass) and Bill Stevenson (drums).

| 10/12/96 | 132 | 1 | | 1 **Everything Sucks** .... | | Epitaph 86481 |
| 4/10/04 | 143 | 1 | | 2 **Cool To Be You** .... | | Fat Wreck Chords 672 |

DESERT ROSE BAND, The
Country band formed in California. Core members: **Chris Hillman** (vocals), John Jorgenson (mandolin) and Herb Pedersen (guitar). Hillman was a founding member of **The Byrds** and the **Flying Burrito Brothers**. Jorgenson left in 1992. Disbanded in early 1994.

| 2/17/90 | 187 | 4 | | 1 **Pages Of Life** .... | | MCA/Curb 42332 |

DeSHANNON, Jackie
Born Sharon Myers on 8/21/1944 in Hazel, Kentucky. Female singer/prolific songwriter. Married **Randy Edelman** on 6/3/1976.

11/1/69	81	15		1 **Put A Little Love In Your Heart**		Imperial 12442
7/22/72	196	2		2 **Jackie**		Atlantic 7231
12/3/77	203	5		3 **You're The Only Dancer**		Amherst 1010

~ ~ ~ ~ ~ ~ ~ ~ ~ ~ *NON-CHARTED ALBUMS* ~ ~ ~ ~ ~ ~ ~ ~ ~ ~ ~
1963 Jackie DeShannon   1965 This Is Jackie DeShannon
1964 Breakin' It Up On The Beatles Tour!

DESMOND, Paul
Born on 11/25/1924 in San Francisco, California. Died on 5/30/1977 (age 52). Jazz alto saxophonist with **Dave Brubeck**.

12/28/63+	129	3		1 **Take Ten** .... [I]		RCA Victor 2569
3/13/71	207	2		2 **Bridge Over Troubled Water** .... [I]		A&M 3032
1/10/76	167	5		3 **1975: The Duets** .... [I]		Horizon 703
				DAVE BRUBECK & PAUL DESMOND		

DE SOUZA, Raul
Born on 8/23/1934 in Rio de Janeiro, Brazil. Trombone player.

| 10/8/77 | 207 | 2 | | 1 **Sweet Lucy** .... [I] | | Capitol 11648 |
| 6/3/78 | 202 | 3 | | 2 **Don't Ask My Neighbors** .... [I] | | Capitol 11774 |

DESPERATION BAND
Collective of Christian singers/musicians based in Colorado Springs, Colorado. Led by Jared Anderson.

| 10/3/09 | 159 | 1 | | 1 **Light Up The World** .... | | Integrity 56278 |

DESPISED ICON
Deathcore band from Montreal, Quebec, Canada: Alexandre Erian (vocals), Steve Marois (vocals), Eric Jarrin (guitar), Ben Landreville (guitar), Max Lavelle (bass) and Alex Pelletier (drums).

| 10/10/09 | 162 | 1 | | 1 **Day Of Mourning** .... | | Century Media 8614 |

DES'REE
Born Des'ree Weeks on 11/30/1968 in London, England (West Indian parentage). Black female singer/songwriter.

11/19/94+	27	45	▲	1 I Ain't Movin'		550 Music 64324
9/5/98	185	2		2 Supernatural		550 Music 69508

DESTINY'S CHILD
Female R&B vocal group from Houston, Texas: **Beyonce** Knowles (born on 9/4/1981), **Kelly Rowland** (born on 2/11/1981), LaTavia Roberson (born on 11/1/1981) and LeToya Luckett (born on 3/11/1981). Roberson and Luckett left in early 2000; replaced by Farrah Franklin (born on 5/3/1981) and **Michelle Williams** (born on 7/23/1980). Franklin left shortly thereafter, leaving trio of Knowles, Rowland and Williams.

3/7/98	67	26	▲	1 Destiny's Child		Columbia 67728
8/14/99+	5	99	▲8	2 The Writing's On The Wall		Columbia 69870
5/19/01	❶2	46	▲4	3 Survivor		Columbia 61063
11/17/01	34	9	●	4 8 Days Of Christmas .... Cat:#23/6 **[X]**		Columbia 86098
				Christmas charts: 3/'01, 18/'02, 37/'05		
3/30/02	29	8		5 This Is The Remix **[K]**		Columbia 86431
11/27/04	2¹	50	▲3	6 Destiny Fulfilled		Columbia 92595
11/12/05	❶¹	30	▲	7 #1's **[G]**		Columbia 97765

DESTRI, Jimmy
Born on 4/13/1954 in Brooklyn, New York. Pop-rock keyboardist. Member of **Blondie**.

1/30/82	201	5		1 Heart On A Wall		Chrysalis 1368

DETECTIVE
Rock band from England: Michael Des Barres (vocals), Michael Monarch (guitar), Tony Kaye (keyboards; **Yes**), Bobby Pickett (bass) and Jon Hyde (drums). Des Barres was a member of **Silverhead**; later joined **Chequered Past**.

5/14/77	135	9		1 Detective		Swan Song 8417
1/14/78	103	12		2 It Takes One To Know One		Swan Song 8504

DETERGENTS, The
Novelty vocal trio from New York: Ron Dante (of **The Archies** and **The Cuff Links**), Tommy Wynn and Danny Jordan.

~ ~ ~ ~ ~ ~ ~ ~ ~ ~ **NON-CHARTED ALBUM** ~ ~ ~ ~ ~ ~ ~ ~ ~ ~ ~ ~
1965 **The Many Faces Of The Detergents**

DETHKLOK
Rock band created for the animated TV series *Metalocalypse* by Brendon Small and Tommy Blancha: Nathan Explosion (vocals), Skwisgaar Skwigelf (guitar), Toki Wartooth (guitar), William Murderface (bass) and Pickles (drums).

10/13/07	21	15		1 The Dethalbum		Williams Street 0002
10/17/09	15	9		2 Metalocalypse: Dethalbum II **[S]**		Williams Street 60008

DETROIT
Rock band from Detroit, Michigan: Mitch Ryder (vocals), Steve Hunter (guitar), Brett Tuggle (guitar), Dirty Ed (congas), Harry Phillips (keyboards), W.R. Cooke (bass) and John Badanjek (drums). Ryder and Badanjek were members of **Mitch Ryder And The Detroit Wheels**. Badanjek later joined the **Rockets**.

1/29/72	176	6		1 Detroit		Paramount 6010

DETROIT EMERALDS
R&B vocal trio from Little Rock, Arkansas: brothers Abrim Tilmon and Ivory Tilmon, with James Mitchell. Abrim Tilmon died of a heart attack on 7/6/1982 (age 37).

6/19/71	151	3		1 Do Me Right		Westbound 2006
2/5/72	78	13		2 You Want It, You Got It		Westbound 2013
4/21/73	181	4		3 I'm In Love With You		Westbound 2018

DeVAUGHN, Raheem
Born in Newark, New Jersey; raised in Maryland. Male R&B singer/songwriter.

7/16/05	46	6		1 The Love Experience		Jive 53723
2/2/08	5	27		2 Love Behind The Melody		Jive 19080

DeVAUGHN, William
Born in 1948 in Washington DC. R&B singer/songwriter/guitarist.

8/3/74	165	11		1 Be Thankful For What You Got		Roxbury 100

DEVICE
Pop-rock trio from Los Angeles, California: Paul Engemann (vocals), Holly Knight (keyboards, bass) and Gene Black (guitar). Engemann joined **Animotion** in 1988. Prolific songwriter Knight was also a member of **Spider**.

7/12/86	73	16		1 22B3		Chrysalis 41526

DEVILDRIVER
Hard-rock band from Los Angeles, California: Brad Fafara (vocals; **Coal Chamber**), Mike Spreitzer (guitar), Jeff Kendrick (guitar), Jon Miller (bass) and John Boecklin (drums). Fafara is the nephew of actor Stanley Fafara (played "Whitey Whitney" on TV's *Leave It To Beaver*).

7/16/05	117	1		1 The Fury Of Our Maker's Hand		Roadrunner 618321
8/18/07	48	4		2 The Last Kind Words		Roadrunner 618010
8/1/09	35	4		3 Pray For Villains		Roadrunner 617875

DeVILLE, Mink — see MINK

DEVIL WEARS PRADA, The
Christian heavy metal band from Dayton, Ohio: Mike Hranica (vocals), Chris Rubey (guitar), Jeremy DePoyster (guitar), Andy Trick (bass) and Daniel Williams (drums).

9/8/07	57	3	1 Plagues		Rise 51
5/23/09	11	13	2 With Roots Above And Branches Below		Ferret 123

DEVIN THE DUDE
Born Devin Copeland on 6/4/1970 in St. Petersburg, Florida; raised in Houston, Texas. Male rapper. Member of **Facemob**.

7/4/98	177	3	1 The Dude		Rap-A-Lot 45938
9/14/02	61	7	2 Just Trying Ta Live		J Prince 42003
			DEVIN (above 2)		
7/31/04	55	4	3 To Tha X-treme		J Prince 42038
4/7/07	30	7	4 Waitin' To Inhale		J Prince 6856
10/25/08	47	3	5 Landing Gear		Cinematic 83000

DeVITO, Karla
Born on 5/29/1953 in Mokena, Illinois. Singer/actress. Starred in the Broadway musical *The Pirates Of Penzance*. Married actor Robby Benson on 7/11/1982.

10/3/81	203	3	1 Is This A Cool World Or What?		Epic 37014

DeVITO, Louie
Born in Brooklyn, New York. Dance DJ/producer.

12/9/00+	93	22	1 New York City Underground Party Volume 3		E-lastik 5002
11/3/01	63	5	2 New York City Underground Party Volume 4		Dee Vee 0001
11/23/02	68	10	3 New York City Underground Party Volume 5		Dee Vee 0004 [2]
5/11/02	92	12	4 Louie DeVito's Dance Factory		Dee Vee 0002
7/5/03	132	5	5 Louie DeVito's Dance Factory Level 2		Dee Vee 0006
9/18/04	131	2	6 Louie DeVito's Dance Factory Level 3		Dee Vee 0011
5/3/03	174	3	7 Dance Divas		Dee Vee 0005
3/20/04	193	1	8 Dance Divas II		Dee Vee 0009

DEVO
Robotic rock-dance band from Akron, Ohio: brothers Mark Mothersbaugh (synthesizers) and Bob Mothersbaugh (vocals, guitar), brothers Jerry Casale (bass) and Bob Casale (guitar), and Alan Myers (drums). David Kendrick replaced Myers by 1988.

10/28/78	78	18	● 1 Q:Are We Not Men? A:We Are Devo!		Warner 3239
			RS500 #447		
6/30/79	73	10	2 Duty Now For The Future		Warner 3337
6/14/80	22	51	▲ 3 Freedom Of Choice		Warner 3435
4/18/81	50	12	4 DEV-O Live	[EP-L]	Warner 3548
10/10/81	23	25	5 New Traditionalists		Warner 3595
11/20/82	47	20	6 Oh, No! It's Devo		Warner 23741
11/3/84	83	6	7 Shout		Warner 25097
7/2/88	189	3	8 Total Devo		Enigma 73303

DeVOL, Frank
Born on 9/20/1911 in Moundsville, West Virginia; raised in Canton, Ohio. Died of heart failure on 10/27/1999 (age 88). Prolific composer/conductor/arranger. Composed the TV theme for *My Three Sons*. Married to singer Helen O'Connell from 1991-93 (her death).

1/6/62	102	2	1 The Old Sweet Songs Of Christmas	[X-I]	Columbia 1543 / 8343

DeVORZON, Barry
Born on 7/31/1934 in Brooklyn, New York. Prolific songwriter/producer/arranger. Leader of Barry & The Tamerlanes.

11/6/76+	42	19	1 Nadia's Theme (The Young And The Restless)	[I]	A&M 3412

3 cuts by DeVorzon and Perry Botkin, Jr.; others by various artists: "Bellavia" and "Chase The Clouds Away" by **Chuck Mangione**; "Emmanuel" by Michael Colombier; "Feelings" by Herb Ohta; "My Reverie" by Ira Sullivan; "Rainbow City" by **Tim Weisberg**; "Zero To Sixty In Five" by **Pablo Cruise**

11/6/76+	133	12	2 Nadia's Theme (The Young And The Restless)	[I]	Arista 4104

cuts by DeVorzon only

DEXYS MIDNIGHT RUNNERS
Pop-rock band from Birmingham, England: Kevin Rowland (vocals), Billy Adams (guitar), Brian Maurice (sax), Paul Speare (flute), Jimmy Patterson (trombone), Micky Billingham (piano), Giorgio Kilkenny (bass) and Seb Shelton (drums). Billingham was later with **General Public**.

2/12/83	14	24	1 Too-Rye-Ay		Mercury 4069

DeYOUNG, Dennis
Born on 2/18/1947 in Chicago, Illinois. Pop-rock singer/songwriter/keyboardist. Member of **Styx**.

10/6/84	29	25	1 Desert Moon		A&M 5006
3/29/86	108	8	2 Back To The World		A&M 5109

DFC
Rap duo from Flint, Michigan: Alpha Breed and T Double E. DFC: Da Funk Clan.

8/31/91	142	10	1 M.C. Breed & DFC		S.D.E.G. 4103
4/9/94	71	11	2 Things In Tha Hood		Assault 92320

DF DUB
Born William Green in Detroit, Michigan. White rapper. Worked as DJ "Billy The Kid" on WILD-FM in Dallas, Texas.

4/5/03	144	1	1 Country Girl		3Sixty 89089

D4, The
Punk-rock band from Auckland, New Zealand: Jimmy Christmas (vocals, guitar), Dion Palmer (vocals, guitar), Vaughan Williams (bass) and Dan Pooley (drums).

4/12/03	164	1		1 6twenty	Flying Nun 162388

D4L
Rap group from Atlanta, Georgia: Lefabian "Fabo" Williams, Dennis "Mook B" Butler, Adrian "Stoney" Parks and Carlos "**Shawty Lo**" Walker. D4L: Down For Life.

11/26/05	22	23	●	1 **Down For Life**	DeeMoney 83890

DFX2
Rock band from San Diego, California: brothers David Farage (vocals, guitar) and Douglas Farage (guitar), Eric Gotthelf (bass) and Frank Hailey (drums).

8/20/83	143	8		1 **Emotion** .... [EP]	MCA 36000

D.H.T.
Electronic-dance duo from Belgium: female singer Edmee Daenen and Flor "DJ Da Rick" Theeuwes. D.H.T.: Danger House Trance.

8/6/05	78	9		1 **Listen To Your Heart**	Robbins 75061

DIAMOND, Neil   1970s: #3 / 1980s: #20 / 1990s: #43 / All-Time: #9
Born on 1/24/1941 in Brooklyn, New York. Pop-rock singer/guitarist/prolific composer. Worked as songplugger/staff writer in New York City; also wrote under pseudonym Mark Lewis. His real name is Neil Diamond, however he considered changing his name to Noah Kaminsky early in his career. First recorded for Duel in 1960. Wrote for **The Monkees** TV show. Wrote score for the movie *Jonathan Livingston Seagull*. Starred in and composed the music for *The Jazz Singer* in 1980. America's top male vocalist from 1966-86.

10/29/66	137	4		1 The Feel Of Neil Diamond	Bang 214
9/16/67	80	19		2 Just For You	Bang 217
5/17/69	82	25	●	3 Brother Love's Travelling Salvation Show	Uni 73047
12/13/69+	30	47	●	4 Touching You Touching Me	Uni 73071
11/21/70	13	45	▲	5 Tap Root Manuscript	Uni 73092
11/13/71	11	25	●	6 Stones	Uni 93106
7/15/72	5	41	▲	7 Moods	Uni 93136
10/26/74	3[2]	27	▲	8 Serenade	Columbia 32919
7/4/76	4	33	▲	9 Beautiful Noise	Columbia 33965
				produced by **Robbie Robertson**	
12/3/77+	6	24	▲[2]	10 I'm Glad You're Here With Me Tonight	Columbia 34990
12/16/78+	4	29	▲[2]	11 You Don't Bring Me Flowers	Columbia 35625
1/12/80	10	20	▲	12 September Morn	Columbia 36121
11/28/81+	17	27	▲	13 On The Way To The Sky	Columbia 37628
10/16/82	9	34	▲	14 Heartlight	Columbia 38359
8/18/84	35	25	●	15 Primitive	Columbia 39199
5/24/86	20	23	●	16 Headed For The Future	Columbia 40368
1/7/89	46	16	●	17 The Best Years Of Our Lives	Columbia 45025
9/14/91	44	32	●	18 Lovescape	Columbia 48610
10/16/93	28	15	●	19 Up On The Roof - Songs From The Brill Building	Columbia 57529
2/24/96	14	18	●	20 Tennessee Moon	Columbia 67382
11/14/98	31	13	●	21 The Movie Album: As Time Goes By	Columbia 69540 [2]
8/11/01	15	14	●	22 Three Chord Opera	Columbia 85500
11/26/05	4	16	●	23 12 Songs	American 97811
5/24/08	❶[1]	18	●	24 Home Before Dark	Columbia 15465
				CHRISTMAS ALBUMS:	
10/24/92	8	15	▲[2]	25 The Christmas Album **Cat:#4/32**	Columbia 52914
				Christmas charts: 3/'92, 7/'93, 17/'94, 26/'95, 31/'96, 23/'97	
11/26/94	51	8	●	26 The Christmas Album Volume II .... **Cat:#19/10**	Columbia 66465
				Christmas charts: 9/'94, 29/'95, 28/'96	
10/31/09	60	11		27 A Cherry Cherry Christmas	Columbia 56892
				Christmas chart: 6/'09	
				GREATEST HITS & COMPILATIONS:	
8/3/68+	100	40		28 Neil Diamond's Greatest Hits	Bang 219
9/12/70	52	25		29 Shilo	Bang 221
2/27/71	100	6		30 Do It!	Bang 224
1/20/73	36	21		31 Double Gold	Bang 227 [2]
9/1/73	35	17	●	32 Rainbow	MCA 2103
6/8/74	29	42	▲[4]	33 Neil Diamond/His 12 Greatest Hits .... **Cat:#9/104**	MCA 2106
10/9/76	102	5		34 And The Singer Sings His Song	MCA 2227
9/19/81	201	4	●	35 Love Songs	MCA 5239
5/29/82	48	42	▲[3]	36 12 Greatest Hits, Vol. II .... **Cat:❶[2]/9**	Columbia 38068
6/25/83	171	7	▲	37 Classics · The Early Years .... **Cat:#16/46**	Columbia 38792

DEBUT	PEAK	WKS	R I A A	ARTIST / Album Title	Catalog	Label & Number
				DIAMOND, Neil — cont'd		
6/6/92	90	23	▲³	38 The Greatest Hits 1966-1992		Columbia 52703 [2]
11/16/96	122	5	●	39 In My Lifetime		Columbia 65013 [3]
8/18/01	26ᶜ	2	●	40 The Best Of Neil Diamond: 20th Century Masters The Millennium Collection		MCA 11947
12/22/01	90	11	▲	41 The Essential Neil Diamond	Cat.#17/5	Legacy 85681 [2]
				LIVE ALBUMS:		
8/22/70	10	56	▲²	42 Neil Diamond/Gold	Cat.#21/32	Uni 73084
				recorded at the Troubadour in Hollywood, California		
12/9/72+	5	78	▲²	43 Hot August Night		MCA 8000 [2]
				recorded on 8/24/1972 at the Greek Theatre in Los Angeles, California		
2/26/77	8	21	▲²	44 Love At The Greek		Columbia 34404 [2]
				recorded August 1976 at the Greek Theatre in Los Angeles, California		
11/21/87+	59	17	▲	45 Hot August Night II		Columbia 40990 [2]
7/16/94	93	4	●	46 Live In America		Columbia 66321 [2]
10/18/03	137	2		47 Stages: Performances		Columbia 90540 [5]
8/29/09	2¹	11		48 Hot August Night/NYC		Columbia 56001 [2]
				SOUNDTRACKS:		
11/3/73	2¹	34	▲²	49 Jonathan Livingston Seagull		Columbia 32550
				Grammy: Soundtrack Album		
11/29/80+	3⁷	115	▲⁵	50 The Jazz Singer		Capitol 12120

~ ~ ~ ~ ~ ~ ~ ~ ~ **NON-CHARTED ALBUMS** ~ ~ ~ ~ ~ ~ ~ ~ ~ ~ ~

1968 **Velvet Gloves And Spit**   1999 **The Neil Diamond Collection**
                                                                    RS500 #222

DIAMOND RIO

Country band formed in Nashville, Tennessee: Marty Roe (vocals; born on 12/28/1960), Jimmy Olander (guitar; born on 8/26/1961), Gene Johnson (mandolin; born on 8/10/1949), Dan Truman (piano; born on 8/29/1956), Dana Williams (bass; born on 5/22/1961) and Brian Prout (drums; born on 12/4/1955).
AWARDS: CMA: Vocal Group 1992, 1993, 1994 & 1997 ★ OPRY: 1998

DEBUT	PEAK	WKS	R I A A	ARTIST / Album Title	Catalog	Label & Number
6/15/91+	83	85	▲	1 Diamond Rio		Arista 8673
11/21/92+	87	21	●	2 Close To The Edge		Arista 18656
8/6/94	100	27	▲	3 Love A Little Stronger		Arista 18745
3/16/96	92	8	●	4 IV		Arista 18812
8/2/97	75	15	▲	5 Greatest Hits	[G]	Arista Nashville 18844
8/15/98	70	34	●	6 Unbelievable		Arista Nashville 18866
2/24/01	36	20	●	7 One More Day		Arista Nashville 67999
9/7/02	23	40	●	8 Completely		Arista Nashville 67046
5/27/06	62	13		9 Greatest Hits II	[G]	Arista Nashville 80981
10/27/07	18ˣ	2		10 A Diamond Rio Christmas: The Star Still Shines	[X]	Word-Curb/War. 887339

DIAMONDS, The

White doo-wop group from Toronto, Ontario, Canada: Dave Somerville (lead), Ted Kowalski (tenor), Phil Levitt (baritone) and Bill Reed (bass). Reed died on 10/22/2004 (age 68).

~ ~ ~ ~ ~ ~ ~ ~ ~ ~ **NON-CHARTED ALBUM** ~ ~ ~ ~ ~ ~ ~ ~ ~ ~ ~

1957 **The Diamonds - America's Number One**
        Singing Stylists

DIBANGO, Manu

Born on 2/10/1934 in Douala, Cameroon, Africa. Jazz-R&B saxophonist/pianist.

DEBUT	PEAK	WKS	R I A A	ARTIST / Album Title	Catalog	Label & Number
6/30/73	79	13		1 Soul Makossa	[I]	Atlantic 7267

DICKINSON, Bruce

Born Paul Bruce Dickinson on 8/7/1958 in Worksop, Nottinghamshire, England; raised in Sheffield, Yorkshire, England. Hard-rock singer. Lead singer of **Iron Maiden**.

DEBUT	PEAK	WKS	R I A A	ARTIST / Album Title	Catalog	Label & Number
5/26/90	100	17		1 Tattooed Millionaire		Columbia 46139
8/13/94	185	1		2 Balls To Picasso		Mercury 522491
6/11/05	180	1		3 Tyranny Of Souls		Sanctuary 84753

DICTATORS

Rock band from New York: Handsome Dick Manitoba (vocals), Ross "The Boss" Funicello (guitar), Scott "Top Ten" Kempner (guitar), Adny Shernoff (keyboards), Mark Mendoza (bass) and Ritchie Teeter (drums). Manitoba, Funicello and Shernoff later formed Manitoba's Wild Kingdom. Kempner formed **The Del-Lords**. Mendoza later joined **Twisted Sister**.

DEBUT	PEAK	WKS	R I A A	ARTIST / Album Title	Catalog	Label & Number
7/30/77	193	2		1 Manifest Destiny		Asylum 1109

DIDDLEY, Bo

Born Otha Ellas Bates McDaniels on 12/30/1928 in McComb, Mississippi; raised in Chicago, Illinois. Died of heart failure on 6/2/2008 (age 79). Highly influential singer/guitarist. Adopted as an infant by his mother's cousin, Mrs. Gussie McDaniel. Name "bo diddley" is a one-stringed African guitar.
AWARDS: Grammy: Lifetime Achievement 1998 ★ R&R Hall of Fame: 1987

DEBUT	PEAK	WKS	R I A A	ARTIST / Album Title	Catalog	Label & Number
11/24/62	117	4		1 Bo Diddley		Checker 2984
5/26/73	208	5		2 The London Bo Diddley Sessions		Chess 50029
2/14/76	207	1		3 The 20th Anniversary Of Rock 'N' Roll		RCA Victor 1229

Billboard			R I A A	ARTIST		
DEBUT	PEAK	WKS		Album Title	Catalog	Label & Number

DIDO
Born Florian Armstrong on 12/25/1971 in London, England. Female pop-rock singer/songwriter.

6/3/00+	4	69	▲⁴	1 No Angel	Cat:#3/27	Arista 19025
10/18/03	4	47	▲²	2 Life For Rent		Arista 50137
12/6/08	13	10		3 Safe Trip Home		Cheeky 30709

DIESEL
Rock band from the Netherlands: Rob Vunderink (vocals, guitar), Mark Boon (guitar), Frank Papendrecht (bass) and Pim Koopman (drums; died on 11/23/2009, age 56).

8/8/81	68	24		1 Watts In A Tank		Regency 19315

DIFFIE, Joe
Born on 12/28/1958 in Tulsa, Oklahoma; raised in Velma, Oklahoma. Country singer/songwriter/guitarist.
AWARD: OPRY: 1993

2/8/92	132	12	●	1 Regular Joe		Epic 47477
5/8/93+	67	53	▲	2 Honky Tonk Attitude		Epic 53002
8/13/94	53	54	▲	3 Third Rock From The Sun		Epic 64357
12/16/95	129	6		4 Mr. Christmas	[X]	Epic 67045
				Christmas chart: 32/'95		
1/13/96	167	7	●	5 Life's So Funny		Epic 67405
6/27/98	131	6		6 Greatest Hits	[G]	Epic 69137
6/19/99	189	1		7 A Night To Remember		Epic 69815

DIFFORD & TILBROOK
Pop-rock duo from London, England: Chris Difford (born on 4/11/1954) and Glenn Tilbrook (born on 8/31/1957).
Both were members of **Squeeze**.

7/14/84	55	15		1 Difford & Tilbrook		A&M 4985

DIFRANCO, Ani   **All-Time: #385**
Born on 9/23/1970 in Buffalo, New York. Adult Alternative singer/songwriter/guitarist. Founded the Righteous Babe record label.

6/8/96	87	4		1 Dilate		Righteous Babe 008
5/10/97	59	5	●	2 Living In Clip	[L]	Righteous Babe 011 [2]
3/7/98	22	10		3 Little Plastic Castle		Righteous Babe 012
2/6/99	29	7		4 Up Up Up Up Up Up		Righteous Babe 013
12/4/99	76	2		5 To The Teeth		Righteous Babe 017
4/28/01	50	6		6 Revelling/Reckoning		Righteous Babe 024 [2]
9/28/02	32	4		7 So Much Shouting/So Much Laughter	[L]	Righteous Babe 029 [2]
3/29/03	30	7		8 Evolve		Righteous Babe 030
2/7/04	37	3		9 Educated Guess		Righteous Babe 034
2/12/05	49	5		10 Knuckle Down		Righteous Babe 042
8/26/06	46	4		11 Reprieve		Righteous Babe 052
9/29/07	89	1		12 Canon	[K]	Righteous Babe 055 [2]
10/18/08	55	2		13 Red Letter Year		Righteous Babe 063

DIG
Rock band from San Diego, California: Scott Hackwith (vocals, guitar), Jon Morris (guitar), Johnny Cornwell (guitar), Phil Friedmann (bass) and Anthony Smedile (drums).

2/19/94	153	6		1 Dig		Radioactive 10916

DIGABLE PLANETS
Hip-hop trio from New York: Ishmael "Butterfly" Butler, Mary Ann "Ladybug" Vierra and Craig "Doodle Bug" Irving.

2/27/93	15	22	●	1 Reachin' (A New Refutation Of Time And Space)		Pendulum 61414
11/5/94	32	7		2 Blowout Comb		Pendulum 30654

DIGBY, Marie
Born on 4/16/1983 in New York; raised in Los Angeles, California. Pop singer/songwriter/guitarist.

4/26/08	29	4		1 Unfold		Hollywood 162610
9/26/09	183	2		2 Breathing Underwater		Hollywood digital

DIGGIN' IN THE CRATES — see D.I.T.C.

DIGITAL UNDERGROUND
Hip-hop group from Oakland, California: Gregory Jacobs (aka "Humpty-Hump" and "Shock-G"), Ron Brooks (aka "Money B"), Earl Cook (aka "Schmoovy-Schmoov"), James Dight (aka "Chopmaster J") and DJ Fuze. Tupac (**2Pac**) Shakur was a member in 1991. Group appeared in the 1991 movie *Nothing But Trouble*.

4/14/90	24	31	▲	1 Sex Packets	Cat:#22/11	Tommy Boy 1026
2/2/91	29	27	●	2 This Is An E.P. Release	[EP]	Tommy Boy 964
11/2/91	44	27	●	3 Sons Of The P		Tommy Boy 1045

DEBUT	PEAK	WKS		ARTIST / Album Title	Catalog	Label & Number
				DIGITAL UNDERGROUND — cont'd		
10/23/93	79	4		4 The Body-Hat Syndrome		Tommy Boy 1080
6/22/96	113	3		5 Future Rhythm		Critique 15452
				DILATED PEOPLES		
				Hip-hop trio from Los Angeles, California: Michael "Evidence" Perretta, Rakaa "Iriscience" Taylor and Christopher "DJ Babu" Oroc.		
6/10/00	74	7		1 The Platform		Capitol 23310
11/10/01	36	11		2 Expansion Team		Capitol 31477
4/24/04	55	9		3 Neighborhood Watch		Capitol 40889
3/11/06	97	2		4 20/20		ABB 11783
				DILLARDS, The		
				Country-rock band from Salem, Missouri: Rodney Dillard (vocals, guitar), Billy Ray Latham (banjo), Dean Webb (mandolin), Mitch Jayne (bass) and Paul York (drums). Also see **The Folkswingers**.		
6/10/72	79	18		1 Roots And Branches		Anthem 5901
1/19/74	211	1		2 Tribute To The American Duck		Poppy 175
				DILLINGER, Daz		
				Born Delmar Arnaud on 5/25/1972 in Long Beach, California. Male rapper. Member of **Tha Dogg Pound**. Cousin of **Snoop Doggy Dogg**.		
4/18/98	8	9		1 Retaliation, Revenge And Get Back		Death Row 53524
6/29/02	109	6		2 This Is The Life I Lead		OCF 0006
9/30/06	35	5		3 So So Gangsta DAZ		So So Def 69308
				DILLINGER ESCAPE PLAN, The		
				Hard-rock band from Morris Plains, New Jersey: Greg Puciato (vocals), Brain Benoit (guitar), Liam Wilson (bass) and Chris Pennie (drums).		
8/7/04	106	2		1 Miss Machine		Relapse 6587
12/1/07	142	1		2 Ire Works		Relapse 6699
				DILLMAN BAND, The		
				Country-rock band formed in Minneapolis, Minnesota: Steve Solmonson (vocals), Pat Frederick (guitar), Michael Wolf (piano), Steve Seamans (bass) and Dan Flaherty (drums). In 1980, Wolf departed; bassist Dik Shopteau joined and Seamans moved from bass to guitar.		
4/1/78	198	2		1 The Daisy Dillman Band		United Artists 838
5/16/81	145	7		2 Lovin' The Night Away		RCA Victor 3909
				DI MEOLA, Al		
				Born on 7/22/1954 in Jersey City, New Jersey. Jazz fusion guitarist. Member of **Return To Forever** from 1974-76.		
3/27/76	129	10		1 Land Of The Midnight Sun [I]		Columbia 34074
5/7/77	58	12	●	2 Elegant Gypsy [I]		Columbia 34461
4/29/78	52	17		3 Casino [I]		Columbia 35277
7/12/80	119	14		4 Splendido Hotel [I]		Columbia 36270 [2]
5/30/81	97	13		5 Friday Night In San Francisco [I-L] JOHN McLAUGHLIN / AL DI MEOLA / PACO DE LUCIA		Columbia 37152
2/6/82	55	13		6 Electric Rendezvous [I]		Columbia 37654
12/25/82+	165	7		7 Tour De Force - "Live" [I-L] recorded on 2/4/1982 at the Tower Theatre in Philadelphia, Pennsylvania		Columbia 38373
8/20/83	171	5		8 Passion, Grace & Fire [I] JOHN McLAUGHLIN / AL DI MEOLA / PACO DE LUCIA		Columbia 38645
10/29/83	128	6		9 Scenario [I]		Columbia 38944
1/23/88	190	1		10 Tirami Su [I] AL DI MEOLA PROJECT		EMI-Manhattan 46995
				DIMMU BORGIR		
				Death-metal band from Oslo, Norway: Shagrath (vocals), Galder (guitar), Silenoz (guitar), Mustis (keyboards), Vortex (bass) and Barker (drums).		
9/27/03	170	1		1 Death Cult Armageddon		Nuclear Blast 1047
5/12/07	43	2		2 In Sorte Diaboli		Nuclear Blast 1862
				DINNER, Michael		
				Born in 1953 in Denver, Colorado. Singer/songwriter/guitarist. Directed the 1985 movie *Heaven Help Us*.		
9/21/74	206	6		1 The Great Pretender		Fantasy 9454
8/28/76	204	4		2 Tom Thumb The Dreamer		Fantasy 9512
				DINNING, Mark		
				Born on 8/17/1933 in Drury, Oklahoma. Died of a heart attack on 3/22/1986 (age 52). Pop singer.		
				~ ~ ~ ~ ~ ~ ~ ~ ~ ~ **NON-CHARTED ALBUM** ~ ~ ~ ~ ~ ~ ~ ~ ~ ~		
				1960 **Teen Angel**		
				DINO		
				Born Dino Esposito on 7/20/1963 in Encino, California; raised in Hawaii and Connecticut. Pop-dance singer.		
3/25/89	34	48	●	1 24/7		4th & B'way 4011
9/8/90	82	21		2 Swingin'		Island 846481

DINO, DESI & BILLY

Vocal trio formed in Los Angeles, California: Dino Martin, Desi Arnaz Jr. and Billy Hinsche. Martin is the son of **Dean Martin**. Arnaz is the son of Lucille Ball and Desi Arnaz. Dino (formerly married to actress Olivia Hussey and to Olympic skater Dorothy Hamill) was killed on 3/21/1987 (age 35) when his Air National Guard jet crashed.

DEBUT	PEAK	WKS		Album Title		Label & Number
9/25/65	51	24		1 I'm A Fool		Reprise 6176
2/12/66	119	6		2 Our Time's Coming		Reprise 6194

DINOSAUR JR.

Rock trio from Amherst, Massachusetts: Joseph Mascis (vocals, guitar), Mike Johnson (guitar) and Patrick Murphy (drums). George Berz replaced Murphy in late 1993.

DEBUT	PEAK	WKS		Album Title		Label & Number
3/30/91	168	6		1 Green Mind		Sire 26479
2/27/93	50	15		2 Where You Been		Sire 45108
9/17/94	44	8		3 Without A Sound		Sire 45719
4/12/97	188	1		4 Hand It Over		Reprise 46506
5/19/07	69	3		5 Beyond		Fat Possum 1081
7/11/09	29	4		6 Farm		Jagjaguwar 150

DIO

Born Ronald Padavona on 7/10/1942 in Portsmouth, New Hampshire. Died of stomach cancer on 5/16/2010 (age 67). Stage name: Ronnie James Dio. Hard-rock singer. Former lead singer of **Black Sabbath** and **Rainbow**. His band: Vivian Campbell (guitar), Jimmy Bain (bass) and Vinnie Appice (drums; Black Sabbath; brother of **Carmine Appice**). Claude Schnell (keyboards) joined in 1984. Campbell left in 1986, replaced by Craig Goldie. Campbell also with **Whitesnake** and **Def Leppard**. Also see **Heaven & Hell**.

DEBUT	PEAK	WKS		Album Title		Label & Number
6/25/83	56	38	▲	1 Holy Diver		Warner 23836
7/21/84	23	35	▲	2 The Last In Line		Warner 25100
8/31/85	29	29	●	3 Sacred Heart		Warner 25292
6/28/86	70	16		4 Intermission	[EP-L]	Warner 25443
				recorded at the San Diego Sports Arena		
8/15/87	43	11		5 Dream Evil		Warner 25612
6/2/90	61	13		6 Lock Up The Wolves		Reprise 26212
2/19/94	142	2		7 Strange Highways		Reprise 45527
6/8/02	199	1		8 Killing The Dragon		Spitfire 15199

DION

Born Dion DiMucci on 7/18/1939 in the Bronx, New York. Formed doo-wop group, Dion & The Belmonts, in 1958. Consisted of Dion, Angelo D'Aleo, Fred Milano and Carlo Mastrangelo. Named for Belmont Avenue in the Bronx. Dion went solo in 1960 as did **The Belmonts**. Brief reunion with The Belmonts in 1967 and 1972, periodically since then.

AWARD: R&R Hall of Fame: 1989

DEBUT	PEAK	WKS		Album Title		Label & Number
11/27/61	11	51		1 Runaround Sue		Laurie 2009
7/14/62	12	22		2 Lovers Who Wander		Laurie 2012
12/15/62+	29	22		3 Dion Sings His Greatest Hits	[G]	Laurie 2013
3/23/63	20	21		4 Ruby Baby		Columbia 8810
6/22/63	115	6		5 Dion Sings To Sandy (and all his other girls)	[K]	Laurie 2017
12/21/68+	128	11		6 Dion		Laurie 2047
3/13/71	210	2		7 You're Not Alone		Warner 1872
1/1/72	200	2		8 Sanctuary		Warner 1945
12/2/72	197	4		9 Suite For Late Summer		Warner 2642
2/24/73	144	8		10 Reunion-Live At Madison Square Garden 1972	[L]	Warner 2664
				DION & THE BELMONTS		
				recorded on 6/2/1972		
3/24/73	194	5		11 Dion's Greatest Hits	[G]	Columbia 31942
5/20/89	130	19		12 Yo Frankie		Arista 8549

~ ~ ~ ~ ~ ~ ~ ~ ~ **NON-CHARTED ALBUMS** ~ ~ ~ ~ ~ ~ ~ ~ ~ ~ ~

1959 **Presenting Dion And The Belmonts**	1963 **Dion Sings The 15 Million Sellers**
1960 **Wish Upon A Star With Dion And The Belmonts**	1963 **Donna The Prima Donna** *[Dion DiMuci]*
1960 **Alone With Dion**	1964 **More Of Dion's Greatest Hits**
1963 **Love Came To Me**	

DION, Celine   1990s: #6 / All-Time: #118

Born on 3/30/1968 in Charlemagne, Quebec, Canada. Adult Contemporary singer. Youngest of 14 children. Began performing at age five. Wrote first song at age 12. Married her longtime manager, Rene Angelil, on 12/17/1994.

DEBUT	PEAK	WKS		Album Title	Catalog	Label & Number
1/19/91	74	26	▲	1 Unison	Cat:#27/5	Epic 46893
4/18/92	34	76	▲²	2 Celine Dion	Cat:#13/12	Epic 52473
11/27/93+	4	149	▲⁶	3 The Colour Of My Love	Cat:#3/64	550 Music 57555
3/30/96	❶³	113	▲¹¹	4 Falling Into You	Cat:#4/67	550 Music 67541
				Grammys: Album of the Year / Pop Vocal Album		
12/6/97+	❶¹	84	▲¹⁰	5 Let's Talk About Love	Cat:#31/4	550 Music 68861
11/21/98	2²	17	▲⁵	6 These Are Special Times	Cat:❶/83 [X]	550 Music 69523
				Christmas charts: 1/'98, 2/'99, 7/'00, 8/'01, 10/'02, 11/'03, 9/'04, 22/'05, 11/'06, 13/'07, 28/'08, 14/'09		

Billboard			R I A A	ARTIST		
DEBUT	PEAK	WKS		Album Title	Catalog	Label & Number

DION, Celine — cont'd

12/4/99	❶³	89	▲⁷	7 All The Way...A Decade Of Song Cat:#2⁵/183 **[G]**		550 Music 63760
11/11/00	28	17	●	8 The Collector's Series Volume One **[K]**		550 Music 85148
4/13/02	❶¹	60	▲³	9 A New Day Has Come		Epic 86400
4/12/03	2¹	32	▲²	10 One Heart		Epic 87185
7/3/04	10	18	●	11 A New Day...Live In Las Vegas **[L]**		Epic 92680
10/30/04	4	22	▲	12 Miracle		Epic 93453
12/1/07	3¹	26	▲	13 Taking Chances		Columbia 08114
11/15/08	8	25		14 My Love: Essential Collection **[G]**		Columbia 35413
12/19/09	149	2		15 These Are Special Times .... **[X-R]**		550 Music 69523

DIPLOMATS, The
Hip-hop group from Harlem, New York: brothers **Cam'ron** Giles, and Ezekiel **"Freekey Zekey"** Giles, with **Jim Jones** and LeRon **"Juelz Santana"** James. Group also recorded as **Dipset**.

4/12/03	8	18	●	1 Diplomatic Immunity		Roc-A-Fella 063211 [2]
12/11/04	46	9		2 Diplomatic Immunity 2		Diplomats 5771
7/30/05	22	5		3 More Than Music, Vol. 1		Diplomats 5835
5/26/07	26	3		4 More Than Music, Vol. 2		Diplomats 5898
				DIPSET (above 2)		

DIPSET — see DIPLOMATS, The

DIR EN GREY
Rock band from Osaka, Japan: Kyo (vocals), Kaoru (guitar), Die (guitar), Toshiya (bass) and Shinya (drums).

11/29/08	114	1		1 Uroboros		The End 123

DIRE STRAITS   **All-Time: #340**
Rock band formed in London, England: **Mark Knopfler** (vocals, guitar; born on 8/12/1949) and his brother David Knopfler (guitar; born on 12/27/1952), with John Illsley (bass) and Pick Withers (drums). David left in mid-1980, replaced by Hal Lindes (left in 1985). Added keyboardist Alan Clark in 1982. Terry Williams replaced drummer Pick Withers in 1983. Guitarist Guy Fletcher added in 1984. Mark and Guy were also members of **The Notting Hillbillies** in 1990. Lineup in 1991: Knopfler, Illsley, Fletcher and Clark, with Chris White (sax), Paul Franklin (pedal steel), Danny Cummings (percussion), Phil Palmer (guitar) and Chris Whitten (drums).

1/6/79	2¹	41	▲²	1 Dire Straits		Warner 3266
6/30/79	11	19	●	2 Communique		Warner 3330
11/15/80	19	31	▲	3 Making Movies		Warner 3480
10/16/82	19	32	●	4 Love Over Gold		Warner 23728
3/12/83	53	15		5 Twisting By The Pool .... **[EP]**		Warner 29800
4/21/84	46	18	●	6 Dire Straits Live - Alchemy .... **[L]**		Warner 25085 [2]
6/8/85	❶⁹	97	▲⁹	7 Brothers In Arms		Warner 25264
				RS500 #351		
11/12/88	62	17	▲	8 Money For Nothing .... **[G]**		Warner 25794
9/28/91	12	32	▲	9 On Every Street		Warner 26680
5/29/93	116	5		10 On The Night .... **[L]**		Warner 45259

DIRKSEN, Senator Everett McKinley
Born on 1/4/1896 in Pekin, Illinois. Died on 9/7/1969 (age 73). U.S. senator from Illinois (1950-69).

1/7/67	16	16		1 Gallant Men .... **[T]**		Capitol 2643
				Grammy: Spoken Word Album		
8/5/67	148	3		2 Man Is Not Alone .... **[T]**		Capitol 2754
12/23/67	52ˣ	2		3 Everett McKinley Dirksen At Christmas Time .... **[X-T]**		Capitol 2792

DIRT BAND, The — see NITTY GRITTY DIRT BAND

DIRTY
Rap duo from Montgomery, Alabama: Daniel Thomas and Tavares Webster.

3/17/01	88	17		1 The Pimp & Da Gangsta		Universal 013557
3/15/03	63	4		2 Keep It Pimp & Gangsta		Universal 018415
10/25/03	160	1		3 Love Us Or Hate Us		Nfinity 42030
9/3/05	186	1		4 Hood Stories		J Prince 68514

DIRTY LOOKS
Hard-rock band formed in Pennsylvania: Dutch-born Henrik Ostergaard (vocals, guitar), Paul Lidel (guitar), Jack Pyers (bass) and Gene Barnett (drums).

5/21/88	134	14		1 Cool From The Wire		Atlantic 81836
8/19/89	118	11		2 Turn Of The Screw		Atlantic 81992

DIRTY PRETTY THINGS
Punk-rock band from London, England: Carl Barat (vocals, guitar), Anthony Rossomando (guitar), Didz Hammond (bass) and Gary Powell (drums). Barat and Powell were members of **The Libertines**.

8/26/06	200	1		1 Waterloo To Anywhere		Interscope 007235

Billboard			R I A A	ARTIST		
DEBUT	PEAK	WKS		Album Title	Catalog	Label & Number

DIRTY PROJECTORS
Experimental-rock band formed in Brooklyn, New York: Haley Dekle (vocals), Dave Longstreth (guitar), Amber Coffman (guitar), Angel Deradoorian (keyboards), Nat Baldwin (bass) and Brian McOmber (drums).

6/27/09	65	5		1 Bitte Orca		Domino 217

DIRTY VEGAS
Electronica trio from England: producers Ben Harris, Paul Harris and Steve Smith.

6/22/02	7	19	●	1 Dirty Vegas		Credence 39986

DISCIPLE
Christian rock band from Knoxville, Tennessee: Kevin Young (vocals), Brad Noah (guitar), Joey Fife (bass) and Tim Barrett (drums).

11/25/06	118	1		1 Scars Remain		SRE 88920
11/8/08	98	1		2 Southern Hospitality		Ino 30462

DISCO TEX & HIS SEX-O-LETTES
Disco studio group assembled by producer **Bob Crewe**. Featuring lead voice Sir Monti Rock III (real name: Joseph Montanez).

5/3/75	36	22		1 Disco Tex & His Sex-O-Lettes		Chelsea 505

DISCOVERY
Alternative-rock duo formed in Brooklyn, New York: Wes Miles (of **Ra Ra Riot**) and Rostam Batmanglij (of **Vampire Weekend**).

7/25/09	89	1		1 LP		XL 446

DISHWALLA
Pop-rock band from Santa Barbara, California: J.R. Richards (vocals), Rodney Cravens (guitar), Scott Alexander (bass) and George Pendergast (drums). Jim Wood (keyboards) added in 1997.

5/18/96	89	34	●	1 Pet Your Friends		A&M 540319
8/29/98	164	1		2 And You Think You Know What Life's About		A&M 540948
5/11/02	192	1		3 Opaline		Immergent 282009

DISPATCH
Alternative-rock trio from Boston, Massachusetts: Brad Corrigan (vocals, guitar), Pete Francis (bass) and Chad Stokes (drums).

11/27/04	187	1		1 All Points Bulletin	[L]	Foundations 003676 [2]

DISTILLERS, The
Punk-rock band formed in Los Angeles, California: Brody Dalle (female vocals, guitar), Tony Bradley (male vocals, guitar), Ryan Sinn (bass) and Andy Granelli (drums). Sinn later joined **Angels And Airwaves**. Dalle was married to **Tim Armstrong** from 1997-2003.

11/1/03	97	1		1 Coral Fang		Hellcat 48586

DISTURBED
Heavy metal band from Chicago, Illinois: David Draiman (vocals), Dan Donegan (guitar), Steve "Fuzz" Kmak (bass) and Mike Wengren (drums). John Moyer (of **The Union Underground**) replaced Kmak in early 2003.

5/13/00	29	103	▲⁴	1 The Sickness	Cat:❶¹⁰/154	Giant 24738
10/5/02	❶¹	53	▲²	2 Believe		Reprise 48320
10/8/05	❶¹	80	▲	3 Ten Thousand Fists	Cat:#13/41	Reprise 49433
6/21/08	❶¹	67	▲	4 Indestructible		Reprise 411132

DISTURBING THA PEACE
Rap group from Atlanta, Georgia: **Ludacris**, **Shawnna**, **I-20**, Tity Boi, Jay Cee and Lil' Fate.

10/5/02	6	10		1 Golden Grain		Def Jam South 063205
12/31/05	11	21	●	2 Ludacris Presents Disturbing Tha Peace		DTP 005786
				LUDACRIS AND DTP		

D.I.T.C.
All-star rap group: **Big L**, **Fat Joe**, **O.C.**, Showbiz & AG, Diamond, Lord Finesse and Buckwild. DITC: Diggin' In The Crates.

3/11/00	141	2		1 D.I.T.C.		Tommy Boy 1304

DIVINE
Female R&B vocal trio from New Jersey: Nikki Bratcher, Kia Thornton and Tonia Tash.

11/14/98+	126	21		1 Fairy Tales		Pendulum 12325

DIVINE HERESY
Hard-rock band formed in Los Angeles, California: Travis Neal (vocals), Dino Cazares (guitar; **Fear Factory**), Joe Payne (bass) and Tim Yeung (drums).

8/15/09	148	1		1 Bringer Of Plagues		Century Media 8626

DIVINYLS
Rock band from Sydney, Australia: Christina Amphlett (vocals), Mark McEntee (guitar), Bjarne Olin (keyboards), Richard Grossman (bass) and J.J. Harris (drums). Grossman joined the **Hoodoo Gurus** in 1989. By 1991, group reduced to a duo of Amphlett and McEntee.

4/9/83	205	9		1 Desperate		Chrysalis 41404
12/7/85+	91	18		2 What A Life!		Chrysalis 41511
2/16/91	15	26	●	3 Divinyls		Virgin 91397

DEBUT	PEAK	WKS	R I A A	ARTIST Album Title	Catalog	Label & Number

DIXIE CHICKS   **All-Time: #437**

Female country trio: Natalie Maines (lead vocals), with sisters Martha "Martie" Erwin (fiddle, mandolin) and Emily Erwin (guitar, banjo). Natalie was born on 10/14/1974 in Lubbock, Texas. Married to Michael Tarabay from 1997-99; married actor Adrian Pasdar on 6/24/2000. Martie was born on 10/12/1969 in York, Pennsylvania. Married to Ted Seidel from 1995-99; married Gareth Maguire (took his last name) on 8/10/2001. Emily was born on 8/16/1972 in Pittsfield, Massachusetts. Married to **Charlie Robison** (took his last name) from 1999-2008. Several radio stations banned their songs after Maines made a controversial statement about President Bush in March 2003. Group named after the **Little Feat** song "Dixie Chicken."

AWARD: CMA: Horizon 1998 / Vocal Group 1998, 1999, 2000 & 2002 / Entertainer 2000

2/14/98+	4	134	▲¹²	1 **Wide Open Spaces**	Cat:❶⁸/168	Monument 68195
				Grammy: Country Album		
9/18/99	❶²	131	▲¹⁰	2 **Fly**	Cat:#2³/66	Monument 69678
				Grammy: Country Album ★ CMA: Album of the Year		
9/14/02	❶⁴	56	▲⁶	3 **Home**	Cat:#37/2	Monument 86840
				Grammy: Country Album		
12/6/03	27	30	●	4 **Top Of The World Tour Live**	[L]	Monument 90794 [2]
6/10/06	❶²	62	▲²	5 **Taking The Long Way**		Columbia 80739
				Grammys: Album of the Year / Country Album		

DIXIE CUPS, The

Black "girl group" from New Orleans, Louisiana: sisters Barbara Ann Hawkins and Rosa Lee Hawkins, with their cousin Joan Marie Johnson.

| 8/29/64 | 112 | 5 | | 1 **Chapel Of Love** .... | | Red Bird 100 |

~ ~ ~ ~ ~ ~ ~ ~ ~ **NON-CHARTED ALBUMS** ~ ~ ~ ~ ~ ~ ~ ~ ~ ~

1965 Iko Iko   1965 **Riding High**

DIXIE DREGS

Instrumental rock band formed in Augusta, Georgia: **Steve Morse** (guitar), T Lavitz (piano), Allen Sloan (violin), Andy West (bass) and Rod Morgenstein (drums). **Mark O'Connor** (violin) replaced Sloan in late 1981. Morse joined **Kansas** in 1986. Morgenstein later joined **Winger**.

5/27/78	182	4		1 **What If**	[I]	Capricorn 0203
5/19/79	111	13		2 **Night Of The Living Dregs**	[I-L]	Capricorn 0216
				side 2 recorded live at the Montreux Jazz Festival		
5/10/80	81	17		3 **Dregs Of The Earth**	[I]	Arista 9528
4/18/81	67	14		4 **Unsung Heroes**	[I]	Arista 9548
3/27/82	56	15		5 **Industry Standard**	[I]	Arista 9588
				DREGS (above 2)		

DIXON, Don

Born on 12/13/1950 in Lancaster, South Carolina. Rock singer/guitarist/producer. Produced albums for **R.E.M.** and **The Smithereens**.

| 3/7/87 | 162 | 8 | | 1 **Most Of The Girls Like To Dance But Only Some Of The Boys Like To** .... | | Enigma 73239 |

DIZE, Tony

Born Tony Cabrera on 12/23/1982 in Boston, Massachusetts (Puerto Rican parents). Reggaeton singer.

| 5/10/08 | 195 | 1 | | 1 **La Melodia De La Calle** .... | [F] | WY 010736 |

DJ CLAY

Born in Detroit, Michigan. Male rapper/producer/DJ.

| 7/26/08 | 156 | 2 | | 1 **Let 'Em Bleed: The Mixx Tape Vol. 2** .... | | Hatchet House 4701 |
| 11/29/08 | 180 | 1 | | 2 **Let 'Em Bleed: The Mixx Tape Vol. 3** .... | | Hatchet House 4705 |

DJ CLUE?

Born Ernesto Shaw on 1/8/1975 in Queens, New York. Male rapper/producer.

1/2/99	26	25	▲	1 **The Professional**		Roc-A-Fella 558891
9/16/00	6	11	●	2 **Backstage Mixtape**		Roc-A-Fella 546641
3/17/01	3¹	16		3 **The Professional 2**		Roc-A-Fella 542325
1/6/07	73	5		4 **The Professional 3**		Roc-A-Fella 006163

DJ DMD AND THE INNER SOUL CLIQUE

Born Dorie Dorsey in Port Arthur, Texas. Male DJ.

| 7/10/99 | 196 | 1 | | 1 **Twenty-Two: P.A. World Wide** .... | | Inner Soul 62428 |

DJ DRAMA

Born Tyree Simmons on 4/22/1978 in Philadelphia, Pennsylvania. Male DJ/producer. Later dropped the "DJ" from his moniker.

| 1/3/09 | 111 | 11 | | 1 **Gangsta Grillz: Dedication 3** .... | | Cash Money 63278 |
| | | | | **LIL WAYNE & DJ DRAMA** | | |

DJ ENVY

Born Raashaun Casey on 9/3/1977 in Queens, New York. Male DJ/remixer. One of the leading "mixtape" producers.

| 3/1/03 | 57 | 4 | | 1 **The Desert Storm Mixtape: Blok Party Vol. 1** ...... | | Desert Storm 86737 |

D.J. JAZZY JEFF & THE FRESH PRINCE

Hip-hop duo from Philadelphia, Pennsylvania: D.J. Jeff Townes (born on 1/22/1965) and rapper/actor **Will Smith** (born on 9/25/1968).

4/25/87+	83	35		1 **Rock The House**		Jive 1026
4/23/88	4	55	▲³	2 **He's The D.J., I'm The Rapper**		Jive 1091 [2]
11/18/89	39	20	●	3 **And In This Corner**...		Jive 1188

D.J. JAZZY JEFF & THE FRESH PRINCE — cont'd

7/27/91	12	42	▲	4 Homebase		Jive 1392
10/30/93	64	15	●	5 Code Red		Jive 41489
6/6/98	144	6		6 Greatest Hits .... [G]		Jive 41640

JAZZY JEFF & FRESH PRINCE (above 2)

DJ KAYSLAY
Born Keith Grayson on 8/14/1966 in Harlem, New York. Male DJ/rapper.

6/7/03	22	8	1 The Streetsweeper Vol. 1		Columbia 87048
4/17/04	27	7	2 The Streetsweeper Vol. 2: The Pain From The Game		Columbia 90700
9/9/06	57	3	3 The Champions: The North Meets The South		Deja 34 5815

DJ KAYSLAY & GREG STREET

DJ KHALED
Born Khaled Khaled on 11/26/1967 in New Orleans, Louisiana. Male DJ/record producer/radio personality.

6/24/06	12	7	1 Listennn: The Album		Terror Squad 4118
6/30/07	8	28	2 We The Best		Terror Squad 4229
10/4/08	7	9	3 We Global		We The Best 4564

DJ KOOL
Born John Bowman in 1959 in Washington DC. Male rapper.

5/18/96	161	5	1 (Let Me Clear My Throat)		CLR 7209

D.J. MAGIC MIKE
Born Michael Hampton in Orlando, Florida. Rap producer.

7/21/90	157	18	●	1 Bass Is The Name Of The Game		Cheetah 9403
1/26/91	153	22	●	2 Back To Haunt You!		Cheetah 9404
				VICIOUS BASE FEATURING D.J. MAGIC MIKE!		
11/23/91+	72	23	●	3 Ain't No Doubt About It		Cheetah 9405
7/25/92	149	7		4 Twenty Degrees Below Zero		Cheetah 9412
				D.J. MAGIC MIKE & M.C. MADNESS (above 2)		
3/27/93	67	18	●	5 Bass: The Final Frontier		Magic 9413
3/27/93	107	7		6 This Is How It Should Be Done		Magic 9411

DJ MUGGS
Born Lawrence Muggerud on 1/28/1968 in Queens, New York. Rap DJ. Member of **Cypress Hill**. Also see **The Soul Assassains**.

11/12/05	180	1	1 Grandmasters		Angeles 1001
			DJ MUGGS vs. GZA/THE GENIUS		

DJ NESTY
Born Ernesto Padilla on 9/5/1973 in Puerto Rico. Reggaeton DJ/producer.

11/29/08	65	6	1 Wisin Y Yandel Presentan La Mente Maestra .... [F]		WY 012278

DJ PAUL
Born Paul Beauregard in Memphis, Tennessee. Male rapper. Member of **Three 6 Mafia**, **Da Headbussaz** and **Prophet Posse**.

6/15/02	127	5	1 Underground Vol. 16: For Da Summa		D-Evil 3600
5/23/09	157	1	2 Scale-A-Ton [Skeleton]		Hypnotize Minds 3620

DJ POOH
Born Mark Jordan in Los Angeles, California. Rap producer.

8/2/97	116	3	1 Bad Newz Travels Fast		Big Beat 92752

DJ QUIK
Born David Blake on 1/18/1970 in Compton, California. Male rapper.

3/2/91	29	42	▲	1 Quik Is The Name		Profile 1402
8/8/92	10	14	●	2 Way 2 Fonky		Profile 1430
3/11/95	14	16	●	3 Safe + Sound		Profile 1462
12/12/98	63	29		4 Rhythm-al-ism		Profile 19034
6/3/00	18	13		5 Balance & Options		Arista 16419
6/22/02	27	7		6 Under Tha Influence		Euponic 970008
10/1/05	43	3		7 Trauma		RBC 11
6/27/09	61	2		8 BlaQKout		Mad Science 17
				DJ QUIK & KURUPT		

DJ SAMMY
Born Samuel Bouriah on 10/29/1969 in Mallorca, Spain. Electronica dance producer.

8/24/02	67	13	1 Heaven		Robbins 75031

DJ SHADOW
Born Josh Davis on 1/1/1973 in Hayward, California; later based in England. Male DJ/producer.

1/31/98	118	4	1 Preemptive Strike		Mo Wax 540867 [2]
6/22/02	44	6	2 The Private Press		MCA 112937
10/7/06	77	2	3 The Outsider		Universal Motown 007443

DJ SKRIBBLE
Born Scott Ialacci on 10/10/1968 in Brooklyn, New York. White DJ/producer. Former member of **Young Black Teenagers**.

9/30/00	158	4	1 Essential Dance 2000		Big Beat 83343
4/28/01	124	6	2 Essential Spring Break - Summer 2001		Big Beat 35065

DLR BAND — see ROTH, David Lee

D-MOB
Dance group assembled by producer Danny D. Lead singer **Cathy Dennis** went solo in late 1990.

1/27/90	82	20	1 A Little Bit Of This, A Little Bit Of That		FFRR 828159

DMX
All-Time: #414
Born Earl Simmons on 12/18/1970 in Baltimore, Maryland; raised in Yonkers, New York. Male rapper/actor. DMX is short for Dark Man X. Acted in the movies *Belly*, *Romeo Must Die*, *Exit Wounds* and *Cradle 2 The Grave*. Member of **Ruff Ryders**.

6/6/98	❶[1]	101	▲[4]	1 It's Dark And Hell Is Hot Cat:#8/34	Ruff Ryders 558227
1/9/99	❶[3]	55	▲[3]	2 Flesh Of My Flesh Blood Of My Blood	Ruff Ryders 538640
1/8/00	❶[1]	74	▲[5]	3 ...And Then There Was X	Ruff Ryders 546933
11/10/01	❶[1]	27	▲	4 The Great Depression	Ruff Ryders 586450
10/4/03	❶[1]	24	▲	5 Grand Champ	Ruff Ryders 063369
8/19/06	2[1]	10		6 Year Of The Dog...Again	Columbia 80742
6/30/07	26	8		7 The Definition Of X: Pick Of The Litter .... [G]	Ruff Ryders 008988

D-NICE
Born Derrick Jones on 6/19/1970 in the Bronx, New York. Male rapper. Member of **Boogie Down Productions**.

8/11/90	75	13	1 Call Me D-Nice		Jive 1202
12/14/91	137	5	2 To Tha Rescue		Jive 41466

D.O.A.
Punk-rock band from Vancouver, British Columbia, Canada: Joe Keithley (vocals), Chris Prohom (guitar), Sunny Boy Roy (bass) and Jon Card (drums).

6/9/90	184	5	1 Murder.		Restless 72376

DOBKINS, Carl Jr.
Born Carl Edward Dobkins on 1/13/1941 in Cincinnati, Ohio. Teen pop singer/songwriter.

~ ~ ~ ~ ~ ~ ~ ~ ~ ~   **NON-CHARTED ALBUM**   ~ ~ ~ ~ ~ ~ ~ ~ ~ ~ ~
1959 **Carl Dobkins, Jr.**

DOBSON, Fefe
Born on 2/27/1985 in Toronto, Ontario, Canada. Black female rock singer/songwriter.

12/27/03+	67	17	1 Fefe Dobson		Island 001244

D.O.C., The
Born Tracy Curry on 6/10/1968 in Houston, Texas. Male rapper.

8/19/89	20	34	▲	1 No One Can Do It Better	Ruthless 91275
2/10/96	30	7		2 Helter Skelter	Giant 24627
3/15/03	184	1		3 Deuce	Silverback 2113

DOC HOLLIDAY
Southern-rock band from Raleigh, North Carolina: Bruce Brookshire (vocals, guitar), Rick Skelton (guitar), Eddie Stone (keyboards), John Samuelson (bass) and Herman Nixon (drums).

4/4/81	201	4	1 Doc Holliday		A&M 4847
3/6/82	204	3	2 Doc Holliday Rides Again...		A&M 4882

DOCTOR AND THE MEDICS
Glam-rock band from London, England: Clive "Doctor" Jackson (lead vocals), brothers Wendi Anadin and Collette Anadin (backing vocals), Steve Maguire (guitar), Richard Searle (bass) and Steve "Vom" Ritchie (drums).

9/13/86	125	8	1 Laughing At The Pieces		I.R.S. 5797

DR. BUZZARD'S ORIGINAL SAVANNAH BAND
Big-band swing/disco band formed in Brooklyn, New York, by brothers Stony Browder (guitar) and Thomas "August Darnell" Browder (bass). Featuring Cory Daye (vocals), Andy Hernandez (vibraphone) **Don Armando** (percussion) and Mickey Sevilla (drums). Darnell and Hernandez left in 1980 to form **Kid Creole & The Coconuts**. Armando died on 11/16/2002 (age 56).

8/21/76+	22	49	●	1 Dr. Buzzard's Original Savannah Band........................	RCA Victor 1504
2/11/78	36	9		2 Dr. Buzzard's Original Savannah Band Meets King Penett..........	RCA Victor 2402

DR. DEMENTO — see VARIOUS ARTIST COMPILATIONS

DR. DOG
Psychedelic-rock band from Philadelphia, Pennsylvania: Scott McMiken (vocals, guitar), Toby Leaman (vocals, bass), Frank McElroy (guitar), Zach Miller (keyboards) and Eric Slick (drums).

8/9/08	86	4	1 Fate...		Park The Van 25

DR. DRE
Born Andre Young on 2/18/1965 in Compton, California. Rapper/producer. Co-founder of **N.W.A.** and **World Class Wreckin' Cru**. Produced several artists. Founded Death Row Records in 1992. Half-brother of **Warren G**. Also see **Various Artists Compilations: *Dr. Dre Presents...The Aftermath***.

1/2/93	3[6]	86	▲[3]	1 The Chronic Cat:#11/30	Death Row 57128
				RS500 #137	
10/8/94	43	8		2 Concrete Roots - Anthology .... [K]	Hitman 51170
6/8/96	52	5		3 First Round Knock Out .... [K]	Triple X 51226
12/4/99	2[4]	93	▲[6]	4 2001 Cat:#43/4	Aftermath 90486

DR. FEELGOOD
Pub-rock band from Canvey Island, Essex, England: Lee Brilleaux (vocals), Wilko Johnson (guitar), John Sparks (bass) and John "The Figure" Martin (drums). Brilleaux died of cancer on 4/7/1994 (age 41).

3/27/76	203	5	1 Malpractice		Columbia 34098

DR. HOOK
Pop-rock band formed in Union City, New Jersey: Ray Sawyer (vocals; born on 2/1/1937; dubbed "Dr. Hook" because of eye patch), Dennis Locorriere (vocals, guitar; born on 6/13/1949), George Cummings (guitar; born on 7/28/1938), Rik Elswit (guitar; born on 7/6/1945), William Francis (keyboards; born on 1/16/1942), Jance Garfat (bass; born on 3/3/1944) and Jay David (drums; born on 8/8/1942). John Wolters (born on 4/28/1945; died of cancer on 6/16/1997, age 52) replaced David in 1973. Bob Henke (of **Goose Creek Symphony**) replaced Cummings in 1975. Group appeared in and performed the music for the 1971 movie *Who Is Harry Kellerman And Why Is He Saying Those Terrible Things About Me?*.

4/29/72	45	23	1 Dr. Hook & The Medicine Show		Columbia 30898
12/2/72+	41	31	2 Sloppy Seconds		Columbia 31622
10/27/73	141	6	3 Belly Up!..		Columbia 32270
			DR. HOOK AND THE MEDICINE SHOW (above 3)		
7/5/75+	141	16	4 Bankrupt		Capitol 11397
5/15/76	62	31	5 A Little Bit More..		Capitol 11522
11/18/78+	66	34	● 6 Pleasure & Pain		Capitol 11859
11/24/79+	71	32	7 Sometimes You Win..		Capitol 12018
12/6/80	175	8	8 Rising		Casablanca 7251
12/20/80+	142	12	9 Dr. Hook/Greatest Hits...	[G]	Capitol 12122
12/5/81	202	2	10 Dr. Hook Live	[L]	Capitol 12114
4/3/82	118	7	11 Players In The Dark		Casablanca 7264

DR. JOHN
Born Malcolm Rebennack on 11/20/1940 in New Orleans, Louisiana. Swamp-rock singer/songwriter/pianist.

10/9/71	184	5	1 Dr. John, The Night Tripper (The Sun, Moon & Herbs)...................		Atco 362
5/13/72	112	11	2 Dr. John's Gumbo		Atco 7006
			RS500 #402		
3/24/73	24	33	3 In The Right Place		Atco 7018
6/16/73	105	12	4 Triumvirate..		Columbia 32172
			MIKE BLOOMFIELD / JOHN PAUL HAMMOND / DR. JOHN		
5/4/74	105	8	5 Desitively Bonnaroo		Atco 7043
12/2/78	207	3	6 City Lights		Horizon 732
5/27/89	142	11	7 In A Sentimental Mood		Warner 25889

~ ~ ~ ~ ~ ~ ~ ~ ~ ~ *NON-CHARTED ALBUM* ~ ~ ~ ~ ~ ~ ~ ~ ~ ~ ~

1968 **Gris-Gris**
RS500 #143

DOCTOR J.R. KOOL
Studio group from New York.

7/20/85	113	13	1 The Complete Story Of Roxanne...The Album		Compleat 1014

DR. STRUT
Jazz band from Los Angeles, California: Tim Weston (guitar), David Woodford (sax), Everett Bryson (percussion), Kevin Bassinson (keyboards), Peter Freiberger (bass) and Claude Pepper (drums).

3/22/80	201	4	1 Struttin'	[I]	Motown 931

DOE, John
Born John Nommensen on 2/25/1953 in Decatur, Illinois. Founded the bands **X** and **The Knitters** with his former wife Exene Cervenka. Appeared in several movies. Took name from the 1941 movie *Meet John Doe*.

6/23/90	193	3	1 Meet John Doe..		DGC 24291

DOG, Tim
Born Timothy Blair on 1/1/1967 in the Bronx, New York. Male rapper.

11/30/91	155	2	1 Penicillin On Wax		Ruffhouse 48707

DOGGETT, Bill
Born on 2/16/1916 in Philadelphia, Pennsylvania. Died on 11/13/1996 (age 80). Leading jazz-R&B organist/pianist.

~ ~ ~ ~ ~ ~ ~ ~ ~ ~ *NON-CHARTED ALBUM* ~ ~ ~ ~ ~ ~ ~ ~ ~ ~ ~

1957 **Everybody Dance The Honky Tonk**

DOGG POUND, Tha
Rap duo from Los Angeles, California: Delmar "**Daz Dillinger**" Arnaud and Ricardo "**Kurupt**" Brown. Arnaud is a cousin of **Snoop Doggy Dogg**. Brown is the older brother of **Roscoe**. Duo also recorded as **D.P.G.**.

11/18/95	❶¹	32	▲² 1 Dogg Food		Death Row 50546
5/26/01	124	6	2 Dillinger & Young Gotti...		D.P.G. 1001
			D.P.G.		
8/18/01	36	8	3 Death Row Presents: Tha Dogg Pound 2002		Death Row 33353
7/15/06	28	5	4 Cali Iz Active		Doggystyle 5919
4/14/07	77	1	5 Dogg Chit		Gangsta Advisory 5539

DOGGYS ANGELS
Female rap trio assembled by **Snoop Dogg**: Chan Gaines, Kim Proby and Kola Marion.

12/9/00	138	2	1 Pleezbaleevit!		Doggy Style 2130
			SNOOP DOGG PRESENTS DOGGYS ANGELS		

Billboard DEBUT	PEAK	WKS	R I A A	ARTIST Album Title	Catalog	Label & Number

DOGGY STYLE ALLSTARS
Rap group formed by **Snoop Dogg**: Mr. Kane, E-White, Soopa Fly and LaToiya Williams.

| 8/31/02 | 19 | 9 | | 1 **Welcome To Tha House, Vol. 1** .... | | Doggy Style 112992 |

DOG'S EYE VIEW
Rock band from Manhattan, New York: Peter Stuart (vocals, guitar), Oren Bloedow (guitar), John Abbey (bass) and Alan Bezozi (drums).

| 3/16/96 | 77 | 19 | | 1 **Happy Nowhere** .... | | Columbia 66882 |

DOKKEN
Hard-rock band formed in Los Angeles, California: **Don Dokken** (vocals; born on 6/29/1953), **George Lynch** (guitar), Juan Croucier (bass) and Mick Brown (drums). Jeff Pilson replaced Croucier in late 1983. Disbanded in 1988. Lynch and Brown formed **Lynch Mob** in 1990. Dokken, Lynch, Pilson and Brown reunited as Dokken in late 1994.

10/15/83	136	13		1 **Breaking The Chains**		Elektra 60290
10/13/84+	49	74	▲	2 **Tooth And Nail**		Elektra 60376
12/21/85+	32	67	▲	3 **Under Lock And Key**		Elektra 60458
12/5/87	13	33	●	4 **Back For The Attack**		Elektra 60735
12/3/88	33	17	●	5 **Beast From The East**	[L]	Elektra 60823 [2]
				recorded April 1988 in Japan		
9/15/90	50	11		6 **Up From The Ashes**		Geffen 24301
				DON DOKKEN		
6/3/95	47	6		7 **Dysfunctional**		Columbia 67075
5/3/97	146	1		8 **Shadowlife**		CMC Int'l. 86210
5/31/08	133	1		9 **Lightning Strikes Again**		Rhino 460028

DOLBY, Thomas
Born Thomas Robertson on 10/14/1958 in London, England. New-wave singer/songwriter/keyboardist.

2/5/83	20	31		1 **Blinded By Science**	[EP]	Harvest 15007
3/19/83	13	28		2 **The Golden Age Of Wireless**		Capitol 12271
3/17/84	35	18		3 **The Flat Earth**		Capitol 12309
5/7/88	70	19		4 **Aliens Ate My Buick**		EMI-Manhattan 48075

DOLCE, Joe
Born in 1947 in Painesville, Ohio. Novelty singer/songwriter.

| 6/27/81 | 181 | 4 | | 1 **Shaddap You Face** .... | [N] | MCA 5211 |

DOMINGO, Placido
Born on 1/21/1941 in Madrid, Spain; raised in Mexico City, Mexico. One of the world's leading operatic tenors. Appeared in several movies. Member of The Three Tenors.

11/7/81+	18	27	▲	1 **Perhaps Love**		CBS 37243
3/13/82	164	6		2 **Domingo-Con Amore**	[F]	RCA Victor 4265
4/9/83	117	11		3 **My Life For A Song**		CBS 37799
8/25/84	210	1		4 **Always In My Heart (Siempre En Mi Corazon) - The Songs Of Ernesto Lecuona**...	[F]	CBS 38828
				songs of Cuban composer-pianist Lecuona; with the Royal Philharmonic Orchestra, Lee Holdridge, director		
3/2/91	171	6		5 **Be My Love...An Album Of Love**		EMI 95468
3/28/09	117	2		6 **Amore Infinito: Songs Inspired By The Poems Of Pope John Paul II**	[F]	DG 012532
				CHRISTMAS ALBUMS:		
12/15/84	9ˣ	1		7 **Christmas With Placido Domingo**		CBS 37245
				with the Vienna Symphony Orchestra conducted by Lee Holdridge; first released in 1981; reissued in 1982 with a different album cover		
12/18/93	154	3		8 **Christmas In Vienna**	[L]	Sony Classical 53358
				PLACIDO DOMINGO / DIANA ROSS / JOSE CARRERAS recorded on 12/23/1992 at the Rathaus in Vienna, Austria		
12/21/96	196	2		9 **A Celebration Of Christmas**	[L]	Elektra 62000
				JOSE CARRERAS / NATALIE COLE / PLACIDO DOMINGO recorded on 12/23/1995 at the Austria Center in Vienna		
12/20/97	192	2		10 **Merry Christmas From Vienna**	[L]	Sony Classical 62970
				PLACIDO DOMINGO / YING HUANG / MICHAEL BOLTON recorded on 12/16/1996 at the Austria Center in Vienna		
12/1/01	102	6		11 **Our Favorite Things**	[L]	Sony Classical 89468
				TONY BENNETT / CHARLOTTE CHURCH / PLACIDO DOMINGO / VANESSA WILLIAMS recorded on 12/21/2000 at the Konzerthaus in Vienna, Austria; Christmas chart: 10/'01		

DOMINO
Born Shawn Ivy in 1972 in St. Louis, Missouri; raised in Long Beach, California. Male rapper.

| 12/25/93+ | 39 | 33 | ● | 1 **Domino** .... | | OutBurst 57701 |
| 6/29/96 | 152 | 1 | | 2 **Physical Funk** .... | | OutBurst 531033 |

DOMINO, Fats   1950s: #48
Born Antoine Domino on 2/26/1928 in New Orleans, Louisiana. Legendary R&B singer/songwriter/pianist. Heavily influenced by Fats Waller and Albert Ammons. Joined the Dave Bartholomew band (mid-1940s). Signed to Imperial record label in 1949. Nicknamed "The Fat Man." Heard on many sessions cut by other R&B artists. In the movies *Shake, Rattle And Rock!*, *Jamboree!*, *The Big Beat* and *The Girl Can't Help It*.
AWARDS: Grammy: Lifetime Achievement 1987 ★ R&R Hall of Fame: 1986 ★ RIAA: American Music Legend

11/10/56+	18	6		1 **Fats Domino - Rock And Rollin'**		Imperial 9009
2/23/57	19	2		2 **This Is Fats Domino!**		Imperial 9028
3/23/57	17	4		3 **Rock And Rollin' With Fats Domino**		Imperial 9004
7/21/62	113	6		4 **Million Sellers By Fats**	[G]	Imperial 9195
10/5/63	130	4		5 **Here Comes...Fats Domino**		ABC-Paramount 455
10/19/68	189	2		6 **Fats Is Back**		Reprise 6304

Billboard			R I A A	ARTIST	Catalog	Label & Number
DEBUT	**PEAK**	**WKS**		**Album Title**		

~ ~ ~ ~ ~ ~ ~ NON-CHARTED ALBUMS by FATS DOMINO ~ ~ ~ ~ ~ ~ ~ ~

1957 **Here Stands Fats Domino**	1960 **Fats Domino Sings Million Record Hits**
1957 **This Is Fats**	1960 **...A Lot Of Dominos!**
1958 **The Fabulous "Mr. D"**	1961 **Let The Four Winds Blow**
1959 **Fats Domino Swings ** 12,000,000 Records**	1962 **What A Party!**
1959 **Let's Play Fats Domino**	

DONAHEW, Casey, Band
Born in Burleson, Texas. Country singer/songwriter/guitarist.

DEBUT	PEAK	WKS			Label & Number
9/19/09	126	1	1	Moving On...........	Almost Country 9205386

DONALDSON, Bo, And The Heywoods
Pop band from Cincinnati, Ohio: Robert "Bo" Donaldson (keyboards), Mike Gibbons (vocals), Scott Baker (guitar), Gary Coveyou (reeds), Rick Joswick (percussion), David Krock (bass) and Nicky Brunetti (drums).

7/6/74	97	16	1	Bo Donaldson And The Heywoods	ABC 824

DONALDSON, Lou
Born on 11/3/1926 in Badin, North Carolina. Black jazz alto saxophonist. Leader of small combos in the East.

6/15/63	141	2	1	The Natural Soul	[I]	Blue Note 84108
10/7/67	141	11	2	Alligator Bogaloo	[I]	Blue Note 84263
10/26/68	182	6	3	Midnight Creeper	[I]	Blue Note 84280
4/5/69	153	7	4	Say It Loud!	[I]	Blue Note 84299
10/4/69	158	6	5	Hot Dog	[I]	Blue Note 84318
7/11/70	190	2	6	Everything I Play Is Funky	[I]	Blue Note 84337
6/9/73	207	3	7	Sophisticated Lou	[I]	Blue Note 024
9/22/73	176	4	8	Sassy Soul Strut	[I]	Blue Note 109
9/28/74	185	3	9	Sweet Lou	[I]	Blue Note 259

DON AND THE GOODTIMES
Rock and roll band from Portland, Oregon: Don Gallucci (vocals, piano; **The Kingsmen**), Joey Newman (guitar), Jeff Hawks (tambourine), Buzz Overman (bass) and Bobby Holden (drums).

8/5/67	109	4	1	So Good	Epic 26311

DONATO, Joao
Born on 8/17/1934 in Rio Branco, Brazil. Male keyboardist.

8/18/73	213	2	1	Donato/Deodato	[I]	Muse 5017

DONNAS, The
Female punk-rock band from Palo Alto, California: Brett "Donna A." Anderson (vocals), Allison "Donna R." Robertson (guitar), Maya "Donna F." Ford (bass) and Torry "Donna C." Castellano (drums).

11/9/02+	62	26	1	Spend The Night...........	Atlantic 83567
11/13/04	76	2	2	Gold Medal	Atlantic 83758
10/6/07	89	1	3	Bitchin'	Purple Feather 1001

DONNER, Ral
Born Ralph Donner on 2/10/1943 in Chicago, Illinois. Died of cancer on 4/6/1984 (age 41). Pop vocalist.

~ ~ ~ ~ ~ ~ ~ ~ ~ ~ NON-CHARTED ALBUM ~ ~ ~ ~ ~ ~ ~ ~ ~ ~ ~

1961 **Takin' Care Of Business**

DONOVAN
All-Time: #218

Born Donovan Leitch on 5/10/1946 in Glasgow, Scotland; raised in Hatfield, England. Pop-rock-folk singer/songwriter/guitarist. Appeared in the movies *The Pied Piper of Hamlin* and *Brother Sun, Sister Moon*. Father of actress Ione Skye and actor Donovan Leitch Jr.

7/17/65	30	23	1	Catch The Wind		Hickory 123
12/18/65+	85	13	2	Fairytale		Hickory 127
10/1/66	96	7	3	The Real Donovan		Hickory 135
4/6/68	177	4	4	Like It Is, Was And Evermore Shall Be...........		Hickory 143
11/8/69	135	7	5	The Best Of Donovan	[G]	Hickory 149
9/24/66	11	29	6	Sunshine Superman		Epic 26217
2/18/67	14	21	7	Mellow Yellow		Epic 26239
12/30/67+	60	15	8	Wear Your Love Like Heaven...........		Epic 26349
1/6/68	19	22	● 9	A Gift From A Flower To A Garden		Epic 171 [2]
				deluxe box set of the albums *Wear Your Love Like Heaven* and *For Little Ones*		
1/13/68	185	3	10	For Little Ones		Epic 26350
7/27/68	18	31	11	Donovan In Concert	[L]	Epic 26386
10/19/68	20	20	12	The Hurdy Gurdy Man		Epic 26420
2/22/69	4	56	▲ 13	Donovan's Greatest Hits	[G]	Epic 26439
9/13/69	23	24	14	Barabajagal		Epic 26481
7/18/70	16	19	15	Open Road		Epic 30125
11/14/70	128	8	16	Donovan P. Leitch	[K]	Janus 3022 [2]
4/3/71	215	3	17	Here Me Now		Janus 3025
3/31/73	25	20	18	Cosmic Wheels		Epic 32156
2/2/74	174	5	19	Essence To Essence		Epic 32800
12/14/74+	135	6	20	7-Tease		Epic 33245
6/5/76	174	3	21	Slow Down World		Epic 33945

DOOBIE BROTHERS, The   All-Time: #179

Rock band formed in San Jose, California: **Patrick Simmons** (vocals, guitar; born on 10/19/1948), **Tom Johnston** (vocals, guitar; born on 8/15/1948), Tiran Porter (bass; born in 1948) and John Hartman (drums; born in 1948). Mike Hossack (percussion; born on 10/17/1946) added in 1972; later replaced by Keith Knudsen (born on 2/18/1948; died of pneumonia on 2/8/2005, age 56). Jeff "Skunk" Baxter (slide guitar; born on 12/13/1948), formerly with **Steely Dan**, added in 1974. **Michael McDonald** (lead vocals, keyboards; born on 2/12/1952), added in 1975. Johnston left in 1978. Baxter and Hartman replaced by Cornelius Bumpus (keyboards, saxophone; born on 1/13/1946; died of a heart attack on 2/3/2004, age 58), John McFee (guitar) and Chet McCracken (drums) in 1979. Johnston wrote majority of hits from 1972-75; McDonald, from 1976-83. Disbanded in 1983. Re-formed in early 1988 with Johnston, Simmons, Hartman, Porter, Hossack, and Bobby LaKind (percussion; died of cancer on 12/24/1992, age 47).

9/11/71	210	1		1 The Doobie Brothers		Warner 1919
8/26/72	21	119	▲	2 Toulouse Street		Warner 2634
3/31/73	7	102	▲²	3 The Captain And Me		Warner 2694
3/16/74+	4	62	▲²	4 What Were Once Vices Are Now Habits		Warner 2750
5/17/75	4	25	●	5 Stampede		Warner 2835
4/3/76	8	44	▲	6 Takin' It To The Streets		Warner 2899
11/20/76+	5	93	▲¹⁰	7 Best Of The Doobies	Cat:#35/19 [G]	Warner 2978
9/10/77	10	21	●	8 Livin' On The Fault Line		Warner 3045
12/23/78+	❶⁵	87	▲³	9 Minute By Minute		Warner 3193
				Grammy: Group Pop Vocal		
10/11/80	3³	28	▲	10 One Step Closer		Warner 3452
11/21/81	39	15	●	11 Best Of The Doobies, Volume II	[G]	Warner 3612
7/23/83	79	9		12 The Doobie Brothers Farewell Tour	[L]	Warner 23772 [2]
6/10/89	17	20	●	13 Cycles		Capitol 90371
5/11/91	82	9		14 Brotherhood		Capitol 94623
9/22/01	142	2		15 Greatest Hits	[G]	Warner Archives 74386

DOOLITTLE, Melinda

Born on 10/6/1977 in Brentwood, Tennessee. R&B singer. Finalist on the sixth season of TV's *American Idol* in 2007.

2/21/09	58	6		1 Coming Back To You		Hi Fi 1004

DO OR DIE

Male rap trio from Chicago, Illinois: Dennis Rounk ("AK"), Anthony Round ("N.A.R.D.") and Darnell Smith ("Belo Zero").

9/21/96	27	29	●	1 Picture This		Rap-A-Lot 42058
4/25/98	13	16	●	2 Headz Or Tailz		Rap-A-Lot 45612
9/16/00	13	9		3 Victory		Rap-A-Lot 49072
8/31/02	64	5		4 Back 2 The Game		Rap-A-Lot 12647
9/6/03+	115	3		5 Pimpin' Ain't Dead		J Prince 42029
2/19/05	40	5		6 D.O.D.		The Legion 93806
4/15/06	159	1		7 Get That Paper		J Prince 68548

DOORS, The   All-Time: #74

Rock band formed in Los Angeles, California: Jim Morrison (vocals; born on 12/9/1943; died of heart failure on 7/3/1971, age 27), Robby Krieger (guitar; born on 1/8/1946), **Ray Manzarek** (keyboards; born on 2/12/1939) and John Densmore (drums; born on 12/1/1944). Controversial onstage performances by Morrison caused several arrests and cancellations. Group appeared in the 1969 movie *A Feast of Friends*. Morrison left group on 12/12/1970; reest of group disbanded in 1973. Val Kilmer portrayed Morrison in the 1991 biographical movie *The Doors*. Also see **Various Artists Compilations:** *Stoned Immaculate - The Music Of The Doors*.

AWARDS: Grammy: Lifetime Achievement 2007 ★ R&R Hall of Fame: 1993

3/25/67	2²	121	▲⁴	1 The Doors	Cat:❶¹⁰/40	Elektra 74007
				Grammy: Hall of Fame ★ RS500 #42		
11/4/67	3⁴	63	▲	2 Strange Days		Elektra 74014
				RS500 #407		
8/10/68	❶⁴	41	▲	3 Waiting For The Sun	Cat:#3/27	Elektra 74024
8/9/69	6	28	▲	4 The Soft Parade	Cat:#4/27	Elektra 75005
3/7/70	4	27	▲	5 Morrison Hotel/Hard Rock Cafe		Elektra 75007
5/8/71	9	34	▲²	6 L.A. Woman		Elektra 75011
				RS500 #362		
11/6/71	31	15		7 Other Voices		Elektra 75017
8/5/72	68	15		8 Full Circle		Elektra 75038
12/16/78+	54	13	▲	9 An American Prayer - Jim Morrison	Cat:❶¹/9	Elektra 502
				GREATEST HITS & COMPILATIONS:		
12/19/70+	25	21	▲	10 13		Elektra 74079
2/12/72	55	11	●	11 Weird Scenes Inside The Gold Mine		Elektra 6001 [2]
9/29/73	158	8		12 The Best Of The Doors		Elektra 5035
11/1/80	17	99	▲³	13 The Doors Greatest Hits	Cat:#13/32	Elektra 515
6/8/85	124	7		14 Classics		Elektra 60417
8/8/87+	32	43	▲¹⁰	15 The Best Of The Doors	Cat:❶³/306	Elektra 60345 [2]
3/23/91	8	20	▲	16 The Doors	[S]	Elektra 61047
11/15/97	65	5	▲	17 The Doors Box Set		Elektra 62123 [4]

				ARTIST / Album Title	Catalog	Label & Number
				DOORS, The — cont'd		
10/6/01	92	6		18 The Very Best Of The Doors		Elektra 78376
8/30/03	63	4	●	19 Legacy: The Absolute Best		Elektra 73889 [2]
10/13/07	113	12	●	20 The Very Best Of The Doors		Elektra 277180 [2]
8/2/08	161	8		21 The Future Starts Here: The Essential Doors Hits	Cat:#35/1	DMC 360060
				LIVE ALBUMS:		
8/8/70	8	20	●	22 Absolutely Live		Elektra 9002 [2]
11/5/83	23	20	●	23 Alive, She Cried .... [K]		Elektra 60269
7/11/87	154	11		24 Live At The Hollywood Bowl .... [EP]		Elektra 60741
				recorded on 7/5/1968		
6/8/91	50	13	▲	25 In Concert .... [K]		Elektra 61082 [2]
8/11/07	145	1		26 Live In Boston 1970		DMC 216124 [3]
12/6/08	191	1		27 Live At The Matrix 1967: San Francisco		DMC 516205 [2]
				DOPE		
				Hard-rock band from Brooklyn, New York: brothers Brian "Edsel Dope" Ebejer (vocals) and "Simon Dope" Ebejer (keyboards), with Emil "Acey Slade" Schmidt (guitar), Andre "Virus" Karkos (guitar), Sloane Jentry (bass) and Racci "Sketchy" Shay (drums). Acey Slade was also a member of **Murderdolls**.		
11/24/01	180	1		1 Life		Flip 85644
8/13/05	128	2		2 American Apathy		3Sixty 51568
3/28/09	88	2		3 No Regrets		E1 4480
				DORATI, Antal		
				Born on 4/9/1906 in Budapest, Hungary. Died on 11/13/1988 (age 82). Principal conductor of BBC Symphony from 1962-66 and of Stockholm Philharmonic from 1966-74. Music director of Washington National Symphony from 1970-77. Principal conductor of Britain's **Royal Philharmonic Orchestra** from 1975-78. Music director of Detroit Symphony from 1977-81.		
3/16/59	3²	54	●	1 Tchaikovsky: 1812 Festival Overture/Capriccio Italien [I]		Mercury 50054
				Grammy: Hall of Fame		
2/27/61	20	16		2 Beethoven: Wellington's Victory/Leonore Overture No. 3/ Prometheus Overture .... [I]		Mercury 9000
				DORE, Charlie		
				Born in 1956 in Pinner, Middlesex, England. Female singer/songwriter.		
4/26/80	145	7		1 Where To Now		Island 9559
9/12/81	204	1		2 Listen!		Chrysalis 1325
				DO-RE-MI CHILDREN'S CHORUS, The		
				Children's chorus that sang with **Tom Glazer** on his 1963 hit single "On Top Of Spaghetti."		
12/9/67	37ˣ	4		1 Do You Hear What I Hear?/Little Drummer Boy, (And More Of The Christmas Songs Children Love To Sing) .... [X]		Kapp 1368 / 3368
				first released in 1963		
12/6/69	11ˣ	1		2 Here Comes Santa Claus & The Christmas Songs Children Love To Sing ... [X]		Kapp 1154 / 3037
				DORO		
				Born Dorothee Pesch on 6/3/1964 in Dusseldorf, Germany. Female hard-rock singer. Member of **Warlock**.		
4/29/89	154	11		1 Force Majeure		Mercury 838016
				DORROUGH		
				Born Dorwin Dorrough on 10/28/1986 in Dallas, Texas. Male rapper.		
8/22/09	36	6		1 Dorrough Music		NGenius 5114
				DORSEY, Jimmy, Orchestra		
				Born on 2/29/1904 in Shenandoah, Pennsylvania. Died of cancer on 6/12/1957 (age 53). Esteemed alto sax and clarinet soloist/ bandleader. Recorded with his brother **Tommy Dorsey** in the Dorsey Brothers Orchestra, 1928-35 and 1953-56.		
10/7/57	19	4		1 The Fabulous Jimmy Dorsey		Fraternity 1008
5/19/58	15	6		2 The Fabulous Dorseys In Hi-Fi .... [I]		Columbia 1190
				TOMMY DORSEY & JIMMY DORSEY		
				DORSEY, Lee		
				Born Irving Lee Dorsey on 12/24/1924 in New Orleans, Louisiana; raised in Portland, Oregon. Died of emphysema on 12/1/1986 (age 61). R&B singer.		
11/12/66	129	5		1 The New Lee Dorsey		Amy 8011
				DORSEY, Tommy, Orchestra		
				Born on 11/19/1905 in Mahanoy Plane, Pennsylvania. Choked to death on 11/26/1956 (age 51). Esteemed trombonist/ bandleader. Tommy and brother **Jimmy Dorsey** recorded together as the Dorsey Brothers Orchestra from 1928-35 and 1953-56. They hosted a musical variety TV show, *Stage Show*, 1954-56. Warren Covington fronted band after Tommy's death.		
5/19/58	15	6		1 The Fabulous Dorseys In Hi-Fi .... [I]		Columbia 1190
				TOMMY DORSEY & JIMMY DORSEY		
5/25/59	38	2		2 Tea For Two Cha Chas .... [I]		Decca 8842
				DOUBLE		
				Pop duo from Switzerland: Kurt Maloo (vocals, guitar) and Felix Haug (keyboards).		
7/26/86	30	21		1 Blue		A&M 5133
				DOUBLE EXPOSURE		
				Disco group from Philadelphia, Pennsylvania: James Williams, Leonard "Butch" Davis, Charles Whittington and Joseph Harris.		
8/21/76	129	11		1 Ten Percent		Salsoul 5503

Billboard			R I A A	ARTIST		
DEBUT	PEAK	WKS		Album Title	Catalog	Label & Number

DOUBLE TROUBLE
Backing duo for **Stevie Ray Vaughan**: Tommy Shannon (bass) and Chris Layton (drums). Also members of **Arc Angels**.

| 2/24/01 | 126 | 2 | | 1 Been A Long Time .... | | Tone-Cool 471180 |

DOUCETTE
Rock band from Montreal, Quebec, Canada: Jerry Doucette (vocals, guitar), Mark Olson (keyboards), Donnie Cummings (bass) and Duris Maxwell (drums).

| 3/25/78 | 159 | 8 | | 1 Mama Let Him Play .... | | Mushroom 5009 |
| 5/26/79 | 202 | 5 | | 2 The Douce Is Loose .... | | Mushroom 5013 |

DOUG AND THE SLUGS
Rock band from Vancouver, British Columbia, Canada: Doug Bennett (vocals), John Burton (guitar), Rick Baker (guitar), Simon Kendall (keyboards), Steve Bosley (bass) and John Wally Watson (drums).

| 2/21/81 | 204 | 2 | | 1 Cognac And Bologna .... | | RCA Victor 3887 |

DOUG E. FRESH & THE GET FRESH CREW
Born Douglas Davis on 9/17/1966 in St. Thomas, Virgin Islands; raised in Brooklyn, New York. Male rapper. The Get Fresh Crew: Barry Bee, Chill Will and **Slick Rick**.

| 6/18/88 | 88 | 13 | | 1 The World's Greatest Entertainer .... | | Reality 9658 |

DOUGHTY, Mike
Born on 6/10/1970 in Fort Knox, Kentucky; later based in New York. Alternative-rock singer/songwriter/guitarist. Leader of **Soul Coughing**.

5/21/05	175	1		1 Haughty Melodic		ATO 21537
3/8/08	87	1		2 Golden Delicious		ATO 0052
10/24/09	138	1		3 Sad Man Happy Man		ATO 0081

DOUGLAS, Carl
Born on 5/10/1942 in Jamaica; raised in California. Disco singer.

| 12/14/74+ | 37 | 17 | | 1 Kung Fu Fighting And Other Great Love Songs .... | | 20th Century 464 |

DOUGLAS, Carol
Born Carol Strickland on 4/7/1948 in Brooklyn, New York. Disco singer.

3/29/75	177	3		1 The Carol Douglas Album		Midland Int'l. 0931
11/6/76	188	6		2 Midnight Love Affair		Midland Int'l. 1798
7/16/77	139	10		3 Full Bloom		Midland Int'l. 2222

DOUGLAS, Mike
Born Michael Dowd on 8/11/1925 in Chicago, Illinois. Died on 8/11/2006 (age 81). Singer for Kay Kyser's band from 1945-50. Hosted own TV talk show from 1961-80.

| 1/29/66 | 46 | 15 | | 1 The Men In My Little Girl's Life .... | | Epic 26186 |

DOVE, Ronnie
Born on 9/7/1935 in Herndon, Virginia; raised in Baltimore, Maryland. White Adult Contemporary singer.

7/24/65	119	41		1 One Kiss For Old Times' Sake		Diamond 5003
4/2/66	35	21		2 The Best Of Ronnie Dove .... [G]		Diamond 5005
10/22/66	122	5		3 Ronnie Dove Sings The Hits For You		Diamond 5006
3/4/67	121	12		4 Cry		Diamond 5007

DOVELLS, The
Rock and roll vocal group from Philadelphia, Pennsylvania: **Len Barry**, Arnie Silver, Jerry Summers and Mike Dennis.

| 7/13/63 | 119 | 7 | | 1 You Can't Sit Down .... | | Parkway 7025 |

~ ~ ~ ~ ~ ~ ~ ~ ~ **NON-CHARTED ALBUMS** ~ ~ ~ ~ ~ ~ ~ ~ ~ ~
1961 **Bristol Stomp**   1962 **For Your Hully Gully Party**
1962 **All The Hits Of The Teen Groups**

DOVES
Pop-rock trio from Manchester, England: Jimi Goodwin (vocals, bass), with twin brothers Jez Williams (guitar) and Andy Williams (drums).

6/22/02	83	3		1 The Last Broadcast		Heavenly 12232
3/19/05	111	2		2 Some Cities		Heavenly 74609
4/25/09	89	2		3 Kingdom Of Rust		Heavenly 93134

DOVE SHACK
Rap trio from Long Beach, California: Mark Makonie, Anthony Blount and Gary Brown.

| 9/9/95 | 68 | 8 | | 1 This Is The Shack .... | | G Funk 527933 |

DOWELL, Joe
Born on 1/23/1940 in Bloomington, Indiana. Pop singer.

~ ~ ~ ~ ~ ~ ~ ~ ~ **NON-CHARTED ALBUM** ~ ~ ~ ~ ~ ~ ~ ~ ~ ~
1961 **Wooden Heart**

DOWN
Hard-rock band formed in New Orleans, Louisiana: Philip Anselmo (vocals; **Pantera**), Pepper Keenan (guitar; **Corrosion Of Conformity**), Kirk Windstein (guitar), Todd Strange (bass) and Jimmy Bower (drums). Anselmo was also with **Superjoint Ritual**.

10/7/95	57	6		1 Nola		EastWest 61830
4/13/02	44	6		2 A Bustle In Your Hedgerow...		Elektra 62745
10/13/07	26	4		3 Over The Under		Down 286176

235

Billboard			ARTIST		
DEBUT	**PEAK**	**WKS**	**Album Title**	**Catalog**	**Label & Number**

DOWNEY, Robert Jr.
Born on 4/4/1965 in Greenwich Village, New York. Popular movie actor. Singer/songwriter/keyboardist.

| 12/11/04 | 121 | 2 | 1 The Futurist .... | | Sony Classical 92654 |

DOWNHERE
Christian rock band formed in Caronport, Saskatchewan, Canada: Marc Martel (vocals, guitar), Jason Germain (guitar), Glenn Lavender (bass) and Jeremy Thiessen (drums).

| 10/24/09 | 8ˣ | 3 | 1 How Many Kings: Songs For Christmas [X] | | Centricity 1092 |

DOWNING, Will
Born in 1963 in Brooklyn, New York. R&B singer/songwriter/producer. Prolific session vocalist.

8/21/93	166	7	1 Love's The Place To Be		Mercury 518086
11/25/95	139	2	2 Moods...		Mercury 528755
11/15/97	127	3	3 Invitation Only		Mercury 536350
10/17/98	169	3	4 Pleasures Of The Night..		Verve Forecast 557613
			WILL DOWNING & GERALD ALBRIGHT		
8/5/00	100	7	5 All The Man You Need		Motown 157881
5/25/02	90	7	6 Sensual Journey		GRP 589610
11/1/03	92	6	7 Emotions..		GRP 000529
11/27/04	37ˣ	1	8 Christmas, Love And You................................... [X]		GRP 002748
10/22/05	85	3	9 Soul Symphony		GRP 005215
11/17/07	37	3	10 After Tonight..		Peak 30221
7/4/09	22	8	11 Classique		Peak 31278

DOZIER, Lamont
Born on 6/16/1941 in Detroit, Michigan. R&B singer/songwriter/producer. With the brothers Brian Holland and Eddie Holland in highly successful songwriting/production team for Motown. Trio left Motown in 1968 and formed own Invictus/Hot Wax label.
AWARDS: Grammy: Trustees 1998 ★ R&R Hall of Fame: 1990 (Non-Performer)

1/26/74	136	13	1 Out Here On My Own		ABC 804
1/25/75	186	2	2 Black Bach..		ABC 839
1/23/82	210	1	3 Lamont...		M&M 104

DRAG-ON
Born Melvin Smalls on 1/4/1979 in the Bronx, New York. Male rapper. Member of **Ruff Ryders**.

| 4/15/00 | 5 | 14 | ● 1 Opposite Of H20 | | Ruff Ryders 490609 |
| 2/28/04 | 47 | 6 | 2 Hell And Back .... | | Ruff Ryders 83583 |

DRAGON
Pop-rock band from Auckland, New Zealand: Marc Hunter (vocals), Robert Taylor (guitar), Alan Mansfield and Paul Hewson (keyboards), Todd Hunter (bass), and Terry Chambers (drums). Hewson died of a drug overdose on 1/9/1985. Hunter died of cancer on 7/17/1998 (age 44).

| 9/15/84 | 208 | 3 | 1 Body And The Beat .... | | Polydor 817874 |

DRAGON, Carmen
Born on 7/28/1914 in Antioch, California. Died on 3/28/1984 (age 69). Conductor of the Capitol Symphony Orchestra. Father of Daryl Dragon (of **Captain & Tennille**). Also see **Leonard Pennario**.

| 4/14/62 | 36 | 8 | 1 Nightfall .... [I] | | Capitol 8575 |

DRAGONFORCE
Hard-rock band formed in London, England: ZP "Zippy" Theart (vocals), Herman Li (guitar), Sam Totman (guitar), Vadim Pruzhanov (keyboards), Frederic Leclercq (bass) and Dave Mackintosh (drums).

| 7/8/06 | 103 | 23 | 1 Inhuman Rampage .... | | Roadrunner 618034 |
| 9/13/08 | 18 | 5 | 2 Ultra Beatdown... | | Roadrunner 617937 |

DRAKE
Born Aubrey Drake Graham on 10/24/1986 in Toronto, Ontario, Canada. Male rapper/singer/actor. Played "Jimmy Brooks" on TV's *Degrassi: The Next Generation*.

| 10/3/09 | 6 | 35↑ | 1 So Far Gone [EP] | | Young Money 013456 |

DRAKE, Nick
Born on 6/19/1948 in Rangoon, Burma; raised in Birmingham, England. Died of a drug overdose on 11/25/1974 (age 26). Folk-rock singer/acoustic guitarist.

~ ~ ~ ~ ~ ~ ~ ~ ~ **NON-CHARTED ALBUMS** ~ ~ ~ ~ ~ ~ ~ ~ ~ ~ ~

1972 **Pink Moon**
    RS500 #320

1976 **Five Leaves Left**
    RS500 #283

1977 **Bryter Layter**
    RS500 #245

DRAKE, Pete, And His Talking Steel Guitar
Born Roddis Drake on 10/8/1932 in Atlanta, Georgia. Died on 7/29/1988 (age 55). Session steel guitarist.

| 5/2/64 | 85 | 14 | 1 Forever .... | | Smash 67053 |

DRAMA
Born Terrence Cook in 1980 in Atlanta, Georgia. Male rapper. Drama stands for Drastic Retaliation Against My Adversaries.

2/26/00	32	26	● 1 Causin' Drama		Atlantic 83306
12/22/07	26	13	2 Gangsta Grillz: The Album		Grand Hustle 185852
6/6/09	26	4	3 Gangsta Grillz: The Album Vol. 2		Embassy 515814

Billboard			R I A A	ARTIST		
DEBUT	PEAK	WKS		Album Title	Catalog	Label & Number

DRAMATICS, The
R&B vocal group from Detroit, Michigan: Ron Banks, William Howard, Larry Demps, Willie Ford and Elbert Wilkins. Howard and Wilkins replaced by L.J. Reynolds and Lenny Mayes in 1973. Wilkins died on 12/13/1992 (age 45). Howard died on 2/22/2000 (age 49). Mayes died on 11/7/2004 (age 53). Banks died on 3/4/2010 (age 58).

DEBUT	PEAK	WKS		Album Title	Catalog	Label & Number
1/22/72	20	24		1 Whatcha See Is Whatcha Get		Volt 6018
10/13/73	86	18		2 A Dramatic Experience		Volt 6019
5/4/74	156	6		3 The Dells vs. The Dramatics		Cadet 60027
3/22/75	31	18		4 The Dramatic Jackpot		ABC 867
11/15/75	93	12		5 Drama V		ABC 916
10/30/76+	103	25		6 Joy Ride		ABC 955
8/13/77	60	19		7 Shake It Well		ABC 1010
5/13/78	44	15	●	8 Do What You Wanna Do		ABC 1072
3/8/80	61	12		9 10 1/2		MCA 3196

DREAD ZEPPELIN
White reggae band from Pasadena, California: Elvis Presley impersonator Greg "Tortelvis" Tortell (vocals), Joe Ramsey and Carl Haasis (guitars), Bryant Fernandez (percussion), Gary Putman (bass) and Paul Masselli (drums). Group specialized in Led Zeppelin songs.

DEBUT	PEAK	WKS		Album Title	Catalog	Label & Number
8/25/90	116	13		1 Un-Led-Ed		I.R.S. 82048

DREAM
Female pop vocal group from Los Angeles, California: Holly Arnstein, Melissa Schuman, Ashley Poole and Diana Ortiz.

DEBUT	PEAK	WKS		Album Title	Catalog	Label & Number
2/10/01	6	34	▲	1 It Was All A Dream		Bad Boy 73037

DREAM, The
Born Terius Nash on 12/12/1978 in Rockingham, North Carolina; raised in Atlanta, Georgia. Male rapper/songwriter. Married to Nivea from 2004-07. Married Christina Milian on 9/4/2009.

DEBUT	PEAK	WKS		Album Title	Catalog	Label & Number
12/29/07	30	40	●	1 Love/Hate		Radio Killa 009872
3/28/09	2[1]	28		2 Love V/S Money		Radio Killa 012579

DREAM ACADEMY, The
Pop-rock trio from England: Nick Laird-Clowes (guitar, vocals), Gilbert Gabriel (keyboards) and Kate St. John (oboe, vocals).

DEBUT	PEAK	WKS		Album Title	Catalog	Label & Number
11/9/85+	20	37		1 The Dream Academy		Warner 25265
11/14/87	181	3		2 Remembrance Days		Reprise 25625

DREAMBOY
R&B group from Oak Park, Michigan: Jeff Stanton (vocals), Jeff Bass (guitar), Jimi Hunt (keyboards), Paul Stewart (bass) and George Twymon (drums).

DEBUT	PEAK	WKS		Album Title	Catalog	Label & Number
1/14/84	168	11		1 Dreamboy [EP]		Qwest 23988

DREAMS
Jazz-rock band formed in New York: brothers Michael Brecker (sax) and Randy Brecker (trumpet), Edward Vernon (vocals), Jeff Kent (guitar), Barry Rogers (trombone), Doug Lubahn (bass) and Billy Cobham (drums). Michael and Randy later recorded as The Brecker Brothers. Michael died on 1/13/2007 (age 57).

DEBUT	PEAK	WKS		Album Title	Catalog	Label & Number
11/28/70	146	6		1 Dreams		Columbia 30225

DREAMS SO REAL
Rock trio from Athens, Georgia: Barry Marler (vocals, guitar), Trent Allen (bass) and Drew Worsham (drums).

DEBUT	PEAK	WKS		Album Title	Catalog	Label & Number
11/26/88+	150	18		1 Rough Night In Jericho		Arista 8555

DREAM STREET
Teen male vocal group from New York: Matt Ballinger, Frankie Galasso, Jesse McCartney, Greg Raposo and Chris Trousdale.

DEBUT	PEAK	WKS		Album Title	Catalog	Label & Number
7/28/01	37	27	●	1 Dream Street		Edel 18304

DREAM SYNDICATE
Rock band from Los Angeles, California: Steve Wynn (vocals, guitar), Karl Precoda (guitar), Dave Provost (bass) and Dennis Duck (drums).

DEBUT	PEAK	WKS		Album Title	Catalog	Label & Number
4/30/83	208	1		1 The Days Of Wine And Roses		Ruby 23844
8/4/84	171	4		2 Medicine Show		A&M 4990

DREAM THEATER   All-Time: #409
Hard-rock band from Los Angeles, California: James LaBrie (vocals), John Petrucci (guitar), Kevin Moore (keyboards), John Myung (bass) and Mike Portnoy (drums). Derek Sherinian replaced Moore in September 1994. Jordan Rudess replaced Sherinian in 1999.

DEBUT	PEAK	WKS		Album Title	Catalog	Label & Number
1/9/93	61	24	●	1 Images And Words		Atco 92148
10/22/94	32	6		2 Awake		EastWest 90126
10/7/95	58	3		3 A Change Of Seasons [EP-L]		EastWest 61842
10/11/97	52	4		4 Falling Into Infinity		EastWest 62060
11/14/98	157	1		5 Once In A Livetime [L]		EastWest 62308 [2]
				recorded on 6/25/1998 in Paris		
11/13/99	73	2		6 Metropolis Pt. 2: Scenes From A Memory		EastWest 62448
9/29/01	120	1		7 Live Scenes From New York [L]		Elektra 62661 [3]
				recorded on 8/30/2000 at the Roseland Ballroom in New York City		
2/16/02	46	2		8 Six Degrees Of Inner Turbulence		Elektra 62742 [2]
11/29/03	53	2		9 Train Of Thought		Elektra 62891
6/25/05	36	3		10 Octavarium		Atlantic 83793
9/16/06	134	1		11 Score: 20th Anniversary World Tour Live [L]		Rhino 74062 [3]
				DREAM THEATER with The Octavarium Orchestra		
6/23/07	19	5		12 Systematic Chaos		Roadrunner 617992

DREAM THEATER — cont'd

4/19/08	122	1	13 Greatest Hit (And 21 Other Pretty Cool Songs)		Atlantic 429948 [2]
7/11/09	6	8	14 **Black Clouds & Silver Linings**		Roadrunner 617883

DREDG
Hard-rock band from Los Gatos, California: Gavin Hayes (vocals, guitar), Mark Engles (guitar), Drew Roulette (bass) and Dino Campanella (drums).

7/9/05	123	1	1 Catch Without Arms..		Interscope 004864
6/27/09	71	1	2 The Pariah, The Parrot, The Delusion		Ohlone 518755

DREGS, The — see DIXIE DREGS

DRESDEN DOLLS, The
Alternative-rock duo from Boston, Massachusetts: **Amanda Palmer** (vocals, piano) and Brian Viglione (guitar, drums).

5/6/06	42	3	1 Yes, Virginia..		Roadrunner 618081
6/7/08	94	1	2 No, Virginia...		Roadrunner 179262

DREW, Kevin
Born in 1976 in Toronto, Ontario, Canada. Alternative-rock singer/songwriter. Formed **Broken Social Scene**.

10/6/07	113	1	1 Spirit If...		Arts & Crafts 02700

D.R.I.
Punk-rock band from Houston, Texas: Kurt Brecht (vocals), Spike Cassidy (guitar), Josh Pappe (bass) and Felix Griffin (drums). John Menor replaced Pappe in 1989. D.R.I.: Dirty Rotten Imbeciles.

7/23/88	116	14	1 Four Of A Kind..		Metal Blade 77304
12/23/89+	140	13	2 Thrash Zone		Metal Blade 73407

DRIFTERS, The
R&B vocal group formed in Harlem, New York: **Ben E. King**, Charlie Thomas, Doc Green and Elsbearry Hobbs, with Reggie Kimber (guitar). Rudy Lewis replaced King in 1961. Lewis died of a heart attack on 5/20/1964 (age 27); replaced by Johnny Moore. Hobbs died on 5/31/1996 (age 60). Moore died of respiratory failure on 12/30/1998 (age 64).

AWARD: R&R Hall of Fame: 1988

6/8/63	110	9	1 Up On The Roof - The Best Of The Drifters .... [G]		Atlantic 8073
8/15/64	40	22	2 Under The Boardwalk		Atlantic 8099
2/6/65	103	6	3 The Good Life With The Drifters		Atlantic 8103
3/16/68	122	8	4 The Drifters' Golden Hits .... [G]		Atlantic 8153
			RS500 #465		

~ ~ ~ ~ ~ ~ ~ ~ ~ **NON-CHARTED ALBUMS** ~ ~ ~ ~ ~ ~ ~ ~ ~ ~
1956 Clyde McPhatter & The Drifters   1962 Save The Last Dance For Me
1958 Rockin' & Driftin'   1964 "Our Biggest Hits"
1960 The Drifters' Greatest Hits

DRISCOLL, Julie — see AUGER, Brian

DRIVE-BY TRUCKERS
Rock band formed in Memphis, Tennessee: **Jason Isbell** (vocals, guitar), Mike Cooley (vocals, guitar), **Patterson Hood** (keyboards), Shonna Tucker (bass) and Brad Morgan (drums). Isbell left in 2007.

9/11/04	147	1	1 The Dirty South		New West 6058
5/6/06	50	3	2 A Blessing And A Curse		New West 6089
2/9/08	37	4	3 Brighter Than Creation's Dark		New West 6135
7/25/09	172	1	4 Live From Austin TX .... [L]		New West 6168
9/19/09	82	1	5 The Fine Print (A Collection of Oddities And Rarities) 2003-2008 .... [K]		New West 6169

DRIVIN' N' CRYIN'
Rock band from Atlanta, Georgia: Kevn Kinney (vocals), Buren Fowler (guitar), Tim Nielsen (bass) and Jeff Sullivan (drums).

4/2/88	130	12	1 Whisper Tames The Lion		Island 90699
1/26/91	90	38	● 2 Fly Me Courageous		Island 848000
3/13/93	95	3	3 Smoke		Island 514319

DROPBOX
Hard-rock band formed in Boston, Massachusetts: John Kosco (vocals), Lee Richards (guitar), Joe Wilkinson (guitar), Jim Preziosa (bass) and Bob Jenkins (drums).

5/1/04	182	1	1 Dropbox		Republic 002057

DROP DEAD, GORGEOUS
Hard-rock band from Denver, Colorado: Danny Stillman (vocals), Kyle BRowning (guitar), Jake Hansen (bass) and Danny Cooper (drums).

9/1/07	139	2	1 Worse Than A Fairy Tale		Suretone 009607
6/20/09	192	1	2 The Hot N' Heavy		Suretone 012943

DROPKICK MURPHYS
Punk-rock band from Boston, Massachusetts: Mike McColgan (vocals), Rick Barton (guitar), Ken Casey (bass) and Matt Kelly (drums). McColgan and Barton left in 2000; replaced by Al Barr (vocals) and James Lynch (guitar). McColgan later formed **Street Dogs**.

4/3/99	184	1	1 The Gang's All Here		Hellcat 80413
2/24/01	144	1	2 Sing Loud, Sing Proud!		Hellcat 80430
9/28/02	155	1	3 Live On St. Patrick's Day From Boston, MA. At The Avalon Ballroom......... [L]		Hellcat 80437

				DROPKICK MURPHYS — cont'd		
6/28/03	83	6		4 Blackout		Hellcat 80446
7/9/05	48	6		5 The Warrior's Code...............................	Cat:#33/3	Hellcat 80472
10/6/07	20	10		6 The Meanest Of Times		Born & Bred 286012

DROWNING POOL
Hard-rock band from Dallas, Texas: Dave Williams (vocals), C.J. Pierce (guitar), Stevie Benton (bass) and Mike Luce (drums). Williams died of a rare heart ailment (cardiomyopathy) on 8/13/2002 (age 30); replaced by Jason "Gong" Jones.

6/23/01	14	50	▲	1 Sinner		Wind-Up 13065
5/8/04	17	10		2 Desensitized		Wind-Up 13080
8/25/07	64	4		3 Full Circle		Eleven Seven 140

D.R.S.
Male R&B vocal group from Sacramento, California: Endo, Pic, Jail Bait, Deuce Deuce and Blunt. D.R.S.: Dirty Rotten Scoundrels.

11/20/93	34	15	●	1 Gangsta Lean		Capitol 81445

DRU DOWN
Born Darnel Robinson in Oakland, California. Male rapper.

9/21/96	54	7		1 Can You Feel Me		Relativity 1531

DRU HILL
Male R&B vocal group from Baltimore, Maryland: Mark **"Sisqo"** Andrews, James **"Woody Rock"** Green, Tamir **"Nokio"** Ruffin and Larry "Jazz" Anthony. Green left in March 1999. Group named after Druid Hill Park in Baltimore.

12/7/96+	23	72	▲	1 Dru Hill		Island 524306
11/14/98	2[1]	53	▲[2]	2 Enter The Dru		Island 524542
12/14/02	21	26	●	3 Dru World Order		Def Soul 063377
10/29/05	72	3		4 Hits .... [G]		Def Soul 005220

D-SHOT
Born Dannell Stevens in San Francisco, California. Male rapper. Member of **The Click**. Brother of **E-40**.

8/16/97	81	2		1 Six Figures		Shot 41602

"D" TRAIN
R&B duo from Brooklyn, New York: James "D Train" Williams (vocals) and Hubert Eaves III (keyboards).

6/26/82	128	9		1 "D" Train		Prelude 14105

D12
Rap group from Detroit, Michigan: Marshall Mathers (**"Eminem"**), DeShaun Holton (**"Proof"**), Denaun Porter (**"Kon Artis"**), Rufus Johnson (**"Bizarre"**), Ondre Moore (**"Swift"**) and Von Carlisle (**"Kuniva"**). D-12 is short for Dirty Dozen. Holton was shot to death on 4/11/2006 (age 30).

7/7/01	❶[2]	22	▲	1 Devil's Night	Cat:#42/1	Shady 490897
5/15/04	❶[1]	28	▲[2]	2 D12 World		Shady 002404

DUALS, The
Rock and roll instrumental duo from Los Angeles, California: Henry Bellinger and Johnny Lageman.

~ ~ ~ ~ ~ ~ ~ ~ ~ ~   *NON-CHARTED ALBUM*   ~ ~ ~ ~ ~ ~ ~ ~ ~ ~
1961 **Stick Shift Twist**

DUBS, The
R&B vocal group from Harlem, New York: Richard Blandon (lead singer), Cleveland Still, Bill Carlyle, Tommy Grate and Jake Miller. Blandon died on 12/20/1991 (age 57).

~ ~ ~ ~ ~ ~ ~ ~ ~ ~   *NON-CHARTED ALBUM*   ~ ~ ~ ~ ~ ~ ~ ~ ~ ~
1962 **The Dubs Meet The Shells**

DUCHIN, Eddy — see MOVIE SOUNDTRACKS: "The Eddy Duchin Story"

DUDEK, Les
Born on 8/2/1952 in Quonset Point, Rhode Island. Rock singer/songwriter/guitarist.

4/17/76	204	3		1 Les Dudek		Columbia 33702
4/23/77	107	12		2 Say No More		Columbia 34397
5/6/78	100	11		3 Ghost Town Parade		Columbia 35088
5/23/81	203	2		4 Gypsy Ride		MCA 36798

DUDES
Rock band from Montreal, Quebec, Canada: Brian Greenway (vocals, guitar), David Henman (guitar), Bob Segarini (guitar), Kootch Trochim (bass), and Ritchie Henman and Wayne Cullen (drums).

10/25/75	208	2		1 We're No Angels...		Columbia 33577

DUELO
Latin band from Mexico: Oscar Trevino, Dimas Lopez, Christian Rivera, Edgar Rodriguez and Juan Barrera.

6/24/06	165	1		1 Relaciones Conflictivas .... [F]		Univision 310724
7/14/07	110	2		2 En Las Manos De Un Angel .... [F]		Univision 311056
2/14/09	88	3		3 Necesito Mas De Ti .... [F]		Fonovisa 353887

Billboard DEBUT	PEAK	WKS	R I A A	ARTIST Album Title	Catalog	Label & Number

DUFF, Hilary
Born on 9/28/1987 in Houston, Texas. Actress/singer. Played the title character in both the TV series and movie *Lizzie McGuire*. Also appeared in several other movies and TV shows.

12/7/02	154	3	●	1 Santa Claus Lane .... Cat:❶¹/13 [X]		Buena Vista 60066
				Christmas charts: 23/'02, 5/'03, 29/'04, 38/'05		
9/13/03	❶¹	77	▲³	2 Metamorphosis	Cat:#35/2	Buena Vista 861006
10/16/04	2¹	33	▲	3 Hilary Duff		Hollywood 162473
9/3/05	❶²	35	▲	4 Most Wanted	[G]	Hollywood 162524
4/21/07	3¹	19	●	5 Dignity		Hollywood 162668
11/29/08	125	1		6 Best Of Hilary Duff	[G]	Hollywood 002195

DUFFY
Born Aimee Duffy on 6/23/1984 in Bangor, Gwynedd, Wales. Pop-rock singer/songwriter.

5/31/08	4	49	●	1 Rockferry		Mercury 010822
				Grammy: Pop Vocal Album		

DUICE
Male rap duo: Ira "L.A. Sno" Brown (from California) and Anthony "Creo-D" Darlington (from Barbados).

2/6/93	84	38	●	1 Dazzey Duks		TMR 71000

DUKE, George
Born on 1/12/1946 in San Rafael, California. Jazz-rock keyboardist. Own group in San Francisco during the mid-1950s. With the Don Ellis Big Band and **Jean-Luc Ponty**. With **Frank Zappa**'s Mothers Of Invention from 1971-75. Also with **Cannonball Adderley** from 1972-75. Own group from 1977. With **Stanley Clarke** in the Clarke/Duke Project.

2/1/75	141	6		1 Feel		MPS/BASF 25355
5/31/75	111	10		2 The Aura Will Prevail		MPS/BASF 25613
1/24/76	169	6		3 I Love The Blues, She Heard My Cry		MPS/BASF 25671
10/23/76	99	9		4 "Live"-On Tour In Europe	[L]	Atlantic 18194
				THE BILLY COBHAM & GEORGE DUKE BAND		
12/4/76	190	2		5 Liberated Fantasies	[I]	MPS/BASF 22835
5/14/77	192	3		6 From Me To You		Epic 34469
10/29/77+	25	24	●	7 Reach For It		Epic 34883
6/3/78	39	14		8 Don't Let Go		Epic 35366
3/17/79	56	11		9 Follow The Rainbow		Epic 35701
11/24/79+	125	11		10 Master Of The Game		Epic 36263
5/31/80	119	9		11 A Brazilian Love Affair		Epic 36483
5/9/81	33	23		12 The Clarke/Duke Project		Epic 36918
				STANLEY CLARKE/GEORGE DUKE		
3/6/82	48	12		13 Dream On		Epic 37532
4/30/83	147	7		14 Guardian Of The Light		Epic 38513
11/26/83+	146	10		15 The Clarke/Duke Project II		Epic 38934
				STANLEY CLARKE/GEORGE DUKE		
4/20/85	183	5		16 Thief In The Night		Elektra 60398
9/13/08	192	1		17 Dukey Treats		BPM 3143

DUKE, Patty
Born Anna Marie Duke on 12/14/1946 in Elmhurst, New York. Movie and TV actress. Married to actor John Astin from 1972-85.

9/18/65	90	12		1 Don't Just Stand There		United Artists 3452

DUKEDAGOD
Born George Moore in Harlem, New York. R&B singer/songwriter. Vice president of A&R for Diplomats record label.

4/29/06	53	5		1 Dipset: The Movement Moves On		Diplomats 68754

DUKE JUPITER
Rock band from Rochester, New York: Marshall James Styler (vocals, keyboards), Greg Walker (guitar), George Barajas (bass) and David Corcoran (drums). Barajas died on 8/17/1982 (age 33). Rickey Ellis (bass) joined in 1983.

4/17/82	204	5		1 Duke Jupiter 1		Coast To Coast 37912
6/2/84	122	12		2 White Knuckle Ride		Morocco 6097

DUKES OF DIXIELAND
Dixieland jazz band from New Orleans, Louisiana: brothers Frank Assunto (trumpet), Fred Assunto (trombone) and Joe Assunto (banjo), with Harold Cooper (clarinet), Stanley Mendelson (piano), Bill Porter (tuba) and Paul Ferrara (drums). Fred Assunto died on 4/21/1966 (age 36). Frank Assunto died on 2/25/1974 (age 42).

9/9/57+	6	26		1 Marching Along With The Dukes Of Dixieland, Vol. 3	[I]	Audio Fidelity 1851
12/11/61+	10	21		2 The Best Of The Dukes Of Dixieland	[G-I]	Audio Fidelity 1956

DULFER, Candy
Born on 9/19/1969 in Amsterdam, Netherlands. Female saxophonist.

6/22/91	22	36	●	1 Saxuality	[I]	Arista 8674

DUNGEON FAMILY
All-star rap group: **Outkast**, **Goodie Mob**, **Backbone**, **Cool Breeze**, **Witchdoctor** and Organized Noize.

12/8/01	42	11		1 Even In Darkness		Arista 14693

Billboard			R I A A	ARTIST		
DEBUT	**PEAK**	**WKS**		**Album Title**	**Catalog**	**Label & Number**

DUNHAM, Jeff
Born on 4/18/1962 in Dallas, Texas. Popular ventriloquist.

| 11/22/08 | 69 | 7 | | 1 Jeff Dunham's Don't Come Home For Christmas .... [X-N] | | Levity 5151 |

Christmas charts: 17/'08, 24/'09

DUNLAP, Gene
Born in Detroit, Michigan. R&B drummer/guitarist/keyboardist. Member of **Earl Klugh**'s group. The Ridgeways vocal group consisted of sisters Gloria, Esther and Gracie with brother Tommy Ridgeway. Esther died of a heart attack on 2/22/2003 (age 43).

| 3/14/81 | 202 | 9 | | 1 It's Just The Way I Feel .... | | Capitol 12130 |

GENE DUNLAP Featuring The Ridgeways

DUNN, Holly
Born on 8/22/1957 in San Antonio, Texas. Country singer/songwriter/guitarist.
AWARDS: CMA: Horizon 1987 ★ OPRY: 1989

| 8/17/91 | 162 | 1 | ● | 1 Milestones - Greatest Hits .... [G] | | Warner 26630 |

DUPREE, Robbie
Born Robert Dupuis on 12/23/1946 in Brooklyn, New York. Pop singer/songwriter.

| 6/14/80 | 51 | 24 | | 1 Robbie Dupree .... | | Elektra 273 |
| 6/13/81 | 169 | 5 | | 2 Street Corner Heroes .... | | Elektra 344 |

DUPREES, The
Italian-American doo-wop group from Jersey City, New Jersey: Joey Vann, Mike Arnone, Tom Bialablow, Joe Santollo and John Salvato. Santollo died of a heart attack on 6/4/1981 (age 37). Vann died on 2/28/1984 (age 40). Arnone died on 10/27/2005 (age 63).

| 12/15/62 | 101 | 5 | | 1 You Belong To Me .... | | Coed 905 |

~ ~ ~ ~ ~ ~ ~ ~ ~ ~ **NON-CHARTED ALBUM** ~ ~ ~ ~ ~ ~ ~ ~ ~ ~
1963 **Have You Heard**

DUPRI, Jermaine
Born Jermaine Dupri Mauldin on 9/23/1972 in Asheville, North Carolina; raised in Atlanta, Georgia. Rapper/prolific producer. Started own So So Def Record label. Discovered **Kris Kross** and **Da Brat**. Acted in the movies *In Too Deep* and *The New Guy*.

| 8/8/98 | 3[1] | 27 | ▲ | 1 Jermaine Dupri Presents Life In 1472 - The Original Soundtrack | | So So Def 69087 |
| 11/17/01 | 15 | 20 | | 2 Instructions .... | | So So Def 85830 |

DURAN DURAN   **1980s: #48 / All-Time: #200**
Synth-pop-dance band from Birmingham, England: Simon LeBon (vocals; born on 10/27/1958), Andy Taylor (guitar; born on 2/16/1961), Nick Rhodes (keyboards; born on 6/8/1962), John Taylor (bass; born on 6/20/1960) and Roger Taylor (drums; born on 4/26/1960). None of the Taylors are related. Group named after a villain in the Jane Fonda movie *Barbarella*. In 1984, Andy and Roger left the group. In 1985, Andy and John recorded with supergroup **The Power Station**; Simon, Nick and Roger recorded as **Arcadia**. Duran Duran reduced to a trio in 1986 of Simon, Nick and John. Expanded to a quintet in 1990 with the addition of guitarist Warren Cuccurullo (**Missing Persons**) and drummer Sterling Campbell (left by 1993; joined **Soul Asylum** in 1995). The original lineup reunited in 2004. Huge popularity helped by their distinctive MTV music videos.

6/5/82+	6	129	▲²	1 Rio		Harvest 12211
10/2/82	98	15		2 Carnival .... [EP]		Harvest 15006
				new mixes of previously released material		
2/19/83	10	87	▲	3 Duran Duran [E]		Capitol 12158
				first released in 1981		
12/10/83+	8	64	▲²	4 Seven And The Ragged Tiger		Capitol 12310
12/1/84+	4	28	▲²	5 Arena [L]		Capitol 12374
12/20/86+	12	34	▲	6 Notorious		Capitol 12540
11/5/88	24	26	●	7 Big Thing		Capitol 90958
12/9/89+	67	16	▲	8 Decade .... [G]		Capitol 93178
9/8/90	46	10		9 Liberty		Capitol 94292
3/13/93	7	47	▲	10 Duran Duran		Capitol 98876
4/22/95	19	10	●	11 Thank You		Capitol 29419
11/1/97	58	3		12 Medazzaland		Capitol 33876
4/24/99	170	1	▲	13 Greatest .... Cat:#7/11 [G]		Capitol 96239
7/1/00	135	1		14 Pop Trash		Hollywood 62266
10/30/04	17	8		15 Astronaut		Epic 92900
12/1/07	36	3		16 Red Carpet Massacre		Epic 07362

DURANTE, Jimmy
Born on 2/10/1893 in Brooklyn, New York. Died of pneumonia on 1/29/1980 (age 86). Legendary comedian. Appeared in several movies and TV shows.

| 9/21/63 | 30 | 19 | | 1 September Song .... | | Warner 1506 |

DURCAL, Rocio
Born Maria Ortiz on 10/4/1944 in Madrid, Spain. Died of cancer on 3/25/2006 (age 61). Latin singer.

5/24/97	152	3		1 Juntos Otra Vez .... [F]		Ariola 47805 [2]
				JUAN GABRIEL & ROCIO DURCAL		
2/18/06	61	10		2 Amor Eterno .... [F]		Sony 77124

DURY, Ian, & The Blockheads

Born on 5/12/1942 in Upminster, Essex, England. Died of cancer on 3/27/2000 (age 57). Punk-rock singer. Crippled by polio during childhood. Known as "The Poet of Punk."

DEBUT	PEAK	WKS		Album Title		Label & Number
5/6/78	168	5		1 New Boots And Panties!!!		Stiff 0002
7/21/79	126	6		2 Do It Yourself		Stiff 36104
2/7/81	159	4		3 Laughter		Stiff 36998
11/21/81	208	2		4 Lord Upminster		Polydor 6337

DWELE

Born Andwele Gardner on 2/14/1978 in Detroit, Michigan. Male R&B singer/songwriter/producer.

6/7/03	108	11		1 Subject		Virgin 80919
10/22/05	54	6		2 Some Kinda...		Virgin 71410
7/12/08	35	6		3 ...Sketches Of A Man		RT 5049

DYING FETUS

Death metal trio from Upper Marlboro, Maryland: John Gallagher (vocals, guitar), Sean Beasley (bass) and Trey Williams (drums).

10/3/09	168	1		1 Descend Into Depravity		Relapse 7054

DYKE AND THE BLAZERS

Funk band from Buffalo, New York: Arlester "Dyke" Christian (vocals), Alvester "Pig" Jacobs (guitar), Bernard Williams (sax), Clarence Towns (sax), Alvin Battle (bass) and Willie Earl (drums). Dyke was shot to death (in Phoenix, Arizona) on 3/13/1971 (age 28).

11/4/67	186	4		1 The Funky Broadway		Original Sound 8876

DYLAN, Bob — 1970s: #17 / 1980s: #43 / 2000s: 22 / All-Time: #8

Born Robert Zimmerman on 5/24/1941 in Duluth, Minnesota; raised in Hibbing, Minnesota. Highly influential singer/songwriter/guitarist/harmonica player. Innovator of folk-rock style. Took stage name from poet Dylan Thomas. To New York City in December 1960. Worked Greenwich Village folk clubs. Signed to Columbia Records in October 1961. Motorcycle crash on 7/29/1966 led to short retirement. Subject of documentaries *Don't Look Back* (1965), *Eat The Document* (1969) and *No Direction Home* (2005). Published novel *Tarantula* in 1970. Acted in movies *Pat Garrett And Billy The Kid* (1973), *Renaldo And Clara* (1978) and *Hearts Of Fire* (1987). Member of the supergroup **Traveling Wilburys**. His son **Jakob Dylan** was lead singer of **The Wallflowers**. Also see **Various Artists Compilations:** *Bob Dylan - The 30th Anniversary Concert Celebration*.

AWARDS: Grammy: Lifetime Achievement 1991 ★ R&R Hall of Fame: 1988

9/7/63	22	32	▲	1 The Freewheelin' Bob Dylan RS500 #97 ★ NRR		Columbia 1986 / 8786
3/7/64	20	21	●	2 The Times They Are A-Changin'		Columbia 2105 / 8905
9/19/64	43	41	●	3 Another Side Of Bob Dylan		Columbia 2193 / 8993
5/1/65	6	43	▲	4 Bringing It All Back Home Grammy: Hall of Fame ★ RS500 #31		Columbia 2328 / 9128
10/2/65	3[1]	47	▲	5 Highway 61 Revisited Grammy: Hall of Fame ★ RS500 #4		Columbia 2389 / 9189
7/23/66	9	34	▲[2]	6 Blonde On Blonde Grammy: Hall of Fame ★ RS500 #9		Columbia 41 / 841 [2]
1/27/68	2[4]	52	▲	7 John Wesley Harding RS500 #301		Columbia 2804 / 9604
5/3/69	3[4]	47	▲	8 Nashville Skyline		Columbia 9825
7/4/70	4	22	●	9 Self Portrait album cover painted by Dylan		Columbia 30050 [2]
11/14/70	7	23	●	10 New Morning		Columbia 30290
2/9/74	❶[4]	21	●	11 Planet Waves BOB DYLAN With The Band		Asylum 1003
2/8/75	❶[2]	24	▲[2]	12 Blood On The Tracks RS500 #16		Columbia 33235
7/26/75	7	14	●	13 The Basement Tapes [E] BOB DYLAN AND THE BAND RS500 #291 recorded in 1967		Columbia 33682 [2]
1/24/76	❶[5]	35	▲[2]	14 Desire RS500 #174		Columbia 33893
7/8/78	11	23	●	15 Street-Legal		Columbia 35453
9/8/79	3[4]	26	▲	16 Slow Train Coming		Columbia 36120
7/12/80	24	11		17 Saved album cover painted by Dylan		Columbia 36553
9/5/81	33	9		18 Shot Of Love		Columbia 37496
11/19/83	20	24	●	19 Infidels		Columbia 38819
6/22/85	33	17		20 Empire Burlesque		Columbia 40110
8/2/86	53	13		21 Knocked Out Loaded		Columbia 40439
6/18/88	61	10		22 Down In The Groove		Columbia 40957
10/7/89	30	23		23 Oh Mercy		Columbia 45281
9/29/90	38	11		24 Under The Red Sky		Columbia 46794
11/21/92	51	8		25 Good As I Been To You		Columbia 53200
11/13/93	70	4		26 World Gone Wrong Grammy: Contemporary Folk Album		Columbia 57590

DYLAN, Bob — cont'd

DEBUT	PEAK	WKS				Catalog	Label & Number
10/18/97	10	29	▲	27	**Time Out Of Mind**		Columbia 68556
					Grammys: Album of the Year / Contemporary Folk Album ★ RS500 #408		
9/29/01	5	26	●	28	**Love And Theft**		Columbia 85975
					Grammy: Contemporary Folk Album ★ RS500 #467		
9/16/06	❶¹	27	▲	29	**Modern Times**		Columbia 87606
5/16/09	❶¹	15		30	**Together Through Life**		Columbia 43893
10/31/09	23	11		31	**Christmas In The Heart** .... [X]		Columbia 57323
					Christmas chart: 1/'09		

GREATEST HITS & COMPILATIONS:

DEBUT	PEAK	WKS				Catalog	Label & Number
5/6/67	10	94	▲⁵	32	**Bob Dylan's Greatest Hits**	**Cat:#37/4**	Columbia 2663 / 9463
12/11/71+	14	36	▲⁵	33	**Bob Dylan's Greatest Hits, Vol. II**		Columbia 31120 [2]
12/22/73+	17	15	●	34	**Dylan**		Columbia 32747
					outtake recordings from 1969-70		
12/7/85+	33	22	▲	35	**Biograph**		Columbia 38830 [5]
4/13/91	49	6	●	36	**The Bootleg Series - Volumes 1-3 [Rare & Unreleased] 1961-1991**		Columbia 47382 [3]
12/3/94	126	2		37	**Greatest Hits Volume 3**		Columbia 66783
11/18/00	67	22	▲	38	**The Essential Bob Dylan**	**Cat:#23/4**	Columbia 85168 [2]
10/20/07	36	9		39	**Dylan**		Legacy 05928
10/20/07	93	1		40	**Dylan: Deluxe Edition**		Legacy 10954 [3]
10/25/08	6	8		41	**The Bootleg Series Volume 8: Tell Tale Signs: Rare And Unreleased 1989-2006**		Columbia 35795 [2]
9/19/09	97	5		42	**Playlist: The Very Best of Bob Dylan '70s**		Columbia 42942

LIVE ALBUMS:

DEBUT	PEAK	WKS				Catalog	Label & Number
7/13/74	3²	19	▲	43	**Before The Flood**		Asylum 201 [2]
					BOB DYLAN/THE BAND		
10/2/76	17	12	●	44	**Hard Rain**		Columbia 34349
5/12/79	13	25		45	**Bob Dylan At Budokan**		Columbia 36067 [2]
					recorded on 3/1/1978 in Japan		
1/5/85	115	9		46	**Real Live**		Columbia 39944
2/18/89	37	11	●	47	**Dylan & The Dead**		Columbia 45056
					BOB DYLAN & GRATEFUL DEAD		
5/20/95	23	10	●	48	**MTV Unplugged**		Columbia 67000
10/31/98	31	5	●	49	**The Bootleg Series Volume 4: Live 1966**		Columbia 65759 [2]
					recorded on 5/17/1966 at the Free Trade Hall in Manchester, England		
12/14/02	56	9	●	50	**The Bootleg Series Volume 5: Bob Dylan Live 1975: The Rolling Thunder Revue** .		Legacy 87047 [2]
4/17/04	28	4		51	**The Bootleg Series Volume 6: Live 1964: The Philharmonic Hall Concert**		Legacy 86882 [2]

SOUNDTRACKS:

DEBUT	PEAK	WKS				Catalog	Label & Number
8/4/73	16	30	●	52	**Pat Garrett & Billy The Kid**		Columbia 32460
9/17/05	16	11	●	53	**No Direction Home: The Soundtrack - The Bootleg Series Vol. 7**		Legacy 93937 [2]

~ ~ ~ ~ ~ ~ ~ ~ ~ ~   *NON-CHARTED ALBUM*   ~ ~ ~ ~ ~ ~ ~ ~ ~ ~ ~

1962 **Bob Dylan** *[Columbia 1779 / 8579]*

DYLAN, Jakob
Born on 12/9/1969 in Greenwich Village, New York. Rock singer/songwriter/guitarist. Son of **Bob Dylan**. Leader of **The Wallflowers**.

DEBUT	PEAK	WKS					Label & Number
6/28/08	24	10		1	**Seeing Things**		Starbucks 02328

DYNAMIC SUPERIORS
R&B vocal group from Washington DC: Tony Washington, George Spann, George Peterbark, Michael McCalphin and Maurice Washington.

DEBUT	PEAK	WKS					Label & Number
4/5/75	201	8		1	**The Dynamic Superiors**		Motown 822
8/9/75	130	10		2	**Pure Pleasure**		Motown 841

DYNAMITE HACK
Rock band from Austin, Texas: Mark Morris (vocals, guitar), Mike Vlahakis (guitar), Chad Robinson (bass) and Chase Scott (drums). Group name taken from a line in the 1980 movie *Caddyshack*.

DEBUT	PEAK	WKS					Label & Number
6/10/00	84	11		1	**Superfast**..		Woppitzer 157884

DYNASTY
R&B-dance trio from Los Angeles, California: Kevin Spencer, Nidra Beard and Linda Carriere.

DEBUT	PEAK	WKS					Label & Number
8/2/80	43	21		1	**Adventures In The Land Of Music**		Solar 3576
10/10/81	119	4		2	**The Second Adventure**		Solar 20

DYSON, Ronnie
Born on 6/5/1950 in Washington DC; raised in Brooklyn, New York. Died of heart failure on 11/10/1990 (age 40). R&B singer/actor. Acted in the Broadway musical *Hair* and the movie *Putney Swope*.

DEBUT	PEAK	WKS					Label & Number
9/5/70	55	18		1	**(If You Let Me Make Love To You Then) Why Can't I Touch You?**...............		Columbia 30223
4/7/73	142	7		2	**One Man Band**		Columbia 32211

Billboard			R I A A	ARTIST		
DEBUT	PEAK	WKS		Album Title	Catalog	Label & Number

E

EAGER, Brenda Lee
Born in Lower Peachtree, Alabama; raised in Chicago, Illinois. Female R&B singer.

| 7/14/73 | 201 | 11 | | 1 The Love We Have, The Love We Had .... | | Mercury 660 |
| | | | | **JERRY BUTLER & BRENDA LEE EAGER** | | |

EAGLES
1970s: #16 / All-Time: #68

Soft-rock band formed in Los Angeles, California: **Glenn Frey** (vocals, guitar; born on 11/6/1948), **Bernie Leadon** (guitar; born on 7/19/1947), **Randy Meisner** (bass; born on 3/8/1946) and **Don Henley** (vocals, drums; born on 7/22/1947). Meisner was a member of **Poco**. Leadon was a member of the **Flying Burrito Brothers**. Frey and Henley were with **Linda Ronstadt**. Debut album recorded in England in 1972. **Don Felder** (guitar; born on 9/21/1947) added in 1975. Leadon replaced by **Joe Walsh** (born on 11/20/1947) in 1975. Meisner replaced by **Timothy B. Schmit** (born on 10/30/1947) in 1977. Frey and Henley were the only members to play on all recordings. Disbanded in 1982. Henley, Frey, Felder, Walsh and Schmit reunited in 1994. Also see **Various Artists Compilations:** *Common Thread: The Songs Of The Eagles*.
AWARD: R&R Hall of Fame: 1998

6/24/72	22	49	▲	1 Eagles		Asylum 5054
				RS500 #374		
5/5/73	41	70	▲²	2 Desperado..		Asylum 5068
				Grammy: Hall of Fame		
4/20/74	17	87	▲²	3 On The Border..	Cat:#10/17	Asylum 1004
6/28/75	❶⁵	56	▲⁴	4 **One Of These Nights**		Asylum 1039
12/25/76+	❶⁸	107	▲¹⁶	5 Hotel California	Cat:#7/158	Asylum 1084
				RS500 #37		
10/20/79	❶⁹	57	▲⁷	6 The Long Run		Asylum 508
11/17/07	❶¹	75	▲⁷	7 Long Road Out Of Eden		ERC 4500 [2]
				GREATEST HITS & COMPILATIONS:		
3/6/76	❶⁵	133	▲²⁹	8 Eagles/Their Greatest Hits 1971-1975	Cat:❶¹⁴/460	Asylum 1052
11/13/82+	52	15	▲¹¹	9 Eagles Greatest Hits, Volume 2....................	Cat:#2⁵/213	Asylum 60205
12/2/00	109	10	▲	10 Selected Works: 1972-1999		Elektra 62575 [4]
11/8/03	3¹	63	▲⁵	11 The Very Best Of	Cat:❶³/98	Warner 73971 [2]
				LIVE ALBUMS:		
11/29/80	6	26	▲⁷	12 Eagles Live	Cat:#25/15	Asylum 705 [2]
11/26/94	❶²	112	▲⁸	13 Hell Freezes Over	Cat:#6/201	Geffen 24725

EAGLES OF DEATH METAL
Rock duo formed in Los Angeles, California: Jesse Hughes (vocals, guitar) and Josh Homme (bass, drums). Homme was also one-half of **Queens Of The Stone Age**.

| 4/29/06 | 113 | 2 | | 1 Death By Sexy... .... | | Records 70001 |
| 11/15/08 | 57 | 2 | | 2 Heart On .... | | Rekords Rekords 70051 |

EAMON
Born Eamon Doyle on 9/19/1984 in Staten Island, New York. Male R&B singer/songwriter.

| 3/6/04 | 7 | 16 | ● | 1 I Don't Want You Back | | Jive 58370 |

EARL, Kate
Born Kate Smithson on 10/8/1981 in Chugiak, Alaska. Female singer/songwriter.

| 9/5/09 | 69 | 1 | | 1 Kate Earl... | | Universal Rep. 0013539 |

EARLAND, Charles
Born on 5/24/1941 in Philadelphia, Pennsylvania. Died of heart failure on 12/11/1999 (age 58). R&B-jazz keyboardist/saxophonist.

7/11/70	108	19		1 Black Talk!..	[I]	Prestige 7758
11/21/70+	131	10		2 Black Drops	[I]	Prestige 7815
5/15/71	176	7		3 Living Black!	[I-L]	Prestige 10009
				recorded at the Key Club in Newark, New Jersey		
4/3/76	155	11		4 Odyssey		Mercury 1049
10/30/76	207	3		5 The Great Pyramid		Mercury 1113
4/3/82	208	3		6 Earland's Jam..	[I]	Columbia 37573

EARLE, Steve
All-Time: #476

Born on 1/17/1955 in Fort Monroe, Virginia; raised in Schertz, Texas. Country-rock singer/songwriter/guitarist. Married singer Allison Moorer on 8/11/2005.

10/25/86	89	20	●	1 Guitar Town		MCA 5713
				RS500 #489		
6/13/87	90	14		2 Exit O		MCA 5998
7/21/90	100	9		3 The Hard Way		MCA 6430
				STEVE EARLE AND THE DUKES (above 2)		
11/12/88+	56	28	●	4 Copperhead Road		Uni 7
3/23/96	106	4		5 I Feel Alright		Warner 46201
10/25/97	126	2		6 El Corazon		Warner 46789
3/13/99	133	3		7 The Mountain		E-Squared 751064
				STEVE EARLE AND THE DEL McCOURY BAND		

Billboard			ARTIST		
DEBUT	PEAK	WKS	Album Title	Catalog	Label & Number

EARLE, Steve — cont'd

6/24/00	66	4	8 Transcendental Blues		E-Squared 751033
4/27/02	109	1	9 Sidetracks .... [K]		E-Squared 751128
			contains songs that were either unreleased or underexposed		
10/12/02	59	3	10 Jerusalem		E-Squared 751147
9/11/04	89	3	11 The Revolution Starts...Now		E-Squared 751565
			Grammy: Contemporary Folk Album		
10/13/07	79	3	12 Washington Square Serenade		New West 6128
			Grammy: Contemporary Folk Album		
5/30/09	19	6	13 Townes		New West 6164
			Grammy: Contemporary Folk Album		
			tribute to songwriter Townes Van Zandt (died on 1/1/1997, age 52)		

EARLS, The
White doo-wop group from the Bronx, New York: Larry Chance, Bob Del Din, Eddie Harder and Jack Wray.

~ ~ ~ ~ ~ ~ ~ ~ ~ ~ **NON-CHARTED ALBUM** ~ ~ ~ ~ ~ ~ ~ ~ ~ ~
1963 **Remember Me Baby**

EARLY NOVEMBER, The
Punk-rock band from Hammonton, New Jersey: Arthur "Ace" Enders (vocals, guitar), Joseph Marro (guitar), Sergio Anello (bass) and Jeff Kummer (drums).

10/25/03	107	1	1 The Room's Too Cold		Drive-Thru 001480
7/29/06	31	5	2 The Mother, The Mechanic, And The Path		Drive-Thru 83630

EARSHOT
Hard-rock band from Los Angeles, California: Wil Martin (vocals), Mike Callahan (guitar), Scott Kohler (guitar), Guy Couturier (bass) and Dieter Hartmann (drums). John Sprague replaced Couturier in 2003.

5/25/02	82	5	1 Letting Go		Warner 47961
7/17/04	127	2	2 Two		Warner 48694

EARTH OPERA
Pop-rock band from Boston, Massachusetts: Peter Rowan (vocals, guitar), **David Grisman** (mandolin), John Nagy (bass) and Paul Dillon (drums). Rowan was also a member of **The Rowans** and **Seatrain**.

3/22/69	181	4	1 The Great American Eagle Tragedy		Elektra 74038

EARTHQUAKE
Rock band from San Francisco, California: John Doukas (vocals), Robbie Dunbar (guitar), Gary Phillips (piano), Stan Miller (bass) and Steve Nelson (drums).

9/4/76	151	4	1 8.5		Beserkley 0047

EARTH, WIND & FIRE   **1970s: #33 / All-Time: #107**

R&B band formed in Chicago, Illinois. Lineup from 1970-72 (on #1-3 below): **Maurice White** (vocals, drums), his brother Verdine White (bass), Wade Flemons (vocals, keyboards), Sherry Scott (vocals), Don Whitehead (keyboards), Michael Beal (guitar), Leslie Drayton (trumpet), Alex Thomas (trombone), Yakov Ben-Israel (congas) and Chet Washington (sax). White disbanded this lineup and moved to Los Angeles, California. Lineup from 1972-73 (on #4-5 below): Maurice White, Verdine White, **Philip Bailey** (vocals, percussion), Ralph Johnson (drums), Larry Dunn (keyboards), Jessica Cleaves (vocals; **Friends Of Distinction**), Roland Bautista (guitar) and **Ronnie Laws** (flute, sax). Lineup from 1974-84 (#6-16 below): Maurice White, Verdine White, Philip Bailey, Ralph Johnson, Larry Dunn, Jessica Cleaves (leaves after #6 below), Johnny Graham (guitar), Al McKay (guitar; former member of **Charles Wright & The Watts 103rd Street Rhythm Band**), Andrew Woolfolk (sax) and another brother, Freddie White (drums). Group appeared in the movies *That's The Way Of The World* (1975) and *Sgt. Pepper's Lonely Hearts Club Band* (1978). Elaborate stage shows featured an array of magic acts and pyrotechnics. Group supported by The Phoenix Horns: Michael Harris, Rahmlee Davis, Louis Satterfield, Don Myrick and Elmar Brown. Lineup from 1987-2005 (#17-23 below): Maurice White, Verdine White, Philip Bailey, Ralph Johnson, Andrew Woolfolk, Sheldon Reynolds (guitar) and Sonny Emory (drums).
AWARD: R&R Hall of Fame: 2000

5/15/71	172	13	1 Earth, Wind & Fire		Warner 1905
1/15/72	89	13	2 The Need Of Love		Warner 1958
9/7/74	97	10	3 Another Time .... [R]		Warner 2798 [2]
			reissue of #1 and #2 above		
11/25/72+	87	25	4 Last Days And Time		Columbia 31702
6/9/73	27	71 ▲	5 Head To The Sky		Columbia 32194
3/30/74	15	37 ▲	6 Open Our Eyes		Columbia 32712
3/15/75	❶³	55 ▲³	7 That's The Way Of The World .... [S]		Columbia 33280
			Grammy: Hall of Fame ★ RS500 #493		
12/6/75+	❶³	54 ▲³	8 Gratitude .... [L]		Columbia 33694 [2]
10/16/76	2²	30 ▲²	9 Spirit		Columbia 34241
12/3/77+	3⁶	47 ▲³	10 All 'N All		Columbia 34905
			Grammy: Group R&B Vocal		
12/2/78+	6	60 ▲⁵	11 The Best Of Earth, Wind & Fire, Vol. I Cat:#27/12 [G]		ARC 35647
6/16/79	3³	38 ▲²	12 I Am		ARC 35730
11/22/80	10	21 ●	13 Faces		ARC 36795 [2]
11/14/81	5	25 ▲	14 Raise!		ARC 37548
3/12/83	12	21 ●	15 Powerlight		Columbia 38367
12/3/83+	40	16	16 Electric Universe		Columbia 38980
11/21/87	33	28 ●	17 Touch The World		Columbia 40596
12/10/88	190	4 ●	18 The Best Of Earth, Wind & Fire, Vol. II .... [G]		Columbia 45013
2/17/90	70	11	19 Heritage		Columbia 45268
10/2/93	39	11	20 Millennium		Reprise 45274

Billboard DEBUT	PEAK	WKS	R I A A	ARTIST / Album Title	Catalog	Label & Number
				EARTH, WIND & FIRE — cont'd		
6/7/03	89	4		21 The Promise...		Kalimba 973002
10/11/03	22^C	7		22 Greatest Hits.. [G]		Legacy 65779
10/8/05	32	6		23 Illumination...		Sanctuary 87513
				EAST COAST FAMILY		
				Grouping of artists assembled by Michael Bivins (**New Edition**, **Bell Biv DeVoe**). Features Bivins, **Another Bad Creation**, **Boyz II Men**, **M.C. Brains**, and **Yo-Yo**, plus newcomers Whytgize, Yvette Brown, Hayden Hajdu, Cali Brock, Tam Rock, Lady V, Tom Boyy, 1010, Fruit Punch, Anthony Velasquez, and Mark Finesse.		
8/15/92	54	28	●	1 East Coast Family Volume One		Biv 10 6352
				EASTON, Elliot		
				Born Elliot Shapiro on 12/18/1953 in Brooklyn, New York. Rock singer/guitarist. Member of **The Cars**.		
3/9/85	99	11		1 Change No Change		Elektra 60393
				EASTON, Sheena		
				Born Sheena Orr on 4/27/1959 in Bellshill, Scotland. Pop singer/actress. Acted on TV's *Miami Vice*.		
				AWARD: Grammy: Best New Artist 1981		
3/14/81	24	38	●	1 Sheena Easton		EMI America 17049
11/28/81+	47	53	●	2 You Could Have Been With Me		EMI America 17061
10/16/82	85	12		3 Madness, Money And Music		EMI America 17080
9/17/83	33	38		4 Best Kept Secret		EMI America 17101
10/20/84+	15	35	▲	5 A Private Heaven		EMI America 17132
11/23/85	40	19	●	6 Do You..		EMI America 17173
12/3/88+	44	26	●	7 The Lover In Me		MCA 42249
4/27/91	90	7		8 What Comes Naturally		MCA 10131
				EASTSIDAZ, Tha		
				Male rap duo from Long Beach, California: Tracy "Tray Deee" Davis and Keiwan "Goldie Loc" Spillman.		
2/19/00	8	31	▲	1 Snoop Dogg Presents Tha Eastsidaz		TVT 2040
8/18/01	4	13	●	2 Duces 'N Trayz - The Old Fashioned Way		TVT 2230
				EASYBEATS, The		
				Rock band formed in Sydney, Australia: Steven Wright (vocals), George Young (guitar), Harry Vanda (guitar), Dick Diamonde (bass) and Gordon Fleet (drums). Young is the older brother of **AC/DC**'s Angus and Malcolm Young. Young and Vanda went on to form **Flash & The Pan**.		
6/10/67	180	5		1 Friday On My Mind		United Artists 6588
				EASY STAR ALL-STARS		
				Reggae band formed in Jamaica: Michael Goldwasser, Victor Axelrod, Patrick Dougher and Victor Rice.		
5/2/09	117	2		1 Easy Star's Lonely Hearts Dub Band		Easy Star 1018
				EAZY-E		
				Born Eric Wright on 9/7/1963 in Compton, California. Died of AIDS on 3/26/1995 (age 31). Rapper/producer. Formerly with **N.W.A.**		
12/10/88+	41	90	▲²	1 Eazy-Duz-It... Cat:#22/4		Ruthless 57100
1/2/93	70	18	●	2 5150 Home 4 Tha Sick .... [EP]		Ruthless 53815
				5150: police code for the criminally insane		
11/6/93	5	38	▲	3 It's On (Dr. Dre) 187um Killa [EP]		Ruthless 5503
				187 is slang for murder		
12/16/95	84	12	●	4 Eternal E... Cat:#2¹/1 [K]		Ruthless 50544
2/17/96	3¹	18	●	5 Str8 Off Tha Streetz Of Muthaphukkin Compton		Ruthless 5504
4/13/02	113	4		6 Impact Of A Legend .... [K]		Ruthless 86461
				EBN/OZN		
				Male duo from New York: Ned "EBN" Liben (synthesizer) and Robert "OZN" Rosen (vocals). Liben died of a heart attack on 2/18/1998 (age 44).		
3/31/84	185	4		1 Feeling Cavalier..		Elektra 60319
				EBONEE WEBB		
				Funk band from Memphis, Tennessee: Michael Winston (vocals), Thomas Brown (guitar), Gregg Davis and Leon Thomas (keyboards), Ron Coleman (trumpet), Charles Liggins (percussion), Ken Coleman (bass) and Roy Munn (drums).		
9/12/81	157	7		1 Ebonee Webb		Capitol 12148
				EBONY EYEZ		
				Born Ebony Williams in 1983 in St. Louis, Missouri. Female rapper.		
10/22/05	137	2		1 7 Day Cycle		Track Masters 66094
				ECHO & THE BUNNYMEN		
				Post-punk band from Liverpool, England: Ian McCulloch (vocals), Will Sergent (guitar), Les Pattinson (bass) and Pete DeFreitas (drums). DeFreitas died in a motorcycle accident on 6/14/1989 (age 27).		
7/25/81	184	2		1 Heaven Up Here..		Sire 3569
				RS500 #471		
3/26/83	137	9		2 Porcupine..		Sire 23770
2/11/84	188	3		3 Echo & The Bunnymen .... [EP-L]		Sire 23987
				recorded on 7/18/1983 at the Royal Albert Hall in London, England		
6/9/84	87	11		4 Ocean Rain		Sire 25084
1/11/86	158	9		5 Songs To Learn & Sing .... [K]		Sire 25360
8/8/87	51	37		6 Echo & The Bunnymen		Sire 25597

Billboard DEBUT	PEAK	WKS	R I A A	ARTIST / Album Title	Catalog	Label & Number

ECKSTINE, Billy
Born on 7/8/1914 in Pittsburgh, Pennsylvania. Died of heart failure on 3/8/1993 (age 78). R&B singer/guitarist/trumpeter. One of the most distinctive baritones in popular music. His son Ed was the president of Mercury Records.

11/17/62	92	6	1 Don't Worry 'Bout Me		Mercury 60736
8/7/71	213	3	2 Feel The Warm		Enterprise 1017

EDDIE, John
Born in 1959 in Richmond, Virginia; raised in New Jersey. Pop-rock singer/songwriter.

6/21/86	83	15	1 John Eddie		Columbia 40181

EDDY, Duane
Born on 4/26/1938 in Corning, New York; raised in Tucson, Arizona. Highly influential guitarist. Best known for his "twangy" guitar sound. His backing band, The Rebels, included top sessionmen: Al Casey (guitar), Larry Knechtel (piano) and Plas Johnson (sax). Eddy appeared in the movies *Because They're Young*, *A Thunder of Drums*, *The Wild Westerners*, *The Savage Seven* and *Kona Coast*. Married to Jessi Colter from 1961-68.

AWARD: R&R Hall of Fame: 1994

1/19/59	5	82	1 Have 'Twangy' Guitar-Will Travel [I]		Jamie 3000
8/3/59	24	24	2 Especially For You [I]		Jamie 3006
1/25/60	18	24	3 The "Twangs" The "Thang" [I]		Jamie 3009
12/26/60+	11	21	4 $1,000,000.00 Worth Of Twang [G-I]		Jamie 3014
7/17/61	93	15	5 Girls! Girls! Girls! [I]		Jamie 3019
5/26/62	82	13	6 Twistin' 'N' Twangin' [I]		RCA Victor 2525
10/27/62	72	6	7 Twangy Guitar-Silky Strings [I]		RCA Victor 2576
1/19/63	47	17	8 Dance With The Guitar Man		RCA Victor 2648
10/5/63	93	8	9 "Twangin'" Up A Storm!		RCA Victor 2700
5/16/64	144	2	10 Lonely Guitar		RCA Victor 2798

vocal background on above 3 albums by the **Anita Kerr Singers**

~ ~ ~ ~ ~ ~ ~ ~ ~ ~ **NON-CHARTED ALBUMS** ~ ~ ~ ~ ~ ~ ~ ~ ~ ~
1960 **Duane Eddy Plays Songs Of Our Heritage**   1965 **Twangsville**
1961 **$1,000,000.00 Worth Of Twang, Volume II**   1965 **Duane A Go Go Go**
1964 **Water Skiing**   1965 **Duane Eddy Does Bob Dylan**
1965 **Twangin' The Golden Hits**

EDELMAN, Randy
Born on 6/10/1947 in Paterson, New Jersey. Pop singer/songwriter/pianist. Married **Jackie DeShannon** on 6/3/1976.

3/22/75	208	2	1 Prime Cuts		20th Century 448

EDEN'S BRIDGE
Christian band from West Yorkshire, England: Sarah Lacy (vocals), David Bird (guitar), Richard Lacy (keyboards), Jon Large (bass) and Terl Bryant (drums).

11/21/98	40ˣ	1	1 Celtic Christmas [X]		StraightWay 20204

EDEN'S CHILDREN
Rock trio from Boston, Massachusetts: Richard Schamach (vocals, guitar), Larry Kiley (bass) and Jimmy Sturman (drums).

3/9/68	196	2	1 Eden's Children		ABC 624

EDEN'S CRUSH
Female pop-dance vocal group: Ana Maria Lombo (from Colombia), Ivette Sosa (from New Jersey), Maile Misajon (from California), Nicole Scherzinger (from Hawaii) and Rosanna Tavarez (from New York). Group assembled for TV series *PopStars*. Scherzinger later joined **The Pussycat Dolls**.

5/19/01	6	13	● 1 PopStars		143 Records 31164

EDER, Linda
Born on 2/3/1961 in Tucson, Arizona; raised in Brainerd, Minnesota. Singer/actress. Starred in the Broadway show *Jekyll & Hyde*.

3/25/00	184	2	1 It's No Secret Anymore		Atlantic 83236
12/16/00	158	3	2 Christmas Stays The Same [X]		Atlantic 83406
			LINDA EDER Featuring The Broadway Gospel Choir		
			Christmas chart: 37/'00		
3/2/02	151	3	3 Gold		Atlantic 83523
3/8/03	115	4	4 Broadway My Way		Atlantic 83580

EDGE, Graeme, Band
Born on 3/30/1941 in Birmingham, England. Rock drummer. Member of **The Moody Blues**. His band consisted of brothers Adrian Gurvitz (vocals, guitar) and Paul Gurvitz (bass). Also see **Baker Gurvitz Army**.

10/11/75	107	9	1 Kick Off Your Muddy Boots		Threshold 15
7/9/77	164	4	2 Paradise Ballroom		London 686
			GRAEME EDGE BAND Featuring Adrian Gurvitz (above 2)		

EDITORS
Alternative-rock band from Birmingham, England: Tom Smith (vocals), Chris Urbanowicz (guitar), Russell Leetch (bass) and Ed Lay (drums).

8/4/07	117	1	1 An End Has A Start		Fader 10703

EDMONDS, Kevon
Born in Indianapolis, Indiana. Male R&B singer. Former member of **After 7**. Brother of **Babyface**.

11/13/99	77	30	1 24/7		RCA 67704
10/31/09	78	3	2 Who Knew		Make 07961

EDMUNDS, Dave

Born on 4/15/1944 in Cardiff, Wales. Singer/songwriter/guitarist/producer. Formed Love Sculpture in 1967. Formed rockabilly band **Rockpile** in 1976. Produced for **Shakin' Stevens**, Brinsley Schwarz and **Stray Cats**.

DEBUT	PEAK	WKS	RIAA	Album Title	Catalog	Label & Number
3/4/72	212	2		1 Rockpile		MAM 3
5/21/77	209	2		2 Get It		Swan Song 8418
10/14/78	202	2		3 Tracks On Wax 4		Swan Song 8505
8/4/79	54	15		4 Repeat When Necessary		Swan Song 8507
5/16/81	48	14		5 Twangin...		Swan Song 16034
1/9/82	163	5		6 The Best Of Dave Edmunds [G]		Swan Song 8510
5/1/82	46	14		7 D.E. 7th		Columbia 37930
5/21/83	51	20		8 Information		Columbia 38651
10/13/84	140	4		9 Riff Raff		Columbia 39273
1/31/87	106	12		10 I Hear You Rockin' [L]		Columbia 40603
				THE DAVE EDMUNDS BAND		
3/24/90	146	6		11 Closer To The Flame		Capitol 90372

ED O. G & DA BULLDOGS

Rap group from Boston, Massachusetts: Edward Anderson, T-Nyne, Gee Man and DJ Cruz. ED O. G: Every Day, Other Girls. BULLDOGS: Black United Leaders Living Directly On Groovin' Sounds.

DEBUT	PEAK	WKS	RIAA	Album Title	Catalog	Label & Number
5/18/91	166	1		1 Life Of A Kid In The Ghetto		PWL America 848326

EDWARD BEAR

Pop trio from Toronto, Ontario, Canada: Larry Evoy (vocals, drums), Roger Ellis (guitar) and Paul Weldon (keyboards). Took name from a character in *Winnie The Pooh*.

DEBUT	PEAK	WKS	RIAA	Album Title	Catalog	Label & Number
2/10/73	63	16		1 Edward Bear		Capitol 11157
7/7/73	183	6		2 Close Your Eyes		Capitol 11192

EDWARDS, Dennis

Born on 2/3/1943 in Birmingham, Alabama. R&B singer. Lead singer of **The Contours** until 1968. Lead singer of **The Temptations** from 1968-77, 1980-84 and 1987-present.

DEBUT	PEAK	WKS	RIAA	Album Title	Catalog	Label & Number
3/3/84	48	27		1 Don't Look Any Further		Gordy 6057
7/27/85	205	5		2 Coolin' Out		Gordy 6148

EDWARDS, Jonathan

Born on 7/28/1946 in Aitkin, Minnesota; raised in Virginia. Singer/songwriter/guitarist.

DEBUT	PEAK	WKS	RIAA	Album Title	Catalog	Label & Number
11/20/71+	42	20		1 Jonathan Edwards		Capricorn 862
11/18/72	167	9		2 Honky-Tonk Stardust Cowboy		Atco 7015
1/19/74	205	3		3 Have A Good Time For Me		Atco 7036
1/11/75	205	2		4 Lucky Day [L]		Atco 104
4/24/76	203	3		5 Rockin' Chair		Reprise 2238

EDWARDS, Kathleen

Born on 7/11/1978 in Ottawa, Ontario, Canada. Adult Alternative singer/songwriter/guitarist.

DEBUT	PEAK	WKS	RIAA	Album Title	Catalog	Label & Number
3/19/05	173	1		1 Back To Me		Zoe 431047
3/22/08	102	1		2 Asking For Flowers		Zoe 431115

EDWARDS, Tommy

Born on 2/17/1922 in Richmond, Virginia. Died on 10/23/1969 (age 47). Black Adult Contemporary singer/pianist/songwriter. Began performing at age nine. First recorded for Top in 1949.

~ ~ ~ ~ ~ ~ ~ ~ ~ ~ ~ **NON-CHARTED ALBUM** ~ ~ ~ ~ ~ ~ ~ ~ ~ ~ ~

1958 It's All In The Game

EDWARDS, Vincent

Born Vincent Edward Zoine on 7/7/1928 in Brooklyn, New York. Died of cancer on 3/11/1996 (age 67). Actor/singer. Star of TV's *Ben Casey*.

DEBUT	PEAK	WKS	RIAA	Album Title	Catalog	Label & Number
7/7/62	5	21		1 Vincent Edwards Sings		Decca 4311
12/29/62+	125	6		2 Sometimes I'm Happy...Sometimes I'm Blue		Decca 4336

EELS

Alternative-rock trio formed in Los Angeles, California: Mark Everett (vocals, guitar), Tommy Walter (bass) and Butch Norton (drums).

DEBUT	PEAK	WKS	RIAA	Album Title	Catalog	Label & Number
9/7/96	114	11		1 Beautiful Freak		DreamWorks 50001
6/21/03	145	1		2 Shootenanny!		DreamWorks 000039
5/14/05	93	1		3 Blinking Lights And Other Revelations		Vagrant 406 [2]
6/20/09	43	3		4 Hombre Lobo: 12 Songs Of Desire		E Works 537

E-40

All-Time: #439

Born Earl Stevens on 11/15/1967 in Vallejo, California. Male rapper. Member of **The Click**.

DEBUT	PEAK	WKS	RIAA	Album Title	Catalog	Label & Number
10/16/93	131	5		1 The Mail Man		Sick Wid' It 7340
4/1/95	13	23	▲	2 In A Major Way		Sick Wid' It 41558
11/16/96	4	20	●	3 Tha Hall Of Game		Sick Wid' It 41591
8/29/98	13	9	●	4 The Element Of Surprise		Sick Wid' It 41645 [2]
11/27/99	28	6		5 Charlie Hustle: The BluePrint Of A Self-Made Millionaire		Sick Wid' It 41691
10/28/00	18	6		6 Loyalty And Betrayal		Sick Wid' It 41719
7/27/02	13	10		7 The Ballatician: Grit & Grind		Sick Wid' It 41808
9/27/03	16	5		8 Breakin News		Sick Wid' It 41857
9/11/04	133	1		9 The Best Of E-40: Yesterday, Today & Tomorrow [G]		Sick Wid' It 62572

E-40 — cont'd

4/1/06	3[1]	30	●	10 My Ghetto Report Card		Sick Wid' It 49963
12/13/08	42	10		11 The Ball Street Journal		Sick Wid' It 412540

EGAN, Walter
Born on 7/12/1948 in Jamaica, New York. Pop-rock singer/songwriter/guitarist.

5/14/77	137	6		1 Fundamental Roll		Columbia 34679
4/15/78	44	31		2 Not Shy		Columbia 35077
8/11/79	201	1		3 Hi Fi		Columbia 35796
5/28/83	187	2		4 Wild Exhibitions		Backstreet 5400

EGG CREAM Featuring Andy Adams
Rock band from Brooklyn, New York. Led by singer/songwriter Andy Adams.

5/28/77	197	4		1 Egg Cream		Pyramid 9008

EGYPTIAN LOVER, The
Born Greg Broussard on 8/31/1963 in Los Angeles, California. Techno-funk singer.

2/9/85	146	10		1 On The Nile		Egyptian Empire 0663

EIFFEL 65
Male dance trio from Italy: Jeffrey Jey, Maurizio Lobina and Gabry Ponte.

12/18/99+	4	42	▲2	1 Europop		Republic 157194

EIGHTBALL
Born Premro Smith in Memphis, Tennessee. Male rapper. One-half of **Eightball & MJG** duo.

6/6/98	5	13	▲2	1 Lost		Suave 53127 [3]
5/12/01	111	3		2 The Slab		JCOR 860924
12/8/01	47	12		3 Almost Famous		JCOR 860964
8/31/02	142	2		4 Lay It Down		Draper 1112

EIGHTBALL & MJG
Rap duo from Memphis, Tennessee: Premro **"Eightball"** Smith and Marlon Jermaine **"MJG"** Goodwin.

6/18/94	106	11		1 On The Outside Looking In		Suave 0002
11/18/95	8	21	●	2 On Top Of The World		Suave House 1521
6/5/99	10	12		3 In Our Lifetime		Suave House 53251
12/9/00	39	17		4 Space Age 4 Eva		JCOR 860916
5/29/04	3[1]	18	●	5 Living Legends		Bad Boy 002389
3/31/07	8	8		6 Ridin High		Bad Boy South 83970

EIGHTEEN VISIONS
Alternative-rock band from Anaheim, California: James Hart (vocals), Keith Barney (guitar), Mick Morris (bass) and Ken Floyd (drums). Hart later formed **Burn Halo**.

7/3/04	147	1		1 Obsession		Trustkill 92458
8/5/06	74	1		2 Eighteen Visions		Trustkill 86449

8TH DAY, The
R&B band from Detroit, Michigan: Melvin Davis (male vocals, drums), Lynn Harter (female vocals), Michael Anthony (guitar), Bruce Nazarian (guitar), Jerry Paul (percussion), Carole Stallings (electric violin), Anita Sherman (vibes) and Tony Newton (bass).

8/7/71	131	16		1 8th Day		Invictus 7306

805
Rock band from New York: Dave Porter (vocals, guitar), Ed Vivenzio (keyboards), Greg Liss (bass) and Frank Briggs (drums).

8/14/82	203	4		1 Stand In Line		RCA Victor 8013

EISLEY
Alternative-rock band from Tyler, Texas: siblings Sherri DuPree (vocals, guitar), Chauntelle DuPree (guitar), Stacy DuPree (keyboards) and Weston DuPree (drums), with Jon Wilson (bass).

2/26/05	189	1		1 Room Noises		Reprise 48990
9/1/07	70	1		2 Combinations		Reprise 223548

ELASTICA
Alternative-rock band from London, England: Justine Frischmann (vocals), Donna Matthews (guitar), Annie Holland (bass) and Justin Welch (drums).

4/1/95	66	27	●	1 Elastica		DGC 24728

EL BAMBINO, Tito
Born Efrain Nevares on 10/5/1981 in Puerto Rico. Latin reggaeton singer.

4/22/06	85	4		1 Top Of The Line	[F]	EMI Latin 49552
10/20/07	167	2		2 It's My Time	[F]	EMI Televisa 02365
4/11/09	138	20		3 El Patron	[F]	Siente 653883

ELBERT, Donnie
Born on 5/25/1936 in New Orleans, Louisiana; raised in Buffalo, New York. Died on 1/26/1989 (age 52). R&B singer.

1/1/72	153	9		1 Where Did Our Love Go		All Platinum 3007

ELBOW
Alternative-pop band from Manchester, England: Gary Garvey (vocals), brothers Mark Potter (guitar) and Craig Potter (keyboards), Pete Turner (bass) and Richard Jupp (drums).

DEBUT	PEAK	WKS				
2/14/04	196	1		1 Cast Of Thousands		V2 27189
5/10/08	109	1		2 Seldom Seen Kid		Fiction 011063

EL CHAPO
Born Ernesto Perez in Sinaloa, Mexico. Latin singer/songwriter/bassist.

| 7/14/07 | 95 | 5 | | 1 Te Va A Gustar | [F] | Disa 724118 |
| 11/29/08 | 117 | 2 | | 2 Para Siempre | [F] | Disa 724141 |

EL CHICANO
Latin band formed in Los Angeles, California. Core members: Mickey Lesperon (guitar), Andre Baeza (congas), Bobby Espinosa (organ), Freddie Sanchez (bass) and Johnny De Luna (drums). Singers included Ersi Arvizu, and brothers Rudy, Steve and Jerry Salas. Rudy and Steve Salas later formed **Tierra**. Espinosa died on 2/27/2010 (age 60).

6/13/70	51	17		1 Viva Tirado	[I]	Kapp 3632
4/17/71	178	9		2 Revolucion		Kapp 3640
5/6/72	173	13		3 Celebration		Kapp 3663
8/4/73	162	16		4 El Chicano		MCA 312
4/6/74	194	3		5 Cinco		MCA 401

EL COCO
Disco studio group led by producers Laurin Rinder and W. Michael Lewis.

| 10/15/77+ | 82 | 23 | | 1 Cocomotion | | AVI 6012 |
| 11/11/78 | 208 | 1 | | 2 Dancing In Paradise | | AVI 6044 |

EL DORADOS, The
Black doo-wop group from Chicago, Illinois: Pirkle Lee Moses (lead), Arthur Bassett, Louis Bradley, Jewel Jones and James Maddox. Moses died of a brain tumor on 12/16/2000 (age 63).

~ ~ ~ ~ ~ ~ ~ ~ ~ ~ ~ ~ ~ ~ *NON-CHARTED ALBUM* ~ ~ ~ ~ ~ ~ ~ ~ ~ ~ ~ ~ ~ ~
1959 **Crazy Little Mama**

ELECTRIC BOYS
Male rock band from Sweden: Conny Bloom (vocals), Franco Santunione (guitar), Andy Christell (bass) and Niclas Sigevall (drums).

| 6/2/90 | 90 | 20 | | 1 Funk-O-Metal Carpet Ride | | Atco 91337 |

ELECTRIC FLAG
Rock-blues band formed in Chicago, Illinois: Nick Gravenites (vocals), **Mike Bloomfield** (guitar), Barry Goldberg (keyboards), Harvey Brooks (bass) and **Buddy Miles** (drums). Brooks went on to join **The Fabulous Rhinestones**. Bloomfield died of a drug overdose on 2/15/1981 (age 36).

| 4/20/68 | 31 | 35 | | 1 A Long Time Comin' | | Columbia 9597 |
| 1/18/69 | 76 | 12 | | 2 The Electric Flag | | Columbia 9714 |

ELECTRIC INDIAN, The
Instrumental studio band from Philadelphia, Pennsylvania: Bobby Eli (guitar), Tim Moore (guitar), **Daryl Hall** (piano), Vincent Montana (vibes), Robert Cupit (percussion), Tom Sellers (bass) and Jim Helmer (drums). Eli and Montana later joined **MFSB**. Sellers formed The Assembled Multitude. Montana formed **The Salsoul Orchestra**. Sellers died in a house fire on 3/9/1988 (age 39).

| 10/4/69 | 104 | 9 | | 1 Keem-O-Sabe | [I] | United Artists 6728 |

ELECTRIC LIGHT ORCHESTRA   All-Time: #215
Orchestral rock band formed in Birmingham, England. Core members: **Jeff Lynne** (vocals, guitar), Richard Tandy (keyboards), Kelly Groucutt (bass) and Bev Bevan (drums). Numerous personnel changes. Group first recorded as **The Move**. **Roy Wood** was a member, left after first album. Bevan also recorded with **Black Sabbath** in 1987. Lynne was also a prolific producer and a member of the supergroup **Traveling Wilburys**. Lynne recorded solo as Electric Light Orchestra in 2001. Grocutt died of a heart attack on 2/19/2009 (age 63).

6/3/72	196	2		1 No Answer		United Artists 5573
3/3/73	172	8		2 Split Ends	[K]	United Artists 5666
				THE MOVE		
4/21/73	62	22		3 Electric Light Orchestra II		United Artists 040
12/29/73+	52	24		4 On The Third Day		United Artists 188
7/20/74	205	2		5 The Best Of The Move	[K]	A&M 3625 [2]
10/19/74	16	32	●	6 Eldorado		United Artists 339
10/25/75+	8	48	●	7 Face The Music		United Artists 546
7/4/76	32	43	●	8 Ole ELO	[K]	United Artists 630
10/30/76+	5	69	▲	9 A New World Record		United Artists 679
11/26/77+	4	58	▲	10 Out Of The Blue		Jet 823 [2]
6/23/79	5	35	▲²	11 Discovery		Jet 35769
12/8/79+	30	15	▲⁴	12 ELO's Greatest Hits	[G]	Jet 36310
7/12/80	4	36	▲²	13 Xanadu	[S]	MCA 6100
				side 1: **Olivia Newton-John**; side 2: Electric Light Orchestra		
8/22/81	16	20	●	14 Time		Jet 37371
7/16/83	36	16		15 Secret Messages		Jet 38490
3/1/86	49	15		16 Balance Of Power		CBS Associated 40048
6/30/01	94	2		17 Zoom		Epic 85336

Billboard DEBUT	PEAK	WKS	R I A A	ARTIST Album Title	Catalog	Label & Number
				ELECTRIC PRUNES, The		
				Psychedelic-rock band from Los Angeles, California: James Lowe (vocals), Ken Williams (guitar), James Spagnola (guitar), Mark Tulin (bass) and Preston Ritter (drums).		
4/15/67	113	12		1 The Electric Prunes		Reprise 6248
9/2/67	172	4		2 Underground		Reprise 6262
1/6/68	135	13		3 Mass In F Minor	[F]	Reprise 6275
				electric rock mass, sung in Latin		
				ELECTRIK RED		
				Female R&B vocal group formed in Los Angeles, California: Kyndra "Binkie" Reevey, Lesley Lewis, Naomi Allen and Sarah Rosete.		
6/13/09	100	1		1 How To Be A Lady: Volume 1		Radio Killa 012397
				ELECTRONIC		
				Dance duo from Manchester, England: Bernard Sumner (of **New Order**) and Johnny Marr (of **The Smiths**).		
6/15/91	109	15		1 Electronic		Warner 26387
7/27/96	143	1		2 Raise The Pressure		Warner 45955
				ELECTRONIC CONCEPT ORCHESTRA		
				Studio group directed by Robin McBride. Features Eddie Higgins on the Moog synthesizer.		
10/18/69	175	2		1 Electric Love	[I]	Limelight 86072
				ELEPHANT MAN		
				Born O'Neil Bryan on 9/11/1977 in Kingston, Jamaica. Dancehall reggae singer.		
12/20/03	74	2		1 Good 2 Go		VP 83681
				ELEPHANT'S MEMORY		
				Jazz-rock band formed in New York: Michal Shapiro (female vocals), Stan Bronstein (male vocals, sax), Richard Ayers (guitar), Richard Sussman (piano), Myron Yules (trombone), John Ward (bass) and Rick Frank (drums). Occasional backing band for **John Lennon**.		
5/10/69	200	2		1 Elephant's Memory		Buddah 5033
10/28/72	205	3		2 Elephant's Memory		Apple 3389
				above 2 are different albums		
				ELEVENTH HOUSE WITH LARRY CORYELL		
				Jazz-rock band formed in Los Angeles, California: **Larry Coryell** (guitar), Randy Brecker (trumpet; **Dreams**, **The Brecker Brothers**), Mike Mandel (piano), Danny Trifan (bass) and **Alphonse Mouzan** (drums). In early 1975, Michael Lawrence replaced Brecker and John Lee replaced Trifan.		
4/13/74	163	11		1 Introducing The Eleventh House With Larry Coryell	[I]	Vanguard 79342
8/9/75	163	4		2 Level One	[I]	Arista 4052
				ELGART, Larry, And His Manhattan Swing Orchestra		
				Born on 3/20/1922 in New London, Connecticut. Alto saxophonist. Brother of **Les Elgart**.		
10/10/64	128	5		1 Command Performance! Les & Larry Elgart Play The Great Dance Hits	[I]	Columbia 2221 / 9021
				LES & LARRY ELGART		
6/19/82	24	41	▲	2 Hooked On Swing	[I]	RCA Victor 4343
2/12/83	89	14		3 Hooked On Swing 2	[I]	RCA Victor 4589
				ELGART, Les, And His Orchestra 1950s: #40		
				Born on 8/3/1917 in New Haven, Connecticut. Died on 7/29/1995 (age 77). Trumpeter/bandleader. Brother of **Larry Elgart**.		
9/3/55	15	1		1 The Dancing Sound	[EP-I]	Columbia 514 [2]
11/3/56	13	7		2 The Elgart Touch	[I]	Columbia 875
8/19/57	14	7		3 For Dancers Also	[I]	Columbia 1008
10/10/64	128	5		4 Command Performance! Les & Larry Elgart Play The Great Dance Hits	[I]	Columbia 2221 / 9021
				LES & LARRY ELGART		
				EL GORILA, Franco		
				Born in Puerto Rico. Male reggaeton singer.		
5/16/09	196	1		1 Welcome To The Jungle	[F]	WY 012845
				ELIEL		
				Born Eliel Osorio on 1/7/1981 in Rio Grande, Puerto Rico. Male reggaeton singer/prolific producer.		
2/12/05	150	1		1 El Que Habla Con Los Manos	[F]	VI 450624
				ELI YOUNG BAND		
				Country band from Denton, Texas: Mike Eli (vocals, guitar), James Young (vocals, guitar), Jon Jones (bass) and Chris Thompson (drums).		
10/4/08	30	9		1 Jet Black & Jealous		Republic 011794
				ELIZALDE, Valentin		
				Born on 2/1/1979 in Navojoa, Sonora, Mexico. Shot to death on 11/25/2006 (age 27). Latin male singer.		
2/10/07	70	10		1 Vencedor	[F]	Universal Latino 006611
2/17/07	44	8		2 Lobo Domesticado	[F]	Universal Latino 008478
				ELLIMAN, Yvonne		
				Born on 12/29/1951 in Honolulu, Hawaii. Female singer/actress. Portrayed Mary Magdalene on the concept album and in the rock opera and movie *Jesus Christ Superstar*. Backing singer for **Eric Clapton**.		
3/12/77	68	16		1 Love Me		RSO 3018
3/11/78	40	17		2 Night Flight		RSO 3031
11/10/79	174	6		3 Yvonne		RSO 3038

251

Billboard			R I A A	ARTIST		
DEBUT	PEAK	WKS		Album Title	Catalog	Label & Number

ELLINGTON, Duke
Born Edward Kennedy Ellington on 4/29/1899 in Washington DC. Died of cancer on 5/24/1974 (age 75). Legendary jazz bandleader/composer/arranger.
AWARD: Grammys: Lifetime Achievement 1966 / Trustees 1968

6/24/57	14	1		1 Ellington At Newport... **[I-L]**		Columbia 934
				Grammy: Hall of Fame		
				recorded on 7/7/1956 at the Newport Jazz Festival		
10/3/64	133	7		2 Ellington '65: Hits Of The 60's/This Time By Ellington.................. **[I]**		Reprise 6122
5/14/66	145	3		3 The Duke At Tanglewood... **[I-L]**		RCA Victor 2857
				DUKE ELLINGTON/BOSTON POPS/ARTHUR FIEDLER		
2/24/68	78	13		4 Francis A. & Edward K..		Reprise 1024
				FRANK SINATRA & DUKE ELLINGTON		
7/25/09	186	1		5 Best Of Duke Ellington... **[K]**		X5 digital

~ ~ ~ ~ ~ ~ ~ ~ ~ **NON-CHARTED ALBUM** ~ ~ ~ ~ ~ ~ ~ ~ ~ ~
1967 Duke Ellington's Far East Suite
Grammys: Jazz Album / Hall of Fame

ELLIOT, Cass — see MAMA CASS

ELLIOTT, Alecia
Born on 12/25/1982 in Muscle Shoals, Alabama. Female country singer.

| 2/12/00 | 172 | 5 | | 1 I'm Diggin' It.. | | MCA 170087 |

ELLIOTT, Missy "Misdemeanor"
Born on 7/1/1971 in Portsmouth, Virginia. Female rapper/songwriter/producer. Former member of group Sista. Childhood friend of rapper/producer **Timbaland**. Started own The Gold Mind record label. Appeared in the movies *Pootie Tang* and *Honey*.

8/2/97	3¹	37	▲	1 Supa Dupa Fly		Gold Mind 62062
7/10/99	10	39	▲	2 Da Real World		Gold Mind 62232
6/2/01	2¹	42	▲	3 Miss E... So Addictive		Gold Mind 62639
11/30/02	3¹	35	▲²	4 Under Construction		Gold Mind 62813
12/13/03	13	19	▲	5 This Is Not A Test!..		Gold Mind 62905
7/23/05	2¹	17	●	6 The Cookbook		Gold Mind 83779

ELLIS, Shirley
Born Shirley Elliston in 1941 in the Bronx, New York. R&B singer/songwriter.

~ ~ ~ ~ ~ ~ ~ ~ ~ ~ **NON-CHARTED ALBUM** ~ ~ ~ ~ ~ ~ ~ ~ ~ ~ ~
1965 The Name Game

ELLIS, Terry
Born on 9/5/1963 in Houston, Texas. Female R&B singer. Member of **En Vogue**.

| 12/2/95 | 116 | 5 | | 1 Southern Gal... | | EastWest 61857 |

ELMO & PATSY
Husband-and-wife team of Elmo Shropshire (born on 10/26/1936 in Lexington, Kentucky) and Patsy Trigg. Divorced in 1985.

| 12/19/87 | 8ˣ | 10 | ▲ | 1 Grandma Got Run Over By A Reindeer **Cat:#42/2 [X]** | | Epic 39931 |
| | | | | Christmas charts: 8/'87, 12/'88, 24/'89, 28/'91 | | |

EL ORIGINAL DE LA SIERRA
Born Jessie Morales in Los Angeles, California. Male Latin singer/songwriter.

| 7/7/01 | 146 | 1 | | 1 Homenaje A Chalino Sanchez .... **[F]** | | Univision 976001 |

EL-P
Born Jaime Meline on 3/4/1975 in Brooklyn, New York. White male rapper/producer. El-P is short for El-Producto.

| 6/1/02 | 198 | 1 | | 1 Fantastic Damage .... | | Definitive Jux 27 |
| 4/7/07 | 78 | 2 | | 2 I'll Sleep When You're Dead .... | | Definitive Jux 137 |

EL RAYO-X — see LINDLEY, David

EL TIGRILLO PALMA
Born Efren Aguilar in Sinaloa, Mexico. Latin singer.

| 3/14/09 | 138 | 2 | | 1 Al Cien Por Millon .... **[F]** | | Fonovisa 353897 |

EL TRONO DE MEXICO
Latin band from Nueva Leon, Mexico: brothers Evarado, Duani and Odilon Marcelino, with Carlos Cruz, Luis Teran and Yovany Morales.

4/12/08	171	1		1 Cruzando Fronteras .... **[F]**		DBC 8701
6/13/09	200	1		2 Almas Gemelas .... **[F]**		Fonovisa 353804
11/21/09	184	2		3 Hasta Mi Final .... **[F]**		Fonovisa 354315

ELVIS BROTHERS, The
Rock trio from Champaign, Illinois: brothers Rob Elvis (vocals, guitar), Graham Elvis (bass) and Brad Elvis (drums).

| 10/22/83 | 209 | 1 | | 1 Movin' Up .... | | Portrait 38865 |

Billboard			R I A A	ARTIST Album Title	Catalog	Label & Number
DEBUT	**PEAK**	**WKS**				

ELY, Joe
Born on 2/9/1947 in Amarillo, Texas; raised in Lubbock, Texas. Country-rock singer/songwriter/guitarist. Member of **The Flatlanders**.

4/11/81	135	11		1 Musta Notta Gotta Lotta		SouthCoast 5183
10/24/81	159	3		2 Live Shots .... [L]		SouthCoast 5262
5/19/84	204	4		3 Hi-Res		MCA 5480

ELY, Rick
Born in Los Angeles, California. Singer/actor. Played "Jeremy Larkin" on the TV series *The Young Rebels* (1970-71).

| 12/26/70 | 202 | 1 | | 1 Rick Ely .... | | RCA Victor 4443 |

EMAROSA
Alternative-rock band from Lexington, Kentucky: Jonny Craig (vocals), E.R. White (guitar), Jonas Ladekjaer (guitar), Jordan Stewart (keyboards), Will Sowers (bass) amd Lukas Koszewski (drums).

| 7/26/08 | 191 | 1 | | 1 Relativity .... | | Rise 066 |

EMERSON, Keith
Born on 11/1/1944 in Todmorden, Lancashire, England. Keyboardist of **Emerson, Lake & Palmer** and **The Nice**.

| 5/2/81 | 183 | 3 | | 1 Nighthawks .... [I-S] | | Backstreet 5196 |

EMERSON DRIVE
Country band from Grande Prairie, Alberta, Canada: Brad Mates (vocals), Danick Dupelle (guitar), Chris Hartman (keyboards), Pat Allingham (fiddle), Jeff Loberg (bass) and Mike Melancon (drums). Hartman and Loberg left in 2002; replaced by Dale Wallace and Patrick Bourque. Allington left in 2003; replaced by David Pichette. Bourque died on 9/25/2007 (age 29).

6/8/02	108	2		1 Emerson Drive		DreamWorks 450272
7/17/04	107	2		2 What If?		DreamWorks 000071
5/26/07	141	8		3 Countrified		Montage 90088

EMERSON, LAKE & PALMER   **All-Time: #287**
Progressive rock trio from England: **Keith Emerson** (keyboards; **The Nice**), **Greg Lake** (vocals, bass, guitars; **King Crimson**) and Carl Palmer (drums; **Atomic Rooster**, **Crazy World of Arthur Brown**). Group split up in 1979, with Palmer joining supergroup **Asia**. Emerson and Lake re-grouped in 1986 with new drummer Cozy Powell (**Whitesnake**). Palmer returned in 1987, replacing Powell who joined **Black Sabbath** in 1990. Powell died in a car crash on 4/5/1998 (age 50).

2/6/71	18	42	●	1 Emerson, Lake & Palmer		Cotillion 9040
7/3/71	9	26	●	2 Tarkus		Cotillion 9900
1/22/72	10	23	●	3 Pictures At An Exhibition [L]		Cotillion 66666
				based on Mussorgsky's classical composition		
7/29/72	5	37	●	4 Trilogy		Cotillion 9903
12/15/73+	11	47	●	5 Brain Salad Surgery		Manticore 66669
9/7/74	4	24	●	6 Welcome Back, My Friends, To The Show That Never Ends - Ladies and Gentlemen [L]		Manticore 200 [3]
4/9/77	12	26	●	7 Works, Volume 1		Atlantic 7000 [2]
12/10/77+	37	14	●	8 Works, Volume 2		Atlantic 19147
				above 2 albums feature mostly solo material		
12/9/78+	55	9	●	9 Love Beach		Atlantic 19211
12/1/79	73	10		10 Emerson, Lake & Palmer In Concert.................................... [L]		Atlantic 19255
11/29/80	108	7		11 The Best Of Emerson, Lake & Palmer .... [G]		Atlantic 19283
6/14/86	23	26		12 Emerson, Lake & Powell		Polydor 829297
6/27/92	78	4		13 Black Moon		Victory 480003

EMERY
Alternative-pop band formed in South Carolina: Toby Morrell (vocals, guitar), Devin SHelton (guitar), Matt Carter (guitar), Josh Head (keyboards), Joel Green (bass) and Seth Studley (drums).

8/20/05	45	3		1 The Question		Tooth & Nail 60604
10/20/07	78	2		2 I'm Only A Man		Tooth & Nail 86641
11/15/08	104	1		3 While Broken Hearts Prevail		Tooth & Nail 21490
6/20/09	50	2		4 ...In Shallow Seas We Sail		Tooth & Nail 44009

EMF
Dance-rock-techno-funk band from Forest of Dean, Gloucestershire, England: James Atkin (vocals), Ian Dench (guitar), Derry Brownson (keyboards, percussion), Zac Foley (bass) and Mark Decloedt (drums). Foley died of a drug overdose on 1/3/2002 (age 31).

| 6/1/91 | 12 | 36 | ▲ | 1 Schubert Dip.. | | EMI 96238 |

EMILIO
Born Emilio Navaira on 8/23/1962 in San Antonio, Texas. Country singer.

| 10/14/95 | 82 | 5 | | 1 Life Is Good .... | | Capitol 32392 |

EMINEM   **2000s: #25 / All-Time: #264**
Born Marshall Mathers III on 10/17/1972 in Kansas City, Missouri; raised in Detroit, Michigan. White male rapper/actor. Protege of **Dr. Dre**. First recorded with the rap group Soul Intent in 1995. Created his alter ego, Slim Shady, for his 1999 album *The Slim Shady LP*. Starred in the 2002 movie *8 Mile*. Member of **D12**.

3/13/99	2³	100	▲⁴	1 The Slim Shady LP	Cat:#3/78	Aftermath 90287
				Grammy: Rap Album ★ RS500 #273		
6/10/00	❶⁸	69	▲⁹	2 The Marshall Mathers LP	Cat:❶²/117	Aftermath 490629
				Grammy: Rap Album ★ RS500 #302		
6/8/02	❶⁶	104	▲⁸	3 The Eminem Show	Cat:#18/35	Aftermath 493290
				Grammy: Rap Album ★ RS500 #317		

Billboard			R I A A	ARTIST		
DEBUT	PEAK	WKS		Album Title	Catalog	Label & Number

EMINEM — cont'd

11/27/04	❶⁴	53	▲⁴	4 Encore	Cat:#46/1	Shady 003771
12/24/05	❶²	70	▲²	5 Curtain Call: The Hits	Cat:#11/24 [G]	Shady 005881
6/6/09	❶²	52↑		6 Relapse		Web 012863
				Grammy: Rap Album		

EMMURE
Deathcore band from Queens, New York: Frankie Palmeri (vocals), Jesse Ketive (guitar), Mike Mulholland (guitar), Mark Davis (bass) and Mike Kaabe (drums).

| 5/31/08 | 141 | 1 | | 1 The Respect Issue | | Victory 449 |
| 9/5/09 | 60 | 2 | | 2 Felony | | Victory 526 |

EMOTIONS, The
Female R&B vocal trio from Chicago, Illinois: sisters Wanda, Sheila and Jeanette Hutchinson. Jeanette replaced by cousin Theresa Davis in 1970, and later by sister Pamela Hutchinson. Jeanette returned to the group in 1978.

8/28/76	45	27	●	1 Flowers		Columbia 34163
6/25/77	7	33	▲	2 Rejoice		Columbia 34762
12/3/77+	88	15		3 Sunshine	[E]	Stax 4100
8/26/78	40	12	●	4 Sunbeam		Columbia 35385
12/8/79	96	10		5 Come Into Our World		ARC 36149
9/26/81	168	4		6 New Affair		ARC 37456
6/23/84	206	2		7 Sincerely		Red Label 001
5/25/85	203	2		8 If I Only Knew		Motown 6136

ENCHANTMENT
R&B vocal group from Detroit, Michigan: Ed Clanton, Bobby Green, Davis Banks, Emanuel Johnson and Joe Thomas.

3/5/77	104	19		1 Enchantment		United Artists 682
1/21/78	46	21		2 Once Upon A Dream		Roadshow 811
3/17/79	145	8		3 Journey To The Land Of...Enchantment		Roadshow 3269
12/6/80+	202	7		4 Soft Lights, Sweet Music		RCA Victor 3824

ENGLAND, Ty
Born on 12/5/1963 in Oklahoma City, Oklahoma. Country singer/songwriter/guitarist.

| 9/2/95 | 95 | 6 | | 1 Ty England | | RCA 66522 |

ENGLAND DAN & JOHN FORD COLEY
Pop duo from Austin, Texas: **Dan Seals** (born on 2/8/1948; died of cancer on 3/25/2009, age 61) and John Ford Coley (born on 10/13/1948). Dan was the brother of Jim Seals of **Seals & Crofts** and cousin of country singers Johnny Duncan, Troy Seals and Brady Seals (of **Little Texas**). Coley appeared in the 1987 movie *Scenes From The Goldmine*.

11/20/76	202	3		1 I Hear The Music	[E]	A&M 4613
				recorded in 1973		
8/21/76	17	31	●	2 Nights Are Forever		Big Tree 89517
4/23/77	80	15		3 Dowdy Ferry Road		Big Tree 76000
4/8/78	61	14		4 Some Things Don't Come Easy		Big Tree 76006
4/14/79	106	12		5 Dr. Heckle And Mr. Jive		Big Tree 76015
1/5/80	194	2		6 Best Of England Dan & John Ford Coley	[G]	Big Tree 76018

ENGLISH BEAT
Ska-rock band formed in Birmingham, England: Dave Wakeling and **Ranking Roger** (vocals), Andy Cox (guitar), Saxa (sax), Dave Steele (bass) and Everett Martin (drums). Split in 1983. Wakeling and Roger formed **General Public**. Cox and Steele formed **Fine Young Cannibals**.

8/9/80	142	14		1 I Just Can't Stop It		Sire 6091
6/27/81	126	6		2 Wha'ppen?		Sire 3567
11/13/82+	39	44		3 Special Beat Service		I.R.S. 70032
12/17/83+	87	22		4 What Is Beat?	[K]	I.R.S. 70040

ENGLISH CONGREGATION, The
Pop vocal group from England. Led by Brian Keith (also a member of **The Kingsway Youth Opera Company**).

| 8/26/72 | 209 | 3 | | 1 Jesahel | | Signpost 8405 |

ENGVALL, Bill
Born on 7/27/1957 in Galveston, Texas. Stand-up comedian/actor. Played "Bill Pelton" on TV's *The Jeff Foxworthy Show*. Member of the **Blue Collar Comedy Tour** and *Blue Collar TV* cast.

3/1/97	50	30	▲	1 Here's Your Sign	[C]	Warner 46263
10/31/98	119	11	●	2 Dorkfish	[C]	Warner 47090
11/20/99	33ˣ	3		3 Here's Your Christmas Album	[X-N]	Warner 47488
				Christmas charts: 33/'99, 36/'05		
9/9/00	133	5		4 Now That's Awesome!	[C]	BNA 69311
11/13/04	183	1		5 A Decade Of Laughs	[C-K]	Warner 48815
3/17/07	93	5		6 15° Off Cool	[C]	Jack 43272
10/24/09	159	1		7 Aged And Confused	[C]	Jack 519708

Billboard DEBUT	PEAK	WKS	R I A A	ARTIST Album Title	Catalog	Label & Number

ENIGMA　　　　　　　　　　　　　　　　　　　　　　　　　　　　**All-Time: #458**
Born Michael Cretu on 5/18/1957 in Bucharest, Romania; later based in Germany. Electronic musician/producer. Worked with **Vangelis** and **The Art Of Noise**. Featured vocalist is Cretu's wife, Sandra.

3/2/91	6	282	▲⁴	1 **MCMXC A.D.**　　　　　　　　　　　　　　Cat:#4/50		Charisma 91642
				title is the Roman numeral for the year 1990		
2/26/94	9	63	▲²	2 **Enigma 2: The Cross of Changes**　　　Cat:#14/53		Charisma 39236
12/14/96	25	29	▲	3 **Enigma 3: Le Roi Est Mort, Vive Le Roi!**		Virgin 42066
2/5/00	33	17	●	4 **The Screen Behind The Mirror**		Virgin 48616
11/10/01	29	18		5 **Love Sensuality Devotion - The Greatest Hits** .... [G]		Virgin 11119
10/18/03	94	5		6 **Voyageur**..		Virgin 90447
10/14/06	95	3		7 **A Posteriori**		Virgin 69994
10/18/08	92	2		8 **Seven Lives Many Faces**		Virgin 37979

ENNIS, Ethel
Born on 11/28/1932 in Baltimore, Maryland. Jazz singer/pianist.

3/21/64	147	2		1 **This Is Ethel Ennis**		RCA Victor 2786

ENO, Brian
Born on 5/15/1948 in Woodbridge, Suffolk, England. Rock producer/keyboardist. Founding member of **Roxy Music**. Production work for **David Bowie**, **Devo**, **Talking Heads** and **U2**. Also see **Passengers**.

8/24/74	151	6		1 **Here Come The Warm Jets**............................		Island 9268
				RS500 #436		
5/27/78	171	5		2 **Before And After Science**		Island 9478
3/21/81	44	13		3 **My Life In The Bush Of Ghosts** .... [I]		Sire 6093
1/17/09	174	2		4 **Everything That Happens Will Happen Today**..........		Opal 002
				DAVID BYRNE & BRIAN ENO (above 2)		

~ ~ ~ ~ ~ ~ ~ ~ ~ ~ **NON-CHARTED ALBUM** ~ ~ ~ ~ ~ ~ ~ ~ ~ ~ ~
1975 **Another Green World**...ENO
RS500 #433

ENRIQUE, Luis
Born on 9/28/1962 in Nicaragua. Latin singer.

6/6/09	126	3		1 **Ciclos** .... [F]		Top Stop 8910
				Grammy: Tropical Latin Album		

ENRIQUEZ, Jocelyn
Born on 12/28/1974 in San Francisco, California. Female R&B-dance singer.

5/31/97	182	1		1 **Jocelyn**		Classified 3049

ENTOUCH
Male R&B vocal duo of Eric McCaine (from Mt. Vernon, New York) and Free (from the Bronx, New York).

2/10/90	177	4		1 **All Nite**		Vintertainment 60858

ENTWISTLE, John
Born on 10/9/1944 in Chiswick, London, England. Died of a heart attack on 6/27/2002 (age 57). Rock singer/bassist. Member of **The Who**.

10/23/71	126	9		1 **Smash Your Head Against The Wall**		Decca 79183
11/18/72+	138	13		2 **Whistle Rymes**.......................................		Track 79190
7/7/73	174	7		3 **Rigor Mortis Sets In**		Track 321
3/1/75	192	1		4 **Mad Dog**		Track 2129
				JOHN ENTWISTLE'S OX		
10/10/81	71	9		5 **Too Late The Hero**....................................		Atco 142

ENUFF Z'NUFF
Rock band from Chicago, Illinois: Chip Z'Nuff (bass), Donnie Vie (vocals), Derek Frigo (guitar) and Vikki Foxx (drums). Frigo died on 5/28/2004 (age 36).

9/30/89	74	34		1 **Enuff Z'nuff**		Atco 91262
4/13/91	143	6		2 **Strength**		Atco 91638

EN VOGUE
Female R&B vocal group formed in Oakland, California: **Terry Ellis** (born on 9/5/1966), Dawn Robinson (born on 11/28/1968), Cindy Herron (born on 9/26/1965) and Maxine Jones (born on 1/16/1966). Herron married pro baseball player Glenn Braggs in June of 1993 and acted in the 1992 movie *Juice*. Reduced to a trio when Robinson went solo in 1997 (she later joined **Lucy Pearl**). Robinson married Andre Allen (of IV Xample) in May 2003.

4/28/90	21	69	▲	1 **Born To Sing**...		Atlantic 82084
4/11/92	8	86	▲³	2 **Funky Divas**		EastWest 92121
10/9/93	49	19		3 **Runaway Love** .... [EP]		EastWest 92296
				3 of 6 songs are remixes from the above album		
7/5/97	8	20	▲	4 **EV3**		EastWest 62057
6/10/00	67	5		5 **Masterpiece Theatre**		EastWest 62416

Billboard			R I A A	ARTIST		
DEBUT	PEAK	WKS		Album Title	Catalog	Label & Number

ENYA
All-Time: #231

Born Eithne Ni Brennan on 5/17/1961 in Gweedore, County Donegal, Ireland. Female New Age singer. Member of the **Clannad** from 1980-82.

2/4/89	25	39	▲⁴	1 Watermark	Cat:❶¹⁷/305	Geffen 24233
12/7/91+	17	238	▲⁵	2 Shepherd Moons	Cat:#22/20	Reprise 26775
				Grammy: New Age Album		
2/15/92+	6ᶜ	148	▲	3 Enya	[E]	Atlantic 81842
				first released in 1987; later released as *The Celts* on Reprise 45681		
12/23/95+	9	66	▲³	4 The Memory Of Trees		Reprise 46106
				Grammy: New Age Album		
11/29/97+	30	40	▲⁴	5 Paint The Sky With Stars - The Best Of Enya	Cat:#2²⁰/125 [G]	Reprise 46835
12/9/00+	2²	103	▲⁷	6 A Day Without Rain	Cat:#18/19	Reprise 47426
				Grammy: New Age Album		
12/10/05	6	33	▲	7 Amarantine		Reprise 49474
11/29/08	8	16	●	8 And Winter Came...	Cat:#18/3 [X]	Reprise 512383
				Christmas charts: 1/'08, 1/'09		
12/5/09	57	6		9 And Winter Came...	[X-R]	Reprise 512383
12/19/09	55	9		10 The Very Best Of Enya	[G]	Reprise 521819
12/19/09	183	1		11 The Very Best Of Enya	[G]	Reprise 1576803 [2]

EPMD

Rap duo from Long Island, New York: **Erick Sermon** and Parrish ("**PMD**") Smith. EPMD: Erick and Parrish Making Dollars.

7/9/88	80	23	●	1 Strictly Business		Fresh 82006
				RS500 #459		
8/19/89	53	14	●	2 Unfinished Business		Fresh 92012
2/2/91	36	21	●	3 Business As Usual		Def Jam 47067
8/15/92	14	18	●	4 Business Never Personal		RAL 52848
10/11/97	16	11	●	5 Back In Business		Def Jam 536389
8/7/99	13	8		6 Out Of Business		Def Jam 558928

EPPS, Preston

Born in 1931 in Oakland, California. Black bongo player.

8/15/60	35	3		1 Bongo Bongo Bongo	[I]	Original Sound 5002

ERASURE
All-Time: #480

Techno-rock-dance duo formed in London, England: Andy Bell (vocals; born on 4/25/1964) and Vince Clarke (instruments; born on 7/3/1960). Clarke was a member of **Depeche Mode** and **Yaz**.

7/18/87	190	3		1 The Circus		Sire 25554
1/16/88	186	3		2 The Two Ring Circus	[K]	Sire 25667 [2]
6/18/88	49	50	▲	3 The Innocents	Cat:#49/1	Sire 25730
5/13/89	73	10		4 Crackers International		Sire 25904
11/11/89	57	23		5 Wild!		Sire 26026
11/2/91	29	17		6 Chorus		Sire 26668
7/18/92	85	22		7 Abba-esque	[EP]	Mute 61386
12/12/92+	112	15	●	8 Pop! - The First 20 Hits	[G]	Sire 45153
6/4/94	18	17		9 I Say I Say I Say		Mute 61633
11/11/95	82	3		10 "Erasure"		Elektra 61852
5/10/97	43	8		11 Cowboy		Maverick 46631
2/15/03	138	1		12 Other People's Songs		Mute 9198
2/12/05	154	1		13 Nightbird		Mute 9260
6/9/07	127	1		14 Light At The End Of The World		Mute 9355

ERIC B. & RAKIM

Rap duo: DJ Eric Barrier (from Elmhurst, New York) and rapper William "**Rakim**" Griffin (from Long Island, New York).

9/12/87	58	38	▲	1 Paid In Full		4th & B'way 4005
				RS500 #227		
8/13/88	22	16	●	2 Follow The Leader		Uni 3
7/7/90	32	14	●	3 Let The Rhythm Hit 'Em		MCA 6416
7/11/92	22	11		4 Don't Sweat The Technique		MCA 10594

ERIKA JO

Born Erika Jo Heriges on 11/2/1986 in Angelton, Texas; raised in Nashville, Tennessee. Country singer. Winner of the third season of TV's *Nashville Star* talent series in 2005.

7/2/05	27	6		1 Erika Jo		Universal South 004522

ERUPTION

Techno-funk-dance band of Jamaican natives based in London, England: Precious Wilson and Lintel (vocals), brothers Gregory and Morgan Petrineau (guitars), Horatio McKay (keyboards) and Eric Kingsley (drums).

4/1/78	133	13		1 Eruption		Ariola 50033

ESCAPE CLUB, The

Pop-rock band formed in London, England: Trevor Steel (vocals), John Holliday (guitar), Johnnie Christo (bass) and Milan Zekavica (drums).

8/27/88	27	38	●	1 Wild Wild West		Atlantic 81871
4/6/91	145	12		2 Dollars And Sex		Atlantic 82198

Billboard	R I A A	ARTIST		
DEBUT	PEAK	WKS	Album Title	Catalog	Label & Number

ESCAPE THE FATE
Hard-rock band from Las Vegas, Nevada: Craig Mabbitt (vocals), Bryan "Monte" Money (guitar), Max Green (bass) and Robert Ortiz (drums).

11/8/08	35	3	1 This War Is Ours .... **Cat**:#34/1	Epitaph 86926

ESCOVEDO, Alejandro
Born on 1/10/1951 in San Antonio, Texas. Latin singer/songwriter/guitarist. Former member of **Rank & File**. Brother of **Coke Escovedo**. Uncle of **Sheila E.**

7/12/08	122	2	1 Real Animal..	Back Porch 82411

ESCOVEDO, Coke
Born Thomas Escovedo on 4/30/1941 in Los Angeles, California. Died on 7/13/1986 (age 45). Latin singer/percussionist. Member of **Azteca**. Brother of **Alejandro Escovedo**. Uncle of **Sheila E.**

3/13/76	195	2	1 Coke	Mercury 1041
5/29/76	190	3	2 Comin' At Ya!..	Mercury 1085
2/12/77	195	1	3 Disco Fantasy	Mercury 1132

ESHAM
Born Rashaam Smith in Long Island, New York; raised in Detroit, Michigan. Male rapper. Member of **Soopa Villainz**.

7/7/01	195	1	1 Tongues	Overcore 2260
5/7/05	176	1	2 A-1 Yola	Psychopathic 4045

ESQUIRE
Rock trio from England: Nikki Squire (vocals), Nigel McLaren (bass) and Charles Olins (keyboards). Nikki is married to **Chris Squire** of **Yes**.

3/28/87	165	4	1 Esquire	Geffen 24101

ESSEX, The
R&B vocal group formed in North Carolina: Anita Humes, Walter Vickers, Rodney Taylor, Billy Hill and Rudolph Johnson.

8/3/63	119	5	1 Easier Said Than Done	Roulette 25234

ESSEX, David
Born David Cook on 7/23/1947 in Plaistow, London, England. Pop-rock singer/actor. Starred in several British movies.

1/5/74	32	21	1 Rock On	Columbia 32560
11/8/75	204	9	2 All The Fun Of The Fair..	Columbia 33813

ESTEBAN
Born Stephen Paul in 1948 in Pittsburgh, Pennsylvania; later based in Phoenix, Arizona. Flamenco guitarist. Became popular after several appearances on the QVC and HSN TV shopping channels.

11/25/00	8^X	1	1 What Child Is This? .... **Cat**:#5/3 [X-I]	Daystar 0007
			first released in 1995	
7/22/00	10^C	2	2 Flamenco Y Rosas [I]	Daystar 0010 [2]
			first released in 1996	
8/19/00	5^C	2	3 Pasion [I]	Daystar 0014
			first released in 1998	
8/19/00+	3^{1C}	3	4 Enter The Heart [I]	Daystar 0016
			first released in 1998	
7/29/00	53	1	5 Heart Of Gold [I]	Daystar 0028
7/29/00	54	2	6 All My Love [I]	Daystar 0022
11/4/00	159	3	7 At Home With Esteban .... [I]	Daystar 8830 [2]
4/14/01	105	2	8 Live! .... [I-L]	Daystar 8832 [2]
7/28/01	192	1	9 Flame, Flamenco & Romance .... [I]	Daystar 8835/36 [2]
8/4/01	118	1	10 By Request .... [I]	Daystar 8841 [4]
12/1/01	179	1	11 Holiday Trilogy .... [X-I]	Daystar 8842 [3]
			Christmas chart: 16/'01	

ESTEFAN, Gloria   1990s: #28 / All-Time: #184
Born Gloria Fajardo on 9/1/1957 in Havana, Cuba; raised in Miami, Florida. Formed **Miami Sound Machine** with her husband Emilio Estefan (keyboards), Juan Avila (bass) and Enrique Garcia (drums). Group eventually grew to nine members. Gloria and Emilio married on 9/2/1978; both were in a serious bus crash on 3/20/1990 (both fully recovered). Gloria played "Isabel Vasquez" in the 1999 movie *Music Of The Heart*.

11/23/85+	21	75	▲³	1 Primitive Love .... **Cat**:#32/9	Epic 40131
				MIAMI SOUND MACHINE	
6/20/87+	6	97	▲³	2 Let It Loose	Epic 40769
				GLORIA ESTEFAN AND MIAMI SOUND MACHINE	
7/29/89	8	69	▲³	3 Cuts Both Ways	Epic 45217
2/16/91	5	68	▲²	4 Into The Light	Epic 46988
11/20/93	43	8	▲	5 Christmas Through Your Eyes................... **Cat**:#12/18 [X]	Epic 57567
				Christmas charts: 9/'93, 18/'94, 22/'95, 28/'96, 40/'97	
11/5/94	9	44	▲²	6 Hold Me, Thrill Me, Kiss Me	Epic 66205
6/22/96	23	40	▲	7 Destiny	Epic 67283

257

ESTEFAN, Gloria — cont'd

DEBUT	PEAK	WKS				Label & Number
6/20/98	23	16	●	8 Gloria!		Epic 69200
10/11/03	39	5		9 Unwrapped		Epic 86790

FOREIGN LANGUAGE ALBUMS:

7/10/93	27	46	▲	10 Mi Tierra		Epic 53807
				Grammy: Tropical Latin Album		
10/14/95	67	16	●	11 Abriendo Puertas		Epic 67284
				Grammy: Tropical Latin Album		
6/10/00	50	9	●	12 Alma Caribena - Caribbean Soul		Epic 62163
				Grammy: Tropical Latin Album		
10/6/07	25	7		13 90 Millas		Burgundy 09055

GREATEST HITS & COMPILATIONS:

11/21/92	15	77	▲⁴	14 Greatest Hits	Cat:#8/40	Epic 53046
2/24/01	92	3		15 Greatest Hits Vol. II		Epic 85396

ESTELLE
Born Estelle Swaray on 1/18/1980 in Hammersmith, West London, England (African mother/Latin father). Female singer/rapper/songwriter.

5/17/08	38	30		1 Shine		Home School 412860

ESTUS, Deon
Born Jeffrey Deon Estus in 1956 in Detroit, Michigan. R&B singer/bassist.

4/1/89	89	15		1 Spell		Mika 835713

ETERNAL
Female R&B vocal group from London, England: sisters Easther Bennett and Vernie Bennett, with Louise Nurding and Kelle Bryan.

3/26/94	152	7		1 Always & Forever		EMI 28212

ETHERIDGE, Melissa   All-Time: #319
Born on 5/29/1961 in Leavenworth, Kansas. Pop-rock singer/songwriter/guitarist. In early 2000, it was announced that David Crosby was the biological father (via artificial insemination) of two children for the couple of Etheridge and Julie Cypher (couple later split). Diagnosed with breast cancer in October 2004 (fully recovered in 2005).

6/18/88+	22	65	▲²	1 Melissa Etheridge	Cat:#23/41	Island 90875
10/7/89	22	58	▲	2 Brave And Crazy	Cat:#50/1	Island 91285
4/4/92	21	26	▲	3 Never Enough		Island 512120
10/9/93+	15	138	▲⁶	4 Yes I Am		Island 848660
12/2/95	6	41	▲²	5 Your Little Secret		Island 524154
10/23/99	12	18	●	6 Breakdown		Island 546518
7/28/01	9	12		7 Skin		Island 548661
2/28/04	15	13		8 Lucky		Island 001822
10/22/05	14	14	●	9 Greatest Hits: The Road Less Traveled	[G]	Island 005137
10/13/07	13	6		10 The Awakening		Island 009463
11/29/08	113	6		11 A New Thought For Christmas	[X]	Island 011475
				Christmas charts: 4/'08, 42/'09		

ETZEL, Roy
Born on 3/6/1925 in Munich, Germany. Trumpet player.

12/18/65	140	5		1 The Silence (Il Silenzio)	[I]	MGM 4330

E.U.
Funk band from Washington DC. Led by singer/bassist Gregory Elliott. E.U.: Experience Unlimited.

4/22/89	158	9		1 Livin' Large		Virgin 91021

EUROGLIDERS
Pop-rock band from Perth, Australia: Grace Knight (vocals), Crispin Akerman (guitar), Amanda Vincent (keyboards), Bernie Lynch (keyboards), Ron Francois (bass) and John Bennetts (drums).

12/22/84+	140	11		1 This Island		Columbia 39588

EUROPE
Hard-rock band from Stockholm, Sweden: Joey Tempest (vocals), Kee Marcello (guitar), John Leven (bass), Mic Michaeli (keyboards) and Ian Haugland (drums).

11/1/86+	8	78	▲³	1 The Final Countdown		Epic 40241
8/27/88	19	25	▲	2 Out Of This World		Epic 44185

EURYTHMICS   All-Time: #397
Pop-rock duo: **Annie Lennox** (vocals, keyboards) and David A. Stewart (guitar). Lennox was born on 12/25/1954 in Aberdeen, Scotland. Stewart was born on 9/9/1952 in Sunderland, England. Both had been in The Tourists from 1977-80. Stewart was married to Siobhan Fahey of **Bananarama** from 1987-96.

5/28/83	15	59	●	1 Sweet Dreams (Are Made Of This)		RCA Victor 4681
2/4/84	7	37	▲	2 Touch		RCA Victor 4917
				RS500 #500		
7/7/84	115	11		3 Touch Dance	[K]	RCA Victor 5086
				vocal and instrumental dance remixes of some cuts from above album		
1/5/85	93	14		4 1984 (For The Love Of Big Brother)	[S]	RCA Victor 5349
5/25/85	9	45	▲	5 Be Yourself Tonight		RCA Victor 5429
8/9/86	12	33	●	6 Revenge		RCA Victor 5847

Billboard			R I A A	ARTIST Album Title	Catalog	Label & Number
DEBUT	PEAK	WKS				

EURYTHMICS — cont'd

DEBUT	PEAK	WKS				
12/26/87+	41	19		7 Savage..		RCA Victor 6794
9/30/89	34	28		8 We Too Are One		Arista 8606
6/15/91	72	23	▲³	9 Greatest Hits .... Cat:#33/2 [G]		Arista 8680
11/6/99	25	12	●	10 Peace		Arista 14617
11/26/05	116	2		11 Ultimate Collection .... [G]		Arista 73799

EVAN AND JARON
Duo of identical twin brothers: Evan and Jaron Lowenstein. Born on 3/18/1974 in Atlanta, Georgia.

1/13/01	156	7		1 Evan And Jaron..		Columbia 69937

EVANESCENCE
Rock band from Little Rock, Arkansas: Amy Lee (vocals), Ben Moody (guitar), Josh LeCompt (bass) and Rocky Gray (drums).
AWARD: Grammy: Best New Artist 2003

3/22/03	3⁷	105	▲⁷	1 Fallen	Cat:❶¹/183	Wind-Up 13063
12/11/04	39	14	●	2 Anywhere But Home .... [L]		Wind-Up 13106
10/21/06	❶¹	48	▲²	3 The Open Door	Cat:#36/1	Wind-Up 13120

EVANS, Bill, Trio
Born on 8/16/1929 in Plainfield, New Jersey. Died after years of drug abuse on 9/15/1980 (age 51). Legendary white jazz pianist. His trio included Scott LaFaro (bass; died in a car crash on 7/6/1961, age 25) and Paul Motian (drums).
AWARD: Grammy: Lifetime Achievement 1994

~ ~ ~ ~ ~ ~ ~ ~ ~ **NON-CHARTED ALBUMS** ~ ~ ~ ~ ~ ~ ~ ~ ~ ~

1960 Portrait In Jazz
Grammy: Hall of Fame
1961 Waltz For Debby
Grammy: Hall of Fame
1963 Conversations With Myself *[Bill Evans]*
Grammys: Jazz Album / Hall of Fame

EVANS, Dan
Born in Frankfort, Illinois. Country singer/songwriter. Contestant on the 2008 TV reality show *The Biggest Loser* (lost 136 pounds).

10/25/08	57	2		1 Goin' All Out		Edje-Executive 1242

EVANS, Faith
Born on 6/10/1973 in Lakeland, Florida; raised in Newark, New Jersey. R&B singer. Married **The Notorious B.I.G.** on 8/4/1994. Acted in the movies *Turn It Up* and *The Fighting Temptations*.

9/16/95	22	32	▲	1 Faith..		Bad Boy 73003
11/14/98	6	45	●	2 Keep The Faith		Bad Boy 73016
11/24/01	14	27	●	3 Faithfully		Bad Boy 73041
4/23/05	2¹	14	●	4 The First Lady		Capitol 77297
1/14/06	7ˣ	2		5 A Faithful Christmas	[X]	Capitol 32191
				Christmas chart: 7/'06		

EVANS, Paul
Born on 3/5/1938 in Brooklyn, New York. Pop singer/songwriter.

~ ~ ~ ~ ~ ~ ~ ~ ~ ~ **NON-CHARTED ALBUM** ~ ~ ~ ~ ~ ~ ~ ~ ~ ~ ~

1960 Paul Evans Sings The Fabulous Teens

EVANS, Sara
Born on 2/5/1971 in New Franklin, Missouri. Country singer/songwriter.

1/23/99	116	13	●	1 No Place That Far..		RCA 67653
10/28/00+	55	85	▲²	2 Born To Fly		RCA 67964
9/6/03	20	47	▲	3 Restless		RCA 67074
10/22/05	3¹	32	▲	4 Real Fine Place		RCA 69486
10/27/07	8	15		5 Greatest Hits	[G]	RCA 08770

EVANS, Tiffany
Born on 8/4/1992 in the Bronx, New York. Pre-teen R&B singer. Won the "junior singer" category on TV's *Star Search*.

5/10/08	134	1		1 Tiffany Evans...		Columbia 91004

EVANS BLUE
Rock band from Toronto, Ontario, Canada: Kevin Matisyn (vocals), Parker Lauzon (guitar), Vlad Tanaskovic (guitar), Joe Pitter (bass) and Darryl Brown (drums).

3/11/06	106	11		1 The Melody And The Energetic Nature Of Volume		The Pocket 162585
8/11/07	44	4		2 The Pursuit Begins When This Portrayal Of Life Ends		The Pocket 000304

EVE
Born Eve Jeffers on 11/10/1978 in Philadelphia, Pennsylvania. Female rapper/songwriter/actress. Appeared in the movie *XXX* as well as both *Barbershop* movies. Starred as "Shelly Williams" in the UPN-TV sitcom *Eve*. Member of **Ruff Ryders**.

10/2/99	❶¹	38	▲²	1 Ruff Ryders' First Lady		Ruff Ryders 490453
3/24/01	4	33	▲	2 Scorpion		Ruff Ryders 490845
9/14/02	6	24	●	3 EVE-Olution		Ruff Ryders 493381

Billboard			R I A A	ARTIST		
DEBUT	PEAK	WKS		Album Title	Catalog	Label & Number

EVERCLEAR
Rock trio formed in Portland, Oregon: Art Alexakis (vocals, guitar), Craig Montoya (bass) and Greg Eklund (drums).

1/13/96	25	38	▲	1 Sparkle And Fade..		Capitol 30929
10/25/97	33	88	▲	2 So Much For The Afterglow		Capitol 36503
7/29/00	9	36	▲	3 Songs From An American Movie Vol. One: Learning How To Smile		Capitol 97061
12/9/00	66	10		4 Songs From An American Movie Vol. Two: Good Time For A Bad Attitude		Capitol 95873
3/29/03	33	4		5 Slow Motion Daydream		Capitol 38270
10/23/04	182	1		6 Ten Years Gone: The Best Of Everclear 1994-2004 .... [G]		Capitol 66481
9/30/06	169	1		7 Welcome To The Drama Club		Eleven Seven 076

EVERETT, Betty
Born on 11/23/1939 in Greenwood, Mississippi; later based in Chicago, Illinois. Died on 8/19/2001 (age 61). R&B singer/pianist.

10/3/64	102	11		1 Delicious Together..		Vee-Jay 1099
				BETTY EVERETT & JERRY BUTLER		

~ ~ ~ ~ ~ ~ ~ ~ ~ ~ **NON-CHARTED ALBUM** ~ ~ ~ ~ ~ ~ ~ ~ ~ ~ ~
1964 It's In His Kiss [Shoop-Shoop]

EVERLAST
Born Erik Schrody on 8/18/1969 in Valley Stream, New York. Singer/songwriter/guitarist/actor. Member of **House Of Pain** and **La Coka Nostra**. Played "Rhodes" in the 1993 movie *Judgment Night*.

10/17/98+	9	55	▲²	1 Whitey Ford Sings The Blues		Tommy Boy 1236
11/4/00	20	15	●	2 Eat At Whitey's		Tommy Boy 1411
6/12/04	56	3		3 White Trash Beautiful		Island 002114
10/11/08	78	1		4 Love, War And The Ghost Of Whitey Ford		Martyr 90126

EVERLIFE
Christian pop-rock trio from Indiana, Pennsylvania: sisters Amber, Sarah and Julia Ross.

3/10/07	121	1		1 Everlife		Buena Vista 861590

EVERLY BROTHERS, The
Rock and roll-pop-country vocal duo/guitarists/songwriters: brothers Don Everly (born Isaac Donald on 2/1/1937 in Brownie, Kentucky) and Phil Everly (born on 1/19/1939 in Chicago, Illinois). Parents were folk and country singers. Don (beginning at age eight) and Phil (age six) sang with parents through high school. Phil married for a time to the daughter of Janet Bleyer (of The Chordettes). Duo split up in July 1973 and reunited in September 1983. Don's daughter Erin was married to Axl Rose of **Guns N' Roses** from 1990-91.

AWARDS: Grammy: Lifetime Achievement 1997 ★ R&R Hall of Fame: 1986 ★ C&W Hall of Fame: 2001 ★ OPRY: 1957

2/10/58	16	3		1 The Everly Brothers		Cadence 3003
8/22/60	23	19		2 The Fabulous Style Of The Everly Brothers .... [K]		Cadence 3040
5/23/60	9	10		3 It's Everly Time!		Warner 1381
12/5/60+	9	24		4 A Date With The Everly Brothers		Warner 1395
8/25/62	35	17		5 The Golden Hits Of The Everly Brothers .... [G]		Warner 1471
9/25/65	141	3		6 Beat & Soul		Warner 1605
7/18/70	180	8		7 The Everly Brothers' Original Greatest Hits .... [G]		Barnaby 350 [2]
2/13/71	205	1		8 End Of An Era .... [K]		Barnaby 30260 [2]
4/1/72	208	4		9 Stories We Could Tell		RCA Victor 4620
3/10/84	162	5		10 The Everly Brothers Reunion Concert .... [L]		Passport 11001 [2]
				recorded September 1983 at the Royal Albert Hall in London, England		
10/13/84	38	17		11 EB 84		Mercury 822431
2/8/86	83	19		12 Born Yesterday...		Mercury 826142

~ ~ ~ ~ ~ ~ ~ ~ ~ ~ **NON-CHARTED ALBUMS** ~ ~ ~ ~ ~ ~ ~ ~ ~ ~ ~
1958 Songs Our Daddy Taught Us	1963 The Everly Brothers Sing Great Country Hits
1959 The Everly Brothers' Best	1964 The Very Best Of The Everly Brothers
1961 The Everly Brothers (Both Sides Of An Evening)	1964 Rock'n Soul
1962 The Everly Brothers Instant Party!	1965 Gone Gone Gone
1962 Christmas With The Everly Brothers And The Boys Town Choir	

EVERSOLE, Archie
Born on 7/26/1984 on a U.S. Army base in Germany; raised in Atlanta, Georgia. Male rapper.

7/6/02	83	7		1 Ride Wit Me Dirty South Style...		Phat Boy 112928

EVERY AVENUE
Punk-pop band from Marysville, Michigan: David Strauchman (vocals), Josh Randall (guitar), Jimmie Deeghan (guitar), Matt Black (bass) and Dennis Wilson (drums).

11/21/09	136	1		1 Picture Perfect..		Fearless 30128

EVERYDAY SUNDAY
Punk-pop band from Columbus, Ohio: Trey Pearson (vocals), Nick Spencer (guitar), Kevin Cramblet (bass) and Tyler Craft (drums).

7/4/09	187	1		1 Best Night Of Our Lives..		Inpop 71455

EVERY MOTHER'S NIGHTMARE
Hard-rock band formed in Nashville, Tennessee: Rick Ruhl (vocals), Steve Malone (guitar), Mark McMurtry (bass) and Jim Phipps (drums).

11/17/90+	146	15		1 Every Mother's Nightmare		Arista 8633

Billboard			R I A A	ARTIST		
DEBUT	PEAK	WKS		Album Title	Catalog	Label & Number

EVERY MOTHERS' SON
Pop-rock band from New York: brothers Dennis Larden (vocals) and Larry Larden (guitar), with Bruce Milner (organ), Schuyler Larsen (bass) and Christopher Augustine (drums).

6/10/67	117	10		1 Every Mothers' Son		MGM 4471

EVERYTHING
Ska-rock band from Sperryville, Virginia: Craig Honeycutt (vocals, guitar), Rich Bradley, Wolfe Quinn and Steve Van Dam (horns), David Slankard (bass) and Nate Brown (drums).

9/5/98	173	8		1 Super Natural		Blackbird 38003

EVERYTHING BUT THE GIRL
Pop-dance duo formed in London, England: **Tracey Thorn** (vocals; born on 9/26/1962) and Ben Watt (instruments; born on 12/6/1962). Group name taken from a furniture store sign on England's Hull University campus.

6/22/85	202	1		1 Love Not Money		Sire 25274
3/17/90	77	18		2 The Language Of Life		Atlantic 82057
8/6/94+	46	32	●	3 Amplified Heart		Atlantic 82605
6/8/96	37	16		4 Walking Wounded		Atlantic 82912
10/16/99	65	7		5 Temperamental		Atlantic 83214

EVERY TIME I DIE
Hard-rock band from Buffalo, New York: brothers Keith Buckley (vocals) and Jordan Buckley (guitar), with Andrew Williams (guitar), Chris Byrnes (bass) and Michael "Ratboy" Novack (drums).

9/10/05	71	2		1 Gutter Phenomenon		Ferret 058
9/22/07	41	2		2 The Big Dirty		Ferret 085
10/3/09	46	2		3 New Junk Aesthetic		Epitaph 87023

EVE 6
Rock trio from Los Angeles, California: Max Collins (vocals, bass), Jon Siebels (guitar) and Tony Fagenson (drums).

6/27/98	33	47	▲	1 Eve 6		RCA 67617
8/12/00	34	28	●	2 Horrorscope		RCA 67713
8/9/03	27	9		3 It's All In Your Head		RCA 52346

EVORA, Cesaria
Born on 8/27/1941 in Mindelo, Sao Vincente, Cape Verde. Female Latin singer.

6/30/01	188	2		1 Sao Vincente .... [F]		Windham Hill 11590

EXCITERS, The
R&B vocal group from Jamaica, New York: Herb Rooney, his wife Brenda Reid, Carol Johnson and Lillian Walker. Rooney and Reid are the parents of prolific producer Antonio "L.A." Reid (of **The Deele**). Johnson died on 5/7/2007 (age 62).

~ ~ ~ ~ ~ ~ ~ ~ ~ **NON-CHARTED ALBUM** ~ ~ ~ ~ ~ ~ ~ ~ ~ ~

1963 **Tell Him**

EXIES, The
Alternative-rock band from Los Angeles, California: Scott Stevens (vocals, guitar), David Walsh (guitar), Freddy Herrera (bass) and Dennis Wolfe (drums).

1/25/03	115	4		1 Inertia		Melisma 13309

EXILE
Pop band formed in Richmond, Kentucky: J.P. Pennington (vocals, guitar), Les Taylor (guitar), Marlon Hargis (keyboards), Sonny Lemaire (bass) and Steve Goetzman (drums). Group had a highly successful country career from 1983-91.

8/19/78	14	26	●	1 Mixed Emotions		Warner/Curb 3205

EXODUS
Hard-rock band from San Francisco, California: Steve Souza (vocals), Rick Hunolt (guitar), Gary Holt (guitar), Rob McKillop (bass) and Tom Hunting (drums). Kirk Hammet of **Metallica** was a member in the early 1980s.

11/28/87+	82	20		1 Pleasures Of The Flesh		Combat 8169
2/25/89	82	17		2 Fabulous Disaster		Combat 2001
8/11/90	137	9		3 Impact Is Imminent		Capitol 90379

EXOTIC GUITARS, The
Studio group featuring the lead guitar of Al Casey.

8/3/68	155	5		1 The Exotic Guitars .... [I]		Ranwood 8002
1/4/69	167	11		2 Those Were The Days .... [I]		Ranwood 8040
5/31/69	162	6		3 Indian Love Call .... [I]		Ranwood 8051
5/8/71	210	2		4 I Can't Stop Loving You .... [I]		Ranwood 8085

EXPLOSIONS IN THE SKY
Instrumental rock band from Austin, Texas: Munaf Rayani (guitar), Mark Smith (guitar), Michael James (bass) and Chris Hrasky (drums).

3/10/07	76	3		1 All Of A Sudden I Miss Everyone .... [I]		Temporary 099

EXPOSE
Female dance trio formed in Miami, Florida: Ann Curless, Jeanette Jurado and Gioia Bruno. Kelly Moneymaker replaced Bruno in 1992.

2/21/87+	16	74	▲²	1 Exposure		Arista 8441
7/1/89	33	50	●	2 What You Don't Know		Arista 8532
11/21/92+	135	13	●	3 Expose		Arista 18577

Billboard			R I A A	ARTIST		
DEBUT	PEAK	WKS		Album Title	Catalog	Label & Number

EXTREME
Pop-rock band from Boston, Massachusetts: Gary Cherone (vocals), Nuno Bettencourt (guitar), Pat Badger (bass) and Paul Geary (drums). Geary replaced by Mike Mangini by 1995. Cherone became lead singer of **Van Halen** in September 1996 (for one album). Bettencourt later joined **Satellite Party**.

4/8/89	80	32		1 Extreme		A&M 5238
8/25/90+	10	75	▲²	2 Pornograffitti		A&M 5313
10/10/92	10	23	●	3 III Sides To Every Story		A&M 540006
2/25/95	40	5		4 Waiting For The Punchline		A&M 540327
8/30/08	78	1		5 Saudades De Rock		Open E 060

EXUMA
Born MacFarlane Mackey on 2/18/1942 in Cat Island, Bahamas. Died on 1/25/1997 (age 54). Male reggae singer/guitarist/drummer.

10/16/71	202	5		1 Do Wah Nanny		Kama Sutra 2040

EYE TO EYE
Pop duo: singer Deborah Berg (from Seattle, Washington) and pianist Julian Marshall (from England).

6/19/82	99	15		1 Eye To Eye		Warner 3570
10/29/83	205	1		2 Shakespeare Stole My Baby		Warner 23919

EZO
Hard-rock band from Sapporo, Japan: Masaki Yamada (vocals), Shoyo Iida (guitar), Taro Takahashi (bass) and Hiro Homma (drums).

6/13/87	150	9		1 E-Z-O		Geffen 24143

F

FABARES, Shelley
Born Michele Fabares on 1/19/1944 in Santa Monica, California. Pop singer/actress. Niece of actress Nanette Fabray. Starred in several movies and TV shows. Married to record producer Lou Adler from 1964-67. Married actor Mike Farrell on 12/31/1984.

7/21/62	106	11		1 Shelley!		Colpix 426
10/27/62	121	5		2 The Things We Did Last Summer		Colpix 431
5/11/63	48	18		3 Teen-Age Triangle .... [G]		Colpix 444
				JAMES DARREN / SHELLY FABARES / PAUL PETERSEN		

~ ~ ~ ~ ~ ~ ~ ~ ~ ~ **NON-CHARTED ALBUM** ~ ~ ~ ~ ~ ~ ~ ~ ~ ~ ~
1964 **More Teenage Triangle**
[w/ James Darren & Paul Petersen]

FABIAN
Born Fabian Forte on 2/6/1943 in Philadelphia, Pennsylvania. Teen idol singer. Acted in several movies.

5/18/59	5	21		1 Hold That Tiger!		Chancellor 5003
12/28/59+	3²	19		2 Fabulous Fabian		Chancellor 5005

~ ~ ~ ~ ~ ~ ~ ~ ~ ~ **NON-CHARTED ALBUMS** ~ ~ ~ ~ ~ ~ ~ ~ ~ ~ ~
1960 **Fabian/Avalon (The Hit Makers)**   1961 **Rockin' Hot!**
1960 **Good Old Summertime**   1962 **Fabian's 16 Fabulous Hits**
1960 **The Fabian Facade: Young And Wonderful**

FABIAN, Lara
Born Lara Crokaert on 1/9/1970 in Etterbeek, Belgium. Female singer/songwriter.

6/17/00	85	16		1 Lara Fabian		Columbia 69053

FABOLOUS
Born John Jackson on 11/18/1979 in Brooklyn, New York. Male rapper.

9/29/01	4	33	▲	1 Ghetto Fabolous		Desert Storm 62679
3/22/03	3¹	35	▲	2 Street Dreams		Desert Storm 62791
11/22/03	28	3		3 More Street Dreams Pt. 2: The Mixtape		Desert Storm 62924
11/27/04	6	16	●	4 Real Talk		Desert Storm 83754
6/30/07	2¹	21	●	5 From Nothin' To Somethin'		Desert Storm 008162
8/15/09	❶¹	16		6 Loso's Way		Desert Storm 013098

FABRIC, Bent, and His Piano
Born Bent Fabricius-Bjerre on 12/7/1924 in Copenhagen, Denmark. Male pianist.

10/27/62+	13	39		1 Alley Cat .... [I]		Atco 148

FABULOUS POODLES
Rock band from England: Tony DeMeur (vocals, guitar), Bobby Valentino (violin), Richie Robertson (bass) and Bryn Burrows (drums).

2/10/79	61	17		1 Mirror Stars		Epic 35666
12/1/79	185	3		2 Think Pink		Epic 36256

Billboard			R I A A	ARTIST Album Title	Catalog	Label & Number
DEBUT	PEAK	WKS				

FABULOUS RHINESTONES, The
Rock trio from Chicago, Illinois: Kal David (vocals, guitar), Harvey Brooks (bass) and Martin Grebb (vocals, keyboards). David was with **Illinois Speed Press**. Brooks was with **Electric Flag**. Grebb was with **The Buckinghams**.

7/29/72	193	6	1 The Fabulous Rhinestones		Just Sunshine 1
9/22/73	193	3	2 Freewheelin'..		Just Sunshine 9
12/27/75+	204	4	3 The Rhinestones		20th Century 489

FABULOUS THUNDERBIRDS, The
Male blues-rock band from Austin, Texas: Kim Wilson (vocals, harmonica), **Jimmie Vaughan** (guitar; older brother of **Stevie Ray Vaughan**), Keith Ferguson (bass) and Fran Christina (drums). Preston Hubbard replaced Ferguson in late 1981. Jimmie appeared in the 1989 movie *Great Balls Of Fire* and recorded in **The Vaughan Brothers** in 1990. Disbanded in June 1990. Reorganized in 1991 with Wilson, Hubbard, Christina and guitarists Duke Robillard and Kid Bangham. Ferguson died of liver failure on 4/29/1997 (age 49).

5/24/80	204	4	1 What's The Word		Chrysalis 1287
3/28/81	176	7	2 Butt Rockin'		Chrysalis 1319
3/15/86	13	53	▲ 3 Tuff Enuff		CBS Associated 40304
7/18/87	49	15	4 Hot Number...		CBS Associated 40818
5/6/89	118	7	5 Powerful Stuff		CBS Associated 45094

FACELESS, The
Death metal band from Encino, California: Derek Rydquist (vocals), Steve Jones (guitar), Michael Keene (guitar), Brandon Giffin (bass) and Lyle Cooper (drums).

11/29/08	119	1	1 Planetary Duality		Sumerian 013

FACEMOB
Rap group from Houston, Texas: Harold Armstrong, **Devin The Dude** Copeland, Gene Dorcy, Loretta Dorsey and Rod Smith.

8/24/96	51	7	1 The Other Side Of The Law		Interface 41336

FACES
Rock band formed in England by former **Small Faces** members **Ronnie Lane** (bass), **Ian McLagan** (organ) and Kenney Jones (drums) with former **Jeff Beck** Group members **Rod Stewart** (vocals) and **Ronnie Wood** (bass). Lane left in 1973; replaced by Tetsu Yamauchi (of **Free**). Disbanded in late 1975. Wood joined **The Rolling Stones** in 1976. Jones joined **The Who** in 1978 and formed **The Law** in 1991. Lane died of multiple sclerosis on 6/4/1997 (age 51).

4/18/70	119	12	1 First Step...		Warner 1851
			SMALL FACES		
3/13/71	29	19	2 Long Player..		Warner 1892
12/18/71+	6	24	● 3 A Nod Is As Good As A Wink...To A Blind Horse		Warner 2574
4/21/73	21	16	4 Ooh La La..		Warner 2665
1/5/74	63	11	5 Rod Stewart/Faces Live - Coast To Coast Overture and Beginners............ [L]		Mercury 697
			ROD STEWART/FACES		
12/11/76	207	1	6 Snakes And Ladders/The Best Of Faces .... [G]		Warner 2897

FACE TO FACE
Rock band from Boston, Massachusetts: Laurie Sargent (vocals), brothers Angelo Kimball (guitar) and Stuart Kimball (guitar), John Ryder (bass) and William Beard (drums).

6/16/84	126	16	1 Face To Face		Epic 38857
6/18/88	176	7	2 One Big Day		Mercury 834376

FACE TO FACE
Punk-rock band from Los Angeles, California: Trevor Keith (vocals), Chad Yaro (guitar), Scott Shiflett (bass) and Rob Kurth (drums). Pete Parada replaced Kurth in 1999.

9/28/96	139	2	1 Face To Face		A&M 540601
8/14/99	162	1	2 Ignorance Is Bliss		Lady Luck 78048
4/27/02	178	1	3 How To Ruin Everything...............................		Vagrant 366

FACTS OF LIFE
R&B vocal trio from Newark, New Jersey: Jean Davis (younger sister of **Tyrone Davis**), Keith William and Chuck Carter.

4/9/77	146	7	1 Sometimes		Kayvette 802

FAGEN, Donald
Born on 1/10/1948 in Passaic, New Jersey. Pop-rock singer/keyboardist. Member of **Steely Dan**.

10/30/82	11	27	▲ 1 The Nightfly		Warner 23696
6/12/93	10	19	● 2 Kamakiriad		Reprise 45230
4/1/06	26	4	3 Morph The Cat		Reprise 49975

FAHEY, John
Born on 2/28/1939 in Cecil County, Maryland. Died of heart failure on 2/22/2001 (age 61). Acoustic guitarist.

8/11/73	208	2	1 After The Ball .... [I]		Reprise 2145

FAINT, The
Eclectic-pop-rock band from Omaha, Nebraska: Maria Taylor, Orenda Fink, Donna Carnes, Kim Salistean, Clark Potter, Scott French, Nate Lefeber and Tracy Sands.

10/2/04	99	2	1 Wet From Birth		Saddle Creek 67
8/23/08	46	2	2 Fascination		Blank Wav 01

FAIRCHILD, Shelly
Born on 8/23/1977 in Clinton, Mississippi. Country singer/songwriter.

5/21/05	162	1	1 Ride		Columbia 90355

Billboard			R I A A	ARTIST	Catalog	Label & Number
DEBUT	PEAK	WKS		Album Title		

FAIRGROUND ATTRACTION
Pop band formed in Glasgow, Scotland: Eddi Reader (female vocals), Mark Nevin (guitar), Simon Edwards (bass) and Roy Dodds (drums).

1/21/89	137	11		1 The First Of A Million Kisses		RCA 8596

FAIRPORT CONVENTION
Folk-rock band formed in London, England. Varying membership included vocalists **Sandy Denny** and **Ian Matthews** (1967-69) and guitarist **Richard Thompson** (1967-71). Denny died of a brain hemorrhage on 4/21/1978 (age 37).

12/4/71	200	1		1 Angel Delight		A&M 4319
3/25/72	195	3		2 "Babbacombe" Lee		A&M 4333
5/5/73	203	3		3 Rosie		A&M 4386
8/16/75	143	8		4 Rising For The Moon		Island 9313
5/22/76	207	1		5 Fairport Chronicles .... [K]		A&M 3530 [2]

FAIR TO MIDLAND
Eclectic-rock band from Sulpher Springs, Texas: Darroh Sudderth (vocals), Cliff Campbell (guitar), Matt Langley (keyboards), Jon Dicken (bass) and Brett Stowers (drums).

6/30/07	137	1		1 Fables From A Mayfly: What I Tell You Three Times Is True		Serjical Strike 008996

FAITH, Percy
1950s: #42 / 1960s: #44 / All-Time: #163

Born on 4/7/1908 in Toronto, Ontario, Canada. Died of cancer on 2/9/1976 (age 67). Orchestra leader. Moved to the U.S. in 1940. Joined Columbia Records in 1950 as conductor/arranger. Also see **Mary Stuart**.

7/28/56	18	2		1 Passport To Romance .... [I]		Columbia 880
5/6/57	8	2		2 My Fair Lady .... [I]		Columbia 895
5/25/59	17	14		3 Porgy And Bess .... [I]		Columbia 1298 / 8105
1/11/60	7	17	●	4 Bouquet .... [I]		Columbia 1322 / 8124
12/19/64	34ˣ	2		5 Music Of Christmas .... [X-I]		Columbia 1381 / 8176
				first released in 1954 on Columbia 588; above release issued in 1959 with a new album cover		
11/28/60+	7	15		6 Jealousy .... [I]		Columbia 1501 / 8292
1/9/61	6	23		7 Camelot .... [I]		Columbia 1570 / 8370
10/9/61	38	7		8 Mucho Gusto! More Music Of Mexico .... [I]		Columbia 1639 / 8439
4/14/62	26	6		9 Bouquet Of Love .... [I]		Columbia 1681 / 8481
9/29/62	105	5		10 The Music Of Brazil! .... [I]		Columbia 1822 / 8622
6/22/63	12	36	●	11 Themes For Young Lovers .... [I]		Columbia 2023 / 8823
10/19/63	80	15		12 Shangri-La! .... [I]		Columbia 2024 / 8824
2/15/64	103	12		13 Great Folk Themes .... [I]		Columbia 2108 / 8908
5/30/64	110	7		14 More Themes For Young Lovers .... [I]		Columbia 2167 / 8967
12/4/65	101	5		15 Broadway Bouquet .... [I]		Columbia 2356 / 9156
12/17/66	24ˣ	7		16 Christmas Is.. [X]		Columbia 2577 / 9377
				Christmas charts: 24/'66, 46/'67, 27/'68		
5/27/67	152	5		17 The Academy Award Winner And Other Great Movie Themes .... [I]		Columbia 2650 / 9450
9/16/67	111	17		18 Today's Themes For Young Lovers		Columbia 2704 / 9504
3/23/68	121	22		19 For Those In Love		Columbia 2810 / 9610
9/21/68	95	11		20 Angel Of The Morning (Hit Themes For Young Lovers).................		Columbia 9706
2/15/69	88	14		21 Those Were The Days		Columbia 9762
5/31/69	194	4		22 Windmills Of Your Mind .... [I]		Columbia 9835
9/27/69	134	11		23 Love Theme From "Romeo & Juliet"..		Columbia 9906
2/14/70	88	14		24 Leaving On A Jet Plane		Columbia 9983
6/13/70	196	2		25 Held Over! Today's Great Movie Themes .... [I]		Columbia 1019
10/17/70	179	4		26 The Beatles Album .... [I]		Columbia 30097
1/23/71	200	2		27 A Time For Love .... [K]		Columbia 30330 [2]
2/27/71	198	2		28 I Think I Love You		Columbia 30502
7/31/71	184	5		29 Black Magic Woman .... [I]		Columbia 30800
12/18/71+	186	6		30 Jesus Christ, Superstar .... [I]		Columbia 31042
4/1/72	176	6		31 Joy.. [I]		Columbia 31301
9/23/72	197	4		32 Day By Day		Columbia 31627
12/16/72+	204	7		33 Percy Faith's All-Time Greatest Hits .... [G-I]		Columbia 31588 [2]
3/24/73	213	3		34 Clair .... [I]		Columbus 32164

FAITH BAND
Pop-rock band from Indianapolis, Indiana: Carl Storie (vocals), David Bennett (guitar), John Cascella (keyboards), Mark Cawley (bass) and David Barnes (drums).

7/7/79	206	4		1 Face To Face		Mercury 3770

Billboard			R I A A	ARTIST	Catalog	Label & Number
DEBUT	PEAK	WKS		Album Title		

FAITHFULL, Marianne
Born on 12/29/1946 in Hampstead, London, England. Pop-rock singer/actress. Involved in a long, tumultuous relationship with **Mick Jagger**. Acted in several stage and screen productions.

6/5/65	12	31		1 Marianne Faithfull		London 423
12/25/65+	81	16		2 Go Away From My World		London 452
11/19/66	147	2		3 Faithfull Forever...		London 482
4/5/69	171	10		4 Marianne Faithfull's Greatest Hits .... [G]		London 547
2/2/80	82	15		5 Broken English		Island 9570
10/17/81	104	9		6 Dangerous Acquaintances		Island 9648
3/26/83	107	7		7 A Child's Adventure		Island 90066
7/7/90	160	9		8 Blazing Away .... [L]		Island 842794
				recorded on 11/25/1989 at St. Anne's Cathedral in New York City		
4/4/09	182	1		9 Easy Come Easy Go		Decca 012708

FAITH, HOPE & CHARITY
R&B vocal trio from Tampa, Florida: Brenda Hilliard, Albert Bailey and Diane Destry.

8/30/75	100	14		1 Faith, Hope & Charity		RCA Victor 1100

FAITH NO MORE
Rock band from San Francisco, California: Mike Patton (vocals), Jim Martin (guitar), Roddy Bottum (keyboards), Billy Gould (bass) and Mike Bordin (drums). Dean Menta replaced Martin in 1994. Jon Hudson replaced Menta in 1995. Patton also formed **Mr. Bungle, Fantomas** and **Tomahawk**.

2/24/90	11	60	▲	1 The Real Thing		Slash 25878
7/4/92	10	19	●	2 Angel Dust		Slash 26785
4/15/95	31	8		3 King For A Day/Fool For A Lifetime		Slash 45723
6/21/97	41	8		4 Album Of The Year		Slash 46629

FALCO
Born Johann Holzel on 2/19/1957 in Vienna, Austria. Died in a car crash on 2/6/1998 (age 40). Dance-pop singer/songwriter.

5/7/83	64	13		1 Einzelhaft		A&M 4951
3/1/86	3[1]	27	●	2 Falco 3		A&M 5105

FALLING UP
Rock band from Albany, Oregon: Jessy Ribordy (vocals), Joe Kisselburgh (guitar), Jeremy Miller (bass) and Josh Shroy (drums).

11/12/05	173	1		1 Dawn Escapes		BEC 60364

FALL OF TROY, The
Hard-rock trio from Mukilteo, Washington: Thomas Erak (vocals, guitar), Frank Ene (bass) and Andrew Forsman (drums).

5/19/07	76	1		1 Manipulator		Equal Vision 140
10/24/09	123	1		2 In The Unlikely Event		Equal Vision 159

FALLON, Jimmy
Born on 9/19/1974 in Brooklyn, New York; raised in Saugerties, New York. Stand-up comedian/actor. Cast member of TV's *Saturday Night Live* from 1998-2004; also starred in several movies. Began hosting TV's *Late Night* talk show in 2009.

9/14/02	47	6		1 The Bathroom Wall .... [C]		DreamWorks 450330

FALL OUT BOY
Punk-rock band from Wilmette, Illinois: Patrick Stump (vocals, guitar), Joe Trohman (guitar), Pete Wentz (bass) and Andy Hurley (drums). Wentz married **Ashlee Simpson** on 5/17/2008.

8/20/05+	10[C]	27	●	1 Take This To Your Grave		Fueled By Ramen 061
				first released in 2003		
6/5/04	153	1		2 My Heart Will Always Be The B-Side To My Tongue .... [EP]		Fueled By Ramen 067
5/21/05	9	77	▲[2]	3 From Under The Cork Tree		Fueled By Ramen 004140
2/24/07	❶[1]	52	▲	4 Infinity On High		Fueled By Ramen 008109
1/3/09	8	23	●	5 Folie A Deux		Decaydance 012196
12/5/09	77	1		6 Believers Never Die: Greatest Hits .... [G]		Decaydance 013703

FALTSKOG, Agnetha
Born on 4/5/1950 in Jonkoping, Sweden. Female singer. Member of **Abba**.

9/17/83	102	11		1 Wrap Your Arms Around Me		Polydor 813242

FAME, Georgie
Born Clive Powell on 6/26/1943 in Leigh, Lancashire, England. Blues-rock singer/pianist.

5/1/65	137	3		1 Yeh Yeh		Imperial 12282
5/11/68	185	4		2 The Ballad Of Bonnie And Clyde		Epic 26368
1/27/96	55	11		3 How Long Has This Been Going On .... [L]		Verve 529136
				VAN MORRISON with Georgie Fame & Friends		
				recorded on 5/3/1995 at Ronnie Scott's Club in London, England		

FAMILY
Rock band from England: Roger Chapman (vocals), John Wetton (guitar, keyboards; **King Crimson, Uriah Heep, U.K., Asia**), Charlie Whitney (guitar), John Palmer (keyboards) and Rob Townsend (drums).

2/5/72	177	7		1 Fearless..		United Artists 5562
10/28/72	183	5		2 Bandstand...		United Artists 5644
3/10/73	207	3		3 Anyway..		United Artists 5527

Billboard DEBUT	PEAK	WKS	R I A A	ARTIST Album Title	Catalog	Label & Number

FAMILY, The
Dance band formed in Minneapolis, Minnesota: Susannah Melvoin (female vocals), Paul "St. Paul" Peterson (vocals, keyboards), Jerome Benton (percussion), Eric Leeds (sax) and Jellybean Johnson (drums). Melvoin is the twin sister of Wendy Melvoin (of **Prince**'s Revolution and **Wendy & Lisa**); their father is jazz pianist Mike Melvoin (**The Plastic Cow**) and their brother was the late Jonathan Melvoin (of **The Smashing Pumpkins**). Peterson, Benton and Johnson were members of **The Time**.

| 9/7/85 | 62 | 22 | | 1 The Family .... | | Paisley Park 25322 |

FAMILY FORCE 5
Christian crunkcore band from Atlanta, Georgia: brothers Solomon, Jacob and Joshua Olds, with Nathen Currin and Derek Mount.

9/6/08	30	3		1 Dance Or Die...		TMG 35471
6/6/09	180	1		2 Dance Or Die With A Vengeance		TMG 97936
10/24/09	3¹ˣ	4		3 Christmas Pageant	[X]	TMG 97937

FAMILY OF MANN
Jazz band formed in New York: **Herbie Mann** (flute), Sam Brown (guitar), David Newman (sax), Pat Rebillot (keyboards), Armen Halburian (percussion), Tony Levin (bass) and Steve Gadd (drums).

| 11/2/74 | 201 | 4 | | 1 First Light .... | [I] | Atlantic 1658 |

FANNY
Female rock band from Los Angeles, California: sisters June Millington (vocals, guitar) and Jean Millington (vocals, bass), with Nicole Barclay (keyboards) and Alice DeBuhr (drums).

| 10/23/71 | 150 | 7 | | 1 Charity Ball .... | | Reprise 6456 |
| 4/1/72 | 135 | 6 | | 2 Fanny Hill .... | | Reprise 2058 |

FANTASIA
Born Fantasia Barrino on 6/30/1984 in High Point, North Carolina. Female R&B singer. Winner on the 2004 season of TV's *American Idol.*

| 12/11/04 | 8 | 42 | ▲ | 1 Free Yourself | | J Records 64235 |
| 12/30/06 | 19 | 38 | ● | 2 Fantasia.. | | J Records 78962 |

FANTASTIC FOUR
R&B vocal group from Detroit, Michigan: James Epps, Joseph Pruitt, Cleveland Horne and Ernest Newsome. Horne died of a heart attack on 4/13/2000. Epps died of a heart attack on 9/7/2000.

| 6/21/75 | 99 | 16 | | 1 Alvin Stone (The Birth And Death Of A Gangster)........................ | | Westbound 201 |

FANTASY
Rock band from Miami, Florida: Vincent DeMeo (male vocals, guitar), Lydia Miller (female vocals), Mario Russo (organ), David Robbins (bass) and Greg Kimple (drums).

| 8/15/70 | 194 | 3 | | 1 Fantasy... | | Liberty 7643 |

FANTASY
Black dance band from New York : Ken Robeson, Tami Hunt, Rufus Jackson and Carolyn Edwards.

| 5/9/81 | 201 | 2 | | 1 Fantasy... | | Pavillion 37151 |

FANTE, Ricky
Born in 1978 in Washington DC. Male R&B singer/songwriter.

| 7/31/04 | 198 | 1 | | 1 Rewind .... | | Virgin 84403 |

FANTOMAS
Hard-rock band formed in Los Angeles, California: Mike Patton (vocals), Buzz Osborne (guitar), Trevor Dunn (bass) and Dave Lombardo (drums). Patton was leader of **Faith No More** and **Tomahawk**. Both Patton and Dunn were members of **Mr. Bungle**. Lombardo was a member of **Slayer**.

2/14/04	183	1		1 Delirivm Cordia..		Ipecac 45
4/23/05	158	1		2 Suspended Animation		Ipecac 62
				album contains a series of 30 cuts titled "04/01/05 Friday" through "4/30/05 Saturday"		

FARGO, Donna
Born Yvonne Vaughan on 11/10/1945 in Mt. Airy, North Carolina. Country singer/songwriter.

7/15/72	47	43	●	1 The Happiest Girl In The Whole U.S.A.		Dot 26000
3/17/73	104	11		2 My Second Album		Dot 26006
1/19/74	204	6		3 All About A Feeling		Dot 26019
12/7/74	207	1		4 Miss Donna Fargo		ABC/Dot 2002

FARQUAHR
Rock band from New Haven, Connecticut: brothers Frank "Flamingo" McGowan, Dennis "Condor" McGowan and Jack "Hummingbird" McGowan, with Doug "Barnswallow" Lapham. All played guitar and all shared vocals. Dennis died on 3/31/2001 (age 57). Frank died on 10/21/2004 (age 65).

| 12/5/70 | 195 | 3 | | 1 Farquahr.. | | Elektra 74083 |

FARRAR, Jay
Born on 12/26/1966 in Millstadt, Illinois. Rock singer/songwriter. Lead singer of **Uncle Tupelo** and **Son Volt**.

10/13/01	137	1		1 Sebastopol..		Artemis 751093
11/7/09	109	1		2 One Fast Move Or I'm Gone: Music From Kerouac's Big Sur	[S]	F-Stop 521477
				JAY FARRAR & BENJAMIN GIBBARD		

FARRELL, Eileen
Born on 2/13/1920 in Willimantic, Connecticut. Died of heart failure on 3/23/2002 (age 82). Opera singer.

| 2/13/61 | 15 | 17 | | 1 I've Got A Right To Sing The Blues .... | | Columbia 1465 |

Billboard			ARTIST		
DEBUT	PEAK	WKS	R I A A Album Title	Catalog	Label & Number

FARRELL, Joe
Born on 12/16/1937 in Chicago Heights, Illinois. Died on 1/10/1986 (age 48). Jazz saxophonist.

| 10/30/76 | 100 | 8 | 1 **Benson & Farrell** .... [I] | | CTI 6069 |
| | | | GEORGE BENSON & JOE FARRELL | | |

FARRELL, Perry
Born Simon Bernstein on 3/29/1959 in Queens, New York; raised in Miami, Florida; later based in Los Angeles, California. Alternative-rock singer/songwriter. Former leader of **Jane's Addiction**, **Porno For Pyros** and **Satellite Party**.

| 8/18/01 | 177 | 1 | 1 **Song Yet To Be Sung** .... | | Virgin 50030 |

FARRENHEIT
Rock trio from Boston, Massachusetts: Charlie Farren (vocals, guitar), David Heit (bass) and Muzz (drums). Farren was lead singer of the **Joe Perry Project**.

| 5/9/87 | 179 | 7 | 1 **Farrenheit** .... | | Warner 25564 |

FARRIS, Dionne
Born in 1969 in Bordentown, New Jersey. Female R&B singer. Former member of **Arrested Development**.

| 3/4/95 | 57 | 20 | 1 **Wild Seed - Wild Flower** .... | | Columbia 57359 |

FASTBALL
Rock trio from Austin, Texas: Miles Zuniga (vocals, guitar), Tony Scalzo (vocals, bass) and Joey Shuffield (drums).

| 3/28/98 | 29 | 52 | ▲ | 1 **All The Pain Money Can Buy** .... | | Hollywood 62130 |
| 10/7/00 | 97 | 3 | | 2 **The Harsh Light Of Day** .... | | Hollywood 62237 |

FASTER PUSSYCAT
Hard-rock band from Los Angeles, California: Taime Downe (vocals), Greg Steele (guitar), Brent Muscat (guitar), Eric Stacy (bass) and Mark Michals (drums). Michals was replaced by Brett Bradshaw in early 1992. Group name taken from the 1965 action movie *Faster Pussycat! Kill! Kill!*

8/29/87	97	35		1 **Faster Pussycat**		Elektra 60730
9/23/89+	48	41	●	2 **Wake Me When It's Over**		Elektra 60883
8/22/92	90	4		3 **Whipped!**		Elektra 61124

FASTWAY
Hard-rock band from England: David King (vocals), Fast Eddie Clarke (guitar), Charlie McCracken (bass) and Jerry Shirley (drums). Clarke was with **Motorhead**. Shirley was with **Humble Pie**.

5/28/83	31	32		1 **Fastway**		Columbia 38662
7/21/84	59	14		2 **All Fired Up**		Columbia 39373
11/22/86+	156	12		3 **Trick Or Treat** .... Cat:#32/24 [S]		Columbia 40549
4/22/89	135	10		4 **On Target**		GWR 75411

FATAL
Born Bruce Washington in Brooklyn, New York. Male rapper.

| 4/18/98 | 50 | 4 | 1 **In The Line Of Fire** .... | | Relativity 1622 |

FATBACK
Funk band from New Jersey: Bill Curtis (vocals, drums), Johnny King (guitar), Saunders McCrae (keyboards), Earl Shelton, George Williams, George Adam and Richard Cromwell (horns) and Johnny Flippin (bass).

2/28/76	158	8		1 **Raising Hell**		Event 6905
8/28/76	182	5		2 **Night Fever**		Spring 6711
				THE FATBACK BAND (above 2)		
8/12/78	73	12		3 **Fired Up 'N' Kickin'**		Spring 6718
9/29/79	89	12		4 **Fatback XII**		Spring 6723
4/19/80	44	27	●	5 **Hot Box**		Spring 6726
11/1/80	91	7		6 **14 Karat**		Spring 6729
6/20/81	102	8		7 **Tasty Jam**		Spring 6731
1/9/82	148	4		8 **Gigolo**		Spring 6734
7/24/82	204	6		9 **On The Floor**		Spring 6736

FAT BOYS
Rap trio from Brooklyn, New York: Mark "Prince Markie Dee" Morales, Darren "The Human Beat Box" Robinson and Damon "Kool Rock" Wimbley. Group starred in the 1987 movie *Disorderlies*. Robinson died of heart failure on 12/10/1995 (age 28).

1/5/85	48	40	●	1 **Fat Boys**		Sutra 1015
8/31/85	63	33	●	2 **The Fat Boys Are Back!**		Sutra 1016
5/24/86	62	19		3 **Big & Beautiful**		Sutra 1017
10/3/87	108	10		4 **The Best Part Of The Fat Boys** .... [K]		Sutra 1018
6/13/87	8	49	▲	5 **Crushin'**		Tin Pan Apple 831948
7/9/88	33	24	●	6 **Coming Back Hard Again**		Tin Pan Apple 835809
10/28/89	175	3		7 **On And On**		Tin Pan Apple 838867

FATBOY SLIM
Born Norman Cook on 7/31/1963 in Bromley, London, England. Techno-house singer/instrumentalist. Former member of **The Housemartins** and **Beats International**.

11/7/98+	34	63	▲	1 **You've Come A Long Way, Baby**		Skint 66247
4/8/00	195	1		2 **The Fatboy Slim/Norman Cook Collection** .... [K]		Hip-O 564787
4/15/00	173	3		3 **On The Floor At The Boutique**		Skint 49130
11/25/00	51	5		4 **Halfway Between The Gutter And The Stars**		Skint 50460
10/23/04	149	1		5 **Palookaville**		Astralwerks 64748

267

Billboard DEBUT	PEAK	WKS	R I A A	ARTIST Album Title	Catalog	Label & Number

F.A.T.E.
Female R&B vocal trio from Jersey City, New Jersey: Tiffany Chisolm, Shaunesa Walker and Patricia McKelvin.
F.A.T.E.: For All That's Endured.

| 6/24/00 | 196 | 1 | | 1 For All That's Endured .... | | Warner 47591 |

FATES WARNING
Hard-rock band from Hartford, Connecticut: John Arch (vocals), Jim Matheos (guitar), Frank Aresti (guitar), Joe DiBiase (bass) and Steve Zimmerman (drums). By 1988, Ray Adler replaced Arch. By 1989, Mark Zonder replaced Zimmerman.

2/7/87	191	4		1 Awaken The Guardian		Enigma 73231
4/23/88	111	13		2 No Exit..		Enigma 73330
9/16/89	141	9		3 Perfect Symmetry...		Enigma 73408

FATHER MC
Born Timothy Brown in Harlem, New York. Dancehall reggae singer.

| 12/1/90+ | 62 | 30 | | 1 Father's Day.. | | Uptown 10061 |
| 9/12/92+ | 185 | 3 | | 2 Close To You.. | | Uptown 10542 |

FAT JOE
Born Joseph Cartagena on 8/19/1970 in the Bronx, New York. Male rapper. Member of **Terror Squad**.

11/11/95	71	3		1 Jealous One's Envy		Relativity 1239
9/19/98	7	10	●	2 Don Cartagena		Mystic 92805
12/22/01+	21	32	▲	3 Jealous One's Still Envy (J.O.S.E.)		Terror Squad 83472
11/30/02	31	11		4 Loyalty..		Terror Squad 83600
7/2/05	6	11		5 All Or Nothing		Terror Squad 83749
12/2/06	14	13		6 Me, Myself & I		Terror Squad 78122
3/29/08	6	5		7 The Elephant In The Room		Terror Squad 14619
10/24/09	73	2		8 Jealous One's Still Envy 2 (J.O.S.E. 2)		Terror Squad 97371

FAT MATTRESS
Rock band from England: Neil Landon (vocals), Noel Redding (guitar), Jimmy Leverton (bass) and Eric Dillon (drums). Redding played bass with the **Jimi Hendrix** Experience.

| 11/15/69 | 134 | 10 | | 1 Fat Mattress .... | | Atco 309 |

FATTY KOO
Teen pop vocal group from Columbus, Ohio: Eddie Brickerman, Marya Barrios, Valure Allison, Ron Riley, Josh Gad and Gabrielle Travis. Group featured in own BET-TV series.

| 7/30/05 | 64 | 2 | | 1 House Of Fatty Koo... | | Columbia 91256 |

FAZE-O
Funk band from Chicago, Illinois: Robert Neal (vocals), Ralph Aikens (guitar), Keith Harrison (keyboards), Fred Crum (bass) and Roger Parker (drums).

| 3/4/78 | 98 | 17 | | 1 Riding High .... | | She 740 |
| 11/11/78 | 145 | 3 | | 2 Good Thang .... | | She 741 |

FEAR BEFORE THE MARCH OF FLAMES
Hard-rock band from Aurora, Colorado: David Marion (vocals), Adam Fisher (guitar), Zachary Hutchings (guitar), Mike Madruga (bass) and Clayton Holyoak (drums).

| 10/7/06 | 153 | 1 | | 1 The Always Open Mouth .... | | Equal Vision 121 |

FEAR FACTORY
Hard-rock band from Los Angeles, California: Burton Bell (vocals), Dino Cazares (guitar), Christian Olde Wolbers (bass) and Ray Herrera (drums). Cazares also formed **Divine Heresy**.

6/7/97	158	1		1 Remanufacture (Cloning Technology)		Roadrunner 8834
8/15/98	77	9	●	2 Obsolete..		Roadrunner 8752
5/12/01	32	5		3 Digimortal		Roadrunner 8487
5/8/04	30	5		4 Archetype..		Liquid 8 12189
9/10/05	45	2		5 Transgression		Calvin 037

FEDERATION
Male rap trio from Fairfield, California: Doonie Baby, Goldie Gold and Mr. Stres.

| 10/23/04 | 200 | 1 | | 1 Federation .... | | Montbello 81218 |

FEDERLINE, Kevin
Born on 3/21/1978 in Fresno, California. Pop singer/songwriter/rapper/actor. Nicknamed "K-Fed." Married to **Britney Spears** from 2004-07; both starred in the TV reality series Britney & Kevin: Chaotic.

| 11/18/06 | 151 | 1 | | 1 Playing With Fire .... | | Federline 01251 |

FEE
Christian rock band from Alpharetta, Georgia: Steve Fee (vocals), Matt Adkins (guitar), Heath Balltzglier (bass) and Brandon Coker (drums).

| 10/24/09 | 101 | 2 | | 1 Hope Rising .... | | Ino 84667 |

FEELIES, The
Rock band from Hoboken, New Jersey: Glenn Mercer (vocals), Bill Million (guitar), Dave Weckerman (percussion), Brenda Sauter (bass) and Stan Demeski (drums).

| 11/19/88 | 173 | 5 | | 1 Only Life .... | | A&M 5214 |

Billboard			R I A A	ARTIST		
DEBUT	PEAK	WKS		Album Title	Catalog	Label & Number
				FEIST Born Leslie Feist on 2/13/1976 in Amherst, Nova Scotia, Canada. Female singer/songwriter.		
5/19/07	16	52	●	1 The Reminder		Cherrytree 008819
10/13/07	49^C	1		2 Let It Die .... [E]		Cherrytree 004442
				FELDER, Don Born on 9/21/1947 in Gainesville, Florida. Rock singer/songwriter/guitarist. Member of the **Eagles** (1975-2003).		
12/3/83+	178	8		1 Airborne		Elektra 60295
				FELDER, Wilton Born on 8/31/1940 in Houston, Texas. R&B reed player. Co-founder of **The Crusaders**.		
12/9/78+	173	14		1 We All Have A Star		ABC 1109
11/8/80	142	13		2 Inherit The Wind		MCA 5144
3/9/85	81	16		3 Secrets .... [I]		MCA 5510
				FELICIANO, Jose Born on 9/8/1945 in Lares, Puerto Rico; raised in Spanish Harlem, New York. Blind since birth. Folk-pop singer/guitarist. Appeared as himself in the movie *Fargo*. AWARD: Grammy: Best New Artist 1968		
7/20/68	2^3	59	●	1 Feliciano!		RCA Victor 3957
12/7/68+	24	19		2 Souled		RCA Victor 4045
7/5/69	16	36	●	3 Feliciano/10 To 23		RCA Victor 4185
12/20/69+	29	14	●	4 Alive Alive-O! .... [L] recorded at the London Palladium		RCA Victor 6021 [2]
5/30/70	57	20		5 Fireworks		RCA Victor 4370
12/1/73	3^{1X}	4		6 Jose Feliciano .... [X] first released in 1970		RCA Victor 4421
4/17/71	92	10		7 Encore! Jose Feliciano's Finest Performances .... [G]		RCA Victor 1005
11/13/71	173	9		8 That The Spirit Needs		RCA Victor 4573
5/19/73	156	8		9 Compartments		RCA Victor 0141
12/21/74+	136	7		10 And The Feeling's Good		RCA Victor 0407
9/6/75	165	4		11 Just Wanna Rock 'N' Roll		RCA Victor APL-1005
5/24/03	173	1		12 Senor Bolero 2 .... [F]		Universal Latino 000083
				FELLINI, Suzanne Born on 8/6/1955 in Manhattan, New York. Rock singer/actress.		
5/17/80	203	4		1 Suzanne Fellini		Casablanca 7205
				FELONY Rock band from Los Angeles, California: brothers Jeffrey Spry (vocals) and Curly Joe Spry (guitar), with Danny Sands (keyboards), Louis Ruiz (bass) and Arty Blea (drums).		
3/26/83	185	5		1 The Fanatic		Rock 'n' Roll 38453
				FELONY, Jayo Born James Savage on 12/31/1969 in San Diego, California. Male rapper.		
9/12/98	46	5		1 Whatcha Gonna Do		Def Jam 558792
				FEMME FATALE Hard-rock band formed in Albuquerque, New Mexico: Lorraine Lewis (vocals), Mazzi Rawd (guitar), Bill D'Angelo (guitar), Rick Rael (bass) and Bobby Murray (drums).		
1/28/89	141	5		1 Femme Fatale		MCA 42155
				FENDER, Freddy Born Baldemar Huerta on 6/4/1937 in San Benito, Texas. Died of cancer on 10/14/2006 (age 69). Country singer/guitarist. Played "Sammy Cantu" in the 1988 movie *The Milagro Beanfield War*. Joined the **Texas Tornados** in 1990.		
4/19/75	20	43	●	1 Before The Next Teardrop Falls		ABC/Dot 2020
10/18/75	41	18		2 Are You Ready For Freddy		ABC/Dot 2044
11/8/75	203	1		3 Since I Met You Baby .... [E] new musical tracks behind Fender's original vocals from 1960		GRT 8005
2/28/76	59	11		4 Rock 'N' Country		ABC/Dot 2050
11/6/76	170	3		5 If You're Ever In Texas		ABC/Dot 2061
5/21/77	155	7		6 The Best Of Freddy Fender .... [G]		ABC/Dot 2079
				FENDERMEN, The Rock and roll duo: Phil Humphrey (from Stoughton, Wisconsin) and Jim Sundquist (from Niagara, Wisconsin). ~ ~ ~ ~ ~ ~ ~ ~ ~ ~ **NON-CHARTED ALBUM** ~ ~ ~ ~ ~ ~ ~ ~ ~ ~ ~ 1960 **Mule Skinner Blues**		
				FENIX*TX Punk-rock band from Houston, Texas: Willie Salazar (vocals, guitar), Damon De La Paz (guitar), Adam Lewis (bass) and Donnie Reyes (drums). Reyes left after first album, guitarist James Love joined and De La Paz moved to drums.		
6/3/00	115	8		1 Fenix*TX		Drive-Thru 12013
6/9/01	87	3		2 Lechuza		Drive-Thru 112484
				FENN, Rick Born on 5/23/1953 in England. Rock singer/guitarist. Member of **10cc**.		
8/31/85	154	5		1 Profiles .... [I] **NICK MASON & RICK FENN**		Columbia 40142

FERGIE
Born Stacy Ferguson on 3/27/1975 in Whittier, California; raised in Hacienda Heights, California. Female singer/songwriter/ actress. Regular on TV's *Kids Incorporated* from 1984-89; also acted in other TV shows and movies. Member of the groups **Wild Orchid** and **Black Eyed Peas**. Married actor Josh Duhamel on 1/10/2009.

10/7/06+	2[1]	94	▲3	1 **The Dutchess**	Cat:#13/9	A&M 007490
6/14/08	46	2		2 **The Dutchess: Deluxe E.P.** [EP]		will.i.am digital

FERGUSON, Jay
Born John Ferguson on 5/10/1947 in Burbank, California. Pop-rock singer/songwriter. Member of **Spirit** and **Jo Jo Gunne**.

3/25/78	72	12		1 **Thunder Island**		Asylum 1115
4/21/79	86	16		2 **Real Life Ain't This Way**		Asylum 158
4/17/82	178	5		3 **White Noise**		Capitol 12196

FERGUSON, Maynard
Born on 5/4/1928 in Verdun, Quebec, Canada. Died of liver failure on 8/23/2006 (age 78). White jazz trumpeter.

7/28/73	128	8		1 **M.F. Horn/3**	[I]	Columbia 32403
4/17/76	75	14		2 **Primal Scream**	[I]	Columbia 33953
4/2/77	22	26	●	3 **Conquistador**	[I]	Columbia 34457
11/26/77	124	8		4 **New Vintage**	[I]	Columbia 34971
10/7/78	113	9		5 **Carnival**	[I]	Columbia 35480
9/1/79	188	3		6 **Hot**	[I]	Columbia 36124
9/27/80	188	2		7 **It's My Time**	[I]	Columbia 36766
5/22/82	185	4		8 **Hollywood**	[I]	Columbia 37713

FERNANDEZ, Alejandro
Born on 4/24/1971 in Jalisco, Mexico. Latin singer. One of the leading romantic singers in Mexico. Son of **Vicente Fernandez**.

10/11/97	125	26	▲	1 **Me Estoy Enamorando**	[F]	Sony Discos 82446
5/29/99	148	3		2 **Mi Verdad**	[F]	Sony Discos 83182
5/13/00	144	5		3 **Entre Tus Brazos**	[F]	Sony Discos 83812
11/8/03	196	1		4 **En Vivo: Juntos Por Ultima Vez**	[F-L]	Sony Discos 91088 [2]
				VICENTE & ALEJANDRO FERNANDEZ		
9/25/04	125	5		5 **A Corazon Abierto**	[F]	Sony Discos 95323
7/14/07	73	5		6 **Viento A Favor**	[F]	Sony 10111
2/2/08	180	2		7 **15 Anos De Exitos**	[F-K]	Discos 605 17948
2/14/09	162	2		8 **De Noche: Clasicos A Mi Manera**	[F-K]	Discos 605 42419
12/26/09	175	2		9 **Dos Mundos: Evolucion**	[F]	Universal Latino 013689
12/26/09	183	1		10 **Dos Mundos: Tradicion**	[F]	Fonovisa 354372

FERNANDEZ, Vicente
Born on 2/17/1940 in Jalisco, Mexico. Latin singer. Known as "The King of The Rancheros." Father of **Alejandro Fernandez**.

11/8/03	196	1		1 **En Vivo: Juntos Por Ultima Vez**	[F-L]	Sony Discos 91088 [2]
				VICENTE & ALEJANDRO FERNANDEZ		
4/16/05	131	5		2 **Mis Corridos Consentidos**	[F]	Sony Discos 95624
12/9/06	182	1		3 **La Tragedia Del Vaquero**	[F]	Sony 02080
4/21/07	81	33		4 **Historia De Un Idolo**	[F]	Sony 07405
10/13/07+	38	60	●	5 **Para Siempre**	[F]	Sony 14602
12/20/08	92	9		6 **Primera Fila**	[F-L]	Sony 40032
7/25/09	58	7		7 **Necesito De Ti**	[F]	Sony Latin 53282
				Grammy: Regional Mexican Album		

FERRANTE & TEICHER
1960s: #32 / All-Time: #144

Piano duo: Arthur Ferrante (born on 9/7/1921 in Manhattan, New York; died on 9/19/2009, age 88) and Louis Teicher (born on 8/24/1924 in Wilkes-Barre, Pennsylvania; died of a heart attack on 8/3/2008, age 83). Met as children while attending Manhattan's Juilliard School. First recorded for Columbia in 1953.

11/20/61+	10	47		1 **West Side Story & Other Motion Picture & Broadway Hits**	[I]	United Artists 6166
12/18/61+	23	16		2 **Love Themes**	[I]	United Artists 8514
2/10/62	30	27		3 **Golden Piano Hits**	[I]	United Artists 8505
3/17/62	11	38		4 **Tonight**	[I]	United Artists 6171
6/16/62	61	11		5 **Golden Themes From Motion Pictures**	[I]	United Artists 6210
9/29/62	43	7		6 **Pianos In Paradise**	[I]	United Artists 6230
12/15/62+	60	11		7 **Snowbound**	[I]	United Artists 6233
6/29/63	23	13		8 **Love Themes From Cleopatra**	[I]	United Artists 6290
12/14/63+	63	17		9 **Concert For Lovers**	[I]	United Artists 6315
3/21/64	128	7		10 **50 Fabulous Piano Favorites**	[I]	United Artists 6343
7/18/64	128	5		11 **The Enchanted World Of Ferrante & Teicher**	[I]	United Artists 6375
11/14/64	145	9		12 **My Fair Lady**	[I]	United Artists 6361
11/28/64+	35	20		13 **The People's Choice**	[I]	United Artists 6385
4/24/65	130	6		14 **Springtime**	[I]	United Artists 6406
6/12/65	120	4		15 **By Popular Demand**	[I]	United Artists 6416

Billboard			R I A A	ARTIST		
DEBUT	PEAK	WKS		Album Title	Catalog	Label & Number

FERRANTE & TEICHER — cont'd

9/11/65	49	13		16 Only The Best .... [I]		United Artists 6434
1/1/66	134	5		17 The Ferrante And Teicher Concert .... [I-L]		United Artists 6444
6/25/66	119	5		18 For Lovers Of All Ages .... [I]		United Artists 6483
9/24/66	57	21		19 You Asked For It! .... [I]		United Artists 6526
12/24/66	52ˣ	4		20 We Wish You A Merry Christmas .... [X-I]		United Artists 6536
				Christmas charts: 52/66, 102/67, 57/68		
2/18/67	133	5		21 A Man And A Woman & Other Motion Picture Themes .... [I]		United Artists 6572
12/2/67	177	2		22 Our Golden Favorites .... [I]		United Artists 6556
12/21/68+	198	4		23 A Bouquet Of Hits .... [I]		United Artists 6659
10/11/69	93	27	●	24 10th Anniversary - Golden Piano Hits .... [G-I]		United Artists 70 [2]
11/22/69+	61	26		25 Midnight Cowboy .... [I]		United Artists 6725
5/30/70	97	10		26 Getting Together .... [I]		United Artists 5501
12/5/70	188	2		27 Love Is A Soft Touch .... [I]		United Artists 6771
3/6/71	134	9		28 The Best Of Ferrante & Teicher .... [I-K]		United Artists 73 [2]
				recordings from 1967-70		
5/8/71	172	4		29 The Music Lovers .... [I]		United Artists 6792
10/9/71	172	5		30 It's Too Late .... [I]		United Artists 5531
1/1/72	186	3		31 Fiddler On The Roof .... [I]		United Artists 5552

FERRELL, Rachelle
Born in 1961 in Berwyn, Pennsylvania. Female R&B singer/keyboardist.

7/16/94	161	8	●	1 Rachelle Ferrell		Manhattan 93769
4/22/95	151	8		2 First Instrument .... [E]		Blue Note 27820
				recorded in 1990		
9/30/00	71	9		3 Individuality (Can I Be Me?)		Capitol 94980

FERRER, Ibrahim
Born on 2/20/1927 in Santiago, Cuba. Died on 8/6/2005 (age 78). Latin singer. Member of the **Buena Vista Social Club**.

6/26/99	137	16	●	1 Buena Vista Social Club Presents Ibrahim Ferrer .... [F]		World Circuit 79532

FERRY, Bryan
Born on 9/26/1945 in Washington, England. Pop-rock singer/songwriter. Lead singer of **Roxy Music**. Married to socialite Lucy Helmore from 1982-2003.

9/7/74	204	5		1 These Foolish Things		Atlantic 7304
10/16/76	160	5		2 Let's Stick Together		Atlantic 18187
4/23/77	126	5		3 In Your Mind		Atlantic 18216
11/4/78	159	5		4 The Bride Stripped Bare		Atlantic 19205
6/29/85	63	25	●	5 Boys And Girls		Warner 25082
11/21/87+	63	31		6 Bete Noire		Reprise 25598
8/26/89	100	11		7 Street Life-20 Great Hits .... [G]		Reprise 25857 [2]
				BRYAN FERRY / ROXY MUSIC		
5/1/93	79	8		8 Taxi		Reprise 45246
10/8/94	94	5		9 Mamouna		Virgin 39838
11/6/99	195	1		10 As Time Goes By		Virgin 48270
6/8/02	189	1		11 Frantic		Virgin 11984
7/14/07	117	2		12 Dylanesque		Virgin 83891

FESTIVAL
Disco studio group assembled by producer Boris Midney.

2/9/80	50	18		1 Evita		RSO 3061

FETCHIN BONES
Rock band from Los Angeles, California: Hope Nicholls (vocals), Aaron Pitkin (guitar), Errol Stewart (guitar), Danna Pentes (bass) and Clay Richardson (drums).

11/18/89	175	8		1 Monster		Capitol 90661

FEVER
Disco band from Ohio: Clydene Jackson (vocals), Dale Reed (sax), Joe Bomback (keyboards) and Dennis Waddington (bass).

12/22/79+	205	5		1 Fever		Fantasy 9580

FEVER TREE
Psychedelic-rock band from Houston, Texas: Dennis Keller (vocals), Michael Knust (guitar), Rob Landes (piano), E.E. Wolfe (bass) and John Tuttle (drums). Knust died of heart failure on 9/15/2003 (age 54).

5/18/68	156	21		1 Fever Tree		Uni 73024
12/28/68+	83	13		2 Another Time, Another Place		Uni 73040
2/7/70	97	6		3 Creation		Uni 73067

FFH
Christian vocal group: husband-and wife Jeromy Deibler and Jennifer Deibler, with Steve Croyle and Brian Smith. Michael Boggs replaced Croyle after first album. FFH: Far From Home.

12/11/99	64	1		1 I Want To Be Like You		Essential 0498
3/25/00	154	2		2 Found A Place		Essential 0529
9/8/01	119	9		3 Have I Ever Told You		Essential 0620
5/3/03	89	5		4 Ready To Fly		Essential 10705

Billboard			R I A A	ARTIST		
DEBUT	PEAK	WKS		Album Title	Catalog	Label & Number

FIASCO, Lupe
Born Wasalu Jaco on 2/17/1982 in Chicago, Illinois. Male rapper/songwriter.

| 10/7/06 | 8 | 13 | | 1 Lupe Fiasco's Food & Liquor | | 1st & 15th 83960 |
| 1/5/08 | 14 | 27 | ● | 2 Lupe Fiasco's The Cool | | 1st & 15th 368316 |

FICTION FAMILY
Alternative-rock duo: Jon Foreman (of Switchfoot) and Sean Watkins (of Nickel Creek).

| 2/7/09 | 71 | 2 | | 1 Fiction Family | | ATO 0065 |

FIEDLER, Arthur — see BOSTON POPS

FIELD, Sally
Born on 11/6/1946 in Pasadena, California. Prolific TV/movie actress.

| 12/23/67+ | 172 | 4 | | 1 The Flying Nun [TV] | | Colgems 106 |

FIELD MOB
Male rap duo from Albany, Georgia: Darion "Smoke" Crawford and "Shawn Jay" Johnson.

1/20/01	194	2		1 613: Ashy To Classy		MCA 112348
11/9/02	33	21		2 From Tha Roota To Tha Toota		MCA 113051
7/8/06	7	9		3 Light Poles And Pine Trees		DTP 006790

FIELDS, Ernie, Orch.
Born on 8/26/1905 in Nacogdoches, Texas. Died on 5/11/1997 (age 91). Black trombonist/pianist/bandleader/arranger.

~ ~ ~ ~ ~ ~ ~ ~ ~ ~ ~ **NON-CHARTED ALBUM** ~ ~ ~ ~ ~ ~ ~ ~ ~ ~ ~ ~
1959 **In The Mood**

FIELDS, Richard "Dimples"
Born on 3/21/1941 in New Orleans, Louisiana; raised in San Francisco, California. Died of a stroke on 1/12/2000 (age 58). R&B singer/songwriter/producer.

| 7/25/81 | 33 | 17 | | 1 Dimples | | Boardwalk 33232 |
| 3/6/82 | 63 | 20 | | 2 Mr. Look So Good! | | Boardwalk 33249 |

FIELDS, W.C.
Born William Claude Dukenfield on 1/29/1880 in Philadelphia, Pennsylvania. Died of pneumonia on 12/25/1946 (age 66). Legendary movie comedian.

1/4/69	30	29		1 The Original Voice Tracks From His Greatest Movies [C]		Decca 79164
10/18/69	197	2		2 W. C. Fields On Radio [C]		Columbia 9890
4/24/76	210	2		3 The Best Of W.C. Fields [C]		Columbia 34144

FIEND
Born Rickey Jones in New Orleans, Louisiana. Male rapper.

| 5/23/98 | 8 | 16 | ● | 1 There's One In Every Family | | No Limit 50715 |
| 7/24/99 | 15 | 12 | | 2 Street Life | | No Limit 50107 |

FIESTA
R&B vocal group: Thomas Bullock, Johnny Burton, Wesley Lee, Carl Sims and Thomas Wiley.

| 2/17/79 | 206 | 2 | | 1 Fiesta | | Arista 4196 |

FIFTH ANGEL
Hard-rock band from Bellevue, Washington: Ted Pilot (vocals), James Byrd (guitar), Ed Archer (guitar), John Macko (bass) and Ken Mary (drums).

| 4/16/88 | 117 | 13 | | 1 Fifth Angel | | Epic 44201 |

5TH DIMENSION, The   **All-Time: #250**
Adult Contemporary-R&B vocal group from Los Angeles, California: Marilyn McCoo, Billy Davis, Jr., Florence LaRue, LaMonte McLemore and Ron Townson. McLemore and McCoo had been in the Hi-Fi's; Townson and Davis had been with groups in St. Louis. First called the Versatiles. McCoo and Davis were married on 7/26/1969 and recorded as a duo since 1976. Townson died of kidney failure on 8/2/2001 (age 68).

6/17/67	8	83	●	1 Up, Up And Away		Soul City 92000
1/13/68	105	31		2 The Magic Garden		Soul City 92001
8/24/68	21	21		3 Stoned Soul Picnic		Soul City 92002
5/31/69	2²	72	●	4 The Age Of Aquarius		Soul City 92005
5/16/70	5	55	●	5 The 5th Dimension/Greatest Hits [G]		Soul City 33900
8/15/70	63	8		6 The July 5th Album		Soul City 33901
5/9/70+	20	50	●	7 Portrait		Bell 6045
3/13/71	17	23		8 Love's Lines, Angles And Rhymes		Bell 6060
10/23/71	32	18	●	9 The 5th Dimension/Live!! [L]		Bell 9000 [2]
11/6/71	112	7		10 Reflections [K]		Bell 6065
4/1/72	58	32		11 Individually & Collectively		Bell 6073
9/30/72	14	24	●	12 Greatest Hits On Earth [G]		Bell 1106
3/24/73	108	11		13 Living Together, Growing Together		Bell 1116
1/11/75	202	7		14 Soul & Inspiration		Bell 1315
8/23/75	136	8		15 Earthbound		ABC 897

Billboard			R I A A	ARTIST Album Title	Catalog	Label & Number
DEBUT	PEAK	WKS				

5TH WARD BOYZ
Rap trio from Houston, Texas: Andre Barnes, Eric Taylor and Richard Nash.

DEBUT	PEAK	WKS				Label & Number
6/5/93	176	3		1 Ghetto Dope		Rap-A-Lot 53859
3/12/94	105	8		2 Gangsta Funk		Rap-A-Lot 53844
12/2/95	189	1		3 Rated G		Rap-A-Lot 40758
12/6/97	180	1		4 Usual Suspects		Rap-A-Lot 45117
9/18/99	125	3		5 P.W.A. The Album...Keep It Poppin'		Rap-A-Lot 50125

5TH WARD JUVENILEZ
Rap trio from Houston, Texas: Frank, Nitty and Daddy Lo.

7/15/95	200	1		1 Deadly Groundz		Rap-A-Lot 40531

50 CENT 2000s: #46 / All-Time: #469
Born Curtis Jackson on 7/6/1975 in Jamaica, Queens, New York. Male rapper/songwriter. Member of **G-Unit**. Starred in the 2005 movie *Get Rich Or Die Tryin'*.

1/11/03	28	10		1 Guess Who's Back?		Full Clip 2003
2/22/03	❶[6]	82	▲[6]	2 Get Rich Or Die Tryin'	Cat:❶[1]/61	Shady 493544
5/3/03	2[1]	17		3 The New Breed		Shady 000108
				no track titles listed		
3/19/05	❶[6]	57	▲[5]	4 The Massacre	Cat:#25/1	Shady 004092
9/29/07	2[1]	27		5 Curtis		Shady 008931
12/5/09	5	20	●	6 Before I Self-Destruct		Shady 012393

54TH PLATOON
Male rap group from New Orleans, Louisiana: Jackie "Big Nut" Washington, Jochan "JS" Scott, Thomas "Nu Black" Valentine and Tevin "TL" Lashley.

5/24/03	128	2		1 All Or N.O.thin		Fubu 9001

50 GUITARS OF TOMMY GARRETT — see GARRETT, Tommy

FIGHT
Hard-rock band formed in England: Rob **Halford** (vocals), Russ Parrish (guitar), Brian Tilse (guitar), Jack "Jay Jay" Brown (bass) and Scott Travis (drums). Mark Chaussee replaced Parrish in 1994. Halford was lead singer of **Judas Priest**.

10/2/93	83	5		1 War Of Words		Epic 57372
5/6/95	120	1		2 A Small Deadly Space		Epic 66649

FILTER
Industrial rock duo from Cleveland, Ohio: Richard Patrick (vocals, guitar, bass) and Brian Liesegang (keyboards, drums). Both worked with Trent Reznor in **Nine Inch Nails**.

5/13/95	59	27	▲	1 Short Bus		Reprise 45864
9/11/99	30	35	▲	2 Title Of Record		Reprise 47388
8/17/02	32	6		3 The Amalgamut		Reprise 47963
5/31/08	60	2		4 Anthems For The Damned		Pulse 90108

FINCH
Rock band from Los Angeles, California: Nate Barcalow (vocals), Randy Strohmeyer (guitar), Alex Linares (guitar), Derek Doherty (bass) and Alex Pappas (drums).

3/30/02+	99	21		1 What It Is To Burn		Drive-Thru 860991
6/25/05	24	4		2 Say Hello To Sunshine		Drive-Thru 004519

FINE FRENZY, A
Born Alison Sudol on 12/23/1984 in Seattle, Washington; raised in Los Angeles, California. Female singer/songwriter/pianist.

8/4/07	91	22		1 One Cell In The Sea		Virgin 73825
9/26/09	28	2		2 Bomb In A Birdcage		Virgin 15721

FINE YOUNG CANNIBALS
Rock trio formed in Birmingham, England: Roland Gift (vocals), Andy Cox (guitar) and David Steele (bass). Cox and Steele were with **English Beat**. Group name taken from the 1960 movie *All The Fine Young Cannibals*. Group appeared in the movie *Tin Men*. Gift acted in the movies *Sammy And Rosie Get Laid* and *Scandal*.

1/25/86	49	28		1 Fine Young Cannibals		I.R.S. 5683
3/11/89	❶[7]	63	▲[2]	2 The Raw & The Cooked		I.R.S. 6273

FINGER ELEVEN
Rock band from Burlington, Ontario, Canada: brothers Scott Anderson (vocals) and Sean Anderson (bass), Rick Jackett (guitar), James Black (guitar) and Rob Gommerman (drums).

7/5/03+	96	43	●	1 Finger Eleven		Wind-Up 13058
3/24/07	31	68	●	2 Them Vs. You Vs. Me		Wind-Up 13112

FINGERPRINTZ
New wave band from Scotland: Jimme O'Neill (vocals), Cha Burns (guitar), Kenny Alton (bass) and Bogdan Wiczling (drums). Burns died of cancer on 3/26/2007 (age 50). O'Neill and Burns later formed **The Silencers**.

10/4/80	206	1		1 Distinguishing Marks		Virgin 13136

FINN, Tim
Born on 6/25/1952 in Te Awamutu, New Zealand. Pop-rock singer/songwriter/guitarist. Former member of **Split Enz**. Brother of Neil Finn (of **Crowded House**). Also see **The Finn Brothers**.

9/17/83	161	5		1 Escapade		A&M 4972

FINN BROTHERS, The
Pop-rock duo from Te Awamutu, New Zealand: brothers **Tim Finn** (born on 6/25/1952) and Neil Finn (born on 5/27/1958). Both were members of **Split Enz** and **Crowded House**.

9/11/04	139	1	1 **Everyone Is Here**		Nettwerk 30376

FINNEY, Albert
Born on 5/9/1936 in Salford, Manchester, England. Prolific movie actor.

9/3/77	199	1	1 **Albert Finney's Album**		Motown 889

FIONA
Born Fiona Flanagan on 9/13/1961 in Manhattan, New York. Female rock singer/actress. Played "Molly McGuire" in the 1987 movie *Hearts Of Fire*.

3/30/85	71	18	1 **Fiona**		Atlantic 81242
11/25/89+	150	16	2 **Heart Like A Gun**		Atlantic 81903

FIONA, Melanie
Born Melanie Fiona Hallim on 7/4/1983 in Toronto, Ontario, Canada. R&B singer/songwriter.

11/7/09+	27	27↑	1 **The Bridge**		SRC 013150

FIORILLO, Elisa
Born on 2/28/1969 in Philadelphia, Pennsylvania. Female dance singer.

2/20/88	163	8	1 **Elisa Fiorillo**		Chrysalis 41608

FIREBALLET
Rock band from New Jersey: Jim Como (vocals), Ryche Chlanda (guitar), Bryan Howe (keyboards), Frank Petto (piano) and Martyn Biglin (bass).

9/6/75	151	8	1 **Night On Bald Mountain**		Passport 98010

FIREBALLS, The
Rock and roll band formed in Raton, New Mexico: Jimmy Gilmer (vocals, piano), George Tomsco (lead guitar), Dan Trammell (rhythm guitar), Stan Lark (bass) and Eric Budd (drums). Doug Roberts replaced Budd in 1962. Roberts died on 11/18/1981.

11/16/63	26	14	1 **Sugar Shack**		Dot 25545
			JIMMY GILMER & THE FIREBALLS		

~ ~ ~ ~ ~ ~ ~ ~ ~ ~ **NON-CHARTED ALBUMS** ~ ~ ~ ~ ~ ~ ~ ~ ~ ~ ~

1960 **The Fireballs**	1961 **Here Are The Fireballs**
1960 **Vaquero**	

FIREFALL
Soft-rock band formed in Boulder, Colorado: Rick Roberts (vocals), Larry Burnett (guitar), Jock Bartley (guitar), Mark Andes (bass) and Mike Clarke (drums). David Muse (keyboards) joined in 1977. Andes was a member of **Spirit** and **Jo Jo Gunne**; joined **Heart** in 1980. Clarke was a member of **The Byrds**. Roberts and Clarke were members of **Flying Burrito Brothers**. Clarke died of liver failure on 12/19/1993 (age 49).

5/8/76	28	67	▲	1 **Firefall**		Atlantic 18174
8/20/77	27	28	●	2 **Luna Sea**		Atlantic 19101
10/28/78+	27	24	▲	3 **Elan**		Atlantic 19183
4/12/80	68	15		4 **Undertow**		Atlantic 16006
1/10/81	102	13		5 **Clouds Across The Sun**		Atlantic 16024
12/26/81+	186	4		6 **The Best Of Firefall** .... **[G]**		Atlantic 19316
3/12/83	199	3		7 **Break Of Dawn**		Atlantic 80017

FIREHOUSE
Pop-metal band from Charlotte, North Carolina: Carl Jeff "C.J." Snare (vocals), Bill Leverty (guitar), Perry Richardson (bass) and Michael Foster (drums).

3/9/91	21	76	▲²	1 **Firehouse**		Epic 46186
7/4/92	23	30	●	2 **Hold Your Fire**		Epic 48615
4/29/95	66	9		3 **3**		Epic 57459

FIREMAN, The — see McCARTNEY, Paul

FIRESIGN THEATRE
Satirical comedy group formed in Los Angeles, California: Phil Austin (born on 4/6/1941), Peter Bergman (born on 11/29/1939), David Ossman (born on 12/6/1936) and Philip Proctor (born on 7/28/1940).

10/18/69	195	2	1 **How Can You Be In Two Places At Once When You're Not Anywhere At All** .... **[C]**		Columbia 9884
9/19/70	106	10	2 **Don't Crush That Dwarf, Hand Me The Pliers** .... **[C]**		Columbia 30102
			NRR		
9/25/71	50	14	3 **I Think We're All Bozos On This Bus** .... **[C]**		Columbia 30737
2/26/72	75	11	4 **Dear Friends** .... **[C-K]**		Columbia 31099 [2]
11/25/72	115	8	5 **Not Insane Or Anything You Want To** .... **[C]**		Columbia 31585
6/2/73	211	2	6 **TV Or Not TV** .... **[C]**		Columbia 32199
			PROCTOR & BERGMAN		
3/2/74	172	5	7 **The Tale Of The Giant Rat Of Sumatra** .... **[C]**		Columbia 32730
11/2/74	147	6	8 **Everything You Know Is Wrong** .... **[C]**		Columbia 33141
10/25/75	201	6	9 **In The Next World, You're On Your Own** .... **[C]**		Columbia 33475
6/11/77	184	2	10 **Just Folks...A Firesign Chat** .... **[C]**		Butterfly 001

FIRE THEFT, The
Rock trio from Seattle, Washington: Jeremy Enigk (vocals, guitar), Nate Mendel (bass) and William Goldsmith (drums). Mendel and Goldsmith were members of **Foo Fighters**; Goldsmith was also with **Sunny Day Real Estate**.

10/11/03	198	1		1 The Fire Theft	Rykodisc 10642

FIRM, The
All-star rock band from England: **Paul Rodgers** (vocals), **Jimmy Page** (guitar), Tony Franklin (bass) and Chris Slade (drums). Rodgers was with **Free** and **Bad Company**. Page was with **The Yardbirds** and **Led Zeppelin**. Disbanded in 1986. Franklin joined **Blue Murder** in 1989. Slade was a member of **AC/DC** from 1990-95. Rodgers joined **The Law** in 1991.

3/2/85	17	33	●	1 The Firm	Atlantic 81239
2/22/86	22	19		2 Mean Business	Atlantic 81628

FIRM, The
All-star rap group: **Nas**, **Foxy Brown**, **AZ** and **Nature**.

11/8/97	❶[1]	22		1 The Firm - The Album	Aftermath 90136

FIRST CHOICE
Female R&B vocal trio from Philadelphia, Pennsylvania: Joyce Jones, Rochelle Fleming and Annette Guest. Ursula Herring replaced Jones in 1977. Debbie Martin replaced Herring in 1979.

10/27/73	184	4		1 Armed And Extremely Dangerous	Philly Groove 1400
10/26/74	143	7		2 The Player	Philly Groove 1502
6/5/76	204	3		3 So Let Us Entertain You	Warner 2934
10/1/77	103	8		4 Delusions	Gold Mind 7501
3/31/79	135	12		5 Hold Your Horses	Gold Mind 9502

FIRST CLASS
Pop studio group formed in England: Tony Burrows (lead vocals), John Carter, Del John and Chas Mills (backing vocals), Spencer James (guitar), Robin Shaw (bass) and Eddie Richards (drums). Burrows was also the vocalist on hits by **The Brotherhood Of Man**, Edison Lighthouse, The Pipkins and **White Plains**.

11/9/74	204	1		1 The First Class	UK 53109

FIRST EDITION, The — see ROGERS, Kenny

FISCHER, Julia
Born on 6/15/1983 in Munich, Germany. Classical violinist.

1/31/09	143	1		1 Bach: Concertos .... [I]	Decca digital

FISCHER, Lisa
Born on 12/1/1958 in Brooklyn, New York. R&B singer.

5/18/91	100	14		1 So Intense	Elektra 60889

FISCHERSPOONER
Electro-pop duo from New York: Warren Fischer and Casey Spooner.

4/23/05	172	1		1 Odyssey	Capitol 94896

FISHBONE
Funk-rock band from Los Angeles, California: Angelo Moore (vocals, sax), Kendall Jones (guitar), Charlie Down (guitar), Christopher Dowd (keyboards), Walter Kibby (trumpet), John Fisher (bass) and Phillip Fisher (drums). Down left in 1991; replaced by John Bigham. Jones left in 1993. Group appeared in several movies.

10/1/88	153	9		1 Truth And Soul	Columbia 40891
5/11/91	49	10		2 The Reality Of My Surroundings	Columbia 46142
6/12/93	99	4		3 Give A Monkey A Brain And He'll Swear He's The Center Of The Universe	Columbia 52764
6/8/96	158	1		4 Chim Chim's Badass Revenge	Rowdy 37010

FISHER, Eddie
Born Edwin Jack Fisher on 8/10/1928 in Philadelphia, Pennsylvania. Pop singer/actor. Married to **Debbie Reynolds** (1955-59), Elizabeth Taylor (1959-64) and **Connie Stevens** (1967-69). Daughter with Debbie is actress/author Carrie Fisher. Daughters with Connie are singer Tricia Leigh Fisher and actress Joely Fisher. Own "Coke Time" 15-minute TV series (1953-57). Acted in several movies.

4/30/55	5	7		1 I Love You	RCA Victor 1097
				EP: RCA Victor EPB-1097 (#5); LP: RCA Victor LPM-1097 (#8)	
3/30/63	128	3		2 Eddie Fisher At The Winter Garden .... [L]	Ramrod 1 [2]
				recorded on 10/2/1962 in New York City	
7/24/65	52	10		3 Eddie Fisher Today!	Dot 25631
11/26/66+	72	10		4 Games That Lovers Play	RCA Victor 3726
7/1/67	193	3		5 People Like You	RCA Victor 3820

FISHER, Matthew
Born on 3/7/1946 in Addiscombe, Croyden, England. Rock singer/songwriter/keyboardist. Member of **Procol Harum** from 1966-70.

11/3/73	210	5		1 Journey's End	RCA Victor 0195

FISHER, Miss Toni
Born in 1931 in Los Angeles, California. Died of a heart attack on 2/12/1999 (age 67). Female singer.

~ ~ ~ ~ ~ ~ ~ ~ ~ ~ **NON-CHARTED ALBUM** ~ ~ ~ ~ ~ ~ ~ ~ ~ ~ ~

1960 **The Big Hurt**

Billboard			R I A A	ARTIST		
DEBUT	PEAK	WKS		Album Title	Catalog	Label & Number

FITZGERALD, Ella
1950s: #25 / All-Time: #488

Born on 4/25/1917 in Newport News, Virginia. Died of diabetes on 6/15/1996 (age 79). The most-honored jazz singer of all time. Discovered after winning on the *Harlem Amateur Hour* in 1934. Hired by Chick Webb and in 1938 created a popular sensation with "A-Tisket, A-Tasket." Following Webb's death in 1939, Ella took over the band for three years. Appeared in several movies.

AWARD: Grammy: Lifetime Achievement 1967

DEBUT	PEAK	WKS		Album Title		Label & Number
9/17/55	7	5		1 Songs From Pete Kelly's Blues		Decca 8166
				PEGGY LEE & ELLA FITZGERALD		
7/28/56	15	1		2 Ella Fitzgerald Sings The Cole Porter Song Book		Verve 4001 [2]
				Grammy: Hall of Fame ★ NRR		
12/15/56	12	2		3 Ella And Louis		Verve 4003
				ELLA FITZGERALD & LOUIS ARMSTRONG		
3/16/57	11	4		4 Ella Fitzgerald Sings The Rodgers And Hart Song Book		Verve 4002 [2]
				Grammy: Hall of Fame		
9/12/60+	11	51		5 Mack The Knife - Ella In Berlin .... [L]		Verve 4041
				Grammys: Female Vocal / Hall of Fame		
11/13/61+	35	34		6 Ella In Hollywood .... [L]		Verve 4052
10/19/63	69	20		7 Ella And Basie!		Verve 4061
				ELLA FITZGERALD & COUNT BASIE		
				Grammy: Hall of Fame		
3/28/64	111	5		8 Ella Fitzgerald Sings The George And Ira Gershwin Song Books		Verve V-29-5 [5]
8/22/64	146	2		9 Hello, Dolly!		Verve 4064
8/19/67	172	2		10 Brighten The Corner		Capitol 2685
12/9/67	27 [X]	4		11 Ella Fitzgerald's Christmas .... [X]		Capitol 2805
10/18/69	196	2		12 Ella		Reprise 6354
8/18/07	97	7		13 Love Letters From Ella .... [K]		Concord Jazz 30213
10/24/09	178	1		14 Golden Voices .... [K]		X5 digital

~ ~ ~ ~ ~ ~ ~ ~ ~ ~   ***NON-CHARTED ALBUM***   ~ ~ ~ ~ ~ ~ ~ ~ ~ ~
1957 **Porgy And Bess** *[w/ Louis Armstrong]*
    Grammy: Hall of Fame

FIVE
Pop vocal group from England: Rich Neville, Scott Robinson, Richard Breen, Jason Brown and Sean Conlon.

DEBUT	PEAK	WKS				
8/22/98+	27	54	▲	1 Five		Arista 19003
6/3/00	108	3		2 Invincible		Arista 14620

FIVE AMERICANS, The
Rock and roll band from Dallas, Texas: Michael Rabon (vocals), Norman Ezell (guitar), John Durrill (keyboards), James Grant (bass) and James Wright (drums). Rabon later joined **Gladstone**. Grant died of a heart attack on 11/29/2004 (age 61). Ezell died of cancer on 5/8/2010 (age 68).

| 4/30/66 | 136 | 5 | | 1 I See The Light | | HBR 9503 |
| 7/8/67 | 121 | 10 | | 2 Western Union | | Abnak 2067 |

5 BROWNS, The
Classical group of siblings: Desirae (born in 1978), Deondra (born in 1980), Gregory (born in 1982), Meloday (born in 1984) and Ryan (born in 1985) Brown. All studied piano simultaneously at Julliard School in New York.

| 2/26/05 | 122 | 2 | | 1 The 5 Browns .... [I] | | RCA Red Seal 66007 |

FIVE FINGER DEATH PUNCH
Hard-rock band formed in Los Angeles, California: Ivan Moody (vocals), Zoltan Bathory (guitar), Darrell Roberts (guitar), Matt Snell (bass) and Jeremy Spencer (drums). Moody was also lead singer of Motograter.

| 8/18/07+ | 107 | 44 | | 1 The Way Of The Fist | Cat:#35/2 | Firm 70116 |
| 10/10/09 | 7 | 29↑ | | 2 War Is The Answer | | Prospect Park 50100 |

FIVE FOR FIGHTING
Born John Ondrasik on 1/7/1968 in Los Angeles, California. Adult Contemporary singer/songwriter/guitarist. Name refers to a penalty in hockey.

8/11/01	54	46	▲	1 America Town		Aware 63759
2/21/04	20	42	▲	2 The Battle For Everything	Cat:#27/1	Aware 86186
8/19/06	8	12		3 Two Lights		Aware 94471
10/31/09	34	4		4 Slice		Aware 18754

FIVE IRON FRENZY
Christian ska-rock band from Denver, Colorado: Reese Roper (vocals), Scott Kerr (guitar), Micah Ortega (guitar), Dennis Culp, Jeff Ortega and Nathanael Dunham (horns), Keith Hoerig (bass) and Andrew Verdecchio (drums). Sonnie Johnston replaced Kerr in 1998.

11/29/97	176	1		1 Our Newest Album Ever!		Sarabellum 46815
11/20/99	190	1		2 Live: Proof That The Youth Are Revolting .... [L]		Five Minute Walk 25248
5/13/00	146	1		3 All The Hype That Money Can Buy		Five Minute Walk 22401

FIVE KEYS, The
R&B vocal group from Newport News, Virginia: brothers Rudy West and Bernie West, Ripley Ingram, Maryland Pierce and Ramon Loper. Ingram died on 3/23/1995 (age 65). Rudy West died of a heart attack on 5/14/1998 (age 65).

~ ~ ~ ~ ~ ~ ~ ~ ~ ~   ***NON-CHARTED ALBUMS***   ~ ~ ~ ~ ~ ~ ~ ~ ~ ~
1956 **The Best Of The Five Keys**   1960 **The Five Keys** *[King label]*
1957 **The Five Keys On Stage!**

Billboard DEBUT	PEAK	WKS	R I A A	ARTIST / Album Title	Catalog	Label & Number

FIVE MAN ELECTRICAL BAND
Rock band from Ottawa, Ontario, Canada: Les Emmerson (vocals, guitar), Ted Gerow (piano), Brian Rading (bass) and brothers Rick Belanger (percussion) and Mike Belanger (drums).

DEBUT	PEAK	WKS		#	Album		Label & Number
7/31/71	148	9		1	Good-Byes & Butterflies		Lionel 1100
2/12/72	199	2		2	Coming Of Age		Lionel 1101

504 BOYZ
All-star rap trio from New Orleans, Louisiana: **Master P** ("Nino Brown"), **Silkk The Shocker** ("Vito") and **Mystikal** ("G Money"). 504 is their local area code.

| 5/20/00 | 2¹ | 26 | ● | 1 | Goodfellas | | No Limit 50722 |
| 12/28/02 | 49 | 9 | | 2 | Ballers | | New No Limit 066372 |

"5" ROYALES, The
R&B vocal group from Winston-Salem, North Carolina: cousins Lowman Pauling, Clarence Pauling and Windsor King, with brothers Eugene Tanner and John Tanner. Lowman Pauling died in December 1973 (age 47). Eugene Tanner died on 12/29/1994 (age 58). Clarence Pauling died on 5/6/1995 (age 67).

~ ~ ~ ~ ~ ~ ~ ~ ~ **NON-CHARTED ALBUMS** ~ ~ ~ ~ ~ ~ ~ ~ ~ ~
1956 **The Rockin' "5" Royales**   1959 **The "5" Royales Sing For You**
1957 **Dedicated To You**

FIVE SATINS, The
R&B vocal group from New Haven, Connecticut: Fred Parris, Al Denby, Jim Freeman and Eddie Martin, with Jessie Murphy (piano).

~ ~ ~ ~ ~ ~ ~ ~ ~ ~ **NON-CHARTED ALBUMS** ~ ~ ~ ~ ~ ~ ~ ~ ~ ~
1957 **The 5 Satins Sing**   1960 **The Five Satins Encore**

FIVE SPECIAL
R&B vocal group from Detroit, Michigan: Bryan Banks, Steve Harris, Greg Finley, Mike Pettilo and Steve Boyd. Banks is brother of Ron Banks of **The Dramatics**.

| 8/11/79 | 118 | 11 | | 1 | Five Special | | Elektra 206 |

FIVE STAIRSTEPS, The
R&B group from Chicago, Illinois: brothers Clarence Burke (vocals), James Burke (guitar), Kenny Burke (bass) and Dennis Burke (drums), with their sister Alohe Burke (vocals). Later joined by their five-year-old brother Cubie Burke. Later became **The Invisible Man's Band**.

3/25/67	139	4		1	The Five Stairsteps		Windy C 6000
1/27/68	195	3		2	Our Family Portrait		Buddah 5008
4/26/69	198	2		3	Love's Happening		Curtom 8002
					5 STAIRSTEPS & CUBIE (above 2)		
6/13/70	83	12		4	Stairsteps		Buddah 5061
12/12/70	199	2		5	Step By Step By Step	[K]	Buddah 5068
4/3/76	203	4		6	2nd Ressurection		Dark Horse 22004
					STAIRSTEPS (above 3)		
5/31/80	90	14		7	The Invisible Man's Band		Mango 9537

FIVE STAR
Family R&B-dance vocal group from Romford, Essex, England: siblings Deniece, Stedman, Doris, Lorraine and Delroy Pearson.

| 9/21/85+ | 57 | 47 | | 1 | Luxury Of Life | | RCA Victor 8052 |
| 10/4/86 | 80 | 25 | | 2 | Silk & Steel | | RCA Victor 5901 |

FIXX, The
Techno-pop band from London, England: Cy Curnin (vocals), Jamie West-Oram (guitar), Rupert Greenall (keyboards), Charlie Barrett (bass) and Adam Woods (drums). Barrett left in early 1983; replaced by Alfred Agies. Agies left in 1985; replaced by Dan Brown.

11/13/82+	106	51		1	Shuttered Room		MCA 5345
5/28/83	8	54	▲	2	Reach The Beach		MCA 39001
9/8/84	19	29	●	3	Phantoms		MCA 5507
6/14/86	30	21		4	Walkabout		MCA 5705
7/18/87	110	7		5	React	[L]	MCA 42008
2/11/89	72	18		6	Calm Animals		RCA 8566
3/16/91	111	10		7	Ink		MCA 10205

FLACK, Roberta   **All-Time: #210**
Born on 2/10/1939 in Black Mountain, North Carolina; raised in Arlington, Virginia. R&B singer/songwriter/pianist. Music scholarship to Howard University at age 15; classmate of **Donny Hathaway**. Worked as a high school music teacher in North Carolina. Discovered by jazz musician **Les McCann**. Signed to Atlantic in 1969.

1/31/70+	❶⁵	54	▲	1	First Take		Atlantic 8230
8/29/70	33	82	●	2	Chapter Two		Atlantic 1569
12/11/71+	18	48	●	3	Quiet Fire		Atlantic 1594
5/13/72	3²	39	●	4	Roberta Flack & Donny Hathaway		Atlantic 7216
9/1/73	3²	53	▲²	5	Killing Me Softly		Atlantic 7271
3/29/75	24	26		6	Feel Like Makin' Love		Atlantic 18131
1/7/78	8	32	●	7	Blue Lights In The Basement		Atlantic 19149
9/30/78	74	10		8	Roberta Flack		Atlantic 19186
3/29/80	25	24	●	9	Roberta Flack Featuring Donny Hathaway		Atlantic 16013

FLACK, Roberta — cont'd

12/20/80+	52	19		10 Live & More .... [L]		Atlantic 7004 [2]

ROBERTA FLACK & PEABO BRYSON
recorded at the Holiday Star Theater in Merrillville, Indiana

6/27/81	161	11		11 Bustin' Loose .... [S]		MCA 5141
11/21/81+	201	11	▲	12 The Best Of Roberta Flack .... [G]		Atlantic 19317
6/19/82	59	21		13 I'm The One		Atlantic 19354
8/13/83	25	42	●	14 Born To Love		Capitol 12284

PEABO BRYSON & ROBERTA FLACK

1/14/89	159	8		15 Oasis		Atlantic 81916
11/9/91	110	10		16 Set The Night To Music		Atlantic 82321

FLAGG, Fannie
Born Patricia Neal on 9/21/1944 in Birmingham, Alabama. TV and movie comedienne/author. Her novel was made into the 1992 movie *Fried Green Tomatoes*.

9/23/67	183	3		1 Rally 'Round The Flagg .... [C]		RCA Victor 3856

FLAME, The
Rock band from Brooklyn, New York: Marge Raymond (vocals), Jimmy Crespo (guitar), Frank Ruby (guitar), Bob Leone (piano), John Paul Fetta (bass) and Eddie Barbato (drums). Crespo was a member of **Aerosmith** from 1979-83.

5/14/77	147	5		1 Queen Of The Neighborhood		RCA Victor 2160

FLAMING EMBER, The
White R&B-rock band from Detroit, Michigan: Joe Sladich (vocals, guitar), Bill Ellis (piano), Jim Bugnel (bass) and Jerry Plunk (drums).

8/29/70	188	3		1 Westbound #9		Hot Wax 702

FLAMING LIPS, The
Rock band from Oklahoma City, Oklahoma: Wayne Coyne (vocals), Ron Jones (guitar), Michael Ivins (bass) and Steven Drozd (drums).

1/21/95	108	11		1 Transmissions From The Satellite Heart		Warner 45334
8/3/02	50	16	●	2 Yoshimi Battles The Pink Robots		Warner 48141
5/10/03	93	2		3 Fight Test .... [EP]		Warner 48433
4/22/06	11	8		4 At War With The Mystics		Warner 49966
9/8/07	185	1		5 U.F.O.S At The Zoo: The Legendary Concert In Oklahoma City .... [L]		Warner 44437
10/31/09	8	6		6 Embryonic		Warner 520857

FLAMINGOS, The
R&B vocal group from Chicago, Illinois: cousins Zeke Carey and Jake Carey, Paul Wilson, Nate Nelson, Tommy Hunt and Terry Johnson. Nelson later joined **The Platters**. Nelson died of a heart attack on 6/1/1984 (age 52). Wilson died in May 1988 (age 53). Jake Carey died of a heart attack on 12/10/1997 (age 74). Zeke Carey died of cancer on 12/24/1999 (age 66).

AWARD: R&R Hall of Fame: 2001

~ ~ ~ ~ ~ ~ ~ ~ ~ **NON-CHARTED ALBUMS** ~ ~ ~ ~ ~ ~ ~ ~ ~ ~ ~

1958 The Flamingos *[Checker label]*　　　　1960 **Requestfully Yours**
1959 Flamingo Serenade　　　　　　　　　　 1962 The Flamingos Meet The Moonglows On The Dusty
1960 Flamingo Favorites　　　　　　　　　　　　　　 Road Of Hits

FLAMIN' GROOVIES
Rock band from San Francisco, California: Cyril Jordan (vocals, guitar), Chris Wilson (vocals, guitar), James Farrell (guitar), George Alexander (bass) and David Wright (drums).

8/21/76	142	7		1 Shake Some Action		Sire 7521

produced by **Dave Edmunds**

FLASH
Rock band formed in England: Colin Carter (vocals), **Peter Banks** (guitar), Ray Bennett (bass) and Michael Hough (drums). Banks had been in **Yes**; later with **After The Fire**.

5/20/72	33	29		1 Flash		Capitol 11040
12/9/72+	121	13		2 Flash In The Can		Capitol 11115
9/1/73	135	8		3 Out Of Our Hands		Capitol 11218

FLASH AND THE PAN
Pop duo formed in Australia: George Young and Harry Vanda (both formerly with **The Easybeats**). George's younger brothers, Angus and Malcolm Young, are members of **AC/DC**.

5/26/79	80	16		1 Flash And The Pan		Epic 36018
5/31/80	159	6		2 Lights In The Night		Epic 36432

FLASH CADILLAC & THE CONTINENTAL KIDS
Fifties-styled rock and roll act from Colorado: Sam "Flash Cadillac" McFadin (vocals, guitar), Linn "Spike" Phillips (guitar), Kris "Angelo" Moe (keyboards), Dwight "Spider" Bement (sax), Warren "Butch" Knight (bass) and Jeff "Wally" Stewart (drums; replaced in 1975 by Paul "Wheaty" Wheatbread). Bement and Wheatbread were with **Gary Puckett & The Union Gap**. Group appeared as the prom band in the 1973 movie *American Graffiti*. Phillips died in 1993 (age 47). McFadin died of a heart attack on 8/31/2001 (age 49). Moe died on 7/8/2005 (age 55).

1/13/73	205	4		1 Flash Cadillac And The Continental Kids		Epic 31787
8/16/75	205	4		2 Sons Of The Beaches		Private Stock 2012

FLATLANDERS, The
All-star country trio: singers/songwriters/guitarists **Joe Ely**, Jimmie Dale Gilmore and Butch Hancock.

7/6/02	168	4		1 Now Again		New West 6040

Billboard DEBUT	PEAK	WKS	R I A A	ARTIST Album Title	Catalog	Label & Number

FLATT & SCRUGGS
Bluegrass duo: Lester Flatt (guitar; born on 6/19/1914 in Overton County, Tennessee; died of a heart attack on 5/11/1979, age 64) and Earl Scruggs (banjo; born on 1/6/1924 in Flintville, North Carolina. Duo formed in 1948 while both were members of Bill Monroe's band. Regulars on TV's *The Beverly Hillbillies*.
AWARDS: C&W Hall of Fame: 1985 ★ OPRY: 1955

4/13/63	115	4		1 Hard Travelin' Featuring The Ballad Of Jed Clampett		Columbia 1951 / 8751
9/28/63	134	6		2 Flatt And Scruggs At Carnegie Hall!.. [L]		Columbia 2045 / 8845
				recorded on 12/8/1962		
3/30/68	194	4		3 Changin' Times Featuring Foggy Mountain Breakdown		Columbia 2796 / 9596
6/8/68	161	4		4 Original Theme From Bonnie & Clyde.. [E]		Mercury 61162
				recordings from 1948-50		
7/6/68	187	5		5 The Story Of Bonnie & Clyde		Columbia 9649

FLAW
Rock band from Louisville, Kentucky: Chris Volz (vocals), Lance Arny (guitar), Jason Daunt (keyboards), Ryan Juhrs (bass) and Chris Ballinger (drums).

3/9/02	119	19		1 Through The Eyes		Republic 014891
5/22/04	42	6		2 Endangered Species		Republic 002396

FLECK, Bela, & The Flecktones
Born on 7/10/1958 in Brooklyn, New York. Male banjo player. The Flecktones: Victor Wooten (bass) and Jeff Coffin (drums).

6/27/98	191	1		1 Left Of Cool .... [I]		Warner 46896
8/30/03	196	1		2 Little Worlds		Columbia 86353 [3]
10/18/08	12ˣ	2		3 Jingle All The Way .... [X-I]		Rounder 610616
				Grammy: Pop Instrumental Album		

FLEET FOXES
Alternative-rock band from Seattle, Washington: Robin Pecknold (vocals, guitar), Skyler Skjelsetey (guitar), Casey Wescott (keyboards), Christian Wargo (bass) and Josh Tillman (drums).

6/21/08+	36	42		1 Fleet Foxes		Sub Pop 777
2/7/09	170	2		2 Sun Giant .... [EP]		Sub Pop 781

FLEETWOOD, Mick
Born on 6/24/1942 in Redruth, Cornwall, England. Blues-rock drummer. Member of **John Mayall**'s Bluesbreakers and **Fleetwood Mac**. Played "Mic" in the 1987 movie *The Running Man*.

7/18/81	43	14		1 The Visitor		RCA Victor 4080

FLEETWOOD MAC

1970s: #13 / All-Time: #53

Pop-rock band formed in England by **Peter Green** (guitar; born on 10/29/1946), **Mick Fleetwood** (drums; born on 6/24/1947), **John McVie** (bass; born on 11/26/1945) and **Jeremy Spencer** (guitar; born on 7/4/1948). Many lineup changes followed as group headed toward rock superstardom. Green and Spencer left in 1970. **Christine McVie** (keyboards; born on 7/12/1943) joined in August 1970. **Bob Welch** (guitar; born on 7/31/1946) joined in April 1971, stayed through 1974. Group relocated to California in 1974, whereupon Americans **Lindsey Buckingham** (guitar; born on 10/3/1949) and **Stevie Nicks** (vocals; born on 5/26/1948) joined in January 1975. Buckingham left in summer of 1987. Guitarists/vocalists **Billy Burnette** and Rick Vito joined in July 1987. Christine McVie and Nicks quit touring with the band at the end of 1990. Vito left in 1991. In early 1993, Nicks and Burnette left. In late 1993, Bekka Bramlett (daughter of **Delaney & Bonnie**) and **Dave Mason** joined Mick, John and Christine in band. The classic lineup of Fleetwood, John & Christine McVie, Buckingham and Nicks reunited in May 1997. Christine McVie retired from the group prior to their 2003 album and tour. Also see **Various Artists Compilations:** *Legacy: A Tribute To Fleetwood Mac's Rumours.*

AWARD: R&R Hall of Fame: 1998

8/17/68	198	3		1 Fleetwood Mac		Epic 26402
2/8/69	184	6		2 English Rose		Epic 26446
7/3/71	190	6		3 Fleetwood Mac In Chicago		Blue Horizon 3801 [2]
				recorded in January 1969		
12/13/69+	109	22		4 Then Play On		Reprise 6368
10/31/70	69	14		5 Kiln House		Reprise 6408
10/30/71	91	12	●	6 Future Games		Reprise 6465
4/22/72	70	27	▲	7 Bare Trees		Reprise 2080
4/28/73	49	13		8 Penguin		Reprise 2138
11/17/73	67	26	●	9 Mystery To Me		Reprise 2158
10/5/74	34	26		10 Heroes Are Hard To Find		Reprise 2196
8/2/75+	❶¹	148	▲⁵	11 Fleetwood Mac	Cat:#25/1	Reprise 2225
				RS500 #183		
2/26/77	❶³¹	134	▲¹⁹	12 Rumours	Cat:#4/133	Warner 3010
				Grammys: Album of the Year / Hall of Fame ★ RS500 #25		
11/3/79	4	37	▲²	13 Tusk	Cat:#30/1	Warner 3350 [2]
7/17/82	❶⁵	45	▲²	14 Mirage		Warner 23607
5/2/87	7	57	▲³	15 Tango In The Night		Warner 25471
4/28/90	18	19	●	16 Behind The Mask...		Warner 26111
5/3/03	3¹	23	●	17 Say You Will		Reprise 48394
				GREATEST HITS & COMPILATIONS:		
3/1/75	138	9		18 Vintage Years		Sire 3706 [2]
				recordings from 1967-69		
12/10/88+	14	26	▲⁸	19 Greatest Hits	Cat:❶³/462	Warner 25801
11/2/02	12	42	▲	20 The Very Best Of Fleetwood Mac		Reprise 73775 [2]

FLEETWOOD MAC — cont'd

LIVE ALBUMS:

12/27/80+	14	18	● 21 Fleetwood Mac Live		Warner 3500 [2]
9/6/97	❶¹	77	▲⁵ 22 The Dance	Cat:#40/9	Reprise 46702
			recorded in June 1997 on a soundstage in Burbank, California		
7/3/04	84	2	23 Live In Boston		Reprise 48726 [2]

REISSUES:

10/16/71	143	7	24 Black Magic Woman		Epic 30632 [2]
			reissue of albums #1 and #2 above		
12/6/75+	118	16	25 Fleetwood Mac In Chicago .... [E]		Sire 3715 [2]
			new cover is eggplant-colored and not the side of a car door		

FLEETWOODS, The
Pop vocal trio from Olympia, Washington: Gary Troxel (born on 11/28/1939), Gretchen Christopher (born on 2/29/1940) and Barbara Ellis (born on 2/20/1940).

12/29/62+	71	6	1 The Fleetwoods' Greatest Hits .... [G]		Dolton 8018

~ ~ ~ ~ ~ ~ ~ ~ ~ **NON-CHARTED ALBUMS** ~ ~ ~ ~ ~ ~ ~ ~ ~ ~ ~
1959 **Mr. Blue**   1960 **The Fleetwoods (Gretchen, Gary and Barbara)**

FLEISCHMAN, Robert
Born in San Francisco, California. Pop-rock singer/songwriter/keyboardist. Became lead singer of the **Vinnie Vincent Invasion** in 1986.

5/19/79	205	2	1 Perfect Stranger		Arista 4220

FLESH FOR LULU
Punk-rock band formed in London, England: Nick Marsh (vocals), Rocco Barker (guitar), Derek Greening (keyboards), Mike Steed (bass) and Hans Perrson (drums).

12/12/87+	89	24	1 Long Live The New Flesh		Capitol 48217

FLESH-N-BONE
Born Stanley Howse on 6/10/1974 in Cleveland, Ohio. Male rapper. Member of **Bone Thugs-N-Harmony**.

12/7/96	23	16	● 1 T.H.U.G.S. - Trues Humbly United Gatherin' Souls		Def Jam 533938
10/28/00	98	3	2 5th Dog Let Loose		Koch 8196

FLESHTONES
New-wave band from Queens, New York: Peter Zaremba (vocals), Keith Streng (guitar), Jan Merek Pakulski (bass) and Bill Milhizer (drums).

3/6/82	174	5	1 Roman Gods		I.R.S. 70018

FLEX
Born Felix Gomez on 8/26/1979 in Panama. Latin male singer/rapper.

2/2/08	70	31	1 Te Quiero .... [F]		Asterisco 15221
2/14/09	104	4	2 La Evolucion Romantic Style .... [F]		EMI Televisa 67917

FLICKERSTICK
Rock band from Dallas, Texas: brothers Brandin Lea (vocals, guitar) and Fletcher Lea (bass), with Rex James Ewing (guitar), Cory Kreig (keyboards) and Dominic Weir (drums).

11/24/01	150	1	1 Welcoming Home The Astronauts		Epic 86132

FLIGHT OF THE CONCHORDS
Comedic folk-rock duo from New Zealand: Bret McKenzie and Jemaine Clement. Starred in own TV series on HBO from 2007-09.

8/25/07	116	7	1 The Distant Future .... [EP]		Sub Pop 746
5/10/08	3¹	22	2 Flight Of The Conchords	[TV]	HBO 715
11/7/09	19	4	3 I Told You I Was Freaky .... [TV]		HBO 800

FLIPMODE SQUAD
Rap collective from Brooklyn, New York: **Busta Rhymes**, **Rampage**, **Rah Digga**, Serious and Spliff Star.

10/10/98	15	8	● 1 The Imperial		Elektra 62238

FLOATERS, The
R&B vocal group from Detroit, Michigan: brothers Paul Mitchell and Ralph Mitchell, Charles Clarke and Larry Cunningham.

6/25/77	10	25	▲ 1 Floaters		ABC 1030
4/22/78	131	8	2 Magic		ABC 1047

FLOBOTS
Alternative-rock/hip-hop band from Denver, Colorado: James "Jonny 5" Laurie and Brer Rabbit (vocals), Andy Guerro (guitar), Joe Ferrone (trumpet), Mackenzie Roberts (viola), Jesse Walker (bass) and Kenny Ortiz (drums).

5/10/08	15	25	1 Fight With Tools		Flobots 15179

FLOCK, The
Rock band from Chicago, Illinois: Fred Glickstein (vocals, guitar), **Jerry Goodman** (violin), Rick Canoff, Tom Webb and Frank Posa (horns), Jerry Smith (bass) and Ron Karpman (drums). Canoff died on 6/18/1988 (age 40).

9/20/69	48	20	1 The Flock		Columbia 9911
10/17/70	96	9	2 Dinosaur Swamps		Columbia 30007

DEBUT	PEAK	WKS	R I A A	ARTIST / Album Title	Catalog	Label & Number
				FLOCK OF SEAGULLS, A		
				New-wave band from Liverpool, England: brothers Mike Score (vocals, keyboards) and Ali Score (drums), with Paul Reynolds (guitar) and Frank Maudsley (bass).		
5/22/82	10	50	●	1 A Flock Of Seagulls		Jive 66000
5/28/83	16	23		2 Listen		Jive 8013
8/25/84	66	10		3 The Story Of A Young Heart		Jive 8250
				FLOETRY		
				Female R&B vocal duo: Marsha Ambrosius (born in London, England) and Natalie Stewart (born in Atlanta, Georgia).		
10/19/02	19	47	●	1 Floetic		DreamWorks 450313
12/6/03	74	3		2 Floacism "Live"	[L]	DreamWorks 001438
11/26/05	7	15		3 Flo'Ology		Erving 005609
				FLOGGING MOLLY		
				Folk-punk band from Los Angeles, California: Dave King (vocals, guitar), Dennis Casey (guitar), Robert Schmidt (banjo), Matt Hensley (accordian), Bridget Regan (fiddle), Nathen Maxwell (bass) and George Schwindt (drums).		
4/6/02+	104	2	●	1 Drunken Lullabies	Cat:#39/1	Side One Dummy 1230
10/2/04	20	7		2 Within A Mile Of Home		Side One Dummy 1251
8/12/06	67	4		3 Whiskey On A Sunday	[L]	Side One Dummy 1287
3/22/08	4	10		4 Float		Side One Dummy 1348
				FLORENCE + THE MACHINE		
				Born Florence Welch on 8/28/1986 in London, England. Experimental-rock singer/songwriter. The Machine is her revolving lineup of backing musicians.		
11/7/09+	130	4↑		1 Lungs		Universal Rep. 013170
				FLO RIDA		
				Born Tramar Dillard on 12/16/1979 in Carol City, Florida. Male rapper/songwriter.		
4/5/08	4	28		1 Mail On Sunday		Poe Boy 442748
4/18/09	8	21		2 R.O.O.T.S. (Route Of Overcoming The Struggle)		Poe Boy 517813
				FLOTSAM AND JETSAM		
				Hard-rock band from Phoenix, Arizona: Eric Knutson (vocals), Ed Carlson (guitar), Mike Gilbert (guitar), Troy Gregory (bass) and Kelly Smith (drums).		
6/18/88	143	8		1 No Place For Disgrace		Elektra 60777
7/7/90	174	7		2 When The Storm Comes Down		MCA 6382
				FLOYD, Eddie		
				Born on 6/25/1937 in Montgomery, Alabama; raised in Detroit, Michigan. R&B singer/songwriter.		
9/4/71	209	2		1 Down To Earth		Stax 2041
				~ ~ ~ ~ ~ ~ ~ ~ ~ ~ **NON-CHARTED ALBUM** ~ ~ ~ ~ ~ ~ ~ ~ ~ ~		
				1966 **Knock On Wood**		
				FLOYD, King		
				Born on 2/13/1945 in New Orleans, Louisiana. Died of diabetes on 3/6/2006 (age 61). R&B singer/songwriter.		
5/29/71	130	5		1 King Floyd		Cotillion 9047
				F.L.Y. (Fast Life Yungstaz)		
				Rap trio from Stone Mountain, Georgia: Myko McFly, Vee and Monk.		
7/11/09	109	1		1 Jamboree		Music Line 013100
				FLYING BURRITO BROTHERS		
				Country-rock band from Los Angeles, California. Various members included **Gram Parsons**, **Chris Hillman** and Mike Clarke (all from **The Byrds**), **Bernie Leadon** (later with the **Eagles**) and Rick Roberts (later with **Firefall**). Parsons died of a drug overdose on 9/19/1973 (age 26). Clarke died of liver failure on 12/19/1993 (age 49).		
5/3/69	164	7		1 The Gilded Palace Of Sin		A&M 4175
				RS500 #192		
6/12/71	176	9		2 The Flying Burrito Bros.		A&M 4295
6/3/72	171	7		3 Last Of The Red Hot Burritos	[L]	A&M 4343
7/13/74	158	5		4 Close Up The Honky Tonks	[K]	A&M 3631 [2]
				recordings from 1968-72		
5/22/76	185	4		5 Sleepless Nights	[E]	A&M 4578
				GRAM PARSONS/THE FLYING BURRITO BROS.		
10/25/75	138	3		6 Flying Again		Columbia 33817
6/26/76	204	1		7 Airborne		Columbia 34222
				FLYING LIZARDS, The		
				New wave band formed in London, England: Patti Palladin (vocals), David Cunningham (guitar, keyboards), Steve Beresford (bass) and J.J. Johnson (drums).		
2/23/80	99	8		1 The Flying Lizards		Virgin 13137
				FLYING MACHINE, The		
				Studio project of British songwriters/producers Tony MacAuley and Geoff Stephens. Touring group featured Tony Newman as lead vocalist. Not to be confused with James Taylor's group.		
12/27/69+	179	7		1 The Flying Machine		Janus 3007

FLYLEAF
Christian hard-rock band formed in Belton, Texas: Lacey Mosley (vocals), Sameer Bhattacharya (guitar), Jared Hartmann (guitar), Pat Seals (bass) and James Culpepper (drums).

3/11/06+	57	133	▲	1 Flyleaf		Octone 50005
11/28/09	8	25		2 Memento Mori		A&M 013512

FLYS, The
Rock band from Los Angeles, California: brothers Adam Paskowitz and Joshua Paskowitz (vocals), Peter Perdichizzi (guitar), James Book (bass) and Nick Lucero (drums).

10/31/98+	109	21		1 Holiday Man		Trauma 74006

FM
Pop-rock trio from Toronto, Ontario, Canada: Cameron Hawkins (vocals, keyboards), Nash The Slash (electric violin) and Martin Deller (drums).

3/3/79	203	4		1 Black Noise		Visa 7007

FM STATIC
Christian rock band formed in Toronto, Ontario, Canada: Trevor McNevan (vocals, guitar), John Bunner (guitar), Justin Smith (bass) and Steve Augustine (drums). McNevan and Augustine are also members of **Thousand Foot Krutch**.

4/25/09	199	1		1 Dear Diary		Tooth & Nail 28552

FOCUS
Progressive-rock band formed in Amsterdam, Holland: **Jan Akkerman** (guitar), **Thijs Van Leer** (keyboards, flute), Martin Dresdan (bass) and Hans Cleuver (drums).

1/20/73	8	38	●	1 Moving Waves [I]		Sire 7401
6/30/73	104	9		2 In And Out Of Focus [I]		Sire 7404
				recorded in 1970		
4/14/73	35	22	●	3 Focus 3 [I]		Sire 3901 [2]
11/17/73	132	10		4 Live At The Rainbow [I-L]		Sire 7408
				recorded on 5/5/1973 at the Rainbow Theatre in London, England		
3/1/75	120	9		5 Dutch Masters - A Selection Of Their Finest Recordings 1969-1973 [I-K]		Sire 7505
6/4/77	163	7		6 Ship Of Memories [I-K]		Sire 7531
8/3/74	66	19		7 Hamburger Concerto [I]		Atco 100
9/27/75	152	6		8 Mother Focus [I]		Atco 117

FOGELBERG, Dan   All-Time: #207
Born on 8/13/1951 in Peoria, Illinois. Died of prostate cancer on 12/16/2007 (age 56). Soft-rock singer/songwriter/guitarist. Worked as a folk singer in Los Angeles, California. With **Van Morrison** in the early 1970s. Session work in Nashville, Tennessee. Fogelberg's backing group is **Fools Gold**.

10/20/73	210	2	▲	1 Home Free	Cat:#2²/97	Columbia 31751
12/7/74+	17	27	▲²	2 Souvenirs	Cat:❶²/185	Full Moon 33137
10/4/75	23	19	▲	3 Captured Angel	Cat:#5/104	Full Moon 33499
6/4/77	13	39	▲²	4 Nether Lands	Cat:#3/117	Full Moon 34185
9/16/78	8	35	▲	5 Twin Sons Of Different Mothers		Full Moon 35339
				DAN FOGELBERG & TIM WEISBERG		
12/8/79+	3²	39	▲²	6 Phoenix		Full Moon 35634
9/12/81	6	62	▲²	7 The Innocent Age		Full Moon 37393 [2]
11/13/82	15	35	▲³	8 Dan Fogelberg/Greatest Hits [G]		Full Moon 38308
2/18/84	15	27	●	9 Windows And Walls		Full Moon 39004
5/11/85	30	23	●	10 High Country Snows		Full Moon 39616
6/20/87	48	19		11 Exiles		Full Moon 40271
9/22/90	103	13		12 The Wild Places		Full Moon 45059
10/16/93	164	3		13 River Of Souls		Full Moon 46934
10/10/09	117	1		14 Love In Time		Full Moon 013368

FOGERTY, John   All-Time: #435
Born on 5/28/1945 in Berkeley, California. Singer/songwriter/multi-instrumentalist. Leader of **Creedence Clearwater Revival**. Brother of **Tom Fogerty**. Went solo in 1972 and recorded as **The Blue Ridge Rangers**.

5/5/73	47	15		1 The Blue Ridge Rangers		Fantasy 9415
10/4/75	78	7		2 John Fogerty		Asylum 1046
1/26/85	❶¹	51	▲²	3 Centerfield		Warner 25203
10/11/86	26	19	●	4 Eye Of The Zombie		Warner 25449
6/7/97	37	31	●	5 Blue Moon Swamp		Warner 45426
				Grammy: Rock Album		
6/27/98	29	16	●	6 Premonition [L]		Reprise 46908
				recorded at The Burbank Studio		
10/9/04	23	5		7 Deja Vu All Over Again		Geffen 003257
11/19/05	13	19	●	8 The Long Road Home: The Ultimate John Fogerty-Creedence Collection	Cat:#8/1 [G]	Fantasy 9686
10/20/07	14	15		9 Revival		Fantasy 30001
9/19/09	24	8		10 Rides Again		Fortunate Son 013286
				THE BLUE RIDGE RANGERS		

FOGERTY, Tom
Born on 11/9/1941 in Berkeley, California. Died of respiratory failure on 9/6/1990 (age 48). Guitarist of **Creedence Clearwater Revival**. Brother of **John Fogerty**. Went solo in 1970.

6/3/72	180	6		1 Tom Fogerty		Fantasy 9407

Billboard			R I A A	ARTIST		
DEBUT	PEAK	WKS		Album Title	Catalog	Label & Number

FOGHAT
All-Time: #401

Rock band formed in England: "Lonesome" Dave Peverett (vocals, guitar; formerly with **Savoy Brown**), Rod Price (guitar), Tony Stevens (bass) and Roger Earl (drums). Settled in New York in 1975, many bass player changes since. Price replaced by Erik Cartwright in 1981. Peverett died of pneumonia on 2/7/2000 (age 57). Price died of head trauma on 3/22/2005 (age 57).

7/15/72	127	22		1 Foghat		Bearsville 2077
3/31/73	67	19	●	2 Foghat		Bearsville 2136
				above 2 are different albums		
2/2/74	34	30	●	3 Energized		Bearsville 6950
11/9/74	40	19	●	4 Rock And Roll Outlaws		Bearsville 6956
10/11/75+	23	52	▲	5 Fool For The City		Bearsville 6959
11/20/76	36	21	●	6 Night Shift		Bearsville 6962
9/10/77	11	29	▲²	7 Foghat Live [L]		Bearsville 6971
5/20/78	25	23	●	8 Stone Blue		Bearsville 6977
10/13/79	35	21		9 Boogie Motel		Bearsville 6990
6/21/80	106	10		10 Tight Shoes		Bearsville 6999
7/25/81	92	9		11 Girls To Chat & Boys To Bounce		Bearsville 3578
11/13/82	162	5		12 In The Mood For Something Rude		Bearsville 23747
6/25/83	192	2		13 Zig-Zag Walk		Bearsville 23888

FOLDS, Ben

Born on 9/12/1966 in Winston-Salem, North Carolina. Adult Alternative singer/songwriter/pianist. His trio included Robert Sledge (bass) and Darren Jessee (drums).

4/5/97+	42	40	▲	1 Whatever And Ever Amen		550 Music 67762
1/31/98	94	4		2 Naked Baby Photos [E-L]		Caroline 7554
				includes recordings from 1995-97		
5/15/99	35	9		3 The Unauthorized Biography Of Reinhold Messner		550 Music 69808
				BEN FOLDS FIVE (above 3)		
9/29/01	42	6		4 Rockin' The Suburbs		Epic 61610
10/26/02	60	3		5 Ben Folds Live [L]		Epic 86863
5/14/05	13	9		6 Songs For Silverman		Epic 94191
11/11/06	114	1		7 SuperSunnySpeedGraphic [K]		Epic 00536
10/18/08	11	5		8 Way To Normal		Epic 09849
5/16/09	94	1		9 Ben Folds Presents: University A Cappella!		Epic 47301

FOLEY, Ellen

Born on 6/5/1951 in St. Louis, Missouri. Rock singer/actress. Vocalist on **Meat Loaf**'s *Bat Out Of Hell* album. Acted in several movies and TV shows.

9/29/79	137	6		1 Nightout		Cleveland Int'l. 36052
4/4/81	152	4		2 Spirit Of St. Louis		Cleveland Int'l. 36984

FOLKSWINGERS, The

Instrumental band formed in Los Angeles, California: **Glen Campbell** (12-string guitar), brothers Rod Dillard (guitar) and Doug Dillard (banjo), and Dean Webb (bass). The latter three were also in **The Dillards**.

9/28/63	132	4		1 12 String Guitar! [I]		World Pacific 1812

FONDA, Jane

Born on 12/21/1937 in Manhattan, New York. Prolific movie actress. Daughter of legendary actor Henry Fonda. Three marriages include movie director Roger Vadim (1965-73), political activist Tom Hayden (1973-90) and media mogul Ted Turner (1991-2001). Albums below contain instructions for aerobic exercises.

5/29/82+	15	120	▲²	1 Jane Fonda's Workout Record		Columbia 38054 [2]
				all cuts also done as instrumentals		
5/21/83	117	7		2 Jane Fonda's Workout Record For Pregnancy, Birth And Recovery		Columbia 38675 [2]
				music by a special studio group; no track titles listed		
8/18/84	135	10	●	3 Jane Fonda's Workout Record - New And Improved		Columbia 39287 [2]
				all cuts also done as instrumentals		
12/15/84+	202	6		4 Jane Fonda's Prime Time Workout		Elektra 60382

FONSI, Luis

Born on 4/15/1978 in Puerto Rico; raised in Orlando, Flordia. Latin singer.

3/30/02	109	2		1 Amor Secreto [F]		Universal Latino 017020
11/15/03	138	1		2 Abrazar La Vida [F]		Universal Latino 001403
7/30/05	62	5		3 Paso A Paso [F]		Universal Latino 004881
12/9/06	192	1		4 Exitos: 98: 06 [G-F]		Universal Latino 008070
9/13/08	15	17		5 Palabras Del Silencio [F]		Universal Latino 011810

FONTAINE, Frank

Born on 4/19/1920 in Cambridge, Massachusetts. Died of a heart attack on 8/4/1978 (age 58). Comedian/singer/actor. Played "Crazy Guggenheim" on **Jackie Gleason**'s TV show.

2/9/63	❶⁵	53	●	1 Songs I Sing On The Jackie Gleason Show		ABC-Paramount 442
8/24/63	44	25		2 Sings Like Crazy		ABC-Paramount 460
3/7/64	92	12		3 How Sweet It Is		ABC-Paramount 470

FONTANA, Wayne — see MINDBENDERS, The

FOO FIGHTERS
All-Time: #428

Rock band formed in Seattle, Washington: Dave Grohl (vocals, guitar), Pat Smear (guitar), Nate Mendel (bass) and William Goldsmith (drums). Taylor Hawkins replaced Goldsmith in 1997. Franz Stahl replaced Smear in 1998. Chris Shiflett replaced Stahl in 2000. Grohl was drummer for **Nirvana**. Group name taken from the fiery UFO-like apparitions seen by U.S. pilots during World War II. Mendel and Goldsmith later formed **The Fire Theft**; Goldsmith was also with **Sunny Day Real Estate**. Shiflett was also a member of **Me First And The Gimme Gimmes**. Grohl assembled the **Probot** project and joined **Them Crooked Vultures**.

7/22/95	23	51	▲	1 Foo Fighters		Roswell 34027
5/11/96	175	1		2 Big Me .... [EP]		Roswell 58530
6/7/97	10	74	▲	3 The Colour And The Shape	Cat:#35/1	Roswell 55832
11/20/99	10	41	▲	4 There Is Nothing Left To Lose		Roswell 67892
				Grammy: Rock Album		
11/9/02	3[1]	50	▲	5 One By One		Roswell 68008
				Grammy: Rock Album		
7/2/05	2[1]	37	▲	6 In Your Honor		Roswell 68038 [2]
11/25/06	21	11		7 Skin And Bones .... [L]		Roswell 88857
				recorded at the Pantages Theater in Los Angeles, California		
10/13/07	3[1]	48	●	8 Echoes, Silence, Patience & Grace		Roswell 11516
				Grammy: Rock Album		
11/21/09	11	24		9 Greatest Hits .... [G]		Roswell 36921

FOOLS, The

Rock band from Boston, Massachusetts: Mike Girard (vocals), brothers Stacey Pedrick (guitar) and Chris Pedrick (drums), Rich Bartlett (guitar) and Doug Forman (bass).

4/5/80	151	8		1 Sold Out		EMI America 17024
3/28/81	158	4		2 Heavy Mental		EMI America 17046

FOOLS GOLD

Pop-rock band formed in Los Angeles, California: Denny Henson (vocals, guitar), Doug Livingston (piano), Tom Kelly (bass) and Ron Grinel (drums). Backing band for **Dan Fogelberg**.

4/24/76	100	13		1 Fools Gold		Morning Sky 5500

FORBERT, Steve

Born on 12/15/1954 in Meridian, Mississippi. Folk-rock singer/songwriter/guitarist.

2/10/79	82	15		1 Alive On Arrival		Nemperor 35538
11/10/79+	20	26		2 Jackrabbit Slim		Nemperor 36191
10/11/80	70	9		3 Little Stevie Orbit		Nemperor 36595
7/24/82	159	6		4 Steve Forbert		Nemperor 37434

FORCE M.D.'S

R&B vocal group from Staten Island, New York: brothers Stevie Lundy and Antoine Lundy, with Jesse Daniels, Charles Nelson and Trisco Pearson. Nelson died of a heart attack on 3/10/1995 (age 30). Antoine Lundy died of ALS on 1/18/1998 (age 33). M.D.: Musical Diversity.

12/15/84	185	4		1 Love Letters		Tommy Boy 1003
2/22/86	69	25		2 Chillin'		Tommy Boy 1010
8/15/87	67	16		3 Touch And Go		Tommy Boy 25631

FORD, Colt

Born James Brown in 1970 in Athens, Georgia. Country singer/songwriter/guitarist. Former professional golfer.

7/11/09	140	20		1 Ride Through The Country .... Cat:#38/7		Average Joe's 1001

FORD, Dee Dee — see GARDNER, Don

FORD, Frankie

Born Francis Guzzo on 8/4/1939 in Gretna, Louisiana. Rock and roll singer.

~ ~ ~ ~ ~ ~ ~ ~ ~ ~ **NON-CHARTED ALBUM** ~ ~ ~ ~ ~ ~ ~ ~ ~ ~
1959 **Let's Take A Sea Cruise**

FORD, Lita

Born Carmelita Ford on 9/19/1958 in London, England; raised in Los Angeles, California. Rock singer/guitarist. Member of **The Runaways** from 1975-79. Married to Chris Holmes (of **W.A.S.P.**) from 1990-92. Married Jim Gillette (lead singer of **Nitro**) on 5/13/1994.

8/4/84	66	16		1 Dancin' On The Edge		Mercury 818864
2/20/88	29	62	▲	2 Lita .... Cat:#50/1		RCA 6397
6/16/90	52	16		3 Stiletto		RCA 2090
11/30/91	132	4		4 Dangerous Curves		RCA 61025

FORD, Rita [Music Boxes]

Born on 10/14/1915 in Manhattan, New York. Died on 10/19/1992 (age 77). Opened own music box shop in 1947. All songs played on Rita Ford's collection of authentic 19th century music boxes, which were an early ancestor of phonographs and juke boxes.

12/21/63	26[X]	8		1 A Music Box Christmas .... [X-I]		Columbia 1698 / 8498
				Christmas charts: 26/'63, 29/'67, 29/'68		
12/23/72	14[X]	1		2 Christmas With Rita Ford's Music Boxes .... [X-I]		Harmony 31577

FORD, Robben

Born on 12/16/1951 in Ukiah, California. Male session guitarist. Also see **Yellowjackets**.

8/6/88	120	13		1 Talk To Your Daughter		Warner 25647

FORD, "Tennessee" Ernie
1950s: #13 / All-Time: #317

Born on 2/13/1919 in Bristol, Tennessee. Died of liver failure on 10/17/1991 (age 72). Legendary country singer/songwriter. Hosted own TV variety show from 1955-65. Known as "The Old Pea Picker."

AWARD: C&W Hall of Fame: 1990

DEBUT	PEAK	WKS			Catalog	Label & Number
4/28/56	12	3		1 This Lusty Land!		Capitol 700
1/5/57	2³	277	▲	2 Hymns		Capitol 756
5/6/57	5	68	●	3 Spirituals		Capitol 818
6/9/58	5	77	●	4 Nearer The Cross		Capitol 1005
5/2/60	23	26		5 Sing A Hymn With Me		Capitol 1332
1/27/62	67	19		6 Hymns At Home		Capitol 1604
5/26/62	110	12		7 Here Comes The Mississippi Showboat		Capitol 1684
11/10/62	43	2		8 I Love To Tell The Story		Capitol 1751
1/5/63	71	12		9 Book Of Favorite Hymns .... [K]		Capitol 1794
4/25/70	192	2		10 America The Beautiful		Capitol 412

CHRISTMAS ALBUMS:

DEBUT	PEAK	WKS			Catalog	Label & Number
12/22/58+	4	3	▲	11 The Star Carol		Capitol 1071
				Christmas charts: 15/'64, 25/'65, 56/'66, 41/'67		
12/28/59+	7	2		12 The Star Carol [R]		Capitol 1071
12/31/60	28	1		13 The Star Carol [R]		Capitol 1071
12/25/61+	110	3		14 The Star Carol [R]		Capitol 1071
12/22/62	48	2		15 The Star Carol [R]		Capitol 1071
12/14/63	14ˣ	8		16 The Story Of Christmas .... [TV]		Capitol 1964
				TENNESSEE ERNIE FORD & THE ROGER WAGNER CHORALE		
				Christmas charts: 14/'63, 19/'64, 28/'68		
12/25/65	31ˣ	1		17 Sing We Now Of Christmas		Capitol 2394

FORD, Willa

Born Amanda Lee Williford on 1/22/1981 in Ruskin, Florida. Female pop singer/actress. Married professional hockey player Mike Modano on 8/25/2007. Played "Chelsea" in the 2009 movie *Friday The 13th*.

DEBUT	PEAK	WKS			Catalog	Label & Number
8/4/01	56	9		1 Willa Was Here		Lava 83437

FORDHAM, Julia

Born on 8/10/1962 in Portsmouth, Hampshire, England. Female singer/songwriter.

DEBUT	PEAK	WKS			Catalog	Label & Number
12/3/88+	118	25		1 Julia Fordham		Virgin 90955
2/17/90	74	20		2 Porcelain		Virgin 91325

FOREIGNER
All-Time: #220

British-American rock band formed in New York: **Lou Gramm** (vocals), **Mick Jones** (guitar), Ian McDonald (guitar, keyboards), Al Greenwood (keyboards), Ed Gagliardi (bass) and Dennis Elliott (drums). Gagliardi, Gramm and Greenwood are from New York. Most of material written by Jones (**Spooky Tooth**) and Gramm. Rick Wills (**Roxy Music**, **Small Faces**) replaced Gagliardi in 1979. Greenwood and McDonald (**King Crimson**) left in 1980. Gramm left in 1991 to form Shadow King; replaced by Johnny Edwards (**Montrose**). Gramm returned in mid-1992; replaced by Kelly Hansen in 2005. Wills left in 1992 to join **Bad Company**; Elliott left to open woodworking business. Jones not to be confused with Mick Jones of The Clash and Big Audio Dynamite.

DEBUT	PEAK	WKS			Catalog	Label & Number
3/26/77	4	113	▲⁵	1 Foreigner		Atlantic 18215
7/8/78	3⁸	88	▲⁷	2 Double Vision		Atlantic 19999
9/29/79	5	41	▲⁵	3 Head Games		Atlantic 29999
7/25/81	❶¹⁰	81	▲⁶	4 4		Atlantic 16999
1/5/85	4	45	▲³	5 Agent Provocateur		Atlantic 81999
12/26/87+	15	37	▲	6 Inside Information		Atlantic 81808
7/6/91	117	9		7 Unusual Heat		Atlantic 82299
3/11/95	136	6		8 Mr. Moonlight		Generama 53961
10/17/09	29	7		9 Can't Slow Down		PLM 521324 [2]

GREATEST HITS & COMPILATIONS:

DEBUT	PEAK	WKS			Catalog	Label & Number
12/25/82+	10	25	▲⁷	10 Foreigner Records Cat:#20/43		Atlantic 80999
10/10/92	123	20	▲²	11 The Very Best...And Beyond .... Cat:#16/8		Atlantic 89999
5/25/02	80	7	▲	12 Complete Greatest Hits		Atlantic 78266
8/2/08	132	9		13 No End In Sight: The Very Best Of Foreigner		Atlantic 512130 [2]
9/12/09	45ᶜ	1		14 Hot Blooded And Other Hits		Rhino 78137

FOREMAN, Jon

Born on 10/22/1976 in San Diego, California. Christian rock singer/songwriter/guitarist. Leader of **Switchfoot** and **Fiction Family**.

DEBUT	PEAK	WKS			Catalog	Label & Number
6/28/08	162	1		1 Summer .... [EP]		Credential digital

FORESTER SISTERS, The

Country family vocal group from Lookout Mountain, Georgia: Kathy, Kim, June and Christy Forester.

DEBUT	PEAK	WKS			Catalog	Label & Number
4/20/91	137	7		1 Talkin' 'Bout Men		Warner 26500

FOREST FOR THE TREES

Born Carl Stephenson in Los Angeles, California. Eclectic singer/songwriter/multi-instrumentalist.

DEBUT	PEAK	WKS			Catalog	Label & Number
9/27/97	190	1		1 Forest For The Trees		DreamWorks 50002

FOREVER MORE

Rock band from Scotland: Alan Gorrie (vocals, bass), Mick "Travis" Strode (vocals, guitar), Onnie "Mair" McIntyre (guitar, vocals) and Stuart Francis (drums). Strode had been in Band Of Joy with **Robert Plant**. Gorrie and McIntyre later formed **AWB**.

DEBUT	PEAK	WKS			Catalog	Label & Number
3/7/70	180	3		1 Yours Forever More		RCA Victor 4272

FOREVER THE SICKEST KIDS
Punk-rock band from Dallas, Texas: Jonathan Cook (vocals), Caleb Turman (guitar), Marc Stewart (guitar), Kent Garrison (keyboards), Austin Bello (bass) and Kyle Burns (drums).

5/17/08	45	6		1 Underdog Alma Mater		Universal Motown 011105
12/5/09	107	1		2 The Weekend: Friday .... [EP]		Universal Motown 013673

FORMAT, The
Rock duo from Phoenix, Arizona: Nate Ruess and Sam Means. Ruess also formed **Fun**.

7/29/06	77	2		1 Dog Problems...		The Vanity Label 30592

FOR SQUIRRELS
Rock band from Gainesville, Florida: John Francis Vigliatura (vocals), Travis Michael Tooke (guitar), William Richard White (bass) and Thomas Jacob Griego (drums). Vigliatura (age 20) and White (age 22) were killed in a car crash on 9/8/1995.

2/3/96	171	4		1 Example		550 Music 67150

FORTE, John
Born on 1/30/1975 in Brooklyn, New York. Male rapper.

8/1/98	84	3		1 Poly Sci		Ruffhouse 68639

FORT MINOR
Solo side project for **Linkin Park** member Mike Shinoda. Combines electronic beats with hip-hop music.

12/10/05+	51	26		1 The Rising Tied		Machine Shop 49388

FORTUNE, James, & FIYA
Born in Houston, Texas. Gospel singer/songwriter. FIYA: Free In Yahweh's Abundance.

4/4/09	119	3		1 The Transformation		Blacksmoke 3045

FORTUNES, The
Pop band formed in England: Shel MacRae and Barry Pritchard (vocals, guitars), David Carr (keyboards), Rod Allen (bass) and Andy Brown (drums). Pritchard died of heart failure on 1/11/1999 (age 54). Bainbridge died of liver cancer on 1/10/2008 (age 63).

7/10/71	134	10		1 Here Comes That Rainy Day Feeling Again..		Capitol 809

40 CAL
Born Calvin Byrd on 8/31/1981 in Harlem, New York. Male rapper.

9/29/07	151	1		1 Broken Safety 2		Dipset 4436

FOSTER, David
Born on 11/1/1949 in Victoria, British Columbia, Canada. Prolific producer/keyboardist. Member of the groups **Skylark** and **Attitudes**.

7/19/86	195	3		1 David Foster		Atlantic 81642
2/20/88	111	8		2 The Symphony Sessions... [I-L]		Atlantic 81799
				recorded on 6/26/1987 at the Orpheum Theater in Vancouver, British Columbia, Canada		
12/11/93	48	5		3 The Christmas Album .... [X]		Interscope 92295
				Christmas chart: 13/'93		
11/29/08	46	22		4 Hit Man: David Foster & Friends..		143 Records 511933

FOSTER & LLOYD
Country vocal duo of songwriters Radney Foster and Bill Lloyd.

5/13/89	142	6		1 Faster & Llouder..		RCA 9587

FOTOMAKER
Pop-rock band from New York: Wally Bryson (guitar), Lex Marchesi (guitar), Frankie Vinci (keyboards), Gene Cornish (bass) and Dino Danelli (drums). All share vocals. Bryson was a member of **The Raspberries**. Cornish and Danelli were members of **The Rascals**.

3/25/78	88	13		1 Fotomaker...		Atlantic 19165

FOUNDATIONS, The
R&B-pop band formed in England: Colin Young (vocals), Alan Warner (guitar), Eric Allendale, Pat Burke and Michael Elliott (horns), Anthony Gomez (keyboards), Peter McBeth (bass) and Tim Harris (drums).

3/8/69	92	11		1 Build Me Up Buttercup.. [L]		Uni 73043
				side 1: live; side 2: studio		

FOUNTAIN, Pete
All-Time: #438
Born on 7/3/1930 in New Orleans, Louisiana. Top jazz clarinetist. Member of **Al Hirt**'s band from 1956-57. Performed on **Lawrence Welk**'s weekly TV show from 1957-59. Owned The French Quarter Inn club in New Orleans.

2/22/60	8	87		1 Pete Fountain's New Orleans [I]		Coral 57282
5/9/60	31	4		2 Pete Fountain Day .... [I-L]		Coral 57313
				recorded on 10/29/1959 at the Municipal Auditorium in New Orleans, Louisiana		
9/11/61	43	4		3 Pete Fountain's French Quarter .... [I]		Coral 57359
				Fountain's nightclub at 231 Bourbon St. in New Orleans, Louisiana		
2/3/62	41	2		4 Bourbon Street.. [I]		Coral 57389
				PETE FOUNTAIN & AL HIRT		
7/28/62	30	6		5 Music From Dixie .... [I]		Coral 57401
9/7/63	91	9		6 South Rampart Street Parade.................................... [I]		Coral 57440
6/13/64	53	14		7 New Orleans At Midnight .... [I]		Coral 57429
8/22/64	48	44		8 Licorice Stick .... [I]		Coral 57460
1/2/65	121	7		9 Pete's Place .... [I-L]		Coral 57453
				recorded at Fountain's French Quarter Inn		
5/8/65	64	14		10 Mr. Stick Man.. [I]		Coral 57473

Billboard			R I A A	ARTIST Album Title	Catalog	Label & Number
DEBUT	PEAK	WKS				

FOUNTAIN, Pete — cont'd

4/23/66	100	8	11 A Taste Of Honey		Coral 57486
12/23/67	100 X	2	12 "Candy Clarinet" Merry Christmas From Pete Fountain [X]		Coral 57487
6/15/68	187	2	13 For The First Time		Decca 74955
			BRENDA LEE & PETE FOUNTAIN		
3/22/69	186	6	14 Those Were The Days [I]		Coral 57505
7/21/73	217	3	15 Pete Fountain's Crescent City [I]		MCA 336

FOUNTAINS OF WAYNE
Pop-rock band from New York: Chris Collingwood (vocals, guitar), Jody Porter (guitar), Adam Schlesinger (bass) and Brian Young (drums). Schlesinger also joined **Tinted Windows**.

6/28/03	115	28	1 Welcome Interstate Managers		S-Curve 90875
7/16/05	168	1	2 Out-Of-State Plates [K]		Virgin 76987 [2]
4/21/07	97	2	3 Traffic And Weather		Virgin 74420

4 BY FOUR
R&B vocal group from Queens, New York: brothers Damen Heyward and Lance Heyward, with Steve Gray and Jeraude Jackson.

6/27/87	141	7	1 4 By Four		Capitol 12560

FOUR FRESHMEN, The   1950s: #15
Jazz-styled vocal/instrumental group from Indianapolis, Indiana: brothers Ross Brabour and Don Barbour, their cousin Bob Flanigan and Ken Albers. Don Barbour died in a car crash on 10/5/1961 (age 32). **Brian Wilson** (of **The Beach Boys**) has often cited them as a major influence.

2/25/56	6	32	1 Four Freshmen And 5 Trombones		Capitol 683
10/13/56	11	8	2 Freshmen Favorites [G]		Capitol 743
3/2/57	9	7	3 4 Freshmen And 5 Trumpets		Capitol 763
11/18/57	25	1	4 Four Freshmen And Five Saxes		Capitol 844
9/29/58	17	1	5 The Four Freshmen In Person [L]		Capitol 1008
11/3/58	11	6	6 Voices In Love		Capitol 1074
1/11/60	40	1	7 The Four Freshmen And Five Guitars		Capitol 1255

4 HIM
Christian vocal group from Mobile, Alabama: Mark Harris, Marty Magehee, Kirk Sullivan and Andy Chrisman.

7/13/96	115	4	1 The Message		Benson 4321
4/25/98	95	5	2 Obvious		Benson 2205
4/10/99	123	1	3 Best Ones [G]		Benson 2395

FOUR JACKS AND A JILL
Pop band from South Africa: Glenys Lynne (vocals), Bruce Bark (guitar), Till Hannamann (organ), Clive Harding (bass) and Tony Hughes (drums).

6/22/68	155	6	1 Master Jack		RCA Victor 4019

FOUR LADS, The
Vocal group from Toronto, Ontario, Canada: Bernie Toorish, Jimmie Arnold, Frankie Busseri and Connie Codarini. Arnold died of lung cancer on 6/15/2004 (age 72). Codarini died on 4/28/2010 (age 80).

10/6/56	14	2	1 On The Sunny Side		Columbia 912

4 NON BLONDES
Pop-rock band from San Francisco, California: Linda Perry (vocals), Roger Rocha (guitar), Christa Hillhouse (bass) and Dawn Richardson (drums).

4/3/93	13	59	▲ 1 Bigger, Better, Faster, More!		Interscope 92112

4 OUT OF 5 DOCTORS
Rock band from Washington, D.C.: George Pittaway (guitar), Jeff Severson (keyboards), Cal Everett (bass) and Tom Ballew (drums).

2/28/81	202	2	1 4 Out Of 5 Doctors		Nemperor 36575

FOURPLAY
All-star jazz band formed in Los Angeles, California: **Lee Ritenour** (guitar), **Bob James** (keyboards), Nathan East (bass) and **Harvey Mason** (drums). **Larry Carlton** replaced Ritenour in 1997.

10/12/91	97	33	● 1 Fourplay [I]		Warner 26656
9/4/93	70	17	● 2 Between The Sheets [I]		Warner 45340
9/9/95	90	10	● 3 Elixir [I]		Warner 45922
6/27/98	146	5	4 4 [I]		Warner 46921
9/9/00	135	5	5 Fourplay...Yes, Please! [I]		Warner 47694
8/10/02	128	5	6 Heartfelt		Bluebird 63916
8/26/06	146	1	7 X		Bluebird 86399
10/11/08	147	1	8 Energy		Heads Up 3146

4 P.M.
R&B vocal group from Baltimore, Maryland: brothers Rene Pena and Roberto Pena, with Larry McFarland and Marty Ware.

2/4/95	126	9	1 Now's The Time		Next Plateau 828579

Billboard			R I A A	ARTIST Album Title	Catalog	Label & Number
DEBUT	PEAK	WKS				

FOUR PREPS, The
Vocal group from Hollywood, California: Bruce Belland, Ed Cobb, Marvin Inabnett and Glen Larson. Inabnett died of a heart attack on 3/7/1999 (age 60). Cobb died of leukemia on 9/19/1999 (age 61).

8/21/61	8	26	1 The Four Preps On Campus	[L]	Capitol 1566
3/24/62	40	17	2 Campus Encore	[L]	Capitol 1647

~ ~ ~ ~ ~ ~ ~ ~ ~ **NON-CHARTED ALBUMS** ~ ~ ~ ~ ~ ~ ~ ~ ~ ~ ~
1958 **The Four Preps**   1960 **Early In The Morning**

4 RUNNER
Country vocal group formed in Nashville, Tennessee: Craig Morris, Billy Simon, Lee Hilliard and Jim Chapman.

5/27/95	144	5	1 4 Runner		Polydor 527379

4 SEASONS, The   1960s: #28 / All-Time: #136
Vocal group formed in Newark, New Jersey: **Frankie Valli** (born on 5/3/1937), Bob Gaudio (born on 11/17/1942), Nick Massi (born on 9/19/1927) and Tommy DeVito (born on 6/19/1928). In 1965, Nick Massi was replaced by Charlie Calello and then by Joe Long. Group disbanded in the early 1970s. Re-formed in 1975: Valli (vocals), Gerry Polci (vocals, drums), John Pavia (guitar), Lee Shapiro (keyboards) and Don Ciccone (bass; formerly with **The Critters**). Massi died of cancer on 12/24/2000 (age 73). Also recorded as The Wonder Who?.
     AWARD: R&R Hall of Fame: 1990

10/27/62	6	27	1 Sherry & 11 Others		Vee-Jay 1053
3/2/63	8	19	2 Big Girls Don't Cry And Twelve Others		Vee-Jay 1056
7/13/63	47	12	3 Ain't That A Shame And 11 Others		Vee-Jay 1059
6/6/64	100	5	4 Stay & Other Great Hits		Vee-Jay 1082
			originally titled *Folk-Nanny*		
2/29/64	84	9	5 Born To Wander		Philips 129
3/28/64	6	25	6 Dawn (Go Away) And 11 Other Great Songs		Philips 124
10/10/64	142	3	7 The Beatles vs. The Four Seasons	[R]	Vee-Jay 30 [2]
			reissue of *Golden Hits Of The 4 Seasons* and *Introducing...The Beatles*		
8/8/64	7	26	8 Rag Doll		Philips 146
4/10/65	77	13	9 The 4 Seasons Entertain You		Philips 164
12/18/65+	106	10	10 Big Hits By Burt Bacharach...Hal David...Bob Dylan...		Philips 193
1/29/66	50	15	11 Working My Way Back To You		Philips 201
6/24/67	37	25	12 New Gold Hits		Philips 243
2/15/69	85	11	13 The Genuine Imitation Life Gazette		Philips 290
6/13/70	190	2	14 Half & Half		Philips 600341
			half the songs by **Frankie Valli** (see Valli for tracks), half by The 4 Seasons		
11/29/75+	38	31	15 Who Loves You		Warner/Curb 2900
5/14/77	168	5	16 Helicon		Warner/Curb 3016

CHRISTMAS ALBUMS:

12/7/63	13ˣ	1	17 The 4 Seasons Greetings		Vee-Jay 1055
12/24/66+	28ˣ	6	18 The 4 Seasons' Christmas Album	[R]	Philips 600-223
			reissue of #17 above; Christmas charts: 72/'66, 28/'67		

GREATEST HITS & COMPILATIONS:

9/7/63	15	56	19 Golden Hits Of The 4 Seasons		Vee-Jay 1065
9/5/64	105	5	20 More Golden Hits By The Four Seasons		Vee-Jay 1088
12/11/65+	10	88	● 21 The 4 Seasons' Gold Vault of Hits		Philips 196
12/3/66+	22	53	● 22 2nd Vault Of Golden Hits		Philips 221
12/17/66+	107	9	23 Lookin' Back		Philips 222
			recordings from the group's first 3 Vee-Jay albums		
12/28/68+	37	21	● 24 Edizione D'Oro (The 4 Seasons Gold Edition-29 Gold Hits)		Philips 6501 [2]
12/13/75+	51	17	25 The Four Seasons Story		Private Stock 7000 [2]

~ ~ ~ ~ ~ ~ ~ ~ ~ **NON-CHARTED ALBUMS** ~ ~ ~ ~ ~ ~ ~ ~ ~ ~ ~
1956 **Joyride** [The Four Lovers]   1965 **Girls Girls Girls We Love Girls**

FOUR TOPS   All-Time: #126
Legendary R&B vocal group from Detroit, Michigan: Levi Stubbs (lead singer; born on 6/6/1936; died on 10/17/2008, age 72), Renaldo "Obie" Benson (born on 6/14/1937; died of cancer on 7/1/2005, age 68), Lawrence Payton (born on 3/2/1938; died of cancer on 6/20/1997, age 59) and Abdul "Duke" Fakir (born on 12/26/1935). Stubbs was the voice of the killer plant in the 1986 movie *Little Shop of Horrors*. Stubbs is the brother of Joe Stubbs (of **100 Proof Aged In Soul**).
     AWARDS: Grammy: Lifetime Achievement ★ R&R Hall of Fame: 1990

2/27/65	63	27	1 Four Tops		Motown 622
11/13/65+	20	35	2 Four Tops Second Album		Motown 634
8/27/66	32	22	3 4 Tops On Top		Motown 647
12/17/66+	17	43	4 Four Tops Live!	[L]	Motown 654
			recorded at the Roostertail in Detroit, Michigan		
4/8/67	79	15	5 4 Tops On Broadway		Motown 657

Billboard			ARTIST		
DEBUT	**PEAK**	**WKS**	**Album Title**	Catalog	**Label & Number**

FOUR TOPS — cont'd

DEBUT	PEAK	WKS		Album Title	Catalog	Label & Number
8/12/67	11	59	6	Four Tops Reach Out...		Motown 660
9/30/67	4	73	7	The Four Tops Greatest Hits [G]		Motown 662
9/28/68	91	16	8	Yesterday's Dreams..		Motown 669
7/5/69	74	10	9	Four Tops Now!..		Motown 675
12/13/69+	163	6	10	Soul Spin...		Motown 695
4/11/70	21	42	11	Still Waters Run Deep...		Motown 704
10/17/70	109	12	12	Changing Times..		Motown 721
10/17/70	113	16	13	The Magnificent 7..		Motown 717
6/26/71	154	6	14	The Return Of The Magnificent Seven.....................		Motown 736
1/8/72	160	6	15	Dynamite...		Motown 745
				SUPREMES & FOUR TOPS (above 3)		
9/25/71	106	10	16	Four Tops Greatest Hits, Vol. 2 [G]		Motown 740
5/27/72	50	28	17	Nature Planned It..		Motown 748
5/12/73	103	9	18	The Best Of The 4 Tops [G]		Motown 764 [2]
8/10/74	203	4	19	Anthology [K]		Motown 809 [3]
11/11/72+	33	31	20	Keeper Of The Castle...		Dunhill/ABC 50129
9/22/73	66	14	21	Main Street People...		Dunhill/ABC 50144
4/27/74	118	11	22	Meeting Of The Minds..		Dunhill/ABC 50166
10/26/74	92	9	23	Live & In Concert [L]		Dunhill/ABC 50188
6/14/75	148	5	24	Night Lights Harmony..		ABC 862
11/13/76	124	8	25	Catfish..		ABC 968
11/25/78	208	2	26	At The Top..		ABC 1092
9/12/81	37	21	27	Tonight!..		Casablanca 7258
11/5/83	202	7	28	Back Where I Belong..		Motown 6066
6/29/85	140	9	29	Magic...		Motown 6130
9/24/88	149	7	30	Indestructible..		Arista 8492

FOUR TUNES, The
R&B vocal group formed in Harlem, New York: Danny Owens, Pat Best, Jimmy Gordon and Jimmie Nabbie. Nabbie died on 9/12/1992 (age 72). Gordon died on 10/27/1993 (age 80). Best died on 10/14/2004 (age 81).

~ ~ ~ ~ ~ ~ ~ ~ ~ ~ ~ **NON-CHARTED ALBUM** ~ ~ ~ ~ ~ ~ ~ ~ ~ ~ ~
1957 **12 x 4**

FOUR YEAR STRONG
Punk-rock band from Worcester, Massachusetts: Dan O'Connor (vocals), Alan Day (guitar), Josh Lyford (keyboards), Joe Weiss (bass) and Jake Massucco (drums).

DEBUT	PEAK	WKS		Album Title	Catalog	Label & Number
8/8/09	115	1	1	Explains It All..		Decaydance 11

FOWLER, Kevin
Born in Amarillo, Texas. Country singer/songwriter/guitarist.

DEBUT	PEAK	WKS		Album Title	Catalog	Label & Number
8/21/04	195	1	1	Loose, Loud & Crazy		Equity 3003
10/13/07	111	1	2	Bring It On...		Equity 3017

FOWLEY, Kim
Born on 7/21/1939 in Manila, Phillipines (father was in US Navy); raised in Los Angeles, California. Male producer/songwriter/manager.

DEBUT	PEAK	WKS		Album Title	Catalog	Label & Number
4/19/69	198	3	1	Outrageous...		Imperial 12423

FOX, Samantha
Born on 4/15/1966 in London, England. Dance singer. Former topless model.

DEBUT	PEAK	WKS			Album Title	Catalog	Label & Number
11/29/86+	24	28	●	1	Touch Me		Jive 1012
10/24/87+	51	25	●	2	Samantha Fox...		Jive 1061
11/26/88+	37	34	●	3	I Wanna Have Some Fun		Jive 1150

FOX, Virgil
Born on 5/3/1912 in Princeton, Illinois. Died of cancer on 10/25/1980 (age 68). Male organist.

DEBUT	PEAK	WKS		Album Title		Catalog	Label & Number
12/24/66	69[X]	1	1	The Christmas Album	[X-I]		Command 11032
5/29/71	183	2	2	Bach Live At Fillmore East	[I-L]		Decca 75263
				recorded on 12/1/1970 in New York City			

FOXWORTHY, Jeff
Born on 9/6/1958 in Atlanta, Georgia; raised in Hapeville, Georgia. Stand-up comedian/actor/author. Starred in own TV sitcom, 1995-97. Began hosting own radio countdown show in April 1999. Member of the **Blue Collar Comedy Tour** and *Blue Collar TV* cast. Host of TV game show *Are You Smarter Than A 5th Grader?*

DEBUT	PEAK	WKS			Album Title		Catalog	Label & Number
8/27/94+	38	75	▲³	1	You Might Be A Redneck If...	[C]		Warner 45314
8/5/95	8	59	▲³	2	Games Rednecks Play	[C]		Warner 45856
8/12/95	155	7		3	The Redneck Test - Volume 43.............................	[C-E]		Laughing Hyena 2043
8/19/95	184	2		4	The Original - Volume 79....................................	[C-E]		Laughing Hyena 2079
9/14/96	21	20	▲	5	Crank It Up - The Music Album	[N]		Warner 46361
6/6/98	50	13	●	6	Totally Committed...	[C]		Warner 46861
11/6/99	189	1	●	7	Greatest Bits..	[C-G]		Warner 47427
5/13/00	143	7		8	Big Funny...	[C]		DreamWorks 50200
9/20/03	76	5		9	The Best Of Jeff Foxworthy: Double Wide, Single Minded	[C-K]		Warner 73903
7/24/04	47	7		10	Have Your Loved Ones Spayed Or Neutered	[C]		Warner 48772

Billboard			R I A A	ARTIST		
DEBUT	PEAK	WKS		Album Title	Catalog	Label & Number

FOXX
Born Jonathan Reed in Baton Rouge, Louisiana. Male rapper.

| 10/20/07 | 144 | 1 | | 1 Street Gossip .... | | Trill 290476 |

FOXX, Inez
Born on 9/9/1942 in Greensboro, North Carolina. Black female singer. Accompanied vocally by her brother Charlie Foxx (died on 9/18/1998, age 68).

~ ~ ~ ~ ~ ~ ~ ~ ~ ~ **NON-CHARTED ALBUM** ~ ~ ~ ~ ~ ~ ~ ~ ~ ~
1963 Mockingbird

FOXX, Jamie
Born Eric Bishop on 12/13/1967 in Terrell, Texas. R&B singer/actor/comedian. Acted in several movies and TV shows. Won Best Actor Oscar for portraying **Ray Charles** in the 2004 movie *Ray*.

8/6/94	78	10		1 Peep This		Fox 66436
1/7/06	❶³	34	▲²	2 Unpredictable		J Records 71779
1/3/09	3¹	40	▲	3 Intuition		J Records 41294

FOXX, Redd
Born John Sanford on 12/9/1922 in St. Louis, Missouri. Died of a heart attack on 10/11/1991 (age 68). Stand-up comedian/actor. Starred in several movies and TV shows. Best known as "Fred Sanford" on TV's *Sanford and Son*. Several of his 1950s and 1960s X-rated "party" albums were never sold in mainstream record shops.

6/3/72	198	3		1 Sanford & Foxx .... [C]		Dooto 853
7/29/72	155	8		2 Sanford And Son .... [C-TV]		RCA Victor 4739
1/3/76	87	13		3 You Gotta Wash Your Ass.. [C]		Atlantic 18157
				no track titles listed on this album		

FOXXX, Freddie
Born James Campbell in 1969 in Westbury, New York. Male rapper. Member of The Flavor Unit MCs. Also records as **Bumpy Knuckles**.

| 7/15/00 | 179 | 4 | | 1 Industry Shakedown .... | | Kjac 2000 |
| | | | | **FREDDIE FOXXX (BUMPY KNUCKLES)** | | |

FOXY
Latin dance band from Miami, Florida: Ish "Angel" Ledesma (vocals, guitar), Richie Puente (percussion), Charlie Murciano (keyboards), Arnold Pasiero (bass) and Joe Galdo (drums). Puente is the son of famous bandleader **Tito Puente**; died on 7/18/2004 (age 48). Ledesma later formed **Oxo**.

7/22/78	12	27		1 Get Off		Dash 30005
4/14/79	29	16		2 Hot Numbers		Dash 30010
1/26/80	207	3		3 Party Boys		Dash 30015

FRAMING HANLEY
Hard-rock band from Nashville, Tennessee: Kenneth Nixon (vocals), Ryan Belcher (guitar), Brandon Wootten (guitar), Luke McDuffee (bass) and Chris Vest (drums).

| 1/24/09 | 169 | 7 | | 1 The Moment .... | | Silent Majority 1001 |

FRAMPTON, Peter　　　　　　　　　　　　　　　　　　　　　　　　**All-Time: #378**
Born on 4/22/1950 in Beckenham, Kent, England. Rock singer/songwriter/guitarist. Former member of **Humble Pie**. Played "Billy Shears" in the 1978 movie *Sgt. Pepper's Lonely Hearts Club Band*.

10/7/72	177	6		1 Wind Of Change		A&M 4348
6/9/73	110	22		2 Frampton's Camel		A&M 4389
3/30/74	125	9		3 Somethin's Happening		A&M 3619
3/29/75	32	64	●	4 Frampton..		A&M 4512
1/31/76	❶¹⁰	97	▲⁶	5 Frampton Comes Alive! [L]		A&M 3703 [2]
6/25/77	2⁴	32	▲	6 I'm In You		A&M 4704
6/23/79	19	16	●	7 Where I Should Be		A&M 3710
6/13/81	43	13		8 Breaking All The Rules		A&M 3722
8/28/82	174	8		9 The Art Of Control		A&M 4905
2/8/86	80	14		10 Premonition		Atlantic 81290
10/14/89	152	6		11 When All The Pieces Fit		Atlantic 82030
9/30/06	129	2		12 Fingerprints .... [I]		A&M 007219
				Grammy: Pop Instrumental Album		

FRANCHI, Sergio
Born on 4/6/1926 in Cremona, Italy. Died of cancer on 5/1/1990 (age 64). Romantic tenor.

11/24/62	17	18		1 Romantic Italian Songs .... [F]		RCA Victor 2640
				also see #7 below		
2/9/63	66	21		2 Our Man From Italy		RCA Victor 2657
7/6/63	103	5		3 Broadway...I Love You		RCA Victor 2674
1/25/64	97	7		4 The Dream Duet..		RCA Victor 2675
				ANNA MOFFO & SERGIO FRANCHI		
3/27/65	114	4		5 Live At The Cocoanut Grove .... [L]		RCA Victor 3310
				recorded on 10/15/1964		
12/18/65	25ˣ	7		6 The Heart Of Christmas (Cuor' Di Natale) .... [X]		RCA Victor 3437
				Christmas charts: 25/'65, 48/'66, 108/'67, 55/'68		
9/5/98	167	1		7 Romantic Italian Songs .... [F-R]		RCA Victor 68902

Billboard			R I A A	ARTIST		
DEBUT	PEAK	WKS		Album Title	Catalog	Label & Number

FRANCIS, Connie
1960s: #27 / All-Time: #165

Born Concetta Rosa Maria Franconero on 12/12/1938 in Newark, New Jersey. Pop singer/actress. Appeared in the movies *Where The Boys Are, Follow The Boys, Looking For Love* and *When The Boys Meet The Girls*. Pop music's top female vocalist from 1958-64.

5/8/61	65	19		1 Connie Francis At The Copa .... [L]		MGM 3913
10/30/61	11	34		2 Never On Sunday And Other Title Songs From Motion Pictures		MGM 3965
4/14/62	47	17		3 Do The Twist...		MGM 4022
10/13/62	22	14		4 Country Music Connie Style		MGM 4079
6/15/63	108	5		5 Award Winning Motion Picture Hits		MGM 4048
10/5/63	94	17		6 Greatest American Waltzes		MGM 4145
12/14/63	16[X]	5		7 Christmas In My Heart .... [X]		MGM 3792
				first released in 1959; Christmas charts: 16/'63, 33/'64		
2/1/64	126	2		8 In The Summer Of His Years		MGM 4210
				a tribute to President **John F. Kennedy**		
12/5/64	149	2		9 A New Kind Of Connie...		MGM 4253
5/1/65	78	15		10 Connie Francis Sings For Mama		MGM 4294
				FOREIGN LANGUAGE ALBUMS:		
2/8/60	4	81		11 Italian Favorites		MGM 3791
12/12/60+	9	20		12 More Italian Favorites		MGM 3871
5/29/61	69	10		13 Jewish Favorites		MGM 3869
2/16/63	103	5		14 Modern Italian Hits		MGM 4102
10/19/63	70	13		15 Mala Femmena & Connie's Big Hits From Italy		MGM 4161
				GREATEST HITS & COMPILATIONS:		
2/22/60	17	100		16 Connie's Greatest Hits...		MGM 3793
7/3/61	39	17		17 More Greatest Hits		MGM 3942
8/25/62	111	9		18 Connie Francis Sings		MGM 4049
11/2/63+	68	23	●	19 The Very Best Of Connie Francis		MGM 4167
				SOUNDTRACKS:		
3/30/63	66	11		20 Follow The Boys..		MGM 4123
8/1/64	122	9		21 Looking For Love		MGM 4229
1/29/66	61	9		22 When The Boys Meet The Girls		MGM 4334

~ ~ ~ ~ ~ ~ ~ ~ ~ ~ **NON-CHARTED ALBUMS** ~ ~ ~ ~ ~ ~ ~ ~ ~ ~ ~

1958 **Who's Sorry Now**   1959 **My Thanks To You**
1959 **The Exciting Connie Francis**   1960 **Rock N' Roll Million Sellers**

FRANCIS, Sage
Born Paul Francis on 11/18/1977 in Providence, Rhode Island. Male rapper.

5/26/07	97	1		1 Human The Death Dance		Anti 86858

FRANCISCO, Don
Born Mario Kreutzberger on 12/28/1940 in Talca, Chile. Latin singer. Began hosting popular TV variety show in Chile in 1962.

11/20/04	192	1		1 Mi Homenaje Gigante A La Musica Nortena .... [F]		Univision 310171

FRANKE & THE KNOCKOUTS
Soft-rock band from New Brunswick, New Jersey: Franke Previte (vocals), Billy Elworthy (guitar), Blake Levinsohn (keyboards), Leigh Foxx (bass) and Claude LeHenaff (drums).

3/28/81	31	27		1 Franke & The Knockouts		Millennium 7755
4/10/82	48	18		2 Below The Belt		Millennium 7763

FRANKENREITER, Donavon
Born on 12/10/1972 in Downey, California; later based in Hawaii. Singer/songwriter/guitarist. Former professional surfer.

5/29/04	165	1		1 Donavon Frankenreiter..		Brushfire 002438
6/24/06	105	2		2 Move By Yourself		Lost Highway 006402
9/6/08	98	1		3 Pass It Around		Lost Highway 011589

FRANKIE GOES TO HOLLYWOOD
Dance-rock band from Liverpool, England: William "Holly" Johnson and Paul Rutherford (vocals), Brian Nash (guitar), Mark O'Toole (bass) and Peter Gill (drums). Group's name inspired by publicity recounting **Frank Sinatra**'s move into the movie industry.

11/24/84	33	41		1 Welcome To The Pleasuredome		Island 90232 [2]
11/15/86	88	13		2 Liverpool		Island 90546

FRANKIE J
Born Francisco Javier Bautista on 12/14/1978 in Tijuana, Mexico; raised in San Diego, California. Latino singer/songwriter/producer.

6/14/03	53	15		1 What's A Man To Do?		Columbia 90073
4/9/05	3[1]	36	▲	2 The One		Columbia 90945
7/1/06	198	1		3 Un Nuevo Dia .... [F]		Columbia 96494
11/4/06	30	3		4 Priceless		Columbia 85084

FRANKLIN, Aretha   1960s: #48 / 1970s: #32 / All-Time: #21

Born on 3/25/1942 in Memphis, Tennessee; raised in Detroit, Michigan. Legendary R&B singer/songwriter/pianist. Known as "The Queen of Soul." Daughter of famous gospel preacher Rev. Cecil L. Franklin, pastor of Detroit's New Bethel Baptist Church. Signed to Columbia Records in 1960 as a jazz-styled singer. Dramatic turn in style and success after signing with Atlantic in 1966 and working with producer Jerry Wexler. Her sisters Carolyn and **Erma Franklin** also recorded. Married to her manager/co-writer Ted White (1961-69) and actor Glynn Turman (1978-84). Appeared in the 1980 movie *The Blues Brothers*.

AWARDS: Grammys: Legend 1991 / Lifetime Achievement 1994 ★ R&R Hall of Fame: 1987

DEBUT	PEAK	WKS					Label & Number
11/17/62	69	12		1	The Tender, The Moving, The Swinging Aretha Franklin		Columbia 1876 / 8676
12/19/64+	84	13		2	Runnin' Out Of Fools		Columbia 2281 / 9081
8/6/66	132	4		3	Soul Sister		Columbia 2521 / 9321
4/8/67	2^3	79	●	4	I Never Loved A Man The Way I Love You		Atlantic 8139
					Grammy: Hall of Fame ★ RS500 #83		
8/26/67	5	41		5	Aretha Arrives		Atlantic 8150
2/24/68	2^2	52	●	6	Aretha: Lady Soul		Atlantic 8176
					RS500 #84		
7/13/68	3^2	35	●	7	Aretha Now		Atlantic 8186
2/15/69	15	32		8	Aretha Franklin: Soul '69		Atlantic 8212
2/14/70	17	30		9	This Girl's In Love With You		Atlantic 8248
9/12/70	25	22		10	Spirit In The Dark		Atlantic 8265
2/19/72	11	31	●	11	Young, Gifted & Black		Atlantic 7213
					Grammy: Female R&B Vocal		
7/14/73	30	20		12	Hey Now Hey (The Other Side Of The Sky)		Atlantic 7265
3/16/74	14	25		13	Let Me In Your Life		Atlantic 7292
12/21/74+	57	13		14	With Everything I Feel In Me		Atlantic 18116
11/15/75	83	11		15	You		Atlantic 18151
6/19/76	18	24	●	16	Sparkle [S]		Atlantic 18176
6/18/77	49	19		17	Sweet Passion		Atlantic 19102
5/13/78	63	11		18	Almighty Fire		Atlantic 19161
10/13/79	146	6		19	La Diva		Atlantic 19248
10/25/80	47	30		20	Aretha		Arista 9538
8/29/81	36	17		21	Love All The Hurt Away		Arista 9552
8/14/82	23	30	●	22	Jump To It		Arista 9602
7/30/83	36	18		23	Get It Right		Arista 8019
					above 2 produced by Luther Vandross		
7/27/85	13	51	▲	24	Who's Zoomin' Who?		Arista 8286
11/15/86+	32	39	●	25	Aretha		Arista 8442
					Grammy: Female R&B Vocal		
5/20/89	55	18		26	Through The Storm		Arista 8572
8/10/91	153	7		27	What You See Is What You Sweat		Arista 8628
4/11/98	30	15	●	28	A Rose Is Still A Rose		Arista 18987
10/4/03	33	11		29	So Damn Happy		Arista 50174
12/1/07	54	7		30	Jewels In The Crown: Duets With The Queen		Arista 78668
11/29/08+	102	7		31	This Christmas [X]		DMI 516593
					Christmas charts: 26/'08, 37/'09		
12/26/09	199	1		32	This Christmas [X-R]		DMI 516593
					GREATEST HITS & COMPILATIONS:		
6/10/67	94	14		33	Aretha Franklin's Greatest Hits		Columbia 2673 / 9473
10/21/67	173	8		34	Take A Look		Columbia 2754 / 9554
6/24/72	160	9		35	In The Beginning/The World Of Aretha Franklin 1960-1967		Columbia 31355 [2]
10/3/81	209	2		36	The Legendary Queen Of Soul		Columbia 37377 [2]
					compilation of her Columbia recordings from 1960-66		
7/19/69	18	33		37	Aretha's Gold		Atlantic 8227
9/25/71	19	34		38	Aretha's Greatest Hits		Atlantic 8295
12/25/76+	135	8		39	Ten Years Of Gold		Atlantic 18204
3/12/94	85	29	▲	40	Greatest Hits (1980-1994)		Arista 18722
11/11/00	45^C	1	▲	41	The Very Best Of Aretha Franklin, Vol. 1		Rhino 71598
					first released in 1994		
					LIVE ALBUMS:		
7/10/65	101	8		42	Yeah!!!		Columbia 2351 / 9151
11/23/68+	13	20		43	Aretha In Paris		Atlantic 8207
					recorded on 5/7/1968 at the Olympia Theatre		
6/5/71	7	34	●	44	Aretha Live At Fillmore West		Atlantic 7205
6/17/72	7	23	▲^{2}	45	Amazing Grace		Atlantic 906 [2]
					Grammys: Soul Gospel Album / Hall of Fame		
					recorded at the New Temple Missionary Baptist Church in Los Angeles, California		
12/26/87+	106	16		46	One Lord, One Faith, One Baptism		Arista 8497 [2]
					Grammy: Soul Gospel Album		
					recorded in July 1987 at the New Bethel Baptist Church in Detroit, Michigan		

Billboard			R I A A	ARTIST Album Title	Catalog	Label & Number
DEBUT	PEAK	WKS				

FRANKLIN, Erma
Born on 3/13/1938 in Memphis, Tennessee; raised in Detroit, Michigan. Died of cancer on 9/7/2002 (age 64). R&B singer. Sister of **Aretha Franklin**.

| 10/18/69 | 199 | 2 | | 1 Soul Sister | | Brunswick 754147 |

FRANKLIN, Kirk
Born on 1/26/1970 in Fort Worth, Texas. Gospel singer/choir leader. Also see **God's Property** and **1NC**.

3/12/94+	58	36	▲	1 Kirk Franklin And The Family .... **[L]**		GospoCentric 2119
				recorded on 7/25/1992 at Grace Temple Church in Fort Worth, Texas		
11/25/95	60	8	●	2 Christmas.. Cat:#30/5 **[X]**		GospoCentric 72130
				Christmas charts: 9/'95, 25/'96, 26/'97		
5/18/96	23	58	▲	3 Whatcha Lookin' 4 .... **[L]**		GospoCentric 72127
				KIRK FRANKLIN AND THE FAMILY (above 3)		
				Grammy: Soul Gospel Album		
				recorded at the Calvary Temple in Dallas, Texas		
10/17/98	7	49	▲²	4 The Nu Nation Project		GospoCentric 90178
				Grammy: Soul Gospel Album		
3/9/02	4	47	▲	5 The Rebirth Of Kirk Franklin		GospoCentric 70037
10/22/05	13	57	▲	6 Hero		Fo Yo Soul 71019
11/25/06	74	6		7 Songs From The Storm, Volume 1		Fo Yo Soul 88401
1/5/08	33	23		8 The Fight Of My Life		Fo Yo Soul 16772
				Grammy: Contemporary R&B Gospel Album		

FRANKLIN, Rodney
Born on 9/16/1958 in Berkeley, California. Jazz pianist.

4/19/80	104	13		1 You'll Never Know .... **[I]**		Columbia 36122
11/29/80	207	1		2 Rodney Franklin .... **[I]**		Columbia 36747
10/17/81	204	6		3 Endless Flight		Columbia 37154
1/22/83	190	3		4 Learning To Love		Columbia 38198
2/25/84	187	3		5 Marathon		Columbia 38953

FRANKS, Michael
Born on 9/18/1944 in La Jolla, California. Jazz-pop singer/songwriter.

7/31/76	131	13	●	1 The Art Of Tea .... Cat:#13/8		Reprise 2230
2/19/77	119	9	●	2 Sleeping Gypsy		Warner 3004
4/8/78	90	10		3 Burchfield Nines..		Warner 3167
3/17/79	68	16		4 Tiger In The Rain		Warner 3294
5/10/80	83	21		5 One Bad Habit		Warner 3427
1/30/82	45	14		6 Objects Of Desire		Warner 3648
10/29/83	141	11		7 Passionfruit		Warner 23962
6/15/85	137	27		8 Skin Dive		Warner 25275
8/1/87	147	11		9 The Camera Never Lies		Warner 25570
7/7/90	121	17		10 Blue Pacific		Reprise 26183

FRANTI, Michael, & Spearhead
Hip-hop band from San Francisco, California: Michael Franti (male vocals; born on 4/21/1966), Trinna Simmons (female vocals), Ras Zulu (chanter), David James (guitar), Carl Young (keyboards), Oneida James (bass) and James Gray (drums).

| 8/12/06 | 125 | 3 | | 1 Yell Fire! .... | | Anti 86807 |
| 9/27/08 | 39 | 13 | | 2 All Rebel Rockers.. | | Boo Boo Wax 86906 |

FRANZ FERDINAND
Punk-rock band from Glasgow, Scotland: Alex Kapranos (vocals, guitar), Nick McCarthy (guitar), Bob Hardy (bass) and Paul Thomson (drums). Group named after the Austrian archduke whose murder helped spark World War I.

3/27/04	32	56	▲	1 Franz Ferdinand		Domino 27
10/22/05	8	16	●	2 You Could Have It So Much Better		Domino 94800
2/14/09	9	9		3 Tonight: Franz Ferdinand		Domino 37255

FRASER, Andy
Born on 8/7/1952 in London, England. Rock singer/bassist. Formerly with **John Mayall**'s Bluesbreakers, **Free** and **Sharks**.

| 7/7/84 | 209 | 1 | | 1 Fine Fine Line .... | | Island 90153 |

FRASER, Brooke
Born on 12/15/1983 in Wellington, New Zealand. Adult Alternative singer/songwriter.

| 7/19/08 | 90 | 1 | | 1 Albertine .... | | Wood And Bone 001 |

FRASER & DEBOLT
Folk duo from Canada: Anthony Fraser and Donna DeBolt.

| 2/13/71 | 206 | 1 | | 1 Fraser & DeBolt .... | | Columbia 30381 |

FRATELLIS, The
Alternative-rock trio from Glasgow, Scotland: John Lawler (vocals, guitar), Barry Wallace (bass) and Gordon McRory (drums).

| 3/31/07 | 48 | 12 | | 1 Costello Music .... | | Cherrytree 008561 |
| 6/28/08 | 80 | 2 | | 2 Here We Stand .... | | Cherrytree 011372 |

FRATIANNE, Linda
Born on 8/2/1960 in Los Angeles, California. World champion figure skater.

| 2/20/82 | 174 | 7 | | 1 Dance & Exercise With The Hits .... | | Columbia 37653 |
| | | | | music performed by The Beachwood All-Stars (studio group) | | |

FRAY, The
Alternative pop-rock band from Denver, Colorado: Isaac Slade (vocals, piano), Joe King (guitar), Dave Welsh (bass) and Ben Wysocki (drums).

DEBUT	PEAK	WKS			
10/1/05+	14	92	▲² 1 How To Save A Life.. Cat:#18/14		Epic 93931
2/21/09	❶¹	50	● 2 The Fray		Epic 10202

FRAYSER BOY
Born Cedric Coleman in Memphis, Tennessee. Male rapper.

| 9/13/03 | 178 | 1 | 1 Gone On That Bay.. | | Hypnotize Minds 3606 |
| 7/30/05 | 124 | 2 | 2 Me Being Me .... | | Hypnotize Minds 68559 |

FREAK NASTY
Born Eric Timmons in Puerto Rico; raised in New Orleans, Louisiana. Male rapper.

| 4/19/97 | 132 | 12 | 1 Controversee...That's Life...And That's The Way It Is... | | Power 2111 |

FREBERG, Stan
Born on 8/7/1926 in Pasadena, California. Top pop music satirist. Did several cartoon voices. Later had a highly successful advertising career.

| 7/3/61 | 34 | 24 | 1 Stan Freberg Presents The United States Of America .... [C] | | Capitol 1573 |

Grammy: Hall of Fame

~ ~ ~ ~ ~ ~ ~ ~ ~ ~ ~ **NON-CHARTED ALBUMS** ~ ~ ~ ~ ~ ~ ~ ~ ~ ~ ~
1957 **A Child's Garden Of Freberg**   1964 **The Best Of Stan Freberg**

FRED, John, & His Playboy Band
Born John Fred Gourrier on 5/8/1941 in Baton Rouge, Louisiana. Died on 4/15/2005 (age 63). Pop-rock singer/songwriter.

| 2/3/68 | 154 | 10 | 1 Agnes English .... | | Paula 2197 |

later released as Judy In Disguise With Glasses

FREDDIE AND THE DREAMERS
Pop band from Manchester, England: Freddie Garrity (vocals; born on 11/14/1936; died of emphysema on 5/19/2006, age 69), Derek Quinn (guitar), Roy Crewsdon (guitar), Peter Birrell (bass) and Bernie Dwyer (drums; died of cancer on 12/4/2002, age 62).

4/17/65	19	19	1 Freddie & The Dreamers.......................................		Mercury 61017
5/8/65	86	10	2 I'm Telling You Now		Tower 5003
6/19/65	85	12	3 Do The Freddie		Mercury 61026

FREDDY JONES BAND, The
Rock band formed in Chicago, Illinois: Marty Lloyd (vocals, guitar), Wayne Healy (vocals, guitar), brothers Rob Bonaccorsi (guitar) and Jim Bonaccorsi (bass) and Simon Horrocks (drums).

| 8/26/95 | 186 | 1 | 1 North Avenue Wake Up Call.................................... | | Capricorn 42040 |

FREE
Rock band formed in England: **Paul Rodgers** (vocals), **Paul Kossoff** (guitar), **Andy Fraser** (bass) and Simon Kirke (drums). Kossoff and Fraser left in 1972, replaced by Tetsu Yamauchi (bass, later with **Faces**) and John "Rabbit" Bundrick (keyboards). Kossoff (died on 3/19/1976 of heart failure) formed **Back Street Crawler**. Rodgers and Kirke formed **Bad Company** in 1974. Rodgers was also lead singer of **The Firm** and **The Law**.

9/13/69	197	2	1 Tons Of Sobs...		A&M 4198
9/5/70	17	27	2 Fire And Water..		A&M 4268
2/27/71	190	2	3 Highway		A&M 4287
9/11/71	89	8	4 Free Live!.. [L]		A&M 4306
5/27/72	69	16	5 Free At Last		A&M 4349
2/3/73	47	16	6 Heartbreaker		Island 9217
5/24/75	120	7	7 Best Of Free.. [G]		A&M 3663

FREE BEER
Male rock trio formed in Los Angeles, California: Sandy Allen (vocals, guitar), Michael Packer (bass) and Caleb Potter (drums).

| 8/30/75 | 203 | 3 | 1 Free Beer... | | Southwind 6402 |

FREED, Alan — see VARIOUS ARTIST COMPILATIONS

FREEKEY ZEKEY
Born Ezekiel Giles in Harlem, New York. Male rapper. Brother of **Cam'ron**. Member of **The Diplomats**.

| 8/11/07 | 154 | 1 | 1 Book Of Ezekiel .... | | Diplomatic Man 196924 |

FREEMAN, Bobby
Born on 6/13/1940 in San Francisco, California. Black rock and roll singer.

~ ~ ~ ~ ~ ~ ~ ~ ~ ~ ~ **NON-CHARTED ALBUMS** ~ ~ ~ ~ ~ ~ ~ ~ ~ ~ ~
1959 **Do You Wanna Dance?**   1964 **C'mon And S-W-I-M**
1962 **Twist With Bobby Freeman**

FREEMAN, Russ — see RIPPINGTONS, The

FREE MOVEMENT, The
R&B vocal group from Los Angeles, California: brothers Adrian Jefferson and Claude Jefferson, Godoy Colbert, Cheryl Conley, Josephine Brown and Jennifer Gates.

| 1/29/72 | 167 | 8 | 1 I've Found Someone Of My Own .... | | Columbia 31136 |

FREEWAY
Born Leslie Pridgen on 7/8/1979 in Philadelphia, Pennsylvania. Male rapper.

DEBUT	PEAK	WKS		Album		Label & Number
3/15/03	5	14		1 Philadelphia Freeway		Roc-A-Fella 586920
12/8/07	42	3		2 Free At Last		Roc-A-Fella 004853
6/6/09	99	1		3 Philadelphia Freeway 2		Real Talk 64

FREHLEY, Ace
Born Paul Frehley on 4/27/1951 in the Bronx, New York. Rock singer/guitarist. Member of **Kiss**.

DEBUT	PEAK	WKS		Album		Label & Number
10/14/78+	26	23	▲	1 Ace Frehley		Casablanca 7121
5/23/87	43	25		2 Frehley's Comet		Megaforce 81749
2/27/88	84	10		3 Live + 1	[L]	Megaforce 81826
				recorded on 9/4/1987 at the Aragon Ballroom in Chicago, Illinois		
6/11/88	81	13		4 Second Sighting		Megaforce 81862
				FREHLEY'S COMET (above 2)		
11/11/89	102	9		5 Trouble Walkin'		Megaforce 82042
10/3/09	27	4		6 Anomaly		Bronx Born 90176

FREIBERG, David
Born on 8/24/1938 in Boston, Massachusetts; later based in San Francisco, California. Rock bassist. Member of **Quicksilver Messenger Service** and **Jefferson Starship**.

DEBUT	PEAK	WKS		Album		Label & Number
6/23/73	120	12		1 Baron Von Tollbooth & The Chrome Nun		Grunt 0148
				PAUL KANTNER, GRACE SLICK & DAVID FREIBERG		

FRENCH, Nicki
Born on 9/26/1964 in Carlisle, Cumbria, England; raised in Tenterden, Kent, England. Female dance singer.

DEBUT	PEAK	WKS		Album		Label & Number
7/8/95	151	4		1 Secrets		Critique 15436

FRENCH KISS
Disco trio from New York: Lamarr Stevens, Muffi Durham and Yvette Johnson.

DEBUT	PEAK	WKS		Album		Label & Number
6/2/79	210	1		1 Panic		Polydor 6197

FRENTE!
Folk-pop band from Melbourne, Australia: Angie Hart (vocals), Simon Austin (guitar), Tim O'Connor (bass) and Mark Picton (drums). Band name is Spanish for "Front."

DEBUT	PEAK	WKS		Album		Label & Number
5/14/94	75	20		1 Marvin The Album		Mammoth 92390

FRESH, Mannie
Born Byron Thomas on 3/20/1974 in New Orleans, Louisiana. Male rapper. Member of **Big Tymers** and **Cash Money Millionaires**.

DEBUT	PEAK	WKS		Album		Label & Number
1/8/05	47	7		1 The Mind Of Mannie Fresh		Cash Money 002808

FRESH PRINCE — see D.J. JAZZY JEFF

FREY, Glenn
Born on 11/6/1948 in Detroit, Michigan. Rock singer/songwriter/guitarist. Founding member of the **Eagles**.

DEBUT	PEAK	WKS		Album		Label & Number
6/26/82	32	38	●	1 No Fun Aloud		Asylum 60129
7/14/84+	22	65	●	2 The Allnighter		MCA 5501
9/3/88	36	19		3 Soul Searchin'		MCA 6239

FRIDA
Born Anni-Frid Lyngstad on 11/15/1945 in Narvik, Norway. Female singer. Member of **Abba**.

DEBUT	PEAK	WKS		Album		Label & Number
11/13/82+	41	28		1 Something's Going On		Atlantic 80018
				produced by **Phil Collins**		

FRIDAY NIGHT BOYS, The
Punk-rock band from Fairfax, Virginia: Andrew Goldstein (vocals), Mike Toohey (guitar), Robby Reider (bass) and Chris Barrett (drums).

DEBUT	PEAK	WKS		Album		Label & Number
6/27/09	198	1		1 Off The Deep End		Photo Finish 518477

FRIEDMAN, Dean
Born on 4/21/1955 in Paramus, New Jersey. Pop singer/songwriter/pianist.

DEBUT	PEAK	WKS		Album		Label & Number
6/4/77	192	6		1 Dean Friedman		Lifesong 6008

FRIEDMAN, Kinky
Born Richard Friedman on 10/31/1944 in Chicago, Illinois; raised in Austin, Texas. Country singer/songwriter/guitarist.

DEBUT	PEAK	WKS		Album		Label & Number
2/1/75	132	6		1 Kinky Friedman		ABC 829

FRIENDS OF DISTINCTION, The
R&B vocal group from Los Angeles, California: Floyd Butler, Harry Elston, Jessica Cleaves and Barbara Jean Love. Butler died of a heart attack on 4/29/1990 (age 49).

DEBUT	PEAK	WKS		Album		Label & Number
5/3/69	35	25		1 Grazin'		RCA Victor 4149
10/25/69	173	6		2 Highly Distinct		RCA Victor 4212
3/28/70	68	21		3 Real Friends		RCA Victor 4313
10/31/70	179	3		4 Whatever		RCA Victor 4408
8/7/71	166	7		5 Friends & People		RCA Victor 4492

FRIJID PINK
Male rock band from Detroit, Michigan: Kelly Green (vocals), Gary Thompson (guitar), Tom Beaudry (bass) and Rich Stevens (drums).

1/24/70	11	30	1 Frijid Pink		Parrot 71033
10/31/70	149	12	2 Defrosted		Parrot 71041

FRIPP, Robert
Born on 5/16/1946 in Wimbourne, Dorset, England. Rock guitarist. Founder of **King Crimson**.

5/26/79	79	14	1 Exposure		EG 6201
4/26/80	110	6	2 God Save The Queen/Under Heavy Manners	[I]	Polydor 6266
4/4/81	90	7	3 The League Of Gentlemen	[I]	Polydor 6317
11/6/82	60	11	4 I Advance Masked	[I]	A&M 4913
10/20/84	155	5	5 Bewitched	[I]	A&M 5011

ANDY SUMMERS & ROBERT FRIPP (above 2)

FROM AUTUMN TO ASHES
Rock band from Long Island, New York: Benjamin Perri (vocals), Scott Gross (guitar), Brian Deneeve (guitar), Mike Pilato (bass) and Francis Mark (drums).

9/27/03	73	2	1 The Fiction We Live		Vagrant 386
9/17/05	58	2	2 Abandon Your Friends		Vagrant 414
4/28/07	74	2	3 Holding A Wolf By The Ears		Vagrant 459

FROM FIRST TO LAST
Hard-rock band formed in Los Angeles, California: Matt Good (vocals, guitar), Travis Richter (guitar), Matt Manning (bass) and Derek Bloom (drums).

4/8/06	25	5	1 Heroine		Epitaph 86779
5/24/08	81	2	2 From First To Last		Suretone 010671

FRONT, The
Hard-rock band from Kansas City, Missouri: brothers Michael Franano (vocals) and Bobby Franano (keyboards), Mike Greene (guitar), Randy Jordan (bass) and Shane Miller (drums).

2/3/90	118	14	1 The Front		Columbia 45260

FRONT 242
Industrial dance band from Brussels, Belgium: vocalists Jean-Luc De Meyer and Richard Jonckheere with instrumentalists Daniel Bressanutti and Patrick Codenys.

2/16/91	95	12	1 Tyranny For You		Epic 46998
6/12/93	166	1	2 06:21:03:11 Up Evil		Epic 53433

FROST
Psycheldelic-rock band from Detroit, Michigan: **Richard Wagner** (vocals, guitar), Don Hartman (guitar), Gordy Garris (bass) and Bob Riggs (drums).

6/21/69	168	10	1 Frost Music		Vanguard 6520
11/29/69+	148	8	2 Rock And Roll Music	[L]	Vanguard 6541
			recorded at the Grande Ballroom in Detroit, Michigan		
10/17/70	197	2	3 Through The Eyes Of Love		Vanguard 6556

FROST — see KID FROST

FROZEN GHOST
Pop-rock duo from Canada: Arnold Lanni (vocals, guitar, keyboards) and Wolf Hassel (bass). Both were members of **Sheriff**.

4/11/87	107	13	1 Frozen Ghost		Atlantic 81736

FRUSCIANTE, John
Born on 3/5/1970 in Queens, New York; raised in Santa Monica, California. Rock singer/guitarist. Member of the **Red Hot Chili Peppers**.

3/13/04	191	1	1 Shadows Collide With People		Warner 48660
2/7/09	151	2	2 The Empyrean		Record Collection 101118

FRYE, David
Born in June 1934 in Brooklyn, New York. Comedian/impressionist. Best known for his impression of President Nixon.

12/27/69+	19	18	1 I Am The President	[C]	Elektra 75006
3/27/71	123	6	2 Radio Free Nixon	[C]	Elektra 74085
12/11/71+	60	13	3 Richard Nixon Superstar	[C]	Buddah 5097
8/11/73	45	15	4 Richard Nixon: A Fantasy	[C]	Buddah 1600

FUEL
Rock band from Harrisburg, Pennsylvania: Brett Scallions (vocals), Carl Bell (guitar), Jeff Abercrombie (bass) and Kevin Miller (drums).

4/18/98	77	35	▲ 1 Sunburn		550 Music 68554
10/7/00	17	60	▲² 2 Something Like Human		550 Music 69436
10/11/03	15	14	3 Natural Selection		Epic 86392
8/25/07	42	3	4 Angels & Devils		Epic 00952

Billboard			R I A A	ARTIST		
DEBUT	PEAK	WKS		Album Title	Catalog	Label & Number

FUGAZI
Punk-rock band from Washington DC: Ian MacKaye (vocals, guitar), Guy Picciotto (guitar), Joe Lally (bass) and Brendan Canty (drums).

7/3/93	153	4		1 **In On The Kill Taker**		Dischord 70
7/1/95	126	5		2 **Red Medicine**		Dischord 90
5/16/98	138	2		3 **End Hits**...		Dischord 110
11/3/01	151	1		4 **The Argument**		Dischord 130

FUGEES (REFUGEE CAMP)
Two-man, one-woman hip-hop group: rappers/producers/cousins **Wyclef Jean** and **Pras Michel** (both of Haitian descent), and rapper/singer **Lauryn Hill** (from East Orange, New Jersey). Fugees is short for refugees.

3/2/96	❶⁴	64	▲⁶	1 **The Score** .... **Cat:#40/4**		Ruffhouse 67147
				Grammy: Rap Album ★ RS500 #477		
12/14/96+	127	13		2 **Bootleg Versions**.. **[K]**		Ruffhouse 67904

FUGS, The
Eclectic-rock trio formed in New York: Tuli Kupferberg (vocals), Ed Sanders (guitar) and Ken Weaver (drums).

10/29/66	142	4		1 **The Fugs First Album**		ESP 1018
7/2/66	95	26		2 **The Fugs**		ESP 1028
10/19/68	167	10		3 **It Crawled Into My Hand, Honest**		Reprise 6305

FULL BLOODED
Born in New Orleans, Louisiana. Male rapper.

12/19/98	112	1		1 **Memorial Day**		No Limit 50027

FULLER, Bobby, Four
Born on 10/22/1942 in Baytown, Texas. Died mysteriously of asphyxiation on 7/18/1966 (age 23). Rock and roll singer/guitarist. His group included his brother Randy Fuller (bass), Jim Reese (guitar) and DeWayne Quirico (drums).

4/2/66	144	2		1 **The Bobby Fuller Four**..		Mustang 901
				~ ~ ~ ~ ~ ~ ~ ~ ~ ~ **NON-CHARTED ALBUM** ~ ~ ~ ~ ~ ~ ~ ~ ~ ~		
				1965 **KRLA King Of The Wheels**		

FULLER, Jerry
Born Jerrell Lee Fuller on 11/19/1938 in Fort Worth, Texas. Pop-rock and roll singer/songwriter/producer.

				~ ~ ~ ~ ~ ~ ~ ~ ~ ~ **NON-CHARTED ALBUM** ~ ~ ~ ~ ~ ~ ~ ~ ~ ~		
				1960 **Teenage Love**		

FULL FORCE
Rap group from Brooklyn, New York: brothers Brian George, Paul George and "Bow Legged" Lou George, with their cousins Gerry Charles, Hugh "Junior" Clarke and Curt Bedeau. Assembled and produced **Lisa Lisa & Cult Jam**. Production work for numerous others.

2/15/86	160	8		1 **Full Force**		Columbia 40117
8/30/86	141	13		2 **Full Force Get Busy 1 Time!**...		Columbia 40395
12/5/87	126	11		3 **Guess Who's Comin' To The Crib?**		Columbia 40894

FULL MOON
Jazz-rock band formed in Los Angeles, California: Buzz Feiten (vocals, guitar), **Neil Larsen** (keyboards), Willie Weeks (bass) and Art Rodriguez (drums). The first two formed the **Larsen-Feiten Band**; both are prolific session musicians.

2/6/82	206	6		1 **Full Moon**		Warner 3585
				FULL MOON Featuring Neil Larsen & Buzz Feiten		

FUN
Pop-punk trio formed in New York: Nate Ruess (vocals, guitar), Andrew Dost (bass) and Jack Antonoff (drums).

9/12/09	71	1		1 **Aim And Ignite**..		Nettwerk 30847

FUN BOY THREE
Ska-rock trio from England: Neville Staples and Terry Hall (vocals), with Lynval Golding (guitar). All were members of the **Specials**.

7/30/83	104	7		1 **Waiting**		Chrysalis 41417

FUNERAL FOR A FRIEND
Hard-rock band from Bridgend, South Wales: Matt "The Rat" Davies (vocals), Kris Roberts (guitar), Darren Smith (guitar), Gareth Davies (bass) and Randy Richards (drums).

7/2/05	139	1		1 **Hours**...		Ferret 62386
6/2/07	135	1		2 **Tales Don't Tell Themselves**		Might 13060

FUNKADELIC
Ensemble of nearly 40 musicians assembled by **George Clinton** (producer/songwriter/lead singer) that also recorded as **Parliament**. In 1968, Clinton formed Funkadelic with rhythm section of his soul group The Parliaments. Although on different labels, Funkadelic and Parliament shared the same personnel which included former members of **The JB's**: brothers Phelps "Catfish" (guitar) and William **"Bootsy"** Collins (bass), Frank **"Kash" Waddy** (drums) and horn players Maceo Parker and **Fred Wesley**. Known as "A Parliafunkadelicament Thang," this funk corporation fostered various offshoot bands, including **The Brides Of Funkenstein**. Concert tours featured elaborate stagings and characters. In 1977, vocalists Clarence "Fuzzy" Haskins, Calvin Simon and Grady Thomas split from Clinton and recorded as **Funkadelic** for LAX in 1981. The corporation disassembled in the early 1980s. Clinton signed his first solo recording contract in 1982.

AWARD: R&R Hall of Fame: 1997

3/21/70	126	17		1 **Funkadelic**		Westbound 2000
10/31/70	92	11		2 **Free Your Mind...And Your Ass Will Follow**		Westbound 2001
8/14/71	108	16		3 **Maggot Brain**		Westbound 2007
				RS500 #486		

FUNKADELIC — cont'd

6/17/72	123	15		4 America Eats Its Young		Westbound 2020 [2]
7/21/73	112	13		5 Cosmic Slop		Westbound 2022
9/7/74	163	5		6 Standing On The Verge Of Getting It On...................................		Westbound 1001
7/19/75	102	16		7 Let's Take It To The Stage		Westbound 215
10/9/76	103	10		8 Tales Of Kidd Funkadelic		Westbound 227
11/27/76	96	12		9 Hardcore Jollies		Warner 2973
10/7/78	16	22	▲	10 One Nation Under A Groove		Warner 3209
				RS500 #177		
10/13/79	18	17	●	11 Uncle Jam Wants You..		Warner 3371
8/29/81	105	4		12 The Electric Spanking Of War Babies		Warner 3482

FUNKADELIC
Group features three original vocalists of The Parliaments: Clarence "Fuzzy" Haskins, Calvin Simon and Grady Thomas. Split from **George Clinton's Parliament/Funkadelic** corporation in 1977.

4/11/81	151	4		1 Connections & Disconnections		LAX 37087

FUNKDOOBIEST
Rap trio from Los Angeles, California: Ralph Medrano, Jason Vasquez and Tyrone Pacheno.

5/22/93	56	9		1 Which Doobie U B?..		Immortal 53212
7/22/95	115	3		2 Brothas Doobie		Immortal 64195

FUNK INC.
Instrumental funk band from Indianapolis, Indiana: Steve Weakley (guitar), Bobby Watley (organ), Eugene Barr (sax), Cecil Hunt (congas) and Jimmy Munford (drums).

2/26/72	211	2		1 Funk Inc.	[I]	Prestige 10031

FUNKMASTER FLEX
Born Aston Taylor in Brooklyn, New York. Black rap DJ/producer.

11/25/95	108	14		1 Funkmaster Flex: The Mix Tape Volume I...............................		Loud 66805
3/1/97	19	16	●	2 Funkmaster Flex: The Mix Tape Volume II..............................		Loud 67472
8/29/98	4	11	●	3 Funkmaster Flex: The Mix Tape Volume III.............................		Loud 67647
12/23/00	26	17	●	4 Funkmaster Flex: The Mix Tape Volume IV		Loud 1961
12/25/99	35	15	●	5 The Tunnel		Def Jam 538258
				FUNKMASTER FLEX & BIG KAP		

FUNKY COMMUNICATION COMMITTEE
Pop band formed in Los Angeles, California: Dennis Clifton (vocals, guitar), J.B. Christman (vocals, keyboards), Steve Gooch (guitar), Lonnie Ledford (bass) and Jim "Be-Bop" Evans (drums). Clifton died of cancer on 1/1/2008 (age 54).

9/8/79	192	2		1 Baby I Want You..		Free Flight 3405

FUN LOVIN' CRIMINALS
Eclectic hip-hop trio formed in Manhattan, New York: Huey Morgan (vocals, guitar), Brian Leiser (bass, keyboards) and Steve Borgovini (drums).

10/5/96	144	12		1 Come Find Yourself		EMI 35703

FURAY, Richie
Born on 5/9/1944 in Yellow Springs, Ohio. Folk-rock singer/songwriter. Member of **Buffalo Springfield**, **Poco**, and **The Souther, Hillman, Furay Band**.

8/7/76	130	8		1 I've Got A Reason		Asylum 1067

FURTADO, Nelly
Born on 12/2/1978 in Victoria, British Columbia, Canada (of Portugese parentage). Female Adult Alternative singer/songwriter.

1/13/01	24	79	▲²	1 Whoa, Nelly!...		DreamWorks 450217
12/13/03	38	11	●	2 Folklore		DreamWorks 001007
7/8/06	❶¹	70	▲	3 Loose		Mosley 006300
10/3/09	39	3		4 Mi Plan	[F]	Nelstar 013318

FURTHER SEEMS FOREVER
Rock band from Pompano Beach, Florida: Jason Gleason (vocals), Josh Colbert (guitar), Derick Cordoba (guitar), Chad Neptune (bass) and Steve Kleisath (drums).

3/1/03	133	2		1 How To Start A Fire		Tooth & Nail 39418
9/11/04	122	1		2 Hide Nothing		Tooth & Nail 97788

FU-SCHNICKENS
Hip-hop trio from Brooklyn, New York: Larry "Poc Fu" Maturine, Rod "Chip Fu" Roachford and James "Moc Fu" Jones.

4/4/92	64	20	●	1 F.U. "Don't Take It Personal"		Jive 41472
11/12/94	81	4		2 Nervous Breakdown		Jive 41519

FUSE ONE
All-star jazz band: **George Benson**, **Tom Browne**, **Stanley Clarke**, Ronnie Foster, **Eric Gale**, **Wynton Marsalis**, Ndugu, **Stanley Turrentine** and **Dave Valentin**.

2/13/82	139	8		1 Silk	[I]	CTI 9006

FUTURE LEADERS OF THE WORLD
Rock band from Buffalo, New York: Phil Tayler (vocals), Jake Stutevoss (guitar), Bill Hershey (bass) and Carl Messina (drums).

10/23/04	153	1		1 LVL IV		Epic 89192

DEBUT	PEAK	WKS		ARTIST / Album Title	Catalog	Label & Number
				FUZZ, The		
				Female R&B vocal trio from Washington DC: Sheila Young, Barbara Gilliam and Val Williams.		
10/2/71	196	3		1 The Fuzz		Calla 2001

G

DEBUT	PEAK	WKS		ARTIST / Album Title	Catalog	Label & Number
				GABEL, Tom		
				Born on 11/8/1980 in Gainesville, Florida. Punk-rock singer/songwriter. Lead singer of **Against Me!**		
11/15/08	185	1		1 Heart Burns .... [EP]		Sire 516456
				GABRIEL, Ana		
				Born Maria Young on 12/10/1955 in Guamuchil, Mexico. Latin singer. No relation to Juan Gabriel.		
9/17/05	173	10		1 Historia De Una Reina .... [F-K]		Sony Discos 95902
11/25/06	166	1		2 La Reina Canta A Mexico .... [F-K]		Sony 01721
11/24/07	192	1		3 Los Gabriel...Simplemente Amigos .... [F-K]		Sony 17489
4/12/08	119	10		4 Los Gabriel...Cantan A Mexico .... [F]		Sony 24734
				JUAN GABRIEL & ANA GABRIEL (above 2)		
				GABRIEL, Juan		
				Born Alberto Valadez on 1/7/1950 in Cotija, Mexico. Latin singer. No relation to Ana Gabriel.		
5/24/97	152	3		1 Juntos Otra Vez .... [F]		Ariola 47805 [2]
				JUAN GABRIEL & ROCIO DURCAL		
4/22/06	92	11		2 La Historia Del Divo .... [F-K]		Sony 81079
11/24/07	192	1		3 Los Gabriel...Simplemente Amigos .... [F-K]		Sony 17489
4/12/08	119	10		4 Los Gabriel...Cantan A Mexico .... [F]		Sony 24734
				JUAN GABRIEL & ANA GABRIEL (above 2)		
				GABRIEL, Peter **All-Time: #270**		
				Born on 2/13/1950 in Woking, Surrey, England. Pop-rock singer/songwriter. Lead singer of **Genesis** from 1966-75. Scored movies *Birdy* and *The Last Temptation Of Christ*. In 1982, financed the World of Music Arts and Dance (WOMAD) festival.		
3/12/77	38	17		1 Peter Gabriel .... Cat:#28/33		Atco 147
7/22/78	45	10		2 Peter Gabriel		Atlantic 19181
6/21/80	22	29		3 Peter Gabriel		Mercury 3848
10/2/82	28	31	●	4 Peter Gabriel (Security)		Geffen 2011
				all of above are different albums		
6/25/83	44	16	●	5 Peter Gabriel/Plays Live .... [L]		Geffen 4012 [2]
4/20/85	162	7		6 Birdy .... [I-S]		Geffen 24070
6/14/86	2³	93	▲⁵	7 So Cat:#14/32		Geffen 24088
				RS500 #187		
7/1/89	60	14	●	8 Passion: Music For The Last Temptation Of Christ .... [I-S]		Geffen 24206 [2]
				Grammy: New Age Album		
12/22/90+	48	28	▲²	9 Shaking The Tree - Sixteen Golden Greats .... Cat:#33/9 [G]		Geffen 24326
10/17/92	2¹	53	▲	10 Us		Geffen 24473
10/1/94	23	12	●	11 Secret World Live .... [L]		Geffen 24722 [2]
				recorded on 11/16/1993 in Modena, Italy		
10/12/02	9	9		12 Up		Real World 493388
11/22/03	100	3		13 Hit .... [G]		Real World 001486 [2]
				GAELIC STORM		
				Celtic-rock band from Santa Monica, California: Patrick Murphy, Steve Twigger, Jessie Burns, Ryan Lacey and Peter Purvis.		
7/26/08	177	1		1 What's The Rumpus?		Lost Again 20081
				GAFFIGAN, Jim		
				Born on 7/7/1966 in Chesterton, Indiana. Stand-up comedian.		
4/18/09	56	5		1 King Baby .... [C]		Comedy Central 0079
				GAHAN, Dave		
				Born on 5/9/1962 in Epping, Essex, England. Lead singer of **Depeche Mode**.		
6/21/03	127	1		1 Paper Monsters		Mute 48471
11/10/07	120	1		2 Hourglass...		Mute 08721
				GAINSBOURG, Charlotte		
				Born on 7/21/1971 in London, England; raised in Paris, France. Pop singer. Daughter of **Jane Birkin & Sergie Gainsbourg**.		
5/12/07	196	1		1 5:55		Because 94703
				GAITHER, Bill & Gloria, And Their Homecoming Friends		
				Legendary gospel artist Bill Gaither (born on 3/28/1936 in Alexandria, Indiana) formed the **Gaither Vocal Band** in the early 1990s, and his group, along with dozens of guest gospel artists ("Their Homecoming Friends"), perform live inspirational concerts throughout the year. Gloria Sickal was born on 3/4/1942. They were married in 1962.		
4/10/99	93	2		1 Kennedy Center Homecoming .... [L]		Spring House 42213
				Grammy: Southern Gospel Album		
11/13/99	98	3		2 Mountain Homecoming .... [L]		Spring House 42220
11/13/99	122	2		3 I'll Meet You On The Mountain .... [L]		Spring House 42221
3/4/00	163	5		4 Good News .... [L]		Spring House 42253
5/13/00	126	3		5 Memphis Homecoming .... [L]		Spring House 42266
5/13/00	145	2		6 Oh, My, Glory! .... [L]		Spring House 42267

DEBUT	PEAK	WKS	R I A A	ARTIST / Album Title	Catalog	Label & Number
				GAITHER, Bill & Gloria, And Their Homecoming Friends — cont'd		
8/26/00	116	1		7 Homecoming Hymns With The Homecoming Friends .... [L]		Spring House 42272
11/11/00	141	1		8 Irish Homecoming .... [L]		Spring House 42268
11/11/00	157	1		9 Whispering Hope .... [L]		Spring House 42269
3/3/01	149	2		10 What A Time! .... [L]		Spring House 42322
9/1/01	172	2		11 London Homecoming .... [L]		Spring House 42317
10/27/01	87	5		12 A Billy Graham Homecoming Volume One .... [L]		Spring House 42366
				Grammy: Southern Gospel Album		
10/27/01	97	4		13 A Billy Graham Homecoming Volume Two .... [L]		Spring House 42351
2/16/02	86	2		14 Freedom Band .... [L]		Spring House 42352
3/30/02	147	1		15 I'll Fly Away .... [L]		Spring House 42368
3/30/02	152	1		16 New Orleans Homecoming .... [L]		Spring House 42367
5/11/02	118	1		17 Bill Gaither's Best Of Homecoming 2001 .... [L]		Spring House 42354
9/28/02	35	5		18 Let Freedom Ring: Live From Carnegie Hall [L]		Spring House 42413
9/28/02	44	3		19 God Bless America: Live From Carnegie Hall .... [L]		Spring House 42414
2/15/03	55	5		20 Heaven .... [L]		Spring House 42415
2/15/03	64	2		21 Going Home .... [L]		Spring House 42416
10/4/03	99	1		22 Red Rocks Homecoming .... [L]		Spring House 42418
10/4/03	121	1		23 Rocky Mountain Homecoming .... [L]		Spring House 42417
2/14/04	169	1		24 We Will Stand .... [L]		Gaither 42461
2/14/04	173	1		25 Build A Bridge .... [L]		Gaither 42462
				BILL GAITHER & T.D. JAKES (above 2)		
7/31/04	150	1		26 A Tribute To Howard & Vestal Goodman .... [L]		Gaither 42570
7/31/04	169	1		27 A Tribute To Jake Hess .... [L]		Gaither 42571
2/12/05	80	3		28 Church In The Wildwood .... [L]		Gaither 42370
2/12/05	93	2		29 Hymns .... [L]		Gaither 42369
3/19/05	85	3		30 Israel Homecoming .... [L]		Gaither 42609
3/19/05	86	3		31 Jerusalem .... [L]		Gaither 42608
9/17/05	112	1		32 A Tribute To George Younce .... [L]		Gaither 42642
11/12/05	119	1		33 Bill Gaither		Gaither 42646
2/25/06	113	2		34 Gaither Homecoming Tour: Live From Toronto .... [L]		Gaither 42643
2/25/06	114	2		35 Canadian Homecoming .... [L]		Gaither 42644
9/15/07	88	2		36 Amazing Grace .... Cat:#50/1 [L]		Gaither 42725
9/15/07	95	2		37 How Great Thou Art .... [L]		Gaither 42726
2/23/08	130	1		38 A Campfire Homecoming .... [L]		Gaither 42723
2/23/08	134	1		39 Homecoming Picnic .... [L]		Gaither 42724
5/3/08	153	1		40 Rock Of Ages .... [L]		Gaither 42771
9/6/08	150	2		41 Country Bluegrass Homecoming: Volume One .... [L]		Gaither 42736
9/6/08	169	2		42 Country Bluegrass Homecoming: Volume Two .... [L]		Gaither 42737
9/12/09	122	1		43 Nashville Homecoming .... [L]		Gaither 42728
9/12/09	131	2		44 Joy In My Heart .... [L]		Gaither 42727
				CHRISTMAS ALBUMS:		
11/30/96	36ˣ	2		45 Joy To The World .... [L]		Spring House 25388
				Christmas charts: 36/'96, 45/'08		
12/2/00	105	3		46 Christmas In The Country .... [L]		Spring House 42316
				Christmas charts: 29/'00, 36/'06		
11/17/01	21ˣ	3		47 Christmas: A Time For Joy .... [L]		Spring House 42350
				Christmas charts: 21/'01, 41/'06		
11/18/06	27ˣ	5		48 Homecoming Christmas: From South Africa .... [L]		Gaither 42651
				Christmas charts: 27/'06, 48/'08		
11/18/06	35ˣ	3		49 Christmas In South Africa .... [L]		Gaither 42696
10/11/08	43ˣ	1		50 A Christmas Homecoming .... [L]		Sparrow 88818
10/24/09	10ˣ	5		51 Christmas [L]		Gaither 42741
				GREATEST HITS & COMPILATIONS:		
3/27/04	109	1		52 Bill Gaither's 20 All-Time Favorite Homecoming Songs And Performances Volume 1 .... [L]		Gaither 42523
3/27/04	125	1		53 Bill Gaither's 20 All-Time Favorite Homecoming Songs And Performances Volume 2 .... [L]		Gaither 42524
8/5/06	171	2		54 Bill Gaither Remembers Homecoming Heroes .... [L]		Gaither 42641
8/5/06	190	2		55 Bill Gaither Remembers Old Friends .... [L]		Gaither 42607

GAITHER VOCAL BAND, The

Gospel group formed in 1980. Lineup by 1999: **Guy Penrod** (lead), **David Phelps** (tenor), **Mark Lowry** (baritone) and **Bill Gaither** (bass). Russ Taff replaced Lowry in 2001. Marshall Hall replaced Taff in 2004. Wes Hampton replaced Phelps in 2005. By 2009, "reunited" lineup consisted of Michael English (lead), Phelps (first tenor), Hampton (second tenor), Lowry (baritone) and Gaither (bass).

DEBUT	PEAK	WKS	R I A A	ARTIST / Album Title	Catalog	Label & Number
6/5/99	162	1		1 God Is Good		Spring Hill 25475
3/3/01	121	2		2 I Do Believe		Spring Hill 21009
8/31/02	159	5		3 Everything Good		Spring House 42412
10/18/03	174	1		4 A Cappella		Spring House 42516
10/23/04	177	3		5 Best Of The Gaither Vocal Band .... [K]		Gaither 42569 [2]
2/11/06	129	5		6 Give It Away		Gaither 42648
11/10/07	91	2		7 Together		Gaither 42729
				GAITHER VOCAL BAND AND ERNIE HAASE & SIGNATURE SOUND		

Billboard DEBUT	PEAK	WKS	R I A A	ARTIST / Album Title	Catalog	Label & Number
				GAITHER VOCAL BAND, The — cont'd		
5/3/08	123	1		8 Lovin' Life		Gaither 42746
				Grammy: Country Gospel Album		
10/18/08	8ˣ	8		9 Christmas Gaither Vocal Band Style	[X]	Gaither 42786
				Christmas charts: 8/'08, 17/'09		
2/14/09	53	3		10 Reunion Volume One	[L]	Gaither 42788
2/14/09	60	2		11 Reunion Volume Two	[L]	Gaither 42795
9/26/09	67	5		12 Reunited		Gaither 46044
				GALBAN, Manuel		
				Born in 1931 in Havana, Cuba. Jazz pianist.		
2/15/03	52	8		1 Mambo Sinuendo	[I]	Perro Verde 79691
				RY COODER & MANUEL GALBAN		
				Grammy: Pop Instrumental Album		
				GALE, Arlyn		
				Born in Chicago, Illinois. Black male singer/songwriter/guitarist.		
10/7/78	206	1		1 Back To The Midwest Night		ABC 1096
				GALE, Eric		
				Born on 9/20/1938 in Brooklyn, New York. Died of cancer on 5/25/1994 (age 55). Jazz guitarist. Member of **Fuse One** and **Stuff**.		
4/9/77	148	12		1 Ginseng Woman	[I]	Columbia 34421
7/21/79	154	5		2 Part Of You	[I]	Columbia 35715
11/8/80	201	5		3 Touch Of Silk	[I]	Columbia 36570
				GALLAGHER		
				Born Leo Gallagher on 7/24/1946 in Fort Bragg, North Carolina; raised in South Tampa, Florida. Stand-up comedian.		
3/15/80	206	5		1 Gallagher..	[C]	United Artists 1019
				GALLAGHER, Rory		
				Born on 3/2/1949 in Ballyshannon, Ireland; raised in Cork, Ireland. Died of liver failure on 6/14/1995 (age 46). Blues-rock singer/guitarist. Leader of **Taste**.		
8/26/72	101	15		1 Rory Gallagher/Live!	[L]	Polydor 5513
4/21/73	147	7		2 Blueprint		Polydor 5522
12/1/73+	186	7		3 Tattoo		Polydor 5539
9/14/74	110	11		4 Irish Tour '74	[L]	Polydor 9501 [2]
2/22/75	156	5		5 Sinner...And Saint		Polydor 6510
11/29/75+	121	13		6 Against The Grain		Chrysalis 1098
10/30/76+	163	11		7 Calling Card		Chrysalis 1124
11/4/78+	116	15		8 Photo-Finish		Chrysalis 1170
10/6/79	140	4		9 Top Priority		Chrysalis 1235
11/15/80	206	3		10 Stage Struck...	[L]	Chrysalis 1280
				recorded on his 1979 world tour		
				GALLAGHER AND LYLE		
				Pop duo from Largs, Ayrshire, Scotland: Benny Gallagher & Graham Lyle. Both formerly with **McGuiness Flint**.		
6/26/76	210	1		1 Breakaway		A&M 4566
				GALLERY		
				Pop band from Detroit, Michigan: Jim Gold (vocals), Brent Anderson (lead guitar), Cal Freeman (steel guitar), Bill Nova (percussion), Dennis Korvarik (bass) and Danny Brucato (drums).		
8/5/72	75	15		1 Nice To Be With You		Sussex 7017
				GALWAY, James		
				Born on 12/8/1939 in Belfast, Ireland. Classical flutist.		
3/3/79	153	5		1 Annie's Song And Other Galway Favorites......................	[I]	RCA Victor 3061
7/26/80	150	6		2 Sometimes When We Touch		RCA Victor 3628
				CLEO LAINE & JAMES GALWAY		
12/14/91	144	1		3 The Wind Beneath My Wings...................................	[I]	RCA Victor 60862
3/30/96	199	1		4 The Celtic Minstrel	[I]	RCA Victor 68393
4/5/97	186	1		5 Legends	[I]	RCA Victor 68776
				JAMES GALWAY & PHIL COULTER		
				GAMBINO FAMILY		
				Male rap duo from New Orleans, Louisiana: Gotti and Feno.		
11/7/98	17	4		1 Ghetto Organized		No Limit 50718
				GAMBLE, Dee Dee Sharp — see **SHARP, Dee Dee**		
				GAME, The		
				Born Jayceon Taylor on 11/29/1979 in Compton, California. Male rapper.		
2/5/05	❶²	35	▲²	1 The Documentary		Aftermath 003562
12/2/06	❶¹	20		2 Doctor's Advocate		Geffen 007933
9/13/08	2¹	28		3 LAX		Geffen 011465
				EARLY ALBUMS:		
11/6/04	146	3		4 Untold Story..		Get Low 7
4/16/05	53	3		5 West Coast Resurrection		Get Low 4570

Billboard			R I A A	ARTIST Album Title	Catalog	Label & Number
DEBUT	PEAK	WKS				
				GAME, The — cont'd		
8/13/05	61	2		6 Untold Story: Volume II		Fast Life 41
4/8/06	151	1		7 G.A.M.E.		Fast Life 65
				GAMMA		
				Rock band formed in San Francisco, California: Davey Pattison (vocals), Ronnie **Montrose** (guitar), Mitchell Froom (keyboards), Glenn Letsch (bass) and Denny Carmassi (drums). Carmassi later joined **Heart**. Pattison later recorded with **Robin Trower**. Froom was married to **Suzanne Vega** from 1995-98; married **Vonda Shepard** in 2004.		
9/22/79	131	17		1 Gamma 1		Elektra 219
9/13/80	65	19		2 Gamma 2		Elektra 288
3/20/82	72	12		3 Gamma 3		Elektra 60034
				GANG OF FOUR		
				Punk-rock band from Leeds, England: Jon King (vocals), Andy Gill (guitar), Dave Allen (bass) and Hugo Burnham (drums).		
11/29/80	201	7		1 Gang Of Four... [EP]		Warner 3494
6/6/81	190	2		2 Solid Gold		Warner 3565
2/13/82	195	2		3 Another Day/Another Dollar............................... [EP]		Warner 3646
6/26/82	175	3		4 Songs Of The Free		Warner 23683
10/8/83	168	4		5 Hard		Warner 23936
				~ ~ ~ ~ ~ ~ ~ ~ ~ ~ **NON-CHARTED ALBUM** ~ ~ ~ ~ ~ ~ ~ ~ ~ ~ ~ 1979 **Entertainment!** *RS500 #490*		
				GANGSTA BOO		
				Born Lola Mitchell on 8/7/1979 in Memphis, Tennessee. Female rapper. Former member of **Prophet Posse**, **Three 6 Mafia** and **Hypnotize Camp Posse**.		
10/17/98	46	6		1 Enquiring Minds		Relativity 1685
8/18/01	29	8		2 Both Worlds, *69		Hypnotize Minds 1925
				GANG STARR		
				Rap duo from Brooklyn, New York: Christopher "DJ Premier" Martin and Keith "**Guru**" Elam (died of cancer on 4/19/2010, age 43).		
3/16/91	121	12		1 Step In The Arena...		Chrysalis 21798
5/23/92	65	10		2 Daily Operation...		Chrysalis 21910
3/26/94	25	12		3 Hard To Earn		Chrysalis 28435
4/18/98	6	13	●	4 Moment Of Truth		Noo Trybe 45585
7/31/99	33	7	●	5 Full Clip: A Decade Of Gang Starr .... [K]		Noo Trybe 47279 [2]
7/12/03	18	8		6 The Ownerz		Virgin 80247
				GANKSTA NIP		
				Born Rowdy Lewayne on 8/28/1969 in Houston, Texas. Male rapper.		
7/24/93	151	2		1 Psychic Thoughts (Are What I Conceive?)		Rap-A-Lot 53860
				GAP BAND, The		
				R&B-funk trio of brothers from Tulsa, Oklahoma: Ronnie Wilson (vocals, horns, keyboards), Robert Wilson (vocals, bass) and **Charlie Wilson** (vocals, drums). Group named for three streets in Tulsa: Greenwood, Archer and Pine.		
5/19/79	77	18		1 The Gap Band		Mercury 3758
12/22/79+	42	28	●	2 The Gap Band II...		Mercury 3804
12/27/80+	16	37	▲	3 The Gap Band III..		Mercury 4003
6/12/82	14	52	▲	4 Gap Band IV		Total Experience 3001
9/10/83	28	43	●	5 Gap Band V - Jammin'		Total Experience 3004
1/19/85	58	23		6 Gap Band VI		Total Experience 5705
3/9/85	103	16	▲	7 Gap Gold/Best Of The Gap Band .... [G]		Total Experience 824343
2/1/86	159	15		8 Gap Band VII		Total Experience 5714
12/9/89+	189	7		9 Round Trip		Capitol 90799
				GARBAGE		
				Alternative-rock band formed in Madison, Wisconsin: Shirley Manson (vocals, guitar; native of Edinburgh, Scotland), Doug Erikson (guitar, bass, keyboards), Steve Marker (guitar, samples) and Butch Vig (drums). Vig produced albums for **Nirvana**, **Soul Asylum**, **Sonic Youth** and **Smashing Pumpkins**.		
9/30/95+	20	81	▲²	1 Garbage..		Almo Sounds 80004
5/30/98	13	70	▲	2 Version 2.0		Almo Sounds 80018
10/20/01	13	8		3 Beautiful Garbage		Almo Sounds 493115
4/30/05	4	11		4 Bleed Like Me		Almo Sounds 004195
8/11/07	68	2		5 Absolute Garbage .... [G]		Almo Sounds 009337
				GARCIA, Jerry		
				Born on 8/1/1942 in San Francisco, California. Died of a heart attack on 8/9/1995 (age 53). Founder/lead guitarist of the **Grateful Dead** and **Old & In The Way**. Produced and acted in the movie *Hells Angels Forever*. Ben & Jerry's "Cherry Garcia" ice cream named after him.		
10/9/71	201	1		1 Hooteroll? .... **HOWARD WALES & JERRY GARCIA**		Douglas 30859
1/29/72	35	14		2 Garcia		Warner 2582
6/22/74	49	15		3 Garcia .... *album later became known as Compliments*		Round 102
2/14/76	42	14		4 Reflections...		Round 565
4/15/78	114	5		5 Cats Under The Stars...		Arista 4160
11/20/82	100	8		6 Run For The Roses		Arista 9603

Billboard DEBUT	PEAK	WKS	R I A A	ARTIST / Album Title	Catalog	Label & Number
				GARCIA, Jerry — cont'd		
11/16/96	135	1		7 Shady Grove		Acoustic Disc 21
				JERRY GARCIA & DAVID GRISMAN		
				GREATEST HITS & COMPILATIONS:		
5/8/04	175	1		8 All Good Things: Jerry Garcia Studio Sessions		Jerry Garcia 78063 [6]
				contains a 128-page booklet		
10/14/06	166	1		9 The Very Best Of Jerry Garcia		J Garcia 73391 [2]
				LIVE ALBUMS:		
9/14/91	97	5		10 Jerry Garcia Band		Arista 18690 [2]
5/3/97	81	5		11 How Sweet It Is...		Grateful Dead 14051
				recorded in 1990 at the Warfield Theater in San Francisco, California		
2/10/01	137	2		12 Don't Let Go		Grateful Dead 14078 [2]
				recorded on 5/21/1976 at the Orpheum Theatre in San Francisco, California		
4/7/01	194	1		13 Shining Star		Grateful Dead 14079 [2]
10/16/04	118	1		14 After Midnight: Kean College, 2/28/80		Rhino 76536 [3]
				JERRY GARCIA BAND (above 5)		
9/10/05	190	1		15 The Jerry Garcia Collection, Vol. 1: Legion Of Mary .... [K]		J Garcia 74692 [2]
				GARCIA, Kany		
				Born on 9/25/1982 in Toa Alta, Puerto Rico. Female Latin singer.		
10/10/09	193	1		1 Boleto De Entrada .... [F]		Sony 47340
				GARDNER, Dave		
				Born on 6/11/1926 in Jackson, Tennessee. Died of a heart attack on 9/22/1983 (age 57). Comedian known as "Brother Dave."		
6/20/60	5	69		1 Rejoice, Dear Hearts! [C]		RCA Victor 2083
8/29/60	5	56		2 Kick Thy Own Self [C]		RCA Victor 2239
9/18/61	15	30		3 Ain't That Weird? .... [C]		RCA Victor 2335
9/1/62	49	13		4 Did You Ever? .... [C]		RCA Victor 2498
3/9/63	52	10		5 All Seriousness Aside .... [C]		RCA Victor 2628
5/4/63	28	13		6 It Don't Make No Difference .... [C]		Capitol 1867
				no track titles listed on any of the albums above		
				GARDNER, Don, and Dee Dee Ford		
				R&B vocal duo from Philadelphia, Pennsylvania.		
				~ ~ ~ ~ ~ ~ ~ ~ ~ ~ *NON-CHARTED ALBUM* ~ ~ ~ ~ ~ ~ ~ ~ ~ ~		
				1962 Need Your Lovin'		
				GARDOT, Melody		
				Born on 2/2/1985 in Mount Laurel, New Jersey. Jazz singer/songwriter.		
3/22/08	80	4		1 Worrisome Heart		Verve 010468
5/16/09	42	6		2 My One And Only Thrill		Verve 012563
				GARFUNKEL, Art		
				Born on 11/5/1941 in Forest Hills, New York. One-half of **Simon & Garfunkel** duo. Appeared in movies *Catch 22*, *Carnal Knowledge* and *Bad Timing*. Has Master's degree in mathematics from Columbia University.		
9/29/73	5	25	●	1 Angel Clare		Columbia 31474
10/25/75	7	28	▲	2 Breakaway		Columbia 33700
2/4/78	19	16	●	3 Watermark		Columbia 34975
4/7/79	67	14		4 Fate For Breakfast		Columbia 35780
9/12/81	113	8		5 Scissors Cut		Columbia 37392
4/16/88	134	8		6 Lefty		Columbia 40942
				GARLAND, Judy 1950s: #39 / All-Time: #441		
				Born Frances Gumm on 6/10/1922 in Grand Rapids, Minnesota. Died of an accidental sleeping pill overdose on 6/22/1969 (age 47). Legendary actress/singer. Hosted own TV variety series (1963-64). Married to **David Rose** from 1941-45 and movie director Vincente Minnelli from 1945-51. Mother of **Liza Minnelli** and Lorna Luft.		
				AWARD: Grammy: Lifetime Achievement 1997		
10/29/55	5	4		1 Miss Show Business		Capitol 676
11/10/56	17	5		2 Judy		Capitol 734
6/17/57	17	3		3 Alone		Capitol 835
8/25/62	33	14		4 The Garland Touch		Capitol 1710
5/11/63	45	6		5 I Could Go On Singing .... [S]		Capitol 1861
				GREATEST HITS & COMPILATIONS:		
1/4/64	136	2		6 The Best Of Judy Garland		Decca 7172 [2]
8/16/69	161	3		7 Judy Garland's Greatest Hits		Decca 75150
				LIVE ALBUMS:		
7/31/61	❶¹³	95	●	8 Judy At Carnegie Hall Cat:#26/1		Capitol 1569 [2]
				Grammys: Album of the Year / Female Vocal / Hall of Fame ★ NRR		
				recorded on 4/23/1961		
9/4/65	41	14		9 "Live" At The London Palladium		Capitol 2295 [2]
				recorded on 11/8/1964		
6/9/73	164	8		10 "Live" At The London Palladium .... [R]		Capitol 11191
				JUDY GARLAND & LIZA MINNELLI (above 2)		
				condensed version of #7 above		
9/16/67	174	3		11 Judy Garland At Home At The Palace - Opening Night		ABC 620
				recorded at the Palace Theatre in New York City		

GARNER, Erroll
Born on 6/15/1923 in Pittsburgh, Pennsylvania. Died on 1/2/1977 (age 53). Jazz pianist/songwriter.

11/25/57	16	2	1 Other Voices .... [I]	Columbia 1014
3/10/58	12	7	2 Concert By The Sea .... [I-L]	Columbia 883
			Grammy: Hall of Fame recorded in 1956 in Carmel, California	
6/26/61	35	31	3 Dreamstreet .... [I]	ABC-Paramount 365
7/6/63	94	6	4 One World Concert .... [I-L]	Reprise 6080
			recorded at Seattle World's Fair	

GARNETT, Gale
Born on 7/17/1942 in Auckland, New Zealand. Female singer/songwriter.

9/26/64	43	22	1 My Kind Of Folk Songs	RCA Victor 2833

GARRETT, David
Born on 9/4/1981 in Aachen, Germany. Classical violinist.

6/20/09	116	6	1 David Garrett .... [I]	Decca 012872

GARRETT, Leif
Born on 11/8/1961 in Hollywood, California. Pop singer/actor. Appeared in several movies.

12/17/77+	37	24	● 1 Leif Garrett	Atlantic 19152
11/25/78+	34	19	● 2 Feel The Need	Scotti Brothers 7100
12/15/79+	129	22	3 Same Goes For You	Scotti Brothers 16008
12/12/81+	185	7	4 My Movie Of You	Scotti Brothers 37625

GARRETT, Tommy, 50 Guitars Of
Born on 7/5/1939 in Dallas, Texas. Prolific producer. Better known as "Snuff" Garrett. 50 Guitars featured guitar solos by Tommy Tedesco. Also see **Midnight String Quartet** and **The Renaissance**.

12/18/61+	36	6	1 50 Guitars Go South Of The Border .... [I]	Liberty 14005
12/14/63+	94	8	2 Maria Elena .... [I]	Liberty 14030
6/13/64	142	2	3 50 Guitars Go Italiano .... [I]	Liberty 14028
11/26/66	99	5	4 50 Guitars In Love .... [I]	Liberty 14037
7/8/67	168	3	5 More 50 Guitars In Love .... [I]	Liberty 14039
5/3/69	147	9	6 The Best Of The 50 Guitars Of Tommy Garrett .... [G-I]	Liberty 14045

GARY, John
All-Time: #322
Born John Gary Strader on 11/29/1932 in Watertown, New York. Died of cancer on 1/4/1998 (age 65). Adult Contemporary singer.

11/9/63+	19	63	1 Catch A Rising Star	RCA Victor 2745
2/22/64	16	46	2 Encore	RCA Victor 2804
8/15/64	42	28	3 So Tenderly	RCA Victor 2922
11/14/64	141	4	4 David Merrick Presents Hits From His Broadway Hits	RCA Victor 2947
			JOHN GARY & ANN-MARGRET	
12/5/64	3[1X]	17	5 The John Gary Christmas Album [X]	RCA Victor 2940
			Christmas charts: 3/'64, 11/'65, 18/'66, 32/'67, 20/'67	
1/23/65	17	33	6 A Little Bit Of Heaven	RCA Victor 2994
7/24/65	11	29	7 The Nearness Of You	RCA Victor 3349
10/30/65	21	25	8 Your All-Time Favorite Songs	RCA Victor 3411
3/12/66	51	20	9 Choice	RCA Victor 3501
7/9/66	65	12	10 Your All-Time Country Favorites	RCA Victor 3570
10/8/66	73	17	11 A Heart Filled With Song	RCA Victor 3666
2/11/67	117	14	12 Especially For You	RCA Victor 3695
5/13/67	90	11	13 Spanish Moonlight	RCA Victor 3785
10/7/67	76	19	14 The John Gary Carnegie Hall Concert .... [L]	RCA Victor 1139
4/19/69	192	3	15 Love Of A Gentle Woman	RCA Victor 4134

GARY'S GANG
Disco band from Queens, New York: Gary Turnier (drums), Eric Matthew (vocals, guitar), Al Lauricella and Rino Minetti (keyboards), Bill Catalano (percussion), Bob Forman (sax) and Jay Leon (trombone).

3/31/79	42	10	1 Keep On Dancin'	Columbia 35793

GASCA, Luis
Born on 3/3/1940 in Houston, Texas. Jazz trumpet player.

5/27/72	195	3	1 Luis Gasca .... [I]	Blue Thumb 37

GASLIGHT ANTHEM, The
Punk-rock band from New Brunswick, New Jersey: Brian Fallon (vocals, guitar), Alex Rosamilia (guitar), Alex Levine (bass) and Benny Horowitz (drums).

9/6/08	70	1	1 The '59 Sound	Side One Dummy 1358

GATES, David
Born on 12/11/1940 in Tulsa, Oklahoma. Pop singer/songwriter. Lead singer of **Bread**.

10/27/73	107	10	1 First	Elektra 75066
2/15/75	102	9	2 Never Let Her Go	Elektra 1028
8/12/78	165	4	3 Goodbye Girl	Elektra 148

Billboard	R I A A	ARTIST		
DEBUT **PEAK** **WKS**		Album Title	**Catalog**	**Label & Number**

GATLIN, Larry
Born on 5/2/1948 in Seminole, Texas. Country singer/songwriter/guitarist.
AWARD: OPRY: 1976

4/1/78	175	5		1	Love Is Just A Game	Monument 7616
7/22/78	140	8		2	Oh! Brother	Monument 7626
12/23/78+	171	9	●	3	Larry Gatlin's Greatest Hits .... [G]	Monument 7628
7/5/80	204	2		4	The Pilgrim	Columbia 36541
					recorded and first released in 1974 on Monument 32571	
11/17/79+	102	16	▲	5	Straight Ahead	Columbia 36250
11/1/80	118	4		6	Help Yourself	Columbia 36582
10/17/81	184	2		7	Not Guilty...	Columbia 37464
					LARRY GATLIN & THE GATLIN BROTHERS BAND (above 3)	

GATTON, Danny
Born on 9/4/1945 in Washington DC. Died of self-inflicted gunshot wound on 10/4/1994 (age 49). Rock guitarist.

4/27/91	121	4		1	88 Elmira St. .... [I]	Elektra 61032

GAYE, Marvin
1970s: #38 / All-Time: #83

Born on 4/2/1939 in Washington DC. Shot to death by his father after a quarrel on 4/1/1984 (one day before his 45th birthday). R&B singer/songwriter/producer. Sang in his father's Apostolic church. In vocal groups the Rainbows, Marquees and **Moonglows**. Session work as a drummer at Motown; married to Berry Gordy's sister Anna from 1961-75. First recorded under own name for Tamla in 1961. In seclusion for several months following the death of Tammi Terrell in 1970. Problems with drugs and the IRS led to his moving to Europe for three years. Also see **Various Artists Compilations:** *Inner City Blues - The Music Of Marvin Gaye* and *Marvin Is 60 - A Tribute Album*.
AWARDS: Grammy: Lifetime Achievement 1996 ★ R&R Hall of Fame: 1987

5/16/64	42	16		1	Together	Motown 613
					MARVIN GAYE & MARY WELLS	
2/27/65	128	10		2	How Sweet It Is To Be Loved By You	Tamla 258
7/16/66	118	10		3	Moods Of Marvin Gaye	Tamla 266
10/7/67	69	44		4	United	Tamla 277
9/21/68	60	21		5	You're All I Need	Tamla 284
					MARVIN GAYE & TAMMI TERRELL (above 2)	
11/2/68+	63	27		6	In The Groove	Tamla 285
6/14/69	33	18		7	M.P.G.	Tamla 292
10/18/69	184	2		8	Easy	Tamla 294
					MARVIN GAYE & TAMMI TERRELL	
11/1/69+	189	3		9	That's The Way Love Is	Tamla 299
6/12/71	6	53	●	10	What's Going On .... Cat:#30/29	Tamla 310
					Grammy: Hall of Fame ★ RS500 #6	
12/30/72+	14	21		11	Trouble Man .... [I-S]	Tamla 322
9/15/73	2[1]	61		12	Let's Get It On .... Cat:#7/36	Tamla 329
					Grammy: Hall of Fame ★ RS500 #165	
11/17/73	26	47		13	Diana & Marvin	Motown 803
					DIANA ROSS & MARVIN GAYE	
7/13/74	8	28		14	Marvin Gaye Live! .... [L]	Tamla 333
					recorded at the Alameda County Coliseum in Oakland, California	
4/3/76	4	28		15	I Want You	Tamla 342
4/2/77	3[3]	26		16	Marvin Gaye Live At The London Palladium .... [L]	Tamla 352 [2]
1/6/79	26	21		17	Here, My Dear	Tamla 364 [2]
					RS500 #462	
2/7/81	32	17		18	In Our Lifetime	Tamla 374
11/20/82	7	41	▲[3]	19	Midnight Love	Columbia 38197
					GREATEST HITS & COMPILATIONS:	
5/30/64	72	14		20	Marvin Gaye/Greatest Hits	Tamla 252
9/30/67	178	5		21	Marvin Gaye/Greatest Hits, Vol. 2	Tamla 278
6/14/69	183	7		22	Marvin Gaye And His Girls	Tamla 293
6/13/70	171	3		23	Marvin Gaye & Tammi Terrell Greatest Hits	Tamla 302
11/7/70	117	6		24	Marvin Gaye Super Hits	Tamla 300
4/20/74	61	29		25	Marvin Gaye Anthology	Motown 791 [3]
10/2/76	44	8		26	Marvin Gaye's Greatest Hits .... Cat:#4/188	Tamla 348
10/22/83+	80	16	▲	27	Every Great Motown Hit Of Marvin Gaye .... Cat:#11/65	Motown 6058
5/5/84	203	2		28	Great Songs And Performances That Inspired The Motown 25th Anniversary Television Special	Motown 5311
5/19/84	208	1		29	Motown Superstar Series Volume 15 .... Cat:#18/20	Motown 115
6/8/85	41	15		30	Dream Of A Lifetime	Columbia 39916
5/3/86	193	2		31	Motown Remembers Marvin Gaye	Tamla 6172
8/4/01	167	3	●	32	The Very Best Of Marvin Gaye	Motown 014367 [2]
3/9/02	34[C]	2		33	The Best Of Marvin Gaye: 20th Century Masters The Millennium Collection Volume 2 The '70s	Motown 153732
					first released in 2000	

~ ~ ~ ~ ~ ~ ~ ~ ~ ~ **NON-CHARTED ALBUMS** ~ ~ ~ ~ ~ ~ ~ ~ ~ ~ ~

1961 The Soulful Moods Of Marvin Gaye	1963 Recorded Live, Marvin Gaye On Stage
1963 That Stubborn Kinda Fellow	1964 When I'm Alone I Cry

GAYLE, Crystal
Born Brenda Gail Webb on 1/9/1951 in Paintsville, Kentucky; raised in Wabash, Indiana. Country singer. Youngest sister of **Loretta Lynn**. Known for her trademark ankle-length hair.
AWARD: CMA: Female Vocalist 1977 & 1978

DEBUT	PEAK	WKS				Label & Number
9/3/77	12	35	▲	1 We Must Believe In Magic		United Artists 771
7/15/78	52	39	▲	2 When I Dream		United Artists 858
8/11/79	128	8		3 We Should Be Together		United Artists 969
11/17/79+	62	22	●	4 Classic Crystal	[G]	United Artists 982
5/3/80	149	6		5 Favorites	[K]	United Artists 1034
9/29/79	36	28	●	6 Miss The Mississippi		Columbia 36203
9/27/80	79	11	●	7 These Days		Columbia 36512
9/19/81	99	16		8 Hollywood, Tennessee		Columbia 37438
9/10/83	169	8	●	9 Crystal Gayle's Greatest Hits	[G]	Columbia 38803
12/4/82+	120	12		10 True Love		Elektra 60200
11/12/83	171	6		11 Cage The Songbird		Warner 23958

GAYLORD & HOLIDAY
Italian-American duo: Ronnie "Gaylord" Fredianelli and Burt "Holiday" Bonaldi. With pianist/arranger Don Rea. Recorded in the late 1950s as The Gaylords.

2/21/76	180	8		1 Second Generation		Prodigal 10009

GAYNOR, Gloria
Born Gloria Fowles on 9/7/1949 in Newark, New Jersey. Disco singer.

2/1/75	25	15		1 Never Can Say Goodbye		MGM 4982
10/11/75	64	21		2 Experience Gloria Gaynor		MGM 4997
8/14/76	107	14		3 I've Got You		Polydor 6063
3/19/77	183	4		4 Glorious		Polydor 6095
1/6/79	4	34	▲	5 Love Tracks		Polydor 6184
10/20/79	58	11		6 I Have A Right		Polydor 6231
5/24/80	178	4		7 Stories		Polydor 6274
7/11/81	206	5		8 I Kinda Like Me		Polydor 6324
1/8/83	210	1		9 Gloria Gaynor		Atlantic 80033

G. DEP
Born Trevell Coleman on 9/12/1978 in Harlem, New York. Male rapper. Stage name is short for Ghetto Dependant.

12/8/01	106	6		1 Child Of The Ghetto		Bad Boy 73042

GEIGER, Teddy
Born John Theodore Geiger II on 9/16/1988 in Buffalo, New York; raised in Pittsford, New York. Male singer/songwriter/guitarist.

4/8/06	8	19		1 Underage Thinking		Columbia 94964

GEILS, J., Band
All-Time: #248
Rock band from Boston, Massachusetts: Jerome Geils (guitar; born on 2/20/1946), **Peter Wolf** (vocals; born on 3/7/1946), "Magic Dick" Salwitz (harmonica; born on 5/13/1945), Seth Justman (keyboards, vocals; born on 1/27/1951), Danny Klein (bass; born on 5/13/1946) and Stephen Jo Bladd (drums; born on 7/13/1942). Wolf left in the fall of 1983.

1/30/71	195	2		1 The J. Geils Band		Atlantic 8275
11/6/71	64	17		2 The Morning After		Atlantic 8297
10/21/72	54	26	●	3 "Live" - Full House	[L]	Atlantic 7241
				recorded on 4/21/1972 at the Cinderella Ballroom in Detroit, Michigan		
4/28/73	10	44	●	4 Bloodshot		Atlantic 7260
12/1/73+	51	18		5 Ladies Invited		Atlantic 7286
10/19/74	26	22		6 Nightmares...And Other Tales From The Vinyl Jungle		Atlantic 18107
9/27/75	36	9		7 Hotline		Atlantic 18147
5/22/76	40	11		8 Live - Blow Your Face Out	[L]	Atlantic 507 [2]
				recorded on 11/15/1975 at the Boston Garden and on 11/19/1975 at Cobo Hall in Detroit, Michigan		
7/9/77	51	17		9 Monkey Island		Atlantic 19103
7/21/79	129	5		10 Best Of The J. Geils Band	Cat:#20/8 [G]	Atlantic 19234
12/6/80	201	5		11 Best Of The J. Geils Band Two	[G]	Atlantic 19284
12/16/78+	49	22	●	12 Sanctuary		EMI America 17006
2/9/80	18	42	●	13 Love Stinks		EMI America 17016
11/14/81+	❶⁴	70	▲	14 Freeze-Frame		EMI America 17062
12/4/82+	23	19	●	15 Showtime!	[L]	EMI America 17087
				recorded September 1982 at the Pine Knob Music Theater in Detroit, Michigan		
11/24/84	80	10		16 You're Gettin' Even While I'm Gettin' Odd		EMI America 17137

GELDOF, Bob
Born on 10/5/1951 in Dublin, Ireland. Rock singer. Leader of **The Boomtown Rats**. Played "Pink" in the **Pink Floyd** movie *The Wall*. Organized British superstar benefits Band Aid, Live Aid and Live 8.

12/13/86+	130	12		1 Deep In The Heart Of Nowhere		Atlantic 81687

GENE LOVES JEZEBEL
Techno-rock band formed in England: twin brothers Jay Aston and Michael Aston (vocals), James Stevenson (guitar), Peter Rizzo (bass) and Chris Bell (drums) joined. Michael Aston left in early 1989.

10/18/86+	155	19		1 Discover		Geffen 24118
11/14/87+	108	22		2 The House Of Dolls		Geffen 24171
8/18/90	123	14		3 Kiss Of Life		Geffen 24260

GENERAL PUBLIC
Pop band from Birmingham, England: Dave Wakeling (vocals, guitar), **Ranking Roger** (vocals, keyboards), Kevin White (guitar), Micky Billingham (keyboards), Horace Panter (bass) and Stoker (drums). Wakeling and Roger had been in **English Beat**. Billingham was with **Dexys Midnight Runners**. General Public disbanded in March 1987. Wakeling and Roger reunited in 1994.

10/27/84+	26	39		1 **...All The Rage**		I.R.S. 70046
10/25/86	83	16		2 **Hand To Mouth**		I.R.S. 5782

GENERATION J
Contemporary gospel group from Atlanta, Georgia: brothers Aaron Sanders and Pierre Sanders, with sisters Adrienne Hudson and Leslie Hudson. J: Justified.

7/31/04	164	1		1 **Secret Place**		Word/Curb 886294

GENERATION UNLEASHED
Worship project featuring various teenage singers and musicians.

2/16/08	199	1		1 **Live Worship**	**[L]**	Maranatha! 971950

GENESIS   All-Time: #138
Formed as a progressive-rock band in England in 1967. Consisted of **Peter Gabriel** (vocals), **Anthony Phillips** (guitar), **Tony Banks** (keyboards), **Mike Rutherford** (guitar, bass) and Chris Stewart (drums; replaced by John Silver in 1968, then John Mayhew in 1969). Phillips and Mayhew left in 1970, replaced by **Steve Hackett** (guitar) and **Phil Collins** (drums). Gabriel left in June 1975, with Collins replacing him as new lead singer. Hackett went solo in 1977, leaving group as a trio: Collins, Rutherford and Banks. Added regular members for touring: Americans Chester Thompson (drums), in 1977, and guitarist Daryl Stuermer, in 1978. Collins also recorded in jazz-fusion group **Brand X**. Rutherford also in own group, **Mike + The Mechanics**, formed in 1985. Hackett later formed group **GTR**. Collins announced his departure from the group in April 1996; Ray Wilson joined as lead singer in June 1997.
AWARD: R&R Hall of Fame: 2010

10/12/74	170	4		1 **From Genesis To Revelation**	**[E]**	London 643
				released in 1969		
12/15/73+	70	29	●	2 **Selling England By The Pound**		Charisma 6060
12/14/74+	41	16	●	3 **The Lamb Lies Down On Broadway**		Atco 401 [2]
3/20/76	31	19	●	4 **A Trick Of The Tail**		Atco 129
1/22/77	26	21	●	5 **Wind & Wuthering**	**Cat:#22/22**	Atco 144
4/15/78	14	33	▲	6 **And Then There Were Three...**	**Cat:#25/20**	Atlantic 19173
4/26/80	11	31	▲	7 **Duke**		Atlantic 16014
10/17/81	7	64	▲²	8 **Abacab**		Atlantic 19313
10/29/83	9	50	▲⁴	9 **Genesis**	**Cat:#18/33**	Atlantic 80116
6/28/86	3²	85	▲⁶	10 **Invisible Touch**	**Cat:#23/4**	Atlantic 81641
11/30/91	4	72	▲⁴	11 **We Can't Dance**		Atlantic 82344
9/20/97	54	5		12 **Calling All Stations**		Atlantic 83037
				GREATEST HITS & COMPILATIONS:		
11/13/99	65	9	●	13 **Turn It On Again - The Hits**	**Cat:#7/23**	Atlantic 83244
9/29/07	132	3		14 **Turn It On Again - The Hits: The Tour Edition**		Atlantic 281852 [2]
10/1/05	100	3		15 **Platinum Collection**		Atlantic 78446 [3]
				LIVE ALBUMS:		
5/18/74	105	14		16 **Genesis Live**		Charisma 1666
				recorded February 1973 in Manchester, England		
12/3/77	47	16		17 **Seconds Out**		Atlantic 9002 [2]
6/26/82	10	25	●	18 **Three Sides Live**		Atlantic 2000 [2]
				side 4: studio cuts from 1979-81		
12/5/92	35	23	●	19 **Live/The Way We Walk - Volume One: The Shorts**		Atlantic 82452
2/27/93	20	9		20 **Live/The Way We Walk - Volume Two: The Longs**		Atlantic 82461

GENTLE GIANT
Progressive-rock band formed in England: brothers Ray Shulman (bass, guitar), Derek Shulman (sax, vocals) and Phil Shulman (sax, trumpet), with Kerry Minnear (keyboards), Gary Green (guitar) and John Weathers (drums). Phil Shulman left in 1973.

10/21/72	197	5		1 **Three Friends**		Columbia 31649
3/31/73	170	9		2 **Octopus**		Columbia 32022
10/12/74	78	13		3 **The Power And The Glory**		Capitol 11337
8/16/75	48	11		4 **Free Hand**		Capitol 11428
5/29/76	137	5		5 **Interview**		Capitol 11532
2/19/77	89	6		6 **The Official "Live" Gentle Giant - Playing The Fool**	**[L]**	Capitol 11592 [2]
10/15/77	81	7		7 **The Missing Piece**		Capitol 11696
4/5/80	203	2		8 **Civilian**		Columbia 36341

GENTRY, Bobbie
Born Roberta Streeter on 7/27/1944 in Chickasaw County, Mississippi; raised in Greenwood, Mississippi. Singer/songwriter. Formerly married to **Jim Stafford**.
AWARD: Grammy: Best New Artist 1967

9/16/67	❶²	30	●	1 **Ode To Billie Joe**		Capitol 2830
3/23/68	132	12		2 **The Delta Sweete**		Capitol 2842
10/12/68	11	47	●	3 **Bobbie Gentry & Glen Campbell**		Capitol 2928
8/9/69	164	4		4 **Touch 'Em With Love**		Capitol 155
12/27/69+	180	2		5 **Bobbie Gentry's Greatest!**	**[G]**	Capitol 381
5/9/70	96	17		6 **Fancy**		Capitol 428
5/22/71	221	2		7 **Patchwork**		Capitol 494

Billboard			R I A A	ARTIST Album Title	Catalog	Label & Number
DEBUT	PEAK	WKS				

GENTRYS, The
Garage-rock band from Memphis, Tennessee: Larry Raspberry, Jimmy Hart and Bruce Bowles (vocals), Bobby Fisher (guitar), Jimmy Johnson (trumpet), Pat Neal (bass) and Larry Wall (drums). Hart later became a professional wrestling manager, known as "The Mouth of The South."

| 12/18/65+ | 99 | 10 | | 1 Keep On Dancing | | MGM 4336 |

GEORGE, Barbara
Born on 8/16/1942 in New Orleans, Louisiana. R&B singer/songwriter.

~ ~ ~ ~ ~ ~ ~ ~ ~ ~ ~ **NON-CHARTED ALBUM** ~ ~ ~ ~ ~ ~ ~ ~ ~ ~ ~
1962 I Know (You Don't Love Me No More)

GEORGE, Lowell
Born on 4/13/1945 in Hollywood, California. Died of drug-related heart failure on 6/29/1979 (age 34). Lead singer of **Little Feat**.

| 4/14/79 | 71 | 9 | | 1 Thanks I'll Eat It Here | | Warner 3194 |

GEORGIA SATELLITES
Rock band from Atlanta, Georgia: Dan Baird (vocals, guitar), Rick Richards (guitar), Rich Price (bass) and Mauro Magellan (drums). Richards later joined **Izzy Stradlin And The Ju Ju Hounds**.

11/1/86+	5	42	▲	1 Georgia Satellites		Elektra 60496
7/2/88	77	13		2 Open All Night		Elektra 60793
11/11/89	130	13		3 In The Land Of Salvation And Sin		Elektra 60887

GEORGIO
Born Georgio Allentini in 1966 in San Francisco, California. Black dance-funk singer/songwriter/keyboardist/guitarist.

| 4/25/87+ | 117 | 52 | | 1 Sexappeal | | Motown 6229 |

GERARDO
Born Gerardo Mejia on 4/16/1965 in Guayaquil, Ecuador; raised in Glendale, California. Rapper/actor. Raps in Spanglish (half Spanish, half English). Appeared in the movies *Can't Buy Me Love* and *Colors*.

| 2/23/91 | 36 | 32 | ● | 1 Mo' Ritmo | | Interscope 91619 |

GERONIMO, Mic
Born in 1973 in Queens, New York. Male rapper.

| 11/22/97 | 112 | 2 | | 1 Vendetta | | Blunt 4930 |

GERRY AND THE PACEMAKERS
Pop-rock band from Liverpool, England: brothers Gerry Marsden (vocals, guitar; born on 9/24/1942) and Freddie Marsden (drums), with Leslie Maguire (piano) and John Chadwick (bass). Freddie Marsden died on 12/9/2006 (age 66).

7/11/64	29	12		1 Don't Let The Sun Catch You Crying		Laurie 2024
11/21/64	129	9		2 Gerry & The Pacemakers Second Album		Laurie 2027
2/27/65	13	20		3 Ferry Cross The Mersey	[S]	United Artists 6387
2/27/65	120	7		4 I'll Be There!		Laurie 2030
5/15/65	44	22		5 Gerry & The Pacemakers Greatest Hits	[G]	Laurie 2031

GERSHWIN, George
Born Jacob Gershowitz on 9/26/1898 in Brooklyn, New York. Died of a brain tumor on 7/11/1937 (age 38). Legendary composer of numerous Broadway and movie scores, most with brother Ira's lyrics. Also see **Various Artists Compilations:** *The Glory Of Gershwin*.

AWARD: Grammy: Trustees Award 1986 (w/ Ira)

| 2/12/94 | 156 | 4 | | 1 Gershwin Plays Gershwin: The Piano Rolls | [I] | Nonesuch 79287 |

digital recordings of 12 of Gershwin's original player piano rolls; realized by Artis Wodehouse

GETO BOYS, The
Rap group from Houston, Texas: Richard "**Bushwick Bill**" Shaw, William "**Willie D**" Dennis, Brad "**Scarface**" Jordan and "**Big Mike**" Barnett.

3/24/90	166	10		1 Grip It! On That Other Level		Rap-A-Lot 103
				GHETTO BOYS		
10/20/90	171	7		2 The Geto Boys		Rap-A-Lot 24306
7/27/91	24	42	▲	3 We Can't Be Stopped		Rap-A-Lot 57161
12/5/92	147	9		4 Best Uncut Dope	[K]	Rap-A-Lot 57183
3/27/93	11	27	●	5 Till Death Do Us Part		Rap-A-Lot 57191
4/20/96	6	18	●	6 The Resurrection		Rap-A-Lot 41555
12/5/98	26	12		7 Da Good Da Bad & Da Ugly		Rap-A-Lot 46780
2/12/05	19	8		8 The Foundation		Rap-A-Lot 68502

GET UP KIDS, The
Pop-rock band from Kansas City, Missouri: brothers Rob Pope (bass) and Ryan Pope (drums), with Matt Pryor (vocals, guitar) and Jim Suptic (guitar). Rob Pope later joined **Spoon**.

| 6/1/02 | 57 | 3 | | 1 On A Wire | | Vagrant 370 |
| 3/20/04 | 58 | 2 | | 2 Guilt Show | | Vagrant 392 |

GETZ, Stan
Born Stan Gayetsky on 2/2/1927 in Philadelphia, Pennsylvania. Died of liver cancer on 6/6/1991 (age 64). Jazz tenor saxophonist. With **Stan Kenton** (1944-45), **Jimmy Dorsey** (1945-46), **Benny Goodman** (1946) and **Woody Herman** (1947-49).

9/15/62+	❶¹	70		1 Jazz Samba	[I]	Verve 8432
				STAN GETZ & CHARLIE BYRD *Grammy: Hall of Fame*		
12/22/62+	13	23		2 Big Band Bossa Nova	[I]	Verve 8494

Billboard			R I A	ARTIST		
DEBUT	PEAK	WKS	A	Album Title	Catalog	Label & Number

GETZ, Stan — cont'd

5/18/63	88	11		3 Jazz Samba Encore!	[I]	Verve 8523
4/11/64	122	6		4 Reflections	[I]	Verve 8554
6/6/64	2²	96	●	5 Getz/Gilberto		Verve 8545

STAN GETZ/JOAO GILBERTO
Grammys: *Album of the Year / Jazz Album / Hall of Fame* ★ RS500 #454

12/19/64+	24	46		6 Getz Au Go Go	[L]	Verve 8600

THE NEW STAN GETZ QUARTET Featuring Astrud Gilberto
recorded on 8/19/1964 at the Cafe Au Go Go in Greenwich Village

9/2/67	195	2		7 Sweet Rain	[I]	Verve 8693
3/1/75	191	1		8 Captain Marvel	[I]	Columbia 32706
6/26/76	208	1		9 The Best Of Two Worlds	[I]	Columbia 33703

~ ~ ~ ~ ~ ~ ~ ~ ~ **NON-CHARTED ALBUM** ~ ~ ~ ~ ~ ~ ~ ~ ~ ~
1961 Focus
Grammy: Hall of Fame

GHETTO BOYS — see GETO

GHETTO COMMISSION
Rap group from New Orleans, Louisiana: Gary Arnold, Byron Dolliole, Dwayne Lawrence, Carlos Stephens and Walter Valerio.

11/28/98	59	2		1 Wise Guys		No Limit 50011

GHETTO MAFIA
Rap duo from Decatur, Georgia: Rod Barber and Fred Pilgrim.

11/7/98	169	2		1 On Da Grind		Rap Artist 2061

GHETTO TWIINZ
Rap duo from New Orleans, Louisiana: twin sisters Tonya Jupiter and Tremethia Jupiter.

10/10/98	191	1		1 No Pain/No Gain		Rap-A-Lot 46259

GHOSTFACE KILLAH
Born Dennis Coles on 5/9/1970 in Staten Island, New York. Male rapper/songwriter. Member of **Wu-Tang Clan**.

11/16/96	2¹	26	▲	1 Ironman		Razor Sharp 67729
2/26/00	7	19	●	2 Supreme Clientele		Razor Sharp 69325
12/8/01	34	6		3 Bulletproof Wallets		Epic 61589
5/8/04	6	7		4 The Pretty Tony Album		Def Jam 002169
4/15/06	4	12		5 FishScale		Def Jam 006155
12/30/06	71	4		6 More Fish		Def Jam 008165
12/22/07	41	5		7 The Big Doe Rehab		Def Jam 009499
10/17/09	28	5		8 Ghostdini: Wizard Of Poetry In Emerald City		Def Jam 013396

GIANT
Rock band formed in Nashville, Tennessee: brothers Dan Huff (vocals, guitar) and David Huff (drums), with Alan Pasqua (keyboards) and Mike Brignardello (bass).

10/14/89+	80	36		1 Last Of The Runaways		A&M 5272

GIANT STEPS
Pop duo from England: Colin Campsie (vocals) and George McFarlane (instruments).

11/12/88	184	5		1 The Book Of Pride		A&M 5190

GIBB, Andy
Born on 3/5/1958 in Manchester, England. Died of heart failure on 3/10/1988 (age 30). Pop singer/songwriter. Youngest brother of Robin, Maurice and **Barry Gibb** (**The Bee Gees**). Hosted TV's *Solid Gold* from 1981-82.

7/2/77	19	68	▲	1 Flowing Rivers		RSO 3019
6/17/78	7	43	▲	2 Shadow Dancing		RSO 3034
3/1/80	21	15	●	3 After Dark		RSO 3069
12/6/80+	46	18		4 Andy Gibb's Greatest Hits	[G]	RSO 3091

GIBB, Barry
Born on 9/1/1946 in Manchester, England. Member of the **Bee Gees**.

10/20/84	72	8		1 Now Voyager		MCA 5506

GIBB, Robin
Born on 12/22/1949 in Manchester, England. Member of the Bee Gees.

7/28/84	204	4		1 Secret Agent		Mirage 90170

GIBBONS, Steve, Band
Born on 7/13/1941 in Harborne, Birmingham, England. Rock singer/guitarist. His band: Bob Wilson (guitar), Trevor Burton (bass) and Bob Lamb (drums).

9/9/78	207	2		1 Down In The Bunker		Polydor 6154

GIBBS, Terri
Born on 6/15/1954 in Miami, Florida; raised in Grovetown, Georgia. Female country singer/pianist. Blind since birth.
AWARD: CMA: Horizon 1981

2/14/81	53	25		1 Somebody's Knockin'		MCA 5173
10/24/81	202	3		2 I'm A Lady		MCA 5255

Billboard DEBUT	PEAK	WKS	R I A A	ARTIST Album Title	Catalog	Label & Number

GIBSON, Debbie
Born on 8/31/1970 in Brooklyn, New York; raised in Merrick, Long Island, New York. Pop singer/songwriter/pianist/actress. Acted in the Broadway shows *Les Miserables* and *Grease*.

9/5/87+	7	89	▲³	1 Out Of The Blue		Atlantic 81780
2/11/89	❶⁵	51	▲²	2 Electric Youth		Atlantic 81932
12/1/90	41	17	●	3 Anything Is Possible		Atlantic 82167
2/6/93	109	3		4 Body Mind Soul		Atlantic 82451

GIBSON, Don
Born on 4/3/1928 in Shelby, North Carolina. Died on 11/17/2003 (age 75). Country singer/songwriter/guitarist.
AWARDS: C&W Hall of Fame: 2001 ★ OPRY: 1958

| 11/2/63 | 134 | 3 | | 1 I Wrote A Song... | | RCA Victor 2702 |

featuring new versions of Gibson's biggest hits

~ ~ ~ ~ ~ ~ ~ ~ ~ ~ **NON-CHARTED ALBUM** ~ ~ ~ ~ ~ ~ ~ ~ ~ ~

1958 Oh Lonesome Me

GIBSON BROTHERS
Disco trio from the West Indies: brothers Chris (guitar), Alex (keyboards) and Patrick (drums) Gibson. All share vocals.

| 7/28/79 | 185 | 2 | | 1 Cuba | | Island 9579 |

GIFFORD, Kathie Lee
Born Kathryn Epstein on 8/16/1953 in Paris, France; raised in Bowie, Maryland. TV personality. Married former pro football player/sportscaster Frank Gifford on 10/18/1986. Co-hostess of TV show *Live With Regis & Kathie Lee* from 1989-2000.

5/15/93	108	3		1 Sentimental..		Warner 45084
12/11/93+	125	5		2 It's Christmastime .... [X]		Warner 45346
				Christmas chart: 23/'93		
5/20/00	139	2		3 Born For You		On The Lamb 15115
11/11/00	170	1		4 Heart Of A Woman		Universal 159690
				KATHIE LEE		

GILBERTO, Astrud
Born on 3/30/1940 in Salvador, Brazil. Female singer. Married to **Joao Gilberto** from 1960-64.

12/19/64+	24	46		1 Getz Au Go Go .... [L]		Verve 8600
				THE NEW STAN GETZ QUARTET Featuring Astrud Gilberto		
				recorded on 8/19/1964 at the Cafe Au Go Go in Greenwich Village		
5/15/65	41	18		2 The Astrud Gilberto Album		Verve 8608
10/9/65	68	18		3 The Shadow Of Your Smile		Verve 8629

GILBERTO, Bebel
Born on 5/12/1966 in Manhattan, New York. Latin singer. Daughter of **Joao Gilberto**.

| 6/26/04 | 154 | 3 | | 1 Bebel Gilberto .... [F] | | Six Degrees 1101 |
| 5/12/07 | 169 | 1 | | 2 Momento .... [F] | | Six Degrees 1133 |

GILBERTO, Joao
Born on 6/10/1931 in Juazeiro, Brazil. Male singer. Father of **Bebel Gilberto**. Married to **Astrud Gilberto** from 1960-64.

6/6/64	2²	96	●	1 Getz/Gilberto		Verve 8545
				STAN GETZ/JOAO GILBERTO		
				Grammys: Album of the Year / Jazz Album / Hall of Fame ★ RS500 #454		

GILDER, Nick
Born on 12/21/1951 in London, England; raised in Vancouver, British Columbia, Canada. Pop-rock singer/songwriter.

| 9/23/78 | 33 | 20 | | 1 City Nights .... | | Chrysalis 1202 |
| 7/7/79 | 127 | 8 | | 2 Frequency .... | | Chrysalis 1219 |

GILL, Johnny
Born on 5/22/1966 in Washington DC. R&B singer. Joined **New Edition** in 1988. His brother Randy and cousin Jermaine Mickey are members of **II D Extreme**. Member of **LSG**.

3/31/84	139	8		1 Perfect Combination		Cotillion 90136
				STACY LATTISAW & JOHNNY GILL		
5/5/90	8	60	▲²	2 Johnny Gill		Motown 6283
6/26/93	14	20	●	3 Provocative		Motown 6355
10/26/96	32	26	●	4 Let's Get The Mood Right		Motown 0646

GILL, Vince   1990s: #13 / All-Time: #238
Born on 4/12/1957 in Norman, Oklahoma. Country singer/guitarist. Member of **Pure Prairie League** from 1979-83. Married to Janis Oliver of the Sweethearts Of The Rodeo from 1980-97. Married **Amy Grant** on 3/10/2000. Member of **The Notorious Cherry Bombs**.
AWARDS: C&W Hall of Fame: 2007 ★ CMA: Male Vocalist 1991, 1992, 1993, 1994 & 1995 / Entertainer 1993 & 1994 ★ OPRY: 1991

7/28/90	67	78	▲²	1 When I Call Your Name .... Cat:#44/1		MCA 42321
3/23/91+	37	98	▲²	2 Pocket Full of Gold................................		MCA 10140
10/19/91	19ᶜ	11	▲	3 The Best Of Vince Gill .... [G]		RCA 9814
9/19/92	10	100	▲⁵	4 I Still Believe In You		MCA 10630
				CMA: Album of the Year		
10/9/93	14	16	▲²	5 Let There Be Peace On Earth .... Cat:#4/33 [X]		MCA 10877
				Christmas charts: 1/'93, 6/'94, 9/'95, 9/'96, 29/'97, 25/'99, 34/'00		
6/25/94	6	112	▲⁴	6 When Love Finds You	Cat:#42/6	MCA 11047
12/9/95	11	36	▲³	7 Souvenirs.. [G]		MCA 11394

GILL, Vince — cont'd

DEBUT	PEAK	WKS	RIAA		Catalog	Label & Number
6/15/96	24	44	▲	8 High Lonesome Sound		MCA 11422
8/29/98	11	27	●	9 The Key		MCA Nashville 70017
11/14/98	39	9	▲	10 Breath Of Heaven .... Cat:#9/8 [X]		MCA Nashville 70038
				with Patrick Williams & His Orchestra; Christmas charts: 3/'98, 13/'99, 34/'03		
5/6/00	39	7	●	11 Let's Make Sure We Kiss Goodbye		MCA Nashville 70098
3/1/03	14	9		12 Next Big Thing		MCA Nashville 70286
11/4/06	17	19	▲	13 These Days		MCA Nashville 006021 [4]
				Grammy: Country Album		

GILLAN

Born Ian Gillan on 8/19/1945 in Hounslow, Middlesex, England. Lead singer of **Deep Purple**. Portrayed Jesus in the rock opera *Jesus Christ Superstar*. Joined **Black Sabbath** for *Born Again* album.

DEBUT	PEAK	WKS	RIAA		Catalog	Label & Number
12/6/80	183	3		1 Glory Road		RSO 1001

GILLETTE

Born Sandra Gillette on 9/16/1973 in Chicago, Illinois. Female rapper.

DEBUT	PEAK	WKS	RIAA		Catalog	Label & Number
4/15/95	155	4		1 On The Attack		SOS 11102

GILLEY, Mickey

Born on 3/9/1936 in Natchez, Mississippi; raised in Ferriday, Louisiana. Country singer/pianist. First cousin to both **Jerry Lee Lewis** and Reverend Jimmy Swaggart. Owner of Gilleys nightclub in Pasadena, Texas. Gilley and the club were featured in the movie *Urban Cowboy*. The club closed in 1989.

DEBUT	PEAK	WKS	RIAA		Catalog	Label & Number
8/30/80	177	3		1 That's All That Matters To Me		Epic 36492
8/22/81	170	6		2 You Don't Know Me		Epic 37416
9/11/82	202	6		3 Put Your Dreams Away		Epic 38082

GILMAN, Billy

Born on 5/24/1988 in Westerly, Rhode Island; raised in Hope Valley, Rhode Island. Teenage country singer.

DEBUT	PEAK	WKS	RIAA		Catalog	Label & Number
7/8/00	22	48	▲²	1 One Voice		Epic 62086
11/4/00	42	10	●	2 Classic Christmas .... Cat:#15/6 [X]		Epic 61594
				Christmas charts: 5/'00, 20/'01		
5/26/01	45	11	●	3 Dare To Dream		Epic 62087
5/3/03	109	2		4 Music Through Heartsongs: Songs Based On The Poems Of Mattie J.T. Stepanek		Epic 86954
				Stepanek was a young poet and advocate who died of muscular dystrophy on 6/22/2004 (age 13)		

GILMER, Jimmy — see FIREBALLS, The

GILMOUR, David

Born on 3/6/1946 in Cambridge, England. Rock singer/guitarist. Member of **Pink Floyd**.

DEBUT	PEAK	WKS	RIAA		Catalog	Label & Number
7/1/78	29	18	●	1 David Gilmour		Columbia 35388
3/17/84	32	28	●	2 About Face		Columbia 39296
3/25/06	6	11		3 On An Island		Columbia 80280
10/11/08	26	4		4 Live In Gdansk [L]		Columbia 34546

GILSTRAP, Jim

Born in 1948 in Pittsburg, Texas. R&B singer.

DEBUT	PEAK	WKS	RIAA		Catalog	Label & Number
8/30/75	179	7		1 Swing Your Daddy		Roxbury 102

GIN BLOSSOMS

Alternative-rock band from Tempe, Arizona: Robin Wilson (vocals), Jesse Valenzuela (guitar), Scott Johnson (guitar), Bill Leen (bass) and Phillip Rhodes (drums). Early guitarist and principal songwriter Doug Hopkins died of a self-inflicted bullet wound on 12/5/1993 (age 32).

DEBUT	PEAK	WKS	RIAA		Catalog	Label & Number
5/1/93+	30	102	▲⁴	1 New Miserable Experience .... Cat:#36/3		A&M 5403
3/2/96	10	20	▲	2 Congratulations I'm Sorry		A&M 540469
8/26/06	159	1		3 Major Lodge Victory		Hybrid 20050

GINUWINE

Born Elgin Lumpkin on 10/15/1970 in Washington DC. Male R&B singer/songwriter.

DEBUT	PEAK	WKS	RIAA		Catalog	Label & Number
10/26/96+	26	68	▲²	1 Ginuwine...The Bachelor		550 Music 67685
4/3/99	5	54	▲²	2 100% Ginuwine		550 Music 69598
4/21/01	3¹	47	▲	3 The Life		Epic 69622
4/26/03	6	27	●	4 The Senior		Epic 86960
12/3/05	12	9		5 Back II Da Basics		Epic 93455
7/11/09	9	13		6 A Man's Thoughts		Asylum 519147

GIORGIO — see MORODER, Giorgio

GIOVANNI

Born Giovanni Marradi in Italy. Classically-trained pianist.

DEBUT	PEAK	WKS	RIAA		Catalog	Label & Number
3/1/97	170	2		1 Romance [I]		NewCastle 5527

GIOVANNI, Nikki, & The New York Community Choir

Born Yolande Goivanni on 6/7/1943 in Knoxville, Tennessee; raised in Lincoln Heights, Ohio. Female poet.

DEBUT	PEAK	WKS	RIAA		Catalog	Label & Number
8/21/71	165	13		1 Truth Is On Its Way [T]		Right-On 5001
				Giovanni recites her poems to the music of famous spirituals performed by various gospel artists		

Billboard			R I A A	ARTIST		
DEBUT	PEAK	WKS		Album Title	Catalog	Label & Number

GIPSY KINGS
Flamenco guitar group formed in Arles, France: brothers Andre, Chico and Nicolas Reyes, with brothers Diego, Paci and Tonino Baliardo.

12/17/88+	57	42	▲	1 Gipsy Kings .... [F]	Elektra Musician 60845
12/16/89+	95	19	●	2 Mosaique .... [F]	Elektra Musician 60892
8/3/91	120	7		3 Este Mundo .... [F]	Elektra Musician 61179
4/22/95	105	22	▲	4 The Best Of The Gipsy Kings .... [F-G]	Nonesuch 79358
3/30/96	143	3		5 Tierra Gitana .... [F]	Nonesuch 79399
8/30/97	97	7		6 Compas .... [F]	Nonesuch 79466
4/3/04	166	6		7 Roots	Nonesuch 79841

GIRL AUTHORITY
Female teen pop vocal group from Sudbury, Massachusetts: Alex "Fashion Girl" Bilbo, Jacqueline "All-Star Girl" Laviolette, Carly "Glamour Girl" Grayson, Jess "Boho Girl" Bonner, Gina "Urban Girl" Miele, Crystal "Country Girl" Evans, Kate "Party Girl" Barker, Zoë "Preppy Girl" Virant and Jessica "Party Girl" Tarr.

| 4/29/06 | 167 | 1 | | 1 Girl Authority .... | Zoe 431088 |

GIRLS
Alternative-rock band from San Francisco, California: Christopher Owens (vocals, guitar), Chet "JR" White (guitar), John Anderson (bass) and Garrett Godard (drums).

| 10/10/09 | 136 | 2 | | 1 Album .... | Fantasy Trashcan 010 |

GIRLSCHOOL
Female hard-rock band from England: Kim McAuliffe (vocals, guitar), Kelly Johnson (guitar), Enid Williams (bass) and Denise Dufort (drums). Johnson died of spinal cancer on 7/15/2007 (age 49).

5/22/82	182	5		1 Hit And Run	Stiff 18
11/27/82	207	2		2 Screaming Blue Murder	Mercury 4066
1/14/84	207	2		3 Play Dirty	Mercury 814689

GIUFFRIA
Rock band from California: Gregg Giuffria (keyboards; **Angel**), David Glen Eisley (vocals), Craig Goldy (guitar), Chuck Wright (bass) and Alan Krigger (drums). Lanny Cordola and David Sikes replaced Goldy and Wright in late 1985. Giuffria, Wright and Cordola joined **House Of Lords** in 1988.

| 12/8/84+ | 26 | 29 | | 1 Giuffria .... | MCA 5524 |
| 5/24/86 | 60 | 14 | | 2 Silk + Steel .... | MCA 5742 |

GLADSTONE
Pop band from Tyler, Texas: H.L. Voelker (vocals), Michael Rabon and Doug Rhone (guitars), Jerry Scheff (bass) and Ron Tutt (drums). Rabon was leader of **The Five Americans**.

| 9/23/72 | 208 | 4 | | 1 Gladstone .... | ABC 751 |

GLASS, Philip
Born on 1/31/1937 in Baltimore, Maryland. New Age composer.

| 4/10/82 | 121 | 6 | | 1 Glassworks .... [I] | CBS 37265 |
| 4/12/86 | 91 | 13 | | 2 Songs From Liquid Days .... | CBS 39564 |

GLASS HARP
Rock trio from Youngstown, Ohio: Phil Keaggy (vocals, guitar), Dan Pecchio (bass) and John Sferra (drums).

2/27/71	216	7		1 Glass Harp	Decca 75261
11/27/71	192	3		2 Synergy	Decca 75306
9/23/72	203	4		3 It Makes Me Glad	Decca 75358

GLASSJAW
Rock band from Long Island, New York: Daryl Palumbo (vocals), Justin Beck (guitar), Todd Weinstock (guitar), Manuel Carrero (bass) and Larry Gorman (drums). Palumbo was also a member of **Head Automatica**.

| 7/27/02 | 82 | 3 | | 1 Worship And Tribute .... | Warner 48286 |

GLASS MOON
Pop-rock band from Raleigh, North Carolina: Dave Adams (vocals, keyboards), Jaime Glaser (guitar), Nestor Nunez (bass) and Chris Jones (drums).

| 5/10/80 | 148 | 9 | | 1 Glass Moon .... | Radio 2003 |

GLASS TIGER
Pop-rock band from Newmarket, Ontario, Canada: Alan Frew (vocals), Al Connelly (guitar), Sam Reid (keyboards), Wayne Parker (bass) and Michael Hanson (drums).

| 7/19/86+ | 27 | 51 | ● | 1 The Thin Red Line .... | Manhattan 53032 |
| 5/7/88 | 82 | 15 | | 2 Diamond Sun .... | EMI-Manhattan 48684 |

GLASVEGAS
Alternative-rock band from Glasgow, Scotland: cousins James Allan (vocals, guitar) and Rob Allan (guitar), with Paul Donoghue (bass) and Caroline McKay (drums).

| 1/24/09 | 126 | 3 | | 1 Glasvegas .... | Columbia 43565 |

GLAZER, Tom, And The Do-Re-Mi Children's Chorus
Born on 9/3/1914 in Philadelphia, Pennsylvania. Died on 2/21/2003 (age 88). Folk singer. Hosted own ABC radio program (1945-47).

| 7/27/63 | 114 | 8 | | 1 On Top Of Spaghetti .... [N] | Kapp 3331 |

Billboard			R I A A	ARTIST Album Title	Catalog	Label & Number
DEBUT	PEAK	WKS				

GLEASON, Jackie   **1950s: #10 / All-Time: #253**

Born Herbert John Gleason on 2/26/1916 in Brooklyn, New York. Died of cancer on 6/24/1987 (age 71). Legendary movie and TV comedian. Father of actress Linda Miller. Grandfather of actor Jason Patric. His albums featured dreamy "mood music" played by studio orchestras, conducted by Gleason with trumpet solos by Bobby Hackett and Pee Wee Erwin; much of the music was written by Gleason.

1/28/56	**7**	5		1 **Music For Lovers Only/Music To Make You Misty** **[E-I]**		Capitol 475 [2]
				reissue of 2 albums: *Music For Lovers Only* (#1 for 23 weeks in 1953 on Capitol 352) and *Music To Make You Misty* (#2 in 1954 on Capitol 455)		
3/5/55	**5**	8		2 **Music To Remember Her** **[I]**		Capitol 570
				LP: Capitol W-570 (#5); EP: Capitol EBF-570 (#6)		
6/25/55	**❶**¹	12		3 **Lonesome Echo** **[I]**		Capitol 627
				LP: Capitol W-627 (#1); EP: Capitol EAP-627 (#2)		
11/12/55	**2**¹	7		4 **Romantic Jazz** **[I]**		Capitol 568
				LP: Capitol W-568 (#2); EP: Capitol EBF-568 (#6)		
2/25/56	**8**	4		5 **Music To Change Her Mind** **[I]**		Capitol 632
6/9/56	**10**	10		6 **Night Winds** **[I]**		Capitol 717
12/8/56	**16**	3		7 **Merry Christmas** **[X-I]**		Capitol 758
				also see #19 below; Christmas charts: 25/'63, 70/'66, 32/'67		
8/26/57	**13**	2	●	8 **Music For The Love Hours** **[I]**		Capitol 816
9/9/57	**16**	10		9 **Velvet Brass** **[I]**		Capitol 859
12/9/57	**14**	4		10 **Jackie Gleason Presents "Oooo!"** **[I]**		Capitol 905
8/10/63	**82**	5		11 **Movie Themes - For Lovers Only** **[I]**		Capitol 1877
12/7/63	**115**	8		12 **Today's Romantic Hits/For Lovers Only** **[I]**		Capitol 1978
6/6/64	**82**	10		13 **Today's Romantic Hits/For Lovers Only, Vol. 2** **[I]**		Capitol 2056
2/5/66	**141**	4		14 **Silk 'N' Brass** **[I]**		Capitol 2409
11/26/66	**71**	11		15 **How Sweet It Is For Lovers** **[I]**		Capitol 2582
6/24/67	**200**	2		16 **A Taste Of Brass For Lovers Only** **[I]**		Capitol 2684
12/23/67	**37**ˣ	2		17 **'Tis The Season** **[X-I]**		Capitol 2791
				also see #19 below		
8/23/69	**192**	2		18 **Close-Up** **[E-I]**		Capitol 255 [2]
				reissue of *Music For Lovers Only* (#1 in 1953 on Capitol 352) and *Music, Martinis and Memories* (#1 in 1954 on Capitol 509)		
12/20/69	**13**ˣ	3		19 **All I Want For Christmas** **[X-I-R]**		Capitol 346 [2]
				reissue of albums #7 and #17 above; Christmas charts: 13/'69, 21/'70		

GLEE CAST

Albums below feature various cast members of the Fox-TV musical comedy series *Glee*.

11/21/09	**4**	28↑	●	1 **Glee: Season One: The Music Volume 1** **[TV]**		Fox 54090
12/26/09	**3**¹	23↑	●	2 **Glee: Season One: The Music Volume 2** **[TV]**		Fox 61705

GLITTER, Gary

Born Paul Gadd on 5/8/1944 in Banbury, Oxfordshire, England. Glam-rock singer. In March 2006, sentenced to three years in a Vietnam prison for sexually abusing two underage girls.

10/28/72	**186**	8		1 **Glitter**		Bell 1108

GLORIANA

Country band formed in Nashville, Tennessee: brothers Tom Gossin and Mike Gossin, with Rachel Reinert and **Cheyenne Kimball**.

8/22/09	**3**¹	14		1 **Gloriana**		Emblem 519780

GLOVER, Roger

Born on 11/30/1945 in Brecon, Powys, Wales. Rock singer/bassist. Member of **Deep Purple** and **Rainbow**.

1/24/76	**142**	8		1 **The Butterfly Ball and the Grasshopper's Feast**		UK 56000
6/16/84	**101**	12		2 **Mask**		21 Records 9009

GNARLS BARKLEY

Collaboration between R&B producer Brian "Danger Mouse" Burton and singer Thomas "Cee-Lo" Callaway (of **Goodie Mob**).

5/27/06	**4**	47	▲	1 **St. Elsewhere**		Downtown 70003
4/5/08	**12**	14		2 **The Odd Couple**		Downtown 450236

GO, Gary

Born Gary Baker in 1985 in Wembley, London, England. Pop-rock singer/songwriter/producer.

8/29/09	**153**	1		1 **Gary Go**		Canvas Room 013156

GOANNA

Rock band from Australia: Shane Howard (vocals), Warrick Harwood (guitar), Graham Davidge (guitar), Peter Coughlan (bass) and Robert Ross (drums). Group named after an Australian reptile species.

6/25/83	**179**	5		1 **Spirit Of Place**		Atco 90081

GOAPELE

Born Goapele Mohlabane on 7/11/1977 in Oakland, California (African father/American mother). Female R&B singer/songwriter. Name pronounced: gwa-pa-lay.

1/14/06	**139**	3		1 **Change It All**		Skyblaze 92910

GOATWHORE

Death metal band from New Orleans, Louisiana: Louis Falgoust (vocals), Sammy Duet (guitar), Nathan Bergeron (bass) and Zack Simmons (drums).

7/11/09	**190**	1		1 **Carving Out The Eyes Of God**		Metal Blade 14743

Billboard			R I A A	ARTIST		
DEBUT	PEAK	WKS		Album Title	Catalog	Label & Number

GODFATHERS, The
Rock band formed in London, England: brothers Peter Coyne (vocals) and Chris Coyne (bass), with Mike Gibson (guitar), Kris Dollimore (guitar) and George Mazur (drums).

| 2/20/88 | 91 | 16 | | 1 Birth, School, Work, Death .... | | Epic 40946 |
| 5/20/89 | 174 | 6 | | 2 More Songs About Love & Hate .... | | Epic 45023 |

GOD FORBID
Heavy metal band from East Brunswick, New Jersey: Byron Davis (vocals), brothers Doc Coyle and Dallas Coyle (guitars), John Outcalt (bass) and Corey Pierce (drums).

| 10/8/05 | 119 | 1 | | 1 IV: Constitution Of Treason .... | | Century Media 8266 |
| 3/14/09 | 110 | 1 | | 2 Earthsblood .... | | Century Media 8519 |

GODFREY, Arthur — see QUINN, Carmel

GODHEAD
Hard-rock band from Washington DC: Jason Miller (vocals, guitar), Mike Miller (guitar), Ulrich "Method" Hepperlin (bass) and James O'Connor (drums).

| 2/10/01 | 153 | 1 | | 1 2000 Years Of Human Error .... | | Posthuman 27289 |

GOD HELP THE GIRL
Studio project assembled by Stuart Murdoch (of **Belle And Sebastian**).

| 7/11/09 | 145 | 1 | | 1 God Help The Girl .... | | Matador 866 |

GODLEY & CREME
Duo from Manchester, England: Kevin Godley (born on 10/7/1945) and Lol Creme (born on 9/19/1947). Both were members of Hotlegs and **10cc**.

| 8/17/85 | 37 | 15 | | 1 The History Mix Volume 1 .... | | Polydor 825981 |

GOD LIVES UNDERWATER
Techno-rock duo from Los Angeles, California: David Reilly and Jeff Turzo.

| 4/11/98 | 137 | 2 | | 1 Life In The So-Called Space Age .... | | A&M 540871 |

GODSMACK
Heavy-metal band formed in Boston, Massachusetts: Salvatore "Sully" Erna (vocals; born on 2/7/1968), Tony Rombola (guitar; born on 11/24/1964), Robbie Merrill (bass; born on 6/13/1963) and Tommy Stewart (drums; born on 5/26/1966). Shannon Larkin (born on 4/24/1967) replaced Stewart in late 2002. Stewart joined **Fuel** in 2005.

1/23/99	22	92	▲⁴	1 Godsmack Cat:❶³/69		Republic 53190
11/18/00	5	52	▲²	2 Awake		Republic 159688
4/26/03	❶¹	57	▲	3 Faceless		Republic 067854
4/3/04	5	19	●	4 The Other Side [EP]		Republic 001539
5/13/06	❶¹	27	●	5 IV		Universal 006548
12/22/07	35	23		6 Good Times, Bad Times...Ten Years Of Godsmack .... [G]		Universal Rep. 010296

GOD'S PROPERTY
Funk-rap-gospel collective of 50 young singers (ages 16-26) founded by Linda Searight in Dallas, Texas. Members of mentor **Kirk Franklin**'s Nu Nation.

| 6/14/97 | 3¹ | 54 | ▲³ | 1 God's Property | | B-Rite 90093 |
| | | | | *Grammy: Gospel Album* | | |

GODZ, The
Rock band from Columbus, Ohio: Bob Hill (guitar), Mark Chatfield (guitar), Eric Moore (bass) and Glen Cataline (drums). All share vocals.

| 4/8/78 | 191 | 5 | | 1 The Godz .... | | Millennium 8003 |
| 2/17/79 | 189 | 2 | | 2 Nothing Is Sacred .... | | Casablanca 7134 |

GOFFIN, Louise
Born in 1960 in Brooklyn, New York. Pop singer/songwriter. Daughter of prolific songwriters Gerry Goffin and **Carole King**.

| 8/4/79 | 87 | 13 | | 1 Kid Blue .... | | Asylum 203 |

GOGOL BORDELLO
Multi-ethnic gypsy punk-rock band formed in New York: Eugene Hutz, Sergey Ryabtsev, Yuri Lemeshev, Oren Kaplan, Thomas Gobena, Pamela Racine, Elizabeth Sun, Pedro Erazo and Oliver Charles.

| 7/28/07 | 115 | 1 | | 1 Super Taranta! .... | | Side One Dummy 1334 |

GO-GO'S
Female rock band formed in Los Angeles, California: **Belinda Carlisle** (vocals; born on 8/17/1958), **Jane Wiedlin** (guitar; born on 5/20/1958), Charlotte Caffey (guitar; born on 10/21/1953), Kathy Valentine (bass; born on 1/7/1959) and Gina Schock (drums; born on 8/31/1957). Disbanded in 1984. Reunions in 1990, 1994 and 2001. Caffey formed **The Graces** in 1989.

8/1/81+	❶⁶	72	▲²	1 Beauty And The Beat Cat:#24/1		I.R.S. 70021
				RS500 #413		
8/14/82	8	28	●	2 Vacation Cat:#28/36		I.R.S. 70031
4/7/84	18	32		3 Talk Show		I.R.S. 70041
11/17/90	127	4		4 Greatest [G]		I.R.S. 44797
6/2/01	57	3		5 God Bless The Go-Go's		Beyond 578182

GOJIRA
Death metal band from Bayonne, France: brothers Joe Duplantier (vocals, guitar) and Mario Duplantier (drums), with Christian Andreu (guitar) and Jean-Michael Labadie (bass). Joe Duplantier is also the bassist for **Cavalera Conspiracy**.

| 11/1/08 | 138 | 1 | | 1 The Way Of All Flesh .... | | Prosthetic 10064 |

Billboard			R I A A	ARTIST		
DEBUT	PEAK	WKS		Album Title	Catalog	Label & Number

GOLD, Andrew
Born on 8/2/1951 in Burbank, California. Pop singer/songwriter/pianist. Son of composer Ernest Gold and singer Marni Nixon. Member of **Wax**.

1/10/76	190	2		1 Andrew Gold		Asylum 1047
5/7/77	95	16		2 What's Wrong With This Picture?		Asylum 1086
2/25/78	81	14		3 All This And Heaven Too		Asylum 116

GOLD, Marty
Born on 12/26/1915 in Brooklyn, New York. Composer/conductor/pianist.

4/13/63	10	18		1 Soundpower!	[I]	RCA Victor 2620

GOLDDIGGERS, The
Female singing/dancing troupe from **Dean Martin**'s TV show: Pauline Antony, Wanda Bailey, Jackie Chidsey, Paula Cinko, Rosetta Cox, Michelle Fave, Tara Leigh, Susan Lund, Micki McGlone and Patricia Mickey.

8/2/69	142	7		1 The Golddiggers		Metromedia 1009

GOLDEN EARRING
Rock band from The Hague, Netherlands: Barry Hay (vocals), George Kooymans (guitar), Rinus Gerritsen (bass) and Cesar Zuiderwijk (drums).

8/3/74	203	5		1 The Golden Earrings .... recorded in 1967	[E]	Capitol 11315
5/4/74	12	29	●	2 Moontan		Track 396
4/12/75	108	8		3 Switch		Track 2139
2/28/76	156	4		4 To The Hilt		MCA 2183
5/28/77	182	2		5 Mad Love		MCA 2254
10/22/77	203	4		6 Live	[L]	MCA 8009 [2]
11/4/78	204	3		7 Grab It For A Second		MCA 3057
12/11/82+	24	30		8 Cut		21 Records 9004
3/17/84	107	9		9 N.E.W.S.		21 Records 9008
11/24/84	158	6		10 Something Heavy Going Down - Live From The Twilight Zone	[L]	21 Records 823717
7/12/86	196	2		11 The Hole		21 Records 90514

GOLDEN GATE STRINGS
Studio group produced by Stu Phillips and conducted by Sid Feller. Phillips earlier conducted **The Hollyridge Strings**.

5/27/67	200	2		1 The Monkees Song Book	[I]	Epic 26248

GOLDEN SMOG
Alternative-rock band formed in Minneapolis, Minnesota: Jeff Tweedy (vocals, guitar), Gary Louris (guitar), Marc Perlman (bass) and Kraig Johnson (drums). Tweedy is also the leader of **Wilco**. Louris and Perlman are also members of **The Jayhawks**.

8/5/06	95	2		1 Another Fine Day		Lost Highway 006029

GOLDFINGER
Rock band from Santa Monica, California: John Feldman (vocals, guitar), Charlie Paulson (guitar), Simon Williams (bass) and Darrin Pfeiffer (drums). Kelly LeMieux replaced Williams in 1999.

5/11/96	110	14		1 Goldfinger		Mojo 53007
9/27/97	85	4		2 Hang-Ups		Mojo 53079
4/15/00	109	2		3 Stomping Ground		Mojo 157531
6/8/02	136	1		4 Open Your Eyes		Mojo 41806

GOLDFRAPP
Eclectic-pop duo from Bath, England: singer/songwriter/keyboardist Alison Goldfrapp and songwriter Will Gregory.

3/25/06	138	2		1 Supernature		Mute 9296
3/15/08	48	3		2 Seventh Tree		Mute 9381

GOLDIE
Born Clifford Price on 9/19/1965 in Wolverhampton, Warwickshire, England. Male techno performer.

2/21/98	178	1		1 Saturnzreturn		London 828983 [2]

GOLDSBORO, Bobby
Born on 1/18/1941 in Marianna, Florida. Singer/songwriter/guitarist. Hosted own TV variety show from 1972-75.

5/6/67	165	3		1 Solid Goldsboro - Bobby Goldsboro's Greatest Hits	[G]	United Artists 6561
4/20/68	5	48	●	2 Honey		United Artists 6642
9/21/68	116	13		3 Word Pictures Featuring Autumn Of My Life		United Artists 6657
6/7/69	60	13		4 Today		United Artists 6704
1/17/70	139	11		5 Muddy Mississippi Line		United Artists 6735
7/4/70	103	10		6 Bobby Goldsboro's Greatest Hits	[G]	United Artists 5502
1/23/71	120	13		7 We Gotta Start Lovin' .... also released as *Watching Scotty Grow*		United Artists 6777
8/28/71	142	5		8 Come Back Home		United Artists 5516
5/27/72	214	3		9 California Wine		United Artists 5578
3/31/73	207	2		10 Brand New Kind Of Love		United Artists 019
9/29/73	150	11		11 Summer (The First Time)		United Artists 124
11/16/74	174	3		12 Bobby Goldsboro's 10th Anniversary Album	[G]	United Artists 311 [2]

~ ~ ~ ~ ~ ~ ~ ~ ~ ~ **NON-CHARTED ALBUMS** ~ ~ ~ ~ ~ ~ ~ ~ ~ ~ ~ ~ ~

1964 **The Bobby Goldsboro Album**   1965 **Little Things**

Billboard			R I A A	ARTIST		
DEBUT	PEAK	WKS		Album Title	Catalog	Label & Number

GOMEZ
Alternative-pop band from Southport, Merseyside, England: Ben Ottewell (vocals, guitar), Ian Ball (guitar), Tom Gray (keyboards), Paul Blackburn (bass) and Olly Peacock (drums).

6/5/04	191	1	1 Split The Difference		Hut 98492
5/20/06	106	3	2 How We Operate		ATO 21547
4/18/09	60	3	3 A New Tide		ATO 0070

GOMEZ, Selena
Born on 7/22/1992 in New York; raised in Grand Prairie, Texas. Pop singer/actress. Plays "Alex Russo" on TV's *Wizards Of Waverly Place*.

10/17/09	9	33↑ ●	1 Kiss And Tell		Hollywood 002831
			SELENA GOMEZ & THE SCENE		

GOMM, Ian
Born on 3/17/1947 in Ealing, London, England. Pop-rock singer/songwriter/guitarist.

9/22/79	104	12	1 Gomm With The Wind		Stiff 36103
3/21/81	210	2	2 What A Blow		Stiff/Epic 36433

GONZALEZ
Disco band formed in London, England: Linda Taylor and Alan Marshall (vocals), Jim Cansfield (guitar), Roy Davies (keyboards), Bobby Stignac (percussion), Mick Eve, Chris Mercer, Bud Beadle, Colin Jacas, Ron Carthy and Martin Drover (horn section), Hugh Bullen (bass) and Sergio Castillo (drums).

1/20/79	67	14	1 Shipwrecked		Capitol 11855

GONZALEZ, Jose
Born in Gothenburg, Sweden. Folk-rock singer/songwriter/guitarist.

10/13/07	132	1	1 In Our Nature		Imperial 9367

GOOD CHARLOTTE
Alternative-rock band from Waldorf, Maryland: twin brothers Joel Madden (vocals) and Benji Madden (guitar), with Billy Martin (guitar), Paul Thomas (bass) and Aaron Escolopio (drums). Chris Wilson replaced Escolopio in 2000. Dean Butterworth replaced Wilson in 2006.

10/14/00	185	2 ●	1 Good Charlotte	Cat:❶¹/57	Daylight 61452
10/19/02	7	95 ▲³	2 The Young And The Hopeless	Cat:#6/24	Daylight 86486
10/23/04	3¹	34 ▲	3 The Chronicles Of Life And Death		Daylight 92425
4/14/07	7	13	4 Good Morning Revival		Daylight 76940

GOODIE MOB
Male rap group from Atlanta, Georgia: Thomas **"Cee-Lo"** Callaway, Willie "Khujo" Knighton, Cameron **"Big Gipp"** and Robert "T-Mo" Barnett. Members of **Dungeon Family**.

11/25/95	45	29 ●	1 Soul Food		LaFace 26018
4/25/98	6	20 ●	2 Still Standing		LaFace 26047
1/8/00	48	12 ●	3 World Party		LaFace 26064
7/17/04	85	2	4 One Monkey Don't Stop No Show		Koch 8480

GOOD LIFE, The
Alternative-rock band from Omaha, Nebraska: Tim Kasher (vocals, guitar), Ryan Fox (guitar), Stefanie Drootin (bass) and Roger Lewis (drums). Kasher is also the leader of **Cursive**.

9/29/07	195	1	1 Help Wanted Nights		Saddle Creek 108

GOODMAN, Benny, and his Orchestra
Born on 5/30/1909 in Chicago, Illinois. Died of a heart attack on 6/13/1986 (age 77). Legendary clarinetist/orchestra leader. Known as "The King of Swing."
    AWARD: Grammy: Lifetime Achievement 1986

3/19/55	7	8	1 B.G. In Hi-Fi [I]		Capitol 565
			LP: Capitol W-565 (#7); EP: Capitol EAP-565 (#11)		
3/24/56	4	10	2 The Benny Goodman Story [I-S]		Decca 8252/3 [2]
11/10/62	80	6	3 Benny Goodman In Moscow [I-L]		RCA Victor 6008 [2]
3/7/64	90	10	4 Together Again! [I]		RCA Victor 2698
4/3/71	189	7	5 Benny Goodman Today [I-L]		London Phase 4 21 [2]
			recorded in Stockholm, Sweden		

GOODMAN, Dickie
Born Richard Goodman on 4/19/1934 in Brooklyn, New York. Died of a self-inflicted gunshot wound on 11/6/1989 (age 55). Goodman and partner Bill Buchanan originated the novelty "break-in" recordings featuring bits of the original versions of Top 40 hits interwoven throughout the recording. Buchanan died of cancer on 8/1/1996 (age 66).

12/6/75+	144	8	1 Mr. Jaws And Other Fables [G-N]		Cash 6000

GOODMAN, Jerry
Born on 3/16/1949 in Chicago, Illinois. Jazz-rock violinist. Member of **The Flock**.

2/8/75	150	3	1 Like Children		Nemperor 430
			JERRY GOODMAN & JAN HAMMER		

GOODMAN, Steve
Born on 7/25/1948 in Chicago, Illinois. Died of leukemia on 9/20/1984 (age 36). Folk singer/songwriter/guitarist.

2/24/73	214	3	1 Somebody Else's Troubles		Buddah 5121
8/23/75	144	6	2 Jessie's Jig & Other Favorites		Asylum 1037
5/15/76	175	4	3 Words We Can Dance To		Asylum 1061

GOODMAN, Vestal
Born on 12/13/1929 in Fyffe, Alabama. Died of complications from the flu on 12/27/2003 (age 74). Mother of the Happy Goodman Family gospel group. Known as the "Queen of Gospel."

| 5/27/00 | 177 | 1 | | 1 Vestal & Friends .... | | Pamplin 2058 |

GOOD RATS
Rock band from Long Island, New York: brothers Peppi Marchello (vocals) and Mickey Marchello (guitar), with John Gatto (guitar), Lenny Kotke (bass) and Joe Franco (drums).

| 2/10/79 | 210 | 1 | | 1 Birth Comes To Us All .... | | Passport 9830 |

GOODREM, Delta
Born on 11/9/1984 in Sydney, New South Wales, Australia. Female singer/actress. Played "Nina Tucker" on the popular Australian soap opera *Neighbours*.

| 8/2/08 | 116 | 1 | | 1 Delta .... | | Mercury 011262 |

GOOD, THE BAD & THE QUEEN, The
Rock band formed in England: Damon Albarn (vocals, keyboards; **Blur**), Simon Tong (guitar), Paul Simonon (bass; **The Clash**) and Tony Allen (drums).

| 2/10/07 | 49 | 7 | | 1 The Good, The Bad & The Queen .... | | Parlophone 73067 |

GOODY GOODY
Disco studio group assembled by producer Vincent Montana. Also see **Salsoul Orchestra**.

| 11/11/78 | 210 | 1 | | 1 Goody Goody .... | | Atlantic 19197 |

GOO GOO DOLLS
Adult Alternative rock trio from Buffalo, New York: John Rzeznik (vocals, guitar; born on 12/5/1965), Robby Takac (bass; born on 9/30/1964) and Mike Malinin (drums; born on 10/10/1967).

9/9/95+	27	54	▲²	1 A Boy Named Goo		Warner 45750
10/10/98	15	104	▲²	2 Dizzy Up The Girl	Cat.#15/11	Warner 47058
6/16/01	164	1		3 What I Learned About Ego, Opinion, Art & Commerce (1987-2000) .... [K]		Warner 47945
4/27/02	4	25	●	4 Gutterflower		Warner 48206
12/11/04	161	1		5 Live In Buffalo - July 4th 2004 .... [L]		Warner 48867
5/13/06	9	20		6 Let Love In		Warner 49748
12/1/07	33	19		7 Greatest Hits Volume One: The Singles .... [G]		Warner 144444
9/6/08	158	1		8 Vol. 2 .... [K]		Warner 288252

GOOSE CREEK SYMPHONY
Country rock band formed in Phoenix, Arizona: Ritchie Hart (vocals, guitar), Paul Howard (guitar), Bob Henke (keyboards), Ellis Schweid (fiddle), Chris Mostert (sax), Dave Birkett (bass) and Dennis Kenmore (drums). Henke later joined **Dr. Hook**.

| 6/3/72 | 167 | 8 | | 1 Words Of Earnest .... | | Capitol 11044 |
| 11/23/74 | 201 | 7 | | 2 Do Your Thing But Don't Touch Mine .... | | Columbia 32918 |

GORDON, Mike
Born on 6/3/1965 in Sudbury, Massachusetts. Alternative-rock singer/bassist. Member of **Phish**.

| 8/23/08 | 170 | 1 | | 1 The Green Sparrow .... | | Rounder 619083 |

GORDON, Nina
Born Nina Shapiro (Gordon is her mother's maiden name) on 11/14/1967 in Washington DC; raised in Chicago, Illinois. Female singer/songwriter/guitarist. Former member of **Veruca Salt**.

| 8/12/00 | 123 | 10 | | 1 Tonight And The Rest Of My Life .... | | Warner 47746 |

GORDON, Robert
Born on 3/29/1947 in Bethesda, Maryland. Rockabilly singer. Member of **Tuff Darts** until 1976.

10/1/77	142	8		1 Robert Gordon With Link Wray		Private Stock 2030
3/18/78	124	7		2 Fresh Fish Special		Private Stock 7008
				above 2 feature guitarist **Link Wray**		
3/24/79	106	12		3 Rock Billy Boogie		RCA Victor 3294
2/2/80	150	9		4 Bad Boy		RCA Victor 3523
4/18/81	117	15		5 Are You Gonna Be The One		RCA Victor 3773
8/28/82	201	6		6 Too Fast To Live Too Young To Die		RCA Victor 4380

GORE, Lesley
Born on 5/2/1946 in Manhattan, New York; raised in Tenafly, New Jersey. Pop singer. Appeared in the movies *Girls On The Beach*, *Ski Party* and *The T.A.M.I. Show*.

7/13/63	24	15		1 I'll Cry If I Want To		Mercury 60805
1/25/64	125	8		2 Lesley Gore Sings Of Mixed-Up Hearts		Mercury 60849
7/18/64	127	6		3 Boys, Boys, Boys		Mercury 60901
12/12/64	146	2		4 Girl Talk		Mercury 60943
7/17/65	95	24		5 The Golden Hits Of Lesley Gore .... [G]		Mercury 61024
12/4/65	120	4		6 My Town, My Guy & Me		Mercury 61042
5/13/67	169	5		7 California Nights		Mercury 61120

GORE, Martin L.
Born Martin Lee Gore on 7/23/1961 in Basildon, Essex, England. Member of **Depeche Mode**.

| 8/12/89 | 156 | 5 | | 1 Counterfeit .... [EP] | | Sire 25980 |

GORILLAZ
Animated hip-hop/rock band created by Jamie Hewlett and Damon Albarn (of **Blur**): 2-D (vocals, keyboards), Noodle (guitar), Murdoc (bass) and Russel (drums).

7/7/01	14	42	▲	1 Gorillaz .... **Cat:**#31/8		Parlophone 33748
3/16/02	84	4		2 G Sides		Parlophone 11967
8/3/02	156	1		3 Spacemonkeyz Versus Gorillaz - Laika Come Home.................		Parlophone 40362
6/11/05	6	68	▲²	4 Demon Days		Parlophone 73838
12/8/07	166	1		5 D-Sides .... [K]		Virgin 10558 [2]

GORILLA ZOE
Born Alonzo Mathis on 11/28/1980 in Atlanta, Georgia. Male rapper/songwriter.

10/13/07	18	7		1 Welcome To The Zoo		Block 293180
4/4/09	8	13		2 Don't Feed Da Animals		Block 514278

GORKY PARK
Rock band from Russia: Nikolai Noskov (vocals), Alexei Belov (guitar), Jan Ianenkov (guitar), "Big" Sasha Minkov (bass) and "Little" Sasha Lvov (drums). Group named after a famous park in Moscow.

9/9/89	80	21		1 Gorky Park		Mercury 838628

GORME, Eydie   1950s: #28 / All-Time: #368
Born Edith Gormezano on 8/16/1931 in the Bronx, New York. Adult Contemporary singer. Vocalist with the big bands of Tommy Tucker and Tex Beneke in the late 1940s. Featured on **Steve Allen's** The Tonight Show. Married **Steve Lawrence** on 12/29/1957.

5/6/57	14	10		1 Eydie Gorme		ABC-Paramount 150
10/28/57	19	4		2 Eydie Swings The Blues..		ABC-Paramount 192
3/31/58	19	4		3 Eydie Gorme Vamps The Roaring 20's		ABC-Paramount 218
11/3/58	20	1		4 Eydie In Love..		ABC-Paramount 246
4/6/63	22	22		5 Blame It On The Bossa Nova		Columbia 2012 / 8812
2/15/64	143	3		6 Gorme Country Style		Columbia 2120 / 8920
9/12/64	54	22		7 Amor .... [F]		Columbia 2203 / 9003
8/28/65	53	11		8 More Amor .... [F]		Columbia 2376 / 9176
6/4/66	22	37		9 Don't Go To Strangers		Columbia 2476 / 9276
12/3/66	9ˣ	4		10 Navidad Means Christmas .... [X-F]		Columbia 2557 / 9357
				EYDIE GORME AND THE TRIO LOS PANCHOS		
2/18/67	85	18		11 Softly, As I Leave You		Columbia 2594 / 9394
5/20/67	136	6		12 Together On Broadway...		Columbia 2636 / 9436
				STEVE LAWRENCE & EYDIE GORME		
12/2/67+	148	9		13 Eydie Gorme's Greatest Hits... [G]		Columbia 2764 / 9564
3/8/69	141	6		14 What It Was, Was Love		RCA Victor 4115
5/10/69	188	3		15 Real True Lovin'...		RCA Victor 4107
				STEVE LAWRENCE & EYDIE GORME (above 2)		
3/7/70	105	12		16 Tonight I'll Say A Prayer		RCA Victor 4303
7/24/71	213	3		17 It Was A Good Time		MGM 4780
7/1/72	208	1		18 The World Of Steve & Eydie..		MGM 4803
				STEVE LAWRENCE & EYDIE GORME with The Mike Curb Congregation		

GOSSIP, The
Punk-rock trio formed in Olympia, Washington: Beth Ditto (vocals), Brace Paine (guitar) and Hannah Blilie (drums).

10/24/09	164	1		1 Music For Men		Columbia 06230

GO! TEAM, The
Alternative-rock band formed in England: Kaori Tsuchida (vocals), Ian Parton (guitar), Sam Dook (guitar), Nkechi Egenamba (percussion), Jamie Bell (bass) and Chi Taylor (drums).

9/29/07	142	1		1 Proof Of Youth		Sub Pop 750

GOUDREAU, Barry
Born on 11/29/1951 in Lynn, Massachusetts. Rock guitarist. Member of **Boston**, **Orion The Hunter** and **RTZ.**

9/20/80	88	8		1 Barry Goudreau		Portrait 36542

GOULD, Morton
Born on 12/10/1913 in Richmond Hill, New York. Died on 2/21/1996 (age 82). Prolific conductor/arranger.
    AWARD: Grammy: Lifetime Achievement 2005

11/9/59	5	52		1 Tchaikovsky: 1812 Overture/Ravel: Bolero .... [I]		RCA Victor 2345
7/18/60	3¹	41		2 Grofe: Grand Canyon Suite/Beethoven: Wellington's Victory ..... [I]		RCA Victor 2433

GOULDMAN, Graham
Born on 5/10/1946 in Manchester, England. Singer/songwriter/bassist. Member of **10cc.**

8/16/80	209	1		1 Animalympics .... [S]		A&M 4810

GOULET, Robert   1960s: #39 / All-Time: #247
Born on 11/26/1933 in Lawrence, Massachusetts (French Canadian parents). Died of lung failure on 10/30/2007 (age 73). Adult Contemporary singer/actor. Appeared in several movies and Broadway shows. Best known for playing Sir Lancelot in Broadway's Camelot.
    AWARD: Grammy: Best New Artist 1962

3/17/62+	43	65		1 Always You		Columbia 1676 / 8476
9/1/62	20	55		2 Two Of Us		Columbia 1826 / 8626

Billboard			R I A A	ARTIST	Catalog	Label & Number
DEBUT	PEAK	WKS		Album Title		

GOULET, Robert — cont'd

DEBUT	PEAK	WKS		ARTIST / Album Title	Catalog	Label & Number
1/5/63	9	48		3 Sincerely Yours...		Columbia 1931 / 8731
4/27/63	11	29		4 The Wonderful World Of Love		Columbia 1993 / 8793
10/19/63	16	23		5 Robert Goulet In Person .... [L]		Columbia 2088 / 8888
				recorded at the Chicago Opera House		
11/30/63	4ˣ	16		6 This Christmas I Spend With You [X]		Columbia 2076 / 8876
				Christmas charts: 4/'63, 5/'64, 17/'65, 90/'67, 30/'68		
5/2/64	31	22		7 Manhattan Tower/The Man Who Loves Manhattan		Columbia 6050 / 2450
				composed and conducted by Gordon Jenkins		
10/17/64	72	16		8 Without You		Columbia 2200 / 9000
12/26/64+	5	29	●	9 My Love Forgive Me		Columbia 2296 / 9096
6/5/65	69	16		10 Begin To Love		Columbia 2342 / 9142
8/14/65	31	19		11 Summer Sounds		Columbia 2380 / 9180
12/11/65+	33	22		12 Robert Goulet On Broadway		Columbia 2418 / 9218
4/30/66	73	12		13 I Remember You		Columbia 2482 / 9282
3/11/67	145	3		14 Robert Goulet On Broadway, Volume 2		Columbia 2586 / 9386
9/14/68	162	15		15 Woman, Woman		Columbia 9695
4/12/69	135	13		16 Both Sides Now		Columbia 9763
9/6/69	174	3		17 Souvenir d'Italie		Columbia 9874
11/14/70	198	2		18 I Wish You Love .... [K]		Columbia 30011 [2]

GOURDIN, Noel
Born in Boston, Massachusetts. R&B singer.

DEBUT	PEAK	WKS		ARTIST / Album Title	Catalog	Label & Number
8/9/08	36	6		1 After My Time		Epic 80645

GOV'T MULE
Southern-rock trio from Macon, Georgia: **Warren Haynes** (vocals, guitar), Allen Woody (bass) and Matt Abts (drums). Haynes and Woody were both members of **The Allman Brothers Band**. Woody died of a heart attack on 8/26/2000 (age 44).

DEBUT	PEAK	WKS		ARTIST / Album Title	Catalog	Label & Number
11/10/01	128	1		1 The Deep End Volume 1		ATO 21502
10/26/02	117	1		2 The Deep End Volume 2		ATO 21507
10/25/03	153	1		3 The Deepest End: Live In Concert .... [L]		ATO 21517 [2]
10/2/04	86	1		4 Deja Voodoo		ATO 21528
9/9/06	62	2		5 High & Mighty		ATO 21555
11/3/07	106	1		6 Mighty High		ATO 21585
11/14/09	34	3		7 By A Thread		Evil Teen 12052

GO WEST
Pop-rock duo from England: Peter Cox (vocals) and Richard Drummie (guitar, vocals).

DEBUT	PEAK	WKS		ARTIST / Album Title	Catalog	Label & Number
3/23/85	60	35		1 Go West		Chrysalis 41495
8/22/87	172	9		2 Dancing On The Couch		Chrysalis 41550
1/30/93	154	11		3 Indian Summer		EMI 94230

GQ
Disco band from the Bronx, New York: Emmanuel LeBlanc (vocals, guitar), Herb Lane (keyboards), Keith Crier (bass) and Paul Service (drums).

DEBUT	PEAK	WKS		ARTIST / Album Title	Catalog	Label & Number
4/7/79	13	35	▲	1 Disco Nights		Arista 4225
4/5/80	46	20		2 Two		Arista 9511
11/14/81	140	8		3 Face To Face		Arista 9547

GRACES, The
Female vocal trio formed in Los Angeles, California: Charlotte Caffey (guitarist of the **Go-Go's**), **Meredith Brooks** and Gia Ciambotti.

DEBUT	PEAK	WKS		ARTIST / Album Title	Catalog	Label & Number
9/9/89	147	9		1 Perfect View		A&M 5265

GRACIN, Josh
Born on 10/18/1980 in Westland, Michigan. Country singer/songwriter. Finalist on the 2003 season of TV's *American Idol*. Served as a lance corporal in the United States Marines.

DEBUT	PEAK	WKS		ARTIST / Album Title	Catalog	Label & Number
7/3/04	11	48	●	1 Josh Gracin		Lyric Street 165045
4/19/08	33	4		2 We Weren't Crazy		Lyric Street 165063

GRAHAM, Larry/GRAHAM CENTRAL STATION
Born on 8/14/1946 in Beaumont, Texas; raised in Oakland, California. R&B singer/bassist. Member of **Sly & The Family Stone** from 1966-72. Formed **Graham Central Station** in 1973: Hershall Kennedy and Robert Sam (keyboards), Willie Sparks and Patrice Banks (percussion), and David Vega (guitar). Graham went solo in 1980.

GRAHAM CENTRAL STATION:

DEBUT	PEAK	WKS		ARTIST / Album Title	Catalog	Label & Number
2/9/74	48	26		1 Graham Central Station		Warner 2763
10/5/74	51	18		2 Release Yourself		Warner 2814
8/2/75	22	24	●	3 Ain't No 'Bout-A-Doubt It		Warner 2876
6/26/76	46	16		4 Mirror		Warner 2937
4/23/77	67	10		5 Now Do U Wanta Dance		Warner 3041

LARRY GRAHAM & GRAHAM CENTRAL STATION:

DEBUT	PEAK	WKS		ARTIST / Album Title	Catalog	Label & Number
7/1/78	105	11		6 My Radio Sure Sounds Good To Me		Warner 3175
7/14/79	136	4		7 Star Walk		Warner 3322

LARRY GRAHAM:

6/21/80	26	24	●	8 One In A Million You		Warner 3447
8/8/81	46	13		9 Just Be My Lady		Warner 3554
6/26/82	142	9		10 Sooner Or Later		Warner 3668
7/30/83	173	4		11 Victory		Warner 23878

GRAMM, Lou
Born Lou Grammatico on 5/2/1950 in Rochester, New York. Lead singer of **Foreigner**.

2/28/87	27	26		1 Ready Or Not		Atlantic 81728
11/11/89+	85	23		2 Long Hard Look		Atlantic 81915

GRAMMER, Billy
Born on 8/28/1925 in Benton, Illinois. Country singer/guitarist.

AWARD: OPRY: 1959

~ ~ ~ ~ ~ ~ ~ ~ ~ ~ **NON-CHARTED ALBUM** ~ ~ ~ ~ ~ ~ ~ ~ ~ ~ ~

1959 Travelin' On

GRANDADDY
Rock band from Modesto, California: Jason Lytle (vocals), Jim Fairchild (guitar), Tim Dryden (keyboards), Kevin Garcia (bass) and Aaron Burtch (drums).

6/28/03	84	3		1 Sumday		V2 27155
5/27/06	171	1		2 Just Like The Fambly Cat		V2 27277

GRAND FUNK RAILROAD
1970s: #25 / All-Time: #177

Hard-rock band formed in Flint, Michigan: Mark Farner (guitar; born on 9/29/1948), Mel Schacher (bass; born on 4/3/1951) and Don Brewer (drums; born on 9/3/1948). All share vocals. Brewer and Farner had been in **Terry Knight and The Pack**; Schacher was bassist with **? & The Mysterians**. Knight became producer/manager for Grand Funk, until his firing in March 1972. Craig Frost (keyboards) added in 1973. Disbanded in 1976. Re-formed in 1981, with Farner, Brewer and Dennis Bellinger (bass). Disbanded again shortly thereafter.

10/11/69	27	55	●	1 On Time		Capitol 307
1/31/70	11	67	▲	2 Grand Funk		Capitol 406
7/11/70	6	63	▲²	3 Closer To Home		Capitol 471
12/5/70	5	62	▲²	4 Live Album	[L]	Capitol 633 [2]
5/1/71	6	40	▲	5 Survival		Capitol 764
12/4/71+	5	30	▲	6 E Pluribus Funk		Capitol 853
5/13/72	17	27	●	7 Mark, Don & Mel 1969-71	[K]	Capitol 11042 [2]
10/14/72	7	27	●	8 Phoenix		Capitol 11099
8/18/73	2²	35	▲	9 We're An American Band		Capitol 11207
3/30/74	5	29	●	10 Shinin' On		Capitol 11278
12/21/74+	10	24	●	11 All The Girls In The World Beware!!!		Capitol 11356

GRAND FUNK (above 3)

9/13/75	21	10		12 Caught In The Act	[L]	Capitol 11445 [2]
1/31/76	47	11		13 Born To Die		Capitol 11482
11/20/76	126	5		14 Grand Funk Hits	[G]	Capitol 11579
8/28/76	52	9		15 Good Singin' Good Playin'		MCA 2216
10/17/81	149	5		16 Grand Funk Lives		Full Moon 3625
3/27/99	40ᶜ	1	●	17 Capitol Collectors Series	[G]	Capitol 90608

first released in 1991

GRANDMASTER FLASH & THE FURIOUS FIVE
Born Joseph Saddler on 1/1/1958 in Barbados; raised in the Bronx, New York. Pioneer rap DJ/producer. The Furious Five consisted of Melvin "Grandmaster Melle Mel" Glover, Nathaniel Glover, Guy WIlliams, Keith Wiggins and Eddie Morris. Wiggins died on 9/8/1989 (age 28).

AWARD: R&R Hall of Fame: 2007

10/16/82	53	24		1 The Message		SugarHill 268
7/13/85	201	5		2 They Said It Couldn't Be Done		Elektra 60389
5/17/86	145	6		3 The Source		Elektra 60476
4/25/87	197	1		4 Ba-Dop-Boom-Bang		Elektra 60723

GRANDMASTER FLASH (above 2)

4/30/88	189	3		5 On The Strength		Elektra 60769

GRAND PUBA
Born Maxwell Dixon on 3/4/1966 in the Bronx; raised in New Rochelle, New York. Male rapper. Former member of **Brand Nubian**.

11/7/92	28	14		1 Reel To Reel		Elektra 61314
7/8/95	48	8		2 2000		Elektra 61619

GRANT, Amy
Born on 11/25/1960 in Augusta, Georgia. Pop singer/songwriter. Began career as a top Christian singer. Married to **Gary Chapman** from 1982-99. Married **Vince Gill** on 3/10/2000.

All-Time: #204

4/20/85	133	20	●	1 Straight Ahead		A&M 5058
6/15/85	35	38	▲	2 Unguarded		A&M 5060
				Grammy: Female Gospel Vocal		
7/23/88	71	13	●	3 Lead Me On		A&M 5199
				Grammy: Female Gospel Vocal		
3/23/91	10	105	▲⁵	4 Heart In Motion		A&M 5321
9/10/94	13	52	▲²	5 House Of Love	Cat:#13/5	A&M 540230
9/27/97	8	24	●	6 Behind The Eyes		A&M 540760
6/8/02	21	21	●	7 Legacy...Hymns & Faith		Word 86211
9/6/03	23	6		8 Simple Things		A&M 000612
5/21/05	42	9		9 Rock Of Ages...Hymns & Faith		Word-Curb 86391
				Grammy: Southern Gospel Album		
10/14/06	87	1		10 Time Again...Amy Grant Live	[L]	Word-Curb 886849
				CHRISTMAS ALBUMS:		
12/21/85+	5ˣ	23	▲	11 A Christmas Album	Cat:#5/20	A&M 5057
				Christmas charts: 9/'85, 12/'87, 13/'88, 25/'89, 5/'91, 16/'92, 28/'93, 37/'94		
10/24/92	2¹	14	▲³	12 Home For Christmas	Cat:#3/46	A&M 540001
				Christmas charts: 1/'92, 6/'93, 7/'94, 8/'95, 13/'96, 13/'97, 18/'98, 42/'05		
11/6/99	36	12	●	13 A Christmas To Remember	Cat:#10/8	A&M 490462
				Christmas charts: 3/'99, 9/'00, 27/'01, 29/'02		
12/20/03	166	1		14 The Best Of Amy Grant The Christmas Collection 20th Century Masters	Cat:#31/3	A&M 000695
				Christmas charts: 25/'03, 31/'04		
11/1/08	41	11	●	15 The Christmas Collection	Cat:#23/1	Sparrow 13781
				Christmas charts: 5/'08, 19/'09		
12/5/09	98	5		16 The Christmas Collection	[R]	Sparrow 13781
				GREATEST HITS & COMPILATIONS:		
9/20/86+	66	33	▲	17 Amy Grant - The Collection		A&M 3900
10/30/04	48	4		18 Greatest Hits: 1986-2004		A&M 003415
10/27/07	196	2		19 Greatest Hits		Sparrow 02797

GRANT, Earl
Born on 1/20/1933 in Idabel, Oklahoma. Died in a car crash on 6/11/1970 (age 37). Black singer/songwriter/pianist.

8/21/61	7	45	●	1 Ebb Tide	[I]	Decca 74165
4/7/62	17	32		2 Beyond The Reef	[I]	Decca 74231
12/1/62	92	10		3 Earl Grant At Basin Street East	[L]	Decca 74299
				recorded in New York City		
1/4/64	139	5		4 Fly Me To The Moon	[I]	Decca 74454
7/11/64	149	2		5 Just For A Thrill	[I]	Decca 74506
5/15/65	143	4		6 Trade Winds	[I]	Decca 74623
12/17/66+	14ˣ	11		7 Winter Wonderland	[X-I]	Decca 74677
				Christmas charts: 35/'66, 16/'67, 16/'68, 14/'69		
3/23/68	192	2		8 Gently Swingin'	[I]	Decca 74937

GRANT, Eddy
Born Edmond Grant on 3/5/1948 in Plaisance, Guyana; raised in London, England. Rock-reggae singer. Member of The Equals.

4/23/83	10	30	●	1 Killer On The Rampage		Portrait 38554
6/23/84	64	17		2 Going For Broke		Portrait 39261

GRANT, Natalie
Born on 12/21/1978 in Seattle, Washington. Christian singer/songwriter.

7/9/05	141	16	●	1 Awaken	Cat:#3/5	Curb 78860
1/21/06+	34ˣ	2		2 Believe	[X]	Curb 78927
				Christmas charts: 47/'05, 34/'06		
3/1/08	81	16		3 Relentless	Cat:#32/1	Curb 79025

GRAPPELLI, Stephane
Born on 1/26/1908 in Paris, France. Died on 12/1/1997 (age 89). Jazz violinist.

6/6/81	108	10		1 Live	[I-L]	Warner 3550
				STEPHANE GRAPPELLI & DAVID GRISMAN		
				recorded on 9/20/1979 at the Berklee Center in Boston, Massachusetts		

GRASS ROOTS, The
Pop-rock band formed in Los Angeles, California: Rob Grill (vocals, bass), Warren Entner (guitar), Creed Bratton (guitar) and Rick Coonce (drums). New lineup in 1971 included Grill, Entner, Reed Kailing and Virgil Webber (guitars), and Joel Larson (drums). Bratton plays "Creed" on TV's *The Office*.

8/19/67	75	15		1 Let's Live For Today		Dunhill 50020
11/23/68+	25	43	●	2 Golden Grass	[G]	Dunhill/ABC 50047
3/29/69	73	16		3 Lovin' Things		Dunhill/ABC 50052
12/6/69	36	21		4 Leaving It All Behind		Dunhill/ABC 50067
10/24/70+	152	27		5 More Golden Grass	[G]	Dunhill/ABC 50087
10/2/71	58	20	●	6 Their 16 Greatest Hits	[G]	Dunhill/ABC 50107
6/24/72	86	14		7 Move Along		Dunhill/ABC 50112
5/19/73	222	2		8 Alotta' Mileage		Dunhill 50137

GRATEFUL DEAD
1970s: #28 / All-Time: #35

Legendary improvisatory-style rock band formed in San Francisco, California: **Jerry Garcia** (vocals, guitar; born on 8/1/1942; died of a heart attack on 8/9/1995, age 53), **Bob Weir** (vocals, guitar; born on 10/16/1947), Ron "Pigpen" McKernan (organ, harmonica; born on 9/8/1945; died of liver failure on 3/6/1973, age 27), **Phil Lesh** (bass; born on 3/15/1940) and Bill Kreutzmann (drums; born on 5/7/1946). **Mickey Hart** (drums; born on 9/11/1943) and Tom Constanten (keyboards) added in 1968. Constanten left in 1970; Hart in 1971. Keith Godchaux (piano; born on 7/19/1948; died in a motorcycle crash on 7/22/1980, age 32) and his wife Donna Godchaux (vocals; born on 8/23/1947) joined in 1972. Hart returned in 1975. Brent Mydland (keyboards; born on 10/21/1952; died of a drug overdose on 7/26/1990, age 37) added in 1979, replacing Keith and Donna Godchaux. Mydland was a member of **Silver**. Weir and Mydland also recorded as **Bobby & The Midnites**. After Mydland's death, **Bruce Hornsby** took over keyboards on tour until **Tubes** keyboardist Vince Welnick joined band. Welnick died on 6/2/2006 (age 55). Incessant touring band with faithful followers known as "Deadheads." Weir, Lesh, Hart and Hornsby formed **The Other Ones**. Also see **Various Artists Compilations:** *Deadicated*.

AWARDS: Grammy: Lifetime Achievement 2007 ★ R&R Hall of Fame: 1994

DEBUT	PEAK	WKS	RIAA	#	Album Title	Catalog	Label & Number
5/6/67	73	28		1	The Grateful Dead		Warner 1689
8/31/68	87	17		2	Anthem Of The Sun RS500 #287		Warner 1749
6/21/69	73	11	●	3	Aoxomoxoa		Warner 1790
6/27/70	27	26	▲	4	Workingman's Dead Grammy: Hall of Fame ★ RS500 #262	Cat:#35/1	Warner 1869
12/12/70+	30	19	▲²	5	American Beauty RS500 #258	Cat:#6/8	Warner 1893
10/27/73	18	19		6	Wake Of The Flood		Grateful Dead 01
7/13/74	16	20		7	Grateful Dead From The Mars Hotel	Cat:#44/1	Grateful Dead 102
9/6/75	12	13		8	Blues For Allah		Grateful Dead 494
8/20/77	28	16	●	9	Terrapin Station		Arista 7001
12/9/78+	41	19		10	Shakedown Street		Arista 4198
5/17/80	23	21		11	Go To Heaven		Arista 9508
7/25/87	6	34	▲²	12	In The Dark	Cat:#22/5	Arista 8452
11/18/89	27	15	●	13	Built To Last		Arista 8575
					EARLY ALBUMS:		
10/31/70	127	10		14	Vintage Dead [L] recorded in 1966 at the Avalon Ballroom in San Francisco, California		Sunflower 5001
6/26/71	154	7		15	Historic Dead [L] more recordings from 1966		Sunflower 5004
					GREATEST HITS & COMPILATIONS:		
3/9/74	75	10	▲³	16	The Best Of/Skeleton's From The Closet	Cat:❶³/205	Warner 2764
11/12/77	121	8	▲	17	What A Long Strange Trip It's Been: The Best Of The Grateful Dead	Cat:#40/1	Warner 3091 [2]
11/2/96	95	2		18	The Arista Years		Arista 18934 [2]
7/5/97	83	3		19	Fallout From The Phil Zone [L] recorded from 1967-1995		Grateful Dead 4052 [2]
11/27/99	170	1	●	20	So Many Roads (1965-1995) [L]		Grateful Dead 14066 [5]
11/3/01	191	1	●	21	The Golden Road (1965-73) contains all of the group's albums recorded for Warner, including several outtakes and live versions; contains a 76-page booklet		Warner 74401 [12]
4/6/02	120	1		22	Postcards Of The Hanging: Grateful Dead Perform The Songs Of Bob Dylan [L] recordings from 1973-90		Grateful Dead 4069
10/4/03	69	4		23	The Very Best Of Grateful Dead		Warner 73899
					LIVE ALBUMS:		
1/3/70	64	15	●	24	Live/Dead RS500 #244 recorded in San Francisco at the Avalon Ballroom (1/26/1969) and Fillmore West (2/27/1969 and 3/2/1969)		Warner 1830 [2]
10/16/71	25	12	●	25	Grateful Dead recorded at various locations; due to its iconic artwork, album known among fans as *Skull & Roses*	Cat:#21/4	Warner 1935 [2]
12/2/72+	24	24	▲²	26	Europe '72		Warner 2668 [3]
7/28/73	60	11		27	History Of The Grateful Dead, Vol. 1 (Bear's Choice) recorded February 1970 at the Fillmore East in New York City		Warner 2721
7/4/76	56	9		28	Steal Your Face recorded October 1974 at Winterland in San Francisco, California		Grateful Dead 620 [2]
4/18/81	43	16		29	Reckoning		Arista 8604 [2]
9/19/81	29	11		30	Dead Set above 2 recorded on the band's 1980 tour		Arista 8606 [2]
2/18/89	37	11	●	31	Dylan & The Dead **BOB DYLAN & GRATEFUL DEAD**		Columbia 45056
10/13/90	43	12	●	32	Without A Net	Cat:#41/1	Arista 8634 [2]
5/11/91	106	2		33	One From The Vault recorded on 8/13/1975 at the Great American Music Hall in San Francisco, California		Grateful Dead 40132
5/30/92	119	3		34	Two From The Vault recorded on 8/23/1968 at the Shrine Auditorium in Los Angeles, California		Grateful Dead 40162 [2]
10/14/95	26	13	●	35	Hundred Year Hall recorded on 4/26/1972 in Frankfurt, Germany		Grateful Dead 40202 [2]
11/16/96	74	4	●	36	Dozin' At The Knick recorded on 3/25/1990 at the Knickerbocker Arena in Albany, New York		Arista 4025 [3]
11/15/97	77	2		37	Fillmore East 2-11-69		Grateful Dead 4054 [2]
10/28/00	165	2	●	38	Ladies And Gentlemen...Fillmore East: New York City: April 1971		Grateful Dead 14075 [4]
10/13/01	196	1		39	Nightfall Of Diamonds recorded on 10/16/1989 at the Meadowlands Arena in East Rutherford, New Jersey		Grateful Dead 14081 [2]
7/27/02	160	2		40	Steppin' Out With The Grateful Dead England '72		Grateful Dead 4084 [4]

Billboard DEBUT	PEAK	WKS	R I A A	ARTIST / Album Title	Catalog	Label & Number

GRATEFUL DEAD — cont'd

DEBUT	PEAK	WKS			Catalog	Label & Number
6/12/04	75	1		41 Rockin' The Rhein With The Grateful Dead		Grateful Dead 78921 [3]
				recordings from the group's 1972 European tour		
7/30/05	137	1		42 Truckin' Up To Buffalo, July 4, 1989....................................		Grateful Dead 73139 [2]
2/10/07	48	1		43 Live At The Cow Palace: New Year's Eve 1976		Grateful Dead 74816 [3]
7/14/07	112	1		44 Three From The Vault		Grateful Dead 162812 [2]
				recorded on 2/19/1971 at the Capitol Theater in Port Chester, New York		
10/18/08	35	1		45 Rocking The Cradle: Egypt 1978		Grateful Dead 512959 [2]
4/25/09	59	2		46 To Terrapin: Hartford '77		Grateful Dead 6008 [3]
				recorded on 5/28/1977 at the Civic Center in Hartford, Connecticut		

GRAVEDIGGAZ

Male rap group: Robert "**RZA**" Diggs (of **Wu-Tang Clan**), Anthony Berkeley, Paul Huston and Arnold Hamilton. Berkeley died of cancer on 7/15/2001 (age 35).

8/27/94	36	11		1 6 Feet Deep		Gee Street 524016
11/1/97	20	6		2 The Pick, The Sickle And The Shovel		Gee Street 32501

GRAVITY KILLS

Heavy-metal rock band from Jefferson City, Missouri: Jeff Scheel (vocals), Matt Dudenhoeffer (guitar), Douglas Firley (keyboards) and Kurt Kerns (bass, drums).

3/23/96	89	25		1 Gravity Kills		TVT 5910
6/27/98	107	4		2 Perversion		TVT 5920

GRAY, David

Born on 6/13/1968 in Sale, England; raised in Solva, Wales. Rock singer/songwriter/guitarist.

9/2/00+	35	83	▲	1 White Ladder .... Cat:#12/20		ATO 69351
5/5/01	153	3		2 Lost Songs 95-98 .... [E]		ATO 69375
11/23/02	17	23	●	3 A New Day At Midnight		ATO 68154
10/1/05	16	19		4 Life In Slow Motion		ATO 71068
12/1/07	96	9		5 Greatest Hits .... [G]		ATO 21591
10/10/09	12	8		6 Draw The Line		IHT 70109

GRAY, Dobie

Born Lawrence Brown on 7/26/1940 in Brookshire, Texas. Black singer/songwriter.

3/10/73	64	21		1 Drift Away		Decca 75397
11/10/73	188	3		2 Loving Arms		MCA 371
11/16/74	203	1		3 Hey Dixie		MCA 449
2/17/79	174	4		4 Midnight Diamond		Infinity 9001

GRAY, Glen, & The Casa Loma Orchestra

Born Glen Gray Knoblaugh on 6/7/1906 in Metamora, Illinois. Died on 8/23/1963 (age 57). Alto saxophonist/bandleader. Formed the Casa Loma Orchestra in 1927.

2/23/57	18	9		1 Casa Loma In Hi-Fi! .... [I]		Capitol 747
6/29/59	28	2		2 Sounds Of The Great Bands! .... [I]		Capitol 1022
2/2/63	63	13		3 Themes Of The Great Bands .... [I]		Capitol 1812
10/19/63	69	15		4 Today's Best .... [I]		Capitol 1938

GRAY, Macy

Born Natalie McIntyre on 9/9/1970 in Canton, Ohio. Female R&B singer/songwriter.

8/14/99+	4	89	▲³	1 Macy Gray On How Life Is		Epic 69490
10/6/01	11	16	●	2 The Id		Epic 85200
8/2/03	44	6		3 The Trouble With Being Myself		Epic 86535
4/14/07	39	8		4 Big		will.i.am 008576

GRAY, Tamyra

Born on 7/26/1979 in Takoma Park, Maryland; raised in Norcross, Georgia. Black singer. Finalist on the first season of TV's *American Idol* in 2002. Had a recurring role on TV's *Boston Public* in 2003.

6/12/04	23	5		1 The Dreamer		19 Records 002817

GREAN, Charles Randolph, Sounde

Born on 10/1/1913 in Manhattan, New York. Died of heart failuire on 12/20/2003 (age 90). Conductor/arranger. Formerly married to singer Betty Johnson.

7/26/69	23	15		1 Quentin's Theme .... [I]		Ranwood 8055

GREASE BAND

Rock band formed in England: Henry McCullough (vocals, guitar), Neil Hubbard (guitar), Phil Plunk (keyboards), Alan Spenner (bass) and Bruce Rowland (drums). Backing band for **Joe Cocker**. McCullough was a member of **Paul McCartney**'s Wings from 1972-1973. Hubbard and Spenner later joined **Kokomo**.

4/17/71	190	3		1 Grease Band		Shelter 8904

GREAT SOCIETY — see SLICK, Grace

GREAT WHITE

Hard-rock band formed in Los Angeles, California: Jack Russell (vocals), Mark Kendall (guitar), Lorne Black (bass) and Gary Holland (drums). Audie Desbrow replaced Holland in 1986. Michael Lardie (keyboards) joined in 1987. Tony Montana replaced Black in 1987. Many personnel changes since 1991. The band's pyrotechnic show during a Rhode Island club concert set off a fire that killed nearly 100 people on 2/21/2003, including the band's guitarist, Ty Longley.

3/24/84	144	12		1 Great White		EMI America 17111
8/16/86	82	13		2 Shot In The Dark		Capitol 12525

Billboard DEBUT	PEAK	WKS	R I A A	ARTIST Album Title	Catalog	Label & Number

GREAT WHITE — cont'd

DEBUT	PEAK	WKS		Album Title		Label & Number
7/18/87	23	53	▲	3 Once Bitten		Capitol 12565
2/13/88	99	12		4 Recovery: Live! .... [L]		Enigma 73295
5/6/89	9	50	▲²	5 ...Twice Shy		Capitol 90640
3/16/91	18	25	●	6 Hooked		Capitol 95330
10/10/92	107	6		7 Psycho City		Capitol 98835
5/28/94	168	1		8 Sail Away		Zoo 11080 [2]
7/24/99	192	1		9 Can't Get There From Here		Portrait 69547

GREAVES, R.B.
Born Ronald Bertram Greaves on 11/28/1944 at the U.S. Air Force base in Georgetown, British Guyana. R&B singer. Nephew of **Sam Cooke**.

| 1/3/70 | 85 | 14 | | 1 R.B. Greaves .... | | Atco 311 |

GREBENSHIKOV, Boris
Born on 11/27/1953 in Leningrad, Russia. Rock singer/songwriter/guitarist.

| 8/26/89 | 198 | 2 | | 1 Radio Silence .... | | Columbia 44364 |

GRECH, Rick
Born on 11/1/1946 in Bordeaux, France. Died of liver failure on 3/17/1990 (age 43). Rock bassist. Member of **Family**, **Traffic**, **Blind Faith**, **Ginger Baker's Air Force** and **KGB**.

| 9/29/73 | 195 | 3 | | 1 The Last Five Years .... [K] | | RSO 876 |

GREELEY, George
Born on 7/23/1917 in Westerly, Rhode Island. Died on 5/26/2007 (age 89). Conductor/pianist.

| 5/22/61 | 29 | 16 | | 1 The Best Of The Popular Piano Concertos .... [I-K] | | Warner 1410 |

GREEN, Al   1970s: #40 / All-Time: #129
Born Albert Greene on 4/13/1946 in Forrest City, Arkansas. R&B singer/songwriter. With gospel group the Greene Brothers. To Grand Rapids, Michigan, in 1959. First recorded for Fargo in 1960. In group The Creations from 1964-67. Sang with his brother Robert Green and Lee Virgins in the group Soul Mates from 1967-68. Went solo in 1969. Wrote most of his songs. Became an ordained minister and returned to gospel music in 1980.
AWARDS: Grammy: Lifetime Achievement 2002 ★ R&R Hall of Fame: 1995

DEBUT	PEAK	WKS		Album Title		Label & Number
1/6/73	19	28		1 Green Is Blues .... [E]		Hi 32055
				released in 1969		
8/28/71+	58	43		2 Al Green Gets Next To You		Hi 32062
2/12/72	8	56	●	3 Let's Stay Together		Hi 32070
9/16/72	162	9		4 Al Green .... [E]		Bell 6076
				recordings from 1967-68		
10/21/72	4	67	▲	5 I'm Still In Love With You	Cat:#50/1	Hi 32074
				RS500 #285		
5/19/73	10	41	●	6 Call Me		Hi 32077
				RS500 #289		
12/29/73+	24	30	●	7 Livin' For You		Hi 32082
11/23/74+	15	33	●	8 Al Green Explores Your Mind		Hi 32087
9/13/75	28	23		9 Al Green Is Love		Hi 32092
3/20/76	59	16		10 Full Of Fire		Hi 32097
11/27/76+	93	14		11 Have A Good Time		Hi 32103
12/24/77+	103	12		12 The Belle Album		Hi 6004
5/2/87	131	14		13 Soul Survivor		A&M 5150
12/6/03	53	12		14 I Can't Stop		Blue Note 93556
1/17/04	45ˣ	1		15 Feels Like Christmas .... [X]		Right Stuff 33603
4/2/05	50	7		16 Everything's OK		Blue Note 74584
6/14/08	9	15		17 Lay It Down		Blue Note 48449
				GREATEST HITS & COMPILATIONS:		
3/22/75	17	21		18 Al Green/Greatest Hits	Cat:#20/82	Hi 32089
				RS500 #52		
7/2/77	134	9		19 Al Green's Greatest Hits, Volume II		Hi 32105
8/19/95	127	29	▲²	20 Al Green/Greatest Hits	Cat:#12/188 [R]	Right Stuff 30800
10/7/00	186	1		21 Take Me To The River		Right Stuff 28679 [2]
2/15/03	91	3		22 The Love Song Collection		Right Stuff 80327
2/3/07	46	11		23 The Definitive Greatest Hits		Hi 82040
2/23/08	196	2		24 What Makes The World Go 'Round?		Starbucks 073

GREEN, Anthony
Born on 4/15/1982 in Doylestown, Pennsylvania. Punk-rock singer/songwriter. Lead singer of **Circa Survive** and **The Sound Of Animals Fighting**.

| 8/23/08 | 44 | 2 | | 1 Avalon .... | | Photo Finish 511321 |

GREEN, Grant
Born on 6/6/1931 in St. Louis, Missouri. Died on 1/31/1979 (age 47). Jazz guitarist.

| 10/16/71 | 151 | 9 | | 1 Visions .... [I] | | Blue Note 84373 |

Billboard			R I A A	ARTIST		
DEBUT	PEAK	WKS		Album Title	Catalog	Label & Number

GREEN, Jack
Born on 3/12/1951 in Glasgow, Scotland. Rock singer/guitarist. Former member of **T. Rex** and **Pretty Things**.

10/18/80	121	8		1 Humanesque...		RCA Victor 3639

GREEN, Pat
Born on 4/5/1972 in San Antonio, Texas; raised in Waco, Texas. Male country singer/songwriter/guitarist.

11/3/01	86	3		1 Three Days		Republic 016016
8/2/03	10	24	●	2 Wave On Wave		Republic 000562
11/6/04	28	4		3 Lucky Ones		Republic 003522
9/9/06	20	6		4 Cannonball..		BNA 84583
2/14/09	18	5		5 What I'm For		BNA 26909

GREEN, Peter
Born Peter Greenbaum on 10/29/1946 in London, England. Blues-rock guitarist. Member of **John Mayall**'s Bluesbreakers and Fleetwood Mac.

2/20/71	205	1		1 The End Of The Game	[I]	Reprise 6436
12/8/79	201	11		2 In The Skies	[I]	Sail 0110
10/25/80	186	5		3 Little Dreamer		Sail 0112

GREEN, Steve
Born on 8/1/1956 in Portland, Oregon. Contemporary Christian singer/songwriter.

11/23/96	40ˣ	1		1 The First Noel	[X]	Sparrow 51585

GREEN, Vivian
Born in 1979 in Philadelphia, Pennsylvania. R&B singer/songwriter.

11/30/02+	51	27	●	1 A Love Story		Columbia 86357
7/16/05	18	9		2 Vivian...		Columbia 90761

GREENBAUM, Norman
Born on 11/20/1942 in Malden, Massachusetts. Pop-rock singer/songwriter.

2/28/70	23	25		1 Spirit In The Sky		Reprise 6365

GREEN DAY 2000s: #50 / All-Time: #222
Punk-rock trio formed in Rodeo, California: Billie Joe Armstrong (vocals, guitar; born on 2/17/1972), Mike "Dirnt" Pritchard (bass; born on 5/4/1972) and Frank "Tre Cool" Wright (drums; born on 12/9/1972). Also recorded as **Foxboro Hot Tubs**.

10/8/94+	4ᶜ	34	●	1 1,039/Smoothed Out Slappy Hours	[E]	Lookout 22
				released in 1990		
10/1/94+	❶²ᶜ	43	▲	2 Kerplunk!	[E]	Lookout 46
				released in 1992		
2/19/94+	2²	113	▲¹⁰	3 Dookie	Cat:#10/67	Reprise 45529
				Grammy: Alternative Album ★ RS500 #193		
10/28/95	2¹	39	▲²	4 Insomniac		Reprise 46046
11/1/97	10	70	▲²	5 Nimrod		Reprise 46794
10/21/00	4	25	●	6 Warning		Reprise 47613
12/1/01	40	31	▲	7 International Superhits!..............................	Cat:❶⁴/88 [G]	Reprise 48145
7/20/02	27	5		8 Shenanigans		Reprise 48208
10/9/04	❶³	101	▲⁵	9 American Idiot	Cat:#10/10	Reprise 48777
12/3/05	8	14		10 Bullet In A Bible	[L]	Reprise 49466
6/7/08	21	3		11 Stop Drop And Roll!!!		Jingle Town 471100
				FOXBORO HOT TUBS		
5/30/09	❶¹	38	●	12 21st Century Breakdown		Reprise 517153
				Grammy: Rock Album		
11/28/09	198	1		13 Last Night On Earth (Live In Tokyo)	[EP-L]	Reprise digital

GREENE, Jack
Born on 1/7/1930 in Maryville, Tennessee. Country singer/songwriter/guitarist. Nicknamed the "Jolly Green Giant."
AWARDS: CMA: Male Vocalist 1967 ★ OPRY: 1967

2/25/67	66	21		1 There Goes My Everything................................		Decca 74845
				CMA: Album of the Year		
7/22/67	151	12		2 All The Time		Decca 74904

GREENE, Lorne
Born on 2/12/1915 in Ottawa, Ontario, Canada. Died of heart failure on 9/11/1987 (age 72). Acted in several movies. Starred in TV's *Bonanza* and *Battlestar Galactica*.

11/28/64+	35	19		1 Welcome To The Ponderosa		RCA Victor 2843
12/25/65	54ˣ	1		2 Have A Happy Holiday	[X]	RCA Victor 3410

GREENE, Mike
Born in Los Angeles, California. Jazz singer/saxophonist.

9/6/75	206	3		1 Pale, Pale Moon...		GRC 10013

GREEN JELLY
Novelty hard-rock band formed in Kenmore, New York: Moronic Dicktator (lead vocals), Joey Blowey, Rootin', Jesus Quisp, Coy Roy, Sadistica, Hotsy Menshot, Tin Titty, Sven Seven, Reason Clean, Mother Eucker, Roof D.H. and Daddy Longlegs. Group originally known as Green Jello.

4/3/93	23	26	●	1 Cereal Killer Soundtrack		Zoo 11038

Billboard			R I A A	ARTIST		
DEBUT	PEAK	WKS		Album Title	Catalog	Label & Number

GREEN ON RED
Country-rock band from Tucson, Arizona: Dan Stuart (vocals), Chuck Prophet (guitar), Alex MacNicol (keyboards), Jack Waterson (bass) and Chris Cacavas (drums).

5/3/86	177	6		1 No Free Lunch		Mercury 826346

GREENSLADE
Rock band from England: Dave Greenslade (vocals, guitar; born on 1/18/1943), Dave Lawson (keyboards), Tony Reeves (bass) and Andrew McCulloch (drums).

7/28/73	218	2		1 Greenslade..		Warner 2698

GREENWOOD, Lee
Born on 10/27/1942 in Los Angeles, California. Country singer/songwriter/multi-instrumentalist. The 9/11 terrorist attacks renewed interest in Greenwood's anthem "God Bless The USA."

AWARD: CMA: Male Vocalist 1983 & 1984

6/5/82	204	5	●	1 Inside And Out...		MCA 5305
5/28/83	73	21	●	2 Somebody's Gonna Love You		MCA 5403
6/9/84	150	20	●	3 You've Got A Good Love Comin'		MCA 5488
9/8/84	89	13		4 Meant For Each Other		MCA 5477
				BARBARA MANDRELL & LEE GREENWOOD		
9/29/01	❶⁹ᶜ	26	▲	5 American Patriot		Liberty 98568
				first released in 1992		
				GREATEST HITS & COMPILATIONS:		
5/18/85	163	8	▲	6 Greatest Hits..		MCA 5582
9/29/01	13ᶜ	1		7 Super Hits		Epic 67572
10/20/01	3²ᶜ	7		8 Best Of Lee Greenwood: God Bless The USA		Curb 77862
				above 2 first released in 1996		
10/20/01	21ᶜ	4		9 Lee Greenwood: God Bless The U.S.A.		Madacy 504
				first released in 1999		
10/20/01	32ᶜ	2		10 God Bless The USA		MCA 20605
				first released in 1990		

GREGG, Ricky Lynn
Born on 8/22/1961 in Longview, Texas. Country-rock singer/songwriter/guitarist.

5/15/93	190	1		1 Ricky Lynn Gregg		Liberty 80135

GREGGAINS, Joanie
Born in Los Angeles, California. Fitness instructor.

6/18/83	177	4		1 Aerobic Shape-Up II		Parade 106
1/14/84	201	8		2 Aerobic Shape-Up III		Parade 112
				includes a 16-page book		

GREGORY, Dick
Born on 10/12/1932 in St. Louis, Missouri. Stand-up comedian/civil rights activist.

6/5/61	23	27		1 In Living Black & White .... [C]		Colpix 417
8/16/69+	182	8		2 The Light Side: The Dark Side .... [C]		Poppy 60001 [2]

GREY, JJ, & Mofro
Funk band from Jacksonville, Florida: JJ Grey (vocals), Daryl Hance (guitar), Anthony Farrell (keyboards), Dennis Marion (trumpet), Art Edmaiston (sax), Andrew Trube (bass) and Anthony Cole (drums).

9/13/08	186	1		1 Orange Blossoms		Alligator 4925

GREY, Joel
Born Joel Katz on 4/11/1932 in Cleveland, Ohio. Singer/actor. Starred in several movies and Broadway shows. Son of comedic bandleader Mickey Katz. Father of actress Jennifer Grey.

6/30/73	217	3		1 Live! .... [L]		Columbia 32252
				recorded at the Waldorf Astoria Hotel in New York City		

GREY & HANKS
R&B-dance vocal duo from Chicago, Illinois: Zane Grey and Len Ron Hanks.

2/3/79	97	11		1 You Fooled Me...		RCA Victor 3069
2/23/80	195	3		2 Prime Time		RCA Victor 3477

GRIFFIN, Kathy
Born on 11/4/1960 in Oak Park, Illinois. Stand-up comedian/actress. Acted in several movies and TV shows.

7/5/08	85	2		1 For Your Consideration .... [C]		Music With A Twist 28847

GRIFFIN, LaShell
Born in Detroit, Michigan. Female R&B singer. Winner of Oprah Winfrey's *Pop Star Challenge* talent contest.

6/12/04	166	1		1 Free...		Epic 92499

GRIFFIN, Patty
Born on 3/16/1964 in Boston, Massachusetts. Adult Alternative singer/songwriter/guitarist.

4/27/02	101	3		1 1000 Kisses...		ATO 21504
5/8/04	67	5		2 Impossible Dream		ATO 21520
2/24/07	34	7		3 Children Running Through		ATO 0036

Billboard DEBUT	PEAK	WKS	R I A A	ARTIST / Album Title	Catalog	Label & Number
				GRIFFITH, Andy		
				Born on 6/1/1926 in Mount Airy, North Carolina. Actor/comedian. Starred in several movies and Broadway shows. Star of TV's *The Andy Griffith Show* and *Matlock*.		
4/20/96	55	28	▲	1 I Love To Tell The Story - 25 Timeless Hymns		Sparrow 51440
				Grammy: Southern Gospel Album		
5/16/98	143	3		2 Just As I Am - 30 Favorite Old Time Hymns.........................		Sparrow 51666
12/20/03	141	1		3 The Christmas Guest: Stories And Songs Of Christmas .... [X]		Sparrow 51815
				Christmas chart: 27/'03		
				GRIFFITH, Nanci		
				Born on 7/16/1954 in Seguin, Texas; raised in Austin, Texas. Folk singer/songwriter/guitarist.		
9/16/89	99	14		1 Storms..		MCA 6319
10/12/91	185	1		2 Late Night Grande Hotel		MCA 10306
3/20/93	54	14	●	3 Other Voices - Other Rooms		Elektra 61464
				Grammy: Contemporary Folk Album		
10/1/94	48	8		4 Flyer..		Elektra 61681
4/12/97	119	6		5 Blue Roses From The Moons		Elektra 62015
8/8/98	85	7		6 Other Voices, Too (A Trip Back To Bountiful)		Elektra 62235
8/18/01	149	3		7 Clock Without Hands		Elektra 62660
				GRIGGS, Andy		
				Born on 8/13/1973 in Monroe, Louisiana. Country singer/songwriter/guitarist.		
5/1/99	142	16	●	1 You Won't Ever Be Lonely..................................		RCA 67596
7/27/02	77	3		2 Freedom		RCA 67006
8/28/04	59	7		3 This I Gotta See		RCA 59630
				GRIM REAPER		
				Heavy metal band from Droitwich, Worcestershire, England: Steve Grimmett (vocals), Nick Bowcott (guitar), Dave Wanklin (bass) and Lee Harris (drums). In 1985, Mark Simon replaced Harris.		
8/25/84	73	27		1 See You In Hell		RCA Victor 8038
7/6/85	108	14		2 Fear No Evil		RCA Victor 5431
8/1/87	93	21		3 Rock You To Hell		RCA Victor 6250
				GRIN		
				Rock band formed in Maryland: **Nils Lofgren** (vocals, guitar), Bob Gordon (bass) and Bob Berberich (drums). Lofgren's brother, guitarist Tom Lofgren, joined in mid-1972. Disbanded in 1973.		
8/7/71	192	3		1 Grin		Spindizzy 30321
2/5/72	180	6		2 1 + 1		Spindizzy 31038
3/10/73	186	7		3 All Out		Spindizzy 31701
				GRINDERMAN — see CAVE, Nick		
				GRINDER SWITCH		
				Southern-rock band from Macon, Georgia: Dru Lombar (vocals, guitar), Larry Howard (guitar), Stephen Miller (keyboards), Joe Dan Petty (bass) and Rick Burnett (drums). Petty died in a plane crash on 1/8/2000 (age 52). Miller died on 8/17/2003 (age 60).		
11/19/77	144	8		1 Redwing		Atco 152
				GRISMAN, David		
				Born on 3/23/1945 in Hackensack, New Jersey. Jazz-bluegrass mandolin player. Member of **Earth Opera** and **Old & In The Way**.		
9/13/80	152	8		1 David Grisman - Quintet '80 .... [I]		Warner 3469
6/6/81	108	10		2 Live .... [I-L]		Warner 3550
				STEPHANE GRAPPELLI & DAVID GRISMAN / recorded on 9/20/1979 at the Berklee Center in Boston, Massachusetts		
10/24/81	174	3		3 Mondo Mando .... [I]		Warner 3618
5/7/83	204	4		4 David Grisman's Dawg Jazz/Dawg Grass..................... [I]		Warner 23804
11/16/96	135	1		5 Shady Grove		Acoustic Disc 21
				JERRY GARCIA & DAVID GRISMAN		
				GRIZZLY BEAR		
				Alternative-rock band formed in Brooklyn, New York: Edward Droste (vocals, guitar), Daniel Rossen (vocals, guitar), Chris Taylor (bass) and Christopher Bear (drums). Rossen also formed **Department Of Eagles**.		
6/13/09	8	20		1 Veckatimest		Warp 0182
				GROBAN, Josh 2000s: #27 / All-Time: #371		
				Born on 2/27/1981 in Los Angeles, California. Classical-styled Adult Contemporary singer.		
12/29/01+	8	101	▲⁴	1 Josh Groban Cat:❶⁷/89		143 Records 48154
12/21/02+	34	17	●	2 Josh Groban In Concert.................................. [L]		143 Records 48413
11/29/03+	❶¹	98	▲⁵	3 Closer Cat:❶¹/118		143 Records 48450
12/18/04	24	12	●	4 Live At The Greek .... [L]		143 Records 48939
11/25/06	2¹	71	▲²	5 Awake		143 Records 44435
5/24/08	8	9		6 Awake Live .... [L]		143 Records 412668
10/27/07	❶⁵	14	▲⁵	7 Noel Cat:❶⁸/18 [X]		143 Records 231548
				Christmas charts: 1/'07, 1/'08, 2/'09		
12/5/09	14	6		8 Noel.. [X-R]		143 Records 231548

GROCE, Larry
Born on 4/22/1948 in Dallas, Texas. Pop-folk singer/songwriter.

3/27/76	187	2		1 Junkfood Junkie .... [L]		Warner/Curb 2933

GROOTNA
Rock band from San Francisco, California: Anna Rizzo (vocals), Vic Smith (guitar), Slim Chance (guitar), Richard Sussman (piano), Kelly Bryan (bass) and Dewey DaGrease (drums).

1/29/72	213	1		1 Grootna		Columbia 31032

GROOVE THEORY
Male-female R&B duo: Bryce Wilson and **Amel Larrieux**. Wilson, then known as Bryce Luvah, was a member of **Mantronix**.

11/11/95	69	20	●	1 Groove Theory		Epic 57421

GROSS, Henry
Born on 4/1/1951 in Brooklyn, New York. Pop-rock singer/songwriter/guitarist.

3/9/74	204	3		1 Henry Gross		A&M 4416
2/8/75	26	23		2 Plug Me Into Something		A&M 4502
2/14/76	64	28		3 Release...		Lifesong 6002
3/12/77	176	7		4 Show Me To The Stage		Lifesong 6010

GROUCH & ELIGH, The
Male rap duo from Oakland, California: Corey "The Grouch" Scoffern and Eligh.

5/9/09	186	1		1 Say G&E!		Legendary Music 50027

GROUNDHOGS
Blues-rock trio from England: Tony McPhee (vocals, guitar), Pete Cruikshank (bass) and Ken Pustelnik (drums).

7/22/72	202	6		1 Who Will Save The World? - The Mighty Groundhogs		United Artists 5570

GROVES, Sara
Born Sara Colbaugh on 9/10/1972 in Vineland, New Jersey; raised in Springfield, Missouri. Contemporary Christian singer/songwriter.

11/24/07+	72	6		1 Tell Me What You Know...		Sponge 84302
11/29/08	175	1		2 O Holy Night.. [X]		Sponge 84521
				Christmas chart: 47/08		

GRUPO BRYNDIS
Latin vocal group from Santa Paula, California: Mauro Posadas, Jose Guevara, Gerardo Izaguirre, Claudio Pablo and Juan Guevara.

7/21/01	152	11		1 Historica Musical Romantica .... [F]		Disa 727012
10/13/01	169	3		2 En El Idioma Del Amor .... [F]		Disa 727016
7/3/04	190	1		3 El Quinto Trago .... [F]		Disa 720369
8/20/05	79	6		4 Por Muchas Razones Te Quiero... [F]		Disa 726819
9/10/05	181	1		5 Le Mejor...Coleccion .... [F-K]		Disa 720561
4/22/06	135	2		6 Recordandote .... [F]		Disa 720786
4/14/07	97	5		7 Solo Pienso En Ti .... [F]		Disa 721017

GRUPO MONTEZ DE DURANGO
Latin group from Mexico: Jose Terrazas, his son Jose Terrazas Jr., Daniel Avila, Francisco Lopez, Armando Ramirez, Alfredo Corral and Ismael Miljarez.

10/18/03	88	6	●	1 De Durango A Chicago .... [F]		Disa 724088
4/10/04	91	7		2 En Vivo Desde Chicago .... [F-L]		Disa 720358
2/19/05	34	12	●	3 Y Sigue La Mata Dando .... [F]		Disa 720464
9/17/05	118	2		4 Vive .... [F-L]		Disa 726823
5/20/06	66	8		5 Borron Y Cuenta Nueva .... [F]		Disa 726699
7/21/07	41	11		6 Agarrese .... [F]		Disa 724115
10/13/07	185	1		7 En Directo De Mexico A Guatemala .... [F-L]		Disa 721111
11/8/08	65	4		8 Nosotros Somos .... [F]		Disa 724140

GRUPO PESADO
Latin band from Mexico: Beto Zapata, Pepe Elizondo, July Tarnez, Luis Garza and Tono Little.

12/6/08	128	1		1 Solo Contigo .... [F]		Disa 724143

GRUSIN, Dave
Born on 6/26/1934 in Littleton, Colorado. Jazz pianist. Composer/producer of numerous movie and TV soundtracks.

1/12/80	52	25	●	1 The Electric Horseman .... [S]		Columbia 36327
				side 1: songs performed by **Willie Nelson**; side 2: instrumental score by Grusin		
3/21/81	74	18		2 Mountain Dance .... [I]		GRP 5010
7/18/81	140	7		3 Dave Grusin and the GRP All-Stars/Live In Japan .... [I-L]		GRP 5506
				recorded on 3/16/1980 in Osaka, Japan		
8/7/82	88	9		4 Out Of The Shadows .... [I]		GRP 5510
4/16/83	181	6		5 Dave Grusin and the NY/LA Dream Band .... [I-L]		GRP 1001
10/5/85	192	2		6 Harlequin .... [I]		GRP 1015
				DAVE GRUSIN & LEE RITENOUR		
2/25/89	110	12		7 Dave Grusin Collection .... [G-I]		GRP 9579
10/21/89	145	8		8 Migration .... [I]		GRP 9592
11/18/89	74	13		9 The Fabulous Baker Boys .... [I-S]		GRP 2002
				Grammy: Movie Soundtrack		
12/14/91	170	2		10 The Gershwin Connection .... [I]		GRP 2005

Billboard			R I A A	ARTIST		
DEBUT	PEAK	WKS		Album Title	Catalog	Label & Number

GRYPHON
Jazz-rock band from England: Graeme Taylor (guitar), Richard Harvey (keyboards), Brian Gulland (bassoon), Philip Nestor (bass) and David Oberle (drums).

12/14/74	201	4		1 Red Queen To Gryphon Three.. [I]	Bell 1316

GTR
Rock band formed in England: Max Bacon (vocals), **Steve Hackett** (guitar), **Steve Howe** (guitar), Phil Spalding (bass) and Jonathan Mover (drums). Hackett was with **Genesis**. Howe was with **Yes** and **Asia**. Band name is short for guitar.

5/17/86	11	26	●	1 GTR...	Arista 8400

GUADALCANAL DIARY
Rock band formed in Marietta, Georgia: Murray Attaway (vocals), Jeff Walls (guitar), Rhett Crowe (bass) and John Poe (drums). Group named after a 1943 war movie.

8/3/85	202	3		1 Walking In The Shadow Of The Big Man..	Elektra 60429
1/16/88	183	7		2 2 X 4...	Elektra 60752
3/25/89	132	13		3 Flip-Flop..	Elektra 60848

GUARALDI, Vince, Trio
Born on 7/17/1928 in San Francisco, California. Died of a heart attack on 2/6/1976 (age 47). Jazz pianist. Formerly with **Woody Herman** and **Cal Tjader**. Wrote the music for the *Peanuts* TV specials.

2/2/63	24	28		1 Jazz Impressions of Black Orpheus .... [I]	Fantasy 3337
11/10/07	40ˣ	2		2 A Charlie Brown Christmas .... [X]	Fantasy 53161 [3]
10/11/08	37ˣ	1		3 Charlie Brown's Holiday Hits .... [X]	Fantasy 9682
12/5/09	79	6	▲³	4 A Charlie Brown Christmas................................... Cat:❶¹/103 [X-I]	Fantasy 8431

soundtrack of the classic Christmas TV special; first released in 1965 on Fantasy 5019; Christmas charts: 13/'87, 9/'88, 9/'89, 9/'90, 18/'91, 16/'92, 23/'93, 22/'94, 17/'95, 17/'96, 15/'97, 18/'98, 25/'99, 15/'00, 8/'01, 8/'02, 9/'03, 12/'04, 6/'05, 2/'06, 4/'07, 6/'08, 12/'09

GUARD, Dave, & The Whiskeyhill Singers
Born on 11/19/1934 in Honolulu, Hawaii. Died of cancer on 3/22/1991 (age 56). Member of **The Kingston Trio** from 1957-61.

6/30/62	92	11		1 Dave Guard & The Whiskeyhill Singers	Capitol 1728

GUARINI, Justin
Born on 10/28/1978 in Columbus, Georgia. Finished in second place on the first season of TV's *American Idol* in 2002.

6/28/03	20	5		1 Justin Guarini	RCA 68188

GUCCI CREW II
Rap trio from Miami, Florida: Rick Taylor, Cleveland Bell and Victor May.

9/23/89	173	6		1 Everybody Wants Some	Gucci 3314

GUCCI MANE
Born Radric Davis on 2/2/1980 in Birmingham, Alabama; later based in Decatur, Georgia. Male rapper.

6/11/05	101	7		1 Trap House	LaFlare 3016
11/11/06	76	2		2 Hard To Kill	Big Cat 3080
10/13/07	69	4		3 Trap-A-Thon..	Big Cat 4000
12/29/07	57	12		4 Back To The Traphouse	Czar 313516
10/11/08	197	1		5 Hood Classics	Big Cat 4026
4/11/09	172	1		6 Bird Money..	Big Cat 7345
5/30/09	23	6		7 Murder Was The Case...	Big Cat 4029
12/26/09	10	23↑		8 The State vs. Radric Davis	Brick Squad 520540

GUERILLA BLACK
Born Charles Williamson in 1977 Chicago, Illinois; raised in Compton, California. Male rapper.

10/16/04	20	12		1 Guerilla City	Virgin 81786

GUERRA, Juan Luis, Y 440
Born on 6/7/1957 in Santo Domingo, Dominican Republic. Latin singer.

9/18/04	110	6	●	1 Para Ti .... [F]	Vene 651000
4/7/07	77	6		2 La Llave De Mi Corazon .... [F]	EMI Televisa 88392

GUESS WHO, The   **All-Time: #276**
Rock band formed in Winnipeg, Manitoba, Canada: Chad Allan (vocals, guitar), Randy Bachman (guitar), Bob Ashley (piano), Jim Kale (bass) and Garry Peterson (drums). Recorded as Chad Allan & The Expressions. Ashley replaced by new lead singer **Burton Cummings** in 1966. Allan left shortly thereafter. Bachman left in 1970 to form **Bachman-Turner Overdrive**; replaced by Kurt Winter and Greg Leskiw. Leskiw and Kale left in 1972; replaced by Don McDougall and Bill Wallace. Domenic Troiano replaced both Winter and McDougall in 1973. Group disbanded in 1975; several reunions since then. Winter died of a bleeding ulcer on 12/14/1997 (age 51). Troiano died of cancer on 5/25/2005 (age 59).

4/26/69	45	19		1 Wheatfield Soul	RCA Victor 4141
10/4/69	91	17		2 Canned Wheat Packed by The Guess Who	RCA Victor 4157
2/14/70	9	55	●	3 American Woman	RCA Victor 4266
10/17/70	14	25	●	4 Share The Land	RCA Victor 4359
4/17/71	12	45	●	5 The Best Of The Guess Who .... Cat:#10/227 [G]	RCA Victor 1004
8/21/71	52	16		6 So Long, Bannatyne	RCA Victor 4574
3/18/72	79	10		7 Rockin'	RCA Victor 4602
8/19/72	39	21		8 Live At The Paramount (Seattle) .... [L]	RCA Victor 4779
				recorded on 5/22/1972	
1/20/73	110	12		9 Artificial Paradise..	RCA Victor 4830
7/14/73	155	8		10 #10	RCA Victor 0130
1/12/74	186	4		11 The Best Of The Guess Who, Volume II .... [G]	RCA Victor 0269

Billboard DEBUT	PEAK	WKS	R I A A	ARTIST Album Title	Catalog	Label & Number

GUESS WHO, The — cont'd

5/11/74	60	26		12 Road Food		RCA Victor 0405
2/1/75	48	9		13 Flavours		RCA Victor 0636
7/26/75	87	7		14 Power In The Music..........................		RCA Victor 0995
4/30/77	173	4		15 The Greatest Of The Guess Who .... [G]		RCA Victor 2253

GUETTA, David
Born on 11/7/1967 in Paris, France. White DJ/producer.

9/12/09	70	11		1 One Love..		Gum 86847

GUIDED BY VOICES
Rock band from Dayton, Ohio: Robert Pollard (vocals), Doug Gillard (guitar), Nate Farley (guitar), Tim Tobias (bass) and Jim MacPherson (drums).

4/21/01	168	1		1 Isolation Drills		TVT 2160
7/6/02	160	1		2 Universal Truths And Cycles		Matador 0547
9/6/03	193	1		3 Earthquake Glue		Matador 574

GUIDRY, Greg
Born on 1/23/1950 in St. Louis, Missouri. Died in a car fire on 7/28/2003 (age 53). Pop singer/songwriter/pianist.

4/17/82	147	7		1 Over The Line		Columbia 37735

GUINEY, Bob
Born on 5/8/1971 in Riverview, Michigan. Star of the first season of the TV reality series *The Bachelor*.

12/13/03	114	1		1 3 Sides...		Wind-Up 13090

GUN
Rock band from Glasgow, Scotland: Mark Rankin (vocals), Giuliano Gizzi (guitar), Baby Stafford (guitar), Dante Gizzi (bass) and Scott Shields (drums).

3/31/90	134	8		1 Taking On The World		A&M 5285

G UNIT
Male rap trio from Jamaica, Queens, New York: Curtis "**50 Cent**" Jackson, Christopher **Lloyd Banks** and David "**Young Black**" Brown.

11/29/03	2[1]	41	▲[2]	1 Beg For Mercy		G-Unit 001594
7/19/08	4	11		2 T*O*S (Terminate On Sight)		G Unit 011461

GUNNE, Jo Jo — see JO JO

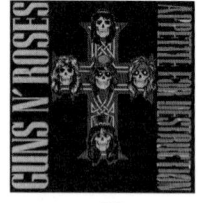

GUNS N' ROSES   All-Time: #187
Hard-rock band formed in Los Angeles, California: William "Axl Rose" Bailey (vocals; born on 2/6/1962), Saul "Slash" Hudson (guitar; born on 7/23/1965), Jeffrey "**Izzy Stradlin'**" Isbell (guitar; born on 4/8/1962), Michael "**Duff**" McKagen (bass; born on 2/5/1964) and Steven Adler (drums; born on 1/22/1965). Rose married Erin Everly (daughter of Don Everly of **The Everly Brothers**) briefly in 1990. Matt Sorum replaced Adler in 1990. Keyboardist Dizzy Reed joined in 1990. Gilby Clarke replaced Stradlin' in late 1991. Slash married model Renee Surran in November 1992. Clarke left band in January 1995. Slash, Sorum and Clarke recorded in 1995 in **Slash's Snakepit**. Rose recorded *Chinese Democracy* (album #8 below) with various other musicians.

8/29/87+	❶[5]	147	▲[18]	1 Appetite For Destruction Cat:❶[1]/418		Geffen 24148
				RS500 #61		
12/17/88+	2[1]	53	▲[5]	2 G N' R Lies Cat:#21/40		Geffen 24198
10/5/91	2[2]	108	▲[7]	3 Use Your Illusion I		Geffen 24415
10/5/91	❶[2]	106	▲[7]	4 Use Your Illusion II		Geffen 24420
12/11/93	4	22	▲	5 The Spaghetti Incident?		Geffen 24617
12/18/99	45	13	●	6 Live Era '87-'93 .... [L]		Geffen 490514 [2]
4/10/04	3[1]	160↑	▲[4]	7 Greatest Hits Cat:❶[12]/157 [G]		Geffen 001714
12/13/08	3[1]	15	▲	8 Chinese Democracy		Black Frog 012356

GURU
Born Keith Elam on 7/17/1966 in Boston, Massachusetts. Died of cancer on 4/19/2010 (age 43). Male rapper/songwriter. Member of **Gang Starr**. Guru stands for Gifted Unlimited Rhymes Universal.

6/5/93	94	19		1 Jazzmatazz Volume I..........................		Chrysalis 21998
8/5/95	71	9		2 Jazzmatazz Volume II: The New Reality		Chrysalis 34290
10/21/00	32	7		3 Jazzmatazz Streetsoul		Virgin 50189
10/13/01	122	4		4 Baldhead Slick & Da Click		Ill Kid 9205

GURVITZ, Adrian — see BAKER GURVITZ ARMY / EDGE, Graeme, Band

GUSTER
Rock trio from Boston, Massachusetts: Adam Gardner (vocals, guitar), Ryan Miller (guitar) and Brian Rosenworcel (drums).

10/16/99	169	1		1 Lost And Gone Forever		Hybrid 31064
7/12/03	35	12		2 Keep It Together		Palm 48306
6/5/04	180	1		3 On Ice: Live From Portland Maine .... [L]		Palm 48710
7/8/06	25	6		4 Ganging Up On The Sun......................		Reprise 49965

Billboard DEBUT	PEAK	WKS	R I A A	ARTIST Album Title	Catalog	Label & Number
				GUTHRIE, Arlo		
				Born on 7/10/1947 in Brooklyn, New York. Folk singer/songwriter. Son of **Woody Guthrie**. Starred as himself in the 1969 movie *Alice's Restaurant*, which was based on his 1967 song "Alice's Restaurant Massacree." Often performed in concert with Pete Seeger.		
11/18/67+	17	99	▲	1 **Alice's Restaurant**		Reprise 6267
10/26/68	100	12		2 **Arlo**	[L]	Reprise 6299
				recorded at the Bitter End in New York City		
10/18/69	63	17		3 **Alice's Restaurant**	[S]	United Artists 5195
10/25/69	54	19		4 **Running Down The Road**		Reprise 6346
11/7/70	33	17		5 **Washington County**		Reprise 6411
6/10/72	52	38		6 **Hobo's Lullabye**		Reprise 2060
4/28/73	87	14		7 **Last Of The Brooklyn Cowboys**		Reprise 2142
6/8/74	165	10		8 **Arlo Guthrie**		Reprise 2183
5/17/75	181	4		9 **Together In Concert**	[L]	Reprise 2214 [2]
				PETE SEEGER & ARLO GUTHRIE		
10/2/76	133	6		10 **Amigo**		Reprise 2239
1/28/78	202	3	●	11 **The Best Of Arlo Guthrie**	[G]	Warner 3117
6/27/81	184	3		12 **Power Of Love**		Warner 3558
				GUTHRIE, Gwen		
				Born on 7/9/1950 in Newark, New Jersey. Died of cancer on 2/4/1999 (age 48). R&B singer/songwriter.		
11/27/82	208	2		1 **Gwen Guthrie**		Island 90004
8/30/86	89	13		2 **Good To Go Lover**		Polydor 829532

GUTHRIE, Woody — see VARIOUS ARTISTS COMPILATIONS: "A Tribute To..."

Billboard DEBUT	PEAK	WKS	R I A A	ARTIST Album Title	Catalog	Label & Number
				GUTTER TWINS, The		
				Alternative-rock duo formed in Los Angeles, California: Greg Dulli (of **Afghan Whigs**) and Mark Lanegan (of **Screaming Trees**).		
3/22/08	117	1		1 **Saturnalia**		Sub Pop 761
				GUY		
				R&B vocal trio from Harlem, New York: brothers **Aaron Hall** and **Damion Hall**, with Teddy Riley. Riley also formed **BLACKstreet**.		
7/30/88+	27	70	▲²	1 **Guy**		Uptown 42176
12/1/90+	16	46	▲	2 **The Future**		MCA 10115
2/12/00	13	10		3 **III**		MCA 112054
				GUY, Buddy		
				Born George Guy on 7/30/1936 in Lettsworth, Louisiana. Blues singer/guitarist. Popular concert attraction. Father of **Shawnna**.		
				AWARDS: R&R Hall of Fame: 2005 ★ Billboard Century: 1993		
10/19/91	136	6	●	1 **Damn Right, I've Got The Blues**		Silvertone 41462
				Grammy: Contemporary Blues Album		
3/27/93	145	7		2 **Feels Like Rain**		Silvertone 41498
				Grammy: Contemporary Blues Album		
11/12/94	180	1		3 **Slippin' In**		Silvertone 41542
				Grammy: Contemporary Blues Album		
5/4/96	186	1		4 **Live! The Real Deal**	[L]	Silvertone 41543
				BUDDY GUY WITH G.E. SMITH & THE SATURDAY NIGHT LIVE BAND recorded at Irving Plaza in New York City and at Legend's in Chicago, Illinois		
6/20/98	163	1		5 **Heavy Love**		Silvertone 41632
6/2/01	162	1		6 **Sweet Tea**		Silvertone 41751
6/21/03	188	1		7 **Blues Singer**		Silvertone 41843
				Grammy: Contemporary Blues Album		
10/15/05	152	1		8 **Bring 'Em In**		Silvertone 72426
8/9/08	68	5		9 **Skin Deep**		Silvertone 31629
				GUY, Jasmine		
				Born on 3/10/1964 in Boston, Massachusetts; raised in Atlanta, Georgia. R&B singer/actress. Acted in several movies. Played "Whitley Gilbert" on TV's *A Different World*.		
11/3/90	143	13		1 **Jasmine Guy**		Warner 26021
				GWAR		
				Hard-rock band formed in Richmond, Virginia: David "Odorus Urungus" Brockie (vocals), Michael "Balsac the Jaws of Death" Derks (guitar), Peter "Flattus Maximus" Lee (guitar), Danyelle "Slymenstra Hymen" Stampe (whips), Charles "Sexicutioner" Varga (chains), Michael "Beefcake the Mighty" Bishop (bass) and Brad "Jizmak the Gusha" Roberts (drums). Group name stands for "God What an Awful Racket."		
4/18/92	177	1		1 **America Must Be Destroyed**		Metal Blade 26807
9/5/09	96	1		2 **Lust In Space**		Metal Blade 14751
				GYM CLASS HEROES		
				Alternative hip-hop band from Geneva, New York: Travie McCoy (vocals), Disashi Lumumba-Kasongo (guitar), Eric Roberts (bass) and Matt McGinley (drums).		
8/12/06+	35	41	●	1 **As Cruel As School Children**		Decaydance 086
9/27/08	14	6		2 **The Quilt**		Decaydance 511260

331

GYPSY

Rock band formed in Minneapolis, Minnesota: James "Owl" Walsh (vocals, keyboards), James Johnson (guitar), Enrico Rosenbaum (guitar), Doni Larson (bass) and Jay Epstein (drums). In early 1971, Willie Weeks replaced Larson and William Lordan replaced Epstein. Walsh re-formed the band in 1978 as the **James Walsh Gypsy Band**.

DEBUT	PEAK	WKS				
10/10/70	44	20		1 Gypsy		Metromedia 1031 [2]
8/7/71	173	8		2 In The Garden		Metromedia 1044
11/18/78	203	5		3 James Walsh Gypsy Band		RCA Victor 2914

GZA/GENIUS

Born Gary Grice on 8/22/1966 in Brooklyn, New York. Male rapper. Member of **Wu-Tang Clan**. Pronounced: jizz-ah.

11/25/95	9	24	●	1 Liquid Swords GENIUS/GZA	Geffen 24813
7/17/99	9	10	●	2 Beneath The Surface	Wu-Tang 11969
12/28/02	75	7		3 Legend Of The Liquid Sword	MCA 113083
11/12/05	180	1		4 Grandmasters DJ MUGGS vs. GZA/THE GENIUS	Angeles 1001
9/6/08	52	2		5 Pro Tools	Babygrande 0372

H

HAASE, Ernie, & Signature Sound

Christian vocal group formed in Evansville, Indiana: Ernie Haase (tenor; born on 12/12/1964), Ryan Seaton (lead), Doug Anderson (baritone), Tim Duncan (bass) and Roy Webb (piano). Haase was a member of **Old Friends Quartet**.

11/12/05	91	1		1 Ernie Haase & Signature Sound	Gaither 42619
2/10/07	59	2		2 Get Away, Jordan	Gaither 42700
11/10/07	91	2		3 Together	Gaither 42729
				GAITHER VOCAL BAND AND ERNIE HAASE & SIGNATURE SOUND	
11/15/08	85	2		4 Dream On	Gaither 42749
10/24/09	2 [1X]	8		5 Every Light That Shines At Christmas [X]	Gaither 42794

HACKETT, Steve

Born on 2/12/1950 in London, England. Rock guitarist. Former member of **Genesis** (1970-77). Formed **GTR** in 1986.

4/17/76	191	4		1 Voyage Of The Acolyte	Chrysalis 1112
4/29/78	103	14		2 Please Don't Touch	Chrysalis 1176
7/7/79	138	4		3 Spectral Mornings	Chrysalis 1223
8/30/80	144	6		4 Defector	Charisma 3103
10/24/81	169	3		5 Cured	Epic 37632

HADDAWAY

Born Nester Haddaway on 1/9/1965 in Tobago, West Indies; raised in Chicago, Illinois. Black dance singer/choreographer.

1/15/94	111	12		1 Haddaway	Arista 18743

HADDON, Deitrick

Born on 5/17/1973 in Detroit, Michigan. Male gospel singer.

9/11/04	178	1		1 Crossroads	Verity 59482
10/28/06	135	2		2 7 Days	Tyscot 88166
9/20/08	98	3		3 Revealed	Verity 23471

HADEN, Charlie

Born on 8/6/1937 in Shenandoah, Iowa. Jazz bassist. Member of **Ornette Coleman**'s band.

10/11/08	100	2		1 Rambling Boy	Decca 011639

HAGAR, Sammy   All-Time: #246

Born on 10/13/1947 in Monterey, California. Rock singer/songwriter/guitarist. Nicknamed "The Red Rocker." Lead singer of **Montrose** (1973-75), **Van Halen** (1985-96) and **Chickenfoot**. The Waboritas: Vic Johnson (guitar), Jesse Harms (keyboards; REO Speedwagon), Mona (bass) and David Lauser (drums). Also see **Hagar, Schon, Aaronson, Shrieve**.

2/26/77	167	9		1 Sammy Hagar	Capitol 11599
1/21/78	100	11		2 Musical Chairs	Capitol 11706
9/8/79	71	13		3 Street Machine	Capitol 11983
6/21/80	85	12		4 Danger Zone	Capitol 12069
1/30/82	28	32	▲	5 Standing Hampton	Geffen 2006
12/25/82+	17	34	●	6 Three Lock Box	Geffen 2021
8/11/84	32	36	▲	7 VOA	Geffen 24043
7/11/87	14	23	●	8 Sammy Hagar	Geffen 24144
				as a result of an MTV contest, album title changed to *I Never Said Goodbye*; however, no vinyl copies were pressed with the new title	
6/7/97	18	17		9 Marching To Mars	MCA 11627
4/10/99	22	14		10 Red Voodoo	MCA 11872
11/11/00	52	2		11 Ten 13	Cabo Wabo 78110
				title derived from his birthdate	
10/26/02	181	1		12 Not 4 Sale	33rd Street 3315
8/12/06	50	2		13 Livin' It Up	Cabo Wabo 74097
				SAMMY HAGAR AND THE WABORITAS (above 4)	
12/6/08	95	1		14 Cosmic Universal Fashion	Loud & Proud 617891

HAGAR, Sammy — cont'd

GREATEST HITS & COMPILATIONS:

DEBUT	PEAK	WKS	RIAA		Catalog	Label & Number
1/8/83	171	9		15 Rematch		Capitol 12238
4/2/94	51	11	●	16 Unboxed		Geffen 24702
8/28/04	75	2		17 The Essential Red Collection		Hip-O 002760

LIVE ALBUMS:

8/19/78	89	9		18 All Night Long		Capitol 11812
11/19/83	203	4		19 Live 1980		Capitol 12299
				recorded at Hammersmith Odeon in London		
6/7/03	152	1		20 Sammy And The Wabo's Live: Hallelujah		Sanctuary 84608
				SAMMY HAGAR AND THE WABORITAS		

HAGAR, SCHON, AARONSON, SHRIEVE
All-star rock band formed in Los Angeles, California: **Sammy Hagar** (vocals), **Neal Schon** (guitar), Kenny Aaronson (bass) and **Michael Shrieve** (drums).

3/31/84	42	18		1 Through The Fire [L]		Geffen 4023

HAGEN, Nina
Born on 3/11/1955 in East Berlin, Germany. Dance-punk singer/actress.

6/5/82	184	3		1 Nunsexmonkrock		Columbia 38008
1/28/84	151	8		2 Fearless		Columbia 39214
6/15/85	201	5		3 Nina Hagen In Ekstasy		Columbia 40004

HAGGARD, Merle   All-Time: #271
Born on 4/6/1937 in Bakersfield, California. Country singer/songwriter/guitarist. Served nearly three years in San Quentin prison for burglary, from 1957-60. Granted a full pardon by Governor Ronald Reagan on 3/14/1972. Formed his backing band, The Strangers, in 1965. Acted in several movies and TV shows.
AWARDS: Grammy: Lifetime Achievement 2006 ★ C&W Hall of Fame: 1994 ★ CMA: Male Vocalist 1970 / Entertainer 1970 / Vocal Duo (w/ Willie Nelson) 1983

5/13/67	165	10		1 I'm A Lonesome Fugitive		Capitol 2702
10/21/67	167	4		2 Branded Man		Capitol 2789
				RS500 #484		
3/15/69	189	7		3 Pride In What I Am		Capitol 168
6/14/69	67	18		4 Same Train, A Different Time		Capitol 223 [2]
8/23/69	140	6		5 Close-Up [R]		Capitol 259 [2]
				reissue of *Strangers* and *Swinging Doors* albums		
10/18/69	99	11		6 A Portrait Of Merle Haggard		Capitol 319
1/24/70	46	52	▲	7 Okie From Muskogee [L]		Capitol 384
				CMA: Album of the Year		
				recorded in Muskogee, Oklahoma		
7/25/70	68	33	●	8 The Fightin' Side Of Me [L]		Capitol 451
				recorded at the Civic Center Hall in Philadelphia, Pennsylvania		
12/19/70+	58	9		9 A Tribute To The Best Damn Fiddle Player In The World (Or, My Salute To Bob Wills)		Capitol 638
4/17/71	66	15		10 Hag		Capitol 735
9/18/71	108	10		11 Someday We'll Look Back		Capitol 835
4/8/72	166	8		12 Let Me Tell You About A Song		Capitol 882
				CMA: Album of the Year		
10/7/72	137	9	▲	13 The Best Of The Best Of Merle Haggard [G]		Capitol 11082
8/25/73	126	11		14 I Love Dixie Blues...So I Recorded "Live" In New Orleans [L]		Capitol 11200
12/8/73	4ˣ	3		15 Merle Haggard's Christmas Present (Something Old, Something New) [X]		Capitol 11230
3/23/74	190	3		16 If We Make It Through December		Capitol 11276
6/28/75	129	9		17 Keep Movin' On		Capitol 11365
11/19/77	133	5		18 My Farewell To Elvis		MCA 2314
11/7/81+	161	28	●	19 Big City		Epic 37593
9/25/82	123	12		20 A Taste Of Yesterday's Wine		Epic 38203
				MERLE HAGGARD & GEORGE JONES		
2/12/83	37	53	▲	21 Pancho & Lefty		Epic 37958
				MERLE HAGGARD & WILLIE NELSON		
11/11/06	119	4		22 Jones Sings Haggard, Haggard Sings Jones: Kickin' Out The Footlights... Again		Bandit 79816
				GEORGE JONES & MERLE HAGGARD		
4/7/07	64	4		23 Last Of The Breed		Lost Highway 008530 [2]
				WILLIE NELSON / MERLE HAGGARD / RAY PRICE		

HAIRCUT ONE HUNDRED
Pop-rock band from Beckenham, Kent, England: **Nick Heyward** (vocals), Graham Jones (guitar), Phil Smith (sax), Mark Fox (percussion), Les Nemes (bass) and Blair Cunningham (drums).

4/24/82	31	37		1 Pelican West		Arista 6600

HALESTORM
Hard-rock band from York, Pennsylvania: sister-and-brother Lizzy Hale (vocals) and Arejay Hale (drums), with Joe Hottinger (guitar) and Josh Smith (bass).

5/16/09	40	23		1 Halestorm		Atlantic 518222

			R I A A	ARTIST		
Billboard						
DEBUT	PEAK	WKS		Album Title	Catalog	Label & Number

HALEY, Bill, And His Comets
1950s: #38

Born on 7/6/1925 in Highland Park, Michigan. Died of a heart attack on 2/9/1981 (age 55). Began career as a country singer. His Comets consisted of Billy Williamson (guitar), Joey D'Ambrosio (sax), Johnny Grande (piano), Marshall Lytle (bass) and Billy Gussack (drums). D'Ambrosio, Richards and Lytle left in September 1955 to form the Jodimars. Comets lineup on subsequent recordings included Williamson, Grande, Franny Beecher (guitar), Rudy Pompilli (sax), Al Rex (bass), Ralph Jones (drums). Pompilli died of cancer on 2/5/1976 (age 47). Grande died on 6/2/2006 (age 55).

AWARD: R&R Hall of Fame: 1987

2/19/55	5	15		1 Shake Rattle And Roll .... [EP]		Decca 2168
1/28/56	12	2		2 Rock Around The Clock .... [G]		Decca 8225
10/13/56	18	5		3 Rock 'N Roll Stage Show		Decca 8345

~ ~ ~ ~ ~ ~ ~ ~ ~ **NON-CHARTED ALBUMS** ~ ~ ~ ~ ~ ~ ~ ~ ~ ~ ~
1955 **Rock With Bill Haley And The Comets** *[Essex label]*   1958 **Rockin' Around the World**
1955 **Shake Rattle and Roll** *[10" LP]*   1958 **Rockin' The Joint!**
1956 **Rockin' The "Oldies"!**

HALFORD

Born Rob Halford on 8/25/1951 in Walsall, Staffordshire, England. Hard-rock singer. Former lead singer of **Judas Priest**, **Fight** and **Two**.

8/26/00	140	1		1 Resurrection		Metal-Is 85200
7/13/02	144	1		2 Crucible		Metal-Is 85233

HALFWAY TO HAZARD

Duo formed in Nashville, Tennessee: Chad Warrix (from Jackson, Kentucky) and David Tolliver (from Hindman, Kentucky).

9/1/07	87	2		1 Halfway To Hazard		Stylesonic 008870

HALIFAX

Pop-punk band from Thousand Oaks, California: Mike Hunau (vocals), Chris Brandt (guitar), Adam Charles (guitar), Doug Peyton (bass) and Tommy Guindon (drums).

6/10/06	130	1		1 The Inevitability Of A Strange World		Drive-Thru 83637

HALL, Aaron

Born on 8/10/1964 in Brooklyn, New York. R&B singer. Member of **Guy** with younger brother **Damion Hall**.

10/16/93	47	55	▲	1 The Truth		Silas 10810
11/7/98	55	5		2 Inside Of You		Silas 11778

HALL, Arsenio — see CHUNKY A

HALL, Carol

Born in Abilene, Texas. Female singer/songwriter.

4/8/72	215	2		1 Beads And Feathers		Elektra 75018

HALL, Charlie

Born in Oklahoma City, Oklahoma. Christian singer/songwriter/worship leader.

2/11/06	184	1		1 Flying Into Daybreak		Six Steps 43917
9/6/08	134	1		2 The Bright Sadness		Six Steps 22222

HALL, Damion "Crazy Legs"

Born Albert Damion Hall on 6/6/1968 in Brooklyn, New York. R&B singer. Member of **Guy** with older brother **Aaron Hall**.

5/14/94	147	2		1 Straight To The Point		Silas 10996

HALL, Daryl

Born Daryl Hohl on 10/11/1946 in Philadelphia, Pennsylvania. "Blue-eyed soul" singer/songwriter/keyboardist. Member of **The Electric Indian** and one half of **Hall & Oates** duo.

3/29/80	58	12		1 Sacred Songs		RCA Victor 3573
9/6/86	29	26		2 Three Hearts In The Happy Ending Machine		RCA Victor 7196
9/25/93	177	3		3 Soul Alone		Epic 53937

HALL, Daryl, & John Oates
1980s: #35 / All-Time: #110

"Blue-eyed soul" pop duo: **Daryl Hall** (see previous entry) and John Oates (guitar, vocals; born on 4/7/1948 in Brooklyn, New York). Met while students at Temple University in 1967. Hall played with **The Electric Indian** and sang backup for many top soul groups before teaming up with Oates in 1972. They passed **The Everly Brothers** as the #1 charting duo of the rock era.

2/23/74+	33	38	▲	1 Abandoned Luncheonette		Atlantic 7269
10/26/74	86	10		2 War Babies		Atlantic 18109
				produced by **Todd Rundgren**		
3/26/77	92	6		3 No Goodbyes .... [K]		Atlantic 18213
9/13/75+	17	76	●	4 Daryl Hall & John Oates		RCA Victor 1144
8/28/76	13	57	●	5 Bigger Than Both Of Us		RCA Victor 1467
9/17/77	30	17		6 Beauty On A Back Street		RCA Victor 2300
5/27/78	42	10		7 Livetime .... [L]		RCA Victor 2802
9/9/78	27	22	●	8 Along The Red Ledge		RCA Victor 2804
10/27/79	33	24		9 X-Static		RCA Victor 3494

Billboard			R I A A	ARTIST		
DEBUT	PEAK	WKS		Album Title	Catalog	Label & Number
				HALL, Daryl, & John Oates — cont'd		
8/16/80+	17	100	▲	10 Voices..		RCA Victor 3646
9/26/81+	5	61	▲	11 Private Eyes		RCA Victor 4028
10/30/82+	3[15]	68	▲²	12 H2O		RCA Victor 4383
11/19/83+	7	44	▲²	13 Rock 'N Soul, Part 1	Cat:#45/5 [G]	RCA Victor 4858
10/27/84	5	51	▲²	14 Big Bam Boom		RCA Victor 5309
9/28/85	21	18	●	15 Live At The Apollo With David Ruffin & Eddie Kendrick .... [L]		RCA Victor 7035
				recorded at the re-opening of New York's Apollo Theater; side 1 features guest vocalists Ruffin and Kendrick		
5/21/88	24	26	▲	16 Ooh Yeah!		Arista 8539
10/27/90	60	29	●	17 Change Of Season		Arista 8614
10/18/97	95	5		18 Marigold Sky		Push 90200
3/1/03	77	7		19 Do It For Love		U-Watch 80100
4/3/04	63	3		20 Ultimate Daryl Hall + John Oates... [G]		BMG 57355 [2]
11/13/04	69	2		21 Our Kind Of Soul		U-Watch 80103
10/31/09	89	1		22 Do What You Want Be What You Are: The Music Of Daryl Hall & John Oates .... [K]		RCA 36974 [4]
				HALL, Jimmy Born on 4/26/1949 in Mobile, Alabama. Lead singer of **Wet Willie**.		
11/22/80	183	2		1 Touch You...		Epic 36516
				HALL, John, Band Born on 10/25/1948 in Baltimore, Maryland. Rock singer/guitarist. Leader of **Orleans**. Band includes Bob Leinbach (keyboards), John Troy (bass) and Eric Parker (drums). Hall was elected to the U.S. House of Representatives (in New York) in 2006.		
5/19/79	203	4		1 Power		Columbia 35790
12/5/81	158	13		2 All Of The Above		EMI America 17058
3/5/83	147	5		3 Searchparty		EMI America 17082
				HALL, Lani Born on 11/1/1945 in Chicago, Illinois. Lead vocalist with **Sergio Mendes & Brasil '66**. Married **Herb Alpert** on 12/15/1974.		
11/18/72	203	12		1 Sundown Lady..		A&M 4359
3/14/81	206	3		2 Blush		A&M 4829
				HALL, Larry Born on 6/30/1940 in Hamlett, Ohio. Died of cancer on 9/24/1997 (age 57). Teen rock and roll singer.		
				~ ~ ~ ~ ~ ~ ~ ~ ~ ~ *NON-CHARTED ALBUM* ~ ~ ~ ~ ~ ~ ~ ~ ~ ~		
				1960 Sandy		
				HALL, Tom T. Born on 5/25/1936 in Olive Hill, Kentucky. Country singer/songwriter/guitarist. AWARDS: C&W Hall of Fame: 2008 ★ OPRY: 1980		
10/9/71	137	6		1 In Search Of A Song		Mercury 61350
6/9/73	181	4		2 The Rhymer And Other Five And Dimers		Mercury 668
1/26/74	149	11		3 For The People In The Last Hard Town.......................................		Mercury 687
4/19/75	180	2		4 Songs Of Fox Hollow		Mercury 500
1/31/76	202	3	●	5 Greatest Hits-Vol. 2 .... [G]		Mercury 1044
				HALL, Trevor Born in South Carolina. Singer/songwriter/guitarist.		
8/15/09	199	1		1 Trevor Hall		Vanguard 79941
				HALLIWELL, Geri Born Geraldine Halliwell on 8/6/1972 in Watford, Hertfordshire, England. Former member of the **Spice Girls** (as "Ginger Spice").		
7/3/99	42	7	●	1 Schizophonic		Capitol 21009
				HALOS, The R&B vocal group from Harlem, New York: Harold Johnson, Al Cleveland, Phil Johnson and Arthur Crier. Crier died of heart failure on 7/22/2004 (age 59).		
				~ ~ ~ ~ ~ ~ ~ ~ ~ ~ *NON-CHARTED ALBUM* ~ ~ ~ ~ ~ ~ ~ ~ ~ ~		
				1962 The Halos		
				HAMILTON, Anthony Born on 6/29/1971 in Charlotte, North Carolina. R&B singer/songwriter.		
10/11/03	33	76	▲	1 Comin' Where I Come From		So So Def 52107
7/16/05	12	12		2 Soulife		So So Def 74695
12/31/05	19	25	●	3 Ain't Nobody Worryin'..		So So Def 74278
4/21/07	90	3		4 Southern Comfort		Merovingian 002
1/3/09	12	42	●	5 The Point Of It All		Mister's Music 23387
				HAMILTON, Chico Born Foreststorn Hamilton on 9/21/1921 in Los Angeles, California. Jazz drummer. Brother of actor Bernie Hamilton.		
12/19/64+	145	4		1 Man From Two Worlds .... [I]		Impulse! 59

HAMILTON, George IV
Born on 7/19/1937 in Winston-Salem, North Carolina. Country singer/songwriter/guitarist. Hosted own TV series in 1959.
AWARD: OPRY: 1960

| 10/5/63 | 77 | 8 | | 1 Abilene .... | | RCA Victor 2778 |

~ ~ ~ ~ ~ ~ ~ ~ ~ ~ **NON-CHARTED ALBUMS** ~ ~ ~ ~ ~ ~ ~ ~ ~ ~ ~
1958 **George Hamilton IV On Campus**   1963 **George Hamilton IV Big 15**

HAMILTON, Russ
Born Ronald Hulme on 1/19/1932 in Liverpool, England. Died on 10/11/2008 (age 76). Pop singer/songwriter.
~ ~ ~ ~ ~ ~ ~ ~ ~ ~ **NON-CHARTED ALBUM** ~ ~ ~ ~ ~ ~ ~ ~ ~ ~ ~
1957 **Rainbows**

HAMILTON, JOE FRANK & REYNOLDS
Pop vocal trio formed in Los Angeles, California: Dan Hamilton, Joe Frank Carollo and Tommy Reynolds. All were members of **The T-Bones**. Reynolds left group in 1972 and was replaced by Alan Dennison. Although Reynolds had left, group still recorded as Hamilton, Joe Frank & Reynolds until July 1976. Hamilton died on 12/23/1994 (age 48).

6/19/71	59	15		1 Hamilton, Joe Frank & Reynolds		Dunhill/ABC 50103
2/19/72	191	4		2 Hallway Symphony		Dunhill/ABC 50113
12/13/75+	82	14		3 Fallin' In Love		Playboy 407

HAMLISCH, Marvin
Born on 6/2/1944 in Brooklyn, New York. Pianist/composer/conductor.
AWARD: Grammy: Best New Artist 1974

| 1/26/74 | ❶⁵ | 41 | ● | 1 The Sting | [I-S] | MCA 390 |
| 8/31/74 | 170 | 5 | | 2 The Entertainer .... | [I] | MCA 2115 |

HAMMER — see M.C. HAMMER

HAMMER, Jan
Born on 4/17/1948 in Prague, Czechoslovakia. Jazz-rock keyboardist.

| 2/8/75 | 150 | 3 | | 1 Like Children .... | | Nemperor 430 |

JERRY GOODMAN & JAN HAMMER

| 7/4/76 | 201 | 7 | | 2 Oh, Yeah? .... | [I] | Nemperor 437 |

JAN HAMMER GROUP

| 4/2/77 | 23 | 15 | ● | 3 Jeff Beck With The Jan Hammer Group Live .... | [I-L] | Epic 34433 |
| 3/31/79 | 209 | 1 | | 4 Black Sheep .... | [I] | Asylum 173 |

HAMMER

| 10/17/81 | 115 | 8 | | 5 Untold Passion .... | | Columbia 37600 |
| 2/5/83 | 122 | 12 | | 6 Here To Stay .... | | Columbia 38428 |

NEAL SCHON & JAN HAMMER (above 2)

HAMMOND, Albert
Born on 5/18/1944 in London, England; raised in Gibraltar, Spain. Pop-rock singer/songwriter. Father of **Albert Hammond Jr.**

| 12/9/72+ | 77 | 15 | | 1 It Never Rains In Southern California................................ | | Mums 31905 |
| 9/1/73 | 193 | 4 | | 2 The Free Electric Band .... | | Mums 32267 |

HAMMOND, Albert, Jr.
Born on 4/9/1980 in Los Angeles, California. Rock singer/songwriter/guitarist. Member of **The Strokes**. Son of **Albert Hammond**.

| 3/24/07 | 117 | 2 | | 1 Yours To Keep.. | | Scratchie 3908 |
| 7/26/08 | 145 | 1 | | 2 Como Te Llama? .... | | Black Seal 32563 |

HAMMOND, Fred
Born on 12/27/1960 in Detroit, Michigan. Black gospel singer. Former member of **Commissioned**.

| 5/16/98 | 51 | 21 | ▲² | 1 Pages Of Life - Chapters I & II.. | | Verity 43110 [2] |
| 4/8/00 | 46 | 17 | ● | 2 Purpose By Design .... | | Verity 43140 |

FRED HAMMOND & RADICAL FOR CHRIST (above 2)

| 11/17/01 | 23ˣ | 2 | | 3 Christmas...Just Remember .... | [X] | Verity 43174 |

Christmas chart: 23/'01

9/28/02	38	8		4 Speak Those Things: POL Chapter 3		Verity 43197
6/26/04	35	13	●	5 Somethin' 'Bout Love..		Verity 58744
10/21/06	29	7		6 Free To Worship		Verity 85990

Grammy: Contemporary R&B Gospel Album

| 10/17/09 | 26 | 11 | | 7 Love Unstoppable .... | | Verity 43341 |

HAMMOND, John Paul
Born on 11/13/1942 in Manhattan, New York. Blues-rock singer/songwriter/guitarist.

| 6/16/73 | 105 | 12 | | 1 Triumvirate .... | | Columbia 32172 |

MIKE BLOOMFIELD / JOHN PAUL HAMMOND / DR. JOHN

HAMMOND, Johnny
Born John Smith on 12/16/1933 in Louisville, Kentucky. Died on 6/4/1997 (age 63). Jazz organist.

| 9/11/71 | 125 | 14 | | 1 Breakout .... | [I] | Kudu 01 |
| 5/20/72 | 174 | 6 | | 2 Wild Horses/Rock Steady .... | [I] | Kudu 04 |

Billboard			R I A A	ARTIST		
DEBUT	PEAK	WKS		Album Title	Catalog	Label & Number

HANCOCK, Herbie — All-Time: #235
Born on 4/12/1940 in Chicago, Illinois. Jazz electronic keyboardist. Pianist with the **Miles Davis** band from 1963-68. Scored several movies. Hancock's vocals are synthesized through the use of a Vocoder machine. Also see **Headhunters** and **V.S.O.P.**

DEBUT	PEAK	WKS		Album Title	Catalog	Label & Number
5/13/67	192	2		1 Blow-Up .... [I-S]		MGM 4447
6/2/73	176	6		2 Sextant .... [I]		Columbia 32212
1/12/74	13	47	▲	3 Head Hunters .... [I]		Columbia 32731
				Grammy: Hall of Fame ★ NRR		
10/5/74	13	23		4 Thrust .... [I]		Columbia 32965
10/12/74	158	3		5 Treasure Chest .... [E-I]		Warner 2807 [2]
10/18/75	21	24		6 Man-Child .... [I]		Columbia 33812
9/11/76	49	17		7 Secrets .... [I]		Columbia 34280
5/7/77	79	7		8 V.S.O.P. .... [I-L]		Columbia 34688 [2]
				V.S.O.P.: Very Special Onetime Performance; recorded on 6/29/1976 at the Newport Jazz Festival		
7/8/78	58	13		9 Sunlight		Columbia 34907
3/17/79	38	22		10 Feets Don't Fail Me Now		Columbia 35764
3/31/79	100	8		11 An Evening With Herbie Hancock & Chick Corea ...... [I-L]		Columbia 35663 [2]
11/24/79	175	2		12 An Evening With Chick Corea & Herbie Hancock ...... [I-L]		Polydor 6238 [2]
1/19/80	202	2		13 The Best Of Herbie Hancock .... [G-I]		Columbia 36309
4/19/80	94	18		14 Monster		Columbia 36415
11/29/80	117	6		15 Mr. Hands .... [I]		Columbia 36578
10/3/81	140	6		16 Magic Windows		Columbia 37387
5/29/82	151	6		17 Lite Me Up		Columbia 37928
2/12/83	202	4		18 Quartet .... [I]		Columbia 38275 [2]
9/3/83	43	65	▲	19 Future Shock .... [I]		Columbia 38814
9/1/84	71	14		20 Sound-System .... [I]		Columbia 39478
				Grammy: R&B Instrumental Album		
9/17/05	22	14		21 Possibilities		Hear 70013
10/13/07+	5	14		22 River: The Joni Letters		Verve 009791
				Grammy: Album of the Year / Contemporary Jazz Album tribute to **Joni Mitchell**		

~ ~ ~ ~ ~ ~ ~ ~ ~ ~   **NON-CHARTED ALBUM**   ~ ~ ~ ~ ~ ~ ~ ~ ~ ~

1965 **Maiden Voyage**
Grammy: Hall of Fame

HANDSOME BOY MODELING SCHOOL
Alternative hip-hop duo formed in New York: producers/musicians Paul Huston and Dan Nakamura. Huston was also a member of **Stetsasonic** and **Gravediggaz**. Nakamura also formed **Gorillaz** and **Head Automatica**.

DEBUT	PEAK	WKS		Album Title	Catalog	Label & Number
11/27/04	168	1		1 White People		Elektra 62941

HANDY, John
Born on 2/3/1933 in Dallas, Texas. Jazz saxophonist.

DEBUT	PEAK	WKS		Album Title	Catalog	Label & Number
6/5/76	43	21		1 Hard Work .... [I]		ABC/Impulse 9314
4/16/77	200	2		2 Carnival .... [I]		ABC/Impulse 9324

HANNIGAN, Lisa
Born on 2/12/1981 in Kilcloon, Ireland. Folk singer/songwriter.

DEBUT	PEAK	WKS		Album Title	Catalog	Label & Number
3/28/09	135	1		1 Sea Saw		ATO 0068

HANSARD, Glen, & Marketa Irglova
Male singer/actor Hansard was born on 4/21/1970 in Dublin, Ireland. Female singer/actress Irglova was born on 2/28/1988 in Valasske Mezirici, Czechoslovakia. Duo also recorded as **The Swell Season**. Both starred in the 2007 movie *Once*.

DEBUT	PEAK	WKS		Album Title	Catalog	Label & Number
3/15/08	194	1		1 The Swell Season		Overcoat 25
11/14/09	15	4		2 Strict Joy		Anti 87048
				THE SWELL SEASON		

HANSEN, Randy
Born on 12/8/1954 in Seattle, Washington. Rock singer/songwriter.

DEBUT	PEAK	WKS		Album Title	Catalog	Label & Number
11/22/80	210	2		1 Randy Hansen		Capitol 12119

HANSON
Pop trio of brothers from Tulsa, Oklahoma: Taylor Hanson (lead vocals, keyboards; born on 3/14/1983), Isaac Hanson (guitar, vocals; born on 11/17/1980) and Zac Hanson (drums, vocals; born on 10/22/1985). Taylor also joined **Tinted Windows**.

DEBUT	PEAK	WKS		Album Title	Catalog	Label & Number
5/24/97	2[1]	58	▲4	1 Middle Of Nowhere		Mercury 534615
12/6/97	7	9	▲	2 Snowed In Cat:#23/7 [X]		Mercury 536717
				Christmas charts: 1/97, 12/98		
5/30/98	6	19	▲	3 3 Car Garage: The Indie Recordings '95-'96 ...... [E]		Mercury 558399
11/21/98	32	9	●	4 Live From Albertane .... [L]		Mercury 538240
				recorded on 7/21/1998 at the Key Arena in Seattle, Washington		
5/27/00	19	16	●	5 This Time Around		Island 542383
5/8/04	25	5		6 Underneath		3CG 10402
10/29/05	182	1		7 The Best Of Hanson: Live And Electric .... [L]		3CG 10515
8/11/07	56	2		8 The Walk		3CG 10702

HANSON, Jennifer
Born on 8/10/1973 in La Habra, California. Country singer/songwriter.

DEBUT	PEAK	WKS		Album Title	Catalog	Label & Number
3/8/03	125	2		1 Jennifer Hanson		Capitol 35247

Billboard DEBUT	PEAK	WKS	R I A A	ARTIST / Album Title	Catalog	Label & Number
				HANSSON, Bo Born on 4/10/1943 in Gothenberg, Sweden. Died on 4/24/2010 (age 67). Male organist.		
5/5/73	154	8		1 Lord Of The Rings .... [I]		Charisma 1059
				HAPPENINGS, The Vocal group from Paterson, New Jersey: Bob Miranda, Tom Giuliano, Ralph DiVito and Dave Libert.		
10/15/66	61	12		1 The Happenings		B.T. Puppy 1001
7/22/67	134	6		2 Back To Back..		B.T. Puppy 1002
				THE TOKENS / THE HAPPENINGS side 1: **The Tokens**; side 2: The Happenings		
8/10/68	156	4		3 The Happenings Golden Hits!.. [G]		B.T. Puppy 1004
9/6/69	181	2		4 Piece Of Mind		Jubilee 8028
				HAPPY MONDAYS Dance-rock band formed in Manchester, England: brothers Shaun Ryder (vocals) and Paul Ryder (bass), Mark Day (guitar), Paul Davis (keyboards), Mark Berry (percussion) and Gary Whelan (drums).		
2/23/91	89	13		1 Pills 'N' Thrills And Bellyaches		Elektra 60986
				HARBOR, Pearl — see PEARL		
				HARDCASTLE, Paul Born on 12/10/1957 in London, England. Keyboardist/producer. Also see **The Jazzmasters**.		
3/23/85	63	25		1 Rain Forest .... [I]		Profile 1206
4/30/94	182	6		2 Hardcastle..		JVC 2033
2/23/08	176	1		3 Hardcastle 5		Trippin 'N' Rhythm 24
				HARDEN TRIO, The Country vocal trio from England, Arkansas: siblings Bobby, Robbie and Arlene Harden.		
6/25/66	146	5		1 Tippy Toeing..		Columbia 2506 / 9306
				HARDIN, Tim Born on 12/23/1941 in Eugene, Oregon. Died of a drug overdose on 12/29/1980 (age 39). Folk-blues singer/songwriter. Relative of notorious outlaw John Wesley Hardin.		
4/26/69	129	8		1 Suite For Susan Moore And Damion-We Are-One, One, All In One		Columbia 9787
7/31/71	189	1		2 Bird On A Wire..		Columbia 30551
11/25/72	209	2		3 Painted Head		Columbia 31764
				HARDY, Hagood Born on 2/26/1937 in Angola, Indiana; raised in Toronto, Ontario, Canada. Died of cancer on 1/1/1997 (age 59). Male vibraphonist. Sideman for **Herbie Mann** and **George Shearing**.		
1/3/76	112	14		1 The Homecoming.. [I]		Capitol 11468
				HARDY BOYS, The Studio band used in the animated cartoon TV series *The Hardy Boys*: brothers Frank Hardy (guitar) and Joe Hardy (bass), Wanda Kay Breckinridge (piano), Chubby Morton (sax) and Pete Jones (drums). All share vocals.		
11/15/69	199	2		1 Here Come The Hardy Boys..		RCA Victor 4217
				HARGROVE, Roy Born on 10/16/1969 in Waco, Texas. Trumpet player.		
6/7/03	185	1		1 Hard Groove .... [I]		Verve 065192
				ROY HARGROVE PRESENTS THE RH FACTOR		
				HARLEM WORLD Rap group from Harlem, New York: Baby Stase (twin sister of **Mase**), Blinky-Blink (brother of Mase), **Loon**, Cardan, Meeno and Huddy.		
3/27/99	11	9	●	1 The Movement		All Out 69503
				HARMONICATS Harmonica trio formed in Chicago, Illinois: Jerry Murad (died on 5/11/1996, age 80), Al Fiore (died on 10/25/1996, age 73) and Don Les (died on 8/25/1994, age 79).		
3/27/61	17	4		1 Cherry Pink And Apple Blossom White.. [I]		Columbia 8356
				Jerry Murad's "Fabulous" HARMONICATS		
				HARNELL, Joe, His Piano And Orchestra Born Joseph Hittelman on 8/2/1924 in the Bronx, New York. Died of heart failure on 7/14/2005 (age 80). "Bossa Nova" conductor/arranger.		
1/26/63	3²	36		1 Fly Me To The Moon and the Bossa Nova Pops .... [I]		Kapp 3318
				HARPER, Ben Born on 10/28/1969 in Empire, California. Folk-rock singer/guitarist. The Innocent Criminals: Juan Nelson (bass) and Dean Butterworth (drums).		
7/5/97	89	11		1 The Will To Live..		Virgin 44178
10/9/99	67	22	●	2 Burn To Shine..		Virgin 48151
4/14/01	70	9	●	3 Live From Mars .... [L]		Virgin 10079 [2]
				BEN HARPER & THE INNOCENT CRIMINALS (above 2)		
3/29/03	19	23		4 Diamonds On The Inside		Virgin 80640
10/9/04	81	6		5 There Will Be A Light..		Virgin 71206
				BEN HARPER AND THE BLIND BOYS OF ALABAMA		
4/8/06	7	15		6 Both Sides Of The Gun		Virgin 57446

Billboard DEBUT	PEAK	WKS	R I A A	ARTIST Album Title	Catalog	Label & Number
				HARPER, Ben — cont'd		
9/15/07	9	9		7 Lifeline **BEN HARPER & THE INNOCENT CRIMINALS**		Virgin 93385
5/23/09	9	7		8 White Lies For Dark Times **BEN HARPER & RELENTLESS7**		Virgin 64786
				HARPERS BIZARRE Vocal group from Santa Cruz, California: Ted Templeman, Eddie James, Dick Yount, John Petersen and Dick Scoppettone. Petersen was a member of **The Beau Brummels**. Templeman later produced many albums for **The Doobie Brothers** and **Van Halen**.		
5/6/67	108	7		1 Feelin' Groovy		Warner 1693
12/9/67+	76	13		2 Anything Goes		Warner 1716
				HARPO, Slim Born James Moore on 1/11/1924 in Lobdell, Louisiana. Died of a heart attack on 1/31/1970 (age 46). Blues singer/harmonica player.		
				~ ~ ~ ~ ~ ~ ~ ~ ~ **NON-CHARTED ALBUMS** ~ ~ ~ ~ ~ ~ ~ ~ ~ ~ 1961 **Slim Harpo Sings Raining In My Heart** 1966 **Baby Scratch My Back**		
				HARRIS, Eddie Born on 10/20/1936 in Chicago, Illinois. Died of cancer on 11/5/1996 (age 60). Jazz tenor saxophonist.		
5/29/61	2[1]	37		1 Exodus To Jazz [I]		Vee-Jay 3016
4/13/68	36	41		2 The Electrifying Eddie Harris [I]		Atlantic 1495
8/3/68	120	16		3 Plug Me In [I]		Atlantic 1506
2/22/69	199	2		4 Silver Cycles [I]		Atlantic 1517
8/16/69	122	9		5 High Voltage [I-L] recorded at the Village Gate in New York City and at Shelly's Manne-Hole in Hollywood, California		Atlantic 1529
12/13/69+	29	38	●	6 Swiss Movement [I-L] recorded June 1969 at the Montreaux Jazz Festival in Switzerland		Atlantic 1537
5/29/71	41	27		7 Second Movement [I] **LES McCANN & EDDIE HARRIS** (above 2)		Atlantic 1583
4/18/70	191	3		8 The Best Of Eddie Harris [G-I]		Atlantic 1545
11/27/71	164	10		9 Eddie Harris Live At Newport [I-L]		Atlantic 1595
7/22/72	185	7		10 Instant Death [I]		Atlantic 1611
2/16/74	150	11		11 E.H. in the U.K. [I]		Atlantic 1647
10/12/74	100	11		12 Is It In [I]		Atlantic 1659
4/19/75	125	9		13 I Need Some Money [I]		Atlantic 1669
9/27/75	133	6		14 Bad Luck Is All I Have [I]		Atlantic 1675

				HARRIS, Emmylou **All-Time: #133** Born on 4/2/1947 in Birmingham, Alabama. Country singer/songwriter/guitarist. Worked as a folk singer in Washington DC in the late 1960s. First recorded for Jubilee in 1969. Toured with the **Flying Burrito Brothers** and **Gram Parsons** until 1973. Own band from 1975. Married to producer Brian Ahern from 1977-84. Married to British songwriter Paul Kennerley from 1985-93. AWARDS: C&W Hall of Fame: 2008 ★ CMA: Female Vocalist 1980 ★ Billboard Century: 1999 ★ OPRY: 1992		
3/15/75	45	15	●	1 Pieces Of The Sky		Reprise 2213
1/24/76	25	23	●	2 Elite Hotel *Grammy: Female Country Vocal*		Reprise 2236
1/22/77	21	21	●	3 Luxury Liner		Warner 3115
2/4/78	29	18	●	4 Quarter Moon In A Ten Cent Town		Warner 3141
12/2/78+	81	17	●	5 Profile: Best Of Emmylou Harris [G]		Warner 3258
5/5/79	43	22	●	6 Blue Kentucky Girl *Grammy: Female Country Vocal*		Warner 3318
5/24/80	26	34	●	7 Roses In The Snow		Warner 3422
11/29/80	102	9		8 Light Of The Stable: The Christmas Album [X]		Warner 3484
2/21/81	22	24	●	9 Evangeline		Warner 3508
12/12/81+	46	20		10 Cimarron		Warner 3603
11/13/82	65	17		11 Last Date [L]		Warner 23740
11/19/83+	116	13		12 White Shoes		Warner 23961
10/6/84	176	6		13 Profile II: The Best Of Emmylou Harris [G]		Warner 25161
5/25/85	171	4		14 The Ballad Of Sally Rose		Warner 25205
3/8/86	157	6		15 Thirteen		Warner 25352
3/28/87	6	48	▲	16 Trio **DOLLY PARTON, LINDA RONSTADT, EMMYLOU HARRIS** *Grammy: Group Country Vocal / Country Vocal Collaboration*		Warner 25491
8/1/87	166	4		17 Angel Band		Warner 25585
2/1/92	174	3		18 At The Ryman [L] **EMMYLOU HARRIS & THE NASH RAMBLERS** *Grammy: Group Country Vocal* recorded on 4/30/1991 in Nashville, Tennessee		Reprise 26664
10/16/93	152	5		19 Cowgirl's Prayer		Asylum 61541

Billboard			R I A A	ARTIST		
DEBUT	PEAK	WKS		Album Title	Catalog	Label & Number

HARRIS, Emmylou — cont'd

10/14/95	94	7		20 Wrecking Ball		Asylum 61854
				Grammy: Contemporary Folk Album		
8/29/98	180	2		21 Spyboy		Eminent 25001
2/27/99	62	14	●	22 Trio II		Asylum 62275
				EMMYLOU HARRIS, LINDA RONSTADT, DOLLY PARTON		
9/11/99	73	7		23 Western Wall: The Tucson Sessions		Asylum 62408
				LINDA RONSTADT & EMMYLOU HARRIS		
9/30/00	54	18		24 Red Dirt Girl		Nonesuch 79616
				Grammy: Contemporary Folk Album		
10/11/03	58	7		25 Stumble Into Grace		Nonesuch 79805
8/6/05	133	3		26 The Very Best Of Emmylou Harris: Heartaches & Highways .... [G]		Warner 73123
5/13/06	17	20		27 All The Roadrunning		Nonesuch 44154
				MARK KNOPFLER & EMMYLOU HARRIS		
6/28/08	22	10		28 All I Intended To Be..		Nonesuch 480444

HARRIS, Major
Born on 2/9/1947 in Richmond, Virginia. R&B singer. Member of **The Delfonics** from 1971-74.

| 3/29/75 | 28 | 22 | | 1 My Way .... | | Atlantic 18119 |
| 2/28/76 | 153 | 6 | | 2 Jealousy .... | | Atlantic 18160 |

HARRIS, Richard
Born on 10/1/1930 in Limerick, Ireland. Died of cancer on 10/25/2002 (age 72). Began prolific acting career in 1958. Portrayed "King Arthur" in the long-running stage production and movie version of *Camelot*.

5/18/68	4	42		1 A Tramp Shining		Dunhill/ABC 50032
11/16/68+	27	15		2 The Yard Went On Forever...................................		Dunhill/ABC 50042
12/18/71+	71	14		3 My Boy		Dunhill/ABC 50116
12/16/72+	181	6		4 Slides...		Dunhill/ABC 50133
5/12/73	203	5		5 His Greatest Performances .... [G]		Dunhill/ABC 50139
9/8/73	25	27		6 Jonathan Livingston Seagull .... [T]		Dunhill/ABC 50160
				Grammy: Spoken Word Album		
				narration from the book; music composed by Terry James		
12/28/74+	29	15		7 The Prophet By Kahlil Gibran .... [T]		Atlantic 18120
				Harris recites Gibran's classic work		

HARRIS, Rolf
Born on 3/30/1930 in Perth, Australia. White novelty singer. Played piano from age nine. Moved to England in the mid-1950s. Developed his unique "wobble board sound" out of a sheet of masonite. Own BBC-TV series from 1970.

| 8/3/63 | 29 | 9 | | 1 Tie Me Kangaroo Down, Sport & Sun Arise................. [N] | | Epic 26053 |

HARRIS, Sam
Born on 6/4/1961 in Cushing, Oklahoma. Pop singer/actor. Winner of TV's *Star Search* male vocalist category in 1984.

| 9/29/84 | 35 | 29 | ● | 1 Sam Harris .... | | Motown 6103 |
| 2/15/86 | 69 | 14 | | 2 Sam-I-Am .... | | Motown 6165 |

HARRISON, Don, Band
Rock band formed in California: Don Harrison (vocals), Russell DaShiell (guitar), Stu Cook (bass) and Doug Clifford (drums). Cook and Clifford were members of **Creedence Clearwater Revival**.

| 5/1/76 | 159 | 6 | | 1 The Don Harrison Band .... | | Atlantic 18171 |

HARRISON, George   **All-Time: #170**
Born on 2/24/1943 in Wavertree, Liverpool, England. Died of cancer on 11/29/2001 (age 58). Singer/songwriter/guitarist. Formed his first group, the Rebels, at age 13. Joined **John Lennon** and **Paul McCartney** in The Quarrymen in 1958; group later evolved into **The Beatles**, with Harrison as lead guitarist. Organized the Bangladesh benefit concerts at Madison Square Garden in 1971. Member of the 1988 supergroup **Traveling Wilburys**. Also see **Various Artists Compilations:** *Concert For George*.
AWARDS: R&R Hall of Fame: 2004 ★ Billboard Century: 1992

1/11/69	49	16		1 Wonderwall Music .... [I]		Apple 3350
				Indian-influenced instrumentals for the unreleased movie *Wonderwall*		
7/5/69	191	2		2 Electronic Sound .... [I]		Zapple 3358
				sounds made by a Moog synthesizer		
12/19/70+	❶⁷	38	▲⁶	3 All Things Must Pass	Cat:#3/19	Apple 639 [3]
				RS500 #437		
1/8/72	2⁶	41	●	4 The Concert For Bangla Desh	Cat:#8/1 [L]	Apple 3385 [3]
				Grammy: Album of the Year		
				recorded on 8/1/1971 at Madison Square Garden		
6/16/73	❶⁵	26	●	5 Living In The Material World	Cat:#36/1	Apple 3410
12/28/74+	4	17	●	6 Dark Horse		Apple 3418
10/11/75	8	11	●	7 Extra Texture (Read All About It)		Apple 3420
11/27/76	31	15	●	8 The Best Of George Harrison	Cat:#9/8 [G]	Capitol 11578
12/11/76+	11	21	●	9 Thirty-Three & 1/3...		Dark Horse 3005
3/17/79	14	18	●	10 George Harrison		Dark Horse 3255
6/20/81	11	13		11 Somewhere In England		Dark Horse 3492
11/27/82	108	7		12 Gone Troppo		Dark Horse 23734

Billboard			R I A A	ARTIST Album Title	Catalog	Label & Number
DEBUT	PEAK	WKS				

HARRISON, George — cont'd

DEBUT	PEAK	WKS				Label & Number
11/21/87+	8	31	▲	13 Cloud Nine		Dark Horse 25643
11/4/89	132	6		14 Best Of Dark Horse 1976-1989 .... [G]		Dark Horse 25726
8/1/92	126	2		15 Live In Japan .... [L]		Dark Horse 26964 [2]
12/7/02	18	9	●	16 Brainwashed		Dark Horse 41969
7/4/09	24	13		17 Let It Roll: Songs By George Harrison .... [G]		Dark Horse 65019

HARRISON, Jerry: Casual Gods
Born on 2/21/1949 in Milwaukee, Wisconsin. Rock keyboardist/producer. Member of **The Modern Lovers** and **Talking Heads**. The Casual Gods are 13 backing musicians.

2/6/88	78	20		1 Casual Gods		Sire 25663
6/9/90	188	3		2 Walk On Water		Sire 25943

HARRISON, Noel
Born on 1/29/1934 in London, England. Singer/actor. Son of actor Rex Harrison.

12/9/67+	135	9		1 Collage		Reprise 6263

HARRISON, Wes
Born on 1/31/1925 in Spartanburg, South Carolina. Sound effects comedian.

11/2/63	83	5		1 You Won't Believe Your Ears .... [C]		Philips 103

HARRISON, Wilbert
Born on 1/5/1929 in Charlotte, North Carolina. Died of a stroke on 10/26/1994 (age 65). R&B singer/songwriter.

1/24/70	190	2		1 Let's Work Together		Sue 8801

HARRY, Debbie
Born on 7/1/1945 in Miami, Florida; raised in Hawthorne, New Jersey. Singer/actress. Member of **The Wind In The Willows**. Lead singer of **Blondie**. Acted in several movies.

8/29/81	25	12	●	1 KooKoo		Chrysalis 1347
12/13/86+	97	13		2 Rockbird		Geffen 24123
10/14/89	123	8		3 Def, Dumb & Blonde		Sire 25938
				DEBORAH HARRY		

HART, Beth
Born on 1/24/1972 in Santa Monica, California. Blues-rock singer/songwriter.

1/29/00	143	6		1 Screamin' For My Supper		143 Records 83192

HART, Corey
Born on 5/31/1962 in Montreal, Quebec, Canada; raised in Malaga, Spain and Mexico City. Male singer/songwriter/keyboardist.

7/14/84	31	36	●	1 First Offense		EMI America 17117
7/20/85	20	37	●	2 Boy In The Box		EMI America 17161
10/18/86	55	27	●	3 Fields Of Fire		EMI America 17217
7/9/88	121	8		4 Young Man Running		EMI-Manhattan 48752
4/28/90	134	5		5 Bang!		EMI 92513

HART, Freddie
Born Fred Segrest on 12/21/1926 in Loachapoka, Alabama. Country singer/songwriter/guitarist.

10/9/71	37	20	●	1 Easy Loving		Capitol 838
3/18/72	89	11		2 My Hang-Up Is You		Capitol 11014
7/1/72	93	16		3 Bless Your Heart		Capitol 11073
9/22/73	188	6		4 Trip To Heaven		Capitol 11197

HART, Mickey
Born on 9/11/1943 in Long Island, New York. Rock drummer. Member of the **Grateful Dead**.

10/21/72	190	4		1 Rolling Thunder		Warner 2635

HARTFORD, John
Born on 12/30/1937 in Brooklyn, New York; raised in St. Louis, Missouri. Died of cancer on 6/4/2001 (age 63). Singer/songwriter/banjo player. Regular on **The Smothers Brothers** TV show.

6/14/69	137	9		1 John Hartford		RCA Victor 4156
11/27/71	193	4		2 Aereo-Plain		Warner 1916

HARTLEY, Keef, Band
Born on 3/8/1944 in Preston, Lancashire, England. Jazz-rock drummer. Member of **John Mayall**'s Bluesbreakers and **Vinegar Joe**.

11/28/70	191	3		1 The Time Is Near		Deram 18047
7/10/71	203	7		2 Overdog		Dream 18057

HARTMAN, Dan
Born on 12/8/1950 in Harrisburg, Pennsylvania. Died of a brain tumor on 3/22/1994 (age 43). Pop-disco singer/songwriter/producer/multi-instrumentalist. Member of the **Edgar Winter Group** from 1972-76.

12/16/78+	80	19		1 Instant Replay		Blue Sky 35641
3/15/80	189	2		2 Relight My Fire		Blue Sky 36302
11/3/84	55	28		3 I Can Dream About You		MCA 5525

HARVEY, PJ
Born Polly Jean Harvey on 10/9/1969 in Yeovil, England. Female singer/guitarist. Had own trio, also named PJ Harvey, which included bassist Stephen Vaughan and drummer Rob Ellis.

DEBUT	PEAK	WKS		Album Title	Catalog	Label & Number
5/22/93	158	1		1 Rid Of Me		Island 514696
				RS500 #405		
3/18/95	40	15		2 To Bring You My Love		Island 524085
				RS500 #435		
10/12/96	178	1		3 Dance Hall At Louse Point		Island 524278
				JOHN PARISH & POLLY JEAN HARVEY		
10/17/98	54	4		4 Is This Desire?		Island 524563
11/18/00	42	9		5 Stories From The City, Stories From The Sea		Island 548144
6/26/04	29	5		6 Uh Huh Her		Island 002751
10/20/07	65	3		7 White Chalk		Island 009972
4/18/09	80	3		8 A Woman A Man Walked By		Island 012811
				PJ HARVEY & JOHN PARISH		

HARVEY, Sensational Alex, Band
Born on 2/5/1935 in Glasgow, Scotland. Died of a heart attack on 2/4/1982 (one day before his 47th birthday). His band: Zal Cleminson (guitar), Hugh McKenna (keyboards), Chris Glen (bass) and Ted McKenna (drums).

DEBUT	PEAK	WKS		Album Title	Catalog	Label & Number
3/1/75	197	1		1 The Impossible Dream		Vertigo 2000
6/21/75	204	2		2 Tomorrow Belongs To Me		Vertigo 2004
11/1/75	100	4		3 "Live"	[L]	Atlantic 18148
				recorded on 5/24/1975 at the Hammersmith Odeon in London, England		

HARVEY DANGER
Rock band from Seattle, Washington: Sean Nelson (vocals), Jeff Lin (guitar), Aaron Huffman (bass) and Evan Sult (drums).

DEBUT	PEAK	WKS		Album Title	Catalog	Label & Number
6/20/98	70	20	●	1 Where Have All The Merrymakers Gone?		Slash 556000

HASLAM, Annie
Born on 6/8/1947 in Bolton, Lancashire, England. Lead singer of **Renaissance**.

DEBUT	PEAK	WKS		Album Title	Catalog	Label & Number
12/24/77+	167	13		1 Annie In Wonderland		Sire 6046

HASTE THE DAY
Christian punk-rock band from Carmel, Indiana: Jimmy Ryan (vocals), brothers Brennan Chaulk (guitar) and Devin Chaulk (drums), Jason Barnes (guitar) and Mike Murphy (bass). Stephen Keech replaced Ryan in early 2006.

DEBUT	PEAK	WKS		Album Title	Catalog	Label & Number
7/16/05	175	1		1 When Everything Falls		Solid State 60567
4/7/07	89	2		2 Pressure The Hinges		Solid State 71671
11/1/08	68	1		3 Dreamer		Solid State 15653

HATEBREED
Hard-rock band from New Haven, Connecticut: Jamey Jasta (vocals), Lou "Boulder" Richards (guitar), Sean Martin (guitar), Chris Beattie (bass) and Rigg Ross (drums).

DEBUT	PEAK	WKS		Album Title	Catalog	Label & Number
4/13/02	50	6		1 Perseverance		Universal 017105
11/15/03	30	3		2 The Rise Of Brutality		No Name 001442
9/16/06	31	4		3 Supremacy		Roadrunner 618054
5/23/09	58	2		4 For The Lions		E1 4557
10/17/09	37	5		5 Hatebreed	[L]	No Name 2053

HATFIELD, Juliana, Three
Born on 7/2/1967 in Wiscasset, Maine. Female rock singer/guitarist. Group also included bassist Dean Fisher and drummer Todd Philips.

DEBUT	PEAK	WKS		Album Title	Catalog	Label & Number
8/21/93	119	12		1 Become What You Are		Atlantic 92278
4/15/95	96	7		2 Only Everything		Mammoth 92540
				JULIANA HATFIELD		

HATHAWAY, Donny
Born on 10/1/1945 in Chicago, Illinois; raised in St. Louis, Missouri. Committed suicide by jumping from the 15th floor of New York City's Essex House hotel on 1/13/1979 (age 33). R&B singer/songwriter/keyboardist. Father of **Lalah Hathaway**.

DEBUT	PEAK	WKS		Album Title	Catalog	Label & Number
5/29/71	73	25		1 Everything Is Everything	[E]	Atco 332
				released in 1970		
5/15/71	89	21		2 Donny Hathaway		Atco 360
3/4/72	18	38	●	3 Donny Hathaway Live	[L]	Atco 386
				recorded at the Bitter End in New York City		
7/21/73	69	13		4 Extension Of A Man		Atco 7029
5/13/72	3²	39	●	5 Roberta Flack & Donny Hathaway		Atlantic 7216
9/20/80	201	4		6 In Performance	[L]	Atlantic 19278

HATHAWAY, Lalah
Born on 12/16/1968 in Chicago, Illinois. R&B singer. Daughter of **Donny Hathaway**.

DEBUT	PEAK	WKS		Album Title	Catalog	Label & Number
10/20/90	191	2		1 Lalah Hathaway		Virgin 91382
5/29/99	196	1		2 The Song Lives On		GRP 9956
				JOE SAMPLE Featuring Lalah Hathaway		
6/21/08	63	3		3 Self Portrait		Stax 30308

HAVANA 3 A.M.
Rock band formed in England: Nigel Dixon (vocals, guitar), **Gary Myrick** (guitar), Paul Simonon (bass) and Travis Williams (drums). Simonon was a member of **The Clash**.

DEBUT	PEAK	WKS		Album Title	Catalog	Label & Number
5/4/91	169	3		1 Havana 3 A.M.		I.R.S. 13069

Billboard			R I A A	ARTIST		
DEBUT	PEAK	WKS		Album Title	Catalog	Label & Number

HAVE HEART
Punk-rock band from New Bedford, Massachusetts: Patrick Flynn (vocals), Ryan Hudon (guitar), Kei Yasui (guitar), Ryan Biggs (bass) and Shawn Costa (drums).

7/26/08	193	1		1 Songs To Scream At The Sun		Bridge Nine 096

HAVENS, Richie
Born on 1/21/1941 in Brooklyn, New York. Black folk singer/guitarist.

11/30/68	192	3		1 Electric Havens [E]		Douglas 780
				released in 1966		
7/6/68	182	2		2 Mixed Bag [E]		Verve Forecast 3006
				released in 1967; also see #6 below		
2/24/68	184	7		3 Something Else Again		Verve Forecast 3034
1/11/69	80	11		4 Richard P. Havens, 1983		Verve Forecast 3047 [2]
1/10/70	155	14		5 Stonehenge		Stormy Forest 6001
11/7/70	190	2		6 Mixed Bag [R]		MGM 4698
1/9/71	29	34		7 Alarm Clock		Stormy Forest 6005
11/13/71	126	11		8 The Great Blind Degree		Stormy Forest 6010
9/23/72	55	18		9 Richie Havens On Stage [L]		Stormy Forest 6012 [2]
6/9/73	182	4		10 Portfolio		Stormy Forest 6013
10/12/74	186	3		11 Mixed Bag II		Stormy Forest 6201
10/2/76	157	4		12 The End Of The Beginning		A&M 4598
10/3/87	173	4		13 Simple Things		RBI 400

HAVOC
Born Kejuan Muchita on 5/21/1974 in Queens, New York. Male rapper. Member of **Mobb Deep**.

10/6/07	173	1		1 The Kush		Nature Sounds 133

HAWKINS, Dale
Born Delmar Hawkins on 8/22/1936 in Goldmine, Louisiana. Died of cancer on 2/13/2010 (age 73). Rockabilly singer/guitarist. First cousin to **Ronnie Hawkins**.

~ ~ ~ ~ ~ ~ ~ ~ ~ ~   *NON-CHARTED ALBUM*   ~ ~ ~ ~ ~ ~ ~ ~ ~ ~
1958 Oh! Suzy-Q

HAWKINS, Edwin, Singers
Born on 8/18/1943 in Oakland, California. Formed gospel group with Betty Watson in 1967 as the Northern California State Youth Choir. Member Dorothy Morrison went on to a solo career.

5/3/69	15	23		1 Let Us Go Into The House Of The Lord		Pavilion 10001
10/2/71	180	8		2 Children (Get Together)		Buddah 5086
5/27/72	171	4		3 I'd Like To Teach The World To Sing		Buddah 5101

HAWKINS, Ronnie
Born on 1/10/1935 in Huntsville, Arkansas. White rockabilly singer. Formed The Hawks in 1952. Moved to Canada in 1958. First cousin to **Dale Hawkins**. Assembled group later known as **The Band**.

~ ~ ~ ~ ~ ~ ~ ~ ~   *NON-CHARTED ALBUMS*   ~ ~ ~ ~ ~ ~ ~ ~ ~ ~
1959 Ronnie Hawkins   1960 Mr. Dynamo

HAWKINS, Screamin' Jay
Born Jalacy J. Hawkins on 7/18/1929 in Cleveland, Ohio. Died of an aneurysm on 2/12/2000 (age 70). R&B singer/songwriter/pianist. Former amatuer boxing champion. Known for his bizarre antics and props used in his stage shows.

~ ~ ~ ~ ~ ~ ~ ~ ~ ~   *NON-CHARTED ALBUMS*   ~ ~ ~ ~ ~ ~ ~ ~ ~ ~
1958 At Home With Screamin' Jay Hawkins   1958 I Put A Spell On You

HAWKINS, Sophie B.
Born Sophie Ballantine Hawkins on 11/1/1967 in Manhattan, New York. Female singer/songwriter.

5/16/92	51	24	●	1 Tongues And Tails		Columbia 46797
8/26/95	65	32	●	2 Whaler		Columbia 53300

HAWK NELSON
Christian rock band from Peterborough, Ontario, Canada: Jason Dunn (vocals, paino), Jonathan Steingard (guitar), Daniel Biro (bass) and Aaron "Skwid" Tosti (drums).

4/22/06	75	4		1 Smile, It's The End Of The World		Tooth & Nail 45613
4/19/08	34	3		2 Hawk Nelson...Is My Friend		BEC 15346
10/10/09	54	3		3 Live Life Loud!		BEC 67306

HAWKWIND
Space-rock band formed in London, England. Featured a fluctuating lineup with lead guitarist Dave Brock the only constant.

11/24/73	179	8		1 Space Ritual/Alive In Liverpool And London [L]		United Artists 120 [2]
10/5/74	110	12		2 Hall Of The Mountain Grill		United Artists 328
6/14/75	150	5		3 Warrior On The Edge Of Time		Atco 115
2/25/78	208	5		4 Quark Strangeness And Charm		Sire 6047

HAWTHORNE, Mayer
Born Andrew Mayer Cohen on 2/2/1979 in Ann Arbor, Michigan. Hip-hop singer/songwriter/rapper.

9/19/09	147	2		1 A Strange Arrangement		Stones Throw 2230

Billboard			R I A A	ARTIST		
DEBUT	PEAK	WKS		Album Title	Catalog	Label & Number

HAWTHORNE HEIGHTS
Alternative-rock band from Dayton, Ohio: JT Woodruff (vocals, guitar), Casey Calvert (guitar), Micah Carli (guitar), Matt Ridenour (bass) and Eron Bucciarelli (drums). Calvert died of a drug overdose on 11/24/2007 (age 26).

10/9/04+	56	67	●	1 The Silence In Black And White		Victory 220
3/18/06	3[1]	17		2 If Only You Were Lonely		Victory 265
8/23/08	23	5		3 Fragile Future		Victory 456

HAY, Colin James
Born on 6/29/1953 in Scotland; raised in Melbourne, Australia. Lead singer/guitarist of **Men At Work**.

2/21/87	126	9		1 Looking For Jack		Columbia 40611

HAYES, Bonnie, with The Wild Combo
Born in San Francisco, California. Female new wave singer/songwriter. The Wild Combo: Kevin Hayes, Hank Manniger and Paul Davis.

8/7/82	206	2		1 Good Clean Fun		Slash 112

HAYES, Darren
Born on 5/8/1972 in Brisbane, Queensland, Australia. One half of **Savage Garden** duo.

4/6/02	35	4		1 Spin		Columbia 86250

HAYES, Isaac
1970s: #23 / All-Time: #147
Born on 8/20/1942 in Covington, Tennessee. Died on 8/10/2008 (age 65). R&B singer/songwriter/keyboardist/actor. Session musician for the Stax label. Teamed with songwriter **David Porter** to write many classic songs. Acted in several movies. Voice of "Chef" on TV's *South Park*.
AWARD: R&R Hall of Fame: 2002

2/26/72	102	12		1 In The Beginning .... [E]		Atlantic 1599
				first released in 1968 as Presenting Isaac Hayes on Enterprise 100		
7/12/69	8	81	●	2 Hot Buttered Soul		Enterprise 1001
4/18/70	8	75		3 The Isaac Hayes Movement		Enterprise 1010
12/5/70	11	56		4 To Be Continued		Enterprise 1014
8/21/71	❶[1]	60	●	5 Shaft [I-S]		Enterprise 5002 [2]
				Grammy: Soundtrack Album		
12/11/71+	10	34		6 Black Moses [I]		Enterprise 5003 [2]
				Grammy: Pop Instrumental Album		
5/19/73	14	26	●	7 Live At The Sahara Tahoe [L]		Enterprise 5005 [2]
10/27/73	16	27	●	8 Joy		Enterprise 5007
6/15/74	146	8		9 Tough Guys [I-S]		Enterprise 7504
				music from the movie Three Tough Guys		
8/3/74	156	9		10 Truck Turner [I-S]		Enterprise 7507 [2]
8/23/75	165	4		11 The Best Of Isaac Hayes [G]		Enterprise 7510
6/21/75	18	19	●	12 Chocolate Chip		HBS 874
1/17/76	85	17		13 Disco Connection		HBS 923
2/21/76	45	12		14 Groove-A-Thon		HBS 925
7/24/76	124	7		15 Juicy Fruit (Disco Freak)		HBS 953
2/19/77	49	13		16 A Man And A Woman [L]		HBS 996 [2]
				ISAAC HAYES & DIONNE WARWICK		
12/17/77+	78	12		17 New Horizon		Polydor 6120
11/18/78+	75	18		18 For The Sake Of Love		Polydor 6164
9/29/79+	39	30	●	19 Don't Let Go		Polydor 6224
10/20/79	80	19		20 Royal Rappin's		Polydor 6229
				MILLIE JACKSON & ISAAC HAYES		
5/17/80	59	15		21 And Once Again		Polydor 6269
11/19/05	171	1		22 Ultimate Isaac Hayes: Can You Dig It? [G]		Stax 8043 [2]

HAYES, Wade
Born on 4/20/1969 in Bethel Acres, Oklahoma. Country singer/songwriter.

1/28/95	99	44	●	1 Old Enough To Know Better		Columbia 66412
7/13/96	91	10	●	2 On A Good Night		Columbia 67563
2/14/98	92	6		3 When The Wrong One Loves You Right		Columbia 68037

HAYNES, Warren
Born on 4/6/1960 in Asheville, North Carolina; later based in Macon, Georgia. Rock singer/songwriter/guitarist. Member of **The Allman Brothers Band** and **Gov't Mule**.

6/26/04	172	1		1 Live At Bonnaroo [L]		ATO 21521

HAYSTAK
Born Jason Winfree on 11/4/1974 in Nashville, Tennessee. White male rapper.

8/10/02	164	2		1 The Natural		In The Paint 8344
4/7/07	186	1		2 Crackavelli		Street Flavor 7920 [2]

Billboard			R I A A	ARTIST		
DEBUT	PEAK	WKS		Album Title	Catalog	Label & Number

HAYWARD, Justin
Born on 10/14/1946 in Swindon, Wiltshire, England. Lead singer/guitarist of **The Moody Blues**.

3/29/75	16	23		1 Blue Jays		Threshold 14
				JUSTIN HAYWARD & JOHN LODGE		
3/12/77	37	16		2 Songwriter		Deram 18073
8/9/80	166	5		3 Night Flight		Deram 4801

HAYWOOD, Leon
Born on 2/11/1942 in Houston, Texas. R&B singer/songwriter/keyboardist.

| 8/16/75 | 140 | 13 | | 1 Come And Get Yourself Some .... | | 20th Century 476 |
| 5/17/80 | 92 | 10 | | 2 Naturally .... | | 20th Century 613 |

HAZA, Ofra
Born on 11/19/1957 in Tel Aviv, Israel. Died of AIDS on 2/23/2000 (age 42). Female singer/songwriter/actress.

| 1/21/89 | 130 | 9 | | 1 Shaday .... | | Sire 25816 |
| 2/10/90 | 156 | 5 | | 2 Desert Wind .... | | Sire 25976 |

HAZARD, Robert
Born Robert Rimato on 8/21/1948 in Philadelphia, Pennsylvania. Died of cancer on 8/5/2008 (age 59). Rock singer/songwriter.
Wrote **Cyndi Lauper**'s "Girls Just Want To Have Fun."

| 3/26/83 | 102 | 11 | | 1 Robert Hazard .... [EP] | | RCA Victor 8500 |

HAZLEWOOD, Lee
Born Barton Lee Hazlewood on 7/9/1929 in Mannford, Oklahoma; raised in Texas. Died of kidney cancer on 8/4/2007 (age 78).
Male singer/songwriter/producer.

4/13/68	13	44	●	1 Nancy & Lee...		Reprise 6273
2/26/72	213	1		2 Nancy & Lee Again..		RCA Victor 4645
				NANCY SINATRA & LEE HAZLEWOOD (above 2)		

HEAD, Roy
Born on 9/1/1941 in Three Rivers, Texas. Rock-country singer/guitarist.

| 12/4/65+ | 122 | 8 | | 1 Treat Me Right .... | | Scepter 532 |

HEAD AUTOMATICA
Alternative-rock duo formed in New York: singer Daryl Palumbo (of **Glassjaw**) and producer/musician Dan Nakamura
(of **Gorillaz**, **Deltron 3030** and **Handsome Boy Modeling School**).

| 9/4/04 | 169 | 1 | | 1 Decadence .... | | Warner 48631 |
| 6/24/06 | 69 | 5 | | 2 Popaganda .... | | I Am 44237 |

HEADBOYS, The
Rock band from Edinburgh, Scotland: Lou Lewis (guitar), Calum Malcolm (keyboards), George Boyter (bass) and Davy Ross
(drums). All share vocals.

| 11/10/79 | 113 | 15 | | 1 The Headboys.. | | RSO 3068 |

HEAD EAST
Rock band from St. Louis, Missouri: John Schlitt (vocals), Michael Sommerville (guitar), Roger Boyd (keyboards), Dan Birney
(bass) and Steve Huston (drums). Schlitt, Sommerville and Birney were replaced by Dan Odum, Tony Gross and Mark Boatman
in early 1980.

8/30/75	126	17	●	1 Flat As A Pancake		A&M 4537
5/22/76	161	6		2 Get Yourself Up		A&M 4579
4/2/77	136	7		3 Gettin' Lucky..		A&M 4624
3/11/78	78	14		4 Head East		A&M 4680
2/3/79	65	14		5 Head East Live! .... [L]		A&M 6007 [2]
11/17/79	96	16		6 A Different Kind Of Crazy		A&M 4795
11/8/80	137	6		7 U.S. 1		A&M 4826

HEADHUNTERS
Backing band for **Herbie Hancock**: Blackbird McKnight (guitar), Bennie Maupin (sax), **Bill Summers** (percussion), Paul Jackson
(bass) and Mike Clark (drums).

| 4/19/75 | 126 | 10 | | 1 Survival Of The Fittest... [I] | | Arista 4038 |

HEADLEY, Heather
Born on 10/5/1974 in Barataria, Trinidad; raised in Fort Wayne, Indiana. R&B singer/actress. Starred in the Broadway musical *Aida*.

10/26/02	38	44	●	1 This Is Who I Am		RCA 69376
2/18/06	5	28	●	2 In My Mind		RCA 64492
1/31/09	27	10		3 Audience Of One		EMI Gospel 26512
				Grammy: Contemporary R&B Gospel Album		

HEADPINS
Rock group from Canada: Darby Mills (female vocals), Brian MacLeod (guitar), Ab Bryant (bass) and Bernie Aubin (drums).
MacLeod and Bryant were with **Chilliwack**. Bryant was also with **Prism**. MacLeod died of brain cancer on 4/25/1992 (age 41).

| 1/21/84 | 114 | 9 | | 1 Line Of Fire .... | | Solid Gold 9031 |

HEADS HANDS AND FEET
Rock band formed in England: Tony Colton (vocals), Albert Lee (guitar), Ray Smith (guitar), Chas Hodges (bass) and Pete Gavin
(drums). Smith died on 11/29/1979 (age 45).

| 5/19/73 | 221 | 3 | | 1 Old Soldiers Never Die .... | | Atco 7025 |

Billboard			R I A A	ARTIST		
DEBUT	PEAK	WKS		Album Title	Catalog	Label & Number

HEADSTONE
Rock band formed in England: Mark Ashton (vocals), Steve Bolton (guitar), Philip Chen (bass) and Chilli Charles (drums). Ashton was a member of **Rare Bird**.

| 10/12/74 | 201 | 5 | | 1 Bad Habits .... | | ABC/Dunhill 50174 |

HEALEY, Jeff, Band
Born Norman Jeffrey Healey on 3/25/1966 in Toronto, Ontario, Canada. Died of cancer on 3/2/2008 (age 41). Blues-rock singer/guitarist. Blind since age one. Formed own group with Joe Rockman (bass) and Tom Stephen (drums). Band appeared in the 1989 movie *Road House*.

10/8/88+	22	69	▲	1 See The Light..		Arista 8553
6/16/90	27	39	●	2 Hell To Pay		Arista 8632
11/28/92	174	2		3 Feel This		Arista 18706

HEAP, Imogen
Born on 12/9/1977 in Essex, England. Female singer/songwriter/pianist.

| 11/19/05+ | 145 | 9 | | 1 Speak For Yourself .... | | RCA Victor 72532 |
| 9/12/09 | 5 | 9 | | 2 Ellipse | | Megaphonic 50605 |

HEAR 'N AID
Collection of 40 hard-rock artists formed to raise money for famine relief efforts in Africa and around the world.

| 7/5/86 | 80 | 7 | | 1 Hear 'N Aid .... | | Mercury 826044 |

HEART   All-Time: #164
Rock band formed in Seattle, Washington: sisters **Ann Wilson** (vocals; born on 6/19/1950) and Nancy Wilson (guitar; born on 3/16/1954), brothers Roger Fisher (guitar; born on 2/14/1950) and Mike Fisher (guitar), Steve Fossen (bass; born on 11/15/1949) and Mike DeRosier (drums; born on 8/24/1951). The Fishers left in 1979. Howard Leese (guitar; born on 6/13/1951) joined in 1980. Fossen and DeRosier left by 1982, replaced by Mark Andes (of **Spirit**, **Jo Jo Gunne** and **Firefall**) and Denny Carmassi (of **Montrose** and **Gamma**). In 1990, former members Fossen, DeRosier and Roger Fisher joined **Alias**. Andes left by 1993. Carmassi left in 1994 to join **Whitesnake**. Nancy married movie director Cameron Crowe on 7/27/1986.

4/10/76	7	100	▲	1 Dreamboat Annie		Mushroom 5005
4/22/78	17	25	▲	2 Magazine...		Mushroom 5008
5/28/77	9	41	▲³	3 Little Queen	Cat:#18/59	Portrait 34799
10/7/78+	17	36	▲²	4 Dog & Butterfly..	Cat:#26/64	Portrait 35555
3/8/80	5	22	●	5 Bebe Le Strange		Epic 36371
12/6/80	13	25	▲²	6 Greatest Hits/Live .... [G-L]		Epic 36888 [2]
				6 of 18 tracks are live		
6/12/82	25	14		7 Private Audition...		Epic 38049
9/17/83	39	21		8 Passionworks		Epic 38800
7/13/85	❶¹	92	▲⁵	9 Heart		Capitol 12410
6/13/87	2³	50	▲³	10 Bad Animals		Capitol 12546
4/21/90	3⁴	49	▲²	11 Brigade		Capitol 91820
10/12/91	107	7		12 Rock The House Live! .... [L]		Capitol 95797
				recorded on 11/28/1990 in Worcester, Massachusetts		
12/4/93	48	17	●	13 Desire Walks On		Capitol 99627
9/16/95	87	6	●	14 The Road Home .... [L]		Capitol 30489
				recorded on 8/12/1994 at The Backstage in Seattle, Washington		
3/29/97	131	13		15 Greatest Hits .... [G]		Capitol 53376
7/10/04	94	4		16 Jupiters Darling		Sovereign Artists 1953
6/9/07	48ᶜ	1	●	17 The Essential Heart.. [G]		Legacy 61557 [2]

HEART AND SOUL ORCHESTRA, The
Disco studio group assembled by DJ/VJ Frankie Crocker.

| 9/11/76 | 210 | 1 | | 1 Frankie Crocker's Heart & Soul Orchestra Presents The Disco Suite | | |
| | | | | Symphony No. 1 .... [I] | | Casablanca 7031 [2] |

HEARTBEATS, The
R&B vocal group from Queens, New York: James "Shep" Sheppard, Wally Roker, Walter Crump, Robbie Adams and Vernon Walker. Group disbanded in 1960. Sheppard formed **Shep & The Limelites** in 1961; was murdered on 1/24/1970 (age 34).

~ ~ ~ ~ ~ ~ ~ ~ ~ ~ **NON-CHARTED ALBUM** ~ ~ ~ ~ ~ ~ ~ ~ ~ ~ ~

1960 **A Thousand Miles Away**

HEARTLAND
Country band from Huntsville, Alabama: Jason Albert (vocals), brothers Craig Anderson (guitar) and Todd Anderson (drums), Mike Myerson (guitar), Chuck Crawford (fiddle) and Keith West (bass).

| 10/28/06 | 11 | 11 | | 1 I Loved Her First... | | Lofton Creek 9006 |

HEARTLESS BASTARDS
Alternative-rock band from Cincinnati, Ohio: Erika Wennerstrom (vocals, guitar), Mark Nathan (guitar), Jesse Ebaugh (bass) and Dave Colvin (drums).

| 2/21/09 | 150 | 1 | | 1 The Mountain... | | Fat Possum 1125 |

Billboard			R I A A	ARTIST		
DEBUT	PEAK	WKS		Album Title	Catalog	Label & Number
				HEARTSFIELD		
				Rock band from Chicago, Illinois: J.C. Heartsfield (vocals), Fred Dobbs, Perry Cordell and Phil Lucafo (guitars), Greg Biela (bass) and Artie Baldacci (drums).		
8/10/74	202	8		1 The Wonder Of It All		Mercury 1003
8/16/75	159	7		2 Foolish Pleasures		Mercury 1034
				HEAT		
				Dance band led by saxophonist/keyboardist Tom Saviano and vocalist Jean Marie Arnold.		
5/10/80	208	1		1 Heat		MCA 3225
				HEAT, Reverend Horton — see REVEREND HORTON HEAT		
				HEATH, Brandon		
				Born Brandon Heath Knell in Nashville, Tennessee. Contemporary Christian singer/songwriter/guitarist.		
9/6/08	73	32		1 What If We		Reunion 10127
				HEATH, Ted, And His Music		
				Born Edward Heath on 3/30/1900 in London, England. Died on 11/18/1969 (age 69). Trombonist/bandleader.		
10/9/61	28	10		1 Big Band Percussion .... [I]		London Phase 4 44002
9/15/62	36	2		2 Big Band Bash .... [I]		London Phase 4 44017
				HEATH BROTHERS, The		
				Jazz duo: brothers Jimmy Heath (sax; born on 10/25/1926 in Philadelphia, Pennsylvania) and Percy Heath (bass; born on 4/30/1923 in Wilmington, North Carolina).		
5/17/80	207	1		1 Live At The Public Theater .... [I-L]		Columbia 36374
7/11/81	202	2		2 Expressions Of Life .... [I]		Columbia 37126
				HEATHERLY, Eric		
				Born on 2/21/1970 in Chattanooga, Tennessee. Country singer/songwriter/guitarist.		
5/6/00	157	15		1 Swimming In Champagne		Mercury 170124
				HEATHERTON, Joey		
				Born Johanna Heatherton on 9/14/1944 in Rockville Centre, Long Island, New York. Movie/TV actress.		
10/21/72	154	13		1 The Joey Heatherton Album		MGM 4858
				HEATWAVE		
				Multi-national, interracial group formed in Germany. Core members: brothers Johnnie Wilder and Keith Wilder (vocals), Eric Johns and William Jones (guitars), Rod Temperton and Calvin Duke (keyboards), Derek Bramblz (bass) and Ernest Berger (drums). Johnnie Wilder died on 5/13/2006 (age 56).		
8/6/77	11	45	▲	1 Too Hot To Handle		Epic 34761
4/22/78	10	26	▲	2 Central Heating		Epic 35260
5/12/79	38	14	●	3 Hot Property		Epic 35970
12/13/80+	71	10		4 Candles		Epic 36873
7/10/82	156	6		5 Current		Epic 38065
				HEAVEN & HELL		
				Heavy metal band formed in Los Angeles, California: Ronnie James **Dio** (vocals), Tony Iommi (guitar), Terry "Geezer" Butler (bass) and Vinny Appice (drums). This band recorded as **Black Sabbath** from 1980-82 and 1991-92. Dio died of stomach cancer on 5/16/2010 (age 67).		
9/15/07	99	1	●	1 Live From Radio City Music Hall .... [L]		Rhino 255484 [2]
5/16/09	8	6		2 The Devil You Know		Rhino 518862
				HEAVENS		
				Alternative-rock duo formed in Chicago, Illinois: Matt Skiba (of **Alkaline Trio**) and Josiah Steinbrick.		
9/30/06	146	1		1 Patent Pending		Epitaph 86828
				HEAVENS EDGE		
				Rock band from Philadelphia, Pennsylvania: Mark Evans (vocals), Reggie Wu (guitar), Steven Parry (guitar), G.G. Guidotti (bass) and David Rath (drums).		
6/23/90	141	12		1 Heavens Edge		Columbia 45262
				HEAVEN 17		
				Electro-pop trio from England: Glenn Gregory (vocals), Martyn Ware and Ian Craig Marsh (synthesizers). Ware and Marsh were founding members of **Human League**.		
2/12/83	68	28		1 Heaven 17		Arista 6606
6/4/83	72	13		2 The Luxury Gap		Arista 8020
4/4/87	177	3		3 Pleasure One		Virgin 90569
				HEAVY D & THE BOYZ		
				Born Dwight Meyers on 5/24/1967 in Jamaica; raised in Mt. Vernon, New York. Male rapper/actor. Former president of Uptown Records. Played "Peaches" in the 1999 movie *The Cider House Rules*. The Boyz consisted of Glen Parrish, Troy Dixon and Edward Ferrell. Dixon died on 7/15/1990 (age 22) from an accidental fall in Indianapolis, Indiana.		
11/14/87	92	16		1 Living Large		MCA 5986
7/1/89	19	51	▲	2 Big Tyme		Uptown 42302
7/20/91	21	41	▲	3 Peaceful Journey		Uptown 10289
1/30/93	40	18	●	4 Blue Funk		Uptown 10734
6/11/94	11	25	▲	5 Nuttin' But Love		Uptown 10998

Billboard			R I A A	ARTIST Album Title	Catalog	Label & Number
DEBUT	PEAK	WKS				

HEAVY D:

| 5/10/97 | 9 | 22 | ● | 6 Waterbed Hev | | Uptown 53033 |
| 7/3/99 | 60 | 6 | | 7 Heavy .... | | Uptown 53260 |

HEAVY PETTIN
Heavy metal band from England: Steve "Hamie" Hayman (vocals), Gordon Bonnar (guitar), Punky Mendoza (guitar), Brian Waugh (bass) and Gary Moat (drums).

| 8/10/85 | 209 | 1 | | 1 Rock Ain't Dead .... | | Polydor 825897 |

HEBB, Bobby
Born on 7/26/1938 in Nashville, Tennessee. R&B singer/songwriter.

| 9/10/66 | 103 | 12 | | 1 Sunny .... | | Philips 212 |

HECTOR EL FATHER
Born on 9/4/1978 in Carolina, Puerto Rico. Latin reggae rapper.

| 12/9/06 | 81 | 1 | ▲ | 1 The Bad Boy .... [F] | | VI 008043 |
| 11/8/08 | 113 | 2 | | 2 Julicio Final .... [F] | | VI 011959 |

HEDBERG, Mitch
Born on 2/24/1968 in St. Paul, Minnesota. Died of a drug overdose on 3/29/2005 (age 37). Stand-up comedian.

| 9/27/08 | 18 | 7 | | 1 Do You Believe In Gosh? .... [C] | | Comedy Central 0063 |

HEDGE & DONNA
Interracial husband-and-wife vocal duo from San Francisco, California: Hedge Capers and Donna Carson.

| 8/7/71 | 212 | 2 | | 1 Evolution .... | | Polydor 4063 |

(HED)PLANET EARTH
Rap-rock band from Huntington Beach, California: Paolo "Jahred Shane" Gomes (vocals), Doug "DJ Product" Boyce (DJ), Wes "Wesstyle" Geer (guitar), Chad "Chizad" Benekos (guitar), Mark "Mawk" Young (bass) and Ben "B.C." Vaught (drums).

9/9/00	63	8		1 Broke		Volcano 41710
4/5/03	33	6		2 Blackout		Volcano 41817
3/12/05	186	1		3 Only In Amerika		Koch 9632
6/24/06	154	1		4 Back 2 Base X		Suburban Noize 58
8/4/07	138	1		5 Insomnia		Suburban Noize 78
1/31/09	72	2		6 New World Orphans		Suburban Noize 100

HEFTI, Neal
Born on 10/29/1922 in Hastings, Nebraska. Died of a heart attack on 10/11/2008 (age 85). Conductor/trumpeter.

| 2/5/55 | 8 | 1 | | 1 Music Of Rudolf Friml [I]
NEAL HEFTI AND HIS ORCHESTRA
10" album | | RCA Victor 3021 |
| 3/12/66 | 41 | 21 | | 2 Batman Theme .... [I] | | RCA Victor 3573 |

HEIGHTS, The
Band made up of cast members from the Fox-TV network prime time TV show of the same name. Show was based on fictional adventures featuring the band. Led by actors/vocalists Shawn Thompson and **Jamie Walters**.

| 11/7/92 | 40 | 15 | ● | 1 The Heights .... [TV] | | Capitol 80328 |

HEINDORF, Ray, & Matty Matlock
Ray Heindorf was born on 8/25/1908 in Haverstraw, New York. Died on 2/3/1980 (age 71). Longtime musical director for the Warner Brothers Orchestra. Julian "Matty" Matlock was born on 4/27/1909 in Paducah, Kentucky. Died on 6/14/1978 (age 69). Clarinet player with numerous TV and radio appearances.

| 9/3/55 | 9 | 4 | | 1 Pete Kelly's Blues [I]
LP: Columbia CL-690 (#9); EP: Columbia B-2103 (#9); songs from the movie; also see vocal recording by **Peggy Lee** and **Ella Fitzgerald**, and narrated recording by **Jack Webb** | | Columbia 690 |

HEINTJE
Born Hendrik Simons on 8/12/1955 in Heerlen, Netherlands. Popular male teen idol in Germany.

| 12/5/70+ | 108 | 11 | | 1 Mama .... | | MGM 4739 |

HE IS LEGEND
Hard-rock band from Wilmington, North Carolina: Schuylar Croom (vocals), Adam Tanbouz (guitar), Mitch Marlow (guitar), Matt Williams (bass) and Steven Bache (drums).

| 10/21/06 | 158 | 1 | | 1 Suck Out The Poison .... | | Solid State 46616 |
| 8/8/09 | 126 | 1 | | 2 It Hates You .... | | Tragic Hero 052 |

HELFGOTT, David
Born on 5/19/1947 in Melbourne, Australia. Classical pianist. The 1996 movie *Shine* was based on his life.

| 2/15/97 | 103 | 8 | | 1 David Helfgott Plays Rachmaninov .... [I] | | RCA Victor 40378 |

HELIX
Hard-rock band from Waterloo, Ontario, Canada: Brian Vollmer (vocals), Brent Doerner (guitar), Paul Hackman (guitar), Mike Uzelac (bass; replaced by Daryl Gray in 1984) and Greg Hinz (drums). Doerner left in mid-1990. Hackman was killed in a bus crash on 7/5/1992 (age 39).

10/22/83	186	4		1 No Rest For The Wicked		Capitol 12281
8/18/84	69	16		2 Walkin' The Razor's Edge		Capitol 12362
6/29/85	103	17		3 Long Way To Heaven		Capitol 12411
11/7/87	179	2		4 Wild In The Streets		Capitol 46920
8/18/90	179	6		5 Back For Another Taste		Grudge 4521

HELL, Richard, & The Voidoids
Born Lester Meyers on 10/2/1949 in Lexington, Kentucky. Punk-rock singer/bassist. Formerly married to **Patty Smyth**. The Voidoids consisted of guitarists Robert Quine and Ivan Julian with drummer Marc Bell.

12/3/77	208	3	1 Blank Generation		Sire 6037

HELLOGOODBYE
Pop-rock band from Huntington Beach, California: Forrest Kline (vocals, guitar), Jesse Kurvink (keyboards), Marcus Cole (bass) and Chris Profeta (drums).

8/26/06	13	36	1 Zombies! Aliens! Vampires! Dinosaurs!		Drive-Thru 83645

HELLO PEOPLE
White-faced, mime-rock band formed in New York: Bobby Sedita (guitar), Larry Tassi (keyboards), Greg Geddes (bass) and N.D. Smart (drums). All shared vocals.

11/30/74	145	13	1 The Handsome Devils..		Dunhill/ABC 50184
			produced by **Todd Rundgren**		

HELLOWEEN
Hard-rock band from Hamburg, Germany: Michael Kiske (vocals), Kai Hansen and Michael Weikath (guitars), Markus Grosskopf (bass) and Ingo Schwichtenberg (drums). Schwichtenberg committed suicide on 3/8/1995 (age 29).

7/4/87	104	21	1 Keeper Of The Seven Keys - Part I		RCA Victor 6399
10/29/88	108	16	2 Keeper Of The Seven Keys - Part II		RCA 8529
4/22/89	123	7	3 I Want Out - Live .... [L]		RCA 9709

HELL RELL
Born Durrell Mohammad in Harlem, New York. Male rapper.

10/13/07	55	2	1 For The Hell Of It		Diplomatic Man 5952
8/9/08	131	1	2 Black Mask Black Gloves		Babygrande 0357

HELLYEAH
All-star rock band: Chad Gray (vocals), Greg Tribbett (guitar), Tom Maxwell (guitar), Bob "Zilla" Kakaha (bass) and Vinnie Paul Abbott (drums). Gray and Tribbett were with **Mudvayne**. Maxwell was with **Nothingface**. Kakaha and Abbott were with **Damageplan**. Abbott was also with **Pantera**.

4/28/07	9	36	1 HellYeah		Epic 07408

HELM, Levon
Born on 5/26/1942 in Marvell, Arkansas. Singer/drummer/actor. Member of **The Band**. Portrayed **Loretta Lynn**'s father in the 1980 movie *Coal Miner's Daughter*. The RCO All-Stars: **Booker T.**, **Paul Butterfield**, **Steve Cropper**, **Dr. John** and Donald "Duck" Dunn.

11/19/77	142	10	1 Levon Helm & The RCO All-Stars		ABC 1017
10/7/78	206	2	2 Levon Helm		ABC 1089
11/17/07	102	5	3 Dirt Farmer		Dirt Farmer 79844
			Grammy: Traditional Folk Album		
7/18/09	36	9	4 Electric Dirt		Dirt Farmer 79861
			Grammy: Americana Album		

HELMET
Rock band from New York: Page Hamilton (vocals, guitar), Peter Mengede (guitar), Henry Bogdan (bass) and John Stanier (drums). Rob Echeverria replaced Mengede in 1993. Chris Traynor replaced Echeverria in 1996. Traynor later recorded with **Institute**.

8/22/92	68	29	● 1 Meantime..		Interscope 92162
7/9/94	45	12	2 Betty		Interscope 92404
4/5/97	47	5	3 Aftertaste		Interscope 90073
10/23/04	121	1	4 Size Matters		Interscope 002968
8/5/06	159	1	5 Monochrome..		Warcon 11

HELMS, Bobby
Born on 8/15/1935 in Bloomington, Indiana. Died of emphysema on 6/19/1997 (age 61). Country singer/guitarist.

~ ~ ~ ~ ~ ~ ~ ~ ~ ~ *NON-CHARTED ALBUM* ~ ~ ~ ~ ~ ~ ~ ~ ~ ~ ~
1957 **Bobby Helms Sings To My Special Angel**

HELTAH SKELTAH
Male rap duo from Brooklyn, New York: **Sean Price** ("Ruck") and Jahmal Bush ("Rock"). Members of **Boot Camp Clik**.

7/6/96	35	11	1 Nocturnal		Duck Down 50532
10/31/98	34	4	2 Magnum Force..		Duck Down 53543
10/18/08	122	1	3 D.I.R.T. (Da Incredible Rap Team)..		Boot Camp 2080

HENDERSON, Eddie
Born on 10/26/1940 in Harlem, New York. Jazz trumpeter/flugelhorn player.

10/15/77	207	5	1 Comin' Through .... [I]		Capitol 11671

HENDERSON, Finis
Born in Chicago, Illinois. White male singer. Former member of Weapons Of Peace. Pronounced: FINE-us.

8/6/83	208	1	1 Finis..		Motown 6036

HENDERSON, Joe
Born in 1937 in Como, Mississippi; raised in Gary, Indiana. Died of a heart attack on 11/7/1964 (age 27). R&B singer.

10/13/62	93	5	1 Snap Your Fingers		Todd 2701

HENDERSON, Luther — see BROADWAY SYMPHONY ORCHESTRA

Billboard			R I A A	ARTIST		
DEBUT	PEAK	WKS		Album Title	Catalog	Label & Number

HENDERSON, Michael
Born on 7/7/1951 in Yazoo City, Mississippi; raised in Detroit, Michigan. R&B singer/bassist. Featured vocalist with **Norman Connors**.

12/4/76+	173	7		1 Solid		Buddah 5662
8/27/77	49	13		2 Goin' Places		Buddah 5693
7/8/78	38	28	●	3 In The Night-Time		Buddah 5712
8/4/79	64	12		4 Do It All...		Buddah 5719
8/30/80	35	18		5 Wide Receiver		Buddah 6001
9/19/81	86	11		6 Slingshot		Buddah 6002
6/4/83	169	5		7 Fickle		Buddah 6004

HENDERSON, Skitch
Born Lyle Henderson on 1/27/1918 in Halstad, Minnesota. Died on 11/1/2005 (age 87). Conductor for TV's *The Tonight Show* from 1962-66.

10/9/65	103	8		1 Skitch...Tonight! .... [I]		Columbia 9167

HENDERSON, Wayne
Born on 9/24/1939 in Houston, Texas. R&B trombone player. Former member of **The Crusaders**.

7/5/80	205	2		1 Prime Time		Polydor 6276
				ROY AYERS & WAYNE HENDERSON		

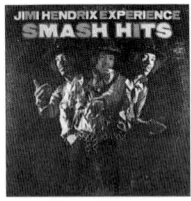

HENDRIX, Jimi   1990s: #16 / All-Time: #40
Born on 11/27/1942 in Seattle, Washington. Died of asphyxiation on 9/18/1970 (age 27). Legendary psychedelic-blues guitarist. Began career as a studio guitarist. Created The Jimi Hendrix Experience with Noel Redding (bass; died on 5/12/2003, age 57) and Mitch Mitchell (drums; died on 11/12/2008, age 61). Formed new group in 1969, Band of Gypsys, with **Buddy Miles** (drums) and Billy Cox (bass). Also see **Various Artists Compilations:** *Stone Free: A Tribute To Jimi Hendrix*.

AWARDS: R&R Hall of Fame: 1992 ★ Grammy: Lifetime Achievement 1992

8/26/67+	5	109	▲⁴	1 **Are You Experienced?**	Cat:#11/6	Reprise 6261
				Grammy: Hall of Fame ★ RS500 #15 ★ NRR		
2/10/68	3³	55	▲	2 **Axis: Bold As Love**	Cat:#11/22	Reprise 6281
				Grammy: Hall of Fame ★ RS500 #82		
10/19/68	❶²	39	▲²	3 **Electric Ladyland**	Cat:#18/2	Reprise 6307 [2]
				THE JIMI HENDRIX EXPERIENCE (above 3)		
				Grammy: Hall of Fame ★ RS500 #54		
3/6/71	3²	39	▲	4 The Cry Of Love		Reprise 2034
10/9/71	15	21	●	5 Rainbow Bridge .... [S]		Reprise 2040
				EARLY ALBUMS:		
12/30/67+	75	12		6 Get That Feeling		Capitol 2856
3/13/71	202	5		7 In The Beginning...		T-Neck 3007
				THE ISLEY BROTHERS & JIMI HENDRIX		
				recorded in 1964; all songs feature then-session guitarist Jimi Hendrix		
3/20/71	127	4		8 Two Great Experiences Together! .... [I]		Maple 6004
				JIMI HENDRIX & LONNIE YOUNGBLOOD		
				recorded in 1965		
9/2/72	82	11		9 Rare Hendrix		Trip 9500
				recorded on 6/10/1966 with Lonnie Youngblood		
				GREATEST HITS & COMPILATIONS:		
8/2/69	6	35	▲²	10 Smash Hits	Cat:#2¹/85	Reprise 2025
				THE JIMI HENDRIX EXPERIENCE		
12/9/72+	48	18		11 War Heroes		Reprise 2103
3/22/75	5	20	●	12 Crash Landing		Reprise 2204
11/29/75	43	11		13 Midnight Lightning		Reprise 2229
8/12/78	114	15		14 The Essential Jimi Hendrix		Reprise 2245 [2]
8/18/79	156	7		15 The Essential Jimi Hendrix, Volume Two		Reprise 2293
4/26/80	127	7		16 Nine To The Universe .... [I]		Reprise 2299
11/17/84	148	5		17 Kiss The Sky		Reprise 25119
12/3/88+	119	17		18 Radio One		Rykodisc 0078 [2]
				THE JIMI HENDRIX EXPERIENCE		
				3-sided album compiled from 5 sessions broadcast on BBC Radio in 1967		
1/5/91	174	5		19 Lifelines/The Jimi Hendrix Story		Reprise 26435 [4]
5/15/93	72	77	▲³	20 The Ultimate Experience	Cat:#4/170	MCA 10829
5/14/94	45	18	▲	21 Blues		MCA 11060
4/29/95	66	7		22 Voodoo Soup		MCA 11236
5/10/97	49	13		23 First Rays Of The New Rising Sun..................................	Cat:#38/1	Exp. Hendrix 11599
10/25/97	51	6		24 South Saturn Delta		Exp. Hendrix 11684
11/21/98+	133	40	▲²	25 Experience Hendrix: The Best Of Jimi Hendrix	Cat:#8/268	Exp. Hendrix 11671
9/30/00	78	3	▲	26 The Jimi Hendrix Experience		Exp. Hendrix 112316 [4]
5/26/01	112	4	●	27 Voodoo Child: The Jimi Hendrix Collection		Exp. Hendrix 112603 [2]
				disc 1: studio recordings; disc 2: live recordings		

HENDRIX, Jimi — cont'd

LIVE ALBUMS:

DEBUT	PEAK	WKS	RIAA	#	Album Title	Catalog	Label & Number
5/2/70	5	61	▲²	28	Band Of Gypsys	Cat:#13/5	Capitol 472
					recorded on 12/31/1969 at the Fillmore East in New York City		
9/19/70	16	20	●	29	Monterey International Pop Festival .... [S]		Reprise 2029
					OTIS REDDING & THE JIMI HENDRIX EXPERIENCE		
					recorded June 1967 and featured in the movie Monterey Pop; side 1: songs performed by The Jimi Hendrix Experience; side 2: songs performed by Otis Redding		
3/4/72	12	19	●	30	Hendrix In The West...		Reprise 2049
7/14/73	89	18		31	Sound Track Recordings From The Film Jimi Hendrix .... [S]		Reprise 6481 [2]
9/25/82	79	8		32	The Jimi Hendrix Concerts...		Reprise 22306 [2]
3/8/86	192	3		33	Jimi Plays Monterey .... [S]		Reprise 25358
					recorded on 6/18/1967		
8/20/94	37	8		34	Jimi Hendrix: Woodstock		MCA 11063
					recorded on 8/18/1969; also see #34 below		
6/20/98	50	9	●	35	BBC Sessions .... [E]		Exp. Hendrix 11742 [2]
					THE JIMI HENDRIX EXPERIENCE		
3/13/99	65	4		36	Live At The Fillmore East		Exp. Hendrix 11931 [2]
					recorded on 12/31/1969		
7/24/99	90	3	●	37	Live At Woodstock..		Exp. Hendrix 11987 [2]
					recorded on 8/18/1969		
11/30/02	200	1		38	Blue Wild Angel: Jimi Hendrix Live At The Isle Of Wight................		Exp. Hendrix 113086 [2]
					recorded on 8/30/1970		
10/4/03	191	1		39	Live At Berkeley		Exp. Hendrix 001102
					THE JIMI HENDRIX EXPERIENCE		
					recorded on 5/3/1970 at the Berkeley Communtity Theatre		
11/3/07	171	1		40	Live At Monterey		Exp. Hendrix 009843

HENDRYX, Nona
Born on 10/9/1944 in Trenton, New Jersey. R&B singer. Member of **Patti LaBelle** & The Blue-Belles from 1961-77.

DEBUT	PEAK	WKS	RIAA	#	Album Title	Catalog	Label & Number
4/23/83	83	19		1	Nona		RCA Victor 4565
5/5/84	167	7		2	The Art Of Defense..		RCA Victor 4999
5/23/87	96	13		3	Female Trouble...		EMI America 17248

HENLEY, Don
Born on 7/22/1947 in Gilmer, Texas. Rock singer/songwriter/drummer. Member of the **Eagles**. Married model Sharon Summerall on 5/20/1995.

DEBUT	PEAK	WKS	RIAA	#	Album Title	Catalog	Label & Number
9/4/82	24	35	●	1	I Can't Stand Still...		Asylum 60048
12/15/84+	13	63	▲³	2	Building The Perfect Beast		Geffen 24026
7/15/89	8	148	▲⁶	3	The End Of The Innocence	Cat:#36/2	Geffen 24217
					Grammy: Male Rock Vocal ★ RS500 #389		
12/9/95	48	26	▲	4	Actual Miles - Henley's Greatest Hits .... [G]		Geffen 24834
6/10/00	7	32	▲	5	Inside Job		Warner 47083

HENRY, Clarence "Frogman"
Born on 3/19/1937 in Algiers, Louisiana. R&B singer/pianist/songwriter. Nicknamed "Frog Man" because of his frog sounds in his 1957 hit "Ain't Got No Home."

~ ~ ~ ~ ~ ~ ~ ~ ~ **NON-CHARTED ALBUM** ~ ~ ~ ~ ~ ~ ~ ~ ~ ~ ~
1961 You Always Hurt The One You Love

HENSEL, Carol
Born in New York. Fitness instructor.

DEBUT	PEAK	WKS	RIAA	#	Album Title	Catalog	Label & Number
3/21/81	56	55		1	Carol Hensel's Exercise & Dance Program		Vintage 7713
12/19/81+	70	28		2	Carol Hensel's Exercise & Dance Program, Volume 2		Vintage 7733
1/22/83	104	12		3	Carol Hensel's Exercise & Dance Program, Volume 3		Vintage 30004

HENSLEY, Ken
Born on 8/24/1945 in London, England. Rock keyboardist. Member of **Uriah Heep**.

DEBUT	PEAK	WKS	RIAA	#	Album Title	Catalog	Label & Number
4/7/73	173	7		1	Proud Words On A Dusty Shelf		Mercury 661

HEPTONES, The
Reggae vocal trio from Kingston, Jamaica: Barry Llewellyn, Earl Morgan and Leroy Sibbles.

DEBUT	PEAK	WKS	RIAA	#	Album Title	Catalog	Label & Number
8/21/76	207	1		1	Night Food		Island 9381

HERCULES AND LOVE AFFAIR
Dance duo from New York: Kim Foxman (vocals) and Andy Butler (instruments).

DEBUT	PEAK	WKS	RIAA	#	Album Title	Catalog	Label & Number
7/12/08	191	1		1	Hercules And Love Affair		Dia 9392

HERMAN, Woody
Born on 5/16/1913 in Milwaukee, Wisconsin. Died of heart failure on 10/29/1987 (age 74). Legendary saxophonist/clarinetist/bandleader.

AWARD: Grammy: Lifetime Achievement 1987

DEBUT	PEAK	WKS	RIAA	#	Album Title	Catalog	Label & Number
2/19/55	11	1		1	The 3 Herds .... [I-K]		Columbia 592
					recordings from 1945-54		
8/17/63	136	4		2	Encore: Woody Herman - 1963 .... [I-L]		Philips 092
					Grammy: Jazz Album		
					recorded at the Basin Street in Hollywood, California		
3/21/64	148	2		3	Woody Herman: 1964 .... [I]		Philips 118

Billboard			R I A A	ARTIST Album Title	Catalog	Label & Number
DEBUT	PEAK	WKS				

HERMAN'S HERMITS
All-Time: #383

Teen pop-rock band from Manchester, England: Peter "Herman" Noone (vocals; born on 11/5/1947), Derek Leckenby (guitar; born on 5/14/1943; died of cancer on 6/4/1994, age 51), Keith Hopwood (guitar; born on 10/26/1946), Karl Green (bass; born on 7/31/1947) and Barry Whitwam (drums; born on 7/21/1946). Group name derived from cartoon character "Sherman" of TV's *The Bullwinkle Show*. Noone later formed **The Tremblers**.

DEBUT	PEAK	WKS				Label & Number
2/20/65	2⁴	40	●	1 Introducing Herman's Hermits		MGM 4282
6/19/65	2⁶	39	●	2 Herman's Hermits On Tour		MGM 4295
3/26/66	14	26		3 Hold On!	[S]	MGM 4342
8/20/66	48	21		4 Both Sides Of Herman's Hermits		MGM 4386
3/18/67	13	35	●	5 There's A Kind Of Hush All Over The World		MGM 4438
10/7/67	75	9		6 Blaze		MGM 4478
9/28/68	182	3		7 Mrs. Brown, You've Got A Lovely Daughter	[S]	MGM 4548

GREATEST HITS & COMPILATIONS:

11/20/65	5	105	●	8 The Best Of Herman's Hermits		MGM 4315
12/3/66+	20	32	●	9 The Best Of Herman's Hermits, Volume 2		MGM 4416
1/13/68	102	8		10 The Best Of Herman's Hermits, Volume III		MGM 4505
8/11/73	202	5		11 Herman's Hermits XX (Their Greatest Hits)		Abkco 4227 [2]

HERNANDEZ, Larry
Born in San Antonio, Texas. Latin singer.

9/5/09	179	1		1 16 Narco Corridos	[F]	Mendieta 570037

HERNANDEZ, Marcos
Born in 1982 in Phoenix, Arizona; raised in Dallas, Texas. Latin singer.

11/12/05	158	1		1 C About Me		Ultrax 6120

HERNANDEZ, Patrick
Born on 4/6/1949 in Paris, France. Disco singer.

7/28/79	61	15		1 Born To Be Alive		Columbia 36100

HERNDON, Ty
Born Boyd Tyrone Herndon on 5/2/1962 in Meridian, Mississippi; raised in Butler, Alabama. Country singer/songwriter/guitarist.

5/6/95	68	13	●	1 What Mattered Most		Epic 66397
8/31/96	65	10	●	2 Living In A Moment		Epic 67564
6/13/98	140	3		3 Big Hopes		Epic 68167
11/20/99	124	2		4 Steam		Epic 69899

HERON, Mike
Born James Michael Heron on 12/12/1942 in Glasgow, Scotland. Singer/songwriter/multi-instrumentalist. Leader of the **Incredible String Band**.

6/26/71	218	2		1 Smiling Men With Bad Reputations		Elektra 74093

HERSH, Kristin
Born on 8/7/1966 in Atlanta, Georgia. Singer/guitarist. Member of **Throwing Muses**. Stepsister of Tanya Donnelly (of **Belly**).

2/19/94	197	1		1 Hips And Makers		Sire 45413

HESITATIONS, The
R&B vocal group from Cleveland, Ohio: brothers George "King" Scott and Charles Scott, Fred Deal, Robert Sheppard, Arthur Blakely, Phillip Dorroh and Leonard Veal. George Scott was accidentally shot to death in February 1968 (age 38).

2/24/68	193	3		1 The New Born Free		Kapp 3548

HEWETT, Howard
Born on 10/1/1957 in Akron, Ohio. R&B singer. Member of **Shalamar** (1979-85). Married to **Nia Peeples** from 1989-93.

11/1/86+	159	16		1 I Commit To Love		Elektra 60487
4/16/88	110	12		2 Forever and Ever		Elektra 60779
4/14/90	54	21		3 Howard Hewett		Elektra 60904
2/25/95	181	2		4 It's Time		Caliber 1008

HEWITT, Jennifer Love
Born on 2/21/1979 in Waco, Texas. Pop singer/actress. Starred in several movies and TV shows.

10/26/02	37	3		1 BareNaked		Jive 41821

HEYWARD, Nick
Born on 5/20/1961 in Beckenham, Kent, England. Pop-rock singer/guitarist. Member of **Haircut One Hundred** (1981-83).

1/14/84	178	4		1 North of a Miracle		Arista 8106

HEYWOOD, Eddie
Born on 12/4/1915 in Atlanta, Georgia. Died on 1/2/1989 (age 73). Jazz pianist.

5/25/59	16	4		1 Canadian Sunset	[I]	RCA Victor 1529

HIATT, John
Born on 8/20/1952 in Indianapolis, Indiana. Eclectic-rock singer/songwriter/guitarist. Member of **Little Village**.

7/7/79	202	4		1 Slug Line		MCA 3088
5/8/82	203	4		2 All Of A Sudden		Geffen 2009
2/16/85	210	1		3 Warming Up To The Ice Age		Geffen 24055
7/4/87	107	17		4 Bring The Family		A&M 5158
9/24/88	98	31		5 Slow Turning		A&M 5206

Billboard			R I A A	ARTIST		
DEBUT	PEAK	WKS		Album Title	Catalog	Label & Number
				HIATT, John — cont'd		
7/7/90	61	19		6 Stolen Moments		A&M 5310
9/25/93	47	11		7 Perfectly Good Guitar		A&M 540135
11/11/95	48	9		8 Walk On...		Capitol 33416
7/19/97	111	4		9 Little Head		Capitol 54672
10/14/00	110	4		10 Crossing Muddy Waters		Vanguard 79576
9/29/01	89	5		11 The Tiki Bar Is Open		Vanguard 79593
5/24/03	73	4		12 Beneath This Gruff Exterior		New West 6045
				JOHN HIATT & THE GONERS		
7/9/05	126	3		13 Master Of Disaster		New West 6076
6/14/08	84	3		14 Same Old Man		New West 6145
				HIBBLER, Al Born on 8/16/1915 in Tyro, Mississippi. Died on 4/24/2001 (age 85). Blind since birth. R&B singer.		
8/4/56	20	2		1 Starring Al Hibbler		Decca 8328
				HI-C Born in 1972 in Louisiana; raised in California. Male rapper.		
1/25/92	152	12		1 Skanless...		Skanless 61235
				HICKS, Dan, & His Hot Licks Born on 12/9/1941 in Little Rock, Arkansas; raised in Santa Rosa, California. Singer/songwriter/guitarist.		
10/2/71	195	8		1 Where's The Money?.. [L]		Blue Thumb 29
				recorded at the Troubadour in Los Angeles, California		
5/20/72	170	5		2 Striking It Rich!		Blue Thumb 36
6/9/73	67	18		3 Last Train To Hicksville...The Home Of Happy Feet		Blue Thumb 51
3/25/78	165	3		4 It Happened One Bite		Warner 3158
				DAN HICKS		
				HICKS, Taylor Born on 10/7/1976 in Birmingham, Alabama. Winner on the 2006 season of TV's *American Idol*.		
12/30/06	2[1]	14	▲	1 Taylor Hicks		Arista 87984
3/28/09	58	4		2 The Distance		Modern Whomp 01913
				HIDDEN IN PLAIN VIEW Punk-rock band from Plainview, New Jersey: Joe Reo (vocals), Rob Freeman (guitar), Mike Saffert (guitar), Chris Amato (bass) and Spencer Perterson (drums).		
3/12/05	154	1		1 Life In Dreaming		Drive-Thru 83622 [2]
				HIDDEN STRENGTH Jazz-funk band formed in Los Angeles, California: Roy Herring (vocals), Grover Underwood (keyboards), Ken Sullivan (keyboards), Ray Anderson (trombone), Robert Leach (sax), Alvin Brown (bass) and Al Thomas (drums).		
3/6/76	208	3		1 Hidden Strength		United Artists 555
				HIEROGLYPHICS Rap group from Oakland, California: A Plus, Tajai, Del, Pep Love, Jay Biz, Opio, Phesto, Casual, Domino and Toure.		
10/25/03	155	1		1 Full Circle...		Hiero Imperium 230109
				HI-FIVE R&B vocal group from Waco, Texas: **Tony Thompson**, Roderick Clark, Russell Neal, Marcus Sanders and Toriano Easley (left after release of first album, replaced by Treston Irby). Clark and Neal left by 1993; Shannon and Terrance joined. Thompson died of a drug overdose on 6/1/2007 (age 31).		
12/8/90+	38	45	●	1 Hi-Five		Jive 1328
8/29/92	82	28	●	2 Keep It Goin' On		Jive 41474
11/13/93	105	4		3 Faithful		Jive 41528
				HIGGINS, Bertie Born Elbert Higgins on 12/8/1944 in Tarpon Springs, Florida. Pop singer/songwriter.		
2/27/82	38	25		1 Just Another Day In Paradise		Kat Family 37901
				HIGGINS, Missy Born Melissa Higgins on 8/19/1983 in Melbourne, Australia. Adult Contemporary singer/songwriter.		
3/28/09	193	1		1 On A Clear Night		Eleven 422652
				HIGH & MIGHTY, The Rap duo from Philadelphia, Pennsylvania: Eric "Mr. Eon" Meltzer and Milo "DJ Mighty Mi" Berger. Members of **Smut Peddlers**.		
9/11/99	193	2		1 Home Field Advantage		Rawkus 50121
				HIGH INERGY R&B vocal group from Pasadena, California: sisters Barbara Mitchell and Vernessa Mitchell, Linda Howard and Michelle Rumph. Vernessa left in 1978; group continued as a trio.		
11/5/77+	28	25		1 Turnin' On		Gordy 978
7/22/78	42	13		2 Steppin' Out..		Gordy 982
5/26/79	147	5		3 Shoulda Gone Dancin'		Gordy 987
11/10/79	205	2		4 Frenzy...		Gordy 989
9/27/80	208	1		5 Hold On		Gordy 996
6/13/81	203	5		6 High Inergy		Gordy 1005
6/4/83	206	3		7 Groove Patrol		Motown 6041

HIGH KINGS, The
Male group that performs traditional Celtic music: Darren Holden, Martin Furey, Finbarr Clancy and Brian Dunphy.

3/29/08	150	2		1 The High Kings .... Manhattan 21344

HIGH ON FIRE
Heavy metal trio from Oakland, California: Matt Pike (vocals, guitar), Jeff Matz (bass) and Des Kensel (drums).

10/6/07	142	1		1 Death Is This Communion .... Relapse 6705

HIGH SCHOOL MUSICAL CAST
Albums below feature the six main cast members of the highly popular Disney TV movie series: Zac Efron, **Vanessa Hudgens**, **Ashley Tisdale**, Lucas Grabeel, **Corbin Bleu** and Monique Coleman. Efron starred in the 2009 movie *17 Again*.

1/28/06	❶²	108	▲⁴	1 High School Musical Cat:#8/10 [TV]	Walt Disney 861426
12/16/06+	127	8		2 High School Musical: Disney's Karaoke Series	Walt Disney 861634
5/19/07	28	13		3 High School Musical: The Concert .... [L]	Walt Disney 000370
9/1/07	❶⁴	61	▲³	4 High School Musical 2 [TV]	Walt Disney 000651
10/27/07	98	10		5 High School Musical 2: Disney's Karaoke Series	Walt Disney 00689
12/29/07	42	3		6 High School Musical 2: Hits Remixed	Walt Disney 001083
1/12/08	52	10		7 High School Musical 2: Non-Stop Dance Party	Walt Disney 001089
2/16/08	65	4		8 High School Musical 2: Be Mine .... [EP]	Walt Disney 001229
11/8/08	2¹	37	▲	9 High School Musical 3: Senior Year [S]	Walt Disney 002714

HIGHWAYMEN
All-star gathering of legendary artists: **Waylon Jennings**, **Willie Nelson**, **Johnny Cash** and **Kris Kristofferson**.

6/1/85	92	35	▲	1 Highwayman	Columbia 40056
3/17/90	79	13		2 Highwayman 2	Columbia 45240

HIGHWAYMEN, The
Folk group formed in Middletown, Connecticut: Dave Fisher, Bob Burnett, Chan Daniels, Steve Trott and Steve Butts. Daniels died of pneumonia on 8/2/1975 (age 35). Fisher died on 5/7/2010 (age 70).

10/9/61	42	22		1 The Highwaymen	United Artists 3125
3/24/62	99	14		2 Standing Room Only!	United Artists 6168
9/7/63	79	9		3 Hootenanny With The Highwaymen .... [L]	United Artists 6294

HILL, Dan
Born on 6/3/1954 in Toronto, Ontario, Canada. Pop singer/songwriter.

12/6/75+	104	17		1 Dan Hill	20th Century 500
12/10/77+	21	24	●	2 Longer Fuse	20th Century 547
1/21/78	79	14		3 Hold On	20th Century 526
9/23/78	118	6		4 Frozen In The Night	20th Century 558
8/8/87	90	19		5 Dan Hill	Columbia 40456

HILL, Faith   All-Time: #355
Born on 9/21/1967 in Jackson, Mississippi. Adopted at less than a week old and raised as Audrey Faith Perry in Star, Mississippi. Country singer/actress. Briefly married to musician Daniel Hill in the late 1980s (took his last name). Married **Tim McGraw** on 10/6/1996. Played "Sarah Sunderson" in the 2004 movie *The Stepford Wives*.
AWARD: CMA: Female Vocalist 2000

1/29/94	59	54	▲³	1 Take Me As I Am .... Cat:#32/1	Warner 45389
9/16/95+	29	80	▲⁴	2 It Matters To Me .... Cat:#43/1	Warner 45872
5/9/98	7	99	▲⁶	3 Faith Cat:#16/38	Warner 46790
11/27/99	❶¹	103	▲⁸	4 Breathe Cat:#13/39	Warner 47373
				Grammy: Country Album
11/2/02	❶¹	39	▲²	5 Cry	Warner 48001
8/20/05	❶¹	67	▲²	6 Fireflies	Warner 48794
10/20/07	12	13		7 The Hits .... [G]	Warner 44230
10/18/08	13	14	●	8 Joy To The World .... Cat:#12/2 [X]	Warner 511500
				Christmas charts: 2/'08, 12/'09
12/5/09	54	6		9 Joy To The World	[X-R]	Warner 511500

HILL, Lauryn
Born on 5/25/1975 in South Orange, New Jersey. R&B singer/songwriter/actress. Member of **The Fugees**. Acted on TV's *As The World Turns* and in the movie *Sister Act 2*.
AWARD: Grammy: Best New Artist 1998

9/12/98	❶⁴	81	▲⁸	1 The Miseducation Of Lauryn Hill Cat:#37/5	Ruffhouse 69035
				Grammys: Album of the Year / R&B Album ★ RS500 #312
5/25/02	3¹	14	▲	2 MTV Unplugged No. 2.0 [L]	Columbia 86580 [2]

HILL, Z.Z.
Born Arzel Hill on 9/30/1935 in Naples, Texas. Died of a heart attack on 4/27/1984 (age 48). Blues singer/guitarist.

1/22/72	194	2		1 The Brand New Z.Z. Hill	Mankind 201
10/2/82	209	2		2 Down Home	Malaco 7406
2/5/83	165	5		3 The Rhythm & The Blues	Malaco 7411
1/7/84	170	9		4 I'm A Blues Man	Malaco 7415

HILLAGE, Steve
Born on 8/2/1951 in London, England. Rock singer/guitarist.

1/15/77	130	9		1 L	Atlantic 18205

Billboard DEBUT	PEAK	WKS	R I A A	ARTIST Album Title	Catalog	Label & Number

HILLMAN, Chris
Born on 12/4/1942 in Los Angeles, California. Folk-rock singer/bassist. Member of **The Byrds**, **Flying Burrito Brothers**, **The Souther, Hillman, Furay Band**, **McGuinn, Clark & Hillman** and **The Desert Rose Band**.

Billboard DEBUT	PEAK	WKS		Album Title		Label & Number
6/19/76	152	6		1 Slippin' Away		Asylum 1062
9/17/77	188	3		2 Clear Sailin'		Asylum 1104

HILLSIDE SINGERS, The
Pop vocal group: Lori Ham, Mary Mayo, Joelle Marino, Bill Marino, Frank Marino, Laura Marino, Rick Shaw, Ron Shaw and Susan Wiedenmann. The Marinos are siblings. Mary Mayo was the wife of producer Al Ham; Lori Ham is their daughter. Rick and Ron Shaw are brothers.

1/8/72	71	16		1 I'd Like To Teach The World To Sing		Metromedia 1051

HILLSONG UNITED
Gathering of various Christian singers and musicians affiliated with the Hillsong Church in Sydney, Australia.

10/5/02	144	2		1 Hillsong Live Worship: Blessed [L]		Hillsong 23182
4/22/06	162	2		2 United We Stand		Hillsong 80535
6/9/07	60	3		3 All Of The Above		Hillsong 09012
9/22/07	114	3		4 Saviour King		Hillsong 11984
4/19/08	117	6		5 The I Heart Revolution: With Hearts As One		Integrity 20858 [2]
8/23/08	55	6		6 This Is Our God [L]		Integrity 30993
6/13/09	21	14		7 Across The Earth: Tear Down The Walls		Hillsong digital
8/22/09	47	7		8 Faith + Hope + Love: Live [L]		Hillsong 54533

HI-LO'S, The   1950s: #44
Vocal group formed in Chicago, Illinois: Gene Puerling, Clark Burroughs, Bob Morse and Bob Strasen. Morse died on 4/20/2002 (age 74). Puerling died on 3/26/2008 (age 80). Numerous appearances on **Rosemary Clooney**'s TV show.

4/13/57	13	3		1 Suddenly It's The Hi-Lo's		Columbia 952
7/22/57	14	7		2 Ring Around Rosie		Columbia 1006
				ROSEMARY CLOONEY AND THE HI-LO'S		
10/14/57	19	4		3 Now Hear This		Columbia 1023

~ ~ ~ ~ ~ ~ ~ ~ ~ ~ **NON-CHARTED ALBUM** ~ ~ ~ ~ ~ ~ ~ ~ ~ ~ ~
1958 **The Hi-Lo's And All That Jazz**
Grammy: Hall of Fame

HILSON, Keri
Born on 10/27/1982 in Atlanta, Georgia. Female R&B singer/songwriter.

4/11/09	4	33	●	1 In A Perfect World...		Mosley 012000

HILTON, Paris
Born on 2/17/1981 in Manhattan, New York. Female singer/actress/socialite. One of the heirs to the Hilton Hotel dynasty. Starred in the 2003 reality series *The Simple Life* with friend Nicole Richie (adopted daughter of **Lionel Richie**); also acted in several movies. In June 2007, served time in jail on probation violation.

9/9/06	6	6		1 Paris		Warner 44138

HIM
Goth-rock band from Finland: Ville Valo (vocals), Mikko "Linde" Lindstrom (guitar), Emerson Burton (keyboards), Mige Amour (bass) and Gas Lipstick (drums). HIM: His Infernal Majesty.

10/16/04	190	1		1 Deep Shadows And Brilliant Highlights		Jimmy Franks 003431
2/19/05	117	1		2 Love Metal		Jimmy Franks 003363
12/2/06	162	1		3 Uneasy Listening Vol. I		Jimmy Franks 007962
10/15/05	18	37	●	4 Dark Light		Sire 49284
10/6/07	12	4		5 Venus Doom		Sire 105980
5/17/08	168	1		6 Digital Versatile Doom: Live At The Orpheum Theatre [L]		Sire 299196

HINDER
Grunge-rock band from Oklahoma City, Oklahoma: Austin Winkler (vocals), Joe Garvey (guitar), Mark King (guitar), Mike Rodden (bass) and Cody Hanson (drums).

10/15/05+	6	96	▲³	1 Extreme Behavior		Universal 005390
11/22/08	4	38	●	2 Take It To The Limit		Universal Rep. 012201

HINDU LOVE GODS
One-time gathering: **Warren Zevon** (vocals) with **R.E.M.** members: Peter Buck (guitar), Mike Mills (bass) and Bill Berry (drums).

11/10/90	168	10		1 Hindu Love Gods		Giant 24406

HINTON, Joe
Born on 11/15/1929 in Evansville, Indiana. Died of cancer on 8/13/1968 (age 38). R&B singer.

~ ~ ~ ~ ~ ~ ~ ~ ~ ~ **NON-CHARTED ALBUM** ~ ~ ~ ~ ~ ~ ~ ~ ~ ~ ~
1964 **Funny (How The Time Slips Away)**

HIPSWAY
Pop band from Scotland: Graham Skinner (vocals), Pim Jones (guitar), John McElhone (bass) and Harry Travers (drums). McElhone later joined **Texas**.

2/21/87	55	18		1 Hipsway		Columbia 40522

HIRES, Matt
Born on 8/5/1985 in Tampa, Florida. Eclectic singer/songwriter/guitarist.

8/15/09	96	1		1 Take Us To The Start		F-Stop 519718

HIROSHIMA
Jazz-pop band from Los Angeles, California: Teri Koide (vocals), Dan Kuramoto and Kimo Cornwell (keyboards), Dean Cortez (bass) and Danny Yamamoto (drums).

12/22/79+	51	27		1 Hiroshima		Arista 4252
11/15/80	72	18		2 Odori		Arista 9541
8/20/83	142	9		3 Third Generation	[I]	Epic 38708
11/30/85+	79	45	●	4 Another Place		Epic 39938
8/15/87	75	32	●	5 Go		Epic 40679
3/25/89	105	19		6 East		Epic 45022

HIRT, Al   1960s: #30 / All-Time: #175
Born Alois Maxwell Hirt on 11/7/1922 in New Orleans, Louisiana. Died of liver failure on 4/27/1999 (age 76). Trumpet virtuoso. Toured with **Jimmy Dorsey**, **Tommy Dorsey**, Ray McKinley and Horace Heidt. Formed own Dixieland combo (with **Pete Fountain**) in the late 1950s.

5/15/61	21	32		1 The Greatest Horn In The World	[I]	RCA Victor 2366
10/9/61	61	11		2 Al (He's The King) Hirt And His Band	[I]	RCA Victor 2354
2/3/62	41	2		3 Bourbon Street	[I]	Coral 57389
				PETE FOUNTAIN & AL HIRT		
2/10/62	24	25		4 Horn A-Plenty	[I]	RCA Victor 2446
1/19/63	96	7		5 Trumpet And Strings	[I]	RCA Victor 2584
3/23/63	44	3		6 Our Man In New Orleans	[I]	RCA Victor 2607
9/21/63+	3[8]	104	●	7 Honey In The Horn		RCA Victor 2733
2/29/64	83	9		8 Beauty And The Beard		RCA Victor 2690
				AL HIRT & ANN-MARGRET		
5/23/64	6	53	●	9 Cotton Candy	[I]	RCA Victor 2917
8/22/64	9	48	●	10 Sugar Lips		RCA Victor 2965
9/26/64	18	31		11 "Pops" Goes The Trumpet	[I]	RCA Victor 2729
				AL HIRT/BOSTON POPS/ARTHUR FIEDLER		
1/30/65	13	43	●	12 The Best Of Al Hirt	[G-I]	RCA Victor 3309
3/13/65	28	27		13 That Honey Horn Sound		RCA Victor 3337
7/24/65	47	22		14 Live At Carnegie Hall	[I-L]	RCA Victor 3416
				recorded on 4/22/1965		
12/11/65	12[X]	8		15 The Sound Of Christmas	[X-I]	RCA Victor 3417
				Christmas charts: 12/'65, 57/'66, 48/'67		
2/12/66	39	18		16 They're Playing Our Song	[I]	RCA Victor 3492
7/30/66	125	6		17 The Happy Trumpet	[I]	RCA Victor 3579
3/18/67	127	5		18 Music To Watch Girls By	[I]	RCA Victor 3773
2/10/68	116	13		19 Al Hirt Plays Bert Kaempfert	[I]	RCA Victor 3917

HITCHCOCK, Robyn, & The Egyptians
Born on 3/3/1952 in London, England. Male rock singer/guitarist. The Egyptians: Andy Metcalfe (bass) and Morris Windsor (drums).

3/5/88	111	15		1 Globe Of Frogs		A&M 5182
4/1/89	139	9		2 Queen Elvis		A&M 5241

HIT CREW, The
Studio band from New Jersey.

10/27/01	50	8		1 Proud To Be American		Turn Up The Music 1294
11/13/04+	37[C]	2		2 Drew's Famous Haunted House Horrors	[I]	Turn Up The Music 1107

HI-TEK
Born Tony Cottrell in Cincinnati, Ohio. Male rapper.

5/26/01	66	10		1 Hi-Teknology		Rawkus 50171
11/4/06	38	2		2 Hi-Teknology 2: The Chip		Babygrande 302

HITMAN SAMMY SAM
Born Sammy King in Atlanta, Georgia. Male rapper.

5/17/03	116	4		1 The Step Daddy		Collipark 000380

HIT THE LIGHTS
Punk-rock band from Lima, Ohio: Nick Thompson (vocals), Omar Zehery (guitar), David Bermosk (bass) and Nathan Van Dame (drums).

7/26/08	97	2		1 Skip School Start Fights		Triple Crown 3079

HIVES, The
Alternative-rock band from Fagersta, Sweden: brothers Pelle Almqvist (vocals) and Niklas Almqvist (guitar), with Mikael "Vigilante Carlstroem" Astrom (guitar), Mattias "Dr. Matt Destruction" Bernvall (bass) and Christian "Chris Dangerous" Grahn (drums).

5/11/02	63	25		1 Veni Vidi Vicious		Epitaph 48327
8/7/04	33	7		2 Tyrannosaurus Hives		Interscope 002756
12/1/07	65	2		3 The Black And White Album		A&M 010030

Billboard			R I A A	ARTIST Album Title	Catalog	Label & Number
DEBUT	PEAK	WKS				

HO, Don, and The Aliis
Born on 8/13/1930 in Kakaako, Oahu, Hawaii. Died of heart failure on 4/14/2007 (age 76). Popular nightclub singer/actor. Father of **Hoku**.

DEBUT	PEAK	WKS				
3/5/66	117	5		1 Don Ho-Again!	[L]	Reprise 6186
12/17/66+	15	50		2 Tiny Bubbles		Reprise 6232
5/27/67	115	5		3 East Coast/West Coast	[L]	Reprise 6244
3/22/69	199	3		4 Suck 'Em Up	[L]	Reprise 6331
8/23/69	162	6	●	5 Don Ho-Greatest Hits!	[G]	Reprise 6357
10/18/69	188	2		6 The Don Ho TV Show	[TV]	Reprise 6367

HODGES, Johnny, & Wild Bill Davis
Jazz saxophonist Hodges was born on 7/25/1906 in Cambridge, Massachusetts. Died of a heart attack on 5/11/1970 (age 63). Jazz organist Davis was born on 11/24/1918 in Glasgow, Missouri; raised in Parsons, Kansas. Died of a stroke on 8/17/1995 (age 76).

DEBUT	PEAK	WKS				
2/20/65	148	2		1 Blue Rabbit	[I]	Verve 8599

HODGSON, Roger
Born on 5/21/1950 in Portsmouth, England. Pop-rock singer/songwriter/guitarist/pianist. Lead singer of **Supertramp**.

DEBUT	PEAK	WKS				
10/27/84	46	22		1 In The Eye Of The Storm		A&M 5004
10/31/87	163	6		2 Hai Hai		A&M 5112

HOFFS, Susanna
Born on 1/17/1959 in Newport Beach, California. Lead singer of **The Bangles**. Starred in the 1987 movie *The Allnighter*. Daughter of movie director Tamara Hoffs. Married movie director Jay Roach on 4/17/1993.

DEBUT	PEAK	WKS				
2/16/91	83	11		1 When You're A Boy		Columbia 46076
5/6/06	192	1		2 Under The Covers		Shout! Factory 97654
8/8/09	106	1		3 Under The Covers: Vol. 2		Shout! Factory 11306
				MATTHEW SWEET & SUSANNA HOFFS (above 2)		

HOGAN, Brooke
Born Brooke Bollea on 5/2/1988 in Tampa, Florida. Teen female singer. Daughter of legendary professional wrestler Terry "Hulk Hogan" Bollea. Appeared with the rest of her family on the VH-1 reality series *Hogan Knows Best*.

DEBUT	PEAK	WKS				
11/11/06	28	4		1 Undiscovered		SMC 44909
8/8/09	144	1		2 The Redemption		Sobe 72485

HOG HEAVEN
Rock band formerly known as **Tommy James**'s Shondells: Eddie Gray (guitar), Ronnie Rosman (keyboards), Mike Vale (bass) and Pete Lucia (drums). All share vocals.

DEBUT	PEAK	WKS				
4/17/71	210	5		1 Hog Heaven		Roulette 42057

HOKU
Born Hoku Ho on 6/10/1981 in Oahu, Hawaii. Daughter of **Don Ho**.

DEBUT	PEAK	WKS				
5/20/00	151	3		1 Hoku		Geffen 490646

HOLDEN, Ron
Born on 8/7/1939 in Seattle, Washington. Died of a heart attack on 1/22/1997 (age 57). R&B singer.

~ ~ ~ ~ ~ ~ ~ ~ ~ ~ **NON-CHARTED ALBUM** ~ ~ ~ ~ ~ ~ ~ ~ ~ ~
1960 **Love You So...**

HOLD STEADY, The
Alternative-rock band formed in Brooklyn, New York: Craig Finn (vocals, guitar), Tad Kubler (guitar), Franz Nicolay (keyboards), Galen Polivka (bass) and Bobby Drake (drums).

DEBUT	PEAK	WKS				
10/21/06	124	2		1 Boys And Girls In America		Vagrant 442
7/5/08	30	6		2 Stay Positive		Vagrant 501
4/25/09	140	1		3 A Positive Rage		Vagrant 533

HOLE
Rock band formed in Los Angeles, California: **Courtney Love** (vocals, guitar), Eric Erlandson (guitar), Kristen Pfaff (bass) and Patty Schemel (drums). Love acted in several movies; married to Kurt Cobain (of **Nirvana**) from 2/24/1992 until his death on 4/8/1994. Pfaff was found dead in her bathtub on 6/16/1994 (age 27); replaced by Melissa Auf Der Maur.

DEBUT	PEAK	WKS				
4/30/94+	52	68	▲	1 Live Through This		DGC 24631
				RS500 #466		
10/14/95	172	2		2 Ask For It	[E-EP]	Caroline 1470
				recordings from 1991-92		
9/26/98	9	41	▲	3 Celebrity Skin		DGC 25164

HOLIDAY, Billie
Born Eleanor Gough on 4/7/1915 in Philadelphia, Pennsylvania. Died on 7/17/1959 (age 44). Legendary jazz singer. Nicknamed "Lady Day." Subject of the 1972 movie *Lady Sings The Blues* starring **Diana Ross**.
AWARDS: Grammy: Lifetime Achievement 1987 ★ R&R Hall of Fame: 2000 (Early Influence)

DEBUT	PEAK	WKS				
12/23/72+	85	21		1 The Billie Holiday Story	[K]	Decca 161 [2]
				recordings from 1944-50		
1/13/73	108	16		2 Strange Fruit	[K]	Atlantic 1614
				recordings from 1939 and 1944		
2/24/73	135	9		3 The Original Recordings	[K]	Columbia 32060
				recordings from 1935-58		
2/10/01	174	2		4 Ken Burns Jazz - The Definitive Billie Holiday	[K-TV]	Verve 549081
9/19/09	122	1		5 The Complete Billie Holiday	[K]	X5 digital

Billboard			R I A A	ARTIST		
DEBUT	PEAK	WKS		Album Title	Catalog	Label & Number
				~ ~ ~ ~ ~ ~ ~ **NON-CHARTED ALBUM by BILLIE HOLIDAY** ~ ~ ~ ~ ~ ~ ~		
				1958 **Lady In Satin**		
				Grammy: Hall of Fame		
				HOLIDAY, J.		
				Born Nahom Grymes on 12/12/1982 in Washington DC. Male R&B singer/songwriter.		
10/20/07	5	31	●	1 **Back Of My Lac'**		Music Line 11805
3/28/09	4	8		2 **Round 2**		Music Line 27532
				HOLIDAY EXPRESS		
				All-volunteer, nonprofit, nonsectarian organization, whose royalties go toward helping the needy.		
1/20/01	16^X	2		1 **Greatest Hits * Holiday Express**.. **[X]**		Oglio 89120
				Christmas charts: 16/'01, 40/'08		
				HOLLAND, Amy		
				Born on 5/15/1955 in Los Angeles, California. Pop singer. Married **Michael McDonald** on 5/21/1983.		
8/30/80	146	14		1 **Amy Holland**		Capitol 12071
				HOLLAND, Eddie		
				Born on 10/30/1939 in Detroit, Michigan. R&B singer/songwriter/producer. Teamed with brother Brian Holland and **Lamont Dozier** in successful songwriting/production team for Motown; wrote many of Motown's greatest hits.		
				AWARDS: Grammy: Trustees 1998 ★ R&R Hall of Fame: 1990 (Non-Performer)		
				~ ~ ~ ~ ~ ~ ~ ~ ~ ~ **NON-CHARTED ALBUM** ~ ~ ~ ~ ~ ~ ~ ~ ~ ~		
				1963 **Eddie Holland**		
				HOLLIDAY, Jennifer		
				Born on 10/19/1960 in Riverside, Texas. R&B singer/actress. Appeared in several Broadway musicals.		
10/22/83	31	22		1 **Feel My Soul**		Geffen 4014
9/14/85	110	14		2 **Say You Love Me**..		Geffen 24073
11/9/91	184	1		3 **I'm On Your Side**		Arista 18578
				HOLLIES, The **All-Time: #471**		
				Pop-rock band from Manchester, England: Allan Clarke (vocals), **Graham Nash** (guitar), Tony Hicks (guitar), Eric Haydock (bass) and Bobby Elliott (drums). Haydock left in 1966; replaced by Bernie Calvert. Nash left in December 1968 to join **David Crosby** and **Stephen Stills** in new trio; replaced by Terry Sylvester, formerly in **The Swinging Blue Jeans**. Shuffling personnel since then. Clarke, Nash, Hicks and Elliott regrouped briefly in 1983.		
				AWARD: R&R Hall of Fame: 2010		
2/12/66	145	3		1 **Hear! Here!**		Imperial 12299
10/22/66	75	11		2 **Bus Stop**		Imperial 12330
2/25/67	91	8		3 **Stop! Stop! Stop!**		Imperial 12339
6/3/67	11	40		4 **The Hollies' Greatest Hits** **[G]**		Imperial 12350
8/5/67	43	14		5 **Evolution**		Epic 26315
4/4/70	32	14		6 **He Ain't Heavy, He's My Brother**...		Epic 26538
2/13/71	183	2		7 **Moving Finger**...		Epic 30255
7/15/72	21	21		8 **Distant Light**		Epic 30958
1/27/73	84	12		9 **Romany**		Epic 31992
10/20/73	157	7		10 **The Hollies' Greatest Hits** .... **[G]**		Epic 32061
5/11/74	28	23	●	11 **Hollies**		Epic 32574
3/29/75	123	10		12 **Another Night**		Epic 33387
7/9/83	90	9		13 **What Goes Around**..		Atlantic 80076
				HOLLISTER, Dave		
				Born on 8/17/1970 in Chicago, Illinois. R&B singer/songwriter. Former member of **BLACKstreet**.		
6/12/99	34	28	●	1 **Ghetto Hymns**...		Def Squad 50047
12/9/00	49	28	●	2 **Chicago '85... The Movie**..		Def Squad 50278
11/2/02	10	7		3 **Things In The Game Done Changed**		Motown 018747
11/29/03	42	2		4 **Real Talk**		DreamWorks 450500
9/9/06	140	1		5 **The Definitive Collection** .... **[G]**		Hip-O 006310
10/14/06	98	1		6 **The Book Of David: Vol. 1 The Transition**		Gospo Centric 85334
8/23/08	88	2		7 **Witness Protection**...		Gospo Centric 28731
				HOLLOWAY, Brenda		
				Born on 6/21/1946 in Atascadero, California. R&B singer/songwriter.		
				~ ~ ~ ~ ~ ~ ~ ~ ~ ~ ~ **NON-CHARTED ALBUM** ~ ~ ~ ~ ~ ~ ~ ~ ~ ~ ~		
				1964 **Every Little Bit Hurts**		
				HOLLOWAY, Loleatta		
				Born on 11/5/1946 in Chicago, Illinois. Female disco singer.		
12/2/78	187	2		1 **Queen Of The Night**		Gold Mind 9501

HOLLY, Buddy / The Crickets

Born Charles Hardin Holley on 9/7/1936 in Lubbock, Texas. One of rock and roll's most original and innovative performers. In February 1957, Holly assembled his backing group, **The Crickets**: Niki Sullivan (rhythm guitar), Joe B. Mauldin (bass) and Jerry Ivan Allison (drums). Signed to Brunswick and Coral labels (subsidiaries of Decca Records). Because of contract arrangements, all Brunswick records were released as The Crickets, and all Coral records were released as Buddy Holly. Holly split from The Crickets in Fall 1958. Holly (age 22), **Ritchie Valens** and the **Big Bopper** were killed in a plane crash near Mason City, Iowa, on 2/3/1959. Gary Busey starred in the 1978 biographical movie *The Buddy Holly Story*. Also see **Bobby Vee**. Also see **Various Artists Compilations**: *Not Fade Away (Remembering Buddy Holly*.

AWARDS: Grammy Lifetime Achievement 1997 ★ R&R Hall of Fame: 1986

DEBUT	PEAK	WKS				Catalog	Label & Number
4/27/59	11	181	●	1	The Buddy Holly Story	[G]	Coral 57279
					includes 4 songs with **The Crickets**		
3/16/63	40	17		2	Reminiscing...	[K]	Coral 57426
					BUDDY HOLLY		
					instrumental backing by The Fireballs dubbed in (1962)		
8/5/78	55	12	●	3	Buddy Holly & The Crickets 20 Golden Greats .... Cat:#35/12	[G]	MCA 3040
					RS500 #92		
11/19/05	37^C	2		4	Greatest Hits..	[G]	MCA 11536
					released in 1996		
3/15/08	101	4		5	Not Fade Away	[G]	Universal 009424
3/21/09	17^C	1		6	The Definitive Collection	[G]	MCA 004710

~ ~ ~ ~ ~ ~ ~ ~ ~ ~ **NON-CHARTED ALBUMS** ~ ~ ~ ~ ~ ~ ~ ~ ~ ~ ~

1957 **The "Chirping" Crickets**	1959 **The Buddy Holly Story, Vol. II**
RS500 #421	1964 **Buddy Holly Showcase**
1958 **That'll Be The Day**	1965 **Holly In The Hills**
1958 **Buddy Holly** [Coral label]	1967 **Buddy Holly's Greatest Hits**

HOLLY & THE ITALIANS

Rock band from Los Angeles, California: Holly Vincent (vocals, guitar), Colin White (guitar), Mark Sidgwick (bass) and Steve Young (drums).

DEBUT	PEAK	WKS				Catalog	Label & Number
7/11/81	177	3		1	The Right To Be Italian		Virgin 37359

HOLLYRIDGE STRINGS, The

Arranged and conducted by Stu Phillips, later of the **Golden Gate Strings**.

DEBUT	PEAK	WKS				Catalog	Label & Number
6/20/64	15	25		1	The Beatles Song Book...	[I]	Capitol 2116
10/10/64	82	12		2	The Beach Boys Song Book..	[I]	Capitol 2156
2/13/65	144	3		3	Hits Made Famous By Elvis Presley	[I]	Capitol 2221
4/24/65	136	3		4	The Nat King Cole Song Book	[I]	Capitol 2310
6/4/66	142	3		5	The New Beatles Song Book	[I]	Capitol 2429

HOLLYWOOD ARGYLES

Gary Paxton recorded "Alley-Oop" as a solo artist; since he was still under contract to Brent Records, where he recorded as Flip of "Skip & Flip," he made up the name Hollywood Argyles after street signs at Hollywood & Argyle. After the song was a hit, Paxton assembled a Hollywood Argyles group. Formed Garpax Records. Paxton is now a gospel artist.

~ ~ ~ ~ ~ ~ ~ ~ ~ ~ **NON-CHARTED ALBUM** ~ ~ ~ ~ ~ ~ ~ ~ ~ ~ ~

1960 **The Hollywood Argyles** ["Alley-Oop"]

HOLLYWOOD STUDIO ORCHESTRA, The

Conducted by Mitchell Powell.

DEBUT	PEAK	WKS				Catalog	Label & Number
1/23/61	23	17		1	Exodus..	[I]	United Artists 6123

HOLLYWOOD UNDEAD

Rap-rock band from Hollywood, California: Charlie Scene, Johnny 3 Tears, J-Dog, Da Kurtzz, Funny Man and Deuce. All perform wearing hockey masks.

DEBUT	PEAK	WKS				Catalog	Label & Number
9/20/08	22	76	●	1	Swan Songs .... Cat:#32/7		A&M 011331
7/11/09	124	1		2	Swan Songs B-Sides EP	[EP]	A&M digital
11/28/09	29	4		3	Desperate Measures	[K]	A&M 013514

HOLMAN, Eddie

Born on 6/3/1946 in Norfolk, Virginia; raised in New York and Philadelphia, Pennsylvania. R&B singer/songwriter.

DEBUT	PEAK	WKS				Catalog	Label & Number
2/21/70	75	13		1	I Love You		ABC 701

HOLMES, Cecil, Soulful Sounds

Born in New York. R&B songwriter/producer. Founded the Chocolate City record label.

DEBUT	PEAK	WKS				Catalog	Label & Number
4/28/73	141	10		1	The Black Motion Picture Experience...............................	[I]	Buddah 5129

HOLMES, Clint

Born on 5/9/1946 in Bournemouth, England; raised in Farnham, England. Pop singer.

DEBUT	PEAK	WKS				Catalog	Label & Number
5/26/73	122	12		1	Playground In My Mind...		Epic 32269

HOLMES, "Groove"

Born Richard Holmes on 5/2/1931 in Camden, New Jersey. Died of prostate cancer on 6/29/1991 (age 60). Jazz organist.

DEBUT	PEAK	WKS				Catalog	Label & Number
5/14/66	89	26		1	Soul Message...	[I]	Prestige 7435
10/29/66	143	3		2	Living Soul	[I-L]	Prestige 7468
12/24/66+	134	6		3	Misty		Prestige 7485
7/10/76	206	2		4	I'm In The Mood For Love...		Flying Dutchman 1537

HOLMES, Jake
Born on 12/28/1939 in San Francisco, California. Folk-rock singer/songwriter.

11/14/70	135	6		1 So Close, So Very Far To Go		Polydor 4034

HOLMES, Leroy, And His Orchestra
Born Alvin Holmes on 9/22/1913 in Pittsburgh, Pennsylvania. Died on 7/27/1986 (age 72). Orchestra conductor/arranger.

9/9/67	42	29		1 For A Few Dollars More And Other Motion Picture Themes .... [I]		United Artists 6608
6/1/68	138	8		2 The Good, The Bad And The Ugly And Other Motion Picture Themes .... [I]		United Artists 6633

HOLMES, Rupert
Born David Goldstein on 2/24/1947 in Northwich, Cheshire, England; raised in Manhattan, New York. Pop singer/songwriter.

11/10/79+	33	31	●	1 Partners In Crime		Infinity 9020
12/20/80	208	1		2 Adventure		MCA 5129

HOLY, Steve
Born on 2/23/1972 in Dallas, Texas. Country singer/songwriter.

12/29/01+	63	17	●	1 Blue Moon		Curb 77972
8/26/06	19	11		2 Brand New Girlfriend		Curb 78758

HOMBRES, The
Garage-rock band from Memphis, Tennessee: B.B. Cunningham (vocals, organ), Gary McEwen (guitar), Jerry Masters (bass) and Johnny Hunter (drums). Hunter committed suicide in February 1976 (age 34). Cunningham's brother, Bill, was a member of **The Box Tops**.

12/9/67	180	4		1 Let It Out (Let It All Hang Out)		Verve Forecast 3036

HOME GROWN
Punk-rock trio from Anaheim, California: Adam Lohrbach (vocals, bass), John Trash (guitar) and Darren Reynolds (drums).

7/13/02	189	1		1 Kings Of Pop		Drive-Thru 060060

HONDELLS, The
Producer Nick Venet and arranger Gary Usher recorded various studio musicians in Southern California under different group names. "Little Honda" featured Usher, Chuck Girard (vocals), **Glen Campbell** and Richie Podolor (guitars), Hal Blaine (drums) and Ritchie Burns (backing vocals). Usher died of cancer on 5/25/1990 (age 51).

11/28/64	119	4		1 Go Little Honda		Mercury 60940

HONEYCOMBS, The
Rock and roll band from London, England: Dennis D'ell (vocals), Allan Ward (guitar), Martin Murray (guitar), John Lantree (bass) and his sister Ann "Honey" Lantree (drums).

1/2/65	147	2		1 Here Are The Honeycombs		Interphon 88001

HONEY CONE, The
Female R&B vocal trio from Los Angeles, California: Carolyn Willis, Edna Wright (sister of Darlene Love) and Shellie Clark.

6/19/71	137	8		1 Sweet Replies		Hot Wax 706
12/11/71+	72	20		2 Soulful Tapestry		Hot Wax 707
9/23/72	189	4		3 Love, Peace & Soul		Hot Wax 713

HONEYDRIPPERS, The
All-star rock band: **Robert Plant** (vocals), **Jimmy Page** and **Jeff Beck** (guitars), and **Nile Rodgers** (bass). Plant and Page are from **Led Zeppelin** and Rodgers is from **Chic**.

10/20/84	4	31	▲	1 Volume One **[EP]**		Es Paranza 90220

HONEYMOON SUITE
Rock band from Toronto, Ontario, Canada: Johnnie Dee (vocals), Dermot Grehan (guitar), Ray Coburn (keyboards), Garry Lalonde (bass) and Dave Betts (drums). Rob Preuss replaced Coburn in 1987.

8/25/84	60	17		1 Honeymoon Suite		Warner 25098
3/15/86	61	35		2 The Big Prize		Warner 25293
5/14/88	86	10		3 Racing After Midnight		Warner 25652

HONOR SOCIETY
Pop-rock band formed in New Jersey: Michael Bruno (vocals, guitar), Jason Rosen (guitar), Andrew Lee (bass) and Alexander Noyes (drums).

10/3/09	18	2		1 Fashionably Late		Hollywood 0047710

HOOBASTANK
Rock band from Agoura Hills, California: Doug Robb (vocals), Dan Estrin (guitar), Markku Lappalainen (bass) and Chris Hesse (drums). Josh Moreau replaced Lappalainen in 2005.

12/8/01+	25	50	▲	1 Hoobastank		Island 586435
12/27/03+	3[1]	68	▲[2]	2 The Reason		Island 001488
6/3/06	12	11	●	3 Every Man For Himself		Island 006162
2/14/09	26	4		4 For(n)ever		Island 012399

HOOD, Patterson
Born in Memphis, Tennessee. Rock singer/keyboardist. Member of **Drive-By Truckers**.

7/11/09	153	1		1 Murdering Oscar (And Other Love Songs)		Ruth St. 60002

Billboard DEBUT	PEAK	WKS	R I A A	ARTIST / Album Title	Catalog	Label & Number
				HOODOO GURUS		
				Rock band from Sydney, Australia: Dave Faulkner (vocals), Brad Shepherd (guitar), Clyde Bramley (bass) and Mark Kingsmill (drums). Rick Grossman (of the **Divinyls**) replaced Bramley in 1989.		
12/1/84	209	1		1 Stoneage Romeos		A&M 5012
5/10/86	140	7		2 Mars Needs Guitars!		Elektra 60485
5/2/87	120	13		3 Blow Your Cool!		Elektra 60728
8/12/89	101	15		4 Magnum Cum Louder		RCA 9781
5/18/91	172	1		5 Kinky		RCA 3009
				HOODOO RHYTHM DEVILS		
				Vocal duo from Oakland, California: Joe Crane and Glenn Walters.		
3/25/78	208	1		1 All Kidding Aside		Fantasy 9543
				HOOKER, John Lee		
				Born on 8/22/1917 in Coahoma County, Mississippi. Died on 6/21/2001 (age 83). Legendary blues singer/guitarist.		
				AWARDS: Grammy: Lifetime Achievement 2000 ★ R&R Hall of Fame: 1991		
2/27/71	73	16		1 Hooker 'N Heat		Liberty 35002 [2]
				CANNED HEAT & JOHN LEE HOOKER		
3/27/71	126	13		2 Endless Boogie		ABC 720 [2]
3/18/72	130	6		3 Never Get Out Of These Blues Alive		ABC 736
10/7/89+	62	38		4 The Healer		Chameleon 74808
9/28/91	101	11		5 Mr. Lucky		Charisma 91724
3/11/95	135	8		6 Chill Out		Pointblank 40107
				Grammy: Traditional Blues Album		
3/22/97	163	3		7 Don't Look Back		Pointblank 42771
				Grammy: Traditional Blues Album		

~ ~ ~ ~ ~ ~ ~ ~ ~ **NON-CHARTED ALBUMS** ~ ~ ~ ~ ~ ~ ~ ~ ~ ~

1959 **I'm John Lee Hooker**   1991 **The Ultimate Collection: 1948-1990**
1962 **Burnin'** *["Boom Boom"]*   *RS500 #375*

Billboard DEBUT	PEAK	WKS	R I A A	ARTIST / Album Title	Catalog	Label & Number
				HOOKFOOT		
				Rock band from England: Caleb Quaye (vocals), Ian Duck (guitar), Dave Glover (bass) and Roger Pope (drums).		
9/25/71	205	4		1 Hookfoot		A&M 4316
				HOOPER, Stix		
				Born Nesbert Hooper on 8/15/1938 in Houston, Texas. R&B drummer. Member of **The Crusaders**.		
11/10/79	166	5		1 The World Within	[I]	MCA 3180
				HOOTERS		
				Pop-rock band from Philadelphia, Pennsylvania: Eric Bazilian (vocals, guitar), Rob Hyman (vocals, keyboards), John Lilley (guitar), Andy King (bass) and David Uosikkinen (drums). Fran Smith replaced King in early 1989.		
5/25/85+	12	74	▲²	1 Nervous Night		Columbia 39912
8/8/87	27	26	●	2 One Way Home		Columbia 40659
12/2/89+	115	16		3 Zig Zag		Columbia 45058
				HOOTIE & THE BLOWFISH		
				Pop-rock band formed in South Carolina: Darius Rucker (vocals; born on 5/13/1966), Mark Bryan (guitar; born on 5/6/1967), Dean Felber (bass; born on 6/9/1967) and Jim Sonefeld (drums; born on 10/20/1964). Rucker began Country career in 2008.		
				AWARD: Grammy: Best New Artist 1995		
7/23/94+	❶⁸	129	▲¹⁶	1 Cracked Rear View	Cat:#10/18	Atlantic 82613
5/11/96	❶²	44	▲³	2 Fairweather Johnson		Atlantic 82886
10/3/98	4	23	▲	3 Musical Chairs		Atlantic 83136
11/11/00	71	3		4 Scattered, Smothered & Covered	[K]	Atlantic 83408
3/22/03	46	6		5 Hootie & The Blowfish		Atlantic 83564
3/20/04	62	6		6 The Best Of Hootie & The Blowfish (1993 Thru 2003)	[G]	Atlantic 78083
8/27/05	47	6		7 Looking For Lucky		Sneaky Long 79784
				HOPE, Bob		
				Born Leslie Townes Hope on 5/29/1903 in Eltham, London, England; raised in Cleveland, Ohio. Died of pneumonia on 7/27/2003 (age 100). Legendary movie/TV/radio comedian. Starred in a series of "Road" movies with **Bing Crosby**.		
7/4/76	175	4		1 America Is 200 Years Old...And There's Still Hope!	[C]	Capitol 11538
				HOPKIN, Mary		
				Born on 5/3/1950 in Pontardawe, Glamorganshire, Wales. Pop singer. Married to record producer Tony Visconti from 1971-81.		
3/29/69	28	20		1 Post Card		Apple 3351
				produced by **Paul McCartney**		
12/4/71	204	3		2 Earth Song/Ocean Song		Apple 3381
11/25/72	201	5		3 Those Were The Days	[G]	Apple 3595
				HOPKINS, Nicky		
				Born on 2/24/1944 in London, England. Died of an intestinal disorder on 9/6/1994 (age 50). Session pianist. Member of **Sweet Thursday** and **Night**.		
2/12/72	33	11		1 Jamming With Edward!	[I]	Rolling Stones 39100
5/5/73	108	10		2 The Tin Man Was A Dreamer		Columbia 32074

HORNE, Jimmy "Bo"
Born on 9/28/1949 in West Palm Beach, Florida. R&B-disco singer.

| 7/1/78 | 122 | 10 | | 1 Dance Across The Floor .... | | Sunshine Sound 7801 |

HORNE, Lena
1950s: #43
Born on 6/30/1917 in Brooklyn, New York. Died on 5/9/2010 (age 92). Jazz-styled singer/actress. Starred in several movies and Broadway shows.
AWARD: Grammy: Lifetime Achievement 1989

9/16/57	24	2		1 Lena Horne At The Waldorf Astoria .... [L]		RCA Victor 1028
				recorded on 12/31/1956		
11/17/58	20	1		2 Give The Lady What She Wants		RCA Victor 1879
6/22/59	13	22		3 Porgy & Bess...		RCA Victor 1507
				LENA HORNE & HARRY BELAFONTE		
4/14/62	102	8		4 Lena On The Blue Side		RCA Victor 2465
2/9/63	102	5		5 Lena...Lovely And Alive		RCA Victor 2587
12/24/66	74ˣ	1		6 Merry From Lena .... [X]		United Artists 6546
5/16/70	162	10		7 Lena & Gabor		Skye 15
				LENA HORNE & GABOR SZABO		
9/26/81	112	9		8 Lena Horne: The Lady And Her Music .... [OC]		Qwest 3597 [2]
				Grammys: Cast Album / Female Pop Vocal		

HORNHEADS, The
Instrumental horn band from Minneapolis, Minnesota: Michael B. Nelson, Steve Strand, Dave Jensen, Kenni Holmen and Kathy Jensen.

| 1/19/08 | 194 | 1 | | 1 'Tis The Season: Jingle Bell Jazz .... [X-I] | | Compass 39785 |
| | | | | no track titles listed on this album; Christmas chart: 13/'07 | | |

HORNSBY, Bruce
Born on 11/23/1954 in Williamsburg, Virginia. Pop-rock singer/songwriter/pianist. The Range: George Marinelli (guitar), David Mansfield (guitar), Joe Puerta (bass) and John Molo (drums). Puerta was a member of **Ambrosia**. Hornsby later toured as a member of the **Grateful Dead** and **The Other Ones**.
AWARD: Grammy: Best New Artist 1986

6/21/86+	3⁴	73	▲³	1 The Way It Is	Cat.#38/1	RCA Victor 5904
5/21/88	5	27	▲	2 Scenes From The Southside		RCA 6686
7/7/90	20	21	●	3 A Night On The Town..		RCA 2041
				BRUCE HORNSBY AND THE RANGE (above 3)		
4/24/93	46	16	●	4 Harbor Lights...		RCA 66114
8/5/95	68	12		5 Hot House		RCA 66584
10/31/98	148	2		6 Spirit Trail		RCA 67468 [2]
11/11/00	167	1		7 Here Come The Noise Makers .... [L]		RCA 69308 [2]
9/4/04	86	2		8 Halcyon Days		Columbia 92652
10/3/09	116	1		9 Levitate..		Verve 013115
				BRUCE HORNSBY & THE NOISEMAKERS		

HOROWITZ, Vladimir
Born Vladimir Gorowicz on 10/3/1903 in Kiev, Russia. Died of a heart attack on 11/5/1989 (age 86). Legendary classical pianist. Moved to the United States in 1928.

11/10/62	14	22		1 Vladimir Horowitz (Chopin, Schumann, Rachmaninoff, Liszt) .... [I]		Columbia 6371
6/22/63	129	8		2 The Sound Of Horowitz .... [I]		Columbia 6411
				Grammy: Classical Album		
7/24/65	22	32		3 Horowitz at Carnegie Hall - An Historic Return .... [I-L]		Columbia 728 [2]
				Grammys: Classical Album / Hall of Fame		
				recorded on 5/9/1965		
11/16/68	185	4		4 Horowitz On Television .... [I-L]		Columbia 7106
				Grammy: Classical Album		
				recorded on 2/1/1968 at Carnegie Hall		
4/29/78	102	14		5 Golden Jubilee Concert - Rachmaninoff Concerto No. 3 .... [I-L]		RCA Victor 2633
				Grammy: Hall of Fame		
				recorded on 1/8/1978 at Carnegie Hall; with **Eugene Ormandy & The New York Philharmonic**		

HORRORPOPS
Punk-rock trio from Copenhagen, Denmark: Patricia Day (vocals, guitar), Kim Nekroman (bass) and Henrik Niedermeier (drums).

| 2/23/08 | 149 | 1 | | 1 Kiss Kiss Kill Kill.. | | Hellcat 80498 |

HORSLIPS
Rock band from Dublin, Ireland: John Fean (vocals, guitar), Jim Lockhart (keyboards), Charles O'Connor (fiddle), Barry Devlin (bass) and Eamon Carr (drums).

| 2/25/78 | 98 | 9 | | 1 Aliens .... | | DJM 16 |
| 3/10/79 | 155 | 9 | | 2 The Man Who Built America.. | | DJM 20 |

HORTON, Johnny
Born on 4/30/1925 in Los Angeles, California; raised in Tyler, Texas. Died in a car crash on 11/5/1960 (age 35). Country singer.

| 2/27/61 | 8 | 34 | ▲ | 1 Johnny Horton's Greatest Hits .... [G] | | Columbia 8396 |
| 4/28/62 | 104 | 10 | | 2 Honky-Tonk Man .... [K] | | Columbia 8779 |

Billboard			R I A A	ARTIST		
DEBUT	PEAK	WKS		Album Title	Catalog	Label & Number

HOT
Interracial female vocal trio from Los Angeles, California: Gwen Owens, Cathy Carson and Juanita Curiel.

5/28/77	125	15		1 **Hot**		Big Tree 89522

HOT APPLE PIE
Country band formed in Nashville, Tennessee: Brady Seals (vocals, guitar), Mark "Sparky" Matekja (guitar), Keith Horne (bass) and Trey Landry (drums). Seals was leader of **Little Texas**.

7/16/05	60	9		1 **Hot Apple Pie**		DreamWorks 003866

HOT BOYS
All-star rap group from New Orleans, Louisiana: **B.G.**, **Juvenile**, **Lil' Wayne** and **Turk**.

8/14/99	5	44	●	1 **Guerilla Warfare**		Cash Money 53264
4/12/03	14	6		2 **Let 'Em Burn**		Cash Money 860966

HOT BUTTER
Group is actually Moog synthesizer player Stan Free (born on 4/12/1922; died on 8/17/1995, age 73).

10/21/72	137	7		1 **Popcorn** .... [I]		Musicor 3242

HOT CHIP
Electro-pop band from London, England: Alexis Taylor (female vocals, keyboards), Joe Goddard (male vocals, keyboards), Al Doyle (guitar), Owen Clarke (bass) and Felix Martin (drums).

2/23/08	109	1		1 **Made In The Dark**		DFA 18094

HOT CHOCOLATE
Interracial rock-soul band formed in London, England: Errol Brown (vocals), Harvey Hinsley (guitar), Larry Ferguson (keyboards), Patrick Olive (bass) and Tony Connor (drums).

3/1/75	55	17		1 **Cicero Park**		Big Tree 89503
11/22/75+	41	21		2 **Hot Chocolate**		Big Tree 89512
9/18/76	172	6		3 **Man To Man**		Big Tree 89519
1/6/79	31	16		4 **Every 1's A Winner**		Infinity 9002
7/28/79	112	6		5 **Going Through The Motions**		Infinity 9010

HOTEL
Pop-rock band from Birmingham, Alabama: Marc Phillips (vocals, keyboards), Tommy Calton (guitar), Mike Reid (guitar), Lee Bargeron (keyboards), George Creasman (bass) and Michael Cadenhead (drums).

8/18/79	204	2		1 **Hotel**		MCA 3158

HOT HOT HEAT
Rock band from Victoria, British Columbia, Canada: Steve Bays (vocals, keyboards), Dante DeCaro (guitar), Dustin Hawthorne (bass) and Paul Hawley (drums). DeCaro later joined **Wolf Parade**.

7/26/03	146	9		1 **Make Up The Breakdown**		Sub Pop 70599
4/23/05	34	10		2 **Elevator**		Sire 48988
9/29/07	86	1		3 **Happiness Ltd.**		Sire 162108

HOTHOUSE FLOWERS
Folk-rock band from Dublin, Ireland: Liam O'Maonlai (vocals), Fiachna O'Braonain (guitar), Peter O'Toole (bass) and Jerry Fehily (drums).

8/27/88	88	33		1 **people**		London 828101
7/14/90	122	16		2 **Home**		London 828197
4/10/93	156	3		3 **Songs From The Rain**		London 828350

HOT TUNA
Rock band formed in San Francisco, California: **Jorma Kaukonen** (vocals, guitar), Jack Casady (vocals, bass), Nikki Buck (keyboards) and Sammy Piazza (drums). Bob Steeler replaced Piazza in late 1974. Kaukonen and Casady were members of **Jefferson Airplane**. Violinist **Papa John Creach** was a member from 1971-73.

7/18/70	30	19		1 **Hot Tuna** .... [L]		RCA Victor 4353
				recorded at New Orleans House in Berkeley, California		
6/26/71	43	13		2 **First Pull Up Then Pull Down** .... [L]		RCA Victor 4550
3/18/72	68	23		3 **Burgers**		Grunt 1004
2/9/74	148	7		4 **The Phosphorescent Rat**		Grunt 0348
5/10/75	75	11		5 **America's Choice**		Grunt 0820
11/29/75	97	9		6 **Yellow Fever**		Grunt 1238
11/20/76	116	10		7 **Hoppkorv**		Grunt 1920
4/15/78	92	10		8 **Double Dose** .... [L]		Grunt 2545 [2]
				recorded at Theatre 1839 in San Francisco, California		

HOUGH, Julianne
Born on 7/20/1988 in Salt Lake City, Utah. Country singer/dancer. Winner (along with partner Apolo Anton Ohno) on season 4 and (along with partner Helio Castroneves) on the season 5 of TV's *Dancing With The Stars*.

6/7/08	3¹	24		1 **Julianne Hough**		Mercury Nashville 011052
11/22/08+	24	10		2 **NBC Sounds Of The Season: The Julianne Hough Holiday Collection** .... [X-EP]		Mercury 012047
				Christmas chart: 2/'08		

HOUSEMARTINS, The
Pop-rock band from Hull, Humberside, England: Paul Heaton (vocals), Norman Cook (guitar), Stan Collimore (bass) and Hugh Whitaker (drums). Dave Hemmingway replaced Whitaker in late 1987. Cook formed **Beats International** and later recorded as **Fatboy Slim**.

2/7/87	124	14	1 London 0 Hull 4		Elektra 60501
1/16/88	177	6	2 The People Who Grinned Themselves To Death		Elektra 60761

HOUSE OF FREAKS
Rock duo from Richmond, Virginia: singer/guitarist Bryan Harvey and drummer Johnny Hott. Harvey (age 49) and his wife and two daughters were brutally murdered on 1/1/2006.

5/6/89	154	10	1 Tantilla		Rhino 70846

HOUSE OF LORDS
Hard-rock band formed in Los Angeles, California: James Christian (vocals), Lanny Cordola (guitar), Gregg Giuffria (keyboards), Chuck Wright (bass) and Ken Mary (drums). Cordola was with **Ozzy Osbourne**. Giuffria was with **Angel**. Giuffria and Wright were both with **Giuffria**; Wright was also with **Quiet Riot**. Mary was with **Alice Cooper**. Michael Guy replaced Cordola in 1990.

11/19/88+	78	27	1 House Of Lords		RCA 8530
10/20/90+	121	18	2 Sahara		RCA 2170

HOUSE OF LOVE, The
Pop-rock band formed in Camberwall, London, England: Guy Chadwick (vocals, guitar), Simon Walker (guitar), Chris Groothuizen (bass) and Pete Evans (drums).

9/17/88	156	7	1 The House Of Love		Relativity 8245
5/5/90	148	8	2 The House Of Love		Fontana 842293
			above 2 are different albums		

HOUSE OF PAIN
White hip-hop group from Los Angeles, California: Erik Schrody, Dan O'Connor and Leor DiMant. Schrody later recorded solo as **Everlast**. All three were also members of **La Coka Nostra**.

8/15/92	14	58	▲	1 House Of Pain		Tommy Boy 1056
7/16/94	12	15	●	2 Same As It Ever Was		Tommy Boy 1089
11/9/96	47	4		3 Truth Crushed To Earth Shall Rise Again		Tommy Boy 1161

HOUSER, Randy
Born Shawn Randolph Houser in Lake, Mississippi. Country singer/songwriter/guitarist.

12/6/08	101	19	1 Anything Goes		Universal South 011699

HOUSTON
Born Houston Summers on 10/26/1983 in Los Angeles, California. Male R&B singer/songwriter.

8/28/04	14	8	●	1 It's Already Written		Capitol 90432

HOUSTON, Cissy
Born Emily Drinkard on 9/30/1933 in Newark, New Jersey. R&B singer. Mother of **Whitney Houston**.

9/16/78	205	6	1 Think It Over		Private Stock 7015

HOUSTON, David
Born on 12/9/1938 in Bossier City, Louisiana. Died of a brain aneurysm on 11/30/1993 (age 54). Country singer/songwriter/guitarist.

AWARD: OPRY: 1972

8/6/66	57	20	1 Almost Persuaded		Epic 26213
9/13/69	143	5	2 David		Epic 26482
4/18/70	194	2	3 Baby, Baby		Epic 26539
9/26/70	170	3	4 Wonders Of The Wine		Epic 30108
6/12/71	218	2	5 A Woman Always Knows		Epic 30657

HOUSTON, Marques
Born on 8/4/1981 in Los Angeles, California. R&B singer. Member of **Immature**.

11/8/03	18	9	1 MH		T.U.G. 62935
6/11/05	13	22	2 Naked		T.U.G. 004696
4/7/07	5	10	3 Veteran		T.U.G. 007925
10/17/09	65	2	4 Mr. Houston		Musicworks 001

HOUSTON, Thelma
Born on 5/7/1946 in Leland, Mississippi. R&B singer/actress.

12/25/76+	11	37	1 Any Way You Like It		Tamla 345
6/18/77	53	12	2 Thelma & Jerry		Motown 887
			THELMA HOUSTON & JERRY BUTLER		
11/12/77	64	11	3 The Devil In Me		Tamla 358
7/21/79	204	3	4 Ride To The Rainbow		Tamla 365
2/2/80	201	4	5 Breakwater Cat		RCA Victor 3500
5/30/81	144	6	6 Never Gonna Be Another One		RCA Victor 3842

Billboard			R I A A	ARTIST		
DEBUT	PEAK	WKS		Album Title	Catalog	Label & Number

HOUSTON, Whitney
1990s: #37 / All-Time: #142
Born on 8/9/1963 in Newark, New Jersey. R&B singer/actress. Daughter of **Cissy Houston** and cousin of **Dionne Warwick**. Former fashion model. Married to **Bobby Brown** from 1992-2007. Starred in the movies *The Bodyguard*, *Waiting To Exhale* and *The Preacher's Wife*.

3/30/85+	❶[14]	163	▲[13]	1 Whitney Houston		Arista 8212
				RS500 #254		
6/27/87	❶[11]	85	▲[9]	2 Whitney		Arista 8405
11/24/90	3[1]	51	▲[4]	3 I'm Your Baby Tonight		Arista 8616
12/5/92	❶[20]	141	▲[17]	4 The Bodyguard	Cat:#17/16 [S]	Arista 18699
				Grammy: Album of the Year		
12/14/96	3[2]	38	▲[3]	5 The Preacher's Wife	[S]	Arista 18951
12/5/98	13	75	▲[4]	6 My Love Is Your Love		Arista 19037
6/3/00	5	29	▲[3]	7 The Greatest Hits	Cat:#25/4 [G]	Arista 14626 [2]
12/28/02	9	24	▲	8 Just Whitney...		Arista 14747
12/6/03	49	6		9 One Wish The Holiday Album	[X]	Arista 50996
				Christmas charts: 5/'03, 38/'04, 50/'05, 50/'09		
9/19/09	❶[1]	25	▲	10 I Look To You		Arista 10033

HOWARD, Adina
Born on 11/14/1974 in Grand Rapids, Michigan. Female R&B singer.

3/18/95	39	26	●	1 Do You Wanna Ride?		Mecca Don 61757

HOWARD, George
Born on 9/15/1956 in Philadelphia, Pennsylvania. Died of cancer on 3/22/1998 (age 41). Jazz saxophonist.

9/1/84	178	4		1 Steppin' Out	[I]	TBA 201
7/27/85	169	4		2 Dancing In The Sun	[I]	TBA 205
4/19/86	142	11		3 Love Will Follow	[I]	TBA 210
12/27/86+	109	26		4 A Nice Place To Be	[I]	MCA 5855
6/18/88	109	8		5 Reflections	[I]	MCA 42145
3/24/90	128	11		6 Personal	[I]	MCA 6335
3/16/91	131	10		7 Love And Understanding	[I]	GRP 9629
5/2/92	137	9		8 Do I Ever Cross Your Mind	[I]	GRP 9669
8/20/94	180	4		9 A Home Far Away	[I]	GRP 9780

HOWARD, Miki
Born on 9/30/1961 in Chicago, Illinois. R&B singer/actress. Portrayed **Billie Holiday** in the 1992 movie *Malcolm X*.

3/14/87	171	6		1 Come Share My Love		Atlantic 81688
2/20/88	145	16		2 Love Confessions		Atlantic 81810
3/3/90	112	16		3 Miki Howard		Atlantic 82024
10/3/92	110	11		4 Femme Fatale		Giant 24452

HOWARD, Rebecca Lynn
Born on 4/24/1979 in Salyersville, Kentucky. Country singer/songwriter.

9/28/02	29	11		1 Forgive		MCA Nashville 170288

HOWARD, Terrence
Born on 3/11/1969 in Chicago, Illinois; raised in Cleveland, Ohio. R&B singer/actor/rapper. Acted in several movies.

9/20/08	31	3		1 Shine Through It		Gentry 09596

HOWE, Steve
Born on 4/8/1947 in London, England. Rock guitarist. Member of **Yes**, **Asia** and **GTR**.

12/20/75+	63	11		1 Beginnings		Atlantic 18154
2/16/80	164	4		2 The Steve Howe Album	[I]	Atlantic 19243

HOWLIN' WOLF
Born Chester Arthur Burnett on 6/10/1910 in West Point, Mississippi. Died of cancer on 1/10/1976 (age 65). Legendary blues singer/guitarist.
AWARD: R&R Hall of Fame: 1991 (Early Influence)

8/21/71	79	15		1 The London Howlin' Wolf Sessions		Chess 60008

~ ~ ~ ~ ~ ~ ~ ~ ~ ~ **NON-CHARTED ALBUMS** ~ ~ ~ ~ ~ ~ ~ ~ ~ ~ ~
1959 **Moanin' In The Moonlight**   1962 **Howlin Wolf**
RS500 #153   *RS500 #223*

H-TOWN
R&B vocal trio from Houston, Texas: twin brothers Solomon "Shazam" Connor and Delando "Dino" Conner, with cousin Darryl "G.I." Jackson. Dino Connor died in a car crash on 1/28/2003 (age 28).

4/24/93	16	27	▲	1 Fever For Da Flavor		Luke 126
11/26/94+	98	23	●	2 Beggin' After Dark		Luke 212
11/15/97	53	11		3 Ladies Edition		Relativity 1596

HUANG, Ying
Born on 11/8/1968 in Shanghai, China. Female soprano opera singer/actress. Starred in the 1995 movie *Madame Butterfly*.

12/20/97	192	2		1 Merry Christmas From Vienna .... [X-L]		Sony Classical 62970

PLACIDO DOMINGO / YING HUANG / MICHAEL BOLTON
recorded on 12/16/1996 at the Austria Center in Vienna

HUBBARD, Freddie
Born on 4/7/1938 in Indianapolis, Indiana. Died of a heart attack on 12/29/2008 (age 70). Jazz trumpeter.

3/10/73	165	7		1 Sky Dive.. [I]		CTI 6018
1/19/74	186	5		2 Keep Your Soul Together .... [I]		CTI 6036
1/11/75	127	7		3 The Baddest Hubbard... [I-K]		CTI 6047
5/17/75	167	4		4 Polar AC .... [I]		CTI 6056
9/14/74	153	7		5 High Energy .... [I]		Columbia 33048
7/19/75	149	6		6 Liquid Love .... [I]		Columbia 33556
9/4/76	85	9		7 Windjammer .... [I]		Columbia 34166
10/29/77	149	6		8 Bundle Of Joy .... [I]		Columbia 34902
7/15/78	131	5		9 Super Blue .... [I]		Columbia 35386

HUDGENS, Vanessa
Born on 12/14/1988 in Salinas, California. Teen actress/singer. Played "Gabriella Montez" in the TV movie **High School Musical**.

10/14/06	24	32	●	1 V		Hollywood 162638
7/19/08	23	8		2 Identified		Hollywood 002052

HUDSON, David
Born in Miami, Florida. R&B singer.

8/23/80	184	2		1 To You Honey, Honey With Love..		Alston 4412

HUDSON, Jennifer
Born on 9/12/1981 in Chicago, Illinois. R&B singer/actress. Placed sixth in voting on the third season of *American Idol*. Won the Best Supporting Actress Oscar for playing "Effie White" in the 2006 movie *Dreamgirls*.

10/18/08	2[1]	37	●	1 Jennifer Hudson		Arista 06303

Grammy: R&B Album

HUDSON AND LANDRY
Comedy duo from Los Angeles, California: "Emperor" Bob Hudson (born on 10/7/1929; died on 9/20/1997, age 67) and Ron Landry (born on 10/24/1934; died on 9/16/2002, age 67). Both were popular radio DJs.

4/10/71	30	26		1 Hanging In There .... [C]		Dore 324
11/27/71+	33	23		2 Losing Their Heads .... [C]		Dore 326
1/6/73	147	9		3 Right-Off! .... [C]		Dore 329

HUDSON BROTHERS
Pop vocal trio from Portland, Oregon: Bill, Brett and Mark Hudson. Hosted own TV variety show during the summer of 1974; also hosted kiddie TV show *The Hudson Brothers Razzle Dazzle Comedy Show*. Bill was married to actress Goldie Hawn from 1976-79; their daughter is actress Kate Hudson.

11/30/74	179	4		1 Totally Out Of Control		Rocket 460
12/7/74	176	4		2 Hollywood Situation...		Casablanca 7004
12/13/75+	165	6		3 Ba-Fa		Rocket 2169

HUES CORPORATION, The
R&B-disco vocal trio from Los Angeles, California: H. Ann Kelly, Bernard Henderson and Fleming Williams. Group appeared in the 1972 movie *Blacula*.

6/29/74	20	18		1 Freedom For The Stallion		RCA Victor 0323
7/5/75	147	5		2 Love Corporation		RCA Victor 0938

HUEY
Born Lawrence Franks on 1/1/1989 in Kinloch, Missouri. Male rapper.

7/7/07	26	5		1 Notebook Paper		Hitz Committee 08534

HUFF, Leon
Born on 4/8/1942 in Camden, New Jersey. R&B keyboardist/producer/songwriter. Formed Philadelphia International Records with partner Kenny Gamble in 1971.

AWARD: R&R Hall of Fame: 2008 (Non-Performer)

11/8/80	204	1		1 Here To Create Music .... [I]		Philadelphia I. 36758

HUGH, Grayson
Born in Hartford, Connecticut. "Blue-eyed soul" singer/songwriter/pianist.

10/15/88+	71	24		1 Blind To Reason		RCA 7661

HUGO & LUIGI
Duo of producers/songwriters/label executives: Hugo Peretti (born on 12/6/1916 in Italy; died on 5/1/1986, age 69) and Luigi Creatore (born on 12/21/1920 in Manhattan, New York). Owned record labels Roulette and Avco/Embassy.

4/27/63	14	13		1 The Cascading Voices Of The Hugo & Luigi Chorus............................		RCA Victor 2641
10/26/63	125	2		2 Let's Fall In Love		RCA Victor 2717

HULLABALLOOS, The
Rock and roll band from England: Ricky Knight (vocals, guitar), Andy Woonton (guitar), Geoff Mortimer (bass) and Harry Dunn (drums).

~ ~ ~ ~ ~ ~ ~ ~ ~ ~ ~ **NON-CHARTED ALBUM** ~ ~ ~ ~ ~ ~ ~ ~ ~ ~ ~
1965 **England's Newest Singing Sensations**

Billboard			R I A A	ARTIST		
DEBUT	PEAK	WKS		Album Title	Catalog	Label & Number

HUM
Rock band from Champaign, Illinois: Matt Talbott (vocals), Tim Lash (guitar), Jeff Dimpsey (bass) and Bryan St. Pere (drums).

7/15/95	105	12		1 You'd Prefer An Astronaut		RCA 66577
2/14/98	150	1		2 Downward Is Heavenward		RCA 67446

HUMAN ABSTRACT, The
Hard-rock band from Los Angeles, California: Andrew Tapley (vocals, guitar), Dean Herrera (guitar), Henry Selva (bass) and Brett Powell (drums).

9/6/08	164	1		1 Midheaven..		Hopeless 697

HUMAN BEINZ, The
Rock and roll band from Youngstown, Ohio: Dick Belly (vocals, guitar), Joe Markulin (guitar), John Pachuta (bass) and Mike Tatum (drums).

3/9/68	65	10		1 Nobody But Me..		Capitol 2906

HUMAN LEAGUE, The
Electro-pop trio from Sheffield, England: lead singer/synthesist **Philip Oakey**, with female vocalists Joanne Catherall and Susanne Sulley. Early members Martyn Ware and Ian Craig Marsh left to form **Heaven 17**.

2/27/82	3[3]	38	●	1 Dare		A&M 4892
9/18/82	135	7		2 Love And Dancing .... [I]		A&M 3209
				THE LEAGUE UNLIMITED ORCHESTRA		
				instrumental versions of songs from album #1 above		
6/18/83	22	29		3 Fascination!.. [EP]		A&M 2501
6/16/84	62	13		4 Hysteria		A&M 4923
10/4/86	24	25		5 Crash		A&M 5129

HUMBLE PIE
Hard-rock band from England: **Peter Frampton** (vocals, guitar), **Steve Marriott** (vocals, guitar; **Small Faces**), Greg Ridley (bass; **Spooky Tooth**) and Jerry Shirley (drums). Frampton left in October 1971; replaced by Clem Clempson (**Rough Diamond**). Disbanded in 1975. Reunited from 1980-81 with Marriott, Shirley, Bobby Tench (guitar) and Anthony Jones (bass). Shirley later joined **Fastway**. Marriott died in a house fire on 4/20/1991 (age 44).

5/8/71	118	23		1 Rock On		A&M 4301
11/6/71	21	32	●	2 Performance-Rockin' The Fillmore .... [L]		A&M 3506 [2]
4/1/72	6	34	●	3 Smokin'		A&M 4342
9/30/72	37	20		4 Lost And Found .... [E]		A&M 3513 [2]
3/24/73	13	21		5 Eat It		A&M 3701 [2]
3/9/74	52	14		6 Thunderbox		A&M 3611
4/26/75	100	8		7 Street Rats		A&M 4514
4/12/80	60	14		8 On To Victory...		Atco 122
5/9/81	154	6		9 Go For The Throat..		Atco 131

HUMMINGBIRD
Jazz-rock band formed in England: Bobby Tench (guitar), Bernie Holland (guitar), Max Middleton (keyboards), Clive Chaman (bass) and Bernard "Pretty" Purdie (drums).

9/4/76	206	5		1 We Can't Go On Like This .... [I]		A&M 4595

HUMPERDINCK, Engelbert   **All-Time: #225**
Born Arnold Dorsey on 5/2/1936 in Madras, India; raised in Leicester, England. Pop singer. First recorded for Decca in 1958. Met **Tom Jones**'s manager, Gordon Mills, in 1965, who suggested his name change to Engelbert Humperdinck (a famous German opera composer). Starred in his own musical variety TV series in 1970.

6/17/67	7	118	●	1 Release Me		Parrot 71012
12/23/67+	10	60	●	2 The Last Waltz		Parrot 71015
8/24/68	12	78	●	3 A Man Without Love..		Parrot 71022
3/22/69	12	33	●	4 Engelbert..		Parrot 71026
1/3/70	5	41	●	5 Engelbert Humperdinck		Parrot 71030
7/11/70	19	40	●	6 We Made It Happen		Parrot 71038
2/20/71	22	24	●	7 Sweetheart		Parrot 71043
9/11/71	25	15	●	8 Another Time, Another Place...............................		Parrot 71048
1/1/72	45	13		9 Live At The Riviera, Las Vegas .... [L]		Parrot 71051
8/19/72	72	14		10 In Time...		Parrot 71056
8/11/73	113	10		11 King Of Hearts..		Parrot 71061
12/21/74+	103	14		12 His Greatest Hits...................................... [G]		Parrot 71067
11/27/76+	17	28	▲[2]	13 After The Lovin'		Epic 34381
6/4/77	201	10		14 Engelbert Sings For You .... [K]		London 688 [2]
7/16/77	167	5		15 Miracles by Engelbert Humperdinck		Epic 34730
12/24/77+	156	4	●	16 Christmas Tyme .... [X]		Epic 35031
5/19/79	164	4		17 This Moment In Time		Epic 35791
6/20/81	203	5		18 Don't You Love Me Anymore?		Epic 37128
11/25/95	23[X]	1		19 The Magic of Christmas .... [X]		Core 9462
				ENGELBERT		

HUMPHREY, Bobbi
Born Barbara Ann Humphrey on 4/25/1950 in Dallas, Texas. Jazz flutist.

3/30/74	84	21	1 Blacks and Blues	[I]	Blue Note 142
12/7/74+	30	18	2 Satin Doll		Blue Note 344
11/29/75	133	5	3 Fancy Dancer	[I]	Blue Note 550
11/6/76	208	4	4 Bobbi Humphrey's Best	[G-I]	Blue Note 699
7/1/78	89	14	5 Freestyle		Epic 35338

HUMPHREY, Paul, & His Cool Aid Chemists
Born on 10/12/1935 in Detroit, Michigan. R&B drummer. The Cool Aid Chemists were Clarence MacDonald, **David T. Walker** and Bill Upchurch.

6/12/71	170	6	1 Paul Humphrey & The Cool Aid Chemists	[I]	Lizard 20106

HUNG, William
Born on 1/13/1983 in Hong Kong, China. Gained notoriety after his failed audition on TV's *American Idol*.

4/24/04	34	10	1 Inspiration		Koch 9579

HUNT, Van
Born on 3/8/1977 in Dayton, Ohio; later based in Atlanta, Georgia. Male R&B singer.

4/22/06	123	1	1 On The Jungle Floor		Capitol 74851

HUNTER, Ian
Born on 6/3/1939 in Oswestry, England. Rock singer/songwriter/guitarist. Leader of **Mott The Hoople** from 1969-74.

5/17/75	50	14	1 Ian Hunter		Columbia 33480
5/22/76	177	7	2 All-American Alien Boy		Columbia 34142
4/28/79	35	24	3 You're Never Alone With A Schizophrenic		Chrysalis 1214
11/3/79	202	6	4 Shades Of Ian Hunter (The Ballad Of Ian Hunter & Mott The Hoople)	[K]	Columbia 36251 [2]
			record 1: **Mott The Hoople**; record 2: solo Ian Hunter		
4/26/80	69	17	5 Ian Hunter Live/Welcome To The Club	[L]	Chrysalis 1269 [2]
8/29/81	62	11	6 Short Back N' Sides		Chrysalis 1326
8/6/83	125	8	7 All Of The Good Ones Are Taken		Columbia 38628
10/28/89+	157	20	8 Y U I ORTA		Mercury 838973
			IAN HUNTER & MICK RONSON		

HUNTER, Ivory Joe
Born on 10/10/1914 in Kirbyville, Texas. Died of cancer on 11/8/1974 (age 60). R&B singer/songwriter/pianist.

~ ~ ~ ~ ~ ~ ~ ~ ~ **NON-CHARTED ALBUMS** ~ ~ ~ ~ ~ ~ ~ ~ ~ ~ ~

1957 **I Get That Lonesome Feeling** *[MGM label]*
1957 **Ivory Joe Hunter** *[Atlantic label]*
1958 **Ivory Joe Hunter Sings Sixteen Of His Greatest Hits** *[King label]*

HUNTER, James
Born on 10/2/1962 in Colchester, Essex, England. "Blue-eyed soul" singer/songwriter.

6/28/08	197	1	1 The Hard Way		Go 30669

HUNTER, John
Born in Chicago, Illinois. Rock singer/keyboardist/songwriter.

2/9/85	148	9	1 Famous At Night		Private I 39626

HUNTER, Robert
Born on 6/23/1941 in San Luis Obispo, California. Rock singer/songwriter/guitarist. Non-performing lyricist for the **Grateful Dead**.

7/6/74	204	4	1 Tales Of The Great Rum Runners		Round 101

HUNTLEY, Chet, & David Brinkley
Co-anchors of TV's *NBC Nightly News* from 1955-70. Brinkley was born on 7/10/1920 in Wilmington, North Carolina; died on 6/11/2003 (age 82). Huntley was born on 12/10/1911 in Cardwell, Montana; died on 3/20/1974 (age 62).

3/14/64	115	7	1 A Time To Keep: 1963	[T]	RCA Victor 1088
			a recall of the voices and events of 1963		

HURRICANE
Hard-rock band from Los Angeles, California: Kelly Hansen (vocals), Robert Sarzo (guitar), Tony Cavazo (bass) and Jay Schellen (drums). Sarzo is the brother of **Whitesnake**'s Rudy Sarzo. Cavazo is the brother of **Quiet Riot**'s Carlos Cavazo. Sarzo left the band in 1989; replaced by Doug Aldrich.

4/30/88	92	36	1 Over The Edge		Enigma 73320
4/14/90	125	10	2 Slave To The Thrill		Enigma 73511

HURRICANE CHRIS
Born Christopher Dooley in 1989 in Shreveport, Louisiana. Male rapper.

11/10/07	24	10	1 51/50 Ratchet		Polo Grounds 18697

HURT
Alternative-rock band from Culpepper, Virginia: J. Loren Wince (vocals, guitar), Paul Spatola (guitar), Josh Ansley (bass) and Evan Johns (drums).

4/8/06	175	1	1 Vol. I		Capitol 41137
10/13/07	101	1	2 Vol. II		Capitol 94656
4/25/09	112	2	3 Goodbye To The Machine		Amusement 1485243

HUSH SOUND, The
Alternative-rock band from Lisle, Illinois: Bob Morris (vocals, guitar), Greta Salpeter (keyboards), Mike LeBlanc (bass) and Darren Wilson (drums).

4/5/08	75	2	1 Goodbye Blues		Decaydance 424956

HUSKER DU
Punk-rock trio from Minneapolis, Minnesota: **Bob Mould** (vocals, guitar), Greg Norton (bass) and Grant Hart (drums). Mould later formed **Sugar**.

4/12/86	140	10	1 Candy Apple Grey		Warner 25385
2/14/87	117	10	2 Warehouse: Songs And Stories		Warner 25544 [2]

~ ~ ~ ~ ~ ~ ~ ~ ~ ~ **NON-CHARTED ALBUM** ~ ~ ~ ~ ~ ~ ~ ~ ~ ~
1985 **New Day Rising**
RS500 #495

HUTCH, Willie
Born Willie Hutchinson on 12/6/1944 in Los Angeles, California; raised in Dallas, Texas. Died on 9/19/2005 (age 60). R&B producer/songwriter. Uncle of Don Hutchinson of **Above The Law**.

6/2/73	114	16	1 The Mack	[S]	Motown 766
10/13/73	183	6	2 Fully Exposed		Motown 784
5/18/74	179	4	3 Foxy Brown	[S]	Motown 811
11/15/75	150	6	4 Ode To My Lady		Motown 838
4/3/76	163	6	5 Concert In Blues		Motown 854

HUTCHENCE, Michael
Born on 1/22/1960 in Sydney, Australia. Committed suicide on 11/22/1997 (age 37). Lead singer of **INXS**.

3/11/00	200	1	1 Michael Hutchence		V2 27064

recorded shortly before his death in 1997

HUTCHINSON, Eric
Born on 9/8/1980 in Washington DC; raised in Takoma Park, Maryland. Pop-rock singer/songwriter.

9/22/07	134	5	1 Sounds Like This		Let's Break Records 0158

HUTSON, Leroy
Born on 6/4/1945 in Newark, New Jersey. R&B singer. Member of **The Impressions** from 1971-73.

3/6/76	170	8	1 Feel The Spirit		Curtom 5010

HYDE, Paul, And The Payolas
Pop-rock band from Canada: Paul Hyde (vocals), Bob Rock (guitar), Alex Boynton (bass) and Chris Taylor (drums). Hyde and Rock later recorded as the duo **Rock and Hyde**.

6/8/85	144	10	1 Here's The World For Ya		A&M 5025

HYDRA
Southern-rock band from Georgia: Wayne Bruce (vocals), Spencer Kirkpatrick (guitar), Orville Davis (bass) and Steve Pace (drums).

9/14/74	202	5	1 Hydra		Capricorn 0130
9/27/75	207	2	2 Land Of Money		Capricorn 0157

HYLAND, Brian
Born on 11/12/1943 in Queens, New York. Pop singer.

4/19/69	160	5	1 Tragedy/A Million To One		Dot 25926
1/30/71	171	4	2 Brian Hyland		Uni 73097

produced by **Del Shannon**

~ ~ ~ ~ ~ ~ ~ ~ ~ ~ **NON-CHARTED ALBUMS** ~ ~ ~ ~ ~ ~ ~ ~ ~ ~
1960 **The Bashful Blond**   1964 **Here's To Our Love**
1961 **Let Me Belong To You**   1965 **Rockin' Folk**
1962 **Sealed With A Kiss**   1966 **The Joker Went Wild/Run Run Look And See**

HYMAN, Dick
Born on 3/8/1927 in New York City, New York. Pianist/conductor/arranger.

11/25/57	21	2	1 60 Great All Time Songs, Vol. 3	[I]	MGM 3537
11/9/63	117	7	2 Electrodynamics	[I]	Command 856
4/4/64	132	5	3 Fabulous	[I]	Command 862
4/27/68	179	2	4 Mirrors - Reflections Of Today	[I]	Command 924
			DICK HYMAN AND "THE GROUP"		
4/19/69	30	30	5 Moog - The Electric Eclectics Of Dick Hyman	[I]	Command 938
9/27/69	110	11	6 The Age Of Electronicus	[I]	Command 946

HYMAN, Phyllis
Born on 7/6/1950 in Philadelphia, Pennsylvania; raised in Pittsburgh, Pennsylvania. Committed suicide on 6/30/1995 (age 44). R&B-dance singer/actress/model. Starred in the Broadway musical *Sophisticated Ladies*.

4/30/77	107	14	1 Phyllis Hyman		Buddah 5681
2/3/79	70	17	2 Somewhere In My Lifetime		Arista 4202
12/8/79+	50	21	3 You Know How To Love Me		Arista 9509
8/1/81	57	13	4 Can't We Fall In Love Again		Arista 9544
6/18/83	112	12	5 Goddess Of Love		Arista 8021
10/11/86+	78	41	6 Living All Alone		Philadelphia Int'l. 53029
8/10/91	117	12	7 Prime Of My Life		Philadelphia Int'l. 11006
11/25/95	67	9	8 I Refuse To Be Lonely		Philadelphia Int'l. 11040

Billboard			R I A A	ARTIST		
DEBUT	PEAK	WKS		Album Title	Catalog	Label & Number

HYPNOTIZE CAMP POSSE
Gathering of rappers from Memphis, Tennessee: **Gangsta Boo**, **Project Pat**, **Three 6 Mafia** and T-Rock.

2/12/00	36	15		1 Three 6 Mafia Presents Hypnotize Camp Posse		Hypnotize Minds 1883

I

IAN, Janis
Born Janis Eddy Fink on 4/7/1951 in Brooklyn, New York. Folk singer/songwriter/pianist/guitarist.

6/17/67	29	28		1 Janis Ian...		Verve Forecast 3017
12/30/67+	179	5		2 For All The Seasons Of Your Mind		Verve Forecast 3024
4/10/71	223	2		3 Present Company...		Capitol 683
6/1/74+	83	20		4 Stars		Columbia 32857
3/22/75	❶¹	64	▲	5 Between The Lines		Columbia 33394
1/24/76	12	19		6 Aftertones...		Columbia 33919
1/29/77	45	12		7 Miracle Row...		Columbia 34440
9/16/78	120	11		8 Janis Ian..		Columbia 35325
7/4/81	156	3		9 Restless Eyes..		Columbia 37360

IAN & SYLVIA
Folk duo from Canada: Ian Tyson (born on 9/25/1933 in Victoria, British Columbia) and wife Sylvia Fricker (born on 9/19/1940 in Chatham, Ontario). Began performing together in 1959. Married from 1964-73.

9/28/63	115	6		1 Four Strong Winds..		Vanguard 79133
9/5/64	70	12		2 Northern Journey		Vanguard 79154
6/19/65	77	18		3 Early Morning Rain		Vanguard 79175
5/28/66	142	6		4 Play One More		Vanguard 79215
4/1/67	130	7		5 So Much For Dreaming		Vanguard 79241
7/8/67	148	10		6 Lovin' Sound...		MGM 4388
9/11/71	201	4		7 Ian & Sylvia...		Columbia 30736

ICE CUBE   1990s: #34 / All-Time: #261
Born O'Shea Jackson on 6/15/1969 in Los Angeles, California. Male rapper/actor. Former member of **N.W.A.** Acted in several movies. Cousin of **Del The Funkyhomosapien**.

6/2/90	19	26	▲	1 AmeriKKKa's Most Wanted		Priority 57120
1/5/91	34	43	▲	2 Kill At Will .... [EP]		Priority 7230
11/16/91	2¹	33	▲	3 Death Certificate		Priority 57155
12/5/92	❶¹	52	▲²	4 The Predator		Priority 57185
12/25/93	5	48	▲	5 Lethal Injection		Priority 53876
12/10/94	19	24	●	6 Bootlegs & B-Sides .... [K]		Priority 53921
1/3/98	116	14		7 Featuring...Ice Cube .... [K]		Priority 51037
12/5/98	7	20	▲	8 War & Peace Vol. 1 (The War Disc)		Priority 50700
4/8/00	3¹	25	●	9 War & Peace Vol. 2 (The Peace Disc)		Best Side 50015
12/22/01	54	16		10 Greatest Hits... [G]		Priority 29091
6/24/06	4	21	●	11 Laugh Now, Cry Later		Lench Mob 65939
9/22/07	169	1		12 In The Movies .... [K]		Priority 97253
9/6/08	5	11		13 Raw Footage		Lench Mob 34635

ICED EARTH
Hard-rock band from Tampa, Florida: Tim Owens (vocals), Jon Schaffer (guitar), James MacDonough (bass) and Richard Christy (drums).

1/31/04	145	1		1 The Glorious Burden		Steamhammer 74970 [2]
9/29/07	79	2		2 Framing Armageddon		Steamhammer 9818
9/27/08	79	1		3 The Crucible Of Man		Steamhammer 9159

ICEHOUSE
Rock band formed in Sydney, Australia: Iva Davies (vocals, guitar), Anthony Smith (keyboards), Keith Welsh (bass) and John Lloyd (drums). Numerous personnel changes through the 1980s, with Davies the only constant. Group name is Australian slang for an insane asylum.

7/25/81	82	15		1 Icehouse..		Chrysalis 1350
10/9/82	129	6		2 Primitive Man..		Chrysalis 1390
5/24/86	55	24		3 Measure For Measure		Chrysalis 41527
10/17/87+	43	44		4 Man Of Colours		Chrysalis 41592

ICE-T
Born Tracy Morrow on 2/16/1958 in Newark, New Jersey; raised in Los Angeles, California. Male rapper/actor. Acted in several movies; plays "Fin Tutuola" on TV's *Law & Order: Special Victims Unit*. Formed band **Body Count**.

8/15/87	93	27	●	1 Rhyme Pays..		Sire 25602
10/1/88	35	33	▲	2 Power		Sire 25765
10/28/89	37	28	●	3 Freedom Of Speech...Just Watch What You Say		Sire 26028
6/1/91	15	33	●	4 O.G. Original Gangster		Sire 26492
4/10/93	14	11	●	5 Home Invasion..		Rhyme Syndicate 53858
6/22/96	89	4		6 VI: Return Of The Real		Rhyme Syndicate 53933

ICICLE WORKS
Rock trio from Liverpool, England: Robert Ian McNabb (vocals, guitar), Chris Layhe (bass) and Chris Sharrock (drums).

4/21/84	40	18		1 Icicle Works	Arista 8202

ICON
Rock band from Phoenix, Arizona: Stephen Clifford (vocals), Dan Wexler (guitar), John Aquilino (guitar), Tracy Wallach (bass) and Pat Dixon (drums).

6/9/84	190	2		1 Icon...	Capitol 12336

ICONZ
Rap group from Miami, Florida: Luc Duc, Stage McCloud, Bull Dog, Chapter, Tony Manshino, Screwface and Supastar.

3/3/01	64	10		1 Street Money	Landmark 62617

IDEAL
R&B vocal group from Houston, Texas: J-Dante, Maverick, PZ and Swab.

10/9/99+	83	37	●	1 Ideal	Noontime 47882

IDES OF MARCH, The
Rock band from Chicago, Illinois: Jim Peterik (vocals, guitar), Ray Herr (guitar), Larry Millas (keyboards), John Larson and Chuck Soumar (horns), Bob Bergland (bass) and Mike Borch (drums). Group named after a line in Shakespeare's *Julis Caesar*. Peterik later formed **Survivor**.

6/27/70	55	12		1 Vehicle..	Warner 1863
7/24/71	207	5		2 Common Bond	Warner 1896

IDOL, Billy
All-Time: #373
Born William Broad on 11/30/1955 in Stanmore, Middlesex, England. Leader of the London punk band Generation X from 1977-81. Suffered serious leg injuries in a motorcycle crash on 2/6/1990. Appeared in the movies *The Doors* and *The Wedding Singer*.

10/24/81+	71	68		1 Don't Stop .... [EP]	Chrysalis 4000
7/31/82+	45	104	●	2 Billy Idol	Chrysalis 41377
12/3/83+	6	82	▲²	3 Rebel Yell	Chrysalis 41450
11/8/86	6	47	▲	4 Whiplash Smile	Chrysalis 41514
10/10/87	10	29	▲	5 Vital Idol [K]	Chrysalis 41620
5/19/90	11	39	▲	6 Charmed Life	Chrysalis 21735
7/17/93	48	7		7 Cyberpunk	Chrysalis 26000
4/14/01	74	26	▲	8 Greatest Hits .... Cat:#32/15 [G]	Chrysalis 28812
4/9/05	46	5		9 Devil's Playground	CS 84735
7/12/08	73	2		10 Idolize Yourself: The Very Best Of Billy Idol .... [G]	Capitol 15140

IF
Jazz-rock band from England: J.W. Hodkinson (vocals), Terry Smith (guitar), Dick Morrissey and Dave Quincy (reeds), John Mealing (keyboards), Jim Richardson (bass) and Dennis Elliot (drums).

10/31/70	187	2		1 If	Capitol 539
1/30/71	203	8		2 If 2	Capitol 676
9/25/71	171	3		3 If 3	Capitol 820
10/28/72	195	4		4 Waterfall	Metromedia 1057

IFIELD, Frank — see BEATLES, The

IGLESIAS, Enrique
All-Time: #388
Born on 5/8/1975 in Madrid, Spain; raised in Miami, Florida. Latin singer. Son of **Julio Iglesias**.

12/11/99	33	49	▲	1 Enrique...	Interscope 490540
11/17/01	2¹	64	▲³	2 Escape	Interscope 493148
12/13/03	31	10		3 Seven	Interscope 001711
6/30/07	17	16		4 Insomniac	Interscope 008964
				FOREIGN LANGUAGE ALBUMS:	
5/25/96	148	18	▲	5 Enrique Iglesias...	Fonovisa 0506
				Grammy: Latin Pop Vocal	
2/15/97	33	18	▲	6 Vivir	Fonovisa 0001
10/10/98	64	16	●	7 Cosas Del Amor	Fonovisa 80002
10/5/02	12	8	●	8 Quizas	Universal Latino 064385
				GREATEST HITS & COMPILATIONS:	
6/19/99	65	22	●	9 Bailamos - Greatest Hits .... [F]	Fonovisa 0517
3/4/00	175	2	●	10 The Best Hits .... [F]	Fonovisa 0518
4/12/08	18	32		11 95/08... [F]	Universal Latino 010974
11/29/08	80	2		12 Greatest Hits	Interscope 012265

IGLESIAS, Julio
Born on 9/23/1943 in Madrid, Spain. Latin singer. Father of **Enrique Iglesias**.

AWARD: CMA: Vocal Duo (w/ Willie Nelson) 1984

9/1/84	5	34	▲⁴	1 1100 Bel Air Place	Columbia 39157
6/4/88	52	17	●	2 Non Stop	Columbia 40995
12/1/90+	37	31	●	3 Starry Night	Columbia 46857
6/4/94	30	19	●	4 Crazy	Columbia 57584
10/7/06	43	3		5 Romantic Classics	Burgundy 78380

IGLESIAS, Julio — cont'd
FOREIGN LANGUAGE ALBUMS:

4/2/83	32	89	▲²	6 Julio		Columbia 38640
8/25/84	159	9		7 In Concert .... [L]		Columbia 39570 [2]
9/1/84	179	6	●	8 Hey!		Columbia 39567
9/1/84	181	6		9 From A Child To A Woman..............................		Columbia 39569
9/15/84	191	4		10 Moments		Columbia 39568
				above 3 recorded from 1980-82		
8/24/85	92	12	●	11 Libra		Columbia 40180
6/6/92	186	2		12 Calor		Sony Discos 80763
12/7/96+	81	18	●	13 Tango		Columbia 67899

IHA, James
Born on 3/26/1968 in Elk Grove, Illinois. Rock guitarist. Member of **Smashing Pumpkins** and **Tinted Windows**.

2/28/98	171	1	1 Let It Come Down		Virgin 45411

IL DIVO
Classical vocal group formed in London, England: David Miller (from America), Sebastien Izambard (from France), Urs Buhler (from Switzerland) and Carlos Martin (from Spain). Formed by *American Idol's* Simon Cowell after a two year search. Group sings mainly in Italian.

5/7/05	4	84	▲	1 Il Divo	Cat:#4/9 [F]	Syco 93963
11/12/05	14	10	▲	2 The Christmas Collection .... Cat:❶³/30 [X]		Syco 97715
				Christmas charts: 1/'05, 2/'06, 13/'07, 14/'08, 8/'09		
2/11/06	❶¹	40	●	3 Ancora [F]		Syco 76914
12/9/06	6	22	▲	4 Siempre [F]		Syco 02673
12/6/08	5	29	●	5 The Promise [F]		Syco 39968
12/5/09	86	5		6 The Christmas Collection .... [X-R]		Syco 97715

ILL AL SKRATCH
Male rap duo from Brooklyn, New York: ILL (I Lyrical Lord) and Al Skratch.

8/20/94	137	12	1 Creep Wit' Me..		Mercury 522661

ILLEGAL
Male teen rap duo from Atlanta, Georgia: Malik Edwards and **Jamal** Phillips.

9/11/93	119	8	1 The Untold Truth		Rowdy 37002

ILLINOIS SPEED PRESS, The
Rock band from Chicago, Illinois: Kal David (vocals, guitar; **The Fabulous Rhinestones**), Paul Cotton (guitar; **Poco**), Mike Anthony (organ), Rob Lewine (bass) and Fred Page (drums).

5/24/69	144	4	1 The Illinois Speed Press...		Columbia 9792

ILL NINO
Rock band from New Jersey: Cristian Machado (vocals), Arhue Luster (guitar), Jardel Paisante (guitar), Danny Couto (percussion), Lazaro Pina (bass) and Dave Chavarri (drums).

10/18/03	37	3	1 Confession..		Roadrunner 618391
10/15/05	101	1	2 One Nation Underground		Roadrunner 61817
3/29/08	145	1	3 Enigma		Cement Shoes 2003

ILLUSION
Jazz-rock band formed in England: Jane Relf (vocals), Jim McCarty (vocals, guitar; **The Yardbirds**), John Knightsbridge (guitar), John Hawken (keyboards), Louis Cennamo (bass) and Eddie McNeil (drums). Relf, McCarty and Hawken were also members of **Renaissance**.

7/2/77	163	7	1 Out Of The Mist		Island 9489

ILLUSION, The
Rock band from Long Island, New York: John Vinci (vocals), Richie Cerniglia (guitar), Mike Maniscalco (keyboards), Chuck Adler (bass) and Mike Ricciardella (drums).

5/10/69	69	27	1 The Illusion		Steed 37003

IMAGINATION
Male R&B-dance trio from London, England: Leee John (vocals), Ashley Ingram (keyboards, bass) and Errol Kennedy (drums).

3/31/84	205	2	1 New Dimension		Elektra 60316

IMBRUGLIA, Natalie
Born on 2/4/1975 in Sydney, Australia. Female pop-rock singer/songwriter. Married Daniel Johns (lead singer of **Silverchair**) on 12/31/2003.

3/28/98	10	52	▲²	1 Left Of The Middle		RCA 67634
3/23/02	35	7		2 White Lilies Island..		RCA 68082

IMMATURE
Teen male R&B vocal trio from Los Angeles, California: **Marques Houston**, Jerome "**Young Rome**" Jones and Kelton Kessee. Later shortened group name to **IMx**.

8/27/94+	88	37	●	1 Playtyme Is Over		MCA 11068
12/23/95+	76	30	●	2 We Got It		MCA 11385
10/11/97	92	3		3 The Journey		MCA 11668
11/13/99	101	4		4 Introducing IMx		MCA 112061
2/9/02	126	15		5 IMx		Tug 39009

Billboard DEBUT	PEAK	WKS	R I A A	ARTIST / Album Title	Catalog	Label & Number

IMMORTAL
Heavy metal band from Bergen, Norway: Olve Eikemo (vocals), Harold Naevdal (guitar), Ole Moe (bass) and Reidar Horghagen (drums).

| 10/24/09 | 162 | 1 | | 1 **All Shall Fall** .... | | Nuclear Blast 2303 |

IMMORTAL TECHNIQUE
Born Felipe Coronel on 8/10/1978 in Lima, Peru; raised in Harlem, New York. Male rapper.

| 7/12/08 | 99 | 3 | | 1 **The 3rd World** .... | | Viper 08 |
| | | | | **IMMORTAL TECHNIQUE & DJ GREEN LATERN** | | |

IMPACT
R&B vocal group from Baltimore, Maryland: Damon Otis Harris, John Simms, Charles Timmons and Donald Tilghman. Harris was a member of **The Temptations** from 1971-75.

| 7/10/76 | 205 | 5 | | 1 **Impact** .... | | Atco 135 |

IMPALAS, The
Doo-wop group from Brooklyn, New York: Joe "Speedo" Frazier, Richard Wagner, Lenny Renda and Tony Carlucci. All members, except black lead singer Frazier, are white.

~ ~ ~ ~ ~ ~ ~ ~ ~ ~ **NON-CHARTED ALBUM** ~ ~ ~ ~ ~ ~ ~ ~ ~ ~

   1959 **Sorry (I Ran All The Way Home)**

IMPELLITTERI
Hard-rock band: Chris Impellitteri (guitar; born on 9/25/1964), Graham Bonnet (vocals; **Rainbow** and **Alacatraz**), Phil Wolfe (keyboards), Chuck Wright (bass; **Quiet Riot**), Pat Torpey (drums; **Ted Nugent** and **Mr. Big**).

| 6/25/88 | 91 | 20 | | 1 **Stand In Line** .... | | Relativity 8225 |

IMPENDING DOOM
Christian heavy metal band from Riverside, California: Brook Reeves (vocals), Greg Pewthers (guitar), David Sittig (bass) and Chad Blackwell (drums).

| 4/18/09 | 144 | 1 | | 1 **The Serpent Servant** .... | | Facedown 078 |

IMPRESSIONS, The   **All-Time: #390**
R&B vocal group from Chicago, Illinois: **Jerry Butler** (born on 12/8/1939), **Curtis Mayfield** (born on 6/3/1942; died on 12/26/1999, age 57), Sam Gooden (born on 9/2/1939) and brothers Arthur Brooks and Richard Brooks. Butler left for a solo career in 1958; replaced by Fred Cash. The Brooks brothers left in 1962, leaving Mayfield as the trio's leader. Mayfield left in 1970 for a solo career; replaced by **Leroy Hutson**. In 1973, Hutson was replaced by Reggie Torian and Ralph Johnson.
AWARD: R&R Hall of Fame: 1991

8/31/63+	43	33		1 **The Impressions**		ABC-Paramount 450
3/28/64	52	22		2 **The Never Ending Impressions**		ABC-Paramount 468
8/8/64	8	34		3 **Keep On Pushing**		ABC-Paramount 493
3/6/65	23	19		4 **People Get Ready**		ABC-Paramount 505
9/18/65	104	9		5 **One By One**		ABC-Paramount 523
3/5/66	79	10		6 **Ridin' High**		ABC-Paramount 545
7/15/67	184	11		7 **The Fabulous Impressions**		ABC 606
3/2/68	35	27		8 **We're A Winner**		ABC 635
12/7/68+	107	13		9 **This Is My Country**		Curtom 8001
5/24/69	104	18		10 **The Young Mods' Forgotten Story**		Curtom 8003
4/29/72	192	2		11 **Times Have Changed**		Curtom 8012
3/17/73	204	5		12 **Preacher Man**		Curtom 8016
7/6/74	176	3		13 **Finally Got Myself Together**		Curtom 8019
10/26/74	202	1		14 **Three The Hard Way** .... [S]		Curtom 8602
8/9/75	115	5		15 **First Impressions**		Curtom 5003
3/13/76	195	3		16 **Loving Power**		Curtom 5009
				GREATEST HITS & COMPILATIONS:		
3/20/65	83	15		17 **The Impressions Greatest Hits**		ABC-Paramount 515
9/21/68+	172	15		18 **The Best Of The Impressions**		ABC 654
3/20/71	180	6		19 **16 Greatest Hits**		ABC 727
3/3/73	180	6		20 **Curtis Mayfield/His Early Years With The Impressions** ..		ABC 780 [2]
2/5/77	199	2		21 **The Vintage Years**		Sire 3717 [2]

~ ~ ~ ~ ~ ~ ~ ~ ~ ~ ~ **NON-CHARTED ALBUM** ~ ~ ~ ~ ~ ~ ~ ~ ~ ~

   1992 **The Anthology 1961-1977**
     RS500 #179

IMUS IN THE MORNING
Born John Donald Imus on 7/23/1940 in Riverside, California. Radio talk-show host. DJ at WGAR in Cleveland at the time of album below.

| 5/27/72 | 201 | 3 | | 1 **1200 Hamburgers To Go** .... [C] | | RCA Victor 4699 |

IMx — see IMMATURE

INC., The
All-star rap group assembled by producer Irv Gotti. Featuring **Ja Rule**, **Ashanti**, **Charli Baltimore** and Vita.

| 7/20/02 | 3¹ | 16 | ● | 1 **Irv Gotti Presents The Inc.** | | Murder Inc. 063033 |

Billboard			R I A A	ARTIST Album Title	Catalog	Label & Number
DEBUT	PEAK	WKS				

INCOGNITO
Jazz-funk trio from England: Maysa Leak (female vocals), Jean Paul Maunick (guitar) and Patrick Clahar (sax).

| 6/24/95 | 149 | 6 | | 1 100 Degrees And Rising .... | | Talkin Loud 528000 |

INCREDIBLE BONGO BAND, The
Instrumental studio band assembled by producer Michael Viner in Los Angeles, California.

| 8/18/73 | 197 | 2 | | 1 Bongo Rock .... [I] | | Pride 0028 |

INCREDIBLE STRING BAND
Folk band from Scotland. Formed by **Mike Heron** and Robin Williamson. Numerous personnel changes with Heron and Williamson the only constants.

7/20/68	161	9		1 The Hangman's Beautiful Daughter		Elektra 74021
3/22/69	174	3		2 Wee Tam		Elektra 74036
3/22/69	180	3		3 The Big Huge		Elektra 74037
12/6/69	166	3		4 Changing Horses		Elektra 74057
7/25/70	196	2		5 I Looked Up		Elektra 74061
1/23/71	183	3		6 'U'		Elektra 2002 [2]
2/19/72	189	3		7 Liquid Acrobat As Regards The Air		Elektra 74112
7/20/74	208	2		8 Hard Rope & Silken Twine		Reprise 2198

INCUBUS
Hard-rock band from Calabasas, California: Brandon Boyd (vocals), Mike Einziger (guitar), Chris Kilmore (DJ), Alex Katunich (bass) and Jose Pasillas (drums). Ben Kenney replaced Katunich in 2003.

11/13/99+	47	98	▲²	1 Make Yourself .... Cat:#4/46		Immortal 63652
9/9/00	41	5		2 When Incubus Attacks Vol. 1 .... [EP]		Immortal 61395
11/25/00	116	1		3 Fungus Amongus .... [E]		Immortal 61497
11/10/01	2¹	60	▲²	4 Morning View .... Cat:#29/5		Immortal 85227
2/21/04	2¹	31	▲	5 A Crow Left Of The Murder...		Immortal 90890
12/16/06	❶¹	42	●	6 Light Grenades		Immortal 83852
7/4/09	5	13		7 Monuments And Melodies .... [G]		Immortal 45317 [2]

INDECENT OBSESSION
Pop band from Brisbane, Australia: David Dixon (vocals), Andrew Coyne (guitar), Michael Szumowski (keyboards) and Darryl Sims (drums).

| 9/1/90 | 148 | 6 | | 1 Indecent Obsession .... | | MCA 6426 |

INDEPENDENTS, The
R&B vocal group from Chicago, Illinois: Chuck Jackson, Maurice Jackson, Helen Curry and Eric Thomas. Chuck Jackson, not to be confused with the same-named solo singer, is the brother of civil rights leader Jesse Jackson.

| 5/19/73 | 127 | 9 | | 1 The First Time We Met .... | | Wand 694 |
| 12/21/74 | 209 | 1 | | 2 Discs Of Gold .... [G] | | Wand 699 |

INDIA.ARIE
Born India Arie Simpson on 10/3/1975 in Denver, Colorado; raised in Atlanta, Georgia. Female R&B singer/songwriter/guitarist.

4/14/01	10	75	▲²	1 Acoustic Soul		Motown 013770
10/12/02	6	32	▲	2 Voyage To India		Motown 064755
				Grammy: R&B Album		
7/15/06	❶¹	20	●	3 Testimony: Vol. 1, Life & Relationship		Universal Motown 006141
2/28/09	3¹	21		4 Testimony: Vol. 2, Love & Politics		Soulbird 012572

INDIGO GIRLS   **All-Time: #327**
Folk-rock duo from Decatur, Georgia: singers/songwriters/guitarists Amy Ray (born on 4/12/1964) and Emily Saliers (born on 7/22/1963).

4/15/89	22	35	▲²	1 Indigo Girls .... Cat:#18/31		Epic 45044
				Grammy: Contemporary Folk Album		
11/25/89+	159	14	●	2 Strange Fire .... [E]		Epic 45427
				songs recorded in 1987		
10/13/90	43	29	●	3 Nomads-Indians-Saints		Epic 46820
5/30/92	21	34	▲	4 Rites Of Passage		Epic 48865
5/28/94	9	26	▲	5 Swamp Ophelia		Epic 57621
10/28/95	40	14	▲	6 1200 Curfews .... [L]		Epic 67229 [2]
5/17/97	7	22	●	7 Shaming Of The Sun		Epic 67891
10/16/99	34	7		8 Come On Now Social		Epic 69914
10/21/00	128	4		9 Retrospective .... [G]		Epic 61602
3/30/02	30	11		10 Become You		Epic 86401
3/6/04	35	7		11 All That We Let In		Epic 91003
7/2/05	159	1		12 Rarities .... [K]		Epic 94442
10/7/06	47	5		13 Despite Our Differences		Hollywood 162635
4/11/09	29	5		14 Poseidon And The Bitter Bug		IG 79896

INDO G
Born Tobian Tools in 1973 in Memphis, Tennessee. Male rapper. Former member of **Prophet Posse**.

| 9/12/98 | 105 | 3 | | 1 Angel Dust .... | | Relativity 1683 |

Billboard			R I A A	ARTIST Album Title	Catalog	Label & Number
DEBUT	PEAK	WKS				

INDUSTRY
Rock band from Long Island, New York: Jon Carin (vocals), Brian Unger (guitar), Rudy Perrone (bass) and Mercury Caronia (drums).

| 1/21/84 | 207 | 1 | | 1 Industry .... [EP] | Capitol 15011 |

INFAMOUS MOBB
Male rap trio from Long Island, New York: Ty Nitty, Gambino and Godfather.

| 4/13/02 | 118 | 5 | | 1 Special Edition .... | LandSpeed 9209 |

IN FEAR AND FAITH
Hard-rock band from San Diego, California: Cody Anderson (vocals), brothers Ramin Niroomand (guitar) and Mehdi Niroomand (drums), Noah Slifka (guitar) and Tyler McElhaney (bass).

| 1/24/09 | 193 | 1 | | 1 Your World On Fire .... | Rise 074 |

INFECTED MUSHROOM
Electronic-rock duo from Haifa, Israel: Erez Eisen and Amit Duvdevani.

| 10/10/09 | 172 | 1 | | 1 The Legend Of The Black Shawarma .... | Perfecto 101140 |

INFECTIOUS GROOVES
Rock-funk band from Los Angeles, California: Mike Muir (vocals), Dean Pleasants (guitar), Adam Siegel (guitar), Dave Dunn (keyboards), Robert Trujillo (bass) and Stephen Perkins (drums). Muir and Trujillo were formerly with **Suicidal Tendencies**. Trujillo joined **Metallica** in 2003.

| 2/22/92 | 198 | 1 | | 1 The Plague That Makes Your Booty Move...It's The Infectious Grooves .... | Epic 47402 |
| 3/6/93 | 109 | 5 | | 2 Sarsippius' Ark .... | Epic 53131 |

IN FLAMES
Hard-rock band from Sweden: Anders Fridan (vocals), Jesper Stromblad (guitar), Bjorn Gelotte (guitar), Peter Iwers (bass) and Daniel Svensson (drums).

4/24/04	145	2		1 Soundtrack To Your Escape	Nuclear Blast 1231
2/25/06	58	4		2 Come Clarity	Ferret 062
4/19/08	28	4		3 A Sense Of Purpose	Koch 4498

INFORMATION SOCIETY
Techno-dance band formed in Minneapolis, Minnesota: Kurt Harland (vocals), Paul Robb (guitar), Amanda Kramer (keyboards) and James Cassidy (bass). Reduced to a trio in 1990 with departure of Kramer.

| 8/20/88 | 25 | 38 | ● | 1 Information Society .... | Tommy Boy 25691 |
| 11/3/90 | 77 | 14 | | 2 Hack .... | Tommy Boy 26258 |

INGMANN, Jorgen, & His Guitar
Born Jorgen Ingmann-Pedersen on 4/26/1925 in Copenhagen, Denmark. White male guitarist.

~ ~ ~ ~ ~ ~ ~ ~ ~ ~   **NON-CHARTED ALBUM**   ~ ~ ~ ~ ~ ~ ~ ~ ~ ~ ~

1961 **Apache**

INGRAM, Jack
Born on 11/15/1970 in Houston, Texas. Country singer/guitarist.

| 4/14/07 | 34 | 6 | | 1 This Is It... | Big Machine 13060 |
| 9/12/09 | 61 | 2 | | 2 Big Dreams & High Hopes... | Big Machine 10300 |

INGRAM, James
Born on 2/16/1952 in Akron, Ohio. R&B singer/songwriter/pianist.

11/12/83+	46	42	●	1 It's Your Night	Qwest 23970
9/13/86	123	9		2 Never Felt So Good	Qwest 25424
10/6/90	117	10		3 It's Real	Warner 25924
10/19/91	168	3	●	4 The Power Of Great Music .... [G]	Warner 26700
5/1/99	165	1		5 Forever More (Love Songs, Hits & Duets)................... [G]	Private Music 82174

INGRAM, Luther
Born on 11/30/1937 in Jackson, Tennessee. Died of diabetes on 3/19/2007 (age 69). R&B singer/songwriter.

| 1/15/72 | 175 | 11 | | 1 I've Been Here All The Time .... | Koko 2201 |
| 9/30/72 | 39 | 21 | | 2 If Loving You Is Wrong I Don't Want To Be Right .... | Koko 2202 |

INJECTED
Rock band from Atlanta, Georgia: Danny Grady (vocals, guitar), Jade Lemmons (guitar), Steve Slovisky (bass) and Chris Wojtal (drums).

| 3/16/02 | 149 | 4 | | 1 Burn It Black .... | Island 548878 |

INMATES, The
Rock band from England: Bill Hurley (vocals), Peter "Gunn" Staines and Tony Oliver (guitars), Ben Donnelly (bass) and Jim Russell (drums).

| 12/1/79+ | 49 | 17 | | 1 First Offence .... | Polydor 6241 |
| 11/8/80 | 206 | 1 | | 2 Shot In The Dark.. | Polydor 6302 |

INNER CIRCLE
Reggae band formed in Kingston, Jamaica: Calton Coffie (vocals), Touter Harvey, Lancelot Hall, brothers Ian and Roger Lewis, and Lester Adderly.

| 5/22/93 | 64 | 49 | ▲ | 1 Bad Boys.. | Big Beat 92261 |
| | | | | *Grammy: Reggae Album* | |

Billboard			R I A A	ARTIST		
DEBUT	PEAK	WKS		Album Title	Catalog	Label & Number

INNER CITY
Techno-funk band led by producer/songwriter/mixer Kevin Saunderson (from Detroit, Michigan) and female vocalist Paris Grey (from Glencove, Illinois).

6/24/89	162	4		1 Big Fun...	Virgin 91242

INNOCENCE MISSION, The
Rock band from Lancaster, Pennsylvania: Karen Peris (vocals), her husband Don Peris (guitar), Mike Bitts (bass) and Steve Brown (drums).

3/24/90	167	10		1 The Innocence Mission...	A&M 5274

INNOCENTS, The
Pop trio from Sun Valley, California: James West (lead singer), Al Candelaria (bass) and Darron Stankey (guitar, tenor). Backup vocal group for **Kathy Young**. First recorded as The Echoes for Andex in 1959.

~ ~ ~ ~ ~ ~ ~ ~ ~ ~ *NON-CHARTED ALBUM* ~ ~ ~ ~ ~ ~ ~ ~ ~ ~ ~

1961 Innocently Yours

INSANE CLOWN POSSE   **All-Time: #352**
White rap duo from Detroit, Michigan: Joe "**Violent J**" Bruce (born on 4/28/1972) and Joe "**Shaggy 2 Dope**" Utsler (born on 10/14/1974). Both wear clown makeup. Members of **Dark Lotus** and **Soopa Villainz**.

7/12/97	63	88	▲	1 The Great Milenko.. Cat:#22/15		Island 524442
6/12/99	4	18	▲	2 The Amazing Jeckel Brothers		Island 524661
11/18/00	20	6		3 Bizaar		Psychopathic 548174
11/18/00	21	5		4 Bizzar...		Psychopathic 548175
				above 2 are different albums		
11/23/02	15	5		5 The Wraith: Shangri-La..		Psychopathic 9912
9/18/04	12	5		6 Hell's Pit..		Psychopathic 4032
6/4/05	32	3		7 The Calm .... [EP]		Psychopathic 4050
4/7/07	20	4		8 The Tempest...		Psychopathic 4063
9/19/09	4	8		9 Bang! Pow! Boom!		Psychopathic 4102
				GREATEST HITS & COMPILATIONS:		
9/5/98	46	5	●	10 Forgotten Freshness Volumes 1 & 2...		Island 524552 [2]
12/3/05	88	1		11 Forgotten Freshness: Volume 4		Psychopathic 4055 [2]
12/2/06	158	1		12 The Wraith: Remix Albums		Psychopathic 4062 [2]
11/17/07	124	1		13 Jugganauts: The Best Of Insane Clown Posse		Psychopathic 009925

INSIDERS
Rock band from Chicago, Illinois: John Siegle (vocals), Jay O'Rourke (guitar), Gary Yerkins (guitar), Jim DeMonte (bass) and Ed Breckenfeld (drums).

10/10/87	167	5		1 Ghost On The Beach...	Epic 40630

INSPECTAH DECK
Born Jason Hunter on 7/6/1970 in Staten Island, New York. Male rapper. Member of **X-Clan** and **Wu-Tang Clan**.

10/23/99	19	5		1 Uncontrolled Substance..	Loud 1865
6/28/03	137	1		2 The Movement	Koch 8660

INSTANT FUNK
Dance-funk band from Philadelphia, Pennsylvania: James Carmichael (vocals), brothers Kim Miller (guitar) and Scotty Miller (drums), George Bell (guitar), Dennis Richardson (keyboards), Charles Williams (percussion), Larry Davis (trumpet), Johnny Onderline (sax) and Raymond Earl (bass).

2/17/79	12	22	●	1 Instant Funk	Salsoul 8513
12/8/79+	129	13		2 Witch Doctor	Salsoul 8529
10/18/80	130	6		3 The Funk Is On	Salsoul 8536
4/10/82	147	7		4 Looks So Fine	Salsoul 8545

INSTITUTE
Band is actually a project by former **Bush** lead singer **Gavin Rossdale**. Includes guitarist Chris Traynor (of **Helmet**) and bassist Cache Tolman.

10/1/05	81	1		1 Distort Yourself	Interscope 004968

INSYDERZ, The
Christian ska-rock band from Detroit, Michigan: Joe Yerke (vocals), Kyle Wasil (guitar), Bram Roberts and Mike Rowland (horns), Beau McCarthy (bass) and Nate Sjogren (drums).

3/21/98	200	1		1 The Insyderz Present...Skalleluia!	Squint 7035

INTERNATIONAL ALL STARS
Studio group directed by Harry Frekin.

12/4/61	47	2		1 Percussion Around The World .... [I]	London Phase 4 44010

INTERPOL
Rock band formed in New York: Dan Kessler (vocals, guitar), Paul Banks (guitar), Carlos Dengler (bass) and Sam Fogarino (drums). Banks also recorded as **Julian Plenti**.

9/28/02	158	5		1 Turn On The Bright Lights	Matador 545
10/16/04	15	24	●	2 Antics	Matador 616
7/28/07	4	10		3 Our Love To Admire	Capitol 76538

IN THIS MOMENT
Heavy metal band from Los Angeles, California: Maria Brink (vocals), Chris Howorth (guitar), Blake Bunzel (guitar), Kyle Konkiel (bass) and Jeff Fabb (drums).

DEBUT	PEAK	WKS			Catalog	Label & Number
10/18/08	73	1		1 The Dream		Century Media 8517

INTOCABLE
Tejano group from Zapata, Texas: Ricardo Munoz, Daniel Sanchez, Rene Martinez, Felix Salinas, Sergio Serna and Juan Hernandez. Group name is Spanish for Untouchable.

8/14/99	173	1		1 Contigo	[F]	EMI Latin 21502
4/27/02	131	2		2 Suenos	[F]	EMI Latin 537745
3/1/03	161	9		3 La Historia	[F-G]	EMI Latin 80818
3/1/03	60	5		4 La Historia	[F-G]	EMI Latin 80819 [2]
9/6/03	95	4		5 Nuestro Destino Estaba Escrito	[F]	EMI Latin 90524
3/13/04	151	4	●	6 Intimamente: En Vivo Live	[F-L]	EMI Latin 96290
3/5/05	62	7		7 X	[F]	EMI Latin 98613
11/10/06	59	4		8 Crossroads: Cruce De Caminos	[F]	EMI Televisa 58875
6/28/08	90	7		9 2C	[F]	EMI Televisa 07725

INTRO
R&B vocal trio from Brooklyn, New York: Kenny Greene, Clinton Wike and Jeff Sanders.

4/24/93	65	45	●	1 Intro	Atlantic 82463
11/18/95	86	2		2 New Life	Atlantic 82662

INTRUDERS, The
R&B vocal group from Philadelphia, Pennsylvania: Sam "Little Sonny" Brown, Eugene "Bird" Daughtry, Phil Terry and Robert "Big Sonny" Edwards. Daughtry died on 12/25/1994 (age 55).

7/27/68	112	9		1 Cowboys To Girls		Gamble 5004
1/25/69	144	6		2 The Intruders Greatest Hits	[G]	Gamble 5005
5/19/73	133	18		3 Save The Children		Gamble 31991
7/21/73	205	4		4 Super Hits	[G]	Gamble 32131

INXS   **All-Time: #294**
Alternative-rock band from Sydney, Australia: Michael Hutchence (vocals; born on 1/22/1960; committed suicide on 11/22/1997, age 37), Kirk Pengilly (guitar, saxophone; born on 7/4/1958), Garry Beers (bass, born on 6/22/1957) and brothers Tim Farris (guitar; born on 8/16/1957), Andy Farris (keyboards, guitar; born on 3/27/1959) and Jon Farris (drums; born on 8/10/1961). Hutchence starred in the movies *Dogs In Space* and *Frankenstein Unbound*; formed the group *Max Q*. Jon Farriss married actress Leslie Bega (TV's *Head Of The Class*) on 2/14/1992. Canadian Jason Dean "J.D. Fortune" Bennison became new lead singer in 2005 after winning the reality TV series *Rock Star: INXS*.

3/19/83	46	31	●	1 Shabooh Shoobah		Atco 90072
10/1/83	148	6		2 Dekadance	[EP]	Atco 90115
				4 extended tracks from above album		
5/26/84	52	28	▲	3 The Swing	Cat:#39/20	Atco 90160
8/18/84	164	3		4 INXS	[E]	Atco 90184
				recorded in 1980		
11/2/85+	11	55	▲²	5 Listen Like Thieves	Cat:#13/50	Atlantic 81277
11/14/87+	3⁴	81	▲⁶	6 Kick	Cat:#15/17	Atlantic 81796
10/6/90	5	43	▲²	7 X		Atlantic 82140
11/23/91	72	11	▲	8 Live Baby Live	[L]	Atlantic 82294
8/22/92	16	31	▲	9 Welcome To Wherever You Are		Atlantic 82394
11/20/93	53	5		10 Full Moon, Dirty Hearts		Atlantic 82541
11/19/94	112	3	▲	11 The Greatest Hits	[G]	Atlantic 82622
5/3/97	41	8		12 Elegantly Wasted		Mercury 534531
11/2/02	144	1	●	13 The Best Of INXS	Cat:❶¹/17 [G]	Atlantic 78251
12/17/05	17	16		14 Switch		Burnett 97727

IOMMI
Born Tony Iommi on 2/19/1948 in Birmingham, England. Hard-rock guitarist. Member of **Black Sabbath**.

11/4/00	129	1		1 Iommi	Divine 27857

IRAHETA, Allison
Born on 4/27/1992 in Glendale, California. Female singer. Finalist on the eighth season of TV's *American Idol* in 2009.

12/19/09	35	6		1 Just Like You	19 Records 55969

IRIS, Donnie
Born Dominic Ierace on 2/28/1943 in Beaver Falls, Pennsylvania. Rock singer/songwriter/guitarist. Former member of **The Jaggerz**.

12/13/80+	57	23		1 Back On The Streets	MCA 3272
9/26/81	84	31		2 King Cool	MCA 5237
11/27/82	180	4		3 The High And The Mighty	MCA 5358
7/2/83	127	12		4 Fortune 410	MCA 5427
3/16/85	115	15		5 No Muss...No Fuss	HME 39949

IRISH ROVERS, The
Irish-born folk band formed in Calgary, Alberta, Canada: Jimmy Ferguson (vocals), brothers Will Millar (vocals, guitar) and George Millar (guitar), their cousin Joe Millar (bass) and Wilcil McDowell (accordian). Ferguson died in October 1997 (age 57). Group also recorded as **The Rovers**.

4/6/68	24	43		1 The Unicorn	Decca 74951
11/9/68	119	8		2 All Hung Up	Decca 75037

Billboard			ARTIST		
DEBUT	PEAK	WKS	R I A A Album Title	Catalog	Label & Number

IRISH ROVERS, The — cont'd

5/10/69	182	5	3 Tales To Warm Your Mind		Decca 75081
4/25/81	157	8	4 Wasn't That A Party		Cleveland Int'l. 37107
			THE ROVERS		

IRISH TENORS, The
All-star classical vocal trio: John McDermott, Anthony Kearns and **Ronan Tynan**. Karl Scully replaced Tynan in 2006.

4/3/99	151	10	● 1 The Irish Tenors	[L]	Point 8552
			recorded at the Royal Dublin Society Hall in Dublin, Ireland		
12/4/99	111	6	2 Home For Christmas	Cat:#44/2 [X]	Point 8870
			Christmas charts: 20/'99, 35/'00		
3/25/00	122	3	3 Live In Belfast	[L]	Point 9018
			recorded on 2/5/2000 at Waterfront Hall in Belfast, Ireland		
3/24/01+	66	5	4 Ellis Island		Music Matters 9020
12/27/03	112	1	5 We Three Kings	[X]	Razor & Tie 82897
			Christmas chart: 22/'03		
4/10/04	69	3	6 Heritage		Razor & Tie 82910
10/24/09	11ˣ	1	7 Christmas	[X]	Razor & Tie 83054

IRON AND WINE
Born Samuel Beam on 7/26/1974 in Columbia, South Carolina; later based in Florida. Alternative-pop singer/songwriter.

4/10/04	158	1	1 Our Endless Numbered Days		Sub Pop 630
3/12/05	128	2	2 Woman King	[EP]	Sub Pop 70665
10/1/05	135	1	3 In The Reins	[EP]	Overcoat 28
			CALEXICO / IRON & WINE		
10/13/07	24	11	4 The Shepherd's Dog		Sub Pop 710
6/6/09	25	8	5 Around The Well		Sub Pop 808 [2]

IRON BUTTERFLY
Psychedelic-rock band from San Diego, California: Doug Ingle (vocals, keyboards), Erik Braunn (guitar), Lee Dorman (bass) and Ron Bushy (drums). Braunn left in late 1969; replaced by Mike Pinera (leader of **Blues Image**) and Larry Reinhardt. Split in mid-1971. Braunn and Bushy regrouped in early 1975 with Phil Kramer (bass) and Howard Reitzes (keyboards). Kramer, who later earned a physics degree and became a mutimedia executive, mysteriously disappeared on 2/12/1995; his remains were found at the bottom of a Malibu canyon on 5/29/1999. Braunn died of heart failure on 7/25/2003 (age 52).

3/9/68	78	49	1 Heavy		Atco 227
7/20/68+	4	140	▲⁴ 2 In-A-Gadda-Da-Vida		Atco 250
2/15/69	3¹	44	● 3 Ball		Atco 280
5/23/70	20	23	4 Iron Butterfly Live	[L]	Atco 318
8/29/70	16	23	5 Metamorphosis		Atco 339
12/25/71+	137	6	6 The Best Of Iron Butterfly/Evolution	[G]	Atco 369
2/15/75	138	6	7 Scorching Beauty		MCA 465
1/3/76	207	2	8 Sun And Steel		MCA 2164

IRON CITY HOUSEROCKERS
Rock band from Pittsburgh, Pennsylvania: Joe Grushecky (vocals), Gary Scalese (guitar), Marc Reisman (harmonica), Gil Snyder (keyboards), Art Nardini (bass) and Ned Rankin (drums). Ed Britt replaced Scalese in early 1980.

| 6/30/79 | 201 | 6 | 1 Love's So Tough | | MCA 3099 |
| 8/30/80 | 204 | 5 | 2 Have A Good Time (But Get Out Alive) | | MCA 5111 |

IRONHORSE
Rock band from Canada: Randy Bachman (vocals, guitar), Tom Sparks (guitar), John Pierce (bass) and Mike Baird (drums). Bachman was a member of **Guess Who** and **Bachman-Turner Overdrive**.

| 4/7/79 | 153 | 10 | 1 Ironhorse | | Scotti Brothers 7103 |

IRON MAIDEN   **All-Time: #181**
Heavy-metal band formed in London, England: Paul Di'anno (vocals), Dave Murray (guitar; born on 3/12/1957), Adrian Smith (guitar; born on 2/27/1957), Steve Harris (bass; born on 3/12/1957) and Clive Burr (drums). **Bruce Dickinson** (born on 8/7/1958) replaced Di'anno in early 1982. Nicko McBrain replaced Burr in early 1983. Blaze Bayley replaced Dickinson in September 1993. Janick Gers replaced Smith in 1994. Dickinson returned to replace Bayley in 1999; Adrian Smith returned that same year. Their demonic mascot, which appears on album covers and in concert, is named "Eddie."

6/6/81	78	23	● 1 Killers		Harvest 12141
4/10/82	33	65	▲ 2 The Number Of The Beast		Harvest 12202
6/11/83	14	45	▲ 3 Piece Of Mind		Capitol 12274
9/29/84	21	34	▲ 4 Powerslave		Capitol 12321
10/11/86	11	39	● 5 Somewhere In Time		Capitol 12524
4/30/88	12	23	6 Seventh Son Of A Seventh Son		Capitol 90258
10/20/90	17	18	● 7 No Prayer For The Dying		Epic 46905
5/30/92	12	13	8 Fear Of The Dark		Epic 48993
10/28/95	147	3	9 The X Factor		CMC Int'l. 8003
4/11/98	124	1	10 Virtual XI		CMC Int'l. 86240
6/17/00	39	10	11 Brave New World		Portrait 62208
9/27/03	18	4	12 Dance Of Death		Columbia 89061

Billboard DEBUT	PEAK	WKS	R I A A	ARTIST / Album Title	Catalog	Label & Number
				IRON MAIDEN — cont'd		
9/23/06	9	7		13 **A Matter Of Life And Death**		Sanctuary 84768
5/31/08	58	6		14 **Somewhere Back In Time: The Best Of 1980-1989** .... [G]		UME 30478
				LIVE ALBUMS:		
10/31/81	89	30		15 **Maiden Japan** .... [EP]		Harvest 15000
				recorded on May 23, 1981 at Kosei Nenkin Hall in Nagoya, Japan		
11/16/85	19	22	▲	16 **Live After Death**		Capitol 12441 [2]
4/10/93	106	2		17 **A Real Live One**		Capitol 81456
11/20/93	140	1		18 **A Real Dead One**		Capitol 89248
4/13/02	186	1		19 **Rock In Rio**		Portrait 86000 [2]
6/27/09	34	3		20 **Flight 666** .... [S]		UME 50398 [2]
				ISAAK, Chris		
				Born on 6/26/1956 in Stockton, California. Singer/songwriter/guitarist/actor. Acted in several movies.		
4/11/87	194	2		1 **Chris Isaak**		Warner 25536
7/15/89+	7	74	▲²	2 **Heart Shaped World**		Reprise 25837
5/1/93	35	24	●	3 **San Francisco Days**		Reprise 45116
6/10/95	31	41	▲	4 **Forever Blue** .... Cat:#41/3		Reprise 45845
10/26/96	33	17	●	5 **Baja Sessions**		Reprise 46325
10/10/98	41	9		6 **Speak Of The Devil**		Reprise 46849
3/2/02	24	12		7 **Always Got Tonight**		Reprise 48016
12/4/04	109	6		8 **Chris Isaak Christmas** .... [X]		Wicked Game 48899
				Christmas charts: 13/'04, 48/'05		
5/27/06	54	15		9 **Best Of Chris Isaak** .... [G]		Wicked Game 49418
3/14/09	29	6		10 **Mr. Lucky**		Wicked Game 518008
				ISBELL, Jason		
				Born on 2/1/1979 in Greenhill, Alabama. Alternative-country singer/songwriter/guitarist.		
3/7/09	131	1		1 **Jason Isbell And The 400 Unit**		Lightning Rod 9968
				I SEE STARS		
				Hard-rock band from Warren, Michigan: Devin Oliver (vocals), Brent Allen (guitar), Jimmy Gregerson (guitar), Chris Moore (keyboards), Jeff Valentine (bass) and Andrew Oliver (drums).		
5/2/09	176	1		1 **3-D**		Sumerian 017
				ISIS		
				Female R&B-funk group: Stella Bass (vocals, bass), Suzi Ghezzi (guitar), Jeanie Fineberg, Lauren Draper and Lolly Bienenfeld (horns), and Liberty Mata (drums).		
9/28/74	208	2		1 **Isis**		Buddah 5605
				ISIS		
				Hard-rock band formed in Boston, Massachusetts: Aaron Turner (vocals, guitar), Mike Gallagher (guitar), Bryant Meyer (keyboards), Jeff Caxide (bass) and Aaron harris (drums).		
5/23/09	98	2		1 **Wavering Radiant**		Ipecac 113
				ISLANDS		
				Alternative-rock band formed in Montreal, Quebec, Canada: Nick Thorburn (vocals), brothers Evan Gordon (guitar) and George Gordon (bass), and Jamie Thompson (drums).		
6/7/08	200	1		1 **Arm's Way**		Anti 86966
				ISLE OF MAN		
				Multi-ethnic pop band (members are from France, Nicaragua, Italy and U.S.): Robere Parlez (vocals), Raun (guitar), Jamie Roberto (bass) and Ronnie Lee Sage (drums).		
7/19/86	110	18		1 **Isle Of Man**		Pasha 40319
				ISLEY, Ernie		
				Born on 3/7/1952 in Cincinnati, Ohio. R&B singer/guitarist. Member of **The Isley Brothers** and **Isley, Jasper, Isley**.		
3/31/90	174	11		1 **High Wire**		Elektra 60902

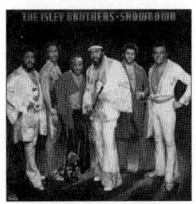

ISLEY BROTHERS, The   All-Time: #73

R&B vocal trio of brothers from Cincinnati, Ohio: O'Kelly Isley, Ronald Isley and Rudolph Isley. Formed own T-Neck label in 1969. Officially added their younger brothers Marvin Isley (bass, percussion) and **Ernie Isley** (guitar, drums) and brother-in-law **Chris Jasper** (keyboards) in 1973. Ernie, Marvin and Chris began recording as the trio **Isley, Jasper, Isley** in 1984. O'Kelly died of a heart attack on 3/31/1986 (age 48); Ronald and Rudolph continued on as The Isley Brothers through 1990. Ernie, Marvin and Ronald reunited as The Isley Brothers in 1991. Ronald married **Angela Winbush** on 6/26/1993. By 2001, Ronald was the featured vocalist under the alter-ego of "Mr. Biggs." Marvin died of diabetes on 6/6/2010 (age 56).

    AWARD: R&R Hall of Fame: 1992

Billboard DEBUT	PEAK	WKS	R I A A	ARTIST / Album Title	Catalog	Label & Number
9/29/62	61	13		1 **Twist & Shout**		Wand 653
6/18/66	140	5		2 **This Old Heart Of Mine**		Tamla 269
5/3/69	22	18		3 **It's Our Thing**		T-Neck 3001
10/18/69	180	3		4 **The Brothers: Isley**		T-Neck 3002
3/13/71	202	5		5 **In The Beginning...** .... [E]		T-Neck 3007
				THE ISLEY BROTHERS & JIMI HENDRIX		
				recorded in 1964; all songs feature then-session guitarist Jimi Hendrix		
9/25/71	71	25		6 **Givin' It Back**		T-Neck 3008

Billboard DEBUT	PEAK	WKS	R I A A	ARTIST Album Title	Catalog	Label & Number
				ISLEY BROTHERS, The — cont'd		
7/1/72	29	33		7 Brother, Brother, Brother		T-Neck 3009
3/17/73	139	13		8 The Isleys Live .... [L]		T-Neck 3010 [2]
9/8/73	8	37	▲	9 3 + 3		T-Neck 32453
12/22/73	195	3		10 Isleys' Greatest Hits .... [G]		T-Neck 3011
9/7/74	14	28	●	11 Live It Up		T-Neck 33070
6/14/75	❶¹	40	▲²	12 The Heat Is On		T-Neck 33536
5/29/76	9	26	▲	13 Harvest For The World		T-Neck 33809
4/16/77	6	34	▲²	14 Go For Your Guns		T-Neck 34432
8/27/77	58	11		15 Forever Gold .... [G]		T-Neck 34452
4/22/78	4	21	▲	16 Showdown		T-Neck 34930
11/18/78	204	4		17 Timeless .... [G]		T-Neck 35650 [2]
6/16/79	14	20	●	18 Winner Takes All		T-Neck 36077 [2]
4/19/80	8	22	▲	19 Go All The Way		T-Neck 36305
3/21/81	28	17	●	20 Grand Slam		T-Neck 37080
10/31/81	45	13		21 Inside You		T-Neck 37533
8/21/82	87	12		22 The Real Deal		T-Neck 38047
6/4/83	19	23	▲	23 Between The Sheets		T-Neck 38674
3/26/94	48ᶜ	2	▲²	24 Isley's Greatest Hits, Vol. 1 .... [G] first released in 1984		T-Neck 39240
12/7/85+	140	12		25 Masterpiece		Warner 25347
6/20/87	64	17		26 Smooth Sailin'		Warner 25586
9/2/89	89	13		27 Spend The Night		Warner 25940
6/13/92	140	3		28 Tracks Of Life		Warner 26620
6/1/96	31	45	▲	29 Mission To Please		Island 524214
				THE ISLEY BROTHERS FEATURING RONALD ISLEY:		
8/25/01	3¹	29		30 Eternal		DreamWorks 450291
5/24/03	❶¹	23	●	31 Body Kiss		DreamWorks 450409
11/29/03	73	2		32 Here I Am: Isley Meets Bacharach.................................... RONALD ISLEY / BURT BACHARACH		DreamWorks 001005
9/11/04	135	1		33 Taken To The Next Phase (Reconstructions)		Legacy 86669
5/27/06	5	18		34 Baby Makin' Music		Def Soul Classics 004812
10/27/07	41ˣ	1		35 I'll Be Home For Christmas .... [X]		Def Soul Classics 009913
				~ ~ ~ ~ ~ ~ ~ ~ ~ ~ **NON-CHARTED ALBUM** ~ ~ ~ ~ ~ ~ ~ ~ ~ ~ ~ ~ 1959 Shout!		

ISLEY, JASPER, ISLEY
R&B trio: Ernie Isley, Chris Jasper and Marvin Isley. See above **Isley Brothers** biography. Marvin died of diabetes on 6/6/2010 (age 56).

2/9/85	135	10		1 Broadway's Closer To Sunset Blvd.		CBS Associated 39873
11/2/85	77	26		2 Caravan Of Love		CBS Associated 40118

ISRAEL AND NEW BREED
Born Israel Houghton in 1971 in San Diego, California; later based in Houston, Texas. Contemporary gospel singer/songwriter. Formed New Breed Ministries in 1995. His backing group includes several singers and musicians.

5/22/04	146	7	●	1 Live From Another Level .... [L]		Integrity Gospel 91263 [2]
11/12/05	62	7	●	2 Alive In South Africa .... [L]		Integrity Gospel 36472 [2]
9/22/07	48	7		3 A Deeper Level: Live .... [L] Grammy: Pop/Contemporary Gospel Album		Integrity 11986
4/11/09	34	11		4 The Power Of One .... Grammy: Contemporary Gospel Album		Integrity 42584
10/24/09	32ˣ	2		5 A Timeless Christmas .... [X] ISRAEL HOUGHTON (above 2)		Integrity 87935

ISYSS
Female R&B vocal group from Los Angeles, California: Lamyia Good, Letecia Harrison, Ardena Clark and Quierra Davis-Martin.

10/19/02	55	7		1 The Way We Do		Arista 14731

IT DIES TODAY
Hard-rock band from Buffalo, New York: Jason Wood (vocals), Mike Hatalak (guitar), Chris Cappelli (guitar), Steve Lemke (bass) and Nick Mirusso (drums).

11/4/06	174	1		1 Sirens		Trustkill 87

IT'S A BEAUTIFUL DAY
Folk-rock band from San Francisco, California. Core members: **David LaFlamme** (male vocals, violin), Pattie Santos (female vocals), Fred Webb (keyboards) Bud Cockrell (bass) and Val Fuentes (drums). LaFlamme left in 1973. Cockrell later joined **Pablo Cruise**. Santos died in a car crash on 12/14/1989 (age 40).

6/14/69	47	70	●	1 It's A Beautiful Day..		Columbia 9768
7/4/70	28	21		2 Marrying Maiden		Columbia 1058
12/11/71+	130	16		3 Choice Quality Stuff/Anytime		Columbia 30734
11/11/72	144	9		4 It's A Beautiful Day At Carnegie Hall .... [L]		Columbia 31338
4/7/73	114	10		5 It's A Beautiful Day...Today		Columbia 32181

Billboard DEBUT	PEAK	WKS	R I A A	ARTIST / Album Title	Catalog	Label & Number
				I-20 Born Bobby Sandimanie in Decatur, Georgia. Male rapper.		
10/23/04	42	5		1 Self Explanatory		Capitol 82114
				IVERS, Eileen Born on 7/13/1965 in the Bronx, New York. Female singer/fiddle player.		
10/18/08	43ˣ	1		1 An Nollaig: An Irish Christmas .... [X]		Musical Bridge 4467
				IVES, Burl Born on 6/14/1909 in Huntington Township, Illinois. Died of cancer on 4/14/1995 (age 85). Folk singer/actor. Acted in several movies. Narrated the animated TV classic *Rudolph The Red-Nosed Reindeer*.		
2/17/62	35	34		1 The Versatile Burl Ives!		Decca 4152
6/2/62	24	36		2 It's Just My Funny Way Of Laughin'		Decca 4279
12/5/64+	65	15		3 Pearly Shells		Decca 74578
12/25/65	32ˣ	1		4 Have A Holly Jolly Christmas .... [X]		Decca 74689
12/23/67	93ˣ	2		5 Christmas Eve With Burl Ives .... [X]		Decca 78391
12/19/09	176	2	●	6 Rudolph The Red-Nosed Reindeer .... Cat:#4/59 [X-TV]		MCA 322177
				soundtrack of the classic Christmas TV show; first released in 1966 on Decca 74815; Christmas charts: 30/'98, 32/'99, 23/'00, 17/'01, 23/'02, 9/'03, 5/'04, 8/'05, 9/'06, 29/'07, 43/'08, 31/'09		
				IVY QUEEN Born Martha Pesante on 3/4/1972 in Anasco, Puerto Rico. Female reggae singer.		
4/14/07	105	6		1 Sentimiento .... [F]		Univision 311140
				I WRESTLED A BEAR ONCE Hard-rock band from Shreveport, Louisiana: Krysta Cameron (vocals), Steve Bradley (guitar), John Ganey (guitar), Mike Martin (bass) and Mike Montgomery (drums).		
6/20/09	122	1		1 It's All Happening		Century Media 8604
				IZIBOR, Laura Born on 5/13/1987 in Dublin, Ireland (Irish mother; African father). Female R&B singer/songwriter.		
7/4/09	27	12		1 Let The Truth Be Told		Atlantic 512240

J

Billboard DEBUT	PEAK	WKS	R I A A	ARTIST / Album Title	Catalog	Label & Number
				JACKA, The Born in Pittsburg, California. Male rapper.		
7/4/09	93	1		1 Tear Gas		SMC 349
				JACKI-O Born Angela Kohn in Miami, Florida. Female rapper.		
11/13/04	95	2		1 Poe Little Rich Girl		Poe Boy 2660
				JACKS, Terry Born on 3/29/1944 in Winnipeg, Manitoba, Canada. Folk-pop singer/songwriter/guitarist. Recorded with his wife Susan Jacks (married from 1968-73) as **The Poppy Family**.		
3/16/74	81	9		1 Seasons In The Sun		Bell 1307
				JACK'S MANNEQUIN Band is actually an experimental solo side project for **Something Corporate** lead singer Andrew McMahon.		
9/10/05	37	2		1 Everything In Transit		Maverick 49320
10/18/08	8	7		2 The Glass Passenger		Sire 371452
				JACKSON, Alan **1990s: #7 / 2000s: #7 / All-Time: #67** Born on 10/17/1958 in Newnan, Georgia. Country singer/songwriter/guitarist. Former car salesman and construction worker. Formed own band, Dixie Steel. Signed to **Glen Campbell**'s publishing company in 1985. AWARDS: CMA: Entertainer 1995, 2002 & 2003 / Male Vocalist 2002 & 2003 ★ OPRY: 1991		
3/31/90+	57	110	▲²	1 Here In The Real World		Arista 8623
6/1/91	17	118	▲⁴	2 Don't Rock The Jukebox		Arista 8681
10/24/92+	13	122	▲⁶	3 A Lot About Livin' (And A Little 'Bout Love)		Arista 18711
7/16/94	5	69	▲⁴	4 Who I Am		Arista 18759
11/16/96	12	73	▲³	5 Everything I Love		Arista 18813
9/19/98	4	40	▲	6 High Mileage		Arista Nashville 18864
11/13/99	9	51	▲	7 Under The Influence		Arista Nashville 18892
11/25/00	15	45	▲	8 When Somebody Loves You		Arista Nashville 69335
2/2/02	❶⁴	76	▲⁴	9 Drive		Arista Nashville 67039
				CMA: Album of the Year		
9/25/04	❶¹	24	▲	10 What I Do		Arista Nashville 63103

JACKSON, Alan — cont'd

DEBUT	PEAK	WKS	RIAA	#	Album Title	Catalog	Label & Number
3/18/06	4	83	▲	11	Precious Memories	Cat:#12/9	Arista Nashville 80281
10/14/06	4	39	●	12	Like Red On A Rose		Arista Nashville 88172
4/21/07	11	11		13	Live At Texas Stadium .... [L]		MCA Nashville 005894
					ALAN JACKSON / GEORGE STRAIT / JIMMY BUFFETT		
3/22/08	❶¹	82	▲	14	Good Time	Cat:#47/2	Arista Nashville 19943

CHRISTMAS ALBUMS:

DEBUT	PEAK	WKS	RIAA	#	Album Title	Catalog	Label & Number
11/6/93	42	12	▲	15	Honky Tonk Christmas	Cat:#17/14	Arista 18736
					Christmas charts: 4/'93, 15/'94, 31/'95, 41/'02, 8/'03, 21/'04, 39/'05, 19/'06		
11/23/02	27	8	●	16	Let It Be Christmas	Cat:#4/19	Arista Nashville 67062
					Christmas charts: 2/'02, 9/'03, 18/'04, 43/'05, 23/'06, 37/'07		

GREATEST HITS & COMPILATIONS:

DEBUT	PEAK	WKS	RIAA	#	Album Title	Catalog	Label & Number
11/11/95	5	104	▲⁶	17	The Greatest Hits Collection	Cat:#11/124	Arista 18801
8/30/03	❶¹	35	▲⁶	18	Greatest Hits Volume II And Some Other Stuff		Arista Nashville 53097 [2]
1/3/04	19	61	▲⁶	19	Greatest Hits Volume II	Cat:#30/9	Arista Nashville 54860
8/25/07+	141	12		20	16 Biggest Hits		Legacy 12228
11/21/09	34	6		21	Songs Of Love And Heartache		Cracker Barrel 759184

JACKSON, Brian — see SCOTT-HERON, Gil

JACKSON, Chuck

Born on 7/22/1937 in Latta, South Carolina; raised in Pittsburgh, Pennsylvania. R&B singer. With **The Dell-Vikings** from 1957-59.

~ ~ ~ ~ ~ ~ ~ ~ ~ ~ ~ ~ *NON-CHARTED ALBUMS* ~ ~ ~ ~ ~ ~ ~ ~ ~ ~ ~ ~

1961 **I Don't Want To Cry**   1965 **Saying Something** *[w/ Maxine Brown]*
1962 **Any Day Now**

JACKSON, Freddie

Born on 10/2/1956 in Harlem, New York. R&B singer/songwriter.

DEBUT	PEAK	WKS	RIAA	#	Album Title	Catalog	Label & Number
5/25/85	10	62	▲	1	Rock Me Tonight		Capitol 12404
11/15/86+	23	51	▲	2	Just Like The First Time		Capitol 12495
8/13/88	48	30	●	3	Don't Let Love Slip Away		Capitol 48987
11/24/90	59	30	●	4	Do Me Again		Capitol 92217
8/29/92	83	12		5	Time For Love		Capitol 96859
2/5/94	66	8		6	Here It Is		Orpheus 66318
3/18/95	187	2		7	Private Party		Street Life 75457

JACKSON, Janet

All-Time: #178

Born on 5/16/1966 in Gary, Indiana. Sister of **The Jackson 5**. R&B singer/songwriter/actress. Regular on TV's *Good Times*, *Diff'rent Strokes* and *Fame*. Co-starred in the movies *Poetic Justice* and *Nutty Professor 2: The Klumps*. Married to James DeBarge (of **DeBarge**) from 1984-85 (annulled). Secretly married to producer Rene Elizondo from 1991-2000. Caused controversy with her performance at the Super Bowl half-time show in February 2004.

DEBUT	PEAK	WKS	RIAA	#	Album Title	Catalog	Label & Number
11/20/82+	63	25		1	Janet Jackson		A&M 4907
10/27/84	147	6		2	Dream Street		A&M 4962
3/8/86	❶²	106	▲⁵	3	Control		A&M 5106
10/7/89	❶⁴	108	▲⁶	4	Janet Jackson's Rhythm Nation 1814		A&M 3920
					RS500 #275		
10/28/95	3¹	29	▲²	5	Design Of A Decade 1986/1996	Cat:#3/14 [G]	A&M 540399
6/5/93	❶⁶	106	▲⁶	6	janet.	Cat:#35/2	Virgin 87825
10/25/97	❶¹	74	▲³	7	The Velvet Rope	Cat:#30/2	Virgin 44762
					RS500 #256		
5/12/01	❶¹	52	▲²	8	All For You		Virgin 10144
4/17/04	2¹	19	▲	9	Damita Jo		Virgin 84404
10/14/06	2¹	15	▲	10	20 Y.O.		Virgin 30416
3/15/08	❶¹	16		11	Discipline		Island 010735
12/5/09	22	9		12	Number Ones	[G]	A&M 013612 [2]

JACKSON, Jermaine

Born on 12/11/1954 in Gary, Indiana. R&B singer/bassist. Member of **The Jackson 5** until group left Motown in 1976. Married to Hazel Gordy (daughter of Berry Gordy) from 1973-87. Rejoined The Jacksons in 1984 for the group's *Victory* album and tour.

DEBUT	PEAK	WKS	RIAA	#	Album Title	Catalog	Label & Number
8/12/72	27	36		1	Jermaine		Motown 752
6/16/73	152	6		2	Come Into My Life		Motown 775
9/25/76	164	11		3	My Name Is Jermaine		Motown 842
8/27/77	174	3		4	Feel The Fire		Motown 888
4/12/80	6	29	●	5	Let's Get Serious		Motown 928
12/6/80+	44	23		6	Jermaine		Motown 948
9/26/81	86	10		7	I Like Your Style		Motown 952
8/21/82	46	16		8	Let Me Tickle Your Fancy		Motown 6017

Billboard DEBUT	PEAK	WKS	R I A A	ARTIST / Album Title	Catalog	Label & Number
				JACKSON, Jermaine — cont'd		
5/19/84	19	49	●	9 Jermaine Jackson		Arista 8203
3/22/86	46	22		10 Precious Moments		Arista 8277
12/2/89+	115	16		11 Don't Take It Personal		Arista 8493
				JACKSON, Joe		**All-Time: #312**
				Born on 8/11/1954 in Burton-on-Trent, England. Eclectic pop-rock singer/songwriter/pianist.		
4/7/79	20	39	●	1 Look Sharp! .... Cat:#2^6/211		A&M 4743
10/27/79	22	25		2 I'm The Man		A&M 4794
11/8/80	41	16		3 Beat Crazy		A&M 4837
8/1/81	42	13		4 Joe Jackson's Jumpin' Jive		A&M 4871
7/17/82	4	57	●	5 Night And Day		A&M 4906
9/24/83	64	13		6 Mike's Murder .... [S]		A&M 4931
4/7/84	20	29		7 Body And Soul		A&M 5000
4/19/86	34	25		8 Big World .... [L]		A&M 6021 [2]
5/2/87	131	8		9 Will Power .... [I]		A&M 3908
5/21/88	91	12		10 Live 1980/86 .... [L]		A&M 6706 [2]
5/6/89	61	21		11 Blaze Of Glory		A&M 5249
5/18/91	116	4		12 Laughter & Lust		Virgin 91628
2/16/08	133	1		13 Rain		Rykodisc 10921
				JACKSON, LaToya		
				Born on 5/29/1956 in Gary, Indiana. R&B singer. Sister of **The Jacksons**.		
10/18/80	116	13		1 LaToya Jackson		Polydor 6291
9/12/81	175	3		2 My Special Love		Polydor 6328
6/9/84	149	6		3 Heart Don't Lie		Private I 39361
				JACKSON, Luscious — see LUSCIOUS JACKSON		
				JACKSON, Mahalia		
				Born on 10/26/1911 in New Orleans, Louisiana. Died of heart failure on 1/27/1972 (age 60). Legendary gospel singer.		
				AWARDS: Grammy: Lifetime Achievement 1972 ★ R&R Hall of Fame: 1997 (Early Influence)		
1/6/62	130	2		1 Sweet Little Jesus Boy .... [X]		Columbia 702
				first released in 1955		
12/14/63+	11^X	17		2 Silent Night – Songs For Christmas .... [X]		Columbia 1903 / 8703
				Christmas charts: 16/'63, 34/'64, 17/'65, 11/'66, 15/'67, 13/'68		
12/21/68+	2^{1X}	5		3 Christmas With Mahalia .... [X]		Columbia 9727
				Christmas charts: 18/'68, 2/'69		
12/18/93	35^C	1		4 Silent Night – Gospel Christmas With Mahalia Jackson .... [X]		LaserLight 15300
				JACKSON, Marlon		
				Born on 3/12/1957 in Gary, Indiana. Member of **The Jacksons**.		
11/28/87	175	7		1 Baby Tonight		Capitol 46942

JACKSON, Michael   1980s: #8 / 2000s: #29 / All-Time: #41

Born on 8/29/1958 in Gary, Indiana. Died of cardiac arrest on 6/25/2009 (age 50). R&B-pop singer/songwriter/actor. Lead singer of **The Jackson 5**. Played "The Scarecrow" in the 1978 movie musical *The Wiz*. Starred in the 15-minute movie *Captain Eo*, which was shown exclusively at Disneyland and Disneyworld. His 1988 autobiography, *Moonwalker*, became a movie the same year. Married to **Lisa Marie Presley** from 1994-96.

AWARDS: Grammy: Legend 1993 / Lifetime Achievement 2010 ★ R&R Hall of Fame: 2001

Billboard DEBUT	PEAK	WKS	R I A A	Album Title	Catalog	Label & Number
2/19/72	14	23		1 Got To Be There		Motown 747
8/26/72	5	32		2 Ben		Motown 755
5/5/73	92	12		3 Music & Me		Motown 767
2/15/75	101	9		4 Forever, Michael		Motown 825
9/1/79+	3^3	170	▲^{8}	5 Off The Wall .... Cat:#4/43		Epic 35745
				Grammy: Hall of Fame ★ RS500 #68		
12/25/82+	●^{37}	144	▲^{29}	6 Thriller .... Cat:●^{11}/164		Epic 38112
				Grammys: Album of the Year / Male Pop Vocal / Hall of Fame ★ RS500 #20 ★ NRR		
9/26/87	●^{6}	94	▲^{8}	7 Bad .... Cat:#4/53		Epic 40600
				RS500 #202		
12/14/91	●^{4}	118	▲^{7}	8 Dangerous .... Cat:#5/25		Epic 45400
11/17/01	●^{1}	28	▲^{2}	9 Invincible .... Cat:#9/14		Epic 69400
				released with 5 different colored covers: blue, green, orange, red and white		
11/14/09	●^{1}	29↑	▲^{2}	10 Michael Jackson's This Is It .... [S]		MJJ 76067 [2]
11/14/09	91	1		11 Michael Jackson's This Is It: Selections From .... [EP-S]		MJJ digital
				EARLY ALBUMS:		
4/25/81	144	10		12 One Day In Your Life		Motown 956
				recordings from 1973-75		
6/2/84	46	15		13 Farewell My Summer Love 1984		Motown 6101
				recordings from 1973		

JACKSON, Michael — cont'd

GREATEST HITS & COMPILATIONS:

9/27/75	156	5		14 The Best Of Michael Jackson .... Cat:#12/24		Motown 851
12/3/83+	7^C	50		15 Great Songs And Performances That Inspired The Motown 25th Anniversary Television Special MICHAEL JACKSON & THE JACKSON 5		Motown 5312
6/23/84	168	7		16 Michael Jackson And The Jackson 5 - 14 Greatest Hits .... picture disc		Motown 6099
7/8/95	❶²	36	▲⁷	17 HIStory: Past, Present And Future - Book I .... Cat:#10/6 disc 1: greatest hits; disc 2: new recordings		Epic 59000 [2]
6/7/97	24	9	▲	18 Blood On The Dance Floor - HIStory In The Mix .... Cat:#10/12		MJJ Music 68000
12/1/01	85	27	●	19 Greatest Hits: HIStory - Volume 1 .... Cat:#8/29		Epic 85250
12/6/03	13	57↑	▲³	20 Number Ones Cat:❶¹⁸/105		Epic 88998
12/4/04	154	1		21 The Ultimate Collection .... Cat:#4/8		MJJ/Epic 92600 [4]
8/6/05+	54	32↑	▲²	22 The Essential Michael Jackson Cat:❶¹/28		Legacy 94287 [2]
7/11/09	139	3		23 Gold		Motown 011431 [2]
7/25/09	57	6		24 The Stripped Mixes		Motown 013303
8/1/09	46^C	1		25 The Best Of Michael Jackson: 20th Century Masters: The Millenium Collection ...		Motown 159917
9/12/09	39	10		26 The Definitive Collection		Motown 013297
10/24/09	9^C	1		27 7 CD Album Mega Bundle		MJJ 08404 [7]
11/7/09	175	1		28 The Remix Suite		Universal Motown 013517

JACKSON, Millie
Born on 7/15/1944 in Thomson, Georgia; raised in Newark, New Jersey. R&B singer/songwriter.

9/16/72	166	11		1 Millie Jackson		Spring 5703
9/29/73	175	6		2 It Hurts So Good		Spring 5706
11/2/74	21	21	●	3 Caught Up		Spring 6703
7/26/75	112	16		4 Still Caught Up		Spring 6708
2/19/77	175	6		5 Lovingly Yours		Spring 6712
10/22/77+	34	23	●	6 Feelin' Bitchy		Spring 6715
7/22/78	55	14	●	7 Get It Out'cha System		Spring 6719
4/21/79	144	6		8 A Moment's Pleasure		Spring 6722
10/20/79	80	19		9 Royal Rappin's .... MILLIE JACKSON & ISAAC HAYES		Polydor 6229
12/22/79+	94	18		10 Live & Uncensored .... [L] recorded at The Roxy in Los Angeles, California		Spring 6725 [2]
6/21/80	100	10		11 For Men Only		Spring 6727
2/7/81	137	4		12 I Had To Say It		Spring 6730
8/15/81	201	5		13 Just A Lil' Bit Country		Spring 6732
3/13/82	113	13		14 Live And Outrageous (Rated XXX) .... [L] recorded at Mr. Vees Figure 8 in Atlanta, Georgia		Spring 6735
12/4/82	201	11		15 Hard Times		Spring 6737
12/27/86+	119	17		16 An Imitation Of Love		Jive 1016

JACKSON, Randy
Born on 6/23/1956 in Baton Rouge, Louisiana. R&B bassist/producer. Judge on TV talent show *American idol*. Member of **Journey** from 1986-87.

3/29/08	50	2		1 Randy Jackson's Music Club: Volume One		Dream Merchant 30277

JACKSON, Rebbie
Born Maureen Jackson on 5/29/1950 in Gary, Indiana. R&B singer. Sister of **The Jacksons**.

10/27/84	63	18		1 Centipede		Columbia 39238

JACKSON, Stonewall
Born on 11/6/1932 in Emerson, North Carolina. Country singer/songwriter/guitarist.
AWARD: OPRY: 1956

~ ~ ~ ~ ~ ~ ~ ~ ~ ~ **NON-CHARTED ALBUM** ~ ~ ~ ~ ~ ~ ~ ~ ~ ~ ~
1959 **The Dynamic Stonewall Jackson** *["Waterloo"]*

JACKSON, Walter
Born on 3/19/1938 in Pensacola, Florida; raised in Detroit, Michigan. Died of a cerebral hemorrhage on 6/20/1983 (age 45). R&B singer.

6/24/67	194	5		1 Speak Her Name		Okeh 14120
10/9/76	113	18		2 Feeling Good		Chi-Sound 656
4/30/77	141	5		3 I Want To Come Back As A Song		Chi-Sound 733
6/6/81	206	5		4 Tell Me Where It Hurts		Columbia 37132

JACKSON, Wanda
Born on 10/20/1937 in Maud, Oklahoma. Country-rockabilly singer/songwriter/guitarist.
AWARD: R&R Hall of Fame: 2009 (Early Influence)

~ ~ ~ ~ ~ ~ ~ ~ ~ ~ **NON-CHARTED ALBUMS** ~ ~ ~ ~ ~ ~ ~ ~ ~ ~ ~
1958 **Wanda Jackson**   1961 **There's A Party Goin' On**
1960 **Rockin' With Wanda!**

JACKSON, Willis
Born on 4/25/1932 in Miami, Florida. Died of heart failure on 10/25/1987 (age 55). Jazz tenor saxophonist.

7/23/66	137	4	1 Together Again! .... [I]		Prestige 7364
			WILLIS JACKSON & JACK McDUFF		
8/30/75	182	3	2 The Way We Were .... [I]		Atlantic 18145

JACKSON 5, The   1970s: #18 / All-Time: #100
R&B group of brothers from Gary, Indiana: **Michael Jackson** (born on 8/29/1958; died on 6/25/2009, age 50), **Jermaine Jackson**, **Marlon Jackson**, Tito Jackson and Jackie Jackson. Known as **The Jackson 5** from 1968-75. Randy Jackson replaced Jermaine in 1976. Jermaine rejoined the group for 1984's highly publicized *Victory* album and tour. Marlon left for a solo career in 1987. Their sisters **Rebbie Jackson**, **La Toya Jackson** and **Janet Jackson** backed the group; each had solo hits. Michael and Janet emerged with superstar solo careers in the 1980s. Group lineup since 1989: Jackie, Tito, Jermaine and Randy Jackson. Tito's sons recorded as **3T**.
AWARD: R&R Hall of Fame: 1997

THE JACKSON 5:

1/17/70	5	32	1 Diana Ross Presents The Jackson 5		Motown 700
6/6/70	4	50	2 ABC		Motown 709
9/26/70	4	50	3 Third Album		Motown 718
5/1/71	11	41	4 Maybe Tomorrow		Motown 735
10/9/71	16	26	5 Goin' Back To Indiana .... [TV]		Motown 742
6/3/72	7	33	6 Lookin' Through The Windows		Motown 750
4/14/73	44	16	7 Skywriter		Motown 761
10/6/73	100	29	8 Get It Together		Motown 783
10/5/74	16	21	9 Dancing Machine		Motown 780
6/14/75	36	15	10 Moving Violation		Motown 829

THE JACKSONS:

12/4/76+	36	27	●	11 The Jacksons		Epic 34229
10/29/77	63	11		12 Goin' Places		Epic 34835
12/16/78+	11	41	▲	13 Destiny		Epic 35552
10/18/80	10	29	▲	14 Triumph		Epic 36424
11/28/81+	30	19	●	15 Jacksons Live .... Cat:#17/2 [L]		Epic 37545 [2]
7/21/84	4	30	▲[2]	16 Victory		Epic 38946
6/17/89	59	11		17 2300 Jackson Street		Epic 40911

CHRISTMAS ALBUMS:

12/5/70	❶[6X]	16	18 Jackson 5 Christmas Album		Motown 713
			Christmas charts: 1/'70, 2/'71, 1/'72, 1/'73		
1/17/04+	26[X]	4	19 The Best Of Jackson 5 The Christmas Collection 20th Century Masters..........		Motown 000706
			Christmas charts: 42/'04, 26/'05, 26/'09		
11/14/09	108	9	20 Ultimate Christmas Collection		Motown 013448
			Christmas chart: 9/'09		

GREATEST HITS & COMPILATIONS:

1/1/72	12	41		21 Jackson 5 Greatest Hits .... Cat:#4/69		Motown 741
7/17/76	84	9		22 Jackson Five Anthology		Motown 868 [3]
12/3/83+	7[C]	50		23 Great Songs And Performances That Inspired The Motown 25th Anniversary Television Special		Motown 5312
				MICHAEL JACKSON & THE JACKSON 5		
6/23/84	168	7		24 Michael Jackson And The Jackson 5 - 14 Greatest Hits		Motown 6099
				picture disc		
4/13/02+	8[C]	21	●	25 The Best Of The Jackson 5: 20th Century Masters The Millennium Collection		Motown 153364
7/11/09	5[C]	15		26 The Ultimate Collection		Motown 530558
7/11/09	19[C]	3		27 The Jacksons Story: Number 1's		Hip-O 009599
8/8/09	48[C]	1		28 Super Hits		Sony 21343
8/8/09	186	1		29 Love Songs		Motown 012464

JACKYL
Hard-rock band from Atlanta, Georgia: Jesse James Dupree (vocals), Jimmy Stiff (guitar) and Jeff Worley (guitar), Tom Bettini (bass) and Chris Worley (drums).

10/10/92+	76	65	▲	1 Jackyl		Geffen 24489
8/20/94	46	11	●	2 Push Comes To Shove		Geffen 24710
8/9/97	133	1		3 Cut The Crap		Epic 67948

JACOBI, Lou
Born Louis Jacobivitch on 12/28/1913 in Toronto, Ontario, Canada. Died on 10/23/2009 (age 95). Actor/comedian. Acted in several movies and TV shows.

11/12/66	134	3	1 Al Tijuana And His Jewish Brass .... [I-N]		Capitol 2596

JACOBS, Debbie
Born in Baltimore, Maryland. Black disco singer.

9/1/79	153	8	1 Undercover Lover		MCA 3156
2/9/80	178	7	2 High On Your Love		MCA 3202

Billboard			R I A A	ARTIST		
DEBUT	PEAK	WKS		Album Title	Catalog	Label & Number

JADAKISS
Born Jayson Phillips on 3/27/1975 in Yonkers, New York. Male rapper/actor. Member of **The Lox** and **Ruff Ryders**. Played "Killer Ben" in the 2003 movie *Ride Or Die*.

8/25/01	5	14	●	1 Kiss Tha Game Goodbye		Ruff Ryders 493011
7/10/04	❶¹	22	●	2 Kiss Of Death		Ruff Ryders 002746
4/25/09	3¹	19		3 The Last Kiss		Ruff Ryders 012391

JADE
Female R&B vocal trio: Joi Marshall, Tonya Kelly and Diane Reed.

| 1/23/93 | 56 | 37 | ▲ | 1 Jade To The Max | | Giant 24466 |
| 10/15/94 | 80 | 22 | ● | 2 Mind, Body & Song | | Giant 24558 |

JADE WARRIOR
Progressive-rock trio from England: Glyn Havard (vocals, bass), Tony Duhig (guitar) and Jon Field (percussion). Duhig died of a heart attack on 11/11/1990 (age 49).

| 5/6/72 | 194 | 2 | | 1 Released | | Vertigo 1009 |
| 2/24/73 | 211 | 3 | | 2 Last Autumn's Dream | | Vertigo 1012 |

JAGGED EDGE
R&B vocal group from Atlanta, Georgia: identical twin brothers Brian "Brasco" Casey and Brandon "Case Dinero" Casey, with Richard "Dollar" Wingo and Kyle "Quick" Norman.

3/7/98	104	36	●	1 A Jagged Era		So So Def 68181
2/5/00	8	74	▲²	2 J.E. Heartbreak		So So Def 69862
7/14/01	3¹	41	▲	3 Jagged Little Thrill		So So Def 85646
11/1/03	3¹	26	●	4 Hard		Columbia 87017
5/15/04	131	1		5 The Ultimate Video Collection [G]		Columbia 58514
5/27/06	4	10		6 Jagged Edge		Columbia 93616
10/13/07	8	8		7 Baby Makin' Project		So So Def 009493

JAGGER, Chris
Born on 12/19/1947 in Dartford, Kent, England. Pop-rock singer. Younger brother of **Mick Jagger**.

| 11/3/73 | 186 | 4 | | 1 Chris Jagger | | Asylum 5069 |

JAGGER, Mick
Born Michael Phillip Jagger on 7/26/1943 in Dartford, Kent, England. Lead singer of **The Rolling Stones**. Appeared in the movies *Ned Kelly* and *Freejack*. Married to model Bianca Jagger from 1971-80. Married to actress/model Jerry Hall from 1990-99. Knighted by Queen Elizabeth in 2002. Older brother of **Chris Jagger**.

3/16/85	13	29	▲	1 She's The Boss		Columbia 39940
10/3/87	41	20		2 Primitive Cool		Columbia 40919
2/27/93	11	16	●	3 Wandering Spirit		Atlantic 82436
12/8/01	39	8		4 Goddess In The Doorway		Virgin 11288
10/20/07	77	2		5 The Very Best Of Mick Jagger [G]		Atlantic 74640

JAGGERZ, The
Pop-rock band from Pittsburgh, Pennsylvania: **Donnie Iris** (vocals, trumpet), Jimmy Ross (vocals, trombone), Billy Maybray (vocals, bass), Benny Faiella (guitar), Thom Davis (organ) and Jim Pugliano (drums). Maybray died of cancer on 12/5/2004 (age 60).

| 4/11/70 | 62 | 11 | | 1 We Went To Different Schools Together | | Kama Sutra 2017 |

JAGS, The
Rock band from Scarborough, England: Nick Watkinson (vocals, guitar), John Alder (guitar), Steve Prudence (bass) and Alex Baird (drums).

| 5/31/80 | 205 | 3 | | 1 Evening Standards | | Island 9603 |

JAGUARES
Alternative-rock band from Mexico: Saul Hernandez (vocals), Cesar Lopez (guitar), Federico Fong (bass) and Alfonso Andre (drums).

7/28/01	139	1		1 Cuando La Sangre Galopa [F]		BMG Latin 86742
11/9/02	95	2		2 El Primer Instinto [F]		RCA 96656
6/18/05	198	1		3 Cronicas De Un Laberinto [F]		Sony Discos 94044

JAHEIM
Born Jaheim Hoagland on 5/26/1978 in New Brunswick, New Jersey. Male R&B singer.

3/31/01	9	68	▲	1 Ghetto Love		Divine Mill 47452
11/23/02	8	41	▲	2 Still Ghetto		Divine Mill 48214
3/4/06	❶¹	14	●	3 Ghetto Classics		Divine Mill 48802
1/5/08	11	26	●	4 The Makings Of A Man		Divine Mill 377532
12/13/08	168	1		5 Classic Jaheim Vol. 1 [G]		Divine Mill 516814

JAKE JONES
Rock band from St. Louis, Missouri: Phil Jost, Mike Krenski, Joe Marshall and Charles Sabatino. Sabatino died on 2/19/1996 (age 45).

| 5/15/71 | 228 | 1 | | 1 Jake Jones | | Kapp 3648 |

JAKES, Bishop T.D.
Born Thomas Dexter Jakes on 6/9/1957 in South Charleston, West Virginia. Famous TV evangelist. Albums below feature vocals by The Potter's House Mass Choir.

3/29/97	183	2		1 **T.D. Jakes Presents Music From Woman, Thou Art Loosed!** .... [L]		Integrity 10502
				recorded at the Superdome in New Orleans, Louisiana		
4/24/99	118	10		2 **Sacred Love Songs**		Island 524630
3/31/01	56	10		3 **The Storm Is Over** .... [L]		Dexterity Sounds 20303
				recorded on 12/3/2000 at The Potter's House in Dallas, Texas		
2/16/02	83	5		4 **Woman Thou Art Loosed: Worship 2002 - Run To The Water...The River Within**...		Dexterity Sounds 20334
4/12/03	63	4		5 **A Wing And A Prayer**		Dexterity Sounds 20378
				Grammy: Gospel Choir Album		
2/14/04	169	1		6 **We Will Stand** .... [L]		Gaither 42461
2/14/04	173	1		7 **Build A Bridge** .... [L]		Gaither 42462
				BILL GAITHER & T.D. JAKES (above 2)		
5/5/07	151	1		8 **Live In Kenya: Grace: The Kenya Experience** .... [L]		Dexterity Sounds 103420

JAM, The
Punk-rock trio from Woking, England: Paul Weller (vocals, bass; born on 5/25/1958), Bruce Foxton (guitar; born on 9/1/1955) and Rick Buckler (drums; born on 12/6/1955). Disbanded in 1982. Weller formed **The Style Council**.

1/28/78	201	4		1 **This Is The Modern World**		Polydor 6129
5/5/79	204	2		2 **All Mod Cons**		Polydor 6188
2/16/80	137	8		3 **Setting Sons**		Polydor 6249
2/7/81	72	11		4 **Sound Affects**		Polydor 6315
12/19/81	176	7		5 **The Jam** .... [EP]		Polydor 503
3/27/82	82	16		6 **The Gift**		Polydor 6349
11/27/82	135	14		7 **The Bitterest Pill (I Ever Had To Swallow)** .... [EP]		Polydor 506
1/15/83	131	9		8 **Dig The New Breed** .... [L]		Polydor 6365
4/9/83	171	4		9 **Beat Surrender** .... [EP]		Polydor 810751
11/26/83	201	6		10 **Snap!** .... [K]		Polydor 815537 [2]

JAMAL
Born Jamal Phillips on 4/26/1979 in Philadelphia, Pennsylvania; raised in Atlanta, Georgia. Male rapper. Member of the **Illegal** rap duo.

11/25/95	198	1		1 **Last Chance, No Breaks**		Rowdy 37008

JAMAL, Ahmad   **1950s: #50**
Born Fritz Jones on 7/2/1930 in Pittsburgh, Pennsylvania. Jazz pianist.

9/22/58	3[1]	107		1 **But Not For Me/Ahmad Jamal At The Pershing**	[I-L]	Argo 628
11/17/58	11	18		2 **Ahmad Jamal, Volume IV**	[I-L]	Argo 636
				recorded on 9/6/1958 at the Spotlite Club in Washington DC		
2/1/60	32	7		3 **Jamal At The Penthouse** .... [I]		Argo 646
12/30/67+	168	8		4 **Cry Young**		Cadet 792
				vocals by the Howard Roberts Chorale		
3/16/74	201	5		5 **Jamalca** .... [I]		20th Century 432
2/15/75	203	1		6 **Jamal Plays Jamal** .... [I]		20th Century 459
3/15/80	173	5		7 **Genetic Walk** .... [I-K]		20th Century 600
11/15/80	201	3		8 **Night Song** .... [I]		Motown 945

JAMES
Rock band from Manchester, England: Tim Booth (vocals), James Gott (guitar), Mark Hunter (keyboards), Saul Davies (violin), Andy Diagram (trumpet), Jim Glennie (bass) and David Baynton-Power (drums).

1/29/94	72	26	●	1 **Laid**		Fontana 514943
3/15/97	158	1		2 **Whiplash**		Fontana 534354

JAMES, Bob   **All-Time: #196**
Born on 12/25/1939 in Marshall, Missouri. Jazz fusion keyboardist. Discovered by **Quincy Jones** in 1962. Was **Sarah Vaughan**'s musical director for four years. In 1973, became arranger of CTI records. In 1976, appointed director of progressive A&R at CBS Records. Formed own label, Tappan Zee, in 1977. Wrote and performed theme for the TV show *Taxi* (titled "Angela"). Joined **Fourplay** in 1991.

11/2/74	85	14		1 **One**.. [I]		CTI 6043
4/12/75	75	14		2 **Two**... [I]		CTI 6057
7/4/76	49	27		3 **Three**.. [I]		CTI 6063
4/9/77	38	17		4 **BJ4**... [I]		CTI 7074
11/26/77+	47	31		5 **Heads**... [I]		Tappan Zee 34896
12/16/78+	37	29	●	6 **Touchdown**... [I]		Tappan Zee 35594
8/25/79	42	14		7 **Lucky Seven**... [I]		Tappan Zee 36056
11/3/79	23	33	●	8 **One On One**.. [I]		Tappan Zee 36241
				BOB JAMES & EARL KLUGH		
				Grammy: Pop Instrumental Album		
7/12/80	47	18		9 **"H"**.. [I]		Tappan Zee 36422
2/21/81	66	16		10 **All Around The Town** .... [I-L]		Tappan Zee 36786 [2]
9/12/81	56	14		11 **Sign Of The Times**..		Tappan Zee 37495

				JAMES, Bob — cont'd		
7/17/82	72	17		12 Hands Down .... [I]		Tappan Zee 38067
11/6/82	44	29		13 Two Of A Kind .... [I]		Capitol 12244
				EARL KLUGH & BOB JAMES		
6/4/83	77	11		14 The Genie (Themes & Variations From The TV Series "Taxi") .... [I-TV]		Columbia 38678
10/8/83	106	13		15 Foxie .... [I]		Tappan Zee 38801
10/27/84	136	10		16 12 .... [I]		Tappan Zee 39580
6/14/86	50	64	▲	17 Double Vision .... [I]		Warner 25393
				BOB JAMES & DAVID SANBORN		
				Grammy: Jazz Fusion Album		
11/22/86+	142	27		18 Obsession .... [I]		Warner 25495
9/10/88	196	2		19 Ivory Coast .... [I]		Warner 25757
8/29/92	170	3		20 Cool .... [I]		Warner 26939
				BOB JAMES & EARL KLUGH		
3/26/94	168	2		21 Restless .... [I]		Warner 45536

JAMES, Etta
Born Jamesetta Hawkins on 1/25/1938 in Los Angeles, California. R&B singer. Nicknamed "Miss Peaches."
AWARDS: Grammy: Lifetime Achievement 2003 ★ R&R Hall of Fame: 1993

8/21/61	68	12		1 At Last!		Argo 4003
				RS500 #116		
8/24/63	117	4		2 Etta James Top Ten .... [G]		Argo 4025
2/1/64	96	10		3 Etta James Rocks The House .... [L]		Argo 4032
				recorded on 9/27/1963 at the New Era Club in Nashville, Tennessee		
3/9/68	82	13		4 Tell Mama		Cadet 802
9/15/73	154	9		5 Etta James		Chess 50042
5/24/03	195	1		6 Let's Roll		Private Music 11646
				Grammy: Contemporary Blues Album		

JAMES, Harry, and His Orchestra
Born on 3/15/1916 in Albany, Georgia. Died of cancer on 7/5/1983 (age 67). Legendary trumpet player/bandleader.
Achieved fame playing with **Benny Goodman** in the late 1930s. Married to actress Betty Grable from 1943-65.

11/12/55	10	1		1 Harry James In Hi-Fi .... [I]		Capitol 654

JAMES, Jessie
Born on 4/12/1988 in Vicenza, Italy (U.S. military base); raised in Georgia. Female country singer/songwriter.

8/29/09	23	5		1 Jessie James		Mercury 013204

JAMES, Jimmy, & The Vagabonds
Born on 9/15/1940 in Jamaica. R&B singer. The Vagabonds: Count Prince Miller (vocals), Wallace Wilson (guitar), Carl Noel (keyboards), Matt Fredericks and Milton James (horns), Phil Chen (bass) and Rupert Balgobin (drums).

11/29/75+	139	16		1 You Don't Stand A Chance If You Can't Dance		Pye 12111

JAMES, Joni
Born Giovanna Carmello Babbo on 9/22/1930 in Chicago, Illinois. Pop singer.

4/2/55	15	2		1 Little Girl Blue .... [EP]		MGM 272 [2]

JAMES, Leela
Born on 6/2/1983 in Los Angeles, California. Female R&B singer.

7/23/05	148	5		1 A Change Is Gonna Come		Warner 48027
4/11/09	84	2		2 Let's Do It Again		Shanachie 5775

JAMES, Melvin
Born in Des Moines, Iowa. Rock singer/songwriter/guitarist.

10/3/87	146	8		1 The Passenger		MCA 5663

JAMES, Rick
All-Time: #370
Born James Johnson on 2/1/1948 in Buffalo, New York. Died of a heart attack on 8/6/2004 (age 56). Funk-rock singer/songwriter/guitarist/producer. Also see **Stone City Band**.

6/24/78	13	36	●	1 Come Get It!		Gordy 981
2/10/79	16	27		2 Bustin' Out Of L Seven		Gordy 984
11/3/79	34	20		3 Fire It Up		Gordy 990
8/23/80	83	10		4 Garden Of Love		Gordy 995
5/2/81	3²	74	▲	5 Street Songs		Gordy 1002
6/5/82	13	23	●	6 Throwin' Down		Gordy 6005
8/27/83	16	29	●	7 Cold Blooded		Gordy 6043
8/25/84	41	19		8 Reflections .... [G]		Gordy 6095
5/11/85	50	26		9 Glow		Gordy 6135
7/5/86	95	12		10 The Flag		Gordy 6185
7/23/88	148	8		11 Wonderful		Reprise 25659
11/8/97	170	1		12 Urban Rapsody		Private I 417070
6/2/07	185	1		13 Deeper Still		Stone City 015

Billboard			R I A A	ARTIST		
DEBUT	PEAK	WKS		Album Title	Catalog	Label & Number

JAMES, Sonny
Born James Loden on 5/1/1929 in Hackleburg, Alabama. Country singer/songwriter/guitarist. Nicknamed "The Southern Gentleman."
AWARDS: C&W Hall of Fame: 2006 ★ OPRY: 1965

DEBUT	PEAK	WKS				
12/24/66	73ˣ	1		1 My Christmas Dream	[X]	Capitol 2589
12/24/66+	141	4		2 The Best Of Sonny James	[G]	Capitol 2615
4/12/69	161	3		3 Only The Lonely		Capitol 193
8/23/69	184	3		4 Close-Up	[R]	Capitol 258 [2]
				reissue of *True Love's A Blessing* and *I'll Never Find Another You* albums		
10/18/69	83	13		5 The Astrodome Presents In Person Sonny James	[L]	Capitol 320
4/11/70	177	4		6 It's Just A Matter Of Time		Capitol 432
9/19/70	197	2		7 My Love / Don't Keep Me Hangin' On		Capitol 478
11/28/70+	187	4		8 #1		Capitol 629
4/24/71	150	5		9 Empty Arms		Capitol 734
9/11/71	197	2		10 The Sensational Sonny James		Capitol 804
9/23/72	190	5		11 When The Snow Is On The Roses		Columbia 31646

JAMES, Tommy, And The Shondells
Born Thomas Jackson on 4/29/1947 in Dayton, Ohio; raised in Niles, Michigan. Pop-rock singer/songwriter. The Shondells: Eddie Gray (guitar), Ronnie Rosman (organ), Mike Vale (bass) and Pete Lucia (drums).

DEBUT	PEAK	WKS				
7/30/66	46	15		1 Hanky Panky		Roulette 25336
4/29/67	74	18		2 I Think We're Alone Now		Roulette 25353
2/24/68	174	5		3 Something Special! The Best Of Tommy James & The Shondells	[G]	Roulette 25355
7/27/68	193	2		4 Mony Mony		Roulette 42012
2/1/69	8	35		5 Crimson & Clover		Roulette 42023
10/25/69	141	6		6 Cellophane Symphony		Roulette 42030
12/13/69+	21	41		7 The Best Of Tommy James & The Shondells	[G]	Roulette 42040
4/11/70	91	9		8 Travelin'		Roulette 42044
9/11/71	131	8		9 Christian Of The World		Roulette 3001
3/4/72	216	1		10 My Head, My Bed & My Red Guitar		Roulette 3007
3/22/80	134	7		11 Three Times In Love		Millennium 7748
				TOMMY JAMES (above 2)		

JAMES GANG, The
Rock band from Cleveland, Ohio: **Joe Walsh** (guitar, keyboards, vocals), Jim Fox (drums) and Tom Kriss (bass; replaced by Dale Peters in 1970). Walsh left in late 1971; replaced by Dominic Troiano and Roy Kenner. Troiano left in 1973 to join **The Guess Who**; replaced by **Tommy Bolin** (died on 12/4/1976, age 25). Many personnel changes from 1974 until group disbanded in 1976. Troiano died of cancer on 5/25/2005 (age 59).

DEBUT	PEAK	WKS				
11/1/69+	83	24		1 Yer' Album		BluesWay 6034
7/25/70	20	66	●	2 James Gang Rides Again		ABC 711
4/17/71	27	30	●	3 Thirds		ABC 721
9/11/71	24	16	●	4 James Gang Live In Concert	[L]	ABC 733
				recorded on 5/15/1971 at Carnegie Hall		
3/18/72+	58	19		5 Straight Shooter		ABC 741
10/7/72	72	15		6 Passin' Thru		ABC 760
2/10/73	79	16		7 The Best Of The James Gang Featuring Joe Walsh	[G]	ABC 774
12/8/73	181	5		8 16 Greatest Hits	[G]	ABC 801 [2]
1/5/74	122	18		9 Bang		Atco 7037
9/14/74	97	10		10 Miami		Atco 102
5/31/75	109	9		11 Newborn		Atco 112

JAMIROQUAI
Interracial alternative dance group led by singer/songwriter Jason Kay (born on 12/30/1969 in Stretford, Manchester, England).

DEBUT	PEAK	WKS				
2/1/97	24	62	▲	1 Travelling Without Moving		Work 67903
6/26/99	28	11		2 Synkronized		Work 69973
9/29/01	44	6		3 A Funk Odyssey		Epic 85954
10/8/05	145	2		4 Dynamite		Epic 97716

JAN & DEAN
White surf-rock male vocal duo from Los Angeles, California: Jan Berry (born on 4/3/1941) and Dean Torrence (born on 3/10/1940). Jan was critically injured in a car crash on 4/12/1966. Their biographical movie *Dead Man's Curve* aired on TV in 1978. Jan died of a seizure on 3/26/2004 (age 62).

DEBUT	PEAK	WKS				
6/22/63	71	10		1 Jan & Dean Take Linda Surfin'		Liberty 7294
8/10/63	32	21		2 Surf City And Other Swingin' Cities		Liberty 7314
1/18/64	22	14		3 Drag City		Liberty 7339
5/23/64	80	21		4 Dead Man's Curve/The New Girl In School		Liberty 7361
10/10/64+	40	20		5 The Little Old Lady From Pasadena		Liberty 7377
10/17/64+	66	19		6 Ride The Wild Surf	[S]	Liberty 7368
2/27/65	33	16		7 Command Performance/Live In Person	[L]	Liberty 7403
10/2/65	107	6		8 Jan & Dean Golden Hits, Volume 2	[G]	Liberty 7417
1/15/66	145	3		9 Folk 'N Roll		Liberty 7431
5/14/66	127	5		10 Filet Of Soul	[L]	Liberty 7441

~ ~ ~ ~ ~ ~ ~ ~ ~ ~ **NON-CHARTED ALBUMS** ~ ~ ~ ~ ~ ~ ~ ~ ~ ~

1960 Jan & Dean [Dore label] 1966 Jan & Dean Golden Hits, Volume Three
1962 Jan & Dean's Golden Hits 1966 Popsicle
1966 Jan And Dean Meet Batman

JANE'S ADDICTION
Alternative-rock band from Los Angeles, California: **Perry Farrell** (vocals), **Dave Navarro** (guitar), Eric Avery (bass) and Stephen Perkins (drums). Farrell and Perkins later formed **Porno For Pyros**. Navarro later joined **Red Hot Chili Peppers**; married actress Carmen Electra on 11/22/2003.

9/17/88+	103	35	▲	1 Nothing's Shocking	**Cat:**#36/6	Warner 25727
				RS500 #309		
9/8/90	19	60	▲²	2 Ritual de lo Habitual		Warner 25993
				RS500 #453		
11/22/97	21	17	●	3 Kettle Whistle		Warner 46752
8/9/03	4	10	●	4 Strays		Capitol 90186
10/7/06	188	1		5 Up From The Catacombs: The Best Of Jane's Addiction	[G]	Warner 73222

JANIS, Tim
Born in 1968 in Maine. New Age pianist.

2/2/02	36^C	1		1 Along The Shore Of Acadia	[I]	Tim Janis Ensemble 1203
				first released in 1998		

JANKEL, Chas
Born on 4/16/1952 in England. Former keyboardist/guitarist with **Ian Dury & The Blockheads**.

3/6/82	126	14		1 Questionnaire		A&M 4885

JANKOWSKI, Horst
Born on 1/30/1936 in Berlin, Germany. Died of cancer on 6/29/1998 (age 62). Jazz pianist.

5/22/65	18	31		1 The Genius Of Jankowski!	[I]	Mercury 60993
12/4/65+	65	13		2 More Genius Of Jankowski	[I]	Mercury 61054
12/3/66	107	2		3 So What's New?	[I]	Mercury 61093

JAPAN
New wave band from London, England: David Sylvian (vocals, guitar), Mick Karn (sax), Richard Barbieri (keyboards) and Steve Jansen (drums). Sylvian and Jansen (real last name: Batt) are brothers.

3/27/82	204	6		1 Japan		Epic 37914

JARRE, Jean-Michel
Born on 8/24/1948 in Lyon, France. Electronic keyboardist.

10/15/77	78	19		1 Oxygene	[I]	Polydor 6112
2/3/79	126	8		2 Equinoxe	[I]	Polydor 6175
7/11/81	98	12		3 Magnetic Fields	[I]	Polydor 6325
5/3/86	52	20		4 Rendez-Vous	[I]	Dreyfus 829125

JARREAU, Al   All-Time: #318
Born on 3/12/1940 in Milwaukee, Wisconsin. R&B/jazz-styled singer. Son of a vicar; began performing in the church choir as a child. Has master's degree in psychology from the University of Iowa. Started professional career in the 1960s; worked clubs in California with **George Duke**.

9/20/75	209	1		1 We Got By		Reprise 2224
8/28/76	132	11		2 Glow		Reprise 2248
6/25/77	49	15	●	3 Look To The Rainbow/Live In Europe	[L]	Warner 3052 [2]
				Grammy: Jazz Vocal		
10/14/78	78	28		4 All Fly Home		Warner 3229
				Grammy: Jazz Vocal		
6/21/80	27	35	●	5 This Time		Warner 3434
8/22/81	9	103	▲	6 Breakin' Away		Warner 3576
				Grammy: Male Pop Vocal		
4/16/83	13	43	▲	7 Jarreau		Warner 23801
11/24/84	49	35		8 High Crime		Warner 25106
9/21/85	125	9		9 Al Jarreau In London	[L]	Warner 25331
				recorded November 1984 at Wembley Arena		
10/4/86	81	28	●	10 L Is For Lover		Warner 25477
12/3/88+	75	23	●	11 Heart's Horizon		Reprise 25778
7/4/92	105	9		12 Heaven And Earth		Reprise 26849
				Grammy: Male R&B Vocal		
6/11/94	114	8		13 Tenderness		Reprise 45422
3/25/00	137	6		14 Tomorrow Today		GRP 547884
10/5/02	137	1		15 All I Got		GRP 589777
11/11/06	58	7		16 Givin' It Up		Monster 2316
				GEORGE BENSON & AL JARREAU		

JARRETT, Keith
Born on 5/8/1945 in Allentown, Pennsylvania. Jazz pianist.

8/24/74	208	1		1 Treasure Island	[I]	ABC/Impulse 9274
8/2/75	160	5		2 El Juicio (The Judgement)	[I]	Atlantic 1673
12/13/75+	202	11		3 Backhand	[I]	ABC/Impulse 9305
2/28/76	201	8		4 The Koln Concert	[I-L]	ECM 1064 [2]
				no track titles listed on this album		
3/13/76	195	1		5 In The Light	[I]	ECM 1033 [2]
7/10/76	179	3		6 Arbour Zena	[I]	ECM 1070
7/17/76	184	2		7 Mysteries	[I]	ABC/Impulse 9315
2/12/77	174	4		8 Shades	[I]	ABC/Impulse 9322
8/6/77	141	12		9 Staircase/Hourglass/Sundial/Sand	[I]	ECM 1090 [2]

Billboard			R I A A	ARTIST		
DEBUT	PEAK	WKS		Album Title	Catalog	Label & Number

JARRETT, Keith — cont'd

10/1/77	117	6		10 Byablue	[I]	ABC/Impulse 9331
11/19/77	206	1		11 The Survivor's Suite	[I]	ECM 1085
				no track titles listed on this album		
5/27/78	201	15		12 Bop-Be	[I]	ABC/Impulse 9334
9/2/78	174	2		13 My Song	[I]	ECM 1115
10/28/78	203	1		14 The Best Of Keith Jarrett	[G-I]	ABC/Impulse 9348

JARS OF CLAY   **All-Time: #482**

Christian alternative pop-rock band formed in Greenville, Illinois: Dan Haseltine (vocals), Steve Mason (guitar), Matt Odmark (guitar) and Charlie Lowell (keyboards).

9/23/95+	46	70	▲²	1 Jars Of Clay	Cat:#19/13	Essential 5573
12/9/95	101	4		2 Drummer Boy	Cat:#32/2 [X-EP]	Essential 5622
				Christmas charts: 29/'96, 19/'99		
10/4/97	8	19	▲	3 Much Afraid		Essential 41612
				Grammy: Pop Gospel Album		
11/27/99	44	12	●	4 If I Left The Zoo		Essential 0499
				Grammy: Pop Gospel Album		
3/23/02	28	11		5 The Eleventh Hour		Essential 10629
				Grammy: Pop Gospel Album		
2/22/03	64	9	●	6 Furthermore: From The Studio, From The Stage	[L]	Essential 10689 [2]
11/22/03	103	5		7 Who We Are Instead		Essential 10709
4/9/05	71	9		8 Redemption Songs		Essential 10758
9/23/06	58	6		9 Good Monsters		Essential 10820
12/8/07	130	4		10 Christmas Songs	[X]	Gray Matters 30725
				Christmas charts: 11/'07, 39/'08		
5/9/09	29	8		11 The Long Fall Back To Earth		Gray Matters 10903

JA RULE

Born Jeffrey Atkins on 2/29/1976 in Queens, New York. Male rapper/actor. Appeared in the movies *Turn It Up*, *The Fast And The Furious*, *Half Past Dead* and *Scary Movie 3*. Member of **The Inc.** and **The Murderers**.

6/19/99	3¹	31	▲	1 Venni Vetti Vecci		Def Jam 538920
10/28/00	❶¹	54	▲³	2 Rule 3:36		Murder Inc. 542934
10/20/01	❶²	53	▲³	3 Pain Is Love		Murder Inc. 586437
12/7/02	4	26	▲	4 The Last Temptation		Murder Inc. 063487
11/22/03	6	10		5 Blood In My Eye		Murder Inc. 001577
11/27/04	7	17	●	6 R.U.L.E.		The Inc. 002955
12/24/05	107	1		7 Exodus	[G]	The Inc. 005813

JASON & THE SCORCHERS

Rock band from Nashville, Tennessee: Jason Ringenberg (vocals), Warner Hodges (guitar), Jeff Johnson (bass) and Perry Baggs (drums).

3/10/84	116	23		1 Fervor	[EP]	EMI America 19008
3/30/85	96	15		2 Lost & Found		EMI America 17153
11/22/86+	91	19		3 Still Standing		EMI America 17219

JASPER, Chris

Born on 12/30/1951 in Cincinnati, Ohio. R&B singer. Member of **The Isley Brothers** from 1969-84. Formed trio (**Isley, Jasper, Isley**) with cousins Marvin Isley and **Ernie Isley**.

3/5/88	182	3		1 Superbad		CBS Associated 44053

JAVIER

Born Javier Colon in 1978 in Hartford, Connecticut. R&B singer/songwriter/guitarist.

8/23/03	91	5		1 Javier		Capitol 39843

JAY & THE AMERICANS

Vocal group formed in New York: John "Jay" Traynor, Sandy Yaguda, Kenny Vance and Howie Kane, with Marty Sanders (guitar). Traynor left in 1962; replaced by lead singer Jay Black (born David Blatt on 11/2/1938).

12/12/64	131	4		1 Come A Little Bit Closer		United Artists 6407
6/12/65	113	17		2 Blockbusters		United Artists 6417
11/20/65+	21	20		3 Jay & The Americans Greatest Hits!	[G]	United Artists 6453
3/19/66	141	4		4 Sunday And Me		United Artists 6474
3/15/69	51	21		5 Sands Of Time		United Artists 6671
2/28/70	105	11		6 Wax Museum		United Artists 6719

~ ~ ~ ~ ~ ~ ~ ~ ~ ~ **NON-CHARTED ALBUMS** ~ ~ ~ ~ ~ ~ ~ ~ ~ ~ ~

1962 **She Cried**   1966 **Jay And The Americans Greatest Hits, Volume 2**

JAY AND THE TECHNIQUES

Interracial R&B-rock band from Allentown, Pennsylvania: Jay Proctor (lead vocals; born on 10/28/1940), George "Lucky" Lloyd (vocals), Dante Dancho (guitar), Ronnie Goosley (sax), Jon Walsh (trumpet), Chuck Crowl (bass) and Karl Landis (drums).

10/28/67+	129	13		1 Apples, Peaches, Pumpkin Pie		Smash 67095

JAYE, Jerry

Born Gerald Jaye Hatley on 10/19/1937 in Manila, Arkansas. Rockabilly singer.

7/29/67	195	2		1 My Girl Josephine		Hi 32038

JAYE, Miles
Born Miles Davis in Brooklyn, New York. R&B singer/songwriter.

12/12/87+	125	12	1 Miles		Island 90615
6/10/89	160	9	2 Irresistible		Island 91235

JAYHAWKS, The
Rock band from Minneapolis, Minnesota: **Mark Olson** (vocals), **Gary Louris** (guitar), Marc Perlman (bass) and Ken Callahan (drums). Olson left in 1996. Louris took over lead vocals. Louris and Perlman also formed **Golden Smog**.

2/27/93	192	2	1 Hollywood Town Hall		Def American 26829
3/4/95	92	9	2 Tomorrow The Green Grass		American 43006
5/10/97	112	1	3 Sound Of Lies		American 43114
5/27/00	129	2	4 Smile		Columbia 69522
4/26/03	51	6	5 Rainy Day Music		American 000076
7/25/09	71	1	6 Music From The North Country: The Jayhawks Anthology	[K]	American 47056

JAYNETTS, The
Female R&B vocal group from the Bronx, New York: Ethel Davis, Mary Sue Wells, Yvonne Bushnell and Ada Ray.

~ ~ ~ ~ ~ ~ ~ ~ ~ ~ **NON-CHARTED ALBUM** ~ ~ ~ ~ ~ ~ ~ ~ ~ ~ ~ ~

1963 **Sally Go 'Round The Roses**

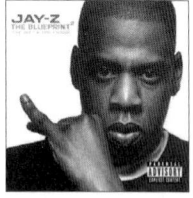

JAY-Z
2000s: #1 / All-Time: #101

Born Shawn Carter on 12/4/1969 in Brooklyn, New York. Male rapper/songwriter. Founded the Roc-A-Fella record label. Appeared in the movies *Streets Is Watching* and *State Property*. Started own clothing line of "Roca Wear." Nicknames include "Hova" (short for Jehovah) and "Jigga." Married **Beyonce** on 4/4/2008.

7/13/96	23	18	▲	1 Reasonable Doubt .... Cat:#2^1/11		Roc-A-Fella 50592
				RS500 #248		
11/22/97	3^1	24	▲	2 In My Lifetime, Vol. 1		Roc-A-Fella 536392
10/17/98	❶^5	69	▲^{5}	3 Vol. 2...Hard Knock Life		Roc-A-Fella 558902
				Grammy: Rap Album		
1/15/00	❶^1	47	▲^{3}	4 Vol. 3...Life And Times Of S. Carter		Roc-A-Fella 546822
11/18/00	❶^1	33	▲^{2}	5 The Dynasty Roc La Familia (2000 —)		Roc-A-Fella 548203
9/29/01	❶^3	35	▲^{2}	6 The Blueprint		Roc-A-Fella 586396
				RS500 #464		
1/5/02	31	17		7 Unplugged	[L]	Roc-A-Fella 586614
4/6/02	2^1	17	▲	8 The Best Of Both Worlds		Roc-A-Fella 586783
				R. KELLY & JAY-Z		
11/30/02	❶^1	26	▲^{3}	9 The Blueprint 2: The Gift And The Curse		Roc-A-Fella 063381 [2]
4/26/03	17	13		10 Blueprint 2.1		Roc-A-Fella 000297
11/29/03	❶^2	58	▲^{3}	11 The Black Album		Roc-A-Fella 001528
5/29/04	106	2		12 The Black Album: Acappella		Roc-A-Fella 002482
11/13/04	❶^1	11	▲	13 Unfinished Business		Jive 003690
				R. KELLY & JAY-Z		
12/18/04	❶^1	25	▲	14 Collision Course		Machine Shop 48962
				JAY-Z/LINKIN PARK		
12/9/06	❶^1	19	▲^{2}	15 Kingdom Come		Roc-A-Fella 008045
11/24/07	❶^1	26		16 American Gangster		Roc-A-Fella 010229
9/26/09	❶^2	36↑	▲	17 The Blueprint 3		Roc Nation 520856
9/26/09	30	3		18 The Blueprint: Collector's Edition	[K]	Roc-A-Fella 013335 [3]

JAZZ CRUSADERS, The — see CRUSADERS, The

JAZZMASTERS, The
Studio project featuring multi-instrumentalist **Paul Hardcastle** and vocalist Helen Rogers.

8/12/95	132	8	1 The Jazzmasters II		JVC 2049

JB's, The
Funk band led by **Fred Wesley**. Backing band for **James Brown**.

7/28/73	77	13	1 Doing It To Death		People 5603
6/29/74	197	3	2 Damn Right I Am Somebody		People 6602
			FRED WESLEY & THE J.B.'s		

J DILLA
Born James Dewitt Yancey on 2/7/1974 in Detroit, Michigan. Died of heart failure on 2/10/2006 (age 32). Highly influential hip-hop singer/songwriter/producer.

9/9/06	103	2	1 The Shining		BBE 076
4/7/07	112	1	2 Ruff Draft		Stones Throw 2153
6/20/09	96	1	3 Jay Stay Paid		Nature Sounds 142

DEBUT	PEAK	WKS	R I A A	**ARTIST** Album Title	Catalog	Label & Number

JEAN, Wyclef

Born on 10/17/1972 in Croix Des Bouquets, Haiti; raised in Brooklyn, New York. Hip-hop singer/songwriter/guitarist/producer. Member of **The Fugees**.

DEBUT	PEAK	WKS				
7/12/97	16	67	▲²	1 Wyclef Jean Presents The Carnival Featuring Refugee Allstars		Ruffhouse 67974
9/9/00	9	30	▲	2 The Ecleftic: 2 Sides II A Book		Columbia 62180
7/6/02	6	14		3 Masquerade		Columbia 86542
11/22/03	22	5		4 The Preacher's Son		Yclef 55425
12/22/07	28	14		5 Carnival Vol. II: Memories Of An Immigrant		In Ya Face 03947
11/28/09	171	1		6 Toussaint St. Jean: From The Hut, To The Projects, To The Mansion		Carnival House 01

JEDI MIND TRICKS

Male rap duo from Brooklyn, New York: Vince "Vinnie Paz" Luvineri (rapper) and Kevin "Stoupe" Baldwin (producer).

10/7/06	140	1		1 Servants In Heaven, Kings In Hell		Babygrande 1002
11/29/08	169	1		2 A History Of Violence		Babygrand 0388

JEFFERSON AIRPLANE / STARSHIP   1970s: #41 / 1980s: #47 / All-Time: #66

Rock band formed as **Jefferson Airplane** in San Francisco, California: **Marty Balin** (vocals, piano; born on 1/30/1942), **Grace Slick** (vocals; born on 10/30/1939), **Paul Kantner** (vocals, guitar; born on 3/17/1941), **Jorma Kaukonen** (guitar; born on 12/23/1940), Jack Casady (bass; born on 4/13/1944) and Spencer Dryden (drums; born on 4/7/1943). Original drummer Skip Spence formed **Moby Grape**. Dryden left in 1970 to join **New Riders Of The Purple Sage**; replaced by Joey Covington. Casady and Kaukonen left by 1974 to go full time with **Hot Tuna**. Balin left in 1971, rejoined in 1975, by which time group was renamed **Jefferson Starship** and consisted of Slick, Kantner, **Papa John Creach** (violin; died on 2/22/1994, age 76), Craig Chaquico (guitar), Pete Sears (keyboards), **David Freiberg** (bass) and John Barbata (drums). Slick left group from June 1978 to January 1981. In 1979, singer Mickey Thomas joined (replaced Balin), along with Aynsley Dunbar (**John Mayall**'s Bluesbreakers, **Frank Zappa**'s Mothers Of Invention, **Journey**) who replaced Barbata. Donnie Baldwin (formerly with **Snail**) replaced Dunbar (later with **Whitesnake**) in 1982. Kantner left in 1984, and, due to legal difficulties, band's name was shortened to **Starship**, whose lineup included Slick, Thomas, Sears, Chaquico and Baldwin. Slick left in early 1988. In 1989, the original 1966 lineup of Balin, Slick, Kantner, Kaukonen and Casady reunited as Jefferson Airplane with Kenny Aronoff (from **John Cougar Mellencamp**'s band) replacing Dryden. Continuing as Starship were Thomas, Chaquico, Baldwin, Brett Bloomfield (bass) and Mark Morgan (keyboards). Starship disbanded in 1990.

AWARD: R&R Hall of Fame: 1996

JEFFERSON AIRPLANE:

9/17/66	128	11		1 Jefferson Airplane Takes Off		RCA Victor 3584
3/25/67	3¹	56	●	2 Surrealistic Pillow		RCA Victor 3766
				Grammy: Hall of Fame ★ RS500 #146		
12/23/67+	17	23		3 After Bathing At Baxter's..		RCA Victor 1511
9/7/68	6	25	●	4 Crown Of Creation		RCA Victor 4058
3/1/69	17	20		5 Bless Its Pointed Little Head .... [L]		RCA Victor 4133
11/22/69	13	44	●	6 Volunteers...		RCA Victor 4238
				RS500 #370		
12/12/70+	12	40	▲	7 The Worst Of Jefferson Airplane........................... Cat:#16/18 [G]		RCA Victor 4459
12/19/70+	20	23	●	8 Blows Against The Empire...		RCA Victor 4448
				PAUL KANTNER/JEFFERRSON STARSHIP		
9/18/71	11	21	●	9 Bark		Grunt 1001
8/19/72	20	21	●	10 Long John Silver		Grunt 1007
4/14/73	52	16		11 Thirty Seconds Over Winterland .... [L]		Grunt 0147
5/4/74	110	8		12 Early Flight .... [K]		Grunt 0437
4/18/87	138	9		13 2400 Fulton Street - An Anthology .... [K]		RCA Victor 5724 [2]
9/23/89	85	7		14 Jefferson Airplane		Epic 45271
				reunion of the 1966-74 lineup		

JEFFERSON STARSHIP:

10/26/74	11	37	●	15 Dragon Fly		Grunt 0717
7/19/75	❶⁴	87	▲²	16 Red Octopus		Grunt 0999
7/10/76	3⁶	38	▲	17 Spitfire		Grunt 1557
1/29/77	37	15	●	18 Flight Log (1966-1976) .... [K]		Grunt 1255 [2]
3/18/78	5	34	▲	19 Earth		Grunt 2515
2/17/79	20	14		20 Gold .... [G]		Grunt 3247
12/1/79+	10	28	●	21 Freedom At Point Zero		Grunt 3452
4/18/81	26	33	●	22 Modern Times..		Grunt 3848
10/30/82	26	31	●	23 Winds Of Change		Grunt 4372
6/16/84	28	23	●	24 Nuclear Furniture		Grunt 4921

STARSHIP:

10/5/85+	7	50	▲	25 Knee Deep In The Hoopla		Grunt 5488
7/25/87	12	25	●	26 No Protection..		Grunt 6413
8/19/89	64	18		27 Love Among The Cannibals		RCA 9693

JEFFREYS, Garland

Born on 6/29/1943 in Brooklyn, New York. Black rock and roll singer.

3/26/77	140	10		1 Ghost Writer		A&M 4629
4/15/78	99	10		2 One-Eyed Jack		A&M 4681
9/22/79	151	5		3 American Boy & Girl		A&M 4778
3/21/81	59	18		4 Escape Artist		Epic 36983
10/31/81	163	4		5 Rock & Roll Adult .... [L]		Epic 37436
2/26/83	176	4		6 Guts For Love		Epic 38190

Billboard			R I A A	ARTIST		
DEBUT	PEAK	WKS		Album Title	Catalog	Label & Number

JELEN, Ben
Born on 7/8/1979 in Edinburgh, Scotland; raised in Bristol, England. Later moved to Texas and relocated to New York. Pop-rock singer/songwriter/guitarist.

5/1/04	113	1	1 Give It All Away		Maverick 48455

JELLYBEAN
Born John Benitez on 11/7/1957 in the Bronx, New York. Renowned club DJ/remixer/producer.

10/20/84	206	1	1 Wotupski!?! .... [EP]		EMI America 19011
9/5/87	101	11	2 Just Visiting This Planet		Chrysalis 41569

JELLYFISH
Rock band from San Francisco, California: Andy Sturmer (vocals, drums), Jason Falkner (guitar), and brothers Chris Manning (bass) and Roger Manning (keyboards). Falkner and Chris Manning left by 1993; bassist Tim Smith joined.

11/17/90+	124	27	1 Bellybutton		Charisma 91400
2/27/93	164	1	2 Spilt Milk		Charisma 86459

JEM
Born Jemma Griffiths on 6/18/1975 in Penarth, Wales; later based in London, England. Female Adult-Alternative singer/songwriter.

5/29/04	197	1	1 Finally Woken		ATO 21519
10/4/08	43	3	2 Down To Earth		ATO 21630

JENCARLOS
Born Jencarlos Canela on 4/21/1988 in Miami, Florida. Male Latin singer/actor.

11/28/09	91	1	1 Buscame .... [F]		Bullseye 8914

JENKINS, Gordon
Born on 5/12/1910 in Webster Groves, Missouri. Died of ALS (Lou Gehrig's disease) on 5/1/1984 (age 73). Pianist/arranger/composer.

11/24/56	13	4	1 Gordon Jenkins Complete Manhattan Tower		Capitol 766
			Grammy: Hall of Fame		
			a musical narrative originally composed by Jenkins in 1945 and first released in 1949 on Decca 723		

JENNINGS, Lyfe
Born Chester Jennings on 6/3/1973 in Toledo, Ohio. Male R&B singer/songwriter/guitarist. Served a prison sentence for arson from 1993-2002.

10/2/04+	39	60	▲	1 Lyfe 268-192 .... Cat:#39/1		Columbia 90946
9/2/06	2¹	17	●	2 The Phoenix		Columbia 96405
5/17/08	4	15		3 Lyfe Change		Columbia 07966

JENNINGS, Mason
Born on 3/19/1975 in Honolulu, Hawaii; raised in Pittsburgh, Pennsylvania; later based in Minneapolis, Minnesota. Singer/songwriter/guitarist.

6/3/06	146	1	1 Boneclouds		Epic 94690
6/7/08	133	1	2 In The Ever		Brushfire 011240
10/3/09	147	1	3 Blood Of Man		Brushfire 013339

JENNINGS, Shooter
Born Waylon Albright Jennings on 5/19/1979 in Nashville, Tennessee. Country singer/songwriter/guitarist. Son of **Waylon Jennings** and **Jessi Colter**. Played his father in the 2005 movie *Walk The Line*.

6/4/05	124	14	1 Put The O Back In Country		Universal South 003816
4/22/06	64	5	2 Electric Rodeo		Universal South 005499
11/10/07	52	2	3 The Wolf		Universal South 008887

JENNINGS, Waylon   **All-Time: #183**
Born on 6/15/1937 in Littlefield, Texas. Died of diabetes on 2/13/2002 (age 64). Legendary country singer/songwriter/guitarist. Bass player for **Buddy Holly** on the fateful "Winter Dance Party" tour in 1959 (gave up his plane seat to the Big Bopper). Established himself in the mid-1970s as a leader of the "outlaw" movement in country music. Married **Jessi Colter** in October 1969. Father of **Shooter Jennings**. Narrator for TV's *The Dukes Of Hazzard*. Also see **Highwaymen** and **Various Artists** Compilations: *I've Always Been Crazy: A Tribute To Waylon Jennings*.
AWARDS: C&W Hall of Fame: 2001 ★ CMA: Male Vocalist 1975 / Vocal Duo (w/ Willie Nelson) 1976

10/4/69	169	4	1 Country-Folk		RCA Victor 4180
			WAYLON JENNINGS & THE KIMBERLYS		
5/16/70	192	2	2 Waylon		RCA Victor 4260
5/26/73	214	5	3 Lonesome, On'ry & Mean		RCA Victor 4854
8/11/73	185	5	4 Honky Tonk Heroes		RCA Victor 0240
10/5/74	105	17	5 The Ramblin' Man		RCA Victor 0734
7/5/75	49	21	●	6 Dreaming My Dreams	RCA Victor 1062
4/17/76	189	4	7 Mackintosh & T.J. .... [S]		RCA Victor 1520
7/17/76	34	35	●	8 Are You Ready For The Country	RCA Victor 1816
12/18/76+	46	17	●	9 Waylon Live .... [L]	RCA Victor 1108
5/21/77	15	33	▲	10 Ol' Waylon	RCA Victor 2317
2/4/78	12	29	▲²	11 Waylon & Willie	RCA Victor 2686
			WAYLON JENNINGS & WILLIE NELSON		
10/21/78	48	24	●	12 I've Always Been Crazy	RCA Victor 2979

Billboard DEBUT	PEAK	WKS	R I A A	ARTIST / Album Title	Catalog	Label & Number
				JENNINGS, Waylon — cont'd		
11/10/79	49	28	●	13 **What Goes Around Comes Around**		RCA Victor 3493
6/7/80	36	43	●	14 **Music Man**		RCA Victor 3602
3/21/81	43	19	●	15 **Leather And Lace**		RCA Victor 3931
				WAYLON JENNINGS & JESSI COLTER		
3/6/82	39	23		16 **Black On Black**		RCA Victor 4247
10/30/82	57	22	●	17 **WWII**		RCA Victor 4455
				WAYLON JENNINGS & WILLIE NELSON		
4/30/83	109	11		18 **It's Only Rock & Roll**		RCA Victor 4673
5/21/83	60	16	●	19 **Take It To The Limit**		Columbia 38562
				WILLIE NELSON & WAYLON JENNINGS		
9/29/84	208	1		20 **Never Could Toe The Mark**		RCA Victor 5017
8/18/90	172	5		21 **The Eagle**		Epic 46104
8/3/91	193	3		22 **Clean Shirt**		Epic 47462
				WAYLON JENNINGS & WILLIE NELSON		
11/8/08	142	1		23 **Waylon Forever**		Black Country Rock 514
				WAYLON JENNINGS & THE 357'S		
				GREATEST HITS & COMPILATIONS:		
5/5/79	28	115	▲⁵	24 **Greatest Hits** Cat:#7/6		RCA Victor 3378
11/24/84	202	4		25 **Waylon's Greatest Hits Vol. 2**		RCA Victor 5325
3/2/02	49ᶜ	1		26 **Super Hits**		RCA 66849
4/20/02	155	1		27 **RCA Country Legends: Waylon Jennings**		RCA 99788 [2]
4/10/04	139	1		28 **Ultimate Waylon Jennings**		RCA 57267
				JENSEN, Kris		
				Born Peter Jensen on 4/4/1942 in New Haven, Connecticut. Pop singer/guitarist.		
				~ ~ ~ ~ ~ ~ ~ ~ ~ ~ ~ **NON-CHARTED ALBUM** ~ ~ ~ ~ ~ ~ ~ ~ ~ ~ ~		
				1962 **Torture**		
				JEREMIH		
				Born Jeremih Felton on 7/17/1987 in Chicago, Illinois. Male R&B singer/rapper/producer.		
7/18/09	6	20		1 **Jeremih**		Def Jam 013095
				JERKY BOYS, The		
				Prank telephone callers from New York: John Brennan and Kamal Ahmed. Duo starred in the 1995 movie *The Jerky Boys*.		
4/17/93+	75	95	▲	1 **The Jerky Boys**	[C]	Select 61495
9/3/94	12	34	▲	2 **The Jerky Boys 2**	[C]	Select 92411
9/7/96	18	12	●	3 **The Jerky Boys 3**	[C]	Ratchet 532893
10/25/97	63	8		4 **The Jerky Boys 4**	[C]	Ratchet 536357
6/5/99	117	4		5 **Stop Staring At Me!**	[C]	Ratchet 546063
				JEROME, Henry		
				Born on 11/12/1917 in Brooklyn, New York. Bandleader/composer.		
10/9/61	42	2		1 **Brazen Brass Goes Hollywood**	[I]	Decca 4085
				JERU THE DAMAJA		
				Born Kendrick Jeru Davis on 2/14/1972 in Brooklyn, New York. Male rapper.		
6/11/94	36	9		1 **The Sun Rises In The East**		Payday 124011
11/2/96	35	5		2 **Wrath Of The Math**		Payday 124119
				JESUS & MARY CHAIN, The		
				Alternative pop-rock band from East Kilbride, Scotland: brothers William Reid and Jim Reid (vocals, guitars), with Douglas Hart (bass) and Murray Dalgish (drums). Numerous personnel changes with the Reid brothers the only constants.		
2/22/86	188	4		1 **Psycho Candy**		Reprise 25383
				RS500 #268		
10/17/87	161	4		2 **Darklands**		Warner 25656
6/18/88	192	3		3 **Barbed Wire Kisses**		Warner 25729
11/25/89+	105	25		4 **Automatic**		Warner 26015
5/2/92	158	2		5 **Honey's Dead**		Def American 26830
9/10/94	98	6		6 **Stoned & Dethroned**		American 45573
				JESUS JONES		
				Alternative pop-rock band formed in London, England: Mike Edwards (vocals, guitar), Jerry DeBorg (guitar), Iain Baker (keyboards), Al Jaworski (bass) and Simon Matthews (drums).		
2/23/91	25	52	▲	1 **Doubt**		Food 95715
2/13/93	59	6		2 **Perverse**		Food 80647
				JET		
				Hard-rock band from Melbourne, Australia: brothers Nick Cester (guitar) and Chris Cester (drums), with Cameron Muncey (vocals, guitar) and Mark Wilson (bass).		
10/25/03+	26	85	▲	1 **Get Born**		Elektra 62892
10/21/06	16	5		2 **Shine On**		Atlantic 83806
9/12/09	27	3		3 **Shaka Rock**		Real Horror 720
				JETBOY		
				Hard-rock band from San Francisco, California: Mickey Finn (vocals), Fernie Rod (guitar), Billy Rowe (guitar), Sam Yaffa (bass) and Ron Tostenson (drums).		
11/12/88	135	10		1 **Feel The Shake**		MCA 42235

JETHRO TULL
1970s: #20 / All-Time: #84

Progressive-rock band formed in Blackpool, England: **Ian Anderson** (vocals, flute; born on 8/10/1947), Mick Abrahams (guitar; born on 4/7/1943), Glenn Cornick (bass; born on 4/24/1947) and Clive Bunker (drums; born on 12/12/1946). Group named after 18th-century agriculturist/inventor of seed drill. Abrahams left after recording of first album (in 1968) to form **Blodwyn Pig**; replaced by Martin Barre on 11/17/1946). Added keyboardist John Evans in 1970. Cornick replaced by Jeffrey Hammond-Hammond in 1971. Bunker left in late 1971; replaced by Barriemore Barlow. John Glascock replaced Hammond-Hammond by 1976. Glascock died on 11/17/1979 (age 28); replaced by bassist David Pegg. Since 1980, Anderson and Barre have fronted several lineups that have included Pegg and drummer Doane Perry.

3/1/69	62	17		1 This Was		Reprise 6336
10/11/69	20	40	●	2 Stand Up		Reprise 6360
5/9/70	11	41	●	3 Benefit		Reprise 6400
5/15/71	7	76	▲³	4 Aqualung		Reprise 2035
				RS500 #337		
5/20/72	❶²	46	●	5 Thick As A Brick		Reprise 2072
11/11/72	3³	31	●	6 Living In The Past	[K]	Chrysalis 1035 [2]
7/21/73	❶¹	32	●	7 A Passion Play		Chrysalis 1040
10/26/74	2³	31	●	8 War Child		Chrysalis 1067
9/27/75	7	14	●	9 Minstrel In The Gallery		Chrysalis 1082
1/24/76	13	23	▲	10 M.U. - The Best Of Jethro Tull	[G]	Chrysalis 1078
5/29/76	14	21		11 Too Old To Rock 'N' Roll: Too Young To Die!		Chrysalis 1111
3/5/77	8	22	●	12 Songs From The Wood		Chrysalis 1132
12/3/77	94	6		13 Repeat-The Best Of Jethro Tull, Vol. II............	[G]	Chrysalis 1135
4/29/78	19	17	●	14 Heavy Horses		Chrysalis 1175
10/21/78	21	15	●	15 Jethro Tull Live - Bursting Out	[L]	Chrysalis 1201 [2]
10/6/79	22	17	●	16 Stormwatch...............................		Chrysalis 1238
9/13/80	30	12		17 "A"		Chrysalis 1301
5/1/82	19	17		18 The Broadsword And The Beast.............		Chrysalis 1380
10/27/84	76	12		19 Under Wraps		Chrysalis 41461
10/10/87	32	28	●	20 Crest Of A Knave...........................		Chrysalis 41590
				Grammy: Hard Rock Album		
8/13/88	97	15		21 20 Years Of Jethro Tull	[K]	Chrysalis 41653 [5]
9/30/89	56	18		22 Rock Island		Chrysalis 21708
9/28/91	88	5		23 Catfish Rising		Chrysalis 21863
10/10/92	150	2		24 A Little Light Music	[L]	Chrysalis 21954
9/30/95	114	1		25 Roots To Branches		Chrysalis 35418
9/11/99	161	1		26 J-Tull Dot Com............................		Fuel 2000 1043
11/15/03	35ˣ	2		27 The Jethro Tull Christmas Album	[X]	Fuel 2000 061340
				Christmas chart: 35/'03, 46/'08		

JETS, The

Family group from Minneapolis, Minnesota: siblings Leroy, Eddie, Eugene, Haini, Rudy, Kathi, Elizabeth and Moana Wolfgramm. Their parents are from the South Pacific country of Tonga. All members play at least two instruments. Eugene left group and formed duo **Boys Club** in 1988.

4/5/86	21	70	▲	1 The Jets...............................		MCA 5667
11/7/87+	35	50	●	2 Magic		MCA 42085
12/10/88	30ˣ	2		3 Christmas With The Jets	[X]	MCA 5856
9/2/89	107	7		4 Believe...............................		MCA 6313

JETT, Joan, & The Blackhearts

Born Joan Larkin on 9/22/1958 in Philadelphia, Pennsylvania. Rock singer/guitarist. Member of **The Runaways** from 1975-78. The Blackhearts: Ricky Byrd (guitar; **Susan**), Gary Ryan (bass) and Lee Crystal (drums). **Kasim Sulton** and Thommy Price (of **Scandal**) replaced Ryan and Crystal in 1987. Jett starred in the 1987 movie *Light Of Day* as the leader of a rock band called The Barbusters.

3/14/81+	51	21		1 Bad Reputation...........................		Boardwalk 37065
12/19/81+	2³	59	▲	2 I Love Rock-N-Roll		Boardwalk 33243
7/16/83	20	20	●	3 Album		Blackheart 5437
10/27/84	67	21		4 Glorious Results Of A Misspent Youth		Blackheart 5476
10/25/86	105	16		5 Good Music		Blackheart 40544
5/28/88	19	46	▲	6 Up Your Alley............................		Blackheart 44146
2/3/90	36	18		7 The Hit List..............................		Blackheart 45473
				JOAN JETT		

JEWEL
All-Time: #464

Born Jewel Kilcher on 5/23/1974 in Payson, Utah; raised in Homer, Alaska. Singer/songwriter/guitarist. Wrote own book of poetry. Played "Sue Lee Shelley" in the movie *Ride With The Devil*. Married rodeo champion Ty Murray on 8/7/2008.

2/17/96+	4	114	▲¹²	1 Pieces Of You	Cat:#4/61	Atlantic 82700
12/5/98	3¹	51	▲⁴	2 Spirit		Atlantic 82950
11/20/99	32	9	▲	3 Joy: A Holiday Collection	Cat:#5/13 [X]	Atlantic 83250
				Christmas charts: 2/'99, 11/'00, 24/'01, 50/'02		
12/1/01	9	33	▲	4 This Way		Atlantic 83519
6/21/03	2¹	21	●	5 0304		Atlantic 83638
5/20/06	8	13		6 Goodbye Alice In Wonderland		Atlantic 83799
6/21/08	8	16		7 Perfectly Clear		Valory 0100
5/23/09	117	1		8 Lullaby..................................		Somerset 2434

Billboard			R I A A	ARTIST		
DEBUT	PEAK	WKS		Album Title	Catalog	Label & Number

JEWELL, Buddy
Born on 4/2/1961 in Lepanto, Arkansas. Country singer/songwriter. Winner of TV's first *Nashville Star* talent series in 2003.

7/19/03	13	25	●	1 Buddy Jewell		Columbia 90131
5/14/05	31	4		2 Times Like These		Columbia 92873

JIBBS
Born Jovan Campbell on 11/1/1990 in St. Louis, Missouri. Teen rapper.

11/11/06	11	21		1 Jibbs Feat. Jibbs		Beasta 007855

JIGSAW
Pop band from England: Des Dyer (vocals, drums), Tony Campbell (guitar), Clive Scott (keyboards) and Barrie Bernard (bass). Scott died of a stroke on 5/10/2009 (age 64).

12/13/75+	55	19		1 Sky High		Chelsea 509

JIMENEZ, Jose
Born William Szathmary on 10/5/1924 in Quincy, Massachusetts. Stage name: Bill Dana. Head comedy writer for **Steve Allen**'s TV show (created the Latin American comic character Jose Jimenez). Star of own TV series from 1963-65.

8/1/60	15	29		1 My Name...Jose Jimenez .... [C]		Signature 1013
7/17/61	5	51		2 Jose Jimenez - The Astronaut (The First Man In Space) [C]		Kapp 1238
12/25/61+	109	9		3 More...Jose Jimenez .... [C]		Kapp 1215
1/13/62	32	22		4 Jose Jimenez In Orbit/Bill Dana On Earth .... [C]		Kapp 1257
10/13/62	16	20		5 Jose Jimenez Talks To Teenagers Of All Ages .... [C]		Kapp 1304
2/23/63	30	14		6 Jose Jimenez - Our Secret Weapon .... [C]		Kapp 1320
12/14/63	128	4		7 Jose Jimenez In Jollywood .... [C]		Kapp 1332

JIMMIE'S CHICKEN SHACK
Rock band from Bowie, Maryland: James Davies (vocals), David Dowling (guitar), Che Lemon (bass) and Mike Sipple (drums).

9/11/99	153	7		1 Bring Your Own Stereo		Rocket 546382

JIMMY EAT WORLD
Rock band from Mesa, Arizona: Jim Adkins (vocals), Tom Linton (guitar), Rick Burch (bass) and Zach Lind (drums).

8/11/01+	31	70	▲	1 Jimmy Eat World		DreamWorks 450334
				originally titled *Bleed American* (title changed after 9/11 terrorist attacks)		
11/6/04	6	28	●	2 Futures		Interscope 003358
11/3/07	5	10		3 Chase This Light		Tiny Evil 009924

JIN
Born Jin Auyeung on 6/4/1982 in China; raised in Miami, Florida. Male rapper.

11/6/04	54	3		1 The Rest Is History		Ruff Ryders 84087

JINGLE CATS, The
The sounds of real cats digitally mastered into song by Mike Spalla. The cats are Cheese Puff, Max, Sprocket, Binky, Clara, Cueball, Graymer, Twizzler and Petunia.

12/25/93+	86	3		1 Meowy Christmas .... Cat:#10/6 [X-N]		Jingle Cats 41226
				Christmas charts: 19/'93, 14/'94, 40/'95		
12/31/94	182	1		2 Here Comes Santa Claws .... [X-N]		Jingle Cats 41229
				Christmas chart: 39/'94		

JIVE BUNNY AND THE MASTERMIXERS
Dance group from England: DJ Les Hemstock and mixers John Pickles, his son Andy Pickles and Ian Morgan.

1/6/90	26	18	●	1 The Album		Music Factory 91322

JIVE FIVE, The
R&B vocal group from Brooklyn, New York: Eugene Pitt (lead singer; born on 11/6/1937), Jerome Hanna and Billy Prophet (tenors), Richard Harris (baritone) and Norman Johnson (bass).

~ ~ ~ ~ ~ ~ ~ ~ ~   ***NON-CHARTED ALBUM***   ~ ~ ~ ~ ~ ~ ~ ~ ~ ~ ~
1965 **I'm A Happy Man**

J.J. FAD
Female rap trio from Los Angeles, California: Juana Burns, Dania Birks and Michelle Franklin. J.J. FAD stands for Just Jammin' Fresh And Def.

7/23/88	49	30	●	1 Supersonic - The Album		Ruthless 90959
				produced by **Dr. Dre**		

J-KWON
Born Jerrell Jones on 12/3/1982 in St. Louis, Missouri. Male rapper.

4/17/04	7	21	●	1 Hood Hop		So So Def 57613

JO, Damita — see DAMITA JO

JOBE, Kari
Born on 4/6/1981 in Dallas, Texas. Female Contemporary Christian singer/songwriter.

2/28/09	67	7		1 Kari Jobe		Integrity 42583

JOB FOR A COWBOY
Death metal band from Glendale, Arizona: Jonny Davy (vocals), Bobby Thompson (guitar), Ravi Bhadriraju (guitar), Brent Riggs (bass) and Jon Rice (drums). Al Glassman replaced Bhadriraju in 2008.

6/2/07	54	2		1 Genesis		Metal Blade 14614
7/25/09	42	5		2 Ruination		Metal Blade 14744

Billboard			R I A A	ARTIST		
DEBUT	PEAK	WKS		Album Title	Catalog	Label & Number

JOBIM, Antonio Carlos
Born on 1/25/1927 in Rio de Janerio, Brazil. Died on 12/8/1994 (age 67). Latin singer/songwriter/guitarist.

9/11/65	57	14		1 The Wonderful World Of Antonio Carlos Jobim		Warner 1611
4/15/67	19	28		2 Francis Albert Sinatra & Antonio Carlos Jobim		Reprise 1021
1/13/68	114	11		3 Wave .... [I]		A&M 3002
1/9/71	196	2		4 Stone Flower .... [I]		CTI 6002

JoBOXERS
Pop band formed in London, England: Dig Wayne (vocals), Rob Marche (guitar), Dave Collard (keybaords), Chris Bostock (bass) and Sean McLusky (drums).

10/15/83	70	15		1 Like Gangbusters		RCA Victor 4847

JODECI
R&B vocal group. Two pairs of brothers from Charlotte, North Carolina: Joel "JoJo" and Cedric "K-Ci" Hailey, with Dalvin and Donald "DeVante Swing" DeGrate. Also see **K-Ci & JoJo**.

9/14/91+	18	83	▲³	1 Forever My Lady		Uptown 10198
1/8/94	3¹	36	▲²	2 Diary Of A Mad Band		Uptown 10915
8/5/95	2¹	46	▲	3 The Show - The After-Party - The Hotel		Uptown 11258
6/25/05	27	8		4 Back To The Future: The Very Best Of Jodeci .... [G]		Universal 001812

JOE   All-Time: #498
Born Joseph Thomas on 7/5/1973 in Columbus, Georgia; raised in Opelika, Alabama. R&B singer/songwriter/guitarist.

9/11/93	105	11		1 Everything		Mercury 518016
8/16/97	13	46	▲	2 All That I Am .... Cat:#44/2		Jive 41603
5/6/00	2¹	60	▲³	3 My Name Is Joe		Jive 41703
12/29/01	32	26	●	4 Better Days		Jive 41786
1/3/04	26	19	●	5 And Then...		Jive 53707
5/12/07	2¹	12		6 Ain't Nothing Like Me		Jive 06704
11/1/08	125	1		7 Greatest Hits .... [G]		Jive 37024
10/11/08	8	9		8 Joe Thomas, New Man		563 Records 00003
8/1/09	7	10		9 Signature		563 Records 00005

JOE & EDDIE
Black folk duo from Berkeley, California: Joe Gilbert and Eddie Brown. Gilbert died on 8/6/1966 (age 25).

1/18/64	119	7		1 There's A Meetin' Here Tonite .... [L]		Crescendo 86
2/15/64	140	4		2 Coast To Coast		Crescendo 96

JOEL, Billy   1980s: #10 / All-Time: #64
Born William Martin Joel on 5/9/1949 in the Bronx, New York; raised in Hicksville, Long Island, New York. Pop-rock singer/songwriter/pianist. Member of The Hassles in the late 1960s. Involved in a serious motorcycle accident in Long Island in 1982. Married to supermodel Christie Brinkley from 1985-94.

AWARDS: Grammy: Legend 1991 ★ R&R Hall of Fame: 1999 ★ Billboard Century: 1994

4/8/72	202	3		1 Cold Spring Harbor		Family 2700
				album was mastered at the wrong speed		
1/14/84	158	8		2 Cold Spring Harbor .... [R]		Columbia 38984
				remix of #1 above (now at the correct speed)		
1/5/74	27	40	▲⁴	3 Piano Man Cat:❶⁴/257		Columbia 32544
11/2/74	35	18	▲	4 Streetlife Serenade		Columbia 33146
6/5/76	122	12	▲	5 Turnstiles .... Cat:#28/40		Columbia 33848
10/8/77+	2⁶	137	▲¹⁰	6 The Stranger Cat:❶¹/16		Columbia 34987
				Grammy: Hall of Fame ★ RS500 #67		
10/28/78	❶⁸	76	▲⁷	7 52nd Street		Columbia 35609
				Grammys: Album of the Year / Male Pop Vocal ★ RS500 #352		
3/22/80	❶⁶	73	▲⁷	8 Glass Houses		Columbia 36384
				Grammy: Male Rock Vocal		
10/16/82	7	35	▲²	9 The Nylon Curtain		Columbia 38200
8/20/83	4	111	▲⁷	10 An Innocent Man		Columbia 38837
8/16/86	7	47	▲²	11 The Bridge		Columbia 40402
11/4/89	❶¹	69	▲⁴	12 Storm Front		Columbia 44366
8/28/93	❶³	56	▲⁵	13 River Of Dreams		Columbia 53003
10/20/01	83	6		14 Fantasies & Delusions .... [I]		Columbia 85397
				Billy Joel's first classical compositions; performed by Richard Joo		
				GREATEST HITS & COMPILATIONS:		
7/20/85	6	65	▲²¹	15 Greatest Hits, Volume I & Volume II .... Cat:#8/224		Columbia 40121 [2]
9/6/97	9	28	▲	16 Greatest Hits Volume III		Columbia 67347
10/20/01	29	16	▲²	17 The Essential Billy Joel .... Cat:#19/10		Columbia 86005 [2]
12/10/05	171	2		18 My Lives		Columbia 93520 [4]

Billboard		R I	ARTIST		
DEBUT	PEAK	WKS	A A	Album Title	Catalog	Label & Number

JOEL, Billy — cont'd

LIVE ALBUMS:

DEBUT	PEAK	WKS	RIAA	#	Album Title	Catalog	Label & Number
10/3/81	8	27	▲³	19	Songs In The Attic		Columbia 37461
11/7/87	38	18	▲	20	Kohu,ept		Columbia 40996 [2]
					recorded in Leningrad (St. Petersburg), Russia; title translates roughly to: "In Concert"		
5/20/00	40	8	●	21	2000 Years - The Millennium Concert		Columbia 63792 [2]
					recorded on 12/31/1999 at Madison Square Garden		
7/1/06	14	6		22	12 Gardens Live		Columbia 85176 [2]

JOE PUBLIC

R&B vocal group from Buffalo, New York: Kevin Scott, Joe Carter, Joe Sayles and Dwight Wyatt.

4/11/92	111	17		1	Joe Public		Columbia 48628

JOEY + RORY

Country vocal duo: wife-and-husband Joey Feek and Rory Feek. Finalists on CMT's *Can You Duet* talent show in 2008.

11/15/08	61	27		1	The Life Of A Song		Sugar Hill 4050

JOHANSEN, David

Born on 1/9/1950 in Staten Island, New York. Rock singer/actor. Leader of the **New York Dolls** from 1971-75. Recorded jazz-pop as **Buster Poindexter**. Acted in several movies.

9/29/79	177	4		1	In Style		Blue Sky 36082
7/11/81	160	3		2	Here Comes The Night		Blue Sky 36589
7/3/82	148	15		3	Live It Up	[L]	Blue Sky 38004
1/9/88	90	15		4	Buster Poindexter		RCA 6633
					BUSTER POINDEXTER AND HIS BANSHEES OF BLUE		

JOHANSSON, Scarlett

Born on 11/22/1984 in Manhattan, New York. Adult Alternative-pop singer/actress. Acted in several movies.

6/7/08	126	1		1	Anywhere I Lay Me Head		Atco 454524
10/3/09	41	9		2	Break Up		Boyletown 511166
					PETE YORN & SCARLETT JOHANSSON		

JOHN, Elton   1970s: #1 / 1980s: #17 / All-Time: #7

Born Reginald Kenneth Dwight on 3/25/1947 in Pinner, Middlesex, England. Pop-rock singer/songwriter/pianist. Formed his first group Bluesology. Took the name of Elton John from the first names of Bluesology members Elton Dean and **Long John Baldry**. Teamed up with lyricist Bernie Taupin beginning in 1967. Formed Rocket Records in 1973. Played the "Pinball Wizard" in the movie version of *Tommy*. Knighted by Queen Elizabeth on 2/24/1998. Elton was the #1 pop artist of the 1970s. Also see **Various Artists Compilations:** *Two Rooms - Celebrating The Songs Of Elton John & Bernie Taupin.*

AWARDS: Grammy: Legend 1999 ★ R&R Hall of Fame: 1994

DEBUT	PEAK	WKS	RIAA	#	Album Title	Catalog	Label & Number
10/3/70+	4	51	●	1	Elton John		Uni 73090
					RS500 #468		
1/23/71	5	37	▲	2	Tumbleweed Connection		Uni 73096
					RS500 #463		
3/27/71	36	19	●	3	"Friends"	[S]	Paramount 6004
11/27/71+	8	51	▲²	4	Madman Across The Water		Uni 93120
6/17/72	●⁵	61	▲	5	Honky Chateau		Uni 93135
					RS500 #357		
2/10/73	●²	89	▲³	6	Don't Shoot Me I'm Only The Piano Player		MCA 2100
10/20/73	●⁸	103	▲⁷	7	Goodbye Yellow Brick Road	Cat:#3/16	MCA 10003 [2]
					Grammy: Hall of Fame ★ RS500 #91		
7/6/74	●⁴	54	▲²	8	Caribou		MCA 2116
2/1/75	6	18		9	Empty Sky	[E]	MCA 2130
					his first album, originally released in 1969		
6/7/75	●⁷	43	▲³	10	Captain Fantastic And The Brown Dirt Cowboy		MCA 2142
					RS500 #158		
11/8/75	●³	26	▲	11	Rock Of The Westies		MCA 2163
11/13/76	3³	22	▲	12	Blue Moves		MCA/Rocket 11004 [2]
11/11/78	15	18	▲	13	A Single Man		MCA 3065
6/30/79	51	18		14	The Thom Bell Sessions	[EP]	MCA 13921
10/27/79	35	10		15	Victim Of Love		MCA 5104
5/31/80	13	21	●	16	21 At 33		MCA 5121
6/6/81	21	19		17	The Fox		Geffen 2002
5/8/82	17	33	●	18	Jump Up!		Geffen 2013
6/11/83+	25	54	▲	19	Too Low For Zero		Geffen 4006
7/21/84	20	34	▲	20	Breaking Hearts		Geffen 24031
11/30/85+	48	28	●	21	Ice On Fire		Geffen 24077
12/6/86	91	9		22	Leather Jackets		Geffen 24114
7/9/88	16	29	●	23	Reg Strikes Back		MCA 6240
9/16/89	23	53	▲	24	Sleeping With The Past		MCA 6321
7/11/92	8	53	▲²	25	The One		MCA 10614
12/11/93	25	22	▲	26	Duets		MCA 10926
4/8/95	13	46	▲	27	Made In England		Rocket 526185

JOHN, Elton — cont'd

DEBUT	PEAK	WKS	RIAA	#	Album Title	Catalog	Label & Number
10/11/97	9	23	▲	28	The Big Picture		Rocket 536266
4/1/00	63	8		29	The Road To El Dorado .... [S]		DreamWorks 50219
10/20/01	15	24	●	30	Songs From The West Coast		Rocket 586330
11/27/04	17	10	●	31	Peachtree Road		Rocket 003647
10/7/06	18	6		32	The Captain & The Kid		Rocket 007545

GREATEST HITS & COMPILATIONS:

DEBUT	PEAK	WKS	RIAA	#	Album Title	Catalog	Label & Number
11/23/74	❶^{10}	104	▲^{16}	33	Elton John - Greatest Hits — RS500 #135	Cat:❶^{101}/681	MCA 2128
10/22/77	21	20	▲^{5}	34	Elton John's Greatest Hits, Volume II	Cat:#3/282	MCA 3027
10/3/87	84	23	▲^{2}	35	Elton John's Greatest Hits, Volume III, 1979-1987	Cat:#26/6	Geffen 24153
11/24/90	82	13	▲	36	To Be Continued...		MCA 10110 [4]
11/28/92+	4^C	71	▲^{2}	37	Greatest Hits 1976-1986		MCA 10693
10/12/96	24	76	▲^{3}	38	Love Songs................	Cat:#17/26	MCA 11481
11/30/02	12	67	▲^{3}	39	Greatest Hits 1970-2002	Cat:#12/46	Rocket 063478 [2]
4/14/07	9	36	●	40	Rocket Man: Number Ones	Cat:#21/16	Rocket 008661

LIVE ALBUMS:

DEBUT	PEAK	WKS	RIAA	#	Album Title	Catalog	Label & Number
5/29/71	11	23		41	11-17-70 — title is date of a New York City concert broadcast on WABC-FM		Uni 93105
5/22/76	4	20	▲	42	Here And There		MCA 2197
7/25/87+	24	41	▲	43	Live In Australia — recorded on 12/14/1986 in Sydney with the Melbourne Symphony Orchestra		MCA 8022 [2]
12/9/00	65	18	●	44	One Night Only–The Greatest Hits — recorded in October 2000 at Madison Square Garden		Universal 13050

JOHN, Little Willie

Born William Edgar John on 11/15/1937 in Cullendale, Arkansas; raised in Detroit, Michigan. Died of a heart attack on 5/26/1968 (age 30). R&B singer/songwriter.

AWARD: R&R Hall of Fame: 1996

~ ~ ~ ~ ~ ~ ~ ~ ~ ~ **NON-CHARTED ALBUMS** ~ ~ ~ ~ ~ ~ ~ ~ ~ ~ ~

1956 **Fever**   1958 **Talk To Me**

JOHN, Robert

Born Robert John Pedrick on 1/3/1946 in Brooklyn, New York. Pop singer.

DEBUT	PEAK	WKS		#	Album Title		Label & Number
8/25/79	68	14		1	Robert John		EMI America 17007
9/13/80	205	4		2	Back On The Street		EMI America 17027

JOHNNY & THE DISTRACTIONS

Rock band from Portland, Oregon: Johnny Koonce (vocals), Mark Spangler (guitar), Gregg Perry (keyboards), Laure Todd (bass) and Kevin Jarvis (drums).

DEBUT	PEAK	WKS		#	Album Title		Label & Number
2/20/82	152	9		1	Let It Rock		A&M 4884

JOHNNY AND THE HURRICANES

Rock and roll instrumental band from Toledo, Ohio: leader Johnny "Paris" Pocisk (saxophone), Dave Yorko (guitar), Paul Tesluk (organ), Lionel Mattice (bass) and Bo Savich (drums). Savich died of cancer on 1/4/2002 (age 62). Pocisk died of leukemia on 5/1/2006 (age 65).

DEBUT	PEAK	WKS		#	Album Title		Label & Number
4/18/60	34	3		1	Stormsville .... [I]		Warwick 2010

~ ~ ~ ~ ~ ~ ~ ~ ~ ~ **NON-CHARTED ALBUMS** ~ ~ ~ ~ ~ ~ ~ ~ ~ ~ ~

1959 **Johnny And The Hurricanes Featuring Red River Rock**   1960 **The Big Sound Of Johnny And The Hurricanes**

JOHNNY HATES JAZZ

Pop trio formed in England: Clark Datchler (vocals), Calvin Hayes (keyboards, drums) and Mike Nocito (guitar, bass). Hayes is the son of producer Mickie Most.

DEBUT	PEAK	WKS		#	Album Title		Label & Number
4/16/88	56	25		1	Turn Back The Clock		Virgin 90860

JOHNS, Michael

Born Michael Lee John on 10/20/1978 in Perth, Australia. "Blue-eyed soul" singer/songwriter. Finalist on the seventh season of TV's *American Idol* in 2008.

DEBUT	PEAK	WKS		#	Album Title		Label & Number
7/11/09	97	2		1	Hold Back My Heart		Downtown 70096

JOHNS, Sammy

Born on 2/7/1946 in Charlotte, North Carolina. Pop singer/songwriter/guitarist.

DEBUT	PEAK	WKS		#	Album Title		Label & Number
3/29/75	148	12		1	Sammy Johns		GRC 5003

JOHNS, Sarah

Born in Pollard, Kentucky. Country singer/songwriter.

DEBUT	PEAK	WKS		#	Album Title		Label & Number
9/15/07	198	1		1	Big Love In A Small Town		BNA 09636

JOHNSON, Carolyn Dawn

Born on 4/30/1971 in Grand Prairie, Alberta, Canada. Country singer/songwriter/guitarist.

DEBUT	PEAK	WKS		#	Album Title		Label & Number
8/25/01	87	12		1	Room With A View		Arista Nashville 69336
5/22/04	65	2		2	Dress Rehearsal		Arista Nashville 57500

JOHNSON, Don
Born on 12/15/1949 in Flatt Creek, Missouri. Actor/singer. Played "Sonny Crockett" on TV's *Miami Vice* and title role on TV's *Nash Bridges*. Starred in several movies. Twice married to and divorced from actress Melanie Griffith.

DEBUT	PEAK	WKS		Album Title	Catalog	Label & Number
9/13/86	17	27	●	1 Heartbeat..		Epic 40366

JOHNSON, Eric
Born on 8/17/1954 in Austin, Texas. Rock guitarist.

4/21/90+	67	60	▲	1 Ah Via Musicom .... [I]		Capitol 90517
9/21/96	51	6		2 Venus Isle .... [I]		Capitol 98331
6/21/97	108	3		3 G3 - Live In Concert .... [I-L]		Epic 67920
				JOE SATRIANI / ERIC JOHNSON / STEVE VAI		

JOHNSON, Howard
Born in Miami, Florida. R&B singer.

| 9/11/82 | 122 | 9 | | 1 Keepin' Love New.. | | A&M 4895 |

JOHNSON, Jack   **2000s: #28 / All-Time: #375**
Born on 5/18/1975 in Oahu, Hawaii. Adult Alternative pop-rock singer/songwriter. Former professional surfer.

2/23/02	34	59	▲	1 Brushfire Fairytales .... Cat:#6/114		Enjoy 860994
5/24/03	3¹	55	▲	2 On And On	Cat:#9/67	Moonshine Con. 075012
3/19/05	2¹	103	▲²	3 In Between Dreams	Cat:#11/100	Jack Johnson 004149
2/25/06	❶¹	44	▲	4 Curious George .... [S]		Brushfire 006116
				JACK JOHNSON & FRIENDS		
2/23/08	❶³	65	▲	5 Sleep Through The Static		Brushfire 010580
3/21/09	118	1		6 Sleep Through The Static: Remixed .... [EP]		Jack Johnson digital
11/14/09	11	15		7 En Concert .... [L]		Brushfire 012973

JOHNSON, Jamey
Born on 7/14/1975 in Enterprise, Alabama; raised in Montgomery, Alabama. Male country singer/songwriter.

| 2/18/06 | 87 | 2 | | 1 The Dollar... | | BNA 72690 |
| 8/23/08 | 28 | 90 | ● | 2 That Lonesome Song .... Cat:#27/3 | | Mercury 011237 |

JOHNSON, Jesse
Born on 5/29/1960 in Rock Island, Illinois. R&B guitarist. Member of **The Time**.

3/16/85	43	43	●	1 Jesse Johnson's Revue..		A&M 5024
10/18/86	70	20		2 Shockadelica		A&M 5122
4/16/88	79	13		3 Every Shade Of Love		A&M 5188

JOHNSON, Michael
Born on 8/8/1944 in Alamosa, Colorado; raised in Denver, Colorado. Singer/guitarist.

9/1/73	213	1		1 There Is A Breeze		Atco 7028
7/15/78	81	17		2 The Michael Johnson Album		EMI America 17002
9/15/79	157	12		3 Dialogue		EMI America 17010
9/13/80	203	2		4 You Can Call Me Blue		EMI America 17035

JOHNSON, Robert
Born on 5/8/1911 in Hazlehurst, Mississippi. Died of strychnine poisoning on 8/16/1938 (age 27). Highly influential Delta blues singer/guitarist/songwriter. His landmark recordings from 1936-37 have caused critics to label him the "Grandfather of Rock 'n' Roll."
AWARDS: Grammy: Lifetime Achievement 2006 ★ R&R Hall of Fame: 1986 (Early Influence)

12/12/87	34ᶜ	5		1 King Of The Delta Blues Singers .... [K]		Columbia 1654
				RS500 #27		
				first released in 1961; recordings from 1936-37		
10/13/90+	80	31	▲	2 The Complete Recordings.. [K]		Columbia 46222 [2]

~ ~ ~ ~ ~ ~ ~ ~ ~ ~ **NON-CHARTED ALBUM** ~ ~ ~ ~ ~ ~ ~ ~ ~ ~
1970 **King Of The Delta Blues Singers, Vol. II**
RS500 #424

JOHNSON, Robert
Born in Memphis, Tennessee. White rock and roll session guitarist. Member of **John Entwistle**'s group Ox in 1974.

| 1/13/79 | 174 | 8 | | 1 Close Personal Friend .... | | Infinity 9000 |

JOHNSON, Syleena
Born on 9/2/1976 in Harvey, Illinois. Female R&B singer. Daughter of singer Syl Johnson.

6/2/01	101	9		1 Chapter 1: Love, Pain & Forgiveness...................................		Jive 41700
12/14/02+	104	19		2 Chapter 2: The Voice		Jive 41815
10/1/05	75	2		3 Chapter 3: The Flesh..		Jive 61093

JOHNSTON, Freedy
Born on 3/7/1961 in Kinsley, Kansas; later based in New York. Male Adult Alternative pop-rock singer/songwriter.

| 3/15/97 | 184 | 1 | | 1 Never Home .... | | Elektra 61920 |

JOHNSTON, Tom
Born on 8/15/1948 in Visalia, California. Rock singer/songwriter/guitarist. Member of **The Doobie Brothers**.

| 10/20/79 | 100 | 13 | | 1 Everything You've Heard Is True .... | | Warner 3304 |
| 5/16/81 | 158 | 7 | | 2 Still Feels Good .... | | Warner 3527 |

Billboard			R I A A	**ARTIST**		
DEBUT	**PEAK**	**WKS**		Album Title	Catalog	**Label & Number**

JOJO
Born Joanna Levesque on 12/20/1990 in Foxboro, Massachusetts. Female teen pop singer.

7/10/04	4	41	▲	1 JoJo	Da Family 002672
11/4/06	3¹	18	●	2 The High Road	Da Family 007500

JO JO GUNNE
Rock band from Los Angeles, California: **Jay Ferguson** (keyboards), brothers Matthew Andes (guitar) and Mark Andes (bass), and Curly Smith (drums). Both Ferguson and Mark Andes had been in **Spirit**. By 1973, Jimmie Randall had replaced Mark Andes. By 1974, John Staehely had replaced Matthew Andes. Group named after the 1958 **Chuck Berry** hit. Mark Andes was later with **Firefall** and **Heart**.

2/26/72	57	22		1 Jo Jo Gunne	Asylum 5053
3/17/73	75	17		2 Bite Down Hard	Asylum 5065
12/22/73+	169	7		3 Jumpin' The Gunne	Asylum 5071
12/28/74	198	1		4 So...Where's The Show?	Asylum 1022

JOLI, France
Born in 1963 in Montreal, Quebec, Canada. White female dance singer.

9/8/79	26	17		1 France Joli	Prelude 12170
6/28/80	175	3		2 Tonight	Prelude 12179

JOLLY, Pete, Trio and Friends
Born Peter Ceragioli on 6/5/1932 in New Haven, Connecticut. Died on 11/6/2004 (age 72). Jazz pianist.

6/8/63	139	2		1 Little Bird ... [I]	Ava 22

JOLSON, Al
Born Asa Yoelson on 3/26/1886 in St. Petersburg, Russia; raised in Washington DC. Died on 10/23/1950 (age 64). One of the most popular entertainers of the 20th century. Starred in several movies and Broadway shows. Married to actress Ruby Keeler from 1928-39.

9/22/62+	40	42		1 The Best Of Jolson ... [G]	Decca 169 [2]

JON & VANGELIS
Duo of **Jon Anderson** (lead singer of **Yes**; born on 10/25/1944 in Lancashire, England) and **Vangelis** (born on 3/29/1943 in Valos, Greece).

5/31/80	125	15		1 Short Stories	Polydor 6272
8/8/81	64	34		2 The Friends Of Mr. Cairo	Polydor 6326
8/13/83	148	7		3 Private Collection	Polydor 813174

JONAS BROTHERS
Teen idol pop-rock trio from Wyckoff, New Jersey: brothers Kevin Jonas (born on 11/5/1987), Joe Jonas (born on 8/15/1989) and Nick Jonas (born on 9/16/1992). Starred in the 2008 Disney Channel movie *Camp Rock*.

8/26/06	91	1		1 It's About Time		Daylight 86716
8/25/07	5	78	▲	2 Jonas Brothers	Cat:#33/3	Hollywood 000282
8/30/08	❶²	35	▲	3 A Little Bit Longer		Hollywood 001944
3/14/09	3¹	14		4 Music From The 3D Concert Experience	[L-S]	Hollywood 002829
4/4/09	150	1		5 iTunes Live From Soho	[EP-L]	Hollywood digital
7/4/09	❶¹	27		6 Lines, Vines And Trying Times		Hollywood 002820
11/28/09	139	1		7 Walmart Soundcheck: Live	[EP-L]	Hollywood 005153

JON B
Born Jonathan Buck on 11/11/1974 in Rhode Island. R&B singer/songwriter.

6/10/95	79	24	●	1 Bonafide	Yab Yum 66436
10/4/97+	33	59	▲	2 Cool Relax	Yab Yum 67805
4/7/01	6	13		3 Pleasures U Like	Edmonds 69998
10/23/04	140	3		4 Stronger Everyday	E2 Records 87520
11/15/08	109	1		5 Helpless Romantic	Vibezelect 39803

JONES, Canton
Born in Deerfield Beach, Florida. Christian hip-hop singer/songwriter.

2/23/08	187	3		1 Kingdom Business	Arrow 4234091
10/24/09	195	1		2 Kingdom Business Pt. 2	Cajo 0020

JONES, Davy
Born on 12/30/1945 in Manchester, England. Pop singer/actor. Member of **The Monkees**.

5/27/67	185	6		1 David Jones	Colpix 493
10/30/71	205	1		2 Davy Jones	Bell 6067

JONES, Donell
Born on 5/22/1973 in Chicago, Illinois. R&B singer/songwriter.

10/19/96	180	4		1 My Heart	LaFace 26025
10/30/99	35	51	▲	2 Where I Wanna Be	LaFace 26060
6/22/02	3¹	19	●	3 Life Goes On	Untouchables 14760
7/8/06	15	11		4 Journey Of A Gemini	LaFace 52138
10/13/07	123	1		5 The Best Of Donell Jones ... [G]	LaFace 15490

Billboard			R I A A	ARTIST		
DEBUT	PEAK	WKS		Album Title	Catalog	Label & Number

JONES, Etta
Born on 11/25/1928 in Aiken, South Carolina. Died of cancer on 10/16/2001 (age 72). Jazz singer.

~ ~ ~ ~ ~ ~ ~ ~ ~ ~ ~ **NON-CHARTED ALBUM** ~ ~ ~ ~ ~ ~ ~ ~ ~ ~ ~

1960 **Don't Go To Strangers**
Grammy: Jazz Album

JONES, Freddy, Band — see FREDDY JONES BAND

JONES, George   All-Time: #344
Born on 9/12/1931 in Saratoga, Texas. Legendary country singer/songwriter/guitarist. Married to **Tammy Wynette** from 1969-75. Known as "No Show Jones" (due to several missed shows in the late 1970s) and "Possum."

AWARDS: C&W Hall of Fame: 1992 ★ CMA: Male Vocalist 1980 & 1981 ★ OPRY: 1956

3/20/65	141	4		1 George Jones & Gene Pitney		Musicor 3044
8/2/69	185	5		2 I'll Share My World With You		Musicor 3177
6/26/65	149	2		3 The Race Is On		United Artists 3422
11/13/71	169	6		4 We Go Together		Epic 30802
				TAMMY WYNETTE & GEORGE JONES		
1/19/80	206	4		5 My Very Special Guests		Epic 35544
6/13/81	132	14	▲	6 I Am What I Am		Epic 36586
11/28/81+	115	14	●	7 Still The Same Ole Me		Epic 37106
9/25/82	123	12		8 A Taste Of Yesterday's Wine		Epic 38203
				MERLE HAGGARD & GEORGE JONES		
10/10/92+	25[C]	15	▲²	9 Super Hits	[G]	Epic 40776
11/2/91	148	10		10 And Along Came Jones		MCA 10398
11/14/92+	77	20	●	11 Walls Can Fall		MCA 10652
12/18/93+	124	11	●	12 High-Tech Redneck		MCA 10910
1/28/95	142	4		13 The Bradley Barn Sessions		MCA 11096
7/8/95	117	13		14 One		MCA 11248
				GEORGE JONES & TAMMY WYNETTE		
9/7/96	171	2		15 I Lived To Tell It All		MCA 11478
7/10/99	53	25	●	16 Cold Hard Truth		Asylum 62368
10/20/01	65	7		17 The Rock: Stone Cold Country 2001		Bandit 67029
4/19/03	131	7		18 The Gospel Collection: George Jones Sings The Greatest Stories Ever Told		Bandit 67063 [2]
11/27/04	118	3	●	19 50 Years Of Hits	[G]	Bandit 220 [3]
10/1/05	79	7		20 Hits I Missed...And One I Didn't		Bandit 79792
11/11/06	119	4		21 Jones Sings Haggard, Haggard Sings Jones: Kickin' Out The Footlights...Again .		Bandit 79816
				GEORGE JONES & MERLE HAGGARD		
9/6/08	79	4		22 Burn Your Playhouse Down: The Unreleased Duets		Bandit 79842
9/19/09	88	4		23 A Collection Of My Best Recollection	[G]	Cracker Barrel 013358

JONES, Glenn
Born in 1962 in Jacksonville, Florida. R&B singer/songwriter.

10/10/87	94	17		1 Glenn Jones		Jive 1062

JONES, Grace
Born Grace Mendoza on 5/19/1948 in Spanishtown, Jamaica; raised in Syracuse, New York. Dance singer/actress/model. Acted in several movies.

10/22/77	109	20		1 Portfolio		Island 9470
8/5/78	97	8		2 Fame		Island 9525
9/1/79	156	7		3 Muse		Island 9538
6/21/80	132	10		4 Warm Leatherette		Island 9592
5/23/81	32	20		5 Nightclubbing		Island 9624
12/11/82	86	20		6 Living My Life		Island 90018
11/23/85	73	20		7 Slave To The Rhythm		Manhattan 53021
1/18/86	161	7		8 Island Life	[G]	Island 90491
12/13/86+	81	16		9 Inside Story		Manhattan 53038

JONES, Howard
Born John Howard Jones on 2/23/1955 in Southampton, Hampshire, England. Pop singer/songwriter/keyboardist.

3/24/84	59	43		1 Human's Lib		Elektra 60346
4/20/85	10	45	▲	2 Dream Into Action		Elektra 60390
5/3/86	34	24		3 Action Replay	[EP-K]	Elektra 60466
11/1/86	56	21		4 One To One		Elektra 60499
4/15/89	65	22		5 Cross That Line		Elektra 60794

JONES, Jack   All-Time: #333
Born on 1/14/1938 in Los Angeles, California. Adult Contemporary singer. Son of actress Irene Hervey and actor/singer Allan Jones. Performed the theme for TV's *Love Boat*. Married to actress Jill St. John from 1967-69.

6/29/63+	98	25		1 Call Me Irresponsible		Kapp 3328
12/28/63+	18	53		2 Wives And Lovers		Kapp 3352
6/20/64	43	19		3 Bewitched		Kapp 3365
8/29/64	62	23		4 Where Love Has Gone		Kapp 3396
12/19/64+	15[X]	11		5 The Jack Jones Christmas Album	[X]	Kapp 3399
				Christmas charts: 17/'64, 30/'65, 15/'66, 26/'67		
1/9/65	11	25		6 Dear Heart		Kapp 3415

JONES, Jack — cont'd

5/8/65	29	22		7 My Kind Of Town		Kapp 3433
9/18/65	86	13		8 There's Love & There's Love & There's Love		Kapp 3435
3/26/66	147	2		9 For The "In" Crowd		Kapp 3465
7/16/66	9	64		10 The Impossible Dream		Kapp 3486
11/26/66+	75	12		11 Jack Jones Sings		Kapp 3500
3/25/67	23	25		12 Lady		Kapp 3511
10/14/67	148	7		13 Our Song		Kapp 3531
2/24/68	167	6		14 What The World Needs Now Is Love!	[K]	Kapp 3551
12/16/67+	146	7		15 Without Her		RCA Victor 3911
4/27/68	198	3		16 If You Ever Leave Me		RCA Victor 3969
9/21/68	195	3		17 Where Is Love?		RCA Victor 4048
8/16/69	183	4		18 A Time For Us		RCA Victor 4209
11/20/71	201	1		19 Song For You		RCA Victor 4613

JONES, Jake — see JAKE JONES

JONES, Jesus — see JESUS

JONES, Jim
Born Joseph Jimmy Jones on 7/15/1976 in the Bronx, New York. Male rapper/songwriter. Member of **The Diplomats**.

9/11/04	18	7		1 On My Way To Church		Diplomats 5770
9/10/05	5	11		2 Harlem: Diary Of A Summer		Diplomats 5830
11/25/06	6	21		3 Hustler's P.O.M.E. (Product Of My Environment)		Diplomats 5964
1/20/07	5ˣ	2		4 A Dipset Xmas	[X]	Diplomats 5957
3/8/08	19	5		5 Harlem's American Gangster		Koch 5073
7/19/08	29	3		6 M.O.B.: The Album		BG 372284
				JIM JONES & BYRD GANG		
4/11/09	9	6		7 Pray IV Reign		Columbia 19376

JONES, Jimmy
Born on 6/2/1937 in Birmingham, Alabama. R&B singer.

~ ~ ~ ~ ~ ~ ~ ~ ~ ~   *NON-CHARTED ALBUM*   ~ ~ ~ ~ ~ ~ ~ ~ ~ ~
1960 Good Timin'

JONES, Joe
Born on 8/12/1926 in New Orleans, Louisiana. Died on 11/27/2005 (age 79). R&B singer/songwriter.

~ ~ ~ ~ ~ ~ ~ ~ ~ ~   *NON-CHARTED ALBUM*   ~ ~ ~ ~ ~ ~ ~ ~ ~ ~
1960 You Talk Too Much

JONES, Jonah   1950s: #35
Born Robert Jones on 10/31/1909 in Louisville, Kentucky. Died on 4/30/2000 (age 90). Jazz trumpeter.

3/10/58	7	17		1 Muted Jazz	[I]	Capitol 839
4/28/58	7	19		2 Swingin' On Broadway	[I]	Capitol 963
9/8/58	14	5		3 Jumpin' With Jonah	[I]	Capitol 1039
				THE JONAH JONES QUARTET (above 2)		

JONES, Mick
Born on 12/27/1944 in London, England. Rock guitarist. Member of **Spooky Tooth** and **Foreigner**. Not to be confused with Mick Jones of The Clash and Big Audio Dynamite.

9/23/89	184	3		1 Mick Jones		Atlantic 81991

JONES, Mike
Born on 1/6/1981 in Houston, Texas. Rapper/songwriter.

5/7/05	3¹	38	▲	1 Who Is Mike Jones?		Swishahouse 49340
12/8/07	183	1		2 The American Dream	[EP]	Ice Age 368764
5/16/09	12	5		3 The Voice		Ice Age 517389

JONES, Norah   2000s: #41 / All-Time: #463
Born on 3/30/1979 in Manhattan, New York; raised in Dallas, Texas. Jazz-styled singer/pianist. Daughter of legendary sitar player **Ravi Shankar**. Member of **The Little Willies**.
AWARD: Grammy: Best New Artist 2002

3/16/02+	❶⁴	153	▲¹⁰	1 Come Away With Me	Cat:❶⁶/175	Blue Note 32088
				Grammys: Album of the Year / Pop Vocal Album		
7/26/03	54	11		2 New York City		Koch 8678
				THE PETER MALICK GROUP Featuring Norah Jones		
2/28/04	❶⁶	71	▲⁴	3 Feels Like Home	Cat:#11/5	Blue Note 84800
2/17/07	❶³	34	▲²	4 Not Too Late	Cat:#46/1	Blue Note 74516
12/5/09	3¹	25	▲	5 The Fall		Blue Note 99286

JONES, Oran "Juice"
Born on 3/28/1957 in Houston, Texas; raised in Harlem, New York. R&B singer/rapper.

9/20/86	44	22		1 Oran "Juice" Jones		Def Jam 40367

JONES, Quincy
All-Time: #219

Born on 3/14/1933 in Chicago, Illinois; raised in Bremerton, Washington. Songwriter/conductor/producer/arranger. Began as a jazz trumpeter with Lionel Hampton (1950-53). Music director for Mercury Records in 1961, then vice president in 1964. Wrote scores for many movies. Scored TV series *Roots* in 1977. Arranger/producer for hundreds of successful singers and orchestras. Produced **Michael Jackson**'s mega-albums *Off The Wall*, *Thriller* and *Bad*. Established own Qwest label in 1981. Married to actress Peggy Lipton (TV's *Mod Squad*) from 1974-89. His biographical movie *Listen Up: The Lives Of Quincy Jones* was released in 1990.

AWARD: Grammys: Trustees 1989 / Legend 1991

12/29/62+	112	8		1 Big Band Bossa Nova	[I]	Mercury 60751
3/4/72	173	9		2 Ndeda	[I-K]	Mercury 623 [2]
11/22/69+	56	39		3 Walking In Space	[I]	A&M 3023
				Grammy: Jazz Album		
9/5/70	63	16		4 Gula Matari	[I]	A&M 3030
10/16/71	56	33		5 Smackwater Jack	[I]	A&M 3037
				Grammy: Pop Instrumental Album		
6/2/73	94	24		6 You've Got It Bad Girl		A&M 3041
5/25/74	6	43	●	7 Body Heat		A&M 3617
8/23/75	16	30		8 Mellow Madness		A&M 4526
10/2/76	43	15		9 I Heard That!!	[K]	A&M 3705 [2]
2/19/77	21	14	●	10 Roots	[TV]	A&M 4626
6/24/78	15	20	▲	11 Sounds...And Stuff Like That!!		A&M 4685
4/4/81+	10	80	▲	12 The Dude	Cat:#23/89	A&M 3721
				Grammy: Group R&B Vocal		
7/17/82	122	17		13 The Best	[G]	A&M 3200
12/9/89+	9	40	▲	14 Back On The Block		Qwest 26020
				Grammy: Album of the Year		
11/25/95	32	38	▲	15 Q's Jook Joint		Qwest 45875
2/20/99	72	8		16 From Q, With Love	[K]	Qwest 46490 [2]

JONES, Rickie Lee
Born on 11/8/1954 in Chicago, Illinois. Female singer/songwriter/guitarist.

AWARD: Grammy: Best New Artist 1979

4/7/79	3²	36	▲	1 Rickie Lee Jones		Warner 3296
8/8/81	5	29	●	2 Pirates		Warner 3432
7/2/83	39	16		3 Girl At Her Volcano	[EP]	Warner 23805
10/13/84	44	21		4 The Magazine		Warner 25117
10/14/89	39	25	●	5 Flying Cowboys		Geffen 24246
10/12/91	121	5		6 Pop Pop		Geffen 24426
10/2/93	111	7		7 Traffic From Paradise		Geffen 24602
10/7/95	121	2		8 Naked Songs - Live And Acoustic	[L]	Reprise 45950
7/5/97	159	1		9 Ghostyhead		Reprise 46557
9/30/00	148	2		10 It's Like This		Artemis 751054
10/25/03	189	1		11 The Evening Of My Best Day		V2 27171
2/24/07	158	1		12 The Sermon On Exposition Boulevard		New West 6108

JONES, Sharon, & The Dap-Kings
Born on 5/4/1956 in Augusta, Georgia; raised in Harlem, New York. Female R&B singer/songwriter.

10/20/07	194	1		1 100 Days, 100 Nights		Daptone 012

JONES, Shirley
Born in Detroit, Michigan. R&B singer. Member of **The Jones Girls**.

8/23/86	128	10		1 Always In The Mood		Philadelphia Int'l. 53031

JONES, Spike
Born Lindley Armstrong Jones on 12/14/1911 in Long Beach, California. Died of emphysema on 5/1/1965 (age 53). Novelty bandleader. Known as "The King of Corn."

11/23/63	113	4		1 Washington Square	[I]	Liberty 3338
				THE NEW BAND OF SPIKE JONES		

JONES, Steve
Born on 9/3/1955 in London, England. Rock guitarist. Member of the **Sex Pistols** and **Chequered Past**.

10/21/89	169	4		1 Fire And Gasoline		MCA 6298

JONES, Tamiko
Born Barbara Tamiko Ferguson in 1945 in Kyle, West Virginia; raised in Detroit, Michigan. R&B singer.

5/17/75	204	5		1 Love Trip		Arista 4040

JONES, Tom
All-Time: #171

Born Thomas Jones Woodward on 6/7/1940 in Pontypridd, Glamorgan, Wales. Pop singer. Worked local clubs as Tommy Scott; formed own trio The Senators in 1963. Began solo career in London in 1964. Host of own TV musical variety series from 1969-71. Knighted by Queen Elizabeth in 2006.

AWARD: Grammy: Best New Artist 1965

DEBUT	PEAK	WKS			Catalog	Label & Number
7/3/65	54	42		1 It's Not Unusual		Parrot 71004
9/18/65	114	5		2 What's New Pussycat?		Parrot 71006
3/4/67+	65	45	●	3 Green, Green Grass Of Home		Parrot 71009
6/15/68+	14	82	●	4 The Tom Jones Fever Zone		Parrot 71019
2/1/69	5	54	●	5 Help Yourself		Parrot 71025
3/15/69	13	58	●	6 Tom Jones Live! .... [L]		Parrot 71014
				originally recorded and released in 1967		
6/14/69	4	43	●	7 This Is Tom Jones		Parrot 71028
11/15/69	3[5]	51	●	8 Tom Jones Live In Las Vegas [L]		Parrot 71031
				recorded at The Flamingo hotel		
5/9/70	6	26	●	9 Tom		Parrot 71037
11/14/70	23	40	●	10 I (Who Have Nothing)		Parrot 71039
5/22/71	17	20	●	11 She's A Lady		Parrot 71046
11/6/71	43	14	●	12 Tom Jones Live At Caesars Palace .... [L]		Parrot 71049 [2]
6/17/72	64	20		13 Close Up		Parrot 71055
6/16/73	93	10		14 The Body And Soul Of Tom Jones		Parrot 71060
1/5/74	185	4		15 Tom Jones' Greatest Hits .... [G]		Parrot 71062
3/5/77	76	16		16 Say You'll Stay Until Tomorrow		Epic 34468
3/5/77	191	3		17 Tom Jones Greatest Hits .... [G]		London 50002
5/23/81	179	3		18 Darlin'		Mercury 4010
11/1/03	127	10		19 Reloaded: Greatest Hits .... [G]		Decca 001421
12/13/08	105	3		20 24 Hours		S-Curve 55001

JONESES, The
R&B vocal group from Pittsburgh: brothers Reggie and Wendall Noble, Harold Taylor, Sam White and Glenn Dorsey.

12/7/74+	202	12		1 Keepin' Up With The Joneses		Mercury 1021

JONES GIRLS, The
R&B vocal trio from Detroit, Michigan: sisters Brenda Jones, Valorie Jones and **Shirley Jones**. Valorie died on 12/2/2001 (age 45).

6/9/79	50	16		1 The Jones Girls		Philadelphia Int'l. 35757
10/18/80	96	24		2 At Peace With Woman		Philadelphia Int'l. 36767
12/5/81+	155	15		3 Get As Much Love As You Can		Philadelphia Int'l. 37627
5/5/84	201	1		4 Keep It Comin'		Philadelphia Int'l. 38555

JONZUN CREW, The
Electronic funk band from Boston, Massachusetts: brothers Michael Johnson (vocals) and Soni Johnson (keyboards), with Gordy Worthy (bass) and Steve Thorpe (drums).

5/14/83	66	20		1 Lost In Space		Tommy Boy 1001

JOPLIN, Janis
All-Time: #420

Born on 1/19/1943 in Port Arthur, Texas. Died of a heroin overdose on 10/4/1970 (age 27). White blues-rock singer. Nicknamed "Pearl." To San Francisco in 1966, joined **Big Brother & The Holding Company**. Left band to go solo in 1968. The **Bette Midler** movie *The Rose* was inspired by Joplin's life.

AWARDS: Grammy: Lifetime Achievement 2005 ★ R&R Hall of Fame: 1995

10/11/69	5	28	▲	1 I Got Dem Ol' Kozmic Blues Again Mama!		Columbia 9913
1/30/71	❶[9]	42	▲[4]	2 Pearl	Cat:#18/38	Columbia 30322
				Grammy: Hall of Fame ★ RS500 #122		
5/13/72	4	27	●	3 Joplin In Concert [L]		Columbia 31160 [2]
				side 1: with **Big Brother & The Holding Company**; side 2: with Full Tilt Boogie Band		
7/14/73	37	22	▲[7]	4 Janis Joplin's Greatest Hits .... Cat:#2[1]/454 [G]		Columbia 32168
5/17/75	54	9		5 Janis .... Cat:#39/2 [S]		Columbia 33345 [2]
2/13/82	104	11		6 Farewell Song .... [K]		Columbia 37569

JORDAN, Jeremy
Born Don Henson on 9/19/1973 in Hammond, Indiana: raised in Calumet City, Illinois. Pop singer.

5/15/93	176	2		1 Try My Love		Giant 24483

JORDAN, Jerry
Born in 1944 in Austin, Texas. Country-religious comedian. Later became a professional artist in Taos, New Mexico.

5/31/75	79	12		1 Phone Call From God .... [C]		MCA 473

JORDAN, Lonnie
Born LeRoy Jordan on 11/21/1948 in San Diego, California. R&B singer/keyboardist. Member of **War**.

2/25/78	158	5		1 Different Moods Of Me		MCA 2329

Billboard			R I A A	ARTIST		
DEBUT	PEAK	WKS		Album Title	Catalog	Label & Number

JORDAN, Montell
Born on 12/3/1968 in Los Angeles, California. Male R&B singer/songwriter.

4/22/95	12	36	▲	1 This Is How We Do It		Def Jam 527179
9/14/96	47	24	●	2 More...		Def Jam 533191
4/18/98	20	26	●	3 Let's Ride		Def Jam 536987
11/27/99	32	26	●	4 Get It On...Tonite		Def Soul 546714

JORDAN, Sass
Born on 12/23/1962 in Birmingham, England; raised in Montreal, Quebec, Canada. Female rock singer. One of the judges on the TV talent show *Canadian Idol*.

| 8/29/92 | 174 | 7 | | 1 Racine | | Impact 10524 |
| 3/19/94 | 158 | 4 | | 2 Rats | | Impact 10980 |

JORDAN, Stanley
Born on 7/31/1959 in Chicago, Illinois. Jazz guitarist.

5/25/85	64	66	●	1 Magic Touch	[I]	Blue Note 85101
2/14/87	116	18		2 Standards, Volume 1	[I]	Blue Note 85130
10/15/88	131	9		3 Flying Home	[I]	EMI 48682

JOSEPH, Margie
Born in 1950 in Gautier, Mississippi. R&B singer.

| 2/6/71 | 67 | 14 | | 1 Margie Joseph Makes A New Impression | | Volt 6012 |
| 8/17/74 | 165 | 3 | | 2 Sweet Surrender | | Atlantic 7277 |

JOURNEY   1980s: #6 / All-Time: #82
Rock band formed in San Francisco, California: Gregg Rolie (vocals, keyboards), **Neal Schon** (guitar), George Tickner (guitar), Ross Valory (bass) and Aynsley Dunbar (drums; **John Mayall** and **Frank Zappa**'s Mothers Of Invention). Schon and Rolie had been in **Santana**. Tickner left in 1975. **Steve Perry** (lead vocals) added by 1978. In 1979, **Steve Smith** replaced Dunbar, who later joined **Jefferson Starship**, then **Whitesnake**. **Jonathan Cain** (keyboards; **The Babys**) added in 1981, replacing Rolie. In 1986 group pared down to a three-man core: Perry, Schon and Cain. **Randy Jackson** (of TV's *American idol*) was a member from 1986-87. Schon and Cain hooked up with **Bad English** in 1989. Smith, Valory and Rolie joined **The Storm** in 1991. Schon with Hardline in 1992. Reunion in 1996 of Perry, Schon, Cain, Valory and Smith. Steve Augeri replaced Perry in 1998.

5/3/75	138	9		1 Journey		Columbia 33388
2/14/76	100	15		2 Look Into The Future		Columbia 33904
2/19/77	85	10		3 Next		Columbia 34311
2/11/78	21	123	▲³	4 Infinity		Columbia 34912
4/14/79	20	96	▲³	5 Evolution		Columbia 35797
1/5/80	152	8		6 In The Beginning	[K]	Columbia 36324 [2]
3/22/80	8	57	▲³	7 Departure		Columbia 36339
2/21/81	9	69	▲²	8 Captured	[L]	Columbia 37016 [2]
8/8/81	❶¹	146	▲⁹	9 Escape	Cat:#9/19	Columbia 37408
2/19/83	2⁹	85	▲⁶	10 Frontiers		Columbia 38504
5/10/86	4	67	▲²	11 Raised On Radio		Columbia 39936
12/3/88+	10	118↑	▲¹⁵	12 Greatest Hits	Cat:❶⁵/744 [G]	Columbia 44493
12/26/92+	90	4	●	13 Time 3	[K]	Columbia 48937 [3]
11/9/96	3¹	27	▲	14 Trial By Fire		Columbia 67514
4/11/98	79	7	●	15 Greatest Hits Live	[G-L]	Columbia 69139
				recorded from 1981-83		
4/21/01	56	6		16 Arrival		Columbia 69864
11/3/01	47	5	▲	17 The Essential Journey	[G]	Columbia 86080 [2]
10/22/05	170	1		18 Generations		Nomota 84774
6/21/08	5	42	▲	19 Revelation		Nomota 4506

JOY DIVISION
Post-punk band formed in Manchester, England: Ian Curtis (vocals), Bernard Albrecht (guitar), Peter Hook (bass) and Stephen Morris (drums). Curtis committed suicide on 5/18/1980 (age 23). Group became **New Order**, recruiting keyboardist/guitarist Gillian Gilbert in December 1980.

| 8/27/88 | 146 | 8 | | 1 Substance | [K] | Qwest 25747 |

~ ~ ~ ~ ~ ~ ~ ~ ~ ~ **NON-CHARTED ALBUM** ~ ~ ~ ~ ~ ~ ~ ~ ~ ~ ~
1980 **Closer**
RS500 #157

JOYFUL NOISE, A
Studio project formed by songwriters Dani Davis and Jason Howland. Features lead vocals by Mig Ayesa, LaChanze and J. Robert Spencer.

| 10/24/09 | 30ˣ | 3 | | 1 Handel's Messiah Rocks | [X] | Integrity 50243 |

JOY OF COOKING
Country-rock band from Berkeley, California: Terry Garthwaite (vocals), Toni Brown (vocals, keyboards), Ron Wilson (percussion), Jeff Neighbor (bass) and Fritz Kasten (drums). Also see **Toni & Terry**.

3/6/71	100	17		1 Joy Of Cooking		Capitol 661
10/9/71	136	7		2 Closer To The Ground		Capitol 828
6/10/72	174	6		3 Castles		Capitol 11050

JS
R&B vocal duo from Los Angeles, California: sisters Kim Johnson and Kandy Johnson. JS: Johnson Sisters.

DEBUT	PEAK	WKS		Album Title	Catalog	Label & Number
8/16/03	33	9		1 Ice Cream		DreamWorks 450332

J-SHIN
Born Jonathan Shinhoster in 1978 in Miami, Florida. Male R&B singer.

3/18/00	71	6		1 My Soul, My Life		Slip-N-Slide 83256

JT THE BIGGA FIGGA
Born Joseph Tom in San Francisco, California. Male rapper.

10/28/95	168	1		1 Dwellin' In Tha Labb...............................		Get Low 53981

JUANES
Born Juan Aristizabal on 8/9/1972 in Medellin, Colombia. Latin singer.

10/5/02+	110	21	●	1 Un Dia Normal.................................... [F]		Surco 017532
10/16/04	33	49	●	2 Mi Sangre .... [F]		Surco 003475
11/10/07	13	19		3 La Vida...Es Un Ratico......................... [F]		Universal Latino
				Grammy: Latin Pop Album		

JUDAS PRIEST　　　　　　　　　　　　**All-Time: #227**
Heavy metal band formed in Birmingham, England: Rob **Halford** (vocals; born on 8/25/1951), Ken "K.K." Downing (guitar; born on 8/25/1951), Glenn Tipton (guitar; born on 10/25/1948), Ian Hill (bass; born on 1/20/1952) and Dave Holland (drums). Scott Travis replaced Holland in 1990. Halford left in 1992 to form **Fight** and **Two**. New lead singer Tim "Ripper" Owens joined in 1996.

8/28/76	204	6		1 Sad Wings Of Destiny.................. **Cat:**#10/83		Ovation 1751
7/30/77	207	1	●	2 Sin After Sin.......................... **Cat:**#15/108		Columbia 34787
4/8/78	173	3	●	3 Stained Class.......................................		Columbia 35296
3/31/79	128	7	●	4 Hell Bent For Leather		Columbia 35706
10/6/79	70	11	▲	5 Unleashed In The East (Live In Japan)........ [L]		Columbia 36179
5/31/80	34	19↑	●	6 British Steel		Columbia 36443
4/4/81	39	25	●	7 Point Of Entry		Columbia 37052
7/24/82	17	53	▲²	8 Screaming For Vengeance		Columbia 38160
2/4/84	18	37	▲	9 Defenders Of The Faith		Columbia 39219
4/12/86	17	36	▲	10 Turbo		Columbia 40158
6/20/87	38	15	●	11 Priest...Live! .... [L]		Columbia 40794 [2]
6/4/88	31	19	●	12 Ram It Down		Columbia 44244
10/6/90	26	20	●	13 Painkiller		Columbia 46891
6/5/93	155	2		14 Metal Works '73-'93........................... [K]		Columbia 53932 [2]
11/15/97	82	2		15 Jugulator		CMC Int'l. 86224
8/18/01	165	1		16 Demolition		Atlantic 83508
3/19/05	13	6		17 Angel Of Retribution		Epic 93966
7/5/08	11	7		18 Nostradamus		Epic 30708
8/1/09	87	1		19 A Touch Of Evil: Live .... [L]		Epic 55266

JUDD, Cledus T.
Born Barry Poole on 12/18/1964 in Crowe Springs, Georgia. Country novelty singer.

9/21/96+	173	9	●	1 I Stoled This Record .... [N]		Razor & Tie 2825
4/18/98	181	2		2 Did I Shave My Back For This? .... [N]		Razor & Tie 82835
12/2/00	198	2		3 Just Another Day In Parodies .... [N]		Monument 85106
5/18/02	136	2		4 Cledus Envy .... [N]		Monument 85897
5/17/03	130	1		5 A Six Pack Of Judd .... [EP-N]		Monument 89223
9/11/04	98	5		6 Bipolar And Proud .... [N]		Koch 9809

JUDD, Wynonna — see WYNONNA

JUDDS, The
Country duo from Ashland, Kentucky: Naomi Judd (born Diana Ellen Judd on 1/11/1946) and her daughter **Wynonna** Judd (born Christina Ciminella on 5/30/1964). Moved to Hollywood in 1968. Moved to Nashville in 1979. Naomi's chronic hepatitis forced duo to split at the end of 1991. Naomi's daughter and Wynonna's half-sister is actress Ashley Judd.
AWARD: CMA: Horizon 1984 / Vocal Group 1985, 1986 & 1987 / Vocal Duo 1988, 1989, 1990 & 1991

12/1/84+	71	26	▲²	1 Why Not Me		RCA/Curb 5319
				Grammy: Group Country Vocal		
12/8/84+	153	15		2 The Judds .... [EP]		RCA/Curb 8515
11/16/85+	66	57	▲	3 Rockin' With The Rhythm		RCA/Curb 7042
4/4/87	52	31	▲	4 Heartland .... **Cat:**#34/7		RCA/Curb 5916
12/19/87	9ˣ	20	▲	5 Christmas Time With The Judds　**Cat:**#21/12 [X]		RCA/Curb 6422
				Christmas charts: 9/'87, 9/'88, 29/'89, 26/'90, 12/'91, 24/'92, 29/'93, 36/'99		
4/22/89	51	20	●	6 River Of Time		RCA/Curb 9595
9/29/90+	62	53	▲	7 Love Can Build A Bridge		RCA/Curb 2070
5/27/00	107	2		8 Reunion Live .... [L]		Curb 170134 [2]
				recorded 12/31/1999 at America West Arena in Phoenix		
				GREATEST HITS & COMPILATIONS:		
8/27/88	76	97	▲²	9 Greatest Hits .... **Cat:**#10/2		RCA/Curb 8318
9/28/91+	54	32	●	10 Greatest Hits Volume Two .... **Cat:**#14/2		RCA/Curb 61018
6/1/91	25ᶜ	3	●	11 Collector's Series		RCA/Curb 2278
6/3/95	187	1	●	12 Number One Hits .... **Cat:**#22/4		RCA/Curb 66489

DEBUT	PEAK	WKS	RIAA	ARTIST / Album Title	Catalog	Label & Number
				JUICY J Born Jordan Houston on 4/5/1975 in Memphis, Tennessee. Male rapper. Member of **Da Headbussaz** and **Three 6 Mafia**.		
8/3/02	93	4		1 **Chronicles Of The Juice Man: Underground**		North North 3601
7/4/09	106	2		2 **Hustle Till I Die**		Hypnotize Minds 3621
				JULES, Gary Born Gary Jules Aguirre on 3/19/1969 in San Diego, California. Alternative-pop singer/songwriter.		
4/10/04	144	2		1 **Trading Snakeoil For Wolftickets**		Universal 002275
				JULIANA THEORY, The Rock band from Greensburg, Pennsylvania: Brett Detar (vocals), Josh Fiedler (guitar), Josh Kosker (guitar), Chad Alan (bass) and Neil Hebrank (drums).		
2/22/03	71	5		1 **Love**		Epic 86163
				JULUKA Interracial pop band from South Africa: **Johnny Clegg** and Sipho Mchunu (vocals, guitars), Cyril Mnculwane and Glenda Miller (keyboards), Scorpion Madondo (horns), Gary Van Zyl (bass) and Derrick DeBeer (drums).		
8/13/83	186	5		1 **Scatterlings**		Warner 23898
11/3/84	209	1		2 **Stand Your Ground**		Warner 25155
				JUMP5 Teen pop vocal group from Nashville, Tennessee: siblings Brandon Hargest and Brittany Hargest, with Lesley Moore, Libby Hodges and Christopher Fedun.		
8/31/02	86	19		1 **All The Time In The World**		Sparrow 51992
11/30/02	31ˣ	3		2 **All The Joy In The World** [X] Christmas chart: 28/'03		Sparrow 40440
10/25/03	150	3		3 **Accelerate**		Sparrow 83553
				JUNGKLAS, Rob Born in Boston, Massachusetts; raised in Memphis, Tennessee. Rock singer/songwriter/guitarist.		
6/14/86	102	22		1 **Closer To The Flame**		Manhattan 53017
				JUNIE Born Walter Morrison in 1954 in Dayton, Ohio. Former keyboardist with the **Ohio Players**.		
6/20/81	205	1		1 **Five**		Columbia 37133
				JUNIOR Born Norman Giscombe on 11/10/1961 in London, England. Funk singer/songwriter.		
5/8/82	71	16		1 **"Ji"**		Mercury 4043
7/23/83	177	6		2 **Inside Lookin' Out**		Mercury 812325
				JUNIOR M.A.F.I.A. Rap group from New York: **Lil' Kim**, Klepto, Trife, Larceny, **Lil' Cease**, Chico and Nino Brown. Proteges of **The Notorious B.I.G.** M.A.F.I.A.: Masters At Finding Intelligent Attitudes.		
9/16/95	8	31	●	1 **Conspiracy**		Undeas 92614
				JUNIOR SENIOR White trip-hop duo from Jutland, Denmark: Jesper "Junior" Mortensen and Jeppe "Senior" Laursen.		
8/23/03	94	4		1 **D-D-Don't Don't Stop The Beat**		Crunchy Frog 83663
				JUNKYARD Hard-rock band formed in Los Angeles, California: David Roach (vocals), Chris Gates (guitar), Brian Baker (guitar), Clay Anthony (bass) and Pat Muzingo (drums).		
8/12/89	105	11		1 **Junkyard**		Geffen 24227
				JUPITER, Duke — see DUKE		
				JURASSIC 5 Interracial hip-hop group from Los Angeles, California: Dante "Akil" Givens, Courtenay "Soup" Henderson, Lucas "DJ Cut Chemist" MacFadden, Mark "DJ Nu-Mark" Potsic, Charles "Chali 2na" Stewart and "Marc 7" Stuart.		
7/8/00	43	15		1 **Quality Control**		Rawkus 490664
10/26/02	15	12		2 **Power In Numbers**		Interscope 493437
8/12/06	15	8		3 **Feedback**		Interscope 006906
				JUSTIS, Bill Born on 10/14/1926 in Birmingham, Alabama. Died on 7/15/1982 (age 55). Session saxophonist/arranger/producer.		
11/24/62	94	8		1 **Bill Justis Plays 12 Big Instrumental Hits** (Alley Cat/Green Onions) [I]		Smash 67021
2/23/63	89	6		2 **Bill Justis Plays 12 More Big Instrumental Hits** (Telstar/The Lonely Bull) [I]		Smash 67030
				~ ~ ~ ~ ~ ~ ~ ~ **NON-CHARTED ALBUM** ~ ~ ~ ~ ~ ~ ~ ~ ~ ~ ~ 1959 **Cloud 9** ["Raunchy"]		
				JUVENILE Born Terius Gray on 3/25/1975 in New Orleans, Louisiana. Male rapper. Member of **Cash Money Millionaires** and **Hot Boys**. Appeared in the movies *Baller Blockin'* and *Hood Angels*.		
6/5/99	137	2		1 **Being Myself** (Remixed) [E]		Warlock 2809
11/21/98+	9	100	▲⁴	2 **400 Degreez** Cat:#37/2		Cash Money 53162
1/1/00	10	26	▲	3 **Tha G-Code**		Cash Money 542179
9/8/01	2¹	18	●	4 **Project English**		Cash Money 860913

Billboard			R I A A	ARTIST	Catalog	Label & Number
DEBUT	PEAK	WKS		Album Title		

				JUVENILE — cont'd		
1/10/04	28	41	▲	5 Juve The Great		Cash Money 001718
11/6/04	31	6		6 The Greatest Hits	[G]	Cash Money 003548
6/5/04	122	4		7 The Beginning Of The End...		J Prince 42046
				JUVENILE • WACKO • SKIP		
3/25/06	**❶**¹	14	●	8 Reality Check		UTP 83790
12/19/09	49	4		9 Cocky & Confident		UTP 511263

JUVET, Patrick
Born on 8/21/1950 in Montreux, Switzerland. Disco singer.

7/1/78	125	14		1 Got A Feeling		Casablanca 7101

K

KADISON, Joshua
Born on 2/8/1963 in Los Angeles, California. Adult Contemporary singer/songwriter/pianist.

1/29/94	69	52	▲	1 Painted Desert Serenade		SBK 80920

KAEMPFERT, Bert, And His Orchestra   1960s: #38 / All-Time: #213
Born on 10/16/1923 in Hamburg, Germany. Died of a stroke on 6/21/1980 (age 56).
Multi-instrumentalist/bandleader/producer/arranger for Polydor Records in Germany. Composed "Strangers In The Night" and "Spanish Eyes" among others. Produced first **Beatles** recording session in Hamburg ("Cry For A Shadow"/"Ain't She Sweet").

12/31/60+	**❶**⁵	40	●	1 Wonderland By Night	[I]	Decca 74101
11/20/61	92	6		2 Dancing In Wonderland	[I]	Decca 74161
4/21/62	82	13		3 Afrikaan Beat And Other Favorites	[I]	Decca 74273
9/29/62	14	17		4 That Happy Feeling	[I]	Decca 74305
7/6/63	87	12		5 Living It Up!	[I]	Decca 74374
11/30/63	6ˣ	16		6 Christmas Wonderland	[X-I]	Decca 74441
				Christmas charts: 6/'63, 34/'64, 38/'65, 21/'66, 62/'67, 38/'68		
11/30/63	79	6		7 Lights Out, Sweet Dreams	[I]	Decca 74265
1/23/65	5	55	●	8 Blue Midnight	[I]	Decca 74569
7/10/65	42	22		9 Three O'Clock In The Morning	[I]	Decca 74670
9/4/65	27	23		10 The Magic Music Of Far Away Places	[I]	Decca 74616
3/12/66	46	28		11 Bye Bye Blues	[I]	Decca 74693
7/9/66	39	21		12 Strangers In The Night	[I]	Decca 74795
10/8/66	30	40	●	13 Bert Kaempfert's Greatest Hits	[G-I]	Decca 74810
5/13/67	122	7		14 Hold Me	[I]	Decca 74860
10/7/67	136	7		15 The World We Knew	[I]	Decca 74925
11/2/68	186	2		16 My Way Of Life	[I]	Decca 75059
3/29/69	194	5		17 Warm And Wonderful	[I]	Decca 75089
11/1/69	153	10		18 Traces Of Love	[I]	Decca 75140
3/28/70	87	7		19 The Kaempfert Touch	[I]	Decca 75175
2/13/71	140	6		20 Orange Colored Sky	[I]	Decca 75256
9/25/71	188	2		21 Bert Kaempfert Now!	[I]	Decca 75305
5/27/72	218	1		22 6 Plus 6	[I]	Decca 75322

KAISER CHIEFS
Punk-rock band from Leeds, England: Ricky Wilson (vocals), Andrew White (guitar), Nick Baines (keyboards), Simon Rix (bass) and Nick Hodgson (drums).

4/2/05	86	7		1 Employment		B-Unique 004215
4/14/07	45	6		2 Yours Truly, Angry Mob		B-Unique 008588
11/15/08	55	2		3 Off With Their Head		B-Unique 012106

KAJAGOOGOO
Pop-synth band formed in Leighton Buzzard, Hertfordshire, England: Christopher "**Limahl**" Hamill (vocals), Steve Askew (guitar), Stuart Neale (keyboards), Nick Beggs (bass) and Jez Strode (drums). Limahl left in late 1983; Beggs took over lead vocals.

6/11/83	38	20		1 White Feathers		EMI America 17094
4/27/85	185	4		2 Extra Play		EMI America 17157

KALEIDOSCOPE
Folk-rock band from Los Angeles, California: **David Lindley** (vocals, guitar), Solomon Feldthouse (clarinet), Templeton Parcely (violin), Stuart Brotman (bass) and Paul Lagos (drums).

6/14/69	139	8		1 Incredible Kaleidoscope		Epic 26467

KALIKO, Krizz
Born Samuel Watson in Kansas City, Missouri. Male rapper.

5/24/08	167	1		1 Vitiligo		Strange 45
8/1/09	85	1		2 Genius		Strange 57

KALIN TWINS
White pop vocal duo of twins Herbert Kalin and Harold Kalin. Born on 2/16/1934 in Port Jervis, New York. Harold died in a car crash on 8/23/2005 (age 71). Herbert died of a heart attack on 7/21/2006 (age 72).

~ ~ ~ ~ ~ ~ ~ ~ ~ ~ ~ **NON-CHARTED ALBUM** ~ ~ ~ ~ ~ ~ ~ ~ ~ ~ ~ ~
1959 **The Kalin Twins** ["When"]

Billboard			R I A A	ARTIST	Catalog	Label & Number
DEBUT	PEAK	WKS		Album Title		

KALLMANN, Gunter, Chorus
Born on 11/19/1927 in Berlin, Germany. Choral director.

5/1/65	97	10		1 Serenade For Elisabeth.. [F]		4 Corners 4209
12/24/66+	126	8		2 Wish Me A Rainbow		4 Corners 4235
12/30/67	76ˣ	1		3 The Gunter Kallman Chorus Sings 28 Christmas Songs .... [X-F]		4 Corners 4245

KALYAN
Disco-reggae band from Trinidad. Led by singer Olsop David.

4/16/77	173	4		1 Kalyan		MCA 2245

KAM
Born Craig Miller in 1971 in Los Angeles, California. Male rapper.

3/6/93	110	7		1 Neva Again...		Street Knowledge 92208
4/1/95	158	1		2 Made In America..		EastWest 61754

KAMAE, Eddie, And The Sons Of Hawaii
Born on 8/4/1927 in Honolulu, Hawaii. legendary ukulele player.

10/27/07	38ˣ	1		1 Christmas Time With Eddie Kamae And The Sons Of Hawaii .... [X]		Hawaii Sons 1014

KAMAKAWIWO'OLE, Israel
Born on 5/20/1959 in Kaimuki, Hawaii. Died of respiratory failure on 6/26/1997 (age 38). Male singer/ukulele player.

7/27/02	25ᶜ	2	▲	1 Facing Future... [E]		Big Boy 5901
				recordings from 1993		
10/13/01	135	5	●	2 Alone In Iz World		Big Boy 5907
7/14/07	44	6		3 Wonderful World		Big Boy 5911

KANDI
Born Kandi Burruss on 5/17/1976 in Atlanta, Georgia. Female R&B singer/songwriter. Former member of **Xscape**.

10/7/00	72	8		1 Hey Kandi..		Columbia 63753
11/21/09	197	1		2 Fly Above .... [EP]		Kandi Koated digital

KANE, Big Daddy
Born Antonio Hardy on 9/10/1968 in Brooklyn, New York. Male rapper. Acted in the movies *The Meteor Man* and *Posse*.

7/16/88	116	19	●	1 Long Live The Kane		Cold Chillin' 25731
10/7/89	33	30	●	2 It's A Big Daddy Thing		Cold Chillin' 25941
11/17/90	37	16		3 Taste Of Chocolate		Cold Chillin' 26303
11/16/91	57	8		4 Prince Of Darkness		Cold Chillin' 26715
6/12/93	52	9		5 Looks Like A Job For...		Cold Chillin' 45128
10/1/94	155	1		6 Daddy's Home		MCA 11102

KANE & ABEL
Male rap duo from Oakland, California: twin brothers David Garcia and Daniel Garcia.

11/9/96	179	1		1 The 7 Sins		No Limit 50634
7/25/98	5	13	●	2 Am I My Brothers Keeper		No Limit 50720
10/9/99	61	6		3 Rise To Power		EastWest 62450
10/14/00	194	2		4 Most Wanted		Most Wanted 0001

KANE GANG, The
Pop trio formed in England: vocalists Martin Brammer and Paul Woods with guitarist David Brewis.

11/21/87	115	20		1 Miracle..		Capitol 48176

KANO
Disco group from Italy: Rosanna Casale, Lella Esposito, Piero Cairo, Bruno Gergonzi, Luciano Nenzatti and Stefano Pulga.

1/9/82	189	4		1 New York Cake		Mirage 19327

KANSAS All-Time: #348
Pop-rock band from Topeka, Kansas: Steve Walsh (vocals, keyboards), Kerry Livgren (guitar, keyboards), Rich Williams (guitar), Robby Steinhardt (violin), Dave Hope (bass) and Phil Ehart (drums). Walsh left in 1981; replaced by John Elefante. Revised lineup in 1986: Walsh, Ehart, Williams, Steve Morse (guitar; Dixie Dregs) and Billy Greer (bass).

6/15/74	174	10	●	1 Kansas		Kirshner 32817
3/22/75	57	15	●	2 Song For America		Kirshner 33385
12/27/75+	70	20	●	3 Masque...		Kirshner 33806
11/6/76+	5	42	▲⁴	4 Leftoverture		Kirshner 34224
10/15/77+	4	51	▲⁴	5 Point Of Know Return		Kirshner 34929
11/18/78+	32	19	▲	6 Two For The Show .... [L]		Kirshner 35660 [2]
6/9/79	10	24	●	7 Monolith		Kirshner 36008
10/4/80	26	21	●	8 Audio-Visions		Kirshner 36588
6/12/82	16	20		9 Vinyl Confessions		Kirshner 38002
8/13/83	41	21		10 Drastic Measures		CBS Associated 38733
9/8/84	154	5	▲⁴	11 The Best Of Kansas .... Cat:#37/6 [G]		CBS Associated 39283
11/15/86+	35	27		12 Power		MCA 5838
11/5/88	114	6		13 In The Spirit Of Things...		MCA 6254

KANTNER, Paul
Born on 3/17/1941 in San Francisco, California. Rock guitarist. Member of **Jefferson Airplane/Starship** and **KBC Band**.

12/19/70+	20	23	●	1 Blows Against The Empire		RCA Victor 4448
				PAUL KANTNER/JEFFERSON STARSHIP		
12/25/71+	89	9		2 Sunfighter		Grunt 1002
				PAUL KANTNER & GRACE SLICK		
6/23/73	120	12		3 Baron Von Tollbooth & The Chrome Nun		Grunt 0148
				PAUL KANTNER, GRACE SLICK & DAVID FREIBERG		
10/29/83	201	3		4 The Planet Earth Rock And Roll Orchestra		RCA Victor 4320

KAOMA
Multi-national group of singers, musicians and dancers based in Paris, France. Fronted by keyboardist/arranger Jean-Claude Bonaventure.

1/27/90	40	21	●	1 World Beat .... [F]		Epic 46010

KAPLAN, Gabriel
Born on 3/31/1945 in Brooklyn, New York. Comedian/actor. Star of TV's *Welcome Back Kotter*.

7/20/74	210	2	1 Holes And Mellow Rolls .... [C]		ABC 815

KARDINAL OFFISHALL
Born Jason Harrow on 5/12/1976 in Toronto, Ontario, Canada. Male reggae rapper/producer.

9/27/08	40	2	1 Not 4 Sale		Konlive 011640

KAREN O AND THE KIDS
Born Karen Orzalek on 11/22/1978 in South Korea; raised in Englewood, New Jersey. Lead singer of the **Yeah Yeah Yeahs**.

10/17/09	35	7	1 Where The Wild Things Are .... [S]		DGC 013164

KARINA
Born Karina Paisan in Brooklyn, New York. Female R&B singer.

9/6/08	57	2	1 First Love		Def Jam 009538

KASABIAN
Rock band from Leicester, England: Tom Meighan (vocals), Sergio Pizzorno (guitar), Chris Edwards (bass) and Chris Karloff (drums). Band named after Manson Family member Linda Kasabian.

3/26/05	94	2	1 Kasabian		RCA 66428
10/7/06	114	1	2 Empire		RCA 88323
6/27/09	126	1	3 West Ryder Pauper Lunatic Asylum		RCA 51831

KaSANDRA
Born John Anderson on 7/30/1936 in Panama City, Florida. R&B singer/songwriter.

11/23/68	142	8	1 John W. Anderson Presents KaSandra		Capitol 2957

KASHIF
Born Michael Jones in 1959 in Brooklyn, New York. Techno-funk singer/musician. Member of **B.T. Express** from 1976-79.

4/9/83	54	33	1 Kashif		Arista 9620
7/21/84	51	21	2 Send Me Your Love		Arista 8205
12/21/85+	144	14	3 Condition Of The Heart		Arista 8385
12/5/87	118	19	4 Love Changes		Arista 8447

KATINAS, The
Contemporary Christian band from American Samoa: siblings John, Jesse, Sam, James and Joseph Katina.

9/13/08	168	1	1 Still		Destiny 1241

KATRINA AND THE WAVES
Pop-rock band formed in Cambridge, England: Katrina Leskanich (vocals; born on 4/10/1960 in Topeka, Kansas), Kimberley Rew (guitar), Vince Dela Cruz (bass) and Alex Cooper (drums).

4/13/85	25	32	1 Katrina And The Waves		Capitol 12400
4/12/86	49	16	2 Waves		Capitol 12478
9/2/89	122	8	3 Break Of Hearts		SBK 92649

KAUKONEN, Jorma, & Vital Parts
Born on 12/23/1940 in Washington DC. Rock guitarist. Member of **Jefferson Airplane** and **Hot Tuna**. Vital Parts: Denny DeGorio (bass) and John Stench (drums).

2/14/81	163	6	1 Barbeque King		RCA Victor 3725

KAY, John
Born Joachim Krauledat on 4/12/1944 in Tilsit, Germany. Hard-rock singer/songwriter. Leader of **Steppenwolf**.

4/29/72	113	11	1 Forgotten Songs & Unsung Heroes		Dunhill/ABC 50120
7/14/73	200	2	2 My Sportin' Life		Dunhill/ABC 50147

KAYAK
Rock band from Holland: Max Werner (vocals), Johan Slager (guitar), Ton Scherpenzeel (keyboards), Theo DeJong (bass) and Charles Schouten (drums).

1/17/76	199	2	1 Royal Bed Bouncer		Janus 7023
3/4/78	117	9	2 Starlight Dancer		Janus 7034
3/3/79	145	7	3 Phantom Of The Night		Janus 7039

Billboard			R I A A	ARTIST		
DEBUT	PEAK	WKS		Album Title	Catalog	Label & Number

KAYE, Sammy
Born on 3/13/1910 in Lakewood, Ohio. Died of cancer on 6/2/1987 (age 77). Leader of popular "sweet" dance band with the slogan "Swing and Sway with Sammy Kaye." Also played clarinet and alto sax.

8/4/56	20	1		1 My Fair Lady (For Dancing) .... [I]		Columbia 885
11/17/56	19	1		2 What Makes Sammy Swing and Sway .... [I]		Columbia 891
5/30/64	97	9		3 Come Dance To The Hits .... [I]		Decca 74502

KAY-GEES, The
Disco band from Jersey City, New Jersey: Kevin Bell (guitar), Kevin Lassiter (keyboards), Wilson Beckett (percussion), Peter Duarte, Ray Wright and Dennis White (horns), Michael Cheek (bass) and Callie Cheek (drums). Bell is the brother of Ronald Bell of **Kool & The Gang**, band is named for that group.

3/1/75	199	1		1 Keep On Bumpin' & Masterplan..		Gang 101
7/31/76	210	2		2 Find A Friend		Gang 102

KBC BAND
Rock trio of former **Jefferson Airplane** bandmates: **Paul Kantner** (guitar), **Marty Balin** (vocals) and Jack Casady (bass).

11/8/86+	75	24		1 KBC Band		Arista 8440

KC AND THE SUNSHINE BAND
Disco band from Hialeah, Florida. Formed by Harry Wayne "KC" Casey (vocals, keyboards; born on 1/31/1951) and Richard Finch (bass; born on 1/23/1954). Other members included Jerome Smith (guitar), Fermin Coytisolo (congas), Robert Johnson (drums), and Ronnie Smith, Denvil Liptrot, James Weaver and Charles Williams (horn section). Smith died in a construction accident on 7/28/2000 (age 47).

8/2/75	4	47		1 KC And The Sunshine Band		TK 603
10/4/75	131	8		2 The Sound Of Sunshine .... [I]		TK 604
				THE SUNSHINE BAND		
10/23/76	13	77		3 Part 3		TK 605
8/19/78	36	13		4 Who Do Ya (Love)		TK 607
7/7/79	50	37		5 Do You Wanna Go Party		TK 611
3/22/80	132	11		6 Greatest Hits.. [G]		TK 612
2/4/84	93	18		7 KC Ten		Meca 8301
				KC		

K-CI & JOJO
R&B vocal duo from Charlotte, North Carolina: brothers Cedric "K-Ci" Hailey (born on 9/2/1969) and Joel "JoJo" Hailey (born on 6/10/1971). Both were founding members of **Jodeci**.

7/5/97+	6	90	▲³	1 Love Always		MCA 11613
7/10/99	8	29	▲	2 It's Real		MCA 11937
12/23/00+	20	30	▲	3 X		MCA 112398
12/14/02	61	9		4 Emotional		MCA 113069
2/26/05	52	7		5 All My Life: Their Greatest Hits .... [G]		Geffen 004059

K-DOE, Ernie
Born Ernest Kador on 2/22/1936 in New Orleans, Louisiana. Died on 7/5/2001 (age 65). R&B singer/songwriter.

~ ~ ~ ~ ~ ~ ~ ~ ~ ~ ~   *NON-CHARTED ALBUM*   ~ ~ ~ ~ ~ ~ ~ ~ ~ ~ ~
1961 **Mother-In-Law**

KEAK DA SNEAK
Born Charles Bowens on 10/21/1977 in Oakland, California. Male rapper. Member of **3XKrazy**.

6/28/08	196	1		1 Deified		Allndadoe 5016

KEANE
Alternative-rock trio from Battle, East Sussex, England: Tom Chaplin (vocals), Tim Rice-Oxley (piano) and Richard Hughes (drums).

6/12/04+	45	54	●	1 Hopes And Fears..		Interscope 002507
7/8/06	4	14		2 Under The Iron Sea		Interscope 006855
11/1/08	7	7		3 Perfect Symmetry		Interscope 012105

KEARNEY, Mat
Born on 2/1/1978 in Eugene, Oregon. Contemporary Christian singer/songwriter/guitarist.

5/6/06+	109	23		1 Nothing Left To Lose		Aware 94177
6/6/09	13	19		2 City Of Black & White		Aware 19597

KEATS
Rock band formed in England: Colin Blunstone (vocals; **The Zombies**), Ian Baimson (guitar), **Pete Bardens** (keyboards), David Paton (bass) and Stuart Elliott (drums).

11/3/84	209	2		1 Keats		EMI America 17136

KEB' MO'
Born Kevin Moore on 10/3/1951 in Los Angeles, California. Blues singer/songwriter/guitarist.

7/6/96	197	1		1 Just Like You		Okeh 67316
				Grammy: Contemporary Blues Album		
9/12/98	109	6		2 Slow Down		Okeh 69376
				Grammy: Contemporary Blues Album		
10/28/00	122	4		3 The Door		Okeh 61428
6/30/01	199	1		4 Big Wide Grin		Okeh 63829
2/28/04	149	5		5 Keep It Simple		Okeh 86408

Billboard			R I A A	ARTIST		
DEBUT	PEAK	WKS		Album Title	Catalog	Label & Number

KEB' MO' — cont'd

10/9/04	174	1		6 Peace...Back By Popular Demand		Okeh 92687
7/1/06	176	1		7 Suitcase		One Haven 77621

KEEL
Hard-rock band from New York: Ron Keel (vocals), Bryan Jay (guitar), Marc Ferrari (guitar), Kenny Chaisson (bass) and Dwain Miller (drums).

3/9/85	99	21		1 The Right To Rock		Gold Mountain 5041
4/19/86	53	18		2 The Final Frontier		MCA 5727
6/27/87	79	13		3 Keel		MCA 42005

KEEN, Robert Earl
Born on 1/11/1956 in Houston, Texas. Alternative-country singer/songwriter/guitarist. Cousin of **Lee Roy Parnell**.

5/17/97	160	1		1 Picnic		Arista 18834
11/14/98	149	1		2 Walking Distance		Arista 18876
9/29/01	111	2		3 Gravitational Forces		Lost Highway 170198
10/25/03	172	1		4 Farm Fresh Onions		Audium 8191
5/28/05	122	1		5 What I Really Mean		Rosetta 9810
10/17/09	83	1		6 The Rose Hotel		Lost Highway 013332

KEEN, Speedy
Born John Keen on 3/29/1945 in London, England. Died on 3/12/2002 (age 56). Rock singer/songwriter/drummer. Former member of **Thunderclap Newman**.

6/16/73	206	4		1 Previous Convictions		Track/MCA 331

KEENE, Tommy
Born in 1957 in Bethesda, Maryland. Rock singer/songwriter/guitarist.

3/29/86	148	17		1 Songs From The Film		Geffen 24090

KEITH
Born James Keefer on 5/7/1949 in Philadelphia, Pennsylvania. Pop singer/songwriter.

3/25/67	124	5		1 98.6/Ain't Gonna Lie		Mercury 61102

KEITH, Toby
2000s: #2 / All-Time: #102
Born Toby Keith Covel on 7/8/1961 in Clinton, Oklahoma; raised in Moore, Oklahoma. Country singer/songwriter/guitarist. Former oil field worker, rodeo hand and defensive end for the Oklahoma Drillers semipro football team. Lead singer of group Easy Money from 1984-88. Formed own Show Dog record label in 2005. Acted in the movies *Broken Bridges* and *Beer For My Horses*.
   AWARD: CMA: 2001 Male Vocalist

5/15/93	99	62	▲	1 Toby Keith		Mercury 514421
10/15/94	46	30	▲	2 Boomtown		Polydor 523407
5/4/96	51	18	▲	3 Blue Moon		A&M 531192
7/12/97	107	12	●	4 Dream Walkin'		Mercury 534836
1/22/00+	56	92	▲	5 How Do You Like Me Now?!	Cat:#27/6	DreamWorks 450209
9/15/01	9	66	▲²	6 Pull My Chain	Cat:#44/2	DreamWorks 450297
8/10/02	❶¹	104	▲⁴	7 Unleashed	Cat:#18/16	DreamWorks 450254
11/22/03	❶¹	66	▲⁴	8 Shock'n Y'all		DreamWorks 450435
6/4/05	2¹	39	▲	9 Honkytonk University		DreamWorks 004300
4/29/06	2¹	40	▲	10 White Trash With Money		Show Dog 006270
6/30/07	❶¹	28	●	11 Big Dog Daddy		Show Dog 005
11/15/08	5	33	●	12 That Don't Make Me A Bad Guy		Show Dog 022
10/24/09	3¹	27		13 American Ride		Show Dog 027
				CHRISTMAS ALBUMS:		
11/15/03+	7ˣ	26		14 Christmas To Christmas	Cat:#14/12	Mercury 527909
				Christmas charts: 40/'03, 9/'04, 24/'05, 7/'06		
11/3/07	23	11		15 A Toby Keith Classic Christmas: Volumes One & Two		Show Dog 015 [2]
				Christmas chart: 2/'07		
				GREATEST HITS & COMPILATIONS:		
11/7/98	61	20	▲²	16 Greatest Hits Volume One	Cat:#18/38	Mercury 558962
5/3/03	45	11	●	17 The Best Of Toby Keith: 20th Century Masters: The Millennium Collection	Cat:#29/2	Mercury 170351
11/27/04	3¹	104	▲³	18 Greatest Hits 2	Cat:#20/47	DreamWorks 002323
5/24/08	2¹	76	▲	19 35 Biggest Hits		Show Dog 010334 [2]

KELIS
Born Kelis Rogers on 8/21/1979 in Harlem, New York. Female R&B singer. Married **Nas** on 1/8/2005 (filed for divorce in April 2009).

1/22/00	144	6		1 Kaleidoscope		Virgin 47911
12/27/03	27	15	●	2 Tasty		Star Trak 52132
9/9/06	10	6		3 Kelis Was Here		Jive 83258

KELLEM, Manny
Born on 11/1/1916 in Philadelphia, Pennsylvania. Died on 11/5/2002 (age 86). Prolific record producer.

4/13/68	197	2		1 Love Is Blue		Epic 26367

KELLER, Jerry
Born on 6/20/1937 in Fort Smith, Arkansas; raised in Tulsa, Oklahoma. Pop singer/songwriter.

~ ~ ~ ~ ~ ~ ~ ~ ~ ~ **NON-CHARTED ALBUM** ~ ~ ~ ~ ~ ~ ~ ~ ~ ~ ~ ~
1959 **Here Comes Jerry Keller**

KELLEY, Josh
Born on 1/30/1980 in Augusta, Georgia. Pop singer/songwriter/keyboardist.

8/2/03	159	11		1 For The Ride Home		Hollywood 162377
9/10/05	114	1		2 Almost Honest		Hollywood 162504

KELLOGG, Stephen, & The Sixers
Born in Boston, Massachusetts. Rock singer/songwriter. The Sixers: Sam Getz (guitar), Kit Karlson (bass) and Boots Factor (drums).

9/26/09	189	1		1 The Bear		Vanguard 79902

KELLY, Casey
Born Daniel Cohen in Baton Rouge, Louisiana. Singer/songwriter/pianist/guitarist.

10/14/72	201	4		1 Casey Kelly		Elektra 75040

KELLY, R.   **2000s: #11 / All-Time: #153**
Born Robert Kelly on 1/8/1967 in Chicago, Illinois. R&B singer/songwriter/producer/multi-instrumentalist. Married **Aaliyah** on 7/31/1994 (marriage later annulled). **Public Announcement** was his assembly of backing singers and dancers. Charged with 21 counts of child pornography in 2001. One of the most in-demand songwriters/producers of the past decade.

2/15/92	42	62	▲	1 Born Into The 90's		Jive 41469
				R. KELLY and Public Announcement		
11/27/93+	2[1]	65	▲[6]	2 12 Play		Jive 41527
12/2/95	❶[1]	68	▲[5]	3 R. Kelly		Jive 41579
11/28/98	2[1]	51	▲[8]	4 R.		Jive 41625 [2]
11/25/00	❶[1]	58	▲[4]	5 TP-2.com		Jive 41705
4/6/02	2[1]	17	▲	6 The Best Of Both Worlds		Roc-A-Fella 586783
				R. KELLY & JAY-Z		
3/8/03	❶[1]	60	▲[2]	7 Chocolate Factory		Jive 41849
10/11/03	4	35	▲	8 The R. In R&B Collection Volume One [G]		Jive 55214
11/8/03	135	2	●	9 The R. In R&B: The Video Collection .... [G]		Jive 53709
9/11/04	2[1]	15	▲[3]	10 Happy People/U Saved Me		Jive 60356 [2]
11/13/04	❶[1]	11	▲	11 Unfinished Business		Jive 003690
				R. KELLY & JAY-Z		
7/23/05	❶[2]	20	▲	12 TP.3 Reloaded		Jive 70214
12/3/05	72	4		13 Remix City Volume 1 .... [K]		Jive 74688
6/16/07	❶[1]	21	▲	14 Double Up		Jive 08537
12/19/09	4	17		15 Untitled		Jive 31136

KELLY, Roberta
Born in 1942 in Los Angeles, California. Black disco singer.

7/31/76	209	1		1 Trouble-Maker		Oasis 5005

KELLY, Sarah
Born in Rockford, Illinois. Contemporary Christian singer/songwriter.

9/2/06	165	1		1 Where The Past Meets Today		Gotee 72942

KELLY, Sean
Born in Toronto, Ontario, Canada. Classical guitarist.

10/17/09	10[X]	1		1 Christmas Guitar [X-I]		Opening Day digital

KEM
Born Kem Owens in Nashville, Tennessee; raised in Detroit, Michigan. Male R&B singer/songwriter.

3/15/03	90	46	●	1 Kemistry .... Cat:#25/1		Motown 067516
6/4/05	5	26	●	2 Album II		Motown 004232

KEMP, Johnny
Born in 1959 in Nassau, Bahamas; raised in Harlem, New York. R&B singer/dancer/actor/songwriter.

6/11/88	68	19		1 Secrets Of Flying		Columbia 40770

KEMP, Tara
Born on 5/11/1964 in San Francisco, California. R&B singer/songwriter/pianist.

DEBUT	PEAK	WKS			
2/16/91	109	14	1	Tara Kemp	Giant 24408

KENDALLS, The
Country duo from St. Louis: father-and-daughter Royce and Jeannie Kendall. Royce died of a heart attack on 5/22/98 (age 63).

1/31/81	205	5	1	The Best Of The Kendalls .... [G]	Ovation 1756

KENDRICKS, Eddie
Born on 12/17/1939 in Union Springs, Alabama; raised in Birmingham, Alabama. Died of cancer on 10/5/1992 (age 52). Lead singer of **The Temptations** from 1960-71. Kendricks later dropped letter "s" from his last name.

5/22/71	80	32	1	All By Myself	Tamla 309
6/3/72	131	14	2	People...Hold On	Tamla 315
6/16/73	18	40	3	Eddie Kendricks	Tamla 327
3/16/74	30	17	4	Boogie Down!	Tamla 330
12/7/74+	108	14	5	For You	Tamla 335
7/12/75	63	25	6	The Hit Man	Tamla 338
1/31/76	38	19	7	He's A Friend	Tamla 343
10/9/76	144	7	8	Goin' Up In Smoke	Tamla 346
4/22/78	180	3	9	Vintage '78	Arista 4170
8/22/81	207	2	10	Love Keys	Atlantic 19294

KENEALLY, Mike, and Beer For Dolphins
Born on 12/20/1961 in San Diego, California. Rock singer/guitarist. Beer For Dolphins: Rick Musallam (guitar), Evan Francis (sax), Chris Opperman (trumpet), Tricia Williams (percussion), Marc Ziegenhagen (keyboards), Bryan Beller (bass) and Jason Smith (drums).

10/14/00	167	1	1	Dancing	Exowax 2404

KENNA
Born Kenna Zemedkun in Addis Ababa, Ethiopia; raised in Virginia Beach, Virginia. Male alternative-funk singer/musician.

11/3/07	124	1	1	Make Sure They See My Face	Star Trak 008809

KENNEDY, John Fitzgerald
Born on 5/29/1917 in Brookline, Massachusetts. Assassinated on 11/22/1963 (age 46) in Dallas, Texas. Brother of **Robert Francis Kennedy**. Elected president of the United States in 1960. Albums below are tributes to his life and career. Also see **Leonard Bernstein** and the **Boston Symphony Orchestra**.

12/28/63+	5	15	1	That Was The Week That Was [T]	Decca 9116

Grammy: Spoken Word Album
the BBC telecast tribute to Kennedy on 11/23/1963

12/28/63+	8	14	2	The Presidential Years 1960-1963 [T]	20th Century Fox 3127

narrated by David Teig

1/11/64	42	8	3	JFK The Man, The President .... [T]	Documentaries Unlim.

narrated by Barry Gray; no record label number

1/18/64	18	9	●	4 A Memorial Album .... [T]	Premier 2099

narrated by Ed Brown; a broadcast on 11/22/1963 by WMCA in New York

1/18/64	109	5	5	Actual Speeches of Franklin D. Roosevelt And John F. Kennedy .... [T]	Somerset 16100

side 1: Kennedy's complete Inaugural Address (1/20/1961); side 2: Roosevelt speeches

1/25/64	101	4	6	John F. Kennedy - A Memorial Album .... [T]	Diplomat 10000
1/25/64	119	4	7	The Presidential Years (1960-1963) .... [T]	Pickwick 169
2/8/64	29	10	8	Four Days That Shocked The World .... [T]	Colpix 2500

narrated by Reid Collins

12/26/64+	49	11	9	The Kennedy Wit .... [T]	RCA Victor 101

narrated by David Brinkley; introduction by Adlai E. Stevenson

12/11/65+	93	8	10	John Fitzgerald Kennedy...As We Remember Him .... [T]	Legacy 1017 [2]

Grammy: Spoken Word Album
narrated by Charles Kuralt; includes a 240-page book

KENNEDY, Joyce
Born in Chicago, Illinois. R&B singer. Member of **Mother's Finest**.

9/8/84	79	13	1	Lookin' For Trouble	A&M 4996

KENNEDY, Robert Francis
Born on 11/20/1925 in Brookline, Massachusetts. Assassinated on 6/5/1968 (pronounced dead one day later; age 42) in Los Angeles, California. Senator from New York. Brother of **John Fitzgerald Kennedy**. Was running for president when he was killed.

1/11/69	187	4	1	A Memorial .... [T]	Columbia 792 [2]

record 1: highlights of speeches 1964-68; record 2: excerpts from the High Requiem Mass at St. Patrick's Cathedral on 6/9/1968

KENNER, Chris
Born on 12/25/1929 in Kenner, Louisiana. Died of a heart attack on 1/28/1976 (age 46). Male R&B singer/songwriter.

~ ~ ~ ~ ~ ~ ~ ~ ~ ~ **NON-CHARTED ALBUM** ~ ~ ~ ~ ~ ~ ~ ~ ~ ~ ~ ~

1964 **Land Of 1000 Dances** *["I Like It Like That"]*

KENNY G
1990s: #19 / All-Time: #94

Born Kenneth Gorelick on 6/5/1956 in Seattle, Washington. Soprano/tenor saxophonist. Joined **Love Unlimited Orchestra** in 1973. With **Jeff Lorber**'s fusion group from 1979-81.

DEBUT	PEAK	WKS	RIAA	#	Title	Catalog	Label & Number
3/24/84	62	21	▲	1	G Force .... [I]		Arista 8192
6/1/85	97	12	▲	2	Gravity .... [I]		Arista 8282
					KENNY G & G FORCE		
9/6/86+	6	102	▲5	3	**Duotones**	Cat:#37/21 [I]	Arista 8427
10/22/88	8	57	▲4	4	**Silhouette**	Cat:#33/10 [I]	Arista 8457
12/9/89+	16	122	▲4	5	**Live** .... Cat:#33/32 [I-L]		Arista 8613 [2]
					recorded on 8/26/1989 in Seattle, Washington		
12/5/92+	2[11]	214	▲12	6	**Breathless**	Cat:#6/14 [I]	Arista 18646
10/19/96	2[1]	51	▲4	7	**The Moment**	[I]	Arista 18935
12/6/97	19	37	▲3	8	**Greatest Hits** .... Cat:#24/9 [G-I]		Arista 18991
7/17/99	17	33	▲	9	**Classics In The Key Of G** .... [I]		Arista 19085
10/5/02	9	18	●	10	**Paradise**	[I]	Arista 14738
6/28/03	42	10		11	**Ultimate Kenny G** .... [G-I]		Arista 50997
12/11/04	40	18	●	12	**At Last...The Duets Album**		Arista 62470
12/2/06	37	14		13	**I'm In The Mood For Love...The Most Romantic Melodies Of All Time** .... [I]		Arista 82690
2/23/08	14	11		14	**Rhythm & Romance** .... [I]		Starbucks 30670
					CHRISTMAS ALBUMS:		
11/19/94	❶[3]	14	▲8	15	**Miracles – The Holiday Album**	Cat:❶[27]/71 [I]	Arista 18767
					Christmas charts: 1/'94, 1/'95, 1/'96, 3/'97, 5/'98, 9/'99, 11/'00, 12/'01, 31/'02, 49/'04		
12/4/99+	6	9	▲3	16	**Faith – A Holiday Album**	Cat:❶[8]/24 [I]	Arista 19090
					Christmas charts: 1/'99, 2/'00, 5/'01, 14/'02, 49/'03		
11/9/02	29	10	●	17	**Wishes – A Holiday Album** .... Cat:#10/7 [I]		Arista 14753
					Christmas charts: 2/'02, 15/'03, 42/'04		
11/19/05	39	8		18	**The Greatest Holiday Classics** .... Cat:#16/17 [K]		Arista 72234
					Christmas charts: 3/'05, 12/'06, 27/'07, 48/'08		
11/25/06	85	6		19	**Holiday Collection** .... Cat:#25/12 [I]		Arista 86734
					Christmas charts: 18/'06, 32/'07, 33/'08, 26/'09		
12/5/09	136	5		20	**Holiday Collection** .... [I-R]		Arista 86734

KENOLY, Ron
Born on 12/6/1944 in Coffeyville, Kansas. Gospel singer.

DEBUT	PEAK	WKS		#	Title		Label & Number
9/9/95	134	4		1	**Sing Out With One Voice** .... [L]		Integrity 02392
					recorded at Carpenter's Home Church in Lakeland, Florida		

KENSRUE, Dustin
Born on 11/18/1980 in Anaheim, California. Punk-rock singer/songwriter/guitarist. Leader of band **Thrice**.

DEBUT	PEAK	WKS		#	Title		Label & Number
2/10/07	144	1		1	**Please Come Home**		Equal Vision 133

KENTON, Stan
Born on 12/15/1911 in Wichita, Kansas. Died of a stroke on 8/25/1979 (age 67). Jazz bandleader/pianist/composer.

DEBUT	PEAK	WKS		#	Title		Label & Number
9/8/56	13	2		1	**Kenton In Hi-Fi** .... [I]		Capitol 724
9/15/56	17	4		2	**Cuban Fire!** .... [I]		Capitol 731
10/23/61	16	28		3	**Kenton's West Side Story** .... [I]		Capitol 1609
					Grammy: Jazz Album		
7/1/72	146	14		4	**Stan Kenton Today** .... [I-L]		London Ph. 4 44179 [2]
					recorded in London, England		
10/10/09	11[X]	3		5	**A Merry Christmas!** .... [X-I-K]		Capitol Jazz 84646

KENTUCKY HEADHUNTERS, The
Country-rock band from Edmonton, Kentucky: brothers Ricky Lee Phelps (vocals) and Doug Phelps (bass), brothers Richard Young (guitar) and Fred Young (drums), and their cousin Greg Martin (guitar). The Phelps brothers left in 1992 to form **Brother Phelps**; replaced by Mark Orr (vocals) and Anthony Kenney (bass). Doug Phelps (vocals) returned in 1996, replacing Orr.

AWARD: CMA: Vocal Group 1990 & 1991

DEBUT	PEAK	WKS		#	Title		Label & Number
12/16/89+	41	96	▲2	1	**Pickin' On Nashville**		Mercury 838744
					Grammy: Country Vocal Group ★ CMA: Album of the Year		
4/20/91	29	30	●	2	**Electric Barnyard**		Mercury 848054
3/13/93	102	6		3	**Rave On!!**		Mercury 512568

KERLI
Born Kerli Koiv on 2/7/1987 in Elva, Estonia. Female electro-pop singer.

DEBUT	PEAK	WKS		#	Title		Label & Number
7/26/08	126	4		1	**Love Is Dead**		Island 009539

Billboard			R I A A	ARTIST		
DEBUT	PEAK	WKS		Album Title	Catalog	Label & Number

KERR, Anita, Singers
Born Anita Jean Grob on 10/13/1927 in Memphis, Tennessee. Formed her group of session singers in 1949.
Also see **Living Voices** and **The San Sebastian Strings**.

3/22/69	162	6		1 The Anita Kerr Singers Reflect On The Hits Of Burt Bacharach & Hal David		Dot 25906
9/20/69	172	3		2 Velvet Voices And Bold Brass		Dot 25951
9/20/75	203	1		3 The Anita Kerr Singers		RCA Victor 1166

KERSH, David
Born on 12/9/1970 in Humble, Texas. Country singer/songwriter.

3/15/97	169	10		1 Goodnight Sweetheart		Curb 77848
3/7/98	134	6		2 If I Never Stop Loving You		Curb 77905

KERSHAW, Doug
Born on 1/24/1936 in Tiel Ridge, Louisiana. Cajun singer/songwriter/fiddler.

2/19/72	206	4		1 Swamp Grass		Warner 2581
9/22/73	214	2		2 Douglas James Kershaw		Warner 2725

KERSHAW, Nik
Born on 3/1/1958 in Bristol, Somerset, England. Pop-rock singer/songwriter/guitarist.

5/5/84	70	20		1 Human Racing		MCA 39020
4/27/85	113	10		2 The Riddle		MCA 5548

KERSHAW, Sammy
Born on 2/24/1958 in Abbeville, Louisiana; raised in Kaplan, Louisiana. Country singer/songwriter/guitarist. Married **Lorrie Morgan** on 9/29/2001.

1/25/92	95	57	▲	1 Don't Go Near The Water		Mercury 510161
3/27/93	57	59	▲	2 Haunted Heart		Mercury 514332
7/9/94	73	27	●	3 Feelin' Good Train		Mercury 522125
9/30/95	131	18	●	4 The Hits: Chapter 1 .... [G]		Mercury 528536
5/25/96	115	36	●	5 Politics, Religion And Her		Mercury 528893
11/22/97+	49	30	▲	6 Labor Of Love		Mercury 536318
5/1/99	99	7		7 Maybe Not Tonight		Mercury 538889
5/5/01	114	3		8 I Finally Found Someone		RCA 67004
				LORRIE MORGAN & SAMMY KERSHAW		

KESNER, Dick, & His Stradivarius Violin
Born on 10/26/1912 in Sioux City, Iowa. Died in a car crash on 1/8/1962 (age 49). Violin player. Regular on **Lawrence Welk**'s TV show (1955-60).

1/12/59	22	2		1 Lawrence Welk Presents Dick Kesner .... [I]		Brunswick 54044

KETCHUM, Hal
Born on 4/9/1953 in Greenwich, New York. Country singer/songwriter/guitarist.
AWARD: OPRY: 1994

2/1/92	45	39	●	1 Past The Point Of Rescue		Curb 77450
10/10/92	151	10		2 Sure Love		Curb 77581
6/18/94	146	6		3 Every Little Word		Curb 77660

KEVIN & BEAN
Morning radio show DJ team from Los Angeles, California: Kevin Ryder and Gene "Bean" Baxter.

12/24/94	57	1		1 Kevin & Bean/No Toys For OJ .... [X-C]		KROQ 59337
				Christmas chart: 17/'94		

KEYS, Alicia
Born Alicia Cook on 1/25/1980 in Hell's Kitchen, Manhattan, New York (Irish-Italian mother/Jamaican father). R&B singer/songwriter/keyboardist.
AWARD: Grammy: Best New Artist 2001

7/14/01	❶³	68	▲⁶	1 Songs In A Minor Cat:#24/21		J Records 20002
				Grammy: R&B Album		
12/20/03	❶²	87	▲⁴	2 The Diary Of Alicia Keys		J Records 55712
10/29/05	❶¹	22	▲	3 Unplugged [L]		J Records 67424
12/1/07	❶⁴	63	▲³	4 As I Am		MBK Records 11513

KGB
All-star rock band: Ray Kennedy (vocals), **Rick Grech** (bass; died on 3/17/1990, age 43), **Mike Bloomfield** (guitar; died on 2/15/1981, age 36), Barry Goldberg (keyboards) and **Carmine Appice** (drums).

3/6/76	124	6		1 KGB		MCA 2166

KHAN, Chaka
Born Yvette Marie Stevens on 3/23/1953 in Great Lakes, Illinois. R&B singer. Became lead singer of **Rufus** in 1972. Sister of **Taka Boom**.

11/4/78	12	21	●	1 Chaka		Warner 3245
6/21/80	43	16		2 Naughty		Warner 3385
5/9/81	17	18	●	3 What Cha' Gonna Do For Me		Warner 3526
12/18/82+	52	18		4 Chaka Khan		Warner 23729
				Grammy: Female R&B Vocal		
10/20/84	14	49	▲	5 I Feel For You		Warner 25162
8/23/86	67	12		6 Destiny		Warner 25425

DEBUT	PEAK	WKS	RIAA	ARTIST / Album Title	Catalog	Label & Number
				KHAN, Chaka — cont'd		
12/17/88	125	12		7 C.K.		Warner 25707
5/2/92	92	9		8 The Woman I Am		Warner 26296
				Grammy: Female R&B Vocal		
11/30/96	84	10	●	9 Epiphany: The Best Of Chaka Khan Volume One	[G]	Reprise 45865
10/13/07	15	8		10 Funk This		Burgundy 09022
				Grammy: R&B Album		
				KHAN, Steve		
				Born on 4/28/1947 in Los Angeles, California. Jazz guitarist/producer. Son of famed songwriter Sammy Cahn.		
2/4/78	157	5		1 Tightrope	[I]	Tappan Zee 34857
				KHIA		
				Born Khia Finch on 11/8/1977 in Philadelphia, Pennsylvania; raised in Tampa, Florida. Female rapper.		
6/1/02	33	25	●	1 Thug Misses		Dirty Down 751132
				KHIA Featuring: DSD		
				KICK AXE		
				Heavy metal band from Regina, Saskatchewan, Canada: George Criston (vocals), Raymond Harvey (guitar), Larry Gillstrom (guitar), Victor Langen (bass) and Brian Gillstrom (drums).		
6/30/84	126	15		1 Vices		Pasha 39297
				KID CAPRI		
				Born David Love on 2/7/1970 in the Bronx, New York. DJ/rapper.		
12/5/98	135	1		1 Soundtrack To The Streets		Track Masters 68781
				KID CREOLE & THE COCONUTS		
				Born August Darnell Browder on 8/12/1950 in Montreal, Quebec, Canada. Singer/songwriter/producer. With his brother Stony Browder in **Dr. Buzzard's Original Savannah Band** during the mid-1970s. Formed The Coconuts with his wife, Adriana "Addy" Kaegi, and Andy "Coati Mundi" Hernandez (also in Dr. Buzzard's; appeared in the movie *Who's That Girl*). Group appeared in the movie *Against All Odds*.		
7/18/81	180	2		1 Fresh Fruit In Foreign Places		Sire 3534
7/3/82	145	12		2 Wise Guy		Sire 3681
10/22/83	204	1		3 Doppelganger		Sire 23977
				KID CUDI		
				Born Scott Mescudi on 1/30/1984 in Cleveland, Ohio; raised in Shaker Heights, Ohio. Male rapper.		
10/3/09	4	31↑		1 Man On The Moon: The End Of Day		Dream On 013195
				KIDDO		
				Funk band from Long Beach, California: Donnie Sterling (vocals), Michael Hampton (guitar), Willie Jenkins (percussion), Leroy Davis (sax), Fred "Juice" Johnson (bass) and Leon "Rock" Goodin (drums).		
5/21/83	206	4		1 Kiddo		A&M 4924
				KID FROST		
				Born Arturo Molina on 5/31/1964 in Los Angeles, California. Male rapper. Later shortened name to **Frost**. Member of **Latin Alliance**.		
7/28/90	67	14		1 Hispanic Causing Panic		Virgin 91377
5/9/92	73	10		2 East Side Story		Virgin 92097
				FROST:		
11/11/95	119	3		3 Smile Now, Die Later		Ruthless 1504
7/19/97	154	3		4 When HELL.A. Freezes Over		Ruthless 1578
5/11/02	183	2		5 Still Up In This $#*+!		Hit A Lick 8399
				KIDJO, Angelique		
				Born on 7/14/1960 in Ouidah, Benin, Africa. Eclectic-dance singer.		
5/19/07	58	5		1 Djin Djin		Starbucks 82967
				KID 'N PLAY		
				Male rap duo: Christopher "Kid" Reid (born on 4/5/1964 in the Bronx, New York) and Christopher "Play" Martin (born on 7/10/1962 in Queens, New York). Starred in the *House Party* movies and *Class Act*. Starred in own Saturday morning cartoon show.		
12/17/88+	96	47	●	1 2 Hype		Select 21628
3/31/90	58	12	●	2 Kid 'N Play's Funhouse		Select 21638
10/19/91	144	11		3 Face The Nation		Select 61206
				KID ROCK 2000s: #32 / All-Time: #415		
				Born Robert Ritchie on 1/17/1971 in Romeo, Michigan. White hip-hop/rock singer. Acted in the movies *Joe Dirt* and *Biker Boyz*.		
1/16/99	4	95	▲11	1 Devil Without A Cause	Cat:#3/194	Lava 83119
6/17/00	2¹	41	▲2	2 The History Of Rock	[K]	Lava 83314
				recordings from 1991-2000		
12/8/01+	3¹	104	▲5	3 Cocky	Cat:#3/69	Lava 83482
11/29/03	8	35	▲	4 Kid Rock		Top Dog 83685
3/18/06	12	10		5 'Live' Trucker	[L]	Top Dog 83914
				KID ROCK & THE TWISTED BROWN TRUCKER BAND		
10/27/07	❶¹	97	▲3	6 Rock N Roll Jesus	Cat:#19/8	Top Dog 290556

KID SENSATION
Born Steven Spence in Seattle, Washington. Male DJ/keyboardist.

8/4/90	175	8	1 Rollin' With Number One		Nastymix 70180

KIDS FROM "FAME", The
Studio musicians featuring cast members of the TV series *Fame*: Debbie Allen, Erica Gimpel, Gene Anthony Ray, Valerie Landsburg, Lee Curreri, Lori Singer, Albert Hague and Carlo Imperato. Singer/actress/director Allen's sister is actress Phylicia Rashad and husband is former basketball player Norm Nixon. Hague died of cancer on 11/12/2001 (age 81). Ray died of a stroke on 11/14/2003 (age 39).

4/3/82	146	8	1 The Kids From "Fame"		RCA Victor 4249
1/15/83	181	4	2 Songs		RCA Victor 4525
3/26/83	98	11	3 The Kids From "Fame" Live! .... [L]		RCA Victor 4674
			recorded at the Royal Albert Hall in London, England		

KIDZ BOP KIDS
Studio group of children assembled by producer Michael Anderson.

10/27/01	76	34	● 1 Kidz Bop..		Razor & Tie 89042
9/7/02	37	35	● 2 Kidz Bop 2		Razor & Tie 89055
3/22/03	17	25	● 3 Kidz Bop 3		Razor & Tie 89060
8/30/03	14	27	● 4 Kidz Bop 4		Razor & Tie 89074
3/13/04	34	16	5 Kidz Bop 5		Razor & Tie 89079
8/28/04	23	22	6 Kidz Bop 6		Razor & Tie 89083
3/12/05	7	25	● 7 Kidz Bop 7		Razor & Tie 89089
8/20/05	6	30	● 8 Kidz Bop 8		Razor & Tie 89104
3/11/06	2[1]	25	● 9 Kidz Bop 9		Razor & Tie 89112
8/19/06	3[1]	28	● 10 Kidz Bop 10		Razor & Tie 89124
3/10/07	4	19	11 Kidz Bop 11		Razor & Tie 89141
8/18/07	7	23	12 Kidz Bop 12		Razor & Tie 89151
3/8/08	4	18	13 Kidz Bop 13		Razor & Tie 89172
8/16/08	8	26	14 Kidz Bop 14		Razor & Tie 89181
2/21/09	7	26	15 Kidz Bop 15		Razor & Tie 89195
8/22/09	8	21	16 Kidz Bop 16		Razor & Tie 89200
			CHRISTMAS ALBUMS:		
11/23/02	66	7	● 17 Kidz Bop Christmas................................ Cat:#3/27		Razor & Tie 89056
			Christmas charts: 8/'02, 9/'03, 12/'04, 21/'05, 10/'06		
12/3/05	128	5	18 A Very Merry Kidz Bop		Razor & Tie 89090
			Christmas charts: 1/'05, 8/'06		
11/24/07	57	7	19 The Coolest Kidz Bop Christmas Ever! .... Cat:#26/4		Razor & Tie 89155
			Christmas charts: 19/'07, 42/'08, 50/'09		
12/19/09	197	1	20 The Coolest Kidz Bop Christmas Ever! .... [R]		Razor & Tie 89155
11/28/09	120	5	21 Kidz Bop Christmas		Razor & Tie 89206
			Christmas chart: 26/'09; different album than #17 above		
			GREATEST HITS & COMPILATIONS:		
6/10/06	176	4	22 More Kidz Bop Gold..		Razor & Tie 89115
7/18/09	94	7	23 Kidz Bop Greatest Hits		Razor & Tie 89201
			SPECIALTY ALBUM:		
11/13/04	132	1	24 Kidz Bop Halloween............................... Cat:#2[1]/22		Razor & Tie 89086

KIHN, Greg, Band
Born on 7/10/1949 in Baltimore, Maryland. White pop-rock singer/songwriter/guitarist. His band consisted of Dave Carpender (guitar), Gary Phillips (keyboards), Steve Wright (bass) and Larry Lynch (drums). Greg Douglas replaced Carpender in late 1982. Kihn went solo in late 1984. Disc jockey at KUFX radio in San Jose since 1996.

9/16/78	145	12	1 Next Of Kihn		Beserkley 0056
8/11/79	114	10	2 With The Naked Eye		Beserkley 10063
4/26/80	167	5	3 Glass House Rock		Beserkley 10068
4/11/81	32	32	4 Rockihnroll		Beserkley 10069
4/10/82	33	17	5 Kihntinued		Beserkley 60101
3/12/83	15	24	6 Kihnspiracy		Beserkley 60224
6/16/84	121	9	7 Kihntagious		Beserkley 60354
3/23/85	51	13	8 Citizen Kihn		EMI America 17152
			GREG KIHN		

KILLAH PRIEST
Born Walter Reed in Brooklyn, New York. Male rapper. Member of **Sunz Of Man**.

3/28/98	24	6	1 Heavy Mental		Geffen 24971
5/27/00	73	3	2 View From Masada		MCA 112177

KILLARMY
Male rap group from Staten Island, New York: Killa Sin, Shogun Assassin, Ninth Prince, Baretta Nine, Islord and Dom Pachino.

8/23/97	34	8	1 Silent Weapons For Quiet Wars		Wu-Tang 50633
8/29/98	40	5	2 Dirty Weaponry		Wu-Tang 50014
9/29/01	122	1	3 Fear Love & War		Loud 1927

KILLER DWARFS
Hard-rock band from Toronto, Ontario, Canada: Russ Graham (vocals), Mike Hall (guitar), Ron Mayer (bass) and Darrell Millar (drums).

5/28/88	165	6		1 Big Deal		Epic 44098
4/28/90	151	9		2 Dirty Weapons		Epic 45139

KILLER MIKE
Born Michael Render on 4/20/1975 in Adamsville, Georgia. Male rapper. Discovered by **OutKast**. Member of **Purple Ribbon All-Stars**.

3/29/03	10	10		1 Monster		Aquemini 86862
7/26/08	178	1		2 I Pledge Allegiance To The Grind II		Grind Time 275

KILLERS, The
Alternative-rock band from Las Vegas, Nevada: Brandon Flowers (vocals, keyboards), David Keuning (guitar), Mark Stoermer (bass) and Ronnie Vannucci (drums).

7/3/04+	7	94	▲³	1 Hot Fuss	Cat:#6/37	Island 002468
10/21/06	2¹	42	▲	2 Sam's Town		Island 007026
12/1/07	12	17		3 Sawdust		Island 010226
12/13/08	6	42	●	4 Day & Age		Island 012197

KILL HANNAH
Rock band from Chicago, Illinois: Mat Devine (vocals), Jonathan Radtke (guitar), Dan Wiese (guitar), Greg Corner (bass) and Elias Mallin (drums).

8/19/06	178	1		1 Until There's Nothing Left Of Us		Atlantic 83972

KILLING JOKE
Dance-rock band from England: Jeremy Coleman (vocals), Geordie Walker (guitar), Paul Raven (bass) and Paul Ferguson (drums). Raven died of a heart attack on 10/20/2007 (age 46).

4/11/87	194	1		1 Brighter Than A Thousand Suns		Virgin 90568

KILLS, The
Alternative-rock duo formed in Florida: Alison Mosshart and Jamie Hince.

4/5/08	133	1		1 Midnight Boom		Domino 164

KILLSWITCH ENGAGE
Hard-rock band from New York: Jesse Leach (vocals), Joel Stroetzel (guitar), Mike D'Antonio (bass) and Adam Dutkiewitz (drums).

5/29/04	21	11	●	1 The End Of Heartache		Roadrunner 618373
12/9/06	32	22	●	2 As Daylight Dies		Roadrunner 618058
7/18/09	7	12		3 Killswitch Engage		Roadrunner 617889

KILO ALI
Born Andrell Rogers on 5/1/1973 in Atlanta, Georgia. Male bass musician/rapper.

8/16/97	173	1		1 Organized Bass		Death Row 90128

KILZER, John
Born on 4/10/1963 in Jackson, Tennessee; raised in Memphis, Tennessee. Rock singer/songwriter/guitarist.

6/11/88	110	15		1 Memory In The Making		Geffen 24190

KIM, Andy
Born Androwis Jovakim on 12/5/1952 in Montreal, Quebec, Canada. Pop singer/songwriter.

8/2/69	82	14		1 Baby I Love You		Steed 37004
9/14/74	21	17		2 Andy Kim		Capitol 11318
12/21/74	190	6		3 Andy Kim's Greatest Hits	[G]	Dunhill/ABC 50193

KIMBALL, Cheyenne
Born on 7/27/1990 in Frisco, Texas. Female singer/songwriter/guitarist. Won *America's Most Talented Kid* TV talent competition in 2003. Starred in the 2006 MTV reality series *Cheyenne*. Joined the country band **Gloriana** in 2008.

7/29/06	15	7		1 The Day Has Come		Daylight 81126

KIMBERLYS, The
Country vocal group from Oklahoma: brothers Harold and Carl Kimberly, with their spouses, sisters Verna and Vera Kimberly.

10/4/69	169	4		1 Country-Folk		RCA Victor 4180
				WAYLON JENNINGS & THE KIMBERLYS		

KIME, Warren, & His Brass Impact Orchestra
Born in New York; later based in Chicago, Illinois. Orchestra leader/arranger/flugelhorn player.

4/15/67	89	12		1 Brass Impact	[I]	Command 910
11/11/67+	177	7		2 Explosive Brass Impact	[I]	Command 919

KIMMEL, Tom
Born Thomas Hobbs in 1953 in Memphis, Tennessee. Rock singer/songwriter.

7/4/87	104	15		1 5 To 1		Mercury 832248

KINDRED THE FAMILY SOUL
Husband-and-wife R&B vocal duo from Philadelphia, Pennsylvania: Fatin Dantzler and Aja Graydon.

4/12/03	159	2		1 Surrender To Love		Hidden Beach 86491
10/8/05	77	4		2 In This Life Together		Hidden Beach 96512
11/8/08	67	2		3 The Arrival		Hidden Beach 00074

KINFOLK KIA SHINE
Born Nakia Shine Coleman on 10/17/1980 in Memphis, Tennessee. Male rapper.

8/18/07	84	1	1 Due Season...	Rap Hustlaz 009150

KING
Pop-rock band from Coventry, England: Paul King (vocals; born on 1/20/1960), Jim Lantsbery (guitar), Mick Roberts (keyboards), Tony Wall (bass) and Adrian Lillywhite (drums).

8/17/85	140	9	1 Steps In Time..	Epic 40061

KING, Albert
Born Albert Nelson on 4/25/1923 in Indianola, Mississippi; raised in Forrest City, Arkansas. Died of a heart attack on 12/21/1992 (age 69). Blues singer/guitarist.

11/16/68	150	10	1 Live Wire/Blues Power.. **[I-L]**	Stax 2003
			recorded at the Fillmore in San Francisco, California	
3/1/69	194	5	2 King Of The Blues Guitar	Atlantic 8213
5/24/69	133	4	3 Years Gone By..	Stax 2010
7/12/69	171	5	4 Jammed Together .... **[I]**	Stax 2020
			ALBERT KING / STEVE CROPPER / POP STAPLES	
7/3/71	188	6	5 Lovejoy...	Stax 2040
10/7/72	140	8	6 I'll Play The Blues For You	Stax 3009
3/20/76	166	6	7 Truckload Of Lovin'...	Utopia 1387
3/12/77	182	3	8 Albert Live .... **[L]**	Utopia 2205 [2]

~ ~ ~ ~ ~ ~ ~ ~ ~ ~ **NON-CHARTED ALBUM** ~ ~ ~ ~ ~ ~ ~ ~ ~ ~ ~ ~
1967 **Born Under A Bad Sign**
RS500 #499

KING, B.B.   **All-Time: #132**
Born Riley King on 9/16/1925 in Itta Bena, Mississippi. Legendary blues singer/guitarist. His guitar named "Lucille." Moved to Memphis in 1946. Own radio show on WDIA-Memphis, 1949-50, where he was dubbed "The Beale Street Blues Boy," later shortened to "Blues Boy," then simply "B.B." First recorded for Bullet in 1949. Appeared in the movies *Into The Night* and *Amazon Women On The Moon*.

AWARDS: **Grammy: Lifetime Achievement 1987 ★ R&R Hall of Fame 1987**

10/12/68	192	3	1 Lucille...	BluesWay 6016
12/27/69+	38	30	2 Completely Well	BluesWay 6037
4/11/70	193	2	3 The Incredible Soul Of B.B. King	Kent 539
10/17/70	26	28	4 Indiana Mississippi Seeds	ABC 713
10/16/71	57	17	5 B.B. King In London	ABC 730
2/26/72	53	17	6 L.A. Midnight	ABC 743
9/9/72	65	20	7 Guess Who	ABC 759
9/8/73	71	25	8 To Know You Is To Love You	ABC 794
8/17/74	153	6	9 Friends	ABC 825
11/8/75	140	5	10 Lucille Talks Back	ABC 898
2/12/77	154	7	11 King Size	ABC 977
5/20/78	124	24	12 Midnight Believer	ABC 1061
8/25/79	112	12	13 Take It Home	MCA 3151
2/28/81	131	10	14 There Must Be A Better World Somewhere	MCA 5162
			Grammy: Traditional Blues Album	
5/15/82	179	5	15 Love Me Tender	MCA 5307
7/2/83	172	4	16 Blues 'N' Jazz..	MCA 5413
			Grammy: Traditional Blues Album	
9/11/93	182	1	17 Blues Summit	MCA 10710
			Grammy: Traditional Blues Album	
11/22/97+	73	30	● 18 Deuces Wild	MCA 11711
11/7/98	186	2	19 Blues On The Bayou	MCA 11879
			Grammy: Traditional Blues Album	
7/1/00	3[1]	43	▲2 20 Riding With The King	Reprise 47612
			B.B. KING & ERIC CLAPTON	
			Grammy: Traditional Blues Album	
12/15/01	151	3	21 A Christmas Celebration of Hope .... **[X]**	MCA 112756
			Grammy: Traditional Blues Album	
			Christmas chart: 21/'01	
6/28/03	165	2	22 Reflections	MCA 000532
10/1/05	45	4	23 80	Geffen 005263
			B.B. KING & FRIENDS	
			Grammy: Traditional Blues Album	
9/13/08	37	5	24 One Kind Favor	Geffen 011791
			Grammy: Traditional Blues Album	

GREATEST HITS & COMPILATIONS:

2/24/73	101	11	25 The Best Of B.B. King	ABC 767
1/13/01	145	2	26 The Best Of B.B. King: The Millennium Collection................ **Cat**#16/6	MCA 111939
4/2/05	96	1	27 The Ultimate Collection	Geffen 003854

KING, B.B. — cont'd
LIVE ALBUMS:

6/14/69	56	34		28 Live & Well		BluesWay 6031
				side 1: live; side 2: studio		
2/20/71	25	33		29 Live In Cook County Jail		ABC 723
				recorded on 9/10/1970 in Chicago, Illinois		
9/25/71	78	8		30 Live At The Regal		ABC 724
				Grammy: Hall of Fame ★ RS500 #141 ★ NRR		
				recorded on 11/21/1964 in Chicago, Illinois		
10/26/74+	43	20	●	31 Together For The First Time...Live		Dunhill/ABC 50190 [2]
7/17/76	73	14		32 Together Again...Live		ABC/Impulse 9317
				B.B. KING & BOBBY BLAND (above 2)		
4/26/80	162	4		33 "Now Appearing" At Ole Miss		MCA 8016 [2]
				recorded at the University of Mississippi		

KING, Ben E.
Born Benjamin Earl Nelson on 9/28/1938 in Henderson, North Carolina; raised in Harlem, New York. R&B singer. Lead singer of **The Drifters** from 1959-60.

8/7/61	57	7		1 Spanish Harlem		Atco 133
5/3/75	39	14		2 Supernatural		Atlantic 18132
7/23/77	33	21		3 Benny And Us		Atlantic 19105
				AVERAGE WHITE BAND & BEN E. KING		

~ ~ ~ ~ ~ ~ ~ ~ ~ **NON-CHARTED ALBUMS** ~ ~ ~ ~ ~ ~ ~ ~ ~ ~

1962 Ben E. King Sings For Soulful Lovers   1964 Ben E. King's Greatest Hits
1962 Don't Play That Song

KING, Carole   1970s: #9 / All-Time: #115
Born Carole Klein on 2/9/1942 in Brooklyn, New York. Singer/songwriter/pianist. Married to songwriting partner Gerry Goffin from 1958-68; their daughter is **Louise Goffin**. One of the most successful female songwriters of the rock era. Also see **Various Artists Compilations:** *Tapestry Revisited - A Tribute To Carole King*.
AWARDS: Grammy: Trustees 2004 ★ R&R Hall of Fame: 1990 (Non-Performer, w/ Gerry Goffin)

5/1/71	84	27		1 Writer: Carole King	[E]	Ode 77006
4/10/71	❶ 15	302	▲10	2 Tapestry	Cat:❶12/301	Ode 77009
				Grammys: Album of the Year / Female Pop Vocal / Hall of Fame ★ RS500 #36 ★ NRR		
12/11/71+	❶ 3	44	▲	3 Music		Ode 77013
11/4/72	2 5	31	●	4 Rhymes & Reasons		Ode 77016
6/23/73	6	37	●	5 Fantasy		Ode 77018
9/28/74	❶ 1	29	●	6 Wrap Around Joy		Ode 77024
3/8/75	20	15		7 Really Rosie	[TV]	Ode 77027
2/7/76	3 3	21	●	8 Thoroughbred		Ode 77034
4/1/78	47	13	▲	9 Her Greatest Hits	[G]	Ode 34967
8/6/77	17	14	●	10 Simple Things		Capitol 11667
6/17/78	104	8		11 Welcome Home		Capitol 11785
6/23/79	104	9		12 Touch The Sky		Capitol 11953
6/7/80	44	17		13 Pearls-Songs Of Goffin And King		Capitol 12073
4/3/82	119	11		14 One To One		Atlantic 19344
5/6/89	111	16		15 City Streets		Capitol 90885
4/2/94	160	3		16 In Concert	[L]	King's X 53878
11/10/01	158	1		17 Love Makes The World		Rockingale 8346
7/30/05	17	15		18 The Living Room Tour	[L]	Rockingale 6200 [2]

~ ~ ~ ~ ~ ~ ~ ~ ~ ~ **NON-CHARTED ALBUM** ~ ~ ~ ~ ~ ~ ~ ~ ~ ~

1964 The Dimension Dolls (volume 1)
[w/ The Cookies & Little Eva]

KING, Claude
Born on 2/5/1923 in Keithville, Louisiana. Country singer/songwriter/guitarist.

8/11/62	80	7		1 Meet Claude King		Columbia 8610

KING, Diana
Born on 11/8/1970 in St. Catherine, Jamaica. Reggae singer.

8/19/95	179	4	●	1 Tougher Than Love		Work 64189

KING, Evelyn "Champagne"
Born on 6/29/1960 in the Bronx, New York; raised in Philadelphia, Pennsylvania. Disco singer.

5/27/78	14	45	●	1 Smooth Talk		RCA Victor 2466
4/14/79	35	17	●	2 Music Box		RCA Victor 3033
10/11/80	124	7		3 Call On Me		RCA Victor 3543
7/25/81	28	18		4 I'm In Love		RCA Victor 3962
9/11/82	27	32	●	5 Get Loose		RCA Victor 4337
				EVELYN KING (above 2)		

Billboard			R I A A	ARTIST		
DEBUT	PEAK	WKS		Album Title	Catalog	Label & Number

KING, Evelyn "Champagne" — cont'd

DEBUT	PEAK	WKS				
12/24/83+	91	20		6 Face To Face		RCA Victor 4725
12/22/84+	203	8		7 So Romantic		RCA Victor 5308
6/25/88	192	3		8 Flirt		EMI-Manhattan 46968

KING, Freddie
Born Freddie Christian on 9/3/1934 in Gilmer, Texas. Died of a heart attack on 12/28/1976 (age 42). Blues singer/guitarist.

| 7/21/73 | 158 | 8 | | 1 Woman Across The River.. | | Shelter 8919 |

~ ~ ~ ~ ~ ~ ~ ~ ~ **NON-CHARTED ALBUMS** ~ ~ ~ ~ ~ ~ ~ ~ ~ ~
1961 Freddie King Sings The Blues   1961 Let's Hide Away And Dance
                                                                 Away With Freddy King

KING, Morgana
Born on 6/4/1930 in Pleasantville, New York. Jazz singer/actress. Played "Mama Corleone" in the movie *The Godfather*.

| 8/22/64 | 118 | 15 | | 1 With A Taste Of Honey .... | | Mainstream 6015 |
| 10/27/73 | 184 | 5 | | 2 New Beginnings... .... | | Paramount 6067 |

KING, Rev. Martin Luther
Born on 1/15/1929 in Atlanta, Georgia. Assassinated on 4/4/1968 (age 39) in Memphis, Tennessee. America's civil rights leader. The third Monday in January is a principal U.S. holiday: Martin Luther King Day.

10/26/63	141	9		1 The Great March To Freedom... [T]		Gordy 906
				recorded on 6/23/1963 in Detroit, Michigan		
11/2/63	102	5		2 The March On Washington .... [T]		Mr. Maestro 1000
				side 1: History of Negro Contributions; side 2: recorded on 8/28/1963 in Washington DC		
11/9/63	119	5		3 Freedom March On Washington .... [T]		20th Century Fox 3110
				recorded on 8/28/1963		
5/4/68	69	8		4 I Have A Dream .... [T]		Creed 3201
				NRR		
				recorded on 8/28/1963 in Washington DC		
5/18/68	173	4		5 The American Dream... [T]		Dooto 841
				recorded during a Freedom Rally at the Los Angeles Coliseum; no track titles listed on above 3 albums		
6/8/68	150	3		6 In Search Of Freedom .... [T]		Mercury 61170
				speeches from 1964-68		
6/8/68	154	3		7 In The Struggle For Freedom And Human Dignity .... [T]		Unart 21033
				recorded on 12/17/1964 in New York City		

KINGBEES, The
Rock trio from Los Angeles, California: Jamie James (vocals, guitar), Michael Rummons (bass) and Rex Roberts (drums).

| 5/31/80 | 160 | 12 | | 1 The Kingbees.. | | RSO 3075 |

KING BISCUIT BOY WITH CROWBAR
Born Richard Newell on 3/9/1944 in Hamilton, Ontario, Canada. Died on 1/5/2003 (age 58). Blues-rock singer/guitarist. Crowbar: Rheal Lanthier (guitar), Richard Bell (piano), Roland Greenway (bass) and Larry Atamanuik (drums).

| 12/26/70+ | 194 | 2 | | 1 Official Music .... | | Paramount 5030 |
| 2/26/72 | 218 | 3 | | 2 Gooduns .... | | Paramount 6023 |

KING CRIMSON   **All-Time: #426**
Progressive-rock band formed in England by guitarist **Robert Fripp**. Group featured an everchanging lineup of top British artists, among them Ian McDonald (sax; **Foreigner**), **Emerson, Lake & Palmer**), **Greg Lake** (bass, vocals; **Emerson, Lake & Palmer**), Bill Bruford (drums; **Yes**), Boz Burrell (bass, vocals; **Bad Company**), John Wetton (bass, vocals; **Family**, **Uriah Heep**, **U.K.**, **Asia**) and American **Adrian Belew** (vocals, guitar). Burrell died on 9/21/2006 (age 60).

12/13/69+	28	25	●	1 In The Court Of The Crimson King - An Observation By King Crimson Cat:#9/16		Atlantic 8245
9/12/70	31	13		2 In The Wake Of Poseidon		Atlantic 8266
3/20/71	113	10		3 Lizard		Atlantic 8278
2/5/72	76	12		4 Islands..		Atlantic 7212
5/5/73	61	14		5 Larks' Tongues In Aspic		Atlantic 7263
5/4/74	64	11		6 Starless And Bible Black		Atlantic 7298
11/23/74	66	11		7 Red		Atlantic 18110
5/24/75	125	5		8 USA .... [L]		Atlantic 18136
10/31/81	45	17		9 Discipline		Warner 3629
7/3/82	52	14		10 Beat		Warner 23692
4/7/84	58	17		11 Three of a Perfect Pair		Warner 25071
5/13/95	83	2		12 THRAK .... [I]		Virgin 40313
3/22/03	150	1		13 The Power To Believe		Sanctuary 84585

KING CURTIS
Born Curtis Ousley on 2/7/1934 in Fort Worth, Texas. Stabbed to death on 8/13/1971 (age 37). Prolific R&B session saxophonist.
AWARD: R&R Hall of Fame: 2000 (Sideman)

6/13/64	103	12		1 Soul Serenade .... [I]		Capitol 2095
6/3/67	185	12		2 The Great Memphis Hits .... [I]		Atco 211
12/9/67+	168	9		3 King Size Soul .... [I]		Atco 231
8/17/68	198	2		4 Sweet Soul .... [I]		Atco 247
12/21/68	190	4		5 The Best of King Curtis .... [G-I]		Atco 266
7/19/69	160	3		6 Instant Groove .... [I]		Atco 293
8/29/70	198	2		7 Get Ready .... [I]		Atco 338
8/21/71	54	15		8 Live At Fillmore West .... [I-L]		Atco 359
3/25/72	189	3		9 Everybody's Talkin' .... [I]		Atco 385

~ ~ ~ ~ ~ ~ ~ **NON-CHARTED ALBUMS by KING CURTIS** ~ ~ ~ ~ ~ ~ ~ ~
1962 **Soul Twist With King Curtis**   1962 **The Shirelles & King Curtis Give A Twist Party**

KING DIAMOND
Hard-rock band from Denmark: King Diamond (vocals), Andy LaRocque (guitar), Michael Denner (guitar), Timi Hansen (bass) and Mikkey Dee (drums). First recorded as **Mercyful Fate**. By 1988, Pete Blakk had replaced Denner and Hal Patino had replaced Hansen.

1/5/85	210	1	1 Don't Break The Oath...	Combat 8011
			MERCYFUL FATE	
7/11/87	123	13	2 Abigail	Roadracer 9622
7/23/88	89	12	3 Them...	Roadracer 9550
9/30/89	111	8	4 Conspiracy...	Roadracer 9461
12/15/90+	179	8	5 "The Eye"...	Roadracer 9346
7/14/07	174	1	6 Give Me Your Soul Please	Metal Blade 14666

KINGDOM COME
Hard-rock band formed in Los Angeles, California: Lenny Wolf (vocals; from Hamburg, Germany), Danny Stag (guitar), Rick Steier (guitar), Johnny Frank (bass), and James Kottak (drums; **Montrose**). In 1984, Wolf formed and fronted **Stone Fury**.

3/19/88	12	29	● 1 Kingdom Come..	Polydor 835368
5/13/89	49	15	2 In Your Face..	Polydor 839192

KINGDOM OF SORROW
Hard-rock band from New Orleans, Louisiana: Jamey Jasta (vocals), Kirk Windstein (guitar), Steve Gibb (guitar), Matt Brunson (bass) and Derek Kerswill (drums).

3/8/08	131	1	1 Kingdom Of Sorrow	Relapse 7012

KING FAMILY, The
The daughters of William King Driggs, with their families, numbering nearly 40. The extended family had own variety TV series in 1965. Included the Four King Sisters (Alyce, Yvonne, Donna and Louise Driggs). Accompanied by the Alvino Rey Orchestra (the husband of Luise Driggs).

7/10/65	34	16	1 The King Family Show!..	Warner 1601
10/2/65	142	3	2 The King Family Album	Warner 1613
12/18/65	8ˣ	2	3 Christmas With The King Family [X]	Warner 1627

KINGFISH
Rock band formed in San Francisco, California: **Bob Weir** (vocals, guitar; **Grateful Dead**), Robby Hoddinott (guitar), Matthew Kelly (guitar), Dave Torbert (bass; **New Riders Of The Purple Sage**) and Chris Herold (drums).

3/27/76	50	9	1 Kingfish	Round 564
5/21/77	103	10	2 Live 'N' Kickin' .... [L]	Jet 732
			recorded at the Roxy in Hollywood, California	

KING HARVEST
Pop-rock band from Olcott, New York: Ron Altback (vocals, piano), Eddie Tuleja (guitar), Rod Novack (sax), Dave Robinson (trombone), Tony Cahill (bass) and David Montgomery (drums).

1/27/73	136	10	1 Dancing In The Moonlight	Perception 36
10/4/75	209	1	2 King Harvest	A&M 4540

KINGOFTHEHILL
Rock band from St. Louis, Missouri: Frankie Muriel (vocals), Jimmy Griffin (guitar), George Potsos (bass) and Vito Bono (drums).

4/13/91	139	6	1 Kingofthehill	SBK 95827

KING RICHARD'S FLUEGEL KNIGHTS
Instrumental band led by Dick "King Richard" Behrke. **Peter Cincotti** portrayed Behrke in the 2004 movie *Beyond The Sea*.

1/27/68	198	2	1 Something Super! .... [I]	MTA 5005

KINGS, The
Rock band from Toronto, Ontario, Canada: David Diamond (vocals, bass), Aryan Zero (guitar), Sonny Keyes (keyboards) and Max Styles (drums).

8/16/80	74	26	1 The Kings Are Here...	Elektra 274
9/26/81	170	4	2 Amazon Beach	Elektra 543

KINGSMEN, The
Rock and roll band from Portland, Oregon: Jack Ely (vocals, guitar), Lynn Easton (drums), Mike Mitchell (guitar), Bob Nordby (bass) and Don Gallucci (keyboards). After release of "Louie Louie" (featuring lead vocal by Ely), Easton took over leadership of band and replaced Ely as lead singer.

1/18/64	20	131	1 The Kingsmen In Person .... [L]	Wand 657
9/26/64	15	37	2 The Kingsmen, Volume II.. [L]	Wand 659
2/20/65	22	18	3 The Kingsmen, Volume 3.. [L]	Wand 662
10/30/65+	68	17	4 The Kingsmen On Campus.. [L]	Wand 670
8/20/66	87	8	5 15 Great Hits .... [K]	Wand 674

KINGS OF CONVENIENCE
Folk-pop duo from Bergen, Norway: Erland Oye and Erik Boe.

11/7/09	112	1	1 Declaration Of Dependence	Source 06840

KINGS OF LEON
Rock band from Nashville, Tennessee: brothers Caleb Followill (vocals, guitar), Jared Followill (bass) and Nathan Followill (drums), with their cousin Matthew Followill (guitar).

9/6/03	113	5		1 Youth & Young Manhood		RCA 52394
3/12/05	55	9		2 Aha Shake Heartbreak.......................................	Cat:#18/19	RCA 64544
4/21/07	25	9		3 Because Of The Times	Cat:#11/29	RCA 03776
10/11/08+	4	86↑	▲	4 Only By The Night		RCA 32712

KINGS OF THE SUN
Hard-rock band from Sydney, Australia: brothers Jeffrey Hoad (vocals) and Clifford Hoad (drums), Glen Morris (guitar) and Anthony Ragg (bass).

4/30/88	136	16	1 Kings Of The Sun		RCA 6826
6/9/90	130	7	2 Full Frontal Attack...		RCA 9889

KINGSPADE
Rap-rock duo from Los Angeles, California: Dustin "D-Loc" Miller and Timothy "Johnny Richter" McNutt. Both are also members of **Kottonmouth Kings**.

5/12/07	110	1	1 P.T.B..		Suburban Noize 77

KINGSTON, Sean
Born Kisean Anderson on 2/3/1990 in Miami, Florida; raised in Kingston, Jamaica. R&B singer/songwriter/rapper.

8/18/07	6	38	●	1 Sean Kingston	Beluga Heights 12999
10/10/09	37	5		2 Tomorrow..	Beluga Heights 33847

KINGSTON TRIO, The
1950s: #9 / 1960s: #13 / All-Time: #37

Folk trio formed in San Francisco, California: **Dave Guard** (born on 11/19/1934; died of cancer on 3/22/1991, age 56), Bob Shane (born on 2/1/1934) and Nick Reynolds (born on 7/27/1933; died of acute respiratory disease on 10/1/2008, age 75). Big break came at San Francisco's Purple Onion, where the group stayed for eight months. Guard left in 1961 to form the Whiskeyhill Singers; **John Stewart** (born on 9/5/1939; died of a stroke on 1/19/2008, age 68) replaced him. Disbanded in 1968, Shane formed New Kingston Trio. Originators of the folk music craze of the 1960s.

11/3/58	❶[1]	195	●	1 The Kingston Trio		Capitol 996
6/22/59	❶[15]	118	●	2 The Kingston Trio At Large		Capitol 1199
				Grammy: Folk Album		
11/9/59	❶[8]	126	●	3 Here We Go Again!		Capitol 1258
4/25/60	❶[12]	73	●	4 Sold Out		Capitol 1352
8/15/60	❶[10]	60	●	5 String Along		Capitol 1407
12/5/60	11	4		6 The Last Month Of The Year.................................... [X]		Capitol 1446
2/27/61	2[1]	39		7 Make Way!		Capitol 1474
7/3/61	3[2]	41		8 Goin' Places..		Capitol 1564
10/9/61	3[2]	46		9 Close-Up		Capitol 1642
6/9/62	7	105	●	10 The Best Of The Kingston Trio [G]		Capitol 1705
8/18/62	7	37		11 Something Special		Capitol 1747
12/15/62+	16	36		12 New Frontier		Capitol 1809
3/30/63	4	29		13 The Kingston Trio #16		Capitol 1871
8/17/63	7	25		14 Sunny Side!..		Capitol 1935
1/11/64	69	14		15 Sing A Song with The Kingston Trio .... [I]		Capitol 2005
2/1/64	18	21		16 Time To Think..		Capitol 2011
1/16/65	53	13		17 The Kingston Trio (Nick-Bob-John)		Decca 74613
6/19/65	126	10		18 Stay Awhile..		Decca 74656
				LIVE ALBUMS:		
2/16/59	2[4]	178	●	19 From The Hungry i		Capitol 1107
				recorded in San Francisco, California		
9/5/60	15	15		20 Stereo Concert		Capitol 1183
				recorded at Liberty Hall in El Paso, Texas		
3/10/62	3[2]	51		21 College Concert		Capitol 1658
				recorded at UCLA		
5/30/64	22	20		22 Back In Town		Capitol 2081
				recorded at the Hungy i in San Francisco, California		
7/12/69	163	6		23 Once Upon A Time		Tetragrammaton 5101 [2]
				recorded at the Sahara-Tahoe Hotel in Las Vegas, Nevada		

KING SWAMP
Rock band formed in London, England: Walter Wray (vocals), Steve Halliwell (guitar), Dominic Miller (guitar), Dave Allen (bass) and Martin Barker (drums). Halliwell, Allen and Barker were members of **Shriekback**. Miller, who was replaced by Nick Lashley, was a member of **World Party**.

6/3/89	159	14	1 King Swamp..		Virgin 91069

KINGSWAY YOUTH OPERA COMPANY, The
Vocal group from England: John Goodison, Brian Keith, Jenny Mason, Norman Smith and Martin Jay. Keith was leader of **The English Congregation**.

8/28/71	217	2	1 Jesus Christ Superstar		Deram 18060

Billboard DEBUT	PEAK	WKS	R I A A	ARTIST / Album Title	Catalog	Label & Number

KING'S X
Rock trio from Houston, Texas: Douglas Pinnick (vocals, bass), Ty Tabor (guitar) and Jerry Gaskill (drums).

5/7/88	144	11		1 Out Of The Silent Planet.................................		Megaforce 81825
8/5/89	123	18		2 Gretchen Goes To Nebraska...........................		Megaforce 81997
11/10/90+	85	24		3 Faith Hope Love By King's X.........................		Megaforce 82145
3/28/92	138	3		4 King's X...		Atlantic 82372
2/5/94	88	4		5 Dogman...		Atlantic 82558
6/8/96	105	1		6 Ear Candy..		Atlantic 82880
6/7/08	145	1		7 XV...		Inside Out 79690

KING TEE
Born Roger McBride on 12/14/1968 in Los Angeles, California. Male rapper.

1/21/89	125	15		1 Act A Fool...		Capitol 90544
10/20/90	175	4		2 At Your Own Risk.....................................		Capitol 92359
2/13/93	95	6		3 Tha Triflin' Album....................................		Capitol 99354
4/15/95	171	1		4 IV Life...		MCA 11146

KINISON, Sam
Born on 12/8/1953 in Peoria, Illinois. Died in a car crash on 4/10/1992 (age 38). Controversial stand-up comedian/actor. Acted in the movie *Back To School* and the TV show *Charlie Hoover*.

11/8/86	175	5		1 Louder Than Hell............................... [C]		Warner 25503
11/26/88	43	17	●	2 Have You Seen Me Lately?..................... [C]		Warner 25748
4/14/90	95	8		3 Leader Of The Banned.......................... [C]		Warner 26073

KINKADE, Thomas — see CHRISTMAS (Various Artists)

KINKS, The   All-Time: #90
Rock band formed in London, England: brothers **Ray Davies** (vocals, guitar; born on 6/21/1944) and **Dave Davies** (guitar, vocals; born on 2/3/1947), with Peter Quaife (bass; born on 12/31/1943) and Mick Avory (drums; born on 2/15/1944). Numerous personnel changes during the 1970s. Ray appeared in the 1986 movie *Absolute Beginners*. Longtime members included the Davies brothers, Ian Gibbons (keyboards, 1979-88), Jim Rodford (bass; from 1978) and Bob Henrit (drums; from 1984; **Charlie**). Henrit and Rodford were members of **Argent**.
   AWARD: R&R Hall of Fame: 1990

12/12/64+	29	26		1 You Really Got Me...............................		Reprise 6143
4/3/65	13	29		2 Kinks-Size..		Reprise 6158
8/28/65	60	9		3 Kinda Kinks......................................		Reprise 6173
12/25/65+	47	17		4 Kinks Kinkdom...................................		Reprise 6184
4/30/66	95	12		5 The Kink Kontroversy..........................		Reprise 6197
2/11/67	135	3		6 Face To Face....................................		Reprise 6228
3/2/68	153	2		7 Something Else By The Kinks.................		Reprise 6279
				RS500 #288		
11/22/69	105	20		8 Arthur (Or The Decline And Fall Of The British Empire)...		Reprise 6366
12/26/70+	35	12		9 Lola Versus Powerman And The Moneygoround, Part One...		Reprise 6423
12/18/71+	100	14		10 Muswell Hillbillies............................		RCA Victor 4644
12/15/73+	177	6		11 Preservation Act 1.............................		RCA Victor 5002
6/15/74	114	11		12 Preservation Act 2.............................		RCA Victor 5040 [2]
5/17/75	51	13		13 Soap Opera.....................................		RCA Victor 5081
12/6/75+	45	14		14 Schoolboys In Disgrace......................		RCA Victor 5102
2/26/77	21	16		15 Sleepwalker....................................	Cat:#47/4	Arista 4106
6/3/78	40	21		16 Misfits..	Cat:#28/4	Arista 4167
7/28/79	11	18	●	17 Low Budget....................................		Arista 4240
9/12/81	15	36	●	18 Give The People What They Want.........		Arista 9567
6/11/83	12	25		19 State Of Confusion...........................		Arista 8018
12/15/84+	57	20		20 Word Of Mouth................................		Arista 8264
12/20/86+	81	16		21 Think Visual...................................		MCA 5822
11/25/89	122	8		22 UK Jive..		MCA 6337
5/1/93	166	1		23 Phobia..		Columbia 48724
				GREATEST HITS & COMPILATIONS:		
8/27/66	9	64	●	24 The Kinks Greatest Hits!		Reprise 6217
4/15/72	94	13		25 The Kink Kronikles............................		Reprise 6454 [2]
				RS500 #231		
2/24/73	145	5		26 The Great Lost Kinks Album.................		Reprise 2127
				recordings which were never released in the U.S.		
6/26/76	144	5		27 The Kink's Greatest-Celluloid Heroes.....		RCA Victor 1743
9/20/80	177	4		28 Second Time Around.........................		RCA Victor 3520
3/31/84	209	2		29 A Compleat Collection........................		Compleat 2001 [2]
7/19/86	159	4		30 Come Dancing With The Kinks - The Best Of The Kinks 1977-1986...		Arista 8428 [2]
				LIVE ALBUMS:		
9/9/67	162	4		31 The Live Kinks.................................		Reprise 6260
				recorded in Scotland		
9/23/72	70	14		32 Everybody's In Show-Biz.....................		RCA Victor 6065 [2]
				record 1: studio recordings; record 2: live recordings		

KINKS, The — cont'd

6/28/80	14	33	●	33 One For The Road		Arista 8401 [2]
2/6/88	110	7		34 The Road		MCA 42107

~ ~ ~ ~ ~ ~ ~ ~ ~ ~ **NON-CHARTED ALBUM** ~ ~ ~ ~ ~ ~ ~ ~ ~ ~ ~
1968 **The Kinks Are The Village Green Preservation Society**
RS500 #255

KINLEYS, The
Country vocal duo of identical twin sisters Heather Kinley and Jennifer Kinley (born on 11/5/1970 in Philadelphia, Pennsylvania).

10/18/97	153	14	●	1 Just Between You And Me		Epic 67965
8/5/00	177	1		2 II		Epic 69593

KIROV ORCHESTRA
Symphony orchestra located in St. Petersburg, Russia; conducted by Valery Gergiev.

10/11/08	12ˣ	8		1 The Nutcracker .... [X-I]		Philips 462114

no track titles listed; Christmas charts: 12/'08, 18/'09

KIRWAN, Danny
Born on 5/13/1950 in London, England. Blues-rock singer/guitarist. Member of **Fleetwood Mac** from 1968-71.

1/17/76	207	4		1 Second Chapter		DJM 1

KISS   **1980s: #40 / All-Time: #52**

Hard-rock theatrical band formed in New York: **Gene Simmons** (bass; born on 8/25/1949), **Paul Stanley** (guitar; born on 1/20/1952), **Ace Frehley** (guitar; born on 4/27/1951) and **Peter Criss** (drums; born on 12/20/1947). All shared vocals. Noted for elaborate makeup and highly theatrical stage shows; Simmons was made up as "The Bat Lizard," Stanley as "Star Child," Frehley as "Space Man" and Criss as "The Cat." Criss replaced by Eric Carr in 1981. Frehley replaced by **Vinnie Vincent** in 1982. Group appeared without makeup for the first time in 1983 on album cover *Lick It Up*. Mark St. John replaced Vincent in 1984. Bruce Kulick, brother of Bob Kulick of **Balance**, replaced St. John in 1985. Carr died of cancer on 11/24/1991 (age 41). St. John died on 4/5/2007 (age 51). Drummer Eric Singer joined in 1991. The original group reunited in 1996. Lineup in 2009: Simmons, Stanley, Singer and Tommy Thayer (guitar). Also see **Various Artists Compilations:** *Kiss My Ass: Classic Kiss Regrooved*.

4/20/74	87	23	●	1 Kiss		Casablanca 9001
11/16/74	100	15	●	2 Hotter Than Hell		Casablanca 7006
4/19/75	32	29	●	3 Dressed To Kill		Casablanca 7016
4/3/76	11	78	▲	4 Destroyer		Casablanca 7025
				RS500 #496		
8/21/76	36	17		5 The Originals .... [R]		Casablanca 7032 [3]
				reissue of albums #1-3 above		
11/20/76	11	45	▲	6 Rock And Roll Over		Casablanca 7037
7/9/77	4	26	▲	7 Love Gun		Casablanca 7057
6/23/79	9	25	▲	8 Dynasty		Casablanca 7152
6/21/80	35	14	●	9 Kiss Unmasked		Casablanca 7225
12/5/81+	75	11		10 Music From The Elder		Casablanca 7261
11/20/82+	45	19	●	11 Creatures Of The Night		Casablanca 7270
10/15/83	24	30	▲	12 Lick It Up		Mercury 814297
10/6/84	19	38	▲	13 Animalize		Mercury 822495
10/5/85	20	29	●	14 Asylum		Mercury 826099
10/10/87	18	34	▲	15 Crazy Nights		Mercury 832626
11/4/89	29	36	●	16 Hot In The Shade		Mercury 838913
6/6/92	6	23	●	17 Revenge		Mercury 848037
11/15/97	27	4		18 Carnival Of Souls - The Final Sessions ...		Mercury 536323
10/10/98	3¹	14	●	19 Psycho-Circus		Mercury 558992
10/24/09	2¹	12		20 Sonic Boom		Kiss 200901

GREATEST HITS & COMPILATIONS:

5/20/78	22	24	▲	21 Double Platinum		Casablanca 7100 [2]
12/3/88+	21	27	▲²	22 Smashes, Thrashes & Hits		Mercury 836427
4/26/97	77	4		23 Greatest Kiss		Mercury 534725
12/8/01	128	1	●	24 The Box Set		Mercury 586561 [5]
				includes a 120-page booklet; special edition housed in a full-size guitar case available on Mercury 586555		
9/14/02	52	6		25 The Very Best Of Kiss .... Cat:#29/9		Island 063122
8/23/03	132	1		26 The Best Of Kiss: 20th Century Masters - The Millennium Collection		Mercury 000827

LIVE ALBUMS:

10/11/75	9	110	●	27 Alive!		Casablanca 7020 [2]
				RS500 #159		
11/26/77+	7	33	▲²	28 Alive II		Casablanca 7076 [2]
6/5/93	9	12	●	29 Alive III		Mercury 514777
3/30/96	15	10	●	30 MTV Unplugged		Mercury 528950
7/13/96	17	11	●	31 You Wanted The Best, You Got The Best!! ..		Mercury 532741
8/9/03	18	4		32 Symphony: Alive IV		Kiss 84624 [2]
				recorded on 2/28/2003 with the Melbourne Symphony Orchestra		
12/9/06	167	1		33 Kiss Alive! 1975-2000		Mercury 7586 [4]

KISSING THE PINK
Synth-pop dance band from England: Nick Whitecross (vocals, guitar), Jon Hall and George Stewart (keyboards), Josephine Wells (sax), Pete Barnett (bass) and Steve Cusack (drums). Shortened name to KTP in 1985.

8/13/83	203	6	1 Naked		Atlantic 80080

KITARO
Born Masanori Takahashi on 2/4/1953 in Toyohashi City, Japan. New Age synthesizer player.

11/30/85	191	2	1 Asia	[I-L]	Geffen 24087
			recorded in Shanghai, China		
5/10/86	141	10	2 My Best	[I-K]	Gramavision 7016
4/4/87	183	1	3 Tenku	[I]	Geffen 24112
5/12/90	159	5	4 Kojiki	[I]	Geffen 24255
9/9/95	199	1	5 An Enchanted Evening	[I-L]	DOMO 71005
12/28/96	185	1	6 Peace On Earth	[X-I]	DOMO 71014

KITCHELL, Sonya
Born on 3/1/1989 in Ashfield, Massachusetts. Jazz singer/songwriter.

4/22/06	172	3	1 Words Came Back To Me		Hear 0501
9/20/08	162	2	2 This Storm		Velour 011456

KITTIE
Female rock band from London, Ontario, Canada: sisters Morgan Lander (vocals, guitar) and Mercedes Lander (drums), with Fallon Bowman (guitar) and Talena Atfield (bass).

1/29/00	79	37	● 1 Spit		Artemis 1002
12/1/01	57	5	2 Oracle		Artemis 751088
8/14/04	105	2	3 Until The End		Artemis 51538
3/10/07	101	1	4 Funeral For Yesterday		X Of Infamy 0001
10/3/09	133	1	5 In The Black		E1 2050

KITTYHAWK
Jazz band from Los Angeles, California: Daniel Bortz (guitar), Paul Edwards (keyboards), Richard Elliot (sax) and Michael Jochum (drums).

5/10/80	207	2	1 Kittyhawk	[I]	EMI America 17029
8/8/81	207	3	2 Race For The Oasis	[I]	EMI America 17053

KIX
Hard-rock band from Hagerstown, Maryland: Steve Whiteman (vocals), Ronnie Younkins (guitar), Brian Forsythe (guitar), Donnie Purnell (bass) and Jimmy Chalfant (drums).

10/10/81	207	4	1 Kix		Atlantic 19307
5/28/83	177	8	2 Cool Kids		Atlantic 80056
10/15/88+	46	60	▲ 3 Blow My Fuse		Atlantic 81877
7/27/91	64	11	4 Hot Wire		EastWest 91714

K'JON
Born in Detroit, Michigan. Male R&B singer/songwriter.

8/22/09	12	15	1 I Get Around		Up&Up 013162

KLAATU
Pop trio from Toronto, Ontario, Canada: Dee Long (vocals, guitar), Terry Draper (keybaords) and John Woloschuck (drums). Anonymous first release led to speculation that they were **The Beatles**. Name taken from alien character in the classic 1951 sci-fi movie *The Day The Earth Stood Still*.

4/2/77	32	11	1 Klaatu		Capitol 11542
10/15/77	83	7	2 Hope		Capitol 11633

KLANG, Donnie
Born on 1/23/1985 in Brooklyn, New York. R&B singer.

9/20/08	19	3	1 Just A Rolling Stone		Bad Boy 511253

KLEEER
R&B-disco band from New York: Isabelle Coles (vocals), Paul Crutchfield (vocals, percussion), Richard Lee (guitar), Norman Durham (bass) and Woody Cunningham (drums).

7/7/79	208	4	1 I Love To Dance		Atlantic 19237
4/26/80	140	10	2 Winners		Atlantic 19262
3/7/81	81	16	3 License To Dream		Atlantic 19288
2/20/82	139	8	4 Taste The Music		Atlantic 19334

KLEIN, Robert
Born on 2/8/1942 in Brooklyn, New York. Stand-up comedian/actor/writer. Appeared in several movies and TV shows. Married to opera singer Brenda Boozer from 1973-89.

4/28/73	191	3	1 Child Of The 50's	[C]	Brut 6001
5/18/74	205	3	2 Mind Over Matter	[C]	Brut 6600
6/28/75	203	3	3 New Teeth	[C]	Epic 33535

KLEMMER, John
Born on 7/3/1946 in Chicago, Illinois. Jazz saxophonist/flutist.

9/13/69	176	5	1 Blowin' Gold	[I]	Cadet Concept 321
12/27/75+	90	40	2 Touch	[I]	ABC 922
9/18/76	66	16	3 Barefoot Ballet	[I]	ABC 950

Billboard			R I A	ARTIST		
DEBUG	PEAK	WKS	A	Album Title	Catalog	Label & Number

DEBUT	PEAK	WKS		ARTIST / Album Title	Catalog	Label & Number
				KLEMMER, John — cont'd		
6/18/77	51	17		4 LifeStyle (Living & Loving)	[I]	ABC 1007
6/17/78	83	10		5 Arabesque	[I]	ABC 1068
11/18/78	178	3		6 Cry	[I]	ABC 1106
6/2/79	172	9		7 Brazilia	[I]	ABC 1116
11/24/79	187	2		8 The Best Of John Klemmer, Volume One/Mosaic	[I-K]	MCA 8014 [2]
8/9/80	146	11		9 Magnificent Madness	[I]	Elektra 284
6/13/81	99	9		10 Hush	[I]	Elektra 527
12/12/81+	202	8		11 Solo Saxophone II - Life	[I]	Elektra 566
				KLF, The		
				Dance duo formed in England: Bill Drummond and Jim Cauty (formerly with **Zodiac Mindwarp**). KLF: Kopyright Liberation Front.		
6/29/91	39	50	●	1 The White Room		Arista 8657
				KLIQUE		
				R&B vocal trio: Howard Huntsberry, Isaac Suthers and his sister Deborah Hunter.		
10/8/83	70	14		1 Try It Out		MCA 39008
				KLOWNS, The		
				Four-man, two-woman vocal group produced by Jeff Barry: Barry Bostwick, John Perry, Peter Lee, Robin Field, Vicky Belmonte and Carolyn Mignini. Bostwick later appeared in several movies. Perry (father of actor Matthew Perry) played the Old Spice sailor in several TV commercials. Group hosted own ABC-TV special on 11/15/1970.		
12/12/70	184	2		1 The Klowns		RCA Victor 4438
				KLUGH, Earl **1980s: #39 / All-Time: #266**		
				Born on 9/16/1953 in Detroit, Michigan. Jazz guitarist/keyboardist. Taught guitar from age 15. Worked Baker's Keyboard Lounge. Toured with **Return To Forever** and **George Benson**. First solo recording for Blue Note in 1976.		
7/10/76	124	6		1 Earl Klugh	[I]	Blue Note 596
12/11/76	188	2		2 Living Inside Your Love	[I]	Blue Note 667
7/9/77	84	8		3 Finger Paintings	[I]	Blue Note 737
7/1/78	139	9		4 Magic In Your Eyes	[I]	United Artists 877
5/19/79	49	21		5 Heart String	[I]	United Artists 942
11/3/79	23	33	●	6 One On One	[I]	Tappan Zee 36241
				BOB JAMES & EARL KLUGH *Grammy: Pop Instrumental Album*		
4/19/80	42	19		7 Dream Come True	[I]	United Artists 1026
9/27/80	134	4		8 How To Beat The High Cost Of Living	[I-S]	Columbia 36741
				HUBERT LAWS & EARL KLUGH		
12/6/80+	98	23		9 Late Night Guitar	[I]	Liberty 1079
11/14/81	53	27		10 Crazy For You	[I]	Liberty 51113
11/6/82	44	29		11 Two Of A Kind	[I]	Capitol 12244
				EARL KLUGH & BOB JAMES		
5/7/83	38	24		12 Low Ride	[I]	Capitol 12253
1/14/84	204	2		13 Marvin & Tige	[I-S]	Capitol 12307
3/31/84	69	23		14 Wishful Thinking	[I]	Capitol 12323
10/27/84	107	17		15 Nightsongs	[I]	Capitol 12372
5/4/85	202	3		16 Key Notes	[I]	Capitol 12405
5/11/85	110	17		17 Soda Fountain Shuffle	[I]	Warner 25262
8/30/86	143	11		18 Life Stories	[I]	Warner 25478
7/11/87	59	31	●	19 Collaboration	[I]	Warner 25580
				GEORGE BENSON & EARL KLUGH		
5/20/89	150	5		20 Whispers And Promises	[I]	Warner 25902
4/6/91	189	3		21 Midnight In San Juan	[I]	Warner 26293
8/29/92	170	3		22 Cool	[I]	Warner 26939
				BOB JAMES & EARL KLUGH		
				KLYMAXX		
				Female R&B band from Los Angeles, California: Lorena Porter (vocals), Cheryl Cooley (guitar), Lynn Malsby (keyboards), Robbin Grider (keyboards), Joyce Irby (bass) and Bernadette Cooper (drums).		
2/2/85+	18	67	●	1 Meeting In The Ladies Room		Constellation 5529
12/6/86+	98	31		2 Klymaxx		Constellation 5832
6/23/90	168	4		3 The Maxx Is Back		MCA 6376
				KMFDM		
				Industrial-electronica-dance rock band from Germany; based in Chicago, Illinois: Cheryl Wilson, Chris Connelly, Dorona Alberti, Nicole Blackman and Jennifer Ginsberg (vocals), Gunter Schulz, En Esch and Mark Durante (guitars), Sascha Konietzko (bass), F.M. Einheit and John Van Eaton (various instruments) and William Rieflin (drums). KMFDM is an acronym: Kein Mehrheit Fur Die Mitleid, which is German for: No Pity For The Majority. Konietzko left to form **MDFMK**.		
7/13/96	92	3		1 Xtort		Wax Trax! 7242
10/11/97	137	2		2 KMFDM		Wax Trax! 7245
5/8/99	189	1		3 Adios		Wax Trax! 7258
				K'NAAN		
				Born Keinan Warsame in 1978 in Mogadishu, Somalia; raised in Toronto, Ontario, Canada. Male rapper.		
3/14/09	32	4		1 Troubadour		A&M 012478

KNACK, The

Rock band formed in Los Angeles, California: Doug Fieger (vocals, guitar), Berton Averre (guitar), Prescott Niles (bass) and Bruce Gary (drums). Fieger was a member of the Detroit rock trio **Sky**. Gary died of cancer on 8/22/2006 (age 55). Fieger died of cancer on 2/14/2010 (age 57).

6/30/79	❶[5]	40	▲[2]	1 Get The Knack		Capitol 11948
3/1/80	15	14	●	2 But The Little Girls Understand		Capitol 12045
11/7/81	93	6		3 Round Trip		Capitol 12168

KNAPP, Jennifer

Born on 4/12/1974 in Chanute, Kansas. Christian folk-rock singer/songwriter/guitarist.

3/18/00	77	7	1 Lay It Down		Gotee 2816
12/8/01	130	2	2 The Way I Am		Gotee 2843

KNICKERBOCKERS, The

Rock band from Bergenfield, New Jersey: Bill "Buddy Randell" Crandall (vocals, sax; The Royal Teens), brothers Bob "Beau Charles" Cecchino (guitar; vocals) and "Johnny Charles" Cecchino (bass, vocals), and Jimmy Walker (drums). Walker replaced **Bill Medley**, for a time, in **The Righteous Brothers**. Band named after Knickerbocker Avenue in their hometown. Crandall died in 1998 (age 57).

2/12/66	134	5	1 Lies		Challenge 622

KNIGHT, Gladys, & The Pips
1970s: #37 / All-Time: #92

R&B family group from Atlanta, Georgia: Gladys Knight (born on 5/28/1944), her brother Merald "Bubba" Knight (born on 9/4/1942), and cousins William Guest (born on 6/2/1941) and Edward Patten (born on 8/2/1939; died of a stroke on 2/25/2005, age 65). Named "Pips" for their manager, cousin James "Pip" Woods. First recorded for Brunswick in 1958. Due to legal problems, Gladys could not record with the Pips from 1977-80. Gladys was a cast member of the 1985 TV series *Charlie & Co.*

AWARD: R&R Hall of Fame: 1996

10/14/67	60	24		1 Everybody Needs Love		Soul 706
6/8/68	158	13		2 Feelin' Bluesy		Soul 707
1/11/69	136	16		3 Silk N' Soul		Soul 711
10/25/69	81	10		4 Nitty Gritty		Soul 713
5/15/71	35	26		5 If I Were Your Woman		Soul 731
1/8/72	60	24		6 Standing Ovation		Soul 736
3/10/73	9	30		7 Neither One Of Us		Soul 737
7/14/73	70	21		8 All I Need Is Time		Soul 739
10/27/73	9	61	●	9 Imagination		Buddah 5141
3/23/74	35	34	●	10 Claudine	[S]	Buddah 5602
11/16/74	17	41	●	11 I Feel A Song		Buddah 5612
1/25/75	207	1		12 In The Beginning	[E]	Bell 1323
10/18/75	24	16	●	13 2nd Anniversary		Buddah 5639
11/27/76	94	12		14 Pipe Dreams	[S]	Buddah 5676
4/23/77	51	21		15 Still Together		Buddah 5689
9/16/78	145	6		16 The One And Only...		Buddah 5701
4/7/79	201	3		17 Gladys Knight		Columbia 35704
5/31/80	48	18		18 About Love		Columbia 36387
9/5/81	109	8		19 Touch		Columbia 37086
5/21/83	34	33	●	20 Visions		Columbia 38205
3/23/85	126	12		21 Life		Columbia 39423
12/12/87+	39	27	●	22 All Our Love		MCA 42004
7/20/91	45	15		23 Good Woman		MCA 10329
10/1/94	53	24	●	24 Just For You		MCA 10946
3/17/01	98	5		25 At Last		MCA 112397

Grammy: Traditional R&B Album

10/21/06	93	5	26 Before Me		Verve 006225

GLADYS KNIGHT (above 4)

12/16/06+	155	4	27 A Christmas Celebration	[X-L]	Many Roads 4964378

GLADYS KNIGHT AND THE SAINTS UNIFIED VOICES
Christmas charts: 22/'06, 9/'09

GREATEST HITS & COMPILATIONS:

4/4/70	55	16	28 Gladys Knight & The Pips Greatest Hits		Soul 723
2/16/74	77	23	29 Anthology		Motown 792 [2]
3/16/74	139	11	30 Knight Time		Soul 741
4/26/75	164	4	31 A Little Knight Music		Soul 744
2/7/76	36	15	32 The Best Of Gladys Knight & The Pips		Buddah 5653

~ ~ ~ ~ ~ ~ ~ ~ ~ ~ **NON-CHARTED ALBUM** ~ ~ ~ ~ ~ ~ ~ ~ ~ ~
1962 **Letter Full Of Tears**

KNIGHT, Jean

Born on 1/26/1943 in New Orleans, Louisiana. Female R&B singer.

8/21/71	60	11	1 Mr. Big Stuff		Stax 2045
8/3/85	180	4	2 My Toot Toot		Mirage 90282

Billboard			R I A A	ARTIST Album Title	Catalog	Label & Number
DEBUT	PEAK	WKS				
				KNIGHT, Jerry		
				Born on 4/14/1952 in Los Angeles, California. R&B singer/bassist. Former member of **Raydio**.		
5/24/80	165	7		1 Jerry Knight		A&M 4788
4/11/81	146	6		2 Perfect Fit		A&M 4843
				KNIGHT, Jordan		
				Born on 5/15/1970 in Worcester, Massachusetts. Pop singer. Former member of **New Kids On The Block**.		
6/12/99	29	16	●	1 Jordan Knight		Interscope 90322
				KNIGHT, Robert		
				Born on 4/21/1945 in Franklin, Tennessee. R&B singer.		
12/16/67	196	2		1 Everlasting Love		Rising Sons 17000
				KNIGHT, Terry, and The Pack		
				Rock band from Flint, Michigan: Terry Knight (vocals; born on 4/9/1943; stabbed to death on 11/1/2004, age 61), Curt Johnson (guitar), Bob Caldwell (organ), Mark Farner (bass) and Don Brewer (drums). Knight formed, managed and produced **Grand Funk Railroad**, which included Farner and Brewer.		
11/26/66+	127	13		1 Terry Knight And The Pack		Lucky Eleven 8000
11/4/72	192	3		2 Mark, Don & Terry 1966-67 .... [K]		Abkco 4217 [2]
				Mark Farner, Don Brewer (both of **Grand Funk**) and Terry Knight		
				K-9 POSSE		
				Rap duo from Teaneck, New Jersey: Vernon Lynch and Wardell Mahone.		
3/4/89	98	14		1 K-9 Posse		Arista 8569
				KNITTERS, The		
				Rock band from Los Angeles, California: Christine "Exene" Cervenka (vocals), "**John Doe**" Nommensen (vocals, guitar), **Dave Alvin** (guitar), Jonny Ray Bartel (bass) and Done "D.J." Bonebrake (drums). Cervenka and Doe were married for a time. Cervenka, Doe, Alvin and Bonebrake were also members of **X**. Alvin was also with **The Blasters**.		
6/15/85	204	4		1 Poor Little Critter On The Road		Slash 25310
				KNOBLOCK, Fred		
				Born J. Fred Knobloch on 4/28/1953 in Jackson, Mississippi. Pop-country singer/songwriter.		
10/4/80	179	5		1 Why Not Me		Scotti Brothers 7109
				KNOC-TURN'AL		
				Born Royal Harbor in Wilmington, California. Male rapper. Protege of **Dr. Dre**.		
8/17/02	74	2		1 L.A. Confidential Presents Knoc-Turn'Al .... [EP]		Elektra 62817
4/10/04	36	4		2 The Way I Am		Elektra 62928
				KNOPFLER, Mark		
				Born on 8/12/1949 in Glasgow, Scotland; raised in Newcastle, England. Rock singer/songwriter/guitarist. Leader of **Dire Straits** and **The Notting Hillbillies**.		
5/21/83	201	4		1 Local Hero .... [I-S]		Warner 23827
11/3/90	127	25		2 Neck And Neck .... [I]		Columbia 45307
				CHET ATKINS & MARK KNOPFLER		
4/13/96	105	12		3 Golden Heart		Warner 46026
10/14/00	60	22	●	4 Sailing To Philadelphia		Warner 47753
10/19/02	38	6		5 The Ragpicker's Dream		Warner 48318
10/16/04	66	6		6 Shangri-La		Warner 48858
5/13/06	17	20		7 All The Roadrunning		Nonesuch 44154
				MARK KNOPFLER & EMMYLOU HARRIS		
10/6/07	26	7		8 Kill To Get Crimson		Warner 281660
10/3/09	17	8		9 Get Lucky		Reprise 520206
				KNOX, Buddy		
				Born on 7/20/1933 in Happy, Texas. Died of cancer on 2/14/1999 (age 65). Rockabilly singer/guitarist.		
				~ ~ ~ ~ ~ ~ ~ ~ ~ *NON-CHARTED ALBUMS* ~ ~ ~ ~ ~ ~ ~ ~ ~ ~ ~		
				1957 **Buddy Knox** 1962 **Buddy Knox's Golden Hits**		
				1959 **Buddy Knox & Jimmy Bowen**		
				KOFFEE BROWN		
				Male-female R&B duo from Minneapolis, Minnesota: Fonz and Vernell "Vee" Sales.		
3/24/01	32	11		1 Mars/Venus		Arista 14662
				KOKOMO		
				Jazz-dance band from London, England: Dyan Birch, Paddie McHugh and Frank Collins (vocals), Neil Hubbard and Jim Mullen (guitars), Tony O'Malley (piano), Joan Linscott (percussion), Mel Collins (sax), Alan Spenner (bass) and Terry Stannard (drums). Hubbard and Spenner were members of **Grease Band**.		
6/7/75	159	9		1 Kokomo		Columbia 33442
4/17/76	194	2		2 Rise And Shine!		Columbia 34031
				KOLOC, Bonnie		
				Born in Waterloo, Iowa; later based in Chicago, Illinois. Female singer/songwriter.		
8/26/72	204	7		1 Hold On To Me		Ovation 1426
8/24/74	209	2		2 You're Gonna Love Yourself In The Morning		Ovation 1438

DEBUT	PEAK	WKS	R I A A	ARTIST Album Title	Catalog	Label & Number
				KONGAS Disco studio group assembled by **Cerrone**.		
3/18/78	120	8		1 **Africansim**		Polydor 6138
				KONGOS, John Born on 9/6/1945 in Johannesburg, South Africa. Pop-rock singer/songwriter.		
2/26/72	204	2		1 **Kongos**		Elektra 75019
				KOOKS, The Rock band from Brighton, East Sussex, England: Luke Pritchard (vocals, guitar), Hugh Harris (guitar), Max Rafferty (bass) and Paul Garred (drums).		
6/16/07	165	1		1 **Inside In / Inside Out**		Virgin 50723
5/3/08	41	8		2 **Konk**		Astralwerks 19375

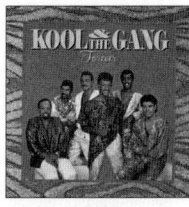

KOOL & THE GANG   All-Time: #188

R&B-funk band formed in Jersey City, New Jersey. Nucleus of group: Robert "Kool" Bell (bass), his brother Ronald Bell (sax), Claydes Smith (guitar), Rick Westfield (keyboards), Dennis Thomas (sax), Robert Mickens (trumpet) and George Brown (drums). All shared vocals. Added lead singer James "J.T." Taylor in 1978. Earl Toon replaced Westfield in 1978. Taylor left in 1988. Smith died on 6/20/2006 (age 57).

DEBUT	PEAK	WKS	R I A A	Album Title	Catalog	Label & Number
2/27/71	122	19		1 Live At The Sex Machine .... [I-L]		De-Lite 2008
9/25/71	157	8		2 The Best Of Kool And The Gang .... [G]		De-Lite 2009
1/1/72	171	7		3 Live At P.J.'S .... [I-L]		De-Lite 2010
				recorded on 5/29/1971 in Hollywood, California		
3/17/73	142	7		4 Good Times		De-Lite 2012
10/13/73+	33	60	●	5 Wild And Peaceful		De-Lite 2013
1/12/74	187	4		6 Kool Jazz .... [I-K]		De-Lite 4001
10/5/74	63	34	●	7 Light Of Worlds		De-Lite 2014
3/8/75	81	23		8 Kool & The Gang Greatest Hits! .... [G]		De-Lite 2015
8/30/75	48	14		9 Spirit Of The Boogie		De-Lite 2016
3/20/76	68	20		10 Love & Understanding		De-Lite 2018
11/20/76+	110	18		11 Open Sesame		De-Lite 2023
1/28/78	142	7		12 The Force		De-Lite 9501
4/15/78	208	2		13 Kool & The Gang Spin Their Top Hits .... [G]		De-Lite 9507
11/11/78	207	2		14 Everybody's Dancin'		De-Lite 9509
9/22/79	13	45	▲	15 Ladies' Night		De-Lite 9513
10/18/80+	10	44	▲	16 Celebrate!		De-Lite 9518
10/17/81	12	67	▲	17 Something Special		De-Lite 8502
10/9/82	29	24	●	18 As One		De-Lite 8505
12/10/83+	29	37	●	19 In The Heart		De-Lite 8508
12/15/84+	13	74	▲²	20 Emergency		De-Lite 822943
12/6/86+	25	42	●	21 Forever		Mercury 830398
8/20/88	109	11		22 Everything's Kool & The Gang: Greatest Hits & More .... [G]		Mercury 834780
				KOOL G RAP Born Nathaniel Wilson on 7/20/1968 in Elmhurst, Queens, New York. Name is short for Kool Genius of Rap.		
12/12/92	185	1		1 Live And Let Die		Cold Chillin' 5001
				KOOL G RAP & D.J. POLO		
10/14/95	24	6		2 4,5,6		Cold Chillin' 57808
				KOOL KEITH Born Keith Thornton in the Bronx, New York. Male rapper.		
8/28/99	180	1		1 Black Elvis/Lost In Space		Ruffhouse 52000
				KOOL MOE DEE Born Mohandas DeWese on 8/8/1962 in Harlem, New York. Male rapper.		
4/18/87	83	21		1 Kool Moe Dee		Jive 1025
11/28/87+	35	50	▲	2 How Ya Like Me Now		Jive 1079
6/17/89	25	23	●	3 Knowledge Is King		Jive 1182
6/29/91	72	9		4 Funke Funke Wisdom		Jive 1388
				KOOPER, Al Born on 2/5/1944 in Brooklyn, New York. Top session keyboardist/guitarist/vocalist. Founded **Blood, Sweat & Tears** in 1968; left in 1969. A member of The Royal Teens in 1959. Founded **The Blues Project** in 1967.		
8/31/68	12	37	●	1 Super Session		Columbia 9701
				MIKE BLOOMFIELD / AL KOOPER / STEVE STILLS		
2/8/69	18	20		2 The Live Adventures Of Mike Bloomfield And Al Kooper .... [L]		Columbia 6 [2]
				MIKE BLOOMFIELD & AL KOOPER recorded on 9/27/1968 at the Fillmore in San Francisco, California		
2/8/69	54	13		3 I Stand Alone		Columbia 9718
10/11/69	125	6		4 You Never Know Who Your Friends Are		Columbia 9855
1/24/70	182	5		5 Kooper Session		Columbia 9951
				AL KOOPER Introduces SHUGGIE OTIS		

DEBUT	PEAK	WKS	RIAA		Album Title	Catalog	Label & Number
				KOOPER, Al — cont'd		
9/19/70	105	6		6	Easy Does It		Columbia 30031 [2]
7/3/71	198	3		7	New York City (You're A Woman)		Columbia 30506
5/6/72	200	2		8	A Possible Projection Of The Future/Childhood's End		Columbia 31159
1/8/77	182	5		9	Act Like Nothing's Wrong		United Artists 702

KORGIS, The
Pop trio formed in England: James Warren (vocals, bass), Stuart Gordon (guitar) and Andy Davis (drums). Warren and Davis were with **Stackridge**.

DEBUT	PEAK	WKS	RIAA		Album Title	Catalog	Label & Number
11/8/80	113	12		1	Dumb Waiters		Asylum 290

KORN   **All-Time: #230**
Heavy metal band formed in Bakersfield, California: Jonathan Davis (vocals; born on 1/18/1971), **Brian "Head" Welch** (guitar; born on 6/19/1970), James "Munky" Shaffer (guitar; born on 6/6/1970), Reggie "Fieldy" Arvizu (bass; born on 11/2/1969) and David Silveria (drums; born on 9/21/1972). Davis is the half brother of Mark Chavez (of **Adema**). Welch left in February 2005.

DEBUT	PEAK	WKS	RIAA		Album Title	Catalog	Label & Number
8/26/95+	72	64	▲²	1	Korn	Cat:#5/92	Immortal 66633
11/2/96	3¹	50	▲²	2	Life Is Peachy	Cat:#8/51	Immortal 67554
9/5/98	❶¹	89	▲⁵	3	Follow The Leader		Immortal 69001
12/4/99	❶¹	47	▲²	4	Issues		Immortal 63710
6/29/02	2¹	34	▲	5	Untouchables		Immortal 61488
12/6/03	9	26	▲	6	Take A Look In The Mirror		Immortal 90335
10/23/04	4	39	▲	7	Greatest Hits Vol. I	Cat:#20/33 [G]	Immortal 92700
5/27/06	51	4		8	Live & Rare	[K-L]	Immortal 82247
12/24/05	3¹	49	▲	9	See You On The Other Side		Virgin 45889
3/24/07	9	7		10	MTV Unplugged	[L]	Virgin 86027
8/18/07	2¹	20	●	11	Untitled		Virgin 03878

K-OS
Born Kevin Brereton on 2/20/1972 in Toronto, Ontario, Canada. Hip-hop singer/songwriter/rapper.

DEBUT	PEAK	WKS	RIAA		Album Title	Catalog	Label & Number
3/10/07	152	1		1	Atlantis: Hymns For Disco		Virgin 80224

KOSSOFF, Paul
Born on 9/14/1950 in Hampstead, London, England. Died of heart failure on 3/19/1976 (age 25). Rock guitarist. Member of **Free** and **Back Street Crawler**.

DEBUT	PEAK	WKS	RIAA		Album Title	Catalog	Label & Number
9/6/75	191	2		1	Back Street Crawler	[E-I]	Island 9264
					recorded in 1973; Kossoff formed new band (named after album title) in 1975		

KOSTELANETZ, Andre, & His Orchestra
Born on 12/22/1901 in St. Petersburg, Russia. Died on 1/13/1980 (age 78). Conductor/arranger.

DEBUT	PEAK	WKS	RIAA		Album Title	Catalog	Label & Number
10/1/55	4	6		1	Meet Andre Kostelanetz	[I-K]	Columbia KZ 1
12/28/63	30ˣ	2		2	Wonderland Of Christmas	[X-I]	Columbia 2068 / 8868
					Christmas charts: 30/'63, 52/'65		
5/23/64	68	7		3	New York Wonderland	[I]	Columbia 2138 / 8938
12/17/66	36ˣ	2		4	Wishing You A Merry Christmas	[X]	Columbia 6779
					with The St. Kilian Boychoir and Phyllis Curtin, soloist		
12/2/67	30ˣ	5		5	Joy To The World (Music For Christmas)	[X]	Harmony 7432 / 11232
					with Earl Wrightson, baritone; originally released in 1960 on Columbia 1528 / 8328		
6/7/69	200	2		6	Traces	[I]	Columbia 9823
11/1/69	194	2		7	Sounds Of Love	[I-K]	Columbia 10 [2]
4/10/71	183	2		8	Love Story	[I]	Columbia 30501

KOTTKE, Leo
Born on 9/11/1945 in Athens, Georgia. Eclectic singer/songwriter/acoustic guitarist.

DEBUT	PEAK	WKS	RIAA		Album Title	Catalog	Label & Number
6/19/71	168	7		1	Mudlark		Capitol 682
2/12/72	127	9		2	Greenhouse		Capitol 11000
4/7/73	108	11		3	My Feet Are Smiling	[I-L]	Capitol 11164
					recorded on 12/19/1972 at the Guthrie Theater in Minneapolis, Minnesota		
2/2/74	69	18		4	Ice Water		Capitol 11262
11/9/74	45	12		5	Dreams and all that stuff	[I]	Capitol 11335
10/25/75	114	7		6	Chewing Pine		Capitol 11446
11/27/76	153	4		7	Leo Kottke 1971-1976 - Did You Hear Me?	[I-K]	Capitol 11576
1/29/77	107	9		8	Leo Kottke	[I]	Chrysalis 1106
9/2/78	143	12		9	Burnt Lips		Chrysalis 1191

KOTTONMOUTH KINGS
Rap-rock band from Los Angeles, California: Brad "Daddy X" Xavier, Dustin "D-Loc" Miller, Timothy "Johnny Richter" McNutt, Robert "Bobby B" Adams, Lou Dog and Pakelika. Also see **Kingspade**.

DEBUT	PEAK	WKS	RIAA		Album Title	Catalog	Label & Number
7/15/00	65	9		1	High Society		Suburban Noize 21480
10/27/01	100	2		2	Hidden Stash II: The Kream Of The Krop		Suburban Noize 24165
10/26/02	51	2		3	Rollin' Stoned		Suburban Noize 34286
5/8/04	42	2		4	Fire It Up		Suburban Noize 28
6/18/05	50	2		5	Kottonmouth Kings		Suburban Noize 44
12/3/05	193	1		6	Joint Venture		Suburban Noize 49
6/24/06	39	3		7	Koast II Koast		Suburban Noize 60
12/9/06	199	1		8	Hidden Stash III		Suburban Noize 73 [2]
9/15/07	44	3		9	Cloud Nine		Suburban Noize 79

Billboard DEBUT	PEAK	WKS	R I A A	ARTIST / Album Title	Catalog	Label & Number
				KOTTONMOUTH KINGS — cont'd		
2/2/08	168	1		10 Greatest Highs.. [K]		Suburban Noize 17529 [2]
11/15/08	42	2		11 The Green Album		Suburban Noize 101
10/31/09	103	1		12 Hidden Stash 420		Suburban Noize 115 [2]
				KOZ, Dave		
				Born David Kozlowski on 3/27/1963 in Los Angeles, California. Pop-jazz saxophonist. Hosts own syndicated radio show.		
3/23/91	128	9		1 Dave Koz... [I]		Capitol 91643
8/14/93	176	5	●	2 Lucky Man .... [I]		Capitol 98892
9/21/96	182	2		3 Off The Beaten Path .... [I]		Capitol 32798
10/16/99	190	1	●	4 The Dance .... [I]		Capitol 99458
12/15/01	140	3		5 A Smooth Jazz Christmas .... [X-I]		Capitol 33837
				DAVE KOZ & FRIENDS		
				Christmas chart: 19/'01		
10/25/03	129	3		6 Saxophonic .... [I]		Capitol 34226
2/17/07	86	5		7 At The Movies .... [I]		Capitol 11405
10/4/08	184	1		8 Greatest Hits .... [G-I]		Capitol 34163
				K-PAZ DE LA SIERRA		
				Latin band formed in Chicago, Illinois: Luis Corral, Sergio Gomez, Yair Loredo, Arming Rodriguez, Rafael Soli, Simon Valtierre and Oscar Zepeda. Group name is Spanish for "K-Peace Of The Mountain." Gomez was found murdered on 12/3/2007 (age 34).		
11/6/04	119	3		1 Pensando En Ti.. [F]		Univision 310291
10/22/05	70	6		2 Mas Capaces Que Nunca .... [F]		Disa 726804
12/2/06	136	1		3 Conquistando Corazones .... [F]		Disa 720970
12/8/07	93	14		4 Capaz De Todo Por Ti .... [F]		Disa 721130
3/8/08	80	6		5 En Vivo Desde El Auditorio Nac 09/07 .... [F]		Disa 726617
				KRAFTWERK		
				Progressive-rock band formed in Dusseldorf, Germany: Ralf Hutter (keyboards; born on 8/20/1946), Florian Schneider (woodwinds; born on 4/7/1947), Klaus Roeder-Bartos (guitar; born on 5/31/1952) and Wolfgang Flur (drums; born on 7/17/1947).		
2/8/75	5	22		1 Autobahn [I]		Vertigo 2003
9/20/75	160	5		2 Ralf And Florian .... [I]		Vertigo 2006
12/13/75+	140	8		3 Radio-Activity		Capitol 11457
4/16/77	119	10		4 Trans-Europe Express		Capitol 11603
				RS500 #253		
5/13/78	130	9		5 The Man-Machine .... [I]		Capitol 11728
6/6/81	72	42		6 Computer-World .... [I]		Warner 3549
11/29/86	156	14		7 Electric Cafe		Warner 25525
				KRALL, Diana All-Time: #449		
				Born on 11/16/1964 in Nanaimo, British Columbia, Canada. Jazz singer/pianist. Married **Elvis Costello** on 12/6/2003.		
9/13/97+	109	8	▲	1 Love Scenes... Cat:#29/2		Impulse! 233
6/26/99+	56	60	▲	2 When I Look In Your Eyes .... Cat:#27/11		Verve 304
				Grammy: Jazz Vocal Album		
10/6/01	9	53	▲	3 The Look Of Love	Cat:#34/1	Verve 549846
10/19/02	18	30	●	4 Live In Paris .... [L]		Verve 065109
				Grammy: Jazz Vocal Album		
				recorded at the Paris Olympia		
5/15/04	4	25	●	5 The Girl In The Other Room		Verve 001826
10/7/06	7	16		6 From This Moment On		Verve 007323
10/6/07	19	16		7 The Very Best Of Diana Krall .... [G]		Verve 009412
4/18/09	3[1]	25		8 Quiet Nights		Verve 012433
				CHRISTMAS ALBUMS:		
11/21/98	35[X]	1		9 Have Yourself A Merry Little Christmas .... [EP]		Impulse! 3111
11/19/05	17	9	●	10 Christmas Songs .... Cat:#16/13		Verve 004717
				Christmas charts: 1/'05, 17/'06, 31/'07, 28/'08, 44/'09		
12/19/09	142	1		11 Christmas Songs .... [R]		Verve 004717
				DIANA KRALL Featuring The Clayton/Hamilton Jazz Orchestra (above 2)		
				KRAMER, Billy J., With The Dakotas		
				Born William Ashton on 8/19/1943 in Bootle, Merseyside, England. Pop singer. The Dakotas: Mike Maxfield (guitar), Robin McDonald (guitar), Ray Jones (bass) and Tony Mansfield (drums).		
6/20/64	48	15		1 Little Children		Imperial 12267
				KRAUSS, Alison, & Union Station All-Time: #465		
				Born on 7/23/1971 in Decatur, Illinois; raised in Champaign, Illinois. Bluegrass singer/songwriter/fiddler. Union Station: Dan Tyminski (guitar), Ron Block (banjo), Adam Steffey (mandolin) and Barry Bales (bass).		
				AWARDS: CMA: Horizon 1995 / Female Vocalist 1995 ★ OPRY: 1993		
2/25/95	13	66	▲[2]	1 Now That I've Found You: A Collection .... [K]		Rounder 610325
4/12/97	45	14	●	2 So Long So Wrong..		Rounder 610365
				Grammy: Bluegrass Album		
8/21/99	60	8	●	3 Forget About It		Rounder 610465
9/1/01	35	53	●	4 New Favorite		Rounder 610495
				Grammy: Bluegrass Album		
11/23/02	36	70	▲[2]	5 Live .... Cat:#32/5 [L]		Rounder 610515 [2]
				Grammy: Bluegrass Album		
				recorded at the Louisville Palace		

KRAUSS, Alison, & Union Station — cont'd

12/11/04	29	30	●	6 Lonely Runs Both Ways		Rounder 610525
				Grammy: Country Album		
4/21/07	10	45	●	7 A Hundred Miles Or More: A Collection	[K]	Rounder 610555
11/10/07	2²	72	▲	8 Raising Sand	Cat:#11/8	Rounder 619075
				ROBERT PLANT & ALISON KRAUSS		
				Grammys: Album of the Year / Contemporary Folk Album		

KRAVITZ, Lenny
All-Time: #365
Born on 5/26/1964 in Brooklyn, New York; raised in Los Angeles, California. Pop-rock singer/songwriter/guitarist. Married to actress Lisa Bonet from 1987-93. Son of actress Roxie Roker (played "Helen Willis" on TV's *The Jeffersons*).

11/25/89+	61	28	●	1 Let Love Rule		Virgin 91290
4/20/91	39	40	▲	2 Mama Said	Cat:#17/2	Virgin 91610
3/27/93	12	60	▲²	3 Are You Gonna Go My Way		Virgin 86984
9/30/95	10	16	●	4 Circus		Virgin 40696
5/30/98+	28	110	▲²	5 5.	Cat:#3/19	Virgin 45605
11/11/00	2¹	94	▲³	6 Greatest Hits	Cat:#9/44 [G]	Virgin 50316
11/17/01	12	17	▲	7 Lenny		Virgin 11233
6/5/04	14	33	●	8 Baptism		Virgin 84145
2/23/08	4	9		9 It Is Time For A Love Revolution		Virgin 63786

KRAYZIE BONE
Born Anthony Henderson on 6/17/1973 in Cleveland, Ohio. Male rapper. Member of **Bone Thugs-N-Harmony**.

4/24/99	4	13	▲	1 Thug Mentality 1999		Mo Thugs 1671 [2]
9/15/01	27	6		2 Thug On Da Line		Thugline 85784
2/26/05	69	3		3 Gemini: Good Vs. Evil		Ball'r 01191

KREATOR
Heavy metal band from Essen, Germany: Miland Petrozza (vocals), Sami Yli-Sirnio (guitar), Christian Giesler (bass) and Jurgen Reil (drums).

1/31/09	165	1		1 Hordes Of Chaos		Steamhammer 9197

KREVIAZUK, Chantal
Born on 5/18/1973 in Winnipeg, Manitoba, Canada. Female Adult Alternative singer/pianist.

5/10/03	119	2		1 What If It All Means Something		Columbia 86482

KRIS KROSS
Male teen rap duo from Atlanta, Georgia: Chris "Mack Daddy" Kelly (born on 5/1/1978) and Chris "Daddy Mack" Smith (born on 1/10/1979). Appeared in the 1993 movie *Who's The Man?*

4/18/92	❶²	65	▲⁴	1 Totally Krossed Out		Ruffhouse 48710
8/21/93	13	25	▲	2 Da Bomb		Ruffhouse 57278
1/27/96	15	22	●	3 Young, Rich & Dangerous		Ruffhouse 67441

KRISTOFFERSON, Kris
All-Time: #392
Born on 6/22/1936 in Brownsville, Texas. Country singer/songwriter/guitarist. Attended England's Oxford University on a Rhodes scholarship. Married to **Rita Coolidge** from 1973-80. Wrote numerous hit songs. Starred in several movies. Also see **Highwaymen**.
AWARD: C&W Hall of Fame: 2004

7/31/71	21	28	●	1 The Silver Tongued Devil And I		Monument 30679
9/11/71	43	22	●	2 Me And Bobby McGee		Monument 30817
3/18/72	41	16		3 Border Lord		Monument 31302
11/25/72+	31	54	●	4 Jesus Was A Capricorn		Monument 31909
9/22/73	26	33	●	5 Full Moon		A&M 4403
				KRIS KRISTOFFERSON & RITA COOLIDGE		
5/25/74	78	14		6 Spooky Lady's Sideshow		Monument 32914
12/21/74+	103	12		7 Breakaway		Monument 33278
				KRIS KRISTOFFERSON & RITA COOLIDGE		
12/6/75+	105	11		8 Who's To Bless...And Who's To Blame		Monument 33379
8/21/76	180	2		9 Surreal Thing		Monument 34254
5/7/77	45	18	●	10 Songs Of Kristofferson	[K]	Monument 34687
4/1/78	86	7		11 Easter Island		Monument 35310
2/3/79	106	9		12 Natural Act		A&M 4690
				KRIS KRISTOFFERSON & RITA COOLIDGE		
11/10/84	152	5		13 Music From SongWriter	[S]	Columbia 39531
				WILLIE NELSON & KRIS KRISTOFFERSON		
3/25/06	172	1		14 This Old Road		New West 6088
10/17/09	167	1		15 Closer To The Bone		New West 6171

KROKUS
Hard-rock band from Solothurn, Switzerland: Marc Storace (vocals), Fernando Von Arb (guitar), Tommy Kiefer (guitar), Chris Von Rohr (bass) and Freddy Steady (drums). Kiefer was replaced by Mark Kohler in late 1981. Steady was replaced by Steve Pace in late 1982. Pace was replaced by Jeff Klaven in 1984. Von Rohr left in 1984.

7/5/80	201	7		1 Metal Rendez-Vous		Ariola America 1502
4/4/81	103	12		2 Hardware		Ariola 1508
4/10/82	53	20		3 One Vice At A Time		Arista 9591
4/16/83	25	41	●	4 Headhunter		Arista 9623
9/8/84	31	27	●	5 The Blitz		Arista 8243

Billboard			R I A A	ARTIST		
DEBUT	PEAK	WKS		Album Title	Catalog	Label & Number

KROKUS — cont'd

5/3/86	45	17		6 Change Of Address		Arista 8402
11/22/86	97	12		7 Alive And Screamin' .... [L]		Arista 8445
5/7/88	87	11		8 Heart Attack		MCA 42087

KRS-ONE
Born Laurence Krisna Parker on 8/20/1965 in Harlem, New York. Male rapper. Co-founder of **Boogie Down Productions**. Considered one of the most socially and politically aware rappers. Nicknamed "The Teacher."

10/16/93	37	8		1 Return Of The Boom Bap		Jive 41517
10/28/95	19	6		2 KRS One		Jive 41570
6/7/97	3¹	13	●	3 I Got Next		Jive 41601
9/9/00	200	1		4 A Retrospective .... [G]		Jive 41718
5/12/01	43	6		5 The Sneak Attack		Front Page 8242
7/12/03	186	1		6 Kristyles		Koch 8342
6/9/07	140	1		7 Hip Hop Lives		Koch 4109
				KRS-ONE & MARLEY MARL		
10/3/09	62	2		8 Survival Skills		Duck Down 2120
				KRS-ONE & BUCKSHOT		

KRYSTAL
Born Krystal Harris on 11/7/1981 in Anderson, Indiana. Singer/songwriter/pianist.

7/28/01	86	6		1 Me & My Piano		Geffen 493046

K'S CHOICE
Rock band from Belgium: Sarah Bettens (vocals), her brother Gert Bettens (vocals, keyboards), Jan Van Sichem (guitar) and Bart Van Der Zeeuw (drums).

5/24/97	121	16		1 Paradise In Me		550 Music 67720

K7
Born Louis Sharpe on 8/25/1969 in Harlem, New York. Male rapper/dancer.

1/29/94	96	33	●	1 Swing Batta Swing		Tommy Boy 1071

KSM
Female pop-punk band from Los Angeles, California: Shelby Cobra (vocals), Shae Padilla (guitar), Katie Cecil (guitar), Sophia Melon (bass) and Kate Cabebe (drums).

10/10/09	145	1		1 Read Between The Lines		Disneysound 002855

K-SOLO
Born Kevin Madison in Central Islip, New York. Male rapper. K-Solo stands for Kevin Self Organization Left Others.

6/20/92	135	2		1 Times Up		Atlantic 82388

KUBAN, Bob, And The In-Men
Pop-rock band from St. Louis, Missouri: Bob Kuban (drums), Walter Scott (vocals), Ray Schulte (guitar), Greg Hoeltzel (keyboards), Pat Hixton (trumpet), Harry Simon (sax), Skip Weisser (trombone) and Mike Krenski (bass). Scott disappeared on 12/27/1983; his ex-wife and her husband were charged with Scott's murder after his body was found three years later with a gunshot wound to the back.

4/23/66	129	5		1 Look Out For The Cheater		Musicland 3500

KULA SHAKER
Rock band from London, England: Crispian Mills (vocals, guitar), Jay Darlington (keyboards), Alonza Bevan (bass) and Paul Winter-Hart (drums). Mills is the son of actress/singer **Hayley Mills**.

2/1/97	200	1		1 K		Columbia 67822

KUMBIA KINGS
Latin band formed in Texas: Jason Cano, Roy Ramirez and Andrew Maes (vocals), Jorge Pena (percussion), Alex Ramirez and Cruz Martinez (keyboards), A.B. Quintanilla (bass) and Robert Del Moral (drums). Quintanilla is the brother of **Selena**. Martinez also formed **Los Super Reyes**.

3/17/01	92	14	●	1 Shhh! .... [F]		EMI Latin 29745
11/16/02	137	2		2 All Mixed Up: Los Remixes ...... [F-K]		EMI Latin 42526
3/15/03	86	9		3 4 .... [F]		EMI Latin 40514
11/8/03	109	6		4 La Historia .... [F-G]		EMI Latin 93488
10/23/04	89	6		5 Fuego .... [F]		EMI Latin 90595
10/21/06	68	11		6 Ayer Fue Kumbia Kings, Hoy Es Kumbia All Starz		EMI Televisa 73597
4/21/07	147	4		7 Greatest Hits: Album Versions ...... [F-G]		EMI Televisa 90331
4/19/08	148	2		8 Planeta Kumbia ...... [F]		EMI Televisa 08677
				KUMBIA ALL STARZ		

KURUPT
Born Ricardo Brown on 11/23/1972 in Philadelphia, Pennsylvania; raised in Hawthorne, California. Male rapper/songwriter. Member of **Tha Dogg Pound**. Older brother of **Roscoe**. Appeared in the movies *The Wash*, *Dark Blue* and *Hollywood Homicide*.

10/24/98	8	6		1 Kuruption!		A&M 540963 [2]
12/4/99	31	15		2 Tha Streetz Iz A Mutha		Antra 2001
8/4/01	10	11		3 Space Boogie: Smoke Oddessey		Antra 751083
9/10/05	60	2		4 Against The Grain		Death Row 63058
6/27/09	61	2		5 BlaQKout		Mad Science 17
				DJ QUIK & KURUPT		

			ARTIST		
Billboard		R I A A			
DEBUT	PEAK	WKS	Album Title	Catalog	Label & Number

KUT KLOSE
Female R&B vocal trio from Atlanta, Georgia: Tabitha Duncan, Athena Cage and LaVonn Battle.

4/1/95	66	20	1 Surrender		Elektra 61668

KUTLESS
Christian rock band from Portland, Oregon: Jon Micah Sumrall (vocals), James Mead (guitar), Ryan Shrout (guitar), Kyle Zeigler (bass) and Kyle Mitchell (drums). Dave Luetkenholter and Jeffrey Gilbert repalced Zeigler and Mitchell in 2005. Nick DePartee replaced Shrout in 2007.

3/13/04	97	4	1 Sea Of Faces..		BEC 97789
3/19/05	87	7	● 2 Strong Tower		BEC 75391
4/8/06	45	7	3 Hearts Of The Innocent...		BEC 73906
7/12/08	64	6	4 To Know That You're Alive		BEC 07161
11/7/09	42	22	5 It Is Well...		BEC 67174

KWAME AND A NEW BEGINNING
Born Kwame Holland in Queens, New York. Male rapper.

5/27/89	114	18	1 The Boy Genius Featuring A New Beginning...		Atlantic 81941
6/16/90	113	15	2 "A Day In The Life" A Pokadelick Adventure		Atlantic 82100

KWELI, Talib
Born Talib Kweli Greene on 10/3/1975 in Brooklyn, New York. Male rapper. Member of **Black Star**.

11/4/00	17	21	1 Reflection Eternal... **TALIB KWELI & HI-TEK**		Rawkus 26143
12/7/02	21	29	2 Quality		Rawkus 113048
10/16/04	14	10	3 The Beautiful Struggle		Rawkus 003407
12/10/05	113	1	4 Right About Now		Koch 5963
9/8/07	2[1]	10	5 Eardrum		Blacksmith 277244

KWELLER, Ben
Born on 6/16/1981 in Greenville, Texas. Male singer/songwriter/guitarist.

4/24/04	83	2	1 On My Way..		ATO 59174
10/7/06	115	1	2 Ben Kweller		ATO 21559
2/21/09	92	1	3 Changing Horses		ATO 0069

KWICK
R&B vocal group from Memphis, Tennessee: Terry Bartlett, Bertram Brown, William Sumlin and Vince Williams.

6/7/80	197	2	1 Kwick...		EMI America 17025

K.W.S.
Dance trio from Nottingham, England: Chris King, Winnie Williams and Meg St. Joseph.

10/17/92	143	5	1 Please Don't Go (The Album)...		Next Plateau 828368

KYPER
Born Randall Kyper in Baton Rouge, Louisiana. Male rapper.

8/4/90	82	12	1 Tic Tac Toe		Atlantic 82116

L

LA ARROLLADORA BANDA EL LIMON
Latin band from Sinaloa, Mexico. Led by Rene Camacho.

11/10/07	200	1	1 Y Que Quede Claro .... [F]		Disa 721127
4/11/09	66	6	2 Mas Adelante.. [F-K]		Disa 724160

LaBELLE, Patti   **All-Time: #169**
Born Patricia Holt on 5/24/1944 in Philadelphia, Pennsylvania. Began singing career as leader of the Ordettes which evolved into The Blue Belles. The quartet, formed in 1962, included **Nona Hendryx**, **Sarah Dash** and Cindy Birdsong. Birdsong left in 1967 to join **The Supremes**. Group continued as a trio. In 1971, group shortened its name to **LaBelle**. In 1977, group disbanded and Patti recorded solo.

12/21/74+	7	28	● 1 Nightbirds *RS500 #272*		Epic 33075
9/20/75	44	13	2 Phoenix		Epic 33579
9/25/76	94	10	3 Chameleon... **LaBELLE** (above 3)		Epic 34189
9/24/77	62	16	4 Patti LaBelle..		Epic 34847
6/24/78	129	7	5 Tasty		Epic 35335
3/31/79	145	16	6 It's Alright With Me		Epic 35772
4/12/80	114	13	7 Released		Epic 36381
10/3/81	156	4	8 The Spirit's In It		Philadelphia Int'l. 37380
1/7/84	40	35	● 9 I'm In Love Again		Philadelphia Int'l. 38539
8/10/85	72	29	10 Patti		Philadelphia Int'l. 40020

DEBUT	PEAK	WKS	R I A A	ARTIST Album Title	Catalog	Label & Number
				LaBELLE, Patti — cont'd		
5/24/86	❶¹	30	▲	11 Winner In You		MCA 5737
7/22/89	86	26		12 Be Yourself		MCA 6292
12/22/90+	18ˣ	5		13 This Christmas	[X]	MCA 10113
10/19/91+	71	36	●	14 Burnin'		MCA 10439
				Grammy: Female R&B Vocal		
11/28/92	135	3		15 Live!	[L]	MCA 10691
				recorded at the Apollo Theatre in New York City		
6/25/94	48	22	●	16 Gems		MCA 10870
7/12/97	39	21	●	17 Flame		MCA 11642
10/10/98	182	1		18 Live! One Night Only	[L]	MCA 11814 [2]
				Grammy: Traditional R&B Vocal recorded at the Hammerstein Ballroom in New York City		
11/11/00	63	5		19 When A Woman Loves		MCA 112267
5/22/04	18	10		20 Timeless Journey		Def Soul Classics 002433
7/9/05	24	9		21 Classic Moments		Def Soul Classics 004639
12/9/06	86	9		22 The Gospel According To Patti LaBelle		Umbrella 970109
12/15/07	174	1		23 Miss Patti's Christmas	[X]	Def Soul Classics 009871
				Christmas charts: 29/'07, 13/'09		
11/8/08	45	2		24 Back To Now		Verve 011511
				LaBELLE		

~ ~ ~ ~ ~ ~ ~ ~ ~ ~ **NON-CHARTED ALBUMS** ~ ~ ~ ~ ~ ~ ~ ~ ~ ~ ~

1963 **Sweethearts Of The Apollo**   1963 **Sleigh Bells, Jingle Bells And Bluebelles**

				L.A. BOPPERS		
				R&B band from Los Angeles, California: Vance Tennort (vocals, drums), Kenny Styles (guitar), Stan Martin (trumpet) and Ed Reddick (bass).		
3/15/80	85	11		1 L.A. Boppers		Mercury 3816
				LA BOUCHE		
				Black male-female dance duo: Lane McCray and Melanie Thornton. Thornton died in a plane crash on 11/24/2001 (age 34); replaced by Kayo Shekoni. La Bouche is French for "mouth."		
2/3/96	28	55	▲	1 Sweet Dreams		RCA 66759
7/11/98	194	1		2 S.O.S.		RCA 67439
				LACE		
				R&B vocal trio: Lisa Frazier, Vivian Ross and Kathy Merrick.		
1/23/88	187	5		1 Shades Of Lace		Wing 833451
				LA' CHAT		
				Born Chastity Daniels in Memphis, Tennessee. Female rapper.		
11/10/01	78	4		1 Murder She Spoke		Hypnotize Minds 8239
				LACHEY, Nick		
				Born on 11/9/1973 in Harlan, Kentucky. Pop singer/songwriter. Member of 98°. Married to **Jessica Simpson** from 2002-06 (they appeared as themselves in the 2003 MTV reality series *Newlyweds).*		
11/29/03	51	2		1 SoulO		Universal 000190
5/27/06	2¹	23	●	2 What's Left Of Me		Jive 83257
				LA COKA NOSTRA		
				Rap group formed in Boston, Massachusetts: Erik "Everlast" Schrody, Dan O'Connor, Leor DiMant, Bill Braunstein and George Carroll. Schrody, O'Connor and DiMant also recorded as **House Of Pain.**		
8/1/09	84	1		1 Brand You Can Trust		Uncle Howie 125
				LACUNA COIL		
				Goth-rock band from Milan, Italy: Cristina Scabbia (female vocals), Andrea Ferro (male vocals), Cristiano Migliore (guitar), Marco Zelati (bass) and Cristiano Mozzati (drums).		
8/7/04	178	4		1 Comalies		Century Media 8160
4/22/06	28	9		2 Karmacode		Century Media 8360
5/9/09	16	6		3 Shallow Life		Century Media 8580
				LADD, Cheryl		
				Born Cheryl Stoppelmoor on 7/12/1951 in Huron, South Dakota. Singer/actress. Starred in several movies and TV shows. Married to David Ladd (son of actor Alan Ladd) from 1973-80. Married producer/songwriter Brian Russell (Brian & Brenda) on 1/3/1981.		
8/12/78	129	11		1 Cheryl Ladd		Capitol 11808
4/28/79	179	3		2 Dance Forever		Capitol 11927
				L.A. DREAM TEAM		
				Rap duo: Rudy Pardee (from Cleveland, Ohio) and Chris Wilson (from Los Angeles, California).		
9/13/86	138	7		1 Kings Of The West Coast		MCA 5779
11/14/87	162	4		2 Bad To The Bone		MCA 42042
				LADY ANTEBELLUM		
				Country trio formed in Augusta, Georgia: Charles Kelley (male vocals), Hillary Scott (female vocals) and Dave Haywood (guitar). Scott is the daughter of singer **Linda Davis.**		
				AWARD: CMA: New Artist 2008 / Vocal Group 2009		
5/3/08	4	109↑	▲	1 Lady Antebellum		Capitol 03206

Billboard			R I A A	ARTIST		
DEBUT	PEAK	WKS		Album Title	Catalog	Label & Number

LADY GAGA
Born Stefani Germanotta on 3/28/1986 in Yonkers, New York. Dance singer/songwriter.
AWARD: Billboard Rising Star: 2009

DEBUT	PEAK	WKS		ARTIST / Album Title	Catalog	Label & Number
11/15/08+	2[1]	81↑	▲[3]	1 The Fame		Streamline 011805
				Grammy: Dance Album		
12/12/09	5	25↑	▲	2 The Fame Monster [EP]		Streamline 013872

LADY OF RAGE, The
Born Robin Allen on 6/11/1968 in Farmville, Virginia. Female rapper.

| 7/12/97 | 32 | 6 | | 1 Necessary Roughness | | Death Row 90109 |

LADY SOVEREIGN
Born Louise Harman on 12/19/1985 in Wembley, London, England. White female rapper/songwriter.

| 11/18/06 | 48 | 3 | | 1 Public Warning | | Def Jam 007625 |

LADYTRON
Electro-pop band formed in Liverpool, England: Helen Marnie and Mira Aroyo (vocals), Reuben Wu (DJ) and Daniel Hunt (instruments).

| 6/21/08 | 131 | 1 | | 1 Velocifero | | Nettwerk 30790 |

L.A. EXPRESS
Backing band for **Tom Scott**: Robben Ford (guitar), David Luell (sax), Victor Feldman (keyboards), Max Bennett (bass) and John Guerin (drums). Guerin died of heart failure on 1/12/2004 (age 64).

| 3/6/76 | 167 | 8 | | 1 L.A. Express [I] | | Caribou 33940 |

LAFLAMME, David
Born on 4/5/1941 in Salt Lake City, Utah. Electric violinist/singer. Leader of **It's A Beautiful Day**.

| 12/25/76+ | 159 | 6 | | 1 White Bird | | Amherst 1007 |

L.A. GUNS
Hard-rock band from Los Angeles, California: Philip Lewis (vocals), Tracii Guns (guitar), Mick Cripps (guitar), Kelly Nickels (bass), and Steve Riley (drums). Guns was also a member of **Contraband** in 1991.

2/6/88	50	33	●	1 L.A. Guns		Vertigo 834144
9/16/89+	38	56	●	2 Cocked & Loaded		Vertigo 838592
7/13/91	42	18		3 Hollywood Vampires		Polydor 849485

LAGWAGON
Punk-rock band from Goleta, California: Joey Cape (vocals), Chris Flippin (guitar), Chris Rest (guitar), Jesse Buglione (bass) and Dave Raun (drums). Cape and Raun were also members of **Me First And The Gimme Gimmes**.

| 4/26/03 | 172 | 1 | | 1 Blaze | | Fat Wreck Chords 642 |

LAID BACK
Synth-pop duo from Denmark: Tim Stahl (keyboards) and John Guldberg (guitar).

| 3/31/84 | 67 | 15 | | 1 ...Keep Smiling | | Sire 25058 |

LAINE, Cleo
Born Clementina Campbell on 10/28/1927 in Southall, Middlesex, England (Jamaican father; British mother). Jazz singer. Married bandleader Johnny Dankworth in 1958.

2/9/74	219	3		1 I Am A Song		RCA Victor 5000
4/6/74	157	8		2 Cleo Laine Live!!! At Carnegie Hall [L]		RCA Victor 5015
				recorded on 10/17/1973		
7/20/74	199	1		3 Day By Day		Buddah 5607
12/28/74+	168	5		4 A Beautiful Thing		RCA Victor 5059
2/7/76	158	10		5 Born On A Friday		RCA Victor 5113
12/4/76	138	11		6 Porgy & Bess		RCA Victor 1831 [2]
				RAY CHARLES & CLEO LAINE		
9/30/78	201	3		7 Gonna Get Through		RCA Victor 2926
7/26/80	150	6		8 Sometimes When We Touch		RCA Victor 3628
				CLEO LAINE & JAMES GALWAY		

LAINE, Frankie
Born Francesco LoVecchio on 3/30/1913 in Chicago, Illinois. Died on 2/6/2007 (age 93). One of the most popular singers of the early 1950s.

4/20/57	13	12		1 Rockin'		Columbia 975
10/23/61	71	37		2 Hell Bent For Leather!		Columbia 8415
5/13/67	16	29		3 I'll Take Care Of Your Cares		ABC 604
10/14/67	162	2		4 I Wanted Someone To Love		ABC 608
3/23/68	127	9		5 To Each His Own		ABC 628
4/19/69	55	11		6 You Gave Me A Mountain		ABC 682

L.A. JETS
Rock band from Los Angeles, California: Karen Lawrence (vocals), Harlin McNees (guitar), Ron Cindrich (bass) and John DeSautels (drums).

| 6/19/76 | 210 | 1 | | 1 L.A. Jets | | RCA Victor 1547 |

LAKE
Rock band from Hamburg, Germany: James Hopkins-Harrison (vocals), Alex Conti (guitar), Geoffrey Peacey (keyboards), Martin Tiefensee (bass) and Dieter Ahrendt (drums). Hopkins-Harrison died of a drug overdose on 5/16/1991 (age 41).

DEBUT	PEAK	WKS		Album Title	Catalog	Label & Number
8/20/77	92	15		1 Lake		Columbia 34763
7/22/78	201	3		2 Lake II		Columbia 35289

LAKE, Greg
Born on 11/10/1948 in Bournemouth, Dorset, England. Rock singer/guitarist. Member of **King Crimson** and **Emerson, Lake & Palmer**.

10/31/81	62	17		1 Greg Lake		Chrysalis 1357
10/1/83	209	1		2 Manoeuvres		Chrysalis 41392

LAKESIDE
R&B-funk band from Dayton, Ohio: Tiemeyer McCain, Thomas Shelby, Otis Stokes and Mark Wood (vocals), Steve Shockley (guitar), Fred Lewis (percussion), Norman Beavers (keyboards), Marvin Craig (bass) and Fred Alexander (drums).

1/6/79	74	19		1 Shot Of Love		Solar 2937
11/3/79	141	18		2 Rough Riders		Solar 3490
11/29/80+	16	35	●	3 Fantastic Voyage		Solar 3720
12/12/81	109	10		4 Keep On Moving Straight Ahead		Solar 3974
1/9/82	58	23		5 Your Wish Is My Command		Solar 26
5/28/83	42	18		6 Untouchables		Solar 60204
7/28/84	68	15		7 Outrageous		Solar 60355

LAMBERT, Adam
Born on 1/29/1982 in Indianapolis, Indiana; raised in San Diego, California. Finished in second place on the 2009 season of TV's *American Idol*.

6/6/09	33	3		1 Season 8 Favorite Performances	[L]	19 Records digital
12/5/09	72	1		2 Take One		Rufftown 2009
12/12/09	3[1]	25↑		3 For Your Entertainment		19 Records 54801

LAMBERT, Miranda
Born on 11/10/1983 in Longview, Texas; raised in Lindale, Texas. Country singer/songwriter/guitarist. Placed third on the first season of TV's *Nashville Star* talent series in 2003.

4/2/05	18	70	▲	1 Kerosene		Epic 92026
5/19/07	6	100	●	2 Crazy Ex-Girlfriend	Cat:#12/13	Columbia 78932
10/17/09	8	33↑	●	3 Revolution		Columbia 46854

LAMBERT, HENDRICKS & ROSS
Jazz vocal trio formed in New York: Dave Lambert (born on 6/19/1917; died after being hit by a car on 10/3/1966, age 49), Jon Hendricks (born on 9/16/1921) and Annie Ross (born on 7/25/1930). Sang lyricized versions of actual **Count Basie** band arrangements.

~ ~ ~ ~ ~ ~ ~ ~ ~ ~ **NON-CHARTED ALBUM** ~ ~ ~ ~ ~ ~ ~ ~ ~ ~ ~

1958 Sing A Song Of Basie
Grammy: Hall of Fame

LAMB OF GOD
Hard-rock band from Richmond, Virginia: Randy Blythe (vocals), Willie Adler (guitar), Mark Morton (guitar), John Campbell (bass) and Chris Adler (drums).

9/18/04	27	5		1 Ashes Of The Wake		Prosthetic 90702
9/9/06	8	8		2 Sacrament		Prosthetic 87804
3/14/09	2[1]	12		3 Wrath		Epic 37592

LaMOND, George
Born George Garcia on 2/25/1967 in Washington DC; raised in the Bronx, New York. Pop singer.

8/18/90	104	10		1 Bad Of The Heart		Columbia 45488

LaMONTAGNE, Ray
Born on 6/18/1974 in Nashua, New Hampshire; later based in Wilton, Maine. Folk-rock singer/songwriter/guitarist.

2/5/05	189	2		1 Trouble		RCA 63459
9/16/06	28	9		2 Till The Sun Turns Black		RCA 83328
11/1/08	3[1]	30		3 Gossip In The Grain		RCA 32670
1/17/09	119	1		4 Live Session	[EP-L]	RCA digital

LAMONT CRANSTON BAND
Rock band from Minneapolis, Minnesota: Pat Hayes (vocals, harmonica), Larry Hayes and Charlie Bingham (guitars), Rick O'Dell and Jim Greenwell (horns), Bruce McCabe (keyboards), Terry Grant (bass) and Jim Novack (drums). Band named after the true identity of the fictional character "The Shadow".

4/24/82	201	4		1 Shakedown		RCA Victor 4313

LAMPA, Rachael
Born on 1/8/1985 in Ann Arbor, Michigan; raised in Louisville, Colorado. Christian pop singer.

8/19/00	120	5		1 Live For You		Word 61068
3/23/02	114	4		2 Kaleidoscope		Word 86182

Billboard			R I A A	ARTIST Album Title	Catalog	Label & Number
DEBUT	PEAK	WKS				

LANCE, Major
Born on 4/4/1939 in Winterville, Mississippi; raised in Chicago, Illinois. Died of heart disease on 9/3/1994 (age 55). R&B singer.

10/5/63	113	3		1 The Monkey Time		Okeh 12105
3/28/64	100	9		2 Um, Um, Um, Um, Um, Um/The Best Of Major Lance	[G]	Okeh 12106
9/4/65	109	6		3 Major's Greatest Hits	[G]	Okeh 12110

LANE, Robin, & The Chartbusters
Born in 1947 in Los Angeles, California; later based in in Boston, Massachusetts. Female rock singer. Daughter of **Dean Martin**'s pianist, Ken Lane. The Chartbusters: Asa Brebner (guitar), Leroy Radcliffe (keyboards), Scott Baerenwald (bass) and Tim Jackson (drums).

5/24/80	207	1		1 Robin Lane & The Chartbusters		Warner 3424
4/25/81	172	4		2 Imitation Life		Warner 3537

LANE, Ronnie
Born on 4/1/1946 in London, England. Died of multiple sclerosis on 6/4/1997 (age 51). Rock singer/bassist. Member of **Small Faces** and **Faces**.

10/15/77	45	12		1 Rough Mix		MCA 2295
				PETE TOWNSHEND & RONNIE LANE		

LANG, Jonny
Born Jon Langseth on 1/29/1981 in Fargo, North Dakota. White blues-rock singer/guitarist. Nicknamed "Kid."

2/15/97	44	62	▲	1 Lie To Me		A&M 540640
11/7/98	28	29	▲	2 Wander This World		A&M 540984
11/1/03	17	17		3 Long Time Coming		A&M 001145
10/7/06	35	7		4 Turn Around		A&M 007292

lang, k.d.   All-Time: #400
Born Kathryn Dawn Lang on 11/2/1961 in Consort, Alberta, Canada. Eclectic singer/songwriter/actress. Played "Hilary" in the 1999 movie *Eye Of The Beholder*.

5/28/88	73	25	●	1 Shadowland		Sire 25724
6/17/89+	69	56	●	2 Absolute Torch And Twang		Sire 25877
				k.d. lang and THE RECLINES		
				Grammy: Female Country Vocal		
4/4/92+	18	90	▲²	3 Ingenue		Sire 26840
11/20/93	82	14		4 Even Cowgirls Get The Blues	[S]	Sire 45433
10/28/95	37	20	●	5 All You Can Eat		Warner 46034
6/28/97	29	16	●	6 Drag		Warner 46623
7/8/00	58	11		7 Invincible Summer		Warner 47605
9/1/01	94	5		8 Live By Request	[L]	Warner 48108
11/23/02	41	18	●	9 A Wonderful World		RPM 86734
				TONY BENNETT & K.D. LANG		
				Grammy: Traditional Pop Album		
8/14/04	55	13		10 Hymns Of The 49th Parallel		Nonesuch 79847
2/23/08	8	9		11 Watershed		Nonesuch 110460

LANGE, Artie
Born on 10/11/1967 in Livingston, New Jersey. Stand-up comedian/actor. Regular on Howard Stern's radio show. Acted in several movies.

11/28/09	154	1		1 Jack And Coke	[C]	Shout! Factory 11757

LANIN, Lester, And His Orchestra   1950s: #17
Born Nathaniel Lester Lanin on 8/26/1907 in Philadelphia, Pennsylvania. Died on 10/27/2004 (age 97). Orchestra leader.

6/24/57	7	10		1 Dance To The Music Of Lester Lanin	[I]	Epic 3340
11/11/57	18	2		2 Lester Lanin And His Orchestra	[I]	Epic 3242
2/3/58	17	2		3 Lester Lanin At The Tiffany Ball	[I]	Epic 3410
6/9/58	19	3		4 Lester Lanin Goes To College	[I]	Epic 3474
11/17/58	12	4		5 Have Band, Will Travel	[I]	Epic 3520
1/20/62	37	20		6 Twistin' In High Society!	[I]	Epic 3825

LANOIS, Daniel
Born on 9/19/1951 in Hull, Quebec, Canada. Prolific producer.

1/20/90	166	5		1 Acadie		Opal 25969
5/10/03	143	2		2 Shine		Anti 86661

LANZ, David
Born on 6/28/1950 in Seattle, Washington. New Age pianist.

1/30/88	125	12		1 Natural States	[I]	Narada Equinox 63001
				DAVID LANZ & PAUL SPEER		
11/5/88	180	6	●	2 Cristofori's Dream	[I]	Narada Lotus 61021
11/26/94	39ˣ	1		3 Christmas Eve	[X-I]	Narada Lotus 61046

LANZA, Mario   1950s: #33
Born Alfredo Cocozza on 1/31/1921 in Philadelphia, Pennsylvania. Died of a heart attack on 10/7/1959 (age 38). Operatic tenor/actor.

4/28/56	9	6		1 Serenade	[S]	RCA Victor 1996
3/17/58	7	8		2 Seven Hills Of Rome	[S]	RCA Victor 2211
11/2/59	5	46		3 For The First Time	[S]	RCA Victor 2338

Billboard			R I A A	ARTIST Album Title	Catalog	Label & Number
DEBUT	PEAK	WKS				
				LANZA, Mario — cont'd		
12/14/59+	4	4		4 Lanza Sings Christmas Carols [X]		RCA Victor 2333
				first released in 1956 on RCA Victor 2029		
12/18/61+	67	5		5 Lanza Sings Christmas Carols [X-R]		RCA Victor 2333
12/21/63+	15ˣ	12		6 Christmas Hymns And Carols [X]		RCA Camden 777
				reissue of #4 & #5 above (with a slightly different song selection); Christmas charts: 24/'63, 15/'64, 56/'65, 51/'66, 36/'67		
5/16/60	4	53		7 Mario Lanza Sings Caruso Favorites [F]		RCA Victor 2393
10/6/62+	64	41		8 I'll Walk With God [E]		RCA Victor 2607
8/8/64	87	15		9 The Best Of Mario Lanza [G]		RCA Victor 2748
				LA OREJA DE VAN GOGH Latin band from Spain: Pablo Benegas, Alvaro Fuentes, Xabi San Martin, Haritz Garde and Amaia Montero.		
5/20/06	114	3		1 Guapa [F]		Sony 79923
				LA QUINTA ESTACION Latin trio from Madrid, Spain: Natalia Jimenez, Angel Reyero and Pablo Dominguez. Originally name La 5A Estacion.		
4/4/09	120	1		1 Sin Frenos [F]		Sony 44947
				Grammy: Latin Pop Album		
				LARKIN, Billy, & The Delegates Born in Los Angeles, California. Jazz organist. The Delegates: Hank Swarn (guitar), Clifford Scott (sax) and Mel Brown (drums). Scott died on 4/19/1993 (age 64).		
4/2/66	148	2		1 Hole In The Wall [I]		World Pacific 1837
				LARKS, The R&B vocal trio from Los Angeles, California: Don Julian, Ted Walters and Charles Morrison. Julian died of pneumonia on 11/6/1998 (age 61).		
1/23/65	143	4		1 The Jerk		Money 1102
				LA ROUX Electro-pop duo from London, England: Eleanor Jackson and Ben Langmaid.		
10/10/09+	121	6↑		1 La Roux		Polydor 013389
				LARRIEUX, Amel Born on 3/8/1973 in Manhattan, New York. Female R&B singer/songwriter. Former member of **Groove Theory**.		
3/4/00	79	9		1 Infinite Possibilities		550 Music 69741
2/7/04	166	1		2 Bravebird		Bliss Life 0001
5/13/06	74	2		3 Morning		Blisslife 002
6/9/07	195	1		4 Lovely Standards		Blisslife 00003
				LARRY THE CABLE GUY Born Daniel Whitney on 2/17/1963 in Pawnee City, Nebraska. "Redneck" stand-up comedian. Starred in the 2006 movie *Larry The Cable Guy: Health Inspector*. Famous catch phrase: "Git-R-Done!" Also see **Blue Collar Comedy Tour**.		
1/24/04	❶¹ᶜ	59	●	1 Lord, I Apologize [C]		Spank-Um 810076
				first released in 2001		
12/4/04	43	5	▲	2 A Very Larry Christmas Cat:❶²/30 [X-C]		Jack 48931
				Christmas charts: 4/'04, 4/'05, 3/'06, 10/'07, 31/'08, 47/'09		
4/16/05	7	27	●	3 The Right To Bare Arms [C]		Jack 49300
4/21/07	16	12		4 Morning Constitutions [C]		Jack 73273
11/17/07	42	9		5 Christmastime In Larryland [X-C]		Jack 276156
				Christmas chart: 8/'07		
10/10/09	71	2		6 Tailgate Party [C]		Jack 519711
				LARSEN, Blaine Born on 2/2/1986 in Tacoma, Washington. Country singer/songwriter/guitarist.		
2/12/05	79	16		1 Off To Join The World		Giantslayer 66012
7/1/06	93	2		2 Rockin' You Tonight		Giantslayer 78715
				LARSEN, Neil Born on 8/7/1948 in Cleveland, Ohio; raised in Siesta Key, Florida. Session keyboardist. Member of **Larsen-Feiten Band**.		
1/20/79	206	4		1 Jungle Fever [I]		Horizon 733
9/1/79	139	7		2 High Gear [I]		Horizon 738
				LARSEN-FEITEN BAND Duo of session musicians: **Neil Larsen** (keyboards) and Buzz Feiten (guitar). Both were also members of **Full Moon**.		
9/13/80	142	10		1 Larsen-Feiten Band		Warner 3468
				LARSON, Nicolette Born on 7/17/1952 in Helena, Montana; raised in Kansas City, Missouri. Died of a cerebral edema on 12/16/1997 (age 45). Former session singer. Married session drummer Russ Kunkel in 1990.		
11/18/78+	15	37	●	1 Nicolette		Warner 3243
11/3/79	47	21		2 In The Nick Of Time		Warner 3370
1/24/81	62	12		3 Radioland		Warner 3502
8/14/82	75	10		4 All Dressed Up & No Place To Go		Warner 3678

Billboard			R I A A	ARTIST		
DEBUT	**PEAK**	**WKS**		**Album Title**	**Catalog**	**Label & Number**

LaRUE, D.C.
Born David Charles L'Heureux on 4/26/1948 in Meriden, Connecticut. Disco singer/songwriter.

| 6/26/76 | 139 | 13 | | 1 Cathedrals | | Pyramid 9003 |
| 1/8/77 | 115 | 11 | | 2 The Tea Dance | | Pyramid 9006 |

LA'S, The
Rock band from Liverpool, England: brothers Lee Mavers (vocals) and Neil Mavers (drums), with Peter Camell (guitar), and John Power (bass). Group name is slang for lads.

| 7/6/91 | 196 | 1 | | 1 The La's | | London 828202 |

LaSALLE, Denise
Born Denise Craig on 7/16/1939 in LeFlore County, Mississippi. R&B singer/songwriter.

2/5/72	120	9		1 Trapped By A Thing Called Love		Westbound 2012
8/4/79	205	3		2 Unwrapped		MCA 3098
4/14/84	204	5		3 Right Place, Right Time		Malaco 7417

LAS KETCHUP
Female pop vocal trio from Cordoba, Spain: sisters Lola, Lucia and Pilar Munoz.

| 10/12/02 | 65 | 16 | | 1 Las Ketchup | [F] | Columbia 86980 |

LAST, James
Born on 4/17/1929 in Bremen, Germany. Producer/arranger/conductor.

2/19/72	160	5		1 Music From Across The Way		Polydor 5505
8/16/75	172	3		2 Well Kept Secret	[I]	Polydor 6040
6/28/80	148	8		3 Seduction	[I]	Polydor 6283
				JAMES LAST BAND		

LAST POETS, The
Black protest group from Harlem, New York: Abiodun Oyewole, Alafia Pudim, Omar Ben Hassen, Nilaja, David Nelson, Felipe Luciano and Gylan Kain. Nelson, Luciano and Kain split from the others to record as **The Original Last Poets**.

6/20/70	29	30		1 The Last Poets		Douglas 3
3/6/71	106	6		2 Right On!	[S]	Juggernaut 8802
				THE ORIGINAL LAST POETS		
4/3/71	104	15		3 This Is Madness		Douglas 30583

LAST SHADOW PUPPETS, The
Alternative-rock trio formed in England: Alex Turner (vocals, guitar), Miles Kane (bass) and James Ford (drums). Turner is also leader of the **Arctic Monkeys**.

| 5/24/08 | 111 | 1 | | 1 The Age Of The Understatement | | Domino 181 |

LASWELL, Greg
Born on 4/26/1974 in Long Beach, California; raised in San Diego, California. Singer/songwriter/producer.

| 7/11/09 | 181 | 1 | | 1 Three Flights From Alto Nido | | Vanguard 79854 |

LATEEF, Yusef
Born William Evans on 10/9/1920 in Chattanooga, Tennessee; raised in Detroit, Michigan. Jazz tenor saxophonist/flutist. After high school graduation, played with Lucky Millinder. Worked with Dizzy Gillespie in 1949, then **Charles Mingus** in the early 1960s.

| 8/16/69 | 183 | 5 | | 1 Yusef Lateef's Detroit | [I] | Atlantic 1525 |

LATHUN
Born Lathun Grady in 1975 in Detroit, Michigan. Male R&B singer/songwriter/guitarist/keyboardist.

| 6/29/02 | 179 | 1 | | 1 Fortunate | | Motown 016704 |

LATIMORE
Born Benjamin Latimore on 9/7/1939 in Charleston, Tennessee. R&B singer/songwriter.

| 3/26/77 | 181 | 5 | | 1 It Ain't Where You Been... | | Glades 7509 |

LATIN ALLIANCE
All-star rap trio: **Kid Frost**, **Mellow Man Ace** and ALT.

| 8/24/91 | 133 | 8 | | 1 Latin Alliance | | Virgin 91625 |

LaTOUR
Born William LaTour in Lowell, Massachusetts; raised in Phoenix, Arizona. Techno-dance artist.

| 5/11/91 | 145 | 4 | | 1 LaTour | | Smash 848323 |

LATTIMORE, Kenny
Born on 4/10/1970 in Washington DC. R&B singer. Married **Chante Moore** on 1/1/2002.

7/20/96+	92	34	●	1 Kenny Lattimore		Columbia 67125
11/7/98	71	8		2 From The Soul Of Man		Columbia 68854
10/27/01	63	4		3 Weekend		Arista 14668
3/1/03	31	15		4 Things That Lovers Do		Arista 14751
10/28/06	95	2		5 Uncovered/Covered		Verity 67926 [2]
				KENNY LATTIMORE & CHANTE MOORE (above 2)		
9/27/08	54	2		6 Timeless		Verve 011500

Billboard			R I A A	ARTIST		
DEBUT	PEAK	WKS		Album Title	Catalog	Label & Number

LATTISAW, Stacy
Born on 11/25/1966 in Washington DC. Female R&B singer. Her brother Jerome "Goldee" is a member of **Prophet Jones**.

7/5/80	44	28	1 Let Me Be Your Angel		Cotillion 5219
7/25/81	46	15	2 With You..		Cotillion 16049
8/28/82	55	16	3 Sneakin' Out		Cotillion 90002
8/27/83	160	8	4 Sixteen		Cotillion 90106
3/31/84	139	8	5 Perfect Combination		Cotillion 90136
			STACY LATTISAW & JOHNNY GILL		
10/11/86	131	22	6 Take Me All The Way		Motown 6212
3/5/88	153	10	7 Personal Attention		Motown 6247

LAUPER, Cyndi
Born on 6/22/1953 in Brooklyn, New York; raised in Queens, New York. Pop-rock singer. Acted in the movies *Vibes* and *Life With Mikey*. Married actor David Thornton on 11/24/1991.
   AWARD: Grammy: Best New Artist 1984

12/24/83+	4	96	▲⁶ 1 **She's So Unusual**		Portrait 38930
			RS500 #494		
10/4/86	4	44	▲² 2 **True Colors**		Portrait 40313
5/27/89	37	21	3 A Night To Remember		Epic 44318
7/3/93	112	4	4 Hat Full Of Stars		Epic 52878
8/5/95	81	12	● 5 Twelve Deadly Cyns...And Then Some .... [G]		Epic 66100
4/19/97	188	1	6 Sisters Of Avalon		Epic 66433
12/6/03	38	14	7 At Last		Daylight 90760
11/26/05	112	2	8 The Body Acoustic...		Daylight 94569
6/14/08	41	2	9 Bring Ya To The Brink		Epic 06592

LAUREANO, Gustavo
Born in Puerto Rico. Latin singer/songwriter/guitarist.

4/7/07	182	1	1 King Callero Del Amor .... [F]		Universal Latino 008587

LaVETTE, Betty
Born Betty Haskins on 1/29/1946 in Muskegon, Michigan; raised in Detroit, Michigan. R&B singer/actress.

2/13/82	207	5	1 Tell Me A Lie		Motown 6000

LAVIGNE, Avril
Born on 9/27/1984 in Belleville, Ontario, Canada; raised in Napanee, Ontario, Canada. Teen pop-rock female singer/songwriter. Married Deryck Whibley (lead singer of rock group **Sum 41**) on 7/15/2006.

6/22/02	2²	97	▲⁶ 1 **Let Go**	Cat:#7/25	Arista 14740
6/12/04	❶¹	66	▲³ 2 **Under My Skin**	Cat:#31/1	Arista 59774
5/5/07	❶²	51	▲ 3 **The Best Damn Thing**		RCA 03774

LAVOE, Hector
Born Hector Martinez on 9/30/1946 in Ponce, Puerto Rico. Died of AIDS on 6/29/1993 (age 46). Latin singer.

8/18/07	144	3	1 El Cantante: The Originals... [F]		Fania 130269

LAW, The
Rock duo from England: vocalist **Paul Rodgers** (**Free**, **Bad Company**, **The Firm**) and drummer Kenney Jones (**Small Faces, Faces, The Who**).

4/13/91	126	6	1 The Law		Atlantic 82195

LAWRENCE, Donald
Born in Spartanburg, South Carolina. Contemporary gospel singer.

4/13/02	170	3	1 Go Get Your Life Back .... [L]		EMI Gospel 20360
			DONALD LAWRENCE & THE TRI-CITY SINGERS recorded at the University Park Baptist Church in Charlotte, North Carolina		
10/30/04	136	1	2 I Speak Life		Verity 62228
			DONALD LAWRENCE & CO.		
4/22/06	149	1	3 Finale: Act One .... [L]		EMI Gospel 33345
4/22/06	190	1	4 Finale: Act Two .... [L]		EMI Gospel 54835
			DONALD LAWRENCE & THE TRI-CITY SINGERS (above 2)		
2/21/09	72	11	5 The Law Of Confession, Part I		Quiet Water 23473
			DONALD LAWRENCE & CO.		

LAWRENCE, Joey
Born on 4/20/1976 in Montgomery, Pennsylvania. Teen actor/singer. Acted on TV's *Gimme A Break*, *Blossom* and *Brotherly Love*. Finished third on season 3 of *Dancing With The Stars*.

3/6/93	74	22	1 Joey Lawrence		Impact 10659

LAWRENCE, Martin
Born on 4/16/1965 in Frankfurt, Germany (father was in U.S. miltary); raised in Landover, Maryland. Black stand-up comedian/ actor. Starred in several movies and TV shows.

10/9/93	76	9	1 Talkin' Shit .... [C]		EastWest 92289

LAWRENCE, Steve
Born Sidney Leibowitz on 7/8/1935 in Brooklyn, New York. Pop singer. Regular performer on **Steve Allen**'s *The Tonight Show*. Married **Eydie Gorme** on 12/29/1957.

6/2/58	19	2	1 Here's Steve Lawrence		Coral 57204
8/14/61	76	10	2 Portrait Of My Love		United Artists 6150

Billboard			R I A A	ARTIST		
DEBUT	PEAK	WKS		Album Title	Catalog	Label & Number

LAWRENCE, Steve — cont'd

2/9/63	27	29		3 Winners!	Columbia 1953 / 8753
2/15/64	135	5		4 Academy Award Losers	Columbia 2121 / 8921
9/12/64	73	9		5 Everybody Knows	Columbia 2227 / 9027
12/11/65	133	2		6 The Steve Lawrence Show	Columbia 2419 / 9219

STEVE LAWRENCE & EYDIE GORME:

5/20/67	136	6		7 Together On Broadway	Columbia 2636 / 9436
3/8/69	141	6		8 What It Was, Was Love	RCA Victor 4115
5/10/69	188	3		9 Real True Lovin'	RCA Victor 4107
7/1/72	208	1		10 The World Of Steve & Eydie	MGM 4803

STEVE LAWRENCE & EYDIE GORME with The Mike Curb Congregation

LAWRENCE, Tracy All-Time: #356

Born on 1/27/1968 in Atlanta, Texas; raised in Foreman, Arkansas. Male country singer/songwriter/guitarist. Wounded in a 1991 shooting incident in Nashville (fully recovered).

1/18/92	71	40	▲	1 Sticks And Stones	Atlantic 82326
3/27/93	25	48	▲²	2 Alibis	Atlantic 82483
10/8/94	28	54	▲	3 I See It Now	Atlantic 82656
10/7/95	151	4		4 Live [L]	Atlantic 82847
2/10/96	25	56	▲²	5 Time Marches On	Atlantic 82866
4/5/97	45	22	●	6 The Coast Is Clear	Atlantic 82985
9/19/98	92	6	●	7 The Best Of Tracy Lawrence [G]	Atlantic 83137
2/19/00	69	6		8 Lessons Learned	Atlantic 83269
11/10/01	136	1		9 Tracy Lawrence	Atlantic 48187
7/28/07	163	1		10 The Very Best Of Tracy Lawrence [G]	Atlantic 171708
4/17/04	17	15		11 Strong	DreamWorks 001032
11/5/05	35	5		12 Then & Now: The Hits Collection [G]	Mercury 004613
2/17/07	53	35		13 For The Love	Rocky Comfort 90012
6/27/09	104	2		14 The Rock	Rocky Comfort 10194

LAWRENCE, Vicki

Born on 3/26/1949 in Inglewood, California. Singer/actress. With **The Young Americans** from 1964-67. Regular on **Carol Burnett**'s CBS-TV series from 1967-78. Also starred in TV's *Mama's Family* (1982-87). Married to **Bobby Russell** from 1972-74.

4/28/73	51	14		1 The Night The Lights Went Out In Georgia	Bell 1120

LAWS, Debra

Born on 9/10/1956 in Houston, Texas. R&B singer. Sister of **Eloise Laws**, **Hubert Laws** and **Ronnie Laws**.

4/11/81	70	27		1 Very Special	Elektra 300

LAWS, Eloise

Born Lavern Eloise Laws on 11/6/1943 in Houston, Texas. R&B singer. Sister of **Debra Laws**, **Hubert Laws** and **Ronnie Laws**.

2/4/78	156	5		1 Eloise	ABC 1022
2/14/81	175	7		2 Eloise Laws	Liberty 1063

LAWS, Hubert

Born on 11/10/1939 in Houston, Texas. Jazz flutist. Brother of **Ronnie Laws**, **Eloise Laws** and **Debra Laws**.

2/24/73	148	9		1 Morning Star [I]	CTI 6022
6/30/73	175	6		2 Carnegie Hall [I-L]	CTI 6025
				recorded on 1/12/1973	
7/13/74	207	1		3 In The Beginning [I]	CTI 3 [2]
6/21/75	42	18		4 The Chicago Theme [I]	CTI 6058
11/6/76	139	6		5 Romeo & Juliet [I]	Columbia 34330
4/8/78	71	18		6 Say It With Silence [I]	Columbia 35022
4/28/79	93	8		7 Land Of Passion	Columbia 35708
9/27/80	134	4		8 How To Beat The High Cost Of Living [I-S]	Columbia 36741
				HUBERT LAWS & EARL KLUGH	
11/8/80	133	13		9 Family [I]	Columbia 36396

LAWS, Ronnie

Born on 10/3/1950 in Houston, Texas. Jazz saxophonist. Brother of **Debra Laws**, **Eloise Laws** and **Hubert Laws**. With **Earth, Wind & Fire** from 1972-73.

9/27/75	73	29		1 Pressure Sensitive [I]	Blue Note 452
6/12/76	46	21		2 Fever [I]	Blue Note 628
5/7/77	37	28	●	3 Friends And Strangers [I]	Blue Note 730
11/4/78	51	22		4 Flame	United Artists 881
2/16/80	24	19		5 Every Generation	United Artists 1001
10/10/81	51	19		6 Solid Ground	Liberty 51087
8/13/83	98	11		7 Mr. Nice Guy	Capitol 12261
1/26/85	201	7		8 Classic Masters [K]	Capitol 12375

LAYZIE BONE

Born Steven Howse on 9/23/1975 in Cleveland, Ohio. Male rapper. Member of **Bone Thugs-N-Harmony** and **Bone Brothers**.

4/7/01	43	6		1 Thug By Nature	Ruthless 85173
				L-BURNA a.k.a. LAYZIE BONE	
6/18/05	96	2		2 It's Not A Game	X-Ray 1464

Billboard			R I A A	ARTIST		
DEBUT	PEAK	WKS		Album Title	Catalog	Label & Number

LCD SOUNDSYSTEM
Born James Murphy on 2/4/1970 in Princeton Junction, New Jersey. Dance-punk singer/musician.

| 4/7/07 | 46 | 3 | | 1 Sound Of Silver .... | | DFA 85114 |

LEADBELLY
Born Huddie Ledbetter on 1/20/1888 in Mooringsport, Louisiana. Died on 12/6/1949 (age 61). Legendary black folk-blues singer/songwriter/guitarist. Also see **Various Artists Compilations:** *Folkways: A Vision Shared - A Tribute To Woody Guthrie And Leadbelly*.
> AWARD: R&R Hall of Fame: 1988 (Early Influence)

~ ~ ~ ~ ~ ~ ~ ~ ~ ~ **NON-CHARTED ALBUM** ~ ~ ~ ~ ~ ~ ~ ~ ~ ~
> 1964 **The Midnight Special**
> *Grammy: Hall of Fame*

LEADERS OF THE NEW SCHOOL
Rap group from Uniondale, New York: **Busta Rhymes**, Charlie Brown, Dinco D and Cut Monitor Milo.

| 8/17/91 | 128 | 6 | | 1 A Future Without A Past... .... | | Elektra 60976 |
| 10/30/93 | 66 | 4 | | 2 T.I.M.E. - The Inner Mind's Eye - The Endless Dispute With Reality .... | | Elektra 61382 |

LEADON, Bernie/Michael Georgiades Band
Leadon was born on 7/19/1947 in Minneapolis, Minnesota. Rock guitarist. Member of the **Flying Burrito Brothers** and the **Eagles**. Brother of Tom Leadon (of **Mudcrutch**). With Georgiades on vocals/guitar.

| 8/20/77 | 91 | 6 | | 1 Natural Progressions .... | | Asylum 1107 |

LEAGUE UNLIMITED ORCHESTRA — see HUMAN LEAGUE, The

LEAPY LEE
Born Graham Pulleyblank on 7/2/1942 in Eastbourne, East Sussex, England. Country-pop singer/actor.

| 1/18/69 | 71 | 12 | | 1 Little Arrows .... | | Decca 75076 |

LEARY, Denis
Born on 8/18/1957 in Worcester, Massachusetts. Stand-up comedian/actor. Starred in several movies and TV shows.

| 2/13/93 | 85 | 13 | ● | 1 No Cure For Cancer .... [C] | | A&M 540055 |
| 12/6/97 | 169 | 1 | | 2 Lock 'N Load .... [C] | | A&M 540832 |

LEATHERWOLF
Hard-rock band from Los Angeles, California: Michael Oliveri (vocals), Carey Howe (guitar), Geoffrey Gayer (guitar), Paul Carman (bass) and Dean Roberts (drums).

| 3/5/88 | 105 | 12 | | 1 Leatherwolf .... | | Island 90660 |
| 4/29/89 | 123 | 8 | | 2 Street Ready .... | | Island 91072 |

LEAVES, The
Garage-rock band from Northridge, California: Robert Arlin (vocals), John Beck (guitar), Robert Lee Reiner (guitar), Jim Pons (bass) and Tom Ray (drums). Pons was later a brief member of **The Turtles**.

| 7/30/66 | 127 | 5 | | 1 Hey Joe .... | | Mira 3005 |

LeBLANC & CARR
Soft-rock duo: Lenny LeBlanc (born on 6/17/1951 in Leominster, Massachusetts) and Pete Carr (born on 4/22/1950 in Daytona Beach, Florida).

| 3/18/78 | 145 | 7 | | 1 Midnight Light .... | | Big Tree 89521 |

LECRAE
Born Lecrae Moore in 1980 in Houston, Texas. Male Christian rapper.

| 10/18/08 | 60 | 4 | | 1 Rebel .... | | Reach 98070 |

LEDISI
Born Ledisi Young in New Orleans, Louisiana. Female R&B singer/songwriter.

9/15/07	78	22		1 Lost & Found		Verve 008909
10/11/08	5^X	5		2 It's Christmas .... [X]		Verve Forecast 011796
9/5/09	14	10		3 Turn Me Loose		Verve Forecast 012677

LeDOUX, Chris
Born on 10/2/1948 in Biloxi, Mississippi; raised in Austin, Texas. Died of liver cancer on 3/9/2005 (age 56). Country singer/songwriter/guitarist. Former rodeo champion.

8/15/92	65	38	●	1 Whatcha Gonna Do With A Cowboy		Liberty 98818
7/31/93	131	8		2 Under This Old Hat		Liberty 80892
9/24/94	128	3		3 Haywire		Liberty 28770
8/1/98	180	1		4 One Road Man		Capitol 21942
6/26/99	145	7	▲	5 20 Greatest Hits .... Cat:#13/8 [G]		Capitol 99781
8/19/00	134	5		6 Cowboy		Capitol 26601
4/27/02	121	2		7 After The Storm		Capitol 34571
8/9/03	162	1		8 Horsepower		Capitol 81580
9/3/05	126	2		9 Anthology Volume I .... [G]		Capitol 30588
5/17/08	175	1		10 Classic: Chris LeDoux .... [G]		Capitol 12872

LED ZEPPELIN
1970s: #19 / All-Time: #48

Hard-rock band formed in England: **Robert Plant** (vocals; born on 8/20/1948), **Jimmy Page** (guitar; born on 1/9/1944), John Paul Jones (bass, keyboards; born John Baldwin on 1/3/1946) and John "Bonzo" Bonham (drums; born on 5/31/1948; died of asphyxiation on 9/25/1980, age 32). First known as the New Yardbirds. Page had been in **The Yardbirds** from 1966-68. Plant and Bonham had been in a group called Band Of Joy. Group formed own Swan Song label in 1974. In concert movie *The Song Remains The Same* in 1976. Group disbanded in December 1980. Plant and Page formed **The Honeydrippers** in 1984. Page also with **The Firm** (1984-86). Jones joined **Them Crooked Vultures**. "Bonham" is the name of group formed by Jason Bonham, John's son, in 1989. Led Zeppelin's most famous recording, "Stairway To Heaven" (on album *Led Zeppelin IV*), was never released as a commercial single.

AWARDS: Grammy: Lifetime Achievement 2005 ★ R&R Hall of Fame: 1995

DEBUT	PEAK	WKS	RIAA	#	Album Title	Catalog	Label & Number
2/15/69	10	95	▲8	1	Led Zeppelin	Cat:#10/105	Atlantic 8216
					Grammy: Hall of Fame ★ RS500 #29		
11/8/69	**❶7**	98	▲12	2	Led Zeppelin II	Cat:#6/149	Atlantic 8236
					RS500 #75		
10/24/70	**❶4**	42	▲6	3	Led Zeppelin III		Atlantic 7201
11/27/71	**24**	259	▲23	4	Led Zeppelin IV	Cat:❶49/347	Atlantic 7208
					Grammy: Hall of Fame ★ RS500 #66		
4/14/73	**❶2**	99	▲11	5	Houses Of The Holy	Cat:#17/70	Atlantic 7255
					RS500 #149		
3/15/75	**❶6**	41	▲16	6	Physical Graffiti		Swan Song 200 [2]
					RS500 #70		
4/24/76	**❶2**	30	▲3	7	Presence	Cat:#14/19	Swan Song 8416
9/8/79	**❶7**	41	▲6	8	In Through The Out Door		Swan Song 16002
					GREATEST HITS & COMPILATIONS:		
12/18/82+	6	16	▲	9	Coda		Swan Song 90051
					previously unreleased recordings from 1969-78		
11/10/90	18	20	▲10	10	Led Zeppelin (Boxed Set)	Cat:#18/12	Atlantic 82144 [4]
3/28/92	47	12	▲2	11	Remasters		Atlantic 82371 [3]
10/9/93	87	2	▲2	12	Boxed Set 2		Atlantic 82477 [2]
12/11/99	71	26	▲	13	Early Days - The Best Of Led Zeppelin Volume One	Cat:#41/1	Atlantic 83268
4/8/00	81	6		14	Latter Days - The Best Of Led Zeppelin Volume Two		Atlantic 83278
12/7/02+	114	68	▲	15	Early Days & Latter Days: The Best Of Led Zeppelin Volume One And Two	Cat:#13/130	Atlantic 83619 [2]
12/1/07	7	90↑	▲2	16	Mothership	Cat:#22/33	Swan Song 313148 [2]
					LIVE ALBUMS:		
11/6/76	**23**	48	▲4	17	The Soundtrack From The Film "The Song Remains The Same"	Cat:#23/4 [S]	Swan Song 201 [2]
					recorded at Madison Square Garden		
12/6/97	12	20	▲2	18	BBC Sessions		Atlantic 83061 [2]
					recorded from 1969-71		
6/14/03	**❶1**	16	▲	19	How The West Was Won		Atlantic 83587 [3]

LEE, Alvin
Born on 12/19/1944 in Nottingham, England. Rock singer/guitarist. Leader of **Ten Years After**.

DEBUT	PEAK	WKS	#	Album Title		Label & Number
1/12/74	138	8	1	On The Road To Freedom		Columbia 32729
				ALVIN LEE & MYLON LeFEVRE		
1/4/75	65	12	2	In Flight	[L]	Columbia 33187 [2]
9/6/75	131	5	3	Pump Iron!		Columbia 33796
6/3/78	115	11	4	Rocket Fuel		RSO 3033
5/26/79	158	5	5	Ride On		RSO 3049
12/20/80+	198	4	6	Free Fall		Atlantic 19287
8/23/86	124	9	7	Detroit Diesel		21 Records 90517

LEE, Amos
Born Ryan Massaro in 1978 in Philadelphia, Pennsylvania; raised in Cherry Hill, New Jersey. Male singer/songwriter.

DEBUT	PEAK	WKS	#	Album Title	Label & Number
3/19/05	113	15	1	Amos Lee	Blue Note 97350
10/21/06	76	5	2	Supply And Demand	Blue Note 50416
7/12/08	29	5	3	Last Days At The Lodge	Blue Note 01225

LEE, Brenda
1960s: #41 / All-Time: #251

Born Brenda Mae Tarpley on 12/11/1944 in Lithonia, Georgia. Professional singer since age six. Signed to Decca Records in 1956. Became known as "Little Miss Dynamite." Successful country singer from 1971-85.

AWARDS: Grammy: Lifetime Achievement 2009 ★ R&R Hall of Fame: 2002 ★ C&W Hall of Fame: 1997

DEBUT	PEAK	WKS	#	Album Title		Label & Number
8/22/60	5	57	1	Brenda Lee		Decca 74039
11/21/60+	4	41	2	This Is.....Brenda		Decca 74082
5/8/61	24	33	3	Emotions		Decca 74104
8/28/61	17	39	4	All The Way		Decca 74176
3/24/62	29	23	5	Sincerely		Decca 74216
11/3/62	20	22	6	Brenda, That's All		Decca 74326
3/9/63	25	31	7	All Alone Am I		Decca 74370
12/21/63+	39	13	8	Let Me Sing		Decca 74439
6/13/64	90	11	9	By Request		Decca 74509
12/5/64+	**7X**	18	10	Merry Christmas From Brenda Lee	[X]	Decca 74583
				Christmas charts: 15/'64, 17/'65, 20/'66, 58/'67, 33/'68, 7/'72		
9/25/65	36	14	11	Too Many Rivers		Decca 74684

Billboard			R I A A	ARTIST		
DEBUT	PEAK	WKS		Album Title	Catalog	Label & Number

LEE, Brenda — cont'd

4/9/66	94	13	12 Bye Bye Blues		Decca 74755
6/25/66	70	14	13 10 Golden Years [G]		Decca 74757
12/24/66+	94	12	14 Coming On Strong		Decca 74825
6/15/68	187	2	15 For The First Time		Decca 74955
			BRENDA LEE & PETE FOUNTAIN		
5/24/69	98	9	16 Johnny One Time		Decca 75111
4/21/73	206	3	17 Brenda		MCA 305

LEE, Dickey
Born Dickey Lipscomb on 9/21/1936 in Memphis, Tennessee. Pop-country singer/songwriter.

11/10/62	50	12	1 The Tale Of Patches		Smash 67020

LEE, Geddy
Born Gary Lee Weinrib on 7/29/1953 in Toronto, Ontario, Canada. Lead singer/bassist of **Rush**.

12/2/00	52	3	1 My Favorite Headache		Anthem 83384

LEE, Jackie
Born Earl Nelson on 9/8/1928 in Lake Charles, Louisiana. Died on 7/12/2008 (age 79). R&B singer. One-half of **Bob & Earl** duo.

2/5/66	85	9	1 The Duck		Mirwood 7000

LEE, Johnny
Born John Lee Ham on 7/3/1946 in Texas City; raised in Alta Loma, Texas. Country singer/songwriter. Married to actress Charlene Tilton (TV's *Dallas*) from 1982-84.

11/15/80	132	21	● 1 Lookin' For Love		Asylum 309
10/24/81	147	8	2 Bet Your Heart On Me		Full Moon 541
8/20/83	201	3	3 Hey Bartender		Warner 23889
11/12/83	210	4	4 Greatest Hits [G]		Warner 23967

LEE, Laura
Born Laura Lee Newton on 3/9/1945 in Chicago, Illinois. R&B singer.

1/29/72	117	11	1 Women's Love Rights		Hot Wax 708
7/15/72	201	5	2 Two Sides Of Laura Lee		Hot Wax 714

LEE, Leapy — see LEAPY LEE

LEE, Murphy
Born Tohri Harper on 12/19/1982 in St. Louis, Missouri. Male rapper. Member of **St. Lunatics**.

10/11/03	8	29	● 1 Murphy's Law		Fo' Reel 001132

LEE, Peggy   1950s: #27 / All-Time: #311
Born Norma Egstrom on 5/26/1920 in Jamestown, North Dakota. Died of a heart attack on 1/21/2002 (age 81). Jazz singer with Jack Wardlow (1936-40), Will Osborne (1940-41) and **Benny Goodman** (1941-43). Went solo in March 1943. In movies *Mister Music* (1950), *The Jazz Singer* (1953) and *Pete Kelly's Blues* (1955). Co-wrote many songs with husband Dave Barbour (married from 1943-52). Awarded nearly $4 million in court for her singing in the animated movie *Lady And The Tramp*.
AWARD: Grammy: Lifetime Achievement 1995

9/17/55	7	5	1 Songs From Pete Kelly's Blues		Decca 8166
			PEGGY LEE & ELLA FITZGERALD		
			LP: Decca DL-8166 (#7); EP: Decca ED-2269 (#7)		
9/23/57	20	1	2 The Man I Love		Capitol 864
7/14/58	15	2	3 Jump For Joy		Capitol 979
12/8/58	16	1	4 Things Are Swingin'		Capitol 1049
4/11/60	11	59	5 Latin Ala Lee!		Capitol 1290
9/11/61	77	22	6 Basin Street East [L]		Capitol 1520
			recorded on 1/12/1961		
8/25/62	85	6	7 Bewitching-Lee! [G]		Capitol 1743
11/17/62+	40	21	8 Sugar 'N' Spice		Capitol 1772
3/9/63	18	26	9 I'm A Woman		Capitol 1857
7/27/63	42	9	10 Mink Jazz		Capitol 1850
9/26/64	97	6	11 In The Name Of Love		Capitol 2096
5/22/65	145	4	12 Pass Me By		Capitol 2320
7/30/66	130	3	13 Big Spender		Capitol 2475
12/30/67	115ˣ	1	14 Happy Holiday [X]		Capitol 2390
12/13/69+	55	18	15 Is That All There Is?		Capitol 386
6/6/70	142	9	16 Bridge Over Troubled Water		Capitol 463
12/19/70	194	2	17 Make It With You		Capitol 622
8/19/72	203	5	18 Norma Deloris Egstrom From Jamestown, North Dakota		Capitol 11077
11/23/74	209	1	19 Let's Love		Atlantic 18103

LEE, Tommy
Born Thomas Lee Bass on 10/3/1962 in Athens, Greece; raised in West Covina, California. Rock singer/drummer. Member of **Motley Crue**. Married to actress Heather Locklear from 1986-93. Married to actress Pamela Anderson from 1995-98.

6/8/02	39	8	1 Never A Dull Moment		MCA 112856
8/27/05	62	7	2 Tommyland: The Ride		TL Educational 90005

LEE, Tracey
Born on 10/22/1970 in Philadelphia, Pennsylvania. Male rapper.

4/26/97	111	6	1 Many Facez	Universal 53036

LEELAND
Christian rock band from Baytown, Texas: brothers Leeland Mooring (vocals, guitar) and Jack Mooring (keyboards), with Matt Campbell (guitar), Jake Holtz (bass) and Mike Smith (drums).

3/15/08	72	2	1 Opposite Way	Essential 10854
9/12/09	84	3	2 Love Is On The Move	Essential 10905

LeFEVRE, Mylon
Born on 10/6/1944 in Gulfport, Mississippi. Rock singer/songwriter. Later turned to Christian music career.

1/12/74	138	8	1 On The Road To Freedom	Columbia 32729
			ALVIN LEE & MYLON LeFEVRE	

LEFEVRE, Raymond
Born on 11/20/1929 in Calais, France. Died on 6/27/2008 (age 78). Conductor/pianist/flutist.

3/30/68	117	16	1 Soul Coaxing (Ame Caline) .... [I]	4 Corners 4244

LEFT BANKE, The
Pop-rock band from Manhattan, New York: Steve Martin (vocals), Rick Brand (guitar), Michael Brown (piano), Tom Finn (bass) and George Cameron (drums). Brown later joined **Stories**.

3/25/67	67	11	1 Walk Away Renee/Pretty Ballerina	Smash 67088

LEGEND, John
Born John Stephens on 12/28/1978 in Springfield, Ohio; later based in Philadelphia, Pennsylvania. R&B singer/songwriter/pianist.
  AWARD: Grammy: Best New Artist 2005

1/15/05	4	65	▲	1 Get Lifted	Cat:#7/16	Columbia 92276
				Grammy: R&B Album		
11/11/06	3[1]	39	▲	2 Once Again		Columbia 80323
2/2/08	7	12		3 Live From Philadelphia .... [L]		G.O.O.D. 21265
11/15/08	4	31	●	4 Evolver		G.O.O.D. 13740

LeGRAND, Michel   **1950s: #37**
Born on 2/24/1932 in Paris, France. Conductor/arranger/pianist.

5/28/55	5	8	1 Holiday In Rome .... [I]	Columbia 647
			LP: Columbia CL-647 (#5); EP: Columbia B-497 (#13)	
9/17/55	13	1	2 Vienna Holiday .... [I]	Columbia 706
6/30/56	9	4	3 Castles In Spain .... [I]	Columbia 888
3/11/72	127	10	4 "Brian's Song" Themes & Variations .... [I]	Bell 6071
7/1/72	173	12	5 Sarah Vaughan/Michel Legrand	Mainstream 361

LEHRER, Tom
Born on 4/9/1928 in Manhattan, New York. Satirical singer/songwriter/pianist.

11/6/65+	18	51	●	1 That Was The Year That Was .... [C]	Reprise 6179
3/26/66	133	8		2 An Evening Wasted With Tom Lehrer .... [C]	Reprise 6199
				recorded March 1959 in Cambridge, Massachusetts	

LEKMAN, Jens
Born on 2/6/1981 in Angered, Sweden. Male singer/songwriter.

10/27/07	192	1	1 Night Falls Over Kortedala	Secretly Canadian 160

LEMONHEADS, The
Pop-rock trio from Boston, Massachusetts: Evan Dando (vocals, guitar), Nic Dalton (bass) and David Ryan (drums).

1/9/93	68	19	●	1 It's A Shame About Ray	Atlantic 82460
10/30/93	56	17	●	2 Come On Feel The Lemonheads	Atlantic 82537
11/2/96	130	2		3 Car Button Cloth	Atlantic 92726
7/11/09	177	1		4 Varshons	The End 137

LEMON PIPERS, The
Psychedelic/bubblegum rock band from Oxford, Ohio: Ivan Browne (vocals, guitar), Bill Bartlett (guitar), R.G. Nave (organ), Steve Walmsley (bass) and Bill Albaugh (drums). Bartlett later joined **Ram Jam**. Albaugh died on 1/20/1999 (age 53).

2/17/68	90	18	1 Green Tambourine	Buddah 5009

LEN
Alternative-rock band from Toronto, Ontario, Canada: Marc Costanzo (vocals), his sister Sharon Costanzo, D. Rock, DJ Moves, Planet Pea and Drunkness Monster.

7/3/99	46	27	●	1 You Can't Stop The Bum Rush	Work 69528

LENKA
Born Lenka Kripac on 3/19/1978 in Sydney, Australia. Female singer/songwriter/pianist/actress.

9/27/08	142	2	1 Lenka	Epic 22732

Billboard			R I A A	ARTIST		
DEBUT	PEAK	WKS		Album Title	Catalog	Label & Number

LENNON, John
All-Time: #124

Born on 10/9/1940 in Woolton, Liverpool, England. Shot to death on 12/8/1980 in Manhattan, New York (age 40). Founding member of **The Beatles**. Married to Cynthia Powell (1962-68); their son is **Julian Lennon**. Met **Yoko Ono** in 1966; married her on 3/20/1969; their son is **Sean Lennon**. Formed Plastic Ono Band in 1969. To New York City in 1971. Fought deportation from the U.S., 1972-76, until he was granted a permanent visa. Also see **Various Artists Compilations**: *Working Class Hero - A Tribute To John Lennon*.

AWARDS: Grammy: Lifetime Achievement 1991 ★ R&R Hall of Fame: 1994

2/8/69	124	8		1 Unfinished Music No. 1: Two Virgins		Apple 5001
6/28/69	174	8		2 Unfinished Music No. 2: Life With The Lions		Zapple 3357
12/13/69	178	3		3 Wedding Album		Apple 3361
12/26/70+	6	33	●	4 John Lennon/Plastic Ono Band		Apple 3372
				RS500 #22		
9/18/71	❶¹	45	▲²	5 Imagine	Cat:#28/1	Apple 3379
				RS500 #76		
11/24/73	9	31	●	6 Mind Games	Cat:#14/45	Apple 3414
10/12/74	❶¹	35	●	7 Walls And Bridges		Apple 3416
3/8/75	6	15	●	8 Rock 'N' Roll	Cat:#17/29	Apple 3419
12/6/80	❶⁸	74	▲³	9 Double Fantasy		Geffen 2001
				Grammy: Album of the Year		
1/14/84	94	12		10 Heart Play - Unfinished Dialogue	[T]	Polydor 817238
				excerpts from a *Playboy* magazine interview done shortly before Lennon's death		
2/11/84	11	19	●	11 Milk And Honey		Polydor 817160
				recorded in 1980		
				GREATEST HITS & COMPILATIONS:		
11/8/75	12	32	▲	12 Shaved Fish		Apple 3421
12/4/82+	33	16	▲³	13 The John Lennon Collection		Geffen 2023
11/22/86	127	4		14 Menlove Ave.		Capitol 12533
				Liverpool street Lennon lived on as a child; comprised of outtakes from *Rock 'N' Roll* and *Walls And Bridges* album sessions		
10/22/88	31	18	●	15 Imagine: John Lennon	[S]	Capitol 90803 [2]
				from the movie documentary of Lennon's life		
3/14/98	65	9	▲	16 Lennon Legend - The Very Best Of John Lennon	Cat:#8/27	Parlophone 21954
11/21/98	99	2	●	17 Anthology		Capitol 30614 [4]
11/20/04	31	8		18 Acoustic		Capitol 74428
10/22/05	135	3		19 Working Class Hero: The Definitive Lennon		Capitol 40391 [2]
				LIVE ALBUMS:		
1/10/70	10	32	●	20 The Plastic Ono Band - Live Peace In Toronto 1969		Apple 3362
				recorded on 9/13/1969		
7/1/72	48	17		21 Some Time In New York City		Apple 3392 [2]
				record 1: studio recordings backed by **Elephants Memory**; record 2: *Live Jam* featuring concert recordings with **Frank Zappa**'s Mothers of Invention		
3/22/86	41	11	●	22 Live In New York City		Capitol 12451
				recorded on 8/30/1972 at Madison Square Garden		

LENNON, Julian
Born John Charles Julian Lennon on 4/8/1963 in Liverpool, England. Pop-rock singer/songwriter/keyboardist. Son of Cynthia and **John Lennon**.

11/10/84+	17	46	●	1 Valotte		Atlantic 80184
4/12/86	32	18	●	2 The Secret Value Of DayDreaming		Atlantic 81640
4/1/89	87	15		3 Mr. Jordan		Atlantic 81928

LENNON, Sean
Born on 10/9/1975 in Manhattan, New York. Rock singer/songwriter/guitarist. Son of **John Lennon** and **Yoko Ono**.

6/6/98	153	1		1 Into The Sun		Grand Royal 94551
10/21/06	152	1		2 Friendly Fire		Capitol 35568

LENNON SISTERS, The
Vocal group from Venice, California: sisters Dianne (born on 12/1/1939), Peggy (born on 4/8/1941), Kathy (born on 8/2/1943) and Janet (born on 6/15/1946) Lennon. With **Lawrence Welk** from 1955-68.

12/25/61+	95	4		1 Christmas With The Lennon Sisters	[X]	Dot 25343
				Christmas charts: 40/'63, 31/'67		
5/27/67	77	18		2 Somethin' Stupid		Dot 25797

LENNOX, Annie
Born on 12/25/1954 in Aberdeen, Scotland. Lead singer of **The Tourists** and the **Eurythmics**. Appeared in the movie *Edward II* and TV movie *The Room*.

AWARD: Billboard Century: 2002

5/30/92	23	72	▲²	1 Diva	Cat:#25/26	Arista 18704
4/1/95	11	60	▲²	2 Medusa		Arista 25717
6/28/03	4	20	●	3 Bare		J Records 52350
10/20/07	9	10		4 Songs Of Mass Destruction		Arista 15260
3/7/09	34	6		5 The Annie Lennox Collection	[G]	Arista 36926

LENNY & SQUIGGY
Duo of actors Michael McKean ("Lenny") and David L. Lander ("Squiggy") of TV's *Laverne & Shirley*. The Squigtones included Christopher Guest (as "Nigel Tufnel"). McKean and Guest went on to form **Spinal Tap**.

5/19/79	205	5		1 Lenny And The Squigtones .... [L]		Casablanca 7149

recorded at The Roxy in Hollywood

LEO, Ted, And The Pharmacists
Born on 9/11/1970 in South Bend, Indiana. Rock singer/songwriter/guitarist. The Pharmacists: Dave Lerner (bass) and Chris Wilson (drums).

4/7/07	109	1		1 Living With The Living		Touch And Go 302

LEONARD, Bishop Dennis
Born in Denver, Colorado. Gospel artist. Pastor of the Heritage Christian Center.

10/13/01	163	1		1 Send It Down .... [L]		EMI Gospel 20341

BISHOP DENNIS LEONARD AND THE HERITAGE CHRISTIAN CENTER MASS CHOIR

LEONTI, Nikki
Born Nichole Leonti on 8/20/1981 in Corona, California. Contemporary Christian singer.

10/3/98	179	1		1 Shelter Me		Pamplin 9829

LE PAMPLEMOUSSE
Disco studio group led by producers Laurin Rinder and W. Michael Lewis. Group name is French for "The Grapefruit."

1/21/78	116	11		1 Le Spank		AVI 6032
2/3/79	207	2		2 Sweet Magic		AVI 6053

LERCHE, Sondre
Born on 9/5/1982 in Bergen, Norway. Male singer/songwriter/guitarist.

9/26/09	178	1		1 Heartbeat Radio		Rounder 619094

LEROI BROTHERS, The
Rock band from Austin, Texas: Steve Doerr (vocals, guitar), Rick Rawls (guitar), Jackie Newhouse (bass) and Mike Buck (drums).

3/28/87	181	5		1 Open All Night		Profile 1224

LE ROUX
Rock band from Baton Rouge, Louisiana: Jeff Pollard (vocals), Tony Haseldon (guitar), Rod Roddy (piano), Bobby Campo (horns), Leon Medica (bass) and David Peters (drums).

7/8/78	135	15		1 Louisiana's Le Roux		Capitol 11734
6/9/79	162	4		2 Keep The Fire Burnin'		Capitol 11926

LOUISIANA'S LeROUX (above 2)

8/23/80	145	6		3 Up		Capitol 12092
2/6/82	64	21		4 Last Safe Place		RCA Victor 4195
4/16/83	203	4		5 So Fired Up		RCA Victor 4510

LESH, Phil, & Friends
Born on 3/15/1940 in Berkeley, California. Rock singer/bassist. Member of the **Grateful Dead**. His Friends: **Warren Haynes** (guitar), Jimmy Herring (guitar), Rob Barraco (keyboards) and John Molo (drums). Haynes was also a member of **The Allman Brothers Band** and **Gov't Mule**.

6/8/02	79	1		1 There And Back Again		Columbia 86406

LESLIE, Ryan
Born Anthony Ryan Leslie on 9/25/1978 in Washington DC; raised in Stockton, California. R&B singer/songwriter.

2/28/09	35	11		1 Ryan Leslie		NextSelection 011473
11/21/09	50	2		2 Transition		NextSelection 013447

LES NUBIANS
R&B vocal duo from Bordeaux, France: sisters Helene Faussart and Celia Faussart.

3/27/99	100	16		1 Princesses Nubiennes .... [F]		Omtown 45997
4/12/03	79	11		2 One Step Forward		Omtown 82569

LESS THAN JAKE
Alternative-rock trio from Gainesville, Florida: Chris DeMakes (vocals, guitar), Roger Manganelli (bass) and Vinnie Fiorello (drums).

10/24/98	80	3		1 Hello Rockview		Capitol 57663
11/11/00	103	1		2 Borders & Boundaries		Fat Wreck Chords 616
6/7/03	45	12		3 Anthem		Sire 48459
8/7/04	157	1		4 B Is For B-Sides		Sire 48788
6/10/06	78	2		5 In With The Out Crowd		Sire 49984
7/12/08	61	2		6 GNV FLA		Sleep It Off 05

LESTER, Ketty
Born Revoyda Frierson on 8/16/1938 in Hope, Arkansas. R&B singer/actress. Acted in several movies and TV shows.

6/9/62	53	11		1 Love Letters		Era 108

LE TIGRE
Alternative-rock trio formed in Portland, Oregon: Kathleen Hanna, Johanna Freeman and J.D. Samson.

11/6/04	130	1		1 This Island		Le Tigre 003385

Billboard			R I A A	ARTIST		
DEBUT	PEAK	WKS		Album Title	Catalog	Label & Number

LeTOYA
Born LeTOYA Luckett on 3/11/1981 in Houston, Texas. Female R&B singer/songwriter. Former member of **Destiny's Child**.

| 8/12/06 | ❶¹ | 15 | ▲ | 1 LeToya | | Capitol 97136 |
| 9/12/09 | 12 | 12 | | 2 Lady Love .... | | Capitol 97259 |

LET'S ACTIVE
Pop-rock trio formed in North Carolina: Mitch Easter (vocals, guitar), Faye Hunter (bass) and Sara Romweber (drums).

2/18/84	154	11		1 Afoot.. [EP]		I.R.S. 70505
11/10/84	138	16		2 Cypress		I.R.S. 70648
4/26/86	111	10		3 Big Plans For Everybody..		I.R.S. 5703

LETTER KILLS
Punk-rock band from Los Angeles, California: Matthew James Shelton (vocals), Timothy Cordova (guitar), Dustin Lovelis (guitar), Kyle Duckworth (bass) and Paul Remund (drums).

| 8/14/04 | 130 | 1 | | 1 The Bridge .... | | Island 002859 |

LETTERMEN, The   1960s: #16 / All-Time: #80
Vocal trio formed in Los Angeles, California: Tony Butala (born on 11/20/1938), Jim Pike (born on 11/6/1936) and Bob Engemann (born on 2/19/1936). Engemann replaced by Gary Pike (Jim's brother) in 1968. The #1 Adult Contemporary vocal group of the 1960s.

2/24/62	6	55		1 A Song For Young Love		Capitol 1669
6/9/62	30	24		2 Once Upon A Time		Capitol 1711
10/13/62+	59	19		3 Jim, Tony And Bob		Capitol 1761
4/13/63	65	10		4 College Standards..		Capitol 1829
2/8/64	31	32		5 A Lettermen Kind Of Love		Capitol 2013
6/20/64	94	10		6 The Lettermen Look At Love		Capitol 2083
11/14/64	41	20		7 She Cried		Capitol 2142
3/13/65	27	23		8 Portrait Of My Love		Capitol 2270
8/21/65	13	24		9 The Hit Sounds Of The Lettermen		Capitol 2359
10/30/65	73	13		10 You'll Never Walk Alone		Capitol 2213
2/19/66	57	17		11 More Hit Sounds Of The Lettermen!....................................		Capitol 2428
6/25/66	52	15		12 A New Song For Young Love		Capitol 2496
12/17/66+	18ˣ	10		13 For Christmas This Year .... [X]		Capitol 2587
				Christmas charts: 25/'66, 41/'67, 47/'68, 18/'70		
2/4/67	58	17		14 Warm		Capitol 2633
7/8/67	31	26		15 Spring!..		Capitol 2711
4/13/68	13	44	●	16 Goin' Out Of My Head		Capitol 2865
12/14/68+	43	21		17 Put Your Head On My Shoulder		Capitol 147
4/5/69	74	18		18 I Have Dreamed		Capitol 202
8/23/69	90	8		19 Close-Up .... [R]		Capitol 251 [2]
				reissue of albums #5 and #6 above		
9/6/69	17	30	●	20 Hurt So Bad		Capitol 269
2/7/70	42	23		21 Traces/Memories..		Capitol 390
9/5/70	134	11		22 Reflections		Capitol 496
2/6/71	119	10		23 Everything's Good About You		Capitol 634
6/26/71	192	6		24 Feelings..		Capitol 781
10/9/71	88	13		25 Love Book		Capitol 836
3/18/72	136	6		26 Lettermen 1		Capitol 11010
				GREATEST HITS & COMPILATIONS:		
10/8/66+	17	27	●	27 The Best Of The Lettermen		Capitol 2554
9/14/68	82	14		28 Special Request		Capitol 2934
2/22/69	128	10		29 The Best Of The Lettermen, Vol. 2......................................		Capitol 138
2/23/74	186	4		30 All-Time Greatest Hits		Capitol 11249
				LIVE ALBUMS:		
8/31/63	76	10		31 The Lettermen In Concert..		Capitol 1936
				recorded at Iona College in New Rochelle, New York		
11/25/67+	10	48	●	32 The Lettermen!!!...And "Live!"		Capitol 2758
6/23/73	193	7		33 "Alive" Again...Naturally		Capitol 11183

LETTERS TO CLEO
Rock band from Boston, Massachusetts: Kay Hanley (vocals), Michael Eisenstein (guitar), Greg McKenna (guitar), Scott Riebling (bass) and Stacy Jones (drums). Jones later became lead singer with **American Hi-Fi**.

| 4/8/95 | 123 | 9 | | 1 Aurora Gory Alice .... | | Giant 24598 |
| 8/26/95 | 188 | 1 | | 2 Wholesale Meats And Fish .... | | Giant 24613 |

Billboard			R I A A	ARTIST		
DEBUT	PEAK	WKS		Album Title	Catalog	Label & Number

LEVEL 42
Pop-rock band formed in London, England: Mark King (vocals, bass), brothers Boon Gould (guitar) and Phil Gould (drums), and Mike Lindup (keyboards). The Goulds left in October 1987; replaced by Alan Murphy (guitar) and Gary Husband (drums). Murphy died of AIDS on 10/19/1989 (age 35).

DEBUT	PEAK	WKS		Album Title	Catalog	Label & Number
3/22/86	18	36		1 World Machine..		Polydor 827487
4/11/87	23	34		2 Running In The Family......................................		Polydor 831593
10/29/88	128	7		3 Staring At The Sun...		Polydor 837247

LEVERT
R&B vocal/instrumental trio from Cleveland, Ohio: brothers **Gerald Levert** (vocals) and **Sean Levert** (vocals, percussion), with Marc Gordon (vocals, keyboards). The Leverts are the sons of Eddie Levert (of **The O'Jays**). Gerald died of a heart attack on 11/10/2006 (age 40). Sean died on 3/30/2008 (age 39).

DEBUT	PEAK	WKS		Album Title	Catalog	Label & Number
10/25/86	192	3		1 Bloodline..		Atlantic 81669
9/5/87	32	24	●	2 The Big Throwdown...		Atlantic 81773
11/26/88+	79	31	●	3 Just Coolin'..		Atlantic 81926
12/1/90	122	34	●	4 Rope A Dope Style...		Atlantic 82164
4/10/93	35	27	●	5 For Real Tho'..		Atlantic 82462
3/29/97	49	8		6 The Whole Scenario..		Atlantic 82986

LEVERT, Gerald   All-Time: #323
Born on 7/13/1966 in Cleveland, Ohio. Died of a heart attack on 11/10/2006 (age 40). R&B singer. Member of **Levert**. Son of Eddie Levert (of **The O'Jays**); brother of **Sean Levert**. Member of **LSG**.

DEBUT	PEAK	WKS		Album Title	Catalog	Label & Number
11/2/91+	48	40	▲	1 Private Line...		EastWest 91777
9/24/94	18	34	▲	2 Groove On...		EastWest 92416
10/14/95	20	30	●	3 Father And Son..		EastWest 61859
				GERALD LEVERT & EDDIE LEVERT SR.		
8/8/98	17	32	▲	4 Love & Consequences.......................................		EastWest 62261
3/25/00	8	28	●	5 G		EastWest 62417
10/6/01	6	11		6 Gerald's World		Elektra 62655
11/2/02	9	10		7 The G Spot		Elektra 62795
11/15/03	6	12		8 Stroke Of Genius		Elektra 62903
12/18/04	29	11		9 Do I Speak For The World.................................		Atlantic 83765
10/22/05	115	2		10 Voices...		Atlantic 73214
3/3/07	2¹	16		11 In My Songs		Atlantic 100341
6/30/07	19	5		12 Something To Talk About..................................		Atlantic 199612
				EDDIE LEVERT SR. & GERALD LEVERT		

LEVERT, Sean
Born on 9/28/1968 in Cleveland, Ohio. Died on 3/30/2008 (age 39). R&B singer. Member of **Levert**. Son of **Eddie Levert** (of **The O'Jays**); brother of **Gerald Levert**.

DEBUT	PEAK	WKS		Album Title	Catalog	Label & Number
7/15/95	146	1		1 The Other Side..		Atlantic 82663

LEWIS, Barbara
Born on 2/9/1943 in Salem, Michigan; raised in South Lyon, Michigan. R&B singer/songwriter/multi-instrumentalist.

DEBUT	PEAK	WKS		Album Title	Catalog	Label & Number
9/25/65	118	7		1 Baby, I'm Yours.. [G]		Atlantic 8110

~ ~ ~ ~ ~ ~ ~ ~ ~ **NON-CHARTED ALBUMS** ~ ~ ~ ~ ~ ~ ~ ~ ~ ~ ~
1963 **Hello Stranger**   1964 **Snap Your Fingers**

LEWIS, Blake
Born on 7/21/1981 in Redmond, Washington. Finished in second place on the 2007 season of TV's *American Idol*.

DEBUT	PEAK	WKS		Album Title	Catalog	Label & Number
12/22/07	10	10		1 Audio Day Dream		19 Records 19935
10/24/09	135	1		2 Heartbreak On Vinyl.......................................		Tommy Boy 1741

LEWIS, Bobby
Born on 2/17/1933 in Indianapolis, Indiana; raised in Detroit, Michigan. R&B singer/songwriter.

~ ~ ~ ~ ~ ~ ~ ~ ~ ~ **NON-CHARTED ALBUM** ~ ~ ~ ~ ~ ~ ~ ~ ~ ~
1961 **Tossin' & Turnin'**

LEWIS, Crystal
Born on 4/29/1970 in Newport Beach, California. Christian singer/songwriter.

DEBUT	PEAK	WKS		Album Title	Catalog	Label & Number
10/26/96	134	2	●	1 Beauty For Ashes..		Myrrh 5036
3/21/98	188	1		2 Gold..		Myrrh 5041

LEWIS, Donna
Born on 8/6/1973 in Cardiff, Wales. Adult Contemporary singer/songwriter.

DEBUT	PEAK	WKS		Album Title	Catalog	Label & Number
7/27/96	31	39	▲	1 Now In A Minute..		Atlantic 82762

LEWIS, Gary, And The Playboys
Born Gary Levitch on 7/31/1945 in Brooklyn, New York. Pop singer/drummer. Son of comedian **Jerry Lewis**. The Playboys: Al Ramsey (guitar), John West (guitar), David Walker (keyboards) and David Costell (bass). Also see **Mae West**.

DEBUT	PEAK	WKS		Album Title	Catalog	Label & Number
3/27/65	26	25		1 This Diamond Ring...		Liberty 7408
9/18/65	18	20		2 A Session With Gary Lewis And The Playboys................		Liberty 7419
12/4/65+	44	16		3 Everybody Loves A Clown..................................		Liberty 7428
3/12/66	71	17		4 She's Just My Style.......................................		Liberty 7435
5/28/66	47	24		5 Hits Again!...		Liberty 7452

Billboard			R I A A	ARTIST		
DEBUT	PEAK	WKS		Album Title	Catalog	Label & Number
				LEWIS, Gary, And The Playboys — cont'd		
10/22/66	10	46	●	6 Golden Greats [G]		Liberty 7468
2/11/67	79	16		7 (You Don't Have To) Paint Me A Picture		Liberty 7487
7/8/67	185	4		8 New Directions		Liberty 7519
8/17/68	150	9		9 Gary Lewis Now!		Liberty 7568
				LEWIS, Glenn		
				Born Glen Ricketts on 3/13/1975 in Toronto, Ontario, Canada. R&B singer/songwriter.		
4/6/02	4	14		1 World Outside My Window		Epic 85787
				LEWIS, Huey, and The News All-Time: #478		
				Born Hugh Cregg III on 7/5/1950 in New York; raised in Danville, California. Pop-rock singer/songwriter. Formed the News in San Francisco, California: Chris Hayes (guitar), Sean Hopper (keyboards), Johnny Colla (sax), Mario Cipollina (bass) and Bill Gibson (drums). Lewis acted in the movies *Back To The Future* and *Short Cuts*.		
8/16/80	203	3		1 Huey Lewis & The News		Chrysalis 1292
2/27/82	13	59	●	2 Picture This		Chrysalis 1340
10/8/83+	❶¹	158	▲⁷	3 Sports		Chrysalis 41412
9/13/86	❶¹	61	▲³	4 Fore!		Chrysalis 41534
8/20/88	11	30	▲	5 Small World		Chrysalis 41622
5/25/91	27	27	●	6 Hard At Play		EMI 93355
5/28/94	55	21		7 Four Chords & Several Years Ago		Elektra 61500
11/16/96	185	1		8 Time Flies...The Best Of Huey Lewis And The News [G]		Elektra 61977
8/11/01	165	1		9 Plan B		Silvertone 41767
6/10/06	70	15		10 Greatest Hits Cat:#30/2 [G]		Capitol 62996
				LEWIS, Jenny, with The Watson Twins		
				Lewis was born on 1/8/1976 in Las Vegas, Nevada. Pop-rock singer/songwriter/actress. Former lead singer of **Rilo Kiley**. As a child, acted in several movies and TV shows. The Watson Twins are identical twin sisters Leigh and Chandra Watson.		
2/11/06	88	2		1 Rabbit Fur Coat		Team Love 80008
10/11/08	24	5		2 Acid Tounge		Warner 508668
				JENNY LEWIS		
				LEWIS, Jerry		
				Born Joseph Levitch on 3/16/1926 in Newark, New Jersey. Comedian/actor. Father of **Gary Lewis**. Formed comedy duo with **Dean Martin** in 1946. Starred in and directed several movies.		
12/22/56+	3²	19		1 Jerry Lewis Just Sings		Decca 8410
				LEWIS, Jerry Lee All-Time: #332		
				Born on 9/29/1935 in Ferriday, Louisiana. Rock and roll singer/pianist. Appeared in the movie *Jamboree!* in 1957. Career waned in 1958 after marriage to 13-year-old cousin, Myra Gale Brown, daughter of his bass player. Made comeback in country music beginning in 1968. Nicknamed "The Killer." Brother of **Linda Gail Lewis**. Cousin to country singer **Mickey Gilley** and former TV evangelist Jimmy Swaggart. Jerry's early career is documented in the 1989 movie *Great Balls Of Fire* starring Dennis Quaid.		
				AWARDS: Grammy: Lifetime Achievement 2005 ★ R&R Hall of Fame: 1986		
3/28/64	116	8		1 The Golden Hits Of Jerry Lee Lewis		Smash 67040
				new recordings of his Sun label hits		
6/5/65	121	5		2 The Return Of Rock		Smash 67063
5/14/66	145	3		3 Memphis Beat		Smash 67079
6/29/68	160	12		4 Another Place Another Time		Smash 67104
2/8/69	149	7		5 She Still Comes Around (To Love What's Left Of Me)		Smash 67112
5/10/69	127	10		6 The Country Music Hall Of Fame Hits, Vol. 1		Smash 67117
5/10/69	124	10		7 The Country Music Hall Of Fame Hits, Vol. 2		Smash 67118
2/28/70	186	2		8 She Even Woke Me Up To Say Goodbye		Smash 67128
1/30/71	190	6		9 There Must Be More To Love Than This		Mercury 61323
1/30/71	213	1		10 In Loving Memories: The Jerry Lee Lewis Gospel Album		Mercury 61318
7/24/71	152	3		11 Touching Home		Mercury 61343
11/27/71	115	12		12 Would You Take Another Chance On Me?		Mercury 61346
4/22/72	105	12		13 The "Killer" Rocks On		Mercury 637
3/3/73	201	2		14 Who's Gonna Play This Old Piano...(Think About It Darlin')		Mercury 61366
3/17/73	37	19		15 The Session		Mercury 803 [2]
4/28/79	186	3		16 Jerry Lee Lewis		Elektra 184
6/21/86	87	12		17 Class Of '55 (Memphis Rock & Roll Homecoming) Cat:#13/2		America Smash 830002
				CARL PERKINS / JERRY LEE LEWIS / ROY ORBISON / JOHNNY CASH		
7/22/89	62	10		18 Great Balls Of Fire! [S]		Polydor 839516
10/14/06	26	9		19 Last Man Standing		Artists First 20001
				GREATEST HITS & COMPILATIONS:		
9/27/69	119	4		20 Original Golden Hits - Volume 1		Sun 102
9/27/69	122	5		21 Original Golden Hits - Volume 2		Sun 103
5/9/70	114	14		22 The Best Of Jerry Lee Lewis		Smash 67131
				LIVE ALBUMS:		
12/5/64+	71	17		23 The Greatest Live Show On Earth		Smash 67056
				recorded on 7/1/1964 in Birmingham, Alabama		
10/10/70	149	6		24 Live At The International, Las Vegas		Mercury 61278
5/22/82	205	3		25 The Survivors		Columbia 37961
				JOHNNY CASH / JERRY LEE LEWIS / CARL PERKINS		
				recorded on 4/23/1981 at the Sporthalle Boeblingen in Stuttgart, West Germany		

Billboard			R I A A	ARTIST	Catalog	Label & Number
DEBUT	PEAK	WKS		Album Title		

DEBUT	PEAK	WKS	R I A A	ARTIST / Album Title	Catalog	Label & Number

~ ~ ~ ~ ~ ~ **NON-CHARTED ALBUMS by JERRY LEE LEWIS** ~ ~ ~ ~ ~ ~ ~

1958 **Jerry Lee Lewis**
1961 **Jerry Lee's Greatest**

1993 **The Jerry Lee Lewis Anthology:**
All Killer, No Filler!
RS500 #242

LEWIS, Leona

Born on 4/3/1985 in Islington, London, England. Pop-R&B singer. Winner on the British TV talent show *The X Factor*.

DEBUT	PEAK	WKS		#	Album Title	Catalog	Label & Number
4/26/08	**❶**[1]	61	▲	1	Spirit		Syco 02554
12/5/09	**13**	10		2	Echo		Syco 59660

LEWIS, Linda

Born on 9/27/1950 in London, England. Black dance singer/actress. Appeared in the movies *A Taste Of Honey* and *A Hard Day's Night*.

9/20/75	**204**	5		1	Not A Little Girl Anymore		Arista 4047

LEWIS, Linda Gail

Born on 7/18/1947 in Ferriday, Louisiana. Country singer. Sister of **Jerry Lee Lewis**.

10/21/00	**161**	2		1	You Win Again		Pointblank 50258
					VAN MORRISON & LINDA GAIL LEWIS		

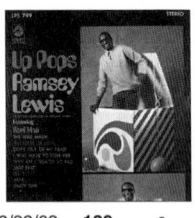

LEWIS, Ramsey   All-Time: #140

Born on 5/27/1935 in Chicago, Illinois. R&B-jazz pianist. First recorded for Argo in 1958. His trio included Eldee Young (bass) and Isaac "Red" Holt (drums). Disbanded in 1965. Young and Holt then formed **The Young-Holt Trio**. Lewis re-formed his trio with Cleveland Eaton (bass) and **Maurice White** (drums; later with **Earth, Wind & Fire**). Reunited with Young and Holt in 1983. Young died on 2/12/2007 (age 71).

RAMSEY LEWIS TRIO:

DEBUT	PEAK	WKS		#	Album Title		Catalog
12/22/62	**129**	2		1	Sound Of Christmas	[X-I]	Argo 687
					Christmas charts: 20/'63, 7/'64, 4/'65, 8/'66, 8/'67, 13/'68, 6/'69		
7/4/64	**125**	7		2	Bach To The Blues	[I]	Argo 732
10/17/64	**103**	13		3	The Ramsey Lewis Trio At The Bohemian Caverns	[I-L]	Argo 741
12/19/64	**8**[X]	15		4	More Sounds Of Christmas	[X-I]	Argo 745
					Christmas charts: 8/'64, 16/'65, 14/'66, 49/'67, 41/'68		
8/14/65	**2**[1]	47		5	The In Crowd	[I-L]	Argo 757
					Grammy: Jazz Album		
					recorded on 5/14/1965 at The Bohemian Caverns in Washington DC		
11/6/65+	**54**	19		6	Choice! The Best Of The Ramsey Lewis Trio	[G-I]	Cadet 755
2/19/66	**15**	27		7	Hang On Ramsey!	[I-L]	Cadet 761
					recorded on 10/15/1965 at The Lighthouse in Hermosa Beach, California		

RAMSEY LEWIS:

DEBUT	PEAK	WKS		#	Album Title		Catalog
9/10/66	**16**	34		8	Wade In The Water	[I]	Cadet 774
3/25/67	**95**	16		9	Goin' Latin	[I]	Cadet 790
7/22/67	**124**	5		10	The Movie Album	[I]	Cadet 782
10/28/67+	**59**	16		11	Dancing In The Street	[I-L]	Cadet 794
3/9/68	**52**	31		12	Up Pops Ramsey Lewis	[I]	Cadet 799
7/20/68	**55**	20		13	Maiden Voyage	[I]	Cadet 811
3/29/69	**156**	14		14	Mother Nature's Son	[I]	Cadet 821
9/6/69	**139**	14		15	Another Voyage	[I]	Cadet 827
3/14/70	**172**	12		16	The Best Of Ramsey Lewis	[G-I]	Cadet 839
3/21/70	**157**	8		17	Ramsey Lewis, The Piano Player	[I]	Cadet 836
10/24/70	**177**	7		18	Them Changes	[I-L]	Cadet 844
					recorded on 5/8/1970 at The Depot in Minneapolis, Minnesota		
6/19/71	**163**	9		19	Back To The Roots	[I]	Cadet 6001
6/24/72	**79**	21		20	Upendo Ni Pamoja	[I]	Columbia 31096
3/3/73	**117**	10		21	Funky Serenity	[I]	Columbia 32030
10/13/73	**198**	3		22	Ramsey Lewis' Newly Recorded All-Time, Non-Stop Golden Hits	[I]	Columbia 32490
12/28/74+	**12**	30	●	23	Sun Goddess		Columbia 33194
10/4/75	**46**	22		24	Don't It Feel Good		Columbia 33800
5/22/76	**77**	11		25	Salongo	[I]	Columbia 34173
5/28/77	**79**	10		26	Love Notes	[I]	Columbia 34696
12/24/77+	**111**	9		27	Tequila Mockingbird	[I]	Columbia 35018
10/28/78	**149**	5		28	Legacy	[I]	Columbia 35483
6/9/79	**203**	8		29	Ramsey	[I]	Columbia 35815
8/23/80	**173**	8		30	Routes	[I]	Columbia 36423
6/20/81	**152**	5		31	Three Piece Suite	[I]	Columbia 37153
3/20/82	**202**	10		32	Live At The Savoy	[I-L]	Columbia 37687
					recorded at The Savoy Theater in New York City		
7/9/83	**206**	5		33	Les Fleurs	[I]	Columbia 38787
9/8/84	**144**	9		34	The Two Of Us		Columbia 39326
					RAMSEY LEWIS & NANCY WILSON		

456

LEWIS, Webster
Born on 9/1/1943 in Baltimore, Maryland. Died on 11/20/2002 (age 59). R&B singer/keyboardist.

| 3/15/80 | 114 | 9 | 1 **8 For The 80's** .... | | Epic 36197 |

LFO
Vocal trio from Orlando, Florida: Rich Cronin, Brad Fischetti and Devin Lima. LFO: Lyte Funky Ones.

| 9/11/99 | 21 | 52 | ▲ | 1 **LFO** .... | | Arista 14605 |
| 7/14/01 | 75 | 17 | | 2 **Life Is Good** .... | | J Records 20006 |

LFT CHURCH CHOIR
Gospel group assembled by **Hezekiah Walker**. LFT: Love Fellowship Tabernacle.

| 4/7/01 | 180 | 1 | 1 **Love Is Live!** .... [L] | Verity 43157 |

LIBERTINES, The
Pop-rock trio from England: Carl Barat (vocals, guitar), John Hassall (bass) and Gary Powell (drums).

| 9/18/04 | 111 | 1 | 1 **The Libertines** .... | Rough Trade 83250 |

LIDELL, Jamie
Born on 9/18/1973 in Huntingdon, Cambridgeshire, England. R&B-funk singer/songwriter/musician.

| 5/17/08 | 183 | 1 | 1 **Jim** .... | Warp 160 |

LIEBERMAN, Lori
Born on 11/18/1949 in Los Angeles, California. Folk singer/songwriter.

| 8/18/73 | 192 | 6 | 1 **Becoming** .... | Capitol 11203 |

LIEBERT, Ottmar
Born in 1959 in Cologne, Germany (of Hungarian and Chinese-German parentage). Flamenco guitarist. Luna Negra (Spanish for Black Moon) are bassist Jon Gagan and drummer Dave Bryant.

5/26/90	134	18	▲	1 **Nouveau Flamenco** .... [I]	Higher Octave 7026
1/5/91	170	2		2 **Poets & Angels: Music 4 The Holidays** .... [X-I]	Higher Octave 7030
				Christmas chart: 22/'90	

OTTMAR LIEBERT + LUNA NEGRA:

7/6/91	176	5	●	3 **Borrasca** .... [I]	Higher Octave 7036
4/11/92	94	25	●	4 **Solo Para Ti** .... [I]	Epic 47848
9/4/93	132	12	●	5 **The Hours Between Night + Day** .... [I]	Epic 53804

LIFEHOUSE
Adult Alternative pop-rock trio trio from Malibu, California: Jason Wade (vocals, guitar), Sergio Andrade (bass) and Rick Woolstenhulme (drums).

11/18/00+	6	73	▲²	1 **No Name Face**	DreamWorks 50231
10/5/02	7	17		2 **Stanley Climbfall**	DreamWorks 50377
4/9/05	10	49	●	3 **Lifehouse**	Geffen 004308
7/7/07	14	76	●	4 **Who We Are**	Geffen 009153

LIFE OF AGONY
Rock band from Brooklyn, New York: Keith Caputo (vocals), "Joey Z" Zampella (guitar), Alan Robert (bass) and Sal Abruscato (drums). Dan Richardson replaced Abruscato in 1997. Joey Z and Richardson later joined **Stereomud**.

10/28/95	153	1	1 **Ugly**	Roadrunner 8924
9/27/97	157	1	2 **Soul Searching Sun**	Roadrunner 8816
7/2/05	147	1	3 **Broken Valley**	Epic 93515

LIGHT, Enoch, & The Light Brigade   1960s: #18 / All-Time: #112
Born on 8/18/1907 in Canton, Ohio. Died on 7/31/1978 (age 70). Conductor of own orchestra, The Light Brigade, since 1935. President of Grand Award label and managing director for Command Records, for whom he produced a long string of hit stereo percussion albums in the 1960s. Enoch's studio musicians variously billed as Terry Snyder And The All-Stars (Terry died on 3/15/1963, age 47), and The Command All-Stars. Also see **Charleston City All-Stars**, **Los Admiradores**, and **Tony Mottola**.

6/15/59	38	4	1 **I Want To Be Happy Cha Cha's** .... [I]	Grand Award 388
1/25/60	❶¹³	124	●	2 **Persuasive Percussion** [I]	Command 800
				TERRY SNYDER & THE ALL-STARS	
1/25/60	2⁵	97	3 **Provocative Percussion** [I]	Command 806
				THE COMMAND ALL-STARS	
8/22/60	3¹	53	4 **Persuasive Percussion, Volume 2** [I]	Command 808
				TERRY SNYDER & THE ALL-STARS	
9/19/60	4	46	5 **Provocative Percussion, Volume 2** [I]	Command 810
4/24/61	3¹	20	6 **Persuasive Percussion, Volume 3** [I]	Command 817
				THE COMMAND ALL-STARS	
10/9/61	❶⁷	57	7 **Stereo 35/MM** [I]	Command 826
2/17/62	8	27	8 **Stereo 35/MM, Volume Two** [I]	Command 831
2/24/62	34	8	9 **Persuasive Percussion, Volume 4** .... [I]	Command 830
				ENOCH LIGHT & THE COMMAND ALL-STARS	
4/21/62	27	13	10 **Great Themes From Hit Films** .... [I]	Command 835

Billboard			R I A A	ARTIST	Catalog	Label & Number
DEBUT	PEAK	WKS		Album Title		

LIGHT, Enoch, & The Light Brigade — cont'd

11/3/62	44	4		11 Enoch Light And His Orchestra At Carnegie Hall Play Irving Berlin .... [I]		Command 840
12/15/62+	8	33		12 Big Band Bossa Nova [I]		Command 844
11/2/63	133	3		13 1963-The Year's Most Popular Themes .... [I]		Command 854
4/4/64	121	7		14 Rome 35/MM.. [I]		Command 863
5/30/64	78	9		15 Dimension "3" .... [I]		Command 867
6/13/64	129	4		16 Command Performances .... [I-K]		Command 868
10/3/64	143	4		17 Great Themes From Hit Films........................... [I]		Command 871
11/7/64+	84	15		18 Discotheque Dance...Dance...Dance .... [I]		Command 873
9/11/65	105	10		19 Magnificent Movie Themes .... [I]		Command 887
5/21/66	144	6		20 Persuasive Percussion 1966 .... [I]		Command 895
4/15/67	173	2		21 Film On Film - Great Movie Themes .... [I]		Project 3 5005
4/22/67	163	4		22 Spanish Strings .... [I]		Project 3 5000
4/26/69	192	7		23 Enoch Light & The Brass Menagerie .... [I]		Project 3 5036
3/21/70	191	4		24 Spaced Out .... [I]		Project 3 5043
2/13/71	211	6		25 The Big Band Hits Of The Thirties .... [I]		Project 3 5049
7/24/71	176	5		26 Big Band Hits Of The 30's & 40's! .... [I]		Project 3 5056

LIGHTER SHADE OF BROWN
Hispanic rap duo from Riverside, California: Robert Gutierrez and Bobby Ramirez.

2/8/92	184	4		1 Brown & Proud		Pump 15154
8/13/94	169	2		2 Layin' In The Cut		Mercury 522479

LIGHTFOOT, Gordon   **All-Time: #277**
Born on 11/17/1938 in Orillia, Ontario, Canada. Adult Contemporary-folk singer/songwriter/guitarist. Worked on *Country Hoedown*, CBC-TV series. Teamed with Jim Whalen as the Two Tones in the mid-1960s. Wrote hit "Early Mornin' Rain" for **Peter, Paul and Mary**. First recorded for Chateau in 1962.

11/15/69	143	6		1 Sunday Concert .... [L]		United Artists 6714
				recorded at Massey Hall in Toronto, Ontario, Canada		
6/26/71	178	5		2 Classic Lightfoot (The Best Of Lightfoot/Volume 2)............................ [K]		United Artists 5510
7/27/74+	155	9		3 The Very Best Of Gordon Lightfoot................................ [K]		United Artists 243
5/30/70+	12	37	●	4 Sit Down Young Stranger		Reprise 6392
				later reissued as If You Could Read My Mind		
5/29/71	38	20		5 Summer Side Of Life...................................		Reprise 2037
3/25/72	42	17		6 Don Quixote		Reprise 2056
11/18/72	95	12		7 Old Dan's Records		Reprise 2116
2/2/74	❶²	42	▲	8 Sundown		Reprise 2177
3/1/75	10	20		9 Cold On The Shoulder		Reprise 2206
11/22/75+	34	24	▲²	10 Gord's Gold .... [G]		Reprise 2237 [2]
6/26/76	12	41	▲	11 Summertime Dream		Reprise 2246
2/4/78	22	20	●	12 Endless Wire		Warner 3149
4/5/80	60	11		13 Dream Street Rose		Warner 3426
2/20/82	87	12		14 Shadows		Warner 3633
8/13/83	175	5		15 Salute		Warner 23901
8/9/86	165	6		16 East Of Midnight.......................................		Warner 25482
4/20/02	128	7	●	17 Complete Greatest Hits .... [G]		Rhino 78287

LIGHTHOUSE
Rock band from Toronto, Ontario, Canada: Bob McBride (vocals), Ralph Cole (guitar), Paul Hoffert (keyboards), Howard Shore (sax), Don Dinovo (viola), Dick Armin (cello), Louie Yacknin (bass) and Skip Prokop (drums). Prokop was a member of **The Paupers**. Shore went on to become the original musical director of TV's *Saturday Night Live*. McBride died on 2/20/1998 (age 51).

5/9/70	133	3		1 Peacing It All Together		RCA Victor 4325
7/24/71	80	21		2 One Fine Morning......................................		Evolution 3007
1/29/72	157	7		3 Thoughts Of Movin' On................................		Evolution 3010
7/29/72	178	7		4 Lighthouse Live! .... [L]		Evolution 3014 [2]
				recorded on 2/6/1972 at Carnegie Hall		
1/13/73	190	9		5 Sunny Days..		Evolution 3016
10/6/73	220	1		6 Can You Feel It		Polydor 5056

LIGHTMAN, Toby
Born in 1978 in Cherry Hill, New Jersey. Female Adult-Alternative singer/songwriter.

4/17/04	200	1		1 Little Things		Lava 83623

LIGHTNING SEEDS, The
Born Ian Broudie on 8/4/1958 in Liverpool, England. Alternative-rock singer/producer. Former member of the **Original Mirrors**.

5/5/90	46	27		1 Cloudcuckooland		MCA 6404
3/14/92	154	6		2 Sense...		MCA 10388

LIGHTS
Born Valerie Poxleitner on 4/11/1987 in Timmins, Ontario, Canada. Synth-pop singer/songwriter/keyboardist.

10/24/09	129	1		1 The Listening...		Warner 519312

LIL BOOSIE
Born Torence Hatch on 11/14/1983 in Baton Rouge, Louisiana. Male rapper/songwriter.

11/11/06	18	15		1 Bad Azz		Trill 68587
6/9/07	17	9		2 Survival Of The Fittest		Trill 100454
				LIL BOOSIE, WEBBIE & FOXX		
10/3/09	7	9		3 SuperBad: The Return Of Boosie Bad Azz		Trill 519781

LIL BOW WOW — see BOW WOW

LIL' CEASE
Born James Lloyd in 1977 in Brooklyn, New York. Male rapper. Member of **Junior M.A.F.I.A.**.

7/31/99	26	6		1 The Wonderful World Of Cease A Leo		Queen Bee 92783

LIL' FLIP
Born Wesley Weston on 3/3/1981 in Houston, Texas. Male rapper.

9/14/02	12	26	▲	1 Undaground Legend		Sucka Free 86521
4/19/03	167	2		2 Lil' Flip And Sucka Free Present 7-1-3 And The Undaground Legend: Remixed ...		Sucka Free 89228 [2]
4/17/04	4	31	▲	3 U Gotta Feel Me		Sucka Free 89143 [2]
4/14/07	15	6		4 I Need Mine $$		Asylum 43269 [2]
3/22/08	137	1		5 All Eyes On Us		Real Talk 46
				LIL' FLIP Featuring Young Noble		

LIL ITALY
Born Clifton Dickson on 12/15/1973 in Vallejo, California. Male rapper.

8/21/99	99	3		1 On Top Of Da World		No Limit 50108

LIL' J
Born Jonathan McDaniel on 5/17/1985 in Long Beach, California. Teen male rapper.

4/20/02	131	5		1 All About J		Hollywood 62322

LIL JON & THE EAST SIDE BOYZ
Born Jonathan Smith on 1/27/1971 in Clarksdale, Mississippi; raised in Atlanta, Georgia. Male rapper/songwriter/producer. Creator of "crunk" style of rap music. The East Side Boyz: "Big Sam" Norris and Wendell "Lil Bo" Neal. Lil Jon became a popular guest rapper in 2003.

6/9/01	43	21	●	1 Put Yo Hood Up		BME 2220
11/16/02+	14	104	▲²	2 Kings Of Crunk	Cat:#10/14	BME 2370
11/22/03	197	1		3 Certified Crunk		Ichiban 01037
12/13/03	37	18		4 Part II		BME 2378
11/27/04	3³	41	▲²	5 Crunk Juice		BME/TVT 2690

LIL' KEKE
Born Marcus Edwards on 3/31/1976 in Houston, Texas. Male rapper.

4/11/98	176	1		1 The Commission		Jam Down 481000
2/9/02	122	3		2 Platinum In Da Ghetto		Koch 8366
12/6/08	120	1		3 Loved By Few Hated By Many		TF 012328

LIL' KIM
Born Kimberly Jones on 7/11/1974 in Brooklyn, New York. Female rapper. Member of **Junior M.A.F.I.A.** Convicted of perjury and sentenced to one year in prison in 2005. Participated on the 2009 season of *Dancing With The Stars.*

11/30/96	11	47	▲²	1 Hard Core		Undeas 92733
7/15/00	4	37	▲	2 The Notorious K.I.M.		Queen Bee 92840
3/22/03	5	29	▲	3 La Bella Mafia		Queen Bee 83572
10/15/05	6	9		4 The Naked Truth		Queen Bee 83818

LILLIX
Female rock band from Cranbrook, British Columbia, Canada: sisters Tasha-Ray Ervin (vocals, guitar) and Lacey-Lee Ervin (keyboards), with Louise Burns (bass) and Kim Urhahn (drums).

6/14/03	188	2		1 Falling Uphill		Maverick 48323

LIL MAMA
Born Niatia Kirkland on 10/4/1989 in Harlem, New York. Female rapper.

5/17/08	25	5		1 VYP: Voice Of The Young People		Familiar Faces 12331

LIL' MO
Born Cynthia Loving on 3/10/1976 in Long Island, New York. Female R&B singer.

7/14/01	14	11		1 Based On A True Story		Elektra 62374
5/17/03	17	10		2 Meet The Girl Next Door		Elektra 62835
9/15/07	112	1		3 Pain & Paper		Drakeweb 2

LIL' O
Born Oreoluwa Magnus-Lawson on 5/20/1981 in Nigeria, Africa; raised in Houston, Texas. Male rapper.

8/4/01	199	1		1 Da Fat Rat Wit Da Cheeze		Game Face 83466

LIL ROB
Born Roberto Flores on 9/22/1975 in San Diego, California. Hispanic rapper/songwriter.

8/13/05	31	8		1 Twelve Eighteen: Part I		Upstairs 1027
11/8/08	101	1		2 1218: Part II		Upstairs 1045
10/17/09	158	1		3 Love & Hate		Upstairs 1048

Billboard			R I A A	ARTIST		
DEBUT	**PEAK**	**WKS**		**Album Title**	**Catalog**	**Label & Number**
				LIL' ROMEO		
				Born Percy Romeo Miller on 8/19/1989 in New Orleans, Louisiana. Male rapper. Son of **Master P**.		
7/21/01	6	24	●	1 Lil' Romeo		Soulja 50198
1/4/03	33	11		2 Game Time		New No Limit 060055
10/9/04	70	8		3 RomeoLand		New No Limit 5753
				LIL SCRAPPY		
				Born Darryl Richardson on 1/19/1984 in North Trenton, New Jersey; raised in Atlanta, Georgia. Male rapper/songwriter.		
3/13/04	12	60	●	1 The King Of Crunk & BME Recordings Present		BME 48556
				TRILLVILLE & LIL SCRAPPY		
12/23/06	24	15		2 Bred 2 Die - Born 2 Live		BME 48568
				LIL SOLDIERS		
				Male rap duo from New Jersey: brothers Ikeim and Freequon.		
5/15/99	80	3		1 Boot Camp		No Limit 50038
				LIL' TROY		
				Born Troy Birklett on 2/24/1966 in Houston, Texas. Male rapper.		
5/1/99	20	51	▲	1 Sittin' Fat Down South		Short Stop 53278
11/10/01	95	4		2 Back To Ballin		Short Stop 8231
				LIL WAYNE **2000s: #42 / All-Time: #386**		
				Born Dwayne Carter on 9/27/1982 in New Orleans, Louisiana. Male rapper/songwriter. Nickname: Weezy. Former member of the **Hot Boys**. Began one year prison sentence for illegal weapon possession charges in March 2010.		
11/20/99	3¹	26	▲	1 Tha Block Is Hot		Cash Money 153919
1/6/01	16	20	●	2 Lights Out		Cash Money 860911
8/10/02	6	14	●	3 500 Degreez		Cash Money 060058
7/17/04	5	36	●	4 Tha Carter	**Cat:#8/1**	Cash Money 001537
12/24/05	2¹	43	▲	5 Tha Carter II	**Cat:#5/39**	Cash Money 005124
11/18/06	3¹	37	●	6 Like Father, Like Son	**Cat:#45/1**	Cash Money 007563
				BIRDMAN & LIL WAYNE		
4/19/08	198	1		7 Happy Fathers Day		BCD 63170
				LIL WAYNE & BIRDMAN		
6/28/08	❶³	96↑	▲³	8 Tha Carter III	**Cat:#5/39**	Cash Money 011033
				Grammy: Rap Album		
1/3/09	111	11		9 Gangsta Grillz: Dedication 3		Cash Money 63278
				LIL WAYNE & DJ DRAMA		
1/24/09	152	1		10 The T-Wayne Show		Guesswhyld digital
				LIL WYTE		
				Born Patrick Lanshaw on 10/6/1982 in Memphis, Tennessee. White male rapper.		
3/22/03	197	1		1 Doubt Me Now		Hypnotize Minds 3604
11/6/04	64	4		2 Phinally Phamous		Hypnotize Minds 68500
6/23/07	46	4		3 The One And Only		Hypnotize Minds 68619
9/12/09	104	2		4 The Bad Influence		Hypnotize Minds 520806
				LIL' ZANE		
				Born Zane Copeland Jr. on 7/11/1982 in Yonkers, New York; raised in Atlanta, Georgia. Male rapper.		
9/9/00	25	20		1 Young World: The Future		Priority 50145
9/6/03	191	1		2 The Big Zane Theory		Priority 50191
				ZANE		
				LIMAHL		
				Born Chris Hamill on 12/19/1958 in England. Former lead singer of **Kajagoogoo**.		
4/27/85	41	20		1 Don't Suppose...		EMI America 17142
				LIMELITERS, The **All-Time: #452**		
				Folk trio formed in Hollywood, California: **Glenn Yarbrough**, Lou Gottlieb and Alex Hassilev. Yarbrough went solo in 1963; replaced by Ernie Sheldon. Gottlieb died of cancer on 7/11/1996 (age 72).		
2/27/61	5	74		1 Tonight: In Person **[L]**		RCA Victor 2272
				recorded on 7/29/1960 at the Ash Grove in Hollywood, California		
9/4/61	40	18		2 The Limeliters		Elektra 7180
10/2/61+	8	36		3 The Slightly Fabulous Limeliters **[L]**		RCA Victor 2393
2/3/62	14	31		4 Sing Out!		RCA Victor 2445
6/9/62	25	29		5 Through Children's Eyes **[L]**		RCA Victor 2512
				recorded on 12/29/1961 at the Berkeley Community Theater		
9/29/62	21	12		6 Folk Matinee		RCA Victor 2547
2/2/63	37	25		7 Our Men In San Francisco **[L]**		RCA Victor 2609
				recorded at the Hungry i in San Francisco, California		
5/25/63	83	6		8 Makin' A Joyful Noise		RCA Victor 2588
9/28/63	73	8		9 Fourteen 14K Folk Songs		RCA Victor 2671
5/9/64	118	5		10 More Of Everything!		RCA Victor 2844

Billboard			R I A A	ARTIST		
DEBUT	PEAK	WKS		Album Title	Catalog	Label & Number

LIMP BIZKIT
All-Time: #456

Alternative-metal band from Jacksonville, Florida: Fred Durst (vocals; born on 8/20/1970), Wes Borland (guitar; born on 2/7/1975), Sam Rivers (bass; born in 1979) and John Otto (drums; born on 3/22/1977). Borland formed **Bigdumbface**. Borland left group in October 2001, replaced by Mike Smith. Borland returned in August 2004, replacing Smith.

DEBUT	PEAK	WKS	RIAA		Album Title	Catalog	Label & Number
4/4/98+	22	77	▲²	1	Three Dollar Bill, Y'all	Cat:❶³/50	Flip 90124
7/10/99	❶⁴	103	▲⁷	2	Significant Other	Cat:#11/23	Flip 90335
11/4/00	❶²	72	▲⁶	3	Chocolate Starfish And The Hot Dog Flavored Water	Cat:#49/1	Flip 490759
12/22/01	26	15	●	4	New Old Songs (Re-Mix)	[K]	Flip 493192
10/11/03	3¹	32	▲	5	Results May Vary		Flip 001235
5/21/05	24	4		6	The Unquestionable Truth (Part 1)		Flip 004703
11/26/05	47	3		7	Greatest Hitz	[G]	Flip 005631

LIND, Bob
Born on 11/25/1942 in Baltimore, Maryland. Folk-rock singer/songwriter.

DEBUT	PEAK	WKS	RIAA		Album Title	Catalog	Label & Number
4/16/66	148	2		1	Don't Be Concerned		World Pacific 1841

LINDLEY, David
Born on 1/1/1944 in San Marino, California. Rock session guitarist. Leader of **Kaleidoscope**. Worked with **James Taylor**, **Linda Ronstadt** and **Jackson Browne**. In 1980, formed El Rayo-X with Jorge Calderon, Walfredo Reyes, William Smith and Ray Woodbury.

DEBUT	PEAK	WKS	RIAA		Album Title	Catalog	Label & Number
5/16/81	83	18		1	El Rayo-X		Asylum 524
11/13/82	202	4		2	Win This Record		Elektra 60178
9/24/88	174	6		3	Very Greasy		Elektra 60768

DAVID LINDLEY & EL RAYO-X (above 2)

LINDSAY, Mark
Born on 3/9/1942 in Eugene, Oregon. Pop singer/songwriter. Lead singer of **Paul Revere & The Raiders**.

DEBUT	PEAK	WKS	RIAA		Album Title	Catalog	Label & Number
3/7/70	36	19		1	Arizona		Columbia 9986
9/5/70	82	10		2	Silverbird		Columbia 30111
10/9/71	180	2		3	You've Got A Friend		Columbia 30735

LINE, Lorie
Born in Reno, Nevada. New Age-light classical pianist.

DEBUT	PEAK	WKS	RIAA		Album Title	Catalog	Label & Number
1/18/03	18ˣ	1		1	Sharing The Season: Volume Four	[X-I]	Time Line 21

LORIE LINE & Her Pop Chamber Orchestra

LINEAR
Pop trio from Miami, Florida: Charlie Pennachio (vocals), Wyatt Pauley (guitar) and Joey Restivo (percussion).

DEBUT	PEAK	WKS	RIAA		Album Title	Catalog	Label & Number
4/28/90	52	20		1	Linear		Atlantic 82090

LINES, Aaron
Born on 11/17/1977 in Fort McMurray, Alberta, Canada. Country singer/songwriter/guitarist.

DEBUT	PEAK	WKS	RIAA		Album Title	Catalog	Label & Number
1/25/03	68	6		1	Living Out Loud		RCA 67057

LINHART, Buzzy
Born William Linhart on 3/3/1943 in Pittsburgh, Pennsylvania. Male singer/songwriter.

DEBUT	PEAK	WKS	RIAA		Album Title	Catalog	Label & Number
10/23/71	210	1		1	The Time To Live Is Now		Kama Sutra 2037

LINK
Born Lincoln Browder on 10/12/1964 in Dallas, Texas. Male rapper.

DEBUT	PEAK	WKS	RIAA		Album Title	Catalog	Label & Number
7/18/98	187	1		1	Sex Down		Relativity 1645

LINKIN PARK
2000s: #13 / All-Time: #284

Alternative-metal band from Los Angeles, California: Chester Bennington (vocals; born on 3/20/1976), Mike Shinoda (rap vocals; born on 2/11/1977), Joseph Hahn (DJ; born on 3/15/1977), Brad Delson (guitar; born on 12/1/1977), David "Phoenix" Farrell (bass; born on 2/8/1977) and Rob Bourdon (drums; born on 1/20/1979). Shinoda also recorded solo side project **Fort Minor**. Bennington also formed **Dead By Sunrise**.

DEBUT	PEAK	WKS	RIAA		Album Title	Catalog	Label & Number
11/11/00+	2⁴	103	▲¹⁰	1	Hybrid Theory	Cat:#2⁵/268	Warner 47755
8/17/02	2¹	33	▲	2	Reanimation	[K]	Warner 48326
					contains new mixes of songs from #1 above		
4/12/03	❶²	104	▲⁴	3	Meteora	Cat:#10/34	Warner 48186
12/6/03	23	35	▲	4	Live In Texas	[L]	Warner 48563
12/18/04	❶¹	25	▲	5	Collision Course		Machine Shop 48962
					JAY-Z/LINKIN PARK		
6/2/07	❶¹	94	▲²	6	Minutes To Midnight	Cat:#8/47	Machine Shop 44477
12/13/08	41	13		7	Road To Revolution: Live At Milton Keynes	[L]	Machine Shop 516748
12/13/08	96	1		8	Songs From The Underground	[EP]	Machine Shop 516991

LINKLETTER, Art
Born Gordon Arthur Kelly on 7/17/1912 in Moose Jaw, Saskatchewan, Canada. Died on 5/26/2010 (age 97). Popular radio and TV personality.

DEBUT	PEAK	WKS	RIAA		Album Title	Catalog	Label & Number
12/31/66+	143	3		1	For The Children Of The World, Art Linkletter Narrates "The Bible.. In The Beginning"	[S-T]	20th Century Fox 3187
					Art adds narration to music, dialogue and sound effects from the soundtrack		

Billboard DEBUT	PEAK	WKS	R I A A	ARTIST / Album Title	Catalog	Label & Number

LINX
Funk band from London, England: David Grant (vocals), Canute Edwards (guitar), Bob Carter (keyboards), Peter Martin (bass) and Andy Duncan (drums).

6/20/81	175	4		1 Intuition		Chrysalis 1332

LIONS & GHOSTS
Rock band from Hollywood, California: Rick Parker (vocals), Michael Lockwood (guitar), Todd Hoffman (bass) and Michael Murphy (drums). Parker is the son of actress Lara Parker.

10/24/87	187	3		1 Velvet Kiss, Lick of the Lime		EMI America 46959

LIPPS, INC.
Funk-dance project from Minneapolis, Minnesota. Formed by producer/songwriter/multi-instrumentalist Steven Greenberg. Vocals by Cynthia Johnson.

4/19/80	5	26	●	1 Mouth To Mouth		Casablanca 7197
10/11/80	63	9		2 Pucker Up		Casablanca 7242

LIPSTIQUE
Disco studio group from Germany assembled by producer Jurgen Korduletsch.

6/3/78	201	12		1 At The Discotheque		Tom N' Jerry 4701

LISA LISA AND CULT JAM
Born Lisa Velez on 1/15/1967 in Harlem, New York. Latin dance singer/actress. Played "Gloria Morales" on the TV series *Taina*. Cult Jam: Alex "Spanador" Moseley and Mike Hughes (drums). Assembled and produced by **Full Force**.

8/31/85	52	66	▲	1 Lisa Lisa & Cult Jam With Full Force		Columbia 40135
5/9/87	7	48	▲	2 Spanish Fly		Columbia 40477
5/13/89	77	13		3 Straight To The Sky		Columbia 44378
9/7/91	133	6		4 Straight Outta Hell's Kitchen		Columbia 46035

LIT
Rock band from Anaheim, California: brothers A. Jay Popoff (vocals) and Jeremy Popoff (guitar), Kevin Blades (bass) and Allen Shellenberger (drums).

3/13/99	31	72	▲	1 A Place In The Sun		RCA 67775
11/3/01	36	4		2 Atomic		RCA 68086
7/10/04	113	1		3 Lit		Dirty Martini 00413

LITTER
Hard-rock band from Detroit, Michigan: Mark Gallagher (vocals), Ray Melina (guitar), Dan Rinaldi (guitar), J. Worthington Kane (bass) and Tom Murray (drums).

8/16/69	175	5		1 Emerge		Probe 4504

LITTLE, Rich
Born on 11/26/1938 in Ottawa, Ontario, Canada. Stand-up comedian/impressionist.

2/13/82	29	13		1 The First Family Rides Again ..... [C]		Boardwalk 33248

with Melanie Chartoff, Michael Richards, Shelley Hack, Jenilee Harrison, Earle Doud (producer) and **Vaughn Meader**

LITTLE AMERICA
Rock band formed in Los Angeles, California: Mike Magrisi (vocals, bass), Andy Logan (guitar), John Hussey (guitar) and Kurt Custer (drums). Custer was a member of **Lynyrd Skynyrd** from 1991-94.

4/25/87	102	14		1 Little America		Geffen 24113

LITTLE ANTHONY AND THE IMPERIALS
R&B vocal group from Brooklyn, New York: Anthony Gourdine (born on 1/8/1940), Ernest Wright, Tracy Lord, Glouster Rogers and Clarence Collins. Sammy Strain, who joined group in 1964, left in 1975 to join **The O'Jays**.
AWARD: R&R Hall of Fame: 2009

1/16/65	135	4		1 I'm On The Outside (Looking In)		DCP 6801
2/20/65	74	13		2 Goin' Out Of My Head		DCP 6808
3/5/66	97	23		3 The Best Of Little Anthony & The Imperials ..... [G]		DCP 6809
10/4/69	172	5		4 Out Of Sight, Out Of Mind		United Artists 6720

~ ~ ~ ~ ~ ~ ~ ~ ~ ~ **NON-CHARTED ALBUM** ~ ~ ~ ~ ~ ~ ~ ~ ~ ~
1959 We Are The Imperials Featuring Little Anthony

LITTLE BIG TOWN
Country vocal group from Georgia: Karen Fairchild, Kimberly Roads, Phillip Sweet and Jimi Westbrook.

10/22/05+	51	98	▲	1 The Road To Here ..... Cat:#28/6		Equity 3010
11/24/07	24	14		2 A Place To Land		Equity 3018

LITTLE BROTHER
Male rap trio from Durham, North Carolina: Phonte Coleman, Thomas "Big Pooh" Jones and Pat "**9th Wonder**" Douthit.

10/1/05	56	3		1 The Minstrel Show		ABB 83783
11/10/07	89	2		2 Getback		ABB 81095

LITTLE CAESAR
Hard-rock band formed in Los Angeles, California: Ron Young (vocals), Apache (guitar), Louren Molinare (guitar), Fidel Paniagua (bass), and Tom Morris (drums). Group named after a 1930 gangster movie.

6/30/90	139	8		1 Little Caesar		DGC 24288

LITTLE CAESAR and The Romans
R&B vocal group from Los Angeles, California: Carl "Little Caesar" Burnett, David Johnson, Early Harris, Leroy Sanders and Johnny Simmons.

~ ~ ~ ~ ~ ~ ~ ~ ~ ~ **NON-CHARTED ALBUM** ~ ~ ~ ~ ~ ~ ~ ~ ~ ~
1961 **Memories Of Those Oldies But Goodies**

LITTLE EVA
Born Eva Narcissus Boyd on 6/29/1943 in Belhaven, North Carolina. Died of cancer on 4/10/2003 (age 59). Discovered by songwriters **Carole King** and Gerry Goffin while babysitting their daughter **Louise Goffin**.

11/3/62	97	6	1 Llllloco-Motion		Dimension 6000

~ ~ ~ ~ ~ ~ ~ ~ ~ ~ **NON-CHARTED ALBUM** ~ ~ ~ ~ ~ ~ ~ ~ ~ ~
1964 **The Dimension Dolls (volume 1)**
[w/ The Cookies & Carole King]

LITTLE FEAT   All-Time: #475
Eclectic rock band formed in Los Angeles, California: **Lowell George** (vocals; **Frank Zappa**'s Mothers Of Invention), Paul Barrere (guitar), Bill Payne (keyboards), Kenny Gradney (bass), Sam Clayton (percussion) and Richie Hayward (drums). Zappa named group after George's shoe size. Disbanded in April 1979. George died of drug-related heart failure on 6/29/1979 (age 34). Reunited briefly in 1985. Regrouped in 1988, adding Craig Fuller (vocals, guitar; **Pure Prairie League**) and Fred Tackett (guitar). Fuller left in 1994; replaced by Shaun Murphy.

5/27/72	203	3	1 Sailin' Shoes		Warner 2600
3/10/73	205	4	● 2 Dixie Chicken..		Warner 2686
9/7/74	36	16	● 3 Feats Don't Fail Me Now		Warner 2784
11/15/75	36	15	4 The Last Record Album		Warner 2884
5/14/77	34	18	● 5 Time Loves A Hero		Warner 3015
3/11/78	18	25	▲ 6 Waiting For Columbus	[L]	Warner 3140 [2]
12/8/79+	29	21	7 Down On The Farm		Warner 3345
8/22/81	39	13	8 Hoy-Hoy!..	[K]	Warner 3538 [2]
8/20/88	36	33	● 9 Let It Roll		Warner 25750
4/28/90	45	16	10 Representing The Mambo		Warner 26163
10/12/91	126	6	11 Shake Me Up		Morgan Creek 20005
5/13/95	154	3	12 Ain't Had Enough Fun		Zoo 11097
9/13/08	81	2	13 Join The Band		429 Records 17735

LITTLE MILTON
Born James Milton Campbell on 9/7/1934 in Inverness, Mississippi. Died of a stroke on 8/4/2005 (age 70). Blues singer/guitarist.

6/5/65	101	14	1 We're Gonna Make It		Checker 2995
6/14/69	159	7	2 Grits Ain't Groceries		Checker 3011
3/28/70	197	2	3 If Walls Could Talk		Checker 3012

LITTLE RICHARD
Born Richard Penniman on 12/5/1932 in Macon, Georgia. R&B-rock and roll singer/pianist. Nicknamed the "Georgia Peach." Appeared in the movies *Don't Knock The Rock*, *The Girl Can't Help It*, *Mister Rock 'n' Roll* and *Down And Out In Beverly Hills*. Earned theology degree in 1961 and was ordained a minister. Left R&B for gospel music, 1959-62, and again in the mid-1970s. One of the key figures in the transition from R&B to rock and roll.

AWARDS: Grammy: Lifetime Achievement 1993 ★ R&R Hall of Fame: 1986

8/5/57	13	5	1 Here's Little Richard	[G]	Specialty 2100
			RS500 #50		
8/19/67	184	3	2 Little Richard's Greatest Hits	[L]	Okeh 14121
11/13/71	193	4	3 King Of Rock And Roll		Reprise 6462

~ ~ ~ ~ ~ ~ ~ ~ ~ ~ **NON-CHARTED ALBUMS** ~ ~ ~ ~ ~ ~ ~ ~ ~ ~
1958 **Little Richard**   1963 **His Biggest Hits**
1958 **The Fabulous Little Richard**

LITTLE RIVER BAND   All-Time: #494
Pop-rock band formed in Melbourne, Australia: **Glenn Shorrock** (vocals), Graham Goble (guitar), Gerard "Beeb Birtles" Bertelkamp (guitar), Rick Formosa (guitar), Roger McLachlan (bass) and Derek Pellici (drums). George McArdle replaced McLachlan in 1977. David Biggs replaced Formosa in 1978. Stephen Housden replaced Briggs in 1981. John Farnham replaced Shorrock in 1982. Steven Prestwich replaced Pellici in 1984.

10/2/76	80	24	1 Little River Band...		Harvest 11512
6/25/77	49	48	● 2 Diamantina Cocktail		Harvest 11645
6/17/78	16	61	▲ 3 Sleeper Catcher		Harvest 11783
8/4/79	10	33	▲ 4 First Under The Wire		Capitol 11954
4/19/80	44	10	5 Backstage Pass	[L]	Capitol 12061 [2]
9/19/81	21	50	● 6 Time Exposure		Capitol 12163
12/4/82+	33	30	▲² 7 Greatest Hits	Cat:#29/1 [G]	Capitol 12247
6/18/83	61	21	8 The Net		Capitol 12273
2/9/85	75	14	9 Playing To Win		Capitol 12365
			LRB		

Billboard DEBUT	PEAK	WKS	R I A A	ARTIST Album Title	Catalog	Label & Number

LITTLE STEVEN AND THE DISCIPLES OF SOUL
Born Steven Lento (later adopted his stepfather's last name) on 11/22/1950 in Winthrop, Massachusetts; raised in New Jersey. Rock singer/guitarist/actor. Formed **Southside Johnny & The Jukes** with co-lead singer Johnny Lyon in 1974. Joined **Bruce Springsteen**'s E Street Band in 1975. Organized **Artists United Against Apartheid**. Played "Silvio Dante" on TV's *The Sopranos*. Hosts own syndicated radio show *Little Steven's Underground Garage*.

DEBUT	PEAK	WKS		#	Album	Label & Number
12/4/82+	118	18		1	Men Without Women..	EMI America 17086
6/9/84	55	17		2	Voice Of America	EMI America 17120
6/13/87	80	12		3	Freedom No Compromise	Manhattan 53048
					LITTLE STEVEN	

LITTLE TEXAS
Country band from Arlington, Texas: Tim Rushlow (vocals), Porter Howell (guitar), Dwayne O'Brien (guitar), Brady Seals (keyboards), Duane Propes (bass) and Del Gray (drums). Seals is the cousin of Jim Seals (of **Seals & Crofts**) and "England" **Dan Seals**. Jeff Huskins replaced Seals in 1995.

3/21/92	99	12	●	1	First Time For Everything...	Warner 26820
6/5/93+	55	71	▲²	2	Big Time	Warner 45276
10/15/94	51	21	▲	3	Kick A Little	Warner 45739
10/14/95	82	16	●	4	Greatest Hits .... [G]	Warner 46017

LITTLE VILLAGE
All-star band formed in Los Angeles, California: **John Hiatt** (vocals), **Ry Cooder** (guitar), **Nick Lowe** (bass) and Jim Keltner (drums).

| 3/7/92 | 66 | 12 | | 1 | Little Village .... | Reprise 26713 |

LITTLE WALTER
Born Marion Walter Jacobs on 5/1/1930 in Marksville, Louisiana. Died of injuries from a street fight on 2/15/1968 (age 37). Blues singer/harmonica player.
AWARD: R&R Hall of Fame: 2008 (sideman)

~ ~ ~ ~ ~ ~ ~ ~ ~ ~ **NON-CHARTED ALBUM** ~ ~ ~ ~ ~ ~ ~ ~ ~ ~ ~
1957 **The Best Of Little Walter**
RS500 #198

LITTLE WILLIES, The
Country band formed in New York: **Norah Jones** (vocals, piano), Richard Julian (vocals, guitar), Jim Campilongo (guitar), Lee Alexander (bass) and Dan Rieser (drums).

| 3/25/06 | 48 | 11 | | 1 | The Little Willies .... | Milking Bull 50671 |

LITTRELL, Brian
Born on 2/20/1975 in Lexington, Kentucky. Pop singer. Former member of **The Backstreet Boys**.

| 5/20/06 | 74 | 4 | | 1 | Welcome Home .... | Reunion 10098 |

LIVE   **All-Time: #490**
Rock band formed in York, Pennsylvania: Ed Kowalczyk (vocals; born on 7/16/1971), Chad Taylor (guitar; born on 11/24/1970), Pat Dahlheimer (bass; born on 5/30/1971) and Chad Gracey (drums; born on 7/23/1971).

1/18/92	73	24	●	1	Mental Jewelry .... Cat:#8/30	Radioactive 10346
5/14/94+	❶¹	121	▲⁸	2	Throwing Copper Cat:#16/15	Radioactive 10997
3/8/97	❶¹	46	▲	3	Secret Samadhi	Radioactive 11590
10/23/99	4	26	▲	4	The Distance To Here	Radioactive 11966
10/6/01	22	8		5	V	Radioactive 12485
6/7/03	28	19		6	Birds Of Pray	Radioactive 000374
11/20/04	65	3		7	Awake: The Best Of Live .... [G]	Radioactive 003514
6/24/06	52	3		8	Songs From Black Mountain..	Epic 96539

LIVGREN, Kerry
Born on 9/18/1949 in Topeka, Kansas. Rock guitarist/keyboardist. Member of **Kansas**.

| 9/20/80 | 209 | 2 | | 1 | Seeds Of Change .... | Kirshner 36567 |

LIVING COLOUR
Black rock band from Brooklyn, New York: Corey Glover (vocals), Vernon Reid (guitar), Muzz Skillings (bass) and William Calhoun (drums). Doug Wimbish replaced Skillings in early 1992. Glover played "Francis" in the 1986 movie *Platoon*.

9/3/88+	6	76	▲²	1	Vivid	Epic 44099
9/15/90	13	35	●	2	Time's Up	Epic 46202
					Grammy: Hard Rock Album	
8/3/91	110	5		3	Biscuits .... [EP]	Epic 47988
3/20/93	26	12		4	Stain	Epic 52780
10/3/09	161	1		5	The Chair In The Doorway	Megaforce 01

LIVING IN A BOX
Pop trio formed in Sheffield, England: Richard Darbyshire (vocals), Marcus Vere (keyboards) and Anthony Critchlow (drums).

| 8/8/87 | 89 | 13 | | 1 | Living In A Box .... | Chrysalis 41547 |

LIVING STRINGS
Studio orchestra from Europe. Arranged and conducted by Hill Bowen.

2/27/61	26	6		1	Living Strings Play All The Music From Camelot .... [I]	RCA Camden 657
2/27/61	42	7		2	Living Strings Play Music Of The Sea .... [I]	RCA Camden 639
12/9/67	30ˣ	6		3	The Spirit Of Christmas .... [X-I]	RCA Camden 783
					Christmas charts: 30/'67, 33/'68	

LIVING TRIO
Studio trio from Europe: an organ, a guitar and an accordion.

12/30/67	78ˣ	1	1 I'll Be Home For Christmas .... [X-I]	RCA Camden 2159

LIVING VOICES
Arranged and conducted by **Anita Kerr**.

12/9/67	35ˣ	4	1 The Little Drummer Boy.. [X]	RCA Camden 911

LIZZY BORDEN
Hard-rock band from Los Angeles, California: Lizzy Borden (vocals), Gene Allen (guitar), Mike Davis (bass) and Joey Scott (drums).

11/1/86	144	10	1 Menace To Society	Enigma 73224
5/2/87	188	6	2 Terror Rising .... [EP]	Enigma 73254
9/26/87	146	7	3 Visual Lies	Enigma 73288
8/26/89	133	10	4 Master Of Disguise	Enigma 73413

LL COOL J
All-Time: #221

Born James Todd Smith on 1/14/1968 in Bay Shore, Long Island, New York; raised in Queens, New York. Male rapper/songwriter/actor. Stage name is abbreviation for Ladies Love Cool James. Acted in several movies. Starred as "Marion Hill" on the 1993 TV series *In The House*.

1/11/86	46	38	▲	1 Radio	Columbia 40239
				RS500 #478	
6/20/87	3¹	53	▲²	2 Bigger And Deffer	Def Jam 40793
7/1/89	6	21	▲	3 Walking With A Panther	Def Jam 45172
10/6/90	16	76	▲²	4 Mama Said Knock You Out	Def Jam 46888
4/17/93	5	24	●	5 14 Shots To The Dome	Def Jam 53325
12/9/95+	20	62	▲²	6 Mr. Smith..	Def Jam 529583
11/23/96	29	28	▲	7 All World .... [G]	Def Jam 534125
11/1/97	7	23	▲	8 Phenomenon	Def Jam 539186
9/30/00	❶¹	12	●	9 G.O.A.T. Featuring James T. Smith The Greatest Of All Time	Def Jam 546819
11/2/02	2¹	29		10 10	Def Jam 063219
9/18/04	4	19	●	11 The DEFinition	Def Jam 002939
4/29/06	6	13	●	12 Todd Smith	Def Jam 006158
9/27/08	9	5		13 Exit 13	Def Jam 011503

LLOYD
Born Lloyd Polite on 1/3/1986 in New Orleans, Louisiana; raised in Atlanta, Georgia. R&B singer.

8/7/04	11	14		1 Southside..	The Inc. 002409
3/31/07	2¹	23	●	2 Street Love	The Inc. 008554
8/23/08	7	9		3 Lessons In Love	The Inc. 011517

LLOYD, Charles, Quartet
Born on 3/15/1938 in Memphis, Tennessee. Jazz tenor saxophonist.

7/15/67	188	4	1 Forest Flower... [I-L]	Atlantic 1473
			recorded on 9/18/1966 at the Monterey Jazz Festival	
8/19/67	171	7	2 Love-In.. [I-L]	Atlantic 1481
			recorded at the Fillmore in San Francisco, California	
1/20/73	208	3	3 Waves .... [I]	A&M 3044

LLOYD, Ian — see STORIES

LMFAO
Male rap duo from Los Angeles, California. Stefan "Redfoo" Gordy and Skyler "Sky Blu" Gordy. Stefan is the son of Motown founder Berry Gordy. Skyler is the grandson of Berry Gordy. Stefan is Skyler's uncle.

7/25/09	33	25	1 Party Rock	Party Rock 012932

LOBO
Born Roland Kent LaVoie on 7/31/1943 in Tallahassee, Florida. Pop singer/songwriter/guitarist.

6/5/71	178	10	1 Introducing Lobo	Big Tree 2003
10/14/72+	37	31	2 Of A Simple Man..	Big Tree 2013
5/5/73	163	5	3 Introducing Lobo .... [R]	Big Tree 2100
			new cover features a picture of Lobo	
6/30/73	128	14	4 Calumet	Big Tree 2101
8/10/74	183	4	5 Just A Singer	Big Tree 89501
4/5/75	151	7	6 A Cowboy Afraid Of Horses	Big Tree 89505
12/15/79	207	2	7 Lobo	MCA 3194

LOCAL H
Rock duo from Zion, Illinois: Scott Lucas (vocals, guitar, bass) and Joe Daniels (drums).

1/11/97	147	7	1 As Good As Dead...	Island 524202
9/19/98	140	2	2 Pack Up The Cats..	Island 524549

LOCKE, Kimberley
Born on 1/3/1978 in Hartsville, Tennessee. Black female singer. Finalist on the 2003 season of TV's *American Idol*.

5/22/04	16	7	1 One Love..	Curb 78845
5/19/07	160	1	2 Based On A True Story	Curb 78883

LOCKLIN, Hank
Born Lawrence Hankins Locklin on 2/15/1918 in McLellan, Florida. Died on 3/8/2009 (age 91). Country singer/songwriter/guitarist.
AWARD: OPRY: 1960

~ ~ ~ ~ ~ ~ ~ ~ ~ ~ **NON-CHARTED ALBUM** ~ ~ ~ ~ ~ ~ ~ ~ ~ ~ ~
1960 **Please Help Me, I'm Falling**

LOCOMOTIV GT
Rock band from Budapest, Hungary: Thomas Barta (vocals, guitar), Gabor Presser (keyboards), Thomas Somlo (bass) and Joseph Laux (drums).

8/17/74	207	1	1 **Locomotiv GT**		ABC 811

LODGE, John
Born on 7/20/1945 in Birmingham, England. Rock singer/bassist. Member of **The Moody Blues**.

3/29/75	16	23	1 **Blue Jays**		Threshold 14
			JUSTIN HAYWARD & JOHN LODGE		
4/23/77	121	9	2 **Natural Avenue**		London 683

LOEB, Lisa
Born on 3/11/1968 in Bethesda, Maryland; raised in Dallas, Texas. Adult Alternative pop-rock singer/songwriter/guitarist. Nine Stories consisted of Tim Bright (guitar), Joe Quigley (bass) and Jonathan Feinberg (drums).

10/14/95	30	23	● 1 **Tails**		Geffen 24734
			LISA LOEB & NINE STORIES		
11/29/97+	88	19	● 2 **Firecracker**		Geffen 25141
3/16/02	199	1	3 **Cake And Pie**		A&M 493242

LOFGREN, Nils
Born on 6/21/1951 in Chicago, Illinois; raised in Garrett Park, Maryland. Pop-rock singer/guitarist/pianist. Leader of **Grin** (1969-1974). Member of **Bruce Springsteen**'s E Street Band from 1984-85.

3/22/75	141	9	1 **Nils Lofgren**		A&M 4509
4/17/76	32	16	2 **Cry Tough**		A&M 4573
3/19/77	36	12	3 **I Came To Dance**		A&M 4628
10/29/77	44	10	4 **Night After Night** .... [L]		A&M 3707 [2]
7/21/79	54	14	5 **Nils**		A&M 4756
9/26/81	99	11	6 **Night Fades Away**		Backstreet 5251
9/17/83	206	1	7 **Wonderland**		Backstreet 5421
6/22/85	150	5	8 **Flip**		Columbia 39982
3/30/91	153	8	9 **Silver Lining**		Rykodisc 10170

LO FIDELITY ALLSTARS
Electronica-dance/rock band from Brighton, Sussex, England: Dave Randall (vocals), Martin Whiteman (keyboards), Andy Dickinson (bass) and Johnny Machin (drums).

5/8/99	115	19	1 **How To Operate With A Blown Mind**		Skint 69654

LOGGINS, Dave
Born on 11/10/1947 in Mountain City, Tennessee. Pop-country singer/songwriter. Cousin of **Kenny Loggins**.

11/2/74	54	16	1 **Apprentice (In A Musical Workshop)**		Epic 32833

LOGGINS, Kenny   All-Time: #295
Born on 1/7/1948 in Everett, Washington. Pop singer/songwriter/guitarist. Cousin of **Dave Loggins**. In band Gator Creek with producer Michael Omartian (later with **Rhythm Heritage**), later in Second Edition. Worked as a songwriter for Wingate Music; wrote **Nitty Gritty Dirt Band**'s "House At Pooh Corner." Signed as a solo artist with Columbia in 1971 where he met and recorded with Jim Messina from 1972-76 (as **Loggins & Messina**).

5/7/77	27	33	▲ 1 **Celebrate Me Home** .... **Cat:**#18/60		Columbia 34655
7/22/78	7	31	▲ 2 **Nightwatch**		Columbia 35387
10/20/79+	16	43	▲ 3 **Keep The Fire**		Columbia 36172
10/4/80	11	31	● 4 **Kenny Loggins Alive** .... [L]		Columbia 36738 [2]
9/25/82	13	44	● 5 **High Adventure**		Columbia 38127
4/20/85	41	31	● 6 **Vox Humana**		Columbia 39174
8/20/88	69	14	7 **Back To Avalon**		Columbia 40535
9/28/91	71	58	● 8 **Leap Of Faith**		Columbia 46140
9/4/93	60	13	● 9 **Outside: From The Redwoods** .... [L]		Columbia 57391
			recorded on 6/23/1993 in Santa Cruz, California		
5/28/94	65	42	▲ 10 **Return To Pooh Corner**		Sony Wonder 57674
4/12/97	39	31	▲ 11 **Yesterday, Today, Tomorrow - The Greatest Hits Of Kenny Loggins** .... [G]		Columbia 67986
7/26/97	107	7	12 **The Unimaginable Life**		Columbia 67865
12/5/98	148	6	13 **December** .... **Cat:**#10/2 [X]		Columbia 69371
			Christmas charts: 7/98, 15/99		

LOGGINS & MESSINA   All-Time: #411
Pop-rock duo of **Kenny Loggins** (see above bio) and **Jim Messina** (born on 12/5/1947 in Maywood, California). Messina was a member of **Buffalo Springfield** and **Poco**.

3/18/72+	70	113	▲ 1 **Sittin' In**		Columbia 31044
11/11/72+	16	61	▲ 2 **Loggins And Messina**		Columbia 31748
11/10/73+	10	49	▲ 3 **Full Sail**		Columbia 32540
5/11/74	5	37	▲ 4 **On Stage** [L]		Columbia 32848 [2]
11/9/74	8	29	● 5 **Mother Lode**		Columbia 33175

Billboard DEBUT	PEAK	WKS	R I A A	ARTIST Album Title	Catalog	Label & Number

LOGGINS & MESSINA — cont'd

DEBUT	PEAK	WKS		Album	Catalog	Label & Number
9/13/75	21	13		6 So Fine		Columbia 33810
1/31/76	16	17	●	7 Native Sons		Columbia 33578
12/11/76+	61	12	▲²	8 The Best Of Friends	Cat:#12/70 [G]	Columbia 34388
11/12/77	83	8		9 Finale	[L]	Columbia 34167 [2]

LOHAN, Lindsay
Born on 7/2/1986 in Cold Spring Harbor, New York. Female actress/singer. Starred in several movies.

| 12/25/04 | 4 | 24 | ▲ | 1 Speak | | Casablanca 003686 |
| 12/24/05 | 20 | 7 | ● | 2 A Little More Personal (Raw) .... | | Casablanca 005782 |

LO-KEY?
Funk band from Minneapolis, Minnesota: Tony "Prof. T" Tolbert and Andre "Dre" Shepard (vocals), Lance Alexander (keyboards), Tyrone "T-Bone" Yarbrough (bass) and Darron "D" Story (drums).

| 11/14/92+ | 121 | 21 | | 1 Where Dey At? .... | | Perspective 1003 |

LOMAX, Jackie
Born on 5/10/1944 in Wallasey, Merseyside, England. Male singer/songwriter.

6/21/69	145	9		1 Is This What You Want?		Apple 3354
7/3/71	211	3		2 Home Is In My Head		Warner 1914
3/25/72	208	2		3 Three		Warner 2591

LOMBARDO, Guy, And His Royal Canadians
Born on 6/19/1902 in London, Ontario, Canada. Died on 11/5/1977 (age 75). Leader of the #1 dance band of the 1930s and 1940s. Known for his classic theme "Auld Lang Syne," which he traditionally played to climax his annual New Year's Eve broadcasts.

1/19/57	18	2		1 Your Guy Lombardo Medley	[I]	Capitol 739
7/28/58	12	4		2 Berlin By Lombardo	[I]	Capitol 1019
12/2/67	24ˣ	5		3 Sing The Songs Of Christmas	[X]	Capitol 1443
				vocals by children from St. Patrick's Parish in Stoneham, Massachusetts		

LONDON, Julie   1950s: #22
Born Julie Peck on 9/26/1926 in Santa Rosa, California. Died of a stroke on 10/18/2000 (age 74). Singer/actress. Played "Dixie McCall" on TV's *Emergency*. Married to **Jack Webb** from 1945-53.

1/28/56	2¹	12		1 Julie Is Her Name		Liberty 3006
8/11/56	16	8		2 Lonely Girl		Liberty 3012
12/15/56+	18	6		3 Calendar Girl		Liberty 9002
7/22/57	15	4		4 About The Blues		Liberty 3043
6/1/63	127	3		5 The End Of The World		Liberty 7300
11/23/63	136	4		6 The Wonderful World Of Julie London		Liberty 7324

LONDON, LaToya
Born on 12/29/1978 in San Francisco, California. Black female singer. Finalist on the third season of TV's *American Idol*.

| 10/8/05 | 82 | 2 | | 1 Love & Life .... | | Peak 8529 |

LONDON, Laurie
Born on 1/19/1944 in London, England. White teen male singer.
~ ~ ~ ~ ~ ~ ~ ~ ~ ~ ~ **NON-CHARTED ALBUM** ~ ~ ~ ~ ~ ~ ~ ~ ~ ~ ~
1958 **England's 14-Year Old Singing Sensation**

LONDONBEAT
R&B-pop group based in England. Vocal trio of Americans Jimmy Helms and George Chandler, with Trinidad native Jimmy Chambers. Backed by British producer/multi-instrumentalist Willy M.

| 3/2/91 | 21 | 25 | ● | 1 In The Blood .... | | Radioactive 10192 |

LONDON PHILHARMONIC ORCHESTRA
Orchestra formed in 1932 in London, England. Conducted by Vladimir Jurowski.

10/20/07+	15ˣ	5		1 Handel's Messiah	[X]	Madacy 53642 [2]
				Christmas charts: 48/'07, 15/'08, 37/'09		
11/10/07	9ᶜ	8		2 Handel: The Messiah	[X]	Sparrow 51560 [2]
10/10/09+	12ˣ	6		3 Thomas Kinkade: Handel's Messiah	[X]	Madacy 53090 [2]

LONDON QUIREBOYS, The
Rock band formed in London, England: Jonathan "Spike" Gray (vocals), Guy Bailey (guitar), Guy Griffin (guitar), Chris Johnstone (keyboards), Nigel Mogg (bass) and Ian Wallace (drums).

| 5/5/90 | 111 | 21 | | 1 A Bit Of What You Fancy .... | | Capitol 93177 |

LONDON SYMPHONY ORCHESTRA
Studio orchestra from England. Performed on many of the top soundtrack scores.

4/21/79	185	2		1 Classic Rock - Volume One	[I]	RSO 3043
3/5/83	145	3		2 Hooked On Rock Classics	[I]	RCA Victor 4608
1/11/86	93	13		3 A Classic Case - The London Symphony Orchestra Plays The Music Of Jethro Tull	[I]	RCA Victor 7067
6/11/94	196	2		4 Symphonic Music Of The Rolling Stones	[I]	RCA Victor 62526

LONE JUSTICE
Country-rock band from Los Angeles, California: **Maria McKee** (vocals), Ryan Hedgecock (guitar), Marvin Etzioni (bass) and Don Heffington (drums). Etzioni and Heffington left in early 1986; Shane Fontayne (guitar), Bruce Brody (keyboards), Gregg Sutton (bass) and Rudy Richman (drums) joined.

5/11/85	56	25		1 Lone Justice		Geffen 24060
11/29/86+	65	30		2 Shelter		Geffen 24122

LONELY ISLAND, The
Novelty trio from Berkeley, California: Andy Samberg, Akira Schaffer and Jorma Taccone. Samberg joined the cast of TV's *Saturday Night Live* in 2005 (Schaffer and Taccone are writers for the show).

2/28/09	13	31		1 Incredibad .... [N]		Universal Rep. 012576

LONESTAR
Country band from Nashville, Tennessee: Richie McDonald (vocals, guitar), Michael Britt (guitar), Dean Sams (keyboards), **John Rich** (bass) and Keech Rainwater (drums). Rich left in January 1998; later formed **Big & Rich**.
AWARD: CMA: Vocal Group 2001

3/2/96	69	17	●	1 Lonestar		BNA 66642
7/5/97	166	3		2 Crazy Nights		BNA 67422
6/19/99	28	96	▲³	3 Lonely Grill	Cat:#21/9	BNA 67762
12/2/00	95	8		4 This Christmas Time .... [X]		BNA 67975
				Christmas charts: 6/'00, 16/'03, 30/'04		
7/14/01	9	64	▲	5 I'm Already There		BNA 67011
6/21/03	7	41	▲	6 From There To Here: Greatest Hits	[G]	BNA 67076
6/12/04	14	34	●	7 Let's Be Us Again		BNA 59751
10/1/05	26	3		8 Coming Home		BNA 70394
11/4/06	37	3		9 Mountains		BNA 87114

LONG, Bishop Eddie L.
Born in Huntersville, North Carolina. Choir director. Senior pastor at the New Birth Missionary Baptist Church in Lithonia, Georgia.

6/5/04	79	2		1 Spirit & Truth		EMI Gospel 76846
6/6/09	109	1		2 The Kingdom Vol. 1		Ultimate 5104
				BISHOP EDDIE LONG & FRIENDS Featuring GW's		

LONG BEACH DUB ALLSTARS
Rock-reggae band from Long Beach, California: Opie Ortiz (vocals), Richard "Ras-1" Smith (guitar), Jack Maness (keyboards), Marshall Goodman (percussion), Tim Wu (sax), Eric Wilson (bass) and Bud Gaugh (drums). Wilson and Gaugh were members of **Sublime**.

10/16/99	67	5		1 Right Back		DreamWorks 50213
9/29/01	59	4		2 Wonders Of The World		DreamWorks 450295

LONGET, Claudine
Born on 1/29/1942 in Paris, France. Female singer/actress. Married to **Andy Williams** from 1961-69. Charged with criminal negligence (served 30 days in jail) in the shooting of boyfriend, Olympic skier Vladimir "Spider" Sabich on 3/21/1976.

4/15/67	11	54	●	1 Claudine		A&M 4121
10/14/67	33	29		2 The Look Of Love		A&M 4129
4/13/68	29	21		3 Love Is Blue		A&M 4142
2/1/69	155	7		4 Colours		A&M 4163

LOOKING GLASS
Pop-rock band formed in New Brunswick, New Jersey: Elliot Lurie (vocals, guitar), Larry Gonsky (keyboards), Piet Sweval (bass) and Jeff Grob (drums). Sweval (who later joined **Starz**) died on 1/23/1990 (age 41).

7/1/72	113	18		1 Looking Glass		Epic 31320
7/21/73	209	9		2 Subway Serenade		Epic 32167

LOON
Born Chauncey Hawkins on 6/20/1975 in Harlem, New York. Male rapper. Member of **Harlem World**.

11/8/03	6	6		1 Loon		Bad Boy 000892

LOOSE ENDS
R&B vocal trio from London, England: Carl McIntosh, Steve Nichol and Jane Eugene. Nichol and Eugene left in 1990; replaced by Sunay Suleyman and Linda Carriere.

7/6/85	46	19		1 A Little Spice		MCA 5588
4/4/87	59	14		2 Zagora		MCA 5745
7/23/88	80	15		3 The Real Chuckeeboo		MCA 42196
12/8/90+	124	16		4 Look How Long		MCA 10044

LOPEZ, Denise
Born in Queens, New York. Female dance singer.

11/26/88	184	4		1 Truth In Disguise		A&M 5226

LOPEZ, George
Born on 4/23/1961 in Los Angeles, California. Latin stand-up comedian/actor. Starred in own TV sitcom from 2002-07.

10/14/06	108	3		1 El Mas Chingon .... [C]		Oglio 89140

LOPEZ, Jennifer
All-Time: #443

Born on 7/24/1969 in the Bronx, New York (Puerto Rican parents). Female singer/actress/dancer. Starred in several movies. Married **Marc Anthony** on 6/5/2004.

DEBUT	PEAK	WKS	RIAA	#	Album Title	Catalog	Label & Number
6/19/99	8	53	▲³	1	On The 6		Work 69351
2/10/01	❶¹	82	▲⁴	2	J.Lo	Cat:#35/6	Epic 63786
2/23/02	❶²	33	▲	3	J To Tha L-O! The Remixes	[K]	Epic 86399
12/14/02+	2¹	40	▲²	4	This Is Me...Then		Epic 86231
12/6/03	69	5		5	The Reel Me	[K]	Epic 90767
3/19/05	2¹	17	▲	6	Rebirth		Epic 90622
4/14/07	10	9		7	Como Ama Una Mujer	[F]	Epic 78149
10/27/07	12	8		8	Brave		Epic 97754

LOPEZ, Trini
1960s: #46 / All-Time: #289

Born Trinidad Lopez on 5/15/1937 in Dallas, Texas. Pop-folk singer/guitarist. Played "Pedro Jiminez" in the 1967 movie *The Dirty Dozen*.

DEBUT	PEAK	WKS	RIAA	#	Album Title	Catalog	Label & Number
7/20/63	2⁶	101	●	1	Trini Lopez At PJ'S	[L]	Reprise 6093
12/7/63+	11	19		2	More Trini Lopez At PJ'S	[L]	Reprise 6103
4/11/64	32	33		3	On The Move	[L]	Reprise 6112
8/22/64	18	24		4	The Latin Album	[F]	Reprise 6125
10/24/64	30	22		5	Live At Basin St. East	[L]	Reprise 6134
1/30/65	18	23		6	The Folk Album		Reprise 6147
6/12/65	32	19		7	The Love Album		Reprise 6165
8/28/65	46	12		8	The Rhythm & Blues Album		Reprise 6171
12/18/65+	101	10		9	The Sing-Along World Of Trini Lopez		Reprise 6183
5/7/66	54	16		10	Trini		Reprise 6196
8/27/66	110	8		11	The Second Latin Album	[F]	Reprise 6215
11/26/66+	47	11		12	Greatest Hits!	[G]	Reprise 6226
3/4/67	114	6		13	Trini Lopez In London		Reprise 6238
9/2/67	162	7		14	Trini Lopez - Now!		Reprise 6255

LORBER, Jeff

Born on 11/4/1952 in Philadelphia, Pennsylvania. Jazz fusion keyboardist. His fusion group included **Kenny G** (flute), Danny Wilson (bass) and Dennis Bradford (drums).

DEBUT	PEAK	WKS	RIAA	#	Album Title	Catalog	Label & Number
9/8/79	119	14		1	Water Sign	[I]	Arista 4234
5/31/80	123	12		2	Wizard Island	[I]	Arista 9516
4/18/81	77	15		3	Galaxian		Arista 9545
					THE JEFF LORBER FUSION (above 3)		
3/27/82	73	13		4	It's A Fact		Arista 9583
5/5/84	106	7		5	In The Heat Of The Night		Arista 8025
3/9/85	90	16		6	Step By Step		Arista 8269
11/15/86+	68	26		7	Private Passion		Warner 25492

LORDS OF ACID

Techno duo from Belgium: Oliver Adams and Praga Khan. Duo also recorded as Channel X and Digital Orgasm.

DEBUT	PEAK	WKS	RIAA	#	Album Title	Catalog	Label & Number
9/6/97	100	6		1	Our Little Secret		Antler Subway 6036
8/14/99	194	1		2	Expand Your Head	[K]	Antler Subway 6047
3/17/01	160	1		3	Farstucker		Antler Subway 6969

LORDS OF THE NEW CHURCH, The

Rock band formed in England: Steven "Stiv Bators" Bator (vocals; born in Youngstown, Ohio), Brian James (guitar), Dave Tregunna (bass) and Nicky Turner (drums). Bator (former lead singer of the **Dead Boys**) died after being struck by a car on 6/4/1990 (age 40).

DEBUT	PEAK	WKS	RIAA	#	Album Title	Catalog	Label & Number
7/23/83	203	3		1	Live For Today	[EP]	I.R.S. 70409
10/29/83	202	2		2	Is Nothing Sacred?		I.R.S. 70039
4/27/85	158	7		3	The Method To Our Madness		I.R.S. 70049

LORDS OF THE UNDERGROUND

Rap trio from Newark, New Jersey: Al "Mr. Funkyman" Wardrick, Dupre "Do It All" Kelly and Bruce "Lord Jazz" Colston.

DEBUT	PEAK	WKS	RIAA	#	Album Title	Catalog	Label & Number
4/17/93	66	25		1	Here Come The Lords		Pendulum 61415
11/19/94	57	3		2	Keepers Of The Funk		Pendulum 30710

LORD SUTCH AND HEAVY FRIENDS

Born David Sutch on 11/10/1940 in Harrow, Middlesex, England. Committed suicide on 6/16/1999 (age 58). Rock singer. Heavy Friends: **Jimmy Page**, **Jeff Beck**, **Nicky Hopkins**, John Bonham (**Led Zeppelin**) and Noel Redding (**The Jimi Hendrix Experience**).

DEBUT	PEAK	WKS	RIAA	#	Album Title	Catalog	Label & Number
2/21/70	84	13		1	Lord Sutch And Heavy Friends		Cotillion 9015

LORD TARIQ & PETER GUNZ

Rap duo from Brooklyn, New York: Sean Hamilton ("Lord Tariq") and Peter Panky ("Peter Gunz").

DEBUT	PEAK	WKS	RIAA	#	Album Title	Catalog	Label & Number
6/20/98	38	10		1	Make It Reign		Columbia 69010

LORENZ, Trey

Born on 1/19/1969 in Florence, South Carolina. Male R&B singer.

DEBUT	PEAK	WKS	RIAA	#	Album Title	Catalog	Label & Number
10/24/92	111	8		1	Trey Lorenz		Epic 47840

LORING, Gloria
Born on 12/10/1946 in Manhattan, New York. Played "Liz Curtis" on TV's *Days Of Our Lives*. Married to Alan Thicke from 1970-83. Mother of **Robin Thicke**. Recorded in 1977 as Cody Jameson.

9/6/86	61	14	1 Gloria Loring	Atlantic 81679

LOS ADMIRADORES
Percussion group produced by **Enoch Light**.

8/29/60	2[1]	50	1 Bongos Bongos Bongos	[I]	Command 809
10/24/60	3[1]	34	2 Bongos/Flutes/Guitars	[I]	Command 812

LOS ANGELES AZULES
Latin vocal group founded by brothers Elias, Jose and Jorge Avante.

8/25/01	161	6	1 Historia Musical .... [F-K]	Disa 727014

LOS BRAVOS
Rock band formed in Spain: Mike Kogel (vocals; born in Germany), Tony Martinez (guitar), Manuel Fernandez (organ), Miguel Danus (bass) and Pablo Gomez (drums).

11/12/66	93	7	1 Black Is Black	Press 83003

LOS BUKIS
Latin vocal group from Mexico: cousins **Marco Antonio Solis** and Joel Solis, brothers Roberto Guadarrama and Pepe Guadarrama, Eusebio Cortez, El Chivo and Pedro Sanchez.

1/25/03	169	4	1 30 Inolvidables .... [F]	Fonovisa 350691
4/19/03	127	7	2 20 Inolvidables .... [F]	Fonovisa 350832
			LOS BUKIS / LOS TEMERARIOS	
8/23/03	121	6	3 25 Joyas Musicales .... Cat:#36/9 [F]	Fonovisa 350895
2/21/04	127	5	4 Cronica De Dos Grandes .... [F]	Fonovisa 351279
			BRONCO / LOS BUKIS	
10/23/04	174	1	5 Lo Mejor De Nosotros 1972 - 1986 .... [F-K]	Fonovisa 351475
2/12/05	120	4	6 Recuerdos Con Amor .... [F]	Fonovisa 351606
1/28/06	166	3	7 Los Inicios De Nuestra Historia .... [F-K]	Fonovisa 352231
			BRONCO / LOS BUKIS (above 2)	
8/19/06	177	2	8 30 Recuerdos .... [F]	Fonovisa 352638 [2]
7/14/07	185	2	9 30 Recuerdos Inolvidables .... [F]	Fonovisa 353283

LOS CAMINANTES
Latin vocal group from Mexico: brothers Agustin Brigado, Horacio Brigado and Martin Brigado, with Hiking Guanajuato and Humberto Navarro.

2/24/07	102	8	1 La Historia .... [F-K]	Sony 05303

LOS CREADOREZ PASITO DURANGUENSE DE ALFREDO RAMIREZ
Latin band from Chicago, Illinois: Alfredo Ramirez (lead vocals), Agustin Delgado (backing vocals), Franscisco Lopez (keyboards), Domingo Llamas, Armando Ramirez and Jose Gomez (horns), Ismael Bustamante (bass) and Miguel Gomez (drums).

2/17/07	31	6	1 Recio, Recio Mis Creadorez .... [F]	Disa 720982
10/20/07	156	1	2 Las Favoritas De Corridos: Rancheras Y Mas............ [F]	Disa 72112
2/23/08	88	5	3 Listos Montados Y Armados .... [F]	Disa 724141
8/15/09	88	3	4 Avanzando En La Vida .... [F]	Disa 721282

LOS DEL RIO
Flamenco guitar duo from Seville, Spain: Antonio Romero Monge and Rafael Ruiz Perdigones. Formed duo in the 1960s. In 1993, they wrote and recorded "Macarena," which became a worldwide dance craze after it was remixed by the Miami production team of The Bayside Boys.

8/24/96	41	20	1 Macarena - Non Stop .... [F]	Ariola 37587

LOS HOROSCOPOS DE DURANGO
Latin group from Mexico. Formed by Armando Terrazas. Members include Armando's daughters Vicky and Marisol and son Leonardo Terrazas. Other members include Braulio Muro, Jorge Banuelos, Alex Gomez and Hector Villasenor.

3/19/05	78	6	1 Y Seguimos Con Duranguense!!! .... [F]	Disa 726869
11/11/06	116	2	2 Desatados .... [F]	Disa 720955
3/22/08	160	1	3 Ayer Hoy Y Siempre .... [F]	Univision 311271

LOS HURACANES DEL NORTE
Latin band from El Centro, Mexico: brothers Rocky Garcia (vocals), Jesus Garcia (accordian), Lupillo Garcia (sax) and Pancho Garcia (bass), with Wico Lopez (drums).

8/19/00	181	1	1 En Que Trabaja El Muchacho .... [F]	Fonovisa 6088

LOS INDIOS TABAJARAS
Indian guitar instrumental duo from Ceara, Brazil: brothers Natalicio (born Musiperi) and Antenor (born Herundy) Lima.

11/16/63+	7	31	1 Maria Elena	[I]	RCA Victor 2822
			originally released in 1958 as *Sweet And Savage* on RCA 1788		
5/16/64	85	10	2 Always In My Heart .... [I]	RCA Victor 2912

LOS INQUIETOS DEL NORTE
Latin band from Mexico: brothers Jose Meza (vocals, guitar), Rosalio Meza (accordian) and Felipe Meza (bass), with Manuel Acevedo (violin) and Jorge Torres (drums).

12/6/08	199	1	1 La Borrachera .... [F]	Siente 653856

LOS LOBOS

Latin rock band formed in Los Angeles, California: David Hildago (vocals; born on 10/6/1954), Cesar Rosas (guitar; born on 9/26/1954), Steve Berlin (sax; born on 9/14/1955), Conrad Lozano (bass; born on 3/21/1951) and Louie Perez (drums; born on 1/29/1953).

DEBUT	PEAK	WKS	RIAA	#	Album Title	Catalog	Label & Number
12/15/84+	47	34		1	How Will The Wolf Survive?		Slash 25177
					RS500 #461		
2/14/87	47	32		2	By The Light Of The Moon		Slash 25523
7/25/87	❶²	44	▲²	3	La Bamba	[S]	Slash 25605
11/5/88	179	4		4	La Pistola Y El Corazon	[F]	Slash 25790
					Grammy: Tejano Album		
9/22/90	103	9		5	The Neighborhood		Slash 26131
6/13/92	143	10		6	Kiko		Slash 26786
9/18/93	196	1		7	Just Another Band From East L.A. - A Collection	[K]	Slash 45367 [2]
4/6/96	81	6		8	Colossal Head		Warner 46172
8/7/99	135	3		9	This Time		Hollywood 62185
6/22/02	82	5		10	Good Morning Aztlán		Mammoth 65518 [2]
5/22/04	75	5		11	The Ride		Mammoth 62443
9/30/06	142	1		12	The Town And The City		Mammoth 162661

LOS LONELY BOYS

Tex-Mex rock trio of brothers from San Angelo, Texas: Henry Garza (guitar), Joey "JoJo" Garza (bass) and Ringo Garza (drums). All share vocals.

DEBUT	PEAK	WKS	RIAA	#	Album Title	Catalog	Label & Number
3/13/04	9	76	▲²	1	Los Lonely Boys	Cat:#39/2	Epic 80305
3/12/05	69	4		2	Live At The Fillmore	[L]	Epic 93990
8/5/06	2¹	11		3	Sacred		Epic 94194
7/19/08	26	7		4	Forgiven		Epic 17428
11/1/08	40ˣ	1		5	Christmas Spirit	[X]	Or 33204
10/31/09	124	1		6	1969	[EP]	Lonely Tune 200902

LOS PIKADIENTES DE CABORCA

Traditional Mexican band from Sonora, Mexico: Pancho (vocals), El Flaco (guitar), El Chino (clarinet), Latigo (sax) and Chalomo (tuba).

DEBUT	PEAK	WKS	RIAA	#	Album Title	Catalog	Label & Number
9/13/08	52	11		1	Vamonos Pa'l Rio	[F]	Sony 36197

LOS PRIMOS DE DURANGO

Latin vocal group from Durango, Mexico: Javier Amaya, Arturo Vargas, Luis Rios and Arturo Duenas.

DEBUT	PEAK	WKS	RIAA	#	Album Title	Catalog	Label & Number
10/13/07	114	4		1	Voy A Convencerte	[F]	ASL 730020

LOS RIELEROS DEL NORTE

Latin group from Chihuahua, Mexico: brothers Daniel, Alfredo and Javier Esquivel, with Pemo Gonzalez.

DEBUT	PEAK	WKS	RIAA	#	Album Title	Catalog	Label & Number
3/20/04	188	1		1	20 Anos De Fuerza Nortena	[F]	Fonovisa 351235
7/14/07	193	1		2	Ven Y Dime	[F]	Fonovisa 353101
6/14/08	136	1		3	Pos Que No...Claro Que Si	[F]	Fonovisa 353575

LOS SUPER REYES

Latin band formed by keyboardist Cruz Martinez (of **Kumbia Kings**) and vocalist Abel Talamantez.

DEBUT	PEAK	WKS	RIAA	#	Album Title	Catalog	Label & Number
9/1/07	130	2		1	El Regrso De Los Reyes	[F]	Warner Latina 262652

LOST BOYZ

Rap group from Queens, New York: Terrance Kelly ("**Mr. Cheeks**"), Ronald Blackwell ("Spigg Nice"), Raymond Rogers ("Freekie Tah") and Eric Ruth ("Pretty Lou"). Rogers was shot to death on 3/29/1999 (age 28).

DEBUT	PEAK	WKS	RIAA	#	Album Title	Catalog	Label & Number
6/22/96	6	23	●	1	Legal Drug Money		Universal 53010
7/5/97	9	19	●	2	Love, Peace And Nappiness		Universal 53080
10/16/99	32	6		3	LB IV Life		Universal 153268

LOS TEMERARIOS

Ranchera band from Fresnillo, Zacatecas, Mexico: brothers Adolfo Angel Alba (keyboards; born in 1963) and Gustavo Angel Alba (guitar; born in 1968), their cousin Fernando Angel (bass), Mario Ortiz (drums) and Carlos Abrego (percussion).

DEBUT	PEAK	WKS	RIAA	#	Album Title	Catalog	Label & Number
2/21/98	175	1	▲	1	Como Te Recuerdo	[F]	Fonovisa 0515
3/18/00	75	5	▲	2	En La Madrugada Se Fue	[F]	Fonovisa 0519
7/13/02	79	7	●	3	Una Lagrima No Basta	[F]	Fonovisa 0529
4/19/03	127	7		4	20 Inolvidables	[F]	Fonovisa 350832
					LOS BUKIS/LOS TEMERARIOS		
12/13/03	179	2		5	Tributo Al Amor	[F]	Fonovisa 351005
7/17/04	91	10		6	Veintisiete	[F]	Fonovisa 51437
10/2/04	121	7		7	La Mejor...Coleccion	[F-K]	Disa 720392 [3]
11/13/04	114	3		8	Regalo De Amor	[F]	Fonovisa 351530
9/17/05	111	4		9	Sueno De Amor	[F]	Fonovisa 352171
10/20/07	59	6		10	Recuerdos Del Alma	[F]	Fonovisa 352162
10/20/07	182	2		11	La Mujer De Los Dos: Exitos De Pelicula	[F]	Disa 726638
7/26/08	26	9		12	Si Tu Te Vas	[F]	Fonovisa 353648
2/14/09	133	3		13	Evolucion De Amor	[F]	Fonovisa 353806

LOS TIGRES DEL NORTE
2000s: #47 / All-Time: #402

Mexican-American band based in California: brothers Jorge Hernandez (vocals, accordian), Eduardo Hernandez, Hernan Hernandez and Raul Hernandez (guitars), with cousin Oscar Lara (drums) and friend Guadalupe Olivio (sax).

DEBUT	PEAK	WKS				Catalog	Label & Number
7/5/97	149	3	▲	1 Jefe De Jefes	[F]		Fonovisa 80711 [2]
7/10/99	92	5		2 Herencia De Familia	[F]		Fonovisa 80761 [2]
10/14/00	92	4	●	3 De Paisano A Paisano	[F]		Fonovisa 6092
9/8/01	116	5	●	4 Uniendo Fronteras	[F]		Fonovisa 6145
11/16/02	54	4		5 La Reina Del Sur	[F]		Fonovisa 50666
7/19/03	67	8		6 Herencia Musical: 20 Corridos Inolvidables	[F-K]		Fonovisa 350871
4/17/04	75	7		7 Pacto De Sangre	[F]		Fonovisa 351245
10/23/04	117	4		8 20 Nortenas Famosas	[F-K]		Fonovisa 351480
4/16/05	48	6		9 Directo Al Corazon	[F]		Fonovisa 351601
9/3/05	129	4		10 Las Mas Pedidas	[F]		Fonovisa 351668
4/22/06	72	4		11 Historias Que Contar	[F]		Fonovisa 352290
11/25/06	175	1		12 La Muerte Del Sopion	[F]		Fonovisa 352922
4/14/07	65	5		13 Detalles Y Emociones	[F]		Fonovisa 353044
9/15/07	137	3		14 20 Corridos Prohibidos	[F]		Fonovisa 353266
3/22/08	68	5		15 Raices	[F]		Fonovisa 353488
				Grammy: Latin Norteno Album			
9/26/09	45	5		16 La Granja	[F]		Fonovisa 354192

LOSTPROPHETS

Rock band formed in Pontypridd, Glamorgan, Wales: Ian Watkins (vocals), Lee Gaze (guitar), Mike Lewis (guitar), Stuart Richardson (bass) and Mike Chiplin (drums). Ilan Rubin replaced Chiplin in early 2006.

DEBUT	PEAK	WKS				Label & Number
4/20/02	186	1		1 The Fake Sound Of Progress		Columbia 85955
2/21/04	33	37	●	2 Start Something		Columbia 86554
7/15/06	33	8		3 Liberation Transmission		Columbia 96531

LOS TRI-O

Latin vocal trio: Andres, Esteban and Manuel.

DEBUT	PEAK	WKS				Label & Number
3/13/99	120	13		1 Nuestro Amor	[F]	Ariola 58436

LOST TRAILERS, The

Country band formed in Atlanta, Georgia: Ryder Lee (vocals, keyboards), Stokes Nielson (vocals, guitar), Manny Medina (guitar), Andrew Nielson (bass) and Jeff Potter (drums).

DEBUT	PEAK	WKS			Label & Number
9/13/08	32	4		1 Holler Back	BNA 09259

LOS TUCANES DE TIJUANA

Tejano band from Tijuana, Mexico: Mario Quintero, Joel Higuera, David Servin and Mario Moreno.

DEBUT	PEAK	WKS				Label & Number
5/24/97	199	1	●	1 Tucanes De Oro, Secuestro De Amor	[F]	EMI Latin 56921
1/27/07	118	3		2 El Papa De Los Pollitos	[F]	Univision 310947
12/6/08	165	1		3 Propiedad Privada	[F]	Fonovisa 311071

LOUDNESS

Hard-rock band from Japan: Minoru Niihara (vocals), Akira Takasaki (guitar), Masayoshi Yamashita (bass) and Munetaka Higuchi (drums). Higuchi died of cancer on 11/30/2008 (age 49).

DEBUT	PEAK	WKS			Label & Number
3/2/85	74	24	1 Thunder In The East		Atco 90246
5/31/86	64	16	2 Lightning Strikes		Atco 90512
8/15/87	190	4	3 Hurricane Eyes		Atco 90619

LOUIE LOUIE

Born Louis Cordero in Los Angeles, California. Dance singer/songwriter.

DEBUT	PEAK	WKS			Label & Number
6/2/90	136	10	1 The State I'm In		WTG 45285

LOUISIANA'S LE ROUX — see LE ROUX

LOUIS XIV

Punk-rock band from San Diego, California: Jason Hill (vocals, guitar), Brian Karscig (guitar), Jimmy Armbrust (bass) and Mark Maigaard (drums).

DEBUT	PEAK	WKS			Label & Number
4/9/05	159	3	1 The Best Little Secrets Are Kept		Pineapple 93825

LOURIS, Gary

Born on 3/10/1955 in Toledo, Ohio; later based in Minneapolis, Minnesota. Folk-rock-pop singer/songwriter/guitarist. Member of **The Jayhawks** and **Golden Smog**.

DEBUT	PEAK	WKS			Label & Number
3/8/08	199	1	1 Vagabonds		Rykodisc 10925
2/14/09	127	1	2 Ready For The Flood		New West 6162
			MARK OLSON & GARY LOURIS		

LOVATO, Demi

Born Demetria Lovato on 8/20/1992 in Dallas, Texas. Teen singer/actress.

DEBUT	PEAK	WKS			Label & Number
10/11/08	2¹	45	1 Don't Forget		Hollywood 002132
8/8/09	❶¹	24	2 Here We Go Again		Hollywood 003493

Billboard			R I A A	ARTIST Album Title	Catalog	Label & Number
DEBUT	PEAK	WKS				

LOVE
Psychedelic folk-rock band from Los Angeles, California. Core members from 1966-68: Arthur Lee (vocals), John Echols (guitar), Bryan MacLean (guitar) and Ken Forssi (bass). In 1969, Lee assembled a new lineup featuring Jay Donnellan (guitar), Frank Fayad (bass) and George Suranovich (drums). Forssi died of cancer on 1/5/1998 (age 63). MacLean died of a heart attack on 12/25/1998 (age 52). Lee died of leukemia on 8/3/2006 (age 61).

DEBUT	PEAK	WKS				
5/14/66	57	18		1 **Love**		Elektra 74001
2/11/67	80	11		2 **Da Capo**		Elektra 74005
1/6/68	154	10		3 **Forever Changes**		Elektra 74013
				Grammy: Hall of Fame ★ RS500 #40		
9/6/69	102	12		4 **Four Sail**		Elektra 74049
12/27/69+	176	5		5 **Out Here**		Blue Thumb 9000 [2]
9/5/70	142	7		6 **Revisited** .... [G]		Elektra 74058
12/26/70	184	3		7 **False Start**		Blue Thumb 8822

LOVE, Courtney
Born on 7/9/1964 in San Francisco, California. Rock singer/songwriter/guitarist/actress. Lead singer of **Hole**. Acted in several movies. Married to Kurt Cobain (lead singer of **Nirvana**) from 1992-94 (his death).

DEBUT	PEAK	WKS				
2/28/04	53	4		1 **America's Sweetheart**		Virgin 91459

LOVE, G. & Special Sauce
Born Garrett Dutton on 10/3/1972 in Philadelphia, Pennsylvania. Blues singer/guitarist. Special Sauce: Jim Prescott (bass) and Jeff Clemens (drums).

DEBUT	PEAK	WKS				
10/7/95	122	1		1 **Coast To Coast Motel**		Okeh 67152
11/15/97	120	2		2 **Yeah, It's That Easy**		Okeh 67784
8/21/99	113	7		3 **Philadelphonic**		Okeh 69746
5/12/01	138	2		4 **Electric Mile**		Okeh 61420
9/11/04	100	4		5 **The Hustle**		Brushfire 003092
8/19/06	39	6		6 **G. Love's Lemonade**		Brushfire 007201
				G. LOVE (above 2)		
7/12/08	63	2		7 **Superhero Brother**		Brushfire 011364

LOVE, Monie
Born Simone Johnson on 7/2/1970 in London, England; raised in Brooklyn, New York. Female rapper.

DEBUT	PEAK	WKS				
11/24/90+	109	12		1 **Down To Earth**		Warner 26358

LOVE AFFAIR
Rock band from Cleveland, Ohio: Rich Spina (vocals, keyboards), Wes Coolbaugh (guitar), John Zdravecky (guitar), Wayne Cukras (bass) and Michal Hudak (drums).

DEBUT	PEAK	WKS				
9/6/80	209	3		1 **Love Affair**		Radio 2004

LOVE AND KISSES
Disco studio group assembled by European producer **Alec R. Costandinos**. Singers included Don Daniels, Elaine Hill, Dianne Brooks and Jean Graham.

DEBUT	PEAK	WKS				
7/30/77	135	14		1 **Love And Kisses**		Casablanca 7063
5/13/78	85	17		2 **How Much, How Much I Love You**		Casablanca 7091

LOVE AND MONEY
Pop trio from Scotland: James Grant (vocals, guitar), Bobby Paterson (bass) and Paul McGeechan (keyboards). Paterson died on 7/23/2006 (age 49).

DEBUT	PEAK	WKS				
3/25/89	175	7		1 **Strange Kind Of Love**		Mercury 836498

LOVE AND ROCKETS
Pop-rock trio formed in England: **Daniel Ash** (guitar, vocals), David Jay (bass) and Kevin Haskins (drums).

DEBUT	PEAK	WKS				
11/1/86+	72	30		1 **Express**		Big Time 6011
10/31/87+	64	28		2 **Earth.Sun.Moon**		Big Time 6058
5/20/89	14	26	●	3 **Love And Rockets**		Beggars Banquet 9715
4/6/96	172	1		4 **Sweet F.A.**		American 43058

LOVE AND THEFT
Country trio formed in Nashville, Tennessee: Brian Bandas, Eric Gunderson and Stephen Liles.

DEBUT	PEAK	WKS				
9/12/09	36	6		1 **World Wide Open**		Carolwood 002135

LOVE CHILDS AFRO CUBAN BLUES BAND
Disco studio group assembled by **Michael Zager**.

DEBUT	PEAK	WKS				
7/12/75	168	5		1 **Out Among 'Em** .... [I]		Roulette 3016

LOVEDRUG
Alternative-rock band from Canton, Ohio: Michael Shepard (vocals, guitar), Jeremy Gifford (guitar), Thomas Bragg (bass) and James Childress (drums).

DEBUT	PEAK	WKS				
3/24/07	162	1		1 **Everything Starts Where It Ends**		Militia Group 050

LOVE/HATE
Rock band from Los Angeles, California: Jim "Jizzy Pearl" Wilkinson (vocal), Jon Love (guitar), Chris "Skid" Rose (bass) and Joey Gold (drums).

DEBUT	PEAK	WKS				
7/14/90	154	5		1 **Blackout In The Red Room**		Columbia 45263

Billboard			R I A A	ARTIST		
DEBUT	PEAK	WKS		Album Title	Catalog	Label & Number

LOVELESS, Patty
Born Patricia Ramey on 1/4/1957 in Pikeville, Kentucky. Country singer/songwriter/guitarist.
AWARDS: CMA: Female Vocalist 1996 ★ OPRY: 1988

9/28/91	151	11		1 Up Against My Heart		MCA 10336
5/8/93+	63	45	▲	2 Only What I Feel		Epic 53236
9/10/94	60	46	▲	3 When Fallen Angels Fly		Epic 64188
				CMA: Album of the Year		
2/10/96	86	43	▲	4 The Trouble With The Truth		Epic 67269
10/18/97	68	16	●	5 Long Stretch Of Lonesome		Epic 67997
4/10/99	99	8	●	6 Classics	[G]	Epic 69809
9/16/00	126	2		7 Strong Heart		Epic 69880
7/14/01	159	7		8 Mountain Soul		Epic 85651
12/21/02	172	2		9 Bluegrass & White Snow: A Mountain Christmas	[X]	Epic 85967
				Christmas chart: 41/'02		
10/4/03	77	3		10 On Your Way Home		Epic 86620
10/1/05	175	1		11 Dreamin' My Dreams		Epic 94481
9/27/08	86	2		12 Sleepless Nights		Saguaro Road 19660
10/17/09	91	4		13 Mountain Soul II		Saguaro Road 24976

LOVERBOY
Rock band formed in Calgary, Alberta, Canada: Mike Reno (vocals), **Paul Dean** (guitar), Doug Johnson (keyboards), Scott Smith (bass; drowned on 11/30/2000, age 45) and Matt Frenette (drums).

1/31/81	13	105	▲²	1 Loverboy		Columbia 36762
11/14/81+	7	122	▲⁴	2 Get Lucky		Columbia 37638
7/2/83	7	39	▲²	3 Keep It Up		Columbia 38703
9/14/85	13	44	▲²	4 Lovin' Every Minute Of It		Columbia 39953
9/12/87	42	21	●	5 Wildside		Columbia 40893
12/23/89	189	2		6 Big Ones	[G]	Columbia 45411

LOVE SPIT LOVE
Rock band formed in England: brothers Richard Butler (vocals) and Tim Butler (bass), with Richard Fortus (guitar) and Frank Ferrer (drums). The Butler brothers were also members of the **Psychedelic Furs**.

10/8/94	195	1		1 Love Spit Love		Imago 21030

LOVETT, Lyle   **All-Time: #484**
Born on 11/1/1957 in Houston, Texas; raised in Klein, Texas. Country singer/songwriter/guitarist. Acted in several movies. Married to actress Julia Roberts from 1993-95.

2/20/88	117	14	●	1 Pontiac		MCA/Curb 42028
2/18/89	62	21	●	2 Lyle Lovett And His Large Band		MCA/Curb 42263
				Grammy: Male Country Vocal		
4/18/92	57	34	●	3 Joshua Judges Ruth		Curb 10475
10/15/94	26	13	●	4 I Love Everybody		Curb/MCA 10808
7/6/96	24	16	●	5 The Road To Ensenada		Curb/MCA 11409
				Grammy: Country Album		
10/10/98	55	7	●	6 Step Inside This House		Curb 11831 [2]
7/17/99	94	9		7 Live In Texas	[L]	Curb 11964
11/10/01	195	1		8 Anthology Volume One: Cowboy Moon	[K]	Curb 170234
3/15/03	106	4		9 Smile: Songs From The Movies		Curb 113184
10/18/03	63	7		10 My Baby Don't Tolerate		Curb 001162
9/15/07	18	8		11 It's Not Big It's Large		Curb/Lost Highway 00896
				LYLE LOVETT AND HIS LARGE BAND		
11/7/09	29	4		12 Natural Forces		Curb 013174

LOVE UNLIMITED
R&B vocal trio from San Pedro, California: sisters Glodean James and Linda James, with Diane Taylor. Glodean was married to **Barry White** from 1974-88.

4/29/72	151	12		1 Love Unlimited		Uni 73131
9/8/73+	3²	44	●	2 Under The Influence Of...		20th Century 414
10/12/74	85	27		3 In Heat		20th Century 443
2/26/77	192	3		4 He's All I've Got		Unlimited Gold 101

LOVE UNLIMITED ORCHESTRA
Forty-piece studio orchestra conducted and arranged by **Barry White**. Formed to back **Love Unlimited**; also heard on some of White's solo hits. **Kenny G** was a member at age 17.

2/9/74	8	25	●	1 Rhapsody In White	[I]	20th Century 433
7/6/74	96	10		2 Together Brothers	[I-S]	20th Century 101
11/9/74+	28	27	●	3 White Gold	[I]	20th Century 458
1/10/76	92	15		4 Music Maestro Please	[I]	20th Century 480
10/30/76	123	8		5 My Sweet Summer Suite	[I]	20th Century 517
2/18/78	201	6		6 My Musical Bouquet	[I]	20th Century 554

Billboard DEBUT	PEAK	WKS	R I A A	ARTIST / Album Title	Catalog	Label & Number
				LOVICH, Lene		
				Born Lili Marlene Premilovich on 3/30/1949 in Detroit, Michigan; raised in England. Singer/actress. Acted in the movies *Cha-Cha* and *Mata Hari*.		
8/4/79	137	10		1 Stateless		Stiff 36102
3/8/80	94	8		2 Flex		Stiff 36308
1/15/83	188	4		3 No-Man's-Land		Stiff 38399
				LOVIN' SPOONFUL, The		
				Jug-rock band formed in New York: **John Sebastian** (vocals, guitar; born on 3/17/1944), Zalman Yanovsky (guitar; born on 12/19/1944; died of a heart attack on 12/13/2002, age 57), Steve Boone (bass; born on 9/23/1943) and Joe Butler (drums; born on 9/16/1941). Sebastian had been with the Even Dozen Jug Band; did session work at Elektra. Yanovsky and Sebastian were members of the Mugwumps with **Mama Cass Elliot** and Denny Doherty (later with **The Mamas & The Papas**). Yanovsky replaced by Jerry Yester (keyboards) in 1967. Disbanded in 1970.		
				AWARD: R&R Hall of Fame: 2000		
12/4/65+	32	35		1 Do You Believe In Magic		Kama Sutra 8050
4/2/66	10	31		2 Daydream		Kama Sutra 8051
9/24/66	126	9		3 What's Up, Tiger Lily? [S]		Kama Sutra 8053
12/17/66+	14	26		4 Hums Of The Lovin' Spoonful		Kama Sutra 8054
3/18/67	3[2]	52	●	5 The Best Of The Lovin' Spoonful [G]		Kama Sutra 8056
4/15/67	160	5		6 You're A Big Boy Now [S]		Kama Sutra 8058
1/20/68	118	7		7 Everything Playing		Kama Sutra 8061
3/30/68	156	5		8 The Best Of The Lovin' Spoonful, Volume 2 [G]		Kama Sutra 8064
4/24/76	183	3		9 The Best...Lovin' Spoonful [G]		Kama Sutra 2608 [2]
				LOW		
				Alternative-rock trio from Duluth, Minnesota: Alan Sparhawk (vocals, guitar), Steve Garrington (bass) and Mimi Parker (drums).		
4/7/07	196	1		1 Drums And Guns		Sub Pop 736
				LOWE, Jim		
				Born on 5/7/1927 in Springfield, Missouri. DJ/vocalist/pianist/composer.		
				~ ~ ~ ~ ~ ~ ~ ~ ~ ~ NON-CHARTED ALBUM ~ ~ ~ ~ ~ ~ ~ ~ ~ ~		
				1956 The Green Door		
				LOWE, Nick		
				Born on 3/24/1949 in Walton, Surrey, England. Rockabilly singer/songwriter/guitarist. Member of **Rockpile**. Married to **Carlene Carter** from 1979-90.		
4/29/78	127	10		1 Pure Pop For Now People		Columbia 35329
				also see #8 below		
7/14/79	31	22		2 Labour Of Lust	Cat:#44/8	Columbia 36087
2/20/82	50	14		3 Nick The Knife		Columbia 37932
4/2/83	129	7		4 The Abominable Showman		Columbia 38589
6/23/84	113	12		5 Nick Lowe & His Cowboy Outfit		Columbia 39371
9/21/85	119	12		6 The Rose Of England		Columbia 39958
				NICK LOWE & HIS COWBOY OUTFIT (above 2)		
4/7/90	182	3		7 Party Of One		Reprise 26132
3/8/08	32[C]	1		8 Jesus Of Cool [R]		Yep Roc 2620
				original British version of album #1 above		
				LOWRY, Mark		
				Born on 6/24/1958 in Houston, Texas. Christian singer/comedian. Member of **The Gaither Vocal Band**.		
5/5/01	130	1		1 On Broadway [C]		Spring House 42270
10/1/05	186	1		2 Mark Lowry Goes To Hollywood [L]		Gaither 42610
				LOX, The		
				Rap trio from Yonkers, New York: David **Styles**, Sean "**Sheek Louch**" Jacobs and Jayson "**Jadakiss**" Phillips. Group name is short for Living Off Xperience. Members of **Ruff Ryders**.		
1/31/98	3[1]	22	▲	1 Money, Power & Respect		Bad Boy 73015
2/12/00	5	16	●	2 We Are The Streets		Ruff Ryders 490599
				L7		
				Female punk-rock band from Los Angeles, California: Suzi Gardner (guitar, vocals), Donita Sparks (guitar, vocals), Jennifer Finch (bass, vocals) and Dee Plakas (drums). Finch left in August 1996.		
8/8/92	160	7		1 Bricks Are Heavy		Slash 26784
7/30/94	117	7		2 Hungry For Stink		Slash 45624
3/15/97	172	1		3 The Beauty Process: Triple Platinum		Slash 46327
				LSG		
				All-star R&B trio: **Gerald Levert**, **Keith Sweat** and **Johnny Gill**.		
11/29/97	4	42	▲[2]	1 Levert - Sweat - Gill		EastWest 62125
8/16/03	6	8		2 LSG2		Elektra 62851

L.T.D.
R&B-funk band from Greensboro, North Carolina: brothers **Jeffrey Osborne** (vocals, drums) and Billy Osborne (keyboards), with John McGhee (guitar), Abraham Miller and Lorenzo Carnegie (saxophones), Jimmie Davis (keyboards), Carle Vickers (trumpet), Jake Riley (trombone), Henry Davis (bass) and Alvino Bennett (drums). The Osborne brothers left in 1980. Leslie Wilson and Andre Ray joined as vocalists. L.T.D.: Love, Togetherness and Devotion.

8/21/76	52	30		1 Love To The World		A&M 4589
8/13/77+	21	34	●	2 Something To Love		A&M 4646
6/17/78	18	26	▲	3 Togetherness		A&M 4705
7/21/79	29	24	●	4 Devotion		A&M 4771
9/6/80	28	28		5 Shine On		A&M 4819
11/28/81+	83	12		6 Love Magic		A&M 4881

L'TRIMM
Female hip-hop duo based in Miami, Florida: Rachel "Tigra" Rougemont and Elana "Bunny" Cager.

11/5/88	132	16		1 Grab It!		Atlantic 81925

LUBOFF, Norman, Choir
Born on 5/14/1917 in Chicago, Illinois. Died of cancer on 9/22/1987 (age 70). Composer/conductor.   **1950s: #29**

10/15/55	14	2		1 Songs Of The West		Columbia 657
				EP: Columbia B-2003 (#14); LP: Columbia CL-657 (#15)		
7/14/56	19	2		2 Songs Of The South		Columbia 860
5/27/57	19	4		3 Calypso Holiday		Columbia 1000
1/13/58	22	1		4 Songs Of Christmas	[X]	Columbia 926
				Christmas charts: 57/'65, and /'66		
12/19/64	28^X	2		5 Christmas With The Norman Luboff Choir	[X]	RCA Victor 2941

LUCAS
Born Lucas Secon in 1970 in Copenhagen, Denmark. Male rapper/producer.

10/22/94	183	4		1 Lucacentric		Big Beat 92467

LUCAS, Carrie
Born in Los Angeles, California. R&B singer.

4/23/77	183	5		1 Simply Carrie		Soul Train 2220
5/19/79	119	10		2 Carrie Lucas In Danceland		Solar 3219
1/31/81	185	3		3 Portrait Of Carrie		Solar 3579
9/11/82	180	3		4 Still In Love		Solar 60008

LUCERO
Country-punk band from Memphis, Tennessee: Ben Nichols (vocals, guitar), Brian Venable (guitar), John Stubblefield (bass) and Roy Berry (drums).

10/24/09	114	1		1 1372 Overton Park		Universal Rep. 013413

LUCIEN, Jon
Born on 1/8/1942 in St. Thomas, Virgin Islands. Died of respiratory failure on 8/18/2007 (age 65). R&B singer.

12/27/75	203	2		1 Song For My Lady		Columbia 33544

LUCIFER'S FRIEND
Rock band from Germany: John Lawton (vocal), Peter Hesslein (guitar), Peter Hecht (keyboards), Dieter Horns (bass) and Joachim Rietenbach (drums).

11/10/73	221	2		1 Lucifer's Friend		Billingsgate 1002
4/19/75	205	1		2 ...Where The Groupies Killed The Blues		Passport 98008

LUCY PEARL
All-star R&B trio: **Raphael Saadiq** (of **Tony Toni Tone**), Dawn Robinson (of **En Vogue**) and Ali Shaheed Muhammad (of **A Tribe Called Quest**). Joi replaced Robinson in 2001. Robinson married Andre Allen (of IV Xample) in May 2003.

6/10/00	26	21	●	1 Lucy Pearl		Pookie 78059

LUDACRIS
Born Christopher Bridges on 9/11/1977 in Champaign, Illinois; raised in Atlanta, Georgia. Male rapper/songwriter/actor. Appeared in the movies *The Wash*, *2 Fast 2 Furious*, *Hustle & Flow* and *Crash*.   **2000s: #39 / All-Time: #461**

10/7/00	179	2		1 Ludacris Presents Incognegro		DTP 911
11/4/00	4	55	▲^{3}	2 Back For The First Time		DTP 548138
12/15/01	3^3	59	▲^{3}	3 Word Of Mouf		DTP 586446
10/25/03	❶^1	45	▲^{2}	4 Chicken*N*Beer		DTP 000930
12/25/04	❶^1	42	▲^{2}	5 The Red Light District		DTP 003483
12/31/05	11	21	●	6 Ludacris Presents Disturbing Tha Peace		DTP 005786
10/14/06	❶^1	32	▲	7 Release Therapy		DTP 007224
12/13/08	5	23	●	8 Theater Of The Mind		DTP 012020

LUDO
Alternative-rock band from St. Louis, Missouri: Andrew Volpe (vocals, guitar), Tim Ferrell (guitar), Tim Convy (keyboards), Adam Brooks (bass) and Matt Palermo (drums).

8/16/08	166	2		1 You're Awful, I Love You		Redbird 009497

LUHRMANN, Baz
Born Bazmark Luhrmann on 9/17/1962 in New South Wales, Australia. Produced and directed the movies *Romeo & Juliet*, *Moulin Rouge* and *Australia*.

3/27/99	24	14	●	1 Something For Everybody		Capitol 57636

LUKE
Born Luther Campbell on 12/22/1960 in Miami, Florida. Male rapper. Leader of **The 2 Live Crew** until 1996.

DEBUT	PEAK	WKS			Label & Number
2/29/92	52	17		1 I Got Shit On My Mind	Luke 91830
6/26/93	54	11		2 In The Nude	Luke 200
7/30/94	174	3		3 Freak For Life 6996	Luke 6996
6/1/96	51	11		4 Uncle Luke	Luke 161000
4/1/00	140	2		5 Luke's Freak Fest 2000	Luke 1876
4/28/01	149	4		6 Something Nasty	Luke 8250
				UNCLE LUKE	

LULU
Born Marie Lawrie on 11/3/1948 in Glasgow, Scotland. Pop singer/actress. Married to Maurice Gibb (of the **Bee Gees**) from 1969-73. Appeared in the 1967 movie *To Sir With Love*.

DEBUT	PEAK	WKS			Label & Number
11/11/67	24	20		1 To Sir With Love	Epic 26339
2/21/70	88	14		2 New Routes	Atco 310
9/26/81	126	10		3 Lulu	Alfa 11006

LUMAN, Bob
Born on 4/15/1937 in Blackjack, Texas; raised in Nacogdoches, Texas. Died on 12/27/1978 (age 41). Country-rockabilly singer/songwriter/guitarist.

AWARD: OPRY: 1965

~ ~ ~ ~ ~ ~ ~ ~ ~ ~ ~   *NON-CHARTED ALBUM*   ~ ~ ~ ~ ~ ~ ~ ~ ~ ~ ~

1960 **Let's Think About Livin'**

LUMIDEE
Born Lumiana Cedeno on 8/24/1984 in Harlem, New York (Puerto Rican parents). Female singer/rapper/songwriter.

DEBUT	PEAK	WKS			Label & Number
7/12/03	22	11		1 Almost Famous	Straight Face 000681
5/5/07	44	3		2 Unexpected	TVT 2900

LUNIZ
Rap duo from Oakland, California: Jarold "**Yukmouth**" Ellis and Garrick "Knumskull" Husband.

DEBUT	PEAK	WKS			Label & Number
7/22/95	20	31	▲	1 Operation Stackola	Noo Trybe 40523
11/29/97	34	11		2 Lunitik Muzik	Noo Trybe 44966

LUNY TUNES
Reggaeton production duo from Puerto Rico: Francisco Saldana and Victor Cabrera.

DEBUT	PEAK	WKS			Label & Number
4/2/05	68	19	●	1 Mas Flow 2 .... [F]	Mas Flow 230007
10/14/06	30	12		2 Mas Flow: Los Benjamins .... [L]	Mas Flow 230013
				LUNY TUNES & TAINY	

LUSCIOUS JACKSON
Female pop-rock band from Manhattan, New York: Jill Cunniff (vocals, bass), Gabrielle Glaser (vocals, guitar), Vivian Trimble (keyboards) and Kate Schellenbach (drums). Trimble left in 1998. Group named after former NBA player Lucious Jackson (played for the Philadelphia 76ers from 1964-72).

DEBUT	PEAK	WKS			Label & Number
9/10/94	114	4		1 Natural Ingredients	Grand Royal 28356
11/16/96+	72	32		2 Fever In Fever Out	Grand Royal 35534
7/17/99	102	6		3 Electric Honey	Grand Royal 96084

LUSH
Rock band from London, England: Miki Berenyi (vocals, guitar), Emma Anderson (guitar), Philip King (bass) and Chris Acland (drums). Acland committed suicide on 10/17/1996 (age 30).

DEBUT	PEAK	WKS			Label & Number
7/2/94	195	1		1 Split	4 A D 45578
3/23/96	189	1		2 Lovelife	4 A D 46170

LUV YOU MADLY ORCHESTRA
Disco studio group assembled by producer Steve James.

DEBUT	PEAK	WKS			Label & Number
9/2/78	207	1		1 Luv You Madly Orchestra	Salsoul 8507

LYMAN, Arthur
Born on 2/2/1932 in Kauai, Hawaii. Died of cancer on 2/24/2002 (age 70). Played vibraphone, guitar, piano and drums. Formerly with **Martin Denny**.

DEBUT	PEAK	WKS			Label & Number
5/12/58+	6	62		1 Taboo .... [I]	HiFi 806
7/24/61	10	30		2 Yellow Bird .... [I]	HiFi 1004
3/30/63	36	6		3 I Wish You Love .... [I]	HiFi 1009

LYMON, Frankie, and The Teenagers
Black doo-wop group from the Bronx, New York. Lead singer Lymon was born on 9/30/1942; died of a drug overdose on 2/27/1968 (age 25). Other members included Herman Santiago, Jimmy Merchant, Joe Negroni (died on 9/5/1978, age 37) and Sherman Garnes (died on 2/26/1977, age 36). Group appeared in the movies *Rock, Rock, Rock* and *Mister Rock 'n' Roll*.

AWARD: R&R Hall of Fame: 1993

DEBUT	PEAK	WKS			Label & Number
1/19/57	19	1		1 The Teenagers Featuring Frankie Lymon	Gee 701

LYNCH, George
Born on 9/28/1954 in Spokane, Washington; raised in Sacramento, California. Hard-rock guitarist. Member of **Dokken** and **Lynch Mob**.

DEBUT	PEAK	WKS			Label & Number
8/21/93	137	1		1 Sacred Groove	Elektra 61422

LYNCH, Ray
Born on 7/3/1943 in Utah; raised in Texas. New Age pianist.

6/24/89	197	2		1 No Blue Thing .... [I]		Music West 103

LYNCH, Stephen
Born on 7/28/1971 in Abington, Pennsylvania; raised in Saginaw, Michigan. Comedic singer/songwriter/guitarist.

10/22/05	129	1	1 The Craig Machine .... [L-N]	What Are? 61006
4/11/09	152	1	2 3 Balloons .... [N]	What Are? 61011

LYNCH MOB
Hard-rock band formed in Los Angeles, California: **George Lynch** (guitar), Oni Logan (vocals), Anthony Esposito (bass) and Mick Brown (drums). Lynch and Brown were members of **Dokken**.

11/10/90	46	23	1 Wicked Sensation	Elektra 60954
5/16/92	56	9	2 Lynch Mob	Elektra 61322

LYNN, Barbara
Born Barbara Lynn Ozen on 1/16/1942 in Beaumont, Texas. R&B singer/songwriter/guitarist.

~ ~ ~ ~ ~ ~ ~ ~ ~ ~ **NON-CHARTED ALBUM** ~ ~ ~ ~ ~ ~ ~ ~ ~ ~
1962 **You'll Lose A Good Thing**

LYNN, Cheryl
Born on 3/11/1957 in Los Angeles, California. R&B-disco singer. Discovered on TV's *The Gong Show*.

11/18/78+	23	30	● 1 Cheryl Lynn	Columbia 35486
1/19/80	167	4	2 In Love...	Columbia 36145
7/11/81	104	13	3 In The Night	Columbia 37034
7/17/82	133	20	4 Instant Love	Columbia 38057
4/28/84	161	5	5 Preppie	Columbia 38961
7/27/85	202	5	6 It's Gonna Be Right...	Columbia 40024

LYNN, Loretta
Born Loretta Webb on 4/14/1935 in Butcher Holler, Kentucky. Country singer/songwriter/guitarist. Sister of **Crystal Gayle**. The 1980 movie *Coal Miner's Daughter* was based on Loretta's autobiography.
AWARDS: Grammy: Lifetime Achievement 2010 ★ C&W Hall of Fame: 1988 ★ CMA: Female Vocalist 1967, 1972 & 1973 / Entertainer 1972 / Vocal Duo (w/ Conway Twitty) 1972, 1973, 1974 & 1975 ★ OPRY: 1962

3/4/67	140	9	1 You Ain't Woman Enough	Decca 74783
4/8/67	80	20	● 2 Don't Come Home A Drinkin'	Decca 74842
12/23/67	103^X	2	3 Country Christmas .... [X]	Decca 74817
4/5/69	168	5	4 Your Squaw Is On The Warpath	Decca 75084
8/9/69	148	4	5 Woman Of The World / To Make A Man	Decca 75113
2/28/70	146	11	6 Wings Upon Your Horns	Decca 75163
2/13/71	81	17	● 7 Coal Miner's Daughter	Decca 75253
3/13/71	78	14	● 8 We Only Make Believe	Decca 75251
			CONWAY TWITTY & LORETTA LYNN	
6/26/71	110	7	9 I Wanna Be Free	Decca 75282
3/4/72	106	13	● 10 Lead Me On	Decca 75326
			CONWAY TWITTY & LORETTA LYNN	
4/8/72	109	9	11 One's On The Way..	Decca 75334
8/25/73	153	9	12 Louisiana Woman, Mississippi Man.......................................	MCA 335
			CONWAY TWITTY & LORETTA LYNN	
9/22/73	183	2	13 Love Is The Foundation	MCA 355
4/19/75	182	2	14 Back To The Country	MCA 471
11/20/93	42	16	● 15 Honky Tonk Angels...	Columbia 53414
			DOLLY PARTON, LORETTA LYNN, TAMMY WYNETTE	
5/15/04	24	15	16 Van Lear Rose	Interscope 002513

Grammy: Country Album

~ ~ ~ ~ ~ ~ ~ ~ ~ ~ **NON-CHARTED ALBUM** ~ ~ ~ ~ ~ ~ ~ ~ ~ ~
2002 **All Time Greatest Hits**
RS500 #485

LYNNE, Gloria
Born Gloria Wilson on 11/23/1931 in Harlem, New York. Black jazz-styled singer.

9/18/61	51	13	1 I'm Glad There Is You..	Everest 5126
10/16/61	101	7	2 He Needs Me..	Everest 5128
10/30/61	57	18	3 This Little Boy Of Mine	Everest 5131
4/7/62	58	22	4 Gloria Lynne At Basin Street East .... [L]	Everest 5137
2/9/63	39	27	5 Gloria Lynne At The Las Vegas Thunderbird .... [L]	Everest 5208
9/21/63+	27	22	6 Gloria, Marty & Strings	Everest 5220
6/6/64	43	19	7 I Wish You Love	Everest 5226
6/5/65	82	10	8 Soul Serenade	Fontana 27541

LYNNE, Jeff
Born on 12/30/1947 in Birmingham, England. Leader of **Electric Light Orchestra** and **The Move**. Otis Wilbury of the **Traveling Wilburys**. Production work for **George Harrison**, **Roy Orbison**, **Tom Petty** and **Del Shannon**.

6/30/90	83	9	1 Armchair Theatre	Reprise 26184

LYNNE, Rockie
Born Rockie Lynne Rash on 11/14/1964 in Statesville, North Carolina; later based in Coon Rapids, Minnesota. Male country singer/songwriter.

5/20/06	163	1		1 Rockie Lynne		Universal South 005363

LYNNE, Shelby
Born Shelby Lynn Moorer on 10/22/1968 in Quantico, Virginia; raised in Jackson, Alabama. Female singer. Played Carrie Cash in the 2005 movie *Walk The Line*.

AWARD: Grammy: Best New Artist 2000

3/10/01	165	1		1 I Am Shelby Lynne		Island 546177
12/1/01	109	1		2 Love, Shelby		Island 586436
10/4/03	160	1		3 Identity Crisis		Capitol 90508
2/16/08	41	8		4 Just A Little Lovin'		Lost Highway 009789

LYNYRD SKYNYRD   All-Time: #104

Southern-rock band formed in Jacksonville, Florida: Ronnie Van Zant (vocals; born on 1/15/1948; died in a plane crash on 10/20/1977, age 29), Allen Collins (guitar; born on 7/19/1952; died of pneumonia on 1/23/1990, age 37), Gary Rossington (guitar; born on 12/4/1951), Ed King (guitar; born on 9/14/1949), Billy Powell (keyboards; born on 6/3/1952; died on 1/27/2009, age 56), Leon Wilkeson (bass; born on 4/2/1952; died on 7/27/2001, age 49) and Robert Burns (drums). King was a member of **Strawberry Alarm Clock**. Group named after their gym teacher Leonard Skinner. Artemus Pyle (born on 7/15/1948) replaced Burns in 1975. Steve Gaines (born on 9/14/1949; died in a plane crash on 10/20/1977, age 28) replaced King in 1976. Steve's sister, Cassie Gaines (born on 1/9/1948; died in a plane crash on 10/20/1977, age 29), joined as backup singer in 1976. Infamous plane crash occurred on 10/20/1977 near Gillsburg, Mississippi. Gary and Allen formed the **Rossington Collins Band** in 1980; split in 1982. Collins was paralyzed in a car crash in 1986. Rossington and vocalist **Johnny Van Zant** (the younger brother of Ronnie and lead singer of **38 Special**, Donnie Van Zant) regrouped with old and new band members for the 1987 Lynyrd Skynyrd Tribute Tour. Rossington, Van Zant, Pyle, Wilkeson, King, Powell regrouped in 1991 with Randall Hall (guitar) and Custer (drums; **Little America**). Pyle left by 1993; replaced by Mike Estes. Custer left by 1994 and Owen Hale joined. Rickey Medlocke (of **Blackfoot**) joined as a guitarist in 1995. Guitarist Hughie Thomasson (of **The Outlaws**) joined in 1996. Also see **Various Artists Compilations:** *Skynyrd Frynds*.

AWARD: R&R Hall of Fame: 2006

9/22/73+	27	79	▲²	1 Lynyrd Skynyrd (pronounced leh-nerd skin-nerd)	Cat:#9/216	MCA/Sounds 363
				RS500 #401		
5/4/74	12	45	▲²	2 Second Helping	Cat:#38/18	MCA/Sounds 413
4/12/75	9	20	▲	3 Nuthin' Fancy		MCA 2137
2/21/76	20	16	●	4 Gimme Back My Bullets		MCA 2170
11/5/77	5	34	▲²	5 Street Survivors	Cat:#34/28	MCA 3029
				album released 3 days before the plane crash; original cover pictured the group engulfed in flames; after the crash, MCA issued a new cover omitting the flames		
9/23/78	15	18	▲	6 Skynyrd's First And...Last	[E]	MCA 3047
				recordings from 1970-72		
6/29/91	64	16		7 Lynyrd Skynyrd 1991		Atlantic 82258
3/6/93	64	7		8 The Last Rebel		Atlantic 82447
8/27/94	115	4		9 Endangered Species		Capricorn 42028
5/17/97	97	6		10 Twenty		CMC Int'l. 86211
8/28/99	96	2		11 Edge Of Forever		CMC Int'l. 86272
6/7/03	30	11		12 Vicious Cycle		Sanctuary 84607
10/17/09	18	8		13 God & Guns		Loud & Proud 617859
				GREATEST HITS & COMPILATIONS:		
12/15/79+	12	65	▲³	14 Gold & Platinum		MCA 11008 [2]
11/20/82	171	7		15 Best Of The Rest		MCA 5370
7/27/91+	11ᶜ	198	▲⁵	16 Skynyrd's Innyrds/Their Greatest Hits		MCA 42293
				first released in 1989		
6/12/99+	146	27	▲²	17 The Best Of Lynyrd Skynyrd - 20th Century Masters - The Millennium Collection	Cat:#6/117	MCA 11941
4/13/02+	11ᶜ	174	▲	18 All Time Greatest Hits		MCA 112229
				first released in 2000		
8/30/03	16	16	▲	19 Thyrty - The 30th Anniversary Collection		UTV 000284 [2]
				LIVE ALBUMS:		
10/2/76	9	43	▲³	20 One More From The Road		MCA 6001 [2]
				recorded July 1976 at the Fabulous Fox Theatre in Atlanta, Georgia		
10/10/87	41	17	●	21 Legend		MCA 42084
				live concert versions of previously unreleased material featuring the vocals of the late Ronnie Van Zant		
4/16/88	68	11		22 Southern By The Grace Of God/Lynyrd Skynyrd Tribute Tour - 1987		MCA 8027 [2]

LYRICS BORN
Born Tsutomu "Tom" Shimura in 1972 in Tokyo, Japan; raised in Berkeley, California. Male rapper.

5/10/08	192	1		1 Everywhere At Once		Anti 86804

LYTLE, Johnny
Born on 10/13/1932 in Springfield, Ohio. Died of kidney failure on 12/15/1995 (age 63). Jazz vibraphonist.

2/26/66	141	2		1 The Village Caller!	[I]	Riverside 480

LYTTLE, Kevin
Born on 9/14/1976 in St. Vincent, West Indies. Reggae-styled singer.

8/14/04	8	12	●	1 Kevin Lyttle		Atlantic 83730

M

M
Born Robin Scott on 4/1/1947 in London, England. Male new-wave singer.

DEBUT	PEAK	WKS	RIAA	Artist / Album Title	Catalog	Label & Number
12/22/79+	79	8		1 **New York-London-Paris-Munich**		Sire 6084

MA, Remy
Born Reminisce Smith on 5/30/1981 in the Bronx, New York. Female rapper/songwriter. Former member of **Terror Squad**. Convicted on assault and weapons charges in March 2008.

2/25/06	33	8		1 **There's Something About Remy: Based On A True Story**		SRC 005122

MA, Yo-Yo
Born on 10/7/1955 in Paris, France (Chinese parents). Classical cellist.

2/15/92	93	18	●	1 **Hush**		Sony 48177
				YO-YO MA & BOBBY McFERRIN		
4/22/00	170	2		2 **Appalachian Journey** .... [I]		Sony Classical 66782
				YO-YO MA / EDGAR MEYER / MARK O'CONNOR		
10/13/01	180	4		3 **Classic Yo-Yo** .... [K]		Sony Classical 89667
6/8/02	153	4		4 **Silk Road Journeys: When Strangers Meet** .... [I]		Sony Classical 89782
				YO-YO MA & THE SILK ROAD ENSEMBLE		
8/16/03	58	14		5 **Obrigado Brazil** .... [I]		Sony Classical 89935
				Grammy: Classical Crossover Album		
4/24/04	175	4		6 **Vivaldi's Cello** .... [I]		Sony Classical 90916
				YO-YO MA & TON KOOPMAN		
				Koopman conducts The Amsterdam Baroque Orchestra		
10/16/04	171	2		7 **Yo-Yo Ma Plays Ennio Morricone** .... [I]		Sony Classical 93456
1/27/07	79	5		8 **Appassionato**		Sony Classical 02668
8/18/07	152	1		9 **New Impossibilities** .... [I]		Sony Classical 10319
11/1/08	20	12		10 **Songs Of Joy & Peace** Cat:#33/3 [X]		Sony Classical 24414
				Christmas charts: 2/'08, 6/'09		
12/5/09+	116	5		11 **Songs Of Joy & Peace** .... [X-R]		Sony Classical 24414
				YO-YO MA & FRIENDS (above 2)		

MABLEY, Moms   **All-Time: #447**
Born Loretta Mary Aiken on 3/19/1894 in Brevard, North Carolina. Died on 5/23/1975 (age 81). Black stand-up comedian/actress. Adopted the stage name of Jackie Mabley from a former boyfriend. Appeared in the movies *Boarding House Blues*, *Emperor Jones* and *Amazing Grace*.

5/1/61	16	57		1 **Moms Mabley At The "UN"** [C]		Chess 1452
7/10/61	121	5		2 **Moms Mabley Onstage** .... [C]		Chess 1447
10/30/61	39	27		3 **Moms Mabley At The Playboy Club** .... [C]		Chess 1460
3/31/62	28	24		4 **Moms Mabley At Geneva Conference** .... [C]		Chess 1463
9/1/62	27	21		5 **Moms Mabley Breaks It Up** .... [C]		Chess 1472
1/12/63	19	18		6 **Young Men, Si - Old Men, No** .... [C]		Chess 1477
6/29/63	41	16		7 **I Got Somethin' To Tell You!** .... [C]		Chess 1479
1/4/64	134	5		8 **The Funny Sides Of Moms Mabley** .... [C]		Chess 1482
7/18/64	118	10		9 **Moms Wows** .... [C]		Chess 1486
				recorded 1961 at the Playboy Club in Chicago, Illinois		
2/29/64	48	24		10 **Out On A Limb** .... [C]		Mercury 60889
9/19/64	128	4		11 **Moms The Word** .... [C]		Mercury 60907
11/13/65	133	3		12 **Now Hear This** .... [C]		Mercury 61012
9/6/69	173	3		13 **The Youngest Teenager** .... [C]		Mercury 61229
				no track titles listed on albums #1-10 & 12-13		

MAC
Born McKinley Phipps on 7/30/1977 in New Orleans, Louisiana. Male rapper. Convicted of manslaughter in 2001; sentenced to 30 years in prison.

8/8/98	11	11		1 **Shell Shocked**		No Limit 50727
10/16/99	44	5		2 **World War III**		No Limit 50109

MacALPINE, Tony
Born on 8/29/1960 in Springfield, Massachusetts. Black hard-rock guitarist.

7/4/87	146	11		1 **Maximum Security** .... [I]		Squawk 832249

MAC BAND
R&B band from Flint, Michigan: brothers Charles, Derrick, Kelvin and Ray McCampbell (vocals), Mark Harper (guitar), Rodney Frazier (keyboards), Ray Flippin (bass) and Slye Fuller (drums).

7/23/88	109	14		1 **Mac Band**		MCA 42090

MacDONALD, Amy
Born on 8/25/1987 in Bishopbriggs, Scotland. Singer/songwriter/guitarist.

9/6/08	92	2		1 **This Is The Life**		Melodramatic 011335

MacDONALD, Jeanette, & Nelson Eddy
Top movie duo of the 1930s. MacDonald was born on 6/18/1903 in Philadelphia, Pennsylvania. Died of a heart attack on 1/14/1965 (age 61). Eddy was born on 6/29/1901 in Providence, Rhode Island. Died of a stroke on 3/6/1967 (age 65).

5/25/59	40	3	●	1 **Favorites In Hi-Fi**		RCA Victor 1738

Billboard			R I A A	ARTIST		
DEBUT	PEAK	WKS		Album Title	Catalog	Label & Number

MacDONALD, Ralph
Born on 3/15/1944 in Harlem, New York. Session percussionist/bandleader.

9/25/76	114	16		1 Sound Of A Drum .... [I]		Marlin 2202
3/4/78	57	17		2 The Path .... [I]		Marlin 2210
7/14/79	110	10		3 Counterpoint		Marlin 2229
10/13/84	108	10		4 Universal Rhythm		Polydor 823323

MacGREGOR, Byron
Born Gary Mack on 3/3/1948 in Calgary, Alberta, Canada. Died on 1/3/1995 (age 46). News director at CKLW-Detroit when he did the narration for "Americans."

2/23/74	208	2		1 Americans .... [T]		Westbound 1000

MacGREGOR, Mary
Born on 5/6/1948 in St. Paul, Minnesota. Pop singer.

1/15/77	17	19		1 Torn Between Two Lovers		Ariola America 50015

MACHINE HEAD
Heavy metal band from Oakland, California: Robb Flynn (vocals), Logan Mader (guitar), Adam Duce (bass) and Dave McClain (drums). Ahrue Luster replaced Mader in 1998.

4/12/97	138	1		1 The More Things Change...		Roadrunner 8860
8/28/99	88	2		2 The Burning Red		Roadrunner 8651
10/20/01	115	1		3 Supercharger		Roadrunner 618500
5/8/04	88	1		4 Through The Ashes Of Empires		Roadrunner 618363
4/14/07	54	2		5 The Blackening........................		Roadrunner 18016

MACHO
Disco studio group assembled by producer Mauro Malavasi.

10/7/78	101	14		1 I'm A Man		Prelude 12160

MACK, Craig
Born on 5/10/1971 in Trenton, New Jersey. Male rapper.

10/8/94	21	19	●	1 Project: Funk Da World		Bad Boy 73001
7/12/97	46	6		2 Operation: Get Down		Street Life 75521

MACK, Jimmie, And The Jumpers
Rock band formed in San Francisco, California: Jimmie Mack (vocals), Flasher (guitar), Gene Leppik (bass) and Steve Merola (drums).

1/17/81	208	2		1 Jimmie Mack And The Jumpers		RCA Victor 3698

MACK, Lonnie
Born Lonnie McIntosh on 7/18/1941 in Harrison, Indiana. Rockabilly guitarist.

11/30/63	103	9		1 The Wham Of That Memphis Man!		Fraternity 1014
6/15/85	130	21		2 Strike Like Lightning		Alligator 4739

MACK 10
Born Dedrick Rolison on 8/9/1971 in Inglewood, California. Male rapper. Married T-Boz (of **TLC**) on 8/19/2000.

7/8/95	33	19	●	1 Mack 10		Priority 53938
10/4/97	14	22	●	2 Based On A True Story		Priority 50675
10/24/98	15	8	●	3 The Recipe		Hoo Bangin' 53512
9/23/00	19	9		4 The Paper Route		Hoo-Bangin' 50148
12/22/01	48	12		5 Bang Or Ball		Cash Money 860968
8/9/03	105	1		6 Ghetto, Gutter & Gangsta		Hoo-Bangin' 970028
10/15/05	65	6		7 Hustla's Handbook		Hoo-Bangin' 73406
10/17/09	141	2		8 Soft White		Hoo-Bangin' 082509

MAC MALL
Born Jamal Rocker in Vallejo, California. Male rapper.

5/11/96	35	8		1 Untouchable		Relativity 1505
4/10/99	185	1		2 Illegal Business? 2000		Don't Give Up 2034

MADAME X
Female R&B vocal trio: Iris Parker, Valerie Victoria and Alisa Randolph.

10/10/87	162	5		1 Madame X		Atlantic 81774

MAD COBRA
Born Ewart Everton Brown on 3/31/1968 in Kingston, Jamaica; raised in St. Mary's, Jamaica. Reggae rapper.

11/7/92	125	15		1 Hard To Wet, Easy To Dry		Columbia 52751

MADD RAPPER, The
Born Deric Angelettie on 7/31/1968 in Brooklyn, New York. Male rapper/producer.

2/5/00	76	3		1 Tell Em Why U Madd		Crazy Cat 69832

MADE MEN
Male rap trio from New York: **Benzino**, Antonio Twice Thou and Mr. Gzus.

9/11/99	61	6		1 Classic Limited Edition		Restless 72981

Billboard			ARTIST		
DEBUT	PEAK	WKS	Album Title	Catalog	Label & Number

MADHOUSE
Jazz-fusion band from Minneapolis, Minnesota: **Prince** (guitar), Matt Fink (keyboards), Eric Leeds (sax), Levi Seacer Jr. (bass) and **Sheila E** (drums). All were members of Prince's band.

2/21/87	107	11	1 **8** .... [I]	Paisley Park 25545

MADINA LAKE
Hard-rock band from Chicago, Illinois: twin brothers Nathan Leone (vocals) and Matthew Leone (bass), with Mateo Camargo (guitar) and Dan Torelli (drums).

4/14/07	154	1	1 **From Them, Through Us, To You**	Roadrunner 18085
5/23/09	153	1	2 **Attics To Eden**	Roadrunner 617931

MAD LADS, The
R&B vocal group from Detroit, Michigan: Julius Green, Sam Nelson, Quincy Billops and Robert Phillips.

8/9/69	180	2	1 **The Mad, Mad, Mad, Mad, Mad Lads**	Volt 6005

MAD LION
Born Oswald Preist in London, England; raised in Jamaica. Male dancehall rapper. Later based in Brooklyn, New York.

5/27/95	114	4	1 **Real Ting**	Weeded 2006

MADNESS
Ska-rock band formed in London, England: Graham McPherson (vocals), Chris Foreman (guitar), Mike Barson (keyboards), Carl Smyth (trumpet), Lee Thompson (sax), Mark Bedford (bass) and Dan Woodgate (drums).

3/8/80	128	9	1 **One Step Beyond...**	Sire 6085
11/22/80	146	4	2 **Absolutely**	Sire 6094
4/30/83	41	29	3 **Madness**	Geffen 4003
3/17/84	109	8	4 **Keep Moving**	Geffen 4022

MADONNA   1980s: #21 / 1990s: #10 / 2000s: #34 / All-Time: #47
Born Madonna Louise Ciccone on 8/16/1958 in Bay City, Michigan. Moved to New York in the late 1970s. Performed with the Alvin Ailey dance troupe. Member of the **Breakfast Club** in 1979. Formed her own band, Emmy, in 1980. Married to actor Sean Penn from 1985-89. Acted in several movies. Appeared in Broadway's *Speed-The-Plow*. Released concert tour documentary movie *Truth Or Dare* in 1991. Married to British movie director Guy Ritchie from 2000-08.
AWARD: R&R Hall of Fame: 2008

9/3/83+	8	168	▲5	1 **Madonna**	Sire 23867
12/1/84+	**❶**3	108	▲10	2 **Like A Virgin**	Sire 25157
7/19/86	**❶**5	82	▲7	3 **True Blue**	Sire 25442
4/8/89	**❶**6	77	▲4	4 **Like A Prayer**	Sire 25844
				RS500 #237	
11/7/92	2¹	53	▲2	5 **Erotica**	Maverick 45154
11/12/94	3¹	48	▲3	6 **Bedtime Stories**	Maverick 45767
3/21/98	2²	78	▲4	7 **Ray Of Light** Cat:#50/1	Maverick 46847
				Grammy: Pop Vocal Album ★ RS500 #363	
10/7/00	**❶**1	55	▲3	8 **Music**	Maverick 47598
				RS500 #452	
5/10/03	**❶**1	14	▲	9 **American Life**	Maverick 48439
12/3/05	**❶**1	37	▲	10 **Confessions On A Dance Floor**	Warner 49460
5/17/08	**❶**1	30	●	11 **Hard Candy**	Warner 421372
				GREATEST HITS & COMPILATIONS:	
12/5/87+	14	22	▲	12 **You Can Dance**	Sire 25535
12/1/90+	2²	141	▲10	13 **The Immaculate Collection** Cat:#8/282	Sire 26440
				RS500 #278	
11/25/95	6	34	▲3	14 **Something To Remember**	Maverick 46100
12/1/01	7	18	▲	15 **GHV2: Greatest Hits Volume 2**	Maverick 48000
12/13/03	115	1		16 **Remixed & Revisited**	Maverick 48624
10/17/09	7	12	●	17 **Celebration**	Warner 289404 [2]
				LIVE ALBUMS:	
7/8/06	33	4		18 **I'm Going To Tell You A Secret**	Warner 49990
2/17/07	15	6		19 **The Confessions Tour**	Warner 44489
				SOUNDTRACKS:	
8/15/87	7	28	▲	20 **Who's That Girl**	Sire 25611
6/9/90	2³	25	▲2	21 **I'm Breathless**	Sire 26209
				songs from and songs inspired by the movie *Dick Tracy*	
11/30/96+	2²	30	▲4	22 **Evita**	Warner 46346 [2]
8/23/97	167	4		23 **Evita**	Warner 46692

MAD RIVER
Folk-rock band from Berkeley, California: David Robinson (guitar), Rick Bockner (guitar), Laurence Hammond (bass) and Greg Dewey (drums). All shared vocals.

8/9/69	192	2	1 **Paradise Bar And Grill**	Capitol 185

MADROX
Born Jamie Spaniolo on 11/5/1975 in Detroit, Michigan. White male rapper. One-half of **Twiztid** duo.

6/3/06	107	1	1 Phatso: The Album		Psychopathic 4058

MAD SEASON
All-star rock project: Layne Staley (vocals, guitar; **Alice In Chains**), Mike McCready (guitar; **Pearl Jam**), John Baker Saunders (bass) and Barrett Martin (drums; **Screaming Trees**). Band name is an English term for the time of year when psilocybin mushrooms are in full bloom. Staley died of a drug overdose on 4/5/2002 (age 34).

4/1/95	24	27	● 1 Above		Columbia 67057

MAD SKILLZ
Born David Lewis in Richmond, Virgina. Male rapper.

3/2/96	154	1	1 From Where???..		Big Beat 92623

MADURA
Folk-rock trio from Chicago, Illinois: Alan DeCarlo (vocals, guitar), David "Hawk" Wolinski (keyboards) and Ross Solomone (drums). DeCarlo and Wolinski were members of **Bangor Flying Circus**. Wolinski was also a member of **Rufus**.

10/30/71	186	2	1 Madura		Columbia 30794 [2]

MADVILLAIN
Collaboration between rapper Daniel "**MF Doom**" Dumile and producer/rapper Otis "Madlib" Jackson (recorded as **Quasimoto**).

4/10/04	179	1	1 Madvillainy...		Stones Throw 2065

MAE
Alternative-rock band from Norfolk, Virginia: Dave Gimenez (vocals, guitar), Zack Gehring (guitar), Rob Sweitzer (keyboards), Matt Padgett (bass) and Jacob Marshall (drums).

4/16/05	51	3	1 The Everglow..		Tooth & Nail 75394
9/1/07	40	2	2 Singularity...		Tooth & Nail 58112

MAGGARD, Cledus, And The Citizen's Band
Born Jay Huguely on 9/21/1947 in Quick Sand, Kentucky. Died on 12/13/2008 (age 61). Recorded "The White Knight" while working at the Leslie Advertising agency in Greenville, South Carolina.

3/13/76	135	8	1 The White Knight... [N]		Mercury 1072

MAGIC
Born Awood Johnson in New Orleans, Louisiana. Male rapper.

10/3/98	15	6	1 Skys The Limit...		No Limit 50017
9/18/99	53	7	2 Thuggin'		No Limit 50110
4/5/03	147	2	3 White Eyes		New No Limit 860993

MAGIC ORGAN, The
The Magic Organ is actually solo organist **Jerry Smith**.

5/6/72	135	7	1 Street Fair... [I]		Ranwood 8092

MAGNETIC FIELDS, The
Alternative-pop band from Boston, Massachusetts: Stephin Merritt (vocals, guitar), John Woo (banjo), Sam Davol (cello) and Claudia Gonson (drums).

5/22/04	152	1	1 i..		Nonesuch 79683
2/2/08	77	2	2 Distortion		Nonesuch 327036

MAGNIFICENT MEN, The
"Blue-eyed soul" band from Harrisburg, Pennsylvania: David Bupp (vocals), Terry Crousore (guitar), Tommy Hoover (organ), Tom Pane (saxophone), Buddy King (trumpet), Jimmy Seville (bass) and Bob "Puff" Angelucci (drums). Hoover died on 1/20/2008 (age 61).

4/8/67	171	2	1 The Magnificent Men...		Capitol 2678
7/29/67	89	9	2 The Magnificent Men "Live!" .... [L]		Capitol 2775

MAGOO — see TIMBALAND

MAHAL, Taj
Born Henry Fredericks on 5/17/1942 in Harlem, New York. Blues singer/guitarist.

2/22/69	160	14	1 The Natch'l Blues		Columbia 9698
10/11/69	85	9	2 Giant Step/De Ole Folks At Home..............................		Columbia 18 [2]
6/12/71	84	13	3 The Real Thing [L]		Columbia 30619 [2]
			recorded at the Fillmore East in New York City		
1/15/72	181	6	4 Happy Just To Be Like I Am		Columbia 30767
11/4/72	177	4	5 Recycling The Blues & Other Related Stuff .... [L]		Columbia 31605
12/1/73	190	5	6 Oooh So Good 'N Blues..		Columbia 32600
10/12/74	165	6	7 Mo' Roots		Columbia 33051
10/18/75	155	7	8 Music Keeps Me Together..		Columbia 33801
6/12/76	201	2	9 Satisfied 'N Tickled Too		Columbia 34103
1/29/77	134	8	10 Music Fuh Ya' (Musica Para Tu).................................		Warner 2994

MAHARIS, George
Born on 9/1/1928 in Astoria, New York. Actor/singer. Played "Buz Murdock" on TV's *Route 66*.

6/2/62	10	30	1 George Maharis Sings!		Epic 26001
9/8/62	32	24	2 Portrait In Music		Epic 26021
3/30/63	129	10	3 Just Turn Me Loose!		Epic 26037
9/14/63	77	7	4 Where Can You Go For A Broken Heart?		Epic 26064

				R I A A	ARTIST Album Title	Catalog	Label & Number
DEBUT	PEAK	WKS					

MAHAVISHNU ORCHESTRA — see McLAUGHLIN, John

MAHER, Matt
Born in St. John's, Newfoundland, Canada. Contemporary Christian singer/songwriter.

4/26/08	168	1	1 Empty & Beautiful		Essential 10857
10/10/09	128	1	2 Alive Again		Essential 10906

MAHOGANY RUSH
Hard-rock trio formed in Montreal, Quebec, Canada: **Frank Marino** (guitar, vocals), Paul Harwood (bass) and Jim Ayoub (drums). Frank's brother Vince Marino (guitar) joined in 1980.

8/24/74	74	15	1 Child Of The Novelty		20th Century 451
3/1/75	159	4	2 Maxoom		20th Century 463
6/21/75	84	13	3 Strange Universe		20th Century 482
6/5/76	175	3	4 Mahogany Rush IV		Columbia 34190

FRANK MARINO & MAHOGANY RUSH:

5/28/77	184	2	5 World Anthem		Columbia 34677
3/11/78	129	11	6 Frank Marino & Mahogany Rush Live	[L]	Columbia 35257
5/12/79	129	10	7 Tales Of The Unexpected	[L]	Columbia 35753
			side 1: studio; side 2: live		
3/8/80	88	9	8 What's Next		Columbia 36204
8/22/81	202	4	9 The Power Of Rock And Roll		Columbia 37099
8/14/82	185	4	10 Juggernaut		Columbia 38023
			FRANK MARINO (above 2)		

MAINE, The
Punk-rock band from Tempe, Arizona: John O'Callaghan (vocals), Jared Monaco (guitar), Kennedy Brock (guitar), Garrett Nickelsen (bass) and Patrick Kirch (drums).

7/26/08	40	5	1 Can't Stop Won't Stop		Fearless 30112
12/27/08	195	1	2 ...And A Happy New Year	[X-EP]	Fearless 30117
			Christmas chart: 39/'09		

MAIN INGREDIENT, The
R&B vocal trio formed in Harlem, New York: Donald McPherson (born on 7/9/1941; died of leukemia on 7/4/1971, age 29), Luther Simmons (born on 9/9/1942) and Tony Sylvester (born on 10/7/1941). Cuba Gooding (born on 4/27/1944; father of actor Cuba Gooding Jr.) replaced McPherson after his death. Sylvester died on 11/26/2006 (age 65).

8/22/70	200	1	1 The Main Ingredient L.T.D.		RCA Victor 4253
3/13/71	146	9	2 Tasteful Soul		RCA Victor 4412
10/2/71	176	5	3 Black Seeds		RCA Victor 4483
6/24/72	79	27	4 Bitter Sweet		RCA Victor 4677
5/5/73	132	13	5 Afrodisiac		RCA Victor 4834
10/20/73	205	13	6 Greatest Hits	[G]	RCA Victor 0314
3/9/74	52	31	7 Euphrates River		RCA Victor 0335
5/10/75	90	12	8 Rolling Down A Mountainside		RCA Victor 0644
12/13/75+	158	8	9 Shame On The World		RCA Victor 1003
9/4/76	201	7	10 Super Hits	[G]	RCA Victor 1858
3/5/77	177	3	11 Music Maximus		RCA Victor 1558
9/20/80	207	3	12 Ready For Love		RCA Victor 3641
			THE MAIN INGREDIENT Featuring Cuba Gooding		

MAINO
Born Jermaine Coleman on 2/21/1973 in Brooklyn, New York. Male rapper.

7/18/09	25	7	1 If Tomorrow Comes...		Hustle Hard 512968

MAJOR FIGGAS
Rap group from Philadelphia, Pennsylvania: female Bianca Jones with males Far'd Nasir, Maurice Brown, Michael Allen, Antonio Walker, Asa Burbage and Rennard East.

9/9/00	115	4	1 Figgas 4 Life		Ruffnation 47749

MAJOR LAZER
Hip-hop duo from Philadelphia, Pennsylvania: Thomas "Diplo" Pentz and David "Switch" Taylor.

7/4/09	169	1	1 Guns Don't Kill People...Lazers Do		Downtown 70088

MAJORS, The
R&B vocal group from Philadelphia, Pennsylvania: Ricky Cordo, Eugene Glass, Frank Troutt, Ronald Gathers and Idella Morris.

~ ~ ~ ~ ~ ~ ~ ~ ~ ~ ~ **NON-CHARTED ALBUM** ~ ~ ~ ~ ~ ~ ~ ~ ~ ~ ~ ~

1963 **Meet The Majors**

MAKAVELI — see 2 PAC

MAKEBA, Miriam
Born Zensi Miriam Makeba on 3/4/1932 in Johannesburg, South Africa. Died of a heart attack on 11/9/2008 (age 76). Married to **Hugh Masekela** from 1964-66.

11/16/63	86	10	1 The World Of Miriam Makeba		RCA Victor 2750
5/30/64	122	4	2 The Voice Of Africa		RCA Victor 2845
7/10/65	85	11	3 An Evening With Belafonte/Makeba		RCA Victor 3420
			HARRY BELAFONTE & MIRIAM MAKEBA		
			Grammy: Folk Album		

Billboard			R I A A	ARTIST		
DEBUT	PEAK	WKS		Album Title	Catalog	Label & Number

MAKEBA, Miriam — cont'd

11/18/67	182	4		4 Miriam Makeba In Concert! .... [L]		Reprise 6253
				recorded at Lincoln Center in New York City		
12/9/67+	74	22		5 Pata Pata		Reprise 6274

MAKEM, Tommy — see CLANCY BROTHERS

MALICE
Hard-rock band from Los Angeles, California: James Neal (vocals), Jay Reynolds (guitar), Mick Zane (guitar), Mark Behn (bass) and Cliff Carothers (drums).

| 4/11/87 | 177 | 6 | | 1 License To Kill .... | | Atlantic 81714 |

MALICK, Peter
Born on 11/28/1951 in Brookline, Massachusetts. White blues guitarist.

| 7/26/03 | 54 | 11 | | 1 New York City .... | | Koch 8678 |
| | | | | THE PETER MALICK GROUP Featuring Norah Jones | | |

MALKMUS, Stephen
Born on 5/30/1966 in Santa Monica, California. Rock singer/songwriter/guitarist. Former member of **Pavement**.

3/3/01	124	2		1 Stephen Malkmus		Matador 444
4/5/03	97	2		2 Pig Lib		Matador 572
				STEPHEN MALKMUS & THE JICKS		
6/11/05	118	1		3 Face The Truth		Matador 650
3/22/08	64	4		4 Real Emotional Trash		Matador 772
				STEPHEN MALKMUS & THE JICKS		

MALMSTEEN, Yngwie J.
Born on 6/30/1963 in Stockholm, Sweden. Hard-rock guitarist. Formerly with **Alcatrazz**. Backed by band Rising Force: **Joe Lynn Turner** (vocals), Jens Johansson (keyboards) and Anders Johansson (drums).

5/4/85	60	43		1 Rising Force		Polydor 825324
9/7/85	52	28		2 Marching Out		Polydor 825733
				YNGWIE J. MALMSTEEN'S RISING FORCE (above 2)		
10/11/86	44	23		3 Trilogy		Polydor 831073
4/23/88	40	18		4 Odyssey		Polydor 835451
				YNGWIE J. MALMSTEEN'S RISING FORCE		
11/11/89	128	8		5 Trial By Fire: Live In Leningrad .... [L]		Polydor 839726
5/26/90	112	6		6 Eclipse		Polydor 843361
2/29/92	121	5		7 Fire And Ice		Elektra 61137

MALO
Latin rock band from San Francisco, California. Core members: Arcelio Garcia (vocals), **Jorge Santana** (guitar; brother of **Carlos Santana**), Richard Kermode (keyboards) and Pablo Tellez (bass). Malo is Spanish for "Bad." Also see **Santana Brothers**.

2/12/72	14	31		1 Malo		Warner 2584
11/11/72	62	14		2 Dos		Warner 2652
4/28/73	101	11		3 Evolution		Warner 2702
3/23/74	188	3		4 Ascencion		Warner 2769
6/12/82	210	1		5 Malo V		Traq 107

MALO, Raul
Born on 8/7/1965 in Miami, Florida. Male singer/songwriter/guitarist. Lead singer of **The Mavericks**.

| 10/20/07 | 11ˣ | 2 | | 1 Marshmallow World & Other Holiday Favorites .... [X] | | New Door 009528 |

MAMA CASS
Born Ellen Naomi Cohen on 9/19/1941 in Baltimore, Maryland. Died of a heart attack (despite rumors, she did not choke to death on a ham sandwich) on 7/29/1974 (age 32). Member of **The Mamas & The Papas**.

10/19/68	87	10		1 Dream A Little Dream		Dunhill/ABC 50040
7/5/69	91	14		2 Bubble Gum, Lemonade &....Something For Mama		Dunhill/ABC 50055
12/6/69+	169	6		3 Make Your Own Kind Of Music .... [R]		Dunhill/ABC 50071
				MAMA CASS ELLIOT		
				reissue of #2 above plus song "Make Your Own Kind Of Music"		
3/13/71	194	1		4 Mama's Big Ones .... [G]		Dunhill/ABC 50093
3/13/71	49	7		5 Dave Mason & Cass Elliot		Blue Thumb 25

MAMAS & THE PAPAS, The   **All-Time: #403**
Folk-pop group formed in Los Angeles, California: **John Phillips** (born on 8/30/1935; died of heart failure on 3/18/2001, age 65), Michelle Phillips (born on 6/4/1944), Denny Doherty (born on 11/29/1940; died on 1/19/2007, age 66) and **Mama Cass** Elliot (born on 9/19/1941; died of a heart attack on 7/29/1974, age 32). Disbanded in 1968; reunited briefly in 1971. John and Michelle were married from 1962-70; their daughter is Chynna Phillips of the **Wilson Phillips** trio. John is also the father of actress MacKenzie Phillips. Michelle Phillips later became a successful actress; briefly married to actor Dennis Hopper in 1970.
AWARD: R&R Hall of Fame: 1998

3/12/66	❶¹	105	●	1 If You Can Believe Your Eyes And Ears		Dunhill 50006
				RS500 #127		
10/1/66	4	76	●	2 The Mamas & The Papas		Dunhill 50010
3/18/67	2⁷	55	●	3 The Mamas & The Papas Deliver		Dunhill 50014
5/25/68	15	34		4 The Papas & The Mamas		Dunhill/ABC 50031
4/10/71	226	2		5 Monterey International Pop Festival .... [L]		Dunhill/ABC 50100
				recorded from 6/16 - 6/18/67 in Monterey, California		
11/6/71	84	8		6 People Like Us		Dunhill/ABC 50106

Billboard			R I A A	ARTIST		
DEBUT	PEAK	WKS		Album Title	Catalog	Label & Number

MAMAS & THE PAPAS, The — cont'd
GREATEST HITS & COMPILATIONS:

11/11/67	5	65	●	7 **Farewell To The First Golden Era**	Cat:#46/2	Dunhill/ABC 50025
9/28/68	53	13		8 **Golden Era, Vol. 2**		Dunhill/ABC 50038
9/27/69	61	26		9 **16 Of Their Greatest Hits**		Dunhill/ABC 50064
3/3/73	186	4		10 **20 Golden Hits**		Dunhill/ABC 50145 [2]

~ ~ ~ ~ ~ ~ ~ ~ ~ ~ **NON-CHARTED ALBUM** ~ ~ ~ ~ ~ ~ ~ ~ ~ ~
1998 **Greatest Hits**
RS500 #423

MAMA'S BOYS
Rock trio from Northern Ireland: brothers Pat McManus (guitar), John McManus (vocals, bass) and Tommy McManus (drums).

8/11/84	172	8	1 **Mama's Boys**		Jive 8214
6/15/85	151	6	2 **Power And Passion**		Jive 8285

MAN
Pub-rock band from Wales: Micky Jones (vocals, guitar), Deke Leonard (guitar), Martin Ace (bass) and Terry Williams (drums).

3/1/75	205	3	1 **Slow Motion**		United Artists 345

MANA
Latin rock band from Mexico: Fher Olvera (vocals), Sergio Vallin (guitar), Juan Calleros (bass) and Alex Gonzalez (drums).

11/1/97	67	4	▲	1 **Suenos Liquidos**	[F]	Warner Latina 20430
7/10/99	83	15	●	2 **MTV Unplugged**	[F-L]	Warner Latina 27864
9/7/02	22	11	●	3 **Revolucion De Amor**	[F]	Warner Latina 48566
12/6/03	181	1		4 **Eclipse**	[F]	Warner Latina 61046
9/9/06	4	36	●	5 **Amar Es Combatir**	[F]	Warner Latina 63661
5/17/08	30	13		6 **Arde El Cielo**	[F-L]	Warner Latina 481788

MANASSAS — see STILLS, Stephen

MANCHESTER, Melissa **All-Time: #424**
Born on 2/15/1951 in the Bronx, New York. Adult Contemporary singer/pianist/composer. Father was a bassoon player with the New York Metropolitan Opera Orchestra. She studied songwriting under **Paul Simon** at the University School of the Arts in the early 1970s. Former backup singer for **Bette Midler**.

6/23/73	156	13		1 **Home To Myself**		Bell 1123
5/4/74	159	5		2 **Bright Eyes**		Bell 1303
3/1/75	12	41	●	3 **Melissa**		Arista 4031
2/21/76	24	17		4 **Better Days & Happy Endings**		Arista 4067
11/20/76+	60	13		5 **Help Is On The Way**		Arista 4095
7/23/77	60	11		6 **Singin'...**		Arista 4136
12/9/78+	33	27		7 **Don't Cry Out Loud**		Arista 4186
11/3/79	63	21		8 **Melissa Manchester**		Arista 9506
9/13/80	68	11		9 **For The Working Girl**		Arista 9533
5/15/82	19	39		10 **Hey Ricky**		Arista 9574
2/26/83	43	21	●	11 **Greatest Hits**	[G]	Arista 9611
12/3/83	135	9		12 **Emergency**		Arista 8094
5/18/85	144	6		13 **Mathematics**		MCA 5587

MANCHESTER ORCHESTRA
Alternative-rock band from Atlanta, Georgia: Andy Hull (vocals, guitar), Robert McDowell (guitar), Chris Freeman (keyboards), Jonathan Corley (bass) and Len Clark (drums).

5/9/09	37	4	1 **Mean Everything To Nothing**		Favorite Gent. 35934

MANCHILD
R&B band from Indianapolis: Flash Ferrell (vocals), Kenneth Edmonds (guitar), Reggie Griffin (reeds), Daryl Simmons (percussion), Chuckie Bush (keyboards), Anthony Johnson (bass) and Robert Parson (drums). Edmonds later formed **The Deele** and recorded solo as **Babyface**.

10/15/77	154	6	1 **Power And Love**		Chi-Sound 765

MANCINI, Henry **1950s: #21 / 1960s: #11 / All-Time: #36**
Born Enrico Mancini on 4/16/1924 in Cleveland, Ohio; raised in Aliquippa, Pennsylvania. Died of cancer on 6/14/1994 (age 70). Leading movie and TV composer/arranger/conductor. Staff composer for Universal Pictures from 1952-58. Married Ginny O'Connor, an original member of **Mel Torme**'s Mel-Tones, on 9/13/1947.
AWARD: Grammy: Lifetime Achievement 1995

3/3/62	28	14		1 **Combo!**	[I]	RCA Victor 2258
				released in 1960		
5/8/61	28	26		2 **Mr. Lucky Goes Latin**	[I]	RCA Victor 2360
2/16/63	12	40		3 **Our Man In Hollywood**		RCA Victor 2604
6/29/63	5	22		4 **Uniquely Mancini**	[I]	RCA Victor 2692
8/1/64	15	19		5 **The Concert Sound Of Henry Mancini**		RCA Victor 2897
1/30/65	11	25		6 **Dear Heart And Other Songs About Love**		RCA Victor 2990

486

DEBUT	PEAK	WKS	R I A A	ARTIST Album Title	Catalog	Label & Number

MANCINI, Henry — cont'd

6/26/65	46	17		7 The Latin Sound Of Henry Mancini .... [I]		RCA Victor 3356
3/12/66	74	13		8 The Academy Award Songs		RCA Victor 6013 [2]
12/3/66+	12ˣ	12		9 A Merry Mancini Christmas .... [X]		RCA Victor 3612
				Christmas charts: 20/'66, 33/'67, 12/'70		
12/17/66+	121	19		10 Music Of Hawaii .... [I]		RCA Victor 3713
3/18/67	65	13		11 Mancini '67 .... [I]		RCA Victor 3694
12/9/67+	126	12		12 Encore! More Of The Concert Sound Of Henry Mancini .... [I]		RCA Victor 3887
5/3/69	5	42	●	13 A Warm Shade Of Ivory .... [I]		RCA Victor 4140
11/1/69	91	16		14 Six Hours Past Sunset .... [I]		RCA Victor 4239
4/25/70	111	17		15 Theme From "Z" And Other Film Music .... [I]		RCA Victor 4350
				Grammy: Instrumental Album		
12/19/70+	91	17		16 Mancini Country .... [I]		RCA Victor 4307
1/23/71	26	22		17 Mancini Plays The Theme From Love Story		RCA Victor 4466
7/31/71	85	11		18 Mancini Concert .... [I]		RCA Victor 4542
1/29/72	109	15		19 Big Screen - Little Screen		RCA Victor 4630
4/29/72	74	19		20 Brass On Ivory .... [I]		RCA Victor 4629
6/9/73	185	3		21 Brass, Ivory & Strings .... [I]		RCA Victor 0098
				HENRY MANCINI & DOC SEVERINSEN (above 2)		
9/23/72	195	5		22 The Mancini Generation .... [I]		RCA Victor 4689
2/14/76	159	6		23 Symphonic Soul .... [I]		RCA Victor 1025
6/11/77	126	8		24 Mancini's Angels .... [I]		RCA Victor 2290
1/10/87	197	2		25 The Hollywood Musicals		Columbia 40372
				JOHNNY MATHIS & HENRY MANCINI		

GREATEST HITS & COMPILATIONS:

8/8/64	42	35	●	26 The Best Of Mancini		RCA Victor 2693
9/26/70	196	2		27 This Is Henry Mancini		RCA Victor 6029 [2]
9/18/76	161	4		28 A Legendary Performer		RCA Victor 1843

SOUNDTRACKS:

2/9/59	❶¹⁰	119	●	29 The Music From Peter Gunn .... [I]		RCA Victor 1956
				Grammys: Album of the Year / Hall of Fame		
6/22/59	7	35		30 More Music From Peter Gunn .... [I]		RCA Victor 2040
3/28/60	2¹	70		31 Music From Mr. Lucky .... [I]		RCA Victor 2198
				Grammy: Pop Instrumental Album		
10/9/61+	❶¹²	96	●	32 Breakfast At Tiffany's .... [I]		RCA Victor 2362
				Grammys: Soundtrack Album / Pop Instrumental Album		
6/2/62	37	12		33 Experiment In Terror .... [I]		RCA Victor 2442
7/21/62	4	50		34 Hatari! .... [I]		RCA Victor 2559
12/28/63+	6	42		35 Charade .... [I]		RCA Victor 2755
4/11/64	8	88	●	36 The Pink Panther .... [I]		RCA Victor 2795
				Grammy: Hall of Fame		
10/2/65	63	22		37 The Great Race .... [I]		RCA Victor 3402
9/10/66	142	4		38 Arabesque .... [I]		RCA Victor 3623
9/10/66	148	2		39 What Did You Do In The War, Daddy? .... [I]		RCA Victor 3648
10/28/67	183	3		40 Two For The Road .... [I]		RCA Victor 3802
8/11/73	215	3		41 Oklahoma Crude .... [I]		RCA Victor 0271

MANCOW

Born Matthew Muller on 6/21/1966 in Kansas City, Missouri. Host of own syndicated morning radio show.

12/2/95	171	1		1 Box Of Sharpies .... [C]		Anon 7400
12/7/96	141	1		2 Fat Boy Pizza Breasts .... [C]		Anon 7500
				no track titles listed		
4/4/98	137	1		3 In The Kingdom Of The Blind The One Eyed Man Is King .... [C]		Anon 7700

MANDEL, Harvey

Born on 3/11/1945 in Detroit, Michigan. Blues-rock guitarist. Member of **Canned Heat** from 1969-74.

5/10/69	187	3		1 Righteous .... [I]		Philips 306
9/20/69	169	4		2 Cristo Redentor .... [I]		Philips 281
2/27/71	213	3		3 Baby Batter .... [I]		Janus 3017
7/22/72	198	3		4 The Snake .... [I]		Janus 3037

MANDEL, Howie

Born on 11/29/1955 in Toronto, Ontario, Canada. Stand-up comedian/actor. Played "Dr. Wayne Fiscus" on TV's *St. Elsewhere* (1982-88) and hosted the TV game show *Deal Or No Deal*.

| 6/21/86 | 148 | 6 | | 1 Fits Like a Glove .... [C] | | Warner 25427 |

MANDELL, Steve — see WEISSBERG, Eric

MANDISA

Born Mandisa Hundley on 10/2/1976 in Citrus Heights, California. Female gospel singer. Finalist on the fifth season of TV's *American Idol* in 2006.

8/18/07	43	7		1 True Beauty .... Cat:#29/1		Sparrow 85720
4/11/09	83	7		2 Freedom		Sparrow 26779
10/10/09	44ˣ	1		3 It's Christmas .... [X]		Sparrow 13780

MANDRE
Born Michael Andre Lewis in Omaha, Nebraska. R&B singer/songwriter/keyboardist/bassist. Member of **Maxayn**.

9/17/77	64	13		1 Mandre		Motown 886
4/22/78	201	13		2 Mandre Two		Motown 900
4/7/79	209	1		3 M3000		Motown 917

MANDRELL, Barbara
Born on 12/25/1948 in Houston, Texas; raised in Oceanside, California. Country singer. Host of own TV variety series from 1980-82.
AWARDS: C&W Hall of Fame: 2009 ★CMA: Female Vocalist 1979 & 1981 / Entertainer 1980 & 1981 ★ OPRY: 1972

2/24/79	170	4	●	1 The Best Of Barbara Mandrell [G]		ABC 1119
5/26/79	132	9		2 Moods		ABC 1088
10/13/79	166	5		3 Just For The Record		MCA 3165
9/27/80	175	6		4 Love Is Fair		MCA 5136
9/5/81	86	24	●	5 Barbara Mandrell Live [L]		MCA 5243
				recorded at the Roy Acuff Theater in Nashville, Tennessee		
5/29/82	153	6		6 In Black & White		MCA 5295
9/3/83	140	4		7 Spun Gold		MCA 5377
6/16/84	204	3		8 Clean Cut		MCA 5474
9/8/84	89	13		9 Meant For Each Other		MCA 5477
				BARBARA MANDRELL & LEE GREENWOOD		
12/15/84	8ˣ	2		10 Christmas At Our House [X]		MCA 5519
5/4/85	210	1		11 Greatest Hits [G]		MCA 5566

MANDRILL
Latin jazz-rock band from Brooklyn, New York: brothers Louis Wilson (trumpet), Richard Wilson (sax) and Carlos Wilson (flute). Omar Mesa (guitar), Claude Cave (keyboards), Fudgie Kae (bass) and Charlie Pardo (drums).

4/24/71	48	22		1 Mandrill		Polydor 4050
4/29/72	56	24		2 Mandrill Is		Polydor 5025
2/17/73	28	30		3 Composite Truth		Polydor 5043
10/13/73	82	15		4 Just Outside Of Town		Polydor 5059
7/26/75	194	2		5 The Best Of Mandrill [G]		Polydor 6047
4/26/75	92	14		6 Solid		United Artists 408
2/7/76	143	8		7 Beast From The East		United Artists 577
11/12/77	124	10		8 We Are One		Arista 4144
1/13/79	154	5		9 New Worlds		Arista 4195

MANFRED MANN
Born Manfred Lubowitz on 10/21/1940 in Johannesburg, South Africa. Formed pop-rock band in England: Mann (keyboards), Paul Jones (vocals), Michael Vickers (guitar), Tom McGuinness (bass) and Mike Hugg (drums). Mike D'Abo replaced Jones in 1967. McGuinness left to form **McGuinness Flint** in 1970. Manfred Mann formed his new Earth Band in 1971: Mann, Mick Rogers (vocals), Colin Pattenden (bass) and Chris Slade (drums). Rogers replaced by Chris Thompson (vocals, guitar) in 1976. Pattenden replaced by Pat King in June 1977. Thompson also recorded with own group **Night** in 1979. Lineup in 1979: Mann, Thompson, King, Steve Waller (guitar, vocals) and Geoff Britton (drums). King replaced by Matt Irving in 1981. Earth Band dissolved in 1986.

11/21/64+	35	18		1 The Manfred Mann Album		Ascot 16015
3/6/65	141	4		2 The Five Faces Of Manfred Mann		Ascot 16018
6/1/68	176	5		3 The Mighty Quinn		Mercury 61168
				MANFRED MANN'S EARTH BAND:		
2/26/72	138	6		4 Manfred Mann's Earth Band		Polydor 5015
6/23/73	196	2		5 Get Your Rocks Off		Polydor 5050
3/2/74	96	15		6 Solar Fire		Polydor 6019
11/30/74	157	3		7 The Good Earth		Warner 2826
9/13/75	120	10		8 Nightingales & Bombers		Warner 2877
9/25/76+	10	37	●	9 The Roaring Silence		Warner 2965
3/11/78	83	6		10 Watch		Warner 3157
5/12/79	144	13		11 Angel Station		Warner 3302
1/24/81	87	16		12 Chance		Warner 3498
1/28/84	40	21		13 Somewhere In Afrika		Arista 8194

MANGIONE, Chuck   All-Time: #307
Born on 11/29/1940 in Rochester, New York. Flugelhorn player/bandleader/composer. Recorded with older brother Gaspare ("Gap") as The Jazz Brothers for Riverside in 1960. To New York City in 1965; played with **Maynard Ferguson**, **Kai Winding**, and **Art Blakey**.

7/15/72	180	6		1 The Chuck Mangione Quartet [I]		Mercury 631
4/26/75	47	19	●	2 Chase The Clouds Away Cat:#9/2 [I]		A&M 4518
11/29/75+	68	15		3 Bellavia [I]		A&M 4557
11/20/76+	86	24		4 Main Squeeze [I]		A&M 4612
10/29/77+	2²	88	▲²	5 Feels So Good [I]		A&M 4658
9/23/78	14	44	●	6 Children Of Sanchez [I-S]		A&M 6700 [2]
				Grammy: Pop Instrumental Album		
2/23/80	8	23	●	7 Fun And Games [I]		A&M 3715
7/17/82	83	10		8 Love Notes [I]		Columbia 38101
1/22/83	202	3		9 70 Miles Young [I]		A&M 4911
6/25/83	154	7		10 Journey To A Rainbow [I]		Columbia 38686
9/15/84	148	8		11 Disguise [I]		Columbia 39479

MANGIONE, Chuck — cont'd

LIVE ALBUMS:

DEBUT	PEAK	WKS	RIAA	Album Title	Catalog	Label & Number
7/3/71	116	11		12 Friends & Love...A Chuck Mangione Concert	[I]	Mercury 800 [2]
11/20/71	194	4		13 Together: A New Chuck Mangione Concert	[I]	Mercury 7501 [2]
				above 2 with the Rochester Philharmonic Orchestra		
12/8/73+	157	12		14 Land Of Make Believe		Mercury 684
				with the Hamilton Philharmonic Orchestra		
12/6/75+	102	10		15 Encore/The Chuck Mangione Concerts	[K]	Mercury 1050
9/16/78	105	6		16 The Best Of Chuck Mangione	[K]	Mercury 8601 [2]
6/30/79	27	23		17 An Evening Of Magic - Chuck Mangione Live At The Hollywood Bowl	[I]	A&M 6701 [2]
5/16/81	55	15		18 Tarantella	[I]	A&M 6513 [2]

MANHATTANS, The

R&B vocal group from Jersey City, New Jersey: Gerald Alston (lead; born on 11/8/1942), Winfred "Blue" Lovett (bass; born on 11/16/1943), Edward "Sonny" Bivins (tenor; born on 1/15/1942), Kenneth "Wally" Kelly (tenor; born on 1/9/1943) and Richard Taylor (baritone; born in 1940; died on 12/7/1987, age 47). Taylor left in 1976.

DEBUT	PEAK	WKS	RIAA	Album Title	Catalog	Label & Number
8/11/73	150	8		1 There's No Me Without You		Columbia 32444
3/1/75	160	4		2 That's How Much I Love You		Columbia 33064
5/1/76	16	27	●	3 The Manhattans		Columbia 33820
2/26/77	68	20	●	4 It Feels So Good		Columbia 34450
3/4/78	78	12		5 There's No Good In Goodbye		Columbia 35252
4/14/79	141	7		6 Love Talk		Columbia 35693
4/19/80	24	26	●	7 After Midnight		Columbia 36411
12/13/80+	87	10		8 Manhattans Greatest Hits	[G]	Columbia 36861
8/8/81	86	10		9 Black Tie		Columbia 37156
8/6/83	104	8		10 Forever By Your Side		Columbia 38600
4/13/85	171	6		11 Too Hot To Stop It		Columbia 39277

MANHATTAN TRANSFER, The   All-Time: #398

Vocal harmony group formed in Manhattan, New York: Tim Hauser (born on 12/12/1941), Alan Paul (born on 11/23/1949), Janis Siegel (born on 7/23/1952) and Laurel Masse (born on 12/29/1951). Cheryl Bentyne (born on 1/17/1954) replaced Masse in 1979. Group hosted own TV variety show on CBS in 1975.

DEBUT	PEAK	WKS	RIAA	Album Title	Catalog	Label & Number
7/12/75	202	2		1 Jukin'	[E]	Capitol 11405
				THE MANHATTAN TRANSFER & GENE PISTILLI		
				recorded in 1971		
5/3/75	33	38	●	2 The Manhattan Transfer		Atlantic 18133
9/18/76	48	9		3 Coming Out		Atlantic 18183
2/18/78	66	10		4 Pastiche		Atlantic 19163
12/8/79+	55	37		5 Extensions		Atlantic 19258
6/13/81	22	27		6 Mecca For Moderns		Atlantic 16036
12/12/81+	103	11	▲	7 The Best Of The Manhattan Transfer	[G]	Atlantic 19319
10/8/83	52	27		8 Bodies And Souls		Atlantic 80104
1/5/85	127	11		9 Bop doo-wopp	[L]	Atlantic 81233
8/10/85	74	40		10 Vocalese		Atlantic 81266
				Grammy: Group Jazz Vocal		
5/30/87	187	3		11 Live	[L]	Atlantic 81723
				recorded in Toyko, Japan		
12/5/87+	96	19		12 Brasil		Atlantic 81803
				Grammy: Group Pop Vocal		
9/21/91	179	2		13 The Offbeat Of Avenues		Columbia 47079
12/12/92	120	4		14 The Christmas Album Cat:#35/4 [X]		Columbia 52968
				Christmas charts: 25/'92, 30/'93		
3/4/95	123	6		15 Tonin'		Atlantic 82661
9/2/95	157	1		16 The Very Best Of The Manhattan Transfer	[G]	Rhino 71560

MANILOW, Barry   1980s: #37 / 2000s: #33 / All-Time: #38

Born Barry Alan Pincus on 6/17/1943 in Brooklyn, New York. Pop singer/songwriter/pianist. Studied at New York's Juilliard School. Music director for the WCBS-TV series *Callback*. Worked at New York's Continental Baths bathhouse/nightclub in New York as **Bette Midler**'s accompanist in 1972; later produced her first two albums. First recorded solo as Featherbed. Wrote numerous commercial jingles in the 1970s.

DEBUT	PEAK	WKS	RIAA	Album Title	Catalog	Label & Number
12/29/73+	206	5		1 Barry Manilow		Bell 1129
8/2/75	28	51	●	2 Barry Manilow I	[R]	Arista 4007
				reissue of #1 above		
11/23/74+	9	58	▲	3 Barry Manilow II		Arista 4016
				first released on Bell 1314 in 1974		
11/8/75+	5	87	▲²	4 Tryin' To Get The Feeling		Arista 4060
8/21/76+	6	60	▲²	5 This One's For You		Arista 4090
2/25/78	3³	58	▲³	6 Even Now		Arista 4164
10/20/79	9	25	▲	7 One Voice		Arista 9505
12/13/80+	15	20	▲	8 Barry		Arista 9537
10/17/81	14	25	●	9 If I Should Love Again		Arista 9573

DEBUT	PEAK	WKS	RIAA	ARTIST / Album Title	Catalog	Label & Number
				MANILOW, Barry — cont'd		
9/25/82	69	9		10 Oh, Julie! .... [EP]		Arista 2500
12/18/82+	32	27	●	11 Here Comes The Night		Arista 9610
12/15/84+	28	20	●	12 2:00 AM Paradise Cafe		Arista 8254
11/30/85	42	24		13 Manilow		RCA Victor 7044
12/12/87+	70	21		14 Swing Street		Arista 8527
5/20/89	64	16		15 Barry Manilow		Arista 8570
10/12/91	68	8		16 Showstoppers		Arista 18687
10/29/94	59	21	●	17 Singin' With The Big Bands		Arista 18771
12/7/96	82	11		18 Summer Of '78		Arista 18809
11/28/98	122	7		19 Manilow Sings Sinatra		Arista 19033
12/1/01	90	3		20 Here At The Mayflower		Concord 2102
10/16/04	47	8		21 Manilow Scores: Songs From Copacabana And Harmony		Concord 2251
2/18/06	❶¹	25	▲	22 The Greatest Songs Of The Fifties		Arista 74509
11/18/06	2¹	12	●	23 The Greatest Songs Of The Sixties		Arista 82640
10/6/07	4	15		24 The Greatest Songs Of The Seventies		Arista 10034
12/13/08	14	6		25 The Greatest Songs Of The Eighties		Arista 37161
				CHRISTMAS ALBUMS:		
12/1/90	40	8	▲	26 Because It's Christmas .... Cat:#14/8		Arista 8644
				Christmas charts: 1/'90, 8/'91, 28/'92, 41/'03, 44/'04		
11/30/02	55	7	●	27 A Christmas Gift Of Love .... Cat:#31/4		Columbia 86976
				Christmas charts: 6/'02, 21/'03		
12/5/09	127	4		28 In The Swing Of Christmas		Arista 57490
				Christmas chart: 11/'09		
				GREATEST HITS & COMPILATIONS:		
12/2/78+	7	75	▲³	29 Greatest Hits		Arista 8601 [2]
12/3/83+	30	19	●	30 Barry Manilow/Greatest Hits, Vol. II		Arista 8102
6/29/85	100	12	●	31 The Manilow Collection - Twenty Classic Hits		Arista 8274
1/2/93	182	1	●	32 The Complete Collection And Then Some...		Arista 18714 [4]
2/23/02	3¹	43	▲²	33 Ultimate Manilow .... Cat:#2¹/68		Arista 10600
				LIVE ALBUMS:		
5/28/77	❶¹	67	▲³	34 Barry Manilow/Live		Arista 8500 [2]
6/30/90	196	1		35 Live On Broadway		Arista 8638
				recorded on 12/3/1989 at the Chicago Theatre		
4/24/04	27	6	●	36 2Nights Live!		Stiletto 59478 [2]

MAN MAN
Alternative-rock band from Philadelphia, Pennsylvania: Ryan Kattner (vocals, keyboards), Russell Higbee (guitar), Jamey Robinson (bass) and Christopher Powell (drums).

| 4/26/08 | 186 | 1 | | 1 Rabbit Habits .... | | Anti 86942 |

MANN, Aimee
Born on 9/8/1960 in Richmond, Virginia. Adult Alternative singer/songwriter. Former lead singer of 'Til Tuesday. Married **Michael Penn** on 12/29/1997.

5/29/93	127	4		1 Whatever		Imago 21017
2/17/96	82	4		2 I'm With Stupid		DGC 24951
1/22/00	58	17	●	3 Magnolia .... [S]		Reprise 47583
5/20/00	134	4		4 Bachelor No. 2 Or, The Last Remains Of The Dodo		SuperEgo 002
9/14/02	35	8		5 Lost In Space		SuperEgo 007
5/21/05	60	3		6 The Forgotten Arm		SuperEgo 182
6/21/08	32	3		7 @#%&*! Smilers		SuperEgo 026

MANN, Barry
Born Barry Iberman on 2/9/1939 in Brooklyn, New York. Pop singer/songwriter. One of pop music's most prolific songwriters in a partnership with wife Cynthia Weil (married in August 1961).

| 2/12/72 | 213 | 1 | | 1 Lay It All Out .... | | New Design 30876 |

~ ~ ~ ~ ~ ~ ~ ~ ~ ~ ~ **NON-CHARTED ALBUM** ~ ~ ~ ~ ~ ~ ~ ~ ~ ~ ~
1963 Who Put The Bomp In The Bomp Bomp Bomp

MANN, Carl
Born on 8/24/1942 in Huntingdon, Tennessee. Rockabilly singer/pianist. Member of the **Carl Perkins** band from 1962-64.

~ ~ ~ ~ ~ ~ ~ ~ ~ ~ ~ **NON-CHARTED ALBUM** ~ ~ ~ ~ ~ ~ ~ ~ ~ ~ ~
1960 Like Mann

MANN, Herbie   **All-Time: #267**
Born Herbert Solomon on 4/16/1930 in Brooklyn, New York. Died of cancer on 7/1/2003 (age 73). Jazz flutist. First recorded with Mat Mathews Quintet for Brunswick in 1953. First recorded as a solo for Bethlehem in 1954. Also see **Family Of Mann**.

11/24/62	100	4		1 Right Now .... [I]		Atlantic 1384
3/2/63	86	7		2 Do The Bossa Nova With Herbie Mann .... [I]		Atlantic 1397
10/8/66	139	6		3 Our Mann Flute .... [I]		Atlantic 1464
2/3/68	151	12		4 Glory Of Love .... [I]		A&M 3003
5/24/69	20	44		5 Memphis Underground .... [I]		Atlantic 1522
3/7/70	184	3		6 Stone Flute .... [I]		Embryo 520
3/28/70	189	2		7 The Best Of Herbie Mann .... [G-I]		Atlantic 1544

DEBUT	PEAK	WKS	RIAA	ARTIST / Album Title	Catalog	Label & Number
				MANN, Herbie — cont'd		
4/17/71	137	3		8 Memphis Two-Step	[I]	Embryo 531
10/30/71	119	23		9 Push Push	[I]	Embryo 532
2/3/73	172	8		10 The Evolution Of Mann	[I-K]	Atlantic 300 [2]
9/22/73	146	8		11 Turtle Bay	[I]	Atlantic 1642
3/30/74	109	10		12 London Underground	[I]	Atlantic 1648
8/17/74	141	11		13 Reggae	[I]	Atlantic 1655
4/19/75	27	18		14 Discotheque	[I]	Atlantic 1670
9/27/75	75	7		15 Waterbed		Atlantic 1676
5/8/76	178	2		16 Surprises		Atlantic 1682
2/12/77	132	7		17 Bird In A Silver Cage	[I]	Atlantic 18209
10/1/77	122	7		18 Herbie Mann & Fire Island		Atlantic 19112
5/27/78	165	5		19 Brazil-Once Again	[I]	Atlantic 19169
2/24/79	77	13		20 Super Mann		Atlantic 19221
				LIVE ALBUMS:		
7/28/62	30	41		21 Herbie Mann At The Village Gate	[I]	Atlantic 1380
12/21/63+	104	8		22 Herbie Mann Live At Newport	[I]	Atlantic 1413
11/27/65	143	3		23 Standing Ovation At Newport	[I]	Atlantic 1445
11/22/69	139	10		24 Live At The Whisky A Go Go	[I]	Atlantic 1536
6/16/73	163	6		25 Hold On, I'm Comin'	[I]	Atlantic 1632
				MANN, Johnny, Singers		
				Born on 8/30/1928 in Baltimore, Maryland. Arranger/conductor. Musical director for Joey Bishop's TV talk show.		
10/12/63	90	4		1 Golden Folk Song Hits, Volume Two		Liberty 7296
10/3/64	77	15		2 Invisible Tears		Liberty 7387
7/15/67	51	23		3 We Can Fly! Up-Up And Away		Liberty 7523
12/16/67	31[X]	3		4 We Wish You A Merry Christmas	[X]	Liberty 7522
				MANN, Manfred — see MANFRED MANN		
				MANN, Tamela		
				Born on 6/9/1966 in Fort Worth, Texas. Gospel singer/actress.		
11/21/09	97	8		1 The Master Plan		Tillymann 8135
				MANNA, Charlie		
				Born on 10/6/1920 in Brooklyn, New York. Died on 11/9/1971 (age 51). Stand-up comedian.		
7/24/61	27	14		1 Manna Overboard!!	[C]	Decca 4159

MANNHEIM STEAMROLLER   2000s: #26 / All-Time: #128

Classical-rock band from Omaha, Nebraska. Under the direction of composer/producer/drummer **Chip Davis**, who founded American Gramaphone Records in 1974. Other members are Jackson Berkey, Amanda Berkey, Ron Cooley and Arnie Roth. Gained recognition through performance on a series of "Old Home Bread" TV commercials. Davis wrote **C.W. McCall**'s "Convoy." Group named after a term from the 1700s meaning crescendo.

DEBUT	PEAK	WKS	RIAA	Album Title	Catalog	Label & Number
12/13/86+	155	14	●	1 Fresh Aire VI	[I]	American Gram. 386
12/19/87+	118	19	●	2 Classical Gas	[I]	American Gram. 800
				MASON WILLIAMS & MANNHEIM STEAMROLLER		
2/17/90	167	8	●	3 Yellowstone - The Music Of Nature	[I]	American Gram. 3089
12/1/90	77	16	●	4 Fresh Aire 7	[I]	American Gram. 777
4/3/99	89	10		5 Mannheim Steamroller Meets The Mouse	[I]	Walt Disney 60641
10/16/99	168	1		6 25 Year Celebration Of Mannheim Steamroller	[I-K]	American Gram. 25 [2]
2/8/03	41	6		7 Romantic Melodies	[I]	American Gram. 214
6/7/03	78	8		8 American Spirit		American Gram. 1776
				MANNHEIM STEAMROLLER & C.W McCALL		
2/26/05	172	1		9 Romantic Themes	[I]	American Gram. 215
				CHRISTMAS ALBUMS:		
12/22/84+	110	6	▲[5]	10 Mannheim Steamroller Christmas ..... Cat:❶[4]/95	[I]	American Gram. 1984
				Christmas charts: 3/'84, 2/'85, 2/'87, 2/'88, 3/'89, 2/'90, 1/'91, 6/'92, 3/'93, 3/'94, 6/'95, 4/'96, 10/'97, 8/'98, 13/'99, 25/'00, 24/'01, 16/'02, 30/'03, 50/'04		
12/21/85	117	5		11 Mannheim Steamroller Christmas	[I-R]	American Gram. 1984
12/20/86	126	5		12 Mannheim Steamroller Christmas	[I-R]	American Gram. 1984
11/26/88+	50	8		13 Mannheim Steamroller Christmas	[I-R]	American Gram. 1984
12/2/89+	54	8		14 Mannheim Steamroller Christmas	[I-R]	American Gram. 1984
12/1/90+	59	7		15 Mannheim Steamroller Christmas	[I-R]	American Gram. 1984
11/26/88	36	8	▲[6]	16 A Fresh Aire Christmas ..... Cat:❶[17]/99	[I]	American Gram. 1988
				Christmas charts: 1/'88, 2/'89, 3/'90, 1/'91, 5/'92, 2/'93, 3/'94, 4/'95, 3/'96, 10/'97, 6/'98, 28/'99, 21/'00, 14/'01, 19/'02, 31/'03, 43/'04, 45/'05		
12/2/89+	43	8		17 A Fresh Aire Christmas	[I-R]	American Gram. 1988
12/1/90+	47	8		18 A Fresh Aire Christmas	[I-R]	American Gram. 1988
9/30/95	3[1]	18	▲[4]	19 Christmas In The Aire ..... Cat:#2[13]/48	[I]	American Gram. 1995
				Christmas charts: 1/'95, 2/'96, 5/'97, 5/'98, 13/'99, 20/'00, 23/'01, 32/'02, 43/'03		

MANNHEIM STEAMROLLER — cont'd

DEBUT	PEAK	WKS	RIAA	#	Album Title	Catalog	Label & Number
11/15/97	24	9	▲	20	Christmas Live .... Cat:#6/18 [I-L]		American Gram. 1997
					recorded on 1/3/1996 at the Orpheum Theater in Omaha, Nebraska; Christmas charts: 1/'97, 14/'99, 19/'00, 11/'02, 16/'03		
11/14/98	25	11	▲	21	The Christmas Angel – A Family Story .... Cat:#11/9 [I]		American Gram. 1998
					story narrated by Olivia Newton-John and Chip Davis; Christmas charts: 2/'98, 10/'99, 41/'02		
11/17/01	5	9	▲³	22	Christmas Extraordinaire .... Cat:❶²/41 [I]		American Gram. 1225
					Christmas charts: 1/'01, 1/'02, 1/'03, 11/'04, 18/'05, 20/'06, 41/'07, 46/'09		
11/17/01	33ˣ	1		23	Mannheim Steamroller Christmas Collection .... [I]		American Gram. 4432 [4]
10/30/04	19	13	▲	24	Christmas Celebration .... Cat:#3/19 [I]		American Gram. 2020
					Christmas charts: 1/'04, 5/'05, 12/'06, 28/'07		
10/27/07	5	12	▲	25	Christmas Song .... Cat:#10/8 [I]		American Gram. 1227
					Christmas charts: 2/'07, 21/'08, 46/'09		
12/19/09	157	2		26	Christmas Song .... [I-R]		American Gram. 1227
11/24/07	92	7		27	Christmas: Traditions .... [I-K]		American Gram. 4525 [3]
					Christmas chart: 23/'07		
11/8/08	48	10		28	Christmasville .... [I]		American Gram. 1231
					Christmas charts: 9/'08, 17/'09		
11/8/08	68	9		29	A Candlelight Christmas .... [I]		American Gram. 1220
					Christmas charts: 8/'08, 31/'09		
10/31/09	29	11		30	Christmas: 25th Anniversary Collection .... [I-K]		American Gram. 2525 [2]
					Christmas chart: 6/'09		
					SPECIALTY ALBUMS:		
10/18/03	53	5		31	Halloween .... Cat:#43/1 [I-N]		American Gram. 1031
11/6/04	65	2		32	Halloween: Monster Mix .... Cat:#17/1 [I-N]		American Gram. 1032
10/28/06	68	4		33	Halloween 2: Creatures Collection .... Cat:#24/3 [I-N]		American Gram. 1033 [2]

MANSON, Marilyn

All-Time: #380

Born Brian Warner on 1/5/1969 in Canton, Ohio. Notorious gothic shock rocker. Band includes: Scott "Daisy Berkowitz" Putesky (guitar), Steve "Madonna Wayne Gacy" Bier (keyboards), Jeordi "Twiggy Ramirez" White (bass) and Ken "Ginger Fish" Wilson (drums).

DEBUT	PEAK	WKS	RIAA	#	Album Title	Catalog	Label & Number
11/11/95+	31	50	▲	1	Smells Like Children		Nothing 92641
10/26/96	3¹	52	▲	2	Antichrist Superstar		Nothing 90086
12/13/97	102	3		3	Remix & Repent .... [EP-K]		Nothing 95017
10/3/98	❶¹	33	▲	4	Mechanical Animals		Nothing 90273
12/4/99	82	4		5	The Last Tour On Earth [L]		Nothing 490524
12/2/00	13	13		6	Holy Wood (In The Shadow Of The Valley Of Death)		Nothing 490832
5/31/03	❶¹	16		7	The Golden Age Of Grotesque		Nothing 000370
10/16/04	9	25	●	8	Lest We Forget: The Best Of [G]		Interscope 003478
6/23/07	8	14		9	Eat Me, Drink Me		Interscope 009054
6/13/09	4	11		10	The High End Of Low		Interscope 012796

MANTOVANI

1950s: #5 / 1960s: #7 / All-Time: #15

Born Annunzio Paolo Mantovani on 11/15/1905 in Venice, Italy. Died on 3/29/1980 (age 74). Classical violinist/bandleader. Known for his 40-piece orchestra and distinctive "cascading strings" sound.

DEBUT	PEAK	WKS	RIAA	#	Album Title	Catalog	Label & Number
11/24/58+	7	68	●	1	Strauss Waltzes .... [I]		London 685
3/24/58	22	1		2	Mantovani Plays Tangos .... [I]		London 768
					above 2 first released in 1953		
3/19/55	14	1		3	Waltz Time .... [I]		London 1094
2/19/55	13	1		4	The Music Of Rudolf Friml [I]		London 1150
7/9/55	8	4	●	5	Song Hits From Theatreland [I]		London 1219
5/26/56	12	7		6	Waltzes Of Irving Berlin .... [I]		London 1452
5/27/57+	❶¹	231	●	7	Film Encores .... [I]		London 1700
5/19/58	5	104	●	8	Gems Forever... [I]		London 3032
2/16/59+	13	46		9	Continental Encores .... [I]		London 3095
6/1/59	6	11		10	Mantovani Stereo Showcase [I-K]		London SS1
6/15/59	14	26		11	Film Encores, Vol. 2 .... [I]		London 3117
1/4/60	8	18		12	All-American Showcase [I-K]		London 3122 [2]
3/28/60	11	30		13	The American Scene .... [I]		London 3136
7/25/60	21	53		14	Songs To Remember .... [I]		London 3149
12/5/60+	2⁵	71	●	15	Mantovani Plays Music From Exodus And Other Great Themes [I]		London 3231
2/20/61	22	12		16	Operetta Memories .... [I]		London 3181
5/29/61	8	50		17	Italia Mia [I]		London 3239
8/14/61	29	10		18	Themes From Broadway .... [I]		London 3250
1/13/62	83	8		19	Songs Of Praise .... [I]		London 245
6/9/62	8	26		20	American Waltzes .... [I]		London 248
10/27/62	24	15		21	Moon River And Other Great Film Themes .... [I]		London 249

MANTOVANI — cont'd

DEBUT	PEAK	WKS		Album Title	Catalog	Label & Number
1/5/63	136	4	22	Stop The World-I Want To Get Off/Oliver!	[I]	London 270
6/1/63	10	18	23	Latin Rendezvous	[I]	London 295
6/8/63	41	12	24	Classical Encores	[I]	London 269
11/9/63+	51	22	25	Mantovani/Manhattan	[I]	London 328
3/14/64	134	3	26	Kismet		London 44043
				vocals by opera stars Robert Merrill and Regina Resnik and chorus		
4/18/64	135	6	27	Folk Songs Around The World	[I]	London 360
11/7/64	37	43	28	The Incomparable Mantovani	[I]	London 392
3/20/65	26	31	29	The Mantovani Sound - Big Hits From Broadway And Hollywood	[I]	London 419
10/23/65	41	21	30	Mantovani Ole	[I]	London 422
3/5/66	23	26	31	Mantovani Magic	[I]	London 448
10/8/66	27	35	32	Mr. Music...Mantovani	[I]	London 474
3/11/67	53	33	● 33	Mantovani's Golden Hits	[G-I]	London 483
9/23/67	49	22	34	Mantovani/Hollywood	[I]	London 516
3/2/68	64	25	35	The Mantovani Touch	[I]	London 526
6/15/68	148	7	36	Mantovani/Tango	[I]	London 532
11/9/68	143	7	37	Mantovani...Memories	[I]	London 542
4/5/69	73	17	38	The Mantovani Scene	[I]	London 548
11/1/69	92	17	39	The World Of Mantovani	[I]	London 565
4/4/70	77	24	40	Mantovani Today	[I]	London 572
11/7/70	167	3	41	Mantovani In Concert	[I-L]	London 578
				recorded at the Royal Festival Hall in London, England		
3/27/71	105	15	42	From Monty, With Love	[I-K]	London 585 [2]
10/30/71	150	9	43	To Lovers Everywhere U.S.A.	[I]	London 598
5/27/72	156	12	44	Annunzio Paolo Mantovani	[I]	London 610
4/7/73	214	2	45	Gypsy Soul	[I]	London 900
				CHRISTMAS ALBUMS:		
12/9/57	4	6	46	Christmas Carols	[I]	London 913
				first released in 1953 and charted in 1954 (#6)		
12/22/58	3[1]	3	47	Christmas Carols	[I-R]	London 913
12/21/59	16	3	48	Christmas Carols	[I-R]	London 913
12/19/60	8	3	49	Christmas Carols	[I-R]	London 913
12/18/61+	36	6	50	Christmas Carols	[I-R]	London 913
12/14/63	7[x]	15	51	Christmas Greetings From Mantovani And His Orchestra	[I]	London 338
				Christmas charts: 7/'63, 23/'65, 42/'66, 20/'67, 10/'68		

MANTRONIX

Hip-hop/dance duo from Brooklyn, New York: Curtis "Mantronik" Kahleel and M.C. Tee. Bryce Wilson replaced Tee in 1989. Wilson later formed **Groove Theory**.

DEBUT	PEAK	WKS		Album Title	Catalog	Label & Number
4/9/88	108	8	1	In Full Effect..		Capitol 48336
3/17/90	161	7	2	This Should Move Ya		Capitol 91119

MANUELLE, Victor

Born on 12/27/1963 in Anasco, Puerto Rico. Latin "salsa" singer.

DEBUT	PEAK	WKS		Album Title	Catalog	Label & Number
10/16/99	96	3	1	Inconfundible	[F]	Sony Discos 83310
2/17/01	197	1	2	Instinto Y Deseo	[F]	Sony Discos 83768
3/20/04	177	2	3	Travesia	[F]	Sony Discos 93272
5/27/06	140	3	4	Decision Unanime	[F]	Sony 76390
12/1/07	184	1	5	Una Navidad A Mi Estilo...	[X-F]	Kiyavi 576696
				Christmas chart: 42/'07		
6/28/08	159	1	6	Soy	[F]	Kiyavi 76697
5/23/09	106	2	7	Muy Personal	[F]	Kiyavi 66992
11/28/09	110	1	8	Yo Mismo..	[F]	Kiyavi 24754

MANZANERA, Phil

Born on 1/31/1951 in London, England. Rock singer/guitarist. Member of **Roxy Music** from 1972-83.

DEBUT	PEAK	WKS		Album Title	Catalog	Label & Number
8/2/75	202	3	1	Diamond Head		Atco 113
2/10/79	176	3	2	K-Scope		Polydor 6178

MANZAREK, Ray

Born on 2/12/1939 in Chicago, Illinois. Rock singer/keyboardist. Member of **The Doors** and **Nite City**.

DEBUT	PEAK	WKS		Album Title	Catalog	Label & Number
2/8/75	150	6	1	The Whole Thing Started With Rock & Roll Now It's Out Of Control		Mercury 1014

MARATHONS, The

The Olympics' Arvee label needed a new single, but since The Olympics were on tour, the label brought in The Vibrations, who were under contract with the Chess/Checker label. The Vibrations recorded "Peanut Butter," and Arvee released it as by The Marathons. Chess discovered the fraud and stopped the Arvee release and then released a re-recorded version on their subsidiary label, Argo. Arvee followed up with a new song by The Marathons, recorded by an unknown non-Vibrations group.

~ ~ ~ ~ ~ ~ ~ ~ ~ ~ ~ ~ **NON-CHARTED ALBUM** ~ ~ ~ ~ ~ ~ ~ ~ ~ ~ ~ ~

1961 **Peanut Butter**

Billboard DEBUT	PEAK	WKS	R I A A	ARTIST Album Title	Catalog	Label & Number

MARCELS, The
Black doo-wop group from Pittsburgh, Pennsylvania: Cornelius Harp, Ronald Mundy, Gene Bricker, Richard Knauss and Fred Johnson. Allen Johnson and Walt Maddox replaced Bricker and Knauss in mid-1961. Mundy left in late 1961. Allen Johnson died of cancer on 9/28/1995.

~ ~ ~ ~ ~ ~ ~ ~ ~ ~ ~ **NON-CHARTED ALBUM** ~ ~ ~ ~ ~ ~ ~ ~ ~ ~ ~
1961 **Blue Moon**

MARCH, Little Peggy
Born Margaret Battivio on 3/8/1948 in Lansdale, Pennsylvania. Pop singer.

| 8/17/63 | 139 | 3 | | 1 **I Will Follow Him** .... | | RCA Victor 2732 |

MARCY PLAYGROUND
Rock trio from Manhattan, New York: John Wozniak (vocals, guitar), Dylan Keefe (bass) and Dan Reiser (drums).

| 12/6/97+ | 21 | 41 | ▲ | 1 **Marcy Playground** .... | | Capitol 53569 |

MARDONES, Benny
Born on 11/9/1946 in Cleveland, Ohio; raised in Savage, Maryland. Pop singer/songwriter.

| 6/7/80 | 65 | 24 | | 1 **Never Run Never Hide** .... | | Polydor 6263 |

MARESCA, Ernie
Born on 4/21/1939 in the Bronx, New York. Rock and roll singer/songwriter.

~ ~ ~ ~ ~ ~ ~ ~ ~ ~ ~ **NON-CHARTED ALBUM** ~ ~ ~ ~ ~ ~ ~ ~ ~ ~ ~
1962 **Shout! Shout! (Knock Yourself Out)**

MARGOT & THE NUCLEAR SO & SO'S
Alternative-rock band from Indianapolis, Indiana: Richard Edwards (vocals), Eric Kang (guitar), Ron Kwansman (guitar), Tyler Watkins (bass) and Brian Deck (drums).

| 10/25/08 | 180 | 1 | | 1 **Not Animal** .... | | Epic 21080 |

MARI, Teairra
Born Teairra Maria Thomas on 12/2/1987 in Detroit, Michigan. Female R&B singer.

| 8/20/05 | 5 | 10 | | 1 Roc-A-Fella Presents Teairra Marí | | Roc-A-Fella 004526 |

MARIACHI BRASS — see BAKER, Chet

MARIE, Teena   **All-Time: #393**
Born Mary Christine Brockert on 3/5/1956 in Santa Monica, California; raised in Venice, California. White R&B singer/songwriter/keyboardist. Discovered by **Rick James**.

5/5/79	94	20		1 **Wild And Peaceful**		Gordy 986
3/15/80	45	23		2 **Lady T**		Gordy 992
9/13/80	38	29		3 **Irons In The Fire**		Gordy 997
6/13/81	23	25	●	4 **It Must Be Magic**		Gordy 1004
11/26/83+	119	24		5 **Robbery**		Epic 38882
12/15/84+	31	35	●	6 **Starchild**		Epic 39528
7/5/86	81	11		7 **Emerald City**		Epic 40318
4/16/88	65	13		8 **Naked To The World**		Epic 40872
10/13/90	132	10		9 **Ivory**		Epic 45101
5/29/04	6	21		10 La Dona		Cash Money 002552
5/27/06	24	10		11 **Sapphire**		Cash Money 006468
6/27/09	20	6		12 **Congo Square**		Stax 31320

MARILLION
Rock group from Aylesbury, England: Derek "Fish" Dick (vocals), Steve Rothery (guitar), Mark Kelly (keyboards), Pete Trewavas (bass) and Mick Pointer (drums). Ian Mosley replaced Pointer in 1984.

6/25/83	175	7		1 **Script For A Jester's Tear**		Capitol 12269
7/21/84	209	1		2 **Fugazi**		Capitol 12331
8/24/85	47	35		3 **Misplaced Childhood**		Capitol 12431
3/22/86	67	10		4 **Brief Encounter** .... [EP-L]		Capitol 15023
7/11/87	103	11		5 **Clutching At Straws**		Capitol 12539

MARILYN MANSON — see MANSON, Marilyn

MARINO, Frank — see MAHOGANY RUSH

MARIO
Born Mario Barrett on 8/27/1986 in Baltimore, Maryland; raised in Teaneck, New Jersey. R&B singer.

8/10/02	9	20	●	1 Mario		J Records 20026
12/25/04	13	31	▲	2 **Turning Point**		3rd Street 61885
12/29/07	21	22		3 **Go**		3rd Street 21569
10/31/09	9	6		4 D.N.A.		J Records 49657

MARJOE
Born Hugh Marjoe Gortner on 1/14/1944 in Long Beach, California. Name is a combination of Mary and Joseph. Toured as a child evangelist starting at age four. Later became an actor, appearing in several movies and TV shows.

| 11/18/72 | 207 | 2 | | 1 **Marjoe** .... [S] | | Warner 2667 |

Billboard			R I A A	ARTIST		
DEBUT	PEAK	WKS		Album Title	Catalog	Label & Number

MARK-ALMOND
Pop-rock duo from England: Jon Mark and Johnny Almond (died of cancer on 11/18/2009, age 63).

6/5/71	154	15	1 Mark-Almond		Blue Thumb 27
1/15/72	87	16	2 Mark-Almond II		Blue Thumb 32
5/26/73	177	7	3 The Best Of Mark-Almond [G]		Blue Thumb 50
10/21/72	103	14	4 Rising		Columbia 31917
8/25/73	73	14	5 Mark-Almond 73 [L]		Columbia 32486
			side 1: live; side 2: studio		
7/31/76	112	14	6 To The Heart		ABC 945

MARK AND BRIAN
Nationally syndicated radio DJ duo of Mark Thompson and Brian Phelps. Based in Los Angeles, California.

11/29/97	48	5	1 You Had To Be There! [C]		Oglio 957 [2]
11/25/00	62	2	2 Mark And Brian/Little Drummer Boys [X-C]		Oglio 86958 [2]

MARKETTS, The
Surf-rock instrumental band from Hollywood, California: Ben Benay (guitar), Mike Henderson (sax), Richard Hobriaco (keyboards), Ray Pohlman (bass) and Gene Pello (drums).

2/8/64	37	14	1 Out Of Limits! [I]		Warner 1537
3/12/66	82	12	2 The Batman Theme [I]		Warner 1642

MAR-KEYS, The
White R&B instrumental band from Memphis, Tennessee: Charles "Packy" Axton (tenor sax), Wayne Jackson (trumpet), Jerry Lee "Smoochie" Smith (keyboards), **Steve Cropper** (guitar), Donald "Duck" Dunn (bass) and Terry Johnson (drums). Staff musicians at Stax/Volt. Cropper and Dunn later joined **Booker T. & The MG's.** Jackson later joined **The Memphis Horns.** Axton died in January 1974 (age 32).

8/26/67	98	4	1 Back To Back [I-L]		Stax 720
			THE MAR-KEYS / BOOKER T. & THE MG's		

~ ~ ~ ~ ~ ~ ~ ~ ~ **NON-CHARTED ALBUM** ~ ~ ~ ~ ~ ~ ~ ~ ~ ~
1961 **Last Night!**

MARKHAM, Pigmeat
Born Dewey Markham on 4/18/1904 in Durham, North Carolina. Died of a stroke on 12/13/1981 (age 77). Black comedian. Regular on TV's *Laugh-In* (1968-69).

7/20/68	109	9	1 Here Come The Judge [C]		Chess 1523

MARKY MARK And The Funky Bunch
Born Mark Wahlberg on 6/5/1971 in Dorchester, Massachusetts. Singer/actor. Starred in several movies. Younger brother of Donnie Wahlberg of **New Kids On The Block.** The Funky Bunch is DJ Terry Yancey and three male and two female dancers.

8/10/91+	21	45	▲ 1 Music For The People		Interscope 91737
10/3/92	67	14	2 You Gotta Believe		Interscope 92203

MARLEY, Bob, & The Wailers   1980s: #27 / All-Time: #114
Born on 2/6/1945 in Rhoden Hall, Jamaica. Died of cancer on 5/11/1981 (age 36). Legendary reggae singer/guitarist. The Wailers included **Peter Tosh** and Bunny Wailer; both left in 1974. Wrote **Eric Clapton**'s hit "I Shot The Sheriff." Father of **Ziggy Marley, Damian "Jr. Gong" Marley** and **Stephen Marley.** In 1990, Marley's birthday proclaimed a national holiday in Jamaica.
AWARDS: Grammy: Lifetime Achievement 2001 ★ R&R Hall of Fame: 1994

11/8/75	171	5	1 Catch A Fire		Island 9241
			Grammy: Hall of Fame ★ RS500 #123		
10/11/75	151	6	● 2 Burnin'		Island 9256
			THE WAILERS		
			RS500 #319 ★ NRR		
5/10/75	92	28	3 Natty Dread		Island 9281
			RS500 #182		
5/15/76	8	22	● 4 Rastaman Vibration		Island 9383
6/11/77	20	24	● 5 Exodus Cat:#50/1		Island 9498
			Grammy: Hall of Fame ★ RS500 #169		
4/22/78	50	17	● 6 Kaya		Island 9517
11/17/79	70	14	7 Survival		Island 9542
8/9/80	45	23	● 8 Uprising		Island 9596
10/31/81	117	6	9 Chances Are [E]		Cotillion 5228
			BOB MARLEY		
			recorded 1968-72		
7/2/83	55	15	● 10 Confrontation		Island 90085
12/4/99+	60	24	● 11 Chant Down Babylon		Tuff Gong 546404
			BOB MARLEY		
			contains newly recorded duets based on Marley's original recordings		

GREATEST HITS & COMPILATIONS:

8/18/84	54	135↑	▲10 12 Legend Cat:❶110/907		Island 90169
			RS500 #46		
9/6/86	140	9	13 Rebel Music		Island 90520
10/24/92	86	15	▲2 14 Songs Of Freedom		Tuff Gong 512280 [4]

Billboard DEBUT	PEAK	WKS	R I A A	ARTIST / Album Title	Catalog	Label & Number
				MARLEY, Bob, & The Wailers — cont'd		
7/30/94	34^C	1		15 At His Best		Special Music 4808
				BOB MARLEY (above 2)		
6/10/95	67	14	●	16 Natural Mystic...		Tuff Gong 524103
6/9/01	60	16		17 One Love: The Very Best Of Bob Marley & The Wailers		UTV 542855
11/26/05	101	4		18 Africa Unite: The Singles Collection		Island 005723
6/30/07	165	1		19 Forever Bob Marley...		Madacy 52245 [3]
7/11/09	77	4		20 B Is For Bob...		Tuff Gong 012564
				LIVE ALBUMS:		
10/23/76	90	9	●	21 Live!..		Island 9376
				recorded on 7/18/1975 at the Lyceum in London, England		
12/16/78+	102	16		22 Babylon By Bus		Island 11 [2]
2/23/91	103	13		23 Talkin' Blues		Tuff Gong 848243
				MARLEY, Damian "Jr. Gong"		
				Born on 7/21/1978 in Kingston, Jamaica. Reggae singer. Son of **Bob Marley**.		
10/1/05	7	34	●	1 Welcome To Jamrock		Ghetto Youths 005416
				Grammy: Reggae Album		
				MARLEY, Stephen		
				Born on 4/20/1972 in Wilmington, Delaware. Reggae singer/songwriter. Son of **Bob Marley**. Former member of **Ziggy Marley And The Melody Makers**.		
4/7/07	35	6		1 Mind Control		Ghetto Youths 008354
				MARLEY, Ziggy, And The Melody Makers		
				Family reggae band from Kingston, Jamaica: David "Ziggy" Marley (vocals, guitar; born on 10/17/1968), **Stephen Marley**, Sharon Marley and Cedella Marley. Children of **Bob Marley**.		
4/23/88	23	42	▲	1 Conscious Party		Virgin 90878
				Grammy: Reggae Album		
8/12/89	26	18	●	2 One Bright Day		Virgin 91256
				Grammy: Reggae Album		
6/15/91	63	19		3 Jahmekya...		Virgin 91626
7/17/93	178	2		4 Joy And Blues		Virgin 87961
7/29/95	170	5		5 Free Like We Want 2 B		Elektra 61702
5/3/03	138	8		6 Dragonfly		Tuff Gong 11636
5/23/09	149	2		7 Family Time		Tuff Gong 0004
				ZIGGY MARLEY		
				Grammy: Children's Music Album		
				MARLEY MARL		
				Born Marlon Williams on 9/30/1962 in Queens, New York. Rapper/producer. Member of **QB Finest**.		
10/8/88	163	5		1 In Control Volume I		Cold Chillin' 25783
10/19/91	152	2		2 In Control Volume II - For Your Steering Pleasure		Cold Chillin' 26257
6/9/07	140	1		3 Hip Hop Lives		Koch 4109
				KRS-ONE & MARLEY MARL		
				MARMALADE, The		
				Pop band from Scotland: Thomas "Dean Ford" McAleese (vocals), Junior Campbell (guitar), Patrick Fairley (piano), Graham Knight (bass) and Alan Whitehead (drums).		
6/20/70	71	13		1 Reflections Of My Life		London 575
				MAROON 5		
				Alternative pop-rock band from Los Angeles, California: Adam Levine (vocals, guitar), James Valentine (guitar), Jesse Carmichael (keyboards), Mickey Madden (bass) and Ryan Dusick (drums).		
				AWARD: Grammy: Best New Artist 2004		
5/31/03+	6	109	▲^{4}	1 Songs About Jane	Cat:❶^1/60	Octone 50001
7/17/04	42	39	●	2 1.22.03.Acoustic .... [EP-L]		Octone 62468
10/8/05	61	2		3 Live: Friday The 13th....................................... [L]		Octone 69952
6/9/07	❶^1	78	▲^{2}	4 It Won't Be Soon Before Long		A&M 008917
7/26/08	117	1		5 Live From Le Cabaret: In Montreal, Quebec .... [L]		A&M digital
12/27/08	73	3		6 Call And Response: The Remix Album .... [K]		A&M 012260
				MARRINER, Neville		
				Born on 4/15/1924 in Lincoln, Lincolnshire, England. Conductor/arranger. Knighted by Queen Elizabeth in 1985.		
11/24/84+	56	78	▲	1 Amadeus .... [S]		Fantasy 1791 [2]
				Grammy: Classical Album		
				MARRIOTT, Steve		
				Born on 1/30/1947 in London, England. Died in a house fire on 4/20/1991 (age 44). Rock singer/guitarist. Former leader of **Small Faces** and **Humble Pie**.		
5/15/76	206	5		1 Marriott..		A&M 4572
				MARSALIS, Branford		
				Born on 8/26/1960 in New Orleans, Louisiana. Jazz saxophonist. Brother of **Wynton Marsalis**. Leader of the *Tonight Show with Jay Leno* band from 1992-95. Appeared in the movies *Bring On The Night*, *Throw Mama From The Train* and *School Daze*.		
5/19/84	164	7		1 Scenes In The City .... [I]		Columbia 38951
8/25/90	63	14		2 Mo' Better Blues .... [S]		Columbia 46792
				THE BRANFORD MARSALIS QUARTET FEATURING TERENCE BLANCHARD		

MARSALIS, Wynton
Born on 10/18/1961 in New Orleans, Louisiana. Jazz trumpeter. Brother of **Branford Marsalis**. Member of **Fuse One**.

3/6/82	165	5		1 Wynton Marsalis .... [I]		Columbia 37574
7/9/83+	102	27		2 Think Of One... .... [I]		Columbia 38641
				Grammy: Jazz Album		
10/13/84	90	39	●	3 Hot House Flowers [I]		Columbia 39530
				Grammy: Jazz Album		
10/19/85	118	10		4 Black Codes (From The Underground).. [I]		Columbia 40009
				Grammy: Jazz Album		
11/1/86	185	4		5 J Mood .... [I]		Columbia 40308
				Grammy: Jazz Album		
9/26/87	153	5	●	6 Marsalis Standard Time - Volume 1 .... [I]		Columbia 40461
				Grammy: Jazz Album		
4/13/91	112	6		7 Standard Time Vol. 2 - Intimacy Calling .... [I]		Columbia 47346
7/7/90	101	16		8 Standard Time Vol. 3 - The Resolution Of Romance....................................... [I]		Columbia 46143
12/23/89	26[X]	3		9 Crescent City Christmas Card .... [X-I]		Columbia 45287
7/26/08	20	8		10 Two Men With The Blues .... [L]		Blue Note 04454
				WILLIE NELSON & WYNTON MARSALIS		

MARSHALL, Amanda
Born on 8/29/1972 in Toronto, Ontario, Canada. Adult Alternative singer/songwriter.

11/2/96	156	7		1 Amanda Marshall		Epic 67562

MARSHALL TUCKER BAND, The   All-Time: #343
Southern-rock band from Spartanburg, South Carolina: Doug Gray (vocals; born on 5/22/1948), brothers Toy Caldwell (guitar; born on 11/13/1947; died of respiratory failure on 2/25/1993, age 45) and Tommy Caldwell (bass; born on 11/9/1949; died in a car crash on 4/28/1980, age 30), George McCorkle (guitar; born on 10/11/1946; died on 6/29/2007, age 60), Jerry Eubanks (sax, flute; born on 3/19/1950) and Paul Riddle (drums; born in 1953). Franklin Wilkie replaced Tommy Caldwell. Toy Caldwell left in 1985. Marshall Tucker was the owner of the band's rehearsal hall.

7/7/73	29	40	●	1 The Marshall Tucker Band		Capricorn 0112
3/9/74	37	28	●	2 A New Life		Capricorn 0124
12/21/74+	54	14	●	3 Where We All Belong .... [L]		Capricorn 0145 [2]
				record 1: studio; record 2: live		
9/13/75	15	34	●	4 Searchin' For A Rainbow		Capricorn 0161
6/26/76	32	20	●	5 Long Hard Ride		Capricorn 0170
2/26/77	23	36	▲	6 Carolina Dreams		Capricorn 0180
5/13/78	22	16	●	7 Together Forever		Capricorn 0205
10/21/78	67	32	▲	8 Greatest Hits .... [G]		Capricorn 0214
5/5/79	30	22		9 Running Like The Wind		Warner 3317
3/22/80	32	15		10 Tenth		Warner 3410
5/23/81	53	12		11 Dedicated		Warner 3525
				in memory of bassist Tommy Caldwell		
6/12/82	95	7		12 Tuckerized		Warner 3684
3/26/83	204	3		13 Just Us		Warner 23803
2/11/84	202	4		14 Greetings From South Carolina		Warner 23997

MARS VOLTA, The
Progressive-rock band from El Paso, Texas: Cedric Bixler-Zavala (vocals), Omar Rodriguez (guitar), Jeremy Ward (keyboards) Jon Theodore (bass) and Ikey Owens (drums). Bixler and Rodriguez were members of **At The Drive-In**. Ward died of a drug overdose on 5/25/2003 (age 27); replaced by Isaiah Owens. Theodore later formed **One Day As A Lion**.

7/12/03	39	11		1 De-Loused In The Comatorium..		Strummer 000593
3/19/05	4	20	●	2 Frances The Mute		Strummer 004129
11/26/05	76	1		3 Scabdates .... [L]		Strummer 005644
9/30/06	9	5		4 Amputechture		GSL 007214
2/16/08	3[1]	7		5 The Bedlam In Goliath		Universal 010616
7/11/09	12	5		6 Octahedron		Warner 519384

MARTHA & THE MUFFINS
New-wave band from Toronto, Ontario, Canada: Martha Johnson (vocals), Mark Gane (guitar), Andy Haas (sax), Carl Finkle (bass) and Tim Gane (drums). By 1984, reduced to duo of Johnson and Gane (recorded as **M+M**).

9/13/80	186	3		1 Metro Music		Virgin 13145
5/21/83	184	4		2 Danseparc		RCA Victor 4664
7/28/84	163	4		3 Mystery Walk		Current 3
				M+M		

MARTHA & THE VANDELLAS
Female R&B vocal trio from Detroit, Michigan: Martha Reeves (born on 7/18/1941), Annette Beard and Rosalind Ashford. Betty Kelly replaced Beard in 1964. Group disbanded from 1969-71; re-formed with Martha and sister Lois Reeves, and Sandra Tilley in 1971. Martha Reeves went solo in late 1972.

AWARD: R&R Hall of Fame: 1995

11/23/63	125	5		1 Heat Wave		Gordy 907
5/29/65	139	3		2 Dance Party		Gordy 915
6/11/66	50	15		3 Greatest Hits .... [G]		Gordy 917
1/21/67	116	8		4 Watchout!..		Gordy 920
10/7/67	140	5		5 Martha & The Vandellas Live!... [L]		Gordy 925
				recorded at the 20-Grand in Detroit, Michigan		

Billboard			R I A A	ARTIST		
DEBUT	PEAK	WKS		Album Title	Catalog	Label & Number

MARTHA & THE VANDELLAS — cont'd

6/1/68	167	8		6 Ridin' High		Gordy 926
4/1/72	146	7		7 Black Magic		Gordy 958

MARTHA REEVES & THE VANDELLAS (above 2)

~ ~ ~ ~ ~ ~ ~ ~ ~ ~ ~ **NON-CHARTED ALBUM** ~ ~ ~ ~ ~ ~ ~ ~ ~ ~ ~

1963 **Come And Get These Memories**

MARTIKA
Born Marta Marrero on 5/18/1969 in Whittier, California. Latin singer/actress. Starred in the TV program *Kids, Incorporated*. Appeared in the 1982 movie musical *Annie*.

2/4/89	15	39	●	1 Martika..		Columbia 44290
9/14/91	111	9		2 Martika's Kitchen...		Columbia 46827

MARTIN, Bobbi
Born Barbara Martin on 11/29/1938 in Brooklyn, New York; raised in Baltimore, Maryland. Died of cancer on 5/2/2000 (age 61). Female pop singer.

3/6/65	127	5		1 Don't Forget I Still Love You		Coral 57472
5/30/70	176	5		2 For The Love Of Him...		United Artists 6700

MARTIN, Dean
1960s: #21 / All-Time: #78

Born Dino Crocetti on 6/7/1917 in Steubenville, Ohio. Died of respiratory failure on 12/25/1995 (age 78). Pop singer/actor. Teamed with comedian **Jerry Lewis** in 1946. Starred in several movies. Hosted own popular TV variety series from 1965-74. His son Dino was in **Dino, Desi & Billy**. Member of **The Rat Pack**.
AWARD: Grammy: Lifetime Achievement 2009

1/8/55	10	3		1 Dean Martin [EP]		Capitol 9123
5/12/62	73	16		2 Dino - Italian Love Songs		Capitol 1659
1/26/63	99	5		3 Dino Latino		Reprise 6054
3/30/63	109	4		4 Country Style..		Reprise 6061
8/15/64	2⁴	49	●	5 Everybody Loves Somebody		Reprise 6130
8/29/64	15	31	●	6 Dream With Dean		Reprise 6123
11/14/64	9	30	●	7 The Door Is Still Open To My Heart		Reprise 6140
2/13/65	13	29	●	8 Dean Martin Hits Again		Reprise 6146
8/28/65	12	39	●	9 (Remember Me) I'm The One Who Loves You		Reprise 6170
11/20/65+	11	34	●	10 Houston...		Reprise 6181
3/12/66	40	27	●	11 Somewhere There's A Someone		Reprise 6201
7/2/66	108	3		12 The Silencers [S]		Reprise 6211
8/27/66	50	25		13 The Hit Sound Of Dean Martin		Reprise 6213
12/3/66+	34	31		14 The Dean Martin TV Show		Reprise 6233
5/13/67	46	25		15 Happiness Is Dean Martin		Reprise 6242
9/2/67	20	48	●	16 Welcome To My World		Reprise 6250
1/4/69	14	25	●	17 Gentle On My Mind..		Reprise 6330
10/4/69	90	17		18 I Take A Lot Of Pride In What I Am		Reprise 6338
9/12/70	97	12		19 My Woman, My Woman, My Wife		Reprise 6403
2/27/71	113	15		20 For The Good Times		Reprise 6428
2/5/72	117	4		21 Dino		Reprise 2053

CHRISTMAS ALBUMS:

12/18/65+	12ˣ	12		22 Holiday Cheer		Capitol 2343

originally issued in 1959 as *A Winter Romance* on Capitol 1285; Christmas charts: 27/65, 17/66, 35/67, 12/68

12/3/66	❶¹ˣ	19	●	23 The Dean Martin Christmas Album		Reprise 6222

Christmas charts: 1/66, 2/67, 4/68, 10/69, 14/70

12/25/04	193	1		24 Christmas With Dino .... Cat:#12/17		Capitol 79764

Christmas charts: 33/04, 43/05, 19/06, 32/07, 48/08

12/19/09	172	2		25 My Kind Of Christmas...		Hip-O 013340

Christmas chart: 39/09

GREATEST HITS & COMPILATIONS:

12/17/66+	95	13	▲	26 The Best Of Dean Martin		Capitol 2601
6/1/68	26	39	●	27 Dean Martin's Greatest Hits! Vol. 1..................................		Reprise 6301
9/7/68	83	21	●	28 Dean Martin's Greatest Hits! Vol. 2..................................		Reprise 6320
2/22/69	145	7		29 The Best Of Dean Martin, Vol. 2		Capitol 140
1/17/04	23ᶜ	7		30 Greatest Hits		Capitol 94961

released in 1998

6/19/04	28	46	▲	31 Dino: The Essential Dean Martin .... Cat:#43/1		Capitol 98487
9/1/07	39	6		32 Forever Cool		Capitol 97441
2/21/09	❶²ᶜ	4		33 Amore!		EMI 793

MARTIN, Eric, Band
Born on 10/10/1960 in San Francisco, California. His band included John Nyman (guitar), Mark Ross (guitar), David Jacobson (keyboards), Tom Duke (bass) and Troy Luccketta (drums; **Tesla**). Martin formed **Mr. Big** in 1988.

9/24/83	191	2		1 Sucker For A Pretty Face		Elektra 60238

DEBUT	PEAK	WKS	R I A A	ARTIST Album Title	Catalog	Label & Number

MARTIN, George
Born on 1/3/1926 in London, England. Prolific producer for **The Beatles**, **Billy J. Kramer**, **Gerry And The Pacemakers**, **America**, **Jeff Beck** and others. Knighted by Queen Elizabeth in 1996.
AWARDS: Grammy: Trustees 1996 ★ R&R Hall of Fame: 1999 (Non-Performer)

| 9/5/64 | 111 | 10 | | 1 Off The Beatle Track .... [I] | | United Artists 3377 |
| 11/7/98 | 158 | 1 | | 2 In My Life .... | | Echo 11841 |

MARTIN, Marilyn
Born on 5/4/1954 in Jellico, Tennessee; raised in Louisville, Kentucky. Adult Contemporary singer/songwriter.

| 2/22/86 | 72 | 11 | | 1 Marilyn Martin .... | | Atlantic 81292 |

MARTIN, Moon
Born John Martin on 10/31/1950 in Oklahoma. Pop-rock singer/songwriter/guitarist.

9/8/79	80	11		1 Escape From Domination		Capitol 11933
11/15/80	138	15		2 Street Fever		Capitol 12099
4/24/82	205	6		3 Mystery Ticket		Capitol 12200

MARTIN, Ray, & His Orchestra
Born on 10/11/1918 in Vienna, Austria; later based in England. Died on 2/7/1988 (age 69). Conductor/arranger.

| 8/14/61 | 43 | 6 | | 1 Dynamica .... [I] | | RCA Victor 2287 |

MARTIN, Ricky
Born Enrique Martin Morales on 12/24/1971 in San Juan, Puerto Rico. Latin singer/actor. Member of **Menudo** from 1984-89. Acted on the TV soap *General Hospital* and on Broadway in *Les Miserables*.

2/28/98+	40	41	▲	1 Vuelve .... [F]		Sony 82653
				Grammy: Latin Pop Album		
5/29/99	❶[1]	67	▲[7]	2 Ricky Martin		Columbia 69891
12/2/00	4	31	▲[2]	3 Sound Loaded		Columbia 61394
3/17/01	83	8		4 La Historia .... [F-K]		Sony Discos 84300
6/7/03	12	9		5 Almas Del Silencio .... [F]		Sony Discos 70439
10/29/05	6	9		6 Life		Columbia 93460
11/25/06	38	8		7 Ricky Martin: MTV Unplugged.. [L]		Sony 00909

MARTIN, Steve
Born on 6/8/1945 in Waco, Texas; raised in Garden Grove, California. Popular stand-up comedian/actor. Comedy writer for the **Smothers Brothers** Comedy Hour TV show and others; frequent appearances on *Saturday Night Live*. Starred in several movies. Married to actress Victoria Tennant from 1986-94.

10/8/77	10	68	▲	1 Let's Get Small [C]		Warner 3090
				Grammy: Comedy Album		
11/4/78	2[6]	26	▲[2]	2 A Wild And Crazy Guy [C]		Warner 3238
				Grammy: Comedy Album		
10/6/79	25	22	●	3 Comedy Is Not Pretty! [C]		Warner 3392
11/14/81	135	4		4 The Steve Martin Brothers .... [C-I]		Warner 3477
				side 1: comedy; side 2: banjo music by Martin		
6/6/09	93	8		5 The Crow: New Songs For The Five-String Banjo .... [I]		Rounder 610647
				Grammy: Bluegrass Album		

MARTINEZ, Angie
Born on 1/9/1972 in the Bronx, New York (Puerto Rican parents). Female rapper. Radio personality at Hot 97 in New York.

| 5/5/01 | 32 | 11 | | 1 Up Close And Personal .... | | Elektra 62366 |
| 9/7/02 | 11 | 9 | | 2 Animal House .... | | Elektra 62780 |

MARTINEZ, Nancy
Born on 8/26/1960 in Quebec City, Quebec, Canada. Dance singer/actress.

| 2/21/87 | 178 | 3 | | 1 Not Just The Girl Next Door .... | | Atlantic 81720 |

MARTINO, Al   1960s: #31 / All-Time: #156
Born Alfred Cini on 10/7/1927 in Philadelphia, Pennsylvania. Died on 10/13/2009 (age 82). Adult Contemporary singer. Encouraged by success of boyhood friend **Mario Lanza**. Winner on *Arthur Godfrey's Talent Scouts* in 1952. Played singer "Johnny Fontane" in the 1972 movie *The Godfather*.

12/1/62	109	6		1 The Exciting Voice Of Al Martino..		Capitol 1774
6/15/63	7	60		2 I Love You Because		Capitol 1914
10/12/63	9	44		3 Painted, Tainted Rose		Capitol 1975
2/8/64	13	28		4 Living A Lie		Capitol 2040
4/18/64	57	15		5 The Italian Voice Of Al Martino		Capitol 1907
6/27/64	31	25		6 I Love You More And More Every Day/Tears And Roses		Capitol 2107
12/5/64	8[X]	11		7 A Merry Christmas [X]		Capitol 2165
				Christmas charts: 8/'64, 19/'65, 59/'66, 23/'67		
2/6/65	41	15		8 We Could		Capitol 2200
6/19/65	42	12		9 Somebody Else Is Taking My Place		Capitol 2312

MARTINO, Al — cont'd

DEBUT	PEAK	WKS		Album Title	Label & Number
9/11/65+	19	47		10 My Cherie	Capitol 2362
2/19/66	8	73	●	11 Spanish Eyes	Capitol 2435
6/18/66	116	6		12 Think I'll Go Somewhere And Cry Myself To Sleep	Capitol 2528
10/29/66+	57	13		13 This Is Love	Capitol 2592
3/25/67	99	12		14 This Love For You	Capitol 2654
6/24/67	23	21		15 Daddy's Little Girl	Capitol 2733
10/14/67+	63	21		16 Mary In The Morning	Capitol 2780
3/30/68	129	4		17 This Is Al Martino	Capitol 2843
4/20/68	56	17		18 Love Is Blue	Capitol 2908
8/31/68	108	16		19 The Best Of Al Martino [G]	Capitol 2946
7/19/69	189	4		20 Sausalito	Capitol 180
12/20/69	196	2		21 Jean	Capitol 379
4/11/70	184	5		22 Can't Help Falling In Love	Capitol 405
11/28/70	172	6		23 My Heart Sings	Capitol 497
3/4/72	204	2		24 Summer Of '42	Capitol 793
6/3/72	138	10		25 Love Theme From "The Godfather"	Capitol 11071
2/8/75	129	8		26 To The Door Of The Sun	Capitol 11366

MARTSCH, Doug

Born on 9/16/1969 in Boise, Idaho. Rock singer/songwriter/guitarist. Former leader of **Built To Spill**.

DEBUT	PEAK	WKS		Album Title	Label & Number
10/5/02	177	1		1 Now You Know	Warner 48338

MARVELETTES, The

Female R&B vocal group from Inkster, Michigan: Gladys Horton, Georgeanna Gordon, Wanda Young, Katherine Anderson and Juanita Cowart. Young and Horton both sang lead. Cowart left in 1962. Gordon left in 1965; died of lupus on 1/6/1980 (age 35). Horton left in 1967, replaced by Anne Bogan. Disbanded in 1969.

DEBUT	PEAK	WKS		Album Title	Label & Number
3/19/66	84	16		1 Greatest Hits [G]	Tamla 253
4/8/67	129	8		2 The Marvelettes	Tamla 274

~ ~ ~ ~ ~ ~ ~ ~ ~ **NON-CHARTED ALBUMS** ~ ~ ~ ~ ~ ~ ~ ~ ~ ~

1961 **Please Mr. Postman**	1962 **Playboy**
1962 **Smash Hits Of 62'**	1963 **The Marvelous Marvelettes**

MARVELOUS 3

Rock trio from Atlanta, Georgia: **Butch Walker** (vocals, guitar), Jayce Fincher (bass) and Doug "Slug" Mitchell (drums).

DEBUT	PEAK	WKS		Album Title	Label & Number
9/30/00	196	1		1 Readysexgo	Elektra 62536

MARX, Groucho

Born Julius Henry Marx on 10/2/1890 in Manhattan, New York. Died of pneumonia on 8/19/1977 (age 86). Legendary TV/movie comedian. Member of **The Marx Brothers** with Chico, Harpo and Zeppo Marx.

DEBUT	PEAK	WKS		Album Title	Label & Number
10/11/69	155	3		1 The Marx Bros. (The Original Voice Tracks From Their Greatest Movies) [C] THE MARX BROTHERS narration by Gary Owens	Decca 79168
11/25/72+	160	15		2 An Evening With Groucho [C] transcription of his one-man concert tour; no track titles listed on this album	A&M 3515 [2]

MARX, Richard

Born on 9/16/1963 in Chicago, Illinois. Pop-rock singer/songwriter. Professional jingle singer since age five. Backing singer for **Lionel Richie**. Married Cynthia Rhodes (of **Animotion**) on 1/8/1989.

DEBUT	PEAK	WKS		Album Title	Label & Number
6/20/87+	8	86	▲³	1 Richard Marx	EMI-Manhattan 53049
5/20/89	❶¹	66	▲⁴	2 Repeat Offender	EMI 90380
11/23/91+	35	58	▲	3 Rush Street	Capitol 95874
2/26/94	37	23	▲	4 Paid Vacation	Capitol 81232
4/26/97	70	6		5 Flesh And Bone	Capitol 31528
11/22/97	140	11		6 Greatest Hits [G]	Capitol 21914
8/28/04	126	1		7 My Own Best Enemy	Manhattan 91719

MARY JANE GIRLS

Female R&B vocal group: Joanne McDuffie, Candice Ghant, Kim Wuletich and Yvette Marina.

DEBUT	PEAK	WKS		Album Title	Label & Number
5/14/83	56	41	●	1 Mary Jane Girls	Gordy 6040
3/16/85	18	38	●	2 Only Four You	Gordy 6092

MARY MARY

Female gospel vocal duo from Inglewood, California: sisters Erica Atkins and Tina Atkins.

DEBUT	PEAK	WKS		Album Title	Label & Number
5/20/00	59	57	▲	1 Thankful	Columbia 63740
				Grammy: Contemporary Gospel Album	
8/3/02	20	16	●	2 Incredible	Columbia 85690
8/6/05	8	45	●	3 Mary Mary	Columbia 92948
12/16/06	148	2		4 A Mary Mary Christmas [X]	Columbia 88650
				Christmas chart: 47/'06	
11/8/08	7	55		5 The Sound	My Block 28087

MAS, Carolyne

Born on 10/20/1955 in Bronxville, New York; raised in Long Island, New York. Rock singer/guitarist.

DEBUT	PEAK	WKS		Album Title	Label & Number
9/22/79	172	3		1 Carolyne Mas	Mercury 3783
7/19/80	203	5		2 Hold On	Mercury 3841

DEBUT	PEAK	WKS	R I A A	ARTIST / Album Title	Catalog	Label & Number

MASE
Born Mason Betha on 8/27/1974 in Jacksonville, Florida; raised in Harlem, New York. Male rapper. In 2000 became a pastor and leader of own ministry in Atlanta, Georgia. Resumed music career in 2004.

11/15/97	❶²	54	▲⁴ 1	Harlem World	Bad Boy 73017
7/3/99	11	11	2	Double Up	Bad Boy 73029
9/11/04	4	12	● 3	Welcome Back	Bad Boy 003063

MASEKELA, Hugh
Born on 4/4/1939 in Witbank, South Africa. R&B-jazz trumpeter/bandleader/arranger. Married to **Miriam Makeba** from 1964-66.

8/5/67	151	10	1	Hugh Masekela's Latest	Uni 73010
1/6/68	90	10	2	Hugh Masekela Is Alive And Well At The Whisky [L]	Uni 73015
6/8/68	17	22	3	The Promise Of A Future	Uni 73028
3/29/69	195	2	4	Masekela	Uni 73041
9/28/74	149	4	5	I Am Not Afraid	Blue Thumb 6015
8/9/75	132	9	6	The Boy's Doin' It	Casablanca 7017
2/11/78	65	19	7	Herb Alpert/Hugh Masekela [I]	Horizon 728

MASKED MARAUDERS, The
Folk-rock band formed in Berekely, California: Phil Marsh (vocals, guitar), Gary Salzman (guitar), Richard Saunders (bass) and Tom Ralston (drums). Project formed after critic Greil Marcus published a ficticious review in *Rolling Stone* magazine about a new album by "The Masked Marauders" (**Bob Dylan**, **Mick Jagger**, **John Lennon** and **Paul McCartney**).

1/3/70	114	12	1	The Masked Marauders	Deity 6378

MASON, Barbara
Born on 8/9/1947 in Philadelphia, Pennsylvania. R&B singer/songwriter.

10/2/65	129	8	1	Yes, I'm Ready	Arctic 1000
2/3/73	95	12	2	Give Me Your Love	Buddah 5117
2/22/75	187	2	3	Love's The Thing	Buddah 5628

MASON, Dave   All-Time: #381
Born on 5/10/1946 in Worcester, West Midland, England. Rock singer/songwriter/guitarist. Original member of **Traffic**. Joined **Delaney & Bonnie** for a short time in 1970. Brief member of **Fleetwood Mac** in 1993.

7/4/70	22	25	● 1	Alone Together	Blue Thumb 19
3/13/71	49	7	2	Dave Mason & Cass Elliot	Blue Thumb 25
11/10/73	50	28	3	It's Like You Never Left	Columbia 31721
11/2/74	25	25	● 4	Dave Mason	Columbia 33096*
10/18/75	27	17	5	Split Coconut	Columbia 33698
4/30/77	37	49	▲ 6	Let It Flow	Columbia 34680
7/1/78	41	19	● 7	Mariposa De Oro	Columbia 35285
6/14/80	74	10	8	Old Crest On A New Wave	Columbia 36144
				GREATEST HITS & COMPILATIONS:	
6/29/74	183	9	9	The Best Of Dave Mason	Blue Thumb 6013
3/22/75	133	3	10	Dave Mason At His Best	Blue Thumb 880
10/28/78	179	4	11	Very Best Of Dave Mason	Blue Thumb 6032
				LIVE ALBUMS:	
2/26/72	51	14	12	Headkeeper	Blue Thumb 34
				side 1: studio; side 2: live	
4/21/73	116	11	13	Dave Mason Is Alive!	Blue Thumb 54
11/27/76+	78	17	14	Certified Live	Columbia 34174 [2]

MASON, Harvey
Born on 2/22/1947 in Atlantic City, New Jersey. R&B session drummer. Joined **Fourplay** in 1991.

4/28/79	149	8	1	Groovin' You	Arista 4227
5/30/81	186	3	2	M.V.P.	Arista 4283

MASON, Jackie
Born Jacob Maza on 6/9/1931 in Sheboygan, Wisconsin. Stand-up comedian/actor. Appeared in several movies and TV shows.

7/14/62	77	7	1	I'm The Greatest Comedian In The World Only Nobody Knows It Yet [C]	Verve 15033
1/9/88	146	9	2	The World According To Me! [C]	Warner 25603

MASON, Nick
Born on 1/27/1945 in Birmingham, England. Rock drummer. Member of **Pink Floyd**.

7/4/81	170	3	1	Nick Mason's Fictitious Sports	Columbia 37307
8/31/85	154	5	2	Profiles [I]	Columbia 40142
				NICK MASON & RICK FENN	

MASON PROFFIT
Country-rock band from Chicago, Illinois: brothers Terry Talbot (vocals, guitar) and John Talbot (guitar, vocals), Bruce "Creeper" Kurnow (piano), Tim Ayres (bass) and Art Nash (drums).

4/17/71	177	8	1	Movin' Toward Happiness	Happy Tiger 1019
11/6/71+	186	14	2	Last Night I Had The Strangest Dream	Ampex 10138
12/9/72	211	3	3	Rockfish Crossing	Warner 2657
5/19/73	198	5	4	Bareback Rider	Warner 2704
1/19/74	203	2	5	Come & Gone [R]	Warner 2746 [2]
				reissue of album #1 above and album *Wanted* (did not chart)	

Billboard			R I A A	ARTIST		
DEBUT	PEAK	WKS		Album Title	Catalog	Label & Number

MASSIVE ATTACK
Electronica-dance band from Bristol, England: Robert "3-D" Del Naja, Andy "Mushroom" Vowles and Grant "Daddy G" Marshall. Neil Davidge replaced Vowles in 1999.

DEBUT	PEAK	WKS		Album Title	Catalog	Label & Number
5/30/98	60	7		1 Mezzanine		Virgin 45599
				RS500 #412		
3/1/03	69	7		2 100th Window		Virgin 81239
4/22/06	198	1		3 Collected		Virgin 60068

~ ~ ~ ~ ~ ~ ~ ~ ~ ~ **NON-CHARTED ALBUM** ~ ~ ~ ~ ~ ~ ~ ~ ~ ~ ~

1991 **Blue Lines**
RS500 #395

MASS PRODUCTION
Disco-funk band from Richmond, Virginia: Agnes "Tiny" Kelly (female vocals), Larry Marshall (male vocals), LeCoy Bryant (guitar), James Drumgole (trumpet), Gregory McCoy (sax), Tyrone Williams (keyboards), Emanual Redding (percussion), Kevin Douglas (bass) and Ricardo Williams (drums).

DEBUT	PEAK	WKS		Album Title	Catalog	Label & Number
1/8/77	142	10		1 Welcome To Our World		Cotillion 9910
8/27/77	83	9		2 Believe		Cotillion 9918
8/12/78	207	1		3 Three Miles High		Cotillion 5205
7/21/79	43	17		4 In The Purest Form		Cotillion 5211
3/29/80	133	9		5 Massterpiece		Cotillion 5218
5/16/81	166	6		6 Turn Up The Music		Cotillion 5226
4/24/82	203	3		7 In A City Groove		Cotillion 5233

MASTA ACE INCORPORATED
Born Duvall Clear on 12/4/1966 in Brownsville, New York. Male rapper.

DEBUT	PEAK	WKS		Album Title	Catalog	Label & Number
5/22/93	134	3		1 SlaughtaHouse		Delicious Vinyl 92249
5/20/95	69	10		2 Sittin' On Chrome		Delicious Vinyl 32873

MASTA KILLA
Born Elgin Turner on 8/18/1968 in Staten Island, New York. Male rapper. Member of **Wu-Tang Clan**.

DEBUT	PEAK	WKS		Album Title	Catalog	Label & Number
6/19/04	136	1		1 No Said Date		Wu-Tang 108
8/26/06	176	1		2 Made In Brooklyn		Nature Sounds 126

MASTERMIND
Disco band from New York: Wendell Derrick (vocals), Joe Frye (guitar), Anselm Scrubb, Mario Ford, Guy Fuertes and Lenny White (horns), Juan Clouden (percussion), Geoffrey Williams (keyboards), Carl Bain (bass) and Brian Wilson (drums).

DEBUT	PEAK	WKS		Album Title	Catalog	Label & Number
11/26/77	207	1		1 Mastermind		Prelude 12147

MASTER P   All-Time: #445
Born Percy Miller on 4/29/1967 in New Orleans, Louisiana. Male rapper/producer. Member of **504 Boyz** and **Tru**. Founder of the No Limit record label. Played professional basketball for the CBA's Fort Wayne Fury in 1998. Brother of **Silkk The Shocker**. Father of **Lil' Romeo**. Also see **Various Artists Compilations: *Master P Presents: No Limit All Stars - Who U Wit?*.**

DEBUT	PEAK	WKS		Album Title	Catalog	Label & Number
5/4/96	26	57	▲	1 Ice Cream Man	Cat:#30/12	No Limit 53978
9/13/97	❶[1]	80	▲[3]	2 Ghetto D	Cat:#44/2	No Limit 50659
11/22/97	❶[2C]	11		3 The Ghettos Tryin To Kill Me!		No Limit 50696
				first released in 1994		
6/13/98	❶[2]	42	▲[4]	4 MP Da Last Don	Cat:#23/1	No Limit 53538 [2]
11/13/99	2[1]	15	●	5 Only God Can Judge Me		No Limit 50092
12/16/00	26	17	●	6 Ghetto Postage		No Limit 26008
1/5/02	53	16		7 Game Face		New No Limit 860977
4/10/04	11	11		8 Good Side/Bad Side		New No Limit 5717 [2]
7/9/05	39	4		9 Ghetto Bill, Vol. 1		New No Limit 5780

MASTODON
Hard-rock band from Atlanta, Georgia: Brent Hinds (vocals, guitar), Bill Kelliher (guitar), Troy Sanders (bass) and Brann Dailor (drums).

DEBUT	PEAK	WKS		Album Title	Catalog	Label & Number
9/18/04	139	1		1 Leviathan		Relapse 6622
9/30/06	32	4		2 Blood Mountain		Relapse 44364
4/11/09	11	10		3 Crack The Skye		Relapse 459132

MATCHBOOK ROMANCE
Punk-rock band from Poughkeepsie, New York: Andrew Jordan (vocals, guitar), Ryan DePaolo (guitar), Ryan Kienle (bass) and Aaron Stern (drums).

DEBUT	PEAK	WKS		Album Title	Catalog	Label & Number
3/4/06	43	3		1 Voices		Epitaph 86774

MATCHBOX TWENTY
Pop-rock band from Orlando, Florida: **Rob Thomas** (vocals; born on 2/14/1972), Kyle Cook (guitar; born on 8/29/1975), Adam Gaynor (guitar; born on 11/26/1963), Brian Yale (bass; born on 10/24/1968) and Paul Doucette (drums; born on 8/22/1972).

DEBUT	PEAK	WKS		Album Title	Catalog	Label & Number
3/22/97	5	118	▲[12]	1 Yourself Or Someone Like You	Cat:❶[1]/111	Lava 92721
				MATCHBOX 20		
6/10/00	3[1]	77	▲[4]	2 Mad Season		Lava 83339
12/7/02	6	72	▲[2]	3 More Than You Think You Are		Atlantic 83612
11/29/03	43	2		4 EP	[EP-L]	Melisma 83701
10/20/07	3[1]	36	●	5 Exile On Mainstream	[G]	Melisma 297340

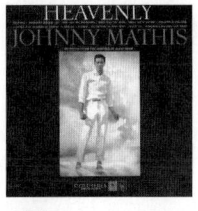

Billboard			R I A A	ARTIST		
DEBUT	PEAK	WKS		Album Title	Catalog	Label & Number

MATCHES, The
Punk-rock band from Oakland, California: Shawn Harris (vocals, guitar), Jonathan Devoto (guitar), Dylan Rowe (bass) and Matt Whalen (drums).

| 4/5/08 | 179 | 1 | | 1 A Band In Hope .... | | Epitaph 86938 |

MATERIAL
Experimental disco band spearheaded by producer/guitarist/percussionist Bill Laswell.

| 1/15/83 | 203 | 7 | | 1 One Down .... | | Elektra 60206 |

MATERIAL ISSUE
Pop trio from Chicago, Illinois: Jim Ellison (vocals, guitar), Ted Ansani (bass) and Mike Zelenko (drums). Ellison committed suicide on 6/20/1996 (age 31).

| 3/16/91 | 86 | 11 | | 1 International Pop Overthrow.................................. | | Mercury 848155 |

MATES OF STATE
Experimental-rock duo from Lawrence, Kansas: husband-and-wife Jason Hammel and Kori Gardner.

| 6/7/08 | 140 | 1 | | 1 Re-Arrange Us .... | | Barsuk 74 |

MATHIESON, Muir
Born on 1/24/1911 in Stirling, Scotland. Died on 8/2/1975 (age 64). Conductor/arranger.

| 5/29/61 | 50 | 21 | | 1 Gone With The Wind............................... [I] | | Warner 1322 |

newly recorded version of the Max Steiner original score

MATHIEU, Mireille
Born on 7/22/1946 in Avignon, France. Female singer.

| 10/4/69 | 118 | 8 | | 1 Mireille Mathieu................................ [F] | | Capitol 306 |

MATHIS, Johnny   1950s: #2 / 1960s: #10 / 1970s: #31 / All-Time: #6
Born on 9/30/1935 in Gilmer, Texas; raised in San Francisco, California. Legendary smooth ballad singer. Studied opera from age 13. Track scholarship at the San Francisco State College. Invited to Olympic tryouts; chose singing career instead. Discovered by George Avakian of Columbia Records. To New York City in 1956. Initially recorded as jazz-styled singer. Columbia A&R executive **Mitch Miller** switched him to singing pop ballads.

AWARD: Grammy: Lifetime Achievement 2003

9/9/57	4	26		1 Wonderful Wonderful		Columbia 1028
12/23/57+	2⁴	113	●	2 Warm		Columbia 1078
4/7/58	10	12		3 Good Night, Dear Lord		Columbia 1119
9/8/58	6	16	●	4 Swing Softly		Columbia 1165
2/9/59	4	96	●	5 Open Fire, Two Guitars		Columbia 1270
9/21/59	❶⁵	295	▲	6 Heavenly		Columbia 1351
1/18/60	2¹	75	●	7 Faithfully		Columbia 1422 / 8219
8/29/60	4	65		8 Johnny's Mood		Columbia 1526 / 8326
10/3/60	6	27		9 The Rhythms And Ballads Of Broadway		Columbia 17 / 803 [2]
5/15/61	38	23		10 I'll Buy You A Star		Columbia 1623 / 8423
2/24/62	14	39		11 Live It Up!		Columbia 1711 / 8511
10/27/62	12	37		12 Rapture		Columbia 1915 / 8715
8/24/63	20	27		13 Johnny		Columbia 2044 / 8844
12/28/63+	23	27		14 Romantically		Columbia 2098 / 8898
2/15/64	13	28		15 Tender Is The Night		Mercury 60890
7/25/64	75	10		16 The Wonderful World Of Make Believe		Mercury 60913
10/17/64	40	20		17 This Is Love		Mercury 60942
3/20/65	52	11		18 Love Is Everything		Mercury 60991
10/16/65	71	26		19 The Sweetheart Tree		Mercury 61041
4/2/66	9	45		20 The Shadow Of Your Smile		Mercury 61073
10/8/66+	50	18		21 So Nice		Mercury 61091
4/1/67	103	11		22 Johnny Mathis Sings		Mercury 61107
12/23/67+	60	20		23 Up, Up And Away		Columbia 2726 / 9526
4/13/68	26	40		24 Love Is Blue		Columbia 9637
12/14/68+	60	21		25 Those Were The Days......................................		Columbia 9705
8/16/69	163	4		26 The Impossible Dream		Columbia 9872
9/13/69	192	2		27 People		Columbia 9871
9/20/69	52	24		28 Love Theme From "Romeo And Juliet"		Columbia 9909
4/4/70	38	26		29 Raindrops Keep Fallin' On My Head		Columbia 1005
10/10/70	61	9		30 Close To You		Columbia 30210
1/23/71	169	7		31 Johnny Mathis Sings The Music Of Bacharach & Kaempfert....		Columbia 30350 [2]
3/13/71	47	18		32 Love Story		Columbia 30499
9/4/71	80	10		33 You've Got A Friend		Columbia 30740
2/5/72	128	7		34 Johnny Mathis In Person .... [L]		Columbia 30979 [2]
				recorded at Caesar's Palace in Las Vegas, Nevada		
6/10/72	71	15		35 The First Time Ever (I Saw Your Face)		Columbia 31342
10/21/72	83	18		36 Song Sung Blue		Columbia 31626

DEBUT	PEAK	WKS	R I A A	ARTIST Album Title	Catalog	Label & Number
				MATHIS, Johnny — cont'd		
2/17/73	83	14		37 Me And Mrs. Jones		Columbia 32114
6/30/73	120	7		38 Killing Me Softly With Her Song		Columbia 32258
11/17/73+	115	22		39 I'm Coming Home		Columbia 32435
12/28/74+	139	7		40 The Heart Of A Woman		Columbia 33251
4/19/75	99	13		41 When Will I See You Again		Columbia 33420
11/8/75+	97	21	●	42 Feelings		Columbia 33887
6/26/76	79	15		43 I Only Have Eyes For You		Columbia 34117
3/19/77	139	5		44 Mathis Is...		Columbia 34441
9/17/77	201	1		45 Hold Me, Thrill Me, Kiss Me		Columbia 34872
4/1/78	9	24	▲	46 You Light Up My Life		Columbia 35259
7/29/78	19	16	●	47 That's What Friends Are For		Columbia 35435
				JOHNNY MATHIS & DENIECE WILLIAMS		
2/24/79	122	7		48 The Best Days Of My Life		Columbia 35649
8/9/80	164	5		49 Different Kinda Different		Columbia 36505
5/8/82	147	9		50 Friends In Love		Columbia 37748
3/10/84	157	19		51 A Special Part Of Me		Columbia 38718
1/10/87	197	2		52 The Hollywood Musicals		Columbia 40372
				JOHNNY MATHIS & HENRY MANCINI		
1/11/92	189	1		53 Better Together - The Duet Album		Columbia 47982
5/25/96	119	1		54 All About Love		Columbia 67509
				CHRISTMAS ALBUMS:		
12/15/58+	3[1]	4	▲[2]	55 Merry Christmas Cat:#10/30		Columbia 1195 / 8021
				Christmas charts: 2/63, 2/64, 7/65, 2/66, 2/67, 5/68, 15/69, 3/73, 18/88, 20/89, 16/90, 17/91, 12/92, 21/93, 35/94, 39/96		
12/21/59+	10	3		56 Merry Christmas [R]		Columbia 1195 / 8021
12/26/60	10	2		57 Merry Christmas [R]		Columbia 1195 / 8021
12/18/61+	31	7		58 Merry Christmas [R]		Columbia 1195 / 8021
12/8/62	12	4		59 Merry Christmas [R]		Columbia 1195 / 8021
11/30/63	2[2X]	20		60 Sounds Of Christmas		Mercury 60837
				Christmas charts: 2/63, 7/64, 13/65, 45/66, 18/67, 11/68		
12/6/69	❶[1X]	20	▲	61 Give Me Your Love For Christmas		Columbia 9923
				Christmas charts: 1/69, 3/70, 5/71, 3/72, 19/73, 19/87, 18/88		
12/12/92	29[X]	1		62 Christmas Eve With Johnny Mathis Cat:#44/2		Columbia 40447
				first released in 1986		
12/18/93	162	3	●	63 The Christmas Music Of Johnny Mathis – A Personal Collection Cat:#30/4 [K]		Columbia/Legacy 57194
				Christmas chart: 29/02		
12/14/02	143	2		64 The Christmas Album		Columbia 86814
				Christmas charts: 23/02, 2/03		
12/30/06	191	1		65 Gold: A 50th Anniversary Christmas Celebration [L]		Legacy 89685
				GREATEST HITS & COMPILATIONS:		
4/14/58	❶[3]	490	▲	66 Johnny's Greatest Hits		Columbia 1133
7/27/59	2[2]	93	●	67 More Johnny's Greatest Hits		Columbia 1344
8/28/61	2[7]	63		68 Portrait Of Johnny		Columbia 1644 / 8444
4/20/63	6	45		69 Johnny's Newest Hits		Columbia 2016 / 8816
5/9/64	35	16		70 I'll Search My Heart And Other Great Hits		Columbia 2143 / 8943
8/1/64	88	10		71 The Great Years		Columbia 34 / 834 [2]
6/24/72	141	15	▲	72 Johnny Mathis' All-Time Greatest Hits		Columbia 31345 [2]
12/27/80+	140	7	●	73 The Best Of Johnny Mathis 1975-1980		Columbia 36871
7/25/81	173	4		74 The First 25 Years - The Silver Anniversary Album		Columbia 37440 [2]
5/10/97	150	1		75 The Global Masters		Columbia 64894 [2]
				all songs recorded from 1963-66		
12/30/06	171	1		76 Gold: A 50th Anniversary Celebration		Legacy 88583
				MATISYAHU		
				Born Matthew Miller on 6/30/1979 in West Chester, Pennsylvania; raised in White Plains, New York. Hasidic reggae rapper/singer. Name is Hebrew for "Gift of God." Wears traditional Hasidic clothing and raps in English, Hebrew and Yiddish.		
11/26/05+	30	26	●	1 Live At Stubb's [L]		Or 96464
3/25/06	4	19	●	2 Youth		Or 81239
1/13/07	146	2		3 No Place To Be [EP]		One Haven 03374
9/12/09	19	6		4 Light		JDub 22170
				MATLOCK, Matty — see HEINDORF, Ray		
				MATT & KIM		
				Dance-punk duo from Brooklyn, New York: Matt Johnson and Kim Schifino.		
6/27/09	165	5		1 Grand		Fader Label 0908
				MATTEA, Kathy		
				Born on 6/21/1959 in South Charleston, West Virginia; raised in Cross Lanes, West Virginia. Country singer/songwriter/guitarist.		
				AWARD: CMA: Female Vocalist 1989 & 1990		
3/3/90	82	19	●	1 Willow In The Wind		Mercury 836950
9/22/90	80	34	▲	2 A Collection Of Hits [G]		Mercury 842330
4/13/91	72	25	●	3 Time Passes By		Mercury 846975
10/24/92	182	7	●	4 Lonesome Standard Time		Mercury 512567

				MATTEA, Kathy — cont'd		
6/4/94	87	8	●	5 Walking Away A Winner		Mercury 518852
2/22/97	121	14		6 Love Travels		Mercury 532899

MATTHEWS, Dave, Band   1990s: #17 / 2000s: #4 / All-Time: #71

Born on 1/9/1967 in Johannesburg, South Africa; raised in Westchester County, New York. Alternative-rock singer/songwriter/guitarist. Formed his band in Charlottesville, Virginia: LeRoi Moore (sax; born on 9/7/1961; died on 8/19/2008, age 46), **Boyd Tinsley** (violin; born on 5/16/1964), Stefan Lessard (bass; born on 6/4/1974) and Carter Beauford (drums; born on 11/2/1957). Popular touring group.

10/15/94+	11	116	▲⁶	1 Under The Table And Dreaming	**Cat:**#8/109	RCA 66449
5/18/96	2¹	104	▲⁷	2 Crash	**Cat:**#2¹/170	RCA 66904
7/19/97	163	9		3 Recently	**[E-EP]**	RCA 67548
				recorded in early 1994		
5/16/98	❶¹	89	▲³	4 Before These Crowded Streets	**Cat:**#10/21	RCA 67660
3/17/01	❶²	78	▲³	5 Everyday		RCA 67988
8/3/02	❶¹	37	▲²	6 Busted Stuff		RCA 68117
10/11/03	2¹	22	▲	7 Some Devil		RCA 55167
				DAVE MATTHEWS		
5/28/05	❶¹	25	▲	8 Stand Up		RCA 68796
11/25/06	10	12	●	9 The Best Of What's Around: Vol. 01	**Cat:**#33/1 **[G]**	Bama Rags 88858 [2]
				disc 1: studio; disc 2: live		
6/20/09	❶¹	43	▲	10 Big Whiskey And The GrooGrux King		Bama Rags 48712
				LIVE ALBUMS:		
11/15/97	3¹	36	▲²	11 Live At Red Rocks 8.15.95		Bama Rags 67587 [2]
				recorded on 8/15/1995 at Red Rocks in Denver, Colorado		
2/6/99	2¹	51	▲³	12 Live At Luther College	**Cat:**#23/2	Bama Rags 67755 [2]
				DAVE MATTHEWS & TIM REYNOLDS		
				recorded on 2/6/1996 in Decorah, Iowa		
12/11/99	15	22	▲²	13 Listener Supported		Bama Rags 67898 [2]
				recorded on 9/11/1999 at Continental Airlines Arena in East Rutherford, New Jersey		
11/10/01	6	14	▲	14 Live In Chicago 12.19.98		Bama Rags 69317 [2]
11/23/02	9	15	▲	15 Live At Folsom Field Boulder Colorado		Bama Rags 68124 [2]
				recorded on 7/11/2001		
12/6/03	14	13	▲	16 The Central Park Concert		Bama Rags 57501 [3]
7/17/04	10	10	●	17 The Gorge		Bama Rags 61633 [2]
12/17/05	37	7		18 Weekend On The Rocks		Bama Rags 75759
10/14/06	37	1		19 Live Trax, Vol. 6: 7/7-7/8/2006 Fenway Park, Boston MA		Bama Rags 01290 [4]
9/1/07	3¹	9		20 Live At Radio City		Bama Rags 13102 [2]
				DAVE MATTHEWS & TIM REYNOLDS		
12/29/07	68	2		21 Live At Piedmont Park		Bama Rags 21444
1/3/09	97	1		22 Live At Miles High Music Festival		Bama Rags 42970

				MATTHEWS, David		
				Born on 4/3/1942 in Sonora, Kentucky. Jazz-dance arranger/composer.		
9/3/77	169	7		1 Dune	**[I]**	CTI 5005

				MATTHEWS, Ian		
				Born on Ian Matthews MacDonald on 6/16/1946 in Scunthorpe, Lincolnshire, England. Founder of **Fairport Convention** and Matthews' Southern Comfort. Also see **Southern Comfort**.		
1/9/71	209	1		1 Second Spring		Decca 75242
4/17/71	72	15		2 Later That Same Year		Decca 75264
				MATTHEWS' SOUTHERN COMFORT (above 2)		
7/10/71	208	6		3 If You Saw Thro' My Eyes		Vertigo 1002
2/12/72	196	3		4 Tigers Will Survive		Vertigo 1010
9/22/73	181	7		5 Valley Hi		Elektra 75061
11/11/78+	80	24		6 Stealin' Home		Mushroom 5012
12/6/80	206	3		7 Spot Of Interference		RSO 3092

				MAURIAT, Paul		
				Born on 3/4/1925 in Marseilles, France; raised in Paris, France. Died on 11/3/2006 (age 81). Orchestra leader.		
12/16/67+	❶⁵	50	●	1 Blooming Hits	**[I]**	Philips 600248
12/23/67+	25ˣ	6		2 The Christmas Album	**[X-I]**	Philips 600255
				Christmas charts: 49/'67, 30/'68, 25/'70		
3/30/68	122	22		3 More Mauriat	**[I]**	Philips 600226
6/8/68	71	18		4 Mauriat Magic	**[I]**	Philips 600270
10/12/68	142	7		5 Prevailing Airs	**[I]**	Philips 600280
3/1/69	77	18		6 Doing My Thing	**[I]**	Philips 600292
5/3/69	157	8		7 The Soul Of Paul Mauriat	**[I]**	Philips 600299
11/1/69	186	3		8 L.O.V.E.	**[I]**	Philips 600320

Billboard			R A A	ARTIST		
DEBUT	PEAK	WKS		Album Title	Catalog	Label & Number

MAURIAT, Paul — cont'd

9/19/70	184	3		9 Gone Is Love	[I]	Philips 600345
5/29/71	180	3		10 El Condor Pasa	[I]	Philips 600352
10/21/72	206	2		11 Theme From A Summer Place	[I]	MGM/Verve 5087

MAVERICKS, The
Country band from Miami, Florida: Raul Malo (vocals, guitar), David Lee Holt (guitar), Robert Reynolds (bass) and Paul Deakin (drums). Nick Kane replaced Holt in early 1995. Reynolds was married to **Trisha Yearwood** from 1994-99.
AWARD: CMA: Vocal Group 1995 & 1996

3/26/94	54	74	▲	1 What A Crying Shame		MCA 10961
10/14/95	58	39	●	2 Music For All Occasions		MCA 11257
3/28/98	96	6		3 Trampoline		MCA 70018

MAXAYN
R&B band formed in Los Angeles, California: Maxayn Lewis (female vocals), Marlo Henderson (guitar), Andre Lewis (keyboards, bass) and Emilio Thomas (drums). Andre Lewis later recorded as **Mandre**.

| 4/7/73 | 206 | 3 | | 1 Mindful | | Capricorn 0110 |

MAX DEMIAN BAND, The
Rock band from Florida: Paul Rose (vocals), Jim LeFevre (guitar), Dan Howe (keyboards), Kirt Pennebaker (bass) and Pete Siegel (drums).

| 3/3/79 | 159 | 5 | | 1 Take It To The Max | | RCA Victor 3273 |

MAX Q
Rock duo formed in Melbourne, Australia: **Michael Hutchence** (of **INXS**) and Ian Olsen. Max Q is the name of Olsen's dog. Hutchence committed suicide on 11/22/1997 (age 37).

| 10/7/89 | 182 | 8 | | 1 Max Q | | Atlantic 82014 |

MAX WEBSTER
Male rock trio from Canada: **Kim Mitchell** (vocals, guitar), Dave Myles (bass) and Gary McCracken (drums). McCracken later joined **Wrabit**.

| 1/10/81 | 202 | 1 | | 1 Universal Juveniles | | Mercury 3855 |

MAXWELL
Born Maxwell Musze on 5/23/1973 in Brooklyn, New York. R&B singer/songwriter/producer.

5/18/96+	37	78	▲²	1 Maxwell's Urban Hang Suite	Cat:#26/2	Columbia 66434
8/2/97	53	15	●	2 MTV Unplugged	Cat:#32/10 [EP-L]	Columbia 68515
7/18/98	3¹	18	▲	3 Embrya		Columbia 68968
9/8/01	❶¹	41	▲	4 Now		Columbia 67136
7/25/09	❶¹	45↑	▲	5 BLACKsummers'night		Columbia 89142
				Grammy: R&B Album		

MAXWELL, Robert, His Harp And Orchestra
Born on 4/19/1921 in Brooklyn, New York. Jazz harpist/composer. Also recorded as Mickey Mozart.

| 4/18/64 | 17 | 24 | | 1 Shangri-La | [I] | Decca 74421 |

MAY, Billy, And His Orchestra
Born on 11/10/1916 in Pittsburgh, Pennsylvania. Died of a heart attack on 1/22/2004 (age 87). Conductor/arranger.

| 3/5/55 | 7 | 3 | | 1 Sorta-May | [I] | Capitol 562 |

MAY, Brian
Born on 7/19/1947 in Twickenham, Middlesex, England. Lead guitarist of **Queen**.

11/19/83	125	9		1 Star Fleet Project	[EP]	Capitol 15014
				BRIAN MAY & FRIENDS		
2/20/93	159	2		2 Back To The Light		Hollywood 61404

MAYALL, John   **All-Time: #325**
Born on 11/29/1933 in Macclesfield, Cheshire, England. Blues-rock singer. His band spawned many of Britain's leading rock musicians.

2/17/68	136	14		1 John Mayall's Blues Breakers Crusade		London 529
6/15/68	128	5		2 The Blues Alone		London 534
9/14/68	59	19		3 Bare Wires		London 537
				JOHN MAYALL'S BLUES BREAKERS		
2/22/69	68	17		4 Blues From Laurel Canyon		London 545
3/14/70	33	19		5 Empty Rooms		Polydor 4010
10/24/70	22	22		6 USA Union		Polydor 4022
4/17/71	52	15		7 Back To The Roots		Polydor 3002 [2]
11/13/71	179	5		8 Memories		Polydor 5012
10/6/73	157	7		9 Ten Years Are Gone		Polydor 3005 [2]
3/15/75	140	4		10 New Year, New Band, New Company		Blue Thumb 6019
8/28/76	205	3		11 A Banquet In Blues		ABC 958
8/25/90	170	8		12 A Sense Of Place		Island 842795
				GREATEST HITS & COMPILATIONS:		
9/13/69	79	12		13 Looking Back		London 562
11/13/71	164	7		14 Thru The Years		London 600 [2]
2/10/73	158	7		15 Down The Line	[L]	London 618 [2]
				record 1: studio cuts 1965-68; record 2: 1964 live concert		

Billboard DEBUT	PEAK	WKS	R I A A	ARTIST Album Title	Catalog	Label & Number

MAYALL, John — cont'd

DEBUT	PEAK	WKS		Album Title	Catalog	Label & Number
2/23/74	201	3		16 The Best Of John Mayall		Polydor 3006 [2]
				LIVE ALBUMS:		
9/20/69	32	55	●	17 The Turning Point		Polydor 4004
2/28/70	93	11		18 The Diary Of A Band		London 570
5/1/71	146	8		19 John Mayall-Live In Europe		London 589
6/17/72	64	18		20 Jazz Blues Fusion		Polydor 5027
10/28/72	116	11		21 Moving On		Polydor 5036

~ ~ ~ ~ ~ ~ ~ ~ ~ ~ **NON-CHARTED ALBUM** ~ ~ ~ ~ ~ ~ ~ ~ ~ ~
1966 **Blues Breakers With Eric Clapton**
RS500 #195

MAYDAY
Rock band from New York: Steve Johnstad (vocals, drums), Randy Fredrix (guitar), David Beck (keyboards) and Charles Mas (bass).

| 11/7/81 | 210 | 1 | | 1 Mayday | | A&M 4873 |

MAYDAY PARADE
Punk-rock band from Tallahassee, Florida: Derek Sanders (vocals), Alex Garcia (guitar), Brooks Betts (guitar), Jeremy Lenzo (bass) and Jake Bundrick (drums).

| 10/24/09 | 31 | 5 | | 1 Anywhere But Here | | Fearless 521114 |

MAYER, John   **2000s: #24 / All-Time: #361**
Born on 10/16/1977 in Bridgeport, Connecticut; raised in Fairfield, Connecticut; later based in Atlanta, Georgia. Adult Alternative singer/songwriter/guitarist. His trio includes Pino Palladino (bass) and Steve Jordan (drums).

DEBUT	PEAK	WKS		Album Title	Catalog	Label & Number
10/6/01+	8	95	▲[4]	1 Room For Squares	Cat:❶[1]/71	Aware 85293
10/5/02	22	9		2 Inside Wants Out [E-EP]		Aware 86861
				first released in 1999		
3/1/03	17	31	▲	3 Any Given Thursday [L]		Aware 87199 [2]
9/27/03	❶[1]	98	▲[2]	4 Heavier Things	Cat:#10/16	Aware 86185
12/10/05	34	13		5 Try! John Mayer Trio Live In Concert [L]		Aware 95115
				JOHN MAYER TRIO		
9/30/06	2[1]	118	▲[2]	6 Continuum	Cat:#22/22	Aware 79019
7/19/08	5	27	●	7 Where The Light Is: John Mayer Live In Los Angeles [L]		Columbia 22665 [2]
12/5/09	❶[1]	26↑	●	8 Battle Studies		Columbia 53087

MAYFIELD, Curtis   **All-Time: #336**
Born on 6/3/1942 in Chicago, Illinois. Died on 12/26/1999 (age 57). R&B singer/songwriter/producer. Leader of **The Impressions** from 1957-70. Started own Curtom record label in 1968. Played "Pappy" in the movie *Short Eyes*. Paralyzed from the chest down when a stage lighting tower fell on him before a concert on 8/13/1990. Also see **Various Artists Compilations:** *A Tribute To Curtis Mayfield.*
AWARDS: Grammys: Legend 1994 / Lifetime Achievement 1995 ★ R&R Hall of Fame: 1999

DEBUT	PEAK	WKS		Album Title	Catalog	Label & Number
10/3/70	19	49	●	1 Curtis		Curtom 8005
5/29/71	21	38		2 Curtis/Live! [L]		Curtom 8008 [2]
				recorded at the Bitter End in New York City		
11/6/71	40	19		3 Roots		Curtom 8009
8/26/72	❶[4]	46	●	4 Superfly [S]		Curtom 8014
				Grammy: Hall of Fame ★ RS500 #69		
3/3/73	180	6		5 Curtis Mayfield/His Early Years With The Impressions [G]		ABC 780 [2]
6/9/73	16	26	●	6 Back To The World		Curtom 8015
11/17/73	135	10		7 Curtis In Chicago [L]		Curtom 8018
5/25/74	39	22		8 Sweet Exorcist		Curtom 8601
11/16/74	76	7		9 Got To Find A Way		Curtom 8604
6/7/75	120	11		10 There's No Place Like America Today		Curtom 5001
7/4/76	171	8		11 Give, Get, Take And Have		Curtom 5007
3/26/77	173	3		12 Never Say You Can't Survive		Curtom 5013
8/11/79	42	16		13 Heartbeat		RSO 3053
7/19/80	180	4		14 The Right Combination		RSO 3084
				LINDA CLIFFORD & CURTIS MAYFIELD		
7/26/80	128	10		15 Something To Believe In		RSO 3077
10/19/96	137	18		16 New World Order		Warner 46348

~ ~ ~ ~ ~ ~ ~ ~ ~ ~ **NON-CHARTED ALBUM** ~ ~ ~ ~ ~ ~ ~ ~ ~ ~
1992 **The Anthology 1961-1977**
RS500 #179

MAYLENE AND THE SONS OF DISASTER
Heavy metal band from Birmingham, Alabama: Dallas Taylor (vocals), Chad Huff (guitar), Kelly Nunn (guitar), Roman Haviland (bass) and Matt Clark (drums).

| 4/7/07 | 156 | 1 | | 1 II | | Ferret 079 |
| 7/11/09 | 71 | 1 | | 2 III | | Ferret 4128 |

MAYSA
Born Maysa Leak on 8/16/1966 in Baltimore, Maryland. Female R&B singer. Member of **Incognito**.

| 11/1/08 | 176 | 1 | | 1 Metamorphosis | | Shanachie 5167 |

Billboard DEBUT	PEAK	WKS	R I A A	ARTIST / Album Title	Catalog	Label & Number

MAZARATI
Funk-rock band from Minneapolis, Minnesota: Sir Casey Terry (vocals), Craig Powell (guitar), Tony Christian (guitar), Aaron Paul Keith and Marr Starr (keyboards), Jerome Cox (bass) and Kevin Patricks (drums).

| 4/19/86 | 133 | 8 | | 1 Mazarati .... | | Paisley Park 25368 |

MAZE Featuring Frankie Beverly   **All-Time: #453**
R&B band formed in Philadelphia, Pennsylvania: Frankie Beverly (vocals; born Howard Beverly on 12/6/1946), Wayne Thomas (guitar), Sam Porter (keyboards), Ronald Lowry (percussion), Robin Duhe (bass) and McKinley Williams (drums).

2/26/77	52	45	●	1 Maze Featuring Frankie Beverly		Capitol 11607
2/4/78	27	22	●	2 Golden Time Of Day		Capitol 11710
4/7/79	33	22	●	3 Inspiration		Capitol 11912
8/2/80	31	23	●	4 Joy And Pain		Capitol 12087
7/4/81	34	27	●	5 Live In New Orleans .... [L]		Capitol 12156 [2]
5/28/83	25	26		6 We Are One		Capitol 12262
3/30/85	45	30	●	7 Can't Stop The Love		Capitol 12377
9/20/86	92	11		8 Live In Los Angeles .... [L]		Capitol 12479 [2]
9/23/89	37	22	●	9 Silky Soul		Warner 25802
9/11/93	37	26	●	10 Back To Basics		Warner 45297

MAZZY STAR
Alternative-rock duo from California: songwriter/guitarist David Roback and vocalist **Hope Sandoval**.

| 7/23/94 | 36 | 31 | ▲ | 1 So Tonight That I Might See .... | | Capitol 98253 |
| 11/16/96 | 68 | 5 | | 2 Among My Swan .... | | Capitol 27224 |

MBULU, Letta
Born on 8/23/1942 in Johannesburg, South Africa. Female R&B singer.

| 3/19/77 | 192 | 3 | | 1 There's Music In The Air .... | | A&M 4609 |

MC/M.C.:

MC BRAINS
Born James Davis on 5/24/1974 in Cleveland, Ohio. Male rapper.

| 4/4/92 | 47 | 17 | | 1 Lovers Lane .... | | Motown 6342 |

MC BREED
Born Eric Breed on 7/12/1971 in Flint, Michigan. Died of kidney failure on 11/22/2008 (age 37). Male rapper.

8/31/91	142	10		1 M.C. Breed & DFC		S.D.E.G. 4103
5/30/92	155	4		2 20 Below		Wrap 8109
5/15/93	156	15		3 The New Breed		Wrap 8120
6/25/94	106	6		4 Funkafied		Wrap 8133
7/8/95	143	2		5 Big Baller		Wrap 8148
4/10/99	180	1		6 It's All Good		Power 5290

MC EIHT
Born Aaron Tyler on 5/22/1971 in Los Angeles, California. Male rapper. Leader of **Compton's Most Wanted** (CMW). Played "A-Wax" in the 1993 movie *Menace II Society*.

8/6/94	5	14	●	1 We Come Strapped		Epic Street 57696
4/27/96	16	8		2 Death Threatz		Epic Street 67139
				MC EIHT FEATURING CMW (above 2)		
11/29/97	64	2		3 Last Man Standing		Epic Street 68041
6/26/99	54	7		4 Section 8		Hoo Bangin' 50021
7/8/00	95	6		5 N' My Neighborhood		Hoo-Bangin' 50103

MC5
Hard-rock band from Detroit, Michigan: Rob Tyner (vocals), Wayne Kramer (guitar), Fred "Sonic" Smith (guitar), Michael Davis (bass) and Dennis Thompson (drums). Tyner died of a heart attack on 9/17/1991 (age 46). Smith married **Patti Smith** on 3/1/1980; died of a heart attack on 11/4/1994 (age 45). MC5 is short for Motor City Five.

3/8/69	30	23		1 Kick Out The Jams .... [L]		Elektra 74042
				RS500 #294		
				recorded on 10/31/1968 at the Grande Ballroom in Detroit, Michigan		
2/21/70	137	7		2 Back In The USA		Atlantic 8247
				RS500 #451		
7/31/71	204	5		3 High Time...		Atlantic 8285

MC HAMMER
Born Stanley Kirk Burrell on 3/30/1963 in Oakland, California. Male rapper. Billed as **Hammer** from 1991-94.

12/3/88+	30	80	▲²	1 Let's Get It Started		Capitol 90924
3/10/90	●¹²¹	108	▲¹⁰	2 Please Hammer Don't Hurt 'Em		Capitol 92857
11/16/91	2²	54	▲³	3 Too Legit To Quit		Capitol 98151
3/19/94	12	25	▲	4 The Funky Headhunter		Giant 24545
				HAMMER (above 2)		
9/30/95	119	3		5 V Inside Out		Giant 24637

Billboard			R I A A	ARTIST		
DEBUT	PEAK	WKS		Album Title	Catalog	Label & Number

MC LYTE
Born Lana Moorer on 10/11/1971 in Queens, New York; raised in Brooklyn, New York. Female rapper.

10/21/89	86	20		1 Eyes On This		First Priority 91304
10/5/91	102	16		2 Act Like You Know		First Priority 91731
7/10/93	90	16		3 Ain't No Other		First Priority 92230
9/14/96	59	6		4 Bad As I Wanna B		EastWest 61781

M.C. MADNESS — see D.J. MAGIC MIKE

MC MAGIC
Born Marco Cardenas in Phoenix, Arizona. Latin rapper. Leader of **NB Ridaz**.

5/27/06	155	1		1 Magic City		Nastyboy 707006

M.C. POOH
Born Lawrence Thomas on 1/25/1971 in Oakland, California. Male rapper.

3/28/92	158	6		1 Funky As I Wanna Be		Jive 41476
				POOH-MAN (MC POOH)		

MC REN
Born Lorenzo Patterson on 6/14/1969 in Los Angeles, California. Male rapper. Former member of **N.W.A.**

7/18/92	12	13	▲	1 Kizz My Black Azz		Ruthless 53802
12/4/93	22	14		2 Shock Of The Hour		Ruthless 5505
4/27/96	31	6		3 The Villain In Black		Ruthless 5544
7/18/98	100	3		4 Ruthless For Life		Ruthless 69313

MC SERCH
Born Michael Berrin on 5/6/1967 in Queens, New York. White rapper. Former member of **3rd Bass**.

9/12/92	103	11		1 Return Of The Product		Def Jam 52964

MC SHY D
Born Peter Jones in the Bronx, New York. Male rapper.

6/27/87	197	1		1 Got To Be Tough		Luke Skyywalker 1004

MC SKAT KAT And The Stray Mob
MC Skat Kat is an animated character featured in **Paula Abdul**'s "Opposites Attract" video. Created by Michael Patterson and Candace Reckinger. Voice of MC Skat Kat: Derrick "Delite" Stevens.

9/28/91	197	2		1 The Adventures Of MC Skat Kat And The Stray Mob		Captive 91396

Mc:

McAULEY SCHENKER GROUP — see SCHENKER, Michael, Group

McBRIDE, Martina   All-Time: #281
Born Martina Schiff on 7/29/1966 in Medicine Lodge, Kansas; raised in Sharon, Kansas. Country singer/songwriter. Married sound technician John McBride on 5/15/1988. Sold T-shirts for **Garth Brooks**'s 1991 concert tour. Signed to RCA in early 1992.
AWARDS: CMA: Female Vocalist 1999, 2002, 2003 & 2004 ★ OPRY: 1995

7/2/94	106	30	▲	1 The Way That I Am		RCA 66288
10/14/95	77	25	▲	2 Wild Angels		RCA 66509
9/13/97+	24	93	▲³	3 Evolution	Cat:#11/17	RCA 67516
11/28/98	68	7	▲	4 White Christmas	Cat:#3/65 [X]	RCA 67654
				Christmas charts: 6/'98, 8/'99, 14/'00, 14/'02, 28/'03, 20/'04, 25/'05, 17/'06, 13/'07, 38/'08, 36/'09		
12/5/09	112	4		5 White Christmas	[X-R]	RCA 67654
10/2/99	19	37	▲	6 Emotion		RCA 67824
10/6/01	5	104	▲³	7 Greatest Hits	Cat:#3/80 [G]	RCA 67012
10/18/03	7	89	▲²	8 Martina		RCA 54207
11/5/05	3²	27	▲	9 Timeless		RCA 72425
4/21/07	4	24	●	10 Waking Up Laughing		RCA 03674
5/17/08	112	2		11 Live In Concert	[L]	RCA 28338
4/11/09	10	9		12 Shine		RCA 34190

McBRIDE & THE RIDE
Country trio formed in Nashville, Tennessee: Terry McBride (vocals, bass), Ray Herndon (guitar) and Billy Thomas (drums).

6/29/91	180	8		1 Burnin' Up The Road		MCA 42343
5/16/92	144	10	●	2 Sacred Ground		MCA 10540

McCAIN, Edwin
Born on 1/20/1970 in Greenville, South Carolina. Adult Alternative singer/songwriter/guitarist.

9/2/95	107	12		1 Honor Among Thieves		Lava 92597
4/18/98	73	42	▲	2 Misguided Roses		Lava 82995
7/3/99	59	22	●	3 Messenger		Lava 83197
7/7/01	105	4		4 Far From Over		Lava 83447
7/10/04	183	1		5 Scream & Whisper		DRT 00409

Billboard			R I A A	ARTIST		
DEBUT	PEAK	WKS		Album Title	Catalog	Label & Number

McCALL, C.W.
Born William Fries on 11/15/1928 in Audubon, Iowa. Country singer/songwriter. The character "C.W. McCall" was created for the Mertz Bread Company (Fries was their advertising man). In 1982, was elected mayor of Ouray, Colorado (served two terms).

4/12/75	143	9		1 Wolf Creek Pass	MGM 4989
11/29/75+	12	19	●	2 Black Bear Road	MGM 5008
5/8/76	143	4		3 Wilderness	Polydor 6069
6/7/03	78	8		4 American Spirit	American Gram. 1776
				MANNHEIM STEAMROLLER & C.W. McCALL	

McCALLUM, David
Born on 9/19/1933 in Glasgow, Scotland. Studio orchestra conductor/actor. Played "Illya Kuryakin" on TV's *The Man From U.N.C.L.E.* and "Dr. Donald 'Ducky' Mallard" on TV's *NCIS*.

2/26/66	27	24		1 Music - A Part Of Me .... [I]	Capitol 2432
6/11/66	79	12		2 Music: A Bit More Of Me .... [I]	Capitol 2498

McCAMPBELL BROTHERS — see MAC BAND

McCANN, Les
Born on 9/23/1935 in Lexington, Kentucky. Jazz keyboardist/singer.

3/29/69	169	10		1 Much Les .... [I]	Atlantic 1516
12/13/69+	29	38	●	2 Swiss Movement .... [I-L]	Atlantic 1537
				recorded June 1969 at the Montreaux Jazz Festival in Switzerland	
5/29/71	41	27		3 Second Movement .... [I]	Atlantic 1583
				LES McCANN & EDDIE HARRIS (above 2)	
4/8/72	141	6		4 Invitation To Openness .... [I]	Atlantic 1603
10/7/72	181	6		5 Talk To The People	Atlantic 1619
1/18/75	166	4		6 Another Beginning	Atlantic 1666
11/22/75	161	4		7 Hustle To Survive	Atlantic 1679

McCANN, Lila
Born on 12/4/1981 in Steilacoom, Washington. Country singer.

7/19/97	86	43	▲	1 Lila	Asylum 62042
4/10/99	85	18		2 Something In The Air	Asylum 62355
7/14/01	152	2		3 Complete	Warner 48002

McCANN, Peter
Born on 1/29/1950 in Bridgeport, Connecticut. Pop singer/songwriter/pianist.

7/30/77	82	12		1 Peter McCann	20th Century 544

McCARLEY, Erin
Born on 1/8/1979 in Garland, Texas. Adult Alternative singer/songwriter/guitarist.

1/17/09	76	3		1 Love, Save The Empty	Universal Rep. 012223

McCARTNEY, Jesse
Born on 4/9/1987 in Manhattan, New York. Teen idol singer/songwriter. Member of **Dream Street**.

10/16/04+	15	69	▲	1 Beautiful Soul	Hollywood 162470
12/3/05	153	6		2 Live: The Beautiful Soul Tour .... [L]	Hollywood 162558
10/7/06	15	14		3 Right Where You Want Me	Hollywood 162614
6/7/08	14	24		4 Departure	Hollywood 001942

McCARTNEY, Paul
1970s: #11 / All-Time: #20

Born James Paul McCartney on 6/18/1942 in Allerton, Liverpool, England. Founding member/bass guitarist of **The Beatles**. Married Linda Eastman on 3/12/1969. First solo album in 1970. Formed group **Wings** in 1971 with Linda (keyboards, backing vocals), Denny Laine (guitar; **Moody Blues**) and Denny Seiwell (drums). Henry McCullough (guitar; **Grease Band**) joined in 1972. Seiwell and McCullough left in 1973. In 1975, Joe English (drums) and **Thunderclap Newman** guitarist Jimmy McCulloch (died on 9/27/1979, age 26) joined; both left in 1977. Wings officially disbanded in April 1981. Backing band since 1989 included Linda, Hamish Stuart (guitar; **AWB**), Robbie McIntosh (guitar; **Night**, **The Pretenders**), Paul Wickens (piano) and Chris Whitten (drums). Blair Cunningham (**Haircut One Hundred**) replaced Whitten by 1993. McCartney starred in own movie *Give My Regards To Broad Street* (1984). Knighted by Queen Elizabeth in 1997. Married to ex-model Heather Mills, 2002-08. Recorded experimental music with Martin "Youth" Glover as **The Fireman**.

AWARDS: Grammy: Lifetime Achievement 1990 ★ R&R Hall of Fame: 1999

5/9/70	❶³	47	▲²	1 McCartney	Apple 3363
6/5/71	2²	37	▲	2 Ram	Apple 3375
				PAUL AND LINDA McCARTNEY	
12/25/71+	10	18	●	3 Wild Life	Apple 3386
				WINGS	
5/12/73	❶³	31	●	4 Red Rose Speedway	Apple 3409
12/22/73+	❶⁴	116	▲³	5 Band On The Run Cat:❶¹/44	Apple 3415
				PAUL McCARTNEY & WINGS (above 2)	
				RS500 #418	
6/14/75	❶¹	77	▲	6 Venus And Mars	Capitol 11419
4/10/76	❶⁷	51	▲	7 Wings At The Speed Of Sound	Capitol 11525
4/15/78	2⁶	28	▲	8 London Town	Capitol 11777
6/30/79	8	24	▲	9 Back To The Egg	Columbia 36057
				WINGS (above 4)	
6/14/80	3⁵	19	●	10 McCartney II	Columbia 36511

McCARTNEY, Paul — cont'd

DEBUT	PEAK	WKS				
1/31/81	158	3		11 The McCartney Interview .... [T]		Columbia 36987
				no track titles listed on this album		
5/15/82	**❶**³	29	▲	12 Tug Of War		Columbia 37462
11/19/83	15	24	▲	13 Pipes Of Peace		Columbia 39149
11/10/84	21	18	●	14 Give My Regards To Broad Street .... [S]		Columbia 39613
9/13/86	30	22		15 Press To Play..		Capitol 12475
6/24/89	21	49	●	16 Flowers In The Dirt		Capitol 91653
11/16/91	109	3		17 CHOBA B CCCP - The Russian Album		Capitol 97615
11/16/91	177	6		18 Paul McCartney's Liverpool Oratorio		EMI 54371 [2]
2/27/93	17	20		19 Off The Ground		Capitol 80362
6/14/97	2¹	20	●	20 Flaming Pie		Capitol 56500
11/1/97	194	1		21 Paul McCartney's Standing Stone		EMI Classics 56484
10/23/99	27	6		22 Run Devil Run		Capitol 22351
12/1/01	26	10		23 Driving Rain		MPL 35510
10/1/05	6	21	●	24 Chaos And Creation In The Backyard		MPL 38299
6/23/07	3²	15	●	25 Memory Almost Full		MPL 30348
12/13/08	67	10		26 Electric Arguments		MPL 0063
				THE FIREMAN		
				GREATEST HITS & COMPILATIONS:		
12/9/78+	29	18	▲	27 Wings Greatest		Capitol 11905
12/19/87+	62	17	▲²	28 All The Best!...	Cat:#36/1	Capitol 48287 [2]
5/26/01	2¹	14	▲²	29 Wingspan: Hits And History		MPL 32946 [2]
				LIVE ALBUMS:		
12/25/76+	**❶**¹	86	▲	30 Wings Over America		Capitol 11593 [3]
11/24/90	26	16		31 Tripping The Live Fantastic		Capitol 94778 [2]
12/15/90+	141	9	▲	32 Tripping The Live Fantastic - Highlights!		Capitol 95379
6/22/91	14	8		33 Unplugged (The Official Bootleg)		Capitol 96413
12/4/93	78	4		34 Paul Is Live		Capitol 27704
12/14/02	8	15	▲²	35 Back In The U.S. Live 2002		MPL 42318 [2]
2/14/09	119	1		36 Amoeba's Secret .... [EP]		MPL 31306
12/5/09	16	10	●	37 Good Evening New York City.............................		MPL 31857

McCLAIN, Alton, & Destiny

Female disco vocal trio: Alton McClain, Delores Warren and Robyrda Stiger. Warren died in a car crash on 2/22/1985 (age 32).

DEBUT	PEAK	WKS				
3/31/79	88	16		1 Alton McClain & Destiny		Polydor 6163

McCLINTON, Delbert

Born on 11/4/1940 in Lubbock, Texas. Blues-rock-country singer/songwriter/guitarist. Recorded as a duo with Glen Clark (see #1 below).

DEBUT	PEAK	WKS				
12/15/73	212	5		1 Subject To Change...		Clean 602
				DELBERT & GLEN		
6/30/79	146	6		2 Keeper Of The Flame		Capricorn 0223
11/22/80+	34	28		3 The Jealous Kind		Capitol 12115
6/6/81	204	4		4 The Best Of Delbert McClinton .... [G]		MCA 5197
12/5/81+	181	9		5 Plain' From The Heart		Capitol 12188
5/30/92	118	13		6 Never Been Rocked Enough		Curb 77521
10/25/97	116	5		7 One Of The Fortunate Few		Curb/Rising Tide 53042
3/24/01	103	3		8 Nothing Personal		New West 6024
				Grammy: Contemporary Blues Album		
10/12/02	84	4		9 Room To Breathe		New West 6042
9/10/05	105	3		10 Cost Of Living..		New West 6079
				Grammy: Contemporary Blues Album		
9/5/09	131	1		11 Acquired Taste		New West 6174
				DELBERT McCLINTON & DICK50		

McCLURKIN, Donnie

Born on 11/9/1959 in Amityville, New York. Black gospel singer.

DEBUT	PEAK	WKS				
9/9/00+	69	73	▲	1 Live In London And More... .... [L]		Verity 43150
				recorded at Fairfield Hall in London, England		
3/22/03	31	16	●	2 Donnie McClurkin...Again		Verity 43199
				Grammy: Contemporary Soul Gospel Album		
4/23/05	12	17	▲	3 Psalms, Hymns & Spiritual Songs....................		Verity 64137 [2]
				Grammy: Traditional Soul Gospel Album		
3/31/07	182	1		4 We Praise You		GospoCentric 69697
				THE McCLURKIN PROJECT		
4/18/09	26	9		5 We All Are One (Live In Detroit) .... [L]		Verity 36108

McCOMAS, Brian

Born on 5/23/1972 in Bethesda, Maryland; raised in Harrison, Arkansas. Country singer/songwriter.

DEBUT	PEAK	WKS				
8/9/03	149	1		1 Brian McComas		Lyric Street 165025

McCOO, Marilyn, & Billy Davis, Jr.
Husband-and-wife R&B vocal duo. McCoo was born on 9/30/1943 in Jersey City, New Jersey. Davis was born on 6/26/1939 in St. Louis, Missouri. Both were members of **The 5th Dimension**. Married on 7/26/1969. Duo hosted own summer variety TV series in 1977. McCoo co-hosted TV's *Solid Gold* from 1981-84.

9/18/76+	30	38	●	1 I Hope We Get To Love In Time		ABC 952
8/20/77	57	8		2 The Two Of Us		ABC 1026
10/7/78	146	6		3 Marilyn & Billy		Columbia 35603

McCORMICK, Gayle
Born in 1949 in St. Louis, Missouri. Former lead singer of **Smith**.

10/16/71	198	3		1 Gayle McCormick		Dunhill/ABC 50109

McCOY, Charlie
Born on 3/28/1941 in Oak Hill, West Virginia. Country harmonica player.
AWARD: C&W Hall of Fame: 2009

5/6/72	98	25		1 The Real McCoy	[I]	Monument 31359
				Grammy: Country Instrumental Album		
11/25/72	120	13		2 Charlie McCoy	[I]	Monument 31910
7/21/73	155	6		3 Good Time Charlie	[I]	Monument 32215
3/23/74	213	4		4 The Fastest Harp In The South	[I]	Monument 32749

McCOY, Neal
Born Hubert Neal McGaughey on 7/30/1958 in Jacksonville, Texas. Country singer.

2/26/94	84	34	▲	1 No Doubt About It		Atlantic 82568
2/11/95	68	24	▲	2 You Gotta Love That!		Atlantic 82727
6/22/96	61	17	●	3 Neal McCoy		Atlantic 82907
6/28/97	55	29	▲	4 Greatest Hits	[G]	Atlantic 83011
11/15/97	135	9		5 Be Good At It		Atlantic 83057
9/10/05	32	7		6 That's Life		903 Records 1001

McCOY, Van
Born on 1/6/1940 in Washington DC. Died of a heart attack on 7/6/1979 (age 39). Disco songwriter/producer.

8/16/75	181	4		1 From Disco To Love	[E]	Buddah 5648
				originally released in 1972		
4/26/75	12	23		2 Disco Baby		Avco 69006
				VAN McCOY & The Soul City Symphony		
10/18/75	80	7		3 The Disco Kid		Avco 69009
5/8/76	106	17		4 The Real McCoy		H&L 69012
10/30/76	202	3		5 Rhythms Of The World		H&L 69014
1/8/77	193	2		6 The Hustle And Best Of Van McCoy	[G]	H&L 69016

McCOYS, The
Pop-rock band from Union City, Indiana: brothers Rick Zehringer (vocals, guitar) and Randy Zehringer (drums), with Randy Hobbs (bass) and Ronnie Brandon (keyboards). Rick later recorded as **Rick Derringer**. Hobbs died on 8/5/1993 (age 45).

11/20/65+	44	19		1 Hang On Sloopy		Bang 212

McCRAE, George
Born on 10/19/1944 in West Palm Beach, Florida. Disco singer. Married to **Gwen McCrae** from 1967-77.

8/3/74	38	15		1 Rock Your Baby		TK 501
7/5/75	152	5		2 George McCrae		TK 602

McCRAE, Gwen
Born on 12/21/1943 in Pensacola, Florida. Disco singer. Married to **George McCrae** from 1967-77.

6/28/75	121	10		1 Rockin' Chair		Cat 2605

McCRARYS, The
R&B vocal group from Los Angeles, California: siblings Linda, Charity, Alfred and Sam McCrary.

9/9/78	138	9		1 Loving Is Living		Portrait 34764

McCREADY, Mindy
Born on 11/30/1975 in Fort Myers, Florida. Country singer.

5/18/96	40	58	▲	1 Ten Thousand Angels		BNA 66806
11/22/97	83	9	●	2 If I Don't Stay The Night		BNA 67504
10/2/99	155	1		3 I'm Not So Tough		BNA 67765

McCREARY, Mary
Born in San Francisco, California. R&B singer/songwriter/pianist. Former member of group Little Sister. Married to **Leon Russell** from 1975-80.

10/26/74	203	8		1 Jezebel		Shelter 2110

McCULLOCH, Ian
Born on 5/5/1959 in Liverpool, England. Lead singer of **Echo & The Bunnymen**.

11/25/89	179	1		1 Candleland		Sire 26012

McCULLOUGH, Ullanda
Born in Detroit, Michigan. Female disco singer.

4/11/81	204	6		1 Ullanda McCullough		Atlantic 19296

McDANIELS, Gene
Born on 2/12/1935 in Kansas City, Missouri; raised in Omaha, Nebraska. R&B-pop singer.

~ ~ ~ ~ ~ ~ ~ ~ ~ ~ ~ **NON-CHARTED ALBUMS** ~ ~ ~ ~ ~ ~ ~ ~ ~ ~ ~

1961 **100 Lbs. Of Clay!**   1962 **Hit After Hit**

McDONALD, Audra
Born on 7/3/1970 in Berlin, Germany; raised in Fresno, California. Classically-trained soprano singer/actress. Starred in several Broadway shows.

| 3/18/00 | 197 | 2 | | 1 How Glory Goes .... | | Nonesuch 79580 |

McDONALD, Country Joe — see COUNTRY JOE

McDONALD, Kathi
Born on 9/25/1948 in Anacortes, Washington. Former session singer.

| 4/6/74 | 156 | 11 | | 1 Insane Asylum .... | | Capitol 11224 |

McDONALD, Michael
Born on 2/12/1952 in St. Louis, Missouri. Pop-rock singer/songwriter/keyboardist. Former lead singer of **The Doobie Brothers**. Married **Amy Holland** on 5/21/1983.

8/28/82	6	32	●	1 If That's What It Takes		Warner 23703
9/7/85	45	15		2 No Lookin' Back		Warner 25291
6/2/90	110	14		3 Take It To Heart		Reprise 25979
7/12/03+	14	57	▲	4 Motown		Motown 000651
2/28/04	19^C	5	●	5 The Very Best Of Michael McDonald .... [G]		Warner 76649
				first released in 2001		
11/13/04	9	17	●	6 Motown Two		Motown 003472
1/15/05	43^X	1		7 The Best Of Michael McDonald: 20th Century Masters The Christmas Collection .... [X]		MCA Nashville 002825
8/27/05	19	8		8 The Ultimate Collection .... [G]		Warner 73167
3/22/08	12	7		9 Soul Speak		Universal Motown 010806
10/17/09	95	3		10 This Christmas .... [X]		Chonin 83036
				Christmas chart: 1/'09		

McDONALD, Richie
Born on 2/6/1962 in Mesquite, Texas; raised in Lubbock, Texas. Christian country singer/songwriter/guitarist. Former lead singer of **Lonestar**.

| 10/18/08 | 126 | 4 | | 1 I Turn To You .... | | Lucid 119186 |

McDONALD, Shawn
Born in 1978 in Eugene, Oregon. Contemporary Christian singer/songwriter.

| 3/25/06 | 116 | 1 | | 1 Ripen .... | | Sparrow 11569 |
| 3/29/08 | 198 | 1 | | 2 Roots .... | | Sparrow 91042 |

McDONALD AND GILES
Keyboardist Ian McDonald was born on 6/25/1946 in Osterley, Middlesex, England. Drummer Michael Giles was born on 3/1/1942 in Waterlooville, Hampshire, England. Both were members of **King Crimson**.

| 2/20/71 | 201 | 11 | | 1 McDonald And Giles .... | | Cotillion 9042 |

McDUFF, Brother Jack
Born Eugene McDuffy on 9/17/1926 in Champaign, Illinois. Died of a heart attack on 1/23/2001 (age 74). Jazz organist.

6/15/63	101	4		1 Screamin'... [I]		Prestige 7259
11/9/63	81	14		2 Live! .... [I-L]		Prestige 7274
7/23/66	137	4		3 Together Again! .... [I]		Prestige 7364
				WILLIS JACKSON & JACK McDUFF		
12/13/69+	192	6		4 Down Home Style .... [I]		Blue Note 84322

McENTIRE, Reba   1990s: #8 / All-Time: #113
Born on 3/28/1955 in Chockie, Oklahoma. Country singer/actress. Competed in rodeos as a horseback barrel rider. Married to rodeo champion Charlie Battles from 1976-87. Married her manager, Narvel Blackstock, in 1989. Acted in the movies *Tremors* and *North*; starred on Broadway in *Annie Get Your Gun*; starred in TV sitcom *Reba* from 2001-07.

AWARDS: CMA: Female Vocalist 1984, 1985, 1986 & 1987 / Entertainer 1986 ★ Billboard Woman of the Year: 2007 ★ OPRY: 1986

10/10/87	102	20	▲	1 The Last One To Know		MCA 42030
5/21/88	118	10	▲	2 Reba	Cat:#50/1	MCA 42134
6/3/89	78	18	▲	3 Sweet Sixteen	Cat:#40/1	MCA 6294
10/14/89	124	8	▲	4 Live .... [L]		MCA 8034
				recorded on 4/3/1989 at the McCallum Theatre in Palm Desert, California		
9/22/90+	39	89	▲³	5 Rumor Has It..		MCA 10016
10/19/91	13	80	▲³	6 For My Broken Heart		MCA 10400
1/2/93	8	56	▲³	7 It's Your Call		MCA 10673
5/14/94	2^1	83	▲³	8 Read My Mind		MCA 10994
10/21/95	5	38	▲	9 Starting Over		MCA 11264

DEBUT	PEAK	WKS	R I A A	ARTIST Album Title	Catalog	Label & Number
				McENTIRE, Reba — cont'd		
11/23/96	15	42	▲	10 What If It's You		MCA 11500
6/20/98	8	30	▲	11 If You See Him		MCA Nashville 70019
12/11/99	28	40	▲	12 So Good Together		MCA Nashville 170119
12/6/03	25	34	▲	13 Room To Breathe		MCA Nashville 000451
10/6/07	❶¹	51	▲	14 Reba: Duets		MCA Nashville 008903
9/5/09	❶¹	39↑	●	15 Keep On Loving You		Valory 0100
				CHRISTMAS ALBUMS:		
12/19/87+	19ˣ	15	▲²	16 Merry Christmas To You	Cat:#15/16	MCA 42031
				Christmas charts: 30/'87, 27/'92, 25/'93, 19/'94, 36/'95, 30/'96, 38/'97, 38/'99		
11/20/99	85	9		17 Secret Of Giving: A Christmas Collection		MCA Nashville 170092
				Christmas charts: 8/'99, 32/'00, 37/'03		
				GREATEST HITS & COMPILATIONS:		
6/6/87	139	23	▲³	18 Reba McEntire's Greatest Hits............	Cat:#20/25	MCA 5979
10/16/93	5	94	▲⁵	19 Greatest Hits Volume Two		MCA 10906
11/10/01	18	15	●	20 Greatest Hits Volume III: I'm A Survivor		MCA Nashville 170202
12/10/05	12	21	▲²	21 Reba: #1's		MCA Nashville 005366 [2]
				McFADDEN & WHITEHEAD		
				R&B duo from Philadelphia, Pennsylvania: Gene McFadden and John Whitehead. Wrote numerous hit songs. Whitehead was shot to death on 5/11/2004 (age 56). McFadden died of cancer on 1/27/2006 (age 56).		
6/2/79	23	17	●	1 McFadden & Whitehead............		Philadelphia Int'l. 35800
10/4/80	153	6		2 I Heard It In A Love Song		TSOP 36773
				McFARLAND, Gary		
				Born on 10/23/1933 in Los Angeles, California. Died of a heart attack on 11/1/1971 (age 38). Jazz vibraphonist.		
4/19/69	189	3		1 America The Beautiful .... [I]		Skye 8
				McFERRIN, Bobby		
				Born on 3/11/1950 in Manhattan, New York. Unaccompanied, jazz-styled improvisation vocalist.		
3/21/87	103	19		1 Spontaneous Inventions		Blue Note 85110
4/23/88	5	55	▲	2 Simple Pleasures		EMI-Manhattan 48059
11/24/90	146	22		3 Medicine Music............		EMI 92048
2/15/92	93	18	●	4 Hush		Sony 48177
				YO-YO MA & BOBBY McFERRIN		
				McGEE, Pat, Band		
				Born on 1/16/1973 in Richmond, Virginia. Male rock singer/guitarist. His band: Al Walsh (guitar), Chardy McEwan (percussion), Jon Williams (keyboards), John Small (bass) and Chris Williams (drums).		
4/29/00	181	1		1 Shine		Giant 24734
				McGILPIN, Bob		
				Born in Fort Dix, New Jersey. Disco singer/songwriter.		
9/16/78	204	4		1 Superstar		Butterfly 010
				McGOVERN, Maureen		
				Born on 7/27/1949 in Youngstown, Ohio. Adult Contemporary singer. Acted in the Broadway show *Pirates Of Penzance*.		
7/28/73	77	16		1 The Morning After		20th Century 419
7/12/75	201	3		2 Academy Award Performance		20th Century 474
9/8/79	162	10		3 Maureen McGovern............		Warner/Curb 3327
				McGRATH, Bob		
				Born on 6/13/1932 in Ottawa, Illinois. Singer/actor. Joined TV's *Sesame Street* in 1969.		
8/15/70	126	11		1 Bob McGrath From Sesame Street............		Affinity 1001

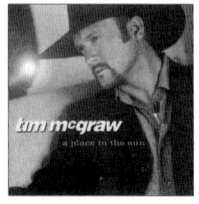

				McGRAW, Tim 2000s: #6 / All-Time: #106		
				Born Samuel Timothy Smith on 5/1/1967 in Delhi, Louisiana; raised in Start, Louisiana. Country singer/songwriter/guitarist. Son of former Major League baseball pitcher Tug McGraw (died on 1/5/2004, age 59). Married **Faith Hill** on 10/6/1996. Acted in the movies *Black Cloud*, *Friday Night Lights* and *Flicka*.		
				AWARD: CMA: Male Vocalist 1999 & 2000 / Entertainer 2001		
4/9/94	❶²	115	▲⁶	1 Not A Moment Too Soon	Cat:#43/1	Curb 77659
10/7/95	4	71	▲³	2 All I Want		Curb 77800
6/21/97	2¹	104	▲⁴	3 Everywhere	Cat:#5/75	Curb 77886
				CMA: *Album of the Year*		
5/22/99	❶¹	86	▲³	4 A Place In The Sun		Curb 77942
				CMA: *Album of the Year*		
5/12/01	2¹	78	▲³	5 Set This Circus Down	Cat:#20/21	Curb 78711
12/14/02	2²	88	▲³	6 Tim McGraw And The Dancehall Doctors		Curb 78746
9/11/04	❶²	86	▲⁴	7 Live Like You Were Dying		Curb 78858

Billboard			R I A A	ARTIST		
DEBUT	PEAK	WKS		Album Title	Catalog	Label & Number
				McGRAW, Tim — cont'd		
4/14/07	**❶**[1]	67	▲	8 Let It Go		Curb 78974
11/7/09	**2**[1]	30↑	●	9 Southern Voice		Curb 79152
				GREATEST HITS & COMPILATIONS:		
12/9/00	**4**	104	▲[6]	10 Greatest Hits	Cat:**❶**[7]/282	Curb 77978
4/15/06	**2**[1]	92	▲[2]	11 Greatest Hits Vol. 2: Reflected	Cat:#18/24	Curb 78891
5/17/08	**10**	50		12 Greatest Hits: Limited Edition		Curb 79086 [2]
10/25/08	**9**	15		13 Greatest Hits 3		Curb 79118
				McGRIFF, Jimmy		
				Born on 4/3/1936 in Philadelphia, Pennsylvania. Died on 5/24/2008 (age 72). Jazz organist.		
12/1/62+	**22**	27		1 I've Got A Woman .... [I]		Sue 1012
11/21/64	**146**	2		2 Topkapi .... [I]		Sue 1033
12/5/64	**15**[X]	4		3 Christmas With McGriff .... [X-I]		Sue 1018
5/29/65	**130**	6		4 Blues For Mister Jimmy .... [I]		Sue 1039
12/28/68+	**161**	19		5 The Worm .... [I]		Solid State 18045
8/7/76	**208**	1		6 The Mean Machine .... [I]		Groove Merchant 3311
				McGRUFF		
				Born in Harlem, New York. Male rapper.		
7/4/98	**169**	1		1 Destined To Be		Uptown 53126
				McGUFFEY LANE		
				Country-rock band from Columbus, Ohio: Bob McNelley (vocals), Terry Efaw (guitar), John Schwab (guitar), Stephen Douglass (keyboards), Stephen Reis (bass) and Dave Rangeler (drums). Group name taken from a street in Athens, Ohio. Douglass died in a car crash on 1/12/1984 (age 33). McNelley died from a self-inflicted gunshot wound on 1/7/1987 (age 36).		
1/31/81	**205**	3		1 McGuffey Lane		Atco 133
1/23/82	**193**	6		2 Aqua Dream		Atco 144
				McGUINN, Mark		
				Born on 8/19/1968 in Greensboro, North Carolina. Country singer/songwriter/guitarist.		
5/26/01	**117**	4		1 Mark McGuinn		VFR 734757
				McGUINN, Roger		
				Born James McGuinn on 7/13/1942 in Chicago, Illinois. Lead singer/guitarist of **The Byrds**. Changed name to Roger in 1968. With **Bobby Darin**'s band and **The Chad Mitchell Trio**, prior to forming The Byrds.		
7/14/73	**137**	9		1 Roger McGuinn		Columbia 31946
9/28/74	**92**	6		2 Peace On You		Columbia 32956
7/5/75	**165**	5		3 Roger McGuinn & Band		Columbia 33541
6/19/76	**204**	5		4 Cardiff Rose		Columbia 34154
5/14/77	**206**	1		5 Thunderbyrd		Columbia 34656
1/26/91	**44**	17		6 Back From Rio		Arista 8648
				McGUINN, CLARK & HILLMAN		
				Pop-rock trio: **Roger McGuinn**, **Gene Clark** and **Chris Hillman**. All were founding members of **The Byrds**. Clark died on 5/24/1991 (age 46).		
2/24/79	**39**	19		1 McGuinn, Clark & Hillman		Capitol 11910
2/16/80	**136**	7		2 City		Capitol 12043
				ROGER McGUINN AND CHRIS HILLMAN FEATURING GENE CLARK		
				McGUINNESS FLINT		
				Rock band formed in England: Tom McGuinness (guitar; **Manfred Mann**), Hughie Flint (drums), Dennis Coulson (vocals), Graham Lyle (guitar) and Benny Gallagher (bass). Also see **Gallagher & Lyle**.		
1/30/71	**155**	8		1 McGuinness Flint		Capitol 625
9/11/71	**198**	2		2 Happy Birthday, Ruthy Baby		Capitol 794
9/1/73	**203**	6		3 Lo & Behold		Sire 7405
				COULSON, DEAN, McGUINNESS, FLINT		
				McGUIRE, Barry		
				Born on 10/15/1937 in Oklahoma City, Oklahoma. Folk-rock singer. Member of **The New Christy Minstrels** from 1962-65.		
9/25/65	**37**	21		1 Eve Of Destruction		Dunhill 50003
				McGUIRE SISTERS, The		
				Vocal trio from Middletown, Ohio: sisters Phyllis McGuire (born on 2/14/1931), Christine McGuire (born on 7/30/1929) and Dorothy McGuire (born on 2/13/1926).		
2/5/55	**2**[1]	8		1 By Request... [EP]		Coral 56123
				EP: Coral EC-81098 (#2); LP: Coral CRL-56123 (#11)		
				~ ~ ~ ~ ~ ~ ~ ~ ~ ~ *NON-CHARTED ALBUM* ~ ~ ~ ~ ~ ~ ~ ~ ~ ~ ~		
				1958 Sugartime		
				McINTYRE, Joey		
				Born on 12/31/1972 in Needham, Massachusetts. Former member of **New Kids On The Block**. Finished third on season 1 on *Dancing With The Stars*.		
4/3/99	**49**	18	●	1 Stay The Same		Columbia 69856

McKAGAN, Duff
Born Michael McKagan on 2/5/1964 in Seattle, Washington. Hard-rock bassist. Member of **Guns N' Roses** and **Velvet Revolver**.

10/16/93	137	2	1 Believe In Me	Geffen 24605

McKAY, Nellie
Born Eleanora Marie on 4/13/1984 in London, England; raised in Manhattan, New York. Adult Alternative singer/songwriter.

3/20/04	181	1	1 Get Away From Me	Columbia 90664 [2]
10/31/09	198	1	2 Normal As Blueberry Pie: A Tribute To Doris Day	Verve 013218

McKEE, Maria
Born on 8/17/1964 in Los Angeles, California. Former lead singer of **Lone Justice**.

7/1/89	120	15	1 Maria McKee	Geffen 24229

McKENDREE SPRING
Folk-pop band from Glens Falls, New York: Fran McKendree (vocals, guitar), Martin Slutsky (guitar), Michael Dreyfuss (violin) and Larry Tucker (bass). By 1974, Tucker had been replaced by Christopher Bishop and drummer Carson Michaels had joined.

11/28/70	192	2	1 Second Thoughts	Decca 75230
5/20/72	163	7	2 McKendree Spring 3	Decca 75332
5/3/75	118	8	3 Get Me To The Country	Pye 12108
3/27/76	193	3	4 Too Young To Feel This Old	Pye 12124

McKENNA, Lori
Born Lorraine Giroux in 1968 in Stoughton, Massachusetts. Country singer/songwriter/guitarist.

9/1/07	109	1	1 Unglamorous	Stylesonic 44299

McKENNITT, Loreena
Born on 2/17/1957 in Morden, Manitoba, Canada. Adult Alternative singer/harpist.

4/9/94	143	11	●	1 The Mask And Mirror	Warner 45420
10/18/97+	17	61	▲²	2 The Book Of Secrets	Warner 46719
12/9/06	83	13		3 An Ancient Muse	Quinlan Road 007920
9/15/07	190	1		4 Nights From The Alhambra [L]	Quinlan Road 009459 [2]
11/22/08	140	6		5 A Midwinter Night's Dream [X]	Quinlan Road 012096
				Christmas charts: 21/'08, 16/'09	

McKENZIE, Bob & Doug
Comedy duo from Canada: Rick "Bob" Moranis (born on 4/18/1953) and Dave "Doug" Thomas (born on 5/20/1949). Characters created for brief segments of *SCTV* television show. Both featured in the 1983 movie *Strange Brew*. Both also appeared in several other movies and TV shows. Thomas is the older brother of **Ian Thomas**.

1/9/82	8	21	●	1 Great White North [C]	Mercury 4034

McKENZIE, Scott
Born Philip Blondheim on 1/10/1939 in Jacksonville, Florida; raised in Virginia. Folk singer.

12/9/67+	127	7	1 The Voice Of Scott McKenzie	Ode 44002

McKNIGHT, Brian   All-Time: #334
Born on 6/5/1969 in Buffalo, New York. R&B singer/songwriter/aranger/producer. Began singing in church choir as a youth (his grandfather was the choir director). Brother of Claude McKnight of **Take 6**.

9/12/92+	58	37	▲	1 Brian McKnight	Mercury 848605
8/26/95	22	27	●	2 I Remember You	Mercury 528280
10/11/97+	13	62	▲²	3 Anytime	Mercury 536215
12/12/98+	95	6		4 Bethlehem .... Cat:#15/1 [X]	Motown 530944
				Christmas charts: 8/'98, 32/'99	
10/9/99	7	52	▲³	5 Back At One	Motown 153708
9/15/01	7	28	●	6 Superhero	Motown 014743
11/23/02	62	4		7 1989-2002: From There To Here [G]	Motown 066114
4/12/03	7	15	●	8 U Turn	Motown 067315
2/26/05	4	15		9 Gemini	Motown 003317
12/23/06	32	13		10 Ten	Warner 44468
12/6/08	109	5		11 I'll Be Home For Christmas [X]	Razor & Tie 83011
				Christmas chart: 35/'08	
11/14/09	20	3		12 Evolution Of A Man	Hard Work 5122

McKUEN, Rod
Born on 4/29/1933 in Oakland, California. Poet/singer/songwriter/producer/actor. Also see **San Sebastian Strings** and **Glenn Yarbrough**.

1/27/68	178	6		1 Listen To The Warm	RCA Victor 3863
11/16/68	175	5		2 Lonesome Cities [T]	Warner 1758
				Grammy: Spoken Word Record	
3/1/69	149	10		3 Greatest Hits Of Rod McKuen [K]	Warner 1772
8/16/69	175	4		4 The Best Of Rod McKuen [K]	RCA Victor 4127
10/11/69	96	16		5 Rod McKuen At Carnegie Hall [L]	Warner 1794 [2]
				recorded on 4/29/1969	
3/14/70	126	13		6 New Ballads	Warner 1837
9/19/70	148	8		7 Rod McKuen's Greatest Hits-2 [K]	Warner 2560
3/20/71	182	4		8 Pastorale	Warner 1894 [2]
7/31/71	201	2		9 Scandalous John [I-S]	Buena Vista 5004
11/6/71	177	3		10 Rod McKuen Grand Tour [L]	Warner 1947 [2]

McLACHLAN, Sarah — All-Time: #272

Born on 1/28/1968 in Halifax, Nova Scotia, Canada. Adult Alternative singer/songwriter/guitarist/pianist. Founded the all-female *Lilith Fair* concert tour in 1997.

DEBUT	PEAK	WKS	RIAA	#	Album Title	Catalog	Label & Number
4/29/89	132	12	●	1	Touch	Cat:#50/1	Arista 8594
4/25/92	167	4	●	2	Solace		Arista 18631
3/5/94	50	100	▲³	3	Fumbling Towards Ecstasy	Cat:#2¹/138	Arista 18725
4/15/95	78	5	●	4	The Freedom Sessions	[EP]	Arista 18784
8/2/97	2¹	108	▲⁸	5	Surfacing	Cat:#2¹/43	Arista 18970
11/22/03	2¹	54	▲²	6	Afterglow		Arista 50150
11/4/06	7	11	▲	7	Wintersong	Cat:#16/9 [X]	Arista 81504
					Christmas charts: 1/'06, 19/'07, 36/'08, 27/'09		
12/19/09	199	1		8	Wintersong	[X-R]	Arista 81504

GREATEST HITS & COMPILATIONS:

DEBUT	PEAK	WKS	RIAA	#	Album Title	Catalog	Label & Number
1/17/04	200	1		9	Remixed		Nettwerk 58763
9/24/05	76	2		10	Bloom: Remix Album		Nettwerk 69798
5/17/08	44	4		11	Rarities, B-Sides, And Other Stuff 2		Nettwerk 29160
10/25/08	11	22		12	Closer: The Best Of Sarah McLachlan		Arista 30263

LIVE ALBUMS:

DEBUT	PEAK	WKS	RIAA	#	Album Title	Catalog	Label & Number
7/3/99	3¹	68	▲³	13	Mirrorball	Cat:#27/6	Arista 19049
12/11/04	107	9		14	Afterglow Live		Arista 64494

McLAGAN, Ian

Born on 5/12/1945 in London, England. Keyboardist of **Small Faces** and **Faces**.

DEBUT	PEAK	WKS	#	Album Title	Label & Number
1/19/80	125	9	1	Troublemaker	Mercury 3786
3/14/81	203	1	2	Bump In The Night	Mercury 4007

McLAREN, Malcolm

Born on 1/22/1946 in London, England. Died of cancer on 4/8/2010 (age 64). British entrepreneur. Former manager of the **New York Dolls** and the **Sex Pistols**.

DEBUT	PEAK	WKS	#	Album Title	Catalog	Label & Number
2/18/84	173	6	1	D'ya Like Scratchin'	[EP]	Island 90124
2/2/85	190	6	2	Fans		Island 90242

McLAUGHLIN, John — All-Time: #477

Born on 1/4/1942 in Doncaster, South Yorkshire, England. Jazz-fusion guitarist. Formed his Mahavishnu Orchestra in 1971 with **Billy Cobham**, **Jan Hammer**, Rick Laird and **Jerry Goodman**. Original group disbanded in 1973.

DEBUT	PEAK	WKS	RIAA	#	Album Title	Catalog	Label & Number
1/29/72	89	26		1	The Inner Mounting Flame	[I]	Columbia 31067
					MAHAVISHNU ORCHESTRA WITH JOHN McLAUGHLIN		
7/1/72	194	4		2	My Goal's Beyond	[I]	Douglas 30766
					MAHAVISHNU JOHN McLAUGHLIN		
10/21/72	152	6		3	Extrapolation	[E-I]	Polydor 5510
					recorded in 1969		
11/11/72	206	2		4	Devotion	[I]	Douglas 31568
2/10/73	15	37	●	5	Birds Of Fire	[I]	Columbia 31996
					MAHAVISHNU ORCHESTRA		
7/7/73	14	24	●	6	Love Devotion Surrender	[I]	Columbia 32034
					CARLOS SANTANA & MAHAVISHNU JOHN McLAUGHLIN		
12/22/73+	41	14		7	Between Nothingness & Eternity	[I-L]	Columbia 32766
					recorded August 1973 in Central Park		
6/1/74	43	14		8	Apocalypse	[I]	Columbia 32957
					with the **London Symphony Orchestra** conducted by Michael Tilson Thomas		
3/22/75	68	11		9	Visions Of The Emerald Beyond	[I]	Columbia 33411
2/21/76	118	7		10	Inner Worlds		Columbia 33908
					MAHAVISHNU ORCHESTRA (above 4)		
6/12/76	194	2		11	Shakti With John McLaughlin	[I]	Columbia 34162
4/2/77	168	4		12	A Handful Of Beauty	[I]	Columbia 34372
					SHAKTI WITH JOHN McLAUGHLIN (above 2)		
5/27/78	105	14		13	Electric Guitarist	[I]	Columbia 35326
					JOHNNY McLAUGHLIN		
4/28/79	147	5		14	Electric Dreams	[I]	Columbia 35785
					JOHN McLAUGHLIN WITH THE ONE TRUTH BAND		
5/30/81	97	13		15	Friday Night In San Francisco	[I-L]	Columbia 37152
					JOHN McLAUGHLIN / AL DI MEOLA / PACO DE LUCIA		
					recorded on 12/5/1980 at the Warfield Theatre		
12/12/81	172	4		16	Belo Horizonte	[I]	Warner 3619
2/5/83	202	2		17	Music Spoken Here	[I]	Warner 23723
8/20/83	171	5		18	Passion, Grace & Fire	[I]	Columbia 38645
					JOHN McLAUGHLIN / AL DI MEOLA / PACO DE LUCIA		

McLAUGHLIN, Jon

Born on 9/27/1982 in Anderson, Indiana. Adult Alternative singer/songwriter/pianist.

DEBUT	PEAK	WKS	#	Album Title	Label & Number
5/19/07	81	2	1	Indiana	Island 008106
10/25/08	49	2	2	OK Now	Island 011612

McLAUGHLIN, Pat

Born in Waterloo, Iowa. Male country singer/songwriter/mandolin player.

DEBUT	PEAK	WKS	#	Album Title	Label & Number
4/16/88	195	1	1	Pat McLaughlin	Capitol 48033

McLEAN, Don
Born on 10/2/1945 in New Rochelle, New York. Adult Contemporary singer/songwriter/guitarist.

2/12/72	111	10		1 Tapestry .... [E]		United Artists 5522
				released in 1971		
11/13/71+	❶⁷	48	▲²	2 American Pie	Cat:#3/266	United Artists 5535
12/23/72+	23	19		3 Don McLean		United Artists 5651
11/23/74	120	8		4 Homeless Brother		United Artists 315
2/14/81	28	21		5 Chain Lightning...		Millennium 7756
11/28/81+	156	11		6 Believers		Millennium 7762

McMURTRY, James
Born on 3/18/1962 in Fort Worth, Texas. Folk-rock singer/songwriter/guitarist. Son of novelist Larry McMurtry.

10/14/89	125	9		1 Too Long In The Wasteland		Columbia 45229
5/3/08	136	1		2 Just Us Kids		Lightning Rod 9502

McNEELY, Larry
Born on 1/3/1948 in Lafayette, Indiana. Singer/songwriter/guitarist/banjo player. Regular on Glen Campbell's TV show.

3/6/71	215	1		1 Glen Campbell Presents Larry McNeely		Capitol 674

McNICHOL, Kristy & Jimmy
Brother-and-sister duo from Los Angeles, California: Kristy (born on 9/11/1962) was a cast member of TV's *Family* and *Empty Nest* and acted in several movies. Jimmy (born on 7/2/1961) also acted in several movies.

8/19/78	116	4		1 Kristy & Jimmy McNichol		RCA Victor 2875

McPHATTER, Clyde
Born on 11/15/1932 in Durham, North Carolina. Died of a heart attack on 6/13/1972 (age 39). R&B singer. Lead singer of The Drifters from 1953-55. One of the most influential and distinctive male voices of the early R&B vocal group era.

AWARD: R&R Hall of Fame: 1987

~ ~ ~ ~ ~ ~ ~ ~ ~ **NON-CHARTED ALBUMS** ~ ~ ~ ~ ~ ~ ~ ~ ~ ~ ~

1958 Love Ballads   1963 The Best Of Clyde McPhatter *[Atlantic label]*
1959 Clyde   1963 Clyde McPhatter's Greatest Hits *[Mercury label]*
1960 Clyde McPhatter's Greatest Hits *[MGM label]*

McPHEE, Katharine
Born on 3/25/1984 in Los Angeles, California. Pop singer. Finished in second place on the 2006 season of TV's *American Idol*.

2/17/07	2¹	17		1 Katharine McPhee		RCA 87983

McRAE, Carmen
Born on 4/8/1922 in Harlem, New York. Died of a stroke on 11/10/1994 (age 72). Jazz singer/pianist.

1/14/67	150	2		1 Alfie		Mainstream 56084

McVIE, Christine
Born Christine Perfect on 7/12/1943 in Bouth, Cumbria, England. Singer/keyboardist with Fleetwood Mac from 1970-2002. Married to Fleetwood Mac bassist John McVie from 1968-77.

8/14/76	104	10		1 The Legendary Christine Perfect Album .... [E]		Sire 7522
				recorded in 1969		
2/18/84	26	23		2 Christine McVie		Warner 25059

MDFMK
Rock trio from Chicago, Illinois: Lucia Cifarelli (vocals), Tim Skold (guitar) and Sascha Konietzko (bass). Konietzko was a member of KMFDM.

4/15/00	182	1		1 MDFMK		Republic 157522

MEADER, Vaughn
Born Abbott Vaughn Meader on 3/20/1936 in Waterville, Maine. Died of heart failure on 10/29/2004 (age 68). President John F. Kennedy impersonator.

12/8/62	❶¹²	49	●	1 The First Family	[C]	Cadence 3060
				Grammys: Album of the Year / Comedy Album		
5/25/63	4	17		2 The First Family Volume Two	[C]	Cadence 3065

MEAT LOAF   All-Time: #433
Born Marvin Lee Aday on 9/27/1947 in Dallas, Texas. Pop-rock singer. Sang lead vocals on Ted Nugent's 1976 *Free-For-All* album. Played "Eddie" in the Los Angeles production and movie of *The Rocky Horror Picture Show*. Appeared in several other movies.

10/29/77+	14	82	▲¹⁴	1 Bat Out Of Hell Cat:❶²²/371		Cleveland Int'l. 34974
				RS500 #343		
9/19/81	45	11		2 Dead Ringer		Cleveland Int'l. 36007
5/18/85	74	10		3 Bad Attitude..		RCA Victor 5451
10/2/93	❶¹	55	▲⁵	4 Bat Out Of Hell II: Back Into Hell		MCA 10699
12/2/95	17	14	▲	5 Welcome To The Neighborhood		MCA 11341
10/2/99	129	5		6 VH1 Storytellers .... [L]		Beyond 78065
				recorded on 10/5/1998 in New York City		
10/11/03	85	4		7 Couldn't Have Said It Better		Sanctuary 84653
11/18/06	8	11	●	8 Bat Out Of Hell III: The Monster Is Loose		Virgin 63147

Billboard DEBUT	PEAK	WKS	R I A A	ARTIST / Album Title	Catalog	Label & Number
				MEAT PUPPETS		
				Rock trio from Phoenix, Arizona: brothers Curt Kirkwood (vocals, guitar) and Cris Kirkwood (bass), with Derrick Bostrom (drums).		
4/2/94	62	27	●	1 Too High To Die		London 828484
10/21/95	183	1		2 No Joke!		London 828665
				MECO		
				Born Domenico Monardo on 11/29/1939 in Johnsonburg, Pennsylvania. Disco producer.		
8/6/77	13	28	▲	1 Star Wars And Other Galactic Funk	[I]	Millennium 8001
1/14/78	62	13		2 Encounters Of Every Kind	[I]	Millennium 8004
9/23/78	68	12		3 The Wizard Of Oz	[I]	Millennium 8009
				the single "Themes From The Wizard Of Oz" hit #35 on the *Hot 100*		
8/2/80	140	8		4 Meco Plays Music From The Empire Strikes Back	[EP-I]	RSO 3086
12/13/80	61	6		5 Christmas In The Stars/Star Wars Christmas Album	[X-N]	RSO 3093
4/3/82	68	9		6 Pop Goes The Movies	[I]	Arista 9598
				the single "Pop Goes The Movies" hit #35 on the *Hot 100*		
8/27/83	202	3		7 Ewok Celebration	[I]	Arista 8098
				MEDEIROS, Glenn		
				Born on 6/24/1970 in Lihue, Kauai, Hawaii (of Portugese parents). Pop singer.		
6/13/87	83	17		1 Glenn Medeiros		Amherst 3313
6/23/90	82	18		2 Glenn Medeiros		MCA 6399
				MEDESKI, MARTIN & WOOD		
				Jazz trio from New York: John Medeski (organ), Bill Martin (percussion) and Chris Wood (bass). Sometimes joined by **John Scofield**.		
8/29/98	174	1		1 Combustication	[I]	Blue Note 93011
4/27/02	169	1		2 Uninvisible	[I]	Blue Note 35870
9/25/04	162	1		3 End Of The World Party (Just In Case)	[I]	Blue Note 95633
10/14/06	188	1		4 Out Louder	[I]	Indirecto 01
				MEDESKI, SCOFIELD, MARTIN & WOOD		
				MEDLEY, Bill		
				Born on 9/19/1940 in Santa Ana, California. Half of **The Righteous Brothers** duo.		
10/12/68	188	4		1 Bill Medley 100%		MGM 4583
4/5/69	152	4		2 Soft And Soulful		MGM 4603
				ME FIRST AND THE GIMME GIMMES		
				Punk-rock band from San Francisco, California: Spike Slawson (vocals), Chris Shiflett (guitar), Joey Cape (guitar), Fat Mike Burkett (bass) and Dave Raun (drums).		
7/19/03	131	2		1 Take A Break		Fat Wreck Chords 650
11/6/04	197	1		2 Ruin Jonny's Bar Mitzvah		Fat Wreck Chords 674
11/4/06	169	1		3 Love Their Country		Fat Wreck Chords 712
7/26/08	163	1		4 Have Another Ball: The Unearthed A-Sides Album		Fat Wreck Chords 729
				MEGADETH **All-Time: #236**		
				Thrash-metal band formed in Los Angeles, California: Dave Mustaine (vocals, guitar; born on 9/13/1961), Marty Friedman (guitar; born on 12/8/1962), Dave Ellefson (bass; born on 11/12/1964) and Nick Menza (drums; born on 7/23/1964). Jimmy DeGrasso replaced Menza in 1998. Al Pitrelli replaced Friedman in 2000. Mustaine was an early guitarist with **Metallica**.		
10/25/86	76	47	▲	1 Peace Sells...But Who's Buying?		Capitol 12526
2/6/88	28	23	▲	2 So Far, So Good...So What!		Capitol 48148
10/20/90	23	30	▲	3 Rust In Peace		Capitol 91935
8/1/92	2¹	58	▲²	4 Countdown To Extinction		Capitol 98531
11/19/94	4	23	▲	5 Youthanasia		Capitol 29004
8/5/95	90	7		6 Hidden Treasures	[EP-K]	Capitol 33670
7/5/97	10	29	●	7 Cryptic Writings		Capitol 38262
9/18/99	16	8		8 Risk		Capitol 99134
11/11/00	66	3		9 Capitol Punishment: The Megadeth Years	[G]	Capitol 25916
6/2/01	16	6		10 The World Needs A Hero		Sanctuary 84503
4/6/02	115	1		11 Rude Awakening	[L]	Sanctuary 84544 [2]
10/2/04	18	5		12 The System Has Failed		Sanctuary 84708
7/16/05	65	8		13 Greatest Hits: Back To The Start	[G]	Capitol 73929
6/2/07	8	6		14 United Abominations		Roadrunner 618029
10/3/09	9	8		15 Endgame		Roadrunner 617885
				MEG & DIA		
				Rock duo of sisters from Draper, Utah: Meg Frampton and Dia Frampton.		
5/9/09	103	1		1 Here, Here And Here		Doghouse 511850
				MEHTA, Zubin		
				Born on 4/29/1936 in Bombay, India. Conductor of the Los Angeles Philharmonic Orchestra.		
6/10/72	175	10		1 Gustav Holst: The Planets	[I]	London 6734
3/4/78	130	8		2 Star Wars And Close Encounters Of The Third Kind	[I]	London 1001
				M83		
				Electro-pop band from Antibes, France: Morgan Kibby (vocals, keyboards), Anthony Gonzalez (guitar), Pierre Maulini (bass) and Loic Maurin (drums).		
5/3/08	107	2		1 Saturdays=Youth		Mute 9384

Billboard			R I A A	ARTIST		
DEBUT	PEAK	WKS		Album Title	Catalog	Label & Number

MEIKO
Born on 2/25/1982 in Roberta, Georgia. Female Adult Alternative singer/songwriter.

12/6/08	159	1		1 Meiko		Lucky Ear 10035

MEISNER, Randy
Born on 3/8/1946 in Scottsbluff, Nebraska. Rock singer/bassist. Member of **Poco** (1968-69), **Rick Nelson**'s Stone Canyon Band (1969-71) and the **Eagles** (1971-77).

7/22/78	204	3		1 Randy Meisner...		Asylum 140
11/1/80+	50	33		2 One More Song...		Epic 36748
8/21/82	94	11		3 Randy Meisner...		Epic 38121

MELACHRINO, George, And His Orchestra
Born George Militiades on 5/1/1909 in London, England (of Greek parents). Died on 6/18/1965 (age 56). Conductor/arranger.

1/8/55	10	1		1 Christmas In High Fidelity	[X-I]	RCA Victor 1045
5/25/59	30	1		2 Under Western Skies..	[I]	RCA Victor 1676

MEL AND TIM
R&B vocal duo from Holly Springs, Mississippi: cousins Mel Hardin and Tim McPherson.

1/6/73	175	7		1 Starting All Over Again...		Stax 3007

MELANIE
Born Melanie Safka on 2/3/1947 in Queens, New York. Folk-pop singer/songwriter/guitarist. Formed Neighborhood record label.

11/15/69	196	2		1 Melanie		Buddah 5041
5/9/70	17	37	●	2 Candles In The Rain..		Buddah 5060
9/26/70	33	19		3 Leftover Wine...	[L]	Buddah 5066
2/27/71	80	10		4 The Good Book		Buddah 95000
12/4/71+	115	12		5 Garden In The City...		Buddah 5095
4/1/72	103	9		6 Four Sides Of Melanie	[K]	Buddah 95005 [2]
11/13/71+	15	27	●	7 Gather Me		Neighborhood 47001
11/11/72	70	20		8 Stoneground Words..		Neighborhood 47005
5/12/73	109	11		9 Melanie At Carnegie Hall..	[L]	Neighborhood 49001 [2]
5/11/74	192	4		10 Madrugada		Neighborhood 48001
2/1/75	208	3		11 As I See It Now		Neighborhood 3000
2/17/79	207	2		12 Ballroom Streets		Tomato 9003 [2]

MELLENCAMP, John Cougar
1980s: #23 / All-Time: #105

Born on 10/7/1951 in Seymour, Indiana. Rock singer/songwriter/producer. Given name Johnny Cougar by **David Bowie**'s manager, Tony DeFries. First recorded for MCA in 1976. Directed and starred in the 1992 movie *Falling From Grace*. Married model Elaine Irwin on 9/5/1992.
AWARDS: R&R Hall of Fame: 2008 ★ Billboard Century: 2001

JOHN COUGAR:

8/18/79+	64	29	●	1 John Cougar		Riva 7401
10/4/80+	37	55	▲	2 Nothin' Matters And What If It Did		Riva 7403
5/8/82	❶⁹	106	▲⁵	3 American Fool	Cat:#27/11	Riva 7501

JOHN COUGAR MELLENCAMP:

11/5/83+	9	66	▲³	4 Uh-Huh		Riva 7504
9/14/85	2³	75	▲⁵	5 Scarecrow	Cat:#30/7	Riva 824865
9/19/87	6	53	▲³	6 The Lonesome Jubilee		Mercury 832465
5/27/89	7	23	▲	7 Big Daddy		Mercury 838220

JOHN MELLENCAMP:

10/26/91	17	46	▲	8 Whenever We Wanted..		Mercury 510151
9/25/93	7	24	▲	9 Human Wheels		Mercury 518088
7/9/94	13	30	▲	10 Dance Naked		Mercury 522428
9/28/96	9	30	▲	11 Mr. Happy Go Lucky		Mercury 532896
12/6/97	33	63	▲³	12 The Best That I Could Do 1978-1988	Cat:#24/54 [G]	Mercury 536738
9/4/99	99	4		13 Rough Harvest...		Mercury 558355
				contains new acoustic versions of previous hits		
10/24/98	41	20	●	14 John Mellencamp		Columbia 69602
11/3/01	15	15	●	15 Cuttin' Heads		Columbia 85098
6/21/03	31	7		16 Trouble No More		Columbia 90133
11/6/04	13	18	▲	17 Words & Music: John Mellencamp's Greatest Hits	[G]	Island 003311 [2]
2/10/07	5	9		18 Freedom's Road		Universal Rep. 008249
8/2/08	7	8		19 Life Death Love And Freedom		Hear 30822

MELLO-KINGS
White teen doo-wop group from Mount Vernon, New York: Bob Scholl (lead; died on 8/27/1975, age 30), Jerry Scholl and Eddie Quinn (tenors), Neil Arena (baritone) and Larry Esposito (bass).

~ ~ ~ ~ ~ ~ ~ ~ ~ ~ **NON-CHARTED ALBUM** ~ ~ ~ ~ ~ ~ ~ ~ ~ ~
1960 Tonight-Tonight

Billboard			R I A A	ARTIST Album Title	Catalog	Label & Number
DEBUT	PEAK	WKS				

MELLOW MAN ACE
Born Ulpiano Sergio Reyes on 4/12/1967 in Cuba; raised in Southgate, California. Male rapper. His brother Senen is a member of **Cypress Hill**.

| 6/2/90 | 69 | 16 | | 1 Escape From Havana .... | | Capitol 91295 |

MELUA, Katie
Born Ketevan Melua on 9/16/1984 in Kutaisi, Georgia Republic; raised in Northern Ireland and England. Female singer/songwriter.

| 6/26/04 | 161 | 1 | | 1 Call Off The Search .... | | Dramatico 002666 |
| 6/24/06 | 108 | 2 | | 2 Piece By Piece .... | | Dramatic 006868 |

MELVIN, Harold, And The Blue Notes
Born on 6/25/1939 in Philadelphia, Pennsylvania. Died of a stroke on 3/24/1997 (age 57). R&B singer. The Blue Notes: **Teddy Pendergrass**, Lawrence Brown, Jerry Cummings and Bernard Wilson. Brown died on 4/6/2008 (age 63). Pendergrass died on 1/13/2010 (age 59).

9/2/72	53	31		1 Harold Melvin & The Blue Notes		Philadelphia Int'l. 31648
11/10/73+	57	20		2 Black & Blue		Philadelphia Int'l. 32407
3/1/75	26	32	●	3 To Be True		Philadelphia Int'l. 33148
12/13/75+	9	24	▲	4 Wake Up Everybody		Philadelphia Int'l. 33808
7/4/76	51	14		5 All Their Greatest Hits! .... [G]		Philadelphia Int'l. 34232
2/5/77	56	10		6 Reaching For The World		ABC 969
3/22/80	95	20		7 The Blue Album		Source 3197

MELVINS
Punk-rock trio from Montesano, Washington: Buzz Osborne (vocals, guitar), Jared Warren (bass) and Coady Willis (drums).

| 7/26/08 | 148 | 1 | | 1 Nude With Boots .... | | Ipecac 105 |

MEMBERS, The
Pop-rock band from Surrey, England: Nicky Tesco (vocals), Jean-Marie Carroll and Nigel Bennett (guitars), Simon Lloyd and Steve Thompson (horns), Chris Payne (bass) and Adrian Lillywhite (drums).

| 4/2/83 | 202 | 5 | | 1 Uprhythm, Downbeat .... | | Arista 6605 |

MEMPHIS BLEEK
Born Malik Cox on 6/23/1978 in Brooklyn, New York. Male rapper/songwriter/actor.

8/21/99	7	9	●	1 Coming Of Age		Roc-A-Fella 538991
12/23/00	16	20	●	2 The Understanding		Roc-A-Fella 542587
1/3/04	35	15		3 M.A.D.E.		Roc-A-Fella 000322
6/4/05	11	6		4 534		Roc-A-Fella 004164

MEMPHIS HORNS, The
Studio band from Memphis, Tennessee: Wayne Jackson (trumpet), Andrew Love (tenor sax), James Mitchell (baritone sax), Lewis Collins (soprano sax) and Jack Hale (trombone). Jackson was a member of the **Mar-Keys**.

9/17/77	201	17		1 Get Up & Dance		RCA Victor 2198
				vocalists include James Gilstrap, John Valenti and Deniece Williams		
6/10/78	163	9		2 The Memphis Horns Band II		RCA Victor 2643
10/6/90	51	32	●	3 Midnight Stroll		Mercury 846652
				THE ROBERT CRAY BAND FEATURING THE MEMPHIS HORNS		

MENA, Maria
Born on 2/19/1986 in Oslo, Norway. Pop-rock singer/songwriter.

| 8/7/04 | 102 | 1 | | 1 White Turns Blue .... | | Columbia 92557 |

MEN AT LARGE
R&B vocal duo from Cleveland, Ohio: David Tolliver and Jason Champion.

| 2/20/93 | 122 | 13 | | 1 Men At Large .... | | EastWest 92159 |
| 11/5/94 | 151 | 1 | | 2 One Size Fits All .... | | EastWest 92459 |

MEN AT WORK
Pop-rock band from Melbourne, Australia: **Colin James Hay** (vocals, guitar), Ron Strykert (guitar), Greg Ham (sax, keyboards), John Rees (bass) and Jerry Speiser (drums). Speiser and Rees left in 1984.
AWARD: Grammy: Best New Artist 1982

7/3/82	❶¹⁵	90	▲⁶	1 Business As Usual		Columbia 37978
5/7/83	3⁵	49	▲³	2 Cargo		Columbia 38660
6/22/85	50	13	●	3 Two Hearts		Columbia 40078

MENDES, Sergio, & Brasil '66   **All-Time: #223**
Born on 2/11/1941 in Niteroi, Brazil. Pianist/bandleader. Brasil '66 consisted of **Lani Hall** and Janis Hansen (vocals), Joses Soares (percussion), Bob Matthews (bass) and Jao Palma (drums). The latter four later recorded as **The Carnival**.

9/10/66	7	126	●	1 Sergio Mendes & Brasil '66		A&M 4116
4/29/67	24	46	●	2 Equinox		A&M 4122
3/9/68	5	51	●	3 Look Around		A&M 4137
6/8/68	197	4		4 Sergio Mendes' Favorite Things .... [E-I]		Atlantic 8177
12/7/68+	3¹	30	●	5 Fool On The Hill		A&M 4160
8/16/69	33	17		6 Crystal Illusions		A&M 4197
12/13/69+	71	16		7 Ye-Me-Le		A&M 4236
7/4/70	101	20		8 Greatest Hits .... [G]		A&M 4252
1/9/71	130	9		9 Stillness		A&M 4284

Billboard			R I A A	ARTIST Album Title	Catalog	Label & Number
DEBUT	PEAK	WKS				

DEBUT	PEAK	WKS		ARTIST / Album Title	Catalog	Label & Number
				SERGIO MENDES & BRASIL '77:		
10/16/71	166	6		10 Pais Tropical		A&M 4315
7/15/72	164	5		11 Primal Roots		A&M 4353
6/2/73	116	15		12 Love Music		Bell 1119
5/18/74	176	5		13 Vintage 74		Bell 1305
2/15/75	105	10		14 Sergio Mendes		Elektra 1027
3/27/76	180	2		15 Homecooking		Elektra 1055
8/20/77	81	12		16 Sergio Mendes And The New Brasil '77		Elektra 1102
				SERGIO MENDES:		
5/7/83	27	27		17 Sergio Mendes		A&M 4937
5/19/84	70	22		18 Confetti		A&M 4984
3/4/06	44	10		19 Timeless		Hear 2263
6/28/08	60	8		20 Encanto		Hear 30278

MEN OF VIZION
R&B vocal group from Brooklyn, New York: George Spencer, Corley Randolph, Spanky Williams, Brian Deramus and Desmond Greggs.

7/6/96	186	4		1 Personal		MJJ Music 66947

MENTAL AS ANYTHING
Rock band from Sydney, Australia: brothers Chris "Reg Mombassa" O'Doherty (guitar) and Pete O'Doherty (bass), Martin Plaza (vocals, guitar), Andrew "Greedy" Smith (keyboards) and Wayne Delisle (drums).

10/1/83	203	1		1 Creatures Of Leisure		A&M 4946

MENUDO
Teen vocal group from Puerto Rico. Many personnel changes due to rule that members must retire at age 16. **Ricky Martin** was a member from 1984-88.

3/10/84	108	12		1 Reaching Out		RCA Victor 4993
5/25/85	100	19		2 Menudo		RCA Victor 5420
8/4/07	190	1		3 La Historia	[F-K]	Sony 09631

MEN WITHOUT HATS
Techno-rock band from Montreal, Quebec, Canada: brothers Ivan Doroschuk (vocals), Stefan Doroschuk (guitar) and Colin Doroschuk (keyboards), with Allan McCarthy (drums; died of AIDS on 8/11/1995, age 38).

8/6/83	13	26	●	1 Rhythm Of Youth		Backstreet 39002
10/6/84	127	4		2 Folk Of The '80s (Part III)		MCA 5487
11/14/87+	73	25		3 Pop Goes The World		Mercury 832730

MENZEL, Idina
Born on 5/30/1971 in Queens, New York. Female actress/singer. Appeared in several movies and Broadway shows. Married actor Taye Diggs on 1/11/2003.

2/16/08	58	3		1 I Stand		Warner 44423

MERCEDES
Born Raquel Miller in 1978 in New Orleans, Louisiana. Female rapper.

7/17/99	72	5		1 Rear End		No Limit 50085

MERCER, Roy D.
Roy D. Mercer is a fictional character invented by DJ's Phil Stone and Brent Douglas of KMOD in Tulsa, Oklahoma. Albums contain crank phone calls.

5/9/98	160	5		1 How Big'a Boy Are Ya? Volume 4	[C]	Capitol 94301
2/13/99	138	4		2 How Big'a Boy Are Ya? Volume 5	[C]	Virgin 46854
11/6/99	164	3		3 How Big'a Boy Are Ya? Volume 6	[C]	Virgin 48214
6/24/06	146	2		4 Black & Blue	[C]	Capitol 73921

MERCHANT, Natalie
Born on 10/26/1963 in Jamestown, New York. Adult Alternative singer/songwriter. Lead singer of **10,000 Maniacs** from 1981-93.

7/8/95	13	92	▲5	1 Tigerlily		Elektra 61745
6/6/98	8	51	▲	2 Ophelia		Elektra 62196
11/27/99	82	7		3 Live In Concert	[L]	Elektra 62444
				recorded on 6/13/1999 at the Neil Simon Theater in New York City		
12/1/01	30	11	●	4 Motherland		Elektra 62721

MERCURY, Freddie
Born Farrokh Bulsara on 9/5/1946 in Zanzibar, Tanzania. Died of AIDS on 11/24/1991 (age 45). Lead singer of **Queen**.

5/18/85	159	6		1 Mr. Bad Guy		Columbia 40071

MERCY
Pop group from Florida: James Marvell, Ronnie Caudill, Roger Fuentes, Buddy Good, Debbie Lewis and Brenda McNish.

6/21/69	38	15		1 The Mercy & Love (Can Make You Happy)		Sundi 803

MERCYFUL FATE — see KING DIAMOND

Billboard DEBUT	PEAK	WKS	R I A A	ARTIST Album Title	Catalog	Label & Number

MERCYME
Christian pop-rock band formed in Oklahoma City, Oklahoma: **Bart Millard** (vocals), Mike Scheuchzer (guitar), Nathan Cochran (bass) and Robby Shaffer (drums).

Billboard DEBUT	PEAK	WKS	RIAA	ARTIST / Album Title	Catalog	Label & Number
12/22/01+	37	96	▲²	1 Almost There	Cat:#3/63	INO/Curb 85725
10/19/02	41	29	●	2 Spoken For	Cat:#6/1	INO/Curb 86218
5/8/04	12	30	●	3 Undone		INO/Curb 82947
11/26/05	64	7		4 The Christmas Sessions	Cat:#8/4 [X]	INO/Epic 96414
				Christmas charts: 10/'05, 11/'06, 30/'07, 33/'08		
5/13/06	13	24	●	5 Coming Up To Breathe		INO/Columbia 80646
12/8/07	15	26	●	6 All That Is Within Me	Cat:#6/6	INO 12573
4/25/09	18	15		7 10	[G]	INO 46605

MERRITT, Bishop Andrew
Born in 1950 in Detroit, Michigan. Founded the Straight Gate Church in 1978. Elevated to Bishop in 1990.

Billboard DEBUT	PEAK	WKS	RIAA	ARTIST / Album Title	Catalog	Label & Number
10/21/00	68	1		1 Faith In The House	[L]	Integrity 14482
				BISHOP ANDREW MERRITT & THE STRAIGHT GATE MASS CHOIR		

MERRITT, Tift
Born Catherine Tift Merritt on 1/8/1975 in Houston, Texas; raised in Bynum, North Carolina. Country singer/songwriter/guitarist.

Billboard DEBUT	PEAK	WKS	RIAA	ARTIST / Album Title	Catalog	Label & Number
3/15/08	156	1		1 Another Country		Fantasy 30455

MERRY-GO-ROUND, The
Pop-rock band from Hawthorne, California: **Emitt Rhodes** (vocals), Gary Kato (guitar), Bill Rinehart (bass; **The Leaves**) and Joel Larson (drums: **The Grass Roots**).

Billboard DEBUT	PEAK	WKS	RIAA	ARTIST / Album Title	Catalog	Label & Number
11/18/67	190	2		1 The Merry-Go-Round		A&M 4132

MERRYWEATHER & FRIENDS
Born Neil Merryweather on 12/27/1945 in Winnipeg, Manitoba, Canada. Rock singer/bassist. Friends: **Steve Miller**, **Dave Mason** and Barry Goldberg.

Billboard DEBUT	PEAK	WKS	RIAA	ARTIST / Album Title	Catalog	Label & Number
10/4/69	199	2		1 Word Of Mouth		Capitol 278 [2]

MESHUGGAH
Hard-rock band from Umea, Sweden: Jens Kidman (vocals), Marten Hagstrom (guitar), Fredrik Thordendal (guitar), Jorgen Lindmark (bass) and Per Sjogren (drums).

Billboard DEBUT	PEAK	WKS	RIAA	ARTIST / Album Title	Catalog	Label & Number
8/24/02	165	1		1 Nothing		Nuclear Blast 6542
6/18/05	170	1		2 Catch Thirty-Three		Nuclear Blast 1311
3/29/08	59	3		3 Obzen		Nuclear Blast 11937

MESSINA, Jim
Born on 12/5/1947 in Maywood, California; raised in Harlingen, Texas. Member of **Buffalo Springfield** (1967-68) and **Poco** (1968-70). Formed **Loggins & Messina** duo with **Kenny Loggins**. Joined the re-formed Poco in 1989.

Billboard DEBUT	PEAK	WKS	RIAA	ARTIST / Album Title	Catalog	Label & Number
10/20/79	58	14		1 Oasis		Columbia 36140
				JIMMY MESSINA		
6/20/81	95	11		2 Messina		Warner 3559

MESSINA, Jo Dee
Born on 8/25/1970 in Framingham, Massachusetts; raised in Holliston, Massachusetts. Country singer.
AWARD: CMA: Horizon 1999

Billboard DEBUT	PEAK	WKS	RIAA	ARTIST / Album Title	Catalog	Label & Number
5/4/96	146	5	●	1 Jo Dee Messina		Curb 77820
4/4/98	61	104	▲²	2 I'm Alright	Cat:#2²/19	Curb 77904
8/19/00	19	66	▲	3 Burn	Cat:#45/1	Curb 77977
12/7/02	147	4		4 A Joyful Noise	[X]	Curb 78755
				Christmas chart: 3/'02		
6/7/03	14	20	●	5 Greatest Hits	[G]	Curb 78790
5/14/05	7	16	●	6 Delicious Surprise		Curb 78770

MEST
Punk-rock band from Chicago, Illinois: cousins Tony Lovato (vocals, guitar) and Matt Lovato (bass), Jeremiah Rangel (guitar) and Nick Gigel (drums).

Billboard DEBUT	PEAK	WKS	RIAA	ARTIST / Album Title	Catalog	Label & Number
6/28/03	64	10		1 Mest		Maverick 48456
11/5/05	116	1		2 Photographs		Maverick 49421

METAL CHURCH
Hard-rock band from Kent, Washington: David Wayne (vocals), Craig Wells (guitar), Kurdt Vanderhoof (guitar), Duke Erikson (bass) and Kirk Arrington (drums). By 1989, Mike Howe had replaced Wayne and John Marshall had replaced Vanderhoof.

Billboard DEBUT	PEAK	WKS	RIAA	ARTIST / Album Title	Catalog	Label & Number
11/8/86+	92	23		1 The Dark		Elektra 60493
3/11/89	75	15		2 Blessing In Disguise		Elektra 60817

METALLICA
1980s: #7 / 1990s: #5 / All-Time: #46

Heavy metal band formed in Los Angeles, California: James Hetfield (vocals, guitar; born on 8/3/1963), Kirk Hammett (guitar; born on 11/18/1962), Cliff Burton (bass; born on 2/10/1962) and Lars Ulrich (drums; born on 12/26/1963). Original guitarist Dave Mustaine left in 1982 to form **Megadeth**. Burton was killed in a bus crash on 9/27/1986 (age 24); replaced by Jason Newsted (born on 3/4/1963). Newsted left in 2001; replaced by Robert Trujillo (of **Suicidal Tendencies**) in 2003. Group's life from 2001-03 was chronicled in the 2004 documentary movie *Some Kind Of Monster*.

AWARD: R&R Hall of Fame: 2009

4/5/86	155	10		1 Kill 'Em All..			Megaforce 069
				first released in 1983			
2/13/88	120	8	▲³	2 Kill 'Em All..	Cat:#20/85 **[R]**		Elektra 60766
				features 2 bonus tracks not included on #1 above			
9/29/84+	100	50	▲⁴	3 Ride The Lightning	Cat:#5/417		Elektra 60396
				first released on Megaforce 769			
3/29/86	29	72	▲⁶	4 Master Of Puppets	Cat:#6/461		Elektra 60439
				RS500 #167			
9/12/87	28	30	▲	5 The $5.98 E.P.: Garage Days Re-Revisited	Cat:#11/25 **[EP]**		Elektra 60757
9/24/88	6	83	▲⁸	6 ...And Justice For All	Cat:#3/508		Elektra 60812 [2]
8/31/91	❶⁴	281	▲¹⁵	7 Metallica	Cat:❶⁴⁰/623		Elektra 61113
				Grammy: Metal Performance with Vocal ★ RS500 #252			
				due to the all black cover, also known among fans as The Black Album			
12/11/93	26	7		8 Live Shit: Binge & Purge	Cat:#41/1 **[L]**		Elektra 61594 [3]
				recorded at Mexico City's Sports Palace; includes 3 videocassettes of concerts in San Diego (1992) and Seattle (1989) plus a 72-page booklet and a "scary guy" stencil; packaged in a cardboard touring trunk replica			
6/22/96	❶⁴	98	▲⁵	9 Load	Cat:#31/12		Elektra 61923
12/6/97	❶¹	75	▲³	10 Reload	Cat:#41/3		Elektra 62126
12/12/98	2¹	44	▲⁵	11 Garage Inc.	**[K]**		Elektra 62299 [2]
				disc 1: new recordings; disc 2: songs released from 1984-1995			
12/11/99	2¹	49	▲⁴	12 S&M	**[L]**		Elektra 62504 [2]
				with the San Francisco Symphony Orchestra; recorded on 4/21/1999 at the Berkeley Community Theater			
6/21/03	❶¹	23	▲²	13 St. Anger			Elektra 62853
7/31/04	37	6		14 Some Kind Of Monster	**[EP-S]**		Elektra 48835
9/27/08	❶³	50	▲	15 Death Magnetic			Warner 508732

METERS, The

R&B instrumental band formed in New Orleans, Louisiana: Arthur Neville (keyboards; brother of **Aaron Neville**), Leo Nocentelli (guitar), George Porter (bass) and Joseph Modeliste (drums). Group disbanded in 1977, when Art, Aaron, and brothers Charles and Cyril formed **The Neville Brothers**.

6/21/69	108	15		1 The Meters..	**[I]**	Josie 4010
1/24/70	198	2		2 Look-Ka Py Py	**[I]**	Josie 4011
				RS500 #218		
7/18/70	200	2		3 Struttin'...		Josie 4012
9/6/75	179	3		4 Fire On The Bayou		Reprise 2228
7/23/77	209	1		5 New Directions		Warner 3051

~ ~ ~ ~ ~ ~ ~ ~ ~ ~ ~ **NON-CHARTED ALBUM** ~ ~ ~ ~ ~ ~ ~ ~ ~ ~ ~

1974 Rejuvenation
RS500 #138

METHENY, Pat, Group
All-Time: #233

Born on 8/12/1955 in Kansas City, Missouri. Male jazz guitarist. Revolving lineup of group has included Lyle Mays (piano), Mark Egan (bass), Dan Gottlieb (drums), Nana Vasconcelos (vocals), Steve Rodby (bass), Pedro Aznar (percussion), Paul Wertico (drums), Armando Marcal (percussion), David Blamires (vocals) and Mark Ledford (vocals, trumpet).

8/26/78	123	12		1 Pat Metheny Group...	**[I]**	ECM 1114
5/5/79	44	22		2 New Chautauqua	**[I]**	ECM 1131
				PAT METHENY		
11/24/79+	53	24		3 American Garage	**[I]**	ECM 1155
11/1/80	89	14		4 80/81	**[I]**	ECM 1180 [2]
				PAT METHENY		
6/20/81	50	21		5 As Falls Wichita, So Falls Wichita Falls	**[I]**	ECM 1190
				PAT METHENY & LYLE MAYS		
5/22/82	50	28		6 Offramp...	**[I]**	ECM 1216
				Grammy: Jazz Fusion Album		
6/25/83	62	17		7 Travels	**[I-L]**	ECM 23791 [2]
				Grammy: Jazz Fusion Album		
5/12/84	116	9		8 Rejoicing..	**[I]**	ECM 25006
				PAT METHENY		
10/13/84	91	35		9 First Circle..	**[I]**	ECM 25008
				Grammy: Jazz Fusion Album		
3/9/85	54	10		10 The Falcon And The Snowman	**[I-S]**	EMI America 17150
8/22/87	86	15	●	11 Still Life (Talking)	**[I]**	Geffen 24145
				Grammy: Jazz Fusion Album		
7/22/89	66	18	●	12 Letter From Home	**[I]**	Geffen 24245
				Grammy: Jazz Fusion Album		
7/7/90	154	6		13 Question And Answer	**[I]**	Geffen 24293
				PAT METHENY / DAVE HOLLAND / ROY HAYNES		

Billboard DEBUT	PEAK	WKS	R I A A	ARTIST Album Title	Catalog	Label & Number
				METHENY, Pat, Group — cont'd		
8/1/92	110	17	●	14 Secret Story	[I]	Geffen 24468
				PAT METHENY		
				Grammy: Contemporary Jazz Album		
8/7/93	170	2		15 The Road To You	[I-L]	Geffen 24601
				Grammy: Contemporary Jazz Album		
4/23/94	181	2		16 I Can See Your House From Here	[I]	Blue Note 27765
				JOHN SCOFIELD & PAT METHENY		
2/4/95	83	10		17 We Live Here	[I]	Geffen 24729
				Grammy: Contemporary Jazz Album		
12/7/96	187	1		18 "Quartet"	[I]	Geffen 24978
10/25/97	124	4		19 Imaginary Day	[I]	Warner 46791
				Grammy: Contemporary Jazz Album		
3/2/02	101	3		20 Speaking Of Now	[I]	Warner 48025
				Grammy: Contemporary Jazz Album		
6/14/03	167	1		21 One Quiet Night	[I]	Warner 48473
				PAT METHENY		
				Grammy: New Age Album		
2/12/05	99	2		22 The Way Up	[I]	Nonesuch 79876
				Grammy: Contemporary Jazz Album		
2/16/08	138	1		23 Day Trip	[I]	Nonesuch 376828
				PAT METHENY with Christian McBride & Antonio Sanchez		
				METHOD MAN		
				Born Clifford Smith on 4/1/1971 in Staten Island, New York. Male rapper. Member of **Wu-Tang Clan**.		
12/3/94	4	43	▲	1 Tical		Def Jam 523839
12/5/98	2¹	24	▲	2 Tical 2000: Judgement Day		Def Jam 558920
10/16/99	3¹	33	▲	3 Blackout!		Def Jam 546609
6/6/09	7	13		4 Blackout! 2		Wu-Tang 012400
6/6/09	90	1		5 Blackout!: 10th Anniversary Collector's Edition	[R]	Def Jam 012992 [2]
				METHOD MAN & REDMAN (above 3)		
				reissue of #3 & #4 above		
6/5/04	2¹	12		6 Tical 0: The Prequel		Def Jam 548405
9/16/06	8	9		7 4:21...The Day After		Def Jam 006986
				METHODS OF MAYHEM		
				Band consists of **Motley Crue** member **Tommy Lee** (vocals, guitar, drums) and male rapper Ti-Lo.		
12/25/99	71	19	●	1 Methods Of Mayhem		MCA 112020
				METHRONE		
				Born Carlos Methrone Reynolds on 11/6/1975 in Plant City, Florida. R&B singer.		
7/22/00	129	10		1 My Life		Claytown 27567
10/6/01	168	2		2 Picture Me		Claytown 2010
				METRIC		
				Alternative-rock band from Toronto, Ontario, Canada: Emily Haines (vocals, guitar), James Shaw (guitar), Josh Winstead (bass) and Joules Scott-Key (drums).		
4/18/09	76	7		1 Fantasies		Metric 80019
				METRO STATION		
				Pop band formed in Los Angeles, California: Mason Musso (vocals), Trace Cyrus (guitar), Blake Healy (bass) and Anthony Improgo (drums). Cyrus is the son of **Billy Ray Cyrus** and the brother of **Miley Cyrus** (**Hannah Montana**). Musso is the older brother of **Mitchel Musso**.		
5/10/08	39	41		1 Metro Station		Red Ink 10521
				MEW		
				Alternative-rock trio from Hellerup, Denmark: Jonas Bjerre (vocals, guitar), Bo Madsen (bass) and Silas Jorgensen (drums).		
9/5/09	130	2		1 No More Stories/Are Told Today/I'm Sorry/They Washed Away/ No More Stories/The World Is Grey/I'm Tired/Let's Wash Away		Evil Office 19942
				MEWITHOUTYOU		
				Punk-rock band from Philadelphia, Pennsylvania: brothers Aaron Weiss (vocals) and Michael Weiss (guitar), Chris Kleinberg (guitar), Greg Jehanian (bass) and Rich Mazzotta (drums).		
10/14/06	116	1		1 Brother, Sister		Tooth & Nail 60429
6/6/09	72	1		2 It's All Crazy! It's All False! It's All A Dream! It's Alright		Tooth & Nail 28896
				MEYER, Edgar		
				Born on 11/24/1960 in Oak Ridge, Tennessee. Bluegrass bassist.		
4/22/00	170	2		1 Appalachian Journey	[I]	Sony Classical 66782
				YO-YO MA / EDGAR MEYER / MARK O'CONNOR		
				MF DOOM		
				Born Daniel Dumile in Brooklyn, New York; later based in London, England. Male rapper. Also see **Madvillain**.		
8/11/07	21ᶜ	1		1 MM...Food?		Rhymesayers 0084
4/11/09	52	4		2 Born Like This		Lex 069
				DOOM		

MFSB
R&B band of studio musicians based at Sigma Sound Studios in Philadelphia, Pennsylvania. MFSB: Mother, Father, Sister, Brother.

DEBUT	PEAK	WKS		Title		Label & Number
4/21/73	131	10	1	MFSB	[I]	Philadelphia Int'l. 32046
1/19/74	4	35	● 2	Love Is The Message	[I]	Philadelphia Int'l. 32707
6/14/75	44	13	3	Universal Love	[I]	Philadelphia Int'l. 33158
12/6/75+	39	12	4	Philadelphia Freedom	[I]	Philadelphia Int'l. 33845
7/10/76	106	9	5	Summertime		Philadelphia Int'l. 34238

MGMT
Electronic-rock duo from Brooklyn, New York: Ben Goldwasser and Andrew VanWyngarden.

2/16/08+	38	99↑	● 1	Oracular Spectacular	Cat:#30/7	Columbia 19512

M.I.A.
Born Mathangi "Maya" Arulpragasam on 7/17/1977 in London, England; raised in India. Female techno artist.

4/9/05	190	2	1	Arular		XL 186
9/8/07	18	45	● 2	Kala	Cat:#23/3	XL 009659

MIAMI SOUND MACHINE — see ESTEFAN, Gloria

MIA X
Born Mia Young in New Orleans, Louisiana; moved to Queens, New York. Female rapper. Member of **Tru**.

7/12/97	21	17	● 1	Unlady Like	No Limit 50705
11/21/98	7	10	2	Mama Drama	No Limit 53502

MICHAEL, George
All-Time: #418
Born Georgios Panayiotou on 6/25/1963 in East Finchley, North London, England; raised in Radlett, Hertfordshire, England (Greek parents). Pop singer/songwriter. One half of the **Wham!** duo.

11/21/87+	❶ 12	87	▲10	1 Faith		Columbia 40867
				Grammy: Album of the Year ★ RS500 #480		
9/29/90	2 1	42	▲2	2 Listen Without Prejudice		Columbia 46898
5/8/93	46	15		3 Five Live	[EP-L]	Hollywood 61479
				GEORGE MICHAEL & QUEEN		
6/1/96	6	24	▲	4 Older		DreamWorks 50000
11/28/98	24	23	▲2	5 Ladies & Gentlemen - The Best Of George Michael	Cat:#44/1 [G]	Epic 69635 [2]
1/1/00	157	7		6 Songs From The Last Century		Virgin 48740
6/5/04	12	16		7 Patience		Epic 92080
4/19/08	23	9		8 Twentyfive	[G]	Aegean 02492 [2]
4/19/08	125	1		9 Twentyfive	[G]	Aegean 10785 [3]

MICHAELS, Bret
Born Bret Michael Sychak on 3/15/1963 in Harrisburg, Pennsylvania. Male singer/songwriter. Lead singer of **Poison**.

6/21/08	40	5	1	Rock My World	VH1 Classic 00121

MICHAELS, Lee
Born on 11/24/1945 in Los Angeles, California. Rock singer/organist.

8/30/69	53	26	1	Lee Michaels		A&M 4199
8/1/70	51	19	2	Barrel		A&M 4249
6/5/71	16	36	3	"5th"		A&M 4302
3/25/72	78	13	4	Space & First Takes		A&M 4336
4/7/73	135	8	5	Lee Michaels Live	[L]	A&M 3518 [2]
6/2/73	172	5	6	Nice Day For Something		Columbia 32275
3/23/74	210	4	7	Tailface		Columbia 32846

MICHAELSON, Ingrid
Born on 12/8/1979 in Staten Island, New York. Female Adult Alternative-pop singer/songwriter.

10/13/07+	63	20	1	Girls And Boys	Cabin 24 03
11/1/08	35	4	2	Be OK	Cabin 24 10
9/12/09	18	10	3	Everybody	Cabin 24 013217

MICHEL, Pras
Born Prakazrel Michel on 10/19/1972 in Harlem, New York. Member of **The Fugees**.

11/14/98	55	5	1	Ghetto Supastar	Ruffhouse 69516
				PRAS	

MICHELE, Chrisette
Born Chrisette Michele Payne on 12/8/1982 in Long Island, New York. R&B singer.

7/7/07	29	41	1	I Am	Def Jam 008774
5/23/09	❶ 1	43	2	Epiphany	Def Jam 012797

MICHEL'LE
Born Michel'le Toussant in 1970 in Los Angeles, California. R&B singer.

1/13/90	35	43	● 1	Michel'le	Ruthless 91282

MICKEY AND SYLVIA

R&B-rock and roll duo: McHouston "Mickey" Baker and **Sylvia** Vanderpool. Baker (born on 10/15/1925 in Louisville, Kentucky) was a prolific session guitarist. Sylvia (born on 3/6/1936 in Harlem, New York) began solo career in 1973. Their son Joey was leader of West Street Mob.

~ ~ ~ ~ ~ ~ ~ ~ ~ ~ **NON-CHARTED ALBUM** ~ ~ ~ ~ ~ ~ ~ ~ ~ ~
1957 **New Sounds**

MIDLER, Bette   All-Time: #121

Born on 12/1/1945 in Honolulu, Hawaii (Jewish parents from New Jersey). Popular singer/actress. In the Broadway show *Fiddler On The Roof* from 1967-70. **Barry Manilow** was her arranger/accompanist in early years. Starred in several movies.
AWARD: Grammy: Best New Artist 1973

12/9/72+	9	76	▲	1	The Divine Miss M		Atlantic 7238
12/8/73+	6	27	●	2	Bette Midler		Atlantic 7270
					above 2 co-produced by **Barry Manilow**		
1/31/76	27	15		3	Songs For The New Depression		Atlantic 18155
5/28/77	49	11		4	Live At Last	[L]	Atlantic 9000 [2]
					recorded at the Cleveland Music Hall		
12/17/77+	51	14		5	Broken Blossom		Atlantic 19151
9/22/79	65	17		6	Thighs And Whispers		Atlantic 16004
12/22/79+	12	45	▲²	7	The Rose	Cat:#42/6 [L-S]	Atlantic 16010
11/29/80	34	14		8	Divine Madness	[L-S]	Atlantic 16022
					recorded at the Pasadena Civic Auditorium		
8/27/83	60	13		9	No Frills		Atlantic 80070
12/21/85+	183	6		10	Mud Will Be Flung Tonight!	[C]	Atlantic 81291
1/21/89	2³	176	▲³	11	Beaches	[S]	Atlantic 81933
10/13/90+	6	73	▲²	12	Some People's Lives		Atlantic 82129
11/30/91	22	21	●	13	For The Boys	[S]	Atlantic 82329
7/10/93	50	37	▲	14	Experience The Divine - Greatest Hits	Cat:#26/18 [G]	Atlantic 82497
12/25/93+	183	2		15	Gypsy	[TV]	Atlantic 82551
					aired on 12/12/1993		
8/5/95	45	35	▲	16	Bette Of Roses		Atlantic 82823
10/3/98	32	16	●	17	Bathhouse Betty		Warner 47078
10/28/00	69	11		18	Bette		Warner 47843
10/18/03	14	22	●	19	Bette Midler Sings The Rosemary Clooney Songbook		Columbia 90350
11/12/05	10	9		20	Bette Midler Sings The Peggy Lee Songbook		Columbia 95107
11/25/06	33	7		21	Cool Yule	[X]	Columbia 86266
					Christmas charts: 6/'06, 25/'09		
10/11/08	66	3		22	Jackpot!: The Best Bette	[G]	Atlantic 73196

MIDNIGHT OIL

Rock band formed in Sydney, Australia: Peter Garrett (vocals), Martin Rotsey (guitar), James Moginie (keyboards), Peter Gifford (bass) and Rob Hirst (drums). Dwayne Hillman replaced Gifford in 1987. Garrett later became involved in politics and was named Australian Arts and Environment Minister in November 2007.

2/4/84	178	5		1	10,9,8,7,6,5,4,3,2,1	Cat:#34/1	Columbia 38996
8/3/85	177	6		2	Red Sails In The Sunset		Columbia 39987
2/13/88	21	55	▲	3	Diesel And Dust		Columbia 40967
3/17/90	20	29	●	4	Blue Sky Mining		Columbia 45398
5/30/92	141	3		5	Scream In Blue Live	[L]	Columbia 52731
5/8/93	49	15		6	Earth And Sun And Moon		Columbia 53793
11/2/96	155	1		7	Breathe		Work 67822

MIDNIGHT STAR

R&B-dance band from Louisville, Kentucky: Belinda Lipscomb (vocals), brothers Reggie and Vince Calloway (horns), Jeff Cooper (guitar), Ken Gant (keyboards), Melvin Gentry (bass) and Bill Simmons (drums). The Calloway brothers later formed **Calloway**.

9/11/82	205	3		1	Victory		Solar 60145
7/30/83+	27	96	▲²	2	No Parking On The Dance Floor		Solar 60241
12/8/84+	32	32	●	3	Planetary Invasion		Solar 60384
6/14/86	56	27	●	4	Headlines		Solar 60454
11/5/88	96	15		5	Midnight Star		Solar 72564

MIDNIGHT STRING QUARTET

Studio group assembled by producer "Snuff" **Tommy Garrett**.

11/19/66+	17	59		1	Rhapsodies For Young Lovers	[I]	Viva 6001
4/8/67	76	12		2	Spanish Rhapsodies For Young Lovers	[I]	Viva 36004
7/29/67	67	15		3	Rhapsodies For Young Lovers, Volume Two	[I]	Viva 36008
12/9/67	18ˣ	4		4	Christmas Rhapsodies For Young Lovers	[X-I]	Viva 36010
3/30/68	129	17		5	Love Rhapsodies	[I]	Viva 36013
8/17/68	194	3		6	The Look Of Love And Other Rhapsodies For Young Lovers	[I]	Viva 36015

Billboard DEBUT	PEAK	WKS	R I A A	ARTIST Album Title	Catalog	Label & Number

MIDON, Raul
Born on 3/14/1966 in Embudo, New Mexico; raised in New York. R&B-jazz singer/songwriter/guitarist. Blind since birth.

| 7/16/05 | 195 | 1 | | 1 State Of Mind .... | | Manhattan 71330 |

MIDTOWN
Punk-rock band formed in New Jersey: Heath Saraceno (guitar), Tyler Rann (guitar), Gabe Saporta (bass) and Rob Hitt (drums). All share vocals.

| 5/4/02 | 90 | 1 | | 1 Living Well Is The Best Revenge .... | | Drive-Thru 112857 |
| 7/17/04 | 109 | 2 | | 2 Forget What You Know .... | | Columbia 92584 |

MIGHTY CLOUDS OF JOY
Black gospel vocal group from Los Angeles, California: Willie Joe Ligon, Johnny Martin, Elmo Franklin, Richard Wallace, Leon Polk and David Walker. Martin died in 1987.

| 10/26/74 | 165 | 5 | | 1 It's Time .... | | Dunhill/ABC 50177 |
| 1/24/76 | 168 | 6 | | 2 Kickin' .... | | ABC 899 |

MIGHTY LEMON DROPS, The
Pop band from Wolverhampton, England: Paul Marsh (vocals), David Newton (guitar), Marcus Williams (bass) and Keith Rowley (drums).

| 3/10/90 | 195 | 2 | | 1 Laughter .... | | Sire 26017 |

MIGHTY MIGHTY BOSSTONES, The
Ska-rock band from Boston, Massachusetts: Dicky Barrett (vocals), Nate Albert (guitar), Ben Carr (dancer), Kevin Lenear, Tim Burton and Dennis Brockenborough (horns), Joe Gittleman (bass) and Joe Sirois (drums). Lawrence Katz replaced Albert and Roman Fleysher replaced Lenear in 1999.

6/5/93	187	1		1 Don't Know How To Party		Mercury 514836
10/22/94	138	1		2 Question The Answers		Mercury 522845
3/29/97	27	50	▲	3 Let's Face It		Mercury 534472
11/7/98	144	1		4 Live From The Middle East .... [L]		Mercury 538247
				recorded in December 1997 at the Middle East club in Cambridge, Massachusetts		
5/20/00	74	4		5 Pay Attention		Big Rig 542451
7/27/02	131	1		6 A Jackknife To A Swan		Big Rig 71234

MIGUEL, Luis   All-Time: #417
Born on 4/19/1970 in San Juan, Puerto Rico; later based in Veracruz, Mexico. Latin singer/actor.

7/10/93	182	3		1 Aries .... [F]		WEA Latina 92993
				Grammy: Latin Pop Album		
9/17/94	29	12	▲	2 Segundo Romance .... [F]		WEA Latina 97234
				Grammy: Latin Pop Album		
11/4/95	45	6	●	3 El Concierto .... [F-L]		WEA Latina 11212 [2]
9/7/96	43	8	●	4 Nada Es Igual .... [F]		WEA Latina 15947
8/30/97	14	19	▲	5 Romances .... [F]		WEA Latina 19798
				Grammy: Latin Pop Album		
10/2/99	36	8		6 Amarte Es Un Placer .... [F]		WEA Latina 29288
10/21/00	93	4		7 Vivo .... [F]		WEA Latina 84573
12/8/01	115	7		8 Mis Romances .... [F]		WEA Latina 41572
11/2/02	125	4		9 Mis Boleros Favoritos .... [F]		Warner Latina 49277 [2]
10/18/03	43	6		10 33 .... [F]		Warner Latina 60873
11/27/04	37	10		11 Mexico En La Piel .... [F]		Warner Latina 61977
				Grammy: Mexican Album		
12/2/06	51	6		12 Navidades Luis Miguel .... [X-F]		Warner Latina 64038
				Christmas chart: 7/06		
5/24/08	10	6		13 Complices .... [F]		Warner Latina 503996
10/10/09	180	1		14 No Culpes A La Noche: Club Remixes .... [F-K]		Warner Latina 521318

MIKA
Born Mica Penniman on 8/18/1983 in Beirut, Lebanon; later based in London, England. Male pop-rock singer/songwriter.

| 4/14/07 | 29 | 26 | | 1 Life In Cartoon Motion .... | | Casablanca 008352 |
| 10/10/09 | 19 | 5 | | 2 The Boy Who Knew Too Much .... | | Casablanca 013312 |

MIKE + THE MECHANICS
Pop-rock band formed in England: Mike Rutherford (bass; Genesis), Paul Carrack and Paul Young (vocals; Sad Cafe), Adrian Lee (keyboards) and Peter Van Hooke (drums). Young, not to be confused with the same-named solo singer, died of a heart attack on 7/15/2000 (age 53).

11/23/85+	26	53	●	1 Mike + The Mechanics		Atlantic 81287
11/19/88+	13	37	●	2 Living Years		Atlantic 81923
4/20/91	107	5		3 Word Of Mouth		Atlantic 82233

MILES, Buddy
Born George Miles on 9/5/1947 in Omaha, Nebraska. Died on 2/26/2008 (age 60). R&B singer/drummer. Member of Electric Flag and Jimi Hendrix's Band of Gypsies. Was the voice of The California Raisins.

6/7/69	145	4		1 Electric Church		Mercury 61222
				BUDDY MILES EXPRESS		
				co-produced by Jimi Hendrix		
7/4/70	35	74		2 Them Changes		Mercury 61280
11/14/70	53	26		3 We Got To Live Together		Mercury 61313
4/10/71	60	24		4 A Message To The People		Mercury 608
10/2/71	50	24		5 Buddy Miles Live .... [L]		Mercury 7500 [2]

528

Billboard			R I A A	ARTIST		
DEBUT	PEAK	WKS		Album Title	Catalog	Label & Number
				MILES, Buddy — cont'd		
7/8/72	8	33	▲	6 Carlos Santana & Buddy Miles! Live! [L]		Columbia 31308
				recorded in Hawaii's Diamond Head volcano crater		
3/10/73	123	9		7 Chapter VII		Columbia 32048
				THE BUDDY MILES BAND		
1/19/74	194	3		8 Booger Bear		Columbia 32694
				BUDDY MILES EXPRESS		
8/23/75	68	11		9 More Miles Per Gallon		Casablanca 7019
				MILES, John		
				Born on 4/23/1949 in Jarrow, England. Rock singer/guitarist/keyboardist. Guest vocalist with the **Alan Parsons Project**.		
5/22/76	171	4		1 Rebel		London 669
3/19/77	93	15		2 Stranger In The City		London 682
8/5/78	210	1		3 Zaragon		Arista 4176
4/5/80	202	2		4 Sympathy		Arista 4261
				MILES, Robert		
				Born Roberto Concina on 11/3/1969 in Fleurier, Switzerland; raised in Fagagna, Italy. Electronic dance DJ/musician.		
8/17/96	54	23	●	1 Dreamland [I]		Arista 18930
				MILIAN, Christina		
				Born Christina Flores on 9/26/1981 in Jersey City, New Jersey; raised in Waldorf, Maryland. R&B singer/songwriter. Married Terius "**The Dream**" Nash on 9/4/2009.		
7/3/04	14	16		1 It's About Time		Island 002223
6/3/06	11	8		2 So Amazin'		Island 006481
				MILLARD, Bart		
				Born in Greenville, Texas. Contemporary Christian singer/songwriter. Leader of **MercyMe**.		
9/6/08	126	1		1 Hymned Again		INO 30475
				MILLER, Buddy & Julie		
				Husband-and-wife duo. Both are singers/songwriters/guitarists. Buddy was born Steven Miller on 9/6/1952 in Fairborn, Ohio; was a member of the **Emmylou Harris** band. Julie was born on 7/12/1956 in Dallas, Texas; recorded Christian music from 1989-94. Married in 1981.		
3/21/09	159	1		1 Written In Chalk		New West 6158
				MILLER, Frankie		
				Born on 11/2/1949 in Glasgow, Scotland. Blues-tinged rock singer/songwriter.		
6/18/77	124	12		1 Full House		Chrysalis 1128
5/13/78	177	10		2 Double Trouble		Chrysalis 1174
6/9/79	209	1		3 A Perfect Fit		Chrysalis 1220
6/26/82	135	9		4 Standing On The Edge		Capitol 12206
				MILLER, Glenn, and his Orchestra 1950s: #47		
				Born Alton Glenn Miller on 3/1/1904 in Clarinda, Iowa. Disappeared on a plane flight from England to France on 12/15/1944 (age 40). Leader of most popular big band of all time. Played trombone for Ben Pollack, Red Nichols, **Benny Goodman** and **Jimmy & Tommy Dorsey**. Started own band in 1937.		
				AWARD: Grammy: Lifetime Achievement 2003		
9/16/57	16	6		1 Marvelous Miller Moods [E]		RCA Victor 1494
				GLENN MILLER ARMY AIR FORCE BAND		
				with Johnny Desmond (vocals); from radio broadcasts during 1943-44		
12/9/57	17	4		2 The New Glenn Miller Orchestra In Hi Fi		RCA Victor 1522
				directed by Ray McKinley (leader of the orchestra after Miller's death)		
2/24/58	19	3		3 The Glenn Miller Carnegie Hall Concert [E-L]		RCA Victor 1506
				recorded on 10/6/1939		
1/25/75	115	9		4 A Legendary Performer [E]		RCA Victor 0693 [2]
				previously unreleased performances from 1939-42		
12/7/91	27[X]	7		5 In The Christmas Mood Cat:#38/10 [X-I]		LaserLight 15418
				recorded in 1988 by alumni of the Glenn Miller Orchestra; Christmas charts: 27/91, 29/'92, 38/'94		
12/25/93	199	1		6 In The Christmas Mood II Cat:#38/2 [X-I]		LaserLight 12200
				MILLER, Jody		
				Born Myrna Joy Brooks on 11/29/1941 in Phoenix, Arizona; raised in Blanchard, Oklahoma. Country singer.		
6/26/65	124	6		1 Queen Of The House		Capitol 2349
8/28/71	117	8		2 He's So Fine		Epic 30659
				MILLER, Marcus		
				Born on 6/14/1959 in Brooklyn, New York. R&B-jazz singer/bassist. Member of **S.M.V.**		
7/14/84	204	4		1 Marcus Miller		Warner 25074
3/22/08	191	1		2 Marcus		3 Deuces 30264

MILLER, Mitch, & The Gang   1950s: #12 / 1960s: #26 / All-Time: #76
Born on 7/4/1911 in Rochester, New York. Producer/conductor/arranger. A&R executive for both Columbia and Mercury Records. Best known for his sing-along albums and TV show (1961-64).

AWARD: Grammy: Lifetime Achievement 2000

7/14/58	**0**[8]	204	●	1 Sing Along With Mitch		Columbia 1160
11/10/58+	4	171	●	2 More Sing Along With Mitch		Columbia 1243
3/23/59	4	130	●	3 Still More! Sing Along With Mitch		Columbia 1283
6/1/59+	11	89	●	4 Folk Songs Sing Along With Mitch		Columbia 1316
8/31/59+	7	100	●	5 Party Sing Along With Mitch		Columbia 1331
12/28/59+	10	91		6 Fireside Sing Along With Mitch		Columbia 1389
4/4/60+	8	89	●	7 Saturday Night Sing Along With Mitch		Columbia 1414
6/27/60	5	107	●	8 Sentimental Sing Along With Mitch		Columbia 1457
10/10/60	40	16		9 March Along With Mitch	[I]	Columbia 1475
10/31/60	5	78	●	10 Memories Sing Along With Mitch		Columbia 1542 / 8342
3/13/61	5	73	●	11 Happy Times! Sing Along With Mitch		Columbia 1568 / 8368
3/13/61	9	27		12 Mitch's Greatest Hits	[G]	Columbia 1544 / 8344
5/29/61	3[1]	46		13 TV Sing Along With Mitch		Columbia 1628 / 8428
9/18/61	6	44		14 Your Request Sing Along With Mitch		Columbia 1671 / 8471
3/10/62	21	23		15 Rhythm Sing Along With Mitch		Columbia 1727 / 8527
6/9/62	27	15		16 Family Sing Along With Mitch		Columbia 1773 / 8573
				CHRISTMAS ALBUMS:		
12/8/58	**0**[2]	5	●	17 Christmas Sing-Along With Mitch		Columbia 1205 / 8027
12/14/59	8	4		18 Christmas Sing-Along With Mitch	[R]	Columbia 1205 / 8027
12/19/60	6	3		19 Christmas Sing-Along With Mitch	[R]	Columbia 1205 / 8027
12/4/61+	9	8		20 Christmas Sing-Along With Mitch	[R]	Columbia 1205 / 8027
12/22/62	37	2		21 Christmas Sing-Along With Mitch	[R]	Columbia 1205 / 8027
11/6/61+	**0**[1]	18	●	22 Holiday Sing Along With Mitch		Columbia 1701 / 8501
				Christmas charts: 9/'63, 15/'64, 22/'65, 14/'66, 17/'67, 37/'68		
12/8/62	33	4		23 Holiday Sing Along With Mitch	[R]	Columbia 1701 / 8501

MILLER, Mrs.
Born Elva Miller on 10/5/1907 in Joplin, Missouri. Died on 6/28/1997 (age 89). Tone-deaf singer.

5/7/66	15	17		1 Mrs. Miller's Greatest Hits	[N]	Capitol 2494

MILLER, Ned
Born Henry Ned Miller on 4/12/1925 in Rains, Utah. Country singer/songwriter.

3/30/63	50	13		1 From A Jack To A King		Fabor 1001

MILLER, Rhett
Born Stewart Ransom Miller on 9/6/1970 in Dallas, Texas. Rock singer/songwriter/guitarist. Former leader of the **Old 97's**.

10/12/02	126	1		1 The Instigator		Elektra 62788
3/18/06	138	1		2 The Believer		Verve Forecast 005616
6/27/09	128	1		3 Rhett Miller		Shout! Factory 11356

MILLER, Roger
Born on 1/2/1936 in Fort Worth, Texas; raised in Erick, Oklahoma. Died of cancer on 10/25/1992 (age 56). Country singer/songwriter/guitarist. Hosted own TV show in 1966. Songwriter of 1985's Broadway musical *Big River*.

AWARDS: Grammy: Best New Country Artist 1964 ★ C&W Hall of Fame: 1995

6/27/64	37	46	●	1 Roger And Out		Smash 67049
				Grammy: Country Album		
				album also released as *Dang Me/Chug-A-Lug*		
2/6/65	4	47	●	2 The Return Of Roger Miller		Smash 67061
				Grammy: Country Album		
7/24/65	13	24		3 The 3rd Time Around		Smash 67068
11/13/65+	6	57	●	4 Golden Hits	[G]	Smash 67073
11/19/66+	108	13		5 Words And Music		Smash 67075
7/1/67	118	8		6 Walkin' In The Sunshine		Smash 67092
8/24/68	173	8		7 A Tender Look At Love		Smash 67103
8/30/69	163	7		8 Roger Miller		Smash 67123
2/14/70	200	2		9 Roger Miller 1970		Smash 67129

MILLER, Steve, Band
1970s: #45 / All-Time: #111

Born on 10/5/1943 in Milwaukee, Wisconsin; raised in Dallas, Texas. Pop-rock singer/songwriter/guitarist. Formed band in high school, The Marksmen, which included **Boz Scaggs**. Moved to San Francisco in 1966; formed the Steve Miller Band, which featured a fluctuating lineup, including long-term members Lonnie Turner (bass) and Gary Mallaber (drums).

DEBUT	PEAK	WKS				
6/15/68	134	18		1 Children Of The Future		Capitol 2920
11/2/68	24	17		2 Sailor		Capitol 2984
6/28/69	22	26		3 Brave New World		Capitol 184
11/29/69+	38	14		4 Your Saving Grace		Capitol 331
7/25/70	23	26		5 Number 5		Capitol 436
10/9/71	82	9		6 Rock Love		Capitol 748
4/1/72	109	10		7 Recall The Beginning...A Journey From Eden		Capitol 11022
11/18/72+	56	39	●	8 Anthology	[K]	Capitol 11114 [2]
10/20/73	2[1]	38	▲	9 The Joker		Capitol 11235
5/29/76	3[2]	97	▲[4]	10 Fly Like An Eagle		Capitol 11497
				RS500 #450		
5/21/77	2[2]	68	▲[3]	11 Book Of Dreams		Capitol 11630
12/9/78+	18	18	▲[13]	12 Greatest Hits 1974-78	Cat:❶[3]/553 [G]	Capitol 11872
11/14/81	26	17	●	13 Circle Of Love		Capitol 12121
6/26/82	3[6]	33	▲	14 Abracadabra		Capitol 12216
4/30/83	125	7		15 Steve Miller Band - Live!	[L]	Capitol 12263
11/10/84	101	10		16 Italian X Rays		Capitol 12339
11/15/86+	65	23		17 Living In The 20th Century		Capitol 12445
10/8/88	108	10		18 Born 2B Blue		Capitol 48303
				STEVE MILLER		
6/26/93	85	15		19 Wide River		Polydor 519441
10/4/03	37	13	●	20 Young Hearts: Complete Greatest Hits	[G]	Capitol 90509

MILLIONS LIKE US
Pop-rock duo from England: John O'Kane (vocals) and Jeep MacNichol (guitar, keyboards).

12/19/87+	171	12		1 ...Millions Like Us		Virgin 90602

MILLI VANILLI
Europop act formed in Germany by producer Frank Farian (creator of **Boney M**). Originally thought to be Rob Pilatus (from Germany) and Fabrice Morvan (from France). Actual vocalists are Charles Shaw, John Davis and Brad Howe. Pilatus died of a drug overdose on 4/2/1998 (age 32).

AWARD: Grammy: Best New Artist 1989 (later revoked)

3/25/89	❶[8]	78	▲[6]	1 Girl You Know It's True		Arista 8592
6/16/90	32	20	●	2 The Remix Album	[K]	Arista 8622

MILLS, Frank
Born on 6/27/1942 in Toronto, Ontario, Canada. Adult Contemporary pianist/composer/producer/arranger.

3/17/79	21	16	●	1 Music Box Dancer	[I]	Polydor 6192
11/24/79+	149	9		2 Sunday Morning Suite	[I]	Polydor 6225

MILLS, Hayley
Born on 4/18/1946 in London, England. Teen actress/singer. Daughter of actor John Mills.

~ ~ ~ ~ ~ ~ ~ ~ ~ ~ ~ **NON-CHARTED ALBUM** ~ ~ ~ ~ ~ ~ ~ ~ ~ ~ ~
1961 **Let's Get Together With Hayley Mills**

MILLS, Stephanie
Born on 3/22/1957 in Brooklyn, New York. R&B singer/actress. Played "Dorothy" in Broadway's *The Wiz*. Briefly married to Jeffrey Daniels of **Shalamar** in 1980.

5/19/79	22	34	●	1 Whatcha Gonna Do...With My Lovin'?		20th Century 583
5/3/80	16	44	●	2 Sweet Sensation		20th Century 603
5/16/81	30	23	●	3 Stephanie		20th Century 700
8/7/82	48	19		4 Tantalizingly Hot		Casablanca 7265
9/17/83	104	19		5 Merciless		Casablanca 811364
10/13/84	73	15		6 I've Got The Cure		Casablanca 822421
3/29/86	47	22		7 Stephanie Mills		MCA 5669
6/27/87	30	36	●	8 If I Were Your Woman		MCA 5996
7/22/89	82	38		9 Home		MCA 6312

MILLS BROTHERS, The
Legendary black family vocal group from Piqua, Ohio: father John Mills (died on 12/8/1967, age 78), with sons Herbert Mills (died on 4/12/1989, age 67), Harry Mills (died on 6/28/1982, age 68) and Donald Mills (died on 11/13/1999, age 84).

AWARD: Grammy: Lifetime Achievement 1998

12/21/68	36[X]	2		1 Merry Christmas	[X]	Dot 25232
				first released in 1959		
3/16/68	21	26		2 Fortuosity		Dot 25809

DEBUT	PEAK	WKS	R I A A	ARTIST Album Title	Catalog	Label & Number
				MILLS BROTHERS, The — cont'd		
4/6/68	145	6		3 The Board Of Directors..		Dot 25838
				COUNT BASIE & THE MILLS BROTHERS		
8/10/68	190	3		4 My Shy Violet..		Dot 25872
5/24/69	184	5		5 Dream		Dot 25927
8/18/73	208	2		6 The Best Of The Mills Brothers .... [G]		Paramount 1010 [2]
				MILSAP, Ronnie **All-Time: #407**		
				Born on 1/16/1943 in Robbinsville, North Carolina. Country singer/songwriter/pianist. Blind since birth. Formed the Apparitions while in high school. Joined **J.J. Cale**'s band. Played session keyboards for **Elvis Presley** in 1969. AWARDS: CMA: Male Vocalist 1974, 1976 & 1977 / Entertainer 1977 ★ OPRY: 1976		
2/15/75	138	7		1 A Legend In My Time		RCA Victor 0846
				CMA: Album of the Year		
11/29/75	191	2		2 Night Things		RCA Victor 1223
9/10/77	97	15	●	3 It Was Almost Like A Song..		RCA Victor 2439
				CMA: Album of the Year		
6/24/78	109	12	●	4 Only One Love In My Life		RCA Victor 2780
6/16/79	98	15		5 Images		RCA Victor 3346
4/5/80	137	13		6 Milsap Magic		RCA Victor 3563
10/25/80+	36	41	▲²	7 Greatest Hits.. [G]		RCA Victor 3772
4/18/81	89	29		8 Out Where The Bright Lights Are Glowing		RCA Victor 3932
9/5/81	31	31	●	9 There's No Gettin' Over Me		RCA Victor 4060
7/3/82	66	14		10 Inside Ronnie Milsap		RCA Victor 4311
4/30/83	36	19		11 Keyed Up..		RCA Victor 4670
6/2/84	180	3		12 One More Try For Love		RCA Victor 5016
8/31/85	102	20	▲	13 Greatest Hits, Vol. 2 .... [G]		RCA Victor 5425
5/3/86	121	12	●	14 Lost In The Fifties Tonight		RCA Victor 7194
				CMA: Album of the Year		
5/25/91	172	2		15 Back To The Grindstone		RCA 2375
1/27/01	178	2	●	16 40 #1 Hits.. [G]		Virgin 48871 [2]
3/28/09	127	1		17 Then Sings My Soul: 24 Favorite Hymns & Gospel Songs		Star Song 42255 [2]
				MIMMS, Garnet, & The Enchanters		
				Born Garrett Mimms on 11/26/1933 in Ashland, West Virginia. R&B singer. The Enchanters: Zola Pearnell, Sam Bell and Charles Boyer.		
11/23/63	91	5		1 Cry Baby And 11 Other Hits		United Artists 3305
				MIMS		
				Born Shawn Mims on 3/22/1981 in Manhattan, New York. Male rapper.		
4/14/07	4	18		1 Music Is My Savior		Capitol 84824
4/25/09	53	3		2 Guilt..		American King 27279
				MINDBENDERS, The		
				Rock and roll band from Manchester, England: Wayne Fontana (vocals), Eric Stewart (guitar, vocals), Bob Lang (bass) and Ric Rothwell (drums). Stewart later formed **10cc**.		
5/1/65	58	9		1 The Game Of Love		Fontana 27542
				WAYNE FONTANA & THE MINDBENDERS		
7/16/66	92	9		2 A Groovy Kind Of Love..		Fontana 27554
				MINDLESS SELF INDULGENCE		
				Punk-rock band from New York: James "Jimmy Urine" Euringer (vocals), Steven "Steve Righ?" Montano (guitar), Lindsey "Lyn Z" Way (bass) and Jennifer "Kitty" Dunn (drums).		
4/30/05	107	2		1 You'll Rebel To Anything		Metropolis 365
5/17/08	27	5		2 If		UCR 099
				MINEO, Sal		
				Born Salvatore Mineo on 1/10/1939 in the Bronx, New York. Stabbed to death on 2/12/1976 (age 37). Singer/actor. Starred with James Dean in the 1955 movie classic *Rebel Without A Cause*.		
				~ ~ ~ ~ ~ ~ ~ ~ ~ ~ **NON-CHARTED ALBUM** ~ ~ ~ ~ ~ ~ ~ ~ ~ ~ ~		
				1958 **Sal**		
				MINGUS, Charles		
				Born on 4/22/1922 in Nogales, Arizona; raised in Los Angeles, California. Died of a heart attack on 1/5/1979 (age 56). Jazz bass guitarist/composer.		
				~ ~ ~ ~ ~ ~ ~ ~ ~ ~ **NON-CHARTED ALBUMS** ~ ~ ~ ~ ~ ~ ~ ~ ~ ~ ~		
				1959 **Mingus Ah Um** 1960 **Mingus Dynasty**		
				NRR *Grammy: Hall of Fame*		
				MINISTRY		
				Industrial-rock band formed by Chicago-based producer/performer Alain Jourgensen (born on 10/8/1958 in Cuba).		
6/25/83	96	14		1 With Sympathy		Arista 6608
4/5/86	194	3		2 Twitch..		Sire 25309
11/5/88	164	4	●	3 The Land Of Rape And Honey		Sire 25799
12/9/89	163	10	●	4 The Mind Is A Terrible Thing To Taste		Sire 26004
8/1/92	27	36	▲	5 Psalm 69		Sire 26012
2/17/96	19	10		6 Filth Pig..		Warner 45838
6/26/99	92	2		7 Dark Side Of The Spoon		Warner 47311

DEBUT	PEAK	WKS	R I A A	ARTIST Album Title	Catalog	Label & Number

MINISTRY — cont'd

DEBUT	PEAK	WKS			
3/8/03	157	1	8 Animositisomina		Sanctuary 84568
5/20/06	134	1	9 Rio Grande Blood		13th Planet 001
10/6/07	130	1	10 The Last Sucker		13th Planet 005

MINK DeVILLE

Rock trio formed in San Francisco, California: Willy DeVille (vocals, guitar), Ruben Siguenza (bass) and Thomas Allen (drums). DeVille died of cancer on 8/6/2009 (age 55)

DEBUT	PEAK	WKS			
8/13/77	186	2	1 Mink DeVille		Capitol 11631
6/10/78	126	5	2 Return To Magenta		Capitol 11780
9/13/80	163	3	3 Le Chat Bleu		Capitol 11955
10/24/81	161	5	4 Coup De Grace		Atlantic 19311
2/18/84	208	3	5 Where Angels Fear To Tread		Atlantic 80115

MINNELLI, Liza

Born on 3/12/1946 in Los Angeles, California. Singer/actress. Daughter of **Judy Garland** and movie director Vincente Minnelli. Starred in several movies and Broadway shows. Married to **Peter Allen** from 1967-73. Married to movie producer Jack Haley, Jr. from 1974-79.

AWARD: Grammy: Living Legends 1989

DEBUT	PEAK	WKS			
11/21/64	115	8	1 Liza! Liza!		Capitol 2174
11/28/70	158	3	2 New Feelin'		A&M 4272
9/30/72	19	23	● 3 Liza With A "Z" [TV]		Columbia 31762
			recorded at the Lyceum Theater in New York City		
3/24/73	38	20	4 Liza Minnelli The Singer		Columbia 32149
12/8/73	207	6	5 The Liza Minnelli Foursider [K]		A&M 3524 [2]
11/11/89	128	10	6 Results		Epic 45098
			features backing and co-production by the **Pet Shop Boys**		
7/6/96	156	1	7 Gently		Angel 35470
			LIVE ALBUMS:		
9/4/65	41	14	8 "Live" At The London Palladium		Capitol 2295 [2]
6/9/73	164	8	9 "Live" At The London Palladium		Capitol 11191
			JUDY GARLAND & LIZA MINNELLI (above 2) condensation of album above		
5/18/74	150	4	10 Live At The Winter Garden		Columbia 32854
11/14/87	156	8	11 Liza Minnelli At Carnegie Hall		Telarc 15502 [2]

MINOGUE, Kylie

Born on 5/28/1968 in Melbourne, Australia. Singer/actress. Regular on the Australian soap opera *Neighbours*.

DEBUT	PEAK	WKS			
9/10/88+	53	28	● 1 Kylie		Geffen 24195
3/16/02	3[1]	44	▲ 2 Fever		Capitol 37670
2/28/04	42	8	3 Body Language		Capitol 95645
4/19/08	139	1	4 X		Astralwerks 14780

MINOR DETAIL

Pop-rock duo from Ireland: brothers John and Willie Hughes.

DEBUT	PEAK	WKS			
10/1/83	187	2	1 Minor Detail		Polydor 815004

MINT CONDITION

R&B band from Minneapolis, Minnesota: Stokley Williams (vocals, drums), Homer O'Dell (guitar), Larry Waddell and Keri Lewis (keyboards), Jeff Allen (sax) and Ricky Kinchen (bass). Lewis married **Toni Braxton** on 4/21/2001.

DEBUT	PEAK	WKS			
2/8/92	63	22	1 Meant To Be Mint		Perspective 1001
1/29/94	104	13	2 From The Mint Factory		Perspective 9005
10/12/96	76	25	● 3 Definition Of A Band		Perspective 9028
12/4/99	64	9	4 Life's Aquarium		Elektra 62353
5/14/05	45	5	5 Livin' The Luxury Brown		Caged Bird 0474
5/24/08	119	2	6 E-Life		Caged Bird 3636

MINUS THE BEAR

Alternative-rock band from Seattle, Washington: Jake Snider (vocals, guitar), Dave Knudson (guitar), Alex Rose (keyboards), Cory Murchy (bass) and Erin Tate (drums).

DEBUT	PEAK	WKS			
9/8/07	74	3	1 Planet Of Ice		Suicide Squeeze 065

MINUTEMEN

Punk-rock band from San Pedro, California: Dennis "D." Boon (vocals, guitar), **Mike Watt** (bass) and George Hurley (drums). Boon died in a van accident on 12/22/1985 (age 27).

~ ~ ~ ~ ~ ~ ~ ~ ~ ~ *NON-CHARTED ALBUM* ~ ~ ~ ~ ~ ~ ~ ~ ~ ~ ~

1984 **Double Nickels On The Dime**
RS500 #411

MIRABAI

Born in Brooklyn, New York. Female folk singer.

DEBUT	PEAK	WKS			
8/30/75	128	6	1 Mirabai		Atlantic 18144

MIRACLE

Born Peter Evans in Augusta, Georgia. Male rapper.

DEBUT	PEAK	WKS			
5/27/00	56	9	1 Miracle		Sound Of Atl. 153283

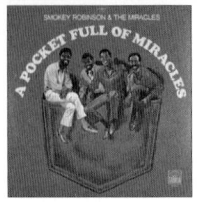

MIRACLES, The   All-Time: #139

R&B vocal group from Detroit, Michigan: **Smokey Robinson**, Claudette Rogers, Bobby Rogers, Ronnie White and Warren Moore. Claudette Rogers retired in 1964; married to Robinson from 1958-86. Bobby Rogers married Wanda Young of **The Marvelettes**. Robinson went solo in 1973; replaced by Billy Griffin. White died of leukemia on 8/26/1995 (age 56).

6/8/63	118	8	1 The Fabulous Miracles		Tamla 238
1/4/64	113	4	2 Doin' Mickey's Monkey		Tamla 245
			SMOKEY ROBINSON & THE MIRACLES:		
11/27/65+	8	40	3 Going To A Go-Go		Tamla 267
			RS500 #271		
12/17/66+	41	27	4 Away We A Go-Go		Tamla 271
9/30/67	28	23	5 Make It Happen		Tamla 276
12/26/70+	143	12	6 The Tears Of A Clown .... [R]		Tamla 276
			reissue (new title) of album above		
10/5/68+	42	23	7 Special Occasion		Tamla 290
8/9/69	25	19	8 Time Out For Smokey Robinson & The Miracles		Tamla 295
12/6/69+	78	12	9 Four In Blue		Tamla 297
5/30/70	97	11	10 What Love Has...Joined Together		Tamla 301
10/24/70	56	11	11 A Pocket Full Of Miracles		Tamla 306
9/25/71	92	10	12 One Dozen Roses		Tamla 312
8/19/72	46	22	13 Flying High Together		Tamla 318
			THE MIRACLES:		
6/2/73	174	4	14 Renaissance		Tamla 325
9/14/74	41	21	15 Do It Baby		Tamla 334
2/8/75	96	9	16 Don't Cha Love It..		Tamla 336
10/25/75+	33	30	17 City Of Angels		Tamla 339
10/16/76	178	3	18 The Power Of Music		Tamla 344
3/19/77	117	5	19 Love Crazy		Columbia 34460
			CHRISTMAS ALBUMS:		
12/19/64+	15^X	8	20 Christmas With The Miracles....................................		Tamla 236
			first released in 1963; Christmas charts: 29/'64, 15/'65, 59/'67		
12/19/70	13^X	2	21 The Season For Miracles		Tamla 307
			GREATEST HITS & COMPILATIONS:		
4/17/65	21	25	22 Greatest Hits From The Beginning............................		Tamla 254 [2]
2/24/68	7	44	23 Greatest Hits, Vol. 2		Tamla 280
2/16/74	97	17	24 Smokey Robinson & The Miracles' Anthology		Motown 793 [3]
9/3/77	209	2	25 Greatest Hits		Tamla 6357
			LIVE ALBUMS:		
10/5/63	139	5	26 The Miracles On Stage..		Tamla 241
2/15/69	71	14	27 Live!		Tamla 289
1/6/73	75	16	28 1957-1972		Tamla 320 [2]
			recorded on 7/14/1972 at the Carter Barron Ampitheatre in Washington DC		

~ ~ ~ ~ ~ ~ ~ ~ ~ ~ **NON-CHARTED ALBUMS** ~ ~ ~ ~ ~ ~ ~ ~ ~ ~ ~ ~
1961 **Hi We're The Miracles**   1962 **I'll Try Something New**
1962 **Cookin' With The Miracles**

MISFITS

Hard-rock band from Lodi, New Jersey: Michale Graves (vocals), Doyle Wolfgang Von Frankenstein (guitar), Jerry Only (bass) and Dr. Chud (drums).

5/31/97	117	2	1 American Psycho		Geffen 25126
10/23/99	138	1	2 Famous Monsters		Roadrunner 8658
8/16/03	133	1	3 Project 1950		Misfits 10643

MISSETT, Judi Sheppard

Born in 1946 in Iowa. Created the Jazzercise fitness routine.

12/5/81	117	20	●	1 Jazzercise		MCA 5272
1/8/83	209	1		2 More Jazzercise..		MCA 5375
				includes instruction poster		

MISSING PERSONS

New-wave band formed in Los Angeles, California: Dale Bozzio (vocals), her then-husband Terry Bozzio (drums), Warren Cuccurullo (guitar), Patrick O'Hearn (bass, synthesizer) and Chuck Wild (keyboards). All but Wild were with **Frank Zappa**'s band. Disbanded in 1986. Terry Bozzio worked with **Jeff Beck** in 1989. Cuccurullo joined **Duran Duran** in 1990.

5/15/82	46	47		1 Missing Persons .... [EP]		Capitol 15001
10/30/82+	17	40	●	2 Spring Session M		Capitol 12228
				title is an anagram of group's name		
3/31/84	43	16		3 Rhyme & Reason		Capitol 12315
8/9/86	86	11		4 Color In Your Life		Capitol 12465

	Billboard		R I A A	ARTIST		
DEBUT	PEAK	WKS		Album Title	Catalog	Label & Number

MISSION U.K., The
Rock band formed in Leeds, England: Wayne Hussey (vocals, guitar), Simon Hinkler (guitar), Craig Adams (bass) and Mick Brown (drums). Hussey and Adams were members of **The Sisters Of Mercy**.

3/7/87	108	18		1 Gods Own Medicine		Mercury 830603
4/30/88	126	10		2 Children		Mercury 834263
3/17/90	101	16		3 Carved In Sand		Mercury 842251

MISSISSIPPI MASS CHOIR
Gospel group based in Jackson, Mississippi.

3/12/05	191	2		1 Not By Might, Nor By Power		Malaco 6035

MISSOURI
Rock band from St. Louis, Missouri: Ron West (vocals, guitar), Web Waterman (guitar), Randall Platt (keyboards), Alan Cohen (bass) and Dan Billings (drums). Billlings died of injuries suffered in a fall on 11/2/2007 (age 51).

6/23/79	174	4		1 Welcome Two Missouri		Polydor 6206

MISTA
R&B vocal group from Atlanta, Georgia: Darryl Allen, Bobby Wilson, Brandon Brown and Byron Reeder. Wilson later recorded solo as **Bobby Valentino**.

8/17/96	183	3		1 Mista		EastWest 61912

MISTAH F.A.B.
Born Stanley Cox on 1/23/1983 in North Oakland, California. Male rapper. F.A.B.: Forever After Bread.

6/2/07	177	1		1 Da Baydestrain		Faeva Afta 181

MIS-TEEQ
Female R&B vocal trio from London, England: Alesha Dixon, Sabrina Washington and Su-Elise Nash.

8/7/04	125	2		1 Mis-Teeq		Reprise 48804

MR. BIG
Rock band from San Francisco, California: **Eric Martin** (vocals), Paul Gilbert (guitar), Billy Sheehan (bass) and Pat Torpey (drums; **Impellitteri**).

7/22/89	46	18		1 Mr. Big		Atlantic 81990
4/20/91+	15	38	▲	2 Lean Into It	Cat:#25/1	Atlantic 82209
10/9/93	82	6		3 Bump Ahead		Atlantic 82495

MR. BUNGLE
Rock band from Eureka, California: Mike Patton (vocals), Trey Spruance (guitar), Trevor Dunn (bass) and Danny Heifetz (drums). Patton was also leader of **Faith No More** and **Tomahawk**. Patton and Dunn later formed **Fantomas**.

10/28/95	113	1		1 Disco Volante		Warner 45963
7/31/99	144	1		2 California		Warner 47447

MR. CHEEKS
Born Terrance Kelly on 3/28/1971 in Queens, New York. Male rapper. Former member of **Lost Boyz**.

11/3/01	32	14		1 John P. Kelly		Universal 014929
4/5/03	75	4		2 Back Again!		Universal 067615

MR. C THE SLIDE MAN
Born William Perry on 6/23/1971 in Chicago, Illinois. R&B singer/rapper.

1/13/01	64	19	●	1 Cha-Cha Slide		M.O.B. 159807

MR. MARCELLO (FROM THE GHETTO)
Born Jerome Hicks in New Orleans, Louisiana. Male rapper.

8/12/00	172	1		1 Brick Livin		Priority 26159

MR. MIKE
Born Michael Walls in Corpus Christi, Texas. Male rapper. Member of **South Circle**.

8/17/96	29	8		1 Wicked Wayz		Suave House 1519
9/25/99	172	2		2 Rhapsody		Priority 50031

MR. MISTER
Pop-rock band formed in Los Angeles, California: Richard Page (vocals, bass), Steve Farris (guitar), Steve George (keyboards) and Pat Mastelotto (drums).

4/14/84	170	7		1 I Wear The Face		RCA Victor 4864
8/31/85+	❶[1]	58	▲	2 Welcome To The Real World		RCA Victor 8045
9/26/87	55	17		3 Go On...		RCA Victor 6276

MR. SERV-ON
Born Edward Smith in New Orleans, Louisiana. Male rapper.

8/23/97	23	12		1 Life Insurance		No Limit 50717
3/6/99	14	5		2 Da Next Level		No Limit 50045

MR. SHORT KHOP
Born Lionel Hunt in Los Angeles, California. Male rapper. Discovered by **Ice Cube**.

4/7/01	154	6		1 Da Khop Shop		Heavyweight 2150

MISTRESS
Pop-rock band from Georgia: Charlie Williams (vocals), Kenny Hopkins (guitar), Danny Chauncey (guitar), David Brown (bass) and Chris Paulsen (drums).

9/15/79	100	14	1 Mistress..		RSO 3059

MITCHELL, Chad, Trio
Born on 12/5/1936 in Portland, Oregon. Folk singer. His trio included Mike Koluk and Joe Frazier. Mitchell left in 1964. **John Denver** joined and group was renamed **The Mitchell Trio**.

3/24/62	39	21	1 Mighty Day On Campus .... [L]		Kapp 3262
			recorded at Brooklyn College		
9/1/62	81	9	2 The Chad Mitchell Trio At The Bitter End............................ [L]		Kapp 3281
			recorded on 3/19/1962 in New York City		
4/13/63	87	30	3 Blowin' In The Wind		Kapp 3313
9/28/63	63	28	4 The Best Of Chad Mitchell Trio.. [G]		Kapp 3334
11/9/63	39	22	5 Singin' Our Mind...		Mercury 60838
3/7/64	29	30	6 Reflecting..		Mercury 60891
11/14/64+	128	11	7 The Slightly Irreverent Mitchell Trio		Mercury 60944
5/1/65	130	3	8 Typical American Boys..		Mercury 60992
			THE MITCHELL TRIO (above 2)		

MITCHELL, Guy
Born Al Cernik on 2/27/1927 in Detroit, Michigan. Died on 7/1/1999 (age 72). Popular singer during the 1950s.

~ ~ ~ ~ ~ ~ ~ ~ ~ ~ ~ **NON-CHARTED ALBUM** ~ ~ ~ ~ ~ ~ ~ ~ ~ ~ ~

1959 **Guy's Greatest Hits**

MITCHELL, Joni   All-Time: #135
Born Roberta Joan Anderson on 11/7/1943 in Fort McLeod, Alberta, Canada; raised in Saskatoon, Saskatchewan. Folk-rock-pop singer/songwriter/guitarist/pianist. Married to her producer/bassist, Larry Klein, from 1982-94.
AWARDS: Grammy: Lifetime Achievement 2002 ★ R&R Hall of Fame: 1997 ★ Billboard Century: 1995

5/18/68	189	9		1 Joni Mitchell	Reprise 6293
6/14/69	31	36	●	2 Clouds	Reprise 6341
				Grammy: Folk Album	
4/11/70	27	33	▲	3 Ladies Of The Canyon	Reprise 6376
7/3/71	15	28	▲	4 Blue	Reprise 2038
				Grammy: Hall of Fame ★ RS500 #30	
12/2/72+	11	28	●	5 For The Roses	Asylum 5057
				NRR	
2/9/74	2⁴	64	▲²	6 Court And Spark	Asylum 1001
				Grammy: Hall of Fame ★ RS500 #111	
12/14/74+	2¹	22	●	7 Miles Of Aisles .... [L]	Asylum 202
12/6/75+	4	17	●	8 The Hissing Of Summer Lawns	Asylum 1051
12/11/76+	13	18	●	9 Hejira	Asylum 1087
1/7/78	25	13	●	10 Don Juan's Reckless Daughter....................................	Asylum 701 [2]
7/7/79	17	18		11 Mingus..	Asylum 505
10/4/80	38	16		12 Shadows And Light .... [L]	Asylum 704 [2]
11/20/82	25	21		13 Wild Things Run Fast	Geffen 2019
11/23/85	63	19		14 Dog Eat Dog...	Geffen 24074
4/9/88	45	16		15 Chalk Mark In A Rain Storm	Geffen 24172
3/23/91	41	14		16 Night Ride Home	Geffen 24302
11/12/94	47	9		17 Turbulent Indigo	Reprise 45786
				Grammy: Pop Vocal Album	
11/16/96	161	2		18 Hits .... [G]	Reprise 46326
10/17/98	75	4		19 Taming The Tiger	Reprise 46451
4/8/00	66	11		20 Both Sides Now	Reprise 47620
				Grammy: Traditional Pop Vocal Album	
10/2/04	177	1		21 Dreamland..	Asylum 76520
10/13/07	14	14		22 Shine..	Hear 30457

MITCHELL, Kim
Born Joseph Kim Mitchell on 7/10/1952 in Sarnia, Ontario, Canada. Male rock singer/guitarist. Lead singer of **Max Webster**.

5/18/85	106	15	1 Akimbo Alogo..		Bronze 90257

MITCHELL, Rubin
Born in Charleston, South Carolina. Jazz pianist.

4/15/67	164	2	1 Presenting Rubin Mitchell.. [I]		Capitol 2658

Billboard			R I A A	ARTIST Album Title	Catalog	Label & Number
DEBUT	**PEAK**	**WKS**				

MITCHELL, Willie
Born on 1/3/1928 in Ashland, Mississippi; raised in Memphis, Tennessee. Died on 1/5/2010 (age 81). R&B keyboardist/arranger/producer. Led house band and later became president of Hi Records.
AWARD: Grammy: Trustees 2007

3/16/68	172	5		1 Willie Mitchell Live .... [I-L]		Hi 32042
				recorded at the Manhattan Club in Memphis, Tennessee		
5/11/68	151	7		2 Soul Serenade.. [I]		Hi 32039
11/7/70	188	2		3 Robbin's Nest.. [I]		Hi 32058

MJG
Born Marlon Jamal Goodwin in Memphis, Tennessee. Male rapper. Half of **Eightball & MJG** duo.

12/6/97	20	13	●	1 No More Glory		Suave House 53105

MOB, The
Brassy pop-rock band from Chicago, Illinois: brothers Artie Herrera (vocals) and Al Herrera (sax), with Mike Sistak (guitar), Tony Nedza (keyboards), Gary Beisber (trombone), Jimmy Franz (trumpet), Jimmy Holvay (bass) and Bobby Ruffino (drums).

2/6/71	204	1		1 The Mob		Colossus 1006

MOBB DEEP
Rap duo from Queens, New York: Kejuan "**Havoc**" Muchita and Albert "**Prodigy**" Johnson. Both are members of **QB Finest**.

5/13/95	18	18	●	1 The Infamous...		Loud 66480
12/7/96	6	16	●	2 Hell On Earth		Loud 66992
9/4/99	3[1]	17	▲	3 Murda Muzik		Loud 63715
12/29/01	22	23	●	4 Infamy..		Loud 85889
5/10/03	21	9		5 Free Agents: The Murda Mix Tape		Landspeed 9222
8/28/04	4	10		6 Amerikaz NightMare		Infamous 53730
5/20/06	3[1]	10		7 Blood Money		G-Unit 006376

MO B. DICK
Born Raymond Poole in Morgan City, Louisiana. Male rapper. Cousin of **Master P**. Member of **Tru**.

5/1/99	66	2		1 Gangsta Harmony		No Limit 50721

MOBY
Born Richard Melville Hall on 9/11/1965 in Harlem, New York; raised in Darien, Connecticut. Techno-dance singer/musician/producer/remixer.

8/5/00	137	8		1 Mobysongs (1993-1998) .... [K]		Elektra 62554
6/19/99+	38	94	▲[2]	2 Play .... Cat:#2[2]/23		V2 27049
				RS500 #341		
11/25/00	165	2		3 Play: The B-Sides..		V2 27085
6/1/02	4	18	●	4 18		V2 27127
4/9/05	28	8		5 Hotel		V2 27243
11/11/06	153	1		6 Go-The Very Best Of Moby .... [G]		V2 27347
4/19/08	27	5		7 Last Night..		Mute 9383
7/18/09	22	4		8 Wait For Me .... [I]		Little Idiot 9416

MOBY GRAPE
Rock band from San Francisco, California: Alexander "Skip" Spence (vocals, guitar), Jerry Miller (guitar), Peter Lewis (guitar), Bob Mosley (bass) and Don Stevenson (drums). Spence, former drummer with **Jefferson Airplane**, left in 1968. Lewis is the son of actress Loretta Young. Spence died of cancer on 4/16/1999 (age 52).

7/1/67	24	27		1 Moby Grape		Columbia 2698 / 9498
				RS500 #121		
5/4/68	20	28		2 Wow..		Columbia 9613 [2]
3/1/69	113	10		3 Moby Grape '69..		Columbia 9696
9/20/69	157	6		4 Truly Fine Citizen		Columbia 9912
9/18/71	177	5		5 20 Granite Creek		Reprise 6460

MOCEDADES
Vocal group from Bilbao, Spain: siblings Amaya, Izaskum and Roberto Amezaga, with Jose Urien, Carlos Uribarri and Javier Barrenechea.

3/16/74	152	7		1 Eres Tu "Touch The Wind" .... [F]		Tara 53000

M.O.D.
Hard-rock band from Los Angeles, California: Billy Milano (vocals), Tim McMurtrie (guitar), Ken Ballone (bass) and Keith Davis (drums). All but Milano left in 1988; replaced by Louie Svitek, Tim Mallare and John Monte. M.O.D.: Method Of Destruction.

11/7/87	153	5		1 U.S.A. For M.O.D.		Megaforce 1344
9/17/88	186	6		2 Surfin' With M.O.D.		Megaforce 1359
3/11/89	151	8		3 Gross Misconduct..		Megaforce 1360

MODELS
Pop-rock band formed in Melbourne, Australia: Sean Kelly (vocals, guitar), Roger Mason (keyboards), James Valentine (sax), James Freud (bass) and Barton Price (drums).

5/3/86	84	18		1 Out Of Mind Out Of Sight		Geffen 24100

MODERN ENGLISH
New-wave band formed in Colchester, England: Robbie Grey (vocals), Gary McDowell (guitar), Stephen Walker (keyboards), Michael Conroy (bass) and Richard Brown (drums).

3/19/83	70	28	●	1 After The Snow	Sire 23821
3/24/84	93	12		2 Ricochet Days	Sire 25066
4/5/86	154	7		3 Stop Start	Sire 25343
6/30/90	135	12		4 Pillow Lips	TVT 2810

MODERN LOVERS, The
Punk-rock band formed in Boston, Massachusetts: Jonathan Richman (vocals, guitar), **Jerry Harrison** (keyboards), Ernie Brooks (bass) and David Robinson (drums). Harrison joined **Talking Heads**. Robinson joined **The Cars**.

~ ~ ~ ~ ~ ~ ~ ~ ~ ~ **NON-CHARTED ALBUM** ~ ~ ~ ~ ~ ~ ~ ~ ~ ~ ~

1976 **The Modern Lovers**
RS500 #381

MODEST MOUSE
Alternative-rock trio from Isaaquah, Washington: Isaac Brock (vocals, guitar), Eric Judy (bass) and Jeremiah Green (drums).

7/1/00	120	2	●	1 The Moon & Antarctica .... **Cat:#19/13**	Epic 63871
10/13/01	147	1		2 Everywhere And His Nasty Parlour Tricks	Epic 62104
4/24/04	18	57	▲	3 Good News For People Who Love Bad News	Epic 87125
4/7/07	❶[1]	25	●	4 We Were Dead Before The Ship Even Sank	Epic 86139
8/22/09	15	9		5 No One's First, And You're Next .... **[EP]**	Epic 46289

MODUGNO, Domenico
Born on 1/9/1928 in Polignano a Mare, Italy. Died of a heart attack on 8/6/1994 (age 66). Singer/actor.

9/15/58	8	6		1 Nel Blu Dipinto Di Blu **(Volare)** And Other Italian Favorites **[F]**	Decca 8808

MOE.
Alternative-rock band from Utica, New York: Rob Derhak (vocals, bass), Al Schnier (guitar), Chuck Garvey (guitar) and Vinnie Amico (drums).

2/10/07	120	1		1 The Conch	Fatboy 6645
2/9/08	119	1		2 Sticks And Stones	Fatboy 6649

MOEN, Don
Born on 6/29/1950 in Minneapolis, Minnesota; later based in Tulsa, Oklahoma. Christian singer/songwriter/choral director.

11/4/00	104	3		1 I Will Sing	Hosanna! 17822

MOFFATTS, The
Family pop vocal group from Tumbler Ridge, British Columbia, Canada: Scott (born on 3/30/1984) with his triplet brothers, Dave, Bob and Clint (born on 3/8/1985) Moffatt.

6/26/99	124	2		1 Chapter I: A New Beginning	Capitol 97939

MOFFO, Anna
Born on 6/27/1932 in Wayne, Pennsylvania. Died of cancer on 3/10/2006 (age 73). Operatic soprano.

1/25/64	97	7		1 The Dream Duet	RCA Victor 2675
				ANNA MOFFO & SERGIO FRANCHI	

MOGWAI
Rock band from Glasgow, Scotland: Stuart Braithwaite (vocals, guitar), Dominic Aitchison (guitar), John Cummings (guitar), Brandan O'Hare (bass) and Martin Bulloch (drums).

7/5/03	182	1		1 Happy Songs For Happy People	Matador 567
3/25/06	128	1		2 Mr. Beast	Matador 681
10/11/08	97	1		3 The Hawk Is Howling	Wall Of Sound 832

MOKENSTEF
Female R&B vocal trio from Los Angeles, California: Monifa Bethune, Kenya Hadley and Stephanie Sinclair.

7/22/95	117	12		1 Azz Izz	OutBurst 527364

MOLLY HATCHET
Southern-rock band formed in Jacksonville, Florida: **Danny Joe Brown** (vocals), Dave Hlubek, Duane Roland and Steve Holland (guitars), Banner Thomas (bass) and Bruce Crump (drums). Jimmy Farrar replaced Brown in 1980; Brown returned and replaced Farrar in 1983. Holland and Thomas left in 1983; John Galvin (keyboards) and Riff West (bass) joined. Brown died of diabetes complications on 3/10/2005 (age 53). Roland died on 6/19/2006 (age 53).

11/11/78+	64	42	▲	1 Molly Hatchet .... **Cat:#49/4**	Epic 35347
9/29/79	19	48	▲[2]	2 Flirtin' With Disaster	Epic 36110
9/20/80	25	21	▲	3 Beatin' The Odds	Epic 36572
12/5/81+	36	14		4 Take No Prisoners	Epic 37480
3/26/83	59	20		5 No Guts...No Glory	Epic 38429
11/24/84	117	13		6 The Deed Is Done	Epic 39621
12/7/85	130	9		7 Double Trouble Live .... **[L]**	Epic 40137 [2]

MOM'S APPLE PIE
Rock band from Warren, Ohio: Bob Fiorino and Tony Gigliotti (vocals), Bob Miller and Joe Ahladis (guitars), Bob Pinti and Fred Marzulla (horns), Dave Mazzochi (keyboards), Greg Yochman (bass) and Pat Aulizia (drums).

12/2/72	203	5		1 Mom's Apple Pie	Brown Bag 14200
				label quickly replaced the original cover art with a less offensive version	

MOM & DADS, The
Polka band from Spokane, Washington: Quentin Ratliff (sax), Harold Hendren (drums), Les Welch (accordian) and Doris Crow (piano).

11/13/71+	85	23		1 The Rangers Waltz.. [I]		GNP Crescendo 2061
5/6/72	165	6		2 In The Blue Canadian Rockies .... [I]		GNP Crescendo 2063

MOMENTS, The / RAY, GOODMAN & BROWN
R&B vocal trio from Hackensack, New Jersey: Harry Ray, Al Goodman and Billy Brown. Changed group name to **Ray, Goodman & Brown** in 1978. Ray died of a stroke on 10/1/1992 (age 45).

3/27/71	184	7		1 Moments Greatest Hits.. [G]		Stang 1004
5/15/71	147	8		2 The Moments Live at the New York State Womans Prison .... [L]		Stang 1006
7/12/75	132	8		3 Look At Me...		Stang 1026
				RAY, GOODMAN & BROWN:		
1/26/80	17	23	●	4 Ray, Goodman & Brown		Polydor 6240
10/4/80	84	12		5 Ray, Goodman & Brown II		Polydor 6299
1/9/82	151	7		6 Stay..		Polydor 6341

MONAE, Janelle
Born Janelle Monae Robinson on 12/1/1985 in Kansas City, Missouri. Female R&B singer.

8/30/08	115	1		1 Metropolis: The Chase Suite		Wondaland 511234

MONAHAN, Pat
Born on 2/28/1969 in Waterford, Pennsylvania. Male singer/songwriter. Lead singer of **Train**.

10/6/07	92	1		1 Last Of Seven		Columbia 80082

MONCHY & ALEXANDRA
Male-female Latin vocal duo from the Dominican Republic: Ramon "Monchy" Rijo (born on 9/19/1977) and Alexandra Cabrera (born on 10/19/1978).

11/6/04	193	1		1 Hasta El Fin .... [F]		J&N 95422
4/15/06	181	1		2 Exitos Y Mas .... [F]		J&N 50078

MONET, Jerzee
Born Tanisha Carey in Bordentown, New Jersey. Female R&B singer/songwriter.

8/3/02	60	5		1 Love & War		DreamWorks 450870

MONEY, Eddie
Born Edward Mahoney on 3/2/1949 in Brooklyn, New York. Rock singer/songwriter. Discovered and subsequently managed by the late West Coast promoter Bill Graham. Formerly an officer with the New York Police Department.

1/7/78	37	49	▲²	1 Eddie Money.. **Cat:#44/24**		Columbia 34909
1/27/79	17	26	▲	2 Life For The Taking		Columbia 35598
8/9/80	35	17		3 Playing For Keeps		Columbia 36514
7/10/82	20	44	▲	4 No Control		Columbia 37960
11/5/83	67	19		5 Where's The Party?		Columbia 38862
8/30/86	20	58	▲	6 Can't Hold Back		Columbia 40096
10/22/88	49	29		7 Nothing To Lose		Columbia 44302
12/2/89+	53	18	●	8 Greatest Hits Sound Of Money .... [G]		Columbia 45381
2/1/92	160	10		9 Right Here		Columbia 46756

MONEY, JT
Born Jeff Tompkins in Florida. Male rapper. One-half of **Poison Clan**.

6/12/99	28	13		1 Pimpin On Wax		Freeworld 50060
5/19/01	48	8		2 Blood Sweat And Years		Freeworld 27069

MONGE, Yolandita
Born on 9/16/1955 in Trujillo Alto, Puerto Rico. Female Latin pop singer.

6/23/07	112	2		1 Demasiado Fuerte .... [F]		La Calle 330048
12/13/08	159	1		2 Mala .... [F]		Universal Latino 678764

MONHEIT, Jane
Born in 11/3/1977 in Oakdale, Long Island, New York. Jazz singer.

6/30/01	153	2		1 Come Dream With Me		N-Coded 4219
10/5/02	173	1		2 In The Sun		N-Coded 4234
9/25/04	94	7		3 Taking A Chance On Love..		Sony Classical 92495
1/21/06	12	1		4 The Season .... [X]		Epic 77711
				Christmas chart: 12/05		

MONICA
Born Monica Arnold on 10/24/1980 in Atlanta, Georgia. R&B singer.

8/5/95	36	61	▲³	1 Miss Thang		Rowdy 37006
8/1/98	8	58	▲³	2 The Boy Is Mine		Arista 19011
7/5/03	❶¹	37	●	3 After The Storm		J Records 20031
10/21/06	8	10		4 The Makings Of Me		J Records 78960

Billboard DEBUT	PEAK	WKS	R I A A	ARTIST Album Title	Catalog	Label & Number

MONIFAH
Born Monifah Carter on 1/28/1968 in Harlem, New York. Female R&B singer/actress.

6/8/96	42	15		1 Moods...Moments	Uptown 53004
9/12/98+	96	32	●	2 Mo'Hogany	Uptown 53155
11/18/00	151	2		3 Home	Universal 157999

MONK, T.S.
Born Thelonious Sphere Monk on 12/27/1949 in Harlem, New York. R&B singer/drummer. Son of **Thelonious Monk**.

1/31/81	64	22		1 House Of Music	Mirage 19291
1/9/82	176	8		2 More Of The Good Life	Mirage 19324

MONK, Thelonious
Born on 10/10/1917 in Rocky Mount, North Carolina. Died on 2/17/1982 (age 64). Legendary jazz pianist. Father of **T.S. Monk**.
AWARD: Grammy: Lifetime Achievement 1993

11/30/63	127	3		1 Criss-Cross ... [I]	Columbia 2038 / 8838
10/15/05	107	14		2 At Carnegie Hall ... [L]	Thelonious 35173
				THELONIOUS MONK QUARTET WITH JOHN COLTRANE recorded on 11/29/1957	
10/18/08	41 C	1		3 Thelonious Monk With John Coltrane ... [I]	Original Jazz Cl. 86039
				Grammy: Hall of Fame	

~ ~ ~ ~ ~ ~ ~ ~ ~ **NON-CHARTED ALBUMS** ~ ~ ~ ~ ~ ~ ~ ~ ~ ~ ~
1956 **Brilliant Corners**   1957 **Monk's Music**
Grammy: Hall of Fame ★ *NRR*   *Grammy: Hall of Fame*

MONKEES, The   **1960s: #37 / All-Time: #98**
Pop group formed in 1965 in Los Angeles, California. Members chosen from over 400 applicants for new Columbia TV series. Consisted of **Davy Jones** (vocals; born on 12/30/1945 in Manchester, England), **Michael Nesmith** (guitar, vocals; born on 12/30/1942 in Houston, Texas), Peter Tork (bass, vocals; born on 2/13/1944 in Washington DC) and Micky Dolenz (drums, vocals; born on 3/8/1945 in Tarzana, California). Jones had been a racehorse jockey, and appeared in London musicals *Oliver* and *Pickwick*. Nesmith had done session work for Stax/Volt. Tork had been in the Phoenix Singers. Dolenz had appeared in TV series *Circus Boy*, using the name Mickey Braddock in 1956. Group starred in the movie *Head* and 58 episodes of *The Monkees* TV show, 1966-68. Tork left in 1968. Group disbanded in 1970. Re-formed (minus Nesmith) in 1986 and again (with Nesmith) in 1996.

10/8/66	❶13	78	▲5	1 The Monkees	Colgems 101
2/4/67	❶18	70	▲5	2 More Of The Monkees	Colgems 102
6/10/67	❶1	51	▲2	3 Headquarters	Colgems 103
11/25/67	❶5	47	▲2	4 Pisces, Aquarius, Capricorn & Jones Ltd.	Colgems 104
5/11/68	34	39	▲	5 The Birds, The Bees & The Monkees	Colgems 109
12/21/68+	45	15		6 Head ... [S]	Colgems 5008
3/1/69	32	15		7 Instant Replay	Colgems 113
11/1/69	100	14		8 The Monkees Present	Colgems 117
9/19/87	72	9		9 Pool It!	Rhino 70706
				GREATEST HITS & COMPILATIONS:	
6/28/69	89	12		10 The Monkees Greatest Hits	Colgems 115
2/6/71	207	2		11 Barrel Full Of Monkees	Colgems 1001
8/7/76	58	30	▲	12 The Monkees Greatest Hits ... Cat:#4/259	Arista 4089
7/26/86	21	34	▲	13 Then & Now...The Best Of The Monkees	Arista 8432
7/15/00	21 C	2		14 The Monkees Greatest Hits	Rhino 72190
				first released in 1995	
5/17/03	51	6		15 The Best Of The Monkees	Rhino 73875
				REISSUES:	
8/16/86	92	24		16 The Monkees	Rhino 70140
8/16/86	96	26		17 More Of The Monkees	Rhino 70142
8/16/86	121	17		18 Headquarters	Rhino 70143
8/16/86	124	17		19 Pisces, Aquarius, Capricorn & Jones Ltd.	Rhino 70141
9/13/86	145	11		20 The Birds, The Bees & The Monkees	Rhino 70144
11/8/86	152	4		21 Changes	Rhino 70148
				first released in 1970 on Colgems 119	

MONO
Dance duo from England: Siobahn DeMare (female vocals) and Martin Virgo (instruments).

3/7/98	137	7		1 Formica Blues	Echo 536676

MONOXIDE
Born Paul Methric on 7/14/1973 in Detroit, Michigan. White male rapper. Member of **Dark Lotus** and **Twiztid**.

12/4/04	191	1		1 Chainsmoker LP	Psychopathic 4044

MONRO, Matt
Born Terrence Parsons on 12/1/1930 in London, England. Died of liver cancer on 2/7/1985 (age 54). Pop singer.

10/2/61	87	14		1 My Kind Of Girl	Warwick 2045
3/13/65	126	3		2 Walk Away	Liberty 7402
5/13/67	86	22		3 Invitation To The Movies/Born Free	Capitol 2730

MONROE, Marilyn
Born Norma Jean Baker on 6/1/1926 in Los Angeles, California. Died of a drug overdose on 8/5/1962 (age 36). Legendary Hollywood actress/sex symbol. Married to baseball player Joe DiMaggio (1954) and playwright Arthur Miller (1956-61).

| 10/20/62 | 111 | 10 | | 1 Marilyn.. | | 20th Century Fox 5000 |

MONROE, Michael
Born Matt Fagerholm on 6/17/1960 in Helsinki, Finland. Hard-rock singer.

| 10/7/89 | 161 | 8 | | 1 Not Fakin' It... | | Mercury 838627 |

MONROES, The
Pop-rock band from San Diego, California: Jesus Ortiz (vocals), Rusty Jones (guitar), Eric Denton (keyboards), Bob "Monroe" Davis (bass) and Jonnie Gilstrap (drums).

| 6/19/82 | 109 | 9 | | 1 The Monroes.. [EP] | | Alfa 15015 |

MONSTER MAGNET
Hard-rock band from Red Bank, New Jersey: David Wyndorf (vocals), Ed Mundell (guitar), Joe Calandra (bass) and Joe Kleiman (drums). Phil Caivano (guitar) joined in 2000.

| 7/4/98 | 97 | 23 | ● | 1 Powertrip.. | | A&M 540908 |
| 4/28/01 | 153 | 1 | | 2 God Says No.. | | A&M 490749 |

MONSTERS OF FOLK
Adult Alternative band formed in Los Angeles, California: **Yim Yames** (of **My Morning Jacket**), Conor "**Bright Eyes**" Oberst, **M. Ward** and Mike Mogis.

| 10/3/09 | 15 | 9 | | 1 Monsters Of Folk.. | | Shangri-La 101044 |

MONTANA ORCHESTRA
Studio group assembled by producer Vincent Montana. Also see **Salsoul Orchestra**.

| 12/19/81+ | 195 | 4 | | 1 Merry Christmas/Happy New Year's .... [X] | | MJS 3302 |

side 1: Christmas medley; side 2: New Year's Eve party medley

MONTE, Lou
Born on 4/2/1917 in Lyndhurst, New Jersey. Died on 6/12/1989 (age 72). Italian-styled novelty singer/guitarist.

| 12/22/62+ | 9 | 25 | | 1 Pepino The Italian Mouse & Other Italian Fun Songs [N] | | Reprise 6058 |

MONTENEGRO, Hugo
Born on 9/2/1925 in Brooklyn, New York. Died of emphysema on 2/6/1981 (age 55). Conductor/composer/arranger.

1/29/66	52	20		1 Original Music From The Man From U.N.C.L.E. .... [I-TV]		RCA Victor 3475
2/17/68	9	39	●	2 Music From "A Fistful Of Dollars" & "For A Few Dollars More" & "The Good, The Bad And The Ugly" [I]		RCA Victor 3927
9/21/68	166	5		3 Hang 'Em High .... [I]		RCA Victor 4022
8/30/69	182	4		4 Moog Power .... [I]		RCA Victor 4170

MONTERO, German
Born in Mexico City, Mexico. Male Latin singer.

| 5/16/09 | 190 | 1 | | 1 Comprendeme .... [F] | | Fonovisa 354007 |

MONTEZ, Chris
Born Ezekiel Christopher Montanez on 1/17/1943 in Los Angeles, California. Pop-rock singer.

| 7/2/66 | 33 | 24 | | 1 The More I See You/Call Me .... | | A&M 4115 |
| 1/14/67 | 106 | 11 | | 2 Time After Time .... | | A&M 4120 |

~ ~ ~ ~ ~ ~ ~ ~ ~ **NON-CHARTED ALBUM** ~ ~ ~ ~ ~ ~ ~ ~ ~ ~
1963 Let's Dance And Have Some Kinda Fun!!!

MONTGOMERY, John Michael
All-Time: #367

Born on 1/20/1965 in Danville, Kentucky. Country singer/songwriter/guitarist. Brother of Eddie Montgomery of **Montgomery Gentry**.
AWARD: CMA: Horizon 1994

1/23/93	27	77	▲³	1 Life's A Dance..		Atlantic 82420
2/12/94	❶¹	82	▲⁴	2 Kickin' It Up		Atlantic 82559
4/15/95	5	65	▲⁴	3 John Michael Montgomery		Atlantic 82728
10/12/96	39	40	▲	4 What I Do The Best		Atlantic 82947
11/1/97	33	29	▲	5 Greatest Hits .... [G]		Atlantic 83060
5/23/98	95	5	●	6 Leave A Mark		Atlantic 83104
6/12/99	135	4		7 Home To You		Atlantic 83185
10/14/00	15	19	●	8 Brand New Me		Atlantic 83378
10/26/02	110	1		9 Pictures		Warner 48341
9/13/03	77	4		10 The Very Best Of John Michael Montgomery............................. [G]		Warner 73918
5/8/04	31	11		11 Letters From Home		Warner 48729
11/1/08	172	1		12 Time Flies..		Stringtown 00200

MONTGOMERY, Wes
Born John Montgomery on 3/6/1925 in Indianapolis, Indiana. Died on 6/15/1968 (age 43). Jazz guitarist.

12/11/65+	116	13		1 Bumpin'... [I]		Verve 8625
9/3/66	51	32		2 Tequila .... [I]		Verve 8653
3/25/67	65	32		3 California Dreaming.. [I]		Verve 8672
5/20/67	129	23		4 Jimmy & Wes The Dynamic Duo .... [I]		Verve 8678

JIMMY SMITH & WES MONTGOMERY

| 12/9/67+ | 56 | 38 | | 5 The Best Of Wes Montgomery .... [I-K] | | Verve 8714 |

MONTGOMERY, Wes — cont'd

9/7/68	187	8		6 The Best Of Wes Montgomery, Vol. 2 .... [I-K]		Verve 8757
10/7/67	13	67	●	7 A Day In The Life [I]		A&M 3001
5/4/68	38	30		8 Down Here On The Ground.. [I]		A&M 3006
11/16/68	94	16		9 Road Song .... [I]		A&M 3012
4/4/70	175	9		10 Greatest Hits .... [G-I]		A&M 4247

~ ~ ~ ~ ~ ~ ~ ~ ~ ~ **NON-CHARTED ALBUM** ~ ~ ~ ~ ~ ~ ~ ~ ~ ~ ~ ~
1960 **The Incredible Jazz Guitar Of Wes Montgomery**
Grammy: Hall of Fame

MONTGOMERY GENTRY

Country vocal duo of Eddie Montgomery and Troy Gentry. Montgomery was born Gerald Edward Montgomery on 9/30/1963 in Danville, Kentucky; raised in Nicholasville, Kentucky. Older brother of **John Michael Montgomery**. Gentry was born on 4/5/1967 in Lexington, Kentucky.
  AWARDS: CMA: Vocal Duo 2000 ★ OPRY: 2009

4/24/99	131	8	▲	1 Tattoos & Scars	Columbia 69156
5/19/01	49	19	●	2 Carrying On	Columbia 62167
9/14/02	26	73	▲	3 My Town	Columbia 86520
6/5/04	10	71	▲	4 You Do Your Thing	Columbia 90558
11/19/05	20	24	●	5 Something To Be Proud Of: The Best Of 1999-2005 .... [G]	Columbia 94982
11/11/06	23	47		6 Some People Change	Columbia 94888
6/28/08	20	10		7 Back When I Knew It All	Columbia 22817
6/13/09	11	9		8 For Our Heroes .... [K]	Cracker Barrel 49446

MONTROSE

Hard-rock band from San Francisco, California: Ronnie Montrose (guitar; **Edgar Winter Group**, **Gamma**), Sammy Hagar (vocals), Bill Church (bass) and Denny Carmassi (drums; Gamma, **Heart**). Church left after first album, replaced by Alan Fitzgerald (**Night Ranger**). Hagar left after second album; replaced by Bob James. Fitzgerald left after third album; replaced by Jim Alcivar. Group disbanded in 1977. Montrose formed new group in 1987 with Johnny Edwards (vocals; **Foreigner**), Glenn Letsch (bass) and James Kottak (drums).

5/11/74	133	12	▲	1 Montrose	Warner 2740
11/16/74	65	14		2 Paper Money	Warner 2823
10/18/75	79	7		3 Warner Bros. Presents Montrose!	Warner 2892
9/25/76	118	7		4 Jump On It	Warner 2963
2/11/78	98	10		5 Open Fire	Warner 3134
				RONNIE MONTROSE	
5/30/87	165	7		6 Mean	Enigma 73264

MONTY PYTHON

Comedy troupe from England: Eric Idle, John Cleese, Terry Jones, Graham Chapman, Michael Palin and Terry Gilliam. Starred in TV's *Monty Python's Flying Circus* from 1969-74. Chapman died of cancer on 10/4/1989 (age 48). Also see **The Rutles**.

5/12/73	217	3		1 Money Python's Previous Record .... [C]	Charisma 1063
				also see #5 below	
5/24/75	48	13		2 Matching Tie & Handkerchief .... [C]	Arista 4039
8/2/75	83	15		3 Monty Python's Flying Circus .... [C]	Pye 12116
8/23/75	87	11		4 The Album Of The Soundtrack Of The Trailer Of The Film Of	
				"Monty Python And The Holy Grail" .... [C-S]	Arista 4050
3/13/76	202	6		5 The Worst Best...Monty Python .... [C-K]	Buddah 5626 [2]
				record 2 is a reissue of #1 above	
6/5/76	186	3		6 Monty Python Live! At City Center .... [C]	Arista 4073
11/10/79	155	2		7 Life Of Brian .... [C-S]	Warner 3396
				individual skit names not shown on above 2 albums	
11/15/80	164	9		8 Monty Python's Contractual Obligation Album.................... [C]	Arista 9536
2/27/82	204	5		9 Instant Record Collection .... [C-K]	Arista 9580

MOODY BLUES, The   **All-Time: #108**

Pop-rock band formed in Birmingham, England: Denny Laine (guitar, vocals; born on 10/29/1944), **Ray Thomas** (flute, vocals; born on 12/29/1942), **Michael Pinder** (keyboards, vocals; born on 12/27/1941), Clint Warwick (bass; born on 6/25/1939; died of liver failure on 5/15/2004, age 64) and **Graeme Edge** (drums; born on 3/30/1942). Laine and Warwick left in the summer of 1966; replaced by **Justin Hayward** (vocals, guitar; born on 10/14/1946) and **John Lodge** (vocals, bass; born on 7/20/1945). Laine joined **Wings** in 1971. Switzerland-born **Patrick Moraz** (former keyboardist of **Yes**) replaced Pinder in 1978; left group in early 1992.

5/4/68+	3[5]	106	▲	1 Days Of Future Passed	Cat:#29/24	Deram 18012
				with The London Festival Orchestra		
9/14/68	23	29	●	2 In Search Of The Lost Chord	Cat:#27/30	Deram 18017
5/31/69	20	136	▲	3 On The Threshold Of A Dream	Cat:#23/38	Deram 18025
1/10/70	14	44	●	4 To Our Children's Children's Children................................	Cat:#36/14	Threshold 1
9/12/70	3[1]	74	▲	5 A Question Of Balance	Cat:#26/18	Threshold 3
8/21/71	2[3]	43	●	6 Every Good Boy Deserves Favour		Threshold 5
11/18/72	❶[5]	44	●	7 Seventh Sojourn		Threshold 7
7/1/78	13	30	▲	8 Octave		London 708
6/13/81	❶[3]	39	▲	9 Long Distance Voyager		Threshold 2901

DEBUT	PEAK	WKS	R I A A	ARTIST / Album Title	Catalog	Label & Number
				MOODY BLUES, The — cont'd		
9/10/83	26	22		10 **The Present**		Threshold 2902
5/17/86	9	42	▲	11 **The Other Side Of Life**		Threshold 829179
6/25/88	38	19		12 **Sur La Mer**		Polydor 835756
7/13/91	94	11		13 **Keys Of The Kingdom**		Polydor 849433
9/4/99	93	5		14 **Strange Times**		Threshold 153565
11/15/03	10[X]	2		15 **December** [X]		Universal 001563
				GREATEST HITS & COMPILATIONS:		
11/23/74+	11	25	●	16 **This Is The Moody Blues**		Threshold 12/13 [2]
3/23/85	132	9		17 **Voices In The Sky/The Best Of The Moody Blues**		Threshold 820155
12/9/89+	113	16	●	18 **Greatest Hits**		Threshold 840659
				LIVE ALBUMS:		
6/4/77	26	15		19 **Caught Live +5**		London 690/1 [2]
				first 3 sides recorded live at the Royal Albert Hall in 1969; side 4: previously unreleased studio recordings		
3/27/93	93	5	●	20 **A Night At Red Rocks With The Colorado Symphony Orchestra**		Polydor 517977
				recorded on 9/9/1992 at Red Rocks Amphitheater in Colorado		
8/26/00	185	1		21 **Hall Of Fame: Recorded Live At The Royal Albert Hall**		Ark 21 810059
				recorded on 5/1/2000		
				~ ~ ~ ~ ~ ~ ~ ~ ~ *NON-CHARTED ALBUM* ~ ~ ~ ~ ~ ~ ~ ~ ~ ~		
				1965 **Go Now - The Moody Blues #1**		
				MOOG MACHINE, The		
				Group is actually synthesizer player Kenny Ascher (born on 10/26/1944 in Washington DC).		
9/27/69	170	8		1 **Switched-On Rock** [I]		Columbia 9921
				MOON, Keith		
				Born on 8/23/1946 in London, England. Died of a drug overdose on 9/7/1978 (age 32). Rock drummer. Member of **The Who**.		
4/5/75	155	3		1 **Two Sides Of The Moon**		Track/MCA 2136
				MOONGLOWS, The		
				R&B vocal group formed in Cleveland, Ohio: Harvey Fuqua, Bobby Lester, Alexander Graves and Prentiss Barnes, with Billy Johnson (guitar). Lester died on 10/15/1980 (age 50). Johnson died on 4/29/1987 (age 63). Barnes died on 9/30/2006 (age 81). Graves died on 10/15/2006 (age 76).		
				AWARD: R&R Hall of Fame: 2000		
8/5/72	193	4		1 **The Return Of The Moonglows**		RCA Victor 4722
				~ ~ ~ ~ ~ ~ ~ ~ ~ *NON-CHARTED ALBUMS* ~ ~ ~ ~ ~ ~ ~ ~ ~ ~		
				1959 **Look! - It's The Moonglows** / 1962 **The Flamingos Meet The Moonglows On The**		
				1962 **The Best Of Bobby Lester And The Moonglows** / **Dusty Road Of Hits**		
				MOORE, Bob, and His Orch.		
				Born on 11/30/1932 in Nashville, Tennessee. Top session bass player.		
11/13/61	33	18		1 **Mexico And Other Great Hits!** [I]		Monument 4005
				MOORE, Chante		
				Born on 2/17/1967 in San Francisco, California. Female R&B singer. Married to actor Kadeem Hardison from 1996-2000. Married **Kenny Lattimore** on 1/1/2002.		
1/30/93	101	27	●	1 **Precious**		Silas 10605
12/3/94	64	12		2 **A Love Supreme**		Silas 11157
6/12/99	31	10		3 **This Moment Is Mine**		Silas 11674
12/2/00	50	11		4 **Exposed**		Silas 112377
3/1/03	31	15		5 **Things That Lovers Do**		Arista 14751
10/28/06	95	2		6 **Uncovered/Covered**		Verity 67926 [2]
				KENNY LATTIMORE & CHANTE MOORE (above 2)		
7/5/08	110	1		7 **Love The Woman**		Peak 30122
				MOORE, Dorothy		
				Born on 10/13/1946 in Jackson, Mississippi. R&B singer.		
5/29/76	29	23		1 **Misty Blue**		Malaco 6351
8/6/77	120	13		2 **Dorothy Moore**		Malaco 6353
				MOORE, Gary		
				Born on 4/4/1952 in Belfast, Ireland. Rock singer/guitarist. Member of **Thin Lizzy**.		
4/23/83	149	13		1 **Corridors Of Power**		Mirage 90077
6/9/84	172	5		2 **Victims Of The Future**		Mirage 90154
3/15/86	146	7		3 **Run For Cover**		Mirage 90482
5/16/87	139	15		4 **Wild Frontier**		Virgin 90588
3/25/89	114	9		5 **After The War**		Virgin 91066
7/14/90+	83	42	●	6 **Still Got The Blues**		Charisma 91369
3/28/92	145	8		7 **After Hours**		Charisma 91825
				MOORE, Justin		
				Born on 3/30/1984 in Poyen, Arkansas. Country singer/songwriter.		
8/29/09	10	33		1 **Justin Moore**		Valory 0100

MOORE, Mandy
Born Amanda Moore on 4/10/1984 in Nashua, New Hampshire. Pop singer/actress. Starred in the movies *A Walk To Remember*, *Chasing Liberty* and *License To Wed*.

12/25/99+	31	23	▲	1 So Real		550 Music 69917
5/27/00	21	28	●	2 I Wanna Be With You		550 Music 62195
7/7/01	35	16	●	3 Mandy Moore		Epic 61430
11/8/03	14	13		4 Coverage		Epic 90127
12/4/04	148	1		5 The Best Of Mandy Moore	[G]	Epic 93458
7/7/07	30	7		6 Wild Hope		Firm 70112
6/13/09	25	2		7 Amanda Leigh		Storefront 99463

MOORE, Melba
Born Melba Hill on 10/29/1945 in Harlem, New York. R&B singer/actress. Appeared in several movies and Broadway shows.

2/20/71	157	5		1 Look What You're Doing To The Man		Mercury 61321
7/5/75	176	4		2 Peach Melba		Buddah 5629
5/8/76	145	5		3 This Is It		Buddah 5657
12/25/76+	177	7		4 Melba		Buddah 5677
11/18/78+	114	18		5 Melba		Epic 35507
				above 2 are different albums		
11/21/81	201	6		6 What A Woman Needs		EMI America 17060
11/13/82+	152	19		7 The Other Side Of The Rainbow		Capitol 12243
12/24/83+	147	14		8 Never Say Never		Capitol 12305
4/27/85	130	10		9 Read My Lips		Capitol 12382
8/23/86+	91	29		10 A Lot Of Love		Capitol 12471

MOORE, Tim
Born in Manhattan, New York. Pop singer/songwriter/guitarist/keyboardist.

10/12/74	119	9		1 Tim Moore		Asylum 1019
8/2/75	181	3		2 Behind The Eyes		Asylum 1042

MOORE, Vinnie
Born on 4/14/1964 in Newcastle, Delaware. Hard-rock guitarist.

6/18/88	147	7		1 Time Odyssey	[I]	Squawk 834634

M.O.P.
Rap duo from Brooklyn, New York: Jamal "Lil' Fame" Grinnage and Billy Danzenie. M.O.P.: Mashed Out Posse.

11/9/96	94	2		1 Firing Squad		Relativity 1555
8/29/98	80	4		2 First Family 4 Life		Relativity 1618
10/28/00	25	5		3 Warriorz		Loud 1778

MORALES, Michael
Born on 4/25/1963 in San Antonio, Texas. Pop singer/songwriter.

6/17/89	113	20		1 Michael Morales		Wing 835810

MORAZ, Patrick
Born on 6/24/1948 in Morges, Switzerland. Keyboardist for **Yes** (1974-78) and **The Moody Blues** (1978-92).

6/5/76	132	5		1 i		Atlantic 18175

MORCHEEBA
Trip-hop trio from Hythe, Kent, England: brothers Ross Godfrey and Paul Godfrey, with Skye Edwards.

8/19/00	113	5		1 Fragments Of Freedom		Sire 31137

MORGAN, Craig
Born Craig Morgan Greer on 7/17/1964 in Kingston Springs, Tennessee. Country singer/songwriter.
AWARD: OPRY: 2008

5/3/03	124	15		1 I Love It		Broken Bow 75672
3/26/05	40	29	●	2 My Kind Of Livin'		Broken Bow 75472
11/18/06	57	29		3 Little Bit Of Life	Cat:#48/1	Broken Bow 7797
10/18/08	113	4		4 Greatest Hits	[G]	Broken Bow 7737
11/8/08	39	3		5 That's Why		BNA 31308

MORGAN, Jane
Born Florence Currier on 12/25/1920 in Newton, Massachusetts; raised in Daytona Beach, Florida. Pop singer.

12/9/57	13	3		1 Fascination		Kapp 1066
				JANE MORGAN AND THE TROUBADORS		
11/26/66	134	4		2 Fresh Flavor		Epic 26211

MORGAN, Lee
Born on 7/10/1938 in Philadelphia, Pennsylvania. Shot to death on 2/19/1972 (age 33). Male jazz trumpeter.

10/10/64+	25	30		1 The Sidewinder	[I]	Blue Note 84157
				Grammy: Hall of Fame		
11/26/66	143	3		2 Search For The New Land	[I]	Blue Note 84169
3/1/69	190	3		3 Caramba!	[I]	Blue Note 84289

MORGAN, Lorrie
1990s: #46

Born Loretta Lynn Morgan on 6/27/1959 in Nashville, Tennessee. Country singer. Daughter of country singer George Morgan. Married to **Keith Whitley** from 1986-89 (his death). Married to singer Jon Randall from 1996-99. Married **Sammy Kershaw** on 9/29/2001 (since separated).

AWARD: OPRY: 1984

1/27/90	117	33	▲	1 Leave The Light On..		RCA 9594
5/25/91+	53	95	▲	2 Something In Red...		RCA 3021
10/31/92	65	65	▲	3 Watch Me		BNA 66047
12/11/93	115	5		4 Merry Christmas From London.................................. [X]		BNA 66282
				Christmas chart: 22/'93		
5/28/94	48	21	●	5 War Paint...		BNA 66379
7/15/95	46	37	▲²	6 Greatest Hits [G]		BNA 66508
6/22/96	62	20	●	7 Greater Need..		BNA 66847
8/30/97	98	11	●	8 Shakin' Things Up		BNA 67499
5/1/99	116	5		9 My Heart		BNA 67763
5/5/01	114	3		10 I Finally Found Someone..		RCA 67004
				LORRIE MORGAN & SAMMY KERSHAW		

MORGAN, Meli'sa
Born in Queens, New York. Female R&B singer.

2/8/86	41	36		1 Do Me Baby		Capitol 12434
12/19/87+	108	19		2 Good Love		Capitol 46943

MORISSETTE, Alanis
All-Time: #350

Born on 6/1/1974 in Ottawa, Ontario, Canada. Adult Alternative pop-rock singer/songwriter. At age 12, acted on the Nickelodeon cable-TV kids series *You Can't Do That On Television*. Played God in the 1999 movie *Dogma*.

7/1/95	❶¹²	113	▲¹⁶	1 Jagged Little Pill Cat:#2¹/120	Maverick 45901
				Grammys: Album of the Year / Rock Album ★ *RS500 #327*	
11/21/98	❶²	28	▲³	2 Supposed Former Infatuation Junkie	Maverick 47094
12/11/99	63	14	●	3 MTV Unplugged .... [L]	Maverick 47589
3/16/02	❶¹	24	▲	4 Under Rug Swept	Maverick 47988
12/28/02	194	1		5 Feast On Scraps	Maverick 48409
				contains leftover songs from the *Under Rug Swept* sessions	
6/5/04	5	14		6 So-Called Chaos	Maverick 48555
8/13/05	50	9		7 Jagged Little Pill: Acoustic	Maverick 49345
12/3/05	51	10		8 The Collection [G]	Maverick 49490
6/28/08	8	11		9 Flavors Of Entanglement	Maverick 269308

MORMON TABERNACLE CHOIR, The
Popular 375-voice choir directed by Richard Condie (died on 12/22/1985). Jerold Ottley took over after Condie's death.

10/19/59+	❶¹	80	●	1 The Lord's Prayer	Columbia 6068
1/5/63	49	8		2 The Lord's Prayer, Volume II..	Columbia 6367
10/30/61	47	1		3 Songs Of The North & South 1861-1865	Columbia 6259
4/15/06	140	2		4 Then Sings My Soul	Mormon Tab. 70036
4/26/08	179	2		5 Called To Serve	Mormon Tab. 5004111
1/17/09	102	1		6 Praise To The Man: Songs Honoring The Prophet Joseph Smith......................	Mormon Tab. 5012323
4/18/09	124	3		7 Come, Thou Fount Of Every Blessing: American Folk Hymns & Spirituals.......	Mormon Tab. 5014332
				CHRISTMAS ALBUMS:	
12/28/59+	5	2		8 The Spirit Of Christmas	Columbia 5423 / 6100
				Christmas charts: 26/'63, 26/'65, 60/'67	
12/25/61+	118	3		9 The Spirit Of Christmas .... [R]	Columbia 5423 / 6100
11/30/63	6ˣ	7	●	10 The Mormon Tabernacle Choir Sings Christmas Carols	Columbia 5222
				first released in 1957; Christmas charts: 6/'63, 48/'67	
12/21/63+	8ˣ	12	●	11 The Joy Of Christmas	Columbia 5899 / 6499
				LEONARD BERNSTEIN/NEW YORK PHILHARMONIC/THE MORMON TABERNACLE CHOIR	
				Christmas charts: 12/'63, 32/'64, 8/'65, 62/'66, 106/'67, 28/'68, 20/'70	
12/12/64	22ˣ	3		12 Christmas With The Mormon Tabernacle Organ And Chimes .... [I]	Columbia 6037 / 6637
				Alexander Schreiner (organist)	
12/18/65+	3¹ˣ	11		13 Handel: Messiah	Columbia 263 / 607 [2]
				THE PHILADELPHIA ORCHESTRA/EUGENE ORMANDY/THE MORMON TABERNACLE CHOIR	
				NRR	
				Christmas charts: 21/'65, 3/'69, 8/'70, 12/'71, 5/'72	
12/18/65	30ˣ	4		14 Christmas Carols Around The World	Columbia 5684 / 6284
				first released in 1961; Christmas charts: 30/'65, 48/'66	
12/21/91	29ˣ	1		15 Silent Night/The Greatest Hits Of Christmas	CBS Masterworks 37206
				with the Columbia Brass and Percussion Ensemble; first released in 1981	
12/11/93	171	3		16 Christmas With The Mormon Tabernacle Choir................ Cat:#14/17	LaserLight 12198
				Christmas charts: 19/'94, 25/'95, 21/'96	
11/13/04	40ˣ	1		17 Sing, Choirs Of Angels!	Mormon Tab. 1063
12/23/06	187	1		18 The Wonder Of Christmas .... [L]	Mormon Tab. 70047
				Christmas chart: 43/'06	
12/15/07	154	3		19 Spirit Of The Season	Mormon Tab. 0711
				Christmas chart: 20/'07	
10/18/08	18ˣ	3		20 Rejoice And Be Merry!	Mormon Tab. 5007325
10/10/09	4ˣ	8		21 Ring Christmas Bells	Mormon Tab. 5023338

Billboard DEBUT	PEAK	WKS	R I A A	ARTIST / Album Title	Catalog	Label & Number

MORNINGWOOD
Alternative-rock band from New York: Chantal Claret (vocals), Richard Steele (guitar), Pedro Yanowitz (bass) and Japa Keenon (drums).

| 1/28/06 | 102 | 2 | | 1 Morningwood .... | | Capitol 64753 |

MORODER, Giorgio
Born on 4/26/1940 in Ortisei, Italy. Electronic composer/conductor/producer.

10/29/77	130	7		1 From Here To Eternity		Casablanca 7065
				GIORGIO		
8/24/85	201	1		2 Philip Oakey & Giorgio Moroder		A&M 5080

MORPHINE
Rock trio from Boston, Massachusetts: Mark Sandman (vocals, bass), Dana Colley (sax) and Billy Conway (drums). Both Sandman and Conway were members of **Treat Her Right**. Sandman died of a heart attack on 7/4/1999 (age 46).

4/8/95	101	4		1 Yes		Rykodisc 10320
3/29/97	67	6		2 Like Swimming		DreamWorks 50009
2/19/00	137	4		3 The Night		DreamWorks 50056

MORRIS, Gary
Born on 12/7/1948 in Fort Worth, Texas. Country singer/songwriter/guitarist.

| 10/15/83 | 174 | 8 | ● | 1 Why Lady Why .... | | Warner 23738 |

MORRISON, James
Born on 8/13/1984 in Rugby, Warwickshire, England. Alternative-pop singer/songwriter/guitarist.

| 3/31/07 | 24 | 9 | | 1 Undiscovered .... | | Polydor 008253 |
| 10/18/08 | 49 | 6 | | 2 Songs For You, Truths For Me .... | | Polydor 012070 |

MORRISON, Mark
Born on 5/12/1974 in Hanover, Germany; raised in Leicester, England. R&B singer.

| 3/29/97 | 76 | 24 | | 1 Return Of The Mack .... | | Atlantic 82963 |

MORRISON, Van   **1990s: #12 / All-Time: #32**
Born George Ivan Morrison on 8/31/1945 in Belfast, Ireland. "Blue-eyed soul"-rock singer/songwriter/multi-instrumentalist. Member of The Javelins skiffle band from 1958-59. Member of The Monarchs from 1960-62. Formed group **Them** in 1963; group disbanded in 1966. Wrote the classic rock hit "Gloria."
AWARD: R&R Hall of Fame: 1993

10/7/67	182	7		1 Blowin' Your Mind!		Bang 218
1/26/74	181	4		2 T.B. Sheets		Bang 400
3/14/09	13C	3	●	3 Astral Weeks		Warner 1768
				Grammy: Hall of Fame ★ RS500 #19		
3/14/70	29	22	▲3	4 Moondance	Cat:#21/66	Warner 1835
				Grammy: Hall of Fame ★ RS500 #65		
12/26/70+	32	17		5 His Band And The Street Choir		Warner 1884
10/30/71	27	24	●	6 Tupelo Honey		Warner 1950
8/5/72	15	28		7 Saint Dominic's Preview		Warner 2633
8/11/73	27	19		8 Hard Nose The Highway		Warner 2712
11/9/74	53	10		9 Veedon Fleece		Warner 2805
5/7/77	43	11		10 A Period Of Transition		Warner 2987
10/14/78	28	23		11 Wavelength		Warner 3212
9/8/79	43	13		12 Into The Music		Warner 3390
9/20/80	73	10		13 Common One		Warner 3462
3/6/82	44	11		14 Beautiful Vision		Warner 3652
4/9/83	116	8		15 Inarticulate Speech Of The Heart		Warner 23802
3/9/85	61	17		16 A Sense Of Wonder		Mercury 822895
8/16/86	70	13		17 No Guru, No Method, No Teacher		Mercury 830077
10/10/87	90	22		18 Poetic Champions Compose		Mercury 832585
7/23/88	102	13		19 Irish Heartbeat		Mercury 834496
				VAN MORRISON & THE CHIEFTAINS		
7/1/89	91	39	●	20 Avalon Sunset		Mercury 839262
11/24/90+	62	25		21 Enlightenment		Mercury 847100
10/12/91	99	17	●	22 Hymns To The Silence		Polydor 849026 [2]
6/26/93	29	16		23 Too Long In Exile		Polydor 519219
7/8/95	33	16	●	24 Days Like This		Polydor 527307
3/22/97	32	16		25 The Healing Game		Polydor 537101
3/27/99	28	20	●	26 Back On Top		Pointblank 47148
10/21/00	161	2		27 You Win Again		Pointblank 50258
				VAN MORRISON & LINDA GAIL LEWIS		
6/1/02	25	12		28 Down The Road		Exile 589177
11/8/03	32	10		29 What's Wrong With This Picture?		Blue Note 90167
6/4/05	25	13		30 Magic Time		Exile 004662
3/25/06	26	12		31 Pay The Devil		Polydor 005968

Billboard DEBUT	PEAK	WKS	R I A A	ARTIST / Album Title	Catalog	Label & Number
				MORRISON, Van — cont'd		
3/3/07	35	17		32 Van Morrison At The Movies		Manhattan 84224
4/19/08	10	10		33 Keep It Simple		Exile 010658
				GREATEST HITS & COMPILATIONS:		
5/26/90	41	242	▲⁴	34 The Best Of Van Morrison	Cat:#3/298	Mercury 841970
3/27/93	176	3		35 The Best Of Van Morrison Volume Two		Polydor 517760
7/4/98	87	4		36 The Philosopher's Stone		Polydor 531789 [2]
				previously unreleased tracks recorded from 1971-1988		
7/7/07	149	1		37 The Best Of Van Morrison Volume 3		Exile 78968 [2]
11/24/07	48	26		38 Still On Top: The Greatest Hits		Exile 010070
				LIVE ALBUMS:		
3/16/74	53	17		39 It's Too Late To Stop Now		Warner 2760 [2]
6/4/94	125	4		40 A Night In San Francisco		Polydor 521290 [2]
				recorded on 12/18/1993 at The Masonic Auditorium in San Francisco, California		
1/27/96	55	11		41 How Long Has This Been Going On		Verve 529136
				VAN MORRISON with Georgie Fame & Friends		
				recorded on 5/3/1995 at Ronnie Scott's Club in London, England		
3/14/09	33	6		42 Astral Weeks: Live At The Hollywood Bowl		Listen To The Lion 93423
				MORRISSEY All-Time: #430		
				Born Steven Morrissey on 5/22/1959 in Davyhulme, Lancashire, England. Alternative singer/songwriter. Leader of The Smiths.		
4/9/88	48	20	●	1 Viva Hate		Sire 25699
11/24/90	59	16	●	2 Bona Drag		Sire 26221
3/23/91	52	10		3 Kill Uncle		Sire 26514
8/15/92	21	14		4 Your Arsenal		Sire 26994
4/9/94	18	10		5 Vauxhall And I		Sire 45451
3/11/95	134	1		6 World Of Morrissey [K]		Sire 45879
9/30/95	66	2		7 Southpaw Grammar		Reprise 45939
8/30/97	61	3		8 Maladjusted		Mercury 536036
6/5/04	11	7		9 You Are The Quarry		Attack 86001
4/16/05	119	1		10 Live At Earls Court [L]		Attack 86012
4/22/06	27	4		11 Ringleader Of The Tormentors		Attack 86014
4/12/08	178	1		12 Greatest Hits [G]		Decca 6009
3/7/09	11	6		13 Years Of Refusal		Attack 012578
				MORSE, Steve, Band		
				Born on 7/28/1954 in Hamilton, Ohio. Lead guitarist of the Dixie Dregs. Also a backing guitarist with Kansas.		
9/1/84	101	12		1 The Introduction [I]		Musician 60369
6/24/89	182	3		2 High Tension Wires [I]		MCA 6275
				STEVE MORSE		
				MORTON, Bishop Paul S., & The FGBCF Mass Choir		
				Born Paul Sylvester Morton on 7/30/1950 in Windsor, Ontario, Canada; later based in New Orleans, Louisiana. Leader of the Greater St. Stephens Full Gospel Church.		
8/9/03	169	1		1 Let It Rain [L]		Tehillah 5497
11/15/08	117	2		2 Cry Your Last Tear [L]		Tehillah 7209
				MOSBY, Johnny and Jonie		
				Country vocal duo: Johnny Mosby (born on 4/26/1933 in Fort Smith, Arkansas) and wife Jonie Mosby (born on 8/10/1940 in Van Nuys, California).		
10/11/69	197	1		1 Hold Me		Capitol 286
				MOS DEF		
				Born Dante Smith on 12/11/1973 in Brooklyn, New York. Male rapper. Member of the rap duo Black Star.		
10/30/99	25	16	●	1 Black On Both Sides		Rawkus 50141
10/30/04	5	13		2 The New Danger		Rawkus 003558
1/13/07	77	5		3 True Magic		Goodtree 007515
6/27/09	9	11		4 The Ecstatic		Downtown 70055
				MOSES, Annie, Band		
				Classical-pop-country band from Texas: husband-and-wife Bill (piano) and Robin (vocals) Wolaver, with their children Annie (violin), Alex (viola), Benjamin (cello), Camille (harp), Gretchen (mandolin) and Jeremiah (banjo).		
10/25/08	17ˣ	1		1 This Glorious Christmas [X]		Man Alive 10130
				MOSES, Teedra		
				Born on 12/17/1976 in New Orleans, Louisiana; raised in Los Angeles, California. Female singer.		
8/28/04	168	1		1 Complex Simplicity		TVT 2450
				MOSS, J.		
				Born James Moss on 12/25/1971 in Detroit, Michigan. Gospel singer.		
4/21/07	84	5		1 V2		Pajam 87214
9/12/09	74	4		2 Just James		Pajam 47910
				MOTE, Gordon		
				Born in Alabama. Contemporary Christian singer/songwriter/pianist. Blind since birth.		
11/10/07	170	1		1 Don't Let Me Miss The Glory		Spring Hill 21131

MOTELS, The

Pop-rock band formed in Berkeley, California: **Martha Davis** (vocals), Guy Perry (guitar), Marty Jourard (keyboards), Michael Goodroe (bass) and Brian Glascock (drums). Scott Thurston (guitar) joined in 1983. Group disbanded in 1987.

12/1/79	175	2	1 Motels		Capitol 11996
7/12/80	45	20	2 Careful		Capitol 12070
4/24/82	16	41	● 3 All Four One		Capitol 12177
10/15/83	22	24	● 4 Little Robbers		Capitol 12288
8/17/85	36	16	5 Shock		Capitol 12378

MOTHER EARTH

Country-rock band from Nashville, Tennessee: **Tracy Nelson** (vocals), Robert Cardwell (guitar), John Andrews (guitar), Andrew McMahon (keyboards), Tim Drummond (bass) and Karl Himmel (drums).

2/22/69	144	8	1 Living With The Animals		Mercury 61194
8/23/69	95	9	2 Make A Joyful Noise		Mercury 61226
5/15/71	199	2	3 Bring Me Home		Reprise 6431
2/26/72	205	1	4 Tracy Nelson/Mother Earth		Reprise 2054
4/14/73	210	5	5 Poor Man's Paradise		Columbia 3175
			TRACY NELSON/MOTHER EARTH (above 2)		

MOTHERLODE

Pop-rock band from in London, Ontario, Canada: William Smith (vocals, keyboards), Ken Marco (guitar), Steve Kennedy (sax) and Wayne Stone (drums). Smith died of a heart attack on 12/1/1997 (age 53).

10/4/69	93	12	1 When I Die		Buddah 5046

MOTHER LOVE BONE

Alternative-rock band from Seattle, Washington: Andrew Wood (vocals), Bruce Fairweather (guitar), Stone Gossard (guitar), Jeff Ament (bass), and Greg Gilmore (drums). Wood died of a drug overdose on 3/16/1990 (age 24). Gossard and Ament recorded with other Seattle notables as **Temple Of The Dog**, in tribute to Wood, then formed **Pearl Jam**.

10/10/92	77	12	1 Mother Love Bone		Stardog 512884 [2]

MOTHER'S FINEST

R&B band formed in Fort Lauderdale, Florida: husband-and-wife Glenn Murdock and **Joyce Kennedy** (vocals), Gary Moore (guitar), Michael Keck (keyboards), Jerry Seay (bass) and Barry Borden (drums).

9/11/76	148	8	1 Mother's Finest		Epic 34179
9/17/77	134	8	2 Another Mother Further		Epic 34699
9/30/78	123	21	3 Mother Factor		Epic 35546
11/17/79	203	4	4 Mother's Finest Live	[L]	Epic 35976
			recorded on the group's 1979 tour		
5/23/81	168	8	5 Iron Age		Atlantic 19302

MOTHERS OF INVENTION, The — see ZAPPA, Frank

MO THUGS FAMILY

Gathering of rap acts from Cleveland, Ohio. Assembled by **Bone Thugs-N-Harmony**. Acts include Tré, Graveyard Shift, Souljah Boy, Ken Dawg and **Il Tru**.

11/23/96	2[1]	23	▲ 1 Family Scriptures		Mo Thugs 1561
6/13/98	25	28	● 2 Family Scriptures Chapter II: Family Reunion		Mo Thugs 1632
7/15/00	45	8	3 Layzie Bone Presents Mo Thugs III: The Mothership		Mo Thugs 8111

MOTION CITY SOUNDTRACK

Punk-rock band from Minneapolis, Minnesota: Justin Pierre (vocals, guitar), Joshua Cain (guitar), Jesse Johnson (keyboards), Matthew Taylor (bass) and Tony Thaxton (drums).

6/25/05	72	6	1 Commit This To Memory		Epitaph 86765
10/6/07	16	6	2 Even If It Kills Me		Epitaph 86862

MOTLEY CRUE   All-Time: #197

Hard-rock band formed in Los Angeles, California: **Vince Neil** (vocals; born Vince Wharton on 2/8/1961), Mick Mars (guitar; born Bob Deal on 5/4/1951), Nikki Sixx (bass; born Frank Ferrana on 12/11/1958) and **Tommy Lee** (drums; born Thomas Bass on 10/3/1962). John Corabi replaced Neil for one album (#7 below) in 1994. Sixx married actress Donna D'Errico on 12/23/1996. Lee was married to actress Heather Locklear from 1986-93 and to actress Pamela Anderson from 1995-98. Lee left group in April 1999; formed **Methods Of Mayhem**. Drummer Randy Castillo joined in early 2000. Castillo died of cancer on 3/26/2002 (age 51). Sixx formed **Sixx: AM**.

12/17/83+	77	62	▲ 1 Too Fast For Love		Elektra 60174
10/15/83+	17	111	▲4 2 Shout At The Devil		Elektra 60289
7/13/85	6	72	▲4 3 Theatre Of Pain		Elektra 60418
6/13/87	2[1]	46	▲4 4 Girls, Girls, Girls		Elektra 60725
9/23/89	❶[2]	109	▲6 5 Dr. Feelgood	Cat:#43/1	Elektra 60829
4/2/94	7	10	● 6 Motley Crue		Elektra 61534
7/12/97	4	9	● 7 Generation Swine		Elektra 61901
12/11/99	133	2	8 Live: Entertainment Or Death	[L]	Motley 78034 [2]
7/29/00	41	6	9 New Tattoo		Motley 78120
7/12/08	4	12	10 Saints Of Los Angeles		Motley 240

Billboard			R I A A	ARTIST		
DEBUT	PEAK	WKS		Album Title	Catalog	Label & Number

MOTLEY CRUE — cont'd

GREATEST HITS & COMPILATIONS:

10/19/91	2¹	37	▲²	11 Decade Of Decadence - '81-'91		Elektra 61204
11/14/98	20	20	●	12 Greatest Hits	Cat:#40/1	Beyond 78002
2/19/05	6	19	▲	13 Red, White & Crue		Hip-O 003908 [2]
12/5/09	94	17↑		14 Greatest Hits		Motley 380

MOTORHEAD

Heavy metal band formed in London, England: Ian "Lemmy" Kilminster (vocals, bass; **Hawkwind**), "Fast Eddie" Clarke (guitar) and Phil Taylor (drums). Clarke left in May 1982 (later formed **Fastway**), replaced by Brian Robertson (**Thin Lizzy**). Taylor and Robertson left in August 1983. Kilminster then organized new foursome with guitarists Phil Campbell and Michael Burston, and drummer Pete Gill (**Saxon**). Taylor replaced Gill in 1991.

12/27/80+	201	10	1 Ace Of Spades		Mercury 4011
9/19/81	204	3	2 No Sleep 'Til Hammersmith	[L]	Mercury 4023
5/22/82	174	6	3 Iron Fist		Mercury 4042
7/23/83	153	7	4 Another Perfect Day		Mercury 811365
12/8/84	205	5	5 No Remorse	[K]	Bronze 90233 [2]
11/29/86	157	11	6 Orgasmatron		GWR/Profile 1223
10/24/87	150	6	7 Rock 'N' Roll		GWR/Profile 1240
3/23/91	142	9	8 1916		WTG 46858
9/13/08	82	2	9 Motorizer		Steamhammer 9163

MOTORS, The

New wave-rock duo from England: Andy McMaster and Nick Garvey.

4/12/80	174	8	1 Tenement Steps		Virgin 13139

MOTTOLA, Tony

Born on 4/18/1918 in Kearney, New Jersey. Died on 8/9/2004 (age 86). Latin-style guitarist.

4/7/62	26	26	1 Roman Guitar	[I]	Command 816
7/21/62	41	6	2 Roman Guitar, Volume Two	[I]	Command 836
12/11/65+	85	13	3 Love Songs - Mexico/S.A.	[I]	Command 889
12/2/67	198	3	4 A Latin Love-In	[I]	Project 3 5010
5/16/70	189	3	5 Tony Mottola's Guitar Factory	[I]	Project 3 5044
1/30/71	212	1	6 Close To You	[I]	Project 3 5050
4/8/72	214	2	7 Superstar Guitar	[I]	Project 3 5062

MOTT THE HOOPLE

Glam-rock band formed in England: **Ian Hunter** (vocals), Mick Ralphs (guitar), Pete Watts (bass) and Dale Griffin (drums). Group name taken from a Willard Manus novel. Ralphs left in 1973 to join **Bad Company**; guitarists Morgan Fisher and Ariel Bender joined. **Mick Ronson** was briefly a member in late 1974. Hunter left in 1976; Fisher, Watts and Griffin formed the **British Lions**.

6/15/74	112	11	1 Rock And Roll Queen		Atlantic 7297
7/4/70	185	2	2 Mott The Hoople		Atlantic 8258
4/17/71	207	6	3 Wildlife		Atlantic 8284
2/19/72	208	3	4 Brain Capers		Atlantic 8304
11/11/72+	89	19	5 All The Young Dudes		Columbia 31750
			RS500 #491		
			produced by **David Bowie**		
8/25/73	35	29	6 Mott		Columbia 32425
			RS500 #366		
4/27/74	28	23	7 The Hoople		Columbia 32871
11/30/74+	23	13	8 Mott The Hoople Live	[L]	Columbia 33282
			recorded on 5/9/1974 at the Uris Theatre in New York City		
11/1/75	160	5	9 Drive On		Columbia 33705
			MOTT		
11/27/76	206	1	10 Greatest Hits	[G]	Columbia 34368

MOULD, Bob

Born on 10/12/1960 in Malone, New York; later based in Minneapolis, Minnesota. Alternative-rock singer/songwriter/guitarist. Member of **Husker Du** and **Sugar**.

5/27/89	127	14	1 Workbook		Virgin 91240
9/15/90	123	10	2 Black Sheets Of Rain		Virgin 91395
5/18/96	101	1	3 Bob Mould		Rykodisc 10342
9/12/98	164	1	4 The Last Dog And Pony Show		Rykodisc 10443 [2]
2/23/08	191	1	5 District Line		Granary 86910

MOULIN ROUGE

Female disco vocal trio: Stephanie Spruill, Julia Tillman and Lorna Willard.

2/24/79	209	3	1 Moulin Rouge		ABC 1120

MOUNTAIN

Power-rock band formed in New York: **Leslie West** (vocals, bass), **Felix Pappalardi** (guitar), Steve Knight (keyboards) and Corky Laing (drums). Pappalardi was shot to death on 4/17/1983 (age 43). Also see **West, Bruce & Laing**.

3/14/70	17	39	●	1 Mountain Climbing!		Windfall 4501
2/6/71	16	29	●	2 Nantucket Sleighride		Windfall 5500
12/18/71+	35	16		3 Flowers Of Evil		Windfall 5501
5/13/72	63	18		4 Mountain Live (the road goes ever on)	[L]	Windfall 5502
2/24/73	72	16	●	5 The Best Of Mountain	[G]	Columbia 32079

				MOUNTAIN — cont'd		
3/9/74	142	8		6 Twin Peaks .... [L]		Columbia 32818 [2]
				recorded on 8/30/1973 in Osaka, Japan		
8/10/74	102	9		7 Avalanche		Columbia 33088
4/27/85	166	6		8 Go For Your Life		Scotti Brothers 40006
				MOUNTAIN GOATS, The Born John Darnielle on 3/16/1967 in Bloomington, Indiana; raised in California. Folk-rock singer/songwriter/guitarist.		
9/9/06	193	1		1 Get Lonely		4AD 2614
10/24/09	110	2		2 The Life Of The World To Come		4AD 2932
				MOUSKOURI, Nana Born on 10/13/1934 in Athens, Greece. Female singer.		
4/9/66	124	8		1 An Evening With Belafonte/Mouskouri .... HARRY BELAFONTE & NANA MOUSKOURI		RCA Victor 3415
10/5/91	141	6		2 Only Love - The Very Best Of Nana Mouskouri.......................... [K]		Philips 510229
				MOUTH & MACNEAL Pop vocal duo from Holland: Willem "Mouth" Duyn and Maggie MacNeal (real name: Sjoukje Van't Spijker). Duyn died of a heart attack on 12/3/2004 (age 67).		
7/1/72	77	16		1 How Do You Do?		Philips 700000
				MOUZON, Alphonse Born on 11/21/1948 in Charleston, South Carolina. R&B singer/pianist/drummer.		
8/27/77	205	3		1 Back Together Again .... LARRY CORYELL & ALPHONSE MOUZON		Atlantic 18220
12/4/82+	146	11		2 Distant Lover		Highrise 100
				MOVE, The — see ELECTRIC LIGHT ORCHESTRA		
				MOVIELIFE, The Punk-rock band from Long Island, New York: Vinnie Caruana (vocals), Brandon Reilly (guitar), Dan Navetta (guitar), Phil Navetta (bass) and Evan Baken (drums).		
3/15/03	164	1		1 Forty Hour Train Back To Penn		Drive-Thru 060092
				MOVING PICTURES Pop band from Sydney, Australia: Alex Smith (vocals), Garry Frost (guitar), Andrew Thompson (sax), Charlie Cole (keyboards), Ian Lees (bass) and Paul Freeland (drums).		
12/4/82+	101	16		1 Days Of Innocence..		Network 60202
				MOYET, Alison Born Genevieve Alison-Jane Moyet on 6/18/1961 in Basildon, Essex, England. Female singer. Member of **Yaz**.		
4/6/85	45	25		1 Alf		Columbia 39956
6/20/87	94	17		2 Raindancing...		Columbia 40653
4/9/94	194	1		3 Essex		Columbia 57448
				MRAZ, Jason Born on 10/20/1977 in Mechanicsville, Virginia. Alternative pop-rock singer/songwriter/guitarist.		
4/5/03	55	56	▲	1 Waiting For My Rocket To Come		Elektra 62829
9/11/04	49	4		2 Tonight, Not Again: Jason Mraz Live At The Eagles Ballroom .... [L]		Elektra 62936
				recorded on 10/28/2003 in Milwaukee, Wisconsin		
8/13/05	5	9		3 Mr. A-Z		Atlantic 83833
4/5/08	101	2		4 We Sing .... [EP]		Atlantic 448316
5/3/08	52	2		5 We Dance .... [EP]		Atlantic 448380
5/31/08	3[1]	95	▲	6 We Sing. We Dance. We Steal Things.	Cat:#24/5	Atlantic 448508
11/28/09	35	2		7 Jason Mraz's Beautiful Mess—Live On Earth .... [L]		Atlantic 520745
				MS. DYNAMITE Born Niomi McLean-Daley on 4/26/1981 in London, England. Female R&B singer.		
3/29/03	179	1		1 A Little Deeper...		Polydor 076043
				MS. JADE Born Chevon Young on 8/3/1979 in Philadelphia, Pennsylvania. Female rapper.		
11/23/02	51	2		1 Girl Interrupted		Beat Club 493442
				MTUME Funk band formed in Philadelphia: James Mtume (male vocals, drums), Tawatha Agee (female vocals), Reggie Lucas (guitar), Phil Fields (keyboards) and Ray Johnson (bass).		
10/18/80	119	4		1 In Search Of The Rainbow Seekers		Epic 36017
5/28/83	26	22	●	2 Juicy Fruit...		Epic 38588
9/15/84	77	19		3 You, Me And He		Epic 39473
7/5/86	135	8		4 Theater Of The Mind		Epic 40262
				M2M Female teen pop vocal duo from Lorenskog, Norway: Marion Ravn and Marit Larsen.		
4/22/00	89	14		1 Shades Of Purple		Atlantic 83258

Billboard DEBUT	PEAK	WKS	R I A A	ARTIST Album Title	Catalog	Label & Number

MUDCRUTCH
Southern-rock band formed in 1970 in Gainesville, Florida: **Tom Petty** (vocals, bass), Mike Campbell (guitar), Tom Leadon (guitar), Benmont Tench (keyboards) and Randall Marsh (drums). Forerunner of Tom Petty & The Heartbreakers. Leadon is the brother of **Bernie Leadon** (of the **Eagles**).

5/17/08	8	11		1 Mudcrutch		Reprise 455868

MUDHONEY
Rock band formed in Seattle, Washington: Mark Arm (vocals), Steve Turner (guitar), Matt Lukin (bass) and Dan Peters (drums).

10/31/92	189	1		1 Piece Of Cake		Reprise 45090

MUDVAYNE
Heavy-metal band from Peoria, Illinois: Chad Gray (vocals), Greg Tribbett (guitar), Ryan Martinie (bass) and Matt McDonough (drums).

9/16/00+	85	36	●	1 L.D. 50		No Name 63821
12/8/01	122	1		2 The Beginning Of All Things To End .... [E]		No Name 85995
				first released in 1997 as *Kill, I Oughtta*		
12/7/02	17	41	●	3 The End Of All Things To Come .... Cat:#24/1		Epic 86487
4/30/05	2[1]	24	●	4 Lost And Found		Epic 90784
12/15/07	51	5		5 By The People, For The People .... [G]		Epic 19023
12/6/08	15	18		6 The New Game		Epic 01295

MUHAMMAD, Idris
Born Leo Morris on 11/13/1939 in New Orleans, Louisiana. Black dance/disco drummer.

6/18/77	127	19		1 Turn This Mutha Out .... [I]		Kudu 34
1/20/79	208	1		2 You Ain't No Friend Of Mine! .... [I]		Fantasy 9566

MULDAUR, Maria
Born Maria D'Amato on 9/12/1943 in the Bronx, New York. Female jazz-styled singer.

9/22/73+	3[3]	56	●	1 Maria Muldaur		Reprise 2148
11/9/74+	23	26		2 Waitress In The Donut Shop		Reprise 2194
3/13/76	53	12		3 Sweet Harmony		Reprise 2235
4/8/78	143	5		4 Southern Winds..		Warner 3162

MULL, Martin
Born on 8/18/1943 in Chicago, Illinois. Comedian/movie and TV actor.

7/14/73	203	5		1 Martin Mull And His Fabulous Furniture In Your Living Room.................. [C]		Capricorn 0117
3/26/77	184	2		2 I'm Everyone I've Ever Loved .... [C]		ABC 997
1/21/78	209	1		3 No Hits, Four Errors - The Best Of Martin Mull.............. [C-K]		Capricorn 0195
6/17/78	157	3		4 Sex & Violins .... [C]		ABC 1064
7/7/79	208	2		5 Near Perfect/Perfect .... [C]		Elektra 200

MULLEN, Nicole C.
Born on 1/3/1964 in Cincinnati, Ohio. Black gospel singer.

9/15/01	123	10	●	1 Talk About It		Word/Curb 85822
11/30/02	42[X]	3		2 Christmas In Black And White .... [X]		Word/Curb 886213

MULLIGAN('S), Gerry, Jazz Combo
Born on 4/6/1927 in Brooklyn, New York. Died on 1/20/1996 (age 68). Jazz saxophonist. Combo included Shelly Manne (drums), Art Farmer (trumpet), **Bud Shank** (sax), Frank Rosolino (trombone), **Pete Jolly** (piano) and Red Mitchell (bass).

5/25/59	39	10		1 I Want To Live! .... [I-S]		United Artists 5006

MULLINS, Rich
Born on 10/21/1955 in Richmond, Indiana. Died in a car crash on 9/19/1997 (age 41). Christian singer/songwriter.

10/11/97	143	1	●	1 Songs		Reunion 16205
7/18/98	113	14		2 The Jesus Record		Word 69309 [2]
5/24/03	179	1		3 Here In America .... [L]		Reunion 10052

MULLINS, Shawn
Born on 3/8/1968 in Atlanta, Georgia. Male singer/songwriter/guitarist. Member of **The Thorns**.

10/3/98	54	35	●	1 Soul's Core		Columbia 69637
3/29/08	199	1		2 Honeydew		Vanguard 79830

MUMBA, Samantha
Born on 1/18/1983 in Dublin, Ireland. R&B singer.

11/18/00+	67	22		1 Gotta Tell You...		Wild Card 549799

MUNGO JERRY
Skiffle band formed in England: Ray Dorset (vocals, guitar), Colin Earl (piano), Paul King (banjo) and Mike Cole (bass).

9/12/70	64	11		1 Mungo Jerry...		Janus 7000

MUNICH MACHINE
Disco studio group formed by producers **Giorgio Moroder** and Pete Bellotte. Vocals by Chris Bennett.

7/1/78	190	3		1 A Whiter Shade Of Pale		Casablanca 7090

MUNIZZI, Martha
Born in 1968 in Lakeland, Florida. Contemporary Christian singer/songwriter.

10/23/04+	179	2		1 The Best Is Yet To Come	[L]	Martha Munizzi 0001
11/20/04	30^X	2		2 When He Came	[X]	Martha Munizzi 0002
4/1/06	60	7		3 No Limits...Live	[L]	Integrity 38602 [2]
4/19/08	135	4		4 Change The World		Integrity 38610

MURAD, Jerry — see HARMONICATS

MURDERDOLLS
Hard-rock band from Des Moines, Iowa: Joseph "Wednesday 13" Poole (vocals), Joey Jordison (guitar), Emil "Acey Slade" Schmidt (guitar), Eric Griffin (bass) and Ben Graves (drums). Jordison is also the drummer of **Slipknot**. Slade was a member of **Dope**.

9/7/02	102	2	1 Beyond The Valley Of The Murderdolls		Roadrunner 618426

MURDERERS, The
Rap group from New York City: **Ja Rule**, Vita, Black Child and Tah Murdah.

4/8/00	15	10	1 Irv Gotti Presents...The Murderers		Murder Inc. 542258

MURDER SQUAD
Project of rapper/producer Prodeje.

3/4/95	106	5	1 S.C.C. Presents Murder Squad Nationwide		DJ West 124040

MURDOCK, Shirley
Born in 1957 in Toledo, Ohio. R&B singer.

2/14/87	44	26	●	1 Shirley Murdock!		Elektra 60443
7/23/88	137	15		2 A Woman's Point Of View		Elektra 60791

MURPHEY, Michael
Born on 3/14/1945 in Oak Cliff, Texas. Country-pop singer/songwriter. Recorded as Travis Lewis of The Lewis & Clarke Expedition in 1967. Worked as a staff writer for Screen Gems. Appeared in the movies *Take This Job And Shove It* and *Hard Country*. In 1984, changed his artist billing to Michael Martin Murphey.

9/23/72	160	9		1 Geronimo's Cadillac		A&M 4358
6/16/73	196	2		2 Cosmic Cowboy Souvenir		A&M 4388
2/22/75	18	38	●	3 Blue Sky-Night Thunder		Epic 33290
12/6/75+	44	13		4 Swans Against The Sun		Epic 33851
11/20/76	130	5		5 Flowing Free Forever		Epic 34220
4/1/78	99	6		6 Lonewolf		Epic 35013
4/28/79	206	2		7 Peaks Valleys Honky-Tonks & Alleys		Epic 35742
9/4/82	69	16		8 Michael Martin Murphey		Liberty 51120
10/29/83	187	3		9 The Heart Never Lies		Liberty 51150

MICHAEL MARTIN MURPHEY (above 2)

MURPHY, David Lee
Born on 1/7/1959 in Herrin, Illinois. Country singer/songwriter/guitarist.

7/29/95	52	36	●	1 Out With A Bang		MCA 11044
6/8/96	104	6		2 Gettin' Out The Good Stuff		MCA 11423

MURPHY, Eddie
Born on 4/3/1961 in Brooklyn, New York. Comedian/actor. Former cast member of TV's *Saturday Night Live*. Starred in several movies. Was married to model Nicole Mitchell from 1993-2006.

8/14/82	52	53	▲	1 Eddie Murphy	[C]	Columbia 38180
11/19/83+	35	44	▲²	2 Eddie Murphy: Comedian	[C]	Columbia 39005
				Grammy: Comedy Album		
10/12/85+	26	26		3 How Could It Be		Columbia 39952
8/26/89	70	9		4 So Happy		Columbia 40970

MURPHY, Peter
Born on 7/11/1957 in Northampton, England. Alternative-rock singer/songwriter. Member of **Bauhaus**.

5/14/88	135	19	1 Love Hysteria		Beggars Banquet 7634
2/3/90	44	22	2 Deep		Beggars Banquet 9877
5/2/92	108	3	3 Holy Smoke		Beggars Banquet 66007

MURPHY, Walter
Born on 12/19/1952 in Manhattan, New York. Studied classical and jazz piano at Manhattan School of Music. Former arranger for **Doc Severinsen** and *The Tonight Show* orchestra.

9/4/76	15	29	●	1 A Fifth Of Beethoven		Private Stock 2015
				THE WALTER MURPHY BAND		
7/16/77	175	3		2 Rhapsody In Blue		Private Stock 2028

MURRAY, Anne
1980s: #29 / All-Time: #97

Born Morna Anne Murray on 6/20/1945 in Springhill, Nova Scotia, Canada. Female singer. High school gym teacher for one year after college. With CBC-TV show *Sing Along Jubilee*. First recorded for ARC in 1968. Regular on **Glen Campbell**'s TV series.
AWARD: CMA: Vocal Duo (w/ Dave Loggins) 1985

DEBUT	PEAK	WKS			Album Title	Catalog	Label & Number
10/3/70	41	31	●	1	Snowbird		Capitol 579
4/3/71	121	9		2	Anne Murray		Capitol 667
10/9/71	179	4		3	Talk It Over In The Morning		Capitol 821
12/11/71+	128	8		4	Anne Murray / Glen Campbell		Capitol 869
5/20/72	143	8		5	Annie		Capitol 11024
4/28/73	39	24		6	Danny's Song		Capitol 11172
3/9/74	24	33		7	Love Song		Capitol 11266
					Grammy: Female Country Vocal		
8/31/74	32	16	●	8	Country	[K]	Capitol 11324
12/14/74+	70	13		9	Highly Prized Possession		Capitol 11354
12/6/75+	142	11		10	Together		Capitol 11433
10/2/76	96	6		11	Keeping In Touch		Capitol 11559
3/4/78	12	52	▲	12	Let's Keep It That Way		Capitol 11743
2/17/79	23	29	▲	13	New Kind Of Feeling		Capitol 11849
11/3/79+	24	23	●	14	I'll Always Love You		Capitol 12012
2/9/80	73	9		15	A Country Collection	[K]	Capitol 12039
5/3/80	88	15		16	Somebody's Waiting		Capitol 12064
10/4/80	16	64	▲⁴	17	Anne Murray's Greatest Hits	Cat:#15/23 [G]	Capitol 12110
5/2/81	55	15	●	18	Where Do You Go When You Dream		Capitol 12144
11/28/81+	54	8	▲²	19	Christmas Wishes	Cat:#25/11 [X]	Capitol 16232
					Christmas charts: 4/'83, 6/'84, 21/'88, 20/'91, 19/'92, 30/'93		
8/28/82	90	12		20	The Hottest Night Of The Year		Capitol 12225
10/15/83+	72	24	●	21	A Little Good News		Capitol 12301
					CMA: Album of the Year		
10/27/84	92	25	●	22	Heart Over Mind		Capitol 12363
2/15/86	68	23	●	23	Something To Talk About		Capitol 12466
6/20/87	149	6		24	Harmony		Capitol 12562
12/24/88+	25ˣ	3		25	Anne Murray Christmas	[X]	Capitol 90886
11/27/99+	38	38	▲	26	What A Wonderful World		StraightWay 20231 [2]
11/24/01	83	8		27	What A Wonderful Christmas	Cat:#19/8 [X-K]	StraightWay 20335 [2]
					Christmas charts: 5/'01, 18/'02, 20/'03		
11/9/02	109	6	●	28	Country Croonin'		StraightWay 39779 [2]
2/12/05	66	7		29	All Of Me		StraightWay 63231 [2]
2/2/08	42	10		30	Duets: Friends & Legends		Manhattan 86278
12/20/08	169	1		31	Anne Murray's Christmas Album	[X]	StraightWay 27642
					Christmas chart: 21/'08		

MURRAY, Keith
Born on 9/13/1974 in Long Island, New York. R&B singer/rapper.

11/26/94	34	19	●	1	The Most Beautifullest Thing In This World		Jive 41555
12/14/96	39	11		2	Enigma		Jive 41595
1/30/99	39	6		3	It's A Beautiful Thing		Jive 41646
8/2/03	40	4		4	He's Keith Murray		Def Jam 000316
8/18/07	52	2		5	Rap-Murr-Phobia (The Fear Of Real Hip-Hop)		Def Squad 5858

MURRAY THE "K" — see VARIOUS ARTIST COMPILATIONS

MURS
Born Nick Carter on 3/16/1978 in Los Angeles, California. Hardcore male rapper.

4/8/06	166	1		1	Murray's Revenge		Record Collection 49412
10/18/08	45	2		2	Murs For President		Warner 176828
12/5/09	131	1		3	Felt 3: A Tribute To Rosie Perez		Rhymesayers 0116
					SLUG & MURS WITH AESOP ROCK		

MUSCLE SHOALS HORNS
R&B-funk band from Muscle Shoals, Alabama: Harrison Calloway (vocals, trumpet), Ronnie Eades (sax), Charles Rose (trombone) and Harvey Thompson (flute).

7/4/76	154	8		1	Born To Get Down		Bang 403

MUSE
Rock trio from Teignmouth, Devon, England: Matthew Bellamy (vocals, guitar), Chris Wolstenholme (bass) and Dominic Howard (drums).

5/15/04	107	28	●	1	Absolution	Cat:#17/1	Warner 48733
7/29/06	9	32	●	2	Black Holes And Revelations	Cat:#23/18	Warner 44284
4/19/08	46	3		3	H.A.A.R.P.: Live From Wembley	[L]	Helium-3 378364
10/3/09	3¹	35↑	●	4	The Resistance		Warner 521130

Billboard			R I A A	ARTIST		
DEBUT	PEAK	WKS		Album Title	Catalog	Label & Number

MUSHROOMHEAD
Hard-rock band from Cleveland, Ohio: Jeff "Jeffrey Nothing" Hatrix (lead vocals), Jason "J Mann" Popson (vocals), Marko "Bronson" Vukcevich (guitar), Dave "Gravy" Felton (guitar), Rick "Stitch" Thomas (samples), Tom "Shmotz" Schmitz (keyboards), Jack "Pig Benis" Kilcoyne (bass) and Steve "Skinny" Felton (drums).

3/9/02	178	3		1 XX		Universal 016430
11/1/03	40	40		2 XIII		Filthy Hands 001036
10/7/06	50	2		3 Savior Sorrow		Filthy Hands 902

MUSIC, The
Rock band from Kippax, Leeds, England: Robert Harvey (vocals), Adam Nutter (guitar), Stuart Coleman (bass) and Phil Jordan (drums).

| 3/15/03 | 128 | 2 | | 1 The Music .... | | Capitol 80328 |

MUSICAL YOUTH
Pop-reggae band from Birmingham, England: Dennis Seaton (vocals), with brothers Kelvin Grant (guitar) and Michael Grant (keyboards), and Patrick Waite (bass) and Junior Waite (drums). Patrick Waite died on 2/18/1993 (age 24).

| 1/8/83 | 23 | 22 | | 1 The Youth Of Today .... | | MCA 5389 |
| 12/17/83+ | 144 | 12 | | 2 Different Style! .... | | MCA 5454 |

MUSIC EXPLOSION, The
Garage-rock band from Mansfield, Ohio: Jamie Lyons (vocals), Don Atkins (lead guitar), Richard Nesta (rhythm guitar), Burton Stahl (bass) and Bob Avery (drums). Lyons died on 9/25/2006 (age 57).

| 8/26/67 | 178 | 2 | | 1 Little Bit O' Soul .... | | Laurie 2040 |

MUSIC MACHINE, The
Rock band from Los Angeles, California: Sean Bonniwell (vocals, guitar), Mark Landon (guitar), Doug Rhodes (organ), Keith Olsen (bass) and Ron Edgar (drums). Olsen became a top record producer in the 1980s.

| 1/21/67 | 76 | 16 | | 1 (Turn On) The Music Machine .... | | Original Sound 5015 |

MUSIQ
Born Taalib Johnson on 9/16/1977 in Philadelphia, Pennsylvania. Male R&B singer/songwriter. Also recorded as **Musiq Soulchild**.

12/2/00+	24	41	●	1 AIJUSWANASEING (I Just Want To Sing)		Def Soul 548289
				MUSIQ SOULCHILD		
5/25/02	❶[1]	35	▲	2 JUSLISEN (Just Listen)		Def Soul 586772
12/27/03	13	23	●	3 soulstar		Def Soul 001616
3/31/07	❶[1]	24	●	4 Luvanmusiq		Atlantic 105404
12/20/08+	86	3		5 A Philly Soul Christmas .... [X]		Atlantic 512993
				Christmas chart: 9/'08		
12/27/08	11	29		6 OnMyRadio		Atlantic 512335
				MUSIQ SOULCHILD (above 3)		

MUSIQUE
Disco trio: Christine Wiltshire, Gina Tharps and Mary Seymour.

| 9/30/78 | 62 | 17 | | 1 Keep On Jumpin' .... | | Prelude 12158 |

MUSSO, Mitchel
Born on 7/9/1991 in Garland, Texas. Teen singer/actor. Plays "Oliver Oken" on TV's **Hannah Montana**. Younger brother of Mason Musso (lead singer of **Metro Station**).

| 6/20/09 | 19 | 11 | | 1 Mitchel Musso .... | | Walt Disney 003103 |

MUTEMATH
Rock band formed in New Orleans, Louisiana: Paul Meany (vocals), Greg Hill (guitar), Roy Mitchell-Cardenas (bass) and Darren King (drums).

| 9/5/09 | 18 | 5 | | 1 Armistice .... | | Warner 519783 |

MXPX
Christian punk-rock trio from Bremerton, Washington: Mike Herrera (vocals, bass), Tom Wisniewski (guitar) and Yuri Ruley (drums).

7/4/98	99	7	●	1 Slowly Going The Way Of The Buffalo		A&M 540910
12/5/98	161	1		2 Let It Happen .... [K]		Tooth & Nail 1122
8/14/99	189	1		3 Live At The Show .... [L]		Tooth & Nail 1147
6/3/00	56	13		4 The Ever Passing Moment		A&M 490656
6/9/01	128	1		5 The Renaissance EP		Fat Wreck Chords 631
6/8/02	147	1		6 Ten Years And Running .... [K]		Tooth & Nail 1196
10/4/03	51	2		7 Before Everything & After		A&M 000941
6/25/05	77	3		8 Panic		Side One Dummy 1269
8/4/07	76	2		9 Secret Weapon		Tooth & Nail 90117

MYA
Born Mya Harrison on 10/10/1979 in Washington DC. Female R&B singer/actress. Appeared in several movies. Finished second on season 9 on *Dancing With The Stars*.

5/9/98	29	53	▲	1 Mya		University 90166
5/13/00	15	52	●	2 Fear Of Flying		University 490853
8/9/03	3[1]	18	●	3 Moodring		A&M 000734

Billboard			R I A A	ARTIST		
DEBUT	PEAK	WKS		Album Title	Catalog	Label & Number

MY BLOODY VALENTINE
Rock band formed in Dublin, Ireland: Bilinda Butcher (vocals, guitar), Kevin Shields (vocals, guitar), Debbie Googe (bass) and Colm O'Ciosoig (drums) Group named after a 1981 horror movie.

~ ~ ~ ~ ~ ~ ~ ~ ~ ~ ~ **NON-CHARTED ALBUM** ~ ~ ~ ~ ~ ~ ~ ~ ~ ~ ~
1991 Loveless
RS500 #219

MY CHEMICAL ROMANCE
Rock band formed in New Jersey: brothers Gerard Way (vocals) and Mikey Way (bass), with Ray Toro (guitar), Frank Iero (guitar) and Matt Pelissier (drums).

6/26/04+	28	77	●	1 Three Cheers For Sweet Revenge	Cat:#39/1	Reprise 48615
4/8/06	30	4		2 Life On The Murder Scene	[L]	Reprise 49476
11/11/06	2¹	58	▲	3 The Black Parade		Reprise 44427
7/19/08	22	3		4 The Black Parade Is Dead!		Reprise 357436

MYERS, Alicia
Born in Detroit, Michigan. R&B singer. Former lead singer of **One Way**.

12/8/84	186	5		1 I Appreciate		MCA 5485

MYERS, Billie
Born on 6/14/1970 in Coventry, England. Female singer/songwriter.

1/31/98	91	21		1 Growing, Pains		Universal 53100

MYLES, Alannah
Born on 12/25/1955 in Toronto, Ontario, Canada; raised in Buckhorn, Ontario, Canada. Female singer.

1/13/90	5	36	▲	1 Alannah Myles		Atlantic 81956

MY LIFE WITH THE THRILL KILL KULT
Rock band from Chicago, Illinois. Assembled by Mr. Groovie Mann (vocals) and Mr. Buzz McCoy (keyboards).

9/25/93	194	1		1 13 Above The Night		Interscope 92258

MY MORNING JACKET
Rock band formed in Louisville, Kentucky: **Yim Yames** (vocals), Johnny Quaid (guitar), Danny Cash (keyboards), Two-Tone Tommy (bass) and Patrick Hallahan (drums). By 2005, Carl Broemel replaced Quaid and Bo Koster replaced Cash. Yames is also a member of **Monsters Of Folk**.

9/27/03	121	3		1 It Still Moves		ATO 52979
10/22/05	67	6		2 Z		ATO 71067
10/14/06	131	1		3 Okonokos: Double Live Album	[L]	ATO 86210 [2]
6/28/08	9	13		4 Evil Urges		ATO 21626
1/31/09	94	1		5 iTunes Live From Las Vegas: Exclusively At The Palms	[EP-L]	ATO digital
5/2/09	158	1		6 Celebracion De La Ciudad Natal	[EP]	ATO 0006

MYRICK, Gary
Born in Dallas, Texas. Rock guitarist. Joined British group **Havana 3 A.M.** in 1991.

9/27/80	203	1		1 Gary Myrick And The Figures		Epic 36524
8/6/83	186	3		2 Language	[EP]	Epic 38637

MYRON
Born Myron Davis in Cleveland, Ohio. R&B singer/songwriter.

8/15/98	156	2		1 Destiny		Island 524479

MYSTERIOUS FLYING ORCHESTRA
Studio group assembled by producer Bob Thiele.

6/11/77	210	1		1 Mysterious Flying Orchestra	[I]	RCA Victor 2137

MYSTIC
Born in Oakland, California. Female hip-hop singer/rapper.

9/1/01	170	3		1 Cuts For Luck And Scars For Freedom		GoodVibe 860936

MYSTIC MOODS, The
Instrumental studio group assembled by producer Brad Miller.

4/30/66	63	14		1 One Stormy Night	[I]	Philips 600205
10/8/66	110	10		2 Nighttide	[I]	Philips 600213
3/25/67	157	4		3 More Than Music	[I]	Philips 600231
11/25/67	164	3		4 Mexican Trip	[I]	Philips 600250
2/24/68	182	4		5 The Mystic Moods Of Love	[I]	Philips 600260
11/9/68	194	3		6 Emotions	[I]	Philips 600277
5/3/69	155	9		7 Extensions	[I]	Philips 600301
11/22/69+	165	8		8 Love Token	[I]	Philips 600321
5/23/70	165	15		9 Stormy Weekend	[I]	Philips 600342
11/28/70+	174	9		10 English Muffins	[I]	Philips 600349
6/26/71	222	3		11 Country Lovin' Folk	[I]	Philips 351
4/29/72	184	3		12 Love The One You're With	[I]	Warner 2577
5/5/73	190	4		13 Awakening	[I]	Warner 2690
7/5/75	201	24		14 Erogenous	[I]	Warner 2786

MYSTIKAL
Born Michael Tyler on 9/22/1970 in New Orleans, Louisiana. Male rapper/songwriter/actor. Member of **504 Boyz**. Acted in the movies *I Got The Hook Up*, *Makin' Baby* and *13 Dead Men*. Sentenced to six years in prison for sexual battery in January 2004.

10/28/95	103	11	●	1 Mind Of Mystikal		Big Boy 41581
11/29/97	3¹	44	▲	2 Unpredictable		No Limit 41620
1/2/99	5	24	▲	3 Ghetto Fabulous		No Limit 41655
10/14/00	❶¹	37	▲²	4 Let's Get Ready		Jive 41696
1/5/02	25	26	●	5 Tarantula		Jive 41770
8/28/04	140	1		6 Prince Of The South...The Hits	[G]	Jive 53708

N

NABORS, Jim
Born on 6/12/1930 in Sylacauga, Alabama. Singer/actor. Appeared in several movies and TV shows. Best-known for his role of "Gomer Pyle" on both *The Andy Griffith Show* and *Gomer Pyle, U.S.M.C.*

10/15/66	24	56	●	1 Jim Nabors Sings Love Me With All Your Heart		Columbia 2558 / 9358
5/20/67	50	40		2 Jim Nabors By Request		Columbia 2665 / 9465
9/16/67	147	6		3 The Things I Love		Columbia 2703 / 9503
12/2/67+	❶¹ˣ	25	●	4 Jim Nabors' Christmas Album	[X]	Columbia 2731 / 9531
				Christmas charts: 7/'67, 7/'68, 1/'69, 3/'70, 6/'71, 5/'72, 20/'73		
7/13/68	153	26		5 Kiss Me Goodbye		Columbia 9620
11/16/68	173	12	●	6 The Lord's Prayer And Other Sacred Songs		Columbia 9716
6/14/69+	145	19		7 Galveston		Columbia 9817
6/27/70	34	23		8 The Jim Nabors Hour		Columbia 1020
9/5/70	124	26		9 Everything Is Beautiful		Columbia 30129
3/27/71	75	13		10 For The Good Times/The Jim Nabors Hour	[L]	Columbia 30449
7/24/71	122	10		11 Help Me Make It Through The Night		Columbia 30810
10/23/71	166	4		12 How Great Thou Art		Columbia 30671
6/17/72	157	8		13 The Way Of Love		Columbia 31336

NADA SURF
Rock trio formed in New York: Matthew Caws (vocals, guitar), Daniel Lorca (bass) and Ira Elliot (drums).

7/13/96	63	12		1 High/Low		Elektra 61913
10/1/05	167	1		2 The Weight Is A Gift		Barsuk 46
2/23/08	82	2		3 Lucky		Barsuk 70

NAIL, David
Born on 5/18/1979 in Kennett, Missouri. Country singer/songwriter.

9/5/09	71	2		1 I'm About To Come Alive		MCA Nashville 011003

NAILS, The
Rock band from New York: Marc Campbell (vocals), Steve O'Rourke (guitar), David Kaufman (keyboards), Doug Guthrie (sax), George Kaufman (bass) and Mike Ratti (drums). George Kaufman died on 3/8/2009 (age 58).

2/23/85	203	6		1 Mood Swing		RCA Victor 8037
8/23/86	194	2		2 Dangerous Dreams		RCA Victor 5831

NAIM, Yael
Born on 2/6/1978 in Paris, France. Female singer/songwriter.

4/5/08	50	7		1 Yael Naim		Tot Ou Tard 461628

NAJEE
Born Jerome Najee Rasheed in Manhattan, New York; raised in Jamaica, Queens, New York. Jazz saxophonist.

2/28/87	56	45	●	1 Najee's Theme	[I]	EMI America 17241
7/9/88	76	21		2 Day By Day	[I]	EMI-Manhattan 90096
4/28/90	63	17		3 Tokyo Blue	[I]	EMI 92248
7/18/92	107	13	●	4 Just An Illusion	[I]	EMI 99400
10/22/94	163	2		5 Share My World	[I]	EMI 30789
9/24/05	193	1		6 My Point Of View	[I]	Heads Up 3104

NAKED BROTHERS BAND, The
Nickelodeon TV series featuring brothers Nat Wolff (vocals, age 11) and Alex Wolff (drums, age 8).

10/27/07	23	17		1 The Naked Brothers Band	[TV]	Nick 16228
5/3/08	23	10		2 I Don't Want To Go To School	[TV]	Nick 28580

NAKED EYES
Pop duo from England: Pete Byrne (vocals) and Rob Fisher (keyboards, synthesizer). Fisher later formed **Climie Fisher**. Fisher died on 8/25/1999 (age 39).

4/16/83	32	42		1 Naked Eyes		EMI America 17089
9/8/84	83	10		2 Fuel For The Fire		EMI America 17116

NALICK, Anna
Born on 3/30/1984 in Glendora, California. Adult Alternative singer/songwriter.

5/7/05	20	33	●	1 Wreck Of The Day		Columbia 90891

NANTUCKET
Southern-rock band from Jacksonville, North Carolina: Larry Uzzell (vocals), Mark Downing (guitar), Tommy Redd (guitar), Eddie Blair (keyboards), PeeWee Watson (bass) and Kenny Soule (drums).

DEBUT	PEAK	WKS	RIAA		Catalog	Label & Number
8/30/80	206	1		1 Long Way To The Top		Epic 36523

NAPOLEON XIV
Born Jerry Samuels on 5/3/1938 in Brooklyn, New York. Novelty singer/songwriter.

~ ~ ~ ~ ~ ~ ~ ~ ~ ~ ~ **NON-CHARTED ALBUM** ~ ~ ~ ~ ~ ~ ~ ~ ~ ~ ~
1966 **They're Coming To Take Me Away, Ha-Haaa!**

NAPPY ROOTS
Rap group formed in Bowling Green, Kentucky: Brian "B. Stille" Scott, Melvin "Scales" Adams, William "Skinny DeVille" Hughes, Vito "Big V" Tisdale, Ryan "R. Prophet" Anthony and Ron "Clutch" Wilson.

DEBUT	PEAK	WKS	RIAA		Catalog	Label & Number
3/16/02	24	50	▲	1 Watermelon, Chicken & Gritz		Atlantic 83524
9/13/03	12	8		2 Wooden Leather		Atlantic 83646
8/23/08	73	1		3 The Humdinger		Nappy Roots 0001

NAS   All-Time: #265
Born Nasir Jones on 9/14/1973 in Brooklyn, New York. Male rapper. Member of **The Firm** and **QB Finest**. Married **Kelis** on 1/8/2005 (filed for divorce in April 2009).

DEBUT	PEAK	WKS	RIAA		Catalog	Label & Number
5/7/94	12	19	▲	1 Illmatic	Cat:❶¹/7	Columbia 57684
				_RS500 #400_		
7/20/96	❶⁴	34	▲²	2 It Was Written	Cat:#39/1	Columbia 67015
4/24/99	❶²	25	▲²	3 I Am...		Columbia 68773
12/11/99	7	26		4 Nastradamus		Columbia 63930
1/5/02	5	38	▲	5 Stillmatic		Columbia 85736
7/20/02	123	3		6 From Illmatic To Stillmatic: The Remixes	[EP-K]	Columbia 86685
10/12/02	10	8		7 The Lost Tapes	[K]	Columbia 85275
12/28/02+	12	28	▲	8 God's Son		Columbia 86930
12/18/04	5	20	▲	9 Street's Disciple		Ill Will 92065 [2]
1/6/07	❶¹	16	●	10 Hip Hop Is Dead		Def Jam 007229
11/24/07	124	1		11 Greatest Hits	[G]	Ill Will 09550
8/2/08	❶¹	15	●	12 Untitled		Def Jam 011505

N.A.S.A.
Hip-hop duo from Los Angeles, California: Samuel "Squeak E. Clean" Spiegel and DJ Zegon. Spiegel is the brother of acclaimed video director Spike Jonze.

DEBUT	PEAK	WKS	RIAA		Catalog	Label & Number
3/7/09	178	1		1 The Spirit Of Apollo		Anti 87001

NASH, Graham
Born on 2/2/1942 in Blackpool, Lancashire, England. Pop-rock singer/songwriter/guitarist. Former member of **The Hollies**. Formed **Crosby, Stills & Nash** in 1968.

DEBUT	PEAK	WKS	RIAA		Catalog	Label & Number
6/19/71	15	24	●	1 Songs For Beginners		Atlantic 7204
4/22/72	4	26	●	2 Graham Nash/David Crosby		Atlantic 7220
1/26/74	34	14		3 Wild Tales		Atlantic 7288
				DAVID CROSBY/GRAHAM NASH:		
10/11/75	6	31	●	4 Wind On The Water		ABC 902
7/24/76	26	15	●	5 Whistling Down The Wire		ABC 956
11/19/77	52	8		6 Crosby/Nash - Live	[L]	ABC 1042
10/28/78	150	4		7 The Best Of Crosby/Nash	[G]	ABC 1102
				GRAHAM NASH:		
3/8/80	117	5		8 Earth & Sky		Capitol 12014
4/26/86	136	7		9 Innocent Eyes		Atlantic 81633
8/28/04	142	1		10 Crosby & Nash		Sanctuary 84683 [2]

NASH, Johnny
Born on 8/19/1940 in Houston, Texas. R&B singer/guitarist/actor.

DEBUT	PEAK	WKS	RIAA		Catalog	Label & Number
11/23/68+	109	12		1 Hold Me Tight		JAD 1207
10/7/72	23	31		2 I Can See Clearly Now		Epic 31607
7/14/73	169	6		3 My Merry-Go-Round		Epic 32158

~ ~ ~ ~ ~ ~ ~ ~ ~ ~ ~ **NON-CHARTED ALBUM** ~ ~ ~ ~ ~ ~ ~ ~ ~ ~ ~
1958 **Johnny Nash**

NASH, Kate
Born on 7/6/1987 in London, England. Adult Alternative-pop singer/songwriter/guitarist.

DEBUT	PEAK	WKS	RIAA		Catalog	Label & Number
1/26/08	36	13		1 Made Of Bricks		Fiction 010536

NASHVILLE BRASS — see DAVIS, Danny

NASHVILLE STRING BAND
All-star guitar trio: **Chet Atkins**, Homer Haynes and Jethro Burns (Homer & Jethro).

DEBUT	PEAK	WKS	RIAA		Catalog	Label & Number
3/13/71	218	3		1 Identified!	[I]	RCA Victor 4472

			R I A	ARTIST Album Title	Catalog	Label & Number
DEBUT	**PEAK**	**WKS**				

NASHVILLE TEENS, The
Rock band from Weybridge, Surrey, England: Arthur Sharp (vocals), John Allen (guitar), Ramon "Ray" Phillips (harmonica), John Hawkes (keyboards), Pete Shannon (bass) and Barry Jenkins (drums; joined **The Animals** in 1966).

~ ~ ~ ~ ~ ~ ~ ~ ~ ~ **NON-CHARTED ALBUM** ~ ~ ~ ~ ~ ~ ~ ~ ~ ~
1964 Tobacco Road

NATALIE
Born Natalie Alvarado on 9/2/1979 in Clear Lake, Texas. Urban-pop singer/songwriter. Former cheerleader for the NBA's Houston Rockets.

DEBUT	PEAK	WKS		Album	Catalog	Label & Number
6/4/05	16	11		1 Natalie		Lathium 004578

NATE DOGG
Born Nathaniel Hale on 8/19/1969 in Los Angeles, California. Male rapper. Former partner of **Warren G**. Cousin of **Snoop Dogg**.

| 8/8/98 | 58 | 5 | | 1 G-Funk Classics Vol. 1 & 2 .... | | Breakaway 3000 [2] |
| 12/22/01 | 32 | 12 | | 2 Music & Me .... | | Desert Storm 62688 |

NATHANSON, Matt
Born on 3/28/1973 in Lexington, Massachusetts. Adult Alternative-pop singer/songwriter.

| 9/1/07 | 60 | 34 | | 1 Some Mad Hope .... | | Vanguard 79827 |
| 4/11/09 | 185 | 1 | | 2 Live Session EP .... **[EP-L]** | | Acrobat digital |

NATIONAL, The
Alternative-rock band from Brooklyn, New York: brothers Bryce Dessner (guitar) and Aaron Dessner (bass), with Matt Berninger (vocals) and Scott Devendorf (drums).

| 6/9/07 | 68 | 6 | | 1 Boxer .... | | Beggars Banquet 252 |

NATIONAL LAMPOON
Comedy troupe spawned from the magazine of the same name. Featured performers included Chevy Chase, John Belushi (**Blues Brothers**) and Christopher Guest (**Spinal Tap**).

9/2/72	132	12		1 Radio Dinner .... **[C]**		Banana 38
6/23/73	107	13		2 Lemmings .... **[C]**		Banana 6006
3/16/74	118	8		3 Missing White House Tapes .... **[C]**		Banana 6008
5/17/75	206	2		4 Gold Turkey .... **[C-K]**		Epic 33410

NATURAL FOUR
R&B vocal group from San Francisco, California: Chris James, Darryl Canady, Steve Striplin and Delmos Whitley.

| 4/27/74 | 207 | 5 | | 1 Natural Four .... | | Curtom 8600 |
| 7/5/75 | 182 | 3 | | 2 Heaven Right Here On Earth .... | | Curtom 5004 |

NATURE
Born Jermaine Baxter on 12/5/1972 in Brooklyn, New York. Male rapper. Member of **The Firm** and **QB Finest**.

| 10/7/00 | 50 | 4 | | 1 For All Seasons .... | | Track Masters 68926 |
| 7/6/02 | 150 | 3 | | 2 Wild Gremlinz .... | | Sequence 8004 |

NATURE'S DIVINE
R&B band from Detroit, Michigan: Lynn Smith (female vocals), Robert Carter (male vocals), Duane Mitchell (guitar), Charles Woods and Marvin Jones (keyboards), Charles Green and Opelton Parker (horns), Robert Johnson (percussion), Keith Fondren (bass) and Mark Mitchell (drums).

| 11/10/79 | 91 | 8 | | 1 In The Beginning .... | | Infinity 9013 |

NAUGHTY BY NATURE
Rap trio from East Orange, New Jersey: Anthony "Treach" Criss, Vincent Brown and Keir Gist. Appeared in the movies *The Meteor Man* and *Who's The Man?* Treach was married to Sandra "Pepa" Denton (of **Salt-N-Pepa**) from 1999-2001.

9/21/91	16	54	▲	1 Naughty By Nature		Tommy Boy 1044
3/13/93	3[1]	31	▲	2 19 Naughty III		Tommy Boy 1069
6/17/95	3[1]	18	●	3 Poverty's Paradise		Tommy Boy 1111
				Grammy: Rap Album		
5/15/99	22	17	●	4 Nineteen Naughty Nine - Nature's Fury		Arista 19047
5/25/02	15	10		5 Iicons		TVT 2340

NAVARRO, Dave
Born on 6/7/1967 in Santa Monica, California. Rock singer/guitarist. Former member of **Jane's Addiction** and **Red Hot Chili Peppers**. Married to actress Carmen Electra from 2003-07.

| 7/7/01 | 61 | 12 | | 1 Trust No One .... | | Capitol 33280 |

NAZARETH   **All-Time: #489**
Hard-rock band formed in Dunfermline, Fife, Scotland: Dan McCafferty (vocals), Manny Charlton (guitar), Pete Agnew (bass) and Darrell Sweet (drums). **Billy Rankin** (guitar) and John Locke (keyboards) added in 1981. Sweet died of a heart attack on 4/30/1999 (age 51).

8/18/73	157	13		1 Razamanaz..		A&M 4396
3/9/74	150	8		2 Loud 'N' Proud		A&M 3609
7/13/74	157	9		3 Rampant...		A&M 3641
4/26/75+	17	40	▲	4 Hair Of The Dog		A&M 4511
5/8/76	24	14		5 Close Enough For Rock 'N' Roll		A&M 4562
12/4/76	75	9		6 Play 'N' The Game		A&M 4610
7/2/77	120	6		7 Hot Tracks .... **[G]**		A&M 4643
11/19/77+	82	16		8 Expect No Mercy		A&M 4666

			NAZARETH — cont'd		
2/3/79	88	14	9 No Mean City		A&M 4741
2/16/80	41	19	10 Malice In Wonderland		A&M 4799
2/14/81	70	13	11 The Fool Circle		A&M 4844
10/10/81	83	9	12 'Snaz .... [L]		A&M 6703 [2]
7/10/82	122	10	13 2XS		A&M 4901
			NAZARIO, Ednita		
			Born on 4/9/1957 in Ponce, Puerto Rico. Latin singer/actress.		
8/17/02	183	2	1 Acustico .... [F-L]		Sony Discos 84956
12/7/02	136	1	2 Acustico Vol. II .... [F-L]		Sony Discos 87649
12/6/03	116	1	3 Por Ti .... [F]		Sony Discos 70618
7/9/05	68	2	4 Apasionada .... [F]		Sony Discos 95790
4/22/06	177	1	5 Apasionada Live .... [F-L]		Sony 80636 [2]
12/29/07	101	2	6 Real .... [F]		Sony 11621
9/27/08	57	3	7 Real...En Vivo .... [F-L]		Sony 34165
11/14/09	27	3	8 Soy .... [F]		Sony 55934
			NAZZ		
			Rock band from Philadelphia, Pennsylvania: **Todd Rundgren** (guitar), Robert "Stewkey" Antoni (vocals), Carson Van Osten (bass) and Thom Mooney (drums).		
10/19/68+	118	26	1 Nazz		SGC 5001
5/10/69	80	15	2 Nazz Nazz		SGC 5002
			NDEGEOCELLO, Me'Shell		
			Born Michelle Johnson on 8/29/1969 in Berlin, Germany; raised in Oxon Hill, Maryland. Black female R&B-dance singer/bassist.		
3/12/94	166	9	1 Plantation Lullabies		Maverick 45333
7/13/96	63	10	2 Peace Beyond Passion		Maverick 46033
9/11/99	105	4	3 Bitter		Maverick 47439
6/22/02	67	3	4 Cookie: The Anthropolgical Mixtape		Maverick 47989
11/1/03	150	1	5 Comfort Woman		Maverick 48547
10/13/07	186	1	6 The World Has Made Me The Man Of My Dreams ...		Emarcy 009597
10/24/09	185	1	7 Devil's Halo		Mercer Street 70112
			NED'S ATOMIC DUSTBIN		
			Rock band from Stourbridge, West Midlands, England: Jonathan Penney (vocals), Garath Pring (guitar), Alexander Griffin (bass), Matthew Cheslin (bass) and Daniel Worton (drums).		
1/11/92	91	14	1 God Fodder		Columbia 47929
11/28/92	183	1	2 Are You Normal?		Columbia 53154
			NEEDHAM, Jimmy		
			Born in Houston, Texas. Contemporary Christian singer/songwriter/guitarist.		
8/1/09	193	1	1 Not Without Love		Inpop 71405
			NEEDTOBREATHE		
			Christian rock duo from Seneca, South Carolina: brothers Bear Rinehart and Bryant "Bo" Rinehart.		
9/15/07	164	1	1 The Heat		Atlantic 236924
9/12/09	20	8	2 The Outsiders		Atlantic 519702
			NEELY, Sam		
			Born on 8/22/1948 in Cuero, Texas. Died of a heart attack on 7/19/2006 (age 57). Pop-country singer/songwriter/guitarist.		
9/16/72	147	11	1 Loving You Just Crossed My Mind		Capitol 11097
2/10/73	175	6	2 Sam Neely-2		Capitol 11143
10/12/74	202	3	3 Down Home		A&M 3626
			NEIL, Vince		
			Born Vincent Neil Wharton on 2/8/1961 in Hollywood, California. Lead singer of **Motley Crue**.		
5/15/93	13	13	1 Exposed		Warner 45260
9/30/95	139	1	2 Carved In Stone		Warner 45877
			NEKTAR		
			Art-rock band formed in Hamburg, Germany: Roye Albrighton (vocals, guitar), Allan Freeman (keyboards), Derek Moore (bass) and Ron Howden (drums). Dave Nelson replaced Albrighton by 1977.		
7/20/74	19	28	1 Remember The Future		Passport 98002
2/15/75	32	20	2 Down To Earth		Passport 98005
4/3/76	89	14	3 Recycled		Passport 98011
9/18/76	141	4	4 A Tab In The Ocean .... [I]		Passport 98017
11/5/77	172	3	5 Magic Is A Child		Polydor 6115

Billboard			R I A A	**ARTIST**			
DEBUT	PEAK	WKS		Album Title		Catalog	Label & Number

NELLY 2000s: #30 / All-Time: #399
Born Cornell Haynes on 11/2/1974 in Austin, Texas; raised in St. Louis, Missouri. Male rapper. Member of **St. Lunatics**. Acted in the movies *Snipes* and *The Longest Yard*. Started own Vokal Clothing line in 2002.

7/15/00	❶⁵	104	▲⁹	1 Country Grammar	Cat:❶¹/27	Fo' Reel 57743
7/13/02	❶⁴	72	▲⁶	2 Nellyville	Cat:#20/8	Fo' Reel 017747
12/13/03	12	22	▲	3 Da Derrty Versions - The Reinvention.. [K]	Fo' Reel 001665
10/2/04	2¹	26	▲	4 Sweat	Derrty 003314
10/2/04	❶¹	37	▲²	5 Suit	Derrty 003316
12/10/05	26	24	●	6 Sweatsuit .... [K]	Derrty 005825
10/4/08	3¹	10	●	7 Brass Knuckles	Derrty 010150

NELSON
Rock duo from Los Angeles, California: Gunnar Nelson (vocals, bass) and Matthew Nelson (vocals, guitar). The identical twin sons (born on 9/20/1967) of **Ricky Nelson**.

| 7/21/90 | 17 | 64 | ▲² | 1 After The Rain .... | DGC 24290 |

NELSON, Ricky 1950s: #32 / All-Time: #242
Born Eric Hilliard Nelson on 5/8/1940 in Teaneck, New Jersey. Died in a plane crash on 12/31/1985 (age 45) in DeKalb, Texas. Son of bandleader Ozzie Nelson and vocalist Harriet Hilliard. Rick and brother David appeared on Nelson's radio show from March 1949, later on TV, 1952-66. Formed own Stone Canyon Band in 1969. In movies *Rio Bravo*, *The Wackiest Ship In The Army* and *Love And Kisses*. Married to Kristin Harmon (sister of actor Mark Harmon) from 1963-82. Their daughter Tracy is a movie/TV actress. Their twin sons began recording as **Nelson** in 1990. Ricky was one of the first teen idols of the rock era.
AWARD: R&R Hall of Fame: 1987

11/11/57+	❶²	33		1 Ricky	Imperial 9048
7/28/58	7	9		2 Ricky Nelson	Imperial 9050
2/2/59	14	19		3 Ricky Sings Again	Imperial 9061
9/28/59+	22	26		4 Songs By Ricky	Imperial 9082
8/29/60	18	22		5 More Songs By Ricky	Imperial 9122

RICK NELSON:

5/29/61	8	49		6 Rick Is 21	Imperial 9152
4/14/62	27	20		7 Album Seven By Rick	Imperial 9167
3/2/63	112	4		8 Best Sellers By Rick Nelson .... [G]	Imperial 9218
5/4/63	128	5		9 It's Up To You .... [K]	Imperial 9223
6/8/63	20	19		10 For Your Sweet Love	Decca 74419
1/4/64	14	22		11 Rick Nelson Sings "For You"	Decca 74479
2/21/70	54	19		12 Rick Nelson In Concert .... [L]	Decca 75162
				recorded at The Troubadour Club in Los Angeles, California	
11/7/70	196	2		13 Rick Sings Nelson	Decca 75236
11/20/71	204	3		14 Rudy The Fifth	Decca 75297
12/9/72+	32	18		15 Garden Party...	Decca 75391
2/23/74	190	4		16 Windfall	MCA 383
				RICK NELSON & THE STONE CANYON BAND (above 3)	
2/21/81	153	6		17 Playing To Win	Capitol 12109
1/14/06	56	18		18 Greatest Hits... [G]	Capitol 12262

~ ~ ~ ~ ~ ~ ~ ~ ~ ~ **NON-CHARTED ALBUMS** ~ ~ ~ ~ ~ ~ ~ ~ ~ ~
1957 **Teen Time** *[w/ Randy Sparks, Jeff Allen, Rock Murphy*   1964 **The Very Thought Of You**
            & Gary Williams]   1964 **Spotlight On Rick**
1963 **Rick Nelson Million Sellers**   1965 **Best Always, Rick Nelson**
1963 **A Long Vacation**   1965 **Love And Kisses**

NELSON, Sandy
Born Sander Nelson on 12/1/1938 in Santa Monica, California. Male session drummer.

1/20/62	6	48		1 Let There Be Drums	[I]	Imperial 9159
4/14/62	29	24		2 Drums Are My Beat! .... [I]	Imperial 9168
7/14/62	55	11		3 Drummin' Up A Storm .... [I]	Imperial 9189
11/3/62	141	3		4 Compelling Percussion .... [I]	Imperial 9204
12/1/62	106	3		5 Golden Hits .... [I]	Imperial 9202
11/21/64+	122	11		6 Live! In Las Vegas .... [I-L]	Imperial 12272
3/6/65	135	5		7 Teen Beat '65 .... [I]	Imperial 12278
7/10/65	120	8		8 Drum Discotheque .... [I]	Imperial 12283
10/2/65	118	11		9 Drums A Go-Go .... [I]	Imperial 12287
1/8/66	126	7		10 Boss Beat .... [I]	Imperial 12298
4/23/66	148	2		11 "In" Beat .... [I]	Imperial 12305

~ ~ ~ ~ ~ ~ ~ ~ **NON-CHARTED ALBUMS** ~ ~ ~ ~ ~ ~ ~ ~ ~ ~ ~ ~
1960 **Sandy Nelson Plays Teen Beat**   1961 **He's A Drummer Boy!**

NELSON, Tracy
Born on 12/27/1944 in French Camp, California. Lead singer of **Mother Earth**. Not to be confused with Ricky Nelson's actress daughter.

| 10/19/74 | 145 | 5 | | 1 Tracy Nelson.. | Atlantic 7310 |

Billboard			R I A A	ARTIST	Catalog	Label & Number
DEBUT	PEAK	WKS		Album Title		

NELSON, Willie   1980s: #1 / 2000s: #16 / All-Time: #14

Born on 4/30/1933 in Abbott, Texas. Legendary country singer/songwriter/guitarist. Played bass for **Ray Price**. Moved to
Nashville in 1960. Moved back to Texas in 1970. Pioneered the "outlaw" country movement. Acted in several movies.
AWARDS: Grammys: Legend 1990 / Lifetime Achievement 2000 ★ C&W Hall of Fame: 1993 ★
CMA: Vocal Duo (w/ Waylon Jennings) 1976 / Entertainer 1979 / Vocal Duo (w/ Merle Haggard) 1983 /
Vocal Duo (w/ Julio Iglesias) 1984 ★ OPRY: 1964

DEBUT	PEAK	WKS	RIAA	Album Title	Catalog	Label & Number
7/14/73	205	6		1 Shotgun Willie		Atlantic 7262
7/26/75	28	43	▲²	2 Red Headed Stranger		Columbia 33482
				Grammy: Hall of Fame ★ RS500 #184		
3/20/76	48	15	▲	3 The Sound In Your Mind		Columbia 34092
10/16/76	60	7	●	4 The Troublemaker		Columbia 34112
7/9/77	91	12		5 To Lefty From Willie		Columbia 34695
				tribute to Lefty Frizzell		
2/4/78	12	29	▲²	6 Waylon & Willie		RCA Victor 2686
				WAYLON JENNINGS & WILLIE NELSON		
5/13/78	30	117	▲⁵	7 Stardust		Columbia 35305
				RS500 #257		
6/30/79	25	18	●	8 One For The Road		Columbia 36064 [2]
				WILLIE NELSON & LEON RUSSELL		
11/17/79+	42	25	▲	9 Willie Nelson Sings Kristofferson		Columbia 36188
				songs written by **Kris Kristofferson**		
12/1/79+	73	8	▲	10 Pretty Paper [X]		Columbia 36189
				Christmas chart: 9/'83		
3/15/80	150	5		11 Danny Davis & Willie Nelson With The Nashville Brass		RCA Victor 3549
				new instrumental backing for earlier recordings by Nelson		
6/14/80	70	25	●	12 San Antonio Rose		Columbia 36476
				WILLIE NELSON & RAY PRICE		
3/21/81	31	23	▲	13 Somewhere Over The Rainbow		Columbia 36883
3/20/82	2⁴	99	▲⁴	14 Always On My Mind		Columbia 37951
				CMA: Album of the Year		
10/30/82	57	22	●	15 WWII		RCA Victor 4455
				WAYLON JENNINGS & WILLIE NELSON		
2/12/83	37	53	▲	16 Pancho & Lefty		Epic 37958
				MERLE HAGGARD & WILLIE NELSON		
3/19/83	39	20		17 Tougher Than Leather		Columbia 38248
5/21/83	60	16	●	18 Take It To The Limit		Columbia 38562
				WILLIE NELSON & WAYLON JENNINGS		
11/26/83+	54	34	▲	19 Without A Song		Columbia 39110
6/16/84	116	7		20 Angel Eyes		Columbia 39363
8/4/84	69	26	▲	21 City Of New Orleans		Columbia 39145
3/30/85	152	7		22 Me & Paul		Columbia 40008
				title refers to Nelson and his drummer Paul English		
10/12/85	178	3	▲	23 Half Nelson		Columbia 39990
8/3/91	193	3		24 Clean Shirt		Epic 47462
				WAYLON JENNINGS & WILLIE NELSON		
4/10/93	75	16		25 Across The Borderline		Columbia 52752
3/26/94	188	1		26 Moonlight Becomes You		Justice 1601
11/19/94	103	11		27 Healing Hands Of Time		Liberty 30420
6/29/96	132	2		28 Spirit		Island 524242
9/19/98	104	6		29 Teatro		Island 524548
10/7/00	83	7		30 Milk Cow Blues		Island 542517
2/2/02	43	23		31 The Great Divide		Lost Highway 586231
11/13/04	75	3		32 It Will Always Be		Lost Highway 002576
7/30/05	46	7		33 Countryman		Lost Highway 004706
4/1/06	114	4		34 You Don't Know Me: The Songs Of Cindy Walker		Lost Highway 006079
11/18/06	87	2		35 Songbird		Lost Highway 006939
4/7/07	64	4		36 Last Of The Breed		Lost Highway 008530 [2]
				WILLIE NELSON / MERLE HAGGARD / RAY PRICE		
2/16/08	56	4		37 Moment Of Forever		Lost Highway 010453
2/21/09	90	7		38 Willie & The Wheel		Bismeaux 1287
				WILLIE NELSON & ASLEEP AT THE WHEEL		
8/29/09	173	1		39 Lost Highway		Lost Highway 013254
9/12/09	43	6		40 American Classic		Blue Note 67197
				EARLY ALBUMS:		
11/8/75	196	3		41 What Can You Do To Me Now		RCA Victor 1234
6/5/76	187	3		42 Phases And Stages		Atlantic 7291
				recorded in 1964		
5/21/77	78	15		43 Before His Time		RCA Victor 2210
3/3/79	154	5		44 Sweet Memories		RCA Victor 3243
8/1/81	148	7		45 The Minstrel Man		RCA Victor 4045
12/3/83	182	5		46 My Own Way		RCA Victor 4819

Billboard			R I A A	ARTIST		
DEBUT	PEAK	WKS		Album Title	Catalog	Label & Number

NELSON, Willie — cont'd

GREATEST HITS & COMPILATIONS:

9/19/81	27	93	▲⁴	47 Willie Nelson's Greatest Hits (& Some That Will Be).............. **Cat:❶¹/8**		Columbia 37542 [2]
9/25/82	201	5		48 The Best Of Willie..		RCA Victor 4420
1/21/95	193	2	▲²	49 Super Hits... **Cat:#25/9**		Columbia 64184
10/13/01+	15ᶜ	42	▲	50 16 Biggest Hits..		Legacy 69322
4/19/03	179	5	●	51 The Essential Willie Nelson..		Legacy 86740 [2]
3/5/05	64	13		52 Songs..		Lost Highway 002300
4/4/09	193	1		53 Naked Willie..		RCA 20111
				contains new mixes of previously released material from 1966-70		

LIVE ALBUMS:

5/8/76	149	7		54 Willie Nelson Live...		RCA Victor 1487
				originally released in 1966 as *Live Country Music Concert*		
12/2/78+	32	55	▲⁴	55 Willie And Family Live...		Columbia 35642 [2]
				recorded at Harrah's in Lake Tahoe, Nevada		
6/27/98	150	2		56 VH1 Storytellers..		American 69416
				JOHNNY CASH & WILLIE NELSON		
11/23/02	133	3		57 Stars & Guitars..		Lost Highway 170340
				recorded on 5/27/2002 at the Ryman Auditorium in Nashville, Tennessee		
7/12/03	42	8		58 Live And Kickin'..		Lost Highway 000453
10/9/04	69	3		59 Outlaws And Angels..		Lost Highway 002794
				WILLIE NELSON & FRIENDS (above 3)		
5/22/04	168	1		60 Live At Billy Bob's Texas...		Smith Music Group 5029
7/26/08	20	8		61 Two Men With The Blues..		Blue Note 04454
				WILLIE NELSON & WYNTON MARSALIS		

SOUNDTRACKS:

1/12/80	52	25	●	62 The Electric Horseman...		Columbia 36327
				side 1: songs performed by Nelson; side 2: instrumental score by **Dave Grusin**		
9/6/80	11	36	▲²	63 Honeysuckle Rose.. **[L]**		Columbia 36752 [2]
				WILLIE NELSON & FAMILY		
11/10/84	152	5		64 Music From SongWriter..		Columbia 39531
				WILLIE NELSON & KRIS KRISTOFFERSON		

NEMESIS

Rap group from Dallas, Texas: The Snake, M.C. Azim and Big Al. By 1993, group consisted of Big Al, **Ron "C"**, Devo X and M.C. Joe Macc.

7/13/91	183	2		1 Munchies For Your Bass..		Profile 1411
7/24/93	159	2		2 Temple Of Boom...		Profile 1441

NENA

Rock band formed in Berlin, Germany: Gabriele "Nena" Kerner (vocals), Carlo Karges (guitar), Uwe Fahrenkrog-Petersen (keyboards), Jurgen Demel (bass) and Rolf Brendel (drums). Karges died of liver failure on 1/30/2002 (age 50).

3/24/84	27	14		1 99 Luftballons...		Epic 39294

NERD

Male rap/production trio from Virginia Beach, Virginia: Shae Haley, Chad Hugo and **Pharrell** Williams. Also known as The Neptunes.

3/30/02	56	35	●	1 In Search Of...		Virgin 11521
4/10/04	6	12	●	2 Fly Or Die...		Star Trak 91457
6/28/08	7	11		3 Seeing Sounds...		Star Trak 011447

NERO, Peter   1960s: #49 / All-Time: #252

Born Bernard Nierow on 5/22/1934 in Brooklyn, New York. Pop-jazz-classical pianist.

AWARD: Grammy: Best New Artist 1961

7/10/61	34	22		1 Piano Forte... **[I]**		RCA Victor 2334
9/18/61	32	62		2 New Piano In Town... **[I]**		RCA Victor 2383
3/17/62	22	23		3 Young And Warm And Wonderful... **[I]**		RCA Victor 2484
7/7/62	16	38		4 For The Nero-Minded... **[I]**		RCA Victor 2536
2/2/63	40	9		5 The Colorful Peter Nero.. **[I]**		RCA Victor 2618
				Grammy: Orchestral Album		
3/30/63	5	28		6 Hail The Conquering Nero... **[I]**		RCA Victor 2638
9/7/63	31	23		7 Peter Nero In Person.. **[I-L]**		RCA Victor 2710
				recorded at Webster Hall in New York City		
2/29/64	133	4		8 Sunday In New York... **[I-S]**		RCA Victor 2827
6/6/64	38	26		9 Reflections.. **[I]**		RCA Victor 2853
10/10/64	42	21		10 Songs You Won't Forget... **[I]**		RCA Victor 2935
2/20/65	123	4		11 The Best Of Peter Nero.. **[G-I]**		RCA Victor 2978
5/29/65	147	3		12 Career Girls.. **[I]**		RCA Victor 3313
10/23/65	86	16		13 Nero Goes "Pops".. **[I]**		RCA Victor 2821
				PETER NERO/BOSTON POPS/ARTHUR FIEDLER		
2/19/66	114	6		14 The Screen Scene.. **[I]**		RCA Victor 3496
7/16/66	141	3		15 Peter Nero-Up Close... **[I]**		RCA Victor 3550
5/13/67	193	2		16 Peter Nero Plays Born Free And Others................................ **[I]**		RCA Camden 2139
4/20/68	180	4		17 Peter Nero Plays Love Is Blue And Ten Other Great Songs........ **[I]**		RCA Victor 3936
5/10/69	193	3		18 I've Gotta Be Me... **[I]**		Columbia 9800
11/27/71+	23	27	●	19 Summer Of '42... **[I]**		Columbia 31105
7/8/72	172	9		20 The First Time Ever (I Saw Your Face)................................. **[I]**		Columbia 31335

Billboard			R I A A	ARTIST		
DEBUT	PEAK	WKS		Album Title	Catalog	Label & Number

NESBY, Ann
Born on 1/11/1952 in Joliet, Illinois. R&B singer. Member of **Sounds Of Blackness**.

10/19/96	157	13	1 I'm Here For You		Perspective 9022
4/6/02	62	11	2 Put It On Paper		Universal 017391

NESMITH, Michael, & The First National Band
Born on 12/30/1942 in Houston, Texas. Pop-rock singer/songwriter/guitarist. Member of **The Monkees**. Also see **The Wichita Train Whistle**.

10/17/70	143	3	1 Magnetic South		RCA Victor 4371
1/2/71	159	4	2 Loose Salute		RCA Victor 4415
5/22/71	218	2	3 Nevada Fighter		RCA Victor 4497
2/12/72	211	1	4 Tantamount To Treason Volume One		RCA Victor 4563
			MICHAEL NESMITH AND THE SECOND NATIONAL BAND		
8/19/72	208	2	5 And The Hits Just Keep On Comin'		RCA Victor 4695
4/9/77	209	1	6 From A Radio Engine To The Photon Wing		Pacific Arts 107
8/4/79	151	9	7 Infinite Rider On The Big Dogma		Pacific Arts 130
			MICHAEL NESMITH (above 3)		

NESS, Mike
Born on 4/3/1962 in Stoneham, Massachusetts. Lead singer of **Social Distortion**.

5/1/99	80	5	1 Cheating At Solitaire		Time Bomb 43524
11/27/99	174	1	2 Under The Influences		Time Bomb 43536

NETHERLANDS PHILHARMONIC ORCHESTRA, The
Studio orchestra from Holland.

11/21/98	8^C	5	1 Brahms Symphony No. 4/Tragic Overture		LaserLight 14001

NEVER SHOUT NEVER
Born Christofer Ingle on 2/11/1991 in Joplin, Missouri. Adult Alternative singer/songwriter/guitarist.

7/11/09	57	2	1 The Summer EP [EP]		Loveway 520373

NEVIL, Robbie
Born on 10/2/1960 in Los Angeles, California. Pop singer/songwriter/guitarist.

11/29/86+	37	46	1 Robbie Nevil		Manhattan 53006
11/26/88+	118	21	2 A Place Like This		EMI 48359

NEVILLE, Aaron
Born on 1/24/1941 in New Orleans, Louisiana. R&B singer. Member of **The Neville Brothers**. Father of **Ivan Neville**.

10/21/89+	7	58	▲³ 1 Cry Like A Rainstorm - Howl Like The Wind Cat:#37/6		Elektra 60872
			LINDA RONSTADT Featuring Aaron Neville		
6/29/91	44	41	▲ 2 Warm Your Heart		A&M 5354
5/8/93	37	58	▲ 3 The Grand Tour		A&M 540086
11/27/93	36	8	▲ 4 Aaron Neville's Soulful Christmas Cat:#11/19 [X]		A&M 540127
			Christmas charts: 8/'93, 16/'94, 16/'95, 29/'96, 28/'97		
5/6/95	64	20	● 5 The Tattooed Heart		A&M 540349
11/1/97	188	1	6 ...To Make Who I Am		A&M 540784
2/15/03	191	1	7 Believe		Tell It 20381
10/7/06	37	8	8 Bring It On Home...The Soul Classics		Burgundy 85489
			~ ~ ~ ~ ~ ~ ~ ~ ~ ~ **NON-CHARTED ALBUM** ~ ~ ~ ~ ~ ~ ~ ~ ~ ~		
			1967 Tell It Like It Is		

NEVILLE, Ivan
Born on 7/23/1965 in New Orleans, Louisiana. Rock singer/bassist. Son of **Aaron Neville**.

11/12/88+	107	23	1 If My Ancestors Could See Me Now		Polydor 834896

NEVILLE BROTHERS, The
Family group from New Orleans, Louisiana: brothers Art, Charles, Cyril and **Aaron Neville**. Art was a member of **The Meters** (1966-77). Cyril was with The Meters (1975-77). Charles and Aaron also contributed to The Meters (1976-77).

8/29/81	166	3	1 Fiyo On The Bayou		A&M 4866
4/11/87	178	3	2 Treacherous: A History Of The Neville Brothers 1955-1985 [K]		Rhino 71494 [2]
5/2/87	155	9	3 Uptown		EMI America 17249
4/8/89	66	24	● 4 Yellow Moon		A&M 5240
8/25/90	60	15	5 Brother's Keeper		A&M 5312
5/23/92	103	9	6 Family Groove		A&M 5384
5/7/94	126	5	7 Live On Planet Earth [L]		A&M 540225

NEVINS, Nancy
Born in Los Angeles, California. Folk-rock singer. Member of **Sweetwater**.

8/16/75	208	1	1 Nancy Nevins		Tom Cat 1063

NEWBEATS, The
Pop vocal trio formed in Shreveport, Louisiana: Larry Henley (lead vocals), with brothers Dean Mathis and Marc Mathis.

10/3/64	56	19	1 Bread & Butter		Hickory 120
1/22/66	131	4	2 Run Baby Run		Hickory 128

Billboard			R I A A	ARTIST	
DEBUT	PEAK	WKS		Album Title	Catalog	Label & Number

NEW BIRTH, The
R&B band from Louisville, Kentucky. Consisted of 17 members with two vocal groups (The New Birth and Love, Peace & Happiness) and band (**The Nite-Liters**). Band consisted of Tony Churchill, Austin Lander, James Baker, Robert Jackson, Leroy Taylor and Robin Russell. Vocal groups consisted of Ann Bogan, Melvin Wilson, Leslie Wilson, Bobby Downs, Londee Loren and Alan Frye. Bogan was a former member of **The Marvelettes**.

DEBUT	PEAK	WKS		Album Title	Label & Number
7/24/71	167	13		1 Morning, Noon & The Nite-Liters .... [I]	RCA Victor 4493
5/20/72	198	2		2 Instrumental Directions .... [I]	RCA Victor 4580
				THE NITE-LITERS (above 2)	
10/30/71	189	2		3 Ain't No Big Thing, But It's Growing	RCA Victor 4526
3/10/73	31	29		4 Birth Day	RCA Victor 4797
11/17/73+	50	31	●	5 It's Been A Long Time..	RCA Victor 0285
8/17/74	56	15		6 Comin' From All Ends	RCA Victor 0494
7/19/75	175	2		7 The Best Of The New Birth .... [G]	RCA Victor 1021
5/24/75	57	17		8 Blind Baby	Buddah 5636
8/28/76	168	4		9 Love Potion...	Warner 2953
12/10/77+	164	6		10 Behold The Mighty Army	Warner 3071

NEW BOYZ
Male rap duo from Hesperia, California: Dominic "Legacy" Thomas and Earl "Ben J" Benjamin.

DEBUT	PEAK	WKS		Album Title	Label & Number
10/3/09	56	9		1 Skinny Jeanz And A Mic	Shotty 520425

NEWBURY, Mickey
Born Milton Newbury on 5/19/1940 in Houston, Texas. Died on 9/28/2002 (age 62). Pop-country singer/songwriter/guitarist.

DEBUT	PEAK	WKS		Album Title	Label & Number
11/13/71+	58	15		1 'Frisco Mabel Joy	Elektra 74107
3/10/73	173	5		2 Heaven Help The Child	Elektra 75055
8/10/74	209	2		3 I Came To Hear The Music	Elektra 1007
4/5/75	172	3		4 Lovers	Elektra 1030

NEW CACTUS BAND — see CACTUS

NEW CHRISTY MINSTRELS, The   All-Time: #396
Folk group named after the Christy Minstrels (formed in 1842 by Edwin "Pop" Christy). Group founded and led by Randy Sparks, and featured **Barry McGuire** (1963), **Kenny Rogers** (1966) and **Kim Carnes** (1968).

DEBUT	PEAK	WKS		Album Title	Label & Number
10/20/62	19	92		1 The New Christy Minstrels	Columbia 1872 / 8672
				Grammy: Choral Group	
2/23/63	30	20		2 The New Christy Minstrels In Person .... [L]	Columbia 1941 / 8741
5/25/63	20	22		3 Tall Tales! Legends & Nonsense	Columbia 2017 / 8817
8/24/63	15	77	●	4 Ramblin' Featuring Green, Green	Columbia 2055 / 8855
12/21/63	5ˣ	8		5 Merry Christmas! .... [X]	Columbia 2096 / 8896
				Christmas charts: 5/'63, 17/'64, 53/'65, 65/'66, 116/'67	
4/18/64	9	34		6 Today .... [S]	Columbia 2159 / 8959
				featuring songs from the movie Advance To The Rear	
8/29/64	48	23		7 Land Of Giants	Columbia 2187 / 8987
2/13/65	62	11		8 Cowboys And Indians...	Columbia 2303 / 9103
6/26/65	22	22		9 Chim Chim Cher-ee	Columbia 2369 / 9169
10/16/65	125	9		10 The Wandering Minstrels	Columbia 2384 / 9184
6/18/66	76	16		11 Greatest Hits.. [G]	Columbia 2479 / 9279
11/28/70	195	2		12 You Need Someone To Love	Gregar 102

NEWCLEUS
Rap-dance group from Brooklyn, New York: brother and sister Ben "Cozmo D" and Yvette Cenad, with brother and sister Bob "Chilly B" and Monique Crafton. Chilly B died of a stroke on 2/23/2010 (age 47).

DEBUT	PEAK	WKS		Album Title	Label & Number
9/8/84	74	28		1 Jam On Revenge	Sunnyview 4901

NEW COLONY SIX, The
Soft-rock band from Chicago, Illinois: Ray Graffia (vocals), Gerald Van Kollenburg (guitar), Patrick McBride (harmonica), Ronnie Rice (organ), Les Kummel (bass) and Chic James (drums). Kummel died in a car crash on 12/18/1978 (age 33).

DEBUT	PEAK	WKS		Album Title	Label & Number
9/2/67	172	7		1 Colonization...	Sentar 3001
7/20/68	157	6		2 Revelations	Mercury 61165
11/1/69	179	4		3 Attacking A Straw Man	Mercury 61228

~ ~ ~ ~ ~ ~ ~ ~ ~ ~ **NON-CHARTED ALBUM** ~ ~ ~ ~ ~ ~ ~ ~ ~ ~ ~
1966 **Breakthrough**

NEW EDITION
R&B vocal group from Boston, Massachusetts: **Ralph Tresvant**, Ronnie DeVoe, Michael Bivins, Ricky Bell and **Bobby Brown**. **Johnny Gill** replaced Brown in 1986. Bell, Bivins and DeVoe recorded as **Bell Biv DeVoe** in 1990. All six members reunited in 1996 and 2004.

DEBUT	PEAK	WKS		Album Title	Label & Number
9/3/83	90	33		1 Candy Girl	Streetwise 3301
10/13/84+	6	54	▲²	2 New Edition	MCA 5515
12/7/85+	32	48	▲	3 All For Love	MCA 5679
12/21/85	9ˣ	2		4 Christmas All Over the World .... [X]	MCA 39040
12/20/86+	43	23	●	5 Under The Blue Moon	MCA 5912
7/9/88	12	50	▲²	6 Heart Break	MCA 42207
10/19/91	99	6		7 New Edition's Greatest Hits, Volume One .... [G]	MCA 10434
9/28/96	❶¹	32	▲²	8 Home Again	MCA 11480
11/27/04	12	5		9 One Love	Bad Boy 003422

Billboard			R I A A	ARTIST / Album Title	Catalog	Label & Number
DEBUT	PEAK	WKS				

NEW ENGLAND
Rock band formed in New York: John Fannon (vocals, guitar), Jimmy Waldo (keyboards), Gary Shea (bass) and Hirsh Gardner (drums). Waldo and Shea later joined **Alcatrazz**.

DEBUT	PEAK	WKS			Label & Number
5/19/79	50	17		1 New England..	Infinity 9007
11/22/80	202	6		2 Explorer Suite...	Elektra 307
7/18/81	176	4		3 Walking Wild...	Elektra 346

NEW ENGLAND CONSERVATORY RAGTIME ENSEMBLE
Conducted by Gunther Schuller.

5/19/73+	65	36		1 Scott Joplin: The Red Back Book .... [I]	Angel 36060
				Grammy: Chamber Music Album	

NEWFIELD, Heidi
Born on 10/4/1970 in Healdsburg, California. Country singer/songwriter/guitarist. Former lead singer of **Trick Pony**.

8/23/08	10	14		1 What Am I Waiting For	Curb 79087

NEW FOUND GLORY
Punk-rock band from Coral Springs, Florida: Jordan Pundik (vocals), Chad Gilbert (guitar), Steve Klein (guitar), Ian Grushka (bass) and Cyrus Bolooki (drums). Band also recorded as the heavy metal parody International Superheroes Of Hardcore (see album #7 below).

10/14/00+	107	21	●	1 New Found Glory	Drive-Thru 112338
6/29/02	4	39	●	2 Sticks And Stones	Drive-Thru 112916
6/5/04	3¹	19	●	3 Catalyst	Drive-Thru 002383
10/7/06	19	6		4 Coming Home	Suretone 007495
10/6/07	42	2		5 From The Screen To Your Stereo Part II	Drive-Thru 83656
4/5/08	167	1		6 Hits .... [G]	Drive-Thru 010661
5/17/08	136	1		7 Tip Of The Iceberg / Takin' It Ova!	Bridge Nine 91 [2]
				NEW FOUND GLORY / INTERNATIONAL SUPERHEROES OF HARDCORE	
3/28/09	12	4		8 Not Without A Fight	Epitaph 87008

NEWHART, Bob
Born George Robert Newhart on 9/5/1929 in Oak Park, Illinois. Stand-up comedian/actor. Starred in three TV sitcoms: *The Bob Newhart Show* (1972-78), *Newhart* (1982-90) and *Bob* (1992-93). Appeared in several movies.

AWARD: Grammy: Best New Artist 1960

5/16/60	❶¹⁴	108	●	1 The Button-Down Mind Of Bob Newhart [C]	Warner 1379
				Grammy: Album of the Year ★ NRR	
11/14/60+	❶¹	70	●	2 The Button-Down Mind Strikes Back! [C]	Warner 1393
				Grammy: Comedy Album	
10/30/61	10	30		3 Behind The Button-Down Mind Of Bob Newhart [C]	Warner 1417
9/8/62	28	26		4 The Button-Down Mind On TV [C]	Warner 1467
2/29/64	113	11		5 Bob Newhart Faces Bob Newhart (Faces Bob Newhart) .... [C]	Warner 1517
4/24/65	126	5		6 The Windmills Are Weakening .... [C]	Warner 1588

NEW HORIZONS
Family funk band from Dayton, Ohio: brothers Mark Thomas (vocals), Varges Thomas (keyboards), Bart Thomas (bass) and Art Thomas (drums), with cousin Timothy Abrams (guitar).

8/20/83	210	2		1 Something New	Columbia 38709

NEW KIDS ON THE BLOCK   All-Time: #413
Pop vocal group from Boston, Massachusetts: **Joey McIntyre** (born on 12/31/1972), Donnie Wahlberg (born on 8/17/1969), Danny Wood (born on 5/14/1969), and brothers Jon Knight (born on 11/29/1968) and **Jordan Knight** (born on 5/17/1970). Wahlberg is the brother of **Marky Mark** (actor Mark Wahlberg). Shortened group name to **NKOTB** in 1992. McIntyre played teacher "Colin Flynn" on TV's *Boston Public* and finished third on season 1 on *Dancing With The Stars*.

8/27/88+	❶²	132	▲⁸	1 Hangin' Tough	Columbia 40985
8/5/89+	25	80	▲³	2 New Kids On The Block .... [E]	Columbia 40475
				released in 1987	
10/14/89	9	18	▲²	3 Merry, Merry Christmas [X]	Columbia 45280
				Christmas charts: 1/'89, 4/'90, 25/'08	
11/17/90+	48	10		4 Merry, Merry Christmas [X-R]	Columbia 45280
6/23/90	❶¹	49	▲³	5 Step By Step	Columbia 45129
12/8/90+	19	32	●	6 No More Games/The Remix Album .... [K]	Columbia 46959
2/12/94	37	6		7 Face The Music	Columbia 52969
				NKOTB	
8/30/08	22	14		8 Greatest Hits.. [G]	Columbia 30562
9/20/08	2¹	17		9 The Block	Interscope 011792

NEW LIFE COMMUNITY CHOIR FEAT. JOHN P. KEE
Choir formed by John Prince Kee in Charlotte, North Carolina.

2/11/95	147	2	●	1 Show Up!..	New Life 43010
11/15/97	107	3		2 Strength	New Life 43108
11/11/00	102	4	●	3 Not Guilty...The Experience	New Life 43139 [2]
11/30/02	163	1		4 Blessed By Association	Verity 43200
				JOHN P. KEE & NEW LIFE	

NEW LIFE WORSHIP
Christian choir formed by Ross Parsley in Colorado Springs, Colorado.

10/18/08	166	1		1 Counting On God	Integrity 4457

NEWMAN, A.C.
Born Allan Carl Newman on 4/14/1968 in Vancouver, British Columbia, Canada. Rock singer/songwriter/guitarist.

2/7/09	99	1		1 Get Guilty	Matador 834

NEWMAN, Randy
Born on 11/28/1943 in New Orleans, Louisiana; raised in Los Angeles, California. Singer/songwriter/pianist. Nephew of composers Alfred, Emil and Lionel Newman. Scored several movies.
AWARD: Billboard Century: 2000

10/2/71	191	3		1 Randy Newman/Live .... [L]	Reprise 6459
				recorded on 9/18/1970 at the Bitter End in New York City	
6/17/72	163	18		2 Sail Away	Reprise 2064
				RS500 #321	
10/5/74	36	23		3 Good Old Boys	Reprise 2193
				RS500 #393	
10/22/77+	9	29	●	4 Little Criminals	Warner 3079
9/1/79	41	11		5 Born Again	Warner 3346
2/12/83	64	13		6 Trouble In Paradise	Warner 23755
7/7/84	202	5		7 The Natural .... [I-S]	Warner 25116
10/15/88	80	19		8 Land Of Dreams	Reprise 25773
6/19/99	194	1		9 Bad Love	DreamWorks 50115
8/23/08	30	5		10 Harps And Angels	Nonesuch 122812

~ ~ ~ ~ ~ ~ ~ ~ ~ ~ **NON-CHARTED ALBUM** ~ ~ ~ ~ ~ ~ ~ ~ ~ ~ ~
1970 **12 Songs**
RS500 #354

NEW ORDER
Techno-dance band formed in Manchester, England. Formerly known as **Joy Division**. After suicide of lead singer Ian Curtis (May 1980), name changed to New Order and members Bernard Sumner (guitar, vocals), Peter Hook (bass) and Stephen Morris (drums) continued as trio. Female keyboardist Gillian Gilbert joined in October 1980. Sumner was also a member of **Electronic**. Hook also with **Revenge**.

6/8/85	94	22		1 Low-Life	Qwest 25289
10/25/86	117	21		2 Brotherhood	Qwest 25511
9/5/87+	36	60	▲	3 Substance .... [G]	Qwest 25621 [2]
				RS500 #361	
2/11/89	32	28	●	4 Technique	Qwest 25845
5/29/93	11	16	●	5 Republic	Qwest 45250
4/1/95	78	5		6 (The Best Of) NewOrder .... [G]	Qwest 45794
11/3/01	41	5		7 Get Ready	Reprise 89621
5/14/05	46	4		8 Waiting For The Sirens' Call...	Warner 49307

NEW PORNOGRAPHERS, The
Rock band from Vancouver, British Columbia, Canada: **Neko Case** (female vocals), Carl Newman (male vocals), Todd Fancey (guitar), Blaine Thurier (keyboards), John Collins (bass) and Kurt Dahle (drums).

5/24/03	196	1		1 Electric Version	Matador 551
9/10/05	44	3		2 Twin Cinema	Matador 621
9/8/07	34	5		3 Challengers	Matador 770

NEW RADICALS
Born Gregg Alexander on 5/4/1970 in Grosse Point, Michigan. New Radicals is his band project of revolving musicians.

11/28/98+	41	40	▲	1 Maybe You've Been Brainwashed Too..	MCA 11858

NEW RIDERS OF THE PURPLE SAGE
Country-rock band formed in San Francisco, California: John Dawson (vocals, guitar), David Nelson (guitar), Dave Torbert (bass) and Spencer Dryden (drums; **Jefferson Airplane**). Guitarist Buddy Cage joined after first album. Torbert left in 1974 to join **Kingfish**; replaced by Skip Battin (died on 7/6/2003, age 69). Dryden died of cancer on 1/11/2005 (age 66). Dawson died of cancer on 7/21/2009 (age 64).

9/11/71	39	15		1 New Riders Of The Purple Sage	Columbia 30888
5/6/72	33	18		2 Powerglide...	Columbia 31284
12/9/72+	85	13		3 Gypsy Cowboy	Columbia 31930
10/20/73	55	18	●	4 The Adventures Of Panama Red	Columbia 32450
4/27/74	68	12		5 Home, Home On The Road .... [L]	Columbia 32870
11/2/74	68	9		6 Brujo	Columbia 33145
11/8/75	144	4		7 Oh, What A Mighty Time	Columbia 33688
6/12/76	145	8		8 New Riders...	MCA 2196
3/7/81	202	2		9 Feelin' All Right	A&M 4818

NEWSBOYS
Christian rock band from Australia: John James (vocals), Jody Davis (guitar), Duncan Phillips (percussion), Jeff Frankenstein (keyboards), Philip Urry (bass) and Peter Furler (drums). James left the group in late 1997, Furler moved to vocals and Phillips moved to drums. By 1999, Phil Joel had replaced Philip Urry.

3/9/96	35	20	●	1 Take Me To Your Leader..	Star Song 20075
7/18/98	61	20	●	2 Step Up To The Microphone	Virgin 45917
12/4/99	80	6		3 Love Liberty Disco	Sparrow 51720
11/11/00	122	10	●	4 Shine The Hits .... [G]	Sparrow 51787
4/13/02	38	7		5 Thrive	Sparrow 51846
4/26/03	33	17		6 Adoration: The Worship Album	Sparrow 41763

NEWSBOYS — cont'd

11/20/04	56	7	7 Devotion	Sparrow 95547
11/18/06	51	11	8 Go .... Cat:#9/4	Inpop 71383
5/23/09	28	9	9 In The Hands Of God	Inpop 71454

NEW SEEKERS, The
Pop-folk band formed in England: Keith Potger, Eve Graham, Lyn Paul, Peter Doyle, Marty Kristian and Paul Layton. Formed by Potger after the disbandment of **The Seekers**. Doyle died of cancer on 10/13/2001 (age 52).

4/3/71	136	6	1 Beautiful People	Elektra 74088
12/25/71+	37	14	2 We'd Like To Teach The World To Sing	Elektra 74115
7/15/72	166	10	3 Circles	Elektra 75034
1/27/73	211	3	4 Come Softly To Me	MGM/Verve 5090
5/19/73	190	4	5 Pinball Wizards	MGM/Verve 5098

NEWSOM, Joanna
Born on 1/18/1982 in Nevada City, California. Female singer/songwriter/harpist.

12/2/06	134	1	1 Ys .... [EP]	Drag City 303

NEWSONG
Christian pop band formed in Kennesaw, Georgia: Eddie Carswell (vocals), Billy Goodwin (guitar), Leonard Ahlstrom (guitar), Scotty Wilbanks (sax, keyboards), Mark Clay (bass) and Jack Pumphrey (drums).

12/30/00+	130	2	1 Sheltering Tree	Benson 83327
12/1/01	113	6	2 The Christmas Shoes .... Cat:#25/3 [X]	Reunion 10033
			Christmas charts: 10/'01, 30/'02	
9/27/03	172	1	3 More Life	Reunion 10054

NEWTON, Juice
Born Judith Kay Cohen on 2/18/1952 in Lakehurst, New Jersey. Pop-country singer/guitarist.

3/7/81+	22	86	▲	1 Juice	Capitol 12136
5/29/82	20	46	●	2 Quiet Lies	Capitol 12210
9/10/83	52	15		3 Dirty Looks	Capitol 12294
7/14/84	128	10		4 Can't Wait All Night	RCA Victor 4995
7/21/84	178	5	●	5 Greatest Hits .... [G]	Capitol 12353

NEWTON, Wayne
Born on 4/3/1942 in Roanoke, Virginia. Singer/multi-instrumentalist. Top Las Vegas entertainer. Began singing career with regular appearances on **Jackie Gleason**'s variety TV show in 1962. Appeared in the 1989 James Bond movie *License To Kill* and the 1990 movie *The Adventures Of Ford Fairlane*.

10/12/63	55	9	1 Danke Schoen	Capitol 1973
5/1/65	17	20	2 Red Roses For A Blue Lady	Capitol 2335
10/23/65	114	6	3 Summer Wind	Capitol 2389
6/4/66	80	21	4 Wayne Newton - Now!	Capitol 2445
12/3/66	10ˣ	10	5 Songs For A Merry Christmas [X]	Capitol 2588
			Christmas charts: 10/'66, 29/'67, 40/'68	
2/4/67	131	13	6 It's Only The Good Times	Capitol 2635
10/7/67	194	4	7 The Best Of Wayne Newton [G]	Capitol 2797
6/1/68	186	5	8 One More Time	MGM 4549
8/31/68	196	3	9 Walking On New Grass	MGM 4523
6/17/72	34	21	10 Daddy Don't You Walk So Fast	Chelsea 1001
11/18/72+	164	11	11 Can't You Hear The Song?	Chelsea 1003

NEWTON-JOHN, Olivia
All-Time: #155

Born on 9/26/1948 in Cambridge, England; raised in Melbourne, Australia. Pop-rock-country singer. Granddaughter of Nobel Prize-winning German physicist Max Born. Starred in the movies *Grease*, *Xanadu* and *Two Of A Kind*. Married to actor Matt Lattanzi from 1985-95.

AWARD: CMA: Female Vocalist 1974

11/27/71	158	4		1 If Not For You	Uni 73117
12/29/73+	54	20	●	2 Let Me Be There	MCA 389
6/8/74	❶¹	61	●	3 If You Love Me, Let Me Know	MCA 411
2/22/75	❶¹	31	●	4 Have You Never Been Mellow	MCA 2133
10/11/75	12	22	●	5 Clearly Love	MCA 2148
3/20/76	13	24	●	6 Come On Over	MCA 2186
11/6/76	30	28	●	7 Don't Stop Believin'	MCA 2223
7/9/77	34	16		8 Making A Good Thing Better	MCA 2280
12/9/78+	7	39	▲	9 Totally Hot	MCA 3067
7/12/80	4	36	▲²	10 Xanadu [S]	MCA 6100
				side 1: Newton-John; side 2: **Electric Light Orchestra**	
10/31/81	6	57	▲²	11 Physical	MCA 5229
11/2/85	29	16	●	12 Soul Kiss	MCA 6151
9/3/88	67	9		13 The Rumour	MCA 6245

Billboard		R I A A	ARTIST		
DEBUT	PEAK	WKS	Album Title	Catalog	Label & Number

NEWTON-JOHN, Olivia — cont'd

12/2/89+	124	13	14 Warm And Tender		Geffen 24257
5/30/98	59	6	15 Back With A Heart		MCA 70030
12/22/07	187	1	16 Christmas Wish	Cat:#49/1 [X]	ONJ Productions 39792
			Christmas chart: 22/08		

GREATEST HITS & COMPILATIONS:

11/12/77+	13	19	▲² 17 Olivia Newton-John's Greatest Hits		MCA 3028
10/9/82	16	86	▲² 18 Olivia's Greatest Hits, Vol. 2		MCA 5347
6/27/92	121	8	● 19 Back To Basics - The Essential Collection 1971-1992		Geffen 24470
9/29/01	150	2	20 Magic: The Very Best Of Olivia Newton-John		UTV 585233

NEW VAUDEVILLE BAND, The
Studio creation of songwriter/record producer Geoff Stephens (born on 10/1/1934 in London, England). Arrangements similar to Rudy Vallee's hits during the 1930s.

12/10/66+	5	31	● 1 Winchester Cathedral		Fontana 27560

NEW YORK CITY
R&B vocal group from Harlem, New York: Tim McQueen, John Brown, Ed Shell and Claude Johnston.

6/16/73	122	10	1 I'm Doin' Fine Now		Chelsea 0198

NEW YORK DOLLS
Glam/punk-rock band formed in New York: **David Johansen** (vocals), Johnny "Thunders" Genzale (vocals, guitar), **Sylvain Sylvain** (guitar), Arthur Kane (bass) and Jerry Nolan (drums). Disbanded in 1976. Genzale died of a drug overdose on 4/23/1991 (age 38). Nolan died of a stroke on 1/14/1992 (age 45). Kane died of leukemia on 7/13/2004 (age 55). Johansen and Sylvain reunited in 2006 with Steve Conte (guitar), Sami Yaffa (bass) and Brian Delaney (drums).

9/1/73	116	12	1 New York Dolls		Mercury 675
			RS500 #213		
6/1/74	167	5	2 In Too Much Too Soon		Mercury 1001
8/12/06	129	1	3 One Day It Will Please Us To Remember Even This		Roadrunner 618045
5/23/09	159	1	4 'Cause I Sez So		Atco 518926

NEW YORK ROCK ENSEMBLE, The
Classical-baroque rock group from New York City: Michael Kamen (vocals, keyboards), Cliff Nivison (guitar), Dorian Rudnytsky (bass) and Marty Fulterman (drums). Kamen later became a top conductor/arranger for several rock acts; died of a heart attack on 11/18/2003 (age 55).

5/27/72	215	2	1 Freedomburger		Columbia 31317

NEXT
R&B vocal trio from Minneapolis, Minnesota: Robert Lavelle "RL" Huggar, with brothers Raphael "Tweety" Brown and Terry "T-Low" Brown.

10/18/97+	37	60	▲² 1 Rated Next		Arista 18973
7/8/00	12	21	● 2 Welcome II Nextasy		Arista 14643
1/4/03	120	9	3 The Next Episode		J Records 20016

NE-YO
Born Shaffer Smith on 10/18/1979 in Camden, Arkansas; raised in Las Vegas, Nevada. Male R&B singer/songwriter.

3/18/06	❶¹	37	▲ 1 In My Own Words		Def Jam 004934
5/19/07	❶¹	35	▲ 2 Because Of You		Def Jam 008697
			Grammy: Contemporary R&B Album		
10/4/08	2¹	47	▲ 3 Year Of The Gentleman		Def Jam 011410

NICE, The
Classical-rock trio from England: **Keith Emerson** (organ; Emerson, Lake & Palmer), Lee Jackson (vocals, bass) and Brian Davison (drums).

8/29/70	197	5	1 Five Bridges .... [I-L]		Mercury 61295
4/24/71	209	7	2 Elegy .... [I-L]		Mercury 61324
2/26/72	152	8	3 Keith Emerson with The Nice .... [R]		Mercury 6500 [2]
			reissue of above 2 albums		

NICE & SMOOTH
Rap duo from Brooklyn, New York: Greg "Nice" Mays and Darryl "Smooth" Barnes.

10/5/91	141	19	1 Ain't A Damn Thing Changed		RAL 47373
7/16/94	66	4	2 Jewel Of The Nile		RAL 523336

NICHOLS, Joe
Born on 11/26/1976 in Rogers, Arkansas. Country singer/songwriter.

AWARD: CMA: Horizon 2003

8/10/02+	72	52	▲ 1 Man With A Memory		Universal South 170285
7/17/04	23	12	2 Revelation		Universal South 002514
11/13/04+	19ˣ	2	3 A Traditional Christmas .... [X]		Universal South 002588
11/12/05	7	55	● 4 III		Universal South 004796
9/8/07	23	6	5 Real Things		Universal South 008888
11/14/09	71	2	6 Old Things New		Universal South 012989

NICHOLS, Mike, & Elaine May

Improvisational comedy team. Nichols was born Michael Peschkowsky on 11/6/1931 in Berlin, Germany; raised in Manhattan, New York. Prolific movie director. Married network newscaster Diane Sawyer on 4/29/1988. May was born Elaine Berlin on 4/21/1932 in Philadelphia, Pennsylvania. Movie writer/director/actress.

6/1/59	39	7	1 Improvisations To Music .... [C]		Mercury 20376
1/23/61	10	32	2 An Evening With Mike Nichols And Elaine May	[C]	Mercury 2200
			Grammy: Comedy Album		
2/24/62	17	29	3 Mike Nichols & Elaine May Examine Doctors .... [C]		Mercury 20680

NICKELBACK

Rock band formed in Hanna, Alberta, Canada: brothers Chad Kroeger (vocals; born on 11/15/1974) and Mike Kroeger (bass; born on 6/25/1972), with Ryan Peake (guitar; born on 3/1/1973) and Ryan Vikedal (drums; born on 5/9/1975). Daniel Adair (of **3 Doors Down**) replaced Vikedal in January 2005.

8/26/00	130	18	▲	1 The State	Roadrunner 8586
9/29/01	2[1]	80	▲[6]	2 Silver Side Up	Cat:#32/17	Roadrunner 618485
7/13/02	182	1		3 Curb .... [E]	Roadrunner 618440
				recorded and first released in Canada in 1996	
10/11/03	6	80	▲[3]	4 The Long Road	Cat:#11/54	Roadrunner 618400
10/22/05	❶[1]	159	▲[8]	5 All The Right Reasons	Cat:#4/75	Roadrunner 618300
12/6/08	2[2]	78↑	▲[2]	6 Dark Horse	Roadrunner 618028

NICKEL CREEK

Bluegrass trio from Los Angeles, California: brother-and-sister Sean Watkins (guitar) and Sara Watkins (fiddle), with Chris Thile (mandolin). Sean Watkins also formed **Fiction Family**.

4/28/01+	125	38	●	1 Nickel Creek	Cat:#3/31	Sugar Hill 3909
8/31/02	18	19	●	2 This Side	Sugar Hill 3941
				Grammy: Contemporary Folk Album	
8/27/05	17	10		3 Why Should The Fire Die?	Sugar Hill 3990

NICKS, Stevie   All-Time: #359

Born Stephanie Nicks on 5/26/1948 in Phoenix, Arizona; raised in San Francisco, California. Pop-rock singer/songwriter. Teamed up with **Lindsey Buckingham** in 1973. Both joined **Fleetwood Mac** in 1975.

8/15/81	❶[1]	143	▲[4]	1 Bella Donna	Modern 139
1/29/83+	28[C]	22		2 Buckingham Nicks	Polydor 5058
				first released in 1973	
7/2/83	5	52	▲[2]	3 The Wild Heart	Modern 90084
12/14/85+	12	35	▲	4 Rock A Little	Modern 90479
6/10/89	10	21	▲	5 The Other Side Of The Mirror	Modern 91245
9/21/91	30	24	▲	6 TimeSpace - The Best Of Stevie Nicks .... [G]	Modern 91711
6/25/94	45	10	●	7 Street Angel	Modern 92246
5/16/98	85	2		8 Enchanted .... [K]	Atlantic 83093 [3]
5/19/01	5	20	●	9 Trouble In Shangri-La	Reprise 47372
4/14/07	21	12		10 Crystal Visions...The Very Best Of Stevie Nicks .... [G]	Reprise 100363
4/18/09	47	2		11 The Soundstage Sessions .... [L]	Reprise 508028

NICOLE

Born Nicole Wray on 5/2/1981 in Salinas, California; raised in Portsmouth, Virginia. Female R&B singer.

9/12/98	42	9	1 Make It Hot	EastWest 62209

NICOLE, Britt

Born Brittany Nicole Waddell on 8/2/1985 in Kannapolis, North Carolina. Black Contemporary Christian singer.

8/29/09	62	7	1 The Lost Get Found	Sparrow 12358

NIELSEN/PEARSON

Pop duo from Sacramento, California: singers/guitarists Reed Nielsen and Mark Pearson.

10/4/80	205	1	1 Nielsen/Pearson	Capitol 12101

NIGHT

Pop-rock band formed in Los Angeles, California: Stevie Lange (female vocals), Chris Thompson (male vocals; **Manfred Mann's Earth Band**), Robbie McIntosh (guitar), Nicky Hopkins (piano), Billy Kristian (bass) and Rick Marotta (drums). McIntosh later joined **The Pretenders** and **Paul McCartney**'s backing band.

8/11/79	113	10	1 Night	Planet 2
1/24/81	204	2	2 Long Distance	Planet 10

NIGHTCRAWLERS, The

Garage-rock band from Daytona Beach, Florida: Chuck Conlon (vocals, bass), Robbie Rouse (vocals), Sylvan Wells (guitar), Pete Thomason (guitar) and Tom Ruger (drums).

~ ~ ~ ~ ~ ~ ~ ~ ~ ~   **NON-CHARTED ALBUM**   ~ ~ ~ ~ ~ ~ ~ ~ ~ ~ ~ ~

1967 The Little Black Egg

NIGHTHAWKS, The

Blues-rock band from Washington DC: Mark Wenner (vocals), Jim Thackery (guitar), Jan Zukowski (bass) and Pete Ragusa (drums).

7/26/80	166	4	1 The Nighthawks	Mercury 3833

NIGHTINGALE, Maxine
Born on 11/2/1952 in Wembley, London, England. R&B singer/actress.

5/29/76	65	9		1 Right Back Where We Started From		United Artists 626
8/20/77	209	1		2 Night Life		United Artists 731
7/21/79	45	18		3 Lead Me On		Windsong 3404
1/8/83	176	4		4 It's A Beautiful Thing		Highrise 101

NIGHT RANGER
Rock band formed in San Francisco, California: Jack Blades (vocals, bass; born on 4/24/1954), Kelly Keagy (vocals, drums; born on 9/15/1952), Jeff Watson (guitar; born on 11/4/1956), Brad Gillis (guitar; born on 6/15/1957), and Alan Fitzgerald (keyboards; born on 7/16/1949). Blades and Gillis were members of **Rubicon**. Blades later joined **Damn Yankees** and formed duo with **Tommy Shaw**.

12/25/82+	38	69		1 Dawn Patrol		Boardwalk 33259
11/19/83+	15	69	▲	2 Midnight Madness		MCA/Camel 5456
6/8/85	10	45	▲	3 7 Wishes		MCA/Camel 5593
4/11/87	28	18	●	4 Big Life		MCA/Camel 5839
10/22/88	81	8		5 Man In Motion		MCA/Camel 6238

NIGHTWATCHMAN, The
Born Thomas Morello on 5/30/1964 in Harlem, New York. Rock singer/songwriter/guitarist. Member of **Rage Against The Machine**, **Audioslave** and **Street Sweeper Social Club**.

5/12/07	119	1		1 One Man Revolution		Epic 67546
10/18/08	180	1		2 The Fabled City		Red Ink 20396

NIGHTWISH
Hard-rock band from Kitee, Finland: Anette Olzon (vocals), Emo Vuorinen (guitar), Tuomas Holopainen (keyboards), Marzo Hietala (bass) and Jukka Nevalainen (drums).

10/20/07	84	3		1 Dark Passion Play		Roadrunner 617984

NILE
Death metal band from Greenville, South Carolina: Karl Sanders (vocals, guitar), Dallas Toler-Wade (guitar), Chris Lollis (bass) and George Kollias (drums).

8/4/07	162	1		1 Ithyphallic		Nuclear Blast 11721
11/21/09	160	1		2 Those Whom The Gods Detest		Nuclear Blast 2224

NILE, Willie
Born Robert Noonan on 6/7/1948 in Buffalo, New York. Rock singer/songwriter.

4/12/80	145	6		1 Willie Nile		Arista 4260
5/2/81	158	8		2 Golden Down		Arista 4284

NILSSON   All-Time: #462
Born Harry Nelson on 6/15/1941 in Brooklyn, New York. Died of a heart attack on 1/15/1994 (age 52). Pop singer/songwriter.

8/23/69	120	15		1 Harry		RCA Victor 4197
3/6/71	25	32		2 The Point! **[TV]**		RCA Victor 1003
				songs and narration from his animated TV special		
7/17/71	149	3		3 Aerial Pandemonium Ballet **[K]**		RCA Victor 4543
				selections from *Pandemonium Shadow Show* and *Aerial Ballet* albums		
12/4/71+	3³	46	●	4 Nilsson Schmilsson		RCA Victor 4515
7/22/72	12	31	●	5 Son Of Schmilsson		RCA Victor 4717
6/2/73	201	6		6 Nilsson Sings Newman		RCA Victor 0203
				all songs written by **Randy Newman**; first released on RCA Victor 4289 in 1970 ($15)		
6/23/73	46	17		7 A Little Touch Of Schmilsson In The Night		RCA Victor 0097
5/4/74	106	9		8 Son Of Dracula **[S]**		Rapple 0220
9/7/74	60	12		9 Pussy Cats		RCA Victor 0570
				produced by **John Lennon**		
4/5/75	141	7		10 Duit On Mon Dei		RCA Victor 0817
2/7/76	111	7		11 Sandman		RCA Victor 1031
7/10/76	158	6		12 ...That's The Way It Is		RCA Victor 1119
8/6/77	108	10		13 Knnillssonn		RCA Victor 2276
6/17/78	140	5		14 Greatest Hits **[G]**		RCA Victor 2798

NIMOY, Leonard
Born on 3/26/1931 in Boston, Massachusetts. Actor/director. Played "Mr. Spock" on *Star Trek*.

6/10/67	83	25		1 Mr. Spock's Music From Outer Space		Dot 25794
				Nimoy sings 3 songs and narrates 3 others; others are instrumentals by Charles Grean		
2/24/68	97	13		2 Two Sides Of Leonard Nimoy		Dot 25835
				side 1: performs as Mr. Spock; side 2: performs as Leonard Nimoy		

NINA SKY
Female R&B vocal duo from New Jersey: twin sisters Nicole Albino and Natalie Albino.

7/17/04	44	12		1 Nina Sky		Next Plateau 002739

NINE
Born Derrick Keyes on 9/19/1969 in Queens, New York. Male rapper.

3/25/95	90	8		1 Nine Livez		Profile 1460

Billboard			R I A A	ARTIST Album Title	Catalog	Label & Number
DEBUT	PEAK	WKS				

NINEDAYS
Rock band from New York: John Hampson (vocals, guitar), Brian Desveaux (vocals, guitar), Jeremy Dean (keyboards), Nick Dimichino (bass) and Vincent Tattanelli (drums).

6/3/00	67	19	●	1 The Madding Crowd		550 Music 63634

NINE INCH NAILS   1990s: #50 / All-Time: #208
Born Trent Reznor on 5/17/1965 in Mercer, Pennsylvania; later based in Cleveland, Ohio. Formed and fronted Nine Inch Nails as an industrial-rock project with revolving musicians, including Richard Patrick and Brian Liesegang of **Filter**.

2/10/90+	75	113	▲³	1 Pretty Hate Machine	Cat:❶¹⁴/172	TVT 2610
10/10/92	7	30	▲	2 Broken	Cat:#35/12	Nothing 92213
3/26/94	2¹	115	▲⁴	3 The Downward Spiral	Cat:#46/1	Nothing 92346
				RS500 #200		
6/17/95	23	20	●	4 Further Down The Spiral .... [EP]		Nothing 95811
10/9/99	❶¹	19	▲²	5 The Fragile		Nothing 490473 [2]
12/9/00	67	5		6 Things Falling Apart		Nothing 490744
2/9/02	37	6		7 And All That Could Have Been, Live .... [L]		Nothing 493185
2/9/02	26	2		8 And All That Could Have Been, Live: Deluxe Edition .... [L]		Nothing 493186 [2]
5/21/05	❶¹	43	●	9 With Teeth		Nothing 004553
5/5/07	2¹	17		10 Year Zero		Nothing 008764
12/8/07	77	2		11 Y34RZ3R0R3MIX3D		Nothing 010331
4/26/08	14	7		12 Ghosts I-IV .... [I]		Null Corporation 26 [2]
8/9/08	13	7		13 The Slip		Null Corporation 27

999
New-wave band from London, England: Nick Cash (vocals), Guy Davis (guitar), John Watson (bass) and Pablo Labritain (drums). 999 is the emergency telephone number in England.

2/23/80	177	3		1 The Biggest Prize In Sport		Polydor 6256
6/27/81	192	2		2 Concrete		Polydor 6323

9.9
R&B vocal trio from Boston, Massachusetts: Margo Thunder, Leslie Jones and Wanda Perry.

9/14/85	79	22		1 9.9		RCA Victor 8049

1910 FRUITGUM CO.
Bubblegum group from New Jersey: Joey Levine (**Ohio Express**, Crazy Elephant, Reunion; vocals), Mark Gutkowski, Floyd Marcus, Pat Karwan, Steve Mortkowitz and Frank Jeckell. Producers Jerry Kasenetz and Jeff Katz used a revolving-door studio-based membership centered around lead singer Levine.

4/20/68	162	8		1 Simon Says..		Buddah 5010
10/5/68	163	12		2 1,2,3 Red Light..		Buddah 5022
4/5/69	147	8		3 Indian Giver		Buddah 5036

98°
White vocal group from Cincinnati, Ohio: brothers Nick Lachey and Drew Lachey, with Jeff Timmons and Justin Jeffre. Nick Lachey was married to **Jessica Simpson** from 2002-06. Drew and his professional dance partner, Cheryl Burke, won TV's *Dancing With The Stars* second season.

8/23/97	145	9	●	1 98°	Cat:#24/2	Motown 530796
11/14/98+	14	78	▲⁴	2 98° And Rising..		Motown 530956
11/6/99	27	12		3 This Christmas .... Cat:#7/9 [X]		Universal 153918
				Christmas charts: 2/'99, 2/'00		
10/14/00	2¹	24	▲²	4 Revelation		Universal 159354
5/25/02	153	1		5 The Collection .... [G]		Universal 017402

95 SOUTH
Hip-hop/bass duo from Jacksonville, Florida: Artice "AB" Bartley and Carlos "Daddy Black" Spencer.

5/15/93	71	26		1 Quad City Knock		Toy 8117
2/18/95	158	2		2 One Mo' 'Gen		Rip-It 9501

9TH WONDER & BUCKSHOT
Male rap duo: Pat "9th Wonder" Douthit and Kenyatta "Buckshot" Blake. Douthit was a member of **Little Brother**. Blake was a member of **Black Moon**.

5/17/08	137	1		1 The Formula		Duck Down 2070

NIRVANA   1990s: #23 / All-Time: #243
Grunge-rock trio from Aberdeen, Washington: Kurt Cobain (vocals, guitar; born on 2/20/1967), Krist Novoselic (bass; born on 5/16/1965) and Dave Grohl (drums; born on 1/14/1969). Cobain married **Courtney Love** (lead singer of **Hole**) on 2/24/1992. Cobain died of a self-inflicted gunshot wound on 4/5/1994 (age 27). Grohl formed **Foo Fighters** in 1995.

1/4/92	89	20	▲	1 Bleach	Cat:❶²/73	Sub Pop 34
				first album; released in June 1989		
10/12/91+	❶²	252	▲¹⁰	2 Nevermind	Cat:#15/64	DGC 24425
				RS500 #17 ★ NRR		
10/9/93	❶¹	87	▲⁵	3 In Utero	Cat:#48/1	DGC 24607
				RS500 #439		
				GREATEST HITS & COMPILATIONS:		
1/2/93	39	25	▲	4 Incesticide .... Cat:#43/2		DGC 24504
				early recordings on independent labels, unreleased demos and performances on British radio broadcasts		
11/16/02	3¹	31	▲	5 Nirvana	Cat:#26/12	DGC 493507

DEBUT	PEAK	WKS	R I A A	ARTIST Album Title	Catalog	Label & Number

NIRVANA — cont'd

DEBUT	PEAK	WKS	R I A A	Album Title	Catalog	Label & Number
12/11/04	19	9	▲	6 With The Lights Out		DGC 003727 [3]
11/19/05	21	12		7 Sliver: The Best Of The Box		Geffen 005617

LIVE ALBUMS:

11/19/94	❶¹	81	▲⁵	8 MTV Unplugged In New York Cat:#23/3	DGC 24727
				Grammy: Alternative Album ★ RS500 #311 recorded on 11/18/1993	
10/19/96	❶¹	21	▲	9 From The Muddy Banks Of The Wishkah	DGC 25105
				recorded from various performances between December 1989 and January 1994	
11/21/09	37	2		10 Live At Reading	DGC 013503

NITE CITY
Rock band formed in Los Angeles, California: Noah James (vocals), Paul Warren (guitar), **Ray Manzarek** (keyboards; **The Doors**), Nigel Harrison (bass; **Blondie**) and Jimmy Hunter (drums).

| 4/2/77 | 204 | 5 | | 1 Nite City.................................... | 20th Century 528 |

NITRO
Hard-rock band from Los Angeles, California: Jim Gillette (vocals), Michael Angelo (guitar), Anthony "T.J. Racer" Brehmer (bass) and Bobby Rock (drums). Gillette married **Lita Ford** on 5/13/1994.

| 8/12/89 | 140 | 9 | | 1 O.F.R. .... | Rhino 70894 |

NITTY GRITTY DIRT BAND
Country-folk-rock band from Long Beach, California. Led by Jeff Hanna (vocals, guitar) and John McEuen (banjo, mandolin). Changed name to **Dirt Band** in 1976. Resumed using Nitty Gritty Dirt Band name in 1982. Various members included Jimmie Fadden (harmonica), Jim Ibbotson (guitar), Al Garth (violin) and **Bernie Leadon**, who replaced McEuen briefly in early 1987. In the movies *For Singles Only* and *Paint Your Wagon*. Hanna married country singer/songwriter Matraca Berg.

4/8/67	151	8		1 The Nitty Gritty Dirt Band		Liberty 7501
12/5/70+	66	32		2 Uncle Charlie & His Dog Teddy		Liberty 7642
2/5/72	162	10		3 All The Good Times		United Artists 5553
12/30/72+	68	32	▲	4 Will The Circle Be Unbroken..................... Cat:#21/2		United Artists 9801 [3]
				Grammy: Hall of Fame ★ NRR	
7/13/74	28	21		5 Stars & Stripes Forever [L]		United Artists 184 [2]
10/4/75	66	9		6 Dream		United Artists 469
12/18/76+	77	13		7 Dirt, Silver & Gold .... [K]		United Artists 670 [3]
7/8/78	163	6		8 The Dirt Band		United Artists 854
1/26/80	76	14		9 An American Dream		United Artists 974
7/19/80	62	16		10 Make A Little Magic		United Artists 1042
9/5/81	102	9		11 Jealousy		Liberty 1106
				THE DIRT BAND (above 4)	
5/27/89	95	12		12 Will The Circle Be Unbroken, Volume II		Universal 12500 [2]
				Grammy: Country Vocal Group ★ CMA: Album of the Year	
10/19/02	134	5		13 Will The Circle Be Unbroken, Volume III		Capitol 40177 [2]

NITZER EBB
Industrial-rock duo from Chelmsford, Essex, England: Douglas McCarthy and Bon Harris.

| 11/16/91 | 146 | 2 | | 1 Ebbhead .... | Geffen 24456 |

NITZINGER
Rock trio from Texas: John Nitzinger (vocals, guitar), Linda Waring (vocals, drums) and Curly Benton (bass).

| 9/2/72 | 170 | 8 | | 1 Nitzinger..................................... | Capitol 11091 |

NITZSCHE, Jack
Born Bernard Nitzsche on 4/22/1937 in Chicago, Illinois. Died of heart failure on 8/25/2000 (age 63). Arranger/producer.

~ ~ ~ ~ ~ ~ ~ ~ ~ ~   *NON-CHARTED ALBUM*   ~ ~ ~ ~ ~ ~ ~ ~ ~ ~ ~
1963 The Lonely Surfer

NIVEA
Born Nivea Hamilton on 3/24/1982 in Atlanta, Georgia. Female R&B singer. Married to **The-Dream** from 2004-07.

| 12/28/02+ | 80 | 18 | | 1 Nivea..................................... | Jive 41746 |
| 5/21/05 | 37 | 6 | | 2 Complicated..................................... | Jive 67156 |

NIX, Don
Born on 9/27/1941 in Memphis, Tennessee. Singer/guitarist/saxophonist. Also see **The Alabama State Troupers**.

| 1/9/71 | 204 | 1 | | 1 In God We Trust .... | Shelter 8902 |
| 9/11/71 | 197 | 3 | | 2 Living By The Days .... | Elektra 74101 |

NIXON, Mojo, & Skid Roper
Novelty-rock duo. Nixon (vocals, guitar) was born Neill Kirby McMillan on 8/2/1957 in Chapel Hill, North Carolina. Roper (washboard, bass) was born Richard Banke on 10/19/1954 in National City, California. Split in early 1990. Nixon appeared in the 1989 movie *Great Balls Of Fire*.

| 10/10/87 | 189 | 2 | | 1 Bo-Day-Shus!!! .... [N] | Enigma 73272 |
| 5/6/89 | 151 | 7 | | 2 Root Hog Or Die .... [N] | Enigma 73335 |

NIXONS, The
Rock band from Dallas, Texas: Zac Maloy (vocals, guitar), Jesse Davis (guitar), Ricky Brooks (bass) and John Humphrey (drums).

| 3/30/96 | 77 | 23 | | 1 Foma..................................... | MCA 11209 |
| 7/12/97 | 188 | 1 | | 2 The Nixons .... | MCA 11644 |

NKOTB — see NEW KIDS ON THE BLOCK

NO AGE
Alternative-rock duo from Los Angeles, California: Randy Randall and Dean Spunt.

5/24/08	196	1		1 Nouns		Sub Pop 772

NOBLES, Cliff, & Co.
Born on 8/4/1941 in Mobile, Alabama. Died on 10/12/2008 (age 67). R&B bandleader/singer.

| 9/21/68 | 159 | 3 | | 1 The Horse.. | | Phil-L.A. of Soul 4001 |

NOBODY'S ANGEL
Interracial female vocal group from Los Angeles, California: Amy Harding, Sarah Smith, Stacey Harper and Ali Navarro.

| 4/1/00 | 184 | 3 | | 1 Nobody's Angel .... | | Hollywood 62184 |

NOCKELS, Christy
Born in Fort Worth, Texas; raised in Oklahoma City, Oklahoma. Contemporary Christian singer/songwriter.

| 6/20/09 | 136 | 1 | | 1 Life Light Up .... | | Sixsteps 93260 |

NO DOUBT
Ska-rock band from Orange County, California: **Gwen Stefani** (vocals; born on 10/3/1969), Tom Dumont (guitar; born on 1/11/1968), Tony Kanal (bass; born on 8/27/1970) and Adrian Young (drums; born on 8/26/1969). Stefani married Gavin Rossdale (lead singer of **Bush**) on 9/14/2002.

1/20/96	❶[9]	90	▲[10]	1 Tragic Kingdom	Cat:#4/42	Trauma 92580
				RS500 #441		
4/29/00	2[1]	46	▲	2 Return Of Saturn		Trauma 490441
12/29/01	9	76	▲[2]	3 Rock Steady		Interscope 493158
				RS500 #316		
12/13/03	2[1]	45	▲[2]	4 The Singles 1992-2003	Cat:#7/2 [G]	Interscope 001495
10/30/04	182	1		5 Everything In Time (B-Sides, Rarities, Remixes) .... [K]		Interscope 003289

NOEL
Born Noel Pagan in the Bronx, New York. Male Latin-disco singer.

| 10/22/88 | 126 | 13 | | 1 Noel .... | | 4th & B'way 4009 |

NOFX
Punk-rock band formed in Los Angeles, California: "Fat Mike" Burkett (vocals, bass), Eric Melvin (guitar), Aaron "El Hefe" Abeyta (guitar), and Erik Sandin (drums). Burkett was also a member of **Me First And The Gimme Gimmes**.

9/9/95	198	1		1 I Heard They Suck Live!! .... [L]	Fat Wreck Chords 528
2/17/96	63	4		2 Heavy Petting Zoo	Epitaph 86457
11/29/97	79	2		3 So Long And Thanks For All The Shoes..	Epitaph 86518
12/11/99	200	1		4 The Decline .... [EP]	Fat Wreck Chords 605
7/1/00	61	6		5 Pump Up The Valuum	Epitaph 86584
3/23/02	147	1		6 The BYO Split Series / Volume III	BYO 079
				NOFX / RANCID	
6/8/02	80	3		7 45 Or 46 Songs That Weren't Good Enough To Go On Our Other Records .. [K]	Fat Wreck Chords 641 [2]
4/12/03	187	1		8 Regaining Unconsciousness.. [EP]	Fat Wreck Chords 656
5/24/03	44	6		9 The War On Errorism	Fat Wreck Chords 657
4/1/06	186	1		10 Never Trust A Hippy .... [EP]	Fat Wreck Chords 708
5/6/06	46	3		11 Wolves In Wolves' Clothing	Fat Wreck Chords 711
5/16/09	36	5		12 Coaster	Fat Wreck Chords 737

NOISETTES
Alternative-rock trio from London, England: Shingai Shoniwa (vocals, bass), Dan Smith (guitar) and Jamie Morrison (drums).

| 10/10/09 | 98 | 3 | | 1 Wild Young Hearts .... | | Mercury 013227 |

NOLAN, Kenny
Born in Los Angeles, California. Pop singer/songwriter.

| 3/26/77 | 78 | 16 | | 1 Kenny Nolan .... | | 20th Century 532 |

NO MERCY
Male vocal trio: brothers Ariel Hernandez and Gabriel Hernandez (from Florida), with Marty Cintron (from New York).

| 11/30/96+ | 104 | 22 | ● | 1 No Mercy .... | | Arista 18941 |

NONCHALANT
Born Tanya Pointer in Washington DC. Female singer/rapper.

| 5/11/96 | 94 | 6 | | 1 Until The Day .... | | MCA 11265 |

NONPOINT
Rock band from Miami, Florida: Elias Soriano (vocals), Andrew Goldman (guitar), KB (bass) and Robb Rivera (drums).

6/2/01	166	1		1 Statement...	MCA 112364
7/13/02	52	3		2 Development...	MCA 112920
8/21/04	115	1		3 Recoil	Lava 93303
11/26/05	147	1		4 To The Pain	Bieler Bros. 70007
11/24/07	129	1		5 Vengeance	Bieler Bros. 70021

NO QUESTION
R&B vocal group from Philadelphia, Pennsylvania: Damon Core, Nicholas Johnson, Thomas Blackwell and Dante Massey.

10/7/00	178	1	1 No Question		RuffNation 47750

NORDEMAN, Nichole
Born on 1/3/1972 in Colorado Springs, Colorado. Contemporary Christian singer/songwriter/pianist.

10/12/02	136	8	1 Woven & Spun		Sparrow 51934
6/11/05	119	3	2 Brave		Sparrow 63575

NOREAGA
Born Victor Santiago on 9/6/1977 in Queens, New York. Male rapper. One-half of **Capone-N-Noreaga** duo.

7/25/98	3¹	19	● 1 N.O.R.E.		Penalty 3077
9/11/99	9	11	● 2 Melvin Flynt - Da Hustler		Penalty 3097
7/13/02	3¹	16	3 God's Favorite		Def Jam 586502
9/30/06	82	2	4 N.O.R.E. Y La Familia...Ya Tu Sabe .... [F]		Roc-La-Familia 006266
			N.O.R.E. (above 2)		

NORFUL, Smokie
Born William Norful on 2/25/1977 in Little Rock, Arkansas; raised in Muskogee, Oklahoma. Gospel singer/songwriter/organist.

3/8/03	154	9	● 1 I Need You Now		EMI Gospel 20374
11/8/03	90	4	2 Smokie Norful: Limited Edition		EMI Gospel 95086
10/23/04	57	6	● 3 Nothing Without You		EMI Gospel 77795
10/21/06	56	5	4 Life Changing		EMI Gospel 33347
4/25/09	55	6	5 Live .... [L]		TreMyles 12832

NORMA JEAN
Born Norma Jean Wright in Elyria, Ohio. R&B singer. Former member of **Chic**.

8/26/78	134	11	1 Norma Jean		Bearsville 6983

NORMA JEAN
Christian hard-rock band from Douglasville, Georgia: Cory Putman (vocals), Scott Henry (guitar), Chris Day (guitar), Jake Schultz (bass) and Dan Davison (drums).

3/19/05	62	2	1 O' God, The Aftermath		Solid State 75392
9/30/06	38	3	2 Redeemer		Tooth & Nail 63560
8/23/08	29	3	3 Norma Jean vs. The Anti Mother		Solid State 08327

NORMAN, Bebo
Born Jeffrey Norman on 5/29/1973 in Columbus, Georgia. Male Christian singer/songwriter/guitarist.

6/2/01	141	1	1 Big Blue Sky		Watershed 10550
9/28/02	114	1	2 Myself When I Am Real		Essential 10691
9/11/04	159	1	3 Try		Essential 0724
10/7/06	187	1	4 Between The Dreaming And The Coming True		Essential 10799
10/20/07	5ˣ	2	5 Christmas: From The Realms Of Glory [X]		BEC 01270

NORMAN, Jessye — see BATTLE, Kathleen

NORTH, Freddie
Born on 5/28/1939 in Nashville, Tennessee. R&B singer/songwriter/guitarist.

1/1/72	179	5	1 Friend		Mankind 204

NORTH MISSISSIPPI ALLSTARS
Blues-rock trio from Hernando, Mississippi: brothers Luther Dickinson (vocals, guitar) and Cody Dickinson (drums), with Chris Chew (bass).

9/24/05	180	1	1 Electric Blue Watermelon		ATO 21541
2/9/08	142	1	2 Hernando		Songs Of The South 006

NO SECRETS
Female teen pop vocal group from Florida: Angel Faith, Jessica Fried, Erin Tanner, Jade Gaspar and Carly Lewis.

8/24/02	136	3	1 No Secrets		Jive 41781

NOTHINGFACE
Hard-rock band from Washington DC: Matt Holt (vocals), Tom Maxwell (guitar), Bill Gaal (bass) and Chris Houck (drums). Maxwell later joined **HellYeah**.

5/10/03	125	1	1 Skeletons		TVT 5980

NOTORIOUS B.I.G., The
Born Christopher Wallace on 5/21/1972 in Brooklyn, New York. Shot to death on 3/9/1997 (age 24). Male rapper. Also known as Biggy Smallz. Married to singer **Faith Evans** from 1994-97 (his death). Jamal Woolard played Wallace in the 2009 biographical movie *Notorious*.

10/1/94	15	59	▲⁴ 1 Ready To Die Cat:❶⁷/55		Bad Boy 73000
			RS500 #133		
4/5/97	❶⁴	79	▲¹⁰ 2 Life After Death Cat:#22/4		Bad Boy 73011 [2]
			RS500 #483		
12/25/99	❶¹	22	▲² 3 Born Again		Bad Boy 73023
1/7/06	3¹	20	▲ 4 Duets: The Final Chapter		Bad Boy 83885
3/24/07	❶¹	13	5 Greatest Hits Cat:#16/3 [G]		Bad Boy 101830

Billboard DEBUT	PEAK	WKS	R I A A	ARTIST / Album Title	Catalog	Label & Number

NOTORIOUS CHERRY BOMBS, The
All-star country band: **Rodney Crowell** (vocals, guitar), **Vince Gill** (vocals, banjo), Richard Bennett (guitar), Hank DeVito (steel guitar), Tony Brown (piano), John Hobbs (organ), Michael Rhodes (bass) and Eddie Bayers (drums)

8/14/04	135	7		1 The Notorious Cherry Bombs	Universal South 002530

NOTTING HILLBILLIES, The
Band of rock guitarists: **Mark Knopfler** and Guy Fletcher (both of **Dire Straits**), with Brendan Croker and Steve Phillips. Recorded at Knopfler's studio in London's Notting Hill Gate.

3/31/90	52	13		1 Missing...Presumed Having A Good Time	Warner 26147

NOVA, Aldo
Born Aldo Caporuscio on 11/13/1956 in Montreal, Quebec, Canada. Rock singer/songwriter/guitarist.

2/20/82	8	37	▲²	1 Aldo Nova	Portrait 37498
10/15/83	56	20	●	2 Subject: Aldo Nova	Portrait 38721
6/8/91	124	7		3 Blood On The Bricks..	Jambco 848513

NOVA, Heather
Born on 7/6/1968 on an island in the Bermuda Sound. Raised on a 40-foot sailboat in the Caribbean. Later settled in London, England. Adult Alternative singer/songwriter.

11/4/95	179	4		1 Oyster..	Big Cat 67113
10/24/98	176	1		2 Siren..	Big Cat 67953

NOVO COMBO
Rock band formed in New York: Pete Hewlett (vocals), Jack Griffith (guitar), Stephen Dees (bass) and **Michael Shrieve** (drums; **Santana**).

10/10/81	167	6		1 Novo Combo..	Polydor 6331
9/25/82	207	2		2 The Animation Generation	Polydor 6356

NOX ARCANA
Classical-rock duo from Cleveland, Ohio: Joseph Vargo and William Piotrowski.

1/27/07	8ˣ	3		1 Winter's Knight [X]	Monolith Graphics 1003
				Christmas charts: 8/'06, 14/'07	

NRBQ
Blues-rock band formed in Miami, Florida: Frank Gadler (vocals), Steve Ferguson (guitar), Terry Adams (keyboards), Joey Spampinato (bass) and Tom Staley (drums). Lineup in 1990: Adams and Spampinato, with Al Anderson (vocals, guitar) and Tom Ardolino (drums). NRBQ: New Rhythm and Blues Quintet/Quartet. Spampinato was married to **Skeeter Davis** from 1983-96.

7/19/69	162	4		1 NRBQ...	Columbia 9858
5/28/83	202	3		2 Grooves In Orbit	Bearsville 23817
1/6/90	198	2		3 Wild Weekend	Virgin 91291

*NSYNC
"Boy band" formed in Orlando, Florida, three years after manager Lou Pearlman signed the **Backstreet Boys**. Members were Chris Kirkpatrick (born on 10/17/1971), Josh **"JC" Chasez** (born on 8/8/1976), Joey Fatone (born on 1/28/1977), **Justin Timberlake** (born on 1/31/1981) and Lance Bass (born on 5/4/1979). Timberlake and Chasez were regulars on TV's *The Mickey Mouse Club*. Fatone appeared in the 2002 movie *My Big Fat Greek Wedding* and finished second on season 4 of *Dancing With The Stars*. Bass finished third on season 7 of *Dancing With The Stars*.

4/11/98	2³	109	▲¹⁰	1 *NSYNC Cat:#3/52	RCA 67613
11/28/98	7	10	▲²	2 Home For Christmas Cat:❶³/29 [X]	RCA 67726
				Christmas charts: 2/'98, 6/'99, 3/'00, 11/'01	
4/8/00	❶⁸	82	▲¹¹	3 No Strings Attached	Jive 41702
8/11/01	❶¹	43	▲⁵	4 Celebrity	Jive 41758
11/12/05	47	4		5 Greatest Hits... [G]	Jive 73307

N2DEEP
White rap duo from Vallejo, California: Jay Trujilo and T.L. Lyon.

7/11/92	55	37	●	1 Back To The Hotel..	Profile 1427

NUCLEAR ASSAULT
Hard-rock band formed in New York: John Connelly (vocals, guitar), Anthony Bramante (guitar), Danny Lilker (bass; **Anthrax**) and Glenn Evans (drums).

8/13/88	145	11		1 Survive	I.R.S. 42195
11/18/89+	126	24		2 Handle With Care	In-Effect 3010

NUCLEAR VALDEZ
Rock group from Miami, Florida: Froilan Sosa (vocals), Jorge Barcala (guitar), Juan Diaz (bass) and Robert LeMont (drums).

2/24/90	175	5		1 I Am I	Epic 45354

NUGENT, Ted   **All-Time: #300**
Born on 12/13/1948 in Detroit, Michigan. Hard-rock singer/guitarist. Leader of **The Amboy Dukes**. Later joined **Damn Yankees**. An avid game hunter and an active supporter of the National Rifle Association. Nicknamed "The Motor City Madman." Had own *Surviving Nugent* reality TV show.

11/22/75+	28	62	▲²	1 Ted Nugent	Epic 33692
10/2/76	24	32	▲²	2 Free-For-All	Epic 34121
6/25/77	17	39	▲³	3 Cat Scratch Fever	Epic 34700
2/11/78	13	22	▲³	4 Double Live Gonzo! .... [L]	Epic 35069 [2]
11/11/78	24	20	▲	5 Weekend Warriors..	Epic 35551
6/2/79	18	18	●	6 State Of Shock..	Epic 36000

Billboard			R I A A	ARTIST Album Title	Catalog	Label & Number
DEBUT	**PEAK**	**WKS**				
				NUGENT, Ted — cont'd		
5/31/80	13	18	●	7 Scream Dream		Epic 36404
3/21/81	51	10		8 Intensities In 10 Cities .... [L]		Epic 37084
11/28/81	140	8	▲²	9 Great Gonzos! The Best Of Ted Nugent .... Cat:#47/1 [G]		Epic 37667
7/17/82	51	14		10 Nugent		Atlantic 19365
2/18/84	56	15		11 Penetrator		Atlantic 80125
3/22/86	76	14		12 Little Miss Dangerous		Atlantic 81632
3/5/88	112	7		13 If You Can't Lick 'Em...Lick 'Em		Atlantic 81812
5/20/95	86	4		14 Spirit Of The Wild		Atlantic 82611
9/22/07	186	1		15 Love Grenade		Eagle 20119
				NUMAN, Gary Born Gary Webb on 3/8/1958 in Hammersmith, England. Synthesized techno-rock artist.		
9/15/79	124	10		1 Replicas .... GARY NUMAN & TUBEWAY ARMY		Atco 117
2/2/80	16	30		2 The Pleasure Principle		Atco 120
10/4/80	64	10		3 Telekon		Atco 103
7/25/81	204	1		4 First Album .... TUBEWAY ARMY FEATURING GARY NUMAN		Atco 106
10/24/81	167	4		5 Dance		Atco 143
10/23/82	201	4		6 I, Assassin		Atco 90014
				NUNN, Bobby Born in Buffalo, New York. R&B singer/songwriter/keyboardist.		
10/23/82	148	8		1 Second To Nunn		Motown 6022
				NU SHOOZ Husband-and-wife duo from Portland, Oregon: John Smith and Valerie Day.		
5/31/86	27	32	●	1 Poolside		Atlantic 81647
4/23/88	93	14		2 Told U So		Atlantic 81804
				NUTINI, Paolo Born on 1/9/1987 in Paisley, Scotland. Male singer/songwriter.		
2/17/07	48	21		1 These Streets		Atlantic 94634
6/20/09	57	2		2 Sunny Side Up		Atlantic 519282
				N.W.A. Rap group from Los Angeles, California: Eric "**Eazy-E**" Wright, Lorenzo "**M.C. Ren**" Patterson, Andre "**Dr. Dre**" Young, O'Shea "**Ice Cube**" Jackson (left by 1990) and DJ Antoine "**Yella**" Carraby. N.W.A.: Niggaz With Attitude. Eazy-E died of AIDS on 3/26/1995 (age 31). Also see **Various Artists Compilations: N.W.A. - Straight Outta Compton - 10th Anniversary Tribute** and *The N.W.A. Legacy Volume 1 1988-1998*.		
3/4/89	37	81	▲²	1 Straight Outta Compton .... Cat:#39/6 RS500 #144		Ruthless 57102
9/1/90	27	25	▲	2 100 Miles And Runnin' .... [EP]		Ruthless 7224
6/15/91	❶¹	44	▲	3 EFIL4ZAGGIN title actually appears on album as an inverse image of NIGGAZ4LIFE		Ruthless 57126
7/20/96	48	12	●	4 Greatest Hits .... Cat:#50/1 [G]		Ruthless 50561
1/13/07	143	1		5 The Best Of N.W.A.: The Strength Of Street Knowledge .... [G]		Ruthless 77716
				NYLONS, The Acapella group formed in Toronto, Ontario, Canada: Marc Connors, Paul Cooper, Claude Morrison and Arnold Robinson. Connors died on 3/25/1991 (age 41).		
3/29/86	133	16		1 Seamless		Open Air 0304
5/23/87	43	24		2 Happy Together		Open Air 0306
6/10/89	136	10		3 Rockapella		Windham Hill 1085
				NYMAN, Michael Born on 3/23/1944 in London, England. New Age pianist/composer.		
1/22/94	41	34	●	1 The Piano .... [I-S]		Virgin 88274
				NYRO, Laura Born Laura Nigro on 10/18/1947 in the Bronx, New York. Died of cancer on 4/8/1997 (age 49). Singer/prolific songwriter.		
8/10/68	181	7		1 Eli And The Thirteenth Confession		Columbia 9626
11/1/69	32	17		2 New York Tendaberry		Columbia 9737
12/26/70+	51	14		3 Christmas And The Beads Of Sweat		Columbia 30259
12/25/71+	46	17		4 Gonna Take A Miracle		Columbia 30987
2/3/73	97	11		5 The First Songs .... [E] reissue of *More Than A New Discovery* (see non-charted album below)		Columbia 31410
3/13/76	60	14		6 Smile		Columbia 33912
7/2/77	137	5		7 Season of Lights...Laura Nyro in Concert .... [L]		Columbia 34786
8/19/78	209	1		8 Nested		Columbia 35449
3/10/84	182	3		9 Mother's Spiritual		Columbia 39215

~ ~ ~ ~ ~ ~ ~ ~ ~ ~ **NON-CHARTED ALBUM** ~ ~ ~ ~ ~ ~ ~ ~ ~ ~ ~
1966 **More Than A New Discovery**
Grammy: Hall of Fame

Billboard			R I A A	ARTIST		
DEBUT	PEAK	WKS		Album Title	Catalog	Label & Number

O

OAKENFOLD, Paul
Born on 8/30/1963 in London, England. Dance DJ/remixer.

10/21/00	114	5		1 Perfecto Presents Another World		Sire 31035 [2]
6/23/01	102	6		2 Swordfish (The Album)	[I-S]	Warner Sunset 31169
7/6/02	65	12		3 Bunkka		Maverick 48204
8/28/04	180	1		4 Creamfields		Perfecto 90724 [2]
6/24/06	145	1		5 A Lively Mind		Maverick 49900
7/25/09	66	1		6 Perfecto: Vegas		Perfecto 90819 [2]

OAKEY, Philip
Born on 10/2/1955 in Hinckley, Leicestershire, England. Leader of **The Human League**.

8/24/85	201	1		1 Philip Oakey & Giorgio Moroder		A&M 5080

OAK RIDGE BOYS
Country vocal group formed in Oak Ridge, Tennessee: Duane Allen (lead; born on 4/29/1943), Joe Bonsall (tenor; born on 5/18/1948), William Lee Golden (baritone; born on 1/12/1939) and Richard Sterban (bass; born on 4/24/1943).
AWARD: CMA: Vocal Group 1978

2/18/78	120	9	●	1 Y'all Come Back Saloon		ABC/Dot 2093
6/17/78	164	11	●	2 Room Service		ABC 1065
3/29/80	154	6	●	3 Together		MCA 3220
11/22/80	99	21	▲	4 Greatest Hits	[G]	MCA 5150
6/13/81	14	48	▲²	5 Fancy Free		MCA 5209
2/20/82	20	21	●	6 Bobbie Sue		MCA 5294
12/4/82+	73	7	●	7 Christmas	[X]	MCA 5365
2/26/83	51	23	●	8 American Made		MCA 5390
11/19/83	121	14	●	9 Deliver		MCA 5455
9/8/84	71	24	▲	10 Greatest Hits 2	[G]	MCA 5496
4/20/85	156	5		11 Step On Out		MCA 5555
5/9/09	156	1		12 A Gospel Journey	[L]	Gaither 42793
6/6/09	77	1		13 The Boys Are Back		Spring Hill 21145

OAKS BAKER, Jenny
Born in 1975 in Salt Lake City, Utah. Female violinist.

10/20/07	24ˣ	1		1 O Holy Night	[X]	Shadow Mtn. 4988155

OAKTOWN'S 3.5.7
Female rap group from Oakland, California: Djuana Johnican, Tabatha King, Vicious C and Sweet Pea.

5/13/89	126	16		1 Wild & Loose		Capitol 90926

O.A.R.
Pop-rock band from Columbus, Ohio: Marc Roberge (vocals, guitar), Richard On (guitar), Jerry DePizzo (sax), Benj Gershman (bass) and Chris Culos (drums). O.A.R.: Of A Revolution.

6/14/03	54	5		1 In Between Now And Then		Everfine 83643
10/22/05	40	3		2 Stories Of A Stranger		Everfine 94109
8/2/08	13	18		3 All Sides		Everfine 511179
				LIVE ALBUMS:		
5/25/02	156	1	●	4 Any Time Now		Everfine 41123 [2]
9/11/04	80	1		5 34th & 8th		Everfine 40713 [2]
6/23/07	69	1		6 Live From Madison Square Garden		Everfine 170108
5/2/09	180	1		7 Hello, Tomorrow	[EP]	Everfine digital

OASIS   **All-Time: #495**
Rock band from Manchester, England: brothers Liam Gallagher (vocals; born on 9/21/1972) and Noel Gallagher (guitar; born on 5/29/1967), with Paul Arthurs (guitar; born on 6/23/1965), Paul McGuigan (bass; born on 5/9/1971) and Tony McCarroll (drums). Alan White (born on 5/26/1972) replaced McCarroll in 1995.

2/11/95	58	20	▲	1 Definitely Maybe		Epic 66431
10/21/95+	4	76	▲⁴	2 (What's The Story) Morning Glory?		Epic 67351
				RS500 #376		
9/13/97	2¹	26	▲	3 Be Here Now		Epic 68530
11/21/98	51	2		4 The Masterplan		Epic 69647
3/18/00	24	8		5 Standing On The Shoulder Of Giants		Epic 63586
12/9/00	182	1		6 Familiar To Millions	[L]	Epic 85267 [2]
				recorded on 7/21/2000 at Wembley Stadium		
7/20/02	23	5		7 Heathen Chemistry		Epic 86586
6/18/05	12	7		8 Don't Believe The Truth		Epic 94493
12/9/06	89	1		9 Stop The Clocks (Best Of)	[G]	Epic 00754 [2]
10/25/08	5	5		10 Dig Out Your Soul		Big Brother 514078

O'BANION, John
Born on 2/16/1947 in Kokomo, Indiana. Died of injuries suffered in a fall on 2/14/2007 (age 59). Pop singer.

5/16/81	164	4		1 John O'Banion		Elektra 342

OBERNKIRCHEN CHILDREN'S CHOIR, The
Choir of children from Obernkirchen, Germany. Founded and conducted by Edith Moeller in 1950.

12/25/65	50^X	1		1 **Christmas Songs** .... [X-F] · Angel 35914

O'BRYAN
Born O'Bryan Burnett on 12/5/1961 in Burgaw, North Carolina. Male R&B singer.

4/10/82	80	12		1 **Doin' Alright** .... · Capitol 12192
3/12/83	87	27		2 **You And I** .... · Capitol 12256
5/26/84	64	21		3 **Be My Lover** .... · Capitol 12332

O.C.
Born Omar Credle on 5/13/1971 in Brooklyn, New York. Male rapper.

9/6/97	90	4		1 **Jewelz** .... · Payday 524399

OCASEK, Ric
Born Richard Otcasek on 3/23/1949 in Baltimore, Maryland. Lead singer/guitarist/songwriter of **The Cars**. Appeared in the 1987 movie *Made In Heaven*. Married supermodel/actress Paulina Porizkova on 8/23/1989.

1/29/83	28	16		1 **Beatitude** .... · Geffen 2022
10/11/86	31	23		2 **This Side Of Paradise** .... · Geffen 24098

OCEAN
Pop band from London, Ontario, Canada: Janice Morgan (vocals), David Tamblyn (guitar), Greg Brown (keyboards), Jeff Jones (bass) and Charles Slater (drums).

5/29/71	60	13		1 **Put Your Hand In The Hand** .... · Kama Sutra 2033

OCEAN, Billy
Born Leslie Sebastian Charles on 1/21/1950 in Trinidad, West Indies; raised in England. R&B-pop singer.

7/25/81	152	3		1 **Nights (Feel Like Getting Down)** .... · Epic 37406
8/25/84	9	86	▲²	2 **Suddenly** · Jive 8213
5/17/86	6	48	▲²	3 **Love Zone** · Jive 8409
3/19/88	18	31	▲	4 **Tear Down These Walls** .... · Jive 8495
11/4/89	77	16	▲	5 **Greatest Hits** .... [G] · Jive 1271

OCEAN BLUE, The
Pop-rock band formed in Hershey, Pennsylvania: Dave Schelzel (vocals, guitar), Steve Lau (keyboards), Bobby Mittan (bass) and Rob Minnig (drums).

2/3/90	155	8		1 **The Ocean Blue** .... · Sire 25906

OCHS, Phil
Born on 12/19/1940 in El Paso, Texas. Committed suicide on 4/9/1976 (age 35). Folk singer/songwriter.

7/9/66	149	2		1 **Phil Ochs In Concert** .... [L] · Elektra 7310
12/9/67	168	5		2 **Pleasures Of The Harbor** .... · A&M 4133
6/14/69	167	7		3 **Rehearsals For Retirement** .... · A&M 4181
3/14/70	194	2		4 **Phil Ochs Greatest Hits** .... · A&M 4253
				album contains all new recordings
1/15/77	210	1		5 **Chords Of Fame** .... [K] · A&M 4599 [2]

O'CONNOR, Carroll
Born on 8/2/1924 in Manhattan, New York; raised in Forest Hills, New York. Died of a heart attack on 6/21/2001 (age 76). TV/movie actor. Acted in several movies. Played "Archie Bunker" on TV's *All In The Family* and "Chief Bill Gillespie" on *In The Heat Of The Night*.

6/17/72	118	13		1 **Remembering You** .... · A&M 4340

O'CONNOR, Hazel
Born on 5/16/1955 in Coventry, England. Female singer/actress. Starred in the 1980 movie *Breaking Glass*.

9/13/80	202	8		1 **Breaking Glass** .... [S] · A&M 4820

O'CONNOR, Mark
Born on 8/5/1961 in Seattle, Washington. Country fiddle player. Former member of the **Dixie Dregs**.
AWARD: CMA: Musician 1991, 1992, 1993, 1994, 1995 & 1996

4/22/00	170	2		1 **Appalachian Journey** .... [I] · Sony Classical 66782
				YO-YO MA / EDGAR MEYER / MARK O'CONNOR

O'CONNOR, Sinead
Born on 12/8/1966 in Dublin, Ireland. Alternative-pop singer/songwriter.

2/6/88	36	38	●	1 **The Lion And The Cobra** .... · Chrysalis 41612
4/7/90	❶⁶	52	▲²	2 **I Do Not Want What I Haven't Got** · Ensign 21759
				Grammy: Alternative Album ★ RS500 #406
10/10/92	27	9		3 **Am I Not Your Girl?** .... · Ensign 21952
10/1/94	36	8		4 **Universal Mother** .... · Ensign 30549
6/21/97	128	3		5 **Gospel Oak EP** .... [EP] · Chrysalis 58651
7/1/00	55	11		6 **Faith And Courage** .... · Atlantic 83337
10/26/02	139	2		7 **Sean-Nos Nua** .... · Vanguard 79724
7/14/07	168	1		8 **Theology** .... · Koch 4237 [2]

OC SUPERTONES
Christian ska-rock band from Orange County, California: Matt Morginsky (vocals), Brian Johnson (guitar), Dan Spencer, Dave Chevalier and Darrin Mettler (horns), Tony Terusa (bass) and Jason Carson (drums). OC: Orange County.

6/21/97	117	6		1 Supertones Strike Back		BEC 17401
3/13/99	95	5		2 Chase The Sun		BEC 17415
10/28/00	168	1		3 Loud And Clear		BEC 17440

OCTOBER PROJECT
Folk-pop band from New Jersey: Mary Fahl (vocals), Marina Belica (vocals, keyboards), David Sabatino (guitar), Emil Adler (piano) and Julie Flanders (lyricist).

10/7/95	184	1		1 Falling Farther In		Epic 67019

O'DAY, Alan
Born on 10/3/1940 in Hollywood, California. Singer/songwriter/pianist.

9/3/77	109	9		1 Appetizers		Pacific 4300

ODETTA
Born Odetta Holmes on 12/31/1930 in Birmingham, Alabama; raised in Los Angeles, California. Died of heart failure on 12/2/2008 (age 77). Black folk singer.

9/28/63	75	8		1 Odetta Sings Folk Songs		RCA Victor 2643

O'DONIS, Colby
Born Colby O'Donis Colon on 3/14/1989 in Queens, New York (Puerto Rican parents). Male R&B/hip-hop singer/songwriter.

10/4/08	41	2		1 Colby O		Konlive 011290

O'DONNELL, Rosie
Born on 3/21/1962 in Commack, New York. Stand-up comedian/actress. Appeared in several movies; hosted own TV talk show.

11/20/99	20	9	▲	1 A Rosie Christmas Cat:#14/9 [X]		Columbia 63685
				Christmas charts: 1/'99, 9/'00, 6/'02		
11/11/00	45	11	●	2 Another Rosie Christmas Cat:#32/1 [X]		Columbia 85102
				Christmas charts: 3/'00, 4/'02		

ODYSSEY
Disco vocal trio from the Bronx, New York: Manilla-born Tony Reynolds, and sisters Lillian Lopez and Louise Lopez, originally from the Virgin Islands.

10/8/77	36	38		1 Odyssey		RCA Victor 2204
11/11/78	123	5		2 Hollywood Party Tonight		RCA Victor 3031
6/14/80	181	4		3 Hang Together		RCA Victor 3526
7/18/81	175	5		4 I Got The Melody		RCA Victor 3910

OFF BROADWAY USA
Rock band from Oak Park, Illinois: Cliff Johnson (vocals), Rob Harding (guitar), John Ivan (guitar), John Pazdan (bass) and Ken Harck (drums).

2/16/80	101	11		1 On		Atlantic 19263
1/17/81	208	1		2 Quick Turns		Atlantic 19286

OFFSPRING, The   **All-Time: #479**
Punk-rock band from Garden Grove, California: Bryan "Dexter" Holland (vocals; born on 12/29/1966), Kevin "Noodles" Wasserman (guitar; born on 2/4/1963), Greg Kriesel (bass; born on 1/20/1965) and Ron Welty (drums; born on 2/1/1971).

1/14/95	14^C	30	●	1 Ignition		Epitaph 86424
				first released in 1993		
6/4/94	4	101	▲6	2 Smash Cat:#12/45		Epitaph 86432
2/22/97	9	38	▲	3 Ixnay On The Hombre		Columbia 67810
12/5/98+	2^2	67	▲5	4 Americana		Columbia 69661
12/2/00	9	24	▲	5 Conspiracy Of One		Columbia 61419
12/27/03	30	21	●	6 Splinter		Columbia 89026
7/9/05	8	16	●	7 Greatest Hits Cat:#33/1 [G]		Columbia 93459
7/5/08	10	30		8 Rise And Fall, Rage And Grace		Columbia 02908

OF MONTREAL
Alternative-rock band from Athens, Georgia: Kevin Barnes (vocals, guitar), Bryan Poole (guitar), Dottie Alexander (keyboards), James Huggins (bass) and Davey Pierce (drums).

2/10/07	72	3		1 Hissing Fauna, Are you The Destroyers?		Polyvinyl 124
11/8/08	38	3		2 Skeletal Lamping		Polyvinyl 160

OHIO EXPRESS
Bubblegum-pop band from Mansfield, Ohio: Joey Levine (vocals), Dale Powers (guitar), Doug Grassel (guitar), Jim Pflayer (keyboards), Dean Krastan (bass) and Tim Corwin (drums). Levine was lead singer with several studio groups.

7/6/68	126	11		1 Ohio Express		Buddah 5018
2/8/69	191	2		2 Chewy, Chewy		Buddah 5026

OHIO PLAYERS
1970s: #44 / All-Time: #256

R&B-funk band from Dayton, Ohio: Leroy "Sugarfoot" Bonner (vocals, guitar), Clarence "Satch" Satchell (vocals, sax), Walter "Junie" Morrison (keyboards), Ralph "Pee Wee" Middlebrooks, Andrew Noland, Bruce Napier and Marvin Pierce (horns), Marshall "Rock" Jones (bass) and Gary Webster (drums). In 1974, Billy Beck replaced Morrison and Jimmy "Diamond" Williams replaced Webster. Numerous personnel changes from 1979-present. Satchell died of a brain aneurysm on 12/30/1995 (age 55). Middlebrooks died on 10/15/1996 (age 57).

3/4/72	177	7		1 Pain		Westbound 2015
2/24/73	63	22		2 Pleasure		Westbound 2017
9/29/73	70	19		3 Ecstasy		Westbound 2021
4/27/74	11	48	●	4 Skin Tight		Mercury 705
11/23/74+	❶¹	29	●	5 Fire		Mercury 1013
8/23/75	2¹	36	●	6 Honey		Mercury 1038
6/12/76	12	20	●	7 Contradiction		Mercury 1088
4/9/77	41	27		8 Angel		Mercury 3701
12/24/77+	68	10		9 Mr. Mean [S]		Mercury 3707
9/9/78	69	9		10 Jass-Ay-Lay-Dee		Mercury 3730
4/14/79	80	14		11 Everybody Up		Arista 4226
4/11/81	165	3		12 Tenderness		Boardwalk 37090
12/19/81	201	6		13 Ouch!		Boardwalk 33247

GREATEST HITS & COMPILATIONS:

11/2/74	102	8		14 Climax		Westbound 1003
2/22/75	92	7		15 Ohio Players Greatest Hits		Westbound 1005
12/20/75+	61	14		16 Rattlesnake		Westbound 211
11/13/76	31	17	●	17 Ohio Players Gold		Mercury 1122

OH, SLEEPER

Hard-rock band from Fort Worth, Texas: Micah Kinard (vocals), James Erwin (guitar), Shane Blay (guitar), Lucas Starr (bass) and Zac Mayfield (drums).

9/12/09	120	1		1 Son Of The Morning		Solid State 64680

OINGO BOINGO

New-wave rock band formed in Los Angeles, California: Danny Elfman (vocals), Steve Bartek (guitar), John Avila (bass) and Johnny Hernandez (drums). Band appeared in the 1986 movie *Back To School*. Elfman also scored several movies; married actress Bridget Fonda on 11/29/2003.

10/25/80	163	5		1 Oingo Boingo [EP]		I.R.S. 70400
8/15/81	172	5		2 Only A Lad		A&M 4863
9/4/82	148	9		3 Nothing To Fear		A&M 4930
9/10/83	144	7		4 Good For Your Soul		A&M 4959
2/11/89	150	6		5 Skeletons In The Closet: The Best Of Oingo Boingo [G]		A&M 5217
11/16/85	98	16	●	6 Dead Man's Party		MCA 5665
3/21/87	77	16		7 Boi-ngo		MCA 5811
10/22/88	90	11		8 Boingo Alive [L]		MCA 8030 [2]
3/10/90	72	14		9 Dark At The End Of The Tunnel		MCA 6365
6/4/94	71	3		10 Boingo		Giant 24555
5/4/96	188	1		11 Farewell: Live From The Universal Amphitheatre, Halloween 1995 [L]		A&M 540504 [2]

O'JAYS, The
All-Time: #158

R&B vocal trio from Canton, Ohio: **Eddie Levert** (born on 6/16/1942), Walter Williams (born on 8/25/1942) and William Powell (born on 1/20/1942). Named after Cleveland DJ, Eddie O'Jay (died on 4/10/1998). Sammy Strain (of **Little Anthony & The Imperials**) replaced Powell in 1975. Powell died on 5/26/1977 (age 35). Eric Grant replaced Strain in 1996. Levert's sons **Gerald Levert** and **Sean Levert** were members of **Levert**.

AWARD: R&R Hall of Fame: 2005

9/9/72	10	44	●	1 Back Stabbers RS500 #318		Philadelphia Int'l. 31712
4/28/73	156	8		2 The O'Jays In Philadelphia [E] recordings from 1969		Philadelphia Int'l. 32120
11/10/73+	11	48	▲	3 Ship Ahoy		Philadelphia Int'l. 32408
6/29/74	17	24	●	4 The O'Jays Live In London [L] recorded December 1973 at the Hammersmith Odeon in London, England		Philadelphia Int'l. 32953
4/26/75	11	24	●	5 Survival		Philadelphia Int'l. 33150
11/29/75+	7	34	▲	6 Family Reunion		Philadelphia Int'l. 33807
10/2/76	20	22	●	7 Message In The Music		Philadelphia Int'l. 34245
6/4/77	27	16	●	8 Travelin' At The Speed Of Thought		Philadelphia Int'l. 34684
1/7/78	132	6		9 The O'Jays: Collectors' Items [G]		Philadelphia I. 35024 [2]
4/29/78	6	28	▲	10 So Full Of Love		Philadelphia Int'l. 35355
9/15/79	16	30	▲	11 Identify Yourself		Philadelphia Int'l. 36027
8/30/80	36	12		12 The Year 2000		Philadelphia Int'l. 36416
5/15/82	49	13		13 My Favorite Person		Philadelphia Int'l. 37999
8/13/83	142	5		14 When Will I See You Again		Epic 38518
10/19/85	121	12		15 Love Fever		Philadelphia Int'l. 53015

DEBUT	PEAK	WKS	R I A A	ARTIST Album Title	Catalog	Label & Number
				O'JAYS, The — cont'd		
10/10/87	66	25		16 Let Me Touch You		EMI-Manhattan 53036
5/27/89	114	17		17 Serious		FMI 90921
2/16/91	73	20	●	18 Emotionally Yours..		EMI 93390
8/14/93	75	11		19 Heartbreaker		EMI 89740
8/2/97	75	10		20 Love You To Tears		Global Soul 31149
10/27/01	53	5		21 For The Love...		MCA 112718
10/16/04	178	2		22 Imagination		Music World 87515
				O'KAYSIONS, The White pop-soul band from Wilson, North Carolina: Donny Weaver (vocals, organ), Wayne Pittman (guitar), Ron Turner (trumpet), Jim Spidel (sax), Jimmy Hennant (bass) and Bruce Joyner (drums).		
11/9/68	153	4		1 Girl Watcher...		ABC 664
				O'KEEFE, Danny Born in 1943 in Wenatchee, Washington. Pop singer/songwriter.		
9/2/72	87	16		1 O'Keefe		Signpost 8404
8/11/73	172	9		2 Breezy Stories		Atlantic 7264
				OK GO Rock band from Chicago, Illinois: Damian Kulash (vocals), Andy Ross (guitar), Tim Nordwind (bass) and Dan Konopka (drums).		
10/5/02	107	2		1 OK Go		Capitol 33724
9/17/05+	69	16		2 Oh No		Capitol 78800
				OKKERVIL RIVER Alternative-rock band from Austin, Texas: Will Sheff (vocals, guitar), Brian Cassidy (guitar), Jonathan Meiburg (keyboards), Patrick Pestorius (bass) and Travis Nelsen (drums).		
8/25/07	62	3		1 The Stage Names		Jagjaguwar 110
9/27/08	42	3		2 The Stand Ins...		Jagjaguwar 124
				OLD & IN THE WAY Bluegrass band formed in San Francisco, California: **Jerry Garcia** (vocals, banjo; **Grateful Dead**), **David Grisman** (vocals, mandolin), Peter Rowan (vocals, guitar), John Kahn (bass) and Vassar Clements (fiddle).		
3/29/75	99	8		1 Old & In The Way .... [L] recorded on 10/8/1973 at the Boarding House in San Francisco, California		Round 103
				OLD CROW MEDICINE SHOW Bluegrass band formed in New York: Willie Watson, Ketch Secor, Critter Fuqua, Kevin Hayes and Morgan Jahnig.		
9/16/06	125	2		1 Big Iron World		Nettwerk 30431
10/11/08	50	5		2 Tennessee Pusher		Nettwerk 30812
				OLDFIELD, Mike Born on 5/15/1953 in Reading, England. Classical-rock, multi-instrumentalist/composer.		
11/10/73+	3²	45	●	1 Tubular Bells Cat:#15/40 [I]		Virgin 105
9/21/74	87	10		2 Hergest Ridge .... [I]		Virgin 109
3/15/75	203	4		3 The Orchestral Tubular Bells.............................. [I] **THE ROYAL PHILHARMONIC ORCHESTRA WITH MIKE OLDFIELD** conducted by David Bedford; no track titles listed on this album		Virgin 115
12/20/75+	146	7		4 Ommadawn .... [I]		Virgin 33913
6/28/80	210	1		5 Airborn .... [I-L] record 1: new studio recordings; record 2: recorded on his 1979 European tour		Virgin 13143 [2]
7/4/81	174	3		6 QE2 .... [I]		Epic 37358
5/8/82	164	5		7 Five Miles Out		Epic 37983
2/27/88	138	8		8 Islands...		Virgin 90645
				OLD FRIENDS QUARTET Gospel group: **Ernie Haase**, Jake Hess, Wesley Pritchard and George Younce. Haase and Younce were also with **The Cathedrals**.		
6/9/01	159	1		1 Encore		Spring House 42321
				OL' DIRTY BASTARD Born Russell Jones on 11/15/1968 in Brooklyn, New York. Died of a drug overdose on 11/13/2004 (age 35). Male rapper. Member of **Wu-Tang Clan**.		
4/15/95	7	21	●	1 Return To The 36 Chambers: The Dirty Version		Elektra 61659
10/2/99	10	27	●	2 N***a Please		Elektra 62414
4/6/02	33	7		3 The Trials And Tribulations Of Russell Jones		D3 9991
1/22/05	157	1		4 Osirus: The Official Mixtape..............................		JC 9016
				OLD 97's Rock band from Dallas, Texas: **Rhett Miller** (vocals, guitar), Ken Bethea (guitar), Murry Hammond (bass) and Philip Peeples (drums).		
4/7/01	121	1		1 Satellite Rides...		Elektra 62531
8/14/04	120	1		2 Drag It Up		New West 6057
5/31/08	85	3		3 Blame It On Gravity		New West 6147

DEBUT	PEAK	WKS	R I A A	ARTIST / Album Title	Catalog	Label & Number

OLEANDER
Rock band from Sacramento, California: Thomas Flowers (vocals), Ric Ivanisevich (guitar), Doug Eldridge (bass) and Fred Nelson (drums).

DEBUT	PEAK	WKS		ARTIST / Album Title		Label & Number
6/12/99	115	19	●	1 February Son		Republic 53242
3/24/01	94	4		2 Unwind		Republic 013377

OLIVER
Born William Oliver Swofford on 2/22/1945 in North Wilkesboro, North Carolina. Died of cancer on 2/12/2000 (age 54). Adult Contemporary singer.

| 8/2/69 | 19 | 38 | | 1 Good Morning Starshine | | Crewe 1333 |
| 5/16/70 | 71 | 13 | | 2 Oliver Again | | Crewe 1344 |

OLIVER, David
Born on 1/8/1942 in Florida (Jamaican parents). Died on 6/6/1982 (age 40). R&B singer/songwriter.

| 5/27/78 | 128 | 8 | | 1 David Oliver | | Mercury 1183 |

OLIVIA
Born Olivia Longott on 2/15/1981 in Brooklyn, New York; raised in Queens, New York. R&B singer/rapper.

| 6/2/01 | 55 | 6 | | 1 Olivia | | J Records 20008 |

OLIVOR, Jane
Born Linda Cohen on 1/1/1947 in Brooklyn, New York. Adult Contemporary singer.

10/22/77	86	8		1 Chasing Rainbows		Columbia 34917
7/8/78	108	12		2 Stay The Night		Columbia 35437
2/23/80	58	12		3 The Best Side Of Goodbye		Columbia 36355
5/29/82	144	6		4 In Concert [L]		Columbia 37938

recorded on 12/21/1981 at the Berkley School of Music in Boston, Massachusetts

OLSEN, Mary-Kate & Ashley
Fraternal twin sisters who shared the role of "Michelle Tanner" on the TV show *Full House*. Born on 6/13/1986 (Ashley is two minutes older) in Sherman Oaks, California. Starred in several movies.

| 12/11/93 | 149 | 5 | | 1 I Am The Cute One | | Zoom Express 35038 |

MARY-KATE + ASHLEY OLSEN AND FRIENDS

OL SKOOL
R&B band from St. Louis, Missouri: Pookie (vocals), Tony Love (guitar), Curtis Jefferson (bass) and Bobby Crawford (drums).

| 3/14/98 | 49 | 9 | | 1 Ol Skool | | Universal 53104 |

OLSON, Mark
Born on 9/18/1961 in Minneapolis, Minnesota. Folk-rock singer/songwriter/guitarist. Member of **The Jayhawks**.

| 2/14/09 | 127 | 1 | | 1 Ready For The Flood | | New West 6162 |

MARK OLSON & GARY LOURIS

OLSSON, Nigel
Born on 2/10/1949 in Wallasey, Merseyside, England. Rock singer/drummer. Member of **Elton John**'s band from 1971-76.

| 3/24/79 | 140 | 5 | | 1 Nigel | | Bang 35792 |

OLSTEAD, Renee
Born Rebecca Renee Olstead on 6/18/1989 in Houston, Texas. White jazz-styled singer.

| 6/19/04 | 90 | 4 | | 1 Renee Oldstead | | 143 Records 48704 |
| 2/14/09 | 161 | 1 | | 2 Skylark | | 143 Records 44247 |

OLYMPICS, The
R&B vocal group from Compton, California: Walter Ward, Eddie Lewis, Charles Fizer, Melvin King and Walter Hammond. Fizer was killed during the Watts riots on 8/14/1965 (age 25). Ward died on 12/11/2006 (age 69).

~ ~ ~ ~ ~ ~ ~ ~ ~ ~ **NON-CHARTED ALBUMS** ~ ~ ~ ~ ~ ~ ~ ~ ~ ~
1960 **Doin' The Hully Gully**   1961 **Dance By The Light Of The Moon**

OMAR, Don
Born William Omar Landrón on 2/10/1978 in Villa Palmeras, Puerto Rico. Reggaeton/hip-hop singer.

6/26/04	84	2		1 The Last Don Live [F-L]		VI 450618 [2]
5/28/05	165	4	●	2 The Last Don Cat:#28/5 [F]		VI 450587
12/24/05	61	17		3 Da Hitman Presents Reggaeton Latino [F]		VI 005850
6/10/06	7	30	●	4 King Of Kings [F]		VI 006662
5/16/09	32	7		5 iDon [F]		VI 012867

OMAR & THE HOWLERS
Blues-rock trio from Austin, Texas: Kent "Omar" Dykes (vocals, guitar), Bruce Jones (bass) and Gene Brandon (drums).

| 6/27/87 | 81 | 19 | | 1 Hard Times In The Land Of Plenty | | Columbia 40815 |

OMARION
Born Omari Grandberry on 11/12/1984 in Los Angeles, California. Male R&B singer. Member of **B2K**. Older brother of **O'Ryan**.

3/12/05	❶¹	30	●	1 O		T.U.G. 92818
1/13/07	❶¹	16		2 21		T.U.G. 81038
12/29/07	11	13	●	3 Face Off		T.U.G. 11492

BOW WOW & OMARION

OMC
Born Pauly Fuemana on 2/8/1969 in Otara, New Zealand. Died on 1/31/2010 (age 40). Singer/songwriter. OMC: Otara Millionaires Club.

5/31/97	40	25	●	1 How Bizarre		Mercury 533435

ONASIS, Erick — see SERMON, Erick

O'NEAL, Alexander
Born on 11/15/1953 in Natchez, Mississippi; raised in Minneapolis, Minnesota. R&B singer.

4/27/85	92	18		1 Alexander O'Neal		Tabu 39331
8/22/87	29	40	●	2 Hearsay		Tabu 40320
12/17/88+	149	5		3 My Gift To You	[X]	Tabu 45016
				Christmas chart: 9/'88		
2/25/89	185	5		4 All Mixed Up	[K]	Tabu 44492
2/16/91	49	15	●	5 All True Man		Tabu 45349
2/27/93	89	8		6 Love Makes No Sense		Tabu 9501

O'NEAL, Jamie
Born Jamie Murphy on 6/3/1968 in Sydney, Australia; raised in Hawaii and Nevada. Female country singer.

11/18/00+	125	24	●	1 Shiver		Mercury 170132
3/19/05	40	4		2 Brave		Capitol 79894

O'NEAL, Shaquille
Born on 3/6/1972 in Newark, New Jersey. Male rapper/actor/NBA basketball player. Starred in the movies *Blue Chips*, *Kazaam* and *Steel*.

11/13/93	25	30	▲	1 Shaq Diesel		Jive 41529
11/26/94	67	10	●	2 Shaq-Fu: da Return		Jive 41550
12/7/96	82	6		3 You Can't Stop The Reign		T.W.IsM. 90087
10/3/98	58	5		4 Respect		T.W.IsM. 540947

ONE DAY AS A LION
Rap-rock duo formed in Los Angeles, California: Zack DeLa Rocha (of **Rage Against The Machine**) and Jon Theodore (of **The Mars Volta**).

8/9/08	28	10		1 One Day As A Lion	[EP]	Anti 86978

101 STRINGS
European studio orchestra assembled by D.L. Miller.

5/25/59+	9	58		1 The Soul Of Spain	[I]	Somerset 6600
1/9/61	21	19		2 The Soul Of Spain, Volume II	[I]	Somerset 9900
1/9/61	46	15		3 101 Strings Play The Blues	[I]	Somerset 5800
1/9/61	104	13		4 Concerto Under The Stars	[I]	Somerset 6700
10/13/07	48	7		5 Halloween	Cat:#15/3 [I]	Madacy 52906 [2]

100 PROOF AGED IN SOUL
R&B vocal trio from Detroit, Michigan: Steve Mancha, Joe Stubbs and Eddie Anderson. Stubbs is the brother of Levi Stubbs (of the **Four Tops**).

12/12/70+	151	7		1 Somebody's Been Sleeping In My Bed		Hot Wax 704

O'NEILL BROTHERS, The
Instrumental piano duo from New Prague, Minnesota: brothers Tim O'Neill and Ryan O'Neill.

2/19/05+	21 ^C	4		1 From The Heart	[I]	O'Neill Brothers 1401 [3]
				first released in 2000		

1NC
Gospel group from Dallas, Texas: Markita Knight, Jana Bell, Ashley Guilbert, Sheila Ingram, Brandon Kizer, Nate Larson, Frank Lawson, Nate Young and Myron Butler. 1NC: One Nation Crew.

9/2/00	58	10		1 Kirk Franklin Presents 1NC		B-Rite 90325

ONEREPUBLIC
Rock band from Denver, Colorado: Ryan Tedder (vocals), Zach Filkins (guitar), Drew Brown (guitar), Brent Kutzle (bass) and Eddie Fisher (drums).

12/8/07+	14	51	●	1 Dreaming Out Loud		Mosley 010266
12/5/09	21	23		2 Waking Up		Mosley 013607

112
R&B band from Atlanta, Georgia: Daron Jones (keyboards), Marvin **"Slim"** Scandrick (strings), Mike Keith (keyboards) and Quinnes Parker (drums). All share lead vocals. Group name pronounced: One Twelve.

9/14/96	37	55	▲²	1 112		Bad Boy 73009
11/28/98	20	53	▲²	2 Room 112		Bad Boy 73021
4/7/01	2 ¹	37	▲	3 Part III		Bad Boy 73039
12/6/03	22	14		4 Hot & Wet		Bad Boy 000927
4/16/05	4	17	●	5 Pleasure & Pain		Def Soul 004471

ONE WAY
R&B band from Detroit, Michigan: Al Hudson (vocals), Dave Roberson (guitar), Kevin McCord (bass) and Greg Green (drums).

11/17/79	181	5		1 One Way Featuring Al Hudson		MCA 3178
8/2/80	128	12		2 One Way Featuring Al Hudson		MCA 5127
				above 2 are different albums		
3/7/81	157	8		3 Love Is...One Way		MCA 5163
9/26/81	79	19		4 Fancy Dancer		MCA 5247
4/3/82	51	23		5 Who's Foolin' Who		MCA 5279
8/20/83	164	6		6 Shine On Me		MCA 5428
5/26/84	58	20		7 Lady		MCA 5470
8/10/85	156	9		8 Wrap Your Body		MCA 5552

ONO, Yoko
Born on 2/18/1933 in Tokyo, Japan. Moved to New York at age 14. Avant-garde artist/poet in the late 1960s. Married **John Lennon** in Gibraltar on 3/20/1969. Also see **Various Artists Compilations:** *Every Man Has A Woman*.

2/6/71	182	3		1 Yoko Ono/Plastic Ono Band		Apple 3373
11/13/71	199	2		2 Fly		Apple 3380 [2]
2/24/73	193	4		3 Approximately Infinite Universe		Apple 3399 [2]
6/27/81	49	9		4 Season Of Glass		Geffen 2004
12/25/82+	98	13		5 It's Alright (I See Rainbows)		Polydor 6364

ONYX
Hip-hop group from Jamaica, Queens, New York: **"Fredro Starr"** Scruggs, Kirk **"Sticky Fingaz"** Jones, Marlon "Big D.S." Fletcher and Suave Sonny Caesar. Fredro Starr went on to act in several movies. Fletcher left in 1995; died of cancer on 5/22/2003 (age 30).

4/17/93	17	37	▲	1 Bacdafucup		Def Jam 53302
11/11/95	22	6		2 All We Got Iz Us		Def Jam 529265
6/20/98	10	10		3 Shut 'Em Down		Def Jam 536988
7/27/02	46	5		4 Bacdafucup: Part II		Koch 8268

OPERA BABES
Classical female vocal duo from London, England: Karen England and Rebecca Knight.

2/8/03	199	1		1 Beyond Imagination		Sony Classical 87803

OPETH
Hard-rock band from Sweden: Mikael Akerfeldt (vocals, guitar), Peter Lindgren (guitar), Martin Mendez (bass) and Martin Lopez (drums). Per Wiberg (keyboards) joined in 2004.

5/10/03	192	1		1 Damnation		Koch 8652
9/17/05	64	2		2 Ghost Reveries		Roadrunner 618123
6/21/08	23	3		3 Watershed		Roadrunner 617936

OPUS
Pop-rock band from Austria: Herwig Rudisser (vocals), Ewald Pfleger (guitar), Kurt Rene Plisnier (keyboards), Niki Gruber (bass) and Gunter Grasmuck (drums).

3/1/86	64	16		1 Up And Down		Polydor 827952

ORB
Electronic trio: LX Paterson, Andy Hughes and Thomas Fehlmann.

3/29/97	174	1		1 Orblivion	[I]	Island 524347

ORBISON, Roy
All-Time: #313

Born on 4/23/1936 in Vernon, Texas. Died of a heart attack on 12/6/1988 (age 52). Pop-rock singer/songwriter/guitarist. Wife Claudette killed in a motorcycle accident on 6/7/1966; two sons died in a fire in 1968. Member of the **Traveling Wilburys**.

AWARDS: Grammy: Lifetime Achievement 1998 ★ R&R Hall of Fame: 1987

4/7/62	21	31		1 Crying		Monument 4007
8/17/63	35	23		2 In Dreams		Monument 18003
9/4/65	55	17		3 There Is Only One Roy Orbison		MGM 4308
3/5/66	128	3		4 The Orbison Way		MGM 4322
6/21/86	87	12		5 Class Of '55 (Memphis Rock & Roll Homecoming)	Cat:#13/2	America Smash 830002
				CARL PERKINS / JERRY LEE LEWIS / ROY ORBISON / JOHNNY CASH		
2/18/89	5	27	▲	6 Mystery Girl		Virgin 91058
12/2/89	123	12		7 A Black And White Night Live	[L-S]	Virgin 91295
				ROY ORBISON AND FRIENDS		
				GREATEST HITS & COMPILATIONS:		
9/1/62	13	140	●	8 Roy Orbison's Greatest Hits		Monument 4009
8/22/64	19	30		9 More Of Roy Orbison's Greatest Hits		Monument 18024
10/17/64	101	11		10 Early Orbison		Monument 18023
11/6/65+	136	11		11 Orbisongs		Monument 18035
8/13/66	94	9		12 The Very Best Of Roy Orbison		Monument 18045
1/15/83	205	5		13 The All-Time Greatest Hits Of Roy Orbison		Monument 38384 [2]
1/7/89	95	15	●	14 In Dreams: The Greatest Hits		Virgin 90604 [2]
				contains re-recorded versions of his early hits		
1/7/89	110	13		15 For The Lonely: A Roy Orbison Anthology, 1956-1965		Rhino 71493 [2]
12/19/92	179	2		16 King Of Hearts		Virgin 86520
				unissued and posthumously completed tracks		
1/30/93	48^C	1	▲	17 The All-Time Greatest Hits Of Roy Orbison, Volume One		Monument 44348
				first released in 1978		

DEBUT	PEAK	WKS		ARTIST / Album Title	Catalog	Label & Number
				ORBISON, Roy — cont'd		
4/26/97	186	1		18 The Very Best Of Roy Orbison		Virgin 42350
				contains re-recorded versions of his early hits		
2/8/03	48^C	1	●	19 16 Biggest Hits		Monument 69738
				first released in 1999		

~ ~ ~ ~ ~ ~ ~ ~ ~ ~ **NON-CHARTED ALBUMS** ~ ~ ~ ~ ~ ~ ~ ~ ~ ~ ~ ~

1961 **Roy Orbison At The Rock House**   1967 **Roy Orbison Sings Don Gibson**
1961 **Roy Orbison Sings Lonely And Blue**   1967 **Cry Softly Lonely One**
1966 **The Classic Roy Orbison**

DEBUT	PEAK	WKS		ARTIST / Album Title	Catalog	Label & Number
				ORBIT, William		
				Born William Wainwright on 2/15/1956 in England. Techno artist.		
3/18/00	198	1		1 Pieces In A Modern Style .... [I]		Maverick 47596 [2]
				ORBITAL		
				Electronic instrumental dance duo from London, England: brothers Phil Hartnoll and Paul Hartnoll..		
6/26/99	191	1		1 The Middle Of Nowhere		London 31065
				ORCHESTRAL MANOEUVRES IN THE DARK		
				Electro-pop band formed in England: keyboardists/vocalists Andrew McCluskey and Paul Humphreys, multi-instrumentalist Martin Cooper and drummer Malcolm Holmes. Humphreys left in 1989.		
2/6/82	144	12		1 Architecture & Morality		Epic 37721
4/23/83	162	6		2 Dazzle Ships		Epic 38543
11/24/84	182	6		3 Junk Culture		A&M 5027
7/27/85	38	53		4 Crush		A&M 5077
10/18/86	47	23		5 The Pacific Age		A&M 5144
3/26/88	46	29	●	6 In The Dark/The Best Of OMD .... [G]		A&M 5186
7/17/93	169	1		7 Liberator		Virgin 88225
				ORGANIZED KONFUSION		
				Male rap duo from Queens, New York: Troy "**Pharoahe Monch**" Jamerson and Larry "Prince Poetry" Baskerville.		
9/3/94	187	1		1 Stress: The Extinction Agenda		Hollywood Basic 61406
10/11/97	141	1		2 The Equinox		Priority 50560
				ORGY		
				Electronic-rock band from Los Angeles, California: Jay Gordon (vocals), Ryan Shuck (guitar), Amir Derakh (keyboards), Paige Haley (bass) and Bobby Hewitt (drums). Shuck and Derakh also joined **Dead By Sunrise**.		
1/16/99	32	41	▲	1 Candyass		Elementree 46923
10/28/00	16	9	●	2 Vapor Transmission		Elementree 47832
				ORIANTHI		
				Born Orianthi Panagaris on 1/22/1985 in Adelaide, Australia. Female pop-rock singer/songwriter/guitarist. Member of **Michael Jackson**'s band in 2009.		
11/14/09+	77	19		1 Believe		19 Records 013502

ORIGINAL BLUES PROJECT — see BLUES PROJECT

ORIGINAL LAST POETS — see LAST POETS, The

DEBUT	PEAK	WKS		ARTIST / Album Title	Catalog	Label & Number
				ORIGINAL MIRRORS		
				Punk-rock band from Liverpool, England: Steve Allen (vocals), Ian Broudie (guitar), Jonathan Perkins (keyboards), Phil Spalding (bass) and Pete Kircher (drums). Broudie later recorded as **The Lightning Seeds**.		
6/21/80	209	1		1 Original Mirrors		Arista 4269
				ORIGINALS, The		
				R&B vocal group from Detroit, Michigan: Fred Gorman, Crathman Spencer, Henry Dixon and Walter Gaines. Spencer died of a heart attack on 10/20/2004 (age 66). Gorman died on 6/13/2006 (age 67).		
1/17/70	174	4		1 Baby, I'm For Real		Soul 716
7/11/70	198	2		2 Portrait Of The Originals		Soul 724
				ORIGINOO GUNN CLAPPAZ		
				Male rap trio from Brooklyn, New York: DaShawn "Starang Wondah" Yates, Barrett "Louieville Sluggah" Powell and Jack "Top Dog" McNair. Members of **Boot Camp Clik**.		
11/16/96	47	4		1 Da Storm		Duck Down 50577
9/18/99	170	1		2 The M-Pire Shrikez Back		Duck Down 50116
				ORION THE HUNTER		
				Rock band formed in Boston, Massachusetts: Fran Cosmo (vocals), **Barry Goudreau** (guitar), Bruce Smith (bass) and Michael DeRosier (drums). Goudreau was a member of **Boston** and **RTZ**. Cosmo joined Boston in 1994.		
5/19/84	57	14		1 Orion The Hunter		Portrait 39239
				O'RIORDAN, Dolores		
				Born on 9/6/1971 in Limerick, Ireland. Pop-rock singer/songwriter. Leader of **The Cranberries**.		
6/2/07	77	1		1 Are You Listening?		Sanctuary 84795

ORLANDO, Tony — see DAWN

Billboard DEBUT	PEAK	WKS	R I A A	ARTIST / Album Title	Catalog	Label & Number

ORLEANS
Pop-rock band formed in New York: **John Hall** (vocals, guitar), brothers Lawrence Hoppen (vocals, guitar) and Lance Hoppen (bass), Jerry Marotta (keyboards), and Wells Kelly (drums). Hall and Marotta left in 1977, replaced by Bob Leinback (keyboards) and R.A. Martin (horns). Kelly died on 10/28/1984 (age 35). Hall was elected to the U.S. House of Representatives (in New York) in 2006.

3/29/75	**33**	32		1 **Let There Be Music**	Asylum 1029
8/28/76	**30**	16		2 **Waking And Dreaming**	Asylum 1070
5/5/79	**76**	13		3 **Forever**	Infinity 9006

ORLONS, The
R&B vocal group from Philadelphia, Pennsylvania: Rosetta Hightower (lead), Marlena Davis, Shirley Brickley and Steve Caldwell. Brickley was shot to death on 10/13/1977 (age 32). Davis died of lung cancer on 2/27/1993 (age 48).

9/1/62	**80**	10		1 **The Wah-Watusi**	Cameo 1020
7/6/63	**123**	5		2 **South Street**	Cameo 1041

~ ~ ~ ~ ~ ~ ~ ~ ~ ~ **NON-CHARTED ALBUMS** ~ ~ ~ ~ ~ ~ ~ ~ ~ ~ ~
1962 **All The Hits By The Orlons**   1964 **The Orlons' Biggest Hits**
1963 **Not Me Not Me Not Me**   1964 **Down Memory Lane With The Orlons**

ORMANDY, Eugene — see PHILADELPHIA ORCHESTRA

ORPHAN
Folk-pop duo from Boston, Massachusetts: Eric Lilljequist and Dean Adrien.

9/2/72	**212**	3		1 **Everyone Lives To Sing**	London 614

ORPHEUS
Soft-rock band from Boston, Massachusetts: Bruce Arnold (vocals, guitar), Jack McKenes (guitar), John Eric Gulliksen (bass) and Harry Sandler (drums).

3/9/68	**119**	14		1 **Orpheus**	MGM 4524
9/28/68	**159**	12		2 **Ascending**	MGM 4569
10/11/69	**198**	1		3 **Joyful**	MGM 4599

ORR, Benjamin
Born Benjamin Orzechowski on 8/9/1947 in Lakewood, Ohio. Died of cancer on 10/3/2000 (age 53). Bassist/vocalist of **The Cars**.

11/8/86+	**86**	22		1 **The Lace**	Elektra 60460

ORR, Bobby
Born on 4/20/1948 in Parry Sound, Ontario, Canada. Pro hockey player with the Boston Bruins (1966-76) and the Chicago Blackhawks (1976-79).

2/13/71	**214**	1		1 **The Two Sides Of Bobby Orr** .... **[T]**	Cori 3101
				interviewed by Don Earle	

ORRALL, Robert Ellis
Born on 5/4/1955 in Winthrop, Massachusetts. Country-pop singer/songwriter/pianist.

4/16/83	**146**	9		1 **Special Pain** .... **[EP]**	RCA Victor 8502

ORRICO, Stacie
Born on 3/3/1986 in Seattle, Washington. Contemporary Christian-pop singer/songwriter.

9/16/00	**103**	5		1 **Genuine**	ForeFront 25253
11/17/01	**26**^X	3		2 **Christmas Wish** .... **[X-EP]**	ForeFront 32588
				Christmas chart: 26/'01	
4/12/03	**59**	49	●	3 **Stacie Orrico**	ForeFront 32589

ORTEGA, Fernando
Born in Albuquerque, New Mexico. Contemporary Christian singer/songwriter.

3/2/02	**197**	1		1 **Storm**	Word 86109
10/10/09	**36**^X	1		2 **Christmas Songs** .... **[X]**	Curb 79110

ORTEGA, Jeannie
Born on 11/19/1986 in Brooklyn, New York (Puerto Rican parents). Dance singer/songwriter/actress. Appeared in the 2006 movie *Step Up*.

8/19/06	**127**	1		1 **No Place Like Brooklyn**	Hollywood 162532

ORTON, Beth
Born on 12/14/1970 in Norwich, Norfolk, England. Female singer/songwriter.

3/27/99	**110**	11		1 **Central Reservation**	Heavenly 19038
8/17/02	**40**	7		2 **Daybreaker**	Heavenly 39918
2/25/06	**92**	5		3 **Comfort Of Strangers**	Astralwerks 49847

O'RYAN
Born O'Ryan Grandberry on 9/12/1987 in Los Angeles, California. Male R&B singer. Younger brother of **Omarion**.

11/6/04	**75**	1		1 **O'Ryan**	T.U.G. 003153

OSBORNE, Jeffrey
Born on 3/9/1948 in Providence, Rhode Island. R&B singer/songwriter/drummer. Lead singer of **L.T.D.** until 1980.

6/19/82	**49**	43		1 **Jeffrey Osborne**	A&M 4896
8/6/83+	**25**	89	●	2 **Stay With Me Tonight**	A&M 4940
10/20/84	**39**	37	●	3 **Don't Stop**	A&M 5017
6/28/86	**26**	26	●	4 **Emotional**	A&M 5103

586

Billboard DEBUT	PEAK	WKS	R I A A	ARTIST / Album Title	Catalog	Label & Number

OSBORNE, Jeffrey — cont'd

8/27/88	86	16		5 One Love-One Dream		A&M 5205
12/15/90+	95	23		6 Only Human		Arista 8620
3/4/00	191	1		7 That's For Sure		Private Music 82170

OSBORNE, Joan
Born on 7/8/1962 in Anchorage, Kentucky. Adult Alternative singer/songwriter/guitarist.

9/9/95+	9	56	▲³	1 Relish		Blue Gorilla 526699
9/30/00	90	4		2 Righteous Love		Interscope 490737
6/9/07	160	2		3 Breakfast In Bed		Womanly Hips 19433
9/27/08	193	1		4 Little Wild One		Womanly Hips 19666

OSBORNE BROTHERS, The
Bluegrass duo of brothers from Hyden, Kentucky: Bobby (born on 12/7/1931; mandolin) and Sonny (born on 10/29/1937; banjo) Osborne.
AWARDS: CMA: Vocal Group 1971 ★ OPRY: 1964

7/4/70	193	1		1 Ru-beeeee		Decca 75204

OSBOURNE, Kelly
Born on 10/27/1984 in London, England. Daughter of **Ozzy Osbourne**. Finished third on season 9 on *Dancing With The Stars*.

12/14/02	101	6		1 Shut Up		Epic 86870
6/25/05	117	1		2 Sleeping In The Nothing		Sanctuary 84737

OSBOURNE, Ozzy   1980s: #42 / All-Time: #131
Born John Osbourne on 12/3/1948 in Birmingham, England. Hard-rock singer/songwriter. Lead singer of **Black Sabbath**. Controversial in his concert antics. Married his manager Sharon Arden on 7/4/1982. Father of **Kelly Osbourne**. Appeared in the 1986 movie *Trick Or Treat*. *The Osbournes*, a reality show based on his family's home life, ran on MTV from 2002-05. Also see **Various Artists Compilations:** *OzzFest*.

4/18/81	21	104	▲⁴	1 Blizzard Of Ozz		Jet 36812
11/21/81	16	73	▲³	2 Diary Of A Madman		Jet 37492
12/10/83+	19	29	▲³	3 Bark At The Moon		CBS Associated 38987
2/15/86	6	39	▲²	4 The Ultimate Sin		CBS Associated 40026
10/22/88	13	27	▲²	5 No Rest For The Wicked		CBS Associated 44245
10/5/91	7	86	▲⁴	6 No More Tears		Epic/Associated 46795
11/11/95	4	44	▲²	7 Ozzmosis		Epic 67091
11/3/01	4	35	▲	8 Down To Earth		Epic 63580
11/19/05	134	1		9 Under Cover		Epic 97750
6/9/07	3¹	20	●	10 Black Rain		Epic 05334
				GREATEST HITS & COMPILATIONS:		
8/18/90	163	2		11 Ten Commandments		Priority 57129
11/29/97	13	42	▲²	12 The Ozzman Cometh	Cat:#4/16	Epic 67980 [2]
3/1/03	81	6	●	13 The Essential Ozzy Osbourne		Legacy 86812 [2]
4/9/05	36	3	●	14 Prince Of Darkness		Epic 92960 [4]
				LIVE ALBUMS:		
5/8/82	120	18		15 Mr. Crowley [EP]		Jet 37640
12/11/82+	14	20	▲	16 Speak Of The Devil		Jet 38350 [2]
				recorded on 9/26/1982 at The Ritz in New York City		
5/9/87	6	23	▲²	17 Tribute		CBS Associated 40714 [2]
				OZZY OSBOURNE/RANDY RHOADS		
				live recordings from 1981 featuring Ozzy's guitarist, Randy Rhoads, who was killed in an airplane crash on 3/19/1982 (age 25)		
3/3/90	58	13	●	18 Just Say Ozzy [EP]		CBS Associated 45451
7/3/93	22	14	▲	19 Live & Loud		Epic/Associated 48973 [2]
7/13/02	70	5		20 Live At Budokan		Epic 86525
				recorded on 2/15/2002 in Japan		

OSIBISA
Jazz-R&B band formed in London, England. Core members: Ghana natives Teddy Osei (reeds), Nee Daku Adams (percussion), Mac Tontoh (bass) and Sol Amarifo (drums), with West Indian Wendell Richardson (guitar). Adams died of a heart attack on 1/1/1995 (age 59).

7/3/71	55	19		1 Osibisa		Decca 75285
2/12/72	66	17		2 Wcyaya		Decca 75327
10/28/72	125	8		3 Heads		Decca 75368
7/21/73	159	7		4 Super Fly T.N.T. [S]		Buddah 5136
12/15/73	202	12		5 Happy Children		Warner 2732
9/28/74	175	4		6 Osibirock		Warner 2802
4/24/76	200	2		7 Welcome Home		Island 9355

Billboard DEBUT	PEAK	WKS	R I A A	ARTIST / Album Title	Catalog	Label & Number

OSKAR, Lee
Born on 3/24/1948 in Copenhagen, Denmark. Harmonica player. Member of **War**.

4/3/76	29	24		1 Lee Oskar .... [I]		United Artists 594
9/16/78	86	12		2 Before The Rain		Elektra 150
8/1/81	162	6		3 My Road Our Road		Elektra 526

OSLIN, K.T.
Born Kay Toinette Oslin on 5/15/1941 in Crossett, Arkansas; raised in Mobile, Alabama. Country singer/songwriter.
AWARD: CMA: Female Vocalist 1988

12/12/87+	68	32	▲	1 80's Ladies		RCA Victor 5924
9/24/88	75	52	▲	2 This Woman		RCA 8369
11/24/90+	76	26	●	3 Love In A Small Town		RCA 2365
5/22/93	126	7		4 Greatest Hits: Songs From An Aging Sex Bomb .... [G]		RCA 66227

OSMENT, Emily
Born on 3/10/1992 in Los Angeles, California. Female singer/actress. Plays "Lilly Truscott" on TV's **Hannah Montana**. Younger sister of actor Haley Joel Osment.

| 11/14/09 | 117 | 3↑ | | 1 All The Right Wrongs .... [EP] | | Wind-Up 13192 |

OSMOND, Donny   All-Time: #316
Born on 12/9/1957 in Ogden, Utah. Lead singer of **The Osmonds**. Brother of **Marie Osmond** and **Little Jimmy Osmond**. Starred in the stage musical *Joseph and The Amazing Technicolor Dreamcoat*. Finished first on season 9 on *Dancing With The Stars*.

7/10/71	13	37	●	1 The Donny Osmond Album		MGM 4782
11/6/71	12	33	●	2 To You With Love, Donny		MGM 4797
5/27/72	6	36	●	3 Portrait Of Donny		MGM 4820
7/22/72	11	30	●	4 Too Young		MGM 4854
12/16/72+	29	20	●	5 My Best To You .... [G]		MGM 4872
3/24/73	26	29		6 Alone Together		MGM 4886
12/8/73+	58	13		7 A Time For Us		MGM 4930
12/7/74+	57	17		8 Donny		MGM 4978
8/21/76	145	8		9 Disco Train		Polydor 6067
9/3/77	169	5		10 Donald Clark Osmond		Polydor 6109
5/13/89	54	23		11 Donny Osmond		Capitol 92354
11/17/90	177	2		12 Eyes Don't Lie		Capitol 94051
11/21/98+	20ˣ	4		13 Christmas At Home .... Cat:#50/1 [X]		Epic/Legacy 65780
				Christmas charts: 37/'98, 20/'99		
2/24/01	64	6		14 This Is The Moment		Decca 013052
1/29/05	137	2		15 What I Meant To Say		Decca 003737
5/12/07	27	3		16 Love Songs Of The '70s		Decca 008291

OSMOND, Donny And Marie
Brother-and-sister co-hosts of own musical/variety TV series and later of own daytime talk show. Starred in the 1978 movie *Goin' Coconuts*.

9/7/74	35	30	●	1 I'm Leaving It All Up To You		MGM 4968
6/28/75	133	6		2 Make The World Go Away		MGM 4996
4/3/76	60	38	●	3 Donny & Marie - Featuring Songs From Their Television Show		Polydor 6068
11/27/76+	85	14	●	4 Donny & Marie - New Season		Polydor 6083
1/7/78	99	12		5 Winning Combination		Polydor 6127
11/11/78	98	8	●	6 Goin' Coconuts .... [S]		Polydor 6169

OSMOND, Little Jimmy
Born on 4/16/1963 in Canoga Park, California. Youngest member of **The Osmonds**.

| 12/2/72+ | 105 | 14 | | 1 Killer Joe .... | | MGM 4855 |

OSMOND, Marie
Born Olive Marie Osmond on 10/13/1959 in Ogden, Utah. Sister of **The Osmonds**. Hosted own musical/variety series *Marie* (1980-81). Co-hosted the TV series *Ripley's Believe It Or Not* (1985-86). Played "Julia Wallace" on the TV series *Maybe This Time* (1995). Finished third on season 5 on TV's *Dancing With The Stars*.
AWARD: CMA: Vocal Duo (w/ Dan Seals) 1986

9/22/73	59	23		1 Paper Roses		MGM 4910
7/20/74	164	9		2 In My Little Corner Of The World		MGM 4944
3/8/75	152	6		3 Who's Sorry Now		MGM 4979
4/30/77	152	6		4 This Is The Way That I Feel		Polydor 6099
11/24/07	93	6		5 Marie Osmond's Magic Of Christmas .... [X]		HiFi 1003
				Christmas chart: 21/'07		

OSMONDS, The   All-Time: #481
Family group from Ogden, Utah. Alan (born on 6/22/1949), Wayne (born on 8/28/1951), Merrill (born on 4/30/1953), Jay (born on 3/2/1955) and **Donny Osmond**. Regulars on **Andy Williams**'s TV show from 1962-67.

1/30/71	14	43	●	1 Osmonds		MGM 4724
6/26/71	22	34	●	2 Homemade		MGM 4770
1/29/72	10	35	●	3 Phase-III		MGM 4796
6/17/72	13	29		4 The Osmonds "Live" .... [L]		MGM 4826 [2]
10/14/72	14	22		5 Crazy Horses		MGM 4851
7/7/73	58	20		6 The Plan		MGM 4902
11/2/74	47	14		7 Love Me For A Reason		MGM 4939

Billboard DEBUT	PEAK	WKS	R I A A	ARTIST Album Title	Catalog	Label & Number
				OSMONDS, The — cont'd		
8/30/75	160	5		8 **The Proud One**		MGM 4993
12/20/75+	148	8		9 **Around The World - Live In Concert** [L]		MGM 5012 [2]
10/23/76	145	6		10 **Brainstorm**		Polydor 6077
12/18/76+	127	5		11 **The Osmond Christmas Album** [X]		Polydor 8001 [2]
1/14/78	192	3		12 **The Osmonds Greatest Hits** [G]		Polydor 9005 [2]
4/19/08	177	1		13 **50th Anniversary Reunion Concert** [L]		Denon 17678
				O'SULLIVAN, Gilbert Born Raymond O'Sullivan on 12/1/1946 in Waterford, Ireland. Adult Contemporary singer/songwriter.		
8/12/72	9	29		1 Gilbert O'Sullivan-Himself		MAM 4
1/6/73	48	19		2 **Back To Front**		MAM 5
10/13/73	101	10		3 **I'm A Writer, Not A Fighter**		MAM 7
				OSWALT, Patton Born on 1/27/1969 in Portsmouth, Virginia. Stand-up comedian/actor. Appeared in several TV shows and movies.		
7/28/07	137	1		1 **Werewolves And Lollipops** [C]		Sub Pop 737
9/5/09	67	3		2 **My Weakness Is Strong** [C]		Degenerate 518428
				OTEP Born Otep Shamaya on 11/7/1979 in Los Angeles, California. Female heavy metal singer/songwriter.		
7/6/02	145	1		1 **Sevas Tra** title is "Art Saves" spelled backwards		Capitol 33346
8/14/04	93	3		2 **House Of Secrets**		Capitol 91043
11/17/07	81	2		3 **The Ascension**		Koch 5044
9/5/09	47	3		4 **Smash The Control Machine**		Victory 529
				OTHER ONES, The Pop-rock band consisting of Australian siblings Jayney (vocals), Alf (vocals) and Johnny (bass) Klimek, and Germans Andreas Schwarz-Ruszczynski (guitar), Stephen Gottwald (keyboards) and Uwe Hoffmann (drums).		
5/16/87	139	6		1 **The Other Ones**		Virgin 90576
				OTHER ONES, The Rock band consisting of former **Grateful Dead** members **Bob Weir** (vocals, guitar), **Phil Lesh** (bass) and **Mickey Hart** (drums), with **Bruce Hornsby** (vocals, keyboards), Mark Karan (guitar), Steve Kimock (guitar), Dave Ellis (sax) and John Molo (drums).		
2/27/99	112	2		1 **The Strange Remain**		Grateful Dead 14062 [2]
				OTIS, Johnny, Show Born John Veliotes on 12/28/1921 in Vallejo, California (of Greek parents). R&B bandleader/composer. Father of **Shuggie Otis**. AWARD: R&R Hall of Fame: 1994 (Non-Performer) ~ ~ ~ ~ ~ ~ ~ ~ ~ ~ ~ **NON-CHARTED ALBUM** ~ ~ ~ ~ ~ ~ ~ ~ ~ ~ ~ 1958 **The Johnny Otis Show**		
				OTIS, Shuggie Born Johnny Alexander Veliotes on 11/30/1953 in Los Angeles, California. R&B singer/songwriter/guitarist. Son of **Johnny Otis**.		
1/24/70	182	5		1 **Kooper Session** AL KOOPER Introduces SHUGGIE OTIS		Columbia 9951
3/7/70	199	2		2 **Here Comes Shuggie Otis**		Epic 26511
3/22/75	181	3		3 **Inspiration Information**		Epic 33059
				O-TOWN Pop vocal group from Orlando, Florida: Trevor Penick, Jacob Underwood, **Ashley Parker Angel**, Erik-Michael Estrada and Dan Miller. Group was put together while auditioning for the TV series *Making The Band*.		
2/10/01	5	54	▲	1 O-Town		J Records 20000
11/30/02	28	8		2 **O2**		J Records 20033
				OTTO, James Born on 7/29/1973 in Fort Lewis, Washington; raised in Benton City, Washington. Country singer/songwriter/guitarist.		
4/26/08	3[1]	23		1 Sunset Man		Raybaw 49907
				OUR LADY PEACE Rock band from Toronto, Ontario, Canada: Raine Maida (vocals), Mike Turner (guitar), Duncan Coutts (bass) and Jeremy Taggart (drums).		
9/6/97+	76	39	▲	1 Clumsy		Columbia 67940
10/16/99	69	4		2 **Happiness...Is Not A Fish That You Can Catch**		Columbia 63707
3/31/01	81	4		3 **Spiritual Machines**		Columbia 85368
7/6/02	9	27	●	4 Gravity		Columbia 86585
7/19/03	112	1		5 **Live** [L]		Columbia 85855
9/17/05	45	2		6 **Healthy In Paranoid Times**		Columbia 94777
8/8/09	41	2		7 **Burn Burn**		Coalition 519895
				OURS Born James Gnecco on 9/30/1973 in Teaneck, New Jersey. Alternative-rock singer/songwriter/guitarist.		
11/23/02	187	1		1 **Precious**		DreamWorks 450373

OUTFIELD, The
Pop-rock trio formed in London, England: Tony Lewis (vocals, bass), John Spinks (guitar) and Alan Jackman (drums). Jackman left by 1990; Lewis and Spinks continued as a duo.

11/2/85+	9	66	▲²	1 Play Deep		Columbia 40027
7/4/87	18	21	●	2 Bangin'		Columbia 40619
4/15/89	53	23		3 Voices Of Babylon		Columbia 44449
11/24/90+	90	16		4 Diamond Days		MCA 10111

OUTKAST   All-Time: #448
Male hip-hop duo from Atlanta, Georgia: "Andre 3000" Benjamin (born on 5/27/1975) and Antwan "Big Boi" Patton (born on 2/1/1975). Members of **Dungeon Family**. Benjamin played "Silk Brown" in the 2003 movie *Hollywood Homicide*.

5/14/94	20	26	▲	1 Southernplayalisticadillacmuzik		LaFace 26010
9/14/96	2¹	33	▲²	2 ATLiens		LaFace 26029
10/17/98	2¹	43	▲	3 Aquemini		LaFace 26053
11/18/00	2²	46	▲⁴	4 Stankonia		LaFace 26072
				Grammy: Rap Album ★ RS500 #359		
12/22/01+	18	29	▲	5 Big Boi & Dre Present...OutKast	[G]	LaFace 26093
10/11/03	❶⁷	56	▲¹¹	6 Speakerboxxx/The Love Below		Arista 50133 [2]
				Grammys: Album of the Year / Rap Album		
9/9/06	2¹	11	▲	7 Idlewild	[S]	LaFace 75791

OUTLAWS
Southern-rock band formed in Tampa, Florida: **Henry Paul** (vocals, guitar), Hughie Thomasson (guitar), Billy Jones (guitar), Frank O'Keefe (bass) and Monte Yoho (drums). By 1981, Freddie Salem, Rick Cua and David Dix had replaced Paul, O'Keefe and Yoho. Paul was a member of **BlackHawk** by 1993. Thomasson joined **Lynyrd Skynyrd** in 1996. Jones died on 2/7/1995 (age 45). O'Keefe died of a drug overdose on 2/26/1995 (age 44). Thomasson died of a heart attack on 9/9/2007 (age 55).

8/9/75	13	16	●	1 Outlaws		Arista 4042
4/10/76	36	12		2 Lady In Waiting		Arista 4070
5/28/77	51	27		3 Hurry Sundown		Arista 4135
3/25/78	29	21	●	4 Bring It Back Alive	[L]	Arista 8300 [2]
				recorded on 9/9/1977 in Chicago, Illinois		
11/25/78	60	18		5 Playin' To Win		Arista 4205
11/3/79	55	18		6 In The Eye Of The Storm		Arista 9507
12/13/80+	25	26	●	7 Ghost Riders		Arista 9542
5/1/82	77	9		8 Los Hombres Malo		Arista 9584
11/27/82+	136	9		9 Greatest Hits Of The Outlaws/High Tides Forever	[G]	Arista 9614
11/8/86	160	10		10 Soldiers Of Fortune		Pasha 40512

OUTLAWZ
Rap group from Los Angeles, California: Malcolm "E.D.I." Greenidge, Katari "Kastro" Cox, Mutah "Napoleon" Beale and Rufus "Young Noble" Cooper. Beale left in 2003; group continued as a trio. Discovered by **2Pac**.

1/8/00	6	20	▲	1 Still I Rise		Interscope 490413
				2PAC + OUTLAWZ		
11/25/00	95	3		2 Ride Wit Us Or Collide Wit Us		Outlaw 2000
11/24/01	100	2		3 Novakane		Outlaw 8324

OUT OF EDEN
Contemporary gospel trio from Richmond, Virginia: sisters Lisa, Andrea and Danielle Kimmey.

2/16/02	178	3		1 This Is Your Life		Gotee 2850

OUTSIDERS, The
Rock band from Cleveland, Ohio: Sonny Geraci (vocals), Tom King (guitar), Bill Bruno (guitar), Mert Madsen (bass) and Rick Baker (drums). Geraci later formed **Climax**.

5/28/66	37	16		1 Time Won't Let Me		Capitol 2501
9/17/66	90	10		2 The Outsiders Album #2		Capitol 2568
8/26/67	103	10		3 Happening 'Live!'	[L]	Capitol 2745

OVERKILL
Hard-rock band from New York: Bobby Ellsworth (vocals), Bobby Gustafson (guitar), D.D. Verni (bass) and Lee "Rat Skates" Kundrat (drums). By 1988, Sid Falck had replaced Kundrat. Gustafson and Falck left by 1993; guitarists Rob Cannavino and Merritt Gant, and drummer Tim Mallare joined.

4/11/87	191	1		1 Taking Over		Megaforce 81735
7/30/88	142	13		2 Under The Influence		Megaforce 81865
11/18/89+	155	8		3 The Years Of Decay		Megaforce 82045
3/27/93	122	2		4 I Hear Black		Atlantic 82476

OVERSTREET, Paul
Born on 3/17/1955 in Antioch, Mississippi. Country singer/songwriter/guitarist.

2/23/91	163	6		1 Heroes		RCA 2459

OVER THE RHINE
Alternative-rock duo from Cincinnati, Ohio: husband-and-wife Linford Detweiler and Karin Bergquist.

10/20/07	42ˣ	1		1 Snow Angels	[X]	Great Speckled Dog 100

OWEN, Jake
Born Josh Owen on 8/28/1981 in Vero Beach, Florida. Country singer/songwriter.

8/12/06	31	13		1 Startin' With Me		RCA 81172
3/14/09	13	9		2 Easy Does It		RCA 31287

OWEN, Randy
Born on12/13/1949 in Fort Payne, Alabama. Lead singer of **Alabama**.

11/22/08	77	2		1 One On One		Broken Bow 7237

OWENS, Buck, And His Buckaroos
Born Alvis Edgar Owens on 8/12/1929 in Sherman, Texas; raised in Mesa, Arizona. Died on 3/25/2006 (age 76). Country singer/songwriter/guitarist. Co-host of TV's *Hee Haw* (1969-86). Backing group: The Buckaroos.

AWARD: C&W Hall of Fame: 1996

7/18/64	46	31	●	1 The Best Of Buck Owens .... [G]		Capitol 2105
9/5/64	88	18		2 Together Again / My Heart Skips A Beat...		Capitol 2135
				also see #12 below		
12/12/64	135	5		3 I Don't Care		Capitol 2186
4/3/65	43	22		4 I've Got A Tiger By The Tail		Capitol 2283
12/18/65	12ˣ	10		5 Christmas With Buck Owens And His Buckaroos .... [X]		Capitol 2396
				Christmas charts: 12/'65, 23/'66, 23/'67; also see #19 below		
3/12/66	106	10		6 Roll Out The Red Carpet For Buck Owens And His Buckaroos		Capitol 2443
9/24/66	114	10		7 Carnegie Hall Concert .... [L]		Capitol 2556
				recorded on 3/25/1966		
9/30/67	177	7		8 Your Tender Loving Care		Capitol 2760
12/21/68	31ˣ	2		9 Christmas Shopping .... [X]		Capitol 2977
				also see #19 below		
2/15/69	199	2		10 I've Got You On My Mind Again		Capitol 131
7/5/69	113	5		11 Buck Owens In London .... [L]		Capitol 232
				recorded at the London Palladium		
8/16/69	185	5		12 Close-Up .... [R]		Capitol 257 [2]
				reissue of *Together Again* and *No One But You* albums		
11/8/69	122	10		13 Tall Dark Stranger		Capitol 212
2/7/70	141	6		14 Big In Vegas .... [L]		Capitol 413
4/25/70	198	2		15 Your Mother's Prayer		Capitol 439
5/16/70	154	6		16 We're Gonna Get Together		Capitol 448
				BUCK OWENS & SUSAN RAYE		
9/19/70	196	2		17 The Kansas City Song		Capitol 476
11/28/70	190	2		18 I Wouldn't Live In New York City		Capitol 628
12/26/70	34ˣ	1		19 A Merry "Hee Haw" Christmas .... [X-R]		Capitol 486 [2]
				reissue of albums #5 and #9 above		

OWENS, Gary
Born Gary Altman on 5/10/1936 in Mitchell, South Dakota. Comedian/DJ. Best known as the announcer on TV's *Laugh-In*.

8/12/72	204	3		1 Put Your Head On My Finger .... [C]		Pride 0002

OWL CITY
Born Adam Young in Owatonna, Minnesota. Adult Alternative singer/songwriter/musician.

8/1/09	8	44↑	▲	1 Ocean Eyes		Universal Rep. 013141

OXO
Pop-rock band from Miami, Florida: Ish "Angel" Ledesma (vocals; **Foxy**), Orlando (guitar), Frank Garcia (bass) and Freddy Alwag (drums).

4/30/83	117	7		1 Oxo		Geffen 4001

OYSTERHEAD
All-star rock trio: **Trey Anastasio** (of **Phish**), **Les Claypool** (of **Primus**) and **Stewart Copeland** (of **The Police**).

10/20/01	48	5		1 The Grand Pecking Order...		Elektra 62677

OZARK MOUNTAIN DAREDEVILS
Country-rock band from Springfield, Missouri: Larry Lee (vocals, drums), John Dillon (guitar), Steve Cash (harmonica) and Michael Granda (bass).

2/16/74	26	28	●	1 The Ozark Mountain Daredevils..		A&M 4411
12/14/74+	19	31		2 It'll Shine When It Shines..		A&M 3654
11/8/75	57	15		3 The Car Over The Lake Album		A&M 4549
10/2/76	74	10		4 Men From Earth		A&M 4601
11/19/77+	132	10		5 Don't Look Down		A&M 4662
9/30/78	176	3		6 It's Alive .... [L]		A&M 6006 [2]
5/24/80	170	4		7 Ozark Mountain Daredevils		Columbia 36375

OZOMATLI
Rock band from Los Angeles, California: Raul Pacheco (vocals, guitar), Jiro Yamaguchi (percussion), Ulises Bella (sax), Asfru Sierra (trumpet), Wil-Dog Abers (bass) and Justin Poree and Andy Mendoza (drums).

9/29/01	138	1		1 Embrace The Chaos		Interscope 493116
7/10/04	125	2		2 Street Signs		Concord 2200
4/21/07	154	1		3 Don't Mess With The Dragon		Concord 2305

OZONE
Funk band from Nashville, Tennessee: Benny Wallace (vocals, guitar), Herman Brown (guitar), James Stewart (keyboards), Thomas Bumpass (trumpet), William White and Ray Woodard (saxophones), Charles Glenn (bass) and Paul Hines (drums).

DEBUT	PEAK	WKS				
2/28/81	206	1		1 Jump On It		Motown 950
9/4/82	152	6		2 Li'l Suzy		Motown 6011
4/23/83	201	4		3 Glasses		Motown 6037

P

PABLO, Petey
Born Moses Barrett on 7/22/1973 in Greenville, North Carolina. Male rapper/songwriter.

11/24/01	13	28	●	1 Diary Of A Sinner: 1st Entry		Jive 41723
5/22/04	4	22	●	2 Still Writing In My Diary: 2nd Entry		Jive 41824

PABLO CRUISE
Pop-rock band from San Francisco, California: Dave Jenkins (vocals, guitar), Cory Lerios (keyboards), Bud Cockrell (bass; It's A Beautiful Day) and Stephen Price (drums). Bruce Day replaced Cockrell in 1977. John Pierce replaced Day, and Angelo Rossi (guitar) joined in 1980.

8/16/75	174	4		1 Pablo Cruise		A&M 4528
4/17/76+	139	13		2 Lifeline		A&M 4575
3/5/77	19	46	▲	3 A Place In The Sun		A&M 4625
6/17/78	6	43	▲	4 Worlds Away		A&M 4697
11/17/79	39	17		5 Part Of The Game		A&M 3712
7/18/81	34	18		6 Reflector		A&M 3726

PACIFIC GAS & ELECTRIC
Blues-rock group from California: Charles Allen (vocals), Glenn Schwartz (guitar), Tom Marshall (guitar), Brent Block (bass) and Frank Cook (drums). Allen spearheaded a new lineup in 1971; group name shortened to **PG&E**. Allen died on 5/7/1990 (age 48).

2/1/69	159	12		1 Get It On...		Power 701
9/13/69	91	8		2 Pacific Gas And Electric		Columbia 9900
7/4/70	101	11		3 Are You Ready		Columbia 1017
8/28/71+	182	8		4 PG&E		Columbia 30362

PAGE, Gene
Born on 9/13/1938 in Los Angeles, California. Died on 8/24/1998 (age 59). R&B keyboardist/arranger.

2/1/75	156	4		1 Hot City	[I]	Atlantic 18111

PAGE, Jimmy
Born on 1/9/1944 in Heston, Middlesex, England. Rock guitarist. Member of **The Yardbirds** (1966-68). In October 1968, formed The New Yardbirds, which evolved into **Led Zeppelin**. Page produced all of the group's music. Joined **The Honeydrippers** in 1984, also co-founded **The Firm** with vocalist **Paul Rodgers**. Also see **Coverdale/Page**.

4/3/82	50	10		1 Death Wish II	[I-S]	Swan Song 8511
7/9/88	26	20	●	2 Outrider		Geffen 24188
11/26/94	4	23	▲	3 No Quarter		Atlantic 82706
5/9/98	8	13	●	4 Walking Into Clarksdale		Atlantic 83092
				JIMMY PAGE & ROBERT PLANT (above 2)		
7/22/00	64	9	●	5 Live At The Greek	[L]	TVT 2140 [2]
				JIMMY PAGE & THE BLACK CROWES		

PAGE, Martin
Born on 9/23/1959 in Southampton, Hampshire, England. Pop singer/songwriter.

4/1/95	161	11		1 In The House Of Stone And Light		Mercury 522104

PAGE, Patti
Born Clara Ann Fowler on 11/8/1927 in Muskogee, Oklahoma; raised in Tulsa, Oklahoma. Pop singer. Used multi-voice effect on her recordings. Own TV series *The Patti Page Show* (1955-58) and *The Big Record* (1957-58). Acted in the 1960 movie *Elmer Gantry*.

11/24/56	18	2		1 Manhattan Tower		Mercury 20226
9/1/62	115	5		2 Golden Hits Of The Boys		Mercury 20712
9/21/63	83	6		3 Say Wonderful Things		Columbia 2049 / 8849
5/22/65	27	26		4 Hush, Hush, Sweet Charlotte		Columbia 2353 / 9153
12/25/65+	51ˣ	4		5 Christmas With Patti Page	[X]	Columbia 2414 / 9214
				Christmas charts: 60/65, 51/'67		
7/27/68	168	6		6 Gentle On My Mind		Columbia 9666

PAGE, Tommy
Born on 5/24/1969 in West Caldwell, New Jersey. Pop singer/songwriter.

5/6/89	166	5		1 Tommy Page		Sire 25740
3/24/90	38	23		2 Paintings In My Mind		Sire 26148
6/15/91	192	2		3 From The Heart		Sire 26583

PAIGE, Jennifer
Born on 9/3/1973 in Marietta, Georgia. Pop singer.

8/29/98	139	14		1 Jennifer Paige		Edel America 62171

PAIGE, Kevin
Born on 10/10/1966 in Memphis, Tennessee. Dance-pop singer/songwriter.

9/23/89	107	31		1 Kevin Paige		Chrysalis 21683

PAISLEY, Brad
2000s: #31 / All-Time: #404
Born on 10/28/1972 in Glen Dale, West Virginia. Country singer/songwriter/guitarist. Married actress Kimberly Williams on 3/23/2003.

AWARDS: CMA: Horizon 2000 / Male Vocalist 2007, 2008 & 2009 ★ OPRY: 2001

10/9/99+	102	34	▲	1 Who Needs Pictures		Arista Nashville 18871
6/16/01	31	41	▲	2 Part II		Arista Nashville 67008
8/9/03	8	104	▲²	3 Mud On The Tires	Cat:#7/11	Arista Nashville 50605
9/3/05	2¹	104	▲²	4 Time Well Wasted	Cat:#13/27	Arista Nashville 69642
				CMA: Album of the Year		
11/25/06	47	8		5 Brad Paisley Christmas	Cat:#45/1 [X]	Arista Nashville 00533
				Christmas chart: 2/'06		
7/7/07	3¹	78	▲	6 5th Gear	Cat:#35/2	Arista Nashville 07171
11/22/08	9	17		7 Play	[I]	Arista Nashville 26908
7/18/09	2¹	46↑		8 American Saturday Night		Arista Nashville 47352

PALM BEACH BAND BOYS, The
Vocal trio led by Roger Rigney and arranged by guitarist Billy Mure.

1/28/67	149	1		1 Winchester Cathedral		RCA Victor 3734

PALMER, Amanda
Born on 4/30/1976 in New York; raised in Lexington, Massachusetts. Alternative-rock singer/songwriter/pianist. Member of **The Dresden Dolls**.

10/4/08	77	1		1 Who Killed Amanda Palmer		Roadrunner 617925

PALMER, Robert
All-Time: #395
Born on 1/19/1949 in Batley, Yorkshire, England; raised on the Mediterranean island of Malta. Died of a heart attack on 9/26/2003 (age 54). Pop-rock singer. Lead singer of **Vinegar Joe** and **The Power Station**.

6/14/75	107	15		1 Sneakin' Sally Through The Alley		Island 9294
11/22/75	136	8		2 Pressure Drop		Island 9372
10/23/76	68	16		3 Some People Can Do What They Like		Island 9420
4/1/78	45	25		4 Double Fun		Island 9476
7/21/79	19	24		5 Secrets		Island 9544
10/11/80	59	17		6 Clues		Island 9595
5/15/82	148	5		7 Maybe It's Live	[L]	Island 9665
				recorded on 11/10/1980 at the Dominion Theatre in London, England		
4/30/83	112	19		8 Pride		Island 90065
11/23/85+	8	90	▲²	9 Riptide		Island 90471
11/25/89+	79	17	▲	10 "Addictions" Volume I	[G]	Island 91318
7/16/88	13	44	▲	11 Heavy Nova		EMI-Manhattan 48057
12/1/90	88	28		12 Don't Explain		EMI 93935
11/14/92	173	1		13 Ridin' High		EMI 98923

PALUMBO, John
Born on 1/13/1951 in Steubenville, Ohio. Rock singer/songwriter. Lead singer of **Crack The Sky**.

5/25/85	209	2		1 Blowing Up Detroit		HME 39950

PANIC AT THE DISCO
Punk-rock band from Las Vegas, Nevada: Brendon Urie (vocals, guitar), Ryan Ross (guitar), Brent Wilson (bass) and Spencer Smith (drums). Jon Walker replaced Wilson in May 2006.

10/15/05+	13	66	▲	1 A Fever You Can't Sweat Out		Decaydance 077
4/12/08	2¹	18		2 Pretty.Odd.		Decaydance 430524

PANIC CHANNEL, The
Punk-rock band from Japan: Meguru (vocals), Kana (guitar), Mayo (guitar), Kiri (bass) and Kyo-Ya (drums).

9/2/06	110	1		1 One		Capitol 35318

PANTERA
Heavy-metal band formed in Arlington, Texas: Phil Anselmo (vocals), brothers "Dimebag" Darrell Abbott (guitar) and Vinnie Paul Abbott (drums), with Rex Brown (bass). Group name is Spanish for Panther. The Abbott brothers were also members of **Damageplan**. Anselmo also with **Down** and **Superjoint Ritual**. Darrell was shot to death on stage on 12/8/2004 (age 38).

3/18/95	43ᶜ	2	▲	1 Cowboys From Hell		Atco 91372
				first released in 1990		
3/14/92	44	77	▲²	2 Vulgar Display Of Power	Cat:#41/2	Atco 91758
4/9/94	❶¹	29	▲	3 Far Beyond Driven		EastWest 92302
5/25/96	4	16	▲	4 The Great Southern Trendkill		EastWest 61908
8/16/97	15	12	●	5 Official Live: 101 Proof	[L]	EastWest 62068
4/8/00	4	12	●	6 Reinventing The Steel		EastWest 62451
10/11/03	38	5	▲	7 The Best Of Pantera: Far Beyond The Great Southern Cowboys' Vulgar Hits	Cat:#12/4 [G]	Elektra 73932

Billboard			R I A A	ARTIST	Catalog	Label & Number
DEBUT	PEAK	WKS		Album Title		

PAPA ROACH
Hard-rock band from Vacaville, California: Coby Dick (vocals), Jerry Horton (guitar), Tobin Esperance (bass) and Dave Buckner (drums). Buckner was married to Mia Tyler (daughter of **Aerosmith**'s Steven Tyler) from 2003-05. Tony Palermo replaced Buckner in early 2008.

DEBUT	PEAK	WKS			Catalog	Label & Number
5/13/00	5	65	▲³	1 Infest		DreamWorks 50223
7/6/02	2¹	15	●	2 Lovehatetragedy		DreamWorks 50381
9/18/04	17	61	▲	3 Getting Away With Murder		El Tonal 003142
9/30/06	16	36		4 The Paramour Sessions		El Tonal 007486
4/11/09	8	25		5 Metamorphosis		DGC 012651

PAPERBOY
Born Mitchell Johnson in Los Angeles, California. Male rapper.

2/13/93	48	33	●	1 The Nine Yards		Next Plateau 1012

PAPER LACE
Pop band formed in England: Phil Wright (vocals, drums), Michael Vaughan (guitar), Chris Morris (guitar) and Cliff Fish (bass).

9/7/74	124	8		1 Paper Lace		Mercury 1008

PAPPALARDI, Felix, & Creation
Born on 12/30/1939 in the Bronx, New York. Shot to death by his wife, Gail Collins, on 4/17/1983 (age 43). Rock singer/bassist. Former leader of **Mountain**. The Japanese band Creation consisted of Kazuo "Flash" Takeda (guitar), Yoshiaki "Daybreak" Iijima (guitar), Shigeru "Sugar" Matsumoto (bass) and Masayuki "Thunder" Higuchi (drums).

8/21/76	210	1		1 Felix Pappalardi & Creation		A&M 4586

PARACHUTE
Pop-rock band from Charlottesville, Virginia: Will Anderson (vocals, guitar), Nat McFarland (guitar), Kit French (keyboards), Alex Hargrave (bass) and Johnny Stubblefield (drums).

5/30/09	40	17		1 Losing Sleep		Mercury 012917

PARAMOR, Norrie, His Strings and Orchestra
Born on 5/15/1914 in England. Died of cancer on 9/9/1979 (age 65). Conductor/composer/arranger.

9/8/56	18	3		1 In London, In Love...	[I]	Capitol Int'l. 10025

PARAMORE
Rock band formed in Franklin, Tennessee: Hayley Williams (vocals), brothers Josh Farro (guitar) and Zac Farro (drums), with Jeremy Davis (bass).

9/1/07+	8^C	27		1 All We Know Is Falling	[E]	Fueled By Ramen 076
				released in 2005		
6/30/07	15	78	▲	2 Riot!	Cat:#3/45	Fueled By Ramen 159612
12/13/08	88	3		3 The Final Riot!	[L]	Fueled By Ramen 512243
10/17/09	2¹	33↑	●	4 Brand New Eyes		Fueled By Ramen 518250

PARIS
All-star rock trio: **Bob Welch** (guitar; **Fleetwood Mac**), Glenn Cornick (bass; **Jethro Tull**) and Thom Mooney (drums; **Nazz**). Hunt Sales (later with **Tin Machine**) replaced Mooney in 1976.

2/7/76	103	9		1 Paris		Capitol 11464
9/11/76	152	6		2 Big Towne, 2061		Capitol 11560

PARIS
Born Oscar Jackson on 10/29/1967 in San Francisco, California. Male rapper.

12/22/90+	158	8		1 The Devil Made Me Do It		Tommy Boy 1030
12/12/92	182	3		2 Sleeping With The Enemy		Scarface 100
10/22/94	128	4		3 Guerrilla Funk		Priority 53882
3/25/06	180	1		4 Rebirth Of A Nation		Guerilla Funk 31021
				PUBLIC ENEMY Featuring Paris		

PARIS, Mica
Born Michelle Wallen on 4/27/1969 in London, England. R&B singer.

5/13/89	86	23		1 So Good		Island 90970

PARIS, Sarina
Born on 12/22/1973 in Toronto, Ontario, Canada. Female dance-pop singer.

6/23/01	167	1		1 Sarina Paris		Playland 50175

PARIS, Twila
Born on 12/28/1958 in Forth Worth, Texas; raised in Fayetteville, Arkansas. Christian singer.

4/20/96	87	9		1 Where I Stand		Sparrow 51518
5/2/98	129	4		2 Perennial - Songs For The Seasons Of Life		Sparrow 51627
10/9/99	112	5		3 True North		Sparrow 51690

PARISH, John
Born in England. Alternative-rock singer/songwriter/guitarist/producer.

10/12/96	178	1		1 Dance Hall At Louse Point		Island 524278
4/18/09	80	3		2 A Woman A Man Walked By		Island 012811
				PJ HARVEY & JOHN PARISH (above 2)		

Billboard			R I A A	ARTIST	Catalog	Label & Number
DEBUT	PEAK	WKS		Album Title		

PARKER, Graham
Born on 11/18/1950 in Camberley, Surrey, England. Pop-rock singer/songwriter/guitarist. **The Rumour**: Brinsley Schwarz (guitar), Martin Belmont (guitar), Bob Andrews (keyboards), Andrew Bodnar (bass) and Stephen Goulding (drums). The Shot: Brinsley Schwarz (guitar), Huw Gower (guitar), George Small (keyboards), Kevin Jenkins (bass) and Michael Braun (drums).

DEBUT	PEAK	WKS		Album Title	Catalog	Label & Number
1/29/77	169	7		1 Heat Treatment		Mercury 1117
11/5/77	125	5		2 Stick To Me		Mercury 3706
7/1/78	149	3		3 The Parkerilla	[L]	Mercury 100 [2]
4/14/79	40	24		4 Squeezing Out Sparks		Arista 4223
				RS500 #335		
5/31/80	40	15		5 The Up Escalator		Arista 9517
				GRAHAM PARKER AND THE RUMOUR (above 4)		
4/10/82	51	16		6 Another Grey Area		Arista 9589
8/20/83	59	14		7 The Real Macaw		Arista 8023
4/20/85	57	21		8 Steady Nerves		Elektra 60388
				GRAHAM PARKER AND THE SHOT		
5/28/88	77	19		9 The Mona Lisa's Sister		RCA 8316
2/24/90	165	9		10 Human Soul		RCA 9876
3/23/91	131	8		11 Struck By Lightning		BMG 3013

PARKER, Ivan
Born in Sanford, North Carolina. Gospel singer. Member of the Gold City Quartet.

DEBUT	PEAK	WKS		Album Title	Catalog	Label & Number
6/14/08	188	1		1 The Best Of Ivan Parker: From The Homecoming Series	[K-L]	Gaither 42721

PARKER, Ray Jr.   All-Time: #467
Born on 5/1/1954 in Detroit, Michigan. R&B singer/songwriter/guitarist. Prominent session guitarist in California; worked with **Stevie Wonder**, **Barry White** and others. Formed group **Raydio** in 1977 with Arnell Carmichael, Larry Tolbert, Darren Carmichael and Charles Fearing. Parker went solo in 1982. Knight later recorded in duo **Ollie & Jerry**.

DEBUT	PEAK	WKS		Album Title	Catalog	Label & Number
2/11/78	27	23	●	1 Raydio		Arista 4163
4/14/79	45	30	●	2 Rock On		Arista 4212
				RAYDIO (above 2)		
4/12/80	33	21	●	3 Two Places At The Same Time		Arista 9515
4/18/81	13	26	●	4 A Woman Needs Love		Arista 9543
				RAY PARKER JR. & RAYDIO (above 2)		
4/24/82	11	27	●	5 The Other Woman		Arista 9590
12/18/82+	51	22		6 Greatest Hits	[G]	Arista 9612
11/26/83+	45	23		7 Woman Out Of Control		Arista 8087
12/15/84+	60	15	●	8 Chartbusters	[G]	Arista 8266
10/26/85	65	13		9 Sex And The Single Man		Arista 8280
10/10/87	86	9		10 After Dark		Geffen 24124

PARKER, Robert
Born on 10/14/1930 in New Orleans, Louisiana. R&B singer/saxophonist.

~ ~ ~ ~ ~ ~ ~ ~ ~ ~ ~ *NON-CHARTED ALBUM* ~ ~ ~ ~ ~ ~ ~ ~ ~ ~ ~

1966 **Barefootin'**

PARKS, Michael
Born on 4/24/1940 in Corona, California. Singer/actor. Appeared in several movies. Played "Jim Bronson" in the 1969 TV series *Then Came Bronson*.

DEBUT	PEAK	WKS		Album Title	Catalog	Label & Number
11/8/69+	35	46		1 Closing The Gap		MGM 4646
5/23/70	24	21		2 Long Lonesome Highway		MGM 4662
10/10/70	71	8		3 Blue		MGM 4717
3/13/71	195	1		4 Lost And Found		Verve 5079
8/7/71	218	1		5 The Best Of Michael Parks	[G]	MGM 4784

PARLIAMENT
Highly influential and prolific funk aggregation of nearly 40 musicians spearheaded by **George Clinton** (producer/songwriter/lead singer). Clinton founded doo-wop group The Parliaments in 1955 in Newark, New Jersey. By 1967, evolved into a Detroit-based soul group with lineup of vocalists Clinton, Raymond Davis (died on 7/5/2005, age 65), Calvin Simon, Clarence "Fuzzy" Haskins and Grady Thomas. In 1968, Clinton formed **Funkadelic** with rhythm section of The Parliaments and changed The Parliaments name to Parliament. Although on different labels, Parliament and Funkadelic shared the same personnel which included several members of **The JB's**: brothers Phelps "Catfish" (guitar) and William "Bootsy" Collins (bass), Frank "Kash" Waddy (drums) and horn players Maceo Parker and **Fred Wesley**. Known as "A Parliafunkadelicament Thang," this funk corporation hosted various offshoots, including **The Brides Of Funkenstein**, among others. Concert tours featured elaborate staging and characters. Simon, Haskins and Thomas split from Clinton in 1977 and recorded as Funkadelic in 1981. The corporation disassembled in the early 1980s. Clinton signed his first solo recording contract in 1982. Clinton regrouped with The P-Funk Allstars in 1996.

AWARD: R&R Hall of Fame: 1997

DEBUT	PEAK	WKS		Album Title	Catalog	Label & Number
8/24/74	201	2		1 Up For The Down Stroke		Casablanca 7002
5/3/75	91	18		2 Chocolate City		Casablanca 7014
2/21/76	13	37	▲	3 Mothership Connection		Casablanca 7022
				RS500 #274		
10/16/76	20	22	●	4 The Clones Of Dr. Funkenstein		Casablanca 7034
5/21/77	29	19	●	5 Parliament Live/P. Funk Earth Tour	[L]	Casablanca 7053 [2]
12/24/77+	13	34	▲	6 Funkentelechy Vs. The Placebo Syndrome		Casablanca 7084
12/16/78+	23	18	●	7 Motor-Booty Affair		Casablanca 7125
12/22/79+	44	19	●	8 Gloryhallastoopid (Or Pin The Tale On The Funky)		Casablanca 7195
1/10/81	61	7		9 Trombipulation		Casablanca 7249

PARNELL, Lee Roy
Born on 12/21/1956 in Abilene, Texas. Country singer/songwriter/guitarist. Cousin of **Robert Earl Keen**.

| 4/27/96 | 173 | 3 | | 1 **We All Get Lucky Sometimes** | | Arista 18790 |

PARR, John
Born on 11/18/1954 in Nottingham, Nottinghamshire, England. Pop-rock singer/songwriter.

| 12/15/84+ | 48 | 26 | | 1 **John Parr** | | Atlantic 80180 |

PARSONS, Alan, Project   All-Time: #302
Born on 12/20/1948 in London, England. Guitarist/keyboardist/producer. Engineered *Abbey Road* by **The Beatles** and *Dark Side Of The Moon* by **Pink Floyd**. Project features various musicians and vocalists. Eric Woolfson (vocals, keyboards) contributes most of the lyrics. Woolfson died of cancer on 12/2/2009 (age 64).

5/15/76	38	46		1 **Tales Of Mystery And Imagination - Edgar Allan Poe**		20th Century 508
7/16/77	9	54	▲	2 **I Robot**		Arista 7002
7/1/78	26	25	●	3 **Pyramid**		Arista 4180
9/15/79	13	27	●	4 **Eve**	Cat:#12/89	Arista 9504
11/15/80+	13	58	▲	5 **The Turn Of A Friendly Card**		Arista 9518
6/19/82	7	41	▲	6 **Eye In The Sky**		Arista 9599
11/19/83	53	29	●	7 **The Best Of The Alan Parsons Project**	[G]	Arista 8193
3/17/84	15	26	●	8 **Ammonia Avenue**		Arista 8204
3/9/85	46	19		9 **Vulture Culture**		Arista 8263
2/1/86	43	18		10 **Stereotomy**		Arista 8384
2/7/87	57	14		11 **Gaudi**		Arista 8448
11/13/93	122	4		12 **Try Anything Once**		Arista 18741

ALAN PARSONS

PARSONS, Gram
Born Cecil Connor on 11/5/1946 in Winter Haven, Florida. Died of a drug overdose on 9/19/1973 (age 26). Country-rock singer/guitarist. Member of **The Byrds** (1968) and the **Flying Burrito Brothers** (1968-70). Also see **Various Artists Compilations:** *Return To Grievous Angel - A Tribute To Gram Parsons.*

| 2/16/74 | 195 | 3 | | 1 **Grievous Angel** | | Reprise 2171 |

RS500 #429

PARTLAND BROTHERS
Pop-rock duo from Colgan, Ontario, Canada: brothers Chris Partland (vocals, guitars) and George "G.P." Partland (vocals, percussion).

| 6/27/87 | 146 | 5 | | 1 **Electric Honey** | | Manhattan 53050 |

PARTON, Dolly   All-Time: #87
Born on 1/19/1946 in Locust Ridge, Tennessee. Country singer/songwriter/actress. Regular on **Porter Wagoner**'s TV show (1967-74). Starred in the movies *9 To 5*, *The Best Little Whorehouse In Texas*, *Steel Magnolias* and *Straight Talk*. In 1986, opened Dollywood theme park in the Smoky Mountains. Hosted own TV variety show in 1987. Also see **Various Artists Compilations:** *Just Because I'm A Woman: Songs Of Dolly Parton.*

AWARDS: C&W Hall of Fame: 1999 ★ CMA: Vocal Group (w/ Porter Wagoner) 1968 / Vocal Duo (w/ Porter Wagoner) 1970 & 1971 / Female Vocalist 1975 & 1976 / Entertainer 1978 ★ OPRY: 1969

11/22/69	194	2		1 **My Blue Ridge Mountain Boy**		RCA Victor 4188
3/22/69	184	4		2 **Just The Two Of Us**		RCA Victor 4039
8/16/69	162	5		3 **Always, Always**		RCA Victor 4186
4/4/70	137	7		4 **Porter Wayne And Dolly Rebecca**		RCA Victor 4305
10/10/70	191	2		5 **Once More**		RCA Victor 4388
3/13/71	142	3		6 **Two Of A Kind**		RCA Victor 4490

PORTER WAGONER & DOLLY PARTON (above 5)

6/12/71	198	1		7 **Joshua**		RCA Victor 4507
4/2/77	71	21		8 **New Harvest...First Gathering**		RCA Victor 2188
10/29/77+	20	47	▲	9 **Here You Come Again**		RCA Victor 2544

Grammy: Female Country Vocal

8/12/78	27	34	●	10 **Heartbreaker**		RCA Victor 2797
6/23/79	40	17	●	11 **Great Balls Of Fire**		RCA Victor 3361
5/3/80	71	13		12 **Dolly Dolly Dolly**		RCA Victor 3546
12/6/80+	11	34	●	13 **9 To 5 And Odd Jobs**		RCA Victor 3852
4/24/82	106	12		14 **Heartbreak Express**		RCA Victor 4289
6/4/83	127	11		15 **Burlap & Satin**		RCA Victor 4691
2/18/84	73	14		16 **The Great Pretender**		RCA Victor 4940
3/28/87	6	48	▲	17 **Trio**		Warner 25491

DOLLY PARTON, LINDA RONSTADT, EMMYLOU HARRIS
Grammy: Group Country Vocal / Country Vocal Collaboration

12/19/87+	153	8		18 **Rainbow**		Columbia 40968
4/6/91	24	47	▲	19 **Eagle When She Flies**		Columbia 46882
3/13/93	16	25	▲	20 **Slow Dancing With The Moon**		Columbia 53199
11/20/93	42	16	●	21 **Honky Tonk Angels**		Columbia 53414

DOLLY PARTON, LORETTA LYNN, TAMMY WYNETTE

| 9/16/95 | 54 | 14 | | 22 **Something Special** | | Columbia 67140 |
| 10/12/96 | 122 | 10 | | 23 **Treasures** | | Rising Tide 53041 |

				PARTON, Dolly — cont'd		
9/12/98	167	2		24 Hungry Again		Decca 70041
2/27/99	62	14	●	25 Trio II		Asylum 62275
				EMMYLOU HARRIS, LINDA RONSTADT, DOLLY PARTON		
11/20/99	198	1		26 The Grass Is Blue		Blue Eye 3900
				Grammy: Bluegrass Album		
2/10/01	97	9		27 Little Sparrow		Sugar Hill 3927
7/27/02	58	10		28 Halos & Horns		Blue Eye 3946
11/29/03	167	1		29 For God And Country		Blue Eye 79756
10/29/05	48	6		30 Those Were The Days		Blue Eye 4007
3/15/08	17	17		31 Backwoods Barbie		Dolly 925
				CHRISTMAS ALBUMS:		
12/8/84+	31	8	▲²	32 Once Upon A Christmas	**Cat:**#15/13	RCA Victor 5307
				KENNY ROGERS & DOLLY PARTON		
				Christmas charts: 1/'84, 4/'85, 10/'87, 16/'88, 15/'89, 14/'90, 14/'91, 19/'92, 25/'93		
11/26/94	37ˣ	1	●	33 Home For Christmas	**Cat:**#37/4	Columbia 46796
				first released in 1990		
				GREATEST HITS & COMPILATIONS:		
10/16/82	77	23	▲	34 Greatest Hits		RCA Victor 4422
6/21/03	130	2		35 Ultimate Dolly Parton		RCA 52008
				LIVE ALBUMS:		
8/15/70	154	2		36 A Real Live Dolly		RCA Victor 4387
				recorded on 4/25/1970 at Sevier County High School in Tennessee		
10/15/94	87	10		37 Heartsongs: Live From Home		Columbia 66123
				recorded on 4/23/1994 at the Dollywood Celebrity Theater in Tennessee		
10/2/04	161	1		38 Live And Well		Blue Eye 3998 [2]
11/28/09	195	1		39 Live From London		Dolly 925
				SOUNDTRACKS:		
7/21/84	135	7		40 Rhinestone		RCA Victor 5032
4/25/92	138	3		41 Straight Talk		Hollywood 61303
				~ ~ ~ ~ ~ ~ ~ ~ ~ ~ **NON-CHARTED ALBUM** ~ ~ ~ ~ ~ ~ ~ ~ ~ ~		
				1971 **Coat Of Many Colors**		
				RS500 #299		

PARTRIDGE FAMILY, The

Popularized through *The Partridge Family* TV series, broadcast from 1970-74. Recordings by series stars **David Cassidy** (lead singer) and real-life stepmother, Shirley Jones (backing vocals). David, son of actor Jack Cassidy, was born on 4/12/1950 in New York City; raised in California. Shirley, born on 3/31/1934 in Smithton, Pennsylvania, starred in the movie musicals *Oklahoma* and *The Music Man;* married David's father in 1956.

10/31/70+	4	68	●	1 The Partridge Family Album		Bell 6050
4/3/71	3³	53	●	2 Up To Date		Bell 6059
8/28/71	9	35	●	3 The Partridge Family Sound Magazine		Bell 6064
12/4/71	❶⁴ˣ	7	●	4 A Partridge Family Christmas Card [X]		Bell 6066
				Christmas charts: 1/'71, 9/'72		
3/25/72	18	17	●	5 The Partridge Family Shopping Bag		Bell 6072
9/16/72	21	23	●	6 The Partridge Family At Home With Their Greatest Hits [G]		Bell 1107
12/16/72+	41	16		7 The Partridge Family Notebook		Bell 1111
7/7/73	167	5		8 Crossword Puzzle		Bell 1122

PARTY, The

Dance group from Florida: Tiffini Hale, Albert Fields, Chase Hampton, Damon Pampolina and Deedee Magno. All were cast members of TV's *The Mickey Mouse Club* in 1988.

10/6/90	116	20		1 The Party		Hollywood 60980
10/5/91	77	12		2 In The Meantime, In Between Time		Hollywood 61225
9/12/92	163	4		3 Free		Hollywood 61358

PASADENAS, The

R&B vocal group from England: brothers Aaron, David and Michael Milliner, with John Banfield and Hammish Seelochan.

3/18/89	89	12		1 To Whom It May Concern		Columbia 45065

PASSAGE

Contemporary gospel trio from Los Angeles, California: husband-and-wife Louis and Valerie Johnson, with Richard Heath. Louis is one-half of **The Brothers Johnson**.

4/11/81	205	5		1 Passage		A&M 4851

PASSENGERS

Collaboration between **U2** and producer **Brian Eno**.

11/25/95	76	4		1 Original Soundtracks 1		Island 524166

PASSION PIT

Electronic-dance band from Cambridge, Massachusetts: Michael Angelakos, Ian Hultquist, Ayad Adhamy, Jeff Apruzzese and Nate Donmoyer.

6/6/09	51	26		1 Manners		Frenchkiss 038

PASSION WORSHIP BAND
Christian group which brings together various speakers and musicians from around the world. Spearheaded by Matt Redman (from England), **Chris Tomlin** (from Texas) and Charlie Hall (from Oklahoma).

4/1/00	139	1		1 Passion: The Road To OneDay		Sparrow 51740
11/11/00	158	2		2 Passion: OneDay Live .... [L]		Sparrow 51768
4/27/02	77	7		3 Passion: Our Love Is Loud .... [L]		Sparrow 51923
3/13/04	163	3		4 Passion: Hymns Ancient And Modern		Sparrow 83817
9/6/03	107	3		5 Sacred Revolution: The Songs From OneDay03		Sixsteps 84393
4/30/05	74	6		6 Passion: How Great Is Our God		Sixsteps 63574
4/22/06	69	3		7 Passion: Everything Glorious .... [L]		Sixsteps 48094
1/20/07	168	1		8 The Best Of Passion (So Far) .... [G]		Sixsteps 42180
2/23/08	74	3		9 Passion: God Of This City		Sixsteps 15422

PASSPORT
Jazz-fusion band from Germany. Led by Klaus Doldinger (sax, keyboards). Numerous personnel changes with Doldinger the only constant.

3/15/75	137	7		1 Cross-Collateral .... [I]		Atco 107
5/15/76	204	4		2 Infinity Machine .... [I]		Atco 132
4/23/77	191	3		3 Iguacu .... [I]		Atco 149
6/3/78	140	7		4 Sky Blue .... [I]		Atlantic 19177
5/26/79	201	6		5 Garden Of Eden .... [I]		Atlantic 19233
4/5/80	163	4		6 Oceanliner .... [I]		Atlantic 19265
8/29/81	175	3		7 Blue Tattoo .... [I]		Atlantic 19304

PASTORIUS, Jaco
Born on 12/1/1951 in Norristown, Pennsylvania. Died of injuries suffered in a beating on 9/22/1987 (age 35). Jazz-rock bassist. Member of **Weather Report**.

5/8/76	203	6		1 Jaco Pastorius .... [I]		Epic 33949
8/15/81	161	3		2 Word Of Mouth .... [I]		Warner 3535

PASTOR TROY
Born Micah Troy on 11/18/1977 in College Park, Georgia. Male rapper.

8/12/00	102	3		1 Book I		Hendu 00007
				PASTOR TROY AND THE CONGREGATION		
6/9/01	83	11		2 Face Off		Madd Society 014173
10/12/02	13	7		3 Universal Soldier		Madd Society 064652
4/10/04	30	6		4 By Any Means Necessary		Khaotic 002297
3/19/05	112	2		5 Face Off Part II		Money & Power 7800
5/6/06	150	2		6 Stay Tru		845 Records 118
8/12/06	130	1		7 By Choice Or By Force		Money & Power 5904
7/21/07	91	3		8 Tool Muziq		Money & Power 185
3/8/08	116	2		9 Attitude Adjuster		Real Talk 44
5/2/09	121	1		10 Feel Me Or Kill Me		Money & Power 280

PATINKIN, Mandy
Born Mandel Patinkin on 11/30/1952 in Chicago, Illinois. Actor/singer. Appeared in several movies, Broadway and TV shows.

11/11/95	136	5		1 Oscar & Steve		Nonesuch 79392
				all songs written by Oscar Hammerstein II and Stephen Sondheim		

PATRA
Born Dorothy Smith on 11/22/1972 in Kingston, Jamaica. Female dance-reggae singer.

4/23/94	103	25	●	1 Queen Of The Pack		Epic 53763
9/2/95	151	4		2 Scent Of Attraction		550 Music 67094

PATRULLA 81
Latin band from Durango, Mexico: father-and-son Jose Medina and Jose Medina Jr., with Diego Fabela, Arnulfo Tovar, Jose Carrasco and Luis Berumen.

7/31/04	199	1		1 En Vivo Desde: Dallas, Texas .... [F]		Disa 720378
5/7/05	54	11		2 Divinas .... [F]		Disa 726847
6/24/06	125	2		3 Tierra Extrana .... [F]		Disa 720852
3/7/09	66	6		4 Quiereme Mas .... [F]		Disa 724152

PATTERSON, Don
Born on 7/22/1936 in Columbus, Ohio. Died on 2/10/1988 (age 51). Jazz organist.

12/16/67	85 [X]	3		1 Holiday Soul .... [X-I]		Prestige 7415

PATTERSON, Kellee
Born in Gary, Indiana. R&B singer/actress. Crowned Miss Indiana in 1971.

1/21/78	201	4		1 Be Happy		Shadybrook 007

PATTON, Robbie
Born in England. Pop-rock singer/songwriter.

8/15/81	162	6		1 Distant Shores		Liberty 1107

Billboard			R I A A	ARTIST		
DEBUT	**PEAK**	**WKS**		**Album Title**	**Catalog**	**Label & Number**

PATTY, Sandi
Born on 7/12/1956 in Oklahoma City, Oklahoma; raised in Anderson, Indiana. Christian singer.

11/30/96	143	5		1 O Holy Night! .... [X]		Word 67313
				Christmas chart: 13/'96		
11/29/97	155	3		2 Artist Of My Soul		Word 68583

PAUL, Billy
Born Paul Williams on 12/1/1934 in Philadelphia, Pennsylvania. R&B singer.

8/22/70	183	5		1 Ebony Woman		Neptune 201
4/28/73	186	3		2 Ebony Woman .... [R]		Philadelphia Int'l. 32118
				reissue of #1 above		
10/16/71	197	2		3 Going East		Philadelphia Int'l. 30580
11/25/72+	17	27	●	4 360 Degrees Of Billy Paul		Philadelphia Int'l. 31793
11/17/73+	110	26		5 War Of The Gods		Philadelphia Int'l. 32409
7/6/74	187	4		6 Live In Europe.. [L]		Philadelphia Int'l. 32952
3/15/75	140	9		7 Got My Head On Straight		Philadelphia Int'l. 33157
12/27/75+	139	20		8 When Love Is New		Philadelphia Int'l. 33843
1/22/77	88	18		9 Let 'Em In		Philadelphia Int'l. 34389
1/28/78	152	4		10 Only The Strong Survive		Philadelphia Int'l. 34923
2/9/80	205	2		11 Best Of Billy Paul .... [G]		Philadelphia I. 36314 [2]

PAUL, Henry, Band
Born on 8/25/1949 in Kingston, New York. Rock singer/guitarist. Member of the **Outlaws** and **BlackHawk**. His band: Dave Fiester (guitar), Billy Crain (guitar), Wally Dentz (bass) and Bill Hoffman (drums).

6/2/79	107	12		1 Grey Ghost...		Atlantic 19232
8/2/80	120	8		2 Feel The Heat..		Atlantic 19273
12/26/81+	158	8		3 Anytime		Atlantic 19325

PAUL, Les, and Mary Ford
Pop duo. Paul was born Lester Polsfuss on 6/9/1915 in Waukesha, Wisconsin; died of pneumonia on 8/13/2009 (age 94). Ford was born Colleen Summers on 7/7/1924 in Pasadena, California; died on 9/30/1977 (age 53). Les Paul was an innovator in electric guitar and multi-track recordings. Married to vocalist Mary Ford from 1949-63.

AWARDS: (Paul): Grammys: Trustees 1983 / Technical 2001 ★ R&R Hall of Fame: 1988 (Early Influence)

12/25/54+	7	16		1 Les Paul And Mary Ford [EP]		Capitol 9121
5/14/55	10	3		2 Les And Mary		Capitol 577
				EP: Capitol EBF-577 (#10); LP: Capitol W-577 (#15)		
5/29/76	172	5		3 Chester & Lester .... [I]		RCA Victor 1167
				CHET ATKINS & LES PAUL		
				Grammy: Country Instrumental Album		
9/17/05	152	2		4 American Made World Played...		Capitol 34064
				LES PAUL & FRIENDS		

PAUL, Sean
Born Sean Paul Henriques on 1/8/1973 in Kingston, Jamaica. Reggae singer/songwriter.

11/30/02+	9	85	▲²	1 Dutty Rock		VP 83620
				Grammy: Reggae Album		
10/15/05	7	52	▲	2 The Trinity		VP 83788
9/5/09	12	7		3 Imperial Blaze		VP 520047

PAUL & PAULA
Pop vocal duo. Ray "Paul" Hildebrand was born on 12/21/1940 in Joshua, Texas. Jill "Paula" Jackson was born on 5/20/1942 in McCaney, Texas.

2/23/63	9	25		1 Paul & Paula Sing For Young Lovers		Philips 600078
8/10/63	99	5		2 We Go Together		Philips 600089
12/7/63	13ˣ	3		3 Holiday For Teens .... [X]		Philips 600101

PAULSEN, Pat
Born on 7/6/1927 in South Bend, Washington. Died of kidney failure on 4/24/1997 (age 69). Stand-up comedian/actor. Regular on **The Smothers Brothers** TV show. Appeared in several movies. Best-known for his perpetual presidential campaign.

10/19/68	71	10		1 Pat Paulsen For President.. [C]		Mercury 61179

PAUPERS, The
Folk-rock band from Toronto, Ontario, Canada: Skip Prokop (vocals, drums; **Lighthouse**), Adam Mitchell (guitar), Chuck Beal (mandolin) and Dennis Gerrard (bass).

11/11/67	178	2		1 Magic People		Verve Forecast 3026

PAVAROTTI, Luciano
Born on 10/12/1935 in Modena, Italy. Died of pancreatic cancer on 9/6/2007 (age 71). World-renown operatic tenor. Starred in the 1982 movie *Yes, Giorgio*. Member of **The Three Tenors**.

11/24/79+	77	21	●	1 O Sole Mio - Favorite Neapolitan Songs [F]		London 26560
				Grammy: Classical Vocal		
11/6/82	158	3		2 Yes, Giorgio... [F-S]		London 9001
12/17/83+	6ˣ	19	▲	3 O Holy Night	Cat.#25/9 [X-F]	London 26473
				first released in 1976; Christmas charts: 7/'83, 6/'84, 21/'88, 19/'89, 20/'90, 14/'91, 22/'92, 16/'07, 32/'08		
9/8/84	103	14		4 Mamma .... [F]		London 411959
1/4/92	173	1		5 Pavarotti Songbook .... [F]		London 433513
10/11/03	135	2		6 Ti Adoro .... [F]		Decca 001096

Billboard			R I A A	ARTIST		
DEBUT	PEAK	WKS		Album Title	Catalog	Label & Number

PAVAROTTI, Luciano — cont'd

11/29/08	153	2		7 The Duets		Decca 012245
				GREATEST HITS & COMPILATIONS:		
3/26/77	209	1		8 The Great Pavarotti .... [F]		London 26510
6/7/80	94	18		9 Pavarotti's Greatest Hits .... [F]		London 2003 [2]
4/24/82	141	7		10 Luciano .... [F]		London 2013
9/22/07	150	1		11 The Greatest Tenor Of All Time .... [F]		Madacy 52385 [2]
10/6/07+	85	8		12 Pavarotti's Greatest Hits .... [F]		London 009040
10/27/07	137	6		13 Pavarotti Forever .... [F]		Decca 001070 [2]
				LIVE ALBUMS:		
7/1/95	185	1		14 Pavarotti & Friends 2 .... [F]		London 444460
				recorded at the Parco Novi Sad in Modena, Italy		
9/22/07	76	1		15 The Best: Farewell Tour .... Cat:#9/3 [F]		Decca 005183 [2]

PAVEMENT

Rock band formed in Stockton, California: **Stephen Malkmus** (vocals, guitar), Scott Kannberg (guitar), Bob Nastanovich (percussion), Mark Ibold (bass) and Steve West (drums).

3/5/94	121	4		1 Crooked Rain, Crooked Rain		Matador 92343
				RS500 #210		
11/13/04	164	1		2 Crooked Rain, Crooked Rain: L.A.'s Desert Origins .... [R]		Matador 610 [2]
				features the original album, with extra tracks		
4/29/95	117	1		3 Wowee Zowee		Matador 45898
11/25/06	185	1		4 Wowee Zowee: Sordid Sentinels Edition .... [R]		Matador 722 [2]
				features the original album, with extra tracks		
3/1/97	70	4		5 Brighten The Corners		Matador 55226
6/26/99	95	2		6 Terror Twilight		Matador 260
11/9/02	152	1		7 Slanted And Enchanted: Luxe And Reduxe .... [R]		Matador 10557 [2]
				features the original album (see non-charted album below), with extra tracks		

~ ~ ~ ~ ~ ~ ~ ~ ~ ~ ~ **NON-CHARTED ALBUM** ~ ~ ~ ~ ~ ~ ~ ~ ~ ~ ~

1992 **Slanted And Enchanted**
RS500 #134

PAVLOV'S DOG

Rock band from St. Louis, Missouri: David Surkamp (vocals), Steve Scorfina (guitar), David Hamilton (keyboards), Doug Rayburn (flute), Siegfried Carver (violin), Rick Stockton (bass) and Mike Safron (drums).

4/5/75	181	6		1 Pampered Menial		ABC 866

PAVONE, Rita

Born on 8/23/1945 in Turin, Italy. Pop singer.

6/20/64	60	14		1 Rita Pavone		RCA Victor 2900

PAXTON, Tom

Born on 10/31/1937 in Chicago, Illinois. Folk singer/songwriter.

AWARD: Grammy: Lifetime Achievement 2009

8/16/69	155	4		1 The Things I Notice Now		Elektra 74043
6/6/70	184	4		2 Tom Paxton 6		Elektra 74066
5/15/71	213	2		3 The Compleat Tom Paxton .... [L]		Elektra 2003 [2]
8/14/71	120	3		4 How Come The Sun		Reprise 6443
8/26/72	191	4		5 Peace Will Come		Reprise 2096
8/4/73	203	3		6 New Songs For Old Friends .... [L]		Reprise 2144
				recorded at the Marquee Club in London		

PAX217

Rock-rap band from Anaheim, California: brothers Dave Tosti (vocals) and Aaron Tosti (drums), with Jesse Craig (guitar) and Josh Auer (bass).

6/8/02	191	1		1 Engage		ForeFront 25295

PAYCHECK, Johnny

Born Donald Eugene Lytle on 5/31/1938 in Greenfield, Ohio. Died of emphysema on 2/18/2003 (age 64). Country singer/songwriter/guitarist.

AWARD: OPRY: 1997

3/11/72	204	1		1 She's All I Got		Epic 31141
2/18/78	72	14	▲	2 Take This Job And Shove It		Epic 35045
1/20/79	203	2		3 Armed And Crazy		Epic 35444

PAYNE, Freda

Born on 9/19/1945 in Detroit, Michigan. R&B singer. Sister of Scherrie Payne (of **The Supremes**). Married to **Gregory Abbott** from 1976-79.

8/22/70	60	13		1 Band Of Gold		Invictus 7301
6/12/71	76	18		2 Contact		Invictus 7307
4/15/72	152	8		3 The Best Of Freda Payne .... [G]		Invictus 9804

PAZ, Espinoza

Born Isidro Espinoza on 10/29/1981 in Sinaloa, Mexico. Male Latin singer/songwriter.

6/6/09	116	6		1 Yo No Canto, Pero Lo Intentamos .... [F]		ASL 730251

Billboard			R I A A	ARTIST		
DEBUT	PEAK	WKS		Album Title	Catalog	Label & Number

PEACHES
Born Merrill Nisker on 11/11/1968 in Toronto, Ontario, Canada. Female electronic musician.

| 7/29/06 | 168 | 1 | | 1 Impeach My Bush | | XL 201 |
| 5/23/09 | 160 | 1 | | 2 I Feel Cream | | XL 415 |

PEACHES & HERB
R&B vocal duo from Washington DC: Francine "Peaches" Barker (born on 4/28/1947; died on 8/13/2005, age 58) and Herb Fame (born Herbert Feemster on 10/1/1942). Re-formed with Fame and Linda "Peaches" Greene in 1977.

3/25/67	30	25		1 Let's Fall In Love		Date 4004
9/2/67	135	12		2 For Your Love		Date 4005
9/21/68	187	3		3 Peaches & Herb's Greatest Hits	[G]	Date 4012
11/25/78+	2[6]	46	▲	4 2 Hot!		Polydor 6172
11/10/79	31	30	●	5 Twice The Fire		Polydor 6239
10/11/80	120	6		6 Worth The Wait		Polydor 6298
9/12/81	168	3		7 Sayin' Something!		Polydor 6332
7/2/83	204	1		8 Remember		Columbia 38746

PEANUT BUTTER CONSPIRACY, The
Psychedelic-rock band from Los Angeles, California: Barbara "Sandi" Robison (vocals), Lance Fent (guitar), John Merrill (guitar), Al Brackett (bass) and Jim Voigt (drums). Robison died on 4/22/1988 (age 43). Voigt died on 11/7/2000 (age 54).

| 5/20/67 | 196 | 3 | | 1 The Peanut Butter Conspiracy Is Spreading | | Columbia 2654 |

PEARL HARBOR & THE EXPLOSIONS
Rock band from San Francisco, California: Pearl E. Gates (vocals), Peter Bilt (guitar), Hilary Stench (bass) and John Stench (drums).

1/26/80	107	11		1 Pearl Harbor And The Explosions		Warner 3404
2/21/81	170	3		2 Don't Follow Me, I'm Lost Too		Warner 3515
				PEARL HARBOUR		

PEARL JAM   1990s: #21 / 2000s: #9 / All-Time: #93
Rock band formed in Seattle, Washington: **Eddie Vedder** (vocals; born on 12/23/1964), Stone Gossard (guitar; born on 7/20/1966), Mike McCready (guitar; born on 4/5/1965), Jeff Ament (bass; born on 3/10/1963) and Dave Krusen (drums; born on 3/10/1966). Gossard and Ament (born on 5/17/1968) replaced Krusen in 1993. Gossard and Ament were members of **Mother Love Bone**. All except Krusen recorded with **Temple Of The Dog**. Band acted in the 1992 movie *Singles* as Matt Dillon's band, Citizen Dick. Abbruzzese left band in August 1994. Drummer Jack Irons (of the **Red Hot Chili Peppers**; born on 7/18/1962) joined in late 1994. McCready also put together **Mad Season** in 1994. Matt Cameron (born on 11/28/1962) replaced Irons in 1999.

1/4/92	2[4]	250	▲[13]	1 Ten Cat:❶[3]/43	Epic/Associated 47857
				RS500 #207	
11/6/93	❶[5]	67	▲[7]	2 Vs.	Epic/Associated 53136
12/10/94	❶[1]	55	▲[5]	3 Vitalogy	Epic 66900
				RS500 #492	
9/14/96	❶[2]	24	▲	4 No Code	Epic 67500
2/21/98	2[1]	36	▲	5 Yield	Epic 68164
6/3/00	2[1]	17	●	6 Binaural	Epic 63665
11/30/02	5	14	●	7 Riot Act	Epic 86825
11/29/03	15	11	●	8 Lost Dogs [K]	Epic 85738 [2]
12/4/04	16	22	▲	9 Rearviewmirror: Greatest Hits 1991-2003 Cat:#41/2 [G]	Epic 93535 [2]
5/20/06	2[1]	17	●	10 Pearl Jam	J Records 71467
10/10/09	❶[1]	32	●	11 Backspacer	Monkeywrench 8274
				LIVE ALBUMS:	
12/12/98	15	15	▲	12 Live On Two Legs	Epic 69752
10/14/00	103	1		13 16/6/00: Spodek, Katowice, Poland	Epic 85052 [2]
10/14/00	125	1		14 22/6/00: Fila Forum Arena, Milan, Italy	Epic 85064 [2]
10/14/00	134	1		15 20/6/00: Arena Di Verona, Verona, Italy	Epic 85061 [2]
10/14/00	137	1		16 30/5/00: Wembley Arena, London, England	Epic 85012 [2]
10/14/00	175	1		17 26/6/00: Sporthalle, Hamburg, Germany	Epic 85073 [2]
3/17/01	159	1		18 Jones Beach, New York - August 25, 2000	Epic 85545 [2]
3/17/01	163	1		19 Boston, Massachusetts - August 29, 2000	Epic 85551 [2]
3/17/01	174	1		20 Indianapolis, Indiana - August 18, 2000	Epic 85530 [2]
3/17/01	176	1		21 Pittsburgh, Pennsylvania - September 5, 2000	Epic 85566 [2]
3/17/01	179	1		22 Philadelphia, Pennsylvania - September 1, 2000	Epic 85557 [2]
3/17/01	181	1		23 Tampa, Florida - August 12, 2000	Epic 85518 [2]
3/17/01	191	1		24 Memphis, Tennessee - August 15, 2000	Epic 85524 [2]
4/14/01	98	1		25 Seattle, Washington - November 6, 2000	Epic 85641 [3]
4/14/01	152	1		26 Las Vegas, Nevada - October 22, 2000	Epic 85611 [2]
6/28/03	182	1		27 Tokyo, Japan: March 3rd 2003	Epic 90336 [2]
8/2/03	169	1		28 State College Pennsylvania: May 3rd 2003	Epic 90500 [3]
8/14/04	18	9		29 Benaroya Hall: October 22nd 2003	Ten Club 63424 [2]
7/14/07	36	2		30 Live At The Gorge 05/06	Monkeywrench 8796 [7]

Billboard			R I A A	ARTIST		
DEBUT	PEAK	WKS		Album Title	Catalog	Label & Number

PEARLS BEFORE SWINE
Folk-rock band formed in Melbourne, Florida: husband-and-wife Tom Rapp (vocals, guitar) and Elizabeth Rapp (vocals), with Wayne Harley (banjo) and Jim Fairs (guitar).

9/27/69	200	2		1 These Things Too		Reprise 6364
5/15/71	223	2		2 City Of Gold		Reprise 6442

PEARSON, Duke
Born Columbus Pearson on 8/17/1932 in Atlanta, Georgia. Died of multiple sclerosis on 8/4/1980 (age 47). Jazz trumpeter/pianist.

4/5/69	193	2		1 The Phantom		Blue Note 84293

PEASTON, David
Born in St. Louis, Missouri. R&B singer/songwriter. Nephew of **Fontella Bass**.

8/5/89	113	18		1 Introducing...David Peaston..		Geffen 24228

PEBBLES
Born Perri McKissack on 8/29/1965 in Oakland, California. Nicknamed "Pebbles" by her family for her resemblance to cartoon character Pebbles Flintstone. Formerly married to singer/songwriter/producer L.A. Reid (of **The Deele**). Cousin of **Cherrelle**. Assembled/managed **TLC**.

2/13/88	14	38	▲	1 Pebbles		MCA 42094
9/29/90	37	36	●	2 Always		MCA 10025

PECK, Danielle
Born on 9/14/1978 in Jacksonville, North Carolina; raised in Coshocton, Ohio. Country singer/songwriter.

6/24/06	115	2		1 Danielle Peck		Big Machine 010160

PEEBLES, Ann
Born on 4/27/1947 in Kinloch, Missouri; later based in Memphis, Tennessee. R&B singer/songwriter.

4/22/72	188	3		1 Straight From The Heart		Hi 32065
3/9/74	155	7		2 I Can't Stand The Rain		Hi 32079

PEEL, David, & The Lower East Side
Band of street musicians from New York: David Peel (vocals, harmonica), Larry Adam (guitar), Billy Joe White (guitar), George Cori (bass) and Harold Black (percussion).

5/24/69	186	3		1 Have A Marijuana .... **[L]**		Elektra 74032
				recorded on the streets of New York City		
5/27/72	191	3		2 The Pope Smokes Dope		Apple 3391
				produced by **John Lennon** and **Yoko Ono**		

PEEPING TOM
Born Michael Patton on 1/27/1968 in Eureka, California. Hard-rock singer. Leader of **Faith No More**, **Mr. Bungle**, **Fantomas** and **Tomahawk**.

6/17/06	103	1		1 Peeping Tom..		Ipecac 77

PEEPLES, Nia
Born on 12/10/1961 in Hollywood, California. R&B singer/actress. Played "Nicole Chapman" on TV's *Fame*. Hosted *Top Of The Pops* TV show and own syndicated music video dance TV program, *Party Machine*. Married to **Howard Hewett** from 1989-93.

5/14/88	97	21		1 Nothin' But Trouble		Mercury 834303

PEEWEE
Born Irvin Salinas on 12/8/1988 in Othello, Washington. Male Latin singer.

8/29/09	181	1		1 Yo Soy .... **[F]**		EMI Televisa 65737

PENA, Jennifer
Born on 9/17/1983 in Corpus Christi, Texas. Latin pop singer.

6/5/04	162	1		1 Seduccion .... **[F]**		Univision 10263
4/16/05	154	3		2 Confesiones .... **[F]**		Fonovisa 351791
				ANA BARBARA & JENNIFER PENA		

PENDERGRASS, Teddy   **All-Time: #299**
Born on 3/26/1950 in Philadelphia, Pennsylvania. Died on 1/13/2010 (age 59). R&B singer. Lead singer of **Harold Melvin & The Blue Notes** from 1970-76. Acted in the 1982 movie *Soup For One*. Auto accident on 3/18/1982 left him partially paralyzed.

3/19/77	17	35	▲	1 Teddy Pendergrass..		Philadelphia Int'l. 34390
7/1/78	11	35	▲	2 Life Is A Song Worth Singing...		Philadelphia Int'l. 35095
6/23/79	5	31	▲	3 Teddy		Philadelphia Int'l. 36003
12/22/79+	33	15	●	4 Teddy Live! Coast To Coast .... **[L]**		Philadelphia I. 36294 [2]
				side 4: interviews and new studio recordings		
8/23/80	14	34	▲	5 TP..		Philadelphia Int'l. 36745
10/3/81	19	27	●	6 It's Time For Love..		Philadelphia Int'l. 37491
8/21/82	59	15		7 This One's For You		Philadelphia Int'l. 38118
1/7/84	123	9		8 Heaven Only Knows..		Philadelphia Int'l. 38646
6/16/84	38	35	●	9 Love Language		Asylum 60317
12/7/85+	96	23		10 Workin' It Back		Asylum 60447
5/28/88	54	24	●	11 Joy		Elektra 60775
3/23/91	49	16		12 Truly Blessed...		Elektra 60891
10/23/93	92	8		13 A Little More Magic		Elektra 61497
5/3/97	137	5		14 You And I		Surefire 13045

Billboard DEBUT	PEAK	WKS	R I A A	ARTIST Album Title	Catalog	Label & Number

PENGUINS, The
Black doo-wop group from Los Angeles, California: Cleveland Duncan (lead), Dexter Tisby (tenor), Bruce Tate (baritone) and Curtis Williams (bass). Tate died on 6/20/1973 (age 36). Williams died on 8/10/1979 (age 44).

~ ~ ~ ~ ~ ~ ~ ~ ~ ~ **NON-CHARTED ALBUM** ~ ~ ~ ~ ~ ~ ~ ~ ~ ~ ~
1959 **The Cool, Cool Penguins**

PENISTON, Ce Ce
Born on 9/6/1969 in Dayton, Ohio; raised in Phoenix, Arizona. Female R&B singer.

| 2/15/92 | 70 | 36 | ● | 1 Finally .... | A&M 5381 |
| 2/12/94 | 96 | 19 | | 2 Thought 'Ya Knew .... | A&M 540138 |

PENN, Michael
Born on 8/1/1958 in Manhattan, New York. Pop-rock singer/songwriter. Brother of actors Sean and Christopher Penn. Son of actor/director Leo Penn and actress Eileen Ryan. Married **Aimee Mann** on 12/29/1997.

| 11/25/89+ | 31 | 34 | | 1 March.. | RCA 9692 |
| 10/3/92 | 160 | 2 | | 2 Free-For-All .... | RCA 61113 |

PENNARIO, Leonard
Born on 7/9/1924 in Buffalo, New York; raised in Los Angeles, California. Died on 6/27/2008 (age 83). Classical pianist.

| 6/8/59 | 29 | 13 | | 1 Concertos under the Stars.. [I] | Capitol 8326 |

PENNYWISE
Hard-rock band from Hermosa Beach, California: Jim Lindberg (vocals), Fletcher Dragge (guitar), Randy Bradbury (bass) and Byron McMackin (drums). Band named after a character in Stephen King's 1986 novel *It*.

7/1/95	96	6		1 About Time	Epitaph 86437
5/10/97	79	4		2 Full Circle	Epitaph 86489
6/26/99	62	7		3 Straight Ahead...	Epitaph 86553
11/11/00	198	1		4 Live At The Key Club.. [L]	Epitaph 86598
7/7/01	67	9		5 Land Of The Free?	Epitaph 86600
9/27/03	54	2		6 From The Ashes	Epitaph 86664
8/27/05	78	2		7 The Fuse	Epitaph 86769
4/12/08	98	1		8 Reason To Believe	MySpace 10013

PENROD, Guy
Born in Texas; raised in Hobbs, New Mexico. Christian singer. Member of **The Gaither Vocal Band**.

| 8/6/05 | 92 | 3 | | 1 The Best Of Guy Penrod .... Cat:#50/1 [K] | Gaither 42612 |

PENTANGLE
Folk band formed in England: Jacqui McShee (vocals), Bert Jansch (guitar), John Renbourn (guitar), Danny Thompson (bass) and Terry Cox (drums).

12/21/68	192	3		1 The Pentangle...	Reprise 6315
1/31/70	200	2		2 Basket Of Light..	Reprise 6372
3/13/71	193	1		3 Cruel Sister	Reprise 6430
12/4/71	183	3		4 Reflection	Reprise 6463
10/28/72	184	4		5 Solomon's Seal	Reprise 2100

PENTHOUSE PLAYERS CLIQUE
Male rap duo: Playa Hamm and Tweed Cadillac.

| 5/16/92 | 76 | 10 | | 1 Paid The Cost .... | Ruthless 57181 |

PEOPLE
Pop-rock band from San Jose, California: Gene Mason and Larry Norman (vocals), Jeff Levin (guitar), Albert Ribisi (keyboards), Robb Levin (bass) and Denny Friedkin (drums). Norman died of heart failure on 2/24/2008 (age 60).

| 7/27/68 | 128 | 8 | | 1 I Love You .... | Capitol 2924 |

PEOPLE'S CHOICE
R&B-dance band from Philadelphia, Pennsylvania: Frankie Brunson (vocals), Guy Fiske (guitar), Darnell Jordan (guitar), Donald Ford (keyboards), Roger Andrews (bass) and David Thompson (drums).

| 9/6/75 | 56 | 15 | | 1 Boogie Down U.S.A... | TSOP 33154 |
| 6/26/76 | 174 | 3 | | 2 We Got The Rhythm .... | TSOP 34124 |

PEPPER
Ska-rock trio from Hawaii; later based in California: Kaleco Wassman (vocals, guitar), Bret Bollinger (bass) and Yesod Williams (drums).

| 10/21/06 | 96 | 2 | | 1 No Shame.. | Volcom 94536 |
| 8/9/08 | 83 | 2 | | 2 Pink Crustaceans And Good Vibrations .... | Law 218 |

PEPPERMINT RAINBOW, The
Pop band from Baltimore, Maryland: sisters Bonnie Lamdin and Pat Lamdin (vocals), Doug Lewis (guitar), Skip Harris (bass) and Tony Corey (drums).

| 8/2/69 | 106 | 9 | | 1 Will You Be Staying After Sunday .... | Decca 75129 |

PEPSI AND SHIRLIE
Female R&B-dance vocal duo from England: Lawrie "Pepsi" DeMacque and Shirlie Holliman.

| 2/27/88 | 133 | 9 | | 1 All Right Now.. | Polydor 833724 |

PEREZ, Amanda
Born in 1980 in Fort Wayne, Indiana. R&B-dance singer/songwriter.

3/15/03	73	15		1 Angel		Powerhouse 82131
7/31/04	90	4		2 I Pray		Powerhouse 78965

PERFECT CIRCLE, A
Hard-rock duo from Hollywood, California: Maynard James Keenan (vocals) and Billy Howerdel (guitar). Keenan is also lead singer of **Tool**.

6/10/00	4	51	▲	1 Mer De Noms	Cat:#27/1	Virgin 49253
10/4/03	2¹	37	▲	2 Thirteenth Step		Virgin 80918
11/20/04	2¹	24	●	3 eMOTIVe		Virgin 66687
12/4/04	57	2		4 aMOTION		Virgin 44115

PERFECT GENTLEMEN
R&B vocal trio from Boston, Massachusetts: Corey Blakely, Maurice Starr Jr. and Tyrone Sutton. Starr's father managed and produced **New Edition** and **New Kids On The Block**.

5/26/90	72	14		1 Rated PG		Columbia 46070

PERFECT STRANGER
Country band from Carthage, Texas: Steve Murray (vocals), Richard Raines (guitar), Shayne Morrison (bass) and Andy Ginn (drums).

7/29/95	68	14		1 You Have The Right To Remain Silent		Curb 77799

PERKINS, Carl
Born on 4/9/1932 in Ridgely, Tennessee. Died of a stroke on 1/19/1998 (age 65). Rockabilly singer/songwriter/guitarist. Member of **Johnny Cash**'s touring troupe from 1965-75. Appeared in the 1985 movie *Into The Night*.
AWARD: R&R Hall of Fame: 1987

5/22/82	205	3		1 The Survivors .... [L]		Columbia 37961
				JOHNNY CASH / JERRY LEE LEWIS / CARL PERKINS		
				recorded on 4/23/1981 at the Sporthalle Boeblingen in Stuttgart, West Germany		
6/21/86	87	12		2 Class Of '55 (Memphis Rock & Roll Homecoming)	Cat:#13/2	America Smash 830002
				CARL PERKINS / JERRY LEE LEWIS / ROY ORBISON / JOHNNY CASH		

~ ~ ~ ~ ~ ~ ~ ~ ~   **NON-CHARTED ALBUMS**   ~ ~ ~ ~ ~ ~ ~ ~ ~ ~ ~
1957 **Dance Album Of...Carl Perkins**   1958 **Whole Lotta Shakin'**

PERKINS, Elvis
Born on 2/9/1976 in Los Angeles, California. Folk-rock singer/songwriter. Son of actor Anthony Perkins (died on 9/12/1992, age 60).

4/4/09	163	1		1 Elvis Perkins In Dearland		XL 401

PERLMAN, Itzhak
Born on 8/31/1945 in Tel-Aviv, Israel. Classical violinist. Lost use of his legs at age four due to polio.

3/14/81	149	9		1 A Different Kind Of Blues .... [I]		Angel 37780
				ITZHAK PERLMAN & ANDRE PREVIN		
1/17/09	33ᶜ	1		2 Bach: Violin Concertos .... [I]		EMI Classics 74720

PERRY, Joe
Born on 9/10/1950 in Lawrence, Massachusetts. Rock guitarist. Member of **Aerosmith**. His Project included Charlie Farren (guitar), David Hull (bass) and Ronnie Stewart (drums).

4/12/80	47	13		1 Let The Music Do The Talking		Columbia 36388
7/4/81	100	10		2 I've Got The Rock 'N' Rolls Again		Columbia 37364
				THE JOE PERRY PROJECT (above 2)		
5/21/05	110	1		3 Joe Perry		Roman 55447

PERRY, Katy
Born Katheryn Hudson on 10/25/1984 in Santa Barbara, California. Pop-rock singer/songwriter/guitarist. Recorded Christian music in 2001 as Katy Hudson.

7/5/08	9	71	▲	1 One Of The Boys		Capitol 04249
12/5/09	168	1		2 MTV Unplugged .... [EP-L]		MTV 56278

PERRY, Phil
Born on 1/1/1952 in Springfield, Illinois. R&B singer/songwriter.

5/18/91	191	1		1 The Heart Of The Man		Capitol 92115

PERRY, Steve
Born on 1/22/1949 in Hanford, California. Lead singer of **Journey**.

4/28/84	12	60	▲²	1 Street Talk		Columbia 39334
8/6/94	15	14	●	2 For The Love Of Strange Medicine		Columbia 44287

PERSUADERS, The
R&B vocal group formed in Harlem, New York: Doug Scott, Willie Holland, James Barnes and Charles Stodghill.

3/11/72	141	7		1 Thin Line Between Love And Hate		Win Or Lose 387
4/7/73	178	4		2 The Persuaders		Atco 7021

PERSUASIONS
Acappella group formed in Harlem, New York: Jerry Lawson, Jesse Russell, Jayotis Washington, Herb Rhoad and Jimmy Hayes. Rhoad died on 12/8/1988 (age 44).

9/18/71	189	3		1 We Came To Play		Capitol 791
2/12/72	88	12		2 Street Corner Symphony		Capitol 872
11/18/72	195	3		3 Spread The Word		Capitol 11101
6/9/73	178	3		4 We Still Ain't Got No Band		MCA 326
7/20/74	207	2		5 More Than Before		A&M 3635

PETER AND GORDON
Pop vocal duo formed in London, England: Peter Asher (born on 6/22/1944 in London, England) and Gordon Waller (born on 6/4/1945 in Braemar, Scotland; died of heart failure on 7/16/2009, age 64). Asher later went into production and management, including work with **Linda Ronstadt**, **James Taylor** and **10,000 Maniacs**.

7/4/64	21	14		1 A World Without Love		Capitol 2115
1/2/65	95	11		2 I Don't Want To See You Again		Capitol 2220
5/22/65	51	15		3 I Go To Pieces		Capitol 2324
8/14/65	49	13		4 True Love Ways		Capitol 2368
4/16/66	60	14		5 Woman		Capitol 2477
7/30/66	72	12		6 The Best Of Peter And Gordon [G]		Capitol 2549
2/4/67	80	13		7 Lady Godiva		Capitol 2664

PETER, BJORN AND JOHN
Rock trio from Stockholm, Sweden: Peter Moren (vocals, guitar), Bjorn Yttling (bass) and John Eriksson (drums).

3/24/07	155	15		1 Writer's Block		Almost Gold 002
4/18/09	92	3		2 Living Thing		StarTime 005

PETER, PAUL & MARY
1960s: #35 / All-Time: #166

Folk trio formed in Greenwich Village, New York: **Peter Yarrow** (born on 5/31/1938 in Brooklyn, New York), **Paul Stookey** (born on 12/30/1937 in Baltimore, Maryland) and **Mary Travers** (born on 11/9/1936 in Louisville, Kentucky; died of leukemia on 9/16/2009, age 72).

4/28/62	❶7	185	▲2	1 Peter, Paul And Mary		Warner 1449
1/19/63	2⁸	99	●	2 (Moving)		Warner 1473
10/26/63	❶5	80	●	3 In The Wind		Warner 1507
8/15/64	4	54	●	4 Peter, Paul And Mary In Concert [L]		Warner 1555 [2]
4/10/65	8	38	●	5 A Song Will Rise		Warner 1589
10/30/65	11	39	●	6 See What Tomorrow Brings		Warner 1615
8/27/66	22	53		7 Peter, Paul And Mary Album		Warner 1648
9/2/67	15	82	▲	8 Album 1700		Warner 1700
9/14/68	14	22		9 Late Again		Warner 1751
6/14/69	12	25	●	10 Peter, Paul And Mommy		Warner 1785
				Grammy: Children's Album		
6/20/70	15	40	▲2	11 10 Years Together/The Best Of Peter, Paul And Mary [G]		Warner 2552
10/21/78	106	7		12 Reunion		Warner 3231
3/14/87	173	5		13 No Easy Walk To Freedom		Gold Castle 171001
10/3/09	29C	1		14 The Very Best Of Peter, Paul & Mary [G]		Warner 73161
10/10/09	29X	2		15 A Holiday Celebration With The New York Choral Society [X]		Warner 45070

PETERS, Bernadette
Born Bernadette Lazzara on 2/28/1948 in Queens, New York. Actress/singer. Appeared in several movies and Broadway shows.

5/3/80	114	14		1 Bernadette Peters		MCA 3230
10/3/81	151	9		2 Now Playing		MCA 5244

PETERSEN, Paul
Born on 9/23/1945 in Glendale, California. Pop singer/actor. Member of Disney's "Mouseketeers" and played "Jeff Stone" on TV's *Donna Reed Show* (1958-66). Became a paperback novelist in the 1970s.

5/11/63	48	18		1 Teen-Age Triangle [G]		Colpix 444
				JAMES DARREN / SHELLY FABARES / PAUL PETERSEN		

~ ~ ~ ~ ~ ~ ~ ~ ~ ~ *NON-CHARTED ALBUMS* ~ ~ ~ ~ ~ ~ ~ ~ ~ ~ ~ ~

1962 **Lollipops And Roses**   1964 **More Teenage Triangle**
1963 **My Dad**   *[w/ James Darren & Shelley Fabares]*

PETERSON, Andrew
Born in Nashville, Tennessee. Contemporary Christian singer/songwriter.

11/8/08	128	1		1 Resurrection Letters: Volume II		Centricity 1067

PETERSON, Michael
Born on 8/7/1959 in Tucson, Arizona. Country singer/songwriter/guitarist.

8/2/97	115	31	●	1 Michael Peterson		Reprise 46618

PETERSON, Oscar, Trio

Born on 8/15/1925 in Montreal, Quebec, Canada. Died of kidney failure on 12/23/2007 (age 82). Jazz pianist. His trio included Ray Brown (bass) and Ed Thigpen (drums).

AWARD: Grammy: Lifetime Achievement 1997

2/9/63	145	2	1	Bursting Out With The All Star Big Band!	[I]	Verve 8476
6/8/63	127	2	2	Affinity	[I]	Verve 8516
10/31/64	81	12	3	Oscar Peterson Trio + One	[I]	Mercury 60975
				with Clark Terry (trumpet)		

PETERSON, Ray

Born on 4/23/1935 in Denton, Texas. Died of cancer on 1/25/2005 (age 69). Pop singer.

~ ~ ~ ~ ~ ~ ~ ~ ~ ~ ~ **NON-CHARTED ALBUM** ~ ~ ~ ~ ~ ~ ~ ~ ~ ~ ~

1960 Tell Laura I Love Her

PETRA

Christian rock band from Fort Wayne, Indiana: John Schlitt (vocals), Bob Harman (guitar), John Lawry (keyboards), Ronny Cates (bass) and Louie Weaver (drums).

9/9/95	91	8	1	No Doubt	Word 62460
3/22/97	155	8	2	Petra Praise 2 - We Need Jesus	Word 67933

PET SHOP BOYS   All-Time: #345

Synth-pop/dance duo formed in England: Neil Tennant (vocals; born on 7/10/1954) and Chris Lowe (keyboards; born on 10/4/1959). Tennant was a writer for the British fan magazine *Smash Hits*.

4/19/86	7	31	▲	1	Please	EMI America 17193
12/27/86+	95	12		2	Disco	EMI America 17246
10/3/87	25	45	●	3	Actually	EMI-Manhattan 46972
11/5/88	34	22	●	4	Introspective	EMI-Manhattan 90868
11/17/90	45	25		5	Behavior	EMI 94310
11/23/91	111	14		6	Discography - The Complete Singles Collection	[G]	EMI 97097
10/23/93	20	17	●	7	Very	EMI 89721
10/8/94	75	3		8	Disco 2	EMI 28105
9/16/95	103	2		9	Alternative	EMI 34023 [2]
9/28/96	39	6		10	Bilingual	Atlantic 82915
11/20/99	84	3		11	Nightlife	Parlophone 31086
5/11/02	73	2		12	Release	Sanctuary 84553
2/22/03	188	1		13	Disco 3	Sanctuary 84595
7/15/06	150	1		14	Fundamental	Rhino 79525
5/9/09	32	2		15	Yes	Astralwerks 96470

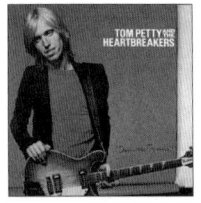

PETTY, Tom, And The Heartbreakers   1980s: #25 / 1990s: #25 / All-Time: #79

Born on 10/20/1950 in Gainesville, Florida. Rock singer/songwriter/guitarist. Formed The Heartbreakers in Los Angeles, California: Mike Campbell (guitar; born on 2/1/1950), Benmont Tench (keyboards; born on 9/7/1953), Ron Blair (bass; born on 9/16/1948) and Stan Lynch (drums; born on 5/21/1955). Howie Epstein (born on 7/21/1955; died of a drug overdose on 2/23/2003, age 47) replaced Blair in 1982; Blair returned in 2002, replacing Epstein. Steve Ferrone replaced Lynch in 1995. Petty appeared in the movies *FM* and *Made In Heaven*. Member of the **Traveling Wilburys**. Also see **Mudcrutch**.

AWARDS: R&R Hall of Fame: 2002 ★ Billboard Century: 2005

9/24/77+	55	42	●	1	Tom Petty & The Heartbreakers	Cat:#4/83	Shelter 52006
6/10/78	23	24	●	2	You're Gonna Get It!	Cat:#13/53	Shelter 52029
11/10/79+	2⁷	66	▲²	3	Damn The Torpedoes	Cat:#8/120	Backstreet 5105
					RS500 #313		
5/23/81	5	31	▲	4	Hard Promises	Cat:#36/32	Backstreet 5160
11/20/82+	9	32	●	5	Long After Dark		Backstreet 5360
4/13/85	7	32	▲	6	Southern Accents		MCA 5486
12/14/85+	22	26		7	Pack Up The Plantation - Live!	[L]	MCA 8021 [2]
5/9/87	20	20	●	8	Let Me Up (I've Had Enough)		MCA 5836
5/13/89	3²	71	▲⁵	9	Full Moon Fever	Cat:#32/18	MCA 6253
					TOM PETTY		
7/20/91	13	41	▲²	10	Into The Great Wide Open		MCA 10317
12/4/93+	5	154	▲¹⁰	11	Greatest Hits	Cat:❶¹/486 [G]	MCA 10813
11/19/94	8	53	▲³	12	Wildflowers		Warner 45759
					TOM PETTY		
8/24/96	15	14	●	13	She's The One	[S]	Warner 46285
5/1/99	10	23	●	14	Echo		Warner 47294
11/18/00	132	2	●	15	Anthology: Through The Years	Cat:#6/3 [G]	MCA 170177 [2]
10/26/02	9	12		16	The Last DJ		Warner 47955
8/12/06	4	14	●	17	Highway Companion		American 44285
					TOM PETTY		
12/12/09	51	7		18	The Live Anthology	[L]	Reprise 512765 [4]
12/12/09+	147	5		19	Greatest Hits	Cat:#9/64 [G]	Geffen 010327

PEYROUX, Madeleine
Born in 1974 in Athens, Georgia. Jazz singer/songwriter.

1/29/05	71	18	●	1 Careless Love		Rounder 613192
9/30/06	33	8		2 Half The Perfect World		Rounder 613252
3/28/09	71	4		3 Bare Bones		Rounder 613272

P.F.M.
Progressive-rock band from Italy: Franco Mussida (vocals, guitar), Flavio Premoli (keyboards), Mauro Pagani (violin), Giorgio Piazza (bass) and Franz DiCioccio (drums). P.F.M.: Premiata Forneria Marconi.

10/20/73	180	6		1 Photos Of Ghosts		Manticore 66668
7/6/74	201	1		2 The World Became The World		Manticore 66673
				PREMIATA FORNERIA MARCONI (above 2)		
12/28/74+	151	8		3 P.F.M. 'Cook'	[I-L]	Manticore 502
8/14/76	206	2		4 Chocolate Kings		Asylum 1071

PFR
Christian rock trio from Minnesota: Joel Hanson (guitar), Patrick Andrew (bass) and Mark Nash (drums). All share vocals. Nash is married to Leigh Nash of **Sixpence None The Richer**. PFR: Pray For Rain.

8/10/96	167	4		1 Them		Vireo 51550

PHAIR, Liz
Born on 4/17/1967 in New Haven, Connecticut. Pop-rock singer/songwriter.

2/5/94	196	1	●	1 Exile In Guyville	Cat:#28/1	Matador 051
				RS500 #328		
10/8/94	27	17	●	2 Whip-Smart		Matador 92429
8/29/98	35	9		3 Whitechocolatespaceegg		Matador 53554
7/12/03	27	18		4 Liz Phair		Capitol 22084
10/22/05	46	2		5 Somebody's Miracle		Capitol 77769

PHANTOM PLANET
Rock band from Los Angeles, California: Alex Greenwald (vocals), Jacques Brautbaur (guitar), Darren Robinson (guitar), Sam Farrar (bass) and Jason Schwartzman (drums). Farrar is the son of prolific songwriter John Farrar. Schwartzman is the son of actress Talia Shire; he starred in the 1998 movie *Rushmore*.

3/16/02	133	6		1 The Guest		Daylight 62066
1/24/04	95	3		2 Phantom Planet		Daylight 86964
5/3/08	119	1		3 Raise The Dead		Fueled By Ramen 442236

PHANTOM, ROCKER & SLICK
Rock trio formed in New York: Slim Jim Phantom (drums) and Lee Rocker (vocals, bass), with Earl Slick (guitar). Phantom and Rocker were members of the **Stray Cats** and Slick was a member of **Silver Condor**.

10/26/85	61	23		1 Phantom, Rocker & Slick		EMI America 17172
10/18/86	181	2		2 Cover Girl		EMI America 17229

PHARCYDE, The
Male rap group from Los Angeles, California: Trevant Hardson, Imani Wilcox, Romye Robinson and Derrick Stewart.

4/17/93	75	19	●	1 Bizarre Ride II The Pharcyde		Delicious Vinyl 92222
12/2/95	37	12		2 Labcabincalifornia		Delicious Vinyl 35102
11/25/00	157	1		3 Plain Rap		Delicious Vinyl 182232

PHAROAHE MONCH
Born Troy Jamerson on 10/31/1972 in Queens, New York. Male rapper. Member of **Organized Konfusion**.

11/6/99	41	5		1 Internal Affairs		Rawkus 50137
7/14/07	58	2		2 Desire		SRC 008096

PHARRELL
Born Pharrell Williams on 4/5/1973 in Virginia Beach, Virginia. Male rapper/producer/songwriter. Member of prolific production trio The Neptunes (recorded as **NERD**).

8/12/06	3¹	11		1 In My Mind		Star Trak 005698

PHELPS, David
Born on 10/21/1969 in Denver, Colorado. Contemporary Christian singer/songwriter. Member of **The Gaither Vocal Band**.

3/13/04	176	1		1 Revelation		Word-Curb 886275
10/20/07	7ˣ	5		2 A David Phelps Christmas: One Wintery Night	[X]	Word-Curb 887232
10/11/08	4ˣ	4		3 O Holy Night: A Live Holiday Celebration	[X-L]	Word-Curb 887774
				Christmas charts: 4/'08, 45/'09		

PHIFE DAWG
Born Malik Taylor on 4/10/1970 in Brooklyn, New York. Male rapper. Member of **A Tribe Called Quest**.

10/14/00	175	4		1 Ventilation: Da LP		Groove Attack 068

PHILADELPHIA BRASS ENSEMBLE, The
First-chair brass virtuosos of **The Philadelphia Orchestra**.

12/30/67+	58ˣ	2		1 A Festival Of Carols In Brass	[X-I]	Columbia 6433 / 7033
				Christmas charts: 113/'67, 58/'68		

PHILADELPHIA ORCHESTRA, The
Conductor Eugene Ormandy was born on 11/18/1899 in Budapest, Hungary; died on 3/12/1985 (age 85). Conducted orchestra from 1938-80. Also see **The Mormon Tabernacle Choir**.

5/19/62	17	13		1 The Magnificent Sound Of The Philadelphia Orchestra............................ [I-K]	Columbia 1 [2]
12/22/62	109	2	●	2 The Glorious Sound Of Christmas .... Cat:#15/22 [X]	Columbia 5769 / 6369

with The Temple University Concert Choir; Christmas charts: 17/'63, 22/'64, 45/'66, 19/'67, 26/'97, 15/'98, 11/'99, 13/'00, 6/'01

12/18/65+	3¹ˣ	11		3 Handel: Messiah [X]	Columbia 263 / 607 [2]

THE PHILADELPHIA ORCHESTRA/EUGENE ORMANDY/THE MORMON TABERNACLE CHOIR
NRR
first released in 1959; Christmas charts: 21/'65, 3/'69, 8/'70, 12/'71, 5/'72

5/6/78	136	8		4 David Bowie Narrates Prokofiev's "Peter And The Wolf"	RCA Victor 2743

DAVID BOWIE/EUGENE ORMANDY & THE PHILADELPHIA ORCHESTRA

PHILBIN, Regis
Born on 8/25/1931 in the Bronx, New York. Popular TV personality.

10/16/04	54	5	1 When You're Smiling	Hollywood 162476
11/19/05	83	7	2 The Regis Philbin Christmas Album .... [X]	Hollywood 162549

Christmas chart: 8/'05

PHILHARMONIA ORCHESTRA
Symphony orchestra formed in 1945 in London, England. Conducted by Esa-Pekka Salonen.

10/17/09+	47ˣ	2	1 Tchaikovsky: The Nutcracker Highlights.................................... [X-I]	Seraphim 73574

PHILLIPS, Anthony
Born on 12/23/1951 in Putney, England. Rock singer/songwriter/guitarist. Member of **Genesis** from 1967-70.

3/26/77	191	3	1 The Geese & The Ghost...	Passport 98020

PHILLIPS, Esther
Born Esther Mae Jones on 12/23/1935 in Galveston, Texas; raised in Los Angeles, California. Died of liver failure on 8/7/1984 (age 48). R&B singer. Recorded with Johnny Otis as "Little Esther."

1/5/63	46	14	1 Release Me!	Lenox 227

"LITTLE ESTHER" PHILLIPS

1/2/71	115	15	2 Burnin' .... [L]	Atlantic 1565
1/31/76	170	4	3 Confessin' The Blues .... [L]	Atlantic 1680

above 2 recorded at Freddie Jett's Pied Piper Club in Los Angeles, California

3/18/72	137	15	4 From A Whisper To A Scream	Kudu 05
12/30/72+	177	8	5 Alone Again, Naturally	Kudu 09
2/9/74	205	6	6 Black-Eyed Blues	Kudu 14
8/2/75	32	17	7 What A Diff'rence A Day Makes	Kudu 23
1/8/77	150	4	8 Capricorn Princess	Kudu 31

PHILLIPS, John
Born on 8/30/1935 in Paris Island, South Carolina. Died of heart failure on 3/18/2001 (age 65). Singer/songwriter/guitarist. Co-founder of **The Mamas & The Papas**. Father of actress MacKenzie Phillips and singer Chynna Phillips (of **Wilson Phillips**).

5/2/70	181	9	1 John Phillips (John The Wolfking Of L.A.)	Dunhill/ABC 50077

PHILLIPS, Sam
Born Leslie Phillips on 1/28/1962 in Glendale, California. Female singer/songwriter/actress. Married to record producer T-Bone Burnett from 1989-2004. Played "Katya" in the 1995 movie *Die Hard With A Vengeance*.

3/26/94	182	1	1 Martinis & Bikinis	Virgin 39438

PHILLIPS, Shawn
Born on 2/3/1943 in Fort Worth, Texas. Male folk-rock singer/songwriter/guitarist.

7/17/71	208	3	1 Second Contribution..	A&M 4282
12/2/72+	57	20	2 Faces	A&M 4363
12/15/73+	72	13	3 Bright White...	A&M 4402
11/30/74+	50	12	4 Furthermore...	A&M 3662
9/13/75	101	9	5 Do You Wonder	A&M 4539
6/5/76	201	4	6 Rumplestiltskin's Resolve	A&M 4582

PHILLIPS, CRAIG & DEAN
Contemporary Christian vocal trio from Austin, Texas: Randy Phillips, Shawn Craig and Dan Dean.

11/23/96	34ˣ	1	1 Repeat The Sounding Joy .... [X]	Star Song 20100
2/15/03	142	4	2 Let Your Glory Fall	Sparrow 51979
10/16/04	179	1	3 Let The Worshippers Arise	Ino/Epic 92879
10/14/06	181	1	4 Top Of My Lungs..	Ino 87933
8/22/09	46	10	5 Fearless..	Ino 84506

PHILLY'S MOST WANTED
Male rap duo from Philadelphia, Pennsylvania: Al "Boobonic" Holly and Joel "Mr. Man" Witherspoon.

8/25/01	69	5	1 Get Down Or Lay Down	Atlantic 83358

PHISH
2000s: #19 / All-Time: #161

Alternative-rock band from Burlington, Vermont: **Trey Anastasio** (guitar; born on 9/30/1964), Page McConnell (keyboards; born on 5/17/1963), **Mike Gordon** (bass; born on 6/3/1965) and Jon Fishman (drums; born on 2/19/1965). All share vocals. Popular "jam band" with several concert appearances.

2/20/93	51	5	●	1 Rift		Elektra 61433
4/16/94	34	13	●	2 (Hoist)		Elektra 61628
11/2/96	7	15	●	3 Billy Breathes		Elektra 61971
11/14/98	8	5		4 The Story Of The Ghost		Elektra 62297
6/3/00	12	18	●	5 Farmhouse		Elektra 62521
12/28/02	46	5		6 Round Room		Elektra 62850
7/3/04	13	4		7 Undermind		Elektra 62969
9/26/09	13	7		8 Joy		Jemp 1049
				LIVE ALBUMS:		
7/15/95	18	14	▲	9 A Live One		Elektra 61777 [2]
11/15/97	17	8		10 Slip Stitch And Pass		Elektra 62121
				recorded on 3/1/1997 at the Markthalle in Hamburg, Germany		
12/11/99	120	2	●	11 Hampton Comes Alive		Elektra 62495 [6]
				recorded on 11/20/1998 at the Coliseum in Hampton, Virginia		
10/6/01	97	1		12 Live Phish 01: 12.14.95, Broome County Arena, Binghamton, New York		Elektra 62702 [2]
10/6/01	93	1		13 Live Phish 02: 7.16.94, Sugarbush Summerstage, North Fayston, Vermont		Elektra 62703 [3]
10/6/01	118	1		14 Live Phish 03: 9.14.00, Darien Lake Performing Arts Center, Darien Center, New York		Elektra 62704 [3]
10/6/01	127	1		15 Live Phish 04: 6.14.00, Drum Logos, Fukuoka, Japan		Elektra 62705 [3]
10/6/01	115	1		16 Live Phish 05: 7.8.00, Alpine Valley Music Theater, East Troy, Wisconsin		Elektra 62706 [3]
11/17/01	105	1		17 Live Phish 06: 11.27.98, The Centrum, Worcester, Massachusetts		Elektra 62707 [3]
5/4/02	128	1		18 Live Phish 07: 8.14.93 World Music Theatre, Tinley Park, Illinois		Elektra 62751 [3]
5/4/02	154	1		19 Live Phish 08: 7.10.99 E Centre, Camden, New Jersey		Elektra 62752 [2]
5/4/02	141	1		20 Live Phish 09: 8.26.89 Townshend Family Park, Townshend, Vermont		Elektra 62753 [3]
5/4/02	147	1		21 Live Phish 10: 6.22.94 Veterans Memorial Auditorium, Columbus, Ohio		Elektra 62754 [3]
5/4/02	145	1		22 Live Phish 11: 11.17.97 McNichols Sports Arena, Denver, Colorado		Elektra 62755 [3]
5/4/02	138	1		23 Live Phish 12: 8.13.96 Deer Creek Music Center, Noblesville, Indiana		Elektra 62756 [3]
11/16/02	112	1		24 Live Phish 13: 10.31.94 Glens Falls Civic Center, Glens Falls, New York		Elektra 62806 [4]
11/16/02	146	1		25 Live Phish 14: 10.31.95 Rosemont Horizon, Rosemont, Illinois		Elektra 62807 [4]
11/16/02	144	1		26 Live Phish 15: 10.31.96 The Omni, Atlanta, Georgia		Elektra 62808 [4]
11/16/02	139	1		27 Live Phish 16: 10.31.98 Thomas & Mack Center, Las Vegas, Nevada		Elektra 62809 [4]
7/29/06	162	1		28 Live In Brooklyn		Jemp 79535 [3]
				recorded on 6/17/2004 at Keyspan Park in Brooklyn, New York		
12/6/08	148	1		29 At The Roxy		Jemp 0141 [8]

PHOENIX
Alternative-rock band from Versailles, France: Thomas Mars (vocals), Chris Mazzalai (guitar), Laurent Brancowitz (guitar), Deck D'Arcy (bass) and Tom Hedlund (drums).

5/30/09	37	52↑		1 Wolfgang Amadeus Phoenix		Loyaute 0105
				Grammy: Alternative Album		

PHOTOGLO, Jim
Born on 4/8/1951 in Los Angeles, California. Pop singer/songwriter.

5/24/80	194	3		1 Photoglo		20th Century 604
6/6/81	119	11		2 Fool In Love With You		20th Century 621

PICKETT, Bobby "Boris", And The Crypt-Kickers
Born on 2/11/1938 in Somerville, Massachusetts. Died of leukemia on 4/25/2007 (age 69). Novelty singer/songwriter. The Crypt-Kickers: **Leon Russell**, Johnny MacCrae, Rickie Page and Gary Paxton.

11/3/62	19	13		1 The Original Monster Mash	[N]	Garpax 57001
9/29/73	173	4		2 The Original Monster Mash	[N-R]	Parrot 71063

PICKETT, Wilson
All-Time: #454

Born on 3/18/1941 in Prattville, Alabama; later based in Detroit, Michigan. Died of a heart attack on 1/19/2006 (age 64). R&B singer/songwriter. Nicknamed the "Wicked Pickett." Sang in local gospel groups. With The Falcons from 1961-63. Career took off after recording in Memphis with guitarist/producer Steve Cropper.

AWARD: R&R Hall of Fame: 1991

10/30/65	107	6		1 In The Midnight Hour		Atlantic 8114
8/27/66	21	29		2 The Exciting Wilson Pickett		Atlantic 8129
1/21/67	42	31		3 The Wicked Pickett		Atlantic 8138
8/12/67	54	11		4 The Sound Of Wilson Pickett		Atlantic 8145
11/11/67+	35	54		5 The Best Of Wilson Pickett	[G]	Atlantic 8151
2/24/68	70	15		6 I'm In Love		Atlantic 8175
7/13/68	91	13		7 The Midnight Mover		Atlantic 8183

DEBUT	PEAK	WKS	R I A A	ARTIST / Album Title	Catalog	Label & Number

PICKETT, Wilson — cont'd

DEBUT	PEAK	WKS			
3/1/69	97	14	8 Hey Jude		Atlantic 8215
4/4/70	197	3	9 Right On		Atlantic 8250
10/3/70	64	19	10 Wilson Pickett In Philadelphia		Atlantic 8270
5/22/71	73	13	11 The Best Of Wilson Pickett, Vol. II	[G]	Atlantic 8290
12/25/71+	132	14	12 Don't Knock My Love		Atlantic 8300
2/10/73	178	8	13 Wilson Pickett's Greatest Hits	[G]	Atlantic 501 [2]
4/28/73	187	3	14 Mr. Magic Man		RCA Victor 4858
9/29/73	212	2	15 Miz Lena's Boy		RCA Victor 0312
12/22/79	205	3	16 I Want You		EMI America 17019

PICKLER, Kellie
Born on 6/28/1986 in Albemarle, North Carolina. Country singer/songwriter. Finalist on the 2006 season of TV's *American Idol*.

11/18/06	9	54	●	1 Small Town Girl	BNA 01797
10/18/08	9	48		2 Kellie Pickler	19 Records 22811

PIECES OF A DREAM
Jazz-styled trio from Philadelphia, Pennsylvania: James Lloyd (keyboards), Cedric Napoleon (bass) and Curtis Harmon (drums).

10/31/81	170	6	1 Pieces Of A Dream		Elektra 350
8/28/82	114	15	2 We Are One		Elektra 60142
2/25/84	90	15	3 Imagine This		Elektra 60270
8/2/86	102	12	4 Joyride		Manhattan 53023

PIGG, Landon
Born on 8/6/1983 in Nashville, Tennessee; raised in Chicago, Illinois. Male Adult Alternative-pop singer/songwriter.

10/17/09	191	1	1 The Boy Who Never		RCA 52874

PILLAR
Christian hard-rock group from Hays, Kansas: Rob Beckley (vocals), Noah Hanson (guitar), Michael "Kalel" Wittig (bass) and Brad Noone (drums).

6/8/02	139	2	1 Fireproof		Flicker 2606
7/3/04	74	7	2 Where Do We Go From Here		Flicker 2631
10/21/06	70	3	3 The Reckoning		Flicker 10825
3/15/08	71	4	4 For The Love Of The Game		Essential 10869
10/10/09	89	2	5 Confessions		Essential 10904

PILOT
Pop-rock trio from Edinburgh, Scotland: David Paton (vocals, guitar), Bill Lyall (keyboards) and Stuart Tosh (drums). Lyall died of AIDS on 12/1/1989 (age 36).

5/31/75	82	14	1 Pilot		EMI 11368

PIMP C
Born Chad Butler on 12/29/1973 in Port Arthur, Texas. Died on 12/4/2007 (age 33). Male rapper. Member of **UGK**. In 2002, sentenced to eight years in prison for illlegal gun possession.

3/19/05	50	6	1 The Sweet James Jones Stories		Rap-A-Lot 68521
7/29/06	3[1]	9	● 2 Pimpalation		Wood Wheel 68634

PINBACK
Alternative-rock duo from San Diego, California: Rob Crow and Armistead Smith.

10/30/04	196	1	1 Summer In Abaddon		Touch And Go 20937
9/29/07	69	2	2 Autumn Of The Seraphs		Touch And Go 300

PINDER, Michael
Born on 12/27/1941 in Birmingham, England. Rock keyboardist. Member of **The Moody Blues**.

5/1/76	133	8	1 The Promise		Threshold 18

PINK
Born Alecia Moore on 9/8/1979 in Doylestown, Pennsylvania; raised in Philadelphia, Pennsylvania. Female singer/songwriter. Nickname derived from a character in the 1992 movie *Reservoir Dogs*. Married professional motocrosser Carey Hart on 1/7/2006.

4/22/00	26	59	▲²	1 Can't Take Me Home		LaFace 26062
12/8/01+	6	90	▲⁵	2 Missundaztood	Cat:#33/10	Arista 14718
11/29/03	9	15	▲	3 Try This		Arista 52139
4/22/06	6	88	▲	4 I'm Not Dead	Cat:#25/11	LaFace 80320
11/15/08	2[1]	81↑	▲	5 Funhouse		LaFace 36759

PINK FLOYD
1970s: #5 / 1980s: #13 / All-Time: #24

Progressive-rock band formed in England: **Syd Barrett** (vocals, guitar; born on 1/6/1046; died on 7/7/2006, age 60), **Roger Waters** (vocals, bass; born on 9/6/1944), **Richard Wright** (keyboards; born on 7/28/1943; died of cancer on 9/15/2008, age 65) and **Nick Mason** (drums; born on 1/27/1945). **David Gilmour** (born on 3/6/1946) replaced Barrett in 1968. Wright left in early 1982. Waters went solo in 1984. Band inactive from 1984-86. Gilmour, Mason and Wright regrouped in 1987. Group name taken from Georgia bluesmen Pink Anderson and Floyd Council.

AWARD: R&R Hall of Fame: 1996

DEBUT	PEAK	WKS	RIAA	#	Album Title	Catalog	Label & Number
12/2/67+	131	11		1	The Piper At The Gates Of Dawn		Tower 5093
					RS500 #347		
11/7/70	55	13	●	2	Atom Heart Mother		Harvest 382
11/6/71	70	73	▲²	3	Meddle		Harvest 832
6/24/72	46	25	●	4	Obscured By Clouds	[S]	Harvest 11078
					music from movie *The Valley*		
3/17/73	❶¹	762↑	▲¹⁵	5	The Dark Side Of The Moon *[HOF / RS500 #43]*	Cat:❶²¹/948	Harvest 11163
					Grammy: Hall of Fame ★ RS500 #43		
9/1/73	153	7		6	More	[E-S]	Harvest 11198
					originally released in 1969		
12/22/73+	36	17	●	7	A Nice Pair	[E]	Harvest 11257 [2]
					reissue of album #1 above and *A Saucerful Of Secrets* (see non-charted album below)		
9/27/75	❶²	39	▲⁶	8	Wish You Were Here	Cat:#11/49	Columbia 33453
					RS500 #209		
2/19/77	3³	28	▲⁴	9	Animals	Cat:#34/1	Columbia 34474
12/15/79+	❶¹⁵	123	▲²³	10	The Wall	Cat:❶¹/454	Columbia 36183 [2]
					Grammy: Hall of Fame ★ RS500 #87		
4/9/83	6	23	▲²	11	The Final Cut		Columbia 38243
9/26/87	3¹	56	▲⁴	12	A Momentary Lapse Of Reason	Cat:#12/18	Columbia 40599
4/23/94	❶⁴	51	▲³	13	The Division Bell		Columbia 64200
					GREATEST HITS & COMPILATIONS:		
7/31/71	152	7		14	Relics		Harvest 759
					recordings from 1967-69		
12/12/81+	31	16	▲²	15	A Collection Of Great Dance Songs	Cat:#6/53	Columbia 37680
6/18/83	68	9		16	Works		Capitol 12276
					Harvest label recordings (1968-73)		
11/24/01	2¹	26	▲⁴	17	Echoes - The Best Of Pink Floyd		Capitol 36111 [2]
					LIVE ALBUMS:		
1/3/70	74	27	▲	18	Ummagumma		Harvest 388 [2]
					record 1: live; record 2: studio		
12/10/88+	11	21	▲³	19	Delicate Sound Of Thunder	Cat:#40/9	Columbia 44484 [2]
6/24/95	❶¹	22	▲²	20	Pulse	Cat:#35/1	Columbia 67065 [2]
5/6/00	19	9	▲	21	Is There Anybody Out There? - The Wall Live 1980-1981		Columbia 62055 [2]

~ ~ ~ ~ ~ ~ ~ ~ ~   *NON-CHARTED ALBUM*   ~ ~ ~ ~ ~ ~ ~ ~ ~ ~
1968 **A Saucerful Of Secrets**

PINK LADY
Female disco duo from Japan: Mie Nemoto and Kei Masuda. Starred in the 1979 TV variety show *Pink Lady & Jeff.*

DEBUT	PEAK	WKS		#	Album Title	Catalog	Label & Number
8/4/79	203	8		1	Pink Lady		Elektra 209

PINK MARTINI
Eclectic-pop band formed in Portland, Oregon. Led by female vocalist China Forbes and pianist Thomas Lauderdale.

DEBUT	PEAK	WKS		#	Album Title		Label & Number
11/6/04	122	4		1	Hang On Little Tomato		Heinz 2
6/2/07	30	7		2	Hey Eugene!		Heinz 3
11/14/09	45	3		3	Splendor In The Grass		Heinz 6

PINK SPIDERS, The
Pop-rock trio from Nashville, Tennessee: Matt Friction (vocals, guitar), Jon Decious (bass) and Bob Ferrari (drums).

DEBUT	PEAK	WKS		#	Album Title		Label & Number
8/19/06	84	5		1	Teenage Graffiti		Suretone 006477

PINMONKEY
Country band formed in Nashville, Tennessee: brothers Chad Jeffers (guitar) and Michael Jeffers (bass), Michael Reynolds (vocals) and Rick Schell (drums). Group name taken from an episode of TV's *The Simpsons.*

DEBUT	PEAK	WKS		#	Album Title		Label & Number
10/26/02	126	1		1	Pinmonkey		BNA 67049

PINSON, Bobby
Born in Tulsa, Oklahoma; raised in Panhandle, Texas. Country singer/songwriter/guitarist.

DEBUT	PEAK	WKS		#	Album Title		Label & Number
6/4/05	108	1		1	Man Like Me		RCA 68173

PIPER, Wardell
Born on 8/25/1945 in Philadelphia, Pennsylvania. Female disco singer.

DEBUT	PEAK	WKS		#	Album Title		Label & Number
7/7/79	203	4		1	Wardell Piper		Midsong Int'l. 009

Billboard			R I A A	ARTIST Album Title	Catalog	Label & Number
DEBUT	PEAK	WKS				

PIPKINS, The
Vocal duo formed in England: Roger Greenaway and Tony Burrows (low voice). Worked together in studio group **White Plains**.

8/8/70	132	4		1 Gimme Dat Ding! .... [N]		Capitol 483

PIRATES OF THE MISSISSIPPI
Country band from Montgomery, Alabama: "Wild" Bill McCorvey (vocals), Rich "Dude" Alves (guitar), Pat Severs (steel guitar), Dean Townson (bass) and Jimmy Lowe (drums).

5/18/91	80	23		1 Pirates Of The Mississippi		Capitol 94389

PISCOPO, Joe
Born on 6/17/1951 in Passaic, New Jersey. Actor/comedian. Cast member of TV's *Saturday Night Live* (1980-84).

7/27/85	168	3		1 New Jersey .... [C]		Columbia 40046

PITBULL
Born Armando Perez on 1/15/1981 in Miami, Florida. Latin male rapper.

9/11/04	14	40	●	1 M.I.A.M.I. (Money Is A Major Issue)		TVT 2650
12/3/05	25	18		2 Money Is Still A Major Issue		TVT 2750
11/18/06	17	10		3 El Mariel		Famous Artists 2820
12/15/07	50	6		4 The Boatlift		TVT 2960
9/19/09	8	11		5 Rebelution		Mr. 305 51991

PITCH BLACK
Male rap group from Brooklyn, New York: DG, Devious, Fast, GOD and Zakee.

2/28/04	124	1		1 Pitch Black Law		Travio 001664

PITNEY, Gene
Born on 2/17/1940 in Hartford, Connecticut; raised in Rockville, Connecticut. Died on 4/5/2006 (age 66). Pop singer. Own band at Rockville High School. Recorded for Decca in 1959 with Ginny Arnell as Jamie & Jane. Recorded for Blaze in 1960 as Billy Bryan. First recorded under own name for Festival in 1960. Wrote "Hello Mary Lou," "He's A Rebel" and "Rubber Ball."
AWARD: R&R Hall of Fame: 2002

12/1/62	48	15		1 Only Love Can Break A Heart		Musicor 3003
5/18/63	85	7		2 Gene Pitney Sings Just For You..		Musicor 3004
11/23/63	105	6		3 Blue Gene		Musicor 3006
11/14/64	42	17		4 It Hurts To Be In Love		Musicor 3019
3/20/65	141	4		5 George Jones & Gene Pitney		Musicor 3044
7/17/65	112	9		6 I Must Be Seeing Things...		Musicor 3056
9/18/65	43	24		7 Looking Through The Eyes Of Love		Musicor 3069
9/14/68	193	3		8 She's A Heartbreaker		Musicor 3164
				GREATEST HITS & COMPILATIONS:		
8/3/63	41	31		9 World-Wide Winners		Musicor 3005
4/4/64	87	9		10 Gene Pitney's Big Sixteen		Musicor 3008
3/19/66	123	8		11 Big Sixteen, Vol. 3		Musicor 3085
12/17/66+	61	51		12 Greatest Hits Of All Times		Musicor 3102

~ ~ ~ ~ ~ ~ ~ ~ ~ ~ **NON-CHARTED ALBUMS** ~ ~ ~ ~ ~ ~ ~ ~ ~ ~
1962 **The Many Sides Of Gene Pitney**   1964 **Gene - Italiano**
1964 **Gene Pitney Meets The Fair Young Ladies Of** 1965 **Gene Pitney's More Big Sixteen**
     Folkland   1966 **Backstage (I'm Lonely)**

PIXIES
Alternative punk-rock band formed in Boston, Massachusetts: **Frank Black** (vocals), Joey Santiago (guitar), Kim Deal (bass) and David Lovering (drums). Deal was also a member of **The Breeders**.

5/6/89	98	27	●	1 Doolittle		Elektra 60856
				RS500 #226		
9/1/90	70	12		2 Bossanova		Elektra 60963
10/26/91	92	8		3 Trompe Le Monde		Elektra 61118
10/25/97	180	1		4 Death To The Pixies .... [K-L]		Elektra 62118 [2]
				contains previous recordings and a 1990 concert recorded in Holland		
5/22/04	161	3		5 Best Of Pixies: Wave Of Mutilation .... [G]		4AD 2406

~ ~ ~ ~ ~ ~ ~ ~ ~ ~ **NON-CHARTED ALBUM** ~ ~ ~ ~ ~ ~ ~ ~ ~ ~
1988 **Surfer Rosa**
   RS500 #315

PLACE, Mary Kay
Born on 8/23/1947 in Tulsa, Oklahoma. Country singer/actress. Appeared in many movies and TV shows. Played "Loretta Haggers" on TV's *Mary Hartman, Mary Hartman* (1976-78).

10/30/76+	202	10		1 Tonite! At The Capri Lounge Loretta Haggers		Columbia 34353
1/7/78	203	6		2 Aimin' To Please...		Columbia 34908

PLACEBO
Punk-pop trio from London, England: Brian Molko (vocals, guitar), Stefan Olsdal (bass) and Steve Hewitt (drums).

4/22/06	180	1		1 Meds		Elevator 53035
6/27/09	51	1		2 Battle For The Sun		Dreambrother 539

PLAIN WHITE T'S
Punk-pop band from Villa Park, Illinois: Tom Higgenson (vocals), Dave Tirio (guitar), Tim Lopez (guitar), Mike Retondo (bass) and De'Mar Hamilton (drums).

DEBUT	PEAK	WKS			Album Title	Catalog	Label & Number
9/30/06+	10	50	●	1	Every Second Counts		Fearless 162637
6/23/07	8C	11		2	All That We Needed		Fearless 30072
10/11/08	33	5		3	Big Bad World		Hollywood 002184

PLANET P
Studio group assembled by German producer Peter Hauke. **Tony Carey** was lead singer.

3/26/83	42	23		1	Planet P		Geffen 4000
12/1/84+	121	14		2	Pink World		MCA 8019 [2]
					PLANET P PROJECT		

PLANET SOUL
Dance duo from Miami: producer George Costa and singer Nadine Renee.

5/11/96	165	3		1	Energy And Harmony		Strictly Rhythm 325

PLANT, Robert   All-Time: #292
Born on 8/20/1948 in West Bromwich, England. Hard-rock singer/songwriter. Member of **Led Zeppelin** and **The Honeydrippers**. Studied accounting before becoming lead singer of such British blues groups as Black Snake Moan, The Banned and The Crawling King Snakes. Also with the groups Listen and Band Of Joy. Fully recovered from a serious auto accident in Greece on 8/4/1975. Regular musicians in the 1980s included Robbie Blunt (guitar) and Paul Martinez (bass). The Strange Sensation: Justin Adams (guitar), Skin Tyson (guitar), John Baggot (keyboards), Billy Fuller (bass) and Clive Dreamer (drums).

7/17/82	5	53	▲	1	Pictures At Eleven		Swan Song 8512
7/30/83	8	40	▲	2	The Principle Of Moments		Es Paranza 90101
6/15/85	20	19	●	3	Shaken 'N' Stirred		Es Paranza 90265
3/12/88	6	48	▲3	4	Now And Zen		Es Paranza 90863
4/7/90	13	25	●	5	Manic Nirvana		Es Paranza 91336
6/12/93	34	24	●	6	Fate Of Nations		Es Paranza 92264
11/26/94	4	23	▲	7	No Quarter		Atlantic 82706
5/9/98	8	13	●	8	Walking Into Clarksdale		Atlantic 83092
					JIMMY PAGE & ROBERT PLANT (above 2)		
8/3/02	40	4		9	Dreamland		Universal 586962
11/22/03	134	1		10	Sixty Six To Timbuktu	[K]	Atlantic 83626 [2]
5/28/05	22	6		11	Mighty Rearranger		Es Paranza 84747
					ROBERT PLANT AND THE STRANGE SENSATION		
11/10/07	2²	72	▲	12	Raising Sand	Cat:#11/8	Rounder 619075
					ROBERT PLANT & ALISON KRAUSS		
					Grammys: Album of the Year / Contemporary Folk Album		

PLASMATICS
Punk-rock band formed in New York: Wendy O. Williams (vocals), Richie Stotts (guitar), Wes Beech (guitar), **Jean Beauvoir** (bass) and Stu Deutsch (drums). Known for their outlandish stage stunts. Williams died of a self-inflicted gunshot wound on 4/6/1998 (age 48).

2/21/81	134	10		1	New Hope For The Wretched		Stiff 9
6/6/81	142	9		2	Beyond The Valley Of 1984		Stiff 11
12/5/81	177	3		3	Metal Priestess	[EP]	Stiff 666

PLASTIC COW, The
Born Michael Melvoin on 5/10/1937 in Oshkosh, Wisconsin. Performs on the moog synthesizer. His son Jonathan Melvoin, a touring keyboardist with **The Smashing Pumpkins**, died of a drug overdose on 7/12/1996 (age 34). Wendy Melvoin (**Prince**'s Revolution, **Wendy & Lisa**) and Susannah Melvoin (**The Family**) are his twin daughters.

11/8/69	184	2		1	The Plastic Cow Goes Mooooooog	[I]	Dot 25961

PLATTERS, The   1950s: #36
R&B vocal group from Los Angeles, California: Tony Williams, David Lynch, Paul Robi, Herb Reed and Zola Taylor. Sonny Turner replaced Williams in 1959. Sandra Dawn and Nate Nelson (of **The Flamingos**) replaced Taylor and Robi in 1965. Lynch died of cancer on 1/2/1981 (age 61). Nelson died of a heart attack on 6/1/1984 (age 52). Robi died of cancer on 2/1/1989 (age 57). Williams died of emphysema on 8/14/1992 (age 64).
AWARD: R&R Hall of Fame: 1990

7/14/56	7	26		1	The Platters		Mercury 20146
1/19/57	12	8		2	The Platters, Volume Two		Mercury 20216
3/30/59	15	8		3	Remember When?		Mercury 20410
3/14/60	6	174	●	4	Encore Of Golden Hits	[G]	Mercury 20472
11/14/60+	20	18	●	5	More Encore Of Golden Hits	[G]	Mercury 20591
7/9/66	100	6		6	I Love You 1,000 Times		Musicor 3091
4/10/93	49C	1		7	20 Greatest Hits	[G]	Federal 4415
					contains re-recordings of their classic hits		

~ ~ ~ ~ ~ ~ ~ ~ ~ ~ **NON-CHARTED ALBUMS** ~ ~ ~ ~ ~ ~ ~ ~ ~ ~ ~
1957 **The Flying Platters**   1960 **Reflections**
1958 **The Flying Platters Around The World**

PLAY
Female teen vocal group from Stockholm, Sweden: Anna Sundstrand, Anais Lameche, Rosie Munter and Faye Hamlin.

7/13/02	74	28	●	1	Play	[EP]	Columbia 86607
6/28/03	67	7		2	Replay		Columbia 87177

PLAYA
R&B vocal trio from Louisville, Kentucky: Ben Bush, John Peacock and Stephen "Static" Garrett. Garrett died on 2/25/2008 (age 33).

4/11/98	86	8		1 Cheers 2 U	Def Jam 536386

PLAYAZ CIRCLE
Male rap duo from College Park, Georgia: Tauheed "Tity Boi" Epps and Earl "Dolla Boy" Conyers.

11/17/07	27	3		1 Supply & Demand	DTP 010083
10/17/09	74	2		2 Flight 360: The Takeoff	DTP 012679

PLAYER
Pop-rock band formed in Los Angeles, California: Peter Beckett (vocals, guitar), John Crowley (vocals, guitar), Wayne Cooke (keyboards), Ronn Moss (bass) and John Friesen (drums). Moss played "Ridge Forrester" on the TV soap *The Bold & The Beautiful*.

11/5/77+	26	34	●	1 Player	RSO 3026
9/9/78	37	23	●	2 Danger Zone	RSO 3036
2/6/82	152	7		3 Spies Of Life	RCA Victor 4186

PLAYMATES, The
Pop vocal trio from Waterbury, Connecticut: Donny Conn, Morey Carr and Chic Hetti.

~ ~ ~ ~ ~ ~ ~ ~ ~ ~ ~ **NON-CHARTED ALBUM** ~ ~ ~ ~ ~ ~ ~ ~ ~ ~ ~
1958 **At Play With The Playmates**

PLAYRADIOPLAY!
Born Daniel Hunter in Aledo, Texas. Experimental-rock singer/songwriter/musician.

4/5/08	157	1		1 Texas	Island 010769

PLEASURE
R&B band from Portland, Oregon: Sherman Davis (vocals), Marlon McClain (guitar), brothers Donald Hepburn and Michael Hepburn (keyboards), Bruce Smith (percussion), Dennis Springer (sax), Nathaniel Phillips (bass) and Bruce Carter (drums).

8/28/76	162	5		1 Accept No Substitutes	Fantasy 9506
4/23/77	113	11		2 Joyous	Fantasy 9526
5/13/78	119	13		3 Get To The Feeling	Fantasy 9550
8/11/79	67	29		4 Future Now	Fantasy 9578
7/12/80	97	14		5 Special Things	Fantasy 9600
5/15/82	164	6		6 Give It Up	RCA Victor 4209

PLEASURE P
Born Marcus Cooper on 12/27/1984 in Miami, Florida. R&B singer. Member of **Pretty Ricky**.

6/27/09	10	15		1 The Introduction Of Marcus Cooper	Atlantic 516393

PLENTI, Julian
Born Paul Julian Banks on 5/3/1978 in Essex, England. Alternative-rock singer/songwriter/guitarist. Member of **Interpol**.

8/22/09	103	1		1 Julian Plenti Is...Skyscraper	Matador 873

PLIES
Born Algernod Washington on 7/1/1976 in Fort Myers, Florida. Male rapper.

8/25/07	2¹	38	●	1 The Real Testament	Big Gates 185340
6/28/08	2¹	21	●	2 Definition Of Real	Big Gates 511238
1/3/09	14	20		3 Da REAList	Big Gates 515812

PLIMSOULS, The
Rock band from Los Angeles, California: Peter Case (vocals), Eddie Munoz (guitar), Dave Pahoa (bass) and Lou Ramirez (drums).

4/4/81	153	4		1 The Plimsouls	Planet 13
7/23/83	186	4		2 Everywhere At Once	Geffen 4002

PLUMB
Born Tiffany Arbuckle on 3/9/1975 in Indianapolis, Indiana; raised in Atlanta, Georgia. Female singer/songwriter.

3/18/06	177	1		1 Chaotic Resolve	Curb 78882

(+44)
Pop-punk band formed in Los Angeles, California: **Blink-182** members Mark Hoppus (vocals, bass) and Travis Barker (drums), with guitarists Shane Gallagher and Craig Fairbaugh.

12/2/06	10	10		1 When Your Heart Stops Beating	Interscope 007754

PLUS ONE
Contemporary Christian vocal group: Gabe Combs, Jeremy Mhire, Nathan Walters, Nate Cole and Jason Perry.

6/10/00	76	51	●	1 The Promise	143 Records 83329
3/16/02	29	12		2 Obvious	Atlantic 83528
11/30/02	47ˣ	2		3 Christmas [X]	Atlantic 83570

PMD
Born Parrish Smith on 5/13/1968 in Smithtown, New York. Male rapper. One-half of **EPMD** duo.

10/15/94	65	3		1 Shade Business	PMD 66475
11/9/96	180	1		2 Business Is Business	Relativity 1569

Billboard DEBUT	PEAK	WKS	R I A A	ARTIST Album Title	Catalog	Label & Number
				PM DAWN		
				Hip-hop duo from Jersey City, New Jersey: brothers Attrell "Prince Be" Cordes (born on 5/19/1970) and Jarrett "DJ Minutemix" Cordes (born on 7/17/1971).		
10/19/91+	48	28	●	1 Of The Heart, Of The Soul And Of The Cross: The Utopian Experience............		Gee Street 510276
4/10/93	30	25	●	2 The Bliss Album...?		Gee Street 514517
10/21/95	119	3		3 Jesus Wept		Gee Street 524147
				POCKETS		
				R&B band from Baltimore, Maryland: Larry Jacobs (vocals), Jacob Sheffer (guitar), Albert McKinney (keyboards), Charles Williams (trumpet), Irving Madison (sax), Kevin Barnes (trombone), Gary Grainger (bass) and George Gray (drums).		
10/22/77	57	24		1 Come Go With Us		Columbia 34879
10/28/78	85	6		2 Take It On Up		Columbia 35384
10/13/79	209	1		3 So Delicious		Columbia 36001
				POCO All-Time: #212		
				Country-rock band formed in Los Angeles, California: Rusty Young (steel guitar), **Richie Furay** (guitar), **Jim Messina** (guitar), **Randy Meisner** (bass) and Geroge Grantham (drums). Furay and Messina had been in **Buffalo Springfield**. Meisner left during recording of first album; replaced by **Timothy B. Schmit** (Schmit would later replace Meisner in the **Eagles**). Messina left in 1970; replaced by Paul Cotton, and Furay left in 1973. Grantham and Schmit left in 1977; replaced by Charlie Harrison, Kim Bullard and Steve Chapman. Disbanded in 1984. In 1989, Young, Furay, Messina, Grantham and Meisner reunited.		
6/28/69	63	21		1 Pickin' Up The Pieces		Epic 26460
6/6/70	58	19		2 Poco		Epic 26522
2/6/71	26	21		3 Deliverin' .... **[L]**		Epic 30209
				recorded at the Boston Music Hall and the Felt Forum in New York City		
9/25/71	52	11		4 From The Inside		Epic 30753
11/25/72+	69	20		5 A Good Feelin' To Know		Epic 31601
9/15/73	38	23		6 Crazy Eyes		Epic 32354
5/11/74	68	13		7 Seven		Epic 32895
11/30/74+	76	11		8 Cantamos		Epic 33192
7/19/75	43	18		9 Head Over Heels		ABC 890
8/2/75	90	8		10 The Very Best Of Poco .... **[G]**		Epic 33537 [2]
4/3/76	169	4		11 Live .... **[L]**		Epic 33336
				recorded November 1974 at Yale University		
5/29/76	89	15		12 Rose Of Cimarron		ABC 946
5/14/77	57	18		13 Indian Summer		ABC 989
11/25/78+	14	52	●	14 Legend **Cat:#46/5**		ABC 1099
7/26/80	46	16		15 Under The Gun		MCA 5132
7/25/81	76	10		16 Blue And Gray		MCA 5227
2/20/82	131	8		17 Cowboys & Englishmen		MCA 5288
12/4/82	195	3		18 Ghost Town		Atlantic 80008
12/4/82	209	1		19 Backtracks .... **[G]**		MCA 5363
5/19/84	167	6		20 Inamorata		Atlantic 80148
9/23/89	40	28	●	21 Legacy		RCA 9694
				P.O.D.		
				Christian hard-rock band from San Diego, California: Paul "Sonny" Sandoval (vocals), Marcos Curiel (guitar), Mark "Traa" Daniels (bass) and Noah "Wuv" Bernardo (drums). Jason Truby replaced Curiel in early 2003. P.O.D.: Payable On Death.		
9/11/99+	51	47	▲	1 The Fundamental Elements Of Southtown		Atlantic 83216
9/29/01	6	71	▲³	2 Satellite		Atlantic 83475
11/22/03	9	13	●	3 Payable On Death		Atlantic 83676
2/11/06	9	10		4 Testify		Atlantic 83857
12/9/06	152	1		5 Greatest Hits: The Atlantic Years .... **[G]**		Atlantic 74790
4/26/08	9	9		6 When Angels & Serpents Dance		Ino 09255
				POE		
				Born Annie Danielewski on 3/3/1968 in Manhattan, New York. Adult Alternative singer/songwriter.		
8/3/96	71	30	●	1 Hello		Modern 92605
11/18/00	115	14		2 Haunted		FEI 83362
				POGUES, The		
				Punk-folk band formed in London, England: Shane MacGowan (vocals), Philip Chevron (guitar), Terry Woods (mandolin), Spider Stacy (tin whistle), James Fearnley (accordion), Jem Finer (banjo), Darryl Hunt (bass) and Andrew Ranken (drums). Original bassist Cait O'Riordan was married to **Elvis Costello** from 1986-2003.		
2/27/88	88	16		1 If I Should Fall From Grace With God		Island 90872
8/12/89	118	9		2 Peace & Love		Island 91225
12/15/90	187	3		3 Hell's Ditch		Island 422846
				~ ~ ~ ~ ~ ~ ~ ~ ~ ~ *NON-CHARTED ALBUM* ~ ~ ~ ~ ~ ~ ~ ~ ~ ~ ~		
				1985 **Rum Sodomy & The Lash** *RS500 #445*		
				POINDEXTER, Buster — see JOHANSEN, David		

POINT BLANK
Southern-rock band from Irving, Texas: John O'Daniel (vocals), Rusty Burns (guitar), Kim Davis (guitar), Bill Randolph (bass) and Peter "Buzzy" Gruen (drums). Bubba Keith replaced O'Daniel in late 1980. Randolph died of a heart attack on 6/19/2001 (age 50).

DEBUT	PEAK	WKS		Album Title	Label & Number
9/11/76	175	3		1 Point Blank	Arista 4087
8/18/79	175	9		2 Airplay	MCA 3160
5/31/80	110	13		3 The Hard Way	MCA 5114
4/25/81	80	24		4 American Excess	MCA 5189
4/17/82	119	17		5 On A Roll	MCA 5312

POINTER, Bonnie
Born on 7/11/1950 in Oakland, California. R&B-disco singer. Member of the **Pointer Sisters** from 1971-78.

DEBUT	PEAK	WKS		Album Title	Label & Number
12/16/78+	96	15		1 Bonnie Pointer	Motown 911
12/22/79+	63	14		2 Bonnie Pointer	Motown 929

POINTER, June
Born on 11/30/1953 in Oakland, California. Died of cancer on 4/11/2006 (age 52). Member of the **Pointer Sisters**.

DEBUT	PEAK	WKS		Album Title	Label & Number
7/2/83	202	3		1 Baby Sister	Planet 4508

POINTER, Noel
Born on 12/26/1954 in Brooklyn, New York. Died of a stroke on 12/19/1994 (age 39). Jazz-fusion violin player.

DEBUT	PEAK	WKS		Album Title		Label & Number
6/18/77	144	8		1 Phantazia	[I]	Blue Note 736
3/18/78	95	13		2 Hold-On		United Artists 848
9/1/79	138	7		3 Feel It	[I]	United Artists 973
8/16/80	167	4		4 Calling		United Artists 1050
4/25/81	201	6		5 All My Reasons		Liberty 1094

POINTER SISTERS   All-Time: #279
R&B vocal group from Oakland, California: sisters Ruth Pointer (born on 3/19/1946), Anita Pointer (born on 1/23/1948), **June Pointer** (born on 11/30/1953; died of cancer on 4/11/2006, age 52) and **Bonnie Pointer** (born on 7/11/1950). Appeared as the "Wilson Sisters" in the 1976 movie *Car Wash*. Bonnie went solo in 1978; group continued as trio in a more contemporary style.

DEBUT	PEAK	WKS			Album Title		Label & Number
6/23/73	13	37	●	1	The Pointer Sisters		Blue Thumb 48
3/9/74	82	10	●	2	That's A Plenty		Blue Thumb 6009
9/14/74	96	15		3	Live At The Opera House	[L]	Blue Thumb 8002 [2]
					recorded on 4/21/1974 in San Francisco, California		
6/14/75	22	22		4	Steppin		Blue Thumb 6021
12/4/76	164	6		5	The Best Of The Pointer Sisters	[G]	Blue Thumb 6026 [2]
12/24/77+	176	3		6	Having A Party		Blue Thumb 6023
12/2/78+	13	32	●	7	Energy		Planet 1
9/22/79	72	8		8	Priority		Planet 9003
8/30/80	34	24		9	Special Things		Planet 9
7/11/81	12	22	●	10	Black & White		Planet 18
7/17/82	59	28		11	So Excited!		Planet 4355
11/13/82	178	3		12	Pointer Sisters' Greatest Hits	[G]	Planet 60203
11/26/83+	8	105	▲²	13	Break Out		Planet 4705
8/10/85	24	34	▲	14	Contact		RCA Victor 5487
11/29/86	48	18		15	Hot Together		RCA Victor 5609
3/19/88	152	6		16	Serious Slammin'		RCA 6562

POINT OF GRACE
Female Contemporary Christian vocal group formed in Arkadelphia, Arkansas: Shelley Phillips, Terry Jones, Denise Jones and Heather Floyd.

DEBUT	PEAK	WKS			Album Title		Label & Number
12/9/95	132	2	●	1	The Whole Truth		Word 5608
9/28/96	46	39	▲	2	Life Love & Other Mysteries		Word 69460
8/22/98	24	27	▲	3	Steady On...		Word 69456
5/27/00	106	5		4	Rarities & Remixes	[K]	Word 63804
5/19/01	20	19	●	5	Free To Fly		Word 86112
4/20/03	136	7	●	6	24		Word/Curb 886251 [2]
10/30/04	85	1		7	I Choose You		Word/Curb 886324
9/15/07	56	22		8	How You Live	Cat:❶²/10	Word/Curb 887090
					CHRISTMAS ALBUMS:		
10/23/99	35	13	●	9	A Christmas Story	Cat:#7/6	Word 63609
					Christmas charts: 4/'99, 30/'00, 10/'01		
11/26/05	113	6		10	Winter Wonderland	Cat:❶²/10	Word/Curb 86413
					Christmas charts: 9/'05, 25/'06, 3/'07, 28/'08, 33/'09		
12/13/08	174	1		11	Tennessee Christmas: A Holiday Collection		Word/Curb 887756
					Christmas charts: 16/'08, 33/'09		

POISON   All-Time: #357
Glam-metal band formed in Harrisburg, Pennsylvania: **Bret Michaels** (vocals; born on 3/15/1963), C.C. DeVille (guitar; born on 5/14/1962), Bobby Dall (bass; born on 11/2/1963) and Rikki Rockett (drums; born on 8/8/1961). Richie Kotzen (born on 3/5/1970) replaced DeVille from 1992-97.

DEBUT	PEAK	WKS			Album Title	Label & Number
8/2/86+	3²	101	▲³	1	Look What The Cat Dragged In	Capitol 12523
5/21/88	2¹	70	▲⁵	2	Open Up And Say...Ahh!	Enigma 48493
7/28/90	2¹	63	▲³	3	Flesh & Blood	Capitol 91813
3/6/93	16	13	●	4	Native Tongue	Capitol 98961
6/8/02	103	1		5	Hollyweird	Cyanide 6975

Billboard DEBUT	PEAK	WKS	R I A A	ARTIST Album Title	Catalog	Label & Number
				POISON — cont'd		
6/23/07	32	4		6 Poison'd!		Capitol 93815
				GREATEST HITS & COMPILATIONS:		
2/6/99	2[1C]	125	▲[2]	7 Poison's Greatest Hits 1986-1996		Capitol 53375
4/1/00	131	1		8 Crack A Smile...And More!		Capitol 24781
8/23/03	141	1		9 Best Of Ballads & Blues		Capitol 91407
4/22/06	17	28	●	10 The Best Of Poison: 20 Years Of Rock .... Cat:#30/27		Capitol 49510
				LIVE ALBUMS:		
11/30/91	51	13	●	11 Swallow This Live		Capitol 98046 [2]
7/1/00	166	1		12 Power To The People		Cyanide 6969
				POISON CLAN Rap duo from Florida: Jeff "**JT Money**" Tompkins and Debonaire.		
9/18/93	97	4		1 Ruff Town Behavior		Luke 202
				POISON THE WELL Hard-rock band from Miami, Florida: Jeff Moreira (vocals), Derek Miller (guitar), Ryan Primack (guitar), Geoff Vegas (bass) and Chris Hornbrook (drums).		
7/19/03	98	3		1 You Come Before You		Atlantic 83645
4/21/07	147	2		2 Versions		Ferret 080
7/25/09	180	1		3 The Tropic Rot		Ferret 131
				POLECATS New-wave band from London, England: Tim Worman (vocals), Martin "Boz" Boorer (guitar), Phil Bloomberg (bass) and Chris Hawkes (drums).		
6/4/83	202	8		1 Make A Circuit With Me .... [EP]		Mercury 812358
				POLICE, The 1980s: #36 / All-Time: #209 Reggae-inflected rock trio formed in England: Gordon "**Sting**" Sumner (vocals, bass; born on 10/2/1951), **Andy Summers** (guitar; born on 12/31/1942) and **Stewart Copeland** (drums; born on 7/16/1952). Sting went on to a highly successful solo career. Copeland later joined **Animal Logic** and **Oysterhead**. Group reunited in 2007. AWARD: R&R Hall of Fame: 2003		
3/3/79	23	63	▲	1 Outlandos D'Amour .... RS500 #434		A&M 4753
11/3/79	25	100	▲	2 Reggatta De Blanc .... RS500 #369		A&M 4792
10/25/80+	5	153	▲[2]	3 Zenyatta Mondatta		A&M 4831
10/24/81	2[6]	109	▲[3]	4 Ghost In The Machine .... RS500 #322		A&M 3730
7/2/83	❶[17]	75	▲[8]	5 Synchronicity		A&M 3735
				Grammy: Rock Vocal Group / Hall of Fame ★ RS500 #455		
7/1/95	86	5	▲	6 Live! .... [L] Disc 1: recorded November 1979 at The Orpheum in Boston, Massachusetts; Disc 2: recorded November 1983 at The Omni in Atlanta, Georgia		A&M 540222 [2]
				GREATEST HITS & COMPILATIONS:		
11/22/86	7	26	▲[5]	7 Every Breath You Take - The Singles Cat:#23/110		A&M 3902
10/16/93	79	5	▲	8 Message In A Box: The Complete Recordings		A&M 540150 [4]
12/13/97	100	13	●	9 The Very Best Of Sting & The Police		A&M 540834
5/13/00+	23[C]	33		10 Every Breath You Take: The Classics		A&M 540380
6/23/07	11	17		11 The Police		A&M 009080 [2]
				POLNAREFF, Michel Born on 7/3/1944 in Nerac, France. Pop singer/guitarist/keyboardist.		
2/21/76	117	13		1 Michel Polnareff		Atlantic 18153
				POLYPHONIC SPREE, The Symphonic-pop band formed in Dallas, Texas. Led by singer/songwriter Tim DeLaughter (former leader of **Tripping Daisy**).		
7/31/04	121	1		1 Together We're Heavy		Hollywood 162455
7/7/07	113	1		2 The Fragile Army		Good Records 2990
				PONTY, Jean-Luc Born on 9/29/1942 in Normandy, France. Jazz-rock violinist. Worked with **Frank Zappa** and **Elton John**. Member of **Mahavishnu Orchestra** from 1973-75.		
7/26/75	158	5		1 Upon The Wings Of Music .... [I]		Atlantic 18138
4/10/76	123	13		2 Aurora .... [I]		Atlantic 18165
12/4/76+	67	23		3 Imaginary Voyage .... [I]		Atlantic 18195
10/1/77	35	16		4 Enigmatic Ocean .... [I]		Atlantic 19110
9/2/78	36	28		5 Cosmic Messenger .... [I]		Atlantic 19189
5/19/79	68	10		6 Jean-Luc Ponty: Live .... [I-L]		Atlantic 19229
10/27/79	54	21		7 A Taste For Passion .... [I]		Atlantic 19253
10/18/80	73	18		8 Civilized Evil .... [I]		Atlantic 16020
2/13/82	44	14		9 Mystical Adventures .... [I]		Atlantic 19333
8/27/83	85	15		10 Individual Choice .... [I]		Atlantic 80098
12/8/84	171	13		11 Open Mind .... [I]		Atlantic 80185
11/2/85	166	4		12 Fables .... [I]		Atlantic 81276

Billboard			R I A A	ARTIST		
DEBUT	PEAK	WKS		Album Title	Catalog	Label & Number

POOR RIGHTEOUS TEACHERS
Rap trio from Trenton, New Jersey: Wise Intelligent, Culture Freedom and Father Shaheed.

6/16/90	142	22		1 Holy Intellect..		Profile 1289
9/21/91	155	3		2 Pure Poverty...		Profile 1415
10/2/93	167	2		3 Black Business..		Profile 1443

POP, The
New-wave band from Los Angeles, California: David Swanson (vocals), Roger Prescott (guitar), Tim Henderson (bass) and Tim McGovern (drums).

| 10/27/79 | 201 | 1 | | 1 Go!... | | Arista 4243 |

POP, Iggy
Born James Osterberg on 4/21/1947 in Muskegon, Michigan. Highly influential punk-rock singer/songwriter. Lead singer of **The Stooges**. Acted in the movies *Cry Baby*, *Hardware* and *The Crow: City Of Angels*. Adopted nickname from his first band, The Iguanas.

4/9/77	72	13		1 The Idiot		RCA Victor 2275
9/17/77	120	6		2 Lust For Life		RCA Victor 2488
4/1/78	204	3		3 Kill City		Bomp 1018
				IGGY POP & JAMES WILLIAMSON		
10/6/79	180	4		4 New Values		Arista 4237
3/8/80	125	7		5 Soldier		Arista 4259
9/19/81	166	5		6 Party		Arista 9572
10/18/86	75	27		7 Blah-Blah-Blah		A&M 5145
7/23/88	110	12		8 Instinct		A&M 5198
7/28/90	90	37		9 Brick By Brick		Virgin 91381
6/20/09	187	1		10 Preliminaires...		Astralwerks 98578

POPE JOHN XXIII
Born Angelo Guiseppe Roncalli on 11/25/1881 in Sotto il Monte, Italy. Died on 6/3/1963 (age 81). Served as Pope from 1958-63.

| 8/3/63 | 126 | 3 | | 1 Pope John XXIII .... [T] | | Mercury 200 |
| | | | | excerpts of the Pope's voice and events during his reign | | |

POPE JOHN PAUL II
Born Karol Jozef Wojtyla on 5/18/1920 in Wadowice, Poland. Died on 4/2/2005 (age 84). Served as Pope from 1978-2005.

| 11/3/79 | 126 | 4 | | 1 Pope John Paul II Sings At The Festival Of Sacrosong .... | | Infinity 9899 |
| 4/10/99 | 175 | 2 | | 2 Abba Pater.. [F] | | Sony Classical 61705 |

POPPER, John
Born on 3/29/1967 in Cleveland, Ohio; raised in Princeton, New Jersey. Lead singer/harmonica player of **Blues Traveler**.

| 9/25/99 | 185 | 1 | | 1 Zygote .... | | A&M 490408 |

POPPY FAMILY, The
Pop band from Canada: Susan Jacks (vocals), her husband **Terry Jacks** (guitar), Craig MacCaw (guitar) and Satwan Singh (percussion). Group and marriage broke up in 1973; Susan and Terry began solo careers.

| 6/20/70 | 76 | 11 | | 1 Which Way You Goin' Billy? .... | | London 574 |

POP WILL EAT ITSELF
Psychedelic-rap-rock band from Stourbridge, England: Clint Mansell and Graham Crabb (vocals), Adam Mole (guitar) and Richard March (bass).

| 8/26/89 | 169 | 6 | | 1 This Is The Day...This Is The Hour...This Is This!................... | | RCA 9742 |

PORCUPINE TREE
Progressive-rock band from Hempstead, Hertfordshire, England: Steven Wilson (vocals, guitar), Richard Barbieri (keyboards), Colin Edwin (bass) and Gavin Harrison (drums).

5/14/05	132	1		1 Deadwing		Lava 93812
5/12/07	59	2		2 Fear Of A Blank Planet		Atlantic 115900
10/3/09	25	3		3 The Incident		Roadrunner 617857

PORNO FOR PYROS
Alternative-rock band formed in Los Angeles, California: **Perry Farrell** (vocals), Peter DiStefano (guitar), Martyn LeNoble (bass) and Stephen Perkins (drums). Farrell and Perkins were with **Jane's Addiction**. Farrell later formed **Satellite Party**.

| 5/15/93 | 3[1] | 21 | ● | 1 Porno For Pyros | | Warner 45228 |
| 6/15/96 | 20 | 11 | | 2 Good God's Urge.. | | Warner 46126 |

PORTER, David
Born on 11/21/1941 in Memphis, Tennessee. R&B singer/songwriter. Songwriting partnership with **Isaac Hayes**.

| 3/28/70 | 163 | 10 | | 1 Gritty, Groovy, & Gettin' It.. | | Enterprise 1009 |
| 1/30/71 | 104 | 9 | | 2 David Porter...Into A Real Thing .... | | Enterprise 1012 |

PORTISHEAD
Alternative pop-rock duo from Bristol, England: multi-instrumentalist Geoff Barrow and vocalist Beth Gibbons. Duo named after a coastal shipping town near Bristol.

1/28/95	79	17	●	1 Dummy		London 828553
				RS500 #419		
10/18/97	21	16		2 Portishead..		London 539189
11/28/98	155	1		3 Roseland NYC Live .... [L]		London 559424
				recorded on 7/24/1997 at the Roseland Ballroom in New York City		
5/17/08	7	11		4 Third		Go! Discs 011141

PORTRAIT
Male R&B vocal group: Eric Kirkland and Michael Saulsberry (from Los Angeles, California), Irving Washington (from Providence, Rhode Island) and Phillip Johnson (from Tulsa, Oklahoma). In 1995, Johnson was replaced by Kurt Jackson (from Aurora, Colorado).

1/9/93	70	21	1 Portrait	Capitol 93496
3/25/95	131	5	2 All That Matters	Capitol 28709

PORTUGAL THE MAN
Alternative-rock band from Wasilla, Alaska: John Gourley (vocals, guitar), Ryan Neighbors (keyboards), Zachary Carothers (bass) and Jason Sechrist (drums).

8/8/09	81	1	1 The Satanic Satanist	Equal Vision 164

P.O.S.
Born Stefon Alexander on 8/18/1981 in Minneapolis, Minnesota. Male rapper.

2/21/09	106	1	1 Never Better	Rhymesayers 0102

POSEY, Sandy
Born on 6/18/1944 in Jasper, Alabama; raised in West Memphis, Arkansas. Pop singer.

12/17/66+	129	7	1 Born A Woman	MGM 4418
9/30/67	182	4	2 I Take It Back	MGM 4480

POSITIVE K
Born Darryl Gibson in the Bronx, New York. Male rapper.

2/20/93	168	10	1 The Skills Dat Pay Da Bills	Island 514057

POST, Mike
Born on 9/29/1944 in Los Angeles, California. Prolific composer of TV theme songs.

11/8/75	195	3	1 Railhead Overture .... [I]	MGM 5005
2/27/82	70	17	2 Television Theme Songs .... [G-I]	Elektra 60028

POSTAL SERVICE, The
Pop-rock duo from Bellingham, Washington: Benjamin Gibbard and James Tamborello. Gibbard also formed **Death Cab For Cutie**.

3/27/04+	114	31	●	1 Give Up .... Cat:#19/9	Sub Pop 595

POTLIQUOR
Rock band from Baton Rouge, Louisiana: George Ratzlaff (vocals), Les Wallace (guitar), Guy Schaeffer (bass) and Jerry Amoroso (drums).

2/19/72	168	7	1 Levee Blues	Janus 3033

POTTER, Grace, And The Nocturnals
Born in 1983 in Waitsfield, Vermont. Rock singer/songwriter/keyboardist. The Nocturnals: Scott Tournet (guitar), Bryan Dondero (bass) and Matt Burr (drums).

8/25/07	119	1	1 This Is Somewhere	Ragged Company 000385

POTTS, Paul
Born on 10/13/1970 in Kingswood, South Gloucestershire, England. Operatic tenor. Winner on the 2007 season of TV's *Britain's Got Talent*.

10/6/07	23	24	1 One Chance	Syco 15517
5/23/09	33	3	2 Passione .... [F]	Syco 47439

POUSETTE-DART BAND
Soft-rock band from Boston, Massachusetts: Jon Pousette-Dart (vocals), John Curtis (guitar), John Troy (bass) and Michael Dawe (drums).

3/19/77	143	7	1 Amnesia	Capitol 11608
6/10/78	161	5	2 Pousette-Dart Band 3	Capitol 11781
8/11/79	203	2	3 Never Enough	Capitol 11935

POVERTYNECK HILLBILLIES
Country band from Fayette County, Pennsylvania: Chris "Abby" Abbondanza (vocals), David "Junior" Guthrie (guitar), Bob "Crafty" Crafton (steel guitar), Chris Higbee (fiddle), Dave Cramer (keyboards), Jeff Volek (bass) and Ryan Lucotch (drums).

6/24/06	159	1	1 Povertyneck Hillbillies	Rust 10801

POWELL, Adam Clayton
Born on 11/29/1908 in New Haven, Connecticut. Died on 4/4/1972 (age 63). Congressman from Harlem, New York (1944-70).

2/25/67	112	9	1 Keep The Faith, Baby! .... [T]	Jubilee 2062

POWELL, Jesse
Born on 9/12/1971 in Gary, Indiana. R&B singer/songwriter.

2/6/99	63	21	●	1 'Bout It	Silas 11789
4/14/01	71	7		2 JP	Silas 112401

POWELL, Roger
Born on 3/14/1949 in San Francisco, California. Rock keyboardist. Former member of **Utopia**.

3/1/80	203	3	1 Air Pocket .... [I]	Bearsville 6994

POWERMAN 5000
Hard-rock band formed in Boston, Massachusetts: Michael "Spider One" Cummings (vocals; younger brother of **Rob Zombie**), Adam Williams (guitar), Mike Tempesta (guitar), Dorian Heartsong (bass) and Al Pahanish (drums). Heartsong and Pahanish left in 2002, replaced by Siggy Siursen (bass) and Adrian Ost (drums).

8/7/99	29	44	▲	1 **Tonight The Stars Revolt!**		DreamWorks 50107
6/7/03	27	9		2 **Transform**		DreamWorks 450433
8/19/06	120	1		3 **Destroy What You Enjoy**		DRT 444

POWERS, Joey
Born in 1939 in Canonsburg, Pennsylvania. Pop singer.

~ ~ ~ ~ ~ ~ ~ ~ ~ ~ ~ **NON-CHARTED ALBUM** ~ ~ ~ ~ ~ ~ ~ ~ ~ ~ ~
1964 **Midnight Mary**

POWER STATION, The
All-star rock band: **Robert Palmer** (vocals), **Andy Taylor** (guitar), John Taylor (bass) and Tony Thompson (drums). The Taylors were members of **Duran Duran**. Thompson was a member of **Chic**. Palmer died of a heart attack on 9/26/2003 (age 54). Thompson died of cancer on 11/12/2003 (age 48).

4/13/85	6	44	▲	1 **The Power Station**		Capitol 12380

POWTER, Daniel
Born on 2/25/1971 in Vancouver, British Columbia, Canada. Adult Alternative-pop singer/songwriter/pianist.

4/29/06	9	22	●	1 **Daniel Powter**		Warner 49332

POZO-SECO SINGERS
Folk-rock trio from Texas: **Don Williams**, Susan Taylor and Lofton Kline. Williams later became a major country star.

7/30/66	127	6		1 **Time**		Columbia 9315
2/4/67	81	10		2 **I Can Make It With You**		Columbia 9400

PRADO, Perez, And His Orchestra
Born Damaso Perez Prado on 12/11/1916 in Mantanzas, Cuba. Died of a stroke on 9/14/1989 (age 72). Bandleader/organist. Known as "The King of The Mambo." Appeared in the movie *Underwater!*

5/25/59	22	3		1 **"Prez"** .... [I]		RCA Victor 1556

~ ~ ~ ~ ~ ~ ~ ~ ~ ~ **NON-CHARTED ALBUMS** ~ ~ ~ ~ ~ ~ ~ ~ ~ ~ ~
1955 **Mambo Mania** *["Cherry Pink And Apple Blossom White"]*   1958 **Dilo Featuring Patricia**

PRAGUE MADRIGAL SINGERS, The
Choral group from Czechoslovakia. Conducted by Miroslav Venhoda.

12/10/66	29[X]	3		1 **The Christmas Carols Of Europe** .... [X-F]		Crossroads 0054

PRAS — see MICHEL, Pras

PRATT, Andy
Born on 1/25/1947 in Boston, Massachusetts. Soft-rock singer/songwriter/keyboardist/guitarist.

5/12/73	192	4		1 **Andy Pratt**		Columbia 31722
7/10/76	104	10		2 **Resolution**		Nemperor 438
8/27/77	90	9		3 **Shiver In The Night**		Nemperor 443

PRATT & McCLAIN
Pop vocal duo: Truett Pratt (from San Antonio, Texas) and Jerry McClain (from Pasadena, California).

7/10/76	190	2		1 **Pratt & McClain Featuring "Happy Days"**		Reprise 2250

PRAY FOR THE SOUL OF BETTY
Hard-rock band from New York: **Constantine** Maroulis (vocals), Joao Joya (guitar), Craig Taylor (bass) and Michael Hamboussi (drums). Maroulis was a finalist on the fourth season of TV's *American Idol* in 2005.

5/28/05	129	1		1 **Pray For The Soul Of Betty**		Koch 5837

PREFAB SPROUT
Pop band from England: brothers Paddy McAloon (vocals, guitar) and Martin McAloon (bass), with Wendy Smith (vocals) and Neil Conti (drums).

11/2/85	178	5		1 **Two Wheels Good**		Epic 40100

PRELUDE
Folk trio formed in England: husband-and-wife Irene Hume (vocals) and Brian Hume (vocals, guitar), with Ian Vardy (guitar).

12/7/74	94	7		1 **After The Gold Rush**		Island 9282
11/22/75+	111	14		2 **Owlcreek Incident**		Pye 12120

PREMIATA FORNERIA MARCONI — see P.F.M.

PREMIERS, The
Latin-rock band from San Gabriel, California: brothers Larry Perez (guitar) and John Perez (drums), with George Delgado (vocals) and Frank Zuniga (bass).

~ ~ ~ ~ ~ ~ ~ ~ ~ ~ **NON-CHARTED ALBUM** ~ ~ ~ ~ ~ ~ ~ ~ ~ ~ ~
1964 **Farmer John Live By The Premiers**

PRESIDENTS, The
R&B vocal trio from Washington DC: Archie Powell, Bill Shorter and Tony Boyd.

1/30/71	158	6		1 **5-10-15-20-25-30 years of love**		Sussex 7005

PRESIDENTS OF THE UNITED STATES OF AMERICA, The
Rock trio from Seattle, Washington: Chris Ballew (vocals), Dave Dederer (guitar) and Jason Finn (drums).

9/2/95+	6	55	▲³	1 **The Presidents Of The United States Of America**		Columbia 67201
11/23/96	31	13	●	2 **II**		Columbia 67577

PRESLEY, Elvis   1950s: #3 / 1960s: #3 / 1970s: #2 / 2000s: #8 / All-Time: #1
Born on 1/8/1935 in Tupelo, Mississippi. Died of heart failure on 8/16/1977 (age 42). Known as "The King of Rock & Roll." Moved to Memphis in 1948. First recorded for Sun in 1954. Signed to RCA Records on 11/22/1955. His backing group included The Jordanaires (vocals), Scotty Moore (guitar), **Bill Black** (bass) and D.J. Fontana (drums). Starred in 31 feature movies. In U.S. Army from 3/24/1958 to 3/5/1960. Married Priscilla Beaulieu on 5/1/1967; divorced on 10/11/1973. Priscilla pursued acting in the 1980s beginning with a role on TV's *Dallas*. Their only child, **Lisa Marie Presley**, (born on 2/1/1968) was married to **Michael Jackson** from 1994-96. Elvis's last "live" performance was in Indianapolis on 6/26/1977.

AWARDS: Grammy: Lifetime Achievement 1971 ★ R&R Hall of Fame: 1986 ★ C&W Hall of Fame: 1998

3/31/56	❶¹⁰	48	●	1 **Elvis Presley**		RCA Victor 1254
				RS500 #55		
				includes 5 Sun recordings from 1954-55		
11/10/56	❶⁵	32	●	2 **Elvis**		RCA Victor 1382
9/30/57	16	1		3 **Just For You** .... [EP]		RCA Victor EPA-4041
3/23/59	19	8		4 **For LP Fans Only**		RCA Victor 1990
				includes 4 Sun recordings from 1954-55		
9/21/59	32	8		5 **A Date With Elvis**		RCA Victor 2011
				includes 5 Sun recordings from 1954-55		
5/9/60	2³	56	●	6 **Elvis Is Back!**		RCA Victor 2231
				recorded within weeks of Elvis's discharge from the Army on 3/5/1960		
7/10/61	❶³	25		7 **Something For Everybody**		RCA Victor 2370
7/14/62	4	31		8 **Pot Luck**		RCA Victor 2523
8/14/65	10	27		9 **Elvis For Everyone!**		RCA Victor 3450
6/14/69	13	34	●	10 **From Elvis In Memphis**		RCA Victor 4155
				RS500 #190		
8/15/09	29ᶜ	1		11 **From Elvis In Memphis: Legacy Edition** .... [R]		RCA 51497 [2]
11/29/69	12	24	●	12 **From Memphis To Vegas / From Vegas To Memphis**		RCA Victor 6020 [2]
				disc one is a live concert recorded in August 1969 at the International Hotel in Las Vegas		
11/21/70	183	3		13 **Elvis Back In Memphis**		RCA Victor 4429
1/23/71	12	21	●	14 **Elvis Country ("I'm 10,000 Years Old")**		RCA Victor 4460
6/26/71	33	15		15 **Love Letters From Elvis**		RCA Victor 4530
2/12/72	43	19	●	16 **Elvis Now**		RCA Victor 4671
7/21/73	52	13		17 **Elvis**		RCA Victor 0283
11/24/73+	50	13		18 **Raised On Rock/For Ol' Times Sake**		RCA Victor 0388
4/6/74	90	8		19 **Good Times**		RCA Victor 0475
2/1/75	47	12		20 **Promised Land**		RCA Victor 0873
6/7/75	57	13		21 **Today**		RCA Victor 1039
4/17/76	76	11		22 **The Sun Sessions**		RCA Victor 1675
				RS500 #11 ★ NRR		
				Elvis's first commercial recordings at the Sun Studio in Memphis from 1954-55		
6/5/76	41	17	●	23 **From Elvis Presley Boulevard, Memphis, Tennessee**		RCA Victor 1506
7/23/77	3³	31	▲²	24 **Moody Blue**		RCA Victor 2428
				includes Elvis's last studio recording on 10/31/1976 ("He'll Have To Go"); pressed on translucent blue vinyl; Elvis died 24 days after this album first charted		

CHRISTMAS ALBUMS:

12/2/57	❶⁴	7	▲⁹	25 **Elvis' Christmas Album**		RCA Victor 1035
				album has a gatefold cover with 10 pages of bound-in color photos of Elvis from *Jailhouse Rock*		
12/31/60	33	1		26 **Elvis' Christmas Album** .... [R]		RCA Victor 1951
1/6/62	120	2		27 **Elvis' Christmas Album** .... [R]		RCA Victor 1951
12/8/62	59	4		28 **Elvis' Christmas Album** .... [R]		RCA Victor 1951
12/28/85	178	2		29 **Elvis' Christmas Album** .... Cat:#10/28 [R]		RCA Victor 5486
				reissue on green vinyl (including the original cover and photos);		
				Christmas charts: 5/'63, 3/'64, 2/'65, 2/'66, 3/'67, 3/'68, 2/'69, 6/'85, 11/'87, 10/'88, 22/'89, 22/'90, 29/'92, 27/'94, 19/'95, 12/'96, 31/'97;		
				Catalog charts: 48/'91, 41/'92, 38/'93, 22/'94, 12/'95, 10/'96, 39/'97		
12/4/71+	❶³ˣ	12	▲³	30 **Elvis Sings The Wonderful World Of Christmas**		RCA Victor 4579
				Christmas charts: 2/'71, 1/'72, 1/'73		
12/5/92+	26ˣ	14	●	31 **Blue Christmas** .... Cat:#19/10 [K]		RCA 59800
				Christmas charts: 27/'92, 26/'93, 36/'04, 43/'06; Catalog charts: 38/'92, 19/'93		
12/3/94	94	6	▲	32 **If Every Day Was Like Christmas** .... Cat:#22/15 [K]		RCA 66482
				Christmas charts: 18/'94, 23/'96, 28/'97, 29/'98; Catalog charts: 50/'95, 22/'96, 24/'97, 31/'98		
11/17/01+	15ˣ	22		33 **White Christmas** .... Cat:#17/15 [K]		RCA 67959
				Christmas charts: 26/'01, 15/'02, 29/'03, 45/'04; Catalog charts: 36/'01, 17/'02, 26/'03, 37/'04		
12/20/03	175	2		34 **Elvis: Christmas Peace** .... [K]		RCA 52393 [2]
				disc one: all 20 Elvis Christmas recordings; disc two: 20 Elvis sacred recordings; Christmas chart: 16/'03		
11/25/06	69	7		35 **Elvis Christmas** .... Cat:#11/2 [K]		RCA 88908
				Christmas charts: 22/'06, 13/'07, 24/'08, 24/'09		
12/5/09	88	5		36 **Elvis Christmas** .... Cat:#31/1 [R]		RCA 88908
11/17/07	81	8		37 **Home For The Holidays** .... [K]		Madacy 52871
				Christmas charts: 12/'07, 50/'08		

PRESLEY, Elvis — cont'd

DEBUT	PEAK	WKS	RIAA	# Album Title	Catalog	Label & Number
11/1/08	17	11		38 Christmas Duets		RCA 35479
				Christmas charts: 4/'08, 22/'09		
12/5/09	111	6		39 Christmas Duets ..... [R]		RCA 35479
12/5/09	80	5	▲²	40 It's Christmas Time ..... Cat:#4/66 [K]		BMG 44931
				Christmas charts: 27/'02, 5/'03, 12/'04, 16/'05, 11/'06; Catalog charts: 23/'99, 21/'00, 13/'01, 4/'02, 4/'03, 12/'04, 13/'05, 10/'06, 27/'08, 25/'09		

GREATEST HITS & COMPILATIONS:

DEBUT	PEAK	WKS	RIAA	# Album Title	Catalog	Label & Number
4/21/58	3²	74	▲⁶	41 Elvis' Golden Records	Cat:#14/32	RCA Victor 1707
2/15/60	31	6	▲	42 Elvis' Gold Records, Volume 2 (50,000,000 Elvis Fans Can't Be Wrong)		RCA Victor 2075
9/14/63	3²	63	▲	43 Elvis' Golden Records, Volume 3		RCA Victor 2765
3/2/68	33	22	●	44 Elvis' Gold Records, Volume 4		RCA Victor 3921
4/21/84	207	2	●	45 Elvis' Gold Records, Volume 5		RCA Victor 4941
8/22/70	45	36	▲²	46 Elvis-Worldwide 50 Gold Award Hits, Vol. 1		RCA Victor 6401 [4]
8/28/71	120	7		47 Elvis-The Other Sides - Worldwide Gold Award Hits, Vol. 2		RCA Victor 6402 [4]
2/2/74	43	28	▲²	48 Elvis-A Legendary Performer, Volume 1		RCA Victor 0341
2/7/76	46	17	▲²	49 Elvis-A Legendary Performer, Volume 2		RCA Victor 1349
1/6/79	113	11	●	50 Elvis-A Legendary Performer, Volume 3		RCA Victor 3082
1/7/84	202	2		51 Elvis-A Legendary Performer, Volume 4		RCA Victor 4848
8/5/78	130	11		52 Elvis Sings For Children And Grownups Too!		RCA Victor 2901
11/4/78	86	7		53 Elvis-A Canadian Tribute		RCA Victor 7065
3/10/79	132	7	●	54 Our Memories Of Elvis		RCA Victor 3279
8/25/79	157	5		55 Our Memories Of Elvis, Volume 2		RCA Victor 3448
8/23/80	27	14	▲	56 Elvis Aron Presley		RCA Victor 3699 [8]
2/14/81	49	12		57 Guitar Man		RCA Victor 3917
12/19/81+	142	7		58 Elvis-Greatest Hits, Volume One		RCA Victor 2347
8/7/82+	32ᶜ	14	▲²	59 Pure Gold		RCA Victor 0971
				originally released in 1975		
11/27/82	133	9		60 The Elvis Medley		RCA Victor 4530
				includes the complete versions of the 6 songs featured in the medley		
5/21/83	103	6		61 I Was The One		RCA Victor 4678
				computer-enhanced stereo versions of rockabilly hits from 1956-61		
11/17/84+	80	19		62 Elvis: A Golden Celebration		RCA Victor 5172 [6]
12/8/84+	154	13		63 Rocker		RCA 5182
				original mono versions of rock 'n roll hits from 1956-57		
3/2/85	154	3		64 A Valentine Gift For You		RCA 5353
				pressed on red vinyl		
5/4/85	208	1		65 Reconsider Baby		RCA Victor 5418
8/8/87	143	9	▲³	66 The Number One Hits	Cat:#16/2	RCA Victor 6382
8/15/87	117	8	▲³	67 The Top Ten Hits		RCA Victor 6383 [2]
8/29/92	159	2	▲²	68 Elvis: The King Of Rock 'N' Roll - The Complete 50's Masters		RCA 66050 [5]
8/2/97	80	3	●	69 Elvis Presley Platinum: A Life In Music		RCA 67469 [4]
7/31/99	163	1		70 Elvis Presley / Artist Of The Century		RCA 67732 [3]
10/14/00	159	4		71 The Elvis Presley Collection: Country		Time-Life/RCA 69403 [2]
9/29/01	150	3		72 The 50 Greatest Love Songs		RCA 68026 [2]
3/2/02	81	8		73 Elvis: The Very Best Of Love		Madacy/BMG 5294
7/13/02	180	1		74 Elvis: Today, Tomorrow & Forever		RCA 65115 [4]
				previously unreleased recordings from 1954-76		
10/12/02	❶³	104	▲⁵	75 Elv1s: 30 #1 Hits	Cat:❶¹/146	RCA 68079
10/25/03	3¹	16	▲	76 Elvis: 2nd To None		RCA 55895
2/12/05	120	4		77 Love, Elvis		RCA 67001
5/21/05	15	8		78 Elvis By The Presleys ..... [TV]		RCA/Sony 67883 [2]
				this CD is a tie-in to the May 2005 CBS-TV documentary special Elvis By The Presleys		
1/20/07	72	5		79 The Essential Elvis Presley		Legacy 89048 [2]
1/26/08	45ᶜ	1		80 HitStory		RCA 71247 [3]
2/16/08	181	3		81 The Very Best Of Love		Madacy 52869
8/30/08	188	1		82 Playlist: The Very Best Of Elvis Presley		RCA 28812

LIVE ALBUMS:

DEBUT	PEAK	WKS	RIAA	# Album Title	Catalog	Label & Number
12/21/68+	8	32	▲	83 Elvis – TV Special ..... [TV]		RCA Victor 4088
				recorded live at Burbank Studios in California; the "comeback" TV special ran on NBC on 12/3/1968		
6/20/70	13	20	▲	84 On Stage-February, 1970		RCA Victor 4362
12/12/70+	21	23	●	85 Elvis-That's The Way It Is		RCA Victor 4445
				soundtrack documentary of Elvis's August 1970 run at the International Hotel in Las Vegas		
7/8/72	11	34	▲³	86 Elvis As Recorded At Madison Square Garden		RCA Victor 4776
2/24/73	❶¹	52	▲⁵	87 Aloha From Hawaii Via Satellite ..... [TV]		RCA 6089 [2]
				TV special recorded in quadraphonic on 1/14/1973 at the Honolulu International Center		
7/27/74	33	13	●	88 Elvis Recorded Live On Stage In Memphis		RCA Victor 0606
11/2/74	130	7		89 Having Fun With Elvis On Stage		RCA Victor 0818
				37 minutes of excerpts of dialogue from Elvis's live concerts		
4/16/77	44	25	▲	90 Welcome To My World		RCA Victor 2274
10/29/77	5	18	▲³	91 Elvis In Concert ..... [TV]		RCA 2587 [2]
3/17/84	163	4		92 Elvis: The First Live Recordings		Music Works 3601
				live recordings from Elvis's appearances on the Louisiana Hayride KWKH radio station in 1955 and 1956		
8/18/07	54	7		93 Elvis: Viva Las Vegas		RCA 11867
				recordings from various Las Vegas shows (1970-72)		

DEBUT	PEAK	WKS	RIAA	#	ARTIST / Album Title	Catalog	Label & Number
					PRESLEY, Elvis — cont'd		
					RELIGIOUS ALBUMS:		
5/13/57	3¹	9	▲	94	Peace In The Valley [EP]		RCA Victor EPA 4054
1/9/61	13	20	▲	95	His Hand In Mine		RCA Victor 2328
3/25/67	18	29	▲²	96	How Great Thou Art		RCA Victor 3758
4/22/72	79	10	▲	97	He Touched Me		RCA Victor 4690
					Grammy: Inspirational Album		
5/13/78	113	8	●	98	He Walks Beside Me (Favorite Songs Of Faith And Inspiration)		RCA Victor 2772
3/24/07	18ᶜ	11	●	99	Elvis: Ultimate Gospel		RCA 57868
1/26/08	4ᶜ	2		100	Peace In The Valley: The Complete Gospel Recordings		RCA 67991 [3]
					SOUNDTRACKS:		
7/22/57	❶¹⁰	29	●	101	Loving You		RCA Victor 1515
9/2/57	18	1	▲	102	Loving You, Vol. II [EP]		RCA Victor EPA 2-1515
9/2/57	22	1	▲	103	Love Me Tender [EP]		RCA Victor EPA-4006
9/15/58	2¹	15	●	104	King Creole		RCA Victor 1884
10/31/60	❶¹⁰	111	▲	105	G.I. Blues		RCA Victor 2256
10/23/61	❶²⁰	79	▲³	106	Blue Hawaii		RCA Victor 2426
12/8/62+	3¹	32	●	107	Girls! Girls! Girls!		RCA Victor 2621
4/20/63	4	26		108	It Happened At The World's Fair		RCA Victor 2697
12/21/63+	3³	24		109	Fun In Acapulco		RCA Victor 2756
4/11/64	6	30		110	Kissin' Cousins		RCA Victor 2894
11/14/64+	❶¹	27	●	111	Roustabout		RCA Victor 2999
4/17/65	8	31	●	112	Girl Happy		RCA Victor 3338
11/13/65+	8	23		113	Harum Scarum		RCA Victor 3468
4/23/66	20	19	▲	114	Frankie And Johnny		RCA Victor 3553
7/16/66	15	19		115	Paradise, Hawaiian Style		RCA Victor 3643
10/29/66	18	32		116	Spinout		RCA Victor 3702
6/24/67	47	20		117	Double Trouble		RCA Victor 3787
12/2/67+	40	14		118	Clambake		RCA Victor 3893
7/6/68	82	13		119	Speedway		RCA Victor 3989
4/25/81	115	10	●	120	This Is Elvis		RCA Victor 4031 [2]
					selections from the movie documentary This Is Elvis		
					RCA CAMDEN - BUDGET ALBUMS:		
4/19/69	96	16	▲	121	Elvis Sings Flaming Star		RCA Camden 2304
					only "Flaming Star" is from the movie		
5/9/70	105	11	▲	122	Let's Be Friends		RCA Camden 2408
11/21/70	65	18	▲	123	Almost In Love		RCA Camden 2440
12/5/70	2³ˣ	7		124	Elvis' Christmas Album		RCA Camden 2428
					Christmas charts: 2/'70, 9/'72, 30/'99		
3/20/71	69	12	▲³	125	You'll Never Walk Alone		RCA Camden 2472
7/24/71	70	11	●	126	C'mon Everybody		RCA Camden 2518
11/27/71	104	8	●	127	I Got Lucky		RCA Camden 2533
7/8/72	87	15		128	Elvis Sings Hits From His Movies, Volume 1		RCA Camden 2567
11/11/72+	22	25	▲²	129	Burning Love And Hits From His Movies, Volume 2		RCA Camden 2595
1/27/73	46	18	▲	130	Separate Ways		RCA Camden 2611

PRESLEY, Lisa Marie

Born on 2/1/1968 in Memphis, Tennessee. Pop-dance singer. Daughter of Priscilla and **Elvis Presley**. Married to **Michael Jackson** from 1994-96. Married to actor Nicolas Cage from 2002-04.

DEBUT	PEAK	WKS		#	Album Title	Catalog	Label & Number
4/26/03	5	18		1	To Whom It May Concern		Capitol 96668
4/23/05	9	7		2	Now What		Capitol 93813

PRESS PLAY

Contemporary Christian band from Los Angeles, California: Paige Adkins (vocals), Dave Hanley (guitar), Tyler Logan (keyboards), Anthony Rick (bass) and Tate Huff (drums). Adkins is the daughter of comedian Sinbad.

DEBUT	PEAK	WKS		#	Album Title	Catalog	Label & Number
6/6/09	45	2		1	Life Is Beautiful		UMCG 001

PRESSURE

Jazz-styled R&B band from Los Angeles, California: Melvin Robinson (vocals), Pat Kelly (guitar), **Ronnie Laws** (sax), Barnaby Finch (keyboards), Bobby Vega (bass) and Art Rodriguez (drums).

DEBUT	PEAK	WKS		#	Album Title	Catalog	Label & Number
2/16/80	207	2		1	Pressure		L.A. 3195

PRESSURE 4-5

Rock band from Santa Barbara, California: Adam Rich (vocals), brothers Joe Schmidt (guitar) and Tom Schmidt (drums), Mark Barry (guitar) and Lyle McKeany (bass).

DEBUT	PEAK	WKS		#	Album Title	Catalog	Label & Number
10/20/01	177	1		1	Burning The Process		DreamWorks 450325

Billboard DEBUT	PEAK	WKS	R I A A	ARTIST Album Title	Catalog	Label & Number

PRESTON, Billy
Born on 9/2/1946 in Houston, Texas; raised in Los Angeles, California. Died of kidney failure on 6/6/2006 (age 59). R&B singer/songwriter/keyboardist. Prolific session musician. Regular on *Shindig* TV show. Appeared in the 1978 movie *Sgt. Pepper's Lonely Hearts Club Band*.

6/12/65	143	3		1 The Most Exciting Organ Ever [I]		Vee-Jay 1123
7/9/66	118	6		2 Wildest Organ In Town! [I]		Vee-Jay 2532
6/10/72	127	12		3 That's The Way God Planned It [E]		Apple 3359
				first released in 1969; produced by George Harrison		
1/22/72	32	38		4 I Wrote A Simple Song		A&M 3507
12/23/72+	32	35		5 Music Is My Life		A&M 3516
10/27/73	52	18		6 Everybody Likes Some Kind Of Music		A&M 3526
9/21/74	17	14		7 The Kids & Me		A&M 3645
7/19/75	43	14		8 It's My Pleasure		A&M 4532
5/5/79	208	2		9 Fast Break [S]		Motown 915
				BILLY PRESTON & SYREETA		
3/8/80	49	18		10 Late At Night		Motown 925
8/8/81	127	9		11 Billy Preston & Syreeta		Motown 958

PRESTON, Johnny
Born John Preston Courville on 8/18/1939 in Port Arthur, Texas. Rock and roll singer.

~ ~ ~ ~ ~ ~ ~ ~ ~ **NON-CHARTED ALBUMS** ~ ~ ~ ~ ~ ~ ~ ~ ~ ~ ~
1960 Running Bear   1960 Come Rock With Me

PRETENDERS, The   All-Time: #351
New-wave rock band formed in England: Chrissie Hynde (vocals, guitar; born on 9/7/1951 in Akron, Ohio), James Honeyman-Scott (guitar), Pete Farndon (bass) and Martin Chambers (drums). Honeyman-Scott died of a drug overdose on 6/16/1982 (age 25); replaced by Robbie McIntosh (of Night). Farndon died of a drug overdose on 4/14/1983 (age 30); replaced by Malcolm Foster. Hynde was married to Jim Kerr of Simple Minds from 1984-90. Lineup in 1994: Hynde, Chambers, Adam Seymour (guitar) and Andy Hobson (bass). Tom Kelly replaced Hobson in 1998.
AWARD: R&R Hall of Fame: 2005

1/26/80	9	78	▲	1 Pretenders Cat:#10/8		Sire 6083
				RS500 #155		
4/18/81	27	29		2 Extended Play Cat:#4/137 [EP]		Sire 3563
8/29/81	10	19	●	3 Pretenders II		Sire 3572
2/4/84	5	42	▲	4 Learning To Crawl		Sire 23980
11/15/86	25	29	●	5 Get Close		Sire 25488
12/5/87	69	15	●	6 The Singles [G]		Sire 25664
6/9/90	48	17		7 Packed!		Sire 26219
5/28/94	41	22	●	8 Last Of The Independents		Warner 45572
11/11/95	100	5		9 The Isle Of View [L]		Warner 46085
7/10/99	158	2		10 Viva El Amor!		Warner 47342
11/30/02	179	1		11 Loose Screw		Artemis 751153
10/25/08	32	4		12 Break Up The Concrete		Shangri-La 101009

PRETTY BOY FLOYD
Male hard-rock band formed in Los Angeles, California: Steve Summers (vocals), Kristy Majors (guitar), Vinnie Chas (bass) and Kari Kane (drums).

3/24/90	130	9		1 Leather Boyz With Electric Toyz		MCA 6341

PRETTY MAIDS
Hard-rock band formed in Denmark: Ronnie Atkins (vocals), Ken Hammer (guitar), Alan Owen (keyboards), Allan Delong (bass) and Phil Moorhead (drums).

6/20/87	165	8		1 Future World		Epic 40713

PRETTYMAN, Tristan
Born on 5/23/1982 in Del Mar, California. Female singer/songwriter/guitarist.

5/3/08	27	3		1 Hello...X		Virgin 66637
8/16/08	115	1		2 Live Session [EP-L]		Virgin digital

PRETTY POISON
Dance band from Philadelphia, Pennsylvania: Jade Starling (vocals), Whey Cooler (keyboards), Louie Franco (guitar) and Bobby Corea (drums).

4/30/88	104	8		1 Catch Me I'm Falling		Virgin 90885

PRETTY RICKY
R&B-rap group from Miami, Florida: Corey Mathis, Diamond Smith, Spectacular Smith and Marcus Cooper.

6/11/05	16	35	●	1 Bluestars		Atlantic 83786
2/10/07	❶¹	19	●	2 Late Night Special		Bluestar 94603
12/5/09	97	1		3 Pretty Ricky		BlueStar 02

PRETTY THINGS
Rock band from England: Jack Green (vocals), Pete Tolson (guitar; T. Rex), Phil May (percussion), John Povey (keyboards), Gordon Edwards (bass) and Skip Alan (drums).

3/1/75	104	9		1 Silk Torpedo		Swan Song 8411
2/21/76	163	6		2 Savage Eye		Swan Song 8414

Billboard		R I A A	ARTIST		
DEBUT	**PEAK**	**WKS**	**Album Title**	**Catalog**	**Label & Number**

PREVIN, Andre
Born on 4/6/1929 in Berlin, Germany. Pianist/conductor/arranger/composer. Musical director for several MGM movies. In the 1970s, served as resident conductor of the **London Symphony Orchestra**. Married to **Dory Previn** from 1959-70. Married to actress Mia Farrow from 1970-79.

AWARD: Grammy: Lifetime Achievement 2010

6/29/59	16	21	1 Secret Songs For Young Lovers .... [I]	MGM 3716
7/4/60+	25	28	2 Like Love .... [I]	Columbia 1437
10/16/61	118	9	3 A Touch Of Elegance .... [I]	Columbia 8449
11/30/63	130	4	4 Andre Previn in Hollywood .... [I]	Columbia 8834
12/19/64	147	4	5 My Fair Lady .... [I]	Columbia 8995
12/2/67	9ˣ	6	6 A Christmas Treasure .... [X]	RCA Victor 3829
			JULIE ANDREWS WITH ANDRE PREVIN	
3/14/81	149	9	7 A Different Kind Of Blues .... [I]	Angel 37780
			ITZHAK PERLMAN & ANDRE PREVIN	

PREVIN, Dory
Born Dory Langan on 10/22/1925 in Rahway, New Jersey. Female folk singer. Married to **Andre Previn** from 1959-70.

4/10/71	218	3	1 Mythical Kings & Iguanas	United Artists 4110
1/8/72	202	5	2 Reflections In A Mud Puddle/Taps Tremors And Timestops	
			(One Last Dance For My Father)	United Artists 5536
7/21/73	220	1	3 Live At Carnegie Hall .... [L]	United Artists 108 [2]
			recorded on 4/18/73	
10/12/74	202	2	4 Dory Previn	Warner 2811

PRICE, Alan
Born on 4/19/1942 in Fatfield, Durham, England. Organist with **The Animals**; left in 1965; rejoined group in 1983.

| 8/11/73 | 117 | 14 | 1 O Lucky Man! .... [S] | Warner 2710 |
| 11/19/77 | 187 | 3 | 2 Alan Price .... | Jet 809 |

PRICE, Kelly
Born on 4/4/1973 in Queens, New York. Female R&B singer.

8/29/98	15	35	▲	1 Soul Of A Woman	Island 524516
7/15/00	5	30	▲	2 Mirror Mirror	Def Soul 542472
12/15/01	176	2		3 One Family - A Christmas Album .... [X]	Def Soul 586222
5/17/03	10	12		4 Priceless	Def Soul 586777
11/11/06	54	4		5 This Is Who I Am	Gospo Centric 88167

PRICE, Leontyne
Born on 2/10/1927 in Laurel, Mississippi. Legendary opera soprano.

12/18/61+	55	5	1 A Christmas Offering .... [X]	London 25280
			Christmas chart: 23/'63	
12/29/62	128	1	2 A Christmas Offering .... [X-R]	London 25280
4/27/63	29	12	3 Giacomo Puccini: Madama Butterfly .... [F]	RCA Victor 6160 [3]
9/7/63	79	6	4 Giacomo Puccini: Tosca .... [F]	RCA Victor 7022 [2]
10/5/63	66	16	5 Great Scenes From Gershwin's "Porgy And Bess"	RCA Victor 2679
			Grammy: Classical Vocal Album	
10/31/64	147	3	6 Georges Bizet: Carmen .... [F]	RCA Victor 6164 [3]

PRICE, Lloyd
Born on 3/9/1933 in Kenner, Louisiana. R&B singer/pianist/composer.

AWARD: R&R Hall of Fame: 1998

~ ~ ~ ~ ~ ~ ~ ~ ~ ~ **NON-CHARTED ALBUMS** ~ ~ ~ ~ ~ ~ ~ ~ ~ ~ ~
1959 **The Exciting Lloyd Price** [*"Stagger Lee"*]   1960 **Mr. Personality Sings The Blues**
1959 **Mr. Personality**   1960 **Mr. Personality's 15 Hits**

PRICE, Ray
Born on 1/12/1926 in Perryville, Texas; raised in Dallas, Texas. Country singer/songwriter/guitarist. Known as "The Cherokee Cowboy."

AWARDS: C&W Hall of Fame: 1996 ★ OPRY: 1952

3/4/67	129	12		1 Touch My Heart	Columbia 2606 / 9406
6/10/67	106	17		2 Danny Boy	Columbia 2677 / 9477
9/12/70+	28	59	▲	3 For The Good Times	Columbia 30106
6/12/71	49	24		4 I Won't Mention It Again	Columbia 30510
				CMA: Album of the Year	
12/4/71	146	5		5 Welcome To My World .... [K]	Columbia 30878 [2]
7/29/72	145	12		6 The Lonesomest Lonesome	Columbia 31546
9/9/72	165	10	●	7 Ray Price's All-Time Greatest Hits .... [G]	Columbia 31364 [2]
4/21/73	161	7		8 She's Got To Be A Saint	Columbia 32033
6/14/80	70	25	●	9 San Antonio Rose	Columbia 36476
				WILLIE NELSON & RAY PRICE	
4/7/07	64	4		10 Last Of The Breed	Lost Highway 008530 [2]
				WILLIE NELSON / MERLE HAGGARD / RAY PRICE	

PRICE, Sean
Born in Brooklyn, New York. Male rapper. One-half of **Heltah Skeltah** duo.

| 2/17/07 | 196 | 1 | 1 Jesus Price Supastar .... | Duck Down 2045 |

PRIDE, Charley — All-Time: #321

Born on 3/18/1938 in Sledge, Mississippi. The first commercially successful black country singer. Played professional baseball in the Negro leagues.

AWARDS: C&W Hall of Fame: 2000 ★ CMA: Male Vocalist 1971 & 1972 / Entertainer 1971 ★ OPRY: 1993

DEBUT	PEAK	WKS		#	Album Title	Catalog	Label & Number
3/30/68	199	2	●	1	The Country Way		RCA Victor 3895
2/15/69	62	43	●	2	Charley Pride: In Person .... [L]		RCA Victor 4094
					recorded at Panther Hall in Fort Worth, Texas		
6/28/69	44	39	●	3	The Sensational Charley Pride		RCA Victor 4153
2/28/70	22	27	●	4	Just Plain Charley		RCA Victor 4290
7/18/70	30	38	●	5	Charley Pride's 10th Album.......................		RCA Victor 4367
12/12/70+	5ˣ	9		6	Christmas In My Home Town [X]		RCA Victor 4406
					Christmas charts: 8/'70, 5/'71, 8/'72, 15/'73		
2/6/71	42	26	●	7	From Me To You		RCA Victor 4468
4/17/71	76	15	●	8	Did You Think To Pray		RCA Victor 4513
					Grammy: Sacred Album		
7/24/71	50	19		9	I'm Just Me		RCA Victor 4560
12/4/71+	38	26	●	10	Charley Pride Sings Heart Songs		RCA Victor 4617
					Grammy: Male Country Vocal		
8/19/72	115	15		11	A Sunshiny Day With Charley Pride		RCA Victor 4742
2/17/73	149	8		12	Songs Of Love By Charley Pride		RCA Victor 4837
7/28/73	166	6		13	Sweet Country		RCA Victor 0217
4/8/78	207	1		14	Someone Loves You Honey		RCA Victor 2478
4/19/80	201	3		15	There's A Little Bit Of Hank In Me		RCA Victor 3548
					GREATEST HITS & COMPILATIONS:		
11/1/69	24	65	●	16	The Best Of Charley Pride		RCA Victor 4223
3/18/72	50	15	●	17	The Best Of Charley Pride, Volume 2 ...		RCA Victor 4682
1/6/73	189	8		18	The Incomparable Charley Pride		RCA Camden 2584
1/22/77	188	2		19	The Best Of Charley Pride, Vol. III		RCA Victor 2023
11/21/81	185	7		20	Greatest Hits		RCA Victor 4151

PRIDE & GLORY

Rock trio formed in New York: Zakk Wylde (vocals, guitar), James LoMenzo (bass) and Brian Tichy (drums). Wylde formerly with **Ozzy Osbourne**'s band, later formed **Black Label Society**.

DEBUT	PEAK	WKS		#	Album Title	Catalog	Label & Number
6/25/94	173	1		1	Pride & Glory		Geffen 24703

PRIEST, Maxi

Born Max Elliott on 6/10/1960 in London, England (of Jamaican parents). Dancehall reggae singer.

DEBUT	PEAK	WKS		#	Album Title	Catalog	Label & Number
12/3/88+	108	17		1	Maxi Priest		Virgin 90957
8/4/90	47	37	●	2	Bonafide		Charisma 91384
12/7/91	189	2		3	Best Of Me [G]		Charisma 91804
12/12/92	191	1		4	Fe Real		Charisma 86500
7/27/96	108	10		5	Man With The Fun		Virgin 41612

PRIESTS, The

Classical vocal trio from Northern Ireland: brothers Eugene and Martin O'Hagen, with David Delargy. All three are actual Catholic priests.

DEBUT	PEAK	WKS		#	Album Title	Catalog	Label & Number
12/20/08	66	9		1	The Priests		RCA Victor 33969

PRIMA, Louis, & Keely Smith — 1950s: #18

Prima was born on 12/7/1911 in New Orleans, Louisiana. Died on 8/24/1978 (age 66). Jazz trumpeter/singer/bandleader. Smith was born on 3/9/1932 in Norfolk, Virginia. Female singer. They were married from 1952-61.

DEBUT	PEAK	WKS		#	Album Title	Catalog	Label & Number
6/23/58	12	4		1	Las Vegas Prima Style [L]		Capitol 1010
					recorded at the Sahara Hotel		
10/20/58	14	8		2	Politely!		Capitol 1073
5/25/59	23	9		3	Swingin' Pretty		Capitol 1145
					KEELY SMITH (above 2)		
5/25/59	37	2		4	Hey Boy! Hey Girl! [S]		Capitol 1160
11/2/59	43	4		5	Louis And Keely!		Dot 3210
1/4/60	40	1		6	Be My Love		Dot 3241
					KEELY SMITH		
1/16/61	9	11		7	Wonderland By Night [I]		Dot 25352
					LOUIS PRIMA		

~ ~ ~ ~ ~ ~ ~ ~ ~ **NON-CHARTED ALBUM** ~ ~ ~ ~ ~ ~ ~ ~ ~ ~

1956 The Wildest! *[Louis Prima]*
Grammy: Hall of Fame

PRIMA J

Female hip-hop duo from Rosemead, California: cousins Janelle and Jessica Martinez.

DEBUT	PEAK	WKS		#	Album Title	Catalog	Label & Number
7/5/08	172	1		1	Prima J		BJH 011224

PRIME MINISTER PETE NICE & DADDY RICH

Rap duo from Queens, New York: "Pete Nice" Nash and "Daddy Rich" Lawson. Former members of **3rd Bass**.

DEBUT	PEAK	WKS		#	Album Title	Catalog	Label & Number
7/31/93	171	1		1	Dust To Dust		Def Jam 53454

DEBUT	PEAK	WKS	R I A A	ARTIST / Album Title	Catalog	Label & Number

PRIMER 55
Rock band from Memphis, Tennessee: Jason Luttrell (vocals), Bobby Burns (guitar), Kobie Jackson (bass) and Preston Nash (drums).

| 9/1/01 | 102 | 2 | | 1 (The) New Release .... | | Island 586183 |

PRIME SUSPECTS
Male rap trio from New Orleans, Louisiana: E, Gangsta T and Skinow.

| 10/24/98 | 36 | 4 | | 1 Guilty Til Proven Innocent .... | | No Limit 50728 |

PRIMITIVE RADIO GODS
Born Christopher O'Connor on 5/7/1965 in Santa Barbara, California. Rock singer/songwriter/guitarist. His touring band includes Luke McAuliffe (guitar), Jeff Sparks (bass) and Tim Lauteiro (drums).

| 7/6/96 | 36 | 17 | ● | 1 Rocket .... | | Ergo 67600 |

PRIMITIVES, The
Pop-rock band from Coventry, West Midlands, England: Tracy Tracey (vocals), Paul Court (guitar), Steve Dullaghan (bass) and Tig Williams (drums).

| 9/10/88 | 106 | 9 | | 1 Lovely .... | | RCA 8443 |
| 12/23/89+ | 113 | 15 | | 2 Pure .... | | RCA 9934 |

PRIMUS
Thrash-jazz-rock trio from San Francisco, California: **Les Claypool** (vocals, bass), Larry LaLonde (guitar) and Tim Alexander (drums).

6/1/91	116	36	▲	1 Sailing The Seas Of Cheese		Interscope 91659
5/8/93	7	34	▲	2 Pork Soda		Interscope 92257
6/24/95	8	19	●	3 Tales From The Punchbowl		Interscope 92553
7/26/97	21	8		4 Brown Album		Interscope 90126
8/29/98	106	2		5 Rhinoplasty		Interscope 90214
11/6/99	44	4		6 Antipop		Interscope 90414
10/25/03	44	2		7 Animals Should Not Try To Act Like People		Interscope 001323
11/4/06	105	1		8 They Can't All Be Zingers .... [K]		Chronicle 005984

PRINCE   1980s: #2 / 1990s: #3 / All-Time: #19
Born Prince Roger Nelson on 6/7/1958 in Minneapolis, Minnesota. R&B singer/songwriter/multi-instrumentalist. Starred in the movies *Purple Rain, Under The Cherry Moon, Sign 'O' The Times* and *Graffiti Bridge.* Founded the Paisley Park record label. The Revolution: Wendy Melvoin (guitar), Lisa Coleman and Matt Fink (keyboards), Eric Leeds (sax), Brownmark (bass) and Bobby Z (drums). Melvoin and Coleman formed duo **Wendy & Lisa** in 1987. The New Power Generation: Rosie Gaines (vocals), Levi Seacer (guitar), Tommy Barbarella (keyboards), Sonny T (bass) and Michael Bland (drums). Also formed jazz-fusion group **Madhouse**. Prince changed his name on 6/7/1993 to a combination male/female "love symbol." By 1994 referred to as "The Artist Formerly Known As Prince" or "The Artist." Announced in May 2000 that he would once again be known as "Prince."
AWARD: R&R Hall of Fame: 2004

10/28/78	163	5		1 For You		Warner 3150
11/17/79+	22	28	▲	2 Prince		Warner 3366
11/8/80	45	52	●	3 Dirty Mind		Warner 3478
				RS500 #204		
11/7/81	21	64	▲	4 Controversy		Warner 3601
11/20/82+	9	153	▲⁴	5 1999	Cat:#6/2	Warner 23720 [2]
				Grammy: Hall of Fame ★ RS500 #163		
2/20/99	150	1		6 1999: The New Master .... [EP-R]		NPG 1999
				7 mixes of "1999"		
5/11/85	❶³	40	▲²	7 Around The World In A Day		Paisley Park 25286
4/18/87	6	54	▲	8 Sign "O" The Times		Paisley Park 25577 [2]
				RS500 #93		
5/28/88	11	21	●	9 Lovesexy		Paisley Park 25720
10/19/91	3¹	45	▲²	10 Diamonds And Pearls		Paisley Park 25379
10/31/92	5	34	▲	11 The Love Symbol Album		Paisley Park 45037
				PRINCE & THE NEW POWER GENERATION (above 2)		
6/4/94	92	12		12 The Beautiful Experience .... [EP]		NPG 71003
				7 mixes of "The Most Beautiful Girl In The World"		
9/3/94	15	10	●	13 Come		Warner 45700
10/14/95	6	8	●	14 The Gold Experience		Warner 45999
7/27/96	26	4		15 Chaos And Disorder		Warner 46317
12/7/96	11	21	▲²	16 Emancipation		NPG 54982 [3]
7/18/98	22	8		17 Newpower Soul		NPG 9872
				PRINCE & THE NEW POWER GENERATION		
11/27/99	18	15	●	18 Rave Un2 The Joy Fantastic		NPG 14624
12/8/01	109	2		19 The Rainbow Children		NPG 70004
5/8/04	3⁴	26	▲²	20 Musicology		NPG 92560
4/8/06	❶¹	16	●	21 3121		Universal 006296
8/11/07	3¹	10		22 Planet Earth		NPG 12970
4/18/09	2¹	16		23 Lotus Flow3r / MPLsoUND / Elix3r		NPG 09549 [3]
				PRINCE / BRIA VALENTE		
				first two are Prince solo; *Elix3r* is a solo album by female singer Valentine		

PRINCE — cont'd

EARLY ALBUMS:

12/10/94	47	11		24 The Black Album		Warner 45793
				recorded in 1987		
9/11/99	85	5		25 The Vault...Old Friends 4 Sale..		Warner 47522
				songs recorded from 1985-94		

GREATEST HITS & COMPILATIONS:

10/2/93	19	12	▲	26 The Hits/The B-Sides		Paisley Park 45440 [3]
				of the 56 tracks, 6 are previously unreleased, 18 are rare B-sides		
10/2/93	46	20	▲	27 The Hits 1	Cat:#3/2	Paisley Park 45431
				disc one of The Hits/The B-Sides		
10/2/93	54	19	▲	28 The Hits 2		Paisley Park 45435
				disc two of The Hits/The B-Sides		
3/14/98	62	5		29 Crystal Ball		NPG 9871 [4]
8/18/01	66	25	▲	30 The Very Best Of Prince	Cat:❶7/72	Warner 74272
9/9/06	61	5		31 Ultimate		Warner 73381 [2]

SOUNDTRACKS:

7/14/84	❶24	72	▲13	32 Purple Rain	Cat:#13/20	Warner 25110
				PRINCE & THE REVOLUTION		
				Grammy: Soundtrack Album / Group Rock Vocal ★ RS500 #72		
4/19/86	3³	28	▲	33 Parade		Paisley Park 25395
				PRINCE & THE REVOLUTION (above 2)		
				music from the movie Under The Cherry Moon		
7/8/89	❶6	34	▲2	34 Batman		Warner 25936
9/8/90	6	24	●	35 Graffiti Bridge		Paisley Park 27493
4/6/96	75	4		36 Girl 6		Warner 46239
				PRINCE & THE NEW POWER GENERATION		

PRINCE PAUL
Born Paul Huston on 4/2/1967 in Long Island, New York. Male rapper. Member of **Gravediggaz**.

3/13/99	138	2		1 A Prince Among Thieves		Tommy Boy 1210
5/24/03	200	1		2 Politics Of The Business		Razor & Tie 82888

PRINE, John
Born on 10/10/1946 in Maywood, Illinois. Folk-rock singer/songwriter.

2/26/72	154	3		1 John Prine...		Atlantic 8296
				RS500 #458		
10/28/72	148	10		2 Diamonds In The Rough		Atlantic 7240
11/24/73	135	11		3 Sweet Revenge		Atlantic 7274
4/26/75	66	10		4 Common Sense		Atlantic 18127
1/15/77	196	2	●	5 Prime Prine-The Best Of John Prine	[G]	Atlantic 18202
7/8/78	116	13		6 Bruised Orange		Asylum 139
9/8/79	152	7		7 Pink Cadillac		Asylum 222
8/30/80	144	7		8 Storm Windows		Asylum 286
4/22/95	159	9		9 Lost Dogs And Mixed Blessings		Oh Boy 013
10/2/99	197	1		10 In Spite Of Ourselves		Oh Boy 019
5/14/05	55	9		11 Fair & Square		Oh Boy 034
				Grammy: Contemporary Folk Album		

PRISM
Rock band formed in Vancouver, British Columbia, Canada: Ron Tabak (vocals), Lindsay Mitchell (guitar), Tom Lavin (guitar), John Hall (keyboards), Ab Bryant (bass; **Chilliwack**, **Headpins**), Rodney Higgs (drums). Bryant and Higgs left after first album; replaced by Allen Harlow and Rocket Norton. Tabak left after second album, replaced by Henry Small. Tabak died in a bicycle accident on 12/6/1984.

10/1/77	137	10		1 Prism		Ariola 50020
7/29/78	158	8		2 See Forever Eyes		Ariola 50034
9/22/79	202	6		3 Armageddon		Ariola America 50063
2/6/82	53	20		4 Small Change		Capitol 12184
8/6/83	202	3		5 Beat Street		Capitol 12266

PRITCHARD, Peter
Born in Wellington, New Zealand. New Age pianist.

9/2/95	149	1		1 Studies For The New Zealand Harmonic Piano	[I]	White Cloud 11001

PRIZE FIGHTER INFERNO, The
Born Claudio Sanchez on 3/12/1978 in Suffern, New York. Hard-rock singer/songwriter/guitarist. Leader of **Coheed And Cambria**.

11/18/06	119	1		1 My Brother's Blood Machine..		Equal Vision 131

PROBOT
Hard-rock project assembled by Dave Grohl (of **Nirvana** and **Foo Fighters**). Each cut features a different lead singer: Cronos (Venom), Max Cavalara (**Sepultura**), Lemmy (**Motorhead**), Mike Dean (**Corrosion Of Conformity**), Kurt Brecht (**D.R.I.**), Lee Dorrian (Napalm Death), Wino (Obsessed), Tom G. Warrior (Celtic Frost), Snake (**Voivod**), Eric Wagner (Trouble) and **King Diamond**.

2/28/04	68	6		1 Probot..		Roswell 30

			R I A A	**ARTIST**		
DEBUT	**PEAK**	**WKS**		**Album Title**	**Catalog**	**Label & Number**

PROCLAIMERS, The
Pop duo from Edinburgh, Scotland: identical twin brothers Craig Reid and Charlie Reid (born on 3/5/1962).

4/8/89+	31	37	●	1 Sunshine On Leith		Chrysalis 41668

PROCOL HARUM **All-Time: #466**
Rock band formed in England: Gary Brooker (vocals, piano), Keith Reid (lyrics), Ray Royer (guitar), Matthew Fisher (organ), Dave Knights (bass) and Bobby Harrison (drums). Royer and Harrison left after first album; replaced by **Robin Trower** and Barrie Wilson. Knights and Fisher left in early 1969; bassist Chris Copping added. Trower left in mid-1971; replaced by Dave Ball; bassist Alan Cartright added while Copping switched to keyboards. Ball left in mid-1972; replaced by Mick Grabham. Cartright left in mid-1976; Copping moved to bass and keyboardist Pete Solley joined. Wilson died of pneumonia in October 1990 (age 43).

9/23/67	47	16		1 Procol Harum..		Deram 18008
12/23/72+	203	5		2 A Whiter Shade Of Pale .... [R]		A&M 4373
				reissue of #1 above		
10/12/68	24	20		3 Shine On Brightly		A&M 4151
5/10/69	32	20		4 A Salty Dog		A&M 4179
7/11/70	34	15		5 Home		A&M 4261
5/8/71	32	20		6 Broken Barricades		A&M 4294
5/13/72	5	28	●	7 Procol Harum Live In Concert with the Edmonton Symphony Orchestra [L]		A&M 4335
				recorded on 11/18/1971 at the Jubilee Auditorium		
10/20/73	131	10		8 The Best Of Procol Harum .... [G]		A&M 4401
3/31/73	21	22		9 Grand Hotel		Chrysalis 1037
4/20/74	86	9		10 Exotic Birds And Fruit		Chrysalis 1058
8/23/75	52	8		11 Procol's Ninth		Chrysalis 1080
3/26/77	147	6		12 Something Magic		Chrysalis 1130

PROCTOR & BERGMAN — see FIRESIGN THEATRE

PROCTOR, Rachel
Born in 1973 in Charleston, West Virginia. Country singer/songwriter.

8/28/04	66	3		1 Where I Belong		BNA 51217

PRODIGY, The
Techno-rave-dance band from England: Maxim Reality and Keith Flint (vocals), Liam Howlett (instruments) and Leeroy Thornhill (dancer). Howlett married Natalie Appleton (of **All Saints**) on 6/6/2002. Also see **Various Artists Compilations:** *Prodigy Present The Dirtchamber Sessions Volume One*.

2/22/97	198	2		1 Music For The Jilted Generation... Cat:#31/5 [I]		Mute 9003
7/19/97	❶¹	57	▲²	2 The Fat Of The Land		Maverick 46606
10/2/04	62	2		3 Always Outnumbered, Never Outgunned		Maverick 47990
3/14/09	58	4		4 Invaders Must Die		Cooking Vinyl 90146

PRODIGY OF MOBB DEEP
Born Albert Johnson on 11/2/1974 in Queens, New York. Male rapper. Member of **Mobb Deep**.

12/2/00	18	15	●	1 H-N-I-C		Loud 1873
4/14/07	32	3		2 Return Of The Mac		Infamous 5534
5/10/08	36	2		3 H.N.I.C. Pt. 2		AAO 40701
				PRODIGY		

PRODUCERS, The
Rock band from Atlanta, Georgia: Van Temple (vocals, guitar), Wayne Famous (keyboards), Kyle Henderson (bass) and Bryan Holmes (drums).

6/6/81	163	2		1 The Producers		Portrait 37097
8/7/82	201	7		2 You Make The Heat		Portrait 38060

PRODUCT, The
Male rap trio from Houston, Texas: Brad **"Scarface"** Jordan (of **The Geto Boys**), Willie Hen and Young Malice.

3/11/06	78	3		1 One Hunid		Underground Rail. 5828

PROFESSOR GRIFF
Born Richard Griffin on 8/1/1960 in Long Island, New York. Male rapper. Former member of **Public Enemy**.

4/14/90	127	8		1 Pawns In The Game		Skyywalker 111

PROFESSOR LONGHAIR
Born Henry Byrd on 12/19/1918 in Bogalusa, Louisiana. Died on 1/30/1980 (age 61). Highly influential blues/R&B piano player.
   AWARD: R&R Hall of Fame: 1992 (Early Influence)

~ ~ ~ ~ ~ ~ ~ ~ ~ ~   **NON-CHARTED ALBUM**   ~ ~ ~ ~ ~ ~ ~ ~ ~ ~
   1972 **New Orleans Piano**
      RS500 #220

PROFYLE
Male R&B vocal group from Shreveport, Louisiana: brothers Hershey and Face, with cousins Baby Boy and L'Jai.

11/4/00	50	10		1 Nothin' But Drama..		Motown 159744

Billboard			ARTIST		
DEBUT	**PEAK**	**WKS**	**Album Title**	**Catalog**	**Label & Number**

PROJECT 86
Christian rock band from Anaheim, California: Andrew Schwab (vocals), Randy Torres (guitar), Steven Dail (bass) and Alex Albert (drums).

10/12/02	146	1	1 Truthless Heros		Atlantic 83568
10/15/05	131	1	2 ...And The Rest Will Follow		Tooth & Nail 77424
7/7/07	124	1	3 Rival Factions..		Tooth & Nail 87131
8/1/09	137	1	4 Picket Fence Cartel		Tooth & Nail 64928

PROJECT PAT
Born Patrick Houston on 2/8/1972 in Memphis, Tennessee. Male rapper. Member of **Hypnotize Camp Posse**. Brother of **Three 6 Mafia** member Juicy J.

10/2/99	52	7	1 Ghetty Green		Hypnotize Minds 1743
8/12/00	176	1	2 Murderers & Robbers Underground....................................		Project 9996
3/17/01	4	26	3 Mista Don't Play - Everythangs Workin		Hypnotize Minds 1950
8/24/02	12	11	4 Layin' Da Smack Down		Loud 86632
12/23/06	64	8	5 Crook By Da Book: The Fed Story		Hypnotize Minds 90910
11/17/07	47	2	6 Walkin' Bank Roll		Hypnotize Minds 5023
3/14/09	70	3	7 Real Recognize Real		Hypnotize Minds 517396

PRONG
Rock trio from New York: Tommy Victor (guitar, vocals), Troy Gregory (bass, vocals) and Ted Parsons (drums). Paul Raven replaced Gregory in 1995. Raven died of a heart attack on 10/20/2007 (age 46).

2/12/94	126	2	1 Cleansing		Epic 53019
6/1/96	107	4	2 Rude Awakening		Epic 66945

PROOF
Born DeShaun Holton on 10/2/1973 in Detroit, Michigan. Shot to death on 4/11/2006 (age 32). Male rapper. Member of **D12**.

8/27/05	65	2	1 Searching For Jerry Garcia		Iron Fist 60297

PROPAGANDHI
Punk-rock band from Portage La Prairie, Manitoba, Canada: Chris Hannah (vocals, guitar), David Guillas (guitar), Todd Kowalski (bass) and Jord Samolesky (drums).

3/28/09	162	1	1 Supporting Caste		Smallman 044

PROPELLERHEADS
Electronic production duo from Bath, England: Alex Gifford and Will White.

4/11/98	100	10	1 Decksandrumsandrockandroll		DreamWorks 50031

PROPHET
Hard-rock band from New York: Russell Arcara (vocals), Ken Dubman (guitar), Joe Zujkowski (keyboards), Scott Metaxas (bass) and Michael Sterlacci (drums).

3/12/88	137	7	1 Cycle Of The Moon...		Megaforce 81822

PROPHET JONES
Hip-hop group from Washington DC: Patrick "P." Rowe, Jerome "Goldee" Lattisaw (brother of **Stacy Lattisaw**), Kevin "K.D." Jackson and Erik "Hollywood" White.

10/6/01	86	9	1 Prophet Jones		University 014551

PROPHET POSSE
Rap group formed in Memphis, Tennessee: **Indo G**, **Gangsta Boo**, **DJ Paul**, **Juicy J**, **Crunchy Black**, M-Child, Scarecrow, The Kaze and Droopy Drew Dog. Gangsta Boo, DJ Paul, Juicy J and Crunchy Black were all members of **Three 6 Mafia**.

3/7/98	168	2	1 Body Parts		Prophet 4406

PROTEST THE HERO
Hard-rock band from Whitby, Ontario, Canada: Rody Walker (vocals), Luke Hoskin (guitar), Tim Millar (guitar), Arif Mirabdolbaghi (bass) and Moe Carlson (drums).

2/16/08	95	1	1 Fortress..		Vagrant 483

PROVINE, Dorothy
Born on 1/20/1935 in Deadwood, South Dakota. Died of emphysema on 4/25/2010 (age 75). Singer/actress. Played "Pinky Pinkham" in the TV series *The Roaring 20's* (1960-62).

5/15/61	34	66	1 The Roaring 20's .... [TV]		Warner 1394

PRU
Born Prudence Renfro on 7/14/1970 in Houston, Texas. Female R&B singer/songwriter.

2/3/01	176	2	1 Pru		Capitol 23120

PRUETT, Jeanne
Born Norma Jean Bowman on 1/30/1937 in Pell City, Alabama. Country singer/songwriter.
AWARD: OPRY: 1973

7/7/73	122	9	1 Satin Sheets..		MCA 338

PRUITT, Jordan
Born on 5/19/1991 in Loganville, Georgia. Teen female singer.

2/24/07	64	3	1 No Ordinary Girl		Hollywood 000260

PRYOR, Richard
Born on 12/1/1940 in Peoria, Illinois. Died of a heart attack on 12/10/2005 (age 65). Black stand-up comedian/actor. Starred in several movies.

DEBUT	PEAK	WKS				Catalog	Label & Number
6/15/74	29	53	●	1	That Nigger's Crazy	[C]	Partee 2404
					Grammy: Comedy Album		
11/2/74	202	4		2	Craps (After Hours)	[C]	Laff 146
5/28/77	58	9		3	Are You Serious???	[C]	Laff 196
9/8/79	176	4		4	Outrageous	[C]	Laff 206
6/4/77	114	5		5	L.A. Jail	[C]	Tiger Lily 14023
8/23/75	12	25	▲	6	Is It Something I Said?	[C]	Reprise 2227
					Grammy: Comedy Album		
10/9/76	22	19	●	7	Bicentennial Nigger	[C]	Warner 2960
					Grammy: Comedy Album		
6/25/77	68	12	▲	8	Richard Pryor's Greatest Hits	[C-K]	Warner 3057
12/16/78+	32	20	●	9	Wanted	[C]	Warner 3364 [2]
4/17/82	21	17		10	Richard Pryor Live On The Sunset Strip	[C-L-S]	Warner 3660
					Grammy: Comedy Album		
					filmed at the Hollywood Palladium		
11/12/83	71	13		11	Richard Pryor: Here And Now	[C-L-S]	Warner 23981
					filmed at the Saenger Theater in New Orleans, Louisiana		

PRYSOCK, Arthur
Born on 1/2/1929 in Spartanburg, South Carolina. Died on 6/14/1997 (age 68). R&B singer.

DEBUT	PEAK	WKS					Label & Number
7/13/63	138	7		1	Coast To Coast		Old Town 2005
12/28/63+	97	7		2	A Portrait Of Arthur Prysock		Old Town 2006
8/15/64	131	8		3	Everlasting Songs For Everlasting Lovers		Old Town 2007
7/17/65	116	7		4	A Double Header With Arthur Prysock		Old Town 2009
3/26/66	107	13		5	Arthur Prysock/Count Basie		Verve 8646
1/29/77	153	4		6	All My Life		Old Town 12-004

PSC
Male rap group from Atlanta, Georgia: AK, Mac Boney, Big Kuntry and C-Rod. PSC: Pimp Squad Clique.

DEBUT	PEAK	WKS					Label & Number
10/8/05	10	6		1	25 To Life		Grand Hustle 83797

PSEUDO ECHO
Pop-rock-dance band formed in Melbourne, Australia: Brian Canham (vocals, guitar), James Leigh (keyboards), Pierre Gigliotti (bass) and Vince Leigh (drums).

DEBUT	PEAK	WKS					Label & Number
3/21/87	54	27		1	Love An Adventure		RCA Victor 5730

PSYCHEDELIC FURS
Techno-rock band formed in England: brothers Richard Butler (vocals) and Tim Butler (bass), John Ashton (guitar), and Vince Ely (drums). Philip Calvert replaced Ely in 1983. The Butler brothers formed **Love Spit Love** in 1994.

DEBUT	PEAK	WKS					Label & Number
11/22/80	140	7		1	The Psychedelic Furs .... **Cat:**#32/10		Columbia 36791
6/27/81	89	14		2	Talk Talk Talk .... **Cat:**#15/72		Columbia 37339
11/13/82+	61	32	●	3	Forever Now		Columbia 38261
5/26/84	43	27	●	4	Mirror Moves .... **Cat:**#29/8		Columbia 39278
3/7/87	29	27		5	Midnight To Midnight		Columbia 40466
9/24/88	102	8		6	All Of This And Nothing	[G]	Columbia 44377
11/25/89	138	4		7	Book Of Days		Columbia 45412

PSYCHO REALM, The
Hip-hop trio formed in Los Angeles, California: Louis "B Real" Freese (of **Cypress Hill**), with brothers Jack "Jackson" Gonzalez and Gustavo "Mr. Duke" Gonzalez.

DEBUT	PEAK	WKS					Label & Number
11/15/97	183	1		1	The Psycho Realm		Ruffhouse 68153

PSYCHOSTICK
Hard-rock trio from Tempe, Arizona: Rob Kersey (vocals, guitar), Josh Key (bass) and Alex Preiss (drums).

DEBUT	PEAK	WKS					Label & Number
10/20/07	18^X	2		1	The Flesh Eating Rollerskate Holiday Joyride	[X]	Rock Ridge 61125

PUBLIC ANNOUNCEMENT
R&B vocal group from Chicago, Illinois: Earl Robinson, Felony Davis, Euclid Gray and Glen Wright. Former backing group for R. Kelly.

DEBUT	PEAK	WKS					Label & Number
4/11/98	81	24		1	All Work, No Play		A&M 540882
2/24/01	89	7		2	Don't Hold Back		RCA 69310

PUBLIC ENEMY
Rap group from Long Island, New York: Carlton Ridenhour ("**Chuck D**"), William Drayton ("Flavor Flav"), Norman Rogers ("**Terminator X**") and William Griffin ("**Professor Griff**"). Griffin left in 1989.

DEBUT	PEAK	WKS					Label & Number
1/23/88	125	12	●	1	Yo! Bum Rush The Show		Def Jam 40658
					RS500 #497		
7/23/88	42	51	▲	2	It Takes A Nation Of Millions To Hold Us Back		Def Jam 44303
					RS500 #48		
4/28/90	10	27	▲	3	Fear Of A Black Planet .... **Cat:**#32/5		Def Jam 45413
					RS500 #300 ★ NRR		
10/19/91	4	37	▲	4	Apocalypse 91...The Enemy Strikes Black		Def Jam 47374
10/3/92	13	14	●	5	Greatest Misses	[K]	Def Jam 53014
9/10/94	14	8	●	6	Muse Sick-N-Hour Mess Age		Def Jam 523362

PUBLIC ENEMY — cont'd

5/16/98	26	10	7 He Got Game .... [S]	Def Jam 558130
8/10/02	110	4	8 Revolverlution	Slam Jamz 8388
8/20/05	69	1	9 Power To The People And The Beats: Public Enemy's Greatest Hits .... [G]	Def Jam 001923
3/25/06	180	1	10 Rebirth Of A Nation	Guerilla Funk 31021
			PUBLIC ENEMY Featuring Paris	

PUBLIC IMAGE LTD.

Punk-rock band formed by lead singer Johnny "Rotten" Lydon (of the **Sex Pistols**). Featured an ever-changing lineup with Lydon the only constant.

5/10/80	171	3	1 Second Edition	Island 3288 [2]
			U.S. retitled version of *Metal Box* (RS500 #469) from Britain (issued in a film canister containing 3 12" records played at 45 rpm)	
5/30/81	114	4	2 The Flowers Of Romance	Warner 3536
3/8/86	115	16	3 Album	Elektra 60438
10/24/87	169	10	4 Happy?	Virgin 90642
6/3/89	106	23	5 9	Virgin 91062

PUCKETT, Gary, And The Union Gap

Born on 10/17/1942 in Hibbing, Minnesota; raised in Yakima, Washington and Twin Falls, Idaho. Pop singer/guitarist. The Union Gap: Gary Withem (keyboards), Dwight Bement (sax), Kerry Chater (bass) and Paul Wheatbread (drums).

2/17/68	22	45	1 Woman, Woman	Columbia 9612
			THE UNION GAP Featuring Gary Puckett	
5/18/68	21	39	● 2 Young Girl	Columbia 9664
11/2/68+	20	20	3 Incredible	Columbia 9715
12/6/69+	50	14	4 The New Gary Puckett And The Union Gap Album	Columbia 9935
7/11/70	50	33	▲ 5 Gary Puckett & The Union Gap's Greatest Hits .... [G]	Columbia 1042
10/16/71	196	2	6 The Gary Puckett Album	Columbia 30862
			GARY PUCKETT	

PUDDLE OF MUDD

Hard-rock band formed in Kansas City, Missouri: Wes Scantlin (vocals, guitar), Paul Phillips (guitar), Doug Ardito (bass) and Greg Upchurch (drums).

9/15/01+	9	88	▲³ 1 Come Clean	Flawless 493074
12/13/03	20	23	● 2 Life On Display	Geffen 001080
10/27/07	27	40	3 Famous	Flawless 009377
12/26/09	95	4	4 Volume 4: Songs In The Key Of Love & Hate	Flawless 013661

PUENTE, Tito

Born Ernest Puente on 4/20/1923 in the Bronx, New York. Died of heart failure on 6/1/2000 (age 77). Top Latin jazz bandleader/instrumentalist.

AWARD: Grammy: Lifetime Achievement 2003

~ ~ ~ ~ ~ ~ ~ ~ ~ ~   **NON-CHARTED ALBUM**   ~ ~ ~ ~ ~ ~ ~ ~ ~ ~

1958 Dance Mania
NRR

PUFF DADDY / P. DIDDY / DIDDY

Born Sean Combs on 11/4/1969 in Harlem, New York. Songwriter/producer/rapper. Founded the Bad Boy record label. Changed performing name to P. Diddy in 2001; shortened to Diddy in 2005. Also see **Various Artists Compilations:** *P. Diddy & Bad Boy Records Present...We Invented The Remix*.

8/9/97	❶⁴	66	▲⁷ 1 No Way Out	Bad Boy 73012
			PUFF DADDY & THE FAMILY	
			Grammy: Rap Album	
9/11/99	2¹	27	▲ 2 Forever	Bad Boy 73033
			PUFF DADDY	
7/28/01	2¹	19	3 The Saga Continues...	Bad Boy 73045
			P. DIDDY & THE BAD BOY FAMILY	
11/4/06	❶¹	33	● 4 Press Play	Bad Boy 83864
			DIDDY	

PUGH, Earnest

Born in Memphis, Tennessee. Gospel singer/songwriter.

8/15/09	110	6	1 Live: Rain On Us .... [L]	EPM 3070

PULP

Pop-rock band from Sheffield, Yorkshire, England: **Jarvis Cocker** (vocals), Russell Senior (guitar), Mark Webber (guitar), Steve Mackey (bass) and Nick Banks (drums).

4/18/98	114	2	1 This Is Hardcore	Island 524492

PUNCH

Pop-rock band from Los Angeles, California: Charlie Merriam, Steve Adler, Dee and Kathy Ward. Merriam, Adler and Ward later formed Sonoma.

8/21/71	225	1	1 Punch	A&M 4307

PURE LOVE & PLEASURE

Pop-rock band from Los Angeles, California: David McAnally and Pegge Ann May (vocals), Bob Bohanna (guitar), John Allair (keyboards) and Dick Rogers (drums).

4/25/70	195	2	1 A Record Of Pure Love & Pleasure	Dunhill/ABC 50076

Billboard			R I A A	ARTIST		
DEBUT	PEAK	WKS		Album Title	Catalog	Label & Number

PURENRG
Teen Christian pop trio from Nashville, Tennessee: Caroline Williams, Laura Myers and Jordan Yates.

5/17/08	103	1		1 Here We Go Again		Fervent 887321
8/1/09	20	1		2 The Real Thing		Fervent 997795

PURE PRAIRIE LEAGUE
Country-rock band formed in Cincinnati, Ohio. Core members: Craig Fuller (vocals, guitar), George Ed Powell (guitar), Larry Goshorn (guitar), Michael Connor (keyboards), Mike Reilly (bass) and Billy Hinds (drums). Fuller left after first album, Powell and Reilly took over lead vocals. Vince Gill joined as lead singer in 1979. Group disbanded in 1983. Fuller joined **Little Feat** by 1988.

2/8/75	34	24	●	1 Bustin' Out .... Cat:#36/8		RCA Victor 4769
6/7/75	24	14		2 Two Lane Highway		RCA Victor 0933
2/7/76	33	16		3 If The Shoe Fits		RCA Victor 1247
11/20/76	99	14		4 Dance		RCA Victor 1924
9/10/77	68	11		5 Live!! Takin' The Stage .... [L]		RCA Victor 2404 [2]
5/13/78	79	11		6 Just Fly		RCA Victor 2590
6/23/79	124	6		7 Can't Hold Back		RCA Victor 3335
5/17/80	37	24		8 Firin' Up		Casablanca 7212
5/2/81	72	15		9 Something In The Night		Casablanca 7255

PURE SOUL
Female R&B vocal group from Washington DC: Shawn Allen, Heather Perkins, Keitha Shepherd and Kirstin Hall.

10/21/95	173	3		1 Pure Soul		Step Sun 92638

PURIFY, James & Bobby
R&B vocal duo from Florida: cousins James Purify and Robert Lee Dickey.

~ ~ ~ ~ ~ ~ ~ ~ ~ ~ *NON-CHARTED ALBUM* ~ ~ ~ ~ ~ ~ ~ ~ ~ ~
1966 **James & Bobby Purify** ["I'm Your Puppet"]

PURIM, Flora
Born on 3/6/1942 in Rio de Janeiro, Brazil. Female jazz singer. Married to **Airto**.

2/15/75	172	5		1 Stories To Tell		Milestone 9058
3/13/76	59	15		2 Open Your Eyes You Can Fly.................................		Milestone 9065
10/16/76	146	5		3 500 Miles High .... [L]		Milestone 9070
				recorded on 7/6/1974 at the Montreaux Jazz Festival		
8/13/77	194	3		4 Encounter		Milestone 9077
3/26/77	163	4		5 Nothing Will Be As It Was...Tomorrow		Warner 2985
6/3/78	174	4		6 Everyday, Everynight		Warner 3168
11/3/79	203	2		7 Carry On...		Warner 3344

PURPLE CITY
Male rap trio from Harlem, New York: Shiest Bub, Agallah and Un Kasa. Best-known for their underground "mix" tapes.

4/9/05	164	1		1 Road To The Riches: The Best Of The Purple City Mixtapes .... [K]		Babygrande 50

PURPLE RIBBON ALL-STARS
All-star rap group: **Big Boi**, **Killer Mike**, **Bubba Sparxxx**, **Sleepy Brown**, **Janelle Monae**, Konkrete and Scar.

12/10/05	49	14		1 Big Boi Presents...Got Purp? Vol. II		Virgin 12207

PURSELL, Bill
Born on 6/9/1926 in Oakland, California; raised in Tulare, California. Adult Contemporary session pianist.

4/6/63	28	14		1 Our Winter Love .... [I]		Columbia 1992

PURSUIT OF HAPPINESS, The
Rock band from Toronto, Ontario, Canada: Moe Berg (male vocals, guitar), Leslie Stanwyck (female vocals), Kris Abbott (guitar), Johnny Sinclair (bass) and Dave Gilby (drums).

12/17/88+	93	21		1 Love Junk		Chrysalis 41675

PUSCIFER
Solo project of Maynard James Keenan (of **Tool** and **A Perfect Circle**). Includes a revolving set of singers and musicians.

11/17/07	25	3		1 V Is For Vagina		Puscifer 88800

PUSSYCAT DOLLS, The
Female pop-dance group formed in Los Angeles, California: Nicole Scherzinger, Carmit Bachar, Ashley Roberts, Jessica Sutta, Melody Thornton and Kimberly Wyatt. Scherzinger was a member of **Eden's Crush**. Scherzinger finished first on season 10 on *Dancing With The Stars*.

10/1/05	5	99	▲	1 PCD		A&M 005374
10/11/08	4	32		2 Doll Domination		Interscope 011770

PYRAMIDS, The
Surf-rock and roll band from Long Beach, California: Skip Mercer and Willie Glover (guitars), Tom Pittman (sax), Steve Leonard (bass) and Ron McMullen (drums). Performed with shaved heads. Appeared in the 1964 movie *Bikini Beach*.

3/14/64	119	6		1 The Original Penetration! And Other Favorites......................		Best 16501

PYTHON LEE JACKSON
Rock band from Australia: David Bently (keyboards), Mick Liber (guitar), Gary Boyle (guitar), Tony Cahill (bass) and David Montgomery (drums).

10/7/72	182	6		1 In A Broken Dream		GNP Crescendo 2066

Billboard			R I A A	ARTIST Album Title	Catalog	Label & Number
DEBUT	PEAK	WKS				

Q

Q
Pop band from Beaver Falls, Pennsylvania: Don Garvin (guitar), Robert Peckman (bass), Bill Thomas (keyboards) and Bill Vogel (drums). All share vocals.

| 6/18/77 | 140 | 2 | | 1 Dancin' Man .... | | Epic 34691 |

QB FINEST
All-star rap group: **Nas**, **Capone**, **Mobb Deep**, Tragedy, MC Shan, **Marley Marl**, **Nature**, **Cormega** and Millennium Thug. QB: Queen's Bridge.

| 1/6/01 | 53 | 23 | ● | 1 Nas & Ill Will Records Presents Queensbridge The Album .... | | Ill Will 63807 |

Q-TIP
Born Jonathan Davis on 11/20/1970 in Harlem, New York. Male rapper. Member of **A Tribe Called Quest**. Cousin of **Consequence**.

12/18/99	28	18	●	1 Amplified		Arista 14619
11/22/08	11	11		2 The Renaissance		Universal Motown 012213
10/3/09	77	1		3 Kamaal The Abstract		Battery 55519

QUAD CITY DJ'S
Hip-hop/bass trio from Orlando, Florida: Nathaniel Orange, Johnny McGowan and Lana LeFleur.

| 7/13/96 | 31 | 42 | ▲ | 1 Get On Up And Dance .... | | Atlantic 82905 |

QUARASHI
Rap-rock band from Reykjavik, Iceland: Solvi Blondal, Hossi Olafsson, Steini Fjelsted and Omar Swarez.

| 4/27/02 | 104 | 3 | | 1 Jinx .... | | Time Bomb 86179 |

QUARTERFLASH
Pop-rock band from Portland, Oregon: husband-and-wife Marv Ross (guitar) and Rindy Ross (vocals, sax), with Jack Charles (guitar), Rick DiGiallonardo (keyboards), Rich Gooch (bass) and Brian David Willis (drums). Group originally known as Seafood Mama.

10/31/81+	8	52	▲	1 Quarterflash		Geffen 2003
7/9/83	34	21		2 Take Another Picture		Geffen 4011
10/5/85	150	5		3 Back Into Blue		Geffen 24078

QUASIMOTO
Born Otis Jackson on 10/24/1973 in Oxnard, California. Male rapper. Better known as Madlib. One half of **Madvillain**.

| 5/21/05 | 174 | 1 | | 1 The Further Adventures Of Lord Quas .... | | Stones Throw 2110 |

QUATEMAN, Bill
Born on 11/4/1947 in Chicago, Illinois. Pop singer/songwriter/guitarist.

| 3/31/73 | 206 | 7 | | 1 Bill Quateman .... | | Columbia 31761 |
| 2/12/77 | 129 | 8 | | 2 Night After Night .... | | RCA Victor 2027 |

QUATRO, Suzi
Born on 6/3/1950 in Detroit, Michigan. Rock singer/songwriter/guitarist. Played "Leather Tuscadero" on TV's *Happy Days* in 1977. Her sister Patti was a member of **Fanny**.

3/30/74	142	13		1 Suzi Quatro		Bell 1302
10/5/74	126	10		2 Quatro		Bell 1313
5/10/75	146	6		3 Your Mama Won't Like Me		Arista 4035
3/24/79	37	20		4 If You Knew Suzi...		RSO 3044
10/6/79	117	14		5 Suzi...And Other Four Letter Words		RSO 3064
11/1/80	165	5		6 Rock Hard		Dreamland 5006

QUAZAR
Funk band from New Jersey: Peachena (female vocals), Kevin Goins (male vocals, guitar), Harvey Banks (guitar), Monica Peters (trumpet), Darryl Dixon (sax), Greg Fitz and Richard Banks (keyboards), Darryl Deliberto (percussion), Eugene Jackson (bass) and Jeff Adams (drums).

| 11/11/78 | 121 | 5 | | 1 Quazar .... | | Arista 4187 |

QUEEN   1990s: #20 / All-Time: #50
Rock band formed in England: **Freddie Mercury** (vocals; born Farrokh Bulsara on 9/5/1946 in Zanzibar, Tanzania; died of AIDS on 11/24/1991, age 45), **Brian May** (guitar; born on 7/19/1947), John Deacon (bass; born on 8/19/1951) and **Roger Taylor** (drums; born on 7/26/1949). Wrote soundtrack for the movie *Flash Gordon* in 1980. **Paul Rodgers** joined band as lead singer in 2005. Also see **Various Artists Compilations:** *Killer Queen: A Tribute To Queen*.
    AWARD: R&R Hall of Fame: 2001

11/3/73+	83	22	●	1 Queen		Elektra 75064
5/11/74	49	13		2 Queen II		Elektra 75082
12/14/74+	12	32	●	3 Sheer Heart Attack		Elektra 1026
12/27/75+	4	56	▲³	4 A Night At The Opera	Cat:#3/35	Elektra 1053
				RS500 #230		
1/15/77	5	19	▲	5 A Day At The Races		Elektra 101
11/26/77+	3²	37	▲⁴	6 News Of The World	Cat:#6/26	Elektra 112

				QUEEN — cont'd		
12/9/78+	**6**	18	▲	7 **Jazz**		Elektra 166
7/19/80	**❶**⁵	43	▲⁴	8 **The Game**		Elektra 513
12/27/80+	**23**	15		9 **Flash Gordon** .... **[S]**		Elektra 518
5/29/82	**22**	21	●	10 **Hot Space**		Elektra 60128
3/17/84	**23**	20	●	11 **The Works**		Capitol 12322
7/19/86	**46**	13	●	12 **A Kind Of Magic**		Capitol 12476
6/24/89	**24**	14		13 **The Miracle**		Capitol 92357
2/23/91	**30**	17	●	14 **Innuendo**		Hollywood 61020
11/25/95	**58**	11	●	15 **Made In Heaven**		Hollywood 62017
11/15/08	**47**	2		16 **The Cosmos Rocks**		Hollywood 002615
				QUEEN & PAUL RODGERS		
				GREATEST HITS & COMPILATIONS:		
11/14/81	**14**	26	▲	17 **Greatest Hits**		Elektra 564
3/28/92	**4**	68	▲³	18 **Classic Queen**	**Cat:#48/2**	Hollywood 61311
10/3/92	**11**	207	▲⁸	19 **Greatest Hits**	**Cat:#2**¹**/563**	Hollywood 61265
1/20/07	**3**¹ᶜ	1		20 **Greatest Hits I & II**		Hollywood 162042 [2]
10/12/02	**48**	1	▲	21 **Greatest Hits I II & III: The Platinum Collection**		Hollywood 162360 [3]
9/4/04	**42**	11		22 **Greatest Hits: We Will Rock You**	**Cat:#28/8**	Hollywood 162465
4/29/06	**45**	11		23 **Stone Cold Classics**		Hollywood 162606
				LIVE ALBUMS:		
7/7/79	**16**	14	▲²	24 **Queen Live Killers**	**Cat:#10/16**	Elektra 702 [2]
6/20/92	**53**	15	▲	25 **Live At Wembley '86**		Hollywood 61104 [2]
				recorded on 7/11/1986		
5/8/93	**46**	15		26 **Five Live** .... **[EP]**		Hollywood 61479
				GEORGE MICHAEL & QUEEN		
10/1/05	**84**	1		27 **Return Of The Champions**		Hollywood 162526 [2]
				recorded on 5/9/2005 at Hallam FM Arena in Sheffield, England		
9/19/09	**111**	1		28 **Live In Ukraine**		Hollywood 004534 [2]
				QUEEN & PAUL RODGERS (above 2)		

QUEEN LATIFAH

Born Dana Owens on 3/18/1970 in Newark, New Jersey. Female singer/rapper/actress. Appeared in several movies.
Played "Khadijah James" on TV's *Living Single*. Latifah is Arabic for delicate and sensitive.

12/16/89+	**124**	17		1 **All Hail The Queen**		Tommy Boy 1022
9/21/91	**117**	23		2 **Nature Of A Sista'**		Tommy Boy 1035
12/4/93+	**60**	31	●	3 **Black Reign**		Motown 6370
7/4/98	**95**	4		4 **Order In The Court**		Motown 530895
10/16/04	**16**	29	●	5 **The Dana Owens Album**		Flavor Unit 003435
10/13/07	**11**	14		6 **Trav'lin' Light**		Flavor Unit 009203
9/12/09	**25**	2		7 **Persona**		Flavor Unit 012972

QUEEN PEN

Born Lynise Walters in 1973 in Harlem, New York. Female rapper.

1/17/98	**78**	20		1 **My Melody**		Lil' Man 90151
6/9/01	**134**	2		2 **Conversations With Queen**		Motown 013785

QUEENS OF THE STONE AGE

Hard-rock duo formed in Palm Desert, California: Josh Homme (vocals, guitar; born on 5/17/1973) and Nick Oliveri (bass;
born on 10/21/1971). Touring band includes several different musicians. Oliveri left in early 2004; Homme continued with
more musicians. Homme also formed **Them Crooked Vultures**.

9/14/02	**17**	50	●	1 **Songs For The Deaf**		Interscope 493425
4/9/05	**5**	12		2 **Lullabies To Paralyze**		Rekords 004186
12/10/05	**186**	1		3 **Over The Years And Through The Woods**		Rekords 005719
6/30/07	**14**	8		4 **Era Vulgaris**		Rekords 009039

QUEENSRYCHE   All-Time: #278

Heavy-metal band from Bellevue, Washington: Geoff Tate (vocals; born on 1/14/1959), Michael Wilton (guitar; born on
2/23/1962), Chris DeGarmo (guitar; born on 6/14/1963), Eddie Jackson (bass; born on 1/29/1961) and Scott Rockenfield
(drums; born on 6/15/1963). Mike Stone (born on 11/30/1969) replaced DeGarmo in 1998.

9/17/83	**81**	22		1 **Queensryche** .... **[EP]**		EMI America 19006
10/13/84	**61**	23	●	2 **The Warning**		EMI America 17134
7/26/86	**47**	21	●	3 **Rage For Order**		EMI America 17197
5/21/88	**50**	52	▲	4 **Operation: Mindcrime**	**Cat:#30/8**	EMI-Manhattan 48640
9/22/90	**7**	129	▲³	5 **Empire**	**Cat:#23/15**	EMI 92806
11/23/91	**38**	11		6 **Operation: Livecrime** .... **[L]**		EMI 97048
11/5/94	**3**¹	19	▲	7 **Promised Land**		EMI 30711
4/12/97	**19**	12		8 **Hear In The Now Frontier**		EMI 56141
10/2/99	**46**	5		9 **Q2K**		Atlantic 83225
7/15/00	**149**	3		10 **Greatest Hits** .... **[G]**		Virgin 49422
10/13/01	**143**	1		11 **Live Evolution** .... **[L]**		Sanctuary 84525 [2]
8/9/03	**56**	2		12 **Tribe**		Sanctuary 84578
4/22/06	**14**	5		13 **Operation: Mindcrime II**		Rhino 73306
12/1/07	**173**	1		14 **Take Cover**		Rhino 334780
4/18/09	**25**	5		15 **American Soldier**		Atco 517967

Billboard			R I A A	ARTIST		
DEBUT	PEAK	WKS		Album Title	Catalog	Label & Number

? (QUESTION MARK) & THE MYSTERIANS
Hispanic garage-rock band formed in Saginaw, Michigan: Rudy "?" Martinez (vocals), Bobby Balderrama (guitar), Frank Rodriguez (organ), Frank Lugo (bass) and Eddie Serrato (drums).

11/19/66	66	15		1 96 Tears..		Cameo 2004

QUICKSAND
Hard-rock band from New York: Walter Schreifels (vocals, guitar), Tom Capone (guitar), Sergio Vega (bass) and Alan Cage (drums).

3/18/95	134	1		1 Manic Compression		Island 526564

QUICKSILVER MESSENGER SERVICE
Rock band formed in San Francisco, California: Gary Duncan (vocals, guitar), John Cipollina (guitar), **David Freiberg** (bass) and Greg Elmore (drums). Dino Valenti joined as lead singer in 1970. Freiberg left in 1973 to join **Jefferson Starship**. Cipollina later joined **Copperhead**. Cipollina died on 5/29/1989 (age 45). Valenti died on 11/16/1994 (age 57).

6/22/68	63	25		1 Quicksilver Messenger Service		Capitol 2904
3/29/69	27	30	●	2 Happy Trails .... [L]		Capitol 120
				RS500 #189		
1/24/70	25	24		3 Shady Grove		Capitol 391
8/22/70	27	24		4 Just For Love..		Capitol 498
1/23/71	26	20		5 What About Me		Capitol 630
12/4/71+	114	9		6 Quicksilver		Capitol 819
5/6/72	134	10		7 Comin' Thru		Capitol 11002
5/19/73	108	10		8 Anthology .... [K]		Capitol 11165 [2]
11/15/75	89	12		9 Solid Silver...		Capitol 11462

QUIET RIOT
Hard-rock band formed in Burbank, California: Kevin DuBrow (vocals), Carlos Cavazo (guitar), Rudy Sarzo (bass) and Frankie Banali (drums). Chuck Wright replaced Sarzo in 1985. DuBrow and Wright left group in 1987; replaced by Paul Shortino (vocals) and Sean McNabb (bass). DuBrow died of a drug overdose on 11/25/2007 (age 52).

4/23/83	❶[1]	81	▲[6]	1 Metal Health		Pasha 38443
8/4/84	15	28	▲	2 Condition Critical		Pasha 39516
8/2/86	31	27		3 QR III		Pasha 40321
11/19/88	119	11		4 Quiet Riot		Pasha 40981

QUINN, Carmel
Born on 7/3/1925 in Dublin, Ireland. Female singer.

4/2/55	3[1]	5		1 Arthur Godfrey Presents Carmel Quinn		Columbia 629
				EP: Columbia B-491 (#3); LP: Columbia CL-629 (#4)		

QUINTANILLA, Beto
Born in 1949 in Nuevo Leon, Mexico. Died on 3/18/2007 (age 58). Male Latin singer.

5/5/07	171	1		1 Tragedias Reales De La Vida................................... [F]		Univision 311143

R

RA
Rock band from Brooklyn, New York: Sahaj Ticotin (vocals, guitar), Ben Carroll (guitar), Sean Corcoran (bass) and Skoota Warner (drums). By 2005, P.J. Farley replaced Corcoran and Andy Ryan replaced Warner.

1/25/03	154	3		1 From One		Republic 066093
7/9/05	137	2		2 Duality		Republic 004836
10/11/08	193	1		3 Black Sun		Sahaja 004

RABBITT, Eddie
Born on 11/27/1941 in Brooklyn, New York; raised in East Orange, New Jersey. Died of cancer on 5/7/1998 (age 56). Country singer/songwriter/guitarist.

6/24/78	143	7		1 Variations..		Elektra 127
6/9/79	91	20		2 Loveline		Elektra 181
11/24/79+	151	12	●	3 The Best Of Eddie Rabbitt................................... [G]		Elektra 235
7/12/80+	19	54	▲	4 Horizon		Elektra 276
8/22/81	23	34	●	5 Step By Step		Elektra 532
11/6/82+	31	25		6 Radio Romance		Elektra 60160
10/1/83	131	11		7 Greatest Hits, Volume II .... [G]		Warner 23925

RABIN, Trevor
Born on 1/13/1954 in Johannesburg, South Africa. Rock singer/songwriter/guitarist. Joined **Yes** in 1982.

12/9/78	192	4		1 Trevor Rabin		Chrysalis 1196
8/19/89	111	10		2 Can't Look Away		Elektra 60781

RACING CARS
Rock band from Manchester, England: Gareth Mortimer (vocals), Ray Ennis (vocals, banjo), Graham Williams (guitar), David Land (bass) and Robert Wilding (drums).

4/2/77	198	3		1 Downtown Tonight...		Chrysalis 1099

DEBUT	PEAK	WKS	R I A A	ARTIST / Album Title	Catalog	Label & Number

Billboard

ARTIST / Album Title

RACONTEURS, The
Rock band formed in Detroit, Michigan: Jack White (vocals, guitar; **The White Stripes**), Brendan Benson (vocals, guitar), Jack Lawrence (bass) and Patrick Keeler (drums). White and Lawrence are also members of **The Dead Weather**.

| 6/3/06 | 7 | 27 | | 1 Broken Boy Soldiers | | Third Man 27306 |
| 4/12/08 | 7 | 19 | | 2 Consolers Of The Lonely | | Third Man 456060 |

RADIATORS, The
Rock band from New Orleans, Louisiana: Dave Malone (vocals), Camile Baudoin (guitar), Ed Volker (keyboards), Glenn Sears (percussion), Reggie Scanlan (bass) and Frank Bua (drums).

| 12/19/87+ | 139 | 16 | | 1 Law Of The Fish | | Epic 40888 |
| 4/1/89 | 122 | 11 | | 2 Zigzagging Through Ghostland | | Epic 44343 |

RADIN, Joshua
Born in Shaker Heights, Ohio. Male singer/songwriter/guitarist.

| 9/27/08 | 34 | 6 | | 1 Simple Times | | Mom & Pop 001 |

RADIOHEAD   All-Time: #338
Alternative-rock band from Oxford, England: Thom Yorke (vocals, guitar; born on 10/7/1968), brothers Jon Greenwood (guitar; born on 11/5/1971) and Colin Greenwood (bass; born on 6/26/1969), Ed O'Brien (guitar; born on 4/15/1968), and Phil Selway (drums; born on 5/23/1967).

5/29/93	32	26	▲	1 Pablo Honey		Capitol 81409
5/13/95+	88	24	▲	2 The Bends ... *RS500 #110*	Cat:#50/1	Capitol 29626
7/19/97	21	55	▲²	3 OK Computer ... *Grammy: Alternative Album ★ RS500 #162*	Cat:#8/19	Capitol 55229
5/9/98	56	3		4 Airbag / How Am I Driving?	[EP]	Capitol 58701
10/21/00	❶¹	28	▲	5 Kid A ... *Grammy: Alternative Album ★ RS500 #428*		Capitol 27753
6/23/01	2¹	16	●	6 Amnesiac		Capitol 32764
12/1/01	44	3		7 I Might Be Wrong: Live Recordings	[L]	Capitol 36616
6/28/03	3¹	20	●	8 Hail To The Thief		Capitol 84543
1/12/08	❶¹	52	●	9 In Rainbows ... *Grammy: Alternative Album*		TBD 21622
6/21/08	81	3		10 The Best Of	[G]	Capitol 16424 [2]
6/21/08	26	11		11 The Best Of	[G]	Capitol 16425

RADNER, Gilda
Born on 6/28/1946 in Detroit, Michigan. Died of cancer on 5/20/1989 (age 42). Actress/comedienne. Appeared in several movies. Cast member of TV's *Saturday Night Live* (1975-80). Married to musician G.E. Smith from 1980-82; married actor Gene Wilder on 9/18/1984.

| 12/1/79+ | 69 | 12 | | 1 Live From New York | [C] | Warner 3320 |

RAEKWON
Born Corey Woods on 1/12/1970 in Staten Island, New York. Male rapper. Member of **Wu-Tang Clan**. Also recorded as **Chef Raekwon**.

8/19/95	4	21	●	1 Only Built 4 Cuban Linx...		Loud 66663
12/4/99	9	9	●	2 Immobilarity		Loud 63844
				CHEF RAEKWON		
1/3/04	102	4		3 The Lex Diamond Story		Ice Water 001716
9/26/09	4	9		4 Only Built 4 Cuban Linx...Pt. II		Ice H2O 68794

RAES, The
Husband-and-wife disco duo: Robbie Rae (born in Resloven, Wales) and Cherrill Rae (born in Carlisle, Wales).

| 3/24/79 | 161 | 5 | | 1 Dancing Up A Storm | | A&M 4754 |

RAFFERTY, Gerry
Born on 4/16/1947 in Paisley, Scotland. Adult Contemporary singer/songwriter/guitarist. Co-leader of **Stealers Wheel**.

5/6/78	❶¹	49	▲	1 City To City		United Artists 840
6/16/79	29	21	●	2 Night Owl		United Artists 958
6/14/80	61	9		3 Snakes And Ladders		United Artists 1039

RAFFI
Born Raffi Cavoukian on 7/8/1948 in Cairo, Egypt; raised in Toronto, Ontario, Canada. Singer/songwriter/guitarist specializing in children's songs.

| 12/19/87 | 22ˣ | 8 | | 1 Raffi's Christmas Album ... *first released in 1983; Christmas charts: 22/'87, 24/'88, 27/'89* | [X] | Shoreline/A&M 0226 |

RAGE AGAINST THE MACHINE
Hard-rock band formed in Los Angeles, California: Zack DeLa Rocha (vocals; born on 1/12/1970), Tom Morello (guitar; born on 5/30/1964), Tim Commerford (bass; born on 2/26/1968) and Brad Wilk (drums; born on 9/5/1968). Morello, Commerford and Wilk later formed **Audioslave**. Morello also recorded as **The Nightwatchman**. DeLa Rocha later formed **One Day As A Lion**.

5/1/93+	45	89	▲³	1 Rage Against The Machine ... *RS500 #368*	Cat:#2²/124	Epic/Associated 52959
5/4/96	❶¹	74	▲³	2 Evil Empire	Cat:#21/15	Epic 57523
11/20/99	❶¹	51	▲²	3 The Battle Of Los Angeles ... *RS500 #426*		Epic 69630

Billboard DEBUT	PEAK	WKS	R I A A	ARTIST / Album Title	Catalog	Label & Number
				RAGE AGAINST THE MACHINE — cont'd		
12/23/00	14	22	▲	4 Renegades		Epic 85289
12/13/03	94	4		5 Live At The Grand Royal Olympic Auditorium .... [L]		Epic 85114
				RAGING SLAB Hard-rock band from New York: Greg Strempka (vocals), Mark Middleton and Elyse Steinman (guitars), Alec Morton (bass) and Bob Pantella (drums).		
10/28/89	113	15		1 Raging Slab		RCA 9680
				RAH DIGGA Born Rashia Fisher on 12/18/1972 in Newark, New Jersey. Female rapper. Member of **Flipmode Squad**.		
4/22/00	18	12		1 Dirty Harriet		Flipmode 62386
				RAHZEL Born Rahzel Brown in the Bronx, New York. Male singer/rapper/songwriter.		
8/28/99	51	5		1 Make The Music 2000		MCA 11938
				RAIDERS — see REVERE, Paul		
				RAIL Hard-rock band from New York: Terry Young (vocals, bass), Richard Knotts (guitar), Andrew Baldwin (guitar) and Kelly Nobles (drums).		
8/25/84	143	10		1 Rail .... [EP]		EMI America 19010
				RAINBOW Hard-rock band led by British guitarist Ritchie Blackmore and bassist **Roger Glover**, both members of **Deep Purple**. Fluctuating lineup included vocalists Ronnie James **Dio**, Graham Bonnet (**Michael Schenker Group, Alcatrazz**) and **Joe Lynn Turner**, keyboardist **Tony Carey** and drummer Cozy Powell (**Emerson, Lake & Powell**). Group split up upon re-formation of Deep Purple in 1984. In 1990, Turner joined Deep Purple and Powell joined **Black Sabbath**. Powell died in a car crash on 4/5/1998 (age 50). Dio died of stomach cancer on 5/16/2010 (age 67).		
9/6/75	30	15		1 Ritchie Blackmore's R-A-I-N-B-O-W		Oyster 6049
6/5/76	48	17		2 Rainbow Rising		Oyster 1601
				BLACKMORE'S RAINBOW (above 2)		
7/16/77	65	9		3 On Stage .... [L]		Oyster 1801 [2]
5/6/78	89	11		4 Long Live Rock 'N' Roll		Polydor 6143
8/25/79	66	15		5 Down To Earth		Polydor 6221
3/7/81	50	16		6 Difficult To Cure		Polydor 6316
11/14/81	147	4		7 Jealous Lover .... [EP]		Polydor 502
5/8/82	30	23		8 Straight Between The Eyes		Mercury 4041
10/1/83	34	21		9 Bent Out Of Shape		Mercury 815305
3/15/86	87	10		10 Finyl Vinyl .... [L]		Mercury 827987 [2]
				recordings from 1978-84		
				RAINDROPS, The White husband-and-wife songwriting team of Ellie Greenwich (born on 10/23/1940; died of a heart attack on 8/26/2009, age 68) and Jeff Barry (born Jeffrey Adelberg on 4/3/1938). Divorced in 1965, but continued to work together. Wrote several hit singles. ~ ~ ~ ~ ~ ~ ~ ~ ~ ~ **NON-CHARTED ALBUM** ~ ~ ~ ~ ~ ~ ~ ~ ~ ~ 1963 The Raindrops		
				RAINMAKERS, The Rock band from Kansas City, Missouri: Bob Walkenhorst (vocals), Steve Phillips (guitar), Rich Ruth (bass) and Pat Tomek (drums).		
9/13/86	85	22		1 The Rainmakers		Mercury 830214
11/28/87	116	19		2 Tornado		Mercury 832795
				RAINWATER, Marvin Born Marvin Percy on 7/2/1925 in Wichita, Kansas. Country-rockabilly singer/songwriter/guitarist. No relation to Jack Rainwater. ~ ~ ~ ~ ~ ~ ~ ~ ~ ~ **NON-CHARTED ALBUM** ~ ~ ~ ~ ~ ~ ~ ~ ~ ~ 1957 Songs By Marvin Rainwater ["Gonna Find Me A Bluebird"]		
				 **RAITT, Bonnie** 1990s: #33 / All-Time: #157 Born on 11/8/1949 in Burbank, California. Blues-rock singer/guitarist. Daughter of Broadway actor/singer John Raitt. Married to actor Michael O'Keefe from 1991-99. AWARD: R&R Hall of Fame: 2000		
10/21/72	138	15		1 Give It Up		Warner 2643
10/27/73	87	20		2 Takin My Time		Warner 2729
11/2/74	80	8		3 Streetlights		Warner 2818
10/11/75	43	12		4 Home Plate		Warner 2864
4/23/77	25	22	●	5 Sweet Forgiveness		Warner 2990
10/13/79	30	21		6 The Glow		Warner 3369
3/6/82	38	18		7 Green Light		Warner 3630

DEBUT	PEAK	WKS			Catalog	Label & Number
				RAITT, Bonnie — cont'd		
8/30/86	115	11		8 Nine Lives		Warner 25486
7/28/90	61	15	●	9 The Bonnie Raitt Collection .... [K]		Warner 26242
4/15/89+	❶³	185	▲⁵	10 Nick Of Time	Cat:#32/8	Capitol 91268
				Grammys: Album of the Year / Female Rock Vocal ★ RS500 #229		
7/13/91	2²	120	▲⁷	11 Luck Of The Draw	Cat:#15/47	Capitol 96111
				Grammy: Female Rock Vocal		
4/9/94	❶¹	47	▲²	12 Longing In Their Hearts		Capitol 81427
				Grammy: Pop Vocal Album		
11/25/95	44	21	●	13 Road Tested .... [L]		Capitol 33705 [2]
4/25/98	17	20	●	14 Fundamental		Capitol 56397
4/27/02	13	23	●	15 Silver Lining		Capitol 31816
10/18/03	47	5		16 The Best Of Bonnie Raitt 1989-2003 .... [G]		Capitol 90491
10/1/05	19	14		17 Souls Alike		Capitol 73628
				RAKIM		
				Born William Griffin on 1/28/1968 in Long Island, New York. Male rapper. One-half of **Eric B. & Rakim** duo.		
11/22/97	4	17	●	1 The 18th Letter		Universal 53113
12/18/99	72	2		2 The Master		Universal 542082
12/5/09	67	1		3 The Seventh Seal		RA 342
				RAKIM & KEN-Y		
				Reggaeton duo from Gurabo, Puerto Rico: Jose "Rakim" Nieves and Kenny "Ken-Y" Vasquez.		
3/4/06	101	24		1 Masterpiece .... [F]		Universal Latino 270183
5/5/07	112	6		2 Masterpiece [Commemorative Edition] .... [F]		Pina 008481
9/27/08	32	6		3 The Royalty/La Realeza .... [F]		Pina 011912
				R.K.M. & KEN-Y		
				RALSTON, Bob		
				Born on 7/2/1938 in Montebello, California. Pianist/organist/arranger. Joined **Lawrence Welk**'s TV show in 1963.		
12/30/67	77ˣ	1		1 Christmas Hymns & Carols .... [X]		RCA Camden 994
				RAMATAM		
				Rock band formed in San Francisco, California: Mike Pinera (vocals, guitar; **Iron Butterfly**, **Blues Image**, **Cactus**), April Lawton (guitar), Tommy Sullivan (keyboards), Russ Smith (bass) and Mitch Mitchell (drums; **Jimi Hendrix** Experience).		
9/2/72	182	7		1 Ramatam		Atlantic 7236
				RAMBEAU, Eddie		
				Born Edward Fluri on 6/30/1943 in Hazleton, Pennsylvania. Pop singer/songwriter.		
7/24/65	148	2		1 Concrete And Clay		DynoVoice 9001
				RAMIN, Sid, and Orchestra		
				Born on 1/22/1924 in Boston, Massachusetts. Conductor/composer/arranger.		
5/25/63	34	6		1 New Thresholds In Sound.................................. [I]		RCA Victor 2658
				RAM JAM		
				Rock band formed in Long Island, New York: Myke Scavone (vocals), Bill Bartlett (guitar), Howie Blauvelt (bass) and Peter Charles (drums). Bartlett was a member of **The Lemon Pipers**. Blauvelt died of a heart attack on 10/25/1993 (age 44).		
9/10/77	34	12		1 Ram Jam		Epic 34885
				RAMMSTEIN		
				Hard-rock band from Berlin, Germany: Till Lindemann (vocals), Richard Kruspe (guitar), Paul Landers (guitar), Flake Lorenz (keyboards), Oliver Riedel (bass) and Christoph Schneider (drums).		
6/27/98	45	31	▲	1 Sehnsucht .... [F]		Motor 539901
9/18/99	179	1		2 Live Aus Berlin .... [F-L]		Motor 547590
				recorded on 8/22/1998 at Parkbuhne Wuhlheide in Berlin, Germany		
4/21/01	77	6		3 Mutter.. [F]		Motor 549639
12/4/04	61	4		4 Reise, Reise .... [F]		Republic 003693
4/15/06	47	5		5 Rosenrot .... [F]		Universal 006385
10/6/07	147	1		6 Volkerball .... [F]		Universal 50716
11/7/09	13	4		7 Liebe Ist Fur Alle Da .... [F]		Pilgrim 2721358
				RAMONE, Joey		
				Born Jeffrey Hyman on 5/19/1951 in Forest Hills, New York. Died of cancer on 4/15/2001 (age 49). Lead singer of the **Ramones**.		
3/9/02	109	2		1 Don't Worry About Me		Sanctuary 84542
				RAMONES		
				Highly influential punk-rock band formed in Brooklyn, New York. Jeffrey "**Joey Ramone**" Hyman (vocals; born on 5/19/1951; died on 4/15/2001, age 49), John "Johnny Ramone" Cummings (guitar; born on 10/8/1948; died of cancer on 9/15/2004, age 55), Douglas "Dee Dee Ramone" Colvin (bass; born on 9/18/1952; died of a drug overdose on 6/5/2002, age 49) and Tom "Tommy Ramone" Erdelyi (drums; born on 1/29/1952). Tommy became the band's co-producer in 1978; replaced by Marc "Marky Ramone" Bell (born on 7/15/1956). Richard "Richie Ramone" Reinhardt (born on 8/11/1957) replaced Marky from 1983-87. Dee Dee left band in 1989 and Chris "C.J. Ramone" Ward (born on 10/8/1965) was added. Group appeared in the 1979 movie *Rock 'n' Roll High School*. Also see **Various Artists Compilations**: *We're A Happy Family: A Tribute To The Ramones*.		
				AWARD: R&R Hall of Fame: 2002		
6/5/76	111	18		1 Ramones		Sire 7520
				RS500 #33		
2/12/77	148	10		2 Leave Home		Sire 7528

Billboard			R I A A	ARTIST		
DEBUT	PEAK	WKS		Album Title	Catalog	Label & Number

RAMONES — cont'd

11/26/77+	49	25	3 Rocket To Russia		Sire 6042
			RS500 #105		
10/21/78	103	11	4 Road To Ruin		Sire 6063
2/23/80	44	14	5 End Of The Century		Sire 6077
8/8/81	58	11	6 Pleasant Dreams		Sire 3571
3/26/83	83	9	7 Subterranean Jungle		Sire 23800
11/3/84	171	6	8 Too Tough To Die..		Sire 25187
6/21/86	143	6	9 Animal Boy		Sire 25433
10/10/87	172	3	10 Halfway To Sanity		Sire 25641
6/25/88	168	5 ●	11 Ramones Mania .... [G]		Sire 25709 [2]
6/17/89	122	6	12 Brain Drain		Sire 25905
9/26/92	190	1	13 Mondo Bizarro		Radioactive 10615
1/29/94	179	1	14 Acid Eaters		Radioactive 10913
7/22/95	148	2	15 Adios Amigos		Radioactive 11273
11/21/09	16 C	1	16 Greatest Hits .... [G]		Sire 70015

RAMPAGE
Born Roger McNair on 8/1/1974 in Brooklyn, New York. Male rapper.

8/16/97	65	4	1 Scouts Honor...By Way Of Blood		Violator 62022

RAMPAL, Jean-Pierre, & Claude Bolling
Flute player Rampal was born on 1/7/1922 in Marseilles, France. Died of heart failure on 5/20/2000 (age 78). Pianist Bolling was born on 4/10/1930 in Cannes, France.

1/31/76	173	4 ●	1 Suite For Flute And Jazz Piano .... [I]		Columbia 33233

RANCID
Punk-rock band from Berkeley, California: **Tim Armstrong** (vocals, guitar), Lars Frederiksen (guitar), Matt Freeman (bass) and Brett Reed (drums). Armstrong is also a member of the **Transplants**.

2/18/95	97	11 ●	1 Let's Go		Epitaph 86434
9/9/95	45	34 ▲	2 ...And Out Come The Wolves		Epitaph 86444
7/18/98	35	5	3 Life Won't Wait		Epitaph 86497
8/19/00	68	4	4 Rancid		Hellcat 80427
3/23/02	147	1	5 The BYO Split Series / Volume III		BYO 079
			NOFX / RANCID		
9/6/03	15	7	6 Indestructible...		Hellcat 48529
6/20/09	11	7	7 Let The Dominoes Fall...		Hellcat 86843

RANDLE, Lynda
Born in 1962 in Washington DC. Gospel singer.

4/11/09	188	1	1 I'm Free...		Gaither 42787

RANDOLPH, Boots
Born Homer Randolph on 6/3/1927 in Paducah, Kentucky. Died of a cerebral hemorrhage on 7/3/2007 (age 80). Session saxophonist.

6/15/63+	79	49 ●	1 Boots Randolph's Yakety Sax .... [I]		Monument 18002
11/13/65	118	5	2 Boots Randolph Plays More Yakety Sax! .... [I]		Monument 18037
1/14/67	36	47 ●	3 Boots With Strings [I]		Monument 18066
2/3/68	189	5	4 Boots Randolph With The Knightsbridge Strings & Voices .... [I]		Monument 18082
3/23/68	76	12	5 Sunday Sax .... [I]		Monument 18092
8/31/68	60	24	6 The Sound Of Boots .... [I]		Monument 18099
5/10/69	82	17	7 ...With Love/The Seductive Sax Of Boots Randolph .... [I]		Monument 18111
12/27/69	16 X	1	8 Boots And Stockings .... [X-I]		Monument 18127
1/10/70	113	18	9 Yakety Revisited .... [I]		Monument 18128
10/10/70	157	9	10 Hit Boots 1970 .... [I]		Monument 18144
1/9/71	168	3	11 Boots With Brass .... [I]		Monument 18147
6/12/71	141	11	12 Homer Louis Randolph, III .... [I]		Monument 30678
11/27/71	144	8	13 The World Of Boots Randolph .... [I-K]		Monument 30963 [2]
12/2/72	192	3	14 Boots Randolph Plays The Great Hits Of Today .... [I]		Monument 31908

RANDOLPH, Robert, & The Family Band
Born in Newark, New Jersey. Black pedal steel guitarist/vocalist. The Family Band: John Ginty (organ), Danyel Morgan (bass) and Marcus Randolph (drums).

8/23/03	145	3	1 Unclassified..		Dare 48472
10/28/06	75	2	2 Colorblind		Warner 44393

RANK & FILE
Country-rock band from Los Angeles, California: brothers Chip Kinman (vocals) and Tony Kinman (bass), **Alejandro Escovedo** (guitar) and Slim Evans (drums).

5/7/83	165	5	1 Sundown		Slash 23833
6/23/84	201	3	2 Long Gone Dead		Slash 25087

RANKIN, Billy
Born on 4/25/1959 in Glasgow, Scotland. Rock singer/guitarist. Member of **Nazareth** from 1981-82.

3/24/84	119	11	1 Growin' Up Too Fast		A&M 4977

RANKIN, Kenny
Born on 2/10/1940 in Manhattan, New York. Died of cancer on 6/7/2009 (age 69). Adult Contemporary singer/songwriter/guitarist.

9/9/72	184	8		1 Like A Seed		Little David 1003
11/16/74+	63	25		2 Silver Morning		Little David 3000
12/13/75+	81	15		3 Inside		Little David 1009
3/12/77	99	23		4 The Kenny Rankin Album		Little David 1013
6/28/80	171	6		5 After The Roses		Atlantic 19271

RANKING ROGER
Born Roger Charley on 2/21/1961 in Birmingham, England. Lead singer of **English Beat** and **General Public**.

8/13/88	151	7		1 Radical Departure		I.R.S. 42197

RANKS, Shabba
Born Rexton Gordon on 1/17/1966 in Sturgetown, Jamaica. Male reggae singer.

6/22/91	89	51	●	1 As Raw As Ever		Epic 47310
				Grammy: Reggae Album		
8/1/92	78	11		2 Rough & Ready - Vol. 1		Epic 52443
10/17/92	64	28	●	3 X-tra Naked		Epic 52464
				Grammy: Reggae Album		
7/1/95	133	4		4 A Mi Shabba		Epic 57801

RANSOME-KUTI, Fela
Born Fela Anikulapo-Kuti on 10/15/1938 in Abeokuta, Nigeria. Died of heart failure on 8/2/1997 (age 58). Male singer.

9/2/72	205	4		1 Live! **[L]**		Signpost 8401
				FELA RANSOME-KUTI AND THE AFRICA '70 WITH GINGER BAKER		

RAPPIN' 4-TAY
Born Anthony Forte on 3/2/1968 in San Francisco, California. Male rapper.

9/24/94	174	7		1 Don't Fight The Feelin' - She's A Sell Out		Rag Top 30889
4/6/96	38	7		2 Off Parole		Rag Top 35509
11/8/97	169	1		3 4 Tha Hard Way		Noo Trybe 57117

RAPTURE, The
Rock band from New York: Luke Jenner (vocals, guitar), Mattie Safer (vocals, bass), Gabriel Andruzzi (sax) and Vito Roccoforte (drums).

11/8/03	121	1		1 Echoes		Strummer 001283
9/30/06	113	1		2 Pieces Of The People We Love		Universal Motown 007438

RA RA RIOT
Alternative-rock band from Syracuse, New York: Wes Miles (vocals), Milo Bonacci (guitar), Alexandra Lawn (cello), Rebecca Zeller (violin), Mathieu Santos (bass) and Gabriel Duquette (drums). Miles also formed **Discovery**.

9/6/08	109	3		1 The Rhumb Line		Barsuk 77

RARE BIRD
Rock band formed in England: Steve Gould (vocals, bass; **Runner**), David Kaffinetti (keyboards), Graham Field (organ) and Mark Ashton (drums). By 1972, Field and Ashton were replaced by Fred Kelly, Ced Curtis, Paul Holland and Paul Karas. Ashton became lead singer of **Headstone**.

3/7/70	117	13		1 Rare Bird		Probe 4514
8/18/73	194	2		2 Epic Forest		Polydor 5530

RARE EARTH
Rock band from Detroit, Michigan: Gil Bridges (vocals, sax), Rod Richards (guitar), Mark Olson (keyboards), Ed Guzman (percussion), John Persh (bass) and Pete Rivera (drums). Numerous personnel changes through the years. Persh died of a staph virus in January 1981 (age 38). Olson died of alcohol-related complications in 1982. Guzman died on 7/29/1993 (age 49).

12/6/69+	12	77	▲	1 Get Ready		Rare Earth 507
7/11/70	15	49	●	2 Ecology		Rare Earth 514
7/17/71	28	25		3 One World		Rare Earth 520
1/1/72	29	21	●	4 Rare Earth In Concert **[L]**		Rare Earth 534 [2]
11/25/72+	90	20		5 Willie Remembers..		Rare Earth 543
6/16/73	65	23		6 Ma		Rare Earth 546
7/12/75	59	11		7 Back To Earth		Rare Earth 548
10/1/77	187	6		8 Rare Earth		Prodigal 10019
6/3/78	156	6		9 Band Together		Prodigal 10025

RASCAL FLATTS
2000s: #15 / All-Time: #301
Country vocal trio formed in Columbus, Ohio: Gary LeVox (born on 7/10/1970), Jay DeMarcus (born on 4/26/1971) and Joe Don Rooney (born on 9/13/1975).

AWARD: CMA: Horizon 2002 / Vocal Group 2003, 2004, 2005, 2006 & 2007

6/24/00+	43	65	▲²	1 Rascal Flatts	Cat:❶³/82	Lyric Street 165011
11/16/02	5	104	▲³	2 Melt	Cat:#5/82	Lyric Street 165031
10/16/04	❶¹	105	▲⁵	3 Feels Like Today	Cat:#2¹/67	Lyric Street 165049
4/22/06	❶³	91	▲⁴	4 Me And My Gang	Cat:#8/39	Lyric Street 165058
10/13/07	❶¹	68	▲²	5 Still Feels Good	Cat:#41/1	Lyric Street 000384
11/15/08	6	67		6 Greatest Hits Volume 1 **[G]**		Lyric Street 002763
4/25/09	❶¹	58↑	▲	7 Unstoppable		Lyric Street 002604

Billboard DEBUT	PEAK	WKS	R I A A	ARTIST Album Title	Catalog	Label & Number

RASCALS, The — All-Time: #460

"Blue-eyed soul" pop-rock band formed in New York: Felix Cavaliere (vocals, organ; born on 11/29/1942), Gene Cornish (vocals, guitar; born on 5/14/1944), Eddie Brigati (vocals, bass; born on 10/22/1945) and Dino Danelli (drums; born on 7/23/1944). All except Danelli had been in **Joey Dee & the Starliters**. Brigati and Cornish left in 1971, replaced by Robert Popwell (bass), Buzzy Feiten (guitar; **Larsen-Feiten Band**) and Ann Sutton (vocals). Group disbanded in 1972. Cavaliere, Cornish and Danelli reunited in June 1988. Also see **Bulldog** and **Fotomaker**.

AWARD: R&R Hall of Fame: 1997

DEBUT	PEAK	WKS	RIAA	#	Album Title	Catalog	Label & Number
5/7/66	15	84	●	1	The Young Rascals		Atlantic 8123
1/21/67	14	74	●	2	Collections		Atlantic 8134
8/12/67	5	59	●	3	Groovin'		Atlantic 8148
					THE YOUNG RASCALS (above 3)		
3/2/68	9	30		4	Once Upon A Dream		Atlantic 8169
7/13/68	❶¹	58	●	5	Time Peace/The Rascals' Greatest Hits	[G]	Atlantic 8190
3/29/69	17	16	●	6	Freedom Suite		Atlantic 901 [2]
1/10/70	45	16		7	See		Atlantic 8246
3/20/71	198	1		8	Search And Nearness		Atlantic 8276
6/5/71	122	12		9	Peaceful World		Columbia 30462 [2]
5/13/72	180	3		10	The Island Of Real		Columbia 31103

RAS KASS

Born John Austin on 9/26/1972 in Watts, California. Male rapper.

DEBUT	PEAK	WKS	RIAA	#	Album Title	Catalog	Label & Number
10/19/96	169	1		1	Soul On Ice		Priority 50529
10/10/98	63	3		2	Rasassination		Priority 50739

RASPBERRIES

Pop-rock band formed in Mentor, Ohio: Eric Carmen (vocals, guitar), Wally Bryson (guitar; **Fotomaker**), David Smalley (bass) and Jim Bonfanti (drums). Smalley and Bonfanti replaced by Scott McCarl and Michael McBride in 1974. Carmen went solo in 1975.

DEBUT	PEAK	WKS	RIAA	#	Album Title	Catalog	Label & Number
5/20/72	51	30		1	Raspberries		Capitol 11036
12/9/72+	36	16		2	Fresh		Capitol 11123
10/6/73	128	7		3	Side 3		Capitol 11220
10/19/74	143	6		4	Starting Over		Capitol 11329
6/12/76	138	4		5	Raspberries' Best Featuring Eric Carmen	[G]	Capitol 11524

RASPUTIN'S STASH

R&B-funk band formed in Los Angeles, California: Martin Dumas (vocals, guitar), Paul Coleman and Vincent Willis (keyboards), Norval Taylor (congas), Wardell Peel and James Whitfield (horns), Bruce Butler (bass) and Frank Donaldson (drums).

DEBUT	PEAK	WKS	RIAA	#	Album Title	Catalog	Label & Number
10/2/71	204	4		1	Rasputin's Stash		Cotillion 9046

RASTUS

Brassy-rock band from Milwaukee, Wisconsin: Danny Magelen (vocals, sax), Marc Roman (vocals, trombone), Tony Corrao and George Sopuch (guitars), Art Appleton, Mike Geraci and Vic Walkuski (horns), Don Nagy (bass) and Dave Smelko (drums).

DEBUT	PEAK	WKS	RIAA	#	Album Title	Catalog	Label & Number
2/20/71	207	3		1	Rastus	[L]	GRT 30004 [2]
					record 1: recorded "live" in Milwaukee; record 2: studio recordings		

RATATAT

Electronic-rock duo from New York: Mike Stroud and Evan Mast.

DEBUT	PEAK	WKS	RIAA	#	Album Title	Catalog	Label & Number
7/26/08	82	2		1	LP3		XL 353

RATCHELL

Rock band from Los Angeles, California: brothers Pat Couchois (vocals) and Chris Couchois (drums), Larry Byrom (guitar) and Howard Messer (bass). Also see **Couchois**.

DEBUT	PEAK	WKS	RIAA	#	Album Title	Catalog	Label & Number
4/15/72	176	3		1	Ratchell		Decca 75330

RAT PACK, The

All-star vocal group: **Frank Sinatra**, **Dean Martin** and **Sammy Davis, Jr.**

DEBUT	PEAK	WKS	RIAA	#	Album Title	Catalog	Label & Number
1/19/02	103	3		1	Eee-O 11: The Best Of The Rat Pack	[K]	Capitol 36452
1/19/02	110	3		2	The Rat Pack Live At The Sands	[L]	Capitol 36615
12/7/02	122	5	▲	3	Christmas With The Rat Pack .... Cat:#2¹/44	[X-K]	Capitol 42210
					Christmas charts: 18/'02, 25/'03, 4/'04, 10/'05, 11/'06, 12/'07, 21/'08, 27/'09		
12/5/09	132	5		4	Christmas With The Rat Pack	[X-K-R]	Capitol 42210
11/1/03	38	8		5	Live And Swingin': The Ultimate Rat Pack Collection	[K-L]	Reprise 73922
10/16/04	49	7		6	The Rat Pack: Boys Night Out	[K]	Capitol 70890
1/13/07	46ˣ	1		7	Christmas With The Rat Pack And Friends	[X-K]	LaserLight 32871

RATT

Hard-rock band formed in Los Angeles, California: Stephen Pearcy (vocals), Warren DeMartini (guitar), Robbin Crosby (guitar), Juan Croucier (bass) and Bobby Blotzer (drums). Pearcy joined **Arcade**. Blotzer joined **Contraband**. Pearcy, DeMartini and Blotzer reunited in 1998 with Robbie Crane (bass). Crosby died of AIDS on 6/6/2002 (age 42).

DEBUT	PEAK	WKS	RIAA	#	Album Title	Catalog	Label & Number
6/30/84	133	19		1	Ratt	[EP]	Time Coast 2203
					first released in 1983		
3/24/84	7	56	▲³	2	Out Of The Cellar		Atlantic 80143
6/29/85	7	42	▲²	3	Invasion Of Your Privacy		Atlantic 81257
10/25/86	26	40	▲	4	Dancing Undercover		Atlantic 81683
11/19/88	17	27	▲	5	Reach For The Sky		Atlantic 81929
9/8/90	23	17	●	6	Detonator		Atlantic 82127
9/21/91	57	18	●	7	Ratt & Roll 81-91	[G]	Atlantic 82260
7/24/99	169	1		8	Ratt		Portrait 69586

Billboard			R I A A	ARTIST		
DEBUT	PEAK	WKS		Album Title	Catalog	Label & Number

RAVAN, Genya
Born Genyusha Zelkowitz on 4/10/1940 in Lodz, Poland; raised in Brooklyn, New York. Lead singer of **Ten Wheel Drive**.

2/19/72	205	3		1 Genya Ravan		Columbia 31001
9/2/78	147	6		2 Urban Desire		20th Century 562
9/29/79	106	6		3 ...And I Mean It!		20th Century 595

RAVEN
Hard-rock trio from Newcastle, England: brothers John Gallagher (vocals, bass) and Mark Gallagher (guitar), with Rob Hunter (drums).

| 3/23/85 | 81 | 15 | | 1 Stay Hard .... | | Atlantic 81241 |
| 3/8/86 | 121 | 10 | | 2 The Pack Is Back .... | | Atlantic 81629 |

RAVEN-SYMONE
Born Raven-Symone Pearman on 12/10/1985 in Atlanta, Georgia. R&B singer/actress. Appeared in several movies. Played "Olivia Kendall" on TV's *The Cosby Show* and starred as "Raven Baxter" on TV's *That's So Raven*.

| 10/9/04 | 51 | 13 | | 1 This Is My Time .... | | Hollywood 162474 |
| 5/17/08 | 159 | 1 | | 2 Raven-Symone .... | | Hollywood 001761 |

RAVEONETTES, The
Male-female rock duo from Copenhagen, Denmark: Sune Rose Wagner (vocals, guitar) and Sharin Foo (vocals, bass).

9/20/03	123	2		1 Chain Gang Of Love		Columbia 90353
5/21/05	152	2		2 Pretty In Black		Columbia 92875
3/8/08	108	3		3 Lust Lust Lust		Vice 80002
10/24/09	126	2		4 In And Out Of Control		Vice 80013

RAWLS, Lou
All-Time: #176

Born on 12/1/1933 in Chicago, Illinois. Died of cancer on 1/6/2006 (age 72). R&B singer known for his very deep voice. Hosted own TV variety show with **The Golddiggers** in 1969. Appeared in the movies *Angel Angel, Down We Go* and *Believe In Me*. Voice of many Budweiser beer ads and featured singer in the *Garfield* TV specials.

4/6/63	130	3		1 Black And Blue		Capitol 1824
				also see #12 below		
5/7/66	4	74	●	2 Lou Rawls Live! **[L]**		Capitol 2459
9/10/66	7	51	●	3 Lou Rawls Soulin'		Capitol 2566
1/21/67	20	31		4 Lou Rawls Carryin' On!		Capitol 2632
5/6/67	18	22		5 Too Much!		Capitol 2713
8/26/67	29	20		6 That's Lou		Capitol 2756
12/2/67	2[1X]	11		7 Merry Christmas Ho! Ho! Ho! **[X]**		Capitol 2790
				Christmas charts: 2/'67, 22/'68, 18/'69, 26/'70		
3/9/68	103	22		8 Feelin' Good		Capitol 2864
7/20/68	165	6		9 You're Good For Me		Capitol 2927
8/31/68	103	16		10 The Best Of Lou Rawls **[G]**		Capitol 2948
6/14/69	71	23		11 The Way It Was - The Way It Is		Capitol 215
8/23/69	191	3		12 Close-Up **[R]**		Capitol 261 [2]
				reissue of Black And Blue and Tobacco Road albums		
12/20/69	200	2		13 Your Good Thing		Capitol 325
4/18/70	172	3		14 You've Made Me So Very Happy		Capitol 427
9/4/71+	68	24		15 Natural Man		MGM 4771
2/26/72	186	4		16 Silk & Soul		MGM 4809 [2]
6/5/76	7	35	▲	17 All Things In Time		Philadelphia Int'l. 33957
4/16/77	41	29	▲	18 Unmistakably Lou		Philadelphia Int'l. 34488
				Grammy: Male R&B Vocal		
12/10/77+	41	34	●	19 When You Hear Lou, You've Heard It All		Philadelphia Int'l. 35036
11/11/78	108	8		20 Lou Rawls Live **[L]**		Philadelphia I. 35517 [2]
				recorded at the Mack Hellinger Theater in New York City		
6/2/79	49	15		21 Let Me Be Good To You		Philadelphia Int'l. 36006
1/12/80	81	18		22 Sit Down And Talk To Me		Philadelphia Int'l. 36304
1/10/81	110	6		23 Shades Of Blue		Philadelphia Int'l. 36774
8/7/82	201	8		24 Now Is The Time		Epic 37488
5/14/83	163	4		25 When The Night Comes		Epic 38553
1/20/07	15[X]	1		26 Lou Rawls Christmas **[X]**		HyLo 19257

RAY, Don
Born Raymond Donnez in Germany. Disco producer/arranger/composer.

| 9/23/78 | 113 | 11 | | 1 The Garden Of Love .... | | Polydor 6150 |

RAY, Jimmy
Born on 10/3/1975 in Walthamstow, East London, England. Pop-rock singer.

| 3/28/98 | 112 | 6 | | 1 Jimmy Ray .... | | Epic 69104 |

Billboard DEBUT	PEAK	WKS	R I A A	ARTIST Album Title	Catalog	Label & Number

RAY, Johnnie
Born on 1/10/1927 in Dallas, Oregon. Died of liver failure on 2/25/1990 (age 63). Pop singer best known for his pleading vocals.

3/2/57	19	2		1 The Big Beat		Columbia 961

RAYDIO — see PARKER, Ray Jr.

RAYE, Collin
Born on 8/22/1960 in DeQueen, Arkansas. Country singer/songwriter/guitarist.

11/30/91+	54	43	▲	1 All I Can Be		Epic 47468
9/12/92	42	50	▲	2 In This Life		Epic 48983
2/12/94	73	45	▲	3 Extremes		Epic 53952
9/9/95	40	95	▲	4 I Think About You		Epic 67033
12/14/96	126	4		5 Christmas: The Gift	[X]	Epic 67751
				Christmas chart: 20/'96		
9/13/97	33	37	▲	6 The Best Of Collin Raye: Direct Hits	[G]	Epic 67893
8/1/98	55	11		7 The Walls Came Down		Epic 68876
5/20/00	81	7		8 Tracks		Epic 69995

RAYE, Susan
Born on 10/18/1944 in Eugene, Oregon. Country singer. Regular on TV's *Hee-Haw*.

5/16/70	154	6		1 We're Gonna Get Together		Capitol 448
				BUCK OWENS & SUSAN RAYE		
9/26/70	190	2		2 One Night Stand		Capitol 543
5/29/71	221	2		3 Willy Jones		Capitol 736

RAY, GOODMAN & BROWN — see MOMENTS, The

RAY J
Born Willie Ray Norwood on 1/17/1981 in McComb, Mississippi; raised in Los Angeles, California. R&B singer/actor. Brother of **Brandy**. Appeared on TV's *The Sinbad Show* and *Moesha* and in the movies *Mars Attacks!* and *Steel*.

7/7/01	21	10		1 This Ain't A Game		Atlantic 83439
10/8/05	48	22		2 Raydiation		Knockout 87521
4/26/08	7	8		3 All I Feel		Deja 34 5041

RAZORLIGHT
Punk-pop band: Johnny Borrell (vocals) and Andy Burrows (drums) from England, with Bjorn Agren (guitar) and Carl Dalemo (bass) from Sweden.

9/9/06	180	1		1 Razorlight		Vertigo 007215

RBD
Latin teen pop vocal group formed in Mexico City, Mexico: Christian Chavez, Anahi Portilla, Alfonso Herrera, Maite Beoriegui, Dulce Maria and Christopher Uckermann. Group stars in the Mexican TV series *Rebelde*.

7/30/05	95	34		1 Rebelde	[F-TV]	EMI Latin 75852
10/22/05	88	27		2 Nuestro Amor	[F]	EMI Latin 35902
4/22/06	120	5		3 Live In Hollywood	[F-L]	EMI Latin 58122
12/9/06	15	19		4 Celestial	[F]	EMI Televisa 75852
1/6/07	40	9		5 Rebels		EMI Televisa 71398
12/8/07	60	5		6 Empezar Desde Cero	[F]	EMI Televisa 11690
4/11/09	192	1		7 Para Olvidarte De Mi	[F]	EMI Televisa 94355

RBL POSSE
Male rap duo from San Francisco, California: Christian "Black C" Mathews and Kyle "Mr. Cee" Church. Church was shot to death on 1/1/1996 (age 21). Ricky "Hitman" Heard replaced Church. Heard was shot to death on 2/4/2003 (age 24). R.B.L: Ruthless By Law.

12/3/94	197	1		1 Ruthless By Law		In-A-Minute 8700
10/18/97	70	3		2 An Eye For An Eye		Big Beat 92771

RBX
Born Eric Collins in Long Beach, California. Male rapper. RBX: Reality Born Unknown.

10/14/95	62	3		1 The RBX Files		Premeditated 45866

REA, Chris
Born on 3/4/1951 in Middlesborough, Cleveland, England. Pop-rock singer/songwriter.

8/12/78	49	12	●	1 Whatever Happened To Benny Santini?		United Artists 879
3/4/89	92	13		2 New Light Through Old Windows		Geffen 24232
3/17/90	107	19		3 The Road To Hell		Geffen 24276
5/18/91	176	1		4 Auberge		Atco 91662

READY FOR THE WORLD
R&B-funk-dance band from Flint, Michigan: **Melvin Riley** (vocals), Gordon Strozier (guitar), Gregory Potts (keyboards), Willie Triplett (percussion), John Eaton (bass) and Gerald Valentine (drums).

6/22/85	17	48	▲	1 Ready For The World		MCA 5594
12/6/86+	32	26	●	2 Long Time Coming		MCA 5829
10/15/88	65	10		3 Ruff 'N' Ready		MCA 42198

Billboard			R I A A	ARTIST Album Title	Catalog	Label & Number
DEBUT	**PEAK**	**WKS**				
				REAL LIFE Pop-rock band from Melbourne, Australia: David Sterry (vocals, guitar), Richard Zatorski (keyboards), Allan Johnson (bass) and Danny Simcic (drums).		
1/7/84	58	24		1 Heart Land		Curb 5459
7/1/89	191	3		2 Send Me An Angel '89 .... [K]		Curb 10614
				REAL McCOY Techno-dance trio: German rapper/songwriter Olaf "O-Jay" Jeglitza with American singers Vanessa Mason and Lisa Cork.		
4/15/95	13	46	▲²	1 Another Night		Arista 18778
4/12/97	79	6		2 One More Time		Arista 18965
				REATARD, Jay Born Jimmy Lindsey on 5/1/1980 in Libourn, Missouri; later based in Memphis, Tennessee. Died of a drug overdose on 1/13/2010 (age 29). Punk-rock singer/songwriter/guitarist.		
9/5/09	182	1		1 Watch Me Fall		Matador 800
				REBEL MEETS REBEL Hard-rock band formed by former **Pantera** members/brothers "Dimebag" Darrell Abbott (guitar) and Vinnie Paul Abbott (drums), with fellow Pantera member Rex Brown (bass) and country singer **David Allan Coe** (vocals). Darrell was shot to death on stage on 12/8/2004 (age 38).		
5/20/06	38	5		1 Rebel Meets Rebel		Big Vin 0001
				REBELS, The — see ROCKIN' REBELS		
				REBELUTION Reggae band from Santa Barbara, California: Eric Rachmany (vocals, guitar), Rory Carey (keyboards), Marley Williams (bass) and Wesley Finley (drums).		
8/22/09	54	2		1 Bright Side Of Life		Hill Kid 87
				RECEIVING END OF SIRENS, The Rock band from Boston, Massachusetts: Brendan Brown (vocals, bass), Nate Patterson (guitar), Alex Bars (guitar), Brian Southall (keyboards) and Andrew Cook (drums).		
8/25/07	130	1		1 The Earth Sings Mi Fa Mi		Triple Crown 03072
				RECKLESS KELLY Country band from Bend, Oregon; later based in Austin, Texas: brothers Willy Braun (vocals, guitar) and Cody Braun (vocals, fiddle), with David Abeyta (guitar), Jimmy McFeeley (bass) and Jay Nazz (drums).		
7/12/08	117	1		1 Reckless Kelly's Bulletproof		Yep Roc 2164
				RECORDS, The Rock band from England: Huw Gower (vocals), John Wicks (guitar), Phil Brown (bass) and Will Birch (drums). **Jude Cole** replaced Gower in late 1979; left in 1981.		
8/25/79	41	14		1 The Records		Virgin 13130
8/9/80	204	3		2 Crashes		Virgin 13140
				RED Christian heavy-metal band from Nashville, Tennessee: Michael Barnes (vocals, keyboards), identical twin brothers Anthony Armstrong (guitar) and Randy Armstrong (bass), Jasen Rauch (guitar) and Hayden Lamb (drums).		
7/21/07	194	1		1 End Of Silence		Essential 10807
2/28/09	15	19		2 Innocence & Instinct		Essential 10863
				REDBONE Native American "swamp-rock" band formed in Los Angeles, California: brothers Lolly Vegas (vocals, guitar) and Pat Vegas (vocals, bass), Anthony Bellamy (guitar) and Peter De Poe (drums). Butch Rillera replaced De Poe in 1973. Lolly died of cancer on 3/4/2010 (age 70).		
11/7/70+	99	17		1 Potlatch		Epic 30109
2/5/72	75	9		2 Message From A Drum		Epic 30815
3/16/74	66	16		3 Wovoka		Epic 32462
10/26/74	174	3		4 Beaded Dreams Through Turquoise Eyes		Epic 33053
				REDBONE, Leon Born Dickran Gobalain on 8/26/1949 in Cyprus; raised in Toronto, Ontario, Canada. White blues singer. Rose to fame in the mid-1970s with appearances on TV's *Saturday Night Live*. Baritone voice of many TV commercials.		
7/31/76	87	15	●	1 On The Track		Warner 2888
1/22/77	38	13		2 Double Time		Warner 2971
9/16/78	163	4		3 Champagne Charlie		Warner 3165
4/11/81	152	11		4 From Branch To Branch		Emerald City 136
				RED CHORD, The Deathcore band from Revere, Massachusetts: Guy Kozowyk (vocals), Mike McKenzie (guitar), Greg Weeks (bass) and Michqael Justian (drums).		
8/11/07	198	1		1 Prey For Eyes		Metal Blade 14629
11/14/09	180	1		2 Fed Through The Teeth Machine		Metal Blade 14770
				REDDING, Gene Born in 1945 in Anderson, Indiana. R&B singer. No relation to Otis Redding.		
8/3/74	208	1		1 Blood Brother		Haven 9200

Billboard DEBUT	PEAK	WKS	R I A A	ARTIST Album Title	Catalog	Label & Number

REDDING, Otis
All-Time: #293

Born on 9/91941 in Dawson, Georgia. Died in a plane crash on 12/10/1967 (age 26) in Lake Monona in Madison, Wisconsin. All-time great soul singer/songwriter. Own record label, Jotis. Plane crash also killed four members of the **Bar-Kays**. Otis's sons formed **The Reddings**.

AWARDS: Grammy: Lifetime Achievement 1999 ★ R&R Hall of Fame: 1989

DEBUT	PEAK	WKS		ARTIST / Album Title		Label & Number
5/2/64	103	8		1 Pain In My Heart		Atco 161
4/10/65	147	3		2 The Great Otis Redding Sings Soul Ballads.............................		Volt 411
10/16/65+	75	34		3 Otis Blue/Otis Redding Sings Soul		Volt 412
				RS500 #74		
4/30/66	54	29		4 The Soul Album		Volt 413
11/26/66+	73	15		5 Complete & Unbelievable....The Otis Redding Dictionary Of Soul		Volt 415
				RS500 #251		
4/22/67	36	31		6 King & Queen		Stax 716
				OTIS REDDING & CARLA THOMAS		
8/19/67	32	42		7 Otis Redding Live In Europe .... [L]		Volt 416
				RS500 #474		
12/2/67+	9	50		8 History Of Otis Redding [G]		Volt 418
3/23/68	4	42		9 The Dock Of The Bay		Volt 419
				RS500 #161		
7/20/68	58	21		10 The Immortal Otis Redding		Atco 252
11/30/68+	82	17		11 Otis Redding In Person At The Whisky A Go Go .... [L]		Atco 265
				recorded April 1966		
7/19/69	46	14		12 Love Man..		Atco 289
8/29/70	200	2		13 Tell The Truth		Atco 333
9/19/70	16	20	●	14 Monterey International Pop Festival .... [L-S]		Reprise 2029

				OTIS REDDING & THE JIMI HENDRIX EXPERIENCE
				    recorded June 1967 and featured in the movie *Monterey Pop*; side 1: songs performed by The **Jimi** Hendrix Experience;
				    side 2: songs performed by Otis Redding		

9/16/72	76	15		15 The Best Of Otis Redding .... [G]		Atco 801 [2]
7/28/07	50ᶜ	1		16 The Very Best Of Otis Redding.................................. [G]		Rhino 71147

~ ~ ~ ~ ~ ~ ~ ~ ~ ~ **NON-CHARTED ALBUM** ~ ~ ~ ~ ~ ~ ~ ~ ~ ~ ~

1998 **Dreams To Remember: The Otis Redding**
    Anthology
    RS500 #147

REDDINGS, The

R&B trio formed in Atlanta, Georgia: **Otis Redding**'s sons Dexter (vocals, bass) and Otis III (guitar), with cousin Mark Locket (vocals, drums, keyboards).

DEBUT	PEAK	WKS		Album Title		Label & Number
12/20/80	174	12		1 The Awakening		Believe 36875
8/1/81	106	5		2 Class		Believe 37175
5/29/82	153	12		3 Steamin' Hot		Believe 37974

REDDY, Helen
All-Time: #419

Born on 10/25/1941 in Melbourne, Victoria, Australia. Adult Contemporary singer. Family was in show business; Helen made stage debut at age four. Own TV series in the early 1960s. Migrated to U.S. in 1966. Acted in the movies *Airport 1975*, *Pete's Dragon* and *Sgt. Pepper's Lonely Hearts Club Band*.

DEBUT	PEAK	WKS		Album Title		Label & Number
6/5/71+	100	37	●	1 I Don't Know How To Love Him		Capitol 762
12/4/71+	167	7		2 Helen Reddy		Capitol 857
12/9/72+	14	62	▲	3 I Am Woman		Capitol 11068
8/11/73	8	43	●	4 Long Hard Climb		Capitol 11213
4/20/74	11	35	●	5 Love Song For Jeffrey		Capitol 11284
11/2/74+	8	28	●	6 Free And Easy		Capitol 11348
7/12/75	11	34	●	7 No Way To Treat A Lady		Capitol 11418
12/6/75+	5	51	▲²	8 Helen Reddy's Greatest Hits [G]		Capitol 11467
8/14/76	16	13	●	9 Music, Music		Capitol 11547
5/21/77	75	19		10 Ear Candy		Capitol 11640

REDEYE

Rock band formed in Los Angeles, California: Douglas "Red" Mark (vocals), Dave Hodgkins (guitar), Bill Kirkham (bass) and Bob Bereman (drums). Mark was a member of **The Sunshine Company**.

DEBUT	PEAK	WKS		Album Title		Label & Number
12/12/70+	113	12		1 Redeye		Pentagram 10003

RED FLAG

Duo from Liverpool, England: brothers Mark Reynolds (vocals) and Chris Reynolds (piano).

DEBUT	PEAK	WKS		Album Title		Label & Number
9/23/89	178	4		1 Naive Art		Enigma 73523

REDHEAD KINGPIN AND THE FBI

Born David Guppy in Englewood, New Jersey. Male rapper. The FBI: Wildstyle, Bo Roc, Lt. Squeak, Buzz and Poochie.

DEBUT	PEAK	WKS		Album Title		Label & Number
4/27/91	182	1		1 The Album With No Name		Virgin 91608

DEBUT	PEAK	WKS	R I A A	ARTIST / Album Title	Catalog	Label & Number

RED HOT CHILI PEPPERS
All-Time: #285

Rock band formed in Los Angeles, California: Anthony Kiedis (vocals; born on 11/1/1962), Hillel Slovak (guitar; born on 4/13/1962; died of a drug overdose on 6/25/1988, age 26), Michael "Flea" Balzary (bass; born on 10/16/1962) and Jack Irons (drums; born on 7/18/1962). Slovak was replaced by **John Frusciante** (born on 3/5/1970). Irons left in 1988 and later joined **Eleven**; then **Pearl Jam**; replaced by Chad Smith (born on 10/25/1962). Frusciante left in May 1992; replaced by Zander Schloss (of **Thelonious Monster** and **The Magnificent Bastards**), then by Arik Marshall, then by Jesse Tobias and finally by **Dave Navarro** (of **Jane's Addiction**) in September 1993. Frusciante returned in 1998, replacing Navarro. Kiedis appeared in the movie *Point Break*. Flea and Kiedis appeared in the movie *The Chase*. Navarro was married to actress Carmen Electra from 2003-07. Smith also joined **Chickenfoot**.

DEBUT	PEAK	WKS		#	Album Title		Label & Number
9/29/84	201	8		1	The Red Hot Chili Peppers		EMI America 17128
11/21/87+	148	18	●	2	The Uplift Mofo Party Plan		EMI-Manhattan 48036
9/16/89	52	42	▲	3	Mother's Milk	Cat:#32/24	EMI 92152
10/17/92	22	30	▲	4	What Hits!?	[K]	EMI 94762
11/19/94	82	2		5	Out In L.A.	[K]	EMI 29665
10/12/91+	3[6]	97	▲[7]	6	Blood Sugar Sex Magik	Cat:#19/3	Warner 26681
					RS500 #310		
9/30/95	4	46	▲[2]	7	One Hot Minute		Warner 45733
6/26/99	3[1]	101	▲[5]	8	Californication	Cat:#2[1]/35	Warner 47386
					RS500 #399		
7/27/02	2[1]	60	▲[2]	9	By The Way		Warner 48140
12/6/03+	18	36	▲	10	Greatest Hits	Cat:#28/36 [G]	Warner 48545
5/27/06	❶[2]	66	▲[2]	11	Stadium Arcadium		Warner 49996 [2]

RED JUMPSUIT APPARATUS, The

Pop-punk band from Middleburg, Florida: Ronnie Winter (vocals), Elias Reidy (guitar), Duke Kitchens (guitar), Joey Westwood (bass) and John Wilkes (drums).

8/5/06	25	62	●	1	Don't You Fake It		Virgin 62829
2/21/09	14	4		2	Lonely Road		Virgin 20106

REDMAN
All-Time: #487

Born Reggie Noble on 4/17/1970 in Newark, New Jersey. Male rapper.

10/24/92	49	24	●	1	Whut? Thee Album		RAL 52967
12/10/94	13	16	●	2	Dare Iz A Darkside		RAL 523846
12/28/96	12	17	●	3	Muddy Waters		Def Jam 533470
12/26/98	11	24	▲	4	Doc's Da Name 2000		Def Jam 558945
10/16/99	3[1]	33	▲	5	Blackout!		Def Jam 546609
6/6/09	7	13		6	Blackout! 2		Wu-Tang 012400
6/6/09	90	1		7	Blackout!: 10th Anniversary Collector's Edition	[R]	Def Jam 012992 [2]
					METHOD MAN & REDMAN (above 3)		
6/9/01	4	16	●	8	Malpractice		Def Jam 548381
4/14/07	13	8		9	Red Gone Wild		Def Jam 003309

REDMAN, Matt

Born in 1974 in Watford, Hertfordshire, England. Contemporary Christian singer/songwriter/guitarist.

1/20/07	154	1		1	Beautiful News		SixSteps 70378
9/12/09	136	1		2	We Shall Not Be Shaken		SixSteps 22220

REDNEX

Euro-dance band from Sweden. Core members: Goran Danielsson, Annika Ljungberg, Cool James and Pat Reiniz (vocals), Bosse Nilsson (fiddle), General Custer (banjo) and Animal (drums).

5/13/95	68	12		1	Sex & Violins		Battery 46000

RED RIDER — see COCHRANE, Tom

RED ROCKERS

Rock band from Algiers, Louisiana: John Griffith (vocals), James Singletary (guitar), Darren Hill (bass) and Jim Reilly (drums). Shawn Paddock replaced Singletary in early 1984.

5/14/83	71	16		1	Good As Gold		Columbia 38629
10/6/84	203	4		2	Schizophrenic Circus		Columbia 39281

RED 7

Rock trio from Los Angeles, California: Gene Stashuk (vocals), Michael Becker (keyboards) and Paul Revelli (drums).

5/25/85	105	10		1	Red 7		MCA 5508
5/30/87	175	3		2	When The Sun Goes Down...		MCA 5792

RED SIREN

Rock band from New York: Kristin Massey (vocals), Robert Haas (guitar), Jon Brant (bass) and Gregg Potter (drums).

4/8/89	124	12		1	All Is Forgiven		Mercury 836776

REED, Dan, Network

Funk-rock band from Portland, Oregon: Dan Reed (vocals; born on 2/17/1963), Brion James (guitar), Blake Sakomoto (keyboards), Melvin Brannon (bass) and Daniel Pred (drums).

4/2/88	95	19		1	Dan Reed Network		Mercury 834309
10/21/89	160	6		2	Slam		Mercury 838868

REED, Jerry
Born Jerry Reed Hubbard on 3/20/1937 in Atlanta, Georgia. Died of emphysema on 9/1/2008 (age 71). Country singer/songwriter/guitarist/actor. Acted in several movies. Regular on TV's *Concrete Cowboys*.
AWARD: CMA: Musician 1970 & 1971

DEBUT	PEAK	WKS		Album Title	Catalog	Label & Number
5/16/70	194	2		1 Cookin'		RCA Victor 4293
3/6/71	102	11		2 Georgia Sunshine		RCA Victor 4391
5/1/71	45	20		3 When You're Hot, You're Hot		RCA Victor 4506
9/18/71	153	5		4 Ko-Ko Joe		RCA Victor 4596
4/1/72	196	2		5 Smell The Flowers		RCA Victor 4660
7/15/72	116	12		6 The Best Of Jerry Reed	[G]	RCA Victor 4729
8/26/72	201	4		7 Jerry Reed		RCA Victor 4750
8/11/73	183	4		8 Lord, Mr. Ford		RCA Victor 0238
9/17/77	203	11		9 East Bound And Down		RCA Victor 2516
10/11/80	208	4		10 Texas Bound And Flyin'		RCA Victor 3771

REED, Jimmy
Born Mathis James Reed on 9/6/1925 in Dunleith, Mississippi. Died from an epileptic seizure on 8/29/1976 (age 50). Blues singer/guitarist.
AWARD: R&R Hall of Fame: 1991

DEBUT	PEAK	WKS		Album Title	Catalog	Label & Number
10/16/61	46	31		1 Jimmy Reed At Carnegie Hall	[G]	Vee-Jay 1035 [2]
				record 1: studio re-creation of his Carnegie Hall program; record 2: The Best of Jimmy Reed		
10/20/62	103	6		2 Just Jimmy Reed		Vee-Jay 1050

~ ~ ~ ~ ~ ~ ~ ~ ~ **NON-CHARTED ALBUMS** ~ ~ ~ ~ ~ ~ ~ ~ ~ ~ ~
1958 **I'm Jimmy Reed** *["Honest I Do"]*   1959 **Rockin' With Reed**

REED, Lou
All-Time: #245
Born on 3/2/1942 in Brooklyn, New York; raised in Freeport, Long Island, New York. Highly influential rock singer/songwriter. Member of **The Velvet Underground**. Regarded as the godfather of punk rock. Appeared in the movie *One Trick Pony*.

DEBUT	PEAK	WKS		Album Title	Catalog	Label & Number
6/24/72	189	2		1 Lou Reed		RCA Victor 4701
12/16/72+	29	31		2 Transformer		RCA Victor 4807
				RS500 #194		
				produced by David Bowie		
10/20/73	98	11		3 Berlin		RCA Victor 0207
				RS500 #344		
3/2/74	45	27	●	4 Rock N Roll Animal	Cat:#24/2 [L]	RCA Victor 0472
				recorded at the Academy of Music in New York City		
10/5/74	10	14		5 Sally Can't Dance		RCA Victor 0611
4/5/75	62	10		6 Lou Reed Live	[L]	RCA Victor 0959
				from same live sessions as album #4		
2/7/76	41	14		7 Coney Island Baby		RCA Victor 0915
4/16/77	156	6		8 Walk On The Wild Side-The Best Of Lou Reed	Cat:#48/4 [G]	RCA Victor 2001
11/13/76	64	8		9 Rock And Roll Heart		Arista 4100
4/8/78	89	9		10 Street Hassle		Arista 4169
6/2/79	130	4		11 The Bells		Arista 4229
5/10/80	158	5		12 Growing Up In Public		Arista 9522
12/20/80	178	4		13 Rock And Roll Diary 1967-1980	[K]	Arista 8603 [2]
2/27/82	169	4		14 The Blue Mask		RCA Victor 4221
4/9/83	159	7		15 Legendary Hearts		RCA Victor 4568
6/16/84	56	32		16 New Sensations		RCA Victor 4998
5/24/86	47	21		17 Mistrial		RCA Victor 7190
1/28/89	40	22	●	18 New York		Sire 25829
5/12/90	103	8		19 Songs For Drella		Sire 26140
				LOU REED & JOHN CALE		
				fictitious account of the life of Andy Warhol		
2/1/92	80	7		20 Magic And Loss		Sire 26662
3/9/96	110	3		21 Set The Twilight Reeling		Warner 46159
4/22/00	183	1		22 Ecstasy		Reprise 47425

REEL BIG FISH
Ska-punk band from Huntington Beach, California: Aaron Barrett (vocals, guitar), Scott Klopfenstein (vocals, trumpet), Tavis Werts (trumpet), Grant Barry and Dan Regan (trombones), Matt Wong (bass) and Andrew Gonzales (drums).

DEBUT	PEAK	WKS		Album Title	Catalog	Label & Number
5/31/97	57	32	●	1 Turn The Radio Off		Mojo 53013
11/7/98	67	3		2 Why Do They Rock So Hard?		Mojo 53159
7/13/02	115	3		3 Cheer Up!		Mojo 41811
4/23/05	155	1		4 We're Not Happy 'Til You're Not Happy		Mojo 68070
7/28/07	106	1		5 Monkeys For Nothin' And The Chimps For Free		Rock Ridge 61122
2/7/09	177	1		6 Fame, Fortune And Fornication		Piss-Off 61204

REEL TIGHT
R&B vocal group from Chattanooga, Tennessee: Reggie Long, Danny Johnson, Bobby Rice and Bobby Torrence.

DEBUT	PEAK	WKS		Album Title	Catalog	Label & Number
6/5/99	197	1		1 Back To The Real		G-Funk 72966

Billboard			R I A A	ARTIST Album Title	Catalog	Label & Number
DEBUT	PEAK	WKS				

REESE, Della
Born Delloreese Patricia Early on 7/6/1931 in Detroit, Michigan. R&B singer/actress. Appeared in several movies and TV shows.

3/7/60	35	2	1 Della..		RCA Victor 2157
10/23/61	113	6	2 Special Delivery..		RCA Victor 2391
4/7/62	94	6	3 The Classic Della..		RCA Victor 2419
10/22/66	149	2	4 Della Reese Live .... [L]		ABC 569

REEVES, Dianne
Born on 10/23/1956 in Detroit, Michigan; raised in Denver, Colorado. Jazz singer.

| 4/23/88 | 172 | 12 | 1 Dianne Reeves .... | | Blue Note 46906 |
| 3/10/90 | 81 | 14 | 2 Never Too Far .... | | EMI 92401 |

REEVES, Jim
Born on 8/20/1923 in Panola County, Texas. Died in a plane crash on 7/31/1964 (age 40). Country singer. Appeared in the 1963 movie *Kimberly Jim*.
AWARDS: C&W Hall of Fame: 1967 ★ OPRY: 1955

5/23/60	18	26	1 He'll Have To Go		RCA Victor 2223
6/16/62	97	11	2 A Touch Of Velvet		RCA Victor 2487
12/14/63	15ˣ	11	3 Twelve Songs Of Christmas.. [X]		RCA Victor 2758
			Christmas charts: 15/'63, 34/'64, 49/'66, 32/'67		
6/13/64	30	30	4 Moonlight And Roses		RCA Victor 2854
8/8/64	9	43	● 5 The Best Of Jim Reeves [G]		RCA Victor 2890
3/6/65	45	13	6 The Jim Reeves Way		RCA Victor 2968
2/12/66	100	6	7 The Best Of Jim Reeves Volume II .... [G]		RCA Victor 3482
6/4/66	21	29	● 8 Distant Drums...		RCA Victor 3542
7/15/67	185	5	9 Blue Side Of Lonesome		RCA Victor 3793
2/13/71	206	8	10 Jim Reeves Writes You A Record.....................................		RCA Victor 4475

REEVES, Martha — see MARTHA & THE VANDELLAS

REFLECTIONS, The
White rock and roll vocal group from Detroit, Michigan: Tony Micale, Danny Bennie, Phil Castrodale, Johnny Dean and Ray Steinberg.

~ ~ ~ ~ ~ ~ ~ ~ ~ ~ **NON-CHARTED ALBUM** ~ ~ ~ ~ ~ ~ ~ ~ ~ ~
1964 **(Just Like) Romeo & Juliet**

RE-FLEX
Techno-rock/dance band formed in London, England: John Baxter (vocals, guitar), Paul Fishman (keyboards), Nigel Ross-Scott (bass) and Roland Kerridge (drums).

| 12/24/83+ | 53 | 28 | 1 The Politics Of Dancing .... | | Capitol 12314 |

REFRESHMENTS, The
Rock band from Tempe, Arizona: Roger Clyne (vocals, guitar), Brian Blush (guitar), Buddy Edwards (bass) and Paul Naffah (drums).

| 6/8/96 | 97 | 19 | 1 Fizzy Fuzzy Big & Buzzy .... | | Mercury 528999 |
| 10/4/97 | 150 | 1 | 2 The Bottle & Fresh Horses .... | | Mercury 536203 |

REGENTS, The
White doo-wop vocal group from the Bronx, New York: Guy Villari (lead), Sal Cuomo, Chuck Fassert, Don Jacobucci and Tony "Hot Rod" Gravagna.

~ ~ ~ ~ ~ ~ ~ ~ ~ ~ **NON-CHARTED ALBUM** ~ ~ ~ ~ ~ ~ ~ ~ ~ ~
1961 **Barbara-Ann**

REGGAETON NINOS
Studio group of child singers similar to the **Kidz Bop Kids** series of albums.

| 1/21/06 | 146 | 13 | 1 Reggaeton Ninos Vol. 1 .... [F] | | Afuego 46957 |
| 9/16/06 | 176 | 2 | 2 Reggaeton Ninos Vol. 2 .... [F] | | Afuego 46381 |

REGINA
Born Regina Richards in Brooklyn, New York. Female dance singer.

| 10/4/86 | 102 | 8 | 1 Curiosity.. | | Atlantic 81671 |

REHAB
Alternative pop-rock duo from Atlanta, Georgia: James "Brooks" Buford and Danny "Boone" Alexander.

| 8/2/08 | 90 | 26 | 1 Graffiti The World .... | | Attica Sound 011555 |

REICHEL, Keali'i
Born in 1961 in Hawaii. Male singer.

| 11/8/97 | 189 | 1 | 1 E O Mai .... [F] | | Punahele 005 |

REID, Terry
Born on 11/13/1949 in Huntingdon, England. Male rock singer/guitarist.

12/21/68+	153	8	1 Bang, Bang You're Terry Reid		Epic 26427
10/18/69	147	5	2 Terry Reid		Epic 26477
4/7/73	172	8	3 River		Atlantic 7259
6/26/76	201	2	4 Seed Of Memory		ABC 935

REINER, Carl, & Mel Brooks

Reiner was born on 3/20/1922 in the Bronx, New York. Actor/writer/director. Appeared in many TV shows and movies. Father of actor/director Rob Reiner. Brooks was born Melvin Kaminsky on 6/28/1926 in Brooklyn, New York. Actor/writer/director. Directed and starred in several movies. Married to actress Anne Bancroft (died on 6/5/2005) from 1964-05.

11/24/73+	150	12		1 2000 And Thirteen .... [C]		Warner 2741
				Grammy: Hall of Fame		
				revival of the 1961 *2000 Year Old Man* act		

RELIENT K

Christian punk-rock band from Canton, Ohio: Matt Thiessen (vocals, guitar), Matt Hoopes (guitar), Brian Pittman (bass) and Dave Douglas (drums). John Warne repalced Pittman in 2004. Ethan Luck replaced Douglas in 2008.

9/15/01	158	1	●	1 The Anatomy Of The Tongue In Cheek		Gotee 2842
3/29/03	38	15	●	2 Two Lefts Don't Make A Right...But Three Do		Gotee 2890
11/20/04	15	52	●	3 Mmhmm		Gotee 72953
11/26/05	94	1		4 Apathetic .... [EP]		Gotee 42009
3/24/07	6	20		5 Five Score And Seven Years Ago		Gotee 70592
11/10/07	96	8		6 Let It Snow Baby...Let It Reindeer .... [X]		Gotee 97420
				Christmas charts: 8/'07, 29/'08, 30/'09		
7/19/08	25	7		7 The Bird And The Bee Sides		Gotee 70009
10/24/09	15	5		8 Forget And Not Slow Down..		Jive 59215

R.E.M.   1980s: #49 / 1990s: #48 / All-Time: #96

Alternative-rock band formed in Athens, Georgia: Michael Stipe (vocals; born on 1/4/1960), Peter Buck (guitar; born on 12/6/1956), Mike Mills (bass; born on 12/17/1958) and Bill Berry (drums; born on 7/31/1958). Developed huge following with college audiences in the early 1980s as one of the first "alternative rock" bands. Buck, Mills and Berry also recorded with **Warren Zevon** as the **Hindu Love Gods**. Berry retired from the group in 1997.
AWARD: R&R Hall of Fame: 2007

5/14/83	36	30	●	1 Murmur		I.R.S. 70604
				RS500 #197		
5/5/84	27	53	●	2 Reckoning		I.R.S. 70044
6/29/85	28	42	●	3 Fables Of The Reconstruction		I.R.S. 5592
8/23/86	21	32	●	4 Lifes Rich Pageant		I.R.S. 5783
9/26/87	10	33	▲	5 R.E.M. No. 5: Document	Cat:#19/4	I.R.S. 42059
				RS500 #470		
11/26/88+	12	40	▲²	6 Green..		Warner 25795
3/30/91	❶²	109	▲⁴	7 Out Of Time	Cat:#36/6	Warner 26496
				Grammy: Alternative Album		
10/24/92	2²	75	▲⁴	8 Automatic For The People	Cat:#19/1	Warner 45138
				RS500 #247		
10/15/94	❶²	54	▲⁴	9 Monster		Warner 45740
9/28/96	2¹	22	▲	10 New Adventures In Hi-Fi		Warner 46320
11/14/98	3¹	16	●	11 Up		Warner 47112
6/2/01	6	10	●	12 Reveal		Warner 47946
10/23/04	13	7		13 Around The Sun		Warner 48894
11/3/07	72	2		14 R.E.M. Live .... [L]		Warner 292668
4/19/08	2¹	18		15 Accelerate		Warner 418620
11/14/09	95	2		16 Live At The Olympia: In Dublin .... [L]		Warner 520872 [2]
				GREATEST HITS & COMPILATIONS:		
5/16/87	52	14		17 Dead Letter Office		I.R.S. 70054
10/22/88	44	19		18 Eponymous..		I.R.S. 6262
10/25/97	185	1		19 R.E.M. In The Attic..		Capitol 21321
11/15/03	8	13	▲	20 In Time 1988-2003: The Best Of R.E.M.	Cat:#32/1	Warner 48381
11/15/03	16	4		21 In Time 1988-2003: The Best Of R.E.M.		Warner 48550 [2]
9/30/06	148	1		22 And I Feel Fine...The Best Of The I.R.S. Years 1982-1987		I.R.S. 69941
9/30/06	116	1		23 And I Feel Fine...The Best Of The I.R.S. Years 1982-1987		I.R.S. 69942 [2]

REMBRANDTS, The

Pop-rock duo from Los Angeles, California: **Danny Wilde** and Phil Solem.

1/19/91	88	24		1 The Rembrandts...		Atco 91412
6/10/95	23	21	▲	2 L.P..		EastWest 61752

REMEDY

Born Ross Filler in 1972 in New York. White male rapper.

5/19/01	130	7		1 The Genuine Article		Fifth Angel 7001

REMEDY DRIVE

Christian rock band from Lincoln, Nebraska: brothers David (vocals, keyboards), Paul (guitar), Philip (bass) and Daniel (drums) Zach.

9/13/08	119	1		1 Daylight Is Coming...		Word-Curb 887341

Billboard	R I A A	ARTIST		
DEBUT	PEAK	WKS	Album Title	Catalog	Label & Number

RENAISSANCE
Classical-rock trio from Surrey, England: **Annie Haslam** (vocals), Michael Dunford (guitar) and Jon Camp (bass).

DEBUT	PEAK	WKS			
9/22/73	171	4	1 Ashes Are Burning		Sovereign 11216
8/3/74	94	21	2 Turn Of The Cards		Sire 7502
8/30/75	48	13	3 Scheherazade And Other Stories		Sire 7510
6/5/76	55	20	4 Live At Carnegie Hall .... [L]		Sire 3902 [2]
2/5/77	46	16	5 Novella		Sire 7526
3/25/78	58	14	6 A Song For All Seasons		Sire 6049
6/16/79	125	9	7 Azure D'or		Sire 6068
12/12/81	196	4	8 Camera Camera		I.R.S. 70019
5/14/83	207	1	9 Time-Line		I.R.S. 70033

RENAISSANCE, The
Studio group assembled by producer **Tommy Garrett**.

1/9/71	198	2	1 Bacharach Baroque .... [I]		Ranwood 8084

RENAY, Diane
Born Renee Diane Kushner on 7/13/1945 in Philadelphia, Pennsylvania. Teen pop singer.

4/4/64	54	11	1 Navy Blue		20th Century Fox 4133

RENE AND ANGELA
R&B vocal duo from Los Angeles, California: Rene Moore and **Angela Winbush**. Winbush married **Ronald Isley** on 6/26/1993.

8/22/81	100	8	1 Wall To Wall		Capitol 12161
7/6/85+	64	70	● 2 Street Called Desire		Mercury 824607

RENE & RENE
Mexican-American duo from Laredo, Texas: Rene Ornelas (born on 8/26/1936) and Rene Herrera (born on 10/2/1935).

1/11/69	129	9	1 Lo Mucho Que Te Quiero		White Whale 7119

REO SPEEDWAGON
1980s: #34 / All-Time: #229

Rock band from Champaign, Illinois: Mike Murphy (vocals), Gary Richrath (guitar), Neal Doughty (keyboards), Gregg Philbin (bass) and Alan Gratzer (drums). Kevin Cronin replaced Murphy in 1976. Bruce Hall replaced Philbin in 1978. Graham Lear replaced Gratzer in 1988. Lineup in 1990: Cronin, Doughty and Hall, joined by new members Dave Amato (guitar), Jesse Harms (keyboards) and Bryan Hitt (drums). Group appeared in the 1978 movie *FM*. Harms later joined **Sammy Hagar**'s Waboritas.

1/12/74+	171	8	▲ 1 Ridin' The Storm Out .... Cat:#49/2		Epic 32378
11/16/74+	98	14	2 Lost In A Dream		Epic 32948
8/2/75	74	10	3 This Time We Mean It		Epic 33338
6/19/76	159	5	4 R.E.O.		Epic 34143
3/19/77	72	50	▲ 5 REO Speedwagon Live/You Get What You Play For .... [L]		Epic 34494 [2]
4/22/78	29	48	▲² 6 You Can Tune A Piano, But You Can't Tuna Fish		Epic 35082
8/11/79	33	23	● 7 Nine Lives		Epic 35988
4/19/80	55	34	▲ 8 A Decade Of Rock And Roll 1970 To 1980 .... [K]		Epic 36444 [2]
12/13/80+	❶¹⁵	101	▲⁹ 9 Hi Infidelity		Epic 36844
7/10/82	7	24	▲ 10 Good Trouble		Epic 38100
11/24/84+	7	49	▲² 11 Wheels Are Turnin'		Epic 39593
2/28/87	28	48	● 12 Life As We Know It		Epic 40444
6/25/88	56	22	▲³ 13 The Hits .... Cat:#40/41 [G]		Epic 44202
8/18/90	129	8	14 The Earth, A Small Man, His Dog And A Chicken		Epic 45246

REPARATA AND THE DELRONS
"Girl group" from Brooklyn, New York: Mary "Reparata" Aiese, Sheila Reillie and Carol Drobnicki.

~ ~ ~ ~ ~ ~ ~ ~ ~ ~ ~ **NON-CHARTED ALBUM** ~ ~ ~ ~ ~ ~ ~ ~ ~ ~ ~
1965 **Whenever A Teenager Cries**

REPLACEMENTS, The
Alternative-rock band from Minneapolis, Minnesota: **Paul Westerberg** (vocals, guitar, piano), brothers Bob Stinson (guitar) and Tommy Stinson (bass), and Chris Mars (drums). Slim Dunlap replaced Bob Stinson in late 1986. Steve Foley replaced Mars in early 1990. Bob Stinson died on 2/18/1995 (age 35). Group nicknamed "The Mats."

2/1/86	183	7	1 Tim		Sire 25330
			RS500 #136		
5/30/87	131	19	2 Pleased To Meet Me		Sire 25557
2/18/89	57	19	3 Don't Tell A Soul		Sire 25831
10/13/90	69	14	4 All Shook Down		Sire 26298
11/15/97	143	1	5 All For Nothing - Nothing For All .... [K]		Reprise 46807 [2]

~ ~ ~ ~ ~ ~ ~ ~ ~ **NON-CHARTED ALBUM** ~ ~ ~ ~ ~ ~ ~ ~ ~ ~
1984 **Let It Be**
RS500 #239

REPUBLICA
Rock band from London, England: Samantha "Saffron" Sprakling (female vocals), Johnny Male (guitar), Tim Dorney (keyboards), Andy Todd (keyboards) and Dave Barbarossa (drums). Barbarossa was also a member of **Adam & The Ants** and **Bow Wow Wow**.

9/28/96	153	16	1 Republica		Deconstruction 66899

RES
Born Shareese Ballard in Philadelphia, Pennsylvania. Female R&B-dance singer. Pronounced: reese.

7/14/01+	115	9	1 How I Do		MCA 112310

Billboard			R I A A	ARTIST		
DEBUT	PEAK	WKS		Album Title	Catalog	Label & Number

RESTLESS HEART
Country band formed in Nashville, Tennessee: Larry Stewart (vocals), Greg Jennings (guitar), Dave Innis (keyboards), Paul Gregg (bass) and John Dittrich (drums). Stewart left in early 1992.

4/11/87	73	25	●	1 Wheels..		RCA Victor 5648
8/27/88	114	11	●	2 Big Dreams In A Small Town		RCA 8317
2/24/90	78	17	●	3 Fast Movin' Train		RCA 9961
11/16/91+	144	12		4 The Best Of Restless Heart.. [G]		RCA 61041
11/7/92+	116	34	●	5 Big Iron Horses		RCA 66049

RETURN TO FOREVER
Jazz-rock band: Al Di Meola (guitar), Chick Corea (keyboards), Stanley Clarke (bass) and Lenny White (drums).

12/8/73	124	15		1 Hymn Of The Seventh Galaxy... [I]		Polydor 5536
9/28/74	32	23		2 Where Have I Known You Before .... [I]		Polydor 6509
3/15/75	39	13		3 No Mystery .... [I]		Polydor 6512
				Grammy: Jazz Album		
4/3/76	35	15	●	4 Romantic Warrior.. [I]		Columbia 34076
4/2/77	38	17		5 Musicmagic		Columbia 34682
3/3/79	155	4		6 Return To Forever Live .... [L]		Columbia 35281
				recorded on 5/20/1977 at the Palladium Theatre in New York City		

RE-UP GANG
Male rap trio from Virginia Beach, Virginia: brothers Gene "Malice" Thornton and Terrance "Pusha T" Thornton, with Ab-Liva. The Thornton brothers also recorded as **Clipse**.

8/23/08	55	2		1 Re-Up Gang		Re-Up Gang 5089

REVENGE
Rock trio from Manchester, England: Peter Hook (vocals, bass; **New Order**), Dave Hicks (guitar) and Chris Jones (keyboards).

9/1/90	190	2		1 One True Passion		Capitol 94053

REVERBERI
Born Gianpiero Reverberi on 7/29/1939 in Genoa, Italy. Classical pianist.

2/21/76	169	7		1 Reverberi & Schumann, Chopin, Liszt............................... [I]		Pausa 7003

REVERE, Paul, And The Raiders   All-Time: #315
Rock and roll band formed in Boise, Idaho: Paul Revere (vocals, born on 1/7/1938), **Mark Lindsay** (vocals; born on 3/9/1942), **Jim Valley** (guitar), Drake Levin (guitar), Phil "Fang" Volk (bass) and Michael Smith (drums). Valley, Levin, Drake and Smith left in 1967; replaced by **Freddy Weller** (guitar), Charlie Coe (bass) and Joe Correro (drums). Smith returned in 1970, replacing Correro. On daily ABC-TV show *Where The Action Is*. Own TV show *Happening* in 1968. Lindsay and Allison recorded with **Steve Alaimo** as **The Unknowns** in 1966. Weller went on to become a prolific Country singer. Smith died on 3/6/2001 (age 58). Levin died of cancer on 7/4/2009 (age 62).

7/3/65+	71	45		1 Here They Come!...		Columbia 2307 / 9107
2/5/66	5	43	●	2 Just Like Us!		Columbia 2451 / 9251
6/11/66	9	43	●	3 Midnight Ride		Columbia 2508 / 9308
12/31/66+	9	33	●	4 The Spirit Of '67		Columbia 2595 / 9395
				also see #12 below		
5/13/67	9	47	●	5 Greatest Hits [G]		Columbia 2662 / 9462
9/2/67	25	21		6 Revolution!		Columbia 2721 / 9521
				also see #12 below		
12/2/67	10ˣ	5		7 A Christmas Present...And Past .... [X]		Columbia 2755 / 9555
3/2/68	61	23		8 Goin' To Memphis		Columbia 2805 / 9605
9/14/68	122	14		9 Something Happening		Columbia 9665
4/5/69	51	19		10 Hard 'N' Heavy (With Marshmallow)		Columbia 9753
8/23/69	48	12		11 Alias Pink Puzz...		Columbia 9905
11/8/69	166	4		12 Two All-Time Great Selling LP's .... [R]		Columbia 12 [2]
				reissue of albums #4 and #6 above		
4/11/70	154	9		13 Collage		Columbia 9964
3/20/71+	209	2		14 The Raiders' Greatest Hits Volume II .... [G]		Columbia 30386
6/19/71	19	20		15 Indian Reservation		Columbia 30768
4/1/72	209	2		16 Country Wine		Columbia 31106
				RAIDERS (above 4)		
7/8/72	143	8		17 All-Time Greatest Hits .... [G]		Columbia 31464 [2]

REVEREND HORTON HEAT
Rock trio from Corpus Christi, Texas: Jim "Reverend" Horton Heath (vocals, guitar), Jimbo Wallace (bass) and Scott Churilla (drums).

7/20/96	165	1		1 It's Martini Time		Interscope 90065
4/11/98	187	1		2 Space Heater		Interscope 90168

REVIS
Rock band from Carbondale, Illinois: Justin Holman (vocals), Robert Davis (guitar), Nathaniel Cox (guitars), Bob Thiemann (bass) and David Piribauer (drums).

6/7/03	115	11		1 Places For Breathing		Epic 86514

REV THEORY
Hard-rock band from Long Island, New York: Rich Luzzi (vocals), Rikki Lixx (guitar), Julien Jorgensen (guitar), Matt McCloskey (bass) and Dave Agoglia (drums).

6/28/08	74	5		1 Light It Up		Van Howes 011064

REYES, Diana
Born on 11/18/1979 in La Paz, Baja, Mexico. Latin singer.

DEBUT	PEAK	WKS			
7/22/06	143	1	1 Las No. 1 De La Reina	[F]	Musimex 708502
2/17/07	94	5	2 Te Voy A Mostrar	[F]	Universal Latino 008411
4/12/08	79	2	3 Insatisfecha	[F]	DBC 8700

REYNOLDS, Debbie
Born Mary Reynolds on 4/1/1932 in El Paso, Texas. Actress/singer. Starred in several movies. Married to **Eddie Fisher** from 1955-59. Mother of actress Carrie Fisher.

4/30/66	23	25	1 The Singing Nun	[S]	MGM 7
5/26/84	182	3	2 Do It Debbie's Way		K-Tel 9190
			music by a "switched on swing" big band; no track titles listed		

REYNOLDS, Tim
Born on 12/15/1957 in Weisbaden, Germany (father in U.S. military); raised in Missouri. Eclectic-rock singer/songwriter/guitarist.

2/6/99	2¹	51	▲³ 1 Live At Luther College	Cat:#23/2 [L]	Bama Rags 67755 [2]
9/1/07	3¹	9	2 Live At Radio City	[L]	Bama Rags 13102 [2]
			DAVE MATTHEWS & TIM REYNOLDS (above 2)		

RHEIMS, Robert
Born in Los Angeles, California. Arranger/conductor.

1/5/59	25	1	1 Merry Christmas in Carols	[X-I]	Rheims 6006 / 7706
			Christmas charts: 16/'63, 67/'66, 23/'67		
1/4/60	39	1	2 We Wish You A Merry Christmas	[X]	Rheims 6008 / 7708
			ROBERT RHEIMS CHORALIERS		
12/21/63+	17ˣ	11	3 For The Whole Family At Christmas	[X-I]	Rheims 6010 / 7710
			Christmas charts: 26/'63, 22/'64, 17/'65, 117/'67, 21/'68		

RHINOCEROS
Rock band from Los Angeles, California: John Finley (vocals), Danny Weis (guitar), Doug Hastings (guitar), Michael Fonfara (keyboards), Alan Gerber (keyboards), Jerry Penrod (bass) and Billy Mundi (drums). By 1969, Peter Hodgson had replaced Penrod. By 1970, Larry Leishman had replaced Hastings and Duke Edwards had replaced Mundi.

12/28/68+	115	22	1 Rhinoceros		Elektra 74030
9/27/69	105	9	2 Satin Chickens		Elektra 74056
7/11/70	178	6	3 Better Times Are Coming		Elektra 74075

RHODES, Emitt
Born on 2/25/1950 in Hawthorne, California. Pop singer/songwriter. Lead singer of **The Merry-Go-Round**.

12/12/70+	29	20	1 Emitt Rhodes		Dunhill/ABC 50089
4/17/71	194	1	2 The American Dream	[E]	A&M 4254
			recordings from 1967-68		
11/27/71	182	4	3 Mirror		Dunhill/ABC 50111

RHYMEFEST
Born Che Smith on 1/1/1977 in Chicago, Illinois. Male rapper.

7/29/06	61	3	1 Blue Collar		Allido 70371

RHYTHM CORPS
Rock band from Detroit, Michigan: Michael Persh (vocals), Greg Apro (guitar), Davey Holmbo (bass) and Richie Lovsin (drums).

8/13/88	104	14	1 Common Ground		Pasha 44159

RHYTHM HERITAGE
Studio group assembled by producers Steve Barri and Michael Omartian. Vocals by Oren and Luther Waters.

3/6/76	40	17	1 Disco-Fied	[I]	ABC 934
2/19/77	138	6	2 Last Night On Earth	[I]	ABC 987
2/25/78	202	5	3 Sky's The Limit		ABC 1037

RIC-A-CHE
Born Rick Dennis in Detroit, Michigan. Male rapper.

7/3/04	179	1	1 Lack Of Communication		SRC 002740

RICE, Chris
Born in Clinton, Maryland. Male Christian singer/songwriter.

10/3/98	167	2	1 Past The Edges		Word 69613
3/22/03	161	2	2 Run The Earth, Watch The Sky		Rocketown 20001

RICE, Damien
Born on 12/7/1973 in Dublin, Ireland; raised in Celbridge, Kildare, Ireland. Male singer/songwriter.

8/23/03+	114	29	● 1 O	Cat:#43/2	DRM 48507
12/2/06	22	16	2 9		Heffa 43249

RICH, Buddy
Born Bernard Rich on 9/30/1917 in Brooklyn, New York. Died of a brain tumor on 4/2/1987 (age 69). Legendary jazz drummer. With **Tommy Dorsey** from 1939-46.

12/31/66+	91	27	1 Swingin' New Big Band	[I-L]	Pacific Jazz 20113
7/15/67	97	21	2 Big Swing Face	[I-L]	Pacific Jazz 20117
11/30/68	186	6	3 Mercy, Mercy	[I-L]	World Pacific 20133
9/13/69	186	3	4 Buddy & Soul	[I-L]	World Pacific 20158

Billboard			R I A A	ARTIST		
DEBUT	PEAK	WKS		Album Title	Catalog	Label & Number

RICH, Buddy — cont'd

5/20/72	180	5		5 Rich In London .... [I-L]		RCA Victor 4666
3/23/74	212	4		6 The Roar Of '74 .... [I]		Groove Merchant 528

RICH, Charlie
Born on 12/14/1932 in Colt, Arkansas. Died of an acute blood clot on 7/25/1995 (age 62). Country singer/songwriter/pianist. Known as "The Silver Fox."

AWARD: CMA: Male Vocalist 1973 / Entertainer 1974

5/4/74	201	7		1 Fully Realized .... [K]		Mercury 7505 [2]
10/19/74	177	4		2 Charlie Rich Sings The Songs Of Hank Williams & Others		Hi 32084
2/23/74	36	27	●	3 There Won't Be Anymore		RCA Victor 0433
10/26/74	84	15		4 She Called Me Baby		RCA Victor 0686
6/21/75	162	4		5 Greatest Hits .... [G]		RCA Victor 0857
2/21/76	204	2		6 The World Of Charlie Rich		RCA Victor 1242
5/19/73+	8	105	▲⁴	7 Behind Closed Doors		Epic 32247

CMA: Album of the Year

3/23/74	24	31	●	8 Very Special Love Songs		Epic 32531

CMA: Album of the Year

4/27/74	89	19		9 The Best Of Charlie Rich		Epic 31933

new recordings of early non-Epic hits

12/7/74+	25	17		10 The Silver Fox		Epic 33250
6/21/75	54	20		11 Every Time You Touch Me (I Get High)		Epic 33455
4/3/76	160	6		12 Silver Linings		Epic 33545
7/4/76	148	6		13 Greatest Hits .... [G]		Epic 34240
10/29/77	180	3		14 Rollin' With The Flow		Epic 34891

~ ~ ~ ~ ~ ~ ~ ~ ~ ~ ~ **NON-CHARTED ALBUM** ~ ~ ~ ~ ~ ~ ~ ~ ~ ~ ~

1960 **Lonely Weekends** [Phillips label]

RICH, John
Born on 1/7/1974 in Amarillo, Texas. Country singer/songwriter/bassist. Former member of **Lonestar**. One-half of **Big & Rich** duo.

4/11/09	16	10		1 Son Of A Preacher Man		Warner 508796

RICH, Tony, Project
Born Antonio Jeffries on 11/19/1971 in Detroit, Michigan. R&B singer/songwriter/keyboardist.

2/3/96	31	47	▲	1 Words		LaFace 26022

RICHARD, Cliff
Born Harry Rodger Webb on 10/14/1940 in Lucknow, India (of British parents); raised in England. Pop singer/guitarist/actor. Appeared in the movies *Expresso Bongo, The Young Ones, Summer Holiday* and *Wonderful Life*. The most successful artist on the British singles charts. Knighted by Queen Elizabeth II in 1995.

4/18/64	115	7		1 It's All In The Game		Epic 26089
8/7/76	76	15		2 I'm Nearly Famous		Rocket 2210
12/8/79+	93	15		3 We Don't Talk Anymore		EMI America 17018
10/11/80	80	34		4 I'm No Hero		EMI America 17039
10/17/81	132	4		5 Wired For Sound		EMI America 17059
10/30/82	209	1		6 Now You See Me, Now You Don't		EMI America 17081

~ ~ ~ ~ ~ ~ ~ ~ ~ **NON-CHARTED ALBUMS** ~ ~ ~ ~ ~ ~ ~ ~ ~ ~ ~

1960 **Cliff Sings**   1961 **Listen To Cliff!**

RICHARDS, Keith
Born on 12/18/1943 in Dartford, Kent, England. Lead guitarist of **The Rolling Stones**. Married model Patti Hansen on 12/18/1983.

10/22/88	24	23	●	1 Talk Is Cheap		Virgin 90973
11/7/92	99	10		2 Main Offender		Virgin 86499

RICHARDSON, Calvin
Born in Monroe, North Carolina. R&B singer/songwriter.

9/27/03	65	10		1 2:35 PM		Hollywood 162351

RICH BOY
Born Marece Richards on 9/2/1983 in Mobile, Alabama. Male rapper/songwriter.

3/31/07	3¹	14		1 Rich Boy		Zone 4 008556

RICHIE, Lionel   **All-Time: #255**
Born on 6/20/1949 in Tuskegee, Alabama. R&B singer/songwriter/pianist. Former lead singer of the **Commodores**. Appeared in the movie *Thank God It's Friday*. His adopted daughter, Nicole Richie, starred with Paris Hilton on the reality TV series *The Simple Life*.

10/23/82	3⁷	140	▲⁴	1 Lionel Richie		Motown 6007
11/12/83	❶³	160	▲¹⁰	2 Can't Slow Down		Motown 6059

Grammy: Album of the Year

8/30/86	❶²	58	▲⁴	3 Dancing On The Ceiling		Motown 6158
5/23/92	19	29	▲	4 Back To Front .... [G]		Motown 6338
5/4/96	28	14	●	5 Louder Than Words		Mercury 532240
7/11/98	152	3		6 Time		Mercury 558518
4/7/01	62	15		7 Renaissance		Island 548225

Billboard			R I A A	ARTIST		
DEBUT	PEAK	WKS		Album Title	Catalog	Label & Number

				RICHIE, Lionel — cont'd		
2/22/03	19	56	▲	8 The Definitive Collection	Cat:#12/69 [G]	Motown 068140
5/22/04	47	9	●	9 Just For You		Island 002558
9/30/06	6	24	●	10 Coming Home		Island 006484
6/6/09	24	8		11 Just Go		Island 011917
				RICHIE RICH		
				Born Richard Serrell on 6/25/1967 in Oakland, California. Male rapper.		
11/23/96	35	17		1 Seasoned Veteran		Def Jam 533471
				RICHTER, Sviatoslav		
				Born on 3/20/1915 in Zhitomir, Ukraine, Russia. Died on 8/1/1997 (age 82). Classical pianist.		
12/12/60+	5	26		1 Brahms: Piano Concerto No. 2	[I]	RCA Victor 2466
				RICKLES, Don		
				Born on 5/8/1926 in Brooklyn, New York. Stand-up comedian/actor. Appeared in several movies and TV shows. Specializes in insult humor. Known as "Mr. Warmth."		
6/15/68	54	29		1 Hello Dummy!	[C]	Warner 1745
				no track titles listed on this album		
4/12/69	180	4		2 Don Rickles Speaks!	[C]	Warner 1779
				RICOCHET		
				Country band formed in Texas: Heath Wright (vocals, guitar), Teddy Carr (guitar), Junior Bryant (fiddle), Eddie Kilgallon (keyboards), Greg Cook (bass) and Jeff Bryant (drums).		
6/15/96	101	17	●	1 Ricochet		Columbia 67223
				RIDDLE, Nelson		
				Born on 6/1/1921 in Oradell, New Jersey. Died on 10/6/1985 (age 64). Trombonist/prolific arranger/conductor.		
5/27/57	20	1		1 Hey...Let Yourself Go!	[I]	Capitol 814
2/17/58	20	1		2 C'mon...Get Happy!	[I]	Capitol 893
10/20/62	48	9		3 Route 66 Theme And Other Great TV Themes	[I]	Capitol 1771
				RIDDLIN' KIDS		
				Punk-rock band from Austin, Texas: Clint Baker (vocals, guitar), Dustin Stroud (guitar), Mark Johnson (bass) and Dave Keel (drums).		
8/24/02	84	4		1 Hurry Up And Wait		Aware 85118
				RIDGELEY, Andrew		
				Born on 1/26/1963 in Bushey, England. Former guitarist of **Wham!**		
6/16/90	130	3		1 Son Of Albert		Columbia 46188
				RIDGWAY, Stan		
				Born on 4/5/1954 in Los Angeles, California. Lead singer of **Wall Of Voodoo** from 1977-83.		
4/12/86	131	9		1 The Big Heat		I.R.S. 5637
				RIFF		
				R&B vocal group from Paterson, New Jersey: Ken Kelly, Steven Capers, Anthony Fuller, Dwayne Jones and Michael Best.		
5/25/91	177	3		1 Riff		SBK 95828
				RIFKIN, Joshua		
				Born on 4/22/1944 in Brooklyn, New York. Classical/jazz/ragtime pianist.		
12/11/65+	83	17		1 The Baroque Beatles Book	[I]	Elektra 7306
2/27/71	223	1		2 Piano Rags By Scott Joplin	[I]	Nonesuch 71248
6/22/74	75	15		3 Piano Rags By Scott Joplin, Volumes I & II	[I]	Nonesuch 73026 [2]
12/14/74	126	5		4 Piano Rags By Scott Joplin, Volume III	[I]	Nonesuch 71305
				RIGHTEOUS BROTHERS, The	**All-Time: #201**	
				"Blue eyed soul" vocal duo: Bill Medley (born on 9/19/1940 in Santa Anna, California) and Bobby Hatfield (born on 8/10/1940 in Beaver Dam, Wisconsin; died of drug related heart failure on 11/5/2003, age 63). Formed duo in 1962. First recorded as the Paramours for Smash in 1962. On *Hullabaloo* and *Shindig* TV shows. Split up from 1968-74. Medley went solo; replaced by Jimmy Walker (**The Knickerbockers**); rejoined Hatfield in 1974.		
				AWARD: R&R Hall of Fame: 2003		
1/2/65	11	21		1 Right Now!		Moonglow 1001
1/16/65	14	20		2 Some Blue-Eyed Soul		Moonglow 1002
6/19/65	39	20		3 This Is New!		Moonglow 1003
1/23/65	4	67		4 You've Lost That Lovin' Feelin'		Philles 4007
5/29/65	9	41		5 Just Once In My Life...		Philles 4008
12/25/65+	16	26		6 Back To Back		Philles 4009
4/30/66	7	32	●	7 Soul & Inspiration		Verve 5001
9/3/66	32	20		8 Go Ahead And Cry		Verve 5004
4/8/67	155	15		9 Sayin' Somethin'		Verve 5010
10/28/67	198	2		10 Souled Out		Verve 5031
12/14/68	187	2		11 One For The Road	[L]	Verve 5058
8/31/74	27	18		12 Give It To The People		Haven 9201
				GREATEST HITS & COMPILATIONS:		
5/21/66	130	11		13 The Best Of The Righteous Brothers		Moonglow 1004
9/16/67	21	50	●	14 Greatest Hits	Cat:#16/70	Verve 5020

Billboard			R I A A	ARTIST		
DEBUT	PEAK	WKS		Album Title	Catalog	Label & Number

RIGHTEOUS BROTHERS, The — cont'd

4/5/69	126	5		15 Greatest Hits, Vol. 2		Verve 5071
8/25/90	31	81		16 Greatest Hits		Verve 823119
10/27/90	178	3	●	17 Anthology (1962-1974)		Rhino 71488 [2]
11/24/90	161	3	▲²	18 Best Of The Righteous Brothers	Cat:❶¹⁹/128	Curb 77381
8/8/92	35ᶜ	8		19 Unchained Melody		Polygram 511078
11/21/92	14ᶜ	1		20 The Very Best Of The Righteous Brothers/Unchained Melody		Verve 847248

RIGHT SAID FRED
Pop-dance-novelty vocal trio from England: brothers Richard Fairbrass (vocals) and Fred Fairbrass (guitar), with Rob Manzoli (guitar).

3/21/92	46	20	●	1 Up		Charisma 92107

RIHANNA
Born Robyn Rihanna Fenty on 2/20/1988 in St. Michael, Barbados. Female dance-pop-R&B singer.

9/17/05	10	35	●	1 Music Of The Sun		SRP 004937
5/13/06	5	45	▲	2 A Girl Like Me		Def Jam 006165
6/23/07	2¹	98	▲²	3 Good Girl Gone Bad	Cat:#12/8	SRP 008968
2/14/09	106	4		4 Good Girl Gone Bad: The Remixes	[K]	SRP 012603
12/12/09	4	25↑	▲	5 Rated R		SRP 013736

RILEY, Cheryl Pepsii
Born on 10/18/1968 in Brooklyn, New York. R&B singer.

11/12/88	128	11		1 Me, Myself And I		Columbia 44409

RILEY, Jeannie C.
Born Jeanne Carolyn Stephenson on 10/19/1945 in Stamford, Texas; raised in Anson, Texas. Country singer.

10/12/68	12	27	●	1 Harper Valley P.T.A.		Plantation 1
3/15/69	187	5		2 Yearbooks And Yesterdays		Plantation 2
9/13/69	142	7		3 Things Go Better With Love		Plantation 3
7/31/71	206	5		4 Jeannie C. Riley's Greatest Hits	[G]	Plantation 13

RILEY, Melvin
Born in Flint, Michigan. Former lead singer of **Ready For The World**.

8/13/94	155	3		1 Ghetto Love		MCA 11016

RILO KILEY
Alternative-pop band from Los Angeles, California: **Jenny Lewis** (vocals), Blake Sennet (guitar), Pierre DeReeder (bass) and Jason Boesel (drums).

9/4/04	161	1		1 More Adventurous		Brute 48876
9/8/07	22	9		2 Under The Blacklight		Warner 189372

RIMES, LeAnn   **All-Time: #244**
Born Margaret LeAnn Rimes on 8/28/1982 in Jackson, Mississippi; raised in Garland, Texas. Country singer/songwriter. Won her first talent show in 1987. Winner on TV's *Star Search* in 1990. Hosted TV talent show *Nashville Star*. Married actor Dean Sheremet on 2/23/2002; separated in 2009.
    AWARDS: Grammy: Best New Artist 1996 ★ CMA: Horizon 1997

7/27/96	3²	97	▲⁶	1 Blue	Cat:#27/7	Curb 77821
3/1/97	❶¹	54	▲²	2 Unchained Melody: The Early Years	[E]	Curb 77856
9/27/97	❶³	55	▲⁴	3 You Light Up My Life: Inspirational Songs		Curb 77885
5/23/98	3¹	37	▲	4 Sittin' On Top Of The World		Curb 77901
11/13/99	8	23	▲	5 LeAnn Rimes		Curb 77947
2/17/01	10	30	●	6 I Need You		Curb 77979
11/3/01	159	3		7 God Bless America		Curb 78726
10/19/02	12	16		8 Twisted Angel		Curb 78747
12/6/03	24	23	▲	9 Greatest Hits	Cat:#22/15 [G]	Curb 78829
10/30/04	81	6		10 What A Wonderful World	Cat:#39/1 [X]	Curb 78779
				Christmas charts: 3/'04, 48/'07, 43/'09		
2/12/05	3¹	47	●	11 This Woman		Curb 78859
10/27/07	4	20		12 Family		Curb 78994

RINGS, The
Rock band from Boston, Massachusetts: Mark Sutton (vocals, guitar), Mike Baker (keyboards), Bob Gifford (bass) and Matt Thurber (drums).

2/21/81	164	6		1 The Rings		MCA 5165

RIOS, Miguel
Born on 6/7/1944 in Granada, Spain. Pop singer.

8/22/70	140	4		1 A Song Of Joy		A&M 4267

RIOS, Waldo De Los
Born on 9/7/1934 in Buenos Aires, Argentina. Committed suicide on 3/28/1977 (age 42). Composer/conductor.

6/5/71	53	16		1 Sinfonias	[I]	United Artists 6802

Billboard			R I A A	ARTIST		
DEBUT	PEAK	WKS		Album Title	Catalog	Label & Number

RIOT
Hard-rock band formed in New York: Rhett Forrester (vocals), Mark Reale (guitar), Rick Ventura (guitar), Kip Leming (bass) and Sandy Slavin (drums). Forrester was shot to death on 1/22/1994 (age 37).

9/12/81	99	11		1 Fire Down Under		Elektra 546
6/19/82	201	7		2 Restless Breed		Elektra 60134
2/5/83	203	6		3 Riot Live .... [EP-L]		Elektra 67969
1/14/84	175	6		4 Born In America		Quality 1008
5/14/88	150	10		5 Thundersteel		CBS Associated 44232

RIP CHORDS, The
Rock and roll band formed in California: Terry Melcher, Bruce Johnston, Phil Stewart, Richard Rotkin, Arnie Marcus and Ernie Bringas. Melcher is the son of **Doris Day**. Johnston went on to join **The Beach Boys**. Melcher died of cancer on 11/19/2004 (age 62).

2/22/64	56	17		1 Hey Little Cobra And Other Hot Rod Hits		Columbia 8951

~ ~ ~ ~ ~ ~ ~ ~ ~ ~ **NON-CHARTED ALBUM** ~ ~ ~ ~ ~ ~ ~ ~ ~ ~
1964 **Three Window Coupe**

RIPERTON, Minnie
Born on 11/8/1947 in Chicago, Illinois. Died of cancer on 7/12/1979 (age 31). R&B singer. Member of **Rotary Connection** from 1967-70. Her daughter Maya Rudolph was a cast member of TV's *Saturday Night Live* from 1999-2007.

11/16/74	160	4		1 Come To My Garden .... [E]		Janus 7011
				recorded in 1969		
8/17/74+	4	47	●	2 Perfect Angel		Epic 32561
5/31/75	18	23		3 Adventures In Paradise		Epic 33454
3/19/77	71	10		4 Stay In Love		Epic 34191
5/19/79	29	27		5 Minnie..		Capitol 11936
9/6/80	35	15		6 Love Lives Forever		Capitol 12097
12/19/81+	203	5		7 The Best Of Minnie Riperton .... [G]		Capitol 12189

RIPPINGTONS Featuring Russ Freeman
Russ Freeman was born on 2/11/1960 in Nashville, Tennessee. Jazz guitarist/keyboardist. The Rippingtons: Jeff Kashiwa (sax), Steve Reid (percussion), Kim Stone (bass) and Tony Morales (drums).

5/7/88	110	15		1 Kilimanjaro .... [I]		Passport Jazz 88042
6/10/89	85	12		2 Tourist In Paradise .... [I]		GRP 9588
8/31/91	148	7		3 Curves Ahead .... [I]		GRP 9651
9/5/92	147	3		4 Weekend In Monaco .... [I]		GRP 9681
3/12/94	118	7		5 The Benoit/Freeman Project .... [I]		GRP 9739
				DAVID BENOIT & RUSS FREEMAN		
9/17/94	192	2		6 Sahara .... [I]		GRP 9781
				RUSS FREEMAN & THE RIPPINGTONS		
10/4/97	147	5		7 Black Diamond .... [I]		Windham Hill 11271

RISE AGAINST
Punk-rock band from Chicago, Illinois: Tim McIlrath (vocals, guitar), Chris Chasse (guitar), Joe Principe (bass) and Brandon Barnes (drums).

8/28/04	136	18	●	1 Siren Song Of The Counter Culture		Geffen 002967
7/22/06	10	27	●	2 The Sufferer & The Witness		Geffen 006976
10/25/08	3[1]	62		3 Appeal To Reason	Cat:#32/5	DGC 011904

RITCHARD, Cyril
Born on 12/1/1897 in Sydney, Australia. Died on 12/18/1977 (age 80). Acted in several movies and Broadway shows.

1/9/61	19	8		1 Alice In Wonderland: The Mad Tea Party/The Lobster Quadrille .... [T]		Riverside 1406

RITCHIE FAMILY, The
Female disco trio from Philadelphia, Pennsylvania: Cheryl Jackson, Cassandra Wooten and Gwen Oliver. Named for producer Ritchie Rome.

10/4/75	53	12		1 Brazil		20th Century 498
7/24/76	30	25		2 Arabian Nights..		Marlin 2201
2/12/77	100	10		3 Life Is Music..		Marlin 2203
7/30/77	164	12		4 African Queens...		Marlin 2206
9/2/78	148	6		5 American Generation		Marlin 2215
5/22/82	203	7		6 I'll Do My Best		RCA Victor 4323

RITENOUR, Lee
Born on 1/11/1952 in Los Angeles, California. Guitarist/composer/arranger. Nicknamed "Captain Fingers." Member of **Fourplay**.

6/4/77	178	5		1 Captain Fingers .... [I]		Epic 34426
6/24/78	121	7		2 The Captain's Journey .... [I]		Elektra 136
6/16/79	136	6		3 Feel The Night .... [I]		Elektra 192
5/9/81	26	23		4 Rit		Elektra 331
4/17/82	163	6		5 Rio .... [I]		Musician 60024
12/4/82	99	14		6 Rit/2		Elektra 60186
6/23/84	145	8		7 Banded Together...		Elektra 60358
10/5/85	192	2		8 Harlequin .... [I]		GRP 1015
				DAVE GRUSIN & LEE RITENOUR		
1/21/89	156	8		9 Festival .... [I]		GRP 9570

RITTER, Josh
Born on 10/21/1976 in Moscow, Idaho. Folk-rock singer/sonwgriter/guitarist.

DEBUT	PEAK	WKS				
9/8/07	79	2		1 The Historical Conquests Of Josh Ritter		Victor 12256

RIVERA, Jenni
Born on 7/2/1969 in Long Beach, California. Latin singer/songwriter.

4/21/07	113	4		1 Mi Vida Loca	[F]	Fonovisa 353001
9/27/08	31	5		2 Jenni	[F]	Fonovisa 353623
12/19/09+	171	3		3 La Gran Senora	[F]	Fonovisa 354398

RIVERA, Lupillo
Born Guadalupe Rivera on 1/30/1972 in La Barca, Jalisco, Mexico; raised in Long Beach, California. Male Latin singer.

3/3/01	163	3	●	1 Despreciado	[F]	Sony Discos 84276
10/12/02	154	2		2 Amorcito Corazon	[F]	Sony Discos 87537
6/12/04	106	3		3 Con Mis Propias Manos	[F]	Univision 10248
6/11/05	164	3		4 El Rey De Las Cantinas	[F]	Univision 310380 [2]

RIVERA, Scarlet
Born in Chicago, Illinois. Female violin player.

9/3/77	206	3		1 Scarlet Rivera	[I]	Warner 3060

RIVERS, Bob
Born in 1952 in North Branford, Connecticut. Hosted own *Twisted Radio* show in Seattle, Washington. Specializes in song parodies.

12/24/88+	19[X]	7	●	1 Twisted Christmas .... **Cat**:#35/6 [X-N]		Critique 90671
				BOB RIVERS COMEDY CORP		
				Christmas charts: 19/'88, 23/'90, 30/'91, 33/'94		
12/18/93+	106	4		2 I Am Santa Claus .... **Cat**:#42/2 [X-N]		Atlantic 82548
				BOB RIVERS & TWISTED RADIO		
				Christmas charts: 23/'93, 34/'94		

RIVERS, Joan
Born Joan Molinsky on 6/8/1933 in Brooklyn, New York. Popular stand-up comedian. Hosted own TV talk show in 1989. Directed the 1978 movie *Rabbit Test*.

4/23/83	22	21		1 What Becomes A Semi-Legend Most?	[C]	Geffen 4007

RIVERS, Johnny   All-Time: #249
Born John Ramistella on 11/7/1942 in Brooklyn, New York; raised in Baton Rouge, Louisiana. Pop-rock singer/songwriter/ guitarist. Recorded with the Spades for Suede in 1957. Named Johnny Rivers by DJ Alan Freed in 1958. To Los Angeles in 1961. Recorded for 12 different labels (1958-64) before his smash debut on Imperial. Began own Soul City label in 1966. Recorded Christian music in the early 1980s.

2/20/65	42	14		1 Johnny Rivers In Action!		Imperial 12280
9/25/65	91	18		2 Johnny Rivers Rocks The Folk		Imperial 12293
12/17/66+	33	46		3 Changes		Imperial 12334
6/24/67	14	21		4 Rewind		Imperial 12341
6/29/68	5	41	●	5 Realization		Imperial 12372
8/8/70	100	9		6 Slim Slo Slider		Imperial 16001
9/11/71	148	4		7 Home Grown		United Artists 5532
11/4/72+	78	20		8 L.A. Reggae		United Artists 5650
7/14/73	212	2		9 Blue Suede Shoes		United Artists 075
9/20/75	147	6		10 New Lovers And Old Friends		Epic 33681
1/14/78	142	8		11 Outside Help		Big Tree 76004
				GREATEST HITS & COMPILATIONS:		
9/24/66	29	36	●	12 Johnny Rivers' Golden Hits		Imperial 12324
6/14/69	26	25	●	13 A Touch Of Gold		Imperial 12427
3/17/73	201	4		14 Superpak		United Artists 93 [2]
				LIVE ALBUMS:		
6/20/64	12	45		15 Johnny Rivers At The Whisky A Go Go		Imperial 12264
10/17/64	38	23		16 Here We A Go Go Again!		Imperial 12274
6/26/65	21	19		17 Meanwhile Back At The Whisky A Go Go		Imperial 12284
4/16/66	52	21		18 "...And I Know You Wanna Dance"		Imperial 12307

RIVIERAS, The
Teen rock and roll group from South Bend, Indiana: Bill Dobslaw (vocals), Jim Boal (guitar), Willie Gout (guitar), Otto Nuss (organ), Doug Gean (bass) and Paul Dennert (drums). Marty Forston was lead singer on "California Sun."

6/13/64	115	5		1 Let's Have A Party		U.S.A. 102

~ ~ ~ ~ ~ ~ ~ ~ ~ ~ **NON-CHARTED ALBUM** ~ ~ ~ ~ ~ ~ ~ ~ ~ ~
1964 **Campus Party**

RIVINGTONS, The
R&B vocal group from Los Angeles, California: Carl White (lead), John "Sonny" Harris, Turner "Rocky" Wilson and Al Frazier. Prolific backing vocalists during the 1950s (known as The Sharps). White died of acute tonsillitis on 1/7/1980 (age 47).

~ ~ ~ ~ ~ ~ ~ ~ ~ ~ **NON-CHARTED ALBUM** ~ ~ ~ ~ ~ ~ ~ ~ ~ ~
1963 **Doin' The Bird**

RJD2
Born Ramble Jon Krohn on 5/27/1976 in Eugene, Oregon; raised in Columbus, Ohio. Male hip-hop DJ/producer.

DEBUT	PEAK	WKS		Album Title		Label & Number
6/5/04	128	1		1 Since We Last Spoke		Definitive Jux 84
3/24/07	190	1		2 The Third Hand		XL 263

R.L.
Born Robert Lavelle Huggar on 4/2/1977 in Minneapolis, Minnesota. R&B singer/songwriter. Member of **Next**.

5/11/02	53	16		1 RL:Ements		J Records 20012

ROACHFORD
R&B-rock band formed in England: Andrew Roachford (vocals, keyboards; born on 1/22/1965), Hawi Gondwe (guitar), Derrick Taylor (bass) and Chris Taylor (drums; **Paul Hyde & The Payolas**).

5/20/89	109	12		1 Roachford		Epic 45097

ROAD, The
Rock band from Buffalo, New York: brothers Jerry Hudson and Phil Hudson (vocals), Ralph Parker (guitar), brothers Jim Hess (organ) and Joe Hess (bass), and Nick Distefano (drums).

1/31/70	199	2		1 The Road		Kama Sutra 2012

ROAD
Rock trio formed in England: Rod Richards (vocals, guitar), Noel Redding (bass) and Leslie Sampson (drums). Redding was a member of The **Jimi Hendrix** Experience.

9/23/72	206	4		1 Road		Nat. Resources 105

ROADRUNNER UNITED
Hard-rock project which unites over 50 artists from the Roadrunner record label.

10/29/05	77	2		1 The All-Star Session		Roadrunner 618157

ROB BASE & D.J. E-Z ROCK
Rap duo from Harlem, New York: Robert "Rob Base" Ginyard with Rodney "D.J. E-Z Rock" Bryce.

10/8/88	31	81	▲	1 It Takes Two		Profile 1267
12/9/89+	50	26	●	2 The Incredible Base		Profile 1285
				ROB BASE		

ROBBINS, Marty
Born Martin Robinson on 9/26/1925 in Glendale, Arizona. Died of a heart attack on 12/8/1982 (age 57). Country singer/songwriter/guitarist. Appeared in the movies *Road To Nashville* and *Guns Of A Stranger*.
AWARDS: C&W Hall of Fame: 1982 ★ OPRY: 1953

12/28/59+	6	57	▲	1 Gunfighter Ballads And Trail Songs		Columbia 1349 / 8158
1/9/61	21	12		2 More Gunfighter Ballads And Trail Songs		Columbia 1481 / 8272
11/3/62+	35	22		3 Devil Woman		Columbia 1918 / 8718
12/2/67	21ˣ	5		4 Christmas With Marty Robbins	[X]	Columbia 2735 / 9535
12/14/68	160	7		5 I Walk Alone		Columbia 9725
7/19/69	194	4		6 It's A Sin		Columbia 9811
5/23/70	117	16		7 My Woman, My Woman, My Wife		Columbia 9978
5/8/71	143	10	●	8 Marty Robbins' Greatest Hits, Vol. III	[G]	Columbia 30571
9/18/71	175	6		9 Today		Columbia 30816
1/22/83	170	9	●	10 Biggest Hits	[G]	Columbia 38309
9/10/83	209	2		11 A Lifetime Of Song 1951-1982	[G]	Columbia 38870 [2]

~ ~ ~ ~ ~ ~ ~ ~ ~ **NON-CHARTED ALBUMS** ~ ~ ~ ~ ~ ~ ~ ~ ~ ~ ~
1956 **Rock'n Roll'n Robbins** [*"Singing The Blues"* / 10" LP]   1958 **Marty Robbins**
1957 **The Song Of Robbins**   1959 **Marty's Greatest Hits**
1957 **Song Of The Islands**

ROBBINS, Rockie
Born Edward Robbins in Minneapolis, Minnesota. R&B singer.

6/16/79	204	3		1 Rockie Robbins		A&M 4758
6/7/80	71	16		2 You And Me		A&M 4805
9/12/81	147	6		3 I Believe In Love		A&M 4869

ROBBS, The
Rock band from Oconomowoc, Wisconsin: brothers David "Dee Robb" Donaldson (vocals, guitar), George "Joe Robb" Donaldson (guitar) and Robert "Bruce Robb" Donaldson (keyboards), with friend "Craig Robb" Krampf (drums).

1/13/68	200	1		1 The Robbs		Mercury 61130

ROBERSON, James
Born in Los Angeles, California. Gospel singer.

9/12/09	97	1		1 Everybody Dance!		JDI 1277

ROBERTINO
Born Robertino Loreti on 10/22/1947 in Rome, Italy. Teen pop singer. Known as "The Singing Baker Boy."

12/1/62	96	6		1 The Young Italian Singing Sensation	[F]	Kapp 3293

ROBERTS, Austin
Born on 9/19/1945 in Newport News, Virginia. Singer/songwriter.

12/16/72+	203	6		1 Austin Roberts		Chelsea 1004

Billboard			R I A A	ARTIST		
DEBUT	PEAK	WKS		Album Title	Catalog	Label & Number

ROBERTS, Julie
Born on 2/1/1979 in Lancaster, South Carolina. Country singer.

| 6/12/04 | 51 | 25 | ● | 1 Julie Roberts | | Mercury 001902 |
| 7/15/06 | 25 | 8 | | 2 Men & Mascara | | Mercury 006327 |

ROBERTSON, Robbie
Born Jaime Robert Klegerman on 7/5/1943 in Toronto, Ontario, Canada. Rock singer/songwriter/guitarist. Member of **The Band**.

11/14/87	38	34	●	1 Robbie Robertson		Geffen 24160
10/19/91	69	10		2 Storyville		Geffen 24303
10/22/94	149	5		3 Music For The Native Americans [TV]		Capitol 28295
				ROBBIE ROBERTSON & THE RED ROAD ENSEMBLE		
				from the TNT-TV special *The Native Americans*		
3/28/98	119	3		4 Contact From The Underworld Of Redboy		Capitol 54243

ROBIN S
Born Robin Stone on 4/27/1962 in Queens, New York. Black female dance singer.

| 7/24/93 | 110 | 15 | | 1 Show Me Love | | Big Beat 82509 |

ROBINS, The
R&B vocal group from Los Angeles, California: Ty Leonard, Billy Richard, Roy Richard and Bobby Nunn. Nunn later joined **The Coasters**. Roy Richard died on 5/1/1983 (age 53). Nunn died of a heart attack on 11/5/1986 (age 61). Billy Richard died on 12/10/2007 (age 79).

~ ~ ~ ~ ~ ~ ~ ~ ~ ~ ***NON-CHARTED ALBUM*** ~ ~ ~ ~ ~ ~ ~ ~ ~ ~ ~
1958 **Rock & Roll Featuring The Robins**

ROBINSON, Chris
Born on 12/20/1966 in Atlanta, Georgia. Lead singer of **The Black Crowes**. Married actress Kate Hudson (daughter of Golide Hawn) on 12/31/2000.

11/9/02	141	1		1 New Earth Mud		Redline 70009
7/17/04	188	1		2 This Magnificent Distance		Vector 48821
				CHRIS ROBINSON & THE NEW EARTH MUD		

ROBINSON, Freddy
Born on 2/24/1939 in Memphis, Tennessee. Died of cancer on 10/8/2009 (age 70). Black jazz-rock guitarist.

| 9/19/70 | 133 | 7 | | 1 The Coming Atlantis [I] | | Pacific Jazz 20162 |

ROBINSON, Smokey   **All-Time: #185**
Born William Robinson on 2/19/1940 in Detroit, Michigan. R&B singer/prolific songwriter. Lead singer of **The Miracles**. Married to Claudette Rogers (also with The Miracles) from 1958-86. Vice president of Motown Records (1985-88).
AWARDS: Grammys: Legend 1990 / Lifetime Achievement 1999 ★ R&R Hall of Fame: 1987

7/14/73	70	19		1 Smokey		Tamla 328
4/13/74	99	17		2 Pure Smokey		Tamla 331
4/19/75	36	42		3 A Quiet Storm		Tamla 337
3/6/76	57	15		4 Smokey's Family Robinson		Tamla 341
2/19/77	47	14		5 Deep In My Soul		Tamla 350
4/15/78	75	19		6 Love Breeze		Tamla 359
1/20/79	165	6		7 Smokin' [L]		Tamla 363 [2]
6/30/79+	17	47		8 Where There's Smoke..		Tamla 366
3/15/80	14	21		9 Warm Thoughts		Tamla 367
3/14/81	10	28	●	10 Being With You		Tamla 375
2/20/82	33	17		11 Yes It's You Lady		Tamla 6001
1/29/83	50	17		12 Touch The Sky		Tamla 6030
9/3/83	124	7		13 Blame It On Love & All The Great Hits [G]		Tamla 6064
6/30/84	141	11		14 Essar		Tamla 6098
2/15/86	104	13		15 Smoke Signals		Tamla 6156
3/28/87	26	58	●	16 One Heartbeat		Motown 6226
3/17/90	112	11		17 Love, Smokey		Motown 6268
10/16/99	134	3		18 Intimate		Motown 153741
5/21/05	64	2		19 My World: The Definitive Collection [G]		Motown 004130
7/8/06	109	3		20 Timeless Love		New Door 006641
9/12/09	59	3		21 Time Flies When You're Having Fun		Robso 400200

ROBINSON, Tom, Band
Born on 6/1/1950 in Cambridge, England. Rock singer/bassist. His band: Danny Kustow (guitar), Mark Ambler (organ) and Dolphin Taylor (drums).

7/15/78	144	8		1 Power In The Darkness		Harvest 11778 [2]
5/12/79	163	7		2 TRB Two		Harvest 11930
2/21/81	209	1		3 Sector 27		I.R.S. 70013

ROBINSON, Vicki Sue
Born on 5/31/1954 in Harlem, New York (African-American father/white mother); raised in Philadelphia, Pennsylvania. Died of cancer on 4/27/2000 (age 45). Disco singer. Appeared in the original Broadway productions of *Hair* and *Jesus Christ Superstar*.

4/10/76	49	39		1 **Never Gonna Let You Go**		RCA Victor 1256
10/23/76	45	16		2 **Vicki Sue Robinson**		RCA Victor 1829
2/11/78	110	9		3 **Half And Half**		RCA Victor 2294

ROBINSON, Wanda
Born on 11/18/1949 in Baltimore, Maryland. Black poet.

10/16/71+	186	13		1 **Black Ivory**	[T]	Perception 18

ROBYN
Born Robyn Carlsson on 6/12/1979 in Stockholm, Sweden. Female dance singer.

7/12/97+	57	54	▲	1 **Robyn Is Here**		RCA 67477
5/17/08	100	1		2 **Robyn**		Konichiwa 010933

ROCHES, The
Folk vocal trio from New York: sisters Maggie Roche, Suzzy Roche and Terre Roche. Suzzy was briefly married to **Loudon Wainwright III** in 1977.

6/16/79	58	11		1 **The Roches**		Warner 3298
11/22/80	130	7		2 **Nurds**		Warner 3475
11/13/82	183	3		3 **Keep On Doing**		Warner 23735

ROCK, Chris
Born on 2/7/1965 in Andrews, South Carolina; raised in Brooklyn, New York. Stand-up comedian/actor. Regular on TV's *Saturday Night Live* from 1989-91. Acted in several movies. Narrator for biographical TV sitcom *Everybody Hates Chris*.

4/26/97	93	7		1 **Roll With The New**	[C]	DreamWorks 50008
7/31/99	44	12		2 **Bigger & Blacker**	[C]	DreamWorks 50055

ROCK, Pete, & C.L. Smooth
Hip-hop duo from Mt. Vernon, New York: Peter "**Pete Rock**" Phillips and Corey "**C.L. Smooth**" Penn.

6/27/92	43	15		1 **Mecca And The Soul Brother**		Elektra 60948
11/26/94	51	4		2 **The Main Ingredient**		Elektra 61661
11/28/98	39	4		3 **Soul Survivor**		Loud 67616
5/29/04	155	1		4 **Soul Survivor II**		BBE 0032
3/15/08	193	1		5 **NY's Finest**		Nature Sounds 135
				PETE ROCK (above 3)		

ROCK, Woody
Born James Green on 9/10/1976 in Baltimore, Maryland. Gospel singer. Former member of **Dru Hill**.

5/4/02	185	3		1 **Soul Music**		Gospo Centric 70030

ROCK AND HYDE
Pop-rock duo from Vancouver, British Columbia, Canada: Paul Hyde (vocals) and Bob Rock (guitar, keyboards). Both formerly with **Paul Hyde & The Payolas**.

5/2/87	94	15		1 **Under The Volcano**		Capitol 12569

ROCK-A-TEENS
Rock and roll teen band from Richmond, Virginia: Vic Mizell (vocals, guitar), Bobby "Boo" Walke (guitar), Bill Cook (guitar), Paul Dixon (bass), Eddie Robinson (sax) and Bill Smith (drums).

~ ~ ~ ~ ~ ~ ~ ~ ~ ~ ~ **NON-CHARTED ALBUM** ~ ~ ~ ~ ~ ~ ~ ~ ~ ~ ~

1960 **Woo-Hoo**

ROCKETS
Rock band from Detroit, Michigan: David Gilbert (vocals), Jim McCarty (guitar), Dennis Robbins (guitar), Donnie Backus (keyboards), Bobby Neil Haralson (bass) and John Badanjek (drums). McCarty and Badanjek were members of **Mitch Ryder & The Detroit Wheels**. Gilbert died of cancer on 8/1/2001 (age 49).

4/14/79	56	26		1 **Rockets**		RSO 3047
2/2/80	53	15		2 **No Ballads**		RSO 3071
8/8/81	165	5		3 **Back Talk**		Elektra 351

ROCKET SUMMER, The
Born Stephen Avery on 12/31/1982 in Colleyville, Texas. Pop-rock singer/songwriter.

8/4/07	44	5		1 **Do You Feel**		Militia Group 008808
11/14/09	114	1		2 **You Gotta Believe**	[EP]	Island digital

ROCKET TO THE MOON, A
Punk-pop band from Braintree, Massachusetts: Nick Santino (vocals, guitar), Justin Richards (guitar), Eric Halvorsen (bass) and Andrew Cook (drums).

10/31/09	82	1		1 **On Your Side**		Fueled By Ramen 520200

ROCKIN' REBELS
Instrumental band from Buffalo, New York: Lee Carroll (guitar), Eddy Jay (sax), Kenny Mills (bass) and Tony DiMaria (drums).

3/23/63	53	19		1 **Wild Weekend**	[I]	Swan 509

ROCKIN' SIDNEY
Born Sidney Semien on 4/9/1938 in Lebeau, Louisiana. Died of cancer on 2/25/1998 (age 59). Zydeco singer/musician.

8/24/85	166	4		1 **My Toot-Toot**	[EP]	Epic 40153
				Grammy: Folk Album		

ROCKO
Born Rodney Hill in 1979 in Atlanta, Georgia. Male rapper.

4/5/08	21	9		1 **Self-Made**	Rocky Road 010773

ROCKPILE
Rock and roll band formed in London, England: **Dave Edmunds** (vocals, guitar), **Nick Lowe** (vocals, bass), Billy Bremner (guitar) and Terry Williams (drums).

11/15/80	27	19		1 **Seconds Of Pleasure**	Columbia 36886

ROCK STAR SUPERNOVA
Hard-rock band formed on the same-named TV reality series: Lukas Rossi (vocals), Gilby Clarke (guitar; **Guns N' Roses**), Jason Newsted (bass; **Metallica**) and Tommy Lee (drums; **Motley Crue**).

12/9/06	101	1		1 **Rock Star Supernova**	Burnett 88414

ROCKWELL
Born Kennedy Gordy on 3/15/1964 in Detroit, Michigan. R&B singer. Son of Motown chairman Berry Gordy.

2/11/84	15	30	●	1 **Somebody's Watching Me**	Motown 6052
2/23/85	120	9		2 **Captured**	Motown 6122

ROCKY FELLERS, The
Rock and roll family band from Manila, Philippines: father Doroteo "Moro" Maligmat, with his sons Eddie, Albert, Tony and Junior Maligmat. Tony died on 3/4/2007 (age 62).

~ ~ ~ ~ ~ ~ ~ ~ ~ **NON-CHARTED ALBUM** ~ ~ ~ ~ ~ ~ ~ ~ ~ ~ ~
1963 **Killer Joe**

RODGERS, Jimmie
Born on 9/18/1933 in Camas, Washington. Pop-folk singer/guitarist. Hosted own TV variety series in 1959. Career hampered following mysterious assault on the San Diego Freeway on 12/1/1967, which left him with a fractured skull. Returned to performing a year later. Starred in movies *The Little Shepherd of Kingdom Come* and *Back Door To Hell*. Not to be confused with the country music pioneer of the same name.

12/16/57	15	3		1 **Jimmie Rodgers**	Roulette 25020
7/30/66	145	4		2 **It's Over**	Dot 25717
1/6/68	162	4		3 **Child Of Clay**	A&M 4130
8/30/69	183	4		4 **Windmills Of Your Mind**	A&M 4187

~ ~ ~ ~ ~ ~ ~ ~ ~ **NON-CHARTED ALBUMS** ~ ~ ~ ~ ~ ~ ~ ~ ~ ~ ~
1958 **The Number One Ballads**   1959 **His Golden Year**
1958 **Jimmie Rodgers Sings Folk Songs**   1959 **It's Christmas Once Again**

RODGERS, Nile
Born on 9/19/1952 in Brooklyn, New York. R&B guitarist/producer. Member of **Chic** and **The Honeydrippers**.

4/16/83	202	4		1 **Adventures In The Land Of The Good Groove**	Mirage 90073
6/22/85	206	3		2 **B-Movie Matinee**	Warner 25290

RODGERS, Paul
Born on 12/17/1949 in Middlesbrough, Cleveland, England. Lead singer of **Free** (1969-73), **Bad Company** (1974-82), **The Firm** (1984-86) and **The Law** (1991). Joined **Queen** for a 2005 album and concert tour.

11/26/83+	135	10		1 **Cut Loose**	Atlantic 80121
5/8/93	91	7		2 **Muddy Water Blues - A Tribute To Muddy Waters**	Victory 480013
10/1/05	84	1		3 **Return Of The Champions** .... [L]	Hollywood 162526 [2]
11/15/08	47	2		4 **The Cosmos Rocks**	Hollywood 002615
9/19/09	111	1		5 **Live In Ukraine** .... [L]	Hollywood 004534 [2]

     QUEEN & PAUL RODGERS (above 3)

RODNEY O & JOE COOLEY
Rap trio from Los Angeles, California: Rodney Oliver, Joe Cooley and Jeff Page.

3/4/89	187	2		1 **Me And Joe**	Egyptian Empire 00777
3/31/90	128	9		2 **Three The Hard Way**	Atlantic 82082

RODRIGO Y GABRIELA
Acoustic guitar duo from Mexico: Rodrigo Sanchez and Gabriela Quintero.

2/3/07	98	9		1 **Rodrigo Y Gabriela** .... [I]	ATO 21557
11/15/08	192	1		2 **Live In Japan** .... [F-I]	ATO 21638
9/26/09	34	9		3 **11:11** .... [I]	Rubyworks 0080

RODRIGUEZ, Daniel
Born on 5/24/1964 in Brooklyn, New York. Operatic tenor. Former member of the New York City Police Department; was on duty during the 9/11 terrorist attacks. Known as "The Singing Policeman."

3/2/02	112	5		1 **The Spirit Of America**	Manhattan 37564

RODRIGUEZ, Johnny
Born Juan Rodriguez on 12/10/1951 in Sabinal, Texas. Country singer/songwriter/guitarist.

4/7/73	156	14		1 **Introducing Johnny Rodriguez**	Mercury 61378
10/27/73	174	4		2 **All I Ever Meant To Do Was Sing**	Mercury 686

RODRIGUEZ, Jose Luis
Born on 1/14/1943 in Caracas, Venezuela. Latin singer/songwriter/actor.

2/28/98	175	1	●	1 **Inolvidable** .... [F]	Sony 82635

Billboard DEBUT	PEAK	WKS	R I A A	ARTIST / Album Title	Catalog	Label & Number

ROE, Tommy
Born on 5/9/1942 in Atlanta, Georgia. Pop-rock singer/songwriter/guitarist.

11/10/62	110	3		1 Sheila		ABC-Paramount 432
11/5/66+	94	13		2 Sweet Pea		ABC-Paramount 575
4/22/67	159	3		3 It's Now Winters Day		ABC 594
4/12/69	25	18		4 Dizzy		ABC 683
12/27/69+	21	29		5 12 In A Roe/A Collection Of Tommy Roe's Greatest Hits [G]		ABC 700
10/31/70	134	6		6 We Can Make Music		ABC 714
11/6/71	202	3		7 Beginnings		ABC 732

~ ~ ~ ~ ~ ~ ~ ~ ~ **NON-CHARTED ALBUMS** ~ ~ ~ ~ ~ ~ ~ ~ ~ ~
1964 **Something For Everybody**   1967 **Phantasy**

ROGER
Born Roger Troutman on 11/29/1951 in Hamilton, Ohio. Shot to death by his brother Larry in a murder-suicide on 4/25/1999 (age 47). R&B singer/songwriter/guitarist. Leader of the family funk group **Zapp**.

10/3/81	26	25	●	1 The Many Facets Of Roger		Warner 3594
6/2/84	64	14		2 The Saga Continues...		Warner 23975
11/28/87+	35	24	●	3 Unlimited!		Reprise 25496
11/13/93	39	29	▲	4 All The Greatest Hits Cat:#26/1 [G]		Reprise 45143
				ZAPP & ROGER		

ROGERS, D.J.
Born DeWayne Julius Rogers in Los Angeles, California. R&B singer/songwriter/keyboardist.

9/18/76	175	5		1 On The Road Again		RCA Victor 1697

ROGERS, Eric, & His Orchestra
Born Eric Gaukroger on 9/25/1921 in Halifax, Yorkshire, England. Died on 4/8/1981 (age 59). Conductor/arranger.

12/4/61	37	8		1 The Percussive Twenties [I]		London Phase 4 44006
11/12/66	114	3		2 Vaudeville!		London Phase 4 44083

ROGERS, Kenny / The First Edition   1980s: #3 / All-Time: #33
Born on 8/21/1938 in Houston, Texas. Country singer/songwriter/guitarist/actor. Member of **The New Christy Minstrels**. Formed and fronted **The First Edition** in 1967. Original lineup included Thelma Camacho, Mike Settle, Terry Williams and Mickey Jones. All but Jones were members of The New Christy Minstrels. Group hosted own syndicated TV variety show *Rollin* in 1972. Rogers split from group in 1973. Starred in movie *Six Pack* and several TV movies. Married to actress Marianne Gordon from 1977-93. Later started the Kenny Rogers Roasters restaurant chain.
    AWARD: CMA: Vocal Duo (w/ Dottie West) 1978 & 1979 / Male Vocalist 1979

1/13/68	118	15		1 The First Edition		Reprise 6276
3/22/69	164	4		2 The First Edition 69		Reprise 6328
				THE FIRST EDITION (above 2)		
10/11/69	48	18		3 Ruby, Don't Take Your Love To Town		Reprise 6352
4/18/70	26	24		4 Something's Burning		Reprise 6385
10/31/70	61	16		5 Tell It All Brother		Reprise 6412
9/25/71	155	3		6 Transition		Reprise 2039
2/5/72	118	14		7 The Ballad Of Calico		Reprise 6476 [2]
				KENNY ROGERS & THE FIRST EDITION (above 5)		
5/7/77	30	25	▲	8 Kenny Rogers		United Artists 689
8/20/77	39	21	▲	9 Daytime Friends		United Artists 754
1/5/80	186	3	●	10 Every Time Two Fools Collide		United Artists 864
				KENNY ROGERS & DOTTIE WEST		
7/29/78	53	12	●	11 Love Or Something Like It		United Artists 903
12/16/78+	12	112	▲5	12 The Gambler		United Artists 934
				CMA: Album of the Year		
4/14/79	82	23	▲	13 Classics		United Artists 946
				KENNY ROGERS & DOTTIE WEST		
9/29/79+	5	53	▲3	14 Kenny		United Artists 979
4/12/80	12	34	▲	15 Gideon		United Artists 1035
7/11/81	6	50	▲	16 Share Your Love		Liberty 1108
				produced by Lionel Richie		
7/24/82	34	24	▲	17 Love Will Turn You Around		Liberty 51124
3/12/83	18	27	▲	18 We've Got Tonight		Liberty 51143
4/20/85	145	7	●	19 Love Is What We Make It		Liberty 51157
9/24/83	6	38	▲2	20 Eyes That See In The Dark		RCA Victor 4697
				produced by Barry Gibb		
9/22/84	31	31	▲	21 What About Me?		RCA Victor 5043
10/19/85	51	28		22 The Heart Of The Matter		RCA Victor 7023
12/13/86+	137	15		23 They Don't Make Them Like They Used To		RCA Victor 5633
9/26/87	163	4		24 I Prefer The Moonlight		RCA Victor 6484
5/27/89	141	8	●	25 Something Inside So Strong		Reprise 25792
8/9/97	193	1		26 Across My Heart		Magnatone 116
2/6/99+	119	6		27 With Love Cat:#15/8		Madacy 0371
5/29/99	60	56	▲	28 She Rides Wild Horses		Dreamcatcher 004

Billboard			R I A A	ARTIST		
DEBUT	PEAK	WKS		Album Title	Catalog	Label & Number

ROGERS, Kenny — cont'd

10/21/00	121	3		29 There You Go Again...		Dreamcatcher 006
4/8/06	14	15		30 Water & Bridges		Capitol 63614

CHRISTMAS ALBUMS:

11/21/81+	34	9	▲²	31 Christmas..		Liberty 51115
				Christmas charts: 1/'83, 3/'84, 27/'88		
12/25/82+	149	4		32 Christmas... [R]		Liberty 51115
12/8/84+	31	8	▲²	33 Once Upon A Christmas... Cat:#15/13		RCA Victor 5307
				KENNY ROGERS & DOLLY PARTON		
				Christmas charts: 1/'84, 4/'85, 10/'87, 16/'88, 15/'89, 14/'90, 14/'91, 19/'92, 25/'93		
12/16/89+	119	6	●	34 Christmas In America		Reprise 25973
				Christmas charts: 12/'89, 28/'91		
12/14/96	63	5	●	35 The Gift .... Cat:#14/6		Magnatone 108
				Christmas charts: 9/'96, 17/'97		
12/19/98	164	3		36 Christmas From The Heart.. Cat:#30/1		Dreamcatcher 001
				Christmas charts: 28/'98, 16/'99, 31/'00		

GREATEST HITS & COMPILATIONS:

2/20/71	57	16	▲	37 Greatest Hits		Reprise 6437
2/4/78	33	103	▲⁴	38 Ten Years Of Gold		United Artists 835
10/18/80	❶²	181	▲¹²	39 Kenny Rogers' Greatest Hits		Liberty 1072
11/12/83+	22	30	▲⁴	40 Twenty Greatest Hits .... Cat:#31/2		Liberty 51152
5/5/84	85	11	▲	41 Duets		Liberty 51154
6/19/04	39	7	●	42 42 Ultimate Hits		Capitol 98794 [2]
2/11/06	14	27	●	43 21 Number Ones		Capitol 40469
6/30/07	180	1		44 Kenny Rogers		Madacy 52554 [3]

ROGERS, Randy, Band

Born in Cleburne, Texas. Male singer/songwriter/guitarist. His band: Geoffrey Hill (guitar), Brady Black (fiddle), Jon Richardson (bass) and Les Lawless (drums).

9/30/06	61	1		1 Just A Matter Of Time		Mercury 007003
10/11/08	29	3		2 Randy Rogers Band		Mercury 011419

ROGERS, Roy

Born Leonard Franklin Slye on 11/5/1911 in Cincinnati, Ohio. Died of heart failure on 7/6/1998 (age 86). Popular "singing cowboy" who starred in several movies. Original member of the famous western group Sons Of The Pioneers. Starred in close to 100 movie Westerns, then in a popular radio and TV series with his wife, Dale Evans.

AWARD: C&W Hall of Fame: 1988

12/23/67	92ˣ	2		1 Christmas Is Always .... [X]		Capitol 2818
				ROY ROGERS & DALE EVANS		
11/9/91	113	9		2 Roy Rogers Tribute		RCA 3024

ROLLING STONES, The   1960s: #22 / 1970s: #8 / 1980s: #12 / All-Time: #5

Blues-influenced rock band formed in London, England: Mick Jagger (vocals; born on 7/26/1943), Keith Richards (lead guitar; born on 12/18/1943) and Brian Jones (guitar; born on 2/28/1942; drowned on 7/3/1969, age 27), Bill Wyman (bass; born on 10/24/1936) and Charlie Watts (drums; born on 6/2/1941). Group took name from a **Muddy Waters** song. Promoted as the bad boys in contrast to **The Beatles**. Mick Taylor (born on 1/17/1949) replaced Jones in 1969. Ronnie Wood (born on 6/1/1947) replaced Taylor in 1975. Movie *Gimme Shelter* is a documentary of the group's performance at the 1969 Altamont concert. Wyman left group in late 1992. Bassist Darryl Jones (born on 12/11/1961; billed as a "side musician") joined in 1994. Considered by many as the world's all-time greatest rock and roll band.

AWARDS: Grammy: Lifetime Achievement 1986 ★ R&R Hall of Fame: 1989

6/27/64	11	35	●	1 England's Newest Hit Makers/The Rolling Stones		London 375
11/14/64	3⁴	38	●	2 12 x 5		London 402
3/20/65	5	53	●	3 The Rolling Stones, Now!		London 420
				RS500 #181		
8/7/65	❶³	66	▲	4 Out Of Our Heads		London 429
				RS500 #114		
12/11/65+	4	33	●	5 December's Children (And Everybody's)		London 451
7/9/66	2²	50	▲	6 Aftermath		London 476
				RS500 #108		
2/18/67	2⁴	47	●	7 Between The Buttons		London 499
				RS500 #355		
12/23/67+	2⁶	30	●	8 Their Satanic Majesties Request		London 2
12/14/68+	5	32	▲	9 Beggars Banquet Cat:#19/2		London 33
				Grammy: Hall of Fame ★ RS500 #57		
12/6/69	3²	44	▲²	10 Let It Bleed Cat:#11/3		London 4
				Grammy: Hall of Fame ★ RS500 #32		
5/15/71	❶⁴	62	▲³	11 Sticky Fingers Cat:#14/12		Rolling Stones 59100
				Grammy: Hall of Fame ★ RS500 #63		
6/10/72	❶⁴	43	▲	12 Exile On Main St. Cat:#16/9		Rolling Stones 2900 [2]
				RS500 #7		
9/29/73	❶⁴	37	▲³	13 Goats Head Soup		Rolling Stones 59101
11/2/74	❶¹	20	▲	14 It's Only Rock 'N Roll		Rolling Stones 79101
5/8/76	❶⁴	24	▲	15 Black And Blue		Rolling Stones 79104

DEBUT	PEAK	WKS	RIAA		Album Title	Catalog	Label & Number
					ROLLING STONES, The — cont'd		
6/24/78	**❶**²	82	▲⁶	16	Some Girls	Cat:#29/11	Rolling Stones 39108
					RS500 #269		
7/19/80	**❶**⁷	51	▲²	17	Emotional Rescue		Rolling Stones 16015
9/12/81	**❶**⁹	58	▲⁴	18	Tattoo You		Rolling Stones 16052
					RS500 #211		
11/26/83	4	23	▲	19	Undercover		Rolling Stones 90120
4/12/86	4	25	▲	20	Dirty Work		Rolling Stones 40250
9/16/89	3⁴	36	▲²	21	Steel Wheels		Rolling Stones 45333
7/30/94	2¹	38	▲²	22	Voodoo Lounge		Virgin 39782
					Grammy: Rock Album		
10/18/97	3¹	27	▲	23	Bridges To Babylon		Virgin 44712
9/24/05	3¹	19	▲	24	A Bigger Bang		Virgin 30067
					GREATEST HITS & COMPILATIONS:		
4/16/66	3³	99	▲²	25	Big Hits (High Tide And Green Grass)		London 1
7/22/67	3⁶	35	●	26	Flowers		London 509
9/13/69	2²	32	●	27	Through The Past, Darkly (Big Hits Vol. 2)		London 3
1/8/72	4	243	▲¹²	28	Hot Rocks 1964-1971	Cat:#16/31	London 606/7 [2]
12/30/72+	9	29	●	29	More Hot Rocks (Big Hits & Fazed Cookies)		London 626/7 [2]
6/21/75	6	17	▲	30	Made In The Shade		Rolling Stones 79102
6/21/75	8	13		31	Metamorphosis	Cat:#50/1	Abkco 1
4/4/81	15	12	●	32	Sucking In The Seventies		Rolling Stones 16028
7/28/84	86	11	●	33	Rewind (1971-1984)		Rolling Stones 90176
9/9/89	91	22	▲	34	Singles Collection: The London Years		Abkco 1218 [4]
10/19/02	2¹	48	▲⁴	35	Forty Licks	Cat:#25/9	Abkco 13378 [2]
9/11/04	30	58	▲	36	The Best Of The Rolling Stones: Jump Back '71-'93	Cat:#34/10	Virgin 64682
12/10/05	76	6		37	Rarities 1971-2003		Virgin 45401
					LIVE ALBUMS:		
12/17/66+	6	48	●	38	Got Live If You Want It!		London 493
					recorded at the Royal Albert Hall in London, England		
10/17/70	6	23	▲	39	'Get Yer Ya-Ya's Out!'	Cat:#24/1	London 5
					recorded in November 1969 at Madison Square Garden		
10/8/77	5	17	●	40	Love You Live		Rolling Stones 9001 [2]
6/26/82	5	23	▲	41	"Still Life" (American Concert 1981)		Rolling Stones 39113
4/20/91	16	17	●	42	Flashpoint		Rolling Stones 47456
12/2/95	9	19	▲	43	Stripped		Virgin 41040
11/2/96	92	3		44	Rock And Roll Circus		Abkco 1268
					recorded in a North London TV studio on 12/10/1968 for a BBC-TV special that never aired		
11/21/98	34	8		45	No Security		Virgin 46740
11/20/04	50	2		46	Live Licks		Virgin 75177 [2]
4/19/08	11	7		47	Shine A Light	[S]	Rolling Stones 010960
					ROLLINS, Sonny		
					Born Theodore Rollins on 9/7/1930 in Harlem, New York. Black jazz tenor saxophonist.		
10/28/78	209	1		1	Don't Stop The Carnival	[I-L]	Milestone 55005 [2]

~ ~ ~ ~ ~ ~ ~ ~ ~ ~ ~ **NON-CHARTED ALBUM** ~ ~ ~ ~ ~ ~ ~ ~ ~ ~ ~
1956 **Saxophone Colossus**
Grammy: Hall of Fame

DEBUT	PEAK	WKS			Album Title		Label & Number
					ROLLINS BAND		
					*Born Henry Garfield on 2/13/1961 in Washington DC. Rock singer/poet/actor. Acted in several movies. Leader of the hardcore punk band **Black Flag**. His band: Chris Haskett (guitar), Andrew Weiss (bass) and Sim Cain (drums). Melvin Gibbs replaced Weiss in 1993. New band in 1999: Jim Wilson (guitar), Marcus Blake (bass) and Jason MacKenroth (drums).*		
4/25/92	160	4		1	The End Of Silence		Imago 21006
4/30/94	33	23		2	Weight		Imago 21034
4/12/97	89	5		3	Come In And Burn		DreamWorks 50007
3/18/00	180	1		4	Get Some - Go Again		DreamWorks 50216
9/8/01	178	1		5	Nice		Sanctuary 84512
					ROMAN HOLLIDAY		
					Pop-rock band formed in Harlow, England: Steve Lambert (vocals), Brian Bonhomme (guitar), Adrian York (keyboards), John Eacott (trumpet), Rob Lambert (sax), Jon Durno (bass) and Simon Cohen (drums). Group named after the 1953 movie starring Audrey Hepburn.		
9/3/83	142	11		1	Roman Holliday	[EP]	Jive 8086
10/22/83	116	6		2	Cookin' On The Roof		Jive 8101
3/2/85	201	4		3	Fire Me Up		Jive 8252

ROMANTICS, The
Pop-rock band from Detroit, Michigan: Wally Palmar (vocals, guitar), Coz Canler (guitar), Mike Skill (bass) and Jimmy Marinos (drums). David Petratos replaced Marinos in early 1985.

2/2/80	61	15		1 The Romantics		Nemperor 36273
12/6/80	176	7		2 National Breakout		Nemperor 36881
11/14/81	182	2		3 Strictly Personal		Nemperor 37435
10/22/83+	14	36	●	4 In Heat		Nemperor 38880
9/21/85	72	11		5 Rhythm Romance		Nemperor 40106

ROME
Born Jerome Woods on 3/5/1970 in Benton Harbor, Michigan. Male R&B singer.

5/3/97	30	30	●	1 Rome		RCA 67441

ROMEO'S DAUGHTER
Rock trio from England: Leigh Matty (vocals), Craig Joiner (guitars, vocals) and Tony Mitman (keyboards).

11/19/88	191	2		1 Romeo's Daughter		Jive 1135

ROMEO VOID
Pop-rock-dance band from San Francisco, California: Debora Iyall (vocals), Peter Woods (guitar), Ben Bossi (sax), Frank Zincavage (bass) and Aaron Smith (drums).

3/6/82	147	6		1 Never Say Never .... [EP]		415 Records 0007
9/4/82	119	13		2 Benefactor		Columbia 38182
8/25/84	68	19		3 Instincts		Columbia 39155

RON "C"
Born Ron Carey in Oakland, California. Male rapper. Member of **Nemesis**.

5/19/90	170	7		1 "C" Ya		Profile 1284
7/25/92	183	3		2 Back On The Street		Profile 1431

RONETTES, The
Black "girl group" from New York: sisters Veronica "Ronnie Spector" Bennett and Estelle Bennett Vann, with cousin Nedra Talley Ross. Veronica was married to **Phil Spector** from 1968-74. Estelle Bennett died on 2/11/2009 (age 67).
AWARD: R&R Hall of Fame: 2007

12/26/64+	96	8		1 ...Presenting The Fabulous Ronettes Featuring Veronica		Philles 4006
				RS500 #427		

~ ~ ~ ~ ~ ~ ~ ~ ~ ~ **NON-CHARTED ALBUM** ~ ~ ~ ~ ~ ~ ~ ~ ~ ~
1965 **The Ronettes Featuring Veronica**

RONNY & THE DAYTONAS
Pop-rock band formed in Tulsa, Oklahoma: Ronny Dayton (vocals), Jimmy Johnson (guitar), Van Evans (bass) and Lynn Williams (drums).

12/5/64	122	6		1 G.T.O.		Mala 4001

~ ~ ~ ~ ~ ~ ~ ~ ~ ~ **NON-CHARTED ALBUM** ~ ~ ~ ~ ~ ~ ~ ~ ~ ~
1966 **Sandy**

RONSON, Mark
Born on 9/4/1975 in London, England; raised in New York. White DJ/producer/remixer.

7/28/07	129	1		1 Version		Allido 10031

RONSON, Mick
Born on 5/26/1946 in Hull, Yorkshire, England. Died of cancer on 4/29/1993 (age 46). Rock singer/guitarist. Member of **David Bowie**'s band from 1969-73 and **Mott The Hoople** in late 1974.

4/6/74	156	5		1 Slaughter On 10th Avenue		RCA Victor 0353
2/8/75	103	9		2 Play Don't Worry		RCA Victor 0681
10/28/89+	157	20		3 Y U I ORTA		Mercury 838973
				IAN HUNTER & MICK RONSON		

RONSTADT, Linda   1970s: #48 / 1980s: #26 / All-Time: #54
Born on 7/15/1946 in Tucson, Arizona. Pop-rock singer. Formed **The Stone Poneys** with Bobby Kimmel (guitar) and Ken Edwards (keyboards). Went solo in 1968. In 1971 formed backing band with **Glenn Frey**, **Don Henley**, **Randy Meisner** and **Bernie Leadon** (later became the **Eagles**). Appeared in the 1978 movie FM. Acted in the Broadway and movie versions of The Pirates of Penzance.

12/2/67+	100	15		1 Evergreen, Vol. 2		Capitol 2763
				THE STONE PONEYS		
10/24/70	103	10		2 Silk Purse		Capitol 407
2/12/72	163	10		3 Linda Ronstadt		Capitol 635
12/7/74+	❶[1]	51	▲[2]	4 Heart Like A Wheel		Capitol 11358
				RS500 #164		
6/14/75	172	4		5 The Stone Poneys Featuring Linda Ronstadt .... [E]		Capitol 11383
				first released in 1967 as The Stone Poneys on Capitol 2666		
10/20/73+	45	56	●	6 Don't Cry Now		Asylum 5064
10/4/75	4	28	▲	7 Prisoner In Disguise		Asylum 1045

DEBUT	PEAK	WKS	RIAA		Catalog	Label & Number
				RONSTADT, Linda — cont'd		
8/28/76	3³	36	▲	8 Hasten Down The Wind		Asylum 1072
				Grammy: Female Pop Vocal		
9/24/77	❶⁵	47	▲³	9 Simple Dreams		Asylum 104
10/7/78	❶¹	32	▲²	10 Living In The USA		Asylum 155
3/15/80	3⁴	36	▲	11 Mad Love		Asylum 510
10/16/82	31	28	●	12 Get Closer		Asylum 60185
10/1/83	3⁵	81	▲³	13 What's New		Asylum 60260
12/8/84+	13	26	▲	14 Lush Life		Asylum 60387
10/11/86	46	27	▲	15 For Sentimental Reasons		Asylum 60474
10/11/86	124	17	●	16 'Round Midnight		Asylum 60489 [3]
				deluxe set of albums #17-19; above 4 arranged and conducted by **Nelson Riddle**		
3/28/87	6	48	▲	17 Trio		Warner 25491
				DOLLY PARTON, LINDA RONSTADT, EMMYLOU HARRIS		
				Grammy: Group Country Vocal / Country Vocal Collaboration		
10/21/89+	7	58	▲³	18 Cry Like A Rainstorm - Howl Like The Wind	Cat:#37/6	Elektra 60872
				LINDA RONSTADT Featuring Aaron Neville		
12/11/93	92	12		19 Winter Light		Elektra 61545
4/1/95	75	12		20 Feels Like Home		Elektra 61703
6/29/96	78	11		21 Dedicated To The One I Love		Elektra 61916
				Grammy: Children's Album		
7/11/98	160	2		22 We Ran		Elektra 62206
2/27/99	62	14	●	23 Trio II		Asylum 62275
				EMMYLOU HARRIS, LINDA RONSTADT, DOLLY PARTON		
9/11/99	73	7		24 Western Wall: The Tucson Sessions		Asylum 62408
				LINDA RONSTADT & EMMYLOU HARRIS		
12/23/00	179	2		25 A Merry Little Christmas	[X]	Elektra 62572
11/27/04	166	1		26 Hummin' To Myself		Verve 000887
8/12/06	146	2		27 Adieu False Heart		Vanguard 79808
				LINDA RONSTADT & ANN SAVOY		
				FOREIGN LANGUAGE ALBUMS:		
12/12/87+	42	35	▲²	28 Canciones De Mi Padre		Elektra 60765
				Grammy: Mexican-American Album		
12/7/91+	88	13		29 Mas Canciones		Elektra 61239
				Grammy: Mexican-American Album		
10/3/92	193	1		30 Frenesi		Elektra 61383
				Grammy: Tropical Latin Album		
				GREATEST HITS & COMPILATIONS:		
2/2/74	92	15		31 Different Drum		Capitol 11269
12/18/76+	6	80	▲⁷	32 Greatest Hits	Cat:#16/23	Asylum 1092
5/21/77	46	9	●	33 A Retrospective		Capitol 11629 [2]
11/8/80	26	21	▲	34 Greatest Hits, Volume Two		Asylum 516
10/12/02	165	3		35 The Very Best Of Linda Ronstadt		Elektra 76019
				RS500 #324		

ROOFTOP SINGERS, The
Folk trio from New York: Erik Darling, Willard Svanoe and Lynne Taylor. Taylor died in 1982 (age 54). Darling died on 8/2/2008 (age 74).

DEBUT	PEAK	WKS	RIAA		Catalog	Label & Number
2/16/63	15	20		1 Walk Right In!		Vanguard 9123

ROONEY
Pop-rock band from Los Angeles, California: Robert Carmine (vocals, guitar), Taylor Locke (guitar), Louie Stephens (keyboards), Matt Winter (bass) and Ned Brower (drums).

DEBUT	PEAK	WKS	RIAA		Catalog	Label & Number
6/7/03+	125	31		1 Rooney		Geffen 000242
8/4/07	42	5		2 Calling The World		Cherrytree 008806

ROOTS, The
Hip-hop band from Philadelphia, Pennsylvania: Tariq "Black Thought" Trotter (vocals), "Malik B" Abdul-Basit (rapper), Leonard "Hub" Hubbard (bass) and Ahmir-Khalib "?uestlove" Thompson (drums).

DEBUT	PEAK	WKS	RIAA		Catalog	Label & Number
2/4/95	104	10		1 Do You Want More?!!!??!		DGC 24708
10/12/96	21	16		2 Illadelph Halflife		DGC 24972
3/13/99	4	18	●	3 Things Fall Apart		MCA 11948
11/20/99	50	3		4 The Roots Come Alive	[L]	MCA 112059
12/14/02	28	38	●	5 Phrenology		MCA 112996
7/31/04	4	13		6 The Tipping Point		Geffen 002573
12/3/05	161	1		7 Home Grown! The Beginner's Guide To Understanding The Roots Volume One	[K]	Geffen 005673
12/3/05	187	1		8 Home Grown! The Beginner's Guide To Understanding The Roots Volume Two	[K]	Geffen 005672
9/16/06	9	7		9 Game Theory		Def Jam 007222
5/17/08	6	9		10 Rising Down		Def Jam 011138

Billboard			R I A A	ARTIST		
DEBUT	**PEAK**	**WKS**		**Album Title**	**Catalog**	**Label & Number**

ROS, Edmundo
Born on 12/7/1910 in Trinidad; later based in London, England. Bandleader/drummer.

5/25/59	28	2		1 Hollywood Cha Cha Cha	[I]	London 152
12/4/61	41	4		2 Bongos From The South	[I]	London Phase 4 44003
9/22/62	31	6		3 Dance Again	[I]	London Phase 4 44015

ROSA, Robi Draco
Born on 6/27/1969 in Long Island, New York. Male Latin singer/songwriter.

| 4/17/04 | 119 | 1 | | 1 Mad Love | | Columbia 86925 |

ROSCOE
Born Cary Brown in 1983 in Philadelphia, Pennsylvania; raised in Hawthorne, California. Male rapper. Younger brother of **Kurupt** (of Tha Dogg Pound).

| 6/28/03 | 148 | 2 | | 1 Young Roscoe Philaphornia | | Priority 28291 |

ROSE, Biff
Born Paul Rose in New Orleans, Louisiana. Singer/songwriter/pianist.

| 2/8/69 | 75 | 14 | | 1 The Thorn In Mrs. Rose's Side | | Tetragrammaton 103 |
| 7/12/69 | 181 | 7 | | 2 Children Of Light | | Tetragrammaton 116 |

ROSE, David, and His Orchestra
Born on 6/15/1910 in London, England; raised in Chicago, Illinois. Died of heart failure on 8/23/1990 (age 80). Conductor/composer/arranger. Married to Martha Raye (1938-41) and **Judy Garland** (1941-45).

| 6/30/62 | 3⁶ | 50 | ● | 1 The Stripper And Other Fun Songs For The Family | [I] | MGM 4062 |

ROSE, Tim
Born on 9/23/1940 in Washington DC. Died on 9/24/2002 (age 62). Singer/songwriter.

| 4/29/72 | 211 | 2 | | 1 Tim Rose | | Playboy 101 |

ROSE GARDEN, The
Pop band formed in Los Angeles, California: Diana Di Rose (vocals), John Noreen (guitar), James Groshong (guitar), William Fleming (bass, piano) and Bruce Boudin (drums).

| 3/16/68 | 176 | 2 | | 1 The Rose Garden | | Atco 225 |

ROSELLI, Jimmy
Born on 12/26/1925 in Hoboken, New Jersey. Male singer.

6/26/65	96	11		1 Life & Love Italian Style	[F]	United Artists 6429
9/11/65	145	2		2 The Great Ones!		United Artists 6438
12/24/66	66ˣ	4		3 The Christmas Album	[X]	United Artists 6538
				Christmas charts: 66/'66, 83/'67		
11/18/67	191	3		4 There Must Be A Way		United Artists 6611
6/21/69	184	3		5 Core Spezzato	[F]	United Artists 6698

ROSE ROYCE
R&B-dance band from Los Angeles, California: Gwen "Rose" Dickey (vocals), Kenji Brown (guitar), Victor Nix (keyboards), Ken Copeland, Fred Dunn and Mike Moore (horns), Terral Santiel (percussion), Lequient Jobe (bass) and Henry Garner (drums).

10/9/76+	14	40	●	1 Car Wash	[S]	MCA 6000 [2]
				Grammy: Soundtrack Album		
8/27/77	9	33	▲	2 Rose Royce II/In Full Bloom		Whitfield 3074
9/9/78	28	24	●	3 Rose Royce III/Strikes Again!		Whitfield 3227
9/8/79	74	8		4 Rose Royce IV/Rainbow Connection		Whitfield 3387
10/4/80	204	1		5 Greatest Hits	[G]	Whitfield 3457
1/24/81	160	7		6 Golden Touch		Whitfield 3512
10/3/81	210	1		7 Jump Street		Whitfield 3620
6/5/82	210	1		8 Stronger Than Ever		Epic 37939

ROSE TATTOO
Hard-rock band from Australia: Gary "Angry" Anderson (vocals), Peter Wells (guitar), Michael Cocks (guitar), Geordie Leech (bass) and Dallas Royall (drums). Wells died of prostate cancer on 3/27/2006. Cocks died of liver cancer on 12/22/2009.

| 11/29/80 | 197 | 3 | | 1 Rock 'N' Roll Outlaw | | Mirage 19280 |
| 1/8/83 | 208 | 1 | | 2 Scarred For Life | | Mirage 90022 |

ROSIE And The Originals
White pop band from San Diego, California. Rosie was born Rosalie Hamlin on 7/21/1945 in Klamath Falls, Oregon; raised in Anchorage, Alaska. The Originals: David Ponci and Noah Tafolla (guitars), Tony Gomez (sax) and Carl Von Goodat (drums).

~ ~ ~ ~ ~ ~ ~ ~ ~ ~ ***NON-CHARTED ALBUM*** ~ ~ ~ ~ ~ ~ ~ ~ ~ ~ ~ ~
1961 **Lonely Blue Nights With Rosie**

ROSS, Diana   1970s: #24 / 1980s: #19 / All-Time: #58

Born Diane Ernestine Ross on 3/26/1944 in Detroit, Michigan. R&B singer/actress. Lead singer of **The Supremes** from 1961-69. Starred in the movies *Lady Sings The Blues*, *Mahogany* and *The Wiz*. Own Broadway show *An Evening With Diana Ross* in 1976. Married to Norwegian shipping magnate Arne Naess from 1986-2000.

DEBUT	PEAK	WKS			Album Title	Catalog	Label & Number
7/11/70	19	28		1	Diana Ross		Motown 711
11/21/70	42	16		2	Everything Is Everything		Motown 724
4/24/71	46	15		3	Diana!	[TV]	Motown 719
8/7/71	56	17		4	Surrender		Motown 723
11/25/72+	❶²	54		5	Lady Sings The Blues	[S]	Motown 758 [2]
7/14/73	5	28		6	Touch Me In The Morning		Motown 772
11/17/73	26	47		7	Diana & Marvin		Motown 803
					DIANA ROSS & MARVIN GAYE		
12/29/73+	52	17		8	Last Time I Saw Him		Motown 812
6/15/74	64	17		9	Diana Ross Live At Caesars Palace	[L]	Motown 801
3/6/76	5	32		10	Diana Ross		Motown 861
2/12/77	29	14		11	An Evening With Diana Ross	[L]	Motown 877 [2]
					recorded at the Ahmanson Theatre in Los Angeles, California		
10/8/77	18	19		12	Baby It's Me		Motown 890
10/21/78	49	17		13	Ross		Motown 907
6/16/79	14	37	●	14	The Boss		Motown 923
6/14/80	2²	52	▲	15	Diana		Motown 936
11/7/81	15	33	▲	16	Why Do Fools Fall In Love		RCA Victor 4153
10/23/82	27	24	●	17	Silk Electric		RCA Victor 4384
7/16/83	32	17		18	Ross		RCA Victor 4677
9/29/84	26	45	●	19	Swept Away		RCA Victor 5009
10/12/85	45	20		20	Eaten Alive		RCA Victor 5422
5/30/87	73	14		21	Red Hot Rhythm & Blues		RCA Victor 6388
6/24/89	116	6		22	Workin' Overtime		Motown 6274
9/28/91	102	3		23	The Force Behind The Power		Motown 6316
12/18/93	154	3		24	Christmas In Vienna	[X-L]	Sony Classical 53358
					PLACIDO DOMINGO / DIANA ROSS / JOSE CARRERAS		
					recorded on 12/23/1992 at the Rathaus in Vienna, Austria		
10/14/95	114	2		25	Take Me Higher		Motown 0586
5/22/99	108	4		26	Every Day Is A New Day		Motown 549522
7/8/06	146	1		27	Blue	[E]	Motown 005694
					recorded in 1972		
2/3/07	32	7		28	I Love You		Manhattan 82652
					GREATEST HITS & COMPILATIONS:		
8/7/76	13	23		29	Diana Ross' Greatest Hits		Motown 869
3/14/81	32	14		30	To Love Again		Motown 951
10/24/81	37	32	●	31	All The Great Hits		Motown 960 [2]
6/11/83	63	12		32	Diana Ross Anthology		Motown 6049 [2]
2/21/04	72	5		33	The No. 1's	Cat:#48/1	Motown 001368
					DIANA ROSS & THE SUPREMES		

ROSS, Rick

Born William Roberts on 1/28/1976 in Coahoma County, Mississippi; raised in Miami, Florida. Male rapper/songwriter. Member of **Triple C's**.

DEBUT	PEAK	WKS			Album Title	Label & Number
8/26/06	❶¹	25	●	1	Port Of Miami	Slip-N-Slide 006984
10/6/07	62	2		2	Rise To Power	Suave House II 70020
3/29/08	❶¹	29	●	3	Trilla	Slip-N-Slide 009536
5/9/09	❶¹	21		4	Deeper Than Rap	Maybach 012772

ROSSDALE, Gavin

Born on 10/30/1967 in London, England. Lead singer of **Bush** and **Institute**. Married **Gwen Stefani** (of **No Doubt**) on 9/14/2002.

DEBUT	PEAK	WKS		Album Title	Label & Number
6/21/08	33	10	1	Wanderlust	Interscope 010882

ROSSINGTON COLLINS BAND

Southern-rock band formed in Jacksonville, Florida: Dale Krantz (vocals), Gary Rossington, Allen Collins and Barry Harwood (guitars), Billy Powell (keyboards), Leon Wilkeson (bass) and Derek Hess (drums). Rossington, Collins, Powell and Wilkeson were members of **Lynyrd Skynyrd**. Disbanded in 1982. Rossington and wife Dale, Jay Johnson (guitar), Ronnie Eades (sax), Tim Sharpton (keyboards), Tim Lindsey (bass) and Mitch Rigel (drums) recorded as **The Rossington Band** in 1988. Collins died of pneumonia on 1/23/1990 (age 37). Wilkeson died on 7/27/2001 (age 49).

DEBUT	PEAK	WKS			Album Title	Label & Number
7/12/80	13	29	●	1	Anytime, Anyplace, Anywhere	MCA 5130
10/10/81	24	16		2	This Is The Way	MCA 5207
7/16/88	140	4		3	Love Your Man	MCA 42166
					THE ROSSINGTON BAND	

Billboard			R I A A	ARTIST		
DEBUT	PEAK	WKS		Album Title	Catalog	Label & Number

ROSSUM, Emmy
Born on 9/12/1986 in Manhattan, New York. Female singer/songwriter/actress. Acted in several movies.

| 11/17/07 | 199 | 1 | | 1 Inside Out.. | | Geffen 010157 |

ROTARY CONNECTION
Multi-racial rock/R&B band formed in Chicago, Illinois: **Minnie Riperton**, Judy Hauff and Sid Barnes (vocals), Bobby Simms (guitar), Charles Stepney (keyboards), Mitch Aliotta (bass) and Kenny Venegas (drums).

3/16/68	37	31		1 Rotary Connection		Cadet Concept 312
10/19/68	176	5		2 Aladdin		Cadet Concept 317
12/28/68+	24ˣ	2		3 Peace .... [X]		Cadet Concept 318
				Christmas charts: 34/'68, 24/'69		

ROTH, Asher
Born on 8/11/1985 in Morrisville, Pennsylvania. White male rapper.

| 5/9/09 | 5 | 12 | | 1 Asleep In The Bread Aisle | | SchoolBoy 012812 |

ROTH, David Lee
Born on 10/10/1954 in Bloomington, Indiana; raised in Pasadena, California. Lead singer of **Van Halen** from 1973-1985 (with brief reunions in 1996, 2000 and 2007). Began hosting own short-lived syndicated morning radio show in January 2006. Nicknamed "Diamond Dave."

2/23/85	15	33	▲	1 Crazy From The Heat .... [EP]		Warner 25222
7/26/86	4	36	▲	2 Eat 'Em And Smile		Warner 25470
2/13/88	6	27	▲	3 Skyscraper		Warner 25671
2/2/91	18	19	●	4 A Little Ain't Enough...		Warner 26477
3/26/94	78	2		5 Your Filthy Little Mouth		Reprise 45391
11/15/97	199	1		6 The Best .... [G]		Rhino 72941
6/27/98	172	1		7 DLR Band..		Wawazat 1217

ROTTIN RAZKALS
Rap trio from East Orange, New Jersey: Chap, Fam and Diesel.

| 4/8/95 | 190 | 1 | | 1 Rottin Ta Da Core .... | | Illtown 0461 |

ROUGH CUTT
Heavy-metal band from Los Angeles, California: Paul Shortino (vocals), Chris Hager and Amir Derakh (guitars), Matt Thorr (bass) and David Alford (drums).

| 3/16/85 | 210 | 1 | | 1 Rough Cutt .... | | Warner 25268 |

ROUGH DIAMOND
Hard-rock band from England: David Byron (vocals; **Uriah Heep**), Clem Clempson (guitar; **Humble Pie**), Damon Butcher (keyboards), Willie Bath (bass) and Geoff Britton (drums). Byron died on 2/28/1985 (age 38).

| 5/7/77 | 103 | 8 | | 1 Rough Diamond .... | | Island 9490 |

ROUGH TRADE
Rock band from Toronto, Ontario, Canada: Carole Pope (vocals), Kevan Staples (guitar), Dave McMorrow (keyboards), Terry Wilkins (bass) and Bucky Berger (drums).

| 2/5/83 | 206 | 7 | | 1 For Those Who Think Young .... | | Boardwalk 33261 |

ROUSSOS, Demis
Born on 6/15/1946 in Alexandria, Egypt (Greek parents). Male singer.

| 8/16/75 | 206 | 1 | | 1 Souvenirs.. | | Big Tree 89509 |
| 6/17/78 | 184 | 6 | | 2 Demis Roussos .... | | Mercury 3724 |

ROUTERS, The
Rock and roll instrumental band formed in Los Angeles, California: Mike Gordon (guitar), Al Kait (guitar), Lynn Frasier (horns), Scott Engel (bass) and Randy Viers (drums).

| 3/2/63 | 104 | 4 | | 1 Let's Go! With The Routers... [I] | | Warner 1490 |

ROVERS, The — see IRISH ROVERS, The

ROWANS, The
Pop trio from Boston, Massachusetts: brothers Peter (vocals, guitar), Lorin (guitar) and Chris (keyboards) Rowan. Peter was a member of **Seatrain**.

| 7/26/75 | 210 | 1 | | 1 The Rowans .... | | Asylum 1038 |

ROWLAND, Kelly
Born Kelendria Rowland on 2/11/1981 in Atlanta, Georgia; raised in Houston, Texas. Female R&B singer/actress. Member of **Destiny's Child**. Played "Kia Waterson" in the 2003 movie *Freddy vs. Jason*.

| 11/9/02 | 12 | 19 | ● | 1 Simply Deep.. | | Columbia 86516 |
| 7/21/07 | 6 | 11 | | 2 Ms. Kelly | | Music World 75588 |

ROWLES, John
Born on 3/26/1947 in Whakatane, New Zealand. Adult Contemporary singer/songwriter.

| 3/20/71 | 197 | 1 | | 1 Cheryl Moana Marie .... | | Kapp 3637 |

Billboard DEBUT	PEAK	WKS	R I A A	ARTIST / Album Title	Catalog	Label & Number

ROXETTE
Pop-rock duo from Sweden: Marie Fredriksson (born on 5/30/1958) and Per Gessle (born on 1/12/1959).

4/22/89+	23	71	▲	1 Look Sharp!		EMI 91098
4/20/91	12	56	▲	2 Joyride		EMI 94435
10/24/92	117	8		3 Tourism	[K]	EMI 99929

old and new tracks recorded live on stage or in studio or hotel rooms during their *Join The Joyride* world tour

ROXY MUSIC
Art-rock band formed in London, England: **Bryan Ferry** (vocals, keyboards), **Phil Manzanera** (guitar), Andy MacKay (horns) and Paul Thompson (drums).

7/28/73	193	2		1 For Your Pleasure		Warner 2696
				RS500 #394		
5/18/74	186	4		2 Stranded		Atco 7045
1/25/75	37	15		3 Country Life		Atco 106
				RS500 #387		
11/29/75+	50	20		4 Siren		Atco 127
				RS500 #371		
8/7/76	81	7		5 Viva! Roxy Music	[L]	Atco 139
1/21/78	206	2		6 Greatest Hits	[G]	Atco 103
3/31/79	23	16		7 Manifesto		Atco 114
6/28/80	35	19		8 Flesh + Blood		Atco 102
1/21/84	183	6		9 The Atlantic Years 1973-1980	[K]	Atco 90122
6/19/82	53	27	▲	10 Avalon		Warner 23686
				RS500 #307		
4/9/83	67	22		11 Musique/The High Road	[EP-L]	Warner 23808

recorded at the Apollo Theatre in Glasgow, Scotland

8/26/89	100	11		12 Street Life-20 Great Hits	[G]	Reprise 25857 [2]

BRYAN FERRY / ROXY MUSIC

ROYAL, Billy Joe
Born on 4/3/1942 in Valdosta, Georgia; raised in Marietta, Georgia. Country-pop singer/guitarist.

9/18/65	96	7		1 Down In The Boondocks		Columbia 9203
1/3/70	100	9		2 Cherry Hill Park		Columbia 9974

ROYAL BLISS
Hard-rock band from Salt Lake City, Utah: Neal Middleton (vocals), Taylor Richards (guitar), Chris Harding (guitar), Tommy Mortensen (bass) and Jake Smith (drums).

1/31/09	151	1		1 Life In-Between		Merovingian 10015

ROYAL CROWN REVUE
Swing band from Los Angeles, California: Eddie Nichols (vocals), James Anchor (guitar), Mando Dorame, Bill Ungerman, Scott Steen (horns), Veikko Lepisto (bass) and Daniel Glass (drums).

9/12/98	172	2		1 The Contender		Warner 47020

ROYAL GUARDSMEN, The
Novelty-pop band from Ocala, Florida: Barry Winslow (vocals, guitar), Chris Nunley (vocals), Tom Richards (guitar), Bill Balough (bass) and Billy Taylor (organ). "Snoopy" songs inspired by Snoopy the Beagle in the "Peanuts" comic strip.

2/11/67	44	22		1 Snoopy vs. The Red Baron	[N]	Laurie 2038
12/23/67+	46	11		2 Snoopy And His Friends	[X-N]	Laurie 2042

Christmas charts: 6/'67, 19/'68

8/31/68	189	2		3 Snoopy For President	[N]	Laurie 2046

~ ~ ~ ~ ~ ~ ~ ~ ~ ~ **NON-CHARTED ALBUM** ~ ~ ~ ~ ~ ~ ~ ~ ~ ~ ~
1967 **The Return Of The Red Baron**

ROYAL PHILHARMONIC ORCHESTRA
Orchestra based in London, England. Conducted by Louis Clark. Founded in 1946 by Sir Thomas Beecham.

3/15/75	203	4		1 The Orchestral Tubular Bells	[I]	Virgin 115

THE ROYAL PHILHARMONIC ORCHESTRA WITH MIKE OLDFIELD
conducted by David Bedford; no track titles listed on this album

11/14/81+	4	68	▲	2 Hooked On Classics	[I]	RCA Victor 4194
8/28/82	33	41	●	3 Hooked On Classics II (Can't Stop The Classics)	[I]	RCA Victor 4373
4/23/83	89	14		4 Hooked On Classics III (Journey Through The Classics)	[I]	RCA Victor 4588

ROYAL SCOTS DRAGOON GUARDS
The military band of Scotland's armored regiment. Led by bagpipe soloist Major Tony Crease.

6/24/72	34	15		1 Amazing Grace	[I]	RCA Victor 4744

ROYCE DA 5'9"
Born Ryan Montgomery on 7/7/1977 in Detroit, Michigan. Male rapper. Name refers to his actual height. Member of Slaughterhouse.

3/13/04	161	1		1 Death Is Certain		Koch 9500
11/7/09	110	1		2 Street Hop		Gracie 0014

ROYKSOPP
Electronic production duo from Tromso, Norway: Torbjorn Brundtland and Svein Berge.

4/11/09	126	1		1 Junior		Wall Of Sound 97748

Billboard DEBUT	PEAK	WKS	R I A A	ARTIST Album Title	Catalog	Label & Number

RTZ
Rock band formed in Boston, Massachusetts: Brad Delp (vocals), **Barry Goudreau** (guitar), Brian Maes (keyboards), Tim Archibald (bass) and David Stefanelli (drums). Delp and Goudreau were members of **Boston**. Goudreau was also with **Orion The Hunter**. RTZ: Return To Zero.

| 3/7/92 | 169 | 5 | | 1 Return To Zero .... | | Giant 24422 |

RUBBER BAND, The
Studio group assembled by producer Michael Lloyd.

| 8/2/69 | 135 | 6 | | 1 Cream Songbook .... [I] | | GRT 10000 |
| 9/6/69 | 116 | 8 | | 2 Hendrix Songbook .... [I] | | GRT 10007 |

RUBBER RODEO
New-wave band from Rhode Island: Trish Milliken (vocals), Bob Holmes (guitar), Mark Tomeo (steel guitar), Gary Leib (keyboards), John Doelp (bass) and Barc Holmes (drums).

| 7/7/84 | 205 | 5 | | 1 Scenic Views .... | | Mercury 818477 |

RUBEN AND THE JETS
Rock band formed in Los Angeles, California: Ruben Guevara (vocals), Tony Duran (guitar), Robert Camarena (guitar), Robert Roberts and Jim Sherwood (horns), Johnny Martinez (keyboards), Bill Wild (bass) and Bob Zamora (drums). Group named after **Frank Zappa**'s 1968 album *Cruising With Ruben & The Jets*.

| 5/5/73 | 205 | 2 | | 1 For Real .... produced by **Frank Zappa** | | Mercury 659 |

RUBICON
Pop-rock band from San Francisco, California: Greg Eckler (vocals, drums), Brad Gillis (guitar), Jerry Martini, Max Haskett and Dennis Marcellino (horns), Jim Pugh (keyboards), and Jack Blades (bass). Martini was a member of **Sly & The Family Stone**. Haskett was a member of **Cold Blood**. Gillis and Blades later formed **Night Ranger**.

| 3/25/78 | 147 | 7 | | 1 Rubicon .... | | 20th Century 552 |

RUBINSTEIN, Arthur
Born on 1/28/1887 in Lodz, Poland. Died on 12/20/1982 (age 95). Classical pianist. Father of Broadway/TV actor John Rubinstein.

| 1/9/61 | 117 | 15 | | 1 Rachmaninoff: Piano Concerto No. 2/ Liszt: Piano Concerto No. 1 .... [I] | | RCA Victor 2068 |
| 2/13/61 | 30 | 12 | | 2 Heart Of The Piano Concerto .... [I] | | RCA Victor 2495 |

RUBIO, Paulina
Born on 6/17/1971 in Mexico City, Mexico. Latin pop-dance singer.

2/17/01	156	15		1 Paulina .... [F]		Universal Latino 543319
7/6/02	11	10	●	2 Border Girl		Universal 153300
2/28/04	105	8		3 Pau-Latina .... [F]		Universal Latino 002036
10/7/06	31	6		4 Ananda .... [F]		Universal Latino 007487
7/11/09	44	3		5 Gran City Pop .... [F]		Universal Latino 013075

RUBY AND THE ROMANTICS
R&B vocal group from Akron, Ohio: Ruby Nash Curtis (born on 11/12/1939), Leroy Fann, Ed Roberts, George Lee and Ronald Mosley. Fann died in November 1973 (age 37). Roberts died of cancer on 8/10/1993 (age 57).

| 5/11/63 | 120 | 6 | | 1 Our Day Will Come .... | | Kapp 3323 |

RUCKER, Darius
Born on 5/13/1966 in Charleston, South Carolina. Black singer/songwriter/guitarist; switched to country music in 2008. Former lead singer of pop-rock band **Hootie & The Blowfish**.
AWARD: CMA: New Artist 2009

| 8/17/02 | 127 | 2 | | 1 Back To Then .... | | Hidden Beach 86492 |
| 10/4/08 | 5 | 87↑ | ▲ | 2 Learn To Live | | Capitol 85506 |

RUDE BOYS
R&B vocal group from Cleveland, Ohio: brothers Ed Banks and J. Little, with Larry Marcus and Melvin Sephus.

| 2/23/91 | 68 | 16 | | 1 Rude Awakenings .... | | Atlantic 82121 |

RUDOLF, Kevin
Born on 2/17/1983 in Manhattan, New York; later based in Miami, Florida. R&B singer/songwriter/guitarist.

| 12/13/08 | 94 | 7 | | 1 In The City .... | | Cash Money 012337 |

RUFF ENDZ
R&B vocal duo from Baltimore, Maryland: David Chance and Dante Jordan.

| 9/9/00 | 52 | 11 | | 1 Love Crimes .... | | Epic 69719 |
| 6/1/02 | 27 | 9 | | 2 Someone To Love You .... | | Epic 85691 |

RUFFIN, David
Born Davis Eli Ruffin on 1/18/1941 in Whynot, Mississippi. Died of a drug overdose on 6/1/1991 (age 50). R&B singer. Brother of **Jimmy Ruffin**. Co-lead singer of **The Temptations** from 1963-68. Also see **Daryl Hall & John Oates**.

6/21/69	31	17		1 My Whole World Ended		Motown 685
12/13/69+	148	7		2 Feelin' Good		Motown 696
11/7/70	178	3		3 I Am My Brother's Keeper .... THE RUFFIN BROTHERS		Soul 728
3/17/73	160	7		4 David Ruffin		Motown 762
1/11/75	201	2		5 Me 'N Rock 'N Roll Are Here To Stay		Motown 818
11/15/75+	31	27		6 Who I Am		Motown 849

				RUFFIN, David — cont'd		
6/12/76	51	12		7 Everything's Coming Up Love		Motown 866
10/27/79	206	2		8 So Soon We Change		Warner 3306
				RUFFIN, Jimmy		
				Born on 5/7/1939 in Collinsville, Mississippi. R&B singer. Brother of **David Ruffin**.		
5/13/67	133	11		1 Top Ten		Soul 704
4/19/69	196	2		2 Ruff'N Ready		Soul 708
11/7/70	178	3		3 I Am My Brother's Keeper		Soul 728
				THE RUFFIN BROTHERS		
5/31/80	152	6		4 Sunrise		RSO 3078
				RUFFNER, Mason		
				Born in Fort Worth, Texas. Rock singer/songwriter/guitarist.		
6/13/87	80	16		1 Gypsy Blood		CBS Associated 40601
				RUFF RYDERS		
				All-star rap group from New York: **DMX**, **Drag-On**, **Eve**, **The Lox** and **Swizz Beatz**.		
5/15/99	❶[1]	37	▲	1 Ruff Ryders - Ryde Or Die Vol. I		Ruff Ryders 90315
7/22/00	2[1]	17	▲	2 Ruff Ryders - Ryde Or Die Vol. II		Ruff Ryders 90625
1/5/02	34	13		3 Ruff Ryders - Ryde Or Die Vol. III		Ruff Ryders 493177
8/13/05	40	4		4 Ruff Ryders - Ryde Or Die Vol. IV: The Redemption		Ruff Ryders 51713
				RUFIO		
				Punk-rock band from Los Angeles, California: Scott Sellers (vocals, guitar), Clark Domae (guitar), Jon Berry (bass) and Mike Jimenez (drums).		
7/5/03	168	1		1 MCMLXXXV		Nitro 15853
7/30/05	199	1		2 The Comfort Of Home		Nitro 15865
				RUFUS Featuring Chaka Khan All-Time: #422		
				R&B group from Chicago, Illinois: **Chaka Khan** (vocals), Tony Maiden (guitar), Nate Morgan and Kevin Murphy (keyboards), Bobby Watson (bass), and Andre Fischer (drums; **American Breed**). Khan has been recording solo and with Rufus since 1978. After 1978, Maiden and David Wolinski also sang lead.		
8/4/73	175	6		1 Rufus		ABC 783
6/29/74	4	30	●	2 Rags To Rufus		ABC 809
				RUFUS (above 2)		
1/4/75	7	24	●	3 Rufusized		ABC 837
12/6/75+	7	32	●	4 Rufus Featuring Chaka Khan		ABC 909
2/5/77	12	25	▲	5 Ask Rufus		ABC 975
2/11/78	14	26	●	6 Street Player		ABC 1049
2/10/79	81	9		7 Numbers		ABC 1098
				RUFUS		
11/17/79	14	26	●	8 Masterjam		MCA 5103
3/28/81	73	11		9 Party 'Til You're Broke		MCA 5159
				RUFUS		
10/31/81	98	14		10 Camouflage		MCA 5270
9/3/83	50	33		11 Live-Stompin' At The Savoy [L]		Warner 23679 [2]
				recorded in February 1982 at the Savoy Theatre in New York City		
				RUMOUR, The		
				Backing band for **Graham Parker**: Brinsley Schwarz (vocals, guitar), Martin Belmont (guitar), Bob Andrews (keyboards), Andrew Bodnar (bass) and Stephen Goulding (drums).		
8/13/77	124	10		1 Max		Mercury 1174
8/4/79	160	3		2 Frogs Sprouts Clogs And Krauts		Arista 4235
				RUNAWAYS, The		
				Female rock band formed in Los Angeles, California: Cherie Currie (vocals), **Joan Jett** (guitar, vocals), **Lita Ford** (guitar, vocals), Micki Steele (bass), and Sandy West (drums). Steele later joined the **Bangles**. West died of cancer on 10/21/2006 (age 47). Biographical movie, *The Runaways*, released in 2010.		
8/21/76	194	2		1 The Runaways		Mercury 1090
2/5/77	172	4		2 Queens Of Noise		Mercury 1126
				RUNDGREN, Todd All-Time: #442		
				Born on 6/22/1948 in Upper Darby, Pennsylvania. Virtuoso rock musician/songwriter/producer/engineer. Leader of groups **Nazz** and **Utopia**. Produced **Meat Loaf**'s *Bat Out Of Hell* album and albums for **Badfinger**, **Grand Funk Railroad**, **The Tubes**, **XTC**, **Patti Smith** and many others.		
1/9/71	185	6		1 Runt		Ampex 10105
7/10/71	214	3		2 Runt - The Ballad Of Todd Rundgren		Bearsville 10116
3/25/72+	29	48	●	3 Something/Anything?		Bearsville 2066 [2]
				RS500 #173		
3/31/73	86	15		4 A Wizard/A True Star		Bearsville 2133
3/16/74	54	17		5 Todd		Bearsville 6952 [2]
6/14/75	86	7		6 Initiation		Bearsville 6957
5/15/76	54	15		7 Faithful		Bearsville 6963
5/6/78	36	26		8 Hermit Of Mink Hollow		Bearsville 6981
12/2/78+	75	15		9 Back To The Bars [L]		Bearsville 6986 [2]
2/21/81	48	13		10 Healing		Bearsville 3522

DEBUT	PEAK	WKS		Album Title	Catalog	Label & Number
				RUNDGREN, Todd — cont'd		
1/22/83	66	13		11 The Ever Popular Tortured Artist Effect		Bearsville 23732
10/12/85	128	8		12 A Cappella		Warner 25128
6/17/89	102	11		13 Nearly Human		Warner 25881
2/16/91	118	8		14 2nd Wind		Warner 26478

RUN-D.M.C.

Highly influential rap trio from Queens, New York: rappers Joseph "Run" Simmons (born on 11/24/1966) and Darryl "D.M.C." McDaniels (born on 5/31/1964) with DJ Jason "Jam Master Jay" Mizell (born on 1/21/1965; shot to death on 10/30/2002, age 37). Group appeared in the movies *Krush Groove* and *Tougher Than Leather*.

AWARD: R&R Hall of Fame: 2009

DEBUT	PEAK	WKS		Album Title	Catalog	Label & Number
6/23/84	53	65	●	1 Run-D.M.C.		Profile 1202
				RS500 #240		
2/23/85	52	56	▲	2 King Of Rock		Profile 1205
6/14/86	3³	71	▲³	3 Raising Hell		Profile 1217
				RS500 #120		
6/4/88	9	28	▲	4 Tougher Than Leather		Profile 1265
12/8/90+	81	15		5 Back From Hell		Profile 1401
12/7/91	199	1		6 Greatest Hits 1983-1991 [G]		Profile 1419
5/22/93	7	16	●	7 Down With The King		Profile 1440
4/21/01	37	6		8 Crown Royal		Arista 16400
9/28/02	117	3		9 Greatest Hits [G]		Profile 10607

RUNNER

Rock band from England: Steve Gould (vocals, guitar; **Rare Bird**), Allan Merrill (guitar), Mickie Feat (bass) and Dave Dowle (drums).

DEBUT	PEAK	WKS		Album Title	Catalog	Label & Number
6/23/79	167	4		1 Runner		Island 9536

RuPAUL

Born RuPaul Andre Charles on 11/17/1960 in San Diego, California. Black male transvestite. Appeared in the movies *Crooklyn* and *The Brady Bunch Movie*. Hosted own talk show on VH-1.

DEBUT	PEAK	WKS		Album Title	Catalog	Label & Number
6/26/93	109	6		1 Supermodel Of The World		Tommy Boy 1058

RUSH   1980s: #22 / All-Time: #61

Hard-rock trio formed in Toronto, Ontario, Canada: **Geddy Lee** (vocals, bass; born on 7/29/1953), Alex Lifeson (guitar; born on 8/27/1953) and John Rutsey (drums; born in 1953; died on 5/11/2008, age 55). Neil Peart (born on 9/12/1952) replaced Rutsey after first album and became band's lyricist. Also see **Victor**.

DEBUT	PEAK	WKS		Album Title	Catalog	Label & Number
9/21/74	105	13	●	1 Rush	Cat:#12/91	Mercury 1011
3/15/75	113	8	▲	2 Fly By Night	Cat:#16/121	Mercury 1023
10/18/75	148	6	●	3 Caress Of Steel	Cat:#13/109	Mercury 1046
4/10/76	61	34	▲³	4 2112		Mercury 1079
9/24/77	33	17	▲	5 A Farewell To Kings		Mercury 1184
4/15/78	121	6	▲	6 Archives [R]		Mercury 9200 [3]
				reissue of albums #1-3 above		
11/18/78	47	21	▲	7 Hemispheres		Mercury 3743
2/2/80	4	36	▲	8 Permanent Waves		Mercury 4001
3/7/81	3³	68	▲⁴	9 Moving Pictures	Cat:#18/8	Mercury 4013
10/2/82	10	33	▲	10 Signals		Mercury 4063
5/5/84	10	27	▲	11 Grace Under Pressure		Mercury 818476
11/9/85	10	28	▲	12 Power Windows		Mercury 826098
9/26/87	13	30	●	13 Hold Your Fire		Mercury 832464
12/2/89	16	27	●	14 Presto		Atlantic 82040
9/21/91	3¹	43	▲	15 Roll The Bones		Atlantic 82293
11/6/93	2¹	26	●	16 Counterparts		Atlantic 82528
9/28/96	5	15	●	17 Test For Echo		Atlantic 82925
6/1/02	6	10		18 Vapor Trails		Anthem 83531
7/17/04	19	6		19 Feedback [EP]		Anthem 83728
5/19/07	3¹	14		20 Snakes & Arrows		Anthem 135484
				GREATEST HITS & COMPILATIONS:		
9/22/90	51	19	▲²	21 Chronicles		Mercury 838936 [2]
3/1/03	62	7	●	22 The Spirit Of Radio: Greatest Hits 1974-1987		Mercury 063335
3/21/09	47	1		23 Retrospective 3: 1989-2008		Anthem 515813
				LIVE ALBUMS:		
10/2/76	40	23	▲	24 All The World's A Stage		Mercury 7508 [2]
				recorded on 6/12/1976 at Massey Hall in Toronto, Ontario, Canada		
11/14/81	10	21	▲	25 Exit...Stage Left		Mercury 7001 [2]
1/28/89	21	15	●	26 A Show Of Hands		Mercury 836346 [2]
11/28/98	35	6	●	27 Different Stages / Live		Atlantic 83122 [3]

Billboard			R I A A	ARTIST		
DEBUT	PEAK	WKS		Album Title	Catalog	Label & Number
				RUSH — cont'd		
11/8/03	33	2	●	28 Rush In Rio		Anthem 83672 [3]
5/3/08	18	3		29 Snakes & Arrows: Live		Anthem 442620 [2]
				RUSH, Jennifer		
				Born Heidi Stern on 9/29/1960 in Queens, New York. Pop singer.		
6/27/87	118	10		1 Heart Over Mind		Epic 40825
				RUSH, Merrilee		
				Born on 1/26/1944 in Seattle, Washington. Female pop singer/keyboardist.		
10/19/68	196	4		1 Angel Of The Morning		Bell 6020
				RUSH, Tom		
				Born on 2/8/1941 in Portsmouth, New Hampshire. Folk-rock-blues singer/songwriter.		
6/11/66	122	7		1 Take A Little Walk With Me..		Elektra 7308
4/20/68	68	14		2 The Circle Game		Elektra 74018
3/27/71	198	1		3 Classic Rush .... [K]		Elektra 74062
3/14/70	76	16		4 Tom Rush...		Columbia 9972
12/26/70+	110	9		5 Wrong End Of The Rainbow		Columbia 30402
4/29/72	128	10		6 Merrimack County		Columbia 31306
10/19/74	124	9		7 Ladies Love Outlaws		Columbia 33054
2/7/76	184	3		8 The Best Of Tom Rush .... [K]		Columbia 33907
				RUSHEN, Patrice		
				Born on 9/30/1954 in Los Angeles, California. R&B singer/songwriter/pianist.		
4/16/77	164	4		1 Shout It Out..		Prestige 10101
2/17/79	98	6		2 Patrice		Elektra 160
11/24/79+	39	22		3 Pizzazz		Elektra 243
11/29/80+	71	18		4 Posh		Elektra 302
5/1/82	14	28		5 Straight From The Heart		Elektra 60015
6/16/84	40	25		6 Now		Elektra 60360
3/28/87	77	19		7 Watch Out!		Arista 8401
				RUSH OF FOOLS		
				Christian rock band from Birmingham, Alabama: Wes Willis (vocals, guitar), Kevin Huguley (guitar), Jacob Chesnut (bass) and Jamie Sharpe (drums).		
5/26/07	181	1		1 Rush Of Fools..		Midas 90150
10/4/08	187	1		2 Wonder Of The World		Midas 90300
				RUSSELL, Bobby		
				Born on 4/19/1941 in Nashville, Tennessee. Died of a heart attack on 11/19/1992 (age 51). Singer/songwriter. Married to **Vicki Lawrence** from 1972-74.		
10/16/71	183	3		1 Saturday Morning Confusion		United Artists 5548
				RUSSELL, Brenda		
				Born Brenda Gordon on 4/8/1949 in Brooklyn, New York. R&B singer/songwriter/pianist.		
9/22/79	65	20		1 Brenda Russell		Horizon 739
4/11/81	107	8		2 Love Life		A&M 4811
3/19/88	49	28		3 Get Here		A&M 5178
				RUSSELL, Leon **1970s: #49 / All-Time: #306**		
				Born Claude Russell Bridges on 4/2/1942 in Lawton, Oklahoma. Rock singer/songwriter/multi-instrumentalist. Prolific session musician. Regular with **Phil Spector**'s "Wall of Sound" session group. Formed Shelter Records in 1970. Recorded as **Hank Wilson** in 1973. Married to **Mary McCreary** from 1975-80. Also see **Joe Cocker**.		
4/8/72	201	8		1 Look Inside The Asylum Choir .... [E]		Smash 67107
12/4/71+	70	20		2 Asylum Choir II .... [E]		Shelter 8910
				LEON RUSSELL & MARC BENNO (above 2)		
				above 2 recorded in 1968-69		
4/11/70	60	19		3 Leon Russell		Shelter 1001
5/29/71	17	29	●	4 Leon Russell & The Shelter People...		Shelter 8903
7/15/72	2⁴	35	●	5 Carney		Shelter 8911
7/7/73	9	26	●	6 Leon Live [L]		Shelter 8917 [3]
				recorded at the Long Beach Arena in California		
9/22/73	28	15		7 Hank Wilson's Back, Vol. I...		Shelter 8923
				HANK WILSON		
6/22/74	34	16		8 Stop All That Jazz		Shelter 2108
5/3/75	30	40	●	9 Will O' The Wisp		Shelter 2138
5/1/76	34	28		10 Wedding Album		Paradise 2943
6/25/77	142	5		11 Make Love To The Music		Paradise 3066
				LEON & MARY RUSSELL (above 2)		
10/23/76	40	16	●	12 Best Of Leon .... [G]		Shelter 52004
8/12/78	115	10		13 Americana		Paradise 3172
6/30/79	25	18	●	14 One For The Road		Columbia 36064 [2]
				WILLIE NELSON & LEON RUSSELL		
7/7/79	204	2		15 Life And Love		Paradise 3341
4/4/81	187	2		16 The Live Album .... [L]		Paradise 3532
				LEON RUSSELL & NEW GRASS REVIVAL		
				recorded on 5/15/1980 at Perkins Palace in Pasadena, California		

RUSTED ROOT
Rock band from Pittsburgh, Pennsylvania: Mike Glabicki (vocals, guitar), John Buynak, Liz Berlin, Jenn Wertz and Jim DiSpirito (percussion), Patrick Norman (bass), and Jim Donovan (drums). Wertz left in 1995.

9/10/94+	51	46	▲	1 When I Woke	Mercury 522713
11/9/96	38	13	●	2 Remember	Mercury 534050
11/21/98	165	2		3 Rusted Root	Mercury 538283
4/27/02	129	1		4 Welcome To My Party	Island 586776

RUSTIX, The
Rock band from Rochester, New York: Albe Galich and Chuck Brucato (vocals), Bob D'Andrea (guitar), Vinnie Strenk (keyboards), Ronny Colins (bass) and David Colon (drums).

11/15/69	200	2	1 Bedlam	Rare Earth 508

RUTHERFORD, Mike
Born on 10/2/1950 in Guildford, Surrey, England. Bassist of **Genesis** and leader of **Mike + The Mechanics**.

4/5/80	163	11	1 Smallcreep's Day	Passport 9843
10/9/82	145	6	2 Acting Very Strange	Atlantic 80015

RUTLES, The
Parody of **The Beatles**: Neil Innes ("Ron Nasty"), Eric Idle ("Dirk McQuickly"), Rikki Fataar ("Stig O'Hara") and John Halsey ("Barry Wom"). Innes was with the **Bonzo Dog Band** and Idle was a member of **Monty Python**. A pseudo-documentary of the group aired on NBC-TV on 3/22/1978.

3/25/78	63	9	1 The Rutles	Warner 3151

RX BANDITS
Ska-punk band from Anaheim, California: Matthew Embree (vocals, guitar), Steve Choi (guitar), Steven Borth (sax), Chris Sheets (trombone), Joseph Troy (bass) and Christopher Tsagakis (drums).

8/2/03	148	1	1 The Resignation	Drive-Thru 000835
8/1/09	117	2	2 Mandala	Sargent House 025

RYAN, Bianca
Born on 9/1/1994 in Philadelphia, Pennsylvania. Pre-teen female singer. Winner on the first season of TV's *America's Got Talent* talent show.

12/2/06	57	4	1 Bianca Ryan	Syco 02093

RYDELL, Bobby
Born Robert Ridarelli on 4/26/1942 in Philadelphia, Pennsylvania. "Teen idol" pop singer/actor. Appeared in the movies *Bye Bye Birdie* and *That Lady From Peking*.

2/27/61	12	34	1 Bobby's Biggest Hits	[G]	Cameo 1009
10/23/61	56	9	2 Rydell At The Copa	[L]	Cameo 1011
			recorded on 7/4/1961		
12/18/61+	7	30	3 Bobby Rydell/Chubby Checker		Cameo 1013
9/1/62	88	11	4 All The Hits		Cameo 1019
12/22/62+	61	12	5 Bobby Rydell/Biggest Hits, Volume 2	[G]	Cameo 1028
1/18/64	67	9	6 The Top Hits Of 1963		Cameo 1070
			includes a bonus 7" single		
3/7/64	98	4	7 Forget Him		Cameo 1080

~ ~ ~ ~ ~ ~ ~ ~ ~ **NON-CHARTED ALBUMS** ~ ~ ~ ~ ~ ~ ~ ~ ~ ~

1959 **We Got Love**	1963 **Bye Bye Birdie**
1960 **Bobby Sings / Bobby Swings**	1963 **Wild (Wood) Days**
1961 **Bobby Rydell....Salutes The "Great Ones"**	1963 **Golden Hits** *[w/ Chubby Checker]*
1963 **All The Hits By Bobby Rydell, Volume 2**	1965 **18 Golden Hits**

RYDER, Mitch, And The Detroit Wheels
Born William Levise on 2/26/1945 in Hamtramck, Michigan. White rock and roll/R&B singer. The Detroit Wheels: Jim McCarty and Joe Cubert (guitars), Earl Elliott (bass) and John Badanjek (drums). Ryder later formed **Detroit**. McCarty and Badanjek formed the **Rockets**.

3/5/66	78	7	1 Take A Ride		New Voice 2000
8/6/66+	23	34	2 Breakout...!!!		New Voice 2002
4/8/67	34	16	3 Sock It To Me!		New Voice 2003
10/14/67+	37	26	4 All Mitch Ryder Hits!	[G]	New Voice 2004
7/9/83	120	9	5 Never Kick A Sleeping Dog		Riva 7503
			MITCH RYDER		
			produced by **John Cougar**		

RYDER, Serena
Born on 12/8/1983 in Toronto, Ontario, Canada. Folk-rock singer/songwriter.

11/21/09	101	1	1 Is It O.K.	Atlantic 516985

RZA
Born Robert Diggs on 7/5/1969 in Brooklyn, New York. Rapper/producer/actor. Member of **Wu-Tang Clan** and **Gravediggaz**. Pronounced: riz-ah. Also recorded as **Bobby Digital**. Also see **Various Artists Compilations**: *The RZA Hits*.

12/12/98	16	12	●	1 RZA As Bobby Digital In Stereo	Gee Street 32521
9/15/01	24	8		2 Digital Bullet	Wu-Tang 8182
7/12/08	111	2		3 Digi Snacks	Wu-Tang 4209
				RZA AS BOBBY DIGITAL (above 3)	
10/25/03	49	4		4 Birth Of A Prince	Wu-Records 84652

S

SAAD, Sue, And The Next
Pop-rock band from Santa Barbara, California: Sue Saad (vocals), Tony Riparetti (guitar), Billy Anstatt (guitar), Bobby Manzer (bass) and James Lance (drums).

3/1/80	131	12		1 Sue Saad And The Next		Planet 4

SAADIQ, Raphael
Born Raphael Wiggins on 5/14/1966 in Oakland, California. R&B singer. Member of **Tony! Toni! Tone!**

6/29/02	25	8		1 Instant Vintage		Universal 016654
11/1/03	182	1		2 All Hits At The House Of Blues [L]		Pookie 1001 [2]
10/23/04	86	1		3 Ray Ray		Pookie 1004
10/4/08	19	41		4 The Way I See It		Columbia 08585

SACRED REICH
Hard-rock band from Phoenix, Arizona: Phil Rind (vocals, bass), Wiley Arnett (guitar), Jason Rainey (guitar) and Greg Hall (drums).

7/28/90	153	9		1 The American Way		Enigma 73560

SADAT X
Born Derek Murphy on 12/29/1968 in New Rochelle, New York. Male rapper. Former member of **Brand Nubian**.

8/3/96	83	3		1 Wild Cowboys		Loud 66922

SAD CAFE
Pop-rock band formed in Manchester, England: Paul Young (vocals), Ashley Mulford (guitar), Ian Wilson (guitar), Vic Emerson (keyboards), John Stimpson (bass) and Tony Cresswell (drums). By 1979, Dave Irving had replaced Cresswell. Young (not to be confused with the solo star) later joined **Mike + The Mechanics**; died of a heart attack on 7/15/2000 (age 53).

1/27/79	94	14		1 Misplaced Ideals [K]		A&M 4737
9/15/79	146	5		2 Facades		A&M 4779
8/15/81	160	6		3 Sad Cafe		Swan Song 16048

SADE   All-Time: #347
Born Helen Folasade Adu on 1/16/1959 in Ibadan, Nigeria; raised in Clacton-on-Sea, England. Jazz-styled singer. Appeared in the 1986 movie *Absolute Beginners*. Also see **Sweetback**.

AWARD: Grammy: Best New Artist 1985

2/23/85	5	81	▲⁴	1 Diamond Life	Cat:#19/40	Portrait 39581
12/21/85+	❶²	46	▲⁴	2 Promise	Cat:#43/4	Portrait 40263
6/4/88	7	45	▲³	3 Stronger Than Pride	Cat:#32/19	Epic 44210
11/21/92	3¹	103	▲⁴	4 Love Deluxe		Epic 53178
11/26/94	9	93	▲⁴	5 Best Of Sade	Cat:#5/172 [G]	Epic 66686
12/2/00	3¹	58	▲³	6 Lovers Rock	Cat:#36/1	Epic 85185
				Grammy: Pop Vocal Album		
2/23/02	3¹	15	●	7 Lovers Live [L]		Epic 86373

SADLER, SSgt Barry
Born on 11/1/1940 in Carlsbad, New Mexico. Died of heart failure on 11/5/1989 (age 49). Staff Sergeant of U.S. Army Special Forces (Green Berets). Served in Vietnam.

2/26/66	❶⁵	32	●	1 Ballads Of The Green Berets		RCA Victor 3547
7/9/66	130	3		2 The "A" Team		RCA Victor 3605

SAFETYSUIT
Alternative-rock band from Tulsa, Oklahoma: Doug Brown (vocals, guitar), Dave Garofalo (guitar), Jeremy Henshaw (bass) and Tate Cunningham (drums).

7/25/09	173	2		1 Life Left To Go		Universal Motown 010978

SA-FIRE
Born Wilma Cosme in 1967 in San Juan, Puerto Rico; raised in East Harlem, New York. Female dance singer.

10/8/88+	79	46		1 Sa-Fire		Cutting 834922

SAGA
Rock band formed in Toronto, Ontario, Canada: Michael Sadler (vocals), brothers Ian Crichton (guitar) and Jim Crichton (bass), Jim Gilmour (keyboards) and Steve Negus (drums).

10/23/82+	29	36	●	1 Worlds Apart		Portrait 38246
10/22/83	92	9		2 Heads Or Tales		Portrait 38999
9/21/85	87	10		3 Behaviour		Portrait 40145

SAGER, Carole Bayer
Born on 3/8/1946 in Manhattan, New York. Singer/prolific songwriter. Married to **Burt Bacharach** from 1982-91.

5/16/81	60	22		1 Sometimes Late At Night		Boardwalk 37069

SAHL, Mort
Born on 5/11/1927 in Montreal, Quebec, Canada. Stand-up comedian/actor. Known for his topical humor.

10/24/60+	22	13		1 Mort Sahl At The Hungry I [C]		Verve 15012
				no track titles listed on this album		
6/30/73	149	7		2 Sing A Song Of Watergate... [C]		GNP Crescendo 2070

Billboard DEBUT	PEAK	WKS	R I A A	ARTIST / Album Title	Catalog	Label & Number
				SAHM, Doug, And Band		
				Born on 11/5/1941 in San Antonio, Texas. Died of heart failure on 11/18/1999 (age 58). Rock singer/songwriter/guitarist. Formed the **Sir Douglas Quintet** and the **Texas Tornados**.		
2/17/73	125	10		1 Doug Sahm And Band		Atlantic 7254
				SAIGON		
				Born Brian Carenard on 6/16/1977 in Newburgh, New York; raised in Brooklyn, New York. Male rapper.		
10/24/09	170	1		1 Warning Shots 2		Amalgam digital
				SAIGON KICK		
				Rock band formed in Miami, Florida: Matt Kramer (vocals), Jason Bieler (guitar), Tom DeFile (bass) and Phil Varone (drums).		
6/20/92	80	26	●	1 The Lizard		Third Stone 92158
				SAILCAT		
				Pop duo from Alabama: Court Pickett (vocals) and John Wyker (vocals, guitar).		
8/12/72	38	14		1 Motorcycle Mama		Elektra 75029
				SAINTE-MARIE, Buffy		
				Born on 2/20/1941 in Piapot Reserve, Saskatchewan, Canada. Folk singer/songwriter.		
5/21/66	97	10		1 Little Wheel Spin And Spin		Vanguard 79211
7/8/67	126	6		2 Fire & Fleet & Candlelight		Vanguard 79250
8/3/68	171	7		3 I'm Gonna Be A Country Girl Again..		Vanguard 79280
10/24/70	142	7		4 The Best Of Buffy Sainte-Marie .... [G]		Vanguard 3/4 [2]
4/10/71	182	6		5 She Used To Wanna Be A Ballerina		Vanguard 79311
5/6/72	134	8		6 Moonshot		Vanguard 79312
				ST. JAMES, Rebecca		
				Born Rebecca Smallbone on 7/26/1977 in Sydney, Australia. Christian singer/songwriter.		
7/13/96	200	1	●	1 God		ForeFront 25141
11/29/97	30^X	1		2 Christmas .... [X]		ForeFront 25176
11/7/98	168	1		3 Pray		ForeFront 25189
11/11/00	166	1		4 Transform		ForeFront 25251
3/16/02	94	11		5 Worship God		ForeFront 32587
3/13/04	187	1		6 Live Worship: Blessed Be Your Name .... [L]		ForeFront 96643
				ST. JOHN, John		
				Born in Florida. Studio musician/producer.		
11/4/06	2^{2C}	12		1 Sounds Of Horror .... [I]		Madacy 51354 [2]
				first released in 2001		
				ST. LUNATICS		
				Hip-hop group from St. Louis, Missouri: Cornell "**Nelly**" Haynes, **Ali** Jones, Tohri "**Murphy Lee**" Harper, Lavell "City Spud" Webb and Robert "Kyjuan" Cleveland.		
6/23/01	3^1	22	▲	1 Free City		Fo' Reel 014119
3/11/06	114	1		2 Who's The Boss		Fast Life 66
				NELLY & THE ST. LUNATICS		
				ST. PETERS, Crispian		
				Born Robin Peter Smith on 4/5/1939 in Swanley, Kent, England. Died on 6/8/2010 (age 71). Pop singer/guitarist.		
				~ ~ ~ ~ ~ ~ ~ ~ ~ ~ ~ **NON-CHARTED ALBUM** ~ ~ ~ ~ ~ ~ ~ ~ ~ ~ ~ ~		
				1966 **The Pied Piper**		
				SAINT TROPEZ		
				Female disco trio: Teresa Burton, Kathy Deckard and Phyllis Rhodes.		
11/26/77	131	10		1 Je T'aime .... [F]		Butterfly 002
5/5/79	65	11		2 Belle De Jour		Butterfly 3100
				ST. VINCENT		
				Born Annie Clark on 9/28/1982 in Tulsa, Oklahoma. Folk-rock singer/songwriter/guitarist.		
5/23/09	90	3		1 Actor..		4AD 2919
				SAKAMOTO, Kyu		
				Born on 11/10/1941 in Kawasaki, Japan. Died in a plane crash on 8/12/1985 (age 43). Male singer.		
6/15/63	14	17		1 Sukiyaki And Other Japanese Hits .... [F]		Capitol 10349
				SALES, Soupy		
				Born Milton Supman on 1/8/1926 in Franklinton, North Carolina. Died on 10/22/2009 (age 83). Slapstick comedian. Hosted own TV show. His sons, Hunt and Tony, were members of the rock group **Tin Machine**.		
4/24/65	102	7		1 Spy With A Pie .... [N]		ABC-Paramount 503
5/15/65	80	7		2 Soupy Sales Sez Do The Mouse And Other Teen Hits .... [N]		ABC-Paramount 517
				SALIVA		
				Hard-rock band from Memphis, Tennessee: Josey Scott (vocals), Wayne Swinny (guitar), Dave Novotny (bass) and Paul Crosby (drums).		
4/14/01	56	33	▲^{2}	1 Every Six Seconds		Island 542959
11/30/02	19	29	●	2 Back Into Your System		Island 063153
9/4/04	20	7		3 Survival Of The Sickest		Island 002957

				SALIVA — cont'd		
2/10/07	19	15		4 Blood Stained Love Story		Island 008107
1/3/09	104	6		5 Cinco Diablo		Island 012398

SALSOUL ORCHESTRA, The
Disco orchestra conducted by producer/arranger Vincent Montana. Vocalists included Phyllis Rhodes, Ronni Tyson, Carl Helm, Philip Hurt and **Jocelyn Brown**. Also see **Montana Orchestra**.

11/29/75+	14	45		1 The Salsoul Orchestra	[I]	Salsoul 5501
10/23/76	61	14		2 Nice 'N' Naasty		Salsoul 5502
12/11/76+	83	6		3 Christmas Jollies	[X]	Salsoul 5507
12/24/77+	48	7		4 Christmas Jollies	[X-R]	Salsoul 5507
6/25/77	61	20		5 Magic Journey		Salsoul 5515
11/26/77+	100	15		6 Cuchi-Cuchi		Salsoul 5519
				CHARO & THE SALSOUL ORCHESTRA		
3/25/78	117	8		7 Up The Yellow Brick Road		Salsoul 8500
9/9/78	97	13		8 Greatest Disco Hits/Music For Non-Stop Dancing	[G]	Salsoul 8508
1/5/80	201	2		9 How High		Salsoul 8528
12/19/81+	170	5		10 Christmas Jollies II	[X]	Salsoul 8547

SALTER, Sam
Born on 2/16/1975 in Los Angeles, California. R&B singer.

10/18/97	199	1		1 It's On Tonight		LaFace 26040

SALT-N-PEPA
Female rap trio from Queens, New York: Cheryl "Salt" James, Sandra "Pepa" Denton and Dee Dee "Spinderella" Roper. Appeared in the 1993 movie *Who's The Man?*. Pepa was married to Treach (of **Naughty By Nature**) from 1999-2001.

8/1/87+	26	53	▲	1 Hot, Cool & Vicious		Next Plateau 1007
8/13/88	38	31	●	2 A Salt With A Deadly Pepa		Next Plateau 1011
4/7/90	38	71	▲	3 Blacks' Magic		Next Plateau 1019
10/5/91+	21 C	33		4 A Blitz Of Salt-N-Pepa Hits: The Hits Remixed	[K]	Next Plateau 1025
10/30/93+	4	89	▲5	5 Very Necessary		Next Plateau 828392
11/8/97	37	12	●	6 Brand New		London 828959

SALTY DOG
Hard-rock band formed in Los Angeles, California: Jimmi Bleacher (vocals), Pete Reveen (guitar), Michael Hannon (bass) and Khurt Maier (drums).

4/7/90	176	3		1 Every Dog Has Its Day		Geffen 24270

SALVADOR
Christian ska-rock band from Austin, Texas: Nic Gonzales (vocals, guitar), Chris Bevins (keyboards), Eliot Torres (percussion), Pablo Gabaldon (trumpet), Billy Griego (trombone), Josh Gonzales (bass) and Art Gonzales (drums).

6/22/02	198	1		1 Into Motion		Word 86134

SAM & DAVE
R&B vocal duo based in Memphis, Tennessee: Sam Moore (born on 10/12/1935 in Miami, Florida) and Dave Prater (born on 5/9/1937 in Ocilla, Georgia; died in a car crash on 4/9/1988, age 50).
AWARD: R&R Hall of Fame: 1992

8/6/66	45	15		1 Hold On, I'm Comin'		Stax 708
1/21/67	118	13		2 Double Dynamite		Stax 712
11/18/67+	62	13		3 Soul Men		Stax 725
2/15/69	87	17		4 The Best Of Sam & Dave	[G]	Atlantic 8218

SAMBORA, Richie
Born on 7/11/1959 in Perth Amboy, New Jersey; raised in Woodbridge, New Jersey. Rock singer/songwriter/guitarist. Member of **Bon Jovi**. Married to actress Heather Locklear from 1994-2007.

9/21/91	36	11		1 Stranger In This Town		Mercury 848895
3/21/98	174	1		2 Undiscovered Soul		Mercury 536972

SAMMIE
Born Sammie Bush on 3/1/1987 in Boynton Beach, Florida. Male R&B singer.

4/1/00	46	31	●	1 From The Bottom To The Top		Freeworld 23168
10/28/06	42	3		2 Sammie		Rowdy 007639

SAMPLE, Joe
Born on 2/1/1939 in Houston, Texas. Jazz keyboardist. Member of **The Crusaders**.

2/25/78	62	25		1 Rainbow Seeker	[I]	ABC 1050
2/10/79	56	26		2 Carmel	[I]	ABC 1126
1/31/81	65	20		3 Voices In The Rain	[I]	MCA 5172
4/16/83	125	14		4 The Hunter	[I]	MCA 5397
4/15/89	129	14		5 Spellbound		Warner 25781
4/10/93	194	1		6 Invitation	[I]	Warner 45209
5/29/99	196	1		7 The Song Lives On		GRP 9956
				JOE SAMPLE Featuring Lalah Hathaway		

SAMPLES, The
Rock band from Boulder, Colorado: Sean Kelly (vocals, guitar), Al Laughlin (keyboards), Andy Sheldon (bass) and Jeep MacNichol (drums).

10/1/94	122	1		1 Autopilot		W.A.R.? 60008
8/3/96	175	1		2 Outpost		MCA 11435

SAM THE SHAM AND THE PHARAOHS
Born Domingo Samudio on 3/6/1939 in Dallas, Texas. The Pharaohs: Ray Stinnet (guitar), Butch Gibson (sax), David Martin (bass) and Jerry Patterson (drums). Martin died on 8/2/1987 (age 50).

6/12/65	26	18		1 Wooly Bully		MGM 4297
9/24/66	82	7		2 Li'l Red Riding Hood		MGM 4407
3/11/67	98	17		3 The Best Of Sam The Sham And The Pharaohs	[G]	MGM 4422

SANBORN, David   All-Time: #362
Born on 7/30/1945 in Tampa, Florida; raised in St. Louis, Missouri. Saxophonist/flutist. Played with **Paul Butterfield** from 1967-71 and with **Stevie Wonder** from 1972-73. Formed own group in 1975.

5/29/76	208	2		1 Taking Off	[I]	Warner 2873
8/28/76	125	8		2 Sanborn	[I]	Warner 2957
7/23/77	208	1		3 Promise Me The Moon	[I]	Warner 3051
6/3/78	151	6		4 Heart To Heart	[I]	Warner 3189
3/8/80	63	19	●	5 Hideaway	[I]	Warner 3379
4/18/81	45	22	●	6 Voyeur	[I]	Warner 3546
7/10/82	70	23		7 As We Speak	[I]	Warner 23650
11/26/83+	81	33	●	8 Backstreet	[I]	Warner 23906
2/9/85	64	32	●	9 Straight To The Heart	[I]	Warner 25150
				Grammy: Jazz Fusion Album		
6/14/86	50	64	▲	10 Double Vision	[I]	Warner 25393
				BOB JAMES & DAVID SANBORN		
				Grammy: Jazz Fusion Album		
2/14/87	74	37	●	11 A Change Of Heart	[I]	Warner 25479
7/16/88	59	28	●	12 Close-Up	[I]	Reprise 25715
				Grammy: Pop Instrumental Album		
7/20/91	170	7		13 Another Hand	[I]	Elektra 61088
5/16/92	107	31	●	14 Upfront	[I]	Elektra 61272
6/25/94	116	8		15 Hearsay	[I]	Elektra 61620
4/15/95	124	11		16 Pearls	[I]	Elektra 61759
10/12/96	180	2		17 Songs From The Night Before	[I]	Elektra 61950
6/21/03	177	1		18 Time Again	[I]	Verve 065578
8/30/08	181	1		19 Here & Gone	[I]	Decca 011152

SANCHEZ, Adan Chalino
Born on 4/14/1984 in Torrance, California. Died in a car crash on 3/27/2004 (age 19). Male Latin singer. Son of popular Latin singer Chalino Sanchez (shot to death on 5/16/1992, age 31).

5/8/04	70	5		1 Amor Y Lagrimas	[F]	Sony Discos 93409

SANCIOUS, David
Born on 11/30/1953 in Asbury Park, New Jersey. Rock keyboardist. Member of **Bruce Springsteen**'s E-Street Band from 1972-74. Later became a prolific session musician.

11/10/79	210	2		1 Just As I Thought	[I]	Arista 4247

SANCTUS REAL
Christian rock band from Toledo, Ohio: Matt Hammitt (vocals), Chris Rohman (guitar), Dan Gartley (bass) and Mark Graalman (drums).

4/22/06	158	2		1 Face Of Love		Sparrow 11574
3/1/08	153	1		2 We Need Each Other		Sparrow 91027

SANDALS, The
Surf-rock band from Los Angeles, California: John Blakeley (guitar), Walter Georis (guitar), Gaston Georis (piano), John Gibson (bass) and Danny Brawner (drums).

2/4/67	110	13		1 The Endless Summer	[I-S]	World Pacific 1832

SANDERS, Pharoah
Born Farrel Sanders on 10/13/1940 in Little Rock, Arkansas. Jazz tenor saxophonist.

8/16/69	188	4		1 Karma	[I]	Impulse! 9181
7/31/71	175	3		2 Thembi	[I]	Impulse! 9206
5/20/78	163	5		3 Love Will Find A Way		Arista 4161

SANDLER, Adam
Born on 9/9/1966 in Brooklyn, New York. Actor/comedian. Cast member of TV's *Saturday Night Live* (1990-95). Starred in several movies.

12/11/93+	129	55	▲²	1 They're All Gonna Laugh At You! ... Cat:#17/17	[C]	Warner 45393
3/2/96	18	57	▲²	2 What The Hell Happened To Me? ... Cat:#17/10	[C]	Warner 46151
10/4/97	18	17	●	3 What's Your Name?	[N]	Warner 46738
10/9/99	16	17	●	4 Stan And Judy's Kid	[C]	Warner 47429
7/31/04	47	4		5 Shhh...Don't Tell	[C]	Warner 48782

SANDLER, Tony, & Ralph Young
Adult Contemporary vocal duo. Sandler was born on 8/18/1933 in Kortrjk, Belgium. Young was born on 7/1/1923 in the Bronx, New York; died on 8/22/2008 (age 85).

12/17/66+	85	19		1 Side By Side		Capitol 2598
4/15/67	166	3		2 On The Move		Capitol 2686
7/5/69	188	4		3 Pretty Things Come In Twos		Capitol 241
7/11/70	199	2		4 Honey Come Back		Capitol 449

SANDOVAL, Hope
Born on 6/4/1966 in Los Angeles, California. Alternative-rock singer/songwriter. Lead singer of **Mazzy Star**.

10/17/09	160	1		1 Through The Devil Softly		Song Bird 30848

SANDPIPERS, The
Adult Contemporary vocal trio from Los Angeles, California: Jim Brady, Michael Piano and Richard Shoff.

10/29/66+	13	37	●	1 Guantanamera		A&M 4117
5/27/67	53	28		2 The Sandpipers		A&M 4125
1/13/68	135	5		3 Misty Roses		A&M 4135
9/7/68	180	5		4 Softly		A&M 4147
5/10/69	194	5		5 The Wonder Of You		A&M 4180
4/18/70	160	10		6 Greatest Hits	[G]	A&M 4246
8/15/70	96	11		7 Come Saturday Morning		A&M 4262

SANDS, Tommy
Born on 8/27/1937 in Chicago, Illinois. Pop singer/actor. Married to **Nancy Sinatra** from 1960-65. Acted in the movies *Sing Boy Sing*, *Mardi Gras*, *Babes In Toyland* and *The Longest Day*.

5/6/57	4	18		1 Steady Date With Tommy Sands		Capitol 848
2/24/58	17	4		2 Sing Boy Sing	[S]	Capitol 929

~ ~ ~ ~ ~ ~ ~ ~ ~ **NON-CHARTED ALBUM** ~ ~ ~ ~ ~ ~ ~ ~ ~ ~
1959 **Sands Storm!**

SANFORD/TOWNSEND BAND, The
Pop-rock duo from Los Angeles, California: Ed Sanford and John Townsend.

8/13/77	57	15		1 The Sanford/Townsend Band		Warner 2966
				album also released as *Smoke From A Distant Fire*		
2/11/78	92	8		2 Duo-Glide		Warner 3081

SAN FRANCISCO SYMPHONY ORCHESTRA
Conducted by Seiji Ozawa (born on 9/1/1935 in Japan).

4/7/73	105	15		1 William Russo: Three Pieces For Blues Band And Orchestra/ Leonard Bernstein: Symphonic Dances From West Side Story	[I]	DG 2530 309

SANG, Samantha
Born on 8/5/1953 in Melbourne, Australia. Pop singer.

3/11/78	29	14	●	1 Emotion		Private Stock 7009

SAN SEBASTIAN STRINGS, The
Music composed by **Anita Kerr** (with sound effects), featuring narration of the poetry of **Rod McKuen**.

3/25/67+	52	143	●	1 The Sea	[I-T]	Warner 1670
9/23/67	115	13		2 The Earth	[I-T]	Warner 1705
2/17/68	68	25		3 The Sky	[I-T]	Warner 1720
1/18/69	20	20		4 Home To The Sea	[I-T]	Warner 1764
11/22/69	84	17		5 For Lovers	[I-T]	Warner 1795
1/17/70	162	5		6 The Complete Sea	[I-T-R]	Warner 1827 [3]
				deluxe set of albums #1, #4 and #7		
9/26/70	171	5		7 The Soft Sea	[I-T]	Warner 1839

SANTA ESMERALDA
Disco studio group assembled by producers Nicolas Skorsky and Jean-Manuel de Scarano. Vocalists include Leroy Gomez and Jimmy Goings.

11/12/77+	25	23	●	1 Don't Let Me Be Misunderstood		Casablanca 7080
2/25/78	41	14		2 The House Of The Rising Sun		Casablanca 7088
9/2/78	141	6		3 Beauty		Casablanca 7109

SANTAMARIA, Mongo
Born Ramon Santamaria on 4/7/1917 in Havana, Cuba. Died of a stroke on 2/1/2003 (age 85). Conga player.

5/4/63	42	10		1 Watermelon Man!	[I]	Battle 96120
3/27/65	112	10		2 El Pussy Cat	[I]	Columbia 9098
8/28/65	79	15		3 La Bamba	[I]	Columbia 9175
6/4/66	135	5		4 Hey! Let's Party	[I]	Columbia 9273
8/10/68	171	18		5 Soul Bag	[I]	Columbia 9653
3/1/69	62	24		6 Stone Soul	[I]	Columbia 9780
11/29/69	193	2		7 Workin' On A Groovy Thing	[I]	Columbia 9937
4/11/70	171	3		8 Feelin' Alright	[I]	Atlantic 8252
10/3/70	195	2		9 Mongo '70	[I]	Atlantic 1567
4/28/79	207	1		10 Red Hot	[I]	Columbia 35696

SANTANA
1970s: #35 / All-Time: #56

Latin-rock band formed by **Carlos Santana** in San Francisco, California. Various members over the years include Alex Ligertwood (vocals), Gregg Rolie (keyboards, vocals), **Neal Schon** (guitar), David Brown (bass) and **Michael Shrieve** (drums). Schon and Rolie formed **Journey**. Shrieve formed **Automatic Man**.
AWARDS: R&R Hall of Fame: 1998 ★ Billboard Century: 1996

DEBUT	PEAK	WKS	RIAA	#	Album Title	Catalog	Label & Number
9/13/69	4	108	▲²	1	Santana		Columbia 9781
					RS500 #150		
10/10/70	❶⁶	88	▲⁵	2	Abraxas		Columbia 30130
					Grammy: Hall of Fame ★ RS500 #205		
10/16/71	❶⁵	39	▲²	3	Santana III		Columbia 30595
11/4/72	8	32	▲	4	Caravanserai		Columbia 31610
12/1/73	25	21	●	5	Welcome		Columbia 32445
11/2/74	20	19	●	6	Borboletta		Columbia 33135
4/10/76	10	26	●	7	Amigos		Columbia 33576
1/22/77	27	19	●	8	Festival		Columbia 34423
11/4/78	27	33	●	9	Inner Secrets		Columbia 35600
10/20/79	25	22	●	10	Marathon		Columbia 36154
4/18/81	9	32	▲	11	Zebop!		Columbia 37158
9/4/82	22	23	●	12	Shango		Columbia 38122
3/23/85	50	21		13	Beyond Appearances		Columbia 39527
3/7/87	95	11		14	Freedom		Columbia 40272
7/21/90	85	11		15	Spirits Dancing In The Flesh		Columbia 46065
5/23/92	102	13		16	Milagro		Polydor 513197
7/3/99	❶¹²	103	▲¹⁵	17	Supernatural	Cat:#8/27	Arista 19080
					Grammys: Album of the Year / Rock Album		
11/9/02	❶¹	56	▲²	18	Shaman		Arista 14737
11/19/05	2¹	20	●	19	All That I Am		Arista 59773
					GREATEST HITS & COMPILATIONS:		
7/27/74	17	21	▲⁷	20	Santana's Greatest Hits	Cat:#12/71	Columbia 33050
4/18/98+	82	20	▲	21	The Best Of Santana	Cat:#7/16	Columbia 65561
11/9/02	125	1	●	22	The Essential Santana		Columbia 86698 [2]
11/3/07	8	30		23	Ultimate Santana		Legacy 06293
11/1/08	82	2		24	Multi Dimensional Warrior		Columbia 10204 [2]
					LIVE ALBUMS:		
11/5/77	10	24	▲²	25	Moonflower		Columbia 34914 [2]
10/29/88	142	6	●	26	Viva Santana		Columbia 44344 [3]
					recordings from 1969-87		
11/20/93	181	1		27	Sacred Fire - Live In South America		Polydor 521082

SANTANA, Carlos
Born on 7/20/1947 in Autlan de Navarro, Mexico. Latin-rock guitarist. Leader of **Santana**. Added "Devadip" to his name in 1973. Also see **Santana Brothers**.

DEBUT	PEAK	WKS	RIAA	#	Album Title		Label & Number
7/8/72	8	33	▲	1	Carlos Santana & Buddy Miles! Live!	[L]	Columbia 31308
					recorded in Hawaii's Diamond Head volcano crater		
7/7/73	14	24	●	2	Love Devotion Surrender	[I]	Columbia 32034
					CARLOS SANTANA & MAHAVISHNU JOHN McLAUGHLIN		
10/12/74	79	8		3	Illuminations	[I]	Columbia 32900
					TURIYA ALICE COLTRANE & DEVADIP CARLOS SANTANA		
3/31/79	87	9		4	Oneness/Silver Dreams-Golden Reality	[I]	Columbia 35686
					DEVADIP		
9/6/80	65	10		5	The Swing Of Delight	[I]	Columbia 36590 [2]
					DEVADIP CARLOS SANTANA		
4/23/83	31	17		6	Havana Moon		Columbia 38642
11/7/87	195	1		7	Blues For Salvador	[I]	Columbia 40875

SANTANA, Jorge
Born on 6/13/1951 in Jalisco, Mexico. Latin-rock singer/guitarist. Younger brother of **Carlos Santana**. Former member of **Malo**. Also see **Santana Brothers**.

DEBUT	PEAK	WKS	RIAA	#	Album Title		Label & Number
10/14/78	202	5		1	Jorge Santana		Tomato 7020

SANTANA, Juelz
Born LaRon James on 2/18/1983 in Harlem, New York. Male rapper. Member of **The Diplomats** and **Skull Gang**.

DEBUT	PEAK	WKS	RIAA	#	Album Title		Label & Number
9/6/03	8	8		1	From Me To U		Roc-A-Fella 000142
12/10/05	9	19	●	2	What The Game's Been Missing!		Diplomats 005426

SANTANA BROTHERS
Latin-rock trio: brothers **Carlos Santana** and **Jorge Santana**, with nephew Carlos Hernandez. Jorge was a member of **Malo**.

DEBUT	PEAK	WKS	RIAA	#	Album Title		Label & Number
10/15/94	191	1		1	Santana Brothers		Island 523677

Billboard			R I A A	ARTIST / Album Title	Catalog	Label & Number
DEBUT	PEAK	WKS				

SANTA ROSA, Gilberto
Born on 8/21/1950 in Carolina, Puerto Rico. Latin singer. Known as "The Salsa Gentleman,"

9/21/02	181	3		1 Viceversa	[F]	Sony Discos 84781
9/11/04	195	1		2 Autentico	[F]	Sony Discos 70623
4/1/06	188	1		3 Directo Al Corazon	[F]	Sony 96814
11/1/08	22ˣ	2		4 Una Navidad Con Gilberto	[X-F]	Day One 33551

SANTO & JOHNNY
Guitar duo from Brooklyn, New York: brothers Santo Farina (born on 10/24/1937) and Johnny Farina (born on 4/30/1941).

1/18/60	20	29		1 Santo & Johnny	[I]	Canadian-Am. 1001
9/26/60	11	36		2 Encore	[I]	Canadian-Am. 1002
6/26/61	80	13		3 Hawaii	[I]	Canadian-Am. 1004

~ ~ ~ ~ ~ ~ ~ ~ ~ **NON-CHARTED ALBUMS** ~ ~ ~ ~ ~ ~ ~ ~ ~ ~
1962 **Come On In...**   1964 **In The Still Of The Night**
1962 **Around The World...With Santo & Johnny**   1965 **The Beatles Greatest Hits**
1963 **Off Shore**

SANTOGOLD
Born Santi White on 9/25/1976 in Philadelphia, Pennsylvania. Male rapper.

5/17/08	74	15		1 Santogold		Lizard King 70034

SANZ, Alejandro
Born Alejandro Sanchez Pizzaro on 12/18/1968 in Madrid, Spain. Latin singer/guitarist.

10/14/00	148	2		1 El Alma Al Aire	[F]	WEA Latina 84774
9/20/03	128	3		2 No Es Lo Mismo	[F]	Warner Latina 60516
				Grammy: Latin Pop Album		
11/25/06	66	2		3 El Tren De Los Momentos	[F]	Warner Latina 64002
11/28/09	84	1		4 Paraiso Express	[F]	Warner Latina 522519

SAOSIN
Alternative-rock band from Newport Beach, California: Cove Reber (vocals), Beau Burchell (guitar), Justin Shekoski (guitar), Chris Sorenson (bass) and Alex Rodriguez (drums).

10/14/06	22	11		1 Saosin		Capitol 73694
9/26/09	19	3		2 In Search Of Soild Ground		Virgin 35009

SAPP, Marvin
Born in 1968 in Grand Rapids, Michigan. Contemporary gospel singer. Member of **Commissioned**.

8/13/05	164	1		1 Be Exalted		Verity 69951
7/21/07+	28	81	●	2 Thirsty	[L]	Verity 09433

SAPPHIRES, The
Black R&B-pop vocal trio from Philadelphia, Pennsylvania: Carol Jackson, George Garner and Joe Livingston.

~ ~ ~ ~ ~ ~ ~ ~ **NON-CHARTED ALBUM** ~ ~ ~ ~ ~ ~ ~ ~ ~ ~
1964 **Who Do You Love**

SARAI
Born Sarai Howard in 1982 in Kingston, New York. White female rapper/songwriter.

8/16/03	187	1		1 The Original		Sweat 85859

SARAYA
Rock band from New Jersey: Sandi Saraya (vocals), Tony Rey (guitar), Gregg Munier (keyboards), Gary Taylor (bass) and Chuck Bonfante (drums). Munier died on 2/3/2006 (age 44).

4/29/89	79	39		1 Saraya		Polydor 837764

SARDUCCI, Father Guido
Born Don Novello on 1/1/1943 in Ashtabula, Ohio. Comedian/actor. Featured on TV's *Saturday Night Live*.

5/10/80	179	2		1 Live At St. Douglas Convent	[C]	Warner 3440

SASHA & JOHN DIGWEED
Duo of dance DJs. Sasha was born Alexander Coe on 9/4/1969 in Bangor, Wales. Digweed was born on 1/1/1967 in Hastings, England.

7/8/00	149	2		1 Communicate	[I]	Kinetic 54657 [2]
8/24/02	157	2		2 Air Drawn Dagger	[I]	Kinetic 54725
7/10/04	200	1		3 Involver		Global Underground 001
				SASHA (above 2)		

SATELLITE PARTY
Alternative-rock band formed in Los Angeles, California: **Perry Farrell** (vocals), Nuno Bettencourt (guitar; of **Extreme**), Carl Restivo (bass) and Kevin Figueredo (drums). Farrell was also leader of **Jane's Addiction** and **Porno For Pyros**.

6/16/07	91	2		1 Ultra Payload		Columbia 87523

SATRIANI, Joe   **All-Time: #387**
Born on 7/15/1956 in Westbury, New York. Rock guitarist. Member of **Chickenfoot**.

11/21/87+	29	75	▲	1 Surfing With The Alien	[I]	Relativity 8193
11/26/88+	42	26	●	2 Dreaming #11	[EP-I-L]	Relativity 8265
				recorded on 6/11/1988 at the California Theater in San Diego, California		
11/18/89	23	39	●	3 Flying In A Blue Dream	[I]	Relativity 1015

Billboard DEBUT	PEAK	WKS	R I A A	ARTIST Album Title	Catalog	Label & Number
				SATRIANI, Joe — cont'd		
8/8/92	22	28	●	4 The Extremist .... [I]		Relativity 1053
11/13/93	95	8	●	5 Time Machine .... [I-K-L]		Relativity 1177 [2]
				recordings from 1984		
10/28/95	51	7		6 Joe Satriani .... [I]		Relativity 1500
6/21/97	108	3		7 G3 - Live In Concert .... [I-L]		Epic 67920
				JOE SATRIANI / ERIC JOHNSON / STEVE VAI		
3/21/98	50	8		8 Crystal Planet .... [I]		Epic 68018
4/1/00	90	3		9 Engines Of Creation .... [I]		Epic 67860
7/13/02	140	1		10 Strange Beautiful Music .... [I]		Epic 86294
5/1/04	80	2		11 Is There Love In Space? .... [I]		Epic 90832
4/1/06	86	2		12 Super Colossal .... [I]		Epic 76755
4/19/08	89	2		13 Professor Satchafunkilus And The Musterion Of Rock .... [I]		Red Ink 21262
				SATTERFIELD, Esther		
				Born in 1946 in North Carolina. Jazz-styled vocalist.		
7/24/76	180	4		1 The Need To Be		A&M 3411
				SATURDAY NIGHT BAND		
				Disco studio group assembled by producers Jesse Boyce and Moses Dillard.		
5/27/78	125	17		1 Come On Dance, Dance		Prelude 12155
				SAUCE MONEY		
				Born Todd Gaither in Brooklyn, New York. Male rapper.		
6/10/00	72	3		1 Middle Finger U.		Priority 24031
				SAUNDERS, Merl		
				Born on 2/14/1934 in San Mateo, California. Died on 10/24/2008 (age 74). Jazz keyboardist.		
6/2/73	197	5		1 Fire Up .... [I]		Fantasy 9421
				SAVAGE, Chantay		
				Born on 7/16/1967 in Chicago, Illinois. Female R&B-dance singer/songwriter.		
3/30/96	106	8		1 I Will Survive (Doin' It My Way)		RCA 66775
				SAVAGE GARDEN		
				Pop duo from Brisbane, Queensland, Australia: **Darren Hayes** and Daniel Jones.		
5/3/97+	3[1]	104	▲7	1 Savage Garden	Cat:#10/63	Columbia 67954
11/27/99	6	59	▲3	2 Affirmation		Columbia 63711
				SAVAGE GRACE		
				Rock band from Detroit, Michigan: Ron Koss (vocals, guitar), John Seanor (keyboards), Al Jacquez (bass) and Larry Zack (drums). Koss died on 10/16/2004.		
6/6/70	182	8		1 Savage Grace		Reprise 6399
				SAVALAS, Telly		
				Born Aristotelis Savalas on 1/21/1924 in Garden City, Long Island, New York. Died of cancer on 1/22/1994 (age 70). Popular TV/movie actor. Gained fame as the star of TV's *Kojak*.		
1/4/75	117	8		1 Telly		MCA 436
				SAVATAGE		
				Hard-rock band from Florida: brothers Jon Olivia (vocals) and Criss Oliva (guitar), with Johnny Lee Middleton (bass) and Steve Wacholz (drums). Criss Oliva died in a car crash on 10/17/1993 (age 30). Producer Paul O'Neill went on to form the **Trans-Siberian Orchestra**.		
6/21/86	158	7		1 Fight For The Rock		Atlantic 81634
10/10/87+	116	23		2 Hall Of The Mountain King		Atlantic 81775
2/24/90	124	12		3 Gutter Ballet		Atlantic 82008
				SAVE FERRIS		
				Ska-rock band from California: Monique Powell (vocals), Brian Mashburn (vocals, guitar), Eric Zamora, T-Bone Willy and Jose Castellanos (horns), Bill Uechi (bass) and Marc Harismendy (drums). Evan Kilbourne replaced Harismendy in 1998.		
9/27/97	75	17		1 It Means Everything		Starpool 68183
11/6/99	136	2		2 Modified		Starpool 69866
				SAVES THE DAY		
				Alternative-rock band from Princeton, New Jersey: Chris Conley (vocals), Ted Alexander (guitar), David Soloway (guitar), Eben D'Amico (bass) and Bryan Newman (drums). Conley and Soloway also formed **Two Tongues**.		
7/28/01	100	2		1 Stay What You Are		Vagrant 860953
10/4/03	27	3		2 In Reverie		Vagrant 001115
9/11/04	160	1		3 Ups & Downs: Early Recordings And B-Sides .... [K]		Vagrant 0398
4/29/06	67	3		4 Sound The Alarm		Vagrant 433
11/17/07	119	1		5 Under The Boards		Vagrant 476
				SAVING ABEL		
				Rock band from Corinth, Mississippi: Jared Weeks (vocals), Jason Null (guitar), Scott Bartlett (guitar), Eric Taylor (bass) and Blake Dixon (drums).		
5/10/08+	49	72	●	1 Saving Abel		Skidco 06053

Billboard			R I A A	ARTIST		
DEBUT	PEAK	WKS		Album Title	Catalog	Label & Number

SAVING JANE
Rock band from Columbus, Ohio: Marti Dodson (vocals), Kris Misevski (guitar), Pat Buzzard (guitar), Joe Cochran (keyboards), Jeremy Martin (bass) and Dak Goodman (drums).

4/29/06	133	2		1 Girl Next Door		Toucan Cove 006469

SAVOY, Ann
Born Ann Allen on 1/20/1952 in Richmond, Virginia. Cajun singer/songwriter/guitarist.

8/12/06	146	2		1 Adieu False Heart		Vanguard 79808
				LINDA RONSTADT & ANN SAVOY		

SAVOY BROWN
Blues-rock band formed in England: **Chris Youlden** (vocals), Lonesome Dave Peverett (vocals, guitar), Kim Simmonds (guitar), Tony Stevens (bass) and Roger Earl (drums). Youlden left in mid-1970. Peverett, Stevens and Earl left in 1971 to form **Foghat**. Many personnel changes thereafter, with Simmonds the only constant member. Peverett died of cancer on 2/7/2000 (age 57).

4/12/69	182	2		1 Blue Matter .... [L]		Parrot 71027
				side 2: recorded live on 12/6/1968 at Leicester College in England		
9/13/69	71	14		2 A Step Further .... [L]		Parrot 71029
				side 2: recorded live on 5/12/1969 at The Cooks Ferry Inn in London, England		
4/25/70	121	18		3 Raw Sienna		Parrot 71036
10/17/70	39	19		4 Looking In		Parrot 71042
9/18/71	75	17		5 Street Corner Talking		Parrot 71047
3/18/72	34	21		6 Hellbound Train		Parrot 71052
11/4/72	151	10		7 Lion's Share		Parrot 71057
6/30/73	84	14		8 Jack The Toad		Parrot 71059
4/20/74	101	8		9 Boogie Brothers		London 638
11/22/75	153	7		10 Wire Fire		London 659
5/22/76	206	5		11 Skin 'N' Bone		London 670
4/9/77	210	1		12 The Best Of Savoy Brown .... [G]		London 5000
9/16/78	208	1		13 Savage Return		London 718
7/25/81	185	4		14 Rock 'N' Roll Warriors		Town House 7002

SAWYER BROWN
Country band formed in Nashville, Tennessee: Mark Miller (vocals), Bobby Randall (guitar), Gregg Hubbard (keyboards), Jim Scholten (bass) and Joe Smyth (drums). Won first prize on TV's *Star Search* in 1984. Duncan Cameron (of **Amazing Rhythm Aces**) replaced Randall in 1991.
AWARD: CMA: Horizon 1985

2/23/85	140	11		1 Sawyer Brown		Capitol/Curb 12391
8/31/91	140	11		2 Buick		Curb 94260
2/1/92	68	30	●	3 The Dirt Road		Curb 95624
9/19/92+	117	20		4 Cafe On The Corner		Curb 77574
8/28/93	81	24	●	5 Outskirts Of Town		Curb 77626
2/11/95	44	29	●	6 Greatest Hits 1990-1995 .... [G]		Curb 77689
9/16/95	77	8		7 This Thing Called Wantin' And Havin' It All		Curb 77785
5/3/97	73	24		8 Six Days On The Road		Curb 77883
3/20/99	99	7		9 Drive Me Wild!		Curb 77902

SAXON
Hard-rock band formed in England: Biff Byford (vocals), Graham Oliver (guitar), Paul Quinn (guitar), Steve Dawson (bass) and Nigel Glocker (drums). Paul Johnson replaced Dawson in 1986.

12/19/81	207	3		1 Denim And Leather		Carrere 37685
7/3/82	208	2		2 Strong Arm Of The Law		Carrere 37679
6/18/83	155	10		3 Power & The Glory		Carrere 38719
4/14/84	174	5		4 Crusader		Carrere 39284
11/2/85	130	8		5 Innocence Is No Excuse		Capitol 12420
2/14/87	149	6		6 Rock The Nations		Capitol 12519

SAY ANYTHING
Alternative-rock band from Los Angeles, California: Max Bemis (vocals), Jake Turner (guitar), Jeff Turner (guitar), Parker Case (keyboards), Alex Kent (bass) and Coby Linder (drums). Bemis and Linder also formed **Two Tongues**.

11/10/07	27	3		1 In Defense Of The Genre		Doghouse 18701 [2]
11/21/09	25	2		2 Say Anything		Doghouse 56410

SAYER, Leo
Born Gerard Sayer on 5/21/1948 in Shoreham, Sussex, England. Pop singer/songwriter.

3/2/74	209	7		1 Silverbird		Warner 2738
2/8/75	16	22		2 Just A Boy		Warner 2836
10/11/75	125	7		3 Another Year		Warner 2885
11/27/76+	10	51	▲	4 Endless Flight		Warner 2962
10/22/77	37	15		5 Thunder In My Heart		Warner 3089
8/19/78	101	14		6 Leo Sayer		Warner 3200
10/18/80+	36	23		7 Living In A Fantasy		Warner 3483

SCAGGS, Boz
All-Time: #331

Born William Scaggs on 6/8/1944 in Canton, Ohio; raised in Plano, Texas. Eclectic singer/songwriter. Recorded in several different styles (pop, rock, soul and jazz). Played in various groups with **Steve Miller** during the 1960s. Based in San Francisco since the early 1970s; owned a restaurant there from 1983-87.

DEBUT	PEAK	WKS		Album Title		Catalog	Label & Number
7/13/74+	171	5		1 Boz Scaggs	[E]		Atlantic 8239
				first released in 1969			
4/8/78	209	1		2 Boz Scaggs	[R]		Atlantic 19166
				remixed version of #1 above			
4/17/71	124	9		3 Moments			Columbia 30454
12/11/71	198	2		4 Boz Scaggs & Band			Columbia 30796
9/23/72	138	9		5 My Time			Columbia 31384
3/23/74	81	20	●	6 Slow Dancer			Columbia 32760
3/20/76	2⁵	115	▲⁵	7 Silk Degrees			Columbia 33920
12/10/77+	11	23	▲	8 Down Two Then Left			Columbia 34729
4/19/80	8	33	▲	9 Middle Man			Columbia 36106
11/29/80+	24	26	▲	10 Hits!	Cat:#3/156 [G]		Columbia 36841
6/4/88	47	18		11 Other Roads			Columbia 40463
4/23/94	91	14		12 Some Change			Virgin 39489
4/26/97	94	10		13 Come On Home			Virgin 42984
9/29/01	146	2		14 Dig			Virgin 10635
5/24/03	167	1		15 But Beautiful			Gray Cat 4000
11/15/08	128	1		16 Speak Low			Decca 012026

SCANDAL

Pop-rock band from New York: **Patty Smyth** (vocals), Zack Smith (guitar), Keith Mack (guitar), Ivan Elias (bass) and Thommy Price (drums). Price later joined **Joan Jett & The Blackhearts** and **Steve Stevens Atomic Playboys**.

DEBUT	PEAK	WKS		Album Title		Catalog	Label & Number
1/29/83	39	32	●	1 Scandal	[EP]		Columbia 38194
8/4/84	17	41	▲	2 Warrior			Columbia 39173
				SCANDAL FEATURING PATTY SMYTH			

SCARBURY, Joey

Born on 6/7/1955 in Ontario, California. Pop singer.

DEBUT	PEAK	WKS		Album Title	Catalog	Label & Number
8/22/81	104	9		1 America's Greatest Hero		Elektra 537

SCARFACE
All-Time: #274

Born Brad Jordan on 11/9/1969 in Houston, Texas. Male rapper. Member of **The Geto Boys**.

DEBUT	PEAK	WKS		Album Title		Catalog	Label & Number
10/26/91	51	27	●	1 Mr. Scarface Is Back			Rap-A-Lot 57167
9/4/93	7	16	●	2 The World Is Yours			Rap-A-Lot 53861
11/5/94	2¹	32	▲	3 The Diary			Rap-A-Lot 39946
3/29/97	❶¹	25	▲	4 The Untouchable			Rap-A-Lot 42799
3/21/98	4	17	▲	5 My Homies			Rap-A-Lot 45471 [2]
10/21/00	7	19	●	6 The Last Of A Dying Breed			Rap-A-Lot 49867
8/24/02	4	14		7 The Fix			Def Jam South 586909
11/9/02	40	5		8 Greatest Hits	[G]		Rap-A-Lot 12646
4/26/03	20	8		9 Balls And My Word			Rap-A-Lot 42024
3/25/06	12	6		10 My Homies Part 2			J Prince 68516
12/22/07	17	13		11 Made			Rap-A-Lot 331772
5/10/08	121	2		12 The Best Of Scarface	[G]		J Prince 461372
12/20/08	24	10		13 Emeritus			J Prince 515832

SCARLETT & BLACK

Electro-pop duo from England: Robin Hild and Sue West.

DEBUT	PEAK	WKS		Album Title	Catalog	Label & Number
3/19/88	107	11		1 Scarlett & Black		Virgin 90647

SCARS ON BROADWAY

Alternative-rock band from Los Angeles, California: Daron Malakian (vocals, guitar), Franky Perez (guitar), Danny Samoun (keyboards), Dominic Cifarelli (bass) and John Dolmayan (drums). Malakian and Dolmayan are also members of **System Of A Down**.

DEBUT	PEAK	WKS		Album Title	Catalog	Label & Number
8/16/08	17	5		1 Scars On Broadway		Velvet Hammer 011592

SCARY KIDS SCARING KIDS

Hard-rock band from Gilbert, Arizona: Tyson Stevens (vocals), Chad Crawford (guitar), Pouyan Afkary (keyboards), D.J. Wilson (bass) and Derek Smith (drums).

DEBUT	PEAK	WKS		Album Title	Catalog	Label & Number
9/15/07	80	3		1 Scary Kids Scaring Kids		Immortal 60039

SCATTERBRAIN

Hard-rock band from New York: Tommy Christ (vocals), Glen Cummings (guitar), Paul Nieder (guitar), Guy Brogna (bass) and Mike Boyko (drums).

DEBUT	PEAK	WKS		Album Title	Catalog	Label & Number
6/16/90	138	16		1 Here Comes Trouble		In-Effect 3012

SCENE 23

Pop vocal group: Laurie Gidosh, Monika Christian, Dorothy Szamborska, Donavan Green and Josh Henderson. Group assembled for TV series *PopStars 2*.

DEBUT	PEAK	WKS		Album Title	Catalog	Label & Number
12/29/01+	146	4		1 PopStars 2		143 Records 31178

SCHAFER, Kermit
Born on 3/24/1923 in Brooklyn, New York. Died on 3/8/1979 (age 55). Compiled several albums made up of radio and TV bloopers.

1/27/58	17	1		1 Pardon My Blooper! Volume 6 .... [C]		Jubilee 6

no track titles listed on this album; Volume 1 charted in 1954 (#9) and Volume 2 charted in 1954 (#12)

SCHENKER, Michael, Group
Born on 1/10/1955 in Savstedt, Germany. Hard-rock guitarist. Former member of **UFO**. Brother of Rudolf Schenker (of the **Scorpions**). Lead singer Robin McAuley joined in 1987; changed name to **McAuley Schenker Group**.

9/20/80	100	14		1 The Michael Schenker Group		Chrysalis 1302
10/24/81	81	8		2 MSG		Chrysalis 1336
4/9/83	151	7		3 Assault Attack		Chrysalis 1393
3/3/84	201	5		4 Built To Destroy		Chrysalis 41441
10/24/87	95	24		5 Perfect Timing		Capitol 46985
2/3/90	92	14		6 Save Yourself		Capitol 92752
				McAULEY SCHENKER GROUP (above 2)		
3/7/92	180	4		7 MSG		Impact 10385
				SCHENKER/McAULEY		

SCHIFRIN, Lalo
Born Boris Schifrin on 6/21/1932 in Buenos Aires, Argentina. Pianist/conductor/composer. Scored several movies.

12/22/62+	35	3		1 Bossa Nova - New Brazilian Jazz .... [I]		Audio Fidelity 1981
12/30/67+	47	31		2 Music From Mission: Impossible.. [I-S]		Dot 25831
				Grammy: Soundtrack Album		
8/7/76	202	3		3 Black Widow.. [I]		CTI 5000

SCHILLING, Peter
Born on 1/28/1956 in Stuttgart, Germany. Pop singer/songwriter.

10/8/83+	61	23		1 Error In The System		Elektra 60265

SCHMIT, Timothy B.
Born Timothy Bruce Schmit on 10/30/1947 in Oakland, California; raised in Sacramento, California. Pop-rock singer/songwriter/bassist. Member of **Poco** and the **Eagles**.

11/10/84	160	5		1 Playin' It Cool..		Asylum 60359
10/3/87	106	11		2 Timothy B		MCA 42049

SCHNEIDER, Bob
Born on 10/12/1965 in Ypsilanti, Michigan; raised in Munich, Germany; later based in Austin, Texas. Pop-rock singer/songwriter/guitarist.

10/17/09	140	1		1 Lovely Creatures		Shockorama 47

SCHNEIDER, John
Born on 4/8/1960 in Mount Kisco, New York. Country singer/actor. Played "Bo Duke" on TV's *The Dukes Of Hazzard* and "Jonathan Kent" on TV's *Smallville*.

6/27/81	37	22		1 Now Or Never		Scotti Brothers 37400
12/5/81+	155	7		2 White Christmas .... [X]		Scotti Brothers 37617
11/17/84	111	12		3 Too Good To Stop Now		MCA 5495

SCHON, Neal
Born on 2/27/1954 in San Mateo, California. Rock singer/guitarist. Member of **Santana**, **Azteca**, **Journey** and **Bad English**. Also see **Hagar, Schon, Aaronson, Shrieve**.

10/17/81	115	8		1 Untold Passion		Columbia 37600
2/5/83	122	12		2 Here To Stay		Columbia 38428
				NEAL SCHON & JAN HAMMER (above 2)		

SCHOOLLY D
Born Jesse Weaver on 6/22/1966 in Philadelphia, Pennsylvania. Male rapper.

8/6/88	180	3		1 Smoke Some Kill		Jive 1101

SCHOOL OF FISH
Pop-rock band from Los Angeles, California: Josh Clayton-Felt (vocals, guitar), Michael Ward (guitar, vocals), Dominic Nardini (bass) and M.P. (drums). Clayton-Felt died of cancer on 1/19/2000 (age 32).

9/14/91	142	7		1 School Of Fish..		Capitol 94557

SCHORY, Dick
Born on 12/13/1931 in Chicago, Illinois; raised in Ames, Iowa. Percussionist/bandleader.

6/29/59+	11	26		1 Music For Bang, Baa-room And Harp.. [I]		RCA Victor 1866
				DICK SCHORY'S New Percussion Ensemble		
4/20/63	13	13		2 Supercussion .... [I]		RCA Victor 2613
				DICK SCHORY'S Percussion Pops Orchestra		

SCHULTZ, Mark
Born on 9/16/1970 in Colby, Kansas. Christian singer/songwriter.

7/28/01	180	1		1 Mark [Schultz]		Word 63839
10/14/06	79	7		2 Broken & Beautiful .... Cat:#3/6		Word-Curb 886570
9/12/09	62	4		3 Come Alive..		Word-Curb 887394

SCHUUR, Diane
Born on 12/10/1953 in Tacoma, Washington. Jazz singer/pianist. Blind since birth.

11/12/88	170	10		1 Talkin' 'Bout You		GRP 9567
2/16/91	148	10		2 Pure Schuur		GRP 9628

SCHWARTZ, Eddie
Born on 12/22/1949 in Toronto, Ontario, Canada. Pop-rock singer/songwriter/producer.

2/6/82	195	6		1 No Refuge		Atco 141

SCIALFA, Patti
Born Vivienne Patricia Scialfa on 7/29/1953 in Deal, New Jersey. Female singer/songwriter. Member of **Bruce Springsteen**'s E-Street Band; married Springsteen on 6/8/1991.

7/3/04	152	2		1 23rd Street Lullaby		Columbia 90371
9/22/07	90	1		2 Play It As It Lays		Columbia 11293

SCISSOR SISTERS
Dance-rock band from New York: Jake Shears (male vocals), Ana Matronic (female vocals), Del Marquis (guitar), Baby Daddy (bass) and Paddy Boom (drums).

8/14/04	102	14		1 Scissor Sisters		Universal 002772
10/14/06	19	6		2 Ta-Dah		Universal Motown 007499

S CLUB 7
Pop vocal group formed in England: Tina Barrett, Paul Cattermole, Jon Lee, Bradley McIntosh, Jo O'Meara, Hannah Spearritt and Rachel Stevens. Group starred in it's own TV series on the Fox Family Channel.

4/29/00	112	18		1 S Club...		Polydor 543103
12/2/00+	69	30	●	2 7		Polydor 549628

SCOFIELD, John
Born on 12/26/1951 in Dayton, Ohio. Jazz guitarist. Also see **Medeski, Martin & Wood**.

4/23/94	181	2		1 I Can See Your House From Here .... [I]		Blue Note 27765
				JOHN SCOFIELD & PAT METHENY		

SCORPIONS   All-Time: #304
Hard-rock band formed in Hanover, Germany: Klaus Meine (vocals; born on 5/25/1948), Rudolf Schenker (guitar; born on 8/31/1948), Matthias Jabs (guitar; born on 10/25/1955), Francis Buchholz (bass; born on 2/19/1954) and Herman Rarebell (drums; born on 11/18/1949). Ralph Rieckermann replaced Buchholz in 1992. Curt Cress replaced Rarebell in 1995. James Kottak replaced Cress in late 1996. Schenker is the brother of Michael Schenker (of **McAuley Schenker Group**).

1/6/79	206	5		1 Tokyo Tapes .... [L]		RCA Victor 3039 [2]
				recorded in April 1978 at Sun Plaza Hall in Tokyo, Japan		
5/7/83+	37^C	24		2 Virgin Killer		RCA Victor 3659
				released in 1977		
7/28/79	55	23	●	3 Lovedrive		Mercury 3795
5/17/80	52	21	▲	4 Animal Magnetism		Mercury 3825
3/27/82	10	74	▲	5 Blackout		Mercury 4039
3/17/84	6	63	▲³	6 Love At First Sting		Mercury 814981
7/13/85	14	43	▲	7 World Wide Live .... [L]		Mercury 824344 [2]
5/7/88	5	43	▲	8 Savage Amusement		Mercury 832963
11/24/90+	21	73	▲²	9 Crazy World		Mercury 846908
10/9/93	24	9		10 Face The Heat		Mercury 518258
6/8/96	99	3		11 Pure Instinct		Atlantic 82913
9/15/07	63	2		12 Humanity: Hour 1		New Door 009777
				GREATEST HITS & COMPILATIONS:		
11/17/79	180	4		13 Best Of Scorpions		RCA Victor 3516
8/4/84	175	4		14 Best Of Scorpions, Vol. 2		RCA Victor 5085
12/2/89+	43	23	▲	15 Best Of Rockers 'N' Ballads .... Cat:#24/16		Mercury 842002
6/22/02	161	1		16 Bad For Good: The Very Best Of Scorpions		Hip-O 548118

SCOTT, Christopher
Born David Mullaney in New York. Moog synthesizer player.

10/4/69	175	3		1 Switched-On Bacharach .... [I]		Decca 75141

SCOTT, Freddie
Born on 4/24/1933 in Providence, Rhode Island. Died on 6/4/2007 (age 74). R&B singer/songwriter.

~ ~ ~ ~ ~ ~ ~ ~ ~ ~ **NON-CHARTED ALBUM** ~ ~ ~ ~ ~ ~ ~ ~ ~ ~ ~
1964 **Freddie Scott Sings And Sings And Sings**

SCOTT, Jack
Born Giovanni Scafone Jr. on 1/28/1936 in Windsor, Ontario, Canada. Rock and roll-ballad singer/songwriter/guitarist.

~ ~ ~ ~ ~ ~ ~ ~ ~ ~ **NON-CHARTED ALBUMS** ~ ~ ~ ~ ~ ~ ~ ~ ~ ~ ~

1959 **Jack Scott**	1961 **The Spirit Moves Me**
1959 **What Am I Living For!**	1964 **Burning Bridges...And More Of The All-Time Great**
1960 **I Remember Hank Williams**	**Hits Of Jack Scott**
1960 **What In The World's Come Over You**	

SCOTT, Jill
Born on 4/13/1972 in Philadelphia, Pennsylvania. R&B singer/songwriter.

8/5/00+	17	70	▲²	1 Who Is Jill Scott? Words And Sounds Vol. 1		Hidden Beach 62137
12/8/01	38	16	●	2 Experience: Jill Scott 826+ .... [L]		Hidden Beach 86150 [2]
				disc 1: recorded on 8/26/2001 in Washington DC; disc 2: new studio tracks		
9/18/04	3¹	27	●	3 Beautifully Human: Words And Sounds Vol. 2		Hidden Beach 92773

Billboard			R I A A	ARTIST		
DEBUT	PEAK	WKS		Album Title	Catalog	Label & Number

SCOTT, Jill — cont'd

2/17/07	12	8		4 Jill Scott Collaborations		Hidden Beach 00019
10/13/07	4	27	●	5 The Real Thing: Words And Sounds Vol. 3		Hidden Beach 00050

SCOTT, Linda
Born Linda Sampson on 6/1/1945 in Queens, New York. Pop singer.

~ ~ ~ ~ ~ ~ ~ ~ ~ **NON-CHARTED ALBUMS** ~ ~ ~ ~ ~ ~ ~ ~ ~ ~
1961 **Starlight Starbright**   1962 **Linda**
1962 **Great Scott!!! Her Greatest Hits**

SCOTT, Marilyn
Born on 12/21/1949 in Alta Dena, California. Adult Contemporary-dance singer.

4/21/79	189	4		1 Dreams Of Tomorrow		Atco 109

SCOTT, Tom
Born on 5/19/1948 in Los Angeles, California. Pop-jazz-fusion saxophonist. Session work for **Joni Mitchell**, **Steely Dan**, **Carole King** and others. Composer of movie and TV scores. Led the house band for TV's *Pat Sajak Show*. Son of Nathan Scott, a composer of TV scores for *Dragnet*, *Wagon Train*, *My Three Sons* and others.

4/27/74	141	16		1 Tom Scott & The L.A. Express .... [I]		Ode 77021
3/15/75	18	27		2 Tom Cat .... [I]		Ode 77029
				TOM SCOTT & THE L.A. EXPRESS (above 2)		
12/20/75+	42	25		3 New York Connection.. [I]		Ode 77033
9/10/77	87	14		4 Blow It Out... [I]		Ode 34966
11/18/78+	123	13		5 Intimate Strangers .... [I]		Columbia 35557
12/15/79	162	6		6 Street Beat .... [I]		Columbia 36137
7/11/81	123	11		7 Apple Juice .... [I-L]		Columbia 37419
				recorded on 1/15/1981 at The Bottom Line in New York City		
9/25/82	164	7		8 Desire .... [I]		Musician 60162

SCOTT-ADAMS, Peggy
Born Peggy Stoutmeyer on 6/25/1948 in Opp, Alabama; raised in Pensacola, Florida. Recorded in the male-female duo **Peggy Scott & Jo Jo Benson**.

3/1/69	196	5		1 Soulshake		SSS Int'l. 1
				PEGGY SCOTT & JO JO BENSON		
2/1/97	72	13		2 Help Yourself		Miss Butch 4003

SCOTT-HERON, Gil, And Brian Jackson
Scott-Heron was born on 4/1/1949 in Chicago, Illinois; raised in Jackson, Tennessee. Keyboardist/singer/songwriter/author/poet. Met keyboardist/singer/songwriter Jackson while attending Lincoln University in Pennsylvania. Duo was together from 1974-80. Scott-Heron then recorded solo.

2/1/75	30	17		1 The First Minute Of A New Day...........................		Arista 4030
11/8/75	103	5		2 From South Africa To South Carolina.....................		Arista 4044
11/13/76	168	5		3 It's Your World .... [L]		Arista 5001 [2]
				recorded on 7/1/1976 at Paul's Mall in Boston, Massachusetts		
10/22/77	130	5		4 Bridges		Arista 4147
9/9/78	61	21		5 Secrets		Arista 4189
3/8/80	82	12		6 1980		Arista 9514
12/20/80+	159	6		7 Real Eyes		Arista 9540
9/26/81+	106	27		8 Reflections		Arista 9566
10/2/82	123	9		9 Moving Target		Arista 9606
				GIL-SCOTT HERON (above 3)		

SCREAMING BLUE MESSIAHS, The
Punk-rock trio from London, England: Bill Carter (vocals, guitar), Chris Thompson (bass) and Kenny Harris (drums).

1/16/88	172	11		1 Bikini Red..		Elektra 60755

SCREAMING TREES
Rock band from Ellensburg, Washington: brothers Van Conner (bass) and Gary Lee Conner (guitar), with Mark Lanegan (vocals) and Barrett Martin (drums). Lanegan also formed **The Gutter Twins**.

1/30/93	141	7		1 Sweet Oblivion		Epic 48996
7/13/96	134	3		2 Dust		Epic 64178

SCREWBALL
Rap group from Queens, New York: Poet, KL, Solo and Hostyle.

7/14/01	185	1		1 Loyalty...		Hydra 9201

SCRIPT, The
Pop-rock trio from Dublin, Ireland: Danny O'Donoghue (vocals, guitar), Mark Sheehan (bass) and Glen Power (drums).

4/4/09+	64	32↑		1 The Script..		Phonogenic 33450

SCRITTI POLITTI
Pop-dance trio formed in England: Green Gartside (vocals), David Gamson (keyboards) and Fred Maher (drums).

8/3/85+	50	28		1 Cupid & Psyche 85...		Warner 25302
7/16/88	113	8		2 Provision...		Warner 25686

Billboard			R I A A	ARTIST		
DEBUT	PEAK	WKS		Album Title	Catalog	Label & Number

SCRUFFY THE CAT
Rock band from Boston, Massachusetts: Charlie Chesterman (vocals), Stephen Fredette (guitar), Burns Stanfield (keyboards), Mac Stanfield (bass) and Randall Gibson (drums).

12/17/88+	177	8		1 Moons Of Jupiter		Relativity 8237

SCRUGGS, Earl, Revue
Born on 1/6/1924 in Flintville, North Carolina. Banjo player. Half of **Flatt & Scruggs** duo. His revue consisted of sons Gary (vocals, bass), Randy (guitar) and Steve (keyboards) Scruggs, with Jim Murphey (steel guitar) and Jody Maphis (drums). Steve Scruggs murdered his wife, then killed himself on 9/23/1992.
AWARD: Grammy: Lifetime Achievement 2008

1/13/73	204	4		1 Live At Kansas State .... [L]		Columbia 31758
				EARL SCRUGGS AND THE EARL SCRUGGS REVUE		
6/2/73	202	8		2 Dueling Banjos .... [I]		Columbia 32268
9/22/73	169	5		3 The Earl Scruggs Revue		Columbia 32426
6/21/75	104	10		4 Anniversary Special, Volume One		Columbia 33416
4/17/76	161	4		5 The Earl Scruggs Revue, Volume II		Columbia 34090
8/9/03	179	4		6 The Three Pickers		Rounder 610526
				EARL SCRUGGS / DOC WATSON / RICKY SKAGGS		

SEA, Johnny
Born John Seay on 7/15/1940 in Gulfport, Mississippi. Country singer/songwriter/guitarist.

8/6/66	147	2		1 Day For Decision		Warner 1659

SEA HAGS
Hard-rock band from San Francisco, California: Ron Yocom (vocals, guitar), Frank Wilsex (guitar), Chris Schlosshardt (bass) and Adam Maples (drums). Wilsex later joined **Arcade**. Schlosshardt died of a drug overdose on 2/1/1991 (age 26).

6/24/89	163	7		1 Sea Hags		Chrysalis 41665

SEAL
Born Sealhenry Samuel on 2/19/1963 in Paddington, London, England (Nigerian/Brazilian parents). Male singer. Married model Heidi Klum on 5/10/2005.

7/20/91	24	63	▲	1 Seal .... **Cat**:#23/46		Sire 26627
6/18/94+	15	118	▲4	2 Seal		ZTT 45415
12/5/98	22	13	●	3 Human Being		Warner 46828
9/27/03	3[1]	42	●	4 Seal IV		Warner 47947
11/27/04	47	16		5 Best: 1991-2004 .... [G]		Warner 48943 [2]
12/1/07	35	10		6 System		Warner 279868
11/29/08	13	42		7 Soul		143 Records 515868

SEA LEVEL
White blues-rock band formed in Macon, Georgia: Chuck Leavell (vocals, keyboards), Jimmy Nalls (guitar), Lamar Williams (bass) and Jai Johanny Johanson (drums). Leavell, Williams and Johanson were also members of **The Allman Brothers Band**. After first album, Randall Bramblett (piano), Davis Causey (guitar) and George Weaver (drums) joined. Johanson and Weaver left after the second album; replaced by Joe English. Matt Greeley (percussion) joined in 1979.

3/5/77	43	15		1 Sea Level		Capricorn 0178
2/4/78	31	16		2 Cats On The Coast		Capricorn 0198
10/28/78	137	16		3 On The Edge		Capricorn 0212
8/23/80	152	6		4 Ball Room		Arista 9531

SEALS, Dan
Born on 2/8/1948 in McCamey, Texas; raised in Rankin, Texas. Died of cancer on 3/25/2009 (age 61). Singer/songwriter/guitarist. One-half of the duo **England Dan & John Ford Coley**. Brother of Jim Seals (of **Seals & Crofts**) and cousin of country singers Johnny Duncan, Troy Seals and Brady Seals (of **Little Texas**).
AWARD: CMA: Vocal Duo (w/ Marie Osmond) 1986

2/8/86	59	15	●	1 Won't Be Blue Anymore		EMI America 17166

SEALS & CROFTS　　　　　　　　　　　　　　　　　　　　　　**All-Time: #349**
Pop duo: Jim Seals (born on 10/17/1941 in Sidney, Texas) and Dash Crofts (born on 8/14/1940 in Cisco, Texas). With The Champs from 1958-65. Jim is the brother of **Dan Seals** and the cousin of country singers Troy Seals (Jo Ann & Troy), Brady Seals (of **Little Texas**) and Johnny Duncan.

10/31/70	122	10		1 Down Home		TA 5004
12/4/71+	133	20		2 Year Of Sunday		Warner 2568
9/2/72	7	109	▲2	3 Summer Breeze		Warner 2629
4/21/73	4	77	●	4 Diamond Girl		Warner 2699
3/2/74	14	34	●	5 Unborn Child		Warner 2761
8/10/74	81	12		6 Seals & Crofts I And II .... [R]		Warner 2809 [2]
				reissue of first 2 albums on TA label: *Seals & Crofts* and *Down Home*		
4/5/75	30	23	●	7 I'll Play For You		Warner 2848
11/15/75+	11	54	▲2	8 Greatest Hits .... [G]		Warner 2886
5/1/76	37	29	●	9 Get Closer		Warner 2907
12/11/76+	73	10		10 Sudan Village		Warner 2976
10/8/77	118	7		11 One On One .... [S]		Warner 3076
5/13/78	78	13		12 Takin' It Easy		Warner 3163

SEAN, Jay
Born Kamaljit Jhooti on 3/26/1983 in London, England. Hip-hop singer/songwriter/rapper.

12/12/09	37	18		1 All Or Nothing		Cash Money 013683

SEARCHERS, The
Rock and roll band from Liverpool, England: Mike Pender and John McNally (vocals, guitars), Tony Jackson (vocals, bass) and Chris Curtis (drums). Jackson died of liver failure on 8/18/2003 (age 63). Curtis died on 2/28/2005 (age 63).

6/20/64	120	8		1 Hear! Hear!..	[E-L]	Mercury 60914
				recorded at the Star Club in Hamburg, Germany		
4/11/64	22	21		2 Meet The Searchers/Needles & Pins		Kapp 3363
8/29/64	97	14		3 This Is Us		Kapp 3409
3/20/65	112	7		4 The New Searchers LP		Kapp 3412
10/23/65	149	2		5 The Searchers No. 4		Kapp 3449
3/15/80	191	2		6 The Searchers		Sire 6082

SEASE, Marvin
Born on 2/16/1946 in Blackville, South Carolina. R&B singer/songwriter/producer.

7/18/87	114	17		1 Marvin Sease	London 830794

SEATRAIN
Fusion-rock band from Marin County, California: John Gregory (vocals, guitar), Jim Roberts (lyricist), Richard Greene (violin), Donald Kretmar (sax), Andy Kulberg (bass) and Roy Blumenfeld (drums). Greene, Kulberg and Blumenfeld were members of **The Blues Project**. Gregory, Kretmar and Blumenfeld left after first album, replaced by Lloyd Baskin (vocals), Peter Rowan (guitar) and Larry Atamanuik (drums). Kulberg died of cancer on 1/30/2002 (age 57). Roberts died of cancer on 10/29/2002 (age 59).

5/17/69	168	4		1 Sea Train	A&M 4171
1/30/71	48	23		2 Seatrain	Capitol 659
10/9/71	91	9		3 The Marblehead Messenger	Capitol 829
4/7/73	201	4		4 Watch	Warner 2692

SEAWIND
Jazz-pop band formed in Hawaii: husband-and-wife Pauline Wilson (vocals) and Bob Wilson (drums), Bud Nuanez (guitar), Larry Williams (keyboards), Kim Hutchcroft (sax), Jerry Hey (trumpet) and Ken Wild (bass). Pauline is the only native Hawaiian in the group.

5/7/77	188	2		1 Seawind..	CTI 5002
1/21/78	122	7		2 Window Of A Child	CTI 5007
3/24/79	143	14		3 Light The Light	Horizon 734
10/25/80	83	11		4 Seawind	A&M 4824

SEA WOLF
Born Alex Church in Los Angeles, California. Alternative-rock singer/songwriter/guitarist.

10/10/09	175	1		1 White Water, White Bloom	DangerBird 039

SEBADOH
Rock trio from Boston, Massachusetts: Lou Barlow (vocals, guitar), Jason Lowenstein (bass) and Bob Fay (drums). Russ Pollard replaced Fay in 1998.

9/7/96	126	2		1 Harmacy	Sub Pop 370
3/13/99	197	1		2 The Sebadoh..	Sup Pop 31044

SEBASTIAN, Joan
Born in 1951 in Juliantla, Mexico. Male Latin singer/songwriter/guitarist.

10/27/01	194	2		1 En Vivo	[F-L]	Musart 2524
				recorded in Guadalajara, Mexico		
7/17/04	125	11		2 Dos Grandes	[F]	Fonovisa 351402
				MARCO ANTONIO SOLÍS & JOAN SEBASTIAN		
7/1/06	189	1		3 Mas Alla Del Soul	[F]	Musart 3771
9/12/09	164	1		4 Pegadito Al Corazon	[F]	Musart 4208

SEBASTIAN, John
Born on 3/17/1944 in Greenwich Village, Manhattan, New York. Pop-rock singer/songwriter. Formed **The Lovin' Spoonful** in 1965.

3/28/70	20	31		1 John B. Sebastian		MGM 4654
10/10/70	129	3		2 John Sebastian Live	[L]	MGM 4720
4/24/71	75	13		3 Cheapo-Cheapo Productions Presents Real Live John Sebastian	[L]	Reprise 2036
9/18/71	93	9		4 The Four Of Us		Reprise 2041
5/15/76	79	10		5 Welcome Back...		Reprise 2249

SEBESKY, Don
Born on 12/10/1937 in Perth Amboy, New Jersey. Jazz arranger/conductor.

1/19/74	206	13		1 Giant Box	[I]	CTI 6031 [2]

SECADA, Jon
Born Juan Secada on 10/4/1961 in Havana, Cuba; raised in Hialeah, Florida. Singer/songwriter. Discovered by **Gloria Estefan**.

6/6/92+	15	103	▲³	1 Jon Secada	Cat:#39/2	SBK 98845
6/11/94	21	46	▲	2 Heart, Soul & A Voice		SBK 29272
4/12/97	40	13		3 Secada...		SBK 55897
8/5/00	173	2		4 Better Part Of Me		550 Music 69840

SECONDHAND SERENADE
Band is actually solo project of pop-rock singer/songwriter/guitarist John Vesely (born in Menlo Park, California).

5/26/07	164	1		1 Awake	Glassnote 63020
3/8/08	44	29		2 A Twist In My Story	Glassnote 405244

2ND II NONE
Male rap duo from Compton, California: cousins Deon "Tha D" Barnett and Kelton "KK" McDonald.

11/16/91+	83	34		1 2nd II None		Profile 1416
10/30/99	162	1		2 Classic 220		Arista 16401

SECRET MACHINES
Rock trio from Dallas, Texas: brothers Brandon (vocals, bass) and Benjamin (guitar) Curtis, with Josh Garza (drums).

5/13/06	159	1		1 Ten Silver Drops		Reprise 49987

SEDAKA, Neil
Born on 3/13/1939 in Brooklyn, New York. Pop singer/songwriter/pianist. Studied piano since elementary school. Formed songwriting team with lyricist Howard Greenfield while attending Lincoln High School (partnership lasted over 20 years). Recorded with **The Tokens** on Melba label in 1956. Attended Juilliard School for classical piano. Prolific hit songwriter. Career revived in 1974 after signing with **Elton John**'s new Rocket label.

12/7/74+	23	62	●	1 Sedaka's Back		Rocket 463
10/11/75	16	32	●	2 The Hungry Years		Rocket 2157
5/1/76	26	22		3 Steppin' Out		Rocket 2195
5/8/76	201	9		4 Sedaka Live In Australia .... [L]		RCA Victor 1540
				recorded at the South Sydney Junior Leagues Club		
9/18/76	159	4		5 Solitaire .... [E]		RCA Victor 1790
				first released in 1972 on Kirshner 117		
5/28/77	59	7		6 A Song		Elektra 102
5/17/80	135	13		7 In The Pocket		Elektra 259
10/25/08+	25ˣ	2		8 The Miracle Of Christmas .... [X]		Razor & Tie 83007
5/30/09	197	1		9 Waking Up Is Hard To Do		Razor & Tie 83008
				GREATEST HITS & COMPILATIONS:		
1/5/63	55	9		10 Neil Sedaka Sings His Greatest Hits		RCA Victor 2627
3/1/75	161	4		11 Neil Sedaka Sings His Greatest Hits .... [R]		RCA Victor 0928
10/22/77	143	5		12 Neil Sedaka's Greatest Hits		Rocket 2297
5/12/07	22	2		13 The Definitive Collection		Razor & Tie 82968

~ ~ ~ ~ ~ ~ ~ ~ **NON-CHARTED ALBUMS** ~ ~ ~ ~ ~ ~ ~ ~ ~ ~ ~

1959 **Neil Sedaka**　　　　　　　　　1961 **Neil Sedaka Sings "Little Devil" And His Other Hits**
1960 **Circulate**

SEDUCTION
Female dance trio from New York: Idalis Leon, April Harris and Michelle Visage.

10/28/89+	36	47	●	1 Nothing Matters Without Love		A&M 5280

SEEDS, The
Garage-rock band from Los Angeles, California: Richard "Sky Saxon" Marsh (vocals, bass), Jan Savage (guitar), Daryl Hooper (keyboards) and Rick Aldridge (drums). Marsh died on 6/25/2009 (age 63).

1/14/67	132	7		1 The Seeds		GNP Crescendo 2023
8/12/67	87	8		2 Future		GNP Crescendo 2038

SEEGER, Pete
Born on 5/3/1919 in Manhattan, New York. Legendary folk singer/songwriter. Formed **The Weavers** in 1948.
AWARDS: Grammy: Lifetime Achievement 1993 ★ R&R Hall of Fame: 1996 (Early Influence)

12/14/63+	42	36		1 We Shall Overcome .... [L]		Columbia 8901
				Grammy: Hall of Fame		
8/14/71	205	5		2 Rainbow Race		Columbia 30739
5/17/75	181	4		3 Together In Concert .... [L]		Reprise 2214 [2]
				PETE SEEGER & ARLO GUTHRIE		

SEEKERS, The
Pop-folk band formed in Australia: Judith Durham (vocals), Keith Potger (guitar), Bruce Woodley (guitar), and Athol Guy (bass). Potger formed **The New Seekers** in 1969.

6/5/65	145	3		1 The Seekers		Marvel 2060
6/12/65	62	16		2 The New Seekers		Capitol 2319
9/25/65	123	6		3 A World Of Our Own		Capitol 2369
2/25/67	10	28		4 Georgy Girl		Capitol 2431
8/19/67	97	10		5 The Best Of The Seekers .... [G]		Capitol 2746

SEETHER
Hard-rock band from Pretoria, Gauteng, South Africa: Shaun Morgan (vocals, guitar; born on 12/21/1978), Pat Callahan (guitar), Dale Stewart (bass) and Nick Oshiro (drums). John Humphrey replaced Oshiro in 2003; Oshiro joined **Static-X**. Callahan left in June 2006.

9/7/02	92	41	●	1 Disclaimer		Wind-Up 13068
7/3/04	53	33	●	2 Disclaimer II		Wind-Up 13100
6/11/05	8	30	●	3 Karma And Effect		Wind-Up 13115
7/29/06	50	6		4 One Cold Night .... [L]		Musketeer 13121
11/10/07	9	93	●	5 Finding Beauty In Negative Spaces	Cat:#26/4	Wind-Up 13127

SEGAL, George
Born on 2/13/1934 in Great Neck, Long Island, New York. Popular TV/movie actor. Accomplished banjo player.

9/2/67	199	2		1 The Yama Yama Man		Philips 242

SEGER, Bob, & The Silver Bullet Band
1900s: #49 / All-Time: #89

Born on 5/6/1945 in Dearborn, Michigan; raised in Detroit, Michigan. Rock singer/songwriter/guitarist. The System: Bob Schultz (keyboards), Dan Honaker (bass) and Pep Perrine (drums). The Silver Bullet Band: Drew Abbott (guitar; of **Third Power**), Alto Reed (horns), Robyn Robbins (keyboards), Chris Campbell (bass) and Charlie Martin (drums).

AWARD: R&R Hall of Fame: 2004

DEBUT	PEAK	WKS	RIAA	#	Album Title	Catalog	Label & Number
2/8/69	62	10		1	Ramblin' Gamblin' Man		Capitol 172
10/31/70	171	4		2	Mongrel		Capitol 499
					BOB SEGER SYSTEM (above 2)		
12/18/71	210	1		3	Brand New Morning		Capitol 731
7/22/72	180	11		4	Smokin' O.P.'s		Palladium 1006
3/3/73	188	6		5	Back In '72		Reprise 2126
4/12/75	131	18	▲²	6	Beautiful Loser		Capitol 11378
					BOB SEGER (above 3)		
5/1/76	34	167	▲⁵	7	'Live' Bullet	[L]	Capitol 11523 [2]
					recorded on 9/4/1975 at Cobo Hall in Detroit, Michigan		
11/13/76+	8	88	▲⁶	8	Night Moves		Capitol 11557
5/27/78	4	110	▲⁶	9	Stranger In Town		Capitol 11698
3/15/80	❶⁶	110	▲⁵	10	Against The Wind		Capitol 12041
					Grammy: Group Rock Vocal		
9/26/81	3⁴	70	▲⁴	11	Nine Tonight	Cat:#24/77 [L]	Capitol 12182 [2]
					recorded in Detroit, Michigan and Boston, Massachusetts		
1/15/83	5	39	▲	12	The Distance		Capitol 12254
4/19/86	3⁴	62	▲	13	Like A Rock		Capitol 12398
9/14/91	7	29	▲	14	The Fire Inside		Capitol 91134
11/12/94	8	131↑	▲⁸	15	Greatest Hits	Cat:❶⁵/661 [G]	Capitol 30334
11/11/95	27	24	●	16	It's A Mystery		Capitol 99774
11/22/03	23	26	●	17	Greatest Hits 2	[G]	Capitol 52772
9/30/06	4	27	▲	18	Face The Promise		Hideout 54506
					BOB SEGER		

SEINFELD, Jerry
Born Jerome Seinfeld on 4/29/1954 in Brooklyn, New York; raised in Massepequa, New York. Stand-up comedian/actor. Starred in own popular TV sitcom from 1990-98.

DEBUT	PEAK	WKS	RIAA	#	Album Title	Catalog	Label & Number
10/10/98	59	14	▲	1	I'm Telling You For The Last Time	[C]	Universal 53175
					recorded at the Broadhurst Theater in New York City		

SELAH
Contemporary Christian trio: siblings Todd Smith and Nicol Smith (vocals; born in Africa to American missionary parents), with Allan Hall (piano).

DEBUT	PEAK	WKS	RIAA	#	Album Title	Catalog	Label & Number
11/30/02+	3²ˣ	17		1	Rose Of Bethlehem	Cat:❶³/9 [X]	Curb 78720
					Christmas charts: 33/'02, 49/'04, 3/'05, 32/'06, 24/'08		
6/12/04	61	21	●	2	Hiding Place	Cat:❶²/10	Curb 78834
9/10/05	117	5		3	Greatest Hymns	Cat:#5/6 [K]	Curb 78890
8/26/06	43	7		4	Bless The Broken Road - The Duets Album		Curb 78944
9/12/09	66	7		5	You Deliver Me		Curb 79138

SELECTER
Ska band from Coventry, England: Pauline Black and Arthur Hendrickson (vocals), Noel Davies and Compton Amanor (guitars), Desmond Brown (keyboards), Charley Anderson (bass) and Charley Bembridge (drums).

DEBUT	PEAK	WKS	RIAA	#	Album Title	Catalog	Label & Number
5/3/80	175	4		1	Too Much Pressure		Chrysalis 1274
3/28/81	201	3		2	Celebrate The Bullet		Chrysalis 1306

SELENA
1990s: #31 / All-Time: #391

Born Selena Quintanilla-Perez on 4/16/1971 in Lake Jackson, Texas; raised in Corpus Christi, Texas. Shot to death by Yolanda Saldivar (founder of Selena's fan club) on 3/31/1995 (age 23). Latin singer. Married her guitarist, Chris Perez. **Jennifer Lopez** starred in the 1997 biographical movie *Selena*. Sister of A.B. Quintanilla (of **Kumbia Kings**).

DEBUT	PEAK	WKS	RIAA	#	Album Title	Catalog	Label & Number
6/18/94+	29	23	▲²	1	Amor Prohibido	[F]	EMI Latin 28803
4/22/95	64	10	●	2	12 Super Exitos	[F]	EMI Latin 30907
4/22/95	79	7	●	3	Live	[F-L]	EMI Latin 42770
					Grammy: Tejano Album		
4/22/95	97	7	●	4	Entre A Mi Mundo	[F]	EMI Latin 42635
4/22/95	147	4		5	Las Reinas Del Pueblo	[F]	EMI Latin 32639
					SELENA & GRACIELA BELTRAN		
5/6/95	❶²ᶜ	9		6	Mis Mejores Canciones-17 Super Exitos	[F]	EMI Latin 27190
5/6/95	22ᶜ	2		7	Ven Conmigo	[F]	EMI Latin 42359
8/5/95	❶¹	49	▲³	8	Dreaming Of You	Cat:#11/19	EMI Latin 34123
3/29/97	7	64	▲	9	Selena	[S]	EMI Latin 55535
4/14/01	176	2		10	Live - The Last Concert	[F-L]	EMI Latin 32119

Billboard			R I A A	**ARTIST** Album Title	Catalog	Label & Number
DEBUT	PEAK	WKS				

SELENA — cont'd

GREATEST HITS & COMPILATIONS:

11/23/96	82	5		11 Siempre Selena	[F]	EMI Latin 53585
4/25/98	131	6		12 Anthology	[F]	EMI Latin 94110 [3]
3/27/98	54	19	●	13 All My Hits - Todos Mis Exitos	[F]	EMI Latin 97886
3/18/00	149	6		14 All My Hits - Todos Mis Exitos Vol. 2	[F]	EMI Latin 23332
10/19/02	159	4	●	15 Ones	[F]	EMI Latin 42096
7/12/03	117	1		16 Greatest Hits		EMI Latin 90398

SEMBELLO, Michael
Born on 4/17/1954 in Philadelphia, Pennsylvania. Pop singer/guitarist. Prolific studio musician.

10/8/83	80	10		1 Bossa Nova Hotel		Warner 23920

SEMISONIC
Rock trio from Minneapolis, Minnesota: Dan Wilson (vocals, guitar), John Munson (bass) and Jacob Slichter (drums).

4/11/98	43	43	▲	1 Feeling Strangely Fine		MCA 11733
3/31/01	103	2		2 All About Chemistry		MCA 112355

SENAY, Eddy
Born Edward Harris in Detroit, Michigan. R&B guitarist/songwriter.

7/1/72	204	4		1 Hot Thang	[I]	Sussex 7013

SENSATIONS, The
R&B vocal group from Philadelphia, Pennsylvania: Yvonne Mills Baker, Sam Armstrong, Alphonso Howell and Richard Curtain. Howell died on 5/7/1998 (age 61).

~ ~ ~ ~ ~ ~ ~ ~ ~ ~ *NON-CHARTED ALBUM* ~ ~ ~ ~ ~ ~ ~ ~ ~ ~ ~

1962 **Let Me In/Music, Music, Music**

SENSES FAIL
Hard-rock band from New Jersey: Buddy Nielsen (vocals), Dave Miller (guitar), Garret Zablocki (guitar), Mike Glita (bass) and Dan Trapp (drums).

5/17/03	144	1		1 From The Depths Of Dreams	[EP]	Drive-Thru 000155
9/25/04	34	6		2 Let It Enfold You		Drive-Thru 0403
10/28/06	15	8		3 Still Searching		Drive-Thru 439
10/25/08	18	5		4 Life Is Not A Waiting Room		Vagrant 512

SEPULTURA
Speed-metal band from Belo Horizonte, Brazil: brothers Max Cavalera (vocals, guitar) and Igor Cavalera (drums), with Andreas Kisser (guitar) and Paulo Jr. (bass). Max Cavalera left in early 1998 to form **Soulfly**; replaced by Derrick Green. Sepultura is Portuguese for grave.

5/4/91	119	4		1 Arise		RC 9328
11/6/93	32	7	●	2 Chaos A.D.		Roadrunner 57458
3/30/96	27	10	●	3 Roots		Roadrunner 8900
6/21/97	162	2		4 Blood-Rooted	[K]	Roadrunner 8821
10/24/98	82	3		5 Against		Roadrunner 8700
4/7/01	134	1		6 Nation		Roadrunner 8560

SEQUENCE, The
Female funk trio from Columbia, South Carolina: Gwendolyn Chisolm, **Angie Stone** and Cheryl Cook.

9/4/82	207	3		1 The Sequence		Sugar Hill 267

SERENDIPITY SINGERS, The
Pop-folk group formed in Boulder, Colorado: Jon Arbenz, Mike Brovsky, Diane Decker, Brooks Hatch, John Madden, Bryan Sennett, Tom Tiemann, Lynne Weintraub and Bob Young.

3/7/64	11	29		1 The Serendipity Singers		Philips 600115
6/27/64	68	15		2 The Many Sides Of The Serendipity Singers		Philips 600134
1/16/65	149	2		3 Take Your Shoes Off with the Serendipity Singers		Philips 600151

SERMON, Erick
Born on 11/25/1968 in Bay Shore, New York. Male rapper. One half of **EPMD** duo. Member of **Def Squad**. Also recorded as **Erick Onasis**. Also see **Various Artists Compilations:** *Insomnia - The Erick Sermon Compilation Album*.

11/6/93	16	6		1 No Pressure		Def Jam 57460
11/25/95	35	4		2 Double Or Nothing		Def Jam 529286
7/15/00	53	7		3 Def Squad Presents Erick Onasis		DreamWorks 450114
11/17/01	33	5		4 Music		J Records 20023
12/7/02	72	4		5 React		J Records 20050
7/10/04	61	2		6 Chilltown, New York		Def Squad 002716

SET YOUR GOALS
Alternative-rock band from Orinda, California: Matt Wilson and Jordan Brown (vocals), Audelio Flores (guitar), Dan Coddaire (guitar), Joe Saucedo (bass) and Michael Ambrose (drums).

8/8/09	65	2		1 This Will Be The Death Of Us		Epitaph 87028

Billboard			R I A A	ARTIST Album Title	Catalog	Label & Number
DEBUT	PEAK	WKS				

SETZER, Brian, Orchestra
Born on 4/10/1959 in Massapequa, Long Island, New York. Lead singer/guitarist of the **Stray Cats**. Played Eddie Cochran in the 1987 movie *La Bamba*. Formed own 16-piece swing orchestra in 1994. Formed trio '68 Comeback Special (named after **Elvis Presley**'s 1968 TV special) with Mark Winchester (bass) and Bernie Dresel (drums).

DEBUT	PEAK	WKS	RIAA	ARTIST / Album Title	Catalog	Label & Number
3/22/86	45	18		1 The Knife Feels Like Justice		EMI America 17178
5/28/88	140	8		2 Live Nude Guitars		EMI-Manhattan 46963
				BRIAN SETZER (above 2)		
4/9/94	158	4		3 The Brian Setzer Orchestra		Hollywood 61565
7/11/98	9	43	▲²	4 The Dirty Boogie		Interscope 90183
8/19/00	62	7		5 Vavoom!		Interscope 490733
6/30/01	152	1		6 Ignition!		Surfdog 67124
				BRIAN SETZER '68 COMEBACK SPECIAL		
10/13/07	141	2		7 Wolfgang's Big Night Out		Surfdog 211388
10/31/09	123	1		8 Songs From Lonely Avenue		Surfdog 521223
				CHRISTMAS ALBUMS:		
12/21/02	141	3		9 Boogie Woogie Christmas	**Cat**:#6/13	Surfdog 44011
				Christmas charts: 17/'02, 11/'03, 12/'04, 50/'05		
11/26/05	56	8		10 Dig That Crazy Christmas	**Cat**:#46/1	Surfdog 44101
				Christmas charts: 4/'05, 43/'06, 29/'07		
10/25/08	20ˣ	2		11 Christmas Rocks!		Surfdog 512780
12/20/08	180	3		12 The Ultimate Christmas Collection	[K]	Surfdog 512781

SEVENDUST
Hard-rock band formed in Atlanta, Georgia: Lajon Witherspoon (vocals), Clint Lowery (guitar), John Connolly (guitar), Vinnie Hornsby (bass) and Morgan Rose (drums). Sonny Mayo replaced Lowery in 2004. Clint is the brother of Corey Lowery (of **Stereomud**); the Lowery brothers later formed **Dark New Day**.

DEBUT	PEAK	WKS	RIAA	ARTIST / Album Title	Catalog	Label & Number
3/28/98	165	16	●	1 Sevendust		TVT 5730
9/11/99	19	14	●	2 Home		TVT 5820
12/1/01	28	13	●	3 Animosity		TVT 5870
10/25/03	14	6		4 Seasons		TVT 5990
5/22/04	90	2		5 Southside Double-Wide: Acoustic Live	[L]	TVT 6050
1/14/06	156	2		6 Best Of Sevendust (Chapter One 1997-2004)	[G]	TVT 6051
10/29/05	20	4		7 Next		Winedark 07
3/24/07	14	7		8 Alpha		7Bros 100437
4/19/08	19	4		9 Chapter VII: Hope & Sorrow		7Bros 429692

SEVEN MARY THREE
Rock band formed in Williamsburg, Virginia: Jason Ross (vocals), Jason Pollock (guitar), Casey Daniel (bass) and Giti Khalsa (drums). Thomas Juliano replaced Pollock in 2000.

DEBUT	PEAK	WKS	RIAA	ARTIST / Album Title	Catalog	Label & Number
11/4/95+	24	52	▲	1 American Standard		Mammoth 92633
6/21/97	75	7		2 Rock Crown		Mammoth 83018
8/1/98	121	2		3 Orange Ave.		Mammoth 83114
6/23/01	178	1		4 The Economy Of Sound		Mammoth 65516

702
Female R&B vocal trio from Las Vegas, Nevada: Kameelah Williams, with sisters Irish and Lemisha Grinstead. Group named after the Las Vegas area code.

DEBUT	PEAK	WKS	RIAA	ARTIST / Album Title	Catalog	Label & Number
2/1/97	82	30	●	1 No Doubt		Biv Ten 0738
7/3/99	34	21	▲	2 702		Motown 549526
4/12/03	45	3		3 Star		Motown 066130

707
Rock band from Detroit, Michigan: Kevin Russell (vocals, guitar), Phil Bryant (bass) and Jim McClarty (drums). Kevin Chalfant (vocals) and Tod Howarth (keyboards) added in 1982. Chalfant co-founded **The Storm** in 1991.

DEBUT	PEAK	WKS	RIAA	ARTIST / Album Title	Catalog	Label & Number
2/7/81	159	6		1 The Second Album		Casablanca 7248
7/3/82	129	9		2 Mega Force		Boardwalk 33253

7 SECONDS
Hard-rock trio from Los Angeles, California: Kevin Seconds (vocals, guitar), Steve Youth (bass) and Troy Mowat (drums).

DEBUT	PEAK	WKS	RIAA	ARTIST / Album Title	Catalog	Label & Number
11/4/89+	153	19		1 Soulforce Revolution		Restless 72344

SEVENTH DAY SLUMBER
Christian hard-rock band from Dallas, Texas: Joseph Rojas (vocals, guitar), Jeremy Holderfield (guitar), Joshua Schwartz (bass) and Elliot Lopes (drums).

DEBUT	PEAK	WKS	RIAA	ARTIST / Album Title	Catalog	Label & Number
3/28/09	141	1		1 Take Everything		BEC 28003

SEVERINSEN, Doc
Born Carl Severinsen on 7/7/1927 in Arlington, Oregon. Legendary trumpeter. Leader of the *The Tonight Show* band (1967-92).

DEBUT	PEAK	WKS	RIAA	ARTIST / Album Title	Catalog	Label & Number
8/27/66	147	2		1 Fever!	[I]	Command 893
11/26/66	133	6		2 Command Performances	[I]	Command 904
10/16/71	185	2		3 Brass Roots	[I]	RCA Victor 4522
4/29/72	74	19		4 Brass On Ivory	[I]	RCA Victor 4629
6/9/73	185	3		5 Brass, Ivory & Strings	[I]	RCA Victor 0098
				HENRY MANCINI & DOC SEVERINSEN (above 2)		
4/17/76	189	4		6 Night Journey	[I]	Epic 34078
11/1/86	65	26		7 The Tonight Show Band With Doc Severinsen	[I]	Amherst 3311
				Grammy: Jazz Album		

Billboard			R I A A	ARTIST		
DEBUT	PEAK	WKS		Album Title	Catalog	Label & Number

SEVERINSEN, Doc — cont'd

| 12/14/91 | 171 | 4 | | 8 Merry Christmas From Doc Severinsen And The Tonight Show Orchestra .. [X-I] | | Amherst 94406 |

Christmas chart: 16/'91

SEVILLE, David
Born Ross Bagdasarian on 1/27/1919 in Fresno, California. Died of a heart attack on 1/16/1972 (age 52). Appeared in the movies *Viva Zapata*, *Stalag 17* and *Rear Window*. Creator of **The Chipmunks**.

~ ~ ~ ~ ~ ~ ~ ~ ~ ~ ~ *NON-CHARTED ALBUM* ~ ~ ~ ~ ~ ~ ~ ~ ~ ~ ~
1958 The Witch Doctor

SEX PISTOLS
Legendary punk-rock band formed in London, England: Johnny "Rotten" Lydon (vocals), **Steve Jones** (guitar), Sid Vicious (bass) and Paul Cook (drums). Disbanded in January 1978. Lydon formed **Public Image Ltd.** in 1978. Vicious died of a drug overdose on 2/2/1979 (age 21), while out on bail for the fatal stabbing of girlfriend Nancy Spungen four months earlier. Jones later joined **Chequered Past**. Movies about group include *The Great Rock 'n' Roll Swindle*, *D.O.A.* and *Sid & Nancy*. Lydon, Jones, Matlock and Cook reunited in 1996.
AWARD: R&R Hall of Fame: 2006

| 12/10/77+ | 106 | 12 | ▲ | 1 Never Mind The Bollocks, Here's The Sex Pistols .... Cat:#14/36 | | Warner 3147 |

RS500 #41

SEXTON, Charlie
Born on 8/11/1968 in San Antonio, Texas. Rock singer/guitarist. Lead guitarist for **Joe Ely**'s band. Co-founder of the **Arc Angels**. Appeared in the 1991 movie *Thelma & Louise*. His brother is the leader of **Will And The Kill**.

| 11/30/85+ | 15 | 34 | | 1 Pictures For Pleasure .... | | MCA 5629 |
| 2/18/89 | 104 | 9 | | 2 Charlie Sexton .... | | MCA 6280 |

SEYMOUR, Phil
Born on 5/15/1952 in Tulsa, Oklahoma. Died of cancer on 8/17/1993 (age 41). Rock singer/drummer. Formerly with the **Dwight Twilley** Band and the **Textones**.

| 2/21/81 | 64 | 16 | | 1 Phil Seymour .... | | Boardwalk 36996 |

SHADES OF BLUE
"Blue-eyed soul" vocal group from Detroit, Michigan: Linda Kerr, Robert Kerr, Ernest Dernai and Nick Marinelli.

~ ~ ~ ~ ~ ~ ~ ~ ~ ~ ~ *NON-CHARTED ALBUM* ~ ~ ~ ~ ~ ~ ~ ~ ~ ~ ~
1966 Happiness Is The Shades Of Blue

SHADOWFAX
Jazz-fusion band from Chicago, Illinois. Core members: G.E. Stinson (guitar), Chuck Greenberg (sax), Phil Maggini (bass) and Stuart Nevitt (drums). Band name taken from J.R.R. Tolkien's novel, *Lord Of The Rings*. Greenberg died of a heart attack on 9/4/1995 (age 45).

11/19/83+	145	19		1 Shadowdance .... [I]		Windham Hill 1029
11/17/84	126	20		2 The Dreams Of Children .... [I]		Windham Hill 1038
7/12/86	114	16		3 Too Far To Whisper .... [I]		Windham Hill 1051
5/14/88	168	5		4 Folksongs For A Nuclear Village .... [I]		Capitol 46924

Grammy: New Age Album

SHADOWS FALL
Hard-rock band from Boston, Massachusetts: Brian Fair (vocals), Jonathan Donais (guitar), Matthew Bachand (guitar), Paul Romanko (bass) and Jason Bittner (drums).

10/9/04	20	8		1 The War Within		Century Media 8228
7/1/06	83	2		2 Fallout From The War		Century Media 8428
4/21/07	46	4		3 Threads Of Life		Atlantic 115516
10/3/09	35	3		4 Retribution		Ferret 520708

SHADOWS OF KNIGHT, The
Garage-rock band from Chicago, Illinois: Jim Sohns (vocals), Joe Kelley (guitar), Jerry McGeorge (guitar), Warren Rogers (bass) and Tom Schiffour (drums).

| 5/14/66 | 46 | 18 | | 1 Gloria .... | | Dunwich 666 |

~ ~ ~ ~ ~ ~ ~ ~ ~ ~ ~ *NON-CHARTED ALBUM* ~ ~ ~ ~ ~ ~ ~ ~ ~ ~ ~
1966 Back Door Men

SHAGGY
Born Orville Richard Burrell on 10/22/1968 in Kingston, Jamaica. Reggae singer.

| 7/29/95 | 34 | 37 | ▲ | 1 Boombastic .... | | Virgin 40158 |

Grammy: Reggae Album

8/26/00+	❶⁶	84	▲⁶	2 Hotshot		MCA 112096
2/23/02	168	1		3 Hotshot: Ultramix (Special Edition) .... [K]		MCA 112827
11/16/02	24	13	●	4 Lucky Day		MCA 113070
10/8/05	144	1		5 Clothes Drop		Big Yard 004180

SHAGGY 2 DOPE
Born Joseph Utsler on 10/14/1974 in Wayne, Michigan. White male rapper. One-half of **Insane Clown Posse**.

| 3/11/06 | 88 | 1 | | 1 F.T.F.O. .... | | Psychopathic 4056 |

F.T.F.O.: Fuck The Fuck Off

Billboard			R I A A	ARTIST Album Title	Catalog	Label & Number
DEBUT	PEAK	WKS				

SHAI
R&B vocal group formed in Washington DC: Garfield Bright, Marc Gay, Carl Martin and Darnell Van Rensalier.

1/9/93	6	52	▲² 1	...If I Ever Fall In Love	Gasoline Alley 10762
1/1/94	127	8	2 Right Back At Cha .... [K]		Gasoline Alley 10945
11/4/95	42	11	3 Blackface		Gasoline Alley 11176

SHAKATAK
Jazz band from London, England: Jill Saward (vocals), Keith Winter (guitar), Bill Sharpe (keyboards), George Anderson (bass) and Roger Odell (drums).

11/27/82	202	3	1 Night Birds		Polydor 6354
4/2/83	204	2	2 Invitations		Polydor 810068
2/23/85	203	7	3 Down On The Street		Polydor 823304

SHAKESPEAR'S SISTER
Female vocal duo: Siobhan Fahey and Marcy "Marcella Detroit" Levy. Fahey was a member of **Bananarama**. Levy was a prominent backing vocalist.

7/18/92	56	29	1 Hormonally Yours		London 828266

SHAKIRA
Born Shakira Isabel Mebarak Ripoll on 2/2/1977 in Barranquilla, Colombia. Female Latin-pop singer.

10/17/98	131	22	● 1 Donde Estan Los Ladrones? .... Cat:#30/2 [F]		Sony Discos 82746
3/18/00	124	8	2 MTV Unplugged .... [F-L]		Sony Discos 83775
			Grammy: Latin Pop Album		
12/1/01	3¹	61	▲³ 3 Laundry Service		Epic 63900
11/30/02	112	10	4 Laundry Service: Limited Edition: Washed And Dried .... [K]		Epic 86962
11/23/02	80	9	5 Grandes Exitos .... [F-G]		Sony Discos 87611
4/17/04	45	6	6 Live & Off The Record .... [F-L]		Epic 91109
6/25/05	4	33	▲ 7 Fijacion Oral Vol. 1 [F]		Epic 94774
			Grammy: Latin Rock Album		
12/17/05	5	57	▲ 8 Oral Fixation Vol. 2		Epic 97708
12/12/09	15	15	9 She Wolf		Epic 61695

SHALAMAR
R&B vocal trio formed in Los Angeles, California: **Jody Watley**, Jeffrey Daniels and **Howard Hewett**.

5/21/77	48	14	1 Uptown Festival		Soul Train 2289
11/4/78	171	4	2 Disco Gardens		Solar 2895
11/10/79+	23	36	● 3 Big Fun		Solar 3479
1/10/81	40	36	● 4 Three For Love		Solar 3577
10/24/81	115	15	5 Go For It		Solar 3984
2/20/82	35	25	● 6 Friends		Solar 28
8/6/83	38	23	7 The Look		Solar 60239
12/8/84+	90	24	8 Heart Break		Solar 60385

SHAMEN, The
Techno-rave dance band from Aberdeen, Scotland: brothers Derek and Keith McKenzie, Richard West, Colin Angus, Will Sinnott and Peter Stephenson. Sinnott drowned on 5/23/1991 (age 31).

2/1/92	138	8	1 En-Tact		Epic 48722

SHANA
Born Shana Petrone on 5/8/1972 in Parkridge, Illinois; raised in Ft. Lauderdale, Florida. Female dance singer.

1/27/90	165	11	1 I Want You		Vision 3316

SHA NA NA
Rock and roll group specializing in 1950's-style music. Core members: Jon "Bowzer" Bauman, Scott Powell, Johnny Contardo, Fred Greene, Don York and Rich Joffe. Group hosted own TV show variety show from 1977-81.

12/13/69	183	7	1 Rock & Roll Is Here To Stay!		Kama Sutra 2010
8/7/71	122	9	2 Sha Na Na .... [L]		Kama Sutra 2034
			side 1: recorded live on 3/1/1971 at Columbia University in New York City; side 2: studio		
7/1/72	156	14	3 The Night Is Still Young		Kama Sutra 2050
4/21/73	38	24	● 4 The Golden Age Of Rock 'N' Roll .... [L]		Kama Sutra 2073 [2]
12/1/73+	140	11	5 From The Streets Of New York .... [L]		Kama Sutra 2075
			recorded on 8/29/1973 in Central Park		
6/1/74	165	6	6 Hot Sox		Kama Sutra 2600
8/9/75	162	4	7 Sha Na Now		Kama Sutra 2605
11/13/99	27ᶜ	1	8 Halloween Oldies Party		Madacy 0358
			first released in 1997		

SHAND, Remy
Born in 1978 in Winnipeg, Manitoba, Canada. Male "blue-eyed soul" singer/songwriter/multi-instrumentalist.

3/30/02	39	21	1 The Way I Feel		Motown 014481

Billboard			R I A A	ARTIST		
DEBUT	PEAK	WKS		Album Title	Catalog	Label & Number

SHANE & SHANE
Christian pop-rock duo from Texas: Shane Barnard and Shane Everett.

4/12/03	149	1		1 Carry Away		Inpop 71264
11/6/04	123	1		2 Clean		Inpop 71290
9/15/07	66	2		3 Pages		Inpop 71403
11/1/08	29ˣ	1		4 Glory In The Highest: A Christmas Record .... [X]		Inpop 71445
11/21/09	96	1		5 Everything Is Different..		Inpop 71453

SHANGRI-LAS, The
"Girl group" formed in Queens, New York. Consisted of two sets of sisters: Mary and Betty Weiss, and twins Mary Ann and Marge Ganser. Mary Ann Ganser died of a drug overdose on 3/14/1970 (age 22). Marge Ganser died of breast cancer on 7/28/1996 (age 48).

3/13/65	109	6		1 Leader Of The Pack..		Red Bird 101
				side 2 has live sounds dubbed in		

~ ~ ~ ~ ~ ~ ~ ~ ~ ~   *NON-CHARTED ALBUMS*   ~ ~ ~ ~ ~ ~ ~ ~ ~ ~
1965 **I Can Never Go Home Anymore**   1966 **Golden Higs Of The Shangri-Las**

SHANICE
Born Shanice Wilson on 5/14/1973 in Pittsburgh, Pennsylvania; raised in Los Angeles, California. Female R&B singer.

11/28/87+	149	18		1 Discovery		A&M 5128
				SHANICE WILSON		
1/18/92	83	26	●	2 Inner Child		Motown 6319
7/9/94	184	3		3 21...Ways To Grow		Motown 0302
3/27/99	56	14		4 Shanice		LaFace 26058
3/11/06	195	1		5 Every Woman Dreams		Imajah 90001

SHANK, Bud
Born Clifford Shank on 5/27/1926 in Dayton, Ohio. Died on 4/2/2009 (age 82). Jazz saxophonist.

2/12/66	56	21		1 Michelle.. [I]		World Pacific 21840

SHANKAR, Ravi
Born on 4/7/1920 in Benares, India. Classical sitarist. Father of **Norah Jones**. Introduced the sitar to rock and roll music.

7/15/67	161	7		1 West Meets East .... [I]		Angel 36418
				YEHUDI MENUHIN & RAVI SHANKAR		
				Grammy: Chamber Music Album		
7/29/67	148	7		2 Ravi Shankar In New York .... [I]		World Pacific 21441
11/18/67+	43	19		3 Ravi Shankar At The Monterey International Pop Festival........................ [I-L]		World Pacific 21442
8/3/68	140	4		4 Ravi Shankar In San Francisco.. [I-L]		World Pacific 21449
4/7/73	213	2		5 In Concert 1972... [I-L]		Apple 3396 [2]
				recorded in New York City		
1/11/75	176	3		6 Shankar Family & Friends		Dark Horse 22002
				produced by **George Harrison**		

SHANNON
Born Brenda Shannon Greene on 5/12/1957 in Washington DC. Black female dance singer.

2/11/84	32	37	●	1 Let The Music Play		Mirage 90134
5/25/85	92	16		2 Do You Wanna Get Away		Mirage 90267

SHANNON, Del
Born Charles Westover on 12/30/1934 in Coopersville, Michigan. Died of a self-inflicted gunshot wound on 2/8/1990 (age 55). Pop singer/songwriter.
AWARD: R&R Hall of Fame: 1999

6/22/63	12	26		1 Little Town Flirt		Big Top 1308
12/12/81+	123	14		2 Drop Down And Get Me		Elektra 568
				produced by **Tom Petty**		

~ ~ ~ ~ ~ ~ ~ ~ ~ ~   *NON-CHARTED ALBUMS*   ~ ~ ~ ~ ~ ~ ~ ~ ~ ~
1961 **Runaway With Del Shannon**   1965 **One Thousand Six Hundred Sixty One Seconds**
1964 **Handy Man**   **With Del Shannon**
1965 **Del Shannon Sings Hank Williams**

SHAREEFA
Born Shareefa Cooper on 1/1/1984 in East Orange, New Jersey. Female R&B singer.

11/11/06	25	5		1 Point Of No Return		DTP 007231

SHARISSA
Born Sharissa Dawes on 8/21/1975 in Brooklyn, New York. Female R&B singer/songwriter.

3/16/02	44	10		1 No Half Steppin'...		Motown 016706

SHARKEY, Feargal
Born on 8/13/1958 in Londonderry, Northern Ireland. Pop-rock singer. Former member of **The Undertones**.

3/8/86	75	11		1 Feargal Sharkey		A&M 5108

SHARKS
Rock band formed in England: Steve "Snips" Parsons (vocals), Chris Spedding (guitar), **Andy Fraser** (bass; **Free**) and Marty Simon (drums).

8/25/73	189	4		1 First Water		MCA 351

Billboard			R I A A	ARTIST		
DEBUT	PEAK	WKS		Album Title	Catalog	Label & Number

SHARP, Dee Dee
Born Dione LaRue on 9/9/1945 in Philadelphia, Pennsylvania. R&B singer. Married record producer Kenny Gamble in 1967.

6/23/62	44	17	1 It's Mashed Potato Time		Cameo 1018
11/17/62	117	4	2 Down To Earth		Cameo 1029
			CHUBBY CHECKER & DEE DEE SHARP		
12/27/80+	204	4	3 Dee Dee		Philadelphia Int'l. 36370
			DEE DEE SHARP GAMBLE		

~ ~ ~ ~ ~ ~ ~ ~ ~ ~ **NON-CHARTED ALBUMS** ~ ~ ~ ~ ~ ~ ~ ~ ~ ~ ~ ~ ~
1962 **All The Hits By Dee Dee Sharp**   1963 **All The Hits By Dee Dee Sharp, Volume II**
1963 **Do The Bird**   1963 **Biggest Hits**

SHARP, Kevin
Born on 12/10/1970 in Weiser, Idaho; raised in Sacramento California. Country singer.

11/23/96+	40	36	● 1 Measure Of A Man		Asylum 61930

SHARPLES, Bob, and His Music
Born on 7/2/1913 in Bury, Lancashire, England. Died on 9/8/1987 (age 74). Bandleader/arranger.

10/9/61	11	25	1 Pass In Review .... [I]		London Phase 4 44001

SHAW, Marlena
Born Marlena Burgess on 9/22/1942 in New Rochelle, New York. Jazz-styled singer.

7/5/75	159	5	1 Who Is This Bitch, Anyway?		Blue Note 397
4/2/77	62	14	2 Sweet Beginnings		Columbia 34458
4/8/78	171	4	3 Acting Up		Columbia 35073

SHAW, Robert, Chorale
Born on 4/30/1916 in Red Bluff, California. Died of a stroke on 1/25/1999 (age 82). Conductor/arranger. Not to be confused with the actor of the same name.

12/23/57+	5	4	● 1 Christmas Hymns And Carols .... [X]		RCA Victor LM-2139
			first charted in 1949 (#5) on RCA Victor 1077; Christmas charts: 9/'63, 31/'64, 41/'66		
12/22/58	13	3	2 Christmas Hymns And Carols .... [X-R]		RCA Victor LM-2139
5/25/59	21	1	3 Deep River And Other Spirituals		RCA Victor 2247
4/27/63	27	10	4 America, The Beautiful		RCA Victor 2662
12/21/63	11ˣ	9	5 The Many Moods of Christmas .... [X]		RCA Victor LSC-2684
			Christmas charts: 11/'63, 29/'65, 68/'66, 28/'67		
12/7/68	8ˣ	6	6 Handel's Messiah .... [X]		RCA Victor LM-6175 [3]
			George Frideric Handel composed this magnificent oratorio in 1741; soloists: Richard Lewis, Thomas Paul, Judith Raskin, Florence Kopleff; Christmas charts: 8/'68, 17/'69		

SHAW, Roland
Born on 5/26/1920 in London, England. Conductor/arranger.

2/27/65	38	25	1 Themes From The James Bond Thrillers .... [I]		London 412
2/5/66	119	5	2 More Themes From The James Bond Thrillers.. [I]		London 445

SHAW, Sandie
Born Sandra Goodrich on 2/26/1947 in Dagenham, Essex, England. Pop singer.

6/12/65	100	4	1 Sandie Shaw		Reprise 6166

SHAW, Tommy
Born on 9/11/1953 in Montgomery, Alabama. Rock singer/guitarist. Member of **Styx** and **Damn Yankees**.

10/20/84	50	25	1 Girls With Guns		A&M 5020
10/26/85	87	9	2 What If		A&M 5097

SHAW/BLADES
Rock duo formed in San Francisco, California: **Tommy Shaw** (of **Styx**) and Jack Blades (of **Night Ranger**). Both were also members of **Damn Yankees**.

4/7/07	117	1	1 Influence		VH1 Classic 00106

SHAWANDA, Crystal
Born in Wikwemikong, Ontario, Canada. Female Country singer.

9/6/08	81	4	1 Dawn Of A New Day		RCA 06762

SHAWNNA
Born Rashawnna Guy on 1/3/1978 in Chicago, Illinois. Female hip-hop singer/rapper. Daughter of **Buddy Guy**.

10/16/04	22	5	1 Worth Tha Weight		Disturb. Tha P. 002950
7/15/06	13	9	2 Block Music		DTP 006909

SHAWTY LO
Born Carlos Walker on 3/31/1976 in Atlanta, Georgia. Male rapper. Member of **D4L**.

3/15/08	13	15	1 Units In The City		D4L 331708

SHEA, George Beverly
Born on 2/1/1909 in Winchester, Ontario, Canada. Legendary gospel singer.

7/12/08	10ᶜ	3	1 How Sweet The Sound: My All-Time Favorites .... [K]		Spring Hill 21060

SHE & HIM
Adult Alternative duo formed in Portland, Oregon: Zooey Deschanel and **M. Ward**. Deschanel has also acted in several movies. Ward is also a member of **Monsters of Folk**.

4/5/08	71	12	1 Volume One... **Cat**:#40/2		Merge 324

SHEAR, Jules
Born on 3/7/1952 in Pittsburgh, Pennsylvania. Pop-rock singer/songwriter.

5/25/85	209	2		1 The Eternal Return		EMI America 17156

SHEARD, Kierra KiKi
Born on 6/20/1987 in Detroit, Michigan. Gospel singer. Daughter of **Karen Clark-Sheard**. Niece of **Dorinda Clark-Cole**.

9/25/04	115	2		1 I Owe You		EMI Gospel 97304
7/15/06	90	2		2 This Is Me		EMI Gospel 32483
11/15/08	114	1		3 Bold Right Life		EMI Gospel 03103
				KIERRA SHEARD		

SHEARING, George, Quintet
Born on 8/13/1919 in London, England. Jazz pianist. Blind since birth.

1950s: #49

10/6/56	20	1		1 Velvet Carpet	[I]	Capitol 720
10/7/57	13	3		2 Black Satin	[I]	Capitol 858
8/25/58	17	2		3 Burnished Brass	[I]	Capitol 1038
7/25/60	11	35		4 White Satin		Capitol 1334
10/30/61	82	14		5 Satin Affair		Capitol 1628
5/5/62	27	16		6 Nat King Cole Sings/George Shearing Plays		Capitol 1675
				NAT KING COLE & GEORGE SHEARING		

SHeDAISY
Country vocal trio from Magna, Utah: sisters Kristyn Osborn (born on 8/24/1970), Kelsi Osborn (born on 11/21/1974) and Kassidy Osborn (born on 10/30/1976).

5/29/99+	70	102	▲	1 The Whole SheBang		Lyric Street 165002
11/25/00	92	8		2 Brand New Year	[X]	Lyric Street 165007
				Christmas chart: 8/'00		
7/13/02	23	10		3 Knock On The Sky		Lyric Street 165015
6/26/04	16	30	●	4 Sweet Right Here		Lyric Street 165044
4/1/06	22	5		5 Fortuneteller's Melody		Lyric Street 165062

SHEEK LOUCH
Born Shawn Jacobs on 11/9/1976 in Yonkers, New York. Male rapper. Member of **The Lox**.

10/4/03	9	6		1 Walk Witt Me		D-Block 001042
11/26/05	23	3		2 After Taxes		D-Block 5833
4/5/08	41	5		3 Silverback Gorilla		D-Block 5595
6/6/09	122	1		4 Life On D-Block		Real Talk 73

SHEIK, Duncan
Born on 11/18/1969 in Montclair, New Jersey; raised in Hilton Head, South Carolina. Alternative pop-rock singer/songwriter/guitarist.

2/1/97	83	36	●	1 Duncan Sheik		Atlantic 82879
10/24/98	163	2		2 Humming		Atlantic 83138
9/14/02	110	4		3 Daylight		Atlantic 83569
2/14/09	181	1		4 Whisper House		Victor 40426

SHEILA E.
Born Sheila Escovedo on 12/12/1957 in Oakland, California. Latin singer/percussionist. With father Pete Escovedo in the band **Azteca** in the mid-1970s. Her brother Peto was in **Con Funk Shun**. Her uncle **Coke Escovedo** was a noted percussionist.

7/7/84	28	46	●	1 The Glamorous Life		Warner 25107
9/21/85+	50	33	●	2 Romance 1600		Paisley Park 25317
3/21/87	56	12		3 Sheila E.		Paisley Park 25498
4/20/91	146	5		4 Sex Cymbal		Warner 26255

SHEKINAH GLORY MINISTRY
Large gospel vocal group based in Chicago, Illinois.

10/13/07	93	6		1 Jesus	[L]	Kingdom 3003
4/11/09	168	1		2 The Best Of Shekinah Glory Ministry	[K]	Kingdom 3023

SHELLEY, Pete
Born Peter McNeish on 4/17/1955 in Leigh, Lancashire, England. Lead singer/guitarist of the **Buzzcocks** (1976-81).

6/26/82	121	10		1 Homosapien		Arista 6602
7/23/83	151	5		2 XL1		Arista 8017

SHELLS, The — see DUBS, The

SHELTON, Blake
Born on 6/18/1976 in Ada, Oklahoma. Country singer/songwriter/guitarist.

8/18/01	45	29	●	1 Blake Shelton		Warner 24731
2/22/03	8	12	●	2 The Dreamer		Warner 48237
11/13/04	20	52	●	3 Blake Shelton's Barn & Grill		Warner 48728
5/19/07	8	40	●	4 Pure BS		Warner 44488
3/22/08	157	2		5 Collector's Edition	[EP]	Warner 439996
12/6/08	34	18		6 Startin' Fires		Warner 512911

Billboard			R I A A	ARTIST	Catalog	Label & Number
DEBUT	PEAK	WKS		Album Title		

SHELTON, Ricky Van
Born on 1/12/1952 in Danville, Virginia; raised in Grit, Virginia. Country singer/songwriter/guitarist.
AWARDS: CMA: Horizon 1988 / Male Vocalist 1989 ★ OPRY: 1988

12/26/87+	76	41	▲	1 Wild-Eyed Dream......................................		Columbia 40602
10/29/88	78	24	▲	2 Loving Proof...		Columbia 44221
12/23/89+	16ˣ	3	●	3 Ricky Van Shelton Sings Christmas.............	[X]	Columbia 45269
2/3/90	53	61	▲	4 RVS III..		Columbia 45250
6/8/91	23	57	▲	5 Backroads...		Columbia 46855
5/23/92	122	24	●	6 Don't Overlook Salvation...........................		Columbia 46854
8/29/92	50	31	▲	7 Greatest Hits Plus...................................	[G]	Columbia 52753
9/11/93	91	8	●	8 A Bridge I Didn't Burn..............................		Columbia 48992

SHENANDOAH
Country band formed in Muscle Shoals, Alabama: Marty Raybon (vocals), Jim Seales (guitar), Stan Thorn (keyboards), Ralph Ezell (bass) and Mike McGuire (drums). Seales was guitarist for the R&B group **Funkadelic**. McGuire was married to actress Teresa Blake (of TV soap *All My Children*) from 1994-98. Rocky Thacker replaced Ezell in 1995. Thorn left in 1996.

7/13/91	186	4	●	1 Extra Mile..		Columbia 45490
2/25/95	182	4		2 In The Vicinity Of The Heart......................		Liberty 31109

SHEP AND THE LIMELITES
R&B vocal trio from Queens, New York: James "Shep" Sheppard (formerly with The Heartbeats), Clarence Bassett and Charles Baskerville. Sheppard was murdered on 1/24/1970 (age 34).

~ ~ ~ ~ ~ ~ ~ ~ ~ ~ ~ **NON-CHARTED ALBUM** ~ ~ ~ ~ ~ ~ ~ ~ ~ ~ ~
1962 **Our Anniversary Featuring "Daddy's Home"**

SHEPARD, Vonda
Born on 7/7/1963 in Manhattan, New York; raised in Los Angeles, California. Singer/songwriter/keyboardist. Had a recurring role as a singer on TV's *Ally McBeal*. Married producer Mitchell Froom (of **Gamma**) in 2004.

5/23/98	7	41	▲	1 Songs From Ally McBeal	[TV]	550 Music 69365
5/8/99	79	9		2 By 7:30..		Jacket 2222
11/27/99	60	14	●	3 Heart And Soul - New Songs From Ally McBeal	[TV]	550 Music 63915
12/2/00	59	6		4 Ally McBeal: A Very Ally Christmas Featuring Vonda Shepard	[X-TV]	550 Music 85196
				Christmas chart: 9/'00		
5/12/01	34	11		5 Ally McBeal: For Once In My Life	[TV]	Epic 85195

SHEPHERD, Ashton
Born on 8/16/1986 in Coffeeville, Alabama. Female country singer/songwriter.

3/22/08	90	2		1 Sounds So Good......................................		MCA Nashville 010039

SHEPHERD, Kenny Wayne, Band
Born on 6/12/1977 in Shreveport, Louisiana. Blues-rock guitarist. His band: Noah Hunt (vocals), Robby Emerson (bass) and Sam Bryant (drums). Keith Christopher replaced Emerson in 1998.

1/27/96	108	33	▲	1 Ledbetter Heights....................................		Giant 24621
10/25/97	74	62	▲	2 Trouble Is...		Giant 24689
10/30/99	52	6	●	3 Live On...		Giant 24729
10/23/04	101	3		4 The Place You're In.................................		Reprise 48866
2/10/07	164	1		5 10 Days Out: Blues From The Backroads......		Reprise 49294

SHEPPARD, T.G.
Born William Browder on 7/20/1944 in Humbolt, Tennessee. Country singer.

4/25/81	119	12		1 I Love 'Em All...		Warner/Curb 3528
1/30/82	152	13		2 Finally!...		Warner/Curb 3600
6/11/83	189	3		3 T.G. Sheppard's Greatest Hits...................	[G]	Warner/Curb 23841
1/14/84	204	4		4 Slow Burn...		Warner/Curb 23911

SHERBS
Pop-rock band from Australia: Daryl Braithwaite (vocals), Harvey James (guitar), Garth Porter (keyboards), Tony Mitchell (bass) and Alan Sandow (drums). Group originally known as Sherbet.

2/28/81	100	16		1 The Skill...		Atco 137
5/22/82	202	4		2 Defying Gravity..		Atco 146

SHERIDAN, Tony — see BEATLES, The

SHERIFF
Pop-rock band from Toronto, Ontario, Canada: Freddy Curci (vocals), Steve DeMarchi (guitar), Arnold Lanni (keyboards), Wolf Hassel (bass) and Rob Elliott (drums). Disbanded in 1983. Hassel and Lanni formed **Frozen Ghost**. Curci and DeMarchi formed **Alias**.

6/25/83	210	1		1 Sheriff...		Capitol 12227
1/7/89	60	14		2 Sheriff...	[R]	Capitol 91216

SHERLEY, Glen
Born on 3/9/1936 in Oklahoma; raised in California. Died of a self-inflicted gunshot on 5/11/1978 (age 42). Country singer/songwriter/guitarist. Was an inmate at the California State Prison in Vacaville at the time of his recordings.

6/5/71	208	1		1 Glen Sherley..	[L]	Mega 1006

Billboard			R I A A	ARTIST		
DEBUT	PEAK	WKS		Album Title	Catalog	Label & Number

SHERMAN, Allan
Born Allan Copelon on 11/30/1924 in Chicago, Illinois. Died of emphysema on 11/21/1973 (age 48). Novelty singer/songwriter. Creator/producer of TV's *I've Got A Secret*.

11/3/62	❶²	51	●	1 My Son, The Folk Singer	[C]	Warner 1475
1/19/63	❶¹	47		2 My Son, The Celebrity	[C]	Warner 1487
8/17/63	❶⁸	32		3 My Son, The Nut	[C]	Warner 1501
4/11/64	25	19		4 Allan In Wonderland	[C]	Warner 1539
11/21/64+	53	14		5 Peter And The Commissar	[C]	RCA Victor 2773
				ALLAN SHERMAN/BOSTON POPS/ARTHUR FIEDLER		
11/28/64+	32	17		6 For Swingin' Livers Only!	[C]	Warner 1569
12/18/65+	88	11		7 My Name Is Allan	[C]	Warner 1604

SHERMAN, Bobby
Born on 7/22/1943 in Santa Monica, California. Teen idol pop singer/actor. Regular on TV's *Shindig*. Played "Jeremy Bolt" on TV's *Here Come The Brides*.

11/8/69+	11	35	●	1 Bobby Sherman		Metromedia 1014
4/11/70	10	48	●	2 Here Comes Bobby		Metromedia 1028
10/24/70	20	26	●	3 With Love, Bobby		Metromedia 1032
4/24/71	48	14		4 Portrait Of Bobby		Metromedia 1040
10/9/71	71	8		5 Getting Together		Metromedia 1045
12/25/71+	2¹ˣ	5		6 Bobby Sherman Christmas Album	[X]	Metromedia 1038
				Christmas charts: 2/'70, 11/'71		
3/25/72	83	9		7 Bobby Sherman's Greatest Hits	[G]	Metromedia 1048

SHERRYS, The
Black "girl group" from Philadelphia, Pennsylvania: sisters Dinell Cook (lead) and Delphine Cook, with Charlotte Butler and Delores "Honey" Wylie. Formed by Joe Cook (Little Joe & The Thrillers).

~ ~ ~ ~ ~ ~ ~ ~ ~ ~ **NON-CHARTED ALBUM** ~ ~ ~ ~ ~ ~ ~ ~ ~ ~ ~
1963 At The Hop With The Sherrys

SHERWOOD
Pop-rock band from San Luis Obispo, California: Nate Henry (vocals, bass), Dan Koch (guitar), Dave Provenzano (guitar), Mike Leibovich (keyboards) and Joe Greenetz (drums).

| 10/31/09 | 91 | 1 | | 1 QU .... | | MySpace 10100 |

SHE WANTS REVENGE
Punk-rock duo formed in Los Angeles, California: Justin Warfield (vocals, guitar) and Adam Bravin (bass, drums).

| 2/18/06 | 38 | 21 | | 1 She Wants Revenge .... | | Flawless 005587 |
| 10/27/07 | 58 | 3 | | 2 This Is Forever .... | | Perfect Kiss 010042 |

SHINEDOWN
Rock band from Jacksonville, Florida: Brent Smith (vocals), Jasin Todd (guitar), Brad Stewart (bass) and Barry Kerch (drums).

8/2/03+	53	60	▲	1 Leave A Whisper	Cat:#48/2	Atlantic 83566
10/22/05	23	39	●	2 Us And Them		Atlantic 83817
7/12/08	8	99↑	▲	3 The Sound Of Madness		Atlantic 511244

SHINEHEAD
Born Edmund Aiken on 4/10/1962 in London, England; raised in Jamaica and the Bronx, New York. Reggae rapper.

| 11/5/88 | 185 | 4 | | 1 Unity .... | | Elektra 60802 |
| 7/28/90 | 155 | 5 | | 2 The Real Rock .... | | Elektra 60890 |

SHINS, The
Pop-rock band from Albuquerque, New Mexico: James Mercer (vocals, guitar), Marty Crandall (keyboards), Neal Langford (bass) and Jesse Sandoval (drums).

9/25/04+	15ᶜ	23	●	1 Oh, Inverted World	[E]	Sub Pop 70550
				released in 2001		
11/8/03	86	6		2 Chutes Too Narrow		Sub Pop 625
2/10/07	2¹	25	●	3 Wincing The Night Away		Sub Pop 705

SHINY TOY GUNS
Alternative-rock band from Los Angeles, California: Carah Faye (female vocals), Chad Petree (male vocals, guitar, bass), Jeremy Dawson (keyboards) and Mikey Martin (drums).

| 11/4/06+ | 90 | 8 | | 1 We Are Pilots .... | | Universal Motown 007615 |
| 11/22/08 | 47 | 2 | | 2 Season Of Poison .... | | Universal Motown 012209 |

SHIPLEY, Ellen
Born on 5/29/1959 in Brooklyn, New York. Female singer/songwriter.

| 10/25/80 | 205 | 5 | | 1 Breaking Through The Ice Age .... | | RCA Victor 3626 |

SHIRELLES, The
R&B-rock and roll "girl group" from Passaic, New Jersey: Shirley Alston (born on 6/10/1941), Beverly Lee (born on 8/3/1941), Doris Kenner (born on 8/2/1941; died of cancer on 2/4/2000, age 58) and Addie "Micki" Harris (born on 1/22/1940; died on 6/10/1982, age 42).

AWARD: R&R Hall of Fame: 1996

5/5/62	59	13		1 Baby It's You		Scepter 504
1/26/63	19	49		2 The Shirelles Greatest Hits	[G]	Scepter 507
6/29/63	68	9		3 Foolish Little Girl		Scepter 511

Billboard			R I A A	ARTIST Album Title	Catalog	Label & Number
DEBUT	PEAK	WKS				

~ ~ ~ ~ ~ ~ NON-CHARTED ALBUMS by THE SHIRELLES ~ ~ ~ ~ ~ ~ ~
1960 **Tonight's The Night**   1963 **It's A Mad, Mad, Mad, Mad World**
1961 **The Shirelles Sing To Trumpets And Strings**   1964 **The Shirelles Sing The Golden Oldies**
1962 **The Shirelles & King Curtis Give A Twist Party** 1967 **The Shirelles Greatest Hits, Vol. II**

SHIRLEY, Don
Born on 1/27/1927 in Kingston, Jamaica. Black pop-jazz-classical pianist/organist.

4/2/55	14	2	1 Tonal Expressions .... [I]	Cadence 1001	

SHIRLEY (AND COMPANY)
Disco band formed in Los Angeles, California: Shirley Goodman (female vocals), Jesus Alvarez (male vocals), Walter Morris (guitar), Bernadette Randle (keyboards), Seldon Powell (sax), Jonathan Williams (bass) and Clarence Oliver (drums). Goodman was one-half of **Shirley & Lee** duo; she died on 7/5/2005 (age 69).

8/2/75	169	3	1 Shame Shame Shame	Vibration 128	

SHIRLEY & LEE
R&B duo from New Orleans, Louisiana: Shirley Goodman (born on 6/19/1936; died on 7/5/2005, age 69) and Leonard Lee (born on 6/29/1935; died on 10/23/1976, age 41). Shirley also formed **Shirley (And Company)**.
~ ~ ~ ~ ~ ~ ~ ~ ~ ~ **NON-CHARTED ALBUM** ~ ~ ~ ~ ~ ~ ~ ~ ~ ~
1956 **Let The Good Times Roll!** [Aladdin label]

SHOCKED, Michelle
Born Michelle Johnston on 2/24/1962 in Dallas, Texas. Folk singer/songwriter.

9/17/88+	73	35	1 Short Sharp Shocked	Mercury 834294	
11/11/89	95	26	2 Captain Swing	Mercury 838878	

SHOCKING BLUE, The
Pop-rock band from The Hague, Holland: Mariska Veres (vocals), Robbie Leeuwen (guitar), Klaasje Wal (bass) and Cor Beek (drums). Beek died on 4/2/1998 (age 49). Veres died on 12/2/2006 (age 59).

2/14/70	31	17	1 The Shocking Blue	Colossus 1000	

SHOES
Rock band from Zion, Illinois: Gary Klebe (vocals), brothers Jeff Murphy (guitar) and John Murphy (bass), and Skip Meyer (drums).

10/13/79	50	12	1 Present Tense...	Elektra 244	
2/7/81	140	7	2 Tongue Twister	Elektra 303	

SHONTELLE
Born Shontelle Layne on 10/3/1985 in Saint James, Barbados. Female R&B singer/rapper.

12/6/08	115	1	1 Shontelligence..	SRP 012343	

SHOOTING STAR
Rock band from Kansas City, Missouri: Gary West (vocals), Van McLain (guitar, vocals), Bill Guffey (keyboards), Charles Waltz (violin), Ron Verlin (bass) and Steve Thomas (drums).

3/15/80	147	14	1 Shooting Star...	Virgin 13133	
9/19/81	92	30	2 Hang On For Your Life..	Epic 37407	
8/7/82	82	9	3 III Wishes	Epic 38020	
7/30/83	162	6	4 Burning	Epic 38683	
11/4/89	151	7	5 Touch Me Tonight-The Best Of Shooting Star .... [G]	Enigma 73549	

SHOP BOYZ
Male rap trio from Atlanta, Georgia: Demetrius "Meanie" Hardin, Richard "Fat" Stevens and Rasheed "Sheed" Hightower.

7/7/07	11	14	1 Rockstar Mentality	OnDeck 009138	

SHORROCK, Glenn
Born on 6/30/1944 in Chatham, Kent, England; raised in Elizabeth, Australia. Former lead singer of **Little River Band**.

10/29/83	207	1	1 Villain Of The Peace...	Capitol 12222	

SHORT, Bobby
Born on 9/15/1924 in Danville, Illinois. Died of leukemia on 3/21/2005 (age 80). Jazz singer/pianist.

3/4/72	169	8	1 Bobby Short Loves Cole Porter..	Atlantic 606 [2]	

SHORTER, Wayne
Born on 8/25/1933 in Newark, New Jersey. Jazz saxophonist. Played with **Art Blakey** (1959-63) and **Miles Davis** (1964-70).

7/12/75	183	3	1 Native Dancer	Columbia 33418	

SHOTGUN
Funk band from Detroit, Michigan: Ernest Lattimore (vocals, guitar), Tyrone Steels (vocals, drums), Billy Talbert (keyboards), Greg Ingram (sax), William Gentry (trumpet), Larry Austin (bass) and Robert Resch (drums).

6/11/77	202	12	1 Shotgun..	ABC 979	
4/29/78	172	5	2 Good, Bad & Funky	ABC 1060	
5/5/79	163	4	3 Shotgun III	MCA 1118	
2/23/80	206	2	4 Shotgun IV	MCA 3201	

Billboard			R I A A	ARTIST		
DEBUT	PEAK	WKS		Album Title	Catalog	Label & Number

SHOTGUN MESSIAH
Hard-rock band from Skovde, Sweden: Zinny San (vocals), Harry Cody (guitar), Tim Skold (bass) and Stixx Galore (drums). San left by 1992 and Skold became vocalist with Bobby Lycon joining on bass.

10/21/89	99	23		1 Shotgun Messiah	Relativity 88561
5/2/92	199	1		2 Second Coming	Relativity 1060

SHOT IN THE DARK
Pop-rock band from England: Krysia Kristianne (vocals), Adam Yurman (guitar), Bryan Savage (sax), Peter White (keyboards) and Robin Lamble (bass). Former backing band for **Al Stewart**.

5/2/81	210	1		1 Shot In The Dark..	RSO 3096

SHOWBREAD
Christian hard-rock band from Savannah, Georgia: Joshua "Josh Dies" Porter (vocals), Ivory Mobley (vocals), Matt Davis (guitar), Mike Jensen (guitar), John Giddens (keyboards), Pat Porter (bass) and Justin Oblinger (drums).

8/19/06	198	1		1 Age Of Reptiles	Tooth & Nail 52479

SHOWDOWN, The
Christian hard-rock band from Elizabethton, Tennessee: David Bunton (vocals), Josh Childers (guitar), Jeremiah Scott (bass) and Andrew Hall (drums).

3/10/07	191	1		1 Temptation Come My Way	Mono vs Stereo 86191

SHRIEKBACK
Pop-rock band formed in London, England. Barry Andrews (**XTC**) fronted fluctuating lineup. Dave Allen (**Gang Of Four**) was bassist from 1983-87. Allen, drummer Martin Barker and guitarist Steve Halliwell formed **King Swamp** in 1988. Disbanded in 1989.

6/25/83	188	3		1 Care	Warner 23874
2/21/87	145	6		2 Big Night Music	Island 90552
7/23/88	169	12		3 Go Bang!	Island 90949

SHRIEVE, Michael
Born on 7/6/1949 in San Francisco, California. Rock drummer. Member of **Santana**, **Automatic Man** and **Novo Combo**. Also see **Hager, Schon, Aaronson, Shrieve**.

8/21/76	60	12		1 Go	Island 9387
				STOMU YAMASHTA / STEVE WINWOOD / MICHAEL SHRIEVE	

SHUPE, Ryan, & The RubberBand
Born in Provo, Utah. Country singer/songwriter/fiddler. The RubberBand: Roger Archibald (guitar), Craig Miner (banjo), Colin Botts (bass) and Bart Olson (drums).

9/24/05	87	3		1 Dream Big	Capitol 37369

SHUST, Aaron
Born in Pittsburgh, Pennsylvania. Contemporary Christian singer/songwriter.

6/3/06+	63	9		1 Anything Worth Saying	Brash 0017
6/23/07	151	1		2 Whispered And Shouted	Brash 0033
8/22/09	197	1		3 Take Over	Brash 0052

SHWAYZE
Born Aaron Smith on 5/29/1986 in Malibu, California. Male rapper.

9/6/08	10	7		1 Shwayze	Suretone 011498
11/21/09	55	1		2 Let It Beat	Bananabeat 013310

SHY
Rock band from Birmingham, England: Tony Mills (vocals), Steve Harris (guitar), Pat McKenna (keyboards), Roy Davis (bass) and Alan Kelly (drums).

6/27/87	193	2		1 Excess All Areas	RCA Victor 6311

SHYHEIM
Born Shyheim Franklin on 11/14/1979 in Brooklyn, New York. Teen male rapper.

5/7/94	52	5		1 AKA The Rugged Child..	Virgin 39385
6/15/96	63	4		2 The Lost Generation	Noo Trybe 41583

SHYNE
Born Jamal Barrow on 11/8/1978 in Belize City, Belize; raised in Brooklyn, New York. Male rapper. Sentenced to ten years in prison on 6/1/2001 for a shooting incident on 12/27/1999.

10/14/00	5	30	●	1 Shyne	Bad Boy 73032
8/28/04	3[1]	11	●	2 Godfather Buried Alive	Gangland 002962

SIA
Born Sia Furler on 12/18/1975 in Adelaide, Australia. Female singer/songwriter.

1/26/08	26	8		1 Some People Have Real Problems	Monkey Puzzle 30629

SIBERRY, Jane
Born on 10/12/1955 in Toronto, Ontario, Canada. Folk singer/songwriter.

6/14/86	149	8		1 The Speckless Sky	Open Air 0305

SICK PUPPIES
Alternative-rock trio from Sydney, Australia: Shimon Moore (vocals, guitar), Emma Anzai (bass) and Mark Goodwin (drums).

4/21/07	181	2		1 Dressed Up As Life	RMR 89752
8/1/09	31	32↑		2 Tri-Polar	RMR 28631

Billboard DEBUT	PEAK	WKS	R I A A	ARTIST Album Title	Catalog	Label & Number

SIDE EFFECT
R&B vocal group from Los Angeles, California: Augie Johnson, Sylvia St. James, Louis Patton and Greg Matta. Their backing band is the **L.A. Boppers**.

3/19/77	115	13		1 **What You Need**		Fantasy 9513
1/7/78	86	15		2 **Goin' Bananas**		Fantasy 9537
1/20/79	135	8		3 **Rainbow Visions**		Fantasy 9569
5/24/80	208	1		4 **After The Rain**		Elektra 261

SIDEWINDERS
Rock band from Tucson, Arizona: Dave Slutes (vocals, guitar), Rich Hopkins (guitar), Mark Perrodin (bass) and Andrea Curtis (drums).

5/13/89	169	5		1 **Witchdoctor**		Mammoth 9663

SIDRAN, Ben
Born on 8/14/1943 in Chicago, Illinois; raised in Racine, Wisconsin. Rock keyboardist. Member of **Steve Miller**'s band.

8/14/76	203	1		1 **Free In America** .... **[I]**		Arista 4081

SIEGEL, Dan
Born in Seattle, Washington; raised in Eugene, Oregon. Jazz pianist.

4/11/81	206	1		1 **The Hot Shot** .... **[I]**		Inner City 1111

SIEGEL-SCHWALL BAND
Blues-rock band from Chicago, Illinois: Corky Siegel (vocals, harmonica), Jim Schwall (guitar), Rollow Radford (bass) and Sheldon Plotkin (drums).

12/18/71	206	3		1 **The Siegel-Schwall Band**		Wooden Nickel 1002
10/20/73	201	7		2 **953 West**		Wooden Nickel 0121

SIGEL, Beanie
Born Dwight Grant on 3/6/1974 in Philadelphia, Pennsylvania. Male rapper.

3/18/00	5	16	●	1 **The Truth**		Roc-A-Fella 546621
7/14/01	5	12		2 **The Reason**		Roc-A-Fella 548838
4/16/05	3[1]	12		3 **The B. Coming**		Roc-A-Fella 003082
11/18/06	192	1		4 **Still Public Enemy #1: Southern Remix Mixtape**		State Property 0017
12/29/07	37	6		5 **The Solution**		Roc-A-Fella 009534
9/19/09	77	2		6 **The Broad Street Bully**		siccness.net 67

SIGLER, Bunny
Born Walter Sigler on 3/27/1941 in Philadelphia, Pennsylvania. R&B singer/songwriter.

2/25/78	77	13		1 **Let Me Party With You**		Gold Mind 7502
4/7/79	119	9		2 **I've Always Wanted To Sing...Not Just Write Songs**		Gold Mind 9503

SIGUE SIGUE SPUTNIK
Rock band formed in England: Martin Degville (vocals), "Neal X" Whitmore (guitar), Tony James (bass; Generation X, **The Sisters Of Mercy**), Miss Yana Ya Ya (effects), Ray Mayhew (drums) and Chris Kavanagh (drums).

8/23/86	96	10		1 **Flaunt It**		Manhattan 53033

SIGUR ROS
Eclectic-ethereal band from Reykjavik, Iceland: Jon Thor Birgisson (vocals, guitar), Kjarten Sveinsson (keyboards), Georg Holm (bass) and Orri Pall Dyrason (drums).

11/16/02	51	4		1 **()** .... no track titles listed on this album		Fat Cat 113091
10/1/05	27	5		2 **Takk...**		Geffen 005345
11/24/07	58	2		3 **Hvarf / Heim**		XL 307
7/12/08	15	11		4 **Med Sud I Eyrum Vid Spilum Endalaust**		XL 364

SILENCERS, The
Rock band from Pittsburgh, Pennsylvania: Frank Czuri (vocals), Warren King (guitar), Dennis Takos (keyboards), Michael Pella (bass) and Ronnie Foster (drums). King died of cancer on 1/29/2010 (age 57).

8/16/80	207	3		1 **Rock 'N' Roll Enforcers**		Precision 36529

SILENCERS, The
Pop-rock band from Scotland: Jimmie O'Neill (vocals, guitar), Cha Burns (guitar), Joe Donnelly (bass) and Martin Hanlin (drums). O'Neill and Burns were also members of **Fingerprintz**. Burns died of cancer on 3/26/2007 (age 50).

8/22/87	147	11		1 **A Letter From St. Paul**		RCA Victor 6442
2/24/90	168	5		2 **A Blues For Buddha**		RCA 9960

SILICON TEENS
Band is actually solo synthesizer player Daniel Miller (born on 2/14/1951 in London, England).

8/16/80	205	1		1 **Music For Parties**		Sire 6092

SILK
Folk-rock band from Cleveland, Ohio: Michael Stanley Gee (vocals, bass), Randy Sabo (vocals, keyboards) and brothers Chris Johns (guitar) and Courtney Johns (drums). Gee dropped his last name and went on to form the **Michael Stanley Band**.

11/8/69	191	2		1 **Smooth As Raw Silk**		ABC 694

SILK
Disco studio group from Philadelphia, Pennsylvania. Vocals by Debra Henry.

8/6/77	208	2		1 **Smooth As Silk**		Prelude 12145

SILK
R&B vocal group from Atlanta, Georgia: Tim Cameron, Jimmy Gates, John Rasboro, Gary Jenkins and Gary Glenn.

12/5/92+	7	47	▲²	1 Lose Control	Elektra 61394
12/2/95	46	18	●	2 Silk	Elektra 61849
4/10/99	21	40	▲	3 Tonight	Elektra 62234
6/30/01	20	11		4 Love Session	Elektra 62642
10/11/03	178	1		5 Silktime	Silk 12147

SILKIE, The
Pop-folk band formed in Hull, England: Silvia Tatler (vocals), Ivor Aylesbury (guitar), Mike Ramsden (guitar) and Kevin Cunningham (bass). Ramsden died on 1/17/2004 (age 60).

~ ~ ~ ~ ~ ~ ~ ~ ~ ~ **NON-CHARTED ALBUM** ~ ~ ~ ~ ~ ~ ~ ~ ~ ~ ~
1965 You've Got To Hide Your Love Away

SILKK THE SHOCKER
Born Vyshonn Miller on 6/18/1975 in New Orleans, Louisiana. Male rapper. Brother of **Master P** and **C-Murder**. Member of **504 Boyz** and **Tru**.

9/7/96	49	9		1 Silkk The Shocker	No Limit 50591
3/7/98	3²	40	▲	2 Charge It 2 Da Game	No Limit 50716
2/6/99	❶¹	20	▲	3 Made Man	No Limit 50003
3/17/01	12	11		4 My World, My Way	No Limit 23221
9/25/04	88	2		5 Based On A True Story	New No Limit 5758

SILLS, Beverly
Born Belle Silverman on 5/25/1929 in Brooklyn, New York. Died of lung cancer on 7/2/2007 (age 78). Legendary opera soprano.

1/3/76	113	6		1 Music of Victor Herbert	Angel 37160

SILOS, The
Rock band formed in New York: Bob Rupe (vocals, bass), Walter Salas-Humara (vocals, guitar), Kenny Margolis (piano), J.D. Foster (bass) and Brian Doherty (drums).

4/21/90	141	9		1 The Silos	RCA 2051

SILVER
Pop-rock band formed in Los Angeles, California: John Batdorf (vocals, guitar; **Batdorf & Rodney**), Greg Collier (guitar), Brent Mydland (keyboards), Tom Leadon (bass) and Harry Stinson (drums). Mydland later joined the **Grateful Dead**; died of a drug overdose on 7/26/1990 (age 37).

9/25/76	142	6		1 Silver	Arista 4076

SILVER, Horace, Quintet
Born on 9/2/1928 in Norwalk, Connecticut. Jazz pianist.

6/12/65	95	10		1 Song For My Father (Cantiga Para Meu Pai) [I]	Blue Note 84185
				Grammy: Hall of Fame	
2/26/66	130	2		2 The Cape Verdean Blues [I]	Blue Note 84220

SILVER APPLES
Electronic rock duo from New York: Danny Taylor and Simeon Coxe. Taylor died of a heart attack on 3/10/2005 (age 56).

8/3/68	193	3		1 Silver Apples	Kapp 3562

SILVERCHAIR
Hard-rock trio from Newcastle, Australia: Daniel Johns (vocals, guitar), Chris Joannou (bass) and Ben Gillies (drums). Johns was married to **Natalie Imbruglia** from 2003-2008.

7/15/95	9	48	▲²	1 Frogstomp	Epic 67247
2/22/97	12	20	●	2 Freak Show	Epic 67905
4/3/99	50	30	●	3 Neon Ballroom	Epic 69816
9/14/02	91	2		4 Diorama	Atlantic 83559
8/11/07	70	3		5 Young Modern	Eleven 255548

SILVER CONDOR
Rock band from New York: Joe Cerisano (vocals), Earl Slick (guitar), John Corey (keyboards), Jay Davis (bass) and Claude Pepper (drums). Slick joined **Phantom, Rocker & Slick** in 1985.

7/4/81	141	12		1 Silver Condor	Columbia 37163

SILVER CONVENTION
Disco studio group from Germany. Assembled by producers Sylvester Levay and Michael Kunze. Vocals by Penny McLean, Ramona Wolf and Linda Thompson.

9/13/75	10	25	●	1 Save Me	Midland Int'l. 1129
4/10/76	13	24		2 Silver Convention	Midland Int'l. 1369
11/13/76	65	12		3 Madhouse	Midland Int'l. 1824
7/16/77	71	10		4 Golden Girls	Midsong Int'l. 2296
8/12/78	208	1		5 Love In A Sleeper	Midsong Int'l. 3038

SILVERHEAD
Rock band from England: Michael Des Barres (vocals), Robbie Blunt (guitar), Rod Davies (guitar), Nigel Harrison (bass) and Pete Thompson (drums). Des Barres later joined **Detective** and **Chequered Past**. Blunt later joined **Robert Plant**'s band. Harrison later joined **Blondie**.

3/9/74	215	4		1 16 And Savaged	MCA 391

DEBUT	PEAK	WKS	R I A A	ARTIST / Album Title	Catalog	Label & Number

				SILVERSTEIN Eclectic-rock band from Burlington, Ontario, Canada: Shane Told (vocals), Neil Boshart (guitar), Josh Bradford (guitar), Billy Hamilton (bass) and Paul Koehler (drums).		
9/3/05	34	6		1 Discovering The Waterfront		Victory 257
6/17/06	148	1		2 18 Candles: The Early Years .... [K]		Victory 291
7/21/07	25	8		3 Arrivals & Departures		Victory 350
4/18/09	33	4		4 A Shipwreck In The Sand		Victory 458

| | | | | **SILVERSTEIN, Shel** Born on 9/25/1930 in Chicago, Illinois. Died of a heart attack on 5/9/1999 (age 68). Satirical songwriter/poet/author/cartoonist. | | |
| 1/20/73 | 155 | 8 | | 1 Freakin' At The Freakers Ball .... [N] | | Columbia 31119 |

				SILVERSUN PICKUPS Alternative-rock band formed in Los Angeles, California: Brian Aubert (vocals, guitar), Joe Lester (keyboards), Nikki Monninger (bass) and Christopher Guanlao (drums).		
2/3/07	80	26		1 Carnavas		DangerBird 009
5/2/09	7	27		2 Swoon		Dangerbird 035

				SIMEONE, Harry, Chorale Born on 5/9/1911 in Newark, New Jersey. Died on 2/22/2005 (age 93). Conductor/arranger.		
1/6/62	119	2	●	1 Sing We Now Of Christmas .... [X]		20th Century Fox 3002
12/22/62	44	2		2 Sing We Now Of Christmas .... [X-R]		20th Century Fox 3002
				album later repackaged as *The Little Drummer Boy* (see #3 below)		
11/30/63+	❶ 4X	32		3 The Little Drummer Boy [X-R]		20th Century Fox 3100
				repackaged version of *Sing We Now Of Christmas*; Christmas charts: 2/'63, 1/'64, 1/'65, 1/'66, 5/'67, 8/'68, 5/'69, 13/'70		
12/11/65+	5 X	11		4 O Bambino/The Little Drummer Boy [X]		Kapp 1450 / 3450
				includes Simeone's new recording of "The Little Drummer Boy"; Christmas charts: 17/'65, 5/'66, 9/'72, 7/'73		

| | | | | **SIMMONS, Gene** Born on 7/10/1937 in Tupelo, Mississippi. Died on 8/29/2006 (age 69). Nicknamed "Jumpin' Gene." | | |
| 11/14/64 | 132 | 5 | | 1 Jumpin' Gene Simmons .... | | Hi 32018 |

				SIMMONS, Gene Born Chaim Witz on 8/25/1949 in Haifa, Israel; raised in Queens, New York. Hard-rock singer/songwriter/bassist. Member of **Kiss**. Appeared in the movies *Runaway* and *Trick Or Treat*. Stars in own TV reality show *Gene Simmons Family Jewels* on A&E.		
10/14/78+	22	22	▲	1 Gene Simmons		Casablanca 7120
6/26/04	86	1		2 ***hole		Simmons 84695

| | | | | **SIMMONS, Patrick** Born on 10/19/1948 in Aberdeen, Washington; raised in San Jose, California. Rock singer/songwriter/guitarist. Member of **The Doobie Brothers**. | | |
| 5/7/83 | 52 | 11 | | 1 Arcade .... | | Elektra 60225 |

				SIMMONS, Richard Born Milton Simmons on 7/12/1948 in New Orleans, Louisiana. Fitness and diet guru.		
6/5/82	44	40	▲	1 Reach		Elektra 60122
				songs sung by Simmons, backed by studio musicians		

				SIMON, Carly **All-Time: #88** Born on 6/25/1945 in Manhattan, New York. Pop singer/songwriter. Father co-founded Simon & Schuster publishing. Folk duo with sister Lucy (The Simon Sisters) in the mid-1960s. Married to **James Taylor** from 1972-83. **AWARD: Grammy: Best New Artist 1971**		
4/24/71	30	25		1 Carly Simon		Elektra 74082
11/27/71+	30	31	●	2 Anticipation		Elektra 75016
12/9/72+	❶ 5	71	▲	3 No Secrets		Elektra 75049
2/2/74	3 1	35	●	4 Hotcakes		Elektra 1002
5/3/75	10	17		5 Playing Possum		Elektra 1033
12/6/75+	17	19	▲ 3	6 The Best Of Carly Simon .... Cat:#46/1 [G]		Elektra 1048
6/26/76	29	13		7 Another Passenger		Elektra 1064
4/22/78	10	29	▲	8 Boys In The Trees		Elektra 128
6/30/79	45	13		9 Spy		Elektra 506
7/12/80	36	32		10 Come Upstairs		Warner 3443
10/17/81	50	24		11 Torch		Warner 3592
10/8/83	69	17		12 Hello Big Man		Warner 23886
7/20/85	88	11		13 Spoiled Girl		Epic 39970
4/25/87	25	60	▲	14 Coming Around Again		Arista 8443
8/27/88	87	13	▲	15 Greatest Hits Live .... Cat:#48/1 [L]		Arista 8526
3/31/90	46	17		16 My Romance		Arista 8582
10/13/90	60	32		17 Have You Seen Me Lately?		Arista 8650
11/19/94	129	8		18 Letters Never Sent		Arista 18752

SIMON, Carly — cont'd

DEBUT	PEAK	WKS			
10/4/97	84	8	19 Film Noir		Arista 18984
6/3/00	90	6	20 The Bedroom Tapes		Arista 14627
12/28/02+	14^X	3	21 Christmas Is Almost Here	[X]	Rhino 78166
			Christmas charts: 49/'02, 14/'03		
5/22/04	22	18	● 22 Reflections: Carly Simon's Greatest Hits	[G]	Arista 59429
8/6/05	7	10	23 Moonlight Serenade		Columbia 94890
1/20/07	13	10	24 Into White		Columbia 86138
5/17/08	15	9	25 This Kind Of Love		Hear 30662
11/14/09	134	2	26 Never Been Gone		Iris 014

SIMON, Joe

Born on 9/2/1943 in Simmesport, Louisiana. R&B singer.

DEBUT	PEAK	WKS			
6/21/69	81	17	1 The Chokin' Kind		Sound Stage 7 15006
11/29/69	192	2	2 Joe Simon...Better Than Ever		Sound Stage 7 15008
4/3/71	153	12	3 The Sounds Of Simon		Spring 4701
3/25/72	71	12	4 Drowning In The Sea Of Love		Spring 5702
12/30/72+	147	8	5 The Best Of Joe Simon	[G]	Sound Stage 7 15009
2/17/73	97	12	6 The Power Of Joe Simon		Spring 5704
10/27/73	207	5	7 Simon Country		Spring 5705
7/19/75	129	12	8 Get Down		Spring 6706

SIMON, Paul   All-Time: #160

Born on 10/13/1941 in Newark, New Jersey; raised in Queens, New York. Singer/songwriter/guitarist. Met **Art Garfunkel** in high school, recorded together as Tom & Jerry in 1957. Worked as Jerry Landis, Tico And The Triumphs, Paul Kane, Harrison Gregory and True Taylor in the early 1960s. To England from 1963-64. Returned to the U.S. and recorded first album with Garfunkel in 1964. Went solo in 1971. Married to actress/author Carrie Fisher from 1983-85. Married singer **Edie Brickell** on 5/30/1992. Acted in the movies *Annie Hall* and *One-Trick Pony*.

AWARD: R&R Hall of Fame: 2001

DEBUT	PEAK	WKS			
2/12/72	4	36	▲ 1 Paul Simon		Columbia 30750
5/26/73	2^2	48	▲ 2 There Goes Rhymin' Simon		Columbia 32280
			RS500 #267		
3/23/74	33	17	● 3 Paul Simon In Concert/Live Rhymin'	[L]	Columbia 32855
10/25/75	❶^1	40	● 4 Still Crazy After All These Years		Columbia 33540
			Grammys: Album of the Year / Male Pop Vocal / Hall of Fame		
9/6/80	12	26	● 5 One-Trick Pony	[S]	Warner 3472
11/19/83+	35	18	6 Hearts And Bones		Warner 23942
9/13/86+	3^1	97	▲^{5} 7 Graceland Cat:#14/33		Warner 25447
			Grammy: Album of the Year ★ RS500 #81 ★ NRR		
11/3/90	4	53	▲^{2} 8 The Rhythm Of The Saints		Warner 26098
11/23/91+	74	11	9 Paul Simon's Concert In The Park	[L]	Warner 26737 [2]
			recorded on 8/15/1991 in Central Park		
12/6/97	42	11	10 Songs From The Capeman		Warner 46814
10/21/00	19	21	● 11 You're The One		Warner 47844
5/27/06	14	13	12 Surprise		Warner 49982
			GREATEST HITS & COMPILATIONS:		
12/3/77+	18	23	▲ 13 Greatest Hits, Etc.		Columbia 35032
11/12/88+	110	14	▲ 14 Negotiations And Love Songs, 1971-1986		Warner 25789 [2]
10/16/93	173	2	● 15 1964/1993		Warner 45394 [3]
11/23/02	108	6	16 The Paul Simon Collection: On My Way, Don't Know Where I'm Goin'		Warner 73774 [2]
7/14/07	42	4	17 The Essential Paul Simon		Warner 159292 [2]
7/18/09	60	5	18 This Better Be Good		Starbucks 8321

SIMON & GARFUNKEL   All-Time: #146

Folk-rock duo from New York: **Paul Simon** and **Art Garfunkel**. Recorded as Tom & Jerry in 1957. Duo split in 1964; Simon was working solo in England; Garfunkel was in graduate school. They re-formed in 1965 and stayed together until 1971. Reunited in 1981 and 2003 for national tours.

AWARDS: Grammy: Lifetime Achievement 2003 ★ R&R Hall of Fame: 1990

DEBUT	PEAK	WKS			
1/22/66	30	31	▲ 1 Wednesday Morning, 3 AM		Columbia 9049
2/19/66+	21	143	▲^{3} 2 Sounds Of Silence Cat:#18/32		Columbia 9269
11/12/66	4	145	▲^{3} 3 Parsley, Sage, Rosemary And Thyme		Columbia 9363
			Grammy: Hall of Fame ★ RS500 #201		
3/16/68	❶^9	69	▲^{2} 4 The Graduate	[S]	Columbia 3180
			Grammy: Soundtrack Album		
4/27/68	❶^7	66	▲^{2} 5 Bookends Cat:#31/40		Columbia 9529
			RS500 #233		

DEBUT	PEAK	WKS	R I A A	ARTIST Album Title	Catalog	Label & Number

SIMON & GARFUNKEL — cont'd

| 2/14/70 | ❶10 | 85 | ▲8 | 6 Bridge Over Troubled Water | Cat:#22/101 | Columbia 9914 |

Grammy: Album of the Year ★ RS500 #51

GREATEST HITS & COMPILATIONS:

| 7/1/72 | 5 | 127 | ▲14 | 7 Simon And Garfunkel's Greatest Hits | Cat:#9/79 | Columbia 31350 |

RS500 #293

| 3/15/03 | 24C | 14 | ▲ | 8 The Best Of Simon & Garfunkel | | Legacy 66022 |

first released in 1999

| 11/1/03 | 27 | 11 | ▲ | 9 The Essential Simon & Garfunkel | | Legacy 90716 [2] |

LIVE ALBUMS:

| 3/13/82 | 6 | 34 | ▲2 | 10 The Concert In Central Park | | Warner 3654 [2] |

recorded on 9/19/1981

| 8/3/02 | 165 | 1 | | 11 Live From New York City, 1967 | | Legacy 61513 |

recorded on 1/22/1967 at Philharmonic Hall

| 12/18/04 | 154 | 2 | | 12 Old Friends: Live On Stage | | Warner 48954 [2] |
| 4/12/08 | 33 | 5 | | 13 Live 1969 | | Legacy 92582 |

SIMONE, Nina
Born Eunice Waymon on 2/21/1933 in Tryon, South Carolina. Died of cancer on 4/21/2003 (age 70). Jazz-styled singer.

6/26/65	99	8		1 I Put A Spell On You		Philips 600172
10/16/65	139	7		2 Pastel Blues		Philips 600187
11/5/66	110	9		3 Wild Is The Wind		Philips 600207
11/25/67	158	4		4 Silk & Soul		RCA Victor 3837
8/21/71	190	4		5 Here Comes The Sun		RCA Victor 4536

GREATEST HITS & COMPILATIONS:

4/19/69	187	3		6 The Best Of Nina Simone		Philips 600298
7/25/70	189	3		7 The Best Of Nina Simone		RCA Victor 4374
9/20/08	31C	4		8 How It Feels To Be Free: Opus Collection		Starbucks 13560

LIVE ALBUMS:

| 3/6/61 | 23 | 5 | | 9 Nina At Newport | | Colpix 412 |

recorded on 6/30/1960

| 9/19/64 | 102 | 11 | | 10 Nina Simone In Concert | | Philips 600135 |
| 3/14/70 | 149 | 12 | | 11 Black Gold | | RCA Victor 4248 |

SIMPLE MINDS
Pop-rock band formed in Glasgow, Scotland: Jim Kerr (vocals), Charles Burchill (guitar, keyboards), Michael MacNeil (keyboards), John Giblin (bass) and Mel Gaynor (drums). MacNeil and Giblin left in 1989. Kerr was married to Chrissie Hynde (of **The Pretenders**) from 1984-90.

2/19/83	69	19		1 New Gold Dream (81-82-83-84)		A&M 4928
2/18/84	64	24		2 Sparkle in the Rain		A&M 4981
11/9/85+	10	42	●	3 Once Upon A Time		A&M 5092
7/18/87	96	10		4 Simple Minds Live: In The City Of Light	[L]	A&M 6850 [2]
5/20/89	70	12		5 Street Fighting Years		A&M 3927
5/4/91	74	11		6 Real Life		A&M 5352
2/25/95	87	7		7 Good News From The Next World		Virgin 39922

SIMPLE PLAN
Punk-rock band from Montreal, Quebec, Canada: Pierre Bouvier (vocals), Jeff Stinco (guitar), Seb Lefebvre (guitar), David Desrosiers (bass) and Chuck Comeau (drums).

12/21/02+	35	69	▲2	1 No Pads, No Helmets...Just Balls	Cat:#2¹/40	Lava 83534
11/13/04	3¹	49	▲	2 Still Not Getting Any...		Lava 93411
10/22/05	119	2		3 MTV Live From The Hard Rock	[L]	Lava 94112
3/1/08	14	8		4 Simple Plan		Lava 384956

SIMPLY RED
Born Mick Hucknall on 6/8/1960 in Denton, Manchester, England. "Blue-eyed soul" singer. Nicknamed "Red" because of his red hair. His backing group included Fritz McIntyre and Tim Kellett (keyboards), Sylvan Richardson (guitar), Tony Bowers (bass) and Chris Joyce (drums). Group disbanded in 1990. Hucknall continued Simply Red as a solo vehicle with various backing musicians.

4/19/86	16	60	▲	1 Picture Book		Elektra 60452
3/28/87	31	26		2 Men And Women		Elektra 60727
3/11/89	22	39	●	3 A New Flame		Elektra 60828
10/19/91+	76	43	●	4 Stars		EastWest 91773
11/11/95	75	13		5 Life		EastWest 61853
11/9/96	116	5		6 Greatest Hits	[G]	EastWest 61993
6/6/98	145	3		7 Blue		EastWest 62222
2/14/04	187	3		8 Home		simplyred.com 0004
5/12/07	156	1		9 Stay		simplyred.com 89935

SIMPSON, Ashlee
Born on 10/3/1984 in Dallas, Texas; raised in Richardson, Texas. Female pop singer/songwriter/actress. Younger sister of **Jessica Simpson**. Played "Cecilia Smith" on TV's *7th Heaven*. Married Pete Wentz (of **Fall Out Boy**) on 5/17/2008.

8/7/04	❶3	40	▲3	1 Autobiography		Geffen 002913
11/5/05	❶1	24	▲	2 I Am Me		Geffen 005436
5/10/08	4	7		3 Bittersweet World		Geffen 010231

SIMPSON, Jessica
Born on 7/10/1980 in Abilene, Texas; raised in Richardson, Texas. Pop-dance singer. Older sister of **Ashlee Simpson**. Married to **Nick Lachey** (of **98°**) from 2002-06 (they appeared as themselves in the 2003 MTV reality series *Newlyweds*). Played "Daisy Duke" in the 2005 movie *The Dukes Of Hazzard*. Older sister of **Ashlee Simpson**.

12/11/99+	25	62	▲²	1 Sweet Kisses		Columbia 69096
6/23/01	6	16	●	2 Irresistible		Columbia 62136
9/6/03+	2¹	75	▲³	3 In This Skin		Columbia 92005
12/11/04	14	5	●	4 Rejovce: The Christmas Album .... **Cat:#30/5** [X]		Columbia 92880
				Christmas charts: 2/'04, 31/'05		
9/16/06	5	9	●	5 A Public Affair		Epic 83215
9/27/08	4	9		6 Do You Know		Epic 21746

SIMPSON, Valerie
Born on 8/26/1946 in Brooklyn, New York. R&B singer/prolific songwriter. Half of husband-and-wife duo **Ashford & Simpson**.

7/31/71	159	6	1 Valerie Simpson Exposed		Tamla 311
8/26/72	162	6	2 Valerie Simpson		Tamla 317

SIMPSONS, The
The voices of the Fox network's animated TV series. Nancy Cartwright is Bart; Dan Castellaneta is Homer; Julie Kavner is Marge; Yeardley Smith is Lisa; and the show's creator Matt Groening is Maggie.

12/22/90+	3¹	39	▲²	1 The Simpsons Sing The Blues	[N]	Geffen 24308
4/5/97	103	12		2 Songs In The Key Of Springfield	[TV]	Rhino 72723
11/20/99	197	1		3 Go Simpsonic With The Simpsons	[TV]	Fox 75480

SINAI BEACH
Christian hard-rock band from Riverside, California: CJ Alderson (vocals), Logan Lambert (guitar), Sean Durham (guitar), Dan Barachkov (bass) and Mike Dunlap (drums).

5/7/05	198	1	1 Immersed		Victory 2722

SINATRA, Frank
1950s: #1 / 1960s: #2 / 1990s: #41 / All-Time: #2

Born on 12/12/1915 in Hoboken, New Jersey. Died of a heart attack on 5/14/1998 (age 82). With Harry James from 1939-40, first recorded for Brunswick in 1939; with **Tommy Dorsey**, 1940-42. Went solo in late 1942. Appeared in many movies from 1941. Won an Oscar for the movie *From Here To Eternity* in 1953. Own TV show in 1957. Own Reprise record company in 1961, sold to Warner Brothers in 1963. Father of **Nancy Sinatra**. Married to actress Ava Gardner from 1951-57. Married to actress Mia Farrow from 1966-68. Regarded by many as the greatest popular singer of the 20th century. Member of **The Rat Pack**.
AWARD: Grammys: Lifetime Achievement 1965 / Trustees 1979 / Legend 1994

1/8/55	11	2		1 Frank Sinatra Sings Songs From "Young At Heart"....................	[EP]	Capitol 571
5/28/55	❶²	29	●	2 In The Wee Small Hours	**Cat:#28/4**	Capitol 581
				Grammy: Hall of Fame ★ RS500 #100		
				EP: Capitol EBF-581 (#1); LP: Capitol W-581 (#2)		
10/15/55	2²	4		3 Our Town	[EP-TV]	Capitol 673
				from the NBC-TV production starring Sinatra and Eva Marie Saint		
3/31/56	2¹	50	●	4 Songs For Swingin' Lovers!		Capitol 653
				Grammy: Hall of Fame ★ RS500 #306		
3/2/57	5	14		5 Close To You		Capitol 789
5/27/57	2¹	36		6 A Swingin' Affair!		Capitol 803
9/23/57	3¹	21		7 Where Are You?		Capitol 855
11/11/57	2¹	27		8 Pal Joey	[S]	Capitol 912
2/3/58	❶⁵	71	●	9 Come Fly With Me		Capitol 920
				Grammy: Hall of Fame		
9/29/58	❶⁵	120	●	10 Frank Sinatra Sings For Only The Lonely	**Cat:#21/1**	Capitol 1053
				Grammy: Hall of Fame		
2/9/59	2⁵	141	●	11 Come Dance With Me!		Capitol 1069
				Grammys: Album of the Year / Male Pop Vocal		
8/24/59	2²	74		12 No One Cares		Capitol 1221
8/22/60	❶⁹	86	●	13 Nice 'N' Easy		Capitol 1417
2/13/61	3¹	36		14 Sinatra's Swingin' Session!!!	**Cat:#14/2**	Capitol 1491
8/14/61	8	39		15 Come Swing With Me!		Capitol 1594
4/21/61	19	29		16 Point Of No Return		Capitol 1676
5/1/61	4	35		17 Ring-A-Ding Ding!		Reprise 1001
8/14/61	6	22		18 Sinatra Swings		Reprise 1002
11/6/61	3¹	42		19 I Remember Tommy...		Reprise 1003
				tribute to **Tommy Dorsey**		
3/17/62	8	31		20 Sinatra & Strings		Reprise 1004
9/1/62	18	16		21 Sinatra And Swingin' Brass		Reprise 1005
11/10/62	25	17		22 All Alone		Reprise 1007
2/2/63	5	42		23 Sinatra-Basie		Reprise 1008
				FRANK SINATRA & COUNT BASIE		
6/22/63	6	35		24 The Concert Sinatra		Reprise 1009

DEBUT	PEAK	WKS	RIAA	ARTIST / Album Title	Catalog	Label & Number
				SINATRA, Frank — cont'd		
10/5/63	8	43	●	25 Sinatra's Sinatra		Reprise 1010
4/11/64	10	24		26 Days Of Wine And Roses, Moon River, And Other Academy Award Winners		Reprise 1011
5/30/64	116	7		27 America, I Hear You Singing		Reprise 2020
				FRANK SINATRA / BING CROSBY / FRED WARING		
8/22/64	13	31		28 It Might As Well Be Swing		Reprise 1012
				FRANK SINATRA & COUNT BASIE		
12/19/64+	19	28		29 Softly, As I Leave You.............		Reprise 1013
7/3/65	9	44		30 Sinatra '65		Reprise 6167
8/21/65+	5	69	●	31 September Of My Years		Reprise 1014
				Grammys: Album of the Year / Hall of Fame		
12/25/65+	9	32		32 A Man And His Music		Reprise 1016
				Grammy: Album of the Year		
12/25/65+	30	16		33 My Kind Of Broadway		Reprise 1015
4/23/66	34	14		34 Moonlight Sinatra		Reprise 1018
6/18/66	❶¹	73	▲	35 Strangers In The Night		Reprise 1017
12/31/66+	6	61	●	36 That's Life		Reprise 1020
4/15/67	19	28		37 Francis Albert Sinatra & Antonio Carlos Jobim		Reprise 1021
9/16/67	24	23		38 Frank Sinatra		Reprise 1022
2/24/68	78	13		39 Francis A. & Edward K.		Reprise 1024
				FRANK SINATRA & DUKE ELLINGTON		
12/28/68+	18	28	●	40 Cycles.............		Reprise 1027
5/10/69	11	19	●	41 My Way		Reprise 1029
9/6/69	30	16		42 A Man Alone & Other Songs Of Rod McKuen		Reprise 1030
4/11/70	101	10		43 Watertown		Reprise 1031
4/24/71	73	15		44 Sinatra & Company		Reprise 1033
10/27/73	13	22	●	45 Ol' Blue Eyes Is Back		Reprise 2155
8/3/74	48	12		46 Some Nice Things I've Missed		Reprise 2195
4/12/80	17	24	●	47 Trilogy: Past, Present, Future		Reprise 2300 [3]
12/5/81+	52	13		48 She Shot Me Down		Reprise 2305
8/25/84	58	13		49 L.A. Is My Lady		Qwest 25145
11/20/93	2³	38	▲³	50 Duets	Cat:#12/2	Capitol 89611
				Grammy: Traditional Pop Album		
12/3/94	9	18	▲	51 Duets II	Cat:#32/1	Capitol 28103
				CHRISTMAS ALBUMS:		
12/30/57+	18	2	▲	52 A Jolly Christmas From Frank Sinatra	Cat:#10/4	Capitol 894
				Christmas charts: 27/'63, 15/'64, 20/'65, 29/'66, 53/'67, 10/'84, 28/'87, 23/'90, 20/'98, 42/'05, 34/'09		
12/22/62	120	2		53 A Jolly Christmas From Frank Sinatra............. [R]		Capitol 894
12/12/64	9ˣ	3		54 12 Songs Of Christmas		Reprise 2022
				BING CROSBY / FRANK SINATRA / FRED WARING And The Pennsylvanians		
12/23/67+	42ˣ	3		55 Have Yourself A Merry Little Christmas.............		Harmony 7400 / 11200
				1944-47 recordings; originally released in 1948 as *Christmas Songs by Sinatra* on Columbia 167 ('78' package); reissued in 1957 as *Christmas Dreaming* on Columbia 1032; Christmas charts: 86/'67, 42/'68		
12/6/69	3¹ˣ	4		56 The Sinatra Family Wish You A Merry Christmas		Reprise 1026
				Frank with daughters Tina and Nancy Sinatra, and son Frank Jr.; first released in 1968		
12/5/92	8ˣ	43		57 It's Christmas Time	Cat:#6/41	LaserLight 15152
				BING CROSBY • FRANK SINATRA • NAT KING COLE		
				Christmas charts: 8/'92, 17/'93, 12/'94, 13/'95, 8/'96, 22/'97		
12/19/98	21ˣ	3		58 It's Christmas Time	Cat:#13/5	LaserLight 15152
				BING CROSBY • FRANK SINATRA • LOUIS ARMSTRONG		
				above 2 released with same title, same packaging and same label number; however, **Louis Armstrong** (2 songs) replaces **Nat King Cole** (6 songs), and only 6 of 33 tracks appear on both releases		
12/26/98	50ᶜ	1	▲	59 The Sinatra Christmas Album .... [K]		Reprise 45743
11/27/04	87	7		60 The Christmas Collection............. [K]	Cat:#32/8	Reprise 76542
				Christmas charts: 7/'04, 32/'05, 46/'06, 50/'08		
				GREATEST HITS & COMPILATIONS:		
12/22/56+	8	17	●	61 This Is Sinatra!		Capitol 768
4/28/58	8	7		62 This Is Sinatra, Volume Two		Capitol 982
				also see #70 below		
6/2/58	12	1		63 The Frank Sinatra Story		Columbia 6 [2]
6/1/59	8	15		64 Look To Your Heart		Capitol 1164
4/10/61	4	60		65 All The Way		Capitol 1538
8/18/62	15	18		66 Sinatra Sings...Of Love And Things		Capitol 1729
9/28/63	129	4		67 Tell Her You Love Her		Capitol 1919
7/29/67	195	2		68 The Movie Songs		Capitol 2700
9/7/68	55	25	▲²	69 Frank Sinatra's Greatest Hits!	Cat:#3/16	Reprise 1025
8/23/69	186	3		70 Close-Up .... [R]		Capitol 254 [2]
				reissue of albums #61 and 62 above		
6/10/72	88	17	▲	71 Frank Sinatra's Greatest Hits, Vol. 2	Cat:#16/1	Reprise 1034
8/3/74	202	3		72 One More For The Road		Capitol 11309
1/4/75	170	3		73 Round #1		Capitol 11357 [2]
12/8/90+	126	11	●	74 The Capitol Years		Capitol 94777 [3]
12/15/90+	98	10	●	75 The Reprise Collection		Reprise 26340 [4]
4/27/91	138	27	▲²	76 Sinatra Reprise - The Very Good Years	Cat:#2⁶/55	Reprise 26501

Billboard DEBUT	PEAK	WKS	R I A A	ARTIST Album Title	Catalog	Label & Number
				SINATRA, Frank — cont'd		
12/9/95	66	5		77 Sinatra 80th - All The Best........................		Capitol 35952 [2]
5/30/98	5ᶜ	4	●	78 The Capitol Collectors Series		Capitol 92160
				first released in 1989		
5/30/98	7ᶜ	10	●	79 The Best Of The Capitol Years		Capitol 99225
				first released in 1992		
6/6/98	124	2	●	80 The Very Best Of Frank Sinatra		Reprise 46589 [2]
2/2/02	32	16	●	81 Greatest Love Songs......................... Cat:#13/4		Reprise 78295
3/1/03	44ᶜ	1		82 Gold..		Capitol 19705
2/3/07	36	7		83 Romance: Songs From The Heart		Capitol 63377
1/19/08	10ᶜ	8		84 The Heart Of The Matter: Frank Sinatra Sings About Love		Starbucks 30872
5/31/08	2¹	87↑		85 Nothing But The Best Cat:#35/11		Reprise 438652
2/7/09	23	7		86 Seduction: Sinatra Sings Of Love		Reprise 516960
				LIVE ALBUMS:		
8/20/66	9	44	●	87 Sinatra At The Sands Cat:#44/1		Reprise 1019 [2]
				with **Count Basie**		
12/7/74+	37	12		88 Sinatra - The Main Event Live		Reprise 2207
				recorded at Madison Square Garden; with **Woody Herman** & The Young Thundering Herd		
12/2/95	61	9	●	89 Sinatra 80th - Live In Concert .... Cat:#19/2		Capitol 31723
5/14/05	199	1		90 Live From Las Vegas		Capitol 60145
12/23/06	165	2		91 Vegas .... [K]		Reprise 74075 [4]
5/23/09	52	8		92 Live At The Meadowlands		Concord 31331
				SINATRA, Nancy		
				Born on 6/8/1940 in Jersey City, New Jersey; raised in Los Angeles, California. Daughter of **Frank Sinatra**. Married to **Tommy Sands** from 1960-65. Appeared in the movies *For Those Who Think Young, Get Yourself A College Girl, The Oscar* and *Speedway*.		
3/12/66	5	42	●	1 Boots		Reprise 6202
6/4/66	41	15		2 How Does That Grab You?....................		Reprise 6207
9/3/66	122	7		3 Nancy In London		Reprise 6221
2/18/67	18	24		4 Sugar		Reprise 6239
9/2/67	43	26		5 Country, My Way		Reprise 6251
1/13/68	37	32		6 Movin' With Nancy .... [TV]		Reprise 6277
4/13/68	13	44	●	7 Nancy & Lee...........................		Reprise 6273
				NANCY SINATRA & LEE HAZLEWOOD		
5/3/69	91	8		8 Nancy		Reprise 6333
10/3/70	99	7		9 Nancy's Greatest Hits .... [G]		Reprise 6409
2/26/72	213	1		10 Nancy & Lee Again		RCA Victor 4645
				NANCY SINATRA & LEE HAZLEWOOD		
				SIN BANDERA		
				Latin pop duo: Leonel Garcia (from Mexico) and Noel Schajris (from Argentina).		
12/10/05	170	2		1 Manana .... [F]		Sony 96872
12/2/06	199	1		2 Pasado .... [F]		Sony 01965
				SINCEROS, The		
				New wave band from London, England: Mark Kjeldsen (vocals, guitar), Don Snow (keyboards), Ron Francois (bass) and Bobby Irwin (drums).		
9/29/79	207	1		1 The Sound Of Sunbathing		Columbia 36134
				SINFIELD, Pete		
				Born on 12/27/1943 in London, England. Rock singer/songwriter.		
10/6/73	190	5		1 Still...................................		Manticore 66667
				SINGING NUN, The		
				Born Jeanine Deckers on 10/17/1933 in Fichermont, Belgium. Committed suicide on 3/31/1985 (age 51). Actual nun; assumed the name Sister Luc-Gabrielle. Recorded under the name Soeur Sourire ("Sister Smile"). **Debbie Reynolds** played Soeur Sourire in fictional 1966 movie about her life.		
11/9/63	❶¹⁰	39	●	1 The Singing Nun .... [F]		Philips 203
4/11/64	90	14		2 Her Joy, Her Songs .... [F]		Philips 209
				SINGLETARY, Daryle		
				Born on 3/10/1971 in Cairo, Georgia. Country singer/songwriter.		
3/14/98	160	3		1 Ain't It The Truth..........................		Giant 24696
				SIOUXSIE AND THE BANSHEES		
				Avant-punk band formed by singer Siouxsie Sioux (Susan Dallion) and bassist Steve Severin (Steve Havoc). Fluctuating personnel around nucleus of group: Sioux, Severin and Peter "Budgie" Clark (drums). Husband-and-wife, Sioux and Budgie, also recorded as **The Creatures**.		
7/7/84	157	7		1 Hyaena		Geffen 24030
5/24/86	88	15		2 Tinderbox...............................		Geffen 24092
4/11/87	188	3		3 Through The Looking Glass		Geffen 24134
10/1/88	68	20		4 Peepshow		Geffen 24205
6/29/91	65	21		5 Superstition		Geffen 24387
3/4/95	127	2		6 The Rapture		Geffen 24630

Billboard DEBUT	PEAK	WKS	R I A A	ARTIST Album Title	Catalog	Label & Number
				SIR DOUGLAS QUINTET		
				Tex-Mex band formed in San Antonio, Texas. **Doug Sahm** (vocals, guitar), Augie Meyers (organ), Frank Morin (horns), Harvey Regan (bass) and John Perez (drums). Re-grouped in 1980 with Sahm, Meyers, Perez, Alvin Crow and Speedy Sparks. Sahm died of heart failure on 11/18/99 (age 58).		
4/19/69	81	11		1 Mendocino	Smash 67115
2/14/81	184	4		2 Border Wave	Takoma 7088
				~ ~ ~ ~ ~ ~ ~ ~ ~ ~ **NON-CHARTED ALBUM** ~ ~ ~ ~ ~ ~ ~ ~ ~ ~ ~ 1966 The Best Of The Sir Douglas Quintet		
				SIR LORD BALTIMORE		
				Rock trio from Brooklyn, New York: John Garner (vocals, drums), Louis Dambra (guitar) and Gary Justin (bass).		
2/6/71	198	2		1 Kingdom Come...	Mercury 61328
				SIR MIX-A-LOT		
				Born Anthony Ray on 8/12/1963 in Seattle, Washington. Male rapper.		
10/22/88+	82	58	▲	1 Swass .... **Cat**:#29/8	Nastymix 70123
11/18/89	67	41	●	2 Seminar	Nastymix 70150
2/22/92	9	61	▲	3 Mack Daddy	Def American 26765
8/6/94	69	9		4 Chief Boot Knocka	Rhyme Cartel 45540
9/14/96	123	4		5 Return Of The Bumpasaurus	Rhyme Cartel 43081
				SISQO		
				Born Mark Andrews on 11/9/1978 in Baltimore, Maryland. R&B singer/songwriter. Member of **Dru Hill**.		
12/18/99+	2[1]	60	▲5	1 Unleash The Dragon	Dragon 546816
7/7/01	7	10	▲	2 Return Of Dragon	Dragon 548836
				SISSEL		
				Born Sissel Kyrkjebo on 6/24/1969 in Bergen, Norway. Female operatic soprano.		
10/11/08	38[X]	1		1 Northern Lights.. **[X-TV]**	Denon 17661
				SISTER HAZEL		
				Rock band formed in Gainesville, Florida: Ken Block (vocals), Ryan Newell (guitar), Andrew Copeland (guitar), Jeff Beres (bass) and Mark Trojanowski (drums).		
6/7/97	47	50	▲	1 ...Somewhere More Familiar..	Universal 53030
7/15/00	63	12		2 Fortress	Universal 157883
2/1/03	177	1		3 Chasing Daylight	Sixth Man 61015
9/11/04	184	1		4 Lift	Sixth Man 61028
10/28/06	86	1		5 Absolutely	Croakin' Poets 40032
10/20/07	39[X]	1		6 Santa's Playlist .... **[X]**	Croakin' Poets 61124
7/5/08	152	1		7 Before The Amplifiers: Live Acoustic .... **[L]**	Croakin' Poets 61169
9/5/09	37	2		8 Release...	Croakin' Poets 61238
				SISTER SLEDGE		
				R&B vocal group from Philadelphia, Pennsylvania: sisters Debra, Joni, Kim and Kathy Sledge.		
2/24/79	3[2]	33	▲	1 We Are Family	Cotillion 5209
3/8/80	31	15		2 Love Somebody Today	Cotillion 16012
2/28/81	42	29		3 All American Girls	Cotillion 16027
2/13/82	69	14		4 The Sisters	Cotillion 5231
6/4/83	169	8		5 Bet Cha Say That To All The Girls	Cotillion 90069
				SISTERS OF MERCY, The		
				Rock duo formed in Leeds, England: Andrew Taylor (vocals) and Patricia Morrison (bass). Morrison left in early 1990; expanded to a quintet which included Tony James (bass; Generation X, **Sigue Sigue Sputnik**), Tim Bricheno and Andreas Bruhn (guitars), and Doktor Avalanche (drums).		
2/6/88	101	16		1 Floodland	Elektra 60762
12/1/90	136	23		2 Vision Thing..	Elektra 61017
				SIXPENCE NONE THE RICHER		
				Pop band from Austin, Texas: Leigh Nash (vocals), Matt Slocum (guitar), Sean Kelly (guitar), Justin Cary (bass) and Dale Baker (drums). Nash is married to Mark Nash of **PFR**.		
3/6/99	89	39	▲	1 Sixpence None The Richer .... **Cat**:#44/2	Squint/Curb/Reprise 7032
11/16/02	154	1		2 Divine Discontent	Squint 86010
				69 BOYZ		
				Bass-rap group from Jacksonville, Florida. Featuring Albert Bryant and Mike Phillips.		
7/16/94+	59	60	▲	1 Nineteen Ninety Quad..	Downlow 6901
8/1/98	114	4		2 The Wait Is Over	QuadraSound 83031
				SIXX: A.M.		
				Rock trio formed in Los Angeles, California: James Michael (vocals, guitar), Nikki Sixx (bass) and Darren Jay "DJ" Ashba (drums). Sixx was a member of **Motley Crue**.		
9/8/07	62	37		1 The Heroin Diaries Soundtrack..................................	Eleven Seven 171
				SIZE, Roni/Reprazent		
				Born Ryan Williams on 10/29/1969 in St. Andrews, Bristol, England (Jamaican parents). Techno artist. Reprazent: Krust, DJ Die, Suv, MC Dynamite and Onallee.		
11/11/00	181	1		1 In The Mode	Talkin' Loud 548201

SKAGGS, Ricky

Born on 7/18/1954 in Cordell, Kentucky. Country singer/songwriter/mandolin player.
AWARDS: CMA: Horizon 1982 / Male Vocalist 1982 / Entertainer 1985 / Vocal Duo (w/ Sharon White) 1987 ★ OPRY: 1982

6/12/82	77	30	●	1 Waitin' For The Sun To Shine		Epic 37193
10/16/82	61	12	▲	2 Highways & Heartaches		Epic 37996
11/10/84	180	5	●	3 Country Boy...		Epic 39410
3/9/85	181	4		4 Favorite Country Songs	[K]	Epic 39409
8/9/03	179	4		5 The Three Pickers		Rounder 610526
				EARL SCRUGGS / DOC WATSON / RICKY SKAGGS		
4/12/08	191	1		6 Honoring The Fathers Of Bluegrass: Tribute To 1946 And 1947.......................		Skaggs Family 901008
				Grammy: Bluegrass Album		

SKEE-LO

Born Anthony Roundtree on 3/5/1975 in Riverside, California. Male rapper.

7/15/95	53	20	●	1 I Wish...		Sunshine 75486

SKELETONWITCH

Death-metal band from Athens, Ohio: brothers Chance Garnette (vocals) and Nate Garnette (guitar), with Scott Hendrick (guitar), Evan Linger (bass) and Derrick Nau (drums).

10/31/09	151	1		1 Breathing The Fire		Prosthetic 10077

SKID ROW

Heavy-metal band formed in Toms River, New Jersey: **Sebastian Bach** (vocals), Dave Sabo (guitar), Scott Hill (guitar), Rachel Bolan (bass) and Rob Affuso (drums).

2/11/89	6	78	▲⁵	1 Skid Row	Cat:#34/9	Atlantic 81936
6/29/91	❶¹	46	▲²	2 Slave To The Grind		Atlantic 82278
10/10/92	58	6	●	3 B-Side Ourselves	[EP]	Atlantic 82431
4/15/95	35	9		4 Subhuman Race		Atlantic 82730

SKILLET

Christian rock band from Memphis, Tennessee: brothers John Cooper (vocals, bass) and Korey Cooper (keyboards), with Ben Kasica (guitar) and Lori Peters (drums).

9/15/01	141	1		1 Alien Youth		Ardent 72507
12/6/03	179	1		2 Collide		Ardent 72522
10/21/06	55	21	●	3 Comatose..		Ardent 94537
11/8/08	164	2		4 Comatose Comes Alive...	[L]	Ardent 512252
9/12/09	2¹	38↑		5 Awake		Ardent 519927

SKINDRED

Punk-rock band from Newport, South Wales: Benji Webbe (vocals), Mikey Dee (guitar), Daniel Pugsley (bass) and Dirty Arya (drums).

10/30/04	189	3		1 Babylon		Lava 93304

SKINNY PUPPY

Industrial-rock trio from Vancouver, British Columbia, Canada: Kevin "Nivek Ogre " Oglivie (vocals), Cevin Key (various instruments) and Dwayne Goettel (keyboards). Goettel died of a drug overdose on 8/23/1995 (age 31).

4/11/92	193	1		1 Last Rights..		Nettwerk 98037
3/16/96	102	1		2 The Process		American 43057
6/12/04	176	1		3 The Greater Wrong Of The Right		SPV 63722
2/17/07	200	1		4 Mythmaker		Hell-O Deathday 63982

SKIP

Born in New Orleans, Louisiana. Male rapper.

11/10/01	155	2		1 Live From Hollygrove		UTP 90100
6/5/04	122	4		2 The Beginning Of The End...		J Prince 42046
				JUVENILE • WACKO • SKIP		

SKRAPE

Hard-rock band from Orlando, Florida: Billy Keeton (vocals), Mike Lynchard (guitar), Brian Milner (keyboards), Pete Sison (bass) and Will Hunt (drums).

4/7/01	157	3		1 New Killer America		RCA 67935

SKULL DUGGERY

Born Andrew Jordan in New Orleans, Louisiana. Male rapper.

9/26/98	21	5		1 These Wicked Streets		Penalty 3082

SKULL GANG

Rap group from Harlem, New York: **Juelz Santana**, Rich Rab, UnKasa and John Depp.

5/23/09	142	1		1 Skull Gang		E1 5109

SKY

Rock trio from Detroit, Michigan: Doug Fieger (vocals, bass), John Coury (guitar) and Rob Stawinski (drums). Fieger was later the leader of **The Knack**; died of cancer on 2/14/2010 (age 57).

12/19/70+	160	6		1 Sky		RCA Victor 4457

			ARTIST		
DEBUT	**PEAK**	**WKS**	**R I A A** / **Album Title**	**Catalog**	**Label & Number**

SKY
Classical-rock band formed in England. John Williams (guitar), Kevin Peek (guitar), Francis Monkman (keyboards), Herb Flowers (bass) and Tristan Fly (drums).

11/1/80+	125	15	1 Sky .... [I]		Arista 8302 [2]
5/2/81	181	3	2 Sky 3 .... [I]		Arista 4288

SKY EATS AIRPLANE
Hard-rock band from Fort Worth, Texas: Bryan Zimmerman (vocals), Zack Ordway (guitar), Lee Duck (guitar), Elliot Coleman (bass) and Travis Orbin (drums).

8/9/08	172	1	1 Sky Eats Airplane		Equal Vision 149

SKYLARK
Pop band from Vancouver, British Columbia, Canada: Donny Gerrard and Bonnie Jean Cook (vocals), with **David Foster** (keyboards) and Duris Maxwell (drums). Foster was later a prolific producer/songwriter.

4/7/73	102	16	1 Skylark		Capitol 11048

SKYLINERS, The
White doo-wop group from Pittsburgh, Pennsylvania: Jimmy Beaumont, Janet Vogel, Wally Lester, Joe VerScharen and Jackie Taylor. Vogel committed suicide on 2/21/1980 (age 37). VerScharen died of cancer on 11/3/2007 (age 67).

~ ~ ~ ~ ~ ~ ~ ~ *NON-CHARTED ALBUM* ~ ~ ~ ~ ~ ~ ~ ~ ~ ~ ~
1959 **The Skyliners**

SKYLIT DRIVE, A
Hard-rock band from Lodi, California: Michael Jagmin (vocals), Joey Wilson (guitar), Nick Miller (guitar), Kyle Simmons (keyboards), Brian White (bass) and Cory LaQuay (drums).

6/7/08	171	1	1 Wires And The Concept Of Breathing		Tragic Hero 476284
6/27/09	64	2	2 Adelphia		Fearless 30123

SKYY
Funk band from Brooklyn, New York: sisters Denise, Delores and Bonne Dunning (vocals), Solomon Roberts (vocals, guitar), Anibal Sierra (guitar), Larry Greenberg (keyboards), Gerald LaBon (bass) and Tommy McConnell (drums). Wayne Wilentz replaced Greenberg in 1982.

5/19/79	117	9	1 Skyy		Salsoul 8517
3/15/80	61	23	2 Skyway		Salsoul 8532
12/6/80+	85	20	3 Skyyport		Salsoul 8537
11/21/81+	18	33	● 4 Skyy Line		Salsoul 8548
11/20/82+	81	13	5 Skyyjammer		Salsoul 8555
8/6/83	183	3	6 Skyylight		Salsoul 8562
5/27/89	155	5	7 Start Of A Romance		Atlantic 81853

SKYZOO
Born Gregory Skyler Taylor on 12/24/1982 in Brooklyn, New York. Male rapper.

10/17/09	126	1	1 The Salvation		Duck Down 2115

SLADE
Hard-rock band formed in Wolverhampton, England: Neville "Noddy" Holder (vocals), David Hill (guitar), Jim Lea (bass, keyboards) and Don Powell (drums). Group starred in the 1975 movie *Flame*.

10/7/72	158	11	1 Slade Alive! .... [L]		Polydor 5508
2/17/73	69	26	2 Slayed?		Polydor 5524
10/20/73	129	7	3 Sladest .... [K]		Reprise 2173
3/9/74	168	5	4 Stomp Your Hands, Clap Your Feet		Warner 2770
7/5/75	93	14	5 Slade In Flame .... [S]		Warner 2865
5/5/84	33	23	6 Keep Your Hands Off My Power Supply		CBS Associated 39336
5/4/85	132	6	7 Rogues Gallery		CBS Associated 39976

SLASH'S SNAKEPIT
Born Saul Hudson on 7/23/1965 in Staffordshire, England; raised in Los Angeles, California. Hard-rock guitarist. Member of **Guns N' Roses** and **Velvet Revolver**.

3/4/95	70	6	1 It's Five O'Clock Somewhere		Geffen 24730

SLATKIN, Felix
Born on 12/22/1915 in St. Louis, Missouri. Died on 2/9/1963 (age 47). Conductor/composer/arranger.

4/6/63	20	12	1 Our Winter Love .... [I]		Liberty 7287

SLAUGHTER
Hard-rock band formed in Las Vegas, Nevada: Mark Slaughter (vocals), Tim Kelly (guitar), Dana Strum (bass) and Blas Elias (drums). Slaughter and Strum were with the **Vinnie Vincent Invasion**. Kelly died in a car crash on 2/5/1998 (age 35).

2/17/90	18	85	▲² 1 Stick It To Ya		Chrysalis 21702
11/24/90+	123	20	2 Stick It Live .... [EP-L]		Chrysalis 21816
5/9/92	8	23	● 3 The Wild Life		Chrysalis 21911
5/20/95	182	1	4 Fear No Evil		CMC 7403

SLAUGHTERHOUSE
All-star rap group: **Joe Budden**, Crooked I, Joell Ortiz and **Royce Da 5'9"**.

8/29/09	25	5	1 Slaughterhouse		E1 2052

Billboard DEBUT	PEAK	WKS	R I A A	ARTIST Album Title	Catalog	Label & Number

SLAVE

Funk band from Dayton, Ohio, formed by Steve Washington (trumpet). Longtime members included Mark Adams (bass), Floyd Miller (vocals, horns) and Danny Webster (vocals, guitar). Washington and members Curt Jones and Starleana Young (vocals) and Tom Lockett (sax) left to form **Aurra** in 1979. **Steve Arrington** (drums, vocals) was a member from 1979-82. Young and Jones later formed **Deja**.

4/9/77	22	28	●	1 Slave		Cotillion 9914
12/17/77+	67	15		2 The Hardness Of The World		Cotillion 5201
8/19/78	78	10		3 The Concept		Cotillion 5206
12/8/79+	92	15		4 Just A Touch Of Love		Cotillion 5217
11/1/80+	53	34	●	5 Stone Jam		Cotillion 5224
10/10/81	46	23		6 Show Time		Cotillion 5227
1/15/83	177	6		7 Visions Of The Lite		Cotillion 90024
10/22/83	168	5		8 Bad Enuff		Cotillion 90118

SLAYER

Hard-rock band formed in Los Angeles, California: Tom Araya (vocals, bass), Jeff Hanneman (guitar), Kerry King (guitar) and Dave Lombardo (drums). Paul Bostaph replaced Lombardo in 1995.

11/15/86	94	18	●	1 Reign In Blood		Def Jam 24131
8/6/88	57	19	●	2 South Of Heaven		Def Jam 24203
10/27/90	40	23	●	3 Seasons In The Abyss		Def American 24307
11/9/91	55	10		4 Live - Decade Of Aggression [L]		Def American 26748 [2]
10/15/94	8	9	●	5 Divine Intervention		American 45522
6/15/96	34	5		6 Undisputed Attitude		American 43072
6/27/98	31	6		7 Diabolus In Musica		American 69192
9/29/01	28	6		8 God Hates Us All		American 586331
8/26/06+	5	6		9 Christ Illusion		American 44300
11/21/09	12	5		10 World Painted Blood		American 41318

SLEATER-KINNEY

Female rock trio from Olympia, Washington: Corin Tucker (vocals, guitar), Carrie Brownstein (bass) and Janet Weiss (drums).

3/13/99	181	1		1 The Hot Rock		Kill Rock Stars 321
5/20/00	177	1		2 All Hands On The Bad One		Kill Rock Stars 360
9/7/02	107	2		3 One Beat		Kill Rock Stars 387
6/11/05	80	3		4 The Woods		Sub Pop 70670

SLEDGE, Percy

Born on 11/25/1940 in Leighton, Alabama. Soul singer/songwriter.

AWARD: R&R Hall of Fame: 2005

6/4/66	37	21		1 When A Man Loves A Woman		Atlantic 8125
11/26/66	136	3		2 Warm & Tender Soul		Atlantic 8132
8/5/67	178	3		3 The Percy Sledge Way		Atlantic 8146
5/25/68	148	6		4 Take Time To Know Her		Atlantic 8180
3/1/69	133	11		5 The Best Of Percy Sledge [G]		Atlantic 8210

SLEEZE BEEZ

Hard-rock group formed in the Netherlands: Andrew Elt (vocals), Chriz Van Jaarsveld (guitar), Don Van Spall (guitar), Ed Jongsma (bass) and Jan Koster (drums).

5/19/90	115	15		1 Screwed Blued & Tattooed		Atlantic 82069

SLICK, Grace

Born Grace Wing on 10/30/1939 in Highland Park, Illinois. Rock singer/songwriter. Member of **Jefferson Airplane/Starship**.

5/4/68	166	4		1 Conspicuous Only In Its Absence [E-L]		Columbia 9624
				THE GREAT SOCIETY WITH GRACE SLICK recorded in 1965		
2/6/71	201	1		2 Grace Slick & The Great Society [K]		Columbia 30459 [2]
12/25/71+	89	9		3 Sunfighter		Grunt 1002
				PAUL KANTNER & GRACE SLICK		
6/23/73	120	12		4 Baron Von Tollbooth & The Chrome Nun		Grunt 0148
				PAUL KANTNER, GRACE SLICK & DAVID FREIBERG		
2/9/74	127	7		5 Manhole		Grunt 0347
4/5/80	32	16		6 Dreams		RCA Victor 3544
2/14/81	48	14		7 Welcome To The Wrecking Ball!		RCA Victor 3851
3/10/84	206	3		8 Software		RCA Victor 4791

SLICK RICK

Born Ricky Walters on 1/14/1965 in London, England (Jamaican parents); raised in the Bronx, New York. Male rapper.

1/21/89	31	40	▲	1 The Great Adventures Of Slick Rick		Def Jam 40513
7/20/91	29	13		2 The Ruler's Back		Def Jam 47372
12/10/94	51	6		3 Behind Bars		Def Jam 523847
6/12/99	8	17	●	4 The Art Of Storytelling		Def Jam 558936

SLIDAWG AND THE REDNECK RAMBLERS

Country novelty band formed in Nashville, Tennessee: Steve Ivey (vocals, guitar), Ray Cole (guitar), Cooter Jenkins (bass) and Melvin Snodgrass (drums).

11/3/07	27	3		1 A Blue Collar Christmas [X-N]		IMI/Madacy 53117
11/3/07	29^X	3		2 A Redneck Christmas [X-N]		IMI/Madacy 53116

Billboard DEBUT	PEAK	WKS	R I A A	ARTIST Album Title	Catalog	Label & Number

SLIGH, Chris
Born on 7/20/1978 in Madison, Tennessee; raised in Greenville, South Carolina. Male rock singer. Finalist on the sixth season of TV's *American Idol* in 2007.

| 5/24/08 | 190 | 1 | | 1 Running Back To You .... | | Brash 0042 |

SLIGHTLY STOOPID
Eclectic-rock band from Ocean Beach, California: Miles Doughty (vocals, guitar), Kyle McDonald (vocals, bass), Oguer Ocon (percussion) and Ryan Moran (drums).

5/7/05	121	1		1 Closer To The Sun		Stoopid 01208
8/25/07	55	3		2 Chronchitis		Stoopid 01
8/9/08	73	3		3 Slightly Not Stoned Enough To Eat Breakfast Yet Stoopid		Stoopid 03

SLIM
Born Marvin Scandrick on 9/25/1979 in Atlanta, Georgia. R&B singer/songwriter. Member of **112**.

| 12/6/08 | 32 | 4 | | 1 Love's Crazy .... | | M3 516391 |

SLIM THUG
Born Stayve Thomas on 2/17/1982 in Houston, Texas. Male rapper.

| 7/30/05 | 2¹ | 12 | | 1 Already Platinum | | Star Trak 003505 |
| 4/11/09 | 15 | 10 | | 2 Boss Of All Bosses .... | | Boss Hogg Outlawz 5093 |

SLIPKNOT
Hard-rock band from Des Moines, Iowa: Corey Taylor (vocals), Mick Thomson (guitar), Jim Root (guitar), Sid Wilson (DJ), Craig Jones (samples), Chris Fehn and Shawn Crahan (percussion), Paul Gray (bass) and Joey Jordison (drums). Taylor, Root and Wilson also formed **Stone Sour**. Jordison is also the guitarist for **Murderdolls**. Gray died on 5/24/2010 (age 38).

7/17/99+	51	77	▲²	1 Slipknot .... Cat:#27/6		I Am 8655
9/15/01	3¹	16	▲	2 Iowa		Roadrunner 8564
6/12/04	2¹	64	▲	3 Vol. 3: (The Subliminal Verses) .... Cat:#37/1		Roadrunner 618388
11/19/05	17	11	●	4 9.0: Live .... [L]		Roadrunner 618115 [2]
9/13/08	❶¹	69	●	5 All Hope Is Gone		Roadrunner 617938

SLUM VILLAGE
Rap trio from Detroit, Michigan: Titus "Baatin" Glover, RL "T3" Altman and Jason "Elzhi" Powers. Glover died on 7/31/2009 (age 35).

8/26/00	180	1		1 Fantastic, Vol. 2		GoodVibe 2025
8/31/02	20	8		2 Trinity (Past, Present And Future)		Barak 38911
7/17/04	37	5		3 Detroit Deli (A Taste Of Detroit)		Barak 83043

SLY & THE FAMILY STONE
Interracial "psychedelic soul" band formed in San Francisco, California: Sylvester "Sly Stone" Stewart (lead vocals; keyboards; born on 3/15/1944 in Dallas, Texas), Sly's brother Freddie Stone (guitar), Cynthia Robinson (trumpet), Jerry Martini (sax), Sly's sister Rose Banks (piano, vocals), Sly's cousin **Larry Graham** (bass) and Gregg Errico (drums).
AWARD: R&R Hall of Fame: 1993

5/4/68	142	7		1 Dance To The Music		Epic 26371
12/7/68	195	5		2 Life		Epic 26397
4/26/69	13	102	▲	3 Stand!		Epic 26456
				RS500 #118		
11/7/70	2¹	79	▲⁵	4 Greatest Hits [G]		Epic 30325
				RS500 #60		
11/13/71	❶²	31	▲	5 There's A Riot Goin' On		Epic 30986
				Grammy: Hall of Fame ★ RS500 #99		
6/30/73	7	33	●	6 Fresh		Epic 32134
				RS500 #186		
7/27/74	15	15	●	7 Small Talk		Epic 32930
11/8/75	45	10		8 High On You		Epic 33835
				SLY STONE		
11/10/79	152	3		9 Back On The Right Track		Warner 3303

SLY FOX
Biracial pop-dance duo: Gary "Mudbone" Cooper and Michael Camacho.

| 3/1/86 | 31 | 22 | | 1 Let's Go All The Way .... | | Capitol 12367 |

SMALL, Millie
Born Millicent Smith on 10/6/1946 in Clarendon, Jamaica. Reggae-ska singer. Nicknamed "The Blue Beat Girl."

| 8/8/64 | 132 | 5 | | 1 My Boy Lollipop .... | | Smash 67055 |

SMALL FACES
Rock band formed in England: **Steve Marriott** (vocals, guitar), **Ian McLagan** (organ), **Ronnie Laine** (bass) and Kenney Jones (drums). In 1968, Marriott formed **Humble Pie**. Remaining members evolved into **Faces** in 1969; disbanded in 1975. Jones joined **The Who** in 1978, formed **The Law** in 1991. Marriott died in a house fire on 4/20/1991 (age 44). Lane died of multiple sclerosis on 6/4/1997 (age 51).

3/16/68	178	3		1 There Are But Four Small Faces		Immediate 52002
9/21/68	159	9		2 Ogdens' Nut Gone Flake		Immediate 52008
				features a round album cover		
3/17/73	189	6		3 Ogdens' Nut Gone Flake .... [R]		Abkco 4225
				new cover is nearly identical to original, inside a square sleeve		
8/5/72	176	10		4 Early Faces .... [E]		Pride 0001

SMALLWOOD, Richard
Born on 11/30/1948 in Atlanta, Georgia. Gospel choral leader based in Washington DC.

8/25/01	189	1		1 Persuaded - Live In D.C. .... [L]		Verity 43172
				RICHARD SMALLWOOD WITH VISION		
6/23/07	162	1		2 Journey: Live In New York		Verity 62226

SMASHING PUMPKINS, The   1990s: #42 / All-Time: #354
Alternative-rock band formed in Chicago, Illinois: **Billy Corgan** (vocals, guitar; born on 3/17/1967), **James Iha** (guitar; born on 3/26/1968), D'Arcy Wretzky (bass; born on 5/1/1968) and Jimmy Chamberlin (drums; born on 6/10/1964). Touring keyboardist Jonathan Melvoin, son of Mike Melvoin (**The Plastic Cow**) and brother of Wendy (**Wendy & Lisa**) and Susannah (**The Family**) Melvoin, died of a drug overdose on 7/12/96 (age 34). Disbanded in 2001. Corgan and Chamberlain formed **Zwan** in 2002. Band reunited in 2006.

9/7/91	195	1	▲	1 Gish	Cat:#20/32	Caroline 1705
8/14/93	10	89	▲⁴	2 Siamese Dream	Cat:#4/69	Virgin 88267
				RS500 #360		
10/22/94	4	23	▲	3 Pisces Iscariot	[K]	Virgin 39834
				contains B-sides and previously unavailable tracks		
11/11/95	❶¹	93	▲⁹	4 Mellon Collie And The Infinite Sadness		Virgin 40861 [2]
				RS500 #487		
5/11/96	46	12	●	5 Zero	[EP]	Virgin 38545
12/14/96	42	6	▲	6 The Aeroplane Flies High	[K]	Virgin 38564 [5]
6/20/98	2¹	25	▲	7 Adore		Virgin 45879
3/18/00	3¹	13	●	8 Machina/The Machines Of God		Virgin 48936
12/8/01	31	14	●	9 (Rotten Apples) Greatest Hits	[G]	Virgin 11316
7/28/07	2¹	14	●	10 Zeitgeist		Martha's Music 138620

SMASH MOUTH
Pop-rock band from San Jose, California: Steve Harwell (vocals), Greg Camp (guitar), Paul DeLisle (bass) and Kevin Coleman (drums). Michael Urbano (of **Bourgeois Tagg**) replaced Coleman in 2000.

8/2/97+	19	60	▲²	1 Fush Yu Mang		Interscope 90142
6/26/99	6	66	▲³	2 Astro Lounge		Interscope 90316
12/15/01	48	10	●	3 Smash Mouth		Interscope 93047
8/23/03	100	2		4 Get The Picture?		Interscope 000795
9/10/05	96	2		5 All Star Smash Hits	[G]	Interscope 005218

SMIF-N-WESSUN — see COCOA BROVAZ

SMILE EMPTY SOUL
Hard-rock trio from Los Angeles, California: Sean Danielsen (vocals, guitar), Ryan Martin (bass) and Derek Gledhill (drums).

7/12/03	94	21	●	1 Smile Empty Soul		ThroBack 83639
11/11/06	169	1		2 Vultures		Bieler Bros. 70012
9/12/09	156	1		3 Consciousness		F.O.F. 11403

SMILEZ & SOUTHSTAR
Male rap duo from Orlando, Florida: Rodney "Smilez" Bailey and Robert "Southstar" Campman.

8/10/02+	91	15		1 Crash The Party		Artist Direct 01030

SMITH
Pop-rock band from Los Angeles, California: **Gayle McCormick** (vocals), Rick Cliburn (guitar), Alan Parker (guitar), Larry Moss (keyboards), Jerry Carter (bass) and Robert Evans (drums).

8/23/69	17	28		1 a group called Smith		Dunhill/ABC 50056
7/4/70	74	12		2 Minus-Plus		Dunhill/ABC 50081

SMITH, Cal
Born Calvin Grant Shofner on 4/7/1932 in Gans, Oklahoma; raised in Oakland. Country singer/guitarist.

9/6/69	170	2		1 Cal Smith Sings		Kapp 3608
4/14/73	191	3		2 I've Found Someone Of My Own		Decca 75369

SMITH, Connie
Born Constance June Meador on 8/14/1941 in Elkhart, Indiana; raised in Hinton, West Virginia, and Warner, Ohio. Country singer. Married **Marty Stuart** on 7/8/1997.
AWARD: OPRY: 1965

5/22/65	105	5		1 Connie Smith		RCA Victor 3341

SMITH, Elliott
Born on 8/6/1969 in Nebraska; raised in Portland, Oregon. Committed suicide on 10/21/2003 (age 34). Rock singer/songwriter/guitarist.

9/12/98	104	3		1 XO		DreamWorks 50048
5/6/00	99	5		2 Figure 8		DreamWorks 50225
11/6/04	19	9		3 From A Basement On The Hill		Anti 86741
5/26/07	24	6		4 New Moon		Kill Rock Stars 455 [2]

SMITH, Frankie
Born in Philadelphia, Pennsylvania. R&B singer/songwriter/producer.

8/8/81	54	10		1 Children Of Tomorrow		WMOT 37391

SMITH, Huey (Piano), And The Clowns
Born on 1/26/1934 in New Orleans, Louisiana. The Clowns featured lead singer Bobby Marchan.

~ ~ ~ ~ ~ ~ ~ ~ ~ ~ **NON-CHARTED ALBUMS** ~ ~ ~ ~ ~ ~ ~ ~ ~ ~ ~

1959 **Having A Good Time**   1962 **'Twas The Night Before Christmas**
1961 **For Dancing**

SMITH, Hurricane
Born Norman Smith on 2/22/1923 in London, England. Died on 3/3/2008 (age 85). Pop singer/producer.

1/6/73	53	18	1 Hurricane Smith		Capitol 1139

SMITH, Jerry, and His Pianos
Born in Philadelphia, Pennsylvania. Male pianist/songwriter. Prolific session musician. Also see **The Magic Organ**.

7/26/69	200	2	1 Truck Stop	[I]	ABC 692

SMITH, Jimmy   1960s: #29 / All-Time: #168
Born on 12/8/1925 in Norristown, Pennsylvania. Died on 2/8/2005 (age 79). Pioneer jazz electric organist. Won Major Bowes Amateur Show in 1934. With father (James Sr.) in song-and-dance team, 1942. With Don Gardner & The Sonotones, recorded for Bruce in 1953. Smith first recorded with own trio for Blue Note in 1956.

DEBUT	PEAK	WKS	Album Title		Label & Number
2/17/62	28	51	1 Midnight Special	[I]	Blue Note 84078
3/9/63	14	22	2 Back At The Chicken Shack	[I]	Blue Note 84117
11/9/63	64	8	3 Rockin' The Boat	[I]	Blue Note 84141
8/1/64	86	20	4 Prayer Meetin'	[I]	Blue Note 84164
11/12/66	121	9	5 "Bucket"!	[I]	Blue Note 84235
6/8/68	128	4	6 Jimmy Smith's Greatest Hits!	[G-I]	Blue Note 89901 [2]
6/2/62	10	34	7 Bashin'	[I]	Verve 8474
5/18/63	11	30	8 Hobo Flats	[I]	Verve 8544
11/9/63	25	33	9 Any Number Can Win	[I]	Verve 8552
11/30/63	108	4	10 Blue Bash!	[I]	Verve 8553
			KENNY BURRELL & JIMMY SMITH		
4/18/64	16	31	11 Who's Afraid Of Virginia Woolf?	[I]	Verve 8583
9/19/64	12	32	12 The Cat	[I]	Verve 8587
12/5/64	8[X]	4	13 Christmas '64	[X-I]	Verve 8604
12/24/66	75[X]	3	14 Christmas Cookin'	[X-I-R]	Verve 8666
			reissue (new title and cover) of album above; Christmas charts: 75/'66, 87/'67		
5/8/65	35	24	15 Monster	[I]	Verve 8618
9/18/65	15	31	16 Organ Grinder Swing...	[I]	Verve 8628
3/12/66	28	27	17 Got My Mojo Workin'	[I]	Verve 8641
9/10/66	77	14	18 Hoochie Coochie Man	[I]	Verve 8667
5/20/67	129	23	19 Jimmy & Wes The Dynamic Duo	[I]	Verve 8678
			JIMMY SMITH & WES MONTGOMERY		
10/7/67	60	20	20 Respect..	[I]	Verve 8705
12/9/67	185	4	21 The Best Of Jimmy Smith	[G-I]	Verve 8721
10/26/68	169	10	22 Livin' It Up!	[I]	Verve 8750
7/26/69	144	3	23 The Boss...	[I]	Verve 8770
5/23/70	197	3	24 Groove Drops	[I]	Verve 8794

SMITH, Kate
Born on 5/1/1907 in Greenville, Virginia. Died on 6/17/1986 (age 79). Legendary soprano singer. Best known for her rendition of "God Bless America."

12/21/63+	83	18	1 Kate Smith at Carnegie Hall..	[L]	RCA Victor 2819
			recorded on 11/2/1963		
10/31/64	145	2	2 The Sweetest Sounds		RCA Victor 2921
1/15/66	36	24	3 How Great Thou Art		RCA Victor 3445
6/25/66	130	3	4 The Kate Smith Anniversary Album		RCA Victor 3535
12/3/66	148	2	5 Kate Smith Today		RCA Victor 3670
12/17/66+	15[X]	9	6 The Kate Smith Christmas Album	[X]	RCA Victor 3607
			Christmas charts: 21/'66, 15/'67, 44/'68		

SMITH, Kathy
Born on 12/11/1951 in New York. Aerobics instructor.

3/13/82	144	13	1 Kathy Smith's Aerobic Fitness		MuscleTone 72151
			music by studio musicians		

SMITH, Keely — see PRIMA, Louis

SMITH, Lonnie
Born on 7/3/1942 in Lackawanna, New York. Jazz organist.

5/16/70	186	2	1 Move Your Hand	[I-L]	Blue Note 84326
			recorded on 8/9/1969 at Club Harlem in Atlantic City, New Jersey		

SMITH, Lonnie Liston
Born on 12/28/1940 in Richmond, Virginia. Jazz keyboardist/trumpeter.

DEBUT	PEAK	WKS				
5/24/75	85	13		1 Expansions		Flying Dutchman 0934
10/18/75	74	15		2 Visions Of A New World		Flying Dutchman 1196
4/10/76	75	14		3 Reflections Of A Golden Dream		Flying Dutchman 1460
12/11/76+	73	20		4 Renaissance		RCA Victor 1822
				LONNIE LISTON SMITH & THE COSMIC ECHOES (above 4)		
7/30/77	58	11		5 Live! [I-L]		RCA Victor 2433
				recorded on 5/19/1977 at Smucker's Cabaret in Brooklyn, New York		
4/22/78	120	13		6 Loveland		Columbia 35332
2/17/79	123	8		7 Exotic Mysteries		Columbia 35654
10/13/79	208	2		8 A Song For The Children		Columbia 36141
5/17/80	202	2		9 Love Is The Answer		Columbia 36373
7/30/83	193	2		10 Dreams Of Tomorrow		Doctor Jazz 38447

SMITH, Michael W.
All-Time: #257

Born Michael Whitaker Smith on 10/7/1957 in Kenova, West Virginia. Contemporary Christian singer/songwriter/keyboardist.

DEBUT	PEAK	WKS				
6/8/91	74	19	▲	1 Go West Young Man		Reunion 24325
9/19/92+	86	29	▲	2 Change Your World		Reunion 24491
9/9/95	16	39	▲	3 I'll Lead You Home		Reunion 83953
				Grammy: Pop Gospel Album		
5/16/98	23	18	●	4 Live The Life		Reunion 10007
12/11/99	21	13	●	5 This Is Your Time		Reunion 0041
12/9/00	70	7	●	6 Freedom [I]		Reunion 0002
10/25/03	38	9		7 The Second Decade: 1993-2003 [G]		Reunion 10080
11/13/04	11	15	●	8 Healing Rain		Reunion 10073
11/25/06+	48	13		9 Stand		Reunion 10109
				CHRISTMAS ALBUMS:		
11/14/98	90	9	●	10 Christmastime	Cat:#2^1/5	Reunion 10015
				Christmas charts: 4/'98, 7/'99		
11/13/04	24^X	5		11 The Christmas Collection		Reunion 10091 [2]
11/3/07	59	10		12 It's A Wonderful Christmas	Cat:#25/6	Reunion 10123
				Christmas charts: 4/'07, 20/'08, 18/'09		
12/12/09	84	1		13 It's A Wonderful Christmas [R]		Reunion 10123
				LIVE ALBUMS:		
9/29/01	20	83	▲	14 Worship		Reunion 10025
				recorded at Carpenter's Home Church in Lakeland, Florida		
11/9/02	14	34	▲	15 Worship Again		Reunion 10074
				Grammy: Pop Gospel Album		
				recorded at Southeast Christian Church in Louisville, Kentucky		
11/15/08	19	40		16 A New Hallelujah		Reunion 10133

SMITH, Mindy
Born on 6/1/1972 in Long Island, New York. Adult-Alternative singer/songwriter.

DEBUT	PEAK	WKS				
2/14/04	143	2		1 One Moment More		Vanguard 79736
10/28/06	167	1		2 Long Island Shores		Vanguard 79797
8/29/09	122	1		3 Stupid Love		Vanguard 79853

SMITH, O.C.
Born Ocie Lee Smith on 6/21/1932 in Mansfield, Louisiana; raised in Los Angeles, California. Died on 11/23/2001 (age 69). Male R&B singer.

DEBUT	PEAK	WKS				
6/15/68	19	42		1 Hickory Holler Revisited		Columbia 9680
3/1/69	50	15		2 For Once In My Life		Columbia 9756
10/18/69	58	16		3 O.C. Smith At Home		Columbia 9908
9/19/70	177	5		4 O.C. Smith's Greatest Hits [G]		Columbia 30227
7/31/71	159	7		5 Help Me Make It Through The Night		Columbia 30664

SMITH, Patti
Born on 12/30/1946 in Chicago, Illinois; raised in New Jersey. Punk-rock singer. Married to Fred "Sonic" Smith of **MC5** from 1980-94 (his death). Her group: Lenny Kaye (guitar), Richard Sohl (keybaords), Ivan Kral (bass) and J.D. Daughtery (drums). Sohl died on 6/3/1990 (age 37). Not to be confused with Patty Smyth of Scandal.

AWARD: R&R Hall of Fame: 2007

DEBUT	PEAK	WKS				
12/13/75+	47	17		1 Horses		Arista 4066
				RS500 #44		
11/27/76+	122	8		2 Radio Ethiopia		Arista 4097
4/8/78	20	23		3 Easter		Arista 4171
5/19/79	18	19		4 Wave		Arista 4221
				PATTI SMITH GROUP (above 3)		
7/30/88	65	15		5 Dream Of Life		Arista 8453
7/6/96	55	5		6 Gone Again		Arista 18747
10/18/97	152	1		7 Peace And Noise		Arista 18986
4/8/00	178	1		8 Gung Ho		Arista 14618
5/15/04	123	1		9 Trampin'		Columbia 90330
5/12/07	60	3		10 Twelve		Columbia 87251

SMITH, Ray
Born on 10/31/1934 in Melber, Kentucky. Committed suicide on 11/29/1979 (age 45). Rockabilly singer/guitarist.

~ ~ ~ ~ ~ ~ ~ ~ ~ ~ **NON-CHARTED ALBUM** ~ ~ ~ ~ ~ ~ ~ ~ ~ ~

1960 **Travelin' With Ray**

SMITH, Rex
Born on 9/19/1956 in Jacksonville, Florida. Actor/singer. Acted in several movies and Broadway shows. Brother of Michael Lee Smith of **Starz**.

DEBUT	PEAK	WKS			Catalog	Label & Number
4/28/79	19	19	●	1 Sooner Or Later		Columbia 35813
1/12/80	165	3		2 Forever, Rex Smith		Columbia 36275
8/22/81	167	4		3 Everlasting Love		Columbia 37494

SMITH, Sammi
Born Jewel Fay Smith on 8/5/1943 in Orange, California; raised in Oklahoma. Died of emphysema on 2/12/2005 (age 61). Female country singer.

2/13/71	33	21		1 Help Me Make It Through The Night		Mega 1000
8/21/71	191	2		2 Lonesome		Mega 1007

SMITH, Steve
Born on 8/21/1954 in Whitman, Massachusetts. Rock drummer. Member of **Journey** and **The Storm**. Vital Information was a jazz fusion band: Eef Albers (guitar), Dean Brown (guitar), Dave Wilczewski (sax) and Tim Landers (bass).

6/16/84	209	2		1 Orion [I]		Columbia 39375
				STEVE SMITH/VITAL INFORMATION		

SMITH, Will
Born on 9/25/1968 in Philadelphia, Pennsylvania. Rapper/actor. One-half of **D.J. Jazzy Jeff and The Fresh Prince** from 1986-93. Starred on TV's *Fresh Prince of Bel Air* and in several movies. Married actress Jada Pinkett on 12/31/1997.

12/13/97+	8	99	▲⁹	1 Big Willie Style Cat:#16/8		Columbia 68683
12/4/99	5	26	▲²	2 Willennium		Columbia 69985
7/13/02	13	8	●	3 Born To Reign		Columbia 86189
4/16/05	6	24	●	4 Lost And Found		Overbrook 004306

SMITHER, Chris
Born on 11/11/1944 in Miami, Florida; raised in New Orleans, Louisiana. Male singer/songwriter/guitarist.

2/13/71	204	1		1 I'm A Stranger Too!		Poppy 40013

SMITHEREENS, The
Power-pop band formed in Carteret, New Jersey: Pat DiNizio (vocals, guitar), Jim Babjak (guitar), Mike Mesaros (bass) and Dennis Diken (drums).

8/16/86+	51	50		1 Especially For You		Enigma 73208
4/9/88	60	31		2 Green Thoughts		Capitol 48375
11/18/89+	41	38	●	3 11		Enigma 91194
9/28/91	120	3		4 Blow Up		Capitol 94963
5/14/94	133	2		5 A Date With The Smithereens		RCA 66391

SMITHS, The
Alternative-rock band formed in Manchester, England: **Morrissey** (vocals), Johnny Marr (guitar), Andy Rourke (bass) and Mike Joyce (drums). Marr later joined **The The** and **Electronic**.

5/5/84	150	11		1 The Smiths Cat:#29/16		Sire 25065
				RS500 #481		
3/2/85	110	32		2 Meat Is Murder		Sire 25269
				RS500 #295		
7/19/86	70	37	●	3 The Queen Is Dead		Sire 25426
				RS500 #216		
10/10/87	55	27	●	4 Strangeways, Here We Come		Sire 25649
10/1/88	77	8		5 Rank [L]		Sire 25786
				recorded October 1986 at The National Ballroom in London, England		
				GREATEST HITS & COMPILATIONS:		
4/25/87	62	25	●	6 Louder Than Bombs		Sire 25569 [2]
				RS500 #365		
10/17/92	139	3		7 Best...I		Sire 45042
11/29/08	98	2		8 The Sound Of The Smiths		Sire 516015

SMOKE RISE
Progressive-rock band from Buffalo, New York: brothers Gary Ruffin (guitar), Hank Ruffin (keyboards) and Stan Ruffin (drums), with Randy Bugg (bass).

8/14/71	203	4		1 The Survival Of St. Joan		Paramount 9000 [2]
				a rock opera based on speculation that Joan of Arc survived		

SMOKESTACK LIGHTNIN'
White blues-rock band from Los Angeles, California: Ron Darling (vocals), Ric Eiserling (guitar), Kelly Green (bass) and Art Guy (drums).

4/12/69	200	2		1 Off The Wall		Bell 6026

Billboard DEBUT	PEAK	WKS	R I A A	ARTIST / Album Title	Catalog	Label & Number
				SMOKIE		
				Pop-rock band from Bradford, Yorkshire, England: Chris Norman (vocals), Alan Silson (guitar), Terry Utley (bass) and Pete Spencer (drums).		
9/13/75	206	1		1 Smokey		MCA 2152
1/22/77	173	6		2 Midnight Cafe		RSO 3005
				SMOOTHE DA HUSTLER		
				Born Damon Smith in Brooklyn, New York. Male rapper.		
5/4/96	93	4		1 Once Upon A Time In America		Profile 1467
				SMOTHERS BROTHERS, The All-Time: #472		
				Comedy team from New York: brothers Tom Smothers (born on 2/2/1937) and Dick Smothers (born on 11/20/1939). Hosted their own TV variety series from 1967-69. Both appeared in several movies. Later founded the highly successful Remick Ridge Vinyards in California.		
7/13/63+	45	50	●	1 The Songs And Comedy Of The Smothers Brothers! .... [C-E]		Mercury 20611
				first released in 1962		
10/20/62	26	66	●	2 The Two Sides Of The Smothers Brothers .... [C]		Mercury 20675
4/6/63+	27	63	●	3 (Think Ethnic!) .... [C]		Mercury 20777
12/14/63+	13	33		4 Curb Your Tongue, Knave! .... [C]		Mercury 20862
5/23/64	23	28		5 It Must Have Been Something I Said! .... [C]		Mercury 20904
12/19/64+	58	20		6 Tour De Farce American History And Other Unrelated Subjects .... [C]		Mercury 20948
6/5/65	57	10		7 Aesop's Fables The Smothers Brothers Way .... [C]		Mercury 20989
10/16/65+	39	28		8 Mom Always Liked You Best! .... [C]		Mercury 21051
8/13/66	119	6		9 Golden Hits Of The Smothers Brothers, Vol. 2 .... [C]		Mercury 21089
11/16/68	164	4		10 Smothers Comedy Brothers Hour .... [C]		Mercury 61193
				SMUT PEDDLERS		
				Male rap trio: Christian "Cage" Palko, Eric "Mr. Eon" Meltzer and Milo "DJ Mighty Mi" Berger. The latter two recorded as The High & Mighty.		
3/10/01	184	1		1 Porn Again		Eastern Con. 50164
				S.M.V.		
				All-star trio of jazz bassists: Stanley Clarke, Marcus Miller and Victor Wooten.		
8/30/08	186	1		1 Thunder .... [I]		Heads Up 3163
				SMYTH, Patty		
				Born on 6/26/1957 in New York. Lead singer of Scandal. Formerly married to Richard Hell (early member of Television); married tennis star John McEnroe in April 1997.		
3/21/87	66	20		1 Never Enough		Columbia 40182
9/5/92	47	34	●	2 Patty Smyth		MCA 10633
				SNAIL		
				Rock band from Santa Cruz, California: Bob O'Neill (vocals, guitar), Ken Kraft (guitar), Jack Register (bass) and Jim Norris (drums). Register and Norris left after first album; replaced by Brett Bloomfield (bass) and Don Baldwin (drums; Jefferson Starship).		
7/8/78	135	12		1 Snail		Cream 1009
11/10/79	186	2		2 Flow		Cream 1012
				SNAP!		
				Studio project assembled by producers Michael Muenzing and Luca Anzilotti. Features a revolving lineup of lead singers including Durron Butler, Jackie Harris, Pennye Ford, Thea Austin, Niki Harris and Paula Brown.		
6/16/90	30	49	●	1 World Power		Arista 8536
10/31/92	121	20		2 The Madman's Return		Arista 18693
				SNEAKER		
				Pop-rock band formed in Los Angeles, California: Mitch Crane (vocals, guitar), Michael Carey Schneider (vocals, keyboards), Tim Torrance (guitar), Jim King (keyboards), Michael Cottage (bass) and Mike Hughes (drums).		
12/12/81+	149	17		1 Sneaker		Handshake 37631
				SNEAKER PIMPS		
				Dance-rock trio from Reading, England: Kelli Drayton (vocals), Chris Comer (guitar) and Liam Howe (keyboards).		
5/31/97	111	23		1 Becoming X		Virgin 42587
				SNIDER, Todd		
				Born on 10/11/1966 in Portland, Oregon. Eclectic-rock singer/songwriter/guitarist.		
8/26/06	173	1		1 The Devil You Know		New Door 006663
6/27/09	144	1		2 Excitement Plan		Yep Roc 2202
				SNIFF 'N' THE TEARS		
				Rock band formed in London, England: Paul Roberts (vocals), Loz Netto (guitar), Mick Dyche (guitar), Alan Fealdman (keyboards), Chris Birkin (bass) and Luigi Salvoni (drums). Disbanded after first album. Roberts led new lineup for second album: Les Davidson (guitar), Mike Taylor (keyboards), Nick South (bass) and Jamie Lane (drums). Roberts joined The Stranglers in 1991.		
7/28/79	35	17		1 Fickle Heart		Atlantic 19242
7/5/80	205	2		2 The Game's Up		Atlantic 19272
9/19/81	192	2		3 Love Action		MCA 5242

			R I A A		ARTIST / Album Title	Catalog	Label & Number
DEBUT	PEAK	WKS					

SNOOP DOGG   2000s: #38 / All-Time: #203

Born Cordozar Calvin Broadus on 10/20/1971 in Long Beach, California. Male rapper/songwriter/actor. Childhood friend of **Dr. Dre** and **Warren G.** Cousin of **Nate Dogg** and Delmar Arnaud (of **Tha Dogg Pound**). Acted in such movies as *Baby Boy*, *Bones*, *The Wash*, *Starsky & Hutch* and *Soul Plane*. Member of **213**. Own TV reality series *Snoop Dogg's Father Hood*.

DEBUT	PEAK	WKS	RIAA	#	Album Title	Catalog	Label & Number
12/11/93	❶³	72	▲⁴	1	Doggy Style	Cat:#7/12	Death Row 92279
11/30/96	❶¹	30	▲²	2	Tha Doggfather		Death Row 90038
					SNOOP DOGGY DOGG (above 2)		
8/22/98	❶²	33	▲²	3	Da Game Is To Be Sold, Not To Be Told		No Limit 50000
5/29/99	2¹	40	▲	4	No Limit Top Dogg		No Limit 50052
11/18/00	24	5		5	Dead Man Walkin		D3 33349
1/6/01	4	36	▲	6	Tha Last Meal		No Limit 23225
11/10/01	28	8		7	Death Row's Snoop Doggy Dogg Greatest Hits	[G]	Death Row 50030
12/14/02	12	36	▲	8	Paid Tha Cost To Be Da Boss		Doggystyle 39157
12/4/04	6	31	▲	9	R&G (Rhythm & Gangsta): The Masterpiece		Doggystyle 003763
10/22/05	121	3		10	The Best Of Snoop Dogg	[G]	Priority 33957
12/9/06	5	21	●	11	Tha Blue Carpet Treatment		Doggystyle 008023
3/29/08	3¹	16		12	Ego Trippin		Doggystyle 010835
10/31/09	129	1		13	Death Row: The Lost Sessions Vol. 1	[K]	Death Row 21013
12/26/09	23	17		14	Malice N Wonderland		Doggystyle 57831

SNOW

Born Darrin O'Brien on 10/30/1969 in Toronto, Ontario, Canada. White male reggae singer/rapper.

DEBUT	PEAK	WKS	RIAA	#	Album Title	Catalog	Label & Number
2/6/93	5	38	▲	1	12 Inches Of Snow		EastWest 92207

SNOW, Hank

Born Clarence Snow on 5/9/1914 in Liverpool, Nova Scotia, Canada. Died of heart failure on 12/20/1999 (age 85). Country singer/songwriter/guitarist. Known as "The Singing Ranger."
AWARDS: C&W Hall of Fame: 1979 ★ OPRY: 1950

DEBUT	PEAK	WKS	RIAA	#	Album Title	Catalog	Label & Number
12/16/67	72ˣ	3		1	Christmas With Hank Snow	[X]	RCA Victor 3826

SNOW, Phoebe

Born Phoebe Laub on 7/17/1952 in New York; raised in New Jersey. Jazz-styled singer.

DEBUT	PEAK	WKS	RIAA	#	Album Title	Catalog	Label & Number
9/7/74+	4	58	●	1	Phoebe Snow		Shelter 2109
11/20/76	202	4		2	Phoebe Snow	[R]	Shelter 52017
2/14/76	13	22	●	3	Second Childhood		Columbia 33952
11/6/76	29	21		4	It Looks Like Snow		Columbia 34387
10/22/77	73	15		5	Never Letting Go		Columbia 34875
10/28/78	100	7		6	Against The Grain		Columbia 35456
4/4/81	51	18		7	Rock Away		Mirage 19297
4/15/89	75	20		8	Something Real		Elektra 60852

SNOW PATROL

Rock band from Dundee, Scotland: Gary Lightbody (vocals, guitar), Nathan Connolly (guitar), Mark McClelland (bass) and John Quinn (drums).

DEBUT	PEAK	WKS	RIAA	#	Album Title	Catalog	Label & Number
8/28/04+	91	31	●	1	Final Straw		Polydor 002271
5/27/06	27	66	▲	2	Eyes Open		Polydor 006675
11/15/08	9	13		3	A Hundred Million Suns		Polydor 012156
11/28/09	182	1		4	Up To Now		Polydor 013606 [2]

SNYPAZ

Male rap group from Chicago, Illinois: Iren Moore, Charles Paxton, Robert Flynn and Dewayne Warren.

DEBUT	PEAK	WKS	RIAA	#	Album Title	Catalog	Label & Number
6/23/01	174	3		1	Livin' In The Scope		Rap-A-Lot 10367

SO

Pop-rock duo from London, England: singer/guitarist Mark Long and multi-instrumentalist Marcus Bell.

DEBUT	PEAK	WKS	RIAA	#	Album Title	Catalog	Label & Number
3/19/88	124	9		1	Horseshoe In The Glove		EMI-Manhattan 46997

SOCCIO, Gino

Born in 1955 in Montreal, Quebec, Canada. Techno-disco singer/multi-instrumentalist.

DEBUT	PEAK	WKS	RIAA	#	Album Title	Catalog	Label & Number
4/21/79	79	13		1	Outline		RFC 3309
5/23/81	96	14		2	Closer		Atlantic 16042

SOCIALBURN

Hard-rock band from Blountstown, Florida: Neil Alday (vocals, guitar), Chris Cobb (guitar), Dusty Price (bass) and Brandon Bittner (drums).

DEBUT	PEAK	WKS	RIAA	#	Album Title	Catalog	Label & Number
3/1/03	178	2		1	Where You Are		Elektra 62790

SOCIAL DISTORTION

Punk-rock band formed in Los Angeles, California: **Mike Ness** (vocals, guitar), Dennis Danell (guitar), John Maurer (bass) and Christopher Reece (drums). Danell died of a brain aneurysm on 2/29/2000 (age 38).

DEBUT	PEAK	WKS	RIAA	#	Album Title	Catalog	Label & Number
5/26/90	128	22	●	1	Social Distortion		Epic 46055
2/29/92	76	16	●	2	Somewhere Between Heaven And Hell		Epic 47978
10/5/96	27	10		3	White Light White Heat White Trash		550 Music 64380
7/18/98	121	2		4	Live At The Roxy	[L]	Time Bomb 43516
					recorded in Hollywood, California		

DEBUT	PEAK	WKS	RIAA	ARTIST / Album Title	Catalog	Label & Number

SOCIAL DISTORTION — cont'd

| 10/16/04 | 31 | 6 | | 5 Sex, Love And Rock 'N' Roll | | Time Bomb 43547 |
| 7/14/07 | 86 | 3 | | 6 Greatest Hits | [G] | Time Bomb 43548 |

SOFT CELL
Techno-pop duo from London, England: **Marc Almond** (vocals) and David Ball (synthesizer).

1/30/82	22	41		1 Non-Stop Erotic Cabaret		Sire 3647
8/14/82	57	14		2 Non-Stop Ecstatic Dancing	Cat:#14/6 [EP]	Sire 23694
2/26/83	84	8		3 The Art Of Falling Apart		Sire 23769 [2]

SOFT MACHINE, The
Experimental rock trio from England: Robert Wyatt (vocals, drums), Michael Ratledge (organ) and Kevin Ayers (guitar).

12/21/68+	160	9		1 The Soft Machine		Probe 4500
6/23/73	210	4		2 Six	[I-L]	Columbia 32260 [2]
				record 1: recorded "live" in London; record 2: studio recording		

SOHO
Interracial dance trio formed in London, England: identical twin sisters Jackie Cuff and Pauline Cuff (vocals), with Tim Brinkhurst (guitar).

| 11/24/90 | 134 | 10 | | 1 Goddess | | Savage 91585 |

SOIL
Hard-rock band from Chicago, Illinois: Ryan McCombs (vocals), Shaun Glass (guitar), Adam Zadel (guitar), Tim King (bass) and Tom Schofield (drums).

| 9/29/01 | 193 | 1 | | 1 Scars | | J Records 20022 |
| 4/10/04 | 78 | 2 | | 2 Redefine | | J Records 59071 |

SOILWORK
Death-metal band from Helsingborg, Sweden: Bjorn Strid (vocals), Peter Wichers (guitar), Sylvain Coudret (guitar), Sven Karlsson (keyboards), Ola Flink (bass) and Dirk Verbeuren (drums).

| 11/10/07 | 148 | 1 | | 1 Sworn To A Great Divide | | Nuclear Blast 1879 |

SOLANGE
Born Solange Knowles on 6/24/1986 in Houston, Texas. Female R&B singer. Sister of **Beyonce** Knowles of **Destiny's Child**.

| 2/8/03 | 49 | 5 | | 1 Solo Star | | Music World 86354 |
| 9/13/08 | 9 | 7 | | 2 Sol-Angel & The Hadley St. Dreams | | Music World 011785 |

SOLDIERZ AT WAR
Rap group from Chicago, Illinois: General Jaymz, C-4, G-Zus, Shotgun Slim, Landmine, Killah C. and Mo' Mike.

| 9/15/01 | 192 | 1 | | 1 Whazzup Joe? | | Millitary 58999 |

SOLE
Born Tonya Johnston on 7/17/1973 in Kansas City, Missouri. Female rapper.

| 10/16/99 | 127 | 13 | | 1 Skin Deep | | DreamWorks 50118 |

SOLEIL, Stella
Born Stella Katsoudas on 11/3/1970 in Chicago, Illinois. Female dance singer.

| 6/9/01 | 106 | 2 | | 1 Dirty Little Secret | | Cherry 013991 |

SOLIS, Javier
Born Gabriel Levario on 9/1/1931 in Mexico. Died after complications from gall bladder surgery on 4/19/1966 (age 34). Latin singer/actor. Appeared in several Mexican movies.

| 9/30/06 | 189 | 2 | | 1 La Historia De Javier Solis | [F-K] | Sony 88292 |
| | | | | recordings from 1950-65 | | |

SOLIS, Marco Antonio   **All-Time: #500**
Born on 12/29/1959 in Ario de Rosales, Michoacan, Mexico. Latin singer. Member of **Los Bukis**.

2/13/99	157	4	▲	1 Trozos De Mi Alma	[F]	Fonovisa 350516
6/16/01	104	6	●	2 Mas De Mi Alma	[F]	Fonovisa 350527
5/31/03	59	5		3 Tu Amor O Tu Desprecio	[F]	Fonovisa 350840
7/17/04	125	11		4 Dos Grandes	[F]	Fonovisa 351402
				MARCO ANTONIO SOLÍS & JOAN SEBASTIAN		
11/20/04	58	5		5 Razon De Sobra	[F]	Fonovisa 351483
10/22/05	198	1		6 Dos Idolos	[F]	Fonovisa 310540
				MARCO ANTONIO SOLIS & PEPE AGUILAR		
10/14/06	52	10		7 Trozos De Mi Alma 2	[F]	Fonovisa 352490
6/28/08	41	13		8 Una Noche En Madrid	[F-L]	Fonovisa 353530
10/25/08	19	8		9 No Molestar	[F]	Fonovisa 353748
11/21/09	174	2		10 Mas De Marco Antonio Solis	[F]	Fonovisa 354216
				GREATEST HITS & COMPILATIONS:		
11/15/03	114	3		11 La Historia Continua...	[F]	Fonovisa 350950
6/11/05	92	9		12 La Historia Continua...Parte II	[F]	Fonovisa 351643
3/17/07	91	5		13 La Historia Continua...Parte III	[F]	Fonovisa 353066
6/2/07	92	66		14 La Mejor...Coleccion	[F]	Fonovisa 353133

Billboard DEBUT	PEAK	WKS	R I A A	ARTIST Album Title	Catalog	Label & Number

SOLO
R&B vocal group from Brooklyn, New York: Eunique Mack, Darnell Chavis, Daniele Stokes and Robert Anderson.

| 9/30/95+ | 52 | 40 | ● | 1 Solo .... | | Perspective 549017 |
| 10/10/98 | 123 | 2 | | 2 4 Bruthas & A Bass | | Perspective 549040 |

SOME, Belouis
Born Neville Keighley on 12/12/1959 in England. Techno-dance singer/multi-instrumentalist.

| 6/1/85 | 201 | 6 | | 1 Some People .... | | Capitol 12345 |

SOMERVILLE, Jimmy
Born on 6/22/1961 in Glasgow, Scotland. Former lead singer of **Bronski Beat** and **Communards**.

| 5/5/90 | 192 | 2 | | 1 Read My Lips .... | | London 828166 |

SOMETHIN' FOR THE PEOPLE
R&B vocal trio from Oakland, California: Jeff Young, Curtis Wilson and Rochad Holiday.

| 10/11/97 | 154 | 15 | | 1 This Time It's Personal .... | | Warner 46753 |
| 8/5/00 | 124 | 1 | | 2 Issues .... | | Warner 47354 |

SOMETHING CORPORATE
Rock band from Anaheim, California: Andrew McMahon (vocals, piano), Josh Partington (guitar), Clutch (bass) and Brian Ireland (drums). McMahon also recorded as **Jack's Mannequin**.

| 6/8/02 | 101 | 2 | | 1 Leaving Through The Window... | | Drive-Thru 112887 |
| 11/8/03 | 24 | 8 | | 2 North... | | Drive-Thru 001190 |

SOMETIMES, Charlotte
Born Jessica Charlotte Poland on 1/15/1988 in Wall Township, New Jersey. Alternative-pop singer/songwriter.

| 6/14/08 | 145 | 1 | | 1 Waves & The Both Of Us .... | | Geffen 011134 |

SOMMERS, Joanie
Born Joan Drost on 2/24/1941 in Buffalo, New York. Pop singer. Appeared in the movies *Everything's Duckie* and *The Lively Set*.

| 9/22/62 | 103 | 3 | | 1 Johnny Get Angry .... | | Warner 1470 |

SON BY FOUR
Latin vocal group from Puerto Rico: brothers Javier Montes and George Montes, with cousin Pedro Quiles and friend Angel Lopez.

| 4/29/00 | 94 | 28 | ● | 1 Son By Four .... [F] | | Sony Discos 83943 |

SONGZ, Trey
Born Tremaine Neverson on 11/28/1984 in Petersburg, Virginia. Male R&B singer/songwriter.

8/13/05	20	26		1 I Gotta Make It..		Song Book 83721
10/20/07	11	23		2 Trey Day		Song Book 135740
9/19/09	3[1]	37↑	●	3 Ready		Song Book 518794

SONICFLOOD
Christian rock band formed in Nashville, Tennessee: Jeff Deyo (vocals), Dwayne Larring (guitar), Jason Halbert (keyboards), Rick Heil (bass) and Aaron Blanton (drums).

10/23/99	158	2		1 Sonicflood..		Gotee 2802
4/28/01	172	3		2 Sonicpraise .... [L]		Gotee 2827
10/20/01	168	2		3 Resonate		Word 86012

SONIC YOUTH
Post-punk art rock band formed in New York: husband-and-wife Thurston Moore (guitar; born on 7/25/1958) and Kim Gordon (bass; born on 4/28/1953), with Lee Ranaldo (guitar; born on 2/3/1956) and Steve Shelley (drums; born on 6/23/1963). All share vocals. Moore and Gordon married in 1984.

7/14/90	96	15		1 Goo		DGC 24297
8/8/92	83	11		2 Dirty		DGC 24493
5/28/94	34	10		3 Experimental Jet Set, Trash And No Star		DGC 24632
10/14/95	58	3		4 Washing Machine		DGC 24825
5/30/98	85	2		5 A Thousand Leaves		DGC 25203
7/13/02	126	1		6 Murray Street		DGC 493319
6/3/00	172	1		7 NYC Ghosts & Flowers		Geffen 490650
6/26/04	64	2		8 Sonic Nurse		Geffen 002549
7/1/06	71	4		9 Rather Ripped...		Geffen 006757
6/27/09	18	6		10 The Eternal		Matador 829

~ ~ ~ ~ ~ ~ ~ ~ ~ ~ **NON-CHARTED ALBUM** ~ ~ ~ ~ ~ ~ ~ ~ ~ ~ ~
1988 **Daydream Nation**
RS500 #329 ★ NRR

SONIQUE
Born Sonia Clarke on 6/21/1968 in London, England. Black female dance-pop singer. Popular DJ in England.

| 3/4/00 | 67 | 26 | | 1 Hear My Cry .... | | Serious 157536 |

Billboard DEBUT	PEAK	WKS	R I A A	ARTIST / Album Title	Catalog	Label & Number

SONNY & CHER · *All-Time: #394*

Husband-and-wife duo: Sonny Bono (born on 2/16/1935 in Detroit, Michigan; died in a skiing accident on 1/5/1998, age 62) and **Cher** (born on 5/20/1946 in El Centro, California). Began career as session singers for **Phil Spector**. First recorded as Caesar & Cleo for Vault in 1963. Married from 1969-75. In the movies *Good Times* (1967) and *Chastity* (1969). Own CBS-TV variety series from 1971-74. Brief TV reunion in 1975. Sonny was mayor of Palm Springs, California, from 1988-92; elected to the U.S. Congress in 1994.

10/23/65	69	16		1 Baby Don't Go		Reprise 6177
8/21/65	2⁸	44	●	2 Look At Us		Atco 177
				also see #7 below		
4/16/66	34	20		3 The Wondrous World Of Sonny & Cher		Atco 183
3/25/67	45	29		4 In Case You're In Love		Atco 203
				also see #7 below		
5/27/67	73	18		5 Good Times	[S]	Atco 214
8/12/67	23	64		6 The Best Of Sonny & Cher	[G]	Atco 219
9/9/72	122	12		7 The Two Of Us	[R]	Atco 804 [2]
				reissue of albums #2 & #4 above		
10/2/71	35	40	●	8 Sonny & Cher Live	[L]	Kapp 3654
2/26/72	14	29	●	9 All I Ever Need Is You		Kapp 3660
6/30/73	132	6		10 Mama Was A Rock And Roll Singer Papa Used To Write All Her Songs		MCA 2101
12/22/73+	175	7		11 Sonny & Cher Live In Las Vegas, Vol. 2	[L]	MCA 8004 [2]
9/28/74	146	6		12 Greatest Hits	[G]	MCA 2117

SONS OF CHAMPLIN

Pop-rock band from San Francisco, California: Bill Champlin (vocals, guitar), Terry Haggerty (guitar), Geoffrey Palmer (keyboards), David Schallock (bass) and James Preston (drums). Champlin joined **Chicago** in 1982.

6/14/69	137	9		1 Loosen Up Naturally		Capitol 200 [2]
11/8/69	171	6		2 The Sons		Capitol 332
6/9/73	186	5		3 Welcome To The Dance		Columbia 32341
10/11/75	207	5		4 The Sons Of Champlin		Ariola America 50002
6/5/76	117	10		5 A Circle Filled With Love		Ariola America 50007
5/28/77	188	4		6 Loving Is Why		Ariola America 50017

SONS OF FUNK

Rap group from Richmond, California: brothers G-Smooth and Dez with their cousins Renzo and Rico.

5/9/98	44	6		1 The Game Of Funk		No Limit 50725

SON VOLT

Alternative country-rock band formed in New Orleans, Louisiana: Jay Farrar (vocals), brothers Dave Boquist (guitar) and Jim Boquist (bass), and Mike Heidorn (drums). Farrar and Heidorn were members of **Uncle Tupelo**.

10/7/95	166	1		1 Trace		Warner 46010
5/10/97	44	3		2 Straightaways		Warner 46518
10/24/98	93	2		3 Wide Swing Tremolo		Warner 47059
7/30/05	89	2		4 Okemah And The Melody Of Riot		Transmit Sound 94743
3/24/07	81	1		5 The Search		Transmit Sound 03232
7/25/09	44	3		6 American Central Dust		Rounder 613274

SOOPA VILLAINZ

Male rap group from Detroit, Michigan: Mr. Heart (Lavel), Mr. Diamond (**Violent J**), Mr. Club (**Shaggy 2 Dope**) and Mr. Spade (**Esham**). Diamond and Club are better known as **Insane Clown Posse**.

9/3/05	92	1		1 Furious		Psychopathic 4053

SOPWITH "CAMEL", The

Pop band from San Francisco, California: Peter Kraemer (vocals, sax), Terry MacNeil (guitar), William Sievers (guitar), Martin Beard (bass), and Norman Mayell (drums). Named after a type of airplane used in World War I.

10/28/67	191	2		1 Sopwith Camel		Kama Sutra 8060
10/20/73	203	6		2 The Miraculous Hump Returns From The Moon		Reprise 2108

S.O.S. BAND, The

Funk-R&B-disco band from Atlanta, Georgia: Mary Davis (vocals, keyboards), Bruno Speight (guitar), Willie Killebrew (sax), Bill Ellis (flute), Jason Bryant (keyboards), John Simpson (bass) and James Earl Jones III (drums).

6/28/80	12	20	●	1 S.O.S.		Tabu 36332
8/22/81	117	6		2 Too		Tabu 37449
12/25/82+	172	8		3 S.O.S. III		Tabu 38352
8/27/83	47	29	●	4 On The Rise		Tabu 38697
9/1/84	60	27		5 Just The Way You Like It		Tabu 39332
5/24/86	44	20	●	6 Sands Of Time		Tabu 40279
11/4/89	194	2		7 Diamonds In The Raw		Tabu 44147
11/4/95	185	1		8 The Best Of The S.O.S. Band	[G]	Tabu 0594

SOUL, David

Born David Solberg on 8/28/1943 in Chicago, Illinois. Actor/singer. Played "Joshua Bolt" on TV's *Here Come The Brides* and "Ken Hutchinson" on TV's *Starsky & Hutch*.

1/22/77	40	22		1 David Soul		Private Stock 2019
9/10/77	86	7		2 Playing To An Audience Of One		Private Stock 7001

SOUL, Jimmy
Born James McCleese on 8/24/1942 in Weldon, North Carolina. Died of a heart attack on 6/25/1988 (age 45). Calypso-styled singer.

~ ~ ~ ~ ~ ~ ~ ~ ~ ~ ~ **NON-CHARTED ALBUM** ~ ~ ~ ~ ~ ~ ~ ~ ~ ~ ~ ~

1963 **If You Wanna Be Happy**

SOUL ASSASSINS, The
Collective of revolving rappers assembled by producer **DJ Muggs**.

DEBUT	PEAK	WKS			Catalog	Label & Number
10/21/00	178	1		1 Muggs Presents The Soul Assassins II		RuffLife 60002
3/22/97	20	9		2 Soul Assassins - Chapter I		Columbia 66820

SOUL ASYLUM
Rock band from Minneapolis, Minnesota: Dave Pirner (vocals, guitar), Dan Murphy (guitar), Karl Mueller (bass) and Grant Young (drums). Pirner appeared in the movie *Reality Bites*. Sterling Campbell (**Duran Duran**) replaced Young in 1995. Mueller died of throat cancer on 6/17/2005 (age 41).

DEBUT	PEAK	WKS	RIAA		Catalog	Label & Number
11/21/92+	11	76	▲²	1 Grave Dancers Union		Columbia 48898
6/24/95	6	21	▲	2 Let Your Dim Light Shine		Columbia 57616
5/30/98	121	2		3 Candy From A Stranger		Columbia 67618
7/29/06	155	1		4 The Silver Lining		Legacy 75161

SOUL CHILDREN, The
R&B vocal group from Memphis, Tennessee: Anita Louis, Shelbra Bennett, John Colbert and Norman West.

DEBUT	PEAK	WKS			Catalog	Label & Number
9/6/69	154	6		1 Soul Children		Stax 2018
3/25/72	203	1		2 Best Of Two Worlds		Stax 2043
4/29/72	159	6		3 Genesis		Stax 3003

SOUL COUGHING
Alternative-rock band formed in New York: **Mike Doughty** (vocals, guitar), Mark Antoni (keyboards), Sebastian Steinberg (bass) and Yuval Gabay (drums).

DEBUT	PEAK	WKS			Catalog	Label & Number
7/27/96	136	4		1 Irresistible Bliss		Slash 46175
10/17/98	49	10		2 El Oso		Slash 46800

SOULDECISION
Male vocal trio from Vancouver, British Columbia, Canada: David Bowman, Ken Lewko and Trevor Guthrie.

DEBUT	PEAK	WKS			Catalog	Label & Number
9/9/00	103	29		1 No One Does It Better		MCA 112361

SOULFLY
Hard-rock band formed in Phoenix, Arizona: Max Cavalera (vocals; **Sepultura**), Jackson Bandeira (guitar), Marcello Rapp (bass) and Roy Mayorga (drums). Mickey Doling and Joe Nuñez replaced Bandeira and Mayorga in 1999.

DEBUT	PEAK	WKS			Catalog	Label & Number
5/9/98	79	3	●	1 Soulfly		Roadrunner 8748
10/14/00	32	5		2 Primitive		Roadrunner 8565
7/13/02	46	4		3 3		Roadrunner 618455
4/17/04	82	1		4 Prophecy		Roadrunner 618304
10/22/05	155	1		5 Dark Ages		Roadrunner 618191
8/16/08	66	2		6 Conquer		Roadrunner 617942

SOUL FOR REAL
R&B vocal group from Long Island, New York: brothers Chris, Andre, Brian and Jason Dalyrimple.

DEBUT	PEAK	WKS	RIAA		Catalog	Label & Number
4/15/95	23	30	▲	1 Candy Rain		Uptown 11125
10/12/96	119	2		2 For Life...		Uptown 53012

SOULFUL STRINGS, The
Instrumental studio band from Chicago, Illinois: Lennie Druss (oboe, flute), Bobby Christian (vibes), Philip Upchurch and Ron Steel (guitars). Arranged and conducted by Richard Evans.

DEBUT	PEAK	WKS				Catalog	Label & Number
8/26/67	166	15		1 Paint It Black	[I]	Cadet 776
11/11/67+	59	34		2 Groovin' With The Soulful Strings	[I]	Cadet 796
8/3/68	189	4		3 Another Exposure	[I]	Cadet 805
12/28/68	35ˣ	1		4 The Magic Of Christmas	[X-I]	Cadet 814
5/3/69	125	6		5 In Concert/Back By Demand	[I-L]	Cadet 820
				recorded on 11/6/1968 at The London House in Chicago, Illinois		
11/29/69+	183	4		6 Spring Fever	[I]	Cadet 834

SOULJA BOY TELL'EM
Born DeAndre Way on 7/28/1990 in Batesville, Mississippi. Male rapper.

DEBUT	PEAK	WKS			Catalog	Label & Number
10/20/07	4	36		1 souljaboytellem.com		ColliPark 009962
1/3/09	43	36		2 iSouljaBoyTellem		ColliPark 012388

SOULJA SLIM
Born James Tapp on 9/9/1977 in New Orleans, Louisiana. Shot to death on 11/26/2003 (age 26). Male rapper.

DEBUT	PEAK	WKS			Catalog	Label & Number
6/6/98	13	10		1 Give It 2 'Em Raw		No Limit 53547
9/1/01	188	1		2 The Streets Made Me		No Limit South 2001

SOUL SEARCHERS — see BROWN, Chuck

SOULS OF MISCHIEF
Hip-hop group from Oakland, California: Tajai Massey, Opio Lindsey, Damani Thompson and Adam Carter.

DEBUT	PEAK	WKS			Catalog	Label & Number
10/16/93	85	8		1 93 'Til Infinity		Jive 41514
10/28/95	111	2		2 No Man's Land		Jive 41551

SOUL SURVIVORS
White garage-rock band from New York and Philadelphia, Pennsylvania: brothers Charles Ingui and Richard Ingui (vocals), Ken Jeremiah (vocals), Ed Leonetti (guitar), Paul Venturini (organ) and Joe Forigone (drums).

11/18/67+	123	13	1 When The Whistle Blows Anything Goes		Crimson 502

SOUL II SOUL
R&B-dance group from London, England, led by the duo of Beresford Romeo and Nellee Hooper. Features female vocalists **Caron Wheeler**, Do'Reen Waddell and Rose Windross, and musical backing by the Reggae Philharmonic Orchestra. Wheeler left in 1990. Waddell died after being struck by a car on 3/1/2002 (age 36).

7/8/89	14	51	▲² 1 Keep On Movin'		Virgin 91267
6/16/90	21	19	● 2 Vol II - 1990 - A New Decade		Virgin 91367
5/16/92	88	8	3 Volume III Just Right		Virgin 91771

SOUNDGARDEN
Hard-rock band formed in Seattle, Washington: **Chris Cornell** (vocals), Kim Thayil (guitar), Hiro Yamamoto (bass) and Matt Cameron (drums). Ben Shepherd replaced Yamamoto in 1991. Cornell and Cameron also recorded with **Temple Of The Dog**. Group disbanded on 4/9/1997.

1/27/90	108	16	1 Louder Than Love		A&M 5252
10/26/91+	39	58	▲² 2 Badmotorfinger		A&M 5374
3/26/94	❶¹	75	▲⁵ 3 Superunknown RS500 #336	Cat:#50/1	A&M 540198
6/8/96	2¹	43	▲ 4 Down On The Upside		A&M 540526
11/22/97	63	11	5 A-Sides	[G]	A&M 540833

SOUND OF ANIMALS FIGHTING, The
Progressive-rock band formed in California: **Anthony Green** (vocals), Matthew Embree (guitar), Joseph Troy (bass) and Christopher Tsagakis (drums). Green is also lead singer of **Circa Survive**. The latter three are also members of **RX Bandits**.

6/17/06	183	1	1 Lover, The Lord Has Left Us...		Equal Vision 127
9/27/08	141	1	2 The Ocean And The Sun		Epitaph 86939

SOUNDS, The
Pop-rock band from Helsingborg, Sweden: Maja Ivarsson (vocals, guitar), Felix Rodriguez (guitar), Jesper Anderberg (keyboards), Johan Bengtsson (bass) and Fredrik Nilsson (drums).

4/8/06	107	2	1 Dying To Say This To You		Scratchie 39060
6/20/09	64	2	2 Crossing The Rubicon		Arnioki 012941

SOUNDS OF BLACKNESS
Gospel group from Minneapolis, Minnesota. Directed by Gary Hines. Featured vocalist is **Ann Nesby**.

11/16/91	176	2	● 1 The Evolution Of Gospel		Perspective 1000
12/19/92+	129	4	2 The Night Before Christmas - A Musical Fantasy Christmas chart: 20/'92	[X]	Perspective 9000
5/7/94	109	18	● 3 Africa To America: The Journey Of The Drum		Perspective 9006
5/24/97	144	5	4 Time For Healing		Perspective 9029

SOUNDS OF SUNSHINE
Pop vocal trio from Los Angeles, California: brothers Walt, Warner and George Wilder.

8/14/71	187	8	1 Love Means You Never Have To Say You're Sorry		Ranwood 8089

SOUNDS ORCHESTRAL
Studio trio from England: John Pearson (piano), Tony Reeves (bass) and Ken Clare (drums).

5/29/65	11	28	1 Cast Your Fate To The Wind	[I]	Parkway 7046

SOUNDTRACK OF OUR LIVES, The
Punk-rock band from Sweden: Ebbot Lundberg (vocals), Mattias Barjed (guitar), Bjorn Olsson (guitar), Martin Hederos (keyboards), Ian Person (percussion), Kalle Gustafsson (bass) and Fredrik Sandsten (drums).

4/2/05	179	1	1 Origin Vol. I		Republic 004217

SOUP DRAGONS, The
Rock-dance fusion band from Glasgow, Scotland: Sean Dickson (vocals), Jim McCulloch (guitar), Sushil Dade (bass) and Paul Quinn (drums).

10/20/90	88	29	1 Lovegod		Big Life 842985
6/27/92	97	22	2 Hotwired		Big Life 13178

SOUTH, Joe
Born Joe Souter on 2/28/1940 in Atlanta, Georgia. Pop-country singer/songwriter/guitarist.

2/8/69	117	14	1 Introspect		Capitol 108
1/17/70	60	23	2 Don't It Make You Want To Go Home?		Capitol 392
9/12/70	125	11	3 Joe South's Greatest Hits	[G]	Capitol 450
12/11/71	207	2	4 Joe South		Capitol 845

SOUTH CENTRAL CARTEL
Rap group from Los Angeles, California: Cary Calvin, Austin Patterson, Brian West, Larry Sanders, Greg Scott and Perry Rayson. By 1997, reduced to duo of Patterson and West.

5/28/94	32	15	1 'N Gatz We Truss		GWK 57294
6/21/97	178	1	2 All Day Everyday		Def Jam 531159

SOUTH CIRCLE
Rap trio from Houston, Texas: Suave House, **Mr. Mike** Walls and Rex Robinson.

7/22/95	63	7	1 Anotha Day Anotha Balla		Suave 1518

Billboard DEBUT	PEAK	WKS	R I A A	ARTIST Album Title	Catalog	Label & Number

SOUTHER, J.D.
Born John David Souther on 11/2/1945 in Detroit, Michigan; raised in Amarillo, Texas. Pop-rock singer/songwriter/guitarist. Member of **The Souther, Hillman, Furay Band**.

9/23/72	206	3		1 **John David Souther**		Asylum 5055
5/8/76	85	11		2 **Black Rose**		Asylum 1059
				JOHN DAVID SOUTHER (above 2)		
9/22/79	41	22		3 **You're Only Lonely**		Columbia 36093
9/1/84	203	6		4 **Home By Dawn**		Warner 25081

SOUTHER, HILLMAN, FURAY BAND, The
Country-rock trio: **J.D. Souther**, **Chris Hillman** and **Richie Furay**.

7/20/74	11	22	●	1 **The Souther, Hillman, Furay Band**		Asylum 1006
6/21/75	39	11		2 **Trouble In Paradise**		Asylum 1036

SOUTHERN COMFORT
Backing band for **Ian Matthews**: Mark Griffiths, Carl Barnwell and Gordon Huntley (guitars), Andy Leigh (bass) and Ray Duffy (drums).

8/14/71	196	2		1 **Frog City**		Capitol 800

SOUTH SHORE COMMISSION
R&B-funk band from Washington DC: Frank McCurry (male vocals), Sheryl Henry (female vocals), Sidney Lennear (guitar), Eugene Rogers (guitar), David Henderson (bass) and Warren Haygood (drums).

12/27/75+	205	5		1 **South Shore Commission**		Wand 6100

SOUTHSIDE JOHNNY & THE ASBURY JUKES
Born John Lyon on 12/4/1948 in Neptune, New Jersey. Rock singer/harmonica player. Core members of The Asbury Jukes: Billy Rush (guitar), Kevin Kavanaugh (keyboards) and Alan Berger (bass).

7/10/76	125	9		1 **I Don't Want To Go Home**		Epic 34180
5/7/77	85	9		2 **This Time It's For Real**		Epic 34668
11/4/78+	112	20		3 **Hearts Of Stone**		Epic 35488
8/18/79	48	14		4 **The Jukes**		Mercury 3793
6/14/80	67	15		5 **Love Is A Sacrifice**		Mercury 3836
5/9/81	80	12		6 **Reach Up And Touch The Sky** [L]		Mercury 8602 [2]
10/1/83	154	6		7 **Trash It Up!**		Mirage 90113
9/8/84	164	8		8 **In The Heat**		Mirage 90186
6/21/86	189	4		9 **At Least We Got Shoes**		Atlantic 81654
				SOUTHSIDE JOHNNY & THE JUKES (above 3)		
12/3/88	198	1		10 **Slow Dance**		Cypress 0115
				SOUTHSIDE JOHNNY		
11/16/91	96	7		11 **Better Days**		Impact 10445
				SOUTHSIDE JOHNNY & THE JUKES		

SOUTHSIDE MOVEMENT, The
R&B-funk band from Chicago, Illinois: Melvin Moore (vocals), Bobby Pointer (guitar), Milton Johnson, Stephen Hawkins and Bill McFarland (horns), Morris Beeks (keyboards), Ronald Simmons (bass) and Willie Hayes (drums).

8/25/73	207	1		1 **The South Side Movement**		Wand 695

SOVINE, Red
Born Woodrow Wilson Sovine on 7/17/1918 in Charleston, West Virginia. Died of a heart attack on 4/4/1980 (age 61). Country singer/songwriter/guitarist.
AWARD: OPRY: 1954

9/11/76	119	6		1 **Teddy Bear**		Starday 968

SPACE
Rock band from Liverpool, England: Tommy Scott (vocals, bass), Jamie Murphy (guitar), Franny Griffith (keyboards) and Andy Parle (drums). Parle died on 8/1/2009 (age 42).

3/8/97	189	5		1 **Spiders**		Universal 53028

SPACEHOG
Rock band from Leeds, England: brothers Royston Langdon (vocals, bass) and Antony Lagdon (guitar), with Richard Steel (guitar) and Jonny Cragg (drums). Royston Langdon married actress Liv Tyler on 3/25/2003.

1/27/96	49	22	●	1 **Resident Alien**		Sire 61834

SPACEK, Sissy
Born Mary Elizabeth Spacek on 12/25/1949 in Quitman, Texas. Actress/singer. Starred in several movies.

9/24/83	204	5		1 **Hangin' Up My Heart**		Atlantic 90100

SPACEY, Kevin
Born Kevin Spacey Fowler on 7/26/1959 in South Orange, New Jersey; raised in California. Prolific movie actor. Played **Bobby Darin** in the 2004 movie *Beyond The Sea*.

1/22/05	141	3		1 **Beyond The Sea** [S]		Atco 78444

SPANDAU BALLET
Pop band formed in London, England: Tony Hadley (vocals), brothers Gary Kemp (guitar) and Martin Kemp (bass), Steve Norman (sax) and John Keeble (drums). The Kemps starred in the 1990 movie *The Krays*. Gary Kemp was married to actress Sadie Frost from 1988-97.

5/16/81	209	1		1 **Journeys To Glory**		Chrysalis 1331
5/14/83	19	37		2 **True**		Chrysalis 41403
8/18/84	50	16		3 **Parade**		Chrysalis 41473

729

Billboard			R I A A	ARTIST		
DEBUT	PEAK	WKS		Album Title	Catalog	Label & Number

SPANIELS, The
Black doo-wop group from Gary, Indiana: James "Pookie" Hudson, lead singer. First recorded for Chance in 1953; then became the first artist to sign with Vee-Jay Records. Bass singer Gerald Gregory died on 2/12/1999 (age 64). Hudson died of cancer on 1/16/2007 (age 72).

~ ~ ~ ~ ~ ~ ~ ~ ~ ~   **NON-CHARTED ALBUM**   ~ ~ ~ ~ ~ ~ ~ ~ ~ ~
1958 **Goodnite, It's Time To Go**

SPANKY AND OUR GANG
Folk-pop band formed in Chicago, Illinois: Elaine "Spanky" McFarlane (vocals; born on 6/19/1942 in Peoria, Illinois), Malcolm Hale, Lefty Baker and Nigel Pickering (guitars), Kenny Hodges (bass), and John Seiter (drums). Spanky became lead singer of the new **Mamas & The Papas** in the early 1980s. Hale died of liver failure on 10/31/1968 (age 27). Baker died of liver failure on 8/11/1971 (age 29).

DEBUT	PEAK	WKS		Album Title	Catalog	Label & Number
9/9/67	77	15		1 Spanky And Our Gang		Mercury 61124
4/27/68	56	25		2 Like To Get To Know You		Mercury 61161
2/15/69	101	7		3 Anything You Choose/Without Rhyme Or Reason		Mercury 61183
11/1/69+	91	17		4 Spanky's Greatest Hit(s)	[G]	Mercury 61227

SPANOS, Danny
Born in Detroit, Michigan. Rock singer/songwriter/guitarist.

9/24/83	201	6		1 Passion In The Dark	[EP]	Epic 38805
3/16/85	208	1		2 Looks Like Trouble		Epic 39459

SPARKLE
Born Stephanie Edwards on 8/12/1975 in Chicago, Illinois. Female R&B singer.

6/6/98	3¹	17	●	1 Sparkle		Rock Land 90149
11/11/00	121	2		2 Told You So		Motown 159743

SPARKS
Pop-rock-dance duo from Los Angeles, California: brothers Ron Mael (born on 8/12/1948) and Russell Mael (born on 10/5/1953).

8/24/74	101	14		1 Kimono My House		Island 9272
2/8/75	63	13		2 Propaganda		Island 9312
11/29/75+	169	6		3 Indiscreet		Island 9345
6/2/79	204	8		4 No. 1 In Heaven		Elektra 186
8/15/81	182	2		5 Whomp That Sucker		RCA Victor 4091
5/22/82	173	6		6 Angst In My Pants		Atlantic 19347
4/30/83	88	17		7 Sparks In Outer Space		Atlantic 80055
8/4/84	202	4		8 Pulling Rabbits Out Of A Hat		Atlantic 80160

SPARKS, Jordin
Born on 12/22/1989 in Staten Island, New York; raised in Glendale, Arizona. Winner on the 2007 season of TV's *American Idol*.

12/8/07	10	54	▲	1 Jordin Sparks		19 Records 18752
8/8/09	7	11		2 Battlefield		19 Records 44668

SPARTA
Rock band from El Paso, Texas: Jim Ward (vocals, guitar), Paul Hinojos (guitar), Matt Miller (bass) and Tony Hajjar (drums). Ward, Hinojos and Hajjar are also members of **At The Drive-In**.

8/31/02	71	4		1 Wiretap Scars		DreamWorks 450366
7/31/04	60	3		2 Porcelain		Geffen 002818
11/11/06	83	1		3 Threes		Hollywood 162613

SPARXXX, Bubba
Born Warren Mathis on 3/6/1977 in LaGrange, Georgia. White rapper. Member of **Purple Ribbon All-Stars**.

10/27/01	3¹	18	●	1 Dark Days, Bright Nights		Beat Club 493127
10/4/03	10	10		2 Deliverance		Beat Club 001147
4/22/06	9	15		3 The Charm		New South 47163

SPEARS, Britney   2000s: #35 / All-Time: #308
Born on 12/2/1981 in Kentwood, Louisiana. Teen idol singer/actress. Regular on TV's *The Mickey Mouse Club* (1992-93). Played "Lucy Wagner" in the 2002 movie *Crossroads*. Married to backing dancer Kevin Federline from 2004-07; they starred in their own 2005 reality series *Britney & Kevin: Chaotic*. Her controversial behavior made her a tabloid headliner since 2004.

1/30/99	❶⁶	103	▲¹⁴	1 ...Baby One More Time	Cat:#9/19	Jive 41651
6/3/00	❶¹	84	▲¹⁰	2 Oops!...I Did It Again	Cat:#40/2	Jive 41704
11/24/01	❶¹	58	▲⁴	3 Britney		Jive 41776
12/6/03	❶¹	45	▲²	4 In The Zone		Jive 53748
11/27/04	4	30	▲	5 Greatest Hits: My Prerogative	[G]	Jive 65294
12/10/05	134	2		6 B In The Mix: The Remixes	[K]	Jive 74062
11/17/07	2¹	34		7 Blackout		Jive 19073
12/20/08	❶¹	42	▲	8 Circus		Jive 40387
11/28/09	22	10		9 The Singles Collection	[G]	Jive 59675

SPECIAL ED
Born Edward Archer on 5/16/1973 in Brooklyn, New York. Male rapper.

6/3/89	73	28		1 Youngest In Charge		Profile 1280
8/18/90	84	13		2 Legal		Profile 1297
7/15/95	107	4		3 Revelations		Profile 1463

SPECIALS
Ska-rock band from Coventry, England: Terry Hall and Novillo Staples (vocals), Lynval Golding and Roddy Radiation (guitars), Jerry Dammers (keyboards), Horace Gentleman (bass) and John Bradbury (drums). Hall, Staples and Golding went on to form **Fun Buy Three**.

| 1/26/80 | 84 | 21 | | 1 The Specials .... | | Chrysalis 1265 |
| 11/8/80 | 98 | 5 | | 2 More Specials .... | | Chrysalis 1303 |

SPECIMEN
Rock band from London, England: Ollie Wisdom (vocals), Jon Klein (guitar), Jonny Melton (keyboards), Kev Mills (bass) and Jonathan Trevenous (drums).

| 2/11/84 | 207 | 1 | | 1 Batastrophe .... [EP] | | Sire 25054 |

SPEED KNOT MOBSTAZ
Rap duo from Chicago, Illinois: Mayz and Liffy Stokes.

| 10/24/98 | 34 | 6 | | 1 Mobstability .... | | Creator's Way 83142 |

SPEEDY KEEN — see KEEN, Speedy

SPEER, Paul
Born in 1952 in Lewiston, Idaho. New Age guitarist.

| 1/30/88 | 125 | 12 | | 1 Natural States .... [I] | | Narada Equinox 63001 |
| | | | | **DAVID LANZ & PAUL SPEER** | | |

SPEKTOR, Regina
Born on 2/18/1980 in Moscow, Russia; raised in the Bronx, New York. Female singer/songwriter/pianist.

| 7/1/06+ | 20 | 34 | ● | 1 Begin To Hope .... | | Sire 44112 |
| 7/11/09 | 3[1] | 19 | | 2 Far | | Sire 519396 |

SPENCE, Judson
Born on 4/29/1965 in Pascagoula, Mississippi. Pop-rock singer/songwriter/multi-instrumentalist.

| 12/10/88 | 168 | 13 | | 1 Judson Spence .... | | Atlantic 81902 |

SPENCER, Jeremy, Band
Born on 7/4/1948 in Hartlepool, County Durham, England. Rock singer/guitarist. Member of **Fleetwood Mac** from 1967-70.

| 9/8/79 | 208 | 2 | | 1 Flee .... | | Atlantic 19236 |

SPENCER, Jon, Blues Explosion
Born in Hanover, New Hampshire. Blues-rock singer/guitarist. His group included Judah Bauer (guitar) and Russell Simins (drums).

11/2/96	121	1		1 Now I Got Worry		Matador 53553
11/7/98	180	1		2 Acme		Matador 95566
4/27/02	196	1		3 Plastic Flag		Matador 542

SPENCER, Tracie
Born on 7/12/1976 in Waterloo, Iowa. Female R&B singer.

6/25/88	146	21		1 Tracie Spencer		Capitol 48186
2/23/91	107	11		2 Make The Difference		Capitol 92153
7/17/99	114	7		3 Tracie		Capitol 34287

SPHEERIS, Jimmie
Born on 11/5/1949 in Greece; raised in California. Died in a car crash on 7/4/1984 (age 34). Singer/songwriter/guitarist.

| 9/20/75 | 135 | 6 | | 1 The Dragon Is Dancing .... | | Epic 33565 |

SPICE GIRLS
Female dance-pop vocal group from England: Victoria Adams (Posh Spice; born on 4/17/1974), Melanie Brown (Scary Spice; born on 5/29/1975), Emma Bunton (Baby Spice; born on 1/21/1976), **Geri Halliwell** (Ginger Spice; born on 8/6/1972) and Melanie Chisholm (Sporty Spice; born on 1/12/1974). Group starred in the movie *Spiceworld*. Halliwell left group in May 1998. Adams married soccer star David Beckham on 7/4/1999. Brown finished second on season 5 on *Dancing With The Stars*.

2/22/97	❶[5]	105	▲[7]	1 Spice	Cat:#2[2]/15	Virgin 42174
11/22/97+	3[2]	74	▲[4]	2 Spiceworld .... [S]		Virgin 45111
11/25/00	39	7		3 Forever		Virgin 50467
2/2/08	93	4		4 Greatest Hits .... [G]		Virgin 07767

SPICE 1
Born Robert Green in 1970 in Bryan, Texas; raised in Oakland, California. Hardcore rapper.

5/2/92	82	31	●	1 Spice 1		Jive 41481
10/16/93	10	18	●	2 187 He Wrote		Jive 41513
				187 is slang for murder		
12/10/94	22	18	●	3 AmeriKKKa's Nightmare		Jive 41547
12/23/95	30	10		4 1990-Sick		Jive 41583
11/15/97	28	4		5 The Black Bossalini (aka Dr. Bomb From Da Bay)		Jive 41596
10/30/99	111	2		6 Immortalized		Jive 41690

SPIDER
Rock band formed in New York: Amanda Blue (vocals), Keith Lentin (guitar), Holly Knight (keyboards), Jimmy Lowell (bass) and Anton Fig (drums). Knight, later joined **Device**. Fig joined house band of TV's *Late Night With David Letterman*.

| 5/17/80 | 130 | 10 | | 1 Spider .... | | Dreamland 5000 |
| 7/11/81 | 185 | 2 | | 2 Between The Lines .... | | Dreamland 5007 |

SPIDERS FROM MARS
Backing band for **David Bowie**: Pete McDonald (vocals), Dave Black (guitar), Trevor Bolder (bass) and Woody Woodmansey (drums).

4/3/76	197	2		1 Spiders From Mars		Pye 12125

SPILL CANVAS, The
Alternative-rock band from Sioux Falls, South Dakota: Nick Thomas (vocals, guitar), Dan Ludeman (guitar), Landon Heil (bass) and Joe Beck (drums).

10/20/07	143	1		1 No Really, I'm Fine		One Eleven 162428

SPINAL TAP
Parody heavy-metal trio introduced in the 1984 mock documentary movie *This Is Spinal Tap*. Actor Michael McKean portrays "David St. Hubbins," Christopher Guest is "Nigel Tufnel" and Harry Shearer is "Derek Smalls". Guest married actress Jamie Lee Curtis on 12/18/1984. McKean played "Lenny" on TV's *Laverne & Shirley*. All three have been regular castmembers of *Saturday Night Live*. Also see **Lenny & Squiggy**.

4/28/84	121	10		1 This Is Spinal Tap .... [S]		Polydor 817846
4/4/92	61	6		2 Break Like The Wind		MCA 10514
7/4/09	52	2		3 Back From The Dead		Label Industry 10196

SPIN DOCTORS
Rock band formed in New York: Christopher Barron (vocals), Eric Schenkman (guitar), Mark White (bass) and Aaron Comess (drums). Anthony Krizan replaced Schenkman in 1993.

7/4/92+	3[2]	115	▲[5]	1 Pocket Full Of Kryptonite		Epic/Associated 47461
1/9/93	145	15		2 Homebelly Groove...Live .... [L]		Epic/Associated 53309
7/2/94	28	16	▲	3 Turn It Upside Down		Epic 52907

SPINESHANK
Hard-rock band from Los Angeles, California: Johnny Santos (vocals), Mike Sarkisyan (guitar), Robert Garcia (bass) and Tom Decker (drums).

10/28/00	183	1		1 The Height Of Callousness		Roadrunner 8563
9/27/03	89	2		2 Self-Destructive Pattern		Roadrunner 618454

SPINNERS   All-Time: #310
R&B vocal group formed in Detroit, Michigan: G.C. Cameron, Henry Fambrough (baritone; born on 5/10/1938), Billy Henderson (tenor; born on 8/9/1939) and Pervis Jackson (bass; born on 5/16/1938). Philippe Wynne (tenor; born on 4/3/1941) replaced Cameron in early 1972. John Edwards replaced Wynne in 1977. Wynne died of a heart attack on 7/13/1984 (age 43). Henderson died of diabetes on 2/2/2007 (age 67). Jackson died of cancer on 8/18/2008 (age 70).

11/14/70	199	2		1 2nd Time Around		V.I.P. 405
5/12/73	124	10		2 The Best Of The Spinners .... [G]		Motown 769
4/21/73	14	28	●	3 Spinners..		Atlantic 7256
3/16/74	16	35	●	4 Mighty Love		Atlantic 7296
12/14/74+	9	26	●	5 New And Improved		Atlantic 18118
8/9/75	8	26	●	6 Pick Of The Litter		Atlantic 18141
12/13/75+	20	21		7 Spinners Live! .... [L]		Atlantic 910 [2]
7/31/76	25	30	●	8 Happiness Is Being With The Detroit Spinners.................		Atlantic 18181
4/2/77	26	13		9 Yesterday, Today & Tomorrow		Atlantic 19100
12/24/77+	57	13		10 Spinners/8		Atlantic 19146
5/20/78	115	9		11 The Best Of The Spinners .... [G]		Atlantic 19179
5/26/79	165	4		12 From Here To Eternally		Atlantic 19219
1/19/80	32	20		13 Dancin' And Lovin'...		Atlantic 19256
6/21/80	53	13		14 Love Trippin'		Atlantic 19270
4/4/81	128	6		15 Labor Of Love		Atlantic 16032
1/16/82	196	4		16 Can't Shake This Feelin'		Atlantic 19318
1/8/83	167	6		17 Grand Slam		Atlantic 80020
4/28/84	201	7		18 Cross Fire		Atlantic 80150

~ ~ ~ ~ ~ ~ ~ ~ ~ ~   **NON-CHARTED ALBUM**   ~ ~ ~ ~ ~ ~ ~ ~ ~ ~ ~
1967 The Original Spinners

SPINOZZA, David
Born in New Jersey. Singer/songwriter/guitarist.

4/8/78	202	13		1 Spinozza		A&M 4677

SPIRAL STARECASE
Pop-rock band from Sacramento, California: Pat Upton (vocals, guitar), Harvey Kaplan (organ), Dick Lopes (sax), Bobby Raymond (bass) and Vinny Parello (drums). Kaplan is the father of **Brenda K. Starr**.

6/14/69	79	16		1 More Today Than Yesterday		Columbia 9852

SPIRIT
Rock band from Los Angeles, California: **Jay Ferguson** (vocals), Randy California (guitar), John Locke (keyboards), Mark Andes (bass) and Ed Cassidy (drums). Ferguson and Andes left to form **Jo Jo Gunne** in mid-1971. Andes became an original member of **Firefall** in 1975; joined **Heart** in 1983. California drowned in Hawaii on 1/2/1997 (age 45). Locke died on 8/4/2006 (age 62).

4/20/68	31	32		1 Spirit		Ode 44004
				<small>also see #8 below</small>		
1/18/69	22	21		2 The Family That Plays Together		Ode 44014
7/22/72	189	7		3 The Family That Plays Together .... [R]		Epic 31461
				<small>new cover does not include the original additional flap</small>		
8/23/69	55	15		4 Clear Spirit		Ode 44016
				<small>also see #8 below</small>		

Billboard DEBUT	PEAK	WKS	R I A A	ARTIST / Album Title	Catalog	Label & Number
				SPIRIT — cont'd		
12/26/70+	63	14	●	5 Twelve Dreams Of Dr. Sardonicus		Epic 30267
3/18/72	63	14		6 Feedback		Epic 31175
7/21/73	119	12		7 The Best Of Spirit	[G]	Epic 32271
8/25/73	191	4		8 Spirit	[R]	Epic 31457 [2]
				reissue of albums #1 & 4 above		
6/7/75	147	9		9 Spirit Of '76		Mercury 804 [2]
7/31/76	179	4		10 Farther Along		Mercury 1094
9/1/84	206	1		11 Spirit Of '84		Mercury 818514
				SPIRITUALIZED Group is actually British solo artist Jason "Spaceman" Pierce with several studio musicians.		
10/13/01	133	1		1 Let It Come Down		Arista 14722
6/14/08	157	1		2 Songs In A&E		Spaceman 542
				SPLENDER Interracial rock band formed in New York: Waymon Boone (vocals), Jonathan Svec (guitar), James Cruz (bass) and Mike Slutsky (drums).		
7/29/00	200	1		1 Halfway Down The Sky		Columbia 69144
				SPLINTER Pop-rock vocal duo from England: Bill Elliott and Bob Purvis.		
10/26/74	81	14		1 The Place I Love		Dark Horse 22001
11/8/75+	202	9		2 Harder To Live		Dark Horse 22006
				SPLIT ENZ New-wave pop band formed in Auckland, New Zealand: brothers **Tim Finn** (vocals) and Neil Finn (guitar, vocals), Eddie Rayner (keyboards), Noel Crombie (percussion), Nigel Griggs (bass) and Malcolm Green (drums; left in 1983). **The Finn Brothers** were later members of **Crowded House**.		
8/30/80	40	25		1 True Colours		A&M 4822
5/23/81	45	19		2 Waiata		A&M 4848
5/8/82	58	20		3 Time And Tide		A&M 4894
7/21/84	137	10		4 Conflicting Emotions		A&M 4963
				SPM Born Carlos Coy on 10/5/1970 in Houston, Texas. Male rapper. SPM: South Park Mexican.		
9/2/00	57	8		1 The Purity Album		Dope House 153292
12/30/00	170	3		2 Time Is Money		Dope House 013336
12/22/01	168	1		3 Never Change		Dope House 016017
5/18/02	149	2		4 Reveille Park		Dope House 6000
10/21/06	46	5		5 When Devils Strike		Dope House 6035
12/6/08	59	3		6 The Last Chair Violinist		Dope House 6037 [2]
				SOUTH PARK MEXICAN		
				SPONGE Alternative-rock band from Detroit, Michigan: Vinnie Dombrowski (vocals), Mike Cross (guitar), Joe Mazzola (guitar), Tim Cross (bass) and Jimmy Paluzzi (drums). Charlie Grover replaced Paluzzi in early 1996.		
2/18/95	58	40	●	1 Rotting Pinata		Work 57800
7/20/96	60	10		2 Wax Ecstatic		Columbia 67578
				SPOOKY TOOTH Rock band formed by keyboardists/vocalists **Gary Wright** and Mike Harrison. Varying personnel. Wright left from 1970-72 to recorded with the group Wonderwheel. Guitarist Luther Grosvenor left in 1972, joined **Stealers Wheel**, then changed name to Ariel Bender and joined **Mott the Hoople** and **Widowmaker**. **Mick Jones**, later of **Foreigner**, was guitarist from 1972-74.		
8/16/69	44	19		1 Spooky Two		A&M 4194
3/21/70	92	14		2 Ceremony		A&M 4225
8/15/70	84	13		3 The Last Puff		A&M 4266
6/5/71	152	7		4 Tobacco Road	[E]	A&M 4300
				reissue of their first album It's All About...		
5/19/73	84	14		5 You Broke My Heart So I Busted Your Jaw		A&M 4385
11/10/73	99	10		6 Witness		Island 9337
9/21/74	130	8		7 The Mirror		Island 9292
4/24/76	172	4		8 That Was Only Yesterday	[K]	A&M 3528 [2]
				GARY WRIGHT/SPOOKY TOOTH		
				SPOON Alternative-rock band from Austin, Texas: Britt Daniel (vocals, guitar), Eric Harvey (keyboards), Josh Zarbo (bass) and Jim Eno (drums).		
5/28/05	44	5		1 Gimme Fiction		Merge 565
7/28/07	10	19		2 Ga Ga Ga Ga Ga		Merge 295
				SPORTS, The Rock band formed in Melbourne, Australia: Stephen Cummings (vocals), Andrew Pendlebury (guitar), Martin Armiger (guitar), James Niven (keyboards), Robert Glover (bass) and Paul Hitchins (drums).		
11/24/79	194	2		1 Don't Throw Stones		Arista 4249
8/16/80	207	1		2 Suddenly...		Arista 4266

SPRINGFIELD, Dusty

Born Mary O'Brien on 4/16/1939 in London, England. Died of cancer on 3/2/1999 (age 59). Blue-eyed soul singer. Member of **The Springfields**.
AWARD: R&R Hall of Fame: 1999

DEBUT	PEAK	WKS	RIAA	Album Title	Catalog	Label & Number
6/27/64	62	13		1 Stay Awhile/I Only Want To Be With You		Philips 600133
12/5/64	136	3		2 Dusty		Philips 600156
7/16/66	77	10		3 You Don't Have To Say You Love Me		Philips 600210
12/24/66	137	3		4 Dusty Springfield's Golden Hits	[G]	Philips 600220
12/23/67+	135	7		5 The Look Of Love		Philips 600256
3/15/69	99	14		6 Dusty In Memphis		Atlantic 8214
				Grammy: Hall of Fame ★ RS500 #89		
2/28/70	107	13		7 A Brand New Me		Atlantic 8249
3/24/73	212	2		8 Cameo		Dunhill 50128

SPRINGFIELD, Rick   1980s: #41 / All-Time: #364

Born Richard Springthorpe on 8/23/1949 in Sydney, New South Wales, Australia. Pop-rock singer/songwriter/guitarist/actor. Played "Dr. Noah Drake" on the TV soap opera *General Hospital*. Starred in the 1984 movie *Hard To Hold*.

DEBUT	PEAK	WKS	RIAA	Album Title	Catalog	Label & Number
8/12/72	35	17		1 Beginnings		Capitol 11047
3/14/81	7	73	▲	2 Working Class Dog		RCA Victor 3697
3/27/82	2³	35	▲	3 Success Hasn't Spoiled Me Yet	Cat:#4/122	RCA Victor 4125
12/18/82+	159	8		4 Wait For Night	[E]	RCA Victor 4235
				first released in 1976 on Chelsea 515		
4/30/83	12	57	▲	5 Living In Oz		RCA Victor 4660
4/7/84	16	36	▲	6 Hard To Hold	[S]	RCA Victor 4935
12/8/84+	78	13		7 Beautiful Feelings	[E]	Mercury 824107
				vocals recorded in 1978 with new music tracks added in 1984		
4/27/85	21	27	●	8 Tao		RCA Victor 5370
2/20/88	55	16		9 Rock Of Life		RCA 6620
5/1/99	189	1		10 Karma		Platinum 9561
7/30/05	197	1		11 The Day After Yesterday		Gomer 481200
8/16/08	28	2		12 Venus In Overdrive		Gomer 011347
1/17/09	7ˣ	1		13 Christmas With You	Cat:#6/2 [X]	Gomer 43737

SPRINGFIELDS, The

Folk trio from London, England: **Dusty Springfield**, her brother Tom Springfield and Tim Feild.

DEBUT	PEAK	WKS	RIAA	Album Title	Catalog	Label & Number
10/27/62	91	4		1 Silver Threads & Golden Needles		Philips 600052

SPRINGSTEEN, Bruce   1980s: #28 / 2000s: #12 / All-Time: #28

Born on 9/23/1949 in Freehold, New Jersey. Rock singer/songwriter/guitarist. Nicknamed "The Boss." His E-Street Band: **Little Steven** Van Zant (guitar), **Clarence Clemons** (sax), Roy Bittan (keyboards), Gary Tallent (bass) and Max Weinberg (drums). Married to model/actress Julianne Phillips from 1985-89. Married backing singer **Patti Scialfa** on 6/8/1991. One of the most popular live concert attractions of all-time. Also see **Various Artists Compilations:** *One Step Up/Two Steps Back: The Songs Of Bruce Springsteen.*
AWARD: R&R Hall of Fame: 1999

DEBUT	PEAK	WKS	RIAA	Album Title	Catalog	Label & Number
7/26/75	60	43	▲²	1 Greetings From Asbury Park, N.J.	Cat:#3/136 [E]	Columbia 31903
				RS500 #379 — first released on 1/5/1973		
7/26/75	59	34	▲²	2 The Wild, The Innocent & The E Street Shuffle	Cat:#27/45 [E]	Columbia 32432
				RS500 #132 — first released on 9/11/1973		
9/13/75	3²	110	▲⁶	3 Born To Run		Columbia 33795
				Grammy: Hall of Fame ★ RS500 #18 ★ NRR		
12/3/05	18	6		4 Born To Run: 30th Anniversary Edition	[R]	Columbia 94175
				reissue includes 2 bonus DVDs featuring concert footage and a making of documentary		
6/17/78	5	97	▲³	5 Darkness On The Edge Of Town		Columbia 35318
				RS500 #151		
11/1/80	❶⁴	108	▲⁵	6 The River		Columbia 36854 [2]
				RS500 #250		
10/9/82	3⁴	29	▲	7 Nebraska		Columbia 38358
				RS500 #224		
6/23/84	❶⁷	139	▲¹⁵	8 Born In The U.S.A.	Cat:#22/1	Columbia 38653
				RS500 #85		
10/24/87	❶¹	45	▲³	9 Tunnel Of Love		Columbia 40999
				Grammy: Male Rock Vocal ★ RS500 #475		
4/18/92	2²	27	▲	10 Human Touch		Columbia 53000
4/18/92	3¹	23	▲	11 Lucky Town		Columbia 53001
12/9/95	11	14	●	12 The Ghost Of Tom Joad		Columbia 67484
				Grammy: Contemporary Folk Album		
8/17/02	❶²	37	▲²	13 The Rising	Cat:#34/1	Columbia 86600
				Grammy: Rock Album		
5/14/05	❶¹	13	●	14 Devils & Dust		Columbia 93990

SPRINGSTEEN, Bruce — cont'd

DEBUT	PEAK	WKS	RIAA	#	Album Title	Catalog	Label & Number
5/13/06	3[1]	22	●	15	We Shall Overcome: The Seeger Sessions		Columbia 82867
10/20/07	❶[2]	26	▲	16	Magic		Columbia 17060
2/14/09	❶[1]	18	●	17	Working On A Dream		Columbia 41355

GREATEST HITS & COMPILATIONS:

DEBUT	PEAK	WKS	RIAA	#	Album Title	Catalog	Label & Number
3/18/95	❶[2]	32	▲[4]	18	Greatest Hits	Cat:#3/129	Columbia 67060
11/28/98	27	7	▲	19	Tracks		Columbia 69475 [4]
					contains unreleased songs and B-sides previously issued as singles only		
5/1/99	64	6		20	18 Tracks		Columbia 69476
					15 of 18 songs from the above album with 3 previously unreleased tracks		
11/29/03	14	13	▲	21	The Essential Bruce Springsteen	Cat:#13/2	Legacy 90773 [3]
1/31/09	43	8		22	Greatest Hits		Columbia 43930

LIVE ALBUMS:

DEBUT	PEAK	WKS	RIAA	#	Album Title	Catalog	Label & Number
11/29/86	❶[7]	26	▲[13]	23	Bruce Springsteen & The E Street Band Live/1975-85		Columbia 40558 [5]
9/13/97	189	1		24	In Concert / MTV Plugged		Columbia 68730
					recorded on 11/11/1992		
4/21/01	5	8	▲	25	Live In New York City		Columbia 85490 [2]
					recorded on 6/29/2000 at Madison Square Garden		
3/18/06	93	2		26	Hammersmith Odeon, London '75		Columbia 77995 [2]
					BRUCE SPRINGSTEEN & THE E STREET BAND (above 2)		
6/23/07	23	5		27	Live In Dublin		Columbia 09582 [2]
					BRUCE SPRINGSTEEN with The Sessions Band		
8/2/08	48	1		28	Magic Tour Highlights [EP]		Columbia digital
					BRUCE SPRINGSTEEN & THE E-STREET BAND		

SPYRO GYRA
1980s: #31 / All-Time: #262

Jazz-pop band formed in Buffalo, New York. Led by saxophonist Jay Beckenstein (born on 5/14/1951). **The Brecker Brothers** (Michael and Randy) were longtime members.

DEBUT	PEAK	WKS	RIAA	#	Album Title	Catalog	Label & Number
5/20/78	99	12		1	Spyro Gyra	[I]	Amherst 1014
4/7/79	27	41	▲	2	Morning Dance	Cat:#3/213 [I]	Infinity 9004
3/22/80	19	29	●	3	Catching The Sun	[I]	MCA 5108
11/1/80	49	30		4	Carnaval	[I]	MCA 5149
8/29/81	41	27		5	Freetime	[I]	MCA 5238
10/23/82	46	24		6	Incognito	[I]	MCA 5368
8/13/83	66	16		7	City Kids	[I]	MCA 5431
7/14/84	59	19		8	Access All Areas	[I-L]	MCA 6893 [2]
					recorded on 11/18/1983 in Florida		
6/29/85	66	23		9	Alternating Currents	[I]	MCA 5606
7/12/86	71	19		10	Breakout	[I]	MCA 5753
9/26/87	84	9		11	Stories Without Words	[I]	MCA 42046
7/16/88	104	8		12	Rites Of Summer	[I]	MCA 6235
7/8/89	120	6		13	Point Of View	[I]	MCA 6309
6/23/90	117	8		14	Fast Forward	[I]	GRP 9608
7/6/91	156	2		15	Collection	[I-K]	GRP 9642
10/11/08	14[X]	3		16	A Night Before Christmas	[X-I]	Heads Up 3145

SPYS

Rock band from New York: John Blanco (vocals), John DiGaudio (guitar), Al Greenwood (keyboards), Ed Gagliardi (bass) and Billy Milne (drums). Greenwood and Gagliardi were members of **Foreigner**.

DEBUT	PEAK	WKS	RIAA	#	Album Title	Catalog	Label & Number
8/14/82	138	10		1	Spys		EMI America 17073

SQUEEZE

Pop-rock band formed in London by vocalists/guitarists Chris Difford and Glenn Tilbrook. Originally known as UK Squeeze due to confusion with American band Tight Squeeze. **Paul Carrack** (of **Ace** & **Mike + The Mechanics**) was keyboardist/vocalist in 1981 of fluctuating lineup; re-joined in 1993. Also see **Difford & Tilbrook**.

DEBUT	PEAK	WKS	RIAA	#	Album Title	Catalog	Label & Number
4/26/80	71	24		1	Argybargy		A&M 4802
5/30/81	44	25		2	East Side Story		A&M 4854
5/29/82	32	30		3	Sweets From A Stranger		A&M 4899
1/8/83	47	21	▲	4	Singles-45's And Under	[K]	A&M 4922
9/21/85	57	20		5	Cosi Fan Tutti Frutti		A&M 5085
10/3/87	36	29		6	Babylon And On		A&M 5161
10/7/89	113	10		7	Frank		A&M 5278
6/9/90	163	5		8	A Round And A Bout	[L]	I.R.S. 82040
10/2/93	182	1		9	Some Fantastic Place		A&M 540140

SQUIER, Billy

Born on 5/12/1950 in Wellesley Hills, Massachusetts. Hard-rock singer/songwriter/guitarist.

DEBUT	PEAK	WKS	RIAA	#	Album Title	Catalog	Label & Number
6/7/80	169	12		1	The Tale Of The Tape		Capitol 12062
5/2/81	5	111	▲[3]	2	Don't Say No		Capitol 12146
8/7/82	5	50	▲[2]	3	Emotions In Motion		Capitol 12217
8/4/84	11	29	▲	4	Signs Of Life		Capitol 12361
10/18/86	61	16		5	Enough Is Enough		Capitol 12483
7/15/89	64	17		6	Hear & Now		Capitol 48748
4/27/91	117	6		7	Creatures Of Habit		Capitol 94303

Billboard DEBUT	PEAK	WKS	R I A A	ARTIST Album Title	Catalog	Label & Number

SQUIRE, Chris
Born on 3/4/1948 in London, England. Rock singer/bassist. Member of **Yes**.

| 1/24/76 | 69 | 12 | | 1 Fish Out Of Water.. | | Atlantic 18159 |

SQUIRREL NUT ZIPPERS
Eclectic-jazz band from Chapel Hill, North Carolina: Jim Mathus (vocals, guitar, trombone), Katharine Whalen (vocals, banjo), Ken Mosher (guitar, sax), Tom Maxwell (sax, clarinet), Je Widenhouse (trumpet), Don Raleigh (bass) and Chris Phillips (drums). Stuart Cole replaced Mosher in 1998. Tim Smith replaced Mosher, David Wright replaced Maxwell and Reese Gray (keyboards) joined in 1999. Group name taken from a brand of candy.

2/22/97	27	51	▲	1 Hot..	Cat:#50/1	Mammoth 0137
9/27/97	165	1		2 Sold Out..	[EP]	Mammoth 0177
8/22/98	18	13	●	3 Perennial Favorites..		Mammoth 980169
12/5/98	117	6		4 Christmas Caravan..	[X]	Mammoth 980192
				Christmas chart: 12/'98		
11/4/00	195	1		5 Bedlam Ballroom..		Mammoth 65502

SRC
Psychedelic-rock band from Detroit, Michigan: Scott Richardson (vocals), Steve Lyman (guitar), brothers Gary Quackenbush (guitar) and Glenn Quackenbush (organ), Robin Dale (bass) and Elmer Clawson (drums). Al Wilmont had replaced Dale by 1969. SRC: Scott Richardson Case.

| 9/28/68 | 147 | 4 | | 1 SRC.. | | Capitol 2991 |
| 6/14/69 | 134 | 9 | | 2 Milestones.. | | Capitol 134 |

SR-71
Punk-rock band from Baltimore, Maryland: Mitch Allan (vocals, guitar), Mark Beauchemin (guitar), Jeff Reid (bass) and Dan Garvin (drums).

| 7/8/00 | 81 | 19 | ● | 1 Now You See Inside.. | | RCA 67845 |
| 11/9/02 | 138 | 1 | | 2 Tomorrow.. | | RCA 68130 |

STABBING WESTWARD
Rock band from Macomb, Illinois: Christopher Hall (vocals, guitar), Walter Flakus (keyboards), Jim Sellers (bass) and Andy Kubiszewski (drums).

3/9/96	67	40	●	1 Wither Blister Burn + Peel..		Columbia 66152
4/25/98	52	16	●	2 Darkest Days..		Columbia 69329
6/9/01	47	5		3 Stabbing Westward..		Koch 8204

STACEY, Phil
Born Joel Philip Stacey on 1/21/1978 in Richmond, Kentucky; raised in Fairfield, Ohio. Country singer.

| 5/17/08 | 43 | 3 | | 1 Phil Stacey.. | | Lyric Street 001680 |

STACEY Q
Born Stacey Swain on 11/30/1958 in Los Angeles, California. Female dance singer.

| 9/27/86 | 59 | 39 | | 1 Better Than Heaven.. | | Atlantic 81676 |
| 3/5/88 | 115 | 11 | | 2 Hard Machine.. | | Atlantic 81802 |

STACKRIDGE
Rock band formed in Bristol, England: Mike Slater (vocals, flute), James Warren (guitar), Andy Davis (keyboards), Jim Walter (bass) and Billy Sparkle (drums).

| 12/28/74+ | 191 | 9 | | 1 Pinafore Days.. | | Sire 7503 |
| 11/1/75 | 209 | 1 | | 2 Extravaganza.. | | Sire 7509 |

STAFFORD, Jim
Born on 1/16/1944 in Eloise, Florida. Singer/songwriter/guitarist. Hosted own summer TV show in 1975 and *Those Amazing Animals*. Formerly married to **Bobbie Gentry**.

| 3/16/74 | 55 | 33 | | 1 Jim Stafford.. | [N] | MGM 4947 |

STAFFORD, Jo
Born on 11/12/1917 in Coalinga, California. Died of heart failure on 7/16/2008 (age 90). Female pop singer. Member of The Pied Pipers from 1940-43. Married to **Paul Weston** from 1952-96. Hosted own TV musical series from 1954-55.

| 12/29/56 | 13 | 8 | | 1 Ski Trails.. | | Columbia 910 |

STAFFORD, Terry
Born on 11/22/1941 in Hollis, Oklahoma; raised in Amarillo, Texas. Died on 3/17/1996 (age 54). Male pop singer.

| 5/16/64 | 81 | 11 | | 1 Suspicion!.. | | Crusader 1001 |

STAGE DOLLS
Rock trio from Trondheim, Norway: Torstein Flakne (vocals), Terje Storli (bass) and Steinar Krokstad (drums).

| 8/19/89 | 118 | 12 | | 1 Stage Dolls.. | | Chrysalis 21716 |

STAIND
Alternative-rock band from Boston, Massachusetts: Aaron Lewis (vocals), Mike Mushok (guitar), Johnny April (bass) and Jon Wysocki (drums).

5/1/99	74	56	▲²	1 Dysfunction..	Cat:❶⁵/24	Flip 62356
6/9/01	❶³	70	▲⁵	2 Break The Cycle	Cat:#16/17	Flip 62626
6/7/03	❶¹	43	▲	3 14 Shades Of Grey		Flip 62882
8/27/05	❶¹	48	▲	4 Chapter V		Flip 62982
12/2/06	41	11		5 The Singles 1996-2006..	[G]	Flip 94558
9/6/08	3¹	28		6 The Illusion Of Progress		Flip 511769

Billboard			R I A A	ARTIST Album Title	Catalog	Label & Number
DEBUT	PEAK	WKS				

STAIRSTEPS — see FIVE STAIRSTEPS, The

STALLING, Carl, Project
Born on 11/10/1891 in Lexington, Missouri. Died on 11/29/1972 (age 81). Worked at Disney in the early 1920s where he invented the process of scoring for animation. Joined Warner Brothers in 1936 and scored over 600 cartoons in his 22 years with the company.

11/10/90	188	2	1 Music From Warner Bros. Cartoons 1936-1958 .... [I]	Warner 26027

STALLION
Pop-rock band from Denver, Colorado: Buddy Stephens (vocals), Danny O'Neil (guitar), Wally Damrick (keyboards), Jorg Gonzalez (bass) and Larry Thompson (drums).

3/26/77	191	9	1 Stallion	Casablanca 7040

STAMPEDERS
Pop-rock trio from Calgary, Alberta, Canada: Rick Dodson, Ronnie King and Kim Berly. All share vocals.

10/23/71	172	6	1 Sweet City Woman	Bell 6068

STAMPLEY, Joe
Born on 6/6/1943 in Springhill, Louisiana. Country singer.
AWARD: CMA: Vocal Duo (w/ Moe Bandy) 1980

4/11/81	170	4	1 Hey Joe! / Hey Moe!	Columbia 37003
7/21/84	205	3	2 The Good Ol' Boys - Alive And Well	Columbia 39426
			MOE BANDY & JOE STAMPLEY (above 2)	

STAN & DOUG
Comedy duo from Seattle, Washington: Stan Boreson (born on 5/25/1925) and Doug Setterberg.

12/26/70	19^X	1	1 Stan And Doug Yust Go Nuts At Christmas .... [X-N]	Golden Crest 31021

STANDELLS, The
Garage-rock band from Los Angeles, California: Dick Dodd (vocals, drums), Larry Tamblyn (guitar), Tony Valentino (guitar) and Gary Lane (bass). Dodd was an original Mouseketeer of TV's *The Mickey Mouse Club*. Tamblyn is the brother of actor Russ Tamblyn.

7/2/66	52	16	1 Dirty Water	Tower 5027

STANKY BROWN GROUP, The
Rock band from New York: James Brown (vocals, keyboards), Jeff Leynor (guitar), Allan Ross (sax), Richard Bunkiewicz (bass) and Jerry Cordasco (drums).

5/15/76	192	3	1 Our Pleasure To Serve You	Sire 7516
3/5/77	195	2	2 If The Lights Don't Get You The Helots Will	Sire 7529
4/29/78	192	5	3 Stanky Brown	Sire 6053

STANLEY, Michael, Band
Born Michael Stanley Gee on 3/25/1948 in Cleveland, Ohio. Rock singer/guitarist. Former member of **Silk**. His band: Kevin Raleigh (vocals, keyboards), Bob Pelander (keyboards), Gary Markshay (guitar), Rick Bell (sax), Mike Gismondi (bass) and Tom Dobeck (drums). Don Powers replaced Markshay in 1982.

5/5/73	206	4	1 Michael Stanley	Tumbleweed 106
2/16/74	207	4	2 Friends & Legends	MCA 372
			MICHAEL STANLEY (above 2)	
9/13/75	184	3	3 You Break It...You Bought It!	Epic 33492
4/30/77	207	2	4 Stagepass .... [L]	Epic 34661 [2]
7/8/78	99	18	5 Cabin Fever	Arista 4182
8/4/79	148	5	6 Greatest Hints	Arista 4236
9/27/80+	86	32	7 Heartland	EMI America 17040
8/1/81	79	15	8 North Coast	EMI America 17056
9/4/82	136	6	9 MSB	EMI America 17071
9/24/83	64	17	10 You Can't Fight Fashion	EMI America 17100

STANLEY, Paul
Born Paul Stanley Eisen on 1/20/1952 in Queens, New York. Rock singer/songwriter/guitarist. Member of **Kiss**.

10/14/78	40	18	▲	1 Paul Stanley	Casablanca 7123
11/11/06	53	2		2 Live To Win	New Door 007580

STANLEY, Ralph
Born on 2/25/1927 in Stratton, Virginia. Legendary bluegrass singer/banjo player. One-half of the Stanley Brothers.
AWARD: OPRY: 2000

6/29/02	163	1	1 Ralph Stanley	DMZ 86625

STANSFIELD, Lisa
Born on 4/11/1966 in Rochdale, Manchester, England. Dance singer.

3/10/90	9	39	▲	1 Affection	Arista 8554
11/30/91+	43	40	●	2 Real Love	Arista 18679
8/16/97	55	10		3 Lisa Stansfield	Arista 18738

STAPLES, Mavis
Born on 7/10/1939 in Chicago, Illinois. R&B singer. Member of **The Staple Singers**. Appeared in the 1990 movie *Graffiti Bridge*.

9/12/70	188	4	1 Only For The Lonely	Volt 6010
6/2/07	180	2	2 We'll Never Turn Back	Anti 86830

Billboard			ᴿ ᴵ ᴬ ᴬ	ARTIST		
DEBUT	**PEAK**	**WKS**		Album Title	Catalog	Label & Number

STAPLES, Pop
Born Roebuck Staples on 12/28/1915 in Winona, Mississippi. Died on 12/19/2000 (age 84). R&B guitarist. Patriarch of **The Staple Singers**.

7/12/69	171	5		1 Jammed Together .... [I]		Stax 2020
				ALBERT KING / STEVE CROPPER / POP STAPLES		

STAPLE SINGERS, The
Family R&B vocal group formed in Chicago, Illinois: Roebuck **Pop Staples** (guitar; born on 12/28/1915 in Winona, Mississippi; died on 12/19/2000, age 84), with his son Pervis Staples (born on 11/18/1935; left in 1971) and daughters Cleotha Staples (born on 4/11/1934), Yvonne Staples (born on 10/23/1938) and lead singer **Mavis Staples** (born on 7/10/1939). Group combined both gospel and secular styles.
AWARDS: Grammy: Lifetime Achievement 2005 ★ R&R Hall of Fame: 1999

3/20/71	117	11		1 The Staple Swingers		Stax 2034
2/26/72	19	37		2 Bealtitude: Respect Yourself		Stax 3002
8/25/73	102	21		3 Be What You Are		Stax 3015
12/15/73	11ˣ	2		4 The Twenty-Fifth Day Of December.. [X]		Fantasy 9442
				originally released in 1962 on Riverside 3513		
9/14/74	125	9		5 City In The Sky		Stax 5515
11/1/75+	20	18		6 Let's Do It Again .... [S]		Curtom 5005
9/25/76	155	5		7 Pass It On		Warner 2945
				THE STAPLES		

STAPP, Scott
Born on 8/8/1973 in Orlando, Florida. Rock singer. Former lead singer of **Creed**.

12/10/05	19	10	▲	1 The Great Divide		Wind-Up 13099

STAR, Jeffree
Born Jeffrey Steininger on 11/15/1986 in Anaheim, California. White male dance singer/transvestite.

10/10/09	122	1		1 Beauty Killer		Popsicle 5004

STARBUCK
Pop-rock band from Atlanta, Georgia: Bruce Blackman (vocals, keyboards), Bo Wagner (marimbas), Sloan Hayes (keyboards), Tommy Strain and Ron Norris (guitars), Jim Cobb (bass) and Dave Snavely (drums). Strain, Norris and Snavely left after first album, replaced by Darryl Kutz (guitar), David Shaver (keyboards) and Ken Crysler (drums).

7/24/76	78	14		1 Moonlight Feels Right..		Private Stock 2013
6/11/77	182	2		2 Rock 'n Roll Rocket..		Private Stock 2027

STARCASTLE
Progressive-rock band from Chicago, Illinois: Terry Luttrell (vocals), Matthew Stewart (guitar), Stephen Hagler (guitar), Herb Schildt (keyboards), Gary Strater (bass) and Stephen Tassler (drums).

3/13/76	95	15		1 Starcastle		Epic 33914
2/5/77	101	11		2 Fountains Of Light		Epic 34375
11/19/77	156	3		3 Citadel		Epic 34935

STARFIELD
Christian rock band from Winnipeg, Manitoba, Canada: brothes Tim Neufeld (vocals) and Jon Neufeld (guitar), Dave Lalonde (bass) and James Johnston (drums).

4/12/08	179	1		1 I Will Go..		Sparrow 11091

STARGARD
Disco trio: Rochelle Runnells, Debra Anderson and Janice Williams. Appeared as "The Diamonds" in the movie *Sgt. Pepper's Lonely Hearts Club Band*.

3/4/78	26	13		1 Stargard		MCA 2321
12/2/78	206	1		2 What You Waitin' For		MCA 3064
7/4/81	186	2		3 Back 2 Back		Warner 3456

STARLAND VOCAL BAND
Pop group formed in Washington DC: Bill and wife Taffy Danoff, John Carroll and future wife Margot Chapman. Bill and Taffy had fronted the folk group Fat City (backed **John Denver** on "Take Me Home, Country Roads"). Hosted own TV variety series in 1977.
AWARD: Grammy: Best New Artist 1976

5/29/76	20	25		1 Starland Vocal Band		Windsong 1351
6/11/77	104	13		2 Rear View Mirror..		Windsong 2239
4/15/78	208	3		3 Late Nite Radio		Windsong 2598

STARLITE ORCHESTRA AND SINGERS, The
Group of studio musicians from Canada.

5/3/97	184	1		1 The Best Of Andrew Lloyd Webber		Madacy 0331
1/13/07	17ˣ	2		2 Christmas Shoes .... [X]		Madacy 52455
11/8/08	31ˣ	3		3 Christmas Favorites... Cat:#46/1 [X]		Madacy 53113 [3]
11/22/08	97	7		4 Christmas Holidays.. [X]		Madacy 54021
				Christmas charts: 20/'08, 42/'09		
12/26/09	186	2		5 Christmas Holidays .... [X-R]		Madacy 54021

STARPOINT
R&B-dance band from Maryland: brothers George Phillips (male vocals), Ernesto Phillips (guitar), Orlando Phillips (bass) and Gregory Phillips (drums), with Renee Diggs (female vocals) and Kayode Adeyemo (percussion).

5/9/81	138	8		1 Keep On It		Chocolate City 2018
9/4/82	208	1		2 All Night Long..		Chocolate City 2022

DEBUT	PEAK	WKS		ARTIST / Album Title	Catalog	Label & Number
				STARPOINT — cont'd		
10/5/85+	60	47	●	3 Restless		Elektra 60424
3/21/87	95	14		4 Sensational		Elektra 60722

STARR, Brenda K.
Born Brenda Kaplan on 10/15/1966 in Manhattan, New York. Singer/actress. Daughter of Harvey Kaplan (of **Spiral Starecase**).

| 5/21/88 | 58 | 24 | | 1 Brenda K. Starr | | MCA 42088 |

STARR, Edwin
Born Charles Hatcher on 1/21/1942 in Nashville, Tennessee; raised in Cleveland, Ohio. Died of a heart attack on 4/2/2003 (age 61). R&B singer.

5/17/69	73	13		1 25 Miles		Gordy 940
9/5/70	52	13		2 War & Peace		Gordy 948
7/31/71	178	7		3 Involved		Gordy 956
1/24/76	210	1		4 Free To Be Myself		Granite 1005
1/20/79	80	14		5 Clean		20th Century 559
7/28/79	115	8		6 Happy Radio		20th Century 591
5/17/80	203	5		7 Stronger Than You Think I Am		20th Century 615

STARR, Fredro
Born Fredro Scruggs on 1/1/1970 in Jamaica, Queens, New York. Male rapper/actor. Member of **Onyx**. Acted in several movies.

| 3/3/01 | 76 | 7 | | 1 Firestarr | | Koch 8180 |

STARR, Ringo   **All-Time: #423**
Born Richard Starkey on 7/7/1940 in Dingle, Liverpool, England. Rock drummer. Played with Rory Storm and the Hurricanes before joining **The Beatles** in 1962. Acted in the movies *Candy*, *The Magic Christian*, *200 Motels*, *Born To Boogie*, *Blindman*, *That'll Be The Day*, *Cave Man* and *Give My Regards To Broad Street*. Played "Mr. Conductor" on PBS-TV's *Shining Time Station* from 1989-91. Married actress Barbara Bach on 4/27/1981.

5/16/70	22	14		1 Sentimental Journey		Apple 3365
10/17/70	65	15		2 Beaucoups of Blues		Apple 3368
11/17/73	2²	37	▲	3 Ringo		Apple 3413
11/30/74+	8	25	●	4 Goodnight Vienna		Apple 3417
12/6/75+	30	11		5 Blast From Your Past	[G]	Apple 3422
10/16/76	28	9		6 Ringo's Rotogravure		Atlantic 18193
10/15/77	162	6		7 Ringo The 4th		Atlantic 19108
5/20/78	129	6		8 Bad Boy		Portrait 35378
11/14/81	98	12		9 Stop And Smell The Roses		Boardwalk 33246
7/4/98	61	4		10 Vertical Man		Mercury 558598
4/12/03	113	2		11 Ringo Rama		Koch 8429
9/15/07	130	2		12 Photograph: The Very Best Of Ringo	[G]	Capitol 93827
2/2/08	94	2		13 Liverpool 8		Capitol 17388

STARR, Ruby, And Grey Ghost
Born Constance Mierzwiak on 11/30/1949 in Toledo, Ohio. Died of lung cancer on 1/14/1995 (age 45). Grey Ghost: Gary Levin (guitar), Marius Penczner (keyboards), David Mayo (bass) and Joel Williams (drums).

| 9/27/75 | 206 | 1 | | 1 Ruby Starr And Grey Ghost | | Capitol 11427 |

STARSAILOR
Rock band from Chorley, Lancashire, England: James Walsh (vocals, guitar), Barry Westhead (keyboards), James Stelfox (bass) and Ben Byrne (drums).

| 1/26/02 | 129 | 8 | | 1 Love Is Here | | Capitol 36448 |

STARSHIP — see JEFFERSON AIRPLANE

STARS ON
Studio group assembled in Holland by producer Jaap Eggermont.

5/9/81	9	24	●	1 Stars On Long Play		Radio 16044
				side 1: medley of **Beatles** songs; the singles "Stars on 45" (#1) and "Stars on 45 II" (#67) both made the *Hot 100*		
10/31/81	120	6		2 Stars On Long Play II		Radio 19314
				the single "More Stars on 45" made the *Hot 100* (#55)		
5/8/82	163	6		3 Stars On Long Play III		Radio 19349
				side 1: **Rolling Stones** medley; side 2: **Stevie Wonder** medley; the single "Stars on 45 III" made the *Hot 100* (#28)		

STARTING LINE, The
Punk-rock band from Churchville, Pennsylvania: Kenny Vasoli (vocals, bass), Matt Watts (guitar), Mike Golla (guitar), and Tom Gryskiewicz (drums).

8/3/02	109	5		1 Say It Like You Mean It		Drive-Thru 060063
5/28/05	18	6		2 Based On A True Story		Drive-Thru 004686
8/18/07	30	4		3 Direction		Virgin 53613

STARZ
Rock band formed in New York: Michael Lee Smith (vocals), Rich Ranno (guitar), Brendan Harkin (guitar), Piet Sweval (bass; **Looking Glass**) and Joe Dube (drums). Smith is the brother of **Rex Smith**. Group first recorded as Fallen Angels. Sweval died on 1/23/1990 (age 41).

9/11/76	123	13		1 Starz		Capitol 11539
4/16/77	89	8		2 Violation		Capitol 11617
2/11/78	105	9		3 Attention Shoppers!		Capitol 11730
12/9/78	208	1		4 Coliseum Rock		Capitol 11861

STATE RADIO
Alternative-rock trio from Sherborn, Massachusetts: Chad Urmston (vocals, guitar), Chuck Fay (bass) and Mike Najarian (drums).

| 10/17/09 | 96 | 1 | | 1 Let It Go | | Ruff Shod 30851 |

STATIC LULLABY, A
Hard-rock band formed in Chino Hills, California: Joe Brown (vocals), Dan Arnold (guitar), Nate Lindeman (guitar), Phil Pirrone (bass) and Brett Dinovo (drums).

| 4/23/05 | 129 | 1 | | 1 Faso Latido | | Columbia 92772 |
| 10/28/06 | 173 | 1 | | 2 A Static Lullaby | | Fearless 30094 |

STATIC-X
Alternative-metal rock band formed in Los Angeles, California: Wayne "Static" Wells (vocals, guitar), Koichi Fukuda (guitar, keyboards), Tony Campos (bass) and Ken Jay (drums). Fukada left in 2000; Static took over keyboards and Tod "Tripp Eisen" Salvador (guitar) joined. Nick Oshiro (of **Seether**) replaced Lacey in early 2003. Salvador was fired in 2005; Fukada returned.

9/4/99+	107	43	▲	1 Wisconsin Death Trip		Warner 47271
6/9/01	11	14	●	2 Machine		Warner 47948
10/25/03	20	6		3 Shadow Zone		Warner 48427
8/7/04	139	1		4 Beneath...Between...Beyond		Warner 48796
7/2/05	29	6		5 Start A War		Warner 49373
4/21/07	36	10		6 Cannibal		Reprise 101710
4/4/09	16	6		7 Cult Of Static		Reprise 517449

STATLER BROTHERS, The
Country vocal group from Staunton, Virginia: brothers Don Reid (born on 6/5/1945) and Harold Reid (born on 8/21/1939), Philip Balsley (born on 8/8/1939) and Lew DeWitt (born on 3/8/1938; died of Crohn's disease on 8/15/1990, age 52). Hosted their own variety show on TNN. Jimmy Fortune (born on 3/11/1955) replaced DeWitt in 1983.
AWARDS: Grammy: Best New Country Artist 1965 ★ C&W Hall of Fame: 2008 ★ CMA: Vocal Group 1972, 1973, 1974, 1975, 1976, 1977, 1979, 1980 & 1984

2/26/66	125	3		1 Flowers On The Wall		Columbia 2449 / 9249
1/30/71	126	11		2 Bed Of Rose's		Mercury 61317
10/16/71	181	2		3 Pictures Of Moments To Remember		Mercury 61349
9/13/75+	121	20	▲³	4 The Best Of The Statler Bros. [G]		Mercury 1037
6/10/78	155	9	●	5 Entertainers...On And Off The Record		Mercury 5007
12/16/78	183	4	▲	6 The Statler Brothers Christmas Card [X]		Mercury 5012
7/14/79	183	2		7 The Originals		Mercury 5016
2/2/80	153	11	●	8 The Best Of The Statler Bros. Rides Again, Volume II [G]		Mercury 5024
9/6/80	169	5	●	9 10th Anniversary		Mercury 5027
7/11/81	103	9		10 Years Ago		Mercury 6002
7/17/82	201	5		11 The Legend Goes On...		Mercury 4048
6/25/83	193	5	●	12 Today		Mercury 812184
5/26/84	177	4	●	13 Atlanta Blue		Mercury 818652
8/9/86	183	2		14 Four For The Show		Mercury 826782

STATON, Candi
Born Canzata Staton on 5/13/1940 in Hanceville, Alabama. Female R&B singer. Formerly married to **Clarence Carter**.

2/27/71	188	2		1 Stand By Your Man		Fame 4202
6/26/76	129	14		2 Young Hearts Run Free		Warner 2948
7/28/79	129	6		3 Chance		Warner 3333

STATON, Dakota   **1950s: #24**
Born Aliyah Rabia on 6/3/1932 in Pittsburgh, Pennsylvania. Died on 4/10/2007 (age 74). Jazz singer.

2/24/58	4	52		1 The Late, Late Show		Capitol 876
10/27/58	22	1		2 Dynamic!		Capitol 1054
6/1/59	23	9		3 Crazy He Calls Me		Capitol 1170
11/16/59	47	3		4 Time To Swing		Capitol 1241

STATUS QUO, The
Psychedelic-rock band from London, England: Francis Rossi (vocals, guitar), Rick Parfitt (guitar), Roy Lynes (organ), Alan Lancaster (bass) and John Coughlin (drums).

9/14/74	201	8		1 Quo		A&M 3649
4/5/75	205	7		2 On The Level		Capitol 11381
4/17/76	148	7		3 Status Quo		Capitol 11509

STEADY B
Born Warren McGlone on 9/17/1969 in Philadelphia, Pennsylvania. Male rapper.

| 10/31/87 | 149 | 7 | | 1 What's My Name | | Jive 1060 |
| 10/22/88 | 193 | 1 | | 2 Let The Hustlers Play | | Jive 1122 |

STEADY MOBB'N
Male rap duo from New Orleans, Louisiana: Billy Bathgate and Crooked Eye.

| 5/24/97 | 29 | 9 | | 1 Pre-Meditated Drama | | No Limit 50704 |
| 12/12/98 | 82 | 2 | | 2 Black Mafia | | No Limit 50026 |

Billboard			ARTIST		
DEBUT	PEAK	WKS	Album Title	Catalog	Label & Number

STEALERS WHEEL
Pop-rock duo from Scotland: **Gerry Rafferty** (vocals, guitar) and Joe Egan (vocals, keyboards).

2/24/73	50	22	1 Stealers Wheel..		A&M 4377
4/13/74	181	3	2 Ferguslie Park		A&M 4419
5/10/75	201	6	3 Right Or Wrong		A&M 4517

STEALIN HORSES
Rock-country band from Lexington, Kentucky: Kiya Heartwood (vocals), Mandy Meyer (guitar), John Durno (bass) and Kopana Terry (drums). Band name is an ancient Native American rite of passage in which young warriors stole horses from nearby tribes.

6/25/88	146	12	1 Stealin Horses		Arista 8520

STEAM
Pop-rock band from Bridgeport, Connecticut. "Na Na Hey Hey Kiss Him Goodbye" was recorded by the trio of Gary DeCarlo, Paul Leka and Dale Frashur, and released as by Steam. After the song became a hit, Leka assembled an actual Steam group to record the rest of the album: Bill Steer (vocals), Jay Babins (guitar), Tom Zuke (guitar), Hank Schorz (keyboards), Mike Daniels (bass) and Ray Corries (drums).

1/10/70	84	13	1 Steam		Mercury 61254

STEEL BREEZE
Pop-rock band from Sacramento, California: Ric Jacobs (vocals), Ken Goorabian (guitar), Waylin Carpenter (guitar), Rod Toner (keyboards), Vinnie Pantleoni (bass) and Barry Lowenthal (drums).

9/18/82	50	28	1 Steel Breeze		RCA Victor 4424

STEELE, Maureen
Born in Los Angeles, California. White pop-dance singer/songwriter.

6/8/85	210	1	1 Nature Of The Beast		Motown 6141

STEELEYE SPAN
Folk band formed in London, England: Maddy Prior (vocals), Tim Hart (guitar), Martin Carthy (guitar), John Kilpatrick (accordian), Rick Kemp (bass) and Nigel Pegrum (drums). Hart died on 12/24/2009 (age 61).

5/12/73	201	6	1 Parcel Of Rogues		Chrysalis 1046
4/27/74	208	3	2 Now We Are Six		Chrysalis 1053
12/6/75	143	6	3 All Around My Hat		Chrysalis 1091
10/30/76	205	4	4 Rocket Cottage		Chrysalis 1123
3/25/78	191	3	5 Storm Force Ten		Chrysalis 1151

STEELHEART
Hard-rock band from Norwalk, Connecticut: Michael Matijevic (vocals), Chris Risola (guitar), Frank Dicostanzo (guitar), Jimmy Ward (bass) and John Fowler (drums). Fowler died on 3/21/2008 (age 42).

9/22/90+	40	59	●	1 Steelheart		MCA 6368
6/27/92	144	7		2 Tangled In Reins		MCA 10426

STEEL PANTHER
Parody heavy metal band formed in Los Angeles, California: Ralph "Michael Starr" Saenz (vocals), Russ "Satchel" Parrish (guitar), Travis "Lexxi Foxxx" Haley (bass) and Darren "Stix Zadinia" Leader (drums).

10/17/09	98	4	1 Feel The Steel		Universal Rep. 012849

STEEL PULSE
Reggae band formed in Birmingham, England: David Hinds (vocals, guitar), Selwyn Brown (keyboards), Alphonso Martin (percussion), Alvin Ewen (bass) and Steve Nesbitt (drums).

7/17/82	120	13	●	1 True Democracy		Elektra 60113
3/31/84	154	12	●	2 Earth Crisis		Elektra 60315
7/23/88	127	7		3 State of...Emergency		MCA 42192

STEELY DAN   **1970s: #50 / All-Time: #143**
Jazz-rock band formed in Los Angeles, California, by **Donald Fagen** (keyboards, vocals; born on 1/10/1948 in Passaic, New York) and Walter Becker (bass, vocals; born on 2/20/1950 in Queens, New York). Group, primarily known as a studio unit, featured Fagen and Becker with various studio musicians. Duo split from 1981-92.
 AWARD: R&R Hall of Fame: 2001

12/2/72+	17	59	▲	1 Can't Buy A Thrill	**Cat:**#13/181	ABC 758
				RS500 #238		
7/21/73	35	34	●	2 Countdown To Ecstasy	**Cat:**#20/43	ABC 779
3/30/74	8	36	▲	3 Pretzel Logic	**Cat:**#24/30	ABC 808
				RS500 #385		
4/12/75	13	26	▲	4 Katy Lied	**Cat:**#19/77	ABC 846
5/22/76	15	29	▲	5 The Royal Scam	**Cat:**#22/53	ABC 931
10/15/77	3[7]	60	▲[2]	6 Aja	**Cat:**#2[2]/278	ABC 1006
				Grammy: Hall of Fame ★ RS500 #145		
12/6/80+	9	36	▲	7 Gaucho	**Cat:**#11/186	MCA 6102
11/4/95	40	5		8 Alive In America	[L]	Giant 24634
3/18/00	6	30	▲	9 Two Against Nature		Giant 24719
				Grammys: Album of the Year / Pop Vocal Album		
6/28/03	9	12		10 Everything Must Go		Reprise 48435

Billboard			R I A A	ARTIST Album Title	Catalog	Label & Number
DEBUT	PEAK	WKS				

STEELY DAN — cont'd
GREATEST HITS & COMPILATIONS:

11/18/78+	30	22	▲	11 **Greatest Hits**		ABC 1107 [2]
7/3/82	115	9	●	12 **Gold**..	Cat:#20/88	MCA 5324
4/21/01	50^C	1	●	13 **A Decade Of Steely Dan**		MCA 5570
				first released in 1985		
8/19/06	92	6		14 **The Definitive Collection**		Geffen 006752

STEFANI, Gwen
Born on 10/3/1969 in Fullerton, California. Lead singer of **No Doubt**. Played Jean Harlow in the 2004 movie *The Aviator*. Married **Gavin Rossdale** (lead singer of **Bush**) on 9/14/2002.

12/11/04+	5	78	▲³	1 **Love.Angel.Music.Baby.**	Cat:#50/1	Interscope 003469
12/23/06	3¹	51	▲	2 **The Sweet Escape**		Interscope 008099

STEINBERG, David
Born on 8/9/1942 in Winnipeg, Manitoba, Canada. Stand-up comedian known for his catchphrase "booga booga!" Hosted own Canadian TV series in the mid-1970s. Later became a prolific TV sitcom director.

1/23/71	182	6		1 **Disguised As A Normal Person** .... [C]		Elektra 74065

STEINER, Tommy Shane
Born on 10/9/1973 in Austin, Texas. Country singer.

4/27/02	71	6		1 **Then Came The Night**		RCA 67041

STEINMAN, Jim
Born on 11/1/1948 in Brooklyn, New York. Songwriter/pianist/producer. Longtime recording partnership with **Meat Loaf**.

5/16/81	63	17		1 **Bad For Good**		Cleveland Int'l. 36531

STELLAR KART
Christian punk-rock band from Phoenix, Arizona: Adam Agee (vocal, guitar), Cody Pellerin (guitar), Brian Calcara (bass) and Jordan Messer (drums).

8/12/06	135	1		1 **We Can't Stand Sitting Down**		Word-Curb 86526
3/15/08	66	1		2 **Expect The Impossible**		Word-Curb 887296

STEPHENSON, Van
Born on 11/4/1953 in Hamilton, Ohio. Died of cancer on 4/8/2001 (age 47). Singer/songwriter. Member of **Blackhawk**.

6/2/84	54	20		1 **Righteous Anger**		MCA 5482

STEPPENWOLF   All-Time: #237
Hard-rock band formed in Los Angeles, California: Joachim "**John Kay**" Krauledat (vocals, guitar; born on 4/12/1944), brothers Dennis "Mars Bonfire" Edmonton (guitar; born on 4/21/1943) and Jerry Edmonton (drums; born on 10/24/1946; died in a car crash on 11/28/1993, age 47), John "Goldy McJohn" Goadsby (keyboards; born on 5/2/1945) and Klaus "Nick St. Nicholas" Kassbaum (bass; born on 9/28/1943). The Edmonton brothers changed both last names from McCrohan. Many personnel changes with Kay the only constant member. Group named after a Herman Hesse novel.

3/9/68	6	87	●	1 **Steppenwolf**		Dunhill/ABC 50029
10/5/68+	3¹	52	●	2 **The Second**		Dunhill/ABC 50037
3/15/69	7	29		3 **At Your Birthday Party**		Dunhill/ABC 50053
7/5/69	29	19		4 **Early Steppenwolf** .... [E-L]		Dunhill/ABC 50060
				recorded in 1967 when band was known as Sparrow		
11/15/69+	17	46	●	5 **Monster**		Dunhill/ABC 50066
4/18/70	7	53	●	6 **Steppenwolf 'Live'** .... [L]		Dunhill/ABC 50075 [2]
11/21/70	19	17	●	7 **Steppenwolf 7**		Dunhill/ABC 50090
3/6/71	24	36	●	8 **Steppenwolf Gold/Their Great Hits** .... [G]		Dunhill/ABC 50099
10/2/71	54	11		9 **For Ladies Only**		Dunhill/ABC 50110
6/17/72	62	13		10 **Rest In Peace** .... [K]		Dunhill/ABC 50124
2/24/73	152	9	▲	11 **16 Greatest Hits** .... Cat:#4/254 [G]		Dunhill/ABC 50135
9/21/74	47	12		12 **Slow Flux**		Mums 33093
9/20/75	155	4		13 **Hour Of The Wolf**		Epic 33583
9/26/87	171	4		14 **Rock & Roll Rebels**		Qwil 1560
				JOHN KAY & STEPPENWOLF		

STEPS
Dance-pop vocal group from England: Lisa Scott-Lee, Ian Watkins, Claire Richards, Lee Latchford-Evans and Faye Tozer.

3/4/00	79	10		1 **Step One**		Jive 41688

STEREOLAB
Experimental-rock band formed in London, England: Laetitia Sadier and Mary Hansen (vocals), Tim Gane (guitar), Morgane Lhote (organ), Richard Harrison (bass) and Andy Ramsay (drums). Hansen died after being struck by a car on 12/9/2002 (age 36).

10/11/97	111	2		1 **Dots And Loops**		Elektra 62065
10/9/99	154	1		2 **Cobra And Phases Group Play Voltage In The Milky Night**		Elektra 62409
9/15/01	178	1		3 **Sound-Dust**		Elektra 62676
2/14/04	174	1		4 **Margerine Eclipse**		Elektra 62926
9/6/08	170	1		5 **Chemical Chords**..		4AD 2815

STEREO MC'S
Dance trio from London, England: Rob Birch, Nick Hallam and Owen Rossiter.

3/27/93	92	29		1 **Connected**..		Gee Street 514061

			R I A A	ARTIST Album Title	Catalog	Label & Number
DEBUT	PEAK	WKS				

STEREOMUD

Hard-rock band formed in New York: Eric Rogers (vocals), John Fattoruso (guitar), "Joey Z" Zampella (guitar), Corey Lowery (bass) and Dan Richardson (drums). Joey Z and Richardson were members of **Life Of Agony**. Lowery is the brother of Clint Lowery (of **Sevendust**); the Lowery brothers later formed **Dark New Day**.

DEBUT	PEAK	WKS		#	Title		Label & Number
6/9/01	142	3		1 Perfect Self			Loud 85483
4/19/03	146	1		2 Every Given Moment			Columbia 86488

STEREOPHONICS

Rock trio from Cwmaman, South Wales: Kelly Jones (vocals, guitar), Richard Jones (bass) and Stuart Cable (drums).

5/5/01	188	1		1 Just Enough Education To Perform		V2 27092

STEVENS, April — see TEMPO, Nino

STEVENS, Cat   1970s: #46 / All-Time: #195

Born Steven Georgiou on 7/21/1948 in London, England. Pop-folk singer/songwriter/guitarist. Began career playing folk music at Hammersmith College in 1966. Contracted tuberculosis in 1968 and spent over a year recuperating. Adopted new style when he re-emerged. Lived in Brazil in the mid-1970s. Converted to Muslim religion in 1979; took name Yusuf Islam.

DEBUT	PEAK	WKS	RIAA	#	Title	Catalog	Label & Number
4/3/71	173	12		1 Matthew & Son/New Masters ..... **[E]**		Deram 18005/10 [2]
				Matthew & Son first released in 1967 on Deram 18005 / New Masters first released in 1968 on Deram 18010		
1/8/72	94	10		2 Very Young And Early Songs ..... **[E]**		Deram 18061
3/20/71	164	16	●	3 Mona Bone Jakon		A&M 4260
				first released in 1970		
2/6/71	8	79	▲³	4 Tea For The Tillerman		A&M 4280
				RS500 #206		
10/9/71	2¹	67	▲³	5 Teaser And The Firecat		A&M 4313
10/14/72	❶³	48	▲	6 Catch Bull At Four		A&M 4365
7/28/73	3¹	43	●	7 Foreigner		A&M 4391
4/13/74	2³	36	▲	8 Buddha And The Chocolate Box		A&M 3623
7/12/75	6	45	▲⁴	9 Greatest Hits	Cat:#8/17 **[G]**	A&M 4519
12/13/75+	13	19	●	10 Numbers		A&M 4555
5/21/77	7	23	●	11 Izitso		A&M 4702
12/23/78+	33	15		12 Back To Earth		A&M 4735
12/15/84	165	8	●	13 Footsteps In The Dark - Greatest Hits, Volume Two ..... **[K]**		A&M 3736
4/15/00	58	38	●	14 The Very Best Of Cat Stevens ..... **[G]**		A&M 541387
12/2/06	52	11		15 An Other Cup		YA 94550
5/23/09	41	9		16 Roadsinger		Eder 012794
				YUSUF (above 2)		

STEVENS, Connie

Born Concetta Ingolia on 8/8/1938 in Brooklyn, New York. Pop singer/actress. Played "Cricket Blake" on TV's *Hawaiian Eye* from 1959-63. Appeared in several movies. Married to **Eddie Fisher** from 1967-69.

~ ~ ~ ~ ~ ~ ~ ~ ~ ~   **NON-CHARTED ALBUM**   ~ ~ ~ ~ ~ ~ ~ ~ ~ ~

1960 **The New Singing Sensation Of Television**

["Sixteen Reasons"]

STEVENS, Dodie

Born Geraldine Ann Pasquale on 2/17/1946 in Chicago, Illinois; raised in Temple City, California. Pop singer.

~ ~ ~ ~ ~ ~ ~ ~ ~ ~   **NON-CHARTED ALBUM**   ~ ~ ~ ~ ~ ~ ~ ~ ~ ~

1961 **Pink Shoelaces**

STEVENS, Ray

Born Harold Ray Ragsdale on 1/24/1939 in Clarksdale, Georgia. Country-novelty singer/songwriter. Hosted own TV variety show in 1970. Also recorded as Henhouse Five Plus Too.

DEBUT	PEAK	WKS	RIAA	#	Title	Catalog	Label & Number
9/15/62	135	2		1 1,837 Seconds Of Humor ..... **[N]**		Mercury 60732
6/21/69	57	13		2 Gitarzan ..... **[N]**		Monument 18115
6/13/70	35	19		3 Everything Is Beautiful		Barnaby 35005
12/12/70+	141	8		4 Ray Stevens...Unreal!!!		Barnaby 30092
9/4/71	95	8		5 Ray Stevens' Greatest Hits	Cat:#28/6 **[G]**	Barnaby 30770
2/5/72	175	9		6 Turn Your Radio On		Barnaby 30809
6/15/74	159	11		7 Boogity Boogity ..... **[N]**		Barnaby 6003
6/28/75	106	14		8 Misty		Barnaby 6012
12/27/75+	173	4		9 The Very Best Of Ray Stevens ..... **[G]**		Barnaby 6018
3/15/80	132	8		10 Shriner's Convention ..... **[N]**		RCA Victor 3574
1/19/85	118	19	▲	11 He Thinks He's Ray Stevens ..... **[N]**		MCA 5517
1/23/93	36ᶜ	3	●	12 His All-Time Greatest Comic Hits ..... **[G-N]**		Curb 77312
				first released in 1990		

~ ~ ~ ~ ~ ~ ~ ~ ~ ~   **NON-CHARTED ALBUMS**   ~ ~ ~ ~ ~ ~ ~ ~ ~ ~

1963 **This Is Ray Stevens**   1968 **The Best Of Ray Stevens**

STEVENS, Shakin'
Born Michael Barratt on 3/4/1948 in Cardiff, Wales. Rockabilly singer/songwriter.

6/19/82	210	1		1 You Drive Me Crazy		Epic 38022

STEVENS, Steve, Atomic Playboys
Born Steven Schneider on 5/5/1959 in Brooklyn, New York. Rock guitarist. Member of **Billy Idol**'s band. The Atomic Playboys: Perry McCarty (vocals), Phil Ashley (keyboards) and Thommy Price (drums). Price was also a member of **Scandal** and **Joan Jett & The Blackhearts**.

9/2/89	119	12		1 Steve Stevens Atomic Playboys		Warner 25920

STEVENS, Sufjan
Born on 7/1/1975 in Detroit, Michigan. Male eclectic pop-rock singer/songwriter/guitarist.

7/23/05	121	8		1 Illinois		Asthmatic Kitty 014
7/29/06	71	2		2 The Avalanche		Asthmatic Kitty 022
12/9/06	122	3		3 Songs For Christmas [X]		Asthmatic Kitty 6028 [5]
				Christmas charts: 7/'06, 37/'07, 23/'08		
11/7/09	171	1		4 The BQE		Asthmatic Kitty 278

STEVENSON, B.W.
Born Louis Stevenson on 10/5/1949 in Dallas, Texas. Died of heart failure on 4/28/1988 (age 38). B.W. is short for Buck Wheat.

5/27/72	206	1		1 B.W. Stevenson		RCA Victor 4685
9/15/73	45	14		2 My Maria		RCA Victor 0088
4/20/74	206	2		3 Calabasas		RCA Victor 0410
2/28/76	201	1		4 We Be Sailin'		Warner 2901

STEVIE B
Born Steven Bernard Hill in Miami, Florida. Dance-pop singer/multi-instrumentalist.

7/23/88	78	21	●	1 Party Your Body		LMR 5500
3/11/89	75	46	●	2 In My Eyes		LMR 5531
7/21/90+	54	43	●	3 Love & Emotion		LMR 2307

STEWART, Al
Born on 9/5/1945 in Glasgow, Scotland. Pop singer/songwriter/guitarist. Also see **Shot In The Dark**.

6/1/74	133	14		1 Past, Present And Future		Janus 3063
3/1/75	30	23		2 Modern Times		Janus 7012
10/9/76+	5	48	▲	3 Year Of The Cat		Janus 7022
10/7/78	10	31	▲	4 Time Passages		Arista 4190
9/13/80	37	13		5 24 Carrots		Arista 9520
11/14/81	110	11		6 Live/Indian Summer [L]		Arista 8607 [2]
				recorded on 4/29/1981 at the Roxy in Hollywood, California		

STEWART, Amii
Born on 1/29/1956 in Washington DC. Disco singer/dancer/actress. In the Broadway musical *Bubbling Brown Sugar*.

3/17/79	19	23	●	1 Knock On Wood		Ariola 50054
11/24/79	207	3		2 Paradise Bird		Ariola America 50072

STEWART, Billy
Born on 3/24/1937 in Washington DC. Died in a car crash on 1/17/1970 (age 32). R&B singer/keyboardist. Nicknamed "Fat Boy."

7/3/65	97	10		1 I Do Love You		Chess 1496
5/7/66+	138	6		2 Unbelievable		Chess 1499

STEWART, Gary
Born on 5/28/1944 in Jenkins, Kentucky; raised in Fort Pierce, Florida. Committed suicide on 12/16/2003 (age 59). Country singer/songwriter/pianist.

8/16/80	165	3		1 Cactus And A Rose		RCA Victor 3627

STEWART, Jermaine
Born on 9/7/1957 in Columbus, Ohio. Died of cancer on 3/17/1997 (age 39). R&B-dance singer.

3/2/85	90	11		1 The Word Is Out		Arista 8261
6/14/86	32	25		2 Frantic Romantic		Arista 8395
4/23/88	98	12		3 Say It Again		Arista 8455

STEWART, John
Born on 9/5/1939 in San Diego, California. Died of a stroke on 1/19/2008 (age 68). Folk-pop singer/songwriter. Member of **The Kingston Trio** from 1961-67. Brother of Mike Stewart (of **We Five**).

6/21/69	193	3		1 California Bloodlines		Capitol 203
1/15/72	195	2		2 The Lonesome Picker Rides Again		Warner 1948
4/28/73	202	6		3 Cannons In The Rain		RCA Victor 4827
7/6/74	195	2		4 The Phoenix Concerts-Live [L]		RCA Victor 0265 [2]
				recorded March 1974 at the Phoenix Symphony Hall		
5/17/75	150	6		5 Wingless Angels		RCA Victor 0816
11/26/77	126	8		6 Fire In The Wind		RSO 3027
5/19/79	10	28		7 Bombs Away Dream Babies		RSO 3051
4/12/80	85	10		8 Dream Babies Go Hollywood		RSO 3074
1/22/83	210	1		9 Blondes		Allegiance 431

Billboard DEBUT	PEAK	WKS	R I A A	ARTIST / Album Title	Catalog	Label & Number

STEWART, Rod   1970s: #26 / 1980s: #50 / 1990s: #38 / 2000s: #17 / All-Time: #13

Born on 1/10/1945 in Highgate, London, England. Pop-rock singer/songwriter. Member of the **Jeff Beck** Group from 1967-69. Member of **Faces** from 1969-75. Married to actress Alana Hamilton from 1979-84. Married to supermodel Rachel Hunter from 1990-2003.

AWARDS: Grammy: Legend 1989 ★ R&R Hall of Fame: 1994

DEBUT	PEAK	WKS	RIAA	#	Album Title	Cat	Label & Number
12/13/69+	139	27		1	The Rod Stewart Album		Mercury 61237
6/20/70	27	57		2	Gasoline Alley		Mercury 61264
6/19/71	❶⁴	52	▲	3	Every Picture Tells A Story	Cat:#45/4	Mercury 609
					RS500 #172		
8/12/72	2³	36	●	4	Never A Dull Moment		Mercury 646
10/26/74	13	14		5	Smiler		Mercury 1017
9/6/75	9	29	●	6	Atlantic Crossing		Warner 2875
7/17/76	2⁵	57	▲²	7	A Night On The Town		Warner 2938
11/26/77+	2⁶	47	▲³	8	Foot Loose & Fancy Free		Warner 3092
12/23/78+	❶³	37	▲⁴	9	Blondes Have More Fun		Warner 3261
12/6/80	12	21	▲	10	Foolish Behaviour		Warner 3485
11/21/81	11	31	▲	11	Tonight I'm Yours		Warner 3602
6/25/83	30	22		12	Body Wishes		Warner 23877
6/30/84	18	35	●	13	Camouflage		Warner 25095
7/12/86	28	19		14	Rod Stewart		Warner 25446
6/4/88+	20	72	▲²	15	Out Of Order		Warner 25684
4/13/91	10	81	▲	16	Vagabond Heart		Warner 26300
6/24/95	35	16	●	17	A Spanner In The Works		Warner 45867
6/20/98	44	14		18	When We Were The New Boys		Warner 46792
2/24/01	50	8		19	Human		Atlantic 83411
11/9/02	4	86	▲³	20	It Had To Be You...The Great American Songbook	Cat:#2²/27	J Records 20039
11/8/03	2²	64	▲²	21	As Time Goes By...The Great American Songbook Vol. II	Cat:#7/4	J Records 55710
11/6/04	❶¹	34	▲	22	Stardust...The Great American Songbook Vol. III	Cat:#46/1	J Records 62182
11/5/05	2¹	24	▲	23	Thanks For The Memory...The Great American Songbook Vol. IV		J Records 69286
10/28/06	❶¹	21	●	24	Still The Same...Great Rock Classics Of Our Time		J Records 82641
11/14/09	4	16		25	Soulbook		J Records 30256
					GREATEST HITS & COMPILATIONS:		
7/7/73	31	25	●	26	Sing It Again Rod		Mercury 680
5/15/76	90	26	●	27	The Best Of Rod Stewart		Mercury 7507 [2]
12/11/76	202	9		28	The Best Of Rod Stewart Vol. 2		Mercury 7508 [2]
11/24/79+	22	19	▲³	29	Rod Stewart Greatest Hits	Cat:#30/7	Warner 3373
12/2/89+	54	18	▲²	30	Storyteller/The Complete Anthology: 1964-1990		Warner 25987 [4]
3/24/90	20	27	▲²	31	Downtown Train: Selections From The Storyteller Anthology	Cat:#15/45	Warner 26158
11/30/96	19	41	▲	32	If We Fall In Love Tonight		Warner 46452
12/1/01+	40	49	▲	33	The Very Best Of Rod Stewart	Cat:#8/72	Warner 78328
9/13/03	66	5		34	Encore: The Very Best Of Rod Stewart Vol. 2		Warner 73911
12/6/08+	53	18		35	The Definitive Rod Stewart		Warner 514093 [2]
					LIVE ALBUMS:		
1/5/74	63	11	●	36	Rod Stewart/Faces Live - Coast To Coast Overture And Beginners		Mercury 697
11/20/82	46	13	●	37	Absolutely Live		Warner 23743 [2]
6/12/93	2⁵	63	▲³	38	Unplugged...And Seated		Warner 45289

STEWART, Sandy
Born Sandra Galitz on 7/10/1937 in Philadelphia, Pennsylvania. Pop singer.

4/6/63	138	2		1	My Coloring Book		Colpix 441

STEWART, Sandy
Born on 1/13/1958 in San Francisco, California; raised in Houston, Texas. Pop-rock singer/songwriter.

3/31/84	208	2		1	Cat Dancer		Modern 90133

STEWART, Wynn
Born on 6/7/1934 in Morrisville, Missouri. Died of a heart attack on 7/17/1985 (age 51). Country singer/songwriter/guitarist.

7/22/67	158	8		1	It's Such A Pretty World Today		Capitol 2737

STICKY FINGAZ
Born Kirk Jones on 4/3/1970 in Jamaica, Queens, New York. Male rapper. Member of **Onyx**.

6/9/01	44	5		1	[Black Trash] The Autobiography Of Kirk Jones		Universal 157990
5/17/03	176	1		2	Decade		D3 9916

STIGERS, Curtis
Born on 10/18/1965 in Hollywood, California; raised in Boise, Idaho. Pop singer/saxophonist.

11/9/91+	101	28		1	Curtis Stigers		Arista 18660

STILLS, Stephen — All-Time: #346

Born on 1/3/1945 in Dallas, Texas. Singer/songwriter/guitarist. Member of **Buffalo Springfield** and **Crosby, Stills & Nash**. Manassas included **Chris Hillman** (guitar; **The Byrds**), Dallas Taylor (drums), Fuzzy Samuels (bass), Paul Harris (organ), Al Perkins (guitar) and Joe Lala (percussion).

DEBUT	PEAK	WKS			Catalog	Label & Number
8/31/68	12	37	●	1 Super Session		Columbia 9701
				MIKE BLOOMFIELD / AL KOOPER / STEVE STILLS		
11/28/70+	3³	39	●	2 Stephen Stills		Atlantic 7202
7/17/71	8	20	●	3 Stephen Stills 2		Atlantic 7206
4/29/72	4	30	●	4 Manassas		Atlantic 903 [2]
5/12/73	26	18		5 Down The Road		Atlantic 7250
				STEPHEN STILLS & MANASSAS (above 2)		
7/5/75	19	17		6 Stills..		Columbia 33575
12/27/75+	42	11		7 Stephen Stills Live .... [L]		Atlantic 18156
5/15/76	31	15		8 Illegal Stills		Columbia 34148
10/9/76	26	18	●	9 Long May You Run		Reprise 2253
				STILLS-YOUNG BAND		
1/8/77	127	5		10 Still Stills-The Best Of Stephen Stills .... [G]		Atlantic 18201
11/11/78	83	4		11 Thoroughfare Gap		Columbia 35380
9/1/84	75	12		12 Right By You		Atlantic 80177

STILLWATER

Rock band from Warner Robins, Georgia: Jimmy Hall (vocals; not to be confused with leader of Wet Willie), Bobby Golden, Michael Causey and Rob Walker (guitars), Bob Spearman (keyboards), Allison Scarborough (bass) and Sebie Lacey (drums).

DEBUT	PEAK	WKS			Catalog	Label & Number
2/10/79	204	1		1 I Reserve The Right..		Capricorn 0210

STING — All-Time: #199

Born Gordon Sumner on 10/2/1951 in Wallsend, Newcastle, England. Pop singer/songwriter/bassist. Lead singer of **The Police**. Acted in the movie *Quadrophenia*, *Dune*, *The Bride* and *Plenty*. Married actress/producer Trudie Styler on 8/20/1992. Nicknamed "Sting" because of a yellow and black jersey he liked to wear.

AWARD: Billboard Century: 2003

DEBUT	PEAK	WKS			Catalog	Label & Number
7/13/85	2⁶	58	▲³	1 The Dream Of The Blue Turtles		A&M 3750
10/31/87	9	52	▲²	2 ...Nothing Like The Sun		A&M 6402 [2]
2/9/91	2¹	39	▲	3 The Soul Cages		A&M 6405
3/27/93	2¹	68	▲³	4 Ten Summoner's Tales		A&M 540070
10/9/93	162	5		5 Demolition Man .... [EP-L]		A&M 540162
				recorded on 7/25/1993 in Italy		
11/26/94	7	38	▲²	6 Fields Of Gold - The Best Of Sting 1984-1994 [G]		A&M 540269
3/30/96	5	34	▲	7 Mercury Falling		A&M 540483
12/13/97	100	13	●	8 The Very Best Of Sting & The Police .... [G]		A&M 540834
10/16/99+	9	90	▲³	9 Brand New Day		A&M 490443
				Grammy: Pop Vocal Album		
12/8/01	32	22	●	10 ...All This Time .... [L]		A&M 493169
				recorded in front of 200 invited guests on 9/11/2001 at Sting's retreat in Tuscany, Italy		
10/19/02	46	6		11 The Very Best Of...Sting & The Police .... Cat:#43/2 [G]		A&M 493252
10/18/03	3¹	27	▲	12 Sacred Love		A&M 001141
10/28/06	25	11		13 Songs From The Labyrinth		DG 007220
11/14/09	6	12	●	14 If On A Winter's Night... [X]		Cherrytree 013329
				Christmas chart: 1/09		

STITES, Gary

Born on 7/23/1940 in Denver, Colorado. Pop singer/songwriter/guitarist.

~ ~ ~ ~ ~ ~ ~ ~ ~ ~ ~ **NON-CHARTED ALBUM** ~ ~ ~ ~ ~ ~ ~ ~ ~ ~ ~ ~
1960 **Lonely For You**

STITT, Sonny

Born Edward Stitt on 2/2/1924 in Boston, Massachusetts. Died on 7/22/1982 (age 58). Jazz saxophonist.

DEBUT	PEAK	WKS			Catalog	Label & Number
4/8/67	172	2		1 What's New!!! .... [I]		Roulette 25343

STONE, Angie

Born on 1/30/1961 in Columbia, South Carolina. R&B singer/keyboardist. Former member of **The Sequence**.

DEBUT	PEAK	WKS			Catalog	Label & Number
10/16/99+	46	34	●	1 Black Diamond		Arista 19092
11/24/01	22	37	●	2 Mahogany Soul		J 20013
7/24/04	14	11		3 Stone Love		J Records 56215
11/3/07	11	8		4 The Art Of Love & War		Stax 30146
12/12/09	133	2		5 Unexpected		Stax 31288

Billboard			R I A A	ARTIST		
DEBUT	PEAK	WKS		Album Title	Catalog	Label & Number

STONE, Doug
Born Douglas Brooks on 6/19/1956 in Marietta, Georgia. Country singer/guitarist. Starred in the 1995 movie *Gordy*.

5/19/90+	97	51	▲	1 Doug Stone		Epic 45303
8/31/91+	74	51	▲	2 I Thought It Was You	Cat:#47/1	Epic 47357
8/29/92	99	34	●	3 From The Heart		Epic 52436
1/23/93	186	1		4 The First Christmas	[X]	Epic 52844
12/4/93+	88	15	●	5 More Love		Epic 57271
12/17/94+	142	12	●	6 Greatest Hits Volume 1	[G]	Epic 66803

STONE, Joss
Born Joscelyn Stoker on 4/11/1987 in Dover, Kent, England. White female soul-styled singer.

10/4/03+	39	49	●	1 The Soul Sessions	[EP]	S-Curve 42234
10/16/04	11	57	▲	2 Mind Body & Soul		S-Curve 94897
4/7/07	2¹	29	●	3 Introducing Joss Stone		Virgin 76268
11/7/09	10	4		4 Colour Me Free!		Virgin 67059

STONE, Kirby, Four
Born on 4/27/1918 in Manhattan, New York. Died on 7/13/1981 (age 63). His vocal group included Eddie Hall, Larry Foster and Mike Gardner.

8/25/58	13	9		1 Baubles, Bangles And Beads		Columbia 1211

STONE, Sly — see SLY & THE FAMILY STONE

STONEBOLT
Pop band from Vancouver, British Columbia, Canada: David Willis (vocals), Ray Roper (guitar), John Webster (keyboards), Dan Atchison (bass) and Brian Lousley (drums).

8/12/78	210	1		1 Stonebolt		Parachute 9006
1/17/81	206	1		2 New Set Of Changes		RCA Victor 3825

STONE CITY BAND
R&B-funk backing band for **Rick James**: Levi Ruffin (vocals), Tom McDermott (guitar), OBX and Erskine Williams (keyboards), Oscar Alston (bass) and Lanise Hughes (drums).

3/22/80	122	8		1 In 'N' Out		Gordy 991
2/7/81	205	3		2 The Boys Are Back		Gordy 1001
				produced by Rick James		

STONE FURY
Hard-rock band formed in Los Angeles, California: Lenny Wolf (vocals), Bruce Gowdy (guitar), Rick Wilson (bass) and Jody Cortez (drums). Wolf formed **Kingdom Come** in 1987.

11/24/84+	144	12		1 Burns Like A Star		MCA 5522

STONEGROUND
Folk-rock band from San Francisco, California: Lynne Hughes, Deirdre LaPorte, Lydia Moreno and Annie Sampson (female vocals), Brian Godula and Cory Lerios (male vocals), Tim Barnes and Sal Valentino (guitars), John Blakeley (bass) and Stephen Price (drums).

1/29/72	205	1		1 Family Album	[L]	Warner 1956 [2]
				recorded on 8/8/1971 in San Francisco, California		

STONE PONEYS — see RONSTADT, Linda

STONE ROSES, The
Alternative-rock band from Manchester, England: Ian Brown (vocal), John Squire (guitar), Gary Mounfield (bass) and Alan Wren (drums).

1/20/90	86	26		1 The Stone Roses	Cat:#48/1	Silvertone 1184
2/4/95	47	13		2 Second Coming		Geffen 24503

STONE SOUR
Hard-rock band formed by **Slipknot** members Corey Taylor (vocals), Jim Root (guitar) and Sid Wilson (bass), with Josh Rand (guitar) and Joel Eckman (drums). By 2006, Shawn Economaki replaced Wilson and Roy Mayorga replaced Eckman.

9/14/02	46	27	●	1 Stone Sour		Roadrunner 618425
8/19/06	4	38	●	2 Come What(ever) May		Roadrunner 618073

STONE TEMPLE PILOTS
Hard-rock band formed in San Diego, California: **Scott Weiland** (vocals; born on 10/27/1967), brothers Dean DeLeo (guitar; born on 8/23/1961) and Robert DeLeo (bass; born on 2/2/1966), and Eric Kretz (drums; born on 6/7/1966). Also see **The Magnificent Bastards** and **Talk Show**.

1/9/93	3²	114	▲⁸	1 Core	Cat:#32/4	Atlantic 82418
6/25/94	❶³	64	▲⁶	2 Purple		Atlantic 82607
4/13/96	4	50	▲²	3 Tiny Music...Songs From The Vatican Gift Shop		Atlantic 82871
11/13/99	6	40	▲	4 No.4		Atlantic 83255
7/7/01	9	10	●	5 Shangri-La Dee Da		Atlantic 83449
11/29/03	26	11		6 Thank You	[G]	Atlantic 83586

Billboard			R I A A	ARTIST		
DEBUT	PEAK	WKS		Album Title	Catalog	Label & Number

STOOGES, The
Highly-influential punk-rock band formed in Detroit, Michigan: **Iggy Pop** (vocals), brothers Ron Asheton (guitar) and Scott Asheton (drums), and Dave Alexander (bass). Disbanded in 1974; reunited in late 2006. Ron Asheton died on 1/6/2009 (age 60).

8/23/69	106	11		1 The Stooges...		Elektra 74051
4/28/73	182	3		2 Raw Power..		Columbia 32111
				IGGY & THE STOOGES		
3/24/07	130	1		3 The Weirdness..		Virgin 64648

~ ~ ~ ~ ~ ~ ~ ~ ~ ~ **NON-CHARTED ALBUM** ~ ~ ~ ~ ~ ~ ~ ~ ~ ~
1970 **Fun House**
RS500 #191

STOOKEY, Paul
Born on 12/30/1937 in Baltimore, Maryland. Folk singer/songwriter/guitarist. Member of **Peter, Paul & Mary**.

| 8/21/71 | 42 | 15 | | 1 Paul And... | | Warner 1912 |
| 2/3/73 | 204 | 4 | | 2 One Night Stand .... [L] | | Warner 2674 |

STORCH, Jeremy
Born in 1947 in Brooklyn, New York. Singer/songwriter/pianist. Later became a rabbi.

| 2/13/71 | 209 | 1 | | 1 From A Naked Window .... | | RCA Victor 4445 |

STORIES
Rock band from Brooklyn, New York: Ian Lloyd (vocals, bass), Steve Love (guitar), Michael Brown (keyboards) and Bryan Madey (drums). Brown was a member of **Left Banke**.

7/1/72	182	9		1 Stories		Kama Sutra 2051
7/28/73	29	19		2 About Us		Kama Sutra 2068
1/19/74	208	2		3 Traveling Underground		Kama Sutra 2078
				IAN LLOYD & STORIES		

STORM, The
Rock band formed in San Francisco, California: Kevin Chalfant (vocals), Gregg Rolie (vocals, keyboards), Josh Ramos (guitar), Ross Valory (bass) and Steve Smith (drums). Rolie was a member of **Santana**. Rolie, Valory and Smith were members of **Journey**. Chalfant was a member of **707**.

| 11/16/91+ | 133 | 17 | | 1 The Storm .... | | Interscope 91741 |

STORM, Gale
Born Josephine Cottle on 4/5/1922 in Bloomington, Texas. Died on 6/27/2009 (age 87). Pop singer/actress. Starred in numerous movie musicals. Star of TV's *My Little Margie* (1952-55) and *The Gale Storm Show* (1956-62). Married to actor Lee Bonnell from 1941-86 (his death).

~ ~ ~ ~ ~ ~ ~ ~ ~ **NON-CHARTED ALBUMS** ~ ~ ~ ~ ~ ~ ~ ~ ~ ~ ~
1956 **Gale Storm**   1958 **Gale's Great Hits**

STORY OF THE YEAR
Rock band from St. Louis, Missouri: Dan Marsala (vocals), Ryan Phillips (guitar), Philip Sneed (guitar), Adam Russell (bass) and Josh Wills (drums).

10/4/03+	51	43	●	1 Page Avenue..		Maverick 48438
5/28/05	138	1		2 Live In The Lou .... [L]		Maverick 48841
10/29/05	19	5		3 In The Wake Of Determination		Maverick 49390
5/10/08	18	5		4 The Black Swan		Epitaph 86928

STRADLIN, Izzy, And The Ju Ju Hounds
Born Jeffrey Isbell on 4/8/1962 in Lafayette, Indiana. Rock singer/guitarist. Former member of **Guns N' Roses**. The Ju Ju Hounds: Rick Richards (guitar), Jimmy Ashhurst (bass) and Charlie Quintana (drums). Richards was a member of the **Georgia Satellites**.

| 10/31/92 | 102 | 9 | | 1 Izzy Stradlin And The Ju Ju Hounds .... | | Geffen 24490 |

STRAIGHT NO CHASER
Acapella group formed in Bloomington, Indiana: Dan Ponce, Mike Itkoff, Randy Stine, Charlie Mechling, Steve Morgan, Jerome Collins, Dave Roberts, Walter Chase, Mike Luginbill and Ryan Ahlwardt.

11/15/08+	46	6		1 Holiday Spirits .... [X]		Atco 515785
				Christmas charts: 4/'08, 7/'09		
12/5/09	68	6		2 Holiday Spirits .... [X-R]		Atco 515785
11/21/09	38	9		3 Christmas Cheers... [X]		Atco 520740
				Christmas chart: 6/'09		

STRAIT, George   **1990s: #4 / 2000s: #3 / All-Time: #22**
Born on 5/18/1952 in Poteet, Texas; raised in Pearsall, Texas. Country singer/guitarist. Served in the U.S. Army from 1972-74. Graduated from Southwest Texas State with a degree in agriculture. Formed the Ace In The Hole band in 1975. Starred as "Dusty Chandler" in the 1992 movie *Pure Country*.
     AWARDS: C&W Hall of Fame: 2006 ★ CMA: Male Vocalist 1985, 1986, 1996 & 1997 / Entertainer 1989 & 1990

3/3/84	163	7	▲	1 Right Or Wrong		MCA 5450
11/10/84	139	16	▲	2 Does Fort Worth Ever Cross Your Mind		MCA 5518
				CMA: Album of the Year		
7/5/86	126	11	▲	3 #7		MCA 5750
2/14/87	117	28	▲²	4 Ocean Front Property		MCA 5913

DEBUT	PEAK	WKS	R I A A	ARTIST Album Title	Catalog	Label & Number
				STRAIT, George — cont'd		
3/19/88	87	14	▲	5 If You Ain't Lovin' (You Ain't Livin')............		MCA 42114
3/4/89	92	24	▲	6 Beyond The Blue Neon....................		MCA 42266
6/2/90	35	42	▲	7 Livin' It Up		MCA 6415
4/6/91	45	49	▲	8 Chill Of An Early Fall		MCA 10204
5/9/92	33	24	▲	9 Holding My Own		MCA 10532
10/3/92	6	129	▲⁵	10 Pure Country	Cat:#47/1 [S]	MCA 10651
10/16/93	5	53	▲²	11 Easy Come, Easy Go		MCA 10907
11/26/94	26	44	▲²	12 Lead On		MCA 11092
5/11/96	7	57	▲²	13 Blue Clear Sky		MCA 11428
				CMA: Album of the Year		
5/10/97	❶¹	57	▲³	14 Carrying Your Love With Me		MCA 11584
				CMA: Album of the Year		
5/9/98	2¹	36	▲²	15 One Step At A Time		MCA Nashville 70020
3/20/99	6	40	▲	16 Always Never The Same		MCA Nashville 70050
10/7/00	7	14	●	17 George Strait		MCA Nashville 170143
11/24/01	9	42	▲	18 The Road Less Traveled		MCA Nashville 170220
6/28/03	5	45	▲	19 Honkytonkville		MCA Nashville 000114
7/16/05	❶¹	34	▲	20 Somewhere Down In Texas		MCA Nashville 004446
10/21/06	3¹	58	▲	21 It Just Comes Natural		MCA Nashville 006023
				CMA: Album of the Year		
4/19/08	❶¹	78	▲	22 Troubadour		MCA Nashville 010826
				Grammy: Country Album ★ CMA: Album of the Year		
8/29/09	❶¹	29	●	23 Twang		MCA Nashville 013173
				CHRISTMAS ALBUMS:		
12/19/87+	17ˣ	14	▲²	24 Merry Christmas Strait To You!	Cat:#17/13	MCA 5800
				Christmas charts: 24/'87, 25/'88, 17/'92, 24/'93, 29/'94		
11/20/99	78	9	●	25 Merry Christmas Wherever You Are	Cat:#45/2	MCA 170093
				Christmas charts: 9/'99, 26/'00, 34/'02, 42/'03		
11/29/08	86	7		26 Classic Christmas		MCA Nashville 011920
				Christmas chart: 5/'08		
				GREATEST HITS & COMPILATIONS:		
4/20/85	157	8	▲⁴	27 Greatest Hits	Cat:#34/5	MCA 5567
9/26/87	68	31	▲³	28 Greatest Hits, Volume Two	Cat:#23/34	MCA 42035
1/18/92	46	19	▲	29 Ten Strait Hits		MCA 10450
9/30/95+	43	39	▲⁸	30 Strait Out Of The Box		MCA 11263 [4]
3/25/00	2¹	34	▲²	31 Latest Greatest Straitest Hits		MCA Nashville 170100
4/13/02	76	18	▲	32 The Best Of George Strait: 20th Century Masters: The Millennium Collection	Cat:#10/21	MCA Nashville 170280
10/23/04	❶²	82	▲⁷	33 50 Number Ones	Cat:❶¹/64	MCA Nashville 000459 [2]
12/1/07	13	26	●	34 22 More Hits	Cat:#13/2	MCA Nashville 010258
				LIVE ALBUMS:		
3/1/03	7	22	●	35 For The Last Time: Live From The Astrodome		MCA Nashville 170319
4/21/07	11	11		36 Live At Texas Stadium		MCA Nashville 005894
				ALAN JACKSON / GEORGE STRAIT / JIMMY BUFFETT		
				STRANGE, Billy Born on 9/29/1930 in Long Beach, California. Session guitarist.		
10/24/64	135	5		1 The James Bond Theme	[I]	GNP Crescendo 2004
7/3/65	146	3		2 English Hits Of '65	[I]	GNP Crescendo 2009
				STRANGELOVES, The Pop trio from New York: writers/producers Bob Feldman, Jerry Goldstein and Richard Gottehrer.		
11/13/65	141	2		1 I Want Candy		Bang 211
				STRANGLERS, The Pop-rock band formed in London, England: Hugh Cornwell (vocals, guitar), Dave Greenfield (keyboards), Jean-Jacques Burnel (bass) and Jet Black (drums).		
7/8/78	210	2		1 Black And White............		A&M 4706
5/2/87	172	4		2 Dreamtime............		Epic 40607
				STRAPPING YOUNG LAD Hard-rock band from Canada: Devin Townsend (vocals, guitar), Jed Simon (guitar), Byron Stroud (bass) and Gene Hoglan (drums).		
7/29/06	200	1		1 The New Black............		Century Media 8427
				STRAWBERRY ALARM CLOCK Psychedelic-rock band formed in Glendale, California: Greg Munford (vocals), Ed King (guitar), Lee Freeman (guitar), Mark Weitz (keyboards), Gary Lovetro (bass) and Randy Seol (drums). King later joined **Lynyrd Skynyrd**. Freeman died of cancer on 2/14/2010 (age 61).		
11/4/67+	11	24		1 Incense And Peppermints		Uni 73014

STRAWBS
Progressive-rock band formed in Leicester, England: David Cousins (vocals), Dave Lambert (guitar), John Hawken (keyboards), Chas Cronk (bass) and Rod Coombes (drums).

7/15/72	191	5	1 Grave New World		A&M 4344
4/28/73	121	9	2 Bursting At The Seams...		A&M 4383
3/2/74	94	17	3 Hero And Heroine..		A&M 3607
3/8/75	47	13	4 Ghosts		A&M 4506
10/11/75	147	6	5 Nomadness		A&M 4544
10/30/76	144	5	6 Deep Cuts		Oyster 1603
8/6/77	175	4	7 Burning For You		Oyster 1604

STRAY CATS
Rockabilly trio from Long Island, New York: **Brian Setzer** (vocals, guitar), Lee Rocker (bass) and Slim Jim Phantom (drums). Also see **Phantom, Rocker & Slick**.

7/3/82	2^{15}	74	▲	1 Built For Speed	EMI America 17070
9/10/83	14	29	●	2 Rant N' Rave With The Stray Cats	EMI America 17102
9/27/86	122	5		3 Rock Therapy	EMI America 17226
4/29/89	111	9		4 Blast Off	EMI 91401

STRAY DOG
Blues-rock band from Texas: Snuffy Walden (vocals, guitar), Timmy Dulaine (guitar), Luis Cabaza (keyboards), Alan Roberts (bass) and Leslie Sampson (drums).

1/4/75	210	1	1 While You're Down There		Manticore 501

STRAYLIGHT RUN
Alternative-rock band from Long Island, New York: brother-and-sister John Nolan (male vocals, guitar) and Michelle Nolan (female vocals, guitar), with Shaun Cooper (bass) and Will Noon (drums).

10/30/04	100	2	1 Straylight Run		Victory 229
10/22/05	168	1	2 Prepare To Be Wrong .... [EP]		Victory 281
7/7/07	72	2	3 The Needles The Space		Universal Rep. 009106

STREEP, Meryl
Born Mary Streep on 6/22/1949 in Summit, New Jersey. Popular movie actress.

4/20/85	180	4	1 The Velveteen Rabbit .... [TV]		Dancing Cat 3007
			MERYL STREEP & GEORGE WINSTON from the PBS-TV animated children's special		

STREET, Greg
Born in Atlanta, Georgia. Rap DJ/producer.

11/3/01	72	4	1 Six O'Clock, Vol. 001		Atlantic 83348
9/9/06	57	3	2 The Champions: The North Meets The South		Deja 34 5815
			DJ KAYSLAY & GREG STREET		

STREET, Janey
Born in Manhattan, New York. Pop-rock singer/songwriter.

11/3/84	145	6	1 Heroes, Angels & Friends		Arista 8219

STREET DOGS
Punk-rock band from Boston, Massachusetts: Mike McColgan (vocals), Marcus Hollar (guitar), Tobe Bean (guitar), Johnny Rioux (bass) and Paul Rucker (drums). McColgan was lead singer of **Dropkick Murphys**.

7/26/08	174	1	1 State Of Grace		Hellcat 80503

STREETLIGHT MANIFESTO
Ska-rock band from East Brunswick, New Jersey: Tom Kalnoky (vocals, guitar), Matt Stewart, Mike Brown and Jim Conti (horns), Pete McCullough (bass) and Chris Thatcher (drums).

12/1/07	154	1	1 Somewhere In The Between..		Victory 329

STREETS
Rock band formed in Atlanta, Georgia: **Steve Walsh** (vocals, keyboards), Mike Slamer (guitar), Billy Greer (bass) and Tim Gehrt (drums). Walsh was a member of **Kansas**.

12/3/83+	166	11	1 1st...		Atlantic 80117
4/13/85	204	3	2 Crimes In Mind		Atlantic 81246

STREETS, The
Born Michael Skinner on 11/27/1978 in Birmingham, England. Electronic musician/composer.

6/5/04	82	4	1 A Grand Don't Come For Free..		Vice 61534
5/13/06	68	2	2 The Hardest Way To Make An Easy Living........................		Vice 63186
10/25/08	154	1	3 Everything Is Borrowed		Vice 80008

STREET SWEEPER SOCIAL CLUB
Rap-rock duo: Robert "Boots" Riley (vocals) and Tom Morello (guitar). Morello (member of **Rage Against The Machine** and **Audioslave**) also recorded as **The Nightwatchman**.

7/4/09	37	3	1 Street Sweeper Social Club..		SSSC 519745

STREISAND, Barbra   1960s: #25 / 1970s: #4 / 1980s: #15 / All-Time: #4

Born on 4/24/1942 in Brooklyn, New York. Popular singer/actress. Starred in several movies and Broadway shows. Nicknamed "Babs." Married to actor Elliott Gould from 1963-71. Married actor James Brolin on 7/1/1998. Recorded in several different styles.

AWARD: Grammys: Legend 1992 / Lifetime Achievement 1995

DEBUT	PEAK	WKS	RIAA	#	Album Title	Catalog	Label & Number
4/13/63	8	101	●	1	**The Barbra Streisand Album**		Columbia 2007 / 8807
					Grammys: Album of the Year / Female Pop Vocal / Hall of Fame		
9/14/63	2³	74	●	2	**The Second Barbra Streisand Album**		Columbia 2054 / 8854
2/29/64	5	74	●	3	**The Third Album**		Columbia 2154 / 8954
10/3/64	❶⁵	84	▲	4	**People**		Columbia 2215 / 9015
					Grammy: Female Pop Vocal		
11/6/65	2³	48	▲	5	**My Name Is Barbra, Two...**		Columbia 2409 / 9209
11/19/66+	5	29	●	6	**Je M'appelle Barbra**		Columbia 2547 / 9347
11/11/67+	12	23	●	7	**Simply Streisand**		Columbia 2682 / 9482
9/6/69	31	17		8	**What About Today?**		Columbia 9816
2/20/71	10	29	▲	9	**Stoney End**		Columbia 30378
9/18/71	11	26	●	10	**Barbra Joan Streisand**		Columbia 30792
2/16/74	❶²	31	▲²	11	**The Way We Were**		Columbia 32801
11/16/74+	13	24	●	12	**ButterFly**		Columbia 33095
11/1/75	12	20	●	13	**Lazy Afternoon**		Columbia 33815
3/6/76	46	14	●	14	**Classical Barbra** [F]		Columbia 33452
7/2/77	3⁴	25	▲²	15	**Streisand Superman**		Columbia 34830
6/17/78	12	27	▲	16	**Songbird**		Columbia 35375
11/3/79	7	26	▲	17	**Wet**		Columbia 36258
10/11/80	❶³	49	▲⁵	18	**Guilty** Cat:#11/4		Columbia 36750
10/27/84	19	28	▲	19	**Emotion**		Columbia 39480
11/23/85+	❶³	50	▲⁴	20	**The Broadway Album**		Columbia 40092
					Grammy: Female Pop Vocal		
11/12/88	10	26	▲	21	**Till I Loved You**		Columbia 40880
7/17/93	❶¹	49	▲²	22	**Back To Broadway**		Columbia 44189
11/29/97	❶¹	27	▲³	23	**Higher Ground**		Columbia 66181
10/9/99	6	23	▲	24	**A Love Like Ours**		Columbia 69601
11/1/03	5	14	●	25	**The Movie Album**		Columbia 89018
10/8/05	5	19	●	26	**Guilty Pleasures**		Columbia 93559
10/17/09	❶¹	14	●	27	**Love Is The Answer**		Columbia 43354
					CHRISTMAS ALBUMS:		
12/19/81+	108	5	▲⁵	28	**A Christmas Album** Cat:#5/52		Columbia 9557
					originally released in 1967; Christmas charts: 1/'67, 3/'68, 15/'69, 7/'70, 6/'71, 1/'73, 2/'83, 5/'84, 3/'85, 5/'87, 5/'88, 8/'89, 9/'90, 6/'91, 9/'92, 17/'93, 13/'94, 16/'95, 17/'96, 16/'97, 31/'98, 31/'99, 19/'07		
12/15/90	167	4		29	**A Christmas Album** [R]		Columbia 9557
11/17/01	15	9	▲	30	**Christmas Memories** Cat:#2¹/9		Columbia 85920
					Christmas charts: 3/'01, 1/'02, 15/'03		
					GREATEST HITS & COMPILATIONS:		
2/28/70	32	30	▲²	31	**Barbra Streisand's Greatest Hits**		Columbia 9968
12/2/78+	❶³	46	▲⁵	32	**Barbra Streisand's Greatest Hits, Volume 2**		Columbia 35679
12/12/81	10	104	▲⁵	33	**Memories** Cat:#44/1		Columbia 37678
10/21/89	26	25	▲²	34	**A Collection Greatest Hits...And More** Cat:#38/8		Columbia 45369
10/12/91	38	16	▲	35	**Just For The Record**		Columbia 44111 [4]
2/16/02	15	9	▲	36	**The Essential Barbra Streisand**		Columbia 86123 [2]
12/14/02	38	14	●	37	**Duets**		Columbia 86126
					LIVE ALBUMS:		
10/12/68	30	20	●	38	**A Happening In Central Park**		Columbia 9710
					recorded on 6/17/1967		
11/18/72+	19	27	▲	39	**Live Concert At The Forum**		Columbia 31760
					recorded on 4/15/1972		
5/9/87	9	28	▲	40	**One Voice**		Columbia 40788
					recorded on 9/6/1986 at her Malibu ranch		
10/15/94	10	22	▲³	41	**The Concert**		Columbia 66109 [2]
5/27/95	81	7	●	42	**The Concert-Highlights**		Columbia 67100
					above 2 recorded in June 1994 at Madison Square Garden in New York City		
10/7/00	21	17	▲	43	**Timeless - Live In Concert**		Columbia 63778 [2]
5/26/07	7	6		44	**Live In Concert 2006**		Columbia 01922

Billboard			R I A A	ARTIST		
DEBUT	PEAK	WKS		Album Title	Catalog	Label & Number

STREISAND, Barbra — cont'd

SOUNDTRACKS:

DEBUT	PEAK	WKS				Label & Number
5/2/64	2³	51	●	45 Funny Girl [OC]		Capitol 2059 / 8859
				Grammys: Cast Album / Hall of Fame		
5/22/65	2³	68	●	46 My Name Is Barbra [TV]		Columbia 2336 / 9136
				Grammy: Female Pop Vocal		
				aired on 4/28/1965		
4/9/66	3²	36	●	47 Color Me Barbra [TV]		Columbia 2478 / 9278
				aired on 3/30/1966		
9/28/68+	12	108	▲	48 Funny Girl		Columbia 3220
11/15/69+	49	33		49 Hello, Dolly!		20th Century Fox 5103
7/25/70	108	24		50 On A Clear Day You Can See Forever		Columbia 30086
2/6/71	186	6		51 The Owl And The Pussycat [T]		Columbia 30401
				comedy dialogue highlights from the movie; background music by **Blood, Sweat & Tears**		
11/24/73	64	16		52 Barbra Streisand...And Other Musical Instruments [TV]		Columbia 32655
				aired on 11/2/1973		
3/29/75	6	25	●	53 Funny Lady		Arista 9004
12/11/76+	❶⁶	51	▲⁴	54 A Star Is Born		Columbia 34403
7/7/79	20	18	●	55 The Main Event		Columbia 36115
11/26/83+	9	26	▲	56 Yentl		Columbia 39152

STRIKERS, The

Funk band from New York: Ruben Faison (vocals), Robert Gilliom (guitar), Robert Rodriguez (guitar), Darryl Gibbs (sax), Howie Young (keyboards), Willie Slaughter (bass) and Milton Brown (drums).

8/29/81	174	3		1 The Strikers		Prelude 14100

STRING-A-LONGS, The

Guitar rock and roll instrumental band from Plainview, Texas: Keith McCormack, Aubrey Lee de Cordova, Richard Stephens and Jimmy Torres (guitars) and Don Allen (drums).

~ ~ ~ ~ ~ ~ ~ ~ ~ ~ ***NON-CHARTED ALBUM*** ~ ~ ~ ~ ~ ~ ~ ~ ~ ~ ~

1961 **Pick A Hit Featuring "Wheels"**

STRING CHEESE INCIDENT, The

Rock band from Boulder, Colorado: Michael Kang (vocals), Bill Nershi (guitar), Kyle Hollingsworth (keyboards), Keith Moseley (bass) and Michael Travis (drums).

6/2/01	147	1		1 Outside Inside		Sci Fidelity 1009
10/11/03	157	1		2 Untying The Not		Sci Fidelity 1015

STROKE 9

Rock band from San Francisco, California: Luke Esterkyn (vocals), John McDermott (guitar), Greg Gueldner (bass) and Eric Stock (drums).

12/18/99+	83	28	●	1 Nasty Little Thoughts		Cherry 53157

STROKES, The

Rock band from Manhattan, New York: **Julian Casablancas** (vocals), **Albert Hammond Jr.** (guitar; son of **Albert Hammond**), Nick Valensi (guitar), Nikolai Fraiture (bass) and Fab Moretti (drums).

10/27/01+	33	58	●	1 Is This It		RCA 68101
				RS500 #367		
11/15/03	4	13	●	2 Room On Fire		RCA 55497
1/21/06	4	11		3 First Impressions Of Earth		RCA 73177

STRUMMER, Joe, & The Mescaleros

Born John Mellor on 8/21/1952 in Ankara, Turkey (British parents). Died of a heart attack on 12/22/2002 (age 50). Punk-rock singer/songwriter/guitarist. Leader of legendary punk band **The Clash**. The Mescaleros: Martin Slattery, Tymon Dogg, Simon Stanford and Scott Shields.

11/8/03	160	1		1 Streetcore		Hellcat 80454

STRUNG OUT

Punk-rock band from Los Angeles, California: Jason Cruz (vocals), Jake Kiley (guitar), Rob Ramos (guitars), Chris Aiken (bass) and Jordan Burns (drums).

5/11/02	185	1		1 An American Paradox		Fat Wreck Chords 633
10/17/09	196	1		2 Agents Of The Underground		Fat Wreck Chords 739

STRUNK, Jud

Born Justin Strunk on 6/11/1936 in Jamestown, New York; raised in Farmington, Maine. Killed in a plane crash on 10/15/1981 (age 45). Singer/songwriter. Regular on TV's *Laugh In*.

5/5/73	138	9		1 Daisy A Day		MGM 4898

STRUNZ & FARAH

Male flamenco guitar duo of Costa Rican Jorge Strunz (of **Caldera**) and Iranian Ardeshir Farah.

3/9/91	164	6		1 Primal Magic [I]		Mesa 79023

STRYPER
Christian hard-rock band from Orange County, California: brothers Michael Sweet (vocals) and Robert Sweet (drums), with Richard "Oz Fox" Martinez (guitar) and Tim Gaines (bass). Disbanded In 1992. Original lineup (minus Gaines) reunited in 2004 with new bass player Tracy Ferrie.

DEBUT	PEAK	WKS	RIAA		Catalog	Label & Number
9/28/85	84	64	●	1 Soldiers Under Command		Enigma 72077
8/23/86	103	30		2 The Yellow And Black Attack! [E]		Enigma 73207
				recordings from 1984		
11/22/86+	32	74	▲	3 To Hell With The Devil		Enigma 73237
7/16/88	32	25	●	4 In God We Trust		Enigma 73317
9/8/90	39	12		5 Against The Law		Enigma 73527
9/3/05	111	1		6 Reborn		Big3 Records 36779
8/8/09	73	2		7 Murder By Pride		Big3 Records 36868

STUART, Marty
Born John Marty Stuart on 9/30/1958 in Philadelphia, Mississippi. Country singer/guitarist. Married **Connie Smith** on 7/8/1997.
AWARD: OPRY: 1992

DEBUT	PEAK	WKS	RIAA		Catalog	Label & Number
5/16/92	193	1	●	1 Tempted		MCA 10106
7/25/92	77	30	●	2 This One's Gonna Hurt You		MCA 10596
4/2/94	141	2		3 Love And Luck		MCA 10880
7/13/96	196	1		4 Honky Tonkin's What I Do Best		MCA 11429

STUART, Mary
Born Mary Stuart Houchins on 7/4/1926 in Miami; raised in Oklahoma City. Died of a stroke on 2/28/2002 (age 75). Actress/singer. Played "Joanne Barron" on TV's *Search For Tomorrow* when she recorded her album below.

DEBUT	PEAK	WKS	RIAA		Catalog	Label & Number
3/19/55	12	2		1 Joanne Sings [EP]		Columbia 487 [2]
				with **Percy Faith** and His Orchestra		

STUDDARD, Ruben
Born on 7/14/1978 in Frankfurt, Germany (U.S. Army base); raised in Birmingham, Alabama. Black male vocalist. Winner on the second season of TV's *American Idol* in 2003.

DEBUT	PEAK	WKS	RIAA		Catalog	Label & Number
12/27/03	❶¹	27	▲	1 Soulful		J Records 54639
12/11/04	20	16	●	2 I Need An Angel		J Records 62623
11/4/06	8	9		3 The Return		J Records 78961
6/6/09	36	4		4 Love Is		19 Records 30100

STUFF
R&B band formed in New York: Richard Tee (keyboards), Gordon Edwards (bass), Cornell Dupree (guitar), **Eric Gale** (guitar), Christopher Parker (drums) and Stephen Gadd (drums). Tee died of cancer on 7/21/1993 (age 49). Gale died of cancer on 5/25/1994 (age 55).

DEBUT	PEAK	WKS	RIAA		Catalog	Label & Number
11/27/76	163	3		1 Stuff [I]		Warner 2968
7/30/77	61	13		2 More Stuff [I]		Warner 3061
5/31/80	205	2		3 Live In New York [I-L]		Warner 3417

STYLE COUNCIL, The
Pop duo from England: Paul Weller (vocals; **The Jam**) and Mick Talbot (keyboards).

DEBUT	PEAK	WKS	RIAA		Catalog	Label & Number
10/22/83	172	5		1 Introducing The Style Council [EP]		Polydor 815277
4/7/84	56	22		2 My Ever Changing Moods		Geffen 4029
6/29/85	123	11		3 Internationalists		Geffen 24061
4/18/87	122	10		4 The Cost Of Loving		Polydor 831443
8/13/88	174	6		5 Confessions Of A Pop Group		Polydor 835785

STYLES
Born David Styles on 11/28/1974 in Corona, Queens, New York. Hardcore rapper. Former member of **The Lox**.

DEBUT	PEAK	WKS	RIAA		Catalog	Label & Number
7/27/02	6	16	●	1 A Gangster And A Gentleman		Ruff Ryders 493339
1/6/07	79	6		2 Time Is Money		Ruff Ryders 005707
12/22/07	52	5		3 Super Gangster (Extraordinary Gentleman)		Phantom 5557
				STYLES P (above 2)		

STYLISTICS, The
R&B vocal group from Philadelphia, Pennsylvania: Russell Thompkins Jr. (lead; born on 3/21/1951), Airrion Love (born on 8/8/1949), James Smith (born on 6/16/1950), James Dunn (born on 2/4/1950) and Herbie Murrell (born on 4/27/1949).

DEBUT	PEAK	WKS	RIAA		Catalog	Label & Number
12/18/71+	23	38	●	1 The Stylistics		Avco 33023
11/11/72+	32	38	●	2 Round 2: The Stylistics		Avco 11006
11/24/73+	66	44		3 Rockin' Roll Baby		Avco 11010
5/25/74	14	31	●	4 Let's Put It All Together		Avco 69001
11/2/74	43	16		5 Heavy		Avco 69004
2/22/75	41	30		6 The Best of The Stylistics	Cat:#34/21 [G]	Avco 69005
6/14/75	72	13		7 Thank You Baby		Avco 69008
11/8/75	99	11		8 You Are Beautiful		Avco 69010
6/19/76	117	6		9 Fabulous		H&L 69013
1/29/77	209	1		10 Once Upon A Jukebox		H&L 69015
11/8/80	127	12		11 Hurry Up This Way Again		TSOP 36470
9/19/81	210	1		12 Closer Than Close		TSOP 37458

STYX
All-Time: #173

Pop-rock band from Chicago, Illinois: **Dennis DeYoung** (vocals, keyboards; born on 2/18/1947), James "J.Y." Young (guitar; born on 11/14/1949), John "J.C." Curulewski (guitar; born on 10/3/1950; died of a brain aneurysm on 2/13/1988, age 37), and twin brothers Chuck Panozzo (bass; born on 9/20/1947) and John Panozzo (drums; born on 9/20/1947; died of a bleeding ulcer on 7/16/1996, age 48). **Tommy Shaw** (vocals, guitar; born on 9/11/1953) replaced Curulewski in 1976. Disbanded in 1984. Reunited in 1990 with guitarist **Glen Burtnick** replacing Shaw, who joined **Damn Yankees**. Todd Sucherman (drums) joined in 1997. Lawrence Gowan replaced DeYoung in 2000. Shaw returned in 2004 to replace Burtnick. In Greek mythology, Styx is a river of Hades.

10/7/72	207	4		1 Styx..	Wooden Nickel 1008
1/25/75	20	19	●	2 Styx II..	Wooden Nickel 1012
				originally released in 1973	
2/9/74	192	2		3 The Serpent Is Rising..	Wooden Nickel 0287
11/9/74	154	12		4 Man Of Miracles..	Wooden Nickel 0638
12/20/75+	58	50	●	5 Equinox..	A&M 4559
10/30/76	66	18	●	6 Crystal Ball..	A&M 4604
7/30/77+	6	127	▲³	7 The Grand Illusion Cat:#22/80	A&M 4637
9/30/78	6	92	▲³	8 Pieces Of Eight	A&M 4724
10/13/79	2¹	60	▲²	9 Cornerstone	A&M 3711
1/31/81	❶³	61	▲³	10 Paradise Theater Cat:#26/60	A&M 3719
3/19/83	3²	34	▲	11 Kilroy Was Here	A&M 3734
10/27/90	63	38	●	12 Edge Of The Century..	A&M 5327
7/17/99	175	1		13 Brave New World..	CMC Int'l. 86275
3/8/03	127	1		14 Cyclorama..	Sanctuary 86337
5/28/05	46	2		15 Big Bang Theory..	New Door 004414
				GREATEST HITS & COMPILATIONS:	
4/15/78	201	17		16 Best Of Styx..	Wooden Nickel 2250
7/5/80	201	7	●	17 Best Of Styx [R]	RCA Victor 3597
9/23/95	138	5	▲²	18 Greatest Hits Cat:#5/76	A&M 540387
5/22/04	136	1		19 Come Sail Away: The Styx Anthology	A&M 002104 [2]
				LIVE ALBUMS:	
4/21/84	31	15		20 Caught In The Act - Live..	A&M 6514 [2]
5/24/97	139	1	●	21 Return To Paradise..	CMC Int'l. 86212 [2]
				recorded at the Rosemont Horizon in Chicago, Illinois	

SUAVE
Born Waymond Anderson Jr. on 2/22/1966 in Los Angeles, California. R&B singer. Son of Waymond Anderson (of **GQ**).

4/23/88	101	12		1 I'm Your Playmate	Capitol 48686

SUBLIME
1990s: #45 / All-Time: #497

Ska-rock trio from Long Beach, California: Brad Nowell (vocals, guitar; born on 2/22/1968; died of a drug overdose on 5/25/1996, age 28), Eric Wilson (bass; born on 2/21/1969) and Floyd "Bud" Gaugh (drums; born on 10/2/1967). After Nowell's death, Wilson and Gaugh formed **Long Beach Dub Allstars**. Also see **Various Artists Compilations:** *Look At All The Love We Found: A Tribute To Sublime.*

8/17/96+	13	104	▲⁵	1 Sublime Cat:#5/309	Gasoline Alley 11413
9/2/06	28ᶜ	1		2 Sublime: 10th Anniversary Deluxe Edition................ [R]	Gasoline Alley 007041 [2]
9/28/96+	140	9	▲²	3 40 Oz. To Freedom .... Cat:#3/125 [E]	Gasoline Alley 11474
				originally released on Skunk 1 in 1992	
10/11/97	169	3		4 What I Got...The 7 Song EP .... [EP]	Gasoline Alley 11678
12/13/97	28	19	▲	5 Second-Hand Smoke	Gasoline Alley 11714
7/11/98	49	10		6 Stand By Your Van - Live In Concert .... [L]	Gasoline Alley 11798
				GREATEST HITS & COMPILATIONS:	
12/5/98	107	2		7 Acoustic - Bradley Nowell And Friends	Gasoline Alley 11889
11/27/99	114	9	●	8 Greatest Hits	Gasoline Alley 112125
12/13/03	190	1	●	9 The Best Of Sublime: 20th Century Masters: The Millennium Collection	Gasoline Alley 112921
12/3/05+	165	4		10 Gold	Chronicles 005667 [2]
12/2/06	97	1		11 Everything Under The Sun	Skunk 007040 [3]

SUBWAY
R&B vocal group from Chicago, Illinois: Eric McNeal, Roy Jones, Keith Thomas and Trerail Puckett.

2/11/95	101	21		1 Good Times	Biv 10 0354

SUE ANN
Born Sue Ann Carwell in Minneapolis, Minnesota. R&B singer.

8/22/81	208	4		1 Sue Ann..	Warner 3562

SUFFOCATION
Death metal band from Long Island, New York: Frank Mullen (vocals), Terrance Hobbs (guitar), Guy Marchais (guitar), Derek Boyer (bass) and Mike Smith (drums).

8/1/09	135	1		1 Blood Oath	Nuclear Blast 2302

SUGA FREE
Born Dejuan Rice on 1/17/1970 in Pomona, California. Male rapper.

3/27/04	72	3		1 The New Testament: The Truth..	Bungalo 00580
5/27/06	194	1		2 Just Add Water	Laneway 970095

Billboard			R I A A	ARTIST		
DEBUT	PEAK	WKS		Album Title	Catalog	Label & Number

SUGAR
Rock trio formed in Athens, Georgia: **Bob Mould** (vocals, guitar), David Barbe (bass) and Malcolm Travis (drums). Mould was a member of **Husker Du**.

4/24/93	130	3		1 Beaster .... **[EP]**		Rykodisc 50260
9/24/94	50	6		2 File Under: Easy Listening		Rykodisc 10300
8/12/95	122	3		3 Besides .... **[K]**		Rykodisc 10321 [2]

SUGAR BEARS
Bubblegum-pop studio production by Jimmy Bowen. **Kim Carnes** wrote and performed vocals for the group. Based on General Foods' "Sugar Crisp" cereal character.

1/22/72	209	1		1 Presenting The Sugar Bears		Big Tree 2009

SUGARCUBES, The
Alternative-rock band from Reykjavik, Iceland: Bjork Gudmundsottir (vocals), Einar Orn Benediktsson (vocals, trumpet), Thor Eldon Jonsson (guitar), Margret Ornolfsdottir (keyboards), Bragi Olafsson (bass) and Siggi Baldursson (drums). Group began as an artist's collective called Kukl (an Icelandic term for witches). Bjork and Thor were married for a time. Thor and Margret married in 1989.

6/18/88	54	29		1 Life's Too Good		Elektra 60801
10/14/89	70	9		2 Here Today, Tomorrow Next Week!		Elektra 60860
3/7/92	95	11		3 Stick Around For Joy		Elektra 61123

SUGARCULT
Rock band from Santa Barbara, California: Tim Pagnotta (vocals, guitar), "Marko 72" DeSantis (guitar), Airin Older (bass) and Ben Davis (drums). Kenny Livingston replaced Davis in 2004.

11/9/02	194	2		1 Start Static		Ultimatum 076673
5/1/04	46	20		2 Palm Trees And Power Lines		Fearless 51512
9/30/06	64	2		3 Lights Out		Fearless 27324

SUGARHILL GANG
Pioneering rap trio from Harlem, New York: Michael "Wonder Mike" Wright, Guy "Master Gee" O'Brien and Henry "Big Bank Hank" Jackson. The first commercially successful rap group.

1/30/82	50	18		1 8th Wonder		SugarHill 249

SUGARLAND
Country trio from Atlanta, Georgia: Jennifer Nettles (vocals), Kristen Hall (guitar) and Kristian Bush (mandolin). Hall left trio in early 2006.
AWARD: CMA: Vocal Duo 2007, 2008 & 2009

2/5/05	16	92	▲³	1 Twice The Speed Of Life .... **Cat:#8/41**		Mercury 002172
11/25/06	4	102	▲³	2 Enjoy The Ride	**Cat:#3/49**	Mercury 007411
8/9/08	❶¹	90	▲²	3 Love On The Inside	**Cat:#31/5**	Mercury 011273
8/22/09	❶¹	16		4 Live On The Inside	**[L]**	Mercury 013191
10/31/09	24	11		5 Gold And Green .... **[X]**		Mercury 013326
				Christmas chart: 3/'09		

SUGARLOAF
Rock band from Denver, Colorado: Jerry Corbetta (vocals, keyboards), Bob Webber (guitar), Bob Raymond (bass) and Bob MacVittie (drums). Myron Pollock replaced MacVittie in 1974.

8/15/70	24	29		1 Sugarloaf		Liberty 7640
2/13/71	111	9		2 Spaceship Earth		Liberty 11010
4/12/75	152	6		3 Don't Call Us-We'll Call You		Claridge 1000
				SUGARLOAF/JERRY CORBETTA		

SUGAR RAY
Rock band from Los Angeles, California: Mark McGrath (vocals), Craig Bullock (DJ), Rodney Sheppard (guitar), Murphy Karges (bass) and Stan Frazier (drums). McGrath was anchor of TV entertainment magazine *Extra* from 2004-08.

7/12/97	12	42	▲²	1 Floored		Lava 83006
1/30/99	17	66	▲³	2 14:59		Lava 83151
6/30/01	6	21	●	3 Sugar Ray		Lava 83414
6/21/03	29	7		4 In The Pursuit Of Leisure		Atlantic 83616
7/9/05	136	3		5 The Best Of Sugar Ray .... **[G]**		Atlantic 74628
8/8/09	80	1		6 Music For Cougars		Pulse 90163

SUGA T
Born Tenina Stevens in San Francisco, California. Female rapper. Member of **The Click**. Sister of **E-40**.

3/16/96	193	1		1 Paper Chasin' (4eva Hustlin')		Jive 41578

SUICIDAL TENDENCIES
Hard-rock band from Venice, California: Mike Muir (vocals), Rocky George (guitar), Mike Clark (guitar), and Robert Trujillo (bass). Muir and Trujillo went on to form **Infectious Grooves**. Trujillo joined **Metallica** in 2003.

5/23/87	100	13		1 Join The Army		Carol 1336
10/1/88	111	12		2 How Will I Laugh Tomorrow When I Can't Even Smile Today		Epic 44288
10/28/89	150	5	●	3 Controlled By Hatred/Feel Like Shit...Deja-Vu		Epic 45244
7/21/90	101	15	●	4 Lights...Camera...Revolution		Epic 45389
7/18/92	52	10		5 The Art Of Rebellion		Epic 48864
7/3/93	117	3		6 Still Cyco After All These Years		Epic 46230
7/2/94	82	3		7 Suicidal For Life		Epic 57774

SUICIDE
Pioneering synth-punk duo from Brooklyn, New York: Alan Vega (vocals) and Martin Rev (electronics).

~ ~ ~ ~ ~ ~ ~ ~ ~ ~ **NON-CHARTED ALBUM** ~ ~ ~ ~ ~ ~ ~ ~ ~ ~ ~
1977 **Suicide**
RS500 #446

SUICIDE MACHINES, The
Rock band from Detroit, Michigan: Jason Navarro (vocals), Dan Lukacinsky (guitar), Royce Nunley (bass) and Derek Grant (drums). Ryan Vandeberghe replaced Grant in 1999.

4/25/98	127	2		1 Battle Hymns		Hollywood 62060
3/4/00	188	1		2 The Suicide Machines		Hollywood 62189

SUICIDE SILENCE
Deathcore band from Riverside, California: Mitch Lucker (vocals), Christopher Garza (guitar), Mark Heylmun (guitar), Daniel Kenny (bass) and Alex Lopez (drums).

10/6/07	94	1		1 The Cleansing..................		Century Media 8388
7/18/09	32	7		2 No Time To Bleed..................		Century Media 8603

SULLIVAN, Jazmine
Born on 4/9/1987 in Philadelphia, Pennsylvania. R&B singer/songwriter.

10/11/08	6	34		1 Fearless		J Records 32713

SULTON, Kasim
Born in 1950 in Brooklyn, New York. Rock singer/bassist. Member of **Utopia** and **Joan Jett & The Blackhearts**.

2/27/82	197	2		1 Kasim		EMI America 17063

SUMAC, Yma
Born Zoila Castillo on 9/10/1922 in Ichocan, Peru. Died of colon cancer on 11/1/2008 (age 86). Female singer. Known for her four-octave singing voice.

4/8/72	205	3		1 Miracles..................		London 608

SUM 41
Punk-rock band from Ajax, Ontario, Canada: Deryck Whibley (vocals, guitar), Dave Baksh (guitar), Jason "Cone" McCaslin (bass) and Steve Jocz (drums). Whibley married **Avril Lavigne** on 7/15/2006.

5/26/01	13	49	▲	1 All Killer No Filler		Island 548662
8/4/01	176	1		2 Half Hour Of Power .... [EP]		Island 542419
12/14/02	32	27	●	3 Does This Look Infected?		Island 063491
10/30/04	10	26	●	4 Chuck		Island 003492
8/11/07	7	9		5 Underclass Hero		Island 008987
4/4/09	154	1		6 All The Good Sh**: 14 Solid Gold Hits .... [G]		Island 012744

SUMMER, Donna
All-Time: #130

Born LaDonna Andrea Gaines on 12/31/1948 in Boston, Massachusetts. R&B singer/songwriter. Dubbed "The Queen of Disco." Acted in European productions of *Hair*, *Godspell*, *The Me Nobody Knows* and *Porgy And Bess*. Married Bruce Sudano (of **Alive & Kicking** and **Brooklyn Dreams**) on 7/16/1980.

11/1/75+	11	30	●	1 Love To Love You Baby		Oasis 5003
3/27/76	21	27	●	2 A Love Trilogy		Oasis 5004
11/6/76	29	26	●	3 Four Seasons Of Love		Casablanca 7038
6/4/77	18	40	●	4 I Remember Yesterday		Casablanca 7056
11/26/77+	26	58	●	5 Once Upon A Time.......................		Casablanca 7078 [2]
9/16/78	❶1	75	▲	6 Live And More [L]		Casablanca 7119 [2]
5/12/79	❶6	49	▲2	7 Bad Girls		Casablanca 7150 [2]
11/3/79+	❶1	39	▲2	8 On The Radio-Greatest Hits-Volumes I & II [G]		Casablanca 7191 [2]
10/11/80	50	15		9 Walk Away - Collector's Edition (The Best Of 1977-1980) .... [G]		Casablanca 7244
11/8/80	13	18	●	10 The Wanderer		Geffen 2000
8/14/82	20	37	●	11 Donna Summer		Geffen 2005
7/16/83	9	32	●	12 She Works Hard For The Money		Mercury 812265
9/22/84	40	17		13 Cats Without Claws		Geffen 24040
10/10/87	122	6		14 All Systems Go		Geffen 24102
5/20/89	53	20		15 Another Place And Time..................		Atlantic 81987
7/10/99	43	13		16 VH1 Presents Donna Summer - Live & More Encore! .... [L]		Epic 69910
10/18/03	111	4		17 The Journey: The Very Best Of Donna Summer .... [G]		Mercury 001009
10/20/07	40	1		18 The Best Of Donna Summer: 20th Century Masters - The Christmas Collection .... [X]		Mercury 005126
6/7/08	17	6		19 Crayons..................		Burgundy 22992

SUMMER, Henry Lee
Born on 7/5/1955 in Brazil, Indiana. Rock singer/songwriter/guitarist.

3/12/88	56	23	1 Henry Lee Summer .... CBS Associated 40895
5/27/89	78	17	2 I've Got Everything .... CBS Associated 45124

SUMMERS, Andy
Born on 12/31/1942 in Lancashire, England. Lead guitarist of **The Police**.

11/6/82	60	11	1 I Advance Masked .... [I] A&M 4913
10/20/84	155	5	2 Bewitched .... [I] A&M 5011
			ANDY SUMMERS & ROBERT FRIPP (above 2)

SUMMERS, Bill, And Summers Heat
Born on 5/20/1948 in Detroit, Michigan. R&B singer/songwriter/percussionist. Formerly with **Herbie Hancock**'s Head Hunters.

4/4/81	129	15	1 Call It What You Want .... MCA 5176
12/12/81+	92	16	2 Jam The Box! .... MCA 5266

SUMMER SET, The
Pop-rock band from Scottsdale, Arizona: Brian Dales (vocals), brothers John Gomez (keyboards) and Stephen Gomez (bass), Josh Montgomery (guitar) and Jess Bowen (drums).

10/31/09	173	1	1 Love Like This .... Razor & Tie 83047

SUN
R&B-funk band from Dayton, Ohio: Byron Byrd (vocals), Sheldon Reynolds (guitar), Anthony Thompson (guitar), Dean Francis (keyboards), Ernie Knisley (percussion), Robert Arnold, Gary King and Larry Hatchet (horns), Don Taylor (bass) and Kym Yancey (drums).

5/6/78	69	22	● 1 Sunburn .... Capitol 11723
7/21/79	85	10	2 Destination: Sun .... Capitol 11941
7/5/80	207	3	3 Sun Over The Universe .... Capitol 12088
5/9/81	205	4	4 Sun: Force Of Nature .... Capitol 12142

SUNDAYS, The
Pop-rock band from London, England: Harriet Wheeler (vocals), David Gavurin (guitar), Paul Brindley (bass) and Patrick Hannan (drums).

5/26/90	39	23	● 1 Reading, Writing And Arithmetic .... DGC 24277
11/7/92	103	25	● 2 Blind .... DGC 24479
10/11/97	33	17	3 Static & Silence .... DGC 25131

SUN KIL MOON
Born Mark Kozelek on 1/24/1967 in Massillon, Ohio. Pop-rock singer/songwriter.

4/19/08	127	2	1 April .... Caldo Verde 006

SUNNY & THE SUNLINERS
Latin group from San Antonio, Texas: Sunny Ozuna, with brothers Jesse, Oscar and Ray Villanueva, Tony Tostado, Gilbert Fernandez and Alred Luna. Originally known as Sunny & The Sunglows.

11/2/63	142	2	1 Talk To Me .... Tear Drop 2000
8/14/65	148	2	2 The Original Peanuts .... [I] Sunglow 103
			THE SUNGLOWS

SUNNY DAY REAL ESTATE
Rock trio from Seattle, Washington: Dan Hoerner (vocals, guitar), Jeff Palmer (bass) and William Goldsmith (drums). Goldsmith later joined the **Foo Fighters**.

10/10/98	132	1	1 How It Feels To Be Something On .... Sub Pop 409
7/8/00	97	2	2 The Rising Tide .... Time Bomb 43541

SUNRIZE
Soul-funk band from Cincinnati, Ohio: Ronnie Scruggs (vocals), Dave Townsend (guitar), Kevin Jones (congas), Tony Herbert (bass) and Everett Collins (drums). Former backing band for **The Isley Brothers**.

10/23/82	206	3	1 Sunrize .... Boardwalk 33257

SUNSCREEM
Techno-pop band from Essex, England: Lucia Holm (vocals), Darren Woodford (guitar), Paul Carnell (keyboards), Rob Fricker (bass) and Sean Wright (drums).

3/20/93	141	5	1 O3 .... Columbia 53449

SUNSET RUBDOWN
Art-rock band formed in Montreal, Quebec, Canada: Spencer Krug (male vocals), Camilla Wynne Ingr (female vocals), Michael Doerksen (guitar), Mark Nicol (bass) and Jordan Robson-Cramer (drums).

7/11/09	108	1	1 Dragonslayer .... Jagjaguwar 140

SUNSHINE BAND, The — see KC

SUNSHINE COMPANY, The
Adult Contemporary band formed in Los Angeles, California: Mary Nance (vocals), Doug "Red" Mark (guitar), Maury Manseau (guitar), Larry Sims (bass) and Merle Brigante (drums). Mark later formed **Redeye**.

10/21/67	126	10	1 Happy Is The Sunshine Company .... Imperial 12359

SUNZ OF MAN
Rap group from Brooklyn, New York: **Killah Priest**, 60 Second Assassin, Prodigal Sunn and Hell Razah.

8/8/98	20	7	1 The Last Shall Be First .... Red Ant 12305

SUPERCHICK
Christian rock band from Los Angeles, California: sisters Tricia Brock (vocals) and Melissa Brock (guitar), with Max Hsu (keyboards), Dave Ghazarian (guitar), Matt Dally (bass) and Brandon Estelle (drums).

4/16/05	126	1		1 Beauty From Pain..		Inpop 71279
7/12/08	65	2		2 Rock What You Got...		Inpop 71436

SUPERDRAG
Rock band from Knoxville, Tennessee: John Davis (vocals), Brandon Fisher (guitar), Tom Pappas (bass) and Don Coffey (drums).

8/3/96	158	5		1 Regretfully Yours		Elektra 61900

SUPERGRASS
Rock band from Oxford, England: brothers Gareth "Gaz" Coombes (vocals, guitar) and Rob Coombes (keyboards), with Mick Quinn (bass) and Danny Goffey (drums).

3/1/03	195	1		1 Life On Other Planets		Island 063685

SUPERJOINT RITUAL
Hard-rock band formed in Texas: Phil Anselmo (vocals, guitar; **Pantera**), Jimmy Bower (guitar), Kevin Bond (guitar), **Hank Williams III** (bass) and Joe Fazzio (drums). Anselmo and Bower were also with **Down**. Williams is the son of **Hank Williams Jr.** and the grandson of **Hank Williams**.

6/8/02	87	3		1 Use Once And Destroy		Sanctuary 70001
8/9/03	55	4		2 A Lethal Dose Of American Hatred		Sanctuary 70022

SUPERNAW, Doug
Born on 9/26/1960 in Bryan, Texas. Country singer/songwriter/guitarist.

8/7/93+	147	28	●	1 Red And Rio Grande		BNA 66133

SUPERSAX
Jazz band formed in Los Angeles, California: Med Flory, Bill Perkins, Warne Marsh and Jay Migliori (saxophones), Conte Candoli (trumpet), Ron Bright (piano), Bud Clark (bass) and Jake Hanna (drums). Flory was also a popular character actor. Hanna died on 2/13/2010 (age 78).

7/14/73	169	7		1 Supersax Plays Bird .... [I]		Capitol 11177
				Grammy: Jazz Album		
4/6/74	182	3		2 Supersax Plays Bird, Volume 2/Salt Peanuts .... [I]		Capitol 11271

SUPERSTAR KIDZ
Studio group featuring vocalists Michele Fischer, Renee Sandstrom, Marco Marinangeli, Julie Griffin, Kelly Hansen, Michael Morabito, Chaka Blackmon and Randy Crenshaw. Sandstrom was a member of **Wild Orchid**.

8/23/03	59	5		1 Superstar Kidz		Walt Disney 860087

SUPERTRAMP
All-Time: #429

Pop-rock band formed in England: **Roger Hodgson** (vocals, guitar; born on 2/3/1950), Rick Davies (vocals, keyboards; born on 7/22/1944), John Helliwell (sax; born on 2/15/1945), Dougie Thomson (bass; born on 3/24/1951) and Bob Siebenberg (drums; born on 10/31/1949). Thomson is the brother of **Ali Thomson**. Hodgson left in 1983.

3/4/78	158	5		1 Supertramp .... [E]		A&M 4665
				recorded in 1970		
12/7/74+	38	76	●	2 Crime Of The Century		A&M 3647
12/13/75+	44	28		3 Crisis? What Crisis?		A&M 4560
4/23/77	16	49	●	4 Even In The Quietest Moments...		A&M 4634
3/31/79	❶⁶	88	▲⁴	5 Breakfast In America		A&M 3708
10/11/80	8	26	●	6 Paris .... [L]		A&M 6702 [2]
				recorded on 11/29/1979 at the Paris Pavillon		
11/13/82	5	28	●	7 Famous Last Words		A&M 3732
6/1/85	21	22		8 Brother Where You Bound		A&M 5014
10/31/87	101	11		9 Free As A Bird		A&M 5181

SUPREMES, The
1960s: #14 / All-Time: #34

R&B vocal trio from Detroit, Michigan: Diana Ross (born on 3/26/1944), **Mary Wilson** (born on 3/6/1944) and Florence Ballard (born on 6/30/1943; died of heart failure on 2/22/1976, age 32). Cindy Birdsong (of **Patti LaBelle**'s Blue Belles) replaced Ballard in 1967. Jean Terrell replaced Ross in late 1969. Lynda Laurence replaced Birdsong in 1972. Terrell and Laurence left in 1973. Mary Wilson re-formed group with Scherrie Payne (sister of **Freda Payne**) and Cindy Birdsong.
AWARD: R&R Hall of Fame: 1988

9/19/64+	2⁴	89		1 Where Did Our Love Go		Motown 621
11/28/64+	21	21		2 A Bit Of Liverpool..		Motown 623
3/20/65	79	8		3 The Supremes Sing Country Western & Pop		Motown 625
5/8/65	75	19		4 We Remember Sam Cooke..		Motown 629
8/21/65	6	37		5 More Hits By The Supremes		Motown 627
12/11/65	6ˣ	12		6 Merry Christmas .... [X]		Motown 638
				Christmas charts: 6/'65, 13/'66, 19/'67, 26/'70		
3/19/66	8	55		7 I Hear A Symphony		Motown 643
9/24/66	❶²	60		8 The Supremes A' Go-Go		Motown 649
2/18/67	6	29		9 The Supremes Sing Holland-Dozier-Holland		Motown 650
6/17/67	20	19		10 The Supremes Sing Rodgers & Hart		Motown 659

DEBUT	PEAK	WKS	RIAA	ARTIST / Album Title	Catalog	Label & Number
				DIANA ROSS & THE SUPREMES:		
4/27/68	18	29		11 Reflections		Motown 665
10/5/68	150	12		12 Funny Girl		Motown 072
11/30/68+	2[1]	32	●	13 Diana Ross & The Supremes Join The Temptations		Motown 679
				DIANA ROSS & THE SUPREMES WITH THE TEMPTATIONS		
12/14/68+	14	21		14 Love Child		Motown 670
12/28/68+	❶[1]	34	●	15 TCB [TV]		Motown 682
				DIANA ROSS & THE SUPREMES WITH THE TEMPTATIONS		
6/21/69	24	18		16 Let The Sunshine In		Motown 689
10/25/69	28	18		17 Together		Motown 692
				DIANA ROSS & THE SUPREMES WITH THE TEMPTATIONS		
11/29/69+	33	20		18 Cream Of The Crop		Motown 694
12/6/69	38	12		19 On Broadway [TV]		Motown 699
				DIANA ROSS & THE SUPREMES WITH THE TEMPTATIONS		
6/6/70	25	19		20 Right On		Motown 705
10/17/70	113	16		21 The Magnificent 7		Motown 717
				SUPREMES & FOUR TOPS		
10/24/70+	68	17		22 New Ways But Love Stays		Motown 720
6/26/71	85	10		23 Touch		Motown 737
6/26/71	154	6		24 The Return Of The Magnificent Seven		Motown 736
1/8/72	160	6		25 Dynamite		Motown 745
				SUPREMES & FOUR TOPS (above 2)		
5/27/72	54	15		26 Floy Joy		Motown 751
11/25/72+	129	13		27 The Supremes		Motown 756
6/28/75	152	8		28 The Supremes		Motown 828
5/22/76	42	15		29 High Energy		Motown 863
				GREATEST HITS & COMPILATIONS:		
9/30/67	❶[5]	89		30 Diana Ross And The Supremes Greatest Hits		Motown 663 [2]
1/10/70	31	25		31 Diana Ross & The Supremes Greatest Hits, Volume 3		Motown 702
6/29/74	66	15	●	32 Anthology (1962-1969)		Motown 794 [3]
				RS500 #431		
4/7/84	35[C]	8		33 Great Songs And Performances That Inspired The Motown 25th Anniversary Television Special		Motown 5313
5/17/86	112	17		34 25th Anniversary		Motown 5381 [3]
2/21/04	72	5		35 The No. 1's Cat:#48/1		Motown 001368
3/28/09	142	1		36 The Definitive Collection		Universal Motown 011732
				LIVE ALBUMS:		
11/13/65+	11	54		37 The Supremes At The Copa		Motown 636
10/5/68+	57	18		38 Live At London's Talk Of The Town		Motown 676
5/16/70	46	18		39 Farewell		Motown 708 [2]
				recorded on 1/14/1970 at the Frontier Hotel in Las Vegas, Nevada		

~ ~ ~ ~ ~ ~ ~ ~ ~ ~ **NON-CHARTED ALBUM** ~ ~ ~ ~ ~ ~ ~ ~ ~ ~

1962 **Meet The Supremes**

SURFACE

R&B trio from New Jersey: Bernard Jackson (vocals, bass), David Townsend (guitar, keyboards) and Dave Conley (drums, sax). Townsend died on 10/26/2005 (age 50).

DEBUT	PEAK	WKS	RIAA	Album Title	Label & Number
5/30/87	55	19		1 Surface	Columbia 40374
11/26/88+	56	39	▲	2 2nd Wave	Columbia 44284
11/24/90+	65	34	●	3 3 Deep	Columbia 46772

SURFARIS, The

Teen rock and roll-surf band from Glendora, California: Ron Wilson (drums), Jim Fuller (guitar), Bob Berryhill (guitar), Pat Connolly (bass) and Jim Pash (sax, clarinet). Wilson died of a brain aneurysm on 5/19/1989 (age 44).

DEBUT	PEAK	WKS	Album Title	Label & Number
8/10/63	15	51	1 Wipe Out [I]	Dot 25535
11/30/63	94	11	2 The Surfaris Play Wipe Out And Others [I]	Decca 74470
3/7/64	120	5	3 Hit City 64	Decca 74487

SURVIVOR

Pop-rock band formed in Chicago, Illinois: Dave Bickler (vocals), Frankie Sullivan (guitar), Jim Peterik (keyboards), Stephan Ellis (bass) and Marc Droubay (drums). Peterik was lead singer for **Ides Of March**. Jimi Jamison replaced Bickler in 1983. Droubay and Ellis left in early 1988.

DEBUT	PEAK	WKS	RIAA	Album Title	Label & Number
3/29/80	169	7		1 Survivor	Scotti Brothers 7107
10/24/81	82	25		2 Premonition	Scotti Brothers 37549
6/26/82	2[4]	41	▲	3 Eye Of The Tiger	Scotti Brothers 38062
10/22/83	82	9		4 Caught In The Game	Scotti Brothers 38791
9/29/84+	16	61	▲	5 Vital Signs	Scotti Brothers 39578
11/8/86	49	24		6 When Seconds Count	Scotti Brothers 40457
11/5/88	187	2		7 Too Hot To Sleep	Scotti Brothers 44282

SUSAN

Rock band from Boston, Massachusetts: brothers Charles Leland (vocals, bass) and Mick Leland (drums), with Ricky Byrd (guitar) and Tom Dickie (guitar). Byrd later joined **Joan Jett & The Blackhearts**.

DEBUT	PEAK	WKS	Album Title	Label & Number
5/5/79	169	5	1 Falling In Love Again	RCA Victor 3372

Billboard			R I A A	ARTIST Album Title	Catalog	Label & Number
DEBUT	PEAK	WKS				
				SUSAN OF SESAME STREET		
				Born Loretta Long on 6/3/1940 in Paw Paw, Michigan; later based in Boston, Massachusetts. Joined the cast of TV's *Sesame Street* (as "Susan Robinson") in 1969.		
8/1/70	86	13		1 Susan Sings Songs From Sesame Street		Scepter 584
				SUTHERLAND, Joan		
				Born on 11/7/1926 in Sydney, Australia. Legendary opera singer.		
12/18/65	22ˣ	2		1 Joy Of Christmas... [X]		London 25943
				with the New Philharmonia Orchestra; Richard Bonynge, conductor		
				SUTHERLAND BROTHERS AND QUIVER		
				Rock and roll band formed in England: brothers Iain Sutherland (vocals, guitar) and Gavin Sutherland (vocals, bass), with their four-piece group Quiver: Tim Renwick (guitar), Pete Wood (keyboards), Bruce Thomas (bass) and Willie Wilson (drums). Quiver disbanded in 1977 and Thomas joined **Elvis Costello**'s Attractions.		
8/18/73	77	17		1 Lifeboat		Island 9326
5/11/74	193	3		2 Dream Kid		Island 9341
5/8/76	195	2		3 Reach For The Sky..		Columbia 33982
				SWAMP DOGG		
				Born Jerry Williams on 7/12/1942 in Portsmouth, Virginia. R&B singer/producer. Member of **Xmas Balls**.		
5/8/71	205	2		1 Rat On!		Elektra 74089
				SWAN, Billy		
				Born on 5/12/1942 in Cape Girardeau, Missouri. Singer/songwriter/keyboardist.		
12/7/74+	21	16		1 I Can Help..		Monument 33279
11/1/75	205	3		2 Rock 'N' Roll Moon..		Monument 33805
				SWANN, Bettye		
				Born Betty Jean Champion on 10/24/1944 in Shreveport, Louisiana. R&B singer.		
				~ ~ ~ ~ ~ ~ ~ ~ ~ ~ **NON-CHARTED ALBUM** ~ ~ ~ ~ ~ ~ ~ ~ ~ ~ ~ ~		
				1967 **Make Me Yours**		
				SWANSON, Brad, & His Whispering Organ Sound		
				Born in Buffalo, New York. Male organist.		
10/18/69	185	2		1 Quentin's Theme... [I]		Thunderbird 9004
				SWARDSON, Nick		
				Born on 10/9/1976 in Minneapolis, Minnesota. Stand-up comedian/actor.		
11/10/07	156	2		1 Party .... [C]		Comedy Central 0056
11/7/09	191	1		2 Seriously, Who Farted? .... [C]		Comedy Central 0089
				SWAY & KING TECH		
				Male rap duo from San Francisco, California: rapper Sway Calloway and DJ King Tech.		
7/3/99	107	7		1 This Or That		Interscope 90292
				SWEAT, Keith **All-Time: #326**		
				Born on 7/22/1961 in Harlem, New York. R&B singer/songwriter/producer. Graduate of New York City College. Worked as a commodities broker for Paine Webber. Member of the short-lived funk group, Jamilah, in 1984. Member of **LSG**.		
1/9/88	15	67	▲³	1 Make It Last Forever		Vintertainment 60763
6/30/90	6	62	▲²	2 I'll Give All My Love To You		Vintertainment 60861
12/14/91	19	33	▲	3 Keep It Comin'		Elektra 61216
7/16/94	8	23	▲	4 Get Up On It		Elektra 61550
7/13/96	5	62	▲⁴	5 Keith Sweat		Elektra 61707
10/10/98	6	27	▲	6 Still In The Game		Elektra 62262
12/2/00	16	19	●	7 Didn't See Me Coming		Elektra 62515
8/31/02	14	12		8 Rebirth...		Elektra 62785
2/22/03	86	4		9 Keith Sweat Live .... [L]		Elektra 62855
1/31/04	31	24	●	10 The Best Of Keith Sweat: Make You Sweat...................................... Cat:#24/7 [G]		Elektra 73954
5/31/08	10	8		11 Just Me		Keia 106556
				SWEAT BAND		
				Spin-off of **George Clinton**'s Parliament/Funkadelic groups. Core members: **Bootsy** Collins, **Fred Wesley**, Maceo Parker, Bernie Worrell, Joel Johnson and Carl Smalls. Parker had been with **James Brown**. Smalls had been in **The Undisputed Truth** and **The Dramatics**.		
12/13/80+	150	8		1 Sweat Band..		Uncle Jam 36857
				SWEATHOG		
				Rock band formed in Los Angeles, California: Lenny Goldsmith (vocals, keyboards), Bob Morris (guitar), Dave Johnson (bass) and Barry Frost (drums).		
7/10/71	216	1		1 Sweathog		Columbia 30601
2/19/72	211	4		2 Hallelujah		Columbia 31144
				SWEET		
				Rock and roll band formed in England: Brian Connolly (vocals; born on 10/5/1944; died of liver failure on 2/9/1997, age 51), Andy Scott (guitar, keyboards; born on 7/30/1949), Steve Priest (bass; born on 2/23/1950) and Mick Tucker (drums; born on 7/17/1947; died of leukemia on 2/14/2002, age 54).		
7/28/73	191	4		1 The Sweet		Bell 1125
7/26/75	25	44	●	2 Desolation Boulevard		Capitol 11395

Billboard DEBUT	PEAK	WKS	R I A A	ARTIST Album Title	Catalog	Label & Number
				SWEET — cont'd		
3/6/76	27	13		3 Give Us A Wink..		Capitol 11496
5/14/77	151	4		4 Off The Record		Capitol 11636
2/18/78	52	28		5 Level Headed		Capitol 11744
5/12/79	151	5		6 Cut Above The Rest		Capitol 11929
				SWEET, Matthew Born on 10/6/1964 in Lincoln, Nebraska. Pop-rock singer/bassist/drummer. Member of **The Thorns**.		
2/29/92	100	29	●	1 Girlfriend		Zoo 11015
7/31/93	75	7		2 Altered Beast		Zoo 11050
4/1/95	65	25	●	3 100% Fun		Zoo 11081
4/12/97	66	5		4 Blue Sky On Mars		Volcano 31130
10/30/99	188	1		5 In Reverse		Volcano 31154
5/6/06	192	1		6 Under The Covers		Shout! Factory 97654
8/8/09	106	1		7 Under The Covers: Vol. 2		Shout! Factory 11306
				MATTHEW SWEET & SUSANNA HOFFS (above 2)		
9/13/08	162	1		8 Sunshine Lies		Shout! Factory 31094
				SWEET, Rachel Born on 7/28/1962 in Akron, Ohio. Pop singer/actress.		
8/4/79	97	9		1 Fool Around		Stiff 36101
3/22/80	123	11		2 Protect The Innocent		Stiff 36337
9/5/81	124	7		3 ...And Then He Kissed Me		ARC 37077
				SWEETBACK Trio consisting of the musicians from **Sade**'s band: Stuart Matthewman (guitar, sax), Andrew Hale (keyboards) and Paul Denman (bass).		
3/8/97	169	5		1 Sweetback .... [I]		Epic 67492
				SWEET F.A. Hard-rock band from New York: Steve DeLong (vocals), Jon Huffman (guitar), James Thunder (guitar), Jim Quick (bass) and Tricky Lane (drums).		
9/15/90	161	10		1 Stick To Your Guns		MCA 6400
				SWEET INSPIRATIONS, The R&B vocal group formed in New Jersey: **Cissy Houston**, Estelle Brown, Sylvia Shemwell and Myrna Smith. Houston is the mother of **Whitney Houston**.		
4/6/68	90	6		1 The Sweet Inspirations		Atlantic 8155
				SWEETNAM, Skye Born on 5/5/1988 in Bolton, Ontario, Canada. Female teen pop-rock singer.		
10/9/04	124	1		1 Noise From The Basement		Capitol 81681
				SWEET SENSATION R&B band from Manchester, England: Marcel King (lead vocals), St. Clair Palmer, Vincent James and Junior Daye (backing vocals), Garry Shaughnessy (guitar), Leroy Smith (keyboards), Barry Johnson (bass) and Roy Flowers (drums). King died on 10/5/1995 (age 37). Smith died on 1/15/2009 (age 57).		
5/3/75	163	7		1 Sad Sweet Dreamer		Pye 12110
				SWEET SENSATION Female dance trio from the Bronx, New York: Betty LeBron, and sisters Margie and Mari Fernandez. Sheila Bega replaced Mari in 1989.		
10/8/88+	63	32		1 Take It While It's Hot		Atco 90917
4/28/90	78	23		2 Love Child		Atco 91307
				SWEET TEE Born Toi Jackson in Queens, New York. Female rapper.		
2/25/89	169	13		1 It's Tee Time...		Profile 1269
				SWEET THUNDER R&B band from Youngstown, Ohio: Booker Newberry (vocals, keyboards), Charles Buie (guitar), Rudell Alexander (bass) and John Aaron (drums).		
7/15/78	125	11		1 Sweet Thunder		Fantasy 9547
				SWEET THURSDAY Rock band from England: Jon Mark (vocals, guitar), Alun Davies (guitar), **Nicky Hopkins** (keyboards), Brian Odgers (bass) and Harvey Burns (drums). Hopkins died on 9/6/1994 (age 50).		
5/12/73	214	2		1 Sweet Thursday...		Great Western G 32039
				SWEETWATER Folk-rock band from Los Angeles, California: **Nancy Nevins** (vocals), R.G. Carlyle (guitar), Albert Moore (flute), Pete Cobain (conga), August Burns (cello), Alex Del Zeppo (keyboards), Fred Herrera (bass) and Alan Malarowitz (drums). The 1999 VH-1 TV movie *Sweetwater* was based on the band's career.		
9/13/69	200	2		1 Sweetwater		Reprise 6313
1/23/71	202	2		2 Just For You		Reprise 6417

SWELL SEASON, The — see HANSARD, Glen, & Marketa Irglova

Billboard DEBUT	PEAK	WKS	RIAA	ARTIST / Album Title	Catalog	Label & Number

SWIFT, Taylor
Born on 12/13/1989 in Reading, Pennsylvania. Female teen country singer/songwriter/guitarist. Played "Samantha Kenny" in the 2010 movie *Valentine's Day*.
AWARD: CMA: Horizon 2007 / Entertainer 2009 / Female Vocalist 2009

DEBUT	PEAK	WKS	RIAA	Album Title	Catalog	Label & Number
11/11/06+	5	186↑	▲⁴	1 Taylor Swift		Big Machine 120702
12/8/07	46	4		2 Sounds Of The Season: The Taylor Swift Holiday Collection.. Cat:#2¹/7 [X-EP]		Big Machine 70012
				Christmas charts: 14/'07, 27/'08, 1/'09		
12/5/09	20	8		3 Sounds Of The Season: The Taylor Swift Holiday Collection .... [X-EP-R]		Big Machine 70012
8/2/08	9	21		4 Beautiful Eyes [EP]		Big Machine 0140
11/29/08	❶¹¹	79↑	▲⁶	5 Fearless		Big Machine 0200
				Grammy: Album / Country Album		

SWIMMING POOL Q's, The
Rock band from Atlanta, Georgia: Anne Richmond Boston (vocals, keyboards), Jeff Calder (guitar), Bob Elsey (guitar), J.E. Garnett (bass) and Billy Burton (drums).

DEBUT	PEAK	WKS	RIAA	Album Title	Catalog	Label & Number
10/20/84	202	5		1 The Swimming Pool Q's		A&M 5015

SWINGING BLUE JEANS, The
Rock and roll band from Liverpool, England: Ray Ennis (vocals, guitar), Ralph Ellis (guitar), Les Braid (bass) and Norman Kuhlke (drums). Braid died of cancer on 7/31/2005 (age 64).

DEBUT	PEAK	WKS	RIAA	Album Title	Catalog	Label & Number
5/30/64	90	9		1 Hippy Hippy Shake		Imperial 12261

SWINGIN' MEDALLIONS
Rock and roll band from Greenwood, South Carolina: John McElrath (vocals), Jimbo Dores (guitar), Brent Forston (organ), Carroll Bledsoe, Charlie Webber and Steve Caldwell (horns), Jim Perkins (bass) and Joe Morris (drums). Caldwell died of cancer on 1/28/2002 (age 54). Webber died of cancer on 1/17/2003 (age 57).

DEBUT	PEAK	WKS	RIAA	Album Title	Catalog	Label & Number
7/30/66	88	12		1 Double Shot (Of My Baby's Love)		Smash 67083

SWINGLE SINGERS, The
Born Ward Swingle on 9/21/1927 in Mobile, Alabama; later based in Paris, France. Pianist/saxophonist. Formed his scat-singing group in 1962.
AWARD: Grammy: Best New Artist 1963

DEBUT	PEAK	WKS	RIAA	Album Title	Catalog	Label & Number
10/26/63+	15	74		1 Bach's Greatest Hits		Philips 600097
				Grammy: Choral Group		
5/30/64	65	17		2 Going Baroque		Philips 600126
				Grammy: Choral Group		
2/20/65	140	6		3 Anyone For Mozart?		Philips 600149
				Grammy: Choral Group		

SWING OUT SISTER
Pop-dance trio formed in England: Corinne Drewery (vocals), Andy Connell (keyboards) and Martin Jackson (drums). Jackson left in 1989.

DEBUT	PEAK	WKS	RIAA	Album Title	Catalog	Label & Number
8/29/87+	40	43	●	1 It's Better To Travel		Mercury 832213
5/27/89	61	19		2 Kaleidoscope World		Fontana 838293
9/19/92	113	11		3 Get In Touch With Yourself		Fontana 512241

SWITCH
R&B-funk band from Mansfield, Ohio: Philip Ingram (vocals), brothers Bobby DeBarge (keyboards) and Tommy DeBarge (bass), Greg Williams and Eddie Fluellen (horns) and Jody Sims (drums). The DeBarges are brothers to the family group **DeBarge**. Bobby DeBarge died of AIDS on 8/16/1995 (age 36).

DEBUT	PEAK	WKS	RIAA	Album Title	Catalog	Label & Number
9/2/78	37	33		1 Switch		Gordy 980
6/2/79	37	36		2 Switch II		Gordy 988
4/12/80	57	14		3 Reaching For Tomorrow		Gordy 993
11/15/80+	85	17		4 This Is My Dream		Gordy 999
11/21/81	174	4		5 Switch V		Gordy 1007

SWITCHFOOT
Christian hard-rock band from San Diego, California: brothers **Jon Foreman** (vocals, guitar) and Tim Foreman (bass), with Jerome Fontamillas (keyboards) and Chad Butler (drums). Jon Foreman also formed **Fiction Family**.

DEBUT	PEAK	WKS	RIAA	Album Title	Catalog	Label & Number
3/15/03+	16	118	▲²	1 The Beautiful Letdown .... Cat:#7/10		Red Ink 71083
10/1/05	3¹	20	●	2 Nothing Is Sound		Columbia 94581
1/13/07	18	10		3 Oh! Gravity		Columbia 82880
11/22/08	123	1		4 The Best Yet [G]		Columbia 38346
11/28/09	13	11		5 Hello Hurricane		Atlantic 522070

SWIZZ BEATZ
Born Kasseem Dean on 8/30/1978 in the Bronx, New York; raised in Atlanta, Georgia. Male rap producer. Member of **Ruff Ryders**.

DEBUT	PEAK	WKS	RIAA	Album Title	Catalog	Label & Number
9/8/07	7	6		1 One Man Band Man		Universal Motown 008895

SWOLLEN MEMBERS
Hip-hop trio from Vancouver, British Columbia, Canada: Shane "Mad Child" Bunting, Prevail and Rob The Viking.

DEBUT	PEAK	WKS	RIAA	Album Title	Catalog	Label & Number
11/14/09	146	1		1 Armed To The Teeth		Battle Axe 136

SWORD, The
Heavy metal band from Austin, Texas: John Cronise (vocals, guitar), Kyle Shutt (guitar), Bryan Richie (bass) and Trivett Wingo (drums).

DEBUT	PEAK	WKS	RIAA	Album Title	Catalog	Label & Number
4/19/08	102	3		1 Gods Of The Earth		Kemado 071

Billboard DEBUT	PEAK	WKS	R I A A	ARTIST / Album Title	Catalog	Label & Number
				SWV (Sisters With Voices) Female R&B vocal trio from Brooklyn, New York. Cheryl "**Coko**" Gamble, Tamara Johnson and Leanne Lyons. Johnson married professional football player Eddie George on 6/20/2004 and was a contestant on the 2009 TV show *Survivor: Tocantins.*		
1/23/93	8	71	▲³	1 It's About Time		RCA 66074
5/28/94	92	10	●	2 The Remixes [EP-K]		RCA 66401
5/11/96	9	25	▲	3 New Beginning		RCA 66487
8/30/97	24	25	●	4 Release Some Tension		RCA 67525
				SYBIL Born Sybil Lynch on 6/2/1965 in Paterson, New Jersey. R&B singer.		
10/21/89	75	24		1 Sybil		Next Plateau 1018
				SYKES, Keith Born in 1948 in Murray, Kentucky; raised in Memphis, Tennessee. Rockabilly singer/songwriter.		
11/22/80	147	11		1 I'm Not Strange I'm Just Like You		Backstreet 3265
2/6/82	205	3		2 It Don't Hurt To Flirt		Backstreet 5277
				SYLK-E. FYNE Born in Los Angeles, California. Female rapper.		
4/11/98	121	12		1 Raw Sylk		RCA 67551
				SYLVAIN, Sylvain Born Sylvain Mizrahi on 2/14/1951 in Cairo, Egypt; raised in Brooklyn, New York. Rock singer/guitarist. Member of the **New York Dolls** (1973-74).		
2/16/80	123	8		1 Sylvain Sylvain		RCA Victor 3475
				SYLVERS, Foster Born on 2/25/1962 in Memphis, Tennessee. Member of **The Sylvers**.		
7/21/73	159	7		1 Foster Sylvers		Pride 0027
				SYLVERS, The R&B family vocal group from Memphis, Tennessee: Olympia-Ann, Leon, Charmaine, James, Edmund, Ricky, Angelia, Pat, Jonathon and **Foster Sylvers**. Leon formed the group **Dynasty** in 1979. Edmund died of lung cancer on 3/11/2004 (age 47).		
3/3/73	180	7		1 The Sylvers		Pride 0007
8/4/73	164	5		2 The Sylvers II		Pride 0026
2/14/76	58	25		3 Showcase		Capitol 11465
11/20/76	80	18		4 Something Special		Capitol 11580
11/26/77+	134	13		5 New Horizons		Capitol 11705
9/16/78	132	8		6 Forever Yours		Casablanca 7103
				SYLVESTER Born Sylvester James on 9/6/1947 in Los Angeles, California. Died of AIDS on 12/16/1988 (age 41). Male disco singer.		
8/5/78	28	42	●	1 Step II		Fantasy 9556
4/28/79	63	15		2 Stars		Fantasy 9579
11/24/79+	123	12		3 Living Proof [L] recorded on 3/11/1979 in San Francisco, California		Fantasy 79010 [2]
9/27/80	147	8		4 Sell My Soul		Honey 9601
7/11/81	156	4		5 Too Hot To Sleep		Honey 9606
3/19/83	168	5		6 All I Need		Megatone 1005
2/14/87	164	5		7 Mutual Attraction		Warner 25527
				SYLVIA Born Sylvia Vanderpool on 3/6/1936 in Harlem, New York. R&B singer/songwriter/producer. One-half of **Mickey & Sylvia** duo.		
6/2/73	70	12		1 Pillow Talk		Vibration 126
				SYLVIA Born Sylvia Kirby on 12/9/1956 in Kokomo, Indiana. Country singer/songwriter.		
5/9/81	139	11		1 Drifter		RCA Victor 3986
8/7/82	56	33	●	2 Just Sylvia		RCA Victor 4312
6/18/83	77	11		3 Snapshot		RCA Victor 4672
4/28/84	178	4		4 Surprise		RCA Victor 4960
				SYMPHONY X Hard-rock band from Middletown, New Jersey: Russell Allen (vocals), Michael Romeo (guitar), Michael Pinnella (keyboards), Michael Lepond (bass) and Jason Rullo (drums).		
7/14/07	123	1		1 Paradise Lost		Inside Out 7925
				SYNDICATE OF SOUND Garage-rock band from San Jose, California: Don Baskin (vocals), Jim Sawyers (guitar), John Sharkey (guitar), Bob Gonzalez (bass) and John Duckworth (drums).		
8/27/66	148	2		1 Little Girl		Bell 6001
				SYNERGY Electronic equipment performed and programmed by New Jersey native Larry Fast.		
6/21/75	66	18		1 Electronic Realizations For Rock Orchestra [I]		Passport 98009
6/26/76	144	11		2 Sequencer [I]		Passport 98014
9/16/78	146	6		3 Cords [I]		Passport 6000

			R I A	ARTIST Album Title	Catalog	Label & Number
DEBUT	PEAK	WKS				

SYREETA
Born Syreeta Wright on 2/28/1946 in Pittsburgh, Pennsylvania. Died of cancer on 7/6/2004 (age 58). R&B singer/songwriter. Married to **Stevie Wonder** from 1972-74.

8/12/72	185	8		1 Syreeta		MoWest 113
7/20/74	116	17		2 Stevie Wonder Presents Syreeta		Motown 808
				above 2 produced by Stevie Wonder		
5/17/80	73	15		3 Syreeta		Tamla 372
8/8/81	127	9		4 Billy Preston & Syreeta		Motown 958
1/30/82	189	3		5 Set My Love In Motion		Tamla 376

SYSTEM, The
Techno-funk-dance duo based in New York: Mic Murphy (vocals, guitar) and David Frank (synthesizer).

3/12/83	94	23		1 Sweat		Mirage 90062
3/31/84	182	5		2 X-Periment		Mirage 90146
4/18/87	62	25		3 Don't Disturb This Groove		Atlantic 81691

SYSTEMATIC
Hard-rock band from San Francisco, California: Adam Ruppel (vocals, guitar), Tim Narducci (guitar), Nick St. Dennis (bass) and Shaun Bannon (drums).

| 6/9/01 | 143 | 1 | | 1 Somewhere In Between | | TMC 62595 |

SYSTEM OF A DOWN
Alternative-metal rock band from Los Angeles, California: **Serj Tankian** (vocals; born on 8/21/1967), Daron Malakian (guitar; born on 7/18/1975), Shavo Odadjian (bass; born on 4/22/1974) and John Dolmayan (drums; born on 7/15/1973). Malakian and Dolmayan also formed **Scars On Broadway**.

10/2/99+	124	33	▲	1 System Of A Down	Cat:#9/65	American 68924
9/22/01	❶[1]	91	▲[3]	2 Toxicity	Cat:❶[1]/64	American 62240
12/14/02	15	22	▲	3 Steal This Album!	Cat:#23/1	American 87062
6/4/05	❶[1]	44	▲	4 Mezmerize		American 90648
12/10/05	❶[1]	28	▲	5 Hypnotize		American 93871

SZABO, Gabor
Born on 3/8/1936 in Budapest, Hungary. Died on 2/26/1982 (age 45). Jazz guitarist.

1/28/67	140	4		1 Spellbinder	[I]	Impulse! 9123
1/13/68	194	2		2 The Sorcerer	[I-L]	Impulse! 9146
				recorded on 4/14/1967 at The Jazz Workshop in Boston, Massachusetts		
6/15/68	157	3		3 Bacchanal	[I]	Skye 3
8/16/69	143	7		4 Gabor Szabo 1969	[I]	Skye 9
5/16/70	162	10		5 Lena & Gabor		Skye 15
				LENA HORNE & GABOR SZABO		
5/19/73	202	6		6 Mizrab	[I]	CTI 6026

T

TACO
Born Taco Ockerse on 7/21/1955 in Jakarta, Indonesia (to Dutch parents). Techno-pop singer.

| 7/23/83 | 23 | 24 | | 1 After Eight | | RCA Victor 4818 |

TAG TEAM
Hip-hop duo from Atlanta, Georgia: Cecil "DC The Brain Supreme" Glenn and "Steve Roll'n" Gibson.

| 8/7/93 | 39 | 40 | ● | 1 Whoomp! (There It Is) | | Life 78000 |

TAINTSTICK
Hard-rock band from Hollywood, California: Jason Ellis (vocals), Michael Tully (guitar), Josh Richmond (bass) and Christian Hand (drums).

| 11/14/09 | 120 | 1 | | 1 6lbs. Of Sound | | Suburban Noize 157 |

TAKE 6
Contemporary gospel group from Alabama: Claude McKnight, Mark Kibble, Mervyn Warren, Cedric Dent, David Thomas and Alvin Chea. McKnight is older brother of **Brian McKnight**.

3/11/89	71	19	▲	1 Take 6		Reprise 25670
				Grammy: Soul Gospel Album		
9/29/90	72	18		2 So Much 2 Say		Reprise 25892
				Grammy: Soul Gospel Album		
12/7/91+	100	6		3 He Is Christmas	Cat:#48/2 [X]	Reprise 26665
				Grammy: Jazz Vocal Album		
				Christmas charts: 11/'91, 23/'92		
7/16/94	86	13	●	4 Join The Band		Reprise 45497
				Grammy: Soul Gospel Album		

TAKE THAT
"Boy band" from England: Gary Barlow, Howard Donald, Jason Orange, Mark Owen and **Robbie Williams**.

| 9/16/95 | 69 | 19 | | 1 Nobody Else | | Arista 18800 |

TAKING BACK SUNDAY
Punk-rock band from Amityville, Long Island, New York: Adam Lazzara (vocals), Ed Reyes (guitar), Mark O'Connell (keyboards), Shaun Cooper (bass) and John Nolan (drums).

2/1/03	183	1	●	1 Tell All Your Friends .... Cat:#23/13	Victory 176
8/14/04	3[1]	26	●	2 Where You Want To Be	Victory 228
11/17/07	141	1		3 Notes From The Past .... [K]	Victory 381
5/13/06	2[1]	26	●	4 Louder Now	Warner 49424
6/20/09	7	8		5 New Again	Warner 516894

TALKING HEADS
All-Time: #309
New-wave/rock band formed in New York: **David Byrne** (vocals, guitar; born on 5/14/1952), **Jerry Harrison** (keyboards, guitar; born on 2/21/1949), Tina Weymouth (bass; born on 11/22/1950) and Chris Frantz (drums; born on 5/8/1951). Harrison was a member of **The Modern Lovers**. Husband-and-wife Weymouth and Frantz (married on 6/18/1977) also formed **Tom Tom Club**.

AWARD: R&R Hall of Fame: 2002

10/8/77+	97	29		1 Talking Heads: 77 .... Cat:#25/25	Sire 6036
				RS500 #290	
8/12/78	29	42	●	2 More Songs About Buildings And Food .... Cat:#19/18	Sire 6058
				RS500 #382	
9/1/79	21	30	●	3 Fear Of Music	Sire 6076
11/1/80	19	27	●	4 Remain In Light	Sire 6095
				RS500 #126	
4/17/82	31	14		5 The Name Of This Band Is Talking Heads .... Cat:#23/1 [L]	Sire 3590 [2]
6/25/83	15	51	▲	6 Speaking In Tongues	Sire 23883
9/22/84	41	118	▲[2]	7 Stop Making Sense .... [L-S]	Sire 25121
				RS500 #345	
				recorded December 1983 at The Pantages Theatre in Hollywood, California	
7/6/85	20	77	▲[2]	8 Little Creatures	Sire 25305
10/4/86	17	29	●	9 True Stories	Sire 25512
4/2/88	19	21	●	10 Naked	Sire 25654
10/31/92	158	2		11 Popular Favorites 1976-1992: Sand In The Vaseline .... [G]	Sire 26760 [2]
9/4/04	36[C]	3		12 The Best Of Talking Heads .... [G]	Sire 76488
5/30/09	73	2		13 Same As It Ever Was .... [G]	Starbucks 8319

TALK SHOW
Rock band formed in Los Angeles, California: Dave Coutts (vocals), brothers Dean DeLeo (guitar) and Robert DeLeo (bass), and Eric Kretz (drums). The latter three were members of **Stone Temple Pilots**. The DeLeo brothers later formed **Army Of Anyone**.

9/20/97	131	3	1 Talk Show	Atlantic 83040

TALK TALK
Pop-rock band from England: Mark Hollis (vocals), Simon Brenner (keyboards), Paul Webb (bass) and Lee Harris (drums). Brenner left in 1983.

9/18/82	132	16	1 The Party's Over	EMI America 17083
4/7/84	42	22	2 It's My Life	EMI America 17113
3/22/86	58	17	3 The Colour Of Spring	EMI America 17179

TAMAR
Born Tamar Braxton on 3/17/1977 in Severn, Maryland. Female R&B singer. Sister of **Toni Braxton**. Member of **The Braxtons**.

4/8/00	127	4	1 Tamar	DreamWorks 50110

TA MARA & THE SEEN
Dance band from Minneapolis, Minnesota: Margaret "Ta Mara" Cox (vocals), Oliver Leiber (guitar), Gina Fellicetta (keyboards), Keith Woodson (bass) and Jamie Chez (drums). Leiber is the son of songwriter Jerry Leiber (of Leiber & Stoller).

11/2/85+	54	25	1 Ta Mara & The Seen	A&M 5078

TAMIA
Born Tamia Washington on 5/9/1975 in Windsor, Ontario, Canada. Female R&B singer.

5/2/98	67	24		1 Tamia..	Qwest 46213
11/11/00	46	28	●	2 A Nu Day	Elektra 62516
4/24/04	17	9		3 More..	Elektra 62847
12/2/06	66	15		4 Between Friends	Plus 1 3784

TAMS, The
R&B "beach music" group from Atlanta, Georgia: brothers Charles and Joseph (lead singer) Pope, with Robert Smith, Floyd Ashton and Horace Key. Ashton replaced by Albert Cottle in 1963. Joseph Pope died on 3/16/1996 (age 63).

~ ~ ~ ~ ~ ~ ~ ~ ~ ~ **NON-CHARTED ALBUM** ~ ~ ~ ~ ~ ~ ~ ~ ~ ~

1964 **Presenting The Tams**

TANEGA, Norma
Born on 1/30/1939 in Vallejo, California. White pop-folk singer/songwriter/pianist/guitarist.

~ ~ ~ ~ ~ ~ ~ ~ ~ ~ **NON-CHARTED ALBUM** ~ ~ ~ ~ ~ ~ ~ ~ ~ ~

1966 **Walkin' My Cat Named Dog**

TANGERINE DREAM
Progressive-rock band formed in Germany by Edgar Froese. Varying lineup also included Christopher Franke (1971-87), Peter Baumann (1972-77), Steve Jollife (1978-84), Klaus Kreiger (1978), Johannes Schmoelling (1979-84) and Paul Haslinger (1985).

7/6/74	196	2	1 Phaedra.. [I]	Virgin 13108
4/2/77	158	7	2 Stratosfear .... [I]	Virgin 34427

Billboard			R I A A	ARTIST		
DEBUT	PEAK	WKS		Album Title	Catalog	Label & Number

TANGERINE DREAM — cont'd

7/23/77	153	6		3 Sorcerer	[I-S]	MCA 2277
12/3/77	178	2		4 Encore	[I-L]	Virgin 35014 [2]
5/9/81	115	10		5 Thief	[I-S]	Elektra 521
11/21/81	195	2		6 Exit	[I]	Elektra 557
5/17/86	96	7		7 Legend	[I-S]	MCA 6165

TANGIER
Hard-rock band from Philadelphia, Pennsylvania: Bill Mattson (vocals), Doug Gordon (guitar), Gari Saint (guitar), Garry Nutt (bass) and Bobby Bender (drums).

| 7/29/89 | 91 | 17 | | 1 Four Winds .... | | Atco 91251 |
| 3/16/91 | 187 | 5 | | 2 Stranded... | | Atco 91603 |

TANK
Born Durrell Babbs on 1/1/1976 in Milwaukee, Wisconsin; raised in Clinton, Maryland. Male R&B singer/songwriter.

3/31/01	7	25	●	1 Force Of Nature		Blackground 50404
11/16/02	20	6		2 One Man		Blackground 064692
6/2/07	2¹	18		3 Sex Love And Pain		Blackground 008982

TANKIAN, Serj
Born on 8/21/1967 in Beirut, Lebanon; later based in Los Angeles, California. Lead singer of **System Of A Down**.

| 11/10/07 | 4 | 20 | | 1 Elect The Dead | | Serjical Strike 286076 |

TANNER, Marc, Band
Born on 8/20/1952 in Hollywood, California. Pop-rock singer/songwriter/guitarist.

| 3/3/79 | 140 | 8 | | 1 No Escape .... | | Elektra 168 |

TANON, Olga
Born on 4/13/1967 in San Juan, Puerto Rico. Female singer. Married to pro baseball player Juan Gonzalez from 1997-99.

5/4/96	170	2	●	1 Nuevos Senderos	[F]	WEA Latina 13667
5/24/97	175	1		2 Llevame Contigo	[F]	WEA Latina 18733
11/14/98	111	2		3 Te Acordaras De Mi	[F]	WEA Latina 25098
5/21/05	196	1		4 Una Nueva Mujer	[F]	Sony Discos 95679
10/28/06	126	2		5 Soy Como Tu	[F]	La Calle 330023

TANTRIC
Rock band from Louisville, Kentucky: Hugo Ferreira (vocals), Todd Whitener (guitar), Jesse Vest (bass) and Matt Taul (drums). The latter three were members of **Days Of The New**.

3/3/01	71	46	●	1 Tantric		Maverick 47978
3/13/04	56	4		2 After We Go		Maverick 48351
5/10/08	91	2		3 The End Begins		Silent Majority 30844
8/22/09	101	1		4 Mind Control		Silent Majority 10007

TANTRUM
Rock band from Chicago, Illinois: Barb Erber, Sandy Caulfield and Pam Bradley (vocals), Ray Sapko (guitar), Phil Balsano (keyboards), Bill Syniar (bass) and Vern Wennerstrom (drums).

| 3/17/79 | 209 | 2 | | 1 Tantrum.. | | Ovation 1735 |
| 1/19/80 | 199 | 3 | | 2 Rather Be Rockin' .... | | Ovation 1747 |

TAPES 'N TAPES
Rock band from Minneapolis, Minnesota: Josh Grier (vocals, guitar), Matt Kretzman (keyboards), Erik Appelwick (bass) and Jeremy Hanson (drums).

| 4/26/08 | 116 | 1 | | 1 Walk It Off .... | | XL 338 |

TAPROOT
Hard-rock band from Ann Arbor, Michigan: Steve Richards (vocals), Mike DeWolf (guitar), Phil Lipscomb (bass) and Jarrod Montague (drums).

7/15/00	160	2		1 Gift		Atlantic 83341
11/2/02	17	21		2 Welcome		Atlantic 83561
9/3/05	33	6		3 Blue-Sky Research...		Velvet Hammer 83720
10/4/08	65	1		4 Our Long Road Home		Velvet Hammer 001

TARNEY/SPENCER BAND, The
Pop-rock duo from Australia: Alan Tarney (vocals, guitar, keyboards) and Trevor Spencer (drums).

| 7/29/78 | 174 | 4 | | 1 Three's A Crowd .... | | A&M 4692 |
| 5/12/79 | 181 | 4 | | 2 Run For Your Life.. | | A&M 4757 |

TARRIERS, The
Folk trio formed in New York: Erik Darling (tenor, banjo), Bob Carey (bass, guitar) and future movie actor Alan Arkin (baritone, guitar). Darling replaced **Pete Seeger** in **The Weavers**, 1958-62, then formed **The Rooftop Singers**. Darling died on 8/2/2008 (age 74).

~ ~ ~ ~ ~ ~ ~ ~ ~ ~ **NON-CHARTED ALBUM** ~ ~ ~ ~ ~ ~ ~ ~ ~ ~ ~ ~
1957 **The Tarriers** [*"The Banana Boat Song"*]

TASH
Born Rico Smith in 1971 in Los Angeles, California. Male rapper. Member of **Tha Alkaholiks**.

| 12/11/99 | 148 | 2 | | 1 Rap Life .... | | Loud 63836 |

TASTE
Rock trio from Ireland: **Rory Gallagher** (vocals, guitar), Richard McCracken (bass) and John Wilson (drums).

8/16/69	133	9		1 Taste		Atco 296

TASTE OF HONEY, A
R&B-disco band from Los Angeles, California: Janice Johnson (vocals, guitar), Hazel Payne (vocals, bass), Perry Kibble (keyboards) and Donald Johnson (drums). By 1980, reduced to a duo Janice Johnson and Hazel Payne. Kibble died of heart failure on 2/23/1999 (age 49).
AWARD: Grammy: Best New Artist 1978

6/17/78	6	27	▲	1 A Taste of Honey		Capitol 11754
7/14/79	59	13		2 Another Taste		Capitol 11951
8/2/80+	36	32		3 Twice As Sweet		Capitol 12089
4/24/82	73	12		4 Ladies Of The Eighties		Capitol 12173

T.A.T.U.
Female teen dance-rock duo from Moscow, Russia: Julia Volkova and Lena Katina.

1/18/03	13	33	●	1 200 KM/H In The Wrong Lane		Interscope 064107
10/29/05	131	1		2 Dangerous And Moving		Interscope 005381

TAUPIN, Bernie
Born on 5/22/1950 in Sleaford, Lincolnshire, England. Singer/songwriter. Main lyricist for **Elton John** since 1969.

3/4/72	217	1		1 Bernie Taupin		Elektra 75020

TAVARES
Family R&B vocal group from New Bedford, Massachusetts: brothers Ralph Tavares (born on 12/10/1941), Antone "Chubby" Tavares (born on 6/2/1945), Feliciano "Butch" Tavares (born on 5/18/1948), Arthur "Pooch" Tavares (born on 11/12/1943) and Perry Lee "Tiny" Tavares (born on 10/24/1949). Butch was formerly married to actress/singer Lola Falana.

2/9/74	160	8		1 Check It Out		Capitol 11258
9/21/74+	121	23		2 Hard Core Poetry		Capitol 11316
8/9/75	26	17		3 In The City		Capitol 11396
6/12/76	24	31		4 Sky High!		Capitol 11533
4/30/77	59	22		5 Love Storm		Capitol 11628
10/15/77	72	10		6 The Best Of Tavares .... [G]		Capitol 11701
5/13/78	115	8		7 Future Bound		Capitol 11719
2/3/79	92	11		8 Madam Butterfly		Capitol 11874
3/8/80	75	7		9 Supercharged		Capitol 12026
1/10/81	205	1		10 Love Uprising		Capitol 12117
12/11/82+	137	11		11 New Directions		RCA Victor 4357
10/15/83	208	1		12 Words And Music		RCA Victor 4700

TAVERNER CONSORT
Orchestra formed in England in 1973 by Andrew Parrott. Named after 16th century composer John Taverner.

10/11/08	8^X	3		1 Christmas Carols [X]		Virgin Classics 03680 [4]

TAXXI
Rock trio from England: David Cumming (vocals, guitar), Colin Payne (keyboards) and Jeff Nead (drums).

12/25/82+	161	11		1 States Of Emergency		Fantasy 9617
10/15/83	210	1		2 Foreign Tongue		Fantasy 9628

TAYLOR, Alex
Born on 2/28/1947 in Boston, Massachusetts. Died of a heart attack on 3/12/1993 (age 46). Singer/songwriter/guitarist. Brother of **James Taylor**, **Kate Taylor** and **Livingston Taylor**.

3/20/71	190	2		1 With Friends And Neighbors		Capricorn 860

TAYLOR, Andy
Born on 2/16/1961 in Cullercoats, England; raised in Wolverhampton, England. Rock singer/guitarist. Member of **Duran Duran** and **The Power Station**.

3/28/87	46	17		1 Thunder		MCA 5837

TAYLOR, James   1970s: #14 / All-Time: #59
Born on 3/12/1948 in Boston, Massachusetts. Singer/songwriter/guitarist. Brother of **Alex Taylor**, **Kate Taylor** and **Livingston Taylor**. Married to **Carly Simon** from 1972-83 and actress Kathryn Walker from 1985-95. Appeared in the 1971 movie *Two Lane Blacktop*.
AWARDS: R&R Hall of Fame: 2000 ★ Billboard Century: 1998

2/6/71	74	8		1 James Taylor And The Original Flying Machine-1967 .... [E]		Euphoria 2
10/3/70	62	28		2 James Taylor .... [E]		Apple 3352
				recorded in 1968		
3/14/70	3^4	102	▲^3	3 Sweet Baby James		Warner 1843
				Grammy: Hall of Fame ★ RS500 #103		
5/8/71	2^4	45	▲^2	4 Mud Slide Slim And The Blue Horizon		Warner 2561
11/25/72+	4	25	●	5 One Man Dog		Warner 2660

Billboard			R I A A	ARTIST		
DEBUT	PEAK	WKS		Album Title	Catalog	Label & Number

TAYLOR, James — cont'd

DEBUT	PEAK	WKS	RIAA	#	Album Title	Catalog	Label & Number
7/13/74	13	18		6	Walking Man		Warner 2794
5/31/75	6	27	●	7	Gorilla		Warner 2866
7/4/76	16	24	●	8	In The Pocket		Warner 2912
12/4/76+	23	42	▲11	9	Greatest Hits	Cat:❶5/751 [G]	Warner 2979
7/9/77	4	39	▲3	10	JT		Columbia 34811
5/12/79	10	23	▲	11	Flag		Columbia 36058
3/21/81	10	23	▲	12	Dad Loves His Work		Columbia 37009
11/23/85	34	30	▲	13	That's Why I'm Here		Columbia 40052
2/13/88	25	34	▲	14	Never Die Young		Columbia 40851
10/19/91	37	47	▲	15	New Moon Shine		Columbia 46038
8/28/93	20	24	▲2	16	(Live)	[L]	Columbia 47056 [2]
6/7/97	9	24	▲	17	Hourglass		Columbia 67912
					Grammy: Pop Vocal Album		
11/25/00	97	12	●	18	Greatest Hits Volume 2	[G]	Columbia 85223
8/31/02	4	25	▲	19	October Road		Columbia 63584
4/26/03	11	42	●	20	The Best Of James Taylor	Cat:#42/2 [G]	Warner 73837
10/28/06	16	12	●	21	James Taylor At Christmas	Cat:#6/15 [X]	Columbia 00323
					Christmas charts: 3/06, 9/07, 21/08, 36/09		
12/19/09	146	3		22	James Taylor At Christmas	[X-R]	Columbia 00323
12/1/07	17	13	●	23	One Man Band		Starcon 30516
10/18/08	4	16		24	Covers		Hear 30829
4/25/09	122	2		25	Other Covers	[EP]	Hear 31385

TAYLOR, Johnnie
Born on 5/5/1938 in Crawfordsville, Arkansas. Died of a heart attack on 5/31/2000 (age 62). R&B singer. With gospel group the Highway QC's in Chicago, early 1950s. In vocal group the Five Echoes; recorded for Sabre in 1954. In the Soul Stirrers gospel group before going solo. First solo recording for SAR in 1961. Nicknamed "The Soul Philosopher."

DEBUT	PEAK	WKS	RIAA	#	Album Title		Label & Number
1/25/69	42	18		1	Who's Making Love...		Stax 2005
4/26/69	126	9		2	Raw Blues		Stax 2008
7/5/69	109	6		3	The Johnnie Taylor Philosophy Continues		Stax 2023
12/19/70	141	5		4	Johnnie Taylor's Greatest Hits	[G]	Stax 2032
4/17/71	112	11		5	One Step Beyond		Stax 2030
7/14/73	54	20		6	Taylored In Silk		Stax 3014
6/8/74	182	8		7	Super Taylor		Stax 5509
3/13/76	5	28	▲	8	Eargasm		Columbia 33951
3/19/77	51	11		9	Rated Extraordinaire		Columbia 34401
1/7/78	202	4		10	Disco 9000		Columbia 35004
5/6/78	164	6		11	Ever Ready		Columbia 35340
7/27/96	108	18		12	Good Love		Malaco 7480
6/17/00	140	15		13	Gotta Get The Groove Back		Malaco 7499

TAYLOR, Kate
Born on 8/15/1949 in Boston, Massachusetts. Singer/songwriter/guitarist. Sister of **James Taylor**, **Alex Taylor** and **Livingston Taylor**.

DEBUT	PEAK	WKS		#	Album Title		Label & Number
3/27/71	88	8		1	Sister Kate		Cotillion 9045

TAYLOR, Kathy
Born in Houston, Texas. Contemporary Christian singer/songwriter.

DEBUT	PEAK	WKS		#	Album Title		Label & Number
2/14/09	190	1		1	Live: The Worship Experience	[L]	Katco 984178

TAYLOR, Little Johnny
Born Johnny Merrett on 2/11/1943 in Gregory, Arkansas; raised in Memphis, Tennessee and Los Angeles, California. Died of diabetes on 5/17/2002 (age 59). Blues singer/songwriter/harmonica player.

DEBUT	PEAK	WKS		#	Album Title		Label & Number
11/9/63	140	2		1	Little Johnny Taylor		Galaxy 203

TAYLOR, Livingston
Born on 11/21/1950 in Boston, Massachusetts. Singer/songwriter/guitarist. Brother of **James Taylor**, **Alex Taylor** and **Kate Taylor**.

DEBUT	PEAK	WKS		#	Album Title		Label & Number
7/25/70	82	20		1	Livingston Taylor		Atco 334
12/18/71+	147	10		2	Liv		Capricorn 863
11/3/73	189	5		3	Over The Rainbow		Capricorn 0114
12/23/78+	202	13		4	3-Way Mirror		Epic 35540

TAYLOR, Mick
Born on 1/17/1949 in Hatfield, Herefordshire, England. Rock singer/guitarist. Member of **The Rolling Stones** from 1969-74.

DEBUT	PEAK	WKS		#	Album Title		Label & Number
7/21/79	119	5		1	Mick Taylor		Columbia 35076

TAYLOR, R. Dean
Born Richard Dean Taylor in 1939 in Toronto, Ontario, Canada. Pop singer/songwriter.

DEBUT	PEAK	WKS		#	Album Title		Label & Number
2/20/71	198	1		1	I Think, Therefore I Am		Rare Earth 522

Billboard			R I A A	ARTIST Album Title	Catalog	Label & Number
DEBUT	PEAK	WKS				

TAYLOR, Roger
Born on 7/26/1949 in Norfolk, England. Rock drummer. Member of **Queen**.

| 5/9/81 | 121 | 10 | | 1 Fun In Space .... | | Elektra 522 |

T-BONES, The
Instrumental studio group: Danny Hamilton (guitar), Joe Frank Carollo (bass) and Tommy Reynolds (drums). Later recorded as **Hamilton, Joe Frank & Reynolds**. Hamilton died on 12/23/1994 (age 48).

| 2/12/66 | 75 | 12 | | 1 No Matter What Shape (Your Stomach's In) .... [I] | | Liberty 7439 |

TCHAIKOVSKY, Bram — see BRAM TCHAIKOVSKY

T-CONNECTION
Disco band from Nassau, Bahamas: brothers Theo Coakley (vocals, keyboards) and Kirk Coakley (bass), with Dave Mackey (guitar) and Tony Flowers (drums).

5/14/77	109	11		1 Magic		Dash 30004
1/21/78	139	11		2 On Fire..		Dash 30008
1/27/79	51	19		3 T-Connection		Dash 30009
11/24/79	188	3		4 Totally Connected		Dash 30014
3/21/81	138	8		5 Everything Is Cool		Capitol 12128
3/20/82	123	10		6 Pure & Natural		Capitol 12191

TEAM SLEEP
Alternative-rock band formed in Los Angeles, California: Chico Moreno (vocals, guitar), Todd Wilkinson (guitar), John "DJ Crook" Molina (DJ), Rick Verrett (bass) and Zach Hill (drums). Moreno is also lead singer of the **Deftones**.

| 5/28/05 | 52 | 2 | | 1 Team Sleep .... | | Maverick 48160 |

TEAR DA CLUB UP THUGS
Rap trio from Memphis, Tennessee: "DJ Paul" Beauregard, Jordan "Juicy J" Houston and Ricky "Lord Infamous" Dunigan. All are members of **Three 6 Mafia**.

| 2/20/99 | 18 | 13 | ● | 1 CrazyNDaLazDayz .... | | Hypnotize Minds 1716 |

TEARDROP EXPLODES
Pop-rock band from England: **Julian Cope** (vocals, bass), Alan Gill (guitar), David Balfe (keyboards) and Gary Dwyer (drums).

| 2/28/81 | 156 | 6 | | 1 Kilimanjaro.. | | Mercury 4016 |
| 2/6/82 | 176 | 4 | | 2 Wilder .... | | Mercury 4035 |

TEARS FOR FEARS
Pop-rock duo from England: Roland Orzabal (vocals, guitar, keyboards; born on 8/22/1961) and Curt Smith (vocals, bass; born on 6/24/1961). Adopted name from Arthur Janov's book *Prisoners of Pain* in 1981. Assisted by Manny Elias (drums) and Ian Stanley (keyboards). Smith left in 1992.

5/7/83	73	69	●	1 The Hurting		Mercury 811039
3/30/85	❶⁵	83	▲⁵	2 Songs From The Big Chair		Mercury 824300
10/7/89	8	34	▲	3 The Seeds Of Love		Fontana 838730
4/4/92	53	13	▲	4 Tears Roll Down (Greatest Hits 82-92) .... [G]		Fontana 510939
7/10/93	45	21	●	5 Elemental		Mercury 514875
10/28/95	79	5		6 Raoul And The Kings Of Spain		Epic 67318
10/2/04	46	3		7 Everybody Loves A Happy Ending...................................		New Door 003042

TECHMASTER P.E.B.
Born Neil Case in Florida. Techno-bass artist.

| 2/29/92 | 132 | 30 | | 1 Bass Computer.. | | Newtown 2208 |
| 8/28/93 | 186 | 2 | | 2 It Came From Outer Bass II .... [I] | | Newtown 2211 |

TECH N9NE
Born Aaron Yates on 11/8/1971 in Kansas City, Missouri. Male rapper.

9/15/01	59	1		1 Anghellic		JCOR 860949
10/12/02	79	2		2 Absolute Power		Strange 1001
11/25/06	50	2		3 Everready (The Religion)		Strange 01
8/4/07	49	3		4 Misery Loves Kompany		Strange 04
7/19/08	12	7		5 Killer		Strange 48
5/16/09	19	6		6 Sickology 101		Strange 54
11/14/09	14	4		7 K.O.D.		Strange 64

TECHNOTRONIC
Dance studio group created by Belgian DJ/producer Thomas DeQuincey and female rapper Ya Kid K.

| 12/23/89+ | 10 | 55 | ▲ | 1 Pump Up The Jam - The Album | **Cat:#25/2** | SBK 93422 |

TEDASHII
Born Tedashii Anderson in Dallas, Texas. Male Christian rapper.

| 6/13/09 | 137 | 1 | | 1 Identity Crisis .... | | Reach 8078 |

Billboard			R I A A	ARTIST Album Title	Catalog	Label & Number
DEBUT	PEAK	WKS				

TEDDY BEARS, The
White doo-wop trio from Los Angeles, California: Phil Spector (born on 12/26/1940 in the Bronx, New York), Carol Connors (lead singer; born Annette Kleinbard) and Marshall Leib (born on 1/26/1939). Spector became a superstar writer and producer; owner of Philles Records. Connors co-wrote "Gonna Fly Now" (theme from the movie *Rocky*). Leib died of a heart attack on 3/15/2002 (age 63).
    AWARD: R&R Hall of Fame: 1989 (Spector)

~ ~ ~ ~ ~ ~ ~ ~ ~ ~ **NON-CHARTED ALBUM** ~ ~ ~ ~ ~ ~ ~ ~ ~ ~
1959 **The Teddy Bears Sing!**

TEDESCHI, Susan
Born on 11/7/1970 in Norwell, Massachusetts. White blues singer/songwriter/guitarist.

2/13/99	181	4	●	1 Just Won't Burn .... **Cat:**#7/5		Tone-Cool 1164
12/7/02	91	12		2 Wait For Me		Tone-Cool 751146
10/29/05	189	1		3 Hope And Desire		Verve Forecast 005111
11/15/08	71	3		4 Back To The River		Verve Forecast 011513

TEENAGE FANCLUB
Pop-rock band from Glasgow, Scotland: Norman Blake (vocals, guitar), Ray McGinley (guitar), Gerry Love (bass) and Brendan O'Hare (drums).

3/7/92	137	4		1 Bandwagonesque		DGC 24461

TEENAGERS, The — see LYMON, Frankie

TEEN QUEENS, The
Black teen doo-wop duo from Los Angeles, California: sisters Betty and Rosie Collins. Sisters of Aaron Collins of **The Cadets/The Jacks**.

~ ~ ~ ~ ~ ~ ~ ~ ~ ~ **NON-CHARTED ALBUM** ~ ~ ~ ~ ~ ~ ~ ~ ~ ~
1956 **Eddie, My Love**

TEE SET, The
Pop band from Delft, Netherlands: Peter Tetteroo (vocals), Hans Van Eijck (organ), Dill Bennink (guitar), Franklin Madjid (bass) and Joop Blom (drums). Tetteroo died of cancer on 9/5/2002 (age 55).

5/16/70	158	6		1 Ma Belle Amie		Colossus 1001

TEGAN AND SARA
Female alternative-pop duo from Calgary, Alberta, Canada: identical twin sisters Tegan and Sara Quin (born on 9/19/1980).

8/11/07	34	8		1 The Con		Vapor 257532
11/14/09	21	3		2 Sainthood		Vapor 521124

TE KANAWA, Kiri
Born on 3/6/1944 in Gisborne, New Zealand. Operatic soprano.

12/7/85+	136	16		1 Blue Skies		London 414666

TELA
Born Winston Rogers in Memphis, Tennessee. Male rapper.

11/23/96+	70	23		1 Piece Of Mind		Suave House 1553
10/24/98	49	5		2 Now Or Never		Rap-A-Lot 46588
10/7/00	47	7		3 The World Ain't Enuff		Rap-A-Lot 49856
10/26/02	116	2		4 Double Dose		Rap-A-Lot 42004

TELEVISION
Punk-rock band from New York: **Tom Verlaine** (vocals, guitar), Richard Lloyd (guitar), Fred Smith (bass) and Billy Ficca (drums). Ficca later joined **The Waitresses**. Early member Richard Hell was once married to **Patty Smyth**.

6/10/78	201	1		1 Adventure		Elektra 133

~ ~ ~ ~ ~ ~ ~ ~ ~ ~ **NON-CHARTED ALBUM** ~ ~ ~ ~ ~ ~ ~ ~ ~ ~
1977 **Marquee Moon**
RS500 #128

TEMPLE OF THE DOG
Gathering of musicians in tribute to Andrew Wood, lead singer of **Mother Love Bone**, who died of a drug overdose on 3/16/1990 (age 24). Features Stone Gossard, Jeff Ament, Eddie Vedder and Mike McCready of **Pearl Jam**, with **Chris Cornell** and Matt Cameron of **Soundgarden**. Gossard and Ament were members of Mother Love Bone.

6/27/92	5	47	▲	1 Temple Of The Dog		A&M 5350

TEMPO
Born David Badillo in Ponce, Puerto Rico. Latin rapper.

7/18/09	189	1		1 Free Tempo .... **[F]**		Free Tempo 80100

TEMPO, Nino, & April Stevens
Brother-and-sister duo from Niagara Falls, New York: Nino Tempo (born on 1/6/1935) and April Stevens (born on 4/29/1936).

11/23/63+	48	14		1 Deep Purple		Atco 156

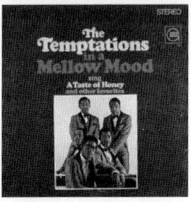

TEMPTATIONS, The   1960s: #23 / 1970s: #27 / All-Time: #10

R&B vocal group from Detroit, Michigan: **Eddie Kendricks**, **David Ruffin**, Paul Williams, Melvin Franklin and Otis Williams. **Dennis Edwards** replaced Ruffin in 1968. Ricky Owens and Richard Street replaced Kendricks and Paul Williams in 1971. Damon Harris replaced Owens in early 1972. Glenn Leonard replaced Harris in 1975. Edwards left group, 1977-79, replaced by Louis Price. Ali Ollie Woodson replaced Edwards from 1984-87. Lineup in 1988: Otis Williams, Franklin, Street, Edwards and Ron Tyson. Lineup in 1998: Otis Williams (the only original member remaining), Ron Tyson, Terry Weeks, Harry McGilberry and Barrington Henderson. Paul Williams died of a self-inflicted gunshot on 8/17/1973 (age 34). Ruffin died of a drug overdose on 6/1/1991 (age 50). Kendricks died of cancer on 10/5/1992 (age 52). Franklin died of heart failure on 2/23/1995 (age 52). Woodson died on 5/30/2010 (age 59).

AWARD: R&R Hall of Fame: 1989

DEBUT	PEAK	WKS		#	Album Title		Label & Number
5/9/64	95	11		1	Meet The Temptations		Gordy 911
4/3/65	35	26		2	The Temptations Sing Smokey		Gordy 912
11/27/65+	11	37		3	Temptin' Temptations		Gordy 914
7/9/66	12	35		4	Gettin' Ready		Gordy 918
8/12/67	7	36		5	With A Lot O' Soul		Gordy 922
12/23/67+	13	44		6	The Temptations in a Mellow Mood		Gordy 924
5/25/68	13	41		7	Wish It Would Rain		Gordy 927
11/30/68+	2¹	32	●	8	Diana Ross & The Supremes Join The Temptations		Motown 679
12/28/68+	❶¹	34	●	9	TCB [TV]		Motown 682
					DIANA ROSS & THE SUPREMES WITH THE TEMPTATIONS (above 2)		
3/15/69	4	40	●	10	Cloud Nine		Gordy 939
8/9/69	24	16		11	The Temptations Show [TV]		Gordy 933
10/11/69	5	41	●	12	Puzzle People		Gordy 949
10/25/69	28	18		13	Together		Motown 692
12/6/69	38	12		14	On Broadway [TV]		Motown 699
					DIANA ROSS & THE SUPREMES WITH THE TEMPTATIONS (above 2)		
4/4/70	9	30	●	15	Psychedelic Shack		Gordy 947
5/8/71	16	35	●	16	Sky's The Limit		Gordy 957
1/29/72	24	22		17	Solid Rock		Gordy 961
8/19/72	2²	44	●	18	All Directions		Gordy 962
3/10/73	7	28	●	19	Masterpiece		Gordy 965
12/29/73+	19	22		20	1990		Gordy 966
2/8/75	13	36	●	21	A Song For You		Gordy 969
11/29/75	40	20		22	House Party		Gordy 973
4/3/76	29	20		23	Wings Of Love		Gordy 971
9/11/76	53	14		24	The Temptations Do The Temptations		Gordy 975
12/10/77+	113	13		25	Hear To Tempt You		Atlantic 19143
11/4/78	205	1		26	Bare Back		Atlantic 19188
5/17/80	45	14		27	Power		Gordy 994
8/29/81	119	9		28	The Temptations		Gordy 1006
5/1/82	37	18		29	Reunion		Gordy 6008
3/19/83	159	9		30	Surface Thrills		Gordy 6032
4/21/84	152	9		31	Back To Basics		Gordy 6085
11/17/84+	55	34		32	Truly For You		Gordy 6119
1/25/86	146	10		33	Touch Me		Gordy 6164
8/2/86	74	33		34	To Be Continued...		Gordy 6207
10/24/87	112	21		35	Together Again		Motown 6246
9/5/98	44	44	▲	36	Phoenix Rising		Motown 530937
6/3/00	54	12		37	Ear-Resistible		Motown 157742
					Grammy: Traditional R&B Album		
12/8/01	140	2		38	Awesome		Motown 016330
6/26/04	163	1		39	Legacy		Motown 002589
2/18/06	80	2		40	Reflections		New Door 005170
11/10/07	108	1		41	Back To Front		New Door 009451
					CHRISTMAS ALBUMS:		
12/5/70+	4ˣ	7	●	42	The Temptations' Christmas Card		Gordy 951
					Christmas charts: 7/'70, 7/'71, 4/'72		
12/17/83	6ˣ	39	▲	43	Give Love At Christmas Cat:#22/33		Motown 2842
					first released in 1980 on Gordy 998; Christmas charts: 6/'83, 14/'87, 12/'88, 17/'89, 13/'90, 20/'92, 22/'93, 25/'94, 37/'95, 37/'96, 29/'97, 29/'98, 36/'99, 23/'03		
12/13/03+	14ˣ	9		44	The Best Of The Temptations The Christmas Collection 20th Century Masters [K]		Motown 000620
					Christmas charts: 18/'03, 40/'04, 14/'05		
					GREATEST HITS & COMPILATIONS:		
12/17/66+	5	120	▲²	45	The Temptations Greatest Hits Cat:#5/2		Gordy 919
9/26/70	15	70	●	46	Temptations Greatest Hits II		Gordy 954
9/15/73	65	26	▲	47	Anthology		Motown 782 [3]
					RS500 #398		
5/17/86	140	16		48	25th Anniversary		Motown 5389 [2]
11/21/98	7ᶜ	2	●	49	Great Songs And Performances That Inspired The Motown 25th Anniversary Television Special		Motown 5315
11/21/98	15ᶜ	1	▲	50	All The Million-Sellers		Motown 5212
11/21/98	137	1	●	51	The Ultimate Collection		Motown 530562

TEMPTATIONS, The — cont'd

DEBUT	PEAK	WKS	RIAA	Album Title	Catalog	Label & Number
12/8/01+	29 C	8	●	52 The Best Of The Temptations Volume 1 The 60's		Motown 53362
5/4/02	167	1		53 My Girl: The Very Best Of The Temptations		Motown 017298 [2]
				LIVE ALBUMS:		
4/1/67	10	51		54 Temptations Live!		Gordy 921
1/4/69	15	24		55 Live At The Copa		Gordy 938
8/22/70	21	18		56 Live At London's Talk Of The Town		Gordy 953

TENACIOUS D

Novelty rock duo: Jack Black (born on 8/28/1969) and Kyle Gass (born on 7/14/1961). Black acted in several movies.

DEBUT	PEAK	WKS	RIAA	Album Title	Catalog	Label & Number
10/13/01	33	43	▲	1 Tenacious D .... Cat:#30/8 [N]		Epic 86234
12/2/06	8	13		2 The Pick Of Destiny [N-S]		Epic 94891

10cc

Art-rock band formed in Manchester, England: Eric Stewart (vocals, guitar), Lol Creme (guitar, keyboards), Graham Gouldman (bass) and Kevin Godley (drums). Stewart and Gouldman were members of **The Mindbenders**. **Godley & Creme** left in 1976; replaced by drummer Paul Burgess. Added members **Rick Fenn**, Stuart Tosh and Duncan MacKay in 1978. Gouldman later in duo **Wax**.

DEBUT	PEAK	WKS	RIAA	Album Title	Catalog	Label & Number
12/1/73	201	7		1 10cc		UK 53105
8/10/74	81	14		2 Sheet Music		UK 53107
4/19/75	15	25		3 The Original Soundtrack		Mercury 1029
9/13/75	161	5		4 100cc [K]		UK 53110
2/14/76	47	13		5 How Dare You!		Mercury 1061
5/14/77	31	20		6 Deceptive Bends		Mercury 3702
12/24/77+	146	6		7 Live And Let Live [L]		Mercury 8600 [2]
10/14/78	69	17		8 Bloody Tourists		Polydor 6161
12/22/79+	188	4		9 Greatest Hits 1972-1978 [G]		Polydor 6244
5/17/80	180	2		10 Look Hear?		Warner 3442
6/26/82	209	1		11 Ten Out Of 10		Warner 3575

TENNILLE, Toni

Born on 5/8/1943 in Montgomery, Alabama. One half of **Captain & Tennille** duo.

DEBUT	PEAK	WKS	RIAA	Album Title	Catalog	Label & Number
6/9/84	142	11		1 More Than You Know		Mirage 90162
12/26/87	198	2		2 All Of Me		Gaia 139001

TENTH AVENUE NORTH

Contemporary Christian trio from West Palm Beach, Florida: Mike Donehey (vocals, guitar), Jeff Owen (bass) and Jason Jamison (drums).

DEBUT	PEAK	WKS	RIAA	Album Title	Catalog	Label & Number
6/7/08+	39	38		1 Over And Underneath		Reunion 10126

10,000 MANIACS

Alternative-rock band formed in Jamestown, New York: **Natalie Merchant** (vocals), Robert Buck (guitar), Dennis Drew (keyboards), Steven Gustafson (bass) and Jerome Augustyniak (drums). Mary Ramsey replaced Merchant in 1994. Buck died of liver failure on 12/19/2000 (age 42).

DEBUT	PEAK	WKS	RIAA	Album Title	Catalog	Label & Number
9/19/87+	37	77	▲²	1 In My Tribe .... Cat:#47/1		Elektra 60738
6/3/89	13	28	▲	2 Blind Man's Zoo		Elektra 60815
11/3/90	102	10		3 Hope Chest - The Fredonia Recordings 1982-1983 [E]		Elektra 60962
				remixes of early songs recorded at Fredonia State University in New York		
10/17/92+	28	56	▲²	4 Our Time In Eden		Elektra 61385
11/13/93	13	45	▲³	5 MTV Unplugged [L]		Elektra 61569
7/5/97	104	14		6 Love Among The Ruins		Geffen 25009

TEN WHEEL DRIVE With Genya Ravan

Jazz-rock band from New York: **Genya Ravan** (vocals), **Michael Zager** (keyboards), Aram Schefrin (guitar), Steve Satten, John Gatchell, Dave Liebman, John Eckert and Dennis Parisi (horns), Bob Piazza (bass) and Allen Herman (drums).

DEBUT	PEAK	WKS	RIAA	Album Title	Catalog	Label & Number
1/10/70	151	16		1 Construction #1		Polydor 4008
8/1/70	161	8		2 Brief Replies		Polydor 4024
6/19/71	190	5		3 Peculiar Friends		Polydor 4062

10 YEARS

Hard-rock band from Knoxville, Tennessee: Jesse Hasek (vocals), Ryan Johnson (guitar), Matt Wantland (guitar), Lewis Cosby (bass) and Brian Vodinh (drums).

DEBUT	PEAK	WKS	RIAA	Album Title	Catalog	Label & Number
9/3/05	72	29		1 The Autumn Effect		Republic 005018
5/31/08	12	10		2 Division		Universal Rep. 010979

TEN YEARS AFTER   **All-Time: #434**

Blues-rock band formed in Nottingham, England: **Alvin Lee** (vocals, guitar; born on 12/19/1944), Chick Churchill (keyboards; born on 1/2/1949), Leo Lyons (bass; born on 11/30/1943) and Ric Lee (drums; born on 10/20/1945).

DEBUT	PEAK	WKS	RIAA	Album Title	Catalog	Label & Number
8/10/68	115	14		1 Undead [L]		Deram 18016
2/22/69	61	18		2 Stonedhenge		Deram 18021
8/30/69	20	23		3 SSSSH		Deram 18029
4/18/70	14	30		4 Cricklewood Green		Deram 18038
12/12/70+	21	16		5 Watt		Deram 18050
4/8/72	55	18		6 Alvin Lee & Company [K]		Deram 18064
7/19/75	174	5		7 Goin' Home! Their Greatest Hits [K]		Deram 18072
8/28/71	17	26	▲	8 A Space In Time		Columbia 30801
10/14/72	43	25		9 Rock & Roll Music To The World		Columbia 31779

Billboard			R I A A	ARTIST Album Title	Catalog	Label & Number
DEBUT	PEAK	WKS				

TEN YEARS AFTER — cont'd

6/23/73	39	21		10 Recorded Live .... [L]		Columbia 32290 [2]
5/18/74	81	14		11 Positive Vibrations		Columbia 32851
9/16/89	120	10		12 About Time		Chrysalis 21722

TEPPER, Robert
Born Antoine Roberto Teppardo in Bayonne, New Jersey. Rock singer/songwriter.

4/19/86	144	8		1 No Easy Way Out		Scotti Brothers 40128

TERMINATOR X
Born Norman Rogers on 8/25/1966 in Long Island, New York. Male rapper. Member of **Public Enemy**.

5/25/91	97	11		1 Terminator X & The Valley Of The Jeep Beets		P.R.O. Division 46896
7/9/94	189	1		2 Super Bad		P.R.O. Division 523343
				TERMINATOR X AND THE GODFATHERS OF THREATT		

TERRELL, Tammi
Born Thomasina Montgomery on 4/29/1945 in Philadelphia, Pennsylvania. Died of a brain tumor on 3/16/1970 (age 24). Female R&B singer. First recorded for Wand in 1961. Worked with the **James Brown** Revue. Tumor diagnosed after collapsing on stage in 1967.

MARVIN GAYE & TAMMI TERRELL:

10/7/67	69	44		1 United		Tamla 277
9/21/68	60	21		2 You're All I Need		Tamla 284
10/18/69	184	2		3 Easy		Tamla 294
6/13/70	171	3		4 Marvin Gaye & Tammi Terrell Greatest Hits .... [G]		Tamla 302

TERROR SQUAD
Hip-hop group formed in the Bronx, New York: **Fat Joe**, Prospect, Armageddon, **Remy Ma** and Tony Sunshine.

10/9/99	22	8		1 Terror Squad: The Album		Big Beat 83232
8/14/04	7	15		2 True Story		SRC 002806

TERRY, Sonny, & Brownie McGhee
Blues harmonica player Terry was born Saunders Terrell on 10/24/1911 in Greensboro, Georgia. Blinded as a youth. Died on 3/11/1986 (age 74). Blues guitarist McGhee was born Walter Brown McGhee on 11/30/1915 in Knoxville, Tennessee. Died of cancer on 2/16/1996 (age 80).

4/7/73	185	5		1 Sonny & Brownie		A&M 4379

TERRY, Tony
Born on 3/12/1964 in Pinehurst, North Carolina; raised in Washington DC. R&B singer.

1/9/88	151	20		1 Forever Yours		Epic 40890
6/22/91	184	6		2 Tony Terry		Epic 45015

TESH, John
Born on 7/9/1952 in Garden City, Long Island, New York. New Age/Contemporary Christian multi-instrumentalist. Former host of TV's *Entertainment Tonight*. Appeared in the 1989 movie *Shocker*. Married actress Connie Sellecca on 4/4/1992. Hosts own syndicated radio show.

6/19/93	181	3		1 Monterey Nights .... [I]		GTS 4570
3/18/95	160	4		2 Sax On The Beach .... [I]		GTS 4578
				THE JOHN TESH PROJECT		
3/25/95	54	33	●	3 Live At Red Rocks .... [I-L]		GTS 4579
				with the Colorado Symphony Orchestra		
3/30/96	114	2		4 Discovery .... [I]		GTSP 532125
				THE JOHN TESH PROJECT		
3/22/97	55	18		5 Avalon .... [I]		GTSP 537112
2/14/98	45	18		6 Grand Passion .... [I]		GTSP 539804
2/27/99	121	7		7 One World .... [I]		GTSP 559673
2/2/02	147	2		8 Pure Hymns .... [I]		Garden City 34581
				THE JOHN TESH PROJECT		
3/16/02	56	21		9 A Deeper Faith .... [I]		Garden City 34591
9/11/04	180	1		10 Worship At Red Rocks .... [I-L]		Garden City 34608
				CHRISTMAS ALBUMS:		
12/12/92+	50	5	●	11 A Romantic Christmas .... Cat:#2¹/18 [I]		GTS 4569
				Christmas charts: 9/'92, 9/'93, 35/'94, 3/'95		
12/10/94	103	5		12 A Family Christmas .... Cat:#3/5 [I]		GTS 4575
				Christmas charts: 26/'94, 4/'95		
11/30/02	136	5		13 Christmas Worship .... [I]		Garden City 34595
				Christmas chart: 10/'02, 30/'03		
12/20/08	127	2		14 Grand Piano Christmas .... [I]		Garden City 4600
				Christmas chart: 12/'08		

TESLA
Hard-rock band formed in Sacramento, California: Jeff Keith (vocals), Frank Hannon (guitar), Tommy Skeoch (guitar), Brian Wheat (bass) and Troy Luccetta (drums). Band named after the inventor of the alternating current generator, Nikola Tesla.

1/31/87	32	61	▲	1 Mechanical Resonance		Geffen 24120
2/18/89	18	67	▲²	2 The Great Radio Controversy		Geffen 24224
12/1/90+	12	48	▲	3 Five Man Acoustical Jam .... [L]		Geffen 24311
				recorded on 7/2/1990 at the Trocadero in Philadelphia, Pennsylvania		
9/28/91	13	56	▲	4 Psychotic Supper		Geffen 24424
9/10/94	20	10	●	5 Bust A Nut		Geffen 24713

TESLA — cont'd

1/20/96	197	1	● 6 Time's Makin' Changes: The Best Of Tesla .... [G]		Geffen 24833
3/27/04	31	4	7 Into The Now		Sanctuary 84637
6/23/07	48	2	8 Real To Reel		Tesla Electric Co. 001
10/25/08	33	3	9 Forever More		Tesla Electric Co. 007

TESTAMENT

Hard-rock band formed in San Francisco, California: Chuck Billy (vocals), Eric Peterson (guitar), Alex Skolnick (guitar), Greg Christian (bass) and Louie Clemente (drums). Skolnick and Clemente left in 1992, replaced by Glen Abelais (guitar) and John Tempesta (drums). Abelais and Tempesta left in 1994; replaced by James Murphy (guitar) and John Dette (drums).

6/25/88	136	14	1 The New Order		Megaforce 81849
9/2/89	77	12	2 Practice What You Preach		Megaforce 82009
10/27/90	73	8	3 Souls Of Black		Megaforce 82143
5/30/92	55	9	4 The Ritual		Atlantic 82392
10/22/94	122	2	5 Low		Atlantic 82645
5/17/08	59	4	6 Formation Of Damnation		Nuclear Blast 2005

TEX, Joe

Born Joseph Arrington Jr. on 8/8/1933 in Rogers, Texas. Died of a heart attack on 8/13/1982 (age 49). R&B singer. Sang with local gospel groups. Won recording contract during Apollo Theater talent contest in 1954. First recorded for King in 1955. Converted to the Muslim faith; changed name to "Joseph Hazziez" in July 1972.

2/6/65	124	7	1 Hold What You've Got		Atlantic 8106
11/27/65	142	7	2 The New Boss		Atlantic 8115
5/7/66	108	8	3 The Love You Save		Atlantic 8124
9/2/67	168	4	4 The Best Of Joe Tex .... [G]		Atlantic 8144
2/24/68	84	17	5 Live And Lively .... [L]		Atlantic 8156
7/27/68	154	7	6 Soul Country		Atlantic 8187
7/19/69	190	5	7 Buying A Book		Atlantic 8231
5/20/72	201	2	8 From The Roots Came The Rapper		Atlantic 8292
4/22/72	17	21	9 I Gotcha		Dial 6002
5/7/77	108	9	10 Bumps & Bruises		Epic 34666

TEXAS

Pop-rock band from Glasgow, Scotland: Sharleen Spiteri (vocals, guitar), Ally McErlaine (guitar), John McElhone (bass) and Stuart Kerr (drums). McElhone was a member of **Hipsway**. Kerr was an early member of **Love And Money**.

8/19/89	88	16	1 Southside		Mercury 838171

TEXAS TORNADOS

All-star band: **Freddy Fender**, **Doug Sahm**, Augie Myers and Flaco Jimenez. Sahm and Meyers were members of the **Sir Douglas Quintet**. Sahm died of heart failure on 11/18/1999 (age 58). Fender died of cancer on 10/14/2006 (age 69).

9/8/90	154	10	1 Texas Tornados		Reprise 26251

TEXTONES

Rock band formed in Texas: Carla Olson (vocals, guitar), George Callins (guitar), Tom Morgan (keyboards), Joe Read (bass) and **Phil Seymour** (drums). Seymour died of cancer on 8/17/1993 (age 41).

11/24/84+	176	8	1 Midnight Mission		Gold Mountain 86010

THALIA

Born Ariadna Thalia Sodi Miranda on 8/26/1971 in Mexico City, Mexico. Female Latin singer. Married record executive Tommy Mottola (former husband of **Mariah Carey**) on 12/2/2000.

9/15/01	167	2	1 Con Banda Grandes Exitos .... [F]		EMI Latin 34722
6/8/02	126	2	2 Thalia .... [F]		EMI Latin 39573
7/26/03	11	9	3 Thalia		EMI Latin 81023
2/28/04	128	5	4 Greatest Hits .... [F-G]		EMI Latin 93043
8/6/05	63	2	5 El Sexto Sentido .... [F]		EMI Latin 75589
12/19/09	198	1	6 Primera Fila .... [F-L]		Sony 56091

THE, The

Born Matthew Johnson on 8/15/1961 in London, England. Eclectic-rock singer/songwriter. His band features an ever-changing lineup of musicians.

2/14/87	89	18	1 Infected		Epic 40471
6/27/87	38 C	4	2 Soul Mining .... [E]		Epic 39266
			released in 1985		
7/22/89	138	12	3 Mind Bomb		Epic 45241
2/13/93	142	4	4 Dusk		Epic 53164

THEE MIDNITERS

Mexican-American rock band from Los Angeles, California: Willie Garcia (vocals), Roy Marquez (guitar), George Dominguez (guitar), Ronnie Figueroa (organ), Romeo Prado (trombone), Larry Rendon (sax), Jimmy Espinoza (bass) and George Salazar (drums).

~ ~ ~ ~ ~ ~ ~ ~ ~ ~ **NON-CHARTED ALBUM** ~ ~ ~ ~ ~ ~ ~ ~ ~ ~

1965 **Thee Midniters**

THEE PROPHETS

Pop band from Milwaukee, Wisconsin: Brian Lake (vocals, keyboards), Jim Anderson (guitar), Dave Leslie (bass) and Chris Michaels (drums).

6/28/69	163	3	1 Playgirl		Kapp 3596

THEM
Rock band from Belfast, Northern Ireland: **Van Morrison**, brothers Jackie McAuley (piano) and Pat McAuley (drums), Billy Harrison (guitar), Alan Henderson (bass) and **Pete Bardens** (keyboards).

7/24/65	54	23		1 Them		Parrot 71005
4/16/66	138	6		2 Them Again		Parrot 71008
7/22/72	154	11		3 Them Featuring Van Morrison	[R]	Parrot 71053 [2]
				reissue (condensed) of the first 2 albums above		
11/2/74	202	4		4 Backtrackin'	[K]	London 639
				THEM FEATURING VAN MORRISON (above 2)		

THEM CROOKED VULTURES
All-star rock trio: Josh Homme (vocals, guitar), John Paul Jones (bass) and Dave Grohl (drums). Homme also with **Queens Of The Stone Age**. Jones also with **Led Zeppelin**. Grohl also with **Nirvana** and **Foo Fighters**.

12/5/09	12	24		1 Them Crooked Vultures		DGC 013783

THEODORE, Mike, Orchestra
Born in Detroit, Michigan. White disco producer.

10/1/77	178	2		1 Cosmic Wind		Westbound 305

THEORY OF A DEADMAN
Rock band from Delta, British Columbia, Canada: Tyler Connolly (vocals, guitar), David Brenner (guitar), Dean Back (bass) and Tim Hart (drums).

10/5/02	85	6		1 Theory Of A Deadman		Roadrunner 618421
4/16/05	58	9		2 Gasoline		Roadrunner 618323
4/19/08	26	107	●	3 Scars & Souvenirs		604 Records 618009

THEO VANESS — see VANESS, Theo

THERE FOR TOMORROW
Alternative-rock band from Orlando, Florida: Maika Maile (vocals), Christian Climer (guitar), Jay Enriquez (bass) and Christopher Kamrada (drums).

6/27/09	181	1		1 A Little Faster		Hopeless 709

THERMALS, The
Punk-rock trio from Portland, Oregon: Hutch Harris (vocals, guitar), Kathy Foster (bass) and Jordan Hudson (drums).

4/25/09	191	1		1 Now We Can See		Kill Rock Stars 504

THEY EAT THEIR OWN
Pop-rock band formed in Los Angeles, California: Laura Baricevic (vocals), Kevin Dixon (guitar), Shark Darkwater (guitar), J.D. Dotson (bass) and Juno Brown (drums).

3/23/91	184	5		1 They Eat Their Own		Relativity 1042

THEY MIGHT BE GIANTS
Alternative-rock duo from Boston, Massachusetts: John Flansburgh (guitar; born on 5/6/1960) and John Linnell (accordian; born on 6/12/1959). Supported by various musicians. Group named after the 1971 movie starring George C. Scott.

12/24/88+	89	19		1 Lincoln		Bar/None 72600
2/10/90	75	22	▲	2 Flood		Elektra 60907
4/11/92	99	6		3 Apollo 18		Elektra 61257
10/1/94	61	4		4 John Henry		Elektra 61654
10/26/96	89	2		5 Factory Showroom		Elektra 61862
8/29/98	186	1		6 Severe Tire Damage	[L]	Restless 72965
9/29/01	134	1		7 Mink Car		Restless 73744
7/31/04	130	1		8 The Spine		Idlewild 431041
7/28/07	118	2		9 The Else		Idlewild 431117
2/23/08	172	1		10 Here Come The 123s With They Might Be Giants		Idlewild 000681
				Grammy: Children's Musical Album		
9/26/09	91	4		11 Here Comes Science		Idlewild 004566

THICKE, Robin
Born on 3/10/1977 in Los Angeles, California. "Blue-eyed soul" singer/songwriter. Son of actress **Gloria Loring** and actor Alan Thicke.

5/3/03	152	1		1 A Beautiful World		Nu America 493375
10/21/06+	5	56	▲	2 The Evolution Of Robin Thicke		Overbrook 006146
10/18/08	3[1]	28		3 Something Else		Star Trak 011793

THIEVERY CORPORATION
Instrumental trip-hop duo from Washington DC: Rob Garza and Eric Hilton.

10/19/02	150	2		1 The Richest Man In Babylon	[I]	18th Street Lounge 060
3/12/05	94	4		2 The Cosmic Game	[I]	18th Street Lounge 0081
10/11/08	35	5		3 Radio Retaliation		ESL 140

THIN LIZZY
Rock band from Dublin, Ireland: Phil Lynott (vocals, bass; born on 8/20/1951; died of heart failure on 1/4/1986, age 34), Brian Robertson (guitar), Scott Gorham (guitar) and Brian Downey (drums). Numerous personnel changes. **Gary Moore** was a member from 1978-79.

4/17/76	18	28	●	1 Jailbreak		Mercury 1081
11/13/76	52	11		2 Johnny The Fox		Mercury 1119
9/24/77	39	11		3 Bad Reputation		Mercury 1186

THIN LIZZY — cont'd

7/22/78	84	12		4 Live And Dangerous.. [L]		Warner 3213 [2]
6/2/79	81	12		5 Black Rose/A Rock Legend..		Warner 3338
11/29/80	120	10		6 Chinatown..		Warner 3496
2/20/82	157	11		7 Renegade..		Warner 3622
5/28/83	159	5		8 Thunder And Lightning..		Warner 23831
1/28/84	185	3		9 'Life'-Live.. [L]		Warner 23986 [2]
3/21/09	189	1		10 Still Dangerous: Live At The Tower Theater Philadelphia 1977 .... [L]		VH1 Classic 00131

3RD BASS

White rap duo from Queens, New York: Michael "**MC Serch**" Berrin and "**Prime Minister Pete Nice**" Nash. Supported by black DJ Richard Lawson.

12/2/89+	55	30	●	1 The Cactus Album..		Def Jam 45415
7/6/91	19	22	●	2 Derelicts Of Dialect		Def Jam 47369

THIRD DAY   2000s: #44 / All-Time: #369

Christian rock band from Marietta, Georgia: Mac Powell (vocals; born on 12/25/1972), Mark Lee (guitar; born on 5/29/1973), Brad Avery (guitar; born on 8/20/1971), Tai Anderson (bass; born on 6/11/1976) and David Carr (drums; born on 11/15/1974).

9/13/97	50	7		1 Conspiracy No. 5..		Reunion 10006
9/11/99	63	9	●	2 Time..		Essential 0528
7/29/00	66	34	▲	3 Offerings: A Worship Album...		Essential 10670
11/24/01	31	33	●	4 Come Together...		Essential 10668
				Grammy: Rock Gospel Album		
3/22/03	18	31	●	5 Offerings II: All I Have To Give...		Essential 10706
5/22/04	12	17		6 Wire..		Essential 10728
11/19/05	8	36	●	7 Wherever You Are		Essential 10795
10/28/06	78	10		8 Christmas Offerings .... Cat:#2² /12 [X]		Essential 10828
				Christmas charts: 10/'06, 44/'07, 2/'08, 22/'09		
12/12/09	112	1		9 Christmas Offerings .... [X-R]		Essential 10828
4/14/07	61	10		10 Chronology: Volume One.. [K]		Essential 10838
8/25/07	73	6		11 Chronology: Volume Two (2001-2006) .... [K]		Essential 10839
8/16/08	6	64		12 Revelation Cat:#42/2		Essential 10853
4/25/09	145	2		13 Live Revelations: On Stage. Off Stage. Backstage. .... [L]		Essential 10298
				Grammy: Rock Gospel Album		

THIRD EYE BLIND

Rock band from San Francisco, California: Stephan Jenkins (vocals), Kevin Cadogan (guitar), Arion Salazar (bass) and Brad Hargreaves (drums). Tony Fredianelli replaced Cadogan in 2002.

4/26/97+	25	104	▲⁶	1 Third Eye Blind .... Cat:#4/18		Elektra 62012
12/11/99	40	53	▲	2 Blue..		Elektra 62415
5/31/03	12	9		3 Out Of The Vein..		Elektra 62888
8/5/06	103	3		4 A Collection.. [G]		Elektra 78779
9/5/09	3¹	7		5 Ursa Major		Mega Collider 01

THIRD POWER

Rock trio from Detroit, Michigan: Drew Abbott (guitar), Jem Targal (vocals, bass) and Jim Craig (drums). Abbott later joined **Bob Seger**'s Silver Bullet Band.

7/4/70	194	2		1 Believe..		Vanguard 6554

3RD STOREE

R&B vocal group from Los Angeles, California: Dante Clark, Gavin Rhone, Barry Reed, Jason Thomas and Kevontay Jackson.

10/19/02	91	5		1 Get With Me		Def Soul 586977

3RD STRIKE

Rock band from Los Angeles, California: Jim Karthe (vocals), Todd Deguchi (guitar), Erik Carlsson (guitar), Gabe Hammersmith (bass) and P.J. McMullan (drums).

6/1/02	72	8		1 Lost Angel		Hollywood 62344

THIRD WORLD

Reggae band from Jamaica: William Clarke (vocals), Stephen Coore (guitar), Michael Cooper (keyboards), Irvin Jarrett (percussion), Richard Daley (bass) and Willie Stewart (drums). Jarrett left by 1989.

2/25/78	203	3		1 96° In The Shade		Island 9443
11/25/78+	55	24		2 Journey To Addis		Island 9554
7/21/79	157	5		3 The Story's Been Told		Island 9569
6/14/80	206	2		4 Arise In Harmony		Island 9574
8/30/80	186	2		5 Third World, Prisoner in The Street .... [L-S]		Island 9616
7/25/81	186	3		6 Rock The World		Columbia 37402
3/20/82	63	27		7 You've Got The Power		Columbia 37744
10/1/83	137	7		8 All The Way Strong		Columbia 38687
4/13/85	119	11		9 Sense Of Purpose		Columbia 39877
7/15/89	107	14		10 Serious Business		Mercury 836952

THIRTEENTH FLOOR ELEVATORS, The

Garage-rock band from Austin, Texas: Roky Erickson (vocals), Stacy Sutherland (guitar), Tommy Hall (guitar), Dan Galindo (bass) and Danny Thomas (drums). Sutherland was murdered on 8/24/1978 (age 32). Galindo died of liver failure on 5/17/2001 (age 51).

~ ~ ~ ~ ~ ~ ~ ~ ~ ~ ~ **NON-CHARTED ALBUM** ~ ~ ~ ~ ~ ~ ~ ~ ~ ~ ~ ~

1967 Psychedelic Sounds

38 SPECIAL
Southern-rock band formed in Jacksonville, Florida: Donnie **Van Zant** (vocals), Don Barnes (guitar), Jeff Carlisi (guitar), Larry Junstrom (bass), Steve Brookins (drums) and Jack Grondin (drums). By 1988, Barnes and Brookins replaced by Danny Chauncey (guitar) and Max Carl (keyboards). Barnes returned in 1992 to replace Carl. Van Zant is the brother of **Lynyrd Skynyrd**'s Ronnie Van Zant.

5/28/77	148	5		1	38 Special	Cat:#36/2	A&M 4638
4/29/78	207	5		2	Special Delivery		A&M 4684
1/5/80	57	19		3	Rockin' Into The Night		A&M 4782
2/21/81	18	57	▲	4	Wild-Eyed Southern Boys		A&M 4835
5/29/82	10	42	▲	5	Special Forces		A&M 4888
12/3/83+	22	39	▲	6	Tour De Force		A&M 4971
5/17/86	17	31	●	7	Strength In Numbers		A&M 5115
8/22/87	35	17	▲	8	Flashback	[G]	A&M 3910
10/22/88+	61	41		9	Rock & Roll Strategy		A&M 5218
8/10/91	170	7		10	Bone Against Steel		Charisma 91640

30 SECONDS TO MARS
Rock band formed in Los Angeles, California: brothers Jared Leto (vocals, guitar) and Shannon Leto (drums), with Solon Bixler (guitar) and Matt Wachter (bass). Jared Leto is also a popular actor (played "Jordan Catalano" on TV's *My So-Called Life*).

9/14/02	107	4		1	30 Seconds To Mars		Immortal 12424
9/17/05+	36	74	▲	2	A Beautiful Lie		Virgin 90992
12/26/09	19	23		3	This Is War		Immortal 65111
					THIRTY SECONDS TO MARS		

36 CRAZYFISTS
Heavy metal band from Anchorage, Alaska: Brock Lindow (vocals), Steve Holt (guitar), Brett Makowski (bass) and Thomas Noonan (drums).

6/14/08	155	1		1	The Tide And Its Takers		Ferret 098

33MILES
Contemporary Christian trio from Franklin, Tennessee: Jason Barton, Chris Lockwood and Collin Stoddard.

10/4/08	161	1		1	One Life		Ino 30461

THIS PROVIDENCE
Punk-rock band from Seattle, Washington: Dan Young (vocals, guitar), Gavin Phillips (guitar), David Blaise (bass) and Andy Horst (drums).

4/4/09	176	1		1	Who Are You Now?		Fueled By Ramen 516824

THOMAS, B.J.
Born Billy Joe Thomas on 8/7/1942 in Hugo, Oklahoma; raised in Rosenberg, Texas. Pop-country singer. Joined band, The Triumphs, while in high school. Also recorded gospel music since 1976.
AWARD: OPRY: 1981

1/18/69	133	12		1	On My Way		Scepter 570
11/8/69+	90	28		2	Greatest Hits, Volume 1	[G]	Scepter 578
1/3/70	12	41	●	3	Raindrops Keep Fallin' On My Head		Scepter 580
5/2/70	72	20		4	Everybody's Out Of Town		Scepter 582
12/12/70+	67	24		5	Most Of All		Scepter 586
11/20/71	92	13		6	Greatest Hits, Volume Two	[G]	Scepter 597
5/20/72	145	9		7	Billy Joe Thomas		Scepter 5101
11/18/72	209	2		8	Country		Scepter 5108
6/9/73	221	5		9	Songs		Paramount 6052
3/29/75	59	14		10	Reunion		ABC 858
8/27/77	114	12		11	B.J. Thomas		MCA 2286
5/21/83	193	3		12	New Looks		Cleveland Int'l. 38561

~ ~ ~ ~ ~ ~ ~ ~ ~ **NON-CHARTED ALBUMS** ~ ~ ~ ~ ~ ~ ~ ~ ~ ~
1965 **I'm So Lonesome I Could Cry** *[Pacemaker label]*   1967 **B.J. Thomas Sings For Lovers And Losers**
1966 **Tomorrow Never Comes**

THOMAS, Carl
Born on 6/15/1970 in Aurora, Illinois. R&B singer/songwriter.

5/6/00	9	49	▲	1	Emotional		Bad Boy 73025
4/10/04	4	12	●	2	Let's Talk About It		Bad Boy 001188
6/23/07	25	6		3	So Much Better		Umbrella 970118

THOMAS, Carla
Born on 12/21/1942 in Memphis, Tennessee. R&B singer. Daughter of **Rufus Thomas**.

3/5/66	134	10		1	Comfort Me		Stax 706
10/15/66	130	5		2	Carla		Stax 709
4/22/67	36	31		3	King & Queen		Stax 716
					OTIS REDDING & CARLA THOMAS		
7/1/67	133	6		4	The Queen Alone		Stax 718
7/5/69	151	5		5	Memphis Queen		Stax 2019
7/19/69	190	4		6	The Best Of Carla Thomas	[G]	Atlantic 8232
8/28/71	213	2		7	Love Means		Stax 2044

~ ~ ~ ~ ~ ~ **NON-CHARTED ALBUM by CARLA THOMAS** ~ ~ ~ ~ ~ ~ ~
1961 **Gee Whiz**

THOMAS, Ian
Born on 7/23/1950 in Hamilton, Ontario, Canada. Pop singer/songwriter. Brother of comedian Dave Thomas ("**Doug McKenzie**").

12/8/73	203	6		1 Ian Thomas		Janus 3058

THOMAS, Irma
Born Irma Lee on 2/18/1941 in Ponchatoula, Louisiana. R&B singer. Nicknamed "The Soul Queen of New Orleans."

6/27/64	104	8		1 Wish Someone Would Care		Imperial 12266

THOMAS, Lillo
Born in 1961 in Brooklyn, New York. Male R&B singer/songwriter.

9/24/83	201	4		1 Let Me Be Yours		Capitol 12290
10/6/84	186	3		2 All Of You		Capitol 12346

THOMAS, Mickey
Born on 12/3/1949 in Cairo, Georgia. Lead singer of **Jefferson Starship/Starship** from 1979-90.

10/17/81	203	3		1 Alive Alone		Elektra 530

THOMAS, Ray
Born on 12/29/1942 in Birmingham, England. Flute/harmonica player of **The Moody Blues**.

8/9/75	68	11		1 From Mighty Oaks		Threshold 16
8/14/76	147	5		2 Hopes Wishes & Dreams		Threshold 17

THOMAS, Rob
Born on 2/14/1972 in Landstuhl, Germany (U.S. military base); raised in Daytona, Florida. Pop-rock singer/songwriter.
Lead singer of **Matchbox Twenty**.

5/7/05	❶[1]	57	▲	1 ...Something To Be		Melisma 83723
7/18/09	3[1]	28		2 Cradlesong		Emblem 517814

THOMAS, Rufus
Born on 3/26/1917 in Cayce, Mississippi; raised in Memphis, Tennessee. Died on 12/15/2001 (age 84). R&B singer/songwriter.
Father of **Carla Thomas**.

12/28/63+	138	3		1 Walking The Dog		Stax 704
4/3/71	147	5		2 Rufus Thomas Live/Doing The Push & Pull At P.J.'s .... [L]		Stax 2039
4/29/72	203	2		3 Did You Heard Me?		Stax 3004

THOMAS, Tasha
Born in 1950 in Jeutyn, Alaska. Died of cancer on 11/8/1984 (age 34). R&B singer/actress. Played "Auntie Em" in Broadway's
The Wiz.

4/21/79	204	1		1 Midnight Rendezvous		Atlantic 19223

THOMAS, Timmy
Born on 11/13/1944 in Evansville, Indiana. R&B singer/songwriter/keyboardist.

1/20/73	53	15		1 Why Can't We Live Together		Glades 6501
6/9/84	205	4		2 Gotta Give A Little Love (Ten Years After)..		Gold Mountain 80006

THOMPSON, Richard
Born on 4/3/1949 in London, England. Singer/songwriter/guitarist. Formed **Fairport Convention** in 1969. Went solo in 1971.
Married to singer **Linda Thompson** (born Linda Pettifer on 8/23/1947 in London, England) from 1972-82.

3/5/83	203	5		1 Shoot Out The Lights		Hannibal 1303
				RICHARD & LINDA THOMPSON		
				RS500 #333		
7/30/83	186	5		2 Hand Of Kindness		Hannibal 1313
2/23/85	202	6		3 One Clear Moment		Warner 25164
				LINDA THOMPSON		
3/9/85	102	13		4 Across A Crowded Room		Polydor 825421
10/25/86	142	6		5 Daring Adventures		Polydor 829728
11/5/88	182	5		6 Amnesia		Capitol 48845
2/26/94	109	3		7 Mirror Blue		Capitol 81492
5/4/96	97	1		8 You? Me? Us?		Capitol 33704 [2]
5/24/03	121	2		9 The Old Kit Bag		Cooking Vinyl 126
8/27/05	197	1		10 Front Parlour Ballads		Cooking Vinyl 4725
6/16/07	111	1		11 Sweet Warrior		Shout! Factory 10555

~ ~ ~ ~ ~ ~ ~ ~ ~ ~ **NON-CHARTED ALBUM** ~ ~ ~ ~ ~ ~ ~ ~ ~ ~ ~
1974 **I Want To See The Bright Lights Tonight**
[w/ Linda Thompson]
RS500 #479

THOMPSON, Robbin, Band
Pop-rock band from Richmond, Virginia: Robbin Thompson (vocals, guitar; born in 1949), Velpo Robertson (guitar), Eric Heiberg
(keyboards), Michael Lanning (bass) and Bob Antonelli (drums). Thompson played in **Bruce Springsteen**'s early Steel Mill band.

10/25/80	168	11		1 Two B's Please		Ovation 1759

Billboard			R I A A	ARTIST		
DEBUT	PEAK	WKS		Album Title	Catalog	Label & Number

THOMPSON, Sue
Born Eva Sue McKee on 7/19/1926 in Nevada, Missouri; raised in San Jose, California. Pop-country singer.

| 3/20/65 | 134 | 3 | | 1 Paper Tiger .... | | Hickory 121 |

~ ~ ~ ~ ~ ~ ~ ~ ~ ~ **NON-CHARTED ALBUMS** ~ ~ ~ ~ ~ ~ ~ ~ ~ ~
1962 **Meet Sue Thompson**   1963 **Golden Hits**
1962 **Two Of A Kind**

THOMPSON, Tony
Born on 9/2/1975 in Waco, Texas; raised in Oklahoma City, Oklahoma. Died of a drug overdose on 6/1/2007 (age 31). R&B singer. Member of **Hi-Five**.

| 7/15/95 | 99 | 5 | | 1 Sexsational .... | | Giant 24596 |

THOMPSON TWINS
Pop-rock trio from England: Tom Bailey (vocals, synthesizer; born on 6/18/1957), Alannah Currie (xylophone, percussion; born on 9/20/1959) and Joe Leeway (conga, synthesizer; born on 11/15/1957). Leeway left in 1986.

6/26/82	148	8		1 In The Name Of Love		Arista 6601
2/26/83	34	25		2 Side Kicks		Arista 6607
3/17/84	10	53	▲	3 Into The Gap		Arista 8200
10/19/85+	20	35	●	4 Here's To Future Days		Arista 8276
4/25/87	76	14		5 Close To The Bone		Arista 8449
8/27/88	175	6		6 Greatest Mixes/The Best Of Thompson Twins .... [K]		Arista 8542
10/21/89	143	6		7 Big Trash		Warner 25921

THOMSON, Ali
Born in 1959 in Glasgow, Scotland. Pop singer/songwriter. Brother of **Supertramp**'s Dougie Thomson.

| 7/5/80 | 99 | 15 | | 1 Take A Little Rhythm .... | | A&M 4803 |
| 4/11/81 | 201 | 2 | | 2 Deception Is An Art .... | | A&M 4846 |

THOMSON, Cyndi
Born on 10/19/1976 in Tifton, Georgia. Country singer/songwriter.

| 8/18/01 | 81 | 23 | ● | 1 My World .... | | Capitol 26010 |

THORN, Paul
Born on 7/13/1964 in Kenosha, Wisconsin. Adult Alternative singer/songwriter/guitarist.

| 3/8/08 | 191 | 1 | | 1 A Long Way From Tupelo.. | | Perpetual 20089 |

THORN, Tracey
Born on 9/26/1962 in Hatfield, Hertfordshire, England. Pop-dance singer. Lead singer of **Everything But The Girl**.

| 4/7/07 | 172 | 1 | | 1 Out Of The Woods... | | Astralwerks 83901 |

THORNLEY
Rock band formed in Toronto, Ontario, Canada: Ian Thornley (vocals, guitar), Tavis Stanley (guitar), Ken Tizzard (bass) and Sekou Lumumba (drums).

| 5/29/04 | 167 | 1 | | 1 Come Again .... | | 604 Records 618325 |

THORNS, The
All-star pop-rock trio: **Matthew Sweet** (vocals, bass), **Shawn Mullins** (vocals, guitar) and Pete Droge (vocals, drums).

| 6/7/03 | 62 | 9 | | 1 The Thorns .... | | Aware 86958 |

THORNTON, Big Mama
Born Willie Mae Thornton on 12/11/1926 in Montgomery, Alabama. Died of heart failure on 7/25/1984 (age 67). Legendary blues singer.

| 8/30/69 | 198 | 2 | | 1 Stronger Than Dirt .... | | Mercury 61225 |

THOROGOOD, George, & The Destroyers   **All-Time: #408**
Born on 12/31/1952 in Wilmington, Delaware. Blues-rock singer/guitarist. The Destroyers: Ron Smith (guitar), Billy Blough (bass) and Jeff Simon (drums). By 1980, Smith left and Hank Carter (sax) joined. Guitarist Steve Chrismar joined in 1986.

9/1/79	78	10		1 Better Than The Rest .... [E]		MCA 3091
				recorded in 1974		
12/9/78+	33	47	●	2 Move It On Over..		Rounder 3024
11/8/80	68	12		3 More George Thorogood And The Destroyers.................................		Rounder 3045
8/28/82	43	48	●	4 Bad To The Bone		EMI America 17076
3/2/85	32	42		5 Maverick		EMI America 17145
8/23/86	33	42	▲	6 Live .... [L]		EMI America 17214
				recorded on 5/23/1986 at the Cincinnati Gardens		
2/6/88	32	24	●	7 Born To Be Bad		EMI-Manhattan 46973
3/16/91	77	13		8 Boogie People		EMI 92514
8/15/92	100	20	▲	9 The Baddest Of George Thorogood And The Destroyers............ [G]		EMI 97718
8/14/93	120	10		10 Haircut..		EMI 89529
6/5/04	55	18	●	11 Greatest Hits: 30 Years Of Rock .... [G]		Capitol 98430
8/15/09	169	1		12 The Dirty Dozen		Capitol 84082

THORPE, Billy
Born on 3/29/1946 in Manchester, England; raised in Australia. Died of a heart attack on 2/28/2007 (age 60). Rock singer/guitarist. Member of **Mick Fleetwood**'s Zoo.

| 5/5/79 | 39 | 23 | | 1 Children Of The Sun .... | | Polydor 6228 |
| 11/8/80 | 151 | 5 | | 2 21st Century Man .... | | Elektra 294 |

THOUSAND FOOT KRUTCH
Christian rock trio from Peterborough, Ontario, Canada: Trevor McNevan (vocals, guitar), Joel Bruyere (bass) and Steve Augustine (drums). McNevan and Augustine also formed **FM Static**.

8/6/05	67	3		1 The Art Of Breaking		Tooth & Nail 74819
10/6/07	58	3		2 The Flame In All Of Us		Tooth & Nail 88247
9/26/09	35	4		3 Welcome To The Masquerade		Tooth & Nail 64783

THP ORCHESTRA
Disco duo from Canada: Barbara Fry (vocals) and W. Michael Lewis (synthesizer). THP: Two Hot People.

2/4/78	65	19		1 Two Hot For Love!		Butterfly 005

3
Rock trio formed by **Emerson, Lake & Palmer** alumni: **Keith Emerson** and Carl Palmer (both British) with California songwriter/guitarist Robert Barry.

3/19/88	97	10		1 To The Power Of Three		Geffen 24181

3-D
Rock band from New York: Rick Zivic (vocals), Keiv Ginsberg (guitar), Ted Wender (keyboards), Nick Stevens (bass) and Mike Fink (drums).

3/1/80	206	2		1 3-D		Polydor 6254

THREE DAYS GRACE
Hard-rock trio from Norwood, Ontario, Canada: Adam Gontier (vocals, guitar), Brad Walst (bass) and Neil Sanderson (drums).

10/25/03+	69	82	▲	1 Three Days Grace		Jive 53479
7/1/06	5	128	▲	2 One-X	Cat:#15/24	Jive 83504
10/10/09	3^1	34		3 Life Starts Now		Jive 46256

THREE DEGREES, The
Female R&B vocal trio from Philadelphia, Pennsylvania: Fayette Pinkney, Sheila Ferguson and Valerie Holiday. Group appeared in the 1971 movie *The French Connection* and an episode of TV's *Sanford & Son*. Pinkney died on 6/27/2009 (age 61).

8/8/70	139	7		1 "Maybe"		Roulette 42050
12/14/74+	28	15		2 The Three Degrees		Philadelphia Int'l. 32406
6/21/75	99	8		3 International		Philadelphia Int'l. 33162
1/17/76	199	1		4 The Three Degrees Live .... [L]		Philadelphia Int'l. 33840
				recorded at Bailey's in London, England		
12/23/78+	169	8		5 New Dimensions		Ariola 50044

THREE DOG NIGHT
All-Time: #198
Pop-rock vocal trio formed in Los Angeles, California: Danny Hutton (born on 9/10/1942), Cory Wells (born on 2/5/1942) and Chuck Negron (born on 6/8/1942). Their regular backing band: Michael Allsup (guitar), Jimmy Greenspoon (keyboards), Joe Schermie (bass) and Floyd Sneed (drums). Named for the coldest night in the Australian outback. Disbanded in the mid-1970s. Re-formed in the mid-1980s.

1/25/69	11	62	▲	1 Three Dog Night		Dunhill/ABC 50048
7/12/69	16	74	●	2 Suitable For Framing		Dunhill/ABC 50058
11/29/69	6	72	●	3 Was Captured Live At The Forum .... [L]		Dunhill/ABC 50068
5/2/70	8	48	●	4 It Ain't Easy		Dunhill/ABC 50078
12/12/70+	14	64	●	5 Naturally		Dunhill/ABC 50088
2/27/71	5	61	●	6 Golden Bisquits .... [G]		Dunhill/ABC 50098
10/23/71	8	34	●	7 Harmony		Dunhill/ABC 50108
7/29/72	6	40	●	8 Seven Separate Fools		Dunhill/ABC 50118
3/17/73	18	27	●	9 Around The World With Three Dog Night .... [L]		Dunhill/ABC 50138 [2]
10/20/73	26	17	●	10 Cyan		Dunhill/ABC 50158
4/6/74	20	22	●	11 Hard Labor		Dunhill/ABC 50168
12/21/74+	15	17	●	12 Joy To The World-Their Greatest Hits .... [G]		Dunhill/ABC 50178
6/21/75	70	12		13 Coming Down Your Way		ABC 888
4/24/76	123	6		14 American Pastime		ABC 928
9/10/83	210	1		15 It's A Jungle .... [EP]		Passport 5001
6/19/04	178	1		16 The Complete Hit Singles .... [G]		Geffen 001779

3 DOORS DOWN
Rock band from Escatawpa, Mississippi: Brad Arnold (vocals), Matt Roberts (guitar), Chris Henderson (guitar), Todd Harrell (bass) and Daniel Adair (drums). Adair left in January 2005 to join **Nickelback**; replaced by Greg Upchurch (of **Puddle Of Mudd**).

2/26/00	7	93	▲[5]	1 The Better Life	Cat:#30/16	Republic 153920
11/30/02	8	97	▲[4]	2 Away From The Sun	Cat:#13/38	Republic 066165
11/29/03	21	28	●	3 Another 700 Miles .... [EP-L]		Republic 001603
2/26/05	❶[1]	42	▲	4 Seventeen Days		Republic 004018
6/7/08	❶[1]	65	●	5 3 Doors Down		Universal Rep. 011065

Billboard			R I A A	ARTIST Album Title	Catalog	Label & Number
DEBUT	**PEAK**	**WKS**				

311
Alternative rap-metal-reggae band from Omaha, Nebraska: Nick Hexum (vocals, guitar; born on 4/12/1970), Doug "SA" Martinez (vocals, DJ; born on 10/29/1969), Tim Mahoney (guitar; born on 2/17/1970), Aaron "P-Nut" Wills (bass; born on 6/5/1974) and Chad Sexton (drums; born on 9/7/1970). 311 (pronounced: three-eleven) is the police code for indecent exposure.

All-Time: #379

DEBUT	PEAK	WKS			Catalog	Label & Number
9/14/96	20^C	12	●	1 Music .... [E]		Capricorn 42008
				released in 1993		
7/30/94	193	1	●	2 Grassroots .... Cat:#23/9		Capricorn 42026
8/12/95+	12	72	▲³	3 311 .... Cat:#13/10		Capricorn 42041
11/23/96	95	1		4 Enlarged To Show Detail		Capricorn 010039
8/23/97	4	33	▲	5 Transistor		Capricorn 536181
11/21/98	77	2		6 Live .... [L]		Capricorn 538263
10/30/99	9	13	●	7 Soundsystem		Capricorn 546645
7/7/01	10	29	●	8 From Chaos		Volcano 32184
8/9/03	7	10		9 Evolver		Volcano 53714
6/26/04	7	17	●	10 Greatest Hits '93-'03 .... Cat:#30/3 [G]		Volcano 60009
9/3/05	5	7		11 Don't Tread On Me		Volcano 69522
6/20/09	3¹	7		12 Uplifter		Volcano 48091

3 INCHES OF BLOOD
Hard-rock band from Vancouver, British Columbia, Canada: Cam Pipes (vocals), Justin Hagberg (guitar), Shane Clark (guitar), Nick Cates (bass) and Ash Pearson (drums).

| 7/14/07 | 147 | 1 | | 1 Fire Up The Blades............................... | | Roadrunner 618023 |
| 9/26/09 | 195 | 1 | | 2 Here Waits Thy Doom .... | | Century Media 8639 |

3LW
Female R&B vocal trio from New Jersey: Naturi Naughton, Kiely Williams and Adrienne Bailon. 3LW: 3 Little Women.

| 12/23/00+ | 29 | 40 | ▲ | 1 3LW.. | | Nine Lives 63961 |
| 11/9/02 | 15 | 6 | | 2 A Girl Can Mack................................... | | Epic 86200 |

THREE O'CLOCK, The
Rock band from Los Angeles, California: Michael Quercio (vocals, bass), Louis Gutierrez (guitar), Mike Mariano (keyboards) and Danny Benair (drums).

| 5/25/85 | 125 | 10 | | 1 Arrive Without Travelling .... | | I.R.S. 5591 |

3OH!3
White electronic-rock/hip-hop duo from Boulder, Colorado: Sean Foreman and Nathaniel Motte.

| 7/26/08+ | 44 | 51 | | 1 Want .... Cat:#36/1 | | Photo Finish 511181 |

THREE 6 MAFIA
Hip-hop group from Memphis, Tennessee: female Lola "**Gangsta Boo**" Mitchell, with males Jordan "Juicy J" Houston, Darnell "Crunchy Black" Carlton, "DJ Paul" Beauregarde, Robert "Koopsta Knicca" Cooper and Ricky "Lord Infamous" Dunigan. Houston, Carlton and Beauregard are the core members on all recordings. Also see **Hypnotize Camp Posse** and **Tear Da Club Up Thugs**.

11/18/00	130	2		1 Kings Of Memphis: Underground Vol. 3 .... [E]		Smoked Out 9997
				TRIPLE SIX MAFIA		
				recordings from the early 1990s		
3/29/97	126	3		2 The End..		Prophet 4405
11/22/97	40	29	●	3 Chpt. 2: "World Domination"		Relativity 1644
7/1/00	6	23	▲	4 When The Smoke Clears Sixty 6, Sixty 1		Loud 1732
11/17/01	19	12		5 Choices..		Loud 1972
7/12/03	4	14	●	6 Da Unbreakables		Hypnotize Minds 89030
5/7/05	10	8		7 Choices II: The Setup		Hypnotize Minds 58884
10/15/05	3¹	49	▲	8 Most Known Unknown		Hypnotize Minds 94724
12/3/05	154	1		9 Most Known Hits.. [G]		Hypnotize Minds 75007
7/12/08	5	18		10 Last 2 Walk		Hypnotize Minds 88580

THREE SUNS, The
Instrumental trio from Philadelphia, Pennsylvania: brothers Al Nevins (guitar) and Morty Nevins (accordian), with cousin Artie Dunn (organ). Al Nevins died on 1/25/1965 (age 48). Morty Nevins died on 7/23/1990 (age 63). Dunn died on 1/15/1996 (age 73).

1950s: #46

5/28/55	13	5		1 Soft And Sweet .... [I]		RCA Victor 1041
				LP: RCA Victor LPM-1041 (#13); EP: RCA Victor EPB-1041 (#13)		
8/18/56	19	1		2 High Fi And Wide .... [I]		RCA Victor 1249
1/26/57	16	6		3 Midnight For Two .... [I]		RCA Victor 1333

3T
R&B teen vocal trio: brothers Taryll, T.J. and Taj Jackson. Sons of Tito Jackson (of **The Jacksons**).

| 1/20/96 | 127 | 15 | | 1 Brotherhood .... | | MJJ Music 57450 |

THREE TENORS, The
All-star trio of operatic tenors: **Jose Carreras**, **Placido Domingo** and **Luciano Pavarotti**.

10/6/90+	35	100	▲³	1 Carreras/Domingo/Pavarotti In Concert .... [L]		London 430433
				recorded on 7/7/1990 at the Baths of Caracalla in Rome, Italy		
12/11/93	127	4	●	2 Christmas Favorites From The World's Favorite Tenors.......... Cat:#21/10 [X-K]		Sony Master. 53725
				Christmas charts: 29/'93, 21/'94, 36/'95		
9/17/94	4	33	▲	3 The 3 Tenors In Concert 1994 .... [L]		Atlantic 82614
				recorded on 7/16/1994 at Dodger Stadium in Los Angeles, California		

Billboard			R I A A	ARTIST		
DEBUT	PEAK	WKS		Album Title	Catalog	Label & Number

THREE TENORS, The — cont'd

9/5/98	83	10	●	4 **The 3 Tenors - Paris 1998** .... **[L]**		Atlantic 83110
				recorded on 7/10/1998		
11/25/00	54	8	●	5 **The Three Tenors Christmas** .... Cat:#17/10 **[X-L]**		Sony Classical 89131
				Christmas charts: 9/'00, 31/'01, 19/'02, 41/'03, 33/'07		

THREE TIMES DOPE
Rap trio from Philadelphia, Pennsylvania: Duerwood Beale, Walter Griggs and Robert Waller.

4/22/89	122	18		1 **Original Stylin'**		Arista 8571

3XKRAZY
Rap trio from Oakland, California: **Keak Da Sneak**, Bart and Agerman.

4/26/97	136	4		1 **Stackin Chips**		Noo Trybe 42961

THRICE
Punk-rock band from Anaheim, California: **Dustin Kensrue** (vocals, guitar), brothers Ed Breckenridge (bass) and Riley Breckenridge (drums), and Teppi Teranishi (guitar).

8/9/03	16	12		1 **The Artist In The Ambulance**		Island 000295
11/5/05	15	7		2 **Vheissu**		Sub City 005428
11/3/07	24	3		3 **The Alchemy Index: Vols. I & II: Fire & Water**		Vagrant 478 [2]
5/3/08	17	2		4 **The Alchemy Index: Vols. III & IV: Air & Earth**		Vagrant 480 [2]
8/29/09	47	3		5 **Beggars**		Vagrant 555

THRILLS
Rock band from New York: Dave Fullerton (vocals, guitar), Tony Monaco (keyboards), Bill Gilbert (bass) and Rob Owens (drums).

6/27/81	199	4		1 **First Thrills**		G&P 1002

THRILLS, The
Eclectic-rock band from Dublin, Ireland: Conor Deasy (vocals, harmonica), Daniel Ryan (guitar), Kevin Horan (keyboards), Padraic McMahon (bass) and Ben Carrigan (drums).

10/2/04	152	1		1 **Let's Bottle Bohemia**		Virgin 66953

THRIVING IVORY
Rock band from Santa Barbara, California: Clayton Stroope (vocals), Drew Cribley (guitar), Scott Jason (keyboards), Bret Cohune (bass) and Paul Niedermier (drums).

1/17/09	102	15		1 **Thriving Ivory**		Wind-Up 13150

THROWDOWN
Hard-rock band from Anaheim, California: Dave Peters (vocals), Mark Choiniere (guitar), Matt Mentley (bass) and Ben Dussault (drums).

7/16/05	156	1		1 **Vendetta**		Trustkill 63
8/25/07	81	2		2 **Venom & Tears**		Trustkill 94

THUG LIFE
Rap group formed in Los Angeles, California: Tupac "**2Pac**" Shakur, Big Syke, Macadoshis, Maurice "Mopreme" Harding and The Rated R. Shakur and Harding were half-brothers. Shakur died on 9/13/1996 (age 25) after a shooting in Las Vegas, Nevada.

10/29/94	42	29	●	1 **Volume 1**		Interscope 92360

THUNDER
Hard-rock band from England: Daniel Bowes (vocals), Luke Morley (guitar), Ben Matthews (keyboards), Mark Luckhurst (bass) and Gary James (drums).

6/1/91	114	10		1 **Backstreet Symphony**		Geffen 24384

THUNDER, Johnny
Born Gil Hamilton on 8/15/1941 in Leesburg, Florida. R&B singer.

~ ~ ~ ~ ~ ~ ~ ~ ~ ~ **NON-CHARTED ALBUM** ~ ~ ~ ~ ~ ~ ~ ~ ~ ~
1963 **Loop De Loop**

THUNDERCLAP NEWMAN
Rock trio formed in England: Andy Newman (keyboards), John **Speedy Keen** (vocals, drums) and Jimmy McCulloch (guitar). McCulloch was a member of **Paul McCartney**'s Wings from 1975-77; died of heart failure on 9/27/1979 (age 26). Keen died on 3/21/2002 (age 56).

10/10/70+	161	10		1 **Hollywood Dream**		Track 8264
				produced by **Pete Townshend**		

THURSDAY
Hard-rock band from New Brunswick, New Jersey: Geoff Rickly (vocals), Steve Pedulla (guitar), Tom Keeley (guitar), Tim Payne (bass) and Tucker Rule (drums).

4/6/02	178	1		1 **Full Collapse**		Victory 145
11/9/02	197	1		2 **Five Stories Falling** .... **[EP-L]**		Victory 189
10/4/03	7	9		3 **War All The Time**		Victory 000293
5/20/06	20	6		4 **A City By The Light Divided**		Victory 006482
11/17/07	113	1		5 **Kill The House Lights**		Victory 408
3/7/09	56	2		6 **Common Existence**		Epitaph 87009

T.I.
Born Clifford Harris on 9/25/1080 in Atlanta, Georgia. Male rapper/record producer/songwriter/actor. Starred in the 2006 movie *ATL*. Co-owner of the record label Grand Hustle.

DEBUT	PEAK	WKS	RIAA	#	Album Title	Catalog	Label & Number
10/27/01	98	3		1	I'm Serious		Ghet-O-Vision 14681
9/6/03	4	51	▲	2	Trap Muzik		Grand Hustle 83650
12/18/04	7	43	▲	3	Urban Legend		Grand Hustle 83734
4/15/06	❶¹	47	▲	4	King		Grand Hustle 83800
7/21/07	❶²	33	▲	5	T.I. vs T.I.P.		Grand Hustle 202172
10/18/08	❶²	55	▲²	6	Paper Trail		Grand Hustle 512267
10/18/08	128	1		7	A King Of Oneself [EP]		Grand Hustle 515963

TIERRA
Latin band formed in Los Angeles, California: brothers Steve Salas (trombone, timbales) and Rudy Salas (guitar), Joey Guerra (keyboards), Bobby Navarrete (reeds), Andre Baeza (congas), Steve Falomir (bass) and Phil Madayag (drums). The Salas brothers and Baeza were formerly with **El Chicano**.

DEBUT	PEAK	WKS		#	Album Title		Label & Number
12/27/80+	38	21		1	City Nights		Boardwalk 36995

TIERRA CALI
Latin band from Mexico: brothers Humberto, Rafael, Cruz, Arcadio and Efrain Plancarte.

DEBUT	PEAK	WKS		#	Album Title		Label & Number
6/14/08	158	1		1	Mas Alla De La Distancia [F]		Vene Music 653429
7/25/09	128	1		2	Si Tu Te Vas [F]		Vene Music 653700

TIESTO
Born Tijs Verwerst on 1/17/1969 in Holland. Dance DJ.

DEBUT	PEAK	WKS		#	Album Title		Label & Number
5/13/06	164	1		1	In Search Of Sunrise 5: Los Angeles		Song Bird 09 [2]
4/28/07	71	4		2	Elements Of Life		Ultra 1515
11/3/07	170	1		3	In Search Of Sunrise 6: Ibiza		Black Hole 30759
6/28/08	91	3		4	In Search Of Sunrise 7: Asia		Song Bird 11 [2]
10/24/09	59	4		5	Kaleidoscope		Ultra 2082

TIFFANY
Born Tiffany Darwish on 10/2/1971 in Norwalk, California. Teen pop singer.

DEBUT	PEAK	WKS	RIAA	#	Album Title		Label & Number
9/26/87+	❶²	69	▲⁴	1	Tiffany		MCA 5793
12/10/88+	17	29	▲	2	Hold An Old Friend's Hand		MCA 6267

TIGER ARMY
Punk-rock trio formed in Berkeley, California: "Nick 13" Jones (vocals, guitar), Jeff Roffredo (bass) and James Meza (drums).

DEBUT	PEAK	WKS		#	Album Title		Label & Number
7/17/04	146	1		1	Tiger Army III: Ghost Tigers Rise		Hellcat 80457
6/23/07	49	3		2	Music From Regions Beyond		Hellcat 80492

TIKARAM, Tanita
Born on 12/8/1969 in Munster, West Germany; raised in Basingstoke, England. Female singer/songwriter.

DEBUT	PEAK	WKS		#	Album Title		Label & Number
2/11/89	59	23		1	Ancient Heart		Reprise 25839
2/24/90	124	7		2	The Sweet Keeper		Reprise 26091
4/20/91	142	5		3	Everybody's Angel		Reprise 26486

TILLIS, Pam
Born on 7/24/1957 in Plant City, Florida. Country singer/songwriter/guitarist. Daughter of Mel Tillis.
AWARDS: CMA: Female Vocalist 1994 ★ OPRY: 2000

DEBUT	PEAK	WKS	RIAA	#	Album Title		Label & Number
1/25/92	69	23	●	1	Put Yourself In My Place		Arista 18642
10/17/92	82	42	▲	2	Homeward Looking Angel		Arista 18649
5/14/94	51	37	▲	3	Sweetheart's Dance		Arista 18758
11/25/95	151	2	●	4	All Of This Love		Arista 18799
6/21/97	47	21	▲	5	Greatest Hits [G]		Arista 18836
3/24/01	183	1		6	Thunder & Roses		Arista 67000

TILLOTSON, Johnny
Born on 4/20/1939 in Jacksonville, Florida; raised in Palatka, Florida. Pop singer/songwriter. Appeared in the movie *Just For Fun*.

DEBUT	PEAK	WKS		#	Album Title		Label & Number
4/14/62	120	5		1	Johnny Tillotson's Best [G]		Cadence 3052
7/21/62	8	31		2	It Keeps Right On A-Hurtin'		Cadence 3058
2/22/64	48	14		3	Talk Back Trembling Lips		MGM 4188
2/6/65	148	3		4	She Understands Me		MGM 4270

~ ~ ~ ~ ~ ~ ~ ~ ~ **NON-CHARTED ALBUMS** ~ ~ ~ ~ ~ ~ ~ ~ ~ ~ ~

1963 You Can Never Stop Me Loving You	1965 Johnny Tillotson Sings Our World
1964 The Tillotson Touch	1966 The Christmas Touch
1965 That's My Style	

'TIL TUESDAY
Pop-rock band formed in Boston, Massachusetts: **Aimee Mann** (vocals, bass), Robert Holmes (guitar), Joey Pesce (keyboards) and Michael Hausman (drums). Michael Montes replaced Pesce in 1988.

DEBUT	PEAK	WKS	RIAA	#	Album Title		Label & Number
4/20/85	19	31	●	1	Voices Carry		Epic 39458
10/25/86	49	26	●	2	Welcome Home		Epic 40314
11/19/88	124	19		3	Everything's Different Now		Epic 44041

TIMBALAND
Born Timothy Mosley on 3/10/1971 in Norfolk, Virginia. Male rapper/producer. Magoo was born Melvin Barcliff on 7/12/1973 in Norfolk, Virginia.

11/29/97+	33	37	▲	1 Welcome To Our World	Blackground 92772
				TIMBALAND AND MAGOO	
12/12/98	41	15		2 Tim's Bio: From The Motion Picture: Life From Da Bassment	Blackground 92813
12/8/01	29	14		3 Indecent Proposal	Blackground 10946
12/6/03	50	3		4 Under Construction Part II	Blackground 001185
4/21/07	5	53	▲	5 Timbaland Presents Shock Value	Mosley 008594
12/26/09	36	23		6 Timbaland Presents Shock Value II........................	Mosley 013645

TIMBERLAKE, Justin
Born on 1/31/1981 in Memphis, Tennessee. Member of *NSYNC. Regular on TV's *The Mickey Mouse Club* (1992-93).

11/23/02	2^1	72	▲^{3}	1 Justified	Cat:#41/1	Jive 41823
				Grammy: Pop Vocal Album		
9/30/06	❶^2	80	▲^{4}	2 FutureSex/LoveSounds	Cat:#17/15	Jive 88062

TIMBUK 3
Husband-and-wife duo from Austin, Texas: Patrick MacDonald and Barbara MacDonald.

10/4/86+	50	30		1 Greetings From Timbuk 3...................................	I.R.S. 5739
5/7/88	107	13		2 Eden Alley..	I.R.S. 42124

TIME, The
R&B-funk-dance band from Minneapolis, Minnesota: **Morris Day** (vocals), **Jesse Johnson** (guitar), Jimmy "Jam" Harris (keyboards), Monte Moir (keyboards), Terry Lewis (bass) and Jellybean Johnson (drums). Lewis, Harris and Moir left before band's featured role in movie *Purple Rain*. Paul "St. Paul" Peterson (keyboards) and Jerome Benton (dancer) joined in 1984; group disbanded later that year. Lewis and Harris became highly successful songwriting/producing team. Lewis married **Karyn White**. Original lineup (and Benton) regrouped in 1990.

9/12/81	50	32	●	1 The Time	Warner 3598
9/25/82	26	33	●	2 What Time Is It?...	Warner 23701
7/28/84	24	57	▲	3 Ice Cream Castle	Warner 25109
7/28/90	18	16	●	4 Pandemonium	Paisley Park 27490

TIMES TWO
White male electro-pop duo of from Pt. Reyes, California: Shanti Jones and Johnny Dollar.

4/30/88	137	11		1 X2	Reprise 25624

TIMMY -T-
Born Timmy Torres on 9/21/1967 in Fresno, California. Dance-pop singer/songwriter.

1/26/91	46	23		1 Time After Time	Quality 15103

TING TINGS, The
Alternative pop-rock duo from Manchester, England: Katie White and Jules DeMartino.

6/7/08	78	54		1 We Started Nothing...	Columbia 28925

TIN MACHINE
Rock band formed in Los Angeles, California: **David Bowie** (vocals), Reeves Gabrels (guitar), Tony Sales (bass; **Utopia**, **Chequered Past**) and Hunt Sales (drums; **Utopia**, **Paris**). The Sales brothers are the sons of TV comedian **Soupy Sales**.

6/10/89	28	17		1 Tin Machine	EMI 91990
9/21/91	126	3		2 Tin Machine II	Victory 511216

TINSLEY, Boyd
Born on 5/16/1964 in Charlottesville, West Virginia. Black adult-alternative singer/violinist. Member of the **Dave Matthews Band**.

7/5/03	97	1		1 True Reflections	Bama Rags 52633

TINTED WINDOWS
All-star power-pop band formed in New York: Taylor Hanson (vocals; **Hanson**), James Iha (guitar; **Smashing Pumpkins**), Adam Schlesinger (bass; **Fountains Of Wayne**) and Brad "Bun E. Carlos" Carlson (drums; **Cheap Trick**).

5/9/09	59	2		1 Tinted Windows...	S-Curve 59001

TIN TIN
Pop duo from Australia: Steve Kipner (keyboards) and Steve Groves (guitar).

6/5/71	197	1		1 Tin Tin	Atco 350

TINY TIM
Born Herbert Khaury on 4/12/1930 in Brooklyn, New York. Died of heart failure on 11/30/1996 (age 66). Novelty singer/ukulele player. Shot to national attention with appearances on TV's *Rowan & Martin's Laugh-In*. Married "Miss Vicki" on Johnny Carson's *Tonight Show* on 12/18/1969; divorced in 1977.

5/4/68	7	32		1 God Bless Tiny Tim [N]	Reprise 6292

TIPPIN, Aaron
Born on 7/3/1958 in Pensacola, Florida; raised in Travelers Rest, South Carolina. Country singer/songwriter/guitarist.

5/25/91	153	21	●	1 You've Got To Stand For Something..........................	RCA 2374
3/28/92	50	60	▲	2 Read Between The Lines....................................	RCA 61129
8/28/93	53	39	●	3 Call Of The Wild..	RCA 66251
11/26/94+	114	13	●	4 Lookin' Back At Myself.....................................	RCA 66420
11/11/95	63	23	●	5 Tool Box	RCA 66740
5/3/97	97	5		6 Greatest Hits...And Then Some .... [G]	RCA 67427

TIPPIN, Aaron — cont'd

8/12/00	53	26	●	7 People Like Us..		Lyric Street 165014
9/28/02	62	2		8 Stars & Stripes		Lyric Street 165033
9/23/06	162	1		9 Now & Then		Nippit 11701

TISDALE, Ashley
Born on 7/2/1985 in West Deal, New Jersey. Female singer/actress. Played "Sharpay Evans" in the Disney TV movie series *High School Musical*.

2/24/07	5	33	●	1 Headstrong		Warner 44425
8/15/09	12	6		2 Guilty Pleasure		Warner 518235

TISDALE, Wayman
Born on 6/9/1964 in Tulsa, Oklahoma. Died of cancer on 5/15/2009 (age 44). Jazz bassist. Professional NBA player from 1985-97.

7/15/06	116	1		1 Way Up!	[I]	Rendezvous 5118
6/21/08	121	1		2 Rebound	[I]	Rendezvous 5139

TJADER, Cal
Born Callen Tjader on 7/16/1925 in St. Louis, Missouri. Died on 5/5/1982 (age 56). Jazz vibraphonist.

9/28/63	79	14		1 Several Shades Of Jade	[I]	Verve 8507
4/17/65	52	22		2 Soul Sauce	[I]	Verve 8614

TKA
Latin disco trio from Harlem, New York: Tony Ortiz, Louis "K7" Sharpe and Ralph Cruz.

1/30/88	135	11		1 Scars Of Love		Tommy Boy 1011
4/25/92	131	9		2 Greatest Hits	[G]	Tommy Boy 1040

TKO
Rock band from Seattle, Washington: Brad Sinsel (vocals), Rick Pierce (guitar), Tony Bortko (keyboards), Mark Seidenverg (bass) and Darryl Siguenza (drums).

4/21/79	181	2		1 Let It Roll		Infinity 9005

TLC
Female R&B vocal trio formed in Atlanta, Georgia: Tionne "T-Boz" Watkins (born on 4/26/1970), Lisa "Left Eye" Lopes (born on 5/27/1971; died in a car crash on 4/25/2002, age 30) and Rozonda "Chilli" Thomas (born on 2/27/1971). Founded and managed by **Pebbles**. T-Boz married **Mack 10** on 8/19/2000 (since separated).

3/14/92	14	73	▲[4]	1 Ooooooohhh...On The TLC Tip		LaFace 26003
12/3/94+	3[1]	99	▲[10]	2 CrazySexyCool Cat:#33/1		LaFace 26009
				Grammy: R&B Album ★ *RS500 #377*		
3/13/99	❶[5]	64	▲[6]	3 FanMail		LaFace 26055
				Grammy: R&B Album		
11/30/02	6	20	▲	4 3D		Arista 14780
7/9/05	53	11		5 Now & Forever: The Hits	[G]	LaFace 50208

TMI BOYZ
Rap group from Houston, Texas: BC, Huskey, Dudella and Sayeed.

6/28/08	79	3		1 Grindin' For A Purpose		Track Muzic 0017

TNT
Hard-rock band from Norway: Tony Harnell (vocals), Ronni Le Tekro (guitar), Morty Black (bass) and Diesel Dahl (drums).

5/23/87	100	21		1 Tell No Tales		Mercury 830979
3/18/89	115	12		2 Intuition		Mercury 836777

TOADIES
Rock band from Fort Worth, Texas: Todd Lewis (vocals, guitar), Darrel Herbert (guitar), Lisa Umbarger (bass) and Mark Reznicek (drums). Clark Vogeler replaced Herbert in 2000.

8/12/95	56	49	▲	1 Rubberneck		Interscope 92402
4/7/01	130	1		2 Hell Below / Stars Above		Interscope 490872
9/6/08	59	2		3 No Deliverance		Kirtland 46

TOAD THE WET SPROCKET
Pop-rock band from Santa Barbara, California: Glen Phillips (vocals), Todd Nichols (guitar), Dean Dinning (bass) and Randy Guss (drums). Name taken from a **Monty Python** skit.

7/11/92	49	46	▲	1 Fear		Columbia 47309
6/11/94	34	42	▲	2 Dulcinea		Columbia 57744
11/11/95	37	15	●	3 In Light Syrup		Columbia 67394
6/7/97	19	12		4 Coil		Columbia 67862

TOBY BEAU
Pop band from Texas: Balde Silva (vocals, harmonica), Danny McKenna (guitar), Ron Rose (banjo), Steve Zipper (bass) and Rob Young (drums). McKenna committed suicide on 4/26/2006 (age 54).

6/10/78	40	23		1 Toby Beau...		RCA Victor 2771
9/1/79	204	3		2 More Than A Love Song		RCA Victor 3119

Billboard DEBUT	PEAK	WKS	R I A A	ARTIST Album Title	Catalog	Label & Number
				TOBYMAC Born Kevin McKeehan on 10/22/1964 in Washington DC. Christian singer. Leader of **DC Talk**.		
11/24/01	110	2	●	1 Momentum .... **Cat:**#5/9		ForeFront 25294
10/23/04	54	18	●	2 Welcome To Diverse City .... **Cat:**#25/2		ForeFront 66417
9/17/05	162	1		3 Renovating Diverse City		ForeFront 32644
3/10/07	10	35	●	4 Portable Sounds **Cat:**❶²/13		ForeFront 70379
6/14/08	112	4		5 Alive And Transported .... **[L]** *Grammy: Rock Gospel Album*		ForeFront 15684
				TODAY R&B vocal group from Englewood, New Jersey: Frederick "**Big Bub**" Drakeford, Larry McCain, Wesley Adams and Larry Singletary.		
1/14/89	86	22		1 Today		Motown 6261
10/13/90	132	6		2 The New Formula		Motown 6309
				TOKENS, The Vocal group formed in Brooklyn, New York: brothers Phil Margo and Mitch Margo, with Hank Medress and Jay Siegel. Formed own B.T. Puppy record label in 1964. The Margos and Siegel recorded as **Cross Country** in 1973. Medress died of lung cancer on 6/18/2007 (age 68).		
1/27/62	54	16		1 The Lion Sleeps Tonight		RCA Victor 2514
5/21/66	148	2		2 I Hear Trumpets Blow		B.T. Puppy 1000
7/22/67	134	6		3 Back To Back.. **THE TOKENS / THE HAPPENINGS** side 1: The Tokens; side 2: **The Happenings**		B.T. Puppy 1002

~ ~ ~ ~ ~ ~ ~ ~ ~ ~ **NON-CHARTED ALBUMS** ~ ~ ~ ~ ~ ~ ~ ~ ~ ~ ~
1962 **We The Tokens Sing Folk**   1966 **The Tokens Again**
1964 **Wheels**

Billboard DEBUT	PEAK	WKS	R I A A	ARTIST Album Title	Catalog	Label & Number
				TOKIO HOTEL Rock band from Magdeburg, Germany: identical twin brothers Bill Kaulitz (vocals), Tom Kaulitz (guitar), Georg Listing (bass) and Gustav Schafer (drums).		
5/24/08	39	21		1 Scream		Cherrytree 011127
10/24/09	35	3		2 Humanoid..		Cherrytree 013478
				TOKYO POLICE CLUB Alternative-rock band from Newmarket, Ontario, Canada: Dave Monks (vocals, bass), Josh Hook (guitar), Graham Wright (keyboards) and Greg Alsop (drums).		
5/10/08	106	2		1 Elephant Shell		Saddle Creek 116
				TOMAHAWK Hard-rock band formed San Francisco, California: Mike Patton (vocals), Duane Denison (guitar), Kevin Rutmanis (bass) and John Stainer (drums). Patton was also leader of **Faith No More**, **Fantômas** and **Mr. Bungle**.		
5/24/03	137	2		1 Mit Gas		Ipecac 40
7/7/07	158	1		2 Anonymous		Ipecac 89
				TOMITA Born Isao Tomita on 4/22/1932 in Tokyo, Japan. Classical keyboardist.		
8/31/74	57	25		1 Snowflakes Are Dancing .... **[I]**		RCA Victor 0488
5/24/75	49	12		2 Moussorgsky: Pictures At An Exhibition .... **[I]**		RCA Victor 0838
2/14/76	71	12		3 Firebird .... **[I]**		RCA Victor 11312
1/8/77	67	13		4 Holst: The Planets .... **[I]**		RCA Victor 1919
2/18/78	115	10		5 Kosmos .... **[I]**		RCA Victor 2616
3/3/79	152	6		6 The Bermuda Triangle .... **[I]**		RCA Victor 2885
12/8/79	206	2		7 Tomita's Greatest Hits .... **[I-K]**		RCA Victor 3439
2/9/80	174	5		8 Ravel: Bolero .... **[I]**		RCA Victor 3412
				TOMLIN, Chris Born on 5/4/1972 in Grand Saline, Texas. Male Contemporary Christian singer/songwriter/guitarist. Member of **Passion Worship Band**.		
9/28/02	161	1		1 Not To Us		Sparrow 38661
10/9/04	39	43	▲	2 Arriving .... **Cat:**#2¹/12		Sixsteps 94243
10/14/06	15	65	●	3 See The Morning.. **Cat:**#39/2		Sixsteps 62828
9/20/08	9	60		4 Hello Love		Sixsteps 12359
10/24/09	44	12		5 Glory In The Highest: Christmas Songs Of Worship .... **[X]** Christmas chart: 1/'09		Sixsteps 93261
				TOMLIN, Lily Born Mary Jean Tomlin on 9/1/1939 in Detroit, Michigan. Comic actress. Cast member of TV's *Laugh-In* (1970-73). Starred in several movies.		
3/27/71	15	25		1 This Is A Recording .... **[C]** *Grammy: Comedy Album*		Polydor 4055
3/25/72	41	22		2 And That's The Truth .... **[C]**		Polydor 5023
11/12/77	120	6		3 On Stage .... **[C]**		Arista 4142
				TOMLINSON, Trent Born on 7/3/1975 in Blytheville, Arkansas; raised in Kennett, Missouri. Country singer/songwriter/guitarist.		
3/25/06	95	11		1 Country Is My Rock..		Lyric Street 165060

Billboard			R I A A	ARTIST		
DEBUT	PEAK	WKS		Album Title	Catalog	Label & Number

TOMMY TUTONE
Rock band formed in San Francisco, California: Tommy Heath (vocals), Jim Keller (guitar), Jon Lyons (bass) and Victor Carberry (drums).

5/24/80	68	13		1 Tommy Tutone		Columbia 36372
2/6/82	20	30		2 Tommy Tutone-2		Columbia 37401
10/29/83	179	3		3 National Emotion....................		Columbia 38425

TOMS, Gary, Empire
Disco band formed in New York: Gary Toms (keyboards), Helen Jacobs (vocals), Rick Kenny (guitar), Eric Oliver (trumpet), Les Rose (sax), Warren Tesoro (percussion), John Freeman (bass) and Rick Murray (drums).

| 9/27/75 | 178 | 3 | | 1 7-6-5-4-3-2-1 Blow Your Whistle .... | | PIP 6814 |

TOM TOM CLUB
Studio project formed by husband-and-wife Chris Frantz and Tina Weymouth (married on 6/18/1977). Both were members of **Talking Heads**.

10/24/81+	23	33	●	1 Tom Tom Club		Sire 3628
8/20/83	73	13		2 Close To The Bone		Sire 23916
4/15/89	114	11		3 Boom Boom Chi Boom Boom		Sire 25888

TONE LOC
Born Anthony Smith on 3/3/1966 in Los Angeles, California. Male rapper/actor. Appeared in several movies.

| 2/18/89 | ●[1] | 42 | ▲[2] | 1 Loc-ed After Dark | | Delicious Vinyl 3000 |

TONEX & THE PECULIAR PEOPLE
Gospel group formed by Anthony "Tonex" Williams (born on 5/16/1975 in San Diego, California).

| 6/5/04 | 89 | 4 | | 1 Out The Box .... [L] | | Verity 53713 [2] |

TONEY, Oscar Jr.
Born on 5/26/1939 in Selma, Alabama; raised in Columbus, Georgia. R&B singer.

| 7/29/67 | 192 | 5 | | 1 For Your Precious Love............ | | Bell 6006 |

TONI & TERRY
Country-rock female duo: Toni Brown and Terry Garthwaite. Both from the group **Joy Of Cooking**.

| 3/3/73 | 205 | 3 | | 1 Cross-Country .... | | Capitol 11137 |

TONIC
Rock band from Los Angeles, California: Emerson Hart (vocals, guitar), Jeff Russo (guitar), Dan Rothchild (bass) and Kevin Shepard (drums). Dan Lavery replaced Rothchild in 1998.

4/19/97	28	57	▲	1 Lemon Parade		Polydor 531042
11/27/99	81	8		2 Sugar		Universal 542069
10/12/02	141	1		3 Head On Straight...............		Universal 064397

TONIGHT SHOW BAND, The — see SEVERINSEN, Doc

TONIO K.
Born Antonio Krikorian on 4/15/1949 in Palm Desert, California. Eclectic singer/songwriter.

| 4/14/79 | 203 | 4 | | 1 Life In The Foodchain .... | | Full Moon 35545 |

TONY! TONI! TONE!
R&B-funk trio from Oakland, California: brothers **Raphael Saadiq** (vocals, bass, keyboards) and **Dwayne Wiggins** (vocals, guitar), with cousin Tim Christian (drums). Trio appeared in the 1991 movie *House Party 2*.

5/28/88	69	46	●	1 Who?		Wing 835549
5/26/90	34	64	▲	2 The Revival		Wing 841902
7/10/93	24	43	▲[2]	3 Sons Of Soul...................		Wing 514933
12/7/96+	32	31	▲	4 House Of Music		Mercury 534250

TOOL
Heavy-metal band from Los Angeles, California: Maynard James Keenan (vocals), Adam Jones (guitar), Paul D'Amour (bass) and Danny Carey (drums). Justin Chancellor replaced D'Amour in 1995. Keenan also formed **A Perfect Circle**.

7/17/93	50	62	▲[2]	1 Undertow .... Cat:#10/6		Zoo 11052
6/2/01	48[C]	1	▲	2 Opiate .... [E]		Volcano 31027
				released in 1995		
10/19/96	2[1]	104	▲[3]	3 Aenima .... Cat:#5/91		Volcano 31087
12/30/00	38	11		4 Salival .... [L]		Volcano 31159
6/2/01	●[1]	40	▲[2]	5 Lateralus .... Cat:#11/1		Volcano 31160
5/20/06	●[1]	61	▲	6 10,000 Days		Tool Dissectional 81991

TOO SHORT   **All-Time: #260**
Born Todd Shaw on 4/28/1966 in Los Angeles, California. Male rapper/songwriter/actor. Played "Lew-Loc" in the 1993 movie *Menace II Society*. Formed own Short record label. Also see **Various Artists Compilations:** *Too Short Mix Tape Volume 1 - Nation Riders.*

2/25/89	37	78	▲[2]	1 Life Is...Too Short................		Jive 1149
9/29/90	20	53	▲	2 Short Dog's In The House		Jive 1348
8/1/92	6	21	▲	3 Shorty The Pimp		Jive 41467
11/13/93	4	33	▲	4 Get In Where You Fit In		Jive 41526
2/11/95	6	20	▲	5 Cocktails		Jive 41553

Billboard			R I A A	ARTIST Album Title	Catalog	Label & Number
DEBUT	**PEAK**	**WKS**				

TOO SHORT — cont'd

DEBUT	PEAK	WKS			Label & Number
6/8/96	3[1]	25	▲	6 Gettin' It (Album Number Ten)	Jive 41584
7/31/99	5	14	●	7 Can't Stay Away	Jive 41644
9/30/00	12	9	●	8 You Nasty	Jive 41711
12/8/01	71	3		9 Chase The Cat	Jive 41761
11/16/02	38	4		10 What's My Favorite Word?	Jive 41816
11/22/03	49	8		11 Married To The Game	Short 53722
2/4/06	80	2		12 Pimpin' Incorporated	Up All Nite 0011
9/16/06	14	6		13 Blow The Whistle	Short 83501
12/22/07	160	1		14 Get Off The Stage	Short 19181

TOOTS & THE MAYTALS
Reggae trio from Jamaica: Fred "Toots" Hibbert, Nate "Jerry" Matthias and Henry "Raleigh" Gordon.

DEBUT	PEAK	WKS			Label & Number
11/1/75	164	13		1 Funky Kingston **RS500 #378**	Island 9330
7/17/76	157	5		2 Reggae Got Soul	Mango 9374
4/24/04	177	4		3 True Love	V2 27186

TOP AUTHORITY
Rap duo of cousins from Flint, Michigan: Dia Kanyama Peacock and Diallo Sekou Peacock.

DEBUT	PEAK	WKS			Label & Number
11/25/95	144	3		1 Rated G	Trak 72668
11/8/97	192	2		2 Uncut - The New Yea	Wrap 8160

TORA TORA
Hard-rock band from Memphis, Tennessee: Anthony Corder (vocals), Keith Douglas (guitar), Patrick Francis (bass) and John Patterson (drums).

DEBUT	PEAK	WKS			Label & Number
7/15/89	47	33		1 Surprise Attack	A&M 5261
6/6/92	132	6		2 Wild America	A&M 5371

TORME, Mel
Born on 9/13/1925 in Chicago, Illinois. Died of a stroke on 6/5/1999 (age 73). Jazz singer/songwriter/pianist/drummer/actor. Wrote "The Christmas Song." Frequently appeared as himself on TV's *Night Court*. Nicknamed "The Velvet Fog."
AWARD: Grammy: Lifetime Achievement 1999

DEBUT	PEAK	WKS			Label & Number
12/19/92	170	3		1 Christmas Songs [X]	Telarc 83315

TORNADOES, The
Surf-rock instrumental band formed in England: Alan Caddy (lead guitar), George Bellamy (rhythm guitar), Roger Jackson (keyboards), Heinz Burt (bass) and Clem Cattini (drums). Burt died of muscular dystrophy on 4/7/2000 (age 57).

DEBUT	PEAK	WKS			Label & Number
1/5/63	45	17		1 The Original Telstar [I]	London 3279

TOROK, Mitchell
Born on 10/28/1929 in Houston, Texas. Country singer/songwriter/guitarist.
~ ~ ~ ~ ~ ~ ~ ~ ~ ~ **NON-CHARTED ALBUM** ~ ~ ~ ~ ~ ~ ~ ~ ~ ~ ~
1960 **Caribbean By Mitchell Torok** *["Pink Chiffon"]*

TORONTO
Rock band from Toronto, Ontario, Canada: Holly Woods (vocals), Sheron Alton (guitar), Brian Allen (guitar), Scott Kreyer (keyboards) and Jim Fox (drums).

DEBUT	PEAK	WKS			Label & Number
8/30/80	185	4		1 Lookin' For Trouble	A&M 4821
9/4/82	162	10		2 Get It On Credit	Network 60153

TORRANCE, Richard, & Eureka
Rock band from Los Angeles, California: Richard Torrance (vocals, guitar), Gary Rowles (guitar), Richard Cantu (congas), Duane Scott (keyboards), Jon Lamb (bass) and Dennis Mansfield (drums).

DEBUT	PEAK	WKS			Label & Number
3/8/75	107	17		1 Belle Of The Ball	Shelter 2134

TORTOISE
Punk-rock trio from Chicago, Illinois: John Herndon (vocals, guitar), Doug McCombs (bass) and John McEntire (drums).

DEBUT	PEAK	WKS			Label & Number
3/10/01	200	1		1 Standards [I]	Thrill Jockey 089
7/11/09	149	1		2 Beacons Of Ancestorship	Thrill Jockey 210

TOSH, Peter
Born Winston Hubert MacIntosh on 10/9/1944 in Westmoreland, Jamaica. Fatally shot on 9/11/1987 (age 42) during a robbery at his home in Jamaica. Former member of **Bob Marley & The Wailers**.

DEBUT	PEAK	WKS			Label & Number
7/31/76	199	2	▲	1 Legalize It	Columbia 34253
12/9/78+	104	20		2 Bush Doctor	Rolling Stones 39109
8/4/79	123	10		3 Mystic Man	Rolling Stones 39111
7/18/81	91	13		4 Wanted Dread & Alive	EMI America 17055
6/18/83	59	17		5 Mama Africa	EMI America 17095
9/22/84	152	8		6 Captured Live [L] recorded at the Greek Theatre in Los Angeles, California	EMI America 17126

TOTAL
Female R&B vocal trio from Harlem, New York: Kima Raynor, Keisha Spivey and Pam Long.

DEBUT	PEAK	WKS			Label & Number
3/2/96	23	27	▲	1 Total	Bad Boy 73006
11/21/98	39	30	●	2 Kima, Keisha & Pam	Bad Boy 73120

TOTO

Soft-rock band formed in Los Angeles, California: brothers Steve Porcaro (vocals, keyboards; born on 9/2/1957) and Jeff Porcaro (drums; born on 4/1/1954; died of a heart attack on 8/5/1992, age 38), Bobby Kimball (vocals; born on 3/29/1947), Steve Lukather (guitar; born on 10/21/1957), David Paich (vocals, keyboards; born on 6/21/1954) and David Hungate (bass). Prominent session musicians. Steve and Jeff's brother, Mike Porcaro, replaced Hungate in 1982. Dennis "Fergie" Fredericksen (of Trillion) replaced Kimball in late 1984. Joseph Williams (son of composer John Williams) replaced Fredericksen in early 1986. Jean-Michel Byron replaced Williams in 1990. Kimball returned in 1998.

DEBUT	PEAK	WKS	RIAA	#	Album Title	Catalog	Label & Number
10/21/78+	9	48	▲²	1	Toto	Cat:#3/42	Columbia 35317
11/17/79	37	29	●	2	Hydra	Cat:#24/22	Columbia 36229
2/7/81	41	10		3	Turn Back		Columbia 36813
4/24/82	4	82	▲³	4	Toto IV		Columbia 37728
					Grammy: Album of the Year		
11/24/84	42	21	●	5	Isolation		Columbia 38962
12/22/84+	168	8		6	Dune	[I-S]	Polydor 823770
9/13/86	40	36	●	7	Fahrenheit		Columbia 40273
3/19/88	64	18		8	The Seventh One		Columbia 40873
9/22/90	153	4	▲	9	Past To Present 1977-1990	[G]	Columbia 45368

TOUCH, Tony

Born Joseph Anthony Hernandez on 7/2/1969 in Brooklyn, New York. Male rapper.

DEBUT	PEAK	WKS	RIAA	#	Album Title	Catalog	Label & Number
5/6/00	57	9		1	The Piecemaker		Tommy Boy 1347

TOUPS, Wayne, & Zydecajun

Born on 10/2/1958 in Lafayette, Louisiana. Singer/songwriter/accordianist. Zydecajun: Wade Richard (guitar), Rick Lagneaux (keyboards), Mark Miller (bass) and Troy Gaspard (drums).

DEBUT	PEAK	WKS	RIAA	#	Album Title	Catalog	Label & Number
3/18/89	183	4		1	Blast From The Bayou		Mercury 836518

TOURISTS, The

Rock band from London, England: Annie Lennox (vocals, keyboards), David A. Stewart (guitar), Peet Coombes (guitar), Eddie Chinn (bass) and Jim Toomey (drums). Lennox and Stewart later formed Eurythmics.

DEBUT	PEAK	WKS	RIAA	#	Album Title	Catalog	Label & Number
4/26/80	204	4		1	Reality Effect		Epic 36386
2/28/81	204	3		2	Luminous Basement		Epic 36757

TOUSSAINT, Allen

Born on 1/14/1938 in New Orleans, Louisiana. R&B singer/songwriter/pianist.
AWARDS: Grammy: Trustees 2009 ★ R&R Hall of Fame: 1998 (Non-Performer)

DEBUT	PEAK	WKS	RIAA	#	Album Title	Catalog	Label & Number
4/19/75	204	6		1	Southern Nights		Reprise 2186
6/24/06	103	3		2	The River In Reverse		Verve Forecast 006660
					ELVIS COSTELLO & ALLEN TOUSSAINT		

TOWER OF POWER

Interracial R&B-funk band from Oakland, California: Lenny Williams (vocals), Willie Fulton (guitar), Greg Adams, Mic Gillette, Steve Kupka, Emilio Castillo and Lenny Pickett (horns). Chester Thompson (keyboards), Francis Prestia (bass) and David Garibaldi (drums).

DEBUT	PEAK	WKS	RIAA	#	Album Title	Catalog	Label & Number
4/10/71+	106	12		1	East Bay Grease		San Francisco 204
6/17/72	85	20		2	Bump City		Warner 2616
6/2/73	15	31	●	3	Tower Of Power		Warner 2681
3/9/74	26	35		4	Back To Oakland		Warner 2749
1/25/75	22	16		5	Urban Renewal		Warner 2834
10/11/75	67	11		6	In The Slot		Warner 2880
5/22/76	99	8		7	Live And In Living Color	[L]	Warner 2924
9/11/76	42	17		8	Ain't Nothin' Stoppin' Us Now		Columbia 34302
4/22/78	89	8		9	We Came To Play!		Columbia 34906
8/11/79	106	12		10	Back On The Streets		Columbia 35784

TOWNSEND, Ed

Born on 4/16/1929 in Fayetteville, Tennessee. Died of heart failure on 8/13/2003 (age 74). R&B singer/songwriter.

~ ~ ~ ~ ~ ~ ~ ~ ~ ~ *NON-CHARTED ALBUM* ~ ~ ~ ~ ~ ~ ~ ~ ~ ~
1959 **New In Town**

TOWNSHEND, Pete

Born on 5/19/1945 in London, England. Rock singer/songwriter/guitarist. Member of The Who. Brother of Simon Townshend.

DEBUT	PEAK	WKS	RIAA	#	Album Title	Catalog	Label & Number
11/18/72+	69	17		1	Who Came First		Track 79189
10/15/77	45	12		2	Rough Mix		MCA 2295
					PETE TOWNSHEND & RONNIE LANE		
5/17/80	5	30	▲	3	Empty Glass		Atco 100
7/10/82	26	26		4	All The Best Cowboys Have Chinese Eyes		Atco 149
3/26/83	35	13		5	Scoop	[K]	Atco 90063 [2]
11/30/85+	26	29	●	6	White City - A Novel		Atco 90473
10/25/86	98	9		7	Pete Townshend's Deep End Live!	[L]	Atco 90553
4/4/87	198	1		8	Another Scoop	[K]	Atco 90539 [2]
7/15/89	58	13		9	The Iron Man: The Musical By Pete Townshend		Atlantic 81996
7/3/93	118	2		10	Psychoderelict		Atlantic 82494

TOWNSHEND, Simon
Born on 10/10/1960 in London, England. Pop-rock singer/songwriter. Brother of **Pete Townshend**.

12/3/83+	169	7		1 Sweet Sound		21 Records 815708
				produced by **Pete Townshend**		

TOYA
Born Toya Rodriguez on 7/22/1983 in St. Louis, Missouri. Female R&B singer/rapper.

8/25/01	109	7		1 Toya		Arista 14697

TOY MATINEE
Pop duo formed in Los Angeles, California: Kevin Gilbert (vocals) and Patrick Leonard (instruments). Gilbert formed a songwriting partnership with **Sheryl Crow**; died of accidental asphyxiation on 5/18/1996 (age 29). Leonard did much songwriting and production work for **Madonna**.

1/26/91	129	8		1 Toy Matinee		Reprise 26235

TOYS, The
Female R&B vocal trio from Jamaica, Queens, New York: Barbara Harris, June Montiero and Barbara Parritt.

2/5/66	92	8		1 The Toys sing "A Lover's Concerto" and "Attack!"		DynoVoice 9002

T-PAIN
Born Faheem Najm on 9/30/1985 in Tallahassee, Florida. Male R&B/hip-hop singer/songwriter.

12/24/05+	33	26	●	1 Rappa Ternt Sanga		Jive 73200
6/23/07	❶¹	28		2 Epiphany		Konvict 08719
11/29/08	4	21	●	3 Thr33 Ringz		Konvict 31630
1/24/09	152	1		4 The T-Wayne Show		Guesswhyld digital
				LIL WAYNE & T-PAIN		

T'PAU
Pop-rock-dance band from Shrewsbury, England: Carol Decker (vocals), Dean Howard (guitar), Ronnie Rogers (guitar), Mick Chetwood (keyboards), Paul Jackson (bass) and Tim Burgess (drums). Group named after a Vulcan princess in an episode of the TV series *Star Trek*.

6/6/87	31	24		1 T'Pau		Virgin 90595

TQ
Born Terrance Quaites on 5/24/1976 in Mobile, Alabama; raised in Los Angeles, California. R&B singer/songwriter.

11/28/98	122	10		1 They Never Saw Me Coming		ClockWork 69431

TRACTORS, The
Country-rock band formed in Tulsa, Oklahoma: Casey Van Beek (vocals), Steve Ripley (guitar), Walt Richmond (keyboards), Ron Getman (bass) and Jamie Oldaker (drums).

9/17/94+	19	46	▲²	1 The Tractors		Arista 18728
12/2/95	68	7		2 Have Yourself A Tractors Christmas .... Cat:#40/1 **[X]**		Arista 18805
				Christmas chart: 15/'95		

TRAE
Born Frazier Thompson on 3/5/1981 in Houston, Texas. Male rapper. One-half of **ABN** duo.

8/12/06	87	2		1 Restless		G-Maab 68640
11/10/07	104	2		2 Life Goes On		G-Maab 307388

TRAFFIC   All-Time: #330
Rock group formed in England. Original lineup: **Steve Winwood** (keyboards, guitar), **Dave Mason** (guitar), **Jim Capaldi** (drums) and Chris Wood (flute, sax). Varying personnel also included bassists **Rick Grech**, David Hood and Roscoe Gee, percussionist Reebop Kwaku Baah, and drummers Jim Gordon and Roger Hawkins; disbanded in 1974. Winwood and Capaldi reunited in 1994. Wood died of pneumonia on 7/12/1983 (age 39). Capaldi died of cancer on 1/28/2005 (age 60).
AWARD: R&R Hall of Fame: 2004

4/27/68	88	22		1 Mr. Fantasy		United Artists 6651
				Grammy: Hall of Fame		
11/30/68+	17	26		2 Traffic		United Artists 6676
5/17/69	19	22		3 Last Exit		United Artists 6702
7/11/70	5	38	●	4 John Barleycorn Must Die		United Artists 5504
12/11/71+	7	30	▲	5 The Low Spark Of High Heeled Boys Cat:#24/27		Island 9306
2/3/73	6	29	●	6 Shoot Out At The Fantasy Factory		Island 9323
9/28/74	9	27	●	7 When The Eagle Flies		Asylum 1020
5/21/94	33	9		8 Far From Home		Virgin 39490
				GREATEST HITS & COMPILATIONS:		
1/3/70	48	14		9 Best Of Traffic		United Artists 5500
5/3/75	155	3		10 Heavy Traffic		United Artists 421
9/27/75	193	4		11 More Heavy Traffic		United Artists 526
				LIVE ALBUMS:		
10/2/71	26	19		12 Welcome To The Canteen		United Artists 5550
				TRAFFIC, ETC.		
11/3/73	29	24		13 Traffic-On The Road		Island 9336 [2]

TRAGICALLY HIP, The
Rock band from Kingston, Ontario, Canada: Gordon Downie (vocals), Bobby Baker (guitar), Paul Langlois (guitar), Gord Sinclair (bass) and Johnny Fay (drums).

DEBUT	PEAK	WKS				
5/12/90	170	6		1 Up To Here		MCA 6310
6/1/96	134	1		2 Trouble At The Henhouse		Atlantic 82899
8/1/98	143	1		3 Phantom Power		Sire 31025
7/1/00	139	1		4 Music @ Work		Sire 31135
6/29/02	169	1		5 In Violet Light		Zoë 1006
4/25/09	148	1		6 We Are The Same		Zoe 431129

TRAILER CHOIR
Country vocal trio formed in Nashville, Tennessee: Vinny Hickerson, Crystal Hoyt and Marc Fortney.

8/29/09	170	5		1 Off The Hillbilly Hook .... [EP]		Show Dog 025

TRAIN
Soft-rock band from San Francisco, California: Pat Monahan (vocals), Rob Hotchkiss (guitar), Jimmy Stafford (guitar), Charlie Colin (bass) and Scott Underwood (drums). In late 2003, Brandon Bush replaced Hotchkiss and Johnny Colt (of The Black Crowes) replaced Colin.

7/10/99	76	32	▲	1 Train .... Cat:#6/20		Aware 38052
4/14/01	6	64	▲²	2 Drops Of Jupiter .... Cat:#30/4		Aware 69888
6/21/03	6	45	▲	3 My Private Nation		Columbia 86593
11/20/04	48	4		4 Alive At Last .... [L]		Columbia 92830
2/18/06	10	15		5 For Me, It's You		Columbia 94472
11/14/09	17	27		6 Save Me, San Francisco		Columbia 07736

TRAMMPS, The
R&B-disco vocal group from Philadelphia, Pennsylvania: Jimmy Ellis, Earl Young, brothers Harold Wade and Stanley Wade, and Robert Upchurch.

7/5/75	159	4		1 Trammps		Golden Fleece 33163
5/15/76	50	24		2 Where The Happy People Go		Atlantic 18172
1/22/77	46	49	●	3 Disco Inferno		Atlantic 18211
12/17/77+	85	13		4 The Trammps III		Atlantic 19148
9/9/78	139	6		5 The Best Of The Trammps .... [G]		Atlantic 19194
5/26/79	184	2		6 The Whole World's Dancing		Atlantic 19210

TRANQUILITY
Rock band from England: Terry Shaddick (vocals), Berkeley Wright (guitar), Kevin McCarthy (guitar), Tony Lukyn (keyboards), Bernard Hagley (bass) and Paul Francis (drums).

3/3/73	207	2		1 Tranquility		Epic 31084

TRANSLATOR
Rock band from Los Angeles, California: Steve Barton (vocals), Robert Darlington (guitar), Larry Dekker (bass) and David Scheff (drums).

9/17/83	206	3		1 No Time Like Now		Columbia 38927

TRANSPLANTS
Rock trio formed in Los Angeles, California: Rob Ashton (vocals), Tim Armstrong (guitar, bass) and Travis Barker (drums). Armstrong is a member of Rancid. Barker is also a member of The Aquabats and Box Car Racer.

11/9/02	96	5		1 Transplants		Hellcat 80448
7/9/05	28	6		2 Haunted Cities		LaSalle 93814

TRANS-SIBERIAN ORCHESTRA
Rock opera-styled project formed and produced by Paul O'Neill in Florida. "Christmas Eve Sarajevo 12/24" was originally released as by the hard-rock band Savatage in 1995. O'Neill then produced a Christmas rock opera album in 1996 under the name Trans-Siberian Orchestra and included the original Savatage recording on it.

4/29/00	165	1	●	1 Beethoven's Last Night		Lava 83319
11/14/09	5	13	●	2 Night Castle .... [I]		Atlantic 520271 [2]

CHRISTMAS ALBUMS:

12/28/96+	89	3	▲²	3 Christmas Eve And Other Stories Cat:❶⁵/89		Lava 92736
				Christmas charts: 15/96, 6/97, 11/98, 10/99, 10/00, 5/01, 4/02, 3/03, 5/04, 4/05, 7/06, 4/07, 9/08, 12/09		
12/5/09	53	6		4 Christmas Eve And Other Stories .... [R]		Lava 92736
12/12/98	103	5	▲	5 The Christmas Attic .... Cat:#4/64		Lava 83145
				Christmas charts: 9/98, 26/99, 24/00, 15/01, 9/02, 7/03, 7/04, 7/05, 11/06, 10/07, 21/08, 23/09		
12/5/09	83	6		6 The Christmas Attic .... [R]		Lava 83145
10/30/04	26	12	▲	7 The Lost Christmas Eve .... Cat:❶¹⁰/40 [I]		Lava 93146
				Christmas charts: 1/04, 2/05, 2/06, 3/07, 7/08, 9/09		
12/5/09	45	6		8 The Lost Christmas Eve .... [I-R]		Lava 93146
1/20/07	16ˣ	6		9 The Christmas Trilogy .... [K]		Lava 73994 [3]
				box set of above 3 albums; Christmas charts: 16/06, 46/07, 27/08		
11/17/07	90	8		10 Trans-Siberian Orchestra .... [EP]		Lava 989963
				Christmas chart: 12/07		

TRANSVISION VAMP
Rock band from England: Wendy James (vocals), Nick Sayer (guitar), Tex Axile (keyboards), Dave Parsons (bass) and Pol Burton (drums).

9/24/88	115	8		1 Pop Art		Uni 5

TRAPEZE
Rock band from Wolverhampton, England: Glenn Hughes (vocals, bass; **Deep Purple**), Mel Galley (guitar; died on 7/1/2008, age 60) and Dave Holland (drums). Hughes left in 1974, replaced by Pete Wright. Rob Kendrick (guitar) also joined in 1974.

1/6/73	209	3		1 You Are The Music...We're Just The Band		Threshold 8
11/2/74	172	6		2 The Final Swing		Threshold 11
1/4/75	146	6		3 Hot Wire		Warner 2828

TRAPP
Born John Parker in Atlanta, Georgia. Male rapper/producer.

5/10/97	123	5		1 Stop The Gunfight		Deff Trapp 9268

TRAPT
Hard-rock band from Los Gatos, California: Chris Brown (vocals, guitar), Simon Ormandy (guitar), Peter Charell (bass) and Aaron Montgomery (drums).

2/8/03	42	82	▲	1 Trapt		Warner 48296
10/1/05	14	9		2 Someone In Control		Warner 49445
8/23/08	18	7		3 Only Through The Pain...		Eleven Seven 230

TRASH CAN SINATRAS, The
Pop-rock band from Irvine, Scotland: brothers John Douglas (guitar) and Stephen Douglas (drums), Frank Reader (vocals), Paul Livingston (guitar) and George McDaid (bass).

2/2/91	131	13		1 Cake		Go! Discs 828201

TRASHMEN, The
Garage-surf-rock band from Minneapolis, Minnesota: Tony Andreason, Dal Winslow and Bob Reed (guitars), with Steve Wahrer (drums). Wahrer died of cancer on 1/21/1989 (age 47).

2/15/64	48	15		1 Surfin' Bird		Garrett 200

TRAVELING WILBURYS
Supergroup masquerading as a band of brothers. Spearheaded by Nelson (**George Harrison**), with Lucky (**Bob Dylan**), Otis (**Jeff Lynne** of ELO), Lefty (**Roy Orbison**) and Charlie (**Tom Petty**) Wilbury. Orbison died on 12/6/1988 (age 52). For their second album, *Vol. 3*, the names have changed to Spike (Harrison), Muddy (Petty), Clayton (Lynne) and Boo (Dylan). Harrison died of cancer on 11/29/2001 (age 58).

11/12/88+	3[6]	53	▲[3]	1 Volume One		Wilbury 25796
				Grammy: Rock Album		
11/17/90	11	22	▲	2 Vol. 3		Wilbury 26324
6/30/07	9	13	●	3 The Traveling Wilburys Collection	[K]	Wilbury 167804 [2]

TRAVERS, Mary
Born on 11/9/1936 in Louisville, Kentucky. Died of leukemia on 9/16/2009 (age 72). Folk singer. Member of **Peter, Paul & Mary**.

4/17/71	71	29		1 Mary		Warner 1907
4/29/72	157	5		2 Morning Glory		Warner 2609
2/24/73	169	6		3 All My Choices		Warner 2677
7/20/74	200	1		4 Circles		Warner 2795
3/11/78	186	5		5 It's In Everyone Of Us		Chrysalis 1168

TRAVERS, Pat
Born on 4/12/1954 in Toronto, Ontario, Canada. Rock singer/guitarist.

7/23/77	209	4		1 Makin' Magic		Polydor 6103
12/17/77+	70	22		2 Putting It Straight		Polydor 6121
10/21/78	99	16		3 Heat In The Street		Polydor 6170
7/21/79	29	22		4 Pat Travers Band Live! Go For What You Know	[L]	Polydor 6202
4/5/80	20	25		5 Crash And Burn		Polydor 6262
				PAT TRAVERS BAND (above 2)		
3/28/81	37	15		6 Radio Active		Polydor 6313
11/6/82	74	13		7 Pat Travers' Black Pearl		Polydor 6361
5/5/84	108	8		8 Hot Shot		Polydor 821064

TRAVIS
Rock band from Glasgow, Scotland: Fran Healy (vocals), Andy Dunlop (guitar), Dougie Payne (bass) and Neil Primrose (drums).

4/22/00	135	10		1 The Man Who		Independiente 62151
6/30/01	39	7		2 The Invisible Band		Independiente 85788
11/1/03	41	3		3 12 Memories		Independiente 90672
5/26/07	58	2		4 The Boy With No Name		Independiente 07962
11/22/08	122	1		5 Ode To J. Smith		Red Telephone Box 7622

TRAVIS, Randy
All-Time: #152

Born Randy Traywick on 5/4/1959 in Marshville, North Carolina. Country singer/songwriter/guitarist/actor. Married his manager, Lib Hatcher, on 5/31/1991. Appeared in several movies and TV shows.
AWARDS: CMA: Horizon 1986 / Male Vocalist 1987 & 1988 ★ OPRY: 1986

DEBUT	PEAK	WKS	RIAA		Album Title	Catalog	Label & Number
7/19/86	85	100	▲³	1	Storms Of Life		Warner 25435
5/30/87	19	103	▲⁵	2	Always & Forever	Cat:#31/8	Warner 25568
					CMA: Album of the Year		
7/30/88	35	43	▲²	3	Old 8x10		Warner 25738
					Grammy: Male Country Vocal		
10/14/89	33	47	▲²	4	No Holdin' Back..		Warner 25988
9/29/90	31	41	▲	5	Heroes And Friends		Warner 26310
9/14/91	43	31	▲	6	High Lonesome		Warner 26661
9/11/93	121	6		7	Wind In The Wire .... [TV]		Warner 45319
5/14/94	59	21	●	8	This Is Me		Warner 45501
8/31/96	77	4		9	Full Circle		Warner 46328
5/9/98	49	9		10	You And You Alone		DreamWorks 450034
10/9/99	130	3		11	A Man Ain't Made Of Stone		DreamWorks 450119
11/2/02+	73	23	●	12	Rise And Shine		Word-Curb 886236
					Grammy: Southern Gospel Album		
11/29/03	90	7	●	13	Worship & Faith		Word-Curb 86273
11/27/04	127	5		14	Passing Through..		Word-Curb 886348
11/12/05	128	5		15	Glory Train: Songs Of Faith, Worship And Praise		Word-Curb 886402
8/2/08	14	10		16	Around The Bend		Warner 43254
					CHRISTMAS ALBUMS:		
12/2/89	70	7	●	17	An Old Time Christmas	Cat:#43/3	Warner 25972
					Christmas charts: 5/'89, 14/'90, 26/'91		
11/24/07	131	6		18	Songs Of The Season		Word-Curb 887146
					Christmas chart: 9/'07		
					GREATEST HITS & COMPILATIONS:		
10/3/92	44	24	▲	19	Greatest Hits Volume One...		Warner 45044
10/3/92	67	31	▲	20	Greatest Hits Volume Two...		Warner 45045
8/21/04	80	7		21	The Very Best Of Randy Travis....................................		Warner 78996
4/4/09	21	13		22	I Told You So: The Ultimate Hits Of Randy Travis		Warner 518189 [2]

TRAVOLTA, John
Born on 2/18/1954 in Englewood, New Jersey. Actor/singer. Played "Vinnie Barbarino" on the TV series *Welcome Back Kotter*. Starred in several movies. Married actress Kelly Preston on 9/12/1991.

DEBUT	PEAK	WKS			Album Title		Label & Number
5/22/76	39	22		1	John Travolta...		Midland Int'l. 1563
3/12/77	66	9		2	Can't Let You Go		Midland Int'l. 2211
12/23/78+	161	7		3	Travolta Fever..[R]		Midsong Int'l. 001 [2]
					reissue of first two albums above		

TREAT HER RIGHT
Rock band from Boston, Massachusetts: Mark Sandman (vocals, guitar), David Champagne (guitar), Jim Fitting (harmonica) and Billy Conway (drums). Sandman and Conway later formed **Morphine**. Sandman died of a heart attack on 7/4/1999 (age 46).

4/9/88	127	18		1	Treat Her Right		RCA 6884

TREMBLERS, The
Pop-rock band formed in England: Peter Noone (vocals), George Conner (guitar), Gregg Inhofer (keyboards), Mark Browne (bass) and Robert Williams (drums). Noone was lead singer of **Herman's Hermits**.

8/23/80	209	1		1	Twice Nightly		Johnston 36532

TREMELOES, The
Pop-rock band from England: Len "Chip" Hawkes (vocals, bass), Alan Blakely (guitar), Ricky West (guitar), and Dave Munden (drums). Alan is the brother of Mike Blakely (of **Christie**). Hawkes is the father of singer Chesney Hawkes. Blakely died of cancer on 6/10/1996 (age 54).

6/24/67	119	8		1	Here Comes My Baby		Epic 26310

TRESVANT, Ralph
Born on 5/16/1968 in Roxbury, Massachusetts. R&B singer. Member of **New Edition**.

12/8/90+	17	37	▲	1	Ralph Tresvant		MCA 10116
1/15/94	131	6		2	It's Goin' Down		MCA 10889

TREVI, Gloria
Born on 2/15/1968 in Monterrey, Mexico. Latin pop-rock singer/songwriter.

10/20/07	169	1		1	Una Rosa Blu ....[F]		Univision 311057

TREVINO, Rick
Born on 5/16/1971 in Austin, Texas. Country singer/songwriter/guitarist.

3/12/94	119	18	●	1	Rick Trevino		Columbia 53560
3/25/95	121	18		2	Looking For The Light		Columbia 66771
8/3/96	117	7		3	Learning As You Go...		Columbia 67452

T. REX
Glam-rock band from England: Marc Bolan (vocals, guitar; born Marc Feld on 7/30/1947; died in a car crash on 9/16/1977, age 30), Mickey Finn (guitar; born Thornton Heath on 6/3/1947; died of liver failure on 1/11/2003, age 55), Steve Currie (bass; born on 5/20/1947; died in a car crash on 4/28/1981, age 33) and Bill Legend (drums).

DEBUT	PEAK	WKS			Catalog	Label & Number
10/7/72	113	12		1 Tyrannosaurus Rex (A Beginning)............ [E]		A&M 3514 [2]
				recordings from 1968		
5/1/71	188	5		2 T-Rex		Reprise 6440
11/6/71+	32	34		3 Electric Warrior		Reprise 6466
				RS500 #160		
8/26/72	17	24		4 The Slider		Reprise 2095
4/28/73	102	10		5 Tanx............		Reprise 2132
9/7/74	205	8		6 Light Of Love		Casablanca 9006

TRIBBETT, Tye, & G.A.
Born on 1/26/1977 in Camden, New Jersey. Male gospel singer/choir director.

DEBUT	PEAK	WKS			Catalog	Label & Number
6/10/06	64	16		1 Victory Live! .... [L]		Columbia 77526
5/24/08	16	13		2 Stand Out		Integrity 16114

TRIBE CALLED QUEST, A
Black hip-hop trio from Queens, New York: Jonathan "Q-Tip" Davis, Ali Shaheed Muhammad and Malik "Phife Dawg" Taylor. Muhammad later joined **Lucy Pearl**.

DEBUT	PEAK	WKS			Catalog	Label & Number
4/28/90	91	19	●	1 People's Instinctive Travels And The Paths Of Rhythm............		Jive 1331
10/12/91	45	49	▲	2 The Low End Theory		Jive 1418
				RS500 #154		
11/27/93	8	29	▲	3 Midnight Marauders		Jive 41490
8/17/96	❶[1]	16	▲	4 Beats, Rhymes And Life		Jive 41587
10/17/98	3[1]	11	●	5 The Love Movement		Jive 41638
11/13/99	81	4		6 The Anthology .... [G]		Jive 41679
7/5/03	190	1		7 Hits, Rarities & Remixes .... [K]		Jive 41839

TRICE, Obie
Born on 11/14/1979 in Detroit, Michigan. Male rapper.

DEBUT	PEAK	WKS			Catalog	Label & Number
10/11/03	5	22	●	1 Cheers		Shady 001105
9/2/06	8	8		2 Second Round's On Me		Shady 006845

TRICK DADDY
Born Maurice Young on 9/23/1973 in Miami, Florida. Male "thug" rapper/producer.

DEBUT	PEAK	WKS			Catalog	Label & Number
1/30/99	30	37	●	1 www.thug.com		Slip-N-Slide 2802
3/4/00	26	28	●	2 Book Of Thugs: Chapter A.K., Verse 47		Slip-N-Slide 83275
4/7/01	4	36	▲	3 Thugs Are Us		Slip-N-Slide 83432
8/24/02	6	23	●	4 Thug Holiday		Slip-N-Slide 83556
11/13/04	2[1]	34	●	5 Thug Matrimony: Married To The Streets		Slip-N-Slide 83677
1/6/07	48	13		6 Back By Thug Demand		Slip-N-Slide 83815
10/3/09	34	3		7 Finally Famous: Born A Thug, Still A Thug		Dunk Ryders 001

TRICK PONY
Country trio formed in Nashville, Tennessee: **Heidi Newfield** (vocals), Keith Burns (guitar) and Ira Dean (bass).

DEBUT	PEAK	WKS			Catalog	Label & Number
3/31/01	91	39	●	1 Trick Pony		Warner 47927
11/23/02	61	4		2 On A Mission		Warner 48236
9/10/05	20	4		3 R.I.D.E.		Curb 78864

TRICK-TRICK
Born Christian Mathis in Detroit, Michigan. Male rapper/songwriter.

DEBUT	PEAK	WKS			Catalog	Label & Number
1/14/06	115	3		1 The People vs. Trick-Trick		Wonderboy 005934

TRICKY
Born Adrian Thaws on 1/27/1968 in Bristol, Avon, England. Male techno-dance artist.

DEBUT	PEAK	WKS			Catalog	Label & Number
12/7/96	140	6		1 Pre-Millennium Tension		Island 524302
6/20/98	84	3		2 Angels With Dirty Faces		Island 524520
9/4/99	182	1		3 Juxtapose		Island 546432
7/14/01	138	3		4 Blowback		Hollywood 62285
9/27/08	147	1		5 Knowle West Boy		Domino 194

TRIK-TURNER
Rock-rap band from Phoenix, Arizona: David Bowers and Doug Moore (vocals), Danny Marquez (DJ), Tracy "Tre" Thorstad (guitar), Steve Faulkner (bass) and Sean Garden (drums).

DEBUT	PEAK	WKS			Catalog	Label & Number
3/16/02	98	11		1 Trik Turner		RCA 68073

TRILLION
Rock band formed in Chicago, Illinois: Dennis "Fergie" Frederiksen (vocals), Frank Barbalace (guitar), Patrick Leonard (keyboards), Ron Anaman (bass) and Bill Wilkins (drums). Frederiksen later joined **Toto**.

DEBUT	PEAK	WKS			Catalog	Label & Number
3/3/79	201	7		1 Trillion		Epic 35460

TRILLVILLE
Male rap trio from Atlanta, Georgia: Jamal "Dirty Mouth" Glaze, Donnell "Don P" Prince and Lawrence "Lil LA" Edwards.

DEBUT	PEAK	WKS			Catalog	Label & Number
3/13/04	12	60	●	1 The King Of Crunk & BME Recordings Present		BME 48556
				TRILLVILLE & LIL SCRAPPY		

Billboard		R I A	ARTIST		
DEBUT	PEAK	WKS	A	Album Title	Catalog	Label & Number

TRINA
Born Katrina Taylor on 12/3/1978 in Miami, Florida. Female rapper/singer. Discovered by **Trick Daddy**.

4/8/00	33	29	●	1 Da Baddest B***h	Slip-N-Slide 83212
9/14/02	14	24		2 Diamond Princess	Slip-N-Slide 83517
10/22/05	11	18		3 Glamorest Life	Slip-N-Slide 83710
4/19/08	6	12		4 Still Da Baddest	Slip-N-Slide 72008

TRINERE
Born Trinere Farrington in Miami, Florida. Female dance singer.

9/23/89	196	2		1 Greatest Hits .... [K]	Pandisc 8804
				TRINERE & FRIENDS	

TRIN-I-TEE 5:7
Contemporary gospel female vocal trio from New Orleans, Louisiana: Terri Brown, Chanelle Hayes and Angel Taylor.

8/8/98	139	27	●	1 Trin-I-Tee 5:7	B-Rite 90094
1/29/00	174	12		2 Spiritual Love	B-Rite 490359
8/24/02	85	8		3 The Kiss	B-Rite 70038
10/6/07	102	3		4 T57	Spirit Rising 0402

TRIO
Electronic-dance-rock trio from Grosskneten, Germany: Stephan Remmler, Kralle Krawinkel and Peter Behrens.

1/15/83	207	4		1 Trio .... [EP]	Mercury 509
8/9/97	118	12		2 Da Da Da .... [E]	Mercury 536205
				recorded in 1982; title track featured in a 1997 Volkswagon commercial	

TRIPLE C'S
Male rap group from Miami, Florida: **Rick Ross**, Kevin "Torch" Belnavis, Gunplay and Young Breed.

11/14/09	44	3		1 Custom Cars & Cycles	Maybach 013568

TRIP LEE
Born William Lee Barefield in Dallas, Texas. Christian rapper.

6/14/08	193	1		1 20/20	Reach 8065

TRIPLETS, The
Triplet sisters Diana, Sylvia and Vicky Villegas. Born on 4/18/1965 in Mexico (American mother and Mexican father).

4/20/91	125	5		1 ...Thicker Than Water	Mercury 848290

TRIPPING DAISY
Pop-rock band from Dallas, Texas: Tim DeLaughter (vocals), Wes Berggren (guitar), Mark Pirro (bass) and Bryan Wakeland (drums). Berggren died on 10/27/1999 (age 28). DeLaughter later formed **The Polyphonic Spree**.

7/15/95	95	13		1 I Am An Elastic Firecracker	Island 524112

TRITT, Travis   1990s: #36 / All-Time: #286
Born James Travis Tritt on 2/9/1963 in Marietta, Georgia. Country singer/songwriter/guitarist. Began singing in Atlanta nightclubs in 1981. Married model Theresa Nelson on 4/12/1997.
AWARDS: CMA: Horizon 1991 ★ OPRY: 1992

3/31/90+	70	99	▲²	1 Country Club	Warner 26094
6/15/91	22	94	▲³	2 It's All About To Change..	Warner 26589
9/5/92	27	57	▲²	3 T-R-O-U-B-L-E	Warner 45048
11/28/92+	75	8		4 A Travis Tritt Christmas: Loving Time Of The Year .... [X]	Warner 45029
				Christmas chart: 13/'92	
5/28/94	20	44	▲²	5 Ten Feet Tall And Bulletproof	Warner 45603
9/30/95	21	37	▲	6 Greatest Hits: From The Beginning .... Cat:#43/1 [G]	Warner 46001
9/14/96	53	29	▲	7 The Restless Kind	Warner 46304
10/31/98	119	4		8 No More Looking Over My Shoulder	Warner 47097
2/17/07	124	5		9 The Very Best Of Travis Tritt .... [G]	Warner 74817
10/21/00	51	88	▲	10 Down The Road I Go .... Cat:#28/3	Columbia 62165
10/12/02	27	9		11 Strong Enough	Columbia 86660
9/4/04	50	4		12 My Honky Tonk History	Columbia 92084
9/8/07	28	6		13 The Storm	Category 5 500103

TRIUMPH
Hard-rock trio formed in Toronto, Ontario, Canada: Rik Emmett (vocals, guitar; born on 7/10/1953), Mike Levine (keyboards, bass) and Gil Moore (drums).

5/19/79	185	2		1 Rock & Roll Machine .... Cat:#22/16	RCA Victor 2982
				released in 1978	
5/5/79	48	28	●	2 Just A Game	RCA Victor 3224
3/29/80	32	18		3 Progressions Of Power	RCA Victor 3524
9/19/81	23	59	▲	4 Allied Forces	RCA Victor 3902
1/29/83	26	27	●	5 Never Surrender	RCA Victor 4382
12/8/84+	35	30	●	6 Thunder Seven	MCA 5537
11/2/85	50	18		7 Stages .... [L]	MCA 8020 [2]
9/6/86	33	27		8 The Sport Of Kings	MCA 5786
11/28/87	82	13		9 Surveillance	MCA 42083

Billboard			R I A A	ARTIST		
DEBUT	PEAK	WKS		Album Title	Catalog	Label & Number

TRIUMPH THE INSULT COMIC DOG
Hand puppet dog created and voiced by writer/comedian Robert Smigel (born on 2/7/1960 in Brooklyn, New York). Regular character on Conan O'Brien's *Late Night* TV show. Smigel is also a longtime writer for TV's *Saturday Night Live*.

| 11/22/03 | 141 | 3 | | 1 Come Poop With Me .... [C] | | Warner 48328 |

TRIUMVIRAT
Techno-rock band from Germany: Helmut Kollen (guitar, vocals), Jurgen Fritz (keyboards) and Hans Bathelt (drums). Kollen replaced by Barry Palmer (vocals) and Dick Frangenberg (bass) in 1976. Kollen committed suicide on 5/5/1977 (age 27).

8/10/74	55	17		1 Illusions On A Double Dimple		Harvest 11311
6/7/75	27	17		2 Spartacus		Capitol 11392
8/7/76	85	8		3 Old Loves Die Hard		Capitol 11551

TRIVIUM
Hard-rock band from Orlando, Florida: Matt Heafy (vocals), Corey Beaulieu (guitar), Paolo Gregoletto (bass) and Travis Smith (drums).

4/2/05	151	1		1 Ascendancy		Roadrunner 618251
10/28/06	25	4		2 The Crusade		Roadrunner 618059
10/18/08	23	4		3 Shogun		Roadrunner 617985

TRIXTER
Hard-rock band from Paramus, New Jersey: Peter Loran (vocals), Steve Brown (guitar), P.J. Farley (bass) and Mark Scott (drums).

| 9/1/90+ | 28 | 54 | ● | 1 Trixter .... | | MCA 6389 |
| 10/31/92 | 109 | 3 | | 2 Hear! .... | | MCA 10635 |

TROCCOLI, Kathy
Born on 6/24/1958 in Brooklyn, New York. Christian singer.

| 5/24/97 | 170 | 1 | | 1 Love & Mercy .... | | Reunion 10003 |

TROGGS, The
Rock band from Andover, England: Reg Presley (vocals), Chris Britton (guitar), Pete Staples (bass) and Ronnie Bullis (drums). Bullis died on 11/13/1992 (age 51).

9/3/66	52	16		1 Wild Thing		Fontana 67556
				same album charted simultaneously on Atco 193		
5/18/68	109	9		2 Love Is All Around		Fontana 67576
8/9/75	210	1		3 The Troggs		Pye 12112

TROOP
R&B vocal group from Pasadena, California: lead singers Steve Russell and Allen McNeil, with Rodney Benford, John Harreld and Reggie Warren.

9/3/88	133	9		1 Troop		Atlantic 81851
1/13/90	73	39	●	2 Attitude		Atlantic 82035
6/20/92	78	12		3 Deepa		Atlantic 82393

TROOPER
Rock band from Vancouver, British Columbia, Canada: Ra McGuire (vocals, guitar), Brian Smith (guitar), Frank Ludwig (keyboards), Doni Underhill (bass) and Tommy Stewart (drums).

| 10/11/75 | 207 | 2 | | 1 Trooper .... | | Legend/MCA 2149 |
| 8/26/78 | 182 | 4 | | 2 Thick As Thieves .... | | MCA 2377 |

TROPEA
Born John Tropea in Florida. Jazz guitarist.

| 3/20/76 | 138 | 7 | | 1 Tropea .... [I] | | Marlin 2200 |
| 5/14/77 | 149 | 7 | | 2 Short Trip To Space .... [I] | | Marlin 2204 |

TROUBADOURS DU ROI BAUDOUIN
Choir and percussionists consisting of 45 boys and 15 teachers from the Kamina School in the Congo.

| 8/2/69 | 184 | 5 | | 1 Missa Luba .... [F] | | Philips 600606 |

TROUBLE FUNK
Funk band from Washington DC: Chester Davis (guitar), James Avery (keyboards), Gerald Reed, Robert Reed, Taylor Reed and David Rudd (horns), Mack Carey (percussion), Tony Fisher (bass) and Emmett Nixon (drums). All shared vocals. Robert Reed died of cancer on 4/13/2008 (age 50).

| 5/8/82 | 121 | 14 | | 1 Drop The Bomb .... | | SugarHill 266 |

TROWER, Robin   **All-Time: #376**
Born on 3/9/1945 in London, England. Rock guitarist/songwriter. Original member of **Procol Harum**. James Dewar was his lead singer from 1973-83; replaced by Davey Pattison in 1986.

5/12/73	106	24		1 Twice Removed From Yesterday		Chrysalis 1039
4/20/74	7	31	●	2 Bridge Of Sighs		Chrysalis 1057
3/1/75	5	17	●	3 For Earth Below		Chrysalis 1073
3/27/76	10	20		4 Robin Trower Live! [L]		Chrysalis 1089
				recorded on 2/3/1975 at the Stockholm Concert Hall		
10/9/76	24	19	●	5 Long Misty Days		Chrysalis 1107
10/1/77	25	19	●	6 In City Dreams		Chrysalis 1148
8/26/78	37	17		7 Caravan To Midnight		Chrysalis 1189
3/1/80	34	15		8 Victims Of The Fury		Chrysalis 1215
3/21/81	37	16		9 B.L.T.		Chrysalis 1324
				JACK BRUCE / BILL LORDAN / ROBIN TROWER		

Billboard			R I A A	ARTIST		
DEBUT	PEAK	WKS		Album Title	Catalog	Label & Number

TROWER, Robin — cont'd

1/30/82	109	0		10 Truce		Chrysalis 1352
				JACK BRUCE & ROBIN TROWER		
10/1/83	191	2		11 Back It Up.............................		Chrysalis 41420
12/27/86+	100	25		12 Passion		GNP Crescendo 2187
5/21/88	133	10		13 Take What You Need.....................		Atlantic 81838

TROY, Doris
Born Doris Higgensen on 1/6/1937 in Harlem, New York. Died of emphysema on 2/16/2004 (age 67). R&B singer/songwriter.

~ ~ ~ ~ ~ ~ ~ ~ ~ ~ **NON-CHARTED ALBUM** ~ ~ ~ ~ ~ ~ ~ ~ ~ ~ ~
1963 **Doris Troy Sings Just One Look &**
Other Memorable Selections

TRU
Rap group from New Orleans, Louisiana: brothers **Master P**, **Silkk The Shocker** and **C-Murder**, with **Mia X** and **Mo B Dick**. TRU: The Real Untouchables.

3/8/97	8	48	▲²	1 **Tru 2 Da Game**		No Limit 50660 [2]
6/19/99	5	21	●	2 **Da Crime Family**		No Limit 50010 [2]
3/12/05	54	2		3 The Truth...............................		New No Limit 5790

TRUCKS, Derek, Band
Born on 6/8/1979 in Jacksonville, Florida. Rock-blues guitarist. Nephew of Butch Trucks of **The Allman Brothers Band** (Butch officially joined The Allman Brothers Band in 2003). His band: Mike Mattison (vocals), Kofi Burbridge (keyboards), Count M'Butu (percussion), Todd Smallie (bass) and Yonrico Scott (drums).

3/11/06	164	1		1 Songlines		Columbia 92844
1/31/09	19	9		2 Already Free		Victor 32781
				Grammy: Contemporary Blues Album		

TRUE, Andrea, Connection
Born on 7/26/1943 in Nashville, Tennessee. White female disco singer/actress. Appeared in several X-rated movies in the 1970s.

6/19/76	47	17		1 More, More, More		Buddah 5670

TRUE VIBE
Christian vocal group from Cincinnati, Ohio: Jason Barton, Nathan Gaddis, Jonathan Lippmann and Jordan Roe.

6/2/01	178	2		1 True Vibe		Essential 10619

TRUST COMPANY
Rock band from Montgomery, Alabama: Kevin Palmer (vocals, guitar), James Fukai (guitar), Josh Moates (bass) and Jason Singleton (drums).

8/10/02	11	20	●	1 The Lonely Position Of Neutral		Geffen 493312
4/9/05	32	6		2 True Parallels...........................		Geffen 004332

TRUTH, The
Rock duo from England: Dennis Greaves and Mick Lister.

5/30/87	115	8		1 Weapons Of Love........................		I.R.S. 5981

TRUTH HURTS
Born Shari Watson on 10/10/1971 in St. Louis, Missouri. Female hip-hop singer.

7/13/02	5	14		1 Truthfully Speaking		Aftermath 493331
6/19/04	173	1		2 Ready Now...............................		Pookie 1002

TRYTHALL, Gil
Born Richard Trythall on 7/25/1939 in Knoxville, Tennessee. Moog synthesizer player.

2/7/70	157	6		1 Switched On Nashville: Country Moog...... [I]		Athena 6003

TSOL
Hard-rock band formed in Los Angeles, California: Joe Wood (vocals), Ron Emory (guitar), Mike Roche (bass) and Mitch Dean (drums). TSOL: True Sounds Of Liberty.

7/4/87	184	2		1 Hit And Run		Enigma 73263

TUBES, The
Pop-rock band from San Francisco, California: John "**Fee Waybill**" Waldo (vocals), Bill Spooner (guitar), Roger Steen (guitar), Michael Cotton (keyboards), Vince Welnick (keyboards), Rick Anderson (bass) and Charles "Prairie" Prince (drums). Welnick joined the **Grateful Dead** in 1990. Welnick died on 6/2/2006 (age 55).

8/2/75	113	18		1 The Tubes		A&M 4534
5/15/76	46	15		2 Young And Rich		A&M 4580
5/28/77	122	6		3 Now...................................		A&M 4632
3/11/78	82	8		4 What Do You Want From Live .... [L]		A&M 6003 [2]
				recorded November 1977 at the Hammersmith Odeon in London, England		
3/31/79	46	18		5 Remote Control		A&M 4751
8/29/81	148	6		6 T.R.A.S.H. (Tubes Rarities And Smash Hits) .... [K]		A&M 4870
5/30/81	36	27		7 The Completion Backward Principle		Capitol 12151
4/2/83	18	34		8 Outside Inside		Capitol 12260
3/23/85	87	10		9 Love Bomb.............................		Capitol 12381

TUBEWAY ARMY — see NUMAN, Gary

TUCK & PATTI
Husband-and-wife duo formed in Las Vegas, Nevada: Tuck Andress (guitar) Patti Cathcart (vocals). Met in 1981 and married in 1983.

6/24/89	162	11		1 Love Warriors		Windham Hill 116
5/18/91	186	1		2 Dream		Windham Hill 0130

TUCKER, Louise
Born in 1956 in Bristol, England. Classical-styled vocalist.

8/6/83	127	10		1 Midnight Blue		Arista 8088

TUCKER, Marshall — see MARSHALL

TUCKER, Tanya
Born on 10/10/1958 in Seminole, Texas; raised in Wilcox, Arizona. Country singer/songwriter/actress. Appeared on the *Lew King* TV series in Phoenix from 1969. Acted in the movies *Jeremiah Johnson* and *Hard Country*. Own reality TV series *Tuckerville* began airing in 2005.

AWARD: CMA: Female Vocalist 1991

3/30/74	159	6	●	1 Would You Lay With Me (In A Field Of Stone)		Columbia 32744
3/8/75	201	8	▲	2 Tanya Tucker's Greatest Hits .... [G]		Columbia 33355
5/17/75	113	7	●	3 Tanya Tucker		MCA 2141
10/2/76	203	4		4 Here's Some Love		MCA 2213
4/8/78	210	1		5 Tanya Tucker's Greatest Hits .... [G]		MCA 3032
12/2/78+	54	22	●	6 TNT		MCA 3066
12/1/79	121	8		7 Tear Me Apart		MCA 5106
11/8/80	209	2		8 Dreamlovers		MCA 5140
8/1/81	180	3		9 Should I Do It		MCA 5228
10/2/82	203	3		10 Changes		Arista 9596
7/20/91+	48	70	▲	11 What Do I Do With Me		Capitol 95562
10/24/92	51	39	▲	12 Can't Run From Yourself		Liberty 98987
5/15/93	65	15	▲	13 Greatest Hits 1990-1992 .... [G]		Liberty 81367
11/6/93	87	19	●	14 Soon		Liberty 89048
4/8/95	169	5		15 Fire To Fire		Liberty 28943
4/12/97	124	12		16 Complicated		Capitol 36885
7/18/09	183	1		17 My Turn		Saguaro Road 24553

TUCKER, Tommy
Born Robert Higginbotham on 3/5/1939 in Springfield, Ohio. Died of poisoning on 1/22/1982 (age 42). R&B singer/songwriter/pianist.

~ ~ ~ ~ ~ ~ ~ ~ ~ ~ ~ **NON-CHARTED ALBUM** ~ ~ ~ ~ ~ ~ ~ ~ ~ ~ ~

1964 Hi-Heel Sneakers

TUFANO & GIAMMARESE
Pop-rock duo from Chicago, Illinois: Denny Tufano and Carl Giammarese. Both were members of **The Buckinghams**.

5/12/73	210	5		1 Tufano And Giammarese		Ode 77017

TUFF DARTS
Rock band from New York: Tommy Frenzy (vocals), Jeff Salen (guitar), Bobby Butani (guitar), John DeSalvo (bass) and John Morelli (drums). **Robert Gordon** was a member until 1976. Salen died on 1/26/2008.

3/18/78	156	6		1 Tuff Darts!		Sire 6048

TUNSTALL, KT
Born Kate Tunstall on 6/23/1975 in Edinburgh, Scotland; raised in St. Andrews, Scotland. Adult Alternative pop-rock singer/songwriter/guitarist.

2/25/06	33	83	▲	1 Eye To The Telescope		Restless 50729
10/6/07	9	13		2 Drastic Fantastic		Relentless 95618
12/15/07+	92	2		3 Sounds Of The Season: The KT Tunstall Holiday Collection .... [X-EP]		NBC 07724
				Christmas chart: 6/'07		
6/14/08	199	1		4 iTunes Live From Soho .... [EP-L]		Relentless digital

TURK
Born Virgil Tab in 1981 in New Orleans, Louisiana. Male rapper. Member of **Cash Money Millionaires** and **Hot Boys**.

6/23/01	9	9		1 Young & Thuggin'		Cash Money 860926
11/8/03	193	1		2 Raw & Uncut		Koch 8661

TURNER, "Big Joe"
Born on 5/18/1911 in Kansas City, Missouri. Died of a heart attack on 11/24/1985 (age 74). Blues-R&B-rock and roll singer.

AWARD: R&R Hall of Fame: 1987 (Blues Pioneer)

~ ~ ~ ~ ~ ~ ~ ~ ~ ~ **NON-CHARTED ALBUMS** ~ ~ ~ ~ ~ ~ ~ ~ ~ ~ ~

1957 Joe Turner   1959 Big Joe Is Here
1958 Rockin' The Blues

TURNER, Ike & Tina

Husband-and-wife R&B duo: guitarist Ike Turner (born on 11/5/1931 in Clarksdale, Mississippi; died on 12/12/2007, age 76) and singer **Tina Turner** (born on 11/26/1938 in Brownsville, Tennessee). Married from 1962-78. Ike served time in prison on drug-related charges. Tina later went on to a successful solo career.
AWARD: R&R Hall of Fame: 1991

DEBUT	PEAK	WKS	RIAA	#	Album Title	Catalog	Label & Number
9/27/69	102	8		1	River Deep-Mountain High		A&M 4178
					recorded in 1966		
4/19/69	91	12		2	Outta Season		Blue Thumb 5
11/22/69	176	3		3	The Hunter		Blue Thumb 11
5/16/70	130	19		4	Come Together		Liberty 7637
12/5/70+	25	38		5	Workin' Together		Liberty 7650
3/27/71	201	8		6	Her Man...His Woman		Capitol 571
11/20/71	108	10		7	'Nuff Said		United Artists 5530
7/22/72	160	9		8	Feel Good		United Artists 5598
2/17/73	205	3		9	Let Me Touch Your Mind		United Artists 5660
12/22/73+	163	6		10	Nutbush City Limits		United Artists 180
5/11/85	189	2		11	Get Back! [G]		Liberty 51156

LIVE ALBUMS:

DEBUT	PEAK	WKS	RIAA	#	Album Title	Catalog	Label & Number
2/6/65	126	6		12	Live! The Ike & Tina Turner Show		Warner 1579
7/19/69	142	9		13	In Person		Minit 24018
					recorded at the Basin Street West in San Francisco, California		
7/10/71	25	22	●	14	Live At Carnegie Hall/What You Hear Is What You Get		United Artists 9953 [2]
10/6/73	211	7		15	The World Of Ike & Tina		United Artists 064 [2]
					recorded on their European tour		

~ ~ ~ ~ ~ ~ ~ ~ ~ **NON-CHARTED ALBUMS** ~ ~ ~ ~ ~ ~ ~ ~ ~ ~
1961 **The Soul Of Ike & Tina Turner**   1965 **The Greatest Hits Of Ike & Tina Turner**
1963 **Dynamite!**   1991 **Proud Mary – The Best Of Ike And Tina Turner**
1963 **Don't Play Me Cheap**   *RS500 #212*
1963 **It's Gonna Work Out Fine**

TURNER, Joe Lynn

Born on 8/2/1951 in Hackensack, New Jersey. Rock singer/guitarist. Member of **Rainbow** and **Deep Purple**.

DEBUT	PEAK	WKS	RIAA	#	Album Title	Catalog	Label & Number
11/2/85	143	12		1	Rescue You		Elektra 60449

TURNER, Josh

Born on 11/20/1977 in Florence, South Carolina; raised in Hannah, South Carolina. Country singer/songwriter/guitarist.
AWARD: OPRY: 2007

DEBUT	PEAK	WKS	RIAA	#	Album Title	Catalog	Label & Number
11/1/03+	29	41	▲	1	Long Black Train Cat:#13/16		MCA Nashville 000974
2/11/06	2^1	92	▲^{2}	2	Your Man		MCA Nashville 004744
11/17/07	5	38	●	3	Everything Is Fine		MCA Nashville 008904

TURNER, Ruby

Born on 6/22/1958 in Jamaica; raised in Birmingham, England. R&B singer.

DEBUT	PEAK	WKS	RIAA	#	Album Title	Catalog	Label & Number
3/31/90	194	2		1	Paradise		Jive 1298

TURNER, Sammy

Born Samuel Black on 6/2/1932 in Paterson, New Jersey. Black ballad singer.

~ ~ ~ ~ ~ ~ ~ ~ ~ ~ **NON-CHARTED ALBUM** ~ ~ ~ ~ ~ ~ ~ ~ ~ ~
1959 **Lavender Blue Moods**

TURNER, Spyder

Born Dwight Turner on 2/4/1947 in Beckley, West Virginia; raised in Detroit, Michigan. R&B singer.

DEBUT	PEAK	WKS	RIAA	#	Album Title	Catalog	Label & Number
3/25/67	158	3		1	Stand By Me		MGM 4450

TURNER, Tina   All-Time: #360

Born Anna Mae Bullock on 11/26/1938 in Brownsville, Tennessee. R&B singer/actress. One-half of **Ike & Tina Turner** duo. Married to Ike from 1962-78. Acted in the movies *Tommy* and *Mad Max-Beyond Thunderdome*. Her autobiography *I, Tina* was made into the 1993 movie *What's Love Got To Do With It*.

DEBUT	PEAK	WKS	RIAA	#	Album Title	Catalog	Label & Number
9/20/75	155	5		1	Acid Queen		United Artists 495
6/16/84	3^{11}	106	▲^{5}	2	Private Dancer		Capitol 12330
9/27/86	4	52	▲	3	Break Every Rule		Capitol 12530
10/7/89	31	21	●	4	Foreign Affair		Capitol 91873
7/3/93	17	30	▲	5	What's Love Got To Do With It [S]		Virgin 88189
9/21/96	61	27		6	Wildest Dreams		Virgin 41920
2/19/00	21	16	●	7	Twenty Four Seven		Virgin 23180

GREATEST HITS & COMPILATIONS:

DEBUT	PEAK	WKS	RIAA	#	Album Title	Catalog	Label & Number
11/9/91	113	17	▲	8	Simply The Best Cat:#35/5		Capitol 97152
2/19/05	2^1	16	▲	9	All The Best		Capitol 63536 [2]
10/18/08	61	6		10	Tina!		Capitol 37422

LIVE ALBUMS:

DEBUT	PEAK	WKS	RIAA	#	Album Title	Catalog	Label & Number
4/9/88	86	9		11	Tina Live In Europe		Capitol 90126 [2]
					Grammy: Female Rock Vocal		
11/7/09	169	1		12	Tina Live		Manhattan 88531

TURRENTINE, Stanley
Born on 4/5/1934 in Pittsburgh, Pennsylvania. Died of a stroke on 9/12/2000 (age 66). Jazz fusion tenor saxophonist. Member of **Fuse One**.

DEBUT	PEAK	WKS		Album Title		Label & Number
1/7/67	149	2		1 Rough 'N Tumble	[I]	Blue Note 84240
11/2/68	193	3		2 The Look Of Love	[I]	Blue Note 84286
3/20/71	182	3		3 Sugar	[I]	CTI 6005
11/16/74	185	7		4 The Baddest Turrentine	[I]	CTI 6048
3/8/75	110	13		5 The Sugar Man	[I]	CTI 6052
10/19/74	69	21		6 Pieces Of Dreams	[I]	Fantasy 9465
5/10/75	65	14		7 In The Pocket	[I]	Fantasy 9478
11/1/75	76	16		8 Have You Ever Seen The Rain	[I]	Fantasy 9493
6/12/76	100	14		9 Everybody Come On Out	[I]	Fantasy 9508
11/27/76+	96	14		10 The Man With The Sad Face	[I]	Fantasy 9519
9/10/77	84	9		11 Nightwings	[I]	Fantasy 9534
3/18/78	63	12		12 West Side Highway	[I]	Fantasy 9548
9/16/78	106	13		13 What About You!	[I]	Fantasy 9563
8/11/79	202	8		14 Betcha	[I]	Elektra 217
7/19/80	209	1		15 Inflation	[I]	Elektra 269
10/10/81	162	3		16 Tender Togetherness	[I]	Elektra 534

TURTLES, The
Pop-rock band formed in Los Angeles, California: Mark Volman (vocals; born on 4/19/1947), Howard Kaylan (vocals; born on 6/22/1947), Jim Tucker (guitar; born on 10/17/1946), Al Nichol (keyboards; born on 3/31/1945), Chuck Portz (bass; born on 3/28/1945) and Don Murray (drums; born on 11/8/1945; died on 3/22/1996, age 50). **Mark Volman and Howard Kaylan** (under the names Flo and Eddie) later joined **Frank Zappa**'s group.

DEBUT	PEAK	WKS		Album Title		Label & Number
10/23/65+	98	19		1 It Ain't Me Babe		White Whale 7111
4/29/67	25	22		2 Happy Together		White Whale 7114
11/18/67+	7	39	●	3 The Turtles! Golden Hits	[G]	White Whale 7115
11/16/68	128	12		4 The Turtles Present The Battle Of The Bands		White Whale 7118
11/1/69	117	9		5 Turtle Soup		White Whale 7124
4/11/70	146	9		6 The Turtles! More Golden Hits	[G]	White Whale 7127
12/21/74	194	7		7 The Turtles' Greatest Hits/Happy Together Again	[G]	Sire 3703 [2]

~ ~ ~ ~ ~ ~ ~ ~ ~ ~ **NON-CHARTED ALBUM** ~ ~ ~ ~ ~ ~ ~ ~ ~ ~

1966 You Baby / Let Me Be

TUTONE, Tommy — see TOMMY

TUXEDO JUNCTION
Female disco group: Jamie Edlin, Marilyn Jackson, Sue Allen and Marti McCall.

DEBUT	PEAK	WKS		Album Title		Label & Number
2/18/78	56	32		1 Tuxedo Junction		Butterfly 007

TV ON THE RADIO
Eclectic-rock band from Brooklyn, New York: Kyp Malone (vocals), Tunde Adebimpe (vocals), David Sitek (instruments), Gerard Smith (bass) and Jaleel Bunton (drums).

DEBUT	PEAK	WKS		Album Title		Label & Number
9/30/06	41	10		1 Return To Cookie Mountain		Interscope 007466
10/11/08	12	14		2 Dear Science		DGC 011882

TWAIN, Shania   **All-Time: #432**
Born Eileen Regina Edwards on 8/28/1965 in Windsor, Ontario, Canada; raised in Timmins, Ontario, Canada. Country singer/songwriter. Adopted the name Shania which means "I'm on my way" in the Ojibwa Indian language. Married rock producer Robert John "Mutt" Lange on 12/28/1993 (separated in 2008).
AWARD: CMA: Entertainer 1999

DEBUT	PEAK	WKS			Album Title		Label & Number
2/24/96	35^C	9	▲	1	Shania Twain		Mercury 514422
					first released in 1993		
3/18/95+	5	107	▲^{12}	2	The Woman In Me	Cat:❶^1/156	Mercury 522886
					Grammy: Country Album		
11/22/97	2^2	151	▲^{20}	3	Come On Over	Cat:#2^1/215	Mercury 536003
12/7/02	❶^5	93	▲^{11}	4	Up!		Mercury 170314 [2]
					contains two versions of the same album: a "country mix" and "rocked-up mix"		
12/7/02	190	1		5	Up!		Mercury 170314
					cassette which contains only the "country mix" version of the album		
11/27/04	2^1	67	▲^{4}	6	Greatest Hits	Cat:#12/11 [G]	Mercury 003072

T.W.D.Y.
Rap production presented by **Ant Banks**. T.W.D.Y.: The Whole Damn Yey.

DEBUT	PEAK	WKS		Album Title		Label & Number
5/8/99	135	9		1 Derty Werk		Thump Street 9986

TWEET
Born Charlene Keys on 3/4/1971 in Rochester, New York. Female R&B singer/songwriter.

DEBUT	PEAK	WKS		Album Title		Label & Number
4/20/02	3^1	21	●	1 Southern Hummingbird		The Gold Mind 62746
4/9/05	17	7		2 It's Me Again		The Gold Mind 62872

12 GAUGE
Born Isiah Pinkney in 1968 in Augusta, Georgia. Male hardcore rapper.

DEBUT	PEAK	WKS		Album Title		Label & Number
4/2/94	141	8		1 12 Gauge		Street Life 75439

DEBUT	PEAK	WKS	RIAA	#	Album Title	Catalog	Label & Number

TWELVE GIRLS BAND
Group of 13 classically-trained female musicians from China: Bin Qu Liao, Shuang Zhang, Ting Sun, Song Mei Yang, Ying Lei, Li Jun Zhan, Jing Jing Ma, Yan Yin, Bao Zhong, Jian Nan Zhou, Kun Zhang, Yuan Sun and Jin Jiang.

| 9/4/04 | 62 | 4 | | 1 | Eastern Energy .... [I] | | Platia 64515 |

12 STONES
Hard-rock band from Mandeville, Louisiana: Paul McCoy (vocals), Eric Weaver (guitar), Kevin Dorr (bass) and Aaron Gainer (drums).

5/11/02	147	10		1	12 Stones		Wind-Up 13069
9/11/04	29	6		2	Potter's Field...		Wind-Up 13082
9/1/07	53	4		3	Anthem For The Underdog..		Wind-Up 13126

TWENNYNINE FEATURING LENNY WHITE
R&B-funk band from New York: Donald Blackman (vocals), Eddie Martinez (guitar), Nick Moroch (guitar), Denzil Miller (keyboards), Barry Johnson (bass) and **Lenny White** (drums).

12/8/79+	54	16		1	Best Of Friends		Elektra 223
11/1/80	106	8		2	Twennynine with Lenny White.......................................		Elektra 304
12/5/81	162	5		3	Just Like Dreamin'		Elektra 551

24-7 SPYZ
Black hard-rock band from the Bronx, New York: Peter Forest (vocals), Jimi Hazel (guitar), Rick Skatore (bass) and Anthony Johnson (drums).

| 6/17/89 | 113 | 16 | | 1 | Harder Than You .... | | In-Effect 3006 |
| 7/14/90 | 135 | 11 | | 2 | Gumbo Millennium... | | In-Effect 3014 |

20/20
Pop-rock band from Tulsa, Oklahoma: Steve Allen (vocals, guitar), Chris Silagyi (keyboards), Ron Flynt (bass) and Mike Gallo (drums).

| 11/3/79 | 138 | 13 | | 1 | 20/20 .... | | Portrait 36205 |
| 6/20/81 | 127 | 12 | | 2 | Look Out! .... | | Portrait 37050 |

TWILLEY, Dwight
Born on 6/6/1951 in Tulsa, Oklahoma. Rock singer/songwriter/pianist. Formed the Dwight Twilley Band with **Phil Seymour** (bass, drums) in 1974.

7/31/76	138	14		1	Sincerely		Shelter 52001
10/8/77	70	13		2	Twilley Don't Mind..		Arista 4140
					DWIGHT TWILLEY BAND (above 2)		
3/24/79	113	9		3	Twilley		Arista 4214
3/13/82	109	11		4	Scuba Divers		EMI America 17064
2/18/84	39	21		5	Jungle..		EMI America 17107

TWIN HYPE
Rap duo from New Jersey: twin brothers Glennis Brown and Lennis Brown.

| 8/26/89 | 140 | 11 | | 1 | Twin Hype .... | | Profile 1281 |

TWINZ
Rap duo from Long Beach, California: identical twin brothers Deon Williams and DeWayne Williams.

| 9/9/95 | 36 | 9 | | 1 | Conversation .... | | G Funk 527883 |

TWISTA
Born Carl Mitchell on 11/27/1973 in Chicago, Illinois. Male rapper.

7/12/97	77	17	●	1	Adrenaline Rush..		Creator's Way 92757
10/24/98	34	6		2	Mobstability		Creator's Way 83142
					TWISTA & THE SPEEDKNOT MOBSTAZ		
3/24/01	150	9		3	Twista Presents: New Testament 2K Street Scriptures Compilation.......... [K]		Legit Ballin' 0001
2/14/04	❶¹	37	▲	4	Kamikaze		Atlantic 83598
10/22/05	2¹	17	●	5	The Day After		Atlantic 83820
10/6/07	10	5		6	Adrenaline Rush 2007		Atlantic 274044
8/1/09	8	14		7	Category F5		GMG 96412

TWISTED SISTER
Hard-rock band from Long Island, New York: David "Dee" Snider (vocals; born on 3/15/1955), John "Jay Jay French" Segall (guitar; born on 7/20/1952), Eddie "Fingers" Ojeda (guitar; born on 8/5/1955), Mark "Animal" Mendosa (bass; born on 8/5/1955), and Anthony Jude "A.J." Pero (drums; born on 10/14/1959). Known for their outlandish make-up and stage clothes. Snider hosts syndicated radio show *House Of Hair*.

8/27/83+	130	14	●	1	You Can't Stop Rock 'N' Roll..		Atlantic 80074
7/7/84	15	51	▲³	2	Stay Hungry		Atlantic 80156
7/18/09	50ᶜ	1		3	Stay Hungry: 25th Anniversary Edition .... [R]		Atlantic 519757 [2]
7/6/85	125	11		4	Under The Blade... [E]		Atlantic 81256
					remixed edition of their first album plus bonus track		
12/21/85+	53	17	●	5	Come Out And Play...		Atlantic 81275
8/1/87	74	11		6	Love Is For Suckers..		Atlantic 81772
12/16/06	147	4		7	A Twisted Christmas .... [X]		Razor & Tie 82964
					Christmas charts: 33/'06, 27/'07		

TWITTY, Conway

Born Harold Jenkins on 9/1/1933 in Friars Point, Mississippi; raised in Helena, Arkansas. Died of an abdominal aneurysm on 6/5/1993 (age 59). Legendary country singer. Appeared in the movies *Sexpot Goes To College* and *College Confidential*. Switched from pop to country music in 1965.

AWARDS: C&W Hall of Fame: 1999 ★ CMA: Vocal Duo (w/ Loretta Lynn) 1972, 1973, 1974 & 1975

DEBUT	PEAK	WKS				
8/16/69	161	3		1	I Love You More Today	Decca 75131
7/4/70	65	26	●	2	Hello Darlin'	Decca 75209
1/23/71	140	7		3	Fifteen Years Ago	Decca 75248
3/13/71	78	14	●	4	We Only Make Believe	Decca 75251
					CONWAY TWITTY & LORETTA LYNN	
5/22/71	91	9		5	How Much More Can She Stand	Decca 75276
9/18/71	142	8		6	I Wonder What She'll Think About Me Leaving	Decca 75292
3/4/72	106	13	●	7	Lead Me On	Decca 75326
					CONWAY TWITTY & LORETTA LYNN	
4/8/72	130	9		8	I Can't See Me Without You	Decca 75335
8/25/73	153	9		9	Louisiana Woman, Mississippi Man	MCA 335
					CONWAY TWITTY & LORETTA LYNN	
9/15/73	134	9	●	10	You've Never Been This Far Before / Baby's Gone	MCA 359
1/31/76	202	5		11	Twitty	MCA 2176
					album also known as *This Time I've Hurt Her More Than She Loves Me*	
2/13/82	144	15		12	Southern Comfort	Elektra 60005
7/23/83	203	7		13	Lost In The Feeling	Warner 23869
5/26/84	207	1		14	By Heart	Warner 25078
9/18/93	135	7		15	Final Touches	MCA 10882
					GREATEST HITS & COMPILATIONS:	
6/26/93	15^C	11	▲	16	The Very Best Of Conway Twitty	MCA 31238
6/26/93	43^C	1		17	The Best Of The Best Of Conway Twitty	Federal 6502
6/26/93	44^C	1		18	Greatest Hits Volume III	MCA 6391
9/11/04	183	1		19	25 Number Ones	MCA Nashville 003084

~ ~ ~ ~ ~ ~ ~ ~ ~ ~ **NON-CHARTED ALBUMS** ~ ~ ~ ~ ~ ~ ~ ~ ~ ~ ~

1959 **Conway Twitty Sings**   1960 **Lonely Blue Boy**
1960 **Conway Twitty's Greatest Hits...**   1961 **The Rock And Roll Story**
1960 **Saturday Night With Conway Twitty**   1963 **R&B 63**

TWIZTID

White male rap duo from Detroit, Michigan: Jamie "**Madrox**" Spaniolo and Paul "**Monoxide**" Methric. Members of **Dark Lotus**.

DEBUT	PEAK	WKS			
7/10/99	149	1	1	Mostasteless	Psychopathic 042099
11/18/00	51	2	2	Freek Show	Psychopathic 548179
4/27/02	103	1	3	Mirror Mirror	Psychopathic 3001
7/19/03	52	2	4	The Green Book	Psychopathic 4014
6/5/04	85	1	5	Cryptic Collection 3	Psychopathic 4025
7/16/05	62	2	6	Man's Myth (Vol. 1)	Psychopathic 4051
8/13/05	80	1	7	Mutant (Vol. 2)	Psychopathic 4052
7/21/07	57	2	8	Independents Day	Psychopathic 4200
4/4/09	11	3	9	W.I.C.K.E.D.	Psychopathic 4204

TWO

Rock band formed in Phoenix, Arizona: Rob **Halford** (vocals; **Judas Priest**; **Fight**), John Lowery (guitar), James Woolley (keyboards), Ray Reandeau (bass) and Sid Riggs (drums).

DEBUT	PEAK	WKS			
3/28/98	176	1	1	Voyeurs	Nothing 90155

II D EXTREME

R&B vocal trio from Washington DC: D'Extra Wiley, Randy Gill (brother of **Johnny Gill**) and his cousin Jermaine Mickey.

DEBUT	PEAK	WKS			
11/27/93	115	4	1	II D Extreme	Gasoline Alley 10958

2GE+HER

Male vocal group formed for the same-named MTV series: Evan Farmer ("Jerry O'Keefe"), Michael Cuccione ("Jason McKnight"), Alex Solovitz ("Mickey Parke"), Noah Bastian ("Chad Linus") and Kevin Farley ("Doug Linus"). Farley is the younger brother of the late comedian Chris Farley. Cuccione died of respiratory failure on 1/13/2001 (age 16).

DEBUT	PEAK	WKS				
3/11/00	35	11	1	2Ge+her	[TV]	TVT 6800
9/16/00	15	8	2	2Ge+her Again	[TV]	TVT 6840

2 IN A ROOM

Dance duo from Washington Heights, New York: rapper Rafael Vargas and remixer Roger Pauletta.

DEBUT	PEAK	WKS			
12/22/90+	151	9	1	Wiggle It	Cutting 91594

2 LIVE CREW, The

Rap group from Miami, Florida: Luther "**Luke**" Campbell, David Hobbs, Chris Wong Won and Mark Ross. By 1994, group consisted of Campbell, Wong Won and Larry Dobson; changed name to **The New 2 Live Crew**. Luke went solo in 1996; Hobbs, Wong Won and Ross reunited as **The 2 Live Crew**.

DEBUT	PEAK	WKS				
4/11/87	128	33	●	1	The 2 Live Crew "Is What We Are"	Luke Skyywalker 100
6/4/88	68	42	●	2	Move Somethin'	Luke Skyywalker 101
7/29/89+	29	81	▲	3	As Nasty As They Wanna Be	Luke Skyywalker 107 [2]
8/11/90	21	22	●	4	Banned In The U.S.A.	Luke 91424
1/19/91	92	12		5	Live In Concert	[L]	Effect 3003

Billboard DEBUT	PEAK	WKS	RIAA	ARTIST / Album Title	Catalog	Label & Number
				2 LIVE CREW, The — cont'd		
10/26/91	22	30	●	6 Sports Weekend (As Nasty As They Wanna Be Part II)		Luke 91720
2/19/94	52	14		7 Back At Your Ass For The Nine-4		Luke 207
				THE NEW 2 LIVE CREW		
8/24/96	145	2		8 Shake A Lil' Somethin'		Lil' Joe 215
				2 LIVE JEWS, The Parody of rap group **The 2 Live Crew**: Eric "MC Moisha" Lambert and Joe "Easy Irving" Stone.		
9/15/90	150	9		1 As Kosher As They Wanna Be ..... [N]		Kosher 3328
				2 LOW Born Cedric White on 3/10/1970 in Houston, Texas. Male rapper.		
2/12/94	176	6		1 Funky Lil Brotha		Rap-A-Lot 53884
				213 Hip-hop trio formed in Los Angeles, California: **Snoop Dogg**, **Nate Dogg** and **Warren G**.		
9/4/04	4	13		1 The Hard Way		Doggystyle 2670

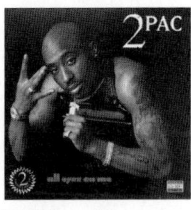

2PAC   1990s: #11 / 2000s: #20 / All-Time: #91

Born Tupac Amaru Shakur on 6/16/1971 in Brooklyn, New York. Died on 9/13/1996 (age 25) of wounds suffered on 9/7/1996 in a shooting in Las Vegas, Nevada. Rapper/actor. Member of **Digital Underground** in 1991. Appeared in the movies *Nothing But Trouble*, *Juice* and *Poetic Justice*. Also recorded as **Makaveli**. Also see **Thug Life**. Also see **Various Artists Compilations:** *The Rose That Grew From Concrete Vol. 1*.

DEBUT	PEAK	WKS	RIAA	ARTIST / Album Title	Catalog	Label & Number
2/29/92	64	23	●	1 2Pacalypse Now ..... Cat:#3/9		Interscope 91767
3/6/93	24	60	▲	2 Strictly 4 My N.I.G.G.A.Z. ..... Cat:#2³/9		Interscope 92209
4/1/95	❶⁴	65	▲²	3 Me Against The World ..... Cat:#12/40		Interscope 92399
3/2/96	❶²	100	▲⁹	4 All Eyez On Me ..... Cat:#13/60		Death Row 524204 [2]
11/23/96	❶¹	63	▲⁴	5 The Don Killuminati - The 7 Day Theory ..... Cat:#24/3		Death Row 90039
				MAKAVELI		
1/8/00	6	20	▲	6 Still I Rise		Interscope 490413
				2PAC + OUTLAWZ		
4/14/01	❶¹	25	▲³	7 Until The End Of Time		Amaru 490840 [2]
12/14/02	5	25	▲²	8 Better Dayz		Amaru 497070 [2]
11/29/03	2¹	22	▲	9 Tupac: Resurrection ..... [S]		Amaru 001533
1/1/05	❶¹	23	▲	10 Loyal To The Game		Amaru 003861
12/9/06	9	15		11 Pac's Life		Amaru 008025
				GREATEST HITS & COMPILATIONS:		
12/13/97	2¹	26	▲⁴	12 R U Still Down? [Remember Me]		Amaru 41628 [2]
8/8/98	112	11		13 In His Own Words		Mecca 8807
12/12/98+	3¹	76	▲⁹	14 Greatest Hits ..... Cat:#15/96		Amaru 490301 [2]
5/6/00	178	1		15 The Lost Tapes		Herb 'N Soul 54377
10/25/03	15	8		16 Nu-Mixx Klazzics		Death Row 9530
9/1/07	45	3		17 Nu Mixx Klazzics Vol. 2 (Evolution: Duets And Remixes)		Death Row 5930
12/22/07	65	12		18 The Best Of 2pac - Part 1: Thug		Amaru 010072
12/22/07	77	5		19 The Best Of 2pac - Part 2: Life		Amaru 010221
				LIVE ALBUMS:		
8/21/04	54	6		20 Live		Death Row 5746
10/22/05	159	1		21 Tupac: Live At The House Of Blues		Death Row 20080
				2 PISTOLS Born Jeremy Saunders on 6/11/1983 in Tarpon Springs, Florida. Male rapper.		
7/5/08	32	4		1 Death Before Dishonor		Justice League 011160
				TWO TONGUES Alternative-rock band formed in Los Angeles, California: Max Bemis (vocals), Chris Conley (guitar), Dave Soloway (bass) and Coby Linder (drums). Bemis and Linder are also members of **Say Anything**. Conley and Soloway are also members of **Saves The Day**.		
2/21/09	111	1		1 Two Tongues		Vagrant 528
				TWO TONS — see WEATHER GIRLS		
				II TRU Female rap duo from Cleveland, Ohio: Jhaz and Brina. Part of the **Mo Thugs Family**.		
10/18/97	194	1		1 A New Breed Of Female		Mo Thugs 1582
				2 UNLIMITED Techno-house dance duo from Amsterdam, Netherlands: Ray Slijngaard (born on 6/28/1971) and Anita Doth (born on 12/25/1971).		
10/17/92	197	1	●	1 Get Ready		Radikal 15407
3/9/96	107	8		2 Hits Unlimited ..... [G]		Radikal 15446

TYCOON
Pop-rock band from New York: Norman Mershon (vocals), Jon Gordon (guitar), Mark Rivera (sax), Michael Fonfara (keyboards), Mark Kreider (bass) and Richard Steinberg (drums).

3/31/79	41	17		1 Tycoon		Arista 4215

TYGA
Born Michael Stevenson on 11/19/1989 in Compton, California. Male rapper.

6/28/08	112	1		1 No Introduction		Bat Squad 8001

TYLER, Bonnie
Born Gaynor Hopkins on 6/8/1953 in Swansea, Wales. Female singer known for her raspy vocals.

6/3/78	16	17	●	1 It's A Heartache		RCA Victor 2821
2/17/79	145	5		2 Diamond Cut		RCA Victor 3072
8/6/83	4	32	▲	3 Faster Than The Speed Of Night		Columbia 38710
4/26/86	106	8		4 Secret Dreams And Forbidden Fire		Columbia 40312

TYMES, The
R&B vocal group from Philadelphia, Pennsylvania: George Williams, George Hilliard, Donald Banks, Albert Berry and Norman Burnett.

8/3/63	15	20		1 So Much In Love		Parkway 7032
12/21/63+	117	10		2 The Sound Of The Wonderful Tymes		Parkway 7038
3/7/64	122	4		3 Somewhere		Parkway 7039
12/7/74	205	2		4 Trustmaker		RCA Victor 0727
2/21/76	202	4		5 Tymes Up		RCA Victor 1072
11/6/76	205	1		6 Turning Point		RCA Victor 1835

~ ~ ~ ~ ~ ~ ~ ~ ~ ~ **NON-CHARTED ALBUM** ~ ~ ~ ~ ~ ~ ~ ~ ~ ~ ~ ~
1964 **18 Golden Hits**

TYNAN, Ronan
Born on 5/14/1960 in Kilkenny, Ireland. Classical tenor. Lost both legs in a 1980 car crash. Member of **The Irish Tenors**.

3/26/05	149	2		1 Ronan		Decca 003863

TYNER, McCoy
Born on 12/11/1938 in Philadelphia, Pennsylvania. Jazz pianist.

6/14/75	161	5		1 Atlantis	[I-L]	Milestone 55002 [2]
				recorded on 8/31/1974 at the Keystone Korner in San Francisco, California		
1/3/76	198	2		2 Trident..	[I]	Milestone 9063
6/12/76	128	11		3 Fly With The Wind	[I]	Milestone 9067
1/22/77	187	3		4 Focal Point	[I]	Milestone 9072
7/9/77	167	5		5 Supertrios	[I]	Milestone 55003 [2]
1/28/78	171	8		6 Inner Voices	[I]	Milestone 9079
10/14/78	170	3		7 The Greeting	[I-L]	Milestone 9085
				recorded on 3/17/1978 at the Great American Music Hall in San Francisco, California		
5/26/79	66	11		8 Together	[I]	Milestone 9087
7/24/82	207	4		9 Looking Out	[I]	Columbia 38053

TYPE O NEGATIVE
Hard-rock band from Brooklyn, New York: Peter Steele (vocals, bass), Kenny Hickey (guitar), Josh Silver (keyboards) and Johnny Kelly (drums). Steele died of heart failure on 4/14/2010 (age 48).

1/14/95	166	11	▲	1 Bloody Kisses		Roadrunner 9100
9/7/96	42	8	●	2 October Rust		Roadrunner 8874
10/9/99	39	6		3 World Coming Down		Roadrunner 8660
11/18/00	99	1		4 The Least Worst Of	[K]	Roadrunner 8510
7/5/03	39	4		5 Life Is Killing Me		Roadrunner 618438
3/31/07	27	3		6 Dead Again		Steamhammer 9919

TYRELL, Steve
Born Stephen Bilao on 12/19/1944 in Houston, Texas. Jazz-styled singer.

1/18/03	7^X	1		1 This Time Of The Year	[X]	Columbia 86638
7/12/08	181	1		2 Back To Bacharach...		New Design 5070

TYRESE
Born Tyrese Gibson on 12/30/1978 in Watts, California. Male R&B singer/songwriter/actor. Starred in the movies *Baby Boy* and *2 Fast 2 Furious*.

11/14/98+	17	36	▲	1 Tyrese		RCA 66901
6/9/01	10	24	●	2 2000 Watts		RCA 68039
1/4/03	16	35	●	3 I Wanna Go There		J Records 20041
12/30/06	23	15		4 Alter Ego		J Records 78963 [2]

TYZIK
Born Jeff Tyzik in Hyde Park, New York. Jazz trumpeter.

9/8/84	172	6		1 Jammin' In Manhattan..		Polydor 821605

U

UB40
Interracial reggae band formed in Birmingham, England: brothers Ali Campbell (lead vocals) and Robin Campbell (guitar, vocals), with Terence "Astro" Wilson (reggae vocals), Norman Hassan (percussion), Michael Virtue (keyboards), Brian Travers (sax), Earl Falconer (bass) and James Brown (drums). Name taken from a British unemployment form.

11/26/83+	14	63	▲	1 Labour Of Love .... Cat:#24/10	A&M 4980
11/10/84	60	26		2 Geffery Morgan...	A&M 5033
8/17/85	40	25		3 Little Baggariddim .... [EP]	A&M 5090
8/30/86	53	17		4 Rat In The Kitchen..	A&M 5137
8/29/87	121	8		5 CCCP: Live In Moscow .... [L]	A&M 5168
8/20/88	44	27		6 UB40	A&M 5213
1/13/90+	30	111	▲	7 Labour Of Love II .... Cat:#18/10	Virgin 91324
8/14/93	6	41	▲	8 Promises And Lies	Virgin 88229
7/19/97	176	2		9 Guns In The Ghetto	Virgin 44402

UBIQUITY
Backing band for **Roy Ayers**: Sylvia Cox (vocals), Greg Moore (vocals, guitar), Philip Woo (keyboards), Justo Almario (sax), John Mosley (trumpet), Chano Oferral (congas), Kerry Turman (bass) and Ricky Lawson (drums).

4/8/78	146	4		1 Starbooty	Elektra 120

UFO
Hard-rock band formed in England: Phil Mogg (vocals), **Michael Schenker** (guitar), Pete Way (bass) and Andy Parker (drums). Paul Raymond (keyboards) joined in 1977. Paul Chapman replaced Schenker in 1979.

8/24/74	202	2		1 Phenomenon	Chrysalis 1059
8/9/75	71	13		2 Force It	Chrysalis 1074
6/19/76	169	4		3 No Heavy Petting...	Chrysalis 1103
6/11/77	23	24		4 Lights Out	Chrysalis 1127
7/29/78	41	18		5 Obsession...	Chrysalis 1182
2/3/79	42	15		6 Strangers In The Night .... [L]	Chrysalis 1209 [2]
1/19/80	51	13		7 No Place To Run	Chrysalis 1239
1/31/81	77	11		8 The Wild The Willing And The Innocent..	Chrysalis 1307
2/20/82	82	14		9 Mechanix	Chrysalis 1360
4/30/83	153	5		10 Making Contact	Chrysalis 41402
4/5/86	106	19		11 Misdemeanor	Chrysalis 41518

UGK
Male rap duo from Port Arthur, Texas: Chad "**Pimp C**" Butler and Bernard "**Bun-B**" Freeman. Butler died on 12/4/2007 (age 33).

9/17/94	95	10		1 Super Tight... UNDERGORUND KINGZ	Jive 41524
8/17/96	15	13	●	2 Ridin' Dirty	Jive 41586
12/1/01	18	15		3 Dirty Money	Jive 41673
10/12/02	70	3		4 Side Hustles	Jive 41826
8/25/07	❶[1]	13		5 Underground Kingz	UGK 02633 [2]
4/18/09	6	11		6 UGK 4 Life	Trill 86966

UGLY KID JOE
Rock band from Isla Vista, California: Whitfield Crane (vocals), Klaus Eichstadt (guitar), Dave Fortman (guitar), Cordell Crockett (bass), and Mark Davis (drums).

2/8/92	4	34	▲	1 As Ugly As They Want To Be [EP]	Stardog 868823
9/26/92+	27	51	▲[2]	2 America's Least Wanted..	Stardog 512571
7/1/95	178	1		3 Menace To Sobriety	Mercury 526997

U-GOD
Born Lamont Hawkins on 11/10/1970 in Brooklyn, New York. Male rapper. Member of **Wu-Tang Clan**.

11/6/99	58	3		1 Golden Arms Redemption	Wu-Tang 50086

U.K.
Art-rock band formed in England: John Wetton (vocals, bass; **Family**, **King Crimson**, **Uriah Heep**, **Asia**), Allan Holdsworth (guitar), **Bill Bruford** (percussion; **Yes**) Eddie Jobson (keyboards; **Roxy Music**) and Terry Bozzio (drums; **Frank Zappa**, **Roxy Music**, **Missing Persons**). Holdsworth and Bruford left after first album.

5/20/78	65	15		1 U.K.	Polydor 6146
3/24/79	45	11		2 Danger Money	Polydor 6194
10/20/79	109	6		3 Night After Night.. [L] recorded June 1979 in Tokyo, Japan	Polydor 6234

U-KREW, The
Rap group from Portland, Oregon: Kevin Morse, Larry Bell, Lavell Alexander, James McClendon and Hakim Muhammad.

2/17/90	93	23		1 The U-Krew	Enigma 73524

ULLMAN, Tracey
Born on 12/30/1959 in Buckinghamshire, England. Actress/singer/comedienne. Hosted own TV show from 1987-90. Acted in several movies.

3/24/84	34	20		1 You Broke My Heart In 17 Places	MCA 5471

Billboard DEBUT	PEAK	WKS	R I A A	ARTIST / Album Title	Catalog	Label & Number

ULTIMATE
Disco studio group assembled by producers Juliano Salerni and Bruce Weeden.

| 3/3/79 | 157 | 11 | | 1 Ultimate .... | | Casablanca 7128 |

ULTIMATE SPINACH
Psychedelic-rock band from Boston, Massachusetts: Ian Bruce-Douglas (vocals, keyboards), Barbara Hudson (vocals, guitar), Geoffrey Winthrop (guitar), Richard Nese (bass) and Keith Lahteinen (drums).

| 2/24/68 | 34 | 24 | | 1 Ultimate Spinach .... | | MGM 4518 |
| 11/9/68 | 198 | 2 | | 2 Behold & See .... | | MGM 4570 |

ULTRAVOX
Electronic-rock band from London, England: **Midge Ure** (vocals, guitar), Billy Currie (keyboards), Chris Cross (bass) and Warren Cann (drums). Ure and Currie also recorded in **Visage**.

9/13/80	164	9		1 Vienna		Chrysalis 1296
10/24/81	144	6		2 Rage In Eden		Chrysalis 1338
3/12/83	61	17		3 Quartet		Chrysalis 1394
5/19/84	115	9		4 Lament		Chrysalis 41459
5/4/85	203	3		5 The Collection .... [K]		Chrysalis 41490

UMPHREY'S McGEE
Alternative-rock band from South Bend, Indiana: Brendan Bayliss (vocals, guitar), Jake Cinninger (vocals, guitar), Joel Cummins (keyboards), Andy Farag (percussion), Ryan Stasik (bass) and Kris Myers (drums).

| 4/22/06 | 186 | 1 | | 1 Safety In Numbers .... | | Sci Fidelity 1032 |
| 2/7/09 | 62 | 1 | | 2 Mantis .... | | Hanging Brains 1117 |

UNCLE KRACKER
Born Matthew Shafer on 6/6/1974 in Mount Clemens, Michigan. White pop-rock singer/DJ. Member of **Kid Rock**'s posse.

7/1/00+	7	49	▲²	1 Double Wide		Lava 83279
10/12/02	43	41	●	2 No Stranger To Shame		Lava 83542
7/17/04	39	8		3 Seventy Two & Sunny		Lava 93195
10/3/09	38	8		4 Happy Hour		Top Dog 519817

UNCLE SAM
Born Sam Turner in Detroit, Michigan. R&B singer.

| 1/17/98 | 68 | 21 | | 1 Uncle Sam .... | | Stonecreek 67731 |

UNCLE TUPELO
Alternative folk-pop trio from Belleville, Illinois: **Jay Farrar**, Jeff Tweedy and Mike Heidorn. Disbanded in 1994. Farrar and Heidorn formed **Son Volt**. Tweedy formed **Wilco**.

| 4/6/02 | 173 | 1 | | 1 83/93: An Anthology .... [K] | | Legacy 62223 |

UNDERGROUND KINGZ — see UGK

UNDERGROUND SUNSHINE
Rock band from Montello, Wisconsin: brothers Egbert Kohl (vocals, bass) and Frank Kohl (drums), with John Dahlberg (guitar) and Jane Little (keyboards).

| 11/8/69 | 161 | 3 | | 1 Let There Be Light .... | | Intrepid 74003 |

UNDEROATH
Christian hard-rock band from Florida: Spencer Chamberlain (vocals), Tim McTague (guitar), James Smith (guitar), Chris Dudley (keyboards), Grant Brandell (bass) and Aaron Gillespie (drums). Gillespie is also lead singer of **The Almost**.

7/3/04+	101	7		1 They're Only Chasing Safety		Solid State 83184
7/8/06	2¹	13	●	2 Define The Great Line		Solid State 42658
6/14/08	81	1		3 Survive, Kaleidoscope .... [L]		Solid State 11710
9/20/08	8	8		4 Lost In The Sound Of Separation		Solid State 08842

UNDER THE INFLUENCE OF GIANTS
Alternative-rock band from Los Angeles, California: Aaron Bruno (vocals), Drew Stewart (guitar), Dave Amezcua (bass) and Jamin Wilcox (drums).

| 8/26/06 | 134 | 2 | | 1 Under The Influence Of Giants .... | | Island 006982 |

UNDERTONES, The
Pop-rock band from Ireland: **Feargal Sharkey** (vocals), brothers Damian O'Neill and John O'Neill (guitars), Mickey Bradley (bass) and Billy Doherty (drums).

| 1/26/80 | 154 | 7 | | 1 The Undertones .... | | Sire 6081 |

UNDERWOOD, Carrie
Born on 3/10/1983 in Checotah, Oklahoma. Female country singer. Winner on the 2005 season of TV's *American Idol*.
AWARDS: Grammy: Best New Artist 2006 ★ CMA: Horizon 2006 / Female Vocalist 2006, 2007 & 2008 ★ OPRY: 2008

12/3/05	2²	151	▲⁷	1 Some Hearts Cat:#2¹/70		Arista Nashville 71197
11/10/07	❶¹	101	▲³	2 Carnival Ride Cat:#15/14		Arista Nashville 11221
11/21/09	❶¹	28	▲	3 Play On		19 Records 49923

806

Billboard DEBUT	PEAK	WKS	R I A A	ARTIST Album Title	Catalog	Label & Number
				UNDERWORLD Rock band from England: Karl Hyde (vocals, guitar), Alfie Thomas (guitar), Rick Smith (keyboards), Baz Allen (bass) and Pascal Console (drums). By 1999, group reduced to trio of Karl Hyde, Darren Emerson and Rick Smith.		
3/19/88	139	19		1 **Underneath The Radar**...		Sire 25627
5/1/99	93	5		2 **Beaucoup Fish**		V2 27042
9/30/00	192	1		3 **Everything, Everything** .... [L]		V2 27078
10/12/02	122	1		4 **A Hundred Days Off**		JBO 27137
11/3/07	169	1		5 **Oblivion With Bells**		Side One 21582
				UNDISPUTED TRUTH, The R&B-disco vocal trio from Detroit, Michigan: Joe Harris, Billie Calvin and Brenda Evans.		
7/24/71	43	18		1 **The Undisputed Truth**..		Gordy 955
2/5/72	114	12		2 **Face To Face With The Truth**		Gordy 959
8/18/73	191	2		3 **Law Of The Land**		Gordy 963
9/14/74	208	3		4 **Down To Earth**		Gordy 968
6/21/75	186	2		5 **Cosmic Truth**		Gordy 970
11/22/75	173	4		6 **Higher Than High**		Gordy 972
1/29/77	66	17		7 **Method To The Madness**		Whitfield 2967
				UNEARTH Hard-rock band from Los Angeles, California: Trevor Phipps (vocals), Buz McGrath (guitar), Ken Susi (guitar), John "Slo" Maggard (bass) and Mike Justian (drums).		
7/17/04	105	2		1 **The Oncoming Storm**...		Metal Blade 14479
8/26/06	35	4		2 **III: In The Eyes Of Fire**		Metal Blade 14574
11/1/08	45	3		3 **The March**		Metal Blade 14692
				UNFORGIVEN, The Rock band from Los Angeles, California: John Henry Jones (vocals), John Hickman, Just Jones and Todd Ross (guitars), Mike Finn (bass) and Alan Waddington (drums).		
8/9/86	185	2		1 **The Unforgiven**...		Elektra 60461
				UNICORN Art-rock band from England: Pete Perrier (vocals, drums), Kevin Smith (guitar), Kenny Baker (keyboards) and Pat Martin (bass).		
10/26/74	129	5		1 **Blue Pine Trees** .... produced by **David Gilmour**		Capitol 11334
				UNION Rock band formed in Canada: Randy Bachman (vocals, guitar), Frank Ludwig (keyboards), Fred Turner (bass) and Chris Leighton (drums). Bachman and Turner were leaders of **Bachman-Turner Overdrive**.		
8/1/81	207	2		1 **On Strike**		Portrait 37368
				UNION GAP, The — see PUCKETT, Gary		
				UNION UNDERGROUND, The Rock band from San Antonio, Texas: Bryan Scott (vocals, guitar), Patrick Kennison (guitar), John Moyer (bass) and Josh Memelo (drums). Moyer joined **Disturbed** in early 2003.		
8/26/00	130	16		1 **...An Education In Rebellion**		Portrait 67778
				UNITED STATES AIR FORCE BAND, The Conducted by Colonel George S. Howard. Formed in 1942 at the direction of President Roosevelt.		
6/29/63	102	6		1 **The United States Air Force Band** .... [I]		RCA Victor 2686
				UNITED STATES MARINE BAND, The Directed by Lieutenant Colonel Albert F. Schoepper. Formed in 1798 at the direction of President Adams.		
6/15/63	22	9		1 **The United States Marine Band** .... [I] *NRR*		RCA Victor 2687
				UNITED STATES NAVY BAND, The Directed by Commander Anthony A. Mitchell. Formed in 1925 at the direction of President Coolidge.		
6/15/63	38	7		1 **The United States Navy Band** .... [I]		RCA Victor 2688
				UNITED STATES OF AMERICA, The Electronic-rock band from Los Angeles: Dorothy Moskowitz (vocals), Gordon Marron (violin), Joseph Byrd (keyboards), Rand Forbes (bass) and Craig Woodson (drums).		
5/4/68	181	9		1 **The United States Of America**............................		Columbia 9614
				UNK Born Anthony Platt on 3/28/1982 in Atlanta, Georgia. Male DJ/rapper.		
10/21/06	109	13		1 **Beat'n Down Yo Block!**		Big Oomp 5973
11/22/08	104	1		2 **2econd Season**		Big Oomp 5098
				UNKLE Experimental hip-hop trio from England: James Lavelle, Tim Goldsworthy and Kudo.		
10/17/98	107	2		1 **Psyence Fiction**		Mo Wax 540970
				UNLIMITED TOUCH R&B band from Brooklyn, New York: Audrey Wheeler and Stephanie James (vocals), Philip Hamilton (guitar), Galen Underwood (keyboards), Samuel Anderson (bass) and Tony Cintron (drums).		
6/20/81	142	7		1 **Unlimited Touch**		Prelude 12184

DEBUT	PEAK	WKS	RIAA	ARTIST / Album Title	Catalog	Label & Number
				UNTOUCHABLES, The		
				Funk band from Los Angeles, California: Jerry Miller and Chuck Askerneese (vocals), Clyde Grimes (guitar), Brewster (keyboards), Derek Breakfield (bass) and Willie McNeil (drums).		
4/1/89	162	9		1 **Agent Double O Soul**		Restless 72342
				U.N.V.		
				R&B vocal group from Detroit, Michigan: brothers John Powe and Shawn Powe, with John Clay and Demetrius Peete. UNV: Universal Nubian Voices.		
7/17/93	59	13		1 **Something's Goin' On**		Maverick 45287
7/15/95	161	3		2 **Universal Nubian Voices**		Maverick 45839
				UNWRITTEN LAW		
				Punk-rock band from Poway, California: Scott Russo (vocals), Rob Brewer (guitar), Steve Morris (guitar), Pat Kim (bass) and Wade Youman (drums). Tony Palermo replaced Youman in 2004.		
2/16/02	69	25		1 **Elva**		Interscope 493139
2/8/03	134	2		2 **Music In High Places**		Lava 83632
2/19/05	51	8		3 **Here's To The Mourning**		Lava 93147
1/27/07	184	1		4 **The Hit List**		Abydos 0009
				UP WITH PEOPLE		
				A "sing-out" musical production featuring various young singing talent.		
7/23/66	61	14		1 **Up With People!**		Pace 1101
				URBAN, Keith — 2000s: #49 / All-Time: #491		
				Born on 10/26/1967 in Whangarei, New Zealand; raised in Caboolture, Queensland, Australia. Country singer/songwriter. Married actress Nicole Kidman on 6/25/2006.		
				AWARD: CMA: Horizon 2001 / Male Vocalist 2004, 2005 & 2006 / Entertainer 2005		
8/26/00+	145	27	▲	1 **Keith Urban**		Capitol 97591
10/26/02	11	111	▲³	2 **Golden Road**	Cat:$\mathbf{O}^8$/99	Capitol 32936
10/9/04	3^1	104	▲⁴	3 **Be Here**	Cat:#3/27	Capitol 77489
11/25/06	3^1	54	▲	4 **Love, Pain & The Whole Crazy Thing**		Capitol 77087
12/8/07	11	63	●	5 **Greatest Hits**	Cat:#40/4 [G]	Capitol 07685
4/18/09	❶^1	59	●	6 **Defying Gravity**		Capitol 35751
8/8/09	153	1		7 **iTunes Originals**		Capitol digital
				URBAN DANCE SQUAD		
				Rap-dance group from Amsterdam, Netherlands: Patrick Remington, Magic Stick, DNA, Silly Sil and Tres Manos.		
8/25/90+	54	39		1 **Mental Floss For The Globe**		Arista 8640
				URE, Midge		
				Born James Ure on 10/10/1953 in Glasgow, Scotland. Rock singer/guitarist. Member of **Ultravox** and **Visage**.		
2/11/89	88	16		1 **Answers To Nothing**		Chrysalis 41649
				URGE, The		
				Ska-rock band from St. Louis, Missouri: Steve Ewing (vocals), Jerry Jost (guitar), Bill Reiter, Matt Kwiatkowski and Todd Painter (horns), Karl Grable (bass) and John Pessoni (drums).		
5/9/98	111	2		1 **Master Of Styles**		Immortal 69152
8/5/00	200	1		2 **Too Much Stereo**		Immortal 49498
				URGE OVERKILL		
				Rock trio from Chicago, Illinois: Nash Kato (guitar), "Eddie" King Roeser (bass) and Blackie Onassis (drums). All share vocals.		
9/18/93	146	9		1 **Saturation**		Geffen 24529
10/14/95	129	1		2 **Exit The Dragon**		Geffen 24818
				URIAH HEEP — All-Time: #457		
				Hard-rock band from England. Core members: David Byron (vocals; later with **Rough Diamond**), Mick Box (guitar), **Ken Hensley** (keyboards; later with **Blackfoot**), Gary Thain (bass) and Keith Baker (drums). Thain died of a drug overdose on 3/19/1976 (age 27). Byron died on 2/28/1985 (age 38).		
10/3/70	186	4		1 **Uriah Heep**		Mercury 61294
1/30/71	103	9		2 **Salisbury**		Mercury 61319
9/25/71	93	20		3 **Look At Yourself**		Mercury 614
6/17/72	23	38	●	4 **Demons And Wizards**		Mercury 630
12/2/72+	31	22	●	5 **The Magician's Birthday**		Mercury 652
5/5/73	37	30	●	6 **Uriah Heep Live**	[L]	Mercury 7503 [2]
10/6/73	33	23	●	7 **Sweet Freedom**		Warner 2724
7/6/74	38	15		8 **Wonderworld**		Warner 2800
8/2/75	85	10		9 **Return To Fantasy**		Warner 2869
3/20/76	145	6		10 **The Best Of Uriah Heep**	[G]	Mercury 1070
6/26/76	161	3		11 **High And Mighty**		Warner 2949
4/30/77	166	3		12 **Firefly**		Warner 3013
11/4/78	186	5		13 **Fallen Angel**		Chrysalis 1204
8/7/82	56	16		14 **Abominog**		Mercury 4057
6/4/83	159	10		15 **Head First**		Mercury 812313

Billboard DEBUT	PEAK	WKS	R I A A	ARTIST Album Title	Catalog	Label & Number

USA-EUROPEAN CONNECTION
Female disco vocal trio: Leza Holmes, Renne Johnson and Sharon Williams.

| 4/8/78 | 66 | 19 | | 1 **Come Into My Heart** .... | | Marlin 2212 |

USA FOR AFRICA
USA: United Support of Artists. Collection of top artists formed to help starving people in Africa.

| 4/20/85 | ❶³ | 22 | ▲³ | 1 **We Are The World** | | Columbia 40043 |

U.S.D.A.
Male rap trio formed in Atlanta, Georgia: **Young Jeezy**, **Blood Raw** and Slick Pulla.

| 6/9/07 | 4 | 17 | | 1 **Cold Summer: The Authorized Mixtape** | | Corporate Thugz 008738 |

USED, The
Rock band from Orem, Utah: Bert McCracken (vocals), Quinn Allman (guitar), Jeph Howard (bass) and Branden Steineckert (drums).

10/19/02+	63	34	●	1 **The Used**		Reprise 48287
8/2/03	84	2		2 **Maybe Memories** .... [K-L]		Reprise 48503
10/16/04	6	36	●	3 **In Love And Death**		Reprise 48789
2/24/07	71	1		4 **Berth** .... [L]		Reprise 49967
6/9/07	5	16		5 **Lies For The Liars**		Reprise 43309
9/19/09	10	9		6 **Artwork**		Reprise 519904

USHER
Born Usher Raymond on 10/14/1978 in Dallas, Texas; raised in Chattanooga, Tennessee and Atlanta, Georgia. Male R&B singer/songwriter/actor. Played "Jeremy Davis" on TV's *Moesha*. Appeared in the movies *The Faculty*, *She's All That* and *Light It Up.*

9/17/94	167	12		1 **Usher**		LaFace 26008
10/4/97+	4	79	▲⁶	2 **My Way**		LaFace 26043
4/10/99	73	9	●	3 **Live** .... [L]		LaFace 26059
8/25/01	4	61	▲⁴	4 **8701**	Cat:#14/24	Arista 14715
4/10/04	❶⁹	96	▲¹⁰	5 **Confessions**	Cat:#8/21	Arista 52141
6/14/08	❶¹	42	▲	6 **Here I Stand**		LaFace 23388

US3
Jazz-rap collaboration by London producers Mel Simpson (keyboards) and Geoff Wilkinson (samples). Samples of recordings on the Blue Note jazz record label serve as the backdrop for new rap solos and jazz playing by some of Britain's top players.

| 1/8/94 | 31 | 33 | ▲ | 1 **Hand On The Torch** .... | | Blue Note 80883 |

UTADA
Born Utada Hikaru on 1/19/1983 in Manhattan, New York (Japanese parents). Female dance singer.

| 10/23/04 | 160 | 1 | | 1 **Exodus** .... | | Island 003185 |
| 4/11/09 | 69 | 3 | | 2 **This Is The One** .... | | Island 012979 |

UTAH SAINTS
Techno-rave duo from England: Jez Willis and Tim Garbutt.

| 11/14/92 | 182 | 4 | | 1 **Something Good** .... | | London 869843 |
| 1/23/93 | 165 | 4 | | 2 **Utah Saints** .... | | London 828374 |

UTFO
Rap group from Brooklyn, New York: Shaun Fequiere, Fred Reeves, Jeff Campbell and Maurice Bailey. UTFO: Un-Touchable Force Organization.

6/15/85	80	20		1 **UTFO**		Select 21614
8/9/86	142	8		2 **Skeezer Pleezer**		Select 21616
10/3/87	67	20		3 **Lethal**		Select 21619
6/10/89	143	4		4 **Doin' It!**		Select 21629

UTOPIA
Pop-rock band formed in New York: **Todd Rundgren** (vocals, guitar), **Roger Powell** (keyboards), **Kasim Sulton** (bass) and John Wilcox (drums).

11/9/74	34	15		1 **Todd Rundgren's Utopia**		Bearsville 6954
11/15/75	66	9		2 **Todd Rundgren's Utopia/Another Live** .... [L]		Bearsville 6961
2/26/77	79	7		3 **RA**		Bearsville 6965
9/24/77	73	8		4 **Oops! Wrong Planet**		Bearsville 6970
1/26/80	32	21		5 **Adventures In Utopia**		Bearsville 6991
10/25/80	65	9		6 **Deface The Music**		Bearsville 3487
3/20/82	102	10		7 **Swing To The Right**		Bearsville 3666
10/16/82	84	19		8 **Utopia**		Network 60183 [2]
2/11/84	74	12		9 **Oblivion**		Passport 6029
3/16/85	161	6		10 **POV**		Passport 6044

U2
1980s: #5 / 1990s: #44 / 2000s: #48 / All-Time: #49

Rock band formed in Dublin, Ireland: Paul "Bono" Hewson (vocals; born on 5/10/1960), Dave "The Edge" Evans (guitar; born on 8/8/1961), Adam Clayton (bass; born on 3/13/1960) and Larry Mullen Jr. (drums; born on 10/31/1961). Released concert tour documentary movie *Rattle And Hum* in 1988. Bono eventually became a social activist and was nominated for the Nobel Peace Prize in 2003 for his efforts to relieve third world debt and to promote AIDS awareness in Africa; he was also named *Time* magazine's 2005 Person of the Year (along with Bill and Melinda Gates). The majority of their recordings were produced by Steve Lillywhite, **Brian Eno** and Daniel Lanois. Also see **Passengers**.

AWARD: R&R Hall of Fame: 2005

DEBUT	PEAK	WKS	RIAA		Album Title	Catalog	Label & Number
3/14/81	63	47	▲	1	Boy		Island 9646
					RS500 #417		
11/7/81	104	38	▲	2	October		Island 9680
3/19/83	12	179	▲⁴	3	War	Cat:#23/33	Island 90067
					RS500 #221		
10/20/84	12	132	▲³	4	The Unforgettable Fire	Cat:#6/5	Island 90231
4/4/87	❶⁹	103	▲¹⁰	5	The Joshua Tree	Cat:#9/246	Island 90581
					Grammys: Album of the Year / Rock Group Vocal ★ RS500 #26		
10/29/88	❶⁶	38	▲⁵	6	Rattle And Hum	Cat:#39/9 [S]	Island 91003 [2]
12/7/91	❶¹	97	▲⁸	7	Achtung Baby		Island 510347
					Grammy: Rock Group ★ RS500 #62		
7/24/93	❶²	40	▲²	8	Zooropa		Island 518047
					Grammy: Alternative Album		
3/22/97	❶¹	28	▲	9	Pop		Island 524334
11/18/00	3¹	94	▲⁴	10	All That You Can't Leave Behind		Interscope 524653
					Grammy: Rock Album ★ RS500 #139		
12/11/04	❶¹	56	▲³	11	How To Dismantle An Atomic Bomb		Interscope 003613
					Grammys: Album of the Year / Rock Album		
3/21/09	❶¹	35	▲	12	No Line On The Horizon		Island 012630
					GREATEST HITS & COMPILATIONS:		
11/21/98	2¹	17	▲²	13	The Best Of 1980-1990/The B-Sides	Cat:#35/1	Island 524612 [2]
11/28/98	45	42	▲²	14	The Best Of 1980-1990	Cat:#2¹/162	Island 524613
11/23/02	3¹	12		15	The Best Of 1990-2000 & B-Sides		Island 063438 [2]
11/30/02	34	14	▲	16	The Best Of 1990-2000		Island 063361
12/9/06	12	45		17	U218: Singles	Cat:#10/5	Island 008027
					LIVE ALBUMS:		
12/10/83+	28	180	▲³	18	Under A Blood Red Sky	Cat:#4/67 [EP]	Island 90127
6/29/85	37	23	▲	19	Wide Awake In America	[EP]	Island 90279
8/9/08	54	2		20	Live From Paris: Hippodrome De Vincennes, Paris, 4th July, 1987		Island digital
					REISSUES:		
12/8/07	20ᶜ	7		21	The Joshua Tree: Deluxe Edition		Island 010285
8/9/08	18ᶜ	1		22	Boy: Deluxe Edition		Island 010946 [2]
8/9/08	24ᶜ	1		23	October: Deluxe Edition		Island 010948 [2]
8/9/08	13ᶜ	1		24	War: Deluxe Edition		Island 010949 [2]

V

VAI, Steve

Born on 6/6/1960 in Long Island, New York. Rock guitarist. With **Frank Zappa**'s band (1979-84), **Alcatrazz** (1985), **David Lee Roth**'s band (1986-88) and **Whitesnake** (1989). Formed **Vai** in 1992 which featured vocalist Devin Townsend and fluctuating band members. Former guitar student of **Joe Satriani**.

DEBUT	PEAK	WKS			Album Title		Label & Number
6/9/90	18	25	●	1	Passion And Warfare	[I]	Relativity 1037
8/14/93	48	8		2	Sex & Religion		Relativity 1132
					VAI		
4/8/95	125	2		3	Alien Love Secrets		Relativity 1245
10/5/96	106	2		4	Fire Garden		Epic 67776
6/21/97	108	3		5	G3 - Live In Concert	[I-L]	Epic 67920
					JOE SATRIANI / ERIC JOHNSON / STEVE VAI		
9/25/99	121	1		6	The Ultra Zone	[I]	Epic 69817
3/12/05	147	1		7	Real Illusions: Reflections		Epic 86800

VAIN

Hard-rock band from San Francisco, California: Davy Vain (vocals), Danny West (guitar), James Scott (guitar), Ashley Mitchell (bass) and Tom Rickard (drums).

DEBUT	PEAK	WKS			Album Title		Label & Number
8/26/89	154	8		1	No Respect		Island 91272

VALE, Jerry
1960s: #50 / All-Time: #288

Born Genaro Vitaliano on 7/8/1932 in the Bronx, New York. Adult Contemporary singer. Acted in the movies *A Wake In Providence* and *No Tomorrow*.

DEBUT	PEAK	WKS			Album Title		Label & Number
8/25/62+	60	48		1	I Have But One Heart		Columbia 1797 / 8597
2/23/63	34	25		2	Arrivederci, Roma		Columbia 1955 / 8755
9/7/63	22	35		3	The Language Of Love		Columbia 2043 / 8843
2/22/64	28	18		4	Till The End Of Time		Columbia 2116 / 8916

Billboard DEBUT	PEAK	WKS	R I A A	ARTIST / Album Title	Catalog	Label & Number
				VALE, Jerry — cont'd		
8/29/64	26	22		5 **Be My Love**		Columbia 2181 / 8981
12/19/64	14[X]	10		6 **Christmas Greetings From Jerry Vale**.................... [X]		Columbia 2225 / 9025
				Christmas charts: 14/64, 51/65, 36/67, 22/68		
1/30/65	55	18		7 **Standing Ovation!**.. [L]		Columbia 2273 / 9073
				recorded on 5/30/1964 at Carnegie Hall		
3/6/65	30	23		8 **Have You Looked Into Your Heart**		Columbia 2313 / 9113
10/16/65	42	17		9 **There Goes My Heart**		Columbia 2387 / 9187
2/12/66	38	17		10 **It's Magic**		Columbia 2444 / 9244
7/2/66	111	4		11 **Great Moments On Broadway**		Columbia 2489 / 9289
3/18/67	117	23		12 **The Impossible Dream**		Columbia 2583 / 9383
9/16/67	128	6		13 **Time Alone Will Tell**		Columbia 2684 / 9484
3/16/68	163	7		14 **You Don't Have To Say You Love Me**		Columbia 2774 / 9574
8/10/68	135	20		15 **This Guy's In Love With You**		Columbia 9694
2/15/69	90	12		16 **Till**		Columbia 9757
7/5/69	180	4		17 **Where's The Playground Susie?**		Columbia 9838
11/1/69	193	2		18 **With Love, Jerry Vale** .... [K]		Columbia 16 [2]
2/14/70	196	2		19 **Jerry Vale Sings 16 Greatest Hits Of The 60's**		Columbia 9982
6/27/70	189	4		20 **Let It Be**		Columbia 1021
2/12/72	200	2		21 **Jerry Vale Sings The Great Hits Of Nat King Cole**		Columbia 31147
				VALENS, Ritchie		
				Born Richard Valenzuela on 5/13/1941 in Pacoima, California. Killed in the plane crash that also took the lives of **Buddy Holly** and the Big Bopper on 2/3/1959 (age 17). Latin-rock singer/songwriter/guitarist. Appeared in the 1959 movie *Go Johnny Go*. The 1987 movie *La Bamba* was based on his life.		
				AWARD: R&R Hall of Fame: 2001		
4/6/59	23	6		1 **Ritchie Valens**		Del-Fi 1201
8/29/87	100	10		2 **The Best Of Ritchie Valens** .... [G]		Rhino 70178
				~ ~ ~ ~ ~ ~ ~ ~ ~ **NON-CHARTED ALBUMS** ~ ~ ~ ~ ~ ~ ~ ~ ~ ~ ~		
				1959 Ritchie 1963 **His Greatest Hits**		
				1960 Ritchie Valens In Concert At Pacoima Jr. High 1965 **His Greatest Hits Vol. 2 Featuring La Bamba!**		
				VALENTIN, Dave		
				Born on 4/29/1952 in the Bronx, New York. Jazz flutist. Member of **Fuse One**.		
10/25/80	194	2		1 **Land Of The Third Eye** .... [I]		GRP 5009
8/8/81	184	4		2 **Pied Piper** .... [I]		GRP 5505
8/7/82	201	5		3 **In Love's Time** .... [I]		GRP 5511
				VALENTINE, Brooke		
				Born on 10/5/1985 in Houston, Texas. Female R&B singer/songwriter.		
4/2/05	16	13		1 **Chain Letter**		Virgin 94229
				VALENTINO, Bobby		
				Born Bobby Wilson on 2/27/1980 in Jackson, Mississippi; raised in Atlanta, Georgia. R&B singer/songwriter. Former member of **Mista**.		
5/14/05	3[1]	23	●	1 **Disturbing Tha Peace Presents Bobby Valentino**		DTP 004293
5/26/07	3[1]	12		2 **Special Occasion**		DTP 007226
2/28/09	7	9		3 **The Rebirth**		Blue Kolla Dreams 66070
				BOBBY V		
				VALJEAN		
				Born Valjean Johns on 11/19/1934 in Shattuck, Oklahoma. Died on 2/10/2003 (age 68). Male pianist.		
7/28/62	113	5		1 **The Theme From Ben Casey** .... [I]		Carlton 143
				VALLI, Frankie		
				Born Francis Castellucio on 5/3/1937 in Newark, New Jersey. Lead singer of **The 4 Seasons**. Suffered from a disease that caused hearing loss in the late 1970s; corrected by surgery. Acted in several movies and played "Rusty Millio" on TV's *The Sopranos*.		
7/22/67	34	23		1 **Frankie Valli-Solo**		Philips 600247
8/10/68	176	5		2 **Timeless**		Philips 600274
6/13/70	190	2		3 **Half & Half**		Philips 600341
				half the cuts by Frankie Valli, half by **The 4 Seasons** (see 4 Seasons for tracks)		
3/29/75	51	28		4 **Closeup**		Private Stock 2000
11/15/75	203	1		5 **Inside You**		Motown 852
12/13/75+	107	8		6 **Our Day Will Come**		Private Stock 2006
12/20/75+	132	8		7 **Frankie Valli Gold** .... [G]		Private Stock 2001
8/26/78	160	7		8 **Frankie Valli...Is The Word**		Warner/Curb 3233
10/27/07	167	2		9 **Romancing The '60s**		Cherry 009908
				VAMPIRE WEEKEND		
				Alternative-rock band formed in Brooklyn, New York: Ezra Koenig (vocals, guitar), Rostam Batmanglij (keyboards), Chris Baio (bass) and Chris Tomson (drums). Batmanglij also formed **Discovery**.		
2/16/08	17	53	●	1 **Vampire Weekend**.. Cat:#32/9		XL 318
				VAN BUUREN, Armin		
				Born on 12/25/1976 in Leiden, Netherlands. Male trance DJ/producer.		
5/24/08	157	1		1 **Imagine**		Ultra 1666
10/25/08	187	1		2 **A State Of Trance 2008**		Armada 1839 [2]

Billboard DEBUT	PEAK	WKS	R I A A	ARTIST Album Title	Catalog	Label & Number

VANDENBERG
Born Adrian Vandenberg on 1/31/1954 in the Netherlands. Hard-rock guitarist. His group: Bert Heerink (vocals), Dick Kemper (bass) and Jos Zoomer (drums). Vandenberg later joined **Whitesnake**.

| 1/8/83 | 65 | 18 | | 1 Vandenberg | | Atco 90005 |
| 1/28/84 | 169 | 7 | | 2 Heading For A Storm | | Atco 90121 |

VANDROSS, Luther 1990s: #29 / All-Time: #120
Born on 4/20/1951 in the Bronx, New York. Died of complications from a stroke on 7/1/2005 (age 54). R&B singer/songwriter/producer. Prolific session singer. Appeared in movie *The Meteor Man*. Also see **Various Artists Compilations:** *So Amazing: An All-Star Tribute To Luther Vandross* and *Forever, For Always, For Luther*.

9/19/81	19	36	▲²	1 Never Too Much		Epic 37451
10/16/82	20	36	▲	2 Forever, For Always, For Love		Epic 38235
12/24/83+	32	41	▲	3 Busy Body		Epic 39196
4/6/85	19	56	▲²	4 The Night I Fell In Love		Epic 39882
10/18/86+	14	53	▲²	5 Give Me The Reason		Epic 40415
10/22/88	9	33	▲	6 Any Love		Epic 44308
5/18/91	7	60	▲²	7 Power Of Love		Epic 46789
				Grammy: Male R&B Vocal		
6/19/93	6	28	▲	8 Never Let Me Go		Epic 53231
10/8/94	5	37	▲²	9 Songs		Epic 57775
10/19/96	9	28	▲	10 Your Secret Love		Epic 67553
8/29/98	26	15	●	11 I Know		Virgin 46089
7/7/01	6	41	▲	12 Luther Vandross		J Records 20007
6/28/03	❶¹	61	▲²	13 Dance With My Father Cat:#3/17		J Records 51885
				Grammy: R&B Album		
11/15/03	22	5		14 Luther Vandross Live: Radio City Music Hall 2003 [L]		J Records 55711
				CHRISTMAS ALBUMS:		
11/25/95	28	8	▲	15 This Is Christmas Cat:#8/16		Epic/LV 57795
				Christmas charts: 4/'95, 11/'96, 25/'97, 44/'02, 8/'03, 38/'04, 33/'05		
11/15/03	57ˣ	1		16 Home For Christmas [K]		Sony 52545
				GREATEST HITS & COMPILATIONS:		
11/4/89+	26	51	▲³	17 The Best Of Luther Vandross...The Best Of Love Cat:#10/61		Epic 45320 [2]
10/18/97	44	24	●	18 One Night With You - The Best Of Love Volume 2		Epic 68220
1/26/02	14ᶜ	19	▲	19 Greatest Hits		Legacy 66068
6/28/03	154	1	●	20 The Essential Luther Vandross Cat:#23/5		Legacy 89167 [2]
9/9/06	9	11	●	21 The Ultimate Luther Vandross Cat:#11/25		Legacy 97700
11/3/07	191	1		22 Love, Luther		LV 11856 [4]

VAN DYK, Paul
Born on 12/16/1971 in Eisenhüttenstadt, East Germany. Techno-dance DJ/producer.

7/8/00	192	1		1 Out There And Back		Mute 9127 [2]
9/1/07	115	2		2 In Between		Mute 9364
6/27/09	115	1		3 Volume: The Best Of Paul Van Dyk		Vandit 2040 [2]

VAN DYKE, Leroy
Born on 10/4/1929 in Spring Fork, Missouri. Country singer/songwriter/guitarist.
AWARD: OPRY: 1962

~ ~ ~ ~ ~ ~ ~ ~ ~ ~ **NON-CHARTED ALBUM** ~ ~ ~ ~ ~ ~ ~ ~ ~ ~ ~
1962 **Walk On By**

VAN EATON, Lon & Derek
Pop-rock duo from England: brothers Lon and Derek Van Eaton.

| 4/19/75 | 210 | 1 | | 1 Who Do You Out Do | | A&M 4507 |

VANESS, Theo
Born on 6/9/1946 in Zoeterwoude, Holland. Male singer.

| 6/16/79 | 145 | 6 | | 1 Bad Bad Boy | | Prelude 12165 |

VANGELIS
Born Evangelos Papathanassiou on 3/29/1943 in Valos, Greece. Keyboardist/songwriter. Also see **Jon & Vangelis**.

3/20/76	204	5		1 Heaven And Hell [I]		RCA Victor 5110
10/17/81+	❶⁴	57	▲	2 Chariots Of Fire [I-S]		Polydor 6335
10/2/82	207	3		3 To The Unknown Man [I]		RCA Victor 4397
12/13/86+	42	39		4 Opera Sauvage [E-I]		Polydor 829663

Billboard DEBUT	PEAK	WKS	R I A A	ARTIST Album Title	Catalog	Label & Number

VAN HALEN
1980s: #30 / All-Time: #125

Hard-rock band formed in Pasadena, California: **David Lee Roth** (vocals; born on 10/10/1955), Eddie Van Halen (guitar, born on 1/26/1955), Michael Anthony (bass; born on 6/20/1954) and Alex Van Halen (drums; born on 5/8/1953). The Van Halen brothers were born in Nijmegen, Netherlands; moved to Pasadena in 1962. **Sammy Hagar** replaced Roth as lead singer in 1985. Eddie was married to actress Valerie Bertinelli, 1981-2007. Hagar left in June 1996. Gary Cherone (**Extreme**) joined as lead singer in September 1996; left after one album (#13 below). Roth briefly rejoined group in 1997. Hagar and Anthony later formed **Chickenfoot**.

AWARD: R&R Hall of Fame: 2007

3/11/78	19	169	▲10	1 Van Halen .... Cat:#19/9		Warner 3075
				RS500 #415		
4/14/79	6	47	▲5	2 Van Halen II		Warner 3312
4/19/80	6	31	▲3	3 Women And Children First	Cat:#10/21	Warner 3415
5/30/81	5	23	▲2	4 Fair Warning		Warner 3540
5/8/82	3³	65	▲4	5 Diver Down		Warner 3677
1/28/84	2⁵	77	▲10	6 1984 (MCMLXXXIV)		Warner 23985
4/12/86	❶³	64	▲6	7 5150	Cat:#42/1	Warner 25394
6/18/88	❶⁴	48	▲4	8 OU812		Warner 25732
7/6/91	❶³	74	▲3	9 For Unlawful Carnal Knowledge		Warner 26594
				Grammy: Hard Rock Album		
3/13/93	5	23	▲2	10 Live: Right Here, Right Now	[L]	Warner 45198 [2]
2/11/95	❶¹	41	▲3	11 Balance		Warner 45760
11/9/96	❶¹	52	▲3	12 Best Of Volume 1	Cat:#21/34 [G]	Warner 46332
4/4/98	4	12	●	13 Van Halen III		Warner 46662
8/7/04	3¹	14	▲	14 The Best Of Both Worlds	[G]	Warner 78961 [2]

VANILLA FUDGE
Psychedelic-rock band formed in New York: Mark Stein (vocals, keyboards), Vinnie Martell (guitar), **Tim Bogert** (bass) and **Carmine Appice** (drums).

9/16/67	6	80	●	1 Vanilla Fudge		Atco 224
3/2/68	17	33		2 The Beat Goes On		Atco 237
7/13/68	20	33		3 Renaissance		Atco 244
3/1/69	16	27		4 Near The Beginning	[L]	Atco 278
10/25/69	34	13		5 Rock & Roll		Atco 303

VANILLA ICE
Born Robert Van Winkle on 10/31/1968 in Miami Lakes, Florida. White rapper. Starred in the 1991 movie *Cool As Ice*.

9/22/90	❶16	67	▲7	1 To The Extreme		SBK 95325
6/22/91	30	30	●	2 Extremely Live	[L]	SBK 96648
11/2/91	89	15		3 Cool As Ice	[S]	SBK 97722

VANITY
Born Denise Matthews on 1/4/1959 in Niagara Falls, Ontario, Canada. Female R&B singer/model/actress. Vanity 6 included Susan Moonsie and Brenda Bennett (also of **Apollonia 6**). Acted in several movies. Married to pro football player Anthony Smith from 1995-96.

10/2/82	45	31	●	1 Vanity 6		Warner 23716
9/22/84	62	23		2 Wild Animal		Motown 6102
3/22/86	66	20		3 Skin On Skin		Motown 6167

VAN LEER, Thijs
Born on 3/31/1948 in Amsterdam, Netherlands. Male flutist. Leader of **Focus**.

10/20/73	208	5		1 Introspection	[I]	Columbia 32346

VANNELLI, Gino
Born on 6/16/1952 in Montreal, Quebec, Canada. Pop singer/songwriter.

9/28/74	60	30		1 Powerful People		A&M 3630
7/19/75	66	23		2 Storm At Sunup		A&M 4533
8/14/76	32	22		3 The Gist Of The Gemini		A&M 4596
11/19/77+	33	16		4 A Pauper In Paradise		A&M 4664
9/30/78	13	35	▲	5 Brother To Brother	Cat:#50/2	A&M 4722
9/19/81	172	2		6 The Best Of Gino Vannelli	[G]	A&M 3729
4/11/81	15	26		7 Nightwalker		Arista 9539
6/29/85	62	25		8 Black Cars		HME 40077
5/23/87	160	7		9 Big Dreamers Never Sleep		CBS Associated 40337

VAN SHELTON, Ricky — see SHELTON

VANWARMER, Randy
Born Randall VanWormer on 3/30/1955 in Indian Hills, Colorado. Died of leukemia on 1/12/2004 (age 48). Pop singer/songwriter/guitarist.

6/2/79	81	10		1 Warmer		Bearsville 6988
6/27/81	205	1		2 Beat Of Love		Bearsville 3561

VAN ZANDT, Miami Steve — see LITTLE STEVEN

VAN ZANT
Country duo from Jacksonville, Florida: brothers Donnie Van Zant and **Johnny Van Zant**. Donnie was lead singer of rock group **38 Special**. Both are the younger brothers of former **Lynyrd Skynyrd** leader Ronnie Van Zant.

5/28/05	21	21	●	1 Get Right With The Man		Columbia 93500
10/27/07	57	3		2 My Kind Of Country		Columbia 06198

VANZANT, Iyanla
Born Ronda Harris on 9/13/1953 in Brooklyn, New York. Female self-help author.

10/2/99	128	6	1 In The Meantime - The Music That Tells The Story		Harmony 1799

VAN ZANT, Johnny, Band
Born on 2/27/1959 in Jacksonville, Florida. Southern-rock singer. Brother of Ronnie (**Lynyrd Skynyrd**) and Donnie (**38 Special**) Van Zant. His band: Robbie Gay and Erik Lundgren (guitars), Danny Clausman (bass) and Robbie Morris (drums). Became lead singer of Lynyrd Skynyrd in 1987. Also see **Van Zant**.

9/6/80	48	15	1 No More Dirty Deals		Polydor 6289
6/13/81	119	10	2 Round Two		Polydor 6322
9/18/82	159	6	3 The Last Of The Wild Ones		Polydor 6355
5/4/85	170	8	4 Van-Zant		Geffen 24059
8/11/90	108	11	5 Brickyard Road		Atlantic 82110
			JOHNNY VAN ZANT		

VAPORS, The
Pub-rock band from Guildford, Surrey, England: David Fenton (vocals), Ed Bazalgette (guitar), Steve Smith (bass) and Howard Smith (drums).

8/16/80	62	28	1 New Clear Days		United Artists 1049
4/4/81	109	9	2 Magnets		Liberty 1090

VASSAR, Phil
Born on 5/28/1965 in Lynchburg, Virginia. Country singer/songwriter/pianist.

8/24/02	44	3	1 American Child		Arista Nashville 67077
10/16/04	69	3	2 Shaken Not Stirred		Arista Nashville 61591
5/20/06+	10	19	3 Greatest Hits Volume 1	[G]	Arista Nashville 78729
5/10/08	10	7	4 Prayer Of A Common Man		Universal South 008907

VAST
Born Jonathan Crosby on 7/25/1976 in Long Beach, California. Eclectic singer/songwriter/guitarist. VAST: Visual Audio Sensory Theater.

9/30/00	142	2	1 Music For People		Elektra 62511

VAUGHAN, Jimmie
Born on 3/20/1951 in Dallas, Texas. White blues-rock singer/guitarist. Member of **The Fabulous Thunderbirds**. Brother of **Stevie Ray Vaughan**. Played "Roland Janes" in the 1989 movie *Great Balls Of Fire*. Recorded with Stevie Ray as **The Vaughan Brothers**.

10/13/90	7	38	▲	1 Family Style		Epic 46225
				THE VAUGHAN BROTHERS		
4/30/94	127	4		2 Strange Pleasure		Epic 57202

VAUGHAN, Sarah   1950s: #26
Born on 3/27/1924 in Newark, New Jersey. Died of cancer on 4/3/1990 (age 66). Jazz singer. Nicknamed "The Divine One."
AWARD: Grammy: Lifetime Achievement 1989

11/24/56	20	2	1 Linger Awhile		Columbia 914
12/1/56	21	1	2 Sassy		EmArcy 36089
4/13/57	14	9	3 Great Songs From Hit Shows		Mercury 100 [2]
8/19/57	14	9	4 Sarah Vaughan Sings George Gershwin		Mercury 101 [2]
7/1/72	173	12	5 Sarah Vaughan/Michel Legrand		Mainstream 361

~ ~ ~ ~ ~ ~ ~ ~ ~ **NON-CHARTED ALBUMS** ~ ~ ~ ~ ~ ~ ~ ~ ~ ~ ~ ~
1955 Sarah Vaughan *[EmArcy label]*   1961 Sarah Vaughan's Golden Hits!!!
Grammy: Hall of Fame

VAUGHAN, Stevie Ray, and Double Trouble   All-Time: #283
Born on 10/3/1954 in Dallas, Texas. Died in a helicopter crash on 8/27/1990 (age 35). White blues-rock singer/guitarist. Brother of **Jimmie Vaughan**. Double Trouble: Reese Wynans (keyboards), Tommy Shannon (bass) and Chris Layton (drums). Recorded with Jimmie as **The Vaughan Brothers**. Shannon and Layton later joined **Arc Angels**. Also see **Various Artists Compilations: A Tribute To Stevie Ray Vaughan**.

7/23/83	38	33	▲²	1 Texas Flood	Cat:#26/5	Epic 38734
6/23/84	31	38	▲²	2 Couldn't Stand The Weather	Cat:#40/1	Epic 39304
10/12/85	34	39	▲	3 Soul To Soul		Epic 40036
7/1/89	33	47	▲²	4 In Step		Epic 45024
				Grammy: Contemporary Blues Album		
10/13/90	7	38	▲	5 Family Style		Epic 46225
				THE VAUGHAN BROTHERS		

GREATEST HITS & COMPILATIONS:

11/23/91	10	48	▲²	6 The Sky Is Crying		Epic 47390
				Grammy: Contemporary Blues Album		
11/18/95	39	35	▲²	7 Greatest Hits	Cat:#33/18	Epic 66217

Billboard DEBUT	PEAK	WKS	R I A A	ARTIST Album Title	Catalog	Label & Number

VAUGHAN, Stevie Ray, and Double Trouble — cont'd

DEBUT	PEAK	WKS		Album Title	Catalog	Label & Number
4/10/99	53	17	●	8 The Real Deal: Greatest Hits Volume 2		Epic 65873
4/22/00	80	8		9 Blues At Sunrise		Legacy 63842
12/9/00	148	5	●	10 SRV		Legacy 65714 [4]
10/19/02	165	2		11 The Essential Stevie Ray Vaughan And Double Trouble		Legacy 86423 [2]

LIVE ALBUMS:

12/20/86+	52	25	▲	12 Live Alive		Epic 40511 [2]
10/24/92	58	12	●	13 In The Beginning		Epic 53168
				recorded on 4/1/1980 in Austin, Texas		
8/16/97	40	12	●	14 Live At Carnegie Hall		Epic 68163
				recorded on 10/4/1984		
12/8/01	178	1		15 Live At Montreux 1982 & 1985		Legacy 86151 [2]

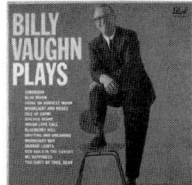

VAUGHN, Billy   1960s: #9 / All-Time: #63

Born Richard Vaughn on 4/12/1919 in Glasgow, Kentucky. Died of cancer on 9/26/1991 (age 72). Orchestra leader. Member of The Hilltoppers vocal group. Musical director for Dot Records.

DEBUT	PEAK	WKS		Album Title		Label & Number
4/21/58+	5	68	●	1 Sail Along Silv'ry Moon	[I]	Dot 3100
10/13/58+	15	47		2 Billy Vaughn Plays The Million Sellers	[I]	Dot 3119
5/4/59	20	3		3 Billy Vaughn Plays	[I]	Dot 3156
5/25/59	7	108	●	4 Blue Hawaii	[I]	Dot 3165
1/18/60	36	1		5 Golden Saxophones	[I]	Dot 3205
3/21/60	❶²	62	●	6 Theme From A Summer Place	[I]	Dot 3276
8/15/60	5	33		7 Look For A Star	[I]	Dot 3322
12/19/60+	5	23		8 Theme From The Sundowners	[I]	Dot 3349
4/24/61	11	43		9 Orange Blossom Special And Wheels	[I]	Dot 3366
10/9/61	17	25		10 Golden Waltzes	[I]	Dot 3280
12/4/61+	20	18		11 Berlin Melody	[I]	Dot 3396
3/24/62	18	12		12 Greatest String Band Hits	[I]	Dot 3409
6/2/62	14	16		13 Chapel By The Sea	[I]	Dot 3424
9/15/62	10	27		14 A Swingin' Safari	[I]	Dot 3458
12/29/62	145	1		15 Christmas Carols	[X-I]	Dot 25148
				released in 1958; Christmas chart: 101/67		
2/16/63	17	32		16 1962's Greatest Hits	[I]	Dot 25497
6/15/63	15	16		17 Sukiyaki And 11 Hawaiian Hits	[I]	Dot 25523
11/9/63	94	8		18 Number 1 Hits, Vol. #1	[I]	Dot 25540
2/1/64	51	17		19 Blue Velvet & 1963's Great Hits	[I]	Dot 25559
6/20/64	144	4		20 Forever	[I]	Dot 25578
8/29/64	141	3		21 Another Hit Album!	[I]	Dot 25593
1/2/65	18	29		22 Pearly Shells	[I]	Dot 25605
4/24/65	45	15		23 Mexican Pearls	[I]	Dot 25628
10/9/65	31	29		24 Moon Over Naples	[I]	Dot 25654
2/12/66	56	14		25 Michelle	[I]	Dot 25679
7/23/66	149	2		26 Great Country Hits	[I]	Dot 25698
10/22/66+	44	35		27 Alfie	[I]	Dot 25751
3/18/67	114	20		28 Sweet Maria		Dot 25782
				THE BILLY VAUGHN SINGERS		
5/13/67	130	7		29 That's Life & Pineapple Market	[I]	Dot 25788
7/29/67	147	2		30 Josephine	[E-I]	Dot 25796
8/12/67	161	5		31 I Love You		Dot 25813
				THE BILLY VAUGHN SINGERS		
9/23/67	159	8		32 Golden Hits/The Best Of Billy Vaughn	[G-I]	Dot 25811
10/28/67	200	2		33 Ode To Billy Joe	[I]	Dot 25828
9/28/68	198	3		34 A Current Set Of Standards	[I]	Dot 25882
5/17/69	95	16		35 The Windmills Of Your Mind	[I]	Dot 25937
3/14/70	188	2		36 Winter World Of Love	[I]	Dot 25975

VAZQUEZ, Mario

Born on 6/15/1977 in the Bronx, New York (Puerto Rican parents). Pop singer. Dropped out of the *American Idol* talent competition before the finals in 2005.

| 10/14/06 | 80 | 2 | | 1 Mario Vazquez | | Arista 81369 |

VEDDER, Eddie

Born Edward Severson III (although he grew up with his step-father's last name of Mueller) on 12/23/1964 in Evanston, Illinois; raised in San Diego, California. Lead singer of **Pearl Jam**. Legally changed his last name to Vedder (his mother's last name).

| 10/6/07 | 11 | 44 | | 1 Into The Wild | [S] | Monkey Wrench 15944 |

VEDERA
Pop-rock band from Kansas City, Missouri: Kristen May (vocals, guitar), brothers Brian Little (guitar) and Drew Little (drums), and Jason Douglas (bass).

DEBUT	PEAK	WKS				
10/24/09	146	1		1 Stages		Epic digital

VEE, Bobby
Born Robert Velline on 4/30/1943 in Fargo, North Dakota. Pop singer. Appeared in the movies *Swingin' Along*, *It's Trad, Dad*, *Play It Cool*, *C'mon Let's Live A Little* and *Just For Fun*.

DEBUT	PEAK	WKS				
3/20/61	18	15		1 Bobby Vee		Liberty 7181
10/30/61	85	8		2 Bobby Vee Sings Hits Of The Rockin' '50's		Liberty 7205
2/3/62	91	14		3 Take Good Care Of My Baby		Liberty 7211
7/21/62	42	23		4 Bobby Vee Meets The Crickets		Liberty 7228
7/21/62	121	6		5 A Bobby Vee Recording Session		Liberty 7232
11/3/62+	24	44		6 Bobby Vee's Golden Greats [G]		Liberty 7245
12/15/62	136	3		7 Merry Christmas From Bobby Vee [X]		Liberty 7267
12/9/67	68ˣ	4		8 The Christmas Album [X-R]		Sunset/Liberty 5186
				reissue of #7 above (minus 2 tracks)		
4/13/63	102	5		9 The Night Has A Thousand Eyes		Liberty 7285
6/1/63	91	8		10 Bobby Vee Meets The Ventures		Liberty 7289
6/27/64	146	2		11 Bobby Vee Sings The New Sound From England!		Liberty 7352
10/7/67	66	12		12 Come Back When You Grow Up		Liberty 7534
4/27/68	187	7		13 Just Today		Liberty 7554

~ ~ ~ ~ ~ ~ ~ ~ **NON-CHARTED ALBUMS** ~ ~ ~ ~ ~ ~ ~ ~ ~ ~

1960 **Bobby Vee Sings Your Favorites**   1964 **30 Big Hits Of The 60's**
1961 **Bobby Vee With Strings And Things**   1966 **30 Big Hits Of The 60's, Volume Two**
1963 **I Remember Buddy Holly**   1966 **Look At Me Girl**

VEGA, Suzanne
Born on 7/11/1959 in Sacramento, California. Folk-pop singer/songwriter/guitarist. Married to record producer Mitchell Froom (of **Gamma**) from 1995-98.

DEBUT	PEAK	WKS				
6/15/85	91	31		1 Suzanne Vega		A&M 5072
5/16/87	11	32	▲	2 Solitude Standing		A&M 5136
5/5/90	50	13		3 Days Of Open Hand		A&M 5293
9/26/92	86	21	●	4 99.9 F		A&M 540005
9/28/96	92	5		5 Nine Objects Of Desire		A&M 540583
10/13/01	178	1		6 Songs In Red And Gray		A&M 493111
8/4/07	129	1		7 Beauty & Crime		Blue Note 68270

VEGA, Tata
Born Carmen Rosa Vega on 10/7/1951 in Queens, New York. Gospel singer.

DEBUT	PEAK	WKS				
4/21/79	170	8		1 Try My Love		Tamla 360

VEGGIETALES
Series of Christian-themed children's albums created by computer animators Phil Vischer and Mike Nawrocki.

DEBUT	PEAK	WKS				
4/25/98+	14ᶜ	32		1 Veggie Tunes		Word 8438
7/18/98	161	4		2 Veggie Tunes 2		Word 5874
7/15/06	191	3		3 Worship Songs		Big Idea 35054
10/17/09	4ˣ	8		4 25 Favorite Christmas Songs! [X]		Big Idea 31148

VELASQUEZ, Jaci
Born on 10/15/1979 in Houston, Texas. Female Latin Christian-pop singer.

DEBUT	PEAK	WKS				
5/10/97	142	16	▲	1 Heavenly Place		Word 67823
6/20/98	56	20	●	2 Jaci Velasquez		Word 69311
9/23/00	49	16	●	3 Crystal Clear		Word 61073
11/17/01	102	7		4 Christmas [X]		Word/Epic 85780
				Christmas charts: 5/'01, 19/'09		
4/12/03	55	8		5 Unspoken		Word/Curb 886223
5/21/05	195	1		6 Beauty Has Grace		Word-Curb 86337

VELEZ, Martha
Born on 8/25/1945 in Harlem, New York. R&B singer/actress. Starred in the Broadway production of *Hair*.

DEBUT	PEAK	WKS				
5/15/76	153	17		1 Escape From Babylon		Sire 7515
				produced by **Bob Marley**		

VELVET REVOLVER
Hard-rock band formed in Los Angeles, California: Scott Weiland (vocals; of **Stone Temple Pilots**) and Dave Kushner (guitar), with former **Guns N' Roses** members Saul "Slash" Hudson (guitar; of **Slash's Snakepit**), Michael "Duff" McKagen (bass) and Matt Sorum (drums).

DEBUT	PEAK	WKS				
6/26/04	❶¹	51	▲²	1 Contraband		RCA 59794
7/21/07	5	13		2 Libertad		RCA 88859

Billboard			R I A	ARTIST		
DEBUT	PEAK	WKS		Album Title	Catalog	Label & Number

VELVET UNDERGROUND, The

Highly influential rock band formed in New York: **Lou Reed** (vocals, guitar), **John Cale** (keyboards), Sterling Morrison (bass) and Maureen Tucker (percussion). Andy Warhol managed the group from 1965-67. Recorded first album with female singer Nico (born Christa Paffgen on 10/16/1939 in Cologne, Germany; died of a brain hemorrhage on 7/18/1988, age 48). Morrison died of cancer on 8/30/1995 (age 53).

AWARD: R&R Hall of Fame: 1996

5/13/67	171	13		1 The Velvet Underground & Nico		Verve 5008
				Grammy: Hall of Fame ★ RS500 #13 ★ NRR		
3/16/68	199	2		2 White Light/White Heat		Verve 5046
				RS500 #292		
4/20/85	197	2		3 The Velvet Underground	[E]	Verve 815454
				RS500 #314		
				first released in 1969 on MGM 4617		
1/30/71	202	1		4 Loaded		Cotillion 9034
				RS500 #109		

GREATEST HITS & COMPILATIONS:

5/19/73	205	4		5 Lou Reed And The Velvet Underground		Pride 0022
3/9/85	85	13		6 VU		Verve 823721
				collection of previously unreleased material from 1968-69		

LIVE ALBUMS:

4/27/74	201	9		7 1969 Velvet Underground Live With Lou Reed		Mercury 7504 [2]
				recorded in Texas and San Francisco in late 1969		
11/13/93	180	1		8 Live MCMXCIII		Sire 45465
				recorded on 6/15/1993 at L'Olympia Theater in Paris, France		

REISSUES:

4/13/85	201	3		9 The Velvet Underground & Nico		Verve 823290
4/6/85	206	1		10 White Light/White Heat		Verve 825119

VENDETTA RED

Hard-rock band from Seattle, Washington: Zach Davidson (vocals, guitar), Justin Cronk (guitar), Erik Chapman (keyboards), Michael Vermillion (bass) and Joseph Lee Childres (drums).

7/12/03	101	8		1 Between The Never And The Now		Epic 86415

VENEGAS, Julieta

Born on 11/24/1970 in Tijuana, Mexico. Female Latin singer.

6/24/06	177	1		1 Limon Y Sal	[F]	Sony 83420
7/5/08	169	1		2 MTV Unplugged	[F-L]	Sony 30821

VENGABOYS

Dance group assembled by Spanish producers Danski and DJ Delmundo: Kim, Robin, Deniece and Roy.

4/24/99	86	30	●	1 The Party Album!		Groovilicious 100

VENTURES, The   1960s: #6 / All-Time: #55

Instrumental rock and roll band from Seattle, Washington: guitarists Nokie Edwards (bass; born on 5/9/1935), Bob Bogle (lead; born on 1/16/1934) and Don Wilson (rhythm; born on 2/10/1933), with drummer Howie Johnson. Johnson suffered serious injuries in a 1961 car accident; replaced by Mel Taylor (born on 9/24/1933; died of heart failure on 8/11/1996, age 62). Johnson died in January 1988 (age 50).

AWARD: R&R Hall of Fame: 2008

12/5/60+	11	37		1 Walk Don't Run	[I]	Dolton 8003
6/26/61	39	14		2 Another Smash!!!	[I]	Dolton 8006
9/18/61	105	14		3 The Ventures	[I]	Dolton 8004
10/2/61	94	17		4 The Colorful Ventures	[I]	Dolton 8008
1/20/62	24	29		5 Twist With The Ventures	[I]	Dolton 8010
5/19/62	41	11		6 The Ventures' Twist Party, Vol. 2	[I]	Dolton 8014
8/11/62	45	12		7 Mashed Potatoes And Gravy	[I]	Dolton 8016
11/24/62	93	8		8 Going To The Ventures Dance Party!	[I]	Dolton 8017
1/5/63	8	40	●	9 The Ventures Play Telstar, The Lonely Bull	[I]	Dolton 8019
5/4/63	30	28		10 "Surfing"	[I]	Dolton 8022
6/1/63	91	8		11 Bobby Vee Meets The Ventures		Liberty 7289
6/8/63	101	14		12 The Ventures Play The Country Classics	[I]	Dolton 8023
8/31/63	30	33		13 Let's Go!	[I]	Dolton 8024
1/25/64	27	18		14 (The) Ventures In Space	[I]	Dolton 8027
7/18/64	32	19		15 The Fabulous Ventures	[I]	Dolton 8029
10/10/64	17	24		16 Walk, Don't Run, Vol. 2	[I]	Dolton 8031
2/13/65	31	24		17 The Ventures Knock Me Out!	[I]	Dolton 8033
6/19/65	27	30		18 The Ventures On Stage	[I-L]	Dolton 8035
8/7/65	96	13		19 Play Guitar With The Ventures	[I-T]	Dolton 16501
9/25/65	16	35		20 The Ventures A Go-Go	[I]	Dolton 8037
12/11/65	9ˣ	9		21 The Ventures' Christmas Album	[X-I]	Dolton 8038
				Christmas charts: 9/'65, 32/'66, 32/'67, 15/'69		
2/12/66	33	22		22 Where The Action Is	[I]	Dolton 8040

Billboard			R I A A	ARTIST	Catalog	Label & Number
DEBUT	PEAK	WKS		Album Title		

VENTURES, The — cont'd

3/5/66	42	21		23 **The Ventures/Batman Theme** .... [I]		Dolton 8042
6/11/66	39	25		24 **Go With The Ventures!** .... [I]		Dolton 8045
9/17/66	33	26		25 **Wild Things!** .... [I]		Dolton 8047
2/18/67	57	26		26 **Guitar Freakout** .... [I]		Dolton 8050
6/3/67	69	15		27 **Super Psychedelics** .... [I]		Liberty 8052
9/2/67	50	44	●	28 **Golden Greats By The Ventures** .... [I]		Liberty 8053
12/23/67+	55	21		29 **$1,000,000.00 Weekend** .... [I]		Liberty 8054
5/25/68	169	6		30 **Flights Of Fantasy** .... [I]		Liberty 8055
8/24/68	128	9		31 **The Horse** .... [I]		Liberty 8057
1/18/69	157	14		32 **Underground Fire** .... [I]		Liberty 8059
5/10/69	11	24	●	33 **Hawaii Five-O** .... [I]		Liberty 8061
12/13/69+	81	12		34 **Swamp Rock** .... [I]		Liberty 8062
3/14/70	154	5		35 **More Golden Greats** .... [I]		Liberty 8060
10/10/70	91	21		36 **The Ventures 10th Anniversary Album** .... [I]		Liberty 35000 [2]
1/15/72	195	3		37 **Theme From Shaft** .... [I]		United Artists 5547
3/18/72	146	3		38 **Joy/The Ventures Play The Classics** .... [I]		United Artists 5575

VERA, Billy
Born William McCord on 5/28/1944 in Riverside, California; raised in Westchester County, New York. Pop singer/songwriter. Acted in the movies *Buckaroo Banzai* and *The Doors*.

5/16/81	118	10		1 **Billy & The Beaters** .... [L]		Alfa 10001
				recorded on 1/15/1981 at the Roxy in Hollywood, California		
12/6/86+	15	26	●	2 **By Request (The Best Of Billy Vera & The Beaters)** .... [E-L]		Rhino 70858

VERGAT, Vic
Born in Switzerland. Rock singer/guitarist.

11/14/81	207	1		1 **Down To The Bone**		Capitol 12187

VERLAINE, Tom
Born Thomas Miller on 12/13/1949 in Mt. Morris, New Jersey. Rock singer. Former member of **Television**.

10/10/81	177	3		1 **Dreamtime**		Warner 3539

VERNE, Larry
Born Larry Vern Erickson on 2/8/1936 in Minneapolis, Minnesota. Photo studio worker-turned-singer by coincidence. A trio of California songwriters who worked in Verne's building selected him to record "Mr. Custer" because of his Southern drawl.

~ ~ ~ ~ ~ ~ ~ ~ ~ ~ **NON-CHARTED ALBUM** ~ ~ ~ ~ ~ ~ ~ ~ ~ ~ ~ ~
1961 **Mister Larry Verne**

VERONICAS, The
Rock duo from Brisbane, Australia: identical twin sisters Lisa and Jessica Origliasso.

3/4/06	133	2		1 **The Secret Life Of...**		Engineroom 49913
1/17/09	107	20		2 **Hook Me Up**		EngineRoom 395260

VERTICAL HORIZON
Rock band from Boston, Massachusetts: Matt Scannell (vocals), Keith Kane (guitar), Sean Hurley (bass) and Ed Toth (drums).

1/22/00	40	71	▲²	1 **Everything You Want**		RCA 67818
10/11/03	61	3		2 **Go**		RCA 68121
10/10/09	158	1		3 **Burning The Days**		Outfall 90170

VERUCA SALT
Rock band from Chicago, Illinois: **Nina Gordon** and Louise Post (vocals, guitars), with Steven Lack (bass) and Jim Shapiro (drums). Name taken from a character in the children's book *Charlie And The Chocolate Factory*.

11/5/94+	69	23	●	1 **American Thighs**		Minty Fresh 7
3/1/97	55	24		2 **Eight Arms To Hold You**		Outpost 30001
6/3/00	171	1		3 **Resolver**		Velveteen 78103

VERVE, The
Rock band from Wigan, England: **Richard Ashcroft** (vocals), Nick McCabe (guitar), Simon Jones (bass) and Peter Salisbury (drums).

10/18/97+	23	46	▲	1 **Urban Hymns**		Virgin 44913
9/13/08	23	4		2 **Forth**		On Your Own 01

VERVE PIPE, The
Rock band from East Lansing, Michigan: brothers Brian Vander Ark (vocals) and Brad Vander Ark (bass), A.J. Dunning (guitar), Doug Corella (keyboards) and Donny Brown (drums).

4/13/96+	24	48	▲	1 **Villains**		RCA 66809
8/14/99	158	1		2 **The Verve Pipe**		RCA 67664

VESTA
Born Vesta Williams in 1963 in Coshocton, Ohio; raised in Los Angeles, California. Female R&B singer.

9/2/89	131	10		1 **Vesta 4 U**		A&M 5223

VIBRATIONS, The
R&B vocal group from Los Angeles, California: Carlton Fisher, James Johnson, Ricky Owens, Dave Govan and Don Bradley. Originally recorded as The Jayhawks (Johnson, Fisher, Govan and Carver Bunkum). Owens joined **The Temptations** for a short time in 1971.

~ ~ ~ ~ ~ ~ ~ ~ ~ ~ ~ **NON-CHARTED ALBUM** ~ ~ ~ ~ ~ ~ ~ ~ ~ ~ ~
1961 **The Watusi**

				V.I.C.		
				Born Victor Owusu on 4/27/1987 in Queens, New York. Male rapper.		
9/13/08	73	2		1 **Beast**		Young Mogul 475004

				VICIOUS BASE		
				Rap duo: D.J. Lace and M.C. Madness.		
1/26/91	153	22	●	1 **Back To Haunt You!**		Cheetah 9404
				VICIOUS BASE FEATURING D.J. MAGIC MIKE!		

				VICTOR		
				Studio project formed by **Rush** guitarist Alex Lifeson. Features various studio musicians/vocalists.		
1/27/96	99	3		1 **Victor**		Atlantic 82852

				VICTORY		
				Hard-rock band from Germany: Fernando Garcia (vocals), Herman Frank (guitar), Tommy Newton (guitar), Peter Knorn (bass) and Fritz Randow (drums).		
5/6/89	182	5		1 **Culture Killed The Native**		Rhino 70844

				VILLAGE PEOPLE		
				Disco vocal group formed in Greenwich Village, New York: Victor Willis (policeman), Randy Jones (cowboy), David Hodo (construction worker), Felipe Rose (indian), Glenn Hughes (leather man) and Alexander Briley (army man). Group starred in the 1980 movie *Can't Stop The Music*. Hughes died of cancer on 3/4/2001 (age 50).		
10/1/77+	54	86	●	1 **Village People**		Casablanca 7064
3/25/78	24	69	▲	2 **Macho Man**		Casablanca 7096
10/21/78+	3[4]	45	▲	3 **Cruisin'**		Casablanca 7118
4/14/79	8	21	▲	4 **Go West**		Casablanca 7144
10/20/79	32	20	●	5 **Live And Sleazy**	[L]	Casablanca 7183 [2]
				record 1: live; record 2: studio		
6/21/80	47	12		6 **Can't Stop The Music**	[S]	Casablanca 7220
8/1/81	138	4		7 **Renaissance**		RCA Victor 4105

				VILLAGE STOMPERS, The		
				Dixieland-styled band from Greenwich Village, New York: Dick Brady, Ralph Casale, Don Coates, Frank Hubbell, Mitchell May, Joe Muranyi, Al McManus and Lenny Pogan.		
11/2/63	5	30		1 **Washington Square**	[I]	Epic 26078
4/25/64	139	3		2 **More Sounds of Washington Square**	[I]	Epic 26090

				VILLARREAL, Alicia		
				Born on 8/31/1974 in Monterrey, Mexico. Female Latin singer.		
5/13/06	180	1		1 **Orgullo De Mujer**	[F]	Universal Latino 006605
7/11/09	166	2		2 **La Jefa**	[F]	Fonovisa 354073

				VINCENT, Gene, and His Blue Caps		
				Born Vincent Eugene Craddock on 2/11/1935 in Norfolk, Virginia. Died of a bleeding ulcer on 10/12/1971 (age 36). Rock singer/songwriter/guitarist. Formed the Blue Caps in Norfolk in 1956. Appeared in the movies *The Girl Can't Help It* and *Hot Rod Gang*. Injured in car crash that killed **Eddie Cochran** in 1960.		
				AWARD: R&R Hall of Fame: 1998		
9/29/56	16	2		1 **Bluejean Bop!**		Capitol 764

~ ~ ~ ~ ~ ~ ~ ~ ~ ~ **NON-CHARTED ALBUMS** ~ ~ ~ ~ ~ ~ ~ ~ ~ ~
1957 **Gene Vincent And The Blue Caps**	1959 **Sounds Like Gene Vincent**
1958 **Gene Vincent Rocks! And The Blue Caps Roll**	1960 **Crazy Times!**
1958 **A Gene Vincent Record Date With The Blue Caps**	

				VINCENT, Rhonda		
				Born on 7/13/1962 in Kirksville, Missouri. Bluegrass singer/songwriter/guitarist.		
10/20/07	45[X]	1		1 **Beautiful Star: A Christmas Collection**	[X]	Rounder 610575

				VINCENT, Vinnie, Invasion		
				Born on 8/5/1952 in Bridgeport, Connecticut. Rock guitarist. Member of **Kiss** from 1982-83. His group: **Robert Fleischman** (vocals), Dana Strum (bass) and Bob Rock (drums). Mark Slaughter replaced Fleischman after first album. Strum and Slaughter left in 1989 to form **Slaughter**.		
9/20/86	64	29		1 **Vinnie Vincent Invasion**		Chrysalis 41529
5/21/88	64	15		2 **All Systems Go**		Chrysalis 41626

				VINEGAR JOE		
				Rock band from England: **Robert Palmer** (male vocals), Elkie Brooks (female vocals), Jim Mullen (guitar), Pete Gage (guitar), Mike Deaon (keyboards), Steve York (bass) and **Keef Hartley** (drums). Palmer went on to a successful solo career.		
2/24/73	201	2		1 **Rock 'N Roll Gypsies**		Atco 7016

Billboard DEBUT	PEAK	WKS	R I A A	ARTIST Album Title	Catalog	Label & Number

VINES, The
Alternative-rock trio from Sydney, Australia: Craig Nicholls (vocals, guitar), Patrick Matthews (bass) and David Oliffe (drums).

8/3/02	11	25	●	1 Highly Evolved		Engineroom 37527
4/10/04	23	6		2 Winning Days		Capitol 84338
4/22/06	136	1		3 Vision Valley		Engineroom 31817

VINTON, Bobby   All-Time: #162
Born Stanley Robert Vinton on 4/16/1935 in Canonsburg, Pennsylvania. Pop singer. Father was a bandleader. Formed own band while in high school; toured as leader of the backing band for Dick Clark's "Caravan of Stars" in 1960. Left band for a singing career in 1962. Hosted own musical variety TV series from 1975-78. Dubbed "The Polish Prince."

8/4/62	5	27	1 Roses Are Red		Epic 26020
1/5/63	137	2	2 Bobby Vinton Sings The Big Ones		Epic 26035
8/10/63	10	33	3 Blue Velvet		Epic 26068
2/1/64	8	28	4 There! I've Said It Again		Epic 26081
7/25/64	31	12	5 Tell Me Why		Epic 26113
1/16/65	18	13	6 Mr. Lonely		Epic 26136
7/3/65	116	5	7 Bobby Vinton Sings For Lonely Nights		Epic 26154
2/12/66	110	5	8 Satin Pillows And Careless		Epic 26182
12/16/67+	41	33	9 Please Love Me Forever		Epic 26341
6/15/68	164	8	10 Take Good Care Of My Baby		Epic 26382
1/4/69	21	24	11 I Love How You Love Me		Epic 26437
6/14/69	69	12	12 Vinton		Epic 26471
4/11/70	90	6	13 My Elusive Dreams		Epic 26540
4/8/72	72	15	14 Ev'ry Day Of My Life		Epic 31286
7/29/72	77	14	15 Sealed With A Kiss		Epic 31642
11/30/74+	16	22	● 16 Melodies Of Love		ABC 851
7/19/75	108	5	17 Heart Of Hearts		ABC 891
12/27/75+	161	7	18 The Bobby Vinton Show		ABC 924
6/11/77	183	2	19 The Name Is Love		ABC 981
			CHRISTMAS ALBUMS:		
12/5/64	13[X]	4	20 A Very Merry Christmas		Epic 26122
12/19/87	20[X]	3	21 Santa Must Be Polish And Other Christmas Sounds Of Today		Tapestry 1001
			Christmas charts: 20/'87, 22/'88		
			GREATEST HITS & COMPILATIONS:		
10/3/64+	12	38	● 22 Bobby Vinton's Greatest Hits		Epic 26098
1/17/70	138	8	23 Bobby Vinton's Greatest Hits Of Love		Epic 26517
6/26/71	204	4	24 The Love Album		Epic 30431 [2]
11/25/72+	119	16	25 Bobby Vinton's All-Time Greatest Hits		Epic 31487 [2]
12/7/74	109	5	26 With Love		Epic 32921
6/28/75	154	5	27 Bobby Vinton Sings The Golden Decade Of Love		Epic 33468 [2]
4/13/96	199	1	28 16 Most Requested Songs		Epic/Legacy 47855

VIO-LENCE
Hard-rock band from San Francisco, California: Sean Killian (vocals), Phil Demmel (guitar), Robb Flynn (guitar), Deen Dell (bass) and Perry Strickland (drums).

8/20/88	154	6	1 Eternal Nightmare		Mechanic 42187

VIOLENT FEMMES
Punk-rock trio from Milwaukee, Wisconsin: Gordon Gano (vocals, guitar), Brian Ritchie (bass) and Victor DeLorenzo (drums). Guy Hoffman replaced DeLorenzo in 1992.

8/3/91	171	7	▲	1 Violent Femmes ... Cat:#30/68 [E]		Slash 23845
				released in 1982		
2/15/86	84	24		2 The Blind Leading The Naked		Slash 25340
2/4/89	93	13		3 3		Slash 25819
5/18/91	141	5		4 Why Do Birds Sing?		Slash 26476
10/2/93	146	3	●	5 Add It Up (1981-1993) [K]		Slash 45403
6/4/94	90	4		6 New Times		Elektra 61553

VIOLENT J
Born Joseph Bruce on 4/28/1972 in Detroit, Michigan. White male rapper. Member of **Insane Clown Posse**, **Dark Lotus** and **Soopa Villainz**.

8/9/03	89	2	1 Wizard Of The Hood	[EP]	Psychopathic 4016
5/16/09	48	3	2 The Shining		Pyschopathic 4101

VIRTUES, The
Rock and roll instrumental band from Philadelphia, Pennsylvania: Frank Virtue (guitar), Jimmy Bruno (guitar), Ralph Frederico (piano), Sonny Ferns (sax) and Barry Smith (drums).

~ ~ ~ ~ ~ ~ ~ ~ ~ ~ *NON-CHARTED ALBUM* ~ ~ ~ ~ ~ ~ ~ ~ ~ ~
1959 **Guitar Boogie Shuffle** *[Wynne label]*

VISAGE
Dance-rock band from England: Steve Strange (vocals), **Midge Ure** (guitar), John McGeoch (guitar), Billy Currie (voilin), Dave Formula (keyboards) and Rusty Egan (drums). Ure and Currie were members of **Ultravox**.

8/8/81	178	4	1 Visage .... **[EP]**	Polydor 501
4/17/82	204	1	2 The Anvil	Polydor 6350

VISCOUNTS, The
Instrumental band from New Jersey: Harry Haller (sax), brothers Bobby (guitar) and Joe (bass) Spievak, Larry Vecchio (organ) and Clark Smith (drums).

1/29/66	144	2	1 Harlem Nocturne .... **[I]**	Amy 8008

~ ~ ~ ~ ~ ~ ~ ~ ~ ~ **NON-CHARTED ALBUM** ~ ~ ~ ~ ~ ~ ~ ~ ~ ~ ~
1960 **The Viscounts** *[Madison label]*

VITALE, Joe
Born in 1949 in Dundalk, Maryland. Rock singer/drummer.

3/1/75	204	2	1 Roller Coaster Weekend	Atlantic 18114
7/4/81	181	3	2 Plantation Harbor	Asylum 529

VITAL INFORMATION — see SMITH, Steve

VITAMIN C
Born Colleen Fitzpatrick on 7/20/1972 in Old Bridge, New Jersey. Female singer/songwriter. Former lead singer of Eve's Plum. Played "Amber Von Tussle" in the 1988 movie *Hairspray*.

9/18/99+	29	29	▲ 1 Vitamin C	Elektra 62406
2/17/01	122	1	2 More	Elektra 62584

VITAMIN Z
Pop band from Sheffield, Yorkshire, England: Geoff Barradale (vocals), Neil Hubbard (guitar), David Rhodes (guitar), Nick Lockwood (keyboards, bass) and Jerry Marotta (drums).

8/10/85	183	3	1 Rites Of Passage	Geffen 24057

VITTORIO
Born Vittorio Grigolo on 2/19/1977 in Arezzo, Italy. Operatic tenor.

9/30/06	195	2	1 Vittorio	Polydor 007307

VIVES, Carlos
Born on 8/7/1961 in Santa Marta, Colombia, South America. Latin singer/actor.

9/18/04	192	2	1 El Rock De Mi Pueblo .... **[F]**	EMI Latin 78306

VIXEN
Female hard-rock band formed in Los Angeles, California: Janet Gardner (vocals, guitar), Jan Kuehnemund (guitar), Share Pedersen (bass) and Roxy Petrucci (drums). Pedersen later joined **Contraband**.

10/1/88+	41	40	● 1 Vixen	EMI-Manhattan 46991
8/18/90	52	16	2 Rev It Up	EMI 92923

VNV NATION
Electro-pop duo formed in Hamburg, Germany: Ronan Harris and Mark Jackson.

7/11/09	186	1	1 Of Faith, Power And Glory	Anachron 2

VOEGELE, Kate
Born on 12/8/1986 in Bay Village, Ohio. Adult Alternative-pop singer/songwriter. Played "Mia Catalano" on the TV series *One Tree Hill*.

2/9/08	27	19	1 Don't Look Away... **Cat**:#37/1	MySpace 10012
6/6/09	10	7	2 A Fine Mess	MySpace 012938

VOGUES, The
Pop-Adult Contemporary vocal group formed in Turtle Creek, Pennsylvania: Bill Burkette, Hugh Geyer, Chuck Blasko and Don Miller.

2/12/66	137	7	1 Five O'Clock World	Co & Ce 1230
9/7/68	29	30	2 Turn Around, Look At Me	Reprise 6314
2/15/69	30	23	3 Till	Reprise 6326
9/27/69	115	9	4 Memories	Reprise 6347
1/10/70	148	9	5 The Vogues' Greatest Hits .... **[G]**	Reprise 6371

~ ~ ~ ~ ~ ~ ~ ~ ~ ~ **NON-CHARTED ALBUM** ~ ~ ~ ~ ~ ~ ~ ~ ~ ~
1965 **Meet The Vogues** *(You're The One)*

VOICES OF EAST HARLEM, The
Black choir from Harlem, New York.

10/10/70	191	3	1 Right On Be Free..	Elektra 74080

VOIVOD
Hard-rock band from Jonquiere, Quebec, Canada: Denis Belanger (vocals), Denis "Piggy" D'Amour (guitar), Jean-Yves Theriault (bass) and Michel Langevin (drums). D'Amour died of cancer on 8/26/2005 (age 45).

12/16/89+	114	16	1 Nothingface	Mechanic 6326

VOLCANO CHOIR
Alternative-rock band from Eau Claire, Wisconsin: Justin Vernon (vocals), Jim Schoenecker (guitar), Daniel Speck (guitar), Thomas Wincek (keyboards), Chris Rosenau (bass) and Jon Mueller (drums). Vernon also recorded as **Bon Iver**.

10/10/09	92	1		1 Unmap		Jagjaguwar 156

VOLLENWEIDER, Andreas
Born on 10/4/1953 in Zurich, Switzerland. Electro-acoustic harpist.

12/1/84+	121	18	●	1 ...Behind The Gardens-Behind The Wall-Under The Tree...	[I]	CBS 37793
12/15/84+	149	15	●	2 Caverna Magica (...Under The Tree-In The Cave...)	[I]	CBS 37827
3/2/85	76	39	●	3 White Winds	[I]	FM/CBS 39963
8/2/86	60	39	▲	4 Down To The Moon	[I]	FM/CBS 42255
				Grammy: New Age Album		
4/15/89	52	19		5 Dancing With The Lion	[I]	Columbia 45154
2/29/92	117	5		6 Book Of Roses	[I]	Columbia 48601

VOLMAN, Mark, And Howard Kaylan
Pop-rock duo. Volman was born on 4/19/1947 in Los Angeles, California. Kaylan was born on 6/22/1947 in New York. Both were founding members of **The Turtles**.

10/7/72	211	2		1 The Phlorescent Leech & Eddie		Reprise 2099

VON BONDIES, The
Rock band from Detroit, Michigan: Jason Stollsteimer (vocals, guitar), Marcie Bolen (guitar), Carrie Smith (bass) and Don Blum (drums).

3/27/04	197	1		1 Pawn Shoppe Heart		Sire 48549

VOUDOURIS, Roger
Born on 12/29/1954 in Sacramento, California. Died on 8/3/2003 (age 48). Pop singer/songwriter/guitarist.

7/7/79	171	3		1 Radio Dream		Warner 3290

VOYAGE
Disco band from Europe: Sylvia Mason (vocals), Slim Pezin (guitar), Marc Chantereau (keyboards), Sauver Mallin (bass) and Pierre-Alain Dahan (drums).

4/8/78	40	21		1 Voyage		Marlin 2213
12/16/78+	47	27		2 Fly Away		Marlin 2225

V.S.O.P.
All-star jazz band: **Herbie Hancock** (piano), **Freddie Hubbard** (trumpet), **Wayne Shorter** (sax), **Ron Carter** (bass) and **Tony Williams** (drums). V.S.O.P.: Very Special Onetime Performance.

11/12/77	123	5		1 The Quintet	[I-L]	Columbia 34976 [2]

W

WACKERS, The
Pop-rock band formed in Montreal, Quebec, Canada: Randy Bishop (vocals), Robert Segarini (guitar), J.P. Lauzon (keyboards), Bill "Kootch" Trochim (bass) and Spencer "Ernie" Earnshaw (drums).

1/6/73	211	3		1 Shredder		Elektra 75046

WACKO
Born in New Orleans, Louisiana. Male rapper.

6/5/04	122	4		1 The Beginning Of The End...		J Prince 42046
				JUVENILE • WACKO • SKIP		

WADE, Adam
Born on 3/17/1937 in Pittsburgh, Pennsylvania. Black Adult Contemporary singer.

~ ~ ~ ~ ~ ~ ~ ~ ~ ~ ~ **NON-CHARTED ALBUM** ~ ~ ~ ~ ~ ~ ~ ~ ~ ~ ~
1962 **Adam Wade's Greatest Hits**

WADSWORTH MANSION
Pop-rock band formed in Los Angeles, California: brothers Steve Jablecki (vocals) and Mike Jablecki (drums), with Wayne Gagnon (guitar) and John Poole (bass).

4/10/71	216	3		1 Wadsworth Mansion		Sussex 7008

WAGNER, Jack
Born on 10/3/1959 in Washington, Missouri. Actor/singer. Played "Frisco Jones" on the TV soap opera *General Hospital* (1983-87).

9/22/84+	44	29		1 All I Need	[EP]	Qwest 25089
10/19/85	150	15		2 Lighting Up The Night		Qwest 25318
5/2/87	151	8		3 Don't Give Up Your Day Job		Qwest 25562

WAGNER, Richard
Born on 9/14/1943 in Oelwein, Iowa; raised in Saginaw, Michigan. Rock singer/songwriter/guitarist. Lead singer of **Frost**.

6/3/78	203	7		1 Richard Wagner		Atlantic 19172

Billboard			R I A A	ARTIST		
DEBUT	PEAK	WKS		Album Title	Catalog	Label & Number

WAGONER, Porter
Born on 8/12/1927 in West Plains, Missouri. Died of lung cancer on 10/28/2007 (age 80). Country singer/songwriter/guitarist. Hosted own TV series from 1960-79. Former co-host of TNN's *Opry Backstage*.
AWARDS: C&W Hall of Fame: 2002 ★ CMA: Vocal Group (w/ Dolly Parton) 1968 / Vocal Duo (w/ Dolly Parton) 1970 & 1971 ★ OPRY: 1957

7/1/67	199	1		1 The Cold Hard Facts Of Life		RCA Victor 3797
3/15/69	161	8		2 The Carroll County Accident		RCA Victor 4116
3/22/69	184	4		3 Just The Two Of Us		RCA Victor 4039
8/16/69	162	5		4 Always, Always		RCA Victor 4186
4/4/70	137	7		5 Porter Wayne And Dolly Rebecca		RCA Victor 4305
				PORTER WAGONER & DOLLY PARTON (above 3)		
5/16/70	190	2		6 You Got-ta Have A License		RCA Victor 4286
10/10/70	191	2		7 Once More		RCA Victor 4388
3/13/71	142	3		8 Two Of A Kind		RCA Victor 4490
				PORTER WAGONER & DOLLY PARTON (above 2)		

WAIKIKIS, The
Instrumental studio group from Belgium.

1/16/65	93	9		1 Hawaii Tattoo .... [I]		Kapp 3366

WAILERS, The
Teen rock and roll instrumental bnd from Tacoma, Washington: John Greek (guitar), Rich Dangel (guitar), Mark Marush (sax), Kent Morrill (piano) and Mike Burk (drums). Dangel died on 12/2/2002 (age 60).

6/27/64	127	6		1 Tall Cool One		Imperial 12262

~ ~ ~ ~ ~ ~ ~ ~ ~ ~ **NON-CHARTED ALBUM** ~ ~ ~ ~ ~ ~ ~ ~ ~ ~ ~
1959 **The Fabulous Wailers**

WAILERS, The — see MARLEY, Bob

WAINWRIGHT, Loudon III
Born on 9/5/1946 in Chapel Hill, North Carolina. Satirical folk singer/songwriter. His father was the longtime editor of *Life* magazine. Played "Capt. Calvin Spaulding" in three episodes of TV's *M*A*S*H* (1974-75). Appeared in the movies *The Slugger's Wife* and *Jacknife*. Married briefly to Suzzy Roche (of **The Roches**) in 1977. Father of **Rufus Wainwright**.

3/3/73	102	13		1 Album III		Columbia 31462
12/22/73	213	4		2 Attempted Mustache		Columbia 32710
3/15/75	156	5		3 Unrequited		Columbia 33369
6/19/76	188	4		4 T Shirt		Arista 4063

WAINWRIGHT, Rufus
Born on 7/22/1973 in Montreal, Quebec, Canada. Singer/songwriter. Son of **Loudon Wainwright III**.

6/23/01	117	1		1 Poses		DreamWorks 450237
10/11/03	60	4		2 Want One		DreamWorks 000896
12/4/04	103	1		3 Want Two		DreamWorks 003716
6/2/07	23	5		4 Release The Stars		Geffen 008767
12/22/07	171	1		5 Rufus Does Judy At Carnegie Hall		Geffen 010318 [2]

WAITE, John
Born on 7/4/1955 in London, England. Lead singer of **The Babys** and **Bad English**.

7/17/82	68	23		1 Ignition		Chrysalis 1376
7/14/84	10	43	●	2 No Brakes		EMI America 17124
8/31/85	36	16		3 Mask Of Smiles		EMI America 17164
7/11/87	77	12		4 Rover's Return		EMI America 17227

WAITRESSES, The
Rock band formed in Akron, Ohio: Patty Donahue (vocals), Chris Butler (guitar), Dan Klayman (keyboards), Mars Williams (sax), Tracy Wormworth (bass) and Billy Ficca (drums; of **Television**). Donahue died of cancer on 12/9/1996 (age 40).

2/6/82	41	24		1 Wasn't Tomorrow Wonderful?		Polydor 6346
12/18/82+	128	10		2 I Could Rule The World If I Could Only Get The Parts ..... [EP]		Polydor 507
6/4/83	155	5		3 Bruiseology		Polydor 810980

WAITS, Tom
Born on 12/7/1949 in Pomona, California. Gravelly-voiced song stylist/actor. Appeared in several movies.

All-Time: #455

11/23/74	201	2		1 The Heart Of Saturday Night		Asylum 1015
				RS500 #339		
11/29/75	164	6		2 Nighthawks At The Diner .... [L]		Asylum 2008 [2]
11/6/76	89	5		3 Small Change		Asylum 1078
10/22/77	113	8		4 Foreign Affairs		Asylum 1117
11/18/78	181	4		5 Blue Valentine		Asylum 162
10/4/80	96	10		6 Heartattack And Vine		Asylum 295
10/29/83	167	7		7 Swordfishtrombones		Island 90095
11/16/85	181	7		8 Rain Dogs		Island 90299
				RS500 #397		
9/26/87	115	10		9 Franks Wild Years		Island 90572
10/8/88	152	6		10 Big Time .... [L]		Island 90987
9/26/92	176	3		11 Bone Machine		Island 512580
				Grammy: Alternative Album		
11/20/93	130	2		12 The Black Rider		Island 518559

Billboard			R I A A	ARTIST	Catalog	Label & Number
DEBUT	PEAK	WKS		Album Title		

<table>
<tr><td colspan="7">WAITS, Tom — cont'd</td></tr>
</table>

DEBUT	PEAK	WKS		ARTIST / Album Title	Catalog	Label & Number
5/15/99	30	9		13 Mule Variations		Epitaph 86547
				Grammy: Contemporary Folk Album ★ RS500 #416		
5/25/02	32	6		14 Blood Money		Anti 86629
5/25/02	33	6		15 Alice		Anti 86632
10/23/04	28	6		16 Real Gone		Anti 86678
12/9/06	74	8	●	17 Orphans: Brawlers, Bawlers & Bastards		Anti 86677 [3]
12/12/09	63	5		18 Glitter And Doom: Live [L]		Anti 87053

WAKEMAN, Rick
Born on 5/18/1949 in London, England. Rock keyboardist. Member of **Strawbs** and **Yes**.

3/24/73	30	45	●	1 The Six Wives Of Henry VIII [I]		A&M 4361
6/15/74	3²	27	●	2 Journey To The Centre Of The Earth [L]		A&M 3621
				recorded on 1/18/1974 at the Royal Festival Hall		
4/19/75	21	15		3 The Myths And Legends Of King Arthur And The Knights Of The Round Table		A&M 4515
5/15/76	67	8		4 No Earthly Connection		A&M 4583
2/26/77	126	7		5 White Rock [I-S]		A&M 4614
12/17/77+	128	8		6 Rick Wakeman's Criminal Record [I]		A&M 4660
7/21/79	170	5		7 Rhapsodies [I]		A&M 6501 [2]

WALDEN, Narada Michael
Born Michael Walden on 4/23/1952 in Kalamazoo, Michigan. R&B singer/songwriter/drummer/producer. With **John McLaughlin**'s Mahavishnu Orchestra from 1974-76.

3/10/79	103	16		1 Awakening		Atlantic 19222
1/5/80	74	19		2 The Dance Of Life		Atlantic 19259
10/18/80	103	8		3 Victory		Atlantic 19279
6/5/82	135	6		4 Confidence		Atlantic 19351

WALDMAN, Wendy
Born on 11/29/1950 in Los Angeles, California. Folk-pop singer/songwriter/producer.

5/3/75	207	2		1 Wendy Waldman		Warner 2859
6/3/78	203	10		2 Strange Company		Warner 3178

WALE
Born Olubowale Akintimehin on 9/21/1984 in Washington DC (Nigerian parents). Male rapper.

11/28/09	21	2		1 Attention Deficit		Interscope 013229

WALES, Howard
Born in San Francisco, California. Rock keyboardist.

10/9/71	201	1		1 Hooteroll?		Douglas 30859
				HOWARD WALES & JERRY GARCIA		

WALKER, Butch
Born on 11/14/1969 in Rome, Georgia. Rock singer/songwriter/guitarist. Former member of **Marvelous 3**.

9/11/04	171	1		1 Letters		Epic 92627
7/29/06	140	1		2 The Rise & Fall Of Butch Walker And The Lets-Go-Out-Tonites!		One Haven 84124
11/29/08	173	1		3 Sycamore Meadows		Power Ballad 11

WALKER, Clay
Born Ernest Clayton Walker on 8/19/1969 in Beaumont, Texas. Country singer/songwriter/guitarist.

9/4/93+	52	57	▲	1 Clay Walker		Giant 24511
10/15/94+	42	43	▲	2 If I Could Make A Living		Giant 24582
11/4/95	57	34	▲	3 Hypnotize The Moon		Giant 24640
4/26/97	32	46	▲	4 Rumor Has It		Giant 24674
6/27/98	41	19	●	5 Greatest Hits [G]		Giant 24700
9/11/99	55	21	●	6 Live, Laugh, Love		Giant 24717
4/14/01	129	3		7 Say No More		Giant 24759
9/27/03	23	13		8 A Few Questions		RCA 67068
5/5/07	15	22		9 Fall		Asylum-Curb 78963

WALKER, David T.
Born in Tulsa, Oklahoma; raised in Los Angeles, California. R&B singer/songwriter/guitarist. Member of **Paul Humphrey's Cool Aid Chemists** and **Afrique**.

2/9/74	187	8		1 Press On [I]		Ode 77020
9/4/76	166	5		2 On Love		Ode 77035

WALKER, Hezekiah, & LFC
Born on 12/24/1962 in Brooklyn, New York. Pastor of the Love Fellowship Church in Brooklyn, New York. Assembled the LFT Church Choir.

6/7/97	182	2		1 Live In London At Wembley [L]		Verity 43023
				recorded on 11/15/1996		
11/27/99	151	2		2 Family Affair		Verity 43132
9/7/02	127	5		3 Family Affair II: Live At Radio City Music Hall [L]		Verity 43176
				recorded on 2/16/2002		
10/15/05	123	2		4 20/85 The Experience		Verity 62829
11/22/08	55	14		5 Souled Out		Verity 23487

Billboard			R I A A	ARTIST		
DEBUT	**PEAK**	**WKS**		**Album Title**	**Catalog**	**Label & Number**

WALKER, Jerry Jeff
Born Ronald Clyde Crosby on 3/16/1942 in Oneonta, New York. Country-rock singer/songwriter.

DEBUT	PEAK	WKS		Album	Catalog	Label & Number
2/24/73	208	4		1 Jerry Jeff Walker		Decca 75384
12/15/73+	160	11	●	2 Viva Terlingua!		MCA 382
1/11/75	141	8		3 Walker's Collectibles		MCA 450
10/4/75	119	7		4 Ridin' High		MCA 2156
7/4/76	84	10		5 It's A Good Night For Singin'		MCA 2202
5/28/77	60	21		6 A Man Must Carry On		MCA 6003 [2]
7/1/78	111	9		7 Contrary To Ordinary..		MCA 3041
7/19/80	185	3		8 The Best Of Jerry Jeff Walker............................. [G]		MCA 5128
1/6/79	206	5		9 Jerry Jeff		Elektra 163
6/20/81	188	3		10 Reunion		SouthCoast 5199

WALKER, Jimmie
Born on 6/25/1947 in the Bronx, New York. Stand-up comedian/actor. Played "J.J. Evans" on TV's *Good Times*.

DEBUT	PEAK	WKS		Album	Catalog	Label & Number
5/31/75	130	12		1 Dyn-O-Mite .... [C]		Buddah 5635

WALKER, Jr., & The All Stars
Born Autry DeWalt-Mixom on 6/14/1931 in Blytheville, Arkansas. Died of cancer on 11/23/1995 (age 64). R&B singer/saxophonist. The All Stars: Willie Woods (guitar), Vic Thomas (keyboards) and James Graves (drums). Woods died on 5/27/1997 (age 60).

DEBUT	PEAK	WKS		Album	Catalog	Label & Number
7/10/65	108	35		1 Shotgun		Soul 701
4/9/66	130	7		2 Soul Session .... [I]		Soul 702
9/3/66	64	13		3 Road Runner		Soul 703
10/7/67	119	11		4 "Live!" .... [L]		Soul 705
2/8/69	172	4		5 Home Cookin'		Soul 710
6/28/69	43	18		6 Greatest Hits .... [G]		Soul 718
1/17/70	92	22		7 What Does It Take To Win Your Love......................		Soul 721
10/3/70	110	5		8 A Gasssss..		Soul 726
7/24/71	91	14		9 Rainbow Funk		Soul 732
1/8/72	142	16		10 Moody Jr.		Soul 733
6/9/73	202	3		11 Peace & Understanding Is Hard To Find		Soul 738
9/24/83	210	1		12 Blow The House Down		Motown 6053
				JUNIOR WALKER		

WALKER, Seth
Born in Austin, Texas. Rock singer/songwriter/guitarist.

DEBUT	PEAK	WKS		Album	Catalog	Label & Number
4/11/09	198	1		1 Leap Of Faith		Hyena 9375

WALKER, Tommy
Born in Los Angeles, California. Christian singer/songwriter/guitarist.

DEBUT	PEAK	WKS		Album	Catalog	Label & Number
1/27/01	153	1		1 Never Gonna Stop		Hosanna! 1846

WALKER BROS., The
"Blue-eyed soul" trio from Los Angeles, California: Scott Engel, Gary Leeds and John Maus.

~ ~ ~ ~ ~ ~ ~ ~ ~ ~ **NON-CHARTED ALBUMS** ~ ~ ~ ~ ~ ~ ~ ~ ~ ~ ~ ~
1965 Introducing The Walker Brothers   1966 The Sun Ain't Gonna Shine Anymore

WALKMEN, The
Alternative-rock band from New York: Hamilton Leithauser (vocals, guitar), Paul Maroon (guitar), Walter Martin (keyboards), Peter Bauer (bass) and Matt Barrick (drums).

DEBUT	PEAK	WKS		Album	Catalog	Label & Number
6/10/06	163	1		1 A Hundred Miles Off...		Record Collection 44223
9/6/08	71	3		2 You & Me		Gigantic 17

WALL, Paul
Born Paul Slayton on 3/11/1981 in Houston, Texas. Male rapper/songwriter.

DEBUT	PEAK	WKS		Album	Catalog	Label & Number
10/1/05	❶[1]	39	▲	1 The Peoples Champ		Swishahouse 83808
4/21/07	8	14		2 Get Money Stay True		Swishahouse 101555
5/30/09	15	5		3 Fast Life		SwishaHouse 517397

WALLACE, Jerry
Born on 12/15/1928 in Guilford, Missouri; raised in Glendale, Arizona. Died of heart failure on 5/5/2008 (age 79). Pop-country singer/guitarist.

DEBUT	PEAK	WKS		Album	Catalog	Label & Number
11/7/64	96	7		1 In The Misty Moonlight		Challenge 619
3/3/73	179	8		2 Do You Know What It's Like To Be Lonesome?............		MCA 301

~ ~ ~ ~ ~ ~ ~ ~ ~ ~ **NON-CHARTED ALBUMS** ~ ~ ~ ~ ~ ~ ~ ~ ~ ~ ~ ~
1959 Just Jerry   1962 Shutters And Boards
1961 There She Goes

WALLER, John
Born on 12/12/1970 in Fayetteville, Georgia. Contemporary Christian singer/songwriter.

DEBUT	PEAK	WKS		Album	Catalog	Label & Number
5/2/09	200	1		1 While I'm Waiting...		Beach Street 10142

WALLER, Robert James
Born on 8/1/1939 in Rockford, Iowa. Novelist/songwriter/singer/guitarist.

8/28/93	200	1		1 The Ballads Of Madison County		Atlantic 82511

WALLFLOWERS, The
Rock band formed in Los Angeles, California: **Jakob Dylan** (vocals), Michael Ward (guitar), Rami Jaffe (keyboards), Greg Richling (bass) and Mario Calire (drums). Dylan is the son of **Bob Dylan**. Ward left in 2001. Fred Eltringham replaced Calire in 2004.

7/20/96+	4	98	▲⁴	1 Bringing Down The Horse	Cat:#21/10	Interscope 90055
10/28/00	13	15	●	2 (Breach)		Interscope 490745
11/23/02	32	4		3 Red Letter Days		Interscope 493491
6/11/05	40	4		4 Rebel, Sweetheart		Interscope 004692
7/4/09	137	1		5 Collected: 1996-2005	[G]	Interscope 010666

WALL OF VOODOO
Alternative-rock band formed in Los Angeles, California: **Stan Ridgway** (vocals), Marc Moreland (guitar), Chas Gray (bass) and Joe Nanini (drums). Moreland died of kidney failure on 3/13/2002 (age 44).

1/10/81	204	3		1 Wall Of Voodoo	[EP]	Index 70401
10/17/81	177	2		2 Dark Continent		I.R.S. 70022
1/15/83	45	23		3 Call Of The West		I.R.S. 70026

WALSH, James — see GYPSY

WALSH, Joe
All-Time: #427

Born on 11/20/1947 in Wichita, Kansas; raised in Cleveland, Ohio. Rock singer/songwriter/guitarist. Member of **The James Gang** and the **Eagles**. Had a recurring role on TV's *The Drew Carey Show*.

10/21/72+	79	29		1 Barnstorm		Dunhill/ABC 50130
6/23/73	6	54	●	2 The Smoker You Drink, The Player You Get		Dunhill/ABC 50140
1/4/75	11	22	●	3 So What		Dunhill/ABC 50171
4/10/76	20	18		4 You Can't Argue With A Sick Mind	[L]	ABC 932
10/28/78	71	7		5 The Best Of Joe Walsh	[G]	ABC 1083
6/10/78	8	27	▲	6 But Seriously, Folks...		Asylum 141
5/23/81	20	18		7 There Goes The Neighborhood		Asylum 523
7/9/83	48	14		8 You Bought It-You Name It		Warner 23884
6/1/85	65	19		9 The Confessor		Warner 25281
8/1/87	113	8		10 Got Any Gum?		Warner 25606
5/18/91	112	17		11 Ordinary Average Guy		Pyramid 47384

WALSH, Steve
Born on 6/15/1951 in St. Joseph, Missouri. Rock singer/keyboardist. Member of **Kansas** and **Streets**.

2/16/80	124	6		1 Schemer-Dreamer		Kirshner 36320

WALTER & SCOTTY
R&B vocal duo: twin brothers Walter and Wallace "Scotty" Scott. Born on 9/3/1943 in Fort Worth, Texas. Members of **The Whispers**.

5/22/93	151	7		1 My Brother's Keeper		Capitol 92958

WALTERS, Jamie
Born on 6/13/1969 in Boston, Massachusetts. Male singer/actor. Former lead singer of **The Heights**.

3/11/95	70	18		1 Jamie Walters		Atlantic 82600

WANDERLEY, Walter
Born on 5/12/1932 in Recife, Brazil. Died of cancer on 9/4/1986 (age 54). Samba organist.

9/3/66	22	41		1 Rain Forest	[I]	Verve 8658

WANG CHUNG
Pop-rock trio from London, England: Jack Hues (vocals, guitar, keyboards), Nick Feldman (bass, keyboards) and Darren Costin (drums). Costin left in 1985.

2/25/84	30	37		1 Points On The Curve		Geffen 4004
11/2/85	85	18		2 To Live And Die In L.A.	[S]	Geffen 24081
11/1/86	41	36	●	3 Mosaic		Geffen 24115
6/10/89	123	6		4 The Warmer Side Of Cool		Geffen 24222

WANSEL, Dexter
Born in Philadelphia, Pennsylvania. R&B keyboardist/producer/arranger.

4/30/77	168	3		1 What The World Is Coming To		Philadelphia Int'l. 34487
4/1/78	139	6		2 Voyager		Philadelphia Int'l. 34985

Billboard DEBUT	PEAK	WKS	R I A A	ARTIST / Album Title	Catalog	Label & Number

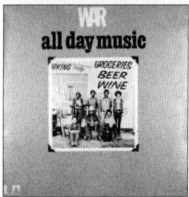

WAR
1970s: #34 / All-Time: #193

Latin band from Long Beach, California: Howard Scott (guitar; born on 3/15/1940), **Lee Oskar** (harmonica; born on 3/24/1948), **Lonnie Jordan** (keyboards; born on 11/21/1948), Charles Miller (sax; born on 6/2/1939), Thomas Allen (percussion; born on 7/19/1931), Morris Dickerson (bass; born on 8/3/1949) and Harold Brown (drums; born on 3/17/1946). All share vocals. **Eric Burdon**'s backup band until 1971. Alice Tweed Smyth (vocals) added in 1978. By 1979, Luther Rabb replaced Dickerson; Pat Rizzo (horns) and Ron Hammond (percussion) joined. Rabb and Hammond were members of **Ballin' Jack**. Smyth left group in 1982. Lineup by 1994: Jordan, Scott, Brown and Hammond with Rae Valentine (music programmer), Charles Green and Kerry Campbell (saxophones), Tetsuya Nakamura (harmonica) and Sal Rodriguez (percussion). Miller was shot to death in June 1980 (age 41). Allen died on 8/30/1988 (age 57). Rabb died on 1/21/2006 (age 63).

DEBUT	PEAK	WKS	●	Album Title	Catalog	Label & Number
5/16/70	18	27		1 Eric Burdon Declares "War"		MGM 4663
12/26/70+	82	9		2 The Black-Man's Burdon		MGM 4710 [2]
12/25/76+	140	5		3 Love Is All Around		ABC 988
				ERIC BURDON AND WAR (above 3)		
4/24/71	190	6		4 War		United Artists 5508
11/20/71+	16	49	●	5 All Day Music		United Artists 5546
11/18/72+	❶²	68	●	6 The World Is A Ghetto		United Artists 5652
				RS500 #449		
9/1/73	6	36	●	7 Deliver The Word		United Artists 128
3/23/74	13	35	●	8 War Live! [L]		United Artists 193 [2]
7/5/75	8	31	●	9 Why Can't We Be Friends?		United Artists 441
8/19/78	69	6		10 Youngblood [S]		United Artists 904
12/3/77+	15	23	●	11 Galaxy		MCA 3030
4/14/79	41	16	●	12 The Music Band		MCA 3085
12/8/79	111	13		13 The Music Band 2		MCA 3193
3/20/82	48	27		14 Outlaw		RCA Victor 4208
7/23/83	164	4		15 Life (Is So Strange)		RCA Victor 4598
7/23/94	200	1		16 Peace Sign		Avenue 71706
				GREATEST HITS & COMPILATIONS:		
9/4/76	6	21	▲	17 Greatest Hits		United Artists 648
7/23/77	23	14	●	18 Platinum Jazz		Blue Note 690 [2]
5/30/87	156	10	▲	19 The Best Of War.....And More	Cat:#18/9	Priority 9467
8/2/03	133	1		20 The Very Best Of War		Avenue 73895 [2]

WARD, Anita
Born on 12/20/1956 in Memphis, Tennessee. Disco singer.

DEBUT	PEAK	WKS	Album Title	Catalog	Label & Number
5/26/79	8	19	1 Songs Of Love		Juana 200,004

WARD, Billy, And His Dominoes
Born on 9/19/1921 in Los Angeles, California. Died on 2/16/2002 (age 80). R&B pianist. His vocal group: Charlie White (tenor), Joe Lamont (baritone) and Bill Brown (bass). Signed by King/Federal in 1950. Lead singers, at various times: **Clyde McPhatter** (1950-53), **Jackie Wilson** (1953-57) and Eugene Mumford.

~ ~ ~ ~ ~ ~ ~ ~ ~ ~ **NON-CHARTED ALBUMS** ~ ~ ~ ~ ~ ~ ~ ~ ~ ~

1958 **Billy Ward And His Dominoes Featuring Clyde McPhatter** *[Federal label]*

1958 **Billy Ward And The Dominoes** *[Decca label]*

1958 **Yours Forever**

WARD, M.
Born Matthew Ward on 10/4/1973 in Newbury Park, California. Adult Alternative singer/songwriter/guitarist. Member of **Monsters Of Folk** and **She & Him**.

DEBUT	PEAK	WKS	Album Title	Catalog	Label & Number
9/16/06	146	1	1 Post-War		Merge 280
3/7/09	31	7	2 Hold Time		Merge 323

WARD, Robin
Born Jacqueline Eloise McDonnell in 1941 in Hawaii; raised in Nebraska. Pop singer.

~ ~ ~ ~ ~ ~ ~ ~ ~ ~ **NON-CHARTED ALBUM** ~ ~ ~ ~ ~ ~ ~ ~ ~ ~

1963 **Wonderful Summer**

WARINER, Steve
Born on 12/25/1954 in Noblesville, Indiana. Country singer/songwriter/guitarist.

AWARD: OPRY: 1996

DEBUT	PEAK	WKS	●	Album Title	Catalog	Label & Number
10/17/87	187	2		1 Greatest Hits [G]		MCA 42032
11/16/91	180	7	●	2 I Am Ready		Arista 18691
5/9/98	41	15	●	3 Burnin' The Roadhouse Down		Capitol 94482
5/22/99	35	12	●	4 Two Teardrops		Capitol 96139

WARING, Fred, And The Pennsylvanians
Born on 6/9/1900 in Tyrone, Pennsylvania. Died on 7/29/1984 (age 84). Orchestra leader.

DEBUT	PEAK	WKS	Album Title	Catalog	Label & Number
9/9/57	25	1	1 Fred Waring And The Pennsylvanians In Hi-Fi		Capitol 845
12/23/57	6	3	2 Now Is The Caroling Season [X]		Capitol 896
12/22/58+	19	3	3 Now Is The Caroling Season [X-R]		Capitol 896
5/30/64	116	7	4 America, I Hear You Singing		Reprise 2020
			FRANK SINATRA/BING CROSBY/FRED WARING		
12/12/64	9ˣ	3	5 12 Songs Of Christmas [X]		Reprise 2022
			BING CROSBY/FRANK SINATRA/FRED WARING		

			R I A A	ARTIST		
DEBUT	**PEAK**	**WKS**		**Album Title**	**Catalog**	**Label & Number**

WARING, Fred, And The Pennsylvanians — cont'd

12/24/66	71ˣ	3		6 A Caroling We Go .... [X]		Decca 74809
				Christmas charts: 71/'66, 74/'67		

WARLOCK
Hard-rock band from Dusseldorf, Germany: **Doro** (vocals), Peter Szigeti (guitar), Rudy Graf (guitar), Frank Rittel (bass) and Michael Eurich (drums).

12/19/87+	80	27		1 Triumph And Agony		Mercury 832804

WARNES, Jennifer
Born on 3/3/1947 in Seattle, Washington; raised in Orange County, California. Adult Contemporary singer/actress.

2/26/77	43	18		1 Jennifer Warnes		Arista 4062
6/9/79	94	23		2 Shot Through The Heart		Arista 4217
2/14/87	72	21		3 Famous Blue Raincoat		Cypress 661111

WARRANT
Male hard-rock band from Los Angeles, California: Jani Lane (vocals), Erik Turner (guitar), Joey Allen (guitar), Jerry Dixon (bass) and Steven Sweet (drums).

3/4/89	10	65	▲²	1 Dirty Rotten Filthy Stinking Rich		Columbia 44383
9/29/90	7	60	▲²	2 Cherry Pie		Columbia 45487
9/12/92	25	13	●	3 Dog Eat Dog		Columbia 52584

WARREN, Rusty
Born Ilene Goldman on 3/17/1931 in Brooklyn, New York; raised in Milton, Massachusetts. Female novelty singer of adults-only songs.

11/7/60+	8	181		1 Knockers Up! .... [C]		Jubilee 2029
5/8/61	55	40		2 Songs For Sinners .... [C]		Jubilee 2024
5/22/61	21	51		3 Sin-Sational .... [C]		Jubilee 2034
12/18/61+	31	50		4 Rusty Warren Bounces Back .... [C]		Jubilee 2039
11/3/62+	22	32		5 Rusty Warren In Orbit .... [C]		Jubilee 2044
10/19/63	52	18		6 Banned In Boston? .... [C]		Jubilee 2049
1/1/66	124	7		7 More Knockers Up! .... [C]		Jubilee 2059
				no track titles listed on albums #2, 4-7		

WARREN G
Born Warren Griffin on 11/10/1970 in Long Beach, California. Male rapper/songwriter. Stepbrother of **Dr. Dre**. Childhood friend of **Snoop Dogg**. Former partner of **Nate Dogg**. Member of **213**.

6/25/94	2¹	53	▲³	1 Regulate...G Funk Era		Violator 523364
4/12/97	11	16	●	2 Take A Look Over Your Shoulder (Reality)..		Def Jam 537254
10/30/99	21	10	●	3 I Want It All		Restless 73710
12/29/01+	83	8		4 The Return Of The Regulator		Universal 016121
10/29/05	80	3		5 In The Mid-Nite Hour		Hawino 54707

WARWICK, Dionne   1960s: #47 / All-Time: #69
Born Marie Dionne Warrick on 12/12/1940 in East Orange, New Jersey. Adult Contemporary/R&B singer. In church choir from age six. With the Drinkard Singers gospel group. Formed the Gospelaires trio with sister **Dee Dee Warwick** and their aunt Cissy Houston (of **Sweet Inspirations**; Dionne is cousin of **Whitney Houston**). Added an "e" to her last name for a time in the mid-1970s. Dionne was **Burt Bacharach**'s and Hal David's main "voice" for the songs they composed. Co-hosted TV's *Solid Gold* 1980-81 and 1985-86. During the 1990s, hosted TV infomercials for the Psychic Friends Network.

9/12/64	68	20		1 Make Way For Dionne Warwick		Scepter 523
3/6/65	107	9		2 The Sensitive Sound Of Dionne Warwick		Scepter 528
1/1/66	45	29		3 Here I Am		Scepter 531
1/7/67	18	66	●	4 Here Where There Is Love		Scepter 555
5/13/67	169	9		5 On Stage and in The Movies		Scepter 559
9/16/67	22	31		6 The Windows Of The World		Scepter 563
3/9/68	6	48	●	7 Valley Of The Dolls		Scepter 568
12/14/68+	18	39		8 Promises, Promises		Scepter 571
4/5/69	11	28		9 Soulful		Scepter 573
5/2/70	23	39		10 I'll Never Fall In Love Again...		Scepter 581
				Grammy: Female Pop Vocal		
12/12/70+	37	24		11 Very Dionne		Scepter 587
1/29/72	54	14		12 Dionne		Warner 2585
2/3/73	178	8		13 Just Being Myself..		Warner 2658
				DIONNE WARWICKE (above 2)		
3/8/75	167	6		14 Then Came You		Warner 2846
12/6/75+	137	15		15 Track Of The Cat		Warner 2893
6/9/79	12	54	▲	16 Dionne		Arista 4230
				produced by **Barry Manilow**		
8/9/80	23	25		17 No Night So Long		Arista 9526
5/22/82	83	12		18 Friends In Love..		Arista 9585
10/30/82+	25	28	●	19 Heartbreaker		Arista 9609
				produced by **Barry Gibb**		

Billboard			R I A A	ARTIST		
DEBUT	PEAK	WKS		Album Title	Catalog	Label & Number

WARWICK, Dionne — cont'd

10/29/83	57	17	20 How Many Times Can We Say Goodbye		Arista 8104
			produced by Luther Vandross		
3/2/85	106	11	21 Finder Of Lost Loves		Arista 8262
12/21/85+	12	26	● 22 Friends		Arista 8398
8/22/87	56	27	23 Reservations For Two		Arista 8446
8/18/90	155	9	24 Dionne Warwick Sings Cole Porter		Arista 8573

GREATEST HITS & COMPILATIONS:

11/18/67	10	69	25 Dionne Warwick's Golden Hits, Part One		Scepter 565
11/1/69	28	28	26 Dionne Warwick's Golden Hits, Part 2		Scepter 577
8/16/69	31	24	● 27 Dionne Warwick's Greatest Motion Picture Hits		Scepter 575
4/8/72	169	5	28 From Within		Scepter 598 [2]
7/2/77	188	7	29 Only Love Can Break A Heart		Musicor 2501
12/23/89+	177	7	30 Greatest Hits 1979-1990		Arista 8540

LIVE ALBUMS:

4/16/66	76	11	31 Dionne Warwick In Paris		Scepter 534
			recorded on 1/18/1966 at the Olympia Theater		
10/30/71	48	17	● 32 The Dionne Warwicke Story		Scepter 596 [2]
2/19/77	49	13	33 A Man And A Woman		HBS 996 [2]
			ISAAC HAYES & DIONNE WARWICK		
6/13/81	72	14	34 Hot! Live and Otherwise		Arista 8605 [2]
			3 of 4 sides are live recordings		

~ ~ ~ ~ ~ ~ ~ ~ ~ **NON-CHARTED ALBUMS** ~ ~ ~ ~ ~ ~ ~ ~ ~ ~
1963 Presenting Dionne Warwick   1964 Anyone Who Had A Heart

WASH, Martha
Born on 12/28/1953 in San Francisco, California. R&B singer. Member of **The Weather Girls**.

3/13/93	169	2	1 Martha Wash		RCA 66052

WASHINGTON, Baby
Born Justine Washington on 11/13/1940 in Bamberg, South Carolina; raised in Harlem, New York. R&B singer/pianist.

~ ~ ~ ~ ~ ~ ~ ~ ~ ~ ~ **NON-CHARTED ALBUM** ~ ~ ~ ~ ~ ~ ~ ~ ~ ~ ~
1963 That's How Heartaches Are Made

WASHINGTON, Deborah
Born on 3/16/1954 in Philadelphia, Pennsylvania. R&B singer/actress.

10/28/78	205	2	1 Any Way You Want It		Ariola America 50040

WASHINGTON, Dinah
Born Ruth Lee Jones on 8/29/1924 in Tuscaloosa, Alabama. Died of an alcohol/pill overdose on on 12/14/1963 (age 39). R&B singer.
AWARD: R&R Hall of Fame: 1993 (Early Influence)

2/1/60	34	22	1 What A Diff'rence A Day Makes!		Mercury 20479
1/23/61	10	14	2 Unforgettable		Mercury 20572
12/18/61+	56	15	3 September In The Rain		Mercury 20638
11/17/62	131	4	4 I Wanna Be Loved		Mercury 20729
6/23/62	33	25	5 Dinah '62		Roulette 25170
10/20/62	78	9	6 Drinking Again		Roulette 25183
2/23/63	61	12	7 Back To The Blues		Roulette 25189
4/4/64	130	6	8 A Stranger On Earth		Roulette 25253

~ ~ ~ ~ ~ ~ ~ ~ ~ ~ **NON-CHARTED ALBUM** ~ ~ ~ ~ ~ ~ ~ ~ ~ ~
1960 The Two Of Us [w/ Brook Benton]

WASHINGTON, Grover Jr.   **All-Time: #194**
Born on 12/12/1943 in Buffalo, New York. Died on 12/17/1999 (age 56). Jazz-R&B saxophonist. Began playing the saxophone at age 10. Left Buffalo and joined first band, the Four Clefs, at age 16. Introduced to drummer **Billy Cobham** while serving in the U.S. Army; this led to much session work in New York City and Philadelphia. Originator of the "smooth jazz" sound.

1/1/72	62	25	1 Inner City Blues	[I]	Kudu 03
9/9/72	111	17	2 All The King's Horses	[I]	Kudu 07
7/14/73	100	14	3 Soul Box	[I]	Kudu 1213 [2]
3/8/75	10	34	4 Mister Magic	[I]	Kudu 20
11/15/75	10	30	5 Feels So Good	[I]	Kudu 24
1/15/77	31	16	6 A Secret Place	[I]	Kudu 32
1/7/78	11	32	7 Live At The Bijou	[I-L]	Kudu 3637 [2]
			recorded May 1977 at the Bijou Cafe in Philadelphia, Pennsylvania		
10/21/78	35	23	8 Reed Seed	[I]	Motown 910
4/28/79	24	19	9 Paradise	[I]	Elektra 182
3/8/80	24	22	10 Skylarkin'	[I]	Motown 933
9/13/80	96	10	11 Baddest	[I-K]	Motown 940 [2]

WASHINGTON, Grover Jr. — cont'd

11/15/80+	5	52	▲² 12	Winelight .... [I]		Elektra 305
				Grammy: Jazz Fusion Album		
10/24/81	149	7	13	Anthology .... [I-K]		Motown 961 [2]
12/12/81+	28	27	14	Come Morning .... [I]		Elektra 562
12/11/82+	50	25	15	The Best Is Yet To Come .... [I]		Elektra 60215
11/10/84	79	23	16	Inside Moves .... [I]		Elektra 60318
8/29/87	66	16	17	Strawberry Moon .... [I]		Columbia 40510
5/16/92	149	11	18	Next Exit .... [I]		Columbia 48530
10/12/96	187	2	19	Soulful Strut .... [I]		Columbia 57505

WASHINGTON, Keith
Born on 11/15/1960 in Detroit, Michigan. R&B singer/songwriter.

5/4/91	48	25	● 1	Make Time For Love		Qwest 26528
10/9/93	100	7	2	You Make It Easy		Qwest 45336
3/28/98	125	8	3	KW		Silas 11744

WAS (NOT WAS)
Interracial pop-dance-R&B group from Detroit, Michigan. Fronted by composer/bassist Don Fagenson ("Don Was") and lyricist/flutist David Weiss ("David Was"). Includes vocalists Sweet Pea Atkinson and Sir Harry Bowens. Group appeared in the 1990 movie *The Freshman*.

10/15/83	134	9	1	Born To Laugh At Tornadoes		Geffen 4016
10/15/88+	43	37	2	What Up, Dog?		Chrysalis 41664
8/18/90	99	11	3	Are You Okay?		Chrysalis 21778

W.A.S.P.
Hard-rock band from Los Angeles, California: Steve "Blackie Lawless" Duren (vocals), Chris Holmes (guitar), Johnny Rod (bass) and Steve Riley (drums). Holmes was married to **Lita Ford** from 1990-92.

10/6/84	74	31	● 1	W.A.S.P.		Capitol 12343
11/23/85	49	23	● 2	The Last Command		Capitol 12435
11/8/86	60	19	3	Inside The Electric Circus		Capitol 12531
10/10/87	77	14	4	Live...In The Raw .... [L]		Capitol 48053
4/22/89	48	13	5	The Headless Children		Capitol 48942

WATERBOYS, The
Rock band formed in London, England, by Mike Scott (vocals, guitar) and Anthony Thistlethwaite (mandolin, sax). Numerous personnel changes. Keyboardist Karl Wallinger left in 1985 to form **World Party**.

12/10/88+	76	26	1	Fisherman's Blues		Chrysalis 41589
10/27/90	180	4	2	Room To Roam		Chrysalis 21768
6/12/93	171	2	3	Dream Harder		Geffen 24476

WATERFRONT
Male pop-rock duo from Cardiff, Wales: Chris Duffy (vocals) and Phil Cillia (guitar).

5/20/89	103	13	1	Waterfront		Polydor 837970

WATERS, Crystal
Born on 10/10/1964 in Philadelphia, Pennsylvania. Black dance singer/songwriter.

7/20/91	197	3	1	Surprise		Mercury 848894
10/8/94	199	1	● 2	Storyteller		Mercury 522105

WATERS, Kim
Born in Baltimore, Maryland. Male saxophonist.

4/14/07	191	1	1	You Are My Lady		Shanachie 5147
11/15/08	200	1	2	I Want You: Love In The Spirit Of Marvin		Shanachie 5166

WATERS, Muddy
Born McKinley Morganfield on 4/4/1915 in Rolling Fork, Mississippi. Died of a heart attack on 4/30/1983 (age 68). Legendary blues singer/guitarist/harmonica player.

AWARDS: Grammy: Lifetime Achievement 1992 ★ R&R Hall of Fame: 1987

11/9/68	127	8	1	Electric Mud		Cadet Concept 314
9/27/69	70	10	2	Fathers And Sons .... [L]		Chess 127 [2]
				record 2: live		
2/19/77	143	7	3	Hard Again		Blue Sky 34449
				Grammy: Blues Album		
2/25/78	157	6	4	I'm Ready		Blue Sky 34928
				Grammy: Blues Album		
4/7/79	203	3	5	Muddy "Mississippi" Waters Live .... [L]		Blue Sky 35712
5/16/81	192	2	6	King Bee		Blue Sky 37064
				above 3 produced by **Johnny Winter**		

~ ~ ~ ~ ~ ~ ~ ~ ~   **NON-CHARTED ALBUMS**   ~ ~ ~ ~ ~ ~ ~ ~ ~ ~

1960 **Muddy Waters At Newport 1960**   2001 **The Anthology**
     RS500 #348   *RS500 #38*
1964 **Folk Singer**
     RS500 #280

Billboard DEBUT	PEAK	WKS	R I A A	ARTIST Album Title	Catalog	Label & Number

WATERS, Roger
Born George Roger Waters on 9/6/1944 in Cambridgeshire, England. Former leader/bassist of **Pink Floyd**. Went solo in 1983.

DEBUT	PEAK	WKS		Album	Catalog	Label & Number
5/19/84	31	18	●	1 The Pros And Cons Of Hitch Hiking		Columbia 39290
7/4/87	50	19		2 Radio K.A.O.S.		Columbia 40795
9/22/90	56	10		3 The Wall - Live In Berlin .... [L]		Mercury 846611 [2]
				recorded on 7/21/1990		
9/19/92	21	10		4 Amused To Death		Columbia 47127
12/23/00	136	1		5 In The Flesh - Live .... [L]		Columbia 85235 [2]

WATLEY, Jody
Born on 1/30/1959 in Chicago, Illinois. R&B singer. Member of **Shalamar** (1977-84). Goddaughter of **Jackie Wilson**.
AWARD: Grammy: Best New Artist 1987

DEBUT	PEAK	WKS		Album	Catalog	Label & Number
3/21/87	10	74	▲	1 Jody Watley		MCA 5898
4/15/89	16	40	●	2 Larger Than Life		MCA 6276
12/2/89	86	13		3 You Wanna Dance With Me? .... [K]		MCA 6343
12/21/91+	124	9		4 Affairs Of The Heart		MCA 10355
11/27/93	164	2		5 Intimacy		MCA 10947

WATSON, Aaron
Born in 1977 in Amarillo, Texas. Country singer/songwriter.

DEBUT	PEAK	WKS		Album	Catalog	Label & Number
4/19/08	175	1		1 Angels & Outlaws		Big Label 5739544

WATSON, Doc
Born Arthel Watson on 3/3/1923 in Deep Gap, North Carolina. Country banjo player.
AWARD: Grammy: Lifetime Achievement 2004

DEBUT	PEAK	WKS		Album	Catalog	Label & Number
8/30/75	193	3		1 Memories		United Artists 423 [2]
8/9/03	179	4		2 The Three Pickers		Rounder 610526
				EARL SCRUGGS / DOC WATSON / RICKY SKAGGS		

WATSON, Johnny "Guitar"
Born on 2/3/1935 in Houston, Texas. Died of a heart attack on 5/17/1996 (age 61). R&B singer/songwriter/guitarist.

DEBUT	PEAK	WKS		Album	Catalog	Label & Number
9/27/75	201	4		1 I Don't Want To Be Alone, Stranger		Fantasy 9484
8/7/76	52	22	●	2 Ain't That A Bitch		DJM 3
4/16/77	20	27	●	3 A Real Mother For Ya		DJM 7
12/24/77+	84	14		4 Funk Beyond The Call Of Duty		DJM 714
4/15/78	154	4		5 Master Funk		DJM 13
				WATSONIAN INSTITUTE		
10/28/78	157	7		6 Giant		DJM 19
8/11/79	204	1		7 What The Hell Is This		DJM 24
7/5/80	115	14		8 Love Jones		DJM 31
6/27/81	177	3		9 Johnny "Guitar" Watson And The Family Clone................		DJM 501

WATSON, Russell
Born on 11/24/1966 in Salford, England. Operatic tenor.

DEBUT	PEAK	WKS		Album	Catalog	Label & Number
5/5/01	90	15		1 The Voice		Decca 468695
10/19/02	114	7		2 Encore		Decca 473160

WATT, Mike
Born on 12/20/1957 in Portsmouth, Virginia. Hard-rock singer/bassist. Former member of the **Minutemen**. Joined **Porno For Pyros** in 1995.

DEBUT	PEAK	WKS		Album	Catalog	Label & Number
3/18/95	129	4		1 Ball-Hog Or Tugboat?		Columbia 67086

WATTS, Ernie
Born on 10/23/1945 in Norfolk, Virginia. R&B saxophonist.

DEBUT	PEAK	WKS		Album	Catalog	Label & Number
2/20/82	161	12		1 Chariots Of Fire.. [I]		Qwest 3637

WATTS 103rd STREET RHYTHM BAND — see WRIGHT, Charles

WA WA NEE
Pop band from Australia: brothers Paul Gray (vocals, keyboards) and Mark Gray (bass), with Steve Williams (guitar) and Chris Sweeney (drums).

DEBUT	PEAK	WKS		Album	Catalog	Label & Number
11/7/87	123	17		1 Wa Wa Nee		Epic 40858

WAX
Pop duo formed in Los Angeles, California: **Andrew Gold** and Graham Gouldman (of **10cc**).

DEBUT	PEAK	WKS		Album	Catalog	Label & Number
4/26/86	101	11		1 Magnetic Heaven...		RCA Victor 9546

WAYBILL, Fee
Born John Waldo on 9/17/1950 in Omaha, Nebraska. Lead singer of **The Tubes**.

DEBUT	PEAK	WKS		Album	Catalog	Label & Number
11/10/84	146	6		1 Read My Lips		Capitol 12369

WAYLON & WILLIE — see JENNINGS, Waylon / NELSON, Willie

WAYNE, Jimmy
Born Jimmy Wayne Barber on 10/23/1972 in Bessemer City, North Carolina; raised in Gastonia, North Carolina. Country singer/songwriter.

DEBUT	PEAK	WKS		Album	Catalog	Label & Number
7/12/03	64	9		1 Jimmy Wayne		DreamWorks 450355
9/13/08	27	8		2 Do You Believe Me Now		Valory 0100

Billboard DEBUT	PEAK	WKS	RIAA	ARTIST Album Title	Catalog	Label & Number

WAYNE, John

Born Marion Morrison on 5/26/1907 in Winterset, Iowa. Died of cancer on 6/11/1979 (age 72). Legendary movie actor. Nicknamed "The Duke."

DEBUT	PEAK	WKS	RIAA	Album Title	Catalog	Label & Number
3/3/73	66	16		1 **America, Why I Love Her** a narrative tribute (with orchestra and chorus) to America	[T]	RCA Victor 4828

WAYSTED

Hard-rock band formed in England: Danny Vaughn (vocals), Paul Chapman (guitar), Pete Way (bass) and John DiTeodoro (drums). Chapman and Way were with **UFO**.

DEBUT	PEAK	WKS	RIAA	Album Title	Catalog	Label & Number
3/21/87	185	2		1 **Save Your Prayers**		Capitol 12538

WC

Born William Calhoun on 8/9/1970 in Los Angeles, California. Male rapper/songwriter. Member of **Westside Connection**. The MAAD Circle: **Coolio**, Big Gee and D.J. Crazy Toons. Coolio left in 1994.

DEBUT	PEAK	WKS	RIAA	Album Title	Catalog	Label & Number
10/21/95	85	3		1 **Curb Servin'** **WC AND THE MAAD CIRCLE**		Payday 828650
5/16/98	19	11		2 **The Shadiest One**		Red Ant 828957
11/9/02	46	5		3 **Ghetto Heisman**		Def Jam 170071
9/1/07	49	3		4 **Guilty By Affiliation**		Lench Mob 03881

WEAKERTHANS, The

Punk-rock band from Winnipeg, Manitoba, Canada: John Samson (vocals, guitar), Stephen Carroll (guitar), Greg Smith (bass) and Jason Tait (drums).

DEBUT	PEAK	WKS	RIAA	Album Title	Catalog	Label & Number
10/13/07	181	1		1 **Reunion Tour**		Anti 86877

WEATHER GIRLS, The

R&B-disco duo from San Francisco, California: Martha Wash and Izora Redman. Formerly known as **The Two Tons** and **Two Tons O' Fun**. Redman died of heart failure on 9/16/2004 (age 62).

DEBUT	PEAK	WKS	RIAA	Album Title	Catalog	Label & Number
5/17/80	91	11		1 **Two Tons O' Fun**		Honey 9584
1/10/81	202	5		2 **Backatcha** **THE TWO TONS**		Fantasy 9615
12/3/83	206	1		3 **Success**		Columbia 38997

WEATHERLY, Jim

Born on 3/17/1943 in Pontotoc, Mississippi. Pop-country singer/songwriter.

DEBUT	PEAK	WKS	RIAA	Album Title	Catalog	Label & Number
9/28/74	94	14		1 **The Songs Of Jim Weatherly**		Buddah 5608

WEATHER REPORT — All-Time: #444

Jazz-fusion band formed by Austrian-born Josef Zawinul (keyboards) and **Wayne Shorter** (sax). Zawinul was a member of **Cannonball Adderley**'s combo for nine years. Various personnel included **Jaco Pastorius** from 1976-82. Zawinul formed the Zawinul Syndicate in 1988. Zawinul died of cancer on 9/11/2007 (age 75).

DEBUT	PEAK	WKS	RIAA	Album Title	Catalog	Label & Number
7/24/71	191	4		1 **Weather Report**	[I]	Columbia 30661
7/15/72	147	6		2 **I Sing The Body Electric** side 2: recorded live in Tokyo, Japan	[I-L]	Columbia 31352
5/26/73	85	17		3 **Sweetnighter**	[I]	Columbia 32210
6/22/74	46	23		4 **Mysterious Traveller**	[I]	Columbia 32494
6/7/75	31	14		5 **Tale Spinnin'**	[I]	Columbia 33417
4/17/76	42	12		6 **Black Market**	[I]	Columbia 34099
4/2/77	30	22	▲	7 **Heavy Weather** Cat:#33/18	[I]	Columbia 34418
10/28/78	52	14		8 **Mr. Gone**	[I]	ARC 35358
10/6/79	47	11		9 **8:30** *Grammy: Jazz Fusion Album*	[I-L]	ARC 36030 [2]
12/13/80+	57	14		10 **Night Passage**	[I]	ARC 36793
2/20/82	68	11		11 **Weather Report**	[I]	ARC 37616
3/19/83	96	10		12 **Procession**	[I]	Columbia 38427
3/24/84	136	8		13 **Domino Theory**	[I]	Columbia 39147
4/27/85	191	3		14 **Sportin' Life**	[I]	Columbia 39908
8/23/86	195	2		15 **This Is This**	[I]	Columbia 40280

WEAVER, Dennis

Born William Dennis Weaver on 6/4/1924 in Joplin, Missouri. Died of cancer on 2/24/2006 (age 81). Actor/singer. Appeared in several TV shows and movies.

DEBUT	PEAK	WKS	RIAA	Album Title	Catalog	Label & Number
5/13/72	191	2		1 **Dennis Weaver**		Im'press 1614

WEAVERS, The

Legendary folk group formed in Greenwich Village, New York: **Pete Seeger** (born on 5/3/1919), Lee Hays (born on 3/14/1914; died on 8/26/1961, age 67), Fred Hellerman (born on 5/13/1927) and female lead Ronnie Gilbert (born on 9/7/1926). Revived and popularized folk music in the early 1950s.

DEBUT	PEAK	WKS	RIAA	Album Title	Catalog	Label & Number
3/13/61	24	7		1 **The Weavers At Carnegie Hall** ***Grammy: Hall of Fame*** recorded on 12/24/1955	[L]	Vanguard 9010
1/23/61	126	13		2 **The Weavers At Carnegie Hall, Vol. 2** recorded on 4/1/1960	[L]	Vanguard 9075

WEBB, Derek

Born on 5/27/1974 in Memphis, Tennessee. Christian folk-rock singer/songwriter/guitarist. Member of **Caedmon's Call**.

DEBUT	PEAK	WKS	RIAA	Album Title	Catalog	Label & Number
9/19/09	66	1		1 **Stockholm Syndrome**		Ino 54009

Billboard			R I A A	ARTIST		
DEBUT	PEAK	WKS		Album Title	Catalog	Label & Number

WEBB, Jack
Born on 4/2/1920 in Santa Monica, California. Died of a heart attack on 12/23/1982 (age 62). Actor/TV producer. Creator/director/star ("Joe Friday") of TV's *Dragnet* and the movie *Pete Kelly's Blues*. Married to **Julie London** from 1945-53.

| 9/3/55 | 2¹ | 8 | | 1 Pete Kelly's Blues **[I-T]** | | RCA Victor 1126 |

LP: RCA Victor LPM-1126 (#2); EP: RCA Victor EPB-1126 (#2)

WEBB, Jimmy
Born on 8/15/1946 in Elk City, Oklahoma. Prolific songwriter.

| 8/12/72 | 202 | 4 | | 1 Letters | | Reprise 2055 |

WEBBER, Andrew Lloyd
Born on 3/22/1948 in London, England. Legendary musical composer. Creator of *Jesus Christ Superstar, Evita, Cats, Phantom Of The Opera, Joseph and The Amazing Technicolor Dreamcoat* and *Requiem*. Collaborated with lyricist Sir Tim Rice. Married to **Sarah Brightman** from 1984-90. Knighted by Queen Elizabeth in 1992.
AWARD: Grammy: Living Legends 1989

5/25/91	130	14	▲	1 The Premiere Collection .... Cat:#23/45 **[K]**		MCA 6284
4/3/93	191	6		2 The Premiere Collection Encore .... **[K]**		Polydor 517336
12/21/96+	155	7		3 The Very Best Of Andrew Lloyd Webber - The Broadway Collection .... **[K]**		Polydor 533064
5/25/02	110	1		4 Gold .... **[G]**		Really Useful 589577

WEBBIE
Born Webster Gradney on 9/6/1985 in Baton Rouge, Louisiana. Male rapper/songwriter.

| 7/23/05 | 8 | 12 | | 1 Savage Life | | Trill 83825 |
| 3/15/08 | 4 | 12 | | 2 Savage Life 2 | | Trill 427836 |

WEBSTER, Max — see MAX WEBSTER

WE CAME AS ROMANS
Hard-rock band from Detroit, Michigan: David Stephens (vocals), Joshua Moore (guitar), Brian Cotton (guitar), Kyle Pavone (keyboards), Andrew Glass (bass) and Eric Choi (drums).

| 11/21/09 | 175 | 1 | | 1 To Plant A Seed | | Equal Vision 175 |

WECHTER, Julius — see BAJA MARIMBA BAND

WEEN
Alternative-rock duo from Lambertville, New Jersey: Mickey "Dean Ween" Melchiondo and Aaron "Gene Ween" Freeman.

7/12/97	159	1		1 The Mollusk		Elektra 62013
5/20/00	121	1		2 White Pepper		Elektra 62449
8/23/03	81	2		3 Quebec		Sanctuary 84591
11/10/07	69	2		4 La Cucaracha		Chocodog 619077

WEEPIES, The
Folk-pop duo from Cambridge, Massachusetts: Steve Tannen and Deb Talan.

| 5/10/08 | 31 | 3 | | 1 Hideaway | | Nettwerk 30777 |

WEEZER
Alternative-rock band formed in Los Angeles, California: **Rivers Cuomo** (vocals, guitar), Brian Bell (guitar), Matt Sharp (bass) and Patrick Wilson (drums). Mikey Welsh replaced Sharp in 1998. Scott Shriner replaced Welsh in early 2002.

8/27/94+	16	76	▲³	1 Weezer .... Cat:#2¹/34		DGC 24629
				RS500 #297		
				also known as *The Blue Album*		
10/12/96	19	16	●	2 Pinkerton .... Cat:#35/2		DGC 25007
6/2/01	4	36	▲	3 Weezer		Geffen 493045
				also known as *The Green Album*		
6/1/02	3¹	19	●	4 Maladroit		Geffen 493241
5/28/05	2¹	47	▲	5 Make Believe		Geffen 004520
6/21/08	4	23		6 Weezer		DGC 011135
				also known as *The Red Album*		
1/3/09	173	1		7 Christmas With Weezer .... **[X-EP]**		DGC digital
				Christmas charts: 47/'08, 15/'09		
11/21/09	7	13		8 Raditude		DGC 013510

WE FIVE
Pop band from San Francisco, California: Beverly Bivens (vocals), Bob Jones (guitar), Jerry Burgan (guitar), Pete Fullerton (bass) and Mike Stewart (drums). Stewart (brother of **John Stewart**) died on 11/13/2002 (age 57).

| 10/16/65 | 32 | 30 | | 1 You Were On My Mind | | A&M 4111 |
| 1/27/68 | 172 | 6 | | 2 Make Someone Happy | | A&M 4138 |

WEILAND, Scott
Born on 10/27/1967 in Santa Cruz, California. Lead singer of **Stone Temple Pilots** and **Velvet Revolver**.

| 4/18/98 | 42 | 5 | | 1 12 Bar Blues | | Atlantic 83084 |
| 12/13/08 | 97 | 1 | | 2 Missing Cleveland | | Softdrive 0002 |

WEIR, Bob
Born Robert Hall on 10/16/1947 in San Francisco, California. Rock singer/guitarist. Co-founder of the **Grateful Dead**. Later formed **Kingfish** and **Bobby & The Midnites**.

| 6/17/72 | 68 | 15 | | 1 Ace | | Warner 2627 |
| 2/11/78 | 69 | 16 | | 2 Heaven Help The Fool | | Arista 4155 |

Billboard			R I A A	ARTIST		
DEBUG	PEAK	WKS		Album Title	Catalog	Label & Number

WEISBERG, Tim
Born on 4/26/1943 in Los Angeles, California. Jazz-pop flutist.

11/4/72	202	3		1 Hurtwood Edge .... [I]		A&M 4352
12/29/73+	160	4		2 Dreamspeaker.. [I-L]		A&M 3045
				side 1: live; side 2: studio		
11/23/74	100	13		3 Tim Weisberg 4 .... [I]		A&M 3658
10/11/75	105	7		4 Listen To The City... [I]		A&M 4545
10/2/76	148	7		5 Live At Last! .... [I-L]		A&M 4600
				recorded on 6/12/1976 at the Troubador in Hollywood, California		
8/20/77	108	12		6 The Tim Weisberg Band .... [I]		United Artists 773
5/6/78	159	6		7 Rotations .... [I]		United Artists 857
9/16/78	8	35	▲	8 Twin Sons Of Different Mothers		Full Moon 35339
				DAN FOGELBERG & TIM WEISBERG		
4/14/79	114	11		9 Night-Rider! .... [I]		MCA 3084
6/9/79	169	4		10 Smile!/The Best Of Tim Weisberg .... [G-I]		A&M 4749
8/2/80	171	7		11 Party Of One .... [I]		MCA 5125
10/17/81	205	3		12 Travelin' Light .... [I]		MCA 5245

WEISSBERG, Eric
Born on 8/18/1939 in New York. Bluegrass banjo player/multi-instrumentalist. Prolific session musician.

1/27/73	❶³	25	▲	1 Dueling Banjos .... [I]		Warner 2683
				ERIC WEISSBERG & STEVE MANDELL		
10/20/73	196	2		2 Rural Free Delivery		Warner 2720
				ERIC WEISSBERG & DELIVERANCE		

WELCH, Bob
Born on 7/31/1946 in Los Angeles, California. Pop-rock singer/guitarist. Member of **Fleetwood Mac** (1971-74) and **Paris**.

10/8/77+	12	46	▲	1 French Kiss...		Capitol 11663
3/10/79	20	17	●	2 Three Hearts		Capitol 11907
12/1/79	105	8		3 The Other One		Capitol 12017
10/11/80	162	5		4 Man Overboard		Capitol 12107
11/14/81	201	4		5 Bob Welch...		RCA Victor 4107

WELCH, Brian "Head"
Born on 6/19/1970 in Bakersfield, California. Hard-rock singer/songwriter/guitarist. Former member of **Korn**.

9/27/08	63	2		1 Save Me From Myself..		Driven 30101

WELCH, Gillian
Born on 10/2/1967 in Manhattan, New York. Eclectic female singer/songwriter/guitarist.

8/15/98	181	1		1 Hell Among The Yearlings...		Almo Sounds 80021
8/18/01	157	3		2 Time (The Revelator)		Acony 0103
6/21/03	107	3		3 Soul Journey		Acony 0305

WELCH, Lenny
Born on 5/31/1938 in Asbury Park, New Jersey. Black Adult Contemporary singer.

2/1/64	73	10		1 Since I Fell For You		Cadence 3068
1/1/66	147	2		2 Since I Fell For You .... [R]		Columbia 9230
				new cover features same photo as original with new artwork		

WELK, Lawrence, And His Orchestra   1950s: #7 / 1960s: #12 / All-Time: #31
Born on 3/11/1903 in Strasburg, North Dakota. Died of pneumonia on 5/17/1992 (age 89). Accordian player/polka bandleader since the mid-1920s. Band's style labeled as "champagne music." Hosted own TV musical variety show from 1955-82.

1/28/56	5	9		1 Lawrence Welk And His Sparkling Strings	[I]	Coral 57011
3/31/56	13	2		2 TV Favorites..		Coral 57025
3/31/56	18	2		3 Shamrocks And Champagne		Coral 57036
5/12/56	6	17		4 Bubbles In The Wine		Coral 57038
8/18/56	10	30		5 Say It With Music	[I]	Coral 57041
8/25/56	17	4		6 Champagne Pops Parade		Coral 57078
10/20/56	18	1		7 Moments To Remember	[I]	Coral 57068
3/16/57	20	1		8 Pick-A-Polka!	[I]	Coral 57067
5/20/57	17	5		9 Waltz With Lawrence Welk	[I]	Coral 57119
10/21/57+	19	2		10 Lawrence Welk Plays Dixieland	[I]	Coral 57146
12/19/60+	4	29		11 Last Date	[I]	Dot 3350
1/30/61	❶¹¹	64	●	12 Calcutta!	[I]	Dot 3359
8/7/61	2¹	49		13 Yellow Bird	[I]	Dot 3389
1/6/62	4	48		14 Moon River	[I]	Dot 3412
5/26/62	6	20		15 Young World	[I]	Dot 3428

			WELK, Lawrence, And His Orchestra — cont'd		
9/15/62	9	15	16 Baby Elephant Walk And Theme From The Brothers Grimm	[I]	Dot 3457
3/9/63	34	25	17 Waltz Time	[I]	Dot 25499
4/6/63	20	28	18 1963's Early Hits	[I]	Dot 25510
8/10/63	33	28	19 Scarlett O'Hara	[I]	Dot 25528
12/7/63+	29	26	20 Wonderful! Wonderful!	[I]	Dot 25552
4/11/64	37	19	21 Early Hits Of 1964	[I]	Dot 25572
4/25/64	127	5	22 A Tribute To The All-Time Greats	[I]	Dot 25544
8/8/64	73	16	23 The Lawrence Welk Television Show 10th Anniversary		Dot 25591
1/9/65	115	6	24 The Golden Millions		Dot 25611
4/3/65	108	12	25 My First Of 1965	[I]	Dot 25616
4/17/65	57	12	26 Apples & Bananas	[I]	Dot 25629
1/29/66	93	6	27 Today's Great Hits	[I]	Dot 25663
3/26/66	106	5	28 Champagne On Broadway	[I]	Dot 25688
12/3/66+	12	41	● 29 Winchester Cathedral	[I]	Dot 25774
4/15/67	72	18	30 Lawrence Welk's "Hits Of Our Time"	[I]	Dot 25790
10/14/67	130	12	31 Golden Hits/The Best Of Lawrence Welk	[G-I]	Dot 25812
4/6/68	130	12	32 Love Is Blue	[I]	Ranwood 8003
2/8/69	173	8	33 Memories	[I]	Ranwood 8044
4/19/69	55	20	34 Galveston	[I]	Ranwood 8049
9/13/69	176	4	35 Lawrence Welk Plays I Love You Truly And Other Songs Of Love	[I]	Ranwood 8053
11/15/69	145	7	36 Jean	[I]	Ranwood 8060
12/12/70+	133	17	37 Candida		Ranwood 8083
5/8/71	219	3	38 No, No, Nanette		Ranwood 8087
2/5/72	202	2	39 Go Away Little Girl		Ranwood 8091
12/23/72+	149	10	40 Reminiscing	[I-K]	Ranwood 5001 [2]
			CHRISTMAS ALBUMS:		
12/22/56	8	3	41 Merry Christmas From Lawrence Welk And His Champagne Music		Coral 57093
12/23/57	18	3	42 Jingle Bells		Coral 57186
1/6/62	100	3	43 Silent Night And 13 Other Best Loved Christmas Songs	[I]	Dot 25397
			Christmas charts: 13/'63, 61/'66, 61/'67		
12/29/62	140	1	44 Silent Night And 13 Other Best Loved Christmas Songs	[I-R]	Dot 25397
			WELLER, Freddy		
			Born on 9/9/1947 in Atlanta, Georgia. Pop-country singer/guitarist. Member of **Paul Revere & The Raiders** (1967-71).		
8/16/69	144	7	1 Games People Play / These Are Not My People		Columbia 9904
			WELLES, Orson		
			Born on 5/6/1915 in Kenosha, Wisconsin. Died of a heart attack on 10/10/1985 (age 70). Legendary movie actor/writer/director.		
8/22/70	66	16	1 The Begatting Of The President	[C]	Mediarts 41-2
			WELLS, Brandi		
			Born in 1955 in Philadelphia, Pennsylvania. Died of cancer on 3/25/2003 (age 48). R&B singer.		
3/20/82	202	7	1 Watch Out		WMOT 37668
			WELLS, Cory		
			Born on 2/5/1942 in Buffalo, New York. Member of **Three Dog Night**.		
3/4/78	210	1	1 Touch Me		A&M 4673
			WELLS, Junior		
			Born Amos Blackmore on 12/9/1934 in Memphis, Tennessee. Died on 1/15/1998 (age 63). Blues singer/harmonica player.		
			~ ~ ~ ~ ~ ~ ~ ~ ~ ~ **NON-CHARTED ALBUM** ~ ~ ~ ~ ~ ~ ~ ~ ~ ~		
			1966 Hoodoo Man Blues		
			Grammy: Blues Album		
			WELLS, Mary		
			Born on 5/13/1943 in Detroit, Michigan. Died of cancer on 7/26/1992 (age 49). R&B singer.		
3/16/63	49	8	1 Two Lovers And Other Great Hits		Motown 607
5/16/64	42	16	2 Together		Motown 613
			MARVIN GAYE & MARY WELLS		
5/30/64	18	37	3 Greatest Hits	[G]	Motown 616
7/25/64	111	12	4 Mary Wells Sings My Guy		Motown 617
5/1/65	145	4	5 Mary Wells		20th Century Fox 4171
			~ ~ ~ ~ ~ ~ ~ ~ ~ ~ **NON-CHARTED ALBUMS** ~ ~ ~ ~ ~ ~ ~ ~ ~		
			1961 Bye Bye Bye/I Don't Want To Take A Chance	1965 Love Songs To The Beatles	
			1962 The One Who Really Loves You	1966 The Two Sides Of Mary Wells	
			1963 Recorded Live On Stage		
			WENDY AND LISA		
			Pop duo from Los Angeles, California: Wendy Melvoin (born on 1/26/1964) and Lisa Coleman (born on 6/8/1960). Formerly with **Prince**'s band, The Revolution. Wendy is the daughter of Michael Melvoin (**The Plastic Cow**).		
9/19/87	88	13	1 Wendy And Lisa		Columbia 40862
4/8/89	119	8	2 Fruit At The Bottom		Columbia 44341

WERNER, David
Born in Pittsburgh, Pennsylvania. Rock singer/guitarist.

| 4/6/74 | 207 | 5 | | 1 Whizz Kid .... | | RCA Victor 0350 |
| 9/1/79 | 65 | 11 | | 2 David Werner .... | | Epic 36126 |

WERTZ, Matt
Born on 2/17/1979 in Kansas City, Missouri. Singer/songwriter/guitarist.

| 10/4/08 | 127 | 1 | | 1 Under Summer Sun.. | | Hand Written 011629 |

WESLEY, Fred, & The Horny Horns
Born on 7/4/1943 in Mobile, Alabama. Funk trombonist. Member of **James Brown**'s band. Also see **The JB's**.

| 4/30/77 | 181 | 5 | | 1 A Blow For Me, A Toot To You.............................. | | Atlantic 18214 |

WEST, Dottie
Born Dorothy Marsh on 10/11/1932 in McMinnville, Tennessee. Died in a car crash on 9/4/1991 (age 58). Country singer.
AWARDS: CMA: Vocal Duo (w/ Kenny Rogers) 1978 & 1979 ★ OPRY: 1964

4/14/79	82	23	▲	1 Classics...		United Artists 946
1/5/80	186	3	●	2 Every Time Two Fools Collide		United Artists 864
				KENNY ROGERS & DOTTIE WEST (above 2)		
4/11/81	126	15		3 Wild West		Liberty 1062

WEST, Kanye
Born on 6/8/1977 in Atlanta, Georgia; raised in Chicago, Illinois. Male rapper/songwriter/producer.

2/28/04	2[3]	74	▲[2]	1 The College Dropout	Cat:#3/2	Roc-A-Fella 002030
9/17/05	❶[2]	37	▲[3]	2 Late Registration	Cat:#6/1	Roc-A-Fella 004813
				Grammy: Rap Album		
9/29/07	❶[1]	52	▲[2]	3 Graduation		Roc-A-Fella 009541
				Grammy: Rap Album		
12/13/08	❶[1]	39	▲	4 808s & Heartbreak		Roc-A-Fella 012198

WEST, Leslie
Born Leslie Weinstein on 10/22/1945 in New York. Male rock singer/guitarist. Founder of **Mountain** and **West, Bruce & Laing**.

9/6/69	72	14		1 Mountain		Windfall 4500
4/19/75	168	6		2 The Great Fatsby		Phantom 0954
11/29/75	203	2		3 The Leslie West Band		Phantom 1258

WEST, Mae
Born Mary Jane West on 8/17/1893 in Brooklyn, New York. Died of a stroke on 11/22/1980 (age 87). Legendary movie actress.

| 7/23/66 | 116 | 5 | | 1 Way Out West .... | | Tower 5028 |
| | | | | backing band (and pictured on album cover): **Gary Lewis And The Playboys** | | |

WEST, Matthew
Born on 4/25/1977 in Downer's Grove, Illinois. Contemporary Christian singer/songwriter/guitarist.

| 2/2/08+ | 95 | 6 | | 1 Something To Say .... | | Sparrow 84520 |

WEST, BRUCE & LAING
All-star rock trio: **Leslie West** (vocals, guitar), **Jack Bruce** (bass) and Corky Laing (drums). West and Laing were with **Mountain**. Bruce was with **Cream**.

11/4/72+	26	20		1 Why Dontcha		Windfall 31929
7/28/73	87	10		2 Whatever Turns You On		Windfall 32216
5/11/74	165	6		3 Live 'N' Kickin' .... [L]		Windfall 33899

WEST COAST BAD BOYZ
Gathering of various rap artists from California.

8/9/97	33[C]	2		1 West Coast Bad Boyz I		No Limit 50695
2/15/97	8	16		2 West Coast Bad Boyz II		No Limit 50658
4/6/02	108	1		3 Poppin' Collars		New No Limit 860975

WEST COAST RAP ALL-STARS, The
All-star rap group: **Above The Law**, **Digital Underground**, **Eazy-E**, **Ice-T**, **J.J. Fad**, **King Tee**, **M.C. Hammer**, **Michel'le**, **N.W.A.**, **Oaktown's 3-5-7**, **Tone Loc** and **Young MC**.

| 7/7/90 | 60 | 12 | | 1 We're All In The Same Gang............................ [V] | | Warner 26241 |

WESTENRA, Hayley
Born on 4/10/1987 in Christchurch, New Zealand. Female classical singer.

| 5/1/04 | 70 | 6 | | 1 Pure .... | | Decca 001866 |
| 3/31/07 | 184 | 1 | | 2 Celtic Treasure .... | | Decca 008560 |

WESTERBERG, Paul
Born on 12/31/1960 in Minneapolis, Minnesota. Rock singer/guitarist. Member of **The Replacements**.

7/3/93	44	10		1 14 Songs		Sire 45255
5/18/96	50	5		2 Eventually		Reprise 46176
3/13/99	104	1		3 Suicaine Gratifaction		Capitol 59004
5/11/02	81	2		4 Stereo		Vagrant 369 [2]
11/8/03	176	1		5 Come Feel Me Tremble		Vagrant 387
9/25/04	178	1		6 Folker		Vagrant 0401

Billboard DEBUT	PEAK	WKS	R I A A	ARTIST / Album Title	Catalog	Label & Number

WESTLIFE
"Boy band" from Dublin, Ireland: Nicky Byrne, Shane Filan, Kian Egan, Mark Feehily and Bryan McFadden.

| 5/6/00 | 129 | 17 | | 1 Westlife .... | | Arista 14642 |

WESTON, Kim
Born Agatha Weston on 12/30/1939 in Detroit, Michigan. R&B singer.

| 9/11/71 | 208 | 1 | | 1 Kim Kim Kim .... | | Volt 6014 |

WESTON, Paul
Born Paul Wetstein on 3/12/1912 in Springfield, Massachusetts. Died on 9/20/1996 (age 84). Conductor/arranger. Married to **Jo Stafford** from 1952-96.

| 10/29/55 | 15 | 1 | | 1 Mood For 12 .... [I] | | Columbia 693 |
| 9/1/56 | 12 | 5 | | 2 Solo Mood .... [I] | | Columbia 879 |

WESTSIDE CONNECTION
All-star rap trio: **Ice Cube**, **Mack 10** and **WC**.

| 11/9/96 | 2[1] | 45 | ▲ | 1 Bow Down | | Priority 50583 |
| 12/27/03 | 16 | 20 | ● | 2 Terrorist Threats .... | | Hoo-Bangin' 24030 |

WESTWIND ENSEMBLE, The
Studio group from California.

| 12/28/96+ | 82 | 3 | | 1 A Christmas Tribute To Mannheim Steamroller........................... Cat:#26/6 [X-I] | | Brentwood 353 |
| | | | | Christmas charts: 12/'96, 17/'97 | | |

WE THE KINGS
Pop-rock band from Bradenton, Florida: brothers Hunter Thomsen (guitar) and Drew Thomsen (bass), with Travis Clark (vocals) and Danny Duncan (drums).

| 2/23/08 | 151 | 15 | | 1 We The Kings .... | | S-Curve 52001 |
| 12/26/09 | 112 | 3 | | 2 Smile Kid .... | | S-Curve 52006 |

WET WET WET
Pop-rock band from Glasgow, Scotland: Marti Pellow (vocals), Neil Mitchell (keyboards), Graeme Clark (bass) and Tom Cunningham (drums).

| 7/16/88 | 123 | 7 | | 1 Popped In Souled Out... | | Uni 5000 |

WET WILLIE
Southern-rock band from Mobile, Alabama: brothers **Jimmy Hall** (vocals) and Jack Hall (bass), with Rick Hirsch (guitar), John Anthony (keyboards) and Lewis Ross (drums). Michael Duke (keyboards, vocals) joined in late 1975.

5/12/73	189	4		1 Drippin' Wet!/Live .... [L]		Capricorn 0113
				recorded on 12/31/1972 at the Warehouse in New Orleans, Louisiana		
6/1/74	41	24		2 Keep On Smilin'		Capricorn 0128
3/8/75	114	7		3 Dixie Rock		Capricorn 0149
4/3/76	133	7		4 The Wetter The Better		Capricorn 0166
6/4/77	191	2		5 Left Coast Live .... [L]		Capricorn 0182
				recorded at the Roxy in Hollywood, California		
1/21/78	118	8		6 Manorisms		Epic 34983
3/18/78	158	6		7 Greatest Hits .... [G]		Capricorn 0200
6/9/79	172	11		8 Which One's Willie?		Epic 35794

WHA-KOO
Pop-rock band from Los Angeles, California: David Palmer (vocals), Danny Douma (guitar), Nick van Maarth (guitar), Richard Kosinski (keyboards), Don Francisco (percussion), Peter Freiberger (bass) and Claude Pepper (drums).

| 3/4/78 | 202 | 10 | | 1 Berkshire... | | ABC 1043 |

WHALUM, Kirk
Born on 7/11/1958 in Memphis, Tennessee. Jazz saxophonist.

| 3/19/88 | 142 | 10 | | 1 And You Know That! .... [I] | | Columbia 40812 |

WHAM!
Pop duo formed in England: **George Michael** and Andrew Ridgeley. First recorded as **Wham! U.K.**

8/20/83	83	44	●	1 Fantastic		Columbia 38911
				WHAM! U.K.		
11/10/84+	❶[3]	80	▲6	2 Make It Big		Columbia 39595
7/19/86	10	28	▲	3 Music From The Edge Of Heaven		Columbia 40285

WHAT IS THIS
Rock trio formed in Los Angeles, California: Alain Johannes (vocals, guitar), Chris Hutchinson (bass) and Jack Irons (drums; **Red Hot Chili Peppers**, **Pearl Jam**).

| 9/14/85 | 187 | 4 | | 1 What Is This .... | | MCA 5598 |
| | | | | produced by **Todd Rundgren** | | |

WHEATUS
Rock band from Long Island, New York: brothers Brendan Brown (vocals, guitar) and Peter Brown (drums), with Phil Jimenez (guitar) and Rich Leigey (bass).

| 9/2/00 | 76 | 9 | | 1 Wheatus .... | | Columbia 62146 |

WHEELER, Billy Edd
Born on 12/9/1932 in Whitesville, West Virginia. Folk singer/songwriter.

| 2/13/65 | 132 | 3 | | 1 Memories Of America / Ode To The Little Brown Shack Out Back .... | | Kapp 3425 |

WHEELER, Caron
Born on 1/19/1963 in London, England (of Jamaican parents). Female R&B singer. Featured vocalist with **Soul II Soul**.

10/27/90	133	7		1 UK Blak	EMI 93497

WHEN IN ROME
Electro-dance trio from England: Clive Farrington and Andrew Mann (vocals), with Michael Floreale (keyboards).

10/15/88+	84	24		1 When In Rome	Virgin 90994

WHISKEY FALLS
Country band formed in Nashville, Tennessee: Seven Williams (vocals), Damon Johnson (guitar, vocals), Wally Brandt (guitar) and Buck Johnson (keyboards). Damon Johnson was the lead singer of the rock band **Brother Cane**.

10/13/07	171	1		1 Whiskey Falls	Midas 90184

WHISKEYTOWN
Rock duo from Jacksonville, North Carolina: **Ryan Adams** (male vocals, guitar) and Caitlin Cary (female vocals, fiddle).

6/9/01	158	1		1 Pneumonia	Lost Highway 170199
3/22/08	40[C]	1		2 Strangers Almanac	Mood Food 009410 [2]

WHISPERS, The — All-Time: #363
R&B-dance vocal group from Los Angeles, California: twin brothers Walter and Wallace Scott, with Leaveil Degree, Marcus Hutson and Nicholas Caldwell. The Scotts also recorded as **Walter & Scotty**.

5/13/72	186	2		1 The Whispers' Love Story	Janus 3041
8/28/76	189	6		2 One For The Money	Soul Train 1450
7/16/77	65	10		3 Open Up Your Love	Soul Train 2270
5/27/78	77	28		4 Headlights	Solar 2774
4/14/79	146	9		5 Whisper In Your Ear	Solar 3105
12/8/79+	201	5		6 Happy Holidays To You .... [X]	Solar 3489
				Christmas charts: 18/'87, 19/'88	
1/5/80	6	35	▲	7 The Whispers	Solar 3521
1/17/81	23	27	●	8 Imagination	Solar 3578
10/3/81	100	9		9 This Kind Of Lovin'	Solar 3976
1/23/82	35	25	●	10 Love Is Where You Find It	Solar 27
3/13/82	180	5		11 The Best Of The Whispers .... [G]	Solar 4242
4/2/83	37	29		12 Love For Love	Solar 60216
12/1/84+	88	26		13 So Good	Solar 60356
5/30/87	22	37	▲	14 Just Gets Better With Time	Solar 72554
8/18/90	83	24	●	15 More Of The Night	Capitol 92957
4/8/95	92	8		16 Toast To The Ladies	Capitol 30270
11/7/09	172	1		17 Thankful	Kingdom 11081

WHITCOMB, Ian
Born on 7/10/1941 in Woking, Surrey, England. Pop singer/songwriter/author.

7/10/65	125	13		1 You Turn Me On!	Tower 5004

WHITE, Alan
Born on 6/14/1949 in Pelton, County Durham, England. Rock drummer. Member of **Yes**.

6/26/76	209	1		1 Ramshackled	Atlantic 18167

WHITE, Barry — All-Time: #167
Born on 9/12/1944 in Galveston, Texas; raised in Los Angeles, California. Died of kidney failure on 7/4/2003 (age 58). R&B singer/songwriter/keyboardist. Formed **Love Unlimited** in 1969, which included future wife Glodean James (married in 1974). Leader of 40-piece **Love Unlimited Orchestra**. Known for his deep voice and romantic subject matter.

4/21/73	16	63	●	1 I've Got So Much To Give	20th Century 407
11/17/73+	20	37	●	2 Stone Gon'	20th Century 423
9/7/74	❶[1]	38	●	3 Can't Get Enough	20th Century 444
				RS500 #281	
4/12/75	17	17	●	4 Just Another Way To Say I Love You	20th Century 466
2/14/76	42	15		5 Let The Music Play	20th Century 502
11/27/76	125	9		6 Is This Whatcha Wont?	20th Century 516
9/17/77	8	33	▲	7 Barry White Sings For Someone You Love	20th Century 543
10/28/78	36	28	▲	8 Barry White The Man	20th Century 571
8/18/79	132	6		9 I Love To Sing The Songs I Sing	20th Century 590
4/28/79	67	9	●	10 The Message Is Love	Unlimited Gold 35763
7/26/80	85	11		11 Barry White's Sheet Music	Unlimited Gold 36208
4/18/81	201	3		12 Barry & Glodean	Unlimited Gold 37054
				BARRY WHITE & GLODEAN WHITE	
10/3/81	207	2		13 Beware!	Unlimited Gold 37176
10/2/82	148	6		14 Change	Unlimited Gold 38048
11/21/87	159	17		15 The Right Night & Barry White	A&M 5154

			R I A A	ARTIST		
DEBUT	PEAK	WKS		Album Title	Catalog	Label & Number
				WHITE, Barry — cont'd		
5/19/90	143	12		16 The Man Is Back!		A&M 5256
11/2/91	96	10		17 Put Me In Your Mix		A&M 5377
10/22/94	20	46	▲²	18 The Icon Is Love		A&M 540115
8/14/99	43	19		19 Staying Power		Private Music 82185
				Grammy: Traditional R&B Album		
				GREATEST HITS & COMPILATIONS:		
11/15/75	23	25	▲	20 Barry White's Greatest Hits	Cat:#2¹/57	20th Century 493
2/6/99	2⁴ᶜ	107	▲²	21 All-Time Greatest Hits		Mercury 522459
				first released in 1995		
5/13/00	148	4	▲	22 The Ultimate Collection	Cat:#25/3	UTV 542291 [2]
9/6/03	100	5		23 The Best Of Barry White: 20th Century Masters The Millennium Collection		Island 000884
				WHITE, Brooke		
				Born on 6/2/1983 in Phoenix, Arizona. Female singer/songwriter.		
8/1/09	50	2		1 High Hopes & Heartbreak		June Baby 90162
				WHITE, Bryan		
				Born on 2/17/1974 in Lawton, Oklahoma; raised in Oklahoma City. Country singer/songwriter/guitarist. Married actress Erika Page on 10/14/2000.		
				AWARD: CMA: Horizon 1996		
8/19/95+	88	42	▲	1 Bryan White		Asylum 61642
4/13/96	52	63	▲	2 Between Now And Forever		Asylum 61880
10/11/97	41	23	●	3 The Right Place		Asylum 62047
9/11/99	81	3		4 How Lucky I Am		Asylum 62278
				WHITE, Karyn		
				Born on 10/14/1965 in Los Angeles, California. R&B-dance singer. Married to producer Terry Lewis (of **The Time**).		
10/15/88+	19	54	▲	1 Karyn White		Warner 25637
9/28/91	53	24	●	2 Ritual Of Love		Warner 26320
10/15/94	99	7		3 Make Him Do Right		Warner 45400
				WHITE, Lari		
				Born on 5/13/1965 in Dunedin, Florida. Country singer.		
1/21/95	125	19	●	1 Wishes		RCA 66395
				WHITE, Lenny		
				Born on 12/19/1949 in Harlem, New York. R&B drummer. Member of **Return To Forever** and **Twennynine**.		
1/31/76	177	3		1 Venusian Summer	[I]	Nemperor 435
3/19/77	203	6		2 Big City	[I]	Nemperor 441
1/27/79	205	2		3 Streamline	[I]	Elektra 164
				WHITE, Maurice		
				Born on 12/19/1941 in Memphis, Tennessee; raised in Chicago, Illinois. R&B singer/songwriter/producer. Percussionist for **Ramsey Lewis** from 1966-71. Founder and co-lead vocalist of **Earth, Wind & Fire**.		
10/5/85	61	19		1 Maurice White		Columbia 39883
				WHITE, Peter		
				Born on 9/20/1954 in Luton, England. Smooth jazz guitarist.		
10/20/07	19ˣ	1		1 Peter White Christmas	[X]	ARTizen 10017
				WHITE, Ron		
				Born on 12/18/1956 in Fritch, Texas. "Redneck" stand-up comedian. Nicknamed "Tater Salad." Also see **Blue Collar Comedy Tour**.		
3/27/04	83	24	●	1 Drunk In Public	[C]	Hip-O 001582
2/25/06	14	11		2 You Can't Fix Stupid	[C]	Image 3061
5/9/09	51	4		3 Behavioral Problems	[C]	Capitol 98425
				WHITE, Tony Joe		
				Born on 7/23/1943 in Goodwill, Louisiana. Bayou-rock singer/songwriter.		
7/26/69	51	16		1 Black And White		Monument 18114
11/22/69	183	3		2 ...Continued		Monument 18133
3/6/71	167	4		3 Tony Joe White		Warner 1900
				WHITECHAPEL		
				Deathcore band from Knoxville, Tennessee: Phil Bozeman (vocals), Ben Savage (guitar), Alex Wade (guitar), Gabe Crisp (bass) and Kevin Lane (drums).		
7/26/08	118	2		1 This Is Exile		Metal Blade 14681
				WHITE LIES		
				Alternative-rock band from London, England: Harry McVeigh (vocals, guitar), Charles Cave (guitar), Jack Lawrence-Brown (bass) and Tommy Bowen (drums).		
4/4/09	146	1		1 To Lose My Life...		Fiction 012590
				WHITE LIGHTNIN'		
				Blues-rock trio from Memphis, Tennessee: brothers Donald Kinsey (vocals, guitar) and Ralph "Woody" Kinsey (drums), with Michael "Busta Cherry" Jones (bass; died on 12/6/1995, age 44).		
8/23/75	205	6		1 White Lightnin'		Island 9325

WHITE LION
Hair-metal band formed in Brooklyn, New York: Mike Tramp (vocals), Vito Bratta (guitar), James Lomenzo (bass) and Greg D'Angelo (drums). Lomenzo and D'Angelo left in 1991; replaced by Tommy Caradonna and Jimmy DeGrasso (of **Y&T**).

9/26/87+	11	86	▲² 1 Pride		Atlantic 81768
4/16/88	151	14	2 Fight To Survive .... [E]		Grand Slam 1
7/1/89	19	27	● 3 Big Game		Atlantic 81969
4/27/91	61	13	4 Mane Attraction		Atlantic 82193

WHITEMAN, Paul
Born on 3/28/1890 in Denver, Colorado. Died of a heart attack on 12/29/1967 (age 77). Legendary orchestra leader.

1/19/57	20	1	1 Paul Whiteman/50th Anniversary		Grand Award 901 [2]

WHITE PLAINS
Studio group from England. Featuring Tony Burrows (vocals), who was also with **The Brotherhood Of Man**, Edison Lighthouse, First Class and **The Pipkins**.

8/22/70	166	4	1 My Baby Loves Lovin'		Deram 18045

WHITE RABBITS
Punk-rock band from Brooklyn, New York: Greg Roberts (vocals, guitar), Alex Even (guitar), Stephen Patterson (keyboards), Brian Betancourt (bass) and Matthew Clark (drums).

6/6/09	184	1	1 It's Frightening		TBD 0006

WHITESNAKE
Former **Deep Purple** vocalist David **Coverdale**, who recorded solo as Whitesnake in 1977, formed British hard-rock band in 1978. Coverdale fronted everchanging lineup. Early members included his Deep Purple bandmates: keyboardist Jon Lord (1978-84) and drummer Ian Paice (1979-81). Players in 1987 included John Sykes (guitar), Neil Murray (bass) and Aynsley Dunbar (former **Jefferson Starship** drummer). Sykes left in 1988 to form **Blue Murder**. Ex-**Dio** guitarist Vivian Campbell was a member from 1987-88, later with Riverdogs, Shadow King and **Def Leppard**. Lineup in 1989 included guitarists **Steve Vai** (**David Lee Roth**'s band) and Adrian **Vandenberg**, Rudy Sarzo (bass) and Tommy Aldridge (drums). Lineup in 1994: Coverdale, Vandenberg, Sarzo, and Warren De Martini (guitar; **Ratt**), Paul Mirkovich (keyboards) and Denny Carmassi (drums; **Heart**). Coverdale was married to actress Tawny Kitaen from 1989-92.

8/16/80	90	16	1 Ready An' Willing		Mirage 19276
12/27/80+	146	12	2 Live....In The Heart Of The City .... [L]		Mirage 19292
			recorded at the Hammersmith Odeon in London, England		
5/30/81	151	6	3 Come An' Get It		Mirage 16043
5/19/84	40	85	▲² 4 Slide It In .... Cat:#4/70		Geffen 4018
4/18/87	2¹⁰	76	▲⁸ 5 Whitesnake		Geffen 24099
11/25/89	10	34	▲ 6 Slip Of The Tongue		Geffen 24249
8/6/94	161	2	▲ 7 Whitesnake's Greatest Hits .... [G]		Geffen 24620
5/10/08	62	3	8 Good To Be Bad		Steamhammer 9813

WHITE STRIPES, The
Alternative-rock duo from Detroit, Michigan: Jack White (vocals, guitar; born John Gillis) and Meg White (drums). Married from 1996-2000. Jack played "Georgia" in the movie *Cold Mountain*. White is also a member of **The Raconteurs** and **The Dead Weather**.

3/23/02	61	52	● 1 White Blood Cells .... Cat:#30/8		Third Man 27124
4/19/03	6	57	▲ 2 Elephant		Third Man 27148
			Grammy: Alternative Album ★ RS500 #390		
6/25/05	3¹	33	3 Get Behind Me Satan		Third Man 27256
			Grammy: Alternative Album		
7/7/07	2¹	32	● 4 Icky Thump		Third Man 162940
			Grammy: Alternative Album		

WHITE TIE AFFAIR, The
Electronica band from Chicago, Illinois: Chris Wallace (vocals), Sean Patwell (guitar), Ryan McClain (keyboards) and Tim McLaughlin (drums).

10/4/08	168	2	1 Walk This Way		Slightly Dangerous 08833

WHITE TOWN
Born Jyoti Mishra on 7/30/1966 in Rourkela, India; raised in England. Male synth-pop singer/multi-instrumentalist.

3/15/97	84	20	1 Women In Technology		Chrysalis 56129

WHITE TRASH
Hard-rock band from New York: Dave Alvin (vocals), Ethan Collins (guitar), Aaron Collins (bass) and Mike Caldarella (drums).

9/21/91	122	7	1 White Trash		Elektra 61053

WHITE WOLF
Hard-rock band from Canada: Don Wilk (vocals), Cam MacLeod (guitar), Rick Nelson (guitar), Les Schwartz (bass) and Loris Bolzon (drums).

2/16/85	162	6	1 Standing Alone		RCA Victor 8042
6/21/86	137	8	2 Endangered Species		RCA Victor 9555

WHITE ZOMBIE
Hard-rock band formed in New York: **Rob Zombie** (vocals), Jay Yuenger (guitar), Sean Yseult (bass) and John Tempesta (drums). Group named after the 1932 Bela Lugosi movie.

7/17/93	26	44	▲² 1 La Sexorcisto: Devil Music Volume One .... Cat:#23/27		Geffen 24460
4/29/95	6	88	▲² 2 Astro-Creep: 2000-Songs Of Love, Destruction And Other Synthetic Delusions Of The Electric Head Cat:#39/7		Geffen 24806
8/31/96	17	19	● 3 Supersexy Swingin' Sounds .... [K]		Geffen 24976
			remixes of songs from #2 above		

Billboard			R I A A	ARTIST Album Title	Catalog	Label & Number
DEBUT	PEAK	WKS				

WHITFIELD, Robert "Goodie"
Born in Dallas, Texas. R&B singer/keyboardist.

| 10/2/82 | 207 | 2 | | 1 Call Me Goodie .... | | Total Experience 3002 |

WHITFORD/ST. HOLMES
Rock duo. Brad Whitford was born on 2/23/52 in Winchester, Massachusetts. Guitarist for **Aerosmith**. Derek St. Holmes was singer/guitarist for **Ted Nugent's** band.

| 9/26/81 | 208 | 2 | | 1 Whitford/St. Holmes .... | | Columbia 37365 |

WHITING, Margaret
Born on 7/22/1924 in Detroit, Michigan; raised in Hollywood, California. Pop singer.

| 2/18/67 | 109 | 8 | | 1 The Wheel Of Hurt .... | | London 497 |

WHITLEY, Keith
Born Jesse Keith Whitley on 7/1/1955 in Sandy Hook, Kentucky. Died of alcohol poisoning on 5/9/1989 (age 33). Country singer/songwriter/guitarist. Married to **Lorrie Morgan** from 1986-89 (his death). Also see **Various Artists Compilations:** *Keith Whitley - A Tribute Album.*

6/3/89	121	14	●	1 Don't Close Your Eyes		RCA 6494
9/2/89	115	7	●	2 I Wonder Do You Think Of Me		RCA 9809
9/1/90	67	45	▲	3 Greatest Hits	[G]	RCA 2277

WHITLOCK, Bobby
Born on 3/18/1948 in Memphis, Tennesee. Rock keyboardist. Member of **Delaney & Bonnie** and **Derek And The Dominos**.

| 4/1/72 | 140 | 10 | | 1 Bobby Whitlock .... | | Dunhill/ABC 50121 |
| 11/4/72 | 190 | 3 | | 2 Raw Velvet .... | | Dunhill/ABC 50131 |

WHITMAN, Slim
Born Otis Whitman on 1/20/1924 in Tampa, Florida. Country yodeller/guitarist.

10/25/80	175	3		1 Songs I Love To Sing		Cleveland Int'l. 36768
12/13/80	184	4		2 Christmas With Slim Whitman	[X]	Cleveland Int'l. 36847
8/29/81	206	3		3 Mr. Songman		Cleveland Int. 37403

WHITTAKER, Roger
Born on 3/22/1936 in Nairobi, Kenya, Africa (of British parents). Adult Contemporary singer.

5/3/75	31	24	●	1 The Last Farewell And Other Hits		RCA Victor 0855
4/24/76	202	8		2 Roger Whittaker		RCA Victor 1313
5/5/79	115	5		3 When I Need You		RCA Victor 3355
12/8/79+	157	10		4 Mirrors Of My Mind		RCA Victor 3501
2/9/80	154	12		5 Voyager		RCA Victor 3518
11/29/80	175	2		6 With Love		RCA Victor 3778
6/13/81	177	3		7 Live In Concert	[L]	RCA Victor 4057 [2]
10/24/81	210	2		8 Changes		RCA Victor 4129

WHO, The   **1970s: #12 / All-Time: #62**
Rock band formed in London, England: **Roger Daltrey** (vocals; born on 3/1/1944), **Pete Townshend** (guitar, vocals; born on 5/19/1945), **John Entwistle** (bass; born on 10/9/1944; died of a heart attack on 6/27/2002, age 57) and **Keith Moon** (drums; born on 8/23/1946; died of a drug overdose on 9/7/1978, age 32). Group starred in the movies *Tommy*, *Quadrophenia* and *The Kids Are Alright*. Kenney Jones (formerly with **Small Faces**) replaced Moon after his death. Eleven fans trampled to death at group's concert in Cincinnati on 12/3/1979. Disbanded in 1982. Regrouped at "Live Aid" in 1986. Daltrey, Townshend and Entwistle reunited with an ensemble of 15 for a U.S. tour in 1989. Jones formed **The Law** with **Paul Rodgers** in 1991.
AWARDS: Grammy: Lifetime Achievement 2001 ★ R&R Hall of Fame: 1990

5/20/67	67	22		1 Happy Jack		Decca 74892
				RS500 #383		
1/6/68	48	23		2 The Who Sell Out		Decca 74950
				RS500 #113		
10/26/68	39	10		3 Magic Bus-The Who On Tour		Decca 75064
6/7/69+	4	126	▲²	4 Tommy		Decca 7205 [2]
				Grammy: Hall of Fame ★ RS500 #96		
8/14/71	4	41	▲³	5 Who's Next	Cat:❶¹⁶/271	Decca 79182
				RS500 #28		
11/10/73	2¹	40	▲	6 Quadrophenia		MCA 10004
				RS500 #266		
10/25/75	8	25	▲	7 The Who By Numbers		MCA 2161
9/9/78	2²	30	▲²	8 Who Are You	Cat:❶⁴/252	MCA 3050
4/4/81	4	20	▲	9 Face Dances		Warner 3516
9/25/82	8	32	●	10 It's Hard		Warner 23731
11/18/06	7	8		11 Endless Wire		Universal Rep. 007846
				GREATEST HITS & COMPILATIONS:		
11/20/71	11	21	▲	12 Meaty Beaty Big And Bouncy	Cat:❶²/91	Decca 79184
10/26/74	15	15	●	13 Odds & Sods	Cat:#17/32	Track 2126
				previously unreleased recordings from 1964-72		
10/17/81	52	19	●	14 Hooligans		MCA 12001 [2]
5/21/83	94	13	▲²	15 Who's Greatest Hits	Cat:#17/97	MCA 5408

WHO, The — cont'd

12/28/85+	116	8		16 Who's Missing		MCA 5641
				contains rare B-sides and previously unreleased selections from 1965-72		
7/23/94	170	1	●	17 Thirty Years Of Maximum R&B		MCA 11020 [4]
6/29/02	31	11	▲	18 The Ultimate Collection		UTV 112877 [2]
4/17/04	57	7		19 The Who Then And Now!: 1964-2004		Geffen 001836

LIVE ALBUMS:

5/30/70	4	44	▲²	20 Live At Leeds ...	Cat:#2³/210	Decca 79175
				RS500 #170		
12/1/84+	81	14		21 Who's Last		MCA 8018 [2]
4/14/90	188	2		22 Join Together		MCA 19501 [2]
11/16/96	194	1		23 Live At The Isle Of Wight Festival 1970		Columbia 65084 [2]
3/4/00	101	3		24 BBC Sessions		MCA 111960
				recorded from 1965-73		

REISSUES:

12/21/74	185	4		25 Magic Bus-The Who On Tour / The Who Sings My Generation		Track 4068 [2]
9/14/02	30ᶜ	1		26 The Who Sings My Generation: Deluxe Edition		MCA 112926 [2]

SOUNDTRACKS:

6/30/79	8	25	▲	27 The Kids Are Alright	[L]	MCA 11005 [2]
10/13/79	46	16		28 Quadrophenia		Polydor 6235 [2]

~ ~ ~ ~ ~ ~ ~ ~ ~ ~ **NON-CHARTED ALBUM** ~ ~ ~ ~ ~ ~ ~ ~ ~ ~
1965 **The Who Sings My Generation**
RS500 #236 ★ NRR

WHODINI
Rap trio from Brooklyn, New York: Jalil "Whodini" Hutchins, John "Ecstacy" Fletcher and Drew "Grandmaster Dee" Carter.

11/24/84+	35	48	▲	1 Escape		Jive 8251
5/17/86	35	39	●	2 Back In Black		Jive 8407
10/17/87	30	22	●	3 Open Sesame		Jive 8494

WICHITA TRAIN WHISTLE, The
A gathering of the top session players in Los Angeles, California.

8/3/68	144	7		1 Mike Nesmith Presents/The Wichita Train Whistle Sings	[I]	Dot 25861

produced by **Mike Nesmith** (of **The Monkees**)

WICKHAM, Phil
Born on 4/5/1984 in San Diego, California. Contemporary Christian singer/songwriter/guitarist.

5/13/06	149	1		1 Phil Wickham		Simple 80644
12/5/09	55	1		2 Heaven & Earth		Ino 84689

WICKS, Chuck
Born on 6/20/1979 in Smyrna, Delaware. Country singer/songwriter. Featured performer on the 2007 TV reality series *Nashville*.

2/9/08	24	9		1 Starting Now		RCA 15468

WIDESPREAD PANIC
Eclectic-rock band from Athens, Georgia: John Bell (vocals, guitar), Michael Houser (guitar), John Hermann (keyboards), Domingo Ortiz (percussion), Dave Schools (bass) and Todd Nance (drums). Houser died of cancer on 8/10/2002 (age 40); replaced by George McConnell.

4/10/93	184	1		1 Everyday		Capricorn 42013
9/24/94	85	3		2 Ain't Life Grand		Capricorn 42027
2/22/97	50	6		3 Bombs & Butterflies		Capricorn 534396
8/14/99	68	4		4 'Til The Medicine Takes		Capricorn 546203
7/7/01	57	6		5 Don't Tell The Band		Sanctuary 84507
5/3/03	61	4		6 Ball		Sanctuary 84606
7/31/04	158	1		7 Uber Cobra		Widespread 84698
10/16/04	169	1		8 Jackassolantern		Widespread 84716
7/1/06	48	3		9 Earth To America		Widespread 84780
3/1/08	78	2		10 Free Somehow		Widespread 0022

LIVE ALBUMS:

5/9/98	67	2		11 Light Fuse Get Away		Capricorn 558145 [2]
6/10/00	161	1		12 Another Joyous Occasion		Widespread 0012
6/29/02	99	2		13 Live In The Classic City		Widespread 84552 [3]
				recorded at the Classic Center in Athens, Georgia		
4/10/04	157	1		14 Night Of Joy		Widespread 84680

WIDOWMAKER
Hard-rock band from England: John Butler (vocals), Ariel Bender (guitar), Huw Lloyd-Langton (guitars), Bob Daisley (bass) and Paul Nicholls (drums). Bender was also with **Spooky Tooth** and **Mott The Hoople**.

8/28/76	205	1		1 Widow Maker		United Artists 642
6/11/77	150	9		2 Too Late To Cry		United Artists 723

WIEDLIN, Jane
Born on 5/20/1958 in Oconomowoc, Wisconsin; raised in Los Angeles, California. Pop-rock singer/guitarist. Member of the Go-Go's.

10/26/85	127	6		1 Jane Wiedlin		I.R.S. 5638
5/28/88	105	21		2 Fur		EMI-Manhattan 48683

Billboard			R I A A	ARTIST		
DEBUT	PEAK	WKS		Album Title	Catalog	Label & Number

WIER, Rusty
Born on 5/3/1944 in Corpus Christi, Texas; raised in Austin, Texas. Died of cancer on 10/9/2009 (age 65). Country-rock singer/songwriter/guitarist.

| 7/19/75 | 103 | 14 | | 1 **Don't It Make You Wanna Dance?** .... | | 20th Century 469 |
| 1/17/76 | 131 | 9 | | 2 **Rusty Wier** .... | | 20th Century 495 |

WIGGINS, Dwayne
Born on 2/14/1963 in Oakland, California. R&B singer/songwriter. Member of **Tony, Toni, Tone**. Brother of **Raphael Saadiq**.

| 5/20/00 | 197 | 1 | | 1 **Eyes Never Lie** .... | | Motown 157594 |

WILBURN BROTHERS
Country duo from Hardy, Arkansas: brothers Virgil "Doyle" Wilburn (born on 7/7/1930; died on 10/16/1982, age 52) and Thurman "Teddy" Wilburn (born on 11/30/1931; died on 11/24/2003, age 71).
AWARD: OPRY: 1953

| 3/28/70 | 143 | 2 | | 1 **Little Johnny From Down The Street** .... | | Decca 75173 |

WILCO
Rock band from Chicago, Illinois: Jeff Tweedy (vocals, guitar), Jay Bennett (guitar), John Stirratt (bass) and Ken Coomer (drums). Glenn Kotche replaced Coomer in early 2002. Tweedy also joined **Golden Smog**. Bennett died on 5/24/2009 (age 45).

11/16/96	73	3		1 **Being There**		Reprise 46236 [2]
3/27/99	78	3		2 **Summerteeth**		Reprise 47282
7/11/98	90	7		3 **Mermaid Avenue**		Elektra 62204
6/17/00	88	4		4 **Mermaid Avenue Vol. II**		Elektra 62522
				BILLY BRAGG & WILCO (above 2)		
5/11/02	13	19	●	5 **Yankee Hotel Foxtrot**		Nonesuch 79669
7/10/04	8	9		6 **A Ghost Is Born**		Nonesuch 79809
12/3/05	47	2		7 **Kicking Television: Live In Chicago** .... [L]		Nonesuch 79903 [2]
				recorded from May 4-7 at the Vic Theatre in Chicago, Illinois		
6/2/07	4	17		8 **Sky Blue Sky**		Nonesuch 131388
7/18/09	4	13		9 **Wilco**		Nonesuch 516608

WILCOX, David
Born on 3/9/1958 in Mentor, Ohio. Singer/songwriter/guitarist.

| 2/26/94 | 165 | 1 | | 1 **Big Horizon** .... | | A&M 540060 |

WILD CHERRY
White funk band from Steubenville, Ohio: Robert Parissi (vocals, guitar), Bryan Bassett (guitar), Mark Avsec (keyboards), Allen Wentz (bass) and Ron Beitle (drums).

7/24/76	5	29	▲	1 **Wild Cherry**		Sweet City 34195
4/2/77	51	9		2 **Electrified Funk**		Sweet City 34462
2/18/78	84	9		3 **I Love My Music**		Sweet City 35011
5/19/79	204	2		4 **Only The Wild Survive**		Epic 35760

WILDE, Danny
Born on 6/3/1956 in Maine; raised in California. Pop-rock singer/songwriter/guitarist. Member of **The Rembrandts**.

| 3/26/88 | 176 | 9 | | 1 **Any Man's Hunger** .... | | Geffen 24179 |

WILDE, Eugene
Born Ronald Broomfield on 12/6/1961 in Miami, Florida. R&B singer/songwriter.

| 1/26/85 | 97 | 15 | | 1 **Eugene Wilde** .... | | Philly World 90239 |

WILDE, Kim
Born Kim Smith on 11/18/1960 in Chiswick, London, England. Pop-rock-dance singer. Daughter of singer Marty Wilde.

6/5/82	86	22		1 **Kim Wilde**		EMI America 17065
2/9/85	84	10		2 **Teases & Dares**		MCA 5550
4/4/87	40	26		3 **Another Step**		MCA 5903
10/1/88	114	6		4 **Close**		MCA 42230

WILDER, Matthew
Born on 1/24/1953 in Manhattan, New York. New-wave singer/songwriter/keyboardist/producer.

| 1/7/84 | 49 | 16 | | 1 **I Don't Speak The Language** .... | | Private I 39112 |

WILDERNESS ROAD
Rock band from Chicago, Illinois: brothers Andy Haban (bass) and Tom Haban (drums), with Warren Leming (guitar) and Nate Herman (keyboards). All share vocals.

| 3/18/72 | 213 | 2 | | 1 **Wilderness Road** .... | | Columbia 31118 |

WILD MAN STEVE
Born Steve Gallon on 9/10/1925 in Monticello, Florida; raised in Waterbury, Connecticut. Died on 9/1/2004 (age 78). Black DJ/comedian. Appeared in the 1977 movie *Petey Wheatstraw*.

11/1/69	185	6		1 **My Man! Wild Man!** .... [C]		Raw 7000
6/6/70	179	2		2 **Wild! Wild! Wild!** .... [C]		Raw 7001
				no track titles listed on above 2 albums		

WILD ONES, The
Garage-rock band from Long Island, New York: Jordan Christopher (vocals), Chuck Alden (guitar), Tom Graves (keyboards), Ed Wright (bass) and Tom Trick (drums). Christopher later acted in several movies.

| 11/20/65 | 149 | 2 | | 1 **The Arthur Sound** .... [L] | | United Artists 3450 |

Billboard			R I A A	ARTIST		
DEBUT	PEAK	WKS		Album Title	Catalog	Label & Number

WILD ORCHID
Teen female vocal trio from Los Angeles, California: Stacy "**Fergie**" Ferguson, Stefanie Ridel and Renee Sandstrom.
Both Ferguson (1984-89) and Sandstrom (1984-87) were regulars on the TV show *Kids Incorporated*. Ferguson later joined
Black Eyed Peas. Sandstrom later joined **Superstar Kidz**.

| 4/12/97 | 153 | 4 | | 1 Wild Orchid .... | | RCA 66894 |

WILD TURKEY
Rock band from England: Gary Pickford-Hopkins (vocals), Tweke Lewis (guitar), Jon Blackmore (guitar), Glenn Cornick (bass;
Jethro Tull) and Jeff Jones (drums).

| 5/6/72 | 193 | 3 | | 1 Battle Hymn .... | | Reprise 2070 |

WILKINSONS, The
Country vocal trio from Belleville, Ontario, Canada: father Steve with children Amanda and Tyler Wilkinson.

| 8/29/98 | 133 | 19 | ● | 1 Nothing But Love .... | | Giant 24699 |
| 4/22/00 | 114 | 3 | | 2 Here And Now .... | | Giant 24736 |

WILL AND THE KILL
Rock band from Austin, Texas: Will Sexton (vocals, guitar), David Grissom (guitar), Alex Napier (bass) and Jeff Boaz (drums).
Sexton is the brother of **Charlie Sexton**.

| 4/9/88 | 129 | 8 | | 1 Will And The Kill .... | | MCA 42054 |

will.i.am
Born William Adams on 3/15/1975 in Los Angeles, California. R&B singer/songwriter/rapper/producer. Founding member of
Black Eyed Peas.

| 10/13/07 | 38 | 4 | | 1 Songs About Girls .... | | will.i.am 009964 |

WILLIAMS, Andy   1960s: #8 / All-Time: #29
Born Howard Andrew Williams on 12/3/1927 in Wall Lake, Iowa. Formed quartet with his brothers and eventually moved to Los
Angeles, California. With **Bing Crosby** on hit "Swingin' On A Star," 1944. With comedienne Kay Thompson in the mid-1940s.
Went solo in 1952. On **Steve Allen**'s *Tonight Show* from 1952-55. Own NBC-TV variety series from 1962-67, 1969-71. Appeared
in the movie *I'd Rather Be Rich* in 1964. Married to singer/actress **Claudine Longet** from 1962-67. One of America's greatest
Adult Contemporary singers. Andy's signature song "Moon River" was recorded in 1962, but was never released as a single.

1/25/60	38	4		1 Lonely Street		Cadence 3030
3/3/62	19	36		2 "Danny Boy" And Other Songs I Love To Sing		Columbia 1751 / 8551
5/12/62+	3[1]	176	●	3 Moon River & Other Great Movie Themes		Columbia 1809 / 8609
10/20/62+	16	44		4 Warm And Willing		Columbia 1879 / 8679
4/20/63	❶[16]	107	●	5 Days Of Wine And Roses		Columbia 2015 / 8815
1/25/64	9	24	●	6 The Wonderful World Of Andy Williams		Columbia 2137 / 8937
5/9/64	5	63	●	7 The Academy Award Winning "Call Me Irresponsible"		Columbia 2171 / 8971
9/26/64	5	33	●	8 The Great Songs From "My Fair Lady" And Other Broadway Hits		Columbia 2205 / 9005
4/10/65	4	65	●	9 Dear Heart		Columbia 2338 / 9138
5/14/66	6	54	●	10 The Shadow Of Your Smile		Columbia 2499 / 9299
1/21/67	21	22		11 In The Arms Of Love		Columbia 2533 / 9333
5/13/67	5	79	●	12 Born Free		Columbia 2680 / 9480
11/18/67+	8	36	●	13 Love, Andy		Columbia 2766 / 9566
6/8/68	9	40	●	14 Honey		Columbia 9662
5/17/69	9	23	●	15 Happy Heart		Columbia 9844
11/8/69	27	21		16 Get Together With Andy Williams		Columbia 9922
6/13/70	43	19		17 Raindrops Keep Fallin' On My Head		Columbia 9896
11/14/70	81	17		18 The Andy Williams Show .... [L]		Columbia 30105
2/20/71	3[1]	33	▲	19 Love Story		Columbia 30497
8/28/71	54	12		20 You've Got A Friend		Columbia 30797
4/8/72	29	26	●	21 Love Theme From "The Godfather"		Columbia 31303
9/30/72	86	18		22 Alone Again (Naturally)		Columbia 31625
11/17/73	185	6		23 Solitaire		Columbia 32383
12/28/74+	150	4		24 You Lay So Easy On My Mind		Columbia 33234
				CHRISTMAS ALBUMS:		
11/30/63	❶[9X]	34	▲	25 The Andy Williams Christmas Album		Columbia 2087 / 8887
				Christmas charts: 1/'63, 1/'64, 1/'65, 60/'66, 6/'67, 17/'68, 30/'69, 4/'70, 4/'71, 8/'72, 6/'73		
12/18/65+	❶[3X]	20	▲	26 Merry Christmas		Columbia 2420 / 9220
				Christmas charts: 5/'65, 1/'66, 20/'67, 4/'68, 1/'69, 19/'70		
12/21/74	203	2		27 Christmas Present		Columbia 33191
12/17/94	137	2		28 The New Andy Williams Christmas Album .... Cat:#32/5 [L]		LaserLight 12326
				Christmas charts: 40/'94, 38/'95, 31/'96		
				GREATEST HITS & COMPILATIONS:		
4/7/62+	59	44		29 Andy Williams' Best		Cadence 3054
1/12/63	54	43		30 Million Seller Songs		Cadence 3061
5/22/65	61	18		31 Hawaiian Wedding Song		Columbia 2323 / 9123
7/3/65	112	6		32 Canadian Sunset		Columbia 2324 / 9124

Billboard			R I A A	ARTIST		
DEBUT	PEAK	WKS		Album Title	Catalog	Label & Number

WILLIAMS, Andy — cont'd

2/5/66	23	23		33 Andy Williams' Newest Hits		Columbia 2383 / 9183
2/1/69	139	7		34 The Andy Williams Sound Of Music		Columbia 5 [2]
3/7/70	42	20	●	35 Andy Williams' Greatest Hits		Columbia 9979
1/8/72	123	5		36 The Impossible Dream		Columbia 31064 [2]
7/7/73	174	5		37 Andy Williams' Greatest Hits, Vol. 2		Columbia 32384

WILLIAMS, Bernie
Born on 9/13/1968 in San Juan, Puerto Rico. Jazz guitarist. Better known as the all-star center fielder for baseball's New York Yankees.

8/2/03	157	2		1 The Journey Within	[I]	GRP 000725
5/2/09	178	1		2 Moving Forward	[I]	Reform 61217

WILLIAMS, Billy
Born on 12/28/1910 in Waco, Texas. Died on 10/17/1972 (age 61). Black singer. Lead singer of The Charioteers from 1930-50.

~ ~ ~ ~ ~ ~ ~ ~ ~ ~   **NON-CHARTED ALBUM**   ~ ~ ~ ~ ~ ~ ~ ~ ~ ~ ~
1957 **Billy Williams** *["I'm Gonna Sit Right Down And Write Myself A Letter"]*

WILLIAMS, Christopher
Born Troy Christopher Williams on 8/22/1967 in the Bronx, New York. R&B singer/songwriter.

1/16/93	63	25		1 Changes		Uptown 10751
3/18/95	104	5		2 Not A Perfect Man		Giant 24564

WILLIAMS, Danny
Born on 1/7/1942 in Port Elizabeth, South Africa. Died on 12/6/2005 (age 63). Black Adult Contemporary singer.

6/13/64	122	5		1 White On White		United Artists 3359

WILLIAMS, Dar
Born Dorothy Williams on 4/19/1967 in Mount Kisco, New York; raised in Chappaqua, New York. Adult Alternative singer/songwriter.

8/2/97	169	1		1 End Of The Summer		Razor & Tie 82830
9/9/00	143	1		2 The Green World		Razor & Tie 82856
3/8/03	120	5		3 The Beauty Of The Rain		Razor & Tie 82886
10/1/05	173	1		4 My Better Self		Razor & Tie 82950
9/27/08	95	2		5 Promised Land		Razor & Tie 82996

WILLIAMS, Deniece
Born Deniece Chandler on 6/3/1951 in Gary, Indiana. R&B singer/songwriter.

10/30/76+	33	36	●	1 This is Niecy		Columbia 34242
11/19/77+	66	20		2 Song Bird		Columbia 34911
7/29/78	19	16	●	3 That's What Friends Are For		Columbia 35435
				JOHNNY MATHIS & DENIECE WILLIAMS		
8/18/79	96	8		4 When Love Comes Calling		ARC 35568
4/4/81	74	32	●	5 My Melody		ARC 37048
4/17/82	20	22		6 Niecy		ARC 37952
6/4/83	54	19		7 I'm So Proud		Columbia 38622
6/9/84	26	19		8 Let's Hear It For The Boy		Columbia 39366

WILLIAMS, Don
Born on 5/27/1939 in Floydada, Texas. Country singer/songwriter/guitarist. Member of the **Pozo-Seco Singers**.
AWARDS: CMA: Male Vocalist 1978 ★ OPRY: 1976

1/27/79	161	7		1 Expressions		ABC 1069
10/4/80	57	31	▲	2 I Believe In You		MCA 5133
				CMA: Album of the Year		
7/25/81	109	11		3 Especially For You		MCA 5210
5/1/82	166	8		4 Listen To The Radio		MCA 5306
4/21/84	208	1	●	5 The Best Of Don Williams Volume III	[G]	MCA 5465

WILLIAMS, Hank
Born Hiram King Williams on 9/17/1923 in Mount Olive, Alabama. Died of alcohol/drug abuse on 1/1/1953 (age 29). Legendary country singer/songwriter/guitarist. Father of **Hank Williams, Jr.** and grandfather of **Hank Williams III**. George Hamilton portrayed Hank in the movie biography *Your Cheatin' Heart*. Also see **Various Artists Compilations: Hank Williams: Timeless**.
AWARDS: Grammy: Lifetime Achievement 1987 ★ R&R Hall of Fame: 1987 (Early Influence) ★ C&W Hall of Fame: 1961 ★ OPRY: 1949

8/7/65	139	3		1 Father & Son		MGM 4276
				HANK WILLIAMS, SR. & HANK WILLIAMS, JR.		
8/7/82	27^C	2		2 Hank Williams, Sr. / Live At The Grand Ole Opry	[L]	MGM 5019
1/23/93	179	1		3 The Best Of Hank & Hank	[G]	Curb 77552
				HANK WILLIAMS, SR. & HANK WILLIAMS, JR.		
6/29/96+	30^C	3	▲	4 24 Of Hank Williams' Greatest Hits	[G]	Polydor 823293 [2]
10/12/96	167	1		5 Men With Broken Hearts		Curb 77868
				THREE HANKS		
10/17/98	41^C	1	●	6 20 Of Hank Williams' Greatest Hits	[G]	Mercury 536029

~ ~ ~ ~ ~ ~ ~ ~ ~ ~   **NON-CHARTED ALBUMS**   ~ ~ ~ ~ ~ ~ ~ ~ ~ ~
1978 **40 Greatest Hits**   1998 **The Complete Hank Williams**
     RS500 #129   *RS500 #225*

WILLIAMS, Hank Jr. 1980s: #14 / All-Time: #117

Born Randall Hank Williams on 5/26/1949 in Shreveport, Louisiana; raised in Nashville, Tennessee. Country singer/songwriter/guitarist. Son of **Hank Williams** and father of **Hank Williams III**. Nicknamed "Bocephus." Starred in the 1968 movie *A Time To Sing*. Richard Thomas starred as Hank in the 1983 biographical TV movie *Living Proof: The Hank Williams Story*.
AWARDS: CMA: Entertainer 1987 & 1988 ★ OPRY: 1962

8/7/65	139	3		1 Father & Son		MGM 4276
				HANK WILLIAMS, SR. & HANK WILLIAMS, JR.		
6/21/69	164	4		2 Songs My Father Left Me		MGM 4621
11/24/79	201	4	●	3 Family Tradition		Elektra/Curb 194
6/21/80	154	17	●	4 Habits Old And New		Elektra/Curb 278
2/21/81	82	15	●	5 Rowdy		Elektra/Curb 330
9/5/81	76	23	▲	6 The Pressure Is On		Elektra/Curb 535
5/8/82	123	20	●	7 High Notes		Elektra/Curb 60100
4/23/83	64	16	●	8 Strong Stuff		Elektra/Curb 60223
11/19/83	116	13	●	9 Man Of Steel		Warner/Curb 23924
6/9/84	100	19	▲	10 Major Moves		Warner/Curb 25088
5/18/85	72	22	●	11 Five-O		Warner/Curb 25267
7/19/86	93	18	●	12 Montana Cafe		Warner/Curb 25412
8/1/87	28	47	▲	13 Born To Boogie		Warner/Curb 25593
				CMA: Album of the Year		
7/16/88	55	19	●	14 Wild Streak		Warner/Curb 25725
2/24/90	71	18	●	15 Lone Wolf		Warner/Curb 26090
5/11/91	50	19	●	16 Pure Hank		Warner/Curb 26536
3/7/92	55	20	●	17 Maverick		Curb/Capricorn 26806
3/27/93	121	4		18 Out Of Left Field		Curb/Capricorn 45225
2/11/95	91	14		19 Hog Wild		Curb 77690
10/12/96	167	1		20 Men With Broken Hearts		Curb 77868
				THREE HANKS		
10/9/99	162	1		21 Stormy		Curb 77953
1/26/02	112	5		22 Almeria Club		Curb 78725
12/6/03	166	1		23 I'm One Of You		Curb 78830
7/4/09	19	6		24 127 Rose Avenue		Curb 79149
				GREATEST HITS & COMPILATIONS:		
11/13/82+	107	70	▲⁵	25 Hank Williams, Jr.'s Greatest Hits Cat:#13/68		Elektra/Curb 60193
1/11/86	183	8	▲	26 Greatest Hits Volume Two		Warner/Curb 25328
2/25/89	61	35	▲	27 Greatest Hits III		Warner/Curb 25834
11/3/90	116	14	●	28 America (The Way I See It)		Warner/Curb 26453
1/23/93	179	1		29 The Best Of Hank & Hank		Curb 77552
				HANK WILLIAMS, SR. & HANK WILLIAMS, JR.		
7/15/06	16	44	●	30 That's How They Do It In Dixie: The Essential Collection		Curb 78881
9/13/08	39ᶜ	4		31 Greatest Hits: Limited Edition		Curb 79115 [2]
				LIVE ALBUMS:		
10/18/69	187	2		32 Live At Cobo Hall, Detroit		MGM 4644
2/14/87	71	24	▲	33 Hank "Live"		Warner/Curb 25538
				SOUNDTRACKS:		
1/2/65	16	37	●	34 Your Cheatin' Heart		MGM 4260
11/2/68	189	3		35 A Time To Sing		MGM 4540

WILLIAMS, Hank III

Born on 12/12/1972 in Nashville, Tennessee. Country singer/guitarist. Son of **Hank Williams Jr.** and grandson of **Hank Williams**. Leader of hard-rock trio **Assjack**.

10/12/96	167	1		1 Men With Broken Hearts		Curb 77868
				THREE HANKS		
2/16/02	156	2		2 Lovesick, Broke & Driftin'		Curb 78728
3/18/06	73	3		3 Straight To Hell		Curb 78869 [2]
11/8/08	18	4		4 Damn Right Rebel Proud		Curb 79027

WILLIAMS, John

Born on 2/8/1932 in Flushing, Long Island, New York. Composer/conductor. Composed numerous movie scores. Conducted the **Boston Pops Orchestra** from 1980-93. His son, Joseph Williams, joined **Toto** in 1986.

2/23/02	98	4		1 American Journey	[I]	Sony Classical 89364

WILLIAMS, Katt

Born Micah Williams on 9/2/1973 in Cincinnati, Ohio; raised in Dayton, Ohio. Black stand-up comedian/actor/rapper.

2/14/09	174	1		1 It's Pimpin' Pimpin'	[C]	Warner 517759

Billboard DEBUT	PEAK	WKS	R I A A	ARTIST / Album Title	Catalog	Label & Number

WILLIAMS, Larry
Born on 5/10/1935 in New Orleans, Louisiana. Committed suicide on 1/2/1980 (age 44). Black rock and roll singer/songwriter/pianist.

~ ~ ~ ~ ~ ~ ~ ~ ~ ~ **NON-CHARTED ALBUM** ~ ~ ~ ~ ~ ~ ~ ~ ~ ~
1958 **Here's Larry Williams**

WILLIAMS, Lee
Born in Tupelo, Mississippi. Male gospel singer/choir leader.

| 8/15/09 | 173 | 1 | | 1 **Fall On Me** .... | | MCG 7065 |

LEE WILLIAMS & THE SPIRITUAL QC'S

WILLIAMS, Lenny
Born on 2/6/1945 in Little Rock, Arkansas; raised in Oakland, California. R&B singer. Member of **Tower Of Power** from 1972-75.

8/6/77	99	26		1 **Choosing You**		ABC 1023
7/22/78	87	25	●	2 **Spark Of Love**		ABC 1073
7/7/79	108	9		3 **Love Current**		MCA 3155
11/15/80	185	2		4 **Let's Do It Today**		MCA 5147

WILLIAMS, Lucinda
Born on 1/26/1953 in Lake Charles, Louisiana. Folk singer/songwriter.

| 7/18/98 | 65 | 20 | ● | 1 **Car Wheels On A Gravel Road** .... | | Mercury 558338 |

Grammy: Contemporary Folk Album ★ RS500 #304

6/23/01	28	11		2 **Essence**		Lost Highway 170197
4/26/03	18	17		3 **World Without Tears**		Lost Highway 170355
5/28/05	66	2		4 **Live At The Fillmore** .... [L]		Lost Highway 002368 [2]
3/3/07	14	11		5 **West**		Lost Highway 006938
11/1/08	9	9		6 **Little Honey**		Lost Highway 001434

WILLIAMS, Mason
Born on 8/24/1938 in Abilene, Texas. Folk guitarist. Comedy writer for **The Smothers Brothers** Comedy Hour (1967-69) and *Saturday Night Live* (1980).

6/29/68	14	34		1 **The Mason Williams Phonograph Record**		Warner 1729
12/28/68+	164	8		2 **The Mason Williams Ear Show**		Warner 1766
5/10/69	44	17		3 **Music By Mason Williams**		Warner 1788
12/19/87+	118	19	●	4 **Classical Gas** .... [I]		American Gram. 800

MASON WILLIAMS & MANNHEIM STEAMROLLER

WILLIAMS, Maurice, & The Zodiacs
Born on 4/26/1938 in Lancaster, South Carolina. R&B singer. The Zodiacs: Wiley Bennett, Henry Gaston, Charles Thomas, Albert Hill and Willie Morrow.

~ ~ ~ ~ ~ ~ ~ ~ ~ ~ **NON-CHARTED ALBUM** ~ ~ ~ ~ ~ ~ ~ ~ ~ ~
1961 **Stay With Maurice Williams And The Zodiacs**

WILLIAMS, Michelle
Born Tenetria Michelle Williams on 7/23/1980 in Rockford, Illinois. R&B singer. Member of **Destiny's Child**.

5/4/02	57	14		1 **Heart To Yours**		Music World 86432
2/14/04	120	1		2 **Do You Know**		Music World 89081
10/25/08	42	2		3 **Unexpected**		Music World 01473

WILLIAMS, Paul
Born on 9/19/1940 in Omaha, Nebraska. Singer/songwriter/actor. Appeared in several movies.

12/25/71+	141	21		1 **Just An Old Fashioned Love Song**		A&M 4327
12/2/72+	159	14		2 **Life Goes On**		A&M 4367
3/2/74	165	10		3 **Here Comes Inspiration**		A&M 3606
11/23/74	95	9		4 **A Little Bit Of Love**		A&M 3655
12/13/75+	146	6		5 **Ordinary Fool**		A&M 4550
8/6/77	155	8		6 **Classics** .... [K]		A&M 4701

WILLIAMS, Robbie
Born on 2/13/1974 in Port Vale, England. Pop-rock singer/songwriter. Former member of **Take That**.

5/22/99	63	28	●	1 **The Ego Has Landed**		Capitol 97726
10/21/00	110	4		2 **Sing When You're Winning**		Capitol 29024
4/19/03	43	7		3 **Escapology**		Chrysalis 81777
11/28/09	160	1		4 **Reality Killed The Video Star**		Chrysalis 87752

WILLIAMS, Robin
Born on 7/21/1952 in Chicago, Illinois. Actor/comedian. Starred in several movies and TV's *Mork & Mindy*.

| 7/21/79 | 10 | 22 | ● | 1 **Reality...What A Concept** .... [C] | | Casablanca 7162 |

Grammy: Comedy Album

| 4/2/83 | 119 | 9 | | 2 **Throbbing Python Of Love** .... [C] | | Casablanca 811150 |

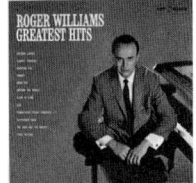

WILLIAMS, Roger — 1950s: #11 / 1960s: #15 / All-Time: #51

Born Louis Weertz on 10/1/1924 in Omaha, Nebraska. Learned to play piano by age three. Educated at Drake University, Idaho State University, and Juilliard School of Music. Took lessons from Lenny Tristano and Teddy Wilson. Win on Arthur Godfrey's TV show led to recording contract.

DEBUT	PEAK	WKS			
3/31/56	19	2		1 Roger Williams ...... [I]	Kapp 1012
				album also released as *Autumn Leaves*	
8/25/56	19	3		2 Daydreams ...... [I]	Kapp 1031
10/27/56	16	2		3 Roger Williams Plays The Wonderful Music Of The Masters ...... [I]	Kapp 1040
3/23/57	6	65	●	4 Songs Of The Fabulous Fifties [I]	Kapp 5000 [2]
10/7/57	20	5		5 Almost Paradise ...... [I]	Kapp 1063
11/4/57+	19	4		6 Songs Of The Fabulous Forties ...... [I]	Kapp 5003 [2]
3/31/58	4	93	●	7 Till [I]	Kapp 1081
2/23/59+	9	70		8 Near You ...... [I]	Kapp 1112
6/15/59	11	24	●	9 More Songs Of The Fabulous Fifties ...... [I]	Kapp 1130
10/26/59+	8	34		10 With These Hands [I]	Kapp 1147
12/28/59+	12	2		11 Christmas Time ...... [X-I]	Kapp 1164
				Christmas charts: 20/'64, 26/'65, 18/'66, 28/'67	
12/25/61+	105	3		12 Christmas Time ...... [X-I-R]	Kapp 1164
4/4/60	25	22		13 Always ...... [I]	Kapp 1172
12/19/60+	5	39		14 Temptation [I]	Kapp 1217
9/11/61	49	15		15 Yellow Bird ...... [I]	Kapp 1244
10/2/61	35	11		16 Songs Of The Soaring '60s ...... [I]	Kapp 1251
3/17/62	9	46		17 Maria [I]	Kapp 3266
9/15/62	27	30		18 Mr. Piano ...... [I]	Kapp 3290
4/20/63	122	13		19 Country Style ...... [I]	Kapp 3305
10/12/63	59	12		20 For You ...... [I]	Kapp 3336
2/8/64	27	19		21 The Solid Gold Steinway ...... [I]	Kapp 3354
9/5/64	126	9		22 Academy Award Winners ...... [I]	Kapp 3406
4/10/65	118	6		23 Roger Williams Plays The Hits ...... [I]	Kapp 3414
10/9/65	63	18		24 Summer Wind ...... [I]	Kapp 3434
12/25/65+	130	7		25 Autumn Leaves-1965 ...... [I]	Kapp 3452
3/26/66	24	67		26 I'll Remember You ...... [I]	Kapp 3470
12/10/66+	7	69	●	27 Born Free [I]	Kapp 3501
5/13/67	51	27		28 Roger! ...... [I]	Kapp 3512
3/2/68	164	5		29 More Than A Miracle ...... [I]	Kapp 3550
1/25/69	131	10		30 Only For Lovers ...... [I]	Kapp 3565
5/31/69	60	11		31 Happy Heart ...... [I]	Kapp 3595
8/9/69	145	10		32 Love Theme From "Romeo & Juliet" ...... [I]	Kapp 3610
3/6/71	112	13		33 Love Story ...... [I]	Kapp 3645
9/18/71	187	3		34 Summer Of '42 ...... [I]	Kapp 3650
4/8/72	187	8		35 Love Theme From "The Godfather" ...... [I]	Kapp 3665
				GREATEST HITS & COMPILATIONS:	
2/3/62	44	23	●	36 Greatest Hits ...... [I]	Kapp 3260
4/4/64	108	8		37 10th Anniversary/Limited Edition ...... [I]	Kapp 1 [3]
9/9/67	87	29		38 Golden Hits ...... [I]	Kapp 3530
3/13/71	203	9		39 Golden Hits Vol. 2 ...... [I]	Kapp 3638

WILLIAMS, Tony

Born on 12/12/1945 in Chicago, Illinois. Died of a heart attack on 2/23/1997 (age 51). Jazz-fusion drummer. Also see **V.S.O.P.**

7/10/71	214	1		1 Ego ...... [I]	Polydor 4065
				THE TONY WILLIAMS LIFETIME	
5/12/79	113	7		2 The Joy Of Flying	Columbia 35705

WILLIAMS, Vanessa

Born on 3/18/1963 in the Bronx, New York; raised in Millwood, New York. R&B singer/actress. In 1983, became the first black woman to win the Miss America pageant; relinquished crown after *Penthouse* magazine scandal. Acted in several movies and Broadway shows. Married to NBA player Rick Fox from 1999-2005.

7/9/88+	38	55	●	1 The Right Stuff	Wing 835694
9/7/91+	17	91	▲³	2 The Comfort Zone	Wing 843522
12/24/94+	57	31	▲	3 The Sweetest Days	Wing 526172
9/13/97	53	9		4 Next	Mercury 536060
2/12/05	159	2		5 Everlasting Love	Lava 83802
6/20/09	91	2		6 The Real Thing	Concord 30816
				CHRISTMAS ALBUMS:	
11/23/96	36	9	●	7 Star Bright ...... Cat:#12/11	Mercury 532827
				Christmas charts: 5/'96, 17/'97, 33/'98	

WILLIAMS, Vanessa — cont'd

12/1/01	102	6	8 Our Favorite Things .... [L]		Sony Classical 89468

TONY BENNETT / CHARLOTTE CHURCH / PLACIDO DOMINGO / VANESSA WILLIAMS
recorded on 12/21/2000 at the Konzerthaus in Vienna, Austria; Christmas chart: 10/'01

12/4/04	120	5	9 Silver And Gold		Lava 93199

Christmas chart: 24/'04

WILLIE AND THE POOR BOYS
All-star rock band: Andy Fairweather Low (vocals, guitar), Mickey Gee (guitar), Geraint Watkins (keyboards), **Bill Wyman** (bass) and Charlie Watts (drums). Wyman and Watts are members of **The Rolling Stones**.

5/25/85	96	12	1 Willie And The Poor Boys		Passport 6047

WILLIE D
Born Willie Dennis on 11/1/1966 in Houston, Texas. Male rapper. Member of **The Geto Boys**.

10/3/92	88	8	1 I'm Goin' Out Lika Soldier..		Rap-A-Lot 57188
11/11/00	124	3	2 Loved By Few, Hated By Many		Rap-A-Lot 50022

WILLIS, Bruce
Born Walter Bruce Willis on 3/19/1955 in Idar-Oberstein, West Germany; raised in Penns Grove, New Jersey. Starred in several movies and TV's *Moonlighting*. Married to actress Demi Moore from 1987-2000.

2/14/87	14	29	● 1 The Return Of Bruno..		Motown 6222

WILLIS, Chuck
Born Harold Willis on 1/31/1928 in Atlanta, Georgia. Died of a bleeding ulcer on 4/10/1958 (age 30). R&B singer/songwriter.

~ ~ ~ ~ ~ ~ ~ ~ ~ ~ **NON-CHARTED ALBUMS** ~ ~ ~ ~ ~ ~ ~ ~ ~ ~

1958 **The King Of The Stroll**   1963 **I Remember Chuck Willis**

WILLMON, Trent
Born on 3/6/1973 in Afton, Texas. Country singer/songwriter/guitarist.

10/30/04	150	1	1 Trent Willmon		Columbia 91257
7/1/06	70	5	2 A Little More Livin'		Columbia 74938

WILLS, Mark
Born Daryl Mark Williams on 8/8/1973 in Cleveland, Tennessee; raised in Blue Ridge, Georgia. Country singer/songwriter/guitarist.

5/30/98	74	56	▲ 1 Wish You Were Here		Mercury 536317
1/29/00	23	29	● 2 Permanently...		Mercury 546296
9/8/01	93	3	3 Loving Every Minute		Mercury 170209
11/23/02	140	14	4 Greatest Hits.. [G]		Mercury 170313
11/8/03	68	3	5 And The Crowd Goes Wild		Mercury 001012

WILL TO POWER
Pop-dance trio from Florida: Bob Rosenberg, Maria Mendez and Dr. J. Rosenberg is the son of singer Gloria Mann. By 1990, reduced to a duo of Rosenberg and Elin Michaels. Group name taken from the work of 19th-century German philosopher Friedrich Nietzsche.

9/10/88	68	29	1 Will To Power..		Epic 40940
2/2/91	178	4	2 Journey Home		Epic 46051

WILMER & THE DUKES
R&B-soul band from Rochester, New York: black vocalist/saxophonist Wilmer Alexander with white band: brothers Ronnie Alberts (bass) and Monte Alberts (drums), with Doug Brown (guitar) and Ralph Gillotte (keyboards). Gillotte died of a heart attack on 2/11/1999 (age 62).

8/16/69	173	3	1 Wilmer & The Dukes		Aphrodisiac 6001

WILSON, Al
Born on 6/19/1939 in Meridian, Mississippi. Died of kidney failure on 4/21/2008 (age 68). R&B singer/drummer.

12/22/73+	70	17	1 Show And Tell		Rocky Road 3601
10/19/74	171	7	2 La La Peace Song		Rocky Road 3700
7/10/76	185	2	3 I've Got A Feeling		Playboy 410

WILSON, Ann
Born on 6/19/1950 in San Diego, California; raised in Bellevue, Washington. Lead singer of **Heart**.

9/29/07	107	2	1 Hope & Glory		Zoe 431085

WILSON, Brian
Born on 6/20/1942 in Hawthorne, California. Pop singer/songwriter. Leader of **The Beach Boys**. His daughters, **Carnie & Wendy Wilson**, formed the trio **Wilson Phillips** with Chynna Phillips in 1989.

7/30/88	54	13	1 Brian Wilson		Sire 25669
7/4/98	88	2	2 Imagination		Paladin 24703
7/10/04	100	1	3 Gettin' In Over My Head		Brimel 76471
10/16/04	13	17	4 Smile..		Nonesuch 79846
12/17/05	200	1	5 What I Really Want For Christmas .... [X]		Arista 70300

Christmas chart: 8/'05

9/20/08	21	4	6 That Lucky Old Sun		Brimel 34147

WILSON, Brian Courtney
Born in Chicago, Illinois. Black gospel singer.

6/20/09	127	1	1 Just Love		Spirit Rising 0662

DEBUT	PEAK	WKS	R I A A	ARTIST Album Title	Catalog	Label & Number
				WILSON, Carl Born on 12/21/1946 in Hawthorne, California. Died of cancer on 2/6/1998 (age 51). Guitarist of **The Beach Boys**.		
5/2/81	185	2		1 Carl Wilson		Caribou 37010
				WILSON, Carnie & Wendy — see WILSON PHILLIPS		
				WILSON, Cassandra Born on 12/4/1955 in Jackson, Mississippi. Jazz singer.		
3/23/96	141	5		1 New Moon Daughter		Blue Note 32861
4/10/99	158	5		2 Traveling Miles		Blue Note 54123
4/13/02	155	3		3 Belly Of The Sun		Blue Note 35072
4/22/06	184	1		4 Thunderbird		Blue Note 63398
				WILSON, Charlie Born on 1/29/1953 in Tulsa, Oklahoma. R&B singer/songwriter. Member of **The Gap Band**. Nicknamed "Uncle Charlie" by **Snoop Dogg**.		
2/10/01	152	10		1 Bridging The Gap		Major Hits 490371
10/1/05	10	18	●	2 Charlie Last Name: Wilson		Jive 69429
3/7/09	2[1]	34		3 Uncle Charlie		Jive 23389
				WILSON, Dennis Born on 12/4/1944 in Inglewood, California. Drowned on 12/28/1983 (age 39). Drummer of **The Beach Boys**.		
9/10/77	96	8		1 Pacific Ocean Blue .... **Cat:**#8/2		Caribou 34353
				WILSON, Flip Born Clerow Wilson on 12/8/1933 in Jersey City, New Jersey. Died of cancer on 11/25/1998 (age 64). Black stand-up comedian. Hosted own TV variety show (1970-74). Also recorded as his female alter ego, Geraldine.		
8/26/67+	34	63		1 Cowboys & Colored People .... [C]		Atlantic 8149
6/1/68	147	7		2 You Devil You .... [C]		Atlantic 8179
2/28/70	17	54	●	3 "The Devil Made Me Buy This Dress" .... [C] **Grammy: Comedy Album**		Little David 1000
1/2/71	45	15		4 "Flip" - The Flip Wilson Show .... [C]		Little David 2000
5/13/72	63	15		5 Geraldine/Don't Fight The Feeling .... [C]		Little David 1001
				WILSON, Gretchen Born on 6/26/1973 in Granite City, Illinois; raised in Pocahontas, Illinois. Country singer/songwriter/guitarist. **AWARD: CMA: Horizon 2004 / Female Vocalist 2005**		
5/29/04	2[1]	102	▲[5]	1 Here For The Party **Cat:**#24/10		Epic 90903
10/15/05	❶[1]	28	▲	2 All Jacked Up		Epic 94169
6/2/07	5	10		3 One Of The Boys		Columbia 89201
				WILSON, J. Frank, and The Cavaliers Born on 12/11/1941 in Lufkin, Texas. Died on 10/4/1991 (age 49). The Cavaliers: Sid Holmes (guitar), Lewis Elliott (bass) and Ray Smith (drums).		
11/14/64	54	14		1 Last Kiss		Josie 4006
				WILSON, Jackie Born on 6/9/1934 in Detroit, Michigan. Died on 1/21/1984 (age 49). Male R&B singer. Collapsed after suffering a stroke on stage on 9/29/1975 at the Latin Casino in Cherry Hill, New Jersey; spent rest of his life in nursing homes. **AWARD: R&R Hall of Fame: 1987**		
11/24/62	137	2		1 Jackie Wilson At The Copa .... [L]		Brunswick 754108
4/27/63	36	21		2 Baby Workout		Brunswick 754110
11/30/63	6[X]	4		3 Merry Christmas From Jackie Wilson [X] Christmas charts: 6/'63, 46/'64		Brunswick 754112
1/14/67	108	7		4 Whispers		Brunswick 754122
11/25/67	163	4		5 Higher And Higher		Brunswick 754130
6/1/68	195	3		6 Manufacturers Of Soul .... JACKIE WILSON & COUNT BASIE		Brunswick 754134

~ ~ ~ ~ ~ ~ ~ ~ ~ ~ **NON-CHARTED ALBUMS** ~ ~ ~ ~ ~ ~ ~ ~ ~ ~

1958 **He's So Fine**	1961 **You Ain't Heard Nothin' Yet**
1959 **Lonely Teardrops**	1961 **By Special Request...**
1960 **So Much**	1962 **Body And Soul**
1960 **Jackie Sings The Blues**	1964 **My Golden Favorites...Vol. 2**
1960 **My Golden Favorites**	1992 **Mr. Excitement!**
1960 **A Woman, A Lover, A Friend**	*RS500 #235*

DEBUT	PEAK	WKS		ARTIST	Catalog	Label & Number
				WILSON, Mary Born on 3/6/1944 in Greeneville, Mississippi; raised in Detroit. R&B singer Member of **The Supremes**.		
11/3/79	208	1		1 Mary Wilson		Motown 927

WILSON, Nancy

1960s: #20 / All-Time: #81

Born on 2/20/1937 in Chillicothe, Ohio; raised in Columbus, Ohio. Jazz-styled singer. Lead singer with Rusty Bryant's Carolyn Club Band. First recorded for Dot in 1956. Not to be confused with Nancy Wilson of the rock group Heart.

5/5/62	30	21	1 Nancy Wilson/Cannonball Adderley		Capitol 1657
9/15/62+	49	18	2 Hello Young Lovers		Capitol 1767
4/6/63	18	46	3 Broadway-My Way		Capitol 1828
			also see #23 below		
8/17/63	11	58	4 Hollywood-My Way		Capitol 1934
			also see #23 below		
1/25/64	4	42	5 Yesterday's Love Songs/Today's Blues		Capitol 2012
5/30/64	10	30	6 Today, Tomorrow, Forever		Capitol 2082
9/5/64	4	31	7 How Glad I Am		Capitol 2155
2/6/65	24	29	8 The Nancy Wilson Show!	[L]	Capitol 2136
			recorded at the Cocoanut Grove in Los Angeles, California		
6/5/65	7	21	9 Today-My Way		Capitol 2321
8/28/65	17	24	10 Gentle Is My Love		Capitol 2351
2/5/66	44	18	11 From Broadway With Love		Capitol 2433
5/28/66	15	33	12 A Touch Of Today		Capitol 2495
8/27/66	35	23	13 Tender Loving Care		Capitol 2555
1/28/67	35	21	14 Nancy-Naturally		Capitol 2634
6/3/67	40	15	15 Just For Now		Capitol 2712
9/2/67	46	19	16 Lush Life		Capitol 2757
			also see #27 below		
2/3/68	115	17	17 Welcome To My Love		Capitol 2844
6/1/68	51	24	18 Easy		Capitol 2909
8/31/68	145	14	19 The Best Of Nancy Wilson	[G]	Capitol 2947
10/12/68	122	7	20 The Sound Of Nancy Wilson		Capitol 2970
2/8/69	117	14	21 Nancy		Capitol 148
7/5/69	122	15	22 Son Of A Preacher Man		Capitol 234
8/23/69	193	2	23 Close-Up	[R]	Capitol 256 [2]
			reissue of albums #3 and #4 above		
11/8/69+	92	18	24 Hurt So Bad		Capitol 353
3/28/70	155	6	25 Can't Take My Eyes Off You		Capitol 429
11/28/70+	54	21	26 Now I'm A Woman		Capitol 541
6/12/71	185	3	27 The Right To Love	[R]	Capitol 763
			reissue (new title) of album #16 above		
7/17/71	185	5	28 But Beautiful		Capitol 798
12/25/71+	151	6	29 Kaleidoscope		Capitol 852
3/17/73	201	7	30 I Know I Love Him		Capitol 11131
9/28/74	97	18	31 All In Love Is Fair		Capitol 11317
7/26/75	119	10	32 Come Get To This		Capitol 11386
5/1/76	126	13	33 This Mother's Daughter		Capitol 11518
7/30/77	198	1	34 I've Never Been To Me		Capitol 11659
9/8/84	144	9	35 The Two Of Us		Columbia 39326
			RAMSEY LEWIS & NANCY WILSON		

WILSON, Shanice — see SHANICE

WILSON PHILLIPS

Pop-Adult Contemporary vocal trio formed in Los Angeles, California: sisters Carnie Wilson (born on 4/29/1968) and Wendy Wilson (born on 10/16/1969), with Chynna Phillips (born on 2/12/1968). Carnie and Wendy's father is **Brian Wilson** (of **The Beach Boys**). Chynna, the daughter of Michelle and **John Phillips** (of **The Mamas & The Papas**), acted in the movie *Caddyshack II* and married actor Billy Baldwin on 9/9/1995. Carnie hosted own TV talk show in 1995.

4/14/90	2[10]	125	▲[5] 1 Wilson Phillips		SBK 93745
6/20/92	4	33	▲ 2 Shadows And Light		SBK 98924
12/25/93	116	3	3 Hey Santa!	[X]	SBK 27113
			CARNIE & WENDY WILSON		
			Christmas chart: 25/'93		
6/12/04	35	8	4 California		Columbia 92103

WINANS, The

Family gospel group from Detroit, Michigan: brothers Michael Winans and Ronald Winans, with twins **Marvin Winans** and Carvin Winans. Brothers of **BeBe & CeCe Winans**. Marvin married **Vickie Winans** and is the father of **Mario Winans**. Also see **Winans Phase2**. Ronald died of heart failure on 6/17/2005 (age 48).

9/26/87	109	11	1 Decisions		Qwest 25510
5/19/90	90	10	● 2 Return		Qwest 26161

WINANS, BeBe

Born Benjamin Winans on 9/17/1962 in Detroit, Michigan. Gospel singer. Brother of **CeCe Winans** and **The Winans**. Uncle of **Mario Winans**.

DEBUT	PEAK	WKS	RIAA	Album Title	Catalog	Label & Number
11/15/97	125	7		1 BeBe Winans		Atlantic 83041
9/16/00	30	12		2 Love And Freedom		Motown 159405
3/23/02	164	1		3 Live And Up Close [L]		Motown 016705
12/11/04	❶^{1C}	5		4 My Christmas Prayer [X]		Hidden Beach 90788
				Christmas chart: 4/'04		
3/12/05	143	1		5 Dream		Still Waters 90727

WINANS, BeBe & CeCe

Brother-and-sister gospel duo from Detroit, Michigan: Benjamin **BeBe Winans** and Priscilla **CeCe Winans**. Siblings of **The Winans**. Uncle and aunt of **Mario Winans**.

DEBUT	PEAK	WKS	RIAA	Album Title	Catalog	Label & Number
3/4/89	95	25	●	1 Heaven		Capitol 90959
7/20/91	74	51	▲	2 Different Lifestyles		Capitol 92078
				Grammy: Contemporary Soul Gospel Album		
12/25/93+	163	2		3 First Christmas [X]		Capitol 89757
10/8/94	111	10	●	4 Relationships		Capitol 28216
10/24/09	12	27		5 Still		B&C 31105

WINANS, CeCe

Born Priscilla Winans on 10/8/1959 in Detroit, Michigan. Gospel singer. Sister of **BeBe Winans** and **The Winans**. Aunt of **Mario Winans**.

DEBUT	PEAK	WKS	RIAA	Album Title	Catalog	Label & Number
10/28/95+	124	9	▲	1 Alone In His Presence		Sparrow 51441
				Grammy: Contemporary Soul Gospel Album		
4/4/98	107	13		2 Everlasting Love		Pioneer 92793
11/21/98+	27^X	2		3 His Gift [X]		Pioneer 92810
11/6/99	129	7	●	4 Alabaster Box		Sparrow 51711
7/7/01	116	17	●	5 CeCe Winans		Sparrow 51826
				Grammy: Contemporary Gospel Album		
9/27/03	32	19	●	6 Throne Room	Cat:#45/1	Pure Springs 90361
10/1/05	41	9		7 Purified		Pure Springs 93997
				Grammy: Contemporary Soul Gospel Album		
4/19/08	57	7		8 Thy Kingdom Come		Pure Springs 84966
				Grammy: Pop Gospel Album		

WINANS, Mario

Born on 3/6/1979 in Orangeburg, South Carolina; raised in Detroit, Michigan. R&B singer/songwriter/keyboardist/drummer. Son of **Marvin Winans** and **Vickie Winans**. Nephew of **BeBe Winans** and **CeCe Winans**.

DEBUT	PEAK	WKS	RIAA	Album Title	Catalog	Label & Number
5/8/04	2^1	17	●	1 Hurt No More		Bad Boy 002392

WINANS, Marvin

Born on 3/5/1958 in Detroit, Michigan. Gospel singer. Married to **Vickie Winans** from 1978-95. Father of **Mario Winans**. Member of **The Winans**.

DEBUT	PEAK	WKS	RIAA	Album Title	Catalog	Label & Number
10/13/07	85	2		1 Alone But Not Alone		Pure Springs 86278

WINANS, Vickie

Born Vickie Bowman on 10/18/1953 in Detroit, Michigan. Gospel singer. Married to **Marvin Winans** from 1978-95. Mother of **Mario Winans**.

DEBUT	PEAK	WKS	RIAA	Album Title	Catalog	Label & Number
5/24/03	110	9		1 Bringing It All Together		Verity 43214
8/26/06	87	6		2 Woman To Woman: Songs Of Life		Verity 85576 [2]
12/22/07	165	1		3 Happy Holidays From Vickie Winans [X]		Destiny Joy 8047
				Christmas chart: 2/'07		
9/12/09	67	5		4 How I Got Over		Destiny Joy 8120

WINANS PHASE2

Family gospel group from Detroit, Michigan, consisting of sons of **The Winans**: Juan and Carvin Jr. (sons of Carvin Winans), Michael Jr. (son of Michael Winans) and Marvin Jr. (son of **Marvin Winans**).

DEBUT	PEAK	WKS	RIAA	Album Title	Catalog	Label & Number
9/25/99	168	2		1 We Got Next		Myrrh 69881

WINBUSH, Angela

Born on 1/28/1955 in St. Louis, Missouri. R&B singer/songwriter. One-half of **Rene & Angela** duo. Married Ronald Isley of The Isley Brothers on 6/26/1993.

DEBUT	PEAK	WKS	RIAA	Album Title	Catalog	Label & Number
11/7/87	81	28		1 Sharp		Mercury 832733
11/11/89	113	17		2 The Real Thing		Mercury 838866
4/2/94	96	14		3 Angela Winbush		Elektra 61591

WINCHESTER, Jesse

Born on 5/17/1944 in Shreveport, Louisiana. Pop singer/songwriter/guitarist.

DEBUT	PEAK	WKS	RIAA	Album Title	Catalog	Label & Number
12/30/72+	193	5		1 Third Down, 110 To Go		Bearsville 2102
11/6/76	210	1		2 Let The Rough Side Drag		Bearsville 6964
5/28/77	115	16		3 Nothing But A Breeze		Bearsville 6968
8/26/78	156	7		4 A Touch On The Rainy Side		Bearsville 6984
6/27/81	188	2		5 Talk Memphis		Bearsville 6989

			R I A A	ARTIST / Album Title	Catalog	Label & Number

WINDING, Kai
Born on 5/18/1922 in Aarhus, Denmark. Died on 5/6/1983 (age 60). Jazz trombonist.

| 8/10/63 | 67 | 24 | | 1 More!!! .... [I] | Verve 8551 |

WIND IN THE WILLOWS, The
Folk-rock band formed in New York: **Debbie Harry** (vocals; **Blondie**), Paul Klein (vocals, guitar), Peter Brittain (guitar), Wayne Kirby (keyboards), Ida Andrews (flute), Steve DePhillips (bass) and Anton Carysforth (drums).

| 8/17/68 | 195 | 3 | | 1 The Wind In The Willows .... | Capitol 2956 |

WINDS OF PLAGUE
Deathcore band from Upland, California: Johnny Cooke (vocals), Nick Eash (guitar), Nick Shearer (guitar), James Cordeey (bass) and Art Cruz (drums).

| 8/29/09 | 72 | 3 | | 1 The Great Stone War.. | Century Media 8571 |

WINEHOUSE, Amy
Born on 9/14/1983 in Southgate, London, England. Female R&B singer.
AWARD: Grammy: Best New Artist 2007

3/31/07+	2¹	78	▲²	1 Back To Black Cat:#18/9	Universal Rep. 008428
				Grammy: Pop Vocal Album	
12/8/07	61	20		2 Frank.. [E]	Universal Rep. 008926

WING AND A PRAYER FIFE AND DRUM CORPS., The
Studio disco group assembled by producer Harold Wheeler. Vocals by Linda November, Vivian Cherry, Arlene Martell and Helen Miles.

| 2/14/76 | 47 | 16 | | 1 Babyface .... | Wing & A Prayer 3025 |

WINGER
Hard-rock band formed in New York: Kip Winger (vocals, bass; born on 6/21/1961), Reb Beach (guitar), Paul Taylor (keyboards; left in 1992) and Rod Morgenstein (drums). Kip was a member of **Alice Cooper**'s band. Morgenstein was a member of **Dixie Dregs**.

9/17/88+	21	64	▲	1 Winger	Atlantic 81867
8/11/90	15	42	▲	2 In The Heart Of The Young	Atlantic 82103
6/5/93	83	5		3 Pull	Atlantic 82485

WINGFIELD, Pete
Born on 5/7/1948 in Kiphook, Hampshire, England. Singer/keyboardist/producer.

| 12/6/75 | 165 | 5 | | 1 Breakfast Special .... | Island 9333 |

WINGS — see McCARTNEY, Paul

WINSTON, George   All-Time: #328
Born in 1949 in Michigan; raised in Miles City, Montana. New Age pianist. Founded Dancing Cat Records in 1983.

6/2/84+	139	44	▲	1 Autumn .... [I]	Windham Hill 1012
				recorded June 1980	
5/12/84	127	32	▲	2 Winter Into Spring.. [I]	Windham Hill 1019
				recorded March 1982	
4/20/85	180	4		3 The Velveteen Rabbit .... [TV]	Dancing Cat 3007
				MERYL STREEP & GEORGE WINSTON	
				from the PBS-TV animated children's special	
10/26/91	55	24	●	4 Summer .... [I]	Windham Hill 11107
10/29/94	62	19	●	5 Forest.. [I]	Dancing Cat 11157
				Grammy: New Age Album	
10/5/96	55	22		6 Linus & Lucy - The Music Of Vince Guaraldi .... [I]	Dancing Cat 11184
4/11/98	137	8		7 All The Seasons Of George Winston - Piano Solos .... [I]	Windham Hill 11266
10/16/99	76	17	●	8 Plains .... [I]	Windham Hill 11465
11/2/02	91	2		9 Night Divides The Day - The Music Of The Doors .... [I]	Windham Hill 11649
10/30/04	146	1		10 Montana - A Love Story.. [I]	Windham Hill 62042
				CHRISTMAS ALBUMS:	
3/12/83+	54	135	▲³	11 December Cat:#7/44 [I]	Windham Hill 1025
				Christmas charts: 5/'85, 3/'87, 2/'88, 6/'89, 6/'90, 5/'91, 10/'92, 18/'93, 23/'94, 30/'95, 38/'96, 38/'97, 29/'00, 33/'01, 21/'06, 20/'07, 9/'08, 50/'09	
11/29/86+	85	15		12 December.. [I-R]	Windham Hill 1025
12/12/87+	89	10		13 December.. [I-R]	Windham Hill 1025
12/17/88+	111	5		14 December.. [I-R]	Windham Hill 1025
12/16/89+	101	6		15 December.. [I-R]	Windham Hill 1025
12/8/90	106	7		16 December.. [I-R]	Windham Hill 1025
10/10/09	9ˣ	6		17 December: 20th Anniversary Edition [I-R]	Windham Hill 11611

WINSTONS, The
R&B band from Washington DC: Richard Spencer (vocals), Quincy Mattison (guitar), Ray Maritano (sax), Phil Tolotta (organ), Sonny Peckrol (bass) and G.C. Coleman (drums).

| 8/2/69 | 78 | 12 | | 1 Color Him Father .... | Metromedia 1010 |

WINTER, Edgar, Group
Born on 12/28/1946 in Beaumont, Texas. Rock singer/keyboardist/saxophonist. Brother of **Johnny Winter**. His group included **Dan Hartman** (1972-76), Ronnie **Montrose** (1972-74) and **Rick Derringer** (1974-76).

DEBUT	PEAK	WKS			Catalog	Label & Number
6/27/70	196	2		1 Entrance		Epic 26503
5/1/71	111	19		2 Edgar Winter's White Trash		Epic 30512
3/25/72	23	25	●	3 Roadwork [L]		Epic 31249 [2]
				EDGAR WINTER'S WHITE TRASH (above 2)		
12/9/72+	3¹	80	▲²	4 They Only Come Out At Night		Epic 31584
5/25/74	13	23	●	5 Shock Treatment		Epic 32461
6/21/75	69	10		6 Jasmine Nightdreams		Blue Sky 33483
10/18/75	124	8		7 The Edgar Winter Group With Rick Derringer		Blue Sky 33798
6/19/76	89	9		8 Together [L]		Blue Sky 34033
				JOHNNY & EDGAR WINTER		

WINTER, Johnny   All-Time: #406
Born on 2/23/1944 in Leland, Mississippi. Blues-rock singer/guitarist. Brother of **Edgar Winter**.

DEBUT	PEAK	WKS			Catalog	Label & Number
4/12/69	40	20		1 The Progressive Blues Experiment		Imperial 12431
9/27/69	111	6		2 The Johnny Winter Story		GRT 10010
5/10/69	24	23		3 Johnny Winter		Columbia 9826
12/6/69	55	17		4 Second Winter		Columbia 9947 [2]
				a 3-sided album (4th side is blank)		
9/26/70	154	4		5 Johnny Winter And		Columbia 30221
3/13/71	40	27	●	6 Live/Johnny Winter And [L]		Columbia 30475
4/7/73	22	24		7 Still Alive And Well		Columbia 32188
2/23/74	42	16		8 Saints & Sinners		Columbia 32715
9/15/73	209	3		9 Austin, Texas		United Artists 139
9/15/73	215	2		10 Before The Storm		Janus 3056 [2]
12/7/74	78	12		11 John Dawson Winter III		Blue Sky 33292
3/6/76	93	12		12 Captured Live! [L]		Blue Sky 33944
6/19/76	89	9		13 Together [L]		Blue Sky 34033
				JOHNNY & EDGAR WINTER		
7/23/77	146	8		14 Nothin' But The Blues		Blue Sky 34813
8/26/78	141	4		15 White, Hot & Blue		Blue Sky 35475
8/4/84	183	4		16 Guitar Slinger		Alligator 4735
10/19/85	156	10		17 Serious Business		Alligator 4742

WINTER, Paul
Born on 8/31/1939 in Altoona, Pennsylvania. Jazz saxophonist.

DEBUT	PEAK	WKS			Catalog	Label & Number
12/29/62+	109	4		1 Jazz Meets The Bossa Nova [I]		Columbia 8725
				PAUL WINTER SEXTET		
8/12/78	209	1		2 Common Ground [I]		A&M 4698
5/3/86	138	11		3 Canyon [I]		Living Music 6

WINTERS, Jonathan
Born on 11/11/1925 in Dayton, Ohio. Improvisational comedian. Appeared in several movies and TV shows.

DEBUT	PEAK	WKS			Catalog	Label & Number
2/1/60	18	53		1 The Wonderful World Of Jonathan Winters [C]		Verve 15009
9/19/60	25	23		2 Down To Earth [C]		Verve 15011
5/29/61	19	42		3 Here's Jonathan [C]		Verve 15025
9/1/62	127	3		4 Another Day, Another World [C]		Verve 15032
3/21/64	145	2		5 Jonathan Winters' Mad, Mad, Mad, Mad World [C]		Verve 15041
12/19/64	148	2		6 Whistle Stopping With Jonathan Winters [C]		Verve 15037

WINTERS, Robert, & Fall
Born in Detroit, Michigan. R&B singer/keyboardist. Stricken with polio at age five; confined to a wheelchair. Own group, Fall, features singer Walter Turner.

DEBUT	PEAK	WKS			Catalog	Label & Number
5/9/81	71	8		1 Magic Man		Buddah 5732

WINWOOD, Steve   All-Time: #282
Born on 5/12/1948 in Birmingham, England. Pop-rock singer/keyboardist/guitarist. Lead singer of **Spencer Davis Group**, **Blind Faith** and **Traffic**.

DEBUT	PEAK	WKS			Catalog	Label & Number
5/29/71	93	8		1 Winwood [K]		United Artists 9950 [2]
				STEVIE WINWOOD		
8/21/76	60	12		2 Go		Island 9387
				STOMU YAMASHTA / STEVE WINWOOD / MICHAEL SHRIEVE		
7/16/77	22	17		3 Steve Winwood		Island 9494
1/17/81	3⁶	43	▲	4 Arc Of A Diver		Island 9576
8/21/82	28	25		5 Talking Back To The Night		Island 9777
7/19/86	3²	86	▲³	6 Back In The High Life		Island 25448
11/21/87+	26	26	▲	7 Chronicles [K]		Island 25660
7/9/88	❶¹	45	▲²	8 Roll With It		Virgin 90946
11/24/90	27	20	●	9 Refugees Of The Heart		Virgin 91405
6/21/97	123	4		10 Junction Seven		Virgin 44059
7/5/03	126	2		11 About Time		Wincraft 0001
5/17/08	12	8		12 Nine Lives		Wincraft 22250
6/6/09	14	11		13 Live From Madison Square Garden [L]		Wincraft 517584 [2]
				ERIC CLAPTON & STEVE WINWOOD		

DEBUT	PEAK	WKS	R I A A	ARTIST Album Title	Catalog	Label & Number

WIRE
Punk-rock band from London, England: Colin Newman (vocals, guitar), Bruce Gilbert (guitar), Graham Lewis (bass) and Mark Field (drums).

DEBUT	PEAK	WKS		ARTIST / Album Title	Catalog	Label & Number
7/8/89	135	10		1 It's Beginning To And Back Again		Enigma 73516

~ ~ ~ ~ ~ ~ ~ ~ ~ ~ **NON-CHARTED ALBUM** ~ ~ ~ ~ ~ ~ ~ ~ ~ ~
1977 **Pink Flag**
RS500 #410

WIRE TRAIN
Rock band formed in San Francisco, California: Kevin Hunter (vocals), Jeff Trott (guitar), Anders Rundblad (bass) and Brian MacLeod (drums).

| 2/18/84 | 150 | 9 | | 1 ...In A Chamber | | Columbia 38998 |
| 5/2/87 | 181 | 4 | | 2 Ten Women | | Columbia 40387 |

WISEGUYS, The
Techno-rock duo from England: Theo "Touche" Keating and Paul "Regal" Eve (left in 1997; Keating continued as a solo act).

| 8/4/01 | 133 | 9 | | 1 The Antidote .... **Cat**:#22/1 | | Ideal 810015 |

WISHBONE ASH
Progressive-rock band from Devonshire, England: Andy Powell (vocals, guitar), Ted Turner (guitar), Martin Turner (bass) and Steve Upton (drums). Male guitarist Laurie Wisefield replaced Ted Turner in 1974.

3/13/71	208	10		1 Wishbone Ash		Decca 75249
9/11/71	174	7		2 Pilgrimage		Decca 75295
6/24/72	169	13		3 Argus		Decca 75437
4/28/73	44	15		4 Wishbone Four		MCA 327
12/1/73	82	18		5 Live Dates .... [L]		MCA 8006 [2]
11/30/74	88	13		6 There's The Rub		MCA 464
3/27/76	136	9		7 Locked In		Atlantic 18164
12/18/76+	154	9		8 New England		Atlantic 18200
11/5/77	166	4		9 Front Page News		MCA 2311
3/29/80	179	2		10 Just Testing		MCA 3221
5/23/81	202	4		11 Number The Brave		MCA 5200
1/23/82	192	4		12 Hot Ash .... [K-L]		MCA 5283

WISIN & YANDEL
Reggaeton duo from Puerto Rico: Juan "Wisin" Luna and Llandel "Yandel" Malave.

11/26/05	30	45	●	1 Pa'l Mundo .... [F]		Mas Flow 561402
10/13/07	184	1		2 Tomando Control: Live .... [F-L]		Machete 010020
11/24/07	14	46		3 Wisin vs Yandel: Los Extraterrestres .... [F]		Machete 010293
				Grammy: Latin Urban Album		
6/13/09	7	23		4 La Revolucion [F]		WY 012967

WITCHDOCTOR
Born in Atlanta, Georgia. Male rapper. Member of **Dungeon Family**.

| 5/9/98 | 157 | 1 | | 1 ...A S.W.A.T Healin' Ritual | | Organized Noize 90146 |

WITCH QUEEN
Studio disco group produced by Peter Alves and **Gino Soccio**.

| 4/28/79 | 158 | 6 | | 1 Witch Queen | | Roadshow 3312 |

WITHERS, Bill
Born on 7/4/1938 in Slab Fork, West Virginia. R&B singer/songwriter/guitarist. Married to actress Denise Nicholas from 1973-74.

6/26/71	39	33		1 Just As I Am		Sussex 7006
5/20/72	4	43	●	2 Still Bill		Sussex 7014
4/21/73	63	21		3 Bill Withers Live At Carnegie Hall .... [L]		Sussex 7025 [2]
4/6/74	67	21		4 +'Justments		Sussex 8032
5/17/75	182	2		5 The Best Of Bill Withers .... [G]		Sussex 8037
11/8/75+	81	15		6 Making Music		Columbia 33704
11/6/76	169	4		7 Naked & Warm		Columbia 34327
10/29/77+	39	26	●	8 Menagerie		Columbia 34903
3/17/79	134	9		9 'Bout Love		Columbia 35596
5/16/81	183	3	●	10 Bill Withers' Greatest Hits .... [G]		Columbia 37199
5/25/85	143	9		11 Watching You Watching Me		Columbia 39887

WITHERSPOON, Jimmy
Born on 8/8/1923 in Gurdon, Arkansas. Died of throat cancer on 9/18/1997 (age 74). Blues singer/bassist.

| 3/8/75 | 176 | 2 | | 1 Love Is A Five Letter Word | | Capitol 11360 |

WITHIN TEMPTATION
Hard-rock band formed in the Netherlands: Sharon Adel (vocals), Robert Westerholt (guitar), Ruud Jolie (guitar), Martin Spierenburg (keyboards), Jeron Veen (bass) and Stephen Haestregt (drums).

| 8/11/07 | 106 | 3 | | 1 The Heart Of Everything | | Roadrunner 618021 |

WOBBLE, Jah
Born John Wardle on 8/11/1958 in London, England. Punk-rock singer/guitarist.

3/31/84	209	1		1 Snake Charmer .... [EP]	Island 90151
				JAH WOBBLE / THE EDGE / HOLGER CZUKAY	

WOLF, Peter
Born Peter Blankfield on 3/7/1946 in the Bronx, New York. Lead singer of the **J. Geils Band**. Married to actress Faye Dunaway from 1974-79. Not to be confused with the producer of the same name.

8/11/84	24	26		1 Lights Out	EMI America 17121
4/18/87	53	15		2 Come As You Are	EMI America 17230
3/31/90	111	7		3 Up To No Good!	MCA 6349

~ ~ ~ ~ ~ ~ ~ ~ ~ ~ **NON-CHARTED ALBUM** ~ ~ ~ ~ ~ ~ ~ ~ ~ ~ ~

2002 Sleepless
RS500 #432

WOLFMAN JACK
Born Robert Weston Smith on 1/21/1938 in Brooklyn, New York. Died of a heart attack on 7/1/1995 (age 57). Legendary DJ with several TV and movie appearances.

10/7/72	210	3		1 Wolfman Jack	Wooden Nickel 1009

WOLFMOTHER
Hard-rock trio from Sydney, Australia: Andrew Stockdale (vocals, guitar), Chris Ross (bass) and Myles Heskett (drums).

5/20/06	22	30	●	1 Wolfmother	Modular 041
11/14/09	16	4		2 Cosmic - Egg	Modular 013365

WOLF PARADE
Alternative-rock band formed in Canada: Dan Boeckner (vocals, guitar), Dante DeCaro (guitar; **Hot Hot Heat**), Hadji Bakaru (DJ), Spencer King (keyboards) and Arlen Thompson (drums).

10/15/05	158	1		1 Apologies To The Queen Mary	Sub Pop 70655
7/5/08	45	4		2 At Mount Zoomer	Sub Pop 720

WOMACK, Bobby
All-Time: #486

Born on 3/4/1944 in Cleveland, Ohio. R&B singer/songwriter/guitarist. Nicknamed "The Preacher."

AWARD: R&R Hall of Fame: 2009

12/28/68	174	2		1 Fly Me To The Moon	Minit 24014
4/17/71	188	5		2 The Womack "Live" .... [L]	Liberty 7645
12/4/71+	83	17		3 Communication	United Artists 5539
6/24/72	43	48		4 Understanding	United Artists 5577
1/13/73	50	20		5 Across 110th Street .... [S]	United Artists 5225
7/7/73	37	21		6 Facts Of Life	United Artists 043
2/9/74	85	19		7 Lookin' For A Love Again	United Artists 199
12/14/74+	142	7		8 Bobby Womack's Greatest Hits .... [G]	United Artists 346
5/24/75	126	4		9 I Don't Know What The World Is Coming To	United Artists 353
1/17/76	147	11		10 Safety Zone	United Artists 544
4/1/78	205	9		11 Pieces	Columbia 35083
6/16/79	206	3		12 Roads Of Life	Arista 4222
12/26/81+	29	23		13 The Poet	Beverly Glen 10000
4/7/84	60	14		14 The Poet II	Beverly Glen 10003
				with guest vocalist **Patti LaBelle**	
6/1/85	207	5		15 Someday We'll All Be Free	Beverly Glen 10006
9/21/85	66	19		16 So Many Rivers	MCA 5617

WOMACK, Lee Ann
Born on 8/19/1966 in Jacksonville, Texas. Country singer.

AWARD: CMA: Female Vocalist 2001

5/31/97	106	23	▲	1 Lee Ann Womack	Decca 11585
10/10/98	136	12	●	2 Some Things I Know	Decca 70040
6/10/00+	16	83	▲³	3 I Hope You Dance .... Cat:#14/18	MCA Nashville 170099
9/7/02	16	11		4 Something Worth Leaving Behind	MCA Nashville 170287
12/14/02	166	2		5 The Season For Romance .... [X]	MCA Nashville 170289
				Christmas chart: 15/'02	
5/22/04	28	8	●	6 Greatest Hits .... [G]	MCA Nashville 001883
2/26/05	12	18	●	7 There's More Where That Came From	MCA Nashville 003073
				CMA: Album of the Year	
11/8/08	23	4		8 Call Me Crazy	MCA Nashville 006025

WOMENFOLK, The
Female folk group from Pasadena, California: Elaine Gealer, Joyce James, Leni Ashmore, Barbara Cooper and Judy Fine. James died on 4/3/2001 (age 69).

5/2/64	118	6		1 The Womenfolk	RCA Victor 2832

Billboard			R I A A	ARTIST		
DEBUT	PEAK	WKS		Album Title	Catalog	Label & Number

WONDER, Stevie   1970s: #29 / All-Time: #43

Born Steveland Morris on 5/13/1950 in Saginaw, Michigan. R&B singer/songwriter/keyboardist. Blind since birth. Signed to Motown in 1960, did backup work. First recorded in 1962, named "Little Stevie Wonder" by Berry Gordy. Married to **Syreeta** Wright from 1970-72. Appeared in the movies *Bikini Beach* and *Muscle Beach Party*. Also see **Various Artists Compilations:** *Conception: An Interpretation Of Stevie Wonder's Songs.*

AWARDS: Grammy: Lifetime Achievement 1996 ★ R&R Hall of Fame: 1989 ★ Billboard Century: 2004

DEBUT	PEAK	WKS	RIAA	#	Album Title	Catalog	Label & Number
7/13/63	❶[1]	20		1	Little Stevie Wonder/The 12 Year Old Genius [L]		Tamla 240
6/18/66	33	25		2	Up-Tight Everything's Alright		Tamla 268
1/28/67	92	7		3	Down To Earth		Tamla 272
9/30/67	45	13		4	I Was Made To Love Her		Tamla 279
1/11/69	50	18		5	For Once In My Life		Tamla 291
10/11/69	34	20		6	My Cherie Amour		Tamla 296
4/11/70	81	15		7	Stevie Wonder Live [L]		Tamla 298
8/29/70	25	16		8	Signed Sealed & Delivered		Tamla 304
5/8/71	62	27		9	Where I'm Coming From		Tamla 308
3/25/72	21	35		10	Music Of My Mind		Tamla 314
					RS500 #284		
11/18/72+	❸[3]	109		11	Talking Book		Tamla 319
					Grammy: Hall of Fame ★ RS500 #90		
8/18/73	4	89		12	Innervisions		Tamla 326
					Grammys: Album of the Year / Hall of Fame ★ RS500 #23		
8/10/74	❶[2]	65		13	Fulfillingness' First Finale		Tamla 332
					Grammys: Album of the Year / Male Pop Vocal		
10/16/76	❶[14]	80	▲[10]	14	Songs In The Key Of Life		Tamla 340 [2]
					Grammys: Album of the Year / Male Pop Vocal / Hall of Fame ★ RS500 #56 ★ NRR		
11/24/79	4	22		15	Journey Through The Secret Life of Plants		Tamla 371 [2]
11/15/80	3[7]	40	▲	16	Hotter Than July		Tamla 373
10/19/85	5	50	▲[2]	17	In Square Circle		Tamla 6134
					Grammy: Male R&B Vocal		
12/5/87	17	31	▲	18	Characters		Motown 6248
4/8/95	16	15	●	19	Conversation Peace		Motown 0238
11/5/05	5	19	●	20	A Time To Love		Motown 002402
					CHRISTMAS ALBUMS:		
12/23/67	81[X]	2		21	Someday At Christmas		Tamla 281
1/15/05	49[X]	1		22	The Best Of Stevie Wonder: 20th Century Masters The Christmas Collection		Motown 002831
					GREATEST HITS & COMPILATIONS:		
4/27/68	37	29		23	Greatest Hits		Tamla 282
11/20/71+	69	12		24	Stevie Wonder's Greatest Hits, Vol. 2		Tamla 313
12/24/77+	34	13		25	Looking Back		Motown 804 [3]
5/29/82	4	28	●	26	Stevie Wonder's Original Musiquarium I		Tamla 6002 [2]
11/16/02	35	49	▲	27	The Definitive Collection Cat:❶[2]/167		Motown 066164
9/22/07	171	2		28	Number 1's		Universal Motown 009479
					SOUNDTRACKS:		
9/22/84	4	40	▲	29	The Woman In Red		Motown 6108
6/15/91	24	21	●	30	Music From The Movie Jungle Fever		Motown 6291

~ ~ ~ ~ ~ ~ ~ ~ ~ ~   **NON-CHARTED ALBUMS**   ~ ~ ~ ~ ~ ~ ~ ~ ~ ~

1962 **Tribute To Uncle Ray**   1964 **With A Song In My Heart**
1962 **The Jazz Soul Of Little Stevie**   1964 **Stevie At The Beach**

WONDER, Wayne

Born VonWayne Charles on 7/26/1972 in Franklin Town, Jamaica. Reggae singer.

3/22/03	29	18		1	No Holding Back		VP 83628

WOOD, Brenton

Born Alfred Smith on 7/26/1941 in Shreveport, Louisiana; raised in San Pedro, California. R&B singer/songwriter/pianist.

7/22/67	184	2		1	Oogum Boogum		Double Shot 5002

WOOD, Lauren

Born in Pittsburgh, Pennsylvania. Pop singer/songwriter/keyboardist.

10/20/79	205	6		1	Lauren Wood		Warner 3278

WOOD, Ronnie

Born on 6/1/1947 in Hillingdon, Middlesex, England. Rock singer/guitarist. Member of the **Jeff Beck** Group from 1967-68. Joined **Faces** in 1969. Joined **The Rolling Stones** in 1975.

7/19/75	118	6		1	Now Look		Warner 2872
5/12/79	45	13		2	Gimme Some Neck		Columbia 35702
					RON WOOD		
9/19/81	164	5		3	1234		Columbia 37473

WOOD, Roy
Born Ulysses Wood on 11/8/1946 in Birmingham, England. Co-founder/cello player of **The Move** and **Electric Light Orchestra**.

5/5/73	201	5	1 Wizzard's Brew	United Artists 042
			ROY WOOD'S WIZZARD	
11/3/73	176	6	2 Boulders..	United Artists 168
2/21/76	205	1	3 Mustard	United Artists 575

WOODBURY, Woody
Born Robert Woodbury in 1927 in St. Paul, Minnesota; later based in Fort Lauderdale, Florida. Adult comedy storyteller.

3/7/60	10	78	1 Woody Woodbury Looks At Love And Life [C]	Stereoddities 1
			no track titles listed on this album	
6/13/60	16	59	2 Woody Woodbury's Laughing Room .... [C]	Stereoddities 2
1/20/62	46	21	3 Woody Woodbury's Saloonatics .... [C]	Stereoddities 4

WOODENTOPS, The
Rock band from Northampton, England: Rolo McGinty (vocals), Simon Mawby (guitar), Alice Thompson (keyboards), Frank DeFreitas (bass) and Benny Staples (drums).

9/20/86	185	6	1 Giant	Columbia 40468

WOODS, Stevie
Born Joseph Stephen Woods on 7/2/1951 in Chatham, Virginia. Male R&B singer/songwriter. Son of jazz great Rusty Bryant.

12/5/81+	153	25	1 Take Me To Your Heaven...	Cotillion 5229

WOODWARD, Lucy
Born on 10/27/1977 in London, England; raised in the Bronx, New York. Pop singer/songwriter.

4/19/03	148	1	1 While You Can	Atlantic 83637

WOOLLEY, Bruce, & The Camera Club
Pop-rock band from England: Bruce Woolley (vocals; born on 11/11/1953), David Birch (guitar), **Thomas Dolby** (keyboards), Matthew Selingman (bass) and Rod Johnson (drums).

3/8/80	184	2	1 Bruce Woolley & The Camera Club	Columbia 36301

WORLD PARTY
Born Karl Wallinger on 10/19/1957 in Prestatyn, Wales. Rock singer/songwriter/keyboardist. Former member of **The Waterboys**.

12/27/86+	39	31	1 Private Revolution...	Chrysalis 41552
6/2/90	73	23	2 Goodbye Jumbo	Ensign 21654
5/8/93	126	8	3 Bang!..	Ensign 21991
7/5/97	167	1	4 Egyptology...	Chrysalis 56482

WORLEY, Darryl
Born on 10/31/1964 in Pyburn, Tennessee; raised in Savannah, Tennessee. Country singer/songwriter/guitarist.

8/3/02	21	13		1 I Miss My Friend	DreamWorks 50351
5/3/03	4	22	●	2 Have You Forgotten?	DreamWorks 000064
11/20/04	72	2		3 Darryl Worley...	DreamWorks 002322
12/9/06	187	1		4 Here And Now	903 Music 1003
6/27/09	172	1		5 Sounds Like Life	Stroudavarious 01002

WORTH DYING FOR
Contemporary Christian band from Modesto, California: Christy Johnson, Sean Loche, Micah Berteau, Josh O'Haire and Nathan Parrish.

5/3/08	166	1	1 Worth Dying For	Integrity 21734

WRABIT
Rock band from Ottawa, Ontario, Canada: Lou Nadeau (vocals), David Aplin (guitar), John Albani (guitar), Les Paulhus (keyboards), Chris Brockway (bass) and Scott "Jeff" Steck (drums).

2/6/82	157	8	1 Wrabit	MCA 5268
10/2/82	210	1	2 Tracks..	MCA 5359

WRATHCHILD AMERICA
Hard-rock band from Baltimore, Maryland: Brad Divens (vocals, bass; **Kix**), Jay Abbene (guitar), Terry Carter (guitar) and Shannon Larkin (drums).

9/30/89	190	6	1 Climbin' The Walls	Atlantic 81889

WRAY, Link, & His Ray Men
Born Frederick Lincoln Wray on 5/2/1929 in Dunn, North Carolina. Died of a heart attack on 11/5/2005 (age 76). Rock and roll guitarist. Also see **Robert Gordon**.

7/24/71	186	4	1 Link Wray	Polydor 4064
			recorded at Wray's 3-track shack in Maryland	

~ ~ ~ ~ ~ ~ ~ ~ ~ ~ **NON-CHARTED ALBUM** ~ ~ ~ ~ ~ ~ ~ ~ ~ ~ ~
1959 **Link Wray & The Wraymen**

WRECKERS, The
Country duo: **Michelle Branch** (born on 7/2/1983 in Sedona, Arizona) and Jessica Harp (born on 2/3/1982 in Kansas City, Missouri).

6/10/06	14	56	●	1 Stand Still, Look Pretty	Maverick 48980

WRECKX-N-EFFECT
Male rap trio from Harlem, New York: Aquil Davidson, Markell Riley and Brandon Mitchell. Riley is brother of **Guy** member/prolific producer Teddy Riley. Mitchell was shot to death in 1990.

1/13/90	103	11		1 Wrecks-N-Effect		Motown 6281
12/12/92+	9	34	▲	2 Hard Or Smooth		MCA 10566

WRIGHT, Bernard
Born in 1963 in Queens, New York. R&B singer/keyboardist.

3/14/81	116	14		1 'Nard		GRP 5011

WRIGHT, Betty
Born on 12/21/1953 in Miami, Florida. R&B singer.

2/26/72	123	6		1 I Love The Way You Love		Alston 388
6/17/78	26	36		2 Betty Wright Live	[L]	Alston 4408
6/2/79	138	6		3 Betty Travelin' In The Wright Circle		Alston 4410
4/23/88	127	13		4 Mother Wit		Ms. B 3301

WRIGHT, Charles, And The Watts 103rd Street Rhythm Band
Born in 1942 in Clarksdale, Mississippi. R&B singer/songwriter/producer. The Watts 103rd Street Rhythm Band: Al McKay (guitar), John Rayford (sax), Bill Cannon (sax), Gabriel Flemings (keyboards), Ray Jackson (trombone), Joe Banks (trumpet), Melvin Dunlap (bass) and James Gadson (drums). McKay later joined **Earth, Wind & Fire**.

4/19/69	140	5		1 Together		Warner 1761
10/18/69	145	4		2 In The Jungle, Babe		Warner 1801
				THE WATTS 103RD STREET RHYTHM BAND (above 2)		
8/8/70	182	10		3 Express Yourself		Warner 1864
5/15/71	147	11		4 You're So Beautiful		Warner 1904

WRIGHT, Chely
Born Richelle Wright on 10/25/1970 in Kansas City, Missouri. Country singer/songwriter/guitarist.

10/4/97	171	7		1 Let Me In		MCA Nashville 70003
6/5/99	124	5	●	2 Single White Female		MCA Nashville 70052
10/13/01	62	3		3 Never Love You Enough		MCA Nashville 70210
3/12/05	96	2		4 The Metropolitan Hotel		Painted Red 12002

WRIGHT, Gary
Born on 4/26/1943 in Creskill, New Jersey. Pop-rock singer/songwriter/keyboardist. Appeared in *Captain Video* TV series in 1950. Member of **Spooky Tooth**.

8/23/75+	7	75	▲[2]	1 The Dream Weaver		Warner 2868
4/24/76	172	4		2 That Was Only Yesterday	[K]	A&M 3528 [2]
				GARY WRIGHT/SPOOKY TOOTH		
1/22/77	23	15		3 The Light Of Smiles		Warner 2951
12/10/77+	117	9		4 Touch And Gone		Warner 3137
3/17/79	147	5		5 Headin' Home		Warner 3244
6/27/81	79	19		6 The Right Place		Warner 3511

WRIGHT, Jaguar
Born in Philadelphia, Pennsylvania. Female R&B singer/songwriter.

2/16/02	56	14		1 Denials Delusions And Decisions		Motive 112683

WRIGHT, Lizz
Born on 1/22/1980 in Hahira, Georgia. Jazz singer.

3/15/08	97	6		1 The Orchard		Verve Forecast 010292

WRIGHT, Michelle
Born on 7/1/1961 in Morpeth, Ontario, Canada. Country singer.

6/13/92	126	14		1 Now & Then		Arista 18685

WRIGHT, Richard
Born on 1/28/1945 in London, England. Died of cancer on 9/15/2008 (age 65). Rock singer/keyboard player. Member of **Pink Floyd**.

11/4/78	203	1		1 Wet Dream		Columbia 35559

WRIGHT, Steven
Born on 12/6/1955 in New York. Stand-up comedian/actor. Known for his "deadpan" delivery. Appeared in several movies.

11/23/85	192	2		1 I Have A Pony	[C]	Warner 25335

WRITER, JR
Born Juan Brito on 9/13/1984 in Manhattan, New York. Latin male rapper.

7/29/06	25	4		1 History In The Making		Diplomatic Man 5839
3/3/07	84	3		2 Writer's Block 4		Diplomatic Man 100461

W'S, The
Christian ska-rock band from Corvallis, Oregon: Andrew Schar (vocals, guitar), Valentine Hellman, Bret Barker and James Carter (horns), Todd Gruener (bass) and Brian Morris (drums).

8/15/98	147	2		1 Fourth From The Last		Sarabellum 25204

WU-SYNDICATE
Male rap duo from Virginia: Myalansky and Joe Mafia.

5/8/99	61	3		1 Wu-Syndicate		Wu-Tang 50056

Billboard DEBUT	PEAK	WKS	R I A A	ARTIST / Album Title	Catalog	Label & Number
				WU-TANG CLAN		
				Rap group from Staten Island, New York: Gary Grice (**Genius/GZA**), Clifford Smith (**Method Man**), Russell Jones (**Ol Dirty Bastard**; died of a drug overdose on 11/13/2004, age 35), Corey Woods (**Raekwon**), Jason Hunter (**Inspectah Deck**), Dennis Coles (**Ghostface Killah**), Lamont Hawkins (**U-God**), Robert Diggs (**RZA**) and Elgin Turner (**Masta Killa**). Diggs was also a member of **Gravediggaz**. Hunter was a member of **X-Clan**.		
11/27/93	41	42	▲	1 Enter The Wu-Tang (36 Chambers)... Cat:#19/23		Loud 66336
				RS500 #386		
6/21/97	❶¹	41	▲⁴	2 Wu-Tang Forever		Loud 66905 [2]
12/9/00	5	17	▲	3 The W		Wu-Tang 62193
7/21/01	72	4		4 Wu-Chronicles Chapter II .... [K]		Wu-Tang 24461
1/5/02	32	13	●	5 Iron Flag		Wu-Tang 86236
10/16/04	82	4		6 Disciples Of The 36 Chambers: Chapter 1 .... [L]		Wu-Tang 84727
11/13/04	72	2		7 Legend Of The Wu-Tang: Wu-Tang Clan's Greatest Hits............... [G]		BMG 61645
12/29/07	25	9		8 8 Diagrams		Wu 010560
7/18/09	49	2		9 Chamber Music		Wu-Tang 4215
				WU-TANG		
				WU-TANG KILLA BEES		
				Rap group from New York. Features **Wu-Tang Clan** members **RZA**, **Method Man**, **Ghostface Killah**, **Raekwon**, **Inspectah Deck** and **Masta Killa**, with **Cappadonna**, **Killarmy** and **Sunz Of Man**.		
8/8/98	4	10	●	1 The Swarm		Wu-Tang 50013
3/30/02	46	6		2 The Sting		Wu-Tang 8362 [2]
				KILLA BEEZ		
				WYATT, Keke		
				Born Ketara Wyatt on 3/10/1982 in Indianapolis, Indiana. Female R&B singer.		
12/1/01+	33	27	●	1 Soul Sista		MCA 112609
				WYMAN, Bill		
				Born William Perks on 10/24/1936 in London, England. Bass guitarist of **The Rolling Stones** from 1962-92.		
6/15/74	99	11		1 Monkey Grip		Rolling Stones 59102
3/27/76	166	5		2 Stone Alone		Rolling Stones 79103
				WYNETTE, Tammy		
				Born Virginia Wynette Pugh on 5/5/1942 in Itawamba County, Mississippi. Died of a blood clot on 4/6/1998 (age 55). Dubbed "The First Lady of Country Music." Married to **George Jones** from 1969-75. Also see **Various Artists Compilations**: *Tammy Wynette Remembered*.		
				AWARDS: C&W Hall of Fame: 1998 ★ CMA: Female Vocalist 1968, 1969 & 1970 ★ OPRY: 1970		
9/7/68+	147	15		1 D-I-V-O-R-C-E		Epic 26392
2/8/69	43	21		2 Stand By Your Man		Epic 26451
5/24/69	189	3		3 Inspiration		Epic 26423
9/6/69	37	61	▲	4 Tammy's Greatest Hits [G]		Epic 26486
2/21/70	83	11		5 The Ways To Love A Man		Epic 26519
5/16/70	85	17		6 Tammy's Touch		Epic 26549
8/15/70	145	2		7 The World Of Tammy Wynette .... [K]		Epic 503 [2]
10/31/70	119	14		8 The First Lady		Epic 30213
12/26/70	30ˣ	1		9 Christmas With Tammy .... [X]		Epic 30343
5/22/71	115	10		10 We Sure Can Love Each Other		Epic 30658
9/18/71	118	8	●	11 Tammy's Greatest Hits, Volume II .... [G]		Epic 30733
11/13/71	169	6		12 We Go Together		Epic 30802
				TAMMY WYNETTE & GEORGE JONES		
4/8/72	133	9		13 Bedtime Story		Epic 31285
2/3/73	201	4		14 My Man		Epic 31717
11/20/93	42	16	●	15 Honky Tonk Angels		Columbia 53414
				DOLLY PARTON, LORETTA LYNN, TAMMY WYNETTE		
7/8/95	117	13		16 One		MCA 11248
				GEORGE JONES & TAMMY WYNETTE		
				WYNONNA **All-Time: #410**		
				Born Christina Ciminella (her biological father was Charlie Jordan) on 5/30/1964 in Ashland, Kentucky. Country singer. One-half of **The Judds** duo with her mother, Naomi. Half-sister of actress Ashley Judd.		
4/18/92	4	86	▲⁵	1 Wynonna		Curb/MCA 10529
5/29/93	5	54	▲	2 Tell Me Why		Curb/MCA 10822
				WYNONNA JUDD (above 2)		
3/2/96	9	26	▲	3 Revelations		Curb/MCA 11090
4/26/97	72	10		4 Collection.. [G]		Curb/MCA 11583
11/8/97	38	19	●	5 The Other Side..		Curb 53061
2/19/00	40	7		6 New Day Dawning		Curb 541067 [2]
8/23/03	8	19		7 What The World Needs Now Is Love		Curb 78811
10/15/05	25	6		8 Her Story: Scenes From A Lifetime .... [L]		Curb 78920 [2]
12/2/06	53	5		9 A Classic Christmas... [X]		Curb 78955
				Christmas chart: 14/'06		
2/21/09	37	3		10 Sing: Chapter 1...		Curb 79133

X

X
Punk-rock band formed in Los Angeles, California: Exene Cervenka (vocals), Billy Zoom (guitar), **John Doe** (bass) and Don Bonebrake (drums). Zoom was replaced by **Dave Alvin** (of **The Blasters**). Tony Gilkyson (son of Canadian singer Terry Gilkyson) joined in early 1987. Cervenka and Doe were married for a time.

DEBUT	PEAK	WKS			Catalog	Label & Number
6/6/81	165	5		1 Wild Gift		Slash 107
				RS500 #334		
7/17/82	76	15		2 Under The Big Black Sun		Elektra 60150
10/8/83	86	23		3 More Fun In The New World		Elektra 60283
8/17/85	89	14		4 Ain't Love Grand		Elektra 60430
7/11/87	107	11		5 See How We Are		Elektra 60492
5/14/88	175	5		6 Live At The Whiskey A Go-Go On The Fabulous Sunset Strip .... [L]		Elektra 60788 [2]

~ ~ ~ ~ ~ ~ ~ ~ ~ ~ **NON-CHARTED ALBUM** ~ ~ ~ ~ ~ ~ ~ ~ ~ ~ ~

1980 **Los Angeles**
RS500 #286

XAVIER
Funk band from Hartford, Connecticut: Ernest "Xavier" Smith (guitar, vocals), Ayanna Little, Emonie Branch and Chuck Hughes (vocals), Jeff Mitchell (guitar), Lyburn Downing (percussion), Ralph Hunt (bass) and Tim Williams (drums).

4/24/82	129	7		1 Point Of Pleasure		Liberty 51116

XAVION
Funk band from Memphis, Tennessee: Dexter Haywood (vocals), Kevan Wilkins (guitar), Johnnie Woods and Derwin Adams (keyboards), Skip Johnson (bass) and Michael Tucker (drums).

10/13/84	201	6		1 Burnin' Hot		Asylum 60375

X-CLAN
Rap group from Brooklyn, New York: Lumumba "Professor X" Carson, Jason "Brother J" Hunter, Anthony "Sugar Shaft" Hardin and Claude "Paradise" Grey. Hunter later joined **Wu-Tang Clan** under the name **Inspectah Deck**. Hardin died of AIDS on 9/1/1995 (age 25). Carson died of spinal meningitis on 3/17/2006 (age 49).

6/2/90	97	25		1 To The East, Blackwards		4th & B'way 4019
6/6/92	31	12		2 Xodus-The New Testament		Polydor 513225

X-ECUTIONERS, The
Rap-DJ production group from Brooklyn, New York: Mista Sinista, Rob Swift, Total Eclipse and Roc Raida (died in a car crash on 9/19/2009, age 37).

3/16/02	15	12		1 Built From Scratch		Loud 86410
6/26/04	118	1		2 Revolutions		Columbia 87136

XMAS BALLS
Novelty trio: Monty Lane Allen, Jerry "**Swamp Dogg**" Williams and Ned McElroy.

1/15/05	37[X]	1		1 She Left Me For Randolph .... [X-N]		S.D.E.G. 1953

XSCAPE
Female R&B vocal group from Atlanta, Georgia: sisters LaTocha Scott and Tamika Scott, with **Kandi** Burruss and Tameka Cottle.

10/30/93	17	36	▲	1 Hummin' Comin' At 'Cha		So So Def 57107
8/5/95	23	42	▲	2 Off The Hook		So So Def 67022
5/30/98	28	33	▲	3 Traces Of My Lipstick		So So Def 68042

XTC
Alternative-rock band formed in Wiltshire, England: Andy Partridge (guitar; born on 11/1/1953), Dave Gregory (keyboards; born on 9/21/1952), Colin Moulding (bass; born on 8/17/1955) and Terry Chambers (drums; born on 7/18/1955). All share vocals. Chambers left in 1986.

1/26/80	176	8		1 Drums And Wires		Virgin 13134
11/22/80+	41	24		2 Black Sea		Virgin 13147
3/20/82	48	20		3 English Settlement		Epic 37943
2/25/84	145	5		4 Mummer		Geffen 4027
11/10/84	178	5		5 The Big Express		Geffen 24054
1/24/87	70	29		6 Skylarking		Geffen 24117
3/18/89	44	21		7 Oranges & Lemons		Geffen 24218 [2]
5/16/92	97	11		8 Nonsuch		Geffen 24474
3/13/99	106	3		9 Apple Venus Volume 1		TVT 3250
6/10/00	108	2		10 Wasp Star (Apple Venus Volume 2)		TVT 3260

XX, The
Electro-pop trio from London, England: Jamie Smith, Romy Croft and Oliver Sim.

9/19/09+	94	22		1 XX		XL 450

XYMOX
Techno-rock/dance trio from Amsterdam, Netherlands: Ronny Moorings (vocals, guitar, keyboards), Pieter Nooten (keyboards) and Anka Wolbert (bass, vocals, keyboards).

6/3/89	165	10		1 Twist Of Shadows		Wing 839233
5/11/91	163	2		2 Phoenix		Wing 848516

XYZ
Hard-rock band from Los Angeles, California: Terry Ilous (vocals), Marc Diglio (guitar), Pat Fontaine (bass) and Paul Monroe (drums).

DEBUT	PEAK	WKS			
12/16/89+	99	24		1 XYZ	Enigma 73525

XZIBIT
Born Alvin Joiner on 9/18/1974 in Detroit, Michigan; raised in New Mexico. Male rapper/songwriter. Hosted MTV's car restoration show *Pimp My Ride*.

DEBUT	PEAK	WKS			
11/2/96	74	4		1 At The Speed Of Life	Loud 66816
9/12/98	58	5		2 40 Dayz & 40 Nightz	Loud 67578
12/30/00+	12	28	▲	3 Restless	Loud 1885
10/19/02	3[1]	12	●	4 Man vs Machine	Loud 85925
1/1/05	43	8	●	5 Weapons Of Mass Destruction	Columbia 92558
11/4/06	50	2		6 Full Circle	Open Bar 4127

Y

YACHTS
Rock band from Liverpool, England: Martin Watson (guitar), Henry Priestman (keyboards), Martin Dempsey (bass) and Bob Bellis (drums). All share vocals.

DEBUT	PEAK	WKS			
10/20/79	179	3		1 S.O.S.	Polydor 6220

YAMAGATA, Rachael
Born on 9/23/1977 in Arlington, Virginia. Female singer/songwriter.

DEBUT	PEAK	WKS			
10/25/08	53	3		1 Elephants...Teeth Sinking Into Heart	Warner 512764

YAMASHTA, Stomu
Born on 3/15/1947 in Kyoto, Japan. Eclectic composer/percussionist.

DEBUT	PEAK	WKS			
8/21/76	60	12		1 Go	Island 9387
				STOMU YAMASHTA / STEVE WINWOOD / MICHAEL SHRIEVE	
10/15/77	156	6		2 Go Too	Arista 4138
8/12/78	205	2		3 Go - Live From Paris .... [L]	Island 10 [2]

YAMES, Yim
Born James Olliges in Louisville, Kentucky. Rock singer/songwriter. Lead singer of **My Morning Jacket**. Member of **Monsters Of Folk**.

DEBUT	PEAK	WKS			
8/22/09	111	1		1 Tribute To .... [EP]	ATO 0074

YAMIN, Elliott
Born on 7/20/1978 in Los Angeles, California; raised in Richmond, Virginia. "Blue-eyed soul" singer/songwriter. Finalist on the fifth season of TV's *American Idol* in 2006.

DEBUT	PEAK	WKS			
4/7/07	3[1]	32	●	1 Elliott Yamin	Hickory 90019
12/8/07+	32	5		2 Sounds Of The Season: The Elliott Yamin Holiday Collection .... [X]	Pulse 70011
				Christmas chart: 1/'07	
3/21/09	162	1		3 My Kind Of Holiday .... [X]	Pulse 901292
				Christmas chart: 34/'10	
5/23/09	26	4		4 Fight For Love	Pulse 30100

Y&T
Hard-rock band from San Francisco, California: Dave Meniketti (vocals, guitar), Joey Alves (guitar), Philip Kennemore (bass) and Leonard Haze (drums). Haze was replaced by Jimmy DeGrasso in 1986. Alves was replaced by Stef Burns in 1989. Band name stands for Yesterday & Today.

DEBUT	PEAK	WKS			
9/10/83	103	12		1 Mean Streak	A&M 4960
8/18/84	46	17		2 In Rock We Trust	A&M 5007
7/20/85	70	17		3 Open Fire .... [L]	A&M 5076
11/23/85	91	12		4 Down For The Count	A&M 5101
7/11/87	78	13		5 Contagious	Geffen 24142
6/2/90	110	8		6 Ten	Geffen 24283

YANKOVIC, "Weird Al"   All-Time: #384
Born on 10/23/1959 in Lynwood, California. Novelty singer/accordionist. Specializes in song parodies. Starred in the movie *UHF*.

DEBUT	PEAK	WKS			
5/21/83	139	8	●	1 "Weird Al" Yankovic .... [N]	Rock 'n' Roll 38679
3/17/84	17	23	▲	2 "Weird Al" Yankovic In 3-D .... [N]	Rock 'n' Roll 39221
7/13/85	50	16	▲	3 Dare To Be Stupid .... [N]	Rock 'n' Roll 40033
11/15/86	177	4		4 Polka Party! .... [N]	Rock 'n' Roll 40520
5/7/88	27	26	▲	5 Even Worse .... [N]	Rock 'n' Roll 44149
8/19/89	146	4		6 UHF/Original Motion Picture Soundtrack And Other Stuff .... [N-S]	Rock 'n' Roll 45265
5/2/92	17	27	▲	7 Off The Deep End .... [N]	Scotti Brothers 75256
10/23/93	46	24	●	8 Alapalooza .... [N]	Scotti Brothers 75415
12/17/94	198	1		9 Greatest Hits Volume II .... [G-N]	Scotti Brothers 75456
3/30/96	14	56	▲	10 Bad Hair Day .... [N]	Rock 'n' Roll 75500
7/17/99	16	32	▲	11 Running With Scissors .... [N]	Way Moby 32118
6/7/03	17	15		12 Poodle Hat .... [N]	Way Moby 31294
				Grammy: Comedy Album	

Billboard			R I A A	ARTIST Album Title	Catalog	Label & Number
DEBUT	PEAK	WKS				

YANKOVIC, "Weird Al" — cont'd

| 10/14/06 | 10 | 20 | ● | 13 Straight Outta Lynwood [N] | | Way Moby 89951 |
| 11/14/09 | 178 | 1 | | 14 The Essential "Weird Al" Yankovic .... [G-N] | | Way Moby 58543 [2] |

YANNI   **1990s: #14 / All-Time: #202**

Born Yiannis Chryssolmalis on 11/14/1954 in Kalamata, Greece; later based in Minneapolis, Minnesota. New Age keyboardist. Long-term relationship (never married) with actress Linda Evans (1989-98).

3/28/92	32	35	▲	1 Dare To Dream .... Cat:#5/80 [I]		Private Music 82096
4/24/93	24	73	▲	2 In My Time .... [I]		Private Music 82106
5/1/99	98	8		3 Love Songs .... [I]		Private Music 82167
10/21/00	20	22	●	4 If I Could Tell You .... [I]		Virgin 49893
3/1/03	27	17		5 Ethnicity... [I]		Virgin 81516
4/11/09	20	15		6 Yanni Voices		Yanni Wake 003659

GREATEST HITS & COMPILATIONS:

8/4/90+	29	93	▲²	7 Reflections Of Passion .... Cat:#3/71 [I]		Private Music 2067
11/30/91+	60	17	●	8 In Celebration Of Life .... Cat:#14/3 [I]		Private Music 2093
5/3/97	17	19	●	9 In The Mirror .... [I]		Private Music 82150
5/24/97	142	2		10 Port Of Mystery .... [I]		Windham Hill 11241
9/13/97	42	22	●	11 Devotion: The Best Of Yanni .... [I]		Private Music 82153
2/8/03	74	5		12 Ultimate Yanni .... [I]		Windham Hill 18106 [2]

LIVE ALBUMS:

3/19/94	5	114	▲⁴	13 Live At The Acropolis [I]		Private Music 82116
				recorded on 9/25/1993 in Athens, Greece		
11/22/97	21	33	▲	14 Tribute .... [I]		Virgin 44981
9/2/06	84	2		15 Yanni Live!: The Concert Event................................ [I]		Yanni 3564

YARBROUGH, Glenn

Born on 1/12/1930 in Milwaukee, Wisconsin. Folk singer. Lead singer of **The Limeliters** (1959-63).

9/19/64	142	4		1 One More Round		RCA Victor 2905
5/8/65	112	8		2 Come Share My Life...		RCA Victor 3301
6/12/65	35	24		3 Baby The Rain Must Fall		RCA Victor 3422
11/6/65	75	12		4 It's Gonna Be Fine		RCA Victor 3472
6/25/66	61	24		5 The Lonely Things		RCA Victor 3539
11/5/66	85	9		6 Live At The Hungry i .... [L]		RCA Victor 3661
5/27/67	159	14		7 For Emily, Whenever I May Find Her		RCA Victor 3801
9/16/67	141	18		8 Honey & Wine		RCA Victor 3860
11/9/68	188	2		9 Each Of Us Alone (The Words And Music Of Rod McKuen) ...		Warner 1736
5/10/69	189	5		10 Glenn Yarbrough Sings The Rod McKuen Songbook .... [K]		RCA Victor 6018 [2]

YARBROUGH & PEOPLES

Male-female R&B-funk vocal duo from Dallas, Texas: Cavin Yarbrough and Alisa Peoples.

| 12/27/80+ | 16 | 24 | ● | 1 The Two Of Us .... | | Mercury 3834 |
| 4/14/84 | 90 | 16 | | 2 Be A Winner .... | | Total Experience 5700 |

YARDBIRDS, The

Rock band formed in England: Keith Relf (vocals, harmonica), **Eric Clapton** and Chris Dreja (guitars), Paul Samwell-Smith (bass, keyboards) and Jim McCarty (drums). **Jeff Beck** replaced Clapton after first album. Samwell-Smith left in 1966; Dreja switched to bass and **Jimmy Page** (guitar) was added. Beck left in December 1966. Group disbanded in July 1968. Page formed the New Yardbirds in October 1968, which evolved into **Led Zeppelin**. Relf died from electrocution on 5/14/1976 (age 33).
AWARD: R&R Hall of Fame: 1992

7/31/65	96	11		1 For Your Love		Epic 26167
12/18/65+	53	33		2 Having A Rave Up With The Yardbirds		Epic 26177
				RS500 #353		
8/27/66	52	16		3 Over Under Sideways Down		Epic 26210
				RS500 #349		
4/29/67	28	37		4 The Yardbirds' Greatest Hits.............................. [G]		Epic 26246
8/12/67	80	8		5 Little Games		Epic 26313
10/3/70	155	6		6 The Yardbirds/Featuring Performances By Jeff Beck, Eric Clapton, Jimmy Page..................................... [K]		Epic 30135 [2]
4/30/77	204	3		7 The Yardbirds Great Hits.................................... [G]		Epic 34491

YARROW, Peter

Born on 5/31/1938 in Brooklyn, New York. Folk singer/songwriter/guitarist. Member of **Peter, Paul & Mary**.

| 3/4/72 | 163 | 8 | | 1 Peter .... | | Warner 2599 |
| 10/13/73 | 203 | 6 | | 2 That's Enough For Me....................................... | | Warner 2730 |

YAYO, Tony

Born Marvin Bernard on 3/31/1978 in Queens, New York. Male rapper. Spent time in prison on weapons charges.

| 9/17/05 | 2¹ | 11 | | 1 Thoughts Of A Predicate Felon | | G-Unit 004873 |

Billboard			R I A A	ARTIST Album Title	Catalog	Label & Number
DEBUT	PEAK	WKS				

YAZ
Synth-dance duo from England: **Alison Moyet** and Vince Clarke (formerly of **Depeche Mode**). Duo formerly named **Yazoo**. Clarke later formed **Erasure**.

10/2/82	92	32	▲	1 Upstairs At Eric's .... Cat:#12/79		Sire 23737
				YAZOO		
8/13/83	69	13		2 You And Me Both		Sire 23903

YEAH YEAH YEAHS
Punk-rock trio from Long Island, New York: Karen Orzolek (vocals), Nick Zinner (guitar) and Brian Chase (drums). Also see **Karen O And the Kids.**

5/17/03+	55	28	●	1 Fever To Tell		Interscope 000349
4/15/06	11	10		2 Show Your Bones		Dress Up 006337
8/11/07	72	3		3 Is Is .... [EP]		Dress Up 009381
3/28/09	22	28		4 It's Blitz!		Dress Up 012735

YEARWOOD, Trisha   1990s: #39 / All-Time: #280
Born Patricia Lynn Yearwood on 9/19/1964 in Monticello, Georgia. Country singer. Married to Robert Reynolds (of **The Mavericks**) from 1994-99. Married **Garth Brooks** on 12/10/2005.
AWARDS: CMA: Female Vocalist 1997 & 1998 ★ OPRY: 1999

7/20/91	31	83	▲2	1 Trisha Yearwood		MCA 10297
9/19/92	46	46	▲	2 Hearts In Armor		MCA 10641
11/13/93	40	20	▲	3 The Song Remembers When		MCA 10911
12/10/94	105	6	●	4 The Sweetest Gift .... Cat:#46/1 [X]		MCA 11091
				Christmas charts: 17/94, 37/99, 39/00		
3/4/95	28	24	▲	5 Thinkin' About You		MCA 11201
9/14/96	52	16	●	6 Everybody Knows		MCA 11477
9/13/97	4	54	▲4	7 Songbook - A Collection Of Hits Cat:#46/1 [G]		MCA Nashville 70011
8/1/98	33	25	▲	8 Where Your Road Leads		MCA Nashville 70023
4/15/00	27	12	●	9 Real Live Woman		MCA Nashville 70102
6/23/01	29	19	●	10 Inside Out...		MCA Nashville 70200
10/1/05	4	19	●	11 Jasper County		MCA Nashville 002326
9/29/07	22	5		12 Greatest Hits .... [G]		MCA Nashville 008776
12/1/07	30	7		13 Heaven, Heartache And The Power Of Love		Big Machine 020302

YELLA
Born Antoine Carraby on 12/11/1967 in Los Angeles, California. Male rapper. Member of **N.W.A.**

| 4/13/96 | 82 | 4 | | 1 One Mo Nigga Ta Go .... | | Street Life 75488 |

YELLO
Computer/synthesizer duo from Zurich, Switzerland: Dieter Meier and Boris Blank.

7/16/83	184	4		1 You Gotta Say Yes To Another Excess...................................		Elektra 60271
9/26/87	92	10		2 One Second		Mercury 832765
4/15/89	152	9		3 Flag		Mercury 836426

YELLOWCARD
Punk-rock band from Jacksonville, Florida: Ryan Key (vocals, guitar), Sean Mackin (violin, vocals), Benjamin E. Harper (guitar), Alex Lewis (bass) and Longineu Parsons (drums).

8/9/03+	23	81	▲	1 Ocean Avenue		Capitol 39844
2/11/06	5	16	●	2 Lights And Sounds		Capitol 70960
8/4/07	13	7		3 Paper Walls		Capitol 98153

YELLOWJACKETS
Pop-jazz band formed in Los Angeles, California: Russell Ferrante (keyboards), Marc Russo (sax), Jimmy Haslip (bass) and Ricky Lawson (drums). Formed as the backing band for **Robben Ford**. Haslip was a member of **Blackjack.**

7/25/81	201	9		1 Yellowjackets .... [I]		Warner 3573
5/28/83	145	10		2 Mirage A Trois .... [I]		Warner 23813
4/13/85	179	4		3 Samurai Samba .... [I]		Warner 25204
9/6/86	195	2		4 Shades .... [I]		MCA 5752

YELLOW MAGIC ORCHESTRA
Electronic instrumental trio from Japan: Ryuichi Sakamoto, Yukihiro Takahashi and Haruomi Hosono.

| 1/26/80 | 81 | 21 | | 1 Yellow Magic Orchestra .... [I] | | Horizon 736 |
| 9/20/80 | 177 | 2 | | 2 X Multiplies .... | | A&M 4813 |

YELLOWMAN
Born Winston Foster on 1/15/1956 in Negril, Jamaica. Albino reggae singer.

| 6/2/84 | 203 | 5 | | 1 King Yellowman .... | | Columbia 39301 |

YES
All-Time: #122

Progressive-rock band formed in London: **Jon Anderson** (vocals), **Peter Banks** (guitar), Tony Kaye (keyboards), **Chris Squire** (bass) and **Bill Bruford** (drums). Banks, who went on to form **Flash** and **After The Fire**, replaced by **Steve Howe** in 1971. Kaye (joined **Badfinger** in 1978) replaced by **Rick Wakeman** in 1971. Bruford left to join **King Crimson**, replaced by **Alan White** in late 1972. Wakeman replaced by **Patrick Moraz** in 1974, re-joined in 1976 when Moraz left. Wakeman and Anderson left in 1980, replaced by **The Buggles'** Trevor Horne (guitar) and Geoff Downes (keyboards). Group disbanded in 1980. Howe and Downes joined **Asia**. Re-formed in 1983 with Anderson, Kaye, Squire, White and South African guitarist **Trevor Rabin**. Anderson left group in 1988. **Anderson, Bruford, Wakeman, Howe** formed self-named group in early 1989. Yes reunited in 1991 with Anderson, Bruford, Wakeman, Howe, Kaye, Squire, White and Rabin. Bruford, Wakeman and Howe had left group by 1994. Lineup in 1996: Anderson, Howe, Squire, Wakeman and White. Billy Sherwood replaced Wakeman in 1997.

7/24/82	36^C	2		1	Yes	[E]	Atlantic 8243
					first released in 1969		
5/8/71+	40	50	▲	2	The Yes Album	Cat:#25/13	Atlantic 8283
1/22/72	4	46	▲²	3	Fragile	Cat:#5/30	Atlantic 7211
10/7/72	3¹	32	▲	4	Close To The Edge	Cat:#25/12	Atlantic 7244
2/2/74	6	27	●	5	Tales From Topographic Oceans		Atlantic 908 [2]
12/28/74+	5	16	●	6	Relayer		Atlantic 18122
7/30/77	8	21	●	7	Going For The One		Atlantic 19106
10/14/78	10	14	▲	8	Tormato		Atlantic 19202
9/13/80	18	19		9	Drama		Atlantic 16019
12/3/83+	5	53	▲³	10	90125		Atco 90125
					title refers to label number		
10/17/87	15	30	▲	11	Big Generator		Atco 90522
7/1/89	30	16	●	12	Anderson, Bruford, Wakeman, Howe		Arista 90126
5/18/91	15	19	●	13	Union		Arista 8643
11/13/93	164	2		14	Symphonic Music Of Yes	[I]	RCA Victor 61938
4/9/94	33	8		15	Talk		Victory 480033
12/13/97	151	1		16	Open Your Eyes		Beyond 3074
10/16/99	99	2		17	The Ladder		Beyond 78046
12/22/01	186	1		18	Magnification		Beyond 578205

GREATEST HITS & COMPILATIONS:

3/22/75	17	12		19	Yesterdays		Atlantic 18103
1/9/82	142	5	▲	20	Classic Yes		Atlantic 19320
2/14/04	131	1		21	The Ultimate Yes: 35th Anniversary Collection		Elektra 78042 [3]

LIVE ALBUMS:

5/26/73	12	32	▲	22	Yessongs		Atlantic 100 [3]
12/20/80+	43	12		23	Yesshows		Atlantic 510 [2]
11/30/85	81	11		24	9012Live - The Solos		Atco 90474
11/16/96	99	1		25	Keys To Ascension		CMC Int'l. 86208 [2]
					recorded on 3/4/1996 at the Fremont Theatre in San Luis Obispo, California		

YING YANG TWINS

Hip-hop duo from Atlanta, Georgia: Deongelo "D-Roc" Holmes (born on 2/13/1979) and Eric "Kaine" Jackson (born on 12/16/1978). They are not related.

4/13/02	58	20		1	Alley: The Return Of The Ying Yang Twins		Collipark 8375
10/4/03	11	54	▲	2	Me & My Brother		Collipark 2480
11/20/04	12	17		3	My Brother & Me		Collipark 2489
7/16/05	2¹	23	▲	4	U.S.A.: United State Of Atlanta		Collipark 2520
1/14/06	45	19		5	U.S.A. Still United		Collipark 2790
12/16/06	40	6		6	Chemically Imbalanced		Collipark 2850

YIPES!!

Rock band from Milwaukee, Wisconsin: Pat McCurdy (vocals), Andy Bartel (guitar), Mike Hoffmann (guitar), Pete Strand (bass) and Teddy Freese (drums).

10/6/79	177	4		1	Yipes!!		Millennium 7745

YOAKAM, Dwight
All-Time: #240

Born on 10/23/1956 in Pikeville, Kentucky. Country singer/songwriter/guitarist/actor. Acted in the movies *Sling Blade*, *The Newton Boys* and *Panic Room*.

4/19/86	61	65	▲²	1	Guitars, Cadillacs, Etc., Etc.		Reprise 25372
5/16/87	55	28	▲	2	Hillbilly Deluxe		Reprise 25567
8/20/88	68	15	▲	3	Buenas Noches From A Lonely Room		Reprise 25749
10/14/89	68	10	▲	4	Just Lookin' For A Hit	[G]	Reprise 25989
11/17/90+	96	75	▲	5	If There Was A Way		Reprise 26344
4/10/93	25	81	▲³	6	This Time		Reprise 45241
6/10/95	56	13	●	7	Dwight Live	[L]	Reprise 45907
11/18/95	30	14	●	8	Gone		Reprise 46051
8/2/97	92	7		9	Under The Covers		Reprise 46690
6/27/98	60	11		10	A Long Way Home		Reprise 46918
6/5/99	80	19	●	11	Last Chance For A Thousand Years - Dwight Yoakam's Greatest Hits From The 90's	[G]	Reprise 47389
6/17/00	195	1		12	dwightyoakamacoustic.net		Reprise 47714
11/18/00	68	4		13	Tomorrow's Sounds Today		Reprise 47827

DEBUT	PEAK	WKS	R I A A	ARTIST / Album Title	Catalog	Label & Number
				YOAKAM, Dwight — cont'd		
7/12/03	75	7		14 Population: Me		Audium 8176
8/14/04	87	12	●	15 The Very Best Of Dwight Yoakam .... [G]		Reprise 78964
7/2/05	54	6		16 Blame The Vain		VIA 6075
11/10/07	42	8		17 Dwight Sings Buck		Via 6129
				YO GOTTI		
				Born Mario Mims on 5/19/1982 in Memphis, Tennessee. Male rapper.		
6/10/06	84	5		1 Back 2 Da Basics		Mouth Of The South 2680
4/25/09	200	1		2 CM2		Inevitable 6273
				YO LA TENGO		
				Alternative-rock trio from Hoboken, New Jersey: Ira Kaplan (vocals, guitar), James McNew (bass) and Georgia Hubley (drums). Kaplan and Hubley are married. Name is Spanish for "I've got it."		
3/11/00	138	2		1 And Then Nothing Turned Itself Inside-Out...............		Matador 371
4/26/03	115	2		2 Summer Sun		Matador 0548
9/30/06	66	4		3 I Am Not Afraid Of You And I Will Beat Your Ass		Matador 692
9/26/09	58	4		4 Popular Songs		Matador 856
				YORKE, Thom		
				Born on 10/7/1968 in Wellingborough, Northamptonshire, England. Alternative-rock singer/songwriter/guitarist. Lead singer of **Radiohead**.		
7/29/06	2[1]	10		1 Eraser		XL 200
				YORN, Pete		
				Born on 7/27/1974 in Montville, New Jersey. Adult Alternative singer/songwriter/guitarist.		
7/14/01+	111	43	●	1 Music For The Morning After		Columbia 62216
5/3/03	18	10		2 Day I Forgot		Columbia 86922
9/16/06	50	3		3 Nightcrawler		Columbia 92892
7/4/09	32	5		4 Back & Forth		Columbia 32162
10/3/09	41	9		5 Break Up		Boyletown 511166
				PETE YORN & SCARLETT JOHANSSON		
				YOST, Dennis — see CLASSICS IV		
				YOULDEN, Chris		
				Born in 1943 in London, England. Male rock-blues singer. Lead singer of **Savoy Brown**.		
7/14/73	210	4		1 Nowhere Road		London 633
				YOUNG, Ace		
				Born Brett Young on 11/15/1980 in Denver, Colorado. "Blue-eyed soul" singer/songwriter.		
8/2/08	160	1		1 Ace Young		Pazzo 00001
				YOUNG, Barry		
				Born in California. Male singer.		
1/1/66	67	12		1 One Has My Name		Dot 25672
				YOUNG, Chris		
				Born on 6/12/1985 in Murfreesboro, Tennessee. Male country singer. Winner on the fourth season of TV's *Nashville Star* talent series in 2006.		
10/21/06	22	6		1 Chris Young..		RCA 87724
9/19/09	19	37		2 The Man I Want To Be		RCA Nashville 22818
				YOUNG, Jesse Colin		
				Born Perry Miller on 11/11/1944 in New York. Folk-rock singer/bassist. Leader of **The Youngbloods**.		
2/9/74	172	6		1 The Soul Of A City Boy .... [E]		Capitol 11267
				first released in 1964 on Capitol 2070		
3/25/72	157	6		2 Together..		Raccoon 2588
10/6/73	51	44		3 Song For Juli		Warner 2734
4/20/74	37	29		4 Light Shine		Warner 2790
3/22/75	26	14		5 Songbird		Warner 2845
3/27/76	34	15		6 On The Road .... [L]		Warner 2913
4/2/77	64	9		7 Love On The Wing...		Warner 3033
12/9/78	165	2		8 American Dreams...		Elektra 157
				YOUNG, John Paul		
				Born on 6/21/1950 in Glasgow, Scotland; raised in Sydney, Australia. Pop singer/songwriter/pianist.		
11/11/78+	119	18		1 Love Is In The Air		Scotti Brothers 7101
				YOUNG, Kathy		
				Born on 10/21/1945 in Santa Ana, California. White teen pop singer.		
				~ ~ ~ ~ ~ ~ ~ ~ ~ ~ **NON-CHARTED ALBUM** ~ ~ ~ ~ ~ ~ ~ ~ ~ ~		
				1961 The Sound Of Kathy Young		
				YOUNG, Loretta		
				Born Gretchen Young on 1/16/1913 in Salt Lake City, Utah. Died of cancer on 8/12/2000 (age 87). Movie/television actress. Won Best Actress Oscar for her role in *The Farmer's Daughter*. Hosted own TV show *The Loretta Young Show* from 1953-61.		
12/24/66	76[X]	1		1 The Littlest Angel .... [T]		Decca DL-8009

YOUNG, Neil   1970s: #30 / 1980s: #38 / 2000s: #23 / All-Time: #17

Born on 11/12/1945 in Toronto, Ontario, Canada. Rock singer/songwriter/guitarist. Member of **Buffalo Springfield** and **Crosby, Stills, Nash & Young**. Appeared in the 1987 movie *Made In Heaven*. Had a relationship (1970-75) and a son with actress Carrie Snodgress (never married).

AWARD: R&R Hall of Fame: 1995

DEBUT	PEAK	WKS	RIAA	#	Album Title	Catalog	Label & Number
6/21/69+	34	98	▲	1	Everybody Knows This Is Nowhere NEIL YOUNG & CRAZY HORSE RS500 #208		Reprise 6349
9/19/70	8	66	▲²	2	After The Gold Rush RS500 #71		Reprise 6383
3/4/72	❶²	41	▲⁴	3	Harvest RS500 #78	Cat:#17/22	Reprise 2032
11/25/72+	45	21		4	Journey Through The Past	[S]	Warner 6480 [2]
8/3/74	16	18	●	5	On The Beach	Cat:#2¹/3	Reprise 2180
7/12/75	25	12		6	Tonight's The Night RS500 #331		Reprise 2221
11/29/75+	25	21	●	7	Zuma NEIL YOUNG & CRAZY HORSE		Reprise 2242
10/9/76	26	18	●	8	Long May You Run STILLS-YOUNG BAND		Reprise 2253
7/2/77	21	15	●	9	American Stars 'N Bars NEIL YOUNG, CRAZY HORSE & THE BULLETS	Cat:#12/1	Reprise 2261
10/21/78	7	30	●	10	Comes A Time		Reprise 2266
7/21/79	8	39	▲	11	Rust Never Sleeps NEIL YOUNG & CRAZY HORSE RS500 #350		Reprise 2295
11/22/80	30	16		12	Hawks & Doves	Cat:#21/1	Reprise 2297
11/21/81	27	17		13	Re-ac-tor NEIL YOUNG & CRAZY HORSE	Cat:#34/1	Reprise 2304
1/22/83	19	17		14	Trans		Geffen 2018
8/20/83	46	15		15	Everybody's Rockin' NEIL & THE SHOCKING PINKS		Geffen 4013
9/7/85	75	12		16	Old Ways		Geffen 24068
8/16/86	46	16		17	Landing On Water		Geffen 24109
7/25/87	75	11		18	Life NEIL YOUNG & CRAZY HORSE		Geffen 24154
4/30/88	61	18		19	This Note's For You NEIL YOUNG & THE BLUENOTES		Reprise 25719
10/21/89	35	28	●	20	Freedom		Reprise 25899
9/29/90	31	25		21	Ragged Glory NEIL YOUNG & CRAZY HORSE		Reprise 26315
11/14/92	16	42	▲²	22	Harvest Moon		Reprise 45057
9/3/94	9	12	●	23	Sleeps With Angels NEIL YOUNG & CRAZY HORSE		Reprise 45749
7/15/95	5	13	●	24	Mirror Ball		Reprise 45934
7/20/96	31	8		25	Broken Arrow NEIL YOUNG & CRAZY HORSE		Reprise 46291
5/13/00	22	13		26	Silver & Gold		Reprise 47305
4/27/02	10	10		27	Are You Passionate?		Reprise 48111
9/6/03	22	6		28	Greendale NEIL YOUNG & CRAZY HORSE		Reprise 48533
10/15/05	11	27	●	29	Prairie Wind		Reprise 49593
5/27/06	15	14		30	Living With War		Reprise 44335
11/10/07	11	9		31	Chrome Dreams II		Reprise 311932
4/25/09	19	6		32	Fork In The Road		Reprise 518040
					GREATEST HITS & COMPILATIONS:		
11/26/77	43	18	▲	33	Decade		Reprise 2257 [3]
12/4/04	27	17	●	34	Greatest Hits		Reprise 48924
6/20/09	102	1		35	Neil Young Archives Vol. 1 (1963 - 1972)		Reprise 175292 [8]
					LIVE ALBUMS:		
10/27/73	22	18	●	36	Time Fades Away		Reprise 2151
12/8/79+	15	24	▲	37	Live Rust		Reprise 2296 [2]
11/9/91	154	4		38	Weld NEIL YOUNG & CRAZY HORSE (above 2)		Reprise 26746 [3]
7/3/93	23	18	●	39	Unplugged recorded on 2/7/1993		Reprise 45310
7/5/97	57	5		40	Year Of The Horse NEIL YOUNG & CRAZY HORSE		Reprise 46652 [2]
12/23/00	169	1		41	Road Rock V 1		Reprise 48036
12/2/06	55	3		42	Live At The Fillmore East: March 6 & 7, 1970 NEIL YOUNG & CRAZY HORSE		Reprise 44429
3/31/07	6	11		43	Live At Massey Hall 1971		Reprise 43328

Billboard			R I A A	ARTIST Album Title	Catalog	Label & Number
DEBUT	PEAK	WKS				
				YOUNG, Neil — cont'd		
12/20/08	40	7		44 Sugar Mountain - Live At Canterbury House 1968		Reprise 516758
12/26/09	193	1		45 Dreamin' Man Live '92		Reprise 511277
				YOUNG, Paul Born on 1/17/1956 in Bedfordshire, England. Pop-rock singer.		
4/14/84	79	23		1 No Parlez		Columbia 38976
5/25/85	19	43	●	2 The Secret Of Association		Columbia 39957
11/22/86	77	17		3 Between Two Fires		Columbia 40543
8/11/90	142	13		4 Other Voices		Columbia 46755
				YOUNG, Steve Born on 7/12/1942 in Newnan, Georgia. Country-rock singer/songwriter.		
9/4/76	201	2		1 Renegade Picker		RCA Victor 1759
				YOUNG AMERICANS, The A 36-member chorus of teenagers and young adults. **Vicki Lawrence** was a member from 1964-67.		
4/19/69	178	3		1 Time For Livin'		ABC 659
				YOUNG & RESTLESS Rap duo from Miami, Florida: Charles Trahan and Leon Johnson.		
5/5/90	104	14		1 Something To Get You Hyped		Pandisc 8809
				YOUNG BLACK TEENAGERS White rap group from New York: Firstborn, Kamron, A.T.A. and **DJ Skribble**.		
2/20/93	158	8		1 Dead Enz Kidz Doin' Lifetime Bidz		Soul 10733
				YOUNG BLEED Born Glenn Clifton on 3/25/1978 in Baton Rouge, Louisiana. Male rapper.		
2/7/98	10	15	●	1 All I Have In This World, Are...My Balls And My Word		No Limit 50738
2/19/00	61	6		2 My Own		Priority 50018
				YOUNGBLOOD, Sydney Born Sydney Ford on 12/2/1960 in San Antonio, Texas. R&B singer.		
10/20/90	185	3		1 Sydney Youngblood		Arista 8651
				YOUNGBLOODS, The Folk-rock band formed in Boston, Massachusetts: **Jesse Colin Young** (vocals, bass), Lowell Levinger (guitar), Jerry Corbitt (guitar) and Joe Bauer (drums). Corbitt left after first album. Bassist Michael Kane joined in 1971. Group disbanded in 1973. Bauer died on 11/7/1982 (age 41).		
3/25/67+	131	8		1 The Youngbloods		RCA Victor 3724
5/10/69	118	29		2 Elephant Mountain		RCA Victor 4150
9/5/70	144	10		3 The Best Of The Youngbloods .... [G]		RCA Victor 4399
8/7/71	186	3		4 Sunlight .... [K]		RCA Victor 4561
10/31/70	80	13		5 Rock Festival .... [L]		Raccoon 1878
7/24/71	157	8		6 Ride The Wind .... [L]		Raccoon 2563
12/4/71	160	5		7 Good And Dusty		Raccoon 2566
12/9/72+	185	10		8 High On A Ridge Top		Raccoon 2653
				YOUNGBLOODZ Rap duo from Atlanta, Georgia: "Sean Paul" Joseph and Jeffrey "J-Bo" Grigsby.		
10/30/99	92	17		1 Against Da Grain		LaFace 26054
9/13/03	5	23	●	2 Drankin' Patnaz		So So Def 50155
12/31/05	44	12		3 Ev'rybody Know Me		LaFace 73175
				YOUNG BUCK Born David Brown on 3/3/1981 in Nashville, Tennessee. Male rapper. Member of **G-Unit**.		
9/11/04	3¹	29	▲	1 Straight Outta Ca$hville		G-Unit 002972
11/26/05	40	2		2 T.I.P.		Mass Appeal 0016
4/14/07	3¹	16		3 Buck The World		G-Unit 008030
				YOUNG DRO Born D'Juan Hart on 1/15/1979 in Atlanta, Georgia. Male rapper/songwriter.		
9/16/06	3¹	13		1 Best Thang Smokin'		Grand Hustle 83949
				YOUNG GUNZ Male rap duo from Philadelphia, Pennsylvania: Chris "Young Chris" Ries and Hanif "Neef" Mohammad.		
3/13/04	3¹	11		1 Tough Luv		Roc-A-Fella 001937
6/11/05	15	5		2 Brothers From Another		Roc-A-Fella 004419
				YOUNG-HOLT UNLIMITED Soul-jazz instrumental band from Chicago, Illinois: Eldee Young (bass), Isaac "Red" Holt (drums) and Don Walker (piano). Both Young and Holt were members of the **Ramsey Lewis Trio**. Walker left by 1968. Young died on 2/12/2007 (age 71).		
1/14/67	132	6		1 Wack Wack .... [I] THE YOUNG HOLT TRIO		Brunswick 754121
1/4/69	9	30		2 Soulful Strut [I]		Brunswick 754144
8/16/69	185	6		3 Just A Melody .... [I]		Brunswick 754150

YOUNG JEEZY
Born Jay Jenkins on 10/12/1977 in South Carolina; raised in Macon, Georgia. Male rapper/songwriter.

8/13/05	2¹	47	▲	1 Let's Get It: Thug Motivation 101		Corporate Thugz 004421
12/30/06	❶¹	30	▲	2 The Inspiration		Corporate Thugz 007227
9/20/08	❶¹	45	●	3 The Recession		CTE 011536

YOUNG LOVE
Rock band formed in New York: Dan Keyes (vocals), Bob Mann (guitar), Ross Tweedy (bass) and Erik Tonneson (drums).

2/17/07	168	1		1 Too Young To Fight It		Island 008101

YOUNG M.C.
Born Marvin Young on 5/10/1967 in London, England; raised in Queens, New York. Male rapper.

9/23/89	9	48	▲	1 Stone Cold Rhymin'		Delicious Vinyl 91309
8/31/91	66	7	●	2 Brainstorm		Capitol 96337

YOUNG ROME
Born Jerome Jones on 10/25/1981 in Los Angeles, California. R&B singer. Former member of **Immature**.

7/10/04	98	2		1 Food For Thought		T.U.G. 002742

YOUNGSTOWN
"Boy band" from Youngstown, Ohio: Sammy Lopez, James Dallas and David Yeager.

3/4/00	96	10		1 Let's Roll		Hollywood 62192

YOUTHFUL PRAISE
Gospel choir from Bridgeport, Connecticut. Directed by James "J.J." Hairston.

9/19/09	141	1		1 Resting On His Promise		Evidence Gospel 7213

YO-YO
Born Yolanda Whitaker on 8/4/1971 in Los Angeles, California. Female rapper.

4/13/91	74	21		1 Make Way For The Motherlode		EastWest 91605
7/11/92	145	2		2 Black Pearl		EastWest 92120
7/10/93	107	5		3 You Better Ask Somebody		EastWest 92252

YUKMOUTH
Born Jarold Ellis on 10/18/1974 in Oakland, California. Male rapper. Member of **Luniz**.

3/13/99	40	7	●	1 Thugged Out: The Albulation		Rap-A-Lot 46720 [2]
4/21/01	71	8		2 Thug Lord: The New Testament		Rap-A-Lot 10042
8/23/03	112	2		3 Godzilla		J Prince 42028

YUNG BERG
Born Christopher Ward on 9/29/1985 in Chicago, Illinois. Male rapper.

8/11/07	32	4		1 Almost Famous: The Sexy Lady EP	[EP]	Yung Boss 10583
8/30/08	20	4		2 Look What You Made Me		Koch 08407

YUNG JOC
Born Jasiel Robinson on 4/2/1983 in Atlanta, Georgia. Male rapper/songwriter.

6/24/06	3¹	27	●	1 New Joc City		Block 83937
9/15/07	3¹	9		2 Hustlenomics		Block 157180

YURO, Timi
Born Rosemary Timothy Yuro on 8/4/1940 in Chicago, Illinois; raised in Los Angeles, California. Died on 3/30/2004 (age 63). White soul singer.

9/18/61	51	13		1 Hurt!!!!!!!		Liberty 3208

~ ~ ~ ~ ~ ~ ~ ~ ~ ~ **NON-CHARTED ALBUM** ~ ~ ~ ~ ~ ~ ~ ~ ~ ~ ~
1962 **What's A Matter Baby**

YUTAKA
Born Yutaka Yokokura in Tokyo, Japan. Male jazz-pop keyboardist.

7/11/81	174	4		1 Love Light	[I]	Alfa 10004

Z

ZAA, Charlie
Born Carlos Sanchez in 1974 in Colombia, South America. Latin singer/songwriter.

9/20/97	185	2	▲	1 Sentimientos	[F]	Sonolux 82136
7/4/98	193	1		2 Un Segundo Sentimiento	[F]	Sonolux 82706

ZACHERLE, John, "The Cool Ghoul"
Born on 9/26/1918 in Philadelphia, Pennsylvania. Hosted horror movies on TV during the 1950s.

11/10/62	44	10		1 Monster Mash	[N]	Parkway 7018

DEBUT	PEAK	WKS	R I A A	ARTIST / Album Title	Catalog	Label & Number
				ZADORA, Pia		
				Born Pia Schipani on 5/4/1954 in Hoboken, New Jersey. Singer/actress. Appeared in several movies.		
3/23/85	201	3		1 When The Rain Begins To Fall		MCA/Curb 5557
3/8/86	113	20		2 Pia & Phil		CBS Associated 40259
				with the **London Philharmonic Orchestra**		
				ZAGER, Michael, Band		
				Born on 1/3/1943 in Passaic, New Jersey. Disco keyboardist/producer. Member of **Ten Wheel Drive** from 1968-73.		
4/22/78	120	13		1 Let's All Chant		Private Stock 7013
				ZAGER & EVANS		
				Folk-rock duo from Lincoln, Nebraska: Denny Zager and Rick Evans (both sing and play guitar).		
8/2/69	30	13		1 2525 (Exordium & Terminus)		RCA Victor 4214
				ZANE — see LIL' ZANE		
				ZANES, Dan		
				Born in 1961 in Exter, New Hampshire; later based in Boston, Massachusetts. Rock singer/songwriter/guitarist. Former leader of **The Del Fuegos**.		
6/3/06	138	2		1 Catch That Train!		Festival Five 009
				DAN ZANES AND FRIENDS		
				ZAPP		
				Funk band from Dayton, Ohio: brothers **Roger** (vocals, guitar), Larry (percussion), Tony (bass) and Lester (drums) Troutman. Roger was shot to death by Larry in a murder-suicide on 4/25/1999. Roger was age 47 and Larry was age 54.		
9/27/80	19	19	●	1 Zapp		Warner 3463
8/14/82	25	19	●	2 Zapp II		Warner 23583
9/3/83	39	22		3 Zapp III		Warner 23875
11/23/85+	110	26	●	4 The New Zapp IV U		Warner 25327
10/7/89	154	4		5 Zapp V		Reprise 25807
11/13/93	39	29	▲	6 All The Greatest Hits	Cat:#26/1 [G]	Reprise 45143
				ZAPP & ROGER		

DEBUT	PEAK	WKS		ARTIST / Album Title	Catalog	Label & Number
				ZAPPA, Frank 1970s: #36 / All-Time: #109		
				Born Francis Vincent Zappa Jr. on 12/21/1940 in Baltimore, Maryland (of Sicilian parentage). Died of prostate cancer on 12/4/1993 (age 52). Rock music's leading satirist. Singer/songwriter/guitarist/activist. Formed **The Mothers Of Invention** in 1965. In the movies *200 Motels* and *Baby Snakes*. Father of Dweezil and Moon Unit Zappa.		
				AWARDS: Grammy: Lifetime Achievement 1997 ★ R&R Hall of Fame: 1995		
2/11/67	130	23		1 Freak Out!		Verve 5005 [2]
				Grammy: Hall of Fame ★ RS500 #243		
7/8/67	41	22		2 Absolutely Free		Verve 5013
3/16/68	30	19		3 We're Only In It For The Money		Verve 5045
				RS500 #296 ★ NRR		
12/21/68+	110	12		4 Cruising With Ruben & The Jets		Verve 5055
				THE MOTHERS OF INVENTION (above 4)		
11/21/70	119	14		5 Chunga's Revenge		Bizarre 2030
10/30/71	59	13		6 Frank Zappa's 200 Motels .... [S]		United Artists 9956 [2]
10/6/73	32	50	●	7 Over-nite Sensation		DiscReet 2149
				THE MOTHERS		
4/20/74	10	43	●	8 Apostrophe (')		DiscReet 2175
7/19/75	26	12		9 One Size Fits All		DiscReet 2216
				FRANK ZAPPA AND THE MOTHERS OF INVENTION		
11/27/76	61	13		10 Zoot Allures		Warner 2970
3/24/79	21	23		11 Sheik Yerbouti		Zappa 1501 [2]
9/22/79	27	25		12 Joe's Garage, Act I		Zappa 1603
12/15/79+	53	12		13 Joe's Garage, Acts II & III		Zappa 1502 [2]
10/3/81	93	7		14 You Are What You Is		Barking Pump. 37537 [2]
6/12/82	23	22		15 Ship Arriving Too Late To Save A Drowning Witch		Barking Pumpkin 38066
4/16/83	153	5		16 The Man From Utopia		Barking Pumpkin 38403
1/18/86	153	6		17 Frank Zappa Meets The Mothers Of Prevention		Barking Pumpkin 74203
				GREATEST HITS & COMPILATIONS:		
4/5/69	151	9		18 Mothermania/The Best Of The Mothers		Verve 5068
7/24/71	201	2		19 The Worst Of The Mothers		MGM 4754
				THE MOTHERS OF INVENTION (above 2)		
				INSTRUMENTAL ALBUMS:		
6/8/68	159	5		20 Lumpy Gravy		Verve 8741
				THE ABNUCEALS EMUUKHA ELECTRIC SYMPHONY ORCHESTRA AND CHORUS		
5/3/69	43	11		21 Uncle Meat		Bizarre 2024 [2]
3/14/70	94	8		22 Burnt Weeny Sandwich		Bizarre 6370
				THE MOTHERS OF INVENTION (above 2)		
11/29/69	173	6		23 Hot Rats		Bizarre 6356
9/9/72	152	7		24 Waka/Jawaka - Hot Rats		Reprise 2094

Billboard			R I A A	ARTIST		
DEBUT	PEAK	WKS		Album Title	Catalog	Label & Number

ZAPPA, Frank — cont'd

10/21/78	147	6		25 Studio Tan		DiscReet 2291
2/17/79	175	4		26 Sleep Dirt		DiscReet 2292
6/2/79	168	4		27 Orchestral Favorites		DiscReet 2294

LIVE ALBUMS:

9/26/70	189	3		28 Weasels Ripped My Flesh		Bizarre 2028
8/21/71	38	15		29 The Mothers/Fillmore East-June 1971		Bizarre 2042
4/22/72	85	9		30 Just Another Band From L.A.		Bizarre 2075

THE MOTHERS (above 3)
recorded on 8/7/1971 at UCLA in Los Angeles, California

| 10/5/74 | 27 | 18 | | 31 Roxy & Elsewhere | | DiscReet 2202 [2] |

ZAPPA/MOTHERS

| 11/1/75 | 66 | 8 | | 32 Bongo Fury | | DiscReet 2234 |

FRANK ZAPPA/CAPTAIN BEEFHEART/THE MOTHERS
recorded on 5/20/1975 in Austin, Texas

| 4/15/78 | 57 | 8 | | 33 Zappa In New York | | DiscReet 2290 [2] |
| 5/30/81 | 66 | 11 | | 34 Tinsel Town Rebellion | | Barking Pump. 37336 [2] |

ZEBRA

Rock trio from New Orleans, Louisiana: Randy Jackson (vocals, guitar), Felix Hanemann (bass) and Guy Gelso (drums).

| 5/14/83 | 29 | 28 | ● | 1 Zebra | | Atlantic 80054 |
| 9/22/84 | 84 | 11 | | 2 No Tellin' Lies | | Atlantic 80159 |

ZEBRAHEAD

Rock-rap band from Los Angeles, California: Justin Mauriello (vocals), Ali Tabatabee (rap vocals), Greg Bergdorf (guitar), Ben Osmundson (bass) and Ed Udhus (drums).

| 9/9/00 | 127 | 2 | | 1 Playmate Of The Year | | Columbia 63817 |

ZENO

Hard-rock trio from Germany: Michael Flexig (vocals, drums), Zeno Roth (guitar) and U. Winsomie Ritgen (bass). Roth's brother Uli is a member of **Scorpions**.

| 5/10/86 | 107 | 10 | | 1 Zeno | | Manhattan 53025 |

ZENTNER, Si, And His Orchestra

Born Simon Zentner on 6/13/1917 in Manhattan, New York. Died of leukemia on 1/31/2000 (age 82). Jazz trombonist.

| 12/18/61+ | 65 | 8 | | 1 Big Band Plays The Big Hits | [I] | Liberty 7197 |
| 3/17/62 | 107 | 12 | | 2 Up A Lazy River (Big Band Plays The Big Hits: Vol. 2) | [I] | Liberty 7216 |

Grammy: Pop Instrumental Album

| 9/1/62 | 108 | 6 | | 3 The Stripper And Other Big Band Hits | [I] | Liberty 7247 |
| 2/9/63 | 139 | 5 | | 4 Desafinado | [I] | Liberty 7273 |

ZEPHYR

Rock band formed in Denver, Colorado: Candy Givens (vocals), her brother David Givens (bass), **Tommy Bolin** (guitar; **Deep Purple**, **The James Gang**), John Faris (keyboards) and Robbie Chamberlain (drums). Bolin died of a drug overdose on 12/4/1976 (age 26). Candy Givens drowned in her hot tub after doing drugs on 1/27/1984 (age 37).

| 12/20/69+ | 48 | 26 | | 1 Zephyr | | Probe 4510 |

ZERO7

Electronic production duo from England: Henry Binns and Sam Hardaker.

3/20/04	139	3		1 When It Falls		Elektra 61558
6/24/06	94	2		2 The Garden		Ultimate Dilemma 63380
10/17/09	142	1		3 Yeah Ghost		Atlantic 520260

ZEVON, Warren

Born on 1/24/1947 in Chicago, Illinois. Died of cancer on 9/7/2003 (age 56). Rock singer/songwriter/pianist. Also see **Hindu Love Gods**. Also see **Various Artists Compilations:** *Enjoy Every Sandwich: The Songs Of Warren Zevon.*

| 8/28/76 | 189 | 2 | | 1 Warren Zevon | Cat:#45/4 | Asylum 1060 |
| 2/25/78 | 8 | 28 | ▲ | 2 Excitable Boy | Cat:#10/14 | Asylum 118 |

above 2 produced by **Jackson Browne**

3/8/80	20	16		3 Bad Luck Streak In Dancing School		Asylum 509
1/17/81	80	10		4 Stand In The Fire	[L]	Asylum 519
8/14/82	93	13		5 The Envoy		Asylum 60159
6/27/87	63	18		6 Sentimental Hygiene		Virgin 90603
5/1/93	198	1		7 Learning To Flinch	[L]	Giant 24493
2/12/00	173	1		8 Life'll Kill Ya		Artemis 751003
9/13/03	12	18		9 The Wind		Artemis 51156

Grammy: Contemporary Folk Album

| 9/27/03 | 168 | 1 | | 10 Genius: The Best Of Warren Zevon | [G] | Elektra 73771 |

ZHANE

Female R&B-dance vocal duo from Philadelphia, Pennsylvania: Renee Neufville and Jean Norris. Pronounced: jah-nay.

| 2/26/94 | 37 | 31 | ▲ | 1 Pronounced Jah-Nay | | Motown 6369 |
| 5/10/97 | 41 | 9 | | 2 Saturday Night | | Illtown 0751 |

ZION

Reggaeton duo from Carolina, Puerto Rico: Felix "Zion" Ortiz and Gabriel "Lennox" Pizzaro.

| 6/23/07 | 53 | 3 | | 1 The Perfect Melody | [F] | Universal Motown 009029 |

Billboard			R I A A	ARTIST		
DEBUT	PEAK	WKS		Album Title	Catalog	Label & Number

ZODIAC MINDWARP & THE LOVE REACTION
Born Mark Manning in England. Rock singer.

3/26/88	132	15		1 Tattooed Beat Messiah		Vertigo 832729

ZOEGIRL
Christian vocal trio formed in California: Alisa Girard, Chrissy Conway and Kristin Swinford.

4/28/01	173	1		1 Zoegirl		Sparrow 51734
12/8/01	111	8		2 Life		Sparrow 51828
10/4/03	149	3		3 Different Kind Of Free		Sparrow 80666
4/2/05	108	2		4 Room To Breathe		Sparrow 73296

ZOMBIE, Rob
Born Robert Cummings on 1/12/1966 in Haverhill, Massachusetts. Founder of **White Zombie**. Wrote and directed several horror movies. Older brother of Michael "Spider One" Cummings of **Powerman 5000**.

9/12/98	5	66	▲3	1 Hellbilly Deluxe		Geffen 25212
11/13/99	38	6		2 American Made Music To Strip By .... [K]		Geffen 490349
12/1/01	8	36	▲	3 The Sinister Urge		Geffen 493147
10/11/03	11	26	▲	4 Past, Present & Future .... Cat:#8/38 [G]		Geffen 001041
4/15/06	5	20		5 Educated Horses		Geffen 006331
11/4/06	166	1		6 The Best of Rob Zombie: 20th Century Masters The Millennium Collection ... [G]		Chronicles 007870
11/10/07	57	2		7 Zombie Live .... [L]		Geffen 009501

ZOMBIES, The
Rock band from Hertfordshire, England: Colin Blunstone (vocals), Paul Atkinson (guitar), Rod **Argent** (keyboards), Chris White (bass) and Hugh Grundy (drums). Atkinson died of liver failure on 4/1/2004 (age 58).

2/27/65	39	17		1 The Zombies		Parrot 71001
3/15/69	95	13		2 Odessey & Oracle		Date 4013
				RS500 #80		
5/25/74	204	6		3 Time Of The Zombies .... [K]		Epic 32861 [2]

Z-RO
Born Joseph McVey on 1/19/1976 in Houston, Texas. Male rapper/songwriter. One-half of **ABN** duo.

3/13/04	170	1		1 The Life Of Joseph W. McVey		J Prince 42035
5/14/05	69	3		2 Let The Truth Be Told		J Prince 68523
11/25/06	75	2		3 I'm Still Livin		J Prince 68612
5/26/07	197	1		4 Power		J Prince 182780
10/11/08	48	3		5 Crack		J Prince 515829
11/14/09	147	1		6 Cocaine		J Prince 522146

Z-TRIP
Born Zachary Sciacca on 7/22/1968 in Phoenix, Arizona. Trip-hop DJ/producer.

5/7/05	90	2		1 Shifting Gears .... [I]		Hard Left 162503

ZUCCHERO
Born Adelmo Fornaciari on 9/25/1955 in Roncocesi, Italy. Male singer. Zucchero is Italian for sugar.

7/30/05	84	7		1 Zucchero & Co. .... [K]		Universal Italia 2301

ZWAN
Alternative-rock band formed by former **Smashing Pumpkins** members **Billy Corgan** (vocals, guitar) and Jimmy Chamberlain (drums), with Matt Sweeney (guitar) and David Pajo (bass).

2/15/03	3[1]	11		1 Mary Star Of The Sea		Martha's Music 48436

ZYDECO, Buckwheat — see BUCKWHEAT

ZZ TOP
All-Time: #159

Boogie-rock trio formed in Houston, Texas: Billy Gibbons (vocals, guitar; born on 12/16/1949), Dusty Hill (vocals, bass; born on 5/19/1949) and Frank Beard (drums; born on 6/11/1949). Gibbons had been lead guitarist in Moving Sidewalks, a Houston psychedelic-rock band. Hill and Beard had played in American Blues, based in Dallas. Group appeared in the movie *Back To The Future III*. Gibbons and Hill are the long-bearded members. Also see **Various Artists Compilations:** *Sharp Dressed Men: A Tribute To ZZ Top.*

> AWARD: R&R Hall of Fame: 2004

1/30/71	201	1		1 ZZ Top's First Album		London 584
5/6/72	104	10		2 Rio Grande Mud		London 612
8/4/73+	8	81	●	3 Tres Hombres .... Cat:#34/6		London 631
				RS500 #498		
5/17/75	10	47	●	4 Fandango! .... [L]		London 656
				side 1: live; side 2: studio		
1/22/77	17	24	●	5 Tejas		London 680
12/17/77+	94	19	▲2	6 The Best Of ZZ Top .... Cat:#21/2 [G]		London 706
11/24/79+	24	43	▲	7 Deguello		Warner 3361
8/8/81	17	22	●	8 El Loco		Warner 3593
4/23/83	9	183	▲10	9 Eliminator .... Cat:#42/3		Warner 23774
				RS500 #396		

Billboard DEBUT	PEAK	WKS	R I A A	ARTIST Album Title	Catalog	Label & Number
				ZZ TOP — cont'd		
11/16/85	**4**	70	▲⁵	10 **Afterburner**		Warner 25342
11/3/90	**6**	37	▲	11 **Recycler**		Warner 26265
5/2/92	**9**	73	▲³	12 **Greatest Hits**	Cat:#12/98 **[G]**	Warner 26846
2/5/94	**14**	23	▲	13 **Antenna**..		RCA 66317
10/5/96	**29**	11		14 **Rhythmeen**..		RCA 66956
10/16/99	**100**	4		15 **XXX**...		RCA 67850
9/27/03	**57**	3		16 **Mescalero**..		RCA 51168
7/3/04	**77**	2		17 **The Very Best Of ZZ Top: Rancho Texicano** .... **[G]**		Warner 78908 [2]

ALBUMS BY CATEGORY

The following categories list charted albums that are not listed in the Main Artist section. The albums within these categories are listed alphabetically by album title.

THE CATEGORIES

Movie Soundtracks
Movie Soundtrack Compilations
Movie-Inspired Compilations
Movie Sing-A-Longs
Television Soundtracks
Original Casts
Christmas (Various Artists)
Various Artists Compilations

CROSS REFERENCES

Many albums are cross referenced in their respective sections and refer back to an artist in the Main Artist section of this book A Movie Soundtrack or Original Cast album is listed in the Main Artist section if one artist contributed a major portion of the album's tracks.

The following are unique to Movie Soundtrack, Original Cast and/or Television Soundtrack albums:

LETTER(S) IN BRACKETS AFTER ALBUM TITLES

Most symbols used in these sections correspond to the symbols used in the Main Artist section (see User's Guide on page xviii). In addition, the following three letter symbols are unique to these sections:

M: Musical   **O:** Oldies   **V:** Various Artists

Two or more letters within brackets separated by a "+" indicate that the symbols apply to different tracks. For example, **[I+V]** means that some of the tracks are Instrumental and the remaining are by Various Artists.

ABBREVIATIONS IN THE TITLE NOTES

cp: Composer   ly: Lyricist   pf: Performer
cd: Conductor   mu: Music writer   sw: Songwriter (music and lyrics)

MOVIE SOUNDTRACK/ORIGINAL CAST STARS

The Movie Soundtrack and Original Cast stars are listed below their respective titles. This information is also included below the Movie Soundtrack and Original Cast cross references.

Billboard DEBUT	PEAK	WKS	R I A A	ARTIST / Album Title .... Catalog	Label & Number

MOVIE SOUNDTRACKS

About A Boy — see BADLY DRAWN BOY
Hugh Grant/Toni Collette/Nicholas Hoult/Sharon Small

| 7/26/86 | 72 | 14 | | 2 **About Last Night**... [V] | EMI America 17210 |

Rob Lowe/Demi Moore/James Belushi/Elizabeth Perkins/George DiCenzo

| 4/9/94 | 2¹ | 36 | ▲² | 3 **Above The Rim** [V] | Death Row 92359 |

Duane Martin/Leon/**2Pac**/Marlon Wayans/Bernie Mac

| 4/12/86 | 62 | 13 | | 4 **Absolute Beginners**... [V] | EMI America 17182 |

Eddie O'Connell/Patsy Kensit/**David Bowie/Ray Davies/Sade**

Across 110th Street — see WOMACK, Bobby
Anthony Quinn/Yaphet Kotto/Anthony Franciosa/Antonio Fargas/Burt Young

| 9/29/07 | 36 | 28 | ▲ | 6 **Across The Universe**.. [V] | Interscope 009801 |

Evan Rachel Wood/Jim Sturgess/Joe Anderson

| 9/29/07+ | 20 | 56 | | 7 **Across The Universe: Deluxe Edition**................ [V] | Interscope 009973 [2] |

Advance To The Rear — see NEW CHRISTY MINSTRELS, The
Glenn Ford/Stella Stevens/Melvyn Douglas/Jim Backus/Joan Blondell

| 7/14/90 | 66 | 9 | | 9 **Adventures Of Ford Fairlane, The**.................... [V] | Elektra 60952 |

Andrew Dice Clay/Wayne Newton/Priscilla Presley/**Morris Day**/Lauren Holly

| 9/17/94 | 106 | 10 | | 10 **Adventures Of Priscilla: Queen Of The Desert, The**............... [O-V] | Mother 516937 |

Terance Stamp/Hugo Weaving/Guy Pearce/Bill Hunter/Julia Cortez

| 3/31/84 | 12 | 22 | ● | 11 **Against All Odds**... [I+V] | Atlantic 80152 |

Rachel Ward/Jeff Bridges/James Woods/Alex Karras/Richard Widmark; cp/pf: **Larry Carlton** and Michel Colombier

| 8/20/94 | 157 | 3 | | 12 **Airheads**... [V] | Fox 11014 |

Brendan Fraser/Steve Buscemi/**Adam Sandler**/Chris Farley/Joe Mantegna

| 4/18/70 | 104 | 19 | | 13 **Airport**... [I] | Decca 79173 |

Burt Lancaster/**Dean Martin**/George Kennedy/Helen Hayes/Maureen Stapleton; cp/cd: Alfred Newman

| 5/13/06 | 193 | 1 | | 14 **Akeelah And The Bee**....................................... [O-V] | Hear 19629 |

Keke Palmer/Laurence Fishburne/Angela Bassett/Curtis Armstrong

| 11/28/92+ | 6 | 74 | ▲³ | 15 **Aladdin** Cat:#30/1 [M] | Disney 60846 |

Grammy: Soundtrack Album
animated movie, voices by: **Robin Williams**/Lea Salonga/Bruce Adler; cp: Alan Menken; ly: Tim Rice/Howard Ashman

| 12/5/60+ | 7 | 47 | | 16 **Alamo, The**.. [I+V] | Columbia 1558 / 8358 |

John Wayne/Richard Widmark/Laurence Harvey/**Frankie Avalon**/Chill Wills; cp/cd: Dimitri Tiomkin

| 11/20/04 | 171 | 2 | | 17 **Alfie**.. [V] | Virgin 63934 |

Jude Law/Marisa Tomei/Omar Epps/Jane Krakowski/Susan Sarandon

| 12/15/01+ | 61 | 16 | | 18 **Ali**... [V] | Interscope 493172 |

Will Smith/**Jamie Foxx**/Jon Voight/Mario Van Peebles/Ron Silver

Alice's Restaurant — see GUTHRIE, Arlo
Arlo Guthrie/Pat Quinn/James Broderick/**Pete Seeger**/Lee Hays

| 7/7/79 | 113 | 8 | | 20 **Alien**.. [I] | 20th Century 593 |

Tom Skerritt/Sigourney Weaver/John Hurt/Harry Dean Stanton/Yaphet Kotto; cp: Jerry Goldsmith; cd: Lionel Newman

| 3/23/02 | 65 | 7 | | 21 **All About The Benjamins**................................. [V] | Slip-N-Slide 39011 |

Ice Cube/Mike Epps/Tommy Flanagan/Anthony Michael Hall/Carmen Chaplin

| 3/22/80 | 36 | 23 | | 22 **All That Jazz**... [M] | Casablanca 7198 |

Roy Scheider/Jessica Lange/Ann Reinking/Ben Vereen/Max Wright; cd: Ralph Burns

| 12/3/83+ | 165 | 7 | | 23 **All The Right Moves**....................................... [V] | Casablanca 814449 |

Tom Cruise/Lea Thompson/Craig T. Nelson/Chris Penn/Mel Winkler

| 11/27/76 | 48 | 9 | | 24 **All This And World War II**............................... [V] | 20th Century 522 [2] |

documentary movie; features **John Lennon** and **Paul McCartney** songs and a book of lyrics

| 9/30/00 | 43 | 29 | ● | 25 **Almost Famous**... [O-V] | Dreamworks 50279 |

Grammy: Soundtrack Album
Frances McDormand/Kate Hudson/Jason Lee/Patrick Fugit/Philip Seymour Hoffman

Alvin And The Chipmunks — see CHIPMUNKS, The
Jason Lee/**David Cross**/Cameron Richardson/Jane Lynch

Alvin And The Chipmunks: The Squeakquel — see CHIPMUNKS, The
Jason Lee/**David Cross**/Zachary Levi/Wendie Malick

Amadeus — see MARRINER, Neville
Tom Hulce/F. Murray Abraham/Elizabeth Berridge/Simon Callow/Jeffrey Jones

| 7/5/86 | 91 | 12 | | 29 **American Anthem**.. [V] | Atlantic 81661 |

Mitch Gaylord/Janet Jones/Michele Phillips/R.J. Williams/Michael Pataki

| 11/24/07 | 36 | 2 | | 30 **American Gangster**.. [V] | Def Jam 010200 |

Denzel Washington/Russell Crowe/Josh Brolin/**RZA**

| 3/1/80 | 7 | 25 | ● | 31 **American Gigolo**... [I+V] | Polydor 6259 |

Richard Gere/Lauren Hutton/Hector Elizondo/Bill Duke/Carol Bruce; cp/pf: **Giorgio Moroder**

| 9/1/73+ | 10 | 60 | ▲³ | 32 **American Graffiti** [O-V] | MCA 8001 [2] |

Richard Dreyfuss/Ron Howard/Cindy Williams/Charles Martin Smith/Harrison Ford

| 4/8/78 | 31 | 11 | | 33 **American Hot Wax**... [O-V] | A&M 6500 [2] |

Tim McIntire/Fran Drescher/Laraine Newman/Jay Leno/Hamilton Camp

| 7/17/99 | 50 | 22 | ● | 34 **American Pie**.. [V] | Universal 53269 |

Jason Biggs/Chris Klein/Tara Reid/Mena Suvari/Eugene Levy

| 8/18/01 | 7 | 17 | ● | 35 **American Pie 2** [V] | Republic 014494 |

Jason Biggs/Chris Klein/Tara Reid/Mena Suvari/Eugene Levy

| 1/31/87 | 42 | 19 | | 36 **American Tail, An**.. [M] | MCA 39096 |

animated movie, voices by: Dom DeLuise/Christopher Plummer/ Madeline Kahn/Laura Carson; cp/cd: James Horner

| 8/9/03 | 23 | 8 | | 37 **American Wedding**... [V] | Universal 000744 |

Jason Biggs/Alyson Hannigan/January Jones/Fred Willard/Eugene Levy

| 1/3/98 | 80 | 6 | | 38 **American Werewolf In Paris, An**....................... [V] | Hollywood 62131 |

Tom Everett Scott/Julie Delpy/Vince Vieluf/Phil Buckman/Julie Bowen

Billboard			R I A A	ARTIST		
DEBUT	PEAK	WKS		Album Title...Catalog	Label & Number	
9/29/79	208	1		39 **Americathon**.. [V]	Lorimar 36174	
				John Ritter/Harvey Korman/Fred Willard/**Meat Loaf/Elvis Costello**		
11/22/97	41	32	●	40 **Anastasia**.. [M]	Atlantic 83053	
				animated movie, voices by: Meg Ryan/John Cusack/Angela Lansbury; ly: Lynn Ahrens; mu: Stephen Flaherty; cp/cd: David Newman		
7/31/04	187	1		41 **Anchorman: The Legend Of Ron Burgundy** .... [O-V]	Republic 002864	
				Will Ferrell/Christina Applegate/Paul Rudd/Steve Carell/Fred Willard		
5/30/09	150	2		42 **Angels & Demons** .... [I]	Sony Classical 52096	
				Tom Hanks/Ewan McGregor/Armin Mueller-Stahl; cp/cd: Hans Zimmer		
9/30/95	96	3		43 **Angus** .... [V]	Reprise 45960	
				George C. Scott/Charlie Talbert/Kathy Bates/Ariana Richards/Rita Moreno		
9/2/78	71	18	▲	44 **Animal House** .... Cat:#14/89 [O-V]	MCA 3046	
				John Belushi/Tim Matheson/John Vernon/Tom Hulce/Donald Sutherland		
				Animalympics — see GOULDMAN, Graham		
				animated movie; voices by: **Gilda Radner/Billy Crystal**/Harry Shearer		
5/29/82	35	31	▲	46 **Annie** .... [M]	Columbia 38000	
				Aileen Quinn/**Carol Burnett**/Albert Finney/**Tim Curry**; mu: Charles Strouse; ly: Martin Charnin; cd: Ralph Burns		
				Annie Get Your Gun — see "Those Glorious MGM Musicals"		
				Betty Hutton/Howard Keel/Louis Calhern/J. Carol Naish/Keenan Wynn		
10/11/08+	116	5		48 **Another Cinderella Story** .... [V]	Warner 83004	
				Selena Gomez/Drew Seeley/Jane Lynch		
1/22/00	28	11		49 **Any Given Sunday** .... [V]	Warner Sunset 83272	
				Al Pacino/Cameron Diaz/Dennis Quaid/James Woods/**Jamie Foxx**		
1/17/81	141	9		50 **Any Which Way You Can** .... [V]	Warner 3499	
				Clint Eastwood/Sondra Locke/Geoffrey Lewis/Ruth Gordon/William Smith		
1/9/61	18	15		51 **Apartment, The**... [I]	United Artists 3105	
				Jack Lemmon/Shirley MacLaine/Fred MacMurray/Ray Walston/Jack Kruschen; cp: Adolph Deutsch; cd: Mitchell Powell		
7/15/95	90	8		52 **Apollo 13** .... [I+O]	MCA 11241	
				Tom Hanks/Ed Harris/Kevin Bacon/Kathleen Quinlan/Gary Sinise; cp: James Horner; cd: Sandy DeCrescent		
3/14/98	175	2		53 **Apostle, The** .... [V]	Rising Tide 53058	
				Robert Duvall/Farrah Fawcett/Billy Bob Thornton/Miranda Richardson/**June Carter** Cash		
				April Love — see BOONE, Pat		
				Pat Boone/Shirley Jones/Dolores Michaels/Arthur O'Connell/Matt Crowley		
4/28/07	126	2		55 **Aqua Teen Hunger Force Colon Movie Film For Theaters** .... [V]	Adult Swim 001	
				animated movie, voices by: Bruce Campbell/Dave Willis/Andy Merrill/Tina Fey		
				Arabesque — see MANCINI, Henry		
				Gregory Peck/Sophia Loren/Alan Badel/Kieron Moore/Carl Duering		
1/23/71	137	10		57 **Aristocats, The**.. Cat:#17/5 [M]	Disneyland 3995	
				animated movie, voices by: Phil Harris/Sterling Holloway/Paul Winchell/Scatman Crothers/Nancy Kulp		
7/11/98	❶²	56	▲⁴	58 **Armageddon** [V]	Columbia 69440	
				Bruce Willis/Liv Tyler/Billy Bob Thornton/Ben Affleck/Steve Buscemi		
4/13/57	❶¹⁰	88		59 **Around The World In 80 Days** [I]	Decca 79046	
				David Niven/Cantinflas/**Noel Coward**/Robert Newton/Shirley MacLaine; cp/cd: Victor Young		
10/21/57	8	4		60 **Around The World In 80 Days** [I]	Stereo-Fidelity 2800	
				pf: New World Theatre Orchestra; not the original soundtrack (see version above)		
9/5/81	32	22		61 **Arthur (The Album)** .... [I+V]	Warner 3582	
				Dudley Moore/**Liza Minnelli**/John Gielgud/Geraldine Fitzgerald/Jill Eikenberry; cp: **Burt Bacharach**		
12/8/07+	33	34		62 **August Rush** .... [V]	Columbia 87796	
				Freddie Highmore/Keri Russell/**Terrence Howard**/**Robin Williams**		
5/31/97	184	4		63 **Austin Powers - International Man Of Mystery** ...... Cat:#14/6 [V]	Hollywood 62112	
				Mike Myers/Elizabeth Hurley/Michael York/Mimi Rogers/Robert Wagner		
6/19/99	5	28	▲	64 **Austin Powers - The Spy Who Shagged Me** [V]	Maverick 47348	
				Mike Myers/Heather Graham/Verne Troyer/Michael York/Robert Wagner		
11/13/99	145	11		65 **Austin Powers - The Spy Who Shagged Me, More Music From**.................. [V]	Maverick 47538	
8/3/02	27	9		66 **Austin Powers In Goldmember** .... [V]	Maverick 48310	
				Mike Myers/**Beyonce**/Seth Green/Michael Caine/Verne Troyer		
11/14/09	168	1		67 **Away We Go** .... [V]	Zero Summer 30859	
				John Krasinski/Maya Rudolph/Catherine O'Hara/Jeff Daniels		
1/20/62	57	18		68 **Babes In Toyland** .... [M]	Buena Vista 4022	
				Tommy Sands/Annette Funicello/Ray Bolger/Ed Wynn/Ann Jillian		
7/7/01	41	8		69 **Baby Boy** .... [V]	Universal 014276	
				Tyrese Gibson/**Snoop Dogg**/A.J. Johnson/Ving Rhames		
8/25/84	203	4		70 **Bachelor Party** .... [V]	I.R.S. 70047	
				Tom Hanks/Adrian Zmed/William Tepper/Tawny Kitaen		
9/5/87	188	2		71 **Back To The Beach** .... [V]	Columbia 40892	
				Frankie Avalon/**Annette** Funicello/Lori Laughlin/Connie Stevens/Demian Slade		
7/27/85	12	32	●	72 **Back To The Future** .... [V]	MCA 6144	
				Michael J. Fox/Christopher Lloyd/Lea Thompson/Crispin Glover/Thomas F. Wilson		
5/7/94	190	1		73 **BackBeat** .... [M]	Virgin 39386	
				Sheryl Lee/Stephen Dorff/Ian Hart/Gary Bakewell/Chris O'Neill; based on the early career of **The Beatles**; pf: Greg Dulli, Don Fleming, Dave Grohl (**Nirvana**), Mike Mills (**R.E.M.**), Thurston Moore (**Sonic Youth**) and Dave Pirner (**Soul Asylum**)		
4/8/95	26	21	▲	74 **Bad Boys** .... [V]	Work 67009	
				Martin Lawrence/Will Smith/Tea Leoni/Theresa Randle/Joe Pantoliano		
8/2/03	❶⁴	25	▲	75 **Bad Boys II** [V]	Bad Boy 000716	
				Martin Lawrence/Will Smith/Peter Stormare/Theresa Randle/Joe Pantoliano		
6/22/02	98	4		76 **Bad Company** .... [V]	Hollywood 162338	
				Anthony Hopkins/**Chris Rock**/Gabriel Macht/Matthew Marsh/Garcelle Beauvais		
				Band Wagon — see "Those Glorious MGM Musicals"		
				Fred Astaire/Cyd Charisse/Oscar Levant/Nanette Fabray		
11/3/01	164	1		78 **Bandits** .... [V]	Columbia 86180	
				Bruce Willis/Billy Bob Thornton/Cate Blanchett/Troy Garity/Stacey Travis		

Billboard DEBUT	PEAK	WKS	R I A A	ARTIST / Album Title / Catalog	Label & Number
12/7/68	183	5		79 **Barbarella** .... [I+M] Jane Fonda/Milo O'Shea/David Hemmings/John Phillip Law/Marcel Marceau; ly/pf: **Bob Crewe**; mu: Charles Fox	DynoVoice 31908
9/14/02	29	10		80 **Barbershop** .... [V] Ice Cube/Cedric The Entertainer/Anthony Anderson/Sean Patrick Thomas/**Eve**	Epic 86575
2/21/04	18	8		81 **Barbershop 2: Back In Business** .... [V] Ice Cube/Cedric The Entertainer/Sean Patrick Thomas/**Eve/Queen Latifah**	Interscope 001945
4/25/98	136	1		82 **Barney's Great Adventure - The Movie** .... [V] Bob West/George Hearn/Shirley Douglas/Trevor Morgan/Diana Rice	Barney 9418
2/14/76	132	15		83 **Barry Lyndon** .... [I] Ryan O'Neal/Marisa Berenson/Patrick Magee/Gay Hamilton/Murray Melvin; cd: Leonard Rosenman	Warner 2903
5/20/95	184	1		84 **Basketball Diaries, The** .... [V] Leonardo DiCaprio/Bruno Kirby/Mark Wahlberg (**Marky Mark**)/Lorraine Bracco/Ernie Hudson	Island 524093
8/26/89	30	12		85 **Batman** .... [I] Michael Keaton/Jack Nicholson/Kim Basinger/Robert Wuhl/Pat Hingle; cp/cd: Danny Elfman; also see **Prince**	Warner 25977
6/28/97	5	22	▲	86 **Batman & Robin** .... [V] Arnold Schwarzenegger/George Clooney/Chris O'Donnell/Uma Thurman/Alicia Silverstone	Warner Sunset 46620
7/2/05	155	2		87 **Batman Begins** .... [I] Christian Bale/Michael Caine/Liam Neeson/Katie Holmes/Gary Oldman; cp/cd: James Newton Howard	Warner Sunset 71324
6/24/95	5	34	▲²	88 **Batman Forever** .... [V] Val Kilmer/Tommy Lee Jones/Jim Carrey/Nicole Kidman/Chris O'Donnell	Atlantic 82759
7/11/92	61	5		89 **Batman Returns** .... [I] Michael Keaton/Michelle Pfeiffer/Danny DeVito/Christopher Walken/Michael Gough	Warner 26972
2/19/00	78	6		90 **Beach, The** .... [V] Leonardo DiCaprio/Tilda Swinton/Virginie Ledoyen/Robert Carlyle/Daniel York	London 31079
				Beach Party — see ANNETTE Annette Funicello/**Frankie Avalon**/Robert Cummings/Harvey Lembeck/Morey Amsterdam	
				Beaches — see MIDLER, Bette Bette Midler/Barbara Hershey/John Heard/Lainie Kazan/Mayim Bialick	
6/2/84	14	21	●	93 **Beat Street, Volume 1** .... [V] Rae Dawn Chong/Guy Davis/John Chardiet/Leon Grant/Lee Chamberlin	Atlantic 80154
9/29/84	137	9		94 **Beat Street, Volume 2** .... [V]	Atlantic 80158
3/2/96	95	5		95 **Beautiful Girls** .... [V] Matt Dillon/Lauren Holly/Timothy Hutton/**Rosie O'Donnell**/Mira Sorvino	Elektra 61888
12/7/91+	19	76	▲²	96 **Beauty And The Beast** .... [M] **Grammy: Soundtrack Album** animated movie, voices by: Robby Benson/Jesse Corti/ Angela Lansbury/Paige O'Hara; cp: Alan Menken; ly: Howard Ashman	Walt Disney 60618
12/6/97	144	3		97 **Beauty And The Beast - The Enchanted Christmas** .... [X-M] mu: Rachel Portman; ly: Don Black; cd: Michael Starobin; Christmas chart: 14/'97	Walt Disney 60948
11/23/96+	20	21	●	98 **Beavis And Butt-Head Do America** .... [V] animated movie, voices by: Mike Judge/Robert Stack/Demi Moore/**Bruce Willis**/David Letterman	Geffen 25002
5/9/64	147	3		99 **Becket** .... [I] Richard Burton/Peter O'Toole/John Gielgud/Gino Cervi/Donald Wolfit; cp: Laurence Rosenthal; cd: Muir Mathieson	Decca 79117
2/17/96	91	16		100 **Bed Of Roses** .... [I+V] Christian Slater/Mary Stuart Masterson/Pamela Segall/Josh Brolin/Debra Monk; cp: Michael Convertino; cd: Artie Kane	Milan 35739
12/18/71	208	5		101 **Bedknobs And Broomsticks** .... [M] Angela Lansbury/David Tomlinson/Roddy McDowall/Sam Jaffe; sw: Richard & Robert Sherman; cd: Irwin Kostal	Buena Vista 5003
8/30/08	74	1		102 **Beer For My Horses** .... [V] Toby Keith/**Rodney Carrington/Ted Nugent/Willie Nelson**	Show Dog 020
6/25/88	118	6		103 **Beetlejuice** .... [I] Michael Keaton/Alec Baldwin/Geena Davis/Jeffrey Jones/Winona Ryder; cp/cd: Danny Elfman	Geffen 24202
11/21/98	5	12	●	104 **Belly** .... [V] Nas/**DMX/Method Man**/Taral Hicks/Tyrin Turner	Def Jam 558925
4/25/60	6	98		105 **Ben-Hur** .... [I] Charlton Heston/Hugh Griffith/Haya Harareet/Stephen Boyd/Sam Jaffe; cp: Miklos Rozsa; cd: Carlo Savina	MGM 1
5/29/93	45	18		106 **Benny & Joon** .... [I] Johnny Depp/Mary Stuart Masterson/Aidan Quinn/Julianne Moore/Oliver Platt; mu: Rachel Portman	Milan 35644
				Benny Goodman Story, The — see GOODMAN, Benny Steve Allen/Donna Reed/Herbert Anderson/Hy Averback/Sammy Davis Sr.	
8/7/82	63	15		108 **Best Little Whorehouse In Texas, The** .... [M] Burt Reynolds/**Dolly Parton**/Dom DeLuise/Charles Durning/**Jim Nabors**; sw: Carol Hall/**Dolly Parton**	MCA 6112
10/30/99	16	29	▲	109 **Best Man, The** .... [V] Taye Diggs/Nia Long/Morris Chestnut/Harold Perrineau/Sanaa Lathan	Columbia 69924
1/12/85	❶²	62	▲²	110 **Beverly Hills Cop** .... [V] **Grammy: Soundtrack Album** Eddie Murphy/Judge Reinhold/Lisa Eilbacher/John Ashton/Ronny Cox	MCA 5547
6/13/87	8	26	▲	111 **Beverly Hills Cop II** .... [V] Eddie Murphy/Judge Reinhold/Brigitte Nielsen/Ronny Cox/Gilbert Gottfried	MCA 6207
6/11/94	158	3		112 **Beverly Hills Cop III** .... [V] Eddie Murphy/Judge Reinhold/Hector Elizondo/Theresa Randle/Alan Young	MCA 11021
				Beyond The Sea — see SPACEY, Kevin Kevin Spacey/Kate Bosworth/Bob Hoskins/John Goodman/**Peter Cincotti**	
11/12/66+	102	13		114 **Bible, The** .... [I] George C. Scott/Ava Gardner/John Huston/**Richard Harris**/Peter O'Toole; cp: Toshiro Mayuzumi; cd: Franco Ferrara; also see **Art Linkletter**	20th Century Fox 4184
10/22/83+	17	161	▲⁶	115 **Big Chill, The** .... Cat:#6/8 [O-V] William Hurt/Glenn Close/Jobeth Williams/Jeff Goldblum/Kevin Kline	Motown 6062
4/28/84	85	49	▲	116 **Big Chill, The (More Songs From The Original Soundtrack)** .... [O-V]	Motown 6094
7/10/99	55	8		117 **Big Daddy** .... [V] **Adam Sandler**/Joey Lauren Adams/Jon Stewart/Rob Schneider/Josh Mostel	American 69947

DEBUT	PEAK	WKS	RIAA	ARTIST Album Title............Catalog	Label & Number
10/24/87	107	9		118 **Big Easy, The** .... [V] Dennis Quaid/Ellen Barkin/Ned Beatty/John Goodman/Gailard Sartain	Antilles 7087
10/26/02	162	2		119 **Big Idea's Jonah - A Veggietales Movie** .... [M] animated movie, voices and songs by: Phil Vischer and Mike Nawrocki	Big Idea 35014
6/17/00	41	13		120 **Big Momma's House** .... [V] Martin Lawrence/Nia Long/Paul Giamatti/**Terrence Howard**/Cedric The Entertainer	So So Def 61076
7/27/91	28	14		121 **Bill & Ted's Bogus Journey** .... [V] Keanu Reeves/Alex Winter/William Sadler/**George Carlin**/Pam Grier	Interscope 91725
4/8/89	170	4		122 **Bill & Ted's Excellent Adventure** .... [V] Keanu Reeves/Alex Winter/**George Carlin**/Bernie Casey/**Jane Wiedlin**	A&M 3915
				Bill Cosby "Himself" — see COSBY, Bill	
10/9/71	135	7		124 **Billy Jack** .... [I+V] Tom Laughlin/Delores Taylor/Julie Webb/Howard Hesseman/Clark Howat; cp/cd: Mundell Lowe	Warner 1926
1/5/74	167	5		125 **Billy Jack** .... [R] see above album for tracks; new cover features solo photo of Billy Jack	Warner 1001
1/5/63	33	22		126 **Billy Rose's Jumbo** .... [M] Doris Day/Stephen Boyd/**Jimmy Durante**/Martha Raye/Dean Jagger; mu: Richard Rodgers; ly: Lorenz Hart; cd: George Stoll	Columbia 2260
11/12/88	169	3		127 **Bird** .... [I] Forest Whitaker/Diane Venora/Sam Wright; features Charlie "Bird" Parker's original solos with instrumental backing	Columbia 44299
				Birdy — see GABRIEL, Peter Matthew Modine/Nicolas Cage/Bruno Kirby/Sandy Baron/John Harkins	
4/15/00	124	3		129 **Black And White** .... [V] Robert Downey Jr./Jared Leto/**Raekwon**/Brooke Shields/Ben Stiller	Loud 62197
				Black And White Night Live, A — see ORBISON, Roy	
				Black Caesar — see BROWN, James Fred Williamson/Art Lund/Julius Harris/Gloria Hendry/James Dixon	
7/31/99	176	2		132 **Black Gangster** .... [V] soundtrack to the novel by Donald Goines	Black Hand 54329
9/5/98	36	22	●	133 **Blade** .... [V] Wesley Snipes/Stephen Dorff/**Kris Kristofferson**/Udo Kier/Traci Lords	TVT Soundtrax 8210
4/6/02	26	9		134 **Blade II** .... [V] Wesley Snipes/**Kris Kristofferson**/Ron Perlman/Leonor Varela/Luke Goss	Immortal 12064
11/27/71	176	10		135 **Bless The Beasts & Children** .... [I+V] Bill Mumy/Barry Robins/Miles Chapin/Jesse White/Ken Swofford; cp/cd: **Barry DeVorzon** & Perry Botkin, Jr.	A&M 4322
5/2/87	198	1		136 **Blind Date** .... [V] Kim Basinger/**Bruce Willis**/John Larroquette/Phil Hartman/William Daniels	Rhino 70705
4/28/01	150	4		137 **Blow** .... [V] Johnny Depp/Penelope Cruz/Ray Liotta/Rachel Griffiths/Paul Reubens	Virgin 10044
				Blow-Up — see HANCOCK, Herbie Vanessa Redgrave/David Hemmings/Sarah Miles/John Castle/Jane Birkin	
8/31/02	136	5		139 **Blue Crush** .... [V] Kate Bosworth/Michelle Rodriguez/Matthew Davis/Sanoe Lake/Mika Boorem	Virgin 13172
				Blue Hawaii — see PRESLEY, Elvis Elvis Presley ("Chad Gates")/Joan Blackman/Angela Lansbury/Nancy Walters/Roland Winters	
9/18/99	31	10	●	141 **Blue Streak** .... [V] Martin Lawrence/Luke Wilson/Dave Chappelle/Peter Greene/Tamala Jones	Epic 63615
				Blues Brothers, The — see BLUES BROTHERS John Belushi/Dan Aykroyd/Carrie Fisher/**James Brown**/Cab Calloway	
				Blues Brothers 2000 — see BLUES BROTHERS Dan Aykroyd/John Goodman/Joe Morton/J. Evan Bonifant/**James Brown**	
10/20/84	207	1		144 **Body Rock** .... [V] Lorenzo Lamas/Vicki Frederick/Cameron Dye/Ray Sharkey	EMI America 17140
				Bodyguard, The — see HOUSTON, Whitney Whitney Houston/Kevin Costner/Gary Kemp (**Spandau Ballet**)/Bill Cobbs/Ralph Waite	
10/27/01	39	5		146 **Bones** .... [V] Snoop Dogg/Pam Grier/Michael T. Weiss/Clifton Powell/Ricky Harris	Doggystyle 50227
4/6/68	12	21		147 **Bonnie And Clyde** .... [I] Warren Beatty/Faye Dunaway/Gene Hackman/Estelle Parsons/Gene Wilder; cp: Charles Strouse	Warner 1742
11/8/97	84	18		148 **Boogie Nights** .... [O-V] Mark Wahlberg (**Marky Mark**)/Julianne Moore/Burt Reynolds/William H. Macy/Heather Graham	Capitol 55631
7/18/92	4	54	▲³	149 **Boomerang** .... [V] Eddie Murphy/Halle Berry/Robin Givens/David Alan Grier/**Martin Lawrence**	LaFace 26006
3/15/97	24	28	▲	150 **Booty Call** .... [V] Jamie Foxx/Tommy Davidson/Vivica A. Fox/Bernie Mac/Tamala Jones	Jive 41604
7/30/66	42	48		151 **Born Free** .... [I] Virginia McKenna/Bill Travers/Geoffrey Keen/Peter Lukoye/Omar Chambati; cp/cd: John Barry	MGM 4368
1/20/90	32	15		152 **Born On The Fourth Of July** .... [I+V] Tom Cruise/Kyra Sedgwick/Raymond J. Barry/Jerry Levine; side A: various artists; side B: instrumental; cp/cd: **John Williams**	MCA 6340
12/2/00	124	3		153 **Bounce** .... [V] Ben Affleck/Gwyneth Paltrow/Jennifer Grey/David Paymer/Natasha Henstridge	Arista 14661
2/18/95	17	29	▲²	154 **Boys On The Side** .... [V] Whoopi Goldberg/Mary-Louise Parker/Drew Barrymore/Matthew McConaughey/Estelle Parsons	Arista 18748
7/27/91	12	18	●	155 **Boyz N The Hood** .... [V] Ice Cube/Cuba Gooding Jr./Morris Chestnut/Laurence Fishburne/Nia Long	Qwest 26643
3/18/95	137	4		156 **Brady Bunch Movie, The** .... [V] Shelley Long/Gary Cole/Michael McKean/Christine Taylor/David Graf	Milan 35698
				Bram Stoker's Dracula — see Dracula	
8/18/07	83	3		158 **Bratz** .... [V] Logan Browning/Janel Parrish/Nathalia Ramos/Skyler Shaye/Jon Voight	Geffen 009481

Billboard DEBUT	PEAK	WKS	R I A A	ARTIST Album Title .... Catalog	Label & Number
6/10/95+	45	64	▲	159 Braveheart .... **Cat:#7/4** **[I]** Mel Gibson/Sophie Marceau/Patrick McGoohan; cp/cd: James Horner; pf: **London Symphony Orchestra**	London 448295
				Breakfast At Tiffany's — see MANCINI, Henry Audrey Hepburn/George Peppard/Patricia Neal/Buddy Ebsen/Martin Balsam	
3/9/85	17	26	●	161 Breakfast Club, The .... **[V]** Molly Ringwald/Anthony Michael Hall/Emilio Estevez/Judd Nelson/Ally Sheedy	A&M 5045
6/2/84	8	23	▲	162 Breakin' **[V]** Lucinda Dickey/Adolfo Quinones/Michael Chambers/Ben Lokey/Chris McDonald	Polydor 821919
1/12/85	52	13		163 Breakin' 2 Electric Boogaloo .... **[V]** Lucinda Dickey/Adolfo Quinones/Michael Chambers/Susie Bono/Harry Caesar	Polydor 823696
				Breaking Glass — see O'CONNOR, Hazel Hazel O'Connor/Phil Daniels/Jonathan Pryce	
6/17/95	47	11	●	165 Bridges Of Madison County, The .... **[V]** Clint Eastwood/**Meryl Streep**/Annie Corley/Victor Slezak/Jim Haynie	Malpaso 45949
4/28/01	36	14		166 Bridget Jones's Diary .... **[V]** Renee Zellweger/Hugh Grant/Colin Firth/Gemma Jones/Jim Broadbent	Island 548797
12/4/04	72	4		167 Bridget Jones: The Edge Of Reason .... **[V]** Renee Zellweger/Hugh Grant/Colin Firth/Jim Broadbent/Gemma Jones	Geffen 003566
4/2/88	67	11		168 Bright Lights, Big City .... **[V]** Michael J. Fox/Kiefer Sutherland/Phoebe Cates/Dianne Wiest/Swoosie Kurtz	Warner 25688
12/11/82+	201	8		169 Brimstone & Treacle .... **[V]** Sting/Denholm Elliott/Joan Plowright/Suzanna Hamilton	A&M 4915
9/9/00	119	16		170 Bring It On .... **[V]** Kirsten Dunst/Eliza Dushku/Jesse Bradford/Gabrielle Union/Claire Kramer	Play-Tone 61431
3/22/03	111	6		171 Bringing Down The House .... **[V]** Steve Martin/**Queen Latifah**/Eugene Levy/Jean Smart/Joan Plowright	Hollywood 162386
12/2/06	156	1		172 Broke Down Melody, A .... **[V]** documentary movie about surfing	Brushfire 007960
1/21/06	54	12		173 Brokeback Mountain .... **[V]** Heath Ledger/Jake Gyllenhaal/Randy Quaid/Anne Hathaway	Focus 005604
9/16/06	35	23		174 Broken Bridges .... **[V]** Toby Keith/Lindsey Haun/Kelly Preston/Burt Reynolds	Show Dog 0001
7/5/80	123	6		175 Bronco Billy .... **[I+V]** Clint Eastwood/Sondra Locke/Geoffrey Lewis/Scatman Crothers/Bill McKinney; cp/cd: Steve Dorff	Elektra 512
11/8/03	52	10		176 Brother Bear .... **[V]** animated movie, voices by: Joaquin Phoenix/Jeremy Suarez/Rick Moranis/Dave Thomas	Walt Disney 860127
4/7/01	32	9		177 Brothers, The .... **[V]** Morris Chestnut/D.L. Hughley/Bill Bellamy/**Tatyana Ali**/Shemar Moore	Warner 48058
10/12/02	16	16		178 Brown Sugar .... **[V]** Taye Diggs/Sanaa Lathan/**Mos Def**/**Queen Latifah**/Boris Kodjoe	MCA 113028
7/22/78	86	13		179 Buddy Holly Story, The .... **[M]** Gary Busey/Don Stroud/Charles Martin Smith/Maria Richwine/Conrad Janis	Epic 35412
8/6/88	157	6		180 Bull Durham .... **[V]** Kevin Costner/Susan Sarandon/Tim Robbins/Trey Wilson/Robert Wuhl	Capitol 90586
9/21/96	85	7		181 Bulletproof .... **[V]** Damon Wayans/**Adam Sandler**/James Farentino/James Caan/Kristen Wilson	MCA Sound. 11498
5/9/98	10	27	●	182 Bulworth **[V]** Warren Beatty/Halle Berry/Sean Astin/Paul Sorvino/Oliver Platt	Interscope 90160
10/15/88+	54	23	●	183 Buster .... **[V]** Phil Collins/Julie Walters/Larry Lamb/Stephanie Lawrence/Ellen Beaven	Atlantic 81905
				Bustin' Loose — see FLACK, Roberta Richard Pryor/Cicely Tyson/Alphonso Alexander/Kia Cooper/Edwin DeLeon	
11/29/69+	16	74	●	185 Butch Cassidy And The Sundance Kid .... **[I+V]** *Grammy: Soundtrack Album* Paul Newman/Robert Redford/Katharine Ross/Strother Martin/Henry Jones; cp/cd: **Burt Bacharach**	A&M 4227
4/27/63	2²	55		186 Bye Bye Birdie **[M]** Ann-Margret/Jesse Pearson/Janet Leigh/Dick Van Dyke; mu: Charles Strouse; ly: Lee Adams; cd: Johnny Green	RCA Victor 1081
3/18/72+	25	72	●	187 Cabaret .... **[M]** *Grammy: Hall of Fame* Liza Minnelli/Michael York/Joel Grey/Helmut Griem/Marisa Berenson; mu: John Kander; ly: Fred Ebb	ABC 752
6/8/96	41	12		188 Cable Guy, The .... **[V]** Jim Carrey/Matthew Broderick/Leslie Mann/**George Segal**/Jack Black	Work 67654
8/23/80	78	12		189 Caddyshack .... **[V]** Chevy Chase/Bill Murray/**Rodney Dangerfield**/Ted Knight/Michael O'Keefe	Columbia 36737
12/20/08	66	17		190 Cadillac Records .... **[V]** Adrien Brody/**Beyonce**/**Mos Def**/Cedric The Entertainer	Music World 36936
11/11/67+	11	87	▲	191 Camelot .... **[M]** Richard Harris/Vanessa Redgrave/David Hemmings; mu: Frederick Loewe; ly: Alan Jay Lerner; cd: Alfred Newman	Warner 1712
6/20/98	25	27	●	192 Can't Hardly Wait .... **[V]** Ethan Embry/Charlie Korsmo/Lauren Ambrose/**Jennifer Love Hewitt**/Seth Green	Elektra 62201
				Can't Stop The Music — see VILLAGE PEOPLE Village People/Valerie Perrine/Bruce Jenner/Steve Guttenberg/Jack Weston	
5/2/60	3¹	68		194 Can-Can **[M]** *Grammy: Movie Soundtrack* Frank Sinatra/Shirley MacLaine/Maurice Chevalier/Louis Jourdan/Juliet Prowse; sw: Cole Porter; cd: **Nelson Riddle**	Capitol 1301
2/1/69	49	16		195 Candy .... **[I+V]** Ewa Aulin/Richard Burton/Marlon Brando/**Ringo Starr**/Charles Aznavour; cp/cd: Dave Grusin	ABC 9
				Car Wash — see ROSE ROYCE Richard Pryor/Franklin Ajaye/Ivan Dixon/**George Carlin**/Sully Boyar	

Billboard DEBUT	PEAK	WKS	R I A A	ARTIST Album Title.. Catalog	Label & Number
2/8/64	100	9		197 **Cardinal, The** .... **[I]** Tom Tryon/John Huston/Carol Lynley/Robert Morse/Ossie Davis; cp/cd: Jerome Moross	RCA Victor 1084
2/25/56	**2**[1]	56	▲	198 **Carousel** **[M]** Gordon MacRae/Shirley Jones/Cameron Mitchell; mu: Richard Rodgers; ly: Oscar Hammerstein II; cd: Alfred Newman	Capitol 694
9/5/64	141	3		199 **Carpetbaggers, The** .... **[I]** George Peppard/Alan Ladd/Carroll Baker/Bob Cummings/Martha Hyer; cp/cd: Elmer Bernstein	Ava 45
				Carry It On — see BAEZ, Joan	
6/24/06	**6**	46	▲	201 **Cars** Cat:#37/1 **[V]** animated movie, voices by: Owen Wilson/Paul Newman/Bonnie Hunt/**Larry The Cable Guy**/**George Carlin**; cp/cd: **Randy Newman**	Walt Disney 861349
5/13/67	22	21		202 **Casino Royale** .... **[I]** Peter Sellers/David Niven/Ursula Andress/**Woody Allen**/**Orson Welles**; cp/cd: **Burt Bacharach**	Colgems 5005
4/17/82	47	14		203 **Cat People** .... **[I]** Nastassia Kinski/Malcolm McDowell/John Heard/Annette O'Toole/John Larroquette; cp: **Giorgio Moroder**	Backstreet 6107
3/14/98	30	5		204 **Caught Up** .... **[V]** Bokeem Woodbine/Cynda Williams/Tony Todd/**Snoop Dogg**/**LL Cool J**	Noo Trybe 45451
3/20/93	41	10		205 **CB4** .... **[V]** Chris Rock/Allen Payne/Phil Hartman/Chris Elliott/Khandi Alexander	MCA 10803
5/27/00	120	8		206 **Center Stage** .... **[V]** Amanda Schull/Zoe Saldana/Susan May Pratt/Peter Gallagher/Donna Murphy	Epic 63969
				Charade — see MANCINI, Henry Cary Grant/Audrey Hepburn/Walter Matthau/James Coburn/George Kennedy	
				Chariots Of Fire — see VANGELIS Ian Charleson/Ben Cross/Nigel Havers/Nick Farrell/Ian Holm	
7/30/05	76	5		209 **Charlie And The Chocolate Factory** .... **[I]** Johnny Depp/Freddie Highmore/David Kelly/Helena Bonham Carter; cp/cd: Danny Elfman	Warner 72264
11/11/00	**7**	36	▲[2]	210 **Charlie's Angels** **[O-V]** Cameron Diaz/Drew Barrymore/Lucy Liu/Bill Murray/Crispin Glover	Columbia 61064
7/12/03	12	8	●	211 **Charlie's Angels: Full Throttle** **[O-V]** Cameron Diaz/Drew Barrymore/Lucy Liu/Bernie Mac/Crispin Glover	Columbia 90132
5/19/73	215	4		212 **Charlotte's Web** **[M]** animated movie, voices by **Debbie Reynolds**/Henry Gibson/Agnes Moorehead; sw: Richard & Robert Sherman	Paramount 1008
2/1/03	**2**[1]	51	▲[2]	213 **Chicago** **[M]** *Grammy: Soundtrack Album* Catherine Zeta-Jones/Renée Zellweger/Richard Gere/**Queen Latifah**/John C. Reilly	Epic 87018
11/19/05	57	12		214 **Chicken Little** .... **[M]** animated movie, voices by: Zach Braff/Don Knotts/Patrick Stewart/Joan Cusack; cp: John Debney	Walt Disney 861372
				Children Of Sanchez — see MANGIONE, Chuck Anthony Quinn/Dolores Del Rio/Katy Jurado/Lupita Ferrer/Lucia Mendez	
11/9/68+	58	28		216 **Chitty Chitty Bang Bang** .... **[M]** Dick Van Dyke/Sally Ann Howes/Lionel Jeffries/Gert Frobe/Benny Hill; sw: Richard M. Sherman and Robert B. Sherman	United Artists 5188
3/3/01	147	7		217 **Chocolat** .... **[I]** Juliette Binoche/Judi Dench/Alfred Molina/Lena Olin/Johnny Depp; cp: Rachel Portman; cd: David Snell	Miramax 89472
12/28/85+	77	12		218 **Chorus Line, A - The Movie** .... **[M]** Michael Douglas/Terrence Mann/Alyson Reed/Cameron English; mu: **Marvin Hamlisch**; ly: Edward Kleban; cd: Ralph Burns	Casablanca 826306
				Christiane F. — see BOWIE, David Natja Brunkhortst/Thomas Haustein/**David Bowie**	
1/21/84	177	5		220 **Christine** .... **[O-V]** Keith Gordon/John Stockwell/Alexandra Paul/Harry Dean Stanton/Robert Prosky	Motown 6086
12/31/05	43	11		221 **Chronicles Of Narnia: The Lion, The Witch And The Wardrobe, The** .... **[I]** Tilda Swinton/Georgie Henley/Skandar Keynes/Anna Popplewell; cp/cd: Harry Gregson-Williams	Walt Disney 861374
5/31/08	26	6		222 **Chronicles Of Narnia: Prince Caspian, The** .... **[I]** Ben Barnes/Georgie Henley/Anna Popplewell/Warwick Davis; cp/cd: Harry Gregson-Williams	Walden Media 000742
10/28/95	176	3		223 **Cinderella** .... **[V]** animated movie, voices by: Ilene Woods/William Phipps/Verna Felton; includes the 1950 movie's original score (#1 album in 1950 on RCA Victor 399) and remakes of songs by contemporary artists	Walt Disney 60886
7/31/04	**9**	27	●	224 **Cinderella Story, A** **[V]** **Hilary Duff**/Jennifer Coolidge/Chad Michael Murray/Regina King	Hollywood 162453
4/18/98	❶[3]	77	▲[5]	225 **City Of Angels** Cat:#35/1 **[V]** Nicolas Cage/Meg Ryan/Dennis Franz/Andre Braugher	Warner Sunset 46867
				Clambake — see PRESLEY, Elvis Elvis Presley ("Scott Heywood")/**Shelley Fabares**/Will Hutchins/Bill Bixby/James Gregory	
				Claudine — see KNIGHT, Gladys/Pips James Earl Jones/Diahann Carroll/Lawrence Hilton-Jacobs/Roxie Roker	
6/22/63	**2**[3]	27		228 **Cleopatra** .... **[I]** Elizabeth Taylor/Richard Burton/Rex Harrison/Roddy McDowall/Martin Landau; cp/cd: Alex North	20th Century Fox 5008
8/18/73	109	10		229 **Cleopatra Jones** .... **[I+V]** Tamara Dobson/Bernie Casey/Shelley Winters/Antonio Fargas/Esther Rolle; cp/cd: J.J. Johnson	Warner 2719
4/13/02	183	1		230 **Clockstoppers** .... **[V]** Jesse Bradford/Paula Garces/French Stewart/Michael Biehn/Robin Thomas	Hollywood 162346
2/5/72	34	31		231 **Clockwork Orange, A** .... **[I]** Malcolm McDowell/Patrick Magee/Michael Bates/Warren Clarke; cp/cd: **Walter Carlos**	Warner 2573
1/7/78	17	16	●	232 **Close Encounters Of The Third Kind** .... **[I]** *Grammy: Soundtrack Album* Richard Dreyfuss/Teri Garr/Francois Truffaut/Melinda Dillon/Bob Balaban; cp/cd: **John Williams**	Arista 9500
				Club Paradise — see CLIFF, Jimmy Robin Williams/Peter O'Toole/Rick Moranis/**Jimmy Cliff**/Twiggy	
8/5/95	49	43	▲	234 **Clueless** .... **[V]** Alicia Silverstone/Wallace Shawn/Brittany Murphy/Paul Rudd/Stacey Dash	Capitol 32617
1/29/05	25	7		235 **Coach Carter** .... **[V]** Samuel L. Jackson/Rob Brown/Robert Ri'chard/Rick Gonzalez/**Ashanti**	Capitol 63164

Billboard			R I A A	ARTIST		
DEBUT	PEAK	WKS		Album Title.. Catalog	Label & Number	
3/29/80	40	20	●	236 Coal Miner's Daughter	MCA 6107	
				Sissy Spacek/Tommy Lee Jones/Beverly D'Angelo/**Levon Helm**		
6/28/86	100	6		237 Cobra .... [V]	Scotti Brothers 40325	
				Sylvester Stallone/Brigitte Nielsen/Reni Santoni/David Rasche/Andrew Robinson		
8/13/88+	2[1]	61	▲⁴	238 Cocktail .... [V]	Elektra 60806	
				Tom Cruise/Bryan Brown/Elisabeth Shue/Gina Gershon/Lisa Barnes		
7/27/85	188	4		239 Cocoon .... [I]	Polydor 827041	
				Don Ameche/Wilford Brimley/Hume Cronyn/Jessica Tandy/Brian Dennehy; cp/cd: James Horner		
1/17/04	51	15		240 Cold Mountain .... [V]	DMZ 86843	
				Jude Law/Nicole Kidman/Renée Zellweger/Philip Seymour Hoffman/Natalie Portman		
11/15/86	81	15		241 Color Of Money, The .... [V]	MCA 6189	
				Paul Newman/Tom Cruise/Mary Elizabeth Mastrantonio/Helen Shaver/John Turturro		
3/8/86	79	13		242 Color Purple, The .... [I]	Qwest 25389 [2]	
				Whoopi Goldberg/Danny Glover/Margaret Avery/Oprah Winfrey; cd: **Quincy Jones**		
5/14/88	31	19	●	243 Colors .... [V]	Warner 25713	
				Sean Penn/Robert Duvall/Maria Conchita Alonso/Don Cheadle/Glenn Plummer		
9/23/72	198	2		244 Come Back Charleston Blue .... [I]	Atco 7010	
				Godfrey Cambridge/Raymond St. Jacques/Adam Wade/Jonelle Allen; cp/cd/pf: **Donny Hathaway**		
7/30/88	177	2		245 Coming To America .... [V]	Atco 90958	
				Eddie Murphy/Arsenio Hall (**Chunky A**)/James Earl Jones/John Amos/Eriq LaSalle		
				Commitments, The — see COMMITMENTS		
				Andrew Strong/Angeline Ball/Robert Arkins/Maria Doyle/Bronagh Gallagher		
6/12/82	162	5		247 Conan The Barbarian.. [I]	MCA 6108	
				Arnold Schwarzenegger/James Earl Jones/Max Von Sydow/Sandahl Bergman; cp/cd: Basil Poledouris		
8/7/93	162	6		248 Coneheads .... [V]	Warner 45345	
				Dan Aykroyd/Jane Curtin/Chris Farley/Michelle Burke/Jason Alexander		
3/6/04	51	11		249 Confessions Of A Teenage Drama Queen .... [V]	Hollywood 162442	
				Lindsay Lohan/Adam Garcia/Glenne Headly/Carol Kane		
3/7/09	135	2		250 Confessions Of A Shopaholic....................................... [V]	Hollywood 002835	
				Isla Fisher/Joan Cusack/John Goodman/John Lithgow		
				Cool As Ice — see VANILLA ICE		
				Vanilla Ice/Kristin Minter/Michael Gross/Naomi Campbell/Dody Goodman		
10/30/93+	111	32	●	252 Cool Runnings .... [V]	Chaos 57553	
				Leon/Doug E. Doug/Rawle Lewis/Malik Yoba/John Candy		
8/1/92	89	6		253 Cool World, Songs From The .... [V]	Warner 45009	
				Kim Basinger/Gabriel Byrne/Brad Pitt		
				Cornbread, Earl And Me — see BLACKBYRDS, The		
				Moses Gunn/Bernie Casey/Keith Wilkes/Madge Sinclair/Laurence Fishburne		
10/8/05	163	2		255 Corpse Bride .... [I]	Warner Sunset 49473	
				animated movie, voices by: Johnny Depp/Helena Bonham Carter/**Tracey Ullman**; cp/cd: Danny Elfman		
9/17/94	173	2		256 Corrina, Corrina .... [V]	RCA 66443	
				Whoopi Goldberg/Ray Liotta/Tina Majorino/Joan Cusack/**Don Ameche**		
3/27/99	44	6		257 Corruptor, The .... [V]	Jive 41671	
				Chow Yun-Fat/Mark Wahlberg (**Marky Mark**)/Ric Young/Paul Ben-Victor/Byron Mann		
1/19/85	93	10		258 Cotton Club, The .... [I]	Geffen 24062	
				Grammy: *Jazz Album*		
				Richard Gere/Gregory Hines/Bob Hoskins/Nicolas Cage/**Tom Waits**; cd: Bob Wilder		
12/1/84+	120	15		259 Country .... [I]	Windham Hill 1039	
				Jessica Lange/Sam Shepard/Wilford Brimley/Matt Clark; cp/cd: Charles Gross		
8/10/02	100	3		260 Country Bears, The .... [V]	Walt Disney 860774	
				animated movie, voices by: Haley Joel Osment/Diedrich Bader/Candy Ford/Stephen Root/Brad Garrett		
8/19/00	10	104	▲⁴	261 Coyote Ugly Cat.:#6/33 [V]	Curb 78703	
				Piper Perabo/Adam Garcia/Maria Bello/Melanie Lynskey/Tyra Banks		
2/15/03	143	2		262 Coyote Ugly: More Music From .... [V]	Curb 78765	
3/8/03	6	16	●	263 Cradle 2 The Grave .... [V]	Bloodline 063615	
				Jet Li/DMX/Anthony Anderson/Kelly Hu/Tom Arnold		
5/18/96	98	8		264 Craft, The .... [V]	Columbia 67626	
				Fairuza Balk/Robin Tunney/Neve Campbell/Rachel True/Skeet Ulrich		
7/21/01	164	2		265 Crazy/Beautiful .... [V]	Hollywood 62292	
				Kirsten Dunst/Jay Hernandez/Bruce Davison/Herman Osorio		
5/28/94	59	8		266 Crooklyn .... [O-V]	40 Acres 11036	
				Alfre Woodard/Delroy Lindo/Spike Lee/Zelda Harris		
				Crossroads — see COODER, Ry		
				Ralph Macchio/Joe Seneca/Jami Gertz/**Steve Vai**/Allan Arbus		
1/27/01	69	17		268 Crouching Tiger, Hidden Dragon .... [I]	Sony Classical 89347	
				Grammy: *Soundtrack Album*		
				Michelle Yeoh/Chow Yun-Fat/Zhang Zi Yi/Chang Cheng; cp/cd: Tan Dun		
4/16/94	❶[1]	44	▲³	269 Crow, The .... [V]	Atlantic 82519	
				Brandon Lee/Ernie Hudson/Rochelle Davis/Michael Wincott/David Patrick Kelly		
8/17/96	8	24	▲	270 Crow - City Of Angels, The .... [V]	Miramax 62047	
				Vincent Perez/Mia Kirshner/Richard Brooks/**Iggy Pop**/Thomas Jane		
4/15/00	104	4		271 Crow - Salvation, The .... [V]	Koch 8070	
				Kirsten Dunst/Eric Mabius/Jodi Lyn O'Keefe/William Atherton/Fred Ward		
3/20/99	60	15	●	272 Cruel Intentions .... [V]	Virgin 47174	
				Ryan Phillippe/Sarah Michelle Gellar/Reese Witherspoon/Selma Blair/Louise Fletcher		
3/22/80	202	4		273 Cruising .... [V]	Lorimar 36410	
				Al Pacino/Paul Sorvino/Karen Allen/Richard Cox		
3/13/93	60	13		274 Crying Game, The.. [I+V]	SBK 89024	
				Stephen Rea/Miranda Richardson/Jaye Davidson/Forest Whitaker; cp: Anne Dudley (**Art Of Noise**)		

Billboard			R I A A	ARTIST		
DEBUT	PEAK	WKS		Album Title.......... Catalog	Label & Number	

				Curious George — see JOHNSON, Jack		
				animated movie, voices by: Will Ferrell/Drew Barrymore/**David Cross**/Eugene Levy		
6/3/06	157	2		276 Da Vinci Code, The .... [I]	Decca 006479	
				Tom Hanks/Audrey Tautou/Ian McKellen/Alfred Molina; cp/cd: Hans Zimmer		
2/3/07	34	12		277 Daddy's Little Girls .... [V]	Atlantic 94676	
				Gabrielle Union/Idris Elba/Lou Gossett Jr./Tasha Smith		
12/1/58	21	1		278 Damn Yankees .... [M]	RCA Victor 1047	
				Tab Hunter/Gwen Verdon/Ray Walston/Jean Stapleton/Russ Brown; sw: Richard Adler and Jerry Ross		
3/28/81	202	4		279 Dance Craze .... [L-V]	Chrysalis 1299	
				concert movie featuring top British ska groups		
8/29/98	54	13		280 Dance With Me .... [F-V]	Epic 68905	
				Vanessa Williams/Chayanne/**Kris Kristofferson**/Joan Plowright/Jane Krakowski		
12/22/90+	48	69	▲	281 Dances With Wolves .... Cat:#24/2 [I]	Epic 46982	
				Grammy: Soundtrack Album		
				Kevin Costner/Mary McDonnell/Graham Greene/Rodney Grant/Robert Pastorelli; cp/cd: John Barry		
3/1/97	20	7		282 Dangerous Ground .... [V]	Jive 41590	
				Ice Cube/Elizabeth Hurley/Ving Rhames		
8/12/95	❶⁴	52	▲³	283 Dangerous Minds .... [V]	MCA 11228	
				Michelle Pfeiffer/George Dzundza/Courtney Vance/Robin Bartlett		
2/22/03	9	24	●	284 Daredevil .... [V]	Wind-Up 13079	
				Ben Affleck/Jennifer Garner/Michael Clarke Duncan/Colin Farrell/Joe Pantoliano		
11/3/07	186	3		285 Darjeeling Limited, The .... [V]	Fox 9240	
				Owen Wilson/Adrien Brody/Jason Schwartzman/Bill Murray		
1/29/83	204	3		286 Dark Crystal, The .... [I]	Warner 23749	
				puppet performers include Jim Henson/Frank Oz/Kathryn Mullen; cp: Trevor Jones; cd: Marcus Dods; pf: **London Symphony Orchestra**		
8/2/08	20	8		287 Dark Knight, The .... [I]	Warner Sunset 511101	
				Christian Bale/Heath Ledger/Aaron Eckhart/Michael Caine/Gary Oldman; cp/cd: Hans Zimmer		
8/1/70	113	7		288 Darling Lili .... [M]	RCA Victor 1000	
				Julie Andrews/Rock Hudson/Jeremy Kemp/Lance Percival/Mike Witney; cp/cd: **Henry Mancini**		
4/1/06	44	3		289 Dave Chappelle's Block Party .... [V]	Geffen 006366	
				movie is a mix of documentary, comedy sketches and musical performances		
7/14/90	27	16	●	290 Days Of Thunder .... [V]	DGC 24294	
				Tom Cruise/Robert Duvall/Randy Quaid/Nicole Kidman/Michael Rooker		
10/30/93+	70	71	▲	291 Dazed And Confused .... Cat:#32/23 [O-V]	Medicine 24533	
				Jason London/Rory Cochrane/Wiley Wiggins/Milla Jovovich/Matthew McConaughey		
2/11/84	181	4		292 D.C. Cab .... [V]	MCA 6128	
				Mr. T/Gary Busey/Anne DeSalvo/Max Gail/Adam Baldwin		
1/27/96	61	13		293 Dead Man Walking .... [V]	Columbia 67522	
				Susan Sarandon/Sean Penn/Robert Prosky/Raymond J. Barry/R. Lee Ermey		
10/14/95	14	18	●	294 Dead Presidents .... [O-V]	Underworld 32438	
				Larenz Tate/Keith David/Chris Tucker/N'Bushe Wright/Bokeem Woodbine		
4/28/07	123	1		295 Death Proof .... [O-V]	Maverick 106172	
				Kurt Russell/Rosario Dawson/Tracie Thoms/Rose McGowan		
				Death Wish II — see PAGE, Jimmy		
				Charles Bronson/Jill Ireland/Vincent Gardenia/Anthony Franciosa/J.D. Cannon		
7/2/77	70	10		297 Deep, The .... [I+V]	Casablanca 7060	
				Nick Nolte/Jacqueline Bisset/Robert Shaw/Louis Gossett/Eli Wallach; cp/cd: John Barry		
5/9/92	166	7		298 Deep Cover .... [V]	Solar 75330	
				Laurence Fishburne/Jeff Goldblum/Gregory Sierra/Clarence Williams III/Charles Martin Smith		
1/22/55	4	9		299 Deep In My Heart [M]	MGM 3153	
				Jose Ferrer/Merle Oberon/Walter Pidgeon/Jim Backus/Russ Tamblyn; cd: Adolph Deutsch; LP: MGM E-3153 (#4); EP: MGM X-276 (#5)		
8/23/97	7	11	●	300 Def Jam's How To Be A Player .... [V]	Def Jam 537973	
				Bill Bellamy/Natalie Desselle/Bernie Mac/Lark Voorhies/Gilbert Gottfried		
1/25/03	88	8		301 Deliver Us From Eva .... [V]	Hollywood 162369	
				LL Cool J/Gabrielle Union/Duane Martin/Essence Atkins/Megan Good		
7/10/04	40	21		302 De-Lovely .... [V]	Columbia 90640	
				Kevin Kline/Ashley Judd/Jonathan Pryce/Kevin McNally		
2/4/95	157	3		303 Demon Knight .... [V]	Atlantic 82725	
				Billy Zane/William Sadler/Jada Pinkett/Thomas Haden Church/CCH Pounder		
6/2/07	98	1		304 Departed, The .... [O-V]	Warner Sunset 43259	
				Leonardo DiCaprio/Matt Damon/Jack Nicholson/Mark Wahlberg (**Marky Mark**)/Martin Sheen		
9/9/95	53	11		305 Desperado .... [V]	Epic Soundtrax 67294	
				Antonio Banderas/Joaquim Almeida/Salma Hayek/Steve Buscemi/Cheech Marin (**Cheech & Chong**)		
8/21/99	68	5		306 Detroit Rock City .... [O-V]	Mercury 546389	
				Edward Furlong/Giuseppe Andrews/James DeBello/Shannon Tweed/**Kiss**		
7/29/06	146	1		307 Devil Wears Prada, The .... [V]	Fox 44383	
				Meryl Streep/Anne Hathaway/Stanley Tucci/Tracie Thoms		
				Devil's Angels — see ALLAN, Davie		
				John Cassavetes/Beverly Adams/Mimsy Farmer/Salli Sachse/Maurice McEndree		
8/13/05	156	1		309 Devil's Rejects, The .... [V]	Hip-O 004794	
				Sid Haig/Bill Moseley/Sheri Moon/Leslie Easterbrook/Geoffrey Lewis/Priscilla Barnes		
1/8/72	74	12		310 Diamonds Are Forever .... [I]	United Artists 5220	
				Sean Connery/Jill St. John/**Jimmy Dean**/Charles Gray/Lana Wood; cp/cd: John Barry		
5/7/05	19	15		311 Diary Of A Mad Black Woman .... [V]	Rowdy 004615	
				Tyler Perry/Kimberly Elise/Steve Harris/Shemar Moore/Cicely Tyson		
6/30/90	108	5		312 Dick Tracy .... [V]	Sire 26236	
				Warren Beatty/Al Pacino/**Madonna**/Glenne Headley/Charlie Korsmo		

Billboard DEBUT	PEAK	WKS	R I A A	ARTIST Album Title.. Catalog	Label & Number
8/4/90	194	1		313 **Dick Tracy** Original Score .... [I] cp/cd: Danny Elfman	Sire 26264
11/30/02	156	3		314 **Die Another Day** .... [I] Pierce Brosnan/Halle Berry/Toby Stephens/John Cleese/Judi Dench; cp/cd: David Arnold	Warner 48348
9/8/73	205	3		315 **Dillinger** .... [I] Warren Oates/Ben Johnson/Michelle Phillips/Cloris Leachman; cp/cd: **Barry DeVorzon**	MCA 360
8/19/00	175	1		316 **Dinosaur** .... [I] animated movie, voices by D.B. Sweeney/Alfre Woodard/Ossie Davis/Max Casella/Julianna Marguiles; cp/cd: James Newton Howard	Walt Disney 860672
9/19/87	❶¹⁸	96	▲¹¹	317 **Dirty Dancing** Cat:#16/22 [O-V] Patrick Swayze/Jennifer Grey/Cynthia Rhodes (**Animotion**)/Jerry Orbach/Jack Weston	RCA Victor 6408
3/19/88	3⁵	52	▲⁴	318 **Dirty Dancing, More** [O-V]	RCA 6965
8/14/99	198	1		319 **Dirty Dancing - The Collector's Edition** .... [O-V]	RCA 67786 [2]
12/27/03	114	6		320 **Dirty Dancing: Ultimate Dirty Dancing** .... [O-V]	RCA 55525
5/19/07	10^C	3		321 **Dirty Dancing: 20th Anniversary** [O-V]	Legacy 69554
3/6/04	46	11		322 **Dirty Dancing: Havana Nights** .... [V] Sela Ward/Diego Luna/Romola Garai/**Mya**	J Records 57758
9/12/87	99	8		323 **Disorderlies** .... [V] **The Fat Boys**/Ralph Bellamy/Tony Plana/Anthony Geary/**Helen Reddy**	Polydor 833274
8/15/98	169	2		324 **Disturbing Behavior** .... [V] James Marsden/Katie Holmes/Nick Stahl/Bruce Greenwood/Steve Railsback	Trauma 74007
				Divine Madness — see MIDLER, Bette	
6/15/02	40	9		326 **Divine Secrets Of The Ya-Ya Sisterhood**................................ [V] Sandra Bullock/Ellen Burstyn/Ashley Judd/James Garner/Maggie Smith	DMZ 86534
7/22/89	68	14		327 **Do The Right Thing** .... [V] Danny Aiello/Ossie Davis/Ruby Dee/Spike Lee/John Turturro	Motown 6272
10/14/67+	55	44	●	328 **Doctor Dolittle** .... [M] Rex Harrison/Samantha Eggar/Anthony Newley/Richard Attenborough/Peter Bull; sw: Leslie Bricusse; cd: Lionel Newman	20th Century Fox 5101
7/4/98	4	37	▲²	329 **Dr. Dolittle** [V] Eddie Murphy/Ossie Davis/Oliver Platt/Peter Boyle/Jeffrey Tambor	Blackground 83113
7/7/01	76	6		330 **Dr. Dolittle 2** .... [V] Eddie Murphy/Kristen Wilson/**Raven-Symone**/Kevin Pollak/Jeffrey Jones	Fox 20005
7/27/63	82	10		331 **Dr. No** .... [I] Sean Connery/Ursula Andress/Joseph Wiseman/Jack Lord/Bernard Lee; cp/cd: Monty Norman	United Artists 5108
11/25/00	52	9		332 **Dr. Seuss' How The Grinch Stole Christmas** .... Cat:#23/6 [X-V] Jim Carrey/Molly Shannon/Jeffrey Tambor/Taylor Momsen/Christine Baranski; Christmas charts: 5/'00, 18/'01	Interscope 490765
3/19/66	❶¹	157	●	333 **Doctor Zhivago** [I] *Grammy: Soundtrack Album* Omar Sharif/Julie Christie/Rod Steiger/Alec Guinness/Ralph Richardson; cp/cd: Maurice Jarre	MGM 6
2/19/72	173	5		334 **Dollar ($)** .... [I+V] Warren Beatty/Goldie Hawn/Gert Frobe/Robert Webber; cp/cd: **Quincy Jones**	Reprise 2051
5/6/95	61	30	●	335 **Don Juan DeMarco** .... [I] Johnny Depp/Marlon Brando/Faye Dunaway; cp: Michael Kamen	A&M 540357
1/27/96	18	19	●	336 **Don't Be A Menace To South Central While Drinking Your Juice In The Hood** .... [V] Shawn Wayans/Marlon Wayans/Tracey Jones/Chris Spencer	Island 524146
				Don't Knock The Twist — see CHECKER, Chubby Chubby Checker/Gene Chandler/**Vic Dana**/Linda Scott/Frank Albertson	
				Doors, The — see DOORS Val Kilmer/Meg Ryan/Kevin Dillon/Kyle MacLachlan/Frank Whaley	
				Double Trouble — see PRESLEY, Elvis Elvis Presley ("Guy Lambert")/Annette Day/John Williams/Yvonne Romain/Leon Askin	
4/5/86	68	7		340 **Down And Out In Beverly Hills** .... [I+V] Nick Nolte/**Bette Midler**/Richard Dreyfuss/Tracy Nelson; cp: **Andy Summers**	MCA 6160
8/11/01	102	15	●	341 **Down From The Mountain**.. [L-V] *Grammy: Traditional Folk Album* documentary movie of a concert recorded on 5/24/2000 at the Ryman Auditorium in Nashville; features several of the bluegrass musicians featured on the soundtrack to the movie *O Brother, Where Art Thou?*	Lost Highway 170221
3/3/01	71	6		342 **Down To Earth** .... [V] Chris Rock/Regina King/Eugene Levy/Frankie Faison/Chazz Palminteri	Epic 61599
6/7/03	191	1		343 **Down With Love** .... [V] Renée Zellweger/Ewan McGregor/David Hyde Pierce/Sarah Paulson/Tony Randall	Reprise 48480
8/25/79	207	4		344 **Dracula**.. [I] Frank Langella/Laurence Olivier/Donald Pleasence/Kate Nelligan; cp/cd: **John Williams**; pf: **London Symphony Orchestra**	MCA 3166
12/12/92	94	6		345 **Dracula, Bram Stoker's** .... [I] Gary Oldman/Winona Ryder/Anthony Hopkins/Keanu Reeves/Sadie Frost; cp: Wojciech Kilar; cd: Anton Coppola	Columbia 53165
12/30/00+	81	9		346 **Dracula 2000** .... [V] Gerard Butler/Jonny Lee Miller/Justine Waddell/Christopher Plummer/Omar Epps	Columbia 61585
7/18/87	137	6		347 **Dragnet**... [I+V] Dan Aykroyd/Tom Hanks/Christopher Plummer/Dabney Coleman/Harry Morgan; cp: Ira Newborn	MCA 6210
4/8/89	94	10		348 **Dream A Little Dream** .... [V] Jason Robards/Corey Feldman/Piper Laurie/Meredith Salenger/Harry Dean Stanton	Cypress 0125
12/23/06+	❶²	31	▲	349 **Dreamgirls** [M] Beyonce/Jamie Foxx/Eddie Murphy/Jennifer Hudson/Danny Glover	Music World 88953
12/23/06+	39	14		350 **Dreamgirls: Deluxe Edition** .... [M]	Music World 02012 [2]
10/16/99	44	7		351 **Drive Me Crazy** .... [V] Melissa Joan Hart/Adrian Grenier/Stephen Collins/Mark Webber/Mark Metcalf	Jive 41692
5/19/01	124	2		352 **Driven** .... [V] Sylvester Stallone/Burt Reynolds/Kip Pardue/Gina Gershon/Stacy Edwards	Curb 78715

Billboard DEBUT	PEAK	WKS	R I A A	ARTIST Album Title.. Catalog	Label & Number
1/11/03	133	8		353 **Drumline** .... **[V]** Nick Cannon/Zoe Saldana/Orlando Jones/Leonard Roberts/Jason Weaver	Fox 41810
4/16/94	105	7		354 **D2: The Mighty Ducks** .... **[V]** Emilio Estevez/Michael Tucker/Jan Rubes/Kathryn Erbe/Carsten Norgaard	Hollywood 61603
9/30/00	102	22	●	355 **Duets** .... **[V]** Huey Lewis/Gwyneth Paltrow/Paul Giamatti/Andre Braugher/Angie Dickinson	Hollywood 62241
8/6/05	26	14		356 **Dukes Of Hazzard, The**.................................. **[V]** Johnny Knoxville/Seann William Scott/**Jessica Simpson**/Burt Reynolds/**Willie Nelson**	Columbia 94894
1/7/95	62	29	●	357 **Dumb And Dumber**.. **[V]** Jim Carrey/Jeff Daniels/Lauren Holly/Karen Duffy/Teri Garr	RCA 66523
				Dune — see TOTO Brad Dourif/Kyle MacLachlan/Kenneth McMillan/Linda Hunt/**Sting**	
7/20/91	50	14		359 **Dying Young** .... **[I]** Julia Roberts/Campbell Scott/Vincent D'Onofrio/Colleen Dewhurst; cp/cd: James Newton Howard	Arista 18692
5/10/03	95	2		360 **DysFunktional Family** .... **[V]** movie is a stand-up performance by comedian Eddie Griffin	Tha Row 63053
1/25/75	204	3		361 **Earthquake** .... **[I]** Charlton Heston/Ava Gardner/George Kennedy/Genevieve Bujold; cp/cd: **John Williams**	MCA 2081
				Easter Parade — see "Those Glorious MGM Musicals" Judy Garland/Fred Astaire/Peter Lawford/Ann Miller/Jules Munshin	
10/22/83	207	1		363 **Easy Money** .... **[V]** Rodney Dangerfield/Joe Pesci/Geraldine Fitzgerald/Candy Azzara	Columbia 38968
9/6/69+	**6**	72	●	364 **Easy Rider** .... **[V]** Peter Fonda/Dennis Hopper/Jack Nicholson/Karen Black/Robert Walker	Dunhill/ABC 50063
6/15/96	119	4		365 **Eddie** .... **[V]** Whoopi Goldberg/Frank Langella/Dennis Farina/Richard Jenkins	Island 524243
				Eddie And The Cruisers — see CAFFERTY, John Michael Pare/Tom Berenger/Ellen Barkin	
				Eddie And The Cruisers II — see CAFFERTY, John Michael Pare/Marina Orsini/Bernie Coulson	
5/26/56	**❶**[1]	99		368 **Eddy Duchin Story, The** .... **[I]** Tyrone Power/Kim Novak/James Whitmore/Victoria Shaw/Jack Albertson; pf: Carmen Cavallaro	Decca 8289
1/26/91	174	3		369 **Edward Scissorhands** .... **[I]** Johnny Depp/Winona Ryder/Dianne Wiest/Anthony Michael Hall/Vincent Price; cp/cd: Danny Elfman	MCA 10133
11/16/02	**❶**[4]	43	▲[4]	370 **8 Mile** .... **[V]** Eminem/Kim Basinger/Mekhi Phifer/Brittany Murphy/Evan Jones	Shady 493508
12/21/02	152	1		371 **8 Mile: More Music From 8 Mile**................... **[O-V]**	Shady 450979
2/5/94	33	18	▲	372 **8 Seconds** .... **[V]** Luke Perry/Stephen Baldwin/Cynthia Geary/Carrie Snodgress/Renee Zellweger	MCA 10927
				El Cantante — see ANTHONY, Marc Marc Anthony/**Jennifer Lopez**/Victor Manuelle/John Ortiz	
8/4/62	35	13		374 **El Cid** .... **[I]** Charlton Heston/Sophia Loren/Raf Vallone/Gary Raymond; cp/cd: Miklos Rozsa	MGM 3977
10/20/73	194	2		375 **Electra Glide In Blue** .... **[I+V]** Robert Blake/Billy Green Bush/Elisha Cook/**Peter Cetera**; cp: James William Guercio	United Artists 062
9/1/84	94	9		376 **Electric Dreams** .... **[V]** Lenny Von Dohlen/Virginia Madsen/Maxwell Caulfield/Bud Cort/Don Fellows	Virgin 39600
				Electric Horseman, The — see NELSON, Willie Robert Redford/**Jane Fonda**/**Willie Nelson**/Valerie Perrine/Allan Arbus	
1/29/05	62	3		378 **Elektra** .... **[V]** Jennifer Garner/Goran Visnjic/Kirsten Prout/Terence Stamp	Wind-Up 13107
12/5/09	102	5		379 **Elf** .... Cat:#11/14 **[X-V]** Will Ferrell/James Caan/Zooey Deschanel/Edward Asner/**Bob Newhart**; Christmas charts: 40/'03, 17/'04, 41/'05, 50/'07, 22/'08, 19/'09	New Line 39028
10/29/05	68	8		380 **Elizabethtown** .... **[V]** Orlando Bloom/Kirsten Dunst/Suasan Sarandon/Alec Baldwin/Bruce McGill	Vinyl Films 71410
4/24/04	112	4		381 **Ella Enchanted**.. **[V]** Anne Hathaway/Hugh Dancy/Cary Elwes/Vivica A. Fox/Minnie Driver	Hollywood 162441
				Elvis-That's The Way It Is — see PRESLEY, Elvis	
2/13/88	150	5		383 **Empire Of The Sun**.. **[I]** Christian Bale/John Malkovich/Miranda Richardson/Nigel Havers/Ben Stiller; cp/cd: **John Williams**	Warner 25668
9/9/95	63	20	●	384 **Empire Records** .... **[V]** Anthony LaPaglia/Maxwell Caulfield/Debi Mazar/Liv Tyler/Renee Zellweger	A&M 540384
5/17/80	**4**	28	●	385 **Empire Strikes Back, The** .... **[I]** *Grammy: Soundtrack Album* Mark Hamill/Harrison Ford/Carrie Fisher/Billy Dee Williams/Alec Guinness; cp/cd: **John Williams**	RSO 4201 [2]
9/6/80	178	4		386 **Empire Strikes Back, The/The Adventures Of Luke Skywalker** .... **[T]** storyline excerpts from the movie (no track titles listed); narrated by Malachi Throne	RSO 3081
2/15/97	60	9		387 **Empire Strikes Back, The** .... **[I-R]** complete score in sequence with previously unreleased music issued in conjunction with the 1997 release of *The Empire Strikes Back* Special Edition movie in theaters	RCA Victor 68747 [2]
12/8/07	39	26		388 **Enchanted** .... **[I+V]** Amy Adams/Patrick Dempsey/**Idina Menzel**/Susan Sarandon/**Julie Andrews**; cp/cd: Michael Kosarin	Walt Disney 000925
6/13/92	130	5		389 **Encino Man** .... **[V]** Sean Astin/Pauly Shore/Brendan Fraser/Megan Ward/Rose McGowan	Hollywood 61330
11/27/99	20	14	▲	390 **End Of Days** .... **[V]** Arnold Schwarzenegger/Gabriel Byrne/Kevin Pollak/Robin Tunney/Rod Steiger	Geffen 490508
8/1/81	**9**	20	●	391 **Endless Love** .... **[I+V]** Brooke Shields/Martin Hewitt/Shirley Knight/Don Murray; cp: Jonathan Tunick/**Lionel Richie**	Mercury 2001

Billboard DEBUT	PEAK	WKS	R I A A	ARTIST Album Title .... Catalog	Label & Number
				Endless Summer, The — see SANDALS, The	
2/8/97	133	5		393 English Patient, The.. [I]	Fantasy 16001
				Grammy: Soundtrack Album	
				Ralph Fiennes/Juliette Binoche/Willem Dafoe/Kristin Scott Thomas; cp: Gabriel Yared; cd: Harry Rabinowitz	
8/10/96	80	6		394 Escape From L.A. .... [V]	Lava 92714
				Kurt Russell/Stacy Keach/Steve Buscemi/Peter Fonda/Cliff Robertson	
7/3/82	37	33	●	395 E.T. - The Extra-Terrestrial .... [I]	MCA 6109
				Grammy: Soundtrack Album	
				Henry Thomas/Peter Coyote/Dee Wallace/Drew Barrymore/Robert MacNaughton; cp/cd: **John Williams**	
2/5/83	201	6		396 E.T. The Extra-Terrestrial .... [T]	MCA 70000
				storybook album with music by **John Williams** and narration by **Michael Jackson**; album was pulled shortly after release due to legal problems	
				Even Cowgirls Get The Blues — see lang, k.d.	
				Uma Thurman/Rain Phoenix/John Hurt/Pat Morita/Keanu Reeves	
8/22/98	100	7		398 Ever After.. [I]	London 460581
				Drew Barrymore/Anjelica Huston/Dougray Scott/Jeanne Moreau; cp/cd: George Fenton	
1/20/79	78	15		399 Every Which Way But Loose .... [V]	Elektra 503
				Clint Eastwood/Sondra Locke/Ruth Gordon/Geoffrey Lewis/Beverly D'Angelo; cd: Steve Dorff	
				Evita — see MADONNA	
				Madonna/Antonio Banderas/Jonathan Pryce/Jimmy Nail	
4/7/01	8	14		401 Exit Wounds [V]	Blackground 10192
				Steven Seagal/**DMX**/Bill Duke/Tom Arnold	
1/16/61	❶14	89	●	402 Exodus [I]	RCA Victor 1058
				Grammy: Soundtrack Album	
				Paul Newman/Eva Marie Saint/Ralph Richardson/Peter Lawford/Lee J. Cobb; cp/cd: Ernest Gold	
				Experiment In Terror — see MANCINI, Henry	
				Glenn Ford/Lee Remick/Stefanie Powers/Roy Poole/Ned Glass	
8/12/78	124	9		404 Eyes Of Laura Mars .... [I+V]	Columbia 35487
				Faye Dunaway/Tommy Lee Jones/Raul Julia/Brad Dourif/Rene Auberjonois; cp/cd: Artie Kane	
7/31/99	133	3		405 Eyes Wide Shut.. [V]	Warner Sunset 47450
				Tom Cruise/Nicole Kidman/Sydney Pollack/Marie Richardson	
				Fabulous Baker Boys, The — see GRUSIN, Dave	
				Jeff Bridges/Michelle Pfeiffer/Beau Bridges/Jennifer Tilly	
1/9/99	47	11		407 Faculty, The.. [V]	Columbia 69762
				Famke Janssen/Bebe Neuwirth/**Usher**/Robert Patrick/Elijah Wood	
				Falcon And The Snowman, The — see METHENY, Pat, Group	
				Timothy Hutton/Sean Penn/Lori Singer/Pat Hingle/Dorian Harewood	
6/13/64	147	2		409 Fall Of The Roman Empire, The.. [I]	Columbia 2460
				Sophia Loren/Stephen Boyd/James Mason/Alec Guinness/Christopher Plummer; cp/cd: Dimitri Tiomkin	
6/7/80	7	82	▲	410 Fame [M]	RSO 3080
				Irene Cara/Eddie Barth/Maureen Teefy/Lee Curreri	
9/12/09	43	10		411 Fame [M]	Lakeshore 340952
				Kay Panabaker/Kelsey Grammer/Bebe Neuwirth/Charles S. Dutton	
9/25/61	88	13		412 Fanny .... [I]	Warner 1416
				Leslie Caron/Maurice Chevalier/**Charles Boyer**/Lionel Jeffries; cp: Harold Rome; cd: Morris Stoloff	
11/17/90	190	2	▲	413 Fantasia, Walt Disney's .... Cat:#33/5 [I]	Buena Vista 60072 [2]
				Grammy: Hall of Fame	
				50th anniversary celebration of the release of the animated movie; cd: Leopold Stokowski; pf: **The Philadelphia Orchestra**	
7/23/05	77	3		414 Fantastic 4 .... [V]	Wind-Up 13114
				Jessica Alba/Michael Chiklis/Ioan Gruffudd/Chris Evans/Julian McMahon	
6/13/92	89	9		415 Far And Away .... [I]	MCA 10628
				Tom Cruise/Nicole Kidman/Thomas Gibson/Robert Prosky/Barbara Babcock; cp/cd: **John Williams**	
4/18/09	116	5		416 Fast & Furious .... [V]	Star Trak 012822
				Vin Diesel/Paul Walker/Michelle Rodriguez/Jordana Brewster	
6/23/01	7	34	▲	417 Fast And The Furious, The [V]	Murder Inc. 548832
				Vin Diesel/Paul Walker/Michelle Rodriguez/Ted Levine/**Ja Rule**	
1/19/02	117	17		418 Fast And The Furious: More Fast And Furious, The................................... [V]	Island 586631
7/8/06	40	9		419 Fast And The Furious: Tokyo Drift, The.. [V]	Motown 007092
				Lucas Black/Zachary Ty Bryan/**Bow Wow**/Nikki Griffin	
				Fast Break — see PRESTON, Billy	
				Gabriel Kaplan/Harold Sylvester/Bernard King	
				Fast Forward — see DECO	
				John Scott Clough/Don Franklin/Tamara Mark/Tracy Silver	
8/28/82	54	20		422 Fast Times At Ridgemont High .... [V]	Full Moon 60158 [2]
				Sean Penn/Phoebe Cates/Jennifer Jason Leigh/Judge Reinhold/Ray Walston	
6/13/98	174	1		423 Fear And Loathing In Las Vegas .... [O-V]	Geffen 25218
				Johnny Depp/Benicio Del Toro/Mark Harmon/Christina Ricci/Gary Busey	
				Ferry Cross The Mersey — see GERRY AND THE PACEMAKERS	
				Gerry and The Pacemakers/Cilla Black/Jimmy Saville	
10/30/71+	30	90	▲	425 Fiddler On The Roof .... [M]	United Artists 10900 [2]
				Topol/Norma Crane/Leonard Frey/Molly Picon; mu: Jerry Bock; ly: Sheldon Harnick; cd: **John Williams**	
6/7/97	99	6		426 Fifth Element, The.. [I]	Virgin 44203
				Bruce Willis/Gary Oldman/Ian Holm/Chris Tucker/Milla Jovovich; cp/cd/pf: Eric Serra	
2/28/04	30	27	●	427 50 First Dates .... [V]	Maverick 48675
				Adam Sandler/Drew Barrymore/Rob Schneider/Sean Astin/Dan Aykroyd	
9/12/98	77	5		428 54 - Volume 1 .... [O-V]	Tommy Boy 1293
				Ryan Phillippe/Salma Hayek/Sela Ward/Mike Myers/Neve Campbell	
9/12/98	74	6		429 54 - Volume 2 .... [O-V]	Tommy Boy 1294
9/27/03	19	23	●	430 Fighting Temptations, The.. [V]	Music World 90286
				Cuba Gooding Jr./**Beyoncé** Knowles/Mike Epps/LaTanya Richardson/**Faith Evans**	

Billboard DEBUT	PEAK	WKS	R I A A	ARTIST / Album Title .... Catalog	Label & Number
7/28/01	193	1		**431 Final Fantasy: The Spirits Within** .... **[I]**	Sony Classical 89697
				animated movie, voices by Ming-Na/Alec Baldwin/Ving Rhames/Steve Buscemi; cp/cd: Elliot Goldenthal	
11/15/03	156	2		**432 Finding Nemo: Ocean Favorites** .... **[M]**	Walt Disney 861022
				animated movie, voices by: Alexander Gould/**Albert Brooks**/Ellen DeGeneres/Geoffrey Rush	
8/23/86	183	3		**433 Fine Mess, A** .... **[V]**	Motown 6180
				Ted Danson/**Howie Mandel**/Richard Mulligan/Stuart Margolin/Paul Sorvino	
10/5/68+	90	26		**434 Finian's Rainbow** .... **[M]**	Warner 2550
				Fred Astaire/**Petula Clark**/Tommy Steele/Keenan Wynn; ly: E.Y. Harburg; mu: Burton Lane; cd: **Ray Heindorf**	
8/1/09	139	3		**435 Fireproof** .... **[I+V]**	Reunion 10143
				Kirk Cameron/Erin Bethea/Ken Bevel/Eric Young	
7/24/93	131	4		**436 Firm, The** .... **[I+V]**	MCA/GRP 2007
				Tom Cruise/Jeanne Tripplehorn/Ed Harris/Holly Hunter/Hal Holbrook; cp: **Dave Grusin**	
10/5/96	90	7		**437 First Wives Club, The** .... **[V]**	Work 67814
				Bette Midler/Goldie Hawn/Diane Keaton/Maggie Smith/Dan Hedaya	
6/24/67	107	28		**438 Fistful Of Dollars, A** .... **[I]**	RCA Victor 1135
				Clint Eastwood/Marianne Koch/Carol Brown/Mario Brega; cp/cd: Ennio Morricone	
4/27/91	58	13	●	**439 Five Heartbeats, The** .... **[V]**	Virgin 91609
				Robert Townsend/Michael Wright/Leon/Harry Lennix/Tico Wells	
8/1/09	42	20		**440 (500) Days Of Summer** .... **[V]**	Fox 518909
				Joseph Gordon-Levitt/Zooey Deschanel/Geoffrey Arend/Chloe Moretz	
10/12/59	22	10		**441 Five Pennies, The** .... **[M]**	Dot 29500
				Danny Kaye/**Louis Armstrong**/Barbara Bel Geddes/Tuesday Weld/Bob Crosby	
				Flame — see SLADE	
2/16/85	130	8		**443 Flamingo Kid, The** .... **[O-V]**	Motown 6131
				Matt Dillon/Richard Crenna/Hector Elizondo/Jessica Walter/Fisher Stevens	
				Flash Gordon — see QUEEN	
				Sam Jones/Max Von Sydow/Melody Anderson/Topol/Timothy Dalton	
4/30/83	❶²	78	▲⁶	**445 Flashdance** .... **[V]**	Casablanca 811492
				Grammy: Soundtrack Album	
				Jennifer Beals/Michael Nouri/Marine Johan/Lilia Skala	
7/27/85	160	4		**446 Fletch** .... **[I+V]**	MCA 6142
				Chevy Chase/Dana Wheeler-Nicholson/Joe Don Baker/Tim Matheson/George Wendt; cp/cd: Harold Faltermeyer	
11/4/06	123	3		**447 Flicka** .... **[V]**	Curb 78962
				Alison Lohman/**Tim McGraw**/Maria Bello/Danny Pino	
5/28/94	73	8		**448 Flintstones, The: Music From Bedrock** .... **[V]**	MCA 11045
				John Goodman/Rick Moranis/Elizabeth Perkins/**Rosie O'Donnell**/Halle Berry	
12/25/61+	15	35		**449 Flower Drum Song** .... **[M]**	Decca 79098
				Nancy Kwan/James Shigeta/Miyoshi Umeki; mu: Richard Rodgers; ly: Oscar Hammerstein II; cd: Alfred Newman	
5/6/78	5	24	▲	**450 FM** .... **[V]**	MCA 12000 [2]
				Michael Brandon/Eileen Brennan/Alex Karras/**Martin Mull**/Cleavon Little	
				Follow The Boys — see FRANCIS, Connie	
				Connie Francis/Paula Prentiss/Ron Randell/Janis Paige/Russ Tamblyn	
4/10/99	32	7	●	**452 Foolish** .... **[V]**	No Limit 50053
				Master P/Eddie Griffin/**Andrew Dice Clay**/Marla Gibbs/Bill Duke	
2/18/84	❶¹⁰	61	▲⁹	**453 Footloose** Cat:#27/25 **[V]**	Columbia 39242
				Kevin Bacon/Lori Singer/John Lithgow/Dianne Wiest/Chris Penn	
9/14/68	192	2		**454 For Love Of Ivy** .... **[I+V]**	ABC 7
				Sidney Poitier/Abbey Lincoln/Beau Bridges/**Carroll O'Connor**; cp/cd: **Quincy Jones**	
10/2/99	72	5		**455 For Love Of The Game** .... **[V]**	MCA 112068
				Kevin Costner/Kelly Preston/John C. Reilly/Jena Malone/Brian Cox	
				For The Boys — see MIDLER, Bette	
				Bette Midler/James Caan/George Segal/Chris Rydell/Patrick O'Neal	
				For The First Time — see LANZA, Mario	
				Mario Lanza/Zsa Zsa Gabor/Kurt Kasznar/Hans Sohnker	
7/25/81	84	19		**458 For Your Eyes Only** .... **[I]**	Liberty 1109
				Roger Moore/Carole Bouquet/Topol/Lynn-Holly Johnson/Julian Glover; cp/cd: Bill Conti	
6/17/95	182	1		**459 Forget Paris** .... **[I+V]**	Elektra 61825
				Billy Crystal/Debra Winger/Joe Mantegna/Julie Kavner/Richard Masur; cp: Marc Shaiman	
7/23/94	2⁵	94	▲¹²	**460 Forrest Gump** Cat:#23/1 **[O-V]**	Epic 66329 [2]
				Tom Hanks/Robin Wright/Gary Sinise/Mykelti Williamson/Sally Field	
9/2/78	102	7		**461 Foul Play** .... **[I+V]**	Arista 9501
				Goldie Hawn/Chevy Chase/Burgess Meredith/Dudley Moore/Billy Barty; cp/cd: Charles Fox	
				Foxy Brown — see HUTCH, Willie	
				Pam Grier/Peter Brown/Terry Carter/Antonio Fargas/Sid Haig	
				Frankie And Johnny — see PRESLEY, Elvis	
				Elvis Presley ("Johnny")/Donna Douglas ("Frankie")/Nancy Kovack/Harry Morgan	
8/16/03	19	37	●	**464 Freaky Friday** .... **[V]**	Hollywood 162404
				Jamie Lee Curtis/**Lindsay Lohan**/Harold Gould/Chad Michael Murray/Mark Harmon	
10/11/08	34ˣ	3		**465 Fred Claus** .... **[X-V]**	Warner 377212
				Vince Vaughn/Paul Giamatti/Miranda Richardson/**Ludacris**; Christmas charts: 34/08, 36/09	
8/30/03	25	6		**466 Freddy vs. Jason** .... **[V]**	Roadrunner 618347
				Robert Englund/Ken Kirzinger/**Kelly Rowland**/Monica Keena/Jason Ritter	
7/31/93	47	35	●	**467 Free Willy** .... **[V]**	MJJ Music 57280
				Jason James Richter/Lori Petty/Jayne Atkinson/Michael Madsen	
6/3/95	170	3		**468 French Kiss** .... **[V]**	Mercury 528136
				Meg Ryan/Kevin Kline/Timothy Hutton	
4/12/03	162	1		**469 Frida** .... **[F-V]**	Universal 474150
				Salma Hayek/Julie Taymor/Alfred Molina/Geoffrey Rush/Roger Rees	
4/29/95	❶²	73	▲²	**470 Friday** .... **[V]**	Priority 53959
				Ice Cube/Chris Tucker/Nia Long/Tiny Lister/John Witherspoon	

Billboard DEBUT	PEAK	WKS	R I A A	ARTIST Album Title.. Catalog	Label & Number
12/7/02	115	2		471 **Friday After Next**... [V] Ice Cube/Mike Epps/John Witherspoon/Anna Marie Horstord/Clifton Powell	Hollywood 162378
2/29/92	181	3		472 **Fried Green Tomatoes** .... [V] Kathy Bates/Jessica Tandy/Mary-Louise Parker/Mary Stuart Masterson/Gailard Sartain	MCA 10461
				Friends — see JOHN, Elton Sean Bury/Anicee Alvina/Ronald Lewis/Toby Robins/Pascale Roberts	
2/10/96	89	6		474 **From Dusk Till Dawn** .... [V] Harvey Keitel/George Clooney/Quentin Tarantino/Juliette Lewis/Cheech Marin (**Cheech & Chong**)	Los Hooligans 67523
5/2/64	27	34		475 **From Russia With Love** .... [I] Sean Connery/Daniela Bianchi/Lotte Lenya/Robert Shaw/Pedro Armendariz; cp/cd: John Barry	United Artists 5114
10/4/97+	99	19	●	476 **Full Monty, The** .... [V] Robert Carlyle/Tom Wilkinson/Mark Addy/Leslie Sharp/Emily Woof	RCA Victor 68904
				Fun In Acapulco — see PRESLEY, Elvis Elvis Presley ("Mike Windgren")/Ursula Andress/Elsa Cardenas/Paul Lukas/Alejandro Rey	
				Funny Girl — see STREISAND, Barbra Barbra Streisand/Omar Sharif/Kay Medford/Anne Francis/Walter Pidgeon	
				Funny Lady — see STREISAND, Barbra Barbra Streisand/James Caan/Omar Sharif/Roddy McDowall/Ben Vereen	
				G.I. Blues — see PRESLEY, Elvis Elvis Presley ("Tulsa McCauley")/Juliet Prowse/James Douglas/Robert Ivers/Leticia Roman	
4/30/83	168	3		481 **Gandhi**.. [I] Ben Kingsley/Candice Bergen/John Gielgud/Trevor Howard; cp/cd: George Fenton; pf: **Ravi Shankar**	RCA Victor 4557
10/25/97	2[1]	20	▲[2]	482 **Gang Related** .... [V] James Belushi/**2Pac**/Lela Rochon/Dennis Quaid/James Earl Jones	Death Row 53509 [2]
8/28/04	20	57	▲	483 **Garden State** .... [V] *Grammy: Soundtrack Album* Zach Braff/Ian Holm/Method Man/Natalie Portman/Peter Sarsgaard	Fox 92843
8/16/97	196	1		484 **George Of The Jungle** .... [V] Brendan Fraser/Leslie Mann/Thomas Haden Church/Holland Taylor/Richard Roundtree	Walt Disney 60806
11/2/96	184	2		485 **Get On The Bus** .... [V] Charles S. Dutton/Ossie Davis/Bernie Mac/Richard Belzer/Andre Braugher	40 Acres 90089
11/26/05	2[1]	30	▲	486 **Get Rich Or Die Tryin'** .... [V] 50 Cent/Joy Bryant/**Terrence Howard**/Bill Duke	G-Unit 005605
11/18/95	170	2		487 **Get Shorty** .... [I+V] John Travolta/Gene Hackman/Rene Russo/Danny DeVito/Dennis Farina; cp: John Lurie; cd: Steven Bernstein	Antilles 529310
9/1/90	8	64	▲	488 **Ghost** .... [I] Patrick Swayze/Demi Moore/Whoopi Goldberg/Tony Goldwyn/Rick Aviles; cp/cd: Maurice Jarre	Varese Sarabande 5276
7/7/84	6	34	▲	489 **Ghostbusters** .... [V] Bill Murray/Dan Aykroyd/Sigourney Weaver/Harold Ramis/Rick Moranis	Arista 8246
7/1/89	14	19	●	490 **Ghostbusters II** .... [V] Bill Murray/Dan Aykroyd/Sigourney Weaver/Harold Ramis/Rick Moranis	MCA 6306
4/29/00	84	3		491 **Ghost Dog: The Way Of The Samurai** .... [V] Forest Whitaker/John Tormey/Cliff Gorman/Henry Silva/Victor Argo	Epic 63794
12/29/56+	16	7		492 **Giant**.. [I] Elizabeth Taylor/Rock Hudson/James Dean/Jane Withers/Sal Mineo; cp/cd: Dimitri Tiomkin	Capitol 773
6/23/58	❶[10]	172	●	493 **Gigi** .... [M] *Grammys: Soundtrack Album / Hall of Fame* Leslie Caron/Maurice Chevalier/Louis Jourdan/Eva Gabor; ly: Alan Jay Lerner; mu: Frederick Loewe; cd: **Andre Previn**	MGM 3641
				Girl Happy — see PRESLEY, Elvis Elvis Presley ("Rusty Wells")/**Shelley Fabares**/Gary Crosby/Jackie Coogan	
				Girl 6 — see PRINCE Theresa Randle/Isaiah Washington/Spike Lee/Debi Mazar	
				Girls! Girls! Girls! — see PRESLEY, Elvis Elvis Presley ("Ross Carpenter")/Stella Stevens/Laurel Goodwin/Jeremy Slate	
				Give My Regards To Broad Street — see McCARTNEY, Paul Paul McCartney/Bryan Brown/**Ringo Starr/Tracey Ullman**/Barbara Bach	
5/20/00	66	24	●	498 **Gladiator** .... [I] Russell Crowe/Joaquin Phoenix/Connie Nielsen/Oliver Reed/**Richard Harris**; cp/cd: Hans Zimmer	Decca 467094
				Glitter — see CAREY, Mariah Mariah Carey/Da Brat/Terrence Howard/Dorian Harewood/**Eric Benét**	
3/17/90	190	2		500 **Glory** .... [I] *Grammy: Soundtrack Album* Matthew Broderick/Denzel Washington/Cary Elwes/Morgan Freeman/Cliff DeYoung; cp/cd: James Horner	Virgin 91329
4/17/99	67	18		501 **Go**.. [V] Katie Holmes/Breckin Meyer/Jay Mohr/Sarah Polley/Scott Wolf	Work 69851
4/8/72	21	35		502 **Godfather, The** .... [I] *Grammy: Soundtrack Album* Marlon Brando/Al Pacino/James Caan/Robert Duvall/Diane Keaton; cp: Nino Rota; cd: Carlo Savina	Paramount 1003
3/8/75	184	2		503 **Godfather, Part II, The** .... [I] Al Pacino/Robert DeNiro/Robert Duvall/Diane Keaton/Lee Strasberg; cp: Nino Rota and Carmine Coppola; cd: Carmine Coppola	ABC 856
1/12/91	102	7		504 **Godfather, Part III, The** .... [I] Al Pacino/Diane Keaton/Talia Shire/Andy Garcia/Sofia Coppola; cp/cd: Carmine Coppola and Nino Rota	Columbia 47078
2/22/03	196	1		505 **Gods And Generals** .... [I] Jeff Daniels/Stephen Lang/Robert Duvall; cp/cd: John Frizzell and Randy Edelman	Sony Classical 87891
4/14/73	50	51		506 **Godspell**.. [M] Victor Garber/David Haskell/Robin Lamont; cp: Stephen Schwartz	Bell 1118
6/6/98	2[1]	26	▲	507 **Godzilla** .... [V] Matthew Broderick/Jean Reno/Hank Azaria/Harry Shearer/Vicki Lewis	Epic 69338
				Goin' Coconuts — see OSMOND, Donny & Marie Donny & Marie Osmond/Kenneth Mars/Ted Cassidy/Herb Edelman/Harold Sakata	

Billboard DEBUT	PEAK	WKS	R I A A	ARTIST Album Title.. Catalog	Label & Number
1/24/87	126	7		509 **Golden Child, The**... **[I+V]** Eddie Murphy/Charlotte Lewis/Charles Dance/Victor Wong/Randall "Tex" Cobb; cp/cd: Michel Colombier	Capitol 12544
12/2/95	180	2		510 **GoldenEye** .... **[I]** Pierce Brosnan/Sean Bean/Izabella Scorupco/Famke Janssen/Joe Don Baker; cp/pf: Eric Serra	Virgin 41048
12/12/64+	❶³	70		511 **Goldfinger** .... **[I]** Sean Connery/Gert Frobe/Honor Blackman/Harold Sakata/Tania Mallet; cp/cd: John Barry	United Artists 5117
7/1/00	69	13		512 **Gone In 60 Seconds** .... **[V]** Nicolas Cage/Angelina Jolie/Giovanni Ribisi/Delroy Lindo/Robert Duvall	Island 542793
7/3/61	64	13		513 **Gone With The Wind** .... **[I]** new recording of movie soundtrack; cp/cd: Max Steiner; originally charted in 1954 (#10) on RCA Victor 3227; also see original soundtrack below	RCA Camden 625
10/14/67+	24	36		514 **Gone With The Wind** .... **[I]** *Grammy: Hall of Fame* Clark Gable/Vivien Leigh/Leslie Howard/Olivia DeHavilland/Hattie McDaniel; taken directly from the movie soundtrack (premiered in 1939); cp/cd: Max Steiner	MGM 10
8/9/97	101	5		515 **Good Burger** .... **[V]** Kel Mitchell/Kenan Thompson/Sinbad/Abe Vigoda/Dan Schneider	Capitol 57955
2/6/88	10	35	▲	516 **Good Morning, Vietnam** .... **[O-V]** *Grammy: Comedy Album* Robin Williams/Forest Whitaker/Tung Thanh Tran/Bruno Kirby/Robert Wuhl	A&M 3913
2/10/68	4	52	●	517 **Good, The Bad And The Ugly, The** .... **[I]** *Grammy: Hall of Fame* Clint Eastwood/Lee Van Cleef/Eli Wallach/Mario Brega; cp/cd: Ennio Morricone	United Artists 5172
				Good Times — see SONNY & CHER Sonny & Cher/George Sanders/Norman Alden	
2/7/98	91	11		519 **Good Will Hunting** .... **[V]** Robin Williams/Matt Damon/Ben Affleck/Minnie Driver	Capitol 23338
				Goodbye, Columbus — see ASSOCIATION, The Richard Benjamin/Jack Klugman/Ali MacGraw	
12/6/69	164	5		521 **Goodbye, Mr. Chips** .... **[M]** Peter O'Toole/**Petula Clark**/Michael Redgrave; sw: Leslie Bricusse; cd: **John Williams**	MGM 19
6/29/85	73	10		522 **Goonies, The** .... **[V]** Sean Astin/Josh Brolin/Jeff Cohen/Corey Feldman/Ke Huy Quan	Epic 40067
10/15/05+	82	19		523 **Gospel, The** .... **[L]** Boris Kodjoe/Nona Gaye/Clifton Powell/**Donnie McClurkin**	Verity 71620
				Gospel Road, The — see CASH, Johnny Johnny Cash/June Carter Cash	
				Graduate, The — see SIMON & GARFUNKEL Dustin Hoffman/Anne Bancroft/Katharine Ross/William Daniels/Murray Hamilton	
				Graffiti Bridge — see PRINCE Prince/Morris Day/Ingrid Chavez/Jerome Benton	
3/18/67	76	28		527 **Grand Prix** .... **[I]** James Garner/Eva Marie Saint/Yves Montand/Toshiro Mifune/Brian Bedford; cp/cd: Maurice Jarre	MGM 8
5/20/78	❶¹²	77	▲⁸	528 **Grease** Cat:❶⁵²/278 **[M]** John Travolta/**Olivia Newton-John**/Stockard Channing/Jeff Conaway/Didi Conn	RSO 4002 [2]
6/19/82	71	13		529 **Grease 2** .... **[M]** Maxwell Caulfield/Michelle Pfeiffer/Adrian Zmed/Lorna Luft	RSO 3803
				Great Balls Of Fire! — see LEWIS, Jerry Lee Dennis Quaid/Winona Ryder/Alec Baldwin/Trey Wilson/**Mojo Nixon**	
9/21/63	50	21	●	531 **Great Escape, The** .... **[I]** Steve McQueen/James Garner/Richard Attenborough/James Coburn/Charles Bronson; cp/cd: Elmer Bernstein	United Artists 5107
1/24/98	25	16	●	532 **Great Expectations** .... **[V]** Ethan Hawke/Gwyneth Paltrow/Anne Bancroft/Robert DeNiro/Hank Azaria	Atlantic 83058
4/20/74	85	16		533 **Great Gatsby, The** .... **[I+V]** Robert Redford/Mia Farrow/Bruce Dern/Karen Black/Scott Wilson; cd: **Nelson Riddle**	Paramount 3001 [2]
7/11/81	66	11		534 **Great Muppet Caper, The** .... **[M]** Jim Henson/Frank Oz/Jerry Nelson/Richard Hunt/Dave Goelz	Atlantic 16047
				Great Race, The — see MANCINI, Henry Tony Curtis/Jack Lemmon/Natalie Wood/Peter Falk/Keenan Wynn	
5/18/96	93	5		536 **Great White Hype, The** .... **[V]** Samuel L. Jackson/Jeff Goldblum/Peter Berg/Jon Lovitz/**Jamie Foxx**	Hudlin Bros. 67636
6/25/77	166	8		537 **Greatest, The** .... **[I+V]** Muhammad Ali (**Cassius Clay**)/Ernest Borgnine/Robert Duvall/James Earl Jones; cp: Michael Masser	Arista 7000
4/17/65	82	13		538 **Greatest Story Ever Told, The** .... **[I]** Charlton Heston/Sidney Poitier/Angela Lansbury/Robert Loggia/Claude Rains; cp/cd: Alfred Newman	United Artists 5120
7/7/84	143	7		539 **Gremlins** .... **[I+V]** Zach Galligan/Phoebe Cates/**Hoyt Axton**/Polly Holliday/Judge Reinhold; cp/cd: Jerry Goldsmith	Geffen 24044
2/15/97	❶¹	12	●	540 **Gridlock'd** .... **[V]** 2Pac/Tim Roth/Thandie Newton/Charles Fleischer/Howard Hesseman	Death Row 90114
4/26/97	31	13	●	541 **Grosse Pointe Blank** .... **[V]** John Cusack/Minnie Driver/Alan Arkin/Dan Aykroyd/Joan Cusack	London 828867
4/27/68	177	3		542 **Guess Who's Coming To Dinner** .... **[I]** Spencer Tracy/Katharine Hepburn/Sidney Poitier/Beah Richards/Isabel Sanford; cp/cd: Frank DeVol	Colgems 108
9/25/61	48	14		543 **Guns Of Navarone, The** .... **[I]** Gregory Peck/David Niven/Anthony Quinn/**James Darren**; cp/cd: Dimitri Tiomkin	Columbia 8455
12/15/62+	10	32		544 **Gypsy** .... **[M]** Rosalind Russell/Natalie Wood/Karl Malden/Ann Jillian/Harvey Korman; mu: Jule Styne; ly: Stephen Sondheim	Warner 1480
4/7/79	65	16	●	545 **Hair** .... **[M]** John Savage/Treat Williams/Beverly D'Angelo; mu/cd: Galt MacDermot; ly: Gerome Ragni and James Rado	RCA Victor 3274 [2]

Billboard			R I A A	ARTIST		
DEBUT	PEAK	WKS		Album Title.. Catalog	Label & Number	
4/2/88	114	6		546 **Hairspray** .... [O-V]	MCA 6228	
				Sonny Bono (**Sonny & Cher**)/**Ruth Brown**/Divine/**Debbie Harry**/Ricki Lake		
7/28/07	2[1]	41	▲	547 Hairspray [M]	New Line 39089	
				John Travolta/Nikki Blonsky/Michelle Pfeiffer/Christopher Walken/Amanda Bynes		
12/8/07	90	6		548 **Hairspray: Collector's Edition** .... [M]	New Line 39098 [2]	
9/8/07	82	3		549 **Halloween**.. [O-V]	Hip-O 009604	
				Scout Taylor-Compton/Malcolm McDowell/Daeg Faerch/Sheri Moon Zombie/Brad Dourif		
9/12/09	159	1		550 **Halloween II**.. [O-V]	Hip-O 013259	
				Scout Taylor-Compton/Malcolm McDowell/Sheri Moon Zombie/Brad Dourif/Caroline Williams		
8/17/68	193	4		551 **Hang 'Em High** .... [I]	United Artists 5179	
				Clint Eastwood/Inger Stevens/Ed Begley/Pat Hingle/Arlene Golonka; cp/cd: Dominic Frontiere		
6/27/09+	72	11		552 **Hangover, The** .... [V]	New Line 39150	
				Bradley Cooper/Ed Helms/Zach Galifianakis/Heather Graham/Jeffrey Tambor		
3/3/01	129	3		553 **Hannibal**... [I]	Decca 467696	
				Anthony Hopkins/Julianne Moore/Gary Oldman/Ray Liotta/Giancarlo Giannini; cp: Hans Zimmer; cd: Gavin Greenaway		
3/23/68	166	9		554 **Happiest Millionaire, The**.. [M]	Buena Vista 5001	
				Fred MacMurray/Tommy Steele/Greer Garson; sw: Richard M. Sherman and Robert B. Sherman; cd: Jack Elliott		
11/25/06	51	25		555 **Happy Feet** .... [V]	Fox 83998	
				animated movie, voices by: **Robin Williams**/Nicole Kidman/Hugh Jackman/Elijah Wood		
				Hard Day's Night, A — see BEATLES, The		
				The Beatles/Wilfrid Brambell		
				Hard To Hold — see SPRINGFIELD, Rick		
				Rick Springfield/Janet Eilber/Patti Hansen/Bill Mumy/Albert Salmi		
9/29/01	55	8		558 **Hardball** .... [V]	So So Def 86025	
				Keanu Reeves/Diane Lane/D.B. Sweeney/John Hawkes		
				Harder They Come, The — see CLIFF, Jimmy		
				Jimmy Cliff/Janet Barkley/Carl Bradshaw		
11/17/01	48	14	●	560 **Harry Potter And The Sorcerer's Stone** .... [I]	Warner Sunset 83491	
				Daniel Radcliffe/Emma Watson/Robbie Coltrane/Maggie Smith/**Richard Harris**; cp/cd: John Williams		
11/30/02	81	6		561 **Harry Potter And The Chamber Of Secrets** .... [I]	Warner Sunset 83574	
				Daniel Radcliffe/Rupert Grint/Emma Watson/Kenneth Branagh/**Richard Harris**; cp/cd: John Williams		
6/12/04	61	6		562 **Harry Potter And The Prisoner Of Azkaban** .... [I]	Warner Sunset 83711	
				Daniel Radcliffe/Rupert Grant/Emma Watson/Robbie Coltrane/Gary Oldman; cp/cd: **John Williams**		
12/3/05	80	4		563 **Harry Potter And The Goblet Of Fire**..................................... [I]	Warner Sunset 49631	
				Daniel Radcliffe/Rupert Grint/Emma Watson/Robbie Coltrane/Maggie Smith; cp/cd: Patrick Doyle		
7/28/07	43	4		564 **Harry Potter And The Order Of The Phoenix**........................... [I]	Warner Sunset 148156	
				Daniel Radcliffe/Emma Watson/Rupert Grint/Ralph Fiennes/Gary Oldman; cp/cd: Nicholas Hooper		
8/1/09	29	4		565 **Harry Potter And The Half-Blood Prince**............................... [I]	New Line 39152	
				Daniel Radcliffe/Emma Watson/Rupert Grint/Helena Bonham Carter/Alan Rickman; cp/cd: Nicholas Hooper		
				Harum Scarum — see PRESLEY, Elvis		
				Elvis Presley ("Johnny Tyronne")/Mary Ann Mobley/Fran Jeffries/Jay Novello/Billy Barty		
				Hatari! — see MANCINI, Henry		
				John Wayne/Red Buttons/Hardy Kruger		
7/4/98	39	8		568 **HavPlenty** .... [V]	Yab Yum 69356	
				Christopher Scott Cherot/Chenoa Maxwell/Hill Harper/Betty Vaughn		
				Having A Wild Weekend — see CLARK, Dave, Five		
				Dave Clark Five/Barbara Ferris		
11/19/66+	85	16		570 **Hawaii** .... [I]	United Artists 5143	
				Julie Andrews/Richard Harris/Max Von Sydow/**Carroll O'Connor**/Gene Hackman; cp/cd: Elmer Bernstein		
				He Got Game — see PUBLIC ENEMY		
				Denzel Washington/Ray Allen/Milla Jovovich/Ned Beatty		
2/21/09	121	4		572 **He's Just Not That Into You**... [V]	New Line 39132	
				Ben Affleck/Jennifer Aniston/Drew Barrymore/**Scarlet Johansson**		
				Head — see MONKEES, The		
				The Monkees/Victor Mature/**Annette** Funicello/Vito Scotti/**Frank Zappa**		
10/29/88	176	2		574 **Heartbreak Hotel** .... [V]	RCA 8533	
				David Keith/Charlie Schlatter/Tuesday Weld		
8/8/81	12	28	▲	575 **Heavy Metal** .... Cat:#28/2 [V]	Asylum 90004 [2]	
				animated movie, voices by: John Candy/Joe Flaherty/Harold Ramis/Richard Romanus/Eugene Levy		
5/6/00	101	4		576 **Heavy Metal 2000** .... [V]	Restless 73717	
				animated movie, voices by **Billy Idol**/Michael Ironside/Julie Strain/Arthur Holden		
2/3/58	25	1		577 **Helen Morgan Story, The**... [M]	RCA Victor 1030	
				Ann Blyth/Paul Newman/Alan King/Gene Evans; vocals performed by Gogi Grant; cd: **Ray Heindorf**		
10/11/69	184	3		578 **Hell's Angels '69** .... [I+V]	Capitol 303	
				Tom Stern/Conny Van Dyke/Jeremy Slate/G.D. Spradlin/Sonny Barger; cp/cd: Tony Bruno		
				Hello, Dolly! — see STREISAND, Barbra		
				Barbra Streisand/Walter Matthau/**Michael Crawford**		
9/30/67	165	2		580 **Hells Angels On Wheels** .... [I]	Smash 67094	
				Adam Roarke/Jack Nicholson/Sabrina Scharf/Jana Taylor/John Garwood; cp/cd: Stu Phillips		
				Help! — see BEATLES, The		
				The Beatles/Leo McKern/Eleanor Bron/Victor Spinetti		
7/9/05	73	7		582 **Herbie: Fully Loaded** .... [V]	Hollywood 162518	
				Lindsay Lohan/Michael Keaton/Matt Dillon/Thomas Lennon/Patrick Cranshaw		
6/14/97	37	15	●	583 **Hercules**.. [M]	Walt Disney 60864	
				animated movie, voices by: Danny DeVito/Tate Donovan/James Woods; mu/cp: Alan Menken; ly: David Zippel		
4/15/00	198	1		584 **Here On Earth** .... [V]	Columbia 63596	
				Chris Klein/Leelee Sobieski/Josh Hartnett/Bruce Greenwood		
				Hey Boy! Hey Girl! — see PRIMA, Louis, & Keely Smith		
				Louis Prima/**Keely Smith**/James Gregory/Henry Slate/Kim Charney		
				Hey, Let's Twist — see DEE, Joey, & The Starliters		
				Joey Dee & The Starliters/Teddy Randazzo/Jo Ann Campbell/Kay Armen/Allan Arbus		

MOVIE SOUNDTRACKS

Billboard DEBUT	PEAK	WKS	R I A A	ARTIST / Album Title	Catalog	Label & Number
12/5/87+	146	13		587 **Hiding Out**	[V]	Virgin 90661
				Jon Cryer/Annabeth Gish/Keith Coogan/Gretchen Cryer/Oliver Cotton		
4/22/00	135	4		588 **High Fidelity**	[V]	Hollywood 62188
				John Cusack/Jack Black/Todd Louiso/Lisa Bonet/Joelle Carter/Joan Cusack/Tim Robbins		
9/28/96	20	12	●	589 **High School High**	[V]	Big Beat 92709
				Jon Lovitz/Tia Carrere/Louise Fletcher/Makhi Phifer		
8/25/56	5	28		590 **High Society**	[M]	Capitol 750
				Bing Crosby/Grace Kelly/**Frank Sinatra**; sw: Cole Porter		
1/21/95	39	17		591 **Higher Learning**	[V]	550 Music 66944
				Jennifer Connelly/**Ice Cube**/Omar Epps/Laurence Fishburne		
				Hit The Deck — see "Those Glorious MGM Musicals"		
				Jane Powell/Tony Martin/**Debbie Reynolds**/Vic Damone		
3/5/05	90	7		593 **Hitch**	[V]	Columbia 93667
				Will Smith/Kevin James/Eva Mendes/Adam Arkin/Amber Valletta		
				Hold On! — see HERMAN'S HERMITS		
				Peter Noone (**Herman's Hermits**)/**Shelley Fabares**/Sue Ane Langdon		
5/10/03	80	16		595 **Holes**	[V]	Walt Disney 860092
				Sigourney Weaver/Jon Voight/Patricia Arquette/Tim Blake Nelson/Shia LaBeouf		
12/12/92	98	5		596 **Home Alone 2 - Lost In New York**	[X-V]	Fox 11000
				Macauley Culkin/Joe Pesci/Daniel Stern/**Tim Curry**/Brenda Fricker; Christmas chart: 15/'92		
				Home Of The Brave — see ANDERSON, Laurie		
4/24/04	151	1		598 **Home On The Range**	[V]	Walt Disney 61066
				animated movie, voices by: Roseanne Barr/Judi Dench/Randy Quaid/Jennifer Tilly		
12/13/03	105	8		599 **Honey**	[V]	Elektra 62925
				Jessica Alba/Mekhi Phifer/Joy Bryant/**Lil' Romeo**/Missy Elliott		
8/29/92	18	38	▲	600 **Honeymoon In Vegas**	[V]	Epic Soundtrax 52845
				James Caan/Nicolas Cage/Sarah Jessica Parker/Pat Morita/Anne Bancroft		
				Honeysuckle Rose — see NELSON, Willie		
				Willie Nelson/Dyan Cannon/Amy Irving/Slim Pickens		
8/30/97	94	6		602 **Hoodlum**	[V]	Loud 90131
				Laurence Fishburne/Tim Roth/Vanessa Williams/Andy Garcia		
1/18/92	182	2		603 **Hook**	[I]	Epic 48888
				Dustin Hoffman/**Robin Williams**/Julia Roberts/Bob Hoskins; cp/cd: **John Williams**; ly: Leslie Briscusse		
5/20/06	194	1		604 **Hoot**	[V]	Mailboat 2116
				Logan Lerman/Luke Wilson/Tim Blake Nelson/Robert Wagner		
6/6/98	4	59	▲²	605 **Hope Floats**	[V]	Capitol 93402
				Sandra Bullock/**Harry Connick Jr.**/Gena Rowlands/Mae Whitman/Michael Pare		
5/16/98	91	8		606 **Horse Whisperer, The**	[V]	MCA 70025
				Robert Redford/Kristin Scott Thomas/Sam Neill/Dianne Wiest		
4/19/03	53	4		607 **House Of 1000 Corpses**	[V]	Geffen 49364
				Sid Haig/Bill Moseley/Sheri Moon/Karen Black/Tom Towles		
4/7/90	104	9		608 **House Party**	[V]	Motown 6296
				Kid 'N Play/Full Force/Martin Lawrence/Robin Harris/Tisha Campbell		
11/9/91	55	12		609 **House Party 2**	[V]	MCA 10397
				Kid 'N Play/Full Force/Martin Lawrence/Tisha Campbell/Iman		
12/29/01+	38	12		610 **How High**	[V]	Def Jam 586628
				Method Man/Redman/Lark Voorhies/Fred Willard/Jeffrey Jones		
8/29/98	8	22	●	611 **How Stella Got Her Groove Back**	[V]	Flyte Tyme 11806
				Angela Bassett/Taye Diggs/Regina King/Whoopi Goldberg		
4/20/63	4	84	●	612 **How The West Was Won**	[I]	MGM 5
				Gregory Peck/Henry Fonda/James Stewart/**Debbie Reynolds**/Lee J. Cobb; cd: Alfred Newman		
				How To Beat The High Cost Of Living — see KLUGH, Earl / LAWS, Hubert		
				Susan St. James/Jane Curtin/Jessica Lange/Richard Benjamin/Fred Willard		
2/22/03	96	15		614 **How To Lose A Guy In 10 Days**	[V]	Virgin 81522
				Kate Hudson/Matthew McConaughey/Adam Goldberg/Michael Michele/Thomas Lennon		
4/22/67	146	4		615 **How To Succeed In Business Without Really Trying**	[M]	United Artists 5151
				Robert Morse/Michele Lee/Rudy Vallee/Anthony Teague; sw: Frank Loesser; cd: **Nelson Riddle**		
6/15/96	11	18	▲	616 **Hunchback Of Notre Dame, The**	[M]	Walt Disney 60893
				animated movie, voices by: Tom Hulce/Heidi Mollenhauer/Jason Alexander; mu: Alan Menken; ly: Stephen Schwartz; cd: Michael Starobin		
4/22/67	153	2		617 **Hurry Sundown**	[I]	RCA Victor 1133
				Michael Caine/**Jane Fonda**/Diahann Carroll/Faye Dunaway; cp/cd: **Hugo Montenegro**		
7/30/05	30	28		618 **Hustle & Flow**	[V]	Grand Hustle 83822
				Terrence Howard/**Ludacris**/Taryn Manning/**Isaac Hayes**		
1/26/02	20	38	●	619 **I Am Sam**	[V]	V2 27119
				Sean Penn/Michelle Pfeiffer/Dakota Fanning/Diane Wiest/Laura Dern		
				I Could Go On Singing — see GARLAND, Judy		
				Judy Garland/Dirk Bogarde/Jack Klugman		
4/25/98	3¹	18	▲	621 **I Got The Hook-Up!**	[V]	No Limit 50745
				Master P/A.J. Johnson/Gretchen Palmer/Tiny Lister		
11/1/97	125	5		622 **I Know What You Did Last Summer**	[V]	Columbia 68696
				Jennifer Love Hewitt/Sarah Michelle Gellar/Ryan Phillippe/Freddie Prinze Jr.		
				I Walk The Line — see CASH, Johnny		
				Gregory Peck/Tuesday Weld/Estelle Parsons/Ralph Meeker		
				I Want To Live! — see MULLIGAN, Gerry		
				Susan Hayward/Simon Oakland/Theodore Bikel		
6/7/97	4	25	▲	625 **I'm Bout It**	[V]	No Limit 50643
				Master P/Anthony Boswell/Moon Jones/Tracy Philpott/**Mack 10**		
11/17/07	95	4		626 **I'm Not There**	[V]	Sony 12038 [2]
				Christian Bale/Cate Blanchett/Richard Gere/Heath Ledger		

DEBUT	PEAK	WKS	R I A A	ARTIST / Album Title / Catalog	Label & Number
4/21/70	174	6		627 **Ice Castles** .... Cat:#35/2 [I] Robby Benson/Lynn-Holly Johnson/Colleen Dewhurst/Tom Skerritt; cp/cd: **Marvin Hamlisch**	Arista 9502
4/2/05	53	7		628 **Ice Princess**.. [V] Michele Trachtenberg/Joan Cusack/Kim Cattrall/Hayden Panettiere	Walt Disney 861227
				Idlewild — see OUTKAST Andre Benjamin/Antwan Patton/**Terrence Howard/Macy Gray**/Ben Vereen	
12/20/80+	130	9		630 **Idolmaker, The** .... [V] Ray Sharkey/Tovah Feldshuh/Peter Gallagher/Paul Land/Olympia Dukakis; sw: Jeff Barry	A&M 4840
				Imagine: John Lennon — see LENNON, John	
1/21/95	63	18	●	632 **Immortal Beloved**.. [I] Gary Oldman/Jeroen Krabbe/Isabella Rossellini; cp: Ludwig Van Beethoven; cd: Sir Georg Solti; pf: **London Symphony Orchestra**	Sony Classical 66301
9/30/67	153	11		633 **In The Heat Of The Night** .... [I+V] Sidney Poitier/Rod Steiger/Warren Oates/Lee Grant/Scott Wilson; cp/cd: **Quincy Jones**	United Artists 5160
2/12/94	114	10		634 **In The Name Of The Father** .... [V] Daniel Day-Lewis/Emma Thompson/Pete Poslethwaite/John Lynch	Island 518841
9/4/99	28	8		635 **In Too Deep** .... [V] Omar Epps/**LL Cool J**/Nia Long/Stanley Tucci/Pam Grier	Columbia 69934
5/1/93	137	6		636 **Indecent Proposal** .... [V] Robert Redford/Demi Moore/Woody Harrelson/Oliver Platt/Seymour Cassel	MCA 10795
7/20/96	73	8		637 **Independence Day** .... [I] *Grammy: Soundtrack Album* **Will Smith**/Bill Pullman/Jeff Goldblum/Mary McDonnell/Judd Hirsch; cp: David Arnold; cd: Nicholas Dodd	RCA Victor 68564
6/16/84	42	10		638 **Indiana Jones And The Temple Of Doom** .... [I] Harrison Ford/Kate Capshaw/Ke Huy Quan; cp/cd: **John Williams**	Polydor 821592
6/7/08	39	3		639 **Indiana Jones And The Kingdom Of The Crystal Skull** .... [I] Harrison Ford/Shia LeBeouf/Karen Allen/Cate Blanchett/John Hurt; cp/cd: **John Williams**	Concord 30825
9/5/09	132	2		640 **Inglourious Basterds** .... [V] Brad Pitt/Christoph Waltz/Eli Roth/Diane Kruger	Reprise 520377
10/19/68	136	5		641 **Interlude** .... [I] Oskar Werner/Barbara Ferris/Donald Sutherland/John Cleese	Colgems 5007
12/31/94	118	6		642 **Interview With The Vampire** .... [I] Tom Cruise/Brad Pitt/Antonio Banderas/Stephen Rea/Kirsten Dunst; cp: Elliot Goldenthal; cd: Jonathan Sheffer	Geffen 24719
4/13/85	118	8		643 **Into The Night** .... [V] Jeff Goldblum/Michelle Pfeiffer/Richard Farnsworth/Dan Aykroyd/Irene Papas	MCA 5561
11/13/65	133	2		644 **Ipcress File, The** .... [I] Michael Caine/Nigel Green/Sue Lloyd; cp/cd: John Barry	Decca 79124
9/14/63	69	11		645 **Irma La Douce** .... [I] Jack Lemmon/Shirley MacLaine/**Lou Jacobi**/Herschel Bernardi; cp/cd: **Andre Previn**	United Artists 5109
2/15/86	54	11		646 **Iron Eagle** .... [V] Louis Gossett Jr./Jason Gedrick/David Suchet/Tim Thomerson	Capitol 12499
5/24/08	158	3		647 **Iron Man** .... [I] Robert Downey Jr./Gwyneth Paltrow/**Terrence Howard**/Jeff Bridges; cp/cd: Ramin Djawadi	Lions Gate 20016
				It Happened At The World's Fair — see PRESLEY, Elvis Elvis Presley ("Mike Edwards")/Joan O'Brien/Gary Lockwood	
12/21/63+	101	11		649 **It's A Mad, Mad, Mad, Mad World** .... [I] Spencer Tracy/Sid Caesar/Milton Berle/**Jonathan Winters**/Buddy Hackett; cp/cd: Ernest Gold	United Artists 5110
11/22/80	137	11		650 **It's My Turn** .... [I+V] Jill Clayburgh/Michael Douglas/Charles Grodin/Beverly Garland/Steven Hill; cp/cd: Patrick Williams	Motown 947
11/2/02	173	2		651 **Jackass The Movie** .... [V] Johnny Knoxville/Bam Margera/Chris Pontius/Steve-O/Wee Man	American 063101
1/17/98	73	7		652 **Jackie Brown** .... [O-V] Pam Grier/Samuel L. Jackson/Robert Forster/Bridget Fonda/Robert DeNiro	Maverick 46841
				Janis — see JOPLIN, Janis	
10/15/94	17	32	▲	654 **Jason's Lyric** .... [V] Forest Whitaker/Allen Payne/Jada Pinkett/Bokeem Woodbine	Mercury 522915
7/26/75	30	17		655 **Jaws** .... [I] *Grammy: Soundtrack Album* Roy Scheider/Richard Dreyfuss/Robert Shaw/Lorraine Gary/Murray Hamilton; cp/cd: **John Williams**	MCA 2087
7/29/78	206	3		656 **Jaws 2** .... [I] Roy Scheider/Lorraine Gary/Murray Hamilton; cp/cd: **John Wiliams**	MCA 3045
8/25/01	28	9		657 **Jay And Silent Bob Strike Back** .... [V] Kevin Smith/Jason Mews/Ben Affleck/Will Ferrell/**Chris Rock**	Universal 016200
				Jazz Singer, The — see DIAMOND, Neil Neil Diamond/Laurence Olivier/Lucie Arnaz/Franklin Ajaye/Sully Boyar	
9/12/09	161	3		659 **Jennifer's Body** .... [V] Megan Fox/Amanda Seyfried/Adam Brody/Johnny Simmons	Fueled By Ramen 518904
2/11/95	79	8		660 **Jerky Boys, The** .... [V] Johnny Brennan/Kamal Ahmed/Alan Arkin/William Hickey/Vincent Pastore	Select 82708
1/4/97	49	36	▲	661 **Jerry Maguire** .... [V] Tom Cruise/Cuba Gooding Jr./Renee Zellweger/Kelly Preston/Jonathan Lipnicki	Epic Soundtrax 67910
6/30/73	21	39	▲	662 **Jesus Christ Superstar**... [M] Ted Neeley/**Yvonne Elliman**/Carl Anderson/Barry Dennen; mu: **Andrew Lloyd Webber**; ly: Sir Tim Rice	MCA 11000 [2]
12/28/85+	55	17		663 **Jewel Of The Nile, The** .... [V] Michael Douglas/Kathleen Turner/Danny DeVito	Jive 8406
				Jimi Hendrix — see HENDRIX, Jimi	
12/22/01+	84	11		665 **Jimmy Neutron: Boy Genius** .... [V] animated movie, voices by Debi Derryberry/Martin Short/Patrick Stewart/Andrea Martin	Nick 48501
				Jonathan Livingston Seagull — see DIAMOND, Neil / HARRIS, Richard James Franciscus/Juliet Mills	
4/14/01	16	18	●	667 **Josie And The Pussycats** .... [M] Rachael Leigh Cook/Tara Reid/Rosario Dawson/Parker Posey/Alan Cumming	Play-Tone 85683

			R I A A	ARTIST		
DEBUT	**PEAK**	**WKS**		**Album Title** .... **Catalog**	**Label & Number**	

				Journey Through The Past — see YOUNG, Neil	
10/2/93	17	20	● 669	Judgment Night .... [V]	Immortal 57144
				Emilio Estevez/Cuba Gooding Jr./**Denis Leary**/Jeremy Piven/**Everlast**	
1/18/92	17	29	● 670	Juice .... [V]	MCA 10462
				Omar Epps/Jermaine Hopkins/Khalil Kain/**2Pac**/Cindy Herron (**En Vogue**)	
11/22/86	159	4	671	Jumpin' Jack Flash .... [V]	Mercury 830545
				Whoopi Goldberg/Carol Kane/Stephen Collins/Annie Potts	
2/3/68	19	34	672	Jungle Book, The .... Cat:#21/2 [M]	Disneyland 3948
				animated movie, voices by: Phil Harris/Sebastian Cabot/**Louis Prima**; sw: Richard M. Sherman and Robert B. Sherman	
				Jungle Fever — see WONDER, Stevie	
				Wesley Snipes/Annabella Sciorra/Spike Lee/Ossie Davis/Ruby Dee	
1/19/08	❶[1]	48	▲ 674	Juno .... [V]	Fox 410236
				Grammy: Soundtrack	
				Ellen Page/Michael Cera/Jennifer Garner/Jason Bateman	
6/12/93	36	26	● 675	Jurassic Park .... [I]	MCA 10859
				Sam Neill/Laura Dern/Jeff Goldblum/Richard Attenborough/Wayne Knight; cp/cd: **John Williams**	
7/21/84	114	12	676	Karate Kid, The .... [V]	Casablanca 822213
				Ralph Macchio/Pat Morita/Elisabeth Shue/Martin Kove	
7/12/86	30	17	677	Karate Kid Part II, The .... [V]	United Artists 40414
				Ralph Macchio/Pat Morita/Tony O'Dell/Danny Kamekona	
				Kids Are Alright, The — see WHO, The	
10/25/03	45	16	● 679	Kill Bill Vol. 1 .... [V]	A Band Apart 48570
				Uma Thurman/Lucy Liu/Vivica Fox/Michael Madsen/Darryl Hannah	
5/1/04	58	5	680	Kill Bill Vol. 2 .... [V]	A Band Apart 48676
				Uma Thurman/David Carradine/Michael Madsen/Daryl Hannah	
7/21/56	❶[1]	277	● 681	King And I, The° .... [M]	Capitol 740
				Yul Brynner/Deborah Kerr/Rita Moreno; mu: Richard Rodgers; ly: Oscar Hammerstein; cd: Alfred Newman	
				King Creole — see PRESLEY, Elvis	
				Elvis Presley ("Danny Fisher")/Carolyn Jones/Walter Matthau/Dean Jagger	
1/8/77	123	8	683	King Kong .... [I]	Reprise 2260
				Jeff Bridges/Jessica Lange/Charles Grodin/John Randolph/Rene Auberjonois; cp/cd: John Barry	
4/16/83	162	6	684	King Of Comedy, The .... [V]	Warner 23765
				Robert DeNiro/**Jerry Lewis**/Tony Randall/Sandra Bernhard/Shelley Hack	
11/6/61+	10	39	685	King Of Kings .... [I]	MGM 2
				Jeffrey Hunter/Siobhan McKenna/Rip Torn; cp/cd: Miklos Rozsa	
4/21/01	61	10	686	Kingdom Come .... [V]	Gospo Centric 70035
				LL Cool J/Jada Pinkett/Vivica A. Fox/Loretta Devine/**Toni Braxton**	
				Kiss Me Kate — see "Those Glorious MGM Musicals"	
				Kathryn Grayson/Howard Keel/Ann Miller/Keenan Wynn	
				Kissin' Cousins — see PRESLEY, Elvis	
				Elvis Presley ("Josh Morgan" & "Jodie Tatum")/Arthur O'Connell/Jack Albertson	
5/26/01	42	18	● 689	Knight's Tale, A .... [O-V]	Columbia 85648
				Heath Ledger/Mark Addy/Rufus Sewell/Shannyn Sossamon/Paul Bettany	
10/26/85	79	20	690	Krush Groove .... [V]	Warner 25295
				Sheila E./Run-DMC/The Fat Boys/Kurtis Blow	
				La Bamba — see LOS LOBOS	
				Lou Diamond Phillips/Esai Morales/Rosana DeSoto/Elizabeth Pena	
				Labyrinth — see BOWIE, David	
				David Bowie/Jennifer Connelly	
8/6/55	14	1	693	Lady And The Tramp .... [EP]	Capitol 3056
				animated movie, voices by Daws Butler/June Foray/Larry Roberts/Barbara Luddy; no track titles listed; includes an 18-page full-color booklet of scenes from the movie	
				Lady Sings The Blues — see ROSS, Diana	
				Diana Ross/Billy Dee Williams/**Richard Pryor**	
5/25/85	203	2	695	Ladyhawke .... [I]	Atlantic 81248
				Matthew Broderick/Michelle Pfeiffer/Rutger Hauer; cp/cd: Andrew Powell; pf: The Philharmonia Orchestra	
6/23/01	32	10	● 696	Lara Croft: Tomb Raider .... [V]	Elektra 62665
				Angelina Jolie/Jon Voight/Iain Glen/Noah Taylor	
8/9/03	177	2	697	Lara Croft Tomb Raider: The Cradle Of Life .... [V]	Hollywood 162417
				Angelina Jolie/Gerard Butler/Noah Taylor/Djimon Hounsou/Chris Barrie	
4/15/06	168	1	698	Larry The Cable Guy: Health Inspector .... [V]	Jack 44109
				Larry The Cable Guy/Joanna Cassidy/Joe Pantoliano/Thomas F. Wilson	
6/26/93	7	21	▲ 699	Last Action Hero .... [V]	Columbia 57127
				Arnold Schwarzenegger/Austin O'Brien/F. Murray Abraham/Art Carney/Anthony Quinn	
3/30/85	58	15	700	Last Dragon, The .... [V]	Motown 6128
				Taimak/Julius J. Carry III/Chris Murney/Leo O'Brien/**Vanity**	
2/27/88	152	10	701	Last Emperor, The .... [I-V]	Virgin 90690
				Grammy: Soundtrack Album	
				John Lone/Joan Chen/Peter O'Toole; cp/cd: David Byrne/Ryuichi Sakamoto/Cong Su	
9/2/06	57	11	702	Last Kiss, The .... [V]	Lakeshore 33869
				Zach Braff/Jacinda Barrett/Casey Affleck/Harold Ramis	
10/24/92	42	65	▲ 703	Last Of The Mohicans, The .... [I]	Morgan Creek 20015
				Daniel Day-Lewis/Madeleine Stowe; cp: Trevor Jones/Randy Edelman; cd: Daniel A. Carlin/Randy Edelman	
				Last Tango In Paris — see BARBIERI, Gato	
				Marlon Brando/Maria Schneider	
				Last Temptation Of Christ, The — see GABRIEL, Peter	
				Willem Dafoe/Harvey Keitel/Barbara Hershey/Harry Dean Stanton	
				Last Waltz, The — see BAND, The	
3/2/63	2[2]	86	707	Lawrence Of Arabia .... [I]	Colpix 514
				Peter O'Toole/Alec Guinness/Anthony Quinn/Omar Sharif; cp/cd: Maurice Jarre; pf: **London Philharmonic Orchestra**	

DEBUT	PEAK	WKS	R I A A	ARTIST Album Title.. Catalog	Label & Number
7/25/92	159	6		708 **League Of Their Own, A** .... [V] Tom Hanks/Geena Davis/**Madonna**/Lori Petty/Jon Lovitz	Columbia 52919
2/17/96	124	13		709 **Leaving Las Vegas** .... [I+V] Nicolas Cage/Elisabeth Shue/Julian Sands/Richard Lewis/Valeria Golino; cp: Mike Figgis	Pangaea 36071
11/18/00	174	1		710 **Left Behind** .... [V] Kirk Cameron/Brad Johnson/Chelsea Noble/Gordon Currie	Reunion 10022
8/4/01	171	1		711 **Legally Blonde** .... [V] Reese Witherspoon/Luke Wilson/Selma Blair/Victor Garber/Jennifer Coolidge	A&M 493078
				Legend — see TANGERINE DREAM Tom Cruise/Mia Sara/**Tim Curry**/Billy Barty	
2/4/95	147	7		713 **Legends Of The Fall** .... [I] Brad Pitt/Anthony Hopkins/Aidan Quinn/Henry Thomas/Julia Ormand; cp/cd: James Horner	Epic Soundtrax 66462
1/18/75	180	3		714 **Lenny** .... [C] Dustin Hoffman/Valerie Perrine; cp/cd: Ralph Burns; based on life of **Lenny Bruce**	United Artists 359
8/12/06	176	1		715 **Leonard Cohen: I'm Your Man** .... [V] documentary movie	Verve Forecast 007169
12/5/87+	**31**	23	●	716 **Less Than Zero** .... [V] Robert Downey Jr./Andrew McCarthy/Jami Gertz/James Spader	Def Jam 44042
				Let It Be — see BEATLES, The	
7/28/73	117	9		718 **Let The Good Times Roll** .... [L-V] Richard Nader's Rock and Roll Revival show	Bell 9002 [2]
				Let's Do It Again — see STAPLE SINGERS, The Sidney Poitier/**Bill Cosby**/**Jimmie Walker**/John Amos	
9/2/89	164	3		720 **Lethal Weapon 2** .... [I+V] Mel Gibson/Danny Glover/Joe Pesci/Joss Ackland; cp/pf: **Eric Clapton** and **David Sanborn**	Warner 25985
6/27/92	101	3		721 **Lethal Weapon 3** .... [I+V] Mel Gibson/Danny Glover/Joe Pesci/Rene Russo; cp/cd: Michael Kamen/**Eric Clapton**/**David Sanborn**	Reprise 26989
4/3/99	**10**	21	▲	722 **Life** .... [V] Eddie Murphy/**Martin Lawrence**/Bernie Mac/Ned Beatty	Rock Land 90314
1/15/05	102	5		723 **Life Aquatic With Steve Zissou, The** .... [V] Bill Murray/Owen Wilson/Cate Blanchett/Anjelica Houston/Willem Dafoe	Hollywood 162494
4/10/99	200	1		724 **Life Is Beautiful** .... [I] Roberto Benigni/Nicoletta Braschi; cp/cd: Nicola Piovani	Virgin 46428
11/1/97	102	4		725 **Life Less Ordinary, A** .... [V] Ewan McGregor/Cameron Diaz/Holly Hunter/Delroy Lindo/Ian Holm	Innerstate 540809
				Life Of Brian — see MONTY PYTHON Graham Chapman/John Cleese/Eric Idle/Michael Palin	
11/27/99	**19**	9	●	727 **Light It Up** .... [V] **Usher**/Forest Whitaker/Judd Nelson/**Vanessa Williams**	Yab Yum 62410
3/14/87	82	10		728 **Light Of Day** .... [V] Michael J. Fox/**Joan Jett**/Gena Rowlands/Michael McKean/Jason Miller	Blackheart 40654
7/20/02	**18**	14		729 **Like Mike** .... [V] Lil Bow Wow/Morris Chestnut/Jonathan Lipnicki/Robert Forster/Crispin Glover	So So Def 86676
5/30/64	110	6		730 **Lilies Of The Field** .... [I] Sidney Poitier/Lilia Skala/Lisa Mann; cp/cd: Jerry Goldsmith	Epic 26094
6/29/02	**11**	40	▲	731 **Lilo & Stitch** .... [V] animated movie, voices by: Daveigh Chase/Chris Sanders/Tia Carrere/Ving Rhames	Walt Disney 60734
5/3/69	182	7		732 **Lion In Winter, The** .... [I] Peter O'Toole/Katharine Hepburn/Timothy Dalton/Anthony Hopkins; cp/cd: John Barry	Columbia 3250
6/18/94	❶[10]	88	▲[11]	733 **Lion King, The** .... Cat:❶[1]/5 [M] animated movie, voices by: Jonathan Taylor Thomas/Jeremy Irons/James Earl Jones; mu: **Elton John**; ly: Tim Rice	Walt Disney 60858
11/8/75	145	6		734 **Lisztomania** .... [M] Roger Daltrey/Rick Wakeman/Ringo Starr; cp: Franz List; ly: **Roger Daltrey** and **Rick Wakeman**	A&M 4546
				Little Fauss And Big Halsy — see CASH, Johnny Robert Redford/Michael J. Pollard/Lauren Hutton/Noah Beery	
12/16/89+	**32**	48	▲[6]	736 **Little Mermaid, The** .... Cat:❶[1]/28 [M] animated movie, voices by: Jodi Benson/Pat Carroll/Samuel E. Wright; mu: Alan Menken; ly: Howard Ashman	Disney 018
11/18/00	95	8		737 **Little Nicky** .... [V] Adam Sandler/Patricia Arquette/Harvey Keitel/**Rodney Dangerfield**/Tiny Lister	Maverick 47856
1/17/87	47	17		738 **Little Shop Of Horrors** .... [M] Rick Moranis/Ellen Greene/Vincent Gardenia/**Steve Martin**; mu: Alan Menken; ly: Howard Ashman	Geffen 24125
7/28/73	**17**	15		739 **Live And Let Die** .... [I] Roger Moore/Jane Seymour/Yaphet Kotto/Clifton James; cp/cd: **George Martin**	United Artists 100
1/27/68	188	7		740 **Live For Life** .... [I] Yves Montand/Candice Bergen/Annie Girardot; cp/cd: Francis Lai	United Artists 5165
5/10/03	**6**	48	▲[2]	741 **Lizzie McGuire Movie, The** .... [V] Hilary Duff/Adam Lamberg/Robert Carradine/Hallie Todd/Jake Thomas	Walt Disney 860080
				Local Hero — see KNOPFLER, Mark Peter Riegert/Burt Lancaster/Fulton MacKay	
9/22/62	63	6		743 **Lolita** .... [I] Peter Sellers/Sue Lyon/Shelley Winters/James Mason; cp/cd: **Nelson Riddle**	MGM 4050
				Long Riders, The — see COODER, Ry David, Keith & Robert Carradine/Stacy & James Keach/Randy & Dennis Quaid/Nicholas & Christopher Guest	
6/11/05	**11**	17		745 **Longest Yard, The** .... [V] Adam Sandler/**Chris Rock**/Burt Reynolds/**Nelly**/Bill Goldberg	Derrty 004552
				Looking For Love — see FRANCIS, Connie Connie Francis/Jim Hutton/Susan Oliver	
11/26/77	134	8		747 **Looking For Mr. Goodbar** .... [V] Diane Keaton/Richard Gere/William Atherton/Tuesday Weld	Columbia 35029

Billboard			R I A A	ARTIST		
DEBUT	PEAK	WKS		Album Title .... Catalog		Label & Number
3/27/65	123	5		748 **Lord Jim** .... [I]		Colpix 521
				Peter O'Toole/James Mason/Curt Jurgens/Eli Wallach; cp: Bronislau Kaper; cd: **Muir Mathieson**		
12/9/78+	39	12		749 **Lord Of The Rings, The** .... [I]		Fantasy 1 [2]
				animated movie, voices by: Christopher Guard/William Squire/John Hurt; cp/cd: Leonard Rosenman		
12/8/01+	29	36	▲	750 **Lord Of The Rings: The Fellowship Of The Ring, The** .... [I]		Reprise 48110
				Grammy: Soundtrack Album		
				Elijah Wood/Ian McKellen/Sean Astin/Liv Tyler/Ian Holm; cp/cd: Howard Shore		
12/28/02+	43	18		751 **Lord Of The Rings: The Two Towers, The** .... [I]		Reprise 48379
				Grammy: Soundtrack Album		
				Elijah Wood/Ian McKellen/Viggo Mortensen/Liv Tyler/Sean Astin; cp/cd: Howard Shore		
12/13/03+	36	22	●	752 **Lord Of The Rings: The Return Of The King, The** .... [I]		Reprise 48521
				Grammy: Soundtrack Album		
				Elijah Wood/Ian McKellen/Liv Tyler/Viggo Mortensen/Sean Astin; cp/cd: Howard Shore		
6/18/05	99	3		753 **Lords Of Dogtown** .... [V]		Geffen 004556
				Heath Ledger/Rebecca DeMornay/John Robinson/Nikki Reed		
8/1/87	15	39	●	754 **Lost Boys, The** .... Cat:#41/1 [V]		Atlantic 81767
				Kiefer Sutherland/Dianne Wiest/Jami Gertz/Jason Patric/Barnard Hughes		
3/8/97	7	18	●	755 **Lost Highway** .... [V]		Nothing 90090
				Bill Pullman/Patricia Arquette/Balthazar Getty/Robert Blake		
2/3/73	58	21		756 **Lost Horizon** .... [M]		Bell 1300
				Peter Finch/Liv Ullmann/**Charles Boyer**/John Gielgud; mu/cd: **Burt Bacharach**; ly: Hal David		
4/18/98	107	4		757 **Lost In Space** .... [I]		TVT Soundtrax 8180
				Gary Oldman/William Hurt/Matt LeBlanc/Mimi Rogers/Heather Graham; cp/cd: Bruce Broughton		
6/7/97	88	4		758 **Lost World: Jurassic Park, The** .... [I]		MCA Soundtrax 11628
				Jeff Goldblum/Julianne Moore/Pete Postlethwaite/Arliss Howard; cp/cd: **John Williams**		
5/14/05	141	2		759 **Lot Like Love, A** .... [V]		Columbia 94223
				Amanda Peet/Ashton Kutcher/Taryn Manning/Linda Hunt		
11/29/03	39	25	●	760 **Love Actually** .... [V]		J Records 56760
				Alan Rickman/Colin Firth/Emma Thompson/Hugh Grant/Rowan Atkinson		
5/6/00	45	12		761 **Love & Basketball** .... [V]		Overbrook 9001
				Omar Epps/Sanaa Lathan/Alfre Woodard/Dennis Haysbert		
3/29/97	16	32	▲	762 **Love Jones** .... [V]		Columbia 67917
				Larenz Tate/Nia Long/Isaiah Washington/Lisa Nicole Carson		
8/28/71	172	6		763 **Love Machine, The** .... [I]		Scepter 595
				Dyan Cannon/John Phillip Law/Robert Ryan/Jackie Cooper/David Hemmings; cp/cd: Artie Butler		
				Love Me Or Leave Me — see DAY, Doris		
				Doris Day/James Cagney/Cameron Mitchell		
				Love Me Tender — see PRESLEY, Elvis		
				Elvis Presley ("Clint Reno")/Richard Egan/Debra Paget		
1/2/71	2[6]	39	●	766 **Love Story** .... [I]		Paramount 6002
				Ali MacGraw/Ryan O'Neal/Ray Milland/John Marley; cp/cd: Francis Lai		
1/17/81	207	1		767 **Loving Couples** .... [V]		Motown 949
				Shirley MacLaine/James Coburn/Susan Sarandon/Stephen Collins		
				Loving You — see PRESLEY, Elvis		
				Elvis Presley ("Deke Rivers")/Lizabeth Scott/Delores Hart		
11/26/94	70	13	●	769 **Low Down Dirty Shame, A** .... [V]		Hollywood 41536
				Keenan Ivory Wayans/Charles S. Dutton/Jada Pinkett/Salli Richardson		
				Mack, The — see HUTCH, Willie		
				Max Julien/**Richard Pryor**/Don Gordon		
				Mackintosh & T.J. — see JENNINGS, Waylon		
				Roy Rogers/Clay O'Brien/Joan Hackett		
				Mad Dogs & Englishmen — see COCKER, Joe		
7/1/95	164	1		773 **Mad Love** .... [V]		Zoo 11111
				Chris O'Donnell/Drew Barrymore/Matthew Lillard/Robert Nadir		
8/24/85	39	13		774 **Mad Max Beyond Thunderdome** .... [I]		Capitol 12429
				Mel Gibson/**Tina Turner**/Angelo Rossitto/Helen Buday/Bruce Spence; cp/cd: Maurice Jarre		
6/11/05	36	19		775 **Madagascar** .... [M]		DreamWorks 004695
				animated movie, voices by: Ben Stiller/**Chris Rock**/David Schwimmer/Jada Pinkett Smith		
11/29/08	148	2		776 **Madagascar 2: Escape 2 Africa** .... [I+V]		will.i.am 012264
				animated movie, voices by: Ben Stiller/**Chris Rock**/David Schwimmer/Jada Pinkett Smith		
6/19/93	196	2		777 **Made In America** .... [V]		Elektra 61498
				Whoopi Goldberg/Ted Danson/**Will Smith**/Nia Long/Paul Rodriguez		
3/11/06	25	13		778 **Madea's Family Reunion** .... [V]		Motown 006212
				Tyler Perry/Blair Underwood/Lynn Whitfield/Cicely Tyson		
3/21/70	106	12		779 **Magic Christian, The** .... [I]		Commonwealth 6004
				Peter Sellers/**Ringo Starr**/Raquel Welch/Christopher Lee/Isabel Jeans; cp/cd: Ken Thorne		
				Magical Mystery Tour — see BEATLES, The		
				Magnolia — see MANN, Aimee		
				Tom Cruise/William H. Macy/Jason Robards/Philip Seymour Hoffman		
11/8/75+	19	26		782 **Mahogany** .... [I]		Motown 858
				Diana Ross/Billy Dee Williams/Anthony Perkins/Beah Richards; cp/cd: Lee Holdridge		
				Main Event, The — see STREISAND, Barbra		
				Barbra Streisand/Ryan O'Neal/Paul Sand/Whitman Mayo/Rory Calhoun		
12/5/92	130	3		784 **Malcolm X** .... [V]		Qwest 45130
				Denzel Washington/Angela Bassett/Albert Hall/Spike Lee/Delroy Lindo		
11/4/95	151	2		785 **Mallrats** .... [V]		MCA Soundtrax 11294
				Shannen Doherty/Jason Lee/Jeremy London/Michael Rooker/Ben Affleck		
3/14/92	50	14	●	786 **Mambo Kings, The** .... [F-V]		Elektra 61240
				Armand Assante/Antonio Banderas/Cathy Moriarty/Maruschka Detmers		
4/13/74	196	3		787 **Mame** .... [M]		Warner 2773
				Lucille Ball/Beatrice Arthur/Bruce Davison/Robert Preston; sw: Jerry Herman		

Billboard DEBUT	PEAK	WKS	R I A A	ARTIST Album Title.. Catalog	Label & Number
7/26/08	**❶**[1]	64	▲	788 **Mamma Mia!** Cat:#48/3 **[M]** Meryl Streep/Amanda Seyfried/Pierce Brosnan/Colin Firth; sw: Benny Andersson & Bjorn Ulvaeus	Decca 011439
11/19/66+	**10**	93	●	789 **Man And A Woman, A** **[I]** Jean-Louis Trintignant/Anouk Aimee/Simone Paris; cp/cd: Francis Lai	United Artists 5147
12/9/72+	**76**	17		790 **Man Of La Mancha** **[M]** Peter O'Toole/Sophia Loren/James Coco; mu: Mitch Leigh; ly: Joe Darion; cd: Laurence Rosenthal	United Artists 9906
1/1/00	**109**	7		791 **Man On The Moon** **[V]** Jim Carrey/Danny DeVito/**Courtney Love**/Paul Giamatti/Jerry Lawler	Warner 47483
3/24/56	**2**[4]	17		792 **Man With The Golden Arm, The** **[I]** Frank Sinatra/Eleanor Parker/Kim Novak/Darren McGavin; cp/cd: Elmer Bernstein	Decca 78257
7/28/79	**94**	11		793 **Manhattan** **[I]** Woody Allen/Diane Keaton/**Meryl Streep**/Mariel Hemingway; cp: **George Gershwin**; cd: **Zubin Mehta**	Columbia 36020
11/4/06	**97**	4		794 **Marie Antoinette** **[V]** Kirsten Dunst/**Marianne Faithfull**/Jason Schwartzman/Judy Davis	Verve Fore. 007822 [2]
				Marjoe — see MARJOE	
10/1/88	**197**	3		796 **Married To The Mob** **[V]** Michelle Pfeiffer/Matthew Modine/Dean Stockwell/Mercedes Ruehl/Alec Baldwin	Reprise 25763
				Marvin & Tige — see KLUGH, Earl John Cassavetes/Gibran Brown/Billy Dee Williams	
10/3/64+	**❶**[14]	114	●	798 **Mary Poppins** **[M]** *Grammys: Soundtrack Album / Children's Album* Julie Andrews/Dick Van Dyke/David Tomlinson/Glynis Johns; sw: Richard M. Sherman and Robert B. Sherman; cd: Irwin Kostal	Buena Vista 4026
8/4/73	**141**	8		799 **Mary Poppins** **[R]** see above album for tracks; new blue cover features new artwork	Buena Vista 5005
4/25/81	**204**	1		800 **Masada** **[I]** Peter O'Toole/Peter Strauss/Barbara Carrera/Anthony Quayle; cp/cd: Jerry Goldsmith	MCA 5168
7/11/70	**120**	16		801 **M*A*S*H** **[I]** Elliott Gould/Donald Sutherland/Tom Skerritt/Sally Kellerman/Robert Duvall; cp: Johnny Mandel	Columbia 3520
8/20/94	**80**	12		802 **Mask, The** **[V]** Jim Carrey/Peter Riegert/Peter Greene/Amy Yasbeck/Richard Jeni	Chaos 66207
8/1/98	**87**	6		803 **Mask Of Zorro, The** **[I]** Antonio Banderas/Anthony Hopkins/Catherine Zeta-Jones; cp/cd: James Horner	Sony Classical 60627
8/9/03	**94**	2		804 **Masked And Anonymous** **[V]** Jeff Bridges/Penelope Cruz/**Bob Dylan**/John Goodman/Jessica Lange	Columbia 90536
4/17/99	**7**	55	▲	805 **Matrix, The** **[V]** Keanu Reeves/Laurence Fishburne/Carrie-Anne Moss/Hugo Weaving	Maverick 47390
5/24/03	**5**	15	●	806 **Matrix Reloaded, The** **[V]** Keanu Reeves/Laurence Fishburne/Carrie-Anne Moss/Jada Pinkett Smith	Warner Sunset 48411 [2]
11/22/03	**69**	2		807 **Matrix Revolutions, The** **[I]** Keanu Reeves/Laurence Fishburne/Carrie-Anne Moss/Jada Pinkett Smith; cp/cd: Don Davis	Warner Sunset 48412
6/4/94	**35**	16	●	808 **Maverick** **[V]** Mel Gibson/Jodie Foster/James Garner/Graham Greene/James Coburn	Atlantic 82595
				Maximum Overdrive — see AC/DC Emilio Estevez/Pat Hingle/Laura Harrington/Yeardley Smith	
				McVicar — see DALTREY, Roger Roger Daltrey/Adam Faith/Cheryl Campbell	
7/8/00	**134**	4		811 **Me, Myself & Irene** **[V]** Jim Carrey/Renee Zellweger/Robert Forster/Chris Cooper	Elektra 62512
8/18/79	**170**	5		812 **Meatballs** **[V]** Bill Murray/Chris Makepeace/Kate Lynch/Jack Blum/Harvey Atkin; mu: Elmer Bernstein	RSO 3056
4/5/08	**116**	2		813 **Meet The Browns** **[V]** Angela Bassett/Rick Fox/Lance Gross/Tyler Perry/David Mann	Atlantic 449020
				Melinda — see BUTLER, Jerry Calvin Lockhart/Rosalind Cash	
2/4/06	**163**	1		815 **Memoirs Of A Geisha** **[I]** Ziyi Zhang/Ken Watanabe/Ted Levine/Mako; cp/cd: **John Williams**	Sony Classical 74708
7/19/97	**❶**[2]	43	▲[3]	816 **Men In Black** **[V]** Tommy Lee Jones/**Will Smith**/Linda Fiorentino/Vincent D'Onofrio/Rip Torn	Columbia 68169
6/12/93	**11**	35	▲	817 **Menace II Society** **[V]** Tyrin Turner/Larenz Tate/Jada Pinkett/Bill Duke/Charles S. Dutton	Jive 41509
1/12/91	**65**	24		818 **Mermaids** **[O-V]** **Cher**/Bob Hoskins/Winona Ryder/Christina Ricci	Geffen 24310
2/27/99	**39**	9		819 **Message In A Bottle** **[V]** Kevin Costner/Robin Wright Penn/John Savage/Paul Newman	Atlantic 83163
8/25/84	**110**	13		820 **Metropolis** **[V]** Gustav Froelich/Brigitte Helm; 1926 movie restored and presented with a contemporary score; cp: **Giorgio Moroder**	Columbia 39526
8/12/06	**104**	4		821 **Miami Vice** **[V]** Colin Farrell/**Jamie Foxx**/Naomie Harris/Justin Theroux	Atlantic 83997
1/11/97	**53**	16		822 **Michael** **[V]** John Travolta/Andie MacDowell/William Hurt/Bob Hoskins/Jean Stapleton	Revolution 24666
8/9/69	**19**	57	●	823 **Midnight Cowboy** **[I+V]** Dustin Hoffman/Jon Voight/Sylvia Miles/Brenda Vaccaro/Barnard Hughes; mu: John Barry	United Artists 5198
11/25/78+	**59**	26		824 **Midnight Express** **[I]** Brad Davis/John Hurt/Randy Quaid/Bo Hopkins; cp/cd: **Giorgio Moroder**	Casablanca 7114
12/13/97	**161**	5		825 **Midnight In The Garden Of Good And Evil** **[V]** Kevin Spacey/John Cusack/Alison Eastwood/Lady Chablis/Jude Law	Warner 46829
				Mighty Ducks — see D2: The Mighty Ducks	
7/8/95	**98**	6		827 **Mighty Morphin Power Rangers: The Movie** **[V]** Karan Ashley/Johnny Yong Bosch/Steve Cardenas	Atlantic 82777

Billboard DEBUT	PEAK	WKS	R I A A	ARTIST Album Title... Catalog	Label & Number
				Mike's Murder — see JACKSON, Joe Debra Winger/Mark Keyloun/Darrell Larson/Paul Winfield	
4/1/00	104	2		829 Million Dollar Hotel, The .... [V] Jeremy Davies/Milla Jovovich/Jimmy Smits/Peter Stormare/Mel Gibson	Interscope 542395
1/13/01	30ˣ	2		830 Miracle On 34th Street .... [X-V] Richard Attenborough/Elizabeth Perkins/Dylan McDermott/J.T. Walsh	Arista/BMG 44980
11/30/96	16	22	▲	831 Mirror Has Two Faces, The .... [I] **Barbra Streisand**/Jeff Bridges/Pierce Brosnan; cp: **Marvin Hamlisch** & **Barbra Streisand**; cd: **Marvin Hamlisch**	Columbia 67887
2/21/87	132	13	●	832 Mission, The .... [I] Robert DeNiro/Jeremy Irons/Liam Neeson/Aidan Quinn; cp/cd: Ennio Morricone	Virgin 90567
6/1/96	16	14	●	833 Mission: Impossible .... [V] Tom Cruise/Jon Voight/Henry Czerny/Emmanuelle Beart/Jean Reno	Mother 531682
5/27/00	2¹	32	▲	834 Mission: Impossible 2 .... [V] Tom Cruise/Dougray Scott/Thandie Newton/Ving Rhames/Anthony Hopkins	Hollywood 62244
				Mo' Better Blues — see MARSALIS, Branford Denzel Washington/Spike Lee/Wesley Snipes/Giancarlo Esposito	
7/11/92	6	19	▲	836 Mo' Money .... [V] Damon Wayans/Marlon Wayans/Stacey Dash/Joe Santos/John Diehl	Perspective 1004
4/17/99	184	1		837 Mod Squad, The .... [V] Claire Danes/Omar Epps/Giovanni Ribisi/Dennis Farina/Josh Brolin	Elektra 62364
2/17/79	201	2		838 Moment By Moment .... [V] Lily Tomlin/John Travolta	RSO 3040
1/10/04	134	5		839 Mona Lisa Smile .... [V] Julia Roberts/Kirsten Dunst/Julia Stiles/Maggie Gyllenhaal	Epic 90737
7/20/63	15	74		840 Mondo Cane .... [I] documentary depicting various cultures around the world; cp/cd: Riz Ortolani and Nino Oliviero	United Artists 5105
9/6/97	37	17	●	841 Money Talks .... [V] Chris Tucker/Charlie Sheen/Heather Locklear/Paul Sorvino	Arista 18975
				Monterey Pop — see HENDRIX, Jimi / REDDING, Otis Monty Python & The Holy Grail — see MONTY PYTHON Graham Chapman/John Cleese/Eric Idle/Carol Cleveland	
8/18/79	159	4		844 Moonraker .... [I] Roger Moore/Lois Chiles/Richard Kiel/Michel Lonsdale; cp/cd: John Barry	United Artists 971
				More — see PINK FLOYD Mimsi Farmer/Klaus Grunberg	
8/11/79	84	12		846 More American Graffiti .... [O-V] Ron Howard/Candy Clark/Bo Hopkins/Cindy Williams	MCA 11006 [2]
10/17/09	81	4		847 More Than A Game .... [V] documentary movie	Harvey Mason 013337
9/9/95	10	46	▲	848 Mortal Kombat .... [V] Christopher Lambert/Linden Ashby/Robin Shou/Bridgette Wilson	TVT 6110
11/15/97	69	13		849 Mortal Kombat: Annihilation .... [V] Robin Shou/Talisa Soto/Brian Thompson/Sandra Hess/James Remar	TVT Soundtrax 8200
5/26/01	3¹	80	▲²	850 Moulin Rouge .... Cat:#33/11 [V] Nicole Kidman/Ewan McGregor/John Leguizamo/Jim Broadbent	Interscope 493035
3/16/02	90	9		851 Moulin Rouge 2 .... [M]	Interscope 493228
				Mr. Mean — see OHIO PLAYERS Fred Williamson/David Mills/Angela Doria	
6/29/02	61	7		853 Mr. Deeds .... [V] **Adam Sandler**/Winona Ryder/John Turturro/Peter Gallagher/Jared Harris	RCA 68118
2/10/96	42	15	●	854 Mr. Holland's Opus .... [O-V] Richard Dreyfuss/Glenne Headly/Jay Thomas/Olympia Dukakis	London 529508
				Mrs. Brown, You've Got A Lovely Daughter — see HERMAN'S HERMITS Herman's Hermits/Stanley Holloway/Mona Washbourne	
6/20/98	24	23	●	856 Mulan .... [M] animated movie, voices by Ming-Na Wen/**Eddie Murphy**/Harvey Fierstein/B.D. Wong; mu: **Matthew Wilder**; ly: David Zippel; cp/cd: Jerry Goldsmith	Walt Disney 60631
12/26/92	189	1		857 Muppet Christmas Carol, The .... [X-M] Michael Caine/Brian Henson/Frank Oz; sw: **Paul Williams** and Miles Goodman	Jim Henson 30017
7/21/79	32	34	●	858 Muppet Movie, The .... [M] *Grammy: Children's Album* Jim Henson/Frank Oz/Jerry Nelson	Atlantic 16001
8/4/84	204	2		859 Muppets Take Manhattan, The .... [M] pf: Jim Henson/Frank Oz/Jerry Nelson/Richard Hunt/Dave Goelz	Warner 25114
11/5/94	❶²	34	▲²	860 Murder Was The Case .... [V] **Snoop Dogg**/Charlie Murphy	Death Row 92484
4/22/95	177	2		861 Muriel's Wedding .... [O-V] Toni Collette/Bill Hunter/Rachel Griffiths	Polydor 527493
3/3/07	63	17		862 Music And Lyrics .... [V] Hugh Grant/Drew Barrymore/Brad garrett/Kristen Johnson/Campbell Scott	Warner Sunset 101537
8/11/62	2⁶	56	●	863 Music Man, The .... [M] Robert Preston/Shirley Jones/Buddy Hackett/Ron Howard; cp: Meredith Willson; cd: **Ray Heindorf**	Warner 1459
10/2/99	51	8	●	864 Music Of The Heart .... [V] **Meryl Streep**/Aidan Quinn/Angela Bassett/**Gloria Estefan**/Cloris Leachman	Miramax 67861
1/5/63	14	19		865 Mutiny On The Bounty .... [I] Marlon Brando/Trevor Howard/**Richard Harris**; cp: Bronislau Kaper; cd: Robert Armbruster	MGM 4
7/5/97	14	66	▲²	866 My Best Friend's Wedding .... [V] Julia Roberts/Dermot Mulroney/Cameron Diaz/Rupert Everett/Philip Bosco	Work 68166
10/10/64+	4	111	●	867 My Fair Lady .... [M] Audrey Hepburn/Rex Harrison/Stanley Holloway; mu: Frederick Loewe; ly: Alan Jay Lerner; cd: **Andre Previn**	Columbia 8000 / 2600

DEBUT	PEAK	WKS	R I A A	ARTIST / Album Title .... Catalog	Label & Number
1/4/92	104	10		868 **My Girl** .... [O-V]	Epic 48732
				Dan Aykroyd/Jamie Lee Curtis/Macauley Culkin/Anna Chlumsky/Richard Masur	
7/18/09	184	1		869 **My Sister's Keeper** .... [V]	New Line 39148
				Cameron Diaz/Abigail Breslin/Sofia Vassilieva/Alec Baldwin	
1/29/05	147	8		870 **Napoleon Dynamite** .... [V]	Lakeshore 33810
				Jon Heder/Jon Gries/Efren Ramirez/Aaron Ruell/Haylie Duff	
7/19/75	80	13		871 **Nashville** .... [M]	ABC 893
				Henry Gibson/**Lily Tomlin**/Shelley Duvall/**Keith Carradine**/Ned Beatty	
				Natural, The — see NEWMAN, Randy	
				Robert Redford/Robert Duvall/Glenn Close/Kim Basinger	
9/10/94	19	31	●	873 **Natural Born Killers** .... [V]	Nothing 92460
				Woody Harrelson/Juliette Lewis/**Robert Downey Jr.**/Tommy Lee Jones/**Rodney Dangerfield**	
4/24/99	161	3		874 **Never Been Kissed** .... [V]	Capitol 98505
				Drew Barrymore/David Arquette/Michael Vartan/Leelee Sobieski	
1/30/61	2[5]	74		875 **Never On Sunday** .... [I]	United Artists 5070
				Melina Mercouri/Jules Dassin/Tito Vandis; cp/cd: Manos Hadjidakis	
3/23/91	2[1]	38	▲	876 **New Jack City** .... [V]	Giant 24409
				Wesley Snipes/**Ice-T**/**Chris Rock**/Mario Van Peebles/Judd Nelson	
4/15/95	22	15	●	877 **New Jersey Drive Vol. 1** .... [V]	Tommy Boy 1114
				Sharron Corley/Gabriel Casseus/Saul Stein/Gwen McGee	
4/29/95	58	4		878 **New Jersey Drive Vol. 2** .... [V]	Tommy Boy 1130
7/16/77	50	14		879 **New York, New York** .... [M]	United Artists 750 [2]
				Liza Minnelli/Robert DeNiro/Lionel Stander/Mary K. Place; sw: John Kander and Fred Ebb; cd: Ralph Burns	
5/2/92	149	1		880 **Newsies** .... [M]	Disney 60832
				Christian Bale/Max Casella/Bill Pullman/Robert Duvall/**Ann-Margret**; mu: Alan Menken; ly: Jack Feldman	
3/11/00	34	8		881 **Next Best Thing, The** .... [V]	Maverick 47595
				Rupert Everett/**Madonna**/Lynn Redgrave/Illeana Douglas	
1/1/00	19	27	●	882 **Next Friday** .... [V]	Priority 23123
				Ice Cube/Mike Epps/John Witherspoon/Tamala Jones	
10/18/08	44	8		883 **Nick & Norah's Infinite Playlist** .... [M]	Atlantic 516007
				Michael Cera/Kat Dennings/Ari Graynor/Alexis Dziena	
10/17/98	95	22	●	884 **Night At The Roxbury, A** .... [V]	DreamWorks 50033
				Will Ferrell/Chris Kattan/Dan Hedaya/Molly Shannon/Richard Grieco	
9/4/82	204	3		885 **Night Shift** .... [V]	Warner 23702
				Henry Winkler/Michael Keaton/Shelley Long	
8/22/81	189	5		886 **Night The Lights Went Out In Georgia, The** ... [V]	Mirage 16051
				Kristy McNichol/Dennis Quaid/Mark Hamill/Don Stroud	
				Nighthawks — see EMERSON, Keith	
				Sylvester Stallone/Rutger Hauer/Billy Dee Williams/Nigel Davenport/Persis Khambatta	
11/6/93	98	9	●	888 **Nightmare Before Christmas, The** .... [X-M]	Walt Disney 60855
				animated movie, voices by: Chris Sarandon/Catherine O'Hara/William Hickey/Paul Reubens; cp/cd: Danny Elfman; Christmas charts: 12/'93, 20/'04, 11/'04, 22/'05	
11/11/06	31	8	●	889 **Nightmare Before Christmas: Special Edition, The** ... Cat:#15/3 [X-M]	Walt Disney 861636 [2]
				Christmas charts: 1/'06, 3/'07, 1/'08, 3/'09	
3/29/86	59	15		890 **9 1/2 Weeks** .... [V]	Capitol 12470
				Mickey Rourke/Kim Basinger/Christine Baranski/Margaret Whitten	
8/5/95	166	5		891 **Nine Months** .... [I+V]	Milan 35726
				Hugh Grant/Julianne Moore/Tom Arnold/**Robin Williams**/Joan Cusack; cp: Hans Zimmer; cd: Nick Glennie-Smith	
12/27/80+	77	15		892 **9 To 5** .... [I]	20th Century 627
				Jane Fonda/Lily Tomlin/**Dolly Parton**/Dabney Coleman/Sterling Hayden; cp/cd: Charles Fox	
				1984 — see EURYTHMICS	
				John Hurt/Richard Burton/Suzanna Hamilton/Cyril Cusack	
12/17/88+	186	6		894 **1969** .... [O-V]	Polydor 837362
				Robert Downey Jr./Kiefer Sutherland/Bruce Dern/Mariette Hartley	
				No Direction Home — see DYLAN, Bob	
				documentary movie	
				Norwood — see CAMPBELL, Glen	
				Glen Campbell/Kim Darby/Joe Namath/Carol Lynley/Pat Hingle	
1/12/02	168	2		897 **Not Another Teen Movie** .... [V]	Maverick 48250
				Chyler Leigh/Jaime Pressly/Ed Lauter/Molly Ringwald/Randy Quaid	
7/17/04	183	2		898 **Notebook, The** .... [V]	New Line 39031
				Ryan Gosling/Rachel McAdams/James Garner/Gena Rowlands	
9/20/86	190	3		899 **Nothing In Common** .... [V]	Arista 8438
				Tom Hanks/**Jackie Gleason**/Eva Marie Saint/Hector Elizondo/Barry Corbin	
7/19/97	12	13	●	900 **Nothing To Lose** .... [V]	Tommy Boy 1169
				Martin Lawrence/Tim Robbins/John C. McGinley/Kelly Preston	
1/31/09	4	9		901 **Notorious** .... [V]	Fox 517001
				Jamal Woolard/Angela Bassett/Derek Luke/Anthony Mackie	
6/5/99	19	40	▲	902 **Notting Hill** .... [V]	Island 546196
				Julia Roberts/Hugh Grant/Hugh Bonneville/Emma Chambers/James Dreyfus	
11/11/95+	103	35	●	903 **Now And Then** .... [O-V]	Columbia 67380
				Christina Ricci/Thora Birch/**Rosie O'Donnell**/Melanie Griffith/Demi Moore	
6/22/96	8	21	▲	904 **Nutty Professor, The** .... [V]	Def Jam 531911
				Eddie Murphy/Jada Pinkett/James Coburn/Dave Chappelle/Larry Miller	
7/29/00	4	18	▲	905 **Nutty Professor II: The Klumps** .... [V]	Def Jam 542522
				Eddie Murphy/Janet Jackson/Larry Miller/John Ales/Anna Maria Horsford	
1/13/01+	❶[2]	102	▲[8]	906 **O Brother, Where Art Thou?** .... Cat:❶1/'96 [V]	Mercury 170069
				Grammys: Album of the Year / Soundtrack Album ★ CMA: Album of the Year	
				George Clooney/John Turturro/Tim Blake Nelson/John Goodman/Charles Durning/Stephen Root	

Billboard			R I A A	ARTIST		
DEBUT	PEAK	WKS		Album Title...Catalog	Label & Number

				O Lucky Man! — see PRICE, Alan Malcolm McDowell/Rachel Roberts/Ralph Richardson		
7/16/83	137	5		908 **Octopussy** .... [I] Roger Moore/Maud Adams/Louis Jourdan/Vijay Amritraj; cp/cd: John Barry	A&M 4967
7/27/68	190	2		909 **Odd Couple, The** .... [I] Jack Lemmon/Walter Matthau/John Fiedler/Herb Edelman; cp/cd: Neal Hefti	Dot 25862
10/30/82	38	23		910 **Officer And A Gentleman, An** .... [V] Richard Gere/Debra Winger/David Keith/Lou Gossett Jr.	Island 90017
9/17/55+	**❶**[2]	283	▲[2]	911 **Oklahoma!** [M] Gordon MacRae/Shirley Jones/Rod Steiger; mu: Richard Rodgers; ly: Oscar Hammerstein II; cd: Jay Blackton	Capitol 595
				Oklahoma Crude — see MANCINI, Henry George C. Scott/Faye Dunaway/Jack Palance		
12/28/68+	20	91	●	913 **Oliver!** .... [M] Mark Lester/Ron Moody/Jack Wild/Oliver Reed; sw: Lionel Bart; cd: John Green	Colgems 5501
1/7/89	170	7		914 **Oliver & Company** .... Cat:#10/4 [M] animated movie, voices by: Joey Lawrence/Bette Midler/Billy Joel/Cheech Marin (Cheech & Chong); cp/cd: J.A.C. Redford	Disney 64101
				On A Clear Day You Can See Forever — see STREISAND, Barbra Barbra Streisand/Yves Montand/Bob Newhart/Jack Nicholson		
2/27/82	147	11		916 **On Golden Pond** .... [I] Henry Fonda/Katharine Hepburn/Jane Fonda/Doug McKeon/Dabney Coleman; cp/cd: Dave Grusin	MCA 6106
2/7/70	103	13		917 **On Her Majesty's Secret Service** .... [I+V] George Lazenby/Diana Rigg/Telly Savalas; cp/cd: John Barry	United Artists 5204
11/3/01	35	4		918 **On The Line** .... [V] Lance Bass/Joey Fatone (both of *NSYNC)/Emmanuelle Chriqui/Dave Foley/Jerry Stiller	Jive 41762
6/16/07+	**7**	53	●	919 **Once** .... Cat:#30/1 [M] Glen Hansard/Marketa Irglova/Bill Hodnett/Marcella Plunkett	Canvasback 10586
10/4/03	174	1		920 **Once Upon A Time In Mexico** .... [F-V] Antonio Banderas/Salma Hayek/Johnny Depp/Mickey Rourke/Enrique Iglesias	Milan 36038
1/4/97	57	25	●	921 **One Fine Day** .... [V] Michelle Pfeiffer/George Clooney/Mae Whitman/Charles Durning/Robert Klein	Columbia 67916
4/17/76	158	7		922 **One Flew Over The Cuckoo's Nest** .... [I] Jack Nicholson/Louise Fletcher/Will Sampson/Scatman Crothers/Danny DeVito; cp: Jack Nitzsche	Fantasy 9500
				101 — see DEPECHE MODE **One On One — see SEALS & CROFTS** Robby Benson/Annette O'Toole/G.D. Spradlin/Gail Strickland/Melanie Griffith **One-Trick Pony — see SIMON, Paul** Paul Simon/Blair Brown/Rip Torn/Joan Hackett/Lou Reed		
1/12/02	62	8		926 **Orange County**.. [V] Colin Hanks/Jack Black/Schuyler Fisk/Lily Tomlin/Chevy Chase	Columbia 85933
5/18/96	41	6		927 **Original Gangstas** .... [V] Fred Williamson/Jim Brown/Pam Grier/Paul Winfield/Isabel Sanford	Noo Trybe 41533
9/9/00	50	6		928 **Original Kings Of Comedy, The** .... [C] Steve Harvey/D.L. Hughley/Bernie Mac/Cedric The Entertainer	Universal 159306
3/20/99	109	5		929 **Other Sister, The**.. [V] Juliette Lewis/Diane Keaton/Tom Skerritt/Giovanni Ribisi	Hollywood 62180
3/19/66	118	5		930 **Our Man Flint** .... [I] James Coburn/Lee J. Cobb/Gila Golan; cp/cd: Jerry Goldsmith	20th Century Fox 4179
2/1/86	38	22	●	931 **Out Of Africa** .... Cat:#22/2 [I] Meryl Streep/Robert Redford/Klaus Maria Brandauer/Michael Gough; cp/cd: John Barry	MCA 6158
3/7/87	120	8		932 **Over The Top** .... [V] Sylvester Stallone/Robert Loggia/Susan Blakely/David Mendenhall/Terry Funk	Columbia 40655
				Owl And The Pussycat, The — see STREISAND, Barbra Barbra Streisand/George Segal/Robert Klein/Roz Kelly **Pagan Love Song — see "Those Glorious MGM Musicals"** Esther Williams/Howard Keel/Rita Moreno		
12/14/02	53	10		935 **Paid In Full** .... [V] Wood Harris/Mekhi Phifer/Esai Morales/Kevin Carroll/Cam'ron	Roc-A-Fella 063201 [2]
10/25/69	28	56	●	936 **Paint Your Wagon** .... [M] Lee Marvin/Clint Eastwood/Jean Seberg/Ray Walston; mu: Frederick Loewe; ly: Alan Jay Lerner; cd: Nelson Riddle	Paramount 1001
9/23/57	9	14		937 **Pajama Game, The** [M] Doris Day/John Raitt/Carol Haney/Reta Shaw; sw: Richard Adler and Jerry Ross; cd: Ray Heindorf	Columbia 5210
				Pal Joey — see SINATRA, Frank Frank Sinatra/Rita Hayworth/Kim Novak		
5/20/95	37	8	●	939 **Panther** .... [V] Kadeem Hardison/Bokeem Woodbine/Tyrin Turner/Joe Don Baker	Mercury 525479
8/4/73	154	12		940 **Paper Moon** .... [O-V] Ryan O'Neal/Tatum O'Neal/Madeline Kahn/John Hillerman	Paramount 1012
2/9/74	210	4		941 **Papillon** .... [I] Steve McQueen/Dustin Hoffman/Victor Jory/Don Gordon; cp/cd: Jerry Goldsmith	Capitol 11260
				Paradise, Hawaiian Style — see PRESLEY, Elvis Elvis Presley ("Rick Richards")/Suzanne Leigh/James Shigeta		
10/23/61	92	8		943 **Parent Trap!, The** .... [I+V] Hayley Mills/Brian Keith/Maureen O'Hara; cd: Tutti Camarata	Buena Vista 3309
2/13/99	180	4		944 **Parent Trap, The** .... [V] Dennis Quaid/Natasha Richardson/Lindsay Lohan/Polly Holliday	Hollywood 62167
				Paris, Texas — see COODER, Ry Harry Dean Stanton/Nastassja Kinski/Dean Stockwell		
9/25/61	45	12		946 **Parrish**... [I] Troy Donahue/Claudette Colbert/Karl Malden/Dean Jagger/Connie Stevens; cp/cd: Max Steiner	Warner 1413

DEBUT	PEAK	WKS	R I A A	ARTIST / Album Title	Catalog	Label & Number
2/5/83	169	6		947 **Party Party** [V] Daniel Peacock/Phoebe Nicholls/Karl Howman/Perry Fenwick/Sean Chapman		A&M 3212
3/13/04	17	13	●	948 **Passion Of The Christ, The** [I] James Caviezel/Maia Morgenstern/Hristo Shopov/Rosalinda Celentano; cp/cd: John Debney		Sony 92046
				Pat Garrett & Billy The Kid — see DYLAN, Bob James Coburn/Bob Dylan/Kris Kristofferson/Jason Robards		
1/23/99	180	2		950 **Patch Adams** [O-V] Robin Williams/Monica Potter/Philip Seymour Hoffman/Bob Gunton		Universal 53245
7/15/00	129	3		951 **Patriot, The** [I] Mel Gibson/Heath Ledger/Joely Richardson/Rene Auberjonois; cp/cd: **John Williams**		Hollywood 62258
5/22/71	117	8		952 **Patton** [I] George C. Scott/Karl Malden/Michael Bates/Edward Binns; cp/cd: Jerry Goldsmith		20th Century Fox 4208
6/9/01	14	18	●	953 **Pearl Harbor** [I] Ben Affleck/Josh Hartnett/Kate Beckinsale/Cuba Gooding Jr.; cp: Hans Zimmer; cd: Gavin Greenaway		Warner 48113
1/23/82	188	2		954 **Pennies From Heaven** [O-V] Steve Martin/Bernadette Peters/Christopher Walken		Warner 3639 [2]
6/29/85	45	12		955 **Perfect** [V] John Travolta/Jamie Lee Curtis/Marilu Henner/Laraine Newman/Jann Wenner		Arista 8278
12/24/77+	131	10		956 **Pete's Dragon** [M] Helen Reddy/Jim Dale/Mickey Rooney/Red Buttons; sw: Al Kasha and Joel Hirschhorn; cd: Irwin Kostal		Capitol 11704
2/23/63	88	7		957 **Phaedra** [I] Melina Mercouri/Anthony Perkins; cp/cd: Mikis Theodorakis		United Artists 5102
12/11/04+	16	49	▲	958 **Phantom Of The Opera, The** [M] Gerard Butler/Emmy Rossum/Patrick Wilson/Minnie Driver		Sony Classical 93521
1/15/05	71	19		959 **Phantom Of The Opera (Special Edition), The** [M] Gerard Butler/Emmy Rossum/Patrick Wilson/Minnie Driver		Really Useful 93522 [2]
3/1/75	194	1	▲	960 **Phantom Of The Paradise** [M] Paul Williams/William Finley/Jessica Harper/Gerrit Graham; sw: **Paul Williams**		A&M 3653
7/20/96	12	43	▲	961 **Phenomenon** [V] John Travolta/Kyra Sedgwick/Forest Whitaker/Robert Duvall		Reprise 46360
1/22/94	12	36	▲	962 **Philadelphia** [V] Tom Hanks/Denzel Washington/Jason Robards/Mary Steenburgen/Antonio Banderas		Epic Soundtrax 57624
				Piano, The — see NYMAN, Michael Holly Hunter/Harvey Keitel/Sam Neill/Anne Paquin		
				Pick Of Destiny, The — see TENACIOUS D Jack Black/Kyle Gass/**Meat Loaf**/Ben Stiller		
5/5/56	6	18		965 **Picnic** [I] William Holden/Kim Novak/Rosalind Russell/Cliff Robertson; cp: George Duning; cd: Morris Stoloff		Decca 78320
				Pink Panther, The — see MANCINI, Henry Peter Sellers/David Niven/Robert Wagner/Capucine		
				Pipe Dreams — see KNIGHT, Gladys/Pips Gladys Knight/Barry Hankerson/Bruce French/Sherry Bain		
				Pirate — see "Those Glorious MGM Musicals" Judy Garland/Gene Kelly/Walter Slezak/Gladys Cooper		
8/28/82	166	6		969 **Pirate Movie, The** [M] Kristy McNichol/Christopher Atkins/Ted Hamilton/Bill Kerr		Polydor 9503 [2]
11/28/09	174	2		970 **Pirate Radio** [O-V] Tom Sturridge/Bill Nighy/Philip Seymour Hoffman/Kenneth Branagh		Universal Rep. 013630 [2]
8/9/03	75	15	●	971 **Pirates Of The Caribbean: The Curse Of The Black Pearl** Cat:#31/3 [I] Johnny Depp/Geoffrey Rush/Orlando Bloom/Keira Knightley; cp: Klaus Badelt; cd: Hans Zimmer		Walt Disney 860089
7/22/06	22	12		972 **Pirates Of The Caribbean: Dead Man's Chest** [I] Johnny Depp/Orlando Bloom/Keira Knightley/Jonathan Pryce; cp/cd: Hans Zimmer		Walt Disney 861447
6/9/07	14	9		973 **Pirates Of The Caribbean: At World's End** [I] Johnny Depp/Orlando Bloom/Keira Knightley/Geoffrey Rush; cp/cd: Hans Zimmer		Walt Disney 000371
7/27/68	195	3		974 **Planet Of The Apes** [I] Charlton Heston/Roddy McDowall/Kim Hunter/Maurice Evans/James Whitmore; cp/cd: Jerry Goldsmith		Project 3 5023
8/11/01	158	2		975 **Planet Of The Apes** [I] Mark Wahlberg/Tim Roth/Helena Bonham Carter/Michael Clarke Duncan/Paul Giamatti; cp: **Danny Elfman**; cd: Pete Anthony		Sony Classical 89666
4/4/87	75	13		976 **Platoon** [O-V] Tom Berenger/Willem Dafoe/Charlie Sheen/Forest Whitaker/John C. McGinley		Atlantic 81742
4/4/98	10	25	▲	977 **Players Club, The** [V] Bernie Mac/Monica Calhoun/Lisa Raye/**Ice Cube**/Jamie Foxx		A&M 540886
6/17/95	❶¹	48	▲³	978 **Pocahontas** [M] animated movie, voices by: Irene Bedard/Judy Kuhn/Mel Gibson; mu: Alan Menken; ly: Stephen Schwartz		Walt Disney 60874
7/17/93	23	15	●	979 **Poetic Justice** [V] Janet Jackson/2Pac/Tyra Ferrell/Regina King/Joe Torry		Epic Soundtrax 57131
11/27/99	8	24	▲²	980 **Pokemon - The First Movie** [V] animated movie, voices by Veronica Taylor/Philip Bartlett/Rachael Lillis/Eric Stuart		Atlantic 83261
8/5/00	85	7		981 **Pokemon The Movie 2000: The Power Of One** [V] animated movie, voices by Veronica Taylor/Ted Lewis/Stan Hart		Atlantic 83370
11/20/04	46	9	●	982 **Polar Express, The** Cat:#24/13 [X-V] animated movie, voices by: Tom Hanks/Leslie Zemeckis/Nona Gaye/Peter Scolari; Christmas charts: 1/04, 11/05, 13/06, 41/07, 19/08, 20/09		Warner Sunset 48897
7/17/82	168	5		983 **Poltergeist** [I] JoBeth Williams/Craig T. Nelson/Heather O'Rourke/Beatrice Straight; cp/cd: Jerry Goldsmith		MGM 5408
12/27/80+	115	10		984 **Popeye** [M] Robin Williams/Shelley Duvall/Ray Walston/Paul Dooley; sw: **Nilsson**		Boardwalk 36880
7/13/59	8	96	●	985 **Porgy And Bess** [M] *Grammy: Soundtrack Album* Sidney Poitier/Dorothy Dandridge; mu: **George Gershwin**; ly: DuBose Heyward and Ira Gershwin; cd: **Andre Previn**		Columbia 2016

Billboard			R I A A	ARTIST		
DEBUT	PEAK	WKS		Album Title..Catalog		Label & Number
4/13/85	122	8		986 **Porky's Revenge!** ....**[V]**		Columbia 39983
				Dan Monahan/Wyatt Knight/Tony Ganios/Mark Herrier/Kaki Hunter		
5/29/93	178	2		987 **Posse** ....**[V]**		A&M 540081
				Mario Van Peebles/**Tone Loc/Big Daddy Kane**/Blair Underwood/Stephen Baldwin		
4/13/96	182	1		988 **Postman (Il Postino), The** ....**[I]**		Miramax 62029
				Massimo Troisi/Philippe Noiret/Maria Grazia Cucinotta; cp/cd: Luis Bacalov		
10/31/98	36	22		989 **Practical Magic** ....**[V]**		Warner Sunset 47140
				Sandra Bullock/Nicole Kidman/Dianne Wiest/Stockard Channing		
7/1/06	160	2		990 **Prairie Home Companion, A** ....**[M]**		New Line 39067
				Garrison Keillor/**Meryl Streep**/Woody Harrelson/Tommy Lee Jones/**Lindsay Lohan**		
				Preacher's Wife, The — see HOUSTON, Whitney		
				Denzel Washington/**Whitney Houston**/Gregory Hines/Courtney Vance		
3/1/86	5	27	●	992 **Pretty In Pink** ....**[V]**		A&M 3901
				Molly Ringwald/Jon Cryer/Andrew McCarthy/Harry Dean Stanton/Annie Potts		
4/7/90	4	91	▲³	993 **Pretty Woman** ....**Cat:#44/1** **[V]**		EMI 93492
				Richard Gere/Julia Roberts/Ralph Bellamy/Jason Alexander/Laura San Giacomo		
12/5/98+	25	20	▲	994 **Prince Of Egypt, The** ....**[V]**		DreamWorks 50041
				animated movie, voices by: Val Kilmer/Ralph Fiennes/Michelle Pfeiffer/Jeff Goldblum; cp: Hans Zimmer; sw: Stephen Schwartz		
1/11/92	84	12		995 **Prince Of Tides, The** ....**[I]**		Columbia 48627
				Barbra Streisand/Nick Nolte/Blythe Danner/Kate Nelligan; cp: James Newton Howard; cd: Marty Paich		
12/26/09+	80	12		996 **Princess And The Frog, The** ....**[V]**		Walt Disney 004585
				animated movie, voices by: Anika Noni Rose/Bruno Campos/Oprah Winfrey/John Goodman		
10/31/87	180	1		997 **Princess Bride, The** ....**[I]**		Warner 25610
				Cary Elwes/Robin Wright/**Mandy Patinkin/Billy Crystal**/Andre The Giant; cp: **Mark Knopfler**		
8/11/01	41	31	●	998 **Princess Diaries, The** ....**[V]**		Walt Disney 860731
				Julie Andrews/Anne Hathaway/**Mandy Moore**/Hector Elizondo		
8/21/04	15	28	●	999 **Princess Diaries 2: Royal Engagement, The** ....**[V]**		Walt Disney 861099
				Julie Andrews/Anne Hathaway/Hector Elizondo/Heather Matarazzo/John Rhys-Davies		
3/15/97	❶¹	9	▲	1000 **Private Parts** ....**[V]**		Warner 46477
				Howard Stern/Robin Quivers/Fred Norris/Mary McCormack/Paul Giamatti		
1/12/08	60	12		1001 **P.S. I Love You** ....**[V]**		Atlantic 362748
				Hilary Swank/Gerard Butler/Lisa Kudrow/Gina Gershon/Kathy Bates		
7/18/09	191	2		1002 **Public Enemies** ....**[O-V]**		Decca 013072
				Johnny Depp/Christian Bale/Marion Cotillard/James Russo		
10/29/94	21	107	▲³	1003 **Pulp Fiction** ....**Cat:#31/8** **[O-V]**		MCA 11103
				John Travolta/Samuel L. Jackson/Uma Thurman/**Bruce Willis**/Tim Roth		
9/8/90	50	34	●	1004 **Pump Up The Volume** ....**[V]**		MCA 8039
				Christian Slater/Scott Paulin/Ellen Greene/Samantha Mathis		
4/10/04	22	22	●	1005 **Punisher, The** ....**[V]**		Wind-Up 13093
				Tom Jane/Russell Andrews/Omar Avila/Samantha Mathis		
				Pure Country — see STRAIT, George		
				George Strait/Lesley Ann Warren/Isabel Glasser		
				Purple Rain — see PRINCE		
				Prince/Apollonia/**Morris Day**/Clarence Williams III		
				Quadrophenia — see WHO, The		
				Phil Daniels/Leslie Ash/**Sting**		
3/9/02	28	19	●	1009 **Queen Of The Damned** ....**[V]**		Warner Sunset 48285
				Aaliyah/Stuart Townsend/Marguerite Moreau/Vincent Perez/Lena Olin		
5/30/98	117	5		1010 **Quest For Camelot** ....**[V]**		Curb 83097
				animated movie, voices by: Pierce Brosnan/Gabriel Byrne/Cary Elwes/Eric Idle/**Don Rickles**		
4/17/82	154	6		1011 **Quest For Fire** ....**[I]**		RCA Victor 4274
				Everett McGill/Rae Dawn Chong/Ron Perlman; cp: Philippe Sarde		
3/1/86	140	5		1012 **Quicksilver** ....**[V]**		Atlantic 81631
				Kevin Bacon/Jami Gertz/Paul Rodriguez/Laurence Fishburne		
6/11/77	209	2		1013 **Raggedy Ann & Andy** ....**[M]**		Columbia 34686
				animated movie, voices by: Didi Conn/Mark Baker/Joe Silver; sw: Joe Raposo		
1/23/82	134	9		1014 **Ragtime** ....**[I]**		Elektra 565
				James Cagney/Howard Rollins/Elizabeth McGovern/Moses Gunn; cp/cd: **Randy Newman**		
7/4/81	62	13		1015 **Raiders Of The Lost Ark** ....**[I]**		Columbia 37373
				Grammy: Soundtrack Album		
				Harrison Ford/Karen Allen/John Rhys-Davies/Denholm Elliott; cp/cd: **John Williams**		
3/11/89	31	16		1016 **Rain Man** ....**[V]**		Capitol 91866
				Dustin Hoffman/Tom Cruise/Valeria Golino/Bonnie Hunt/Barry Levinson		
				Rainbow Bridge — see HENDRIX, Jimi		
6/15/85	204	2		1018 **Rappin'** ....**[V]**		Atlantic 81252
				Mario Van Peebles/Tasia Valenza/Kadeem Hardison		
				Rattle And Hum — see U2		
				Ray — see CHARLES, Ray		
				Jamie Foxx/Regina King/Larenz Tate/Curtis Armstrong		
12/31/94+	29	18	●	1021 **Ready To Wear (Pret-A-Porter)** ....**[V]**		Columbia 66791
				Julia Roberts/Tim Robbins/Sophia Loren/Marcello Mastroianni		
2/26/94	13	52	▲²	1022 **Reality Bites** ....**[V]**		RCA 66364
				Winona Ryder/Ethan Hawke/Ben Stiller/Janeane Garofalo/Steve Zahn		
12/26/81+	202	8		1023 **Reds** ....**[I]**		Columbia 37690
				Warren Beatty/Diane Keaton/Jack Nicholson/Maureen Stapleton; cp: Stephen Sondheim; cd: Paul Gemignani		
				Reggae Sunsplash '81 — see VARIOUS ARTIST COMPILATIONS		
10/21/00+	49	36	▲	1025 **Remember The Titans** ....**[O-V]**		Walt Disney 60687
				Denzel Washington/Will Patton/Wood Harris/Ryan Hurst		
10/15/05	40	18		1026 **Rent** ....**[M]**		Warner 49455 [2]
				Anthony Rapp/Adam Pascal/Rosario Dawson/Idina Menzel/Taye Diggs		

Billboard DEBUT	PEAK	WKS	R I A A	ARTIST Album Title.. Catalog	Label & Number
12/3/05	43	13		1027 **Rent: Selections From The Original Motion Picture**.................... [M]	Warner 49468
3/11/95	24°	33		1028 **Reservoir Dogs**... [O-V]	MCA 10541
				Harvey Keitel/Tim Roth/Chris Penn/Steve Buscemi/Quentin Taratino	
3/30/02	24	9		1029 **Resident Evil**.. [V]	Roadrunner 618450
				Mila Jovovich/Michelle Rodriguez/Eric Mabius/James Purefoy/Martin Crewes	
9/18/04	43	5		1030 **Resident Evil: Apocalypse**.. [V]	Roadrunner 618242
				Milla Jovovich/Sienna Gullory/Oded Fehr/Jared Harris/Mike Epps	
6/11/83	20	17		1031 **Return Of The Jedi**.. [I]	RSO 811767
				Mark Hamill/Harrison Ford/Carrie Fisher/Billy Dee Williams; cp/cd: **John Williams**	
3/29/97	51	4		1032 **Return Of The Jedi**.. [I-R]	RCA Victor 68748 [2]
				complete score in sequence with previously unreleased music issued in conjunction with the 1997 release of the *Return Of The Jedi* Special Edition movie in theaters	
				Rhinestone — see PARTON, Dolly	
				Sylvester Stallone/**Dolly Parton**/Richard Farnsworth/Ron Leibman	
2/1/97	16	13	●	1034 **Rhyme & Reason**... [V]	Priority 50635
				concert movie/documentary	
				Richard Pryor Live On The Sunset Strip — see PRYOR, Richard	
				Richard Pryor: Here And Now — see PRYOR, Richard	
3/7/98	54	7		1037 **Ride**.. [V]	Tommy Boy 1227
				Malik Yoba/Melissa De Sousa/John Witherspoon/**Fredro Starr**	
				Ride The Wild Surf — see JAN & DEAN	
				Tab Hunter/**Fabian/Shelley Fabares**/Barbara Eden	
				Right On! — see LAST POETS	
				David Nelson/Felipe Luciano/Gylan Kain	
6/3/89	67	10		1040 **Road House**... [V]	Arista 8576
				Patrick Swayze/Ben Gazzara/Kelly Lynch/Sam Elliott/Terry Funk	
				Road To El Dorado, The — see JOHN, Elton	
				animated movie, voices by Kevin Kline/Kenneth Branagh/Rosie Perez	
6/21/80	125	8		1042 **Roadie**... [V]	Warner 3441 [2]
				Meat Loaf/Art Carney/Kaki Hunter/Gailard Sartain	
7/18/64	56	14		1043 **Robin And The 7 Hoods**.. [M]	Reprise 2021
				Frank Sinatra/Dean Martin/Bing Crosby/**Sammy Davis, Jr.**; sw: Sammy Cahn and James Van Heusen; cd: **Nelson Riddle**	
2/2/74	216	5		1044 **Robin Hood**... [M]	Disneyland 3810
				animated movie, voices by Peter Ustinov/Phil Harris/Terry-Thomas; sw: **Roger Miller**	
7/20/91	5	45	▲	1045 **Robin Hood: Prince Of Thieves**... [I]	Morgan Creek 20004
				Kevin Costner/Mary Elizabeth Mastrantonio/Morgan Freeman/Christian Slater/Alan Rickman; cp/cd: Michael Kamen	
4/9/05	198	1		1046 **Robots**.. [V]	Virgin 60410
				animated movie, voices by: **Robin Williams**/Halle Berry/Ewan McGregor/Drew Carey/**Paula Abdul**	
6/2/79	118	6		1047 **Rock 'N' Roll High School**.. [V]	Sire 6070
				P.J. Soles/Vincent Van Patten/Dey Young/**Ramones**	
3/9/57	16	9		1048 **Rock, Pretty Baby**.. [M]	Decca 8429
				Sal Mineo/John Saxon/Luana Patten; cp: **Henry Mancini**; pf: Jimmy Daley & The Ding-A-Lings	
9/22/01	102	4		1049 **Rock Star**.. [V]	Posthuman 50238
				Mark Wahlberg (**Marky Mark**)/Jennifer Aniston/Jason Flemyng/Dominic West	
3/5/77	4	34	▲	1050 **Rocky**.. [I]	United Artists 693
				Sylvester Stallone/Talia Shire/Carl Weathers/Burgess Meredith/Burt Young; cp/cd: Bill Conti	
8/25/79	147	5		1051 **Rocky II**... [I]	United Artists 972
				Sylvester Stallone/Talia Shire/Carl Weathers/Burgess Meredith/Burt Young; cp/cd: Bill Conti	
7/10/82	15	19	●	1052 **Rocky III**.. [I+V]	Liberty 51130
				Sylvester Stallone/Talia Shire/Mr. T/Burt Young/Burgess Meredith; cp/cd: Bill Conti	
11/16/85+	10	30	▲	1053 **Rocky IV**.. [V]	Scotti Brothers 40203
				Sylvester Stallone/Talia Shire/Dolph Lundgren/Burt Young/Brigitte Nielsen	
1/13/07	87	5		1054 **Rocky Balboa: The Best Of Rocky**.. [K-V]	Legacy 76267
				Sylvester Stallone/Burt Young/Milo Ventimiglia/Geraldine Hughes/Antonio Tarver	
4/15/78	49	58	●	1055 **Rocky Horror Picture Show** .... Cat:#45/1 [M]	Ode 21653
				Tim Curry/Susan Sarandon/Barry Bostwick/**Meat Loaf**; sw: Richard O'Brien	
10/15/05	168	1		1056 **Roll Bounce**.. [V]	Music World 87539
				Bow Wow/Nick Cannon/Khleo Thomas/Mike Epps	
8/23/75	156	6		1057 **Rollerball**.. [I]	United Artists 470
				James Caan/John Houseman/Maud Adams/John Beck/Moses Gunn; cd: **Andre Previn**	
6/16/62	5	28		1058 **Rome Adventure**.. [I]	Warner 1458
				Troy Donahue/Suzanne Pleshette/Angie Dickinson; cp: Max Steiner	
2/8/69	2²	74	▲	1059 **Romeo & Juliet**.. [I+T]	Capitol 2993
				Leonard Whiting/Olivia Hussey/Michael York/Pat Heywood/John McEnery; cp/cd: Nino Rota	
11/16/96+	2²	48	▲³	1060 **Romeo & Juliet**... [V]	Capitol 37715
				Claire Danes/Leonardo DiCaprio/John Leguizamo/Paul Sorvino/Pete Postlethwaite	
4/26/97	27	18		1061 **Romeo & Juliet Volume 2**.. [I]	Capitol 55567
4/15/00	3¹	29	▲	1062 **Romeo Must Die**... [V]	Blackground 49052
				Jet Li/**Aaliyah**/Russell Wong/**DMX**/Delroy Lindo	
5/17/97	64	17		1063 **Romy And Michele's High School Reunion** .... [O-V]	Hollywood 62098
				Mira Sorvino/Lisa Kudrow/Janeane Garofalo/Alan Cumming	
				Rose Marie — see "Those Glorious MGM Musicals"	
				Ann Blyth/Howard Keel/Fernando Lamas/Bert Lahr	
				Rose, The — see MIDLER, Bette	
				Bette Midler/Alan Bates/Frederic Forrest/Harry Dean Stanton	
1/24/87	196	3		1066 **Round Midnight**.. [I]	Columbia 40464
				Dexter Gordon/Francois Cluzet/Gabrielle Haker/Lonette McKee; cp/cd: **Herbie Hancock**	
				Roustabout — see PRESLEY, Elvis	
				Elvis Presley ("Charlie Rogers")/Barbara Stanwyck/Joan Freeman/Pat Buttram	

Billboard DEBUT	PEAK	WKS	R I A A	ARTIST Album Title........ Catalog	Label & Number
1/26/02	**162**	3		1068 **Royal Tenenbaums, The** .... [V] Gene Hackman/Anjelica Houston/Gwyneth Paltrow/Ben Stiller/Owen Wilson	Hollywood 162347
10/31/70	**148**	6		1069 **R.P.M.** .... [I+V] Anthony Quinn/**Ann-Margret**/Gary Lockwood/Paul Winfield; sw: **Barry DeVorzon** and Perry Botkin Jr.	Bell 1203
7/5/03	**198**	1		1070 **RugRats Go Wild** .... [V] animated movie, voices by: Bruce Willis/Tim Curry/E.G. Dailey/Cheryl Chase	Nickelodeon 162399
11/25/00	**48**	16	●	1071 **RugRats In Paris: The Movie** .... [V] animated movie, voices by Susan Sarandon/E.G. Daily/Christine Cavanaugh/Cheryl Chase	Maverick 47850
11/21/98+	**19**	26	▲	1072 **RugRats Movie, The** .... [V] animated movie, voices by: E.G. Daily/Melanie Chartoff/Whoopi Goldberg/**Busta Rhymes**	Interscope 90181
				Rumble Fish — see COPELAND, Stewart Matt Dillon/Mickey Rourke/Diane Lane/Dennis Hopper/Diana Scarwid	
8/14/99	**4**	33	▲	1074 **Runaway Bride** .... [V] Julia Roberts/Richard Gere/Joan Cusack/Hector Elizondo/Rita Wilson	Columbia 69923
7/5/86	**43**	15		1075 **Running Scared** .... [V] Gregory Hines/**Billy Crystal**/Steven Bauer/Jimmy Smits	MCA 6169
				Rush — see CLAPTON, Eric Jason Patric/Jennifer Jason Leigh/**Gregg Allman**/Sam Elliott/Max Perlich	
10/3/98	**5**	33	▲	1077 **Rush Hour** .... [V] Jackie Chan/Chris Tucker/Tom Wilkinson/Chris Penn/Elizabeth Pena	Def Jam 558663
8/18/01	**11**	9	●	1078 **Rush Hour 2** .... [V] Jackie Chan/Chris Tucker/John Lone/Alan King/Zhang Zi Yi	Def Jam 586216
3/13/99	**191**	1		1079 **Rushmore** .... [O-V] Jason Schwartzman/Olivia Williams/Bill Murray/Brian Cox	London 556074
7/5/86	**20**	16	●	1080 **Ruthless People** .... [V] Danny DeVito/**Bette Midler**/Judge Reinhold/Helen Slater/Anita Morris	Epic 40398
12/19/70+	**199**	4		1081 **Ryan's Daughter** .... [I] Robert Mitchum/Sarah Miles/Trevor Howard; cp/cd: Maurice Jarre	MGM 27
4/12/97	**24**	16		1082 **Saint, The** .... [V] Val Kilmer/Elisabeth Shue/Rade Serbedzija	Virgin 42959
6/25/88	**112**	6		1083 **Salsa** .... [V] Robby Rosa/Rodney Harvey/Magali Alvarado/**Tito Puente**	MCA 6232
10/23/65	**89**	15		1084 **Sandpiper, The** .... [I] *Grammy: Soundtrack Album* Elizabeth Taylor/Richard Burton/Eva Marie Saint/Charles Bronson; cp: Johnny Mandel; cd: Robert Armbruster	Mercury 61032
10/24/92	**200**	1		1085 **Sarafina! The Sound Of Freedom** .... [M] Whoopi Goldberg/Leleti Khumalo/**Miriam Makeba**/John Kani; cp: Mbongeni Ngema and **Hugh Masekela**	Qwest 45060
				Saturday Night Fever — see BEE GEES John Travolta/Karen Gorney/Donna Pescow/Barry Miller/Sal Bisoglio	
1/13/01	**3**⁵	46	▲²	1087 **Save The Last Dance** .... [V] Julia Stiles/Sean Patrick Thomas/**Fredro Starr**	Hollywood 62288
7/7/01	**129**	8		1088 **Save The Last Dance, More** .... [V]	Hollywood 62323
5/6/89	**62**	14		1089 **Say Anything...** .... [V] John Cusack/Ione Skye/John Mahoney/Lili Taylor/Eric Stoltz	WTG 45140
				Scandalous John — see McKUEN, Rod Brian Keith/Michele Carey/Rick Lenz/Harry Morgan	
1/28/84	**203**	3		1091 **Scarface** .... [V] Al Pacino/Steven Bauer/Michelle Pfeiffer/Mary Elizabeth Mastrantonio	MCA 6126
4/9/94	**45**	7	●	1092 **Schindler's List** .... [I] *Grammy: Soundtrack Album* Liam Neeson/Ben Kingsley/Ralph Fiennes/Caroline Goodall; cp/cd: **John Williams**	MCA 10969
3/19/88	**81**	17		1093 **School Daze** .... [V] Laurence Fishburne/Giancarlo Esposito/Tisha Campbell/Spike Lee	EMI-Manhattan 48680
10/18/03	**95**	12		1094 **School Of Rock** .... [V] Jack Black/Joan Cusack/Mike White/Sarah Silverman/Adam Pascal	Atlantic 83694
6/22/02	**28**	14		1095 **Scooby-Doo** .... [V] Freddie Prinze, Jr./Sarah Michelle Gellar/Matthew Lillard/Linda Cardellini/Rowan Atkinson	Lava 83543
4/10/04	**107**	4		1096 **Scooby-Doo 2: Monsters Unleashed** .... [V] Freddie Prinze Jr./Sarah Michelle Gellar/Matthew Lillard/Linda Cardellini/Seth Green	Warner Sunset 48684
4/13/02	**5**	19	●	1097 **Scorpion King, The** .... [V] Dwayne "The Rock" Johnson/Michael Clarke Duncan/Kelly Hu/Bernard Hill/Grant Heslov	Universal 017115
12/20/97+	**50**	10	●	1098 **Scream 2** .... [V] David Arquette/Neve Campbell/Courteney Cox/Sarah Michelle Gellar/Laurie Metcalf	Capitol 21911
2/12/00	**32**	14	●	1099 **Scream 3** .... [V] David Arquette/Neve Campbell/Courtney Cox/Patrick Dempsey	Wind-Up 13056
12/26/70+	**95**	8		1100 **Scrooge** .... [X-M] **Albert Finney**/Alec Guinness/Edith Evans; sw: Leslie Bricusse; cd: Ian Fraser; Christmas chart: 13/'70	Columbia 30258
12/3/88+	**93**	9		1101 **Scrooged** .... [X-V] Bill Murray/Karen Allen/John Forsythe/Bobcat Goldthwait/Carol Kane	A&M 3921
6/13/87	**131**	8		1102 **Secret Of My Success, The** .... [V] Michael J. Fox/Helen Slater/Richard Jordan/Margaret Whitton	MCA 6205
				Selena — see SELENA Jennifer Lopez/Jacob Vargas/Jon Seda/Lupe Ontiveros	
				Serenade — see LANZA, Mario Mario Lanza/Joan Fontaine/Vincent Price/**Vincent Edwards**	
10/20/01	**111**	5		1105 **Serendipity** .... [V] John Cusack/Kate Beckinsale/Jeremy Piven/Molly Shannon/Eugene Levy	Miramax 61583
10/12/96	**4**	38	▲	1106 **Set It Off** .... [V] Jada Pinkett/**Queen Latifah**/Vivica A. Fox/Kimberly Elise	EastWest 61951

Billboard			R I A A	ARTIST		
DEBUT	PEAK	WKS		Album Title.. Catalog		Label & Number
				Seven Brides For Seven Brothers — see "Those Glorious MGM Musicals"		
				Howard Keel/Jeff Richards/Russ Tamblyn/Jane Powell/Julie Newmar		
				Seven Hills Of Rome — see LANZA, Mario		
				Mario Lanza/Renato Roscel/Marisa Allasio		
5/9/09	179	1		1109 17 Again... [V]		New Line 39144
				Zac Efron/Leslie Mann/Thomas Lennon/Matthew Perry		
12/30/72+	163	11		1110 1776.. [M]		Columbia 31741
				William Daniels/Howard DaSilva/Ken Howard/David Ford/Blythe Danner; sw: Sherman Edwards		
10/17/64	148	3		1111 7th Dawn, The.. [I]		United Artists 5115
				William Holden/Susannah York/Capucine; cp/cd: Riz Ortolani		
6/14/08	2[1]	17		1112 Sex And The City... [V]		New Line 39114
				Sarah Jessica Parker/Kim Cattrall/Kristin Davis/Chris Noth/**Jennifer Hudson**		
10/11/08	45	2		1113 Sex And The City: Volume 2.. [V]		New Line 39119
				Sarah Jessica Parker/Kim Cattrall/Kristin Davis/Chris Noth		
8/12/78	5	28	▲	1114 Sgt. Pepper's Lonely Hearts Club Band.................... [M]		RSO 4100 [2]
				Peter Frampton/Bee Gees/George Burns/Steve Martin; sw: **John Lennon** and **Paul McCartney**		
				Shaft — see HAYES, Isaac		
				Richard Roundtree/Moses Gunn/Gwenn Mitchell		
7/1/00	22	12	●	1116 Shaft.. [V]		LaFace 26080
				Samuel L. Jackson/**Vanessa Williams**/Jeffrey Wright/Christian Bale		
7/21/73	147	9		1117 Shaft In Africa.. [I]		ABC 793
				Richard Roundtree/Vonetta McGee/Frank Finlay; cp/cd: Johnny Pate		
8/26/72	100	16		1118 Shaft's Big Score!.. [I]		MGM 36
				Richard Roundtree/Moses Gunn/Joe Santos; cp: Gordon Parks; cd: Dick Hazard		
10/30/04	116	11		1119 Shall We Dance?.. [V]		Casablanca 003494
				Richard Gere/**Jennifer Lopez**/Susan Sarandon/Stanley Tucci/Lisa Ann Walter		
10/9/04	31	18		1120 Shark Tale... [V]		DreamWorks 003468
				animated movie, voices by: **Will Smith**/Robert DeNiro/Renée Zellweger/Jack Black/Angelina Jolie		
1/23/82	171	8		1121 Sharky's Machine.. [V]		Warner 3653
				Burt Reynolds/Rachel Ward/Bernie Casey/Brian Keith		
3/12/88	92	8		1122 She's Having A Baby.. [V]		I.R.S. 6211
				Kevin Bacon/Elizabeth McGovern/Alec Baldwin/Dennis Dugan		
				She's The One — see PETTY, Tom, And The Heartbreakers		
				Jennifer Aniston/Maxine Bahns/Edward Burns/Cameron Diaz		
10/9/65	147	2		1124 Shenandoah... [I]		Decca 79125
				James Stewart/Patrick Wayne/Doug McClure; cp: Frank Skinner; cd: Joseph Gershenson		
1/18/97	59	15		1125 Shine.. [I]		Philips 454710
				Armin Mueller-Stahl/Noah Taylor/Geoffrey Rush/Lynn Redgrave; cp: David Hirschfelder; cd: Ricky Edwards; pf: **David Helfgott**		
11/18/89	97	12		1126 Shocker... [V]		SBK 93233
				Michael Murphy/Peter Berg/Cami Cooper/Mitch Pileggi		
9/2/95	4	21	●	1127 Show, The.. [L-V]		Def Jam 529021
				concert movie/documentary		
				Show Boat — see "Those Glorious MGM Musicals"		
				Kathryn Grayson/Howard Keel/Ava Gardner/Joe E. Brown		
6/2/01	28	84	▲[2]	1129 Shrek... Cat:#29/15 [V]		DreamWorks 450305
				animated movie, voices by Mike Myers/Cameron Diaz/John Lithgow/**Eddie Murphy**		
5/29/04	8	41	●	1130 Shrek 2.. [V]		Geffen 002557
				animated movie, voices by: Mike Myers/Cameron Diaz/**Eddie Murphy**/Antonio Banderas/**Julie Andrews**		
6/2/07	34	6		1131 Shrek The Third.. [V]		Geffen 008898
				animated movie, voices by: Mike Myers/Cameron Diaz/**Eddie Murphy**/Anotnio Banderas/**Julie Andrews**		
				Silencers, The — see MARTIN, Dean		
				Dean Martin/Stella Stevens/Daliah Lavi/**Victor Buono**		
8/11/07	108	3		1133 Simpsons Movie, The.. [M]		Extreme 40088
				animated movie, voices by: Dan Castellaneta/Julie Kavner/Nancy Cartwright/Yeardley Smith/Hank Azaria/Harry Shearer		
4/29/89	196	1		1134 Sing... [V]		Columbia 45086
				Lorraine Bracco/Peter Dobson/Jessica Steen/Louise Lasser		
				Sing Boy Sing — see SANDS, Tommy		
				Tommy Sands/Lili Gentle/Edmond O'Brien		
				Singin' In The Rain — see "Those Glorious MGM Musicals"		
				Gene Kelly/Donald O'Connor/**Debbie Reynolds**		
				Singing Nun, The — see REYNOLDS, Debbie		
				Debbie Reynolds/Ricardo Montalban/Greer Garson		
7/18/92	6	69	▲[2]	1138 Singles... [V]		Epic 52476
				Matt Dillon/Bridget Fonda/Campbell Scott/Kyra Sedgwick		
6/27/92	40	54	●	1139 Sister Act.. [V]		Hollywood 61334
				Whoopi Goldberg/Maggie Smith/Mary Wickes/Kathy Najimi/Harvey Keitel		
12/25/93+	74	14	●	1140 Sister Act 2: Back In The Habit.................................... [V]		Hollywood 61562
				Whoopi Goldberg/Kathy Najimy/James Coburn/Maggie Smith/Mary Wickes		
6/25/05	164	2		1141 Sisterhood Of The Traveling Pants, The...................... [V]		Columbia 94606
				Amber Tamblyn/Alexis Bledel/America Ferrera/Nancy Travis		
				Slade In Flame — see SLADE		
10/31/98	84	3		1143 Slam... [V]		Immortal 69587
				Saul Williams/Sonja Sohn/Bonz Malone/Beau Sia/Lawrence Wilson		
				Slaughter's Big Rip-Off — see BROWN, James		
				Jim Brown/Brock Peters/Ed McMahon/Art Metrano/Don Stroud		
7/10/93	❶[1]	79	▲[4]	1145 Sleepless In Seattle.......................... Cat:#18/6 [V]		Epic Soundtrax 53764
				Tom Hanks/Meg Ryan/**Rosie O'Donnell**/Bill Pullman/Rob Reiner		
6/19/93	23	23	●	1146 Sliver.. [V]		Virgin 88064
				Sharon Stone/William Baldwin/Tom Berenger/Martin Landau		

Billboard			R I A A	ARTIST		
DEBUT	PEAK	WKS		Album Title.. Catalog		Label & Number
1/10/09	4	29		1147 **Slumdog Millionaire** [V] *Grammy: Soundtrack Album* Dev Patel/Freida Pinto/Madhur Mittal/Anil Kapoor		Interscope 012502
7/25/98	103	5		1148 Small Soldiers [O-V] Kirsten Dunst/Gregory Smith/Jay Mohr/Phil Hartman/**Denis Leary**		DreamWorks 50051
9/24/77	202	10		1149 Smokey And The Bandit .... [I+V] Burt Reynolds/Sally Field/Jackie Gleason/**Jerry Reed**; mu: Bill Justis and **Jerry Reed**		MCA 2099
9/6/80	103	11		1150 Smokey And The Bandit 2 [V] Burt Reynolds/Sally Field/**Jackie Gleason/Jerry Reed**		MCA 6101
9/2/06	43	4		1151 Snakes On A Plane [V] Samuel L. Jackson/Juliana Margulies/Nathan Phillips/Keenan Thompson		Decaydance 39069
2/10/01	143	4		1152 Snatch.. [V] Benicio Del Toro/Dennis Farina/Brad Pitt/Vinnie Jones		TVT Soundtrax 6950
3/4/00	183	2		1153 Snow Day [V] Chris Elliott/Mark Webber/Jean Smart/**Chevy Chase**		Geffen 490598
8/14/93	88	7		1154 So I Married An Axe Murderer [V] Mike Myers/Nancy Travis/Anthony LaPaglia/Amanda Plummer/Brenda Fricker		Chaos 57303
				Some Kind Of Monster — see METALLICA		
3/21/87	57	13		1156 Some Kind Of Wonderful [V] Lea Thompson/Eric Stoltz/Mary Stuart Masterson/Craig Sheffer		MCA 6200
1/17/04	132	9		1157 Something's Gotta Give.. [V] Jack Nicholson/Diane Keaton/Keanu Reeves/Frances McDormand/Amanda Peet		Columbia 90911
12/6/80	187	2	▲	1158 Somewhere In Time [I] Christopher Reeve/Jane Seymour/Teresa Wright; cp/cd: John Barry		MCA 5154
				Son Of Dracula — see NILSSON Nilsson/Ringo Starr/Rosanna Lee		
1/23/71	95	8		1160 Song Of Norway .... [M] Florence Henderson/Toralv Maurstad/Edward G. Robinson; cp: Edvard Grieg		ABC 14
				Song Remains The Same, The — see LED ZEPPELIN **SongWriter — see KRISTOFFERSON, Kris / NELSON, Willie** Willie Nelson/**Kris Kristofferson**/Melinda Dillon		
				Sorcerer — see TANGERINE DREAM Roy Scheider/Bruno Cremer/Francisco Rabal		
10/4/97	4	35	▲²	1164 **Soul Food** [V] Vanessa Williams/Vivica A. Fox/Nia Long/Mekhi Phifer		LaFace 26041
10/4/97	73	3		1165 Soul In The Hole [L-V] concert movie/documentary		Loud 67531
11/15/86	138	9		1166 Soul Man... [V] C. Thomas Howell/Rae Dawn Chong/Arye Gross/James Sikking		A&M 3903
9/25/71	112	10		1167 Soul To Soul .... [L-V] concert movie shot in Ghana, West Africa		Atlantic 7207
3/20/65	❶²	233	●	1168 **Sound Of Music, The** [M] *Grammy: Hall of Fame* Julie Andrews/Christopher Plummer/Eleanor Parker; mu: Richard Rodgers; ly: Oscar Hammerstein II; cd: Irwin Kostal		RCA Victor 2005
6/12/82	168	12		1169 Soup For One .... [V] Saul Rubinek/Marcia Strassman/Gerrit Graham; sw: Bernard Edwards and Nile Rodgers (**Chic**)		Mirage 19353
3/31/58	❶³¹	262	●	1170 **South Pacific** [M] Rossano Brazzi/Mitzi Gaynor/John Kerr; mu: Richard Rodgers; ly: Oscar Hammerstein II; cd: Alfred Newman		RCA Victor 1032
7/10/99	28	11	●	1171 South Park: Bigger, Longer & Uncut .... [M] animated movie, voices by: Trey Parker/Matt Stone/Mary Kay Bergman/**Isaac Hayes**		Atlantic 83199
11/30/96+	2¹	82	▲⁶	1172 **Space Jam** [V] Michael Jordan/Bill Murray/Wayne Knight		Warner Sunset 82961
				Sparkle — see FRANKLIN, Aretha Irene Cara/Philip Michael Thomas/Lonette McKee		
8/16/97	7	25	●	1174 **Spawn** [V] John Leguizamo/Michael Jai White/Martin Sheen/Theresa Randle		Immortal 68494
10/29/94	176	1		1175 Specialist, The [V] Sylvester Stallone/Sharon Stone/James Woods/Rod Steiger/Eric Roberts		Crescent Moon 66384
				Speedway — see PRESLEY, Elvis Elvis Presley ("Steve Grayson")/**Nancy Sinatra**/Bill Bixby/Gale Gordon		
				Spiceworld — see SPICE GIRLS		
5/18/02	4	35	▲	1178 Spider-Man [V] Tobey Maguire/Willem Dafoe/Kirsten Dunst/James Franco/Cliff Robertson		Roadrunner 86402
7/10/04	7	20	●	1179 Spider-Man 2 [V] Tobey Maguire/Kirsten Dunst/James Franco/Alfred Molina/Rosemary Harris		Columbia 92628
5/19/07	33	4		1180 Spider-Man 3 .... [V] Tobey Maguire/Kirsten Dunst/James Franco/Topher Grace/Thomas Hayden Church		Record Collection 105788
				Spinout — see PRESLEY, Elvis Elvis Presley ("Mike McCoy")/**Shelley Fabares**/Diane McBain		
6/8/02	40	24	●	1182 Spirit: Stallion Of The Cimarron .... [M] animated movie, music by: **Bryan Adams** and Hans Zimmer		A&M 493304
11/27/04	76	14		1183 SpongeBob SquarePants Movie, The................................ [V] animated movie, voices by: Tom Kenny/Clancy Brown/Bill Fagerbakke/Alec Baldwin/Jeffrey Tambor		Nick 48888
5/17/97	89	10		1184 Sprung [V] Tisha Campbell/Rusty Cundieff/Paula Jai Parker/Joe Torry		Qwest 46541
8/27/77	40	16		1185 Spy Who Loved Me, The... [I] Roger Moore/Barbara Bach/Richard Kiel/Curt Jurgens; cp/cd: **Marvin Hamlisch**		United Artists 774
7/13/85	21	37	●	1186 St. Elmo's Fire [V] Emilio Estevez/Rob Lowe/Andrew McCarthy/Demi Moore/Judd Nelson		Atlantic 81261

Billboard DEBUT	PEAK	WKS	R I A A	ARTIST Album Title .... Catalog	Label & Number
				St. Louis Blues — see COLE, Nat "King"	
				Nat "King" Cole/Eartha Kitt/Pearl Bailey/Cab Calloway	
9/20/86	31	45	● 1188	**Stand By Me** .... [O-V]	Atlantic 81677
				Wil Wheaton/River Phoenix/Corey Feldman/Jerry O'Connell/Richard Dreyfuss	
10/26/68+	98	20	1189	**Star!** .... [M]	20th Century Fox 5102
				Julie Andrews/Richard Crenna/Michael Craig/Robert Reed	
				Star Is Born, A — see STREISAND, Barbra	
				Barbra Streisand/Kris Kristofferson/Gary Busey/Oliver Clark	
1/5/80	50	11	● 1191	**Star Trek - The Motion Picture** .... [I]	Columbia 36334
				William Shatner/Leonard Nimoy/DeForest Kelley/James Doohan/Persis Khambatta; cp/cd: Jerry Goldsmith	
7/17/82	61	9	1192	**Star Trek II - The Wrath Of Khan** .... [I]	Atlantic 19363
				William Shatner/Leonard Nimoy/Ricardo Montalban/DeForest Kelley; cp/cd: James Horner	
6/23/84	82	8	1193	**Star Trek III - The Search For Spock** .... [I]	Capitol 12360
				William Shatner/DeForest Kelley/Christopher Lloyd; cp/cd: James Horner; includes bonus 12" single "The Search For Spock"	
1/4/92	171	1	1194	**Star Trek VI - The Undiscovered Country** .... [I]	MCA 10512
				William Shatner/Leonard Nimoy/DeForest Kelley/James Doohan; Kim Cattrall; cp/cd: Cliff Eidelman	
5/23/09	49	5	1195	**Star Trek** .... [I]	Varese 066966
				Chris Pine/Zachary Quinto/Eric Bana/Leonard Nimoy/Winona Ryder; cp/cd: Michael Giacchino	
6/18/77	2³	53	▲ 1196	**Star Wars** [I]	20th Century 541 [2]
				Grammys: Soundtrack Album / Pop Instrumental ★ *NRR*	
				Mark Hamill/Harrison Ford/Carrie Fisher/Alec Guinness; cp/cd: **John Williams**	
12/17/77+	36	10	● 1197	**Star Wars, The Story Of** .... [T]	20th Century 550
				storyline excerpts from the movie (no track titles listed); narrator: Roscoe Lee Browne	
2/1/97	49	11	● 1198	**Star Wars: A New Hope** .... [I-R]	RCA Victor 68746 [2]
				complete score in sequence with previously unreleased music issued in conjunction with the 20th anniversary release of the *Star Wars* Special Edition movie in theaters	
5/22/99	3¹	16	▲ 1199	**Star Wars Episode I - The Phantom Menace** [I]	Sony Classical 61816
				Liam Neeson/Ewan McGregor/Natalie Portman/Jake Lloyd/Samuel L. Jackson; cp/cd: **John Williams**	
5/11/02	6	11	● 1200	**Star Wars Episode II: Attack Of The Clones** [I]	Sony Classical 89932
				Ewan McGregor/Natalie Portman/Hayden Christensen/Samuel L. Jackson/Christopher Lee; cp/cd: **John Williams**	
5/21/05	6	12	1201	**Star Wars Episode III: Revenge Of The Sith** [I]	Sony Classical 94220
				Hayden Christensen/Natalie Portman/Ewan McGregor/Ian McDiarmid; cp/cd: **John Williams**	
8/30/08	142	1	1202	**Star Wars: The Clone Wars** .... [I]	Sony Classical 35616
				animated movie, voices by: Matt Lanter/Christopher Lee/Samuel L. Jackson/Anthony Daniels; cp/cd: Kevin Kiner	
4/26/75	206	3	1203	**Stardust** .... [O-V]	Arista 5000 [2]
				David Essex/Adam Faith/Larry Hagman/**Keith Moon**	
3/27/04	175	2	1204	**Starsky & Hutch** .... [O-V]	TVT 6700
				Ben Stiller/Owen Wilson/**Snoop Dogg**/Vince Vaughn/Juliette Lewis	
5/12/62	12	19	1205	**State Fair** .... [M]	Dot 29011
				Pat Boone/Ann-Margret/Bobby Darin; mu: Richard Rogers; ly: Oscar Hammerstein II; cd: Alfred Newman	
2/16/02	14	12	1206	**State Property** .... [V]	Roc-A-Fella 586671
				Beanie Sigel/Memphis Bleek/Jay-Z/Omillio Sparks	
				Staying Alive — see BEE GEES	
				John Travolta/Cynthia Rhodes (**Animotion**)/Sarah Miles/Julie Bovasso	
9/6/97	185	1	1208	**Steel** .... [V]	Qwest 46678
				Shaquille O'Neal/Annabeth Gish/Richard Roundtree/Judd Nelson	
8/26/06	6	18	1209	**Step Up** [V]	Jive 88063
				Channing Tatum/Jenna Dewan/Drew Sidora/Rachel Griffiths/**Heavy D**	
2/23/08	5	19	1210	**Step Up 2: The Streets** [V]	Atlantic 409212
				Briana Evigan/Robert Hoffman/Will Kemp/Cassie Ventura	
6/6/70	200	2	1211	**Sterile Cuckoo, The** .... [I]	Paramount 5009
				Liza Minnelli/Wendell Burton/Tim McIntire; cp/cd: Fred Karlin	
				Sting, The — see HAMLISCH, Marvin	
				Paul Newman/Robert Redford/Robert Shaw/Charles Durning/Ray Walston	
				Stop Making Sense — see TALKING HEADS	
				Storytelling — see BELLE AND SEBASTIAN	
				Selma Blair/Leo Fitzpatrick/Paul Giamatti	
				Straight Talk — see PARTON, Dolly	
				Dolly Parton/James Woods/Griffin Dunne/Michael Madsen	
11/4/95	135	1	1216	**Strange Days** .... [V]	Lightstorm 67226
				Ralph Fiennes/Angela Bassett/Juliette Lewis/Tom Sizemore	
10/17/98	185	1	1217	**Strangeland** .... [V]	TVT Soundtrax 8270
				Dee Snider (**Twisted Sister**)/Elizabeth Pena/Kevin Gage/Robert Englund	
9/12/70	91	9	1218	**Strawberry Statement, The** .... [V]	MGM 14 [2]
				Bruce Davison/Kim Darby/James Coco	
1/14/95	135	4	1219	**Street Fighter** .... [V]	Priority 53948
				Jean-Claude Van Damme/Raul Julia/**Kylie Minogue**	
5/30/98	27	12	1220	**Streets Is Watching** .... [V]	Roc-A-Fella 558132
				Jay-Z/Dame Dash/Kareem Burke	
6/16/84	32	21	1221	**Streets Of Fire** .... [V]	MCA 5492
				Michael Pare/Diane Lane/Rick Moranis/Amy Madigan	
7/20/96	152	2	1222	**Striptease** .... [O-V]	EMI 52498
				Demi Moore/Armand Assante/Ving Rhames/Robert Patrick/Burt Reynolds	
8/10/02	122	3	1223	**Stuart Little 2** .... [V]	Epic 86719
				Geena Davis/Hugh Laurie; voices by: Michael J. Fox/Nathan Lane/James Woods	
4/27/96	90	5	1224	**Substitute, The** .... [V]	Priority 50576
				Tom Berenger/Ernie Hudson/Diane Venora/Glenn Plummer/**Marc Anthony**	
3/19/94	169	3	1225	**Sugar Hill** .... [V]	Beacon 11016
				Wesley Snipes/Michael Wright/Theresa Randle/Clarence Williams III	

DEBUT	PEAK	WKS	R I A A	ARTIST Album Title.. Catalog	Label & Number
8/28/82	152	7		1226 **Summer Lovers** .... **[V]** Peter Gallagher/Daryl Hannah/Valerie Quennessen/Barbara Rush	Warner 23695
9/11/71	52	34		1227 **Summer Of '42** .... **[I]** Jennifer O'Neill/Gary Grimes/Jerry Houser; cp/cd: **Michel LeGrand**	Warner 1925
7/24/99	195	1		1228 **Summer Of Sam** .... **[O-V]** John Leguizamo/Adrien Brody/Mira Sorvino/Jennifer Esposito	Hollywood 62190
				Sunday In New York — see NERO, Peter Cliff Robertson/Rod Taylor/Jane Fonda/Robert Culp	
5/11/96	4	13	▲	1230 **Sunset Park** .... **[V]** Rhea Perlman/Carol Kane/**Fredro Starr**	Flavor Unit 61904
				Superfly — see MAYFIELD, Curtis Ron O'Neal/Carl Lee/Julius Harris	
				Super Fly T.N.T. — see OSIBISA Ron O'Neal/Roscoe Lee Browne/Sheila Frazier	
8/17/96	133	5		1233 **Supercop** .... **[V]** Jackie Chan/Michelle Khan/Maggie Cheung/Ken Tsang/Yuen Wah	Interscope 90088
1/13/79	44	13		1234 **Superman - The Movie** .... **[I]** *Grammy: Soundtrack Album* Christopher Reeve/Margot Kidder/Marlon Brando/Gene Hackman/Ned Beatty; cp/cd: **John Williams**	Warner 3257 [2]
7/4/81	133	9		1235 **Superman II** .... **[I]** Christopher Reeve/Margot Kidder/Gene Hackman/Jackie Cooper/Ned Beatty; cp/cd: Ken Thorne	Warner 3505
7/2/83	163	3		1236 **Superman III** .... **[I+V]** Christopher Reeve/**Richard Pryor**/Annette O'Toole; cp: **John Williams**/Ken Thorne/**Giorgio Moroder**	Warner 23879
7/15/06	110	2		1237 **Superman Returns** .... **[I]** Brandon Routh/Kate Bosworth/Frank Langella/Eva Marie Saint/**Kevin Spacey**; cp/cd: John Ottman	Warner 77654
1/5/08	16	24		1238 **Sweeney Todd: The Demon Barber Of Fleet Street** .... **[M]** Johnny Depp/Helena Bonham Carter/Alan Rickman/Sacha Baron Cohen	Nonesuch 368572
3/8/69	72	22		1239 **Sweet Charity** .... **[M]** Shirley MacLaine/**Sammy Davis Jr.**/Ricardo Montalban; mu: Cy Coleman; ly: Dorothy Fields	Decca 71502
				Sweet Dreams — see CLINE, Patsy Jessica Lange/Ed Harris/Ann Wedgeworth	
10/12/02	46	22		1241 **Sweet Home Alabama** .... **[V]** Reese Witherspoon/Patrick Dempsey/Fred Ward/Mary Kay Place/Candice Bergen	Hollywood 162364
2/24/01	66	11		1242 **Sweet November** .... **[V]** Keanu Reeves/Charlize Theron/Jason Isaacs/Frank Langella	Warner Sunset 47944
7/3/71	139	19		1243 **Sweet Sweetback's Baadasssss Song** .... **[I]** Melvin Van Peebles/Rhetta Hughes/John Amos; cp: Melvin Van Peebles	Stax 3001
8/16/97	168	9		1244 **Swingers** .... **[V]** Jon Favreau/Vince Vaughn/Ron Livingston/Patrick Van Horn	Hollywood 62091
				Swordfish — see OAKENFOLD, Paul John Travolta/Hugh Jackman/Halle Berry/Don Cheadle	
4/22/06	148	4		1246 **Take The Lead** .... **[V]** Antonio Banderas/Rob Brown/Alfre Woodard/Jenna Dewan	Universal 006372
7/11/81	210	1		1247 **Take This Job And Shove It!** .... **[V]** Robert Hays/Art Carney/Barbara Hershey/Eddie Albert/**Martin Mull**	Epic 37177
1/29/00	198	1		1248 **Talented Mr. Ripley, The** .... **[V]** Matt Damon/Gwyneth Paltrow/Jude Law/Cate Blanchett/Jack Davenport	Sony Classical 51337
5/27/95	16	11	●	1249 **Tales From The Hood** .... **[V]** Corbin Bernsen/David Alan Grier/Wings Hauser/Clarence Williams III	MCA Sound. 11243
4/15/95	72	10		1250 **Tank Girl** .... **[V]** Lori Petty/**Ice-T**/Naomi Watts/Malcolm McDowell	Elektra 61760
3/11/89	166	4		1251 **Tap** .... **[V]** Gregory Hines/Suzzanne Douglas/Joe Morton/**Sammy Davis Jr.**	Epic 45084
6/5/99	5	67	▲²	1252 **Tarzan** .... **[M]** *Grammy: Soundtrack Album* animated movie, voices by: Tony Goldwyn/Minnie Driver/Glenn Close/**Rosie O'Donnell**; sw: **Phil Collins**; cp: Mark Mancina	Walt Disney 60645
10/27/84	34	16	●	1253 **Teachers** .... **[V]** Nick Nolte/JoBeth Williams/Judd Hirsch/Ralph Macchio/Lee Grant	Capitol 12371
11/20/04	98	2		1254 **Team America: World Police** .... **[M]** animated movie, voices by: Trey Parker/Matt Stone	Atlantic 83759
4/21/90	13	24	▲	1255 **Teenage Mutant Ninja Turtles** .... **[V]** Judith Hoag/Elias Koteas/Ray Serra/Josh Pais	SBK 91066
4/13/91	30	22	●	1256 **Teenage Mutant Ninja Turtles II - The Secret Of The Ooze** .... **[V]** Paige Turco/David Warner/Ernie Reyes/Kenn Troum	SBK 96204
4/10/93	123	6		1257 **Teenage Mutant Ninja Turtles III** .... **[V]** Elias Koteas/Paige Turco/Vivian Wu/Sab Shimono/Stuart Wilson	SBK 89016
1/5/80	80	9		1258 **"10"** .... **[I]** Bo Derek/Dudley Moore/**Julie Andrews**/Robert Webber/Brian Dennehy; cp/cd: **Henry Mancini**	Warner 3399
4/24/99	52	27	●	1259 **10 Things I Hate About You** .... **[V]** Julia Stiles/Heath Ledger/Joseph Gordon-Levitt/Larisa Oleynik	Hollywood 62216
1/21/89	101	13		1260 **Tequila Sunrise** .... **[V]** Mel Gibson/Michelle Pfeiffer/Kurt Russell/Raul Julia/J.T. Walsh	Capitol 91185
8/31/91	70	6		1261 **Terminator 2: Judgment Day** .... **[I]** Arnold Schwarzenegger/Linda Hamilton/Robert Patrick/Edward Furlong; cp: Brad Fiedel	Varese Sarabande 5335
4/21/84	111	10		1262 **Terms Of Endearment** .... **[I+V]** Shirley MacLaine/Debra Winger/Jack Nicholson/Jeff Daniels/John Lithgow; cp: Michael Gore	Capitol 12329
5/13/78	10	27	▲	1263 **Thank God It's Friday** .... **[V]** Jeff Goldblum/Valerie Landsburg/Debra Winger; includes bonus 12" single	Casablanca 7099 [2]
10/12/96	21	30	●	1264 **That Thing You Do!** .... **[V]** Tom Hanks/Tom Everett Scott/Liv Tyler/Johnathon Schaech/Steve Zahn	Play-Tone 67828

Billboard DEBUT	PEAK	WKS	R I A A	ARTIST Album Title.. Catalog	Label & Number
6/22/74	128	14		1265 **That's Entertainment** .... [M] musical highlights from MGM's greatest musicals	MCA 11002 [2]
7/24/76	203	4		1266 **That's Entertainment, Part 2** .... [M] more musical highlights from MGM's greatest musicals	MGM 5301
				That's The Way Of The World — see EARTH, WIND & FIRE Harvey Keitel/Ed Nelson/Cynthia Bostwick/Bert Parks	
6/15/91	54	12		1268 **Thelma & Louise** .... [V] Susan Sarandon/Geena Davis/Harvey Keitel/Brad Pitt/Chris McDonald	MCA 10239
1/22/55	6	4		1269 **There's No Business Like Show Business** [M] Ethel Merman/Donald O'Connor/Dan Dailey/**Marilyn Monroe**; sw: Irving Berlin; LP: Decca DL-8091 (#6); EP: Decca ED-828 (#9)	Decca 8091
8/15/98	132	7		1270 **There's Something About Mary** .... [V] Cameron Diaz/Matt Dillon/Ben Stiller/Lee Evans/Chris Elliott	Capitol 95737
10/23/99	64	5		1271 **Thicker Than Water** .... [V] **Mack 10/Fat Joe/MC Eiht**/Kidada Jones/**Ice Cube**	Hoo Bangin' 50016 [2]
				Thief — see TANGERINE DREAM James Caan/Tuesday Weld/**Willie Nelson**	
12/22/84+	179	4		1273 **Thief Of Hearts**... [I+V] Steven Bauer/Barbara Williams/John Getz/George Wendt; cp/cd: Harold Faltermeyer	Casablanca 822942
3/2/96	22	18	●	1274 **Thin Line Between Love & Hate, A** .... [V] **Martin Lawrence**/Lynn Whitfield/Regina King/**Bobby Brown/Della Reese**	Jac-Mac 46134
5/8/04	41	17		1275 **13 Going On 30** .... [O-V] Jennifer Garner/Mark Ruffalo/Judy Greer/Andy Serkis	Hollywood 162454
12/8/07	53	6		1276 **This Christmas** .... Cat:#50/1 [X-V] Delroy Lindo/Loretta Devine/**Chris Brown**/Regina King; Christmas chart: 14/'07	Jive 19075
				This Is Elvis — see PRESLEY, Elvis **This Is Spinal Tap — see SPINAL TAP** Christopher Guest/Michael McKean/Harry Shearer	
8/31/68	182	6		1279 **Thomas Crown Affair, The** .... [I] Steve McQueen/Faye Dunaway/Paul Burke/Jack Weston; cp/cd: **Michel LeGrand**	United Artists 5182
4/15/67	16	48	●	1280 **Thoroughly Modern Millie** .... [M] **Julie Andrews**/Mary Tyler Moore/Carol Channing/John Gavin; cd: **Andre Previn**	Decca 71500
9/15/73	185	7		1281 **Those Glorious MGM Musicals: Singin' In The Rain/Easter Parade** .... [M]	MGM 40 [2]
9/8/73	211	5		1282 **Those Glorious MGM Musicals: Seven Brides For Seven Brothers/ Rose Marie** .... [M]	MGM 41 [2]
9/15/73	184	6		1283 **Those Glorious MGM Musicals: Show Boat/Annie Get Your Gun** .... [M]	MGM 42 [2]
9/22/73	212	3		1284 **Those Glorious MGM Musicals: Pirate/Pagan Love Song/ Hit The Deck** .... [M]	MGM 43 [2]
8/25/73	205	9		1285 **Those Glorious MGM Musicals: Band Wagon/Kiss Me Kate** .... [M]	MGM 44 [2]
9/1/73	221	1		1286 **Those Glorious MGM Musicals: Till The Clouds Roll By/ Three Little Words** .... [M]	MGM 45 [2]
3/24/07	52	9		1287 **300** .... [I] Gerard Butler/Lena Headey/David Wenham/Dominic West; cp/cd: Tyler Bates	Warner Sunset 101272
				Three Little Words — see "Those Glorious MGM Musicals" Fred Astaire/Red Skelton/Arlene Dahl/Keenan Wynn	
12/4/93+	101	14		1289 **Three Musketeers, The** .... [I] Charlie Sheen/Kiefer Sutherland/Chris O'Donnell/Oliver Platt; cp/cd: Michael Kamen	Hollywood 61581
3/18/00	190	1		1290 **3 Strikes**... [V] Brian Hooks/N'Bushe Wright/Faizon Love/David Alan Grier	Priority 50118
				Three The Hard Way — see IMPRESSIONS, The Jim Brown/Fred Williamson/Jim Kelly	
				Three Tough Guys — see HAYES, Isaac Isaac Hayes/Fred Williamson/Lino Ventura	
4/23/94	49	10		1293 **Threesome** .... [V] Lara Flynn Boyle/Stephen Baldwin/Josh Charles/Alexis Arquette	Epic Soundtrax 57881
12/11/65+	10	28		1294 **Thunderball** [I] Sean Connery/Claudine Auger/Adolfo Celi; cp/cd: John Barry	United Artists 5132
				Till The Clouds Roll By — see "Those Glorious MGM Musicals" June Allyson/**Judy Garland**/Lucille Bremer/Van Heflin	
				Time To Sing, A — see WILLIAMS, Hank Jr Hank Williams Jr./**Shelley Fabares**/Ed Begley	
9/27/80	37	17		1297 **Times Square** .... [V] Tim Curry/Trini Alvarado/Robin Johnson/Anna Maria Horsford	RSO 4203 [2]
9/7/96	82	6		1298 **Tin Cup** .... [V] Kevin Costner/Rene Russo/Cheech Marin (**Cheech & Chong**)/**Don Johnson**	Epic Soundtrax 67609
7/8/00	127	2		1299 **Titan A.E.** .... [V] animated movie, voices by Matt Damon/Bill Pullman/Nathan Lane/Janeane Garofalo	Java 25275
12/27/97+	**❶**[16]	71	▲[11]	1300 **Titanic** [I] Leonardo DiCaprio/Kate Winslet/Billy Zane/Gloria Stuart/Kathy Bates; cp/cd: James Horner	Sony Classical 63213
9/12/98	2[1]	23	▲	1301 **Titanic, Back To** [I] additional music from the movie *Titanic*	Sony Classical 60691
				To Live and Die in L.A. — see WANG CHUNG William L. Peterson/Willem Dafoe/John Turturro/Dean Stockwell	
9/23/67	16	22		1303 **To Sir, With Love** .... [I+V] Sidney Poitier/Judy Geeson/Christian Roberts/**Lulu**; cp/cd: Ron Grainer	Fontana 67569
9/23/95	108	4		1304 **To Wong Foo, Thanks For Everything! Julie Newmar** .... [V] Patrick Swayze/Wesley Snipes/John Leguzamo/Stockard Channing	MCA Sound. 11231
2/23/80	207	4		1305 **Together?** .... [V] Jacqueline Bisset/Maximilian Schell/Terence Stamp	RCA Victor 3541

DEBUT	PEAK	WKS	R I A A	ARTIST Album Title .... Catalog	Label & Number
				Together Brothers — see LOVE UNLIMITED ORCHESTRA Anthony Wilson/Ahmad Nurradin/Glynn Turman/Owen Pace	
3/21/64	38	23		1307 **Tom Jones** .... [I] *Grammy: Soundtrack Album* Albert Finney/Susannah York/Hugh Griffith/David Tomlinson; cp/cd: John Addison	United Artists 5113
9/8/73	214	2		1308 **Tom Sawyer** .... [M] Johnny Whitaker/Jodie Foster/Celeste Holm/Warren Oates	United Artists 057
3/29/75	2[1]	35	●	1309 **Tommy** [M] Roger Daltrey/**Ann-Margret**/Oliver Reed/**Elton John/Tina Turner**; sw: **Pete Townshend**	Polydor 9502 [2]
1/17/98	197	1		1310 **Tomorrow Never Dies** .... [I] Pierce Brosnan/Jonathan Pryce/Michelle Yeoh/Teri Hatcher; cp: David Arnold; cd: Nicholas Dodd	A&M 540830
2/26/83	144	12		1311 **Tootsie** .... [I] Dustin Hoffman/Jessica Lange/Charles Durning/Bill Murray/Sydney Pollack; cp/cd: **Dave Grusin**	Warner 23781
6/7/86	❶[5]	93	▲[9]	1312 **Top Gun** Cat:#8/176 [V] Tom Cruise/Kelly McGillis/Val Kilmer/Anthony Edwards/Tom Skerritt	Columbia 40323
1/9/65	150	2		1313 **Topkapi** .... [I] Melina Mercouri/Peter Ustinov/Maximilian Schell/Robert Morley; cp: Manos Hadjidakis	United Artists 5118
2/1/75	158	3		1314 **Towering Inferno, The** .... [I] Paul Newman/Steve McQueen/William Holden/Faye Dunaway/Fred Astaire; cp/cd: **John Williams**	Warner 2840
12/16/95+	94	10		1315 **Toy Story** .... [I] animated movie, voices by: Tom Hanks/Tim Allen/**Don Rickles**/Jim Varney/Wallace Shawn; cp/pf: **Randy Newman**	Walt Disney 60883
12/4/99	111	6		1316 **Toy Story 2** .... [I] animated movie, voices by: Tom Hanks/Tim Allen/Joan Cusack/Kelsey Grammer/**Don Rickles**; cp/pf: **Randy Newman**	Walt Disney 60647
1/16/93	161	4		1317 **Toys** .... [X-V] Robin Williams/Michael Gambon/Joan Cusack/**LL Cool J**	Geffen 24505
9/29/01	35	14		1318 **Training Day** .... [V] Denzel Washington/Ethan Hawke/Scott Glenn/**Snoop Dogg/Dr. Dre**	Priority 50213
8/10/96	48	26	●	1319 **Trainspotting** .... [V] Ewan McGregor/Ewen Bremner/Jonny Lee Miller/Kevin McKidd	Capitol 37190
7/21/07	21	13		1320 **Transformers** .... [V] Shia LeBeouf/Megan Fox/John Turturro/Josh Duhamel/**Tyrese**	Warner 220348
10/27/07	172	1		1321 **Transformers: The Score** .... [I] cp/cd: Steve Jablonsky	Warner 298812
7/11/09	7	17		1322 **Transformers: Revenge Of The Fallen** [V] Shia LeBeouf/Megan Fox/John Turturro/Josh Duhamel/**Tyrese**	Reprise 519264
7/11/09	49	3		1323 **Transformers: Revenge Of The Fallen: The Score** .... [I] cp/cd: Steve Jablonsky	Reprise 519972
12/12/92+	82	10		1324 **Trespass** .... [V] Bill Paxton/**Ice-T**/William Sadler/**Ice Cube**	Sire 26978
12/21/74+	130	8		1325 **Trial Of Billy Jack, The** .... [I+V] Tom Laughlin/Delores Taylor/Victor Izay; cp/cd: Elmer Bernstein	ABC 853
				Tribute To Jack Johnson, A — see DAVIS, Miles **Trick Or Treat — see FASTWAY** Marc Price/Tony Fields/**Gene Simmons**	
7/31/82	135	5		1328 **Tron** .... [I] Jeff Bridges/Bruce Boxleitner/David Warner/Barnard Hughes; cp: **Walter Carlos**; cd: Douglas Gamley	CBS 37782
				Trouble Man — see GAYE, Marvin Robert Hooks/Paul Winfield/Ralph Waite/Paula Kelly	
5/29/04	102	3		1330 **Troy** .... [I] Brad Pitt/Diane Kruger/Eric Bana/Orlando Bloom/Peter O'Toole; cp/cd: James Horner	Warner Sunset 48798
				Truck Turner — see HAYES, Isaac Isaac Hayes/Yaphet Kotto/Nichelle Nichols/Scatman Crothers	
8/2/69	77	12		1332 **True Grit** .... [I] **John Wayne**/Glen Campbell/Kim Darby/Robert Duvall; cp/cd: Elmer Bernstein	Capitol 263
				Tupac: Resurrection — see 2PAC	
11/22/08	❶[1]	80	▲[2]	1334 **Twilight** [V] Kristen Stewart/Robert Pattinson/Peter Facinelli/Ashley Greene	Summit 515923
12/13/08+	65	19		1335 **Twilight: The Score** .... [I] cp/cd: Carter Burwell	Atlantic 98732
10/31/09	❶[1]	31	▲	1336 **Twilight Saga: New Moon, The** [V] Kristen Stewart/Robert Pattinson/Taylor Lautner/Ashley Greene	Summit 519421
12/5/09	80	5		1337 **Twilight Saga: New Moon: The Score, The** .... [I] cp/cd: Alexandre Desplat	Summit 2075
7/23/83	210	1		1338 **Twilight Zone-The Movie** .... [I] Dan Aykroyd/**Albert Brooks**/Scatman Crothers/John Lithgow; cp/cd: Jerry Goldsmith	Warner 23887
9/19/92	173	1		1339 **Twin Peaks - Fire Walk With Me** .... [I] Sheryl Lee/Kyle MacLachlan/**David Bowie/Chris Isaak**; cp: Angelo Badalamenti/David Lynch	Warner 45019
1/21/89	162	12		1340 **Twins** .... [V] Arnold Schwarzenegger/Danny DeVito/Kelly Preston/Chloe Webb	WTG 45036
5/25/96	28	20	●	1341 **Twister** .... [V] Helen Hunt/Bill Paxton/Jami Gertz/Cary Elwes	Warner Sunset 46254
6/14/03	5	22	●	1342 **2 Fast 2 Furious** [V] Paul Walker/**Tyrese**/Eva Mendes/Cole Hauser/**Ludacris**	Def Jam 000426
				Two For The Road — see MANCINI, Henry Audrey Hepburn/**Albert Finney**/Eleanor Bron/William Daniels	
3/20/99	154	2		1344 **200 Cigarettes** .... [O-V] Ben Affleck/Dave Chappelle/**Courtney Love**/Jay Mohr/Christina Ricci	Mercury 538738
12/3/83+	26	20	▲	1345 **Two Of A Kind** .... [V] **John Travolta/Olivia Newton-John**/Charles Durning/Beatrice Straight/Scatman Crothers	MCA 6127

DEBUT	PEAK	WKS	R I A A	ARTIST Album Title .... Catalog	Label & Number
				200 Motels — see ZAPPA, Frank Frank Zappa/Ringo Starr/Theodore Bikel	
7/13/68	24	120	● 1347	**2001: A Space Odyssey** .... [I] Gary Lockwood/Keir Dullea/William Sylvester/Daniel Richter; features classical music by various orchestras	MGM 13
10/10/70	147	7	1348	**2001: A Space Odyssey (Volume Two)** .... [I]	MGM 4722
2/2/85	173	5	1349	**2010** .... [I] Roy Scheider/John Lithgow/Helen Mirren/Bob Balaban/Keir Dullea; cp: David Shire	A&M 5038
				UHF — see YANKOVIC, "Weird Al" "Weird Al" Yankovic/Kevin McCarthy/Michael Richards/Victoria Jackson	
				Under The Cherry Moon — see PRINCE Prince/Jerome Benton/Kristin Scott Thomas/Steven Berkoff	
6/22/02	125	2	1352	**Undercover Brother** .... [O-V] Eddie Griffin/Chris Kattan/Denise Richards/Dave Chappelle/Billy Dee Williams	Hollywood 162357
9/20/03	55	5	1353	**Underworld** .... [V] Kate Beckinsale/Scott Speedman/Michael Sheen/Shane Brolly/Erwin Leder	Lakeshore 33781
1/28/06	98	6	1354	**Underworld: Evolution** .... [V] Kate Beckinsale/Scott Speedman/Tony Curran/Derek Jacobi	Lakeshore 33846
1/31/09	141	3	1355	**Underworld: Rise Of The Lycans** .... [V] Michael Sheen/Bill Nighy/Kate Beckinsale/Rhona Mitra	Lakeshore 34055
9/7/02	101	2	1356	**Undisputed** .... [V] Wesley Snipes/Ving Rhames/Peter Falk/Michael Rooker/**Master P**	Cash Money 860990
7/18/64	11	33	1357	**Unsinkable Molly Brown, The** .... [M] **Debbie Reynolds**/Harve Presnell/Harvey Lembeck; sw: Meredith Willson; cd: Robert Armbruster	MGM 4232
2/1/92	114	9	1358	**Until The End Of The World** .... [V] William Hurt/Solveig Dommartin/Rudiger Vogler/Sam Neill	Warner 26707
				Up In Smoke — see CHEECH & CHONG Cheech Marin/Tommy Chong (**Cheech & Chong**)/Stacy Keach	
5/12/84	185	3	1360	**Up The Creek** .... [V] Tim Matheson/Jennifer Runyon/Dan Monahan/Stephen Furst	Pasha 39333
				Uptight — see BOOKER T. & THE MG'S Raymond St. Jacques/Ruby Dee/Frank Silvera	
5/17/80	3[2]	47	▲ 1362	**Urban Cowboy** .... [V] John Travolta/Debra Winger/Scott Glenn/Madolyn Smith/Barry Corbin	Asylum 90002 [2]
1/10/81	134	6	1363	**Urban Cowboy II** .... [V] more music from the original soundtrack	Full Moon 36921
2/17/01	101	3	1364	**Valentine** .... [V] David Boreanaz/Denise Richards/Marley Shelton/Jessica Capshaw	Warner Sunset 47943
				Valley, The — see PINK FLOYD Bulle Ogler/Jean-Pierre Kalfon	
3/12/94	155	5	1366	**Valley Girl** .... [V] Deborah Foreman/Nicholas Cage/Michael Bowen/Elizabeth Daily; selections from the original U.S. and British soundtracks, plus songs featured in the 1983 movie but not included on either album	Rhino 71590
2/3/68	11	27	1367	**Valley Of The Dolls** .... [M] Barbara Parkins/**Patty Duke**/Sharon Tate/Susan Hayward; sw: Dory Previn and **Andre Previn**; cd: **John Williams**	20th Century Fox 4196
1/5/02	109	7	1368	**Vanilla Sky** .... [V] Tom Cruise/Penelope Cruz/Kurt Russell/Jason Lee/Cameron Diaz	Reprise 48109
1/30/99	19	23	● 1369	**Varsity Blues** .... [V] James Van Der Beek/Jon Voight/Paul Walker/Ron Lester/Scott Caan	Hollywood 62177
6/5/82	174	4	1370	**Victor/Victoria** .... [M] **Julie Andrews**/James Garner/Robert Preston/Alex Karras; mu/cd: **Henry Mancini**; ly: Leslie Bricusse	MGM 5407
1/4/64	145	3	1371	**Victors, The** .... [I] George Peppard/George Hamilton/Eli Wallach; cp/cd: Sol Kaplan	Colpix 516
6/29/85	38	15	1372	**View To A Kill, A** .... [I] Roger Moore/Tanya Roberts/Christopher Walken/**Grace Jones**; cp/cd: John Barry	Capitol 12413
				Virgin Suicides, The — see AIR Kirsten Dunst/James Woods/Kathleen Turner/Scott Glenn	
3/2/85	11	23	▲ 1374	**Vision Quest** .... [V] Matthew Modine/Linda Fiorentino/Michael Schoeffling/Ronny Cox	Geffen 24063
12/2/95+	❶[5]	49	▲[7] 1375	**Waiting To Exhale** .... [V] **Whitney Houston**/Angela Bassett/Lela Rochon/Loretta Devine	Arista 18796
6/30/62	33	19	1376	**Walk On The Wild Side** .... [I] Laurence Harvey/**Jane Fonda**/Capucine/Anne Baxter/Barbara Stanwyck; cp/cd: Elmer Bernstein	Ava 4
12/3/05+	9	67	▲ 1377	**Walk The Line** .... [M] *Grammy: Soundtrack Album* Joaquin Phoenix/Reese Witherspoon/Robert Patrick/**Shelby Lynne**/**Shooter Jennings**	Fox 13109
2/2/02	34	47	▲ 1378	**Walk To Remember, A** .... Cat:#37/6 [V] Mandy Moore/Shane West/Peter Coyote/Daryl Hannah/Lauren German	Epic 86311
7/12/08	127	3	1379	**WALL-E** .... [I] animated movie, voices by: Ben Burtt/Elissa Knight/Jeff Garlin/Fred Willard; cp/cd: Thomas Newman	Pixar 001743
8/17/68	189	3	1380	**War And Peace** .... [I] Ludmilla Savelyeva/Vyacheslav Tikhonov/Sergei Bondarchuk; cp: Vyacheslav Ovchinnikov	Melodiya 2918
5/5/79	125	8	1381	**Warriors, The** .... [V] Michael Beck/Thomas Waites/James Remar/Deborah Van Valkenburg/Mercedes Ruehl	A&M 4761
11/24/01	19	8	● 1382	**Wash, The** .... [V] Snoop Dogg/**Dr. Dre**/Shaquille O'Neal/Tiny Lister/Pauly Shore	Aftermath 493128
3/21/09	30	5	1383	**Watchmen** .... [O-V] Malin Akerman/Billy Crudup/Matthew Goode/Jackie Earle Haley	Warner Sunset 516751
3/21/09	140	1	1384	**Watchmen: Score** .... [I] cp/cd: Tyler Bates	Warner Sunset 516750

Billboard DEBUT	PEAK	WKS	R I A A	ARTIST Album Title... Catalog	Label & Number
11/28/98	109	7		1385 Waterboy, The.. [V] Adam Sandler/Kathy Bates/Fairuza Balk/**Jerry Reed**/Henry Winkler	Hollywood 62157
2/17/73	28	17	●	1386 Wattstax: The Living Word... [L-V] live concert held in August 1972 in Los Angeles	Stax 3010 [2]
9/15/73	157	5		1387 Wattstaxx 2: The Living Word... [L-V] more songs from the concert	Stax 3018 [2]
2/16/74	20	15	●	1388 Way We Were, The.. [I] **Grammy: Soundtrack Album** Barbra Streisand/Robert Redford/Bradford Dillman/Sally Kirkland/James Woods; cp: **Marvin Hamlisch**	Columbia 32830
3/7/92	❶²	47	▲²	1389 Wayne's World.. [V] Mike Myers/Dana Carvey/Rob Lowe/Tia Carrere/Lara Flynn Boyle	Reprise 26805
1/1/94	78	9		1390 Wayne's World 2.. [V] Mike Myers/Dana Carvey/Tia Carrere/Christopher Walken/Chris Farley	Reprise 45485
3/23/02	126	3		1391 We Were Soldiers.. [V] Mel Gibson/Madeleine Stowe/Greg Kinnear/Sam Elliott/Barry Pepper	Columbia 86403
2/21/98	5	63	▲²	1392 Wedding Singer, The.. [O-V] Adam Sandler/Drew Barrymore/Christine Taylor/Allen Covert/Steve Buscemi	Maverick 46840
8/8/98	22	35	●	1393 Wedding Singer Volume 2, The.................................... [O-V]	Maverick 46984
8/31/85	105	11		1394 Weird Science.. [V] Anthony Michael Hall/Ilan Mitchell-Smith/Kelly LeBrock/Bill Paxton	MCA 6146
10/23/61+	❶⁵⁴	198	▲³	1395 West Side Story.. [M] **Grammys: Soundtrack Album / Hall of Fame** Natalie Wood/Richard Beymer/Rita Moreno/George Chakiris; mu: **Leonard Bernstein**; ly: Steephen Sondheim; cd: Johnny Green	Columbia 2070
4/19/03	106	8		1396 What A Girl Wants... [V] Amanda Bynes/Colin Firth/Eileen Atkins/Anna Chancellor/Jonathan Pryce	Atlantic 83641
				What Did You Do In The War, Daddy? — see MANCINI, Henry James Coburn/Dick Shawn/Aldo Ray/**Carroll O'Connor**	
12/30/00+	30	25	●	1398 What Women Want... [O-V] Mel Gibson/Helen Hunt/Marisa Tomei/Lauren Holly/Alan Alda	Columbia 61595
				What's Love Got To Do With It — see TURNER, Tina Angela Bassett/Laurence Fishburne/Jenifer Lewis/Khandi Alexander	
8/7/65	14	22		1400 What's New Pussycat?... [I+V] Peter Sellers/Peter O'Toole/Capucine/**Woody Allen**; mu: **Burt Bacharach**; ly: Hal David	United Artists 5117
6/16/01	38	10		1401 What's The Worst That Could Happen?.......................... [V] Martin Lawrence/Danny DeVito/John Leguizamo/Glenne Headly	NY.LA 493069
				What's Up, Tiger Lily? — see LOVIN' SPOONFUL Woody Allen/China Lee/Louise Lasser	
6/4/94	133	6		1403 When A Man Loves A Woman.. [I] Andy Garcia/Meg Ryan/Lauren Tom/Ellen Burstyn; cp/cd: Zbigniew Preisner	Hollywood 61606
				When Harry Met Sally — see CONNICK, Harry Jr. Billy Crystal/Meg Ryan/Carrie Fisher/Bruno Kirby	
				When The Boys Meet The Girls — see FRANCIS, Connie Connie Francis/Harve Presnell/**Herman's Hermits**	
6/7/80	208	2		1406 Where The Buffalo Roam.. [V] Bill Murray/Peter Boyle/Bruno Kirby/Rene Auberjonois	Backstreet 5126
5/13/00	126	6		1407 Where The Heart Is... [V] Natalie Portman/Ashley Judd/Stockard Channing/Joan Cusack	RCA 67963
				Where The Wild Things Are — see KAREN O AND THE KIDS Max Records/Catherine Keener/Mark Ruffalo/Steve Mouzakis	
10/17/09	113	3		1409 Whip It.. [O-V] Ellen Page/Marcia Gay Harden/Drew Barrymore/**Jimmy Fallon**	Fox 521759
4/11/92	92	8		1410 White Men Can't Jump... [V] Wesley Snipes/Woody Harrelson/Rosie Perez/Tyra Ferrell	EMI 98414
11/2/85+	17	26	●	1411 White Nights.. [V] Mikhail Baryshnikov/Gregory Hines/Geraldine Page/Helen Mirren	Atlantic 81273
				White Rock — see WAKEMAN, Rick	
8/7/99	145	3		1413 Whiteboys... [V] Danny Hoch/Dash Mihok/Mark Webber/Bonz Malone/**Snoop Dogg**	Offline 8310
9/3/66	119	5		1414 Who's Afraid Of Virginia Woolf?...................................... [I] Elizabeth Taylor/Richard Burton/**George Segal**/Sandy Dennis; cp/cd: Alex North	Warner 1656
				Who's That Girl — see MADONNA Madonna/Griffin Dunne/Haviland Morris/John McMartin	
5/8/93	32	8		1416 Who's The Man?... [V] Doctor Dre/Ed Lover/**Denis Leary**/Bill Bellamy/Ice-T	Uptown 10794
10/20/07	51	5		1417 Why Did I Get Married?... [V] Tyler Perry/**Janet Jackson**/Jill Scott/Malik Yoba	Atlantic 307772
9/26/98	55	4		1418 Why Do Fools Fall In Love... [V] Halle Berry/Vivica A. Fox/Lela Rochon/Larenz Tate/**Little Richard**	EastWest 62265
				Wild Angels, The — see ALLAN, Davie Peter Fonda/**Nancy Sinatra**/Bruce Dern/Dianne Ladd; cp/cd: **Mike Curb**	
10/18/69	192	2		1420 Wild Bunch, The... [I] William Holden/Ernest Borgnine/Robert Ryan/Warren Oates/Strother Martin; cp/cd: Jerry Fielding	Warner 1814
7/6/68	12	32		1421 Wild In The Streets.. [V] Christopher Jones/Diana Varsi/Shelley Winters/**Richard Pryor**; sw: Barry Mann/Cynthia Weil; cd: **Mike Curb**	Tower 5099
10/27/84	201	2		1422 Wild Life, The.. [V] Christopher Penn/Ilan Mitchell-Smith/Eric Stoltz/Lea Thompson	MCA 5523
1/18/03	167	4		1423 Wild Thornberrys Movie, The... [V] animated movie, voices by: Lacey Chabert/**Tim Curry**/Lynn Redgrave/Flea (**Red Hot Chili Peppers**)/Alfre Woodard	Nick/Jive 48503
7/3/99	4	18	▲²	1424 Wild Wild West.. [V] **Will Smith**/Kevin Kline/Kenneth Branagh/Salma Hayek/Ted Levine	Overbrook 90344

Billboard DEBUT	PEAK	WKS	R I A A	ARTIST Album Title.. Catalog	Label & Number
5/14/94	120	6		1425 **With Honors** .... **[V]** Joe Pesci/Brendan Fraser/Moira Kelly/Patrick Dempsey/Josh Hamilton	Maverick 45549
10/21/78	40	17	●	1426 **Wiz, The** .... **[M]** **Diana Ross/Michael Jackson/Lena Horne**/Nipsey Russell/**Richard Pryor**; sw: Charlie Smalls; cd: **Quincy Jones**	MCA 14000 [2]
				Woman in Red, The — see WONDER, Stevie Gene Wilder/Charles Grodin/Judith Ivey/**Gilda Radner**	
3/11/00	155	5		1428 **Wonder Boys** .... **[V]** Michael Douglas/Tobey Maguire/Frances McDormand/Katie Holmes	Columbia 63849
				Wonderwall — see HARRISON, George	
5/23/98	52	7		1430 **Woo** .... **[V]** Jada Pinkett Smith/Tommy Davidson/Dave Chappelle/**LL Cool J**	Untertainment 69364
7/31/99	16	23	●	1431 **Wood, The** .... **[V]** Taye Diggs/Omar Epps/Richard T. Jones/Sean Nelson	Jive 41686
6/6/70	❶[4]	68	▲[2]	1432 **Woodstock** **[L-V]** movie of historic rock festival near Woodstock, New York, on August 15-17, 1969	Cotillion 500 [3]
4/10/71	7	17	●	1433 **Woodstock Two** **[L-V]** more songs from the 1969 festival	Cotillion 400 [2]
7/11/09	10[C]	3		1434 **Woodstock: Music From The Original Soundtrack And More** **[L-S-R]**	Cotillion 518805 [2]
3/11/89	45	14		1435 **Working Girl** .... **[V]** Melanie Griffith/Harrison Ford/Sigourney Weaver/Joan Cusack/Alec Baldwin	Arista 8593
				Xanadu — see NEWTON-JOHN, Olivia / ELECTRIC LIGHT ORCHESTRA Olivia Newton-John/Michael Beck/Gene Kelly	
6/20/98	26	10	●	1437 **X-Files, The** .... **[V]** David Duchovny/Gillian Anderson/Martin Landau/Blythe Danner/Armin Mueller-Stahl	Elektra 62200
8/24/02	9	23	●	1438 **XXX** **[V]** Vin Diesel/Asia Argento/Marton Csokas/Samuel L. Jackson/Michael Roof	Universal 156259 [2]
5/14/05	117	1		1439 **XXX: State Of The Union** .... **[V]** Ice Cube/Samuel L. Jackson/Willem Defoe/**Xzibit**	Jive 67922
8/7/65	82	10		1440 **Yellow Rolls-Royce, The** .... **[I]** Ingrid Bergman/Rex Harrison/Shirley MacLaine/Omar Shariff; cp/cd: Riz Ortolani	MGM 4292
				Yellow Submarine — see BEATLES, The	
				Yentl — see STREISAND, Barbra Barbra Streisand/**Mandy Patinkin**/Amy Irving	
				Yes, Giorgio — see PAVAROTTI, Luciano **Luciano Pavarotti**/Kathryn Harrold/Eddie Albert	
				You Got Served — see B2K	
10/29/77	17	15	●	1445 **You Light Up My Life** .... **[I]** Didi Conn/Joe Silver/Melanie Mayron; cp/cd: Joseph Brooks	Arista 4159
7/15/67	27	26		1446 **You Only Live Twice** .... **[I]** Sean Connery/Donald Pleasence/Akiko Wakabayashi/Mie Hama; cp/cd: John Barry	United Artists 5155
				You're A Big Boy Now — see LOVIN' SPOONFUL Peter Kastner/Rip Torn/Geraldine Page/Julie Harris	
12/26/98+	44	20	●	1448 **You've Got Mail** .... **[O-V]** Tom Hanks/Meg Ryan/Parker Posey/Jean Stapleton/Dave Chappelle	Atlantic 83153
				Young At Heart — see DAY, Doris Doris Day/Frank Sinatra/Gig Young/Ethel Barrymore	
3/22/75	128	8		1450 **Young Frankenstein** .... **[T]** Gene Wilder/Peter Boyle/Marty Feldman/Teri Garr/Cloris Leachman	ABC 870
				Young Guns II — see BON JOVI Emilio Estevez/Kiefer Sutherland/Lou Diamond Phillips	
				Youngblood — also see WAR Lawrence Hilton-Jacobs/Bryan O'Dell/Ren Woods	
3/1/86	166	6		1453 **Youngblood** .... **[V]** Rob Lowe/Ed Lauter/Cynthia Gibb/Patrick Swayze	RCA Victor 7172
				Your Cheatin' Heart — see WILLIAMS, Hank Jr. George Hamilton/Susan Oliver/Red Buttons/Arthur O'Connell	
8/28/04	156	2		1455 **Yu-Gi-Oh!** .... **[V]** animated movie, voices by: Dan Green/Eric Stuart/Wayne Grayson/Tara Jayne	RCA 63950
4/11/70	128	8		1456 **Z** .... **[I]** Yves Montand/Irene Papas; cp: Mikis Theodorakis; cd: Bernard Gerard	Columbia 3370
				Ziggy Stardust — The Motion Picture — see BOWIE, David	
10/13/01	82	4		1458 **Zoolander** .... **[V]** Ben Stiller/Owen Wilson/Will Ferrell/Christine Taylor/Jerry Stiller	Hollywood 162324
5/1/65	26	79		1459 **Zorba The Greek** .... **[I]** Anthony Quinn/Irene Papas/Alan Bates; cp/cd: Mikis Theodorakis	20th Century Fox 4167

Billboard			R I A A	ARTIST
DEBUT	PEAK	WKS		Album Title.. Catalog	Label & Number

MOVIE SOUNDTRACK COMPILATIONS

DEBUT	PEAK	WKS			Label & Number
4/3/99	82	12	●	1 All Time Greatest Movie Songs, The	Sony 69879
2/8/69	198	2		2 Best Of The Soundtracks	Tower 5148
4/22/95	95	46	▲	3 Classic Disney Volume I - 60 Years Of Musical Magic .... Cat.#25/11	Walt Disney 60865
4/29/95	143	15	▲	4 Classic Disney Volume II - 60 Years Of Musical Magic	Walt Disney 60866
8/17/96	178	11	●	5 Classic Disney Volume III - 60 Years Of Musical Magic.....................	Walt Disney 60907
1/23/61	2[3]	81		6 Great Motion Picture Themes [I]	United Artists 3122
9/25/61	129	5		7 Great Motion Picture Themes (More Original Sound Tracks And Hit Music) .... [I]	United Artists 3158
12/28/96+	155	9		8 Movie Luv - The Ultimate Movie Soundtrack Collection........................	EMI-Capitol 54555
3/13/65	72	27		9 Music To Read James Bond By	United Artists 6415
5/19/62	31	16		10 Original Motion Picture Hit Themes	United Artists 3197

MOVIE-INSPIRED COMPILATIONS

DEBUT	PEAK	WKS			Label & Number
10/15/05	110	10		1 Chronicles Of Narnia: The Lion, The Witch And The Wardrobe, Music Inspired By The	Sparrow 11457
12/11/93+	124	13		2 More Songs For Sleepless Nights .... collection of songs inspired by the movie *Sleepless In Seattle*	Epic Soundtrax 57682
9/18/04	37	4		3 Passion Of The Christ: Songs, The	Lost Keyword 13105
4/24/04	59	5		4 Passion Of The Christ, Songs Inspired By The................................	Universal South 002320
12/5/98+	73	15	●	5 Prince Of Egypt - Inspirational, The	DreamWorks 50050
12/5/98+	85	11	●	6 Prince Of Egypt - Nashville, The...	DreamWorks 50045
3/18/95	23	23		7 Rhythm Of The Pride Lands .... collection of songs inspired by the movie *The Lion King*	Walt Disney 60871
10/19/91	160	12		8 Simply Mad About The Mouse .... collection of songs inspired by various Disney movies	Columbia 46019
11/12/88	119	15		9 Stay Awake: Various Interpretations Of Music From Vintage Disney Films	A&M 3918
2/17/96	65	11	●	10 West Side Story, The Songs Of...	RCA Victor 62707
4/5/75	84	10		11 Wolfman Jack/More American Graffiti	MCA 8007 [2]

MOVIE SING-A-LONGS

DEBUT	PEAK	WKS			Label & Number
1/16/99	187	1		1 Bug's Life Sing-Along, A	Walt Disney 60971
7/26/97	191	1		2 Hercules Sing-Along	Walt Disney 60925
7/6/96	180	4	●	3 Hunchback Of Norte Dame Sing-Along, The	Walt Disney 60894
7/2/94	40	53	▲	4 Lion King Sing-Along, The	Walt Disney 60857
12/21/96	160	3		5 101 Dalmatians Sing-Along	Walt Disney 60910
6/17/95	46	16	▲	6 Pocahontas Sing-Along	Walt Disney 60876
7/3/99	152	4		7 Tarzan Sing-Along...	Walt Disney 60991
1/18/97	151	1		8 Toy Story Sing-Along...	Walt Disney 60922
3/9/96	122	7	●	9 Winnie The Pooh Sing-Along	Walt Disney 60889

Billboard DEBUT	PEAK	WKS	R I A A	ARTIST Album Title.. Catalog	Label & Number

TELEVISION SOUNDTRACKS
The stars of the show are listed directly below the title.

11/20/71+	8	22	●	1 **All In The Family** [C]	Atlantic 7210
				Carroll O'Connor/Jean Stapleton/Rob Reiner/Sally Struthers; comedy excerpts from the show	
12/30/72+	129	8		2 **All In The Family - 2nd Album** .... [C]	Atlantic 7232
				more comedy excerpts from the show	
1/11/97	134	6		3 **All That** .... [V]	Loud 67423
				Keenan Thompson/Kel Mitchell/Amanda Bynes	
				Ally McBeal — see SHEPARD, Vonda	
				Calista Flockhart/Peter MacNicol/Lisa Nicole Carson/Jane Krakowski	
5/24/03	48	5		5 **American Dreams: 1963-1964**.................... [O-V]	Hip-O 000231
				Gail O'Grady/Tom Verica/Brittany Snow/Will Estes/Rachel Boston	
10/19/02	4	13	●	6 **American Idol: Greatest Moments** [L-V]	RCA 68141
5/17/03	2[1]	15	●	7 **American Idol Season 2: All-Time Classic American Love Songs** [L-V]	RCA 51169
11/1/03	28	11	●	8 **American Idol: The Great Holiday Classics** .... Cat:#17/6 [X-L-V]	RCA 55424
				Christmas charts: 2/'03, 17/'04	
5/15/04	10	10	●	9 **American Idol Season 3: Greatest Soul Classics** [V]	RCA 61775
6/4/05	6	12	●	10 **American Idol Season 4: The Showstoppers** [L-V]	RCA 68844
6/10/06	3[1]	13		11 **American Idol Season 5: Encores** [V]	RCA 85757
7/18/09	34	8		12 **American Idol: Season 8** [V]	19 Records 55516
8/22/09	17	6		13 **American Idol: Season 8: The 5 Song EP** .... [EP-V]	19 Records 70453
9/27/03	113	2		14 **American Juniors: Kids In America** [L-V]	19 Records 55973
11/27/99	175	1		15 **Annie** [M]	Sony Classical 89008
				Alicia Morton/Kathy Bates/Alan Cumming/Victor Garber	
1/20/01	22[X]	1		16 **Arthur's Perfect Christmas** .... [M]	Rounder 8097
				animated special, voices by: Michael Yarmush/Oliver Grainger/Melissa Altro	
2/9/08	140	3		17 **Backyardigans: Born To Play, The**.................... [M]	Nickelodeon 20878
				Sean Curley/LaShawn Jefferies/Johah Bobo/Naelee Kae	
9/18/93	9	47	▲[3]	18 **Barney's Favorites - Volume 1** Cat:#34/11 [M]	SBK 27114
				Bob West/Julie Johnson/Patty Wirtz/Brice Armstrong/Todd Duffey	
9/17/94	66	20	▲	19 **Barney's Favorites - Volume 2**.................... [M]	EMI 28338
11/29/97	150	5		20 **Barney: Happy Holidays Love, Barney** .... [X-M]	Barney 9517
4/23/66	112	8		21 **Batman** [I+T]	20th Century Fox 4180
				Adam West/Burt Ward; cd: **Nelson Riddle**; music and dialogue excerpts from the show	
10/21/78	144	6		22 **Battlestar Galactica** .... [I]	MCA 3051
				Lorne Greene/Richard Hatch/Dirk Benedict; cp/cd: Stu Phillips	
8/15/09	195	1		23 **Battlestar Galactica: Season 4** [I]	La-La Land 1100 [2]
				Edward James Olmos/Mary McDonnell/Jamie Bamber/James Callis	
6/17/89	157	10		24 **Beauty And The Beast / Of Love And Hope** .... [I+T]	Capitol 91583
				Linda Hamilton/Ron Perlman; cp/cd: Lee Holdridge; includes poetry readings by Perlman	
12/11/93	5	23	▲[2]	25 **Beavis & Butt-head Experience, The** Cat:#40/1 [V]	Geffen 24613
				animated series, voices by: Mike Judge/Tracy Grandstaff/Adam Welch	
				Ben Casey — see VALJEAN	
				Vincent Edwards/Sam Jaffe/Harry Landers/Jeanne Bates	
11/7/92+	76	34	●	27 **Beverly Hills, 90210 - The Soundtrack** [V]	Giant 24465
				Luke Perry/Jason Priestly/Shannon Doherty/Jennie Garth	
11/24/62+	49	9		28 **Bonanza** [M]	RCA Victor 2583
				Lorne Greene/Michael Landon/Dan Blocker/Pernell Roberts	
12/21/63+	15[X]	3		29 **Bonanza - Christmas on the Ponderosa** .... [X-M]	RCA Victor 2757
				Brady Bunch, The — see BRADY	
11/6/99	51	4		31 **Buffy The Vampire Slayer** [V]	TVT Soundtrax 8300
				Sarah Michelle Gellar/Seth Green/Nicholas Brendon/Alyson Hannigan	
10/12/02	49	5		32 **Buffy The Vampire Slayer: "Once More, With Feeling"**............ [M]	Mutant Enemy 619058
7/5/08	3[4]	36	▲	33 **Camp Rock** [M]	Walt Disney 001742
				Demi Lovato/Joe Jonas (**Jonas Brothers**)/Meaghan Martin/Alyson Stoner	
10/11/03	177	1		34 **Charmed** [V]	Private Music 52130
				Alyssa Milano/Holly Marie Combs/Rose McGowan/Brian Krause	
8/30/03+	33	63	▲[2]	35 **Cheetah Girls, The** Cat:#34/10 [M]	Walt Disney 860126
				Raven-Symone/Adrienne Bailon/Kiely Williams/Sabrina Bryan/Lynn Whitfield	
7/10/04	124	7		36 **Cheetah Girls: Special Edition, The** .... [M]	Walt Disney 861104
11/26/05	74	7		37 **Cheetah Girls: Cheetah-licious Christmas, The** .... Cat:#5/9 [X-M]	Walt Disney 861402
				Christmas charts: 15/'05, 5/'06, 45/'07, 32/'08	
9/2/06	5	32	▲	38 **Cheetah Girls 2, The** [M]	Walt Disney 861592
12/23/06	193	2		39 **Cheetah Girls 2: Disney's Karaoke Series, The**....................	Walt Disney 861633
12/12/98	16	21	▲	40 **Chef Aid: The South Park Album** .... [V]	American 69377
				animated show, voices by Trey Parker/Matt Stone/Mary Kay Bergman/**Isaac Hayes**	
12/22/90+	76	15	●	41 **Civil War, The** [I+V]	Elektra N. 79256
				from the documentary series produced by public television; pf: Jay Ungar/Jacquelyn Schwab/New American Brass Band	
12/13/08	74	2		42 **Colbert Christmas: The Greatest Gift Of All, A** .... [X-C]	Comedy Central 0073
				Grammy: Comedy Album	
				Christmas charts: 34/'08, 25/'09	
3/1/86	125	7		43 **Cosby Show, Music From The - A House Full Of Love** .... [I]	Columbia 40270
				Bill Cosby/Phylicia Rashad/Lisa Bonet/Malcolm-Jamal Warner; sw: **Bill Cosby** & Stu Gardner; pf: **Grover Washington, Jr.**	
5/9/81	136	13		44 **Cosmos, The Music Of** .... [I]	RCA Victor 4003
				selections from PBS television series hosted by Carl Sagan; cp/cd: various	
				Dallas — see CRAMER, Floyd	
				Larry Hagman/Victoria Principal/Patrick Duffy/Barbara Bel Geddes/Charlene Tilton	

Billboard			R I A A	ARTIST		
DEBUT	PEAK	WKS		Album Title.. Catalog	Label & Number

DEBUT	PEAK	WKS	RIAA	ARTIST / Album Title	Label & Number
8/2/69	**18**	19		46 **Dark Shadows** .... [I] Jonathan Frid/David Selby/Joan Bennett/Nancy Barrett/Lara Parker; cp/cd: Robert Cobert	Philips 314
5/15/99	**7**	17	●	47 **Dawson's Creek** [V] James Van Der Beek/Katie Holmes/Michelle Williams/Joshua Jackson/Kerr Smith	Columbia 69853
10/21/00	**59**	6		48 **Dawson's Creek Volume 2, Songs From** .... [V]	Columbia 85149
10/8/05	**93**	2		49 **Desperate Housewives** .... [V] Teri Hatcher/Felicity Huffman/Marcia Cross/Eva Longoria	Hollywood 162499
10/16/04	**133**	13	●	50 **Dora The Explorer** .... [M] animated series, voices by: Kathleen Herles/Harrison Chad/Marc Weiner/Sasha Toro	Nick 64435
10/29/05	**193**	1		51 **Dora The Explorer: Dance Fiesta!** .... [M]	Nick 71837
1/13/01	**36**ˣ	1		52 **Dr. Seuss' How The Grinch Stole Christmas! & Horton Hears A Who!**... [X-M] includes the original TV soundtracks for 2 Dr. Seuss classics: *How The Grinch Stole Christmas!* (narrated by Boris Karloff-1966) and *Horton Hears A Who!* (narrated by Hans Conreid-1969)	Rhino 75969
4/17/82	**93**	14		53 **Dukes Of Hazzard, The** .... [M] John Schneider/Tom Wopat/Sorrell Booke/James Best/Catherine Bach; includes songs and narration by cast members	Scotti Brothers 37712
				Fame — see KIDS FROM "FAME" Debbie Allen/Lee Curreri/Albert Hague	
5/14/05	**105**	1		55 **Family Guy: Live In Las Vegas** .... [M] animated series, voices by: Seth MacFarlane/Alex Borstein/Seth Green	Fox 004569
5/29/99	**97**	5		56 **Felicity** .... [V] Keri Russell/Scott Speedman/Amanda Foreman/Scott Foley	Hollywood 62228
6/8/02	**196**	1		57 **Felicity: Senior Year** .... [V]	Nettwerk 30263
				Flying Nun, The — see FIELD, Sally Sally Field/Alejandro Rey/Marge Redmond/Madeleine Sherwood	
10/14/95	**41**	29	▲	59 **Friends** .... [V] Jennifer Aniston/Courteney Cox/Lisa Kudrow/Matt LeBlanc/Matthew Perry/David Schwimmer	Reprise 46008
				Glee Cast — see MAIN ARTIST SECTION	
10/29/05+	**117**	10		61 **Grey's Anatomy** .... [V] Ellen Pompeo/Sandra Oh/Katherine Heigl/Patrick Dempsey/T.R. Knight	Hollywood 162557
9/30/06	**14**	25		62 **Grey's Anatomy: Volume 2** .... [V]	Hollywood 162630
9/29/07	**16**	5		63 **Grey's Anatomy: Volume 3**	Hollywood 000458
				Gypsy — see MIDLER, Bette Bette Midler/Peter Riegert/Cynthia Gibb/Edward Asner	
				Hannah Montana — see CYRUS, Miley Miley Cyrus/Billy Ray Cyrus]/Emily Osment]/Mitchel Musso	
11/3/07	**84**	17		66 **Hannah Montana: Disney's Karaoke Series**	Walt Disney 000491
5/23/70	**196**	4		67 **Hee Haw, The Stars Of** .... [V] Buck Owens/Roy Clark/Archie Campbell/Grandpa Jones/Junior Samples	Capitol 437
				Here's Johnny — see Tonight Show	
				High School Musical Cast — see MAIN ARTIST SECTION	
6/28/08	**28**	13		70 **iCarly** .... [V] Miranda Cosgrove/Jennette McCurdy/Nathan Kress/Jerry Trainor	Nickelodeon 30987
12/5/92	**137**	2		71 **Jacksons: An American Dream, The** .... [V] Lawrence Hilton-Jacobs/Billy Dee Williams/**Vanessa Williams**/Angela Bassett/Jason Weaver	Motown 6356
4/15/00	**79**	14		72 **Jesus - The Epic Mini-Series** .... [V] Jeremy Sisto/Jacqueline Bisset/Armin Mueller-Stahl/Gary Oldman	Sparrow 51730
1/27/07	**3**¹	20	●	73 **Jump In!** .... [V] Corbin Bleu/Keke Palmer/David Reivers/Shanica Knowles	Walt Disney 000117
1/27/01	**99**	7		74 **Ken Burns Jazz, The Best Of** .... [V]	Legacy 61439
1/27/01	**113**	6	▲	75 **Ken Burns Jazz - The Story Of America's Music** .... [V] above 2 feature music from the PBS documentary; the box set includes a 44 page booklet	Legacy 61432 [5]
8/9/03	**125**	5		76 **Kim Possible** .... [V] animated series, voices by: Christy Romano/Will Friedle/Nancy Cartwright/Gary Cole	Walt Disney 860097
10/19/68+	**105**	17		77 **Laugh-In** .... [C] Dan Rowan/Dick Martin/Arte Johnson/Judy Carne/Goldie Hawn	Epic 15118
4/5/69	**88**	10		78 **Laugh-In '69** .... [C] second cast album featuring comedy highlights	Reprise 6335
12/27/69+	**14**ˣ	4		79 **Littlest Angel, The** .... [X-M] Johnny Whitaker/Fred Gwynne/E.G. Marshall/Tony Randall	Mercury 603
8/31/02+	**31**	54	▲	80 **Lizzie McGuire** .... [V] **Hilary Duff**/Lalaine Vergas/Adam Lamberg/Jake Thomas/Robert Carradine	Buena Vista 860791
9/18/04	**146**	3		81 **Lizzie McGuire: Total Party!** .... [V]	Walt Disney 861095
2/14/98	**178**	1		82 **Long Journey Home** .... [V] from the PBS documentary series *The Irish In America: Long Journey Home*	Unisphere 68963
2/24/01	**148**	2		83 **Malcolm In The Middle** .... [V] Frankie Muniz/Jane Kaczmarek/Bryan Cranston/Justin Berfield/Erik Per Sullivan	Restless 73743
				Man From U.N.C.L.E., The — see MONTENEGRO, Hugo Robert Vaughn/**David McCallum**/Leo Carroll	
9/13/03	**92**	9		85 **Martin Scorsese Presents The Best Of The Blues** .... [V] music from the PBS-TV documentary series	UTV 000704
11/5/05	**161**	1		86 **Masters Of Horror** .... [V] music from the Showtime anthology series	Immortal 60011
10/12/85	**❶**¹¹	34	▲⁴	87 **Miami Vice** .... [V] Don Johnson/Philip Michael Thomas/Edward James Olmos	MCA 6150
12/6/86+	**82**	12		88 **Miami Vice II** .... [V] second album of songs featured on the show	MCA 6192
5/3/75	**51**	13		89 **Mickey Mouse Club** .... [M] Jimmie Dodd/**Annette**/Spin & Marty/Mouseketeers	Disneyland 1362

Billboard DEBUT	PEAK	WKS	R I A A	ARTIST Album Title .... Catalog	Label & Number
7/23/66	120	15		90 Mickie Finn's - America's No.1 Speakeasy .... [L]	Dunhill/ABC 50009
				San Diego night club specializing in *Gay '90s* music; featuring pianist Fred Finn and his wife Mickie (banjo)	
				Mission: Impossible — see SCHIFRIN, Lalo	
				Peter Graves/Greg Morris/Martin Landau	
8/8/87	50	14		92 Moonlighting .... [O-V]	MCA 6214
				Cybill Shepherd/**Bruce Willis**/Allyce Beasley/Curtis Armstrong	
12/18/99	138	4		93 Mr. Hankey's Christmas Classics .... [X-N]	American 62224
				songs from the animated TV show *South Park*; Christmas chart: 23/'99	
				Mr. Lucky — see MANCINI, Henry	
				John Vivyan/Ross Martin/Pippa Scott	
1/21/78	153	5		95 Muppet Show, The .... [M]	Arista 4152
				Grammy: Children's Album	
				Frank Oz/Jim Henson/Jerry Nelson/Richard Hunt/Dave Goelz	
5/24/03	174	1		96 Nashville Star: The Finalists .... [L-V]	Columbia 87169
				Native Americans, Music For The — see ROBERTSON, Robbie	
2/28/09	82	6		98 NCIS: The Official TV Soundtrack .... [V]	CBS 022 [2]
				Mark Harmon/Michael Weatherly/**David McCallum**/Pauley Perrette	
11/21/09	130	1		99 NCIS: The Official TV Soundtrack Volume 2 .... [V]	CBS 029
10/7/95	73	6		100 New York Undercover .... [V]	Uptown 11342
				Michael DeLorenzo/Malik Yoba/Patti D'Arbanville-Quinn	
4/17/04	52	10		101 OC: Mix 1, The .... [V]	Warner Sunset 48685
				Peter Gallagher/Kelly Rowan/Ben McKenzie/Adam Brody/Mischa Barton	
11/13/04	90	10		102 OC: Mix 2, The .... [V]	Warner Sunset 48695
11/13/04	39[X]	1		103 OC: Mix 3 - Have A Very Merry Chrismukkah, The .... [X-V]	Warner Sunset 48700
4/23/05	56	4		104 OC: Mix 4, The .... [V]	Warner Sunset 48705
11/26/05	108	2		105 OC: Mix 5, The .... [V]	Warner Sunset 49443
2/26/94	83	5		106 One Life To Live - The Best Of Love .... [V]	SBK 28336
				Erica Slezak/Robin Strasser/Phil Carey/Robert S. Woods/Clint Ritchie	
5/9/60	30	2		107 One Step Beyond, Music From .... [I]	Decca 8970
				from the *Alcoa Presents* TV series hosted by John Newland; cd: Harry Lubin; pf: Berlin Symphony Orchestra	
2/12/05	51	7		108 One Tree Hill .... [V]	Warner Sunset 48981
				Chad Michael Murray/James Lafferty/Hilarie Burton/Barry Corbin	
2/25/06	54	7		109 One Tree Hill Volume 2: Friends With Benefit .... [V]	Warner Sunset 49425
4/17/04	70	3		110 Oprah's Pop Star Challenge .... [V]	Epic 92330
6/29/02	13	7		111 Osbourne Family Album, The .... [V]	Epic 86670
1/27/01	42	10		112 Oz .... [V]	Avatar 10007
				Ernie Hudson/Terry Kinney/Rita Moreno/B.D. Wong	
				Peter Gunn — see MANCINI, Henry	
				Craig Stevens/**Herschel Bernardi**/Lola Albright	
10/10/09	59	21		114 Phineas And Ferb .... [V]	Walt Disney 003007
				animated series, voices by: Vincent Martella/Thomas Sangster/**Ashley Tisdale**	
2/7/04	127	11		115 Pixel Perfect .... [V]	Walt Disney 61056
				Ricky Ullman/Leah Pipes/Spencer Redford	
4/17/99	86	7		116 PJs, The .... [V]	Hollywood 62170
				animated series, voices by: **Eddie Murphy**/Janet DuBois/Loretta Divine	
5/5/01	152	3		117 Queer As Folk .... [V]	RCA Victor 63769
				Randy Harrison/Gale Harold/Hal Sparks/Sharon Gless	
5/25/02	167	2		118 Queer As Folk: The Second Season .... [V]	RCA 63921
6/7/03	173	1		119 Queer As Folk: The Third Season .... [V]	Tommy Boy 1568 [2]
2/28/04	39	6		120 Queer Eye For The Straight Guy .... [V]	Capitol 95912
				Carson Kressley/Ted Allen/Jai Rodriguez/Kyan Douglas/Thom Filicia	
9/18/93	156	18		121 Ren & Stimpy: You Eediot! .... [M]	Nickelodeon 57400
				animated series, voices by Billy West/Cheryl Chase/Vincent Waller	
				Roaring 20's, The — see PROVINE, Dorothy	
				Dorothy Provine/Donald May/Rex Reason	
10/8/05	68	2		123 Rock Star: A Night At The Mayan Theatre .... [L-V]	Burnett 97726
				Roots - see JONES, Quincy	
				LeVar Burton/John Amos/Leslie Uggams/Ben Vereen	
3/16/02	167	1		125 Roswell .... [V]	Nettwerk 30255
				Shiri Appleby/Jason Behr/Katherine Heigl/Majandra Delfino/William Sadler	
1/15/05	45[X]	1		126 RugRats: Holiday Classics! .... [X-M]	Nick 64698
11/14/98	71	16	●	127 Sabrina The Teenage Witch .... [V]	Geffen 25220
				Melissa Joan Hart/Caroline Rhea/Beth Broderick/Nick Bakay	
				Sanford and Son — see FOXX, Redd	
				Redd Foxx/Demond Wilson/LaWanda Page/Whitman Mayo	
12/25/76+	38	13		129 Saturday Night Live .... [C]	Arista 4107
				John Belushi/Dan Aykroyd/Chevy Chase/Jane Curtin/**Gilda Radner**	
10/16/99	183	1		130 Saturday Night Live - The Musical Performances Volume 1 .... [L]	DreamWorks 50205
7/25/70	23	54	●	131 Sesame Street Book & Record, The .... [M]	Columbia 1069
				Grammy: Children's Album	
				Bob McGrath/Loretta Long (**Susan of Sesame Street**)/Jim Henson/Frank Oz/Carroll Spinney	
12/11/71+	78	10		132 Sesame Street 2 .... [M]	Warner 2569
5/6/00	42	5		133 '70s, The .... [O-V]	Island 542473
				Brad Rowe/Guy Torry/Vinessa Shaw/Amy Smart/Kathryn Harrold	
4/20/59	3[1]	28		134 77 Sunset Strip .... [I]	Warner 1289
				Efrem Zimbalist, Jr./Roger Smith/Ed Byrnes; musical director: Warren Barker	
10/4/80	115	6		135 Shogun .... [I]	RSO 3088
				Richard Chamberlain/Toshiro Mifune/Yoko Shimada; cp/cd: Maurice Jarre	

TELEVISION SOUNDTRACKS

DEBUT	PEAK	WKS	R I A A	ARTIST Album Title.. Catalog	Label & Number
9/10/05	74	3		136 **Six Feet Under, Volume Two: Everything Ends**.. [V] Peter Krause/Michael C. Hall/Frances Conroy/Lauren Ambrose/Rachel Griffiths	Astralwerks 11797
2/13/99	22	8		137 **'60s, The**.. [O-V] Julia Stiles/Bill Smitrovich/Jerry O'Connell/Josh Hamilton	PolyGram TV 538743
3/15/03	31	5		138 **Smallville**... [V] Tom Welling/Kristen Kreuk/Michael Rosenbaum/**John Schneider**/Annette O'Toole	Elektra 62792
11/26/05	186	1		139 **Smallville: Volume 2 Metropolis Mix**... [V]	Hollywood 162555
1/22/00	54	26	●	140 **Sopranos, The**.. [V] James Gandolfini/Lorraine Bracco/Michael Imperioli/Edie Falco/**Little Steven**	Play-Tone 63911
5/26/01	38	7	●	141 **Sopranos: Peppers & Eggs, The**... [V]	Play-Tone 85453 [2]
1/20/01	147	4		142 **Soul Food: The Series - The Best R&B Of 2000** .... [V] Rockmond Dunbar/Irma Hall/Aaron Meeks/Darrin Dewitt Henson	Def Soul 548156
2/28/09	44	7		143 **Spectacular!** .... [M] Nolan Funk/Jesse Moss/Britt Irvin/Tammia Sursok	Nickelodeon 30108
9/8/01	171	7		144 **SpongeBob SquarePants Original Theme Highlights**................................. [V] animated series, voices by Tom Kenny/Rodger Bumpass/Bill Faggerbakke/Clancy Brown	Nick 49500
3/21/09	62	9		145 **SpongeBob's Greatest Hits** .... [K]	Nickelodeon 44678
6/9/73	205	5		146 **Strauss Family, The** .... [I] Derek Jacobi/Margaret Whiting/Eric Woofe/Stuart Wilson; cd: Cyril Ornadel; pf: **London Symphony Orchestra**	Polydor 3506 [2]
8/7/04	182	1		147 **Stuck In The Suburbs**... [V] Danielle Panabaker/Ryan Belleville/Shannon Floyd/Ric Reitz/Kristen Nelson	Walt Disney 861106
12/1/73+	34	23		148 **Sunshine** .... [M] Cliff DeYoung/Christina Raines/Brenda Vaccaro/Meg Foster/Bill Mumy; cp: **John Denver**	MCA 387
				Taxi — see JAMES, Bob Judd Hirsch/Tony Danza/Marilu Henner/Danny DeVito/Andy Kaufman	
6/5/04	44	23	●	150 **That's So Raven** .... [V] Raven-Symone/T'Keyah "Crystal" Keymah/Rondell Sheridan/Orlando Brown/Kyle Massey	Walt Disney 861015
3/25/06	44	7		151 **That's So Raven Too!** .... [V]	Walt Disney 861427
12/21/74+	30	11	●	152 **Tonight Show, Here's Johnny - Magic Moments From The** .... [C] actual musical and comedy excerpts from the TV show hosted by Johnny Carson from October 1, 1962-May 22, 1992	Casablanca 1296 [2]
11/21/98	16	27	▲	153 **Touched By An Angel - The Album** .... [V] Roma Downey/**Della Reese**/John Dye	550 Music 68971
12/4/99	86	7		154 **Touched By An Angel – The Christmas Album** .... [X-V] Christmas chart: 9/'99	550 Music 69710
6/6/09	105	13		155 **True Blood** .... [V] Anna Paquin/Stephen Moyer/Sam Trammell/Chris Bauer	HBO 519381
9/29/90	22	25	●	156 **Twin Peaks** .... [I] Kyle McLachlan/Michael Ontkean/Joan Chen/Sherilyn Fenn/Piper Laurie; cp/cd: Angelo Badalamenti	Warner 26316
				Velveteen Rabbit, The — see STREEP, Meryl / WINSTON, George	
11/10/58+	2[4]	89		158 **Victory At Sea, Vol. 2** .... [I]	RCA Victor 2226
9/11/61	7	32		159 **Victory At Sea, Vol. 3** .... [I] above 2 are orchestral suites from the NBC-TV series which featured actual footage of World War II naval battles; cp: Richard Rodgers; cd: Robert Russell Bennett	RCA Victor 2523
12/21/74	125	2		160 **Waltons' Christmas Album, The** .... [X] Richard Thomas/Ralph Waite/Michael Lerned/Will Geer/Ellen Corby	Columbia 33193
10/13/07	136	2		161 **War, The** .... [O-V] period music from the Ken Burns documentary	Legacy 10203 [4]
10/2/04	57	2		162 **Will & Grace: Let The Music Out!** .... [O-V] Eric McCormack/Debra Messing/Sean Hayes/Megan Mullally	BMG 59695
8/22/09	24	12		163 **Wizards Of Waverly Place**.. [V] **Selena Gomez**/David Henrie/Jake Austin/David DeLuise	Walt Disney 003006
1/5/08	66	8		164 **WWE Presents: Raw's Greatest Hits: The Music** .... [V]	WWE 21259
10/6/01	46	6		165 **WWF: Tough Enough** .... [V]	DreamWorks 450336
6/1/02	82	4		166 **WWF: Tough Enough 2** .... [V]	Geffen 493314
4/13/96	47	10		167 **X-Files: Songs In The Key Of X, The**... [V] David Duchovny/Gillian Anderson/Mitch Pileggi/William B. Davis	Warner 46079

		R	ARTIST	
		I		
		A		
DEBUT	PEAK	WKS	Album Title.. Catalog	Label & Number

ORIGINAL CASTS

DEBUT	PEAK	WKS	RIAA	ARTIST / Album Title	Label & Number
9/23/78	161	5		1 Ain't Misbehavin' .... *Grammy: Cast Album* Ken Page/Nell Carter/Andre DeShields; cp: Fats Waller	RCA Victor 2965 [2]
4/21/62	21	16		2 All American .... Ray Bolger/Eileen Herlie/Ron Husmann; mu: Charles Strouse; ly: Lee Adams	Columbia 2160
6/18/77	81	39	▲	3 Annie .... *Grammy: Cast Album* Andrea McArdle/Reid Shelton/Danielle Brisebois; mu: Charles Strouse; ly: Martin Charnin	Columbia 34712
12/30/57+	12	5		4 Annie Get Your Gun .... Mary Martin/John Raitt; sw: Irving Berlin	Capitol 913
8/6/66	113	7		5 Annie Get Your Gun .... Ethel Merman/Bruce Yarnell; sw: Irving Berlin	RCA Victor 1124
5/23/70	168	7		6 Applause .... Lauren Bacall/Robert Mandan/Bonnie Franklin/Brandon Maggert; mu: Charles Strouse; ly: Lee Adams	ABC 11
12/17/66+	113	9		7 Apple Tree, The .... Barbara Harris/Larry Blyden/Alan Alda/**Robert Klein**; mu: Jerry Bock; ly: Sheldon Harnick	Columbia 3020
2/20/65	143	2		8 Bajour .... Chita Rivera/Nancy Dussault/**Herschel Bernardi**/Paul Sorvino; sw: Walter Marks	Columbia 2700
5/8/65	138	4		9 Baker Street (A Musical Adventure Of Sherlock Holmes) .... Fritz Weaver/Inga Swenson; sw: Marian Grudeff and Raymond Jessel	MGM 7000
8/30/80	205	2		10 Barnum .... Jim Dale/Glenn Close/Marianne Tatum/Terri White; mu: Cy Coleman; ly: Michael Stewart	Columbia 36576
2/9/57	20	1		11 Bells Are Ringing .... *Grammy: Hall of Fame* Judy Holliday/Sydney Chaplin; mu: Jule Styne; ly: Betty Comden and Adolph Green	Columbia 5170
12/26/64+	132	8		12 Ben Franklin In Paris .... Robert Preston/Ulla Sallert; mu: Mark Sandrich Jr.; ly: Sidney Michaels	Capitol 2191
12/15/62+	73	20		13 Beyond The Fringe .... Dudley Moore/Alan Bennett/Peter Cook/Jonathan Miller	Capitol 1792
6/14/69	195	3		14 Boys In The Band, The .... Kenneth Nelson/Peter White; no track titles listed	A&M 6001 [2]
7/18/60+	12	61		15 Bye Bye Birdie .... Chita Rivera/Dick Van Dyke/Kay Medford/Dick Gautier; mu: Charles Strouse; ly: Lee Adams	Columbia 5510
1/7/67	37	39		16 Cabaret .... *Grammy: Cast Album* Joel Grey/Jill Haworth/Jack Gilford/Bert Convy/Lotte Lenya; mu: John Kander; ly: Fred Ebb	Columbia 3040
1/23/61	❶⁶	265	●	17 Camelot .... *Grammy: Hall of Fame* Richard Burton/**Julie Andrews**/**Robert Goulet**; mu: Frederick Loewe; ly: Alan Jay Lerner	Columbia 2031
4/19/69	171	4		18 Canterbury Tales .... George Rose/Hermione Baddeley/Martyn Green; mu: Richard Hill and John Hawkins; ly: Nevill Coghill	Capitol 229
5/29/61	❶¹	67		19 Carnival .... Anna Maria Alberghetti/James Mitchell/Kaye Ballard; sw: Bob Merrill	MGM 3946
11/10/62	12	19		20 Carousel .... version of the Rodgers & Hammerstein musical; produced by **Enoch Light** and featuring vocalists Alfred Drake and Roberta Peters	Command 843
11/6/82+	86	22		21 Cats .... Wayne Sleep/Paul Nicholas/Elaine Paige; original London cast; sw: **Andrew Lloyd Webber**	Geffen 2017 [2]
2/26/83	113	64	▲	22 Cats .... *Grammy: Cast Album* Ken Page/Betty Buckley/Timothy Scott/Reed Jones; original Broadway cast	Geffen 2031 [2]
2/26/83	131	14		23 Cats .... selections from the original Broadway cast	Geffen 2026
7/4/09	100	3		24 Chess: In Concert .... **Josh Groban**/**Idina Menzel**/Adam Pascal/Marti Pellow; sw: Benny Andersson, Bjorn Ulvaeus and Tim Rice	Reprise 517635 [2]
8/23/75	73	10		25 Chicago .... Gwen Verdon/Chita Rivera/Jerry Orbach; mu: John Kander; ly: Fred Ebb	Arista 9005
2/15/97	131	2	●	26 Chicago - The Musical .... Cat:#34/3 *Grammy: Cast Album* Ann Reinking/Bebe Neuwirth/James Naughton/Joel Grey; mu: John Kander; ly: Fred Ebb	RCA Victor 68727
8/16/75	98	49	▲²	27 Chorus Line, A .... Pamela Blair/Wayne Cilento/Priscilla Lopez/Donna McKechnie; mu: **Marvin Hamlisch**; ly: Edward Kleban	Columbia 33581
4/29/57	15	1		28 Cinderella .... **Julie Andrews**; mu: Richard Rodgers; ly: Oscar Hammerstein II; a special CBS-TV production (March 31, 1957)	Columbia 5190
2/11/06	150	2		29 Color Purple, The	Angel 42954
6/20/70	178	2		30 Company .... *Grammys: Cast Album / Hall of Fame* Dean Jones/Barbara Barrie; sw: Stephen Sondheim	Columbia 3550
6/13/92	165	2		31 Crazy For You .... Harry Groener/Jodi Benson/Joel Goodness/Ida Henry; mu: **George Gershwin**; ly: Ira Gershwin	Angel 54618
8/2/69	195	2		32 Dames At Sea .... **Bernadette Peters**/David Christmas/Tamara Long/Sally Stark; mu: Jim Wise; ly: George Haimsohn and Robin Miller	Columbia 3330
6/11/55	6	6		33 Damn Yankees .... Gwen Verdon/Stephen Douglass/Ray Walston; sw: Richard Adler and Jerry Ross; LP: RCA Victor LOC-1021 (#6); EP: RCA Victor EOC-1021 (#11)	RCA Victor 1021
4/5/69	128	8		34 Dear World .... Angela Lansbury/Milo O'Shea/Carmen Mathews/Ted Agress; sw: Jerry Herman	Columbia 3260
8/24/59	44	2		35 Destry Rides Again .... **Andy Griffith**/Dolores Gray/Scott Brady/Stuart Damon; sw: Harold Rome	Decca 79075

Billboard			R I A A	ARTIST	
DEBUT	PEAK	WKS		Album Title.. Catalog	Label & Number
5/22/65	81	9		36 **Do I Hear A Waltz?** .... Elizabeth Allen/**Sergio Franchi**/Carol Bruce; mu: Richard Rodgers; ly: Stephen Sondheim	Columbia 2770
3/20/61	12	22		37 **Do Re Mi** .... Phil Silvers/Nancy Walker/Nancy Dussault; mu: Jule Styne; ly: Betty Comden and Adolph Green	RCA Victor 2002
7/31/61	58	9		38 **Donnybrook!** .... Eddie Foy/Art Lund/Joan Fagan; sw: Johnny Burke	Kapp 8500
5/22/82	11	29	●	39 **Dreamgirls** .... *Grammy: Cast Album* Jennifer Holliday/Loretta Devine/Cleavant Derricks; mu: Henry Krieger; ly: Tom Eyen	Geffen 2007
8/23/80	105	19	▲	40 **Evita** .... *Grammy: Cast Album* Patti LuPone/**Mandy Patinkin**/Bob Gunton; mu: **Andrew Lloyd Webber**; ly: Tim Rice	MCA 11007 [2]
7/25/64	96	8		41 **Fade Out-Fade In** .... **Carol Burnett**/Jack Cassidy/**Lou Jacobi**; mu: Jule Styne; ly: Betty Comden/Adolph Green	ABC-Paramount 3
1/22/55	6	1		42 **Fanny** .... Ezio Pinza/Walter Slezak/Florence Henderson; sw: Harold Rome; EP: RCA Victor EOC-1015 (#6); LP: RCA Victor LOC-1015 (#7)	RCA Victor 1015
8/3/63	117	6		43 **Fantasticks, The** .... Kenneth Nelson/Jerry Orbach/Rita Gardner; mu: Harvey Schmidt; ly: Tom Jones	MGM 3872
10/31/64+	7	206	▲²	44 **Fiddler On The Roof** .... *Grammy: Hall of Fame* Zero Mostel/Maria Karnilova/Bea Arthur/Bert Convy; mu: Jerry Bock; ly: Sheldon Harnick	RCA Victor 1093
1/11/60	7	89		45 **Fiorello!** .... Tom Bosley/Patricia Wilson/Ellen Hanley/Howard da Silva; mu: Jerry Bock; ly: Sheldon Harnick	Capitol 1321
7/3/65	111	8		46 **Flora, The Red Menace** .... Liza Minnelli/Bob Dishy/Robert Kaye/Danny Carroll; mu: John Kander; ly: Fred Ebb	RCA Victor 1111
1/12/59	❶³	151	●	47 **Flower Drum Song** .... Miyoshi Umeki/Larry Blyden/Pat Suzuki; mu: Richard Rodgers; ly: Oscar Hammerstein II	Columbia 2009
6/5/71	172	3		48 **Follies** .... Alexis Smith/Gene Nelson/Yvonne De Carlo/Dorothy Collins; sw: Stephen Sondheim	Capitol 761
1/25/86	181	6		49 **Follies - In Concert** .... *Grammy: Cast Album* **Carol Burnett**/George Hearn/Lee Remick/**Mandy Patinkin**; sw: Stephen Sondheim	RCA Victor 7128 [2]
1/17/81	120	11		50 **42nd Street** .... Tammy Grimes/Jerry Orbach/Stan Page/Carole Cook; mu: Harry Warren; ly: Al Dubin	RCA Victor 3891
				Funny Girl — see STREISAND, Barbra	
7/7/62	60	14		52 **Funny Thing Happened On The Way To The Forum, A** .... Zero Mostel/Jack Gilford/David Burns/John Carradine; sw: Stephen Sondheim	Capitol 1717
2/24/62	81	9		53 **Gay Life, The** .... Walter Chiari/Barbara Cook/Jules Munshin; sw: Howard Dietz and Arthur Schwartz	Capitol 1560
5/25/68	161	6		54 **George M!** .... Joel Grey/Betty Ann Grove/**Bernadette Peters**	Columbia 3200
2/9/74	209	4		55 **Gigi** .... Karin Wolfe/Alfred Drake/Agnes Moorehead/Maria Karnilova; mu: Frederick Loewe; ly: Alan Jay Lerner	RCA Victor 0404
1/25/64	33	14		56 **Girl Who Came To Supper, The** .... Jose Ferrer/Florence Henderson; sw: **Noel Coward**	Columbia 2420
8/7/71+	34	79	●	57 **Godspell** .... *Grammy: Cast Album* Stephen Nathan/Robin Lamont; sw: Stephen Schwartz	Bell 1102
12/19/64+	36	16		58 **Golden Boy** .... **Sammy Davis Jr.**/Billy Daniels/Cindy Robbins; mu: Charles Strouse; ly: Lee Adams	Capitol 2124
1/1/66	118	4		59 **Great Waltz, The** .... Giorgio Tozzi/Jean Fenn; cp: Johann Strauss	Capitol 2426
8/1/92	109	5		60 **Guys And Dolls** .... *Grammy: Cast Album* Peter Gallagher/Nathan Lane/Faith Prince; mu: Frank Loesser; Original Cast version charted in 1951 (#1) on Decca 8036	RCA Victor 61317
7/20/59	13	116		61 **Gypsy** .... *Grammys: Cast Album / Hall of Fame* Ethel Merman/Jack Klugman/Sandra Church; mu: Jule Styne; ly: Stephen Sondheim	Columbia 2017
9/6/03	175	1		62 **Gypsy** .... *Grammy: Cast Album* **Bernadette Peters**/David Burtka/Heather Lee; mu: Jule Styne; ly: Stephen Sondheim	Broadway Angel 83858
9/13/08	58	1		63 **Gypsy** .... Patti LuPone/Laura Benanti/Boyd Gaines; mu: Jule Styne; ly: Stephen Sondheim	Time-Life 19659
8/3/68+	❶¹³	151	●	64 **Hair** .... *Grammys: Cast Album / Hall of Fame* Gerome Ragni/James Rado/Lynn Kellogg; mu: Galt MacDermot; ly: Gerome Ragni and James Rado	RCA Victor 1150
5/10/69	186	4		65 **Hair** .... Paul Nicholas/Oliver Tobias; original London cast	Atco 7002
6/13/09	63	3		66 **Hair (The American Tribal Love-Rock Musical)** .... Sasha Allen/Allison Case/Gavin Creel; mu: Galt MacDermot; ly: Gerome Ragni and James Rado	Ghostlight 84467
8/31/02	131	2		67 **Hairspray** .... Cat:#47/1 *Grammy: Cast Album* Marissa Jaret Winokur/Harvey Fierstein/Linda Hart/Dick Latessa; sw: Marc Shaiman and Scott Wittman (based on the 1988 movie)	Sony Classical 87708
6/12/65	103	14		68 **Half A Sixpence** .... Tommy Steele/Polly James/Norman Allen/John Cleese; sw: David Heneker	RCA Victor 1110
8/15/64	128	13		69 **Hamlet** .... Richard Burton/Hume Cronyn/Alfred Drake/Eileen Herlie; 4-album set of dialogue from Shakespeare's play	Columbia 702 [4]
7/3/61	84	6		70 **Happiest Girl In The World, The** .... **Cyril Ritchard**/Janice Rule; mu: Jacques Offenbach; ly: E.Y. Harburg	Columbia 2050

DEBUT	PEAK	WKS	R I A A	ARTIST Album Title... Catalog	Label & Number
2/22/64	❶¹	90	●	71 **Hello, Dolly!** *Grammy: Hall of Fame* Carol Channing/David Burns/Eileen Brennan/Charles Nelson Reilly/Mary Jo Catlett; sw: Jerry Herman	RCA Victor 1087
11/16/63+	38	16		72 **Here's Love** .... Janis Paige/Craig Stevens; sw: Meredith Willson	Columbia 2400
5/16/64	76	20		73 **High Spirits** .... Beatrice Lillie/Tammy Grimes/Edward Woodward; sw: Hugh Martin and Timothy Gray	ABC-Paramount 1
11/27/61+	19	47		74 **How To Succeed In Business Without Really Trying** .... *Grammy: Cast Album* Robert Morse/Rudy Vallee/Bonnie Scott/Charles Nelson Reilly; sw: Frank Loesser	RCA Victor 1066
7/21/62	125	5		75 **I Can Get It For You Wholesale** .... Lillian Roth/Jack Kruschen/Elliott Gould/**Barbra Streisand**; sw: Harold Rome	Columbia 2180
1/14/67	84	16		76 **I Do! I Do!** .... Mary Martin/Robert Preston; mu: Harvey Schmidt; ly: Tom Jones	RCA Victor 1128
1/30/65	126	8		77 **I Had A Ball** .... Buddy Hackett/Richard Kiley; sw: Jack Lawrence and Stan Freeman	Mercury 6210
6/17/67	177	8		78 **Illya Darling** .... Melina Mercouri/Orson Bean; mu: Manos Hadjidakis; ly: Joe Darion	United Artists 9901
6/21/08	82	2		79 **In The Heights** .... *Grammy: Cast Album* Andrea Burns/Tony Chiroldes/Janet Dacal; sw: Lin-Manuel Miranda	Ghostlight 84428 [2]
3/26/88	126	6		80 **Into The Woods** .... *Grammy: Cast Album* Bernadette Peters/Joanna Gleason/Chip Zien/Tom Aldredge; sw: Stephen Sondheim	RCA 6796
5/19/73	203	6		81 **Irene**... Debbie Reynolds/Monte Markham/George S. Irving/Ruth Warrick; mu: Harry Tierney; ly: Joseph McCarthy	Columbia 32266
12/5/60+	9	33		82 **Irma La Douce** Elizabeth Seal/Keith Michell/Clive Revill; mu: Marguerite Monnot; ly: Alexandre Breffort	Columbia 2029
1/20/07	20ˣ	4		83 **Irving Berlin's White Christmas: The Musical** .... [X] Stephen Bogardus/Jeffrey Denman/Kerry O'Malley; sw: Irving Berlin; Christmas charts: 20/'07, 39/'09	Ghostlight 81225
1/4/64	87	5		84 **Jennie** .... Mary Martin/George Wallace/Robin Bailey; mu: Arthur Schwartz; ly: Howard Dietz	RCA Victor 1083
6/24/06	85	47	▲	85 **Jersey Boys** .... Cat:#7/107 John Lloyd Young/Daniel Reichard/Christian Hoff/J. Robert Spencer; mu: Bob Gaudio; ly: Bob Crewe	Rhino 73271
1/8/72	31	10		86 **Jesus Christ Superstar** .... Ben Vereen/Jeff Fenholt/**Yvonne Elliman**/Bob Bingham; mu: **Andrew Lloyd Webber**; ly: Sir Tim Rice	Decca 1503
8/7/82	47ᶜ	2		87 **Joseph And The Amazing Technicolor Dreamcoat** .... Bill Hutton/Stephen Hope/Laurie Beechman/Barry Tarallo; sw: **Andrew Lloyd Webber**	MCA 399
3/14/70	187	4		88 **Joy** .... Oscar Brown Jr./Jean Pace/Sivuca; sw: various	RCA Victor 1166
12/25/61+	80	12		89 **Kean** .... Alfred Drake/Lee Venora; sw: Robert Wright and George Forrest	Columbia 2120
10/24/92	135	4		90 **King And I, The** .... musical score performed in the studio, not on stage; mu: Richard Rogers; ly: Oscar Hammerstein II; cd: John Mauceri; pf: **Julie Andrews**/Ben Kingsley/Lea Salonga/**Peabo Bryson**	Philips 438007
				Kismet — see MANTOVANI Alfred Drake/Doretta Morrow/Richard Kiley	
3/24/62	139	3		92 **Kwamina** .... Sally Ann Howes/Terry Carter; sw: Richard Adler	Capitol 1645
9/24/83	52	15	●	93 **La Cage Aux Folles** .... George Hearn/Gene Barry/David Cahn/Linda Haberman; sw: Jerry Herman	RCA Victor 4824
8/4/07	86	5		94 **Legally Blonde** .... Laura Bell Bundy/Richard Blake/Christian Borle; sw: Laurence O'Keefe and Nell Benjamin	Ghostlight 84423
4/11/87	106	15	▲	95 **Les Miserables** .... Cat:#17/1 Colm Wilkinson/Roger Allam/Rebecca Caine/Patti LuPone; original London cast; mu: Claude-Michel Schonberg; ly: Herbert Kretzmer	Relativity 8140 [2]
6/20/87	117	10	▲⁴	96 **Les Miserables** .... Cat:#21/43 *Grammy: Cast Album* Colm Wilkinson/Terrence Mann/Judy Kuhn/Randy Graff; Broadway cast; mu: Claude-Michel Schonberg; ly: Herbert Kretzmer	Geffen 24151 [2]
1/11/92	184	1	●	97 **Les Miserables: Highlights From The Complete Symphonic** **International Cast Record** .... Cat:#42/1 features performers drawn from worldwide productions of musical; mu: Claude-Michel Schonberg; ly: Alain Boublil & Herbert Kretzmer	First Night 1099
12/29/56	19	3		98 **Li'l Abner** .... Edith Adams/Peter Palmer/Howard St. John/Stubby Kaye; mu: Gene de Paul; ly: Johnny Mercer	Columbia 5150
6/25/05	189	1		99 **Light In The Piazza, The** .... Matthew Morrison/Michael Berresse/Sarah Berry/Mark Harelik; sw: Adam Guettel	Nonesuch 79829
12/6/97	162	10	●	100 **Lion King, The** .... *Grammy: Cast Album* John Vickery/Samuel E. Wright/Geoff Hoyle; mu: **Elton John**; ly: Sir Tim Rice	Walt Disney 60802
1/19/63	44	10		101 **Little Me** .... Sid Caesar/Virginia Martin/Nancy Andrews; mu: Cy Coleman; ly: Carolyn Leigh	RCA Victor 1078
3/15/08	26	2		102 **Little Mermaid, The** .... Sierra Boggess/Derrick Baskin/Trevor Braun; mu: Alan Menken; ly: Howard Ashman and Glenn Slater	Disney 001033
5/5/73	94	12		103 **Little Night Music, A**... *Grammy: Cast Album* Glynis Johns/Len Cariou/Hermione Gingold; sw: Stephen Sondheim	Columbia 32265
3/22/97	116	11		104 **Lord Of The Dance**.. [I] music from the Irish dance production starring world champion dancer Michael Flatley; cp: Ronan Hardiman	Philips 533757
1/11/69	185	2		105 **Maggie Flynn** .... Shirley Jones/Jack Cassidy; sw: Hugo Peretti/Luigi Creatore (**Hugo & Luigi**)/George David Weiss	RCA Victor 2009

Billboard			R I A A	ARTIST	Label & Number
DEBUT	PEAK	WKS		Album Title.. Catalog	

DEBUT	PEAK	WKS	RIAA	ARTIST / Album Title	Label & Number
7/2/66	**23**	66	●	**106 Mame** .... *Grammy: Cast Album* Angela Lansbury/Bea Arthur/Ron Young/Margaret Hall; sw: Jerry Herman	Columbia 3000
11/10/01	**169**	20	▲	**107 Mamma Mia!** .... **Cat**:#4/72 Lisa Stokke/Siobhan McCarthy/Louise Plowright/Andrew Langtree; sw: Benny Andersson, Bjorn Ulvaeus and Stig Anderson (based on the music of **Abba**)	Decca Broadway 543115
1/22/66+	**31**	167	●	**108 Man Of La Mancha**................................. *Grammy: Hall of Fame* Richard Kiley/Irving Jacobson/Joan Diener; mu: Mitch Leigh; ly: Joe Darion	Kapp 4505
10/17/64	**137**	4		**109 Merry Widow, The**................................. Patrice Munsel/Bob Wright; sw: Franz Lehar	RCA Victor 1094
11/20/61+	**10**	41		**110 Milk And Honey** Robert Weede/Mimi Benzell/Molly Picon; sw: Jerry Herman	RCA Victor 1065
3/10/90	**122**	11	▲	**111 Miss Saigon** .... Jonathan Pryce/Claire Moore/Lea Salonga/Simon Bowman; original London cast; mu: Claude-Michel Schonberg and Alain Boublil; ly: Richard Maltby Jr. and Alain Boublil	Geffen 24271 [2]
5/21/05	**69**	8		**112 Monty Python's Spamalot** .... *Grammy: Cast Album* David Hyde Pierce/Hank Azaria/**Tim Curry**/Michael McGrath; mu: John Du Prez; ly: Eric Idle	Decca Broadway 004265
8/4/56	**11**	4		**113 Most Happy Fella, The** .... Robert Weede/Jo Sullivan/Art Lund/Susan Johnson; sw: Frank Loesser	Columbia 2330
12/1/62	**14**	24		**114 Mr. President**...................................... Robert Ryan/Nanette Fabray; sw: Irving Berlin	Columbia 2270
2/24/58	**❶**[12]	245	▲	**115 Music Man, The** *Grammys: Cast Album / Hall of Fame* Robert Preston/Barbara Cook; sw: Meredith Willson	Capitol 990
4/28/56	**❶**[15]	480	▲[3]	**116 My Fair Lady** *Grammy: Hall of Fame ★ NRR* Rex Harrison/**Julie Andrews**/Stanley Holloway/Robert Coote; mu: Frederick Loewe; ly: Alan Jay Lerner	Columbia 5090
6/28/86	**150**	6		**117 Mystery Of Edwin Drood, The** .... Betty Buckley/**Cleo Laine**/George Rose; sw: **Rupert Holmes**	Polydor 827969
8/5/57	**17**	3		**118 New Girl In Town** .... Gwen Verdon/Thelma Ritter/George Wallace; sw: Bob Merrill	RCA Victor 1027
5/30/09	**103**	3		**119 Next To Normal** .... Alice Ripley/J. Robert Spencer/Jennifer Damiano; mu: Tom Kitt; ly: Brian Yorkey	Ghostlight 84433 [2]
1/15/83	**209**	5		**120 Nine** .... Raul Julia/Camille Saviola/Karen Akers/Anita Morris; sw: Maury Yeston	CBS 38325
8/15/09	**130**	1		**121 9 To 5: The Musical** .... Stephanie Block/Megan Hilty/Allison Janney/Marc Kudisch; sw: **Dolly Parton**	Dolly 1
3/13/71	**61**	19		**122 No, No, Nanette** .... Ruby Keeler/Jack Gilford/Bobby Van/Helen Gallagher; mu: Vincent Youmans; ly: Irving Caesar and Otto Harbach	Columbia 30563
4/21/62	**5**	62		**123 No Strings** *Grammy: Cast Album* Richard Kiley/Diahann Carroll/Alvin Epstein/Polly Rowles; sw: Richard Rodgers	Capitol 1695
2/24/73	**211**	2		**124 Oh Coward!** .... Barbara Cason/Roderick Cook/Jamie Ross; sw: Noel Coward	Bell 9001 [2]
11/3/62	**4**	99	●	**125 Oliver!** *[HOF]* Clive Revill/Georgia Brown/Bruce Prochnik; sw: Lionel Bart	RCA Victor 2004
12/11/65+	**59**	32		**126 On A Clear Day You Can See Forever** .... *Grammy: Cast Album* Barbara Harris/John Cullum/Tito Vandis; mu: Burton Lane; ly: Alan Jay Lerner	RCA Victor 2006
1/4/64	**37**	15		**127 110 In The Shade** .... Robert Horton/Inga Swenson/Stephen Douglass; mu: Harvey Schmidt; ly: Tom Jones	RCA Victor 1085
				Over Here! — see ANDREWS SISTERS Patty Andrews/Maxene Andrews/**John Travolta**; sw: Richard M. Sherman/Robert B. Sherman	
				Pajama Game, The — see CONNICK, Harry Jr. **Harry Connick Jr.**/Michael McKean/Kelli O'Hara/Peter Benson	
9/10/94	**103**	2		**130 Passion** .... *Grammy: Cast Album* Marin Mazzie/Donna Murphy/Jere Shea/Gregg Edelman; sw: Stephen Sondheim	Angel 55251
4/2/55	**4**	5		**131 Peter Pan** Mary Martin/**Cyril Ritchard**; mu: Mark Charlap and Jule Styne; ly: Carolyn Leigh/Betty Comden/Adolph Green; LP: RCA Victor LOC-1019 (#4); EP: RCA Victor EOC-1019 (#5)	RCA Victor 1019
5/23/87+	**33**	255	▲[4]	**132 Phantom Of The Opera, The** .... **Cat**:#12/87 **Michael Crawford**/Sarah Brightman/Steve Barton; original London cast; mu: **Andrew Lloyd Webber**; ly: Charles Hart	Polydor 831273 [2]
3/10/90+	**46**	331	▲[4]	**133 Phantom Of The Opera, Highlights From The** .... **Cat**:#23/27 second volume released from the London stage production	Polydor 831563
1/13/73	**129**	10		**134 Pippin** .... Ben Vereen/Jill Clayburgh/Irene Ryan; sw: Stephen Schwartz	Motown 760
6/6/81	**178**	3		**135 Pirates Of Penzance, The** .... Kevin Kline/Estelle Parsons/**Linda Ronstadt/Rex Smith**; ly: W.S. Gilbert; mu: Arthur Sullivan	Elektra 601 [2]
5/5/01	**139**	10		**136 Producers, The** .... *Grammy: Cast Album* Nathan Lane/Matthew Broderick/Roger Bart/Gary Beach/Cady Huffman; sw: **Mel Brooks** (based on his 1968 movie)	Sony Classical 89646
1/25/69	**95**	12		**137 Promises, Promises** .... *Grammy: Cast Album* Jerry Orbach/Jill O'Hara/Edward Winter; mu: **Burt Bacharach**; ly: Hal David	United Artists 9902
6/13/70	**138**	5		**138 Purlie** .... Cleavon Little/**Melba Moore**/Sherman Hemsley/Helen Martin; mu: Gary Geld; ly: Peter Udell	Ampex 40101

Billboard DEBUT	PEAK	WKS	R I A A	ARTIST Album Title.. Catalog	Label & Number
5/25/59	47	1		139 **Redhead**	RCA Victor 1048
				Grammy: Cast Album Gwen Verdon/Richard Kiley/Leonard Stone; mu: Albert Hague; ly: Dorothy Fields	
9/14/96	19	22	▲²	140 **Rent**	DreamWorks 50003 [2]
				Adam Pascal/Anthony Rapp/Daphne Rubin-Vega; sw: Jonathan Larson	
3/30/96+	48	27	▲	141 **Riverdance - Music From The Show**...	Celtic Heartbeat 82816
				Grammy: Cast Album traditional Irish music from the music and dance revue production; sw: Bill Whelan	
4/10/65	54	34		142 **Roar Of The Greasepaint, The-The Smell Of The Crowd**..............	RCA Victor 1109
				Anthony Newley/**Cyril Ritchard**; sw: Anthony Newley and Leslie Bricusse	
6/20/09	118	2		143 **Rock Of Ages**...	New Line 39151
				Constantine Maroulis/Amy Spangler/James Carpinello/Adam Danaheisser; sw: Ethan Popp	
11/16/74	207	1		144 **Rocky Horror Show, The**	Ode 77026
				Tim Curry/**Meat Loaf**/Jamie Donnelly/Boni Enten; sw: Richard O'Brien	
11/27/61+	36	22		145 **Sail Away**	Capitol 1643
				Elaine Stritch/James Hurst/Grover Dale/Evelyn Russell; sw: **Noel Coward**	
7/28/73	201	2		146 **Seesaw**	Buddah 95006
				Michele Lee/Ken Howard; mu: Cy Coleman; ly: Dorothy Fields	
2/24/01	191	1		147 **Seussical: The Musical**	Decca Broadway 159792
				Kevin Chamberlin/Janine LaManna/Michele Pawk/Anthony Blair Hall/David Shiner; mu: Stephen Flaherty; ly: Lynn Ahrens (based on the writings of Dr. Seuss)	
5/17/69	174	6		148 **1776**	Columbia 3310
				William Daniels/Ken Howard/Howard da Silva; sw: Sherman Edwards	
6/22/63	15	17		149 **She Loves Me**	MGM 4118 [2]
				Grammy: Cast Album Barbara Cook/Daniel Massey/Barbara Baxley/Jack Cassidy; mu: Jerry Bock; ly: Sheldon Harnick	
9/15/62	95	6		150 **Show Boat**	Columbia 2220
				John Raitt/Barbara Cook/William Warfield/Anita Darian; mu: Jerome Kern; ly: Oscar Hammerstein II	
4/11/09	88	1		151 **Shrek: The Musical**..	Decca Broadway 012627
				Brian D'Arcy James/Sutton Foster/Daniel Breaker/Christopher Sieber; mu: Jeanine Tesori; ly: David Lindsay-Abaire	
4/16/55	9	3		152 **Silk Stockings**	RCA Victor 1016
				Hildegarde Neff/**Don Ameche**/Gretchen Wyler/Leon Belasco; sw: Cole Porter	
1/8/66	128	8		153 **Skyscraper**	Capitol 2422
				Julie Harris/Peter Marshall/Charles Nelson Reilly; mu: James Van Heusen; ly: Sammy Cahn	
6/16/73	211	2		154 **Sondheim: A Musical Tribute**...	Warner 2705 [2]
				Angela Lansbury/Jack Cassidy/Dorothy Collins/Glynis Johns; sw: Stephen Sondheim	
12/21/59+	❶¹⁶	276	●	155 **Sound Of Music, The**	Columbia 2020
				Grammy: Cast Album Mary Martin/Theodore Bikel; mu: Richard Rodgers; ly: Oscar Hammerstein II	
6/14/08	59	5		156 **South Pacific**	Masterworks 30457
				Kelli O'Hara/Paulo Szot/Loretta Ables Sayre/Danny Burstein; mu: Richard Rogers; ly: Oscar Hammerstein II	
6/30/07	96	2		157 **Spring Awakening**	Decca Broadway 008020
				Skylar Astin/Gerard Canonico/Lilli Cooper; mu: **Duncan Sheik**; ly: Steven Sater	
11/24/62+	3²	76		158 **Stop The World-I Want To Get Off**	London 88001
				Anthony Newley/Anna Quayle; sw: Leslie Bricusse and Anthony Newley	
4/7/62	81	11		159 **Subways Are For Sleeping**	Columbia 2130
				Sydney Chaplin/Carol Lawrence/Orson Bean; mu: Jule Styne; ly: Betty Comden and Adolph Green	
8/25/84	149	11		160 **Sunday In The Park With George**..	RCA Victor 5042 [2]
				Grammy: Cast Album Mandy Patinkin/**Bernadette Peters**/Brent Spiner/Judith Moore; sw: Stephen Sondheim	
11/20/93	170	1		161 **Sunset Boulevard - The Andrew Lloyd Webber Musical**	Polydor 519767 [2]
				Patti LuPone/Kevin Anderson/Daniel Benzali/Meredith Braun; mu: **Andrew Lloyd Webber**	
10/1/94	191	1		162 **Sunset Boulevard, Andrew Lloyd Webber's - American Premiere Recording** ..	Really Useful 3507 [2]
				Glenn Close/Alan Campbell/Judy Kuhn/George Hearn; mu: **Andrew Lloyd Webber**	
6/9/79	78	11		163 **Sweeney Todd-The Demon Barber Of Fleet Street**	RCA Victor 3379 [2]
				Grammy: Cast Album Angela Lansbury/Len Cariou/Victor Garber/Edmund Lyndeck; sw: Stephen Sondheim	
3/12/66	92	16		164 **Sweet Charity**..	Columbia 2900
				Gwen Verdon/John McMartin/Thelma Oliver/Ruth Buzzi; mu: Cy Coleman; ly: Dorothy Fields	
7/15/06	170	2		165 **Tarzan**...	Walt Disney 861541
				Josh Strickland/Jenn Gambatese/Tim Jerome/Merle Dandridge; sw: **Phil Collins**	
1/16/61	15	34		166 **Tenderloin**...	Capitol 1492
				Maurice Evans/Ron Husmann/Wayne Miller/Eileen Rodgers; mu: Jerry Bock; ly: Sheldon Harnick	
3/24/79	167	6		167 **They're Playing Our Song**	Casablanca 7141
				Robert Klein/Lucie Arnaz; mu: **Marvin Hamlisch**; ly: **Carole Bayer Sager**	
6/29/02	175	1		168 **Thoroughly Modern Millie**..	RCA Victor 63959
				Sheryl Lee Ralph/Harriet Harris/Marc Kudisch/Gavin Creel/Angela Christian; sw: Richard Morris and Dick Scanlan (based on the 1967 movie)	
8/6/66	145	2		169 **Time For Singing, A**	Warner 1639
				Ivor Emmanuel/Tessie O'Shea/Shani Wallis; mu: John Morris; ly: Gerald Freedman and John Morris	
7/19/97	158	1		170 **Titanic - A New Musical**	RCA Victor 68834
				David Costabile/John Cunningham/David Garrison; sw: Maury Yeston	
7/31/93	114	2		171 **Tommy, The Who's**	RCA Victor 61874 [2]
				Grammy: Cast Album Michael Cerveris/Marcia Mitzman/Jonathan Dokuchitz/Paul Kandel; sw: **Pete Townshend**	
7/27/63	64	11		172 **Tovarich**	Capitol 1940
				Vivian Leigh/Jean Pierre Aumont/Alexander Scourby; mu: Lee Pockriss; ly: Anne Croswell	
5/8/76	200	2		173 **Treemonisha**..	DG 2707 [2]
				Carmen Balthrop/Betty Allen/Curtis Rayam; sw: Scott Joplin; cd: Gunther Schuller	

Billboard			R I A A	ARTIST		
DEBUT	PEAK	WKS		Album Title.. Catalog	Label & Number
12/26/60+	6	48		174 **Unsinkable Molly Brown, The**	Capitol 1509
				Tammy Grimes/Harve Presnell; sw: Meredith Willson	
3/17/58+	5	191	●	175 **West Side Story**	Columbia 5230
				Grammy: Hall of Fame ★ NRR	
				Carol Lawrence/Larry Kert/Chita Rivera/Art Smith; mu: **Leonard Bernstein**; ly: Stephen Sondheim	
6/20/09	123	2		176 **West Side Story**	Masterworks 52391
				Grammy: Cast Album	
				George Akram/Cody Green/Karen Olivo/Josefina Scaglione; mu: **Leonard Bernstein**; ly: Stephen Sondheim	
4/4/64	28	14		177 **What Makes Sammy Run?**...	Columbia 2440
				Steve Lawrence/Sally Ann Howes/Robert Alda; sw: Ervin Drake	
1/24/04+	128	56	▲	178 **Wicked** .... **Cat:**#3/204	Decca Broadway 001682
				Grammy: Cast Album	
				Idina Menzel/Kristin Chenoweth/Carole Shelley/Joel Grey; mu/ly: Stephen Schwartz	
1/30/61	6	41		179 **Wildcat**	RCA Victor 1060
				Lucille Ball/Keith Andes; mu: Cy Coleman; ly: Carolyn Leigh	
5/3/75	43	16	●	180 **Wiz, The**	Atlantic 18137
				Grammy: Cast Album	
				Stephanie Mills/Tiger Haynes/Ted Ross/Hinton Battle; sw: Charlie Smalls	
6/27/81	196	2		181 **Woman Of The Year**	Arista 8303
				Lauren Bacall/Harry Guardino/Rex Everhart; mu: John Kander; ly: Fred Ebb	
1/26/08	197	1		182 **Xanadu**	PS Classic 858
				Kerry Butler/Cheyenne Jackson/Tony Roberts/Jackie Hoffman; sw: **Jeff Lynne** and John Farrar	
7/1/67	165	5		183 **You're A Good Man, Charlie Brown**...........................	MGM 9
				Gary Burghoff/Bob Balaban/Bill Hinnant/Reva Rose; sw: Clark Gesner	
1/25/69	177	7		184 **Zorba**	Capitol 118
				Herschel Bernardi/Maria Karnilova; mu: John Kander; ly: Fred Ebb	

Billboard DEBUT	PEAK	WKS	R I A A	ARTIST Album Title.. Catalog	Label & Number

CHRISTMAS (Various Artists)

1/13/07	11ˣ	3		1 ABC: A Holiday Affair	Buena Vista 000116
11/13/04+	39ˣ	2		2 Absolute Favorite Christmas	Fervent 30055 [2]
12/9/06+	35ˣ	2		3 Absolute Favorite Christmas For Kids .... Cat:#43/1 Christmas charts: 41/'06, 35/'09	Fervent/Curb 886476
11/29/08+	10	9		4 All Wrapped Up [M] Christmas chart: 1/'08	Hollywood 002724
11/28/09+	87	2		5 All Wrapped Up: Vol. 2 .... [M] Christmas chart: 7/'09	Hollywood 004732
12/16/00	145	3		6 All-Star Christmas .... Christmas chart: 25/'00	Epic 85113
11/20/82	96	9		7 Annie's Christmas .... children's story with music, narration and dialogue; Annie: Robin Ignico; narrator: William Woodson	Columbia 38361
12/20/08	194	1		8 Awesome! 80s Christmas: Holiday Party Starter .... Christmas chart: 33/'08	Compass 39503
1/12/08	16ˣ	3		9 Baby It's Cold Outside............... Cat:#43/3 Christmas charts: 16/'07, 30/'08	Starbucks 39775
10/18/08	22ˣ	2		10 Best Of Christmas Jazz: 20th Century Masters: The Christmas Collection - Volume 1, The	Verve 009214
10/18/08	23ˣ	2		11 Best Of Christmas Jazz: 20th Century Masters: The Christmas Collection - Volume 2, The	Verve 009213
1/14/06	25ˣ	2		12 Best Of Motown Christmas-Volume 2: 20th Century Masters The Christmas Collection, The............... Christmas chart: 25/'05	Motown 005034
1/14/06	21ˣ	2		13 Best Of Smooth Jazz Christmas: 20th Century Masters The Christmas Collection, The .... [I] Christmas chart: 21/'05	Hip-O 005163
12/23/89+	24ˣ	11	●	14 Billboard Greatest Christmas Hits (1935-1954)............... Cat:#37/11 Christmas charts: 28/'89, 25/'90, 24/'91, 35/'97	Rhino 70637
12/23/89+	15ˣ	59	▲	15 Billboard Greatest Christmas Hits (1955-Present) .... Cat:#13/41 Christmas charts: 19/'89, 21/'90, 15/'91, 17/'92, 22/'93, 25/'94, 25/'95, 23/'96, 32/'97, 32/'98, 32/'99, 31/'00	Rhino 70636
12/16/06	196	1		16 Blue Collar Christmas: Redneck Style .... [N] Christmas chart: 37/'06	Madacy 52588
12/4/04	135	3		17 Care Bears: Holiday Hugs!............... Christmas charts: 10/'04, 13/'05	Madacy Kids 50631
12/26/92	196	1		18 Carnegie Hall Christmas Concert, A............... [L] cd: Andre Previn; pf: Kathleen Battle, Frederica von Stade and Wynton Marsalis; recorded on 12/8/1991	Sony Classical 48235
12/14/96	113	5		19 Carols Of Christmas, The............... [I] Christmas chart: 22/'96	Windham Hill 11193
1/13/07	41ˣ	1		20 Celtic Christmas, A...............	Madacy 53051
12/2/95	97	6		21 Celtic Christmas............... Cat:#36/3 Christmas chart: 15/'95	Windham Hill 11178
11/30/96	96	7		22 Celtic Christmas II............... Christmas chart: 14/'96	Windham Hill 11192
11/29/97	103	6		23 Celtic Christmas III............... [I] Christmas charts: 13/'97, 34/'98	Windham Hill 11233
11/21/98	27ˣ	5		24 Celtic Christmas IV............... [I] Christmas chart: 27/'98	Windham Hill 11367
12/15/07	170	2		25 Celtic Ladies Christmas............... Christmas charts: 37/'07, 50/'08	Madacy 53227 [3]
11/30/02	30ˣ	8		26 Children Sing For Children............... songs by various children's choirs from around the world; Christmas charts: 30/'02, 38/'03, 44/'04	United Audio 10991
12/9/72	7ˣ	12		27 Christmas Album, The Cat:#17/6 Christmas charts: 7/'72, 10/'73, 19/'91, 28/'92	Columbia 30763 [2]
12/19/87+	26ˣ	5		28 Christmas Album, A............... all 11 tracks taken from #27 above; Christmas charts: 27/'87, 26/'88	Columbia 39466
11/17/01	21ˣ	10	●	29 Christmas: All-Time Greatest Records............... Cat:#17/7 Christmas charts: 21/'01, 35/'02, 43/'04	Curb 77351
11/20/99	40ˣ	2		30 Christmas: All-Time Greatest Records, Volume 2 .... Christmas charts: 40/'99, 42/'04	Curb 77515
12/12/81	210	1		31 Christmas Country	Elektra 554
12/14/63	13ˣ	3		32 Christmas Gift For You (From Philles Records) .... Grammy: Hall of Fame ★ RS500 #142 also see Phil Spector's Christmas Album	Philles 4005
12/19/87+	22ˣ	10		33 Christmas Gift For You (From Phil Spector) .... [R] reissue of #32 above; Christmas charts: 25/'87, 22/'88, 30/'90; also see Phil Spector's Christmas Album	Phil Spector/Rhino 70235
12/1/73	7ˣ	4		34 Christmas Greetings From Nashville	RCA Victor 0262
12/23/67	98ˣ	2		35 Christmas In Germany .... [F] 10 of 14 songs performed by the 120+ children's choir "Bielefelder Kinderchor"; first released in 1957	Capitol 10095
11/15/03	27ˣ	2		36 Christmas In Nashville...............	Madacy 0496
12/15/07	85	3		37 Christmas Number 1's............... Christmas chart: 33/'07	Hip-O 009212
12/16/95	161	3		38 Christmas Of Hope...............	Columbia 67407
12/28/96	155	2		39 Christmas On Death Row .... Christmas chart: 35/'96	Death Row 90108
12/12/87+	130	8		40 Christmas Rap .... Christmas charts: 4/'87, 4/'88	Profile 1247
11/23/96+	17ˣ	5		41 Christmas: 16 Most Requested Songs .... Christmas charts: 28/'96, 34/'99, 17/'09	Columbia/Legacy 48947

Billboard			R I A A	ARTIST		
DEBUT	PEAK	WKS		Album Title.. Catalog	Label & Number

DEBUT	PEAK	WKS		ARTIST / Album Title	Label & Number
11/3/07+	41ˣ	5		42 **Christmas Songs 4 Kids** .... Christmas charts: 45/'07, 41/'08	Twin Sisters 155
11/30/02+	28ˣ	4		43 **City On A Hill: It's Christmas Time**....................... Cat:#43/1 Christmas chart: 33/'03	Essential 0693
12/20/03	133	2		44 **Classic Country: Christmas** .... Christmas chart: 28/'03	Time-Life 18927
12/19/98	186	2		45 **Colors Of Christmas, The** .... Christmas chart: 32/'98	Windham Hill 11368
11/25/95	173	1		46 **Contemporary Gospel Christmas, A**............... Cat:#3/13 Christmas charts: 20/'95, 5/'96, 15/'99	Regency 20026
12/20/97	159	2		47 **Country Cares For Kids** .... Christmas chart: 28/'97	BNA 67518
12/25/82+	172	4		48 **Country Christmas, A**	RCA Victor 4396
11/29/97	96	6		49 **Country Superstar Christmas, A**............................. Christmas chart: 13/'97	Hip-O 40066
12/12/98	152	3		50 **Country Superstar Christmas II, A**......................... Christmas chart: 27/'98	Hip-O 40124
12/16/00	185	2		51 **Country Superstar Christmas III, A**........................ Christmas chart: 40/'00	Hip-O 541831
11/10/07	32	10		52 **Disney Channel Holiday** .... Cat:#12/6 Christmas charts: 4/'07, 6/'08	Walt Disney 000845
11/29/08+	34	9		53 **Disney: Fairy Tale Holiday** .... [M] Christmas chart: 3/'08	Walt Disney 002051
11/21/09+	64	9		54 **Disney: Holiday Magic 2009** .... Christmas chart: 3/'09	Walt Disney 004580
12/7/91	25ˣ	3		55 **Disney Presents A Family Christmas** .... Christmas charts: 25/'91, 28/'92	Disneyland 005
12/23/67	83ˣ	2		56 **Disney Presents 30 Favorite Songs Of Christmas** .... first released in 1963	Disneyland 1239
11/30/96	192	1		57 **Disney's Christmas Collection** .... Cat:#3/34 Christmas charts: 17/'96, 10/'97, 3/'98, 33/'99, 24/'00, 21/'01, 44/'02, 17/'04	Walt Disney 60887
12/2/95	119	5		58 **Disney's Christmas Sing Along** .... Christmas chart: 22/'95	Walt Disney 60882
11/15/03	35ˣ	3		59 **Disney's Family Christmas Collection**	Walt Disney 60130
12/5/98	187	3		60 **Disney's Favorite Christmas Songs**	Walt Disney 60987
12/1/07+	64	8		61 **Disney's Holiday Celebration 2007** .... Christmas chart: 3/'07	Walt Disney 00855
11/19/05+	21ˣ	3		62 **Disney's Princess Christmas Album** .... Christmas charts: 50/'05, 21/'09	Walt Disney 861378
12/6/97	32ˣ	2		63 **Disney's Season Of Song: A Traditional Holiday Collection** .... [I]	Walt Disney 60843
11/8/08	30	10		64 **Essential Now That's What I Call Christmas, The**.......... Cat:#28/1 Christmas charts: 5/'08, 26/'09	Universal 011941
12/5/09	84	5		65 **Essential Now That's What I Call Christmas, The** .... [R]	Universal 011941
12/7/91	8ˣ	10		66 **50 All Time Christmas Favorites** Cat:#11/15 all songs performed by Canadian studio vocalists and musicians; christmas charts: 8/'91, 16/'92, 39/'94	Madacy 53289 [2]
12/3/05	66	7		67 **40 Years: A Charlie Brown Christmas**....................... Christmas charts: 4/'05, 48/'06, 42/'08	Peak 8534
11/25/95	34ˣ	2		68 **Frosty The Snowman** .... Cat:#45/2	LaserLight 15307
12/25/99	179	2		69 **Gift Of Christmas, A** .... Christmas chart: 39/'99	Foundation 99681
11/29/97	35ˣ	1		70 **God With Us: A Celebration Of Christmas Carols & Classics**	Sparrow 51642
1/7/89	140	2	●	71 **GRP Christmas Collection, A**.............................. [I] Christmas charts: 5/'88, 5/'89, 11/'90	GRP 9574
1/6/90	162	1	●	72 **GRP Christmas Collection, A**........................... [I-R] see album above for tracks	GRP 9574
12/14/91	137	4		73 **GRP Christmas Collection Vol. II, A** .... Christmas chart: 17/'91	GRP 9650
12/25/93	185	1		74 **GRP Christmas Collection Vol. III, A** .... [I]	GRP 9728
12/5/92	82	6		75 **Handel's Messiah - A Soulful Celebration** .... Christmas chart: 12/'92	Reprise 26980
12/8/01+	9ˣ	24		76 **Happy Holidays** Cat:#6/14 Christmas charts: 26/'01, 9/'02, 34/'03, 27/'04	United Audio 10801
1/17/09	175	1		77 **Happy Holidays: A Traditional Christmas: Volume 2** .... Christmas chart: 19/'08	Compass 43728
12/4/04	134	5		78 **Have A Fun Christmas** .... [N] Christmas chart: 30/'04	Time-Life 18951
12/9/67	54ˣ	4		79 **Have A Jewish Christmas...?** .... [C] Lennie Weinrib narrates comedy sketches	Tower 5081
11/22/08	189	1		80 **Have You Heard?**.. Christmas chart: 32/'08	Starbucks 1237346
12/8/07	82	5		81 **Hear Something Country: Christmas** .... Christmas charts: 3/'07, 49/'08	BNA 13016
12/6/03+	29ˣ	5		82 **Heavenly Christmas**	Rhino 73958
1/13/07	34ˣ	1		83 **Here Comes Santa Claus**	United Audio 11341
1/12/08	18ˣ	2		84 **Home For The Holidays: A Traditional Christmas Vol. 1**	Universal 012140
12/6/08	103	5		85 **Hotel Cafe Presents: Winter Songs, The** .... Christmas charts: 13/'08, 29/'09	Hotel Cafe 36111
11/19/05+	26ˣ	7		86 **Incredible Singing Christmas Tree, The**................. Christmas chart: 26/'05	Big Idea 35051

DEBUT	PEAK	WKS	R I A A	ARTIST / Album Title	Catalog	Label & Number
1/27/07	45ˣ	1		87 Integrity's iWorship: A Christmas Offering		Integrity 94558
12/6/03	182	2		88 Integrity's iWorsh!p Christmas: A Total Worship Experience		Integrity 90365 [2]
				Christmas chart: 18/'03		
12/9/95	95	5		89 Jazz To The World	Cat:#36/2	Blue Note 32127
12/10/88	28ˣ	2		90 Jingle Bell Jazz	[I]	Columbia 36803
				originally issued in 1962 on Columbia 8693		
1/19/08	80	1		91 Jingle Bell Jukebox: An Early Rock-N-Roll Christmas	[X]	Sony 17914
				Christmas chart: 4/'07		
12/6/08	177	2		92 Jingle Bell Rock: Malt Shop Merry Christmas		Compass 43725
				Christmas chart: 16/'09		
10/17/09	45ˣ	1		93 John Deere: Smoky Mountain Holiday	[I]	Camden 55
1/1/94	186	2		94 LaFace Family Christmas, A		LaFace 26011
				Christmas chart: 28/'93		
11/28/09+	66	11		95 Letters To Santa: A Holiday Musical Collection		Concord 23190666
				Christmas chart: 1/'09		
12/18/04	195	1		96 Lifetime Of Romance: Christmas		Time-Life 19003
				Christmas chart: 46/'04		
1/17/09	10ˣ	1		97 Looney Tunes Sing-A-Long Christmas, A	Cat:#12/1	Immergent 281145
12/1/07	129	2		98 Love's Holiday: A Gospel Christmas		Time Life 19530
				Christmas chart: 30/'07		
12/5/09	45	6		99 Making Merry		Starbucks 86608
				Christmas chart: 9/'09		
12/17/05	149	3		100 Martha Stewart Living Music: Traditional Songs For The Holidays		Legacy 97702
				Christmas chart: 34/'05		
1/14/06	38ˣ	2		101 Martha Stewart Living Music: Jazz For The Holidays		Legacy 97699
				Christmas chart: 38/'05		
1/19/08	21ˣ	1		102 Martini Merry Christmas		Compass 010126
12/8/07	168	3		103 Mary, Did You Know?		Word-Curb/War. 887317
				Christmas chart: 15/'07		
1/4/03	38ˣ	1		104 Maybe This Christmas		Nettwerk 30295
12/30/57+	19	3		105 Merry Christmas From The Ames Brothers – Don Cornell – Eileen Barton – Johnny Desmond	[EP]	Coral EC 82003 [2]
				7" double-packet EP (originally released as a 10" LP in 1952 on Coral 56080)		
12/28/68	24ˣ	1		106 Merry Christmas From Motown		Motown 681
				reissued in 1970 as Christmas Gift Rap on Motown 725		
12/22/07	199	1		107 Mix Style: Santa Claus Family		Compass 39798
11/25/00+	12ˣ	9		108 Most Wonderful Time Of The Year, The	Cat:#12/14	LaserLight 55610 [3]
				3 CD albums: Merry Christmas from Pat Boone... (LaserLight 15469 in 1992), Home For Christmas (LaserLight 12345 in 1994), and The Most Wonderful Time of the Year (LaserLight 12507 in 1995); Christmas charts: 12/'00, 12/'01		
12/8/73	❶¹ˣ	4		109 Motown Christmas, A		Motown 795 [2]
				Christmas charts: 1/'73, 26/'87		
12/15/01	162	3		110 MTV TRL Christmas		Lava 83512
				Christmas chart: 17/'01		
11/26/05	49ˣ	1		111 My Little Pony: A Very Minty Christmas		Hasbro 88880
				this is actually a children's DVD (no tracks); Christmas chart: 49/'05		
12/24/88+	12ˣ	11		112 Narada The Christmas Collection	[I]	Narada 63902
				Christmas charts: 14/'88, 12/'89, 24/'90		
12/19/92	166	2		113 Narada Christmas Collection Volume 2	[I]	Narada 63909
				Christmas chart: 23/'92		
1/19/91	19ˣ	1		114 Narada Nutcracker, The	[I]	Narada 63904
12/16/06	177	2		115 Nativity Story: Sacred Songs, The		New Line 39073
				Christmas chart: 19/'06		
10/18/08	31	15		116 Nightmare Revisited	Cat:#37/1	Walt Disney 001747
				Christmas charts: 1/'08, 2/'09		
1/13/07	20ˣ	2		117 No Way! It's Like So Christmas		St. Clair 3577
11/10/01	3¹	12	▲⁶	118 Now That's What I Call Christmas!	Cat:❶¹⁴/41	Universal 585620 [2]
				Christmas charts: 1/'01, 1/'02, 3/'03, 6/'04, 3/'05, 41/'06, 25/'07, 25/'08, 35/'09		
12/19/09	177	1	▲⁶	119 Now That's What I Call Christmas!	[R]	Universal 585620 [2]
11/8/03	17	10	▲²	120 Now That's What I Call Christmas! 2 The Signature Collection	Cat:❶³/28	Capitol 83098 [2]
				Christmas charts: 1/'03, 4/'04, 9/'05, 27/'06, 26/'07		
10/28/06	10	12	▲	121 Now That's What I Call Christmas! 3	Cat:#2⁴/19	Sony 89482 [2]
				Christmas charts: 1/'06, 3/'07, 7/'08, 12/'09		
12/5/09	56	5		122 Now That's What I Call Christmas! 3	[R]	Sony 89482
11/14/09	57	9		123 NOW That's What I Call A Country Christmas		EMI 56260 [2]
				Christmas chart: 10/'09		
1/15/00	27ˣ	1		124 Nutcracker & Messiah Highlights		LaserLight 24829 [2]
				2 CD albums: The Nutcracker Highlights by the Berlin Symphony Orchestra (LaserLight 15146 in 1989) and Handel's Messiah by The Oratorio Society Of New York (LaserLight 12346 in 1998)		
11/29/97	22ˣ	7		125 Nutcracker Christmas, A	Cat:#28/4	Intersound 1631
12/25/93+	40ᶜ	5		126 Nutcracker Highlights, The		LaserLight 15146
12/15/79	209	3		127 On This Christmas Night	[X]	MCA Songbird 3184
12/5/70	7ˣ	4		128 Peace On Earth		Capitol 585 [2]
12/7/02	120	4		129 Peaceful Christmas, A	[I]	Time-Life 18858
				Christmas chart: 25/'02		
12/23/72	6ˣ	4		130 Phil Spector's Christmas Album	[R]	Apple 3400
				reissue of A Christmas Gift For You (From Philles Records); Christmas charts: 6/'72, 8/'73		
12/2/00	32	7	▲	131 Platinum Christmas	Cat:#23/5	Arista/Jive 41741
				Christmas charts: 3/'00, 30/'01		

CHRISTMAS (Various Artists)

Billboard DEBUT	PEAK	WKS	R I A A	ARTIST Album Title .... Catalog	Label & Number
12/8/01	24^X	2		**132 Radio Disney Holiday Jams** .... Cat:#19/3	Walt Disney 60696
12/21/02	194	1		**133 Radio Disney Holiday Jams 2** .... Christmas chart: 24/'02	Walt Disney 60988
12/4/04	138	4		**134 Radio Disney Jingle Jams** .... Christmas chart: 8/'04	Walt Disney 861191
12/21/96	189	2		**135 Rudolph, Frosty And Friends Favorite Christmas Songs** .... Christmas chart: 40/'97	Sony Wonder 67766
12/6/08	160	4		**136 Santa Baby: A Romantic Christmas** .... Christmas chart: 15/'09	Compass 43718
12/20/08+	156	3		**137 Santa Claus Is Coming To Town: A Family Christmas** .... Cat:#17/2 Christmas charts: 10/'07, 15/'08	Compass 43723
12/9/67	17^X	4		**138 Santa's Own Christmas** .... [N] Santa (Walt Jacobs) sings and tells stories for children	Capitol 2836
1/19/08	127	1		**139 Season Of Soul: A Classic R&B Christmas, A** .... [X] Christmas chart: 8/'07	Universal 010127
12/25/65	37^X	1		**140 Season's Greetings/A Christmas Festival Of Stars!** .... first released in 1959	Columbia 1394 / 8189
12/18/04	153	2		**141 Shimmy Down The Chimney: A Country Christmas** .... Christmas chart: 25/'04	Capitol 71143
12/10/05+	37^X	2		**142 Shout Praises! Kids Christmas** .... Christmas charts: 47/'05, 37/'06	Integrity 92639
1/16/99	29^X	1		**143 Sleigh Ride: The Joy Of Christmas**	Reader's Digest 9114
12/20/08	185	1		**144 Soft Rock Christmas, A** .... Christmas charts: 37/'08, 27/'09	Compass 43722
1/13/07	33^X	1		**145 Song For A Winter's Night**	Sony 85762
11/29/08	87	6		**146 Songs For A Cause** .... Christmas chart: 28/'08	Sony 35284
11/24/01	116	8		**147 Songs 4 Worship Christmas** .... Cat:#17/2 Christmas charts: 9/'01, 23/'02, 5/'03, 17/'04	Integrity 14804 [2]
10/27/07	30^X	1		**148 Songs 4 Worship Christmas Joy**	Integrity 84294 [2]
11/15/03+	32^X	3		**149 Songs 4 Worship Kids Christmas**	Integrity 18952
12/21/68+	8^X	8		**150 Soul Christmas** Christmas charts: 13/'68, 8/'69, 8/'70	Atco 269
11/24/07	34	10		**151 Stockings By The Fire** .... Christmas chart: 3/'07	EMI 103
11/15/03+	13^X	12		**152 Strawberry Shortcake: Berry, Merry Christmas** .... [M] Christmas charts: 22/'03, 13/'04, 30/'05, 29/'06	Koch 9502
11/29/97	43	7		**153 Superstar Christmas** .... Cat:#10/13 Christmas charts: 5/'97, 18/'98, 36/'99, 35/'00	Epic 68750
12/23/95	182	1		**154 Superstars Of Christmas 1995**	Capitol 35347
11/29/08	152	5		**155 This Warm December: A Brushfire Holiday Vol. 1** .... Christmas chart: 40/'08	Brushfire 012191
11/15/03	40^X	2		**156 Thomas Kinkade Christmas Favorites: Victorian Christmas** .... [I] Christmas charts: 40/'03, 50/'04	Madacy 4460
11/15/03	24^X	3		**157 Thomas Kinkade Home For Christmas: Village Christmas** .... Christmas charts: 24/'03, 44/'06	Madacy 4459
11/15/03	33^X	1		**158 Thomas Kinkade The Best Of Christmas: Silent Night** .... [I]	Madacy 4425
12/13/03	162	3		**159 Thomas Kinkade Treasury Of Christmas: St. Nicholas Circle** .... Christmas chart: 27/'03	Madacy 2219 [2]
11/3/07	49^X	1		**160 Thomas Kinkade: Treasury Of Christmas**	Madacy 53097
11/24/01	65	7		**161 Time-Life Treasury Of Christmas, The** .... Cat:#7/11 Christmas charts: 6/'01, 12/'02, 27/'03, 47/'04	Time-Life 18800 [2]
11/23/02	46	7		**162 Time-Life Treasury Of Christmas: Holiday Memories, The** .... Cat:#8/10 Christmas charts: 6/'02, 13/'03, 35/'04	Time-Life 18857 [2]
12/20/03	144	2		**163 Time-Life Treasury Of Christmas: Evergreen, The** .... Christmas chart: 10/'03	Time-Life 18950
12/16/06	191	1		**164 Time Life-Treasury Of Christmas: The Greatest Holiday Duets, The**	Time Life 73340
12/20/08	158	2		**165 'Tis The Season: Celtic Christmas** .... Christmas charts: 25/'07, 40/'08	Compass 43733
1/19/08	40^X	1		**166 'Tis The Season: Christmas Piano & Harp** .... [I]	Compass 39778 [2]
1/12/08	17^X	2		**167 'Tis The Season: Classical Christmas** .... [I]	Compass 39780
1/17/09	36^X	1		**168 'Tis The Season: Country Christmas**	Compass 43726
1/17/09	27^X	1		**169 'Tis The Season: Deck The Halls**	Compass 43732 [2]
11/22/08	105	4		**170 'Tis The Season: Kids Christmas Sing-Along** .... Cat:#32/1 Christmas charts: 26/'08, 18/'09	Compass 43735
12/5/09	150	3		**171 'Tis The Season: Kids Christmas Sing-Along** .... [R]	Compass 43735
1/17/09	200	1		**172 'Tis The Season: Praise & Worship Christmas** .... Christmas chart: 23/'08	Compass 43717
1/17/09	31^X	1		**173 'Tis The Season: Smooth Jazz Christmas** .... Cat:#48/1	Compass 43734 [2]
12/5/98	71	6	●	**174 Ultimate Christmas** .... Cat:#4/22 Christmas charts: 8/'98, 11/'99, 12/'00, 23/'01, 44/'02	Arista 19019
12/11/04	150	3		**175 Ultimate Christmas 2** .... Christmas chart: 32/'04 songs by Christina Aguilera, Kelly Clarkson, Dido, R. Kelly, Elvis Presley, Santana, and others	BMG 64195
12/17/94	139	4		**176 Ultimate Christmas Album, The** .... Christmas chart: 31/'94	Collectables 2511
12/23/95	147	2		**177 Ultimate Christmas Album Volume II, The**	Collectables 2512
12/20/03	159	2		**178 Very Special Acoustic Christmas, A** .... Christmas charts: 28/'03	Lost Highway 001038

DEBUT	PEAK	WKS	R I A A	ARTIST Album Title... Catalog	Label & Number
11/14/87	20	13	▲⁴	179 **Very Special Christmas, A** **Cat:❶**¹/63	A&M 3911
				Christmas charts: 1/'87, 1/'88, 4/'89, 5/'90, 3/'91, 5/'92, 9/'93, 9/'94, 9/'95, 12/'06, 14/'97, 21/'98, 34/'99, 34/'00, 41/'02, 40/'05, 33/'09	
12/17/88+	57	5		180 **Very Special Christmas, A**... **[R]**	A&M 3911
12/9/89+	55	7		181 **Very Special Christmas, A**... **[R]**	A&M 3911
12/8/90+	58	6		182 **Very Special Christmas, A**... **[R]**	A&M 3911
12/19/09	193	1		183 **Very Special Christmas, A**... **[R]**	A&M 3911 [2]
11/14/92	7	11	▲²	184 **Very Special Christmas 2, A** .... **Cat:#3/34**	A&M 540003
				Christmas charts: 2/'92, 6/'93, 8/'94, 12/'95, 18/'96, 23/'97, 39/'98	
11/8/97	31	10	●	185 **Very Special Christmas 3, A** .... **Cat:#3/14**	A&M 0764
				Christmas charts: 2/'97, 7/'98, 34/'99, 33/'00	
12/1/01	112	6		186 **Very Special Christmas 5, A**..	A&M 3138
				Christmas charts: 12/'01, 21/'02, 38/'03	
12/4/99	100	7		187 **Very Special Christmas Live: From Washington, D.C., A**............. **Cat:#38/1 [L]**	A&M 0484
				Christmas charts: 17/'99, 11/'00	
12/12/09	116	4		188 **Very Special Christmas 7, A**..	A&M 013527
				Christmas chart: 34/'09	
12/5/98	162	1		189 **Very Veggie Christmas, A** .... **Cat:#18/4 [N]**	Lyrick 9456
				Christmas charts: 11/'98, 22/'99, 46/'05	
11/1/08	41ˣ	1		190 **We Wish You A Metal Xmas And A Headbanging New Year**...........................	Armoury 25016
1/19/06	88	1		191 **What A Swingin' Season: A Big Band Christmas** .... **[X]**	Sony 17913
				Christmas chart: 5/'07	
12/20/08	187	1		192 **White Christmas: A Traditional Christmas Volume 2**	Universal 012141
				Christmas chart: 25/'07	
11/16/02	118	7		193 **Windham Hill Christmas, A** .... **[I]**	Windham Hill 11651
				Christmas chart: 13/'02	
11/15/03	11ˣ	5		194 **Windham Hill Christmas II, A** .... **[I]**	Windham Hill 53901
12/4/04	155	3		195 **Windham Hill Christmas: I'll Be Home For Christmas, A**............... **[I]**	Windham Hill 64413
				Christmas chart: 23/'04	
1/14/06	15ˣ	2		196 **Windham Hill Christmas: The Night Before Christmas, A** .... **[I]**	Windham Hill 71888
				Christmas chart: 15/'05	
12/4/99	131	6		197 **Winter Solstice On Ice**.. **[I]**	Windham Hill 11459 [2]
				Christmas charts: 12/'99, 21/'00	
12/5/98	30ˣ	2		198 **Winter Solstice Reunion, A** .... **[I]**	Windham Hill 11369
11/22/08	42	11		199 **Winter Wonderland**	Starbucks 1196825
				Christmas chart: 5/'08	
12/7/85+	77	14	●	200 **Winter's Solstice, A**... **[I]**	Windham Hill 1045
				Christmas charts: 15/'87, 17/'88, 16/'89, 13/'90, 22/'91	
12/20/86+	172	5	●	201 **Winter's Solstice, A**... **[I-R]**	Windham Hill 1045
12/10/88+	108	7		202 **Winter's Solstice II, A** .... **Cat:#39/1 [I]**	Windham Hill 1077
				Christmas charts: 8/'88, 14/'89, 19/'90, 16/'91	
12/1/90	90	8	●	203 **Winter's Solstice III, A**... **Cat:#32/5 [I]**	Windham Hill 1098
				Christmas charts: 8/'90, 11/'91, 29/'92	
11/27/93	55	7	●	204 **Winter's Solstice IV, A** .... **Cat:#20/7 [I]**	Windham Hill 11134
				Christmas charts: 11/'93, 17/'94	
12/2/95	85	6		205 **Winter's Solstice V, A** .... **[I]**	Windham Hill 11174
				Christmas charts: 13/'95, 13/'96	
12/13/97	139	4		206 **Winter's Solstice VI, A** .... **[I]**	Windham Hill 11220
				Christmas chart: 21/'97	
12/1/01	176	3		207 **Winter's Solstice: Silver Anniversary Edition, A** .... **[I]**	Windham Hill 11604
				Christmas charts: 14/'01, 15/'08	
11/15/03	23ˣ	1		208 **WNUA 95.5: Smooth Jazz Sampler Volume 16**..	WNUA 9553 [2]
1/20/07	27ˣ	2		209 **Worship Jamz: Christmas**	Razor & Tie 89119
10/19/02	45	13	▲	210 **WOW Christmas (Red)** .... **Cat:#7/13**	Word 886078 [2]
				Christmas charts: 5/'02, 13/'03, 20/'04, 44/'05	
11/19/05	54	8	●	211 **WOW Christmas (Green)** .... **Cat:#19/10**	Word-Curb 86414 [2]
				Christmas charts: 5/'05, 26/'06, 41/'07	
12/1/07	78	6		212 **WOW Gospel Christmas**	Word-Curb 95761 [2]
				Christmas chart: 9/'07	
1/15/00	28ˣ	1		213 **Yule B' Swingin'**..	Hip-O 40117
				first released in 1998	

Billboard			R I A A	ARTIST	
DEBUT	PEAK	WKS		Album Title.. Catalog	Label & Number

VARIOUS ARTISTS COMPILATIONS

12/5/81	203	8		1 Aerobic Dancing!..	Parade 100
4/3/99	75	11		2 Absolute Hits, The...	Atlantic 83158
3/26/05	187	1		3 Absolute Modern Worship For Kids..	Fervent 30062
3/31/07	172	1		4 Absolute Modern Worship For Kids (Yellow)...	Fervent/Word-Curb 86487
4/3/04	151	2		5 Absolute Worship..	Fervent 30045 [2]
1/19/08	100	5		6 Across The Pond..	Universal 009613
7/16/05	170	2		7 Agarron Durango vs. Tierra Caliente.. [F]	Disa 726829
6/26/04	180	3		8 Agarron Duranguense... [F]	Disa 726970
2/17/62	99	7		9 Alan Freed's Memory Lane...	End 314
8/5/78	151	6		10 Alivemutherforya.. [I-L]	Columbia 35349
4/1/95	40ᶜ	1		11 All The Best From Ireland..	Madacy 71
11/24/62	110	7		12 All The Hits By All The Stars...	Parkway 7013
5/18/91	187	1		13 Alligator Records 20th Anniversary Collection, The	Alligator 105/6 [2]
2/19/94	167	3		14 Alternative NRG.. [L]	Hollywood 61449
7/25/09	165	2		15 Alternative Press: Summer Of Rock 2009: Your Ultimate Guide......................	Red 9471
9/23/95	198	2	▲	16 Amazing Grace: A Country Salute To Gospel...	Sparrow 51445
7/3/04	157	1		17 Amazing Grace 3: A Country Salute To Gospel..	Sparrow 95556
11/22/69	197	1		18 Amazing Mets, The...	Buddah 1969
				featuring the singing voices of the New York Mets; 1969 World Series Champs (note label number)	
12/30/72+	201	7		19 Amazing Spider-Man: From Beyond The Grave!..	Buddah 5119
				5 spoken episodes plus 4 songs performed by The Webspinners	
12/22/01	17	12	●	20 America: A Tribute To Heroes... [L]	Interscope 493188 [2]
				performances from the telethon aired on 9/21/2001 to raise money for the September 11th disaster relief fund	
7/13/96	51	5		21 America Is Dying Slowly...	Red Hot 61925
1/31/76	201	7		22 American Graffiti Vol. III.. [O]	MCA 8008 [2]
5/31/97	198	1		23 ...And Then There Was Bass...	Tony Mercedes 26038
5/19/73	213	3		24 Ann Arbor Blues & Jazz Festival 1972............................... [L]	Atlantic 502 [2]
				recorded from 9/8 - 9/10/1972 at Otis Spann Memorial Field in Ann Arbor, Michigan	
12/28/68	200	2		25 Anthology Of British Blues Vol. 2, An..	Immediate 52014
4/13/96	130	1		26 Antonio Vivaldi, The Four Seasons.................................... [I]	Digital Master. 71847
9/6/69	185	5		27 Apollo 11: Flight To The Moon..	Bell 1100
				actual voice transmissions of America's space missions; narrated by astronaut Wally Schirra	
2/22/64	43	17		28 Apollo Saturday Night... [L]	Atco 159
				recorded on 11/16/1963 at the Apollo Theater in New York City	
2/21/04	157	2		29 Arcoiris Musical Mexicano 2004.. [F]	Univision 310233
3/26/94	184	3		30 Art Laboe's Dedicated To You Vol. 4..	Original Sound 9304
3/15/08	174	1		31 Artist's Choice: Bob Dylan...	Sony 20845
7/30/83	209	1		32 Artists And Songs That Inspired The Motown 25th Anniversary	
				T.V. Special, The...	Motown 5321
2/28/70	180	3		33 Astromusical House Of..., The.. [I]	Astro 1001/1012
				series of 12 albums, each named after a zodiac sign; music selected is supposed to reflect the character of the sign	
12/29/62+	47	12		34 At Home With That Other Family .... [C]	Roulette 25203
7/20/63	99	6		35 At The Hootenanny... [L]	Kapp 3330
7/30/83	205	3		36 Attack Of The Killer B's, Vol. 1...	Warner 23837
				B-sides and non-album tracks	
5/25/02	105	4		37 Atticus: Dragging The Lake..	Side One Dummy 1232
4/5/03	51	8		38 Atticus: Dragging The Lake II...	Side One Dummy 1236
3/12/05	63	4		39 Atticus: Dragging The Lake 3...	Side One Dummy 1252
9/8/07	139	12		40 Bachata #1s... [F]	La Calle 330050
10/31/98	51	7	●	41 Bad Boy Greatest Hits Volume 1	Bad Boy 73022
12/11/04	93	2		42 Bad Boy's R&B Hits..	Bad Boy 003700
3/27/04	2¹	16	●	43 Bad Boy's 10th Anniversary...The Hits	Bad Boy 002112
7/9/05	140	1		44 Bam Margera Presents: Viva La Bands...	456 Records 1410
4/24/04	115	4		45 Barbie Hit Mix	Kid Rhino 78074
8/12/06	171	1		46 Barbie Hit Mix 2..	Kid Rhino 74092
8/1/92	32	12		47 Barcelona Gold..	Warner 26974
11/11/06	154	1		48 B.B.T. .... [F]	Fonovisa 352772 [2]
4/7/07	195	1		49 B.B.T. 2... [F]	Fonovisa 353103 [2]
2/6/71	205	1		50 Beautiful People...	Harmony 11383
9/9/06	142	4		51 Believe: Songs Of Faith From Today's Top Country & Christian Artists...........	Arista Nashville 10822
3/15/08	148	1		52 Bella Luna... Cat:#17/4	Sony 13481
9/4/04	196	1		53 Best Classics 100... [I]	EMI Classics 85842 [6]
7/20/02	187	1		54 Best Of America, The..	Curb 78727
10/12/96+	107	26		55 Best Of Country Sing The Best Of Disney, The...	Walt Disney 60902
2/7/98	82	8		56 Best Of Love - 16 Great Soft Rock Hits...	Madacy 6806
10/23/99	178	3		57 Best Of Rap City...	Fully Loaded 48291
8/14/99	136	1		58 Best Opera Album In The World...Ever!, The...................... [F]	Virgin 42203 [2]
8/14/99	130	1		59 Best Soul Album In The World...Ever!, The..	Virgin 47421
7/17/04	160	2		60 BET Awards *04 Nominees...	Hip-O 002788
4/10/99	102	10		61 BET - Best Of Planet Groove...	Fully Loaded 47109
8/5/00	137	1		62 BET On Jazz Presents: For The Love Of Jazz	NARM 50004
3/17/07	143	1		63 Beth Moore Presents: Songs Of Deliverance	Warner 70003

Billboard DEBUT	PEAK	WKS	R I A A	ARTIST Album Title.. Catalog	Label & Number
1/11/09	190	6		61 Beware Of Greeks Bearing Gifts.. [C]	Musicor 3173
7/12/08	130	2		65 Big Blue Ball	Real World 150
8/8/70	197	2		66 Big Hits Now, The	Dunhill/ABC 50085
12/14/63+	27	18		67 Big Sounds Of The Drags!, The	Capitol 2001
				actual sounds of drag racing at a quarter-mile track; no track titles listed on this album	
4/8/72	191	4		68 Big Sur Festival/One Hand Clapping .... [L]	Columbia 31138
12/31/05	184	1		69 Bigg Snoop Dogg Presents: Welcome To Tha Chuuch - Da Album..................	Doggystyle 5874
8/5/06	161	2		70 Billboard #1s: Classic Country	Rhino 77883 [2]
7/17/04	103	2		71 Bishop T.D. Jakes Presents: He-Motions	Dexterity Sounds 77796
9/13/08	7^C	2		72 Blazin' Reggae	Razor & Tie 89100
4/10/99	199	1		73 Blue's Big Treasure - A Musical Adventure	Kid Rhino 75626
9/11/93	40	11	●	74 Bob Dylan - The 30th Anniversary Concert Celebration........................... [L]	Columbia 53230 [2]
				recorded on 10/16/1992 at Madison Square Garden in New York City	
2/15/03	73	6		75 Body + Soul: Absolute	Time-Life 18882
2/10/07+	11	4		76 Body + Soul Collection: Midnight Fire, A	Sony 21358
4/17/99	92	8		77 Body + Soul: Love Serenade .... Cat:#3/28	Time Life 33972 [2]
2/2/02	129	9		78 Body + Soul: No Control	Time Life 18805
4/18/98	119	5		79 Boom! - 17 Explosive Hits	Beast 54112
4/19/97	93	20		80 Booty Mix 2	Intersound 9510
4/25/98	182	2		81 Booty Mix 3 - Wiggle Patrol	Intersound 9526 [2]
4/22/89	178	4		82 Brazil Classics 1 Beleza Tropical .... [F]	Fly 25805
10/20/79	201	2		83 Bread & Roses .... [L]	Fantasy 79009 [2]
				recorded in October 1977 at the Greek Theater in Berkeley, California	
1/26/85	206	1		84 Breakdancing..	Columbia 39903
3/22/69	105	9		85 Bubble Gum Music Is The Naked Truth	Buddah 5032
8/26/95	91	1		86 Buy-Product - A Tasty Sample Of Choice Cuts From 16 Artists	DGC 24824
5/22/04	138	3		87 Buzz, The..	Warner 89081
8/12/06	77	7		88 Buzz Ballads...	UME 89129
4/5/08	87	6		89 Buzz Cuts	UME 89185
7/22/78	84	10		90 California Jam 2 .... [L]	Columbia 35389 [2]
				recorded on 3/18/1978 in Ontario, California	
12/7/02	88	2		91 Cash Money Records Platinum Hits Volume One	Cash Money 860933
11/13/82	63	19		92 Casino Lights .... [L]	Warner 23718
				recorded at the Montreux Jazz Festival in Switzerland	
2/14/81	204	1		93 Castle Donnington: Monsters Of Rock.. [L]	Polydor 6311
				recorded on 8/16/1980 in Castle Donnington, England	
4/24/71	221	2		94 Celebration .... [L]	Ode 77008
				recorded in 1970 at the Big Sur Folk Festival in Monterey, California	
4/13/96	121	4		95 Cell Block Compilation	Cell Block 50556
3/31/07	133	1		96 Celtic Favorites .... Cat:#44/1	Madacy 52247 [3]
2/24/01	8^C	3		97 Celtic Moods	Virgin 44951
3/16/91	47	21		98 Chess	RCA Victor 5340 [2]
10/18/08	175	1		99 Chicago's Finest: ONXRT: Live From The Archives Volume 11 .... [L]	WXRT 70
6/5/71	148	9		100 Child's Garden Of Grass (A Pre-Legalization Comedy), A .... [C]	Elektra 75012
1/22/05	65	29		101 Chosen Few: El Documental .... [F]	Chosen Few 1015
12/2/06	73	2		102 Chosen Few: El Documental II .... [F]	Chosen Few 76277 [2]
10/21/06	182	1		103 Chrome Children	Stones Throw 2150
5/22/99	11	9		104 Chronic 2000	Death Row 51161 [2]
6/21/03	157	2		105 Church: Songs Of Soul & Inspiration..	DMI 067763
12/6/08	21	1		106 Cities 97 Sampler: Live From Studio C: 20th Anniversary .... [L]	KTCZ 7013
12/5/09	32	1		107 Cities 97 Sampler 21: Live From Studio C... [L]	Cities 97 3015
3/9/02	107	7		108 City On A Hill: Sing Alleluia..	Essential 10622
9/9/00	148	9		109 City On A Hill: Songs Of Worship And Praise	Essential 10607
5/11/02	179	1		110 Classic Chillout Album, The	Epic 86337
9/29/01	60	8		111 Classical Hits	Sony Classical 89702
10/7/95	142	14		112 Club Mix 95 V. 2	Coldfront 6186
2/17/96	51	38	●	113 Club Mix '96 - Volume 1	Cold Front 6218
9/21/96	188	3		114 Club Mix '96 - Volume 2	Cold Front 6236
3/8/97	36	36	▲	115 Club Mix '97	Cold Front 6242 [2]
11/1/97	64	25	▲	116 Club Mix '98	Cold Front 6254 [2]
6/20/98	107	9		117 Club Mix '98 - Volume 2	Cold Front 6340 [2]
11/21/98+	152	7	●	118 Club Mix 99	Cold Front 6366 [2]
5/25/91	38	19	●	119 Club MTV Party To Go - Volume One	Tommy Boy 1037
10/18/03	80	6		120 CMT Most Wanted Volume 1	Capitol 93166
4/22/95	90	11		121 Come Together - America Salutes The Beatles.....................................	Liberty 31712
2/14/04	149	1		122 Committed 2 Rock...	Time Life 19674
10/30/93	3^1	55	▲^{3}	123 Common Thread: The Songs Of The Eagles	Giant 24531
				CMA: Album of the Year	
4/5/03	134	2		124 Conception: An Interpretation Of Stevie Wonder's Songs.................................	Motown 067314
				Concert For Bangla Desh, The — see HARRISON, George	
12/6/03	97	6		126 Concert For George .... [L]	Warner 74546 [2]
				tribute concert to George Harrison; recorded on 11/29/2002 (exactly one year after his death) at Royal Albert Hall	

Billboard DEBUT	PEAK	WKS	R I A A		ARTIST Album Title... Catalog	Label & Number
12/15/01	27	9	▲	127	**Concert For New York City, The** .... [L] recorded on 10/20/2001 at Madison Square Garden (proceeds donated to the Robin Hood 9/11 relief fund)	Columbia 86270 [2]
4/18/81	36	12		128	**Concerts For The People Of Kampuchea** .... [L] recorded in December 1979 in London, England	Atlantic 7005 [2]
6/13/70	175	4		129	**Core Of Rock, The**	MGM 4669
7/26/08	91	3		130	**Country Sings Disney**	Lyric Street 001932
4/11/09	116	1		131	**Creflo Dollar Presents: Heart Of Gold: Change**	Arrow 4234002
7/12/08	107	1		132	**Crue Fest Compilation** .... [L]	Seven Seven 250
12/27/03	161	7		133	**Crunk And Disorderly**	TVT 2500
7/10/04	164	2		134	**Crunk Classics**	TVT 2510
12/3/05	55	11		135	**Crunk Hits**	TVT 2505
9/9/06	48	6		136	**Crunk Hits Vol. 2**	TVT 2508
1/27/07	110	4		137	**Crunk Hits Vol. 3**	TVT 2511
12/22/07	196	1		138	**Crunk Hits Vol. 4**	TVT 2514
11/18/00	143	2		139	**Damizza Presents...Where I Wanna Be**	Baby Ree 31149
6/27/64	102	6		140	**Dance Discotheque**	Decca 74556
9/14/96	60	24		141	**Dance Hits '96 Supermix**	Popular 12001
5/17/97	144	11		142	**Dance Hits Supermix 2**	Popular 12013
3/5/94	167	16	●	143	**Dance Mix USA**	Radikal 6705
9/3/94	127	12		144	**Dance Mix USA Vol. 2**	Radikal 6712
5/6/95	71	19		145	**Dance Mix USA Vol. 3**	Radikal 6727
4/6/96	37	29		146	**Dance Mix USA Vol. 4**	Radikal 6747
10/26/96	101	15		147	**Dance Mix USA Vol. 5**	Radikal 6750
3/29/97	125	8		148	**Dance Mix USA Vol. 6**	Quality 6760
3/7/09	49	7		149	**Dark Was The Night: A Red Hot Compilation**	Red Hot 2835 [2]
11/4/06	72	2		150	**Day Hell Broke Loose 3, The**	Swishahouse 68557
5/11/91	24	16		151	**Deadicated**	Arista 8669
12/14/96	35	24	▲	152	**Death Row - Greatest Hits**	Death Row 50677 [2]
3/17/01	104	5		153	**Def Jam 1985-2001: The History Of Hip Hop, Volume 1**	Def Jam 542951
7/2/05	164	1		154	**Def Jam Recordings: #1 Spot**	Def Jam 004555
10/4/03	83	4		155	**Def Jam Recordings Presents Music Inspired By Scarface**.........................	Def Jam 001196
11/14/98	84	3		156	**Def Jam Survival Of The Illest Live From 125 N.Y.C.** .... [L]	Def Jam 538176
7/23/94	139	10		157	**DGC Rarities Vol. 1**	DGC 24704
10/18/97	36	5		158	**Diana Princess Of Wales 1961-1997** .... [L] the BBC recording of the funeral service held at London's Westminster Abbey on 9/6/1997	BBC/London 460000
12/20/97	15	11	▲	159	**Diana, Princess Of Wales - Tribute**	Columbia 69012 [2]
7/14/73	27	18	●	160	**Dick Clark/20 Years Of Rock N' Roll**	Buddah 5133 [2]
3/13/71	85	7		161	**Different Strokes**	Columbia 12
3/21/98	192	3		162	**Digital Empire - Electronica's Best**	Cold Front 6321 [2]
12/24/77+	115	11		163	**Disco Boogie**	Salsoul 0101 [2]
7/26/75	153	5		164	**Disco Gold**	Scepter 5120
7/15/78	115	12		165	**Disco Party**	Marlin 2207/8 [2]
4/28/79	159	5		166	**Disco Spectacular Inspired By The Film "Hair"**	RCA Victor 3356
6/21/75	206	15		167	**Discotech #1**	Motown 824
7/5/75	206	3		168	**Discotech #2**	Motown 831
2/14/70	95	13		169	**DisinHAIRited** .... songs written for, but not included in the musical *Hair*	RCA Victor 1163
11/20/04+	174	6		170	**Disney Channel Hits: Take 1**	Walt Disney 861230
6/27/09	72	12		171	**Disney Channel Playlist**..	Walt Disney 003713
10/8/94+	18[C]	60		172	**Disney Children's Favorites 1**	Walt Disney 60605
6/25/05	145	10		173	**Disney Girlz Rock**	Walt Disney 861322
9/27/08	154	6		174	**Disney Girlz Rock 2**	Walt Disney 001965
3/31/01	181	2	▲	175	**Disney's Greatest Volume 1**	Walt Disney 860693
10/12/96	193	1		176	**Disney's Music From The Park** .... commemorating the 25th Anniversary of Walt Disney World	Walt Disney 60915
3/23/02	127	6		177	**Disney's Superstar Hits**	Walt Disney 860711
10/5/02+	52	36	●	178	**Disneymania: Superstar Artists Sing Disney...Their Way!**........................	Walt Disney 60785
2/14/04	29	23	●	179	**Disneymania 2: Music Stars Sing Disney...Their Way!**	Walt Disney 61004
3/5/05	30	36	●	180	**Disneymania 3: Music Stars Sing Disney...Their Way!**	Walt Disney 861248
4/22/06	15	24	●	181	**Disneymania 4: Music Stars Sing Disney...Their Way!**	Walt Disney 861453
4/14/07	14	19		182	**Disneymania 5: Music Stars Sing Disney...Their Way!**	Walt Disney 000244
6/7/08	22	13		183	**Disneymania 6: Music Stars Sing Disney...Their Way!**	Walt Disney 001130
10/15/05	146	8		184	**DisneyRemixMania**...	Walt Disney 861354
11/9/02	104	1		185	**DivasLasVegas** .... [L]	Epic 86750
4/11/98	130	5		186	**D.J. Magic Mike Presents Bootyz In Motion**	Jake 90188
8/10/96	168	5		187	**D.J. Mix '96 Volume 1**	Beast 5300
5/17/97	87	13		188	**D.J. Mix '97 Vol. 2**	Beast 53112
10/25/97	178	3		189	**D.J. Mix '98 Vol. 1**	Beast 53332
1/16/99	189	1		190	**D.J. Mix 99**	Beast 54422 [3]
8/31/96	197	1		191	**DMA Dance - Vol. 2: Eurodance**	Interhit 20152
4/14/07	164	1		192	**Don Omar Presents: El Pentagono** .... [F]	VI 000870

Billboard DEBUT	PEAK	WKS	R I A A	ARTIST Album Title.. Catalog	Label & Number
5/4/02	74	10		193 Dove Hits 2002..	Sparrow 38887
4/5/03	98	8		194 Dove Hits 2003..	Reunion 10076
5/22/04	185	1		195 Dove Hits 2004..	Word-Curb 886313
3/20/04	22	8		196 Down Low, Tha...	Razor & Tie 89067
11/18/95	139	1	●	197 Down South Hustlers Bouncin' And Swingin' Tha Value Pack Compilation	No Limit 53993 [2]
11/29/75	198	2		198 Dr. Demento's Delights .... [N]	Warner 2855
12/14/96	6	13	▲	199 Dr. Dre Presents...The Aftermath	Aftermath 90044
9/20/08	39	2		200 Dr. Horrible's Sing-Along Blog	Mutant Enemy digital
12/5/64	129	3		201 Dracula's Greatest Hits .... [N]	RCA Victor 2977
				parodies of popular songs by Dracula (Gene Moss)	
11/15/97+	16^C	3		202 Drew's Famous Halloween Party Music	Turn Up 1023
9/6/03	187	1		203 Drive-Thru Invasion Tour Compilation	Drive-Thru 001028
4/29/95	137	8		204 D-Shot Presents Boss Ballin' Compilation Album - The Best In The Business...	Shot 7000
1/16/71	185	3		205 Earle Doud Presents Spiro T. Agnew Is A Riot! .... [C]	Cadet Concept 1
11/10/01	178	1		206 Easy Rock	Razor & Tie 89039
8/25/07	188	1		207 Echo Presenta: Invasion .... [F]	VI 009207
2/6/82	105	11		208 Echoes Of An Era	Elektra 60021
11/14/98	191	1		209 ECW: Extreme Music	Slab 86262
				ECW: Extreme Championship Wrestling	
10/15/05	124	10		210 El Draft 2005 .... [F]	Chosen Few 1056
2/19/05	182	1		211 El Movimiento De Hip Hop En Espanol Vol. 2 .... [F]	Univision 310361
5/15/04	195	1		212 El Pasito Duranguense .... [F]	Disa 720365
12/8/01	197	1		213 El Ultimo Adios/The Last Goodbye.. [F-M]	Epic 86266
9/8/84	147	9		214 Electric Breakdance	Dominion 2320
3/21/98	166	5		215 Elmopalooza!	Sony Wonder 63432
4/10/99	41	7	●	216 Elton John And Tim Rice's Aida	Rocket 524628
				Grammy: Cast Album	
11/12/94	125	1		217 Elvira Presents Monster Hits...	Rhino 71778
12/23/06	2^1	22	▲	218 Eminem Presents: The Re-Up	Shady 007885
11/30/96	124	6		219 Emmanuel - A Musical Celebration Of The Life Of Christ	Sparrow 51556
				Christmas chart: 16/'96	
8/2/80	168	5		220 Empire Jazz .... [I]	RSO 3085
				adaptation of The Empire Strikes Back	
4/8/95	17	19	●	221 Encomium: A Tribute To Led Zeppelin	Atlantic 82731
2/17/07	129	1		222 Endless Highway: The Music Of The Band..	429 Records 17618
9/9/67	197	1		223 England's Greatest Hits	Fontana 67570
11/6/04	99	3		224 Enjoy Every Sandwich: The Songs Of Warren Zevon	Artemis 51581
8/12/95	30	104	▲²	225 ESPN Presents Jock Jams Volume 1 .... Cat:#6/75	Tommy Boy 1137
9/7/96	10	63	▲²	226 ESPN Presents Jock Jams Volume 2	Tommy Boy 1163
9/27/97	23	41	▲	227 ESPN Presents Jock Jams Volume 3	Tommy Boy 1214
9/12/98	20	35	●	228 ESPN Presents Jock Jams Volume 4	Tommy Boy 1266
11/12/94+	79	30	●	229 ESPN Presents Jock Rock Volume 1 .... Cat:#32/3	Tommy Boy 1100
11/4/95	121	18		230 ESPN Presents Jock Rock Volume 2	Tommy Boy 1136
7/10/99	78	10		231 ESPN Presents Jock Rock 2000	Tommy Boy 1332
5/31/03	149	6		232 ESPN Presents Stadium Anthems: Music For The Fans......................	Hollywood 162387
6/15/96	49	14		233 ESPN Presents X Games - Music From The Edge	Tommy Boy 1173
6/28/97	102	8		234 ESPN Presents X Games - The Soundtrack Album	Tommy Boy 1202
7/8/00	182	2		235 Everlasting Love Songs	UTV 170137
10/13/84	75	10		236 Every Man Has A Woman	Polydor 823490
				all songs written by Yoko Ono	
7/22/72	178	6		237 Everything You Always Wanted To Know About The Godfather - But Don't Ask .... [C]	Columbia 31608
6/20/98	131	4		238 Exodus	Word 69349
6/11/05	151	3		239 Explosion Duranguense .... [F]	Disa 720537
6/27/81	51	9		240 Exposed/A Cheap Peek At Today's Provocative New Rock	CBS 37124 [2]
12/5/81	124	5		241 Exposed II	CBS 37601 [2]
2/17/68	194	4		242 Family Portrait	A&M 19002
4/17/99	7	20	●	243 Family Values Tour 1998, The .... [L]	Immortal 69904
6/10/00	32	33		244 Family Values Tour 1999, The .... [L]	Flawless 490641
5/25/02	55	5		245 Family Values Tour 2001, The .... [L]	The Label 62762
1/13/07	102	2		246 Family Values Tour 2006, The .... [L]	Firm 60010
4/13/96	126	1		247 Famous Overtures III .... [I]	Digital Master. 71855
3/24/01	187	1		248 Fat Music Volume 5: Live Fat, Die Young	Fat Wreck Chords 613
2/15/03	12^C	1		249 Favorite Love Songs From The Slow Jams Collection	EMI-Capitol 24181
10/13/01	52	10		250 FB Entertainment Presents: The Goodlife	FB 014859
1/29/05	175	2		251 15 Duranguenses De Corazon.. [F]	Disa 720488
1/13/07	100	3		252 15 Years On Death Row	Death Row 63077 [2]
1/24/09	179	3		253 50 Most Essential Pieces Of Classical Music .... [I]	X5 digital
7/15/72	40	16		254 Fillmore: The Last Days .... [L]	Fillmore 31390 [3]
6/6/81	203	1		255 Film Classics .... [I]	RCA 4020

Billboard			R I A A	ARTIST	
DEBUT	PEAK	WKS		Album Title.. Catalog	Label & Number
2/14/04	14	14		256 Fired Up!..	Razor & Tie 89077
2/26/05	48	8		257 Fired Up! 2..	Razor & Tie 89091
3/11/06	84	3		258 Fired Up! 3..	Razor & Tie 89118
9/18/71	47	9		259 First Great Rock Festivals Of The Seventies: Isle Of Wight/ Atlanta Pop Festival.. **[L]**	Columbia 30805 [3]
				Isle Of Wight was held August 26-31, 1970 in England; Atlanta Pop Festival was held July 3-5, 1970	
7/11/64	96	14		260 First Nine Months Are The Hardest!, The................ **[C]**	Capitol 2034
5/10/75	208	2		261 Flash Fearless Versus The Zorg Women Parts 5 & 6	Chrysalis 1072
9/17/88	70	10		262 Folkways: A Vision Shared - A Tribute To Woody Guthrie And Leadbelly........	Columbia 44034
10/19/63	87	10		263 Fool Britannia... **[C]**	Acappella 1
6/15/91	31	30	●	264 For Our Children..	Disney 60616
10/5/96	144	4		265 For Our Children Too!...................................	Kid Rhino 72494
8/22/98	69	4		266 For The Masses..	A&M 540919
4/6/02	145	1		267 Forever Country...	Razor & Tie 89044
6/30/07	164	1		268 Forever Country...	Madacy 52383 [3]
8/14/04	144	2		269 Forever, For Always, For Luther.....................	GRP 002426
				tribute to **Luther Vandross**	
6/23/07	131	2		270 Forever Soul R&B..	Madacy 52253 [3]
9/29/01	97	6		271 41st Side, The...	Lake 9204
3/24/01	173	1		272 Fred Hammond Presents: "In Case You Missed It...And Then Some"........	F Hammond 43154
1/6/73+	68	58	●	273 Free To Be...You And Me..............................	Bell 1110
4/12/08	105	3		274 From The Coffeehouse.................................	Rhino 8175
9/4/04	56	1		275 Future Soundtrack For America.....................	Barsuk 37
9/2/06	181	1		276 Gargolas Next Generation........................ **[F]**	VI 007314
8/11/73	208	3		277 Gemini Suite.. **[I]**	Warner 2717
5/26/56	9	9		278 **Gentlemen, Be Seated!**	Epic 3238
				recreation of a complete minstrel show	
9/7/02	150	6		279 Girls Of Grace...	Word 886204
8/16/97	183	1		280 Give 'Em The Boot.......................................	Hellcat 80402
10/18/08	157	2		281 Glam Revolution: The Heyday & Legacy Of Glam Rock...........	Starbucks 08535
3/23/02	173	1		282 Global Hits 2002...	Universal 017004
10/15/94	192	1		283 Glory Of Gershwin, The..............................	Mercury 526091
3/24/07	151	8		284 Glory Revealed: The Word Of God In Worship....	Reunion 10823
8/1/09	163	2		285 Glory Revealed II: The Word Of God In Worship....	Reunion 10137
11/3/01	❶¹	16	●	286 **God Bless America**	Columbia 86300
10/27/01	128	2		287 God Bless America: United We Stand!............	St. Clair 00812
12/7/02	172	1		288 God's Leading Ladies.................................	Dexterity Sounds 20385
10/13/07	104	2		289 Goin' Home: A Tribute To Fats Domino...........	Vanguard 225 [2]
2/10/01	28	31	●	290 Goin' South...	Razor & Tie 89033
2/9/02	122	3		291 Goin' South Volume 2................................	Razor & Tie 89049
2/17/07	145	3		292 Goin' South: Platinum Edition......................	Razor & Tie 89130 [2]
1/21/06	188	1		293 Gold Star Music: Reggaeton Hits................ **[F]**	Gold Star 180016
10/18/08	40	3		294 Golden Age Of Song..................................	Starbucks 011519
7/27/63	97	6		295 Golden Goodies, Vol. 1..............................	Roulette 25207
7/20/63	89	5		296 Golden Goodies, Vol. 2..............................	Roulette 25210
8/3/63	112	4		297 Golden Goodies, Vol. 3..............................	Roulette 25218
7/27/63	124	4		298 Golden Goodies, Vol. 5..............................	Roulette 25215
8/3/63	86	3		299 Golden Goodies, Vol. 6..............................	Roulette 25216
10/14/67	177	4		300 Golden Instrumentals............................. **[I]**	Dot 25820
11/17/01	179	1		301 Good Rockin' Tonight - The Legacy Of Sun Records........	London-Sire 31165
7/18/09	76	5		302 Gospel Truth Presents Gospel Mix Volume III....	Worldwide 3068
4/26/03	73	8		303 Got Hits!...	Virgin 81922
7/23/05	110	3		304 Got Hits 2: More Perfect Pop!.....................	Capitol 162519
11/29/03	187	4	●	305 Gotta Have Gospel!...................................	Integrity Gospel 90671 [2]
10/15/05	150	3		306 Gotta Have Gospel! 3................................	Integrity Gospel 33962 [2]
2/25/95	26	11		307 Grammy Nominees 1995.............................	Grammy 67043
2/24/96	16	13	▲	308 Grammy Nominees 1996.............................	Grammy 67565
3/1/97	14	20	●	309 Grammy Nominees 1997.............................	Grammy 553292
2/28/98	11	12	●	310 Grammy Nominees 1998.............................	Grammy 11752
2/27/99	8	16	●	311 **Grammy Nominees 1999**	Grammy 62381
2/26/00	9	20	▲	312 **Grammy Nominees 2000**	Grammy 67945
2/24/01	12	12	●	313 **Grammy Nominees 2001**	Chrysalis 31520
2/23/02	13	12	●	314 **Grammy Nominees 2002**	Grammy 584705
3/1/03	6	16	●	315 **Grammy Nominees 2003**	Grammy 73843
2/7/04	4	14	●	316 **Grammy Nominees 2004**	Grammy 58022
2/19/05	4	16	●	317 **Grammy Nominees 2005**	Grammy 60944
2/11/06	14	9	●	318 **Grammy Nominees 2006**	Grammy 74277
2/10/07	3¹	19	●	319 **Grammy Nominees 2007**	Grammy 03827
2/16/08	4	10		320 **Grammy Nominees 2008**	Grammy 010630
2/14/09	6	11		321 **Grammy Nominees 2009**	Grammy 517633

DEBUT	PEAK	WKS	R I A A	ARTIST Album Title.. Catalog	Label & Number
2/27/99	54	11		322 Grammy Rap Nominees 1999..	Grammy 62380
3/11/00	151	2		323 Grammy Rap Nominees 2000..	Grammy 67944
2/24/01	43	9		324 Grammy R&B/Rap Nominees 2001...	Grammy 31647
1/19/08	37	8		325 Grammys: 50th Anniversary Collection, The.............................	Grammy 31079
4/25/64	70	15		326 Great Voices Of The Century..	Angel 4
5/13/67	87	18		327 Greatest Hits From England, The..	Parrot 71010
9/27/69	189	2		328 Greatest Hits From Memphis, The..	Hi 32049
5/3/97	129	15		329 Greatest Sports Rock And Jams	Cold Front 6245 [2]
10/4/97	192	4		330 Greatest Sports Rock And Jams Volume 2	Cold Front 6255 [2]
7/15/89	68	24		331 Greenpeace/Rainbow Warriors	Geffen 24236 [2]
2/13/71	212	2		332 Grieg's Greatest Hits Made Popular In Song Of Norway .... [I]	RCA Victor 3198
4/29/00	122	3		333 Guerra De Estados Pesados.. [F]	Lideres 950016
12/17/88	171	8		334 Guitar Speak.. [I]	I.R.S. 42240
11/10/07	107	3		335 Guitar Hero III: Legends Of Rock: Companion Pack	Interscope 010131
1/10/81	209	1		336 Guitar Heroes	Epic 36864
5/23/09	154	1		337 Guitar Heroes .... [I]	Naxos digital
6/9/73	216	2		338 Guitars That Destroyed The World, The	Columbia 31998
11/16/91	190	1		339 Halloween Hits .... Cat:#18/1	Rhino 70535
11/14/09	12 C	1		340 Halloween Party: 16 Scary Songs...	K-Tel digital
10/11/97	73	14		341 Halloween Songs & Sounds .... Cat:#20/5	Walt Disney 60625
10/21/00	176	3		342 Halloween Sound Effects .... Cat:#27/3	LaserLight 21375
11/27/04	162	2		343 Halo 2	Sumthing Else 2103
12/15/07	200	1		344 Halo 3	Sumthing Else 2037
10/10/09	179	1		345 Halo 3: ODST	Bungie 2068
10/13/01	175	2		346 Hank Williams: Timeless	Lost Highway 170239
11/11/89	65	21		347 Happy Anniversary, Charlie Brown!	GRP 9596
11/20/99	105	4	●	348 Hard + The Heavy Volume One, The...	Redline 75997 [2]
11/11/00	152	1		349 Haunted House CD, The	LaserLight 21376
3/21/09	80	3		350 Heading West: Songs For The Open Road	Starbucks 31315
4/5/03	186	1		351 Heart Of Roadrunner Records, The	Roadrunner 618387
6/15/91	198	1		352 Hearts Of Gold - The Classic Rock Collection	Foundation 96647
9/20/97	161	2		353 Heat	Boss 70012
3/27/71	222	3		354 Heavenly Stars	Cotillion 052
8/9/69	151	2		355 Heavy Hits!	Columbia 9840
2/28/70	128	3		356 Heavy Sounds	Columbia 9952
3/14/09	107	1		357 Heroes	War Child 94299
7/21/01	175	2		358 Hey Love... Volume 1	Time Life 18734
10/20/01	196	1		359 Hidden Beach Recordings Presents: Unwrapped Vol. 1	Hidden Beach 85653
7/31/04	163	1		360 Hidden Beach Recordings Presents: Unwrapped Vol. 3	Hidden Beach 90950
4/28/73	160	8		361 History Of British Blues, Volume One	Sire 3701 [2]
6/1/74	198	2		362 History Of British Rock	Sire 3702 [2]
12/21/74+	141	11		363 History Of British Rock, Volume 2	Sire 3705 [2]
11/22/75+	145	10		364 History Of British Rock, Volume 3	Sire 3712 [2]
4/6/68	187	3		365 History Of Rhythm & Blues, Volume 1/The Roots 1947-52	Atlantic 8161
3/30/68	173	5		366 History Of Rhythm & Blues, Volume 2/The Golden Years 1953-55	Atlantic 8162
4/6/68	189	3		367 History Of Rhythm & Blues, Volume 3/Rock & Roll 1956-57	Atlantic 8163
4/6/68	180	4		368 History Of Rhythm & Blues, Volume 4/The Big Beat 1958-60	Atlantic 8164
6/30/07	200	1		369 Hits Of The 70s	Madacy 52389 [3]
7/13/02	181	2		370 Hopelessly Devoted To You - Vol. 4	Helpless 662
6/24/06	173	1		371 Hopelessly Devoted To You - Vol. 6	Sub City 685 [2]
1/18/97	188	2		372 Hot Luv - The Ultimate Dance Songs Collection	EMI-Capitol 54547
2/15/64	138	3		373 Hot Rod Hootenanny .... [N]	Capitol 2010
12/14/63+	62	15		374 Hot Rod Rally	Capitol 1997
8/26/78	208	2		375 Hotels, Motels And Road Shows .... [L]	Capricorn 0208 [2]
5/24/97	113	2		376 House Connection Volume 1	Aqua Boogie 0003
2/23/08	131	6		377 How Great Thou Art: Gospel Favorites From The Grand Ole Opry: Live.... [L]	Opry 20939
1/19/63	56	19		378 How To Strip For Your Husband .... [I]	Roulette 25186
				instrumentals by Sonny Lester, with booklet *How To Strip For Your Husband* by strip-teaser Ann Corio	
6/12/71	224	1		379 Howdy Doody	PIP 6808
				no track titles listed on this album	
4/10/76	177	2		380 Hustle Hits!	De-Lite 2019
11/20/04+	49	10	▲	381 I Can Only Imagine: Ultimate Power Anthems Of The Christian Faith Cat:❶12/62	Time-Life 19223 [2]
9/16/00+	144	6	●	382 I Could Sing Of Your Love Forever..	Worship Tog. 20282 [2]
8/18/01	164	7	●	383 I Could Sing Of Your Love Forever 2 .... [L]	Worship Tog. 20314 [2]
				disc 1: studio; disc 2: live	
4/5/03	133	1		384 I Could Sing Of Your Love Forever: Kids .... Cat:#20/2	Worship Together 20371
7/9/55	5	5		385 I Like Jazz! .... [K]	Columbia 1
10/19/02	60	37	▲	386 iWorsh!p: A Total Worship Experience	Integrity 23362 [2]
9/27/03	134	5		387 iWorsh!p: A Total Worship Experience Vol. 2	Integrity 90362 [2]
10/30/04	154	4		388 iWorsh!p Next: A Total Worship Experience	Integrity 92638 [2]
9/6/03	131	2		389 I've Always Been Crazy: A Tribute To Waylon Jennings	RCA 67064

VARIOUS ARTISTS COMPILATIONS

DEBUT	PEAK	WKS	RIAA	#	ARTIST / Album Title	Catalog	Label & Number
9/30/95	**104**	8		390	Idiot's Guide To Classical Music, The	[I]	RCA Victor 62641
10/4/08	77	6		391	Idolos: De Mexico Para El Mundo	[F]	Fonovisa 353715
10/1/94	70	8		392	If I Were A Carpenter		A&M 540258
10/4/08	59	3		393	Imus Ranch Record, The		New West 6140
1/25/75	208	1		394	In Concert, Volume Two	[I-L]	CTI 6049
1/10/81	156	5		395	In Harmony - A Sesame Street Record		Sesame Street 3481
					Grammy: Children's Album		
11/21/81	129	10		396	In Harmony 2		Columbia 37641
					Grammy: Children's Album		
12/13/97	15	19	●	397	In Tha Beginning...There Was Rap		Priority 50639
11/4/95	106	3		398	Inner City Blues - The Music Of Marvin Gaye		Motown 0452
5/11/96	53	4		399	Insomnia - The Erick Sermon Compilation Album		Interscope 90060
6/30/07	15	10		400	Instant Karma: The Amnesty International Campaign To Save Darfur		Warner 156028
10/30/71	203	3		401	Instant Replay (Two Sides of Football)	[C]	Decca 75300
4/14/07	197	1		402	Interpretations: Celebrating The Music Of Earth, Wind & Fire		Stax 2294
4/29/72	206	2		403	Invictus' Greatest Hits		Invictus 9807
3/31/07	149	1		404	Irish Favorites		Madacy 52835 [3]
2/28/81	201	3		405	I.R.S. Greatest Hits Vols. 2 & 3		I.R.S. 70800 [2]
11/23/02	24	4		406	Irv Gotti Presents: The Remixes		Murder Inc. 063411
12/26/87+	180	6		407	Island Story, 1962-1987: 25th Anniversary, The		Island 90684 [2]
6/12/71	202	6		408	It's Howdy Doody Time!		RCA Victor 4546
10/23/99	58	5		409	J Prince Presents Realest Niggaz Down South		Rap-A-Lot 50119 [2]
3/26/83	205	3		410	Jacki Sorensen's Aerobic Dancing		Lakeside 30005
12/22/90+	131	11		411	Jam Harder - The A&M Underground Dance Compilation		A&M 5339
12/18/65+	93	9		412	James Blonde, Secret Agent 006.95, "The Man From T.A.N.T.E."	[C]	Colpix 495
2/19/00	181	2		413	Jazz For A Rainy Afternoon	[I]	32 Jazz 32061
1/31/09	137	2		414	Jazz Signatures 2: Great Performances By Jazz Masters		Starbucks 1505
8/6/05	43	9		415	Jermaine Dupri Presents...Young, Fly & Flashy Vol. 1		So So Def 73874
11/21/70+	❶³	101	●	416	Jesus Christ Superstar		Decca 7206 [2]
11/6/71	183	7		417	Jewish American Princess, The	[C]	Bell 6063
8/1/98	170	4		418	Jim Brickman's Visions Of Love		Windham Hill 11342
9/11/99	51	13		419	Jock Jams Volume 5		Tommy Boy 1364
11/24/01	188	1		420	Jock Jams: The All Star Jock Jams		Tommy Boy 1524
11/17/07	131	2		421	Joel Osteen Presents: Free To Worship		Joel Osteen 40081
4/13/96	195	1		422	Johannes Brahms, Piano Concerto No. 1 - 16 Waltzes Op. 39	[I]	Digital Master. 71812
6/5/71	225	1		423	Johnny Otis Show Live At Monterey!	[L]	Epic 30473 [2]
4/3/71	84	12		424	Joseph And The Amazing Technicolor Dreamcoat		Scepter 588
					no individual song titles listed		
11/1/03	55	9		425	Just Because I'm A Woman: Songs Of Dolly Parton		Sugar Hill 3980
6/13/09	30	3		426	Just Dance		Ultra 013025
5/13/95	145	8	●	427	Keith Whitley - A Tribute Album		BNA 66416
8/27/05	104	1		428	Killer Queen: A Tribute To Queen		Hollywood 162522
10/12/02	140	2		429	Kindred Spirits: A Tribute To The Songs Of Johnny Cash		Columbia 86310
10/18/08	141	1		430	KINK Live 11	[L]	Kink 11
10/17/09	103	1		431	KINK Live Twelve	[L]	Starbucks 2009
7/9/94	19	12	●	432	Kiss My Ass: Classic Kiss Regrooved		Mercury 522123
9/1/90	92	8		433	Knebworth - The Album	[L]	Polydor 84702 [2]
					recorded on 6/30/1990 in England		
11/27/04	191	1		434	La Misi4n: The Take Over	[F]	Mas Flow 180010 [2]
11/27/04	131	2		435	Las + Bailables: Del Pasito Duranguense	[F]	Disa 720463
9/30/00	125	3		436	Latin Grammy Nominees: 2000	[F]	Epic 85133
10/5/02	181	1		437	Latin Grammy Nominees: 2002	[F]	Warner Latina 49152
8/14/99	152	8		438	Latin Mix USA 2	[F]	Sony Discos 69989
10/4/97	169	1		439	Lawhouse Experience Volume One		Street Life 75525
4/11/98	86	7		440	Legacy: A Tribute To Fleetwood Mac's Rumours		Lava 83054
12/6/80	154	13		441	Legend Of Jesse James, The		A&M 3718
8/6/77	121	9		442	Let's Clean Up The Ghetto		Philadelphia Int. 34659
5/8/99	172	2		443	Life In The Fat Lane - Fat Music Vol. IV		Fat Wreck Chords 585
5/16/98	24	15	▲	444	Lilith Fair: A Celebration Of Women In Music	[L]	Arista 19007 [2]
6/5/99	87	2		445	Lilith Fair: A Celebration Of Women In Music Volume 2	[L]	Arista 19079
6/5/99	98	2		446	Lilith Fair: A Celebration Of Women In Music Volume 3	[L]	Arista 19081
10/25/69	200	2		447	Live At Bill Graham's Fillmore West	[L]	Columbia 9893
10/18/69	169	4		448	Live At Yankee Stadium	[L]	T-Neck 3004 [2]
10/12/02	117	1		449	Live From Bonnaroo	[L]	Sanctuary 84571 [2]
10/31/09	153	1		450	Live From The 305	[L]	Poe Boy 5096
6/7/86	105	7		451	Live! For Life	[L]	I.R.S. 5731
5/3/03	154	2		452	Living The Gospel: Gospel Greats	Cat:#46/1	Time-Life 606
5/6/00	175	2		453	Loaded With Hits		Foundation 99715 [2]
7/9/05	105	3		454	Look At All The Love We Found: A Tribute To Sublime		Cornerstone 44
5/28/05	55	2		455	Los Bandoleros: The First Don Omar Production	[F]	All Star 450673
7/15/06	34	7		456	Los Rompe Discotekas	[F]	Roc-La-Familia 006888
8/11/07	104	4		457	Los Vaqueros: The Wild Wild Mixes	[F]	WY 009208

DEBUT	PEAK	WKS	R I A A	ARTIST / Album Title ... Catalog	Label & Number
9/23/00	108	4		458 **Loud Rocks**	Loud 62201
4/13/96	174	1		459 **Ludwig Van Beethoven, Symphony No. 5 - Violin Romances No. 2+1** [I]	Digital Master. 71805
1/20/68	176	5		460 **Lyndon Johnson's Lonely Hearts Club Band** [C]	Atco 230
5/23/98	167	2		461 **Lyricist Lounge Volume One** [L]	Open Mic 1129 [2]
12/16/00	33	15		462 **Lyricist Lounge Volume Two** [L]	Rawkus 26131
7/27/96	65	20	●	463 **Macarena Club Cutz**	RCA 66745
7/27/96	85	13		464 **Macarena Mix** [F]	BMG 31388
7/28/62	108	14		465 **Mad "Twists" Rock 'N' Roll** [N]	Big Top 1305
1/13/79	207	1		466 **Magical Music Of Walt Disney, The**	Ovation 5000 [4]
12/16/89+	87	15		467 **Make A Difference Foundation: Stairway To Heaven/Highway To Hell** [L] recorded on 8/12/1989 at the Moscow Music Peace Festival	Mercury 842093
10/7/72	186	7		468 **Mar Y Sol** [L] recorded on 4/1/1972 in Puerto Rico	Atco 705 [2]
7/10/99	97	6		469 **Marvin Is 60 - A Tribute Album**	Motown 549520
6/12/99	62	5		470 **Master P Presents: No Limit All Stars - Who U Wit?**	No Limit 50106
10/12/02	174	1		471 **Maxim Rocks!**	UTV 583957
12/11/99	82	1		472 **McCaughey Septuplets: Sweet Dreams, The**	Word 63922
10/17/98	9	7	●	473 **Mean Green - Major Players Compilation**	No Limit 53505
5/29/04	139	15		474 **Mega Movie Mix**	Walt Disney 861089
7/15/72	176	7		475 **Metropolitan Opera Gala Honoring Sir Rudolf Bing** [L]	DG 2530 260
4/12/80	35	27	▲	476 **Mickey Mouse Disco**	Disneyland 2504
12/3/94	173	4		477 **Mickey Unrapped**	Walt Disney 60627
4/26/08	189	1		478 **Midnight Soul: 'Round Midnight**	Time-Life 216992
1/27/79	122	8		479 **Milestone Jazzstars In Concert** [I-L]	Milestone 55006 [2]
3/20/99	195	2		480 **Millennium Classic Rock Party**	Rhino 75628
11/13/99	179	1		481 **Millennium '80s New Wave Party**	Rhino 75923
8/1/98	124	12	●	482 **Millennium Funk Party**	Rhino 75467
5/22/99	63	45	●	483 **Millennium Hip-Hop Party**	Rhino 75699
10/2/82	206	3		484 **Miss Piggy's Aerobique Exercise Workout Album** [N]	Warner 23717
1/20/01	47 C	1		485 **Mob Hits**	Triage 96401 [2]
7/20/96	98	6		486 **MOM - Music For Our Mother Ocean**	Surfdog 90062
8/10/02	22	14		487 **Monsta Jamz**	Razor & Tie 89053
7/17/99	27	39	▲	488 **Monster Ballads**	Razor & Tie 89024
3/10/01	110	6		489 **Monster Ballads Volume 2**	Razor & Tie 89035
2/18/06	18	24		490 **Monster Ballads: Platinum Edition**	Razor & Tie 89107
9/5/09	109	4		491 **Monster Ballads: The Ultimate Set**	Razor & Tie 89208
4/21/01	95	9		492 **Monster Booty**	Razor & Tie 89034
5/11/02	166	1		493 **Monster Disco**	Razor & Tie 89052
3/11/00	171	5		494 **Monster '80s**	Razor & Tie 89026
5/6/00	89	10		495 **Monster Madness**	Razor & Tie 89028
10/18/97	20 C	6		496 **Monster Mash**	Holly Music 19157
11/13/99	12 C	9		497 **Monster Mash And Other Songs Of Horror**	Madacy 0028
8/12/00	52	13	●	498 **Monsters Of Rap**	Razor & Tie 89031
6/27/98	112	58	▲	499 **Monsters Of Rock**	Razor & Tie 89004
3/11/00	145	5		500 **Monsters Of Rock Volume 2**	Razor & Tie 89027
8/11/07	77	8		501 **Monsters Of Rock: Platinum Edition**	Razor & Tie 89163
6/23/07	58	4		502 **Monterey International Pop Festival** [L]	Starbucks 82972 [2]
7/26/97	179	1		503 **More Sun Splashin' - 16 Hot Summer Hits!**	Madacy 6804
4/2/05	106	13		504 **More Than 50 Most Loved Hymns**	Liberty 60812
1/17/04	5 C	14		505 **Most Relaxing Classical Album In The World...Ever!, The** [I]	Virgin 44890 [2]
6/8/63	47	14		506 **Motor-Town Review, Vol. 1, The** [L] recorded at the Apollo Theatre in New York City	Motown 609
5/30/64	102	5		507 **Motor-Town Review, Vol. 2, The** [L] recorded at the Fox Theatre in Detroit, Michigan	Motown 615
12/18/65+	111	7		508 **Motortown Review In Paris** [L] recorded at Olympia Music Hall in Paris, France	Tamla 264
8/23/69	177	5		509 **Motortown Review Live** [L] recorded at the Fox Theatre in Detroit, Michigan	Motown 688
4/11/70	105	4		510 **Motown At The Hollywood Palace** [L]	Motown 703
7/3/71	220	1		511 **Motown Chartbusters Volume 3**	Motown 732
3/7/98	65	12		512 **Motown 40 Forever**	Motown 0849 [2]
5/8/04	83	8		513 **Motown 1's** ... Cat:#2 1/3	Motown 001781
4/11/09	7 C	1		514 **Motown 1's: Vol. 2**	Universal Motown 008388
6/11/05	86	2		515 **Motown: Remixed**	Motown 003900
5/22/71	204	5		516 **Motown Story, The** [5] includes interviews with artists	Motown 726 [5]
7/9/83	114	9		517 **Motown Story: The First Twenty-Five Years, The** narrated by **Lionel Richie** and **Smokey Robinson**	Motown 6048 [5]
2/22/69	159	4		518 **Motown Winners' Circle/No. 1 Hits, Vol. 1**	Gordy 835
2/22/69	135	5		519 **Motown Winners' Circle/No. 1 Hits, Vol. 2**	Gordy 936
10/18/08	44	2		520 **Mountain 103.7 FM: Live From The Mountain Music Lounge Volume 14, The** [L]	The Mountain 14
10/17/09	55	3		521 **Mountain 103.7 FM: Live From The Mountain Music Lounge Volume 15, The** [L]	KMTT 2009

Billboard DEBUT	PEAK	WKS	R I A A	ARTIST Album Title.. Catalog	Label & Number
4/13/02	195	1		522 MTV: Best Of TRL Pop, The..	UTV 584599
5/11/96	75	20		523 MTV Buzz Bin: Volume 1	Mammoth 92672
11/15/97	180	2		524 MTV Grind Volume One	Tommy Boy 1207
6/20/92	19	41	▲	525 MTV: Party To Go Volume 2	Tommy Boy 1053
7/10/93	29	25	●	526 MTV: Party To Go Volume 3	Tommy Boy 1074
7/10/93	35	23	●	527 MTV: Party To Go Volume 4	Tommy Boy 1075
6/18/94	36	24	●	528 MTV: Party To Go Volume 5	Tommy Boy 1097
12/10/94+	54	25	●	529 MTV: Party To Go Volume 6	Tommy Boy 1109
11/18/95	54	25	●	530 MTV: Party To Go Volume 7	Tommy Boy 1138
12/9/95+	47	31	●	531 MTV: Party To Go Volume 8	Tommy Boy 1139
7/27/96	28	16	●	532 MTV: Party To Go Volume 9	Tommy Boy 1164
11/16/96	40	18	●	533 MTV: Party To Go Volume 10	Tommy Boy 1168
12/13/97+	50	21	●	534 MTV: Party To Go '98	Tommy Boy 1234
12/12/98+	60	16	●	535 MTV: Party To Go '99	Tommy Boy 1268
12/25/99+	86	9		536 MTV: Party To Go 2000	Tommy Boy 1365
10/24/98	100	7		537 MTV: Party To Go Platinum Mix	Tommy Boy 1267
3/14/98	152	2		538 MTV Presents: Hip Hop Back In The Day	Priority 51070
7/1/00	42	11		539 MTV: Return Of The Rock, The	Roadrunner 8536
11/25/00	75	10		540 MTV: Return Of The Rock Volume 2, The	Roadrunner 8509
7/28/01	184	2		541 MTV: 20 Years Of Pop	Maverick 48144
10/25/03	34	6	●	542 MTV2: Headbangers Ball	Roadrunner 618327 [2]
10/16/04	43	5		543 MTV2: Headbangers Ball Volume 2	Roadrunner 618256 [2]
4/29/06	60	6		544 MTV2 Headbangers Ball: The Revenge	Roadrunner 618068 [2]
5/24/97	63	12		545 MTV's Amp	Astralwerks 7550
7/11/98	181	3		546 MTV's Amp²	Astralwerks 7558
6/30/01	138	1		547 MTV's Hip Hopera: Carmen	Music World 85846
3/2/85	91	12		548 MTV's Rock 'N Roll To Go	Elektra 60399
12/25/71+	189	4		549 Muppet Alphabet Album, The.. includes blackboard, chalk and a set of letters	Columbia 25503
11/30/63	148	2		550 Murray The K - Live From The Brooklyn Fox .... [L]	KFM 1001
12/25/61+	26	15		551 Murray The K's Blasts From The Past	Chess 1461
8/4/62	124	13		552 Murray The K's Gassers For Submarine Race Watchers	Chess 1470
7/20/63	69	10		553 Murray The K's Nineteen-Sixty Two Boss Golden Gassers	Scepter 510
10/9/61	63	29		554 Murray The K's Sing Along With The Original Golden Gassers	Roulette 25159
3/13/04	148	1		555 Music As A Weapon II	Reprise 48256
8/18/79	171	4		556 Music for UNICEF Concert/A Gift Of Song, The.................................... [L] recorded on 1/9/1979 at the United Nations Hall	Polydor 6214
3/18/72	165	6		557 Music People, The	Columbia 31280 [3]
7/30/05	117	1		558 MVP 2: The Grand Slam .... [F]	MVP 375206
9/9/95	99	18	●	559 My Utmost For His Highest	Myrrh 83410
10/13/90	125	14		560 Narada Wilderness Collection, The .... [I]	Narada 63905
6/8/02	90	3		561 NASCAR On Fox: Crank It Up	MCA 583328
4/29/95	90	11		562 NASCAR: Runnin' Wide Open	Columbia 67020
10/22/94	50	9	●	563 Nativity In Black: A Tribute To Black Sabbath	Columbia 66335
6/24/00	95	3		564 Nativity In Black II: A Tribute To Black Sabbath	Divine 26095
9/6/03	❶¹	13	●	565 Neptunes Present...Clones, The	Star Trak 51295
12/17/66+	72	10		566 New First Family, 1968, The .... [C]	Verve 15054
5/13/00	100	11		567 New Millennium Hip-Hop Party	Rhino 79824
2/17/01	170	3		568 New Millennium Love Songs	Rhino 76699
3/7/70	200	1		569 New Spirit Of Capitol, The	Capitol 6
11/23/91+	170	10		570 New York Rock And Soul Revue - Live At The Beacon, The .... [L] recorded on 3/1/1991 in New York City	Giant 24423
9/26/98	105	18		571 Next Generation Swing	Beast 56532
4/9/05	96	5		572 Nickelodeon Kids' Choice	Nick 67581
4/1/06	108	5		573 Nickelodeon Kids' Choice Vol. 2	Nick 78689
7/28/79	21	25	●	574 Night At Studio 54, A	Casablanca 7161 [2]
10/30/99	142	1		575 Night In Rocketown, A .... [L]	Rocketown 63746
9/24/88	31	17	●	576 1988 Summer Olympics Album/One Moment In Time	Arista 8551
7/4/09	133	1		577 99 Essential Chants .... [F]	Milan digital
10/3/09	76	1		578 99 Most Essential Baroque Masterpieces, The.................................... [I]	X5 digital
1/17/09	29	1		579 99 Most Essential Beethoven Masterpieces, The .... [I]	X5 digital
3/14/09	34	1		580 99 Most Essential Mozart Masterpieces, The .... [I]	X5 digital
9/12/09	77	1		581 99 Most Essential Pieces Of The Romantic Era, The .... [I]	X5 digital
11/14/09	106	1		582 99 Most Essential Vivaldi Masterpieces, The .... [I]	X5 digital
4/11/09	28	1		583 99 Perfectly Relaxing Songs .... [I]	Jade digital
11/27/93	56	12		584 No Alternative	Arista 18737
7/3/99	18	21		585 No Boundaries - A Benefit For The Kosovar Refugees	Epic 63653
12/26/98	19	14		586 No Limit Soldier Compilation - We Can't Be Stopped	No Limit 50724
12/22/79+	19	18	●	587 No Nukes/The MUSE Concerts For A Non-Nuclear Future .... [L] benefit concerts recorded in September 1979 at Madison Square Garden in New York City	Asylum 801 [3]
8/11/90	79	9		588 Nobody's Child - Romanian Angel Appeal	Warner 26280
7/7/01	122	8		589 Non Stop Hip Hop	Razor & Tie 81027 [2]
9/8/01	83	5		590 Non Stop '90's Rock	Razor & Tie 89038

Billboard			R I A A	ARTIST Album Title.. Catalog	Label & Number
DEBUT	PEAK	WKS			
9/20/08	108	4		591 Northern Songs: Canada's Best & Brightest...	Starbucks 8167
2/24/96	119	2		592 Not Fade Away (Remembering Buddy Holly)	Decca 11260
11/14/98+	10	33	▲	593 Now	Virgin 46795
8/14/99	3[1]	29	▲[2]	594 Now 2	Virgin 47910
12/25/99+	4	37	▲[2]	595 Now 3	Universal 545417
8/5/00	❶[3]	43	▲[2]	596 Now 4	Universal 524772
12/2/00	2[2]	42	▲[4]	597 Now 5	Sony 85206
4/21/01	❶[3]	39	▲[3]	598 Now 6	Epic 85663
8/18/01	❶[3]	36	▲[3]	599 Now 7	Virgin 10749
12/8/01	2[5]	34	▲[3]	600 Now 8	EMI 11154
4/6/02	❶[1]	37	▲[2]	601 Now 9	Universal 584408
8/10/02	2[1]	28	▲	602 Now 10	Sony 86788
12/7/02	2[1]	25	▲[2]	603 Now 11	Universal 069720
4/12/03	3[2]	26	▲	604 Now 12	EMI 82344
8/9/03	2[3]	23	▲	605 Now 13	Universal 000556
11/22/03	3[4]	32	▲[3]	606 Now 14	Columbia 90753
4/10/04	2[3]	30	▲[2]	607 Now 15	EMI 76990
8/14/04	❶[2]	35	▲[3]	608 Now 16	Universal 003017
11/20/04	❶[1]	33	▲[3]	609 Now 17	Sony 74203
4/2/05	2[2]	27	▲	610 Now 18	Sony 93863
8/6/05	❶[2]	31	▲[2]	611 Now 19	Sony 12133
11/19/05	❶[2]	32	▲[2]	612 Now 20	Sony 005740
4/22/06	2[2]	31	▲	613 Now 21	Universal 006201
7/29/06	❶[3]	28	▲	614 Now 22	Sony 83563
11/25/06	❶[1]	28	▲[2]	615 Now 23	Sony 01750
4/14/07	❶[2]	25	▲	616 Now 24	EMI 88505
8/4/07	❶[2]	29	▲	617 Now 25	Universal 009055
12/1/07	3[1]	34	▲	618 Now 26	EMI 10765
3/29/08	2[2]	28	▲	619 Now 27	Sony 22781
6/21/08	2[1]	35	▲	620 Now 28	EMI 08144
11/29/08	3[1]	34	▲	621 Now 29	Universal 012100
4/11/09	❶[1]	32	●	622 Now 30	Universal 012654
7/18/09	❶[1]	40	●	623 Now 31	EMI 28617
11/21/09	5	28↑		624 Now 32	EMI 58647
4/8/06	36	22		625 Now Latino .... [F]	EMI 72440
12/9/06	84	10		626 Now Latino 2 .... [F]	Universal Latino 8069
10/27/07	89	6		627 Now Latino 3 .... [F]	Sony 50237
4/11/09	165	2		628 Now Latino 4 .... [F]	EMI 47246
2/11/06	6	25	●	629 Now #1's	Universal 005959
12/1/07	60	18		630 Now Party Hits!..	EMI 10767
11/29/08	32	17		631 Now That's What I Call Music! 10th Anniversary, The Best Of	Universal 012225
6/21/08	20	17		632 Now That's What I Call Classic Rock .... Cat.#45/1	EMI 08145
10/10/09	31	7		633 Now That's What I Call Club Hits	EMI 56256
9/13/08	7	33		634 Now That's What I Call Country	Capitol 011724
9/12/09	10	34		635 Now That's What I Call Country Vol. 2	Universal 56259
11/21/09	108	2		636 Now That's What I Call Dance Classics	EMI 60492
1/31/09	13	9		637 Now That's What I Call Motown	Universal 012489
4/11/09	30	8		638 Now That's What I Call Power Ballads	Universal 012676
3/29/08	11	15		639 Now That's What I Call The 80s	Sony 22784
7/18/09	37	6		640 Now That's What I Call The 80s Vol. 2	EMI 45347
6/23/07	123	2		641 #1 Hits Of The 50s And 60s	Madacy 52251
8/12/00	155	4		642 Nuthin' But A Gangsta Party	Priority 23916
4/10/99	77	8	▲	643 N.W.A. Legacy Volume 1 1988-1998, The	Priority 51111 [2]
9/14/02	154	2		644 N.W.A. Legacy Volume 2, The	Priority 37824
12/19/98	142	2		645 N.W.A. - Straight Outta Compton - 10th Anniversary Tribute	Priority 53532
6/8/02	13	15	●	646 Off The Hook	Sony 86591
7/14/84	92	13		647 Official Music Of The XXIIIrd Olympiad Los Angeles 1984, The	Columbia 39322 [2]
6/5/04	185	1		648 Okayplayer: True Notes Vol. 1	Okayplayer 001
2/5/94	123	19	●	649 Old School	Thump 4010
6/18/94	147	5		650 Old School Volume 2	Thump 4020
9/21/59	12	183		651 Oldies But Goodies	Original Sound 5001
8/14/61	12	54		652 Oldies But Goodies, Vol. 3	Original Sound 5004
6/16/62	15	39		653 Oldies But Goodies, Vol. 4	Original Sound 5005
6/1/63	16	31		654 Oldies But Goodies, Vol. 5	Original Sound 5007
1/25/64	31	11		655 Oldies But Goodies, Vol. 6	Original Sound 5011
1/9/65	121	9		656 Oldies But Goodies, Vol. 7	Original Sound 5012

VARIOUS ARTISTS COMPILATIONS

DEBUT	PEAK	WKS	R I A A	Album Title / Catalog	Label & Number
4/25/98	145	6		657 One And Only Love Album, The	Polydor 555610 [2]
7/19/08	128	2		658 100 Most Essential Pieces Of Classical Music, The .... [I]	X5 digital
10/11/97	193	1		659 One Step Up/Two Steps Back: The Songs Of Bruce Springsteen	Right Stuff 59780 [2]
11/25/06	32	9		660 Only Hits	Atlantic 74798
1/14/06	51	15	●	661 Open The Eyes Of My Heart	INO/Epic 83649 [2]
10/8/66	49	21		662 Opening Nights At The Met	RCA Victor 6171 [3]
				historic recordings by opera stars who performed at New York's old Metropolitan Opera House from 1883-1965	
12/13/69+	166	5		663 Original Hits Of Right Now, The	Dunhill/ABC 50070
8/31/63	128	4		664 Original Hootenanny, The	Crestview 806
12/29/62+	27	13		665 Other Family, The .... [C]	Laurie 5000
12/24/05	146	2		666 Our New Orleans 2005: A Benefit Album	Nonesuch 79934
9/10/66	40	14		667 Our Wedding Album or The Great Society Affair .... [C]	Jamie 3028
5/17/97	192	1		668 OzzFest .... [L]	Red Ant 7000
4/14/01	144	2		669 OzzFest - Second Stage Live .... [L]	Divine 28860 [2]
9/1/01	25	6		670 OzzFest 2001: The Second Millennium ... [L]	Divine 85950
9/21/02	82	3		671 OzzFest Live 2002 .... [L]	Columbia 86830
6/1/02	❶¹	25	▲	672 P. Diddy & Bad Boy Records Present...We Invented The Remix	Bad Boy 73062
2/21/09	60	3		673 Paris Magnifique	Starbucks 00161
1/29/05	184	2		674 Parranda Tequilera 2005 .... [F]	Univision 310389
2/21/98	105	6		675 Party Over Here 98	Elektra 62088
7/3/04	65	6		676 Patriotic Country	Music For A Cause 60923
7/2/05	125	4		677 Patriotic Country 2	Music For A Cause 69078
7/19/08	162	1		678 Patriotic Country 3	Razor & Tie 89189
11/13/76	209	1		679 Peter And The Wolf .... [I]	RSO 3001
4/2/77	208	1		680 Phil Spector's Greatest Hits .... [O]	Warner/Spector 9104 [2]
1/18/64	80	8		681 Pick Hits Of The Radio Good Guys	Laurie 2021
10/17/87	123	20		682 Piledriver: The Wrestling Album II ...... [N]	Epic 40889
9/23/00	59	8		683 Platinum Hits 2000	Columbia 61586
5/16/09	10	14		684 Playing For Change: Songs Around The World	Hear 31130
4/13/02	117	2		685 Pledge Of Allegiance Tour, The .... [L]	Columbia 86417
7/17/99	90	25	●	686 Pokemon - 2.B.A. Master	Koch 8901
10/15/55	8	5		687 Pop Shopper	RCA Victor 12-13
				EP: RCA Victor SPC 7-13 (#8); LP: RCA Victor SPL 12-13 (#9)	
3/8/03	187	1		688 Power, The	Razor & Tie 89061
1/18/97	51	14		689 Power Of Love	Madacy 6803
8/12/00	181	2		690 Powerpuff Girls: Heroes & Villains, The	Rhino 75848
9/15/01	165	3		691 Prayer Of Jabez, The	ForeFront 34274
1/12/63	35	13		692 President Strikes Back!, The .... [C]	Kapp 1322
6/6/87	194	3		693 Prince's Trust 10th Anniversary Birthday Party, The ... [L]	A&M 3906
				recorded on 6/20/1986 at Wembley Arena in London, England	
10/18/08	191	3		694 Princess Disneymania: Music Stars Sing Disney...Their Way!	Walt Disney 002050
4/24/99	136	2		695 Prodigy Present The Dirtchamber Sessions Volume One	Beggars Banquet 128
				no track titles listed	
9/22/79	202	4		696 Propaganda	A&M 4786
10/13/01	43	20		697 Pulse	Razor & Tie 89041
2/16/08	178	1		698 Pulse: Platinum Edition	Razor & Tie 89179
5/26/07	125	1		699 Punk Goes Acoustic 2	Fearless 30098
4/26/08	86	4		700 Punk Goes Crunk	Fearless 30108
5/27/06	186	2		701 Punk Goes '90s	Fearless 30087
3/28/09	15	8		702 Punk Goes Pop Volume Two	Fearless 30119
7/18/98	80	8		703 Punk-O-Rama 3	Epitaph 86534
7/10/99	113	8		704 Punk-O-Rama 4	Epitaph 86563
7/8/00	71	9		705 Punk-O-Rama 5	Epitaph 86588
6/23/01	80	10		706 Punk-O-Rama 6	Epitaph 86615
7/13/02	67	9		707 Punk-O-Rama 7	Epitaph 86646
6/7/03	79	6		708 Punk-O-Rama 8	Epitaph 86673 [2]
6/26/04	68	3		709 Punk-O-Rama 9	Epitaph 86716
6/25/05	93	6		710 Punk-O-Rama 10	Epitaph 86755
5/5/01	161	1		711 Pure Blues	UTV 556176
10/11/97	125	7		712 Pure Dance 1998	Polygram 553847
12/14/96+	83	57	▲	713 Pure Disco .... Cat:#37/1	Polydor 535877
11/8/97+	71	46	●	714 Pure Disco 2	Polydor 555120
10/17/98	150	5		715 Pure Disco 3	PolyGram TV 565357
8/28/99	113	10		716 Pure 80's	UTV 564809
3/31/01	184	1	●	717 Pure 80's Hits	UTV 560784
2/15/03	197	1		718 Pure 80's Love: The #1 Hits	UTV 069612
5/27/06	160	7		719 Pure 80's: #1's	Hip-O 006279
5/23/98	51	29	●	720 Pure Funk	PolyGram TV 558299
5/29/99	147	2		721 Pure Funk Volume 2	PolyGram TV 565550
1/27/01	68	10		722 Pure Jazz	UTV 520191
2/19/00	136	3		723 Pure Love	UTV 541225

Billboard DEBUT	PEAK	WKS	R I A A	ARTIST Album Title........................ Catalog	Label & Number
5/17/97	10	48	▲²	724 **Pure Moods**	Virgin 42186
12/5/98+	154	13		725 **Pure Moods II**	Virgin 46796
2/24/01	66	10		726 **Pure Moods III**	Virgin 50836
10/19/02	138	4		727 **Pure Moods IV**	Virgin 12082
8/15/98	150	8		728 **Pure Reggae**	PolyGram TV 565122
6/21/97	124	5		729 **Pure Soul**	Polygram 553641
3/18/00	92	12	●	730 **Radio Disney Jams 2**	Walt Disney 60980
3/3/01	109	7		731 **Radio Disney Jams 3**	Walt Disney 860692
10/20/01	169	5		732 **Radio Disney Jams 4**	Walt Disney 860737
9/28/02	122	13		733 **Radio Disney Jams 5**	Walt Disney 860787
9/27/03	105	10		734 **Radio Disney Jams 6**	Walt Disney 860088
4/9/05	57	6		735 **Radio Disney Jams 7**	Walt Disney 861280
2/25/06	70	11		736 **Radio Disney Jams 8**	Walt Disney 861429
3/31/07	55	7		737 **Radio Disney Jams 9**	Walt Disney 000118
2/9/08	18	35		738 **Radio Disney Jams 10**	Walt Disney 001099
2/14/09	41	19		739 **Radio Disney Jams 11**	Walt Disney 003128
4/29/06	199	1		740 **Radio Disney: Move It!**	Walt Disney 861341
10/28/06	82	13		741 **Radio Disney: Party Jams**	Walt Disney 861637
4/24/04	75	2		742 **Radio Disney: Ultimate Jams**	Walt Disney 61077
11/8/86+	114	17	●	743 **Rap's Greatest Hits**	Priority 9466
5/2/87	167	4		744 **Rap's Greatest Hits, Volume 2**	Priority 9468
6/7/03	137	4		745 **Rasta Jamz**	Razor & Tie 89062
8/29/92	136	14		746 **Rave 'Til Dawn**	SBK 80070
6/5/99	30	7		747 **Rawkus Presents: Soundbombing II**	Rawkus 50069
6/22/02	23	7		748 **Rawkus Presents: Soundbombing III**	Rawkus 112917
11/17/90+	38	24		749 **Red Hot + Blue**	Chrysalis 21799
10/1/94	183	1		750 **Red Hot + Country**	Mercury 522639
7/25/92	52	11		751 **Red Hot + Dance**	Columbia 52826
11/1/03	143	3		752 **Red Star Sounds Presents Def Jamaica**	Def Jam 001195
10/27/01	129	3		753 **Red Star Sounds - Volume One: Soul Searching**	Red Star 85857
7/5/97	192	2		754 **Reggae Gold 1997**	VP 1509
6/6/98	147	8		755 **Reggae Gold 1998**	VP 1529
6/5/99	131	5		756 **Reggae Gold 1999**	VP 1559
6/10/00	153	10		757 **Reggae Gold 2000**	VP 1599 [2]
6/16/01	196	2		758 **Reggae Gold 2001**	VP 1629 [2]
6/8/02	112	20		759 **Reggae Gold 2002**	VP 1679 [2]
7/5/03	43	12		760 **Reggae Gold 2003**	VP 83654
7/3/04	64	7		761 **Reggae Gold 2004**	VP 93302
7/9/05	97	3		762 **Reggae Gold 2005**	VP 1729
7/8/06	121	3		763 **Reggae Gold 2006**	VP 1759
6/30/07	152	1		764 **Reggae Gold 2007: Treasure Of The Caribbean**	VP 1789
7/18/09	156	1		765 **Reggae Gold 2009**	VP 1849
7/10/82	203	7		766 **Reggae Sunsplash '81 - A Tribute To Bob Marley** .... **[L-S]**	Elektra 60035 [2]
				recorded and filmed at festival honoring late reggae great Marley at Jarrett Park in Montego Bay, Jamaica	
4/16/05	189	1		767 **Reggaeton Hitmakers 2000/2005** .... **[F]**	VI 450713 [2]
9/27/03	71	4		768 **Remembering Patsy Cline**	MCA 170297
4/6/85	77	14		769 **Requiem**	Angel 38218
3/24/90	166	5		770 **Requiem For The Americas - Songs From The Lost World**	Enigma 73354
7/31/99	185	1		771 **Return Of The Grievous Angel - A Tribute To Gram Parsons**	Almo Sounds 80024
4/12/03	34	6		772 **Rewind: The Hip-Hop DVD Magazine Issue 1**	Shadyville 6101
3/19/94	18	31	▲	773 **Rhythm Country And Blues**	MCA 10965
8/10/96	138	3		774 **Rhythm Of The Games - 1996 Olympic Games Album**	LaFace 26026
5/8/04	54	7		775 **Rock Against Bush Vol. 1**	Fat Wreck Chords 675
8/28/04	45	6		776 **Rock Against Bush Vol. 2**	Fat Wreck Chords 677
11/24/56	20	2		777 **Rock & Roll Forever**	Atlantic 1239
1/24/87	121	11		778 **Rock For Amnesty**	Mercury 830617
9/27/08	50	5		779 **Rock Heroes**	Thrive 90787
3/9/02	179	1		780 **Rock This**	Razor & Tie 89043
7/5/69	182	7		781 **Rock's Greatest Hits**	Columbia 11 [2]
2/3/73	205	3		782 **Rock-O-Rama**	Abkco 4222 [2]
6/5/93	135	1		783 **Roll Wit Tha Flava**	Flavor Unit 53615
3/5/94	175	1		784 **Romantic Classics - Intimate Moments** .... **[I]**	Madacy 0330
12/6/75	205	1		785 **Roots Of British Rock**	Sire 3711 [2]
12/9/00	89	4		786 **Rose That Grew From Concrete Vol. 1, The**	Amaru 490813
10/8/05	91	2		787 **Rose Vol. 2: Music Inspired By Tupac's Poetry, The**	Amaru 5836
10/27/90	140	11		788 **Rubaiyat - Elektra's 40th Anniversary**	Elektra 60940 [2]
4/11/98	119	2		789 **Ruthless Records Tenth Anniversary Compilation - Decade Of Game**	Ruthless 68766 [2]
7/10/99	61	5		790 **RZA Hits, The**	Razor Sharp 69610
9/9/78	202	6		791 **Salsoul Saturday Night Disco Party**	Salsoul 8505
6/22/96	197	1		792 **Sanctuary: 20 Years Of Windham Hill** .... **[I]**	Windham Hill 11180 [2]
9/17/05	131	2		793 **Sangre Nueva** .... **[F]**	Gold Star 180000
12/23/95+	67	17	●	794 **Saturday Morning Cartoons' Greatest Hits**	MCA 11348

VARIOUS ARTISTS COMPILATIONS

DEBUT	PEAK	WKS	R I A A	#	ARTIST / Album Title	Catalog	Label & Number
11/7/64	95	8		795	Saturday Night At The Uptown ...... [L]		Atlantic 8101
					recorded at the Uptown Theatre in Philadelphia, Pennsylvania		
4/27/96	70	13		796	Schoolhouse Rock! Rocks		Lava 92681
5/31/08	42	5		797	Second Wave, The		Rhino 8185
5/23/81	106	12		798	Secret Policeman's Ball/The Music, The ...... [L]		Island 9630
3/20/82	29	16		799	Secret Policeman's Other Ball/The Music, The ...... [L]		Island 9698
					above 2 are benefit concerts for Amnesty International		
8/15/81	209	5		800	Seize The Beat (Dance Ze Dance)		Island 9667
3/17/07	63	2		801	Serve & Collect		Boss Hogg Outlawz 5526
9/20/08	47	2		802	Serve & Collect II		Boss Hogg Outlawz 5094
9/9/78	75	10	●	803	Sesame Street Fever		Sesame Street 79005
9/15/73	211	5		804	Sesame Street Live! ...... [L]		Columbia 32343
					"live" show featuring songs by the TV show cast; includes poster		
5/18/02	81	3		805	Sharp Dressed Men: A Tribute To ZZ Top		RCA 67036
11/4/06	121	1		806	She Was Country When Country Wasn't Cool: A Tribute To Barbara Mandrell ..		BNA 00182
3/21/09	101	4		807	She's Got Soul		Starbucks 012600
6/19/99	191	1		808	Short Music For Short People		Fat Wreck Chords 591
					no track titles listed		
6/6/98	38	10	●	809	Short Records - Nationwide - Independence Day: The Compilation		$hort 46100 [2]
6/9/07	50 C	1		810	Shout Praises! Kids Gospel 2		Integrity Gospel 89164
8/22/98	24 C	1		811	Shout To The Lord		Hosanna! 68965
1/30/99	156	3		812	Shout To The Lord 2000 ...... [L]		Hosanna! 69789
1/27/01	168	3	●	813	Shout To The Lord: The Platinum Collection		Hosanna! 1867 [2]
7/13/63	7	46		814	Shut Down		Capitol 1918
12/6/69+	147	15		815	Signs Of The Zodiac		A&M 4211
					series of 12 albums about the signs of the zodiac		
10/17/09	102	3		816	Silky Soul Music...An All-Star Tribute To Maze Featuring Frankie Beverly		Brantera 6165
7/17/99	200	1		817	Sing America		Warner 47245
4/11/64	84	11		818	16 Original Big Hits		Motown 614
1/15/66	108	5		819	16 Original Big Hits, Volume 4		Motown 633
11/5/66	57	19		820	16 Original Big Hits, Volume 5		Motown 651
2/25/67	95	25		821	16 Original Big Hits, Volume 6		Motown 655
10/14/67	79	18		822	16 Original Big Hits, Volume 7		Motown 661
12/30/67+	163	7		823	16 Original Big Hits, Volume 8		Motown 666
11/16/68+	173	9		824	16 Original Big Hits, Volume 9		Motown 668
11/30/59+	2 7	78	●	825	60 Years Of Music America Loves Best		RCA Victor 6074 [2]
10/31/60	6	59		826	60 Years Of Music America Loves Best, Volume II		RCA Victor 6088 [2]
9/4/61	5	40		827	60 Years Of Music America Loves Best, Volume III (Popular)		RCA Victor 1509
9/4/61	6	18		828	60 Years Of Music America Loves Best, Volume III (Red Seal)		RCA Victor 2574
11/12/94	56	12	●	829	Skynyrd Frynds		MCA 11097
2/13/99	111	10		830	Slammin' Wrestling Hits		Beast 54582
7/16/05	37	11		831	Slow Motion		Razor & Tie 89096
4/8/06	87	3		832	Slow Motion 2		Razor & Tie 89121
6/24/06	120	1		833	Smack: The Album: Volume 1		Smack 5857
9/2/06	76	6		834	Smackers Presents: Girl Next		Hollywood 162648
9/9/00	110	3		835	Smooth Grooves: The Essential Collection		Rhino 79885
5/12/07	71	1		836	Snoop Dogg Presents The Big Squeeze		Doggystyle 5545
10/8/05	4	11		837	So Amazing: An All-Star Tribute To Luther Vandross		J Records 62472
7/6/96	32	33	●	838	So So Def Bass All-Stars		So So Def 67532
7/12/97	71	23		839	So So Def Bass All-Stars Volume II		So So Def 67998
10/24/98	129	3		840	So So Def Bass All-Stars Volume III		So So Def 69346
7/20/02	117	6		841	So So Def Presents: Definition Of A Remix		So So Def 86689
11/29/80	204	1		842	Solar Galaxy Of Stars Live ...... [L]		Solar 3780 [2]
					recorded at the Concord Pavilion in Concord, California		
3/19/66	107	19		843	Solid Gold Soul		Atlantic 8116
4/22/00	94	7		844	Solid Gold Soul - Deep Soul		Rhino 79779
1/24/09	9 C	3		845	Something To Believe In		Starbucks 11000328
6/17/06	192	1		846	Somos Americanos ...... [F]		Urban Box Office 1100
10/26/02	160	3		847	Songs For A Purpose Driven Life		Maranatha! 71450
7/20/63	72	12		848	Songs For A Summer Night		Columbia 2 [2]
10/31/98	151	2		849	Songs 4 Life - Embrace His Grace!	Cat:#15/1	Time Life 80403 [2]
10/3/98+	43	19	●	850	Songs 4 Life - Feel The Power!	Cat:#9/3	Time Life 80401 [2]
10/17/98	131	2		851	Songs 4 Life - Lift Your Spirit!	Cat:#13/1	Time Life 80402 [2]
11/21/98	189	1		852	Songs 4 Life - Renew Your Heart!	Cat:#12/1	Time Life 80404 [2]
8/23/08	77	1		853	Songs For Tibet: The Art Of Peace		Art Of Peace digital [2]
6/2/01	91	10	●	854	Songs 4 Worship: Be Glorified		Integrity 61003 [2]
10/27/07+	67	20		855	Songs 4 Worship: Country		Time-Life 19523
5/17/03	149	1		856	Songs 4 Worship En Espanol: Canta Al Senor ...... [F]		Integrity 18629 [2]
10/24/09	58	6		857	Songs 4 Worship: 50 Greatest Praise And Worship Songs		Integrity 24702 [3]
5/5/01	122	14	●	858	Songs 4 Worship: Holy Ground		Integrity 61002 [2]
3/10/01	51	80	▲ 2	859	Songs 4 Worship: Shout To The Lord	Cat:#8/25	Integrity 61001 [2]
4/26/08	154	1		860	Songs 4 Worship: Shout To The Lord: Special Edition		Integrity 19404 [3]

Billboard DEBUT	PEAK	WKS	R I A A	ARTIST Album Title.. Catalog	Label & Number
5/3/08	79	4		861 Songs Of The Siren	Starbucks 89339
3/27/71	176	8		862 Songs Of The Humpback Whale	Capitol 620
				actual recorded sounds of Whales near Bermuda	
4/5/69	172	3		863 Soul Explosion	Stax 2007 [2]
2/23/08	136	3		864 Soulsville USA: Stax Classics 1965-1973	Starbucks 131
5/11/63	39	8		865 Sound of Genius, The	Columbia SGS 1 [2]
9/4/99	53	11		866 Source Hip-Hop Music Awards 1999 - The Album, The.........	UTV 564891
9/2/00	17	21	●	867 Source Hip-Hop Music Awards 2000 - The Album, The.........	Def Jam 542829
9/1/01	28	12		868 Source Hip-Hop Music Awards 2001 - The Album, The.........	Def Jam 586239
1/3/98	38	32		869 Source Presents Hip Hop Hits - Volume 1, The	PolyGram TV 536204
11/28/98+	46	23	●	870 Source Presents Hip Hop Hits - Volume 2, The	PolyGram TV 565668
12/18/99+	45	19		871 Source Presents Hip Hop Hits - Volume 3, The	UTV 545440
12/30/00+	43	20	●	872 Source Presents Hip Hop Hits - Volume 4, The	Def Jam 520062
1/5/02	47	16		873 Source Presents Hip Hop Hits - Volume 5, The	UTV 586662
1/4/03	35	15		874 Source Presents Hip Hop Hits - Volume 6, The	Def Jam 063546
12/27/03	89	13		875 Source Presents Hip Hop Hits - Volume 7, The	Def Jam 001614
7/17/04	45	12		876 Source Presents Hip Hop Hits - Volume 8, The	Source 2522
1/8/05	75	13		877 Source Presents Hip-Hop Hits - Volume 9, The	Source 2523
8/13/05	60	6		878 Source Presents Hip-Hop Hits - Volume 10, The	Source 0956
7/30/77	142	11		879 South's Greatest Hits, The	Capricorn 0187
9/23/78	201	2		880 South's Greatest Hits Volume II, The	Capricorn 0209
9/13/97	23	6		881 Southwest Riders	Sick Wid' It 45009 [2]
6/5/61	❶⁹	40		882 Stars For A Summer Night	Columbia 1 [2]
8/30/03	6	9		883 State Property Presents: The Chain Gang Vol. II	Roc-A-Fella 000971
3/31/07	120	2		884 Stax 50th Anniversary Celebration........................	Stax 30203 [2]
9/2/67	145	4		885 Stax/Volt Revue - Live In London, The .... [L]	Stax 721
8/27/77	203	6		886 Steppin' Out	Midland Int'l. 2423
7/13/02	73	5		887 Steve Harvey Compilation: Sign Of Things To Come........	MCA 112875
10/31/98	170	4		888 Steve Austin's Stone Cold Metal	Mars 44004
4/8/78	202	8		889 Stiffs Live .... [L]	Stiff 0001
				recorded at Leicester University in London, England	
10/25/97	150	3		890 Stone Country: Country Artists Perform The Songs Of The Rolling Stones	Beyond Music 3055
11/27/93	28	19	●	891 Stone Free: A Tribute To Jimi Hendrix	Reprise 45438
12/2/00	72	11		892 Stoned Immaculate -- The Music Of The Doors........	Elektra 62475
2/19/94	129	1		893 Straight From Da Streets Volume 1	Priority 53885
9/14/91	95	11		894 Straight From The Hood	Priority 7063
11/25/00	56	7		895 Strait Up	Immortal 50365
6/19/99	167	3		896 Streams	Word 69875
8/23/97	26	7		897 Suave House	Suave House 1585
7/8/00	158	1		898 Suave House: Off Da Chain	Suave House 751030
5/5/01	145	3		899 Suddenly '70s	Razor & Tie 89036
6/16/62	24	14		900 Summer Festival	RCA Victor 6097 [2]
7/6/96	66	14		901 Sun Splashin' - 16 Hot Summer Hits!	Madacy 26927
9/20/08	93	4		902 Sundown: Music For Unwinding	EMI 19973
3/1/69	178	5		903 Super Groups, The	Atco 279
8/5/67	12	60		904 Super Hits, The	Atlantic 501
7/20/68	76	33		905 Super Hits, Vol. 2, The	Atlantic 8188
11/23/68+	68	19		906 Super Hits, Vol. 3, The	Atlantic 8203
7/19/69	164	10		907 Super Hits, Vol. 4, The	Atlantic 8224
6/29/68	130	9		908 Super Oldies/Vol. 3	Capitol 2910 [2]
7/12/69	196	2		909 Super Oldies/Vol. 5	Capitol 216 [2]
12/13/08	188	1		910 Super 1's .... [F]	Universal Latino 531377
11/14/70	197	2		911 Super Rock	Columbia 30121 [2]
3/30/96	95	1		912 Surrender To The Air .... [I]	Elektra 61905
7/24/93	131	15		913 Sweet Relief: A Benefit For Victoria Williams	Thirsty Ear 57134
8/24/96	115	2		914 Sweet Relief II: Gravity Of The Situation - The Songs Of Vic Chesnutt	Columbia 67573
2/21/09	84	3		915 Sweetheart: Our Favorite Artists Sing Their Favorite Love Songs	Starbucks 00124
2/21/09	63	3		916 Swing, Swing, Swing	Starbucks 00163
8/29/98	146	7		917 Swing This, Baby!	Slimstyle 78000
12/28/02	50	9		918 Swizz Beatz Presents G.H.E.T.T.O. Stories...........	DreamWorks 450326
11/11/00	195	1		919 Take A Bite Outta Rhyme: A Rock Tribute To Rap	Republic 158301
11/18/95	158	6	●	920 Take My Hand - Songs From The 100 Acre Wood ...	Walt Disney 60863
4/20/91	165	5		921 Tame Yourself	R.N.A. 70772
9/26/98	111	5		922 Tammy Wynette Remembered	Asylum 62277
11/18/95+	53	22	●	923 Tapestry Revisited - A Tribute To Carole King.........	Lava 92604
6/10/89	159	18		924 TeeVee Toons: The Commercials	TVT 1400
9/9/00	164	3		925 Teen Riot!	Razor & Tie 89030
11/9/85+	82	34		926 Television's Greatest Hits	TeeVee Tunes 1100 [2]
11/15/86	149	16		927 Television's Greatest Hits, Volume II	TeeVee Tunes 1200 [2]
8/11/84	201	1		928 That's The Way I Feel Now......................... [I]	A&M 6600 [2]
12/4/04	38	3		929 Themeaddict: WWE The Music V6 .... [I]	Columbia 93572

VARIOUS ARTISTS COMPILATIONS

Billboard DEBUT	PEAK	WKS	R I A A	ARTIST Album Title.. Catalog	Label & Number
3/1/69	31	17		930 **Themes Like Old Times**	Viva 36018 [2]
				features 180 of the most famous original radio themes	
10/17/98	156	1		931 **This Is Alice Music Volume 2**	Alice 32
11/3/01	200	1		932 **This Is Alice Music Volume 5**	Alice Radio 9735
				above 2 compiled by San Francisco radio station Alice 97.3	
3/16/68	146	22		933 **This Is Soul**	Atlantic 8170
7/13/02	61	8		934 **This Is Ultimate Dance!**...	J Records 20034
1/31/09	121	2		935 **This Is Us: Songs From Where You Live**	Starbucks 8322
10/20/01	193	2		936 **This Is Your Country**	UTV 585061
12/27/75+	192	3		937 **Threads Of Glory - 200 Years Of America In Words & Music**........................	London Phase 4 14000 [6]
				6 volume boxed set tracing America's history using music, sound effects and many famous guest narrators	
9/16/06	74	31	●	938 **Three Wooden Crosses**	Word-Curb 86582
4/26/08	152	2		939 **ThriveMix Presents: Dance Anthems 2**	ThriveDance 90782
6/17/06	125	2		940 **ThriveMix02**	ThriveDance 90748
2/3/07	101	2		941 **ThriveMix03**	ThriveDance 90758 [2]
9/29/07	194	1		942 **ThriveMix04**	ThriveDance 90766
11/22/97	181	1		943 **Tibetan Freedom Concert** .... [L]	Grand Royal 59110 [3]
5/1/93	125	8		944 **Today's Hit Country**	K-Tel 6068
1/23/93	177	1		945 **Today's Hot Country**	K-Tel 6063
12/18/93+	179	4		946 **Today's Top Country**	K-Tel 6099
11/18/00+	16[C]	27	▲	947 **Toddler Favorites**	Rhino 75262
12/9/72+	5	38	●	948 **Tommy**	Ode 99001 [2]
11/5/05	148	1		949 **Tony Hawk's American Wasteland**	Vagrant 420
10/21/00	171	3		950 **Too Gangsta For Radio**	Death Row 2018
9/11/99	197	1		951 **Too Short Mix Tape Volume 1 - Nation Riders**	$hort 46106
12/9/95	191	1		952 **Too Short Presents The Dangerous Crew - Don't Try This At Home**	Dangerous 41573
9/29/07	164	2		953 **Top Latino V3** .... [F]	Discos 605 14450
6/28/08	30	11		954 **Total Club Hits**	ThriveDance 90784
1/24/09	16	11		955 **Total Club Hits 2**	ThriveDance 90799
8/8/09	36	5		956 **Total Club Hits 3**	Thrive 90814
1/26/08	69	11		957 **Total Dance 2008**	Thrivedance 90780
8/23/08	21	10		958 **Total Dance 2008: Vol. 2**	ThriveDance 90789
3/21/09	13	6		959 **Total Dance 2009**	ThriveDance 90807
2/23/02	12	26	▲	960 **Totally Country**	BNA 67043
11/16/02	23	17	●	961 **Totally Country Vol. 2**	Epic 86920
10/11/03	37	14		962 **Totally Country Vol. 3**	Warner 73955
2/26/05	5	33	▲	963 **Totally Country Vol. 4**	Sony 67287
2/25/06	17	14		964 **Totally Country Vol. 5**	Warner 77145
2/17/07	18	11		965 **Totally Country Vol. 6**	Sony 03828
7/14/01	34	16		966 **Totally Dance**	Warner 14720
7/19/03	48	10		967 **Totally Hip Hop**	Warner 52553
11/27/99	14	36	▲	968 **Totally Hits**	Arista 14625
6/17/00	13	19	▲	969 **Totally Hits 2**	Warner 62529
12/2/00	25	19	▲	970 **Totally Hits 3**	Arista 83412
10/13/01	3[1]	28	▲	971 **Totally Hits 2001**	Warner 14684
6/22/02	2[1]	23	▲	972 **Totally Hits 2002**	Warner 78192
11/16/02	21	12		973 **Totally Hits 2002: More Platinum Hits**	BMG 73768
10/25/03	13	15	●	974 **Totally Hits 2003**	Warner 55777
5/22/04	14	14	●	975 **Totally Hits 2004**	Warner 59211
10/23/04	19	13		976 **Totally Hits 2004 Vol. 2**	Warner 76574
6/4/05	20	11		977 **Totally Hits 2005**	Warner 74691
7/19/03	66	5		978 **Totally R&B**	Warner 52552
10/14/95	198	1		979 **Tower Of Song - The Songs Of Leonard Cohen**......................	A&M 540259
8/22/09	144	3		980 **Town And Country Blues**	Concord 1511
7/7/01	188	4		981 **Trance Party (Volume One)**	Robbins 75022
7/13/02	135	10		982 **Trance Party (Volume Two)**	Robbins 75030
7/26/69	144	7		983 **Treasury Of Great Contemporary Hits, A**.....................	Dunhill/ABC 50057
3/12/94	56	14		984 **Tribute To Curtis Mayfield, A**	Warner 45500
5/12/07	103	3		985 **Tribute To Joni Mitchell, A**	Nonesuch 122620
8/24/96	47	10	●	986 **Tribute To Stevie Ray Vaughan, A** .... [L]	Epic 67599
				recorded on 5/11/1995 at the Austin City Limits Studio in Austin, Texas	
4/29/72	183	2		987 **Tribute To Woody Guthrie - Part One, A** .... [L]	Columbia 31171
4/29/72	189	2		988 **Tribute To Woody Guthrie - Part Two, A** .... [L]	Warner 2586
				above 2 albums used proceeds to benefit Huntington's Disease Research	
9/13/08	57	2		989 **Tropical Thunder**	Warner 89193
12/18/71+	185	7		990 **Truth Of Truths - A Contemporary Rock Opera**	Oak 1001 [2]
2/27/61	19	23		991 **12 + 3 = 15 Hits**	End 310
1/23/82	208	4		992 **20 Aerobic Dance Hits**	Parade 101 [2]
6/4/83	42	28	●	993 **25 #1 Hits From 25 Years** .... Cat:#12/42	Motown 5308 [2]
6/11/83	107	9		994 **25 Years Of Grammy Greats** .... Cat:#45/4	Motown 5309
3/20/65	44	18		995 **20 Original Winners Of 1964**	Roulette 25293
4/12/80	150	6		996 **20/20 - Twenty No. 1 Hits From Twenty Years At Motown**.......................	Motown 937 [2]

Billboard DEBUT	PEAK	WKS	R I A A	ARTIST Album Title..Catalog	Label & Number
11/9/91+	18	32	▲	997 Two Rooms - Celebrating The Songs Of Elton John & Bernie Taupin	Polydor 845750
8/1/98	83	14	●	998 Ultimate Country Party	Arista 18850
5/6/00	141	5		999 Ultimate Country Party 2	Arista 18890
11/30/96+	17	50	▲	1000 Ultimate Dance Party 1997	Arista 18943
11/15/97	38	31	●	1001 Ultimate Dance Party 1998	Arista 18988
11/14/98	69	21	●	1002 Ultimate Dance Party 1999	Arista 19026
6/24/00	70	14		1003 Ultimate Dance Party 2000	Arista 14647
6/26/99	174	1		1004 Ultimate Divas	Arista 19066
9/13/97	46	27	●	1005 Ultimate Hip Hop Party 1998	Arista 18977
9/13/97	124	10		1006 Ultimate New Wave Party 1998	Arista 18985
6/21/03	55	6		1007 Ultimate Smash Hits	Arista 52522
7/20/02	180	3		1008 Ultra.Dance 02	Ultra 1123 [2]
3/22/03	162	3		1009 Ultra.Dance 03	Ultra 1155 [2]
9/13/03	93	4		1010 Ultra.Dance 04	Ultra 1175 [2]
5/8/04	98	4		1011 Ultra.Dance 05	Ultra 1190 [2]
2/12/05	161	2		1012 Ultra.Dance 06	Ultra 1249 [2]
2/11/06	98	2		1013 Ultra.Dance 07	Ultra 1358 [2]
2/10/07	82	3		1014 Ultra.Dance 08	Ultra 1485 [2]
2/9/08	77	8		1015 Ultra.Dance 09	Ultra 1636 [2]
1/24/09	41	5		1016 Ultra.Dance 10	Ultra 1895
6/27/09	75	2		1017 Ultra Hits	Ultra 2043
10/11/08	157	1		1018 Ultra.Mix	Ultra 1784
6/17/06	129	3		1019 Ultra.Weekend 2	Ultra 1411 [2]
6/9/07	171	2		1020 Ultra.Weekend 3	Ultra 1532 [2]
9/27/69	196	2		1021 Underground Gold	Liberty 7625
11/11/00	43	15	●	1022 Universal Smash Hits	Universal 158299
2/26/05	118	2		1023 Universal Smash Hits 3	Universal 003692
12/24/94	97	10	●	1024 Unplugged Collection Volume One, The .... [L]	Warner 45774
6/24/06	172	1		1025 Unsound	Epitaph 86813
7/12/08	173	1		1026 Unwrapped Vol. 5.0: The ColliPark Cafe Sessions	Hidden Beach 00061
11/14/09	103	3		1027 Up, Down, Turn Around: Circa 80	Starbucks 8410
3/15/08	135	4		1028 Upright, Grand And All Right: Masters Of Jazz Piano	Universal 008144
6/19/93	71	16		1029 Uptown MTV Unplugged .... [L]	Uptown 10858
8/23/97	184	3		1030 Urban Beats	Polygram 553764
6/6/98	193	1		1031 Urban Beats 2: The Definitive Guide To Electronic Music	Polygram 555840 [2]
9/26/81	173	3		1032 Urgh! A Music War .... [L]	A&M 6019 [2]
7/6/02	55	11		1033 Vans Warped Tour 2002 Compilation .... [L]	SideOneDummy 1233 [2]
6/21/03	21	12	●	1034 Vans Warped Tour 2003 Compilation .... [L]	SideOneDummy 1237 [2]
6/26/04	8	13	●	1035 Vans Warped Tour 2004 Compilation [L]	SideOneDummy 1248 [2]
6/25/05	13	12	●	1036 Vans Warped Tour 2005 Compilation .... [L]	SideOneDummy 1268 [2]
6/24/06	27	11	●	1037 Vans Warped Tour 2006 Compilation .... [L]	SideOneDummy 1291 [2]
6/23/07	31	13		1038 Vans Warped Tour 2007 Compilation .... [L]	SideOneDummy 1331 [2]
6/21/08	35	12		1039 Vans Warped Tour 2008 Compilation .... [L]	SideOneDummy 1355 [2]
6/27/09	45	12		1040 Vans Warped Tour 2009 Compilation .... [L]	SideOneDummy 1387 [2]
6/1/02	197	1		1041 Verve//Remixed	Verve 589606
9/13/03	149	4		1042 Verve//Remixed2	Verve 000598
4/23/05	165	2		1043 Verve//Remixed3	Verve 004166
5/14/05	94	5		1044 Very Best Of Death Row, The	Death Row 63060
10/21/00	177	4		1045 Very Scary Music: Classic Horror Themes	LaserLight 21378
2/26/05	184	1		1046 VH1 Classic Presents Metal Mania: Stripped!	Immortal 60004
10/24/98	21	20	●	1047 VH1 Divas Live .... [L]	Epic 69600
11/20/99	90	5	●	1048 VH1 Divas Live/99 .... [L]	Arista 14604
9/6/97	174	2		1049 VH1 More Of The Big 80's	Rhino 72820
5/13/00	160	3		1050 VH1 Storytellers .... [L]	Interscope 490511
8/21/99	195	1		1051 VH1 The Big 80's - Big Hair	Rhino 75842
4/12/08	65	4		1052 Vintage Country: The Golden Age Of Country Music	Sony 08651
8/28/99	8	14	●	1053 Violator - The Album	Violator 558941
8/11/01	10	8		1054 Violator The Album V2.0	Violator 85790
4/26/08	127	12		1055 Voices: The Ultimate Gospel Collection	BET 221252
2/14/09	11	7		1056 Voices: WWE The Music Vol. 9	WWE 43882
7/24/76	153	6		1057 Volunteer Jam .... [L] recorded on 9/9/1975 in Murfreesboro, Tennessee	Capricorn 0172
10/21/78	206	3		1058 Volunteer Jam III And IV .... [L] recorded on 1/8/1977 and 1/14/1978 at the Nashville Municipal Auditorium	Epic 35368 [2]
7/19/80	104	9		1059 Volunteer Jam VI .... [L] recorded on 1/12/1980 at the Nashville Municipal Auditorium	Epic 36438 [2]
7/25/81	149	4		1060 Volunteer Jam VII .... [L] recorded on 1/17/1981 at the Nashville Municipal Auditorium	Epic 37178
2/7/76	10	51	▲²	1061 Wanted! The Outlaws CMA: Album of the Year	RCA Victor 1321
8/12/78	98	25		1062 War Of The Worlds, The	Columbia 35290 [2]

VARIOUS ARTISTS COMPILATIONS

Billboard DEBUT	PEAK	WKS	R I A A	ARTIST Album Title	Catalog	Label & Number
6/23/73	62	18		1063 Watergate Comedy Hour, The [C]		Hidden 11202
10/16/71	181	4		1064 Way To Become The Sensuous Woman By "J", The		Atlantic 7209
				no track titles listed		
12/4/99	40	8	●	1065 WCW Mayhem The Music		Tommy Boy 1353
				WCW: World Championship Wrestling		
6/23/07	105	3		1066 We All Love Ella: Celebrating The First Lady Of Song		Verve 008833
4/19/08	163	3		1067 We The Best		MTS 29
3/1/03	43	5		1068 We're A Happy Family: A Tribute To Ramones		DV8 86352
11/27/65	3³	25	●	1069 Welcome To The LBJ Ranch! [C]		Capitol 2423
7/16/05	177	1		1070 Wendy Williams Brings The Heat Vol. 1		Question Mark 60135
6/1/59	5	3		1071 What's New? On Capitol Stereo, Vol. 1		Capitol SN-1
4/2/66	22	18		1072 When You're In Love The Whole World Is Jewish [C]		Kapp 4506
7/22/78	181	4		1073 White Mansions		A&M 6004
12/21/85+	167	12		1074 Windham Hill Records Piano Sampler [I]		Windham Hill 1040
10/20/84	108	25		1075 Windham Hill Records Sampler '84 [I]		Windham Hill 1035
3/29/86	102	18		1076 Windham Hill Records Sampler '86 [I]		Windham Hill 1048
2/27/88	134	16		1077 Windham Hill Records Sampler '88 [I]		Windham Hill 1065
4/15/89	176	4		1078 Windham Hill Records Sampler '89 [I]		Windham Hill 1082
9/6/80	69	7		1079 Winners		I&M 017
1/15/83	109	14		1080 Winning Hand, The		Monument 38389 [2]
4/13/96	175	1		1081 Wolfgang Amadeus Mozart, Piano Concertos No. 22 and No. 24 [I]		Digital Master. 71832
4/13/96	196	1		1082 Wolfgang Amadeus Mozart, Violin Concertos No. 1, 2 + 3 [I]		Digital Master. 71825
11/15/08+	36ᶜ	1		1083 Wolfman Jack's Halloween Fun For Kids [N]		St. Clair 0008
11/10/07	40ᶜ	3		1084 Wolfman Jack's Halloween Special: Monster Mash Bash		St. Clair 1075
5/15/04	67	5		1085 Women & Songs		Warner 78200
3/24/07	3¹ᶜ	4		1086 Wonderful Cross: 12 Modern Worship Songs Celebrating The Cross, The		Worship Together 20357
8/27/94	186	1		1087 Woodstock: Three Days Of Peace And Music - Twenty-Fifth Anniversary Collection [L]		Atlantic 82636 [4]
				recorded from August 15-17, 1969		
11/26/94	50	12	▲	1088 Woodstock 94 [L]		A&M 540289 [2]
				recorded from August 12-14, 1994		
11/6/99	32	6	●	1089 Woodstock 99 [L]		Epic 63770 [2]
				recorded from July 23-25, 1999		
8/29/09	120	2		1090 Woodstock: 40 Years On: Back To Yasgur's Farm [L]		Rhino 519761 [6]
10/28/95	94	3		1091 Working Class Hero - A Tribute To John Lennon		Hollywood 62015
7/18/09	96	4		1092 World Is Africa		Starbucks 012438
7/10/65	107	7		1093 World Of Country Music, The		Capitol 5 [2]
4/8/00	8	17	●	1094 World Wrestling Federation - Aggression		Priority 50120
4/13/02	3¹	13	●	1095 World Wrestling Federation - Forceable Entry		Columbia 85211
10/26/96	184	2		1096 World Wrestling Federation - Full Metal		Edel America 8689
3/7/98	165	17		1097 World Wrestling Federation - The Music Volume 2		Koch 8709
1/23/99	10	30	▲	1098 World Wrestling Federation - The Music Volume 3		Koch 8803
11/20/99	4	22	▲	1099 World Wrestling Federation - The Music Volume 4		Koch 8808
3/10/01	2¹	15	●	1100 World Wrestling Federation - The Music Volume 5		Smack Down! 8830
7/16/05	116	7		1101 Worship Jamz		Razor & Tie 89102
7/29/06	139	5		1102 Worship Jamz 2		Fuseic 89120
6/7/03	103	9		1103 Worship Together: Be Glorified		Time-Life 42011 [2]
2/1/03	39	52	▲	1104 Worship Together: I Could Sing Of Your Love Forever		Time-Life 42010 [2]
12/9/95	144	14	▲	1105 WOW 1996		Sparrow 51516 [2]
11/16/96	71	32	▲	1106 WOW 1997		Sparrow 51562 [2]
11/22/97	52	30	▲	1107 WOW 1998		Sparrow 51629 [2]
11/7/98	51	42	▲²	1108 WOW 1999		Sparrow 51686 [2]
11/13/99	29	37	▲²	1109 WOW 2000		Sparrow 51703 [2]
11/18/00	36	36	▲²	1110 WOW 2001		Sparrow 51779 [2]
7/8/00	111	11	●	1111 WOW Gold		Provident 10533 [2]
2/14/98	100	16	▲	1112 WOW Gospel 1998		Verity 43109 [2]
3/13/99	94	12	▲	1113 WOW Gospel 1999		Verity 43125 [2]
2/26/00	93	11	▲	1114 WOW Gospel 2000		Word 43149 [2]
2/24/01	75	14	▲	1115 WOW Gospel 2001		EMI 43163 [2]
2/23/02	46	14	●	1116 WOW Gospel 2002		EMI Christian 43188 [2]
2/22/03	29	20	▲	1117 WOW Gospel 2003		EMI 43213 [2]
2/14/04	27	16	▲	1118 WOW Gospel 2004		Word 57494 [2]
2/12/05	29	19	●	1119 WOW Gospel 2005		Word-Curb 65344 [2]
2/18/06	20	16	●	1120 WOW Gospel 2006		Word-Curb 75160 [2]
2/17/07	21	14	●	1121 WOW Gospel 2007		Word-Curb 02499 [2]
3/1/08	34	22	●	1122 WOW Gospel 2008		Word-Curb 19290 [2]
2/14/09	27	21		1123 WOW Gospel 2009		Word-Curb 41675 [2]
10/4/08	124	2		1124 WOW Gospel Essentials: All-Time Favorite Songs		Word-Curb 27619
5/26/07	74	4		1125 WOW Gospel #1s: 30 Of The Greatest Gospel Hits Ever!		EMI/Word-Curb 08764 [2]

DEBUT	PEAK	WKS	R I A A	ARTIST / Album Title .... Catalog	Label & Number
4/26/08	99	10		1126 WOW Hits 1	Sony 10879
11/10/01	52	26	▲	1127 WOW Hits 2002	EMI Christian 51850 [2]
10/19/02	34	30	▲	1128 WOW Hits 2003	EMI 39776 [2]
10/25/03	51	31	▲	1129 WOW Hits 2004	EMI 90652 [2]
10/23/04	39	40	▲	1130 WOW Hits 2005	Word 71106 [2]
10/22/05	42	35	▲	1131 WOW Hits 2006	Word-Curb 11247 [2]
10/21/06	38	35	▲	1132 WOW Hits 2007	Word-Curb 67196 [2]
10/20/07	56	37	●	1133 WOW Hits 2008	Word-Curb 96677 [2]
10/25/08	31	52	▲	1134 WOW Hits 2009	Word-Curb 887742 [2]
10/24/09	33	32↑	●	1135 WOW Hits 2010	Word-Curb 14857 [2]
3/24/07	100	5		1136 WOW Hymns	Word-Curb 887145 [2]
4/23/05	58	21	●	1137 WOW #1s	Word-Curb 10769 [2]
8/7/99	84	19	▲	1138 WOW - The 90s	Word 69975 [2]
4/22/06	75	23	●	1139 WOW Worship Aqua	Word-Curb 10814 [2]
7/3/99	70	89	▲²	1140 WOW Worship Blue	Integrity 69974 [2]
4/7/01	78	20	●	1141 WOW Worship Green	Integrity 19552 [2]
4/15/00	65	33	▲	1142 WOW Worship Orange	Integrity 63840 [2]
3/27/04	62	13		1143 WOW Worship Red	EMI 86300 [2]
4/5/03	44	30	▲	1144 WOW Worship Yellow	EMI 80198 [2]
11/30/85+	84	19		1145 Wrestling Album, The .... [N]	Epic 40223
11/5/05	190	1		1146 Wu-Tang Meets The Indie Culture	Wu-Tang 212
4/10/99	25	9		1147 Wu-Tang Records Presents: Wu-Chronicles	Wu-Tang 51143
11/30/02	13	8	▲	1148 WWE Anthology .... [K]	Smack Down! 8832 [3]
1/31/04	12	8		1149 WWE Originals	Columbia 90881
4/12/08	24	4		1150 WWE: The Music Volume 8	WWE 27339
6/10/06	8	9		1151 WWE: Wreckless Intent	WWE 82559
12/13/97	182	2		1152 WWJD .... WWJD: What Would Jesus Do	ForeFront 25183
11/25/06	44	6		1153 WY Records Presents: Los Vaqueros .... [F]	WY 008010
10/14/67	165	5		1154 Yiddish Are Coming! The Yiddish Are Coming!, The .... [C]	Verve 15058
10/23/99	173	2		1155 YM Hot Tracks Vol. 1	Damian 12227
7/12/97	88	8		1156 Yo! MTV Raps	Def Jam 534746
9/18/65	9	34		1157 You Don't Have To Be Jewish .... [C]	Kapp 4503
7/15/67	118	9		1158 Zodiac: Cosmic Sounds, The	Elektra 74009

THE TOP ARTISTS

The Top 500 Album Artists Ranking From 1955-2009

Point System:

Next to each artist's name is their point total. The points are totaled through the May 29, 2010, chart. Each artist's points are accumulated according to the following formula:

1. **Highest chart position** each album reached on *The Billboard 200* or *Bubbling Under* chart:

    #1 = 200 points for its first week at #1, plus 20 points
    for each additional week at #1

    #2 = 190 points for its first week at #2, plus 10 points
    for each additional week at #2

    #3 = 180 points for its first week at #3, plus 5 points
    for each additional week at #3

#4-5	=	170 points	**#111-120**	=	90 points
#6-10	=	160 points	**#121-130**	=	80 points
#11-15	=	155 points	**#131-140**	=	70 points
#16-20	=	150 points	**#141-150**	=	60 points
#21-30	=	145 points	**#151-160**	=	50 points
#31-40	=	140 points	**#161-170**	=	40 points
#41-50	=	135 points	**#171-180**	=	30 points
#51-60	=	130 points	**#181-190**	=	20 points
#61-70	=	125 points	**#191-200**	=	10 points
#71-80	=	120 points	**#201-210**	=	5 points
#81-90	=	115 points	**#211-220**	=	4 points
#91-100	=	110 points	**#221-235**	=	3 points
#101-110	=	100 points			

2. Highest chart position each album reached on *Billboard's* **Top Pop Catalog Albums** chart and special **Christmas Albums** chart <u>exclusively</u> (<u>not</u> included if album also made *The Billboard 200* chart):

> #1 = 50 points for its first week at #1, plus 5 points for each additional week at #1
>
> #2 = 45 points for its first week at #2, plus 3 points for each additional week at #2
>
> #3 = 40 points for its first week at #3, plus 2 points for each additional week at #3

#4-5	= 35 points		#21-30	= 15 points
#6-10	= 30 points		#31-40	= 10 points
#11-15	= 25 points		#41-50	= 5 points
#16-20	= 20 points		#51-75	= 3 points

3. **Total weeks charted** (includes <u>all</u> weeks charted on the Top Pop Catalog Albums chart.

Christmas albums are awarded points for their peak position for their <u>first</u> chart appearance only. Their seasonal re-entries are awarded points for their weeks charted only.

In the case of a tie, the artist listed first is determined by the following tie-breaker rules:

1) Most charted albums   2) Most Top 40 albums   3) Most Top 10 albums

When two artists combine for a hit album, such as Kenny Rogers and Dolly Parton, the full point value is given to both artists. Duos, such as Simon & Garfunkel, Hall & Oates, or Brooks & Dunn, are considered regular recording teams, and their points are not shared by either artist individually.

Headings And Special Symbols:

Old Rank: Artist ranking in *The Billboard Albums 1956-2005* book

New Rank: Artist ranking in *Top Pop Albums 1955-2009* book

HOF **Rock & Roll Hall of Fame Inductee**

● **Denotes deceased Solo Artist**

■ **Denotes one or more deceased Group Member**

★ **Hot Artist**
Hot artist charted 2 or more Top 10 albums since the previous edition. (Greatest Hits, Compilations, Catalog and Christmas albums do not qualify.)

NEW Artist's first ranking in the Top 500

+ Subject to change since an album is still charted as of the 5/29/2010 cut-off date.

TOP 500 ARTISTS (#1-100)

Old Rank	New Rank		Points
(1)	1.	Elvis Presley...● ....HOF....	18,376
(2)	2.	Frank Sinatra...●	14,595 +
(3)	3.	The Beatles...■ ....HOF..	14,445
(4)	★4.	Barbra Streisand	11,091
(5)	5.	The Rolling Stones...■ ....HOF..	10,614
(6)	6.	Johnny Mathis	10,448
(7)	7.	Elton John ....HOF..	10,082
(8)	★8.	Bob Dylan ....HOF..	9,351
(9)	★9.	Neil Diamond	8,240
(10)	10.	The Temptations...■ ....HOF..	7,885
(12)	11.	Eric Clapton ....HOF..	7,797
(11)	12.	The Beach Boys...■ ....HOF..	7,521
(16)	★13.	Rod Stewart ....HOF..	7,434
(14)	14.	Willie Nelson	7,241
(17)	15.	Mantovani...●	7,232
(15)	16.	Ray Charles...● ....HOF..	7,201
(26)	17.	Neil Young ....HOF..	7,100
(13)	18.	Ray Conniff...●	7,059
(21)	★19.	Prince ....HOF..	6,950
(19)	20.	Paul McCartney ....HOF..	6,828
(18)	21.	Aretha Franklin ....HOF..	6,575
(44)	★22.	George Strait	6,468
(32)	23.	Jimmy Buffett	6,372
(23)	24.	Pink Floyd...■ ....HOF..	6,368 +
(28)	25.	Chicago...■	6,296
(20)	26.	David Bowie ....HOF..	6,249
(22)	27.	James Brown...● ....HOF..	6,232
(51)	★28.	Bruce Springsteen ....HOF..	6,189
(24)	29.	Andy Williams	6,146
(27)	30.	Bee Gees...■	6,136
(25)	31.	Lawrence Welk...●	6,134
(43)	32.	Van Morrison ....HOF..	6,113
(34)	33.	Kenny Rogers	6,021
(29)	34.	The Supremes...■ ....HOF..	5,946
(38)	35.	Grateful Dead...■	5,928
(30)	36.	Henry Mancini...●	5,856
(31)	37.	The Kingston Trio...■	5,827
(53)	★38.	Barry Manilow	5,775
(36)	39.	Aerosmith ....HOF..	5,769
(35)	40.	Jimi Hendrix...● ....HOF..	5,768
(66)	41.	Michael Jackson...● ....HOF..	5,692 +
(33)	42.	Herb Alpert ....HOF..	5,663
(37)	43.	Stevie Wonder ....HOF..	5,595
(45)	44.	Nat "King" Cole...● ....HOF..	5,579
(49)	45.	Johnny Cash...● ....HOF..	5,553
(48)	46.	Metallica...■ ....HOF..	5,546
(58)	47.	Madonna ....HOF..	5,538
(42)	48.	Led Zeppelin...■ ....HOF..	5,529 +
(60)	49.	U2 ....HOF..	5,450
(54)	50.	Queen...■ ....HOF..	5,414

Old Rank	New Rank		Points
(39)	51.	Roger Williams	5,401
(46)	52.	Kiss...■	5,395
(40)	53.	Fleetwood Mac ....HOF..	5,271
(47)	54.	Linda Ronstadt	5,184
(41)	55.	The Ventures...■ ....HOF..	5,179
(55)	56.	Santana ....HOF..	5,151
(57)	57.	Garth Brooks	5,131 +
(52)	58.	Diana Ross	5,121
(67)	59.	James Taylor ....HOF..	5,106
(73)	60.	AC/DC...■ ....HOF..	5,095 +
(64)	61.	Rush...■	5,064
(56)	62.	The Who...■ ....HOF..	5,010
(50)	63.	Billy Vaughn...●	4,956
(62)	64.	Billy Joel ....HOF..	4,843
(70)	65.	Alabama	4,807
(59)	66.	Jefferson Airplane/ Starship...■ ....HOF..	4,790
(103)	★67.	Alan Jackson	4,758
(72)	68.	Eagles ....HOF..	4,702
(61)	69.	Dionne Warwick	4,674
(79)	70.	Tony Bennett	4,658
(102)	★71.	Dave Matthews Band...■	4,629
(68)	72.	Harry Belafonte	4,601
(69)	73.	The Isley Brothers...■ ....HOF..	4,582
(76)	74.	The Doors...■ ....HOF..	4,554
(63)	75.	John Denver...●	4,534
(65)	76.	Mitch Miller	4,522
(91)	★77.	Mariah Carey	4,476
(81)	78.	Dean Martin...●	4,417
(85)	79.	Tom Petty/ The Heartbreakers...■ ....HOF..	4,413
(71)	80.	The Lettermen	4,360
(74)	81.	Nancy Wilson	4,319
(84)	82.	Journey	4,308 +
(75)	83.	Marvin Gaye...● ....HOF..	4,300
(77)	84.	Jethro Tull...■	4,262
(104)	★85.	Bon Jovi	4,237 +
(98)	86.	Elvis Costello ....HOF..	4,212
(78)	87.	Dolly Parton	4,175
(99)	88.	Carly Simon	4,095
(100)	89.	Bob Seger ....HOF..	4,061 +
(80)	90.	The Kinks ....HOF..	4,052
(115)	91.	2Pac...●	4,042
(87)	92.	Gladys Knight/The Pips...■ .....HOF..	4,034
(117)	★93.	Pearl Jam	4,022
(109)	94.	Kenny G	4,004
(83)	95.	Joan Baez	3,990
(118)	96.	R.E.M. ....HOF..	3,990
(92)	97.	Anne Murray	3,978
(82)	98.	The Monkees	3,972
(86)	99.	Glen Campbell	3,915
(101)	100.	Jackson 5/Jacksons...■ ....HOF..	3,904

Old Rank	New Rank		Points
(149)★	101.	Jay-Z	3,900 +
(204)★	102.	Toby Keith	3,888
(110)	103.	Creedence Clearwater Revival...■ HOF	3,886 +
(105)	104.	Lynyrd Skynyrd...■ HOF	3,858
(111)★	105.	John Cougar Mellencamp HOF	3,858
(196)★	106.	Tim McGraw	3,849 +
(88)	107.	Earth, Wind & Fire HOF	3,844
(89)	108.	The Moody Blues...■	3,841
(90)	109.	Frank Zappa...● HOF	3,840
(97)	110.	Daryl Hall & John Oates	3,830
(93)	111.	Steve Miller Band	3,786
(94)	112.	Enoch Light...●	3,781
(125)★	113.	Reba McEntire	3,748 +
(119)	114.	Bob Marley...● HOF	3,729 +
(96)	115.	Carole King HOF	3,729
(95)	116.	Cher	3,726
(121)	117.	Hank Williams, Jr.	3,719
(130)	118.	Celine Dion	3,689
(133)	119.	Def Leppard...■	3,669
(116)	120.	Luther Vandross...●	3,648
(120)	121.	Bette Midler	3,624
(106)	122.	Yes	3,568
(107)	123.	Allman Brothers Band...■ HOF	3,559
(108)	124.	John Lennon...● HOF	3,552
(112)	125.	Van Halen HOF	3,525
(113)	126.	Four Tops...■ HOF	3,503
(114)	127.	Bill Cosby	3,481
(197)	128.	Mannheim Steamroller	3,456
(138)	129.	Al Green HOF	3,438
(137)	130.	Donna Summer	3,418
(134)	131.	Ozzy Osbourne	3,385
(127)	132.	B.B. King HOF	3,383
(151)	133.	Emmylou Harris	3,357
(142)	134.	Natalie Cole	3,348
(135)	135.	Joni Mitchell HOF	3,343
(122)	136.	The 4 Seasons...■ HOF	3,334
(146)	137.	Black Sabbath...■ HOF	3,328
(129)	138.	Genesis HOF	3,323
(123)	139.	The Miracles...■	3,307
(124)	140.	Ramsey Lewis	3,302
(152)	141.	George Benson	3,283
(148)	142.	Whitney Houston	3,282
(136)	143.	Steely Dan HOF	3,241
(128)	144.	Ferrante & Teicher...■	3,231
(147)	145.	Perry Como...●	3,225
(144)	146.	Simon & Garfunkel HOF	3,225
(132)	147.	Isaac Hayes...● HOF	3,220
(251)★	148.	Kenny Chesney	3,213 +
(141)	149.	Alice Cooper	3,210
(188)	150.	Harry Connick, Jr.	3,210 +

Old Rank	New Rank		Points
(173)	151.	Brooks & Dunn	3,206 +
(168)	152.	Randy Travis	3,192
(175)★	153.	R. Kelly	3,151
(339)★	154.	Andrea Bocelli	3,131
(139)	155.	Olivia Newton-John	3,109
(143)	156.	Al Martino...●	3,083
(140)	157.	Bonnie Raitt HOF	3,082
(145)	158.	The O'Jays...■ HOF	3,071
(150)	159.	ZZ Top HOF	3,052
(186)	160.	Paul Simon HOF	3,038
(170)	161.	Phish	3,034
(153)	162.	Bobby Vinton	3,032
(155)	163.	Percy Faith...●	3,028
(154)	164.	Heart	3,016
(156)	165.	Connie Francis	3,002
(158)	166.	Peter, Paul & Mary...■	3,002
(157)	167.	Barry White...●	3,001
(159)	168.	Jimmy Smith...●	2,942
(183)	169.	Patti LaBelle	2,941
(169)	170.	George Harrison...● HOF	2,940
(166)	171.	Tom Jones	2,929
(174)	172.	Beastie Boys	2,919
(161)	173.	Styx...■	2,918
(185)	174.	Jackson Browne HOF	2,913
(160)	175.	Al Hirt...●	2,912
(164)	176.	Lou Rawls...●	2,878
(162)	177.	Grand Funk Railroad	2,860
(234)★	178.	Janet Jackson	2,853
(163)	179.	The Doobie Brothers...■	2,851
(179)	180.	Crosby, Stills & Nash (& Young) HOF	2,847
(215)	181.	Iron Maiden	2,840
(165)	182.	Phil Collins	2,838
(126)	183.	Waylon Jennings...●	2,835
(181)	184.	Gloria Estefan	2,822
(191)	185.	Smokey Robinson HOF	2,813
(167)	186.	Chubby Checker	2,809
(218)	187.	Guns N' Roses	2,794 +
(171)	188.	Kool & The Gang...■	2,779
(305)★	189.	Mary J. Blige	2,764
(172)	190.	Commodores...■	2,760
(176)	191.	Deep Purple...■	2,758
(190)	192.	Michael Bolton	2,733
(177)	193.	War...■	2,726
(178)	194.	Grover Washington, Jr. ...●	2,720
(209)	195.	Cat Stevens	2,706
(180)	196.	Bob James	2,690
(217)	197.	Motley Crue...■	2,689 +
(182)	198.	Three Dog Night	2,668
(229)	199.	Sting	2,657
(203)	200.	Duran Duran	2,653

Old Rank	New Rank		Points
(184)	201.	The Righteous Brothers...■	2,649
(221)	202.	Yanni	2,641
(289)★	203.	Snoop Dogg	2,641
(224)	204.	Amy Grant	2,632
(187)	205.	Joe Cocker	2,631
(233)	206.	Cheap Trick	2,627
(192)	207.	Dan Fogelberg...●	2,627
(299)	208.	Nine Inch Nails	2,616
(213)	209.	The Police ....HOF	2,604
(189)	210.	Roberta Flack	2,600
(280)	211.	Dave Brubeck	2,590
(194)	212.	Poco	2,581
(193)	213.	Bert Kaempfert...●	2,580
(195)	214.	Pat Boone	2,565
(198)	215.	Electric Light Orchestra...■	2,557
(214)	216.	The Cure	2,555
(200)	217.	Carpenters...■	2,554
(201)	218.	Donovan	2,543
(199)	219.	Quincy Jones	2,543
(231)	220.	Foreigner	2,540
(248)★	221.	LL Cool J	2,533
(275)	222.	Green Day	2,532
(239)	223.	Sergio Mendes	2,526
(202)	224.	Jeff Beck ....HOF	2,513
(205)	225.	Engelbert Humperdinck	2,507
(241)	226.	Depeche Mode	2,500
(237)	227.	Judas Priest	2,492 +
(223)	228.	America	2,488
(206)	229.	REO Speedwagon	2,487
(317)★	230.	Korn	2,485
(269)	231.	Enya	2,471
(208)	232.	Miles Davis...● ....HOF	2,444
(219)	233.	Pat Metheny Group	2,444
(211)	234.	The Band...■ ....HOF	2,438
(245)	235.	Herbie Hancock	2,433
(278)★	236.	Megadeth	2,417
(210)	237.	Steppenwolf...■	2,416
(238)	238.	Vince Gill	2,414
(212)	239.	Pat Benatar	2,408
(212)	240.	Dwight Yoakam	2,406
(216)	241.	Judy Collins	2,394
(242)	242.	Ricky Nelson...● ....HOF	2,393
(246)	243.	Nirvana...■	2,385
(255)	244.	LeAnn Rimes	2,374
(220)	245.	Lou Reed	2,371
(272)	246.	Sammy Hagar	2,358
(222)	247.	Robert Goulet...●	2,358
(225)	248.	J. Geils Band	2,352
(226)	249.	Johnny Rivers	2,351
(228)	250.	The 5th Dimension...■	2,340
(207)	251.	Brenda Lee ....HOF	2,335
(227)	252.	Peter Nero	2,333
(409)	253.	Jackie Gleason...●	2,317
(230)	254.	The Crusaders	2,315
(307)	255.	Lionel Richie	2,315
(232)	256.	Ohio Players...■	2,301
(332)	257.	Michael W. Smith	2,300
(427)★	258.	The Chipmunks	2,292
(274)	259.	Abba ....HOF	2,285 +
(303)	260.	Too Short	2,282
(323)	261.	Ice Cube	2,274
(240)	262.	Spyro Gyra	2,269
(236)	263.	The Byrds...■ ....HOF	2,254
(318)	264.	Eminem	2,253 +
(351)★	265.	Nas	2,251
(243)	266.	Earl Klugh	2,250
(244)	267.	Herbie Mann...●	2,233
(345)★	268.	Tori Amos	2,230
(358)	269.	Bone Thugs-N-Harmony	2,224
(247)	270.	Peter Gabriel	2,216
(292)	271.	Merle Haggard	2,214
(363)	272.	Sarah McLachlan	2,203
(267)	273.	Paul Anka	2,196
(391)	274.	Scarface	2,194
(277)	275.	Boyz II Men	2,191
(249)	276.	The Guess Who...■	2,190
(250)	277.	Gordon Lightfoot	2,189
(326)	278.	Queensryche	2,189
(252)	279.	Pointer Sisters...■	2,188
(321)	280.	Trisha Yearwood	2,188
(374)★	281.	Martina McBride	2,188
(325)	282.	Steve Winwood	2,187
(253)	283.	Stevie Ray Vaughan...●	2,184
(460)	284.	Linkin Park	2,177
(331)	285.	Red Hot Chili Peppers...■	2,174
(306)	286.	Travis Tritt	2,173
(254)	287.	Emerson, Lake & Palmer...■	2,170
(256)	288.	Jerry Vale	2,164
(257)	289.	Trini Lopez	2,161
(258)	290.	Eddy Arnold...●	2,159
NEW★	291.	Michael Buble	2,158 +
(322)	292.	Robert Plant	2,156
(262)	293.	Otis Redding...● ....HOF	2,149
(260)	294.	INXS...■	2,146
(259)	295.	Kenny Loggins	2,146
(261)	296.	Bad Company...■	2,145
(265)	297.	The Animals...■ ....HOF	2,140
(263)	298.	Cameo	2,138
(264)	299.	Teddy Pendergrass...●	2,137
(270)	300.	Ted Nugent	2,135

TOP 500 ARTISTS (#301-400)

Old Rank	New Rank		Points	Old Rank	New Rank		Points
NEW★	301.	Rascal Flatts	2,134 +	(343)	351.	The Pretenders...■ ... HOF	1,913
(266)	302.	Alan Parsons Project...■	2,130	(457)	352.	Insane Clown Posse	1,905
(268)	303.	Chet Atkins...● ... HOF	2,121	(313)	353.	Cream ... HOF	1,903
(295)	304.	Scorpions	2,111	(369)	354.	The Smashing Pumpkins	1,901
(276)	305.	Boston Pops Orchestra	2,110	(423)	355.	Faith Hill	1,901
(276)	306.	Leon Russell	2,109	(402)	356.	Tracy Lawrence	1,900
(273)	307.	Chuck Mangione	2,105	(415)	357.	Poison	1,898
(439)★	308.	Britney Spears	2,104	NEW	358.	Jim Brickman	1,891
(294)	309.	Talking Heads ... HOF	2,099	(401)	359.	Stevie Nicks	1,888
(279)	310.	Spinners...■	2,093	(359)	360.	Tina Turner	1,881
(316)	311.	Peggy Lee...●	2,091	NEW★	361.	John Mayer	1,881 +
(288)	312.	Joe Jackson	2,089	(329)	362.	David Sanborn	1,876
(281)	313.	Roy Orbison...●	2,086	(324)	363.	The Whispers	1,876
(301)	314.	Bryan Adams	2,082	(370)	364.	Rick Springfield	1,876
(284)	315.	Paul Revere & The Raiders...■	2,075	(377)	365.	Lenny Kravitz	1,867
(314)	316.	Donny Osmond	2,064	(395)	366.	Sheryl Crow	1,866
(283)	317.	Tennessee Ernie Ford...●	2,063	(330)	367.	John Michael Montgomery	1,858
(311)	318.	Al Jarreau	2,062	(328)	368.	Eydie Gorme	1,855
(336)	319.	Melissa Etheridge	2,059	NEW	369.	Third Day	1,849
(285)	320.	Dave Clark Five ... HOF	2,055	(333)	370.	Rick James...●	1,836
(287)	321.	Charley Pride	2,039	NEW★	371.	Josh Groban	1,828
(286)	322.	John Gary...●	2,036	(461)	372.	Creed	1,825
(382)	323.	Gerald Levert...●	2,031	(365)	373.	Billy Idol	1,824
NEW★	324.	Miley Cyrus	2,030 +	NEW	374.	Trace Adkins	1,822
(290)	325.	John Mayall	2,025	NEW★	375.	Jack Johnson	1,818
(327)	326.	Keith Sweat	2,023	(334)	376.	Robin Trower	1,811
(355)	327.	Indigo Girls	2,015	(444)★	377.	Backstreet Boys	1,806
(296)	328.	George Winston	2,006	(357)	378.	Peter Frampton	1,804
(291)	329.	Bobby Darin...● ... HOF	2,003	(396)	379.	311	1,801
(291)	330.	Traffic...■ ... HOF	1,984	(454)★	380.	Marilyn Manson	1,801
(320)	331.	Boz Scaggs	1,980	(337)	381.	Dave Mason	1,798
(335)	332.	Jerry Lee Lewis ... HOF	1,976	(338)	382.	Blood, Sweat & Tears	1,795
(297)	333.	Jack Jones	1,975	(340)	383.	Herman's Hermits...■	1,793
(413)	334.	Brian McKnight	1,973	(404)	384.	"Weird Al" Yankovic	1,790
(372)	335.	Alice In Chains...■	1,968	(479)	385.	Ani DiFranco	1,790
(298)	336.	Curtis Mayfield...● ... HOF	1,963	NEW★	386.	Lil Wayne	1,785 +
(300)	337.	Blue Oyster Cult	1,957	(414)	387.	Joe Satriani	1,784
(467)	338.	Radiohead	1,956	NEW	388.	Enrique Iglesias	1,782
(302)	339.	Clint Black	1,956	(341)	389.	Charlie Daniels Band	1,775
(304)	340.	Dire Straits	1,947	(344)	390.	The Impressions...■ ... HOF	1,774
(425)	341.	The Black Crowes	1,944	(342)	391.	Selena...●	1,772
(315)	342.	Peabo Bryson	1,943	(282)	392.	Kris Kristofferson	1,753
(309)	343.	Marshall Tucker Band...■	1,943	(456)	393.	Teena Marie	1,752
(403)	344.	George Jones	1,937	(346)	394.	Sonny & Cher...■	1,751
(354)	345.	Pet Shop Boys	1,931	(347)	395.	Robert Palmer...●	1,749
(308)	346.	Stephen Stills	1,931	(348)	396.	New Christy Minstrels	1,746
(319)	347.	Sade	1,927	(348)	397.	Eurythmics	1,745
(310)	348.	Kansas	1,922	(352)	398.	The Manhattan Transfer	1,741
(312)	349.	Seals & Crofts	1,918	(416)	399.	Nelly	1,740
(350)	350.	Alanis Morissette	1,914	(408)	400.	k.d. lang	1,737

TOP 500 ARTISTS (#401-500)

Old Rank	New Rank		Points
(353)	401.	Foghat...■	1,732
NEW	402.	Los Tigres Del Norte	1,728
(356)	403.	The Mamas & The Papas...■ .HOF	1,728
NEW★	404.	Brad Paisley	1,728 +
NEW	405.	Counting Crows	1,724
(362)	406.	Johnny Winter	1,720
(389)	407.	Ronnie Milsap	1,718
(380)	408.	George Thorogood	1,717
NEW	409.	Dream Theater	1,713
(463)	410.	Wynonna	1,710
(360)	411.	Loggins & Messina	1,709
(361)	412.	Petula Clark	1,708
NEW	413.	New Kids On The Block	1,708
NEW	414.	DMX	1,708
NEW	415.	Kid Rock	1,708
(—)	416.	Sammy Davis Jr. ...●	1,707
(500)	417.	Luis Miguel	1,705
(446)	418.	George Michael	1,705
(364)	419.	Helen Reddy	1,704
(366)	420.	Janis Joplin...● HOF	1,703
(373)	421.	Bar-Kays...■	1,701
(367)	422.	Rufus Feat. Chaka Khan	1,701
(432)	423.	Ringo Starr	1,700
(368)	424.	Melissa Manchester	1,699
(420)	425.	The B-52's...■	1,695
(375)	426.	King Crimson...■	1,688
(376)	427.	Joe Walsh	1,688
NEW	428.	Foo Fighters	1,683
(378)	429.	Supertramp	1,683
NEW	430.	Morrissey	1,680
(379)	431.	Rita Coolidge	1,680
(383)	432.	Shania Twain	1,680
(433)	433.	Meat Loaf	1,678
(381)	434.	Ten Years After	1,675
NEW	435.	John Fogerty	1,672
NEW	436.	Coldplay	1,671
(496)	437.	Dixie Chicks	1,664
(384)	438.	Pete Fountain	1,661
NEW	439.	E-40	1,660
(388)	440.	The Cars...■	1,660
(438)	441.	Judy Garland...●	1,658
(387)	442.	Todd Rundgren	1,654
NEW	443.	Jennifer Lopez	1,653
(385)	444.	Weather Report...■	1,649
(386)	445.	Master P	1,648
NEW	446.	Billy Ray Cyrus	1,639
(390)	447.	Moms Mabley...●	1,637
(462)	448.	OutKast	1,634
NEW★	449.	Diana Krall	1,631
NEW	450.	Barenaked Ladies	1,629
(392)	451.	Cypress Hill	1,626
(393)	452.	The Limeliters...■	1,624
(394)	453.	Maze Feat. Frankie Beverly	1,619
(399)	454.	Wilson Pickett...● HOF	1,617
NEW	455.	Tom Waits	1,615
(397)	456.	Limp Bizkit	1,610
(398)	457.	Uriah Heep...■	1,604
(495)	458.	Enigma	1,602
NEW	459.	Steven Curtis Chapman	1,600
(400)	460.	The Rascals HOF	1,598
NEW★	461.	Ludacris	1,594
(405)	462.	Nilsson...●	1,586
NEW★	463.	Norah Jones	1,585
NEW★	464.	Jewel	1,582
NEW	465.	Alison Krauss	1,576
(411)	466.	Procol Harum...■	1,574
(406)	467.	Ray Parker Jr./Raydio	1,574
(407)	468.	Ashford & Simpson	1,573
NEW★	469.	50 Cent	1,570
(418)	470.	Sam Cooke...● HOF	1,564
(410)	471.	The Hollies HOF	1,564
(412)	472.	The Smothers Brothers	1,563
(—)	473.	Count Basie...●	1,561
(417)	474.	AWB (Average White Band)...■	1,561
(466)	475.	Little Feat...■	1,560
NEW	476.	Steve Earle	1,560
(419)	477.	John McLaughlin	1,554
(480)	478.	Huey Lewis & The News	1,553
NEW	479.	The Offspring	1,553
(447)	480.	Erasure	1,550
(428)	481.	The Osmonds	1,550
NEW	482.	Jars Of Clay	1,547
(422)	483.	Bread...■	1,547
NEW	484.	Lyle Lovett	1,543
NEW★	485.	Busta Rhymes	1,534
(434)	486.	Bobby Womack HOF	1,532
NEW	487.	Redman	1,532
(—)	488.	Ella Fitzgerald...●	1,530
(421)	489.	Nazareth...■	1,530
(483)	490.	Live	1,530
NEW★	491.	Keith Urban	1,529 +
(424)	492.	Bachman-Turner Overdrive	1,526
NEW★	493.	Beck	1,526
(426)	494.	Little River Band	1,522
NEW	495.	Oasis	1,521
(429)	496.	Anita Baker	1,519
NEW	497.	Sublime...■	1,517
NEW★	498.	Joe	1,516
(430)	499.	The Association...■	1,514
NEW	500.	Marco Antonio Solis	1,513

A-Z — TOP 500 ARTISTS

Due to their special "various artists" nature, there are three acts listed in the Main Artist Section that we have <u>excluded</u> from the Artist Rankings. Below is a list of those artists and where they <u>would</u> have ranked in the 2000s Decade and All-Time lists:

> Bill & Gloria Gaither & Their Homecoming Friends (2000s: #1 / All-Time: #86)
> Kidz Bop Kids (2000s: #2 / All-Time: #121)
> High School Musical Cast (2000s: #38 / All-Time: #443)

The following 47 artists were ranked in the Top 500 Artists of our *Billboard Albums 1956-2005* book, but have now dropped out of the Top 500:

Ed Ames	Duane Eddy	Eddie Money	Charlie Rich
Anthrax	Eddie Harris	Lorrie Morgan	Run-D.M.C.
Joan Armatrading	Hootie & The Blowfish	New Edition	Allan Sherman
Booker T. & The MG's	Jermaine Jackson	Bob Newhart	Nancy Sinatra
Boston	Millie Jackson	Nitty Gritty Dirt Band	Sly & The Family Stone
Toni Braxton	The James Gang	*NSYNC	The Stylistics
Harry Chapin	Ja Rule	Outlaws	Toto
Tracy Chapman	The Judds	Gene Pitney	Tower Of Power
Con Funk Shun	John Fitzgerald Kennedy	Jean-Luc Ponty	UB40
Dawn Feat. Tony Orlando	Loretta Lynn	Richard Pryor	Bobby Vee
Destiny's Child	MC Hammer	Public Enemy	Tammy Wynette
George Duke	Stephanie Mills	Rainbow	

TOP 50 ARTISTS
1955-1959

1.	Frank Sinatra	3,910
2.	Johnny Mathis	2,955
3.	Elvis Presley	2,855
4.	Harry Belafonte	2,368
5.	Mantovani	2,023
6.	Nat "King" Cole	2,015
7.	Lawrence Welk	1,934
8.	Pat Boone	1,879
9.	The Kingston Trio	1,857
10.	Jackie Gleason	1,715
11.	Roger Williams	1,433
12.	Mitch Miller	1,414
13.	Tennessee Ernie Ford	1,303
14.	Perry Como	1,291
15.	The Four Freshmen	980
16.	Dave Brubeck Quartet	803
17.	Lester Lanin	786
18.	Louis Prima & Keely Smith	757
19.	Ray Conniff	731
20.	Doris Day	694
21.	Henry Mancini	694
22.	Julie London	675
23.	Ray Anthony	660
24.	Dakota Staton	660
25.	Ella Fitzgerald	637
26.	Sarah Vaughan	626
27.	Peggy Lee	624
28.	Eydie Gorme	624
29.	The Norman Luboff Choir	609
30.	Crazy Otto	601
31.	Shelley Berman	601
32.	Ricky Nelson	596
33.	Mario Lanza	550
34.	Bing Crosby	539
35.	Jonah Jones	516
36.	The Platters	512
37.	Michel LeGrand	498
38.	Bill Haley & His Comets	497
39.	Judy Garland	482
40.	Les Elgart	480
41.	Martin Denny	479
42.	Percy Faith	478
43.	Lena Horne	475
44.	The Hi-Lo's	474
45.	Les Baxter	467
46.	The Three Suns	467
47.	Glenn Miller	463
48.	Fats Domino	462
49.	George Shearing Quintet	461
50.	Ahmad Jamal	460

1960s

1.	The Beatles	8,238
2.	Frank Sinatra	6,846
3.	Elvis Presley	6,047
4.	Ray Conniff	5,421
5.	Ray Charles	4,857
6.	The Ventures	4,790
7.	Mantovani	4,770
8.	Andy Williams	4,752
9.	Billy Vaughn	4,513
10.	Johnny Mathis	4,463
11.	Henry Mancini	4,087
12.	Lawrence Welk	4,029
13.	The Kingston Trio	3,970
14.	The Supremes	3,921
15.	Roger Williams	3,800
16.	The Lettermen	3,730
17.	Herb Alpert	3,631
17.	Enoch Light	3,578
19.	The Beach Boys	3,559
20.	Nancy Wilson	3,467
21.	Dean Martin	3,454
22.	The Rolling Stones	3,347
23.	The Temptations	3,295
24.	James Brown	3,260
25.	Barbra Streisand	3,133
26.	Mitch Miller	3,108
27.	Connie Francis	3,002
28.	The 4 Seasons	2,949
29.	Jimmy Smith	2,929
30.	Al Hirt	2,912
31.	Al Martino	2,847
32.	Ferrante & Teicher	2,767
33.	Nat "King" Cole	2,737
34.	Chubby Checker	2,727
35.	Peter, Paul & Mary	2,632
36.	Bill Cosby	2,527
37.	The Monkees	2,496
38.	Bert Kaempfert	2,355
39.	Robert Goulet	2,346
40.	Johnny Cash	2,296
41.	Brenda Lee	2,279
42.	Joan Baez	2,268
43.	Tony Bennett	2,253
44.	Percy Faith	2,231
45.	Harry Belafonte	2,220
46.	Trini Lopez	2,161
47.	Dionne Warwick	2,136
48.	Aretha Franklin	2,126
49.	Peter Nero	2,122
50.	Jerry Vale	2,116

TOP 50 ARTISTS
1970s

1.	Elton John	5,691
2.	Elvis Presley	5,563
3.	Neil Diamond	3,617
4.	Barbra Streisand	3,508
5.	Pink Floyd	3,356 +
6.	Chicago	3,280
7.	David Bowie	3,198
8.	The Rolling Stones	3,115
9.	Carole King	3,101
10.	Bee Gees	3,031
11.	Paul McCartney	2,942
12.	The Who	2,928
13.	Fleetwood Mac	2,902
14.	James Taylor	2,902
15.	John Denver	2,896
16.	Eagles	2,884
17.	Bob Dylan	2,870
18.	The Jackson 5	2,802
19.	Led Zeppelin	2,750
20.	Jethro Tull	2,707
21.	James Brown	2,662
22.	Eric Clapton	2,634
23.	Isaac Hayes	2,633
24.	Diana Ross	2,631
25.	Grand Funk Railroad	2,584

26.	Rod Stewart	2,526
27.	The Temptations	2,496
28.	Grateful Dead	2,488
29.	Stevie Wonder	2,488
30.	Neil Young	2,426
31.	Johnny Mathis	2,382
32.	Aretha Franklin	2,375
33.	Earth, Wind & Fire	2,370
34.	War	2,369
35.	Santana	2,355
36.	Frank Zappa	2,335
37.	Gladys Knight & The Pips	2,325
38.	Marvin Gaye	2,302
39.	The Beach Boys	2,300
40.	Al Green	2,300
41.	Jefferson Starship	2,292
42.	The Allman Brothers Band	2,271
43.	The Beatles	2,271
44.	Ohio Players	2,247
45.	Steve Miller Band	2,227
46.	Cat Stevens	2,205
47.	The Band	2,186
48.	Linda Ronstadt	2,151
49.	Leon Russell	2,087
50.	Steely Dan	2,043

1980s

1.	Willie Nelson	2,887
2.	Prince	2,858
3.	Kenny Rogers	2,795
4.	AC/DC	2,702 +
5.	U2	2,580
6.	Journey	2,483 +
7.	Metallica	2,449
8.	Michael Jackson	2,425
9.	Alabama	2,279
10.	Billy Joel	2,177
11.	Aerosmith	2,103
12.	The Rolling Stones	2,026
13.	Pink Floyd	2,022
14.	Hank Williams, Jr.	1,994
15.	Barbra Streisand	1,921
16.	Pat Benatar	1,920
17.	Elton John	1,895
18.	Jimmy Buffett	1,851
19.	Diana Ross	1,804
20.	Neil Diamond	1,790
21.	Madonna	1,780
22.	Rush	1,743
23.	John Cougar Mellencamp	1,740
24.	Elvis Costello	1,733
25.	Tom Petty/The Heartbreakers	1,668

26.	Linda Ronstadt	1,664
27.	Bob Marley & The Wailers	1,650 +
28.	Bruce Springsteen	1,643
29.	Anne Murray	1,596
30.	Van Halen	1,580
31.	Spyro Gyra	1,570
32.	Eric Clapton	1,570
33.	David Bowie	1,566
34.	REO Speedwagon	1,564
35.	Daryl Hall & John Oates	1,563
36.	The Police	1,563
37.	Barry Manilow	1,553
38.	Neil Young	1,546
39.	Earl Klugh	1,540
40.	Kiss	1,518
41.	Rick Springfield	1,507
42.	Ozzy Osbourne	1,498
43.	Bob Dylan	1,494
44.	Cameo	1,471
45.	Def Leppard	1,454
46.	Peabo Bryson	1,447
47.	Starship	1,444
48.	Duran Duran	1,443
49.	R.E.M.	1,422
50.	Rod Stewart	1,419

TOP 50 ARTISTS
1990s

1.	**Garth Brooks**	4,601
2.	**Mariah Carey**	2,886
3.	**Prince**	2,760
4.	**George Strait**	2,638
5.	**Metallica**	2,438
6.	**Celine Dion**	2,282
7.	**Alan Jackson**	2,232
8.	**Reba McEntire**	2,172
9.	**Eric Clapton**	2,077
10.	**Madonna**	2,076
11.	**2Pac**	2,051
12.	**Van Morrison**	1,967
13.	**Vince Gill**	1,934
14.	**Yanni**	1,900
15.	**Michael Bolton**	1,890
16.	**Jimi Hendrix**	1,889
17.	**Dave Matthews Band**	1,839
18.	**Brooks & Dunn**	1,772
19.	**Kenny G**	1,767
20.	**Queen**	1,763
21.	**Pearl Jam**	1,755
22.	**Harry Connick, Jr.**	1,725
23.	**Nirvana**	1,704
24.	**Clint Black**	1,687
25.	**Tom Petty/Heartbreakers**	1,571
26.	**Jimmy Buffett**	1,559
27.	**Alabama**	1,556
28.	**Gloria Estefan**	1,553
29.	**Luther Vandross**	1,548
30.	**Alice In Chains**	1,538
31.	**Selena**	1,529
32.	**Def Leppard**	1,523
33.	**Bonnie Raitt**	1,513
34.	**Ice Cube**	1,510
35.	**Boyz II Men**	1,441
36.	**Travis Tritt**	1,423
37.	**Whitney Houston**	1,421
38.	**Rod Stewart**	1,400
39.	**Trisha Yearwood**	1,376
40.	**Beastie Boys**	1,366
41.	**Frank Sinatra**	1,362
42.	**The Smashing Pumpkins**	1,350
43.	**Neil Diamond**	1,345
44.	**U2**	1,332
45.	**Sublime**	1,325
46.	**Lorrie Morgan**	1,322
47.	**Phil Collins**	1,318
48.	**R.E.M.**	1,314
49.	**Bob Seger**	1,310 +
50.	**Nine Inch Nails**	1,297

2000s

1.	**Jay-Z**	3,173 +
2.	**Toby Keith**	3,108
3.	**George Strait**	2,972
4.	**Dave Matthews Band**	2,790
5.	**Kenny Chesney**	2,707 +
6.	**Tim McGraw**	2,617 +
7.	**Alan Jackson**	2,526
8.	**Elvis Presley**	2,325
9.	**Pearl Jam**	2,267
10.	**Andrea Bocelli**	2,231
11.	**R. Kelly**	2,190
12.	**Bruce Springsteen**	2,182
13.	**Linkin Park**	2,177
14.	**Michael Buble**	2,158 +
15.	**Rascal Flatts**	2,134 +
16.	**Willie Nelson**	2,107
17.	**Rod Stewart**	2,089
18.	**Miley Cyrus**	2,030 +
19.	**Phish**	1,992
20.	**2Pac**	1,991
21.	**The Beatles**	1,978
22.	**Bob Dylan**	1,937
23.	**Neil Young**	1,916
24.	**John Mayer**	1,881 +
25.	**Eminem**	1,865 +
26.	**Mannheim Steamroller**	1,853
27.	**Josh Groban**	1,828
28.	**Jack Johnson**	1,818
29.	**Michael Jackson**	1,746 +
30.	**Nelly**	1,740
31.	**Brad Paisley**	1,728 +
32.	**Kid Rock**	1,708
33.	**Barry Manilow**	1,701
34.	**Madonna**	1,682
35.	**Britney Spears**	1,682
36.	**Coldplay**	1,671
37.	**Bon Jovi**	1,615
38.	**Snoop Dogg**	1,604
39.	**Ludacris**	1,594
40.	**Mariah Carey**	1,590
41.	**Norah Jones**	1,585
42.	**Lil Wayne**	1,579 +
43.	**Mary J. Blige**	1,575
44.	**Third Day**	1,573
45.	**Jimmy Buffett**	1,572
46.	**50 Cent**	1,570
47.	**Los Tigres Del Norte**	1,550
48.	**U2**	1,538
49.	**Keith Urban**	1,529 +
50.	**Green Day**	1,526

TOP ARTIST ACHIEVEMENTS

MOST CHARTED ALBUMS

1. Elvis Presley 130
2. Frank Sinatra 92
3. Johnny Mathis 76
4. Willie Nelson 64
5. Johnny Cash 61
6. James Brown 57
7. Barbra Streisand 56
8. The Temptations 56
9. The Beatles 54
10. Bob Dylan 54
11. Ray Charles 54
12. Ray Conniff 54
13. Neil Diamond 51
14. The Beach Boys 51
15. Mantovani 51
16. The Rolling Stones 47
17. Aretha Franklin 46
18. Grateful Dead 46
19. Neil Young 45
20. Elton John 44
21. Eric Clapton 44
22. Lawrence Welk 44
23. Kenny Rogers 44
24. David Bowie 42
25. Van Morrison 42
26. Henry Mancini 41
27. Tony Bennett 41
28. Dolly Parton 41
29. The Supremes 40
30. Jimi Hendrix 40

MOST TOP 40 ALBUMS

1. Frank Sinatra 57
2. Elvis Presley 52
3. Barbra Streisand 48
4. The Rolling Stones 42
5. Bob Dylan 41
6. The Beatles 38
7. Elton John 36
8. Neil Young 32
9. Eric Clapton 31
10. Neil Diamond 29
11. The Temptations 28
12. Rod Stewart 28
13. Paul McCartney 28
14. Johnny Mathis 27
15. Mantovani 26
16. Ray Conniff 26
17. Lawrence Welk 24
18. Kiss 24
19. Prince 23
20. Aretha Franklin 23
21. The Beach Boys 22
22. George Strait 21
23. David Bowie 21
24. Bruce Springsteen 21
25. Stevie Wonder 21
26. Madonna 21
27. Jefferson Airplane/Starship .. 21
28. Ray Charles 20
29. Barry Manilow 20
30. James Taylor 20
31. Rush 20

MOST TOP 10 ALBUMS

1. The Rolling Stones 36
2. Frank Sinatra 35
3. The Beatles 30
4. Barbra Streisand 30
5. Elvis Presley 27
6. Bob Dylan 19
7. Madonna 18
8. Paul McCartney 17
9. Johnny Mathis 16
10. Elton John 16
11. Neil Diamond 16
12. George Strait 16
13. Bruce Springsteen 16
14. Mariah Carey 15
15. Rod Stewart 14
16. Prince 14
17. The Kingston Trio 14
18. Garth Brooks 14
19. Dave Matthews Band 14
20. Mitch Miller 14
21. The Beach Boys 13
22. Jay-Z 13
23. Tim McGraw 13
24. Van Halen 13
25. Eric Clapton 12
26. Ray Conniff 12
27. Chicago 12
28. Andy Williams 12
29. Led Zeppelin 12
30. R. Kelly 12

MOST #1 ALBUMS

1. The Beatles 19
2. Jay-Z 11
3. Elvis Presley 10
4. Barbra Streisand 9
5. The Rolling Stones 9
6. Bruce Springsteen 9
7. Garth Brooks 8
8. Elton John 7
9. Paul McCartney 7
10. Madonna 7
11. Led Zeppelin 7
12. U2 7
13. Michael Jackson 6
14. Eagles 6
15. Mariah Carey 6
16. R. Kelly 6
17. Janet Jackson 6

MOST WEEKS AT #1

1. The Beatles 132
2. Elvis Presley 67
3. Michael Jackson 51
4. Garth Brooks 51
5. The Kingston Trio 46
6. Whitney Houston 46
7. Elton John 39
8. The Rolling Stones 38
9. Fleetwood Mac 38
10. Harry Belafonte 37
11. The Monkees 37
12. Prince 34
13. Bee Gees 31
14. Eagles 30
15. Mariah Carey 30
16. Led Zeppelin 29
17. Bruce Springsteen 27

MOST GOLD & PLATINUM ALBUMS

1. Elvis Presley 67
2. Barbra Streisand 50
3. The Beatles 44
4. The Rolling Stones 41
5. Neil Diamond 40
6. Elton John 36
7. Bob Dylan 35
8. George Strait 34
9. Frank Sinatra 33
10. Kenny Rogers 28
11. Eric Clapton 27
12. Rod Stewart 26
13. Paul McCartney 26
14. Willie Nelson 24
15. Kiss 24
16. Rush 24
17. Prince 23
18. Aerosmith 23

Ties are broken according to rank in the *Top 500 Artists* section. For all categories except Most Charted Albums, Christmas albums that made the Pop Albums chart are counted for their first chart appearance only; their seasonel re-entries are not added to the totals. Also, for all categories except Most Charted Albums, albums that made the special Christmas Albums chart and the Pop Catalog Albums chart are not counted.

THE TOP ALBUMS

TOP 100 ALBUMS
1955-2009

PK YR	WKS CHR	WKS T40	WKS T10	WKS @ #1	RANK	TITLE	ARTIST
62	198	144	106	54	1.	West Side Story	Movie Soundtrack
83	144	91	78	37	2.	Thriller	Michael Jackson
58	262	161	90	31	3.	South Pacific	Movie Soundtrack
56	99	72	58	31	4.	Calypso	Harry Belafonte
77	134	60	52	31	5.	Rumours	Fleetwood Mac
78	120	54	35	24	6.	Saturday Night Fever	Bee Gees/Movie Soundtrack
84	72	42	32	24	7.	Purple Rain	Prince & The Revolution/Movie Soundtrack
90	108	70	52	21	8.	Please Hammer Don't Hurt 'Em	MC Hammer
92	141	76	40	20	9.	The Bodyguard	Whitney Houston/Movie Soundtrack
61	79	53	39	20	10.	Blue Hawaii	Elvis Presley/Movie Soundtrack
91	132	70	50	18	11.	Ropin' The Wind	Garth Brooks
87	96	68	48	18	12.	Dirty Dancing	Movie Soundtrack
67	70	45	25	18	13.	More Of The Monkees	The Monkees
92	97	59	43	17	14.	Some Gave All	Billy Ray Cyrus
83	75	50	40	17	15.	Synchronicity	The Police
60	276	168	105	16	16.	The Sound Of Music	Original Cast
90	67	39	26	16	17.	To The Extreme	Vanilla Ice
63	107	61	23	16	18.	Days Of Wine And Roses	Andy Williams
98	71	33	20	16	19.	Titanic	Movie Soundtrack
56	480	292	173	15	20.	My Fair Lady	Original Cast
71	302	68	46	15	21.	Tapestry	Carole King
67	184	63	33	15	22.	Sgt. Pepper's Lonely Hearts Club Band	The Beatles
82	90	48	31	15	23.	Business As Usual	Men At Work
59	118	43	31	15	24.	The Kingston Trio At Large	The Kingston Trio
81	101	50	30	15	25.	Hi Infidelity	REO Speedwagon
80	123	35	27	15	26.	The Wall	Pink Floyd
65	114	78	48	14	27.	Mary Poppins	Movie Soundtrack
86	163	78	46	14	28.	Whitney Houston	Whitney Houston
60	108	67	44	14	29.	The Button-Down Mind Of Bob Newhart	Bob Newhart
61	89	55	38	14	30.	Exodus	Movie Soundtrack
76	80	44	35	14	31.	Songs In The Key Of Life	Stevie Wonder
62	101	59	33	14	32.	Modern Sounds In Country And Western Music	Ray Charles
64	52	40	28	14	33.	A Hard Day's Night	The Beatles/Movie Soundtrack
60	124	105	43	13	34.	Persuasive Percussion	Enoch Light/Terry Snyder and The All-Stars
61	95	73	37	13	35.	Judy At Carnegie Hall	Judy Garland
66	78	49	32	13	36.	The Monkees	The Monkees
69	151	59	28	13	37.	Hair	Original Cast
95	113	89	72	12	38.	Jagged Little Pill	Alanis Morissette
58	245	123	66	12	39.	The Music Man	Original Cast
88	87	69	51	12	40.	Faith	George Michael
62	96	69	46	12	41.	Breakfast At Tiffany's	Henry Mancini/Movie Soundtrack
99	103	63	44	12	42.	Supernatural	Santana
60	73	42	29	12	43.	Sold Out	The Kingston Trio
78	77	39	29	12	44.	Grease	Movie Soundtrack
62	49	26	17	12	45.	The First Family	Vaughn Meader
08	79 +	79 +	58 +	11	46.	Fearless	Taylor Swift
91	113	66	49	11	47.	Mariah Carey	Mariah Carey
61	64	50	33	11	48.	Calcutta!	Lawrence Welk
87	85	51	31	11	49.	Whitney	Whitney Houston
69	148	32	27	11	50.	Abbey Road	The Beatles

PK YR	WKS CHR	WKS T40	WKS T10	WKS @ #1	RANK	TITLE	ARTIST
64	71	27	21	11	51.	Meet The Beatles!	The Beatles
85	34	22	18	11	52.	Miami Vice	Television Soundtrack
89	175	78	64	10	53.	Forever Your Girl	Paula Abdul
57	88	88	54	10	54.	Around The World In 80 Days	Movie Soundtrack
58	172	78	54	10	55.	Gigi	Movie Soundtrack
76	97	55	52	10	56.	Frampton Comes Alive!	Peter Frampton
56	48	48	43	10	57.	Elvis Presley	Elvis Presley
59	119	47	43	10	58.	The Music From Peter Gunn	Henry Mancini
99	93	52	37	10	59.	Millennium	Backstreet Boys
81	81	52	34	10	60.	4	Foreigner
94	88	56	31	10	61.	The Lion King	Movie Soundtrack
60	111	46	29	10	62.	G.I. Blues	Elvis Presley/Movie Soundtrack
84	61	27	20	10	63.	Footloose	Movie Soundtrack
60	60	27	20	10	64.	String Along	The Kingston Trio
57	29	29	19	10	65.	Loving You	Elvis Presley/Movie Soundtrack
63	39	22	18	10	66.	The Singing Nun	The Singing Nun
70	85	24	17	10	67.	Bridge Over Troubled Water	Simon & Garfunkel
74	104	20	11	10	68.	Elton John - Greatest Hits	Elton John
04	96	58	41	9	69.	Confessions	Usher
85	97	55	37	9	70.	Brothers In Arms	Dire Straits
96	90	70	36	9	71.	Tragic Kingdom	No Doubt
87	103	58	35	9	72.	The Joshua Tree	U2
66	129	59	32	9	73.	What Now My Love	Herb Alpert & The Tijuana Brass
82	64	35	27	9	74.	Asia	Asia
68	69	47	26	9	75.	The Graduate	Simon & Garfunkel/Movie Soundtrack
82	106	40	22	9	76.	American Fool	John Cougar
81	58	30	22	9	77.	Tattoo You	The Rolling Stones
61	40	39	21	9	78.	Stars For A Summer Night	Various Artist Compilation
79	57	36	21	9	79.	The Long Run	Eagles
60	86	35	19	9	80.	Nice 'N' Easy	Frank Sinatra
70	69	26	19	9	81.	Cosmo's Factory	Creedence Clearwater Revival
65	71	38	16	9	82.	Beatles '65	The Beatles
65	44	33	15	9	83.	Help!	The Beatles/Movie Soundtrack
68	168	25	15	9	84.	The Beatles [White Album]	The Beatles
71	42	23	15	9	85.	Pearl	Janis Joplin
72	51	20	13	9	86.	Chicago V	Chicago
55	15	15	13	9	87.	Love Me Or Leave Me	Doris Day/Movie Soundtrack
65	185	141	61	8	88.	Whipped Cream & Other Delights	Herb Alpert's Tijuana Brass
95	129	73	55	8	89.	Cracked Rear View	Hootie & The Blowfish
58	204	127	53	8	90.	Sing Along With Mitch	Mitch Miller & The Gang
86	95 +	60	46	8	91.	Slippery When Wet	Bon Jovi
89	78	61	41	8	92.	Girl You Know It's True	Milli Vanilli
73	103	43	36	8	93.	Goodbye Yellow Brick Road	Elton John
93	128	50	33	8	94.	Music Box	Mariah Carey
57	94	55	31	8	95.	Love Is The Thing	Nat "King" Cole
00	82	49	31	8	96.	No Strings Attached	*NSYNC
77	107	32	28	8	97.	Hotel California	Eagles
59	126	40	26	8	98.	Here We Go Again!	The Kingston Trio
80	74	27	24	8	99.	Double Fantasy	John Lennon/Yoko Ono
78	76	34	22	8	100.	52nd Street	Billy Joel

TOP 25 ALBUMS BY DECADE
1955-1959

PK YR	WKS CHR	WKS T40	WKS T10	WKS @ #1	RANK	TITLE	ARTIST
58	262	161	90	31	1.	South Pacific	Movie Soundtrack
56	99	72	58	31	2.	Calypso	Harry Belafonte
56	480	292	173	15	3.	My Fair Lady	Original Cast
59	118	43	31	15	4.	The Kingston Trio At Large	The Kingston Trio
58	245	123	66	12	5.	The Music Man	Original Cast
57	88	88	54	10	6.	Around The World In 80 Days	Movie Soundtrack
58	172	78	54	10	7.	Gigi	Movie Soundtrack
56	48	48	43	10	8.	Elvis Presley	Elvis Presley
59	119	47	43	10	9.	The Music From Peter Gunn	Henry Mancini
57	29	29	19	10	10.	Loving You	Elvis Presley/Movie Soundtrack
55	15	15	13	9	11.	Love Me Or Leave Me	Doris Day/Movie Soundtrack
58	204	127	53	8	12.	Sing Along With Mitch	Mitch Miller & The Gang
57	94	55	31	8	13.	Love Is The Thing	Nat "King" Cole
59	126	40	26	8	14.	Here We Go Again!	The Kingston Trio
58	125	76	39	7	15.	Tchaikovsky: Piano Concerto No. 1	Van Cliburn
56	61	61	53	6	16.	Belafonte	Harry Belafonte
59	295	40	38	5	17.	Heavenly	Johnny Mathis
56	32	32	24	5	18.	Elvis	Elvis Presley
58	120	55	19	5	19.	Frank Sinatra Sings For Only The Lonely	Frank Sinatra
59	63	46	19	5	20.	Exotica	Martin Denny
58	71	50	18	5	21.	Come Fly With Me	Frank Sinatra
57	7	7	6	4	22.	Elvis' Christmas Album	Elvis Presley
58	490	178	57	3	23.	Johnny's Greatest Hits	Johnny Mathis
59	151	67	17	3	24.	Flower Drum Song	Original Cast
55	14	14	12	3	25.	Starring Sammy Davis. Jr.	Sammy Davis Jr.

1960s

PK YR	WKS CHR	WKS T40	WKS T10	WKS @ #1	RANK	TITLE	ARTIST
62	198	144	106	54	1.	West Side Story	Movie Soundtrack
61	79	53	39	20	2.	Blue Hawaii	Elvis Presley/Movie Soundtrack
67	70	45	25	18	3.	More Of The Monkees	The Monkees
60	276	168	105	16	4.	The Sound Of Music	Original Cast
63	107	61	23	16	5.	Days Of Wine And Roses	Andy Williams
67	184	63	33	15	6.	Sgt. Pepper's Lonely Hearts Club Band	The Beatles
65	114	78	48	14	7.	Mary Poppins	Movie Soundtrack
60	108	67	44	14	8.	The Button-Down Mind Of Bob Newhart	Bob Newhart
61	89	55	38	14	9.	Exodus	Movie Soundtrack
62	101	59	33	14	10.	Modern Sounds In Country And Western Music	Ray Charles
64	52	40	28	14	11.	A Hard Day's Night	The Beatles/Movie Soundtrack
60	124	105	43	13	12.	Persuasive Percussion	Enoch Light/Terry Snyder and The All-Stars
61	95	73	37	13	13.	Judy At Carnegie Hall	Judy Garland
66	78	49	32	13	14.	The Monkees	The Monkees
69	151	59	28	13	15.	Hair	Original Cast
62	96	69	46	12	16.	Breakfast At Tiffany's	Henry Mancini/Movie Soundtrack
60	73	42	29	12	17.	Sold Out	The Kingston Trio
62	49	26	17	12	18.	The First Family	Vaughn Meader
61	64	50	33	11	19.	Calcutta!	Lawrence Welk
69	148	32	27	11	20.	Abbey Road	The Beatles
64	71	27	21	11	21.	Meet The Beatles!	The Beatles
60	111	46	29	10	22.	G.I. Blues	Elvis Presley/Movie Soundtrack
60	60	27	20	10	23.	String Along	The Kingston Trio
63	39	22	18	10	24.	The Singing Nun	The Singing Nun
66	129	59	32	9	25.	What Now My Love	Herb Alpert & The Tijuana Brass

TOP 25 ALBUMS BY DECADE
1970s

PK YR	WKS CHR	WKS T40	WKS T10	WKS @ #1	RANK	TITLE	ARTIST
77	134	60	52	31	1.	Rumours	Fleetwood Mac
78	120	54	35	24	2.	Saturday Night Fever	Bee Gees/Movie Soundtrack
71	302	68	46	15	3.	Tapestry	Carole King
76	80	44	35	14	4.	Songs In The Key Of Life	Stevie Wonder
78	77	39	29	12	5.	Grease	Movie Soundtrack
76	97	55	52	10	6.	Frampton Comes Alive!	Peter Frampton
70	85	24	17	10	7.	Bridge Over Troubled Water	Simon & Garfunkel
74	104	20	11	10	8.	Elton John - Greatest Hits	Elton John
79	57	36	21	9	9.	The Long Run	Eagles
70	69	26	19	9	10.	Cosmo's Factory	Creedence Clearwater Revival
71	42	23	15	9	11.	Pearl	Janis Joplin
72	51	20	13	9	12.	Chicago V	Chicago
73	103	43	36	8	13.	Goodbye Yellow Brick Road	Elton John
77	107	32	28	8	14.	Hotel California	Eagles
78	76	34	22	8	15.	52nd Street	Billy Joel
76	51	27	21	7	16.	Wings At The Speed Of Sound	Wings
79	41	28	18	7	17.	In Through The Out Door	Led Zeppelin
72	48	26	17	7	18.	American Pie	Don McLean
75	43	24	17	7	19.	Captain Fantastic And The Brown Dirt Cowboy	Elton John
71	38	22	14	7	20.	All Things Must Pass	George Harrison
70	88	40	30	6	21.	Abraxas	Santana
79	88	48	26	6	22.	Breakfast In America	Supertramp
77	51	28	18	6	23.	A Star Is Born	Barbra Streisand/Movie Soundtrack
79	55	26	18	6	24.	Spirits Having Flown	Bee Gees
79	49	26	16	6	25.	Bad Girls	Donna Summer

1980s

PK YR	WKS CHR	WKS T40	WKS T10	WKS @ #1	RANK	TITLE	ARTIST
83	144	91	78	37	1.	Thriller	Michael Jackson
84	72	42	32	24	2.	Purple Rain	Prince & The Revolution/Movie Soundtrack
87	96	68	48	18	3.	Dirty Dancing	Movie Soundtrack
83	75	50	40	17	4.	Synchronicity	The Police
82	90	48	31	15	5.	Business As Usual	Men At Work
81	101	50	30	15	6.	Hi Infidelity	REO Speedwagon
80	123	35	27	15	7.	The Wall	Pink Floyd
86	163	78	46	14	8.	Whitney Houston	Whitney Houston
88	87	69	51	12	9.	Faith	George Michael
87	85	51	31	11	10.	Whitney	Whitney Houston
85	34	22	18	11	11.	Miami Vice	Television Soundtrack
89	175	78	64	10	12.	Forever Your Girl	Paula Abdul
81	81	52	34	10	13.	4	Foreigner
84	61	27	20	10	14.	Footloose	Movie Soundtrack
85	97	55	37	9	15.	Brothers In Arms	Dire Straits
87	103	58	35	9	16.	The Joshua Tree	U2
82	64	35	27	9	17.	Asia	Asia
82	106	40	22	9	18.	American Fool	John Cougar
81	58	30	22	9	19.	Tattoo You	The Rolling Stones
86	95 +	60	46	8	20.	Slippery When Wet	Bon Jovi
89	78	61	41	8	21.	Girl You Know It's True	Milli Vanilli
80	74	27	24	8	22.	Double Fantasy	John Lennon/Yoko Ono
84	139	96	84	7	23.	Born In The U.S.A.	Bruce Springsteen
85	123	70	31	7	24.	No Jacket Required	Phil Collins
89	63	40	27	7	25.	The Raw & The Cooked	Fine Young Cannibals

TOP 25 ALBUMS BY DECADE
1990s

PK YR	WKS CHR	WKS T40	WKS T10	WKS @ #1	RANK	TITLE	ARTIST
90	108	70	52	21	1.	Please Hammer Don't Hurt 'Em	MC Hammer
92	141	76	40	20	2.	The Bodyguard	Whitney Houston/Movie Soundtrack
91	132	70	50	18	3.	Ropin' The Wind	Garth Brooks
92	97	59	43	17	4.	Some Gave All	Billy Ray Cyrus
90	67	39	26	16	5.	To The Extreme	Vanilla Ice
98	71	33	20	16	6.	Titanic	Movie Soundtrack
95	113	89	72	12	7.	Jagged Little Pill	Alanis Morissette
99	103	63	44	12	8.	Supernatural	Santana
91	113	66	49	11	9.	Mariah Carey	Mariah Carey
99	93	52	37	10	10.	Millennium	Backstreet Boys
94	88	56	31	10	11.	The Lion King	Movie Soundtrack
96	90	70	36	9	12.	Tragic Kingdom	No Doubt
95	129	73	55	8	13.	Cracked Rear View	Hootie & The Blowfish
93	128	50	33	8	14.	Music Box	Mariah Carey
95	110	51	20	8	15.	The Hits	Garth Brooks
92	64	35	17	7	16.	The Chase	Garth Brooks
99	103	65	50	6	17.	...Baby One More Time	Britney Spears
93	106	52	36	6	18.	janet.	Janet Jackson
95	81	49	29	6	19.	Daydream	Mariah Carey
90	52	27	16	6	20.	I Do Not Want What I Haven't Got	Sinead O'Connor
94	99	56	43	5	21.	II	Boyz II Men
97	105	60	33	5	22.	Spice	Spice Girls
91	110	49	21	5	23.	Unforgettable With Love	Natalie Cole
96	49	30	21	5	24.	Waiting To Exhale	Movie Soundtrack
99	64	30	16	5	25.	FanMail	TLC

2000s

PK YR	WKS CHR	WKS T40	WKS T10	WKS @ #1	RANK	TITLE	ARTIST
08	79 +	79 +	58 +	11	1.	Fearless	Taylor Swift
04	96	58	41	9	2.	Confessions	Usher
00	82	49	31	8	3.	No Strings Attached	*NSYNC
00	69	33	20	8	4.	The Marshall Mathers LP	Eminem
00	111	27	17	8	5.	1	The Beatles
01	74	27	14	8	6.	Weathered	Creed
03	56	42	24	7	7.	Speakerboxxx/The Love Below	OutKast
03	82	39	27	6	8.	Get Rich Or Die Tryin'	50 Cent
02	104	52	26	6	9.	The Eminem Show	Eminem
01	84	39	22	6	10.	Hotshot	Shaggy
05	57	31	14	6	11.	The Massacre	50 Cent
09	25 +	21	14	6	12.	I Dreamed A Dream	Susan Boyle
04	71	24	11	6	13.	Feels Like Home	Norah Jones
00	104	61	25	5	14.	Country Grammar	Nelly
07	14	12	12	5	15.	Noel	Josh Groban
02	93	16	10	5	16.	Up!	Shania Twain
03	153	100	36	4	17.	Come Away With Me	Norah Jones
02	56	37	26	4	18.	Home	Dixie Chicks
02	72	44	18	4	19.	Nellyville	Nelly
07	63	27	17	4	20.	As I Am	Alicia Keys
04	53	25	17	4	21.	Encore	Eminem
07	61	25	16	4	22.	High School Musical 2	High School Musical Cast
02	43	24	15	4	23.	8 Mile	Movie Soundtrack
02	76	28	11	4	24.	Drive	Alan Jackson
03	25	12	9	4	25.	Bad Boys II	Movie Soundtrack

+: still charted as of 5/29/2010

ALBUMS OF LONGEVITY

Albums that charted 175 weeks or more on the *Billboard 200* chart.

PK YR	PK POS	PK WKS	WKS CHR	RANK	TITLE	ARTIST
73	1	1	762 +	1.	The Dark Side Of The Moon	Pink Floyd
58	1	3	490	2.	Johnny's Greatest Hits	Johnny Mathis
56	1	15	480	3.	My Fair Lady	Original Cast
92	46	1	331	4.	Highlights From The Phantom Of The Opera	Original Cast
71	1	15	302	5.	Tapestry	Carole King
59	1	5	295	6.	Heavenly	Johnny Mathis
56	1	2	283	7.	Oklahoma!	Movie Soundtrack
91	6	2	282	8.	MCMXC A.D.	Enigma
91	1	4	281	9.	Metallica	Metallica
56	1	1	277	10.	The King And I	Movie Soundtrack
57	2	3	277	11.	Hymns	Tennessee Ernie Ford
60	1	16	276	12.	The Sound Of Music	Original Cast
61	1	6	265	13.	Camelot	Original Cast
58	1	31	262	14.	South Pacific	Movie Soundtrack
71	2	4	259	15.	Led Zeppelin IV	Led Zeppelin
88	33	1	255	16.	The Phantom Of The Opera	Original Cast
92	1	2	252	17.	Nevermind	Nirvana
92	2	4	250	18.	Ten	Pearl Jam
58	1	12	245	19.	The Music Man	Original Cast
72	4	2	243	20.	Hot Rocks 1964-1971	The Rolling Stones
90	41	2	242	21.	The Best Of Van Morrison	Van Morrison
92	17	1	238	22.	Shepherd Moons	Enya
65	1	2	233	23.	The Sound Of Music	Movie Soundtrack
59	1	1	231	24.	Film Encores	Mantovani and his orchestra
92	3	2	224	25.	No Fences	Garth Brooks
92	13	1	224	26.	Garth Brooks	Garth Brooks
93	2	11	214	27.	Breathless	Kenny G
92	11	1	207	28.	Greatest Hits	Queen
65	7	2	206	29.	Fiddler On The Roof	Original Cast
58	1	8	204	30.	Sing Along With Mitch	Mitch Miller & The Gang
90	3	3	202	31.	Soul Provider	Michael Bolton
62	1	54	198	32.	West Side Story	Movie Soundtrack
58	1	1	195	33.	The Kingston Trio	The Kingston Trio
62	5	5	191	34.	West Side Story	Original Cast
08	5	2	186 +	35.	Taylor Swift	Taylor Swift
65	1	8	185	36.	Whipped Cream & Other Delights	Herb Alpert's Tijuana Brass
62	1	7	185	37.	Peter, Paul And Mary	Peter, Paul & Mary
90	1	3	185	38.	Nick Of Time	Bonnie Raitt
67	1	15	184	39.	Sgt. Pepper's Lonely Hearts Club Band	The Beatles
83	9	1	183	40.	Eliminator	ZZ Top
59	12	2	183	41.	Oldies But Goodies	Various Artists
80	1	2	181	42.	Kenny Rogers' Greatest Hits	Kenny Rogers
61	8	1	181	43.	Knockers Up!	Rusty Warren
59	11	1	181	44.	The Buddy Holly Story	Buddy Holly
84	28	3	180	45.	Under A Blood Red Sky	U2
83	12	1	179	46.	War	U2
59	2	4	178	47.	From The Hungry i	The Kingston Trio
89	2	3	176	48.	Beaches	Bette Midler
63	3	1	176	49.	Moon River & Other Great Movie Themes	Andy Williams
89	1	10	175	50.	Forever Your Girl	Paula Abdul
74	1	3	175	51.	John Denver's Greatest Hits	John Denver

BEST SELLING ALBUMS
Albums Certified by RIAA That Sold 10 Million or More Units

Millions			Millions		
29	'76	Eagles/Their Greatest Hits 1971-1975...*Eagles*	11	'80	Aerosmith's Greatest Hits...*Aerosmith*
29	'82	Thriller...*Michael Jackson*	11	'67	Sgt. Pepper's Lonely Hearts Club Band... *The Beatles*
23	'71	Led Zeppelin IV (untitled)...*Led Zeppelin*	11	'00	1...*The Beatles*
23	'80	The Wall...*Pink Floyd*	11	'99	Human Clay...*Creed*
22	'80	Back In Black...*AC/DC*	11	'96	Falling Into You...*Celine Dion*
21	'98	Double Live...*Garth Brooks*	11	'82	Eagles Greatest Hits, Volume 2...*Eagles*
21	'85	Greatest Hits, Volume I & Volume II... *Billy Joel*	11	'98	Devil Without A Cause...*Kid Rock*
20	'97	Come On Over...*Shania Twain*	11	'97	Houses Of The Holy...*Led Zeppelin*
19	'68	The Beatles [White Album]...*The Beatles*	11	'00	No Strings Attached...**NSYNC*
19	'77	Rumours...*Fleetwood Mac*	11	'03	Speakerboxxx/The Love Below...*OutKast*
18	'87	Appetite For Destruction...*Guns N' Roses*	11	'76	Greatest Hits...*James Taylor*
17	'76	Boston...*Boston*	11	'94	CrazySexyCool...*TLC*
17	'90	No Fences...*Garth Brooks*	11	'02	Up!...*Shania Twain*
17	'92	The Bodyguard...*Whitney Houston/Soundtrack*	11	'87	Dirty Dancing...*Soundtrack*
16	'73	The Beatles/1967-1970...*The Beatles*	11	'97	Titanic...*Soundtrack*
16	'77	Hotel California...*Eagles*	10	'90	Garth Brooks...*Garth Brooks*
16	'94	Cracked Rear View...*Hootie & The Blowfish*	10	'94	The Hits...*Garth Brooks*
16	'74	Elton John - Greatest Hits...*Elton John*	10	'97	Sevens...*Garth Brooks*
16	'75	Physical Graffiti...*Led Zeppelin*	10	'93	Music Box...*Mariah Carey*
16	'95	Jagged Little Pill...*Alanis Morissette*	10	'95	Daydream...*Mariah Carey*
15	'73	The Beatles/1962-1966...*The Beatles*	10	'92	Unplugged...*Eric Clapton*
15	'78	Saturday Night Fever...*Bee Gees/Soundtrack*	10	'67	Patsy Cline's Greatest Hits...*Patsy Cline*
15	'88	Greatest Hits...*Journey*	10	'83	Pyromania...*Def Leppard*
15	'91	Metallica...*Metallica*	10	'97	Let's Talk About Love...*Celine Dion*
15	'73	The Dark Side Of The Moon...*Pink Floyd*	10	'99	Fly...*Dixie Chicks*
15	'99	Supernatural...*Santana*	10	'76	Best Of The Doobies...*The Doobie Brothers*
15	'84	Born In The U.S.A....*Bruce Springsteen*	10	'87	The Best Of The Doors...*The Doors*
14	'97	Backstreet Boys...*Backstreet Boys*	10	'94	Dookie...*Green Day*
14	'91	Ropin' The Wind...*Garth Brooks*	10	'77	The Stranger...*Billy Joel*
14	'77	Bat Out Of Hell...*Meat Loaf*	10	'02	Come Away With Me...*Norah Jones*
14	'72	Simon And Garfunkel's Greatest Hits... *Simon & Garfunkel*	10	'71	Tapestry...*Carole King*
14	'99	...Baby One More Time...*Britney Spears*	10	'90	Led Zeppelin (Boxed Set)...*Led Zeppelin*
13	'99	Millennium...*Backstreet Boys*	10	'00	Hybrid Theory...*Linkin Park*
13	'85	Whitney Houston...*Whitney Houston*	10	'84	Like A Virgin...*Madonna*
13	'78	Greatest Hits 1974-78...*Steve Miller Band*	10	'90	The Immaculate Collection...*Madonna*
13	'91	Ten...*Pearl Jam*	10	'84	Legend...*Bob Marley & The Wailers*
13	'84	Purple Rain...*Prince/Soundtrack*	10	'90	Please Hammer Don't Hurt 'Em... *MC Hammer*
13	'86	Bruce Springsteen & The E Street Band Live/1975-85...*Bruce Springsteen*	10	'87	Faith...*George Michael*
12	'69	Abbey Road...*The Beatles*	10	'91	Nevermind...*Nirvana*
12	'86	Slippery When Wet...*Bon Jovi*	10	'95	Tragic Kingdom...*No Doubt*
12	'94	II...*Boyz II Men*	10	'97	Life After Death...*The Notorious B.I.G.*
12	'85	No Jacket Required...*Phil Collins*	10	'98	*NSYNC...**NSYNC*
12	'87	Hysteria...*Def Leppard*	10	'93	Greatest Hits...*Tom Petty & The Heartbreakers*
12	'98	Wide Open Spaces...*Dixie Chicks*	10	'83	Can't Slow Down...*Lionel Richie*
12	'95	Pieces Of You...*Jewel*	10	'00	Oops!...I Did It Again...*Britney Spears*
12	'92	Breathless...*Kenny G*	10	'04	Confessions...*Usher*
12	'69	Led Zeppelin II...*Led Zeppelin*	10	'87	The Joshua Tree...*U2*
12	'96	Yourself Or Someone Like You...*Matchbox 20*	10	'78	Van Halen...*Van Halen*
12	'80	Kenny Rogers' Greatest Hits...*Kenny Rogers*	10	'84	1984 (MCMLXXXIV)...*Van Halen*
12	'71	Hot Rocks...*The Rolling Stones*	10	'76	Songs In The Key Of Life...*Stevie Wonder*
12	'95	The Woman In Me...*Shania Twain*	10	'83	Eliminator...*ZZ Top*
12	'94	Forrest Gump...*Soundtrack*	10	'94	The Lion King...*Soundtrack*

#1 ALBUMS

This section lists in chronological order, by peak date, all of the 839 albums which hit the #1 position on *Billboard's Top Pop Albums* chart (currently *The Billboard 200*) from January 1, 1955 through July 3, 2010. (The #1 albums that <u>debuted</u> after the December 26, 2009 research cut-off date are <u>not</u> listed elsewhere in this book.)

For the years 1958 through 1963, when separate stereo and monaural (mono) charts were published each week, the total number of weeks an album held the #1 spot on either or both of these charts is listed below the album. Weeks at #1 on Stereo chart and Mono chart are not totalled together; weeks at #1 is determined by total number of <u>issues</u> that an album held the #1 spot — whether it was #1 on both charts, or on either the stereo or mono chart.

Billboard has not published an issue for the last week of the year since 1976. For the years 1976 through 1991, *Billboard* considered the charts listed in the last published issue of the year to be "frozen" and all chart positions remained the same for the unpublished week. This frozen chart data is included in our tabulations. Since 1992, *Billboard* has <u>compiled</u> *The Billboard 200* chart for the last week of the year, even though an issue is <u>not published</u>. This chart is only available through *Billboard's* computerized information network (BIN). Our tabulations include this unpublished chart data.

See the introduction pages of this book for more details on researching the *Top Pop Albums* charts.

DATE: Date album first peaked at the #1 position

WKS: Total weeks album held the #1 position

↕: Indicates album hit #1, dropped down, and then returned to the #1 spot

> Each year's top #1 album(s) is boxed out for quick reference. The top albums are determined by the most weeks at the #1 position.

#1 ALBUMS

1955

DATE	WKS	

Two albums from 1954 continued into 1955 at the #1 spot: "The Student Prince" by Mario Lanza (18 wks.) and "Music, Martinis And Memories" by Jackie Gleason (2 wks.).

1. 5/28 **1** **Crazy Otto** *Crazy Otto*
2. 6/11 **3** **Starring Sammy Davis, Jr.**
   Sammy Davis, Jr.
3. 6/25 **2** **In The Wee Small Hours** *Frank Sinatra*
4. 7/23 **9** **Love Me Or Leave Me**
   Doris Day/Movie Soundtrack
5. 7/23 **1** **Lonesome Echo** *Jackie Gleason*

1956

DATE	WKS	

Beginning with 3/24/1956, Billboard published the LP chart on a weekly basis. From the first of the year to that date, there were only two published charts.

1. 1/28 **2** **Oklahoma!** *Movie Soundtrack*
2. 3/24 **6** **Belafonte** *Harry Belafonte*
   the first #1 album on the weekly charts
3. 5/5 **10** **Elvis Presley** *Elvis Presley*
4. 7/14 **15↕** **My Fair Lady** *Original Cast*
   peaked at #1 in 4 consecutive years: 1956 (8 weeks), 1957 (1 week), 1958 (3 weeks) and 1959 (3 weeks — stereo charts)
5. 9/8 **31↕** **Calypso** *Harry Belafonte*
6. 10/6 **1** **The King And I** *Movie Soundtrack*
7. 10/13 **1** **The Eddy Duchin Story**
   Carmen Cavallaro/Movie Soundtrack
8. 12/8 **5** **Elvis** *Elvis Presley*

1957

DATE	WKS	

1. 5/27 **8** **Love Is The Thing** *Nat "King" Cole*
2. 7/22 **10↕** **Around The World In 80 Days**
   Movie Soundtrack
3. 7/29 **10** **Loving You** *Elvis Presley/Movie Soundtrack*
4. 12/16 **4↕** **Elvis' Christmas Album** *Elvis Presley*
5. 12/30 **1** **Merry Christmas** *Bing Crosby*

1958

DATE	WKS	

1. 1/20 **2** **Ricky** *Ricky Nelson*
2. 2/10 **5** **Come Fly with me** *Frank Sinatra*
3. 3/17 **12↕** **The Music Man** *Original Cast*
4. 5/19 **31↕** **South Pacific** *Movie Soundtrack*
   includes 28 weeks at #1 on Stereo chart which began on 5/25/1959
5. 6/9 **3↕** **Johnny's Greatest Hits** *Johnny Mathis*
6. 7/21 **10↕** **Gigi** *Movie Soundtrack*
   includes 3 weeks at #1 in 1958, 3 weeks at #1 on solo chart in 1959, and 4 weeks at #1 on mono charts beginning on 5/25/1959
7. 8/11 **7↕** **Tchaikovsky: Piano Concerto No. 1**
   Van Cliburn
8. 10/6 **8↕** **Sing Along With Mitch**
   Mitch Miller & The Gang
9. 10/13 **5** **Frank Sinatra Sings For Only The Lonely** *Frank Sinatra*
10. 11/24 **1** **The Kingston Trio** *The Kingston Trio*
11. 12/29 **2** **Christmas Sing-Along With Mitch**
    Mitch Miller & The Gang

1959

DATE	WKS	

1. 2/2 **3** **Flower Drum Song** *Original Cast*
2. 2/23 **10** **The Music From Peter Gunn**
   Henry Mancini

> **5/25/1959: Billboard splits solo album chart into separate Stereo and Monaural (Mono) charts**

3. 6/22 **5** **Exotica** *Martin Denny*
   Mono: 5 weeks
4. 7/13 **1** **Film Encores** *Mantovani and his orchestra*
   Stereo: 1 week
5. 7/27 **15** **The Kingston Trio At Large**
   The Kingston Trio
   Mono: 15 weeks
6. 11/9 **5** **Heavenly** *Johnny Mathis*
   Mono: 5 weeks
7. 12/14 **8** **Here We Go Again!** *The Kingston Trio*
   Stereo: 2 weeks; Mono: 8 weeks

1960

DATE	WKS	

1. 1/11 **1** **The Lord's Prayer**
   Mormon Tabernacle Choir
   Stereo: 1 week
2. 1/25 **16** **The Sound Of Music** *Original Cast*
   Stereo: 15 weeks; Mono: 12
3. 4/25 **13↕** **Persuasive Percussion**
   Enoch Light/Terry Snyder and The All-Stars
   Stereo: 13 weeks
4. 5/2 **2↕** **Theme From A Summer Place**
   Billy Vaughn and his orchestra
   Mono: 2 weeks
5. 5/9 **12↕** **Sold Out** *The Kingston Trio*
   Stereo: 3 weeks; Mono: 10 weeks
6. 7/25 **14↕** **The Button-Down Mind Of Bob Newhart** *Bob Newhart*
   Mono: 14 weeks
7. 8/29 **10↕** **String Along** *The Kingston Trio*
   Stereo: 10 weeks; Mono: 6 weeks
8. 10/24 **9↕** **Nice 'N' Easy** *Frank Sinatra*
   Stereo: 9 weeks; Mono: 1 week
9. 12/5 **10↕** **G.I. Blues** *Elvis Presley/Movie Soundtrack*
   Stereo: 2 weeks; Mono: 8 weeks

1961

DATE	WKS	

1. 1/9 **1** **The Button-Down Mind Strikes Back!**
   Bob Newhart
   Mono: 1 week
2. 1/16 **5↕** **Wonderland By Night**
   Bert Kaempfert and his orchestra
   Mono: 5 weeks
3. 1/23 **14↕** **Exodus** *Movie Soundtrack*
   Stereo: 14 weeks; Mono: 3 weeks
4. 3/13 **11↕** **Calcutta!** *Lawrence Welk*
   Stereo: 11 weeks; Mono: 8 weeks
5. 6/5 **6** **Camelot** *Original Cast*
   Mono: 6 weeks
6. 7/17 **9** **Stars For A Summer Night**
   Various Artists
   Stereo: 9 weeks; Mono: 4 weeks
7. 7/17 **1** **Carnival** *Original Cast*
   Mono: 1 week
8. 8/21 **3** **Something For Everybody** *Elvis Presley*
   Mono: 3 weeks

#1 ALBUMS

1961 (cont'd)

9. 9/11 **13**   **Judy At Carnegie Hall** *Judy Garland*
Stereo: 9 weeks; Mono: 13 weeks

10. 11/20 **7**   **Stereo 35/MM**
Enoch Light & The Light Brigade
Stereo: 7 weeks

11. 12/11 **20**   **Blue Hawaii** *Elvis Presley/Movie Soundtrack*
Stereo: 4 weeks; Mono: 20 weeks

#1 ALBUMS

1968

	DATE	WKS	
1.	1/6	8	**Magical Mystery Tour**
			The Beatles/Movie Soundtrack
2.	3/2	5	**Blooming Hits** *Paul Mauriat & his orchestra*
3.	4/6	9↕	**The Graduate**
			Simon & Garfunkel/Movie Soundtrack
4.	5/25	7↕	**Bookends** *Simon & Garfunkel*
5.	7/27	2	**The Beat Of The Brass**
			Herb Alpert & The Tijuana Brass
6.	8/10	4	**Wheels Of Fire** *Cream*
7.	9/7	4↕	**Waiting For The Sun** *The Doors*
8.	9/28	1	**Time Peace/The Rascals' Greatest Hits**
			The Rascals
9.	10/12	8↕	**Cheap Thrills**
			Big Brother & The Holding Company
10.	11/16	2	**Electric Ladyland** *Jimi Hendrix Experience*
11.	12/21	5↕	**Wichita Lineman** *Glen Campbell*
12.	12/28	9↕	**The Beatles [White Album]** *The Beatles*

1969

	DATE	WKS	
1.	2/8	1	**TCB** *Diana Ross & The Supremes with*
			The Temptations
2.	3/29	7↕	**Blood, Sweat & Tears** *Blood, Sweat & Tears*
3.	4/26	13	**Hair** *Original Cast*
4.	8/23	4	**Johnny Cash At San Quentin** *Johnny Cash*
5.	9/20	2	**Blind Faith** *Blind Faith*
6.	10/4	4	**Green River** *Creedence Clearwater Revival*
7.	11/1	11↕	**Abbey Road** *The Beatles*
8.	12/27	7↕	**Led Zeppelin II** *Led Zeppelin*

1970

	DATE	WKS	
1.	3/7	10	**Bridge Over Troubled Water**
			Simon & Garfunkel
2.	5/16	1	**Deja Vu** *Crosby, Stills, Nash & Young*
3.	5/23	3	**McCartney** *Paul McCartney*
4.	6/13	4	**Let It Be** *The Beatles/Movie Soundtrack*
5.	7/11	4	**Woodstock** *Movie Soundtrack*
6.	8/8	2	**Blood, Sweat & Tears 3** *Blood, Sweat & Tears*
7.	8/22	9	**Cosmo's Factory**
			Creedence Clearwater Revival
8.	10/24	6↕	**Abraxas** *Santana*
9.	10/31	4	**Led Zeppelin III** *Led Zeppelin*

1971

	DATE	WKS	
1.	1/2	7	**All Things Must Pass** *George Harrison*
2.	2/20	3↕	**Jesus Christ Superstar** *Various Artists*
3.	2/27	9	**Pearl** *Janis Joplin*
4.	5/15	1	**4 Way Street** *Crosby, Stills, Nash & Young*
5.	5/22	4	**Sticky Fingers** *The Rolling Stones*
6.	6/19	15	**Tapestry** *Carole King*
7.	10/2	4	**Every Picture Tells A Story** *Rod Stewart*
8.	10/30	1	**Imagine** *John Lennon*
9.	11/6	1	**Shaft** *Isaac Hayes/Movie Soundtrack*
10.	11/13	5	**Santana III** *Santana*
11.	12/18	2	**There's A Riot Goin' On**
			Sly & The Family Stone

1972

	DATE	WKS	
1.	1/1	3	**Music** *Carole King*
2.	1/22	7	**American Pie** *Don McLean*
3.	3/11	2	**Harvest** *Neil Young*
4.	3/25	5	**America** *America*
5.	4/29	5	**First Take** *Roberta Flack*
6.	6/3	2	**Thick As A Brick** *Jethro Tull*
7.	6/17	4	**Exile On Main St.** *The Rolling Stones*
8.	7/15	5	**Honky Chateau** *Elton John*
9.	8/19	9	**Chicago V** *Chicago*
10.	10/21	4	**Superfly** *Curtis Mayfield/Movie Soundtrack*
11.	11/18	3	**Catch Bull At Four** *Cat Stevens*
12.	12/9	5	**Seventh Sojourn** *The Moody Blues*

1973

	DATE	WKS	
1.	1/13	5	**No Secrets** *Carly Simon*
2.	2/17	2	**The World Is A Ghetto** *War*
3.	3/3	2	**Don't Shoot Me I'm Only The Piano**
			Player *Elton John*
4.	3/17	3	**Dueling Banjos**
			Eric Weissberg & Steve Mandell
5.	4/7	2	**Lady Sings The Blues**
			Diana Ross/Movie Soundtrack
6.	4/21	1	**Billion Dollar Babies** *Alice Cooper*
7.	4/28	1	**The Dark Side Of The Moon** *Pink Floyd*
8.	5/5	1	**Aloha From Hawaii Via Satellite**
			Elvis Presley
9.	5/12	2	**Houses Of The Holy** *Led Zeppelin*
10.	5/26	1	**The Beatles/1967-1970** *The Beatles*
11.	6/2	3	**Red Rose Speedway**
			Paul McCartney & Wings
12.	6/23	5	**Living In The Material World**
			George Harrison
13.	7/28	5↕	**Chicago VI** *Chicago*
14.	8/18	1	**A Passion Play** *Jethro Tull*
15.	9/8	5	**Brothers And Sisters**
			The Allman Brothers Band
16.	10/13	4	**Goats Head Soup** *The Rolling Stones*
17.	11/10	8	**Goodbye Yellow Brick Road** *Elton John*

1974

	DATE	WKS	
1.	1/5	1	**The Singles 1969-1973** *Carpenters*
2.	1/12	5	**You Don't Mess Around With Jim**
			Jim Croce
3.	2/16	4	**Planet Waves** *Bob Dylan*
4.	3/16	2	**The Way We Were** *Barbra Streisand*
5.	3/30	3↕	**John Denver's Greatest Hits**
			John Denver
6.	4/13	4↕	**Band On The Run**
			Paul McCartney & Wings
7.	4/27	1	**Chicago VII** *Chicago*
8.	5/4	5	**The Sting**
			Marvin Hamlisch/Movie Soundtrack
9.	6/22	2	**Sundown** *Gordon Lightfoot*
10.	7/13	4	**Caribou** *Elton John*
11.	8/10	1	**Back Home Again** *John Denver*
12.	8/17	4	**461 Ocean Boulevard** *Eric Clapton*

#1 ALBUMS

1974 (cont'd)

13.	9/14	2	**Fulfillingness' First Finale**	
			Stevie Wonder	
14.	9/28	1	**Bad Company** *Bad Company*	
15.	10/5	1	**Endless Summer** *The Beach Boys*	
16.	10/12	1	**If You Love Me, Let Me Know**	
			Olivia Newton-John	
17.	10/19	1	**Not Fragile** *Bachman-Turner Overdrive*	
18.	10/26	1	**Can't Get Enough** *Barry White*	
19.	11/2	1	**So Far** *Crosby, Stills, Nash & Young*	
20.	11/9	1	**Wrap Around Joy** *Carole King*	
21.	11/16	1	**Walls And Bridges** *John Lennon*	
22.	11/23	1	**It's Only Rock 'N Roll** *The Rolling Stones*	
23.	11/30	10	**Elton John - Greatest Hits** *Elton John*	

1975

DATE	WKS			
1.	2/8	1	**Fire** *Ohio Players*	
2.	2/15	1	**Heart Like A Wheel** *Linda Ronstadt*	
3.	2/22	1	**AWB** *Average White Band*	
4.	3/1	2	**Blood On The Tracks** *Bob Dylan*	
5.	3/15	1	**Have You Never Been Mellow**	
			Olivia Newton-John	
6.	3/22	6	**Physical Graffiti** *Led Zeppelin*	
7.	5/3	2	**Chicago VIII** *Chicago*	
8.	5/17	3	**That's The Way Of The World**	
			Earth, Wind & Fire/Movie Soundtrack	
9.	6/7	7↕	**Captain Fantastic And The Brown Dirt Cowboy** *Elton John*	
			the first album to debut at #1	
10.	7/19	1	**Venus And Mars** *Wings*	
11.	7/26	5	**One Of These Nights** *Eagles*	
12.	9/6	4↕	**Red Octopus** *Jefferson Starship*	
13.	9/13	1	**The Heat Is On** *The Isley Brothers*	
14.	9/20	1	**Between The Lines** *Janis Ian*	
15.	10/4	2	**Wish You Were Here** *Pink Floyd*	
16.	10/18	2	**Windsong** *John Denver*	
17.	11/8	3	**Rock Of The Westies** *Elton John*	
18.	12/6	1	**Still Crazy After All These Years**	
			Paul Simon	
19.	12/13	5	**Chicago IX - Chicago's Greatest Hits**	
			Chicago	

1976

DATE	WKS			
1.	1/17	3	**Gratitude** *Earth, Wind & Fire*	
2.	2/7	5	**Desire** *Bob Dylan*	
3.	3/13	5↕	**Eagles/Their Greatest Hits 1971-1975**	
			Eagles	
4.	4/10	10↕	**Frampton Comes Alive!** *Peter Frampton*	
5.	4/24	7↕	**Wings At The Speed Of Sound** *Wings*	
6.	5/1	2	**Presence** *Led Zeppelin*	
7.	5/15	4↕	**Black And Blue** *The Rolling Stones*	
8.	7/31	2	**Breezin'** *George Benson*	
9.	9/4	1	**Fleetwood Mac** *Fleetwood Mac*	
10.	10/16	14↕	**Songs In The Key Of Life** *Stevie Wonder*	

1977

DATE	WKS			
1.	1/15	8↕	**Hotel California** *Eagles*	
2.	1/22	1	**Wings Over America** *Wings*	
3.	2/12	6	**A Star Is Born**	
			Barbra Streisand/Movie Soundtrack	
4.	4/2	31↕	**Rumours** *Fleetwood Mac*	
5.	7/16	1	**Barry Manilow/Live** *Barry Manilow*	
6.	12/3	5	**Simple Dreams** *Linda Ronstadt*	

1978

DATE	WKS			
1.	1/21	24	**Saturday Night Fever**	
			Bee Gees/Movie Soundtrack	
2.	7/8	1	**City To City** *Gerry Rafferty*	
3.	7/15	2	**Some Girls** *The Rolling Stones*	
4.	7/29	12↕	**Grease** *Movie Soundtrack*	
5.	9/16	2↕	**Don't Look Back** *Boston*	
6.	11/4	1	**Living In The USA** *Linda Ronstadt*	
7.	11/11	1	**Live And More** *Donna Summer*	
8.	11/18	8↕	**52nd Street** *Billy Joel*	

1979

DATE	WKS			
1.	1/6	3	**Barbra Streisand's Greatest Hits, Volume 2** *Barbra Streisand*	
2.	2/3	1	**Briefcase Full Of Blues** *Blues Brothers*	
3.	2/10	3	**Blondes Have More Fun** *Rod Stewart*	
4.	3/3	6↕	**Spirits Having Flown** *Bee Gees*	
5.	4/7	5↕	**Minute By Minute** *The Doobie Brothers*	
6.	5/19	6↕	**Breakfast In America** *Supertramp*	
7.	6/16	6↕	**Bad Girls** *Donna Summer*	
8.	8/11	5	**Get The Knack** *The Knack*	
9.	9/15	7	**In Through The Out Door** *Led Zeppelin*	
10.	11/3	9	**The Long Run** *Eagles*	

1980

DATE	WKS			
1.	1/5	1	**On The Radio-Greatest Hits-Volumes I & II** *Donna Summer*	
2.	1/12	1	**Bee Gees Greatest** *Bee Gees*	
3.	1/19	15	**The Wall** *Pink Floyd*	
4.	5/3	6	**Against The Wind** *Bob Seger*	
5.	6/14	6	**Glass Houses** *Billy Joel*	
6.	7/26	7	**Emotional Rescue** *The Rolling Stones*	
7.	9/13	1	**Hold Out** *Jackson Browne*	
8.	9/20	5	**The Game** *Queen*	
9.	10/25	3↕	**Guilty** *Barbra Streisand*	
10.	11/8	4	**The River** *Bruce Springsteen*	
11.	12/13	2	**Kenny Rogers' Greatest Hits**	
			Kenny Rogers	
12.	12/27	8	**Double Fantasy** *John Lennon/Yoko Ono*	

1981

DATE	WKS			
1.	2/21	15↕	**Hi Infidelity** *REO Speedwagon*	
2.	4/4	3↕	**Paradise Theater** *Styx*	
3.	6/27	4	**Mistaken Identity** *Kim Carnes*	
4.	7/25	3	**Long Distance Voyager**	
			The Moody Blues	
5.	8/15	1	**Precious Time** *Pat Benatar*	

#1 ALBUMS

1981 (cont'd)

6.	8/22	10↕	**4** *Foreigner*
7.	9/5	1	**Bella Donna** *Stevie Nicks*
8.	9/12	1	**Escape** *Journey*
9.	9/19	9	**Tattoo You** *Rolling Stones*
10.	12/26	3	**For Those About To Rock We Salute You** *AC/DC*

	DATE	WKS	## 1982
1.	2/6	4	**Freeze-Frame** *The J. Geils Band*
2.	3/6	6	**Beauty And The Beat** *Go-Go's*
3.	4/17	4	**Chariots Of Fire** *Vangelis/Movie Soundtrack*
4.	5/15	9↕	**Asia** *Asia*
5.	5/29	3	**Tug Of War** *Paul McCartney*
6.	8/7	5	**Mirage** *Fleetwood Mac*
7.	9/11	9	**American Fool** *John Cougar*
8.	11/13	15	Business As Usual *Men At Work*

	DATE	WKS	## 1983
1.	2/26	37↕	Thriller *Michael Jackson*
2.	6/25	2	**Flashdance** *Movie Soundtrack*
3.	7/23	17↕	**Synchronicity** *The Police*
4.	11/26	1	**Metal Health** *Quiet Riot*
5.	12/3	3	**Can't Slow Down** *Lionel Richie*

	DATE	WKS	## 1984
1.	4/21	10	**Footloose** *Movie Soundtrack*
2.	6/30	1	**Sports** *Huey Lewis & The News*
3.	7/7	7↕	**Born In The U.S.A.** *Bruce Springsteen*
4.	8/4	24	Purple Rain *Prince and the Revolution/Movie Soundtrack*

	DATE	WKS	## 1985
1.	2/9	3	**Like A Virgin** *Madonna*
2.	3/2	3	**Make It Big** *Wham!*
3.	3/23	1	**Centerfield** *John Fogerty*
4.	3/30	7↕	**No Jacket Required** *Phil Collins*
5.	4/27	3	**We Are The World** *USA For Africa*
6.	6/1	3	**Around The World In A Day** *Prince & The Revolution*
7.	6/22	2	**Beverly Hills Cop** *Movie Soundtrack*
8.	7/13	5↕	**Songs From The Big Chair** *Tears For Fears*
9.	8/10	2	**Reckless** *Bryan Adams*
10.	8/31	9	**Brothers In Arms** *Dire Straits*
11.	11/2	11↕	Miami Vice *Television Soundtrack*
12.	12/21	1	**Heart** *Heart*

	DATE	WKS	## 1986
1.	1/25	3	**The Broadway Album** *Barbra Streisand*
2.	2/15	2	**Promise** *Sade*
3.	3/1	1	**Welcome To The Real World** *Mr. Mister*

1986 (cont'd)

4.	3/8	14↕	Whitney Houston *Whitney Houston*
5.	4/26	3	**5150** *Van Halen*
6.	7/5	2	**Control** *Janet Jackson*
7.	7/19	1	**Winner In You** *Patti LaBelle*
8.	7/26	5↕	**Top Gun** *Movie Soundtrack*
9.	8/16	5	**True Blue** *Madonna*
10.	9/27	2	**Dancing On The Ceiling** *Lionel Richie*
11.	10/18	1	**Fore!** *Huey Lewis & The News*
12.	10/25	8↕	**Slippery When Wet** *Bon Jovi*
13.	11/1	4	**Third Stage** *Boston*
14.	11/29	7	**Bruce Springsteen & The E Street Band Live/1975-85** *Bruce Springsteen*

	DATE	WKS	## 1987
1.	3/7	7	**Licensed To Ill** *Beastie Boys*
2.	4/25	9	**The Joshua Tree** *U2*
3.	6/27	11	**Whitney** *Whitney Houston*
4.	9/12	2	**La Bamba** *Los Lobos/Movie Soundtrack*
5.	9/26	6	**Bad** *Michael Jackson*
6.	11/7	1	**Tunnel of Love** *Bruce Springsteen*
7.	11/14	18↕	Dirty Dancing *Movie Soundtrack*

	DATE	WKS	## 1988
1.	1/16	12↕	Faith *George Michael*
2.	1/23	2	**Tiffany** *Tiffany*
3.	6/25	4	**OU812** *Van Halen*
4.	7/23	6↕	**Hysteria** *Def Leppard*
5.	8/6	5↕	**Appetite For Destruction** *Guns N' Roses*
6.	8/20	1	**Roll With It** *Steve Winwood*
7.	8/27	1	**Tracy Chapman** *Tracy Chapman*
8.	10/15	4	**New Jersey** *Bon Jovi*
9.	11/12	6	**Rattle And Hum** *U2/Movie Soundtrack*
10.	12/24	4	**Giving You The Best That I Got** *Anita Baker*

	DATE	WKS	## 1989
1.	1/21	6↕	**Don't Be Cruel** *Bobby Brown*
2.	3/11	5	**Electric Youth** *Debbie Gibson*
3.	4/15	1	**Loc-ed After Dark** *Tone Loc*
4.	4/22	6	**Like A Prayer** *Madonna*
5.	6/3	7	**The Raw & The Cooked** *Fine Young Cannibals*
6.	7/22	6	**Batman** *Prince/Movie Soundtrack*
7.	9/2	1	**Repeat Offender** *Richard Marx*
8.	9/9	2	**Hangin' Tough** *New Kids On The Block*
9.	9/23	8↕	**Girl You Know It's True** *Milli Vanilli*
10.	10/7	10↕	Forever Your Girl *Paula Abdul*
11.	10/14	2	**Dr. Feelgood** *Motley Crue*
12.	10/28	4	**Janet Jackson's Rhythm Nation 1814** *Janet Jackson*
13.	12/16	1	**Storm Front** *Billy Joel*

#1 ALBUMS

#1 ALBUMS

1996

	DATE	WKS	
1.	1/20	5	**Waiting To Exhale** *Movie Soundtrack*
2.	3/2	2	**All Eyez On Me** *2Pac*
3.	4/6	1	**Anthology 2** *The Beatles*
4.	5/4	1	**Evil Empire** *Rage Against The Machine*
5.	5/11	2	**Fairweather Johnson** *Hootie & The Blowfish*
6.	5/25	4	**The Score** *Fugees (Refugee Camp)*
7.	6/22	4	**Load** *Metallica*
8.	7/20	4	**It Was Written** *Nas*
9.	8/17	1	**Beats, Rhymes And Life** *A Tribe Called Quest*
10.	9/14	2	**No Code** *Pearl Jam*
11.	9/28	1	**Home Again** *New Edition*
12.	10/5	3↕	**Falling Into You** *Celine Dion*
13.	10/19	1	**From The Muddy Banks Of The Wishkah** *Nirvana*
14.	11/2	1	**Recovering The Satellites** *Counting Crows*
15.	11/9	1	**Best Of Volume 1** *Van Halen*
16.	11/16	1	**Anthology 3** *The Beatles*
17.	11/23	1	**The Don Killuminati - The 7 Day Theory** *Makaveli*
18.	11/30	1	**Tha Doggfather** *Snoop Doggy Dogg*
19.	12/7	2	**Razorblade Suitcase** *Bush*
20.	12/21	9↕	**Tragic Kingdom** *No Doubt*

1997

	DATE	WKS	
1.	2/15	1	**Gridlock'd** *Movie Soundtrack*
2.	3/1	1	**Unchained Melody/The Early Years** *LeAnn Rimes*
3.	3/8	1	**Secret Samadhi** *Live*
4.	3/15	1	**Private Parts** *Movie Soundtrack*
5.	3/22	1	**Pop** *U2*
6.	3/29	1	**The Untouchable** *Scarface*
7.	4/5	1	**Nine Lives** *Aerosmith*
8.	4/12	4	**Life After Death** *The Notorious B.I.G.*
9.	5/10	1	**Share My World** *Mary J. Blige*
10.	5/17	1	**Carrying Your Love With Me** *George Strait*
11.	5/24	5↕	**Spice** *Spice Girls*
12.	6/21	1	**Wu-Tang Forever** *Wu-Tang Clan*
13.	6/28	2	**Butterfly Kisses (Shades Of Grace)** *Bob Carlisle*
14.	7/19	1	**The Fat Of The Land** *Prodigy*
15.	7/26	2	**Men In Black - The Album** *Movie Soundtrack*
16.	8/9	4↕	**No Way Out** *Puff Daddy & The Family*
17.	8/16	1	**The Art Of War** *Bone Thugs-N-Harmony*
18.	9/6	1	**The Dance** *Fleetwood Mac*
19.	9/20	1	**Ghetto D** *Master P*
20.	9/27	3↕	**You Light Up My Life - Inspirational Songs** *LeAnn Rimes*
21.	10/4	1	**Butterfly** *Mariah Carey*
22.	10/11	1	**Evolution** *Boyz II Men*
23.	10/25	1	**The Velvet Rope** *Janet Jackson*
24.	11/8	1	**The Firm - The Album** *The Firm*
25.	11/15	2	**Harlem World** *Mase*

1997 (cont'd)

	DATE	WKS	
26.	11/29	1	**Higher Ground** *Barbra Streisand*
27.	12/6	1	**Reload** *Metallica*
28.	12/13	5	**Sevens** *Garth Brooks*

1998

	DATE	WKS	
1.	1/17	1	**Let's Talk About Love** *Celine Dion*
2.	1/24	16	**Titanic** *Movie Soundtrack*
3.	5/16	1	**Before These Crowded Streets** *Dave Matthews Band*
4.	5/23	2	**The Limited Series** *Garth Brooks*
5.	6/6	1	**It's Dark And Hell Is Hot** *DMX*
6.	6/13	3↕	**City Of Angels** *Movie Soundtrack*
7.	6/20	2	**MP Da Last Don** *Master P*
8.	7/18	2	**Armageddon** *Movie Soundtrack*
9.	8/1	3	**Hello Nasty** *Beastie Boys*
10.	8/22	2	**Da Game Is To Be Sold, Not To Be Told** *Snoop Dogg*
11.	9/5	1	**Follow The Leader** *Korn*
12.	9/12	4↕	**The Miseducation Of Lauryn Hill** *Lauryn Hill*
13.	10/3	1	**Mechanical Animals** *Marilyn Manson*
14.	10/17	5	**Vol. 2...Hard Knock Life** *Jay-Z*
15.	11/21	2	**Supposed Former Infatuation Junkie** *Alanis Morissette*
16.	12/5	5	**Double Live** *Garth Brooks*

1999

	DATE	WKS	
1.	1/9	3	**Flesh Of My Flesh Blood Of My Blood** *DMX*
2.	1/30	6↕	**...Baby One More Time** *Britney Spears*
3.	2/6	1	**Made Man** *Silkk The Shocker*
4.	2/13	1	**Chyna Doll** *Foxy Brown*
5.	3/13	5↕	**Fanmail** *TLC*
6.	4/24	2	**I Am...** *Nas*
7.	5/15	1	**Ruff Ryders - Ryde Or Die Vol. I** *Ruff Ryders*
8.	5/22	1	**A Place In The Sun** *Tim McGraw*
9.	5/29	1	**Ricky Martin** *Ricky Martin*
10.	6/5	10↕	**Millennium** *Backstreet Boys*
11.	7/10	4↕	**Significant Other** *Limp Bizkit*
12.	9/11	1	**Christina Aguilera** *Christina Aguilera*
13.	9/18	2	**Fly** *Dixie Chicks*
14.	10/2	1	**Ruff Ryders' First Lady** *Eve*
15.	10/9	1	**The Fragile** *Nine Inch Nails*
16.	10/16	2	**Human Clay** *Creed*
17.	10/30	12↕	**Supernatural** *Santana*
18.	11/20	1	**The Battle Of Los Angeles** *Rage Against The Machine*
19.	11/27	1	**Breathe** *Faith Hill*
20.	12/4	1	**Issues** *Korn*
21.	12/11	3↕	**All The Way...A Decade Of Song** *Celine Dion*
22.	12/25	1	**Born Again** *The Notorious B.I.G.*

#1 ALBUMS

2000

	DATE	WKS		
1.	1/8	1	...And Then There Was X	DMX
2.	1/15	1	Vol. 3...Life And Times Of S. Carter	
			Jay-Z	
3.	2/12	2	Voodoo	D'Angelo
4.	4/8	8	No Strings Attached	*NSYNC
5.	6/3	1	Oops!...I Did It Again	Britney Spears
6.	6/10	8	The Marshall Mathers LP	Eminem
7.	8/5	3	Now 4	Various Artists
8.	8/26	5	Country Grammar	Nelly
9.	9/30	1	G.O.A.T. Featuring James T. Smith	
			The Greatest Of All Time	LL Cool J
10.	10/7	1	Music	Madonna
11.	10/14	1	Let's Get Ready	Mystikal
12.	10/21	1	Kid A	Radiohead
13.	10/28	1	Rule 3:36	Ja Rule
14.	11/4	2	Chocolate Starfish And The Hot Dog	
			Flavored Water	Limp Bizkit
15.	11/18	1	The Dynasty Roc La Familia (2000 —)	
			Jay-Z	
16.	11/25	1	TP-2.com	R. Kelly
17.	12/2	8↕	1	The Beatles
18.	12/9	2↕	Black & Blue	Backstreet Boys

2001

	DATE	WKS		
1.	2/10	1	J.Lo	Jennifer Lopez
2.	2/17	6↕	Hotshot	Shaggy
3.	3/17	2	Everyday	Dave Matthews Band
4.	4/14	1	Until The End Of Time	2Pac
5.	4/21	3	Now 6	Various Artists
6.	5/12	1	All For You	Janet Jackson
7.	5/19	2	Survivor	Destiny's Child
8.	6/2	1	Lateralus	Tool
9.	6/9	3	Break The Cycle	Staind
10.	6/30	1	Take Off Your Pants And Jacket	
			Blink 182	
11.	7/7	2↕	Devil's Night	D-12
12.	7/14	3↕	Songs In A Minor	Alicia Keys
13.	8/11	1	Celebrity	*NSYNC
14.	8/18	3	Now 7	Various Artists
15.	9/8	1	Now	Maxwell
16.	9/15	1	Aaliyah	Aaliyah
17.	9/22	1	Toxicity	System Of A Down
18.	9/29	3	The Blueprint	Jay-Z
19.	10/20	2	Pain Is Love	Ja Rule
20.	11/3	1	God Bless America	Various Artists
21.	11/10	1	The Great Depression	DMX
22.	11/17	1	Invincible	Michael Jackson
23.	11/24	1	Britney	Britney Spears
24.	12/1	1	Scarecrow	Garth Brooks
25.	12/8	8	Weathered	Creed

2002

	DATE	WKS		
1.	2/2	4↕	Drive	Alan Jackson
2.	2/23	2↕	J To Tha L-O! The Remixes	
			Jennifer Lopez	
3.	3/16	1	Under Rug Swept	Alanis Morissette
4.	3/23	2	O Brother, Where Art Thou?	
			Movie Soundtrack	
5.	4/6	1	Now 9	Various Artists
6.	4/13	1	A New Day Has Come	Celine Dion
7.	4/20	3	Ashanti	Ashanti
8.	5/11	1	No Shoes, No Shirt, No Problems	
			Kenny Chesney	
9.	5/18	1	Hood Rich	Big Tymers
10.	5/25	1	JUSLISEN (Just Listen)	Musiq
11.	6/1	1	P. Diddy & Bad Boy Records	
			Present...We Invented The Remix	
			Various Artists	
12.	6/8	6↕	The Eminem Show	Eminem
13.	7/13	4↕	Nellyville	Nelly
14.	8/3	1	Busted Stuff	Dave Matthews Band
15.	8/10	1	Unleashed	Toby Keith
16.	8/17	2	The Rising	Bruce Springsteen
17.	9/14	4↕	Home	Dixie Chicks
18.	10/5	1	Believe	Disturbed
19.	10/12	3	Elv1s: 30 #1 Hits	Elvis Presley
20.	11/2	1	Cry	Faith Hill
21.	11/9	1	Shaman	Santana
22.	11/16	4↕	8 Mile	Movie Soundtrack
23.	11/30	1	The Blueprint 2: The Gift And The	
			Curse	Jay-Z
24.	12/7	5	Up!	Shania Twain

2003

	DATE	WKS		
1.	1/25	4↕	Come Away With Me	Norah Jones
2.	2/22	6↕	Get Rich Or Die Tryin'	50 Cent
3.	3/8	1	Chocolate Factory	R. Kelly
4.	4/12	2	Meteora	Linkin Park
5.	4/26	1	Faceless	Godsmack
6.	5/3	1	Thankful	Kelly Clarkson
7.	5/10	1	American Life	Madonna
8.	5/24	1	Body Kiss	
			The Isley Brothers Featuring Ronald Isley	
9.	5/31	1	The Golden Age Of Grotesque	
			Marilyn Manson	
10.	6/7	1	14 Shades Of Grey	Staind
11.	6/14	1	How The West Was Won	Led Zeppelin
12.	6/21	1	St. Anger	Metallica
13.	6/28	1	Dance With My Father	Luther Vandross
14.	7/5	1	After The Storm	Monica
15.	7/12	1	Dangerously In Love	Beyoncé
16.	7/19	2	Chapter II	Ashanti
17.	8/2	4	Bad Boys II	Movie Soundtrack
18.	8/30	1	Greatest Hits Volume II and Some	
			Other Stuff	Alan Jackson
19.	9/6	1	The Neptunes Present...Clones	
			Various Artists	

#1 ALBUMS

2003 (cont'd)

20.	9/13	1	**Love & Life** *Mary J. Blige*
21.	9/20	1	**Metamorphosis** *Hilary Duff*
22.	9/27	1	**Heavier Things** *John Mayer*
23.	10/4	1	**Grand Champ** *DMX*
24.	10/11	7↕	**Speakerboxxx/The Love Below** *OutKast*
25.	10/25	1	**Chicken*N*Beer** *Ludacris*
26.	11/1	2	**Measure Of A Man** *Clay Aiken*
27.	11/22	1	**Shock'n Y'all** *Toby Keith*
28.	11/29	2↕	**The Black Album** *Jay-Z*
29.	12/6	1	**In The Zone** *Britney Spears*
30.	12/20	2↕	**The Diary Of Alicia Keys** *Alicia Keys*
31.	12/27	1	**Soulful** *Ruben Studdard*

2004

	DATE	WKS	
1.	1/24	1	**Closer** *Josh Groban*
2.	2/14	1	**Kamikaze** *Twista*
3.	2/21	1	**When The Sun Goes Down** *Kenny Chesney*
4.	2/28	6	**Feels Like Home** *Norah Jones*
5.	4/10	9↕	**Confessions** *Usher*
6.	5/15	1	**D12 World** *D12*
7.	6/12	1	**Under My Skin** *Avril Lavigne*
8.	6/26	1	**Contraband** *Velvet Revolver*
9.	7/3	1	**To The 5 Boroughs** *Beastie Boys*
10.	7/10	1	**Kiss Of Death** *Jadakiss*
11.	7/17	2	**The Hunger For More** *Lloyd Banks*
12.	7/31	1	**License To Chill** *Jimmy Buffett*
13.	8/7	3↕	**Autobiography** *Ashlee Simpson*
14.	8/14	2↕	**Now 16** *Various Artists*
15.	9/11	2	**Live Like You Were Dying** *Tim McGraw*
16.	9/25	1	**What I Do** *Alan Jackson*
17.	10/2	1	**Suit** *Nelly*
18.	10/9	3↕	**American Idiot** *Green Day*
19.	10/16	1	**Feels Like Today** *Rascal Flatts*
20.	10/23	2	**50 Number Ones** *George Strait*
21.	11/6	1	**Stardust...The Great American Songbook Vol. III** *Rod Stewart*
22.	11/13	1	**Unfinished Business** *R. Kelly & Jay-Z*
23.	11/20	1	**Now 17** *Various Artists*
24.	11/27	4↕	**Encore** *Eminem*
25.	12/11	1	**How To Dismantle An Atomic Bomb** *U2*
26.	12/18	1	**Collision Course** *Jay-Z/Linkin Park*
27.	12/25	1	**The Red Light District** *Ludacris*

2005

	DATE	WKS	
1.	1/1	1	**Loyal To The Game** *2Pac*
2.	2/5	2↕	**The Documentary** *The Game*
3.	2/12	1	**Be As You Are: Songs From An Old Blue Chair** *Kenny Chesney*
4.	2/26	1	**Seventeen Days** *3 Doors Down*
5.	3/5	1	**Genius Loves Company** *Ray Charles*
6.	3/12	1	**O** *Omarion*
7.	3/19	6	**The Massacre** *50 Cent*
8.	4/30	2↕	**The Emancipation Of Mimi** *Mariah Carey*

2005 (cont'd)

9.	5/7	1	**...Something To Be** *Rob Thomas*
10.	5/14	1	**Devils & Dust** *Bruce Springsteen*
11.	5/21	1	**With Teeth** *Nine Inch Nails*
12.	5/28	1	**Stand Up** *Dave Matthews Band*
13.	6/4	1	**Mezmerize** *System Of A Down*
14.	6/11	1	**Out Of Exile** *Audioslave*
15.	6/25	3	**X&Y** *Coldplay*
16.	7/16	1	**Somewhere Down In Texas** *George Strait*
17.	7/23	2	**TP.3 Reloaded** *R. Kelly*
18.	8/6	2	**Now 19** *Various Artists*
19.	8/20	1	**Fireflies** *Faith Hill*
20.	8/27	1	**Chapter V** *Staind*
21.	9/3	2	**Most Wanted** *Hilary Duff*
22.	9/17	2	**Late Registration** *Kanye West*
23.	10/1	1	**The Peoples Champ** *Paul Wall*
24.	10/8	1	**Ten Thousand Fists** *Disturbed*
25.	10/15	1	**All Jacked Up** *Gretchen Wilson*
26.	10/22	1	**All The Right Reasons** *Nickelback*
27.	10/29	1	**Unplugged** *Alicia Keys*
28.	11/5	1	**I Am Me** *Ashlee Simpson*
29.	11/12	1	**#1's** *Destiny's Child*
30.	11/19	2↕	**Now 20** *Various Artists*
31.	11/26	1	**The Road And The Radio** *Kenny Chesney*
32.	12/3	1	**Confessions On A Dance Floor** *Madonna*
33.	12/10	1	**Hypnotize** *System Of A Down*
34.	12/24	2	**Curtain Call: The Hits** *Eminem*

2006

	DATE	WKS	
1.	1/7	2↕	**The Breakthrough** *Mary J. Blige*
2.	1/14	3↕	**Unpredictable** *Jamie Foxx*
3.	2/11	1	**Ancora** *Il Divo*
4.	2/18	1	**The Greatest Songs Of The Fifties** *Barry Manilow*
5.	2/25	1	**Curious George** *Jack Johnson*
6.	3/4	1	**Ghetto Classics** *Jaheim*
7.	3/11	2↕	**High School Musical** *Television Soundtrack*
8.	3/18	1	**In My Own Words** *Ne-Yo*
9.	3/25	1	**Reality Check** *Juvenile*
10.	4/8	1	**3121** *Prince*
11.	4/15	1	**King** *T.I.*
12.	4/22	3	**Me And My Gang** *Rascal Flatts*
13.	5/13	1	**IV** *Godsmack*
14.	5/20	1	**10,000 Days** *Tool*
15.	5/27	2	**Stadium Arcadium** *Red Hot Chili Peppers*
16.	6/10	2	**Taking The Long Way** *Dixie Chicks*
17.	6/24	1	**Decemberunderground** *AFI*
18.	7/1	1	**The Big Bang** *Busta Rhymes*
19.	7/8	1	**Loose** *Nelly Furtado*
20.	7/15	1	**Testimony: Vol. 1, Life & Relationship** *India.Arie*
21.	7/22	1	**American V: A Hundred Highways** *Johnny Cash*
22.	7/29	3↕	**Now 22** *Various Artists*

#1 ALBUMS

2006 (cont'd)

23.	8/12	1	**LeToya** *LeToya*
24.	8/26	1	**Port Of Miami** *Rick Ross*
25.	9/2	1	**Back To Basics** *Christina Aguilera*
26.	9/9	1	**Danity Kane** *Danity Kane*
27.	9/16	1	**Modern Times** *Bob Dylan*
28.	9/23	1	**B'Day** *Beyonce*
29.	9/30	2	**FutureSex/LoveSounds** *Justin Timberlake*
30.	10/14	1	**Release Therapy** *Ludacris*
31.	10/21	1	**The Open Door** *Evanescence*
32.	10/28	1	**Still The Same...Great Rock Classics Of Our Time** *Rod Stewart*
33.	11/4	1	**Press Play** *Diddy*
34.	11/11	2	**Hannah Montana** *Hannah Montana*
35.	11/25	1	**Now 23** *Various Artists*
36.	12/2	1	**Doctor's Advocate** *The Game*
37.	12/9	1	**Kingdom Come** *Jay-Z*
38.	12/16	1	**Light Grenades** *Incubus*
39.	12/23	1	**Ciara: The Evolution** *Ciara*
40.	12/30	1	**The Inspiration** *Young Jeezy*

DATE WKS 2007

1.	1/6	1	**Hip Hop Is Dead** *Nas*
2.	1/13	1	**21** *Omarion*
3.	1/20	2	**Dreamgirls** *Movie Soundtrack*
4.	2/3	2↕	**Daughtry** *Daughtry*
5.	2/10	1	**Late Night Special** *Pretty Ricky*
6.	2/17	3↕	**Not Too Late** *Norah Jones*
7.	2/24	1	**Infinity On High** *Fall Out Boy*
8.	3/24	1	**Greatest Hits** *The Notorious B.I.G.*
9.	3/31	1	**Luvanmusiq** *Musiq Soulchild*
10.	4/7	1	**We Were Dead Before The Ship Even Sank** *Modest Mouse*
11.	4/14	1	**Let It Go** *Tim McGraw*
12.	4/21	2	**Now 24** *Various Artists*
13.	5/5	2	**The Best Damn Thing** *Avril Lavigne*
14.	5/19	1	**Because Of You** *Ne-Yo*
15.	5/26	1	**Call Me Irresponsible** *Michael Buble*
16.	6/2	1	**Minutes To Midnight** *Linkin Park*
17.	6/9	1	**It Won't Be Soon Before Long** *Maroon 5*
18.	6/16	1	**Double Up** *R. Kelly*
19.	6/23	1	**Epiphany** *T-Pain*
20.	6/30	1	**Big Dog Daddy** *Toby Keith*
21.	7/7	1	**Lost Highway** *Bon Jovi*
22.	7/14	1	**Hannah Montana 2 / Meet Miley Cyrus** *Hannah Montana / Miley Cyrus*
23.	7/21	2	**T.I. vs T.I.P.** *T.I.*
24.	8/4	2↕	**Now 25** *Various Artists*
25.	8/18	1	**Finding Forever** *Common*
26.	8/25	1	**Underground Kingz** *UGK*
27.	9/1	4	**High School Musical 2** *High School Musical Cast*
28.	9/29	1	**Graduation** *Kanye West*
29.	10/6	1	**Reba: Duets** *Reba McEntire*
30.	10/13	1	**Still Feels Good** *Rascal Flatts*
31.	10/20	2↕	**Magic** *Bruce Springsteen*
32.	10/27	1	**Rock N Roll Jesus** *Kid Rock*

2007 (cont'd)

33.	11/10	1	**Carnival Ride** *Carrie Underwood*
34.	11/17	1	**Long Road Out Of Eden** *Eagles*
35.	11/24	1	**American Gangster** *Jay-Z*
36.	12/1	4↕	**As I Am** *Alicia Keys*
37.	12/8	5	Noel *Josh Groban*

DATE WKS 2008

1.	1/12	1	**Growing Pains** *Mary J. Blige*
2.	1/19	1	**In Rainbows** *Radiohead*
3.	2/9	1	**Juno** *Movie Soundtrack*
4.	2/23	3	**Sleep Through The Static** *Jack Johnson*
5.	3/15	1	**Discipline** *Janet Jackson*
6.	3/22	1	**Good Time** *Alan Jackson*
7.	3/29	1	**Trilla** *Rick Ross*
8.	4/5	1	**Welcome To The Dollhouse** *Danity Kane*
9.	4/12	1	**DAY26** *Day26*
10.	4/19	1	**Troubadour** *George Strait*
11.	4/26	1	**Spirit** *Leona Lewis*
12.	5/3	2	**E=MC2** *Mariah Carey*
13.	5/17	1	**Hard Candy** *Madonna*
14.	5/24	1	**Home Before Dark** *Neil Diamond*
15.	5/31	1	**Narrow Stairs** *Death Cab For Cutie*
16.	6/7	1	**3 Doors Down** *3 Doors Down*
17.	6/14	1	**Here I Stand** *Usher*
18.	6/21	1	**Indestructible** *Disturbed*
19.	6/28	3↕	**Tha Carter III** *Lil Wayne*
20.	7/5	2	**Viva La Vida Or Death And All His Friends** *Coldplay*
21.	8/2	1	**Untitled** *Nas*
22.	8/9	1	**Breakout** *Miley Cyrus*
23.	8/16	1	**Love On The Inside** *Sugarland*
24.	8/23	1	**Mamma Mia!** *Movie Soundtrack*
25.	8/30	2	**A Little Bit Longer** *Jonas Brothers*
26.	9/13	1	**All Hope Is Gone** *Slipknot*
27.	9/20	1	**The Recession** *Young Jeezy*
28.	9/27	3	**Death Magnetic** *Metallica*
29.	10/18	2	**Paper Trail** *T.I.*
30.	11/1	1	**Lucky Old Sun** *Kenny Chesney*
31.	11/8	2	**Black Ice** *AC/DC*
32.	11/22	1	**Twilight** *Movie Soundtrack*
33.	11/29	11↕	Fearless *Taylor Swift*
34.	12/6	1	**I Am...Sasha Fierce** *Beyonce*
35.	12/13	1	**808s & Heartbreak** *Kanye West*
36.	12/20	1	**Circus** *Britney Spears*

DATE WKS 2009

1.	2/14	1	**Working On A Dream** *Bruce Springsteen*
2.	2/21	1	**The Fray** *The Fray*
3.	3/21	1	**No Line On The Horizon** *U2*
4.	3/28	2	**All I Ever Wanted** *Kelly Clarkson*
5.	4/11	1	**Now 30** *Various Artists*
6.	4/18	1	**Defying Gravity** *Keith Urban*
7.	4/25	1	**Unstoppable** *Rascal Flatts*
8.	5/2	1	**Hannah Montana: The Movie** *Miley Cyrus*
9.	5/9	1	**Deeper Than Rap** *Rick Ross*

#1 ALBUMS

2009 (cont'd)

10.	5/16	1	**Together Through Life** *Bob Dylan*
11.	5/23	1	**Epiphany** *Chrisette Michele*
12.	5/30	1	**21st Century Breakdown** *Green Day*
13.	6/6	2	**Relapse** *Eminem*
14.	6/20	1	**Big Whiskey And The GrooGrux King**
			Dave Matthews Band
15.	6/27	2↕	**The E.N.D.** *The Black Eyed Peas*
16.	7/4	1	**Lines, Vines And Trying Times**
			Jonas Brothers
17.	7/18	1	**Now 31** *Various Artists*
18.	7/25	1	**BLACKsummers'night** *Maxwell*
19.	8/1	1	**Leave This Town** *Daughtry*
20.	8/8	1	**Here We Go Again** *Demi Lovato*
21.	8/15	1	**Loso's Way** *Fabolous*
22.	8/22	1	**Live On The Inside** *Sugarland*
23.	8/29	1	**Twang** *George Strait*
24.	9/5	1	**Keep On Loving You** *Reba McEntire*
25.	9/12	1	**Breakthrough** *Colbie Caillat*
26.	9/19	1	**I Look To You** *Whitney Houston*
27.	9/26	2	**The Blueprint 3** *Jay-Z*
28.	10/10	1	**Backspacer** *Pearl Jam*
29.	10/17	1	**Love Is The Answer** *Barbra Streisand*
30.	10/24	2	**Crazy Love** *Michael Buble*
31.	11/7	1	**The Twilight Saga: New Moon**
			Movie Soundtrack

2009 (cont'd)

32.	11/14	1	**Michael Jackson's This Is It**
			Michael Jackson
33.	11/21	1	**Play On** *Carrie Underwood*
34.	11/28	1	**The Circle** *Bon Jovi*
35.	12/5	1	**Battle Studies** *John Mayer*
36.	12/12	6	**I Dreamed A Dream** *Susan Boyle*

	DATE	WKS	**2010**
1.	1/23	1	**Animal** *Kesha*
2.	1/30	1	**Contra** *Vampire Weekend*
3.	2/6	1	**Hope For Haiti Now** *Various Artists*
4.	2/13	4↕	**Need You Now** *Lady Antebellum*
5.	2/27	3	**Soldier Of Love** *Sade*
6.	3/27	1	**Battle Of The Sexes** *Ludacris*
7.	4/10	4↕	**My World 2.0** *Justin Bieber*
8.	4/17	1	**Raymond V Raymond** *Usher*
9.	5/8	1	**Glee: The Music, The Power Of Madonna** *Glee Cast*
10.	5/15	1	**B.o.B. Presents: The Adventures of Bobby Ray** *B.o.B.*
11.	5/22	1	**The Oracle** *Godsmack*
12.	6/5	2	**Glee: The Music, Volume 3: Showstoppers** *Glee Cast*
13.	6/19	1	**To The Sea** *Jack Johnson*
14.	6/26	1	**Glee: The Music, Journey To Regionals** *Glee Cast*
15.	7/3	1*	**Thank Me Later** *Drake*

* #1 album at press time — peak weeks subject to change

THE CHARTS FROM TOP TO BOTTOM

That's because these are the **only** books that get right to the bottom of *Billboard's* major charts, with **complete, fully accurate chart data on every record ever charted**. So they're quoted with confidence by DJ's, music show hosts, program directors, collectors and other music enthusiasts worldwide.

Each book lists every record's significant chart data, such as peak position, debut date, peak date, weeks charted, label, record number and much more, all conveniently arranged for fast, easy reference. Most books also feature artist biographies, record notes, RIAA Platinum/Gold Record certifications, top artist and record achievements, all-time artist and record rankings, a chronological listing of all #1 hits, and additional in-depth chart information.

TOP POP SINGLES 1955-2008
An artist-by-artist listing of every artist & song that made *Billboard's* "Hot 100," "Bubbling Under" & Pop Singles Charts from January, 1955 through December, 2008! 1,344 pages. Hardcover.

ACROSS THE CHARTS: THE SIXTIES
Devoted to all the music from 1960-1969 across all of *Billboard's* singles charts: Hot 100, Bubbling Under, Country, R&B and Adult Contemporary. Listed together in one comprehensive artist section. 496 pages. Hardcover.

A CENTURY OF POP MUSIC
This unique book chronicles the biggest Pop hits of the past 100 years, in yearly rankings of the Top 40 songs of every year from 1900 through 1999. Includes complete artist and title sections, pictures of the top artists, top hits and top artists by decade, and more. 256 pages. Softcover.

TOP POP ALBUMS 1955-2009
An artist-by-artist listing of every artist & album that made *Billboard's* pop albums and "Bubbling Under" charts from January 1, 1955 through December 26, 2009! Also includes research from Pop Catalog Albums chart. 984 pages. Hardcover.

DVD-rom: THE TRACKS of Top Pop Albums 1955-2009
The perfect supplement to our Top Pop Albums 1955-2009 book. For every artist and category (Movie Soundtrack, etc.) that appears within our new Albums book, this DVD-rom contains an alphabetical listing of all the titles of their album and CD tracks and each title's album count according to the companion book. Fully searchable.

ALBUM CUTS 1955-2001
A companion guide to our Top Pop Albums 1955-2001 book — an A-Z list of cut titles along with the artist name and chart debut year of the album on which the cut is first found. 720 pages. Hardcover.

CHART DVD-roms *:

HONOR ROLL OF HITS	View PDFs of all 962 *Billboard* Honor Roll of Hits charts which measured a song's popularity versus a particular hit's popularity, fromMarch 24, 1945 through November 16, 1963. No title section included.
THE SIXTIES 1960-1999 **THE SEVENTIES 1970-1979** **THE EIGHTIES 1980-1989** **THE NINETIES 1990-1999** **THE 2000s 2000-2009**	Five complete collections of the actual weekly Hot 100 charts from each decade. Viewable in PDF format. Now in full color and magnifiable. Searchable title sections included. * DVD-roms do not contain video or audio files. Require a computer with a DVD drive and a photo viewer or Adobe Acrobat Reader. DVD-roms will NOT play on a consumer DVD deck.

BILLBOARD HOT 100 CHARTS:

THE SIXTIES 1960-1969 **THE SEVENTIES 1970-1979** **THE 2000s 2000-2009**	Three complete collections of the actual weekly "Hot 100" charts from each decade; black-and-white reproductions at 70% of original size. Over 550 pages each. Deluxe Hardcover.

BILLBOARD POP ALBUM CHARTS 1965-1969
Every weekly *Billboard* pop albums chart, shown in its entirety, from 1965 through 1969. Black-and-white reproductions at 70% of original size. 496 pages. Deluxe Hardcover.

HOT COUNTRY SONGS 1944-2008
The complete history of the most genuine of American musical genres, with an artist-by-artist listing of every Country single ever charted. 672 pages. Hardcover.

HOT COUNTRY ALBUMS 1964-2007
An artist-by-artist listing of every album to appear on *Billboard's* Top Country Albums chart from its first appearance in 1964 through 2007, with a complete A-Z listing below each artist of tracks from every charted album by that artist. Also includes research from Country Catalog Albums chart. 344 pages. Hardcover.

COUNTRY ANNUAL 1944-1997
A year-by-year ranking, based on chart performance, of over 16,000 Country hits. 704 pages. Hardcover.

ROCK TRACKS 1981-2008
Every song and artist that made *Billboard's* Modern Rock Tracks chart and Mainstream (Album) Rock Tracks chart appear in one main artist listing. 400 pages. Hardcover.

TOP ADULT SONGS 1961-2006
Artist-by-artist listing of every song to appear on *Billboard's* Easy Listening and Hot Adult Contemporary singles charts from July 17, 1961 through July 29, 2006 and now, for the first time, includes the songs and artists that appeared on *Billboard's* Adult Top 40 singles charts from March 16, 1996 through July 29, 2006. 426 pages. Hardcover.

TOP R&B ALBUMS 1965-1998
An artist-by-artist listing of every album to appear on *Billboard's* Top R&B Albums chart from its first appearance in 1965 through 1998. Includes complete listings of all tracks from every Top 10 R&B album. 360 pages. Hardcover.

CHRISTMAS IN THE CHARTS 1920-2004
Every charted Christmas single and album of the past 85 years, arranged by artist. Complete title sections for both singles and albums. Bonus section – 24-page full-color Christmas Photo Album. 272 pages. Softcover.

#1 POP PIX 1953-2003
<u>Full-color</u> pictures of nearly 1,000 *Billboard* Pop/Hot 100 #1 hits of the past 51 years in chronological sequence. 112 pages. Softcover.

#1 ALBUM PIX 1945-2004
<u>Full-color</u> pictures of every #1 Pop, Country and R&B album, in chronological sequence. 176 pages. Softcover.

BILLBOARD TOP 10 SINGLES CHARTS 1955-2000
A complete listing of each weekly Top 10 singles chart from *Billboard's* Best Sellers chart (1955-July 28, 1958) and Hot 100 chart from its inception (August 4, 1958) through 2000. Each chart shows each single's current and previous week's positions, total weeks charted on the entire chart, original label & number, and more. 712 pages. Hardcover.

BILLBOARD TOP 10 ALBUM CHARTS 1963-1998
This books contains more than 1,800 individual Top 10 charts from over 35 years of *Billboard's* weekly Top Albums chart (currently titled The Billboard 200). Each chart shows each album's current and previous week's positions, total weeks charted on the entire Top Albums chart, original label & number, and more. 536 pages. Hardcover.

MUSIC YEARBOOKS 2005-06/2004/2003/2002/2001/2000/1999/1998/1997/1996/1995/1994/1993/1992/1991/1990
A complete review of each year's charted music — Top Pop Singles and Albums, Country Singles and Albums, R&B Singles and Albums, Adult Contemporary Singles, Rock Tracks, and Bubbling Under Singles books. Various page lengths. Softcover.

MUSIC YEARBOOKlet 2007-08
Custom-printed and stapled paper booklet consists of the five most popular Yearbook sections only: one combined 2007-2008 "Hot 100"/"Bubbling Under" Artist Section; separate 2007 and 2008 "Hot 100" Annual rankings; and separate 2007 and 2008 "Hot Country Songs" Annual rankings.